Parkinson's Disease

*Diagnosis and
Clinical Management*

Second Edition

& Info

Parkinson's Disease

Diagnosis and Clinical Management

Second Edition

EDITED BY

STEWART A. FACTOR, DO
Professor and Director Movement Disorder Program
Department of Neurology
Emory University
Atlanta, Georgia

WILLIAM J. WEINER, MD
Professor and Chairman
Department of Neurology
University of Maryland
Baltimore, Maryland

Demos

New York

Acquisitions Editor: R. Craig Percy
Cover Designer: Aimee Davis
Compositor and Indexing: Publication Services, Inc.
Printer: Sheridan Press

Visit our website at www.demosmedpub.com

Library of Congress Cataloging-in-Publication Data

Parkinson's disease : diagnosis and clinical management / edited by Stewart A. Factor, William J. Weiner. —2nd ed.
    p. ; cm.
  Includes bibliographical references and index.
  ISBN-13: 978-1-933864-00-6 (hardcover : alk. paper)
  ISBN-10: 1-933864-00-1 (hardcover : alk. paper)
  1. Parkinson's disease. I. Factor, Stewart A., 1956- II. Weiner, William J.
  [DNLM: 1. Parkinson Disease—diagnosis. 2. Parkinson Disease—therapy. WL 359 P247315 2008]
  RC382.P2644 2008
  616.8'33—dc22
               2007032324

Medicine is an ever-changing science undergoing continual development. Research and clinical experience are continually expanding our knowledge, in particular our knowledge of proper treatment and drug therapy. The authors, editors, and publisher have made every effort to ensure that all information in this book is in accordance with the state of knowledge at the time of production of the book.

Nevertheless, this does not imply or express any guarantee or responsibility on the part of the authors, editors, or publisher with respect to any dosage instructions and forms of application stated in the book. Every reader should examine carefully the package inserts accompanying each drug and check with a physician or specialist whether the dosage schedules mentioned therein or the contraindications stated by the manufacturer differ from the statements made in this book. Such examination is particularly important with drugs that are either rarely used or have been newly released on the market. Every dosage schedule or every form of application used is entirely at the reader's own risk and responsibility. The editors and publisher welcome any reader to report to the publisher any discrepancies or inaccuracies noticed.

Special discounts on bulk quantities of Demos Medical Publishing books are available to corporations, professional associations, pharmaceutical companies, health care organizations, and other qualifying groups. For details, please contact:

Special Sales Department
Demos Medical Publishing
386 Park Avenue South, Suite 301
New York, NY 10016
Phone: 800–532–8663 or 212–683–0072
Fax: 212–683–0118
Email: orderdept@demosmedpub.com

Made in the United States of America
07 08 09 10 5 4 3 2 1

To Ann Marie

—SAF

Abel—welcome
Lisa—"ichigo ichie"

—WJW

Contents

III. BEHAVIORAL AND PSYCHIATRIC MANIFESTATIONS

IV. PATHOLOGY AND NEUROCHEMISTRY

V. BIOMARKERS

VI. PATHOGENESIS AND ETIOLOGY

VII. DRUGS

VIII. TREATMENT ISSUES

IX. SURGERY

X. SUBTYPES OF PARKINSONISM

XI. OTHER ISSUES

Foreword

Parkinson's disease is the second most common neurodegenerative disorder after Alzheimer's disease. It has been suggested that the prevalence of the disease will double over the next 20 years. Since the publication of the first edition of this book, there have been important advances in our understanding of the etiology, pathogenesis, investigation and management of Parkinson's disease. The field is moving ahead rapidly, so a second edition of this important book is readily justified. Exciting advances and new developments have occurred in almost every important area covered in the text. There have been changes in our understanding of the pathology of the disease, where it begins in the nervous system, and how it progresses. Indeed, there is now evidence to suggest that the disease does not affect the dopaminergic substantia nigra pars compacta at the earliest stages but instead begins in the lower brainstem, olfactory bulb, and anterior olfactory nucleus. The early involvement of areas unrelated to the nigrostriatal system highlights the importance of evaluating symptoms including constipation, sleep disorders (such as REM behavior disorder), anosmia, and so on. Not only do these and other nonmotor features become more common and problematic as the disease progresses but some also may serve as early markers for the presence of the disease even before more typical parkinsonian features develop. Recognizing and assaying these features may become particularly important when effective disease-modifying therapy (often termed "neuroprotective therapy") becomes available.

Recent years have seen increasing recognition of the importance of later-stage symptoms believed to be unrelated to nigrostriatal dopamine deficiency. Indeed, after 10 to 15 years of disease, these constitute some of the most difficult and poorly addressed management problems. Symptoms such as speech and swallowing dysfunction, sensory symptoms, gait disturbances and postural instability, autonomic and sleep dysfunction, and cognitive and psychiatric disturbances all contribute considerably to parkinsonian disability. All of these are given appropriate emphasis and coverage in this new edition.

Concepts of disease pathogenesis are actively evolving. Recently, these have been particularly driven by important advances in our understanding of the genetics of Parkinson's disease. Highlighting the importance of these developments is a new chapter dealing exclusively with the genetics of Parkinson's disease (and, for obvious reasons, the elimination of an older chapter entitled "Is There a Familial Form of Parkinson's Disease?"). Indeed, breakthroughs in this area more than any other have encouraged the belief that "Parkinson's disease" is not a uniform, single disease entity and that it may be more appropriate to think in terms of Parkinson's *diseases*.

In the broadest terms, treatment for Parkinson's disease can be subdivided into neuroprotective, neurorestorative, and symptomatic categories. Neuroprotective therapy remains the holy grail of all neurodegenerative diseases. Recent years have seen several disappointments in this area of Parkinson's disease therapeutics, and it remains an important challenge to understand why very promising drugs have failed in human trials. Establishing effective and reliable methods for very early diagnosis and monitoring of disease progression (biomarkers) is a high priority. Recent studies suggest that there may be confounding factors that will have to be resolved before existing and newer imaging modalities can be used as surrogate markers of disease progression.

Despite almost four decades of use, levodopa remains the most effective treatment in Parkinson's disease. Concerns about its potential neurotoxicity have been largely allayed, although motor complications remain an important therapeutic challenge. It is clear that the early use of dopamine agonists can delay some of these problems; however, a number of previously unrecognized side effects have come to light in recent years, including excessive daytime somnolence and a variety of behavioral disorders, which are clearly more common with these drugs. A number of newer symptomatic drug therapies, such as adenosine A2 antagonists, show promise. The management of psychiatric disturbances and cognitive dysfunction has also seen important advances in recent years. All of these topics are addressed in this new edition.

Surgical treatment remains an important option for selected patients with Parkinson's disease. This field has also evolved considerably since the last edition. Pallidotomy and other lesion techniques have been largely replaced by deep brain stimulation (DBS), and the subthalamic nucleus has become the target of choice in most patients. Follow-up for 5 or more years shows contin-

ued marked benefit to levodopa-responsive symptoms, with major improvements in quality of life. However, there is little evidence that this treatment changes the course of the disease, including the later development of the nondopaminergic features mentioned above. In this regard, newer targets are being explored—for example, the pedunculopontine nucleus for treatment-resistant ambulatory disturbances. Double-blind trials of neuro-restorative/neuroregenerative therapies have had disappointing results; however, there is still considerable hope that the understanding of past failures will permit successful advances in the future. Finally, since the last edition, the first trials of different types of gene therapy have been undertaken, with promising initial results.

We also recognize the many gaps in our knowledge and shortcomings of existing treatment. All of these issues are appropriately addressed in this text. The second edition of *Parkinson's Disease: Diagnosis and Clinical Management* edited by Drs. Factor and Weiner, provides a state-of-the-art review of where we've been, where we are now, and where we are going.

Anthony E. Lang, MD, FRCPC
University of Toronto

Preface

When, however, the nature of the subject and the circumstances under which it has been taken up, are considered, it is hoped that the offering of the following pages to the attention of the medical public, will not be severely censured. The disease, respecting which the present inquiry is made, is of a nature highly afflictive. Notwithstanding which, it has not yet obtained a place in the classification of nosologists; some have regarded its characteristic symptoms as distinct and different diseases, and others have given its name to diseases differing essentially from it; whilst the unhappy sufferer has considered it as an evil, from the domination of which he had no prospect of escape.

James Parkinson

The first edition of *Parkinson's Disease: Diagnosis and Clinical Management* was published in 2002. In 1998, when we began preparation of the book, the coming millennium gave us pause to contemplate significant developments in Parkinson's disease (PD) research, which clearly affected the lives of our patients. The result was a comprehensive text including 58 scholarly chapters from many of the leading investigators in the field summarizing the state of current knowledge on clinical features, pathology, neurochemistry, etiology, and treatment. However, 6 years later, further important and dramatic developments have changed our thinking regarding this disease. Our concept of the pathology now focuses not only on the dopaminergic system but also on nondopaminergic nonstriatal systems. The evolution of the synucleinopathy has also attracted increasing attention. New nondopaminergic drugs for the treatment of PD are close to approval, and it is expected that nondopaminergic agents will be the focus of clinical therapeutics for the next decade. In recent years it has come to be believed that PD might have an environmental basis; however, it has now been demonstrated that genetics plays a major role, and several causative and susceptibility genes have been discovered. These and other discoveries led us to embark on the preparation of this second edition, which has 63 chapters, including updates of those from the first edition. Some chapters have been eliminated or replaced, and 23 are entirely new. We feel that this second edition will be useful not only to movement disorder specialists and fellows but also to neurologists, gerontologists, neurosurgeons, neuropsychologists, neuroscience researchers, and neurology residents. Because it provides both theoretical and practical approaches to PD, this text will be an important addition to their libraries.

This edition is organized to provide a comprehensive view of PD and takes the reader through 11 sections covering history, clinical presentation, behavioral and psychiatric manifestations, pathology and neurochemistry, biomarkers, pathogenesis and etiology, drugs, treatment issues, surgery, subtypes of parkinsonism, and other issues. The history section remains largely unchanged. We begin with a chapter on James Parkinson, followed by Louis's chapter delineating the limited references to the shaking palsy cited in the 1817 publication by James Parkinson. Goetz, in his chapter, points out that Charcot expanded the description of PD by adding rigidity to its cardinal features, asserting that PD may be diagnosed without tremor, and coining the term *Parkinson's disease*. In addition, the time line in Chapter 4 reflects important PD discoveries since 1900, including the advances made since the first edition of this volume was published.

The next two sections (15 chapters) provide a clinical description of PD. They are organized to emphasize not only the motor aspects but also the nonmotor aspects of the disease, including its behavioral and psychiatric features. The chapters on autonomic dysfunction and depression have been completely rewritten. As patients live longer, nondopaminergic features including nonmotor symptoms are becoming major issues. Giladi and Nieuwboer, in Chapter 7, discuss freezing of gait, which is highly troublesome and thus far not amenable to therapy. Often nonmotor complaints—such as sensory symptoms (pain, numbness, tingling, and internal tremor), speech dysfunction, gastrointestinal and other autonomic symptoms, or sleep disorders—may dominate the discussion with patients at office visits. For this reason we felt that it was important to address them in separate chapters. In addition, Chapter 8, on sensory symptoms, has a newly added section on olfactory dysfunction and its possible role in early diagnosis. The natural history of PD is also discussed. Feigin and Eidelberg, in Chapter 13, review current knowledge of the progressive nature of PD based on clinical, pathological, and imaging studies, showing, for instance, that the preclinical period may be less than 10 years. Clinical rating scales, which have revolutionized our ability to quantitate the progressive nature of PD and effects of therapy, are also discussed.

Parkinson mistakenly reported that the senses and intellect were uninjured in this disorder. However, the treatment of dementia represents the greatest unmet need in our patients. The definition and concepts concerning the pathogenesis of this phenomenon have changed dramatically in the last decade. Marder and Jacobs, in Chapter 15, present a very cogent survey of the clinical issues of dementia in PD. There is increasing awareness that PD is also associated with a variety of psychiatric disorders. Another new chapter reports on the recently described impulse control disorders. In some patients, these psychiatric features play a significant role (Chapters 15 to 19).

While our knowledge of the clinical syndrome has improved, so has our understanding of the pathology and neurochemistry of PD (Chapters 20 to 23). Chapter 20, discussing pathology, is completely new; Dickson, its author, covers, among other things, the work of Braak and colleagues, who have proposed a new pathological staging system. In Section V, we address the issues of biomarkers, with an emphasis on imaging. Chapter 24 provides an overview of the status of biomarkers, followed by chapters on all the available imaging modalities. All

five chapters are new, including a discussion of current controversies surrounding the use of imaging in clinical trials.

The pathogenesis and etiology of PD remain unknown even after 190 years; however, several well-established theories are a key focus of research. Section VI covers theories on pathogenesis with three new chapters, one discussing animal models, one on protein aggregation, and another on inflammation. the newest of these theories. Beal discusses oxidative stress, mitochondrial dysfunction and excitotoxicity, while Burke covers the concept and terminology of apoptosis. This section also addresses other issues, including Tanner's discussion of epidemiology and Langston's review of MPTP research. These are followed by new chapters on pesticides and genetics. The latter chapter, by Payami and colleagues, discusses both causative and susceptibility genes.

Parkinson's disease remains the only neurodegenerative disorder that has demonstrated significant responsiveness to therapeutic intervention. Over the last 40 years, with the introduction of a wide range of pharmacologic agents and surgical procedures, there has been a revolution in the management of PD. Still other treatments, which are experimental at this time, represent a potential for improved care in the future, including neuroprotection. With the availability of multiple new treatments, a number of new issues have emerged, including the approach to treating early disease, motor fluctuations, and psychosis. All these aspects of therapy are extensively treated in this text and discussed in detail (Chapters 38 to 56). Hurtig and colleagues begin with a detailed discussion of levodopa, including its history and evolution and the controversies surrounding it. Further discussions of amantadine and anticholinergics, MAOIs, dopamine agonists, and COMT inhibitors are included. Three new chapters cover excitatory amino acid antagonists, adenosine A2 antagonists, and complementary and alternative medications. Under treatment issues, we have added a new chapter on the treatment of dementia in PD. In addition, a new chapter on genetic testing details the tests that are now publicly available and the controversies related to them. Interest in surgery was rejuvenated in the 1990s because of improved surgical technology and the progressive nature of PD. Enormous interest in surgery continues, and new chapters covering ablative therapies, DBS, and transplantation are included.

The differential diagnosis of PD is complicated. Section X (Chapters 57 and 58) reviews those disorders that are most important under the titles of "Symptomatic Parkinsonism" and "Parkinson-Plus Disorders." Those covered in the latter chapter include PSP, MSA, CBD, and DLB.

Chapters 59 to 63 cover additional important topics in PD, including a discussion of outcome measures (new), family caregiving, the economics of PD, and driving. This section includes a discussion of the relative role of quality-of-life testing versus disability and outcome measures in clinical trials. We close with a chapter from a patient's perspective written by David Heydrick, a neurologist who developed PD in 2002.

All 63 chapters together form a comprehensive review of the many issues regarding PD which face physicians today. While we have organized the chapters so as to complement one another, providing a lucid text that can be read sequentially from beginning to end, we have also provided extensive cross referencing within each chapter, so that subjects of interest can easily be isolated. Each chapter may also stand on its own as a scholarly review of its particular topic; each is concisely written and heavily referenced for this purpose.

As we move forward in our endeavors to better understand Parkinson's disease, we close in the spirit of James Parkinson:

The disease had escaped particular notice; and the task of ascertaining its nature and cause by anatomical investigation did not seem likely to be taken up by those who, from their abilities and opportunities, were most likely to accomplish it. That these friends to humanity and medical science, who have already unveiled to us many of the morbid processes by which health and life is abridged, might be excited to extend their researches to this malady, was much desired; and it is hoped that this might be procured by the publication of these remarks.

Stewart A. Factor
William J. Weiner

Acknowledgments

We would like to thank all the contributors of this text. We realize that this is a complicated era in medicine and it is becoming more and more difficult to find the time to participate in these endeavors. Despite that, our authors were able to contribute timely, cogent and comprehensive reviews in their area of expertise and for that we are grateful.

We would also like to thank Craig Percy of Demos for his work in moving this book to completion.

Finally, we are indebted to Rosalyn Newman, Eugenia and Michael Brin, Victor and Marilyn Riley, The Sartain Lanier Foundation, and Mrs. Lou Brown Jewell for their extraordinarily generous support of our Parkinson's Disease and Movement Disorder programs.

Contributors

Paul D. Acton, PhD
Associate Professor
Radiology
Thomas Jefferson University
Philadelphia, Pennsylvania
*Chapter 26: Single Photon Emission Computed
    Tomography*

Charles H. Adler, MD, PhD
Professor of Neurology
Mayo Medical School
Chair
Mayo Clinic Division of Movement Disorders
Mayo Clinic
Scottsdale, Arizona
Chapter 39: Amantadine and Anticholinergics

J. Eric Ahlskog, PhD, MD
Professor of Neurology
Mayo Medical School
Consultant in Neurology
Mayo Clinic
Rochester, Minnesota
*Chapter 51: Symptomatic Treatment Approaches for
    Early Parkinson's Disease*

Ron L. Alterman, MD
Associate Professor
Neurosurgery
Mount Sinai School of Medicine
New York, New York
Chapter 54: Deep Brain Stimulation

Karen E. Anderson, MD
Assistant Professor of Psychiatry and Neurology
Department of Neurology, Movement Disorders
University of Maryland School of Medicine
Baltimore, Maryland
Chapter 49: Treatment of Dementia

Patricia G. Archbold, RN, DNSc
Professor Emerita
School of Nursing
Oregon Health and Science University
Portland, Oregon
Chapter 60: Family Caregiving

M. Flint Beal, MD
Chairman
Anne Parrish Titzell Professor of Neurology
Neurology and Neuroscience
Weill Medical College of Cornell University
New York, New York
*Chapter 30: Pathogenesis: Oxidative Stress,
    Mitochondrial Dysfunction, and Excitotoxicity*

Ranjita Betarbet, PhD
Assistant Professor
Department of Neurology
Emory University
Atlanta, Georgia
Chapter 35: Rotenone and Other Toxins

Meredith Broderick, MD
Resident Physician
Department of Neurology
University Hospitals Case Medical Center
Cleveland, Ohio
Chapter 57: Parkinson's-plus Disorders

Robert E. Burke, MD
Professor
Departments of Neurology and Pathology
Columbia University
New York, New York
Chapter 31: The Concept and Mechanisms of Programmed Cell Death

Richard Stanley Burns, MD
Director
Movement Disorders Program
Department of Neurology
Barrow Neurological Institute
Phoenix, Arizona
Chapter 21: Neurochemistry

Mackenzie Carpenter, MD
Resident
Department of Neurology
University of Maryland School of Medicine
Baltimore, Maryland
Chapter 18: Apathy and Amotivation

Julie H. Carter, RN, MS
Professor
Department of Neurology
Oregon Health and Science University
Portland, Oregon
Chapter 60: Family Caregiving

Thomas C. Chelimsky, MD
Professor of Neurology
Director, Autonomic Disorders
Neurological Institute
University Hospitals Case Medical Center
Cleveland, Ohio
Chapter 11: Autonomic Dysfunction

Cynthia Louise Comella, MD
Professor
Department of Neurological Sciences
Rush University Medical Center
Chicago, Illinois
Chapter 12: Sleep Disorders

Ana Maria Cuervo, MD, PhD
Associate Professor
Departments of Anatomy and Structural Biology and Medicine
Albert Einstein College of Medicine
Bronx, New York
Chapter 32: Protein Aggregation

Dennis W. Dickson, MD
Professor
Departments of Pathology and Neuroscience
Mayo Clinic College of Medicine
Jacksonville, Florida
Chapter 20: Neuropathology

E. Ray Dorsey, MD, MBA
Assistant Professor
Department of Neurology
University of Rochester Medical Center
Rochester, New York
Chapter 24: Status of Biological Markers
Chapter 61: Economics

David Eidelberg, MD
Director
Movement Disorders Center
North Shore–Long Island Jewish Health System
Manhasset, New York
Chapter 13: Natural History

Debra Elliott, MD
Associate Professor
Department of Neurology
Health Sciences Center
Louisiana State University
Shreveport, Louisiana
Chapter 8: Sensory Symptoms

Stewart A. Factor, DO
Professor and Director
Movement Disorder Program
Department of Neurology
Emory University
Atlanta, Georgia
Chapter 1: James Parkinson: The Man and the Essay
Chapter 4: Timeline of Parkinson's Disease History Since 1900
Chapter 62: Driving

Andrew Feigin, MD
Associate Professor of Neurology
Movement Disorders Center
North Shore–Long Island Jewish Health System
Manhasset, New York
Chapter 13: Natural History

Paul S. Fishman, MD, PhD
Professor and Research Director
Department of Neurology
University of Maryland School of Medicine
Chief
Neurology Service
Maryland VAHCS
Baltimore, Maryland
Chapter 29: Animal Models

Cynthia M. Fox, PhD, CCC-SLP
Research Associate
National Center for Voice and Speech
Denver, Colorado
Chapter 9: Voice, Speech, and Swallowing Disorders

Susan H. Fox, PhD, MRCP(UK)
Assistant Professor of Neurology
Division of Neurology
University of Toronto
Toronto, Ontario, Canada
Chapter 19: Impulse-control Disorders

Stephen T. Gancher, MD, FAAN
Staff Neurologist
Kaiser Permanente
Adjunct Associate Professor of Neurology
Oregon Health and Sciences University
Portland, Oregon
Chapter 14: Clinical Rating Scales

William T. Garrett, MD
Department of Neurology
Neurology Specialists of Savannah
Savannah, Georgia
Chapter 58: Symptomatic Parkinsonism

Nir Giladi, MD
Professor of Neurology
Chairman, Department of Neurology
Director, Movement Disorders Unit and Parkinson's
    Center
Tel Aviv Sourasky Medical Center
Sackler School of Medicine
Tel Aviv University
Tel Aviv, Israel
Chapter 7: Gait Disturbances

Christopher G. Goetz, MD
Director, Movement Disorders Program
Professor of Neurological Sciences and
    Pharmacology
Rush University Medical Center
Chicago, Illinois
Chapter 3: Charcot and Parkinson's Disease

James G. Greene, MD, PhD
Assistant Professor
Department of Neurology
Emory University
Atlanta, Georgia
Chapter 43: Excitatory Amino Acid Antagonists

Paul Greene, MD
Associate Professor of Clinical Neurology
Department of Neurology
Columbia University
New York, New York
*Chapter 55: Neural Transplantation: Yesterday, Today,
    and Tomorrow*

J. Timothy Greenamyre, MD, PhD
Professor
Department of Neurology
Pittsburgh Institute of Neurodegenerative Diseases
University of Pittsburgh
Pittsburgh, Pennsylvania
Chapter 35: Rotenone and Other Toxins

Robert E. Gross, MD, PhD
Assistant Professor of Neurological Surgery
Department of Neurosurgery
Emory University School of Medicine
Atlanta, Georgia
*Chapter 56: Stereotactic Pallidotomy and
    Thalamotomy*

Steven A. Gunzler, MD
Movement Disorders Fellow
Clinical Instructor
Department of Neurology
Oregon Health and Science University
Portland VA Medical Center
Portland, Oregon
Chapter 46: Motor Fluctuations and Dyskinesia

Mark Hallett, MD
Chief
Human Motor Control Section
Medical Neurology Branch
National Institute of Neurological Disorders and
    Stroke
National Institutes of Health
Bethesda, Maryland
Chapter 27: Magnetic Resonance Imaging

John Hardy, PhD
Chief
Laboratory of Neurogenetics
National Institute on Aging
National Institutes of Health
Bethesda, Maryland
Chapter 53: Genetic Testing

Robert A. Hauser, MD, MBA
Professor
Departments of Neurology, Pharmacology, and
    Experimental Therapeutics
University of South Florida
Director
Parkinson's Disease and Movement Disorders Center
National Parkinson's Foundation Center of Excellence
Tampa, Florida
Chapter 40: Monoamine Oxidase Inhibitors

Claire Henchcliffe, MD, DPhil
Assistant Professor
Department of Neurology and Neuroscience
Weill Medical College of Cornell University
New York, New York
*Chapter 30: Pathogenesis: Oxidative Stress,
    Mitochondrial Dysfunction, and Excitotoxicity*

David S. Heydrick, MD, MS
President
Heydrick NeuroCare, LLC
Frederick, Maryland
Chapter 63: The Patient's Perspective

Robert G. Holloway, MD, MPH
Professor of Neurology and Community and Preventive
    Medicine
Department of Neurology
University of Rochester Medical Center
Rochester, New York
Chapter 24: Status of Biological Markers
Chapter 61: Economics

Howard Hurtig, MD
Chief of Neurology and Co-Director
Parkinson's Disease and Movement Disorders Center
Pennsylvania Hospital
Frank and Gwladys Elliott Professor and Vice Chair
Department of Neurology
University of Pennsylvania School of Medicine
Philadelphia, Pennsylvania
*Chapter 38: Levodopa: A Pharmacologic Miracle Four
    Decades Later*

Sanjay S. Iyer, MD
Director
Movement Disorders Center
Carolinas Medical Center
Charlotte, North Carolina
Chapter 58: Symptomatic Parkinsonism

Diane M. Jacobs, PhD
Neuropsychological Consultant
Del Mar, California
Chapter 15: Dementia

Jorge L. Juncos, MD
Associate Professor
Department of Neurology
Division of Movement Disorders
Emory University School of Medicine
Atlanta, Georgia
Chapter 45: Complementary and Alternative Medicine

Denise M. Kay, PhD
Research Scientist
Division of Genetic Disorders
Wadsworth Center
New York State Department of Health
Albany, New York
Chapter 37: Genetics

Amos D. Korczyn, MD, MSc
Professor and Chair
Department of Neurology
Tel Aviv University
Ramat Aviv, Israel
Chapter 41: Dopamine Agonists

Roger Kurlan, MD
Professor of Neurology
University of Rochester School of Medicine and
    Dentistry
Rochester, New York
Chapter 17: Anxiety and Panic

J. William Langston, MD
Scientific Director and CEO
Parkinson's Institute
Sunnyvale, California
*Chapter 34: The Impact of MPTP on Parkinson's
    Disease Research: Past, Present, and Future*

Elan D. Louis, MD, MSc
Professor
Departments of Neurology and Epidemiology
College of Physicians and Surgeons
Mailman School of Public Health
Columbia University
New York, New York
Chapter 2: Paralysis Agitans in the Nineteenth Century

Andres M. Lozano, BSc, MD, PhD, FRCSC, BMedSci
Senior Scientist
Department of Neuroscience
Division of Brain Imaging and Behaviour Systems
Toronto Western Hospital
Toronto, Ontario, Canada
*Chapter 56: Stereotactic Pallidotomy and
    Thalamotomy*

Norika Malhado-Chang, MD
Clinical Instructor
Department of Neurology
Mount Sinai School of Medicine
New York, New York
Chapter 54: Deep Brain Stimulation

Karen S. Marder, MD, MPH
Professor
Department of Neurology
Sergievsky Center
Taub Institute of Psychiatry
Columbia University
New York, New York
Chapter 15: Dementia

Deborah C. Mash, PhD
Professor
Department of Neurology
Miller School of Medicine
Miami, Florida
Chapter 23: Dopamine Receptor Diversity

William M. McDonald, MD
JB Fuqua Chair for Late-Life Depression
Chief of Geriatric Psychiatry
Department of Psychiatry
Emory University Medical School
Atlanta, Georgia
Chapter 16: Depression

Aideen McInermey-Leo
Chief
Laboratory of Neurogenetics
National Institute on Aging
National Institutes of Health
Bethesda, Maryland
Chapter 53: Genetic Testing

Rukmini Menon, MD
Chief Resident
Department of Neurology
Duke University Medical Center
Durham, North Carolina
Chapter 44: Adenosine A$_{2A}$ Receptor Antagonists

Hideki Mochizuki, MD, PhD
Associate Professor
Department of Neurology
Juntendo University
Tokyo, Japan
Chapter 52: Progress in Gene Therapy

Eric S. Molho, MD
Professor of Neurology
Department of Neurology
Parkinson's Disease and Movement Disorders Center
Albany Medical Center
Albany, New York
Chapter 48: Psychosis and Other Behaviors

Jennifer S. Montimurro, BS
Research Scientist
Division of Genetic Disorders
Wadsworth Center
New York State Department of Health
Albany, New York
Chapter 37: Genetics

Paul Morrish, DM
Consultant Neurologist
Department of Neurology
Gloucestershire Hospitals NHS Foundation Trust
Gloucester Royal Hospital
Gloucester, United Kingdom
Chapter 28: Controversies in Neuroimaging

M. Maral Mouradian, MD
William Dow Lovett Professor of Neurology
Director, Center for Neurodegenerative and
    Neuroimmunologic Diseases
University of Medicine and Dentistry of New Jersey
Robert Wood Johnson Medical School
Piscataway, New Jersey
Chapter 52: Progress in Gene Therapy

Andrew B. Newberg, MD
Associate Professor
Department of Radiology
University of Pennsylvania
Philadelphia, Pennsylvania
*Chapter 26: Single Photon Emission Computed
    Tomography*

Alice Nieuwboer, PhD
Doctor
Rehabilitation Sciences
Katholieke Universiteit Leuven
Leuven, Belgium
Chapter 7: Gait Disturbances

Puiu F. Nisipeanu, MD
Senior Neurologist
Department of Neurology
Hillel Yaffe Hospital
Hadera, Israel
Chapter 41: Dopamine Agonists

John G. Nutt, MD
Professor
Department of Neurology
Oregon Health and Science University
Portland VA Medical Center
Portland, Oregon
Chapter 46: Motor Fluctuations and Dyskinesia

Haydeh Payami, PhD
Professor of Genetics
Division of Genetic Disorders
Wadsworth Center
New York State Department of Health
Albany, New York
Chapter 37: Genetics

Joel S. Perlmutter, MD
Elliot Stein Family Professor of Neurology
Departments of Neurology, Radiology, Neurobiology,
    and Program in Physical Therapy
Washington University
St. Louis, Missouri
Chapter 25: Positron Emission Tomography

Leonard Petrucelli, PhD
Assistant Professor
Department of Neuroscience
Mayo Clinic College of Medicine
Jacksonville, Florida
Chapter 32: Protein Aggregation

Ronald F. Pfeiffer, MD
Professor and Vice Chair
Department of Neurology
University of Tennessee Health Science Center
Memphis, Tennessee
Chapter 36: Inflammation

Michael Pourfar, MD
Assistant Professor
Movement Disorders Center
North Shore–Long Island Jewish Health System
Manhasset, New York
Chapter 13: Natural History

Serge Przedborski, MD, PhD
Page and William Black Professor of Neurology
Department of Neurology and Pathology and Cell
    Biology
Columbia University
New York, New York
Chapter 32: Protein Aggregation

**Eamonn M. M. Quigley, MD, RCP, FACP, FACG,
    FRCPI**
Professor of Medicine and Human Physiology
Department of Medicine
Alimentary Pharmabiotic Centre
National University of Ireland
Cork, County Cork, Ireland
Chapter 10: Gastrointestinal Features

Jose Martin Rabey, MD
Professor and Chairman
Department of Neurology
Assaf Harofe Medical Center
Tel Aviv University
Zerifim, Israel
Chapter 21: Neurochemistry

Alexander Rajput, MD
Associate Professor
Division of Neurology
University of Saskatchewan
Saskatoon, Saskatchewan, Canada
Chapter 5: Epidemiology
Chapter 40: Monoamine Oxidase Inhibitors

Ali H. Rajput, MBBS
Professor Emeritus
Division of Neurology
University of Saskatchewan
Saskatoon, Saskatchewan, Canada
Chapter 5: Epidemiology

Michele L. Rajput, PhD
Research Assistant
Epidemiologist
Neurology Research
University of Saskatchewan
Saskatoon, Saskatchewan, Canada
Chapter 5: Epidemiology

Lorraine O. Ramig, PhD, CCC-SLP
Professor
Department of Speech, Language, and Hearing Sciences
University of Colorado at Boulder
Senior Scientist
National Center for Voice and Speech
Denver, Colorado
Chapter 9: Voice, Speech, and Swallowing Disorders

Bernard M. Ravina, MD, MSCE
Associate Professor
Unit Chief
Movement and Inherited Neurological Disorders Unit
Department of Neurology
University of Rochester
Rochester, New York
Chapter 24: Status of Biological Markers

Irene Hegeman Richard, MD
Associate Professor of Neurology and Psychiatry
University of Rochester School of Medicine and
    Dentistry
Rochester, New York
Chapter 17: Anxiety and Panic

David E. Riley, MD
Director
Movement Disorders Center, Neurological Institute
Department of Neurology
University Hospitals Case Medical Center
Cleveland, Ohio
Chapter 57: Parkinson's-plus Disorders

Jacob I. Sage, MD
Director
Movement Disorders Center
Robert Wood Johnson Medical School
New Brunswick, New Jersey
Chapter 47: Fluctuations of Nonmotor Symptoms

Ali Samii, MD
Associate Professor
Department of Neurology
University of Washington
Clinical Director of the Seattle component of the
    Northwest VA Parkinson's Disease Research
    Education and Clinic Center (PADRECC)
Seattle, Washington
*Chapter 6: Cardinal Features of Early Parkinson's
    Disease*

Shimon Sapir, PhD, CCC-SLP
Professor
Department of Communication Sciences and Disorders
University of Haifa
Haifa, Israel
Chapter 9: Voice, Speech, and Swallowing Disorders

Kapil D. Sethi, MD
Neurologist and Director
Movement Disorders Program
Medical College of Georgia
Augusta, Georgia
Chapter 58: Symptomatic Parkinsonism

Lisa M. Shulman, MD
Associate Professor
Department of Neurology
University of Maryland School of Medicine
Baltimore, Maryland
Chapter 18: Apathy and Amotivation
Chapter 59: Outcome Measures

Andrew D. Siderowf, MD, MSCE
Associate Professor of Neurology
University of Pennsylvania School of Medicine
Philadelphia, Pennsylvania
Chapter 50: Status of Neuroprotective Therapies
Chapter 61: Economics

Tanya Simuni, MD
Associate Professor
Department of Neurology
Director
Parkinson's Disease and Movement Disorders Center
Northwestern University Feinberg School of Medicine
Chicago, Illinois
*Chapter 38: Levodopa: A Pharmacologic Miracle Four
    Decades Later*

Yoland Smith, PhD
Professor
Yerkes National Primate Research Center
Department of Neurology
Emory University
Atlanta, Georgia
Chapter 22: Basal Ganglia: Anatomy and Physiology

Mark A. Stacy, MD
Associate Professor
Departments of Medicine and Neurology
Duke University Medical Center
Durham, North Carolina
Chapter 44: Adenosine A_{2A} Receptor Antagonists

Matthew B. Stern, MD
Parker Family Professor of Neurology
University of Pennsylvania School of Medicine
Philadelphia, Pennsylvania
Chapter 50: Status of Neuroprotective Therapies

Barbara J. Stewart, PhD
Professor Emerita
School of Nursing
Oregon Health and Science University
Portland, Oregon
Chapter 60: Family Caregiving

Michele Tagliati, MD
Associate Professor
Deparment of Neurology
Mount Sinai School of Medicine
New York, New York
Chapter 54: Deep Brain Stimulation

Caroline M. Tanner, MD, PhD
Director
Clinical Research
The Parkinson's Institute
Sunnyvale, California
*Chapter 33: Etiology: The Role of Environment and
    Genetics*

Jerrold L. Vitek, MD, PhD
Director, Neuromodulation Research Center
Department of Neuroscience
Lerner Research Institute
The Cleveland Clinic Foundation
Cleveland, Ohio
Chapter 22: Basal Ganglia: Anatomy and Physiology

Valerie Voon, MD
Clinical Fellow
Human Motor Control Section
National Institute of Neurological Disorders and
    Stroke
National Institute of Health
Bethesda, Maryland
Lecturer
Department of Psychiatry
Toronto Western Hospital
Toronto, Ontario, Canada
Chapter 19: Impulse-control Disorders

Cheryl Waters, MD, FRCP
Albert and Judith Glickman Professor
Department of Neurology
Columbia University
New York, New York
Chapter 42: Catechol-O-Methyltransferase Inhibitors

William J. Weiner, MD
Professor and Chairman
Department of Neurology
University of Maryland
Baltimore, Maryland
Chapter 1: James Parkinson: The Man and the Essay
*Chapter 4: Timeline of Parkinson's Disease History
    Since 1900*
Chapter 62: Driving

Thomas Wichmann, MD
Associate Professor
Yerkes National Primate Center
Department of Neurology
Emory University
Atlanta, Georgia
Chapter 22: Basal Ganglia: Anatomy and Physiology

Tao Wu, MD
Associate Professor
Beijing Institute of Geriatrics
Xuanwu Hospital
Department of Neurology
Capital Medical University
Beijing, China
Chapter 27: Magnetic Resonance Imaging

Theresa A. Zesiewicz, MD
Associate Professor
Department of Neurology, and Pharmacology and
    Experimental Therapeutics
University of South Florida
Parkinson's Disease and Movement Disorders Center
National Parkinson's Foundation Center of Excellence
Tampa, Florida
Chapter 40: Monoamine Oxidase Inhibitors

Richard M. Zweig, MD
Professor
Department of Neurology
Health Sciences Center
Louisiana State University
Shreveport, Louisiana
Chapter 8: Sensory Symptoms

I

HISTORY

James Parkinson:
The Man and the Essay

Stewart A. Factor
William J. Weiner

Movement disorder specialists utter his name on a daily basis—in speaking to patients, interacting with colleagues, and giving lectures at medical colleges and societies to physicians, residents, and students. It was Charcot, in the late nineteenth century, who first suggested that the shaking palsy be given the name "Parkinson's disease" (PD) (1), which has now become a subject of intense interest. PD is the second most common neurodegenerative disorder, affecting over 1 million people in the United States alone; debilitating to patients and costly to society, it is the subject of innumerable scientific papers and is not infrequently mentioned in the lay literature or on the news. PD knows no boundaries with regard to race, nationality, gender, or social class, and we frequently hear about afflicted celebrities. Who was this man whose fame persists nearly 200 years after his seminal publication? Who was James Parkinson? History portrays him as a Renaissance man, who lived from 1755 to 1824. He was not only a practicing general physician who contributed to the medical literature of his time but also had interests as wide as politics, chemistry, and paleontology. We thought it would be appropriate to begin this text by discussing Parkinson the man and his famous *Essay on the Shaking Palsy*, which started it all. We do not provide a detailed biography of his life, since others have already done so; the reader is referred to two interesting books for additional details (2, 3). This chapter is followed by 2 chapters that discuss how PD was perceived in the nineteenth century. There is an emphasis on Charcot and how he was able further define the clinical features of the shaking palsy and separate it from other clinical entities. The history section ends with an outline of important discoveries since that time.

THE MAN

James Parkinson was born on April 11, 1755, to John and Mary Parkinson (3). They resided at number 1 Hoxton Square in the Parish of St. Leonards of Shoreditch, Middlesex County, where Parkinson lived his entire life. He was the oldest of three children, followed by his brother William and sister Mary Sedgewood. His father was a physician and surgeon practicing in Hoxton. At age 20, James studied at London Hospital Medical College for 6 months, followed by an apprenticeship with his father, which lasted 6 years. He qualified as a surgeon in 1784 at the age of 29 (4) and later joined his father in a practice referred to as Parkinson and Son. This was a large, lucrative practice, which also cared for the poor in the parish. Father and son served as attendings at a "private madhouse" for over 30 years. The practice of Parkinson and Son lasted through 80 years and 4 generations.

In 1781, James Parkinson married Mary Dale, and they had 6 children. Two died in infancy or early childhood, their first, James John, and their sixth, Jane Dale. His second child, John William Keys Parkinson, joined him in medical practice, and ultimately John's son James Keys Parkinson joined the practice as well.

We know little about James Parkinson's appearance except that he was "rather below middle stature" (3). An apparent photograph, which was initially identified as this James Parkinson, was published in *Medical Classics* in 1938 (5) (Figure 1-1), but it turned out to be from a group photo taken in 1872, well after Parkinson's death, of the membership of the British Dental Association (2). The subject's name was also James Parkinson. No actual photos or drawings of him exist. James Parkinson died on December 21, 1824, of a dominant hemisphere stroke that initially caused hemiplegia and aphasia. He was buried at the parish of St. Leonards, but his gravestone is not to be found today. A factory occupies the site of his birth on number 1 Hoxton Square (Figure 1-2), and in September 1961, a commemorative blue plaque was placed at the doorway (3) (see Figure 1-3).

Parkinson had a number of talents that served him well in his career. He was fluent in English, Latin, French, and Greek as well as an expert at shorthand, which he used to take verbatim notes at the various lectures he attended. Some of these notes were later used to publish the lectures; for example, the surgical lectures of John Hunter were published in 1833 as *Hunterian Reminiscences* (published by Parkinson's son John William Keys Parkinson). He was also an accomplished artist, a talent he utilized in his many writings and emphasized as important to medical students.

Parkinson was a political activist who found it difficult to remain silent while citizens suffered. He lived under the reign of King George III, at a time when the standard of living was declining as the result of war and rising taxes. Representation in parliament for all citizens was nonexistent, and corruption pervaded the government. The French Revolution, which led to the death of Louis XVI, was ongoing, and the American colonies had recently gained their freedom from British rule, instigating important discussions among British social reformers regarding democracy, suffrage, and representation for all, not just the rich. These social reformers were referred to by Edmund Burke, a conservative political leader of the time, as defenders of the "swinish multitude." It was also the time when Thomas Paine wrote his famous *The Rights of Man*. James Parkinson was a member of two outspoken societies of that time; The London Corresponding Society, started by Thomas Hardy in 1792, and the Society of Constitutional Information. Both king and parliament were exceedingly suspicious of these organizations. There was no freedom of the press or speech, and the right of habeas corpus was suspended

FIGURE 1-1

Photo of a British dentist named James Parkinson. It was taken in 1872 but was misidentified as James Parkinson, author of *An Essay on the Shaking Palsy*, who died in 1824. (Reproduced with permission from Robert E. Krieger Publishing Co.)

to prevent revolution from spilling into Great Britain. Many members of these societies were tried, convicted of treason, and severely punished. The primary objective of the London Corresponding Society was to bring about reform that would provide parliamentary representation for the general public. Although these reformers were suppressed to some extent, their activities may ultimately have helped to bring about more representative democracy in Great Britain (3). Parkinson took part in this as a writer. In a periodical known as *Politics of the People*, he wrote a series of a dozen or more articles under the civil disobedience, unfair imprisonment and poor prison conditions, the education of children from poor families, and making provision for the aged and disabled (3, 6, 8). The proceeds from the sale of the pamphlets were used to support the families of those who were political prisoners (9). Parkinson was identified as their author in an advertisement in the *London Times* and during an investigative cross-examination under oath for the British Privy Council, but he was never accused of wrongdoing. However, the publisher of the periodical was tried and convicted of treason.

Parkinson was also a key character in the "popgun plot" to assassinate King George III. Five members of the London Corresponding Society were arrested for high treason in relation to the apparent plan. In fact, a plan never existed except in the mind of one man, Thomas Upton. Three others were falsely accused based on forged letters (forged by Upton), and one was arrested because of his association with Upton. Only one actually went to trial. The plot involved the firing of a poison-tipped arrow from an air gun. No further details were ever devised. Parkinson's role was threefold. He visited one of the prisoners as physician and pleaded for the his removal from poor prison conditions. He also requested that the prisoner receive regular visits from a physician. He was a spokesperson for the prisoners with regard to

FIGURE 1-2

The building currently located at 1 Hoxton Square, the birthplace of James Parkinson. (Photograph generously provided by Christopher Goetz, MD).

pseudonym "Old Hubert" (3, 6, 7) between 1793 and 1795 (8). These essays were highly critical of the political system and covered a wide range of social topics while at the same time parrying with Edmund Burke. Some of the titles were "Revolutions Without Bloodshed or Reformation Preferable to Revolt"; "Pearls Cast Before Swine by Edmund Burke—Scraped Together by Old Hubert"; "A Vindication of the London Corresponding Society"; and "An Address to the Hon. E. Burke from the Swinish Multitude." These writings dealt with such issues as political corruption, poverty, unfairness of taxes and wages,

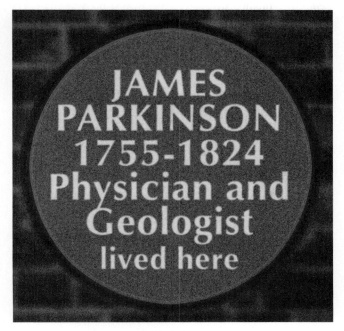

FIGURE 1-3

A closeup of the plaque (actually blue in color) on the building memorializing James Parkinson.

bail. Finally, he was a witness for the defense during the Privy Council's hearings for the 3 falsely accused and in the one trial that was held. He did not appear for Upton. He asserted the innocence of the accused. During the Privy Council's investigation, Parkinson initially refused to take the oath unless he received assurances that he would only be asked questions on the topic at hand. This annoyed the attorney general no end and he was told he would not be asked questions that might incriminate him (he responded that "there was no question you can produce an answer to criminate me"), but he was tricked. He was asked questions on issues regarding society membership and plans and about various writings, including some of his own. He was a formidable witness, disclosing little information, but he did admit to his memberships and his writings under the pseudonym Old Hubert. When asked if he had seen certain members, he always answered that he had seen them in his own home. None of the accused were found guilty and all were ultimately freed. Parkinson, in his writings and appearances before the Privy Council, took significant risks with regard to his own career and life. He could have been prosecuted for his activities in the societies, association with others accused, and for writings against the monarchy. But he was a man of principle and honor who felt that these issues were too important to allow him to remain silent. The members of the Privy Council respected his forthrightness and, as a result, he was not prosecuted. He left the London Corresponding Society shortly after the Popgun trials as more extreme forces took it over. He gave up his political writing in 1795.

Despite leaving the society, he was unwavering in his stance for parliamentary reform. He continued that fight as a trustee of the Vestry for the Liberty of Hoxton (also referred to as a parish councilor), to which he was appointed in 1799 (3). He remained at this post for 25 years, until his death. While the council was concerned about local affairs such as highway upkeep, illumination of the streets, and support of the church of St. Leonard, they were also active in national affairs. Since there was no parliamentary representation, the council took on that role, using town meetings and petitions as a means of protest. The primary concern was parliamentary reform and improvement of representation. The petition sent to the House of Commons from the parish contained many of the points Parkinson had written about in his earlier political papers, indicating his significant role in its composition.

Through the parish council, Parkinson took on other responsibilities, usually with humanitarian goals. He was concerned about the welfare of children who worked as apprentices. In the early nineteenth century, children of the poor and orphans found second homes with the better off, who took them in and put them to work. Some were abused in various ways. Parkinson recommended

the formation of a team of inspectors who would travel to the various households. In fact, he took on this role himself and discovered some of these abuses. Based on his findings, a law that required review and visitation was set into motion. His interest in child abuse issues did not start there. He had written about it in 1800 in his article "The Villagers' Friend and Physician" (10). He also became a trustee for the poor and was appointed surgeon, apothecary, and man-midwife to the poor of the parish in 1813. The latter position was salaried and it required, among other things, that he make house calls on sick paupers. His accomplishments during this time included the formation of separate fever wards for patients with typhus fever. He emphasized the contagious nature of the disease, a view not universally accepted at that time, and ultimately won support. After 4 years of discussion, a 12-bed ward was completed and the impact was significant. His papers entitled "Observations on the Necessity of Parochial Fever Wards, with Remarks on the Present Extensive Spread of Fever," written in 1818, and "On the Treatment of Infectious or Typhoid Fever," written in 1824, led to the construction of fever wards in London and the surrounding area and provided for improved treatment with appropriate hospital care and nursing. When James Parkinson died and his son resigned, it took 6 physicians to fill their positions as parish physicians.

James Parkinson made significant contributions to the medical literature (Figure 1-4) beyond the *Essay on the Shaking Palsy*. These included books, monographs, and case studies written for physicians and the lay public, some of which are worth mentioning. In 1799 he wrote a two-volume book on domestic medicine entitled *Medical Admonitions to Families, Respecting the Preservation of Health and the Treatment of the Sick*. In this 548-page text, he examined the symptoms and physical signs of common ailments of the time and emphasized the need for an experienced physician. A table of symptoms, listed alphabetically, was included in the book. This served to point out the difficulty in providing a definite diagnosis early in the course of an illness. He discussed such topics as the problems associated with the improper indulgence of children, epilepsy and pseudoseizures, and resuscitation of the drowned (3, 10). He wrote a monograph entitled *Observations on the Nature and Cure of Gout* in 1805. This paper included a clinical description, including the presumed experience of his father and himself, both of whom suffered from gout, along with pathology and therapy of the time. He criticized the accepted theories of etiology and treatment. In 1802 he wrote "Hints for the Improvement of Trusses," which included a description of his invention to make their use easier. In this paper, he complained about the high price of these devices, since they were needed mainly by those of modest means.

AN

ESSAY

ON THE

SHAKING PALSY.

BY

JAMES PARKINSON,

MEMBER OF THE ROYAL COLLEGE OF SURGEONS.

LONDON:

PRINTED BY WHITTINGHAM AND ROWLAND,

Goswell Street,

FOR SHERWOOD, NEELY, AND JONES,

PATERNOSTER ROW.

1817.

(a)

CONTENTS.

CHAP. I.

CHAP. II.

CHAP. III.

CHAP. IV.

CHAP. V.

(b)

AN

ESSAY

ON THE

SHAKING PALSY.

CHAPTER I.

DEFINITION—HISTORY—ILLUSTRATIVE CASES.

SHAKING PALSY. *(Paralysis Agitans.)*

Involuntary tremulous motion, with lessened muscular power, in parts not in action and even when supported; with a propensity to bend the trunk forward, and to pass from a walking to a running pace: the senses and intellects being uninjured.

(c)

FIGURE 1-4

(A) Title page of the monograph *An Essay on the Shaking Palsy.* (B) Table of Contents. (C) First page, showing the definition of the disease.

His first paper was a case report entitled "Some Account of the Effects of Lightning," about two men struck by lightning during the same storm. One was outdoors, the other indoors. They both responded to therapy with bleeding, hot brandy and water, and wet flannels. This paper was presented to the Medical Society of London on February 4, 1789. The clinical findings described in this paper are now considered the hallmarks of lightning injuries (11). These findings have often been attributed to Charcot and Lichtenberg, but it has been pointed out that Parkinson was the first to observe the salient features of lightning injuries. He wrote several papers with his son John William Keys Parkinson, including "A Case of Trismus," which was read to the Medical and Chirurgical Society by John on June 18, 1811. The two also coauthored the earliest reference to appendicitis in the English literature in 1812. The paper entitled " A Case of Diseased Vermiform Appendix" was read before the Medical and Chirurgical Society on January 21 of the same year and included a clinical and pathological discussion of a 5-year-old boy who died of a ruptured appendix and resultant peritonitis. Another interesting publication was "Cases of Hydrophobia," which was an account of two cases written from memory, because Parkinson had either given the notes to another physician or lost them. He wrote " I shall be obliged to rely, in the following account, entirely on my memory, which is however so impressed with the most important facts, that although it has to refer to a rather distant period, it will not, I trust, materially mislead me." The case notes, which he had given to another physician, were later published in a book, with some discrepancies.

As a physician, Parkinson was concerned about the education and qualifications of physicians in practice and the easy access of untrained "quacks" to medical practice. In 1800 he wrote an article entitled "The Hospital Pupil: An Essay Intended to Facilitate the Study of Medicine And Surgery," where he addressed qualifications including more than ordinary ability and intelligence and limited levity (6). While it was a guide for medical students, he used the opportunity to criticize the educational program of the time (3, 8, 12) and recommended liberal arts education and the knowledge of multiple languages for use in reviewing the literature. His proposed curriculum was similar to more modern education (3, 12). He was also an active advocate for the Apothecaries Act of 1815, which required licensing examinations for a proper diploma and allowed for prosecution of those who practiced without appropriate qualifications.

Parkinson had a fascination with chemistry, which probably started as early as 1780 and ultimately led to the publication of a well-received textbook (3, 6). It started with his reading of the works of Dr. Richard Watson and persisted with his attendance at the lectures of Sir Humphrey Davy at the Royal Institution of Great Brit-

ain in the early 1800s. In 1800, he wrote *The Chemistry Pocket Book*. A heavily referenced theoretical text, it was nevertheless easy to read and brought chemistry to the level of the "ordinary reader." It was a concise yet comprehensive account of the knowledge in the field and was inexpensive. It sold well, which led to the publication of 4 editions, the last in1807. The last edition was reissued in 1809. The final edition included chapters on geology, with which he was very familiar, and the biology of bodily fluids.

James Parkinson was also an avid collector of minerals, fossils, and seashells and gained notoriety for his knowledge of geology and oryctology (a term changed to "paleontology" about 10 years after his death) (3, 4, 6). He acquired his knowledge by collecting specimens in the field from the gravel and clay pits of Shoreditch, exchanging and trading pieces, and purchasing pieces from dealers and at auctions; thus he became a self educated expert. He apparently became interested in the subject after reading the chemical essays of Richard Watson, the same book which led to his interest in chemistry. He assembled one of the largest, most valuable collections of fossils in Great Britain. It was displayed in his house at 1 Hoxton Square in his own museum. After his death, in 1827, the collection was auctioned off, with many pieces ending up in various museums in Cambridge, Oxford, and Haslemere (3, 4).

In the early 1800s Parkinson took on the enormous task of writing a 3-volume text on oryctology (paleontology) entitled *Organic Remains of a Former World*. It was in these texts that his artistic abilities were utilized to the fullest, as all figures were drawings of his specimens. Volume I, *An Examination of the Mineralized Remains of the Vegetables and Animals of the Antediluvian World Generally Termed Extraneous Fossils*, was published in 1804. There were 1146 pages, 42 plates, and 700 figures. Volume II, *The Fossil Zoophytes*, was published in 1808, and Volume III, *Fossil Starfish, Echini, Shells, Insects, Amphibia, Mammalia, & c.* was published in 1811. This book was the first systematic examination of oryctology in the English language and the first comprehensive text to cover both plants and animals, including vertebrates (3). It was written for the general public to introduce them to the study of this subject. Parkinson made it a practical guide to help students who were digging to identify their findings. He did not use the standard chapter format to write this book but instead used a series of letters to an imaginary friend ("with an inquiring mind") to cover the topics. He apparently used this format not only because he thought it would be easier to follow but also because he thought it would work better with his busy schedule and ability to write only in short time slots. The text included a discussion on the history of the science going back to the Greek and Roman philosophers. He discussed the effect of Noah's flood and provided a theory of petrification, which differed from the accepted theory of his time. In the second volume he described the muriatic acid test, which he devised to demonstrate the presence of organic matter in the fossilized specimen. He also reported on the structure of pebbles. His classification of fossils was a departure from the standard ones. These volumes solidified his place as an expert in the field.

The book sold well and was reprinted several times, even after Parkinson's death, and went out of print in the 1840s. The plates were republished in 1850 in Mantell's *Pictorial Atlas of Fossil Remains.* Parkinson published a follow-up book in 1822 entitled *Outlines of Oryctology,* with 343 pages and 220 figures. A practical field manual for the student. it was an easy-to-read introductory book and was reissued in 1830 with corrections that Parkinson had made prior to his death.

Parkinson was a founding member of the Geological Society and was present at the inaugural meeting in 1807. He was an active member, serving one 2-year term on the society council. In the first issue of the *Transactions of the Geological Society*, published in 1811, he wrote a paper entitled "Observations on Some of the Strata in the Neighborhood of London, and on the Fossil Remains Contained in Them," which gave the first detailed description of the strata of the London basin and led to the new field of stratigraphic geology. He made other contributions to the transactions in the following years. He also made contributions to the *British Encyclopedia and Dictionary of the Arts and Sciences* on the subjects of oryctology and conchology. Because of his many important contributions to the field, Parkinson was made an honorary member of the Wernerian Society of Natural History of Edinburgh and the Imperial Society of Naturalists of Moscow.

Parkinson received several honors in life and posthumously. In 1777, while still an apprentice to his father, he received a silver medal for his part in the rescue of a man who attempted suicide by hanging. This was a case his father ultimately reported. On April 11, 1823, his 68th birthday, he became the first recipient of the Honorary Gold Medal from the Royal College of Surgeons for "his promotion of natural knowledge particularly expressed by his splendid work on Organic Remains . . ." (3, 4, 12). In September 1955, to commemorate the 200th anniversary of Parkinson's birth, a marble tablet with the inscription "*James Parkinson, of Hoxton, Surgeon and Apothecary*" was unveiled and a special service held (4). Among those present were two of his direct descendants and the president of the History of Medicine Section of the Royal Society of Medicine. In that same year a tribute to Parkinson was held at the Second International Congress of Neuropathologists, held at the Royal College of Surgeons of England. J. G. Greenfield gave an address entitled "Historical Landmarks in the Pathology of Involuntary Movement" and referred to Parkinson's contribu-

tion. Also at that meeting, a special exhibit was presented by his biographer A. D. Morris (medical superintendent of St Leonard's Hospital in Shoreditch), reviewing many aspects of his life (4). Because of his work in paleontology, a species of nautilus, a tropical cephalopod mollusk, was named after him: *Nautilus parkinsoni* (3). Also, his name is preserved in geological circles, well-known fossils containing oolite are referred to as the ammonite *Parkinsonia parkinsoni*, the crinoid *Apiocrinus parkinsoni*, a gastropod *Rostellaria parkinsoni*, and a stemless palm *Nipa parkinsoni* (4, 13). And medically, of course, his name is attached to the neurologic disorder that he described so well—*Parkinson's disease.*

Melvin Yahr described Parkinson as a "Physician for all seasons" (6). He was not only a humane physician in a busy practice who cared for the poor and mentally ill but also a talented writer who added substantially to the medical literature of his time, publishing a series of important papers and books on a variety of topics. These publications were directed not only to the medical community but also to the common people. Over 200 years later, he continues to be remembered for some of those contributions. In addition, he was an expert in chemistry, paleontology, and geology, making important strides in these sciences through a number of publications, books, and papers, for which he received due recognition. Finally, he was a political activist, using his talents as a writer to spearhead a battle against corruption and inequity.

COMMENTS ON *AN ESSAY ON THE SHAKING PALSY*

Parkinson published his medical classic *An Essay on the Shaking Palsy* in 1817 at the age of 62 (14) (Figure 1-4). This was a comprehensive treatise containing 5 chapters and 66 pages on the subject (which he called "paralysis agitans"). The review includes his experience with 6 patients. He must have contemplated this subject for some time, because he indicates that the first time he saw the disorder it "was observed in a case which occurred several years back, and which, from the particular symptoms which manifested themselves in its progress: from the little knowledge of its nature, acknowledged to be possessed by the physician who attended: and from the mode of its termination: excited an eager wish to acquire some further knowledge of its nature and cause." This work is considered a medical classic because of the eloquent and detailed description of the clinical features of the disease. It is unlikely that any of us, having the benefit of nearly 200 years of hindsight, could provide as eloquent a description as Parkinson did based solely on 6 patients. It should be noted that of the 6 patients that he reports on, 3 were "casually met on the street" or "only seen at a distance." Despite that, he accumulated a substantial knowledge of the clinical features and natural history of this disorder. We emphasize that anyone interested in Parkinson's disease should take the time to read this gem of the neurologic literature.

He starts in the preface with an apology (as he did in several other works), clearly underestimating his abilities as well as the respect that they engendered. As a clinician and not having had the opportunity to examine the pathology of any of his cases, he wrote "some conciliatory explanation should be offered for the present publication: in which, it is acknowledged that mere conjecture takes the place of experiment: and, that analogy is the substitute for anatomic examination, the only sure foundation for pathological knowledge." He claims to have taken on the task of writing the paper because he felt that the disease was unrecognized and/or poorly classified and he wanted more effort focused on it. He indicates that

> the disease had escaped particular notice: and the task of ascertaining its nature and cause by anatomic investigation, did not seem likely to be taken up by those who, from their abilities and opportunities, were most likely to accomplish it. That these friends of humanity and medical science, who have already unveiled to us many of the morbid processes by which health and life is abridged, might be excited to extend their researches to this malady, was much desired; and it was hoped, that this might be procured by the publication of these remarks.

These words were placed in the preface as an introduction to the paper itself and the paper also concluded similarly. Parkinson also described this paper as being a work in progress; he "considered it to be a duty to submit his opinions to the examinations of others, even in their present state of immaturity and imperfection" (he refers to himself in the third person in the writing of this paper). Other important issues that he discusses in the preface include, from a clinical standpoint, that he recognizes that this is a disease of long duration which progresses to a level of significant disability. He indicates "the disease . . ., is of a nature highly afflictive". He also indicates that the patients themselves understand the chronicity of the disease and the disability associated with it: "whilst the unhappy sufferer has considered it as an evil, from the domination of which he had no prospect of escape". Parkinson indicates that in order to understand the natural history of the disease one needs to either observe patients as they evolve or see patients at various stages of the disease or receive a "correct history of its symptoms even for several years." He notes in the preface that, in fact, he came to understand the nature of the illness from all three. He also indicates in the preface that he may not be the first to have seen this disease and that

there are other publications supporting this possibility (14, 15, 16). But he suggests that very often the authors thought of the individual features of paralysis agitans as separate disorders: "some have regarded its characteristic symptoms as distinct and different diseases, and others have given its name to diseases distinct from it."

The first 2 chapters (Chapter 1: Definition–History–Illustrative Cases; Chapter 2: Pathognomonic Symptoms Examined: Tremor Coactus–Scelotyrbe Festinana) provide the clinical description of the disease and are the portions of the paper that have made it so enduring. It is astounding how much Parkinson gleaned from the small number of cases he saw, especially since half of them were seen only briefly. He notes that the tremor and the gait disorder, the most visually dramatic features, are the pathognomonic symptoms of the disease: "the tremulous agitation, and the almost invincible propensity to run, when wishing only to walk, each of which has been considered by nosologists as distinct diseases, appear to be pathognomonic symptoms of this malady." He indicates quite succinctly that the resting tremor is the characteristic feature and one that could differentiate paralysis agitans from other forms of tremor. And he indicates that the differentiation of tremor is not really that hard: "a small degree of attention will be sufficient to perceive, that Sauvages, by this just distinction, actually separates this kind of tremulous motion, and which is the kind peculiar to this disease, from the Genus Tremor." He wrestled with the appropriate terminology for the tremor to separate it from other forms of tremor that occurred in action. He suggested that the term "palpitation" would be more appropriately utilized. He indicates that "the separation of palpitation of the limbs from tremor, is the more necessary to be insisted on, since the distinction may assist in leading to a knowledge of the seat of the disease." He also points out clearly that tremor alone cannot lead to the diagnosis: "tremor can, indeed, only be considered as a symptom." He then describes in an eloquent fashion the natural history of disease starting from the very earliest points and its insidious nature, "so slight and nearly imperceptible are the first inroads of malady, and so extremely slow is its progress, that it rarely happens, that the patient can form any recollection of the precise period of commencement." He continues; "The first symptoms perceived are, a slight sense of weakness, with a proneness to tremble in some particular part: . . .but most commonly of the hands and arms. . . .These symptoms gradually increase in the part first afflicted; and at an uncertain period, but seldom in less than 12 months or more, the morbid influence is felt in some other part". He continues later writing "after a few months the patient is found to be less strict than usual in preserving an upright posture: this being most observable whilst walking, but sometimes whilst sitting or standing." He points out the benign nature of the early symptoms, indicating that "hitherto the patient will have experienced but little inconvenience." He then goes on to show how the disabling portions of the disease begin to appear:

> But as the disease proceeds similar employments [writing and other dexterous maneuvers] are accomplished with considerable difficulties, the hand failing to answer the exactness to the dictates of the will. Walking becomes a task which cannot be performed without considerable attention. The legs are not raised to that height, or with that promptitude which the will directs, so that utmost care is necessary to prevent frequent falls. At this period the patient experiences much inconvenience, which unhappily is found daily to increase.

The discussion provides even further information on the continued progression, as he notes: "as time and the disease proceed, difficulties increase: writing can now be hardly at all accomplished. Whilst at meals the fork not being duly directed frequently fails to raise the morsel from the plate . . . at this period the patient seldom experiences a suspension of the agitation of his limbs." He then goes on to provide a detailed description of the gait disorder that characterizes paralysis agitans with particular emphasis on festination: "The propensity to lean forward becomes invincible, and the patient is thereby forced to step on the toes and fore part of the feet, whilst the upper part of the body is thrown so far forward as to render it difficult to avoid falling on the face. . . .irresistibly impelled to take much quicker and shorter steps, and thereby to adopt unwillingly a running pace."

In the very late stages he indicates that "the trunk is almost permanently bowed, muscular power is more decidedly diminished, and the tremulous agitation becomes violent. Patients walk now with great difficulty and are unable any longer to support themselves with a stick."

It is suggested that Parkinson did not discuss bradykinesia as a major feature of the disease (8). He does not mention it as a pathognomonic feature; however, he does discuss it in a variety of ways. Bradykinesia is not infrequently described by patients as a feeling of weakness in the later stages, and that is how Parkinson discusses it, as noted in the previous quotation. In his definition, Parkinson indicates that this stage is marked by "lessened muscular power," but he also notices a decrease in general motion by indicating, in his description of Case 5, "the inability for motion." It is frequently noted that Parkinson does not mention rigidity as a major feature of the disease. Possibly he did not actually perform a physical examination on these patients, but he primarily observed them and took their histories.

Parkinson did recognize a variety of other features of the disease, which were not emphasized until much later. Perhaps he did not recognize their high frequency because of the limited number of patients available to him. These features are now considered to be important aspects of PD. With regard to sleep disorders, he writes "in this stage, the sleep becomes much disturbed." The speech disorder is also well recognized: "the power of articulation is lost," and he indicates that in the later stages of disease. "his words are now scarcely intelligible." He vividly describes the features of a masked face and drooling by indicating that "the chin is now almost immovably bent down upon the sternum. The slops with which he is attempted to be fed, with the saliva, are continually trickling from the mouth." The inability to swallow is also alluded to by the use of soft foods in that comment. Constipation, a feature that is present in a large percentage of patients, is well recognized: "the bowels, which had been all along torpid, now, in most cases, demand stimulating medicines of very considerable power."

The observation that Parkinson's disease may occur without tremor is frequently attributed to Charcot (see Chapter 3), but in fact Parkinson himself may have described such a case. In his Case 5, he mentions nothing of tremor in the description but instead recognizes only the akinesia and gait disorder. However, he saw this patient only from a distance. He also probably first described the freezing phenomenon as well, although this is also usually not attributed to his description. A discussion in Case 6 describes it perfectly: "It being asked, if whilst walking he felt much apprehension from the difficulty of raising his feet, if he saw a rising pebble in his path? He avowed, in a strong manner, his alarm on such occasion; and it was observed by his wife, that she believed, that in walking across the room he would consider as a difficulty the having to step over a pin." It is often noted that Parkinson did not recognize any psychiatric or behavioral changes that might be associated with the disease, as indicated by his definition, which states ". . . the senses and intellects being uninjured." It may be that he only believed that to be true for the earlier stages of the disease. Later, in discussing advanced disease, he does note that patients may suffer "with slight delirium." In addition, there is some discussion of the possibility of depression occurring in these patients. In discussing a case described in the literature that he thinks to be very similar to paralysis agitans, there is a comment indicating "a more melancholy object I never beheld. The patient, naturally a handsome, middle-size, sanguine man, of a cheerful disposition, and an active mind, appeared much emaciated, stooped and dejected," There is no further discussion of whether or not Parkinson thought of this as a major feature of the disease. Finally, we have come to recognize, in the last 2 or 3 decades, that sensory symptoms may, in fact, occur in Parkinson's disease, particularly in relation to pain. Pain of various types has been well described. In fact, he does describe pain in a variety of ways in this manuscript, even suggesting that it may be an important early feature. With regard to Case 4, he describes that "his application was on account of considerable degree inflammation over the lower ribs on the left side," and after treating this patient, he indicates that "no change appeared to have taken place in his original complaint." In addition, in Chapter 4 (entitled "Proximate Cause–Remote Causes–Illustrative Cases"), he discusses pain of the radicular type in the arms, which might represent an early feature of the disease. In fact, one female patient he discusses complained of radicular pain similar to that described by other patients, which he thought might also represent paralysis agitans and attributed it to the disease. He states "on meeting with these 2 cases, it was thought that it might not be improbable that attacks of this kind, considered at the time merely as rheumatic affections, might lay the foundation of this lamentable disease, which might manifest itself at some distant period, when the circumstance in which it had originated, had, perhaps, almost escaped the memory."

He also recognizes the more common occurrence of this disease in older patients, since his 6 patients all were 50 years of age or older. He recognizes, while discussing the literature and other similar cases, that younger age of onset might suggest the presence of a different disorder.

Chapter 3 provides his differential diagnosis for the shaking palsy; in fact, he mentions how frequently, and inappropriately, that term is utilized to describe patients: "that the name by which it is here distinguished has been hitherto vaguely applied to diseases very different from each other, as well as from that to which it is now appropriated." He discusses patients with stroke, seizures, and other forms of tremor.

In Chapter 4, Parkinson ventures a guess on the location of the lesion and the etiology of the disease and indicates quite succinctly that it is a guess: "before making the attempt to point out the nature and cause of this disease, it is necessary to plead, that it is made under very unfavorable circumstances. Unaided by previous inquiries immediately directed to this disease, and not having had the advantage, in a single case, of that light which anatomical examination yields, opinions and not facts can only be offered. Conjecture founded on analogy, and an attentive consideration for the peculiar symptoms of the disease, have been the only guides that could be obtained for this research, the result of which is, as it ought to be, offered with hesitation." As in the classic neurologic teaching, Parkinson takes us through the localization process by showing first that it is a nervous disease by writing "by the nature of the symptoms we are taught, that the disease depends upon some irregularity in the direction of the nervous influence"; then he goes on to indicate more specifically that it is a central nervous system disease, and particularly located in the upper cervical spine, instead of a peripheral nervous system disease. He writes "that the injury is rather in the source of this influence than merely in the nerves of the parts; by the situation of the parts

whose actions are impaired, and the order in which they become affected, that the proximate cause of the disease is in the superior part of the medulla spinalis." He also points out that it does not go beyond the brainstem by stating "and by the absence of injury to the senses and to the intellect, that the morbid state does not extend to the encephalon." His primary thoughts on the etiologic process relate to neck trauma and inflammation. It is interesting that he notes that none of his patients had had any significant trauma that might cause the type of damage he was considering. In this chapter he provides discussions of appropriate cases. This is the weakest part of his paper, because those patients that he discusses do not clearly have the symptoms of paralysis agitans. However, he uses them as examples in much the same way as we hypothesize on etiology and location of the lesion by the discussion of obvious symptomatic cases. In relation to this he notes "although it may not mark an identity of the disease, serves at least to show that nearly the same parts were the seat of disease in both instances. Thus we attain something like confirmation of the supposed proximate cause, and of one of the assumed occasional causes." He further discusses the slowly progressive nature of the pathologic process within the brain, leading to the progressive nature of the disease: "but taking all circumstances into due consideration, particularly the very gradual manner in which the disease commences, and proceeds in its attacks; as well as the inability to ascribe its origin to any more obvious cause, we are led to seek for it in some slow morbid change in the structure of the medulla, or its investing membranes, or theca, occasioned by simple inflammation or rheumatic or scrophulous affection." He then discusses the order of spreading as the disease progresses in moving downward and further into the cervical spine or upward into the medulla oblongata.

Finally, in Chapter 5, he addresses possible treatments. He probably is the first person to have discussed neuroprotective therapies: "There appears to be sufficient reason for hoping that some remedial process may ere long be discovered, by which, at least, the progress of the disease may be stopped." He also notes "and even, if unfortunately deferred to a later period, they might then arrest the further progression of the disease, although the removing of the effects already produced, might be hardly to be expected"; which indicates that he did not think much of symptomatic therapies at that time. Parkinson was not impressed by the use of oral therapies: "the employment of internal medicines is scarcely warrantable; unless analogy should point out some remedial trial of which rational hope might authorize." He was concerned, however, that because of the slow progression of the disease and its benign nature in the early stages, that patients might delay treatment; ". . . seldom occurring before the age of 50, and frequently yielding but little inconvenience for several months, it is generally considered as the mere remediable diminution of the nervous influence, naturally resulting from declining life; and remedies therefore are seldom sought for." In discussing the treatments of the day. he actually speaks about the need for clinical trials to prove their usefulness; "experiment has not indeed been yet employed to prove, but analogy certainly warrants the hope, that similar advantages might be derived from the use of the means enumerated, in the present disease."

The essay was well received in the medical community (17). As this was the latter part of an illustrious career, the reviews indicated knowledge of Parkinson's previous work and respect for the man, his modesty, and his contributions. In particular, this report was found to be important and continues to be viewed in the same manner today. Despite this, there was no second printing of the monograph and originals became scarce. In the twentieth century, attention was drawn back to it by its reprinting in several books (2, 3, 5) and in copies provided by pharmaceutical companies.

If one were to look at Parkinson's initial cry for attention to this disease and then the incredible amount of work published in the scientific literature today, it would appear clear that his intent was successful. PD continues to be a disorder that receives substantial research attention as well as publicity in the lay literature. In the preface Parkinson says; "Should the necessary information be thus obtained, the writer will repine to no censure which the precipitated publication of mere conjectural suggestions may incur; but shall think himself fully rewarded by having excited the attention of those, who may point out the most appropriate means of relieving a tedious and most distressing malady." Although we have not yet cured PD, if Parkinson were to see the progress made in the last 2 centuries, as presented in this text, we think he would be "fully rewarded."

References

1. Goetz CG, Chmura TA, Lanska DJ. The history of Parkinson's disease: Part 2 of the MDS-sponsored History of Movement Disorders exhibit, Barcelona, June 2000. *Mov Disord* 2001; 16:156–161.
2. McMenemey WH. James Parkinson 1755–1824: A biographical essay. In: Critchley M (ed). *James Parkinson (1755–1824)*. London: Macmillan, 1955:1–143.
3. Morris AD. James Parkinson: His life and times. In: Clifford, Rose F (ed). *History of Neuroscience*. Boston, MA: Birkhauser, 1989.
4. Kelly EC. James Parkinson. *Medical Classics* 1938; 2:957–997.
5. Eyles JM. James Parkinson (1755–1824). *Nature* 1955; 176:580–581.
6. Tyler KL, Tyler HR. the secret life of James Parkinson (1755–1824): The writings of Old Hubert. *Neurology* 1986; 36:222–224.
7. Jelinek JE. Parkinson and the plum tree. *Arch Neurol* 1994; 51:1182–1183.
8. Yahr MD. A physician for all seasons: James Parkinson, 1755–1824. *Arch Neurol* 1978; 35:185–188.
9. Currier RD, Currier MM. James Parkinson: On child abuse and other things. *Arch Neurol* 1991; 48:95–97.
10. Gibson W. An essay on Dr James Parkinson (1755–1824). From the XIII International Congress on Parkinson's Disease. Vancouver, Canada, July, 1999.
11. Cherington M. James Parkinson: Links to Charcot, Lichtenberg and lightning. *Arch Neurol* 2004; 61:977.
12. Gibson W. Dr James Parkinson (1755–1824). *Neurosci News* 1999; 2:11–14.
13. Pearce JMS. Aspects of the history of Parkinson's disease. *J Neurol Neurosurg Psychiatry* 1989; 52(Special Suppl):6–10.
14. Parkinson J. *An Essay on the Shaking Palsy*. London: Sherwood, Neely, and Jones, 1817.
15. Calne DB, Dubini A, Stern G. Did Leonardo describe Parkinson's disease? *N Engl J Med* 1989; 320:594.
16. Manyam BV. Paralysis agitans and levodopa in "Ayurveda": Ancient Indian medical treatise. *Mov Disord* 1990; 5:47–48.
17. Hertzberg L. An essay on the shaking palsy: Reviews and notes on the journals in which they appeared. *Mov Disord* 1990; 5:162–166.

2 Paralysis Agitans in the Nineteenth Century

Elan D. Louis

ames Parkinson, a general practitioner, published the first pamphlet devoted exclusively to paralysis agitans (*An Essay on the Shaking Palsy*) in 1817 (1). Despite its wide renown in the present day, Parkinson's work is said to have received little immediate attention in his native country, England; when he died in 1824, Parkinson was perhaps better known as a geologist and political pamphleteer (see Chapter 1). As late as 1868, a half century after Parkinson's seminal publication, Sanders implied that nothing new had been added to the literature on this disorder: "Succeeding authors have, in general, simply quoted it [Parkinson's initial publication], or have . . . overlooked the disease altogether" (2). He further added that the original contributions made since his [Parkinson's] time have been few and fragmentary" (2). There are several other indications that, before Charcot's studies beginning in 1861 (3–5), the disease had received little attention. In 1861, Charcot wrote that "paralysis agitans is indisputably a very little known disease" (3), and McHenry wrote in 1958 that "Charcot later named this *hitherto unrecognized* [italics added] entity after Parkinson" (6).

The purpose of this chapter is to examine the medical literature on Parkinson's disease (PD) during the 45-year period from 1817 to 1861 in order to provide an account of the number and type of references to the shaking palsy.

This chapter serves as a supplement to a partial bibliography published elsewhere (7). The year 1861 was chosen as an endpoint because it represents the beginning of Charcot's landmark publications in this area (see Chapter 3) (3–5). This analysis is restricted to the literature published in England.

BACKGROUND

In 1817 (1), Parkinson elegantly described the clinical features of 6 cases of what he termed "the shaking palsy or paralysis agitans," including the resting tremor, flexed posture, festinating gait, and "lessened muscular power" or "paralysis" (1, 6, 8). He did not distinguish what he referred to as "paralysis" or "lessened muscular power" from what would be recognized by later physicians as bradykinesia and paucity of movement. His detailed and insightful view of the disease was based on only 6 cases. Further testament to his ability to astutely observe was the fact that several of these cases (cases 2, 3, and 5) had either been "only seen at a distance," "noticed casually in the street," or "casually met with in the street" (1). In 1865, Sanders suggested alternative names for the shaking palsy, including "Parkinson's disease," "paralysis agitans festinia," "paralysis agitans senilis," and "paralysis agitans parkinsonii" (9). Later, in 1888, Charcot suggested renaming this entity after James Parkinson (Parkinson's disease) (6).

LITERATURE REVIEW

The British literature on paralysis agitans during this 45- year period included 26 references (10–35) apart from Parkinson's treatise (1). These references were published in either general medical textbooks (5), textbooks dealing specifically with disorders of the nervous system (3), or journals (18). Each of these publications was relatively brief, and none provided an original and comprehensive analysis of the clinical signs, treatment, etiology, and pathology of this newly described disorder.

PARKINSON'S DISEASE: DIAGNOSIS AND MEDICAL MANAGEMENT

References to PD may be divided into three categories. The first are those that provide no more than a partial reiteration of Parkinson's initial clinical description, often quoting directly from his 1817 treatise (10–16). Second are those that provide somewhat more than a reiteration of Parkinson's description. These consist either of passing remarks about paralysis agitans or brief descriptions of original case reports (17–29). Third are those describing cases that today we would classify as other neurologic disorders (e.g., convulsive disorders) (30–35). Each of these categories is discussed further below.

A substantial number of the references merely provided a partial reiteration of the detailed clinical descriptions of Parkinson. These references, the majority of them appearing in textbooks, do not provide new clinical observations (10–16). They either quote or paraphrase large sections from Parkinson's treatise. All of these credit Parkinson with the initial description [e.g., "A disease has been lately described by Mr. Parkinson, under the title *paralysis agitans* or shaking palsy, which appears to me to be highly deserving of our attention" (10) or "Mr. Parkinson's description of the disease, however, is the best we have hitherto had and is as follows" (11).]

Several references provide more than a reiteration of Parkinson's description (17–29). These consist either of passing remarks about paralysis agitans or of brief original case reports. The majority of these were published in journals rather than in textbooks. Many were published by Dr. Elliotson, a practitioner at St. Thomas's Hospital in London. In 1827, Elliotson commented on an individual with paralysis agitans whom he had attended at St. Thomas's Hospital. The patient was briefly described as having "constant shaking of the legs and arms" (17). Elliotson further wrote: "The

intensity of the tremor varies. Till within the last week, the agitation would sometimes cease for a few hours or even a whole day, but for the last week has been constant" (17). In 1830 Elliotson described a 38-year-old schoolmaster with right-sided tremor of 18-months' duration. The patient also exhibited a tongue tremor and tachyphemia. Elliotson wrote: "The affection of the tongue is attended by the following very curious result . . . and suddenly he brings out his words with extreme rapidity; and such is the effort that he cannot stop himself. . . . It is a phenomenon analogous to the running which occurs on the attempt to walk" (19). In 1831, in a clinical lecture published in the *Lancet*, Dr. Elliotson remarked on paralysis agitans. He distinguished between "organic" forms of paralysis agitans arising later in life and paralysis agitans resulting from fright:

> There was a case of *acute rheumatism*, and one of *paralysis agitans* from fright. I spoke of this disease before. The patient was a man fifty years of age; and usually, I believe, it arises at such an age from an organic cause, for I have never been able to cure a person of it at or after middle life. I cured one between thirty and forty years of age, but he was the oldest. In this case it came on from fright, and therefore there may be nothing organic . . . (20).

It would seem that Dr. Elliotson had under his care individuals with several distinct disorders, all of which he labeled "paralysis agitans." Among these were cases of paralysis agitans that started in later life and were difficult to cure. These were probably cases of PD. In 1838 (23) and again in 1841 (24), Hall wrote: "I have long had an interesting case under my care" (24). He briefly described a man, 28 years of age, who "is affected by weakness and agitation of the right arm and leg; augmented on any occasion of agitation, and on moving; it is observed as he walks or when he passes his cane from one hand to the other; there is, besides, a peculiar lateral rocking motion of the eyes, and a degree of stammering and defective articulation" (24). Hall referred to this entity as "hemiplegic paralysis agitans" (24). In 1842, Thompson commented in the *Lancet* that treatment with the ergot of rye was beneficial in ". . .the paralysis agitans or tremens in advanced life, where I have seen it of considerable benefit recently myself . . ." (25). One of the lengthier accounts of paralysis agitans was published in the *Guy's Hospital Reports* in 1853. Four cases in individuals ranging in age from 34 to 60 years were briefly described. Each case was reported by a different author. Consistently noted were the gradual and asymmetric onset of this disorder, the subsequent involvement of both ipsilateral limbs, the progression to a more severe and generalized disorder, and the predominance, clinically, of resting tremor (27). The following passages are excerpted from this report:

A fair healthy looking man, by trade a hatter, states that in October, two years ago, the weather being cold at the time, he got very wet, and sat for a long time in a coffee room with his wet clothes upon him, and afterwards embarked on board a steam boat, remaining on deck all night. The next morning on disembarking, he could scarcely walk, his limbs feeling stiff and tired. After four days, his right hand began to tremble so much that he could not write, and gradually the whole arm became similarly affected. After eight months, his right leg began to feel heavy and tremble like the arm on the same side (27).

One of the other four cases was described as follows:

A 34-year-old man who was an engine driver of the one of the steam-tugboats on the river . . . dates his first symptoms from four years ago, when he began to have an aching pain in the left shoulder, soon following by trembling of the muscles, and in the course of a year extending down to the hand. The leg on the same side was similarly affected, and for nine months the disease was hemiplegic. During the last three months the other arm has begun to shake . . .' (27).

Finally, in 1855, Paget reported a man with a palsy of the third cranial nerve and a gait abnormality. The man, a 41-year-old brick maker, had been admitted to Addenbrooke's Hospital. Paget wrote that the patient's "tendency to fall is chiefly forwards; he has a tendency to lean forwards, and fall on his face. . . . Whenever he got out of bed, he likewise fell precipitately forward" (28, 29). Paget noted that the gait abnormality was progressive, writing as follows: "During the earlier part of the time, he could make two or three steps forward before falling; afterwards, the propensity to fall forwards showed itself before he could take a single step" (28). Interestingly, the pathology in this case was attributed to a lesion in the region of the midbrain: "The disease of the crura was the only peculiar and uncommon lesion of the brain, and is therefore naturally associated with the peculiar and unique symptom" (28). He further noted that the lesion "was deeply seated, occupying in both crura the position of the locus niger, and encroaching on the nervous fibrils around it" (28).

Those references that did not merely reiterate what Parkinson had written, consisted either of passing remarks or of brief comments without extensive clinical detail. When original cases were reported, these were isolated cases by single authors. Only one author of this period described having seen more than one case: Elliotson had seen "four or five cases" by 1833 (13).

Several references described cases that today we would classify as other neurologic disorders (30–35). In 1827 a case of "paralysis agitans" was described with unusual features, including the onset of tremor in a leg, which was described as "swollen, dark coloured, and painful" (30). The illness was also accompanied by "giddiness, with some pain in the head" (30). In the Lancet in 1831, Gowry described a case of "paralysis agitans intermittens" (31). The patient, a 26-year old woman "of sanguine temperament" (31), experienced convulsive paroxysms for a period of less than a week. The author wrote:

Involuntary tremor of upper and lower extremities, continuing for about five or six minutes, occurring twice or three times every hour, and attended with complete loss of power of limbs; muscles of lips re [sic] rapidly and spasmodically brought into contact during paroxysm, and tongue partially protruded, with a corresponding sound, and inability to articulate; orbicular muscles of eyelids, during some of the paroxysms, are similarly affected; paroxysm terminates in a heavy sigh. . . . During intermission is able to raise hands to head, but this is done slowly and with great consequent fatigue (31).

In this particular case, the term "paralysis agitans" was used descriptively to refer to the cessation of voluntary movement (paralysis) accompanied by chronic seizure activity (agitans). An anonymous report, dated 1832, described a case seen at St. Thomas's Hospital (32). The diagnosis was given as "paralysis agitans," although the clinical course was unusual. The report described a 54-year old "china-burner, of a spare habit" (32), who had been admitted to the hospital. He had experienced two episodes that were separated by an 18-month period. Each episode was of 6 weeks' duration, during which "the whole of his extremities were in a continual state of tremor; head and jaw also affected" (32). The patient made a "perfect" recovery each time. In 1839 a case of paralysis agitans was reported in the Lancet (33). From the description, it seems more probable that the patient, a 14-year-old girl "of apparently good constitution, though slender make" (33), had transiently experienced either epilepsia partialis continua, chorea, or ballism. The author wrote that the patient ". . . has a constant and violent involuntary motion or shaking of the right forearm, and slightly of the arm; the motion is so violent that it cannot be stopped, though held down. Was seized with the same complaint months ago, and got relief from some medicine taken inwardly" (33). She recovered almost fully from the reported episode after a brief period of 4 days, with the author writing that she was "almost quite well; only a very slight tremulous motion indeed, so slight as to be scarcely perceptible; has good motion of the arm, and thinks in a few days more shall be perfectly restored" (33). Green described tremor disorders in 3 children (34). Reynolds reported a case of a 57-year-old carpenter who had a tremor. However, the tremor seemed to be an action tremor rather than a tremor at rest: "any attempt to move the limb voluntarily at once reproduces the shaking" (35). With the use of galvanic stimulation, the tremor resolved to a great extent. In summary, both "paralysis" and shaking or "agitans" were noted to accompany neurologic disorders other than PD, and the term "paralysis agitans" was often loosely applied to these disorders. The problem was well summarized by Sanders in 1865:

> In regard to paralysis agitans, it is necessary to remark that this name is sometimes loosely and inaccurately applied . . . . It may be questioned, however, whether the term paralysis agitans ought to be confined to the senile form of it, associated with a propensity to fall or move forwards, described by Parkinson. I think, that it would be more useful to reserve for Parkinson's disease the specific name of paralysis agitans festinia, or senilis, or parkinsonii, and thus leave us free to extend the general name of paralysis agitans to other causes occurring at various ages, and not attended by the irresistible impulse to move forwards. Certainly there are many instances of true paralysis (especially spinal paralysis and paraplegia) which are accompanied by jerking and shaking movements without any tendency to move forward, and which require a designation that shall not confound them with Parkinson's disease (9).

It was clear to Parkinson and others that the motor system was one of the systems principally affected in paralysis agitans. The early view was that the paucity and slowness of movement were the result of weakness or paralysis, hence the name paralysis agitans seemed appropriate (1, 10, 24). Parkinson (1817) noted that patients with this disorder had "lessened muscular power" (1), and he further added that "the weakened powers of the muscles in the affected parts is so prominent a symptom, as to be very liable to mislead the inattentive, who may regard the disease a mere consequence of constitutional debility" (1). Similarly, Cooke (1820) wrote that "this disease begins with some degree of weakness" (10), and Hall (1841) wrote that "the first symptom of this *insidious* [his italics] disease is weakness and tremor" (24). However, several authors questioned whether paralysis was indeed present. In 1836 Watson wrote that "I refer to what has been badly called the *shaking palsy* [his italics] . . . badly . . . because there is in truth no paralysis at all" (16). In 1855 Reynolds wrote that "The term paralysis agitans is essentially bad, as paralysis does not necessarily exist in the condition referred to, and when present, as in some cases, is not primary. . . . The patient can do little with his affected limbs; but it is because of their constant agitation, not because of their paralysis" (15). However, a clear separation between signs of pyramidal dysfunction (weakness and spasticity) and extrapyramidal dysfunction (bradykinesia and rigidity) did not arise until the work of Charcot (see Chapter 3). In 1879, Charcot wrote:

"According to that author [Parkinson], decreased muscle strength always accompanies the disease, and it is probably true for a good number of cases. But this is far from being the rule. Many patients, including ours today, maintain, at least for a long time, good muscular strength" (4). In the 1880s Charcot (6) began to call to attention the presence of "slow movements" and "muscular rigidity" in his patients with paralysis agitans, distinguishing rigidity from weakness and bradykinesia:

> More commonly, muscular rigidity only comes on or predominates in the most advanced stage of paralysis agitans. Yet, long before rigidity actually develops, patients have significant difficulty performing ordinary activities; this problem relates to another cause. In some of the various patients I showed you can easily recognize how difficult it is for them to do things even though rigidity or tremor is not the limiting feature. Instead, even a cursory exam demonstrates that their problem relates more to slowness in execution of movement rather than to real weakness. . . .These phenomena have often been interpreted as weakness, but you may be assured that until late in the disease these patients are remarkably strong (6).

Although Parkinson noted that the intellect was "uninjured" in paralysis agitans (1), the prevalence of dementia in Parkinson's disease has been variably estimated to be on the order of 10% to 40% (36–40). During the 45-year period in question, clinicians sometimes made passing remarks about the cognitive compromise observed in later stages of this illness. For example, Reynolds wrote that "the intelligence is enfeebled" (15). However, it was not until after this period that physicians first began to emphasize the presence of cognitive impairment in some of their patients. In 1865, Sanders noted that in the final stages of the disease, "the memory and intellect are weakened" (9). In 1881, Buzzard wrote the following regarding the mental state of one of his patients, a 64-year-old man who had worked as an upholsterer's foreman and who had had paralysis agitans for 2 years: "As regards his mental state, in reply to inquiry he says that 'he feels lost.' He says 'he wants to give his address,' and gives 139 Bow Road, which is not altogether correct. He seems very obtuse, and scarcely speaks at all, though he is always apparently conscious" (41).

During this period there was little new knowledge or understanding of the precise location of the pathology in this disorder. In general, authors reiterated Parkinson's explanation that the pathology lay in the superior part of the medulla spinalis (1). However, as noted previously, in 1855 Paget reported a man with a palsy of the third cranial nerve and the "involuntary tendency to fall precipitately forwards" (28). On autopsy, a mass ". . . came close to the surface at the origin of the left oculo-motor nerve; but elsewhere it was deeply seated, occupying in both crura the position of the locus niger, and encroaching on the nervous fibrils around it" (28). Paget then wrote:

'But, assuming the immediate cause of the falling forward to have been due to the disease of the crura cerebri, we have still some little ambiguity. The structure of each crus is twofold; in its interior is the locus niger, the vesicular substance constituting a nervous centre. The exterior is composed of nervous fibrils, which form the medium of communication between the cerebral and other parts of the nervous system. . . . It may, then, the asked, whether the peculiar symptoms were due to the disease of the nervous centre or of the fibers of communication. . . . The locus niger is, with good reason, regarded as the nervous centre of the oculo-motor nerve; and this seems commonly held to be its function. We have no right to presume that its function is thus limited, although, looking to its moderate dimensions, we may incline to the opinion, that it cannot exercise a very considerable influence over the general movements of the body and so may be justified in concluding that the particular derangement of locomotion was rather caused by disease of the fibres whose function is to keep up a communication between the cerebrum and other parts of the nervous system (28).

For the time being, the central role of the substantia nigra in the pathogenesis of PD remained elusive. Later, in the 1870s and again in 1893, Benedikt, Blocq, and Marinesco reported cases of hemiparkinsonism in the setting of peduncular tuberculomas, and in 1893 Brissaud speculated that the substantia nigra might be the location of the disease process (42–44).

The primary aim of this analysis was to review the literature published in England. During this period, there were also several references to PD in both the German and the French literature. The most notable were those of Romberg (45, 46) and Trousseau (47). These are discussed elsewhere (48).

CONCLUSION

James Parkinson's work in 1817 on the shaking palsy (1) received little initial attention in his country, and before Charcot's work in this area, which began in the early 1860s (3–5), this disease was the subject of little scholarship (2, 3, 6). In the 45-year period between 1817 and 1861, there are a small number of references in the British literature to "shaking palsy." References either (a) merely reiterated word for word what had already been written by Parkinson or quoted directly from his text, (b) provided passing remarks about paralysis agitans, (c) provided relatively sparse clinical descriptions of newly reported cases, and (d) did not separate PD from other disease entities characterized by both "shaking" and "palsy" (e.g., tonic-clonic seizures and ballism). During this period, little new information was added to the original clinical observations made by Parkinson in 1817. The separation of extrapyramidal signs (bradykinesia) from pyramidal signs (weakness) did not become apparent until later work by the French neurologic community.

ACKNOWLEDGMENTS

This work was supported by Federal Grant NIH NS01863 and the Paul Beeson Physician Faculty Scholars in Aging Research Award.

References

1. Parkinson J. *An Essay on the Shaking Palsy.* London: Whittingham and Rowland, 1817.
2. Sanders WR. Paralysis agitans. In: Reynolds JR (ed). *System of Medicine.* Vol. 2. Philadelphia: Lippincott, 1868:184–204.
3. Charcot JM, Vulpian A. De la paralysie agitante. *Gaz Hebdomadaire Med Chirurg* 1861; 8:765–767, 816–820; 9:54–59.
4. Charcot JM. *Lectures on Diseases of the Nervous System.* Philadelphia: H. C. Lea, 1879.
5. Charcot JM. Paralysie agitante, tremblement senile, sclerose en plaque. *Gaz Hopit Paris* 1881; 54:98–100.
6. McHenry LC Jr. James Parkinson, surgeon and paleontologist. *J Okla Med Assoc* 1958; 51:521–523.
7. Reynolds JR. *A System of Medicine.* Philadelphia: Lippincott, 1868:184–204.
8. McMenemey WH. James Parkinson 1755–1824: A biographical essay. In: Critchley M (ed). *James Parkinson (1755–1824).* London: Macmillan, 1955:1–143.
9. Sanders WR. Case of an unusual form of nervous disease, dystaxia or pseudo-paralysis agitans, with remarks. *Edinburgh Med J* 1865; 10:987–997.
10. Cooke J. *A Treatise on Nervous Disease.* London: Longman, 1820:207.
11. Good JM. *The Study of Medicine, with a Physiological System of Nosology.* 2nd ed. Philadelphia: Bennett & Walton, 1824:297–300.
12. Good JM. *The Study of Medicine.* Vol IV. 3rd ed. London: Thomas and George Underwood, 1829:486–490.
13. Elliotson J. Lectures on the theory and practice of medicine. Diseases of the head and nervous system. *London Med Gaz* 1833; January 5:433–537.
14. Todd RB. Paralysis. In: Forbes J (ed). *Cyclopaedia of Practical Medicine.* Vol III. London: Sherwood, Gilbert and Piper, 1833:259–260.
15. Reynolds JR. *The Diagnosis of Diseases of the Brain, Spinal Cord, Nerves and Their Appendages.* London: John Churchill, 1855:163–164.
16. Watson T. *Lectures on the Principles and Practice of Physic Delivered at King's College, London.* Vol. I. 5th ed. Philadelphia: H. C. Lea, 1872:629–631. [A little-revised edition of lectures initially given in 1836–1837].
17. Elliotson J. On the medical properties of the subcarbonate of iron. *Medico-Chirurgic Trans* 1827; 13:232–353.
18. Elliotson J. On the use of subcarbonate of iron in tetanus. *Lancet* 1829:557–559.
19. Elliotson J. Clinical lecture on paralysis agitans. *Lancet* 1830:119–123.
20. Elliotson J. Clinical lecture. *Lancet* 1831; I:289–297.
21. Elliotson J. Clinical lecture. *Lancet* 1831:557.
22. Elliotson J. Clinical lecture. *Lancet* 1831:599.
23. Hall M. Lectures on the theory and practice of medicine. *Lancet* 1838:41.
24. Hall M. *On the Diseases and Derangements of the Nervous System.* London: H Baillière, 1841:320–321.
25. Thompson JB. "Chorea sancti viti," with cases and observations. *Lancet* 1842; I:616–618.
26. Graves RJ. *A System of Clinical Medicine.* Dublin: Fannin, 1843.
27. Birkett EL. Poland A. *Guy's Hospital Reports.* 2nd ser. London: John Churchill, 1853:134–136.
28. Paget GE. Case of involuntary tendency to fall precipitately forwards, with remarks. *Med Times Gaz* 1855; 10:178–180.

29. Reynolds JR. Dr Paget's case of disease in the crura cerebri. *Med Times Gaz* 1855; 10:218–219.

30. Case of paralysis agitans, or shaking palsy, treated with carbonate of iron. *Lancet* 1827:766–767.

31. Gowery TC. Case of paralysis agitans intermittens. *Lancet* 1831; II:651.

32. Hospital reports. St. Thomas's Hospital. Paralysis agitans. *London Med Surg J* 1832; 11:605–607.

33. Gibson M. On spinal irritation. *Lancet* 1839; II:567–571.

34. Green H. Cases of nervous tremor in children. *Prov Med J* 1844:178.

35. Reyonolds JR. Report of a case of paralysis agitans removed by continuous galvanic current. *Lancet* 1859; II:558–559.

36. Celesia GG. Wanamaker WM. Psychiatric disturbances in Parkinson's disease. *Dis Nerv Syst* 1972; 33:577–583.

37. Lieberman A, Dziatolowski M, Kupersmith M, et al. Dementia in Parkinson's disease. *Ann Neurol* 1979; 6:355–359.

38. Martilla RJ, Rinne UK. Dementia in Parkinson's disease. *Acta Neurol Scand* 1976; 54:431–441.

39. Mayeux R, Stern Y, Rosenstein R, et al. An estimate of the prevalence of dementia in idiopathic Parkinson's disease. *Arch Neurol* 1988; 45:260–263.

40. Mayeux R, Chen J, Mirabello E, et al. An estimate of the incidence of dementia in patients with idiopathic Parkinson's disease. *Neurology* 1990; 40:1513–1517.

41. Buzzard T. A clinical lecture on shaking palsy. *Brain* 1881; 4:473–492.

42. Benedikt M. Tremblement avec paralysie croisée du moteur oculaire commune. *Bull Méd* 1889; 3:547–548.

43. Marinesco G. Blocq P. Sur un cas de tremblement parkinsonien hémiplégique d'une tumeur du pédoncule cérébral. *Comp Rend Soc Biol* 1983; 5:105–111.

44. Brissaud E. In: Meige H (ed). *Leçons sur les maladies nerveuses*. Paris: Masson, 1895.

45. Romberg M. *Lehrbuch der Nervenkrankheiten des Menschen*. Berlin: A. Duncker, 1840–1846.

46. Romberg M. *A Manual of the Nervous Diseases of Man*. Vol II. London: New Sydenham Society, 1853.

47. Trousseau A. Tremblement senile et paralysie agitante. *Clinique Médicale de l'Hotel-Dieu de Paris*. Paris: H Baillière, 1861.

48. Tyler KL. A history of Parkinson's disease. In: Koller WC (ed). *Handbook of Parkinson's Disease*. New York: Marcel Dekker, 1987.

3 Charcot and Parkinson's Disease

Christopher G. Goetz

During their early years at the Salpêtrière in the 1860s, J.-M. Charcot and A. Vulpian collaborated so closely in the study of multiple sclerosis and Parkinson's disease (PD) that the exact contribution made by each cannot be determined (Figure 3-1). As early as 1861, they coauthored a three-part summary article in which they reviewed the past medical literature (primarily foreign), referred to a few reports by French colleagues, and added a case that they had observed themselves (1–3). Charcot recalled in 1868 that his well-documented first article still did not clarify the nature and characteristics of multiple sclerosis—an issue that he and Vulpian frequently faced in the large population of Salpêtrière invalids. "In all these descriptions, including our own, there was total confusion between paralysis agitans and multiple sclerosis" (4) (161F, 134E). The separation of PD from other neurologic entities was one of Charcot's major clinical contributions, and in facilitating the proper identification of the disease, these studies set the stage for the eventual anatomic link to midbrain lesions by Brissaud in 1895 (5) and nigral degeneration by Greenfield and Bosanquet in 1953 (6).

Jean-Martin Charcot's focused descriptions of PD, its clinical spectrum, and associated features were amplified throughout his career. His teaching sessions in the amphitheater of the Salpêtrière provided the needed medical and theatrical setting to compare various movement disorders from the vast patient material at Charcot's disposal. Charcot lectured specifically on PD, both in his formal Friday lectures and in his show-and-tell clinical case presentations, known as the "Tuesday lessons." The formal lectures were by and large read from detailed notes that were compiled by his assistant Bourneville into the multivolume complete works (*Oeuvres Complètes*) (4). The Tuesday lessons were impromptu teaching exercises and primarily aimed at showing diagnostic strategies through history-taking and clinical examination. These doctor-patient dialogues were hand-transcribed by his students, Blin, Colin, and Jean Charcot, the professor's son. These lessons were reproduced in lithograph form in limited edition and later edited (and often purged of interesting comments and reflections) for a more widely available printed version (7) (Figure 3-2).

TREMOROUS DISEASES

The origin of clinical confusion between multiple sclerosis and PD was the prominent shaking or tremor that occurred in both conditions. Charcot approached the problem of differential diagnosis by examining tremor as a clinical phenomenon. These studies stand among

FIGURE 3-1

Jean-Marie Charcot (left) and A. Vulpian (right) who worked together in the 1860s at the Salpêtrière hospital in Paris and wrote a series of seminal articles that help to separate PD from other tremorous conditions, most specifically multiple sclerosis.

Charcot's most perceptive clinical investigations and showed his ingenious methods of collecting clinical data with the tools available at the time. Although today tremors are best analyzed with special electronic detectors that are lightweight and sensitive to small amplitude changes in movement, Charcot adapted the available tools of the era to his advantage. His first studies were purely observational; he noted that sometimes tremor occurred when the patient moved the involved extremity, but that it was absent when the limb was completely relaxed and immobile. In contrast, other tremors persisted during rest and often occurred only at rest. Using an adaptation of the bulky apparatus called a sphygmograph, Charcot was able to record various tremors and demonstrate the difference in frequency and amplitude in various groups of patients (Figure 3-3). By comparing groups of patients, Charcot noted that those with rest tremor also had rigidity, balance difficulties, and slowness of movement (Figure 3-4). These features con-

stituted the cluster of signs that would be known as paralysis agitans or PD, a condition previously described by James Parkinson in 1817, but not completely studied until Charcot's seminal descriptions. In contrast, patients with predominant action tremor usually had distinctive multifocal sclerotic lesions of the central nervous system that had been termed *sclérose en taches ou en isles* by Cruveilhier (8). Charcot increasingly ascribed this type of tremor, especially when it clustered with signs of weakness, sensory abnormalities, visual problems, and nystagmus, to multiple sclerosis.

The lectures on comparative features of multiple sclerosis and PD were originally presented in 1868, 1869, and 1871. Thereafter they were repeated in modified form. For many of the studies, Charcot recruited his interns and externs, and the results formed the basis of many medical theses for graduating interns. With his familiar proviso, *"si je ne me trompe pas,"* he remarked on his student's work of 1868: "If I am not mistaken, the line of demarcation

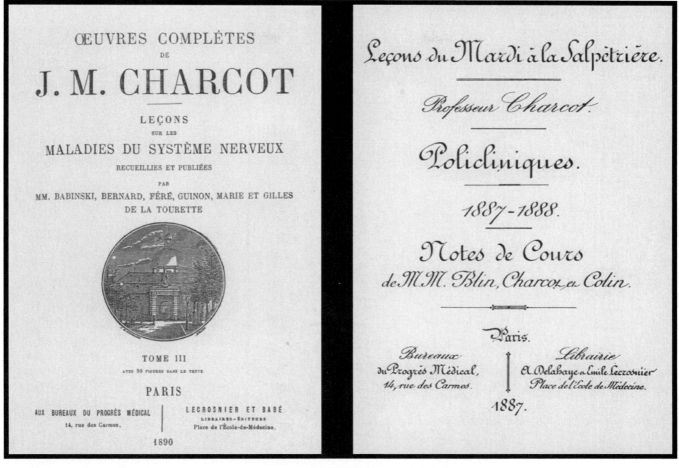

FIGURE 3-2

Charcot's main contributions on PD were coalesced in two series of teaching materials, the *Oeuvres Complètes* (*Complete Works*), based on his formal lectures (left), and his *Leçons du Mardi* (*Tuesday lessons*), which were hand transcriptions of his impromptu show-and-tell clinical presentations (right).

between these was determined by me for the first time in the thesis of Dr. Ordenstein" (4) (161F, 134E).

Parkinson's Disease

After a long and frustrating search, Charcot acquired a copy of Parkinson's *"An Essay on the Shaking Palsy"* (1817) through the help of an English librarian, Dr. Windsor (Figure 3-5). In 1887 there was still no French translation of this work. Speaking during one of in his impromptu Tuesday lessons, he said:

> It is a small pamphlet almost impossible to find . . . . As short as the work is, it contains a number of superb ideas, and I would encourage any one of you to embark on a French translation" (7, *Leçon 9*).'

He described the features identified by Parkinson, citing the strengths and weaknesses of the original description:

> "This is a descriptive and vivid definition that is correct for many cases, most in fact, and will always have the advantage over others of having been the first. But it errs by being too general and being inapplicable to the case where tremor is absent. We also do not find here a reference to the element of rigidity that gives to these patients their characteristic appearance. We could go back and improve on this definition as a starting point for more discussion, although we should not stop at Parkinson's definition. Read the entire book, and it will provide you with the satisfaction and knowledge that one always gleans from a direct clinical description made by an honest and careful observer (7).

Beginning with this essay, Charcot dissected the four cardinal features of PD, and from the definition of archtypal cases, he encouraged his students to define and classify clinical variants.

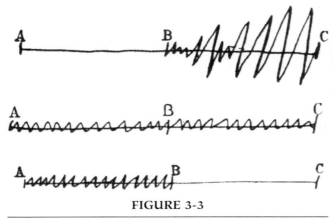

FIGURE 3-3

Tremor drawings from Charcot's lesson on tremor classification. AB indicates rest and BC represents action. Top: multiple sclerosis; middle and bottom, PD.

CHARCOT AND PARKINSON'S DISEASE

Tremor

On the basis of his early work with Vulpian, Charcot divided tremor by using the same features that modern neurologists employ—the frequency of the movements and the actions associated with the tremor's greatest intensity (1). Charcot placed the tremor of both PD and multiple sclerosis in his first category of slow tremors, that is, 4 to 6 oscillations. He differentiated the two by the observation that multiple sclerosis patients have no tremor at rest— and that their tremor becomes evident only with activity and that it increases with effort. In contrast, PD patients show tremor both at rest and during activity, and the intensity does not increase with action (see Figure 3-3). A third type of slow tremor, referred to by others as senile tremor, had the characteristics of Parkinsonian parkinsonian tremor, except that head titubation accompanied the tremorit.

Charcot was tenacious in his stand that PD patients had no head tremor and that any shaking of the head that they might show was entirely secondary to trunk or extremity tremor. This stand was contested by other contemporaries and became the source of heated discussion among clinicians in Paris (10). To prove this point, Charcot brought a series of patients to the amphitheater, each wearing a headband to which Charcot had attached a long thin rod with a feather at the end. Charcot instructed the audience to watch the wavering of the feathers from these many patients (Figure 3-6). As those affected with PD sat or stood, the feathers oscillated like those on the heads

FIGURE 3-4

Statue by Paul Richter, who worked at the Salpêtrière as an artist, physician, and sculptor. This patient shows the flexed posture and joint deformities of PD. The statue today is in the Musée de l'Assitance Publique, Paris.

of patients with other forms of tremor. But if the trunk or arm was suddenly supported or moved, the head tremor promptly ceased. With this famed feather study, Charcot convinced his colleagues that titubation was not an accompanying feature of PD and that any head shaking seen in such patients was mere overflow. However, Charcot clearly recognized jaw and tongue tremors as features of parkinsonism.

The observation that movement or support diminished parkinsonian tremor shows that Charcot realized the importance of movement in the control of parkinsonian tremor. Early in the disease, movement suspended tremor. Later, however, with disease progression, tremor became continual. Parkinsonian tremor was never exacerbated by the patient's movement.

To contrast with the slow forms of tremor, Charcot identified rapid or vibratory tremors, that is, 8 to 9 oscillations. In this group were tremors associated with

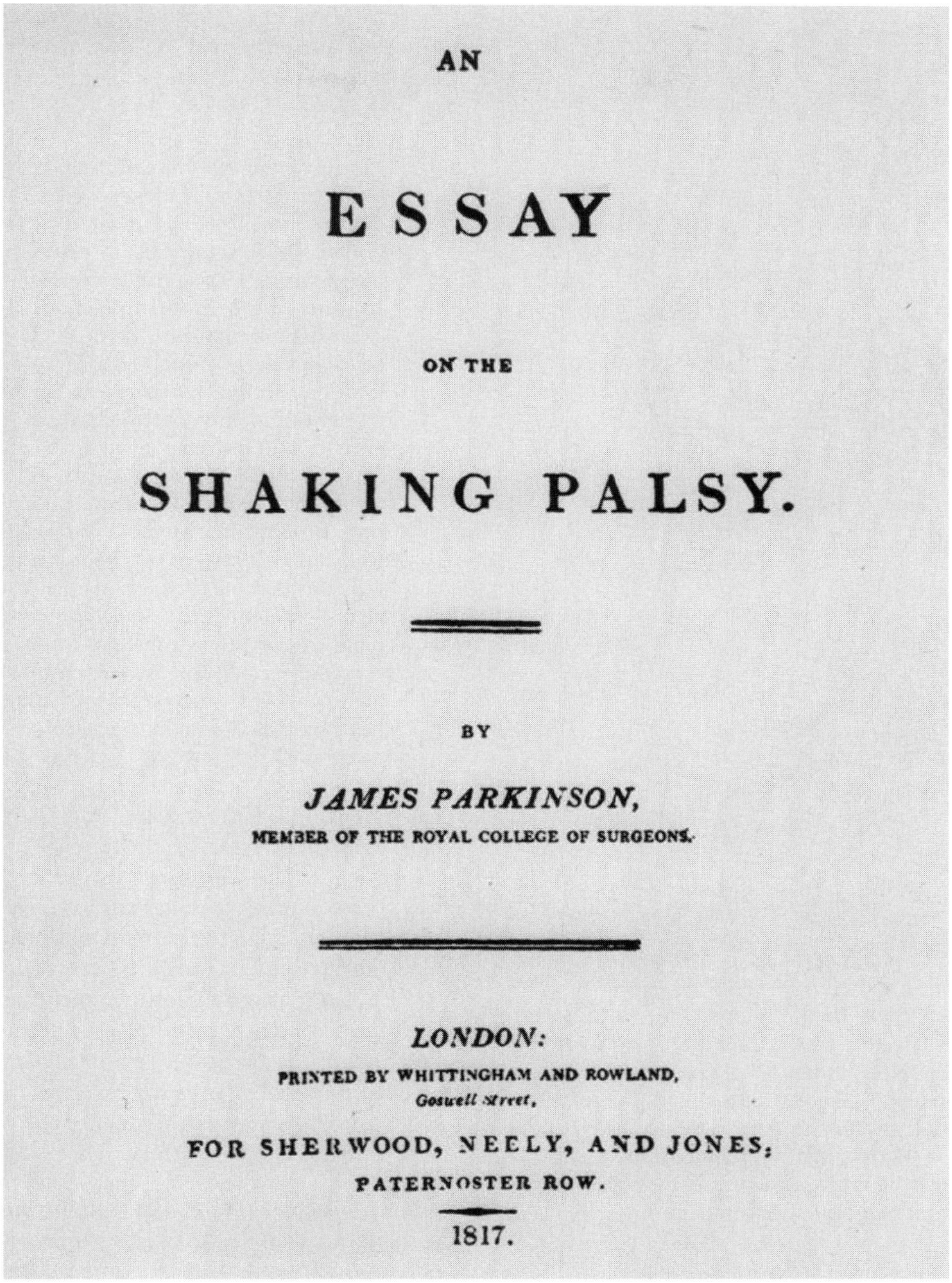

AN

ESSAY

ON THE

SHAKING PALSY.

———

BY

JAMES PARKINSON,
MEMBER OF THE ROYAL COLLEGE OF SURGEONS.

———

LONDON:
PRINTED BY WHITTINGHAM AND ROWLAND,
Goswell Street,

FOR SHERWOOD, NEELY, AND JONES;
PATERNOSTER ROW.

1817.

FIGURE 3-5

Essay on the Shaking Palsy by James Parkinson (1817) was the first medical monograph devoted to the description of PD. Charcot owned a copy of this rare booklet, but the copy at the Bibliothèque Charcot, Paris, has been lost.

alcoholism, Basedow's disease, and general paresis. In his final group of tremors with intermediate oscillatory frequency, he included mainly hysterical tremors and mercurialism. In addition to the frequency, particular characteristics typified the parkinsonian tremor. Charcot described a patient thus: "The parts of the hand oscillate in almost a pathognomonic manner. The fingers approach the thumb as if to spin wool, and simultaneously the wrist and forearm flex to and fro"" (7, *Leçon* 9).

Although Charcot recognized that tremor was a major manifestation of PD, he was insistent that it was

FIGURE 3-6

Drawings from the Salpêtrière of patients with various neurologic conditions. The top two figures are of note for this article: the top figure shows the hunched posture of a patient with PD; the second figure demonstrates Charcot's method of determining titubation and postural head tremor. The patient wore a band around the head with a feather attached to the top, and physicians observed the wavering of the feather when the head was unsupported and supported.

not required for the diagnosis. In this regard he considered the term *paralysis agitans* a misnomer. He recognized that most patients have both rigidity and tremor and divided variants of Parkinsonism parkinsonism into two major categories:– cases with tremor and no rigidity and those with rigidity and no tremor. In those patients without marked tremor, he observed that the posture was often less flexed, with the legs and back held in a stiff and even slightly extended attitude.

Bradykinesia. Although Charcot did not speak of akinesia specifically, he clearly recognized it as distinct

from rigidity in its clinical significance and often in its independent temporal development. Having spoken of the rare situation in which rigidity may be marked early in the disease, he wrote:

> "More commonly, muscular rigidity only comes on or predominates in the most advanced stage of paralysis agitans. Yet, long before rigidity actually develops, patients have significant difficulty performing ordinary activities; this problem relates to another cause. In some of the various patients I showed you, you can easily recognize how difficult it is for them to do things even though rigidity or tremor is not the limiting feature. Instead even a cursory exam demonstrates that their problem relates more to slowness in execution of movement rather than to real weakness. In spite of tremor, a patient is still able to do most things, but he performs them with remarkable slowness. I commented on this a few minutes ago in regard to speaking. Between the thought and the action there is a considerable time lapse. One would think neural activity can only be effected after remarkable effort; in reality, the execution of the slightest movement causes extreme fatigue for the patient. These phenomena have often been interpreted as weakness, but you may be assured that until late in the disease, these patients are remarkably strong" (7, *Leçon* 21).

Commenting on the masked facies or blank stare that is so characteristic of the parkinsonian patient, he continued: ". . . the muscles of the face are motionless, there is even a remarkable fixity of look, and the features present a permanent expression of mournfulness, sometimes of stolidness or stupidity" (4) (167F, 139E). On masked facies, he continued: "This particular facies was not originally appreciated. It is not in Parkinson's description. I believe I am the first to draw attention to its features that are so arresting and that in fact suffice to establish with ease the proper diagnosis" (4), (168F, 140E).

Stance, Posture, and Gait Abnormalities. Charcot considered drawings, photographs, and sculptures to be important medical documents and invested heavily in developing a medical iconography wing of the Salpêtrière service. Charcot himself was an avid sketcher and included his own drawings as part of regular patient notes (*observations*). Although technically crude and rapidly executed, they captured the stature, posture, and gait of PD in its natural evolution (Figure 3-7). Of Charcot's drawings, Henry Meige wrote: "The ability to discern in a country scene or in a human body certain essential contours, to perceive instantly a pattern and to be able to isolate from this pattern the elements necessary for its expression—— and to do it exactly in spite of all irrelevant details—this is the faculty that Charcot possessed to a high degree". "(11, p. 491)."

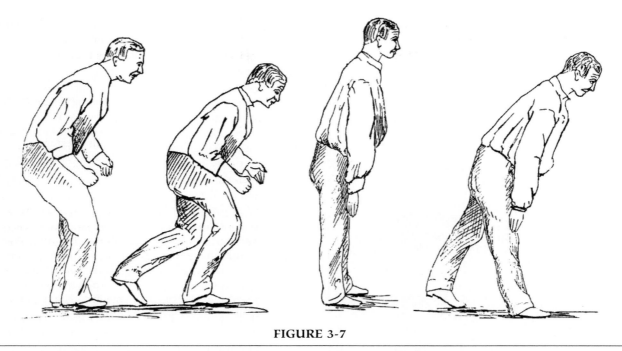

FIGURE 3-7

Drawings by Charcot contrasting the usual flexion posture of PD with one variant of PD with extended posture.

CHARCOT AND PARKINSON'S DISEASE

In Figure 3-8 Charcot captured the posture, facial expression, and hands of a parkinsonian Jewish merchant seen on one of his voyages to Morocco in 1889. With his junior colleagues he developed *La Nouvelle Iconographie de la Salpêtrière*, a journal that contained an extensive photographic and drawing pictorial collection of the neurologic patients at the Salpêtrière during and after Charcot's tenure until 1918.

Charcot described the slow and hesitant walking of the parkinsonian patients and the patient's tendency to retropulse and propulse. "In contrast, if you even tap the second patient, he will propulse forward and his gait will be quite unusual. His head bends forward, he takes a few steps and they become quicker and quicker to the point that he can even bump into the wall and hurt himself. If I pull on his trousers from behind, he will retropulse in the same distinctive way" (7, *Leçon* 21).

Charcot attempted to analyze propulsion and retropulsion and remained unsatisfied with available theories.

> "In this regard, I will make a comment on a rather widespread and respected physiologic explanation of propulsion in patients with paralysis agitans. I willingly agree that the tendency to make running steps relates to the thrust-forward posture, so that in walking, these patients will run after their center of gravity. Evidently, however, this explanation will not account for retropulsion, for the body's forward inclination does not change at all as the patient retropulses. In this case, he cannot be said to run after his center of gravity; in fact, he runs away from it" (7, *Leçon* 21).

Rigidity Parkinson himself did not speak of rigidity in his description. Charcot, however, identified this important sign and differentiated it from spasticity:

> "Spasticity, as you know, is of spinal origin and is more or less directly related to a physiologic or structural dysfunction of the descending spinal pyramidal tracts. What is the physiologic explanation for rigidity in Parkinson's disease? As far as I know, nothing is known and it is just this ignorance that I plan to demonstrate to you today. I have two goals, first to stimulate you to study the phenomenon of rigidity and second to impress on you the essential distinction between rigidity and pyramidal or spinal hypertonicity—, that is, the absence of reflex accentuation in rigidity" (7, *Leçon* 22).

The absence of pyramidal weakness in rigid parkinsonian patients was further emphasized by Charcot: "Sooner or later there is an apparent decrease in strength. Movement is slow and seemingly weak, although testing with a dynamometer shows that this is not really weakness. Such problems seem rather to relate, as we will see, to muscle rigidity" (7, *Leçon* 22).

Etiology and Natural Progression

Charcot classified PD as a *névrose*, a term used to designate neurologic conditions, where no identifiable neuroanatomic lesions were present. Although the onset

FIGURE 3-8

A Moroccan patient afflicted with PD, drawn by Charcot in 1889 while he was on a voyage. As Charcot said to his students, "I have seen such patients everywhere, in Rome, Amsterdam, Spain. They reflect always the same picture. They can be identified from afar. You do not need a medical history" (9, Leçon 21).

was usually insidious, he believed that two precipitating influences could be identified—prolonged exposure to a damp, cold environment, especially a dark first-floor dwelling with poor air ventilation, and a sudden exposure to an intensely emotional crisis. In the case report by Romberg of a patient whose tremor began after he was robbed by Cossacks and left in the snow, the two influences could not be easily separated. The disease affected patients in their forties and fifties and was distinctly not a disease that regularly began in the eldely population. Charcot thought that tremor could cease during the final phase

of illness, even when it had previously been the most prominent feature of the disease in the past (4).

Charcot recognized that most cases of PD had a relentlessly progressive course and that patients became increasingly disabled over time. Because almost all patients at the Salpêtrière were lifelong residents, he had the opportunity to chart their course. He engaged professional artists, like Paul Richer, to document the progressive impairments, and included such documents as part of the patients' medical records (Figure 3-9). In constrast to this usual pattern, however, Charcot also believed that PD could resolve and be cured in certain cases. wever, He doubted however that such cases related in any way to the various pharmacologic therapies used. He cited several reports of patients who were followed by reputable physicians and whose parkinsonism disappeared. Whether there were toxic, encephalitic, or drug-induced forms of reversible parkinsonism in the nineteenth century is not known. After citing the reports of cures coincident with therapy, he wrote: "These citations show that the shaking palsy is not incurable, but we must recognize that we know nothing about nature's role in such cases of reversible disability" (7, Leçon 9).

Treatment

"He disdained therapeutic interventions, considering the irregularities of the human body as an astronomer would watch the movements of the stars." (12). These words were written by the writer Léon Daudet, who had known Charcot in several capacities, as the playmate and boyhood friend of Charcot's son, as a medical student under Charcot's watchful eye, and as the son of Charcot's patient, novelist Alphonse Daudet, who suffered from neurosyphilis. The description evokes an image of a scientific purist and a distant, objective, even emotionally cold researcher, an image reinforced by Charcot's silent manner and stern physical bearing. In spite of their dramatic flair, however, Daudet's words must be reviewed with circumspection, for throughout the height of his career Charcot was not only a world-renowned scientific researcher but also a prominent and highly sought -after practicing physician. As a clinician, Charcot developed aspects of the modern neurologic examination, introduced diagnostic tools and strategies, and treated numerous neurologic conditions, including PD, with traditional, and innovative, even controversial, therapies. Although Daudet suggests that Charcot was a therapeutic nihilist, Charcot's lectures, articles, and personal correspondence with patients demonstrated an active interest in therapeutic interventions.

Charcot's attentiveness to treatment, follow-up, and surveillance is evident in a series of 18 unpublished letters located in the archive collection of the Bibliothéque Charcot, Paris (portfolio MA VIII, Parkinson's disease),

FIGURE 3-9

Portrait of a patient on the Charcot neurological service at the Salpêtrière, drawn by the medical artist Paul Richer, showing the progressive impairment over time. The picture captures the posture and arthritic changes of untreated PD.

which concerns a patient with PD. These unnumbered documents, not all dated, cover a period of at least 15 months, from January 1863 through March 1864, and are kept in an envelope with the patient's name and the diagnosis "paralysis agitans" written in Charcot's large script. As a group, these letters reveal how the doctor—patient relationship arose and evolved, as well as the attentiveness offered to the patient by Charcot. Charcot's letters of reply to the patient were based on the patient's and his family's assessment of response to treatment. Charcot adopted this system as an efficient form of organization for dealing with outpatients, as shown in an undated letter from the series attached with the prescription: "I would be most obliged, Monsieur, if you would remind me of this prescription the next time you write."

In the first letter, dated January 19, 1863, the patient reminded Charcot that he was originally referred by Brown-Séquard and that Charcot had seen him two months earlier. Charcot had prescribed rest and camphor

therapy, which the patient followed, but without respite. Thereafter Charcot embarked on several therapies, and each time he modified his recommendation based on the detailed reports of symptoms and changes. The treatments included hyoscyamine, a centrally active anticholinergic drug that is among the class of agents currently used to treat PD, and ergot products, which are the basis of some modern dopamine agonist drugs. He also used silver nitrate, iron compounds, henbane, pills, and zinc oxide. Charcot was highly specific in his instructions, indicating that quinquina should be diluted with syrup made from orange rind and that pills be made of 0.5 centigrams of silver nitrate impregnated in 9 grams of soft bread to render 100 pills for ingestion.

The documents are particularly revealing of the tone of the doctor—patient relationship. The traditional image, derived from the Tuesday lessons of nearly 25 years later, is Charcot's speaking to the patient, often iimperiously, about his or her symptoms and the patient's generally

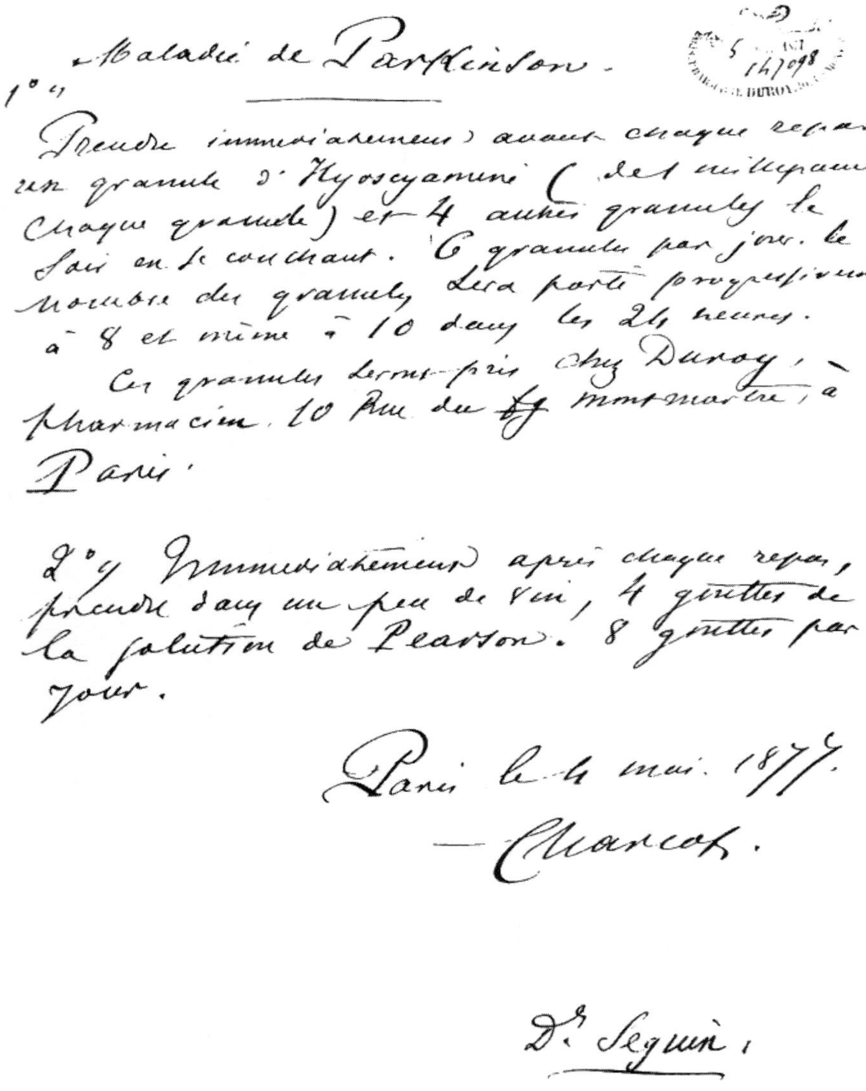

Maladie de Parkinson.

1° Prendre immédiatement avant chaque repas un granule d'Hyoscyamine (de 1 milligramme chaque granule) et 4 autres granules le soir en se couchant. 6 granules par jour. Le nombre des granules sera porté progressivement à 8 et même à 10 dans les 24 heures.

Ces granules seront pris chez Duroy, pharmacien. 10 Rue du Fg Montmartre, à Paris.

2° Immédiatement après chaque repas, prendre dans un peu de vin, 4 gouttes de la solution de Pearson. 8 gouttes par jour.

Paris le 4 mai. 1877.

— Charcot.

Dr Seguin.

FIGURE 3-10

Prescription written by Charcot for a patient with PD. *Translation:* 1. Take immediately before each meal, one granule of hyoscyamine (at one milligram per granule) and four additional granules of the same dose at night before retiring. Start with six pills daily and progressively increase to eight and then ten pills daily. These pills may be bought at the Duroy Pharmacy, 10 rue de Faubourg Montmartre in Paris. 2. Immediately following each meal, take in a small glass of wine, 4 drops of Pearson solution, that is 8 drops each day. Paris, May 4, 1877. Charcot.

accepting his recommendations without comment. These earlier letters document instead a lively interchange between doctor and patient, with the patient assertively evaluating Charcot's treatments and, with some audacity, even recommending that he consider others. When the patient was helped, he openly acknowledged Charcot's contribution, but when he was not, he wrote back promptly asking for better treatments. The tone of Charcot's replies is not known, as his letters are not included, but the dates of the letters demonstrate that he answered the letters quickly and kept them together as a medical dossier. A copy of a prescription written by Charcot for a patient with PD is shown in Figure 3-10.

CHARCOT AND PARKINSON'S DISEASE

Summarizing his views of the state of therapy for PD in the 1870s, he stated: "Everything, or almost everything, has been tried against this disease. Among the medicinal substances that have been extolled, and which I have myself administered to no avail, I need only enumerate a few." (4).

Charcot's Students and the Salpêtrière

Although in the 1880s Charcot's research focus moved increasingly toward the study of hysteria in the 1880s, he maintained a keen interest in PD throughout his career. Several of his students wrote their medical theses on PD and its variants. After Charcot died, the Salpêtrière remained a focus of PD study, and E. Brissaud, who temporarily assumed Charcot's professorial chair in neurology, reported cystic brain stem lesions in the midbrain of PD patients in 1895. Several articles on parkinsonian variants were published in the *Nouvelle Iconographie de la Salpêtrière* and other journals that Charcot had established. These reports remain important medical documents on parkinsonian syndromes and their natural evolution and progression, especially because of the accompanying photographs from the Salpêtrière.

References

1. Charcot J-M, Vulpian A. *La paralysie agitante. Gaz Hebdom Med Chir* 1861; 765–768, 816–823; 1862; 54–64.
2. Charcot J-M, Vulpian A. *Sur deux cas de sclérose des cordons postérieurs de la moelle avec atrophie des racines postérieurs (tabes dorsalis, Romberg; ataxie locomotrice progressive, Duchenne de Boulogne). Comptes-Rendus des Séances et Mémoires de la Société de Biologie* 1862; 4:155–163.
3. Charcot J-M, Vulpian A. *Sur un cas d'atrophie des cordons postérieurs de la moelle épinière et des racines postérieures (ataxie locomotrice progressive). Gaz Hebdom Med Chir* 1862; 9:247–254, 277–283.
4. Charcot J-M. *Oeuvres Complétes.* Vol 1 (*Leçon 5*). Paris: Bureaux du Progrès Médical, 1872. In English: Charcot JM. *The Diseases of the Nervous System Delivered at the Salpêtrière.* (Translator, G. Sigerson.) London: New Sydenham Society, 1877.
5. Brissaud E. *Leçons sur les maladies nerveuses.* Paris: Masson, 1895.
6. Greenfield JG, Bosanquet FD. The brain stem lesions in parkinsonism. *J Neurol Neurosurg Psychiatry* 1953; 16:213–226.
7. Charcot J-M. *Leçons du Mardi à la Salpêtrière 1887–1888.* Paris: Bureaux du Progrès Médical, 1887.
8. Cruveilhier J *L'anatomie pathologique du corps humain.* Paris: Baillière, (1829–1842)
9. Parkinson J. *An Essay on the Shaking Palsy.* London: Whittingham and Rowland for Sherwood, Neeley, and Jones, 1817.
10. Charcot J-M. *Paralysie agitante, tremblement sénile, sclérose en plaque. Gaz Hopit Paris* 1881; 54:98–100.
11. Meige H. *Charcot artiste. Nouvelle iconographie de la Salpêtrière* 1898; 11:489–516.
12. Daudet L. *Devant la douleur.* Paris: Nouvelle Librairie Nationale, 1944.

4 Timeline of Parkinson's Disease History Since 1900

William J. Weiner
Stewart A. Factor

1911
- First synthesis of D/L dopa (1)

1912–1913
- Description of intracytoplasmic eosinophilic inclusions (later referred to as Lewy bodies) in dorsal motor nucleus of vagus and substantia innomita; the substantia nigra was considered unaffected in the original report (2–3)

1913
- Levodopa isolated from broad bean plants at Roche and a simplified manufacturing process described (4)

1917–1926
- First diagnosis of encephalitis lethargica—secondary parkinsonism (5, 6)

1919
- Constancy of nigral lesions in PD noted (7)

1929
- Use of large doses of atropine for PD initiated (8)

1940
- First neurosurgical approach to the basal ganglia for treatment of postencephalitic tremor attempted (9)

1947
- First stereotactic pallidotomy (10)

1950s
- Introduction of synthetic anticholinergics (11)

1951
- Discovery of dopamine ("encephalin") in the brain and the determination that only levodopa could increase its concentration in the central nervous system (12)
- First use of apomorphine in PD (13)

1952–1953
- Substantia nigral lesions essential and the occurrence of Lewy bodies required as definite criteria in neurological definition of PD (14, 15)

1955
- Introduction of ventrolateral (VL) thalamotomy for tremor (16)

1957
- Catechol compounds demonstrated in brains of a variety of animals (17)
- "Reserpine demonstrated to reduce brain dopamine and cause bradykinesia in rabbits; both reversed with levodopa (18)."

1958–1959
- Dopamine demonstrated to be highly concentrated in the caudate/putamen (19, 20)

1959

- Catechol compounds including dopamine demonstrated in human brain (21)

1960

- Description of Shy-Drager syndrome (22)
- Dopamine found to be decreased in the corpus striatum of brain from patients with PD (23)

1961–1962

- First reported successful trials of intravenous and oral low-dose levodopa (24, 25)

1964

- Description of striatonigral degeneration (26)
- Description of progressive supranuclear palsy (PSP) (27)

1964–1965

- Histofluorescence techniques demonstrate that dopamine is concentrated in substantia nigral neurons; existence of nigrostriatal dopaminergic pathway discovered (28, 29)

1967

- First successful oral use of high-dose D/L dopa (30)

1968

- Description of corticobasal degeneration (31)
- First successful use of oral high-dose levodopa (32)
- Multiple system atrophy (MSA)—unifying concept for olivopontocerebellar atrophy (OPCA), striatonigral degeneration, and Shy-Drager syndrome (33)
- Laradopa (levodopa) approved by the FDA for use in PD and distributed worldwide (34)

1969

- First successful use of amantadine (35)

1973

- Introduction of dopa decarboxylase inhibitors: FDA approves carbidopa/levodopa (Sinemet) (36)
- Concept of dopamine agonists introduced (37)

1974

- Identification of dopamine receptors (38)
- First clinical use of bromocriptine, the first oral dopamine agonist (39)

1975

- Introduction of benserizide-levodopa (Madopar) (34)
- First clinical use of L-deprenyl, the first MAO-B inhibitor (34)

1978

- Bromocriptine approved by the FDA for use in PD

1979

- MPTP (1-methyl 4-phenyl 1, 2, 3, 6-tetrahydropyridine)-induced parkinsonism first reported, although it is not recognized (40)
- Dopamine receptors found to exist as subtypes (41)

1983

- MPTP-induced parkinsonism recognized and more fully described (42)

1985

- First use of the atypical antipsychotic clozapine for psychosis in PD (43)

1986

- Parkinson Study Group (PSG) formed

1989

- Thalamic deep brain stimulation (DBS) first used for treatment of tremor (44)
- FDA approves pergolide for use in advanced PD
- FDA approves selegiline for use in advanced PD
- First report of the DATATOP (Deprenyl and Tocopheral Antioxidant Therapy of Parkinsonism) study—a controversial study with several firsts: first PSG trial, first neuroprotective trial, first use of need for dopaminergic therapy as an endpoint (45)

1990

- Contursi kindred described—large autosomal dominant kindred (46)
- First description of diffuse Lewy body disease (47–50)
- Model of basal ganglia circuitry introduced, providing an explanation for the effect of surgical therapy in PD (51–53)

1991

- FDA approves Sinemet CR for use in PD

1992

- Reintroduction of pallidotomy in PD (54)

1993

- Apomorphine approved for use in PD in the United Kingdom

1995

- DBS of the subthalamic nucleus first used for treatment of PD (55)

1997

- FDA approves thalamic DBS to treat parkinsonian tremor
- The new generation of dopamine agonists pramipexole and ropinirole are approved for use in the United States
- Amantadine found to improve dyskinesia (56)
- The first mutation of Park1, alpha-synuclein gene, is identified in Contursi and other kindreds with PD (57)
- The first mutation of Park2, also known as parkin, causing juvenile autosomal recessive parkinsonism, is identified (58)
- Lewy bodies found to stain for alpha-synuclein (59)

1998

- Tolcapone is approved by the FDA for use in stable and fluctuating PD

1999

- Entacapone is approved by the FDA for use in advanced PD
- UCH-L1 (Park5) gene mutation discovered in a sib pair with PD (60)
- First double-blind placebo-controlled trial demonstrating the efficacy of clozapine in the treatment of psychosis in PD (61)

2000

- Rotenone animal model for PD is developed (62)

2001

- The first mutation of Park6, in the PINK1 (PTEN-induced putative kinase-1) gene, causing an autosomal recessive form of parkinsonism, is discovered (63)
- A double-blind, sham surgery–controlled study of fetal transplantation in PD demonstrates lack of efficacy and the development of runaway dyskinesias (64)

2002

- DBS Surgery of the subthalamic nucleus (STN) is approved by the FDA for treatment of fluctuating PD patients
- Proteosomal inhibitors are used to develop an animal model of PD (65)

2003

- The first mutation of Park7 in the DJ1 gene, causing an autosomal recessive form of parkinsonism, is discovered (66)
- Braak and Braak present a schema for ascending progression of Lewy body pathology in PD (67)

2004

- Subcutaneous administration of apomorphine is approved by the FDA as rescue therapy for "off" times in PD (68)
- The first Park8 mutation in the LRRK2 (leucine-rich repeat kinase 2) gene—causing an autosomal dominant form of PD and the only hereditary form of parkinsonism found in typical sporadic late-onset disease—is discovered (69, 70)
- ELLDOPA trial results are reported, producing clinical data suggesting that levodopa might be protective, while imaging data suggest the opposite (71)

2005

- Preliminary results of a pilot trial for the first gene therapy in PD, viral vector delivery of the GAD gene into the STN, is reported (72)

2006

- Rasagiline (an MAO-B inhibitor) is approved by the FDA for use in early and advanced PD (73, 74)
- Orally disintegrating (Zydis) selegiline (an MAO B inhibitor) is approved by the FDA for use in advanced PD (75)
- The results of the first large-scale double-blind, placebo-controlled trial examining an antiapoptotic drug (Cep 1347) as a potential neuroprotective agent in PD are reported, showing the drug's failure (76)
- Intraputamenal infusion of GDNF (glial cell line–derived neurotrophic factor) fails to modify PD in a randomized, placebo-controlled trial (77)

2007

- Rotigotine dopamine agonist patch is approved by the FDA for use in early and advanced PD (78)
- Pergolide is removed from the U.S. market due to cardiac valvulopathy (79)

References

1. Funk C. Synthese des d, 1-3-4, Dioxyphenylalanins. *Chem Zentralbl I*, 1911.
2. Lewy FH. Paralysis agitans. I. Pathologische anatomie. In: Lewandowsky M (ed). *Handbuch der Neurologie*. Berlin: Springer, 1912:920–933.
3. Lewy FH. Zur pathologischen Anatomie der Paralysis agitans. *Dtsch Z Nervenheilk* 1913; 50:50–55.
4. Guggenheim M. Dioxyphenylanin, eine neue Aminosaure aus Vicia faba. *Z Physiol Chem* 1913; 88:276–284.
5. Duvoisin RC, Yahr MD. Encephalitis and parkinsonism. *Arch Neurol* 1965; 12:227–239.
6. Von Economo C. Encephalitis lethargica. *Wien Klin Wochenschr* 1917; 30:581–585.
7. Tretiakoff C. Contribution a l'etude de l'anatomie pathologic du locus niger de soemmering avec quelques deductions relative a la pathogenie des troubles du tunos musculaire et de la maladie de Parkinson. Theses pour le doctorat en Medicine. Paris: These de Paris, 1919:1–24.
8. Kleemann. Zitiert nach Kapp W, Leickert KH. Das Parkinson-Syndrom. Stuttgart: Schattauer, 1971.
9. Meyers R. Surgical procedure for postencephalitic tremor, with notes on the physiology of the premotor fibres. *Arch Neurol Psychiatry* 1949; 44:455–459.
10. Spiegel EE, Wycis HT, Marks M, et al. Stereotaxic apparatus for operations on the human brain. *Science* 1947; 106:349–350.
11. Fahn S. The history of parkinsonism. *Mov Disord* 1989; 4(Suppl 1): S2–S10.
12. Raab W, Gigee W. Concentration and distribution of "encephalin" in the brain of humans and animals. *Proc Soc Exp Biol Med* 1951; 180:1200.
13. Schwab RS, Amador LV, Lettvin JY. Apomorphine in Parkinson's disease. *Trans Am Neurol Assoc* 1951; 76:251–253.
14. Beheim-Schwarzbach D. Uber-zelleib-veranderungen in nucleus coeruleus bei Parkinson symptomen. *J Nerv Ment Dis* 1952; 116:619–632.
15. Greenfield JG, Bosanquet FD. The brain-stem lesions in parkinsonism. *J Neurol Neurosurg Psychiatry* 1953; 16:213–226.
16. Hassler R. The pathological and pathophysiological basis of tremor and parkinsonism. *Second International Congress on Neuropathology*. Amsterdam: Excerpta Medical Foundation, 1955:2940.
17. Montagu KA. Catechol compounds in rat disease and in brains of different animals. *Nature* 1957; 180:244–245.
18. Carlsson A, Lindquist M, Magnusson T. 3,4-dihy-droxyphenylalaninen and 5-hydroxytryptophan as reserpine antagonists. *Nature* 1957; 180:200.
19. Carlsson A, Lindquist M, Magnusson T, et al. On the presence of 3 hydroxytyramine in brain. *Science* 1958; 127:471–472.
20. Bertler A, Rosengren E. Occurrence and distribution of catecholamines in brain. *Acta Physiol Scand* 1959; 47:350–361.
21. Sano I, Gamo T, Kakimoto Y, et al. Distribution of catechol compounds in human brain. *Biochem Biophys Acta* 1959; 32:586–587.
22. Shy GM, Drager GA. A neurological syndrome associated with orthostatic hypotension. *Arch Neurol* 1960; 2:511–527.
23. Ehringer H, Hornykiewicz O. Verteilung von Noradrenalin und Dopamin (3-hydroxytyramin) im Gerhirn des Menschens und ihr Verhalten bei Erkrankugen des extrapyramidalen Systems. *Klin Wochenschr* 1960; 38:1236–1239.
24. Birkmayer W, Hornykiewicz O. Der 1-3,4 Dioxyphenylalanin (D dopa)-Effekt bei der Parkinson-Akinese. *Wien Klin Wochenschr* 1961; 73:787–788.

25. Barbeau A, Sourkes TL, Murphy CF. Les catecholamines dans la maladie de Parkinson, In J de Ajuriaguerra (ed). *Monoamines et Systeme Nerveaux Central*. Geneva: Georg, & Cie SA 1962; 247–262.

26. Adams RD, Van Bogaert L, Van der Eecken H. Striatonigral degeneration. *J Neuropath Exp Neurol* 1964; 23:584–608.

27. Steele JC, Richardson JC, Olszewski J. Progressive supranuclear palsy. *Arch Neurol* 1964; 10:333–359.

28. Anden NE, Carlsson A, Dahlstrom A, et al. Demonstration and mapping of nigroneostriatal dopamine neurons. *Life Sci* 1964; 3:523–530.

29. Poirier LJ, Sourkes TL. Influence of the substantia nigra on the catecholamine content of the striatum. *Brain* 1965; 88:181–192.

30. Cotzias GC, Van Woert MH, Schiffer LM. Aromatic amino acids and modifications of parkinsonism. *N Engl J Med* 1967; 276:374–379.

31. Rebeiz JJ, Kolodny EH, Richardson EP. Corticodentatonigral degeneration with neuronal achromasia. *Arch Neurol* 1968; 18:20–33.

32. Cotzias GC, Papavasiliou PS, Gellene R. Modification of parkinsonism: Chronic treatment with L-dopa. *N Engl J Med* 1969; 280:337–345.

33. Graham JG, Oppenheimer DR. Orthostatic hypotension and nicotine sensitivity in a case of multiple-system atrophy. *J Neurol Neurosurg Psychiatry* 1969; 32:28–34.

34. Kapp W. The history of drugs for the treatment of Parkinson's disease. *J Neural Transm* 1992; 38:1–6.

35. Schwab RS, England AC, Poskanzer DC, Young RR. Amantadine in the treatment of Parkinson's disease. *JAMA* 1969; 208:1168–1170.

36. Rinne UK, Sonninen V, Siirtola T. Treatment of parkinsonism patients with levodopa and extracerebral decarboxylase inhibitor, Ro 4-4062. *Adv Neurol* 1973; 3:59–71.

37. Corrodi H, Fuxe K, Hokfelt T, et al. Effect of ergot drugs on central catecholamine neurons. Evidence for a stimulation of central dopamine neurons. *J Pharm Pharmacol* 1973; 25:409.

38. Seeman P. Brain dopamine receptors. *Pharmacol Rev* 1980; 32:229–313.

39. Calne DB, Teychenne PF, Claveria LE, et al. Bromocriptine in parkinsonism. *Br Med J* 1974; 4:442–444.

40. Davis GC, Williams AC, Markey SP, et al. Chronic parkinsonism secondary to intravenous injection of meperidine analogs. *Psychiatr Res* 1979; 1:249–254.

41. Kebabian JK, Calne DB. Multiple receptors for dopamine. *Nature* 1979; 277:92–96.

42. Langston JW, Ballard P, Tetrud JW, et al. Chronic parkinsonism in humans due to a product or merperidine-analog synthesis. *Science* 1983; 219:979–980.

43. Scholz E, Dichgans J. Treatment of drug-induced exogenous psychosis in parkinsonism with clozapine and fluperlapine. *Eur Arch Psychiatr Neurol Sci* 1985; 235:60–64.

44. Benabid AL, Pollak P, Hommel M, et al. Treatment of Parkinson tremor by chronic stimulation of the ventral intermediate nucleus of the thalamus. *Rev Neurol (Paris)* 1989; 145:320–323.

45. The Parkinson Study Group. Effect of deprenyl on the progression of disability in early Parkinson's disease. *N Engl J Med* 1989;321:1364–1371.

46. Golbe LI, Di Iorio G, Bonavita V, et al. A large kindred with autosomal dominant Parkinson's disease. *Ann Neurol* 1990; 27:276–282.

47. McKeith IG, Galasko D, Kosaka K, et al. Consensus guidelines for the clinical and pathological diagnosis of dementia with Lewy bodies. (DLB): Report of the Consortium on DLB International Workshop. *Neurology* 1996; 47:1113–1124.

48. Kosaka K. Diffuse Lewy body disease in Japan. *J Neurol* 1990;237:197–204.

49. Dickson DW, Ruan D, Crystal H, et al. Hippocampal degeneration differentiates diffuse Lewy body disease (DLBD) from Alzheimer's disease: Light and electron microscopic immunocytochemistry of CA2-3 neurites specific to Lewy body disease. *Neurology* 1991; 41:1402–1409.

50. Hansen LA, Masliah E, Terry RD, Mirra SS. A neuropathological subset of Alzheimer's disease with concomitant Lewy body disease and spongiform change. *Acta Neuropathol* 1989; 78:194–201.

51. DeLong MR. Primate models of movement disorders of basal ganglia origin. *Trends Neurosci* 1990;13:281–285.

52. Albin RL, Young AB, Penney JB, The functional anatomy of basal ganglia disorders. *Trends Neurosci* 1989; 12:366–375.

53. Crossman, AR. Neural mechanisms in disorders of movement. *Comp Biochem Physiol A* 1989; 93:141–149.

54. Latinen LV, Bergenheim AT, Hariz MI. Ventroposterolateral pallidotomy can abolish all parkinsonian symptoms. *Stereotact Funct Neurosurg* 1992; 58:14–21.

55. Limousin O, Pollack P, Benazzouz A, et al. Effect on parkinsonian signs and symptoms of bilateral subthalamic nucleus stimulation. *Lancet* 1995; 345:91–95.

56. Rajput AH, Uitti RJ, Lang AE, et al. Amantadine ameliorates levodopa-induced dyskinesia. *Neurology* 1997; 48:A328.

57. Polymeropoulos MH, Lavedan C, Leroy E, et al. Mutation of α-synuclein identified in families with Parkinson's disease. *Science* 1997; 276:2045–2047.

58. Matsumine H, Saito M, Shimoda-Matsubayashi S, et al. Localization of a gene for an autosomal recessive form of juvenile parkinsonism to chromosome 6q25.2-27. *Am J Hum Genet* 1997; 60:588–596.

59. Spillantini MG, Schmidt ML, Lee VM, et al. Alpha-synuclein in Lewy bodies. *Nature* 1997; 388:839–840.

60. Lincoln S, Vaughhn J, Wood, N. Low frequency of pathogenic mutations in the ubiquitin carboxy-terminal hydrolase gene in familial Parkinson's disease. *Neuroreport* 1999; 10:427–429.

61. Parkinson Study group. Low dose clozapine for the treatment of drug-induced psychosis in Parkinson's disease. *N Engl J Med* 1999; 340:757–763.

62. Betarbet R, Sherer TB, Mackenzie G, et al. Chronic systemic pesticide exposure reproduces features of Parkinson's disease. *Nat Neurosci* 2000; 3:1301–1306.

63. Valente EM, Abou-Sleiman PM, Caputo V, et al. Hereditary early-onset Parkinson's disease caused by mutations in PINK1. *Science* 2004; 304:1158–1160.

64. Freed CR, Greene PE, Breeze RE, et al. Transplantation of embryonic dopamine neurons for severe Parkinson's disease. *N Engl J Med* 2000; 344:710–719.

65. McNaught KS, Bjorklund LM, Belizaire R, et al. Proteasome inhibition causes nigral degeneration with inclusion bodies in rats. *Neuroreport* 2002; 13:1437–1441.

66. Bonifati V, Rizzu P, van Baren M, et al. Mutations in the DJ-1 gene associated with autosomal recessive early-onset parkinsonism. *Science* 2003; 299:256–259.

67. Braak H, Del Tredici K, Rub U, et al. Staging of brain pathology related to sporadic Parkinson's disease. *Neurobiol Aging* 2003; 24:197–211.

68. Dewey RB, Hutton JT, LeWitt PA, Factor SA. A randomized, double-blind, placebo-controlled trial of subcutaneously injected apomorphine for parkinsonian off-states. *Arch Neurol* 2001: 58:1385–1392.

69. Paisan-Ruiz C, Jain S, Evans EW, et al. Cloning of the gene containing mutations that cause PARK8-linked Parkinson's disease. *Neuron* 2004; 44:1–12.

70. Zimprich A, Biskup S, Leitner P, et al. Mutations in LRRK2 cause autosomal dominant parkinsonism with pleomorphic pathology. *Neuron* 2004; 44:601–607.

71. Fahn S, Oakes D, Shoulson I, et al. Levodopa and the progression of Parkinson's disease. *N Engl J Med* 2004; 351:2498–508.

72. Feign A, Kaplitt M, During M, et al. Gene therapy for Parkinson's disease with AAV-GAD: An open-label, dose escalation, safety-tolerability trial. Mov Disord 2005; 20:1236.

73. Parkinson Study Group. A controlled trial of Rasagiline in early Parkinson's disease. *Arch Neurol* 2000; 59:1937–1943.

74. Parkinson Study Group. A randomized placebo-controlled trial of rasagiline in levodopa-treated patients with Parkinson disease and motor fluctuations: The PRESTO study. *Arch Neurol* 2005; 62:241–248.

75. Waters CH, Sethi KD, Hauser RA, et al, Zydis Selegiline Study Group. Zydis selegiline reduces off time in Parkinson's disease patients with motor fluctuations: A 3-month, randomized, placebo-controlled study. *Mov Disord* 2004; 19:426–432.

76. Waldmeier P, Bozyczko-Coyne D, Williams M, Vaught JL. Recent clinical failures in Parkinson's disease with apoptosis inhibitors underline the need for a paradigm shift in drug discovery for neurodegenerative diseases. *Biochem Pharmacol* 2006; 72:1197–206.

77. Lang AE, Gill S, Patel NK, et al. Randomized controlled trial of intraputamenal glial cell line–derived neurotrophic factor infusion in Parkinson's disease. *Ann Neurol* 2006; 59:459–466.

78. Watts RL, Jankovic J, Waters C, et al. Randomized, blind, controlled trial of transdermal rotigotine in early Parkinson disease. *Neurology* 2007; 68:272–276.

79. Zanettini R, Antonini A, Gotto G, et al. Valvular heart disease and the use of dopamine agonists for Parkinson's disease. *N Engl J Med* 2007; 356:39–46.

II

CLINICAL PRESENTATION

5 Epidemiology

Michele L. Rajput
Ali H. Rajput
Alexander Rajput

The epidemiology of Parkinson's disease (PD) can be divided into the broad categories of descriptive, analytic, and experimental. Descriptive epidemiology deals with incidence, mortality, and prevalence rates. Analytic studies identify those factors that influence the frequency of disease, time trends, and their significance. These studies identify associations of different events and factors involved in PD in an effort to determine causes. Experimental epidemiology focuses primarily on treatments and requires careful clinical assessments and documentation.

Most scientific research occurs in laboratories, where a hypothesis is generated and then tested using controlled experiments. By contrast, epidemiology is the study of nature's experiments, which may have been influenced by economic, social, or medical developments. Unlike laboratory experiments, which can be strictly controlled to eliminate confounding variables, epidemiologic studies must continuously navigate potential biases. Major biases may be introduced during case finding, data collection, data analysis, or interpretation of data. If care is not taken, these biases can render conclusions invalid. Planned laboratory experiments can be verified by others using exactly the same methodology and material. However, no two epidemiologic studies are ever identical because they are conducted using human populations over long periods of time.

Compared with laboratory experiments, epidemiologic studies require considerably more time and effort, and the yield—for example, publications or presentations per unit of effort—is far less. Epidemiologic studies must be planned, conducted, and interpreted carefully; patience truly is a virtue in these studies. The disadvantages are balanced by an important fact: the final objective of biomedical research is the application of its findings to human health and disease, and an overwhelming majority of laboratory studies may never reach this goal. In contrast, well-done epidemiologic studies have direct and immediate application.

The connection between an epidemiologic study and daily clinical practice requires interpretation on the part of the clinician. It is important that appropriate significance be given to each aspect of the observations. A large report may have only a small part that is both scientifically valid and clinically applicable. A clinician may have to interpret a one-of-a-kind epidemiologic study. An even more difficult situation is presented when two somewhat similar studies come to different conclusions. In those situations, a rule of thumb is often the best guide: rely on your intuition regardless of who the author is, where the study was conducted, and in which journal the paper was published. If something does not make sense, do not believe it, or at least reserve judgment until further research supports the conclusions. Here we briefly outline some of the issues that are critical for good epidemiologic studies of parkinsonism.

SELECTION OF LOCATION AND POPULATION

There is no community or institution that lends itself to all types of epidemiologic studies. Experimental and clinical studies are conducted in clinic populations. Incidence studies must often focus on physician-diagnosed cases ascertained via health care providers. With appropriate effort, prevalence studies can be conducted in any community. Because there is no biological marker, the diagnosis of PD can be made only by clinical assessment, and it requires a high level of cooperation from those being screened. All individuals in the community may not wish to participate. In spite of some limitations, a door-to-door survey of a community is the best method to ensure accurate ascertainment of all cases for prevalence studies.

The age distribution of the population being studied must also be considered. Parkinsonism is concentrated in older age groups; therefore studies restricted to individuals above a certain age would find inflated rates. Unless rates are adjusted for the age distribution of the community residents, these rates will not be applicable to the general population. Prevalence studies conducted in community residents often exclude the institutional population. Because a large proportion of advanced parkinsonian patients reside in institutions, these studies provide lower prevalence rates and are therefore not generalizable (1, 2).

DIAGNOSIS OF PARKINSONISM
AND VARIANTS

Wide variations in the diagnostic criteria utilized in epidemiologic studies make comparisons difficult if not impossible. While reading the results of a study, it is critical to ascertain the definition used by the researchers to discern exactly which patient population is being described. de Rijk and coworkers carefully reviewed the literature on the diagnostic criteria of PD used in different epidemiologic studies and concluded that the best criteria are the same as those used in clinical studies (3). A patient is diagnosed as having PD if 2 of the 3 following symptoms are documented: bradykinesia, rigidity, and tremor (3, 4). Of course if the objective of the study were to study idiopathic PD alone (4), an accurate diagnosis of PD would require the exclusion of the many variants of parkinsonism (5). These variants include but are not limited to drug-induced parkinsonism (DIP),

progressive supranuclear palsy (PSP), and multiple system atrophy (MSA).

Most epidemiologic studies make no special effort to identify different variants of PS, and this can complicate the interpretation of results and the generalizability of conclusions. A Rochester study of patients diagnosed between 1967 and 1979 elaborated on the variants of parkinsonism: 85.5% PD, 7.2% DIP, 1.4% PSP, 2.1% MSA, and 1% vascular parkinsonism (6). Every recent incidence and prevalence study has noted that the most common parkinsonian variant is PD.

To further complicate matters, the clinical diagnosis of PD is not always accurate (4). In most cases the error involves the misdiagnosis of other variants of parkinsonian syndrome (PS) or of patients with essential tremor as having PD. Even after many years of follow-up, up to 24% percent of the patients clinically diagnosed as having PD had a different diagnosis upon autopsy (4, 7). Most epidemiologic studies probably do not accurately reflect the frequency of the uncommon variants. For instance, DIP is rare in community residents (1) but common in the institutionalized elderly (2). Those epidemiologic studies that are all-inclusive therefore indicate a larger proportion of DIP (6, 8, 9). They reflect the PS variants in the entire population and therefore are more meaningful. With the widespread use of newer antipsychotic agents, it is anticipated that DIP may become less common.

PROGRESSION OF PARKINSONISM
AND STAGING OF DISEASE

The distribution of patients with respect to stage of disease is another important characteristic to know about a study population. The progression of motor symptoms differs in PS variants. The rate of progression of disability is more rapid in MSA and PSP than in idiopathic PD (10, 11). It has been estimated that the progression from one stage—as defined by Hoehn and Yahr (H&Y)—to the next takes approximately 2 to 2.9 years (12), but recent studies indicate that progression in an optimally treated PD patient is much slower. An average nondemented PD patient with onset at age 62 years who is treated appropriately progresses by one H&Y stage in approximately 6 years (13). The progression rate varies widely from patient to patient. Despite these variations, the disease will advance at a relatively constant rate in any given individual (12).

INCIDENCE OF PARKINSON'S DISEASE

Incidence studies are difficult to perform because they require the identification of all new cases in a large, defined population. Most studies to date have used various combinations of hospital records, specialist records, prescription drug databases, and inquiries to physicians, hospitals, and long-term-care facilities. The most complete case ascertainment includes door-to-door surveys and screenings to identify cases not previously diagnosed. Door-to-door surveys can also be used to identify a population without PD that can be followed prospectively to identify new cases as symptoms first appear. By necessity, incidence studies usually report each incident case as of date of diagnosis, since the date of symptom onset is difficult to pinpoint. To avoid year-to-year fluctuations, studies must include all patients diagnosed over several years.

In 2003, Twelves and colleagues completed a systematic review of all PD incidence studies (14). After thoroughly reviewing 94 references, 25 PD incidence studies were identified. These studies used a variety of methods and differing case definitions; moreover, their data came from many different countries, including North and South America, Australia, Europe, Asia, and the Middle East. Crude annual incidence rates ranged from 4.5 per 100, 000 in Libya (15) to 26 per 100, 000 in London (16). Five studies were similar enough and provided sufficient data for the calculation of age-standardized rates (17–21). Ultimately, four of these studies gave annual incidence rates ranging from 16.5 to 18 per 100, 000 population. These studies were from Finland (18, 19), the borough of Manhattan in New York City (20), and the United Kingdom (21). One study from Italy gave a much lower estimated annual incidence rate of 8 per 100, 000 (17). The authors hypothesize that low case ascertainment from 20-year-old medical records and/or the high rate of undiagnosed PD in Italy contributed to the low incidence rate in the Italian study.

The incidence of PD increases with advancing age. It is concentrated in the higher age groups, and only 4% to 10% of patients have onset before age 40. In our clinic-based study of 934 patients over 22 years, 6% had onset before age 40 (11). In the most recent Olmsted County study, the annual incidence per 100, 000 was 1 between the ages of 30 and 39 years, 17 between the ages of 50 and 59 years, and 93 between the ages of 70 and 79 years (8). On the basis of these incidence rates, the lifetime risks of PD are estimated at 2.0% for men and 1.3% for women (22).

If the current survival trends continue, there will be a progressively higher population of elderly in the general population, and the overall incidence of PD will rise. Other developments that contribute to higher incidence are the increasing recognition that PD may begin at a young age and that a significant proportion of demented patients also have parkinsonian features. This is not a true increase in incidence but an effect of improved case ascertainment.

LIFE EXPECTANCY IN PARKINSON'S DISEASE

PD by itself is not fatal; however, it leads to physical disabilities that predispose to deep venous thrombosis, pulmonary embolism, pneumonia (23), falls, and resulting complications (24). Patients with PD have mortality rates 35% to 65% higher than those of matched controls (25, 26). Life expectancy in western countries has progressively increased over the last several decades because of improved socioeconomic conditions and better health care. Parkinson's disease patients of today would share some of those longevity gains; hence the life expectancy of contemporary patients would be longer than that of patients diagnosed 30 to 40 years ago. To overcome that bias in studying mortality, cases and controls must be matched on birth year and gender.

The onset of PD is insidious and difficult to ascertain precisely. The date of onset is established retrospectively, relying on the patient's history; it is only an approximation and not an exact date. The interval between symptom onset and clinical diagnosis may be several years. Because of the uncertainty of the onset date, life expectancy from the onset of symptoms cannot be measured accurately.

By approximating a time of onset retrospectively for survival analysis, survival rates expected in the general population are artificially inflated by not accounting for individuals with PD who die without having been diagnosed (27). When we used the date of onset in our study of 934 PS patients, survival in the PS group was longer than expected in the general population. The observation that patients suffering from a chronic, progressively disabling disease lived longer than the general population of unaffected individuals does not make sense. To overcome this bias, survival must be computed from the date of first patient contact and controls matched as of this date (11, 28). By doing so, the benefits of socioeconomic and medical advancements in the general population would be shared by parkinsonian patients equally and would not be a factor in the PD survival gains (29).

Although expressing survival as a "mean" number of years has value in counseling patients, it does not help to elucidate any survival changes consequent to current methods of management. As life expectancy in the general population increases, one would expect some increase in mean life expectancy in parkinsonian patients as well. Several studies indicate that, in the last three decades, life expectancy in parkinsonian patients has increased significantly. Uitti and coworkers, using a mathematical model, concluded that the use of levodopa increased survival considerably (28). Kurtzke and associates (30) observed changes in age at death between 1970 and 1985 and concluded that patients were now living 5 years longer than they were before levodopa became available. If the recent 5-year increase in mean survival in parkinsonian patients were added to the prelevodopa survival of 9.42 years (excluding postencephalitic parkinsonism) (13), the mean survival today would be approximately 15 years.

Change in life expectancy with time has implications not only for the individual patient but also for the health care system in order to provide services. If the new cases were to emerge at the same rate as before but survival increased, the total number of cases at any given time would be higher than before. If there is indeed an increase in the life expectancy of today's patients compared with the past generations, it may reflect the benefits of modern drug therapy. Some observers have concluded that the life expectancy gain is simply an indicator of improved socioeconomic/general medical care, leading to increased survival (31). To distinguish between these points of view, case-control studies are needed, but they would be unethical. Levodopa, the most potent drug, or any other drug given to control symptoms, cannot be withheld for a prolonged period from any person with the objective of comparing the survival of treated versus untreated patients. By necessity, evaluations of the effect of access to levodopa must be made by other means.

At the Movement Disorder Clinic in Saskatoon, Saskatchewan, 934 patients were studied between 1968 and 1990 (11). The severity of disability and the type of parkinsonism in these patients were comparable to those noted in a large prevalence study (32). These 934 patients could be subdivided into prelevodopa- and levodopa-era cases based on date of first visit to the Movement Disorder Clinic (11). Survival was reduced in both groups, but the most favorable prognosis was noted in 565 cases with onset after 1973 and unrestricted levodopa access. In 1975, the Saskatchewan prescription drug policy was implemented and levodopa was fully funded by the province for all patients. Cases diagnosed before 1974 had a 10-year survival of 46%, compared with the expected 69%. For cases diagnosed in 1974 or later, the observed 10-year survival was 78%, compared with the expected 83%. Thus survival was significantly better in the more recent cases compared with those diagnosed earlier, when levodopa was not available or was severely restricted $P < .025$). Further analysis demonstrated that the survival benefits were realized only when levodopa was initiated before the patients developed postural instability as indicated by modified H&Y stage 2.5.

Survival of PD patients has improved remarkably since levodopa came into widespread use, although it remains shortened compared with that of the general population. It is estimated that the life expectancy of a nondemented patient with onset of idiopathic PD at age 62.4 years will be reduced by approximately 2 years if the disease is treated adequately. Survival is significantly

shorter in other variants of parkinsonism and in those who have dementia at first assessment (11). Shortened survival in patients with dementia has also been reported by several other workers (28, 33).

PREVALENCE OF PARKINSON'S DISEASE

Disease prevalence is a result of incidence and survival. With an aging population and improved medical therapy, PD prevalence can be expected to increase even if age-specific incidence rates remain constant.

There is universal agreement that the prevalence of parkinsonism increases with age. One recent study in Holland found the prevalence of PD to be 0.6% (6 per 1000 people) in those between the ages of 65 and 69 years and 2.6% (26 per 1000) in the those aged 85 to 90 years (34). It is estimated that between 1971 and 1991 there was a doubling in the number of individuals over age 85 in Canada and the United States, thereby markedly enlarging the population at risk for developing parkinsonism. In Finland, the age-adjusted prevalence of PD increased from 139 per 100, 000 in 1971 to 166 per 100, 000 in 1992 (19).

The best prevalence studies are those in which the entire population of a community is directly surveyed. Most studies are restricted to populations 40 years of age and older, thereby excluding the significant portion of the general population below that age, where the prevalence is lower. This gives the impression of higher than actual rates in the general population. Worldwide, prevalence rates range from 57 per 100, 000 in China (56) to 371 per 100, 000 in Sicily (35). A state registry was used to estimate PD prevalence as 329.3 per 100, 000 in Nevada (36). As noted earlier, prevalence studies should not rely only on physician-diagnosed cases. Door-to-door studies have revealed that between 35% and 42% of the parkinsonian patients were undiagnosed before the survey (35, 37).

There are other means of estimating prevalence, but they are not reliable. Death registers as a source of prevalence rates have the lowest yield. In an overwhelming majority of these patients, the patient dies of a related medical condition and the diagnosis of PD is not noted on the death certificate (38). Also, the accurate coding of PD is associated with patient income; PD was recorded in almost 70% of the high-income group compared with just 35% in the group with the lowest income (38). The number of antiparkinsonian drug prescriptions in a population is another indicator of prevalence rates. Drug tracer methodology was used to estimate PD prevalence in British Columbia as ranging between 109 and 125 per 100, 000 (39). However, this is an underestimate, since undiagnosed cases are missed as well as early, mild cases as yet untreated.

RISK FACTORS

Both heredity and the environment have a role in the etiology of PD. These topics are covered in later chapters.

Race and ethnicity may be associated with risk of PD. Some previous studies based on private patients in American hospitals indicated that the risk of parkinsonism differed according to skin color, with whites being at increased risk (40, 41). On the assumption that environmental toxins might cause PD, it has been suggested that MPTP toxicity is more likely in whites than in blacks (42). On the other hand, studies in Copiah County, Mississippi, found no significant differences in PS risk in a mixed-race community consisting of nearly equal number of blacks and whites (37). In another mixed-race U.S. population survey, the incidence was highest among black males, although there was higher mortality in this group, resulting in lower prevalence in blacks (43). When age of population was taken into account, the prevalence of parkinsonism in U.S. blacks was 5-fold higher than in blacks living in Nigeria. (44). It should be noted that the studies of blacks and whites in Copiah County, Mississippi (37), and those in Nigeria (44) were conducted by the same principal investigator (B.S. Schoenberg) using the same methodologic tools and that the results are therefore not attributable to methodologic bias.

A study of a health maintenance organization reported that incidence rates did indeed vary by race/ethnicity (45). The highest rates were among Hispanics (16.6 per 100, 000), followed by non-Hispanic whites (13.6), Asians (11.3), and blacks (10.2). In contrast, the prevalence of PD in China varied greatly by geographic region, with one rural region having a prevalence of 620 per 100, 000 (46). One study of PD in an Inuit population in Greenland reported an age-adjusted PD prevalence of 187.5 per 100, 000, similar to the rate of 209 per 100, 00 in the Faroe Islands but double that of 98.3 per 100, 000 in Als, Denmark (47). The prevalence of PD in elderly care home residents in Bangalore was 19.5% among the Indians compared with just 3.9% among the admixed Anglo-Indian residents (48). Geographic variations were also observed in Alberta, Canada (49). These data suggest some role of race/ethnicity in the risk for PD, but the environment likely plays a larger part.

Risk of PD is also associated with gender. Several studies have reported a higher prevalence in males than in females (19, 20, 50, 51), and large clinical trials often enroll more males than females (52). On the other hand, one study did find a higher prevalence among women (53), and higher prevalence rates have been reported in women than in men in some carefully conducted door-to-door studies (35, 54). The preponderance of the evidence indicates that the relative risk for men of developing PD is 1.5 (50). Although men may develop PD more often than women, their disease course seems to be similar, including age at death, which one would not expect given women's longer life expectancy (55).

Smoking and caffeine are independently associated with a lower risk of PD (56). A review of 6 prospective studies reported a pooled risk of 0.51 for ever smokers and 0.35 for current smokers compared with never smokers (57). Smoking has a dose-response relationship with PD (58). Current heavy smokers had a lower risk (OR = 0.08) than current light smokers (OR = 0.59), and former heavy smokers who had recently quit had a lower risk (OR = 0.37) than those who had quit more than 20 years earlier (OR = 0.86). Caffeine has a similar relationship in men, with about half the PD risk for the highest caffeine intake compared with the lowest (59); however, the relationship in women was U-shaped, with the lowest risk in the moderate intake category. For both smoking and caffeine, the cause-effect relationship with PD has not been established. PD will continue to increase in prevalence. In addition to basic science studies, prospective epidemiologic studies are needed to ascertain what causes PD, so as to identify prevention strategies. By necessity, these studies will be large and time-consuming but also well worth pursuing.

References

1. Moghal S, Rajput AH, D'Arcy C, et al. Prevalence of movement disorders in elderly community residents. *Neuroepidemiology* 1994; 13:175–178.
2. Moghal S, Rajput AH, Meleth R, et al. Prevalence of movement disorders in institutionalized elderly. *Neuroepidemiology* 1995; 14:297–300.
3. de Rijk MC, Rocca WA, Anderson DW et al. A population perspective on diagnostic criteria for Parkinson's disease. *Neurology* 1997; 48:1277–1281.
4. Duvoisin R, Golbe LI. Toward a definition of Parkinson's disease. *Neurology* 1989; 39:746.
5. Rajput AH, Rozdilsky B, Rajput AH. Accuracy of clinical diagnosis in parkinsonism: A prospective study. *Can J Neurol Sci* 1991; 18:275–278.
6. Rajput AH, Offord KP, Beard CM, et al. Epidemiology of parkinsonism: Incidence, classification, and mortality. *Ann Neurol* 1984; 16:278–282.
7. Hughes AJ, Ben-Shlomo Y, Daniel SE, et al. What features improve the accuracy of clinical diagnosis in Parkinson's disease? A clinicopathologic study. *Neurology* 1992; 42:1142–1146.
8. Bower JH, Maraganore DM, McDonnell SK, et al. Incidence and distribution of parkinsonism in Olmsted County, Minnesota, 1976–1990. *Neurology* 1999; 52:1214–1220.
9. Montgomery EB Jr. Pharmacokinetics and pharmacodynamics of levodopa. *Neurology* 1992; 42(Suppl 1):17–22.
10. Rajput AH, Pahwa R, Pahwa P, et al. Prognostic significance of the onset mode in parkinsonism. *Neurology* 1993; 43:829–830.
11. Rajput AH, Uitti RJ, Rajput AH, et al. Timely levodopa (LD) administration prolongs survival in Parkinson's disease. *Parkinsonism Relat Disord* 1997; 3(3):159–165.
12. Marttila RJ, Rinne UK. Disability and progression of Parkinson's disease. *Acta Neurol Scand* 1977; 56:159–169.
13. Alves G, Wentzel-Larsen T, Aarsland D, Larsen JP. Progression of motor impairment and disability in Parkinson disease. *Neurology* 200; 65:1436–1441.
14. Twelves D, Perkins KSM, Counsell C. Systematic review of incidence studies of Parkinson's disease. *Mov Disord* 2003; 18(1):19–31.
15. Ashok PP, Radhakrishnan K, Sridharan R, Mousa ME. Epidemiology of Parkinson's disease in Benghazi, North-East Libya. *Clin Neurol Neurosurg* 1986; 88:109–113.
16. Cockerell OC, Goodridge DM, Brodie D, et al. Neurological disease in a defined population: The results of a pilot study in two general practices. *Neuroepidemiology* 1996; 15:73–82.
17. Granieri E, Carreras M, Casetta I, et al. Parkinson's disease in Ferrara, Italy, 1967 through 1987. *Arch Neurol* 1991; 48:854–857.
18. Martilla RJ, Rinne UK. Epidemiology of Parkinson's disease in Finland. *Acta Neurol Scand* 1976; 53:81–102.

19. Kuopio AM, Marttila RJ, Helenius H, Rinne UK. Changing epidemiology of Parkinson's disease in southwestern Finland. *Neurology* 1999; 52:302–308.

20. Mayeux R, Marder K, Cote LJ, et al. The frequency of idiopathic Parkinson's disease by age, ethnic group, and sex in northern Manhattan, 1988–1993. *Am J Epidemiol* 1995; 142:820–827.

21. MacDonald BK, Cockerell OC, Sander JW, Shorvon SD. The incidence and lifetime prevalence of neurological disorders in a prospective community-based study in the UK. *Brain* 2000; 123:665–676.

22. Elbaz A, Bower JH, Maraganore DM, et al. Risk tables for parkinsonism and Parkinson's disease. *J Clin Epidemiol* 2002; 55(1):25–31.

23. Fall PA, Saleh A, Fredrickson M, Olsson JE, et al. Survival time, mortality, and cause of death in elderly patients with Parkinson's disease: A 9-year follow-up. *Mov Disord* 2003; 18(11):1312–1316.

24. Mosewich RK, Rajput AH, Shuaib A, et al. Pulmonary embolism: An underrecognized yet frequent cause of death in parkinsonism. *Mov Disord* 1994; 9(3):350–352.

25. Herlofson K, Lie SA, Arsland D, Larsen JP. Mortality and Parkinson's disease: Community based study. *Neurology* 2004; 62(6):937–942.

26. Hughes TA, Ross HF, Mindham RH, Spokes EG. Mortality in Parkinson's disease and its association with dementia and depression. *Acta Neurol Scand* 2004; 110(2):118–123.

27. Roos RAC, Jongen JCG, Vander Velde EA. Clinical course of patients with idiopathic Parkinson's disease. *Mov Disord* 1996; 11(3):236–242.

28. Uitti RJ, Ahlskog JE, Maraganore DM, et al. Levodopa therapy and survival in idiopathic Parkinson's: Olmsted County project. Neurology. 1993 Oct;43(10):1918–26.

29. Lilienfeld DE, Sekkor D, Simpson S, et al. Parkinsonism death rates by race, sex and geography: A 1980's update. *Neuroepidemiology* 1990; 9:243–247.

30. Kurtzke JF, Flaten TP, Murphy FM. Death rates from Parkinson's disease in Norway reflect increased survival. *Neurology* 1991; 41:1665–1667.

31. Lilienfeld DE, Chan E, Ehland J, et al. Two decades of increasing mortality from Parkinson's disease among the US elderly. *Arch Neurol* 1990; 47:731–734.

32. Marttila RJ, Rinne UK. Dementia in Parkinson disease. *Acta Neurol Scand* 1976; 54:431–441.

33. Marder K, Mirabello E, Chen J, et al. Death rates among demented and nondemented patients with Parkinson's disease. *Ann Neurol* 1990; 28(2):295.

34. de Rijk MC, Launer LJ, Berger K, et al. Prevalence of Parkinson's disease in Europe: A collaborative study of population-based cohorts. *Neurology* 2000; 54(Suppl 5):S21–S23.

35. Morgante L, Rocca WA, Di Rosa AE, et al. Prevalence of Parkinson's disease and other types of parkinsonism: A door-to-door survey in three Sicilian municipalities. *Neurology* 1992; 42:1901–1907.

36. Strickland D, Bertoni JM. Parkinson's prevalence estimated by a state registry. *Mov Disord* 2004; 19(3):318–323.

37. Schoenberg BS, Anderson DW, Haerer AF. Prevalence of Parkinson's disease in the biracial population of Copiah County, Mississippi. *Neurology* 1985; 35(6):841–845.

38. Pressley JC, Tang MX, Marder K, et al. Disparities in the recording of Parkinson's disease on death certificates. *Mov Disord* 2005; 20(3):325–321.

39. Lai BCL, Schulzer M, Marion S, et al. The prevalence of Parkinson's disease in British Columbia, Canada, estimated by using drug tracer methodology. *Parkinsonism Relat Disord* 2003; 9:233–238.

40. Kessler II. Epidemiologic studies of Parkinson's disease, II. A hospital based survey. *Am J Epidemiol* 1972; 95(4):308–318.

41. Kessler II. Epidemiology study of Parkinson's disease. *Am J Epidemiol* 1972; 96:242–254.

42. Lerner MR, Goldman RS. Skin colour, MPTP, and Parkinson's disease. *Lancet* 1987; 2(8552):212.

43. Mayeux R, Marder K, Cote LJ, et al. The frequency of idiopathic Parkinson's disease by age, ethnic group, and sex in northern Manhattan, 1988–1993. *Am J Epidemiol* 1995; 142:820–827.

44. Schoenberg BS, Osuntokun BO, Adejua AOG, et al. Comparison of the prevalence of Parkinson's disease in black populations in the rural United States and in rural Nigeria: Door-to-door community studies. *Neurology* 1988; 38:645–646.

45. Van Den Eeden SK, Tanner CM, Bernstein AL, et al. Incidence of Parkinson's disease: Variation by age, gender, and race/ethnicity. *Am J Epidemiol* 2003; 157(11):1015–1022.

46. Wang SJ, Fuh JL, Liu CY, et al. Parkinson's disease in Kin-Hu, Kinmen: A community survey by neurologists. *Neuroepidemiol* 1994; 13:69–74.

47. Wermuth L, Pakkenberg H, Jeune B. High age-adjusted prevalence of Parkinson's disease among Inuits in Greenland. *Neurology* 2002; 58:1422–1425.

48. Ragothaman M, Murgod UA, Gururaj G, et al. Lower risk of Parkinson's disease in an admixed population of European and Indian origins. *Mov Disord* 2003; 18(8):912–914.

49. Svenson LW, Platt GH, Woodhead SE. Geographic variations in the prevalence rates of Parkinson's disease in Alberta. *Can J Neurol Sci* 1993; 20(4):307–311.

50. Wooten GF, Currie LJ, Bovbjerg VE, et al. Are men at greater risk for Parkinson's disease then women? *J Neurol Neurosurg Psychiatry* 2004; 75:637–639.

51. Vines JJ, Larumbe R, Gaminde I, et al. Incidence of idiopathic and secondary Parkinson's disease in Navarre. *Neurologia* 1999; 14:16–22.

52. Parkinson Study Group. Effect of deprenyl on the progression of disability in early Parkinson's disease. *N Engl J Med* 1989; 321:1364–1371.

53. Granieri E, Carresas M, Casetta I, et al. Parkinson's disease in Ferra, Italy, 1967–1987. *Arch Neurol* 1991; 48:854–857.

54. de Rijk MC, Breteler MMB, Graveland GA, et al. Prevalence of Parkinson's disease in the elderly: The Rotterdam Study. *Neurology* 1995; 45:2143–2146.

55. Diamond SG, Markham CH, Hoehn MM, et al. An examination of male-female differences in progression and mortality of Parkinson's disease. *Neurology* 1990; 40:763–766.

56. Ragonese P, Salemi G, Morgante L, et al. A case-control study on cigarette, alcohol, and coffee consumption preceding Parkinson's disease. *Neuroepidemiology* 2003; 22:297–304.

57. Allam MF, Campbell MJ, Hofman A, et al. Smoking and Parkinson's disease: Systematic review of prospective studies. *Mov Disord* 2004; 19(6):614–621.

58. Gorell JM, Rybicki BA, Johnson CC, Peterson EL. Smoking and Parkinson's disease: A dose-response relationship. *Neurology* 1999; 52:115–119.

59. Ascherio A, Zhang SM, Hernan MA, et al. Prospective study of caffeine consumption and risk of Parkinson's disease in men and women. *Ann Neurol* 2001; 50:56–63.

6 Cardinal Features of Early Parkinson's Disease

Ali Samii

The term *parkinsonism* has evolved over time to refer to the constellation of signs in the clinical entity described by James Parkinson in 1817 (1). The 3 cardinal signs include resting tremor, rigidity, and bradykinesia. However, there are no specific criteria for the use of this term. For instance, does the presence of any of the core features alone constitute parkinsonism? Or is a threshold of motor signs needed before a patient would be labeled as having parkinsonism?

Parkinson's disease (PD), the most common cause of parkinsonism (2), has a more specific definition, with gradations of diagnostic certainty (3–5). The definitive diagnosis of PD requires autopsy; however more rigorous clinical diagnostic criteria have emerged over the last 2 decades (6). The motor signs of early PD are usually asymmetric, and symptomatic improvement with dopaminergic drugs is significant and sustained. Familial parkinsonism and familial PD are entities that may follow an autosomal dominant (with variable penetrance) or autosomal recessive pattern of inheritance.

EARLY NONSPECIFIC FEATURES

The early symptoms of PD may be nonspecific, such as fatigue, reduced energy, joint stiffness (especially of the shoulder), muscles cramps, or vague sensory disturbances. Unilateral limb dystonia, especially in the foot, may accompany the sensation of limb stiffness (7). Dragging of one foot or tripping after walking a distance even in the absence of dystonia may occur. The patient may take a longer time to perform daily activities. The eyes may feel dry, with a sensation of burning due to the reduced frequency of blinking.

There may be a feeling of internal (usually asymmetric) quivering before the emergence of visible resting tremor (8). Slower and more effortful handwriting, with smaller letters (micrographia) may occur. Typing on the computer keyboard may become slower, with more typographical errors. The patient may complain of hoarseness or a soft voice (hypophonia), especially after speaking for a while. Family members may notice an asymmetrically reduced arm swing in the patient during ambulation. Drooling is usually not an early feature of PD, but it can rarely occur early in the course of the disease.

Sleep disturbances are common in early PD, even before the emergence of motor symptoms. Rapid-eye-movement (REM) sleep behavior disorder is a common manifestation. It is due to the loss of the normal muscle atonia during REM sleep and is characterized by excessive movements while dreaming. The acting out of dreams can be quite violent and even injurious to the patient or the bed partner. One study found that among patients with PD and REM sleep behavior disorder, more than half developed the disorder before motor symptoms were present (9). Others have suggested that REM sleep behavior disorder is actually part of the overall dopamine deficiency syndrome seen in PD (10). Periodic limb movements during sleep, a common complaint usually voiced by the bed partner, may further fragment sleep.

Restless legs syndrome (RLS) and a sense of inner restlessness (restless body syndrome) are common in early PD. The clinical syndrome of akathisia (Greek term meaning "inability to sit still") has similarities to RLS. RLS responds well to dopaminergic therapy, and akathisia is frequently brought on by dopamine antagonists, again suggesting a shared neurotransmitter mechanism. The prevalence of RLS in the general population is nearly 10% (11), while its prevalence in PD patients has been reported to be as high 21%, about twice that in the general population (12). The relationship between brain iron and dopamine deficiency, RLS, and PD remains to be elucidated.

Further early nonmotor manifestations include constipation, seborrheic dermatitis, decreased perception of smell (hyposmia), and dysautonomia, including bladder dysfunction. Constipation is a common early complaint. One study questions whether constipation is part of early PD or whether it is so prevalent before the presence of motor symptoms that it may be a marker of susceptibility to develop PD (13). Constipation may also be exacerbated by drugs, both dopaminergic and anticholinergic agents, used to treat motor symptoms.

The perplexing association between seborrheic dermatitis and PD and its improvement with levodopa treatment has been established for decades (14). The exact mechanism for seborrheic dermatitis is unclear. It is an ill-defined condition characterized by chronic scaling of the skin on the head and trunk, where sebaceous glands are prominent. Theories of why it occurs in PD patients have ranged from increased sebum excretion, to slow emptying of the pilosebaceous canal reservoir, and even to the possibility that a common potential environmental agent may lead to both seborrheic dermatitis and PD (15).

Hyposmia occurs early in PD and may precede motor symptoms by many years. It is such a well-recognized feature of PD that some are proposing olfactory dysfunction as a risk factor for developing PD (16). Hyposmia is bilateral and unrelated to the side of initial motor signs or antiparkinson drug therapy (17). A recent study suggests that a combination of idiopathic REM sleep behavior disorder and olfactory dysfunction had a high correlation with the presence of clinical and neuroimaging signs of nigrostriatal dysfunction (18).

The most common bladder symptoms in early PD are urinary frequency, urgency, and urge incontinence. These symptoms generally correlate with the severity of detrusor hyperreflexia (i.e., excessive detrusor muscle contraction at early stages of bladder filling) as measured by urodynamic testing (19). Obstructive uropathy due to an enlarged prostate further exacerbates bladder symptoms in older men with PD. Erectile dysfunction in men is also extremely common in any stage of PD (20).

Although the presence of early severe dementia together with motor parkinsonism points to a diagnosis other than PD, subtle abnormalities in cognition and executive function are common in early PD. Change in personality, difficulty with concentration, slowed thinking (bradyphrenia), and mood changes—especially depression and anxiety—may be present in early PD (21). Visual perception, recognition deficits, impaired tasks of executive function, planning and working memory, and information processing may all be impaired (22, 23). There is evidence that these cognitive deficits in PD significantly influence quality-of-life measures (24).

CORRELATION BETWEEN SYMPTOMS AND PATHOLOGIC STAGES OF PARKINSON'S DISEASE

Braak et al. have proposed that PD is a synucleinopathy with 6 neuropathologic stages (25, 26). It is believed that the pathologic changes in PD begin years before motor symptoms appear. Table 6-1 summarizes the 6 pathologic stages proposed by Braak and colleagues. During the presymptomatic (with regard to motor symptoms) stages 1 to 2, inclusion-body pathology is confined to the medulla oblongata, the dorsal motor nucleus of the vagus nerve and the reticular formation, the pontine tegmentum, the olfactory bulb, and the anterior olfactory nucleus. In addition, the first Lewy body pathology appears in the locus ceruleus. These pathologic changes may explain hyposmia, early mild dysautonomia, and early mood/cognitive complaints.

In stages 3 to 4, the substantia nigra and the basal portions of the midbrain and forebrain are involved. The pars compacta of the substantia nigra, where the dopaminergic neurons of the nigrostriatal pathway are located, are clearly involved by these stages. Other brain regions that show pathologic change include the cholinergic tegmental pedunculopontine nucleus, raphe nuclei, cholinergic magnocellular nuclei of the basal forebrain, and hypothalamic tuberomamillary nucleus. Braak hypothesizes that by stages 3 to 4, patients cross the threshold to manifest the motor symptoms of PD (26). Motor, cognitive, and autonomic complaints at these stages may be explicable by the underlying pathology.

In stages 5 to 6, the neurodegenerative process is widespread and involves much of the neocortex. The previously described pathologic changes in other regions are more pronounced and inclusion-body pathology is now present in the prefrontal and association cortices and even in primary neocortical areas. Therefore the damage to the

---

TABLE 6-1
Pathologic Stages of PD Proposed by Braak et al.

Stage 1
Medulla oblongata and olfactory bulb lesions in dorsal nucleus of cranial nerves IX and X, intermediate reticular formation, olfactory bulb, and anterior olfactory nucleus

Stage 2
Pontine tegmentum pathology of stage 1 plus lesions in caudal raphe nuclei, gigantocellular reticular nucleus, and ceruleus-subceruleus complex

Stage 3
Midbrain pathology of stage 2 plus lesions in pars compacta of substantia nigra

Stage 4
Basal prosencephalon and mesocortex pathology of stage 3 plus prosencephalic lesions, anteromedial temporal mesocortex, and allocortex (CA-2 plexus)

Stage 5
Neocortex pathology of stage 4 plus lesions in prefrontal cortex and sensory association neocortical areas

Stage 6
Neocortex pathology of stage 5 plus lesions in first-order sensory association areas, premotor cortex, and even primary sensory and motor cortices

---

Source: Adapted from Braak et al. (25, 26). With permission.

---

autonomic, limbic, and somatomotor system that began in stages 1 to 2 is now compounded by the neocortical pathology. In advanced PD, motor symptoms are more severe and dysautonomia and cognitive impairment more pronounced, correlating with the widespread pathologic changes.

CARDINAL MOTOR FEATURES OF EARLY PARKINSON DISEASE

Tremor

Tremor is the most common presenting sign of early PD (27). Approximately 70% of patients notice tremor as the first symptom (28). Onset of tremor is usually in one hand; it may later involve the contralateral upper limb or ipsilateral lower limb. Typically, the tremor is a 3- to 5-Hz rhythmic "pill-rolling" movement of the thumb and index finger while the hand is at rest. There may be abduction and adduction of the thumb or flexion and extension of the wrist or of the metacarpophalangeal joints. The tremor may also extend to the forearm with pronation/supination or even to the elbow and upper arm.

During early disease, tremor is often intermittent and is evident only under stress. Tremor is worsened by anxiety, fatigue, and sleep deprivation. It diminishes with voluntary activity but may reappear with static posture (e.g., outstretched hands) and is absent during sleep. Resting tremor is enhanced by mental task performance, such as "serial 7" subtractions, and by motor task performance in a different body part. The hand tremor may also be enhanced during ambulation. Compared with essential tremor, the resting tremor of PD is generally less likely to be exacerbated by caffeine or improved with alcohol.

The jaw, tongue, head, and trunk are rarely affected by tremor in PD, although the resting tremor in the arm can be so severe as to be "transmitted" to the trunk and head. Tremor limited to the head/neck is more likely a sign of essential tremor rather than of PD. Resting tremor in the ankles or the thighs may be seen only when the patient is supine or keeps the legs in a certain position. Lower limb resting tremor may be exacerbated by motor activity in the upper limbs, but it usually disappears with ambulation.

The mechanism of parkinsonian resting tremor is unknown but is thought to be due unmasking of a pathologic central oscillator at 3 to 5 Hz (29). The anatomic basis for resting tremor is likely different from the suspected classic neuropathology of PD (i.e., nigrostriatal degeneration). Functional neuroimaging of this pathway with positron emission tomography (PET) shows better neuroimaging correlation with bradykinesia and rigidity than with tremor (30). In addition, as in the case of essential tremor, lesioning of the ventral intermediate nucleus of the thalamus (a cerebellar relay nucleus) alleviates parkinsonian resting tremor (31). The exact mechanism by which pallidotomy, pallidal stimulation, or subthalamic stimulation improves resting tremor, in addition to improving rigidity and bradykinesia, is unclear.

Rigidity

Rigidity is an increased resistance to passive stretch (29). This resistance is nearly equal in both agonist and antagonist muscles and generally uniform throughout the range of motion of the joint being tested. It may be sustained (plastic or "lead pipe") or intermittent and ratchety ("cogwheel"). Although cogwheel rigidity is usually thought to be parkinsonian rigidity complicated by parkinsonian tremor, it may occur in the absence of tremor, and the frequency felt by the examiner tends to be higher than that of the visible resting tremor.

Rigidity is only one form of increased tone; it should be differentiated from spasticity, paratonia, pain-related guarding of the joints in arthritic patients, and even a cogwheel phenomenon seen in essential tremor. Spasticity is velocity-dependent ("clasp-knife") and is associated with upper motor neuron signs such as pathologic hypereflexia, Babinski signs, and pyramidal distribution weakness. Gegenhalten or paratonic stiffness as seen in dementia is characterized by a resistance to passive movement proportional to the force applied by the examiner. Joint pain in the setting of arthritis can lead to local muscle spasm and guarding and cause increased tone (32). The cogwheel phenomenon may also be seen in severe essential tremor due to the interruption of passive movement by coarse tremor, especially if the patient fails to relax completely.

Rigidity is usually asymmetric in early PD. It is commonly present at one or both wrists and in the neck. Rigidity may also manifest as a slightly flexed elbow on the more affected side in early disease. Rigidity (and bradykinesia) may even lead to tendon contractures with limited joint range of motion despite dopaminergic therapy. Shoulder rigidity may predispose the patient to develop a frozen shoulder syndrome and early arthritis (33). As the disease progresses, the characteristic stooped posture is manifest, likely in part due to severe rigidity of the flexor musculature of the cervical and thoracic spine (34).

The pathogenesis of rigidity in PD is multifactorial, related to abnormal long-latency reflexes, abnormal background muscle contraction, and even changes in muscle and joint characteristics (29). As opposed to the monosynaptic spinal cord reflexes, long-latency stretch reflexes are mediated by a loop through the sensorimotor cortices, and their enhancement is likely related to abnormal excitability of this central loop (35). The overactivity in the dorsal premotor cortex in PD patients, as measured by transcranial magnetic stimulation (36), helps support the hypothesis that this is a contributor to rigidity.

Assessment of rigidity can be challenging and remains largely qualitative as judged by the examiner (37). Rigidity at the wrist is optimally assessed by passive movements of ± 30 degrees around the midposition with angular velocities of 140 to -190 degrees per second (38). Repeated tone examinations in both the sitting and lying positions may be necessary, as the PD patient does not relax well and there is slight muscle contraction at rest (29). Rigidity may be brought out or enhanced with contralateral motor activity (e.g., examining wrist tone while the patient does finger tapping with the other hand). Quantitative measurements of rigidity are difficult, but responses measured by controlled stretches may be accomplished by torque motors with good clinical correlation (39).

Bradykinesia

Although resting tremor may be the most visible sign of PD, bradykinesia is usually its most disabling component. Bradykinesia describes slowness of voluntary movements and poverty of normal associated movements; akinesia is an extension of bradykinesia implying nearly absent voluntary movement (40). There may be 2 reasons for akinesia: either the movement is too small to be seen or the time to generate movement is extremely long, so that the movement never really occurs. Using this distinction between bradykinesia and akinesia, reaction-time experiments can help evaluate both bradykinesia (through prolongation of movement time) and akinesia (through prolongation of reaction time).

Bradykinesia can be present as an early sign in different body parts. In the eyes it presents with saccadic hypometria (41) and in the face with reduced frequency of blinking and diminished facial animation. Hypophonia is likely a symptom of bradykinesia of the respiratory and the vocal cord muscles (42). In examining the patient for hypophonia, the patient is asked to say the months of the year loudly and clearly. In early PD, the voice lacks the natural fluctuations of volume and pitch and tends to fatigue quickly. In later stages there is slow initiation of speech, which becomes progressively softer (sometimes down to a whisper) and more monotonous. In early PD, dysarthria is usually absent, but it is a common problem in later stages. New-onset of stuttering or reemergence of childhood stuttering may be an early sign of PD (43).

Bradykinesia and rigidity are usually asymmetrically present in the same limb in early PD. Initially bradykinesia may be confined to the distal muscles of the hand, manifesting itself as micrographia (if the dominant hand is involved first) or slow finger tapping and impaired performance on fine motor tasks. Micrographia is best brought out by asking the patient to write continuously in cursive letters without resting or taking the pen off the paper. The proximal limb and truncal muscles tend to be involved later in the disease, but if one considers reduced arm swing to be a sign of bradykinesia, this can certainly be an early presenting sign. Before assessing bradykinesia, the examiner must exclude local arthritic pain, corticospinal tract or cerebellar signs, impaired cardiopulmonary reserve, and auditory, visual, or cognitive disturbances that may affect the patient's comprehension or performance of the motor tasks.

Limb bradykinesia, as measured by the motor part of the Unified Parkinson Disease Rating Scale (44), is rated by having the patient tap the index finger to the thumb repeatedly, do alternating pronation/supination of the forearm, close the hand into a fist and open it sequentially, and tap the sole of the foot rhythmically to the floor while seated by lifting the foot about 10 cm each time. It is important that the patient perform these tasks for a long enough time (at least 15 seconds) per side to allow for motor fatigue to become apparent. The examiner should pay attention to the speed, amplitude, and the rhythmicity of the movements and how they change over the period during which the task is being performed.

Generalized bradykinesia is rated by the overall slowing of all body parts, including an evaluation of how easily the patient stands from a seated position with or without pushing off the arm rests and of the patient's speed of ambulation.

More quantitative objective measures of limb bradykinesia in PD have been used. One of the simplest and most accurate tests is performance on the Purdue pegboard (45). The patient is asked to insert pegs in the holes on the pegboard, first with each hand separately and then with both at once, over a specified period of time. In a comparison between tapping on a contact board with a contact pencil and the insertion of pegs, both tasks proved to be useful tools for the objective evaluation of bradykinesia in PD, but peg insertion correlated better with disease severity (46). The superiority of the pegboard test over a tapping task as a marker of bradykinesia in PD was confirmed (47). Bradykinesia is correlated with nigrostriatal neuroimaging (30). Similarly, the Purdue pegboard score also correlates with nigrostriatal dysfunction measured by PET (48). Rapid alternate tapping with the index and middle fingers on two adjacent keys of a computerized electronic drum with simultaneous contralateral hand activation also showed significant correlation with fluorodopa PET scans (49).

The exact mechanism underlying bradykinesia is unclear (29), but it is thought to be related to decreased cortical activation due to impaired function in the basal ganglia–thalamocortical circuitry (50). Bradykinesia results from a failure of the basal ganglia's output to reinforce the cortical mechanisms that prepare and execute the commands to move (51). Impairment of both motor cortex activation and deactivation measured by transcranial magnetic stimulation is an early feature of PD and may be a physiologic correlate of bradykinesia (52). Other human evidence supporting decreased cortical activation includes somatosensory evoked potential studies (53) and movement-related cortical potentials looking at the Bereitschaftspotential, which is a slow-rising negativity before self-paced voluntary movements (54). In addition, cerebral blood flow studies using PET show abnormal cortical blood flow in PD, which is normalized by stimulation of the subthalamic nucleus (55).

Postural Instability and Gait Disturbance

Although postural instability is included as one of the 4 motor signs of PD (56), only resting tremor, rigidity, and bradykinesia are considered to be the 3 cardinal features (57). Significant impairment of postural reflexes is rare in early PD and usually occurs about 5 years after the onset of the disease (58). In fact, the presence of severe early postural instability points to a diagnosis other than PD. Nevertheless, gait disturbance and mild postural instability can be present in early PD, especially in patients with an older age of onset (59).

In early PD, the posture may show a slight flexion of the neck or trunk with a slight lean to one side. Abnormalities of gait may include asymmetrically reduced arm swing, overall slowing of gait and early fatigue, shortened stride length and intermittent shuffle, or tripping over objects, sometimes in association with ankle dystonia and the inability to turn quickly. As the disease progresses, gait initiation becomes a problem, the steps become shorter and more uncertain, and there is festination. Fear of falling further contributes to a progressively hesitant gait (60). *Freezing* refers to difficulty initiating gait or stoppage of gait when turning or arriving at a real or perceived obstacle (61). Freezing is usually absent in early PD.

The mechanisms underlying postural instability and the gait disturbance are likely multifactorial (62). Many contributors to gait and balance problems—such as arthritic pain, sensory neuropathy, and visual problems—may have nothing to do with PD itself. Clinical tests for the evaluation of postural instability in patients with PD are numerous, but the most valid simple clinical test is an unexpected shoulder pull from behind (63). The patient is asked to stand with eyes open and feet comfortably apart and instructed to resist falling by taking one step back using either foot when necessary. This "pull test" should be performed by the examiner with a moderate pull consistently each time, while being prepared to catch the patient from behind if necessary and counting the number of steps taken by the patient to maintain balance (64). The pull test is usually normal in early PD, with no more that one step backward needed to recover. The timed "up and go" test is a simple and reliable timed ambulation test. The patient is timed and the number of steps counted while he or she rises from an armchair, walks 3 to 6 meters (10 to 20 feet), turns, walks back, and sits down again (65). The total number of steps counted should include all the steps needed to make a 180-degree U-turn.

THE DIFFERENTIAL DIAGNOSIS OF PARKINSON'S DISEASE

The clinical diagnosis of PD relies heavily on history, neurologic examination, and improvement of motor signs with dopaminergic therapy (6). The differential diagnosis of parkinsonian syndromes is extensive (66, 67). It includes normal aging, essential tremor, drug-induced parkinsonism, the Parkinson-plus syndromes (progressive supranuclear palsy, corticobasal degeneration, the multiple-system atrophies, and dementia with Lewy bodies), vascular parkinsonism, normal-pressure hydrocephalus, and other less common diseases (68). Attention to distinct patterns of symptoms and signs and the time course of the disease can help to improve diagnostic accuracy (69).

Normal Aging

There is little agreement on a definition of normal aging (70). Slowness of movement, stooped posture, stiffness, and postural instability are common in the elderly (71). Comorbid conditions such as arthritis can also contribute to reduced mobility and stiffness. Asymmetric motor signs and a more accelerated rate of symptom progression are more suggestive of PD. If the level of suspicion for PD is high enough, a trial of levodopa may be the only way to establish significant and sustained response to dopaminergic therapy and hence the clinical diagnosis of PD.

Essential Tremor

Essential tremor is characterized by action tremor rather than resting tremor (72). It tends to be bilateral but is frequently asymmetric; in half the cases, there is a family history. The frequency (8 Hz) of essential tremor is higher than that of PD, but it decreases with age. In severe cases, essential tremor may seem to be present at rest, making it difficult to differentiate from the tremor seen in PD. The presence of rigidity, bradykinesia, and response to dopaminergic therapy helps differentiate PD from essential tremor. However, some PD patients have a postural rather than a rest tremor or both postural and rest tremor, and some with long-standing essential tremor may develop parkinsonism (73).

Drug-Induced Parkinsonism

Drug-induced parkinsonism usually occurs after exposure to neuroleptics. Antiemetic and promotility agents (e.g., promethazine, prochlorperazine, metoclopramide, and droperidol) (74), reserpine (75), tetrabenazine (76), and even some calcium channel blockers (e.g., flunarizine and cinnarizine) (77) can cause parkinsonism. The symptoms are symmetric, and drug-induced parkinsonism resolves when the offending drug is stopped, although resolution may require weeks to months.

Progressive Supranuclear Palsy

Progressive supranuclear palsy (PSP) is a rapidly progressive degenerative disease belonging to the family of tauopathies, with widespread pathology involving cortical and subcortical structures (78). In PSP, oculomotor disturbance, early postural instability with falls, and frontal dementia predominate. There is symmetric onset of parkinsonism, early postural instability, severe axial rigidity, absence of tremor, and poor response to dopaminergic therapy. Supranuclear gaze palsy, especially of downgaze, is the defining characteristic. Blepharospasm and eyelid opening apraxia are also common (79).

Corticobasal Degeneration

Corticobasal degeneration (CBD) usually manifests with markedly asymmetric parkinsonism and cortical signs (80). There is asymmetric limb dystonia and limb apraxia as well as corticospinal tract signs and earlier dementia than in PD. Cortical myoclonus, early oculomotor and eyelid abnormalities, cortical sensory signs (e.g., agraphesthesia), and the alien limb phenomenon may be present. There is poor response to dopaminergic medications. The variability of presentation of pathologically proven CBD is wide; for example, it can present as a primary frontotemporal dementing illness that can mimic the dementia seen in other neurodegenerative diseases (81).

Multiple-System Atrophy

Multiple-system atrophy (MSA) is a current term lumping together the previously split entities of olivopontocerebellar atrophy (OPCA), Shy-Drager syndrome, and striatonigral degeneration (82). MSA presents with parkinsonism as well as cerebellar, autonomic (orthostatic hypotension, bladder and bowel dysfunction, temperature dysregulation), and pyramidal dysfunction in various combinations (83, 84). MSA-P (formerly striatonigral degeneration) is characterized by symmetric parkinsonism without tremor and early postural instability. MSA-C (formerly OPCA) manifests itself with cerebellar signs and parkinsonism. Corticospinal tract signs and respiratory stridor may be seen in all types of MSA. There is no significant motor improvement with dopaminergic therapy. In fact, the severity of orthostatic hypotension often prevents an adequate trial of dopaminergic drugs.

Dementia with Lewy Bodies

Whether dementia with Lewy bodies (DLB) exists as a distinct clinical entity is controversial. The usual description of DLB indicates that it is characterized by progressive parkinsonism and early dementia. DLB is the second most common cause of neurodegenerative dementia in older people (85). Some estimates suggest that up to 30% of dementias may be due to DLB (86). The current consensus is to restrict a diagnosis of DLB to patients with parkinsonism who develop dementia before or within 12 months of the onset of motor symptoms (87). In DLB, there is minimal or no resting tremor. Early cognitive and psychiatric problems are present. Fluctuating cognition and level of interaction, early recurrent and well-formed hallucinations, REM behavior sleep disorder, and psychosis may be present even prior to dopaminergic therapy. Motor symptoms do not improve and psychiatric symptoms are exacerbated by small doses of dopaminergic medications.

Vascular Parkinsonism

Vascular parkinsonism is due to multiple infarcts in the basal ganglia and the subcortical white matter (88). Since there are no specific diagnostic criteria, true incidence and prevalence rates of vascular parkinsonism are not known, but some estimates suggest that this condition may account for up to12% of all cases of parkinsonism (89). In vascular parkinsonism, the motor signs are symmetric, affecting the lower limbs more than the upper limbs, so-called lower-body parkinsonism. Gait difficulty is a common presentation. Resting tremor is usually absent. Dementia, pseudobulbar affect, urinary symptoms, and pyramidal signs frequently accompany vascular parkinsonism. There is no therapeutic response to dopaminergic therapy. Brain imaging reveals extensive small vessel disease in the basal ganglia and the subcortical white matter. Microvascular lesions are commonly seen on magnetic resonance imaging (MRI) in the older population, and PD patients are no exception. Therefore the mere presence of these lesions on imaging does not necessarily imply vascular parkinsonism.

Normal-Pressure Hydrocephalus

Normal-pressure hydrocephalus (NPH) refers to chronic, communicating adult-onset hydrocephalus. Gait disturbance, urinary incontinence, and cognitive impairment make up the clinical triad of NPH without other signs of raised intracranial pressure (e.g., papilledema). NPH has been the subject of an intensive advertising campaign (90) that has raised patients' concern about whether their parkinsonism is caused by this problem. Hydrocephalus can present with motor signs similar to those seen in vascular parkinsonism. It is hypothesized that the close proximity of the basal ganglia and their connections to the ventricular system may predispose them to mass effect or ischemic injury in the setting of ventriculomegaly (91). The gait disturbance of NPH does not respond to dopaminergic therapy or to external cues, while both are quite effective in improving gait and stride length in PD (92).

NEUROIMAGING IN THE DIAGNOSIS OF EARLY PD

PD is a clinical diagnosis; in typical cases, no laboratory test or neuroimaging is necessary. However, when the history or clinical findings are atypical, MRI may be helpful. Over the last 2 decades, functional neuroimaging of the nigrostriatal dopaminergic pathway with PET and single photon emission computed tomography (SPECT) has been refined as a tool in quantifying functional dopaminergic terminals in the striatum (93, 94).

Functional neuroimaging is still used only experimentally and not for the routine diagnosis of early PD or assessment of disease progression. Both SPECT and PET have been used in therapeutic trials that include disease progression as an outcome measure (95, 96). However, drug-induced changes in radiotracer binding might undermine the reliability of imaging studies of disease progression (97). For this reason, there is much controversy about the interpretation of the neuroimaging findings of those trials (98).

CONCLUSION

The 3 cardinal features of early PD are resting tremor, rigidity, and bradykinesia. Table 6-2 summarizes proposed diagnostic criteria for clinically possible, clinically probable, and clinically definite PD as well as the exclusionary criteria (68). Postural instability is a rare occurrence in early PD and is less specific than the other 3 signs. Asymmetry of motor symptoms and signs is the rule rather that the exception in PD. However, asymmetry may be absent or may not be uniform for the different motor signs (e.g., in the same patient, tremor may be

---

TABLE 6-2
Clinical Criteria for the Diagnosis or Exclusion of Parkinson Disease

1. Diagnostic Criteria
Clinically possible PD
  One of the following: asymmetric resting tremor, asymmetric rigidity, or asymmetric bradykinesia
Clinically probable PD
  Any 2 of the following: asymmetric resting tremor, asymmetric rigidity, or asymmetric bradykinesia
Clinically definite PD
  Criteria for clinically probable PD
  Definitive response to antiparkinsonian medications

2. Exclusionary criteria
Exposure to drugs that can cause parkinsonism, such as neuroleptics, some antiemetic medications, tetrabena zine, reserpine, flunarizine, and cinnarizine
Cerebellar signs
Corticospinal tract signs
Eye movement abnormalities other than a slight limitation of upward gaze
Severe dysautonomia
Early moderate to severe gait disturbance or dementia
Evidence of severe subcortical white matter disease, hydrocephalus, or other structural lesions on MRI that may explain parkinsonian symptomatology

Source: Adapted from Samii et al. (68). With permission.

worse on one side and bradykinesia and rigidity worse on the other) (99). Exposure to drugs that can cause parkinsonism, cerebellar or corticospinal tract signs, oculomotor abnormalities other than slight limitation of upward gaze, severe dysautonomia, early moderate to severe gait disturbance or dementia, severe subcortical white matter disease, and hydrocephalus should point to a diagnosis other than PD. The heterogeneity in early

clinical signs and subsequent disease progression has led some to divide PD into various subtypes depending on age of onset, tremor predominance, and rate of progression (100). Parkinson's disease remains a clinical diagnosis based on its phenotype (101); there is no confirmatory diagnostic test. At present, functional neuroimaging of the nigrostriatal pathway with PET and SPECT are not unequivocal markers of disease progression in PD.

*R*eferences

1. Calne DB. Is "Parkinson's disease" one disease? *J Neurol Neurosurg Psychiatry* 1989; (Suppl):18–21.
2. Nutt JG, Wooten GF. Clinical practice: Diagnosis and initial management of Parkinson's disease. *N Engl J Med* 2005; 353(10):1021–1027.
3. Gibb WR, Lees AJ. The relevance of the Lewy body to the pathogenesis of idiopathic Parkinson's disease. *J Neurol Neurosurg Psychiatry* 1988; 51(6):745–752.
4. Calne DB, Snow B, Lee C: Criteria for diagnosing Parkinson's disease. *Ann Neurol* 1992; 32(Suppl S1):25–27.
5. Gelb DJ, Oliver E, Gilman S. Diagnostic criteria for Parkinson disease. *Arch Neurol* 1999; 56(1):33–39.
6. Calne D. A definition of Parkinson's disease. *Parkinsonism Relat Disord* 2005; 11(Suppl 1): S39–S40.
7. Lees AJ, Hardie RJ, Stern GM. Kinesigenic foot dystonia as a presenting feature of Parkinson's disease. *J Neurol Neurosurg Psychiatry* 1984; 47(8):885.
8. Shulman LM, Singer C, Bean J, Weiner WJ. Internal tremor in patients with Parkinson's disease. *Mov Disord* 1996; 11:3–7.
9. Olson EJ, Boeve BF, Silber MH. Rapid eye movement sleep behaviour disorder: Demographic, clinical and laboratory findings in 93 cases. *Brain* 2000; 123:331–339.
10. Matheson JK, Saper CB. REM sleep behavior disorder: A dopaminergic deficiency disorder? *Neurology* 2003; 61(10):1328–1329.
11. Phillips B, Young T, Finn L, et al. Epidemiology of restless legs symptoms in adults. *Arch Intern Med* 2000; 160(14):2137–2141.
12. Ondo WG, Vuong KD, Jankovic J. Exploring the relationship between Parkinson disease and restless legs syndrome. *Arch Neurol* 2002; 59(3):421–424.
13. Abbott RD, Petrovitch H, White LR, et al. Frequency of bowel movements and the future risk of Parkinson's disease. *Neurology* 2001; 57(3):456–462.
14. Burton JL, Shuster S. Effect of L-dopa on seborrhoea of Parkinsonism. *Lancet* 1970; 2(7662):19–20.
15. Mastrolonardo M, Diaferio A, Logroscino G. Seborrheic dermatitis, increased sebum excretion, and Parkinson's disease: A survey of possible links. *Med Hypotheses* 2003; 60(6):907–911.
16. Ponsen MM, Stoffers D, Booij J, et al. Idiopathic hyposmia as a preclinical sign of Parkinson's disease. *Ann Neurol* 2004; 56(2):173–181.
17. Double KL, Rowe DB, Hayes M, et al. Identifying the pattern of olfactory deficits in Parkinson disease using the brief smell identification test. *Arch Neuro.* 2003; 60(4):545–549.
18. Stiasny-Kolster K, Doerr Y, Moller JC, et al. Combination of "idiopathic" REM sleep behaviour disorder and olfactory dysfunction as possible indicator for alpha-synucleinopathy demonstrated by dopamine transporter FP-CIT-SPECT. *Brain* 2005; 128(Pt 1):126–137.
19. Singer C. Urinary dysfunction in Parkinson's disease. *Clin Neurosci* 1998;(2):78–86.
20. Siddiqui MF, Rast S, Lynn MJ, et al. Autonomic dysfunction in Parkinson's disease: A comprehensive symptom survey. *Parkinsonism Relat Disord* 2002; 8(4):277–284.
21. Uekermann J, Daum I, Peters S, et al. Depressed mood and executive dysfunction in early Parkinson's disease. *Acta Neurol Scand* 2003; 107(5):341–348.
22. Laatu S, Revonsuo A, Pihko L, et al. Visual object recognition deficits in early Parkinson's disease. *Parkinsonism Relat Disord* 2004; 10(4):227–233.
23. Dubois B, Pillon B. Cognitive deficits in Parkinson's disease. *J Neurol* 1997; 244(1):2–8.
24. Schrag A, Jahanshahi M, Quinn N. What contributes to quality of life in patients with Parkinson's disease? *J Neurol Neurosurg Psychiatry* 2000; 69(3):308–312.
25. Braak H, Del Tredici K, Rub U, et al. Staging of brain pathology related to sporadic Parkinson's disease. *Neurobiol Aging* 2003; 24(2):197–211.
26. Braak H, Ghebremedhin E, Rub U, et al. Stages in the development of Parkinson's disease–related pathology. *Cell Tissue Res* 2004; 318(1):121–134.
27. Rajput AH, Rozdilsky B, Ang L. Occurrence of resting tremor in Parkinson's disease. *Neurology* 1991; 41(8):1298–1299.
28. Calne DB, Stoessl AJ. Early parkinsonism. *Clin Neuropharmacol* 1986; (9 Suppl 2): S3–S8.
29. Hallett M. Parkinson revisited: pathophysiology of motor signs. *Adv Neurol* 2003; 91:19–28.
30. Otsuka M, Ichiya Y, Kuwabara Y, et al. Differences in the reduced 18F-Dopa uptakes of the caudate and the putamen in Parkinson's disease: correlations with the three main symptoms. *J Neurol Sci* 1996; 136(1–2):169–173.
31. Jankovic J, Cardoso F, Grossman RG, Hamilton WJ. Outcome after stereotactic thalamotomy for parkinsonian, essential, and other types of tremor. *Neurosurgery* 1995; 37(4):680–686.
32. Ertan S, Fresko I, Apaydin H, et al. Extrapyramidal type rigidity in rheumatoid arthritis. *Rheumatology (Oxford)* 1999; 38(7):627–630.
33. Riley D, Lang AE, Blair RD, et al. Frozen shoulder and other shoulder disturbances in Parkinson's disease. *J Neurol Neurosurg Psychiatry* 1989; 52(1):63–66.
34. Djaldetti R, Mosberg-Galili R, Sroka H, et al. Camptocormia (bent spine) in patients with Parkinson's disease: Characterization and possible pathogenesis of an unusual phenomenon. *Mov Disord* 1999; 14(3):443–447.
35. Rothwell JC, Obeso JA, Traub MM, Marsden CD. The behaviour of the long-latency stretch reflex in patients with Parkinson's disease. *J Neurol Neurosurg Psychiatry* 1983; 46(1):35–44.
36. Buhmann C, Gorsler A, Baumer T, et al. Abnormal excitability of premotor-motor connections in de novo Parkinson's disease. *Brain* 2004; 127:2732–2746.
37. Prochazka A, Bennett DJ, Stephens MJ, et al. Measurement of rigidity in Parkinson's disease. *Mov Disord* 1997; 12(1):24–32.
38. Teravainen H, Tsui JK, Mak E, Calne DB. Optimal indices for testing parkinsonian rigidity. *Can J Neurol Sci* 1989; 16(2):180–183.
39. Hallett M, Berardelli A, Delwaide P, et al. Central EMG and tests of motor control. Report of an IFCN committee. *Electroencephalogr Clin Neurophysiol* 1994; 90(6):404–432.
40. Marsden CD. Slowness of movement in Parkinson's disease. *Mov Disord* 1989; 4(Suppl 1): S26–S37.
41. Rottach KG, Riley DE, DiScenna AO, et al. Dynamic properties of horizontal and vertical eye movements in parkinsonian syndromes. Ann Neurol 1996; 39(3):368–377.
42. Baker KK, Ramig LO, Luschei ES, Smith ME. Thyroarytenoid muscle activity associated with hypophonia in Parkinson disease and aging. *Neurology* 1998; 51(6): 1592–1598.
43. Shahed J, Jankovic J. Re-emergence of childhood stuttering in Parkinson's disease: A hypothesis. *Mov Disord* 2001; 16(1):114–118.
44. Martinez-Martin P, Gil-Nagel A, Gracia LM, Gomez JB, Martinez-Sarries J, Bermejo F. Unified Parkinson's Disease Rating Scale characteristics and structure. The Cooperative Multicentric Group. Mov Disord. 1994;9(1):76–83.
45. Muller T, Benz S. Quantification of the dopaminergic response in Parkinson's disease. *Parkinsonism Relat Disord* 2002; 8(3):181–186.
46. Muller T, Schafer S, Kuhn W, Przuntek H. Correlation between tapping and inserting of pegs in Parkinson's disease. *Can J Neurol Sci* 2000; 27(4):311–315.
47. Kraus PH, Klotz P, Hoffmann A, et al. Analysis of the course of Parkinson's disease under dopaminergic therapy: Performance of "fast tapping" is not a suitable parameter. *Mov Disord* 2005; 20(3):348–354.
48. Vingerhoets FJ, Schulzer M, Calne DB, Snow BJ. Which clinical sign of Parkinson's disease best reflects the nigrostriatal lesion? *Ann Neurol* 1997; 41(1):58–64.
49. Pal PK, Lee CS, Samii A, et al. Alternating two finger tapping with contralateral activation is an objective measure of clinical severity in Parkinson's disease and correlates with PET. *Parkinsonism Relat Disord* 2001; 7(4):305–309.
50. Wichmann T, DeLong MR. Functional neuroanatomy of the basal ganglia in Parkinson's disease. *Adv Neurol.* 2003;91:9–18.
51. Berardelli A, Rothwell JC, Thompson PD, Hallett M. Pathophysiology of bradykinesia in Parkinson's disease. *Brain* 2001; 124:2131–2146.
52. Chen R, Kumar S, Garg RR, Lang AE. Impairment of motor cortex activation and deactivation in Parkinson's disease. *Clin Neurophysiol* 2001; 112(4):600–607.
53. Rossini PM, Babiloni F, Bernardi G, et al. Abnormalities of short-latency somatosensory evoked potentials in parkinsonian patients. *Electroencephalogr Clin Neurophysiol* 1989; 74(4):277–289.
54. Dick JP, Rothwell JC, Day BL, et al. The Bereitschaftspotential is abnormal in Parkinson's disease. *Brain* 1989; 112 (Pt 1):233–244.
55. Strafella AP, Dagher A, Sadikot AF. Cerebral blood flow changes induced by subthalamic stimulation in Parkinson's disease. *Neurology* 2003; 60(6):1039–1042.
56. Bloem BR. Postural instability in Parkinson's disease. *Clin Neurol Neurosurg* 1992; 94(Suppl):S41–S45.
57. Koller WC, Montgomery EB. Issues in the early diagnosis of Parkinson's disease. Neurology 1997; 49(1 Suppl 1):S10–S25.

58. Marttila RJ, Rinne UK. Disability and progression in Parkinson's disease. *Acta Neurol Scand* 1977; 56(2):159–169.

59. Gibb WR, Lees AJ. A comparison of clinical and pathological features of young- and old-onset Parkinson's disease. *Neurology* 1988; 38(9):1402–1406.

60. Adkin AL, Frank JS, Jog MS. Fear of falling and postural control in Parkinson's disease. *Mov Disord* 2003; 18(5):496–502.

61. Bloem BR, Hausdorff JM, Visser JE, Giladi N. Falls and freezing of gait in Parkinson's disease: A review of two interconnected, episodic phenomena. *Mov Disord* 2004; 19(8):871–884.

62. Nallegowda M, Singh U, Handa G, et al. Role of sensory input and muscle strength in maintenance of balance, gait, and posture in Parkinson's disease: A pilot study. *Am J Phys Med Rehabil* 2004; 83(12):898–908.

63. Visser M, Marinus J, Bloem BR, et al. Clinical tests for the evaluation of postural instability in patients with Parkinson's disease. *Arch Phys Med Rehabil* 2003; 84(11):1669–1674.

64. Munhoz RP, Li JY, Kurtinecz M, et al. Evaluation of the pull test technique in assessing postural instability in Parkinson's disease. *Neurology* 2004; 62(1):125–127.

65. Podsiadlo D, Richardson S. The timed "Up & Go": A test of basic functional mobility for frail elderly persons. *J Am Geriatr Soc* 1991; 39(2):142–148

66. Poewe W, Wenning G. The differential diagnosis of Parkinson's disease. *Eur J Neurol* 2002; (9 Suppl 3):23–30.

67. Christine CW, Aminoff MJ. Clinical differentiation of parkinsonian syndromes: Prognostic and therapeutic relevance. *Am J Med* 2004; 117(6):412–419.

68. Samii A, Nutt JG, Ransom BR. Parkinson's disease. *Lancet* 2004; 363:1783–1793.

69. Lachenmayer L. Differential diagnosis of parkinsonian syndromes: Dynamics of time courses are essential. *J Neurol* 2003; 250(Suppl 1):I11–I14.

70. Calne DB, Eisen A, Meneilly G. Normal aging of the nervous system. *Ann Neurol* 1991; 30(2):206–207.

71. Bennett DA, Beckett LA, Murray AM, et al. Prevalence of parkinsonian signs and associated mortality in a community population of older people. *N Engl J Med* 1996; 334(2):71–76.

72. Jankovic J. Essential tremor: Clinical characteristics. *Neurology* 2000; 54(11 Suppl 4):S21–S25.

73. Jankovic J. Essential tremor and Parkinson's disease. *Ann Neurol* 1989; 25(2):211–212.

74. Bateman DN, Darling WM, Boys R, Rawlins MD. Extrapyramidal reactions to metoclopramide and prochlorperazine. *Q J Med* 1989; 71(264):307–311.

75. Ross RT. Drug-induced parkinsonism and other movement disorders. *Can J Neurol Sci* 1990; 17(2):155–162.

76. Giladi N, Melamed E. Levodopa therapy can ameliorate tetrabenazine-induced parkinsonism. *Mov Disord* 1999; 14(1):158–159.

77. Teive HA, Troiano AR, Germiniani FM, Werneck LC. Flunarizine and cinnarizine-induced parkinsonism: A historical and clinical analysis. *Parkinsonism Relat Disord* 2004; 10(4):243–245.

78. Rampello L, Butta V, Raffaele R, et al. Progressive supranuclear palsy: A systematic review. *Neurobiol Dis* 2005; 20(2):179–186.

79. Golbe LI, Davis PH, Lepore FE. Eyelid movement abnormalities in progressive supranuclear palsy. *Mov Disord* 1989; 4(4):297–302.

80. Mahapatra RK, Edwards MJ, Schott JM, Bhatia KP. Corticobasal degeneration. *Lancet Neurol* 2004; 3(12):736–743.

81. Kertesz A, McMonagle P, Blair M, et al. The evolution and pathology of frontotemporal dementia. *Brain* 2005; 128(Pt 9):1996–2005.

82. Shulman LM, Minagar A, Weiner WJ. Multiple system atrophy. In: Watts RL, Koller WC (eds). *Movement Disorders: Neurologic Principles and Practice*, 2nd ed. New York: McGraw Hill, 2004:319–326.

83. Gilman S, Low PA, Quinn N, et al. Consensus statement on the diagnosis of multiple system atrophy. *J Neurol Sci* 1999; 163(1):94–98.

84. Wenning GK, Colosimo C, Geser F, Poewe W. Multiple system atrophy. *Lancet Neurol* 2004; 3(2):93–103.

85. McKeith I, Mintzer J, Aarsland D, et al. Dementia with Lewy bodies. *Lancet Neurol* 2004; 3(1):19–28.

86. Zaccai J, McCracken C, Brayne C. A systematic review of prevalence and incidence studies of dementia with Lewy bodies. *Age Ageing* 2005; 34(6):561–566.

87. Geser F, Wenning GK, Poewe W, McKeith I. How to diagnose dementia with Lewy bodies: State of the art. *Mov Disord* 2005; 20(Suppl 12):S11–S20.

88. Sibon I, Fenelon G, Quinn NP, Tison F. Vascular parkinsonism. *J Neurol* 2004; 251(5):513–524.

89. Thanvi B, Lo N, Robinson T. Vascular parkinsonism: An important cause of parkinsonism in older people. *Age Ageing* 2005; 34(2):114–119.

90. Friedman JH. NPH on TV. *Med Health RI* 2005; 88(8):252.

91. Curran T, Lang AE. Parkinsonian syndromes associated with hydrocephalus: Case reports, a review of the literature, and pathophysiological hypotheses. *Mov Disord* 1994; 9(5):508–520.

92. Stolze H, Kuhtz-Buschbeck JP, Drucke H, et al. Comparative analysis of the gait disorder of normal pressure hydrocephalus and Parkinson's disease. *J Neurol Neurosurg Psychiatry* 2001; 70(3):289–297.

93. Vingerhoets FJ, Snow BJ, Lee CS, et al. Longitudinal fluorodopa positron emission tomographic studies of the evolution of idiopathic parkinsonism. *Ann Neurol* 1994; 36(5):759–764.

94. Lee CS, Samii A, Sossi V, Ruth TJ, et al. In vivo positron emission tomographic evidence for compensatory changes in presynaptic dopaminergic nerve terminals in Parkinson's disease. *Ann Neurol* 2000; 47(4):493–503.

95. Parkinson Study Group. Dopamine transporter brain imaging to assess the effects of pramipexole vs levodopa on Parkinson disease progression. *JAMA* 2002; 287(13):1653–1661.

96. Whone AL, Watts RL, Stoessl AJ, et al. REAL-PET Study Group. Slower progression of Parkinson's disease with ropinirole versus levodopa: The REAL-PET study. *Ann Neurol* 2003; 54(1):93–101.

97. Winogrodzka A, Booij J, Wolters ECh. Disease-related and drug-induced changes in dopamine transporter expression might undermine the reliability of imaging studies of disease progression in Parkinson's disease. *Parkinsonism Relat Disord* 2005; 11(8):475–484.

98. Ravina B, Eidelberg D, Ahlskog JE, et al. The role of radiotracer imaging in Parkinson disease. *Neurology* 2005; 64(2):208–215.

99. Toth C, Rajput M, Rajput AH. Anomalies of asymmetry of clinical signs in parkinsonism. *Mov Disord* 2004; 19(2):151–157.

100. Lewis SJ, Foltynie T, Blackwell AD, et al. Heterogeneity of Parkinson's disease in the early clinical stages using a data driven approach. *J Neurol Neurosurg Psychiatry* 2005; 76(3):343–348.

101. Uitti RJ, Baba Y, Wszolek ZK, Putzke DJ. Defining the Parkinson's disease phenotype: Initial symptoms and baseline characteristics in a clinical cohort. *Parkinsonism Relat Disord* 2005; 11(3):139–145.

7

Gait Disturbances

Nir Giladi
Alice Nieuwboer

In his paper "An Essay on the Shaking Palsy"(1), James Parkinson first described, as follows, the gait disturbances typical of the condition later to be named after him:

> The propensity to lean forward becomes invincible, and the patient is thereby forced to step on the toes and fore part of the feet, whilst the upper part of the body is thrown so far forward as to render it difficult to avoid falling on the face. In some cases, when this state of the malady is attained, the patient can no longer exercise himself by walking in his usual manner, but is thrown on the toes and forepart of the feet; being, at the same time, irresistibly impelled to make much quicker and short steps, and thereby to adopt unwillingly a running pace. In some cases it is found necessary entirely to substitute running for walking; since otherwise the patient, on proceeding only a very few paces, would inevitably fall.

Gait disturbances such as festination are characteristic integral elements of Parkinson's disease (PD). However, it was not until recently that episodic gait disturbance was recognized as a specific parkinsonian feature (2).

Parkinsonian gait is classified as a hypokinetic rigid type of gait disorder (Table 7-1) (3). However, the underlying mechanism of gait disturbance in PD is heterogeneous and complex. It is affected by muscle rigidity, hypokinesia, bradykinesia, decrease in force generation, dysrhythmicity, left/right dyssynchrony, abnormal scaling of step size, abnormal preparation and execution of motor set (4), as well as dysexecutive syndrome. In addition, the ability to initiate and maintain locomotion is heavily dependent on postural reflexes, which are frequently disturbed in PD. The contribution of each disturbance to the final parkinsonian gait abnormality differs from one patient to another and in the same individual at different times of day or stages of the disease.

The purpose of this chapter is to characterize the different subtypes of gait disturbances in PD, correlate them with the clinical syndrome, and discuss the effects of different therapeutic modalities.

GAIT DISTURBANCE AS PART OF THE CLINICAL SYNDROME

Gait disturbance (not including decreased arm swing while walking) is the presenting symptom in 3.5% to 18% of patients clinically diagnosed as having PD (5–7). Gomez and coworkers (8) compared PD patients with symptom onset before the age of 40 years with those with symptom onset after age 60 and found that gait disturbance was the presenting symptom in 39% of the late-onset patients compared with only 3% of the early-onset subgroup. However, a significant number of patients who present

TABLE 7-1
System-Oriented Classification of Gait Syndromes

Peripherally originating gait syndromes

- **Musculoskeletal**
  Joints, bones, ligaments, tendons or muscles,
  peripheral nerves, neuromuscular junction

- **Sensory**
  Proprioceptive, vestibular, visual

Centrally originating gait syndromes

- **Spinal**
  Spastic paraparetic
  Sensory ataxic

- **Pyramidal**
  Spastic
  Paretic

- **Cerebellar**
  Ataxic

- **Extrapyramidal**
  Bradykinetic/hypokinetic
  Rigid
  Dyskinetic
  Episodic

- **Frontal**
  Dysequilibrium
  "Apractic"

- **Unclassified**
  Cautious

with gait disturbance as the initial motor symptom of parkinsonism (frequently in association with postural reflex abnormalities) are eventually diagnosed as having other parkinsonian syndromes, such as progressive supranuclear palsy (PSP), normal-pressure hydrocephalus (NPH), or vascular parkinsonism and not primary PD. In a retrospective analysis of patients with a pathologically confirmed diagnosis of Lewy body PD, none had gait disturbance as the presenting symptom, whereas 100% of those with pathologically observed vascular changes at the level of the basal ganglia and parkinsonism presented with gait disturbance (9). In other clinical-pathologic studies, 13% to 33% of patients presented with postural instability or gait disturbance (PIGD) as the initial motor symptom (10–12). Those patients who present with PIGD as the initial motor symptom are significantly older (10), which concords with our clinical experience.

It is more common for gait disturbance to be a feature of advanced PD. As the disease progresses, all patients lose their ability to walk independently because

of a combination of severe rigidity, akinesia, and postural instability. Hoehn and Yahr (5) based their clinical scale for PD motor progression on this observation, defining the most advanced stages (stages 4 and 5) according to the individual's ability to stand and walk.

Since the introduction of levodopa 40 years ago (13), the relationship between disease progression and deterioration of gait has become more complex. Because of recent therapeutic advances, patients can often walk well in the "on" state even in the advanced stages of the disease, whereas akinesia can be seen at earlier stages as part of the "off" state. Furthermore, the beneficial effect of levodopa treatment has created new types of gait disturbances, such as choreic or dystonic (dyskinetic) gait and "on" freezing. Moreover, the use of levodopa and functional neurosurgery have increased the PD patient's life expectancy and years of mobility. Consequently, disturbed postural reflexes, orthostatic hypotension, severely distorted posture, as well as cognitive disturbances have become major contributory factors in gait disturbance in advanced stages of PD.

ASSESSMENT OF GAIT

Gait should be assessed in every PD patient as part of the basic evaluation at the initial and all follow-up evaluations. Two timed tests of gait can be used to assess performance, the 10-m walk test and the timed "'up-and-go'" (TUG) test (14–16). Both tests have established validity and reliability in both the home and the clinical setting for patients with PD (16–18). In the 10-m walk test, the patient is asked to perform straight-line walking, enabling the measurement of gait speed, step length, and step frequency. In the TUG, the patient is asked to stand up and walk forward for 3 meters, turn around, and return back to his or her chair, providing an opportunity to evaluate turning, gait initiation, and termination. In both tests it is important to be explicit about the speed with which the task should be accomplished: the patient should be asked to walk at whatever speed feels most comfortable (or is preferred). While the patient is performing the task, the examiner should assess the patient's ability to initiate gait, keep an upright position, walk toward a destination, perform a turn in place, and return to the chair correctly. Other features that should be observed are body posture, speed and fluency of stepping, stride length, and the distance between the feet (base). While looking carefully at a single step, one should note the height to which the swinging leg is raised above the ground and how this foot meets the floor (heel strike) and rolls forward. In addition, attention should be paid to the degree of arm swing and axial rotation. Such an examination should be performed in an open space free of obstacles to allow for the patient's best performance. There are several clinical scales in use to evaluate gait. The most widely used is the Tinetti scale, which assesses balance and mobility in two different measurements that yield a maximum of 28 points: 16 for balance and 12 for gait (19). There is no universally accepted scale that specifically assesses parkinsonian gait. However, almost all clinical scales in use for evaluation of parkinsonism include several items to rate gait. If the patient is complaining about freezing, the examiner should try to provoke freezing episodes by asking the patient to perform more turns, walk through narrow spaces, and step up and down the stairs to differentiate between freezing (gait disturbance only) and akinesia (stairs and gait disturbance).

The clinical assessment of gait is ultimately based on the examiner's observational impression. For more detailed and precise evaluation of gait, however, the assessment takes place in a 3-dimensional computerized gait laboratory, where cadence, stride length, velocity, and double limb support are measured while obtaining information on muscle activation, joint movement, and analysis of limb movement in space (20). For the assessment of dynamic aspects of gait, such as stride-to-stride variation, left/right leg synchronization as well as the use of cues or the effect of dual tasking, locomotion should be assessed over a longer period of time and over multiple steps. For such studies either pressure-sensitive insoles or special shoes are frequently used, as well as walkways with sensor pads. Ambulatory monitors are now used for quantifying daily walking and general mobility in daily life (21, 22).

Gait Initiation

Initiation of gait can be subdivided into a movement preparation period and a movement execution phase. Movement preparation represents the "motor planning" phase, in which an overall strategy is taken as to where, when, and how to initiate gait (23). In PD patients, the preparation time was found to be significantly prolonged, with a tendency to become longer as the disease progressed (24). Execution time was prolonged as well, but to a lesser degree (24). Normally the Bereitschafts potential (BP) (the preparatory cortical potential proceeding a motor act) is larger in amplitude when complex sequences of movements are being executed, such as stepping, rather than when simple motor tasks are performed (25). Vidailhet and coworkers (26) found that the BP did not increase in amplitude in PD patients when step initiation in standing was compared with foot tapping in sitting. The abnormal response of the BP in step initiation was interpreted as an indirect neurophysiologic sign for abnormality in the central preparatory phase of gait initiation (26).

During gait initiation, posture is adjusted by first shifting the center of gravity (COG) laterally and rotating the body before weight is taken on the stance foot to allow the leading leg to swing forward while the COG is shifted anteriorly to create the forward momentum (27). This shift in the COG anteriorly is accomplished by bending the ankle and trunk (28). The onset of the anterior shift of the trunk was found to be slow in patients with advanced PD (24). In addition, there is reduced lateral shift of the body mass over the stance limb, decreased propulsive force, and prolonged anticipatory postural adjustment (29, 30). Alterations in postural stability might interfere with the performance of an otherwise intact motor program and movement sequencing and might create specific difficulties in gait initiation (31). Execution time and the relative timing of submovement sequences associated with gait initiation were similar in PD patients and age-matched controls (24).

All of these motor deficits reported in PD patients are most pronounced in self-initiated gait, whereas external cues, attention, and sensory stimulation as well as levodopa treatment can improve these parameters significantly (29). One can conclude that disturbances in gait initiation are directly related to dysfunction of the basal ganglia to control internally cued movement sequences, delaying onset but not slowing down the execution or altering the pattern of movement components of gait initiation (24, 29).

Start hesitation is the classic parkinsonian disturbance experienced at gait initiation. It has been described as the most common type of freezing of gait (FOG) and is considered to be part of the episodic gait disturbances discussed below, under "Freezing of Gait" (6, 32, 33) (Table 7-2).

Start hesitation is best described by patients as a feeling that their feet are "stuck or glued to the ground." It is frequently seen at initiation of gait but also occurs while changing from one mode of movement to another—for example, while completing a turn and trying to move

---

TABLE 7-2
Examples of Episodic Gait Disturbances in Parkinsonism*

Freezing of gait
  Start hesitation
  Turning hesitation
  Tight quarters hesitation
  Hesitation while reaching destination
  Hesitation during mental overload or stressful situations

Festinating gait

---

*It is helpful to distinguish between those gait disturbances that occur continuously, whenever the patient walks (e.g., slowness, reduced foot strike) and those that are transient and episodic.

forward. Although an episode of start hesitation generally lasts a few seconds, it can sometimes last long enough to make gait impossible. During the "on" state, start hesitation usually lasts a few seconds and is easily overcome; during the "off" state, start hesitation lasts much longer and is more difficult to overcome (32). During these episodes, patients are actively trying to overcome the block by making small and ineffective movements with their legs. In the worst case, this situation can lead to falls.

The mechanism responsible for start hesitation is not clear, but it has been associated with a complete lack of initiation of postural adjustments (29). Andrews (34) recorded leg muscle activation of PD patients during freezing episodes and demonstrated coactivation of agonist and antagonist muscles without the temporal activation pattern seen in normal gait initiation. Such a disturbance of muscle activity can explain the inability to initiate a step.

The gait initiation pattern of PD patients is difficult to assess objectively, both in gait laboratories and during the office visit, because it is highly variable and influenced by many sensory and cognitive factors. Several studies attempting to assess start hesitation or other FOG episodes have failed (Table 7-3) (29, 35). We have recently proposed a FOG interview based questionnaire—a validated scale for evaluating severity of freezing episodes and the frequency of start hesitation (36, 37).

Locomotion

Abnormal locomotion is characteristic of parkinsonism. The parkinsonian gait is slow, with reduced stride length, decreased cadence (steps per minute), and increased proportion of the gait cycle spent in the double-limb support phase of stance. Shuffling and festinating gait, freezing episodes, decreased arm swing, and abnormal posture are additional contributory features. Morris and

coworkers (38, 39) demonstrated in a series of experiments that patients with PD have a fundamental disturbance in stride length regulation, whereas cadence control remains intact. However, it becomes increasingly clear that basal ganglia dysfunction affects not only the automatic maintenance of the scale of movement (motor set) but also the running of each component of the motor plan in a timely manner (cue production). Recent findings of higher step-to-step variability of stride duration (32, 40–43) and increased variability of leg muscle activation during stepping (44, 45) may reflect this deficit in cue production. Stride length can become normal by the use of visual cues or strategies that increase attention to gait performance (39, 46). In contrast, tasks that compete for the individual's attention while walking (dual tasking distraction) decrease gait speed and increase stride-to-stride variability (dysrhythmicity) and left/right swing phase synchronization (39, 47–49). Normal locomotion in PD is a motor task influenced by cognition (50). Furthermore, the vulnerability of locomotion during dual tasking in regard to rhythmicity is directly correlated with the performance of the executive functions and attention (48).

Shorter stride length and increased stride-to-stride variability may be indirect signs of a disturbance at the level of the basal ganglia and the premotor/supplementary motor area (SMA)–associated loops, which are important structures for the internal control and automatic running of the gait pattern. In other words, the primary disturbance in parkinsonian gait is in motor set (4, 39), which affects gait as an automatic task.

Freezing of Gait

Freezing episodes while the patient is in motion (motor blocks) represent a special form of locomotive disturbance seen only in parkinsonism. This phenomenon refers to transient episodes, lasting seconds, in which walking is halted. It is a positive symptom that starts with hastened but synchronized activation of leg muscles prior to the actual block (51, 52) and continues with an ineffective activation of the leg muscles during the actual block (53).

Freezing episodes are unrelated to muscle weakness or abnormal muscle tone; once freezing ends, the patient is free to move or perform the task at his or her usual pace (2).

"The pathophysiology of FOG is poorly understood as neuro-imaging of gait itself is not possible. Recent neuro-imaging studies of brain activity during rest in patients with and without FOG have reported conflicting results using 2 different techniques (54). A PET-study of the dopamine and glucose metabolism in the striatum showed no group differences. A SPECT- study of brain perfusion demonstrated that patients with FOG have

TABLE 7-3
Clinical Characteristics of Freezing of Gait (FOG) Episodes as Reported by 390 Parkinson's Patients with Fluctuations in Motor Response

CHARACTERISTICS	
Percentage of Patients with FOG	48
Mainly outdoor	29
Start hesitation	57
Turning hesitation	54
At doorway	34
On open runway	22

Source: From Giladi et al. (39). With permission.

decreased bilateral activity of the orbitofrontal cortex in comparison to their counterparts without FOG(55). Whether this deficit reflects a primary dysfunction of reduced processing of incentive motivation which is associated with the orbitofrontal area, or is evidence of reduced compensatory activity to prevent FOG is unclear."

The severity of freezing is not correlated with any of the other cardinal features of parkinsonism, supporting its unique and independent pathophysiology (56). Freezing of gait can be classified into 2 types according to its relation with dopaminergic treatment: (a) as a symptom of a hypodopaminergic state that will improve with dopaminergic treatment ("off" freezing) (32) and (b) as an event that occurs during relatively normal gait ("on" freezing); the latter does not improve with apomorphine injections and can become worse with dopaminergic treatment (57). Thus freezing while "on" is not necessarily the same as "on" freezing. Another and probably more common explanation is that the treatment dose effectively improves bradykinesia and rigidity but is not high enough to overcome freezing. In such cases higher doses of levodopa might improve gait at the price of the appearance of dyskinesias.

Andrews (34) recorded electromyographic (EMG) activity with surface electrodes in 5 PD patients suffering from frequent freezing episodes. All 5 had similar (EMG) activity during the FOG episodes, which was initial activity of the gastrocnemius-soleus muscles, followed by simultaneous activity of the tibialis anterior muscle. This activity of flexors and, shortly thereafter, the coactivation of flexors and extensors was observed during freezing episodes in the muscles of the knee as well. Subsequent studies showed variable patterns of sometimes reciprocal and sometimes simultaneous EMG activity in leg flexors and extensors in relation to freezing that differed from the muscle activity recorded in resting and postural tremor (58, 59). When EMG activity during the steps preceding freezing was analyzed, premature timing in the tibial and gastrocnemius muscles occurred with overall preservation of reciprocity. This was interpreted as a disturbance of central gait cycle timing, contributing to insufficient generation of step amplitude and eventual breakdown of movement (52).

Freezing phenomena are common in PD (6, 60) and have been reported in most other hypokinetic movement disorders (60). It is part of parkinsonian akinesia (34, 61–63). FOG was reported in about 7% of recently diagnosed untreated parkinsonian patients (6, 64). Later on, however, when levodopa treatment had to be (and not been) initiated because of clinical deterioration, 26% of these patients ultimately experienced FOG (65). This increment in the percentage of "freezers" before levodopa was given, demonstrates that disease progression is a major cause of FOG and is unrelated to treatment.

Barbeau (66, 67) and Ambani and Van Woert (68) were the first to notice a significant increase in freezing starting about a year after the introduction of high-dose levodopa treatment. In advanced PD, it is difficult to differentiate between the contribution of the underlying pathologic process, disease progression, and the possible effect of levodopa treatment on the development of freezing. Several reports have demonstrated an association between FOG and the duration of levodopa treatment (6, 66, 69), although Lamberti and coworkers (65) found no such association. An association between dopamine agonist treatment and freezing of gait has been suggested (70). Such relationships could be attributed to the weaker symptomatic effect of dopamine agonists (ropinerol and pramipexol) when they were compared to levodopa in early stages of PD. The answer to this controversy will come from prospective studies.

Several reports have shown that there is an increased risk of FOG in PD when initial symptoms begin on the left side in association with speech or balance problems (6, 64, 65). In contrast, the risk of developing freezing significantly decreased when the initial motor symptom was tremor (64). Other factors found to be associated with increased freezing episodes were depression (33, 64), increased stride-to-stride variability (32), and left/right leg dyssynchronicity (71). An association of freezing of gait with dysexecutive function further supports the role of cognition in the development of FOG (72).

Freezing episodes have been divided into 3 subtypes: (a) no movement–akinesia (the patient is not making any observed effort to overcome the block), (b) trembling in place (rapid synchronized movement of both legs observed as the patient attempts to overcome the block but no movement forward is seen), and (c) shuffling forward (the patient makes an effort to overcome the block and is partially successful but the steps are very small and rapid and no real step is taken) (32).

Patients can often overcome freezing episodes by paying increased attention to the motor task and using external cues and a variety of behavioral and motor tricks (73). Stressful situations, especially time-limited ones such as entering an elevator or crossing the street when the light is green, exacerbate FOG. Curiously, a visit to the doctor's office or the gait laboratory improves FOG (35)—a phenomenon that may amaze the caregiver and that is probably related to attention and stress. Hence, the clinical evaluation and quantification of FOG during motion is difficult because of the highly variable and transitory nature of this motor disturbance.

Freezing can be a very disabling symptom of parkinsonism. It is especially troublesome when it occurs on every attempt to move. At these times it might be difficult to differentiate it from akinesia during the "off" state. One study has demonstrated that the experience of FOG plays a special and very important role in the decreased quality of life associated with PD, over and above its effect on gait and mobility (74).

Festinating Gait

Festinating gait is another typical disturbance of locomotion in parkinsonian patients. Its frequency is undetermined, but it is known to be more common in older patients and in those with more advanced PD (75). Festinating gait is commonly seen in idiopathic PD and rarely in symptomatic parkinsonism (76). It consists of rapid small steps taken in an attempt to keep the center of gravity (COG) above the feet while the trunk leans forward involuntarily and shifts the COG forward. To compensate and in an attempt to prevent falling, the patient increases stepping velocity and further shortens the stride (77). Rather than representing compensatory steps for an increasing loss of step amplitude, festination may also be a primary deficit related to freezing. The increased step frequency combined with minimal step amplitude, characteristic of festination, may reflect an involuntary rhythmic dyscontrol of gait. Further evidence for the fact that festination and freezing are related phenomena is provided by the finding that freezing preceded by festinating steps is the most common subtype of freezing (32, 51, 78).

Arm Swing

One of the clinical features associated with parkinsonian gait is decreased arm swing. It is frequently a very early sign of the disease. Decreased arm swing was reported as the most bothersome presenting symptom in 2.5% of 800 diagnosed unmedicated patients enrolled in the Deprenyl and Tocopherol Anti-oxidative Therapy of Parkinsonism (DATATOP) study (79). The reduction in upper limb movements in PD patients was associated with a significantly delayed onset of arm swing, reduced length of arm cycle, and reduced velocity of arm swing in the gait cycle (24). Decreased arm swing while walking is part of hypokinesia/bradykinesia and is also influenced by rigidity. All these parameters are further disturbed with progression of the disease (24).

TREATMENT OF PARKINSONIAN GAIT

Levodopa, the most effective and commonly used antiparkinsonian drug, has significant and long-lasting effects on parkinsonian gait. Shortly after levodopa was introduced for the treatment of parkinsonism in the late 1960s, its effect on gait velocity became clear (79–81). Its use led to a significant improvement in stride length, velocity, and synchronization of movements, double-support time, and control of foot landing (82, 83). However, there

was a ceiling effect to the improvements in stride length and double-support time; that is, there was no further improvement above a certain dose (82). The addition of motivational or arousal processes and external cueing yielded further improvements in stride length (39, 84).

The effect of levodopa on locomotion occurs through mechanisms involved in control of force and amplitude rather than rhythmicity or automaticity (82). Levodopa treatment did not affect stride-to-stride variation and had little effect on the ability to produce rhythmic stepping in response to an external cue (41). The symptomatic benefit of levodopa is greater in younger-onset (< 40 years) patients, suggesting that gait disturbances in the older PD population are related to nondopaminergic mechanisms.

The motor complications of long-term treatment with levodopa, especially dyskinesia (dystonia and chorea), have serious implications with regard to gait. Severe painful foot or leg dystonia as well as violent generalized or crural chorea/ballism, frequently aggravated by walking, have become a major problem of advanced PD patients. Patients often have to choose between an akinetic "off" state with freezing or an "on" state with disabling dyskinesias. These hyperkinetic complications are much more common in younger patients (85) and appear initially in the legs, affecting walking.

Dopamine agonists' clinical benefit on gait, as measured by the Unified Parkinson's Disease Rating Scale (UPDRS) (86) and other clinical assessment tools, has been shown. Amantadine, selegiline, rasagilene, tolcapone, and entacapone are all known for their symptomatic benefit on almost all parkinsonian parameters, including gait disturbances. However, there has been no prospective, double blind study that assessed the effect of any of these drugs on parkinsonian gait as the primary outcome.

In addition to medications, it is generally agreed that nonpharmacologic treatment and, in particular, rehabilitation can improve parkinsonian gait disturbances (87).

Treatment of Freezing of Gait

Freezing is considered to be among the more resistant symptoms in PD. "Off" freezing may respond to dopaminergic treatment, whereas "on" freezing sometimes improves by lowering the dosage of dopaminergic medications.

One of the most characteristic features of freezing is its response to "tricks" or attentional strategies. Stern and associates (73) were the first to report such tricks in detail, dividing them into (a) gait modification by the patient alone or with the assistance of another person and (b) assistance by auditory (nonverbal), verbal, or visual stimuli or cueing. Based on clinical observation, motor tricks can be recommended to overcome a freezing episode because of their effectiveness, noninvasiveness, and availability. However, whether training with such strategies is also effective in reducing the occurrence of freezing episodes needs further investigation.

Selegiline was shown to decrease the frequency of FOG in early PD in a subanalysis of the DATATOP study (64). Selegiline's mechanism of action on freezing is poorly understood. Theoretically, the drug might act either by its inhibitory effect on monoamine oxidase type B (MAO-B) to increase dopaminergic activity, through the amphetaminergic activity of its metabolites, or through another undefined mechanism. The possibility that this drug has a specific effect on motor programming was raised by a study demonstrating significantly improved movement control and directional control of arm movement (88). Whether selegiline taken concomitantly with levodopa has the same symptomatic effect on FOG in more advanced cases remains to be determined.

The direct effect of levodopa on FOG has never been assessed. However, it is a common experience that when freezing episodes are directly related to a hypodopaminergic state, any dopaminomimetic treatment that will decrease the severity or duration of the "off" phase will decrease the number of freezing episodes. The effect of dopamine agonist drugs on FOG is not clear. Two studies suggest that treatment with dopamine agonists can exacerbate freezing episodes (70, 89), but these observations have never been confirmed in a large-scale prospective study in advanced patients. In contrast, apomorphine injections have been reported to produce a good symptomatic effect on severe freezing episodes where other antiparkinsonian agents failed (57, 90).

L-threo 3, 4-dihydroxyphenylserine (DOPS) (a chemical precursor of norepinephrine) has been reported to have a moderate symptomatic effect on FOG mainly in patients with "pure freezing syndrome" (91). A similar study (92) reports complete disappearance of freezing in 2 patients with PD lasting for 3 weeks, after which the freezing returned and showed no additional response even when higher doses of L-threo-DOPS were given. Two additional patients had transient subjective improvement for 4 weeks. Another report describes only transient benefit from L-threo-DOPS in a patient with pure akinesia (93). Two small double-blind studies found no benefit from L-threo-DOPS treatment for freezing in advanced PD (S. Fahn, personal communication) (94). Although the role of L-threo-DOPS in FOG in parkinsonian patients is limited, it seems to provide a mild and temporary benefit for patients with "pure freezing syndrome, " an entity believed to be a subtype of PSP (95).

REHABILITATION OF GAIT DISTURBANCES

Physiotherapy for gait disorders in PD can be of benefit, especially by improving the speed of walking through a variety of training methods (96, 97). Treadmill training

has been shown to have an immediate beneficial effect on gait speed (98), at least in patients with early to mid stage PD, with some carryover to normal walking lasting up to 4 months (99). In addition, walking on a treadmill can be used as an external pacemaker, improving the timing variability of gait (100).

To overcome the typical problem of automatic maintenance of appropriate scale and timing of gait, cues have been used as a nonautomatic drive for walking. External cues are temporal or spatial stimuli associated with the initiation and ongoing facilitation of motor activity (gait). In contrast, targeted attention also enhances movement but provides an internal focus, which may be easily diverted and difficult to generate continually. Given the faulty automatic brain circuits of the basal ganglia and the supplementary motor area, it is not surprising that neuroimaging studies show patients with PD tending to make more use of the prefrontal, parietothalamic premotor cerebellar circuitry (101, 102). Cueing may emphasize the activation of these alternative lateral neural pathways, whereas attention may underscore the use of prefrontal and frontal pathways.

Cueing immediately improves the range and timing of movement. Two systematic reviews (17, 103) provide the strongest evidence for the short-term effects of auditory cues (104) and, to a lesser degree, for visual and somatosensory cueing. The clinical application of cues by physiotherapists in the home situation showed carryover of these immediate effects into improved gait and balance performance tested without the presence of cues, as well as a better score on the FOG questionnaire in those suffering from freezing. Effect wore off after training and showed limited carryover to function in the activities of daily living (ADLs) (105). There is some limited evidence that auditory cueing in particular improves the quality of gait during double tasking (21). Although clinically several forms of sensory stimulation ameliorate freezing, auditory cueing with a metronome or visual markers (walking device) have so far not shown any measurable effects on the occurrence of freezing in the "on" phase. Cueing of patients with freezing may require a specific set of cueing techniques to accommodate for the dysregulation of both the scale and timing of stepping; these procedures require study in the "off" phase.

FUNCTIONAL NEUROSURGERY FOR GAIT DISTURBANCES

Stereotactic neurosurgery is an increasingly common approach for treating patients with advanced PD. Unilateral pallidotomy has significant beneficial effect in decreasing "off" duration and severity as well as the severity of dyskinesia (106–110). Some studies also report significant improvement of gait disturbances mainly associated with the "off" state (109, 111). Bilateral high-frequency deep brain stimulation (DBS) of the globus pallidus internus (GPi) has shown that gait can be significantly improved when the dorsal GPi was stimulated, whereas stimulation of the posteroventral GPi causes significant worsening of parkinsonian gait (112). A meta-analysis examining the effects of bilateral stimulation of the subthalamic nucleus and unilateral/ bilateral GPi stimulation showed clear benefits in gait and posture scores, more so during the "off" than the "on" state (113, 114). In one study, 2 patients with PD and gait disturbance received low-frequency (20-Hz) stimulation via DBS at the level of the pedunculopontine nucleus (PPN) in the upper brainstem. The initial report is of interest because of the significant improvement in gait, over 50%, which opens a whole new approach to the treatment of gait in PD (115).

ACKNOWLEDGMENT

This review was supported in part by an unrestricted educational grant from the National Parkinson Foundation, Miami, Florida.

References

1. Parkinson J:. *An Essay on the Shaking Palsy.* London, Sherwood, Neely and Jones, 1817.
2. Giladi N, Fahn S. Freezing phenomenon, the fifth cardinal sign of parkinsonism. In: Fisher A et al. (eds.). *Progress in Alzheimer's and Parkinson's Diseases.* New York and London: Plenum Press, 1998:329–335.
3. Giladi N, Bloem BR, Hausdorff JM. Gait Disturbances and Falls in: *Neurology and Clinical Neuroscience* Ed. A.H.V. Schapira. *Mosby, Inc. (Elsevier Inc.)* Philadelphia, USA, 2007; 455–470.
4. Morris ME, Iansek R, McGinley J, et al. Three-dimensional gait biomechanics in Parkinson's disease: Evidence for a centrally mediated amplitude regulation disorder. *Mov Disord* 2005; 20(1):40–50.
5. Hoehn MM, Yahr MD. Parkinsonism: Onset, progression, and mortality. *Neurology* 1967; 50:318.
6. Giladi N, McMahon D, Przedborski S, et al. Motor blocks in Parkinson's disease. *Neurology* 1992; 42:333–339.
7. Parkinson Study Group. Effect of deprenyl on the progression of disability in early Parkinson's disease. *N Engl J Med* 1989; 321:1364–1371.
8. G. Yogev, M. Plotnik, C. Peretz, N. Giladi, JM. Hausdorff. Gait asymmetry in patients with Parkinson's disease and elderly fallers: When does the bilateral coordination of gait require attention? *Exp Brain Res* 177: 2007; 336–346.
9. Gomez AG, Jorge R, Garcia S, et al. Clinical and pharmacological differences in early-versus late-onset Parkinson's disease. *Mov Disord* 1997; 12:277–284.
10. Yamanouchi H, Nagura H. Neurological signs and frontal white matter lesions in vascular parkinsonism. A clinicopathologic study. *Stroke* 1997; 28:965–969.
11. Gibb WR, Lees AJ. A comparison of clinical and pathological features of young-and old-onset Parkinson's disease. *Neurology* 1988; 38:1402–1406.
12. Rajput AH, Pahwa P, Pahwa P, et al. Prognostic significance of the onset mode in parkinsonism. *Neurology* 1993; 43:829–830.
13. Hughes AJ, Daniel SE, Blankson S, et al. A clinicopathologic study of 100 cases of Parkinson's disease. *ArchNeurol* 1993; 50:140–148.
14. Cotzias GC, Van WM, Schiffer LM. Aromatic amino acids and modification of parkinsonism. *N Engl J Med* 1967; 276:374–379.
15. Podsiadlo D, Richardson S. The timed "up & go": A test of basic functional mobility for frail elderly persons. *J Am Geriatr Soc* 1991; 39:142–148.
16. Mathias S, Nayak U, Isaacs B. Balance in the elderly patient: The "get-up and go" test. *Arch Phys Med Rehabil* 1986; 67:387–389.
17. Morris S, Morris ME, Iansek R. Reliability of measurements obtained with the timed get up & go test in people with Parkinson's disease. *Phys Ther* 1999; 81:810–818.
18. Lim I, van Wegen E, de Goede C, et al. Effects of external rhythmical cueing on gait in patients with Parkinson's disease: A systematic review. *Clin Rehabil* 2005; 19(7):695–713.
19. Brusse KJ, Zimdars S, Zalewski KR, Steffen TM. Testing functional performance in people with Parkinson disease. *Phys Ther* 2005; 85(2):134–141.
20. Tinetti ME. Performance-oriented assessment of mobility problems in elderly patients. *J Am Geriatr Soc* 1986; 34:119–126.
21. Elble J. Clinical and research methodology for study of gait. In: Masdeu J et al. (eds). *Gait Disorders of Aging.* Philadelphia and New York: Lippincott-Raven, 1997:123–113.
22. Rochester L, Hetherington V, Jones D, et al. The effect of external rhythmical cues (auditory and visual) on walking during a functional task in homes people with Parkinson's disease. *Arch Phys Med Rehabil* 2005; 86:999–1006.
23. Rochester L, Hetherington V, Jones D, et al. Attending to the task: Interference effects of functional tasks on walking in Parkinson's disease—Roles of cognition, depression, fatigue, and balance. *Arch Phys Med Rehabil* 2004; 85(10):1578–1585.
24. Marsden CD. What do the basal ganglia tell premotor cortical areas? *Ciba Found Symp* 1987; 132:282–300.
25. Rosin R, Topka H, Dichgans J. Gait initiation in Parkinson's disease. *Mov Disord* 1997; 12:682–690.
26. Simonetta M, Clanet M, Rascol O. Bereitschaftspotential in a simple movement or in a motor sequence starting with the same simple movement. *Electroencephalogr Clin Neurophysiol* 1991; 81:129–134.
27. Vidailhet M, Stocchi F, Rothwell JC, et al. The Bereitschaftspotential preceding simple foot movement and initiation of gait in Parkinson's disease. *Neurology* 1993; 43:1784–1788.
28. Elble J, Moody C, Leffler K, et al. The initiation of normal walking. *Mov Disord* 1994; 9:139–146.
29. Breniere Y, Cuong Do M. Control of gait initiation. *J Mot Behav* 1991; 23:235–240.
30. Burleigh JA, Horak FB, Nutt JG, et al. Step initiation in Parkinson's disease: Influence of levodopa and external sensory triggers. *Mov Disord* 1997; 12:206–215.
31. Crenna P, Frigo C. A motor programme for the initiation of forward-oriented movements in humans. *J Physiol (Lond)* 1991; 437:635–653.
32. Horak F. Postural inflexibility in parkinsonian subjects. *J Neurol Sci* 1992; 111:46–58.
33. Schaafsma D, Giladi N, Balash Y, et al. Gait Dynamics in Parkinson's disease: Relationship to parkinsonian features, falls and response to levodopa. *J Neurol Sci* 2003; 212: 47–53.
34. Giladi N, Rascol O, Brooks OC, et al. Largo study group. Rasagiline treatment can improve freezing of gait in advanced Parkinson's disease: A prospective randomized, double blind placebo and entacapone controlled study. *Mov Disord* 2004; 19(suppl 9):538.
35. Andrews CJ. Influence of dystonia on the response to long-term L-dopa therapy in Parkinson's disease. *J Neurol Neurosurg Psychiatry* 1973; 36:630–636.
36. Nieuwboer A, de Weerdt W, Dom R, et al. A frequency and correlation analysis of motor deficits in Parkinson's disease. *Disabil Rehabil* 1998; 20:142–150.
37. Giladi N, Shabtai H, Simon ES, et al. Construction of freezing of gait questionnaire for patients with Parkinsonism. *Parkinsonism Relat Disord* 2000; 6:165–170.
38. Giladi N, Tal Y, Azulay T, et al. Validation of the freezing of gait questionnaire (FOG-Q) for patients with Parkinson's disease. *Mov Disord* 2007, in press.
39. Morris ME, Iansek R, Matyas TA. The pathogenesis of gait hypokinesia in Parkinson's disease. *Brain* 1994; 117:1169–1181.
40. Morris ME, Lansek R, Matyas TA, et al. Stride length regulation in Parkinson's disease. Normalization strategies and underlying mechanisms. *Brain* 1996; 119:551–568.
41. Vieregge P, Stolze H, Klein C, et al. Gait quantitation in Parkinson's disease: Locomotor disability and correlation to clinical rating scales. *J Neural Transm* 1997; 104:237–248.
42. Hausdorff JM, Cudkowicz ME, Firtion R, et al. Gait variability and basal ganglia disorders: Stride-to-stride variations of gait cycle timing in Parkinson's and Huntington's disease. *MovDisord* 1998; 13:428–437.
43. Baltadjieva R, Giladi N, Balash Y, et al. Gait changes in naive Parkinson's disease patients Eur J Neuroscience 2006; 24(6): 1815–20.
44. Hausdorff JM, Balash J, Giladi N. Effects of cognitive challenge on gait variability in patients with Parkinson's disease. *J Geriatr Psychiatry Neurol* 2003; 16(1):53–58.
45. Miller RA, Thaut MH, McIntosh GC, et al. Components of EMG symmetry and variability in parkinsonian and healthy elderly gait. *Electroencephalogr Clin Neurophysiol* 1996; 101:1–7.
46. Cioni M, Richards CL, Malouin F, et al. Characteristics of the electromyographic patterns of lower limb muscles during gait in patients with Parkinson's disease when OFF and ON L-dopa treatment. *Ital J Neurol Sci* 1997; 18:195–208.
47. Lewis GN, Byblow WD, Walt SE. Stride length regulation in Parkinson's disease: The use of extrinsic, visual cues. *Brain* 2000; 123(Pt 10):2077–2090.
48. Hausdorff JM, Schaafsma J, Balash Y, et al. Impaired regulation of stride variability in Parkinson's disease subjects with freezing of gait. *Exp Brain Res* 2003; 149:187–194.
49. Yogev G, Giladi N, Peretz C, et al. Dual tasking, gait rhythmicity, and Parkinson's disease: Which aspects of gait are attention demanding? *Eur J Neurosci* 2005; 22: 1248–1256.
50. Hausdorff, JM, Yogev G, Springer S, et al. Walking is more like catching than tapping: Gait in the elderly as a complex cognitive task. *Exp Brain Res* 2005; 164:541–548.

51. Nieuwboer A, Dom R, De Weerdt W, et al. Abnormalities of the spatiotemporal characteristics of gait at the onset of freezing in Parkinson's disease. *Mov Disord* 2001; 16(6):1066–1075.

52. Nieuwboer A, Dom R, De Weerdt W, et al. Electromyographic profiles of gait prior to onset of freezing episodes in patients with Parkinson's disease. *Brain* 2004; 127:1650–1660.

53. Hausdorff JM, Balash J, Giladi N. Time series analysis of leg movements during freezing of gait in Parkinson's disease: Akinesia, rhyme or reason? *Physica A* 2003; 321:565–570.

54. Bartel AI, de Jong BM, Giladi N, Schaafsma JD, Maguire RP, Veenmat L, Pruim J, Balash J Youdim MBH, Leenders KL. Striatal dopa and glucose metabolism in PD patients with freezing of gait. *Mov Disord* 2006; 21 (9):1326–32.

55. Matsui H, Udaka F, Myoshi T, et al. Three-dimensional stereotactic surface projection study of freezing of gait and brain perfusion image in Parkinson's disease. *Mov Disord* 2005; 20(10):1272–1277.

56. Bartels AL, Balash Y, Gurevich T, et al. Relation between freezing of gait (FOG) and other features of Parkinson's disease: FOG is not correlated with bradykinesia. *J Clinical Neurosci* 2003; 10(5) :584–588.

57. Linazasoro G. The apomorphine test in gait disorders associated with parkinsonism. *ClinNeuropharmacol* 1996; 19:171–176.

58. Ueno E, Yanagisawa N, Takami M. Gait disorders in parkinsonism. A study with floor reaction forces and EMG. *Adv Neurol* 1993; 60:414–418.

59. Yanagisawa N, Hayashi R, Mitoma H. Pathophysiology of frozen gait in parkinsonism. In: Ruzicka R, Hallett M, Jankovic J (eds). *Advances in Neurology: Gait Disorders*. Philadelphia: Lippincott Williams & Wilkins, 2001; 87:199–207.

60. Giladi N, Kao R, Fahn S. Freezing phenomenon in patients with parkinsonian syndromes. *Mov Disord* 1997; 12:302-306.

61. Schwab R, England A, Peterson E. Akinesia in Parkinson's disease. *Neurology* 1959; 9:65–72.

62. Narabashi H. Clinical analysis of akinesia. *J neural Transm Suppl* 1980;(16):129–36.

63. Martin J. Disorder of locomotion associated with disease of the basal ganglia. In: *The Basal Ganglia and Posture*. Philadelphia: Lippincott, 1967:24–35.

64. Giladi N, McDermott M, Fahn S, et al. and the Parkinson Study Group. Freezing of gait in Parkinson's disease: Prospective assessment of the DATATOP cohort. *Neurology* 2001; 56:1712–1712.

65. Lamberti P, Armenise S, Castaldo V, et al. Freezing gait in Parkinson's disease. *Eur Neurol* 1997; 38:297–301.

66. Barbeau A. Long term appraisal of levodopa therapy. *Neurology* 1972; 22:22–24.

67. Barbeau A. Six years of high level levodopa therapy in severely akinetic parkinsonian patients. *Arch Neurol* 1976; 33:333–338.

68. Ambani L, Van Woert M. Start hesitation: A side effect of long-term levodopa therapy. *N Engl J Med* 1973; 288 (21) :1113–1115.

69. Kizkin S, Ozer F, Ufacik M, et al. Motor blocks in Parkinson's disease. *Mov Disord* 1997; 12(101):378.

70. Ahlskog J, Muenter M, Bailey P, et al. Dopamine agonist treatment of fluctuating parkinsonism: D-2 (controlled release MK-458) vs combined D-1 and D-2 (pergolide). *Arch Neurol* 1992; 49:560–568.

71. Plotnik M, Giladi N, Balash Y, et al. Is freezing of gait in Parkinson's disease related to asymmetric motor function? *Ann Neurol* 2005; 57:656–663.

72. Nieuwboer A, Willems AM, Rochester L, et al. Physical and cognitive characteristics of freezers and non-freezers in Parkinson's disease. *Gait and Mental Function* International Congress 2006, Madrid, Spain. Abstract.

73. Stern GM, Lander CM, Lees AJ. Akinetic freezing and trick movements in Parkinson's disease. *J Neural Transm Suppl* 1980; 16:137–141.

74. Moore O., Peretz C, Giladi N. Freezing of gait affects quality of life of people with Parkinson's disease beyond its relationships with mobility and gait. *Mov Disord* 2007; in press.

75. Imai H. [Festination and freezing]. *Rinsho Shinkeigaku* 1993; 33:1307–1309.

76. Thompson P, Marsden CD. Clinical neurological assessment of balance and gait disorders. In: Bronstein A et al (eds). *Clinical Disorders of Balance. Posture. and Gait*. London: Arnold, 1996:79–84.

77. Brown P, Steiger M. Basal ganglia gait disorders. In: Bronstein A et al (eds). *Clinical Disorders of Balance. Posture. and Gait*. London: Arnold, 1996:156–167.

78. Giladi N, Shabtai H, Rozenberg E, Shabtai E. Gait festination in Parkinson's disease. *Parkinsonism Relat Disord* 2001; 7:135–138.

79. Parkinson Study Group. DATATOP: A multicenter controlled clinical trial in early Parkinson's disease. *Arch Neurol* 1989; 46(10):1052–1060.

80. Mones RJ. An evaluation of L-dopa in Parkinson patients. *Trans Am Neurol Assoc* 1969; 94:307–309.

81. Boshes B, Blonsky ER, Arbit J, et al. Effect of L-dopa on individual symptoms of parkinsonism. *Trans Am Neurol Assoc* 1969; 94:229–231.

82. Ferrandez AM, Blin O. A comparison between the effect of intentional modulations and the action of L-dopa on gait in Parkinson's disease. *Behav Brain Res* 1991; 45:177–183.

83. Pederson S, Oberg B, Larsson L, et al. Gait analysis, isokinetic muscle strength measurement in patients with Parkinson's disease. *Scand J Rehab Med* 1997; 29:67–74.

84. Thaut MH, McIntosh GC, Rice RR, et al. Rhythmic auditory stimulation in gait training for Parkinson's disease patients. *Mov Disord* 1996; 11:193–200.

85. Kostic V, Przedborski S, Flaster E, et al. Early development of levodopa-induced dyskinesias and response fluctuations in young-onset Parkinson's disease. *Neurology* 1991; 41:202–205.

86. Fahn S, Elton R. Members of the UPDRS development committee. Unified Parkinson's Disease Rating Scale. In: Fahn S et al (eds). *Recent Developments in Parkinson's Disease*. Florham Park, NJ: Macmillan Health Care Information, 1987:153–163.

87. Weiner WJ, Singer C. Parkinson's disease and nonpharmacologic treatment programs. *J Am Geriatr Soc* 1989; 37:359–363.

88. Giladi N, Honigman S, Hocherman S. The effect of deprenyl treatment on directional and velocity control of arm movement in patients with early stages of Parkinson's disease. *Clin Neuropharmacol* 1999; 22:54–59.

89. Rascol O, Brooks DJ, Korczyn AD, De Deyn PP, Clarke CE, Lang AE (2000) A five-year study of the incidence in dyskinesia in patients with early Parkinson's disease who were treated with ropinirole or levodopa. 056 Study Group. *N. Engl. J Med*. 342: 1484–1491.

90. Corboy DL, Wagner ML, Sage JI. Apomorphine for motor fluctuations and freezing in Parkinson's disease. *Ann Pharmacother* 1995; 29:282–288.

91. Narabayashi H, Kondo T, Nagatsu T, et al. DL Threo-3,4-Dihydoxyphenylserine for freezing symptom in parkinsonism. In: Hassler R et al (eds). *Advances in Neurology*. New York: Raven Press, 1984:497–552.

92. Oribe E, Kaufman H, Yahr M. Freezing phenomena in Parkinson's disease: Clinical features and effect of treatment with L-threo-DOPS. In: Narabayashi H et al (eds). *Norepinephrine Deficiency and Its Treatment with L-threo DOPS in Parkinson's Disease and the Related Disorders*. New York: Parthenon, 1993:89–96.

93. Yamamoto M, Fujii S, Hatanaka Y. Result of long-term administration of L-threo-3, 4-dihydroxyphenyl-serine in patients with pure akinesia as an early symptom of progressive supranuclear palsy. *ClinNeuropharmacol* 1997; 20:371–373.

94. Quinn N, Perlmutter J,Marsden CD.Acute administration of DL-threo DOPS does not affect the freezing phenomenon in parkinsonian patients. *Neurology* 1984; 34:149.

95. Imai H, Narabayashi H, Sakata E. "Pure akinesia" and the later added supranuclear ophthalmoplegia. *Adv Neurol* 1987; 45:207–212.

96. Dean KOH, Jones D, Ellis-Hill C, et al. A comparison of physiotherapy techniques for patients with Parkinson's disease (Cochrane Review). *Cochrane Database Syst Rev* 2001:1(CD002815).

97. de Goede CJ, Keus SH, Kwakkel G, Wagenaar RC. The effects of physical therapy in Parkinson's disease: A research synthesis. *Arch Phys Med Rehabil* 2001; 82:509–515.

98. Pohl M, Rockstroh G, Ruckriem S, et al. Immediate effects of speed-dependent treadmill training on gait parameters in early Parkinson's disease. *Arch Phys Med Rehabil* 2003; 84(12):1760–1766.

99. Miyai I, Fujimoto Y, Yamamoto H, et al. Long-term effect of body weight-supported treadmill training in Parkinson's disease: A randomized controlled trial. *Arch Phys Med Rehabil* 2002; 83(10):1370–1373.

100. Frenkel-Toledo S, Giladi N, Peretz C, et al. Treadmill walking as an external pacemaker to improve gait rhythm and stability in Parkinson's disease. *Mov Disord*. 2005; 20(9):1109–1114.

101. Wu T, Hallett M. A functional MRI study of automatic movements in patients with Parkinson's disease. *Brain* 2005 ;128:2250–2259.

102. Samuel M, Caballos-Baumann AO, Blin J, et al. Evidence for lateral premotor and parietal overactivity in Parkinson's disease during sequential and bimanual movements. A PET study. *Brain* 1997; 120:963–976.

103. Rubinstein TC, Giladi N, Hausdorff JM. The power of cueing to circumvent dopamine deficits: a review of physical therapy treatment of gait disturbances in Parkinson's disease (review). *Mov Disord* 2002; 17(6):1148–1160.

104. McIntosh GC, Brown SH, Rice RR, et al. Rhythmic auditory-motor facilitation of gait patterns in patients with Parkinson's disease. *J Neurol Neurosurg Psychiatry* 1997; 62:22–26.

105. Nieuwboer A, Kwakkel G, Rochester L, et al . Cueing training in the home improves gait-related mobility in Parkinson's disease: The RESCUE-trial. *J Neurol Neurosurg Psychiatry*. 2007 Feb; 78(2): 134–40.

106. Meyer CH. Unilateral pallidotomy for Parkinson's disease promptly improves a wide range of voluntary activities, especially gait and trunk movements. *Acta Neurochir Suppl Wien* 1997; 68:37–41.

107. Kumar R, Lozano AM, Montgomery E, et al. Pallidotomy and deep brain stimulation of the pallidum and subthalamic nucleus in advanced Parkinson's disease. *Mov Disord* 1998; 13:73–82.

108. Laitinen LV, Bergenheim AT, Hariz MI. Leksell's posteroventral pallidotomy in the treatment of Parkinson's disease. *J Neurosurg* 1992; 76:53–61.

109. Lang AE, Lozano AM, Montgomery E, et al. Posteroventral medial pallidotomy in advanced Parkinson's disease. *N Engl J Med* 1997; 337:1036–1042.

110. Ondo W, Jankovic J, Lai EC, et al. Assessment of motor function after stereotactic pallidotomy. *Neurology* 1998; 50:266–270.

111. Baron MS, Vitek JL, Bakay RA, et al. Treatment of advanced Parkinson's disease by posterior GPi pallidotomy: 1-year results of a pilot study. *Ann Neurol* 1996; 40:355–366.

112. Bejjani B, Damier P, Arnulf I, et al. Pallidal stimulation for Parkinson's disease. Two targets? *Neurology* 1997; 49:1564–1569.

113. Bakker M, Esselink RA, Munneke M, et al. Effects of stereotactic neurosurgery on postural instability and gait in Parkinson's disease. *Mov Disord* 2004; 19(9):1092–1099.

114. Krack P, Pollak P, Limousin P, et al. Subthalamic nucleus or internal pallidal stimulation in young onset Parkinson's disease. *Brain* 1998; 121:451–457.

115. Plaha P, Gill SS. Bilateral deep brain stimulation of the pedunculopontine nucleus for Parkinson's disease. *Neuroreport* 2005; 16(17):1883–1887.

8   Sensory Symptoms

Richard M. Zweig
Debra Elliott

S ensory symptoms are perhaps as common as tremor in Parkinson's disease (PD), but because these symptoms are not seen by physicians and may not be reported by caretakers, they may be overlooked. In discussions of PD, *sensory symptoms* usually refers to painful or nonpainful somatosensory symptoms. Descriptions and classifications have variously included or excluded pain or other sensory symptoms thought not to be directly related to PD (i.e., comorbidities such as an arthritic knee or neuropathic pain in a PD patient with diabetes). However, the relationship can be ambiguous (e.g., low back pain). Other studies have excluded symptoms associated with increased muscle contraction. But although "muscular" symptoms—such as painful dystonic spasms, cramps, aching, heaviness, or stiffness—typically parallel levodopa-related fluctuations in motor signs, other sensory symptoms may also be levodopa-responsive. These include sensory symptoms thought to reflect autonomic disturbances—such as dyspnea, precordalgia, and distal cold sensation—or sensations of an inner restlessness (akathisia). The response to levodopa may be more variable or absent in patients with stabbing, paresthesia-like sensations or an internal tremor, and symptoms may worsen with levodopa in patients with burning sensations (Table 8-1).

The pathophysiologic processes contributing to sensory symptoms in PD are not well understood but are likely multiple, involving dopaminergic and nondopaminergic sytems as well as the basal ganglia and extrastriatal systems. This chapter begins with an illustrative case report followed by a discussion of somatosensory symptoms in patients with PD and a review of dopaminergic and other pathophysiologic processes that may be contributing to these symptoms. This is followed by a brief discussion on another nearly universal sensory symptom in PD: hyposmia. Finally, a brief review of the evaluation and treatment of somatosensory symptoms is included.

FREQUENCY, LOCATION, AND QUALITY OF SOMATOSENSORY SYMPTOMS

Sensory symptoms are present in the majority of individuals with PD. Among a series of 388 consecutive levodopa-responsive PD patients completing an itemized questionnaire, 67% endorsed pain or other sensory symptoms (1). Of these, 94% had pain characterized as "muscular" (mostly endorsed as "stiffness"), and approximately half had pain considered "rheumatologic"—primarily articular or spinal. Whereas 10% of patients had restless legs or akathisia; only 8% had pain characterized as

TABLE 8-1
Somatosensory Symptoms in Parkinson's Disease

SYMPTOM	LOCALIZATION	LEVODOPA RESPONSE	OTHER THERAPY	REFS.
Paresthesia-like: numbness tingling coldness	Extremities, esp.side of greatest motor signs	Variable	Possibly anxiolytics	2, 3, 4, 9, 11
Aching pain	Extremities, joints	variable		2, 3, 4, 5, 6, 11
Burning	Extremities > head or body	May worsen		2, 3, 4, 9
Radicular	Extremities	Variable		5, 6
Cramps, tightness	Neck, calf, paraspinal	Often responsive		5
Painful dystonias	Usually feet	Often responsive	Possibly lithium	5, 6
Genitalia (in women)		Often responsive		4, 8
Unilateral oral (esp. burning)		Usually none	Clozapine, possibly other analgesics	8
Sensory dyspnea		May be responsive		9
Internal tremor	Axial+/− limb	Usually none	Anxiolytics	10
Akathisia		Occasional	Clozapine	11, 12
Headache	Esp. nuchal	Occasional	Amitriptyline	15, 16, 17
Back pain	Mid/lower back	May be responsive		18

paresthesia, dysesthesia, burning, itching, or "ill defined." Localization was mostly segmental or axial, with an occasional radicular or pseudoradicular distribution. Headache, facial pain, anorectal pain, or pain in a visceral distribution was uncommon. Pain was present at disease onset in over 25%, and in those with motor fluctuations, pain often occurred in the "off" phase.

Population-based quality-of-life surveys corroborate the presence of pain and other sensory symptoms in PD (2–4). Unfortunately, the fact that pain and discomfort are also common in the aging general population makes a true disease-specific cause-and-effect association difficult. For example, using a short questionnaire, Schrag and colleagues (2) reported that 46.2% of 461 individuals between the ages of 60 to 69 from the general population endorsed "pain"; this figure increased to over 60% among individuals over 80 years of age. Most of the 124 PD patients from this study were over 60. For these patients, the percentage with pain was only fractionally greater than that in the general population (e.g., 54.5%

CASE REPORT

A 76-year-old man with a 13-year history of PD had a 4-year history of pain in his left lower extremity. This was described as an electric-like, stabbing pain that traveled from the left thigh and groin to his ankle. Before the onset of pain, symptoms consisted primarily of levodopa-responsive hypophonic dysarthria, hypomimia, tremor of his lower lip, and mild generalized bradykinesia. Although gait and posture were mildly affected, he was regularly playing golf. The pain became severe, was unresponsive to conservative therapy, and did not appear to be associated with or affected by levodopa treatment. Spondylitic changes and lumbar disc herniation (LS through S1) were seen on imaging studies. Despite a decompressive laminectomy, pain persisted; it was aggravated by standing and walking but relieved by bending forward. No sensory changes were found on examination, but weakness of the left extensor hallucis longus was noted, as was pain with extension of the lumbar spine and straight leg raising. Repeat imaging and electromyography (EMG) were consistent with L5 radiculopathy and a second surgical procedure was performed, but without success. Following a third unsuccessful procedure less than 2 years after onset of pain, placement of a temporary spinal cord–stimulating electrode was undertaken. Although paresthesias elicited by stimulation corresponded to the distribution of his usual pain, there was no relief from pain. Initially change in posture and reluctance to walk were attributed to pain resulting from the patient's spinal disease. However, a severe parkinsonian gait disorder with frequent freezing evolved.

in the 60- to 69-year-old age group). Pain did increase with disease severity, as reflected in the staging defined by Hoehn and Yahr (5). In another population-based quality-of-life survey of 111 patients evaluated in 1993 and then 4 years later, worsening of motor function [i.e., Unified Parkinson's Disease Rating Scale (UPDRS) motor score] related to increased nonmotor measures, including pain, social isolation, and "emotional reactions"(6). Over 4 years, more than 50% of patients had a greater than 30% increase in pain score.

In an early series of 101 patients, including patients with postencephalitic parkinsonism (7), about 40% reported pain, tingling, numbness, coldness, or burning primarily localized to one or more limbs, typically ipsilateral to the side of the body with the greater motor deficit. There was a paresthesia-like quality to most of the symptoms, and sensory symptoms preceded the onset of motor symptoms in several patients. This series excluded patients with diabetes, arthritis, musculoskeletal diseases, or other medical illnesses. Aching or cramp-like sensations were included, but pains or other sensory symptoms thought to be clearly associated with increased muscle contraction (painful dystonic spasms, cramps) or otherwise caused by the primary motor disorder (heaviness, stiffness) were also excluded. Response to levodopa was variable, with increased pain (especially a burning sensation) occurring more often than pain relief (7). These results were similar to those in a more recent study of 51 consecutive PD patients, 36 with predominantly unilateral symptoms (8). Patients with cognitive impairment or neuropathy were excluded. Of the 36 with unilateral disease, 21 had pain described as burning, itching, or tearing. In 6 patients, pain was the initial symptom. Usually but not always, pain occurred on the more affected side; however, it could sometimes be bilateral or rarely be felt on the less affected side. In a series of 50 patients (9), nerve conduction and studies of somatosensory evoked potentials were within normal limits and did not distinguish between patients with and without somatosensory symptoms.

In contrast to these studies, other authors have emphasized nonmotor symptomatology that specifically parallels levodopa-related fluctuations in motor signs. In a series of 95 patients with PD, 46% reported pain, which was related to motor fluctuations in two-thirds (10). The majority of these patients had cramps or muscle tightness (neck, paraspinal area, calf). Painful foot and other dystonias were also common, while radicular-like pain, joint pain, or akathitic-related sensations occurred less commonly. Quinn and coworkers (11) have proposed a classification of pain in PD primarily based on timing of (and response to) levodopa. In these patients with or without associated dystonic spasms, pain would occur in the early morning, with "beginning of dose," "end of dose," or "wearing-off." They also recognized levodopa-responsive pain preceding the diagnosis of PD and peak-dose pain associated with "on period" dyskinesias (12).

Ford and coworkers (13) reported a series of 8 patients with PD and one case of atypical parkinsonism with severe oral or genital pains of unknown etiology. In the 3 women with genital pain, the pain was generally responsive to levodopa and was associated with motor fluctuations or wearing off. Oral pain was less responsive to levodopa. These sensations were often unilateral and burning in quality. In all cases the pain syndromes were described as having "a relentless and distressing quality that overshadowed the other features of the parkinsonism" (13). Psychiatric disturbances were noted in 6 patients, including depression and anxiety. Other nonmotor "off" symptoms, as described by Hillen and Sage (14), included sensory dyspnea and other sensory-related autonomic disturbances.

A common sensory syndrome in patients with PD—typically associated with aching, tingling, or burning—is "internal tremor." In a series of 100 consecutive patients, 44% reported internal tremor (15). Overall, 69% had internal tremor, other sensory symptoms, or both. Internal tremor was most often localized axially (chest, abdomen, and neck), with or without limb involvement. There was no statistical association of internal tremor with the presence or severity of resting tremor. This symptom was not associated with motor fluctuations and was not relieved by antiparkinsonian medications. There was an association with symptoms of anxiety and response to anxiolytics. The authors recognized the similarity between both internal tremor and paresthesia-like sensory symptoms of Parkinson's patients and somatic symptoms associated with primary anxiety disorders. They distinguished internal tremor from akathisia, another common symptom in Parkinson's patients that can arguably be considered "sensory."

In a series of 100 patients with PD, 68% acknowledged feelings of inner restlessness resulting in a need to move (16). In the majority of patients, this was attributed to parkinsonian motor disturbances or various sensory complaints. However, "pure" akathisia, not attributable to other features of the disease, was reported by 26% of the total group. This symptom, typically found in patients with more advanced disease, was usually not responsive to antiparkinsonian medications and was not associated with motor fluctuations. The authors distinguished akathisia from the restless legs syndrome (RLS); for example, only 2 of the patients with pure akathisia had symptoms primarily in the evening or at night. In another study, clozapine-responsive nocturnal akathisia was reported in 9 patients with PD (17). Five of the patients had stereotyped repetitive movements of the lower extremity that were associated with the akathisia. Because of the lack of lower extremity paresthesias, these patients were also thought not to have RLS.

Typical levodopa-responsive RLS has been described in PD, occurring in up 20% of patients, in contrast to a frequency of 4% to 10% in the general population (18). It is usually not the presenting feature of PD but rather tends to occur after the diagnosis of PD has been made. Sensory discomfort in RLS includes deep, sharp, lancing pain as well as burning or "creepy-crawly" sensations, inducing an urge to move the legs (19). Patients with PD and RLS tend to be older than those with primary or familial RLS; the latter does not predispose to developing PD later in life (20). PD patients with RLS are older than those without RLS and are more likely to develop depression (21).

In 50 patients with motor fluctuations, Witjas and associates (22) divided 54 nonmotor symptoms into autonomic, cognitive/psychiatric, and pain/sensory categories, as originally proposed by Riley and Lang (23). The most common sensory symptom, considered "autonomic" in this study, was a "sensation of being hot," present in 56% of the patients. Akathisia was reported in 54% of patients. Other common symptoms—including dyspnea, a cold sensation (both considered autonomic), and a "tightening" sensation—were present in over 40% of patients. Hot or cold sensations were present in the "off" state in over half of the patients with these complaints but were also not uncommonly independent of state. Other common sensory (or sensory/autonomic) symptoms, seen in over 20% of patients, were tingling sensations, diffuse pain, restlessness (distinguished in this study from akathisia), precordialgia, and abdominal pains. Less common symptoms included neuralgia-like and burning pains. Internal tremor was not mentioned in this study. Six of the patients reported sensory fluctuations as "most incapacitating." The sensations of burning and less often akathisia were occasionally associated with the "on" state. In a similar study of 47 patients (24), of which all but 9 had motor "off" symptoms, 22 had associated nonmotor "off" symptoms. Included in the group of those with "autonomic" symptoms were 7 patients with variously off-state facial flushing or other "hot" sensations, 2 describing cold sensations, and 3 with abdominal bloating or abdominal or genital pain. Other sensory symptoms included 7 patients with dyspnea, and 1 each with pain in the lower extremities or internal tremor. In the course of these studies, an attempt was made to distinguish and exclude sensory symptoms thought to be "muscular."

Frequency and characteristics of headache and back pain have been studied in PD. Headache—more commonly nuchal than occipital, temporal, or frontal but not associated with nuchal (or extremity) rigidity—was present in 35% of a series of 71 patients (25). Although early-morning headache responsive to levodopa has been described (26), larger studies report tension-like headaches responsive to amitriptyline (26, 27).Middle or lower back pain was reported to be present at some stage of the illness in 68% of a series of 60 patients with PD without "conditions well known to cause back pain" (28). Back pain preceded the onset of recognized parkinsonism in almost half of these patients. In several patients, back pain was responsive to levodopa. None of the studies reporting frequency of headache or back pain included control groups without PD. Tension-like headaches and low back pain are among the most common symptoms reported to the general neurologist or primary care physician. Thus the relationship between PD-specific pathology and these symptoms must be considered unclear.

Patients will often endorse more than one sensory symptom and often will have both sensory and other nonmotor symptoms. In a series of 99 nondemented PD patients, Shulman and colleagues (29) used standardized test batteries to determine the frequency of 5 categories of nonmotor symptoms: depression, anxiety, fatigue, sleep disturbance, and sensory symptoms. All but 12% of the patients had a nonmotor symptom in at least 1 category; 60% had symptoms in 2 or more, and nearly 25% endorsed 4 or 5 categories. Sensory symptoms were present in 63% of the patients. Overall, greater nonmotor symptoms correlated with severity of PD as reflected in the UPDRS.

PATHOPHYSIOLOGY OF SENSORY DYSFUNCTION

The basal ganglia are thought to participate in motivationally or behaviorally relevant sensorimotor integration (30, 31). Current models of basal ganglial physiology emphasize somatotopically and functionally segregated parallel circuits (32, 33); less attention has been directed toward defining sensorimotor integrative properties. Basal ganglial output from the traditionally recognized output nuclei—that is, the globus pallidus internus and substantia nigra pars reticulata—is inhibitory (32, 33). Output directed toward regions of the thalamus that project to the frontal lobe is highly segregated somatotopically. In PD, increased activity of the globus pallidus internus and substantia nigra reticulata, due to a shift in balance between "direct" and "indirect" basal ganglial pathways, results in excessive inhibition of thalamocortical activity (34). Frontal hypometabolism—which has been demonstrated in patients with PD using ^{18}F fluorodeoxyglucose positron emission tomography (PET) scanning (35)—is thought to underlie "hypokinetic" features of PD. However, positive symptomatology, in particular somatosensory disturbances, is not well accounted for by the "direct/indirect" model of basal ganglial function (see Figure 8-1).

The striatum receives sensory input from numerous sources (30, 33). As the entire neocortex projects

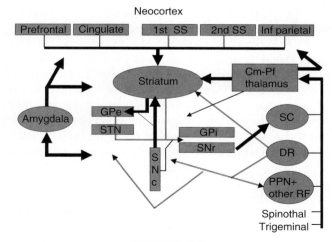

FIGURE 8-1

Possible basal ganglia–related pathways involved in nociceptive and nonnociceptive somatosensory processing. Most of these pathways are described in the text. Thicker arrows reflect relatively larger or better-studied pathways. Excitatory versus inhibitory aspects are not indicated in this figure.

Abbreviations: Cm-Pf = centre median and parafascicular nuclei; DR = dorsal raphe; GPe = globus pallidus externa; GPe = globus pallidus interna; Inf = inferior; PPN = pedunculopontine nucleus; RF = reticular formation; SC = superior colliculus; Spinothal = spinothalamic; SS = somatosensory; SNc = substantia nigra pars compacta; SNr = substantia nigra pars reticulata; STN = subthalamic nucleus.

to the striatum, any cortical area involved in sensory processing could theoretically utilize basal ganglial connectivity. Projections to the striatum from cortical areas involved in somatosensory function include somatotopically organized input from the first somatosensory cortex (30). This input to the putamen parallels input from the primary motor cortex. Dense topographic projections also arise from the second somatosensory cortex and inferior parietal area 7b (36), which contains somatosensory, multisensory, and task-related neurons. All of these regions contain neurons selectively responsive to painful (nociceptive) stimuli. Regions of the prefrontal and cingulate cortex that contain nociceptive neurons also project to the striatum (30, 37). Electrical stimulation of the primary somatosensory cortex produces striatal activity distinct from that due to stimulation of the motor cortex and suggests that the caudate/putaminal response to somatosensory stimuli allows somatotopic somatosensory discrimination and perception (38). In a rat model of PD, functional neuroimaging revealed decreased excitatory input to the sensorimotor cortex due to depletion of dopamine in the substantia nigra pars compacta and striatum and increased spatial homogeneity, suggesting increased neuronal synchronization in the parkinsonian

state (38). In patients with PD (40), disorders of somatosensory discrimination and perception are represented by deficits in tasks requiring perioral 2-point discrimination; poor tactile localization on the tongue, lips, and jaw; and problems in discriminating grating orientation and roughness at the fingertips.

Patients with PD demonstrated abnormal cortical and subcortical activation upon passive sensory stimulation as measured using [15]O PET (39). Decreased vibratory stimulus–induced activation was seen of the contralateral sensorimotor (S1/M1) and lateral premotor cortex, contralateral S2, contralateral posterior cingulate, bilateral prefrontal cortex (Brodmann area 10), and contralateral basal ganglia, along with enhanced activation of ipsilateral sensory cortical areas (caudal S1, S2, and insular cortex). These responses were considered to represent altered central focusing and gating of sensory impulses or enhanced compensatory recruitment of associative sensory areas due to basal ganglial dysfunction.

The principal thalamic input to the striatum arises from the intralaminar nuclei, including the center median and parafascicular nuclei (33, 42). The specific function of this thalamic input is not known; however, in experimental animals, the majority of neurons within these structures (or at least major areas within them) respond to somatosensory and, in particular, nociceptive stimuli (42).

With the exception of the first somatosensory cortex, somatosensory-responsive (particularly nociceptive) neurons within the other cortical areas, as noted earlier, and in the intralaminar thalamic nuclei often have large, bilateral receptive fields or no somatotopic organization (30, 36). This parallels striatal (and pallidal) somatosensory-responsive neurons, which also tend to have large cutaneous receptive fields (31). Nociception-related inputs to the intralaminar thalamic nuclei arise from (or are modulated by inputs from) numerous sites, including spinothalamic and spinoreticulothalamic tracts and their trigeminal equivalents, the superior colliculus (43), pedunculopontine nucleus (cholinergic and noncholinergic neurons located within the mesopontine reticular formation) (44), dorsal raphe, and substantia nigra reticulata (45). Of course many of these sites connect with each other or to other basal ganglia–related structures (30), possibly relaying somatosensory information (e.g., substantia nigra reticulata projections to the superior colliculus, pedunculopontine connections to the substantia nigra, globus pallidus, and subthalamic nucleus)(44).

The majority of dopaminergic substantia nigra neurons are also responsive to somatosensory input, but only if the input is of specific behavioral significance. For example, in a monkey study (46), over 85% of 171 dopaminergic neurons evaluated in the awake animal increased firing rates that followed the spontaneous touch of food but not of nonfood objects hidden behind a box.

In anesthetized monkeys, 68% of 140 dopaminergic neurons responded to painful stimulation by decreasing firing rates. There was no response in this setting to nonpainful somatosensory stimulation (even if intense). Responses in both paradigms (awake and anesthetized) were nonsomatotopic and bilateral. Metabolic mapping studies in rodents and cats—following stimulation of vibrissae corresponding to corticostriate projections—showed a robust neural response in the caudate/putamen. The information processed was thought to be used to determine sensory-dependent postures (i.e., head positioning for feeding) rather than localization. The activity pattern was "patchy" anatomically, representing several functionally different regions of the striatum (47).

There is evidence that dopaminergic substantia nigra neurons can encode stimulus intensity (48). Dopaminergic nigrostriatal projections appear to significantly influence the sensory responsiveness of striatal neurons, although the effect may be indirect (30, 49). Striatal neurons are normally highly responsive to external sensory stimulation. Responsiveness in the caudate nucleus is decreased and altered qualitatively (less selective, larger receptive fields) in cats treated with the dopamine-selective neurotoxin 1-methyl 4-phenyl 1,2,3, 6-tetrahydropyridine (MPTP) (49). The onset of this effect is coincident with that of parkinsonian motor deficits. With recovery of motor function, striatal neuronal responses return to baseline. Decreased responsiveness of striatal neurons to sensory input may contribute to the contralateral sensory neglect that results from the intrastriatal administration of the dopamine-depleting agent 6-hydroxydopamine (30).

The intricate relationship between sensory processing and motor function has been discussed by Kaji and Murase (50). They noted that PD patients can take advantage of external visual or auditory sensory clues to initiate and perform movements. The "sensory trick" in normalizing body posture or movement in dystonia by tactile or proprioceptive input is a similar phenomenon, implying a general sensorimotor mismatch in motor control in this condition. Task specificity in dystonia points to a dysfunction of motor output linked to a fixed sensory input. The basal ganglia encode and "gait" sensory information relevant to motor control and also alter visual and auditory cortical evoked responses. The responsiveness of the trigeminal sensory nucleus is also altered by activation of the caudate nucleus or globus pallidus. These activities are "set-related" or "context-dependent" discharges associated with the movements or postures required by the environment. As a consequence of basal ganglial sensory processing, neurons in the supplementary motor or premotor cortex discharge in response to a sensory cue long before the onset of movement. Lesions of the basal ganglia therefore affect mainly automatic movements that depend on sensory guidance.

Visual stimuli are also processed by the striatum with output mapped from the lateral substantia nigra to area TE of the temporal lobe (51). In monkeys, higher-order visual cortical projections to the caudate/putamen are much more prominent than primary visual cortical projections (52). PD-related deficits in perception of facial expression as well as visual hallucinations seen in other Lewy body diseases and schizophrenia may be manifestations of a deficit in these higher cortical visual connections (47). Testing errors on the effect of visual feedback on pointing can detect changes in the processing of visual proprioceptive information in very mild PD and may even be used in the future for early diagnosis (53).

The coordination of sensory stimuli is relevant to cognition. Striatal cells are particularly active in relation to cues that orient spatial attention (47). In PD, decreased ability to focus on salient stimuli and ignore irrelevant information (54) results in impaired attention, which can cause deficits in working memory, attentional set-shifting, planning and problem solving, and perception. This last can affect sensory symptoms in patients.

DOPAMINERGIC MODULATION OF NOCICEPTION AND PARKINSON'S DISEASE

Dopamine depletion appears to increase nociception (30, 55, 56). Although both basal ganglia–related supraspinal and spinal dopaminergic responses have been implicated, the effect appears to be predominantly supraspinal (30, 36, 57, 58). For example, in a mouse study demonstrating hyperalgesia following systemic administration of MPTP (59), the effect diminished after about 2 weeks, coincident with a marked increase in serotonin activity (despite low dopamine concentrations). Dopamine (and serotonin) mediation of nociception may involve interactions with opiate activity.

Best known for their analgesic properties, opiates are found in high concentrations in the basal ganglia and colocalize with GABA in both "direct" and "indirect" striatopallidal projections (33): direct pathway projections to the globus pallidus internus and substantia nigra reticulata colocalize dynorphin (and substance P), whereas indirect pathway projections to the globus pallidus externus colocalize enkephalin. Kurumaji and coworkers (59) have provided indirect evidence favoring the role of basal ganglial metenkephalin in pain responsiveness by finding a close relationship in the rat between circadian fluctuations in pain responsiveness and metenkephalin–like immunoreactivity in selective brain regions, including the striatum and "mesolimbic" area but not within the thalamus or amygdala.

Mesocorticolimbic dopamine neurons arising in the ventral tegmental area (VTA) respond to opioids (via indirect activation) and psychostimulants (via decreased reuptake and/or reduced release) and play a role in the reward response to these substances. These neurons project to the nucleus accumbens, amygdala, and prefrontal cortex. Although they are not as severely affected as dopaminergic nigral neurons, there is involvement of VTA neurons at least in some patients with PD [e.g., see Zweig and coworkers (60)] . Moreover, dysregulation of this system may contribute to the "dopamine dysregulation syndrome" that sometimes complicates dopaminergic therapy in PD patients (61). Dopamine also modulates opioid antinociception, both at the spinal level and supraspinally, as studied in rodent models using acute phasic (tail flick), tonic pain (formalin), and integrated (hot plate) tests (62). This complex network can augment and/or diminish response to a noxious stimulus. Results from experimental models are sometimes conflicting, which is consistent with the wide variability of PD-associated pain symptoms, ranging from no pain in a limb that is continuously moving or rigid, to aching or otherwise unexplained burning or dysesthetic pain.

Acute and sustained noxious stimuli increase dopamine (DA) in the spinal dorsal horn (63). Although there are conflicting reports (64), in general D2 agonists potentiate spinally mediated antinociception when they are given alone or with opioids (65). D2 agonists selectively interrupt nociceptive reflexes without interfering with monosynaptic motor reflexes. By contrast, D1 agonists elicit pronociceptive effects both alone and when given with D2 agonists or opioids. The anti- and pronociceptive actions of D2 and D1 agonists respectively are expressed via their actions on projection neurons from the dorsal horn and/or primary afferent terminals (63). Nevertheless, on the basis of tail-flick testing for acute pain (presumably spinally mediated) in D2 receptor knockout mice, kappa opioid and to a less degree mu opioid analgesia is enhanced (66).

Dopamine agonists, both in experimental animals and in humans, appear to potentiate the analgesic effect of morphine, whereas depletion of dopamine, for example, by 6-hydroxydopamine lesions of the substantia nigra compacta and adjacent VTA, attenuates morphine analgesia (30, 67–70). In humans, dextroamphetamine has been added to morphine to enhance analgesia—for example, postoperatively (65). The selective D2 dopamine agonist quinpirole, the nonspecific agonist apomorphine, as well as cocaine and amphetamine typically induce analgesia in the formalin test for tonic pain (71). These effects, which are thought to be mediated supraspinally, can be blocked by pretreatment with either D1 or D2 antagonists. Lesions causing DA depletion in the VTA have been found to block the analgesic effects of systemic opioids in tonic pain (formalin test) but not in acute, phasic pain. Also, application of a DA antagonist into the nucleus accumbens blocks analgesia induced by application of opioids into the VTA or amphetamine in the accumbens, supporting a specific role for DA release in this structure

in opioid-mediated analgesia (71). In the rat model, an analgesic effect of dextroamphetamine is blocked by 6-hydroxydopamine lesions (67). Other studies have demonstrated that mu opioid and DA-mediated antinociception requires D1-like receptors supraspinally (62, 72). Dopamine-mediated augmentation of morphine-induced antinociception, at least via D2 receptors, may involve 5-HT2 antagonism, which in turn increases dopamine release (73).

Altier and Stewart (74) noted that morphine injected into the VTA caused analgesia to tonic painful stimuli. Exposure to stress caused release of the naturally occurring opioid metenkephalin in the VTA, resulting in inhibition of tonic pain. This effect could be blocked by the intra-VTA infusion of the opioid antagonist naltrexone. Similar results were found using substance P agonists and antagonists, suggesting a role for this substance in DA-related mesocorticolimbic tonic pain modulation as well (74). DA release in the nucleus accumbens following morphine administration was suppressed in a chronic neuropathic pain model (sciatic nerve lesion in the mouse) (75). The function of mu opioid receptors in the VTA was also downregulated. This has been hypothesized to explain the decreased addictive tendency of chronic opiate use clinically in chronic pain states. In this model, neuropathic pain may activate the ascending inhibitory pathway from the spinal cord projecting indirectly to the VTA, resulting in reduction in morphine-induced DA release in the nucleus accumbens. Although mu opioid agonists stimulate DA release, kappa agonists inhibit DA release in the nucleus accumbens (and dorsal caudate) (76, 77). Thus activation of the kappa opioid system by chronic inflammatory nociception may inhibit dopamine release in the nucleus accumbens, also resulting in the suppression of reward effects produced by morphine (70).

Dopamine levels within the dorsal striatum as well as the nucleus accumbens and other VTA projection sites vary significantly in otherwise normal humans with common polymorphisms of the catechol-O-methyltransferase (COMT) genotype. Individuals homozygous for an allele resulting in greater COMT activity and thus less dopamine (and less D2 receptor binding) have been hypothesized, based on animal models, to have increased enkephalin content in projection sites, resulting in an increased ability to activate mu opioid receptors in response to pain (78). This was demonstrated using PET imaging of a selective mu opioid radiotracer. The clinical consequence was less pain reported following sustained hypertonic saline infusion into the masseter muscle in individuals with this allele (78). More recently, the same group demonstrated activation of mu opioid receptors in the nucleus accumbens and other mesocorticolimbic sites in humans, reporting reduced pain following the administration of a placebo in this pain model (79).

The relevance of these observations for PD is unclear. In principle, as with the COMT allele, untreated or undertreated patients might be expected to experience less pain, but then they might be expected to respond to dopamine-based therapies by experiencing more pain, as can occur with levodopa therapy (7). However, Djaldetti and associates (80), using quantitative measurement of tactile and thermal sensory input via a visual analog scale, found that tactile and warm sensation was unchanged in PD but that heat pain threshold was significantly lowered in both the "on" and "off" states.

In addition to modulating VTA/mesocorticolimbic, spinal, and well-known periaqueductal gray and serotonergic raphe noiciceptive-responsive pathways, morphine injected into various regions of rat pallidum or substantia nigra reticulata also produces a dose-dependent analgesia (inhibited by naloxone) (81, 82). This effect appears to be specific, as responses on nonnociceptive sensorimotor tasks are generally unaffected. At least within the substantia nigra, this effect appears to be mediated by the mu receptor (76). Similarly, intravenous morphine significantly depresses nociception-related responses in additional brain regions—including, in a rat study (83) the ventral globus pallidus and the central nucleus of the amygdala. Putative nociception-related pathways between this region of the amygdala and basal ganglia (including the globus pallidus and substantia nigra) have also been reported (30).

Interestingly, certain pain syndromes similar to those described in patients with PD have also been described in psychiatric patients following neuroleptic use. In a series of 107 psychiatric inpatients (84), 23% of 60 patients being treated with neuroleptics experienced pain, as compared with only 1 of 47 patients being treated with other psychotropic drugs. In general, the pain described was a poorly localized aching in the extremities. Sensory complaints of heaviness, stiffness, or those associated with acute dystonic reactions were excluded. Pain occurred more frequently in patients with parkinsonism, akathisia, or both and tended to correlate with the severity of parkinsonism. Ford and coworkers (85) described 11 patients with tardive oral (9 patients) and genital (2 patients) pain similar in character to that which the same authors described in patients with PD—for example, as severe, relentless, and overshadowing other neurologic symptoms (13). All of the patients also had typical orolingual dyskinesia, and most had tardive dystonia or akathisia as well.

An interesting relationship exists between nociception and RLS involving dopaminergic and opioid systems. Stiasny-Kolster and coworkers (86) showed significant generalized static hyperalgesia to pinprick in the limbs of RLS patients as compared with healthy controls. There was no allodynia to light touch, however, suggesting A-delta fiber high-threshold input central sensitization. This neuropathic hyperalgesia improved with dopaminergic treatment. The authors conclude that the pathophysiology of RLS includes disturbed supraspinal pain modulation involving descending dopaminergic pathways. The role of opioids in the pathophysiology of RLS has been known empirically because of treatment efficacy. Opioid-binding abnormalities in the "medial pain system" (thalamus, amygdala, caudate, anterior cingulated gyrus, insular cortex, and orbitofrontal cortex) was demonstrated by von Spiczak and colleagues (87).

Nondopaminergic mechanisms may also be responsible for some of the sensory symptoms in patients with PD. Neuronal loss occurs within the locus ceruleus (LC) in PD (88). Noradrenergic projections from the LC to the dorsal horn of the spinal cord, along with direct and indirect noradrenergic fibers from A5/A7 groups in the pontine tegmentum, reportedly inhibit ascending nociceptive pathways (89). There is also moderate to severe loss of cholinergic neurons of the pedunculopontine nucleus in PD (90–92). In addition to projections to intralaminar thalamic nuclei, projections to other sites may contribute to a role of this nucleus in nonopiate analgesic systems (93, 94). These cholinergic neurons have also been implicated in an experimental model of morphine addiction (95, 96), possibly via projections to the dopaminergic mesolimbic system.

Studies have reported an association of pain with depression in PD (97, 98). In one study of 95 patients, 46% had pain thought to be associated with the disease. Severe depression was noted in 34% of those with pain but in only 13% of those without pain. Although, as suggested by the authors (97), depression may color "the interpretation of pain" or "pain can exacerbate an already present depression," it is also possible that underlying serotonergic pathology could predispose to both pain and depression. The latter possibility was supported by a study of cerebrospinal fluid from 10 PD patients with pain, 14 PD patients without pain, and 8 non-PD patients with poststroke thalamic pain syndrome (98). In addition to having the highest scores on a self-test depression scale, the PD patients with pain had significantly lower levels of the serotonin metabolite 5-HIAA in their cerebrospinal fluid (CSF) than did the other groups. Low CSF levels 5-HIAA had previously been associated with depression in PD without reference to pain (99).

OLFACTORY SYMPTOMS IN PARKINSON'S DISEASE

Unlike somatosensory symptoms, where variability is the rule, diminished sense of smell is found almost universally in patients with PD. Although initial studies using single odorants suggested hyposmia in less than 50% of patients (100, 101), a comprehensive objective evaluation using The University of Pennsylvania Smell Identification Test

(UPSIT) indicated that greater than 90% of PD patients have a profound olfactory deficit (102). Deficits include odor identification as well as discrimination and odor threshold detection (102–105). Although patients are often unaware of their olfactory dysfunction (102), hyposmia occurs very early in the course of PD; along with rapid-eye-movement (REM) sleep behavior disorder and constipation, it may commonly precede parkinsonian motor signs (106, 107). Although hyposmia is not clearly related to disease duration, odor discrimination was shown to correlate negatively with motor scores on the Unified Parkinson's Disease Rating Scale (UPDRS) (104). Relatively higher UPSIT scores may distinguish patients with tremor-predominant or a more benign PD from those with predominantly postural instability–gait disorder disease (108), at least in those tremor-predominant patients with a family history of tremor (109). Smell identification scores have also been shown to correlate with dopamine transporter imaging in the striatum in patients with early PD (110) and in a percentage of asymptomatic relatives of PD patients, some of whom subsequently developed PD (111, 112).

The early or even "presymptomatic" hyposmia noted in PD is fully consistent with known early alpha synuclein–immunoreactive Lewy body and Lewy neurite pathology as well as neuronal loss involving the anterior olfactory nucleus and olfactory bulb (113, 114). In defining their staging system for PD pathology, Braak and colleagues (114) noted involvement of the olfactory nucleus or bulb in many patients with stage 1 disease, most with stage 2, and all with stages 3 to 6 disease. They also noted subsequent pathology in olfactory-related regions, including the olfactory tubercle, piriform cortex, periamygdaloid cortex, and olfactory portions of the entorhinal cortex. Of note, the olfactory bulb pathology does not appear to include dopaminergic cells within this structure. Rather, a significantly increased number of dopaminergic cells within the olfactory bulb in PD has been reported. As dopamine inhibits the mitral cell response to olfactory input, this paradoxic finding has been hypothesized to contribute to the hyposmia in these patients (115). Consistent with lack of evidence indicating a direct relationship between dopaminergic dysfunction and hyposmia, dopaminergic therapies have not been reported to improve olfactory function in PD (102, 106). In one study, deep brain stimulation (DBS) of the subthalamic nucleus was shown to improve odor discrimination, if not odor thresholds, in PD patients (117), possibly indicating a role for higher-order olfactory-related structures in this function. Impairment in sniffing has also been demonstrated in PD and correlates with poor performance on olfactory tests (118).

Although patients may be unaware of hyposmia, it is possible that decreased smell may contribute to the weight loss often seen in PD. This has not been formally studied, but patients with decreased appetite and weight loss will often indicate that food no longer "tastes good." Finally, hyposmia may be clinically useful in discriminating PD from related conditions. While hyposmia is also an early and almost universal finding in Alzheimer's disease and dementia with Lewy bodies, it appears to be milder in multiple system atrophy and uncommon in progressive supranuclear palsy, corticobasal degeneration, and probably essential tremor [as reviewed by Hawkes (119)]. Olfaction is also reportedly normal in RLS (120) and vascular parkinsonism (121). Olfaction distinguished early-onset patients with the Parkin mutation, who had normal olfaction, from those without the mutation, where the hyposmia typical of older patients was found (122).

TREATMENT OF SENSORY SYMPTOMS IN PARKINSON'S DISEASE

The evaluation and treatment of sensory symptoms in patients with Parkinson's disease still requires the nuanced, subjective, qualitative approach (i.e., the "art of medicine") practiced by many of the best physicians of past eras. Parkinson's is primarily a disease of the elderly, who often have (or develop) multiple medical problems. The treating physician must obviously look for "flags" suggesting other disease processes, such as weakness (focal or out of proportion to that due to deconditioning), axial sensory level, hyperreflexia or reflex loss, astereognosia, or joint deformity. Although a certain restraint in ordering diagnostic studies to evaluate each sensory symptom is warranted, it can be difficult to decide where to draw the line. For example, a normal electromyographic/nerve conduction velocity (EMG/NCV) study can be reassuring in certain situations. However, patients often have several normal or otherwise unhelpful studies. Cervical or lumbar MRI scans are rarely normal in the elderly, yet they are often not helpful.

In evaluating sensory complaints, the physician should always try to determine whether there is a link to levodopa-related fluctuations in motor symptoms or to other aspects of the motor disturbance. Although some somatosensory symptoms would be more likely than others to respond to levodopa (Table 8-1), an increase in the dosage of levodopa (or dopamine agonist) might be remarkably effective in the individual patient. In other patients, levodopa can aggravate or cause pain (e.g., burning). In some patients, pain experienced during the "on" period does not respond to manipulation of oral dopaminergic medications; the only course is to stop levodopa and sacrifice mobility for comfort (12). Transient drug holidays may stop pain, but they do not provide a long-term solution. Two papers have reported on the usefulness of subcutaneous apomorphine injections for "off" period pain refractory to levodopa (123, 124). In this situation the apomorphine injection, with its rapid action, aborts a painful episode early. The effects have been shown to last several years (124). Apomorphine can be effective in patients who are refractory to treatment with other dopamine agonists. Leg edema, a common side effect of amantadine and dopamine agonists, can be associated with sensory symptoms. As in patients with other causes of dystonia, focal dystonia in PD may respond to injections of botulinum toxin (125). Long-acting benzodiazepines (e.g., clonazepam) may be useful for patients with internal tremor and those with nocturnal akathisia (15), particularly if they also have symptoms suggestive of a REM sleep behavior disorder. The atypical neuroleptic clozapine has also been reported to be effective in patients with nocturnal akathisia (18, 126), whereas inconsistent benefits from this medication have been reported in small series of patients with pain of the pelvis, back, or lower extremity (126, 127). Unfortunately the efficacy of narcotics, aspirin, acetaminophen, other nonsteroidal anti-inflammatory drugs, anticonvulsants, or other analgesic agents has not been systematically evaluated for the treatment of sensory symptoms in PD. From practical experience, they often do not appear to be useful.

Treatment of RLS in PD includes diagnosing and treating secondary disorders such as iron deficiency,

although the frequency of iron deficiency as a comorbidity contributing to RLS symptoms in PD patients has not been explored. Nonpharmacologic measures include maintaining regular sleep patterns, avoiding caffeine and alcohol, moderate exercise, and relaxation techniques. It is important that dopamine agonist or levodopa use in these patients be consistent with the overall management of the patient's symptoms.

Invasive procedures for PD also affect nonmotor symptoms. Loher and coworkers (128) reported that unilateral or bilateral deep brain stimulation improved pain by 74% to 90%, cramps by 88% to 90%, and dysesthesia by 88% to 100% at 1 year. The effect was seen within the first week after surgery and was sustained. Honey and associates (129) showed that unilateral pallidotomy was effective in improving or abolishing Parkinson's-related somatic and musculoskeletal pain for up to 1 year (the length of the study) in the majority of patients—an effect that appeared to be greater than that achieved with levodopa alone. Pain symptoms were improved bilaterally even when motor symptoms responded unilaterally, and dramatic pain relief was seen in patients whose rigidity responded only modestly. Thus invasive procedures may improve nonmotor symptoms, adding quality-of-life benefits over and above those achieved for motor symptoms.

References

1. Giuffrida R, Vingerhoets FJ, Bogousslavsky J, et al. Pain in Parkinson's disease. *Rev Neurol (Paris)* 2005; 161:407–418.
2. Schrag A, Jahanshahi M, Quinn N. How does Parkinson's disease affect quality of life? A comparison with quality of life in the general population. *Mov Disord* 2000; 15:1112–1118.
3. Kuopio AM, Marttila RJ, Helenius H, et al. The quality of life in Parkinson's disease. *Mov Disord* 2000; 15:216–223.
4. Quittenbaum BH, Grahn B. Quality of life and pain in Parkinson's disease: A controlled cross-sectional study. *Parkinsonism Relat Disord* 2004; 10:129–136.
5. Hoehn MM, Yahr MD. Parkinsonism; Onset, progression, and mortality. *Neurology* 1967; 17:427–442.
6. Karlsen KH, Tandberg E, Arsland D, et al. Health related quality of life in Parkinson's disease: A prospective longitudinal study. *J Neurol Neurosurg Psychiatry* 2000; 69:584–589.
7. Snider SR, Fahn S, Isgreen WP, et al. Primary sensory symptoms in parkinsonism. *Neurology* 1976; 26:423–429.
8. Djaldetti R, Shifrin A, Rogowski Z, et al. Quantitative measurement of pain sensation in patients with Parkinson disease. *Neurology* 2004; 62:2171–2175.
9. Koller WC. Primary sensory symptoms in Parkinson's disease. *Neurology* 1984; 34:957–959.
10. Goetz CG, Tanner CM, Levy M, et al. Pain in Parkinson's disease. *Mov Disord* 1986; 1:45–49.
11. Quinn NP, Koller WC, Lang AE, et al. Painful Parkinson's disease. *Lancet* 1986; 1:1366–1369.
12. Nutt JG, Carter JH. Sensory symptoms in parkinsonism related to central dopaminergic function. *Lancet* 1984; 2:456–457.
13. Ford B, Louis ED, Greene P, et al. Oral and genital pain syndromes in Parkinson's disease. *Mov Disord* 1996; 11:421–426.
14. Hillen ME, Sage JI. Nonmotor fluctuations in patients with Parkinson's disease. *Neurology* 1996; 47:1180–1183.
15. Shulman LM, Singer C, Bean JA, et al. Internal tremor in patients with Parkinson's disease. *Mov Disord* 1996; 11:3–7.
16. Lang AE, Johnson K. Akathisia in idiopathic Parkinson's disease. *Neurology* 1987; 37:477–481.
17. Linazasoro G, Marti Masso JF, Suarez JA. Nocturnal akathisia in Parkinson's disease: Treatment with clozapine. *Mov Disord* 1993; 8:171–174.
18. Garcia-Borreguero D, Odin P, Serrano C. Restless legs syndrome and PD. A review of the evidence for a possible association. *Neurology* 2003; 61(Suppl 3):S49–S55.
19. Thorpy, MJ. New paradigms in the treatment of restless legs syndrome. *Neurology* 2005; 64 (Suppl 3):S28–S33.
20. Ondo WG, Vuong KD, Jankovic J. Exploring the relationship between Parkinson disease and restless legs syndrome. *Arch Neurol* 2002; 59:421–424..
21. Krishnan PR, Bhatia M, Behari M. Restless legs syndrome in Parkinson's disease: A case-controlled study. *Mov Disord* 2003; 18:181–185.
22. Witjas T, Kaphan E, Azulay JP, et al. Nonmotor fluctuations in Parkinson's disease: Frequent and disabling. *Neurology* 2002; 59:408–413.
23. Riley DE, Lang AE. The spectrum of levodopa-related fluctuations in Parkinson's disease. *Neurology* 1993; 43:1459–1464.
24. Raudino F. Non motor off in Parkinson's disease. *Acta Neurol Scand* 2001; 104:312–315.
25. Indo T, Naito A, Sobue I. Clinical characteristics of headache in Parkinson's disease. *Headache* 1983; 23:211–212.
26. Indo T, Takahashi A. Early morning headache of Parkinson's disease: A hitherto unrecognized symptom? *Headache* 1987; 27:151–154.
27. Indaco A, Carrieri PB. Amitriptyline in the treatment of headache in patients with Parkinson's disease: A double-blind placebo-controlled study. *Neurology*1988; 38:1720–1722.
28. Sandyk R. Back pain as an early symptom of Parkinson's disease. *SA Med J* 1982; 2:3.
29. Shulman LM, Taback RL, Bean J et al. Comorbidity of the nonmotor symptoms of Parkinson's disease. *Movt Disord* 2001; 16:507–510.
30. Chudler EH, Dong WK. The role of the basal ganglia in nociception and pain. *Pain* 1995; 60:3–38.
31. Marsden CD. The mysterious motor function of the basal ganglia: The Robert Wartenberg Lecture. *Neurology* 1982; 32:514–539.
32. Alexander GE, Crutcher MD. Functional architecture of basal ganglia circuits: Neural substrates of parallel processing. *Trends Neurosci* 1990; 13:266–271.
33. Flaherty AW, Graybiel AM. Anatomy of the basal ganglia. In: Marsden CD, Fahn S (eds). *Movement Disorders 3*. Oxford, UK: Butterworth-Heinemann, 1994:3–27.
34. DeLong MR. Primate models of movement disorders of basal ganglia origin. *Trends Neurosci* 1990; 13:281–285.
35. Eidelberg D, Moeller JR, Dhawan V, et al. The metabolic topography of parkinsonism. *J Cereb Blood Flow Metab* 1994; 14:783–801.

36. Dong WK, Chudler EH, Sugiyama K, et al. Somato-sensory, multisensory, and task-related neurons in cortical area 7b (PF) of unanesthetized monkeys. *J Neurophysiol* 1994; 72:542–564.

37. Sathian K, Zangaladze A, Green J, et al. Tactile spatial acuity and roughness discrimination: Impairments due to aging and Parkinson's disease. *Neurology* 1997; 49: 168–177.

38. Brown LL, Sharp FR. Metabolic mapping of rat striatum: somatotopic organization of sensorimotor activity. *Brain Res* 1995; 686:207–222.

39. Pelled G, Bergman H, Ben-Hur T, et al. Reduced basal activity and increased functional homogeneity in sensorimotor and striatum of a Parkinson's disease rat model: a functional MRI study. *Eur J Neurosci* 2005; 21:2227–2232.

40. Schneider JS, Diamond SG, Markham CH. Deficits in orofacial sensorimotor function in Parkinson's disease. *Ann Neurol* 1986; 19:275–282.

41. Boecker H, Ceballos-Baumann A, Bartenstein P, et al. Sensory processing in Parkinson's and Huntington's disease: Investigations with 3D H(2)(15)O-PET. *Brain* 1999; 122:1651–1665.

42. Dong WK, Ryu H, Wagman IH. Nociceptive responses of neurons in medial thalamus and their relationship to spinothalamic pathways. *J Neurophysiol* 1978; 41:1592–1613.

43. Krauthamer GM, Krol JG, Grunwerg BS. Effect of superior colliculus lesions on sensory unit responses in the intralaminar thalamus of the rat. *Brain Res* 1992; 576:277–286.

44. Manaye KF, Zweig R, Wu D, et al. Quantification of cholinergic and select non-cholinergic mesopontine neuronal populations in the human brain. *Neuroscience* 1999; 89: 759–770.

45. Li J, Ji YP, Qiao JT, et al. Suppression of nociceptive responses in parafascicular neurons by stimulation of substantial nigra: An analysis of related inhibitory pathways. *Brain Res* 1992; 591:109–115.

46. Romo R, Schmaltz W. Somatosensory input to dopamine neurones of the monkey midbrain: Responses to pain pinch under anaesthesia and to active touch in behavioural context. *Prog Brain Res* 1989; 80:473–478.

47. Brown LL, Schneider JS, Lidsky TI. Sensory and cognitive functions of the basal ganglia. *Curr Opin Neurobiol* 1997; 7:157–163.

48. Gao DM, Jeaugey L, Pollak P, et al. Intensity-dependent nociceptive responses from presumed dopaminergic neurons of the substantia nigra, pars compacta in the rat and their modification by lateral habenula inputs. *Brain Res* 1990; 529:315–319.

49. Rothblat DS, Schneider JS. Response of caudate neurons to stimulation of intrinsic and peripheral afferents in normal, symptomatic, and recovered MPTP-treated cats. *J Neurosci* 1993; 13:4372–4378.

50. Kaji R, Murase N. Sensory function of basal ganglia. *Mov Disord* 2001; 16:593–594.

51. Middleton FA, Strick PL. The temporal lobe is a target of output from the basal ganglia. *Proc Natl Acad Sci USA* 1995; 93:8683–8687.

52. Saint-Cyr JA, Ungerleider LG, Desimone R. Organization of visual cortical inputs to the striatum and subsequent outputs to the pallido-nigral complex in the monkey. *J Comp Neurol* 1990; 298:129–156.

53. Keijsers NL, Admiral MA, Cools AR, et al. Differential progression of proprioceptive and visual information processing deficits in Parkinson's patients. *Eur J Neurosci* 2005; 21: 239–248.

54. Levin BE, Llabre MM, Weiner WJ. Cognitive impairments associated with early Parkinson's disease. *Neurology* 1989; 39:557–561.

55. Rosland JH, Humskaar S, Broch OJ, et al. Acute and long term effects of 1-methyl-4-phenyl-1,2,3,6-tetrahydropyridine (MPTP) in tests of nociception in mice. *Pharmacol Toxicol* 1992; 70:31–37.

56. Lin MT, Wu JJ, Chandra A, et al. Activation of striatal dopamine receptors induces pain inhibition in rats. *J Neural Transm* 1981; 51:213–222.

57. Sage JI, Kortis HI, Sommer W. Evidence for the role of spinal cord systems in Parkinson's disease-associated pain. *Clin Neuropharmacol* 1990; 13:171–174.

58. Altier N, Stewart J. The role of dopamine in the nucleus accumbens in analgesia. *Life Sci* 1999; 65:2269–2287.

59. Kurumaji A, Takashima M, Ohi K, et al. Circadian fluctuations in pain responsiveness and brain met enkephalin-like immunoreactivity in the rat. *Pharmacol Biochem Behav* 1988; 29:595–599.

60. Zweig RM, Cardillo JE, Cohen M et al. The locus ceruleus and dementia in Parkinson's disease. *Neurology* 1993; 43:986–991.

61. Evans AH, Pavese N, Lawrence AD, et al. Compulsive drug use linked to sensitized ventral striatal dopamine transmission. *Ann Neurol* 2006; 59:852–858.

62. Flores JA, El Banoua F, Galan-Rodriguez B, et al. Opiate anti-nociception is attenuated following lesion of large dopamine neurons of the paeriaqueductal grey: Critical role for D1 (not D2) dopamine receptors. *Pain* 2004; 110:205–214.

63. Millan MJ. Descending control of pain. *Prog Neurobiol* 2002; 66:355–474.

64. Cook CD, Barrett AC, Syvanthong C, et al. Modulatory effects of dopamine D3/2 agonists on kappa opioid-induced antinociception and diuresis in the rat. *Psychopharmacology* 2000; 152:14–23.

65. Nazarian A, Rodarte-Freeman AL, McDougall SA. Dopaminergic modulation of kappa opioid-mediated ultrasonic vocalization, antinociception, and locomotor activity in the preweanling rat. *Behav Neurosci* 1999; 113:816–825.

66. King MA, Bradshaw S, Chang AH, et al. Potentiation of opioid analgesia in dopamine$_2$ receptor knock-out mice: evidence for a tonically active anti-opioid system. *J Neurosci* 2001; 21:7788–7792.

67. Forrest Jr. WH, Brown BW, Brown CR, et al. Dextroamphetamine with morphine for the treatment of postoperative pain. *N Engl J Med* 1977; 296:712–715.

68. Price MTC, Fibiger HC. Ascending catecholamine systems and morphine analgesia. *Brain Res* 1975; 99:189–193.

69. Morgan MJ, Franklin KBJ. 6-Hydroxydopamine lesions of the ventral tegmentum abolish D-amphetamine and morphine analgesia in the formalin test but not in the tail flick test. *Brain Res* 1990; 519:144–149.

70. Gupta YK, Chugh A, Seth SD. Opposing effect of apomorphine on antinociceptive activity of morphine: A dose-dependent phenomenon. *Pain* 1989; 36:263–269.

71. Altier N, Stewart J. The role of dopamine in the nucleus accumbens in analgesia. *Life Sci* 1999; 65:2269–2287.

72. Karper PE, Nazarian A, Crawford CA, et al. Role of dopamine D1 receptors for kappa-opioid-mediated locomotor activity and antinociception during the preweanling period: A study using D1 receptor knockout mice. *Physiol Behav* 2000; 68:585–590.

73. Zarrindast M, Nassiri-Rad S, Pazouki M. Effects of dopaminergic agents on antinociception in formalin test. *Gen Pharmacol* 1999; 32:517–522.

74. Altier N, Stewart J. Dopamine receptor antagonists in the nucleus accumbens attenuate analgesia induced by ventral tegmental area substance P or morphine and by nucleus accumbens amphetamine. *J. Pharmacol Exp Ther* 1998; 285:208–215.

75. Narita M, Suzuki M, Imai S, et al. Molecular mechanism of changes in the morphine-induced pharmacological actions under chronic pain-like state: Suppression of dopaminergic transmission in the brain. *Life Sci* 2004; 74:2655–2673.

76. Di Chiara G, Imperato A. Opposite effects of mu and kappa opiate agonists on dopamine release in the nucleus accumbens and in the dorsal caudate of freely moving rats. *J Pharmacol Exp Ther* 1988; 244:1067–1080.

77. Margolis EB, Hjelmstad GO, Bonci A et al. Kappa-opioid agonists directly inhibit midbrain dopaminergic neurons. *J Neurosci* 2003; 23:9981–9986.

78. Zubieta J, Heitzeg MM, Smith YR, et al. COMT val^{158}met genotype affects mu-opioid neurotransmitter responses to a pain stressor. *Science* 2003; 299:1240–1243.

79. Zubieta J-K, Bueller JA, Jackson LR, et al. Placebo effects mediated by endogenous opioid activity on mu-opioid receptors. *J Neurosci* 2005; 25:7754–7762.

80. Djaldetti R, Shifrin A, Rogowski Z, et al. Quantitative measurement of pain sensation in patients with Parkinson disease. *Neurology* 2004; 62:2171–2175.

81. Baumeister AA. The effects of bilateral intranigral microinjection of selective opioid agonists on behavioral responses to noxious thermal stimuli. *Brain Res* 1981; 557: 136–145.

82. Anagnostakis Y, Zis V, Spyraki C. Analgesia induced by morphine injected into the pallidum. *Behav Brain Res* 1992; 48:135–143.

83. Huang G-F, Besson J-M, Bernard J-F. Intravenous morphine depresses the transmission of noxious messages to the nucleus centralis of the amygdala. *Eur J Pharmacol* 1993; 236:449–456.

84. Decina P, Mukherjee S, Caracci G, et al. Painful sensory symptoms in neuroleptic-induced extrapyramidal syndromes. *Am J Psychiatry* 1989; 149:1075–1080.

85. Ford B, Greene P, Fahn S. Oral and genital tardive pain syndromes. *Neurology* 1994; 44: 2115–2119.

86. Stasny-Kolster K, Magerl W, Oertel WH, et al. Static mechanical hyperalgesia without dynamic tactile allodynia in patients with restless legs syndrome. *Brain* 2004; 127:773–782.

87. Von Spiczak S, Whone AL, Hammers A, et al. The role of opioids in restless legs syndrome: an [^{11}C] diprenorphine PET study. *Brain* 2005; 128:906–917.

88. Zweig RM, Cardillo JE, Cohen M, et al. The locus ceruleus and dementia in Parkinson's disease. *Neurology* 1993; 43:986–991.

89. Buzas B, Max MB. Pain in Parkinson disease. *Neurology* 2004; 62:2156–2157.

90. Hirsch EC, Graybiel AM, Duyckaert C, et al. Neuronal loss in the pedunculopontine tegmental nucleus in Parkinson's disease and progressive supranuclear palsy. *Proc Nat Acad Sci USA* 1987; 84:5976–5980.

91. Jellinger K. The pedunculopontine nucleus in Parkinson's disease, progressive supranuclear palsy and Alzheimer's disease. *J Neurol Neurosurg Psychiatry* 1988; 51:540–543.

92. Zweig RM, Jankel WR, Hedreen JC, et al. The pedunculopontine nucleus in Parkinson's disease. *Ann Neurol* 1989; 26:41–46.

93. Iwamoto ET. Characterization of the antinociception induced by nicotine in the pedunculopontine tegmental nucleus and the nucleus raphe magnus. *J Pharmacol Exp Ther* 1991; 257:120–133.

94. Katayama Y, De Witt DS, Beeker DP, et al. Behavioral evidence for a cholinoceptive pontine inhibitory area: Descending control of spinal motor output and sensory input. *Brain Res* 1984; 296:241–262.

95. Becara A, van der Kooy D. The tegmental pedunuclopontine nucleus: A brainstem output of the limbic system critical for the conditioned place preferences produced by morphine and amphetamine. *J Neurosci* 1989; 9:3400–3409.

96. Klitinick MA, Kalivas P. Behavioral and neurochemical studies of opioid effects in the pedunculopontine nucleus and mediodorsal thalamus. *J Pharmacol Exp Ther* 1994; 269:437–478.

97. Goetz CG, Wilson RS, Tanner CM, et al. Relationships among pain, depression, and sleep alterations in Parkinson's disease. *Adv Neurol* 1986; 45:345–347.

98. Urakami K, Takahashi K, Matsushima E, et al. The threshold of pain and neurotransmitter's change on pain in Parkinson's disease. *Jpn J Psychiatr Neurol* 1990; 44: 589–593.

99. Mayeux R, Stern Y, Williams J, et al. Clinical and biochemical features of depression in Parkinson's diseases. *Am J Psychiatry* 1986; 143:756–759.

100. Ansari KA, Johnson A. Olfactory function in patients with Parkinson's disease. *J Chronic Dis* 1975; 28:493–497.

101. Ward CD, Hess WA, Calne DB. Olfactory impairment in Parkinson's disease. *Neurology* 1983; 33:943–946.

102. Doty RL, Deems DA, Stellar S. Olfactory dysfunction in parkinsonism: a general deficit unrelated to neurologic signs, disease stage, or disease duration. *Neurology* 1988; 38: 1237–1244.

103. Hawkes CH, Shephard BC, Daniel SE. Olfactory dysfunction in Parkinson's disease. *J Neurol Neurosurg Psychiatry* 1997; 62:436–446.

104. Tissingh G, Berendse HW, Bergmans P, et al. Loss of olfaction in de novo and treated Parkinson's disease: Possible implications for early diagnosis. *Mov Dis* 2001; 16: 41–46.

105. Muller A, Reichmann H, Livermore A, et al. Olfactory function in idiopathic Parkinson's disease (IPD): Results from cross-sectional studies in IPD patients and long-term follow-up of de-novo IPD patients. *J Neural Transm* 2002; 109:805–811.

106. Langston JW. The Parkinson's complex: Parkinsonism is just the tip of the iceberg. *Ann Neurol* 2006; 59:591–596.

107. Postuma RB, Lang AE, Massicotte-Marquez J, et al. Potential early markers of Parkinson disease in idiopathic REM sleep behavior disorder. *Neurology* 2006; 28:845–851.

108. Stern MB, Doty RL, Dotti M, et al. Olfactory function in Parkinson's disease subtypes. *Neurology* 1994; 44:266–268.

109. Ondo WG, Dejian Lai. Olfaction testing in patients with tremor-dominant Parkinson's disease: Is this a distinct condition? *Mov Disord* 2005; 20:471–475.

110. Siderowf A, Newberg A, Chou, KL, et al. [^{99m}Tc] TRODAT-1 SPECT imaging correlates with odor identification in early Parkinson disease. *Neurology* 2005; 64:1716–1720.

111. Berendse HW, Booij J, Francot CMJE, et al. Subclinical dopaminergic dysfunction in asymptomatic Parkinson's disease patients' relatives with decreased sense of smell. *Ann Neurol* 2001; 50:34–41.

112. Ponsen MM, Stoffers D, Booij J et al. Idiopathic hyposmia as a preclinical sign of Parkinson's disease. *Ann Neurol* 2004; 56:173–181.

113. Pearce RK, Hawkes CH, Daniel SE. The anterior olfactory nucleus in Parkinson's disease. *Mov Disord* 1995; 10:283–287.

114. Braak H, Del Tredici K, Rub U, et al. Staging of brain pathology related to sporadic Parkinson's disease. *Neurobiol Aging* 2003; 24:197–211.

115. Huisman E, Uylings HBM, Hoogland PV. A 100% increase of dopaminergic cells in the olfactory bulb may explain hyposmia in Parkinson's disease. *Mov Disord* 2004; 19: 687–692.

116. Roth J, Radil T, Ruzicka E, et al. Apomorphine does not influence olfactory thresholds in Parkinson's disease. *Funct Neurol* 1998; 13:99–103.

117. Hummel T, Jahnke U, Sommer U, et al. Olfactory function in patients with idiopathic Parkinson's disease: Effects of deep brain stimulation in the subthalamic nucleus. *J Neural Transm* 2005; 112:669–676.

118. Sobel N, Thomason ME, Stappen I et al. An impairment in sniffing contributes to the olfactory impairment in Parkinson's disease. *Proc Natl Acad Sci USA* 2001; 98:4154–4159.

119. Hawkes C. Olfaction in neurodegerative disorder. *Movement Disorders* 2003; 18: 364–372.

120. Adler CH, Gwinn KA, Newman S. Olfactory function in restless legs syndrome. *Mov Disord* 1998; 13:563–565.

121. Katzenschlager R, Zijlmans J, Evans A et al. Olfactory function distinguishes vascular parkinsonism from Parkinson's disease. *J Neurol Neurosurg Psychiatry* 2004; 75: 1749–1752.

122. Khan NL, Katzenschlager R, Watt H, et al. Olfaction differentiates parkin disease from early-onset parkinsonism and Parkinson disease. *Neurology* 2004; 62:1224–1226.

123. Frankel JP, Lees AJ, Kempster PA, et al. Subcutaneous apomorphine in the treatment of Parkinson's disease. *J Neurol Neurosurg Psychiatry* 1990; 53:96–101.

124. Factor SA, Brown DL, Molho ES. Subcutaneous apomorphine injections as treatment for intractable pain in Parkinson's disease. *Mov Disord* 2000; 15:167–169.

125. Jankovic J, Tintner R. Dystonia and parkinsonism. *Parkinsonism Relat Disord* 2001; 8: 109–121.

126. Trosch RM, Friedman JH, Lannon MC, et al. Clozapine use in Parkinson's disease: A retrospective analysis of a large multicentered clinical experience. *Mov Disord* 1998; 13:37–38.

127. Juncos JL. Clozapine treatment of parkinsonian pain syndromes. *Mov Disord* 1996; 11: 603–604.

128. Loher TJ, Burgunder J-M, Weber S, et al. Effect of chronic pallidal deep brain stimulation on off period dystonia and sensory symptoms in advanced Parkinson's disease. *J Neurol Neurosurg Psychiatry* 2002; 73:395–399.

129. Honey CR, Stoessl AJ, Tsui JKC, et al. Unilateral pallidotomy for reduction of parkinsonian pain. *J Neurosurg* 1999; 91:198–201.

9 Voice, Speech, and Swallowing Disorders

Shimon Sapir
Lorraine O. Ramig
Cynthia M. Fox

Most individuals with Parkinson's disease (PD) develop voice and speech disorders during the course of their illness (1). Reduced vocal loudness, monotone and breathy or hoarse voice, and imprecise, hypokinetic articulation are the main characteristics of Parkinsonian speech (2, 3–13). These voice and speech disorders, collectively termed hypokinetic dysarthria, can be among the first signs of PD (14). Reduced facial expression, body gestures, and voice changes often make individuals with PD seem cold, withdrawn, unintelligent, and moody (15). Hypokinetic dysarthria often impairs effective communication and reduces the ability to socialize, interact with family, and maintain employment, thus adversely affecting the quality of life of these individuals (9, 16, 17).

Most individuals with PD also develop swallowing disorders (dysphagia) during their illness (18). These disorders sometime appear as first signs of the disease (19). The swallowing problems include difficulty with lingual motility, bolus formation, and initiation of swallow as well as delayed pharyngeal response and decreased pharyngeal contraction (18, 20, 21). Weight loss and lack of enjoyment in eating associated with dysphagia have been reported by patients. Aspiration pneumonia may develop during later stages of the disease and in some cases may cause death (22).

Although neuropharmacologic (23, 24) and neurosurgical (25, 26) approaches have proven effective in improving limb motor symptoms in PD, their therapeutic impact on speech production and swallowing has been minimal, adverse, or inconsistent (27, 28). Vocal fold collagen augmentation has been reported to improve glottic closure and phonation in PD (29, 30). Traditional treatment of hypokinetic dysarthria has focused on changing rate, articulation, prosody, or a combination of these (31, 32). Swallowing treatment has focused on behavioral changes and dietary modifications (21). The Lee Silverman Voice Treatment (LSVT) emphasizes increasing amplitude of motor output across the speech mechanism through increased vocal loudness with self-monitoring; it has generated the first short- and long-term efficacy data (33, 34) for successfully treating disordered voice, speech, and swallowing as well as facial expression and tongue mobility in this population (20, 35–38). Improvement in brain function following LSVT has been documented (39–41). In a degenerative disease such as PD, these improvements may be indicative of neural plasticity.

Electronic and computer technology has been adapted to deliver LSVT via a real or a virtual clinician, thus aiding in the accessibility, administration, practice, cost-effectiveness, and overall effectiveness of LSVT in PD.

SPEECH AND VOICE CHARACTERISTICS IN PARKINSON'S DISEASE

Speech and voice disorders in individuals with PD have been attributed to the physical features of the disease, especially muscle rigidity (e.g., refs. 42 and 43). However, the specific pathophysiologic mechanisms underlying these disorders remain unclear (44–46), and studies point to other etiologies, such as reduced muscle activation and deficits in sensorimotor gating, internal cueing, amplitude scaling, and self-regulation of vocal output and effort (47, 48). Perceptual, acoustic, aerodynamic, kinematic, videostroboscopic, electroglottographic, and electromyographic data have documented disorders of laryngeal, respiratory, articulatory, and velopharyngeal function in PD (49–52).

Laryngeal and Respiratory Disorders

Darley and coworkers were among the first to use a cluster analysis and systematic description of perceptual characteristics of speech and voice in PD (53–55). They identified reduced loudness; reduced prosodic pitch inflection (monopitch) and loudness inflection (monoloudness); reduced linguistic stress; breathy, hoarse, or harsh voice quality; imprecise consonant and vowel articulation; and short rushes of speech as the distinctive cluster of features of Parkinsonian speech. Logemann, Boshes, and Fisher (56–57) reported voice quality problems such as hoarseness, roughness, breathiness, and tremor in 89% of 200 unmedicated patients with PD. Ludlow and Bassich (58) reported a harsh voice in 83% and a breathy voice in 17% of individuals with PD. They suggested that harsh voice quality may be associated with drug-related dyskinesias. Aronson (14) and Stewart and coworkers (59) noted that voice disorders may occur very early in the disease process. These clinical observations have been confirmed (1, 57, 60).

Physiologic Studies of Laryngeal Dysfunction in Parkinson's Disease

Disordered laryngeal function has been documented through a number of videoendoscopic studies. Hansen and coworkers (51) reported vocal fold bowing (lack of medial vocal fold closure) together with greater amplitude of vibration and laryngeal asymmetry in 30 of 32 individuals with PD. Blumin and colleagues (61) used videostroboscopy and fiberoptic endoscopic techniques as well as a voice handicap index (VHI) questionnaire to assess laryngeal and swallowing function in 15 individuals with severe PD who were candidates for deep brain stimulation. Thirteen (87%) patients had significant vocal fold bowing, 15 (100%) had some degree of pharyngeal residue of solids noted on evaluation of swallowing, and

14 (93%) had a significant self-reported voice handicap. Smith and coworkers (36) made videostroboscopic observations of individuals with PD and reported that 12 of 21 patients had a form of glottal incompetence (bowing, anterior or posterior chink) on nasal fiberoptic views. Perez and coworkers (62) observed laryngeal tremor in 55% of 29 individuals with PD. The primary site of tremor was vertical laryngeal motion. However, the most striking stroboscopic findings were abnormal phase closure and phase asymmetry. Additional data to support laryngeal closure problems come from analysis of the electroglottographic (EGG) signals. Uziel (13) reported EGG waveforms with reduced amplitude in PD relative to nondisordered speakers. Gerratt and coworkers (63) reported an abnormally large speed quotient and poorly defined closing period in this population. These observations were consistent with slow vocal fold opening relative to the rate of closure and incomplete closure of the vocal folds.

The nature of the laryngeal abnormalities described has been investigated with electromyographic (EMG) techniques. EMG studies of Parkinsonian speech indicate either a reduction of neural drive to the laryngeal muscles (44) or abnormally elevated laryngeal muscle activity (45, 64–66) and poor reciprocal suppression of laryngeal and respiratory muscles (67). Hirose and Joshita (68) studied EMG data derived from the thyroarytenoid (TA) muscles in an individual with PD who had limited vocal fold movement. They observed no reduction in the number of motor unit discharges and no pathologic discharge patterns (such as polyphasic or high-amplitude voltages). They reported loss of reciprocal suppression of the TA during inspiration and interpreted this as evidence of deterioration in the reciprocal adjustment of the antagonist muscles associated with PD rigidity. Gallena and colleagues (64) used TA EMG and nasoendoscopy to compare laryngeal physiology during speech of individuals with PD *on* versus *off* leveodopa, and of individuals without PD. Significant differences were found between patients and nonpatients and in the *on* and *off* conditions: some patients were observed to have higher levels of laryngeal muscle activation, more vocal fold bowing, and greater impairment in voice onset and offset control when they were *off* levodopa than when they were *on* levodopa and in comparison to the healthy controls. Luschei and coworkers (69) studied single motor unit activity in the TA muscle in individuals with PD and found that the firing rate of the TA motor units was decreased in male subjects. The authors interpreted these findings and past reports to suggest that PD affects rate and variability in motor unit firing in the laryngeal musculature. Baker and coworkers (44) found in their EMG study that absolute TA amplitudes during a known-loudness-level task in individuals with PD were the lowest when compared with normal aging controls. Relative TA amplitudes were also decreased in both the aging and PD groups when compared with the young normals. These authors concluded that reduced levels of TA muscle activity may contribute to the reduced vocal fold adduction and the reduced vocal loudness and increased breathiness typically observed in PD and aging populations. The decrease in neural drive to the laryngeal system is incongruent with the suggestion that vocal bowing, glottic incompetence, and hypophonia in PD are all related to rigidity. Moreover, the fact that hypophonic patients with PD can markedly increase vocal loudness when instructed to do so speaks against the notion of rigidity as the cause of hypophonia in PD (48, 70, 71). It may be tentatively concluded that hypophonia and laryngeal dysfunction in PD are related to hypokinesia secondary to sensorimotor gating abnormalities.

Physiologic Studies of Respiratory Dysfunction in Parkinson's Disease

Respiratory studies of Parkinsonian speech have documented reduction or abnormalities in chest wall movements, respiratory muscle activation patterns (50, 72, 73), vital capacity (74–76), intraoral air pressure during consonant or vowel production, and airflow patterns (67, 73, 77–79). Some of these aerodynamic abnormalities may be related to variations in airflow resistance due to abnormal movements of the vocal folds and supraglottic area (67) or to abnormal chest wall movements and respiratory muscle activation patterns (50, 72, 73).

Acoustic Studies of Phonatory Dysfunction in Parkinson's Disease

Acoustic data have been used to describe the speech and voice characteristics of individuals with PD and seem to parallel perceptual descriptions. These acoustic measures include vocal sound pressure level (VocSPL), voice fundamental frequency (Fo) and its variability (expressed in terms of standard deviation of Fo, or SDFo, and standard deviation of semitones, or STSD), phonatory stability (expressed in terms of jitter, shimmer, and/or harmonic-to-noise ratio), and vowel formants.

Early studies (3, 4, 58, 59, 80, 81) failed to find a reduction in VocSPL in spite of perceptual impression of reduced loudness in these individuals. However, reports by Fox and Ramig (82) and Sapir and colleagues (60) documented reduced VocSPL by 2 to 4 decibels (at 30 cm) across a number of speech tasks in comparing individuals with PD with an age- and gender-matched control group. A 2- to 4-decibel change is equal to a 40% change in loudness perception (82).

Voice frequency variability (expressed as SDFo or STSD), necessary for prosodic aspects of speech, has been reported to be consistently lower in individuals with PD when compared with a nondisordered control group (3,

4, 58, 80). These findings support the perceptual characteristics of the reduced prosodic pitch variation (hypoprosodia, monopitch or monotonous speech) that is typically observed (53–55). A reduction in maximum Fo range has also been reported in the speech of individuals PD when compared to the speech of nondisordered speakers (3, 58, 83).

Measures of short-term phonatory instability (e.g., jitter, shimmer, harmonics-to-noise ratio) have also been documented in PD, along with various perceptual characteristics of disordered voice quality (e.g., hoarse, breathy, harsh) (84, 85). Long-term phonatory instability, especially vocal tremor in the range of 3 to 7 Hz, has been documented during sustained vowel phonation in PD (38, 84, 86–88).

Temporal aspects of Parkinsonian speech movements have been investigated using acoustic measures. Such acoustic studies have documented problems with timing of vocal onsets and offsets (voicing during normally voiceless closure intervals of voiceless stops) (13, 49, 89) and spirantization (presence of fricative-like, aperiodic noise during stop closures). These problems most likely reflect laryngeal movement abnormalities (90), but since they are associated with consonant production, these temporal problems may also be related to articulatory control.

Articulatory and Velopharyngeal Disorders

Phonetic and Physiologic Studies. Imprecise consonants have been observed in PD (56–57, 74). Logemann and coworkers (56, 57) used perceptual evaluation and phonetic transcription of articulation problems in 45% of 200 individuals studied. They suggested that articulatory undershoot and inadequate narrowing of the vocal tract may underlie problems with stops (e.g., /p/), affricates (e.g., /ch/), and fricatives (e.g., /s/) in speech in PD. Using similar phonetic analyses techniques, Ho and her colleagues (1) studied 200 individuals with PD and found that, whereas nearly all individuals had a voice problem, approximately half had articulatory and fluency problems. Ho and colleagues found that voice problems typically preceded other speech problems, but as the disease progressed, the articulation and fluency problems became more severe, matching the severity of the voice problems or becoming more severe than the voice problems. Similar observation were made by Sapir and coworkers (60), who studied voice and speech problems in 40 individuals with idiopathic PD (IPD) using perceptual and phonetic analysis techniques. These patients had sought speech therapy and were medicated with levodopa or dopamine agonists.

Kinematic and electromyographic (EMG) studies of orofacial movements during Parkinsonian speech indicate a reduction in the size (to near half of normal)

and peak velocity of jaw movements, increased levels of tonic resting and background neuromuscular activity, and loss of reciprocity between agonist and antagonistic muscle groups in the perioral muscles (49, 91–92). Forrest and colleagues (90) employed acoustic, perceptual, and kinematic analyses of connected speech in geriatric individuals with PD and age-matched healthy controls. As a group, the Parkinsonian speakers had very limited jaw movement, with markedly reduced jaw opening displacements and velocities compared with the normal geriatrics. Lower lip movement amplitude and velocity were also reduced for the Parkinsonian speakers relative to the normal geriatrics, but to a lesser degree than the movement of the jaw. These studies collectively indicate hypokinetic speech movements associated with abnormal neural drive to the speech periphery and abnormal sensorimotor gating.

Importantly, the presence and severity of articulatory impairment in the speech of individuals with PD is related, in many cases, to the speech task being performed. Caligiuri (93) used kinematic analyses of lip displacement amplitude, peak instantaneous velocity, and movement time to assess the effects of rate of speech on articulatory function in PD. He found that lip movements were normal when the individuals spoke at a rate of 3 to 5 syllables per second but became hypokinetic when the rate increased to 5 to 7 syllables per second, which is the typical rate of conversational speech. Kempler and Van Lancker (94) found that the speech of a dysarthric individual with PD was much less intelligible during spontaneous speech than during the production of the same utterances in other modes, such as repetition, reading, or singing. Rosen and colleagues (95) studied decline in vocal intensity in PD and matched controls across different tasks: vowel prolongation, syllable repetition [diadochokinesis (DDK)], isolated sentences, and conversation. They found that the PD speakers had no significant differences in intensity decline from healthy speakers in vowel prolongation. However, vocal intensity of speakers with PD declined more rapidly than that of controls in DDK tasks. Also, although intensity slopes in conversation were more variable in both groups, some individuals with PD exhibited abrupt changes in vocal intensity. Ackermann and Ziegler (49) used acoustic analysis of sentence utterances of the speech of individuals with IPD to provide information on speech tempo and accuracy of articulation. They found that the speech tempo was not significantly different from normal. Also, switching between opening and closing movements of the speech articulators in sentence production seemed undisturbed. However, patients had a reduced capacity to complete articulatory occlusion, which was most likely due to a reduction in the range of articulatory movements. This articulatory "undershoot" was not uniform, in that it was influenced by linguistic demands. Specifically, articulatory closures associated with a stressed syllable were performed at the expense of unstressed ones. Ho and colleagues (1) found that speech articulation in individuals with PD became more impaired (hypokinetic) when these individuals had to utter a series of phonemes that were heterogeneous in terms of place of articulation than when they were homogenous in place of articulation. These findings suggest that to best assess articulatory and other aspects of speech in individuals with PD it is necessary to include a variety of speech tasks that tax dysarthric speakers and thus reveal the specific deficits. Since many studies of speech articulation in PD report conflicting findings, it might be that some of these differences are related to the specific speech tasks used to assess articulatory function (48). It is also possible that differences between individuals and speech tasks reflect different compensatory mechanisms.

Disordered Rate and Effects of Rate on Articulation in Parkinson's Disease.   Individuals with PD may have a tendency to speak in a rapid rate, which is accompanied by hypokinetic and decayed articulatory movements. This tendency is symptomatic of the disease, and it may be related to a combination of temporal processing, scaling, cuing, and sensorimotor gating deficits (37). To prevent this tendency, these individuals may choose, as a compensatory or preventative measure, to slow their rate of speech markedly. Some evidence for this compensatory mechanism comes from kinematic findings by Caligiuri (93), who showed that lip movements were normal when individuals with IPD spoke at a rate of 3 to 5 syllables per second, but became hypokinetic when these individuals were asked speak at a faster rate similar to that of normal speech (to 5 to 7 syllables per second). Ackerman and colleagues (91) described a patient with akinetic-rigid PD who was instructed to synchronize labial diadochokinesis (DDK) to sequences of periodic acoustic stimuli (2.5 to 6 Hz). This individual was able to synchronize his DDK to the stimulus rate up to about 4 Hz, but when the stimulus rate exceeded 4 Hz, his DDK was uncontrollably produced at 8 to 9 Hz, indicating speech hastening. Still another evidence is that when individuals with PD are instructed to speak clearly they are likely to slow their speech (96).

Although rapid rate has been reported in 6% to 13% of individuals (3, 4, 97–99), Canter (80) reported slower than normal rates. To what extent these different findings relate to the pathophysiology of speech disorder or to compensatory mechanisms is difficult to verify.

Aside from rate of speech, there are other prosodic abnormalities in Parkinsonian speech, namely fluency disorders. These include palilalia, stuttering, and other forms of dysfluency, although these disorders are observed in a small percentage of patients with PD (53, 60).

Resonance Disorders in Parkinsonian Speech.
Resonance problems are not common in PD, and when they are present, the voice typically sounds like a "foghorn" (14). This phenomenon is hard to describe. Perceptually, the voice sounds slightly hypernasal and with a "muffled," "back" resonance quality. The acoustic and physiologic nature of this phenomenon is not clear. Aerodynamic and kinematic studies suggest that velopharyngeal movements may be reduced in some of these individuals (52, 100, 101). Abnormal tongue posture may contribute to the percept of "foghorn" resonance in Parkinsonian speech.

Acoustic Studies of Speech Articulation in Parkinson's Disease. Articulatory movements in Parkinsonian speech have been studied indirectly, by means of acoustic analysis, mostly of formant dynamics. Formants are peaks of acoustic energy along the frequency domain in the speech spectrum. The center frequencies of these formants are lawfully related to the position of the speech articulators and the overall configuration of the vocal tract created by the articulators. Because of this relationship, researchers use analysis of formant frequency dynamics to represent articulatory movements.

Sapir and colleagues (48) compared various measures of the first (F1) and second (F2) vowel formants in age-matched individuals with and without IPD. They found that F2 of the vowel /u/ (F2u) was significantly higher, and the ratio of the F2 of the vowel /i/ and the F2 of the vowel /u/ (F2i/F2u) was significantly smaller in the patients compared to the healthy controls. They argued that since F2 reflects articulatory mobility and extent of articulatory movements, these acoustic differences likely indicate a reduction of vowel articulatory motility during speech. McRae and colleagues (102) studied acoustic and perceptual consequences of articulatory rate changes in the speech of individuals with PD and the speech of age-matched healthy controls. They reported that, irrespective of rate condition, the relationship between perceived severity of speech and measures of acoustic working space (constructed by the first and second formants of vowels /i/, /ae/, /u/, and /a/) was such that the PD group exhibited smaller measures of acoustic working space and more severe perceptual estimates of speech articulation than the control speakers. The reduction in working vowel space is indicative of reduced motility of the articulators, consistent with hypokinetic articulation characteristic of Parkinsonian speech. Yunusova and colleagues (103) studied breath-group intelligibility in the dysarthric speech of individuals with PD or ALS in comparison to age-matched healthy individuals. They found in both dysarthric groups fewer average words and reduced interquartile ranges for F2, the latter serving as a global measure of articulatory mobility. Flint and colleagues (104) compared the speech of patients with PD to that of individuals with major depression and neurologically and psychiatrically healthy controls. Both major depression and PD groups had significantly shortened voice onset time and decreased F2 transition compared to controls, suggesting reduced range of articulatory movements. Forrest and colleagues (90) found that in addition to the kinematic findings reviewed earlier Parkinsonian speakers had reduced formant transitions compared to the normal geriatrics. These acoustic abnormalities were greater for the more severe, compared to the milder, dysarthric speakers and were most apparent in the more complex vocalic gestures.

IMPAIRED SENSORY AND HIGH-LEVEL FUNCTIONS AS CAUSES OF HYPOKINETIC DYSARTHRIA

Whereas the speech and voice symptoms associated with PD are generally considered in relation to motor output problems, sensory abnormalities in these individuals have been recognized for years (23, 105, 106) and these abnormalities may bear directly on the motor deficits in Parkinsonian speech. Albin and coworkers (107) and Penny and Young (108) have suggested that basal ganglia excitatory circuits inadequately activate cortical motor centers, and as a result, motor neuron pools are not provided with adequate activation; thus movements are small and weak. Berardelli (109) has suggested that the defect in motor cortex activation is due to a perceptual failure to select the muscle commands to match the external force and speed requirements. Maschke and coworkers (110) and Demirci and coworkers (111) have suggested that this is a problem with kinesthesia secondary to basal ganglia sensory gating dysfunction. Demirci and coworkers (111) also argued that because of this dysfunction, when individuals with PD match their effort to their kinesthetic feedback, they will constantly underscale their movement.

Sensory problems have been studied in relation to speech output in PD (112–114) and may play an important role in motor speech disorders (115). Problems in sensory perception of effort have been identified as an important focus of successful voice treatment for individuals with PD (116). Consistent with suggestions by Hallet and colleagues (110), it has been observed that when individuals with PD are asked to produce "loud" speech (i.e., attempt large movements), they increase their otherwise underscaled soft speech to a level within normal limits. However, when they produce this loud speech these patients will complain that they are talking "too loud." Furthermore, individuals with PD often report people around them "must need hearing aids" rather than recognizing that their own speech has become too soft. It appears that sensory processing deficits may be a factor in speech and voice characteristics observed in PD.

Several research studies provide insights about the nature of hypophonia in PD. Ho and colleagues (70) examined the regulation of speech volume in hypophonic subjects with PD and age- and gender-matched controls. They first investigated the ability of individuals with PD to automatically regulate speech volume in response to two types of implicit cues: background noise and instantaneous auditory feedback. The control subjects demonstrated appropriate speech volume response to these cues; that is, they automatically spoke louder in the presence of competing noise (the Lombard effect), and automatically decreased speech volume when hearing their own voice amplified and fed back to them via headphones instantaneously. The individuals with PD had an overall decrease in speech volume and they were less able than controls to appropriately increase or decrease speech volume in the presence of background noise and when their own voice was instantaneously amplified and fed back to them via headphones. In another experiment, the subjects were given explicit cues regarding adjustment of speech volume, and under these conditions, the ability of subjects with PD to regulate speech volume was normalized in spite of overall low voice intensity. These findings were interpreted by Ho and colleagues to suggest that the individuals with PD fail to respond to the implicit cues integral to scaling speech volume, even though they clearly have the capacity to speak with a normal voice volume, as least at the earlier stages of the disease. The difference in voice loudness regulation with explicit versus implicit cues is extremely important, as it suggests that the hypophonia in individuals with PD is at least partially related to a deficit in internal (implicit) cueing, and that this deficit can be compensated for by external cueing. It also indicates that hypophonia is not necessarily related to peripheral deficits such as muscle rigidity.

In another study, Ho and colleagues (1) examined the automatic regulation of speech volume over distance in hypophonic patients with PD and age- and sex-matched controls. They used two modes of speech: conversation and recitation of sequential material (e.g., counting). During speech production, the controls significantly increased overall speech volume for conversation relative to that for sequential material. The patients were unable to achieve this overall increase for conversation and consistently spoke with a lower voice volume than controls at all distances. However, they were still able to increase speech volume for greater distances in a manner similar to controls for conversation and sequential material, thus demonstrating a normal pattern of speech volume regulation. Ho and colleagues interpreted these findings to suggest that speech volume regulation is intact in PD, although the gain is reduced. They also suggested that these findings are reminiscent of skeletal motor control studies in PD, in which the amplitude of movement is reduced but the pattern of movement is intact. This suggestion is in line with the notion that the main function of the basal ganglia is to serve as an amplifier by controlling the gain, through gating and scaling, of cortically generated movement patterns (48, 117).

In still another study Ho and colleagues (71) contrasted the volume level of speech production with perceived volume in hypophonic individuals with PD and in age-matched healthy individuals with normal voice and speech. To assess the ability to regulate and perceive vocal loudness, the subjects were asked to read aloud (without additional instructions) either in a loud voice or in a quiet voice using the same material and to rate the loudness of their voices immediately after speaking; at a later time, they were asked to do the same by hearing their voices recorded on tape. These perceptual ratings were compared with actual speech volume produced in reading and conversation tasks. Ho and colleagues found that there was less of a difference between patients' production and perception of speech volume compared with that of the controls. Also, even though they spoke more softly than the controls, they perceived their own speech (when rated immediately after speaking and later upon hearing recorded speech) to be louder than did the control subjects. The patients overestimated the volume of their speech during both reading and conversation. Ho and associates interpreted these findings to suggest that either hypophonia is the result of an abnormal perceptual mechanism or the perceptual system is abnormal owing to the generation of quiet speech.

Problems with self-perception of vocal loudness may also be related to motor-to-sensory cortical gating mechanisms. Studies have demonstrated self-initiated, speech-induced inhibitory influences on neuronal activity in the auditory cortex via feed-forward efferent mechanisms (118). Dysfunction of such feed forward mechanisms has been documented in individuals with schizophrenia and has been linked to inner speech and auditory hallucinations (119). Studies by Liotti and colleagues (40) using positron emission tomography (PET) and evoked response potentials (ERPs) have demonstrated the presence of abnormal (excessive) auditory cortex activity during speech in PD, suggesting abnormal collateral gating of auditory neurons. This abnormality has been shown to be partially reversed (reflected in a reduction in excessive auditory activity) in response to intensive voice treatment (LSVT, see below) and in parallel with improvement in voice and speech function and dopaminergic activity in the striatofrontal network. Importantly, the motor-to-sensory gating mechanisms are not specific to the vocal and auditory systems and can involve other sensory systems relevant to speech, such as the somatosensory system and its striatocortical connections (120).

The hypophonia in PD might be related to deficits in internal (implicit) cueing, abnormal scaling or regulation of the gain of movement amplitude, abnormal gating of the somatosensory cortex, abnormal gating of the auditory cortex via feed-forward mechanisms, abnormal perception of one's own voice, or a combination of these. Further research on the role of sensory problems in the speech and voice characteristics of Parkinsonian speech is necessary (115).

SWALLOWING DISORDERS

Swallowing disorders (see Chapter 10) may develop in as many as 90% of individuals with PD (121) and may be among the first signs of the disease (21). Identification of swallowing disorders is extremely important in this population, given the ramifications on nutrition and the ability to take oral medication appropriately. Silent aspiration may be observed, and pneumonia is sometimes the cause of death in individuals in the later stages of the disease (121).

Normal Physiology of Swallowing

In order to understand the nature of swallowing problems in PD, it is important to review the neurophysiology of swallowing. An excellent review has been provided by Jean (122). Swallowing, especially the oropharyngeal stage, is a complex, largely stereotypical, sensorimotor motor activity that is mediated mainly by medullary neural network to serve both alimentary purposes and upper airway protection. It involves hypoglossal, trigeminal, and ambigual motor neurons that are commonly activated in various functions, including deglutition, mastication, respiration, vocalization, and speech. Although the basic swallowing pattern can be elicited without supramedullary influences, physiologically, the swallowing network is subject to influences from higher centers, both cortical and subcortical. Evidence for such higher central mechanisms involvement in swallowing comes from clinical observations that swallowing can be initiated voluntarily and without the need to digest food or protect the airway, and from the presence of swallowing dysfunction secondary to higher levels, cortical and subcortical lesions or diseases. The specific contributions of higher neural centers to swallowing are not well delineated, although they are likely to include control of the timing and initiation of the swallow, modification of the swallow via corticobulbar gating of reflexogenic activity, and co-ordination between swallowing and other oropharyngeal and respiratory-laryngeal functions such as speech. Among the subcortical sites that can trigger or modify swallow are the substantia nigra and subthalamic nuclei, both of which play a major role in the neuropathology of Parkinson's disease. Recent functional magnetic resonance imaging (fMRI) studies of swallowing in healthy humans demonstrate regional activation of the nucleus ambiguus, sensorimotor cortex (M1, S1, and supplementary motor area), S2, premotor cortex, inferior frontal cortex (BA 44 and 45), posterior parietal cortex, the insular cortex, superior temporal gyrus (BA 38), cerebellum, putamen, globus pallidus, thalamus, anterior cingulate gyrus, superior temporal gyrus, and substantia nigra (123–125), with evidence that swallowing control is mediated through parallel loops rather than through a hierarchical organization. Many of these neural regions are also activated during normal speech production (126).

The extensive activation of brain regions during swallowing is not surprising if one considers swallowing as complex behavior rather than merely a brainstem sensorimotor phenomenon. As suggested by Leopold and Kagel (18), swallowing may involve a 5-stage process of ingestion: preoral (anticipatory), preparatory, lingual, pharyngeal, and esophageal. The first stage involves an interaction of preoral motor, cognitive, psychosocial, and somatoesthetic elements engendered by the meal. This model of swallowing behavior, coupled by the multiregional activation of the brain, is important for understanding the swallowing problems in PD.

Physiologic Mechanisms Underlying Swallowing Disorders in Parkinson's Disease

If one also considers the possibility that some of the pathogenic causes of voice and speech disorders in PD—such as deficits in internal cueing, sensorimotor gating, scaling of movement amplitude, and self-regulation of effort—may also affect swallowing, the diagnosis and treatment of swallowing may have to be considered within the framework of the 5-stage model and higher-level deficits. Given that mealtime is often a social event, where swallowing and conversation take place alternately or simultaneously, such a situation might be especially problematic for individuals with PD, both because they have to carefully monitor speech and swallowing while eating and because these two tasks might be defective and difficult to monitor and control in PD.

Swallowing abnormalities have been reported in all stages of the disease (121), and many individuals with PD have more than one type of swallowing dysfunction (18). Disorders in both oral and pharyngeal stages of swallowing have been observed (18, 121, 127). El Sharkawi and coworkers (20) reported dysfunctions of the oral phase of swallowing, with most predominant problems being reduced tongue control and strength and reduced oral transit times. Others have reported a "rocking-like" motion of the tongue during the oral phase (21). This motion seemed to occur when the patients were unable to lower the posterior portion of the tongue to propel the bolus into the pharynx. Inability or delayed ability to trigger the swallowing reflex has also been observed in this population (21). These disorders may limit the ability of the individual with PD to control the food or liquid bolus while in the oral cavity. This may interfere with mastication and the oral phase of swallowing and lead to choking or aspiration of food or liquid. Reduced nutritional intake, lack of enjoyment in eating, and difficulty in taking medications result from oral-phase swallowing dysfunction.

Pharyngeal-stage dysfunction includes residue in the valleculae due to reduced tongue base retraction. El Sharkawi and coworkers (20) reported that this was the most common problem in the pharyngeal stage of swallowing. Aspiration may occur in these patients as a result of the residue left in the pharynx after the swallow is complete (21). Leopold and Kagel (18) found several disorders of laryngeal movement during swallowing. These included slow glottic closure, incomplete glottic closure, absent glottic closure, and slowed or delayed excursion of the vocal folds (18). Increased pharyngeal transit time has been reported. Silent aspiration has been observed in the later stages of the disease and can be a contributory cause of death (128). Dysfunction in the pharyngeal stage of swallowing may also lead to a feeling that food is stuck in the throat, choking, penetration, aspiration, reduced nutritional intake, or reduced ability to self-medicate.

Swallowing dysfunction occurs in this population even when the individual is considered optimally medicated for motor symptoms (121). Evidence in animals indicates significant effects of dopamine agonists and antagonists on the swallow reflex (129, 130). However, the therapeutic effects of dopamine agonists on swallowing dysfunction in PD are either minimal or moderate and appear to take place only in early disease. These findings suggest that swallowing dysfunction in PD might be related, at least partially, to nondopaminergic mechanisms (131, 132).

Referral for swallowing evaluation is extremely important at the first sign of problems. The need for this referral may occur during early disease.

TREATMENT

Medical Treatments

In contrast to the marked therapeutic effects of levodopa, dopamine agonists, and various neurosurgical techniques on major limb motor symptoms of PD such akinesia, tremor, and rigidity (133–139), the magnitude, consistency, and long-term outcome of such treatments on voice, speech, and swallowing disorders is far from satisfactory (140, 141). Some new medical and surgical interventions—such as nondopaminergic medicine, cranial and subdural repetitive magnetic stimulation, and

injections for laryngeal collagen augmentation—seem to offer more positive effects on voice and speech.

Medical Treatment for Voice and Speech Disorders in Parkinson's Disease

Effects of Levodopa on Speech. Gallena and colleagues (64) studied the effects of levodopa on laryngeal function in 6 unmedicated (de novo) patients with early IPD. They found that the administration of levodopa reduced excessive laryngeal muscle activity and vocal fold bowing and improved control of voice onset and offset during speech in some patients. De Letter and colleagues (142) assessed the effects of levodopa on speech intelligibility in 10 dysarthric individuals with PD, using a standardized intelligibility test. They reported significant improvement in speech intelligibility with levodopa *on* compared to *off* medication. Goberman and colleagues (143) examined the acoustic-phonatory characteristics of speech in 9 individuals with PD and fluctuating motor symptoms before and after taking levodopa. When these patients were compared to healthy controls, it was found that the voice Fo variability in vowels and mean Fo were higher and intensity range was lower in the patients compared to controls. It was also found that differences in speech between *on* and *off* medication were small, although in some instances phonation clearly improved. Jiang and colleagues (43) assessed the effects of levodopa on vocal function in 15 individuals with IPD and tremor using airflow and electroglottographic measures. The subjects were recorded as they sustained vowel phonation before and after taking medication. Speed quotient, acoustic shimmer (cycle-to-cycle amplitude perturbation), and extent of tremor derived from acoustic intensity contours were found to significantly decrease and vocSPL to increase after medication. Acoustic jitter (cycle-to-cycle frequency perturbation) and extent of tremor derived from airflow signals did not significantly differentiate between pre- and postmedication voices. Sanabria and colleagues (144) used acoustic measures to study the effects of levodopa treatment on vocal function in 20 patients with PD before and after levodopa. When compared to premedication, postmedication voice Fo significantly increased, and jitter, soft phonation index (noise parameter), and frequency tremor intensity index significantly decreased, indicating improvement in phonatory function with medication. Cahill et al (145) studied the effects of levodopa on lip function in 16 patients with PD, using a computerized semiconductor lip pressure transducer. Lip pressures recorded during both speech and nonspeech tasks tended to improve after levodopa administration.

However, numerous studies (141, 146) have failed to find significant improvement in voice and speech functions with levodopa or dopamine agonists. These negative findings question the role of dopamine in hypokinetic dysarthria and raise the possibility that other nondopaminergic or special dopaminergic mechanisms may play an important etiologic part. Indeed, clonazepam (dosage 0.25 to 0.5 mg/d), a nondopaminergic agent, has been reported to significantly improve speech in 10 of 11 individuals with PD and hypokinetic dysarthria (147).

Effects of Levodopa on Swallowing Disorders in Parkinson's Disease. Hunter and coworkers (131) studied the effect of levodopa therapy on symptomatic dysphagia in 15 individuals with PD. All had motor fluctuations. On 2 separate days, after overnight withdrawal of all anti-Parkinsonian medication, a modified barium swallow using cinefluoroscopy and different food consistencies was performed before and after administration of oral levodopa and subcutaneous apomorphine. The investigators reported that although all patients had an unequivocal motor response to both agents, there were few significant responses in any of the quantitative or qualitative criteria of swallowing dysfunction. They did note that the oral preparatory phase showed a therapeutic response, but not with all consistencies. Also, in a subgroup of patients, the pharyngeal phase time improved. It was concluded that Parkinsonian swallowing dysfunction is not solely related to nigrostriatal dopamine deficiency and it may be due to an additional nondopamine-related disturbance of the central pattern generator for swallowing. Fuh and associates (148) examined the oropharyngeal swallowing ability in 19 PD patients using modified barium swallow before and after administering oral levodopa. They reported that twelve (63.2%) patients demonstrated objective evidence of swallowing abnormalities; although only 6 patients (31.6%) had subjective complaints. In the 12 patients with abnormal swallowing, 6 (50%) showed objective improvement after levodopa treatment, while the remaining six showed no change. Bushmann and coworkers (149) evaluated the presence of dysphagia and the response to levodopa in 20 patients with PD and 13 controls with clinical rating scales and modified barium swallows before and after oral levodopa. They reported that 15 patients and 1 control had abnormal swallows, which included disturbances of oral and pharyngeal phases of swallowing. Patients without dysphagia frequently had abnormal swallows, including silent aspiration. Seven patients (47%) improved swallowing after levodopa, whereas one worsened. Tison and colleagues (132) assessed the effects of apomorphine (in combination with domperidone) on buccolinguofacial motoricity and on various swallowing stages by using videofluoroscopy in 8 patients with dysphagia. Frequent swallowing abnormalities included vallecular stasis, fragmentation of the bolus, and buccal stagnation of the bolus. These investigators reported that apomorphine improved buccal stagnation in all cases and vallecular stasis and fragmentation in about half the cases. Of three individuals with direct laryngeal penetration, two cases improved with apomorphine. Total swallowing duration improved by apomorphine in 5 patients. This improvement correlated with an improvement of the buccolinguofacial motoricity and pharyngeal transit time.

Brain Stimulation

Effects of Deep Brain Stimulation on Speech. Numerous studies have assessed the effects of deep brain stimulation (DBS) of the subthalamic nucleus (STN), ventral intermediate nucleus of the thalamus (Vim), and globus pallidus internus (GPi) on speech and nonspeech functions. These structures are parts of two major loops, the cortex-striatum-GPi-thalamus-cortex loop and the cortex-STN-GPi-thalamus-cortex loop, both of which interact and play a major role in motor, sensory, and executive functions and in the pathophysiology of PD (150). DBS of these neural structures has provided clinical benefits for individuals with PD. Specifically, stimulation of the Vim can relieve tremor, and stimulation of the STN and GPi can each reduce bradykinesia, rigidity, and tremor in individuals with PD (151). The improvement is typically seen some 6 to 12 months after treatment. However, the effects of DBS on voice and speech have been shown to be adverse or inconclusive in most studies.

In a 5-year study of unilateral or bilateral DBS-THAL in 38 individuals with essential tremor (ET) or PD, Pahwa and colleagues (152) reported that Parkinsonian patients with unilateral implants had an 85% improvement in the targeted hand tremor and those with bilateral implants had a 100% improvement in the left hand and 90% improvement in the right hand. However, 75% of individuals with PD treated with bilateral DBS-THAL developed dysarthria as a side effect of the surgery. In a multicenter, 1-year and 3- to 4-year follow-up study of a large cohort of patients with severe PD treated with either bilateral DBS-STN (n = 49) or bilateral DBS-GPi (n = 20), Rodriguez-Oroz and colleagues (153) reported that stimulation of either site induced a significant improvement (50% for the STN group and 39% for the GPi group) of the *off* medication UPDRS-III score at 3 to 4 years with respect to baseline. Stimulation improved cardinal features and activities of daily living (ADL) and prolonged the *on* time spent with good mobility without dyskinesias. Daily dosage of levodopa was significantly reduced only in the STN-treated group (35% reduction). Comparison of stimulation-induced improvement at 1 year with 3 to 4 years showed a significant worsening in the *on* medication motor states of the Unified Parkinson's Disease Rating Scale III (UPDRS-III), ADL, and gait in both groups, and speech and postural stability in the STN-treated group. Adverse events included cognitive decline, speech difficulty, instability, gait disorders, and depression. These were more common in the STN group. Nevertheless, all patients chose to continue with the DBS treatment in spite of these side effects. In another study by Krack and colleagues (154), in a 1-, 3-, and 5-year follow-up prospective study of bilateral DBS-STN of 49 consecutive individuals with advance PD (of whom 7 did not complete the study due to death or loss to follow-up), patients' scores at 5 years for motor function while off medication improved by 54% and those for ADL improved by 49% compared to baseline. Speech was the only motor function for which off-medication scores did not improve. The scores for motor function on medication did not improve 1 year after surgery. On medication, there was worsening of akinesia, speech, postural stability, and freezing of gait between years 1 and 5. At 5 years, the dose of dopaminergic treatment and the duration and severity of levodopa-induced dyskinesia were reduced compared to baseline. The average scores for cognitive performance remained unchanged, but dementia developed in 3 patients after 3 years. Mean depression scores remained unchanged. These two studies clearly indicate long-term improvement with DBS of STN or GPi in motor function while *off* medication and in dyskinesia while *on* medication in patients with advanced PD. The worsening of akinesia, speech, postural stability, freezing of gait, and cognitive function with *on* medication between the first and last follow-up years may reflect natural progression of PD, although this conclusion cannot be ascertained without comparison to control groups.

Several studies examined specific aspects of voice, speech, swallowing, and related orofacial and respiratory-laryngeal functions associated with DBS treatment of PD. Santens and colleagues (155) studied lateralized effects of DBS-STN on different aspects of speech in individuals with PD. They found significant differences between left versus right stimulation. Unlike right-sided stimulation, left-sided stimulation had a profound negative effect on prosody, articulation, and intelligibility. With bilateral stimulation, no differences in speech characteristics were observed between *on* and *off* stimulation. They suggest that a balanced tuning of bilateral basal ganglial networks is necessary for speech, with the left circuit probably playing a dominant role. Wang and colleagues (156) also studied the effects of unilateral DBS-STN on respiratory/phonatory subsystems of speech production in PD. Speech recordings were made in the medication-*off* state at baseline, 3 months post-DBS with stimulation *on*, and with stimulation *of*, in 6 right-handed patients. Stimulation *on* improved UPDRS-III scores in all patients. Three patients who received left DBS-STN showed a significant decline in vocal intensity and vowel duration from their baseline. Wang and colleagues attributed the latter findings to microlesions of the dominant hemisphere for speech.

Gentil and colleagues (157) assessed the effects of bilateral DBS-STN on hypokinetic dysarthria in PD. Using force measurements of the articulatory organs and acoustic analysis in 16 patients, they noted that DBS-STN reduced reaction and movement time of the articulatory organs, increased maximal strength and precision of these organs, and improved respiratory and phonatory functions. Gentil and colleagues (158) also compared the effects of bilateral DBS-STN versus DBS-Vim on oral control in 14 individuals. They used force transducers to sample ramp-and-hold force contractions generated by the upper lip, lower lip, and tongue at 1- and 2-N target force levels as well as maximal force. After an overnight fast, patients were evaluated under two conditions: during bilateral DBS and 1 hour after DBS was off. With STN stimulation, dynamic and static control of the articulatory organs improved greatly, whereas it worsened with Vim stimulation. In another study of 26 patients treated with bilateral DBS-STN, Gentil and colleagues (159), using acoustic analysis of voice, found that, compared with *off* stimulation, *on* stimulation resulted in a longer duration of sustained vowels; shorter duration of sentences, words, and pausesl increased variability in voice F0 in sentences; and increased stability of voice F0 during sustained vowels. There was no difference in vocal intensity between *on*- and *off*-stimulation conditions. In another study, Pinto and colleagues (160) assessed the impact of bilateral DBS-STN on forces and control of the upper lip, lower lip, and tongue in 26 dysarthric patients before and after DBS surgery. The investigators reported that with stimulation *on*, there was improvement in motor examination scores of the UPDRS as well as in the maximal voluntary force, reaction time, movement time, precision of the peak force and the hold phase during an articulatory force task. They also reported that these beneficial effects of DBS on articulatory forces persisted though the different periods of postsurgical follow-up (3-months, 1 to 2 years, 3 to 5 years). However, dysarthria evaluated by the UPDRS was worse in two subgroups of patients with a 1- to 2-year and 3- to 5-year postsurgical follow-up in comparison with a subgroup of patients with a 3-month follow-up. The incongruence between improved articulatory forces and deterioration in dysarthria is puzzling, although it may be related to the idea that dysarthria in PD is related to high-level sensorimotor functions rather than to peripheral deficits and that improvement on the force task may have been related to external cueing induced by the task itself.

Dromey and colleagues (161) studied the effects of bilateral DBS-STN on acoustic measures of voice in 7 individuals with PD. Acoustic recordings of the voice were made before surgery in the medication-*off* and medication-*on* conditions and after surgery with and without stimulation in the medication-*off* and medication-*on* conditions. There were significant improvements in limb motor function in response to medication before surgery and with the DBS-STN *on* after surgery. Six months after surgery, there were statistically significant though small increases in vocSPL and Fo variability with medication and DBS *on*. Rousseaux and colleagues (162) studied the effects of bilateral DBS-STN on speech parameters and intelligibility in 7 patients. Speech was evaluated in 6 conditions: before and 3 months after surgery, with stimulation *off* or *on*, and with and without a suprathreshold levodopa dose. Overall, performance level on the UPDRS-III improved with DBS postimplantation, whereas the effects on speech were minimal or adverse. Modest beneficial effects were reported on several motor speech parameters, especially lip movements. Modulation of voice pitch and loudness improved mildly. Articulation was not affected and speech intelligibility was slightly reduced in the *on*-stimulation condition, especially when patients received levodopa. Marked negative effects on intelligibility were observed in 2 patients owing to increased facial and trunk dyskinesias and not related to electrode position or stimulation parameters.

Saint-Cyr and colleagues (163) studied neuropsychological consequences of chronic bilateral DBS-STN in 11 individuals with advanced PD (age = 67 ± 8 years, verbal IQ = 114 ± 12). They were evaluated in their best "*on* state" with tests assessing frontostriatal function before surgery and at 3 to 6 months and 9 to 12 months (n = 10) after surgery. Saint-Cyr and colleagues noted that despite clinical motor benefits at 3 to 6 months postsurgery, there were significant declines in working memory, speed of mental processing, bimanual motor speed and co-ordination, set switching, phonemic fluency, long-term consolidation of verbal material, and the encoding of visuospatial material. These declines were more consistently observed in individuals who were 69 years of age and older (n = 6). At 9 to 12 months postoperatively, only learning based on multiple trials had recovered and tasks reliant on the integrity of frontostriatal circuitry either did not recover or gradually worsened. Based on these findings it was concluded that bilateral DBS-STN can have a negative impact on various aspects of frontal executive functioning, especially in patients 69 of age and older. Saint-Cyr and colleagues suggest additional studies with a larger number of subjects and with future assessment of the possible reversibility of these adverse effects by turning the DBS off.

The picture that emerges from these studies indicates marked improvement in primary motor deficits (rigidity, akinesia, tremor) with DBS, especially off medication. DBS has only moderate effects on the speech motor system during nonspeech task and minimal therapeutic or adverse effects on voice and speech functions. In some individuals, deterioration in executive functions occurs. Although follow-up studies suggest deterioration in speech and cognition following DBS, it is not clear to what extent this deterioration is due to DBS surgery and to what extent it is related to the progressive nature of the disease. Regarding the effects of surgery, it is conceivable that both stereotaxic lesions and voltage spread

from the stimulating electrodes adversely affect the neural network subserving speech (156, 160, 164). Evidence for voltage spread on speech intelligibility has been provided by Tornqvist and colleagues (165). These investigators assessed the effects of different electrical parameter settings on the intelligibility of speech in 10 patients treated with bilateral DBS-STN. These patients were treated for 15 ± 5 months with symptom reduction in the UPDRS-III. Eleven DBS parameters were manipulated in random order to test their effects. Amplitude was increased and decreased by 25%, frequency was varied in the range 70 to 185 pps, and each of the contacts was tested separately as a cathode. The patients read a standard running text and 5 nonsense sentences per setting. A listener panel transcribed the nonsense sentences as perceived and evaluated the quality of speech on a visual analog scale. With the patients' normally used settings, there was no significant group difference between DBS *off* and *on*. In 4 patients, however, intelligibility deteriorated with DBS ON. The higher frequencies or increased amplitude caused impairments in intelligibility, whereas changing the polarity between the separate contacts did not.

Effects of Transcranial/Subdural Stimulation on Speech and Swallowing. Dias and colleagues (166) studied the effects of repetitive transcranial magnetic stimulation (rTMS) on vocal function in 30 patients. They examined 2 different sets of rTMS parameters: active or sham 15-Hz rTMS of the left dorsolateral prefrontal cortex (LDLPFC) and active 5-Hz rTMS of the primary motor cortex (M1)–mouth area. Acoustic and perceptual analysis of voice and voice-related quality of life (V-RQOL) were employed using a blind rater. Stimulation of the of M1-mouth induced an improvement in the voice Fo and intensity. Stimulation of the LDLPFC resulted in mood amelioration and subjective improvement of the V-RQOL but not in objective measures of voice Fo and intensity.

Pagni and colleagues (167) studied the effects of extradural motor cortex stimulation in 3 patients. They found that unilateral stimulation relieved, partially or dramatically, tremor, akinesia, standing, anteropulsion, gait, speech, and swallowing as well as levodopa-induced symptoms such as dyskinesia and psychiatric complications. They also found that the results of stimulation did not fade away and that drug dosage was reduced by 50%. These 2 studies suggest that transcortical/transdural stimulation of the motor cortex may have therapeutic effects on voice, speech, and swallowing.

Ablative Brain Surgeries: Effects on Speech

Effects of Pallidotomy on Speech. The effects of pallidotomy on speech, language, and cognition have been assessed in several studies, most demonstrating inconsistent or mild-moderate adverse results. Schulz and colleagues

(168) used acoustic analyses to assess the impact of pallidotomy on voice and speech in 6 persons with PD. Acoustic measures were analyzed before surgery and 3 months after surgery. All 6 individuals demonstrated positive changes in at least one acoustic measure. Two individuals consistently demonstrated positive changes in phonatory and articulatory measures, whereas 3 did not improve after surgery. In another study Schulz and colleagues (169) assessed changes in vocSPL following unilateral posteroventral pallidotomy (PVP) in 25 hypokinetic dysarthric patients with PD. These individuals were recorded using a variety of speech tasks, once before and once after PVP. The pre-PVP vocSPL was subtracted from the post-PVP vocSPL to derive a relative change in vocal SPL. It was found that mildly dysarthric individuals had significantly greater relative increases in vocal SPL following PVP, whereas moderately or severely dysarthric individuals had relative decreases in vocSPL following PVP. Uitti and colleagues (170) assessed speech, motor, and neuropsychological effects of unilateral medial pallidotomy in 57 consecutive individuals with PD. Pallidotomy significantly improved motor function. Speech intelligibility was preserved, with a tendency to decline mildly in one-third of patients postoperatively. Performance on measures of letter fluency and semantic fluency declined in patients with left pallidotomies, but otherwise cognitive abilities remained stable following surgery.

Scott and colleagues (171) compared the effects of unilateral versus bilateral posteroventral pallidotomy (UPVP and BPVP, respectively) in individuals with PD. Total UPDRS scores improved by 27% in the UPVP group and by 53% in the BPVP group. Patients also perceived reduced postoperative functional disability and improvements in quality of life, as indicated in physical and psychosocial questionnaire subscales. The only adverse cognitive/language effects noted 3 months after surgery were impaired categorical verbal fluency in both groups and impaired phonemic verbal fluency in the BPVP. These were mild findings that were elucidated through testing and not reported subjectively by the patients. Scott and colleagues observed no other postsurgical sequelae related to pallidotomy. They reported a fall in speech diadochokinetic rates and patients' subjective perception of a worsening of preexisting dysarthria, hypophonia, and hypersalivation/drooling following BPVP, although these changes did not appear to have functional consequences. Troster and colleagues (172) reported verbal fluency declines after unilateral pallidotomy, left or right. The left and right pallidotomy groups were matched on key demographic, cognitive, and disease variables. The nature of this decline and its laterality 4 months post-surgery was studied; the investigators concluded that the decline was in lexical rather than semantic verbal fluency. They also found that this decline was most evident in the group that had undergone left-sided surgery.

They attributed this latter finding to the role that the left frontal-basal ganglionic circuits play in word retrieval processes and/or lexical search and access. Overall these findings indicate mild deficits in speech and language following pallidotomy, restricted primarily to deficits in lexical verbal fluency and to a lesser extent to speech motor functions.

Effects of Thalamotomy on Speech.   Nagulic and colleagues (173) used acoustic analyses to assess the effects of stereotactic thalamotomy in 7 male patients with PD. The patients' voices were recorded a week before and a week after right-sided thalamotomy. The mean vocSPL during the initial segment of the speech signal increased after thalamotomy relative to before from 59.24 dB to 75.04 dB, and the voice Fo increased accordingly from a mean of 104 to mean of 122 Hz. The voice formants F1 and F2 shifted to the higher energy and frequency regions. Overall fluency of pronunciation also improved. Parkin and colleagues (174) studied the effects of bilateral stereotaxic lesioning of the STN on individuals with PD. They found significant improvement in *off* rigidity and *on* tremor following unilateral lesions. Bilateral lesions resulted in 3 major complications: speech disturbance, worsening of gait, and L-dopa–resistant limb dystonia.

The differential effects of right versus left ventrolateral thalamotomy on dichotic listening and language function in PD were studied by Hugdahl and colleagues (175). Patients were tested for asymmetry of language functioning with dichotic presentations of consonant-vowel (CV) syllables. Dichotic listening was performed before and after surgery as well as during electrical stimulation of the VL nucleus just before lesioning. The results indicated a reduction in right ear advantage (REA) in the patient group compared to normative findings in healthy individuals; an increase in REA during left-sided stimulations; and a marked reduction in REA after left-sided lesions. These findings suggest that speech and language function may be more disturbed with left than right thalamotomy in most patients, depending on their language hemispheric dominance.

Farrell and colleagues (176) studied the effects of various neurosurgical procedures (pallidotomy, thalamotomy, DBS) on perceptual speech characteristics, speech intelligibility, and oromotor function in 22 patients with PD. This surgical group was compared with a group of 16 participants with PD who did not undergo neurosurgical management and with a group of 25 neurologically healthy individuals matched for age and gender. Results indicated that that none of the neurosurgical interventions significantly changed perceptual speech dimensions or oromotor function in spite of significant postoperative improvements in ratings of general motor function and disease severity.

Effects of Peripheral Surgery on Speech and Swallowing

Collagen Augmentation of the Vocal Folds for Improved Phonation. Two studies documented improvement in phonation with collagen augmentation of the vocal folds via percutaneous injection and with fiberoptic guidance in some hypophonic patients with PD. Using a telephone interview of 18 patients treated with this procedure, Kim and colleagues (30) reported that 11 (61%) receiving collagen augmentation considered their voices improved for at least 2 months. Of the 7 unimproved patients, 5 were aphonic before and after the collagen injection. Kim and colleagues concluded that although the majority of patients are likely to benefit from the procedure, patients with advanced neurologic disease with aphonia, difficulty with speech initiation, dysphagia, or ambulatory difficulty are less likely to respond. In a study of 35 hypophonic PD patients treated with collagen augmentation. Berke and colleagues (29), using a telephone survey, found that 75% of patients expressed satisfaction with the improvement in their voice, compared with 16% who expressed dissatisfaction with the results of collagen augmentation. Although these preliminary results are encouraging, more objective methods of voice evaluation are needed, as well as long-term follow-up of treatment outcome.

Cricopharyngeal Myotomy for Improved Swallowing. Born and coworkers (177) assessed the effects of cricopharyngeal myotomy in 4 patients with PD and dysphagia associated with cricopharyngeal dysfunction, diagnosed with radiologic and manometric methods. They reported excellent results with the myotomy, with excellent and sustained improvement in swallowing.

Behavioral Speech, Voice, and Swallowing Treatment

General Approach to Treatment. Although the incidence of voice and speech disorders in PD is extremely high (80% to 90%), only a small percentage of these individuals (3% to 4%) are likely to receive speech therapy (5, 8). One explanation for this discrepancy may be that in the past, carryover and long-term treatment outcomes were disappointing. The "conventional wisdom" has been that "changes that occur in the treatment room disappear on the way to the parking lot" (178–181). This challenge of carryover and long-term treatment outcomes has been observed consistently over a wide range of speech treatments applied to this population (97). These approaches included training in rate control, prosody, loudness, articulation, respiration, or a combination of these (32). In addition, some forms of treatment included devices such as delayed auditory feedback (DAF), amplification devices, and pacing boards, although these methods did not yield long-term therapeutic effects (31, 58, 97, 182).

In discussing treatment effects and efficacy in PD, it is important to make a distinction between *stimulation* and *training. Stimulation* refers to situations where the patient is asked or instructed to perform a task, such as speaking in a loud or clear voice. Stimulation induces a transient behavior in response to an external cue. *Training* refers to a systematic and intensive program designed to change a behavior such that it will not depend on external cueing and will be sustained over a protracted time. Training involves learning, memory, and reliance on internal sources (cueing, self-regulation) to maintain the acquired behavior. When individuals with PD are in the treatment room and receiving direct stimulation or feedback from the speech clinician or an instrument (external cue) (97, 183, 184), they are able to improve speech and voice production. However, it has been challenging to maintain these improvements (training the ability to internally cue). This consistent observation provides potential insight into the underlying problems in carryover. One explanation relates to the sensory processing and internal cueing problems frequently experienced by these individuals (23, 109, 112). Recognition of these problems, and addressing them in the training regimen, may improve treatment of motor speech output. Support for these ideas come from the work of Ramig and coworkers (33, 34), who documented that the training sensory perception of effort appears to be a key element in successful speech treatment in PD. In addition, neuropsychological problems, such as deficits in procedural learning (185, 186) and executive functions, even at the early phase of PD (187), may underlie the challenges that individuals with PD have in learning new habits and maintaining them for a protracted time. These therapeutic challenges are further intensified by the fact that PD is a degenerative condition, and PD is often associated with adverse effects of medication, depression, and dementia, especially in the later stages of the disease.

Another important issue is the optimal time in the course of the disease at which behavioral treatment should be initiated. It has been suggested that behavioral treatment (e.g., speech therapy, occupational therapy, physiotherapy) should be provided during the later phases of the disease (188). However, given the increased challenges associated with the advanced stages of the disease, the more optimal time to succeed with behavioral therapy should be at the onset of disease. Neural plasticity and neural protection induced by intensive training is most likely to occur during earlier stages of PD, when the dopaminergic system is not fully degenerated and there is some potential for recovery or development of a compensatory mechanism (189–191). For the training to be most effective, behavioral treatment of voice, speech, and swallowing disorders in PD should be administered as soon as the disease is diagnosed, when these disorders mild or moderate in severity.

Finally, it has been shown that to obtain maximum therapeutic results, the training regimen should include principles of motor plasticity, namely, intensive training of motor tasks, increased practice of motor tasks, active engagement in tasks, and the sensory experience of the motor task (192, 193). Training should address the most prominent etiologic factors underlying the behavior to be changed, with the target behavior having a significant ameliorating impact on these etiologic factors. In voice and speech disorders in PD, training should address deficits in internal cueing, sensorimotor gating, scaling amplitude of speech movement patterns, and self-perception and regulation of vocal effort and output. Lee Silverman Voice Treatment appears to meet these requirements.

Intensive Voice Treatment. In 1988, Ramig and colleagues (194) introduced Lee Silverman Voice Treatment (LSVT), a Parkinson-specific approach that trains amplitude (increased vocal loudness) as a single motor control parameter, thereby targeting the proposed pathophysiologic mechanisms underlying bradykinesia/hypokinesia: mainly inadequate scaling of agonist muscle activation. This approach also trains individuals with PD to "recalibrate" their motor and perceptual systems so that they are less inclined to downscale (reduce amplitude) speech movement parameters. It is geared toward overcoming or compensating for deficits in internal cueing and self-regulation of vocal effort during speech production.

LSVT is delivered in a manner consistent with theories of motor learning (195) and skill acquisition as well as neural plasticity (e.g., intensity, complexity, saliency) (196). Specifically, LSVT uses high-effort but not strenuous loud phonation to encourage maximum phonatory efficiency and coactivation and co-ordination of speech subsystems. Patients are taken through exercises on a daily basis, repeatedly practicing and emphasizing maximum-duration loud phonations, maximum high- and low-pitch phonations, and speech exercises with improved loudness. This improved phonation is carried over into speech and conversation following a standardized hierarchy, with focus on monitoring the amount of effort required to sustain sufficient vocal loudness ("calibration"). No direct attention is given to speech rate, prosodic pitch inflection, or articulation. Therapy is administered 4 times a week over 4 weeks, each session lasting 50 to 60 minutes.

Unlike approaches that focus on speech rate, pitch prosody, or articulation, LSVT focuses on the speech problem observed most often in individuals with PD: soft voice. Ramig and coworkers hypothesize that there are at least 3 features underlying hypophonic voice in PD, including (a) an overall amplitude scale down (23, 107, 108) to the speech mechanism (reduced amplitude of neural drive to the muscles of the speech mechanism); (b) problems in sensory gating and the perception of vocal effort (23, 109) and loudness (71), which prevents the

individual with PD from accurately monitoring his or her vocal output; and (c) difficulty—due to deficits in internal cueing, self-monitoring, amplitude scaling, and regulation—in independently generating and scaling the right amount of effort and movement amplitude to produce adequate loudness (37, 110, 111). These 3 features— which may be augmented by deficits in memory, learning,

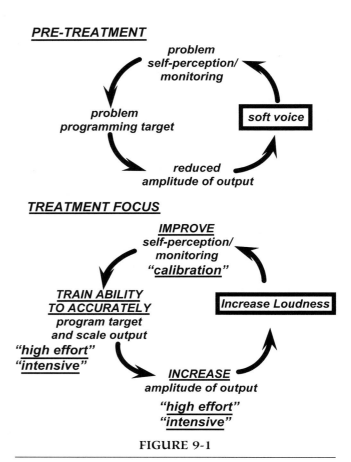

FIGURE 9-1

This figure graphically summarizes the hypothesized neural basis for the LSVT approach to treating individuals with PD. Before treatment (top circle), the "soft" voice of the patient may be a result of reduced amplitude of output to the speech mechanism. The soft voice is maintained because patients have reduced self-perception or self-monitoring and fail to realize that the voice is too soft. Therefore when they program output for another utterance, they downscale the output and continue to produce a soft voice.

The LSVT focus (bottom circle) addresses the soft voice at 3 levels. High-effort, intensive treatment is designed to train increased amplitude of output to the respiratory phonatory system to generate increased loudness. Patients are then trained to improve self-perception or self-monitoring of effort so that they understand the relationship between increased effort and successful communication. In this way, when they generate an utterance on their own, they are able to "carry over" adequate effort and loudness for successful communication outside the treatment room.

and executive functions even early in the disease—may be significant factors that make PD particularly resistant to treatment. LSVT has been designed to address both the primary deficits underlying the voice and speech disorders in PD as well as the sensory, perceptual, and cognitive deficits that interfere with treatment learning and long-term maintenance of treatment gains.

LSVT comprises 5 essential concepts: (a) a single focus on increasing vocal loudness; (b) the improvement of sensory perception, self-monitoring, and self-regulation of vocal effort and loudness—that is, "calibration" of vocal output; (c) treatment administered in a high-effort style; (d) intensive treatment; and (e) the quantification of all speech and voice. Treatment techniques are designed to scale up amplitude to the respiratory and phonatory system and train sensory perception of effort and internal cueing and scaling of adequate output (Figure 9-1). Treatment 4 times a week for ae month is consistent with principles of motor learning and skill acquisition (197, 198) and muscle training (37, 110, 111, 199) (Figure 9-2).

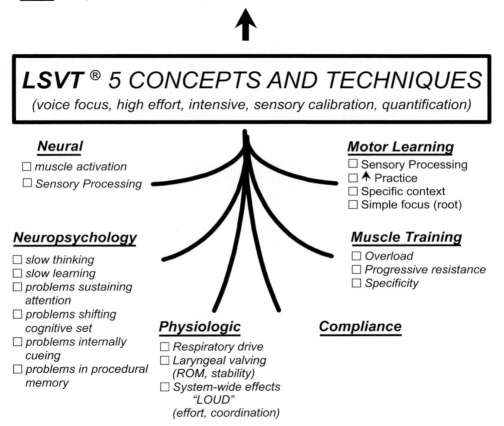

Goal: _Improved functional oral communication that "lasts"_

LSVT ® 5 CONCEPTS AND TECHNIQUES
(voice focus, high effort, intensive, sensory calibration, quantification)

Neural
☐ _muscle activation_
☐ _Sensory Processing_

Motor Learning
☐ Sensory Processing
☐ ↑ Practice
☐ Specific context
☐ Simple focus (root)

Neuropsychology
☐ _slow thinking_
☐ _slow learning_
☐ _problems sustaining attention_
☐ _problems shifting cognitive set_
☐ _problems internally cueing_
☐ _problems in procedural memory_

Muscle Training
☐ _Overload_
☐ _Progressive resistance_
☐ _Specificity_

Physiologic
☐ _Respiratory drive_
☐ _Laryngeal valving (ROM, stability)_
☐ _System-wide effects "LOUD" (effort, coordination)_

Compliance

FIGURE 9-2

This figure graphically summarizes the rationale underlying the 5 essential concepts and techniques of the LSVT from a neural, speech mechanism physiology, motor learning, muscle training, and neuropsychological compliance perspective. The neural bases are the reduction in muscle activation and self-monitoring and consequent problem in programming an output target with adequate amplitude. The physiologic basis is the focus on respiratory drive and laryngeal valving to generate a maximally efficient vocal source. "Loud" is used as the system trigger for improving effort and coordination across the speech mechanism. The LSVT is administered in a manner consistent with principles of motor learning in order to maximize treatment effectiveness. Sensory processing, increased practice, practice within specific context, and a simple "root" focus (e.g., "loud") are key elements of treatment. The LSVT is also administered in a way consistent with principles of muscle training. Treatment technique overloads the muscles, using progressive resistance in specific activities. The neuropsychological aspects of Parkinson's disease that may make learning challenging include slow thinking, slow learning, problems in sustaining attention, problems in shifting cognitive set, problems of internal cueing, and problems in procedural memory. These aspects are also considered in the LSVT through the simplicity and redundancy of treatment. The LSVT is designed to maximize patient compliance. From day 1 of treatment, activities are designed to maximize impact on daily functional communication. Based on those findings, a number of phase 2 experimental studies (e.g., randomized, blinded) were carried out.

To date, physiologic, acoustic, perceptual, and clinical trial studies involving over 200 individuals with PD (including those treated by LSVT , those treated by an alternative speech therapy, and those awaiting therapy) and 40 healthy controls (receiving no treatment) have documented the widespread long-term therapeutic effects of LSVT on respiratory, laryngeal, and orofacial functions. These studies have provided evidence for improved vocal loudness, voice quality, prosodic pitch inflection, speech articulation, and overall speech quality and intelligibility (141). Brain imaging studies using O^{15} positron emission tomography (PET) have documented changes in brain function consistent with speech improvement following LSVT (39–41). LSVT has been described by the members of the U.S. Academy of Neurologic Communications Disorders and Sciences (ANCDS) (200) as the most promising form of behavioral therapy to address the types of speech impairment experienced in PD. Treatment data suggest that those with mild to moderate PD have the most positive outcomes following LSVT . Patients with co-occurring mild to moderate depression and dementia have succeeded in treatment (34). However, the effectiveness of LSVT may be compromised by several factors, including severe depression, dementia, atypical Parkinsonism, or side effects of medication and neurosurgery. Because treatment focuses on voice, all patients must have a laryngeal examination before treatment to rule out any contraindications (vocal nodules, gastric reflux, laryngeal cancer). It is important to clarify that the goal of LSVT is to maximize phonatory efficiency. It is never the goal to teach "tight or pressed" voice but rather to improve vocal fold adduction for optimum loudness and quality.

Effectiveness Data for Lee Silverman Voice Treatment. Lee Silverman Voice Treatment was initially developed during the 1980s. Short- (34) and long-term (33, 35, 201, 202) outcome data have been reported. In one study, 45 patients were randomly assigned to one of two forms of behavioral treatment: respiratory effort treatment or respiratory and voice effort treatment (LSVT). Significant pretreatment to posttreatment improvements were observed for more variables and were of greater magnitude for subjects who received the voice and respiratory effort treatment (LSVT) than the other behavioral treatment. Only subjects who received LSVT rated a significant posttreatment decrease of the impact of PD on their communication. Corresponding perceptual ratings by blinded raters of voice hoarseness and breathiness revealed significant improvement only in those treated with LSVT (203), and only those in LSVT group improved or maintained vocSPL and vocal loudness above pretreatment levels. Perceptual reports by patients and family members supported the positive impact of treatment on functional daily communication. These therapeutic gains

have been shown to be maintained, as evident in 1-year and 2-year follow-up studies (201, 202).

In another study (204), 29 individuals with PD were evaluated over 6 months. Half the group received LSVT and half served as untreated controls. In addition, an age-matched, nondisordered, nontreated control group was also studied. Only subjects who received LSVT demonstrated significant increases in vocSPL (related to loudness), and this increase was on average 8 dB immediately after treatment and 6 dB at 6-month follow-up. The average is across the different speech tasks performed by the subjects (sustaining vowel phonation, reading a passages, and during a monologue). An important aspect of this work was to evaluate the underlying mechanisms of treatment outcomes. A study by Smith and coworkers (36) documented increases in vocal fold closure following treatment in individuals who received LSVT but not in those who received respiratory treatment only. These data were collected outside of the treatment clinic by clinicians not directly involved in the study and therefore support generalization of treatment effects. Consistent with these findings, Ramig and Dromey (205) reported increased subglottal air pressure and maximum flow declination rate accompanying increased vocSPL following LSVT. These findings were interpreted to be consistent with increased respiratory drive and vocal fold adduction accompanying successful treatment.

Increased phonatory effort improves not only vocal characteristics (loudness, pitch variability, vocal quality) but also appears to trigger effort and co-ordination across the speech mechanism. The observation of larger movements in the upper articulatory system following LSVT is consistent with reports of Schulman (206) that, as a speaker talks "louder, " there are accompanying vocal tract and articulatory changes, including increased movements of the articulators. Several other studies (48) demonstrate significant changes in orofacial articulatory functions associated with stimulated vocal loudness increase in neurologically healthy individuals with normal speech. These studies suggest that stimulation of loud speech results in strong coupling of the orofacial with the laryngeal speech systems, such that articulatory movements can potentially increase vocal fold adduction and subglottal pressure, thus enhancing the production of loud phonation. The increased movements of the speech articulation during loud phonation may further increase vocal loudness by enlarging the vocal tract and changing its configuration to increase the acoustic energy generated at the level of the larynx (see ref. 48).

Ramig and coworkers reported improvement in orofacial articulation function with loud phonation in individuals with PD treated with LSVT (133). Sapir and associates (48) compared individuals with PD treated with LSVT (n = 14) with individuals with PD (n = 15) and healthy age-matched controls (n = 14) not receiving LSVT and not receiving any other form of therapy. They used acoustic and perceptual analyses to assess the impact of LSVT on vowel articulation. These analyses were based on vowels extracted from words embedded in phrases. There was a significant improvement in both vowel acoustics and perceptual ratings of vowel goodness as well as in VocSPL in the group receiving LSVT but not in the 2 other groups. These findings are consistent with our previous perceptual study (201), where we documented increased speech loudness and speech quality ratings in individuals with PD following LSVT but not in those who received an alternative (respiratory effort) speech treatment.

Effects of Lee Silverman Voice Treatment on Facial Expression in Parkinson's Disease. Lee Silverman Voice Treatment has also been shown to be effective for the treatment of reduced facial expression (207), an effect that could potentially improve communication, appearance, and quality of life in PD. Video data were taken from recordings of 44 individuals with PD who had received either a month of phonation-based treatment (LSVT) or respiratory effort treatment (RET) as part of a large treatment efficacy study designed to examine the effects of different types of therapy on speech and voice in PD. Twenty-second video samples of all subjects taken before and after treatment were paired and played at random without sound to trained raters, who judged each pair of video clips for facial mobility and engagement. The recordings were made while subjects were engaged in conversational speech. Overall, members of LSVT group received more ratings of increased facial mobility and engagement following treatment relative to members of the RET group. Moreover, the extent of change for facial mobility after treatment was perceived as greater for the LSVT group than for the RET group.

Effects of Lee Silverman Voice Treatment on Brain Function. Brain imaging studies using O¹⁵ PET have also documented marked changes in brain function consistent with speech improvement following LSVT (39–41). Specifically, while stimulated loud phonation prior to the administration of LSVT activated cortical premotor areas, particularly the supplementary motor area (SMA), post-LSVT SMA activity was normalized and activity in the basal ganglia (right putamen) increased, suggesting a shift from abnormal cortical motor activation toward normal subcortical organization of speech-motor output. The post-LSVT changes indicated an increase in activity in right anterior insula and right dorsolateral prefrontal cortex, suggesting that LSVT recruits a phylogenetically old, preverbal communication system involved in vocalization and emotional communication (consistent with multisystem effects of LSVT). Another study (40) involving evoked response potentials (ERPs)

found excessive activity in the auditory cortex prior to LSVT treatment, which was markedly reduced to a near normal level following LSVT.

Effects of Lee Silverman Voice Treatment on Other Neurologic Disorders. To evaluate application of LSVT to other neurologic disorders, a number of case studies were carried out. In one study, LSVT was used in an individual with PD who had had a bilateral thalamotomy (208). In another study, LSVT was used in 3 individuals who had Parkinson-plus syndromes, including multisystem atrophy and progressive supranuclear palsy (209). Although improvements were documented in speech and voice characteristics in these individuals following treatment, the magnitude was not as great as in those with PD.

LSVT has been administered to 2 individuals with multiple sclerosis (MS) (210) and to 1 with cerebellar dysfunction secondary to thiamine deficiency (211). Those with MS showed marked improvement in vocSPL, vocal loudness, vocal fatigue, and sustained duration of vowel phonation. The individual with cerebellar dysfunction also showed therapeutic gains, as well as improvement in prosodic Fo inflection, acoustic correlates of articulatory function, speech intelligibility, and overall communication and employer satisfaction. Most of these improvements were maintained at 6- or 9-month follow-up. These findings suggest that the positive impact of LSVT is not specific to PD.

Lee Silverman Voice Treatment Delivered Through Electronic Devices and the Internet. Studies have begun to assess the effectiveness of electronic devices to promote home practice, augment the effects of LSVT, reduce clinician time, and cut costs of treatment. These devices [e.g., a personal digital assistant (PDA)] have been adapted with special software to deliver LSVT or other types of speech therapy programs (212). One such PDA, named LSVT Companion, or LSVTC, is programmed to collect acoustic data and provide feedback as it guides the patient through LSVT exercises. Instead of the usual 16 treatment sessions of clinician-delivered LSVT, only 9 sessions are with a clinician; the other 7 are completed independently at home by the patient utilizing LSVTC. Pilots studies with patients have demonstrated marked and long-term (6-month follow-up) improvement in voice and speech with LSVTC, these results being comparable to those obtained with the regular, fully clinician-administered LSVT (212). These findings support the feasibility of using state-of-the-art technology to administer speech treatment and keep records of patients' progress.

Still other technologies to self-administer LSVT include Telehealth systems or other web-enabled speech therapy systems. Prototypes of these technologies are now being tested to assess their efficacy. Overall, these new developments are likely to enhance accessibility, allowing the cost-effective, intensive sensorimotor training important for successful speech outcomes.

Behavioral Swallowing Treatment for Individuals with Parkinson's Disease. Treatment of swallowing disorders in PD has not been extensively studied. Conventional treatment techniques have included oral motor exercises to improve muscle strength, range of motion and co-ordination, and behavioral modifications such as the Mendelsohn maneuver, effortful breath-hold, swallow-cough, chin positioning, double swallow, effortful swallow, and diet and liquid modifications (21, 213). The effectiveness of these techniques varies and seems to depend on motivation and co-operation by the patient, family support, and the timeliness of referral for a swallowing evaluation. Research studies regarding the efficacy of these treatment methods suffer from methodologic shortcomings, and there is a need for clinical trials that can verify treatment efficacy (214).

Although LSVT was originally not intended to improve swallowing, 3 studies have documented marked improvement in orofacial function relevant to swallowing following LSVT or a similar treatment regimen. Sharkawi and coworkers (20) found that LSVT reduced swallowing motility disorders in the group they studied by 51%. De Angelis and colleagues (215) documented improvement in vocal function as well as elimination of swallowing complaints in PD treated with an intensive vocal rehabilitation program that emphasized loud phonation and increased sphincteric closure of the glottis. This treatment was administered in 13 group sessions within a month. Ward and colleagues (216) reported increased tongue force and motility in individuals with PD treated with LSVT, which may explain the improvement in swallowing.

CONCLUSION

Speech, voice, and swallowing problems occur in PD and may have a negative effect on communication, health, and overall quality of life. Although all aspects of speech production may be affected, disordered voice is one of the most common problems. Previous forms of treatment for the disorder of speech and voice in PD have had modest effectiveness. LSVT, which addresses increased vocal effort and improved sensory perception of effort and is administered in 16 high-effort sessions in a month, has been documented to be a successful approach in the short and long term.

A wide variety of swallowing disorders in both the oral and pharyngeal stages of swallowing may occur in these patients. There are limited efficacy data on the treatment of these disorders, but behavioral and dietary modification and LSVT may help minimize these difficulties. Although the degenerative course of PD cannot be altered, improvements in oral communication and swallowing function are important components of developing the highest levels of functioning and independence.

Acknowledgment

This chapter was supported by the following grants: NIH-NIDCD RO1-DC01150 and P60 DC-00976.

*R*eferences

1. Ho A, Iansek R, Marigliani C, et al. Speech impairment in a large sample of people with Parkinson's disease. *Behav Neuro.* 1998; 11:131–137.
2. Atarashi J, Uchida E. A clinical study of Parkinsonism. *Rec Adv Res Nerv Syst* 1959; 3:871–882.
3. Canter GJ. Speech characteristics of patients with Parkinson's disease: III. Articulation, diadochokinesis and overall speech adequacy. *J Speech Hear Disord* 1965; 30: 217–224.
4. Canter GJ. Speech characteristics of patients with Parkinson's disease: II. Physiological support for speech. *J Speech Hear Disord* 1965; 30:44–49.
5. Hartelius L, Svensson P. Speech and swallowing symptoms associated with Parkinson's disease and multiple sclerosis: A survey. *Folia Phonia. Logoped* 1994; 46:9–17.
6. Hoberman SG. Speech techniques in aphasia and Parkinsonism. *J Michigan State Med Soc* 1958; 57:1720–1723.
7. Logemann J, Fisher H, Boshes B, Blonsky E. Frequency and concurrence of vocal tract dysfunctions in the speech of a large sample of Parkinson patients. *J Speech Disord* 1978; 43:47–57.
8. Mutch R, Strucwick A, Roy S, et al. Parkinson's disease: Disability review and management. *Br Med J* 1986; 293:675–677.
9. Oxtoby M. *Parkinson's Disease Patients and Their Social Needs.* London: Parkinson's Disease Society, 1982.
10. Scott S, Caird FI, Williams BO. *Communication in Parkinson's Disease.* Rockville, MD: Aspen, 1985.
11. Selby G. Parkinson's disease. In: Vinken PJ, Bruyn GW (eds). *Handbook of Clinical Neurology.* Amsterdam: North Holland, 1968.
12. Streifler M, Hofman S. Disorders of verbal expression in Parkinsonism. In: . Hassler RG, Christ JF (eds). *Advances in Neurology.* New York: Raven Press, 1984.
13. Uziel A, Bohe M, Cadilhac J et al. Les troubles de la voix et de la parole dans les syndromes Parkinson'siens. *Folia Phoniat Logoped* 1975; 27(3):166–176.
14. Aronson AE. *Clinical Voice Disorders.* New York: Thieme-Stratton, 1990.
15. Pitcairn TK, Clemie S, Gray JM, Pentland B. Non-verbal cues in the self-presentation of Parkinsonian patients. *Br J Clin Psychol* 1990; 29:177–184.
16. Rascol O, Payoux P, Ory F, et al., Limitations of current Parkinson's disease therapy. *Ann Neurol.* 2003; 53 Suppl 3:S3–12
17. Miller N, Noble E, Jones D, Burn D. Life with communication changes in Parkinson's disease. *Age Ageing* 2006; 35:235–239.
18. Leopold NA, Kagel MA. laryngeal deglutition movement in Parkinson's disease. *Neurology* 1997; 48:373–375.
19. Potulska A, Friedman A, Krolicki L, et al. Swallowing disorders in Parkinson's disease. *Parkinsonism Relat Disord.* 2003; 9:349–53.
20. Sharkawi AE, Ramig L, Logemann JA, et al. Swallowing and voice effects of Lee Silverman Voice Treatment (LSVT): A pilot study. *J Neurol Neurosurg Psychiatry* 2002; 72:31–33.
21. Logemann JA. *Evaluation and Treatment of Swallowing Disorders.* Austin, TX: Pro-Ed, 1998.
22. Robbins J, Logemann JA, Kirshner H. Swallowing and speech production in Parkinson's disease. *Ann Neurol* 1986; 11:283–287.
23. Barbeau A, Sourkes TL, Murphy CF. Les catecholamines de la maladie de Parkinson's. In: Ajuria Guerra J (ed). *Monoamines et Systeme Nerveux Central.* Geneva: George, 1962.
24. Birkmayer W, Kiewicz GH. Oder l-dioxyphenylanin(l-dopa) Effekt im Parkinson-Syndrom des Menschen. *Arch Psychiatr Nervenkr* 1962; 203:560–574.
25. Freed CR, Breeze RE, Rosenberg NL, et al. Survival of implanted fetal dopamine cells and neurologic improvement 12 to 46 months after transplantation for Parkinson's disease. *N Engl J Med* 1992; 327(22):1549–1555.
26. Svennilson E, Torvik A, Lowe R, et al. Treatment of Parkinsonism by stereotatic thermolesions in the pallidal region. A clinical evaluation of 81 cases. *Acta Psychiatr Scand.* 1960; 35:358–77.

27. Baker K, Ramig LO, Johnson A, et al. Preliminary speech and voice analysis following fetal dopamine transplants in 5 individuals with Parkinson disease. *J Speech Hear Res* 1997; 40:615–626.

28. Larson K, Ramig LO, Scherer RC. Acoustic and glottographic voice analysis during drug-related fluctuations in Parkinson's disease. *J Med Speech Lang Pathol* 1994; 2:211–226.

29. Berke GS, Gerratt B, Kreiman J, Jackson K. Treatment of Parkinson hypophonia with percutaneous collagen augmentation. *Laryngoscope* 1999; 109:1295–1299.

30. Kim SH, Kearney JJ, Atkins JP. Percutaneous laryngeal collagen augmentation for treatment of Parkinsonian hypophonia. *Otolaryngol Head Neck Surg* 2002; 126:653–656.

31. Helm N. Management of palilalia with a pacing board. *J Speech Hear Disord* 1979; 44:350–353.

32. Yorkston KM. Treatment efficacy: Dysarthria. *J Speech Hear Res* 1996; 39:S46–S57.

33. Ramig LO, Countryman S, O'Brien C, et al. Intensive speech treatment for patients with Parkinson's disease: Short and long term comparison of two techniques. *Neurology* 1996; 47:1496–1504.

34. Ramig L, Countryman S, Thompson L, et al. Comparison of two forms of intensive speech treatment for Parkinson disease. *J Speech Hear Res* 1995; 38:1232–1250.

35. Dromey C, Ramig LO, Johnson A. Phonatory and articulatory changes associated with increased vocal intensity in Parkinson disease: A case study. *J Speech Hear Res* 1995; 38:751–763.

36. Smith M, Ramig LO, Dromey C, et al. Intensive voice treatment in Parkinson's disease: Laryngostroboscopic findings. *J Voice* 1995; 9:453–459.

37. Stelmach GE. Basal ganglia impairment and force control. In: Requin J, Stelmach GE (eds). *Tutorial in Motor Neuroscience.* Dordrecht, The Netherlands: Kluwer Academic Publishers, 1991.

38. Winholtz WS, Ramig LO. Vocal tremor analysis with the vocal demodulator. *NCVS Status Prog Rep* 1992; 2:119–137.

39. Liotti M, Ramig LO, Vogel D, et al. Hypophonia in Parkinson's disease. Neural correlates of voice treatment revealed by PET. *Neurology* 2003; 60:432–440.

40. Liotti M, Vogel D, Sapir S, et al. Abnormal auditory gating in Parkinson's disease before & after LSVT. Paper presented at the Annual Meeting of the American Speech, Language and Hearing Association, Washington, DC, November, 2000.

41. Narayana S, Vogel D, Brown S, et al. Mechanism of action of voice therapy in Parkinson's hypophonia: A PET study. Poster presented at the 11th Annual Meeting of the Organization for Human Brain Mapping. Toronto, Ontario, Canada, 2005.

42. Gath I, Yair E. analysis of vocal tract parameters in Parkinsonian speech. *J Acoust Soc Am* 1988; 84:1628–1634.

43. Jiang J, Lin E, Wang J, Hanson DG. Glottographic measures before and after levodopa treatment in Parkinson's disease. *Laryngoscope* 1999; 109:1287–1294.

44. Baker K, Ramig LO, Luschei E, Smith M. Thyroarytenoid muscle activity associated with hypophonia in Parkinson disease and aging. *Neurology* 1998; 51(6):1592–1598.

45. Leanderson R, Meyerson BA, Persson A. Effect of L dopa on speech in Parkinsonism: An EMG study of labial articulatory function. *J Neurol Psychiatry* 1971; 43:679–681.

46. Leanderson R, Meyerson BA, Persson A. Lip muscle function in Parkinsonian dysarthria. *Acta Otolaryngol* 1972; 74:350–357.

47. Sapir S, Ramig L, Fox C. The Lee Silverman Voice Treatment [LSVT®] for Voice, Speech, and Other Orofacial Disorders in People with Parkinson's Disease. *Future Neurol.* 2006; 1:563–570.

48. Sapir S, Spielman J, Ramig L, et al. effects of intensive voice treatment (LSVT) on vowel articulation in dysarthric individuals with idiopathic Parkinson disease: Acoustic and perceptual findings. *J Speech Lang Hear Res.* In press.

49. Ackermann H, Ziegler W. Articulatory deficits in Parkinsonian dysarthria: An acoustic analysis. *J Neurol Neurosurg Psychiatry* 1991; 54:1093–1098.

50. Estenne M, Hubert M, Troyer AD. Respiratory muscle involvement in Parkinson's disease. *N Engl J Med* 1984; 311:1516.

51. Hansen DG, Gerratt BR, Ward PH. Cinegraphic observations of laryngeal function in Parkinson's disease. *Laryngoscope* 1984; 94:348–353.

52. Hoodin RB, Gilbert HR. Nasal airflows in Parkinsonian speakers. *J Commun Disord* 1989; 22:169–180.

53. Darley FL, Aronson AE, Brown JR. Clusters of deviant speech dimensions in the dysarthrias. *J Speech Hear Res* 1969; 12:462–469.

54. Darley FL, Aronson A, Brown J. Differential diagnostic patterns of dysarthria. *J Speech Hear Res* 1969; 12:246–269.

55. Darley FL, Aronson AE, Brown JR. *Motor Speech Disorders.* Philadelphia: Saunders, 1975.

56. Logemann J, Boshes B, Fisher H. The steps in the degeneration of speech and voice control in Parkinson's disease. In: J. Siegfried (ed). *Parkinson's Diseases: Rigidity, Akinesia, Behavior.* Vienna: Hans Huber, 1973.

57. Logemann J, Fisher H, Boshes B, Blonsky E. Frequency and concurrence of vocal tract dysfunctions in the speech of a large sample of Parkinson patients. *J Speech Hear Disord* 1978; 43:47–57.

58. Ludlow CL, Bassich CJ. Relationships between perceptual ratings and acoustic measures of hypokinetic speech. In: McNeil MR, Rosenbek JC, Aronson AE (eds). *The Dysarthrias: Physiology, Acoustics, Perception, Management.* San Diego, CA: College-Hill Press, 1984.

59. Stewart C, Winfield L, Hunt A, et al. Speech dysfunction in early Parkinson's disease. *Mov Disord* 1995; 10(5):562–565.

60. Sapir S, Pawlas AA, Ramig LO, et al. Voice and speech abnormalities in Parkinson disease: Relation to severity of motor impairment, duration of disease, medication, depression, gender, and age. *J Med Speech Lang Pathol* 2001: 9:213–226.

61. Blumin JH, Pcolinsky DE, Atkins JP. Laryngeal findings in advanced Parkinson's disease. *Ann Otol Rhinol Laryngol* 2004; 113:253–258.

62. Perez K, Ramig LO, Smith M, et al. the Parkinson larynx: Tremor and videostroboscopic findings. *J Voice* 1996; 10:354–361.

63. Gerratt BR, Hansen DG, Berke GS. Glottographic measures of laryngeal function in individuals with abnormal motor control. In: Baer T, Sasaki C, Harris K (eds). *Laryngeal Function in Phonation and Respiration.* Boston: College-Hill Press, 1987.

64. Gallena S, Smith PJ, Zeffiro T, Ludlow CL. Effects of levodopa on laryngeal muscle activity for voice onset and offset in Parkinson disease. *J Speech Lang Hear Res* 2001; 44:1284–1299.

65. Hunker CJ Abbs JH. Physiological analyses of Parkinsonian tremors in the orofacial system. In: McNeil MR, Rosenbek JC, Aronson AE (eds). *The Dysarthrias: Physiology, Acoustics, Perception, Management.* San Diego, CA: College-Hill Press, 1984.

66. Netsell R, Daniel B, Celesia GG. Acceleration and weakness in Parkinsonian dysarthria. *J Speech Hear Disord* . 1975: 40:170–178.

67. Vincken WG, Gauthier SG, Dollfuss RE, et al. Involvement of upper-airway muscles in extrapyramidal disorders: Aa cause of airflow limitation. *N Engl J Med* 1984; 311:438–442.

68. Hirose H, Joshita Y. Laryngeal behavior in patients with disorders of the central nervous system. In: Hirano M, Kirchner JA, Bless DM (eds). *Neurolaryngology: Recent Advances.* Boston: Little, Brown, 1987.

69. Luschei ES, Ramig LO, Baker KL, et al. Discharge characteristics of laryngeal single motor units during phonation in young and older adults and in persons with Parkinson disease. *J Neurophysiol* 1999; 81:2131–2139.

70. Ho AK, Bradshaw JL, Iansek R, Alfredson R. Speech volume regulation in Parkinson's disease: Effects of implicit cues and explicit instructions. *Neuropsychologia* 1999; 37:1453–1460.

71. Ho AK, Bradshaw JL, Iansek T. Volume perception in Parkinsonian speech. *Mov Disord* 2000; 15:1125–1131.

72. Murdoch BE, Chenery HJ, Bowler S, et al. Respiratory function in Parkinson's subjects exhibiting a perceptible speech deficit: A kinematic and spirometric analysis. *J Speech Hear Disord* 1989; 54:610–626.

73. Solomon NP, Nixon TJ. Speech breathing in Parkinson's disease. *J Speech Hear Res* 1993; 36:294–310.

74. Cramer W. De spaak bij patienten met Parkinsonisme. *Logop Phoniatr* 1940; 22:17–23.

75. De la Torre R, Mier M, Boshes B. Evaluation of respiratory function: Preliminary observations. *Q Bull Northwest U Med School* 1960; 34:332–336.

76. Laszewski Z. Role of the department of rehabilitation in preoperative evaluation of Parkinsonian patients. *J Am Geriatr Soc* 1956; 4:1280–1284.

77. Marquardt TP. *Characteristics of Speech in Parkinson's Disease: Electromyographic, Structural Movement and Aerodynamic Measurements.* Seattle: University of Washington, 1973.

78. Mueller PB. Parkinson's disease: Motor-speech behavior in a selected group of patients. *Folia Phoniatr Logoped* 1971; 23:333–346.

79. Schiffman PL. A "saw-tooth" pattern in Parkinson's disease. *Chest* 1985; 87:124–126.

80. Canter GJ. Speech characteristics of patients with Parkinson's disease: I. Intensity, pitch and duration. *J Speech Hear Disord* 1963; 28:221–229.

81. Metter E, Hanson WR. Clinical and acoustical variability in hypokinetic dysarthria. *J Commun Disord* 1986; 19:347–66.

82. Fox C, Ramig L. Sound pressure level and self-perception of speech and voice in men and women who have idiopathic Parkinson disease. *Am J Speech Lang Pathol* 1997; 6:85–94.

83. King, J, Ramig, L, Lemke, J, et al. Parkinson's disease: Longitudinal changes in acoustic parameters of phonation. *J Med Speech Lang Pathol* 1994; 2:29–42.

84. Ramig LA, Titze OR, Scherer R, et al. Acoustic analysis of voices of patients with neurologic disease: Rationale and preliminary data. *Ann Otolaryngol Rhinol Laryngol* 1988; 97:164–172.

85. Zwirner P, Murry T, Woodson GE. Phonatory function of neurologically impaired patients. *J Commun Disord* 1991; 24:287–300.

86. Ludlow C, Bassich C, Connor N, et al. Phonatory characteristics of vocal fold tremor. *J Phonet* 1986; 14:509–515.

87. Ramig LA, Shipp T. Comparative measures of vocal tremor and vocal vibrato. *J Voice* 1987; 1:162–167.

88. Philippbar SA, Robin DA, Luschei ES. Limb, jaw and vocal tremor in Parkinson's patients. In: Yorkston KM, Beukelman DR (eds). *Recent Advances in Clinical Dysarthria.* Boston:College-Hill Press, 1989.

89. Weismer G. Articulatory characteristics of Parkinsonian dysarthria: Segmental and phrase-level timing, spirantization and glottal-supraglottal coordination. In: McNeil M, Rosenbek J, Aronson A (eds). *The Dysarthrias: Physiology, Acoustics, Perception and Management.* San Diego, CA: College Hill Press, 1984.

90. Forrest K, Weismer G, Turner GS. Kinematic, acoustic, and perceptual analyses of connected speech produced by Parkinsonian and normal geriatric adults. *J Acoust Soc Am* 1989; 85:2608–2622.

91. Ackermann H, Konczak J, Hertrich I. The temporal control of repetitive articulatory movements in Parkinson's disease. *Brain Lang* 1997; 56:312–319.

92. Hirose H. pathophysiology of motor speech disorders (dysarthria). *Folia Phoniatr (Basel)* 1986; 38:61–88.

93. Caligiuri M. the influence of speaking rate on articulatory hypokinesia in Parkinsonian dysarthria. *Brain Lang* 1989; 36:493–502.

94. Kempler D, Van Lancker D. Effect of speech task on intelligibility in dysarthria: A case study of Parkinson's disease. *Brain Lang* 2002; 80:449–464.

95. Rosen KM, Kent RD, Duffy JR. Task-based profile of vocal intensity decline in Parkinson's disease. *Folia Phoniatr Logoped* 2005; 57:28–37.

96. Goberman AM, Elmer LW. Acoustic analysis of clear versus conversational speech in individuals with Parkinson disease. *J Commun Disord* 2005; 38:215–230.

97. Adams SG. Hypokinetic dysarthria in Parkinson's disease. In: McNeil MR (ed). *Clinical Management of Sensorimotor Speech Disorders*. New York: Thieme, 1997.

98. Hammen VL, Yorkston KM, Beukelman DR. Pausal and speech duration characteristics as a function of speaking rate in normal and Parkinsonian dysarthric individuals. In: Yorkston KM, Beukelman DR (eds). *Recent Advances in Clinical Dysarthria*. Boston: College-Hill Press, 1989.

99. Hanson WR, Metter EJ. DAF speech rate modification in Parkinson's disease: A report of two cases. In: Berry WR (eds). *Clinical Dysarthria*. San Diego, CA: College-Hill Press, 1983.

100. Hirose H, Kiritani S, Ushijima T, et al. Patterns of dysarthric movements in patients with Parkinsonism. *Folia Phoniatr Logoped* 1981; 33(4):204–215.

101. Hoodin RB, Gilbert HR. Parkinsonian dysarthria: An aerodynamic and perceptual description of velopharyngeal closure for speech. *Folia Phoniatr Logoped* 1989; 41:249–258.

102. McRae PA, Tjaden K, Schoonings B. Acoustic and perceptual consequences of articulatory rate change in Parkinson disease. *J Speech Lang Hear Res* 2002; 45:35–50.

103. Yunusova Y, Weismer G, Kent RD, Rusche NM. Breath-group intelligibility in dysarthria: Characteristics and underlying correlates. *J Speech Lang Hear Res* 2005; 48: 1294–310.

104. Flint AJ, Black SE, Campbell-Taylor I, et al. Abnormal speech articulation, psychomotor retardation, and subcortical dysfunction in major depression. *J Psychiatr Res* 1993; 27; 309–319.

105. Koller WC. Sensory symptoms in Parkinson's disease. *Neurology* 1984; 34:957–959.

106. Tatton WG, Eastman MJ, Bedingham W, et al. Defective utilization of sensory input as the basis for bradykinesia, rigidity and decreased movement repertoire in Parkinson's disease: A hypothesis. *Can J Neurosci* 1984; 11:136–143.

107. Albin RL, Young AB, Penny JB. The functional anatomy of basal ganglia disorders. *Trends Neurosci* 1989; 12:366–375.

108. Penny JB, Young AB. Speculations on the functional anatomy of basal ganglia disorders. *Annu Rev Neurosci* 1983; 6:73–94.

109. Berardelli A, Dick JP, Rothwell JC, et al. Scaling of the size of the first agonist EMG burst during rapid wrist movements in patients with Parkinson's disease. *J Neurol Neurosurg Psychiatry* 1986; 49: 1273–1279.

110. Maschke M, Gomez C, Tuite P, et al. Dysfunction of the basal ganglia, but not the cerebellum, impairs kinaesthesia. Brain. 2003; 126:2312–22.

111. Demirci M, Grill S, McShane L, et al. A mismatch between kinesthetic and visual perception in Parkinson's disease. *Ann Neurol*. 1997; 41:781–8.

112. Schneider JS, Diamond SG, Markham CH. Deficits in orofacial sensorimotor function in Parkinson's disease. *Ann Neurol* 1986; 19:275–282.

113. Schneider JS, Lidsky TI. *Basal Ganglia and Behavior: Sensory Aspects of Motor Functioning*. Toronto: Hans Huber, 1987.

114. Solomon N, Robin D. Perceptions of effort during handgrip and tongue elevation in Parkinson's disease. *Parkinsonism Relat Disord*. 2005; 11:353–61.

115. Fox C, Ramig L, Ciucci M, et al., The science and practice of LSVT/LOUD: neural plasticity-principled approach to treating individuals with Parkinson disease and other neurological disorders. *Semin Speech Lang* 2006; 27:283–99.

116. Ramig LO, Pawlas A, Countryman S. The Lee Silverman Voice Treatment (LSVT): A practical guide to treating the voice and speech disorders in Parkinson disease. Iowa City, IA: National Center for Voice and Speech and LSVT Foundation, 1995.

117. Desmurget M, Grafton S, Vindras P, et al. Basal ganglia network mediates the control of movement amplitude. *Exp Brain Res* 2003; 153:197–209.

118. Curio G, Neuloh G, Numminen J, et al. Speaking modifies voice-evoked activity in the human auditory cortex. *Human Brain Mapping* 2000; 9:183–191.

119. Ford JM, Mathalon DH. Electrophysiological evidence of corollary discharge dysfunction in schizophrenia during talking and thinking. *J Psychiatr Res* 2004; 38:37–46.

120. Boecker H, Ceballos-Baumann A, Bartenstein P, et al. Sensory processing in Parkinson's and Huntington's disease: Investigations with 3D H(2)(15)O-PET. *Brain* 1999; 122: 1651–1665.

121. Miller N, Noble E, Jones D, et al. Hard to swallow: dysphagia in Parkinson's disease. *Age Ageing*. 2006; 35:614–8.

122. Jean A. Brain stem control of swallowing: Neuronal network and cellular mechanisms. *Physiol Rev* 2001; 81:929–969.

123. Hartnick CJ, Rudolph C, Willging JP, Holland SK. Functional magnetic resonance imaging of the pediatric swallow: Imaging the cortex and the brainstem. *Laryngoscope* 2001; 111:1183–1191.

124. Mosier K, Bereznaya I. Parallel cortical networks for volitional control of swallowing in humans. *Exp Brain Res* 2001; 140:280–289.

125. Suzuki M, Asada Y, Ito J, et al. Activation of cerebellum and basal ganglia on volitional swallowing detected by functional magnetic resonance imaging. *Dysphagia* 2003; 18(2):71–77.

126. Riecker A, Mathiak K, Wildgruber D, et al. fMRI reveals two distinct cerebral networks subserving speech motor control. *Neurology* 2005; 64:700–706.

127. Stroudley J, Walsh M. Radiographic assessment of dysphagia in Parkinson's disease. *Br J Radiol* 1991; 64:890–893.

128. Robbins J, Logemann JA, Kirshner H: swallowing and speech production in Parkinson's disease. *Ann Neurol* 1986; 11:283–287.

129. Jia YX, Sekizawa K, Ohrui T, et al. Dopamine D1 receptor antagonist inhibits swallowing reflex in guinea pigs. *Am J Physiol* 1998; 274:R76–R80.

130. Kessler JP, Jean A. Effect of catecholamines on the swallowing reflex after pressure microinjections into the lateral solitary complex of the medulla oblongata. *Brain Res* 1986; 386:69–77.

131. Hunter PC, Crameri J, Austin S, et al. Response of Parkinsonian swallowing dysfunction to dopaminergic stimulation. *J Neurol Neurosurg Psychiatry* 1997; 63:579–583.

132. Tison F, Wiart L, Guatterie M, et al. Effects of central dopaminergic stimulation by apomorphine on swallowing disorders in Parkinson's disease. *Mov Disord* 1996; 11:729–732.

133. Critchley EMR. Speech disorders of Parkinsonism: A review. *J Neurol Neurosurg Psychiatry* 1981; 44:751–758.

134. Mawdsley C. Speech and levodopa. *Adv Neurol* 1973; 3:33–47.

135. Mawdsley C, Gamsu CV. Periodicity of speech in Parkinsonism. *Nature* 1971; 231: 315–316.

136. Nakano KK, Zubick H, Tyley HR. Speech defects of Parkinsonian patients. *Neurology* 1973; 23:865–870.

137. Rigrodsky S, Morrison EB. Speech changes in Parkinsonism during L-dopa therapy: Preliminary findings. *J Am Geriatr Soc* 1970; 18:142–151.

138. Wolfe V, Garvin J, Bacon M, et al. Speech changes in Parkinson's disease during treatment with L-dopa. *J Commun Disord*. 1975; 8:271–9.

139. Yaryura-Tobias JA, Diamond B, Merlis S. Verbal communication with L-dopa treatment. *Nature* 1971; 234: 224–225.

140. Goberman A. Correlation between acoustic speech characteristics and non-speech motor performance in Parkinson disease. *Med Sci Monit* 2005; 11:CR109–CR116.

141. Trail M, Fox C, Ramig LO, et al. Speech treatment for Parkinson's disease. *Neuro-Rehabilitation* 2005; 20:205–221.

142. De Letter M, Santens P, Van Borsel J. The effects of levodopa on word intelligibility in Parkinson's disease. *J Commun Disord* 2005; 38:187–196.

143. Goberman A, Coelho C, Robb M. Phonatory characteristics of Parkinsonian speech before and after morning medication: The ON and OFF states. *J Commun Disord* 2002; 35:217–239.

144. Sanabria J, Ruiz PG, Gutierrez R, et al. The effect of levodopa on vocal function in Parkinson's disease. *Clin Neuropharmacol* 2001; 24:99–102.

145. Cahill LM, Murdoch BE, Theodoros DG, et al. Effect of oral levodopa treatment on articulatory function in Parkinson's disease: Preliminary results. *Motor Control* 1998; 2:161–172.

146. Kompoliti K, Wang QE, Goetz CG, et al. Effects of central dopaminergic stimulation by apomorphine on speech in Parkinson's disease. *Neurology* 2000; 54:458–462.

147. Biary N, Pimental PA, Langenberg PW. A double-blind trial of clonazepam in the treatment of Parkinsonian dysarthria. *Neurology* 1988; 38:255–258.

148. Fuh JL, Lee RC, Wang SJ, et al. Swallowing difficulty in Parkinson's disease. *Clin Neurol Neurosurg* 1997; 99:106–112.

149. Bushmann M, Dobmeyer SM, Leeker L, Perlmutter JS. Swallowing abnormalities and their response to treatment in Parkinson's disease. *Neurology* 1989; 39: 1309–1314.

150. Leblois A, Boraud T, Meissner W, et al. Competition between feedback loops underlies normal and pathological dynamics in the basal ganglia. *J Neurosci* 2006; 26: 3567–3583.

151. Perlmutter JS, Mink JW. Deep brain stimulation. *Annu Rev Neurosci*, 2006; 29:229–57.

152. Pahwa R, Lyons KE, Wilkinson SB, et al. Long-term evaluation of deep brain stimulation of the thalamus. *J Neurosurg* 2006; 104:506–512.

153. Rodriguez-Oroz MC, Obeso JA, Lang AE, et al. bilateral deep brain stimulation in Parkinson's disease: A multicentre study with 4 years follow-up. *Brain* 2005; 128: 2240–2249.

154. Krack P, Batir A, Van Blercom N, et al. Five-year follow-up of bilateral stimulation of the subthalamic nucleus in advanced Parkinson's disease. *N Engl J Med* 2003; 349: 1925–1934.

155. Santens P, De Letter M, Van Borsel J, et al. Lateralized effects of subthalamic nucleus stimulation on different aspects of speech in Parkinson's disease. *Brain Lang* 2003; 87:253–258.

156. Wang E, Verhagen Metman L, Bakay R, et al: The effect of unilateral electrostimulation of the subthalamic nucleus on respiratory/phonatory subsystems of speech production in Parkinson's disease: A preliminary report. *Clin Linguist Phonet* 2003; 17:283–239.

157. Gentil M, Pinto S, Pollak P, Benabid AL. Effect of bilateral stimulation of the subthalamic nucleus on Parkinsonian dysarthria. *Brain Lang* 2003; 85:190–196.

158. Gentil M, Garcia-Ruiz P, Pollak P, Benabid AL. Effect of bilateral deep-brain stimulation on oral control of patients with Parkinsonism. *Eur Neurol* 2000; 44:147–152.

159. Gentil M, Chauvin P, Pinto S, et al. Effect of bilateral stimulation of the subthalamic nucleus on Parkinsonian voice. *Brain Lang* 2001; 78:233–240.

160. Pinto S, Gentil M, Fraix V, et al. Bilateral subthalamic stimulation effects on oral force control in Parkinson's disease. *J Neurol* 2003; 250:179–187.

161. Dromey C, Kumar R, Lang AE, Lozano AM. An investigation of the effects of subthalamic nucleus stimulation on acoustic measures of voice. *Mov Disord* 2000; 15:1132–1138.

162. Rousseaux M, Krystkowiak P, Kozlowski O, et al. Effects of subthalamic nucleus stimulation on Parkinsonian dysarthria and speech intelligibility. *J Neurol* 2000; 251: 327–334.

163. Saint-Cyr JA, Trepanier LL, Kumar R, et al. Neuropsychological consequences of chronic bilateral stimulation of the subthalamic nucleus in Parkinson's disease. *Brain* 2000; 123:2091–2108.

164. McIntyre CC, Mori S, Sherman DL, et al. Electric field and stimulating influence generated by deep brain stimulation of the subthalamic nucleus. *Clin Neurophysiol* 2004; 115:589–595.

165. Tornqvist AL, Schalen, L, Rehncrona S. Effects of different electrical parameter settings on the intelligibility of speech in patients with Parkinson's disease treated with subthalamic deep brain stimulation. *Mov Disord* 2005; 20:416–423.

166. Dias AE, Barbosa ER, Coracini K, et al. Effects of repetitive transcranial magnetic stimulation on voice and speech in Parkinson's disease. *Acta Neurol Scand* 2006; 113:92–99.

167. Pagni CA, Zeme S, Zenga F. Further experience with extradural motor cortex stimulation for treatment of advanced Parkinson's disease. Report of 3 new cases. *J Neurosurg Sci* 2003; 47:189–193.

168. Schulz GM, Peterson T, Sapienza CM, et al. Voice and speech characteristics of persons with Parkinson's disease pre- and post-pallidotomy surgery: Preliminary findings. *J Speech Lang Hear Res* 1999; 42:1176–1194.

169. Schulz GM, Greer M, Friedman W. Changes in vocal intensity in Parkinson's disease following pallidotomy surgery. *J Voice* 2000; 14:589–606.

170. Uitti RJ, Wharen RE, Duffy JR, et al. Uunilateral pallidotomy for Parkinson's disease: Speech, motor, and neuropsychological outcome measurements. *Parkinsonism Relat Disord* 2000; 6:133–143.

171. Scott R, Gregory R, Hines N, et al. neuropsychological, neurological and functional outcome following pallidotomy for Parkinson's disease. A consecutive series of eight simultaneous bilateral and twelve unilateral procedures. *Brain* 1998; 121:659–675.

172. Troster AI, Woods SP, Fields JA. Verbal fluency declines after pallidotomy: An interaction between task and lesion laterality. *Appl Neuropsychol* 2003; 10:69–75.

173. Nagulic M, Davidovic J, Nagulic I. Parkinsonian voice acoustic analysis in real-time after stereotactic thalamotomy. *Stereotact Funct Neurosurg* 2005; 83:115–121.

174. Parkin S, Nandi D, Giladi N, et al. Lesioning the subthalamic nucleus in the treatment of Parkinson's disease. *Stereotact Funct Neurosurg* 2001; 77:68–72.

175. Hugdahl K, Wester K, Asbjornsen A. The role of the left and right thalamus in language asymmetry: Dichotic listening in Parkinson patients undergoing stereotactic thalamotomy. *Brain Lang* 1990; 39:1–13.

176. Farrell A, Theodoros D, Ward E, et al. Effects of neurosurgical management of Parkinson's disease on speech characteristics and oromotor function. *J Speech Lang Hear Res* 2005; 48:5–20.

177. Born LJ, Harned RH, Rikkers LF, et al. Cricopharyngeal dysfunction in Parkinson's disease: Role in dysphagia and response to myotomy. *Mov Disord* 1996; 11:53–58.

178. Allan CM. treatment of non-fluent speech resulting from neurological disease: treatment of dysarthria. *Br J Disord Commun* 1970; 5:3–5.

179. Greene HCL. *The Voice and Its Disorders*. London: Pitman Medical, 1980.

180. Weiner WJ, Lang AE. *Movement Disorders; A Comprehensive Survey*. Mount Kisco, NY: Futura, 1989.

181. Sarno MT. Speech impairment in Parkinson's disease. *Arch Phys Med Rehabil* 1968; 49:269–275.

182. Downie AW, Low JM, Lindsay DD. Speech disorders in Parkinsonism: Usefulness of delayed auditory feedback in selected cases. *Br J Disord Commun* 1981; 16:135–139.

183. Rubow RT, Swift E. A microcomputer-based wearable biofeedback device to improve transfer of treatment in Parkinsonian dysarthria. *J Speech Hear Disord* 1985; 50:178–185.

184. Scott S, Caird FL. Speech therapy for Parkinson's disease. *J Neurol Neurosurg Psychiatry* 1983; 46:140–144.

185. McNamara P, Obler LK, Au R, et al. Speech monitoring skills in Alzheimer's disease, Parkinson's disease and normal aging. *Brain Lang* 1992; 42:38–51.

186. Saint-Cyr JA, Taylor AE, Lang AE. Procedural learning and neostriatal dysfunction in man. *Brain* 1988; 111:941–59.

187. Muslimovic D, Post B, Speelman JD, Schmand B: cognitive profile of patients with newly diagnosed Parkinson disease. *Neurology.* 2005; 65:1239–45.

188. Rajput A, Rajput AH. Parkinson's disease management strategies. *Expert Rev Neurother* 2006; 6:91–99.

189. Kleim J, Jones TA, Schallert T. Motor enrichment and the induction of plasticity before or after brain injury. *Neurochem Res* 2003; 28:1757–1769.

190. Taub E. Harnessing brain plasticity through behavioral techniques to produce new treatments in neurorehabilitation. *Am Pscyhol* 2004; 59:692–704.

191. Tillerson J, Caudle WM, Reveron ME, Miller GW. Exercise induces behavioral recovery and attenuates neurochemical deficits in rodent models of Parkinson's disease. *Neuroscience* 2003; 119:899–911.

192. Fisher B, Petzinger GM, Nixon K, et al. Exercise-induced behavioral recovery and neuroplasticity in the 1-methyl-4-phenyl-1, 2, 3, 6-tetrahydropyridine-lesioned mouse basal ganglia. *J Neurosci Res* 2004; 77:378–390.

193. Tillerson J, Cohen AD, Philhower Jet al. Forced limb-use effects on the behavioral and neurochemical effects of 6-hydroxydopamine. *J Neurosci* 2001; 21:4427–4435.

194. Ramig L, Mead C, Scherer R, Horii Y, et al. Voice therapy and Parkinson's disease: A longitudinal study of efficacy. Paper presented at the Clinical Dysarthria Conference, San Diego, CA, February, 1988.

195. Ofer-Noy N, Dudai Y, Karni A. Skill learning in mirror reading: How repetition determines acquisition. *Cog Brain Res* 2003; 17:507–521.

196. Tillerson J, Miller G. Forced limb-use and recovery following brain injury. *Neuroscientist* 2002; 8:574–585.

197. Schmidt RA. A schema theory of discrete motor skill learning. *Psychol Rev* 1975; 82:225–260.

198. Schmidt RA. *Motor Control and Learning*. Champaign, IL: Human Kinetics Publishers, 1988.

199. Astrand PO, Rodahl K: *Textbook of Work Physiology*. New York: McGraw-Hill, 1970.

200. Yorkston K, Spencer KA, Duffy JR. Behavioral management of respiratory/phonatory dysfunction from dysarthria: A systematic review of the evidence. *J Med Speech Lang Pathol* 2003; 11:xiii–xxxviii.

201. Sapir S, Ramig LO, Hoyt P, et al. Speech loudness and quality 12 months after intensive voice treatment (LSVT) for Parkinson's disease: A comparison with an alternative speech treatment. *Folia Phoniatr Logop* 2002; 54:296–303.

202. Ramig LO, Sapir S, Countryman S, et al. Intensive voice treatment (LSVT) for patients with Parkinson's disease: A 2 year follow up. *J Neurol Neurosurg Psychiatry* 2001; 71:493–498.

203. Baumgartner CA, Sapir S, Ramig LO. Voice quality changes following phonatory-respiratory effort treatment (LSVT) versus respiratory effort treatment for individuals with Parkinson disease. *J Voice* 2001; 15:105–114.

204. Ramig LO, Sapir S, Fox C, Countryman S. Changes in vocal loudness following intensive voice treatment (LSVT) in individuals with Parkinson's disease: A comparison with untreated patients and normal age-matched controls. *MovDisord* 2001; 16:79–83.

205. Ramig LO, Dromey C. Aerodynamic mechanisms underlying treatment-related changes in SPL in patients with Parkinson disease. *J Speech Hear Res* 1996; 39:798–807.

206. Schulman R. Articulatory dynamics of loud and normal speech. *J Acoustic Soc Am* 1989; 85:295–312.

207. Spielman J, Borod J, Ramig L. the effects of intensive voice treatment on facial expressiveness in Parkinson disease: Preliminary data. *Cogn Behav Neurol* 2003; 16:177–188.

208. Countryman S, Ramig LO. Effects of intensive voice therapy on speech deficits associated with bilateral thalamotomy in Parkinson's disease: A case study. *J Med Speech-Lang Pathol* 1993; 1(4):233–249.

209. Countryman S, Ramig LO, Pawlas AA. Speech and voice deficits in Parkinsonian plus syndromes: Can they be treated? *J Med Speech-Lang Pathol* 1994; 2:211–225.

210. Sapir S, Pawlas A, Ramig L, et al. Effects of intensive phonatory-respiratory treatment (LSVT) on voice in two individuals with multiple sclerosis. *J Med Speech Lang Pathol* 2001; 9:35–45.

211. Sapir S, Spielman J, Ramig LO, et al. Effects of intensive voice treatment [the Lee Silverman Voice Treatment (LSVT)] on ataxic dysarthria: a case study. *Am J Speech Lang Pathol*2003; 12:387–399.

212. Halpern A, Matos C, Ramig LO, et al. LSVTC—A PDA supported speech treatment for Parkinson's disease. Presented at the 9th International Congress of Parkinson's Disease and Movement Disorders, New Orleans, LA, 2005.

213. Yorkston KM, Miller RM, Strand EA. *Management of Speech and Swallowing in Degenerative Diseases*. Communication Skill Builders, Tucson, Ariz 1995.

214. Deane KH, Whurr R, Clarke CE, et al. Nonpharmacological therapies for dysphagia in Parkinson's disease. *Cochrane Database Syst Rev.* 2001; 1: CD002816.

215. de Angelis EC, Mourao LF, Ferraz HB, et al. Effect of voice rehabilitation on oral communication of Parkinson's disease patients. *Acta Neurol Scand* 1997; 96:199–205.

216. Ward E, Theodoros D, Murdoch B, Silburn P. Changes in maximum capacity tongue function following the Lee Silverman Voice Treatment program. *J Med Speech-Lang Pathol* 2000; 8:331–335.

10 Gastrointestinal Features

Eamonn M. M. Quigley

lthough it has been recognized for some time that gastrointestinal problems are common and frequently distressing to patients with Parkinson's disease (PD), their pathophysiology, evaluation, and management have received relatively little attention. This chapter reviews the current status of our understanding of gastrointestinal function in PD, outlines an approach to the evaluation and management of these symptoms, and speculates on future prospects in this area.

OVERVIEW OF GASTROINTESTINAL MOTOR FUNCTION

Although several gastrointestinal functions could be disturbed in PD in relation either to the disease process itself or to its therapy, this chapter focuses on the gastrointestinal function that has received the greatest attention: gastrointestinal motility. First, however, a brief overview of gastrointestinal motor function is appropriate.

Given its essential role in digestion, absorption, secretion, and excretion, the gastrointestinal tract and its associated organs play an essential role in homeostasis. The various physiologic processes of the gastrointestinal tract serve these functions; thus motility propels food, chyme, and stool and promotes mixing to facilitate both contact time and digestion. Gut muscle and nerve are integrated into a "minibrain" and adapted to subserve these homeostatic functions. Throughout most of the gastrointestinal tract, gut smooth muscle is arranged in two layers: an outer longitudinal layer and an inner circular layer. At the beginning and end of the gut, striated muscle is found in the oropharynx, upper esophageal sphincter, and proximal part of the esophagus and in the external anal sphincter and pelvic floor muscles. In these locations, somatic innervation plays a crucial role in the regulation of swallowing and defecation; these functions are particularly prone to disruption in neurologic disease. Throughout the remainder of the gut, several levels of control are evident. Myogenic regulation of motility refers to intrinsic properties of gut muscle cells and their interactions with one another. Next comes the enteric nervous system, which is now recognized as a distinct and independent division of the autonomic nervous system (1). The enteric nervous system may represent the most important level of neuronal control of motility and is capable of generating and modulating many functions within the gastrointestinal tract without input from the more traditional divisions of the autonomic and central nervous systems. Through variations in neuronal morphology and in the electrophysiologic properties of individual neurons as well as through the presence of a wide variety of neurotransmitters and neuromodulatory peptides, the enteric nervous system demonstrates striking plasticity. Of relevance to any discussion of the gut in central nervous system disorders, it is now recognized that the enteric and central nervous systems share many similarities, both morphologic and functional. For example, almost all neurotransmitters identified within the central nervous system are also found in enteric neurons; the concept of enteric nervous system involvement in neurologic disease is thus not surprising. Although the enteric nervous system is primarily responsible for the generation and modulation of most motor activities within the gut, input from autonomic nerves and the central nervous system also modulates motor activity. Autonomic input is now recognized to be exerted primarily though the modulation of enteric nervous system activity rather than through a direct input to effector cells in the gut, be they smooth muscle or epithelial secretory cells. It is now evident that the gut has important sensory functions. Although these are usually subconscious, gut sensation may be relayed to and perceived within the central nervous system. Sensory input is also fundamental to several reflex events in the gut, such as the viscerovisceral reflexes that coordinate function along the gut (2). Indeed, sensory dysfunction is now believed to play an important role in the pathogenesis of a variety of functional gastrointestinal disorders, such as irritable bowel syndrome (2).

The following is a brief overview of the motor functions of the principal organs of the gastrointestinal tract. Swallowing is a complex and highly organized act, traditionally divided into two phases: oropharyngeal and esophageal. The oropharyngeal phase includes the transfer of the food bolus to the pharynx, pharyngeal peristalsis, and propulsion through the upper esophageal sphincter into the esophageal body. This is accomplished through the precisely coordinated action of several muscle groups, including those of the tongue, pharynx, and upper esophageal sphincter. Cranial nerves V, VII, IX, X, and XII convey the afferent and efferent signals involved in this phase of swallowing, which is coordinated in a swallowing center in the reticular formation in the brainstem (3). The esophageal phase of swallowing is primarily a function of the smooth muscle esophagus and is regulated centrally via vagal afferents and peripherally by the intrinsic properties of esophageal smooth muscle (4). Transport of the bolus from the esophagus to the stomach involves the simultaneous generation of a peristaltic sequence in the esophageal body and complete relaxation of the lower eosphageal sphincter; the latter is mediated by a prominent inhibitory innervation at the sphincter.

The main functions of gastric motility are to accommodate and store the ingested meal, grind down (triturate) solid particles, and then empty the homogenized meal in a regulated fashion into the duodenum (5, 6). Fluctuations in tone in the proximal stomach are critical to the accommodation of the meal, while high-amplitude peristaltic contractions in the antrum generate the forces necessary to disrupt large solid particles. Small intestinal motility should serve to mix the meal with intestinal secretions and, periodically, propel chyme and undigested material in an aboral direction (6). Between meals, a periodic wave of contractions, the migrating motor complex, slowly traverses the small intestine, ensuring clearance of any remaining food debris. By virtue of the specialized intrinsic properties of their musculature as well as a distinctive and predominantly inhibitory innervation, the lower esophageal, pyloric, and ileocecal sphincters regulate transit between adjacent organs and prevent oral reflux.

Colonic motility is less well characterized in humans. Mixing and retropulsion appear to dominate in the right colon, whereas storage and intermittent aborad propulsion are the dominant functions on the left side (7). Finally, the anal canal and distal rectum—another site where somatic and autonomic neural networks intersect—play a crucial role in the regulation of defecation and the maintenance of continence.

GASTROINTESTINAL DYSFUNCTION IN PARKINSON'S DISEASE: HISTORIC BACKGROUND AND PRINCIPAL FEATURES

The cardinal gastrointestinal manifestations of PD were clearly and vividly described in Parkinson's original monograph in 1817 (8). Referring to swallowing difficulties, he stated that "food is with difficulty retained in the mouth until swallowed; and then is difficultly swallowed—the saliva fails of being directed to the back part of the fauces, and hence is continually draining from the mouth." He also recognized problems with constipation and defecation: "The bowels, which all along had been torpid, now in most cases, demand stimulating medicines of very considerable power: the expulsion of the faeces from the rectum sometimes requiring mechanical aid." Thereafter, gastrointestinal manifestations of PD received relatively little attention until the latter half of the twentieth century; they are now recognized as important and at times, from the patient's perspective, dominant features of this disorder (9–11). A number of surveys then described a high frequency of drooling, dysphagia, gastroesophageal reflux, delayed gastric emptying, and constipation (12–17). Various factors were invoked to explain the pathophysiology of these symptoms, including alterations in diet, reduced activity, side effects of antiparkinsonian medications, and associated autonomic dysfunction (18). The true prevalence of gastrointestinal symptoms in PD and their relationship to the disease process itself were not defined until quite recently. In a series of studies that included age- and gender-matched controls and employed validated study instruments as well as follow-up, Edwards and colleagues confirmed a high prevalence of esophageal and colorectal symptoms among patients with PD regardless of therapy (19–21). Among 98 patients, disordered salivation (70%), dysphagia (52%), nausea (24%), constipation (29%), and defecatory dysfunction (66%) emerged as the gastrointestinal symptoms that were truly more common in PD (19). Only PD severity and the duration of disease correlated with gastrointestinal symptoms; patient age, gender, level of activity, dietary fiber intake, and antiparkinsonian therapy did not (19). These findings appeared to support Parkinson's original hypothesis, that gastrointestinal symptoms are a component of the disease process itself. However, attempts to correlate the Parkinson's disease process with objective tests of gastrointestinal motor function have proven more difficult. Constipation and defecatory dysfunction, especially common in PD (22), may predate the onset of the neurologic features. Ueki and Otsuka, in a study documenting a prevalence of constipation of 79% among 94 Japanese PD patients, noted that constipation had predated the onset of PD by an average of 18 years in 45% of the patients (23). They went on to link a tendency to a lower intake of liquids from early life with the ultimate development of constipation and PD. Similarly, Abbott and colleagues found that a history of less than one bowel movement per day was associated with a threefold increased risk of the later development of PD (24).

DYSPHAGIA IN PARKINSON'S DISEASE

Swallowing difficulty is among the most common, distressing, and challenging gastrointestinal problems in PD. Because of the risk of aspiration and its impact on nutrition, as well as intake of orally administered medications, disordered swallowing function is potentially life-threatening. The primary symptoms are drooling, or sialorrhea, and dysphagia, the latter usually described as a sensation of food sticking at the level of the thyroid cartilage. It is crucial to understand that, in PD, drooling and difficulty with saliva are manifestations of disordered swallowing and not of abnormal salivation. Patients with PD do not secrete excess saliva; indeed, salivary output in PD is either normal or decreased (12, 18). Drooling reflects a difficulty in transporting saliva to the posterior pharynx. Up to 30% of patients with PD describe respiratory symptoms such as coughing, choking, or nocturnal dyspnea in association with dysphagia (19). The carefully performed study of Ali and colleagues has considerably clarified the pathogenesis of dysphagia in PD. Among the many components of swallowing studied, lingual tremor, impaired pharyngeal peristalsis, and restricted opening of the upper esophageal sphincter best predicted dysphagia (25). Given the important role of tongue pulsion in generating the force that propels the bolus through the upper esophageal sphincter, the central role of lingual tremor in the pathogenesis of dysphagia in PD can be readily understood. Impaired opening of the upper esophageal sphincter may lead to the appearance of cricopharyngeal "bars" on radiologic studies and to the development of Zenker's diverticula (26). Other studies attest to the high prevalence of abnormalities in the oropharyngeal phase of swallowing as detected on videofluoroscopic studies (27–32) and emphasize impaired lingual and palatal function as a consequence of hypokinesia (31, 32); however, they have failed to describe good correlations between the prevalence or severity of these abnormalities, the degree of disability related to PD, or the severity of its more classic features.

The clinician must be aware of one potential trap in the clinical assessment of the parkinsonian patient with dysphagia: namely, the false localization of dysphagia to the region of the upper esophageal sphincter by PD patients whose disease process lies in the distal esophagus (33). Although the true prevalence of gastroesophageal reflux in PD remains to be determined, it is certainly clear that PD patients are not immune from reflux disease or from complications such as peptic esophageal strictures. For reasons that remain poorly understood, affected patients frequently present with dysphagia, which is indistinguishable in nature of presentation from that associated with the PD process itself. A failure to recognize this and to fully investigate all PD patients with dysphagia will lead to inappropriate therapy. If gastroesophageal reflux is recognized, appropriate therapy may lead to a significant improvement in dysphagia. Studies of motor function of the esophageal body and lower esophageal sphincter function have revealed significant problems in these areas as well (34–36). In one study, esophageal motor abnormalities, including aperistalsis and diffuse esophageal spasm, were documented in 73% of 22 PD patients and were especially prevalent among those who had daily dysphagia (35). Bassotti and colleagues, in a study documenting a high frequency of similar motor abnormalities, found little correlation between symptoms and manometric findings (34).

NAUSEA, VOMITING, DYSPEPSIA, AND GASTRIC FUNCTION IN PARKINSON'S DISEASE

Nausea and vomiting are common symptoms among patients with PD and are the symptoms that may clearly be directly related to the central effects of dopaminergic medications. However, the survey performed by Edwards and colleagues indicated that nausea may be a feature of PD (19) per se, and some studies suggest a high prevalence of gastroparesis in PD (37–43). Formal studies of gastric emptying of solids, using a variety of techniques, have documented delay in from 36% to 88% of patients (39, 40, 43); here again, correlations between gastric emptying rate and either gastrointestinal symptoms or PD severity have been poor. Gastric emptying may play a crucial role in the management of patients with PD, especially in those with prominent "on"-"off" fluctuations. These individuals are dependent on an accurately timed delivery of dopaminergic medications from the stomach to their site of absorption in the small intestine (44). In such individuals, relatively minor fluctuations in gastric emptying rate can significantly disrupt PD control. There is some evidence that prokinetic medications may help to smooth control in these patients (37, 45).

It is surprising that the true status of gastric neuromuscular function in PD remains unclear and that there have been few if any appropriately performed studies of any parameter of gastric motor function in this patient population. Those that have been performed have either not employed appropriate controls or have failed to correct for the possible influence of dopaminergic medications. A study using the noninvasive technique of electrogastrography also indicated that gastric motility may be disturbed in PD, irrespective of dopaminergic therapy (46). Subsequent studies failed, however, to find this noninvasive approach a useful predictor of symptoms (47, 48). Further studies are clearly needed.

Although delayed small bowel transit (49) as well as severe disruption of small intestinal motility, resulting in pseudo-obstruction and ileus, have been reported in PD, we know very little regarding small bowel motility in this disease.

CONSTIPATION, DIFFICULT DEFECATION, AND COLONIC AND ANORECTAL FUNCTION

Constipation and difficult defecation are the most common gastrointestinal symptoms among patients with established PD (19). Symptom assessments and formal tests of colonic and anorectal function suggest that both delayed colonic transit (i.e., abnormal motility of the colon) and defecatory dysfunction (i.e., dysco-ordinate activity in the pelvic floor and sphincter muscles) contribute to symptom development (19, 50, 51). Furthermore, many patients exhibit features of both abnormalities. Slow-transit constipation may progress to megacolon and even fatal perforation.

Formal studies of the defecatory mechanism in these patients suggest that an inability to relax the puborectalis muscle on straining, and thereby "straighten out" the anal canal to facilitate defecation, is a common and important contributing feature (21, 50, 52). A failure to generate sufficient abdominal pressure on straining (50) will contribute to ineffective defecation and lead to increased postdefecatory residuals. Direct electromyographic recordings from the sphincter muscles in affected patients have demonstrated that, although the function of the internal anal sphincter is preserved, the external sphincter, puborectalis, and levator ani muscles are stimulated and may "paradoxically" contract as the patient attempts to defecate (53–55). These abnormalities appear similar to those described in the urinary tract in PD.

THE PATHOPHYSIOLOGY OF GASTROINTESTINAL DYSFUNCTION IN PARKINSON'S DISEASE: AVAILABLE EVIDENCE AND FUTURE PROSPECTS

In the past, gastrointestinal symptoms in PD were largely ascribed to side effects of antiparkinsonian medications, inactivity, and dietary changes. It now appears unlikely that, apart from inducing nausea and vomiting, dopaminergic medications have a central role in the pathogenesis of gastrointestinal dysfunction in PD. The balance of evidence now suggests that most gastrointestinal symptoms reflect the direct involvement of parts of the gastrointestinal tract or their central control mechanisms by the primary disease process. Dysphagia resulting from lingual tremor or impaired opening of the upper esophageal sphincter and obstructive defecation consequent upon an impaired puborectalis response to straining appear to be based on disturbances in skeletal muscle function analogous to other, better recognized manifestations of this disease process. Some (19, 40) but by no means all (31, 35, 43, 51) studies were able to correlate the prevalence and severity of these symptoms to the severity and duration of disease and to parallel disease activity in those with prominent "on"-"off" fluctuations (19, 43, 47). Furthermore, the response of these symptoms to dopaminergic therapy has been either disappointing or entirely absent (25, 56). The basis for this paradox remains unexplained.

Skeletal muscle involvement cannot explain gastrointestinal symptoms originating from most of the gastrointestinal tract, lined as it is by smooth muscle and controlled by the enteric and autonomic nervous systems. Autonomic dysfunction could certainly play a role, given its prevalence in PD and its prominence in some PD-related syndromes such as the Shy-Drager syndrome. Relationships between autonomic dysfunction and gastrointestinal dysfunction in PD have not been examined directly.

Evidence has accumulated to suggest a more direct involvement of the gastrointestinal tract in PD. Lewy bodies have been identified in autonomic neurons supplying the gastrointestinal tract (57) as well as in the enteric nervous system (ENS) of the esophagus and colon (58, 59). Furthermore, Singaram and colleagues have documented severe depletion of dopaminergic neurons in the colon in a small number of patients with PD and severe constipation (60). Further studies are needed to delineate the extent of dopamine depletion in the ENS and to define its relationship to symptoms and motor dysfunction in affected PD patients. It is tempting to speculate that further studies of the ENS may provide valuable insights into the basic mechanisms of disease initiation and progression in PD. The ENS could serve as a window to the central nervous system (61).

The gastrointestinal tract has also been implicated in a theory pointing to infection in the etiology of PD (62), noting the detection of Lewy bodies in the dorsal motor nucleus of the vagus (DMV) prior to their appearance in the substantia nigra, Braak postulated the retrograde transport of an infectious agent from the intestine to the central nervous system. In support of this hypothesis, the same group went on to document the parallel occurrence of α-synuclein intranuclear inclusions, analogous to those that define Lewy bodies in the central nervous system, in neurons of both Meissner's and Auerbach's plexus from the stomach; all patients studied had inclusions in the DMV and ENS; only those with more advanced disease had inclusions in the substantia nigra, mesocortex or neocortex (63). Others have proposed an association with *Helicobacter* infection, either active or past (64–67); although eradication of this organism has been reported to result in symptomatic improvement, this may relate to improved dopaminergic absorption (68) rather than to a direct effect on the disease process per se.

MANAGEMENT OF GASTOINTESTINAL COMPLICATIONS IN PARKINSON'S DISEASE

Few studies have directly addressed the therapy of gastrointestinal symptoms in PD. Those that have examined the symptomatic response to dopaminergic therapy among PD patients with dysphagia have produced disappointing results. For patients with dysphagia, emphasis must be placed, in the first instance, on maneuvers designed to promote efficient deglutition and minimize the risk of aspiration. If aspiration has occurred and is likely to recur, alternate routes of nutrition may need to be considered. Although a percutaneous, endoscopically placed gastrostomy (PEG) may provide an acceptable and safe alternative route for the provision of nutrients and will avoid the need for intravenous access and total parenteral nutrition, it is equally important to recognize that this approach will not prevent aspiration and could promote aspiration in the patient with gastroparesis or gastroesophageal reflux disease. If aspiration is to be avoided in this situation, more distal access routes, such as a jejunostomy, must be employed. A variety of nonpharmacologic approaches and maneuvers have been recommended for the management of oropharyngeal dysphagia in PD; none has been subjected to a randomized controlled clinical trial (69). With respect to sialorrhea, however, a recent randomized controlled study reported good results following the direct injection of botulinum toxin into the parotid and submandibular glands (70).

Nausea and vomiting may present a formidable therapeutic challenge in PD. Metoclopramide and phenothiazines should not be used because of their propensity to cause or exacerbate parkinsonian symptoms. Cisapride, a prokinetic devoid of a central antiemetic action, may accelerate gastric emptying but has not been shown to alleviate nausea and vomiting in this patient population; in any case, it has been withdrawn from most countries because of concerns regarding possible cardiac toxicity. The peripheral dopamine antagonist domperidone, which is not available in the United States, would appear to be the ideal alternative given that it does not cross the blood-brain barrier, yet it is both an antiemetic and a prokinetic. Limited studies support its efficacy, not only as an antiemetic but also as a useful adjunct to dopaminergic therapy in those who may be experiencing impaired delivery of dopaminergic medications to the intestine (37, 38). In patients experiencing nausea and vomiting from levodopa, the use of additional carbidopa (Lodosyn) can be helpful. Tablets contain 25 mg of carbidopa, and one tablet with each levodopa dose may be sufficient to alleviate these adverse symptoms.

The management of constipation and difficult defecation begins with the exclusion of other causes of these symptoms, particularly depression. Given the increased prevalence of depression among patients with PD and the frequency with which elderly patients with depression present with lower gastrointestinal symptoms, this disorder needs to be considered and sought for. The management of constipation can often prove difficult. Although simple measures, such as increasing fluid intake and the ingestion of dietary fiber (71), may prove helpful in some patients, many continue to be symptomatic; some, especially those with difficult defecation, are poorly tolerant of conventional laxative approaches. Few therapeutic strategies have been subjected to formal clinical trials in the PD patient with constipation. There are limited data to suggest efficacy for psyllium (72) and cisapride (73, 74) in those with slow-transit constipation. Newer prokinetics, such as tegaserod or mosapride, offer promise but have not been widely investigated in PD (75). Short-term studies in a small number of patients provide some evidence that the potent dopaminergic agent apomorphine may improve anorectal and pelvic floor co-ordination and promote evacuation (76). A similar approach has been adopted among PD patients with problems with micturition. One approach that we have found helpful is the use of polyethylene glycol–based solutions as laxatives. These agents, commonly used in large volume for bowel cleansing prior to barium enema studies and colonoscopy, are administered on a daily basis in much smaller volumes and increased until a regular soft stool is obtained (77). This approach is generally well tolerated and is usually not complicated by the distention and bloating associated with many osmotic agents. It is important to emphasize that, in the patient with severe constipation, considerable emphasis must be placed on achieving regular evacuation by whatever means. In this way silent progression to impaction, megacolon, and perforation may be avoided (78–81).

In non-PD patients with disturbed defecation and similar abnormalities in anal sphincter/pelvic floor coordination, biofeedback has proved effective. This strategy has not been assessed in PD and may be difficult to achieve, given the prevalence of cognitive dysfunction and significant physical impairment associated with this disease. In one small study, the injection of botulinum toxin into the puborectalis muscle resulted in improved defecatory function in 10 of 18 PD patients with outlet-type constipation (82).

CONCLUSION

Gastrointestinal symptoms are common in patients with established PD, may precede the appearance of overt neurologic symptoms, and may represent a major challenge to the patient, family, and health care providers. The nature of the gastrointestinal symptoms truly associated with PD has been considerably clarified and the prominence of disturbed swallowing and difficult defecation has become ever more evident (84). Although many descriptive studies attest to the frequency and implications of gastrointestinal dysfunction in PD, the precise pathogenesis of these symptoms remains to be clearly elucidated; the balance of evidence currently supports the direct involvement of the gastrointestinal tract by the PD process. However, correlations between tests of gastrointestinal function and PD severity and even gastrointestinal symptomatology are often tenuous, and these symptoms rarely respond to dopaminergic agents. Nevertheless, studies suggesting the direct involvement of the ENS by the PD process are particularly intriguing. There are few trials of any therapeutic modality in the management of the PD patient with gastrointestinal symptoms, and therapy remains largely empiric. Further studies are urgently required. In the meantime, the clinician should remain alert to the importance of gastrointestinal dysfunction in this common degenerative neurologic disease and should be aware of relatively simple management strategies that may serve to avoid complications and significantly alleviate distress.

References

1. Goyal RK, Hirano I. Mechanisms of disease: The enteric system. *N Engl J Med* 1996; 334:1106–1115.
2. Mayer EA, Gebhart GF. Basic and clinical aspects of visceral hyperalgesia. *Gastroenterology* 1994; 107:271–293.
3. Morrell RM. The neurology of swallowing, In: Groher ME (ed). *Dysphagia and Management*. New York: Butterworths, 1984:12–18.
4. Diamant N. Firing up the swallowing mechanism. *Nature Med* 1996; 2:1190–1191.
5. Wood, JD, Schultz SG eds. Malagelada J-R, Azpiroz F. Determinants of gastric emptying and transit in the small intestine. In: *Handbook of Physiology*, 2nd ed. *The Gastrointestinal System*. Vol. 1, Part 2. Washington DC: American Physiological Society, 1989:909–938.
6. Quigley EMM. Gastric motor and sensory function and dysfunction. In: Feldman M, Friedman LS, Brandt LJ (eds). *Sleisenger and Fordtran's Gastrointestinal and Liver Disease*, 8th ed. Philadelphia: Elsevier Science, 2006.
7. Quigley EMM. Colonic motility and colonic function. In: Pemberton JH, Swash M, Henry MM (eds). *The Pelvic Floor. Its Function and Disorders*. Philadelphia: Saunders, 2002:84–93.
8. Parkinson J. *An Essay on the Shaking Palsy*. London: Whittingham and Rowland, 1817.
9. Siddiqui MF, Rast S, Lynn MJ, et al. Autonomic dysfunction in Parkinson's disease: A comprehensive symptom survey. *Parkinsonism Relat Disord* 2002; 8:277–284.
10. Pfeiffer RF. Gastrointestinal dysfunction in Parkinson's disease. *Lancet Neurol* 2003; 2: 107–116.
11. Chaudhuri KR, Healy DG, Scahpira AH, et al. Non-motor symptoms of Parkinson's disease: diagnosis and management. *Lancet Neurol* 2006; 5:235–245.
12. Eadie MJ, Tyrer JH. Alimentary disorder in parkinsonism. *Aust Ann Med* 1965; 14: 13–22.
13. Logemann JA, Blonksy ER, Boshes B. Dysphagia in parkinsonism *JAMA* 1975; 231: 69–70.
14. Bushman M, Dobmeyer SM, Leeker L, et al. Swallowing abnormalities and their response to treatment in Parkinson's disease. *Neurology* 1989; 39:1309–1314.
15. Logemann J, Blonsky ER, Boshes B. Lingual control in Parkinson's disease *Trans Am Neurol Assoc* 1973; 98:276–278.
16. Calne DB, Shaw DG, Spiers ASD, et al. Swallowing in parkinsonism *Br J Radiol* 1970; 43:456–457.
17. Palmer ED. Dysphagia in parkinsonism. *JAMA* 1974; 229:1349.
18. Edwards LL, Quigley EMM, Pfeiffer RF. Gastrointestinal dysfunction in Parkinson's disease: Frequency and pathophysiology. *Neurology* 1992; 42:726–732.
19. Edwards LL, Pfeiffer RF, Quigley EMM, et al. Gastrointestinal symptoms in Parkinson's disease. *Mov Disord* 1991; 6:151–156.
20. Edwards LL, Quigley EMM, Hofman R, et al. Gastrointestinal symptoms in Parkinson's disease: 18-month follow-up study. *Mov Disord* 1993; 8:83–86.
21. Edwards LL, Quigley EMM, Harned RK, et al. Characterization of swallowing and defecation in Parkinson's disease. *Am J Gastroenterol* 1994; 89:15–25.
22. Sakakibara R, Shinotoh H, Uchiyama T, et al. Questionnaire-based assessment of pelvic organ dysfunction in Parkinson's disease. *Auton Neurosci* 2001; 92:76–85.
23. Ueki A, Otsuka M. Life style risks of Parkinson's disease: Association between decreased water intake and constipation. *J Neurol* 2004; 251(Suppl 7):VII18–VII23.
24. Abbott RD, Petrovitch H, White LR, et al. Frequency of bowel movements and the future risk of Parkinson's disease. *Neurology* 2001; 57:456–62.
25. Ali GN, Wallace KI, Schwartz R, et al. Mechanisms of oral-pharyngeal dysphagia in patients with Parkinson's disease. *Gastroenterology* 1996; 110:383–392.
26. Born LJ, Harned RH, Rikkers LF, et al. Cricopharyngeal dysfunction in Parkinson's disease: Role in dysphagia and response to myotomy. *Mov Disord* 1996; 11:53–58.
27. Leopold NA, Kagel MC. Laryngeal deglutition movement in Parkinson's disease. *Neurology* 1997; 48:373–376.
28. Leopold NA, Kagel MC. Pharyngo-esophaegal dysphagia in Parkinson's disease. *Dysphagia* 1997; 12:11–18.
29. Johnston BT, Castell JA, Stumacher S, et al. Comparison of swallowing function in Parkinson's disease and progressive supranuclear palsy. *Mov Disord* 1997; 12:322–327.
30. Nagaya M, Kachi T, Yamada T, et al. Videofluoroscopic study of swallowing in Parkinson's disease. *Dysphagia* 1998; 13:95–100.
31. Ertekin C, Tarlaci S, Aydogdu I, et al. Electrophysiological evaluation of pharyngeal phase of swallowing in patients with Parkinson's disease. *Mov Disord* 2002; 17:942–949.
32. Volonte MA, Porta M, Comi G. Clinical assessment of dysphagia in early phases of Parkinson's disease. *Neurol Sci* 2002; 23(Suppl 2):S121–S122.
33. Byrne KG, Pfeiffer RF, Quigley EMM. Gastrointestinal dysfunction in Parkinson's disease. A report of clinical experience at a single center. *J Clin Gastroenterol* 1994; 19:11–16.
34. Bassotti G, Germani U, Pagliaricci S, et al. Esophageal manometric abnormalities in Parkinson's disease. *Dysphagia* 1998; 13:28–31.
35. Castell JA, Johnston BT, Colcher A, et al. Manometric abnormalities of the esophagus in patients with Parkinson's disease. *Neurogastroenterol Motil* 2001; 13:361–364.
36. Johnston BT, Colcher A, Li Q, et al. Repetitive proximal esophageal contractions: A new manometric finding and a possible further link between Parkinson's disease and achalasia. *Dysphagia* 2001; 16:186–189.
37. Soykan I, Sarosiek I, Schifflet J, et al. The effect of chronic oral domperidone therapy on gastrointestinal symptoms and gastric emptying in patients with Parkinson's disease. *Mov Disord* 1997; 12:952–957.

38. Evans MA, Broe GA, Triggs EJ, et al. Gastric emptying rate and the systemic availability of levodopa in the elderly parkinsonian patient. *Neurology* 1981; 31:1288–1294.

39. Goetze O, Wierczorek J, Mueller T, et al. Impaired gastric emptying of a solid test meal in patients with Parkinson's disease using ^{13}C-sodium octonoate breath test. *Neurosci Let* 2005; 375:170–173.

40. Goetze O, Nikodem AB, Wiezcorek J, et al. Predictors of gastric emptying in Parkinson's disease. *Neurogastroenterol Motil* 2006; 18:369–375.

41. Djaldetti R, Baron J, Ziv I, et al. Gastric emptying in Parkinson's disease: Patients with and without response fluctuations. *Neurology* 1996; 46:1051–1054.

42. Thomaides T, Karapanayiotides T, Zoukos Y, et al. Gastric emptying after semi-solid food in multiple system atrophy and Parkinson's disease. *J Neurol* 2005; 252:1055–1059.

43. Hardoff R, Sula M, Tamir A, et al. Gastric emptying and gastric motility in patients with Parkinson's disease. *Mov Disord* 2001; 16:1041–1047.

44. Kurlan R, Rothfield KP, Woodward WR, et al. Erratic gastric emptying of levodopa may cause "random" fluctuations of parkinsonian mobility. *Neurology* 1988; 38:419–421.

45. Djaldetti R, Koren M, Ziv I, et al. Effect of cisapride on response fluctuations in Parkinson's disease. *Mov Disord* 1995; 10:81–84.

46. Soykan I, Lin Z, Bennett JP, et al. Gastric myoelectrical activity in patients with Parkinson's disease: Evidence of a primary gastric abnormality. *Dig Dis Sci* 1999; 44:927–931.

47. Naftali T, Gadoth N, Huberman M, et al. Electrogastrography in patients with Parkinson's disease. *Can J Neurol Sci* 2005; 32:82–86.

48. Chen CL, Lin HH, Chen SY, et al. Utility of electrogastrography in differentiating Parkinson's disease with or without gastrointestinal symptoms: A prospective controlled study. *Digestion* 2005; 71:187–191.

49. Davies KN, King D, Billington D, et al. Intestinal permeability and orocaecal transit time in elderly patients with Parkinson's disease. *Postgrad Med J* 1996; 72:164–167.

50. Sakakibara R, Odaka T, Uchiyama T, et al. Colonic transit time and rectoanal videomanometry in Parkinson's disease. *J Neurol Neurosurg Psychiatry* 2003; 74: 268–272.

51. Bassotti G, Maggio D, Battaglia E, et al. Manometric investigation of anorectal function in early and late stage Parkinson's disease. *J Neurol Neurosurg Psychiatry* 2000; 68:768–770.

52. Ashraf W, Pfeiffer RF, Quigley EMM. Anorectal manometry in the assessment of anorectal function in Parkinson's disease: A comparison with chronic idiopathic constipation. *Mov Disord* 1004; 9:655–663.

53. Ashraf W, Wszolek ZK, Pfeiffer RF, et al. Anorectal function in fluctuating (on-off) Parkinson's disease: Evaluation by combined anorectal manometry and eclectromyography. *Mov Disord* 1009; 10:650–657.

54. Mathers SE, Kempster PA, Swash M, et al. Constipation and paradoxical puborectalis contraction in anismus and Parkinson's disease: A dystonic phenomenon? *J Neurol Neurosurg Psychiatry* 1988; 51:1503–1507.

55. Mathers SE, Kempster PA, Law PJ, et al. Anal sphincter dysfunction in Parkinson's disease. *Arch Neurol* 1989; 46:1061–1064.

56. Hunter PC, Crameri J, Austin S, et al. Response of parkinsonian swallowing dysfunction to dopaminergic stimulation. *J Neurol Neurosurg Psychiatry* 1997; 63:579–583.

57. Wakabayashi K, Takahashi H, Ohama E, et al. Lewy bodies in the visceral autonomic nervous system in Parkinson's disease. In: Narabayashi H, Yanagisawa N, Mizuno Y (eds). *Parkinson's Disease. From Basic Research to Treatment (Advances in Neurology, Vol 60)*. New York: Raven Press, 1993:609–612.

58. Kupsky WJ, Grimes MM, Sweeting J, et al. Parkinson's disease and megacolon: Concentric hyaline inclusions (Lewy bodies) in enteric ganglion cells. *Neurology* 1987; 37:1253–1255.

59. Wakabayashi K, Takahashi H, Ohama E, et al. Parkinson's disease: An immunohistochemical study of Lewy body–containing neurons in the enteric nervous system. *Acta Neuropathol* 1990; 79:581–583.

60. Singaram C, Ashraf W, Gaumnitz EA, et al. Dopaminergic defect of enteric nervous system in Parkinson's disease patients with chronic constipation. *Lancet* 1995; 346: 861–864.

61. Quigley C, EMM. Epidemiology and pathophysiology of gastrointestinal manifestations in Parkinson's disease. In: Corazziari (ed). *Neurogastroenterology*. Berlin: deGruyter, 1996:167–178.

62. Braak H, Rub U, Gai WP, et al. Idiopathic Parkinson's disease: Possible routes by which vulnerable neuronal types may be subject to neuroinvasion by an unknown pathogen. *J Neurol Transm* 2003; 110:517–536.

63. Braak H, de Vos, RAI, Bohl J, et al. Gastric α-synuclein immunoreactive inclusions in Meissner's and Auerbach's plexus in cases staged for Parkinson's disease-related brain pathology. *Neurosci Lett* 2006; 396:67–72.

64. Dobbs RJ, Dobbs SM, Weller C, et al. Role of chronic infection and inflammation in the gastrointestinal tract in the etiology and pathogenesis of idiopathic parkinsonism. Part 1: Eradication of *Helicobacter pylori* in cachexia of idiopathic parkinsonism. *Helicobacter* 2005; 10:267–275.

65. Bjarnason IT, Charlett A, Dobbs RJ, et al. Role of chronic infection and inflammation in the gastrointestinal tract in the etiology and pathogenesis of idiopathic parkinsonism. Part 2: Response of facets of clinical idiopathic parkinsonism to *Helicobacter pylori* eradication. A randomized, double-blind, placebo-controlled efficacy study. *Helicobacter* 2005; 10:276–287.

66. Weller C, Charlett A, Oxlade NL, et al. Role of chronic infection and inflammation in the gastrointestinal tract in the etiology and pathogenesis of idiopathic parkinsonism. Part 3: Predicted probability and gradients of severity of idiopathic parkinsonism based on *H. pylori* antibody profile. *Helicobacter* 2005; 10:288–297.

67. Weller C, Oxlade N, Dobbs SM, et al. Role of inflammation in the gastrointestinal tract in the etiology and pathogenesis of idiopathic parkinsonism. *FEMS Immunol Med Microbiol* 205; 44:129–135.

68. Pierantozzi M, Pietroiusti A, Brusa L, et al. *Helicobacter pylori* eradication and L-dopa absorption in patients with PD and motor fluctuations. *Neurology* 2006; 66:1824–1829.

69. Deane KH, Whurr R, Clarke CE, et al. Non-pharmacological therapies for dysphagia in Parkinson's disease. *Cochrane Database Syst Rev* 2001; (1):CD002816.

70. Ondo WG, Hunter C, Moore W. A double-blind placebo-controlled trial of botulinum B for sialorrhea in Parkinson's disease. *Neurology* 2004; 62:37–40.

71. Astarloa R, Mena MA, Sanchez V, et al. Clinical and pharmacokinetic effects of a diet rich in insoluble fiber on Parkinson's disease. *Clin Neuropharmacol* 1992; 15:375–380.

72. Ashraf W, Pfeiffer RF, Park F, et al. Constipation in Parkinson's disease: Objective assessment and response to psyllium. *Mov Disord* 1997; 12:946–951.

73. Jost WH, Schimrigk K. Cisapride treatment of constipation in Parkinson's disease. *Mov Disord* 1993; 8:339–343.

74. Jost WH, Schimrigk K. Long-term results with cisapride in Parkinson's disease. *Mov Disord* 1997; 12:423–425.

75. Liu Z, Sakakibara R, Odaka T, et al. Mosapride citrate, a novel 5-HT4 agonist and partial 5-HT3 antagonist, ameliorates constipation in parkinsonian patients. *Mov Disord* 2005 20:680–686.

76. Edwards LL, Quigley EMM, Harned RK, et al. Defecatory function in Parkinson's disease: Response to apomorphine. *Ann Neurol* 1993; 33:490–493.

77. Corazziari E, Badiali D, Bazzocchi G, et al. Long-term efficacy, safety, and tolerability of low daily doses of isomotic polyethylene glycol electrolyte balanced solution (PMF-100) in treatment of functional chronic constipation. *Gut* 2000; 46:522–526.

78. Lewitan A, Nathanson L, Slade WR Jr. Megacolon and dilatation of the small bowel in parkinsonism. *Gastroenterology* 1951; 17:367–374.

79. Rosenthal MJ, Marshall CE. Sigmoid volvolus in association with parkinsonism. Report of four cases. *J Am Geriatr Soc* 1987; 35:683–684.

80. Caplan LH, Jacobson HG, Rubinstein BM, et al. Megacolon and volvulus in Parkinson's disease. *Radiology* 1965; 85:73–79.

81. Bak MP, Boley SJ. Sigmoid volvulus in elderly patients. *Am J Surg* 1986; 151:71–75.

82. Cadeddu F, Bentivoglio AR, Brandara F, et al. Outlet type dysfunction in Parkinson's disease: Results of botulinum toxin treatment. *Aliment Pharmacol Ther* 2005; 22:997–1003.

83. Quigley EMM, Gastrointestinal dysfunction in Parkinson's disease. *Semin Neurol* 1996; 16:245–250.

11 Autonomic Dysfunction

Thomas C. Chelimsky

As understanding of Lewy body pathology evolves, it is becoming clear that Parkinson's disease (PD) should no longer be conceptualized as a disorder involving primarily motor pathways and secondarily other aspects of neural function. The major manifestations of this disorder in any individual are simply a function of the neuraxis localization of the Lewy body, which may involve the substantia nigra, the central and possibly peripheral autonomic centers, and the cortex. The observation that a sleep disorder precedes the onset of motor manifestations in some patients (1) and that autonomic dysfunction may come earlier underlines this view. It may be more useful to consider this disorder as a triad of dysautonomia/dyssomnia, motor dysfunction, and dementia and to assume that every patient will harbor some element of each, understanding that in individual patients one or more of these elements may well be imperceptible. It is my experience that (nonsleep) dysautonomia commonly precedes motor manifestations, although no epidemiologic studies have quantified this occurrence. The purpose of this chapter is to review the epidemiology, pathophysiology, diagnosis, and management of autonomic disturbances in Parkinson's disease.

IS DYSAUTONOMIA COMMON IN PARKINSON'S DISEASE?

Autonomic dysfunction is more prevalent in PD than commonly assumed. The exact prevalence of these disorders is difficult to determine owing to uncertainties in the measurement of the abnormality and in the attribution to the disease process. As an example of measurement uncertainty, one might assume that orthostatic hypotension (OH) would be fairly easy to detect through a simple set of vital signs performed in 2 positions. However, our findings (2) demonstrate that accurate detection required a tilt-table test rather than a simple stand, and major blood pressure drops may not occur until after 10 to 15 minutes in the upright position (3). Placing every patient with PD on a tilt table involves more cost and effort than a simple measurement of lying and standing vital signs and may mean that OH goes undetected. This becomes problematic given that patients with severe OH may report no symptoms at all until they experience a fall or an episode of syncope. Uncertain disease attribution occurs, for example, with bladder dysfunction, which is very common in both men and women in this age group without PD related, respectively, to prostatic hypertrophy and prior child delivery issues.

Nonetheless, a fair estimate of the prevalence of autonomic symptoms found a clinically significant impact on daily life ("a lot" or "very much") in 50% of 141 patients with PD. The major symptoms affecting PD patients "a lot" or "very much" were constipaton (PD vs. control 41% vs. 8%), orthostatic symptoms (53% vs. 0%), and bladder dysfunction (54% vs. 17%) (4). Another study using a 9-item questionnaire on 532 patients with PD detected a prevalence of constipation in 58%, orthostatic symptoms in 22%, and urinary dysfunction in 23% (5). This study excluded patients with Lewy body dementia and may have evaluated a population with more narrow motor-only PD. Surprisingly, this study found no correlation between duration of illness and severity of symptoms. Age and the presence of hypertension were the major predictors. This is not the only study to report this curious finding, which emphasizes the need to adequately evaluate patients for problems related to autonomic nervous system failure at every stage of the disease. OH may even precede the onset of motor symptoms by several years (1) and occurs in about 15% of patients at the onset of PD (6).

The combination of the higher than expected prevalence of OH in patients with PD, the difficulty in identifying OH by a simple standing pressure, and patients' nonreporting of symptoms typical of orthostasis—such as light-headedness or fainting—suggests that OH may result in a large burden of occult morbidity in this population. No study has directly examined how frequently major OH (e.g., drop to a systolic pressure of 70 mm Hg) occurs in the absence of patient awareness, but this is not an uncommon occurrence. Patients may simply report a fall. In one study of a catchment area of 180,000 patients, falls were the most common reason for admission (44 admissions) for 367 patients with PD over a 4-year period (7). Even patients without PD who fall have OH about one-quarter of the time (8) and half of cognitively normal individuals may not recall a faint that occurred 3 months earlier (9).

WHAT IS THE ETIOLOGY OF DYSAUTONOMIA IN PARKINSON'S DISEASE?

While one might have assumed that the origin of autonomic failure in PD is due to central nervous system failure in parallel with other parkinsonian disorders such as multiple system atrophy (MSA), this does not appear to be the case. Early studies found predominant involvement of sympathetic ganglia with Lewy bodies (10). A very extensive postmortem examination of the entire nervous system in patients with PD found Lewy body involvement in both central (hypothalamus, intermediolateral cell horn throughout the cord, vagal nuclei) and confirmed peripheral involvement in the sympathetic ganglia, enteric nervous system, and peripheral plexuses (11).

Growing evidence suggests that the predominant site of failure is the peripheral adrenergic system, with central nervous system involvement being much less clinically meaningful. There is, for example, no reduction in patients with PD compared to controls in the number of tyrosine hydroxylase–positive neurons in the rostral ventrolateral medulla, the primary brainstem nucleus for control of sympathetic pressor outflow (12). This contrasts sharply with the situation for MSA , where the authors found devastation of this nucleus. Cardiac radionuclide imaging provides another line of evidence suggesting peripheral nervous system involvement in PD. The heart is denervated early, even before autonomic testing becomes abnormal (13, 14). In addition, as baroreflex function deteriorates, cardiac denervation is much more prominent in PD than in MSA, where it remains almost normal (15). Radioactive fluorodopamine studies show similar results (16). These findings occur whether PD is sporadic or inherited (at least in the case of excess alpha-synuclein production) (17), suggesting that peripheral autonomic denervation is a common property inherent to the pathophysiology of PD regardless of the underlying etiology.

WHAT TESTS ARE USEFUL TO ASSESS AUTONOMIC FUNCTION IN PARKINSON'S DISEASE?

Patients with PD may present with a large number of complaints, some nonspecific, that suggest the presence of autonomic dysfunction. Common presentations include fatigue, falls, constipation, urinary urgency or dribbling, excessive sweating, or intolerance to hot environments. For unclear reasons, patients will seldom use the words "dizzy" or "light-headed" even in the presence of a severe drop in blood pressure. The first step in the evaluation process is to define the presence and degree of severity of autonomic dysfunction and whether there is occult OH . If formal autonomic testing is not available, then a tilt table test can provide the most critical information required for management.

Autonomic testing in most neurology labs involves 3 tests of cardiovascular autonomic function, and 1 or 2 tests of sudomotor sympathetic function. The tests of cardiovascular autonomic function establish which branches of the autonomic nervous system are affected (afferent, efferent sympathetic, efferent parasympathetic), while the tests of sweating localize any lesions in the neuraxis. The three most commonly performed cardiovascular studies are the cardiac response to deep breathing, the cardiac and vascular responses to the Valsava maneuver, and the cardiac and vascular responses to a 70-degree tilt table.

The cardiac response to deep breathing requires the subject to take 6 deep breaths in 1 minute (a 5-second deep breath in followed by a 5-second breath out) while heart rate is recorded. In normal individuals, the heart accelerates during inspiration and decelerates during expiration, presumably to fill the capacitance of the pulmonary bed that increases from 100 to about 400 mL as a result of full pulmonary expansion. The difference between the peak heart rate during inspiration and the trough heart rate during the ensuing expiration is averaged for the 5 best breaths and compared to age-based norms, which vary from a difference of about 25 beats per minute at age 12 to 5 beats per minute at age 80. As detailed in Table 11-1, this reflex requires both afferent and efferent signals that travel through the vagus nerve and is considered to be a test of cardiac parasympathetic function almost exclusively. It is one of the first cardiovascular autonomic abnormalities encountered in diabetic autonomic neuropathy (18), perhaps because of the length of the vagus and the length-dependent involvement of autonomic nerves in peripheral disorders. The timing of its appearance and prognostic implication has not been so clearly delineated in PD.

The cardiovascular response to the Valsalva maneuver provides a small window view of nearly the entire range of autonomic cardiovascular control. For 15 seconds, the patient holds 40 mm Hg with the mouth against a mercury column connected to a mouthpiece with a small air leak, preventing closure of the glottis. The pressure is translated into the intrathoracic cavity, essentially producing a sudden 40–mm Hg positive gradient or "dam" against which venous blood must still return. In humans venous return is facilitated by a very low intrathoracic pressure, usually between 5 and 10 mm Hg, and an increase to 40 mm Hg constitutes a hefty increase to be overcome. The cardiovascular system normally responds to this challenge through dramatic vasoconstriction accompanied by cardioacceleration (termed "phase II"). When the subject releases pressure after 15 seconds, a large volume of blood surges from the suddenly "undammed" venous pool, resulting in a bradycardia and vasodilation (termed "phase IV"). The maneuver is read as the ratio of the highest heart rate attained in phase II to the lowest attained in phase IV. Reduction in this ratio may result from either cardiac sympathetic or cardiac parasympathetic denervation, and the individual heart rates of each phase require perusal.

Although it is the simplest test of autonomic function from a mechanical perspective, the tilt-table test is probably the most complex to interpret. After blood pressure and heart rate have been recorded for 3 minutes in the supine position, the table is raised to a standing angle, usually around 70 degrees, while vital sign recording continues. A prolonged recording of around 30 to 40 minutes will clearly increase the yield of detection of significant OH (3) and is especially important in this population. In our lab, we perform a 30-minute tilt if the patient complains of dizziness or other potentially orthostatic problems without having lost consciousness or fallen and 40 minutes if they have ever lost consciousness or fallen.

Several rapid compensatory changes work during standing to maintain blood flow to the brain against gravity. It is easiest to conceptualize these events according to the physiology of a pump, considering (a) a preload or capacitance group, including the status of the venous system and available volume for venous return; (b) changes in the heart, the pump itself; and (c) an afterload or resistance group, relating mainly to arterial tone. The 3 cardiovascular vital signs bear a rough relation to each of these, with systolic pressure reflecting cardiac output and therefore the (a) preload factors, assuming a normal pump; while the heart rate reflects (b) activity and autonomic influence on the pump itself; and diastolic pressure is a manifestation of (c) arterioconstriction.

Standing triggers afferent information to flow from 2 main sources: the motor cortex communicates the intent to stand while the atrial low-pressure baroreceptor senses and conveys the resultant reduction in venous return to the right atrium. Upon receipt of this message, the integrating centers, the lateral catecholaminergic brainstem groups and the nucleus tractus solitarius, activate sympathetic fibers to produce vasoconstriction and cardioacceleration and also reduce cardiac parasympathetic flow from the dorsal motor nucleus of the vagus. The normal result is a slight drop (< 10 mm Hg) in systolic pressure, a slight increase in diastolic pressure (< 5 mm Hg), and a mild acceleration in heart rate (< 20 beats per minute). Due to the passive nature of the stimulus, a tilt study differs from standing in 2 main respects: premotor cortex has no opportunity to send the signal of intent to stand, and the active calf muscle pump cannot aid venous return. The tilt is therefore more likely to demonstrate an orthostatic deficit than is a simple stand.

Interpretation of the tilt study is based on distinction of three common patterns. In OH (the first graph in Figure 11-1), there is a gradual decline in both systolic and diastolic pressures with or without a compensatory increase in heart rate. This is the pattern most commonly encountered in PD. Blood pressure may not drop immediately; an extended study may be required to uncover more subtle abnormalities (3). The second pattern is that of a postural tachycardia syndrome (POTS) (the second graph in Figure 11-1), defined as an increase of 30 beats per minute or greater in heart rate in the first 10 minutes of the tilt study in the absence of sustained OH. In contrast to OH, which primarily reflects an inadequate signal for arterial constriction, POTS is generally thought to represent a loss of venous return to due venomotor impairment. It is rarely seen in PD and occurs most often younger women with secondary dysautonomias such as migraine headache, irritable bowel syndrome,

TABLE 11-1
Tests of Autonomic Function

Autonomic Test	Stimulus	Afferent Signal	Integrating Center	Efferent Signal	Response
Cardiac response to deep breathing	Six deep breaths per minute	Pulmonary stretch J-receptors through vagus nerve	Nucleus tractus solitarius	Dorsal motor nucleus of the vagus (DMNX) to vagus nerve	Cardioacceleration during inspiration
Valsalva maneuver	Hold 40 mm Hg pressure through mouth with open glottis for 15 s	Low-pressure atrial baroreceptors through vagus	Nucleus tractus solitarius	*Phase II:* 1. Inhibition of DMNX to ↑ HR 2. Excitation of catecholaminergic cell groups in the ventrolateral medulla to descending sympathetics exiting at T1 to vasoconstrict ↑HR *Phase IV:* Reverse of 1 and 2	*Phase II:* Cardioacceleration and narrowed pulse pressure *Phase IV:* Cardiodeceleration and widened pulse pressure
Tilt-table test	Patient supine for 3 min, then passively tilted up to 70 degrees	Low-pressure atrial baroreceptors through vagus	Nucleus tractus solitarius	1) Inhibition of DMNX to ↑ HR 2) Excitation of catecholaminergic cell groups in the ventrolateral medulla to descending sympathetics exiting at T1 to vasoconstrict	Mild increase in heart rate of 5–10 beats per minute, with mild reduction in systolic pressure 5–10 mm Hg, and mild increase in diastolic pressure of 5–10 mm Hg
Sudo-motor axon reflex test	2 mA for 5 min across a 10% ACh solution in outer of 2-chamber capsule	Sudomotor axon	None	Sudomotor axon (this is an axon reflex)	Sweat rate measured from inner chamber of 2-chamber capsule applied to skin
Thermo-regulatory sweat test	Person placed in 50°C, 50% humidity for 30 min with alizarin Red S indicator powder applied to the skin	Temperature sensors in the anterior hypothalamus and peripheral veins	Anterior hypothalamus	Descending projections from anterior and lateral hypothalamus to intermediolateral cell horn (neuron 1), followed by preganglionic spinal neurons which synapse 1-1 on postganglionic sudomotor axons	Geographic area of sweating on skin and sweat rate quantitation of sweat rates

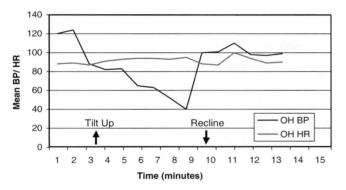

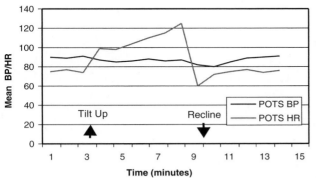

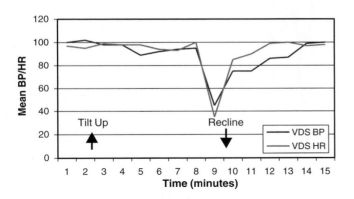

FIGURE 11-1

(A) 90 Degree tilt table in OH, (B) 90 degree tilt table in POTS, and (C) 90 degree tilt table in VDS,

or fibromyalgia. Occasionally, it occurs as a harbinger of orthostatic insufficiency in PD and may reflect venomotor (rather than arteriomotor) denervation.

The last pattern (the third graph in Figure 11-1) depicts reflex syncope where pressure drops rapidly to undetectable levels, often associated with a drop in heart rate. A propensity to syncope may be present in half the population (19). Such a pattern may occur in isolation, but is so common that it is frequently superimposed on OH or POTS or may have been an occult propensity throughout the patient's life and only became manifest with the appearance of PD. This is relevant to the management of syncope in patients with OH and PD, who may require agents that prevent syncope in addition to those that increase pressure.

The tests of sweating provide helpful information regarding the neuraxis localization of a pathologic process. The quantitative sudomotor axon reflex test (20) specifically tests the integrity of the postganglionic sudomotor axon and is the primary test of peripheral autonomic nervous system function. It is performed by iontopheresis of 10% acetylcholine (Ach) across the skin for 10 minutes in the outer chamber of a dual concentric chamber capsule, while the consequent sweat output is recorded from the inner chamber (see Figure 11-1).

In contrast, the thermoregulatory sweat test provides information regarding the entire sudomotor system, including afferent thermal sensing, brainstem integration, and efferent pathways comprising a first-order neuron from the anterior hypothalamus to the intermediolateral (IML) cell horn, a second-order neuron from the IML to a sympathetic ganglion, and the final third-order neuron, the postganglionic axon, the one tested by the Quantitative Sudomotor Axon Reflex Test QSART. These two tests localize the neuraxis lesion, as shown in Table 11-2.

The thermoregulatory sweat test will generally demonstrate loss of sweating in a distal distribution (hands and feet) in a process involving the peripheral autonomic nerves, whereas it may show a "central pattern" with preservation in the hands and feet and loss elsewhere when the central nervous system is involved. However, this is only relative, as previously reported (Figure 11-2); other patients have a peripheral pattern. Further, autonomic testing is incapable of distinguishing MSA from PD (21).

In attempting to distinguish these two disorders, the test with the best evidence-based track record is radionuclide imaging of the noradrenergic terminals in the heart using [123I]-metaiodobenzylguanidine (123I-MIBG) or 6-[18-F]-fluorodopamine (22, 23). PD patients demonstrate near total loss of noradrenergic terminals, likely related to the presence of Lewy bodies in sympathetic ganglia and the production of a postganglionic lesion, while MSA patients consistently demonstrate preservation of postganglionic innervation.

Pupillometry will often show abnormalities of either sympathetic or parasympathetic function, providing information potentially useful specific to an individual patient.

TABLE 11-2		
Localization of Neuraxis Pathophysiology via Sweat Tests		
TEST	PNS (POSTGANGLIONIC LESION)	CNS
QSART	Reduced response	Normal
TST	Reduced in hands and feet	Inverted
QSART = quantative sudomotor avon reflex test. TST = thermoregulatory sweat test.		

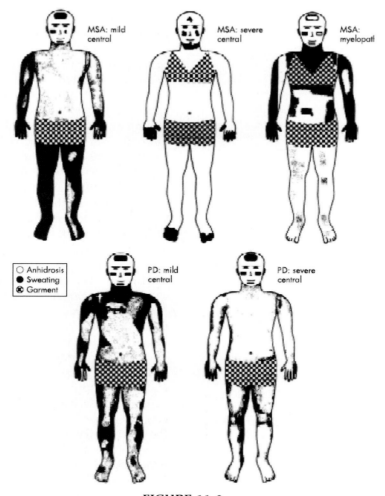

FIGURE 11-2

Thermoregulatory sweat tests in PD and MSA (21).

Although abnormalities are more prevalent in peripheral disorders, no pattern has been shown to consistently distinguish different entities (24). A report suggests that the difference between the response to instillation of cocaine and that to instillation of phenylephrine may have some value in distinguishing PD from MSA. In this report, patients were distinguished on the basis of MIBG scan results. PD patients with a primarily postganglionic pathology, demonstrated a greater response to phenylephrine (supersensitivity) and less response to a block of norepinephrine reuptake. Just the opposite held true for patients with MSA. A difference of > 1 mm between the two responses was consistent with a diagnosis of PD (25).

WHY OBTAIN AUTONOMIC TESTING?

Autonomic testing in PD has great utility. Probably its greatest usefulness is in the patient who falls. It is critical to understand that patients with PD who fall often have no cognitive awareness that they have an orthostatic drop in pressure and may not even realize that they are fainting until an observer provides this information. Thirty percent of cognitively normal patients above 70 years of age do not recall a fall witnessed 3 months earlier (26). Further, we found in our laboratory that almost half of those patients with profound OH (≥ 100 mm Hg drop in systolic pressure during tilt) have no recognizable orthostatic symptoms, and the remainder developed symptoms only very late in the study when pressure had dropped below 80/50 and they were nearly syncopal. In this patient population, orthostatic symptoms may not occur at all (let alone be recalled accurately). For these reasons, clinicians should employ a very low threshold for ordering autonomic testing (especially the tilt portion) in patients with PD or MSA.

A second reason to obtain autonomic testing is to exclude an occult superimposed (potentially treatable) peripheral autonomic disorder. Although axon reflex testing may be reduced in disorders involving the central nervous system (21, 27) and despite the fact that sympathetic ganglia contain Lewy bodies, it is unusual to see a total absence of sudomotor axon reflex responses in PD; such a finding usually signals another concomitant disorder, such as an immune etiology or B_{12} deficiency. During the last 4 years, we examined 4 patients with a parkinsonian syndrome and severe OH whose pressure nearly normalized after treatment with intravenous immunoglobulin. This response is presumably due to the presence of an underlying autonomic neuropathy indicated by the disproportionately low axon reflex responses. Finally, the presence of autonomic dysfunction signals a poorer prognosis and may indicate the need for earlier intervention.

TREATMENT OF AUTONOMIC DYSFUNCTION

Orthostasis

Orthostatic hypotension is defined as a sustained drop of more than 20 mm Hg in systolic blood pressure or more than 10 mm Hg in diastolic (28). However, in patients with PD, there can be much deeper drops in pressure on standing (sometimes more than 100 mm Hg), so that the standing systolic pressure may barely reach 70 to 80 mm Hg while the supine readings are either high (150/80) or very high (200/100). One can usually employ a stepwise approach beginning with nonpharmacologic methods and proceeding to medications, depending on the magnitude of the problem and the response to treatment.

Establishing Clear Numeric and Symptomatic Goals

Prior to embarking on any treatment, the physician and patient must agree on specific goals. These will depend on the level of supine hypertension as well as the drop in blood pressure with standing. One attempts to keep the standing systolic high enough for reasonable continuous function in the upright position for 15 to 30 minutes without allowing excessive supine pressures. A specific functional goal should accompany this plan; for example, shopping for so many minutes, doing the dishes, or gardening. For instance, in a patient who initially drops from 150/90 to 75/50 mm Hg over 5 minutes, one might aim for a standing systolic of 100 mm Hg for 15 to 20 minutes. Lying pressures should generally not often exceed 175/100 mm Hg. One can prohibit lying flat during the time of maximum effect of some medications to aid in this goal. It is critical to have the patient actively participate with these goals. The patient may use an automated blood pressure cuff to take readings once a day lying (or sitting only if supine pressures are too high) and standing about 1 hour after the morning medications. In addition, patients should measure the "standing time" along with the of vitals, defined as the amount of time they can stand without becoming severely light-headed or presyncopal. In patients who do not experience orthostatic symptoms, repeated pressure measurements must replace the sense of impending syncope.

Nonpharmacologic Methods

The cornerstone of nonpharmacologic treatment is dietary salt replacement. This can be done through high-salt foods (e.g., pickles, anchovies, etc.) or through salt tablets available at many sport stores or pharmacies or on the Internet. Total daily supplemental requirements vary from 2 g to as much as 8 g per day or more. A 24-hour urine sodium greater than 170 meq indicates adequate supplementation.

High-pressure stockings combined with an abdominal binder provide a second excellent means of increasing pressure. For optimal benefit to occur, hose should be (1) custom-fitted, (2) a high-pressure type (40 to 50 mmHg), and (3) at least thigh high if used with an abdominal binder, otherwise of abdominal height with a zipper. Patients with PD who find dressing a challenge may like the shorter hose combined with a binder better than the abdominal height.

Conditioning exercises that involve the general musculature as well as the vascular smooth muscles sustain and sometimes improve orthostatic endurance. A number of exercises and positions improve orthostatic tolerance at the time of their employment (29). Although the longer-term benefit of repeated performance of these exercises has not been demonstrated, we recommend that patients practice them twice per day. They include the following:

1. Crossed leg squeeze: While holding onto a chair for support, stand with the right leg crossed in front of left leg and squeeze the legs together for 45 seconds, then relax for 30 seconds. Repeat this set 3 times. This maneuver forces venous blood back into the thoracic cavity.
2. Toe raise: While raised up on the balls of your feet, contract your calf muscles for 10 seconds, then relax 5 seconds. Repeat this cycle 10 times.
3. Squat: Transfer from standing to squat. Remain squatting for 1 minute. Then slowly rise to a standing position again. Repeat 3 times.
4. Sustained handgrip: With arms above heart level, flex the biceps muscles and make fists. Hold for 15 seconds. Relax for 15 seconds. Repeat this cycle 5 times.
5. Self-tilt (30): Repeat tilt-table tests are unreliable and tend to show improved orthostatic tolerance with each repetition of the test. Ector and his colleagues found that repeat tilting does in fact produce significant improvement in orthostatic

tolerance (30). We ask patients to perform this by themselves at home by leaning against a wall at about 70 degrees in a carpeted area with no sharp edges (in case of faint). They should begin at their usual standing time (see "establishing clear numeric goals" above, usually 3 to 10 minutes), perform the exercise twice daily, and attempt to increase by 1 minute per week. They may combine this exercise with the measurement of orthostatic vital signs and of standing time.

The drinking of water profoundly affects blood pressure, raising it anywhere from 25 to 60 mm Hg almost immediately and lasting about an hour (31). This response likely reflects a neural reflex, since intravenous administration of similar volumes of fluid is ineffective. The pathways for this reflex remain unknown. Perhaps afferent vagal sensors signal stomach content to the nucleus tractus solitarius. Solutes such as salt or sugar reduce the impact of the reflex; the optimal stimulus is plain room temperature water. Volumes less than 16 ounces are less effective. From a practical perspective, this reflex provides an excellent window of pressure maintenance until medications or salt intake can take effect. Patients are advised to keep a large 16-oz glass of water at the bedside and to drink it immediately upon awakening in the morning or after a nap.

Both PD and OH lead to deconditioning due to loss of patient mobility and fear of fainting. Water jogging constitutes an excellent environment for exercise in patients with OH because the pressure of the water on the lower extremities and abdomen increases venous return and enhances arterial pressure in a manner similar to high-pressure hose. The water also provides an ideal resistive environment for strengthening and toning. Patients with PD and OH can exercise longer and more efficiently in this way. The water is also helpful for the treatment of low back pain, which is common. Ideally, patients go into water 5 ft deep and walk or jog for 20 minutes initially. This exercise time is gradually increased until they can do 45 minutes 3 times a week. Water jogging classes are often also available at fitness centers for people with arthritis.

Pharmacologic Methods

Pharmacologic approaches become necessary as orthostasis worsens, and several approaches may be required simultaneously. Agents are listed here by their primary operative mechanism, though this is not always known.

Direct alpha adrenoceptor activation. Direct alpha-adrenergic stimulation constitutes an obvious target for increasing blood pressure and substituting for the gradual reduction in available norepinephrine secreted by the postganglionic sympathetic neurons. Midodrine

is the cleanest of these agents (32). With a 4-hour duration of action, little penetration into the CNS, and relatively pure alpha-1 adrenoreceptor agonist selectivity, it provides an ideal profile for increasing blood pressure. By prescribing it only when the patient is planning to be active, one may avert supine hypertension. In younger patients, one can dose it 3 times per day, upon arising, 4 hours later, and 8 hours later to cover a 12-hour period. In older patients who take naps, dosing twice a day may provide more reasonable coverage, at 8 a.m. and 3 p.m., for example. Single-dose requirements vary from 1.25 to 20 mg, depending on response. Blood pressure logs are of great help in adjusting doses for optimal effect. One can expect a 25- to 50-mm Hg pressure rise from best dose.

Pseudoephedrine is another alpha agonist, although it is much less selective, having some affinity for beta receptors (resulting in tachycardia) as well as possessing some ability to cross the blood-brain barrier and procucing CNS stimulation. It is useful primarily when midodrine cannot be utilized (e.g., drug allergy, cost).

Indirect activation of alpha-adrenergic receptors. Several agents increase alpha-adrenergic activation through varying mechanisms. The theoretical advantage of these drugs over direct alpha-adrenergic agonists stems from the physiology of norepinephrine secretion. In the normal individual in the supine position, norepinephrine production is absent, while this agent is secreted in large amounts in the upright position, resulting in a doubling in venous effluent norepinephrine levels. Any drug that utilizes physiologic norepinephrine as a mediator of alpha-adrenoceptor stimulation will lower supine hypertension due to its absence in the supine position. This benefit has been demonstrated with pyridostigmine, but it is only theoretical with the other agents. For example:

1. Blockade of norepinephrine reuptake through amphetamine-related agents, such as methylphenidate, which can effectively increase blood pressure, at doses similar to those used for attention deficit disorder. The newer nonselective reuptake inhibitor antidepressant medications, such as duloxetine and venlafaxine, may also provide some benefit by a similar mechanism.
2. Blockade of the presynaptic autoregulatory alpha-2 receptor. Yohimbine (5 mg bid) will increase norepinephrine release and produce a pressor response.
3. Pyridostigmine is an activator of the sympathetic nervous system at the ganglionic level through inhibition of acetylcholinesterase and increased binding of acetylcholine to the postganglionic nicotinic receptor (33).
4. Fludrocortisone in low dose (0.1 mg per day) upregulates alpha-adrenergic receptors in the vasculature (34), thus sensitizing the vasoconstrictive response

to norepinephrine or to exogenous alpha-adrenergic agonists and increasing the effectiveness of the latter. Fludrocortisone can be an excellent complementary drug to any medication that ultimately has an effect on alpha-receptor–mediated vasoconstriction. In higher dose it produces its better-known aldosterone-like effect on the kidney, increasing overall blood volume.

Volume expansion. It should be emphasized that all of the agents discussed require the presence of salt supplementation for effectiveness. The better-known effect of fludrocortisone consists in volume expansion through an aldosterone-like mechanism. Doses required for this effect range from 0.1 to 0.4 mg per day. Potassium levels should be monitored or supplemented. The accompanying swelling of the lower extremity can be well managed with high-pressure hose.

Indomethacin (35) and other nonsteroidal agents can produce powerful volume expansion through a prostaglandin-mediated fluid-retention effect on the kidney. Finally, erythropoietin (36) provides pressor benefit when anemia is present with OH. Because of its expense, it is considered a measure of last resort.

Treatment sequence. The most common drug strategy depends on whether supine hypertension plays a dominant role in the clinical picture. If not, midodrine and fludrocortisone provide a naturally complementary pair of agents, since midodrine binds to alpha receptors, and fludrocortisone sensitizes them. A next step might consist of the addition of pyridostigmine or indomethacin to increase sympathetic outflow and provide additional volume. In this scenario, treatment would also include every nonpharmacologic method discussed above.

When supine hypertension is a major issue, treatment is mitigated so that hypertensives provide help during the daytime and periods of upright position while antihyperensives may play a role in reducing supine hypertension when the patient reclines. A typical combination might be midodrine (because of its limited time of action), modest doses of salt, and an angiotensin converting enzyme inhibitor at night. Measurements of supine and standing pressures daily—before and 1 hour after medications—critically guide therapy, much as with insulin and sugar levels.

Management of Bladder Dysfunction

Bladder dysfunction in PD may take both an upper or lower motor neuron form and may involve the sphincter, detrusor, or both. Classically, the upper motor neuron defect will produce urgency and frequency, while a lower motor neuron defect will produce retention with overflow incontinence if it involves the detrusor or leakage if it involves the sphincter. From a practical perspective, one determines whether the process poses any risk to the urinary system (through either recurrent urinary tract infections or hydronephrosis) by assessing a postvoid residual. Less than 100 mL residual of urine suggests conservative management and more implies more aggressive measures such as catheterization.

As in OH, physical training of the bladder and the pelvic floor can provide excellent benefit, which may outperform medications (37).

Pharmacologic treatment derives from the physiology of bladder innervation. Simplistically, the parasympathetic nervous system induces both detrusor and sphincter contraction through a muscarinic cholinergic mechanism, while the sympathetic nervous system produces urinary sphincteric contraction through an alpha-adrenergic mechanisim and detrusor relaxation through a beta-adrenergic receptor.

Thus, an overactive bladder will often respond to anticholinergically mediated detrusor relaxation. Many such agents exist: older oxybutinin (Ditropan) and tolteradine (Detrol) and newer agents such as darifenacin (Enablex), solifenacin (Vesicare), and trospium (Sanctura). In contrast, an underactive bladder with mild retention and a weak stream may benefit from a muscarinic cholinergic agonist such are bethanechol (Urecholine), available both orally and by injection. Importantly, cholinergic activation may also increase sphincter tone, and a postvoid residual should be checked after initial dosing.

Sphincteric dysfunction may necessitate an alpha-adrenergic antagonist, such as terazosin. However, one should exercise great caution with the use of this group of agents in patients with PD due to the potential exacerbation or unmasking of occult OH. The patient may not experience orthostatic symptoms even with very low pressures, in which case a pretreatment tilt study may provide valuable information. The converse of this must also be kept in mind: namely, that alpha-adrenergic agonists used in the treatment of OH may exacerbate sphincteric insufficiency and result in urinary retention.

Postvoid residuals in excess of 100 mL despite medical therapy will usually necessitate the institution of self-catheterization. In patients able to void partially, scheduling can occur 2 or 3 times in a day, immediately prior to sleep, upon arising, and in the middle of the day. Total incapacity to void will require a more rigorous catheterization regimen involving catheterization every 6 hours.

Bowel Issues

Bowel issues are common in patients with PD. In fact, constipation itself may constitute a risk factor for the development of PD (38) and occurs with far greater frequency in patients (approximately 60%) than in age-matched controls (20%) (39). A report suggests a benefit from tegasorod (40). Polyethylene glycol 17 g once daily can also provide effective treatment.

Diarrhea reflects a complication of primary constipation, either through a secondary bacterial overgrowth syndrome or due to impaction and liquid stool coursing around the impact area. A flat plate radiograph of the abdomen often provides the diagnosis.

Delayed gastric emptying occurs with great frequency (88% for solids) (41) but is less often clinicallyimportant clinically. Although metoclopramide may provide benefit, its use must be balanced with the risk of worsening PD motor symptoms.

Anal sphincteric dysfunction can occur, with fecal soiling and sometimes frank fecal incontinence. Patients' embarrassment and reticence in voicing these complaints spontaneously contributes to the underestimate of their frequency. It is important for physicians to elicit these problems directly. Fecal incontinence may result from fecal impaction; a flat plate of the abdomen assesses this possibility. The anal sphincter, like the urinary sphincter, receives major excitatory input from sympathetic alpha-adrenergic fibers. For this reason, phenylephrine 1% or 2% cream from a compounding pharmacy will constrict the sphincter for 3 to 4 hours (42, 43).

Thermoregulatory Complaints

The three main issues in this category brought to a physician by patients with PD are (a) hyperhidrosis, (b) inability to tolerate a hot environment, and (c) flushing. A thermoregulatory sweat test provides useful information regarding the location, severity, and pattern of a sweat disorder. Although often related to PD, other contributing factors, such as a vitamin deficiency or neuropathy, should be considered. Focal hyperhidrosis responds well to injections of botulinum toxin. Generalized hyperhidrosis often improves with clonidine 0.1 mg at bedtime or prior to the expected occurrence. Once again, caution regarding exacerbation of OH is advisable. Anticholinergics such as probanthine or glycopyrrolate may also be tried. Biofeedback may produce impressive results.

Poor tolerance to heat is more difficult to manage since it represents the absence of neurologic function rather than excess. One can try using procholinergic medications such as urecholine 10 mg by mouth. Fludrocortisone will sometimes restore some sweat function, but we have found this problem difficult to treat. Finally, flushing of the face or other parts of the body may benefit from measures similar to those taken with hyperhidrosis, including biofeedback, anticholinergics, and clonidine.

*R*eferences

1. Goldstein DS. Orthostatic hypotension as an early finding in Parkinson's disease. Clin Auton Res 2006; 16:46–54.
2. Lambrecht R, McNeeley K, Tusing L, Chelimsky T. Evaluation of a brief cardiovascular autonomic screen. Auton Neurosci 2007; 131:102–6.
3. Gibbons CH, Freeman R. Delayed orthostatic hypotension: a frequent cause of orthostatic intolerance. Neurology 2006; 67:28–32.
4. Magerkurth C, Schnitzer R, Braune S. Symptoms of autonomic failure in Parkinson's disease: prevalence and impact on daily life. Clin Auton Res 2005; 15:76–82.
5. Korchounov A, Kessler KR, Yakhno NN, Damulin IV, Schipper HI. Determinants of autonomic dysfunction in idiopathic Parkinson's disease. J Neurol 2005; 252:1530–6.
6. Bonuccelli U, Lucetti C, Del Dotto P, et al. Orthostatic hypotension in de novo Parkinson disease. Arch Neurol 2003; 60:1400–4.
7. Woodford H, Walker R. Emergency hospital admissions in idiopathic Parkinson's disease. Mov Disord 2005; 20:1104–8.
8. Ooi WL, Hossain M, Lipsitz LA. The association between orthostatic hypotension and recurrent falls in nursing home residents. Am J Med 2000; 108:106–11.
9. Shaw FE, Kenny RA. The overlap between syncope and falls in the elderly. Postgrad Med J 1997; 73:635–9.
10. Rajput AH, Rozdilsky B. Dysautonomia in Parkinsonism: a clinicopathological study. J Neurol Neurosurg Psychiatry 1976; 39:1092–100.
11. Tomomasa T, Kuroume T, Arai H, Wakabayashi K, Itoh Z. Erythromycin induces migrating motor complex in human gastrointestinal tract. Dig Dis Sci 1986; 31:157–61.
12. Benarroch EE, Schmeichel AM, Parisi JE. Involvement of the ventrolateral medulla in parkinsonism with autonomic failure. Neurology 2000; 54:963–8.
13. Courbon F, Brefel-Courbon C, Thalamas C, et al. Cardiac MIBG scintigraphy is a sensitive tool for detecting cardiac sympathetic denervation in Parkinson's disease. Mov Disord 2003; 18:890–7.
14. Oka H, Mochio S, Onouchi K, Morita M, Yoshioka M, Inoue K. Cardiovascular dysautonomia in de novo Parkinson's disease. J Neurol Sci 2006; 241:59–65.
15. Oka H, Mochio S, Yoshioka M, Morita M, Onouchi K, Inoue K. Cardiovascular dysautonomia in Parkinson's disease and multiple system atrophy. Acta Neurol Scand 2006; 113:221–7.
16. Goldstein DS, Holmes CS, Dendi R, Bruce SR, Li ST. Orthostatic hypotension from sympathetic denervation in Parkinson's disease. Neurology 2002; 58:1247–55.
17. Singleton JR, Smith AG, Bromberg MB. Increased prevalence of impaired glucose tolerance in patients with painful sensory neuropathy. Diabetes Care 2001; 24:1448–53.
18. Ewing DJ, Campbell IW, Clarke BF. The natural history of diabetic autonomic neuropathy. Quaterly Journal of Medicine 1980; 193:95.
19. Colman N, Nahm K, Ganzeboom KS, et al. Epidemiology of reflex syncope. Clin Auton Res 2004; 14 Suppl 1:9–17.
20. Low PA, Caskey PE, Tuck RR, Fealey RD, Dyck PJ. Quantitative sudomotor axon reflex in normal and neuropathic subjects. Ann Neurol 1983; 14:573–80.
21. Riley DE, Chelimsky TC. Autonomic nervous system testing may not distinguish multiple system atrophy from Parkinson's disease. J Neurol Neurosurg Psychiatry 2003; 74:56–60.
22. Goldstein D, Holmes C, Li S, Bruce S, Metman L, Cannon R. Cardiac sympathetic denervation in Parkinson disease. Ann Intern Med 2000; 133:338–47.
23. Braune S. The role of cardiac metaiodobenzylguanidine uptake in the differential diagnosis of parkinsonian syndromes. Clin Auton Res 2001; 11:351–5.
24. Bremner F, Smith S. Pupil findings in a consecutive series of 150 patients with generalised autonomic neuropathy. J Neurol Neurosurg Psychiatry 2006; 77:1163–8.
25. Sawada H, Yamakawa K, Yamakado H, et al. Cocaine and phenylephrine eye drop test for Parkinson disease. Jama 2005; 293:932–4.
26. Cummings S, Nevitt M, Kidd S. Forgetting falls: The limited accuracy of recall of falls in the elderly. J Am Geriatr Soc 1988; 36:613–6.
27. Cohen J, Low P, Fealey R, Sheps S, Jiang N-S. Somatic and autonomic function in progressive autonomic failure and multiple system atrophy. Ann Neurol 1987; 22:692–9.
28. Anonymous. Consensus statement on the definition of orthostatic hypotension, pure autonomic failure, and multiple system atrophy. The Consensus Committee of the American Autonomic Society and the American Academy of Neurology. Neurology 1996; 46:1470.
29. Bouvette CM, McPhee BR, Opfer-Gehrking TL, Low PA. Role of physical countermaneuvers in the management of orthostatic hypotension: efficacy and biofeedback augmentation. Mayo Clin Proc 1996; 71:847–53.
30. Reybrouck T, Heidbuchel H, Van De Werf F, Ector H. Long-term follow-up results of tilt training therapy in patients with recurrent neurocardiogenic syncope. Pacing Clin Electrophysiol 2002; 25:1441–6.
31. Jordan J, Shannon JR, Diedrich A, Black B, Robertson D, Biaggioni I. Water potentiates the pressor effect of ephedra alkaloids. Circulation 2004; 109:1823–5.
32. Jankovic J, Gilden JL, Hiner BC, et al. Neurogenic orthostatic hypotension: a double-blind placebo-controlled study with midodrine. Neurology 1991.
33. Singer W, Opfer-Gehrking TL, McPhee BR, Hilz MJ, Bharucha AE, Low PA. Acetylcholinesterase inhibition: a novel approach in the treatment of neurogenic orthostatic hypotension. J Neurol Neurosurg Psychiatry 2003; 74:1294–8.
34. Davies IB, Bannister RG, Sever PS, Wilcox CS. Fludrocortisone in the treatment of postural hypotension: altered sensitivity to pressor agents [proceedings]. Br J Clin Pharmacol 1978; 6:444P-5P.

35. Kochar MS, Itskovitz HD. Treatment of idiopathic orthostatic hypotension (Shy-Drager syndrome) with indomethacin. The Lancet 1978;May 13:1011–4.

36. Hoeldtke RD, Streeten DH. Treatment of orthostatic hypotension with erythropoietin. N Engl J Med 1993; 329:611–5.

37. Burgio KL, Locher JL, Goode PS, et al. Behavioral vs drug treatment for urge urinary incontinence in older women: a randomized controlled trial. Jama 1998; 280:1995–2000.

38. Abbott RD, Ross GW, White LR, et al. Environmental, life-style, and physical precursors of clinical Parkinson's disease: recent findings from the Honolulu-Asia Aging Study. J Neurol 2003; 250 Suppl 3:III30–9.

39. Kaye J, Gage H, Kimber A, Storey L, Trend P. Excess burden of constipation in Parkinson's disease: a pilot study. Mov Disord 2006; 21:1270–3.

40. Morgan JC, Sethi KD. Tegaserod in constipation associated with Parkinson disease. Clin Neuropharmacol 2007; 30:52–4.

41. Goetze O, Nikodem AB, Wiezcorek J, et al. Predictors of gastric emptying in Parkinson's disease. Neurogastroenterol Motil 2006; 18:369–75.

42. Carapeti EA, Kamm MA, Phillips RK. Randomized controlled trial of topical phenylephrine in the treatment of faecal incontinence. Br J Surg 2000; 87:38–42.

43. Cheetham MJ, Kamm MA, Phillips RK. Topical phenylephrine increases anal canal resting pressure in patients with faecal incontinence. Gut 2001; 48:356–9.

12 Sleep Disorders

Cynthia Louise Comella

S leep disturbance is a common yet underdiagnosed feature of Parkinson's disease (PD). The frequency of nighttime sleep disturbances in PD ranges from 60 to greater than 90% (1–3). Comparisons with age-matched controls show that PD patients have more complaints of fragmented sleep despite increased ingestion of nighttime soporific drugs (4). Excessive daytime sleepiness is also increased in PD compared to age-matched controls and is present in approximately 50% of mild to moderate PD (5–7). Sleep disturbances in PD may be primary to the disease itself or secondary to other factors, including medications, depression, and age-related disorders (8).

The frequent occurrence of PD-associated sleep disturbances is largely unrecognized by physicians, who tend to focus primarily on the motor symptoms. Detailed assessments of sleep and sleep disturbances are often omitted. Similarly, patients and caregivers frequently do not realize the importance of reporting sleep disturbances to their physicians unless the disturbance is severe. Without particular attention to sleep and sleep quality, many PD patients may unnecessarily endure treatable sleep disorders for long periods of time. An increased awareness and more aggressive treatment of nighttime problems of PD patients will promote a better quality of life for both patients and caregivers.

NOCTURNAL SLEEP DISTURBANCES IN PARKINSON DISEASE

Nocturnal sleep disturbance in PD may arise for different reasons. Frequently occurring complaints with associated causes are listed in Table 12-1. In early PD, subjective sleep quality does not differ from that of age-matched controls (9). Polysomnography in early PD however, may show an increase in muscle tone, abnormal movements during sleep, including increased blinking, blepharospasm, and tremor (10, 11), periodic limb movements of sleep, REM sleep behavior disorder, and respiratory abnormalities (12). These nocturnal disorders may increase as the disease progresses.

SLEEP FRAGMENTATION

Sleep fragmentation—characterized by frequent awakenings (2)—is very common in PD. A survey study in the United Kingdom reported that in 76% of 220 PD patients, nocturnal sleep was disrupted. Common causes include frequent urination, inability to turn over in bed, painful leg cramps, tremor, and foot dystonia (1).

TABLE 12-1

Sleep Disturbances in Parkinson's Disease

Due to nocturnal recurrence of PD symptoms
• Tremor
• Difficulty turning over in bed
• Rigidity
• Painful cramps

Due to conditions that are associated with PD
• Depression
• Anxiety
• Restless legs syndrome
• Periodic limb movement disorder
• Rapid eye movement (REM) behavior disorder
• Dementia
• Sleep apnea
• Nocturnal urination
• Excessive daytime napping

Due to medications used to treat PD
• Dopamine agonist induced insomnia
• Side effects of selegiline, anticholinergics, amantadine
• Vivid dreams, nightmares
• Hallucinations

Due to other conditions
• Medical conditions
  • Arthritis
  • Cardiac or pulmonary disorders
  • Reflux
  • Infections
  • Prostate hypertrophy
  • Pain not due to PD
• Medication used to treat medical conditions
• Withdrawal from sedative/hypnotics
• Emotional conditions
  • Stress
  • Anxiety
  • Reactions to major life events

Sleep fragmentation may be due to recurrent symptoms of PD, with increased difficulty rolling over, recurrence of tremor, and feelings of stiffness, restlessness, and discomfort. In advanced patients the effect of daytime medication wanes in the evening and night, with consequent increase in muscle rigidity, slowness, stiffness, and tremor. The diagnosis of nocturnal symptoms of PD as the cause of the sleep disturbance can often be made through a careful history.

Sleep fragmentation from recurrent PD symptoms may improve with nocturnal use of levodopa (13–15). In particular, sustained-release levodopa preparations may improve subjective reports of nocturnal awakenings (16). Bedtime administration of these preparations may also improve morning PD disability (15). Other methods to prolong levodopa levels that may be effective in reducing nighttime symptoms include administration of tolcapone or entacapone or catechol-O-methyl transferase (COMT)–inhibiting compounds. These drugs prolong the duration of action of levodopa by preventing enzymatic degradation of levodopa by COMT. COMT inhibitors would be effective only in patients receiving levodopa, having no effect on patients treated with other antiparkinsonian agents (17). Clinical experience has shown this to be an effective approach, although clinical trials addressing this issue have not been done. For patients who awaken in the early morning hours or who experience nocturnal PD symptoms only occasionally, using regular preparations of levodopa at the time of awakening may be preferable because of the drug's rapid onset of action. Typically, small doses (one-half to 1 tablet of immediate-release 25/100 carbidopa/levodopa) are needed.

Although the direct-acting dopamine receptor agonists have a prolonged half-life, the usefulness of these agents for the treatment of nocturnal PD symptoms has not been adequately evaluated. Some studies have found that nocturnal activity is greater in PD patients treated with levodopa or direct-acting dopamine agonists (18–20). Others have reported that although nocturnal sleep may improve with levodopa, daytime sleepiness may increase (12).

Sleep Fragmentation Due to Sleep Apnea

Sleep apnea may be central (airflow ceases due to absence of activation of respiratory muscles), obstructive (airflow is reduced or stopped despite respiratory muscle effort), or mixed (involving elements of both). Sleep apnea is common in elderly men and is a risk factor for stroke and death (21). Sleep apnea has been observed in approximately 20% to 40% of PD patients referred to a sleep laboratory who were assessed by polysomnography (22–25); it is predominantly obstructive sleep apnea syndrome (OSAS). In contrast to nonparkinsonian patients with OSAS, PD patients with OSAS typically have a normal body mass index (22, 26). Patients with sleep apnea may present solely with excessive daytime sleepiness, although caregivers may report loud snoring or gasping and choking during sleep. The presence of snoring is a predictor of daytime sleepiness in PD (27) and indicates that further assessment for apnea is needed. Obstructive sleep apnea is most effectively treated using continuous positive airway pressure (CPAP). Patients who are excessively sleepy during the day without a clear cause or those with a suggestive history should be evaluated for sleep apnea by polysomnography. In particular, patients diagnosed with multiple system atrophy (MSA) may have nocturnal apnea with glottic closure resulting in stridor (28, 29). This variant of obstructive sleep apnea responds poorly to CPAP; use of a tracheostomy at night may be lifesaving.

Sleep Fragmentation Due to Restless Legs Syndrome and Periodic Limb Movements During Sleep

Restless legs syndrome (RLS) is diagnosed through subjective report of an urge to move the legs, usually accompanied or caused by uncomfortable or unpleasant sensations in the legs. The urge to move worsens at rest, is relieved by movement, and occurs or worsens in the evening or night (30). Although RLS is common in PD (7, 27, 31), it may not be more frequent than in an age-matched population without PD (27) and may be related to the lower ferritin levels found in PD (31).

Treatment of RLS in PD has not been assessed. If serum ferritin levels are low, iron replacement can be considered and has been effective in reducing RLS symptoms in nonparkinsonian RLS patients (32). The treatment of choice for moderate to severe RLS symptoms is the use of direct dopamine receptor agonists (33). Levodopa, although an effective treatment for RLS, often leads to a worsening of RLS symptoms, with occurrence earlier in the day (augmentation) (34). Whether augmentation is an issue in patients who receive dopaminergic therapy throughout the day has not been evaluated.

Periodic limb movement during sleep (PLMS) occurs primarily during non-rapid-eye-movement (non-REM) sleep and is marked by an intermittent rhythmic movement of the legs (triple flexion of hip, knee, and ankle) that can result in arousals and awakenings if severe. PLMs appears to be more frequent in PD (35). For RLS and PLMS, the direct-acting dopamine receptor agonists appear to be superior to levodopa, with a reduced occurrence of rebound (RLS symptoms occurring at the end of the effect of a single dose of levodopa) and augmentation (RLS symptoms occurring at an earlier time in the evening, often associated with spread to other body areas and more severe symtpoms). Opiates and benzodiazepines may also be effective (36).

An additional cause of both fragmented and delayed sleep onset is depression. Depression is estimated to affect approximately 40% of PD patients (37). In non-PD patients, depression often causes an associated sleep disturbance. An early REM period is one of the characteristic polysomnographic features. Treatment of depression can improve sleep disturbance in both non-PD and PD patients. When administered in small doses in the evening hours, the tricyclic antidepressants (e.g., trazodone, amitriptyline, and nortriptyline), with their sedating side effects, may be beneficial (38–40). Because these agents may exacerbate RLS symptoms and increase PLMS it is important to differentiate these problems. In addition, in some patients,

tricyclic antidepressants may initiate or worsen night-time hallucinations.

In PD patients with situational anxiety or acute insomnia with no other contributing factor, the short-term use of zolpidem at bedtime may provide relief, often without causing rebound insomnia after discontinuation (41). Melatonin in small doses (less than 3 mg) 1 to 2 hours before bedtime may be of benefit, although loss of this hormone has not been demonstrated in PD (42, 43).

SLEEP DISTURBANCE: HALLUCINATIONS SYNDROME IN PARKINSON'S DISEASE PATIENTS ON CHRONIC DOPAMINERGIC THERAPY

Some 25% to 40% of PD patients develop dopaminergic drug–induced visual hallucinations (44). Factors associated with the occurrence of hallucinations include dementia, sleep disturbance, depression, visual disturbances, and axial predominance of motor signs (45–47). It was postulated that sleep disruption was an early risk factor for hallucinations (48–50), but this has been disputed by more recent longitudinal studies (45) finding that fragmented sleep is not specifically associated with hallucinations, although vivid dreams may be (47).

Polysomnographic findings in PD patients with dysphoric dreams and hallucinations have not been consistent. One study demonstrated an absence of K-complexes and sleep spindles with abnormalities in sleep architecture and variable suppression of REM (50). Another study compared 5 hallucinating patients with 5 nonhallucinating PD patients matched for severity of PD and antiparkinsonian medications. Comparisons revealed that hallucinations were associated with reduced sleep efficiency and a marked reduction in REM sleep (51).

The treatment of dopaminergic drug-induced hallucinations includes discontinuation of drugs with central effects that are not essential to the patient's care. This could include elimination of anticholinergic agents, anxiolytics, centrally active pain medications including codeine compounds, and antidepressants. The provision of a night light may be useful. A reduction in dopamine drug dose and avoidance of evening doses may be beneficial but can also lead to a worsening of motor symptoms. Shifting from direct dopamine agonists to shorter-acting levodopa preparations may also be helpful. If reduction in dopaminergic drugs results in exacerbation of motor symptoms, the atypical antipsychotics can be used. Clozapine has been shown to be an effective treatment for drug-induced hallucinations in PD without causing deterioration in motor symptoms (52). The major adverse effect from clozapine is the development of agranulocytosis. In order to monitor this potentially life-threatening side effect, weekly blood counts are required for the 6 six months of therapy. If the levels are stable after 6 months, blood tests at biweekly intervals must still be continued. Other atypical agents, including quetiapine, are being assessed (53). These agents do not require blood monitoring but have been associated with other significant adverse effects, including diabetes and cardiovascular effects (54).

REM SLEEP BEHAVIOR DISORDER IN PARKINSON'S DISEASE

REM sleep behavior disorder (RBD) has particular relevance to PD and other parkinsonian syndromes. It occurs in association with PD and may predate its onset. Normal REM sleep is marked by cortical desynchronization similar to that seen in the waking state, rapid eye movements, cardiorespiratory irregularities, and skeletal muscle atonia interrupted by phasic muscle twitches. Although dreams may occur during other sleep stages, the dreams during REM sleep are vivid and more internally organized. The anatomic areas involved in the generation and maintenance of REM sleep lie in the brainstem. In animal models, lesions in these REM-related brainstem areas in the pons result in motor behaviors during REM (55–58). The severity of the pontine lesion determines the extent of the behavioral pattern observed. In humans, the occurrence of RBD is similarly thought to reflect damage to these same REM-related areas.

RBD was first described in 1986 by Schenck and colleagues (59–61), who observed abnormal behaviors occurring mostly in elderly men. As subsequent cases were reported, the salient clinical features of this syndrome emerged. The minimal diagnostic criteria for RBD as defined by the revised International Classification of Sleep Disorders (ICSD) includes electromyographic evidence of maintained muscle tone in submental muscles or excessive activity in limb muscles during REM sleep, with one of the following: sleep-related injury or disruptive behavior by history or abnormal sleep behaviors during REM sleep during polysomnography (62). The caregiver may report that dreams appear to be "acted out." The dreams recalled during episodes of RBD are often aggressive or violent and may lead to injury (63–67).

Episodes of RBD may occur sporadically, with a flurry of episodes occurring nightly followed by a period of quiescence. In a patient with RBD, dreams of being chased, threatened, or trapped lead to behaviors such as punching, choking, kicking, or leaping out of bed. Patients have sustained ecchymosis, lacerations, fractures, and dislocations (66, 68, 69). Similarly, the bed partners of RBD patients are at risk for injury and are often frightened by the sudden violent outbursts of a person who may be quiet and mild while awake. Usually it is only on questioning by the physician that these nighttime episodes are revealed. The patient seldom remembers the episode, and the caregiver may believe that the episodes are not part of a neurologic syndrome.

On the basis of clinical criteria, RBD has been observed in 15% to 32% of PD patients (66). However, clinical criteria for evaluation may not be highly reliable (70) and may lack sensitivity (71). When evaluated by polysomnography, 33% of PD patients had RBD, but up to 58% had evidence of loss of muscle atonia during REM sleep (72), suggesting that more than 50% of PD patients may have subclinical or clinically manifest RBD. It has been reported that 33% of PD patients may have RBD symptoms prior to the onset of motor manifestations (73), leading some to suggest that RBD may be a harbinger of PD. This has been supported by observations—by single photon emission computed tomography (SPECT—that primary RBD without PD may be associated with abnormalities in olfaction and with nigrostriatal degeneration (74).

RBD is more frequent in parkinsonian syndromes that have more extensive brainstem or cortical pathology, such as MSA and dementia with Lewy bodies (DLB) (75–77). In addition in these disorders, a greater number of patients may report onset of RBD symptoms prior to parkinsonian motor symptoms. RBD may indicate incipient cognitive dysfunction, with slowing of the electroencephalogram (EEG) and mild abnormalities on cognitive testing (78, 79). Pathologic studies in moderate to severe PD demonstrate a 40% reduction in cholinergic neurons and Lewy body formation in the pedunculopontine tegmental nucleus (80). These observations suggest that certain REM abnormalities may reflect anatomic subcategories of the synucleinopathies with more extensive brainstem involvement (81, 82). This may have prognostic implications, perhaps predicting a poorer outcome. Longitudinal studies have not been done.

Treatment of RBD is indicated when symptoms disrupt sleep of the patient or bedpartner or cause injury. Although adequate controlled trials are lacking, anecdotal and case series suggest that RBD is treatable. Small doses of clonazepam (starting at 0.25 mg) may reduce or eliminate the symptoms (83) but may also cause confusion in an elderly patient. Melatonin has been found to be effective in some patients (84). Donepezil, pramipexole, and quetiapine may also be beneficial (85, 86).

EXCESSIVE DAYTIME SLEEPINESS IN PARKINSON'S DISEASE

Excessive daytime sleepiness (EDS) is frequent in PD (90). Factors associated with EDS include anxiety (87), more advanced PD, longer disease duration (88), nocturnal snoring (89, 90), depression (91), male gender (7), and orthostatic hypotension(92). One of the most consistent factors associated with EDS is the use of dopamine agonists (DA). Following a brief report of 8 patients treated with a DA who fell asleep suddenly (sleep attack) while driving, resulting in motor vehicle accidents (93), concerns over the safety of this class of drugs has led to driving restrictions in some countries. Observations of similar occurrences are numerous (6, 94–97). It has become clear that all dopaminergic drugs used to treat PD can lead to daytime sleepiness and sleep attacks. The use of DA may carry an increased risk (98). Other factors that contributed to EDS are correlated with more advanced disease (7). In one community-based study (90), EDS was seen in 15.5% of PD patients, compared with 4% of patients with diabetes mellitus and 1% of controls. This problem was associated with more advanced PD, greater disability, a higher level of cognitive decline, more frequent hallucinations, and longer duration of levodopa therapy. In PD patients who drive, the degree of daytime sleepiness, occurrence of sudden-onset sleep episodes, and presence of moderate PD were risks for motor vehicle accidents (99).

The occurrence of excess daytime napping followed by nocturnal wakefulness is a frequent complaint of patients and caregivers. In addition to the sleep disorders described, other factors may promote this "reversal" of the normal day-night rhythms. Sedentary PD patients who largely remain indoors during the day may doze frequently. The occurrence of these intermittent sleep periods, especially during the afternoon and evening, may impede the ability to fall asleep at night. Further, antiparkinsonian medications may cause sleepiness. This is particularly true for levodopa and the dopamine receptor agonists (64–66). Other medications for medical indications can aggravate daytime sleepiness. Consultation with the patient's family physician may provide adjustments in these concomitant drugs and eliminate overly sedating ones.

Treatment of day-night reversal relies heavily on the restoration of normal sleep patterns. Good sleep hygiene includes established bedtime and wakeup times with exposure to adequate light during the day and darkness at night. Indoor lighting may not be sufficient to promote a normal circadian rhythm. Exposure to sunlight or its equivalent during the day is needed. This can be accomplished by frequent trips outside, keeping window shades open during the day, or exposure to a light source designed to provide the needed light strength. Physical exercise appropriate to the patient's level of functioning may also promote daytime wakefulness. Strenuous exercise, however, should be avoided for 3 to 4 hours before sleep. A hot bath about an hour before bedtime may be relaxing and promote the onset of sleep by increasing body temperature and allowing the patient to fall asleep during the cooling phase. A light bedtime snack and avoidance of fluid intake in the evening may alleviate nighttime hunger and reduce nocturnal urination. Relaxation techniques may also be useful in reducing nighttime stress and muscle tension.

Sleepiness following antiparkinsonian medications is sometimes difficult to control. A dose reduction may improve postdrug sleepiness but may also lead to an unacceptable increase in parkinsonian symptoms. If the patient is taking a dopamine agonist, changing to another agonist may provide relief. A few patients have reported ae sudden onset of an irresistible urge to sleep associated with pramipexole, ropinirole, and pergolide (93, 100, 101). This may be alleviated by the discontinuing the drug or switching to another agonist (8).

Daytime stimulant medications are reserved for those patients who are unresponsive to other adjustments. The amphetamine metabolites of selegiline may increase alertness. Small doses of methylphenidate administered during the day may also be helpful but can disrupt nighttime sleep. Modafil may be of some benefit.

References

1. Lees, A.J., Blackburn, N.A. and Campbell, V.L. The nighttime problems of Parkinson's disease. Clin Neuropharmacol. 1988; 11:512–9.
2. Factor, S.A., Mcalarney, T., Sanchez-Ramos, J.R. and Weiner, W.J. Sleep disorders and sleep effect in Parkinson's disease. Mov Disord. 1990; 5:280–5.
3. Oerlemans, W.G. and De Weerd, A.W. The prevalence of sleep disorders in patients with Parkinson's disease. A self-reported, community-based survey. Sleep Med. 2002; 3:147–9.
4. Tandberg, E., Larsen, J.P. and Karlsen, K. A community-based study of sleep disorders in patients with Parkinson's disease. Mov Disord. 1998; 13:895–9.
5. Tan, E.K., Lum, S.Y., Fook-Chong, S.M., et al. Evaluation of somnolence in Parkinson's disease: comparison with age- and sex-matched controls. Neurology. 2002; 58:465–8.
6. Hobson, D.E., Lang, A.E., Martin, W.R., et al. Excessive daytime sleepiness and sudden-onset sleep in Parkinson disease: a survey by the Canadian Movement Disorders Group. Jama. 2002; 287:455–63.
7. Ondo, W.G., Dat Vuong, K., Khan, H., et al. Daytime sleepiness and other sleep disorders in Parkinson's disease. Neurology. 2001; 57:1392–6.
8. Comella, C.L. Sleep disturbances in Parkinson's disease. Curr Neurol Neurosci Rep. 2003; 3:173–80.
9. Carter J., Carroll S., Lannon M.C. Sleep disruption in untreated Parkinson's disease. Neurology. 1990; 40(suppl1):220–225.
10. Mouret, J. Differences in sleep in patients with Parkinson's disease. Electroencephalogr Clin Neurophysiol. 1975; 38:653–7.
11. Ferini-Strambi, L., Franceschi, M., Pinto, P., et al. Respiration and heart rate variability during sleep in untreated Parkinson patients. Gerontology. 1992; 38:92–8.
12. Kaynak, D., Kiziltan, G., Kaynak, H., et al. Sleep and sleepiness in patients with Parkinson's disease before and after dopaminergic treatment. Eur J Neurol. 2005; 12:199–207.
13. Van Den Kerchove, M., Jacquy, J., Gonce, M. and De Deyn, P.P. Sustained-release levodopa in parkinsonian patients with nocturnal disabilities. Acta Neurol Belg. 1993; 93:32–9.
14. Askenasy, J.J. and Yahr, M.D. Reversal of sleep disturbance in Parkinson's disease by antiparkinsonian therapy: a preliminary study. Neurology. 1985; 35:527–32.
15. Lees, A.J. A sustained-release formulation of L-dopa (Madopar HBS) in the treatment of nocturnal and early-morning disabilities in Parkinson's disease. Eur Neurol. 1987; 27 Suppl 1:126–34.
16. Jansen, E.N. and Meerwaldtt, J.D. Madopar HBS in nocturnal symptoms of Parkinson's disease. Adv Neurol. 1990; 53:527–31.
17. Stacy, M. Sleep disorders in Parkinson's disease: epidemiology and management. Drugs Aging. 2002; 19:733–9.
18. Van Hilten, B., Hoff, J.I., Middelkoop, H.A., et al. Sleep disruption in Parkinson's disease. Assessment by continuous activity monitoring. Arch Neurol. 1994; 51:922–8.
19. Comella, C.L., Morrissey, M. and Janko, K. Nocturnal activity with nighttime pergolide in Parkinson disease: a controlled study using actigraphy. Neurology. 2005; 64:1450–1.

20. Hogl, B., Rothdach, A., Wetter, T.C. and Trenkwalder, C. The effect of cabergoline on sleep, periodic leg movements in sleep, and early morning motor function in patients with Parkinson's disease. Neuropsychopharmacology. 2003; 28:1866–70.

21. Yaggi, H.K., Concato, J., Kernan, W.N., et al. Obstructive sleep apnea as a risk factor for stroke and death. N Engl J Med. 2005; 353:2034–41.

22. Arnulf, I., Konofal, E., Merino-Andreu, M., et al. Parkinson's disease and sleepiness: an integral part of PD. Neurology. 2002; 58:1019–24.

23. Maria, B., Sophia, S., Michalis, M., et al. Sleep breathing disorders in patients with idiopathic Parkinson's disease. Respir Med. 2003; 97:1151–7.

24. Rye, D.B., Bliwise, D.L., Dihenia, B. and Gurecki, P. FAST TRACK: daytime sleepiness in Parkinson's disease. J Sleep Res. 2000; 9:63–9.

25. Wetter, T.C., Collado-Seidel, V., Pollmacher, T., et al. Sleep and periodic leg movement patterns in drug-free patients with Parkinson's disease and multiple system atrophy. Sleep. 2000; 23:361–7.

26. Stevens, S., Comella, C.L. and Stepanski, E.J. Daytime sleepiness and alertness in patients with Parkinson disease. Sleep. 2004; 27:967–72.

27. Krishnan, P.R., Bhatia, M. and Behari, M. Restless legs syndrome in Parkinson's disease: a case-controlled study. Mov Disord. 2003; 18:181–5.

28. Munschauer, F.E., Loh, L., Bannister, R. and Newsom-Davis, J. Abnormal respiration and sudden death during sleep in multiple system atrophy with autonomic failure. Neurology. 1990; 40:677–9.

29. Vetrugno, R., Provini, F., Cortelli, P., et al. Sleep disorders in multiple system atrophy: a correlative video-polysomnographic study. Sleep Med. 2004; 5:21–30.

30. Hening, W.A. and Allen, R.P. Restless legs syndrome (RLS): the continuing development of diagnostic standards and severity measures. Sleep Med. 2003; 4:95–7.

31. Ondo, W.G., Vuong, K.D. and Jankovic, J. Exploring the relationship between Parkinson disease and restless legs syndrome. Arch Neurol. 2002; 59:421–4.

32. Trenkwalder, C., Paulus, W. and Walters, A.S. The restless legs syndrome. Lancet Neurol. 2005; 4:465–75.

33. Stiasny-Kolster, K., Trenkwalder, C., Fogel, W., et al. Restless legs syndrome–new insights into clinical characteristics, pathophysiology, and treatment options. J Neurol. 2004; 251 Suppl 6:VI/39–43.

34. Hogl, B., Kiechl, S., Willeit, J., et al. Restless legs syndrome: a community-based study of prevalence, severity, and risk factors. Neurology. 2005; 64:1920–4.

35. Happe, S. and Trenkwalder, C. Movement disorders in sleep: Parkinson's disease and restless legs syndrome. Biomed Tech (Berl). 2003; 48:62–7.

36. Thorpy, M.J. and Adler, C.H. Parkinson's disease and sleep. Neurol Clin. 2005; 23:1187–208.

37. Scaravilli, T., Gasparoli, E., Rinaldi, F., et al. Health-related quality of life and sleep disorders in Parkinson's disease. Neurol Sci. 2003; 24:209–10.

38. Adler, C.H. Nonmotor complications in Parkinson's disease. Mov Disord. 2005; 20 Suppl 11:S23–9.

39. Richard, I.H. Depression in Parkinson's Disease. Curr Treat Options Neurol. 2000; 2:263–274.

40. Thorpy, M.J. Sleep disorders in Parkinson's disease. Clin Cornerstone. 2004; 6 Suppl 1A:S7–15.

41. Abe, K., Hikita, T. and Sakoda, S. Sleep disturbances in Japanese patients with Parkinson's disease–comparing with patients in the UK. J Neurol Sci. 2005; 234:73–8.

42. Bubenik, G.A., Blask, D.E., Brown, G.M., et al. Prospects of the clinical utilization of melatonin. Biol Signals Recept. 1998; 7:195–219.

43. Dowling, G.A., Mastick, J., Colling, E., et al. Melatonin for sleep disturbances in Parkinson's disease. Sleep Med. 2005; 6:459–66.

44. Fenelon, G., Mahieux, F., Huon, R. and Ziegler, M. Hallucinations in Parkinson's disease: prevalence, phenomenology and risk factors. Brain. 2000; 123 (Pt 4):733–45.

45. Goetz, C.G., Wuu, J., Curgian, L.M. and Leurgans, S. Hallucinations and sleep disorders in PD: six-year prospective longitudinal study. Neurology. 2005; 64:81–6.

46. Diederich, N.J., Goetz, C.G. and Stebbins, G.T. Repeated visual hallucinations in Parkinson's disease as disturbed external/internal perceptions: focused review and a new integrative model. Mov Disord. 2005; 20:130–40.

47. Pappert, E.J., Goetz, C.G., Niederman, F.G., et al. Hallucinations, sleep fragmentation, and altered dream phenomena in Parkinson's disease. Mov Disord. 1999; 14:117–21.

48. Nausieda, P.A., Weiner, W.J., Kaplan, L.R., et al. Sleep disruption in the course of chronic levodopa therapy: an early feature of the levodopa psychosis. Clin Neuropharmacol. 1982; 5:183–94.

49. Nausieda, P.A., Tanner, C.M. and Klawans, H.L. Serotonergically active agents in levodopa-induced psychiatric toxicity reactions. Adv Neurol. 1983; 37:23–32.

50. Nausieda, P.A., Glantz, R., Weber, S., et al. Psychiatric complications of levodopa therapy of Parkinson's disease. Adv Neurol. 1984; 40:271–7.

51. Comella, C.L., Tanner, C.M. and Ristanovic, R.K. Polysomnographic sleep measures in Parkinson's disease patients with treatment-induced hallucinations. Ann Neurol. 1993; 34:710–4.

52. Friedman, J.H. and Fernandez, H.H. Atypical antipsychotics in Parkinson-sensitive populations. J Geriatr Psychiatry Neurol. 2002; 15:156–70.

53. Juri, C., Chana, P., Tapia, J., et al. Quetiapine for insomnia in Parkinson disease: results from an open-label trial. Clin Neuropharmacol. 2005; 28:185–7.

54. Pacher, P. and Kecskemeti, V. Cardiovascular side effects of new antidepressants and antipsychotics: new drugs, old concerns? Curr Pharm Des. 2004; 10:2463–75.

55. Jones, B.E. Paradoxical sleep and its chemical/structural substrates in the brain. Neuroscience. 1991; 40:637–56.

56. Jones, B.E. The role of noradrenergic locus coeruleus neurons and neighboring cholinergic neurons of the pontomesencephalic tegmentum in sleep-wake states. Prog Brain Res. 1991; 88:533–43.

57. Shiromani P.J., Siegel J.M. Descending projections from the dorsolateral pontine tegmentum to the paramedian reticular nucleus of the caudal medulla in the cat. Brain Res. 1990; 517:224–228.

58. Hendricks J.C., Morrison A.R., Mann G.L. Different behaviors during paradoxical sleep without atonia depend on pontine lesion site. Brain Res. 1982; 239:81–105.

59. Schenck, C.H., Bundlie, S.R., Ettinger, M.G. and Mahowald, M.W. Chronic behavioral disorders of human REM sleep: a new category of parasomnia. Sleep. 1986; 9:293–308.

60. Schenck, C.H., Bundlie, S.R., Patterson, A.L. and Mahowald, M.W. Rapid eye movement sleep behavior disorder. A treatable parasomnia affecting older adults. Jama. 1987; 257:1786–9.

61. Schenck, C.H., Hurwitz, T.D. and Mahowald, M.W. REM sleep behavior disorder. Am J Psychiatry. 1988; 145:652.

62. Medicine, A.A.O. The International Classification of Sleep Disorders, 2nd ed.: Diagnostic and coding manual. Journal. 2005.

63. Fantini, M.L., Corona, A., Clerici, S. and Ferini-Strambi, L. Aggressive dream content without daytime aggressiveness in REM sleep behavior disorder. Neurology. 2005; 65:1010–5.

64. Schenck, C.H., Milner, D.M., Hurwitz, T.D., et al. A polysomnographic and clinical report on sleep-related injury in 100 adult patients. Am J Psychiatry. 1989; 146:1166–73.

65. Schenck, C.H. and Mahowald, M.W. Injurious sleep behavior disorders (parasomnias) affecting patients on intensive care units. Intensive Care Med. 1991; 17:219–24.

66. Comella, C.L., Nardine, T.M., Diederich, N.J. and Stebbins, G.T. Sleep-related violence, injury, and REM sleep behavior disorder in Parkinson's disease. Neurology. 1998; 51:526–9.

67. Boeve, B.F., Silber, M.H. and Ferman, T.J. REM sleep behavior disorder in Parkinson's disease and dementia with Lewy bodies. J Geriatr Psychiatry Neurol. 2004; 17: 146–57.

68. Olson, E.J., Boeve, B.F. and Silber, M.H. Rapid eye movement sleep behaviour disorder: demographic, clinical and laboratory findings in 93 cases. Brain. 2000; 123 (Pt 2): 331–9.

69. Dyken, M.E., Lin-Dyken, D.C., Seaba, P. and Yamada, T. Violent sleep-related behavior leading to subdural hemorrhage. Arch Neurol. 1995; 52:318–21.

70. Vignatelli, L., Bisulli, F., Zaniboni, A., et al. Interobserver reliability of ICSD-R minimal diagnostic criteria for the parasomnias. J Neurol. 2005; 252:712–7.

71. Eisensehr, I., V Lindeiner, H., Jager, M. and Noachtar, S. REM sleep behavior disorder in sleep-disordered patients with versus without Parkinson's disease: is there a need for polysomnography? J Neurol Sci. 2001; 186:7–11.

72. Gagnon, J.F., Bedard, M.A., Fantini, M.L., et al. REM sleep behavior disorder and REM sleep without atonia in Parkinson's disease. Neurology. 2002; 59:585–9.

73. Schenck, C.H., Bundlie, S.R. and Mahowald, M.W. Delayed emergence of a parkinsonian disorder in 38% of 29 older men initially diagnosed with idiopathic rapid eye movement sleep behaviour disorder. Neurology. 1996; 46:388–93.

74. Stiasny-Kolster, K., Doerr, Y., Moller, J.C., et al. Combination of 'idiopathic' REM sleep behaviour disorder and olfactory dysfunction as possible indicator for alpha-synucleinopathy demonstrated by dopamine transporter FP-CIT-SPECT. Brain. 2005; 128:126–37.

75. Iranzo, A., Santamaria, J., Rye, D.B., et al. Characteristics of idiopathic REM sleep behavior disorder and that associated with MSA and PD. Neurology. 2005; 65:247–52.

76. Plazzi, G., Corsini, R., Provini, F., et al. REM sleep behavior disorders in multiple system atrophy. Neurology. 1997; 48:1094–7.

77. Boeve, B.F., Silber, M.H., Parisi, J.E., et al. Synucleinopathy pathology and REM sleep behavior disorder plus dementia or parkinsonism. Neurology. 2003; 61:40–5.

78. Gagnon, J.F., Fantini, M.L., Bedard, M.A., et al. Association between waking EEG slowing and REM sleep behavior disorder in PD without dementia. Neurology. 2004; 62:401–6.

79. Gagnon, J.F., Postuma, R.B., Mazza, S., et al. Rapid-eye-movement sleep behaviour disorder and neurodegenerative diseases. Lancet Neurol. 2006; 5:424–32.

80. Hirsch, E.C., Graybiel, A.M., Duyckaerts, C. and Javoy-Agid, F. Neuronal loss in the pedunculopontine tegmental nucleus in Parkinson disease and in progressive supranuclear palsy. Proc Natl Acad Sci U S A. 1987; 84:5976–80.

81. Iranzo, A., Molinuevo, J.L., Santamaria, J., et al. Rapid-eye-movement sleep behaviour disorder as an early marker for a neurodegenerative disorder: a descriptive study. Lancet Neurol. 2006; 5:572–7.

82. Ferini-Strambi, L., Fantini, M.L., Zucconi, M., et al. REM sleep behaviour disorder. Neurol Sci. 2005; 26 Suppl 3:s186–92.

83. Schenck, C.H. and Mahowald, M.W. REM sleep behavior disorder: clinical, developmental, and neuroscience perspectives 16 years after its formal identification in SLEEP. Sleep. 2002; 25:120–38.

84. Boeve, B.F., Silber, M.H. and Ferman, T.J. Melatonin for treatment of REM sleep behavior disorder in neurologic disorders: results in 14 patients. Sleep Med. 2003; 4:281–4.

85. Ringman, J.M. and Simmons, J.H. Treatment of REM sleep behavior disorder with donepezil: a report of three cases. Neurology. 2000; 55:870–1.

86. Schmidt, M.H., Koshal, V.B. and Schmidt, H.S. Use of pramipexole in REM sleep behavior disorder: Results from a case series. Sleep Med. 2006; 7:418–23.

87. Wegelin, J., Mcnamara, P., Durso, R., et al. Correlates of excessive daytime sleepiness in Parkinson's disease. Parkinsonism Relat Disord. 2005; 11:441–8.

88. Gjerstad, M.D., Aarsland, D. and Larsen, J.P. Development of daytime somnolence over time in Parkinson's disease. Neurology. 2002; 58:1544–6.

89. Hogl, B., Seppi, K., Brandauer, E., et al. Increased daytime sleepiness in Parkinson's disease: a questionnaire survey. Mov Disord. 2003; 18:319–23.

90. Rissling, I., Frauscher, B., Kronenberg, F., et al. Daytime sleepiness and the COMT val158met polymorphism in patients with Parkinson disease. Sleep. 2006; 29:108–11.

91. Barbar, S.I., Enright, P.L., Boyle, P., et al. Sleep disturbances and their correlates in elderly Japanese American men residing in Hawaii. J Gerontol A Biol Sci Med Sci. 2000; 55: M406–11.

92. Rye, D.B. Excessive daytime sleepiness and unintended sleep in Parkinson's disease. Curr Neurol Neurosci Rep. 2006; 6:169–76.

93. Frucht, S., Rogers, J.D., Greene, P.E., et al. Falling asleep at the wheel: motor vehicle mishaps in persons taking pramipexole and ropinirole. Neurology. 1999; 52:1908–10.

94. Ulivelli, M., Rossi, S., Lombardi, C., et al. Polysomnographic characterization of pergolide-induced sleep attacks in idiopathic PD. Neurology. 2002; 58:462–5.

95. Chaudhuri, K.R., Pal, S. and Brefel-Courbon, C. 'Sleep attacks' or 'unintended sleep episodes' occur with dopamine agonists: is this a class effect? Drug Saf. 2002; 25:473–83.

96. Ferreira, J.J., Galitzky, M., Montastruc, J.L. and Rascol, O. Sleep attacks and Parkinson's disease treatment. Lancet. 2000; 355:1333–4.

97. Schapira, A.H. Sleep attacks (sleep episodes) with pergolide. Lancet. 2000; 355:1332–3.

98. Etminan, M., Samii, A., Takkouche, B. and Rochon, P.A. Increased risk of somnolence with the new dopamine agonists in patients with Parkinson's disease: a meta-analysis of randomised controlled trials. Drug Saf. 2001; 24:863–8.

99. Meindorfner, C., Korner, Y., Moller, J.C., et al. Driving in Parkinson's disease: mobility, accidents, and sudden onset of sleep at the wheel. Mov Disord. 2005; 20: 832–42.

100. Razmy, A., Lang, A.E. and Shapiro, C.M. Predictors of impaired daytime sleep and wakefulness in patients with Parkinson disease treated with older (ergot) vs newer (nonergot) dopamine agonists. Arch Neurol. 2004; 61:97–102.

101. Hauser, R.A., Gauger, L., Anderson, W.M. and Zesiewicz, T.A. Pramipexole-induced somnolence and episodes of daytime sleep. Mov Disord. 2000; 15:658–63.

13 Natural History

Michael Pourfar
Andrew Feigin
David Eidelberg

As new therapies for Parkinson's disease (PD) are developed, the need for accurate and comprehensive descriptions of the natural history of the disease becomes increasingly urgent. Specifically, knowledge regarding the length of the preclinical period, age of clinical onset, rates of progression of early and later stages of the disease, and common causes of death is critical for designing clinical trials aimed at neuroprotection. In addition, studies aimed at improving the symptoms of PD will be strengthened by a thorough understanding of the usual causes of disability as well as the typical manner and time at which they present. Over the past two decades, much has been learned regarding the natural history of PD. This chapter reviews this information and its implications for the experimental therapeutics of PD.

PRECLINICAL PERIOD

Estimates of time between the onset of neurophysiologic dysfunction and clinical onset of PD have been derived from postmortem pathologic studies, in vivo neuroimaging studies, and, more recently, by clinically observing select populations based on their genetic predisposition.

Neuropathologic Studies

Neuropathologic studies of PD initially suggested that patients with the earliest signs of disease have already lost as much as 50% of the pigmented dopaminergic neurons in the substantia nigra and 80% of striatal dopamine (1). Subsequent studies modified these findings, suggesting that clinical signs of PD begin to emerge when there has been an approximately 30% reduction in total nigral dopaminergic neurons (2). The most affected ventrolateral region of the substantia nigra, however, has lost greater than 60% of its neurons at clinical onset. Using cross-sectional neuropathologic data from patients with PD at various stages and assuming a nonlinear progression of disease, these authors estimated that the neuropathologic process began approximately 5 years before the clinical onset of symptoms. An earlier postmortem study, utilizing a vesicular monoamine transporter-binding ligand to quantify striatal dopaminergic innervation, found similar reductions in dopaminergic activity but suggested a longer preclinical period of 20 to 30 years (3). The difference is likely due to the absence of patients with very early disease in the latter study; that is, the rate of neuronal loss in PD has been consistently found to be more rapid in the early stages of disease (2, 4). Therefore, if the rate of neuronal loss in middle and advanced disease is extrapolated back to the preclinical period, the length of the preclinical period will be overestimated. However, in focusing on nigral loss as the incipient neuropathologic event, these studies may be underestimating the preclinical period, for it has been demonstrated that the earliest pathologic changes may be occurring not in the nigra but in the dorsal IX/X motor and anterior olfactory nuclei (5). Further complicating retrospective predictions of the preclinical period are neuropathologic case reports of individuals with long-standing rapid-eye-movement (REM) sleep behavior disorder (RBD) without parkinsonism who are found to have Lewy bodies in the substantia nigra on postmortem evaluation (6, 7). Such findings suggest the possibility of a longer preclinical period in at least a subset of patients.

Neuroimaging Studies

Estimates of the preclinical period in PD based on neuroimaging studies have varied. Much of this variation may be accounted for by differences in methodology, the limited number of time points, and the heterogeneity of patient populations being studied (e.g., variations in age of onset, symptom type and severity, and differences in medication status). Preclinical estimates also vary widely depending on whether a linear or nonlinear progression model is utilized. If the progression of PD is nonlinear, with a more rapid rate of decline in early disease and slower progression later, then linear extrapolation from data collected from more advanced PD patient will incorrectly predict a longer preclinical period. Using [^{18}F]-fluorodopa (FDOPA) positron emission tomography (PET), Vingerhoets and coworkers studied 16 patients on two occasions separated by a mean of 7 years (8). Linear regression analysis estimated the preclinical period at 40 to 50 years, although a nonlinear fit of the data predicted a preclinical period of 10 to 15 years. Morrish and coworkers reported a less than 7-year preclinical period utilizing a linear model with serial FDOPA PET scans in 32 PD patients (9). These findings were corroborated by those of Nurmi and coworkers, who performed two FDOPA PET scans in 21 PD patients at a 5-year interval and estimated a preclinical period of 6.5 years (10). Hilker and coworkers, utilizing serial FDOPA PET in 31 PD patients, estimated a nonlinear, preclinical period of 5 to 6 years (11). Longitudinal studies utilizing single photon emission computed tomography (SPECT) scans have also been utilized to estimate the preclinical period. Marek and coworkers performed a SPECT study utilizing [^{123}I] β-CIT, a dopamine transporter ligand, in a cohort of patients with early PD and estimated a preclinical period of approximately 4 years (12). Using [^{18}F]-fluorodeoxyglucose (FDG) PET, Moeller and Eidelberg (13) demonstrated an abnormal dissociation between a brain network associated with aging and the actual age of PD patients. By extrapolating back to when this dissociation equaled zero, they obtained an estimate of the preclinical period of approximately 5 years. Thus,

despite continued controversy as to whether PD progresses linearly or nonlinearly, neuroimaging studies in patients with relatively early PD seem to be consistent in estimating the preclinical period at under 10 years and perhaps at or under 5.

Clinical Studies

Clinical evidence also supports the neuropathologic and neuroimaging estimates of the preclinical period. Gonera and coworkers (14) compared medical records of 60 PD patients during the decade preceding the diagnosis of PD with those of 58 age- and sex-matched controls. They found several signs and symptoms that occurred more frequently in the PD group than in the control group, including mood changes, pain, paresthesias, and hypertension—differences that were identified 4 to 6 years before PD onset. Others have reported depression, malaise, and nonspecific sensory complaints occurring in the years preceding the clinical diagnosis (15). More recently, certain nonspecific clinical findings have been identified as potential preclinical harbingers of PD. A decreased sense of smell in individuals that also have a first-degree relative with PD has been identified as a potential marker. Two studies paired such individuals with imaging modalities and identified a subset of hyposmic patients with dopaminergic deficiency who, in some cases, went on to develop PD during 2 years of follow-up (16, 17). REM sleep behavior disorder has also been identified as a potential preclinical marker, sometimes with a latency of over 10 years (7). Longer prospective studies will be required to more clearly establish the relationship and variability between individual "preclinical" symptoms and the time course to more evident motor findings.

CLINICAL PRESENTATION

Age of Onset and Symptoms at Onset

The average age of PD onset is approximately 50 to 60 years (18–20), but the range is quite broad, extending from childhood to the old age. Approximately 5% of patients present symptoms before the age of 40. The factors that determine age of onset are unknown, but increasing evidence supports a genetic predisposition in many early-onset cases (generally classified as those with onset at age 40 or below). Inzelberg and coworkers reviewed age of onset in 240 PD patients and found an average of 59 years in those with a family history of PD compared with 66 years in those without a family history (21). Even in cases of PD with a known or presumed genetic etiology, however, the age of onset can vary considerably. Khan and coworkers, reviewing the phenotypes of 24 patients with the parkin mutation, found an average

age of onset of 24 but a range of 7 to 54 years (22). In a recently identified cohort of early-onset PD patients with PINK-1 genetic mutations, age of onset was below 36 years in homozygous carriers but up to 45 years in heterozygous carriers (23).

The presenting symptoms of PD can be highly variable. Many subtle signs and symptoms—such as changes in handwriting, mood, sleep, and autonomic function—are identified only retrospectively as early manifestations of PD (24). An asymmetric resting tremor is the most common initial symptom to lead to the diagnosis, accounting for as many as 70% of cases (25–27). Interestingly, some investigators have noted a preponderance of right-sided symptoms at onset (25). In a retrospective study of over 1200 sporadic and 300 familial PD patients, tremor was found to be the most common presenting symptom in both cohorts, occurring in 54% of familial cases and 48% of sporadic ones (20). Tremor was most common in the upper extremity and was asymmetric in 95% of familial and 87% of sporadic cases. The next most common presenting symptoms in both groups were bradykinesia (approximately 29%) and rigidity (approximately 6%). Dystonia and a relatively symmetric onset appear to be more common presenting features in parkin-related cases as compared with cases of sporadic PD (28).

RATE OF PROGRESSION

Pathological Studies

Braak and coworkers described a progressive caudorostral spread of neuropathology (5). In their proposed schema, PD pathology progresses through 6 stages, spreading from the medulla (I) to the pons and upper brainstem (II to III), to the anterior temporal mesocortex (IV) and then to the neocortex (V to VI). The rate of progression between stages, however, has yet to be delineated.

Clinical Studies

Although James Parkinson described aspects of progression in his original account of the disease (29), the first quantitative observations regarding the rate of progression of PD were provided by Hoehn and Yahr in their landmark study of 856 parkinsonian patients (26). Utilizing the Hoehn and Yahr (HY) scale, the authors evaluated the progression of PD disability in a cohort of 183 untreated patients. They found that the median time from symptom onset to HY IV was 9 years and to end-stage HY V was 14 years. Nonetheless, the progression of PD was observed to be highly variable, such that 16% of patients progressed to HY V in less than 5 years while 34% were still in HY I or II 10 or more years after symptom onset. Subsequent studies have confirmed the

extensive variability in the rate of progression of PD (30, 31). Overall, the average amount of time in each HY stage has been estimated to be 2 to 3 years (30).

Clinical trials aimed at slowing the progression of PD have provided valuable data regarding the natural history of the disease. The study of patients in the placebo arm of large, prospective long-term trials—although typically limited to relatively mild cases—yields detailed and accurate information regarding the progression of untreated PD. The Deprenyl and Tocopherol Antioxidant Therapy of Parkinsonism (DATATOP) study enrolled 800 subjects with early (HY I and II) untreated PD and utilized the Unified Parkinson's Disease Rating Scale (UPDRS) (32). Of these 800 subjects, 353 were treated with placebo or placebo plus tocopherol (found to be ineffective). Overall, the total UPDRS score in these individuals worsened by 14% per year (approximately 4 points) and the motor portion of the UPDRS score worsened by 9% per year (approximately 2.5 points). One-third of this group, however, progressed at a slower rate (total UPDRS decline 6% per year; motor UPDRS score decline 4%) and did not require symptomatic therapy during follow-up (33). In the Earlier versus Later Levodopa Therapy in Parkinson's Disease (ELLDOPA) study, 90 of 361 patients with early PD were randomized to placebo for 40 weeks (34). The mean total UPDRS decline in the 70 patients who remained in the study at 42 weeks was approximately 8 points, with a motor UPDRS decline of approximately 5 points. Many subsequent studies using more heterogeneous PD populations have documented motor UPDRS declines ranging from 1 to 5 points per year, with an average decline of approximately 2.5 points per year (9, 11, 35–39). Factors affecting UPDRS scores and accounting for variability in these studies include differences in patient ages, medications, and potential confounds related to drug washout periods of varying length.

Neuroimaging Studies

Neuroimaging studies with positron emission tomography (PET) and single photon emission computed tomography (SPECT) have examined the rate of progression of PD. Several studies established that these methods, utilizing different radioligands, provide objective measures that correlate with clinical measures of PD severity. Nevertheless, there remains controversy regarding the interpretation of neuroimaging-based progression studies due to variations in technique, cohort heterogeneity (e.g., age, disease subtypes, and duration), and medication status (e.g., differing dosages, effects of medications on radiotracer binding, and varying washout periods) (40–42).

[18F]-fluorodopa (FDOPA) is the most extensively utilized PET radiotracer in progression studies. Striatal FDOPA uptake, a measure of decarboxylation and storage in dopaminergic terminals, accurately distinguishes patients with early PD from normal controls (43, 44) and correlates well with UPDRS severity ratings (45–47). Similar cross-sectional results have been observed with radioligands that bind to the dopamine transporter (DAT) (cf. ref. 48). Several longitudinal PD studies, most with only 2 time points, have compared changes in either FDOPA uptake or DAT binding with changes in clinical progression (8–11, 49). Two early studies demonstrated 1.7% and 2.3% per year declines, respectively, in striatal-to-background ratios of FDOPA uptake (8, 50). Several subsequent studies have reported annual striatal declines of 3% to 6.6% compared with 0% to 2.5% in normal controls (9, 11, 51). A number of FDOPA PET studies observed regional differences in the rates of dopaminergic loss within the striatum, with mean annual declines of 8% to 10% in the putamen and 3.5% to 5.9% in the caudate (9, 10). Nurmi and coworkers reported a 10.3% annual decline of FDOPA uptake in the posterior putamen compared with 8.3% in the anterior putamen and 5.9% in the caudate (10). In a subsequent study, they used [18F]-2-β-carbomethoxy-3-β-(4-fluorophenyl) tropane (CFT), a DAT-binding PET ligand, to scan 12 de novo patients at baseline and 2 years later (52). They found greater absolute rate of decline in the anterior putamen, along with a more rapid decline of tracer uptake on the side ipsilateral to the more clinically affected side. These and other findings suggested that the rate of progression is nonlinear, with a faster decline in the initially less deafferented subregions of the striatum. Indeed, Hilker and coworkers (11) used FDOPA PET to scan 31 PD patients over an average of 64.5 months. They found that the putamenal rate of decline was inversely correlated with disease duration. Patients with tremor-predominant PD appeared to have slower rates of progression in the caudate than bradykinesia-predominant patients. In other PET studies, patients with the parkin mutation have also been shown to have a slower loss of FDOPA uptake compared with PD patients (53).

SPECT studies utilizing DAT ligands also examined the rate of progression of PD and have paralleled PET progression findings. The best-studied SPECT ligand has been [123I] β-CIT (54, 55). The annualized rate of loss of [123I] β-CIT striatal uptake has been measured between 5.6% and 12% in several studies (12, 35, 56–60). A nonlinear progression with a more rapid initial decline has also been inferred from some serial SPECT studies. Jennings and coworkers reported a total annual decrease in striatal binding of 7.1% for patients with a 2-year history of PD, compared with a decrease of 3.7% in patients with a 4.5-year history of PD (61). Staffen and coworkers found an inverse relationship between the annual percentage decline of [123I] β-CIT uptake and HY severity (57). In another [123I]β-CIT study, however, Pirker and coworkers performed three SPECT scans over a 5-year period and found a relatively linear 6.6% striatal loss of [123I] β-CIT uptake (58). Long-term imaging studies with multiple time points will be needed to conclusively characterize the decline in nigrostriatal dopaminergic function.

Progressive changes in regional brain function have been described in a longitudinal study of early-PD patients scanned with [18F]-fluorodeoxyglucose (FDG) PET (62). Fifteen PD patients underwent initial PET imaging within 2 years of diagnosis with both FDG and [18F]-fluoropropyl β-CIT, a DAT-binding ligand. These patients subsequently underwent repeat imaging with both tracers at 24 and 48 months. At each time point, the FDG PET scans were used to quantify the activity of 2 reproducible PD-related spatial covariance patterns (i.e., metabolic networks). The expression of a motor-related network (e.g., ref. 63; see ref. 64 for review) increased significantly over time; it correlated with concurrent declines in striatal DAT binding and with increases in UPDRS motor ratings. By contrast, the expression of an independent cognition-related network (65, 66) increased at a comparatively slower rate and did not correlate with changes in nigrostriatal dopaminergic function or motor disability ratings. These findings point to differences in the natural history of motor- and cognition-related neural systems in PD. The data support a future role for network markers in the objective assessment of motor and non-motor progression in parkinsonism.

Clinical Predictors of Progression

Given the variability of the rate of progression of PD, the ability to predict the prognosis for a given patient would be very useful both in clinical practice and for clinical trials. Unfortunately, reliable predictors of disease severity have not yet been identified. Factors that have been associated with a slower rate of progression include tremor predominance and young age at onset (33). Several studies have reported a slower rate of onset of disability in patients presenting with tremor (67–69). This has led to some speculation that tremor-predominant PD, with minimal rigidity or bradykinesia, may constitute a milder subtype (70). Tremor-predominant PD also seems to be associated with less cognitive decline compared with PD associated with more prominent gait and postural instability (71). Alves and coworkers, for example, followed a large tremor-predominant PD cohort for 8 years and found that only those who developed gait and postural impairment developed accelerated cognitive decline (72). Cognitive status, measured with formal neuropsychological testing, appears to be a clinical predictor, with more cognitively impaired patients experiencing more rapid progression of motor function (73). Age of onset of parkinsonian symptoms is another factor that has repeatedly been shown to correlate with rate of progression. Early age of onset has been associated with a relatively good prognosis (68, 74–77). In an 8-year prospective study, patients who were older at onset had a more rapid decline in UPDRS scores, with an average annual decline of 2.6 points for those 50 years of age and 3.8 points for those who were 70 (78).

One factor that may influence both age of onset and rate of progression is genetic susceptibility. It has frequently been reported that many early-onset PD patients with the parkin mutation have a relatively slow rate of progression compared with patients with PD (79–81). Heterogeneous rates of progression even within a given parkin family, however, suggest that the nature of the genetic mutation(s) alone may not serve as a reliable predictor of progression.

Effects of Therapy

Dopaminergic therapy has affected the natural history of PD. First, the course of progression of disability in PD has been altered, and, second, complications of long-term exposure to levodopa must now be considered part of the natural history of the disease.

The rate of progression of PD disability appears to be slower since the advent of levodopa therapy. Hoehn (82) reported that PD patients treated with levodopa spent 3 to 5 years more in each HY stage compared with subjects followed in the prelevodopa era. Furthermore, among PD patients with a disease duration of 10 to 14 years, 38% of levodopa-treated patients had reached HY stage IV or V or had died, compared with 83% of untreated patients. Despite these observations, it remains uncertain whether levodopa actually alters the neuropathologic progression of PD. The results of the ELLDOPA trial demonstrated that patients receiving the highest doses of levodopa maintained the most robust clinical improvement even after a 4-week medication washout (34), suggesting that levodopa may slow clinical progression. By contrast, the β-CIT SPECT findings in the ELLDOPA study suggested a more rapid decline in putamenal DAT binding in the high-dose levodopa treated group. The long-term effects of levodopa on PD progression remain uncertain, as do the effects of dopamine agonists. Two large double-blind controlled trials comparing early treatment with dopamine agonists to levodopa found slower declines in presynaptic dopaminergic function for those on agonists, but in the absence of a placebo group and in light of the ELLDOPA findings, these results are difficult to interpret (56, 83).

Although levodopa has provided dramatic and sustained symptomatic benefits for patients with PD, these benefits appear to occur at the expense of long-term complications such as dyskinesias and motor fluctuations. Several factors appear to affect the likelihood of developing complications of dopaminergic therapy, including duration of exposure to levodopa, levodopa dose, PD severity, and age (84–86). Overall,

between 50% and 100% of all PD patients taking levodopa for more than 6 years will develop peak-dose dyskinesias (25). In an effort to reduce the incidence of dyskinesias, early treatment of PD often focuses on drugs other than levodopa. PD patients initially treated with dopamine agonists show a significantly lower rate of dyskinesias at 5 years even if levodopa is added, although dopamine agonists do not provide the same level of symptomatic improvement as levodopa (87, 88). Finally, in a recent FDOPA PET study on the effects of deep brain stimulation (DBS) on PD progression, 30 patients exhibited a continuous decline in dopaminergic function on the order of that found in previous longitudinal studies, suggesting that DBS does not alter the course of PD progression (89).

Disease Duration and Mortality

Although the overall duration of PD from onset until death may not have changed significantly since the advent of levodopa, mortality in early PD has been dramatically reduced (90, 91). In the prelevodopa era, Hoehn and Yahr found a mean duration of disease of 9.4 years and a mean age at death of 67 in a cohort of 672 PD patients (26). They found a mortality rate 2.9 times that expected for an age-matched population. Subsequently, after the introduction of levodopa, Hoehn (82) reported a mortality ratio of 1.5, and other studies have found similar mortality rates (92, 93). Mean PD duration has been found to be approximately 13 years, and the mean age at death has been reported at 73 (93). Therefore levodopa has reduced the mortality of PD and extended life, although patients with PD still have higher mortality rates than age-matched populations without PD. In a 13-year follow-up of 800 patients who had enrolled in the earlier DATATOP study, PD-specific variables associated with mortality included increased symmetry of parkinsonism at presentation, early gait dysfunction, and a rapid rate of clinical worsening prior to enrollment (94). A poor response to levodopa was also associated with mortality independent of disease severity.

The causes of death in PD patients have not changed since the advent of dopaminergic therapy. Cardiovascular disease is the most common cause of death, followed by pneumonia (93). Malignant neoplasms, although the second most common cause of death in the general population over the age of 65, appears to occur less frequently in PD patients (93, 95).

CONCLUSION

Over the past 4 decades, the development and validation of clinical scales and neuroimaging methods has permitted more quantitative and rigorous descriptions of PD onset and progression. Advances in the understanding of the pathophysiology of PD over the same period have begun to suggest therapeutic strategies aimed at altering the course of the disease. The challenge for the future will be to identify disease-modifying agents. The ability to achieve this will be based both on the strong groundwork of knowledge of the natural history of PD already accumulated as well as on the development of new methods of assessing disease severity and progression.

References

1. Marsden CD. Parkinson's disease. *Lancet* 1990; 335:948–952.
2. Fearnley JM, Lees AJ. Ageing and Parkinson's disease: Substantia nigra regional selectivity. *Brain* 1991; 114 (Pt 5):2283–2301.
3. Scherman D, Desnos C, Darchen F, et al. Striatal dopamine deficiency in Parkinson's disease: Role of aging. *Ann Neurol* 1989; 26:551–557.
4. Lee CS, Schulzer M, Mak EK, et al. Clinical observations on the rate of progression of idiopathic parkinsonism. *Brain* 1994; 117 (Pt 3):501–507.
5. Braak H, Del Tredici K, Rub U, et al. Staging of brain pathology related to sporadic Parkinson's disease. *Neurobiol Aging* 2003; 24:197–211.
6. Uchiyama M, Isse K, Tanaka K, et al. Incidental Lewy body disease in a patient with REM sleep behavior disorder. *Neurology* 1995; 45:709–712.
7. Boeve BF, Silber MH, Parisi JE, et al. Synucleinopathy pathology and REM sleep behavior disorder plus dementia or parkinsonism. *Neurology* 2003; 61:40–45.
8. Vingerhoets FJ, Snow BJ, Lee CS, et al. Longitudinal fluorodopa positron emission tomographic studies of the evolution of idiopathic parkinsonism. *Ann Neurol* 1994; 36:759–764.
9. Morrish PK, Rakshi JS, Bailey DL, et al. Measuring the rate of progression and estimating the preclinical period of Parkinson's disease with [18F]dopa PET. *J Neurol Neurosurg Psychiatry* 1998; 64:314–319.
10. Nurmi E, Ruottinen HM, Bergman J, et al. Rate of progression in Parkinson's disease: a 6-[18F]fluoro-L-dopa PET study. *Mov Disord* 2001; 16:608–615.
11. Hilker R, Schweitzer K, Coburger S, et al. Nonlinear progression of Parkinson disease as determined by serial positron emission tomographic imaging of striatal fluorodopa F18 activity. *Arch Neurol* 2005; 62:378–382.
12. Marek KL, Seibyl J, Fussell B, et al. 123I-betaCIT: Assessment of progression in Parkinson's disease. *Neurology* 1997; 48 (Suppl 2):A207.
13. Moeller JR, Eidelberg D. Divergent expression of regional metabolic topographies in Parkinson's disease and normal ageing. *Brain* 1997; 120:2197–2206.
14. Gonera EG, van't Hof M, Berger HJ, et al. Symptoms and duration of the prodromal phase in Parkinson's disease. *Mov Disord* 1997; 12:871–876.
15. Koller WC. When does Parkinson's disease begin? *Neurology* 1992; 42:27–31; discussion 41–28.
16. Ponsen MM, Stoffers D, Booij J, et al. Idiopathic hyposmia as a preclinical sign of Parkinson's disease. *Ann Neurol* 2004; 56:173–181.
17. Berendse HW, Booij J, Francot CM, et al. Subclinical dopaminergic dysfunction in asymptomatic Parkinson's disease patients' relatives with a decreased sense of smell. *Ann Neurol* 2001; 50:34–41.
18. Hoehn MM. The natural history of Parkinson's disease in the pre-levodopa and post-levodopa eras. *Neurol Clin* 1992; 10:331–339.
19. Rajput AH, Offord KP, Beard CM, et al. Epidemiology of parkinsonism: Incidence, classification, and mortality. *Ann Neurol* 1984; 16:278–282.
20. Baba Y, Markopoulou K, Putzke JD, et al. Phenotypic commonalities in familial and sporadic Parkinson disease. *Arch Neurol* 2006; 63:579–583.
21. Inzelberg R, Schechtman E, Paleacu D, et al. Onset and progression of disease in familial and sporadic Parkinson's disease. *Am J Med Genet A* 2004; 124:255–258.
22. Khan NL, Graham E, Critchley P, et al. Parkin disease: A phenotypic study of a large case series. *Brain* 2003; 126:1279–1292.
23. Bonifati V, Rohe CF, Breedveld GJ, et al. Early-onset parkinsonism associated with PINK1 mutations: Frequency, genotypes, and phenotypes. *Neurology* 2005; 65:87–95.
24. Becker G, Muller A, Braune S, et al. Early diagnosis of Parkinson's disease. *J Neurol* 2002; 249(Suppl 3):III/40–III/48.
25. Poewe WH, Wenning GK. The natural history of Parkinson's disease. *Ann Neurol* 1998; 44:S1–S9.
26. Hoehn MM, Yahr MD. Parkinsonism: Onset, progression and mortality. *Neurology* 1967; 17:427–442.
27. Uitti RJ, Baba Y, Wszolek ZK, et al. Defining the Parkinson's disease phenotype: Initial symptoms and baseline characteristics in a clinical cohort. *Parkinsonism Relat Disord* 2005; 11:139–145.
28. Lohmann E, Periquet M, Bonifati V, et al. How much phenotypic variation can be attributed to parkin genotype? *Ann Neurol* 2003; 54:176–185.
29. Parkinson J. *An Essay on the Shaking Palsy.* London: Sherwood, Neely, and Jones, 1817.
30. Martilla RJ, Rinne UK. Disability and progression in Parkinson's disease. *Acta Neurol Scand* 1977; 56:159.
31. Goetz CG, Stebbins GT, Blasucci LM. Differential progression of motor impairment in levodopa-treated Parkinson's disease. *Mov Disord* 2000; 15:479–484.
32. Parkinson Study Group. Effects of tocopherol and deprenyl on the progression of disability in early Parkinson's disease. *N Engl J Med* 1993; 328:176–183.
33. Jankovic J, McDermott M, Carter J, et al. Variable expression of Parkinson's disease: A base-line analysis of the DATATOP cohort. The Parkinson Study Group. *Neurology* 1990; 40:1529–1534.
34. Fahn S, Oakes D, Shoulson I, et al. Levodopa and the progression of Parkinson's disease. *N Engl J Med* 2004; 351:2498–2508.
35. Marek K, Innis R, van Dyck C, et al. [123I]beta-CIT SPECT imaging assessment of the rate of Parkinson's disease progression. *Neurology* 2001; 57:2089–2094.
36. Colloby SJ, Williams ED, Burn DJ, et al. Progression of dopaminergic degeneration in dementia with Lewy bodies and Parkinson's disease with and without dementia assessed using 123I-FP-CIT SPECT. *Eur J Nucl Med Mol Imaging* 2005; 32:1176–1185.
37. Hilker R, Klein C, Hedrich K, et al. The striatal dopaminergic deficit is dependent on the number of mutant alleles in a family with mutations in the parkin gene: Evidence for enzymatic parkin function in humans. *Neurosci Lett* 2002; 323:50–54.
38. Jankovic J, Kapadia AS. Functional decline in Parkinson disease. *Arch Neurol* 2001; 58:1611–1615.
39. Jennings D, Seibyl J, Oakes D, et al. Clinical determinants of progressive dopamine transporter loss measured by b-CIT and SPECT. *Mov Disord* 2002; 17:1104.
40. Morrish PK. The harsh realities facing the use of SPECT imaging in monitoring disease progression in Parkinson's disease. *J Neurol Neurosurg Psychiatry* 2003; 74:1447.
41. Feigin A. Evidence from biomarkers and surrogate endpoints. *NeuroRx* 2004; 1: 323–330.
42. Winogrodzka A, Booij J, Wolters E. Disease-related and drug-induced changes in dopamine transporter expression might undermine the reliability of imaging studies of disease progression in Parkinson's disease. *Parkinsonism Relat Disord* 2005; 11:475–484.
43. Dhawan V, Ishikawa T, Patlak C, et al. Combined FDOPA and 3OMFD PET studies in Parkinson's disease. *J Nucl Med* 1996; 37:209–216.
44. Dhawan V, Ma Y, Pillai V, et al. Comparative analysis of striatal FDOPA uptake in Parkinson's disease: Ratio method versus graphical approach. *J Nucl Med* 2002; 43: 1324–1330.
45. Eidelberg D, Moeller JR, Dhawan V, et al. The metabolic anatomy of Parkinson's disease: C [18F]fluorodeoxyglucose and [18F]fluorodopa positron emission tomographic studies. *Mov Disord* 1990; 5:203–213.
46. Takikawa S, Dhawan V, Chaly T, et al. Input functions for 6-[fluorine-18]fluorodopa quantitation in parkinsonism: comparative studies and clinical correlations. *J Nucl Med* 1994; 35:955–963.
47. Ishikawa T, Dhawan V, Kazumata K, et al. Comparative nigrostriatal dopaminergic imaging with iodine-123-beta CIT-FP/SPECT and fluorine-18-FDOPA/PET. *J Nucl Med* 1996; 37:1760–1765.
48. Trošt M, Dhawan V, Feigin A, et al. PET and SPECT. In: Beal MF, Lang A, Ludolph A (eds). *Neurodegenerative Diseases: Neurobiology Pathogenesis and Therapeutics.* Cambridge, UK: Cambridge University Press, 2005:290–300.
49. Nurmi E, Ruottinen HM, Kaasinen V, et al. Progression in Parkinson's disease: A positron emission tomography study with a dopamine transporter ligand [18F]CFT. *Ann Neurol* 2000; 47:804–808.
50. Morrish PK, Sawle GV, Brooks DJ. An [18F]dopa-PET and clinical study of the rate of progression in Parkinson's disease. *Brain* 1996; 119(Pt 2):585–591.
51. Dhawan V, Nakamura T, Margouleff C, et al. Double-blind controlled trial of human embryonic dopaminergic tissue transplants in advanced Parkinson's disease: Fluorodopa PET imaging. *Neurology* 1999; 52(Suppl 2):A405–A406.
52. Nurmi E, Bergman J, Eskola O, et al. Progression of dopaminergic hypofunction in striatal subregions in Parkinson's disease using [18F]CFT PET. *Synapse* 2003; 48:109–115.
53. Khan NL, Brooks DJ, Pavese N, et al. Progression of nigrostriatal dysfunction in a parkin kindred: An [18F]dopa PET and clinical study. *Brain* 2002; 125:2248–2256.
54. Marek KL, Seibyl JP, Zoghbi SS, et al. [123I] beta-CIT/SPECT imaging demonstrates bilateral loss of dopamine transporters in hemi-Parkinson's disease. *Neurology* 1996; 46:231–237.
55. Seibyl JP, Marek KL, Quinlan D, et al. Decreased single-photon emission computed tomographic [123I]beta-CIT striatal uptake correlates with symptom severity in Parkinson's disease. *Ann Neurol* 1995; 38:589–598.
56. Parkinson Study Group. Pramipexole vs levodopa as initial treatment for Parkinson disease: A randomized controlled trial. *JAMA* 2000; 284:1931–1938.
57. Staffen W, Mair A, Unterrainer J, et al. Measuring the progression of idiopathic Parkinson's disease with [123I] beta-CIT SPECT. *J Neural Transm* 2000; 107:543–552.
58. Pirker W, Holler I, Gerschlager W, et al. Measuring the rate of progression of Parkinson's disease over a 5-year period with beta-CIT SPECT. *Mov Disord* 2003; 18: 1266–1272.
59. Winogrodzka A, Bergmans P, Booij J, et al. [123I]beta-CIT SPECT is a useful method for monitoring dopaminergic degeneration in early stage Parkinson's disease. *J Neurol Neurosurg Psychiatry* 2003; 74:294–298.
60. Jennings D, Seibyl J, Innis R, et al. [123I]beta-CIT and SPECT imaging assessment of progression of dopamine transporter loss in Parkinson's disease. *Mov Disord* 2000; 15 (Suppl 3):219.

61. Jennings D, Innis R, Seibyl J, et al. [123I]beta-CIT and SPECT assessment of progression of early and late Parkinson's disease. *Neurology* 2001; 56 (Suppl 3):A47.

62. Huang C, Feigin A, Ma Y, et al. Imaging measures of longitudinal change in Parkinson's disease. *Neurology* 2005; 64:A235.

63. Ma Y, Tang C, Spetsieres P, et al. Abnormal metabolic network activity in Parkinson's disease: Test-retest reproducibility. *J Cereb Blood Flow Metab* 2006:in press.

64. Eckert T, Eidelberg D. Neuroimaging and therapeutics in movement disorders. *NeuroRx* 2005; 2:361–371.

65. Mentis MJ, McIntosh AR, Perrine K, et al. Relationships among the metabolic patterns that correlate with mnemonic, visuospatial, and mood symptoms in Parkinson's disease. *Am J Psychiatry* 2002; 159:746–754.

66. Huang C, Carbon M, Mattis P, et al. Metabolic patterns associated with cognitive function in Parkinson's disease. *Mov Disord* 2006; 21:S104.

67. Marttila RJ, Rinne UK. Disability and progression in Parkinson's disease. *Acta Neurol Scand* 1977; 56:159–169.

68. Zetusky WJ, Jankovic J, Pirozzolo FJ. The heterogeneity of Parkinson's disease: Clinical and prognostic implications. *Neurology* 1985; 35:522–526.

69. Roos RA, Jongen JC, van der Velde EA. Clinical course of patients with idiopathic Parkinson's disease. *Mov Disord* 1996; 11:236–242.

70. Josephs KA, Matsumoto JY, Ahlskog JE. Benign tremulous parkinsonism. *Arch Neurol* 2006; 63:354–357.

71. Burn DJ, Rowan EN, Allan LM, et al. Motor subtype and cognitive decline in Parkinson's disease, Parkinson's disease with dementia, and dementia with Lewy bodies. *J Neurol Neurosurg Psychiatry* 2006; 77:585–589.

72. Alves G, Larsen JP, Emre M, et al. Changes in motor subtype and risk for incident dementia in Parkinson's disease. *Mov Disord* 2006; 8:1123–1130.

73. Dujardin K, Defebvre L, Duhamel A, et al. Cognitive and SPECT characteristics predict progression of Parkinson's disease in newly diagnosed patients. *J Neurol* 2004; 251:1383–1392.

74. Goetz CG, Tanner CM, Stebbins GT, et al. Risk factors for progression in Parkinson's disease. *Neurology* 1988; 38:1841–1844.

75. Blin J, Dubois B, Bonnet AM, et al. Does ageing aggravate parkinsonian disability? *J Neurol Neurosurg Psychiatry* 1991; 54:780–782.

76. Diamond SG, Markham CH, Hoehn MM, et al. Effect of age at onset on progression and mortality in Parkinson's disease. *Neurology* 1989; 39:1187–1190.

77. Ghebremedhin E, Del Tredici K, Vuksic M, et al. Relationship of apolipoprotein E and age at onset to Parkinson disease neuropathology. *J Neuropathol Exp Neurol* 2006; 65:1 16–123.

78. Alves G, Wentzel-Larsen T, Aarsland D, et al. Progression of motor impairment and disability in Parkinson disease: A population-based study. *Neurology* 2005; 65:1436–1441.

79. Wu RM, Bounds R, Lincoln S, et al. Parkin mutations and early-onset parkinsonism in a Taiwanese cohort. *Arch Neurol* 2005; 62:82–87.

80. Bertoli-Avella AM, Giroud-Benitez JL, Akyol A, et al. Novel parkin mutations detected in patients with early-onset Parkinson's disease. *Mov Disord* 2005; 20:424–431.

81. Munhoz RP, Sa DS, Rogaeva E, et al. Clinical findings in a large family with a parkin ex3delta40 mutation. *Arch Neurol* 2004; 61:701–704.

82. Hoehn MM. Parkinsonism treated wtih levodopa: Progression and mortality. *J Neural Transm* 1983; (Suppl 19):253–264.

83. Whone AL, Watts RL, Stoessl AJ, et al. Slower progression of Parkinson's disease with ropinirole versus levodopa: The REAL-PET study. *Ann Neurol* 2003; 54:93–101.

84. McDowell FH. Ten-year follow-up study of levodopa-treated patients with Parkinson's disease. *Adv Neurol* 1979; 24:475–480.

85. Quinn N, Critchley P, Marsden CD. Young onset Parkinson's disease. *Mov Disord* 1987; 2:73–91.

86. Horstink MW, Zijlmans JC, Pasman JW, et al. Severity of Parkinson's disease is a risk factor for peak-dose dyskinesia. *J Neurol Neurosurg Psychiatry* 1990; 53:224–226.

87. Rascol O, Brooks DJ, Korczyn AD, et al. A five-year study of the incidence of dyskinesia in patients with early Parkinson's disease who were treated with ropinirole or levodopa. 056 Study Group. *N Engl J Med* 2000; 342:1484–1491.

88. Parkinson Study Group. Pramipexole versus levodopa as initial treatment for Parkinson's Disease: A randomized control trial. *Jama* 2000;284(15):1931–1938.

89. Hilker R, Portman AT, Voges J, et al. Disease progression continues in patients with advanced Parkinson's disease and effective subthalamic nucleus stimulation. *J Neurol Neurosurg Psychiatry* 2005; 76:1217–1221.

90. Curtis L, Lees AJ, Stern GM, et al. Effect of L-dopa on course of Parkinson's disease. *Lancet* 1984; 2:211–212.

91. Uitti RJ, Ahlskog JE, Maraganore DM, et al. Levodopa therapy and survival in idiopathic Parkinson's disease: Olmsted County project. *Neurology* 1993; 43:1918–1926.

92. Shaw KM, Lees AJ, Stern GM. The impact of treatment with levodopa on Parkinson's disease. *Q J Med* 1980; 49:283–293.

93. DiRocco A, Molinari SP, Kollmeier B, et al. Parkinson's disease: Progression and mortality in the L-dopa era. *Adv Neurol* 1996; 69:3–11.

94. Marras C, McDermott MP, Rochon PA, et al. Survival in Parkinson disease: Thirteen-year follow-up of the DATATOP cohort. *Neurology* 2005; 64:87–93.

95. Jansson B, Jankovic J. Low cancer rates among patients with Parkinson's disease. *Ann Neurol* 1985; 17:505–509.

14 Clinical Rating Scales

Stephen T. Gancher

Before the discovery of levodopa, studies that described the efficacy of drug treatment or of surgical therapy largely relied on subjective impressions. In more recent years, standardized ratings have been developed to compare the effectiveness of a variety of interventions and to allow studies of the natural history of disease progression.

Several different measures of disease severity are employed. In addition to motor signs, which are used in all objective scales, a number of symptoms may also be used. These include patient self-reports such as diaries, estimation of functional performance, and measures of impairments of the quality of life.

Another approach is to use biological markers of disease severity, such as the binding of radiolabeled ligands in the basal ganglia. These measures are potentially useful in neuroprotective studies.

EARLY STANDARDIZED RATINGS

A brief, single-item assessment of motor function was reported by Hoehn and Yahr in a paper describing the natural history of Parkinson's disease (PD) (1). Although this scale was used to classify patients broadly, it is very easily administered and a modified form is still widely used in practice and clinical trials. A number of other early scales, such as the Northwestern University Disability Scale (2), employed a general measure of independence or contained a mixture of motor signs and functional status (3–5). Scales for PD are comprehensively reviewed by Martinez-Martin (6).

THE UNIFIED PARKINSON'S DISEASE RATING SCALE

Description

Because of differences in weighting signs and symptoms and variability between scales, a committee chaired by Dr. Stanley Fahn was created in 1984 to develop a standardized scale. This scale, the Unified Parkinson's Disease Rating Scale (UPDRS), is a composite of various previous scales and its use in the United States has largely supplanted others.

The UPDRS is a composite scale consisting of 6 sections. Unless otherwise indicated, each item is defined by a short sentence and is rated from 0–4 (normal to severely affected).

Administration and Content

The UPDRS is administered by a combination of patient interview and physical examination. It can be administered either by a physician, a nurse experienced in PD, or a trained technician. Depending on the skill of the rater and interactions with the patient, the UPDRS takes approximately 20 to 30 minutes to administer. In practice, the motor portion of the UPDRS is the quickest to administer, particularly in mildy affected patients.

Part I of the UPDRS consists of 4 items, assessing cognitive symptoms, mood, motivation, and the presence or absence of a thought disorder. Although helpful as a general screen, these items are inadequate to estimate the severity of dementia or depression; other instruments should be used for their assessment.

Part II consists of 13 items, describing difficulties in performance of a number of activities of daily living such as bathing, dressing, using utensils, as well as any interference in functioning from impairments in walking as a result of tremor or of sensory symptoms. Although these items are useful, 2 limitations should be kept in mind. First, patient perceptions may differ considerably, and it is not unusual to observe large discrepancies between subjective ratings and how the scale relates to objective measures of disease severity. A second difficulty is that functional performance may change during "on" and "off" states. Because patients commonly perform certain daily activities during certain times or only during "on" periods, rating functional performance only during "on" or "off" states may be artificial and difficult for patients to answer accurately.

Part III is a 14-item rating of motor signs based largely on items in the Columbia Disability scale. In addition to ratings of tremor and an assessment of facial and generalized bradykinesia, performance of several tasks is used to rate disease severity, including slowness noted while the patient is repeatedly tapping the index finger against the thumb, clenching and unclenching a fist, rising from a chair, and other tasks. The definitions of impairment with each task are straightforward, and the scale is reproducible. However, this motor scale does not take into account any interference from dyskinesias or dystonias, which may downgrade motor performance in some patients.

Part IV rates complications of therapy. This includes questions about the duration, severity, and timing of dyskinesias and motor fluctuations and the presence or absence of anorexia, sleep disturbance, or orthostatic hypotension.

Part V is a modified version of the Hoehn and Yahr staging system; overall disease severity is divided into unilateral or bilateral signs and whether balance and gait are affected.

Part VI is a disability scale, estimating the degree of dependency in daily activities; this is a modification of an earlier scale (6).

Validation

Validation of Clinical Ratings. Several studies have estimated the interrater reliability of the UPDRS. In an early study (7), the UPDRS scores of 24 patients with PD were rated by 2 neurologists with experience in use of this scale. Overall, ratings closely agreed between raters ($r = 0.8$), although the ratings of some items, such as speech ($r = 0.29$) and facial akinesia ($r = 0.07$), were less reliable; this was attributed to difficulty in grading patients with equivocal hypophonia or facial masking.

Subsequent studies have also found a good correlation between raters. Three nurse clinicians and a neurologist rated motor signs in 75 patients using the motor exam (Part III) of the UPDRS; the nurses readministered the scale 3 weeks later. The ratings were closely correlated between different raters over the 3-week period ($r = 0.7–0.9$), further demonstrating that the scale has good test-retest and interrater reliability (8).

Another study rated 34 patients with advanced PD during "on" as well as "off" periods on each of 2 visits and found a good correlation between repeated "on" ($r = 0.97$) and repeated "off" ($r = 0.84$) periods (9).

The test-retest reproducibility of the UPDRS has also been measured in a large study. Four hundred patients with early stage disease were evaluated by the UPDRS by the same neurologists at 2 times approximately 2 weeks apart. The intraclass coefficient, a measure of reproducibility, was very high for the overall UPDRS score (0.92); measures of specific subscales such as mental, ADL, and motor scores as well as for symptom-based subscales were also quite good, ranging from 0.86 to 0.90 (10).

As the UPDRS is a somewhat lengthy scale to administer, a number of studies have addressed which items are most important. One study found that some items were redundant and less reproducible and could be omitted (11). Another study reported that a 6-item measure of disability, derived from the ADL section of the UPDRS, had a very good correlation (ranging from $r = 0.76$ to $r = 0.92$), with other disability and motor measures (12). A short motor scale with a reduced number of items has been developed. This scale, the short Parkinson's evaluation scale (SPES), which was studied in 85 patients and has very good intra- and interrater reliability, correlates well with the UPDRS and is shorter to administer (13).

SYMPTOM RATINGS

Symptom rating instruments have been less extensively tested. One study (14) found a good correlation between Part II of the UPDRS, Hoehn and Yahr stage ($r = 0.7$), and Part III of the UPDRS ($r = 0.8$). Studies of the ADL section of the UPDRS found good agreement between patients, caregivers, and neurologist (15, 16). However, the correlations between symptom ratings and motor ratings are less clear; while one study found a good correlation (r = 0.8) (14), another study did not (15). Another study of 103 patients compared ratings of a quality-of-life scale with Hoehn and Yahr stage and found a moderate correlation (r = 0.5–0.7) (17).

BIOLOGICAL MARKERS

Ratings of motor impairments have been compared to *in vivo* markers of basal ganglia biochemical abnormalities in patients with PD. Studies using positron emission tomography (PET) have found an increase in glucose metabolism (18) as well as a reduction of fluorodopa uptake and retention in the basal ganglia in PD. These abnormalities are observed early in the disease and have been found in individuals with genetic or environmental risk factors for PD but not yet exhibiting motor signs. More recent studies have been performed with single photon emission computed tomography (SPECT), a technology requiring less specialized equipment and using more stable radioisotopes, such as compounds that bind the dopamine transporter. These two types of studies correlate closely (19), and both correlate moderately well with motor ratings, particularly with measures of rigidity and bradykinesia (19–21).

These studies have been used to estimate disease progression by studying individual patients over time (22, 23). However, the correlation between the loss of signal and motor scores is imperfect. Generally, the loss of signal in the basal ganglia over time is reduced to a greater extent than are clinical measures of PD, and not all studies show a good correlation between changes in basal ganglia radionuclide uptake and changes in motor scores (23) over time.

Recent drug trials that have investigated possible effects of drug treatment in affecting disease progression have yielded conflicting data. In a study designed to determine if levodopa treatment affects disease progression, patients were studied before and after a 9-month period of treatment with either levodopa or placebo. At the end of this treatment period, patients treated with levodopa exhibited a greater loss of striatal dopamine transporter uptake compared to untreated patients, yet they exhibited a slower rate of clinical decline (24). Similar results were seen in studies comparing levodopa and dopamine agonist treatment in early-stage patients; patients treated with levodopa did better clinically, yet they exhibited a greater loss of either dopamine transporter signal (25) or fluorodopa uptake (26) compared to those treated with dopamine agonists.

The interpretation of these studies is problematic. There is evidence that short-term treatment with levodopa or a dopamine agonist substantially reduces the uptake of a dopamine transporter marker (27), and it is unclear if clinical measures or imaging of the dopamine transporter are the "gold standard" to estimate disease progression.

OVERVIEW: ADVANTAGES AND DISADVANTAGES

Because of its wide use and extensive validation, the UPDRS has become the "gold standard" reference scale. It is in common use in multicenter drug trials, in the process of new drug approvals, in trials of neurosurgical treatments, and in neuroprotective trials.

There are some disadvantages to the UPDRS. Although it is used over a wide range of disease severities, it is not ideally designed for very mildly affected patients with subtle physical findings nor in patients with very severe disease. In addition, some items are redundant, not as reproducible or valid across time or with different raters, or are ambiguous.

A more significant limitation of the UPDRS is that a number of associated physical symptoms and signs develop in most patients with PD over time that are not assessed adequately. These include such problems as neuropsychological deficits, sleep disturbances, anxiety, fatigue, depression and executive dysfunction, dysphagia, and dysarthria. In addition, autonomic symptoms such as impotence, orthostatic hypotension, and bladder and bowel dysfunction become major disabling features of patients with advancing PD but are not assessed adequately. A task force has been established to address these limitations and to develop a new version (28).

The Capit Rating Scale

The Core Assessment Program for Intracerebral Transplantation (CAPIT) (29) was devised to standardize the ratings obtained in studies of transplantation in PD and is now commonly used in assessing other neurosurgical treatments.

In addition to utilizing the UPDRS, the CAPIT protocol also includes a rating of dyskinesias. Other items include diary information, timed motor tasks, and videotaped evaluation before and after an oral dose of levodopa. One useful feature is a "practically defined off" period, which is defined as the motor state in the morning after an overnight period without medications at least 1 hour after arising (to avoid confounding effects of a sleep benefit).

RATINGS OF DYSKINESIAS

Several dyskinesia rating scales have been devised. The abnormal involuntary movement scale (AIMS), which was devised for ratings of tardive dyskinesia, has been used in earlier studies but is not well suited for evaluation of

PD in that it concentrates on cranial and oral dyskinesias and is not recommended.

A number of very simple scales have been described. One scale, described in the CAPIT protocol, rates the intensity of dyskinesias and the duration for the waking day (each on a scale of 0–5), and scores overall dyskinesias as the average of these 2 scores. Although simple, the distribution and types of dyskinesias are not specified.

Another simple scale rates dyskinesias in each limb, the trunk, and head and neck on a scale of 0 to 4 (0 = absent; 4 = incapacitating) (30). These scales are easy and quick to administer, take minimal training, and can be used for repeated examinations in pharmacologic studies, but their reproducibility has not been studied.

A more detailed dyskinesia scale based on videotaped ratings of performance of motor task is often used (31). Patients are videotaped performing 4 tasks (walking, drinking from a cup, putting on a coat, and buttoning), and an overall severity score is assigned. In addition, the different types and most severe dyskinesias are identified.

The reliability of this scale has been studied. Videotapes of 20 patients were reviewed on 2 occasions by multiple raters, including physicians and study coordinators. Agreement between raters on the severity, type of dyskinesia, and severity of dyskinesia was good for both groups of raters (r = 0.8–0.9). A follow-up study compared the ratings of 34 patients during two different "on" times and found that the ratings were very close (9).

Although it is useful, there are limitations to this scale. It is relatively fast to administer but still takes several minutes and may not be appropriate for acute pharmacologic studies, in which dyskinetic movements are assessed at very frequent intervals. In addition, this scale does not assess the distribution or amplitude of movements. Further, many dyskinesias occur only at specific times of the day and may not be readily observed during office evaluation. Finally, intensity of pain is not estimated on this scale.

DIARY RATINGS

Another way to assess motor fluctuations is by patient self-report. The patient is instructed to rate motor symptoms, averaging performance over each hour or half hour. In some versions, the patient is asked to distinguish between "on" and "on with dyskinesias', and to note if dyskinesias are troublesome or not. Although helpful, a number of problems are encountered with diary information. Unless the directions are explicit, misleading information can be reported by patients if they are simply asked to rate themselves "on" or "off." Under research conditions, some patient self-reports correlate poorly with nursing or physician motor ratings; patients may rate themselves as "off" because of fatigue or may not be able to distinguish between tremor and dyskinesias.

Limited studies have been conducted to test the reliability of patient self-reports. In one study, 26 patients with motor fluctuations kept diary information, rating their function as "off, " "partially off, " "on, " and "on with dyskinesias." The overall agreement between physician and patient ratings was fair, but several days of diary information were required to achieve reliability (32).

In a larger study (33), patients were asked to rate waking functional status as "off, " "on without dyskinesias, " "on with nontroublesome dyskinesia, " or "on with troublesome dyskinesia" every half hour for 3 consecutive days over each of 2 weeks. At the end of each of these days, patients also provided responses to several questions regarding dyskinesias and motor function using a visual analog scale. The percent of the waking day in which patients rated themselves as either "on" without dyskinesia or without troublesome dyskinesia was very stable over the duration of the study. However, there was only a fair correlation (r = 0.41) between this measure and the answer to the question "How much of the day today did you experience a good response?" The correlation between the diary data, "'on' with troublesome dyskinesias" and the answer to the question "How much of the day today did you have troublesome dyskinesia?" was also only fair (r = 0.57). This study suggests that patient self-perception of motor response over the day may be somewhat inaccurate, but patient diaries, when filled out prospectively, may be a simple and useful way to report some aspects of motor function.

UNIFIED PARKINSON'S DISEASE RATING SCALE

Mentation, Behavior, and Mood

1. Intellectual Impairment:
   0 –None.
   1 –Mild. Consistent forgetfulness with partial recollection of events and no other difficulties.
   2 –Moderate memory loss, with disorientation and moderate difficulty handling complex problems. Mild but definite impairment of function at home with need of occasional prompting.
   3 –Severe memory loss with disorientation of time and often of place. Severe impairment in handling problems.
   4 –Severe memory loss with orientation preserved to person only. Unable to make judgments or solve problems. Requires much help with personal care. Cannot be left alone at all.

2. Thought Disorder (Due to dementia or drug intoxication):
   0 –None.
   1 –Vivid dreaming.

2 –"Benign" hallucinations with insight retained.
3 –Occasional to frequent hallucinations or delusions; without insight; could interfere with daily activities.
4 –Persistent hallucinations, delusions, or florid psychosis. Not able to care for self.

3. Depression:
   0 –Not present.
   1 –Periods of sadness or guilt greater than normal, never sustained for days or weeks.
   2 –Sustained depression (1 week or more).
   3 –Sustained depression with vegetative symptoms (insomnia, anorexia, weight loss, loss of interest).
   4 –Sustained depression with vegetative symptoms and suicidal thoughts or intent.

4. Motivation/Initiative:
   0 –Normal.
   1 –Less assertive than usual; more passive.
   2 –Loss of initiative or disinterest in elective (non-routine) activities.
   3 –Loss of initiative or disinterest in day-to-day (routine) activities.
   4 –Withdrawn, complete loss of motivation.

Activities of Daily Living (Determine for "on/off")

5. Speech:
   0 –Normal.
   1 –Mildly affected. No difficulty being understood.
   2 –Moderately affected. Sometimes asked to repeat statements.
   3 –Severely affected. Frequently asked to repeat statements.
   4 –Unintelligible most of the time.

6. Salivation:
   0 –Normal.
   1 –Slight but definite excess of saliva in mouth; may have nighttime drooling.
   2 –Moderately excessive saliva; may have minimal drooling.
   3 –Marked excess of saliva with some drooling.
   4 –Marked drooling, requires constant tissue or handkerchief.

7. Swallowing:
   0 –Normal.
   1 –Rare choking.
   2 –Occasional choking.
   3 –Requires soft food.
   4 –Requires nasogastric tube or gastrostomy feeding.

8. Handwriting:
   0 –Normal.
   1 –Slightly slow or small.
   2 –Moderately slow or small; all words are legible.
   3 –Severely affected; not all words are legible.
   4 –The majority of words are not legible.

9. Cutting Food and Handling Utensils:
   0 –Normal.
   1 –Somewhat slow and clumsy, but no help needed.
   2 –Can cut most foods, although clumsy and slow; some help needed.
   3 –Food must be cut by someone, but can still feed slowly.
   4 –Needs to be fed.

10. Dressing:
    0 –Normal.
    1 –Somewhat slow, but no help needed.
    2 –Occasional assistance with buttoning, getting arms in sleeves.
    3 –Considerable help required but can do some things alone.
    4 –Helpless.

11. Hygeine:
    0 –Normal.
    1 –Somewhat slow but no help needed.
    2 –Needs help to shower or bathe or very slow in hygienic care.
    3 –Requires assistance for washing, brushing teeth, combing hair, going to bathroom.
    4 –Foley catheter or other mechanical aids.

12. Turning in bed and adjusting bedclothes:
    0 –Normal.
    1 –Somewhat slow but no help needed.
    2 –Can turn alone or adjust sheets but with great difficulty.
    3 –Can initiate but not turn or adjust sheets alone.
    4 –Helpless.

13. Falling (unrelated to freezing).
    0 –None.
    1 –Rare falling.
    2 –Occasional falls, less than once per day.
    3 –Falls an average of once per day.
    4 –Falls more than once per day.

14. Freezing when walking:
    0 –None.
    1 –Rare freezing when walking, may have start-hestitation.
    2 –Occasional freezing when walking.

3 –Frequent freezing. Occasionally falls from freezing.

4 –Frequent falls from freezing.

15. Walking:
0 –Normal.
1 –Mild difficulty. May not swing arms or may tend to drag leg.
2 –Moderate difficulty, but requires little or no assistance.
3 –Severe disturbance of walking, requiring assistance.
4 –Cannot walk at all, even with assistance.

16. Tremor:
0 –Absent.
1 –Slight and infrequently present.
2 –Moderate; bothersome to patient.
3 –Severe; interferes with many activities.
4 –Marked; interferes with most activities.

17. Sensory Complaints Related to Parkinsonism:
0 –None.
1 –Occasionally has numbness, tingling, or mild aching.
2 –Frequently has numbness, tingling, or aching; not distressing.
3 –Frequent painful sensations.
4 –Excruciating pain.

Motor Examination

18. Speech:
0 –Normal.
1 –Slight loss of expression, diction, and volume.
2 –Monotone, slurred but understandable; moderately impaired.
3 –Marked impairment, difficult to understand.
4 –Unintelligible.

19. Facial Expression:
0 –Normal.
1 –Minimal hypomimia, could be normal "poker face."
2 –Slight but definitely abnormal diminution of facial expression.
3 –Moderate hypomimia; lips parted some of the time.
4 –Masked or fixed facies with severe or complete loss of facial expression; lips parted 1/4 inch or more.

20. Tremor at Rest:
0 –Absent.
1 –Slight and infrequently present.

2 –Mild in amplitude and persistent moderate in amplitude, but only intermittently present.
3 –Moderate in amplitude and present most of the time.
4 –Marked in amplitude and present most of the time.

21. Action or Postural Tremor of Hands:
0 –Absent.
1 –Slight; present with action.
2 –Moderate in amplitude, present with action.
3 –Moderate in amplitude, with posture holding as well as action.
4 –Marked in amplitude; interferes with feeding.

22. Rigidity (Judged on passive movement of major joints with patient relaxed in sitting position. Cogwheeling to be ignored):
0 –Absent.
1 –Slight or detectable only when activated by mirror or other movements.
2 –Mild to moderate.
3 –Marked, but full range of motion easily achieved.
4 –Severe, range of motion achieved with difficulty.

23. Finger Taps (Patient taps thumb with index finger in rapid succession with widest amplitude possible, each hand separately):
0 –Normal.
1 –Mild slowing or reduction in amplitude (11–14/5 sec).
2 –Moderately impaired. Definite and early fatiguing. May have occasional arrests in movement (7–10/5 sec).
3 –Severely impaired. Frequent hesitation in initiating movements or arrests in ongoing movement (3–6/5 sec).
4 –Can barely perform the task(0–2/5 sec).

24. Hand Movements (Patient opens and closes hand in rapid succession with widest amplitude possible, each hand separately):
0 –Normal.
1 –Mild slowing or reduction in amplitude.
2 –Moderately impaired. Definite and early fatiguing. May have occasional arrests in movement.
3 –Severely impaired. Frequent hesitation in initiating movements or arrests in ongoing movement.
4 –Can barely perform the task.

25. Rapid Alternating Movements of Hands (Pronation-supination movements of hands, vertically or horizontally, with as large an amplitude as possible, both hands simultaneously):
    0 –Normal.
    1 –Mild slowing or reduction in amplitude.
    2 –Moderately impaired. Definite and early fatiguing. May have occasional arrests in movement.
    3 –Severely impaired. Frequent hesitation in initiating movements or arrests in ongoing movement.
    4 –Can barely perform the task.

26. Foot agility (Patient taps heel on ground in rapid succession, picking up entire foot. Amplitude should be about 3 inches):
    0 –Normal
    1 –Mild slowing and/or reduction in amplitude.
    2 –Moderately impaired. Definite and early fatiguing. May have occasional arrests in movement.
    3 –Severely impaired. Frequent hesitation in initiating movements or arrests in ongoing movement.
    4 –Can barely perform the task.

A new version of this scale also includes the following item:

Toe tapping: subject sits in chair with or without shoes on. Knees should be flexed and legs essentially perpendicular so that heels of feet are placed comfortably about one inch forward of the perpendicular. The patient is instructed as follows: "with your heel on the ground, tap the toes of the foot and don't stop until I tell you to; keep it smooth and regular and as large and as fast as you can." The rater counts the taps to self and has the patient tap 20 times before telling him or her to stop.

    0 –Normal. Height of toes off the ground should be at least 1 inch. There are no haltings or hesitations during the tapping, which is smooth and evenly spaced throughout. The normal amplitude should not decrement with continuous tapping.
    1 –Mildly impaired amplitude maintained without decrementing, but there are 1–2 hesitations or irregularities in otherwise smooth tapping of toes 20 times.
    2 –Moderately impaired. Able to tap the toes the full 20 times with any of the following abnormalities:
       (a) between 2–5 very brief hesitations; or
       (b) at least one longer halting period; or
       (c) decrementing amplitude with tapping.

    3 –Severely impaired. Any of the following abnormalities; (a) cannot tap the toes 20 times but does achieve at least 10 taps; or (b) if 20 taps are achieved they are accomplished with more than 5 hesitations or more than one long halt; or (c) the amplitude never achieved the height of 1 inch or without decrementing further during the 20 taps.
    4 –Markedly impaired. Cannot tap the toes 20 times.

27. Arising from Chair: (Patient attempts to arise from a straight-back wood or metal chair with arms folded across chest.)
    0 –Normal.
    1 –Slow; or may need more than one attempt.
    2 –Pushes self up from arms of seat or may need more than one attempt.
    3 –Tends to fall back and may have to try more than one time but can get up without help.
    4 –Unable to arise without help.

28. Posture:
    0 –Normal erect.
    1 –Not quite erect, slightly stooped posture; could be normal for older person.
    2 –Moderately stooped posture, definitely abnormal; can be slightly leaning to one side.
    3 –Severely stooped posture with kyphosis; can be moderately leaning to one side.
    4 –Marked flexion with extreme abnormality of posture.

29. Gait:
    0 –Normal
    1 –Walks slowly, may shuffle with short steps, but no festination or propulsion.
    2 –Walks with difficulty, but requires little or no assistance; may have some festination, short steps, or propulsion.
    3 –Severe disturbance of gait, requiring assistance.
    4 –Cannot walk at all, even with assistance.

30. Postural Stability (Response to sudden posterior displacement produced by pull on shoulders while patient erect with eyes open and feet slightly apart. Patient is prepared):
    0 –Normal.
    1 –Retropulsion, but recovers unaided.
    2 –Absence of postural response; would fall if not caught by examiner.
    3 –Very unstable, tends to lose balance spontaneously.
    4 –Unable to stand without assistance.

31. Body Bradykinesia and Hypokinesia (Combining slowness, hesitancy, decreased arm swing, small amplitude, and poverty of movement in general):
    0 –None.
    1 –Minimal slowness, giving movement a deliberate character; could be normal for some persons. Possibly reduced amplitude.
    2 –Mild degree of slowness and poverty of movement which is definitely abnormal. Alternatively, some reduced amplitude.
    3 –Moderate slowness, poverty or small amplitude of movement.
    4 –Marked slowness, poverty or small amplitude of movement.

Complications of Therapy (in the past week)

Dyskinesias

32. Duration: What proportion of the waking day are dyskinesias present? (Historical information) 0 = None; 1 = 1–25% of day; 2 = 26–50% of day; 3 = 51–75% of day; 4 = 76–100% of day.
33. Disability: How disabling are the dyskinesia? (Historical information; may be modified by office examination) 0 = Not disabling; 1 = Mildly disabling; 2 = Moderately disabling; 3 = Severely disabling; 4 = Completely disabling.
34. Painful Dyskinesias: How painful are the dyskinesias? 0 = No painful dyskinesias; 1 = Slight; 2 = Moderate; 3 = Severe; 4 = Marked.
35. Presence of Early Morning Dystonia: (Historical information) 0 = No; 1 = Yes.

Clinical Fluctuations

36. Are any "off" periods predictable as to timing after a dose of medication? 0 = No; 1 = Yes.
37. Are any "off" periods unpredictable as to timing after a dose of medication? 0 = No; 1 = Yes.
38. Do any of the "off" periods come on suddenly, for example, over a few seconds? 0 = No; 1 = Yes.
39. What proportion of the waking day is patient "off" on average? 0 = None; 1 = 1–25% of day; 2 = 26–50% of day; 3 = 51–75% of day; 4 = 76–100% of day.

Other Complications

40. Does the patient have anorexia, nausea, or vomiting? 0 = No; 1 = Yes.
41. Does the patient have any sleep disturbances, for example, insomnia or hypersomnolence? 0 = No; 1 = Yes.

42. Does the patient have symptomatic orthostasis? 0 = No; 1 = Yes.

MODIFIED HOEHN AND YAHR STAGING

Stage 0 –No signs of disease.
Stage 1 –Unilateral disease.
Stage 1.5 –Unilateral plus axial involvement.
Stage 2 –Bilateral disease, without impairment of balance.
Stage 2.5 –Mild bilateral disease with recovery on pull test.
Stage 3 –Mild to moderate bilateral disease; some postural instability; physically independent.
Stage 4 –Severe disability; still able to walk or stand unassisted.
Stage 5 –Wheelchair-bound or bedridden unless aided.

MODIFIED SCHWAB AND ENGLAND ACTIVITIES OF DAILY LIVING SCALE

100% –Completely independent. Able to do all chores without slowness, difficulty or impairment. Essentially normal. Unaware of any difficulty.
90% –Completely independent. Able to do all chores with some degree of slowness, difficulty, and impairment. Might take twice as long. Beginning to be aware of difficulty.
80% –Completely independent in most chores. Takes twice as long. Conscious of difficulty and slowness.
70% –Not completely independent. More difficulty with some chores. Three to four times as long in some. Must spend a large part of the day with chores.
60% –Some dependency. Can do most chores, but exceedingly slowly and with much effort. Errors; some impossible.
50% –More dependent. Help with half, slower, etc. Difficulty with everything.
40% –Very dependent. Can assist with all chores, but few alone.
30% –With effort, now and then does a few chores alone or begins alone. Much help needed.
20% –Nothing alone. Can be a slight help with some chores. Severe invalid.
10% –Total dependent, helpless. Complete invalid.
0% –Vegetative functions such as swallowing, bladder, and bowel functions are not functioning. Bedridden.

DYSKINESIA RATING SCALE (31)

Directions:

1. View the patient walk, drink from a cup, put on a coat and button clothing.
2. Rate the severity of dyskinesias. These may include chorea, dystonia, and other dyskinetic movements in combination. Rate the patient's worst function.
3. Check which dyskinesias are observed (more than one response possible).
4. Check the type of dyskinesia that is causing the most disability on the tasks seen on the tape (only one response is permitted).

Severity rating code:

0 Absent
1 Minimal severity, no interference with voluntary motor acts
2 Dyskinesias may impair voluntary movements but patient is normally capable of undertaking most motor acts
3 Intense interference with movement control and daily life activities are greatly limited 4 violent dyskinesias, incompatible with any normal motor tasks

Dyskinesias observed (more than one choice possible): Chorea, dystonia, other most disabling dyskinesia (choose one): Chorea, dystonia, other.

References

1. Hoehn MM, Yahr MD. Parkinsonism: Onset, progression, and mortality. *Neurology* 1967; 17:427–442.
2. Canter CJ, de la Torre R, Mier M. A method of evaluating disability in patients with Parkinson's disease. *J Nerv Ment Dis* 1961; 133:143–147.
3. Schwab RS. Progression and prognosis in Parkinson's disease. *J Nerv Ment Dis* 1960; 130:556–566.
4. Webster DD. Critical analysis of the disability in Parkinson's disease. *Mod Treat* 1968; 5:257–282.
5. Yahr MD, Duvoisin RC, Schear MJ, et al. Treatment of parkinsonism with levodopa. *Arch Neurol* 1969; 21:343–354.
6. Martinez-Martin P. Rating scales in Parkinson's disease. In: Jankovic J, Tolosa E (eds). *Parkinson's Disease and Movement Disorders*. Baltimore: Williams & Wilkins, 1993: 281–292.
7. Richards M, Marder K, Cote L, et al. Interrater reliability of the Unified Parkinson's Disease Rating Scale Motor Examination. *Mov Disord* 1994; 9:89–91.
8. Bennett DA, Shannon KM, Beckett LA, et al. Metric properties of nurses' ratings of parkinsonian signs with a modified Unified Parkinson's Disease Rating Scale. *Neurology* 1997; 49(6):1580–1587.
9. Metman LV, Myre B, Verwey N, et al. Test-retest reliability of UPDRS-III, dyskinesia scales, and timed motor tests in patients with advanced Parkinson's disease: An argument against multiple baseline assessments. *Mov Disord* 2004; 19:1079–1084.
10. Siderowf A, McDermott M, Kieburtz K et al. Test-retest reliability of the Unified Parkinson's Disease Rating Scale in patients with early Parkinson's disease: results from a multicenter clinical trial. *Mov Disord* 2002; 17:758–763.
11. Martinez-Martin P, Gil-Nagel A, Gracia LM, et al. The cooperative multicentric group. Unified Parkinson's Disease Rating Scale characteristics and structure. *Mov Disord* 1994; 9:76–83.
12. Martinez-Martin P, Fontan C, Frades Payo B, et al. Parkinson's disease: Quantification of disability based on the Unified Parkinson's Disease Rating Scale. *Neurologia* 2000; 15:382–387.
13. Marinus J, Visser M, Stiggelbout AM, et al. A short scale for the assessment of motor impairments and disabilities in Parkinson's disease: The SPES/SCOPA. *J Neurol Neurosurg Psychiatry* 2004; 75:388–395.
14. van Hilten JJ, van der Zwan AD, Zwinderman AH, et al. Rating impairment and disability in Parkinson's disease: Evaluation of the Unified Parkinson's Disease Rating Scale. *Mov Disord* 1994; 9:84–88.
15. Louis ED, Lynch T, Marder K, et al. Reliability of patient completion of the historical section of the Unified Parkinson's Disease Rating Scale. *Mov Disord* 1996; 11(2):185–192.
16. Martinez-Martin P, Benito-Leon J, Alonso F, et al. Patients', doctors', and caregivers' assessment of disability using the UPDRS-ADL section: Are these ratings interchangeable? *Mov Disord* 2003; 18:985–992.
17. Martinez-Martin P, Frades Payo B. Quality of life in Parkinson's disease: Validation, study of the PDQ-39 Spanish version. The Grupo Centro for study of Movement Disorders. *J Neurol* 1998; 245(Suppl 1):S34–S38.
18. Eidelberg D, Moeller JR, Ishikawa T, et al. Assessment of disease severity in parkinsonism with fluorine-18-fluorodeoxyglucose and PET. *J Nucl Med* 1995; 36:378–383.
19. Eshuis SA, Maguire RP, Leenders KL, et al. Comparison of FP-CIT SPECT with F-DOPA PET in patients with de novo and advanced Parkinson's disease. *Eur J Nucl Med Mol Imaging* 2006; 33:200–209.
20. Seibyl JP, Marek KL, Quinlan D, et al. Decreased single-photon emission computed tomographic [123I]-beta-CIT striatal uptake correlates with symptom severity in Parkinson's disease. *Ann Neurol* 1995; 38(4):589–598.
21. Eising EG, Muller TT, Zander C, et al. SPECT-evaluation of the monoamine uptake site ligand [123I](1R)-2-beta-carbomethoxy-3-beta-(4-iodo-phenyl)-tropane ([123I]beta-CIT) in untreated patients with suspicion of Parkinson's disease. *J Inves Med* 1997; 45(8):448–452.
22. Pirker W, Holler I, Gerschlager W, et al. Measuring the rate of progression of Parkinson's disease over a 5-year period with beta-CIT SPECT. *Mov Disord* 2003; 18:1266–1272.
23. Marek K, Innis R, van Dyck C, et al. [123I]beta-CIT SPECT imaging assessment of the rate of Parkinson's disease progression. *Neurology* 2001; 57:2089–2094.
24. Fahn S, Oakes D, Shoulson I, et al. Levodopa and the progression of Parkinson's disease *N Engl J Med* 2004; 351:2498–2508.
25. Parkinson Study Group. Dopamine transporter brain imaging to assess the effects of pramipexole vs levodopa on Parkinson's disease progression. *JAMA* 2002; 287:1653–61.
26. Whone AL, Watts RL, Stoessl AJ, et al. Slower progression of Parkinson's disease with ropinirole versus levodopa: The REAL-PET study. *Ann Neurol* 2003; 54:93–101.
27. Guttman M, Stewart D, Hussey D, et al. Influence of L-dopa and pramipexole on striatal dopamine transporter in early PD. *Neurology* 2001; 56:1559–1564.
28. Movement disorder society task force on rating scales for Parkinson's disease. The Unified Parkinson's Disease Rating Scale (UPDRS): Status and recommendations. *Mov Disord* 2003; 18:738–750.
29. Langston JW, Widner H, Goetz CG, et al. Core Assessment Program for Intracerebral Transplantations (CAPIT). *Mov Disord* 1992; 7:2–13.
30. Nutt JG, Woodward WR, Hammerstad JP, et al. The "on-off" phenomenon in Parkinson's disease: Relation to levodopa absorption and transport. *N Engl J Med* 1984; 310: 483–488.
31. Goetz CG, Stebbins GT, Shale HM, et al. Utility of an objective dyskinesia rating scale for Parkinson's disease: Inter- and intrarater reliability assessment. *Mov Disord* 1994; 9:390–394.
32. Reimer J, Grabowski M, Lindvall O, et al. Use and interpretation of on/off diaries in Parkinson's disease. J Neurol Neurosurg Psychiatry 2004; 75:396–400.
33. Hauser R, Deckers F, Lehert P. Parkinson's disease home diary: Further validation and implications for clinical trials. Mov Disord 2004; 19:1409–1413.

III

BEHAVIORAL
AND PSYCHIATRIC
MANIFESTATIONS

15 Dementia

Karen S. Marder
Diane M. Jacobs

Although estimates of the prevalence and incidence of dementia in Parkinson's disease (PD) vary, there is little doubt that it is an important complication both because of the need for reduction or elimination of some of the medications used to treat the motor manifestations of PD and the impact of dementia on morbidity and mortality. The spectrum of cognitive impairment seen in PD may be conceptualized as a continuum. Although some patients with PD never develop cognitive impairment, most have selective impairment in the domains of memory, executive function and visuospatial skills. A proportion of patients with isolated deficits progress to dementia. Several questions remain unresolved: (a) What is the pattern of neuropsychological impairment in PD and how does it evolve in those who become demented? (b) What is the etiology of dementia in PD and to what extent is the dementia due to Alzheimer's disease (AD)? (c) What are the demographic characteristics, genetic influences, and environmental risk factors associated with dementia in PD? (d) What are the currently available treatments for dementia in PD?

DEFINING DEMENTIA IN PARKINSON'S DISEASE

The most widely used criteria for the diagnosis of dementia, from the current edition of the *Diagnostic and Statistical Manual of Mental Disorders* (DSM-IV-TR), require "the development of multiple cognitive deficits . . . sufficiently severe to cause impairment in occupational or social functioning" (1). The cognitive deficits must include impairment of learning or memory plus impaired language, praxis, object recognition, or executive functioning. The cognitive dysfunction must represent a decline from premorbid levels and cannot occur exclusively during the course of delirium. Although previous editions of the DSM stated that "an underlying causative organic factor is always assumed" in cases of dementia, specification of an etiologic factor was not necessary to make the diagnosis. In the DSM-IV-TR (1), however, specific dementia diagnoses are assigned based on the presumed etiology; specifically, dementia of the Alzheimer's type, vascular dementia, or dementia due to other general medical conditions. PD is listed among the general medical conditions to which dementia can be attributed.

According to the DSM-IV-TR (1), "The essential feature of Dementia Due to Parkinson's Disease is the presence of a dementia that is judged to be the direct pathophysiological consequence of PD." In many cases, however, it is difficult or even impossible to determine whether dementia in a patient with PD is due to a "direct pathophysiological consequence of Parkinson's disease" or to a comorbid dementing disorder, such as Alzheimer's disease (AD) or dementia with Lewy bodies (DLB).

One factor determining whether dementia is due to PD is the temporal relationship between the onset of the motor and cognitive symptoms. This temporal relationship is critical in differentiating AD or DLB from PD with dementia (PDD). If dementia is the primary symptom and extrapyramidal motor signs appear only later in the disease course, a diagnosis of AD (with extrapyramidal features) may be warranted. Conversely, although parkinsonism and visual hallucinations are quite common in the advanced stages of AD, if these symptoms are prominent early in the course of dementia, a diagnosis of DLB should be considered.

The temporal distinction between PDD and DLB is more difficult. The original consensus guidelines for the diagnosis of DLB (2) suggest that if the onset of parkinsonian motor symptoms precedes the onset of cognitive symptoms by more than 12 months, the diagnosis of PDD is warranted. If, on the other hand, the cognitive and motor symptoms commence within 12 months of each other, a diagnosis of DLB should be considered. A recent revision of these guidelines (3) acknowledges that

> The 1-year rule distinguishing between DLB and PDD may be difficult to apply in clinical settings and in such cases the term most appropriate to each individual patient should be used. . . . DLB should be diagnosed when dementia occurs before or concurrently with parkinsonism and PDD should be used to describe dementia that occurs in the context of well-established PD. In research studies in which distinction is made between DLB and PDD, the 1-year rule between the onset of dementia and parkinsonism for DLB should be used.

In addition to the temporal relationship between the cognitive and motor symptoms, additional clinical features associated with DLB (e.g., visual hallucinations, rapid-eye-movement (REM) sleep behavior disorder, severe neuroleptic sensitivity, reduced striatal dopamine transporter activity on functional neuroimaging) are helpful in making the distinction between AD, DLB, and PDD (3).

Clinicopathologic studies have found the accuracy of a clinical diagnosis of DLB to be poor, hovering around 50% accurate (4–6). In an analysis of case vignettes describing 15 patients with PD, 14 with DLB, and 76 without PD or DLB, all confirmed by autopsy, PD was predicted by asymmetric presentation (bradykinesia, tremor, and rigidity), levodopa- induced dyskinesias, and absence of cognitive impairment (4). DLB was predicted by the presence of hallucinations and the absence of tremor, bradykinesia, and dystonia. Clinically, DLB was under diagnosed, and was most often misdiagnosed as AD or PD. Less likely entities that could be mistaken for dementia in PD include multi-infarct dementia, progressive supranuclear palsy, multisystem atrophy, and corticobasal degeneration. Early spontaneous motor signs in AD have been associated with false-positive clinical diagnoses of DLB, whereas greater emphasis on hallucinations as a diagnostic feature may improve the clinical distinction between DLB and AD (5). The degree of concomitant AD tangle pathology has been found to have an important influence on the clinical presentation and therefore the clinical diagnostic accuracy of DLB (6).

NEUROPSYCHOLOGICAL CHARACTERISTICS OF DEMENTIA IN PARKINSON'S DISEASE

Numerous studies have examined the pattern of cognitive strengths and weaknesses that characterizes dementia in patients with PD (see refs. 7 and 8 for a review of this literature). PDD has been described as a prototypical "subcortical dementia" characterized by predominant impairment of executive functions (i.e., planning, initiating, sequencing, monitoring, and shifting between responses); psychomotor speed, visuomotor and visuospatial skills, memory retrieval (but not storage); and verbal fluency. Language functions other than verbal fluency are relatively preserved, as are orientation and memory storage. This is in contrast to AD, a prototypical "cortical dementia, " in which impairments in language, orientation, and memory storage are often early and prominent symptoms. Thus, in addition to the chronology of symptom presentation, the pattern of cognitive impairment of the dementia syndrome itself may be useful in clarifying the etiology of dementia, at least in its early stages. An overview of results from these studies is presented in Table 15-1.

Although impairment of learning or memory is a requisite criterion for the diagnosis of dementia, the characteristics of memory impairment vary depending on the etiology of the dementia syndrome. One of the most frequently observed differences between demented patients with PD and AD on neuropsychologic testing is performance on tests of delayed recall and recognition memory. Both PD and AD patients are impaired in their ability to recall new information. Thus, performance on tests of immediate and delayed recall memory is impaired relative to normative data for both patient groups. What distinguishes PD from AD patients is performance on delayed recall testing relative to immediate recall; that is, their retention or "savings" of new material over a delay interval differs. Patients with AD rapidly forget new information, even material that was recalled accurately on

TABLE 15-1

Typical Neuropsychological Test Performance of Patients with Cognitive Impairment Due to Parkinson's Disease, Mild Parkinson's Disease Dementia, and Mild Alzheimer's Disease

	PD	PDD	AD
Memory			
Immediate free recall	Mildly impaired	Impaired	Impaired
Delayed free recall	Mildly impaired	Impaired	Severely impaired
Delayed recognition	Normal	Normal	Severely impaired
Percent retention*	Normal (>70%)	Normal–Mildly impaired (>50%)	Severely impaired (<50%)
Language			
Naming	Normal	Normal to Mildly impaired	Severely impaired
Verbal fluency	Impaired	Severely impaired	Impaired
Orientation	Normal	Normal	Impaired
Visuospatial skills	Impaired	Impaired	Impaired
Executive functions†	Impaired	Severely impaired	Severely impaired

*Percent retention = (immediate free recall/delayed free recall) × 100.
†Executive functions may be disproportionately impaired relative to other cognitive abilities.

immediate memory testing (9, 10). In AD, the percentage of recently learned material retained after a delay interval is very low, often less than 50%. Patients with AD often are unable to recall or even recognize material that was recalled correctly several minutes earlier. In contrast, delayed recall and recognition memory in patients with PD often is commensurate with the level of recall on testing of immediate memory. Hence, PD is associated with relatively good retention of newly acquired information over a delay interval. This difference in performance on memory testing between AD and PD patients is evident even when groups are comparable in terms of overall severity of dementia, and it may be particularly pronounced in the early or mild stages. The fact that long-term retention of new material is relatively maintained in PD but impaired in AD supports the conclusion that the memory impairment associated with PD is primarily a retrieval deficit, while AD is characterized by deficient encoding or consolidation of information. The encoding deficit of AD likely reflects the prominent pathology of the hippocampus and entorhinal cortex associated with this disorder (11, 12), while the poor retrieval of new information by PD patients may be secondary to executive dysfunction (i.e., inability to initiate a systematic search of memory) and reflects dysfunction of subcorticofrontal circuits (13).

Although the distinction between "subcortical" and "cortical" dementia has been a useful heuristic in research on PDD, several reports have suggested that there is considerable heterogeneity in the memory profiles of PD patients. Detailed examinations of performance on word-list learning tasks among patients with PD (not all of whom were demented) suggest that memory functioning is normal in approximately 50% of patients; approximately one-third exhibit the expected retrieval deficit profile while the remainder have encoding deficits more typically associated with AD (14–16). It is important, therefore, to consider performance on memory testing within the context of other neuropsychological and clinical characteristics.

Retrospective autopsy studies have supported a neuropsychological distinction between diagnostic groups. Kraybill and associates (17) compared cognitive data from patients with autopsy-confirmed AD, Lewy body pathology alone (LBP), or both. Results revealed that patients with AD alone and AD plus Lewy body pathology (LBP) had more severe memory impairment than patients with just LBP. In contrast, LBP alone was associated with more severe executive dysfunction. Further, patients with combined AD and LBP had the most rapid rate of cognitive decline. In a similar comparison of patients with AD and DLB, Hamilton and colleagues (18) found that although both DLB and AD patients exhibit significant memory impairment, the ability to consolidate information was less severely impaired in DLB patients than in AD patients.

ROLE OF DOPAMINE IN COGNITIVE DYSFUNCTION

Cognitive impairment in the absence of dementia occurs frequently in PD, even among newly diagnosed patients (19, 20). The mild or relatively circumscribed cognitive dysfunction observed in many patients with PD does not progress to dementia in all affected individuals. There is, however, substantial overlap in the pattern of observed deficits in PDD and nondemented PD patients. As in PDD, impairments of attentional and executive functions, visuospatial skills, recall memory, and verbal fluency are common among nondemented PD patients. This pattern of impaired and preserved cognitive abilities on neuropsychological testing is similar to that associated with damage to the frontal lobes, particularly the prefrontal cortex (13, 21), and is hypothesized to reflect dopamine deficiency and reduced neostriatal outflow to the prefrontal cortex (13). Specifically, loss of dopaminergic neurons in the substantia nigra and nigrostriatal pathway disrupts the physiologic activity of the neostriatum (22) and compromises the functioning of subcortical-cortical functional-anatomic loops.

Neuropsychological examination of patients with MPTP-induced parkinsonism has supported the assumption that at least some of the cognitive symptoms of PD are due to loss of dopaminergic innervation of the basal ganglia. In their comparisons of patients with MPTP-induced parkinsonism to age- and education-matched controls, Stern and Langston (23) found that patients had impaired visuospatial and executive functions as assessed by the Rosen Drawing (24), Stroop Color-Word (25), and verbal fluency tests (26). Similar but less severe changes were seen in MPTP-exposed subjects who were motorically asymptomatic, suggesting that these cognitive abilities may be dopamine-specific and that deficits in these domains might be present even in the absence of parkinsonian motor impairment.

Further support for the role of dopamine in cognitive dysfunction in PD comes from examination of PD patients on and off levodopa therapy. Malapani and colleagues (27) examined the ability of nondemented PD patients to process 2 cognitive tasks simultaneously as assessed by simple (i.e., single presentation) and complex (i.e., concurrent presentation) visual and auditory-choice reaction-time measures. They compared 3 groups of PD patients: a group receiving their usual dose of levodopa, a group of recently diagnosed untreated patients, and a group assessed at the time of maximal ("on" state) and minimal ("off" state—treatment withdrawn for 18 hours) clinical benefit of levodopa therapy. Compared with healthy, age-matched normal control subjects, PD patients receiving their standard dose of levodopa and those tested in the "on" state performed normally on tests of simple- and complex-choice reaction time. In contrast, recently diagnosed untreated patients and those tested in the "off" state were impaired on tests of complex- but not simple-choice reaction time. These results suggest that concurrent processing of cognitive information requires adequate dopaminergic transmission (27). Similar "on-off" differences have been reported on measures of verbal delayed-recall memory (28). A report from the DATATOP study revealed that 6 months after the initiation of levodopa therapy, PD patients performed significantly better on tests of frontal lobe function, including measures of psychomotor speed, set-shifting ability, and verbal fluency (29).

PROGRESSION OF COGNITIVE IMPAIRMENT IN PARKINSON'S DISEASE

It is unclear what factors differentiate PD patients who will develop dementia from those who remain cognitively intact or have mild or circumscribed cognitive impairments. Risk factors for dementia have been identified, as have neuropsychological predictors of later decline. Jacobs and colleagues (30) found that the performance of nondemented patients with PD on tests of letter and category fluency was a highly sensitive neuropsychological predictor of incident dementia. Poor verbal fluency in PD patients likely reflects poor executive function rather than an impairment of language per se. Specifically, patients are impaired in their ability to initiate a systematic retrieval of semantic stores and efficiently generate exemplars. Thus, the poor performance of PD patients on measures of verbal fluency, like other deficits of frontal lobe functions, may be attributable to compromised subcortical-cortical circuitry. In a subsequent examination of the same cohort but with longer follow-up, Levy and colleagues (31) found that baseline measures of verbal memory provided an additional contribution to the identification of PD patients who would later become demented. Using a more comprehensive neuropsychological test battery, Mahieux and colleagues (32) found that, in addition to verbal fluency, several other measures of attention and executive function (performance on the Picture Completion subtest of the Wechsler Adult Intelligence Scale–Revised (33) and the interference section of the Stroop Test (25) also were significant neuropsychological predictors of subsequent dementia. Similarly, Woods and Troster (34) found evidence of frontal/executive dysfunction in PD patients' performance on Digit Span Backward, the Wisconsin Card Sorting Test (perseverative errors), and word-list learning and recognition a year prior to the diagnosis of dementia.

A growing body of evidence suggests that when cognitive impairment progresses to dementia in patients with PD, not only do the relatively circumscribed impairments seen in nondemented PD patients worsen in severity but additional cognitive domains are affected. Specifically, there is a qualitative shift in the pattern of cognitive deficits, with substantial broadening and worsening of memory dysfunction, as dementia emerges (9). In a prospective neuropsychological study of the evolution of cognitive changes associated with dementia in PD and

AD, Stern and colleagues (35) found that performance on tests of visual confrontation naming [Boston Naming Test (36)] and delayed-recall memory worsened as non-demented PD patients developed dementia. PD patients performed worse than healthy elders who subsequently developed AD on category fluency throughout the follow-up period, suggesting either that poor verbal fluency is an early manifestation of dementia in PD but not AD or that dementia is overlaid on this preexisting performance deficit. In contrast, elders who subsequently developed AD consistently performed worse than PD patients on a test of delayed recognition memory, consistent with the conclusion that dementia in AD but not PD is characterized by an encoding deficit.

It is widely hypothesized that as dementia emerges in PD and cognitive deficits expand and worsen, so too the underlying pathology expands beyond the dopaminergic system and subcorticofrontal circuits. In some patients, a cholinergic deficit is superimposed on the dopaminergic deficit of PD. This cholinergic deficit likely reflects atrophy of cholinergic cells in the nucleus basalis of Meynart and may occur independently of histopathologic changes indicative of AD. Other dementia patients, however, do show neuropathologic evidence of PD and AD. Finally, the contribution of cortical Lewy bodies must be considered in the differential etiology of PD dementia.

PREVALENCE OF DEMENTIA

The prevalence of dementia in PD has been reported to be as low as 8% (37) and as high as 93% (38). Methodologic issues that have led to this wide range of prevalence estimates include lack of uniform criteria for dementia, ascertainment from case records rather than formal neuropsychological examination, and failure to adjust for age at the time of assessment. Prevalence estimates may also be influenced by the inclusion of patients who meet critieria for DLB (3) rather than PDD, since the period of parkinsonism preceding dementia cannot be accurately determined in dementia prevalence studies.

In an analysis of 2530 patients participating in 17 studies over a 60-year period, Brown and Marsden (39) suggested that the prevalence of dementia was 15%. However, studies performed subsequent to that analysis suggest that the prevalence of dementia in PD is 20% to 40% (40–45). In a systematic review of 12 prevalence studies that met strict prespecified criteria for PD or dementia in PD including 1767 PD patients, the proportion of PD patients with dementia was 24.5% (95% confidence interval (CI) 17.4 to 31.5) (46). When limited to 4 large studies that focused specifically on PD dementia (40–42, 47), 31.1% (95% CI 20.1 to 42.1)

met criteria for dementia. The estimated prevalence of PDD in the general population was 30 (95% CI 19.0 to 41.1) per 100, 000 and between 150 to 500 per 100, 000 among those aged 65 and above. In 24 prevalence studies of dementia that met prespecified criteria, 3.6% (3.1 to 4.1) of all dementia was attributable to PD.

INCIDENCE OF DEMENTIA

Incidence may provide a more meaningful estimate of the frequency of dementia in PD, because the development of dementia may reduce survival; therefore demented PD patients are less likely to be reflected in prevalence surveys. The incidence of dementia among PD patients ranges from 42.6 (48) to 112.5 (49) per 1000 person-years of observation. The highest incidence rates 112.5 (49), 95.5 (50), and 107.4 (51) were reported from community-based studies in which follow-up was more complete than in hospital-based series.

RISK OF DEMENTIA IN PATIENTS WITH PARKINSON'S DISEASE COMPARED WITH AGE-MATCHED CONTROLS

Several studies have compared the risk of dementia in PD with the risk of dementia among controls and have reported risk ratios from 1.7 to 5.9 (45, 49–54). Despite similar incidence rates of dementia in PD in 2 community-based samples (49, 50), a lower risk ratio (RR 1.7; 95% CI 1.1 to 2.7) was reported in the New York study than in the Norwegian study (RR 5.9; 95% CI 3.9 to 9.1) because of an unusually high incidence of dementia in controls in the New York study. A subsequent study in the same New York cohort followed for a mean of 3.6 years, including a different control sample, reported a 3.7-fold increase in risk of dementia in PD compared with controls after adjustment for age, education, and gender (54). In an analysis of the New York and Norwegian studies of incident dementia, the combined risk of dementia in cases compared with controls was 3.4 (2.7 to 4.2). Age-specific risk of dementia is higher among younger PD patients than in age-matched controls because of the low baseline frequency of dementia at that age (53). Compared with controls, PD patients with more severe extrapyramidal signs (UPDRS part III motor score >24) had a 5-fold higher risk of dementia than controls; however, risk among those with less severe motor signs (≤24) was also significantly elevated (RR 2.4; 95% CI 1.2 to 4.9) compared with controls (55). In the same study (55), compared with controls, men (RR 5.5; 95% CI 2.4 to 12.7) had a higher risk of incident dementia than women (RR 2.5; 95% CI 1.2 to 5.3).

MORTALITY

The relatively high incidence rate of dementia compared with the lower prevalence rate in the hospital-based samples of Mayeux and coworkers (40, 56) prompted the consideration that disease duration was shortened by the development of dementia. In two studies, one clinic-based (57) and one community-based (58), the development of dementia significantly reduced survival after controlling for age and disease duration. Several studies have now confirmed that, after controlling for age and disease duration, the development of dementia in the setting of PD is a risk factor for death, with remarkably similar estimates of a 2- to 3-fold increase in risk when dementia is considered as a time-dependent covariate (45, 54, 58). Incident dementia is associated with an increased risk of mortality (RR 2.2; 95% CI 1.1 to 4.5) even after adjustment for the severity of motor signs at each visit (RR 1.04; 95% CI 1.02 to 1.07) (54), suggesting that dementia and disease severity independently contribute to risk of mortality.

RISK FACTORS FOR DEMENTIA IN PARKINSON'S DISEASE

An approach favored by epidemiologists has been to determine the risk factors for dementia in PD by following nondemented PD patients over time and determining what baseline characteristics are predictive of the development of dementia (43, 49, 59, 60). Age at the time of assessment and severity of motor signs are the 2 risk factors that have been most consistently associated with the development of dementia in PD (48–50, 61–65). Duration of PD tends to be longer in demented than in nondemented PD patients (43); however, it has not emerged as a significant predictor of dementia in multivariate analyses (48, 50). This suggests that disease duration may actually reflect older age or disease severity. Age at onset and current age were highly correlated, however, when both were included in multivariate models; current age but not age at onset was predictive of dementia (48–50), suggesting that current age might be a more important predictor than age at onset. In a prospective cohort study of non-demented PD cases, the combined effect of increasing age (above 72 years) and severity of motor signs (above 24) was associated with a 10-fold risk of dementia, whereas the risk of dementia for PD patients above 72 years of age and motor signs equal to or less than 24 or motor signs above 24 and age equal to or less than 72 years were not significantly elevated (55). Because increasing age in the absence of severe motor signs was not associated with dementia, a pathologic process intrinsic to PD is implicated in the etiology of dementia and is supported by neuropathologic findings that cortical Lewy bodies are integral to the development of dementia (66–69). However, there is also evidence to suggest that specific PD signs such as postural instability and gait impairment, which may be mediated by nondopaminergic pathways and may be less responsive to levodopa, are more strongly associated with the development of dementia than traditional dopa-responsive signs such as rigidity (70). The possibility of subtypes of PD that may appear early in the disease process, including a non-tremor-dominant subgroup with significant cognitive impairment, has been posited (20).

A higher frequency of PDD in men than in women has been reported in some studies (48, 49, 53, 55, 59) but not in others (40, 50, 71). Other risk factors include family history of dementia (72, 73), depression (41, 49, 60), psychological stress (e.g., the Holocaust) (74), and low socioeconomic status/low educational attainment (59).

GENETIC AND ENVIRONMENTAL RISK FACTORS

Investigations of risk factors for dementia in PD have examined whether genetic and environmental influences identified in AD are also associated with dementia in PD. Evidence suggests that there may be shared genetic contributions for AD and PDD when the dementia is due to Alzheimer pathology. In a community-based study in Washington Heights, New York, a 3-fold increased risk of history of AD was demonstrated in siblings of PDD patients compared with siblings of controls, while risk of AD was not elevated among relatives of nondemented PD patients compared with relatives of controls, supporting the possibility of aggregation of AD and PDD. The risk was further elevated (RR: 4.9; 95% CI: 1.1 to 21.4) among siblings above 65 years of age (73). In another study using the same family history interview, the risk of AD was not increased in relatives of nondemented PD patients compared with relatives of controls [hazard ratio (HR): 1.1; 95% CI: 0.7 to 1.6, $P = 0.6$] and did not differ by whether age of onset of PD was early (≤50 years) or late-(above age 50 years), suggesting a lack of shared genetic contributions for AD and PD when not accompanied by dementia (75). Elbaz (76), using a similar approach, found no association of PD and dementia among first-degree relatives, although nondemented and demented probands with PD were not evaluated separately.

There are conflicting results about the risk of dementia in PD associated with ApoE4. With the exception of 3 studies (77–79), a significantly increased frequency of the ApoE-ε4 allele has not been found in individual studies of PDD compared with PD without dementia or controls (80–84). However, a meta-analysis including 10 clinical studies (451 nondemented, 197 demented) found a composite OR of 1.6 (95% CI 1.0 to 2.5) for dementia in cases with an E4 allele (85);

however, it cited evidence for possible publication bias resulting in negative studies not being published. Two neuropathologic studies of PD, each including fewer than 50 PD patients, have assessed the association of the ApoE-ε4 allele with concomitant Alzheimer changes and found conflicting results (84, 86). An increased risk of PD dementia in carriers of the ApoE-ε2 allele has been reported (87) and may be dramatically elevated compared to that in noncarriers (RR 13.5; 95% CI 4.5 to 40.6) (45). A new mutation in the α-synuclein gene (E46K) was found to be responsible for PDD in one family (88). Triplication of α-synuclein was identified in the Iowa kindred (Park 4) and a Swedish-American family with autosomal dominant PDD (89). In all 3 families, DLB but not Alzheimer pathology was seen. These findings support the possibility that alpha synuclein burden alone is sufficient to account for dementia in a rare subset of familial PDD.

Few studies have explored the association of environmental risk factors with PDD. Although an inverse association of smoking and PD has been reported (90), Ebmeier and colleagues found that a history of smoking was associated with a 4-fold higher risk for developing dementia among PD patients over a 3.5-year follow-up (91). In another longitudinal study (92), a history of smoking was associated with a 2-fold increased risk, whereas current smoking was associated with a 5-fold risk of incident dementia. In the same study, history of head injury, diabetes, or cardiovascular disease was not associated with increased risk of dementia. An inverse association between estrogen replacement therapy and PD dementia has been reported (93).

A gene-environment interaction for PDD (94) was demonstrated in one study, in which the interaction of pesticide exposure and the presence of a CYP2D6 29B+ was associated with a 3-fold increase in risk of PDD (OR 3.17; 95% CI = 1.11 to 9.05), although neither pesticide exposure nor CYP2D6 29B+ was independently associated with dementia.

NEUROPATHOLOGY

There are abundant data indicating that the neuropathologic basis of PDD is heterogeneous; however, studies are difficult to interpret owing to methodologic limitations, including the retrospective collection of clinical information, inclusion of patients who may have met clinical criteria for DLB, and reliance on clinic-based or brain-bank samples, which are vulnerable to selection bias. With the advent of alpha synuclein (AS) immunostaining and the use over the past decade of the National Institute of Neurological and Communicative Diseases and Stroke/Alzheimer's Disease and Related Disorders Association (NINCDS/ADRDA) criteria for AD (which

emphasize the importance of neurofibrillary tangles in addition to senile plaques), there has been an increasing appreciation of the role of limbic and cortical Lewy bodies as an important pathologic substrate for PDD. With the exception of 3 large clinicopathologic studies (95–97), all studies have included less than 40 demented patients, with the majority including less than 25 patients who underwent autopsy. Four studies included prospective cognitive assessments proximate to death using screening mental status tests (48, 98, 99), one of which was community-based (69). All other studies including 2 large series reported by Jellinger (96, 97) relied on retrospective information gleaned from chart review.

There are 3 broad concepts regarding the pathologic basis of dementia in PD. First, concomitant AD may be the cause of PDD, since AD pathology is more severe in demented than in nondemented PD patients (100, 101). Second, pathologic studies demonstrating greater numbers of Lewy bodies in the medial substantia nigra (102, 103), ventral tegmental area (104), locus ceruleus (104), and nucleus basalis of Meynert (104–106) in PDD compared with PD support the idea that subcortical Lewy body pathology might be sufficient to cause dementia in PD. Third, since the wider recognition of DLB as a cause of dementia, it has been proposed that cognitive impairment in PD may correlate with the "spread" of the Lewy body pathology from brainstem neurons to higher cortical areas (107, 108). Whether there is a spread of Lewy bodies, implying that PD and DLB are part of a continuum, or whether cortical and subcortical LB pathology occur concurrently remains unknown. Degeneration of subcortical structures may reduce the threshold at which AD changes, which are relatively less severe and widespread than in AD, may cause dementia in PD (109, 110).

Alvord and colleagues(111) were the first to report that PD patients had more AD cortical pathology than age-matched controls. However, some studies suggest that the proportion of PD patients considered to have concomitant AD may not be higher than in controls if stringent pathologic criteria for AD are used (112–116). One study of 28 PD patients found a correlation of cognitive impairment as assessed prospectively by the Mini-Mental State exam (MMS) (117) with AD pathology (98). However, the contribution of subcortical Lewy bodies to cognitive impairment in PD was not assessed. Differences in the severity and distribution of AD pathology have been noted in the brains of PD patients compared with AD patients (110, 114, 115, 118, 119), suggesting that AD changes in PD may differ from AD alone. The largest clinicopathologic series of PDD patients included 200 from an Austrian brain bank who met criteria for brainstem PD. Cases with numerous cortical or limbic Lewy bodies were excluded. AD pathology (primarily neurofibrillary tangles) was associated with dementia determined retrospectively and was also a predictor of poor survival (97). In favor of an essential role of subcortical structures in the dementia of PD, several early reports have provided evidence that subcortical neuronal loss with Lewy body pathology might be associated with dementia in the absence of significant AD pathology (105, 113, 120–123). In particular, loss of cholinergic neurons in the nucleus basalis of Meynert has been observed in PD independently of AD cortical pathology (124, 125), but neuronal loss in the nucleus basalis of Meynert is not necessarily associated with dementia (125). However, these early studies preceded the use of ubiquitin or AS immunostaining to detect cortical LBs. The first quantitative assessment of neuronal loss in the substantia nigra (SN) of PD patients revealed that the number of lateral neurons was inversely correlated with rigidity and hypokinesia, whereas medial SN neuron number was inversely correlated with dementia (126). Stereologic approaches have been used to examine the correlation between loss of pigmented neurons in the SN and clinical findings in 12 PD patients and 12 controls. The number of pigmented neurons was 45% of the control mean ($P < .001$) and was inversely correlated with both duration and stage of disease (127).

Over the past decade, the importance of limbic and cortical Lewy bodies as important contributors to the development of dementia has been recognized. Two studies using AS immunostaining (67, 128) found a stronger association of cortical LBs than AD changes with dementia in PD. In a sample of 20 nondemented and 22 clinically diagnosed demented PD patients, cortical Lewy bodies were the best predictor of dementia, while NFTs, senile plaques (SPs), and dystrophic hippocampal neurites were not independently associated with dementia in PD. No formal assessment of cognitive function was performed. Mattila and associates (128) evaluated cognitive impairment retrospectively from hospital records using a rating scale for dementia (Reisberg's Global Deterioration Scale) and found that the total number of Lewy bodies and NFTs in the temporal cortex were both significant predictors of dementia in PD. The contribution of the degree and extension of subcortical Lewy bodies to dementia in PD was not considered in either of these studies. Two other studies, using anti-ubiquitin immunostaining, assessed limbic and neocortical regions exclusively and found a correlation of cognitive impairment in PD with Lewy neurites in the CA2 hippocampal field (99) and in the periamygdaloid cortex (129). A study comparing 13 PD patients who developed dementia on average 10.5 years after the onset of parkinsonism to 9 nondemented PD patients found that Lewy body counts were increased 10-fold in cortical and limbic areas compared to those in nondemented PD patients ($P < .002$) with only modest AD pathology (66). In the nucleus basalis of Meynert and SN, Lewy body counts were twice as high in the demented individuals, but this

did not reach significance. NFTs were significantly higher in the CA1 field of demented compared with nondemented individuals. In the neocortex, Lewy bodies were correlated with plaques and NFTs; however, plaques and NFTs were not correlated in the neocortex, CA1 field, or entorhinal cortex. The authors concluded that although Lewy body pathology was the most prominent finding in demented PD patients, the mild AD pathology suggested an interplay between these two types of pathology. The largest published prospective study (95) included 65 PD patients with Lewy body pathology but excluded those with AD changes. The authors found that the criterion of > 2 Lewy bodies in the parahippocampal gyrus was the most specific pathology differentiating demented and nondemented PD patients. Aarsland and coworkers (69), conducted a prospective community-based study of 22 PD patients who came to autopsy, 18 of whom met criteria for dementia. These investigators found that the Lewy body score but not the Braak and Braak stage was associated with the annual rate of decline in scores on the Mini-Mental State exam, and none of the cases met NIA-Reagan high-likelihood criteria for AD. Although this study does not preclude Alzheimer changes as contributory to dementia in PD, it does highlight the importance of limbic and neocortical Lewy bodies as contributors to cognitive impairment in PD.

NEUROIMAGING

Structural and functional imaging [(single photon emission computed tomography (SPECT) and positron emission tomography (PET)] have been used to try to determine the neuroanatomic substrate of dementia in PD. Formerly, the primary distinction investigators sought to make was between AD and PD. Currently DLB has also been considered in the differential, and its pattern on functional imaging has been explored.

Using SPECT, a number of investigators have demonstrated a pattern of temporoparietal hypometabolism in PDD (130–132) like that seen in AD. Interestingly, nondemented PD patients did not differ from controls in global or regional hypoperfusion (130, 132, 133). There is a suggestion that SPECT scans show lower 99mTc-HMPAO (99mTc-hexamethyl propylene amine oxime) uptake in the frontal and basal ganglial regions in patients with "early" PDD (average of 2.5 years; stages I and II) compared with nondemented patients (132). Two studies have examined PDD patients longitudinally and suggest that dopaminergic loss may be associated with both motor and cognitive decline. In studies using HMPAO SPECT over 1 year, striatal perfusion was found to increase and to correlate with worsening parkinsonism. This pattern, seen in both PDD and DLB, was believed to reflect a compensatory change associated with decreasing dopaminergic input from the substantia nigra (134). In another study using ^{123}I-FP CIT (^{123}I labeled 2β-carbomethoxy-3β-(4-iodophenyl)-N-(3-fluoropropyl) nortropane) SPECT, DLB and PDD rates of decline were similar and were correlated with both the severity of dementia and motor impairment (135).

PET demonstrates widespread cortical global hypometabolism in PD patients compared with controls (136, 137). Nondemented PD patients had cortical hypometabolism compared with controls while demented PD patients showed more severe hypometabolism in temporoparietal regions, as seen in AD (136, 138). Using the radioligand N11C-methly-4-piperidyl acetate (MP4A), a substrate of cerebral acetylcholinesterase, severe loss of cortical cholinergic activity has been demonstrated in PDD. Performance on tests of attention and working memory correlated with loss of cortical cholinesterase activity in PDD (139). MP4A and related tracers have been used in studies of similar size for patients with PD and PDD, demonstrating cholinergic dysfunction comparable to or greater than that in AD (140). A study that measured both striatal FDOPA uptake and MP4A found that nondemented PD patients had moderate cholinergic dysfunction, but those with PDD had a severe cholinergic deficit affecting the entire cortex, presumably reflecting loss of ascending projections from the nucleus basalis of Meynert. Frontal and temporoparietal FDOPA and MP4A binding covaried in PDD, suggesting a role for both cholinergic denervation and dopaminergic deficits in PDD (141).

TREATMENT OF COGNITIVE IMPAIRMENT

Dementia may limit pharmacotherapy for PD. Once dementia develops, many medications used to treat the motor manifestations of PD must be reduced or discontinued so as to improve cognition. The strategy used in patients with worsening cognitive impairment is to eliminate medications that exacerbate cognitive impairment. This strategy may, however, worsen motor function. The clinician and family must decide on the optimal balance. Patients with PDD are particularly vulnerable to medications that may exacerbate preexisting cognitive impairment. In addition to worsening memory, the medications used to treat PD may induce confusion and hallucinations. One management strategy is to first eliminate anticholinergic medications as well as medications with high anticholinergic activity. Amantadine is another drug that often causes confusion in PD patients with cognitive impairment. If confusion does not remit, a reduction of dopaminergic agents to the lowest possible effective dose should be attempted.

Selegiline, which may delay the development of functional impairment in patients with moderate Alzheimer's disease, was previously examined in PD (142). In a secondary analysis of cognitive test performance in 800 patients with early, untreated PD followed in the DATATOP study, there was no effect of either deprenyl 10 mg or tocopherol 2000 IU on test performance, although cognitive performance was relatively stable over the observation period (143). Until the approval of cholinesterase inhibitors for AD, there were only 2 randomized controlled trials for PDD. Sano and coworkers (144) showed no improvement in cognition with the nootropic piracetam. Cholinesterase inhibitors may be effective in PDD because the cholinergic neurotransmitter system is implicated (145–147). The largest study using rivastigmine, a cholinesterase inhibitor, included 541 patients in whom dementia developed 2 years after PD. Moderate improvement in global measures of dementia, cognition (executive function and attention), and behavioral symptoms were seen at 24 weeks. The most common side effects were nausea, vomiting, and worsening tremor (148). A smaller 10-week randomized clinical trial of donepezil in 22 patients using a crossover design revealed a trend toward improvement on the primary outcome measure (ADAScog) compared to placebo, and a significant improvement in the Mattis Dementia Rating scale (149), and the clinical global impression of change (secondary outcome). Donepezil did not worsen the motor signs of PD (150). Based on these studies and several open-label studies of tacrine (151), donepezil (152–154), rivastigmine (155, 156), and galantamine (157), there appears to be modest benefit in cognition from the use of cholinesterase inhibitors for up to 6 months without major worsening of motor function.

Dementia in PD represents multiple pathologic substrates including PD alone, PD plus AD, and DLB. Neuropsychological, imaging, and pathologic studies suggest a common denominator referable to early dopamine deficiency. Although it has become more apparent which patients are at risk for progression to dementia, the etiologic factors leading to additional involvement of other neurotransmitter systems, with or without the pathologic changes associated with AD, deserve further investigation.

References

1. American Psychiatric Association. *Diagnostic and Statistical Manual of Mental Disorders*, 4th ed, text revision (DSM-IV-TR). Washington, DC: American Psychiatric Association, 2000.
2. McKeith IG, Galasko D, Kosaka K, et al. Consensus guidelines for the clinical and pathologic diagnosis of dementia with Lewy bodies (DLB): Report of the Consortium on DLB International Workshop. *Neurology* 1996; 47:1113–1124.
3. McKeith IG, Dickson DW, Lowe J, et al. Diagnosis and management of dementia with Lewy bodies: Third report of the DLB Consortium. *Neurology* 2005; 65: 1863–1872.
4. Litvan I, MacIntyre A, Goetz CG, et al. Accuracy of the clinical diagnoses of Lewy body disease, Parkinson disease, and dementia with Lewy bodies: A clinicopathologic study. *Arch Neurol* 1998; 55:969–978.

5. Hohl U, Tiraboschi P, Hansen LA, Thal LJ, Corey–Bloom J. Diagnostic accuracy of dementia with Lewy bodies. *Arch Neurol* 2000; 57:347–351.

6. Merdes AR, Hansen LA, Jeste DV, et al. Influence of Alzheimer pathology on clinical diagnostic accuracy in dementia with Lewy bodies. *Neurology* 2003; 60:1586–1590.

7. Raskin SA, Borod JC, Tweedy J. Neuropsychological aspects of Parkinson's disease. *Neuropsychol Rev* 1990; 1:185–221.

8. Stout JC, Johnson SA. Cognitive impairment and dementia in basal ganglia disorders. Curr Neurol Neurosci Rep 2005; 5:355–363.

9. Stern Y, Richards M, Sano M, Mayeux RP. Comparison of cognitive changes in patients with Alzheimer's and Parkinson's disease. *Arch Neurol* 1993; 50:1040–1045.

10. Troster AI, Butters N, Salmon DP, et al. The diagnostic utility of savings scores: Differentiating Alzheimer's and Huntington's diseases with the logical memory and visual reproduction tests. *J Clin Exp Neuropsychol* 1993; 15:773–788.

11. Hyman BT, Van Hoesen GW, Damasio AR, Barnes CL. Alzheimer's disease: Cell-specific pathology isolates the hippocampal formation. *Science* 1984; 225:1168–1170.

12. Braak H, Braak E. Evolution of the neuropathology of Alzheimer's disease. *Acta Neurol Scand Suppl* 1996; 165:3–12.

13. Taylor AE, Saint-Cyr JA, Lang AE. Frontal lobe dysfunction in Parkinson's disease. The cortical focus of neostriatal outflow. *Brain* 1986; 109(Pt 5):845–883.

14. Weintraub D, Moberg PJ, Culbertson WC, et al. Evidence for impaired encoding and retrieval memory profiles in Parkinson disease. *Cogn Behav Neurol* 2004; 17: 195–200.

15. Filoteo JV, Rilling LM, Cole B, et al. Variable memory profiles in Parkinson's disease. *J Clin Exp Neuropsychol* 1997; 19:878–888.

16. Zizak VS, Filoteo JV, Possin KL, et al. The ubiquity of memory retrieval deficits in patients with frontal-striatal dysfunction. *Cogn Behav Neurol* 2005; 18:198–205.

17. Kraybill ML, Larson EB, Tsuang DW, et al. Cognitive differences in dementia patients with autopsy-verified AD, Lewy body pathology, or both. *Neurology* 2005; 64: 2069–2073.

18. Hamilton JM, Salmon DP, Galasko D, et al. A comparison of episodic memory deficits in neuropathologically confirmed dementia with Lewy bodies and Alzheimer's disease. *J Int Neuropsychol Soc* 2004; 10:689–697.

19. Muslimovic D, Post B, Speelman JD, Schmand B. Cognitive profile of patients with newly diagnosed Parkinson disease. *Neurology* 2005; 65:1239–1245.

20. Foltynie T, Brayne CE, Robbins TW, Barker RA. The cognitive ability of an incident cohort of Parkinson's patients in the UK. The CamPaIGN study. *Brain* 2004; 127:550–560.

21. Bondi MW, Kaszniak, AW, Bayles KA, et al. Contributions of frontal system dysfunction ot memory and perceptual abilities in Parkinson's disease. *Neuropsychology* 1993; 7:89–102.

22. Penney JB Jr, Young AB. Speculations on the functional anatomy of basal ganglia disorders. *Annu Rev Neurosci* 1983; 6:73–94.

23. Stern Y, Langston JW. Intellectual changes in patients with MPTP-induced parkinsonism. *Neurology* 1985; 35:1506–1509.

24. Rosen WG. *The Rosen Drawing Test.* Bronx, NY: Department of Veterans Affairs Medical Center, 1981.

25. Stroop JP. Studies of interferences in serial verbal reactions. *J Exp Psychol* 1935; 18: 643–662.

26. Benton AL, Hamsher KD. *Multilingual Aphasia Examination.* Iowa City, IA: University of Iowa, 1976.

27. Malapani C, Pillon B, Dubois B, Agid Y. Impaired simultaneous cognitive task performance in Parkinson's disease: A dopamine-related dysfunction. *Neurology* 1994; 44:319–326.

28. Mohr E, Fabbrini G, Williams J, et al. Dopamine and memory function in Parkinson's disease. *Mov Disord* 1989; 4:113–120.

29. Growdon JH, Kieburtz K, McDermott MP, et al. Levodopa improves motor function without impairing cognition in mild non-demented Parkinson's disease patients. Parkinson Study Group. *Neurology* 1998; 50:1327–1331.

30. Jacobs DM, Marder K, Cote LJ, Sano M, Stern Y, Mayeux R. Neuropsychological characteristics of preclinical dementia in Parkinson's disease. Neurology 1995; 45:1691–1696.

31. Levy G, Jacobs DM, Tang MX, et al. Memory and executive function impairment predict dementia in Parkinson's disease. *Mov Disord* 2002; 17:1221–1226.

32. Mahieux F, Fenelon G, Flahault A, et al. Neuropsychological prediction of dementia in Parkinson's disease. *J Neurol Neurosurg Psychiatry* 1998; 64:178–183.

33. Weschler D. *WAIS-R Manual.* New York: Psychological Corporation, 1981.

34. Woods SP, Troster AI. Prodromal frontal/executive dysfunction predicts incident dementia in Parkinson's disease. *J Int Neuropsychol Soc* 2003; 9:17–24.

35. Stern Y, Tang MX, Jacobs DM, et al. Prospective comparative study of the evolution of probable Alzheimer's disease and Parkinson's disease dementia. *J Int Neuropsychol Soc* 1998; 4:279–284.

36. Kaplan E, Goodglass H, Weintraub S. *Boston Naming Test.* Philadelphia: Lea & Febiger, 1983.

37. Taylor A, Saint-Cyr JA, Lang AE. Dementia prevalence in Parkinson's disease. *Lancet* 1985; 1:1037.

38. Pirozzolo FJ, Hansch EC, Mortimer JA, et al. Dementia in Parkinson disease: A neuropsychological analysis. *Brain Cogn* 1982; 1:71–83.

39. Brown RG, Marsden CD. How common is dementia in Parkinson's disease? *Lancet* 1984; 2:1262–1265.

40. Mayeux R, Denaro J, Hemeneigildo N, et al. A population-based investigation of Parkinson's disease with and without dementia. Relationship to age and gender. *Arch Neurol* 1992; 49:492–497.

41. Aarsland D, Tandberg E, Larsen JP, Cummings JL. Frequency of dementia in Parkinson's disease. Arch Neurol 1996; 53:538–542.

42. Tison F, Dartigues JF, Auriacombe S, et al. Dementia in Parkinson's disease: A population-based study in ambulatory and institutionalized individuals. *Neurology* 1995; 45: 705–708.

43. Biggins CA, Boyd JL, Harrop FM, et al. A controlled, longitudinal study of dementia in Parkinson's disease. *J Neurol Neurosurg Psychiatry* 1992; 55:566–571.

44. Friedman A, Barcikowska M. Dementia in Parkinson's disease. *Dementia* 1994; 5: 12–16.

45. de Lau LM, Schipper CM, Hofman A, et al. Prognosis of Parkinson disease: Risk of dementia and mortality: The Rotterdam Study. *Arch Neurol* 2005; 62:1265–1269.

46. Aarsland D, Zaccai J, Brayne C. A systematic review of prevalence studies of dementia in Parkinson's disease. *Mov Disord* 2005; 20:1255–1263.

47. Marttila RJ, Rinne UKP. Dementia in Parkinson's disease. *Acta Neurol Scand* 1976; 54:431–441.

48. Hughes TA, Ross HF, Musa S, et al. A 10-year study of the incidence of and factors predicting dementia in Parkinson's disease. *Neurology* 2000; 54:1596–1602.

49. Marder K, Tang MX, Cote L, et al. The frequency and associated risk factors for dementia in patients with Parkinson's disease. *Arch Neurol* 1995; 52:695–701.

50. Aarsland D, Andersen K, Larsen JP, et al. Risk of dementia in Parkinson's disease: A community-based, prospective study. *Neurology* 2001; 56:730–736.

51. Hobson P, Meara J. Risk and incidence of dementia in a cohort of older subjects with Parkinson's disease in the United Kingdom. *Mov Disord* 2004; 19:1043–1049.

52. Rajput AH, Offord KP, Beard CM, Kurland LT. A case-control study of smoking habits, dementia, and other illnesses in idiopathic Parkinson's disease. *Neurology* 1987; 37:226–232.

53. Breteler MM, de Groot RR, van Romunde LK, Hofman AP. Risk of dementia in patients with Parkinson's disease, epilepsy, and severe head trauma: A register-based follow-up study. *Am J Epidemiol* 1995; 142:1300–1305.

54. Levy G, Tang MX, Louis ED, et al. The association of incident dementia with mortality in PD. *Neurology* 2002; 59:1708–1713.

55. Levy G, Schupf N, Tang MX, et al. Combined effect of age and severity on the risk of dementia in Parkinson's disease. *Ann Neurol* 2002; 51:722–729.

56. Mayeux R, Chen J, Mirabello E, et al. An estimate of the incidence of dementia in idiopathic Parkinson's disease. *Neurology* 1990; 40:1513–1517.

57. Marder K, Leung D, Tang M, et al. Are demented patients with Parkinson's disease accurately reflected in prevalence surveys? A survival analysis. *Neurology* 1991; 41:1240–1243.

58. Louis ED, Marder K, Cote L, et al. Mortality from Parkinson disease. *Arch Neurol* 1997; 54:260–264.

59. Glatt SL, Hubble JP, Lyons K, et al. Risk factors for dementia in Parkinson's disease: Effect of education. *Neuroepidemiology* 1996; 15:20–25.

60. Starkstein SE, Mayberg HS, Leiguarda R, et al. A prospective longitudinal study of depression, cognitive decline, and physical impairments in patients with Parkinson's disease. *J Neurol Neurosurg Psychiatry* 1992; 55:377–382.

61. Piccirilli M, D'Alessandro P, Finali G, Piccinin GLP. Neuropsychological follow–up of parkinsonian patients with and without cognitive impairment. *Dementia* 1994; 5:17–22.

62. Elizan TS, Sroka H, Maker H, et al. Dementia in idiopathic Parkinson's disease. Variables associated with its occurrence in 203 patients. *J Neural Transm* 1986; 65:285–302.

63. Ebmeier KP, Calder SA, Crawford JR, et al. Clinical features predicting dementia in idiopathic Parkinson's disease: A follow–up study. *Neurology* 1990; 40:1222–1224.

64. Stern Y, Marder K, Tang MX, Mayeux R. Antecedent clinical features associated with dementia in Parkinson's disease. *Neurology* 1993; 43:1690–1692.

65. Hely MA, Morris JG, Reid WG, et al. Age at onset: The major determinant of outcome in Parkinson's disease. *Neurology* 1995; 92:455–463.

66. Apaydin H, Ahlskog JE, Parisi JE, et al. Parkinson disease neuropathology: Later-developing dementia and loss of the levodopa response. *Arch Neurol* 2002; 59:102–112.

67. Hurtig HI, Trojanowski JQ, Galvin J, et al. Alpha-synuclein cortical Lewy bodies correlate with dementia in Parkinson's disease. *Neurology* 2000; 54:1916–1921.

68. Mattila PM, Roytta M, Torikka H, et al. Cortical Lewy bodies and Alzheimer–type changes in patients with Parkinson's disease. *Acta Neuropathol (Berl)* 1998; 95:576–582.

69. Aarsland D, Perry R, Brown A, et al. Neuropathology of dementia in Parkinson's disease: A prospective, community–based study. *Ann Neurol* 2005; 58:773–776.

70. Levy G, Tang MX, Cote LJ, et al. Motor impairment in PD: Relationship to incident dementia and age. *Neurology* 2000; 55:539–544.

71. Diamond SG, Markham CH, Hoehn MM, et al. An examination of male-female differences in progression and mortality of Parkinson's disease. *Neurology* 1990; 40:763–766.

72. Marder K, Flood P, Cote L, Mayeux R. A pilot study of risk factors for dementia in Parkinson's disease. *Mov Disord* 1990; 5:156–161.

73. Marder K, Tang MX, Alfaro B, et al. Risk of Alzheimer's disease in relatives of Parkinson's disease patients with and without dementia. *Neurology* 1999; 52:719–724.

74. Salganik I, Korczyn A. Risk factors for dementia in Parkinson's disease. *Adv Neurol* 1990; 53:343–347.

75. Levy G, Louis ED, Mejia-Santana H, et al. Lack of familial aggregation of Parkinson disease and Alzheimer disease. *Arch Neurol* 2004; 61:1033–1039.

76. Elbaz A, Grigoletto F, Baldereschi M, et al. Familial aggregation of Parkinson's disease: A population-based case-control study in Europe. EUROPARKINSON Study Group. *Neurology* 1999; 52:1876–1882.

77. Arai H, Muramatsu T, Higuchi S, Sasaki H, Trojanowski JQ. Apolipoprotein E gene in Parkinson's disease with or without dementia. *Lancet* 1994; 344:889.

78. Parsian A, Racette B, Goldsmith LJ, Perlmutter JS. Parkinson's disease and apolipoprotein E: Possible association with dementia but not age at onset. *Genomics* 2002; 79:458–461.

79. Pankratz N, Byder L, Halter C, et al. Presence of an APOE4 allele results in significantly earlier onset of Parkinson's disease and a higher risk with dementia. *Mov Disord* 2006; 21:45–49.

80. Marder K, Maestre G, Cote L, et al. The apolipoprotein epsilon 4 allele in Parkinson's disease with and without dementia. *Neurology* 1994; 44:1330–1331.

81. Koller WC, Glatt SL, Hubble JP, et al. Apolipoprotein E genotypes in Parkinson's disease with and without dementia. *Ann Neurol* 1995; 37:242–245.

82. Inzelberg R, Chapman J, Treves TA, et al. Apolipoprotein E4 in Parkinson disease and dementia: New data and meta-analysis of published studies. *Alzheimer Dis Assoc Disord* 1998; 12:45–48.

83. Whitehead AS, Bertrandy S, Finnan F, et al. Frequency of the apolipoprotein E epsilon 4 allele in a case-control study of early onset Parkinson's disease. *J Neurol Neurosurg Psychiatry* 1996; 61:347–351.

84. Mattila PM, Koskela T, Roytta M, et al. Apolipoprotein E epsilon4 allele frequency is increased in Parkinson's disease only with co-existing Alzheimer pathology. *Acta Neuropathol (Berl)* 1998; 96:417–420.

85. Huang X, Chen P, Kaufer DI, et al. Apolipoprotein E and dementia in Parkinson disease: A meta-analysis. *Arch Neurol* 2006; 63:189–193.

86. Egensperger R, Bancher C, Kosel S, et al. The apolipoprotein E epsilon 4 allele in Parkinson's disease with Alzheimer lesions. *Biochem Biophys Res Commun* 1996; 224:484–486.

87. Harhangi BS, de Rijk MC, van Duijn CM, et al. APOE and the risk of PD with or without dementia in a population-based study. *Neurology* 2000; 54:1272–1276.

88. Zarranz JJ, Alegre J, Gomez-Esteban JC, et al. The new mutation, E46K, of alpha-synuclein causes Parkinson and Lewy body dementia. *Ann Neurol* 2004; 55:164–173.

89. Farrer M, Kachergus J, Forno L, et al. Comparison of kindreds with parkinsonism and alpha-synuclein genomic multiplications. *Ann Neurol* 2004; 55:174–179.

90. Morens DM, Grandinetti A, Reed D, et al. Cigarette smoking and protection from Parkinson's disease: False association or etiologic clue? *Neurology* 1995; 45:1041–1051.

91. Ebmeier KP, Calder SA, Crawford JR, et al. Mortality and causes of death in idiopathic Parkinson's disease: Results from the Aberdeen whole population study. *Scott Med J* 1990; 35:173–175.

92. Levy G, Tang MX, Cote LJ, et al. Do risk factors for Alzheimer's disease predict dementia in Parkinson's disease? An exploratory study. *Mov Disord* 2002; 17:250–257.

93. Marder K, Tang MX, Alfaro B, et al. Postmenopausal estrogen use and Parkinson's disease with and without dementia. *Neurology* 1998; 50:1141–1143.

94. Hubble JP, Kurth JH, Glatt SL, et al. Gene-toxin interaction as a putative risk factor for Parkinson's disease with dementia. *Neuroepidemiology* 1998; 17:96–104.

95. Harding AJ, Halliday GM. Cortical Lewy body pathology in the diagnosis of dementia. *Acta Neuropathol (Berl)* 2001; 102:355–363.

96. Jellinger KA. Morphological substrates of dementia in parkinsonism. A critical update. *J Neural Transm Suppl* 1997; 51:57–82.

97. Jellinger KA, Seppi K, Wenning GK, Poewe W. Impact of coexistent Alzheimer pathology on the natural history of Parkinson's disease. *J Neural Transm* 2002; 109:329–339.

98. Bancher C, Braak H, Fischer P, Jellinger KA. Neuropathological staging of Alzheimer lesions and intellectual status in Alzheimer's and Parkinson's disease patients. *Neurosci Lett* 1993; 162:179–182.

99. Churchyard A, Lees AJ. The relationship between dementia and direct involvement of the hippocampus and amygdala in Parkinson's disease. *Neurology* 1997; 49:1570–1576.

100. Hakim AM, Mathieson GP. Dementia in Parkinson disease: A neuropathologic study. *Neurology* 1979; 29:1209–1214.

101. Boller F, Mizutani T, Roessmann U, Gambetti P. Parkinson disease, dementia, and Alzheimer disease: Clinicopathological correlations. *Ann Neurol* 1980; 7:329–335.

102. Rinne JO, Rummukainen J, Paljarvi L, Rinne UK. Dementia in Parkinson's disease is related to neuronal loss in the medial substantia nigra. *Ann Neurol* 1989; 26:47–50.

103. Paulus W, Jellinger K. The neuropathologic basis of different clinical subgroups of Parkinson's disease. *J Neuropathol Exp Neurol* 1991; 50:743–755.

104. Zweig RM, Cardillo JE, Cohen M, et al. The locus ceruleus and dementia in Parkinson's disease. *Neurology* 1993; 43:986–991.

105. Gaspar P, Gray F. Dementia in idiopathic Parkinson's disease. A neuropathological study of 32 cases. Acta Neuropathol (Berl) 1984; 64:43–52.

106. Whitehouse PJ, Hedreen JC, White CL III, Price DL. Basal forebrain neurons in the dementia of Parkinson disease. *Ann Neurol* 1983; 13:243–248.

107. Hurtig HI, Trojanowski JQ, Galvin J, et al. Alpha–synuclein cortical Lewy bodies correlate with dementia in Parkinson's disease. *Neurology* 2000; 54:1916–1921.

108. Braak H, Del Tredici K, Rub U, et al. Staging of brain pathology related to sporadic Parkinson's disease. *Neurobiol Aging* 2003; 24:197–211.

109. Braak H, Rub U, Jansen Steur EN, et al. Cognitive status correlates with neuropathologic stage in Parkinson disease. *Neurology* 2005; 64:1404–1410.

110. Jendroska K, Lees AJ, Poewe W, Daniel SE. Amyloid beta-peptide and the dementia of Parkinson's disease. *Mov Disord* 1996; 11:647–653.

111. Alvord EC Jr. The pathology of Parkinsonism. II. An interpretation with special reference to other changes in the aging brain. *Contemp Neurol Ser* 1971; 8:131–161.

112. Xuereb JH, Tomlinson BE, Irving D, et al. Dementia in Parkinson's disease: Relationship to parkinsonian dementia. *Adv Neurol* 1990; 53:35–40.

113. Ball MJ. The morphological basis of dementia in Parkinson's disease. *Can J Neurol Sci* 1984; 11:180–184.

114. Braak H, Braak EP. Cognitive impairment in Parkinson's disease: Amyloid plaques, neurofibrillary tangles, and neuropil threads in the cerebral cortex. *J Neural Transm Park Dis Dement Sect* 1990; 2:45–57.

115. Ince P, Irving D, MacArthur F, Perry RH. Quantitative neuropathological study of Alzheimer-type pathology in the hippocampus: Comparison of senile dementia of Alzheimer type, senile dementia of Lewy body type, Parkinson's disease and non-demented elderly control patients. *J Neurol Sci* 1991; 106:142–152.

116. Jendroska K. The relationship of Alzheimer-type pathology to dementia in Parkinson's disease. *J Neural Transm Suppl* 1997; 49:23–31.

117. Folstein MF, Folstein SE, McHugh PR. "Mini-mental state": A practical method for grading the cognitive state of patients for the clinician. *J Psychiatr Res* 1975; 12:189–198.

118. Duyckaerts C, Gaspar P, Costa C, et al. Dementia in Parkinson's disease. Morphometric data. *Adv Neurol* 1993; 60:447–455.

119. Vermersch P, Delacourte A, Javoy-Agid F, et al. Dementia in Parkinson's disease: Biochemical evidence for cortical involvement using the immunodetection of abnormal Tau proteins. *Ann Neurol* 1993; 33:445–450.

120. Heilig CW, Knopman DS, Mastri AR, Frey W II. PD dementia without Alzheimer pathology. *Neurology* 1985; 35:762–765.

121. Chui HC, Mortimer JA, Slager U, et al. Pathologic correlates of dementia in Parkinson's disease. *Arch Neurol* 1986; 43:991–995.

122. Torack RM, Morris JCP. The association of ventral tegmental area histopathology with adult dementia. *Arch Neurol* 1988; 45:497–501.

123. Sudarsky L, Morris J, Romero J, Walshe TM. Dementia in Parkinson's disease: The problem of clinicopathological correlation. *J Neuropsychiatry Clin Neurosci* 1989; 1:159–166.

124. Tagliavini F, Pilleri G. Note on the pathology of the basal nucleus of Meynert in degenerative brain disorders. *Schweiz Arch Neurol Neurochir Psychiatr* 1984; 135:277–280.

125. Nakano I, Hirano A. Parkinson's disease: Neuron loss in the nucleus basalis without concomitant Alzheimer's disease. *Ann Neurol* 1984; 15:415–418.

126. Rinne JO, Rummukainen J, Paljarvi L, et al. Neuronal loss in the substantia nigra in patients with Alzheimer's disease and Parkinson's disease in relation to extrapyramidal symptoms and dementia. *Prog Clin Biol Res* 1989; 317:325–332.

127. Ma SY, Roytta M, Rinne JO, et al. Correlation between neuromorphometry in the substantia nigra and clinical features in Parkinson's disease using disector counts. *J Neurol Sci* 1997; 151:83–87.

128. Mattila PM, Rinne JO, Helenius H, et al. Alpha-synuclein-immunoreactive cortical Lewy bodies are associated with cognitive impairment in Parkinson's disease. *Acta Neuropathol (Berl)* 2000; 100:285–290.

129. Mattila PM, Rinne JO, Helenius H, Roytta M. Neuritic degeneration in the hippocampus and amygdala in Parkinson's disease in relation to Alzheimer pathology. *Acta Neuropathol (Berl)* 1999; 98:157–164.

130. Sawada H, Udaka F, Kameyama M, et al. SPECT findings in Parkinson's disease associated with dementia. *J Neurol Neurosurg Psychiatry* 1992; 55:960–963.

131. Pizzolato G, Dam M, Borsato N, et al. [99mTc]-HM-PAO SPECT in Parkinson's disease. *J Cereb Blood Flow Metab* 1988; 8:S101–108.

132. Spampinato U, Habert MO, Mas JL, et al. (99mTc)-HM-PAO SPECT and cognitive impairment in Parkinson's disease: A comparison with dementia of the Alzheimer type. *J Neurol Neurosurg Psychiatry* 1991; 54:787–792.

133. Wang SJ, Liu RS, Liu HC, et al. Technetium-99m hexamethylpropylene amine oxime single photon emission tomography of the brain in early Parkinson's disease: Correlation with dementia and lateralization. *Eur J Nucl Med* 1993; 20:339–344.

134. Firbank MJ, Burn DJ, McKeith IG, O'Brien JT. Longitudinal study of cerebral blood flow SPECT in Parkinson's disease with dementia, and dementia with Lewy bodies. *Int J Geriatr Psychiatry* 2005; 20:776–782.

135. Colloby S, O'Brien J. Functional imaging in Parkinson's disease and dementia with Lewy bodies. *J Geriatr Psychiatry Neurol* 2004; 17:158–163.

136. Peppard RF, Martin WR, Carr GD, et al. Cerebral glucose metabolism in Parkinson's disease with and without dementia. *Arch Neurol* 1992; 49:1262–1268.

137. Vander Borght T, Minoshima S, Giordani B, et al. Cerebral metabolic differences in Parkinson's and Alzheimer's diseases matched for dementia severity. *J Nucl Med* 1997; 38:797–802.

138. Kuhl DE, Minoshima S, Fessler JA, et al. In vivo mapping of cholinergic terminals in normal aging, Alzheimer's disease, and Parkinson's disease. *Ann Neurol* 1996; 40: 399–410.

139. Bohnen NI, Kaufer DI, Ivanco LS, et al. Cortical cholinergic function is more severely affected in parkinsonian dementia than in Alzheimer disease: An in vivo positron emission tomographic study. *Arch Neurol* 2003; 60:1745–1748.

140. Bohnen NI, Kaufer DI, Hendrickson R, et al. Cognitive correlates of cortical cholinergic denervation in Parkinson's disease and parkinsonian dementia. *J Neurol* 2006; 253:242–247.

141. Hilker R, Thomas AV, Klein JC, et al. Dementia in Parkinson disease: Functional imaging of cholinergic and dopaminergic pathways. *Neurology* 2005; 65:1716–1722.

142. Sano M, Ernesto C, Thomas RG, et al. A controlled trial of selegiline, alpha-tocopherol, or both as treatment for Alzheimer's disease. The Alzheimer's Disease Cooperative Study. *N Engl J Med* 1997; 336:1216–1222.

143. Kieburtz K, McDermott M, Como P, et al. The effect of deprenyl and tocopherol on cognitive performance in early untreated Parkinson's disease. Parkinson Study Group. *Neurology* 1994; 44:1756–1759.

144. Sano M, Stern Y, Marder K, Mayeux R. A controlled trial of piracetam in intellectually impaired patients with Parkinson's disease. *Mov Disord* 1990; 5:230–234.

145. Jellinger KAP. Morphological substrates of dementia in parkinsonism. A critical update. *J Neural Transm Suppl* 1997; 51:57–82.

146. Whitehouse PJ, Hedreen JC, White CL III, Price DLP. Basal forebrain neurons in the dementia of Parkinson disease. *Ann Neurol* 1983; 13:243–248.

147. Perry EK, Curtis M, Dick DJ, et al. Cholinergic correlates of cognitive impairment in Parkinson's disease: Comparisons with Alzheimer's disease. *J Neurol Neurosurg Psychiatry* 1985; 48:413–421.

148. Emre M, Aarsland D, Albanese A, et al. Rivastigmine for dementia associated with Parkinson's disease. *N Engl J Med* 2004; 351:2509–2518.

149. Mattis SP. Mental status examination for organic mental syndrome in the elderly patient. In: Bellak L, Karasu T (eds). *Geriatric Psychiatry*. New York: Grune & Stratton, 1976: 77–121.

150. Ravina B, Putt M, Siderowf A, et al. Donepezil for dementia in Parkinson's disease: A randomised, double blind, placebo controlled, crossover study. *J Neurol Neurosurg Psychiatry* 2005; 76:934–939.

151. Hutchinson M, Fazzini EP. Cholinesterase inhibition in Parkinson's disease. *J Neurol Neurosurg Psychiatry* 1996; 61:324–325.

152. Aarsland D, Laake K, Larsen JP, Janvin CP. Donepezil for cognitive impairment in Parkinson's disease: A randomised controlled study. *J Neurol Neurosurg Psychiatry* 2002; 72:708–712.

153. Bergman J, Lerner VP. Successful use of donepezil for the treatment of psychotic symptoms in patients with Parkinson's disease. *Clin Neuropharmacol* 2002; 25:107–110.

154. Fabbrini G, Barbanti P, Aurilia C, et al. Donepezil in the treatment of hallucinations and delusions in Parkinson's disease. *Neurol Sci* 2002; 23:41–43.

155. Korczyn AD, Giladi NP. Acetylcholinesterase inhibitors in the treatment of dementia in Parkinson's disease. In: Bedard MA, Agid Y, Chouinard S, et al (eds). *Mental and Behavioral Dysfunction in Movement Disorders*. Totowa, NJ: Humana Press, 2003:295–301.

156. Reading PJ, Luce AK, McKeith IGP. Rivastigmine in the treatment of parkinsonian psychosis and cognitive impairment: Preliminary findings from an open trial. *Mov Disord* 2001; 16:1171–1174.

157. Aarsland D, Hutchinson MP. Galantamine for Parkinson's disease with dementia. *Eur Neuropsychopharmacol* 2002; 12(Suppl 12):S378–S379.

16 Depression

William M. McDonald

omorbid depression is the most common nonmotor symptom of Parkinson's disease (PD). Depression in PD (dPD) occurs in approximately 40% of patients and is evenly divided between major depression (MD) and minor forms of depression, including dysthymia and other forms of subsyndromal depression (1–4).

Comorbid depression affects both motor and non-motor functioning in PD (5). In one study of 92 patients evaluated at yearly intervals, dPD patients showed a decline in motor function, activities of daily living (ADLs), and cognitive functioning (6). Disability, and particularly the patient's perception of the severity of his or her disability, is correlated with comorbid depressive symptoms (7, 8) and has been shown to have a significant effect on quality of life (9, 10). Depression in PD is also associated with increased caregiver burden (11), with a significant level of both caregiver depression (12) and distress (13).

Not surprisingly, the treatment of depression can have positive effects on motor as well as nonmotor symptoms including cognition (14), sleep onset and maintenance (15, 16), and pain (16). This chapter provides a template for the diagnostic assessment of dPD and review the available data on the efficacy of pharmacotherapy, psychotherapy, and nonsomatic treatments [e.g., electroconvulsive therapy (ECT) and transcranial magnetic stimulation (TMS)] in dPD.

EPIDEMIOLOGY

In a comprehensive literature review of 45 PD depression studies conducted from 1922 through 1998, the overall prevalence of dPD was estimated to be 31% for all PD patients (2). The range of the prevalence of dPD varies with methodology and may be as high as 40% in community samples, with a yearly incidence of 1.9% and a cumulative incidence of 8.4% (17). Dooneief et al. (17) compared this annual incidence rate with published estimates from other studies for otherwise healthy adults over age 50 living in the community and found a rate of only 0.2% per year (vs. 1.9% per year for dPD). This finding demonstrates that the increased incidence of dPD in community samples is not explained by aging alone.

Surveys using more rigorous methodologies have found a lower but nevertheless clinically significant prevalence of dPD. In a Norwegian community sample, researchers identified depression using the criteria of the *Diagnostic and Statistical Manual* (DSM)(18) and quantified depressive symptoms using the Montgomery and Asberg Depression Rating Scale (MADRS) (19). In this very well characterized sample of 245 subjects, 7.7% met

DSM criteria for major depression (MD), with 5.1% of the subjects classified as having moderate to severe depression based on their MADRS score. A total of 45.5% of subjects were assessed by the MADRS as having significant, mild depressive symptoms, although these patients did not necessarily meet DSM criteria for MD. Combining patients with mild, moderate, and severe depression as rated by the MADRS yields a figure for dPD closer to the 47% cited by Dooneief et al. (17). Using a self-report measure, the Beck Depression Inventory (BDI), 24.1% of the PD patients met criteria for significant depressive symptoms (defined as a BDI ≥ 18). This incidence of significant depression was 6 times the rate found in a healthy elderly control group. It was also more than twice the rate of depression in a comparison group of patients with diabetes mellitus, demonstrating that the higher rate of depression found in PD subjects is not simply a reaction to a chronic disease.

Patients with significant depressive symptoms, even those who do not meet criteria for MD, are at risk for developing more severe affective syndromes. In a longitudinal cross-sectional study that followed 92 patients, 11% of PD patients who were initially diagnosed with minor depression (the same criteria as for MD but with fewer than 5 symptoms) met criteria for MD at 1-year follow-up (6). Importantly, a significant number of dPD patients can also develop more chronic symptoms of depression. In one study that followed more than 500 PD patients over a 9-year period, the patients with dPD were assessed using the Geriatric Depression Scale (20). Of the patients who were depressed initially, 35% improved, 34% remained depressed but stable, and 31% worsened. DPD can therefore become a chronic disabling disease, and although this study did not address the effects of treatment on the course of dPD, effective treatment has the potential to improve the long-term outcome of these patients.

ETIOLOGY

Researchers and clinicians have debated the etiology of dPD. Clearly the disability due to motor symptoms of PD is a cause of considerable morbidity and declines in measures of quality of life have been directly correlated with disease progression (21). This trend is most marked in younger PD patients (21). Patients who are affected prior to retirement can become disabled, thus adding to the financial burden. The motor symptoms are a cause of social embarrassment for many patients and may lead to increasing isolation. In fact, many patients and their families argue that any depressive symptoms are clearly the result of the disability associated with motor features of PD. Clinicians are faced with this argument in discussing treatments for dPD and the justification for adding an antidepressant medication.

In comparisons of dPD patients with matched groups of medically disabled patients, the PD patients had significantly higher depression scores (19, 22). Ehmann et al. (22) found that within the PD group, depression was not correlated with age, gender, duration of PD, or clinical ratings of PD symptom severity or functional disability. There is no clear association between disability from the motor symptoms of PD and depression (see "Risk Factors," below). This suggests that there are probably other factors leading to the development of dPD, rather than depression as simply a reaction to the disability and a possible biological connection.

In fact, the incidence of depression in patients later diagnosed with PD as compared with that in a matched control population showed a frequency of depression prior to PD that was 2.4 times greater than that in controls (23). The increased incidence of depression both before and after the development of motor symptoms of PD is further evidence of a pathophysiologic relationship between dPD and MD.

Evidence of a biological component to dPD is supported by an understanding of anatomic and changes in neurotransmitter function associated with the neurodegenerative process of PD. Disruption of the cortical-subcortical neuronal circuit is involved in the regulation of mood (24, 25). Neuroimaging studies have demonstrated smaller volumes of subcortical nuclei in dPD patients than in nondepressed controls; findings in depressed non-PD patients were similar (26, 27).

Studies using 2-[18F]-fluoro-2-deoxy-D-glucose and PET imaging (FDG-PET) also support the hypothesis that cortical-subcortical dysfunction is present in dPD. Mayberg et al. measured regional cerebral glucose metabolism in depressed and nondepressed patients with PD and in normal control subjects of comparable age (28). Compared to both nondepressed PD patients and control subjects, relative metabolic activity in the caudate and orbital-inferior region of the frontal lobe was significantly lower in the dPD patients. The amount of glucose hypometabolism was directly proportional to the score on a standardized depression scale. This pattern of orbitofrontal hypometabolism in dPD patients is distinct from the hypometabolism of the dorsal anterolateral prefrontal cortex in MD patients without PD (29), yet it supports cortical-subcortical dysfunction as a primary etiology in both dPD and idiopathic MD.

There is also support for altered serotonin function as a cause of dPD. The density of the midbrain serotonin transporter is decreased (30). Reductions in content of cerebrospinal fluid (CSF) in the serotonin metabolite 5-hydroxyindole acetic acid (5-HIAA) have also been associated with both idiopathic MD and dPD (31). Depressed mood in a subset of these subjects was responsive to administration of oral 5-hydroxytryptophan (a serotonin precursor) with an associated increase in

CSF 5-HIAA concentrations (31). Other studies have also found an association between depressed mood and decreased serotonin levels (32–34).

Decreased serotonin in the CSF may be related to dysfunction in the serotonin transporter that removes serotonin from the synaptic cleft. Genetic abnormalities in the short arm of the allele coding for the serotonin transporter have been found in MD. The same functional polymorphism in the promoter region of the serotonin transporter gene that is associated with anxiety in non-PD patients was also linked to higher levels of anxiety and depression PD patients (35).

These results regarding central serotonin deficits are supported by an analysis of the personality traits of dPD patients (36). Patients who showed high levels of harm avoidance, a trait related to central serotonergic systems, also had high levels of depressive symptoms. Yet depression was not correlated with novelty seeking, a personality trait related to dopaminergic pleasure and reward systems. This innovative analysis adds further support for the role of serotonin in dPD.

Elucidation of the role of neurotransmitters in dPD is complicated by the fact that patients are being treated with dopaminergic agents, which may have psychoactive effects. To control for the potentially confounding effects of these medications on other neurotransmitter levels, investigators examining CSF serotonin levels often discontinue dopaminergic medications for as long as 10 days to measure metabolites (32). To eliminate the possibility that long-term use of parkinsonian medications may have an effect on neurotransmitter function, 26 drug-naive PD patients were evaluated to determine the levels of biogenic amines in their CSF. Patients were matched for age and disability and diagnosed using DSM criteria. No significant differences were found between CSF levels of dopamine, noradrenaline, 3, 4-dihydroxyphenylacetic acid, homovanillic acid, 3-methoxy-4-hydroxyphenylglycol, and 5-HIAA as determined by high-performance liquid chromatography. These data support the potential influence of anti-PD medications on neurotransmitter function (37).

The degeneration of dopaminergic fibers, particularly those arising from the ventral tegmental area and terminating in the mesolimbic dopamine area, may be central to the expression of depressive symptoms in PD. These fibers are associated with the reward- and pleasure-producing pathways. A loss of ventral tegmental neurons has been demonstrated in PD (38) and is hypothesized to be a cause of apathy (39) and anhedonia (40). In fact, challenges to this system using the noradrenergic and dopamine reuptake inhibitor methylphenidate have demonstrated that PD patients do not show the expected sustained euphorogenic effect of the drug (41).

Using [(11)C]RTI-32 positron emission tomography (PET) as an in vivo marker of both dopamine and noradrenaline transporter binding, Remy et al. studied 8t PD and 12 dPD patients who were matched for age, disease duration, and doses of antiparkinsonian medication (42). The dPD cohort had lower [(11)C]RTI-32 binding in the locus ceruleus and several regions of the limbic system, including the anterior cingulate cortex, thalamus, amygdala, and ventral striatum. The severity of anxiety in dPD patients was inversely correlated with the amount of binding. Using single photon emission computed tomography (SPECT), decreases in striatal dopamine transporter have also been correlated with anxiety and depressive symptoms in patients with PD (43).

RISK FACTORS

Researchers investigating potential risk factors for dPD have usually examined those clinical variables known to be associated with depression in non-PD patients, particularly late-onset depression (44). These studies have been generally inconclusive and difficult to interpret because they comprise such highly diverse samples (i.e., based in the community vs. a research clinic, new-onset vs. chronic PD) and the results are frequently contradictory. Table 16-1 lists some of the most frequently cited studies in this area.

Another approach to understanding the risk factors for dPD is to conceptualize increased risk as resulting from the combination of variables within a subgroup of PD patients. In fact, those PD patients who develop depression appear to represent a distinct subgroup (1). In follow-up over 14 months and 2.5 years (31), those who were depressed at the end of the follow-up period were generally the same patients who were depressed at the beginning. A minority developed new-onset depression or had a resolution of their depressive episode.

Rather than one specific set of risk factors being associated with the development of dPD, there are probably multiple factors that, together, result in the depressive syndromes. For example, Santamaria et al. (45) found that dPD patients were younger, less impaired, and with a higher positive family history of PD than nondepressed PD patients. Other studies have found that older age and comorbid physical disease are associated with dPD (see Table 16-1). Being male has been shown to increase the risk of developing dPD, but only among younger patients (46, 47).

Although there is no clear relationship of disease severity and dPD (see Table 16-1), the effect of motor symptoms may be more complex and dependent upon other factors. For example, patients with akinetic-rigid PD had a significantly higher prevalence of depression (38% vs. 15%) than did patients with tremor-predominant disease (48). Bradykinesia was the extrapyramidal sign most

TABLE 16-1
Risk Factors Associated with Developing Depression in PD

RISK FACTOR	REFERENCES SUPPORTING AN ASSOCIATION WITH dPD	REFERENCES NOT SUPPORTING AN ASSOCIATION WITH dPD
Older age	1	2–7
Female gender	8, 9	1, 2, 4, 10
Personal history of depression	1, 8, 11	
Family history of depression	1, 5, 6	
Comorbid medical disease	1, 4	3
Severity of PD symptoms	2, 5, 7, 8, 10, 12	4, 6, 13

1. Leentjens AF, Lousberg R, Verhey FR. Markers for depression in Parkinson's disease. *Acta Psychiatrica Scandinavica.* 2002; 106(3):196–201.
2. Tandberg E, Larsen JP, Aarsland D, Laake K, Cummings JL. Risk factors for depression in Parkinson disease. *Arch Neurol.* 1997; 54(5):625–630.
3. Hantz P, Caradoc-Davies G, Caradoc-Davies T, et al. Depression in Parkinson's disease. *Am J Psychiatry* 1994; 151(7): 1010–1014.
4. Ehmann TS, Beninger RJ, Gawel MJ, Riopelle RJ. Depressive symptoms in Parkinson's disease: A comparison with disabled control subjects. *J Geriatr Psychiatr Neurol* 1990; 3(1):3–9.
5. Starkstein SE, Preziosi TJ, Bolduc PL, Robinson RG. Depression in Parkinson's disease. *J Nerv Ment Dis* 1990; 178(1):27–31.
6. Santamaria J, Tolosa E, Valles A. Parkinson's disease with depression: A possible subgroup of idiopathic parkinsonism. *Neurology* 1986; 36(8):1130–1133.
7. Kostic VS, Filipovic SR, Lecic D, et al. Effect of age at onset on frequency of depression in Parkinson's disease. *J Neurol Neurosurg Psychiatry* 1994; 57(10):1265–1267.
8. Rojo A, Aguilar M, Garolera MT, et al. Depression in Parkinson's disease: Clinical correlates and outcome. *Parkinsonism Relat Disord* 2003; 10(1):23–28.
9. Kuopio AM, Marttila RJ, Helenius H, et al. The quality of life in Parkinson's disease. *Mov Disord* 2000; 15(2):216–223.
10. Cole SA, Woodard JL, Juncos JL, et al. Depression and disability in Parkinson's disease. *J Neuropsychiatr Clin Neurosci* 1996; 8(1):20–25.
11. Brown RG, MacCarthy B, Gotham AM, et al. Depression and disability in Parkinson's disease: A follow-up of 132 cases. *Psychol Med* 1988; 18(1):49–55.
12. Schrag A, Jahanshahi M, Quinn NP. What contributes to depression in Parkinson's disease? *Psychol Med* 2001; 31(1):65–73.
13. Menza MA, Mark MH. Parkinson's disease and depression: The relationship to disability and personality. *J Neuropsychiatr Clin Neurosci* 1994; 6(2):165–169.

highly correlated with depressive symptoms. Patients with predominantly right-sided motor symptoms have also been shown to have more depressive symptoms (46, 49).

One risk factor—which is, however, supported by only limited data—is a personal or family history of MD (see Table 16-1). As with non-PD patients, having a previous episode of MD or a first-degree relative with MD increases an individual's risk of developing MD. For example, Starkstein et al. found no clear relationship between comorbid depression and age of the patient, duration of disease, gender, or family history of PD (49, 50). The primary predictors of dPD in that study were the severity of motor symptoms and disability and a family history of depression. Again, these factors may predispose an individual to develop MD, and additional risk factors (e.g., right-sided symptoms, increasing motor disability, female gender) may further increase the patient's susceptibility and result in the development of the depressive syndrome.

NONMOTOR SYMPTOMS

The relationship between motor and nonmotor symptoms—including apathy, pain, anxiety, sleep disorders, fatigue, psychosis, cognitive dysfunction, and sensory symptoms—in PD is complicated. One study found that only a small minority of PD patients (12%) did not have at least 1 nonmotor feature and that more than half had 2 or more (51). Another study examining 139 patients who had been diagnosed for at least 4 years found that 61% had at least 1 psychiatric symptom (52). Depression was the most common (in 38% of patients), followed by hallucinations (27%). In this study, the highest mean scores on the Neuropsychiatric Inventory (NPI), which assesses caregiver reports of symptoms over the preceding month, were for depression, hallucinations, and apathy.

Apathy

Apathy (see Chapter 18) may occur either as a separate syndrome or a comorbid disorder with depression. One study found the rates of apathy alone and apathy with comorbid dPD were 12% and 30%, respectively (39). Apathy in PD patients may be difficult to distinguish from depression and, in particular, anhedonia. There are a number of valid rating scales to quantify apathy (e.g., Refs. 39 and 53), including the Apathy Evaluation Scale (54).

Conceptually, apathy should be defined as a loss of interest (or motivation) without the loss of pleasure, whereas anhedonia is the loss of interest *and* pleasure. In PD, distinguishing those patients with loss of pleasure alone from those with anhedonia can significantly decrease the number of patients with depression (40). Apathy in PD may have a different although overlapping etiology and pathophysiology than dPD. The neural mechanisms of apathy are hypothesized to involve the brainstem and forebrain circuits that mediate goal-directed behavior (54).

Cognitive Impairment

Depression in PD appears to be linked with cognitive impairment (see Chapter 15), and the degree of depression has been shown to be the single most important factor associated with increased severity of cognitive impairment (55). Mayeux et al. found a correlation between the severity of depression and cognitive impairment, particularly for calculation, digit span, and visuomotor skills (56). In this study, the severity of parkinsonism, particularly bradykinesia, also correlated with the decline in cognition.

Patients with PD and dementia have an increased risk of depression, and depressed PD patients have an increased risk of developing dementia (57–59). The rate of dPD in patients with a score below 20 on the Mini-Mental State Examination (MMSE) 7 times the rate of MD in PD patients with an MMSE score at or above 20 (19). It correlation was also found between higher MADRS scores (i.e., increased depressive symptoms) and more impairment in ADLs, presence of motor fluctuations, more evidence of atypical parkinsonism, higher daily doses of levodopa, and younger age. In a later study, this group reported that an MMSE score below 24 was associated with a 6.6-fold greater risk of depression (59).

Psychosis

Psychosis (see Chapter 48) is a frequent complication of PD that can occur in up to 40% of patients (60). Hallucinations and psychosis have also been associated with increased caregiver burden (11), earlier nursing home placement (61), as well as dPD. A level 2 or higher on the thought disorder subscale of the Unified Parkinson Disease Rating Scale (UPDRS) increases the probability of MD by a factor of 3.5 (59).

Visual hallucinations are associated with nondopaminergic features including insomnia, visual disorders, and a high axial motor score (62) as well as cognitive impairment (63) and depression (64). Levodopa and dopamine agonists can be a cause of psychosis in PD. However historical data that predate the use of levodopa indicate that hallucinations may be a part of the disease process itself rather than simply a complication of pharmacotherapy, especially when PD is complicated by comorbid dementia, depression, or nonspecific encephalopathy (65).

Minor visual hallucinations [e.g., sensation of a presence (a person), a sideways passage (commonly of an animal), or illusions] are commonly associated with depressive symptoms, whereas formed visual hallucinations are more often associated with cognitive disorders, daytime somnolence, and a long duration of PD (60). Delusions (i.e., a fixed false belief) are less common. When they occur in the context of a depressive disorder, they are usually mood-congruent or associated with mood (i.e., delusions with a strong depressive content, such as nihilistic or self-deprecatory delusions).

Anxiety Disorders

Symptoms of anxiety (see Chapter 17) can be a prominent feature of depression and dPD (66). Anxiety disorders that occur as comorbid conditions in dPD—including panic disorder, social phobia, and generalized anxiety disorder—have been found in up to 40% of dPD patients (67) and are the second most common nonmotor feature in PD (52). Fortunately most anxiety disorders respond to treatment with the selective serotonin reuptake inhibitors (SSRIs), although it may take longer for the patient with comorbid anxiety to have a full and adequate response to somatic treatments.

Mood Fluctuations

PD patients often experience distinct "on" and "off" phases in their response to levodopa (68). "On" states are characterized by a responsiveness to levodopa, leading to decreased bradykinesia, tremor, and rigidity, and may also result in drug-induced dyskinesias. "Off" states are characterized by absence of response to the medication and increased motor symptoms and signs. Many nondepressed patients will describe mood fluctuations that correlate with these "on" and "off" periods.

Parkinson's patients show depression in both "on" and "off" periods; but when evaluated in an "off" phase, they may appear more depressed and will exhibit increased motor symptoms and psychomotor slowing. There may be some improvement in mood when they come "on." As the severity of PD advances, fluctuations increase, with an increase in "off" time. Use of dopamine agonists early in the treatment of PD may decrease the need for levodopa and thereby delay the development of "on/off" phenomena (69).

Nondepressed PD patients with severe "on/off" motor responses often have accompanying changes in mood (70–75). Patients with clinically apparent mood changes during their motor "on" or "off" states are also more likely to be diagnosed with depression (76). Patients with severe "on/off" fluctuations are also more likely to have symptoms of anxiety or panic, particularly as their medication is wearing off (66, 77). Cantello et al. compared PD patients with motor fluctuations to subjects diagnosed with chronic but active rheumatoid arthritis. The latter presented with increased physical disability due to severe morning joint stiffness, with a repetitive pattern of mobile and immobile periods. It was found that the PD patients had more severe mood fluctuations than those with chronic arthritis.

Administration of intravenous levodopa has also been shown to improve mood (78). These fluctuations in mood with levodopa support a role for central dopaminergic function in controlling mood states through mesocortical and mesolimbic dopamine pathways (72). There is, however, little evidence that oral administration of levodopa has a direct effect on mood.

RECOGNITION OF DEPRESSION

The diagnosis of depression is difficult in any medically ill population. but more so in PD because of multiple overlapping symptoms. In one study conducted in a movement disorders clinic at a university hospital, the diagnostic accuracy of neurologists evaluating PD patients for mood, anxiety, fatigue, and sleep disorders was assessed using standardized rating scales (79). The diagnostic accuracy for the treating neurologists was 35% for depression, 42% for anxiety, 25% for fatigue, and 60% for sleep disturbance. The prevalence of depression by the BDI was 44%, yet the neurologists diagnosed depression in less than half of those patients (21%).

PD patients have a number of *pseudodepressive* symptoms as part of their core symptoms, including masked face, bradykinesia, insomnia, gastrointestinal disturbances, sexual dysfunction, and concentration problems. Not surprisingly, nonsomatic core symptoms of depression (e.g., sadness, suicidal ideation) have the highest correlation with a diagnosis of dPD (80). The diagnostic criteria for MD are listed in Table 16-2.

In research settings, somatic symptoms of depression that overlap with the symptoms of PD (e.g., concentration problems, insomnia, fatigue) can discriminate depressed and nondepressed PD patients (81). In the study by Leentjens et al. (80), the only somatic symptoms of depression shown to discriminate depressed from nondepressed patients were early-morning awakening and decreased appetite. Other studies have found a different pattern. Somatic symptoms that discriminate dPD from PD included loss of appetite, initial and middle insomnia, and loss of libido, although no significant between-group differences were found in the frequency of anergia, motor retardation, and early-morning awakening (50).

In a study by Starkstein et al., dPD patients had a significantly higher frequency of nonsomatic symptoms, including worrying, brooding, loss of interest, hopelessness, suicidal tendencies, social withdrawal,

---

TABLE 16-2
Core Symptoms of Major Depression using Diagnostic and Statistical Manual Criteria

The diagnosis of major depression requires a 2-week period of persistent depressed mood and/or anhedonia (loss of interest and pleasure). Once these criteria are met, patients must meet at least 5 of the following 9 criteria, and these symptoms must severe enough to cause significant distress or impairment in daily functioning:

1. Depressed, dysphoric, or sad mood
2. Anhedonia, which should be distinguished from the loss of interest and motivation seen in apathetic PD patients
3. Insomnia or hypersomnia*
4. Anorexia or increased appetite*
5. Poor concentration or indecisiveness
6. Guilt, self-blame, or ruminations of failure
7. Fatigue or loss of energy, which in PD should not simply occur when the patient's medication is wearing off*
8. Psychomotor retardation that must be distinguished from bradykinesia in PD, or psychomotor agitation that must be distinguished from akasthesia and dyskinesia
9. Suicidal ideation or excessive ruminations about death

Associated symptoms of depression not in the criteria:
Anxiety
Irritability
Emotionality and crying spells that are distinguished from the emotional incontinence observed in pseudobulbar states
Decreased libido
Somatization and focus on physical problems
Helplessness
Worthlessness
Pessimism, hopelessness

---

*Somatic symptoms of depression that are distinguished from the cognitive symptoms such as depressed mood and guilt.
Source: American Psychiatric Association. *Diagnostic and Statistical Manual of Mental Disorders,* 4th ed. Washington, DC: APA Press, 2000.

---

self-depreciation, ideas of reference, and anxiety (50). Other researchers have found that dPD patients show a unique pattern of depressive symptoms with prominent anxiety, dysphoria, pessimism, and somatic symptoms but not guilt or self-blame (82). Cummings, in his seminal review of dPD studies, concluded that depression in PD is subtly different from idiopathic mood disorders. He found that pattern of sadness without guilt or self-reproach, a high rate of anxiety symptoms, a relative lack of delusions and hallucinations, and a low suicide rate despite a high frequency of suicidal ideation was the most common presentation of dPD (1).

INCLUSIVE CRITERIA

Research in medically ill depressed populations has supported the inclusive approach to diagnosing dPD. That is, once a patient meets one of the primary criteria for depression (2 weeks or more of persistent anhedonia or depressed mood), the other symptoms of depression should be counted as present or absent without regard to whether the clinician assesses them to be attributed to depression or PD (83).

Using this approach to the diagnosis of depression in PD, the clinician would first determine whether the patient met primary criteria. If that were the case, the clinician would then proceed to ask about the other criteria, including sleep disturbance, guilt, fatigue, concentration problems (or problems with making decisions), appetite disturbance, psychomotor retardation or agitation, and suicidal thoughts or persistent ruminations about death (see Table 16-2). If the patient met 5 of the 9 criteria for the diagnosis of MD, the patient would fulfill criteria for dPD and somatic treatment should be considered. The inclusive criteria were supported as the "gold standard" for confirming a diagnosis of dPD by a joint task force of the National Institute of Mental Health (NIMH) and the National Institute of Neurological Diseases and Stroke (NINDS) (84).

Once the diagnosis of dPD has been made, the clinician should also be alert to the possibility of comorbid anxiety disorders, substance abuse, and bipolar disorder, which all occur with increased frequency in non-PD patients with MD. PD patients with underlying bipolar disorder may present in the depressed phase of their illness; the clinician obtaining the psychiatric history should therefore also include questions about a previous history of mania (e.g., grandiosity, spending sprees, flight of ideas). If a bipolar patient in the depressed phase of the illness is started on antidepressant medication without antimanic medication (e.g., lithium, carbamazepine, or valproic acid), he or she is at risk for cycling into mania. However, there is little evidence to support an increased rate of mania or hypomania in patients with PD, and there are only sporadic case reports of PD patients who developed mania after the onset of their motor symptoms (85, 86).

Rating Scales

Psychiatric rating scales for depression can be particularly useful in screening and following dPD patients. Rating scales for depression include the *observer-rated* Hamilton Depression Rating Scale (HDRS) (87), Montgomery Åsberg Depression Rating Scale (MADRS) (88), part 1 item 3 of the Unified Parkinson's Disease Rating Scale (UPDRS) (89) and the *patient-rated* Geriatric Depression Scale (GDS) (90), Beck Depression Inventory (BDI) (91), Zung Depression Rating Scale (ZDRS) (92), Hospital Anxiety and Depression Rating Scale (HADS) (93), and Center for Epidemiologic Studies Depression Scale (CES-D) (94). The caregiver-rated Cornell Scale for Depression in Dementia (CSDD) (95) is designed to assess mood symptoms in patients with cognitive impairment and may be particularly useful in PD patients with associated dementia. Recently a task force of the Mood Disorders Society evaluated these rating scales in dPD (personal communication, Anette Scragg). This review is presently in preparation and should be completed in 2006–2007.

Most of these scales have been validated in dPD, but some of them are particularly useful in a clinical neurology practice. The GDS has both 30- and 15-item versions, and both have been validated in dPD (96, 97). The scale is an excellent screen for depression, asks simple yes/no questions, and can be completed and scored in about 10 minutes, so it is ideal to use in a general neurology practice during routine evaluations.

The BDI is another patient-rated scale, which is valid in screening for dPD (79), assessing severity of depressed mood (98), and following the response to treatment (99). However, the BDI is probably best used for following treatment response and assessing severity and not as a routine screening instrument. The BDI is much longer and more tedious than the GDS (there are multiple choices for each question), and patients without psychiatric disorders frequently object to completing it because of the nature of the questions. Some of the questions ask about suicide, libido, and self-esteem, and there are others that can feel intrusive to the routine medical patient. For these reasons, the GDS is a better screening instrument. The BDI is a better instrument to use in following patients already identified as depressed, particularly because it does assess suicidal ideation (which the GDS does not).

The MADRS is a 10-item observer-rated questionnaire that can be used to screen for depression and, more importantly, to both rate the severity of depressive symptoms and follow the progression of symptoms during the course of treatment. It is valid in dPD (100) and is perhaps more useful in a general neurology practice than the longer and more detailed observer-rated HDRS, which is also valid in dPD (101) but can take 2 to 3 times longer to complete. The MADRS includes most of the DSM criteria for MD except for reverse neurovegetative symptoms (i.e., hypersomnia and hyperphagia) and psychomotor retardation and agitation.

While most of the scales described above can be used with mild cognitive impairment, the CSDD was designed for evaluating depression in patients with dementia and includes information from the caregiver and other collateral sources of information. The primary problem in using the CSDD is the same as that of any observer who is trying to determine whether a symptom is due to dPD or the motor symptoms of PD: the caregiver may discount symptoms such as insomnia or fatigue if he or she judges that they are not due to depression, and there are no clear guidelines for the caregiver in making these distinctions. The CSDD has not been shown to be valid specifically in dPD patients with dementia, although the CSDD has been shown to be valid in diagnosing depression in Alzheimer's disease (AD) and in following response to treatment in AD (102). The CSDD is a good scale for clinical follow-up of dPD in patients with moderate to severe dementia, particularly when they are unable to respond to the other rating scales appropriately.

The first part of the UPDRS does have a section headed "Mood, Mentation, and Behavior" and is intended as a screening tool. It has only 1 question on mood. The other 3 questions probe for intellectual impairment, thought disorder, and motivation/initiative. The UPDRS is being revised to add more questions to evaluate mood. The present version is only a minimal screen and the GDS is a more sensitive and specific screening tool for dPD.

Evaluation of Depression

Depression in PD patients is often not recognized; when it is, it is undertreated. Researchers evaluated the treatment histories of 100 PD patients seen in the clinic and found that approximately one-third met criteria for depression; however, less than one-third of these were actually being treated with an antidepressant (103). Of the patients who were being treated for depression, almost half were still depressed, yet only about 1 in 10 of these persistently depressed patients were receiving the maximal dose of antidepressant medication. Only one-third of patients with persistent depression had received more than one antidepressant trial. These statistics would indicate that even in a research setting with experienced neurologists and psychiatrists attending to patients, the identification and minimum adequate somatic treatment of dPD are difficult to achieve.

Treatment studies in PD and other medical conditions have recently begun to focus on the group of patients with significant depressive symptoms who do not meet criteria for MD. This group has been defined as having subsyndromal depression (SSD) and meets DSM criteria for minor depression (criteria for MD but fewer than 5 of the 9 symptoms), dysthymia (low-grade chronic depression), recurrent brief depression (criteria for MD but recurrent episodes shorter than the 2 weeks required for MD), or depression not otherwise specified. Non-PD patients with SSD are significantly impaired (104) and SSD syndromes are a major risk factor for the devel-

opment of MD (105, 106). Although the data on the etiology and treatment of SSD in PD are still emerging, researchers have shown that chronic illness poses the risk that SSD will progress to MD (105) and that the treatment of SSD syndromes in non-PD patients can prevent the progression to MD (107).

Whether the clinician treats SSD in PD will probably depend on the clinical factors such as the patient's perception of the severity of the depressive symptoms (e.g., excessive fatigue) and whether there is a previous history of MD. Given the disability associated with depressive symptoms in most PD studies and the known risk of SSD progressing to MD, careful consideration should be given to a trial of antidepressant therapy. Even without research data, the risk/benefit ratio would seem to be weighted toward at least one antidepressant trial.

Screening

As discussed in the section on recognition of depression, there are a number of psychiatric scales with excellent sensitivity and specificity in dPD. The 15-item (or 30-item) GDS has a number of practical advantages for use in a neurology clinic. The scale has established validity in dPD, elicits simple yes/no answers, and takes no more than 5 minutes to complete. The questions are not "psychiatric" (unlike the BDI, which asks questions regarding suicide and self-worth), and patients in a medical setting do not object to completing the scale as part of routine screening. Finally, the scale can be scored by nonmedical personnel and does not take away from time between the clinician and the patient.

Patients who score 5 or higher on the 15-item GDS (or 10 or higher on the 30-item GDS) should be evaluated further by the clinician. The clinician should focus on two questions: Are you feeling depressed, sad, or "blue" over the past 2 weeks? Are you becoming more withdrawn or isolated, or are you having trouble enjoying things that you used to enjoy over the past 2 weeks? If the answer to either of these questions is positive, the clinician should further probe for the other symptoms of MD listed in Table 16-2. As noted earlier, the responses to the symptoms of depression should be considered without regard to whether the clinician feels they are due to PD or any other medical illness (i.e., the inclusive criteria should be used). If the patient scores positive on 5 of 9 criteria, the clinician should initiate the depression treatment protocol.

Evaluating Comorbid Syndromes. Depressed patients without PD have higher rates of anxiety disorders, substance abuse, and mania. Screening for these other disorders can be done with minimal training by a registered nurse or technician using available instruments such as the MINI (108). This scale is available in many languages and can provide a relatively quick assessment of comorbid psychiatric disorders for clinical and research purposes.

Laboratory Workup. Prior to initiating therapy, medical causes of depressive symptoms should be excluded, including dementia, hypothyroidism, B12 or folate deficiency, elevated plasma homocysteine levels, and testosterone deficiency. In addition to causing *pseudodepression*, hypothyroidism and deficiencies in folate, B12, or testosterone may also reduce the response to antidepressant therapy.

Parkinson's patients with depression should be screened for dementia using the MMSE (109). Hypothyroidism is often associated with PD and depression (110); when it occurs in PD, the diagnosis may be confounded by shared symptomatology (111–113). Therefore the evaluation of dPD patients should include a screen for thyroid disease, recognizing that PD medications (such as levodopa) may inhibit the secretion of thyroid-stimulating hormone (TSH) (112, 114), thus masking the laboratory diagnosis of hypothyroidism.

Serum levels of vitamin B12 and folate should be checked when patients screen positive for depression. Deficiency in vitamin B12 is a cause of depressive symptoms (115, 116) and is common in the elderly (117, 118). Homocysteine levels are also increased in patients with depression (119), dementia (120) and PD (121, 122). In particular, long-term treatment with levodopa can increase homocysteine levels (123, 124); it is important to monitor homocysteine levels in PD because elevated levels are associated with vascular disease (125). Treatment with medications that increase the metabolism of homocysteine [e.g., S-adenosylmethionine (SAM-e)] may attenuate the effects of elevated homocysteine levels (124). SAM-e has also been shown to have antidepressant effects in depressed patients with (126) and without PD (127).

Symptoms of testosterone deficiency include fatigue, diminished libido, insomnia, and dysphoria and overlap with the symptoms of MD. Testosterone deficiency has been associated with depressive symptoms in non-PD (128, 129). Testosterone supplementation may provide symptomatic benefit in both non-PD (130) and PD patients (129).

TREATMENT OF DEPRESSION

Antiparkisonian Medications

The mesolimbic dopamine pathways are functionally reward and pleasure pathways; however, there is no evidence that the administration of levodopa has any antidepressant effect. The dopamine agonists have relatively weak antidepressant properties (78, 131, 132) and, like levodopa, have been associated with other psychiatric side effects, including psychosis, agitation, and delirium (133).

Pallidotomy and thalamotomy are surgical treatments utilized for controlling the motor symptoms of PD (134, 135). Both have limited psychiatric sequelae (136–138). Patients with a history of depression are more likely to experience a depressive episode following pallidotomy, although this may be the result of the natural progression of their depressive illness and the known propensity for patients with MD to have recurrent episodes (138, 139). Transient hypomania has been reported in 2 patients following pallidotomy, although pallidal lesions in both patients were located in the anteromedial portion of the GPi rather than the posteroventral portion (140).

Deep brain stimulation (DBS) targeting the subthalamic nucleus (STN) and GPi to reduce "off" period akinesias and dyskinesias (141) and ventrointermedial (Vim) nucleus of the thalamus to reduce tremor (142) have been used successfully in advanced PD patients. A number of psychiatric side effects have been reported with STN DBS, including depression, mania, psychosis, and delirium (143, 144). Recurrent manic episodes were reported in one patient following GPi DBS (145). Thus surgical therapy, with current targets, does not appear to provide benefit for depression in PD.

Selegiline, a monoamine oxidase type B (MAO-B) inhibitor, can have antidepressant effects (1); in an open-label multicenter trial to examine the motor effects of this agent, PD patients were noted to have improvements in mood (146). However it was difficult to determine in this trial whether the antidepressant effect was primarily due to independent mood changes to the effects of selegiline on motor symptoms (which improved significantly), or to an amphetamine effect from drug metabolites.

Generally the studies that have shown an antidepressant effect of selegiline have used doses of 30 to 40 mg (147), far above the dose used to treat the motor symptoms of PD. At such doses, selegiline becomes a nonselective inhibitor of both MAO-A and MAO-B and the patient has to follow a tyramine-free diet and restrict the use of certain medications (e.g., meperidine). The Food and Drug Administration (FDA) has approved a selegiline patch for the treatment of MD. At low doses, there are no dietary or medication restrictions with this patch; however, a tyramine-free diet is required for patients on higher doses.

The D2/3 receptor agonist pramipexole, has been shown to have an antidepressant effect when it is added to an SSRI or tricyclic antidepressant (TCA) (mean dose = 0.97 mg). this was demonstrated in an open-label study in a group of 37 non-PD patients with treatment-resistant MD (148). Ten of the patients dropped out due to intolerance. In a multicenter trial comparing pergolide to pramipexole in the treatment of 41 dPD patients with mild to moderately severe symptoms, patients on both medications showed a significant decrease in the self-rated Zung Depression Rating Scale

TABLE 16-3
Antidepressant Medications

	MINIMUM DOSE	TARGET DOSE	MAXIMUM DOSE
Tricyclics			
Nortriptyline†	50 mg	50–150 mg	Serum level*
Desipramine†	75 mg	100–300 mg	Serum level*
Selective serotonin reuptake inhibitors			
Fluoxetine†	10 mg 20 mg	40 mg	
Sertraline	50 mg	100 mg	200 mg
Paroxetine†	10 mg	20 mg	40 mg
Paroxetine CR (controlled release)	12.5 mg	25 mg	50 mg
Citalopram†	20 mg	40 mg	60 mg
Escitalopram	10 mg	20 mg	40 mg
Serotonin and norepinephrine			
Venlafaxine	75 mg	150 mg	225 mg
Venlafaxine XR (extended release)	75 mg	150 mg	300 mg
Mirtazapine†	30 mg	45 mg	60 mg
Duloxetine	30 mg	60 mg	60 mg
Others			
Bupropion†	300 mg	450 mg	450 mg
Bupropion SR (sustained release)	300 mg	300 mg	400 mg
Bupropion XL (extended release)	300 mg	300 mg	450 mg
Trazodone†	150 mg	400 mg	600 mg
Nefazodone†	200 mg	300 mg	600 mg
Reboxetine‡	4 mg	4 mg	6 mg
Selegiline patch	6 mg	6 mg	12 mg

*The serum levels are obtained 8 to 12 hours after the last dose of medication. The recommended minimum and optimal blood levels for nortriptyline are a plasma concentration greater than 50 ng/mL and 120 ng/mL, respectively. For desipramine the patient should have a blood level of at least 100 ng/mL and optimally around 150 ng/mL.
†Available as a generic medication in the United States.
‡Not available in the United States.

(132). However, only the pramipexole group showed a significant decline in the observer rated MADRS.

Antidepressant Medication

Surprisingly there are few placebo-controlled studies to guide treatment with antidepressant medication in PD. In a Cochrane systematic review, the authors found that there were insufficient data on the effectiveness and safety of antidepressant therapies in PD (149). A more recent meta-analysis of antidepressant trials in elderly patients with PD found that active treatment with an antidepressant and treatment with a placebo both had large effect sizes, and there was no significant difference between the groups (150). This was contrasted with the same type of analysis in geriatric depressed patients without PD, which found a large effect size for active treatment that was statistically different from placebo. It was also determined that in PD, increasing age and a diagnosis of MD were associated with antidepressant response,

and that the TCAs were more effective than the SSRIs. This authors of this study agreed with Chang et al. (149) and concluded that placebo-controlled trials in dPD are needed in order to drawe definitive conclusions.

The commonly used antidepressant medications are listed in Table 16-3.

The TCAs and monoamine oxidase inhibitors (MAOIs) are the oldest in this class of drugs and have a number of side effects that are particularly concerning. The alpha-adrenergic side effects potentially worsen orthostatic hypotension and anticholinergic side effects exacerbate autonomic problems, including increasing dry mouth and constipation. The anticholinergic side effects can also worsen memory and concentration problems and lead to confusion, delirium, and psychosis. The TCAs also can also have effects on cardiac conduction and should be used carefully in older adults. These conduction effects can lead to heart block.

Amitriptyline is a tertiary TCA that may be difficult to tolerate at therapeutic doses (150 to 300 mg/day), but it can be very effective not only for depression but also for chronic pain or disordered sleep even at low doses (25 mg). The metabolite of amitriptyline, nortriptyline, has a better side-effect profile and is the only TCA to be tested in dPD in a placebo-controlled trial (151). In this trial of 19 PD patients, nortriptyline was found to be superior to placebo, but statistical significance was not reported. Menza and colleagues are presently conducting a placebo-controlled trial of nortriptyline in dPD (personal communication).

In clinical practice the SSRIs have replaced TCAs as first-line agents in the treatment of dPD. There are few clinical data to support superior efficacy of the SSRIs; however, these medications are better tolerated. Clinically significant side effects include sexual dysfunction (loss of libido, anorgasmia), agitation and sleep disturbance, anxiety, headache, weight gain, rare bradycardia, and nausea or diarrhea. Some side effects (e.g., agitation, anxiety, headaches, and gastrointestinal symptoms) may diminish with continued treatment and can be limited by slowly titrating the dose. Other side effects (e.g., sleep disturbance and sexual dysfunction) often continue and may interfere with treatment compliance.

One potential side effect of SSRIs that is of particular concern in PD is exacerbation of motor symptoms (152) secondary to modulation of serotonin-mediated dopamine release in nigrostriatal pathways (153, 154). There have been numerous case reports of extrapyramidal side effects (EPS) with SSRIs in non-PD depressed patients (153–164). However, the risk of developing EPS is only modestly increased in larger samples and case-controlled studies (165–167), and a number of studies suggest that EPS is not a clinically relevant side effect for most patients, including those with PD (168–174).

A potentially fatal complication may result from the combination of an SSRIs [(and potentially TCAs(175)] with the MAO-B inhibitor selegiline. This combination can cause a "serotonin syndrome" from the rapid increase in central nervous system serotonin levels. In the syndrome's mildest form, patients may feel only agitation and tremor. These symptoms may progress to delirium, with neurologic abnormalities (muscle rigidity, tremor, hyperreflexia, clonus, seizures), autonomic instability (including diaphoresis, tachypnea, tachycardia, hyperpyrexia, and hypertension)—a syndrome that can eventually result in coma and death. This syndrome will more commonly result when selegiline is given at higher doses than are used to treat the motor symptoms of PD (i.e., higher than 5 to 10 mg/day), since at the higher doses selegiline can nonspecifically inhibit both MAO-A and MAO-B. In practice, this concern may be relatively minor, since the doses of selegiline used to treat PD are relatively low. One study found that the combination of selegiline with antidepressant medications led to symptoms consistent with serotonin syndrome in only 11 (0.24%) of 4568

patients treated with the combination. Only 2 (0.04%) patients experienced serious symptoms, and no deaths were reported (152).

As previously discussed, there are few placebo-controlled trials of the efficacy of antidepressant medications in dPD, with one meta-analysis finding only 3 studies of the 43 reviewed that were methodologically appropriate for analysis (149). Previous reviews (e.g., Refs. 3 and 4) outlined the many methodologic shortcomings of these studies, including small sample size, heterogeneous populations, inadequate antidepressant dosing, and the failure to use standardized diagnostic criteria for depression or rating scales to document symptom change.

Two placebo-controlled trials of SSRIs include one small study using citalopram, which showed no significant difference from placebo (176), and a trial with sertraline, which also showed no statistically significant difference from placebo (177). The sertraline study was underpowered, as the study was stopped prematurely owing to problems with enrollment (177). Aside from these, the majority of studies are open-labeled, and they demonstrate some evidence for the antidepressant efficacy of SSRIs in dPD (164, 170–173, 178, 179) and dPD with comorbid anxiety (180, 181).

The medications that act on both serotonin, norepinephrine, and "other" medications are listed in Table 16-3. Mirtazapine—an alpha-2 antagonist, 5HT-(1A) agonist, and 5HT-(2) antagonist—was hypothesized to decrease medication-induced dyskinesias because of the positive effect on dyskinesias noted in other drugs with 5HT-(1A) agonistic activity, such as buspirone (182). In a small study of 20 PD patients, mirtazapine proved to be moderately effective in reducing levodopa-induced dyskinesias, either alone or in association with amantadine. There are, however, no data to support their use in dPD. In clinical practice, mirtazapine is associated with sedation, particularly at low doses (7.5 to 15 mg) and is frequently given with SSRIs at bedtime as a sedative and augmenting agent. Mirtazapine is also associated with weight gain and may be useful in anorectic dPD patients with significant weight loss.

Nefazodone, a mixed serotonin-receptor antagonist and reuptake inhibitor, was as effective as fluoxetine in treating dPD in a small (n = 15) randomized trial (99). Patients randomized to nefazodone showed an improvement in their UPDRS scores, whereas the fluoxetine group was unchanged. Unfortunately nefazodone has recently received a "black box" warning on its label regarding liver toxicity, and this has limited its use.

Bupropion is a weak reuptake inhibitor for dopamine and norepinephrine (although its exact mechanism of action is unknown) and has long been an interesting medication in the treatment of dPD because of its action on dopamine. In an open study in which bupropion was given to 20 PD patients (12 had depressive symptoms), parkinsonism was decreased by 30% or more in half the patients (183). Of the 12 patients with depressive symptoms, 5 were noted to improve, although many experienced side effects that were dose-limiting.

Reboxetine, a pure noradrenergic reuptake inhibitor, is not available in the United States. In a study of 17 dPD patients followed over 4 months, a significant decrease in depressive symptoms was seen, with no effect on UPDRS motor scores (184).

Electroconvulsive Therapy

Electroconvulsive therapy (ECT) is generally reserved as a third-line treatment for patients with resistant depression, but it can be used earlier in the treatment protocol when the patient is severely depressed and a more immediate intervention is necessary. ECT is effective in treating depression, psychosis, and motor symptoms in PD (185–189) and can be used to treat drug-induced psychosis in levodopa-treated patients (189, 190).

Although ECT is recognized as a safe, effective treatment (191), its use in patients with PD can be challenging, as they are more sensitive to the cognitive side effects (e.g., confusion, memory disturbance, interictal delirium (192, 193). These side effects can be minimized by using unilateral rather than bitemporal ECT, spacing the treatments to no more than twice a week, and holding the morning antiparkinsonian medication until after the treatment (194). In elderly PD patients, ECT may also be associated with an increased risk of falls and cardiovascular complications (191, 195, 196).

Repetitive Transcranial Magnetic Stimulation

Repetitive transcranial magnetic stimulation (rTMS) is effective in the treatment of MD in non-PD patients (197–201) and has shown promise as a treatment in neurologic conditions because of its favorable side-effect profile (202). Open-label trials demonstrate that rTMS has antidepressant effects in dPD patients (203) and that rTMS was as effective as fluoxetine for the treatment of dPD patients in some (204). Like ECT, rTMS improves the motor symptoms of PD (205–212), but not in all studies (213–216). The mechanism for these motor effects as well as possibly the antidepressant effects of rTMS may be related to the consequent release of subcortical dopamine, as shown in both animals and humans (217–221).

At present the use of rTMS in MD and dPD is still considered investigational. However, with the completion in December 2005 of a large multicenter trial in rTMS for the treatment of MD and the submission of data to the Food and Drug Administration, approval for the clinical use of rTMS is imminent, depending on the strength of the results, which have not yet been published.

Vagal nerve stimulation (VNS) is approved for use in both MD and epilepsy. There are, however, no trials in dPD.

Psychotherapy

Cognitive behavioral therapy (CBT) and interpersonal psychotherapy (IPT), either alone or in combination with pharmacotherapy, are established treatments for MD (222–228). In combination with antidepressant medications, psychotherapy may be useful for any level of depression. Psychotherapy can also be effective in depressed cognitively impaired patients (224, 225, 229, 230), although a recent study did not find maintenance interpersonal psychotherapy helpful in preventing relapse in patients above 70 years of age with moderate cognitive impairment (231).

There is evidence that dPD patients tend to use coping strategies that are dysfunctional (such as avoiding or ignoring problems rather than trying to solve them) and that CBT might be useful in helping to treat depressive symptoms by redirecting them (232). Ehman's group (22) found a negative bias in the dPD group, shown in their tendency to view themselves as more disabled than they were objectively. This type of "cognitive distortion" is addressed by CBT techniques. Functional disability is related to depression scores, and helping a patient cope with this disability by using active (e.g., physical therapy, assistive devices, following medication regimens) as opposed to passive (e.g., isolation and withdrawal) coping strategies is a form of CBT practiced by PD treatment teams in routine clinical care. Clinical researchers have described how CBT can be adapted to the treatment of dPD (233), and model treatment programs have been developed specifically for dPD (234).

A Treatment Algorithm

This section outlines an algorithm for the treatment of dPD based on a clinically validated PROSPECT algorithm used to treat elderly depressed patients (235). We recently published the algorithm (236), which is shown in Figure 16-1.

The optimal medication dosages are listed in Table 16-3. In the PROSPECT trial, citalopram was the SSRI used as the first-line antidepressant. Citalopram is generic, has few drug-drug interactions and low protein binding, and is a good choice in the elderly; however, a small placebo-controlled trial was negative in dPD (176). Given the fact that there are no definitive randomized controlled trials of antidepressants in dPD, the clinician should use the SSRI with which he or she has the most familiarity.

In this algorithm, rating scales are used to quantify response, with corresponding cutoffs to indicate standard

Algorithm for Treating Depression in Parkinsonís Disease*

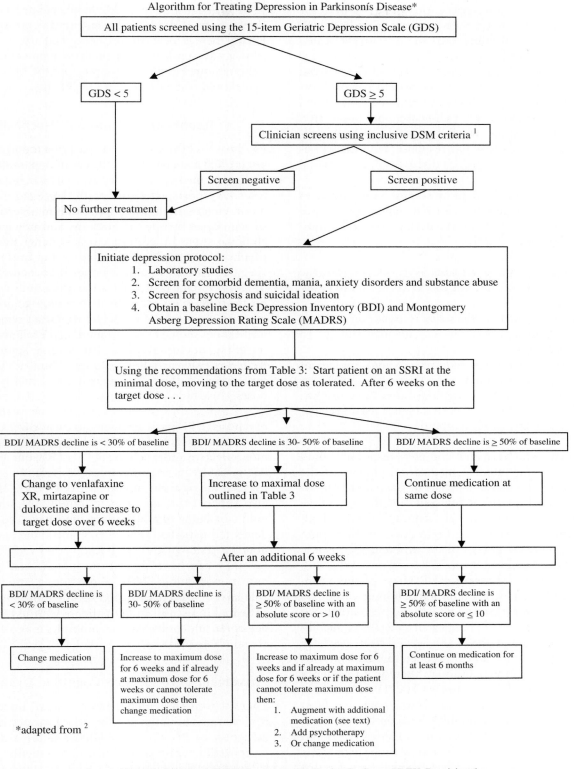

All patients screened using the 15-item Geriatric Depression Scale (GDS)

GDS < 5

GDS ≥ 5

Clinician screens using inclusive DSM criteria [1]

Screen negative

Screen positive

No further treatment

Initiate depression protocol:
1. Laboratory studies
2. Screen for comorbid dementia, mania, anxiety disorders and substance abuse
3. Screen for psychosis and suicidal ideation
4. Obtain a baseline Beck Depression Inventory (BDI) and Montgomery Asberg Depression Rating Scale (MADRS)

Using the recommendations from Table 3: Start patient on an SSRI at the minimal dose, moving to the target dose as tolerated. After 6 weeks on the target dose . . .

BDI/ MADRS decline is < 30% of baseline

BDI/ MADRS decline is 30- 50% of baseline

BDI/ MADRS decline is ≥ 50% of baseline

Change to venlafaxine XR, mirtazapine or duloxetine and increase to target dose over 6 weeks

Increase to maximal dose outlined in Table 3

Continue medication at same dose

After an additional 6 weeks

BDI/ MADRS decline is < 30% of baseline

BDI/ MADRS decline is 30- 50% of baseline

BDI/ MADRS decline is ≥ 50% of baseline with an absolute score or > 10

BDI/ MADRS decline is ≥ 50% of baseline with an absolute score or ≤ 10

Change medication

Increase to maximum dose for 6 weeks and if already at maximum dose for 6 weeks or cannot tolerate maximum dose then change medication

Increase to maximum dose for 6 weeks and if already at maximum dose for 6 weeks or if the patient cannot tolerate maximum dose then:
1. Augment with additional medication (see text)
2. Add psychotherapy
3. Or change medication

Continue on medication for at least 6 months

*adapted from [2]

1. Marsh L, McDonald WM, Cummings JL, Ravina B, Group NNW. Provisional diagnostic criteria for depression in Parkinson's Disease: Report of an NINDS/NIMH Work Group. *Mov Disord*. 2006;21(2):148–158.

2. McDonald WM, Holtzheimer PE, 3rd, Byrd EH. The diagnosis and treatment of depression in Parkinson's disease. *Current Treatment Options in Neurology*. 2006;8(3):245–255.

definitions for partial response (30% to 50% decrease in baseline), response (> 50% decrease from baseline), and remission (an absolute score of < 10 on the scale). The clinician may forgo rating scales and instead use the clinical global impression of the patient. Partial response, response, and remission would roughly correspond to the patient showing a minimal, moderate, and complete response on a clinical global impression scale. The 10-question observer-rated MADRS and self-rated BDI were used to gauge response, but other scales can certainly be substituted, as discussed under "Rating Scales," above.

This algorithm is based on several basic principles in the treatment of geriatric patients, which are outlined in the PROSPECT trial and the data presented on antidepressant efficacy in dPD:

1. None of the antidepressants have a clear advantage in terms of efficacy, but the SSRIs are more easily tolerated.
2. Older patients take longer to respond, on average, and require a 12-week trial at adequate dosages to assess response.
3. Older patients often require maximal dosages of antidepressants to have a full response.
4. Patients should be treated until they have reached remission, or they will be at a higher risk of relapse and chronic residual symptoms.

Patients who have an incomplete response should be considered for either a medication change (if the response is minimal after 6 weeks or the patient cannot tolerate the medication) or augmentation therapy. In the algorithm, the patient is changed from an SSRI to a dual-mechanism medication (see Table 16-3) or bupropion in order to take advantage of the different therapeutic actions of these medications (237).

Augmentation strategies in dPD have not been subjected to clinical trials. The addition of lithium carbonate has perhaps the most clinical data for augmentation, but it is difficult to use in PD because of side effects, including tremor and gait ataxia (238). Several strategies have been used in routine clinical practice to augment antidepressant medications, although there is no evidence for the efficacy of these treatments in dPD and minimal evidence in geriatric depression. Mirtazapine has been shown to be effective in a double-blind controlled trial in patients who had a partial response to SSRIs (239) and may decrease the sexual dysfunction associate with SSRIs (240). Bupropion SR has also been shown to be effective as an augmenting agent to SSRIs in younger (241) and geriatric patients (242). Bupropion has also been shown to decrease SSRI-induced sexual dysfunction (243). The use of low-dose methylphenidate (244, 245) and modafanil (246) has been shown to be effective in augmenting

SSRIs in geriatric patients. Methylphenidate has also been shown to treat apathy independent of depression (247). Finally there is increasing evidence that atypical antipsychotics have a role in antidepressant augmentation (248) although quetiapine or clozapine are the only atypicals that should be considered in PD patients.

Treatment of Comorbid Psychosis

Psychosis in PD may occur as part of a mood syndrome but is often associated with the use of dopamine agonists and other medications used to treat PD motor symptoms. Psychosis associated with depression is usually mood-congruent. In PD, psychosis is more often related to the dopaminergic medications and not mood. The clinician should therefore assess whether the onset of psychosis is temporally related to the initiation of a specific medication and whether that medication can be stopped. One protocol for the order of discontinuing medication (4) is to start by discontinuing anticholinergics and amantadine first. If hallucinations remain, other medications should be discontinued in the following order: selegiline, nocturnal doses of dopamine agonists, controlled-release carbidopa/levodopa (Sinemet CR), daytime doses of dopamine agonists, and finally daytime doses of carbidopa/levodopa.

Atypical antipsychotics are first-line treatments for psychosis in PD patients owing to their lower dopamine D2 receptor blockade (249). Clozapine is arguably the most effective antipsychotic in PD (250), but its use may be limited by its potential to cause agranulocytosis and by need for rigorous monitoring (249, 251–253). Data also support the use of quetiapine (254), although a mild worsening of motor symptoms may occur in more demented patients (255–260). Olanzapine and risperidone have shown antipsychotic efficacy in PD patients, but they can have significant side effects, including motor worsening (249). Ziprasidone and aripiprazole have not been adequately studied in psychotic PD patients (261–263). In PD patients with psychosis and dementia, anticholinesterase inhibitors may also be beneficial (264–268).

Treatment of Associated Cognitive Dysfunction

There is limited evidence from a small uncontrolled trial that galantamine may be beneficial in treating the dementia of PD (269). Galantamine also decreased visual hallucinations in 7 of the 9 patients who had hallucinations and improved parkinsonian motor symptoms in 7 of the 16 patients, while worsening tremor in 3 others. There is additional evidence from double-blind and open trials that cholinesterase inhibitors may be beneficial in the treatment of psychosis in PD patients with dementia (270).

CONCLUSION

Comorbid depression is common in PD and is a cause of considerable morbidity. DPD affects both motor and nonmotor symptoms in PD and has been associated with a worsening of the UPDRS and declines in ADLs and cognitive functioning. DPD is also associated with increased caregiver burden and distress.

Data from samples of elderly living in the community and patients with similar chronic disease (e.g., diabetes mellitus and osteoarthritis) demonstrate that the increased incidence of depression in PD is not simply the result of aging or a reaction to a chronic disabling disease. Studies of the pathophysiology of dPD support the role of the underlying neurodegenerative process in PD leading to a disruption in the cortical-subcortical neuronal circuit involved in mood regulation. Additional studies support the role for abnormal serotonin and dopamine circuits, two neurotransmitters known to have a role in depression and associated affective states such as apathy.

The recognition of dPD is difficult because of the overlap of PD motor symptoms and depressive symptoms. The recommendations from a number of expert panels have been to use inclusive DSM criteria (i.e., include all symptoms without consideration to etiology). Standardized rating scales with proven validity in dPD can also be useful in a neurology practice to identify dPD and associated syndromes and follow dPD patients in treatment.

Certain syndromes occur as relatively common comorbid syndromes, including apathy, cognitive difficulties, psychosis, and anxiety. These associated conditions can cause difficulties in the treatment of dPD and in some cases (e.g., apathy) may be difficult to distinguish from dPD. Depressed PD patients may show a unique pattern of depressive symptoms that is different from those of elders with MD. This symptom profile includes a pattern of sadness without guilt or self-reproach, a high rate of anxiety symptoms, a relative lack of delusions and hallucinations, and a low suicide rate despite a high frequency of suicidal ideation.

The treatment of dPD is complicated by the lack of randomized clinical trials to identify which antidepressant agents are most effective. Available clinical evidence is primarily from open trials and show that TCSs and SSRIs are both effective treatments. There is limited evidence that the dopamine agonists may be effective as augmenting agents. Although there are no clinical trials of psychotherapy, techniques used in CBT have the potential for helping the negative biases observed in many dPD patients. ECT and rTMS are also supported as somatic treatments for dPD. A treatment algorithm is presented for dPD which utilizes lessons learned from geriatric depression. Although this algorithm can be used in general practice, treatment of dPD must be individualized for each patient.

References

1. Cummings JL. Depression and Parkinson's disease: A review. *Am J Psychiatry* 1992; 149(4):443–454.
2. Slaughter JR, Slaughter KA, Nichols D, et al. Prevalence, clinical manifestations, etiology, and treatment of depression in Parkinson's disease. *J Neuropsychiatr Clin Neurosci* 2001; 13(2):187–196.
3. McDonald WM, Richard IH, DeLong MR. Prevalence, etiology, and treatment of depression in Parkinson's disease. *Biol Psychiatry* 2003; 54(3):363–375.
4. Holtzheimer PE, McDonald WM, DeLong MR. Mood disorders in Parkinson's disease. In: Evans D, Charney DS (eds). *The Physician's Guide to Depression and Bipolar Disorders.* New York: McGraw-Hill, 2005:333–354.
5. Weintraub D, Moberg PJ, Duda JE, et al. Effect of psychiatric and other nonmotor symptoms on disability in Parkinson's disease. *J Am Geriatr Soc.* 2004; 52(5):784–788.
6. Starkstein SE, Mayberg HS, Leiguarda R, et al. A prospective longitudinal study of depression, cognitive decline, and physical impairments in patients with Parkinson's disease. *J Neurol Neurosurg Psychiatry* 1992; 55(5):377–382.
7. Schrag A, Jahanshahi M, Quinn NP. What contributes to depression in Parkinson's disease? *Psychol Med* 2001; 31(1):65–73.
8. Liu CY, Wang SJ, Fuh JL, Lin CH, Yang YY, Liu HC. The correlation of depression with functional activity in Parkinson's disease. *Journal of Neurology.* Aug 1997; 244(8):493–498.
9. Schrag A, Jahanshahi M, Quinn N. What contributes to quality of life in patients with Parkinson's disease?[see comment]. *J Neurol Neurosurg Psychiatry* 2000; 69(3): 308–312.
10. Global Parkinson's Disease Study Steering Committee. Factors impacting on quality of life in Parkinson's disease: results from an international survey. *Mov Disord* 2002; 17(1):60–67.
11. Schrag A, Hovris A, Morley D, Quinn N, Jahanshahi M. Caregiver burden in Parkinson's disease is closely associated with psychiatric symptoms, falls, and disability. *Parkinsonism Relat Disord* 2006; 12(1):35–41.
12. Fernandez HH, Tabamo RE, David RR, Friedman JH. Predictors of depressive symptoms among spouse caregivers in Parkinson's disease. *Mov Disord* 2001; 16(6):1123–1125.
13. Aarsland D, Larsen JP, Karlsen K, et al. Mental symptoms in Parkinson's disease are important contributors to caregiver distress. *Int J Geriatr Psychiatry* 1999; 14(10):866–874.
14. Norman S, Troster AI, Fields JA, Brooks R. Effects of depression and Parkinson's disease on cognitive functioning. *J Neuropsychiatr Clin Neurosci* 2002; 14(1):31–36.
15. Happe S, Ludemann P, Berger K. The association between disease severity and sleep-related problems in patients with Parkinson's disease. *Neuropsychobiology* 2002; 46(2):90–96.
16. Starkstein SE, Preziosi TJ, Robinson RG. Sleep disorders, pain, and depression in Parkinson's disease. *Eur Neurol* 1991; 31(6):352–355.
17. Dooneief G, Mirabello E, Bell K, et al. An estimate of the incidence of depression in idiopathic Parkinson's disease. *Arch Neurol* 1992; 49(3):305–307.
18. American Psychiatric Association. *Diagnostic and Statistical Manual of Mental Disorders,* 4th ed. Washington, DC: APA Press, 2000.
19. Tandberg E, Larsen JP, Aarsland D, Cummings JL. The occurrence of depression in Parkinson's disease. A community-based study. *Arch Neurol* 1996; 53(2):175–179.
20. Rojo A, Aguilar M, Garolera MT, et al. Depression in Parkinson's disease: Clinical correlates and outcome. *Parkinsonism Relat Disord* 2003; 10(1):23–28.
21. Schrag A, Jahanshahi M, Quinn N. How does Parkinson's disease affect quality of life? A comparison with quality of life in the general population. *Mov Disord* 2000; 15(6):1112–1118.
22. Ehmann TS, Beninger RJ, Gawel MJ, Riopelle RJ. Depressive symptoms in Parkinson's disease: A comparison with disabled control subjects. *J Geriatr Psychiatr Neurol* 1990; 3(1):3–9.
23. Leentjens AF, Van den Akker M, Metsemakers JF, et al. Higher incidence of depression preceding the onset of Parkinson's disease: A register study. *Mov Disord* 2003; 18(4):414–418.
24. Mayberg HS. Modulating dysfunctional limbic-cortical circuits in depression: Towards development of brain—based algorithms for diagnosis and optimised treatment. *Br Med Bull* 2003; 65:193–207.
25. Sheline YI. Neuroimaging studies of mood disorder effects on the brain. *Biol Psychiatry* 2003; 54(3):338–352.
26. Lisanby SH, McDonald WM, Massey EW, et al. Diminished subcortical nuclei volumes in Parkinson's disease by MR imaging. *J Neural Transm Suppl* 1993; 40:13–21.
27. McDonald WM, Krishnan KR. Magnetic resonance in patients with affective illness. *Eur Arch Psychiatr Clin Neurosci* 1992; 241(5):283–290.
28. Mayberg HS, Starkstein SE, Sadzot B, et al. Selective hypometabolism in the inferior frontal lobe in depressed patients with Parkinson's disease. *Ann Neurol* 1990; 28(1): 57–64.

29. Baxter LR Jr, Schwartz JM, Phelps ME, et al. Reduction of prefrontal cortex glucose metabolism common to three types of depression. *Arch Gen Psychiatry* 1989; 46(3): 243–250.

30. Murai T, Muller U, Werheid K, et al. In vivo evidence for differential association of striatal dopamine and midbrain serotonin systems with neuropsychiatric symptoms in Parkinson's disease. *J Neuropsychiatr Clin Neurosci* 2001; 13(2):222–228.

31. Mayeux R, Stern Y, Sano M, et al. The relationship of serotonin to depression in Parkinson's disease. *Mov Disord* 1988; 3(3):237–244.

32. Mayeux R, Stern Y, Williams JB, et al. Clinical and biochemical features of depression in Parkinson's disease. *Am J Psychiatry* 1986; 143(6):756–759.

33. Kostic VS, Djuricic BM, Covickovic-Sternic N, et a;. Depression and Parkinson's disease: Possible role of serotonergic mechanisms. *J Neurol* 1987; 234(2):94–96.

34. Mayeux R, Stern Y, Cote L, Williams JB. Altered serotonin metabolism in depressed patients with parkinson's disease. *Neurology* 1984; 34(5):642–646.

35. Menza MA, Palermo B, DiPaola R, et al. Depression and anxiety in Parkinson's disease: Possible effect of genetic variation in the serotonin transporter. *J Geriatr Psychiatry Neurol.* 1999; 12(2):49–52.

36. Menza MA, Mark MH. Parkinson's disease and depression: The relationship to disability and personality. *J Neuropsychiatr Clin Neurosci* 1994; 6(2):165–169.

37. Kuhn W, Muller T, Gerlach M, et al. Depression in Parkinson's disease: Biogenic amines in CSF of "de novo" patients. *J Neural Transm* 1996; 103(12):1441–1445.

38. Uhl GR, Hedreen JC, Price DL. Parkinson's disease: Loss of neurons from the ventral tegmental area contralateral to therapeutic surgical lesions. *Neurology* 1985; 35(8):1215–1218.

39. Starkstein SE, Mayberg HS, Preziosi TJ, et al. Reliability, validity, and clinical correlates of apathy in Parkinson's disease. *J Neuropsychiatr Clin Neurosci* 1992; 4(2):134–139.

40. Hoogendijk WJ, Sommer IE, Tissingh G, et al. Depression in Parkinson's disease. The impact of symptom overlap on prevalence. *Psychosomatics* 1998; 39(5):416–421.

41. Cantello R, Aguggia M, Gilli M, et al. Major depression in Parkinson's disease and the mood response to intravenous methylphenidate: Possible role of the "hedonic" dopamine synapse. *J Neurol Neurosurg Psychiatry* 1989; 52(6):724–731.

42. Remy P, Doder M, Lees A, Tet al. Depression in Parkinson's disease: Loss of dopamine and noradrenaline innervation in the limbic system. *Brain* 2005;.

43. Weintraub D, Newberg AB, Cary MS, et al. Striatal dopamine transporter imaging correlates with anxiety and depression symptoms in Parkinson's disease. *J Nucl Med* 2005; 46(2):227–232.

44. McDonald WM, Salzman C, Schatzberg AF. Depression in the elderly. *Psychopharmacol Bull* 2002; 36(Suppl 2):112–122.

45. Santamaria J, Tolosa E, Valles A. Parkinson's disease with depression: A possible subgroup of idiopathic parkinsonism. *Neurology* 1986; 6(8):1130–1133.

46. Cole SA, Woodard JL, Juncos JL, et al. Depression and disability in Parkinson's disease. *J Neuropsychiatr Clin Neurosci* 1996; 8(1):20–25.

47. Kostic VS, Filipovic SR, Lecic D, et al. Effect of age at onset on frequency of depression in Parkinson's disease. *J Neurol Neurosurg Psychiatry* 1994; 57(10):1265–1267.

48. Starkstein SE, Petracca G, Chemerinski E, et al. Depression in classic versus akinetic-rigid Parkinson's disease. *Mov Disord* 1998; 13(1):29–33.

49. Starkstein SE, Preziosi TJ, Bolduc PL, Robinson RG. Depression in Parkinson's disease. *J Nerv Ment Dis* 1990; 178(1):27–31.

50. Starkstein SE, Preziosi TJ, Forrester AW, Robinson RG. Specificity of affective and autonomic symptoms of depression in Parkinson's disease. *J Neurol Neurosurg Psychiatry* 1990; 53(10):869–873.

51. Shulman LM, Taback RL, Bean J, Weiner WJ. Comorbidity of the nonmotor symptoms of Parkinson's disease. *Mov Disord* 2001; 16(3):507–510.

52. Aarsland D, Larsen JP, Lim NG, et al. Range of neuropsychiatric disturbances in patients with Parkinson's disease. *J Neurol Neurosurg Psychiatry* 1999; 67(4):492–496.

53. van der Wurff FB, Beekman AT, Comijs HC, et al. [Apathy syndrome: a clinical entity?]. *Tijdschr Gerontol Geriatr* 2003; 34(4):146–150.

54. Marin RS. Apathy: Concept, syndrome, neural mechanisms, and treatment. *Semin Clin Neuropsychiatry* 1996; 1(4):304–314.

55. Starkstein SE, Preziosi TJ, Berthier ML, et al. Depression and cognitive impairment in Parkinson's disease. *Brain* 1989; 112(Pt 5):1141–1153.

56. Mayeux R, Stern Y, Rosen J, Leventhal J. Depression, intellectual impairment, and Parkinson disease. *Neurology* 1981; 31(6):645–650.

57. Hughes TA, Ross HF, Musa S, et al. A 10-year study of the incidence of and factors predicting dementia in Parkinson's disease. *Neurology* 2000; 54(8):1596–1602.

58. Stern Y, Marder K, Tang MX, Mayeux R. Antecedent clinical features associated with dementia in Parkinson's disease. *Neurology* 1993; 43(9):1690–1692.

59. Tandberg E, Larsen JP, Aarsland D, et al. Risk factors for depression in Parkinson disease. *Arch Neurol* 1997; 54(5):625–630.

60. Fenelon G, Mahieux F, Huon R, Ziegler M. Hallucinations in Parkinson's disease: Prevalence, phenomenology, and risk factors. *Brain* 2000; 123(Pt 4):733–745.

61. Aarsland D, Larsen JP, Tandberg E, Laake K. Predictors of nursing home placement in Parkinson's disease: a population-based, prospective study. *J Am Geriatr Soc* 2000; 48(8):938–942.

62. de Maindreville AD, Fenelon G, Mahieux F. Hallucinations in Parkinson's disease: A follow-up study. *Mov Disord* 2005; 20(2):212–217.

63. Bronnick K, Aarsland D, Larsen JP. Neuropsychiatric disturbances in Parkinson's disease clusters in five groups with different prevalence of dementia. *Acta Psychiatr Scand* 2005; 112(3):201–207.

64. Aarsland D, Larsen JP, Cummins JL, Laake K. Prevalence and clinical correlates of psychotic symptoms in Parkinson disease: A community-based study. *Arch Neurol* 1999; 56(5):595–601.

65. Fenelon G, Goetz CG, Karenberg A. Hallucinations in Parkinson disease in the prelevodopa era. *Neurology* 2006; 66(1):93–98.

66. Menza MA, Robertson–Hoffman DE, Bonapace AS. Parkinson's disease and anxiety: Comorbidity with depression. *Biol Psychiatry* 1993; 34(7):465–470.

67. Richard IH, Schiffer RB, Kurlan R. Anxiety and Parkinson's disease. *J Neuropsychiatr Clin Neurosci* 1996; 8(4):383–392.

68. Friedenberg DL, Cummings JL. Parkinson's disease, depression, and the on–off phenomenon. *Psychosomatics* 1989; 30(1):94–99.

69. Shults CW. Treatments of Parkinson disease: Circa 2003. *Arch Neurol* 2003; 60(12):1680–1684.

70. Brown RG, Marsden CD, Quinn N, Wyke MA. Alterations in cognitive performance and affect-arousal state during fluctuations in motor function in Parkinson's disease. *J Neurol Neurosurg Psychiatry* 1984; 47(5):454–465.

71. Cantello R, Gilli M, Riccio A, Bergamasco B. Mood changes associated with "end–of–dose deterioration" in Parkinson's disease: A controlled study. *J Neurol Neurosurg Psychiatry* 1986; 49(10):1182–1190.

72. Girotti F, Carella F, Grassi MP, et al. Motor and cognitive performances of parkinsonian patients in the on and off phases of the disease. *J Neurol Neurosurg Psychiatry* 1986; 49(6):657–660.

73. Hardie RJ, Lees AJ, Stern GM. On–off fluctuations in Parkinson's disease. A clinical and neuropharmacological study. *Brain* 1984; 107(Pt 2):487–506.

74. Nissenbaum H, Quinn NP, Brown RG, et al. Mood swings associated with the "on–off" phenomenon in Parkinson's disease. *Psychol Med* 1987; 17(4):899–904.

75. Richard IH, Justus AW, Kurlan R. Relationship between mood and motor fluctuations in Parkinson's disease. *J Neuropsychiatr Clin Neurosci* 2001; 13(1):35–41.

76. Racette BA, Hartlein JM, Hershey T, et al. Clinical features and comorbidity of mood fluctuations in Parkinson's disease. *J Neuropsychiatr Clin Neurosci* 2002; 14(4): 438–442.

77. Nuti A, Ceravolo R, Piccinni A, et al. Psychiatric comorbidity in a population of Parkinson's disease patients. *Eur J Neurol* 2004; 11(5):315–320.

78. Maricle RA, Nutt JG, Valentine RJ, Carter JH. Dose-response relationship of levodopa with mood and anxiety in fluctuating Parkinson's disease: A double-blind, placebo-controlled study. *Neurology* 1995; 45(9):1757–1760.

79. Shulman LM, Taback RL, Rabinstein AA, Weiner WJ. Non-recognition of depression and other non-motor symptoms in Parkinson's disease. *Parkinsonism Relat Disord* 2002; 8(3):193–197.

80. Leentjens AF, Marinus J, Van Hilten JJ, et al. The contribution of somatic symptoms to the diagnosis of depressive disorder in Parkinson's disease: A discriminant analytic approach. *J Neuropsychiatr Clin Neurosci* 2003; 15(1):74–77.

81. Levin BE, Llabre MM, Weiner WJ. Parkinson's disease and depression: Psychometric properties of the Beck Depression Inventory. *J Neurol Neurosurg Psychiatry* 1988; 51(11):1401–1404.

82. Brown RG, MacCarthy B, Gotham AM, et al. Depression and disability in Parkinson's disease: a follow–up of 132 cases. *Psychol Med* 1988; 18(1):49–55.

83. Koenig HG, George LK, Peterson BL, Pieper CF. Depression in medically ill hospitalized older adults: Prevalence, characteristics, and course of symptoms according to six diagnostic schemes. *Am J Psychiatry* 1997; 154(10):1376–1383.

84. Marsh L, McDonald WM, Cummings JL, et al. Provisional diagnostic criteria for depression in Parkinson's disease: Report of an NINDS/NIMH Work Group. *Mov Disord* 2006; 21(2):148–158.

85. Keshavan MS, David AS, Narayanen HS, Satish P. "On–off" phenomena and manic–depressive mood shifts: Case report. *J Clin Psychiatry* 1986; 47(2):93–94.

86. Cannas A, Spissu A, Floris GL, et al. Bipolar affective disorder and Parkinson's disease: A rare, insidious and often unrecognized association. *Neurol Sci* 2002; 23(Suppl 2): S67–S68.

87. Hamilton M. A rating scale for depression. *J Neurol Neurosurg Psychiatry* 1960; 23:56–62.

88. Montgomery SA, Asberg M. A new depression scale designed to be sensitive to change. *Br J Psychiatry* 1979; 134:382–389.

89. Lang AET, Fahn S. Assessment of Parkinson's disease. In: Munsat TL (ed). *Quantification of Neurological Deficit.* Boston: Butterworth, 1989:285–309.

90. Yesavage JA, Brink TL, Rose TL, et al. Development and validation of a geriatric depression screening scale: A preliminary report. *J Psychiatr Res* 1982; 17(1):37–49.

91. Beck AT, Ward CH, Mendelsohn M, et al. An inventory for measuring depression. *Arch Gen Psychiatry* 1961; 4:561–571.

92. Zung WW, Richards CB, Short MJ. Self-rating depression scale in an outpatient clinic. Further validation of the SDS. *Arch Gen Psychiatry* 1965; 13(6):508–515.

93. Snaith RP, Zigmond AS. Hospital Anxiety and Depression Scale (HADS). *Handbook of Psychiatric Measures.* Washington, DC: American Psychiatric Association Press, 2000:547–548.

94. Radloff LS. The CES–D Scale: A self–report depression scale for research in the general population. *Appl Psychol Meas* 1977; 1:385–401.

95. Alexopoulos GS, Abrams RC, Young RC, Shamoian CA. Cornell Scale for Depression in Dementia. *Biol Psychiatry* 1988; 23(3):271–284.

96. McDonald WM, Holtzheimer PE, Haber M, et al. Validity of the 30-item Geriatric Depression Scale in patients with Parkinson's disease. *Mov Disord.* 2005.

97. Weintraub D, Oehlberg KA, Katz IR, Stern MB. Test characteristics of the 15–item geriatric depression scale and Hamilton depression rating scale in Parkinson disease. *Am J Geriatr Psychiatry* 2006; 14(2):169–175.

98. Huber SJ, Freidenberg DL, Paulson GW, et al. The pattern of depressive symptoms varies with progression of Parkinson's disease [see comment]. *J Neurol Neurosurg Psychiatry* 1990; 53(4):275–278.

99. Avila A, Cardona X, Martin–Baranera M, et al. Does nefazodone improve both depression and Parkinson disease? A pilot randomized trial. *J Clin Psychopharmacol* 2003; 23(5):509–513.

100. Leentjens AF, Verhey FR, Lousberg R, et al. The validity of the Hamilton and Montgomery-Asberg depression rating scales as screening and diagnostic tools for depression in Parkinson's disease. *Int J Geriatr Psychiatry* 2000; 15(7):644–649.

101. Naarding P, Leentjens AF, van Kooten F, Verhey FR. Disease-specific properties of the Rating Scale for Depression in patients with stroke, Alzheimer's dementia, and Parkinson's disease. *J Neuropsychiatry Clin Neurosci* 2002; 14(3):329–334.

102. Muller-Thomsen T, Arlt S, Mann U, et al. Detecting depression in Alzheimer's disease: Evaluation of four different scales. *Arch Clin Neuropsychol* 2005; 20(2):271–276.

103. Weintraub D, Moberg PJ, Duda JE, et al. Recognition and treatment of depression in Parkinson's disease. *J Geriatr Psychiatr Neurol* 2003; 16(3):178–183.

104. Judd LL, Paulus MP, Wells KB, Rapaport MH. Socioeconomic burden of subsyndromal depressive symptoms and major depression in a sample of the general population. *Am J Psychiatry* 1996; 153(11):1411–1417.

105. Cuijpers P, Smit F. Subthreshold depression as a risk indicator for major depressive disorder: A systematic review of prospective studies [see comment] [review]. *Acta Psychiatr Scand* 2004; 109(5):325–331.

106. Hermens ML, van Hout HP, Terluin B, et al. The prognosis of minor depression in the general population: A systematic review [review]. *Gen Hosp Psychiatry* 2004; 26(6):453–462.

107. Cuijpers P, Van Straten A, Smit F. Preventing the incidence of new cases of mental disorders: A meta-analytic review. *J Nerv Ment Dis* 2005; 193(2):119–125.

108. Sheehan DV, Lecrubier Y, Sheehan KH, et al. The Mini–International Neuropsychiatric Interview (M.I.N.I.): The development and validation of a structured diagnostic psychiatric interview for DSM–IV and ICD–10. *J Clin Psychiatry* 1998; 59(Suppl 20):22–33; quiz 34–57.

109. Folstein MF, Folstein SE, McHugh PR. "Mini–mental state." A practical method for grading the cognitive state of patients for the clinician. *J Psychiatr Res* 1975; 12(3): 189–198.

110. Haggerty JJ Jr, Prange AJ Jr. Borderline hypothyroidism and depression. *Annu Rev Med* 1995; 46:37–46.

111. Garcia-Moreno JM, Chacon-Pena J. Hypothyroidism and Parkinson's disease and the issue of diagnostic confusion. *Mov Disord* 2003; 18(9):1058–1059.

112. Tandeter HB, Shvartzman P. Parkinson's disease camouflaging early signs of hypothyroidism. *Postgrad Med* 1993; 94(5):187–190.

113. Otake K, Oiso Y, Mitsuma T, et al. Hypothalamic dysfunction in Parkinson's disease patients. *Acta Med Hung* 1994; 50(1–2):3–13.

114. Lefebvre J, Loeuille GA, Steinling M, Linquette M. [Comparative action of L–dopa and bromocriptine on thyrostimulating hormone (T.S.H.) in primary hypothyroidism (author's transl)]. *Nouv Presse Med* 1979; 8(38):3033–3036.

115. Lindenbaum J, Healton EB, Savage DG, et al. Neuropsychiatric disorders caused by cobalamin deficiency in the absence of anemia or macrocytosis. *N Engl J Med* 1988; 318(26):1720–1728.

116. Dharmarajan TS, Norkus EP. Approaches to vitamin B12 deficiency. Early treatment may prevent devastating complications. *Postgrad Med* 2001; 110(1):99–105; quiz 106.

117. Dharmarajan TS, Ugalino JT, Kanagala M, et al. Vitamin B12 status in hospitalized elderly from nursing homes and the community. *J Am Med Dir Assoc* 2000; 1(1):21–24.

118. Dharmarajan TS, Adiga GU, Norkus EP. Vitamin B12 deficiency. Recognizing subtle symptoms in older adults. *Geriatrics* 2003; 58(3):30–34, 37–38.

119. Bottiglieri T, Laundy M, Crellin R, et al. Homocysteine, folate, methylation, and monoamine metabolism in depression. *J Neurol Neurosurg Psychiatry* 2000; 69(2):228–232.

120. Reutens S, Sachdev P. Homocysteine in neuropsychiatric disorders of the elderly. *Int J Geriatr Psychiatry* 2002; 17(9):859–864.

121. Kuhn W, Roebroek R, Blom H, et al. Hyperhomocysteinaemia in Parkinson's disease. *J Neurol* 1998; 245(12):811–812.

122. Kuhn W, Roebroek R, Blom H, et al. Elevated plasma levels of homocysteine in Parkinson's disease. *Eur Neurol* 1998; 40(4):225–227.

123. Muller T, Werne B, Fowler B, Kuhn W. Nigral endothelial dysfunction, homocysteine, and Parkinson's disease. *Lancet* 1999; 354(9173):126–127.

124. Muller T, Woitalla D, Hauptmann B, et al. Decrease of methionine and S–adenosylmethionine and increase of homocysteine in treated patients with Parkinson's disease. *Neurosci Lett* 2001; 308(1):54–56.

125. Hankey GJ, Eikelboom JW. Homocysteine and vascular disease. *Lancet* 1999; 354(9176):407–413.

126. Di Rocco A, Rogers JD, Brown R, Werner P, Bottiglieri T. S-Adenosyl-methionine improves depression in patients with Parkinson's disease in an open-label clinical trial. *Mov Disord* 2000; 15(6):1225–1229.

127. Mischoulon D, Fava M. Role of S-adenosyl-L-methionine in the treatment of depression: A review of the evidence. *Am J Clin Nutr* 2002; 76(5):1158S–1161S.

128. Barrett-Connor E, Von Muhlen DG, Kritz-Silverstein D. Bioavailable testosterone and depressed mood in older men: The Rancho Bernardo Study. *J Clin Endocrinol Metab* 1999; 84(2):573–577.

129. Okun MS, McDonald WM, DeLong MR. Refractory nonmotor symptoms in male patients with Parkinson disease due to testosterone deficiency: A common unrecognized comorbidity. *Arch Neurol* 2002; 59(5):807–811.

130. Seidman SN, Rabkin JG. Testosterone replacement therapy for hypogonadal men with SSRI-refractory depression. *J Affect Disord* 1998; 48(2–3):157–161.

131. Jouvent R, Abensour P, Bonnet AM, et al. Antiparkinsonian and antidepressant effects of high doses of bromocriptine. An independent comparison. *J Affect Disord* 1983; 5(2):141–145.

132. Rektorova I, Rektor I, Bares M, et al. Pramipexole and pergolide in the treatment of depression in Parkinson's disease: A national multicentre prospective randomized study. *Eur J Neurol* 2003; 10(4):399–406.

133. Young BK, Camicioli R, Ganzini L. Neuropsychiatric adverse effects of antiparkinsonian drugs. Characteristics, evaluation and treatment. *Drugs Aging* 1997; 10(5):367–383.

134. Vitek JL, Bakay RA, Freeman A, et al. Randomized trial of pallidotomy versus medical therapy for Parkinson's disease. *Ann Neurol* 2003; 53(5):558–569.

135. Burchiel KJ. Thalamotomy for movement disorders. *Neurosurg Clin North Am* 1995; 6(1):55–71.

136. York MK, Levin HS, Grossman RG, Hamilton WJ. Neuropsychological outcome following unilateral pallidotomy. *Brain* 1999; 122(Pt 12):2209–2220.

137. Alegret M, Valldeoriola F, Tolosa E, et al. Cognitive effects of unilateral posteroventral pallidotomy: A 4-year follow-up study. *Mov Disord* 2003; 18(3):323–328.

138. Green J, Barnhart H. The impact of lesion laterality on neuropsychological change following posterior pallidotomy: A review of current findings. *Brain Cogn* 2000; 42(3):379–398.

139. Green J, McDonald WM, Vitek JL, et al. Neuropsychological and psychiatric sequelae of pallidotomy for PD: Clinical trial findings. *Neurology* 2002; 58(6):858–865.

140. Okun MS, Bakay RA, DeLong MR, Vitek JL. Transient manic behavior after pallidotomy. *Brain Cogn* 2003; 52(2):281–283.

141. Vitek JL. Deep brain stimulation for Parkinson's disease. A critical re-evaluation of STN versus GPi DBS. *Stereotact Funct Neurosurg* 2002; 78(3–4):119–131.

142. Limousin P, Speelman JD, Gielen F, Janssens M. Multicentre European study of thalamic stimulation in parkinsonian and essential tremor. *J Neurol Neurosurg Psychiatry* 1999; 66(3):289–296.

143. Bejjani BP, Damier P, Arnulf I, et al. Transient acute depression induced by high-frequency deep-brain stimulation. *N Engl J Med* 1999; 340(19):1476–1480.

144. Herzog J, Volkmann J, Krack P, et al. Two-year follow-up of subthalamic deep brain stimulation in Parkinson's disease. *Mov Disord* 2003; 18(11):1332–1337.

145. Miyawaki E, Perlmutter JS, Troster AI, et al. The behavioral complications of pallidal stimulation: A case report. *Brain Cogn* 2000; 42(3):417–434.

146. Ruggieri S, Denaro A, Meco G, et al. Multicenter trial of L–deprenyl in Parkinson disease. *Ital J Neurol Sci* 1986; 7(1):133–137.

147. Kuhn W, Muller T. The clinical potential of deprenyl in neurologic and psychiatric disorders. *J Neural Transm Suppl* 1996; 48:85–93.

148. Lattanzi L, Dell'Osso L, Cassano P, et al. Pramipexole in treatment-resistant depression: A 16-week naturalistic study. *Bipolar Disord* 2002; 4(5):307–314.

149. Chung TH, Deane KH, Ghazi–Noori S, et al. Systematic review of antidepressant therapies in Parkinson's disease. *Parkinsonism Relat Disord* 2003; 10(2):59–65.

150. Weintraub D, Morales KH, Moberg PJ, et al. Antidepressant studies in Parkinson's disease: A review and meta-analysis [review]. *Mov Disord* 2005; 20(9):1161–1169.

151. Andersen J, Aabro E, Gulmann N, et al. Anti-depressive treatment in Parkinson's disease. A controlled trial of the effect of nortriptyline in patients with Parkinson's disease treated with L–dopa. *Acta Neurol Scand* 1980; 62(4):210–219.

152. Richard IH, Kurlan R. A survey of antidepressant drug use in Parkinson's disease. Parkinson Study Group. *Neurology* 1997; 49(4):1168–1170.

153. Jimenez-Jimenez FJ, Tejeiro J, Martinez-Junquera G, et al. Parkinsonism exacerbated by paroxetine. *Neurology* 1994; 44(12):2406.

154. Meltzer HY, Young M, Metz J, et al. Extrapyramidal side effects and increased serum prolactin following fluoxetine, a new antidepressant. *J Neural Transm* 1979; 45(2):165–175.

155. Lambert MT, Trutia C, Petty F. Extrapyramidal adverse effects associated with sertraline. *Prog Neuropsychopharmacol Biol Psychiatry* 1998; 22(5):741–748.

156. Leo RJ. Movement disorders associated with the serotonin selective reuptake inhibitors. *J Clin Psychiatry* 1996; 57(10):449–454.

157. Jones-Fearing KB. SSRI and EPS with fluoxetine. *J Am Acad Child Adolesc Psychiatry* 1996; 35(9):1107–1108.

158. Simons JA. Fluoxetine in Parkinson's disease. *Mov Disord* 1996; 11(5):581–582.

159. Coulter DM, Pillans PI. Fluoxetine and extrapyramidal side effects. *Am J Psychiatry* 1995; 152(1):122–125.

160. Bouchard R, Pourcher E, Vincent P. Fluoxetine and extrapyramidal side effects. *Am J Psychiatry* 1989; 146(10):1352–1353.

161. Hesselink JM. Serotonin and Parkinson's disease. *Am J Psychiatry* 1993; 150(5): 843–844.

162. Steur EN. Increase of Parkinson disability after fluoxetine medication. *Neurology* 1993; 43(1):211–213.

163. Tate JL. Extrapyramidal symptoms in a patient taking haloperidol and fluoxetine. *Am J Psychiatry* 1989; 146(3):399–400.

164. Tesei S, Antonini A, Canesi M, et al. Tolerability of paroxetine in Parkinson's disease: A prospective study. *Mov Disord* 2000; 15(5):986–989.

165. Schillevoort I, van Puijenbroek EP, de Boer A, et al. Extrapyramidal syndromes associated with selective serotonin reuptake inhibitors: A case-control study using spontaneous reports. *Int Clin Psychopharmacol* 2002; 17(2):75–79.

166. Lane RM. SSRI-induced extrapyramidal side effects and akathisia: Implications for treatment. *J Psychopharmacol* 1998; 12(2):192–214.

167. Gony M, Lapeyre-Mestre M, Montastruc JL. Risk of serious extrapyramidal symptoms in patients with Parkinson's disease receiving antidepressant drugs: a pharmacoepidemiologic study comparing serotonin reuptake inhibitors and other antidepressant drugs. *Clin Neuropharmacol* 2003; 26(3):142–145.

168. Mamo DC, Sweet RA, Mulsant BH, et al. Effect of nortriptyline and paroxetine on extrapyramidal signs and symptoms: A prospective double-blind study in depressed elderly patients. *Am J Geriatr Psychiatry* 2000; 8(3):226–231.

169. Caley CF, Friedman JH. Does fluoxetine exacerbate Parkinson's disease? *J Clin Psychiatry* 1992; 53(8):278–282.

170. Dell'Agnello G, Ceravolo R, Nuti A, et al. SSRIs do not worsen Parkinson's disease: Evidence from an open-label, prospective study. *Clin Neuropharmacol* 2001; 24(4):221–227.

171. Hauser RA, Zesiewicz TA. Sertraline for the treatment of depression in Parkinson's disease. *Mov Disord* 1997; 12(5):756–759.

172. Montastruc JL, Fabre N, Blin O, et al. Does fluoxetine aggravate Parkinson's disease? A pilot prospective study. *Mov Disord* 1995; 10(3):355–357.

173. Rampello L, Chiechio S, Raffaele R, et al. The SSRI, citalopram, improves bradykinesia in patients with Parkinson's disease treated with L-dopa. *Clin Neuropharmacol* 2002; 25(1):21–24.

174. Richard IH, Maughn A, Kurlan R. Do serotonin reuptake inhibitor antidepressants worsen Parkinson's disease? A retrospective case series. *Mov Disord* 1999; 14(1):155–157.

175. Hinds NP, Hillier CE, Wiles CM. Possible serotonin syndrome arising from an interaction between nortriptyline and selegiline in a lady with parkinsonism. *J Neurol* 2000; 247(10).

176. Wermuth L. A double-blind, placebo-controlled, randomized, multi-center study of pramipexole in advanced Parkinson's disease. *Eur J Neurol* 1998; 5(3):235–242.

177. Leentjens AF, Vreeling FW, Luijckx GJ, Verhey FR. SSRIs in the treatment of depression in Parkinson's disease. *Int J Geriatr Psychiatry* 2003; 18(6):552–554.

178. Ceravolo R, Nuti A, Piccinni A, et al. Paroxetine in Parkinson's disease: Effects on motor and depressive symptoms. *Neurology* 2000; 55(8):1216–1218.

179. Rabey JM, Orlov E, Korczyn AD. Comparison of fluvoxamine versus amitriptyline for treatment of depression in Parkinson's disease. *Neurology* 1996; 46:A374.

180. Vaswani M, Linda FK, Ramesh S. Role of selective serotonin reuptake inhibitors in psychiatric disorders: A comprehensive review. *Prog Neuropsychopharmacol Biol Psychiatry* 2003; 27(1):85–102.

181. Zohar J, Westenberg HG. Anxiety disorders: A review of tricyclic antidepressants and selective serotonin reuptake inhibitors. *Acta Psychiatr Scand Suppl* 2000; 403:39–49.

182. Meco G, Fabrizio E, Di Rezze S, et al. Mirtazapine in L-dopa–induced dyskinesias. *Clin Neuropharmacol* 2003; 26(4):179–181.

183. Goetz CG, Tanner CM, Klawans HL. Bupropion in Parkinson's disease. *Neurology* 1984; 34(8):1092–1094.

184. Pintor L, Bailles E, Valldeoriola F, et al. Response to 4–month treatment with reboxetine in Parkinson's disease patients with a major depressive episode. *Gen Hosp Psychiatry* 2006; 28(1):59–64.

185. Pridmore S, Pollard C. Electroconvulsive therapy in Parkinson's disease: 30 month follow up. *J Neurol Neurosurg Psychiatry* 1996; 60(6):693.

186. Friedman J, Gordon N. Electroconvulsive therapy in Parkinson's disease: A report on five cases. *Convuls Ther* 1992; 8(3):204–210.

187. Fall PA, Ekman R, Granerus AK, et al. ECT in Parkinson's disease. Changes in motor symptoms, monoamine metabolites and neuropeptides. *J Neural Transm Park Dis Dement Sect* 1995; 10(2–3):129–140.

188. Moellentine C, Rummans T, Ahlskog JE, et al. Effectiveness of ECT in patients with parkinsonism. *J Neuropsychiatry Clin Neurosci* 1998; 10(2):187–193.

189. Factor SA, Molho ES, Brown DL. Combined clozapine and electroconvulsive therapy for the treatment of drug-induced psychosis in Parkinson's disease. *J Neuropsychiatry Clin Neurosci* 1995; 7(3):304–307.

190. Hurwitz TA, Calne DB, Waterman K. Treatment of dopaminomimetic psychosis in Parkinson's disease with electroconvulsive therapy. *Can J Neurol Sci* 1988; 15(1):32–34.

191. van der Wurff FB, Stek ML, Hoogendijk WJ, Beekman AT. The efficacy and safety of ECT in depressed older adults: A literature review. *Int J Geriatr Psychiatry* 2003; 18(10):894–904.

192. Salzman C, Wong E, Wright BC. Drug and ECT treatment of depression in the elderly, 1996–2001: A literature review. *Biol Psychiatry* 2002; 52(3):265–284.

193. Figiel GS, Hassen MA, Zorumski C, et al. ECT-induced delirium in depressed patients with Parkinson's disease. *J Neuropsychiatry Clin Neurosci* 1991; 3(4):405–411.

194. McDonald W, Thompson T, McCall W, Zorumpski C. Electroconvulsive therapy. In: Schatzberg A, Nemeroff C (eds). *Textbook of Psychopharmacology.* Vol 3. Washington, DC: American Psychiatric Press, 2004:685–717.

195. Datto CJ. Side effects of electroconvulsive therapy. *Depress Anxiety* 2000; 12(3):130–134.

196. Zielinski RJ, Roose SP, Devanand DP, et al. Cardiovascular complications of ECT in depressed patients with cardiac disease. *Am J Psychiatry* 1993; 150(6):904–909.

197. Holtzheimer PE III, Russo J, Avery DH. A meta-analysis of repetitive transcranial magnetic stimulation in the treatment of depression. *Psychopharmacol Bull* 2001; 35(4):149–169. [Erratum in: Psychopharmacol Bull. 2003 Spring; 2037(2002):2005.]

198. Burt T, Lisanby SH, Sackeim HA. Neuropsychiatric applications of transcranial magnetic stimulation: A meta-analysis. *Int J Neuropsychopharmacol.* 2002; 5(1):73–103.

199. Kozel FA, George MS. Meta-analysis of left prefrontal repetitive transcranial magnetic stimulation (rTMS) to treat depression. *J Psychiatr Pract* 2002; 8(5):270–275.

200. Martin JL, Barbanoj MJ, Schlaepfer TE, et al. Repetitive transcranial magnetic stimulation for the treatment of depression: Systematic review and meta-analysis. *Br J Psychiatry* 2003; 182:480–491.

201. Avery DH, Holtzheimer PE III, Fawaz W, et al. A controlled study of repetitive transcranial magnetic stimulation in medication-resistant major depression. *Biol Psychiatry* 2006; 59(2):187–194.

202. McDonald WM, Greenberg BD. Electroconvulsive therapy in the treatment of neuropsychiatric conditions and transcranial magnetic stimulation as a pathophysiological probe in neuropsychiatry. *Depress Anxiety* 2000; 12(3):135–143.

203. Dragasevic N, Potrebic A, Damjanovic A, et al. Therapeutic efficacy of bilateral prefrontal slow repetitive transcranial magnetic stimulation in depressed patients with Parkinson's disease: An open study. *Mov Disord* 2002; 17(3):528–532.

204. Fregni F, Santos CM, Myczkowski ML, et al. Repetitive transcranial magnetic stimulation is as effective as fluoxetine in the treatment of depression in patients with Parkinson's disease. *J Neurol Neurosurg Psychiatry* 2004; 75(8):1171–1174.

205. Pascual-Leone A, Valls-Sole J, Brasil-Neto JP, et al. Akinesia in Parkinson's disease. II. Effects of subthreshold repetitive transcranial motor cortex stimulation. *Neurology* 1994; 44(5):892–898.

206. Siebner HR, Mentschel C, Auer C, Conrad B. Repetitive transcranial magnetic stimulation has a beneficial effect on bradykinesia in Parkinson's disease. *Neuroreport* 1999; 10(3):589–594.

207. Siebner HR, Rossmeier C, Mentschel C, et al. Short-term motor improvement after sub-threshold 5-Hz repetitive transcranial magnetic stimulation of the primary motor hand area in Parkinson's disease. *J Neurol Sc.* 2000; 178(2):91–94.

208. de Groot M, Hermann W, Steffen J, et al. [Contralateral and ipsilateral repetitive transcranial magnetic stimulation in Parkinson patients]. *Nervenarzt* 2001; 72(12):932–938.

209. Sommer M, Kamm T, Tergau F, et al. Repetitive paired-pulse transcranial magnetic stimulation affects corticospinal excitability and finger tapping in Parkinson's disease. *Clin Neurophysiol* 2002; 113(6):944–950.

210. Shimamoto H, Takasaki K, Shigemori M, et al. Therapeutic effect and mechanism of repetitive transcranial magnetic stimulation in Parkinson's disease. *J Neurol* 2001; 248(Suppl 3):III48–III52.

211. Mally J, Stone TW. Therapeutic and "dose-dependent" effect of repetitive microelectroshock induced by transcranial magnetic stimulation in Parkinson's disease. *J Neurosci Res* 1999; 57(6):935–940.

212. Mally J, Stone TW. Improvement in parkinsonian symptoms after repetitive transcranial magnetic stimulation. *J Neurol Sci* 1999; 162(2):179–184.

213. Boylan LS, Pullman SL, Lisanby SH, et al. Repetitive transcranial magnetic stimulation to SMA worsens complex movements in Parkinson's disease. *Clin Neurophysio.* 2001; 112(2):259–264.

214. Okabe S, Ugawa Y, Kanazawa I. 0.2-Hz repetitive transcranial magnetic stimulation has no add-on effects as compared to a realistic sham stimulation in Parkinson's disease. *Mov Disord* 2003; 18(4):382–388.

215. Tergau F, Wassermann EM, Paulus W, Ziemann U. Lack of clinical improvement in patients with Parkinson's disease after low and high frequency repetitive transcranial magnetic stimulation. *Electroencephalogr Clin Neurophysiol Suppl* 1999; 51:281–288.

216. Ghabra MB, Hallett M, Wassermann EM. Simultaneous repetitive transcranial magnetic stimulation does not speed fine movement in PD. *Neurology* 1999; 52(4):768–770.

217. Ohnishi T, Hayashi T, Okabe S, et al. Endogenous dopamine release induced by repetitive transcranial magnetic stimulation over the primary motor cortex: An [11C]raclopride positron emission tomography study in anesthetized macaque monkeys. *Biol Psychiatry* 2004; 55(5):484–489.

218. Kanno M, Matsumoto M, Togashi H, Yoshioka M, Mano Y. Effects of acute repetitive transcranial magnetic stimulation on dopamine release in the rat dorsolateral striatum. *J Neurol Sci.* 2004; 217(1):73–81.

219. Strafella AP, Paus T, Fraraccio M, Dagher A. Striatal dopamine release induced by repetitive transcranial magnetic stimulation of the human motor cortex. *Brain* 2003; 22:22.

220. Keck ME, Welt T, Muller MB, et al. Repetitive transcranial magnetic stimulation increases the release of dopamine in the mesolimbic and mesostriatal system. *Neuropharmacology* 2002; 43(1):101–109.

221. Strafella AP, Paus T, Barrett J, Dagher A. Repetitive transcranial magnetic stimulation of the human prefrontal cortex induces dopamine release in the caudate nucleus. *J Neurosci* 2001; 21(15):RC157.

222. DeRubeis RJ, Gelfand LA, Tang TZ, Simons AD. Medications versus cognitive behavior therapy for severely depressed outpatients: Mega-analysis of four randomized comparisons. *Am J Psychiatry* 1999; 156(7):1007–1013.

223. Scott J. Cognitive therapy for depression. *Br Med Bull* 2001; 57:101–113.

224. Gloaguen V, Cottraux J, Cucherat M, Blackburn IM. A meta-analysis of the effects of cognitive therapy in depressed patients. *J Affect Disord* 1998; 49(1):59–72.

225. Thase ME, Greenhouse JB, Frank E, et al. Treatment of major depression with psychotherapy or psychotherapy-pharmacotherapy combinations. *Arch Gen Psychiatry* 1997; 54(11):1009–1015.

226. Browne G, Steiner M, Roberts J, et al. Sertraline and/or interpersonal psychotherapy for patients with dysthymic disorder in primary care: 6-month comparison with longitudinal 2-year follow-up of effectiveness and costs. *J Affect Disord* 2002; 68(2–3):317–330.

227. Reynolds CF III, Frank E, Perel JM, et al. Nortriptyline and interpersonal psychotherapy as maintenance therapies for recurrent major depression: A randomized controlled trial in patients older than 59 years. *JAMA* 1999; 281(1):39–45.

228. Frank E, Kupfer DJ, Wagner EF, et al. Efficacy of interpersonal psychotherapy as a maintenance treatment of recurrent depression. Contributing factors. *Arch Gen Psychiatry* 1991; 48(12):1053–1059.

229. Cole MG, Elie LM, McCusker J, et al. Feasibility and effectiveness of treatments for depression in elderly medical inpatients: A systematic review. *Int Psychogeriatr* 2000; 12(4):453–461.

230. Miller MD, Cornes C, Frank E, et al. Interpersonal psychotherapy for late-life depression: Past, present, and future. *J Psychother Pract Res* 2001; 10(4):231–238.

231. Reynolds CF III, Dew MA, Pollock BG, et al. Maintenance treatment of major depression in old age [see comment]. *N Engl J Med* 2006; 354(11):1130–1138.

232. Ehmann TS, Beninger RJ, Gawel MJ, Riopelle RJ. Coping, social support, and depressive symptoms in Parkinson's disease. *J Geriatr Psychiatr Neurol* 1990; 3(2):85–90.

233. Cole K, Vaughan FL. The feasibility of using cognitive behaviour therapy for depression associated with Parkinson's disease: a literature review [review]. *Parkinsonism Relat Disord.* 2005; 11(5):269–276.

234. Dobkin RD, Allen LA, Menza M. A cognitive-behavioral treatment package for depression in Parkinson's disease. *Psychosomatics* 2006; 47(3):259–263.

235. Mulsant BH, Alexopoulos GS, Reynolds CF III, et al. Pharmacological treatment of depression in older primary care patients: The PROSPECT algorithm. *Int J Geriatr Psychiatry* 2001; 16(6):585–592.

236. McDonald WM, Holtzheimer PE III, Byrd EH. The diagnosis and treatment of depression in Parkinson's disease. *Curr Treat Options Neurol* 2006; 8(3):245–255.

237. Hirschfeld RM, Montgomery SA, Aguglia E, et al. Partial response and nonresponse to antidepressant therapy: Current approaches and treatment options [review] *J Clin Psychiatry* 2002; 63(9):826–837.

238. McDonald WM, Wermager J. Pharmacologic treatment of geriatric mania. *Curr Psychiatr Rep* 2002; 4(1):43–50.

239. Carpenter LL, Yasmin S, Price LH. A double-blind, placebo-controlled study of antidepressant augmentation with mirtazapine. *Biol Psychiatr* 2002; 51(2):183–188.

240. Fava M, Dunner DL, Greist JH, et al. Efficacy and safety of mirtazapine in major depressive disorder patients after SSRI treatment failure: An open-label trial. *J Clin Psychiatry* 2001; 62(6):413–420.

241. Trivedi MH, Fava M, Wisniewski SR, et al. Medication augmentation after the failure of SSRIs for depression [see comment]. *N Engl J Med* 2006; 354(12):1243–1252.

242. Whyte EM, Basinski J, Farhi P, et al. Geriatric depression treatment in nonresponders to selective serotonin reuptake inhibitors. *J Clin Psychiatry* 2004; 65(12):1634–1641.

243. Labbate LA, Croft HA, Oleshansky MA. Antidepressant-related erectile dysfunction: Management via avoidance, switching antidepressants, antidotes, and adaptation [review]. *J Clin Psychiatr* 2003; 10:11–19.

244. Lavretsky H, Kim MD, Kumar A, Reynolds CF III. Combined treatment with methylphenidate and citalopram for accelerated response in the elderly: An open trial. *J Clin Psychiatry* 2003; 64(12):1410–1414.

245. Masand PS, Anand VS, Tanquary JF. Psychostimulant augmentation of second generation antidepressants: A case series. *Depress Anxiety* 1998; 7(2):89–91.

246. Xiong GL, Christopher EJ, Goebel J. Modafinil as an alternative to methylphenidate as augmentation for depression treatment. *Psychosomatics* 2005; 46(6):578–579.

247. Padala PR, Petty F, Bhatia SC. Methylphenidate may treat apathy independent of depression. *Ann Pharmacother* 2005; 39(11):1947–1949.

248. Holtzheimer PE, Nemeroff CB. Advances in the treatment of depression. *NeuroRX* 2006; 3(1):42–56.

249. Fernandez HH, Trieschmann ME, Friedman JH. Treatment of psychosis in Parkinson's disease: Safety considerations. *Drug Saf* 2003; 26(9):643–659.

250. Wagner ML, Defilippi JL, Menza MA, Sage JI. Clozapine for the treatment of psychosis in Parkinson's disease: Chart review of 49 patients. *J Neuropsychiatr Clin Neurosci* 1996; 8(3):276–280.

251. Trosch RM, Friedman JH, Lannon MC, et al. Clozapine use in Parkinson's disease: A retrospective analysis of a large multicentered clinical experience. *Mov Disord* 1998; 13(3):377–382.

252. The Parkinson Study Group. Low-dose clozapine for the treatment of drug-induced psychosis in Parkinson's disease. *N Engl J Med* 1999; 340(10):757–763.

253. The French Clozapine Parkinson Study Group. Clozapine in drug-induced psychosis in Parkinson's disease. *Lancet* 1999; 353(9169):2041–2042.

254. Menza MM, Palermo B, Mark M. Quetiapine as an alternative to clozapine in the treatment of dopamimetic psychosis in patients with Parkinson's disease. *Ann Clin Psychiatry* 1999; 11(3):141–144.

255. Fernandez HH, Trieschmann ME, Burke MA, et al. Long-term outcome of quetiapine use for psychosis among parkinsonian patients. *Mov Disord* 2003; 18(5):510–514.

256. Reddy S, Factor SA, Molho ES, Feustel PJ. The effect of quetiapine on psychosis and motor function in parkinsonian patients with and without dementia. *Mov Disord* 2002; 17(4):676–681.

257. Bullock R, Saharan A. Atypical antipsychotics: Experience and use in the elderly. *Int J Clin Pract* 2002; 56(7):515–525.

258. Morgante L, Epifanio A, Spina E, et al. Quetiapine versus clozapine: Aa preliminary report of comparative effects on dopaminergic psychosis in patients with Parkinson's disease. *Neurol Sci* 2002; 23(Suppl 2):S89–S90.

259. Wijnen HH, van der Heijden FM, van Schendel FM, et al. Quetiapine in the elderly with parkinsonism and psychosis. *Eur Psychiatry* 2003; 18(7):372–373.

260. Juncos JL, Roberts VJ, Evatt ML, et al. Quetiapine improves psychotic symptoms and cognition in Parkinson's disease. *Mov Disord* 2004; 19(1):29–35.

261. Connemann BJ, Schonfeldt-Lecuona C. Ziprasidone in Parkinson's disease psychosis. *Can J Psychiatry* 2004; 49(1):73.

262. Schonfeldt-Lecuona C, Connemann BJ. Aripiprazole and Parkinson's disease psychosis. *Am J Psychiatry* 2004; 161(2):373–374.

263. Fernandez HH, Trieschmann ME, Friedman JH. Aripiprazole for drug-induced psychosis in Parkinson disease: Preliminary experience. *Clin Neuropharmacol* 2004; 27(1):4–5.

264. McKeith IG, Grace JB, Walker Z, et al. Rivastigmine in the treatment of dementia with Lewy bodies: Preliminary findings from an open trial. *Int J Geriatr Psychiatry* 2000; 15(5):387–392.

265. Bullock R, Cameron A. Rivastigmine for the treatment of dementia and visual hallucinations associated with Parkinson's disease: A case series. *Curr Med Res Opin* 2002; 18(5):258–264.

266. Bergman J, Lerner V. Successful use of donepezil for the treatment of psychotic symptoms in patients with Parkinson's disease. *Clin Neuropharmacol* 2002; 25(2):107–110.

267. Fabbrini G, Barbanti P, Aurilia C, et al. Donepezil in the treatment of hallucinations and delusions in Parkinson's disease. *Neurol Sci* 2002; 23(1):41–43.

268. Reading PJ, Luce AK, McKeith IG. Rivastigmine in the treatment of parkinsonian psychosis and cognitive impairment: Preliminary findings from an open trial. *Mov Disord* 2001; 16(6):1171–1174.

269. Aarsland D, Hutchinson M, Larsen JP. Cognitive, psychiatric and motor response to galantamine in Parkinson's disease with dementia. *Int J Geriatr Psychiatry* 2003; 18(10):937–941.

270. Hanagasi HA, Emre M. Treatment of behavioural symptoms and dementia in Parkinson's disease. *Fundam Clin Pharmacol* 2005; 19(2):133–146.

17 Anxiety and Panic

Irene Hegeman Richard
Roger Kurlan

D ementia and depression have long been recognized as the 2 major behavioral disorders typically associated with Parkinson's disease (PD). However, recent evidence suggests that others, such as anxiety, may be equally important. This chapter focuses on available information supporting a relationship between PD and anxiety, which may help to elucidate pathogenetic mechanisms and appropriate therapy. Recent years have brought an expanded repertoire of pharmacotherapies for primary mood and anxiety disorders that can be utilized in PD patients—as can further experience with surgical approaches in PD and their effects on behavioral features. However, there continues to be a lack of controlled clinical research in the area of anxiety in PD.

Anxiety is a state characterized by a vague and unpleasant sense of apprehension, often accompanied by autonomic symptoms such as palpitations and dry mouth. It may serve as a beneficial alerting signal, warning of impending danger and stimulating appropriate measures, but it may also be pathologic if the symptoms are prolonged or excessive or if they occur at inappropriate times. An anxiety disorder connotes the presence of significant dysfunction due to anxiety. There are many different anxiety disorders, which are distinguished from one another by their constellation of symptoms, response to medications, and, in some cases, presumed etiologic

mechanisms (1). The fourth edition of *The Diagnostic and Statistical Manual of Mental Disorders* (DSM-IV) includes the categories of anxiety disorders, which are listed in Table 17-1. The specific criteria for a panic attack as outlined in DSM-IV are listed in Table 17-2. The anxiety classification scheme has not been modified with the recent text revision of DSM-IV (2).

ANXIETY IN PARKINSON'S DISEASE

Prevalence of Anxiety

One of the first formal studies of anxiety in PD was conducted by Rubin et al. (3), who used a standardized questionnaire and DSM-III-R (4) criteria for anxiety and affective disorders to evaluate 16 PD patients (out of a total PD population of 210 patients) who reported marked episodic anxiety. Of the total population, 8 patients (4%) met the criteria for panic-anxiety disorder and 6 simultaneously met the criteria for major depression or dysthymia. The rate for panic-anxiety disorder was noted to be greater than that estimated for the general population. Subsequent studies have also observed that anxiety in patients with PD occurs more frequently than expected. Stein and coworkers (5) systematically evaluated 24 PD patients for the presence of DSM-III-R axis I syndromes.

TABLE 17-1
Categories of Anxiety Disorders in DSM-IV

Panic disorder with and without agoraphobia
Agoraphobia without a history of panic disorder
Specific and social phobias
Obsessive-compulsive disorder
Posttraumatic stress disorder and acute stress disorder
Generalized anxiety disorder
Anxiety disorder due to a general medical condition
Substance-induced anxiety disorder
Anxiety disorder not otherwise specified (including
    mixed anxiety-depressive disorder)

In this group, 9 subjects (38%) had a clinically significant anxiety disorder, a rate that is much greater than that in the general population (5% to 15%), in primary care clinics (10%), or in patients with chronic medical conditions (11%). Vazquez et al. (6) found that 31 of 131 PD patients (24%) had experienced recurrent panic attacks that fulfilled most of the DSM-III-R criteria (4) for panic disorder. A recent study by Shulman et al. (7) found a similar rate of anxiety and also revealed that anxiety and other nonmotor symptoms may be underrecognized by treating physicians.

In addition to exceeding prevalence rates in the general population, anxiety disorders in PD have been found to be more common than in other neurologic or medical illnesses. Schiffer et al. (8) carried out structured clinical psychiatric interviews for 16 depressed PD patients and 20 depressed multiple sclerosis patients and found that anxiety disorders were more common in the patients with PD. Among these, 75% met the criteria for past or present

---

TABLE 17-2
Possible Symptoms of Panic Attack in DSM-IV

1. Palpirations, pounding heart, or accelerated
       heart rate
2. Sweating
3. Trembling or shaking
4. Sensations of shortness of breath or smothering
5. Feeling of choking
6. Chest pain or discomfort
7. Nausea or abdominal distress
8. Feeling dizzy, unsteady, lightheaded, or faint
9. Derealization (feelings of unreality) or
       depersonalization (being detached from oneself)
10. Fear of losing control or going crazy
11. Fear of dying
12. Paresthesias (numbness or tingling sensations)
13. Chills or hot flushes

---

generalized anxiety disorder (GAD) or panic disorder, whereas only 10% of patients with multiple sclerosis met these criteria.

Menza et al. (9) compared 42 patients with PD and 21 matched medical control subjects (patients with chronic debilitating osteoarthritis matched for age and length of illness) by using DSM-III-R criteria and a variety of psychiatric rating scales. Among the PD patients, 12 (29%) had a formal anxiety disorder, as did only 1 medical control subject (5%). In a subsequent study of 104 PD patients and 61 medical control subjects with equal disability, Menza and Mark (10) noted that PD patients scored higher than control subjects on measures of depression and anxiety. In another study, Gotham et al. (11) found that the frequency of anxiety in PD exceeded that of healthy control subjects but was not greater than that in patients with chronic arthritis. One study revealed that PD patients experienced more complaints related to autonomic function (e.g., postural dizziness, urinary frequency, dry mouth) than controls (12). The authors concluded that some PD patients diagnosed with anxiety or depression may in fact be experiencing the subjective concomitants of autonomic failure and that this might lead to an overdiagnosis of these psychiatric disorders in the PD population. Given the fact that "significance persisted after the autonomic items were removed from the Hamilton scales," it would appear more likely that patients with PD have common neurobiological abnormalities that can result in both emotional and autonomic dysfunction.

Thus, most studies have shown that anxiety occurs commonly in patients with PD and at a higher rate than in normal or other disease-comparison populations.

Clinical Features of Anxiety Disorders

A wide range of anxiety disorders have been reported in patients with PD. In the study by Stein and coworkers (5), of the 9 PD subjects with a clinically significant anxiety disorder, 1 had GAD, 2 had panic disorder, 1 had longstanding panic disorder with recent onset of a superimposed major depressive episode, 1 had panic disorder and social phobia, 3 had social phobia alone, and 1 had anxiety disorder not otherwise specified. The authors judged that 3 additional patients had symptoms of social phobia that appeared to be secondary to self-consciousness about PD symptoms. These patients were not considered to have a clinically significant anxiety disorder because they did not meet DSM-III-R diagnostic criteria for social phobia (where it was specified that a diagnosis of social phobia could not be made if the fear was related to symptoms of a medical disorder) (4); these patients would now meet DSM-IV (1) criteria for anxiety disorder not otherwise specified. Vazquez et al. (6) described only panic disorder, whereas Schiffer et al. (8) reported the presence of panic disorder and GAD. Menza et al. (9) noted that anxiety diagnoses in PD patients are clustered among panic disorder, phobic disorder, and GAD.

Lauterbach and Duvoisin (13) described anxiety disorders in patients with familial parkinsonism and noted the following rates: simple phobia, 34.3%; agoraphobia, 15.8%; obsessive-compulsive disorder (OCD), 13.2%; panic disorder, 7.9%; GAD and social phobia, each 5.3%. The authors noted that their observed rate of GAD was similar to that reported by Stein et al. (5) in their study of patients with PD, whereas a lower rate of panic disorder and higher rates of social phobia and OCD were identified in their familial parkinsonism subjects. In a more recent study comparing patients with two different movement disorders, Lauterbach et al. (14) reported that GAD had a higher prevalence in patients with dystonia, whereas panic disorder was more common in PD.

Thus, a wide range of anxiety disorders may occur in PD patients. Further studies involving larger patient populations and standard psychiatric interviews are needed to clarify the relative frequencies of the various anxiety disorder types.

Time of Onset of Anxiety

Although many investigators have indicated that anxiety symptoms tend to appear after the diagnosis of PD has been established (5, 6, 14, 15), one study involving patients with familial parkinsonism reported that the onset of anxiety preceded the appearance of motor symptoms (13). Furthermore, a large, prospective study involving a cohort of male health professionals found an association between self-reported phobic anxiety and later development of PD (16). Whether this association is causal or the result of a shared diathesis remains to be determined. Regardless, these observations suggest that like depression, anxiety symptoms among parkinsonian patients are not simply related to psychological and social difficulties in adapting to the illness.

Relationship of Anxiety to Antiparkinsonian Medications

The issue of whether antiparkinsonian medications might be responsible for some of the anxiety symptoms seen in PD patients remains unsettled. Henderson et al. (15) noted that among PD subjects taking levodopa and reporting anxiety, 44% had the onset of anxiety before beginning levodopa and 56% had it after treatment was initiated. Stein et al. (5) found no significant difference between anxious and nonanxious patients with PD with regard to the cumulative dose of levodopa. The authors did note, however, that many subjects were taking other antiparkinsonian medications—such as anticholinergics, amantadine, and bromocriptine—and that a potential influence of these drugs could not be excluded.

Siemers and coworkers (17) studied anxiety state and motor performance in 19 patients with PD. All were taking levodopa/carbidopa and most were also receiving adjunctive antiparkinsonian medications, including dopamine receptor agonists, selegiline, and anticholinergics. Two patients were taking benzodiazepines. The authors found no statistical differences in motor, depression, or anxiety scores based on the presence or absence of the additional medications. In the study by Menza and coworkers (9), levodopa dose did not significantly correlate with anxiety measures. The authors also found that there was no difference in measures of anxiety for patients receiving or not receiving selegiline or pergolide. In distinction to the above reports, Vazquez et al. (6) concluded that panic attacks were related to levodopa therapy but not to other agonist drugs. The authors found that 24% of PD patients under chronic levodopa therapy had experienced recurrent panic attacks. It was noted that the PD patients with panic were put on levodopa earlier than the PD patients without panic and that they needed higher dosages. However, these panic attacks occurred primarily in the "off" state. Rondot and coworkers (18) found that anxious PD patients received similar doses of levodopa when compared to the general PD population; it was therefore concluded that anxiety was not caused by chronic treatment with levodopa. However, they noted that anxiety is seen in certain individuals as an acute mental disorder associated with the taking of levodopa. Thus whether treatment with antiparkinsonian medications might influence anxiety symptoms in PD patients remains an unsettled issue.

Relationship of Anxiety to Motor Symptoms

The majority of studies have shown that depression in PD is not closely correlated with the severity of motor symptoms or the degree of disability (19), thus supporting the notion that this behavioral disorder is not a reaction to the illness but is more likely related to central biochemical disturbances that accompany PD. Recent studies have examined the relationship between anxiety and PD motor symptoms. Most studies have identified no significant difference in disability ratings between PD patients with and those without anxiety (5, 9).

Some authors have reported higher degrees of anxiety in patients who experience "on-off" motor fluctuations (9, 15, 20, 21), whereas others have failed to confirm this relationship (5, 13, 22). One could conjecture that the unpredictable nature of the on-off states might result in anxiety behavior similar to that which occurs in laboratory animals after they are exposed to unpredictable aversive stimuli (23). Riley and Lang (24) include anxiety as one of the psychiatric disturbances that vary with parkinsonian motor fluctuations. Most authors have noted that in patients who do experience the on-off phenomenon, anxiety tends to occur most often during the "off" phase (5, 6, 15, 17). It is interesting that as early as 1976, Marsden and Parkes (25) commented that "the off period may be accompanied by panic, flushing and sweating, and leg pain," although they did not specifically discuss the relationship between anxiety and parkinsonian mobility states. One study revealed that in most patients, mood or anxiety improved significantly from "off" to "on" but then worsened again in the "on" state when dyskinesias appeared (26). In a levodopa infusion study, Maricle et al. (27) found that mood, anxiety, and motor fluctuations tended to correlate in that patients experienced greater anxiety and depression during periods of poor mobility and vice versa. They did not find that patients had a recurrence of anxiety and depression with the onset of dyskinesias. Other studies have found a relationship between mood, arousal or psychic activation, and mobility changes during on-off fluctuations but did not specifically address anxiety (28, 29). In an effort to better understand the relationship among motor, mood, and anxiety fluctuations, Richard et al. (20) conducted a prospective study using visual analog scales in 87 patients with PD. The results suggest that PD patients are heterogeneous with regard to the presence, range, and pattern of fluctuations. Among patients with motor fluctuations, 75% had mood and/or anxiety fluctuations. The majority of patients with mood fluctuations also experienced anxiety fluctuations. Many patients reported the "classic pattern" of low mood and high anxiety during periods of immobility. However, not all patients exhibited a temporal correlation between motor and emotional states, and it was not uncommon for mood and anxiety to fluctuate independently of one another.

Lauterbach and Duvoisin (13) noted that for patients with familial parkinsonism who had panic attacks before the diagnosis of the movement disorder, the symptoms lessened as the disease advanced and particularly when "freezing" episodes (sudden immobility that can render a patient motionless) appeared. The attenuation of anxiety symptoms may have resulted from continued noradrenergic cell loss

A variety of questions have been raised regarding the exact relationship between anxiety and motor function. Does decreased mobility cause anxiety? Can anxiety cause decreased mobility? Are both anxiety and decreased mobility the result of common central neurochemical disturbances? Routh et al. (30) described a patient with PD and anxiety characterized by both social phobia and agoraphobia or panic disorder. The patient's motor symptoms could not be controlled by levodopa during periods of increased anxiety, leading the authors to conclude that anxiety may indeed worsen parkinsonian motor features. Arguing against such causality would be the finding that even during experimental yohimbine-induced panic attacks and anxiety (31), patients had no

measured worsening of their parkinsonian motor symptoms. To determine how CNS dopaminergic activity may relate to mood and anxiety, Menza et al. (26) assessed 10 patients with PD and motor fluctuations for mood and anxiety changes during discrete "off," "on," and "on with dyskinesias" periods. Only one patient rated his moods as consistently improving from "off" to "on" to "on with dyskinesias," paralleling presumed increasing striatal and limbic dopaminergic activity. Most of the patients, however, felt depressed and anxious when they were "off" and when they were "on with dyskinesias," leading the authors to conclude that the behavioral responses of most patients probably reflect an emotional reaction to their motor symptoms. An alternative explanation might be that there is an optimal level of dopamine that is necessary to prevent depressed mood and anxiety. In the levodopa infusion study conducted by Maricle and colleagues (27), the emotional changes generally preceded the motor changes by several minutes, thereby making it unlikely that the anxiety and depression represented an emotional reaction to motor impairment. It seems more likely that CNS levodopa depletion results in both mood and motor changes but that the time course of effects might be slightly different.

Some authors have suggested that changes of other neurotransmitters that occur during parkinsonian motor fluctuations may play a role in the occurrence of anxiety. Siemers et al. (17) postulated that an alteration in serotonin may be responsible for the increase in anxiety symptoms related to motor performance. Vazquez et al. (6) suggested that norepinephrine may play a primary role in panic attacks in PD. Further studies are needed to clarify the relationship between motor state and anxiety in PD and to uncover pathogenetic mechanisms.

Epidemiology of Anxiety

Because anxiety occurring in PD involves a population of older individuals, it is of interest that anxiety disorders in psychiatric patients characteristically begin by young adulthood. Thus the onset of anxiety in late age in association with PD is contrary to the expected natural course of this condition and favors an etiologic link between the two disorders. This notion is further supported by current data indicating that anxiety disorders are less common in the elderly than in younger adults (32). The frequency of anxiety in PD exceeds the expected prevalence rates in this age group and this also favors a pathogenetic relationship. It should be noted, however, that some authors believe that an underdiagnosis of anxiety in late life may contribute to low prevalence estimates in the healthy elderly population (33, 34). In reviewing the epidemiology and comorbidity of anxiety disorders in the elderly, Flint (32) concluded that GAD and phobias account for most anxiety in late life and that panic disorder is rare, which is in contrast to the rather frequent occurrence of panic disorder in patients with PD. It was noted that when panic disorder did occur in elderly patients, females accounted for all the cases. In contrast to these observations, it is interesting to note that panic disorder occurring in the setting of PD involves both males and females.

Raj et al. (35) suggest that late-onset panic disorder may be more common than previously thought; they also noted that such patients are more likely to have coexistent medical disorders such as chronic obstructive pulmonary disease (COPD), vertigo, and PD. The authors speculate that medical disorders such as COPD and PD might have a role in the onset of late-life panic disorder.

Relationship Between Anxiety and Depression

It is well known that anxiety and depressive disorders commonly coexist in psychiatric populations. In a review of coexisting depression and anxiety, Lydiard (36) notes that up to 60% of patients with depressive symptoms also have anxiety, and that 20% to 30% of patients with major depression meet criteria for panic disorder. Between 21% and 91% of patients meeting criteria for panic disorder experience an episode of major depression one or more times during their lives. Lidiard also notes that patients with combined panic disorder and major depression are more significantly impaired than patients with either disorder alone.

There appears to be a relationship between anxiety and depression in PD as well. In a review of depression in PD, Cummings (19) notes that the depression in PD is distinguished from other depressive disorders by greater anxiety and less self-punitive ideation. After discovering that the diagnoses of anxiety and panic disorder were significantly more frequent among depressed patients with PD than depressed patients with multiple sclerosis, Schiffer et al. (8) suggested that PD patients may experience an atypical depression, a subtype that includes anxiety. One study showed that 92% of PD patients who had an anxiety disorder also had a depressive disorder, and that 67% of those with a depressive disorder also had an anxiety disorder (9). Another study compared PD patients with age-matched healthy spouse controls and noted that the report of depression plus panic or anxiety (as compared with either condition alone) best distinguished the two populations (15). Although other studies have also shown a close correlation between depression and anxiety in PD (6, 37), anxiety can clearly occur in the absence of depression. A study by Lin et al. (38) revealed that although the degrees of anxiety and depression assessed via standardized rating scales were generally correlated, 14 of 58 (24%) PD patients determined to be free of depressive symptoms fulfilled DSM-III-R criteria for GAD.

Because most patients with PD are elderly, it is important to look at comorbidity in this age group. It was pointed out by Flint (32), in his review of anxiety in the elderly, that studies show considerable comorbidity of anxiety disorders and depression in late life. The rate of comorbidity for GAD and phobias with depression in old age is similar to that quoted for younger patients. However, the depressed elderly appear to have a lower risk for developing panic attacks (32). The frequent occurrence of depression coexisting with panic in PD is of particular interest and suggests that these behavioral responses are etiologically related to the neurobiological changes that accompany PD.

Relationship Between Anxiety and Dementia

Although there is some evidence for an increased rate of anxiety in primary dementia disorders (39), the relationship between anxiety and dementia in PD is not clear. Depression appears to be equally frequent in PD with and without dementia (19). Iruela et al. (40) hypothesized that anxiety may actually lessen in PD patients if they become demented, and there is a significant decrease in brain levels of norepinephrine in the dementia of PD (41); an abnormal activity of noradrenergic cells in the locus ceruleus has been hypothesized to cause anxiety. Addressing this issue, however, Lauterbach (42) studied 38 patients with familial parkinsonism and found no relationship between dementia and anxiety symptoms. Most of the studies that examined anxiety in patients with PD either failed to comment on the cognitive status of the patients (8, 15) or deliberately excluded patients with dementia (5, 9, 17); therefore definite conclusions cannot be reached regarding a relationship between anxiety and cognitive decline in this illness. Fleminger (37) noted that two groups of patients with PD who differed with regard to the presence of anxiety did not differ on their performance on two tests of cognitive function (National Adult Reading Test and Information, Memory, and Concentration Test). Vazquez et al. (6) found that anxious and nonanxious PD patients did not differ with respect to their severity of dementia as assessed by the Unified Parkinson's Disease Rating Scale (UPDRS) but noted that more formal measures of cognitive function were not performed and also that the degree of mental impairment was low in both groups.

Neurobiology of Anxiety as It Relates to Parkinson's Disease

Significant advances have been made in uncovering some of the possible biological mechanisms of anxiety. An examination of this information along with the known neurobiological alterations in PD may shed light on common mechanisms that might be responsible for the apparent relationship between the two conditions.

The main neurotransmitters implicated in the pathogenesis of anxiety include norepinephrine, serotonin, and gamma-aminobutyric acid (GABA) (43, 44). There is strong evidence implicating noradrenergic dysfunction, particularly the alpha-2 adrenergic receptors, and perhaps the locus ceruleus itself, in the development of primary anxiety disorders, especially panic disorder (43–49). Interestingly, many abnormalities of the noradrenergic system have also been discovered in PD patients. The dorsal ascending noradrenergic pathway is particularly affected. This pathway originates in the locus ceruleus and projects to the cerebral cortex, amygdala, hippocampus, and septum (50). Studies have demonstrated catecholaminergic cell loss in the locus ceruleus in PD (51, 52). This loss appears to correlate with the presence of dementia (41, 53, 54) . There appear to be changes in both central and peripheral adrenergic receptors in PD. Studies have shown that alpha-2 receptors are decreased in number in the cerebral cortex (55). Other studies have noted a decrease in alpha-2 adrenoceptors (56) and decreased yohimbine-binding sites (57) in platelets of untreated PD patients. Bernal and coworkers (58) suggest that untreated PD is associated with a significant reduction in alpha-2 adrenergic sensitivity. It is possible that patients with PD are more vulnerable to panic attacks because they have an alteration of alpha-2 adrenergic receptors. It is also possible that the locus ceruleus is disinhibited in PD secondary to changes in other neurotransmitter systems. Lauterbach (42), Lauterbach and Duvoisin (13), and Vazquez and coworkers (6) independently provided data in PD suggesting that locus ceruleus disinhibition may lead to panic attacks.

Further support for a noradrenergic role in the development of anxiety in PD comes from our pilot study of experimental yohimbine-induced panic. Oral yohimbine (an alpha-2 antagonist) was administered to 6 patients with PD who had a history of anxiety or depression, 2 parkinsonian patients without psychiatric illness, and 2 normal controls. Parkinsonian patients with a history of anxiety developed panic attacks at frequencies comparable to those of primary psychiatric patients with panic disorder. Regardless of their history of anxiety and/or depression, parkinsonian patients demonstrated a vulnerability to yohimbine-induced somatic symptoms (31).

Alterations in the serotonin neurotransmitter system have also been postulated to play a role in anxiety disorders, particularly OCD and social phobia (59, 60), posttraumatic stress disorder, GAD, and perhaps panic disorder (61). Some abnormalities of the serotonergic system have been recorded in PD. Studies have demonstrated a loss of large neurons in the median (62) and dorsal raphe nuclei. There is decreased serotonin concentration in the putamen, caudate, globus pallidus, substantia nigra, hypothalamus, and frontal cortex. Less severe declines occur in other areas as well (64) . A decrease in the density of binding sites in the putamen for the serotonin-specific reuptake inhibitors has also been shown (65, 66). It is possible that interactions between noradrenergic and

serotonergic systems may be relevant to the expression of certain anxiety disorders, since serotonin can decrease locus ceruleus firing by its effects on 5-HT2 receptors (61). Results from a study by Menza et al. suggest that variations of the short allele of the serotonin transporter gene may represent significant risk factors for the development of anxiety and depression in PD.

The potential role of GABA in the genesis of anxiety is suggested by the efficacy of benzodiazepines for the treatment of panic disorder and GAD. These drugs produce their effects by activating GABA receptors in the brain (61). In PD brains examined postmortem, an increased concentration of GABA in putamen and pallidum and a decreased concentration in cortical areas have been observed (50).

It has been postulated that a dopaminergic dysregulation may relate to social phobia (68) and panic disorder (69, 70) and that both dopamine and serotonin systems may be involved in OCD (71, 72). Since alterations in dopaminergic function are the hallmark of PD, it is not surprising that patients would have a greater than expected frequency of anxiety disorders. Levodopa infusion studies in patients with PD completed by Maricle et al. (27) clearly implicate a dopaminergic deficiency state in anxiety, at least that which is associated with motor fluctuations. Tomer et al. (73) hypothesized that reduced dopaminergic activity in the striatum may be responsible for obsessive-compulsive symptoms in PD. It has been demonstrated that dopamine decreases the firing rate of the locus ceruleus (74). In turn, several investigators have hypothesized that the dopamine deficiency of PD might result in an alteration of noradrenergic systems and could be responsible for certain anxiety disorders in patients with this illness (6, 40, 42). One recent functional imaging study supported this notion, indicating an association between affective measures (depression and anxiety) and decreased striatal dopamine transporter availability in patients with PD (75).

Aside from classic neurotransmitter systems, neuropeptides may also play a role in anxiety. It is of interest that abnormalities of corticotropin-releasing factor (CRF) have been related to anxiety and depression, possibly via influences on the locus ceruleus (76). Thus, a disturbance of CRF in PD, which has not yet been investigated, might explain the combination of anxious and depressive symptoms.

There is some evidence suggesting that lateralized cerebral factors in PD may be important in the genesis of anxiety. For example, imaging studies have revealed more prominent right hemispheric abnormalities in panic disorder (77). Evidence to date suggests greater involvement of the right side of the brain in PD patients with anxiety. Fleminger (37) examined 17 patients with PD where symptoms were worse on the right side of the body (RHP) and 13 patients whose symptoms were worse on the left side of the body (LHP). Present State Examination symptoms that were more common in the LHP group were panic with autonomic features, depressed mood, and social withdrawal. Similarly, Rubin et al. (3) noted that panic-anxiety disorder in PD patients was associated with early left-right asymmetry of PD motor features. Tomer et al. (73) noted highly significant correlations between the severity of left-sided motor symptoms and obsessive-compulsive symptomatology in patients with PD. In contrast, a recent functional imaging study in PD patients noted an association between decreased dopamine transporter availability in the left anterior putamen and affective symptoms (anxiety and depression) (75). This hypothesis requires further study.

Brain imaging studies in psychiatric patients with anxiety have shown abnormalities in the basal ganglia (78–80). Potts and coworkers (80) found no statistically significant differences between social phobia patients and normal control subjects with regard to cerebral, caudate, putamen, and thalamic volumes but noted an age-related reduction in putamen volumes in patients with social phobia. The authors conjectured that social phobia might be a manifestation of a dopamine-deficiency state and that, as they age, some social phobic patients may be at greater risk of developing the manifestations of parkinsonism. Neuropsychological testing has also demonstrated that patients with OCD and PD have deficits attributable to basal ganglia dysfunction (81, 82). These findings, in addition to recent functional imaging studies (75), suggest that basal ganglia disturbances in PD might explain the development of anxiety in patients suffering from this illness.

There appear to be many demonstrated biological abnormalities in PD that may not only explain the frequent occurrence of anxiety in this disorder but also contribute to our understanding of the mechanisms of anxiety in psychiatric patients.

Treatment of Anxiety in Parkinson's Disease

If anxiety occurs exclusively during "off" period, it would be reasonable to first try to minimize "off" time with adjustment of the antiparkinsonian medication regimen, including the use of subcutaneous apomorphine, which can be particularly effective for rescuing patients from "off"-period panic attacks (see Chapter 47). There have also been some preliminary studies suggesting that the dopamine agonist pramipexole might be effective in alleviating depressive symptoms (83–85). The effects of this medication on anxiety have not yet been studied.

Persistent anxiety despite optimal antiparkinsonian drug therapy may be treated with psychotherapy or specific psychotropic medications. Commonly used drugs to treat anxiety disorders include serotonin-norepinepherine reuptake inhibitors (SNRIs) (e.g., venlafaxine, duloxetine),

selective serotonin reuptake inhibitors (SSRIs), benzodiazepines, and buspirone. Neither the tricyclic antidepressants nor the monoamine oxidase inhibitors (MAOIs) are typically used as first-line agents to treat anxiety. There are very few clinical trials of medication treatment for anxiety in the elderly (86) and none that specifically address the optimal treatment of anxiety in patients with PD. One recent open-label study of citalopram involving 10 patients with PD and major depression found that improvement in depression was associated with improvement in anxiety and functional capacity (87).

Stein et al. (5) have indicated that anxiety disorders in PD may respond to pharmacotherapy with antidepressants and benzodiazepines. Lauterbach and Duvoisin (13) caution, however, that benzodiazepines can at times worsen parkinsonian symptoms. Benzodiazepines can also be problematic with regard to impairment of arousal, cognition, and balance. Benzodiazepines can provide relief of symptoms associated with panic, GAD, and social phobia but are not indicated for OCD. Alprazolam was shown to be effective for anxiety symptoms in mixed anxiety-depressive disorder in patients who were more than 60 years old and had just undergone cardiac bypass surgery (34).

Buspirone can be effective for GAD but is unlikely to help panic, OCD, or social phobia (34). A study of buspirone in PD patients designed to investigate possible antiparkinsonian effects of the drug noted that the agent was well tolerated in doses up to 60 mg but actually caused increased anxiety and worsening of motor function at doses of 100 mg/day. Anxiolytic effects at the well-tolerated doses were not observed, but patients were not selected for the presence of anxiety (88). Another study investigating the efficacy of buspirone for dyskinesias in PD revealed no change in depression or anxiety scores at a dosage of 20 mg/day. These patients were also not selected on the basis of psychological symptoms (89).

One should keep in mind that specific aspects of PD, especially the use of antiparkinsonian medications, may influence the choice of anxiolytic medications. For instance, nonselective MAOIs are contraindicated in patients receiving levodopa because of the risk of hypertensive crisis. Selegiline, a selective MAO type B inhibitor, does not induce hypertensive crisis in PD patients treated with dopaminergic agents. The drug is commonly used in PD to prolong the duration of levodopa action in patients with motor fluctuations and also because of reports that this drug may slow the progression of disease. Selegiline has been found to be an effective antidepressant agent in psychiatric populations, but only at higher doses, where its MAO-B selectivity is lost. Although selegiline has not been specifically tested for its antianxiety effects, it was noted that depressed patients with anxiety or panic actually responded less well to selegiline than did those without anxiety symptoms (90). In addition, selegiline is metabolized to amphetamine, which could enhance the symptoms of anxiety.

The manufacturer of selegiline cautions against the concomitant use of an antidepressants because of potentially serious central nervous system (CNS) toxicity, which may represent the serotonin syndrome. Manifestations of the serotonin syndrome vary but may include changes in mental status as well as in motor and autonomic function. Based on our survey of members of the Parkinson Study Group (PSG) and our review of published case reports and adverse experiences reported to the U.S. Food and Drug Administration and the manufacturer of selegiline (Eldepryl), it appears that serious adverse experiences resulting from the combined use of selegiline and antidepressants in patients with PD are quite rare and that the frequency of the true "serotonin syndrome" is even rarer (91). One patient treated with selegiline developed hypertensive crisis when given buspirone (89). A conservative approach would be to avoid selegiline (or any other MAO-B inhibitor that becomes available, such as rasagaline) in any PD patient who requires a TCA, an SSRI, an SNRI, or perhaps buspirone for the treatment of anxiety or depression. On the other hand, we do not consider the risks of combining such medications unacceptable if the patient could benefit from both selegiline and an antidepressant medication (91). It makes sense to inform patients of the potential risks of combination therapy and to monitor them carefully.

The SSRIs are generally well tolerated and can be effective for almost all types of anxiety, including panic, OCD, social phobia, and GAD (92). There are, however, case reports of SSRIs increasing the level of motor disability in patients with PD (93–95). Other authors have reported that this class of drugs does not appear to be associated with exacerbations of parkinsonian signs and symptoms (96–98). It is advisable to use an SSRI if deemed appropriate but to monitor motor function and discontinue the SSRI (via gradual taper to avoid a possible withdrawal syndrome) if it appears to have been associated with a worsening motor status. The issue of whether SSRIs result in motor dysfunction awaits a formal clinical trial, which would also address the issue of antidepressant and perhaps anxiolytic efficacy of these agents in patients with PD. The more recently available SNRIs have been shown to be effective in treating depression and anxiety, and there is some evidence to suggest that they may be particularly effective in treating depression characterized by a high degree of anxiety. We await the results of a currently active controlled clinical trial to assess efficacy and tolerability of SNRIs in PD.

Elderly patients may be more sensitive to anxiolytic medications by virtue of their altered metabolism, tendency toward falls and oversedation, and concomitant medical conditions (34, 99, 100). Caution is recommended in treating this age group.

The effect that surgical therapies may have on psychiatric symptoms in PD is not clear. There have been some reports of reduced anxiety after surgical interventions, particularly those involving the globus pallidus (101–103). One report described worsened anxiety after bilateral stimulation of the subthalamic nucleus (104).

CONCLUSION

Although few studies have specifically investigated anxiety in patients with PD, some preliminary conclusions can be drawn. Anxiety disorders frequently occur in association with PD and may be important causes of morbidity. Actual prevalence rates are uncertain, but estimates suggest that up to 40% of patients experience significant anxiety. This frequency is greater than expected, particularly for an elderly population. In addition, the age at onset of anxiety in PD patients is later than what would be expected from current information regarding the natural course of anxiety disorders in the general population. It should be noted that most psychiatric rating instruments used to assess anxiety may present some difficulties in interpretation when applied to PD patients, which could confound prevalence studies. Some of the somatic symptoms of anxiety, such as tremor, may be difficult to distinguish from symptoms of the underlying disease.

Virtually all of the types of anxiety disorders have been described in PD, but panic disorder, GAD, and social phobia appear to be the ones most commonly encountered. The frequency of panic disorder in particular is high.

Anxiety frequently appears after the diagnosis of PD is established, but recent evidence suggests that it can also develop years before the motor features. The latter observation suggests that anxiety may not represent psychological and social difficulties in adapting to the illness but rather may be linked to specific neurobiological processes occurring in PD. It is possible that anxiety might represent the first sign of illness for some patients with PD (41), a risk factor for PD, or the result of a shared diathesis toward both conditions. Whether antiparkinsonian medications themselves contribute to anxiety needs clarification.

The relationship between anxiety and motor function remains unclear and may vary among patients. The fact that levodopa infusions resulted in increased anxiety several minutes before motor impairment (27) and the discovery that anxiety and motor fluctuations occur independently in some patients (20) makes the notion of anxiety as a reaction to motor dysfunction less tenable.

Anxiety and depression frequently coexist in PD. It remains to be determined whether anxiety in patients with PD reflects one of the following: (a) an underlying depressive mood disorder, (b) a particular subtype of depression (atypical depression, anxious or agitated depression), or (c) an independent psychiatric disturbance. The association between depression and panic disorder, which is commonly observed in PD patients, is less common in the general elderly population and does suggest a unique relationship in PD.

The relationship between anxiety and dementia in PD is not clear, but current evidence suggests that cognitive dysfunction is not related to the presence of anxiety symptoms in this disorder.

Current information supports the view that specific neurobiological processes associated with PD may be responsible for the development of anxiety in patients with this illness. There is evidence that various neurotransmitter systems and circuits involving the basal ganglia may be involved.

The optimal pharmacologic treatment for anxiety in patients with PD has not been established. Clinicians should be aware that some anxiolytic agents may be contraindicated in PD and others may worsen symptoms of the illness.

References

1. American Psychiatric Association. *Diagnostic and Statistical Manual of Mental Disorders* (DSM-IV-R), 4th ed rev. Washington, DC: American Psychiatric Association, 1994.
2. American Psychiatric Association. *Diagnostic and Statistical Manual of Mental Disorders* (DSM-IV-TR) (Text Revision). Washington, DC: American Psychiatric Association, 2000.
3. Rubin AJ, Kurlan R, Schiffer R, et al. Atypical depression and Parkinson's disease (abstract). *Ann Neurol* 1986; 20:150.
4. American Psychiatric Association. *Diagnostic and Statistical Manual of Psychiatry*, 3rd ed. Washington, DC: American Psychiatric Association, 1987.
5. Stein M, Henser IJ, Juncos JL, et al. Anxiety disorders in patients with Parkinson's disease. *Am J Psychiatry* 1990; 147:217–220.
6. Vazquez A, Jimenez-Jimenez FJ, Garcia-Ruiz P, et al. "Panic attacks" in Parkinson's disease: A long-term complication of levodopa therapy. *Acta Neurol Scand* 1993; 87:14–18.
7. Shulman LM, Taback RL, Rabinstein AA, Weiner WJ. Non-recognition of depression and other non-motor symptoms in Parkinson's disease. *Parkinsonism Relat Disord* 2002; 8:193–197.
8. Schiffer RB, Kurlan R, Rubin A, et al. Evidence for atypical depression in Parkinson's disease. *Am J Psychiatry* 1988; 145:1020–1022.
9. Menza MA, Robertson-Hoffman DE, Bonapace AS. Parkinson's disease and anxiety: Comorbidity with depression. *Biol Psychiatry* 1993; 34:465–470.
10. Menza MA, Mark MH. Parkinson's disease and depression: The relationship to disability and personality. *J Neuropsychiatr Clin Neurosci* 1994; 6:165–169.
11. Gotham A-M, Brown RG, Marsden CD. Depression in Parkinson's disease: A quantitative and qualitative analysis. *J Neurol Neurosurg Psychiatry* 1986; 49:381–389.
12. Berrios GE, Campbell C, Politynska BE. Autonomic failure, depression and anxiety in Parkinson's disease. *Br J Psychiatry* 1995; 166:789–792.
13. Lauterbach EC, Duvoisin RC. Anxiety disorders and familial parkinsonism (letter). *Am J Psychiatry* 1992; 148:274.
14. Lauterbach EC, Freeman A, Vogel RL. Correlates of generalized anxiety and panic attacks in dystonia and Parkinson's disease. *Cogn Behav Neurol* 2003; 16:225–233.
15. Henderson R, Kurlan R, Kersun JM, et al. Preliminary examination of the comorbidity of anxiety and depression in Parkinson's disease. *J Neuropsychiatry Clin Neurosci* 1992; 148:274.
16. Weisskopf MG, Chen H, Schwarzschild MA, et al. Prospective study of phobic anxiety and risk of Parkinson's disease. *Mov Disord* 2003; 18:646–651.
17. Siemers ER, Shekhar A, Quaid K, et al. Anxiety and motor performance in Parkinson's disease. *Mov Disord* 1993; 8:501–506.
18. Rondot P, deRecondo J, Colgnet A, et al. Mental disorders in Parkinson's disease after treatment with L-dopa. *Adv Neurol* 1984; 40:259–269.
19. Cummings JL. Depression and Parkinson's disease: A review. *Am J Psychiatry* 1992; 149:443–454.
20. Richard IH, Frank s, McDermott MP, et al. The ups and down of Parkinson disease: A prospective study of mood and anxiety fluctuations. *Cogn Behav Neurol* 2004; 17:201–207.
21. Factor SA, Molho ES, Podskalny GD, et al. Parkinson's disease: Drug-induced psychiatric states. In: Weiner WJ, Lang AE (eds). *Behavioral Neurology of Movement Disorders: Advances in Neurology.* New York: Raven Press, 1995:115–138.
22. Nissenbaum H, Quinn NP, Brown RG, et al. Mood swings associated with the "on-off" phenomenon in Parkinson's disease. *Psychol Med* 1987; 17:899–904.
23. Seligman MEP. Chronic fear produced by unpredictable shock. *J Comp Physiol Psychol* 1968; 66:402–411.
24. Riley DE, Lang AE. The spectrum of levodopa-related fluctuations in Parkinson's disease. *Neurology* 1993; 43:1459–1464.
25. Marsden CD, Parkes JD. "On-off" effects in patients with Parkinson's disease and chronic levodopa therapy. *Lancet* 1976; 1:292–296.
26. Menza MA, Sage JI, Marshall E, et al. Mood changes and "on-off" phenomena in Parkinson's disease. *Mov Disord* 1990; 5:148–151.
27. Maricle RA, Nutt JG, Valentine RJ, et al. Dose-response relationship of levodopa with mood and anxiety in fluctuating Parkinson's disease: A double-blind, placebo-controlled study. *Neurology* 1995; 45:1757–1760.
28. Brown RG, Marsden CD, Quinn NP. Alterations in cognitive performance and affect-arousal state during fluctuations in motor function in Parkinson's disease. *J Neurol Neurosurg Psychiatry* 1984; 47:454–465.
29. Cantello R, Gilli M, Riccio A, et al. Mood changes associated with "end-of-dose deterioration" in Parkinson's disease: A controlled study. *J Neurol Neurosurg Psychiatry* 1986; 49:1182–1190.
30. Routh LC, Black JL, Shlskog JE. Parkinson's disease complicated by anxiety. *Mayo Clin Proc* 1987; 62:733–735.
31. Richard IH, Kurlan R, Lichter D, et al. Parkinson's disease: A preliminary study of yohimbine challenge in patients with anxiety. *Clin Neuropharmacol* 1999; 22:172–175.
32. Flint AJ. Epidemiology and comorbidity of anxiety disorders in the elderly. *Am J Psychiatry* 1994; 151:640–649.
33. Palmer BW, Jeste DV, Sheikh JI. Anxiety disorders in the elderly: DSM-IV and other barriers to diagnosis and treatment. *J Affect Disord* 1997; 46:183–190.
34. Small GW. Recognizing and treating anxiety in the elderly. *J Clin Psychiatry* 1997; 8:41–47.
35. Raj BA, Corvea MH, Dagon EM. The clinical characteristics of panic disorder in the elderly: A retrospective study. *J Clin Psychiatry* 1993; 54:150–155.
36. Lydiard RB. Coexisting depression and anxiety: Special diagnostic and treatment issues. *J Clin Psychiatry* 1991; 52 (Suppl 6):48–54.
37. Fleminger S. Left-sided Parkinson's disease is associated with greater anxiety and depression. *Psychol Med* 1991; 21:629–638.
38. Lin CY, Yang SJ, Fuh JL, et al. The correlation of depression with functional activity in Parkinson's disease. *J Neurol* 1997; 244:493–498.
39. Wands K, Merskey H, Hachinski VC, et al. A questionnaire investigation of anxiety and depression in early dementia. *J Am Geriatr Soc* 1990; 38:535–538.
40. Iruela LM, Ibanez-Rojo V, Palanca I, Caballero L. Anxiety disorders and Parkinson's disease (letter). *Am J Psychiatry* 1992; 149:719–720.
41. Cash R, Dennis T, L'Heureux R, et al. Parkinson's disease and dementia: Norepinephrine and dopamine in locus ceruleus. *Neurology* 1987; 37:42–46.
42. Lauterbach EC. The locus ceruleus and anxiety disorders in demented and nondemented familial parkinsonism (letter). *Am J Psychiatry* 1993; 150:994.
43. Nutt D, Lawson C. Panic attacks: A neurochemical overview of models and mechanisms. *Br J Psychiatry* 1992; 160:165–178.
44. Heninger GR, Charney DS. Monoamine receptor systems and anxiety disorders. *Psychiatr Clin North Am* 1988; 11:309–326.
45. Charney DS, Heninger GR, Brief A. Noradrenergic function in panic anxiety: Effects of yohimbine in healthy subjects and patients with agoraphobia and panic disorder. *Arch Gen Psychiatry* 1984; 41:751–763.
46. Charney DS, Woods SW, Goodman WK, et al. Neurobiological mechanisms of panic anxiety: Biochemical and behavioral correlates of yohimbine-induced panic attacks. *Am J Psychiatry* 1987; 144:1030–1036.
47. Nutt DJ. Altered alpha-2-adrenoceptor sensitivity in panic disorder. *Arch Gen Psychiatry* 1989; 46:165–169.
48. Uhde T, Stein MB, Vittone BJ, et al. Behavioral and physiologic effects of short-term and long-term administration of clonidine in panic disorder. *Arch Gen Psychiatry* 1989; 46:170–177.
49. Charney DS, Heninger GR. Abnormal regulation of noradrenergic function in panic disorders: Effects of clonidine in healthy subjects and patients with agoraphobia and panic disorder. *Arch Gen Psychiatry* 1986; 43:1042–1054.
50. Agid Y, Cervera P, Hirsch E, et al. Biochemistry of Parkinson's disease 28 years later: A critical review. *Mov Disord* 1989; 4(Suppl 1):S126–S144.
51. Patt S, Gerhard L. A study of human locus ceruleus in normal brains and in Parkinson's disease. *Neuropathol Appl Neurobiol* 1993; 19:519–523.
52. German DC, Manaye KF, White CLI, et al. Disease-specific patterns of locus ceruleus cell loss. *Ann Neurol* 1992; 32:667–676.
53. Chan-Palay V. Depression and dementia in Parkinson's disease: Catecholamine changes in the locus ceruleus, a basis for therapy. *Adv Neurol* 1993; 60:438–446.
54. Zweig RM, Cardillo JE, Cohen M, et al. The locus ceruleus and dementia in Parkinson's disease. *Neurology* 1993; 43:986–991.

55. Cash R, Ruberg M, Raisman R, et al. Adrenergic receptors in Parkinson's disease. *Brain Res* 1984; 322:369–375.

56. Villeneuve A, Berlan M, LaFontan M, et al. Platelet alpha-2-adrenoceptors in Parkinson's disease: Decreased number in untreated patients and recovery after treatment. *Eur J Clin Invest* 1985; 15:403–407.

57. Montastruc J-L, Villeneuve A, Berlan M, et al. Study of platelet alpha-2-adrenoceptors in Parkinson's disease. *Adv Neurol* 1986; 45:253–258.

58. Bernal M, Rascol O, Belin J, et al. Alpha-2 adrenergic sensitivity in Parkinson's disease. *Clin Neuropharmacol* 1989; 12:138–144.

59. Insel TR, Zohar J, Benkelfat C, et al. Serotonin in obsessions, compulsions, and the control of aggressive impulses. *Ann NY Acad Sci* 1990; 600:574–585.

60. Miner CM, Davidson JR. Biological characterization of social phobia (review). *Eur Arch Psychiatry Clin Neurosci* 1995; 244:304–308.

61. Charney DS, Woods SW, Krystal JH, et al. Serotonin function and human anxiety disorders. *Ann NY Acad Sci* 1990; 600:558–572.

62. Halliday GM, Blumbergs PC, Cotton RG, et al. Loss of brainstem serotonin and substance P–containing neurons in Parkinson's disease. *Brain* Res 1990; 510:104–107.

63. Jellinger K. The pathology of parkinsonism. In: Marsden CD, Fahn S, eds. *Movement Disorders*. London: Butterworth, 1987:124–165.

64. Agid Y, Javoy-Agid F, Ruberg M. Biochemistry of neurotransmitters in Parkinson's disease. In: Marsden CD, Fahn S (eds). *Movement Disorders*. London: Butterworth, 1987:166–230.

65. Raisman R, Cash R, Agid Y. Parkinson's disease: Decreased density 3H-imipramine and 3H-paroxetine binding sites in putamen. *Neurology* 1986; 36:556–560.

66. D'Amato RJ, Zweig RM, Whitehouse PJ, et al. Aminergic systems in Alzheimer's disease and Parkinson's disease. *Ann Neurol* 1987; 22:229–236.

67. Menza MA, Palermo B, DiPaola R, et al. Depression and anxiety in Parkinson's disease: Possible effect of genetic variation in the serotonin transporter. *J Geriatr Psychiatry Neurol* 1999; 12:49–52.

68. Potts NLS, Davidson JRT. Social phobia: Biological aspects and pharmacotherapy. *Prog Neuropsychopharmacol Biol Psychiatry* 1992; 16:635–646.

69. Pitchot W, Annsseau M, Gonzalez Moreno A, et al. Dopaminergic function in panic disorder: Comparison with major and minor depression. *Biol Psychiatry* 1992; 32:1004–1011.

70. Argyl N. Panic attacks in chronic schizophrenia. *Br J Psychiatry* 1990; 157:430–433.

71. McDougle CJ, Goodman WK, Price LH. Dopamine antagonists in tic-related and psychotic spectrum obsessive compulsive disorder (literature review). *J Clin Psychiatry* 1994; 55 (Suppl):24–31.

72. Marazziti D, Hollander E, Lensi P, et al. Peripheral markers of serotonin and dopamine function in obsessive-compulsive disorder. *Psychiatr Res* 1992; 42:41–51.

73. Tomer R, Levin BE, Weiner WJ. Obsessive-compulsive symptoms and motor asymmetries in Parkinson's disease. *Neuropsychiatry Neuropsychol Behav Neurol* 1993; 6:26–30.

74. Cedarbaum JM, Aghajanian GK. Catecholamine receptors on locus ceruleus neurons: Pharmacological characterization. *Eur J Pharmacol* 1977; 44:375–385.

75. Weintraub D, Newbrg AB, Cary MS, et al. Striatal dopamine transporter imaging correlates with anxiety and depression symptoms in Parkinson's disease. *J Nucl Med* 2005; 46:227–232.

76. Owens MJ, Nemeroff CB. The role of corticotropin-releasing factor in the pathophysiology of affective and anxiety disorders: Laboratory and clinical studies. *Ciba Found Symp* 1993; 172:296–308.

77. Fontaine R, Breton G, Dery R, et al. Temporal lobe abnormalities in panic disorder: An MRI study. *Biol Psychiatry* 1990; 27:304–310.

78. Faulstich ME, Sullivan DC. Positron emission tomography in neuropsychiatry. *Invest Radiol* 1991; 26:184–194.

79. Davidson JRT, Krishnan KRR, Charles HC, et al. Magnetic resonance spectroscopy in social phobia: Preliminary findings. *J Clin Psychiatry* 1993; 54(Suppl 12):19–24.

80. Potts NLS, Davidson JRT, Krishnan KRR, et al. Magnetic resonance imaging in social phobia. *Psychiatr Res* 1994; 52:35–42.

81. Hollander E, Cohen L, Richards M, et al. A pilot study of the neuropsychology of obsessive-compulsive disorder and Parkinson's disease: Basal ganglia disorders. *J Neuropsychiatr Clin Neurosci* 1993; 5:104–107.

82. Saint-Cyr JA, Taylor AE, Nicholson K. Behavior and the basal ganglia (literature review). *Adv Neurol* 1995; 65:1–28.

83. Pogarell O, Kunig G, Oertel WH. A non-ergot dopamine agonist, pramipexole, in the therapy of advanced Parkinson's disease: Improvement of parkinsonian symptoms and treatment-associated complications. A review of three studies. *Clin Neuropharmacol* 1997; 20:S28–S35.

84. Corrigan M, Evans. Pramipexole, a dopamine agonist, in the treatment of major depression. In: American Society of Neuropsychology Meeting, 1997; Honolulu, Hawaii, 1997.

85. Szegedi A, Hillert A, Wetzel H, et al. Pramipexole, a dopamine agonist, in major depression: Antidepressant effects and tolerability in an open-label study with multiple doses. *Clin Neuropharmacol* 1997; 20:S36–S45.

86. Pearson JL. Research in late-life anxiety. Summary of a National Institute of Mental Health Workshop on Late-Life Anxiety. *Psychopharmacol Bull* 1998; 34:127–138.

87. Menza M, Marin H, Kaufman K, et al. Citalopram treatment of depression in Parkinson's disease: The impact on anxiety, disability, and cognition. *J Neuropsych Clin Neurosci* 2004; 16:315–319.

88. Ludwig CL, Weinberger DR, Bruno G, et al. Buspirone, Parkinson's disease, and the locus ceruleus. *Clin Neuropharmacol* 1986; 9:373–378.

89. Bonifati V, Fabrizio E, Cipriani R, et al. Buspirone in levodopa-induced dyskinesias. *Clin Neuropharmacol* 1994; 17:73–82.

90. Mann JJ, Aarons SF, Wilner PJ, et al. A controlled study of the antidepressant efficacy and side effects of (-)-deprenyl. *Arch Gen Psychiatry* 1989; 46:45–50.

91. Richard IH, Kurlan R, Tanner C, et al and the Parkinson Study Group. Serotonin syndrome and the combined use of deprenyl and an antidepressant in Parkinson's disease. *Neurology* 1997; 48:1070–1077.

92. Stein DJ, Andersen HF, Goodman WK. Escitalopram for the treatment of GAD: Efficacy across different subgroups and outcomes. *Ann Clin Psychiatry* 2005; 17:71–75.

93. Steur ENHJ. Increase in Parkinson disability after fluoxetine medication. *Neurology* 1993; 43:211–213.

94. Jimenez FJ, Tejeiro J, Martinez-Junquera G, et al. Parkinsonism exacerbated by paroxetine. *Neurology* 1994; 44:2406.

95. Chouinard G, Sultan S. A case of Parkinson's disease exacerbated by fluoxetine. *Hum Psychopharmacol* 1992; 7:63–66.

96. Caley CF, Friedman JH. Does fluoxetine exacerbate Parkinson's disease? *J Clin Psychiatry* 1992; 53:278–282.

97. Shulman LM, Singer C, Liefert R, et al. Therapeutic effects of sertraline in patients with Parkinson's. *Mov Disord* 1996; 11:603.

98. Montastruc J-L, Fabre N, Blin O, et al. Does fluoxetine aggravate Parkinson's disease? A pilot prospective study. *Mov Disord* 1995; 10:355–357.

99. Stoudemire A, Moran MG. Psychopharmacologic treatment of anxiety in the medically ill elderly patient: Special considerations. *J Clin Psychiatry* 1993; 54(Suppl 5):27–33.

100. Salzman C. Anxiety in the elderly: Treatment strategies. *J Clin Psychiatry* 1990; 51(Suppl 10):18–21.

101. Higginson CI, Fields JA, Troster AI. Which symptoms of anxiety diminish after surgical interventions for Parkinson's disease? *Neuropsychiatr Neuropsychol Behav Neurol* 2001; 14:117–121.

102. Troster AI, Fields JA, Wilkinson SB, et al. Unilateral disease pallidal stimulation for Parkinson's disease: Neurobehavioral functioning before and 3 months after electrode implantation. *Neurology* 1997; 49:1078–1083.

103. Straits-Troster K, Fields JA, Wilkinson SB, et al. Health-related quality of life in Parkinson's disease after pallidotomy and deep brain stimulation. *Brain Cogn* 2000; 42:399–416.

104. Houeto JL, Mesnage V, Mallet L, et al. Behavioural disorders, Parkinson's disease and subthalamic stimulation. *J Neurol Neurosurg Psychiatry* 2002; 72:701–707.

18 Apathy and Amotivation

Lisa M. Shulman
Mackenzie Carpenter

Think about the role that qualities such as creativity, ambition, imagination, and perseverance play in your life. What kind of an impact would a reduction of energy, drive, and initiative have on your career, personal life, and general sense of fulfillment? It is easy to overlook the capacity that apathy and amotivation have to reduce our productivity and self-satisfaction. Cognitive dysfunction and depression are increasingly regarded as significant sources of functional impairment in Parkinson's disease (PD), but the contribution of loss of motivation to disability is generally not acknowledged. The study of apathy in PD and other medical conditions is still in its infancy; in total around 1200 papers about apathy have appeared in the medical literature over the last 20 years, while 85,000 papers about depression appeared during the same time interval. Of these, about 70 focused on apathy in PD, in contrast to 200 papers during the same period evaluating apathy in AD and 1400 papers investigating depression in PD. We are only beginning to explore the pathophysiology and management of amotivation, and there is still much to be learned about the associations between apathy and the range of motor and nonmotor symptoms of PD. This chapter reviews our current understanding of apathy in the setting of PD, focusing on issues of definition, recognition, clinical correlates, pathophysiology, and treatment.

The word *apathy*, derived from the Greek term *pathos*, or passion, is defined most simply as loss of motivation. Apathy may contribute to disability in a broad range of medical and psychiatric conditions, yet it may also pose a problem in healthy adults, especially the elderly. Since amotivation is commonly an intrinsic personality trait, it is important for the clinician to evaluate a patient's level of motivation relative to his or her previous level of functioning and the standards of the patient's age and culture (1). Silva and Marin (1–3) describe 3 spheres of evidence of the syndrome of apathy, including diminished goal-directed behavior, diminished goal-directed cognition, and diminished emotional concomitants of goal-directed behavior. Reduced goal-directed behavior is manifest by a lack of effort, initiative, and perseverance. A change in goal-directed cognition is evidenced by a lack of interest in experiencing or learning new things and a lack of concern about one's health or functional disability. Last, emotional evidence of apathy includes flat affect or indifference. Loss of motivation may dominate a clinical presentation or may be subordinated by the presence of more overt symptomatology, such as dementia or depression.

There is a complex relationship between emotional intensity and apathy. An absence of emotional intensity is an important element of apathy, yet apathy frequently coexists with depression, which by definition is accompanied by despair and emotional pain. Neurologic disorders such as PD result in disruption of motor function, facial expressivity, body language, and communication that can all interfere with our perception of the patient's emotional state. The patient with PD may appear disinterested while remaining profoundly concerned with his or her goals and responsibilities (4). Neurology is replete with symptoms and signs that may confound the accurate assessment of apathy, including abulia, anhedonia, aprosodia, psychomotor retardation, and bradyphrenia.

CLINICAL CORRELATES OF APATHY IN PARKINSON'S DISEASE

Marsden and Parkes (5) observed in 1977 that some PD patients manifest a "blunting of interest and drive, amounting to apathy." The study of apathy in PD, however, awaited the development of a reliable and valid scale by Marin in the 1990s (3, 6, 7) (Table 18-1). There are two versions of the scale: one that is self-administered

and one scored by the clinician. In 1992, Starkstein et al. (8) administered an abridged version of Marin's Apathy Evaluation Scale along with scales measuring depression, anxiety, cognitive function, and disease severity to 50 PD patients. Of these, 42% had significant apathy; 12% of those with apathy were not depressed, and 30% had both apathy and depression. An additional 26% had depression but no apathy and 32% had neither apathy nor depression. There was no difference in the level of apathy between depressed and nondepressed patients.

Anxiety scores were significantly higher in depressed patients as compared with those with apathy. Apathetic patients (with and without depression) showed a poorer performance on tests of verbal memory and time-dependent tasks. There was no difference between PD patients with and without apathy in terms of age, gender, level of education, PD duration, or severity. The presence of apathy was also not associated with the severity of akinesia or rigidity. The poor performance of PD patients with apathy on time-dependent cognitive tasks suggests a relationship between the concepts of bradyphrenia and apathy.

TABLE 18-1
Apathy Evaluations Scale (Clinician Version)

Name: ———   Date: —/—/—
Rater: ———

Rate each item based on an interview of the subject. The interview should begin with a description of the subject's interests, activities and daily routine. Base your ratings on both verbal and nonverbal information. Ratings should be based on the past four weeks. For each item ratings should be judged:

Not at All Characteristic	Slightly Characteristic	Somewhat Characteristic	A Lot Characteristic
1	2	3	4

— 1. She/he is interested in things.
— 2. She/he gets things done during the day.
— 3. Getting things started on his/her own is important to him/her.
— 4. She/he is interested in learning new things.
— 5. She/he is interested in learning new things.
— 6. She/he puts little effort into anything.
— 7. She/he approaches life with intensity.
— 8. Seeing a job through to the end is important to her/him.
— 9. She/he spends time doing things that interest her/him.
— 10. Someone has to tell her/him what to do each day.
— 11. She/he is less concerned about her/his problems than she should be.
— 12. She/he has friends.
— 13. Getting together with friends is important to him/her.
— 14. When something good happens, she gets excited.
— 15. She/he has an accurate understanding of her/his problems.
— 16. Getting things done during the day is important to her/him.
— 17. She/he has initiative.
— 18. She/he has motivation.

See reference 7.

Recently, Sockeel et al. (9) further modified the Marin Apathy Evaluation Scale (AES) into a structured standardized interview called the Lille Apathy Rating Scale (LARS) with the goal of eliciting accurate self-reports from PD patients and quantifying apathy severity. This interview consists of 33 yes/no questions. Nine domains were identified: reduction in daily productivity, lack of initiative, lack of interest, loss of novelty seeking, loss of motivation, blunting of emotional responses, loss of interest in maintaining social contacts, lack of concern, and loss of self- and social awareness. The authors evaluated 159 PD patients and 58 healthy control subjects, comparing the LARS with the AES and the clinical impressions of examining neurologists. Interrater reliability, internal consistency, and test-retest reliability of the LARS was superior to that of the AES when compared with expert judgment. Theoretically, this scale could be used as an instrument for quantifying and tracking changes in the severity of apathy in PD patients over time so as to assess efficacy of various treatments.

APATHY: NEUROANATOMY AND NEUROCHEMISTRY

Like many common behavioral symptoms, such as depression or anxiety, apathy may be a significant determinant of behavior either as an inherent feature of the adult personality or an acquired symptom associated with neurologic, psychiatric, or medical conditions. Apathetic behavior can be analyzed from a strictly organic biochemical perspective or from a psychological perspective.

Where does motivation reside in the brain? The limbic system has been traditionally viewed as being central to emotion and motivation. In particular, the amygdala is thought to play the role of a "motivational rheostat" (10), filtering environmental stimuli and influencing goal-directed behavior. Duffy (10) proposes 4 different neuronal circuits, all with limbic input, involved in generating motivational valence and translating motivation into behavior. This motivational circuitry makes important connections with the basal ganglia. Key structures of the motivational circuits are believed to be the nucleus accumbens, the ventral pallidum, and the ventral tegmental area. Levy et al. (11) suggest that apathy occurs when the cortex is functionally disconnected from key limbic input and Mayeux et al. (12) suggest that bradyphrenia arises from neuronal depletion of the locus ceruleus.

Apathy syndromes have been described in a range of neurologic disorders that provide a glimpse of the localization of motivation in the brain. In addition to PD, apathy is a common feature of basal ganglia disorders including progressive supranuclear palsy, Huntington's disease, Wilson's disease, carbon monoxide poisoning, dementia pugilistica, and lacunar stroke (13, 14). Diminished motivation ranging from apathy to akinetic

mutism arises from prefrontal syndromes following lesions of the mesiofrontal cortex and its connections to the anterior cingulate cortex. These syndromes result from trauma, meningioma, hydrocephalus, and aneurysm or stroke affecting the anterior cerebral circulation. Lesions of the dorsolateral frontal region related to frontotemporal dementia, AD, alcoholic dementia, tumor, or subdural hematoma give rise to diminished cognitive flexibility, concrete thinking, perseveration, and impersistence, resulting in amotivational behavior. In an imaging study of patients with Alzheimer's disease (AD) using single photon emission computed tomography (SPECT), the presence of apathy was correlated with decreased right temporoparietal perfusion, whereas loss of insight was correlated with decreased right temporooccipital perfusion (15).

Cerebral infarction of the posterior limb of the internal capsule has been associated with apathy, psychic akinesia, motor neglect, and akinetic mutism (16, 17). Starkstein et al. (16) described neural pathways between the internal pallidum and the pedunculopontine nucleus with relays in the posterior limb of the internal capsule and the substantia nigra; these may result in bradyphrenia and apathy. Thalamic infarction has also been associated with motivational disorders (13).

Neuropathology of the deep white matter—including subcortical encephalomalacia, human immunodeficiency virus, multiple sclerosis, diffuse axonal injury, radiation injury, and postanoxic encephalopathy—may result in behavioral changes including amotivation (13). In particular, subcortical encephalomalacia is increasingly recognized as a significant factor in late-onset depression (18) and is likely to also be an important cause of apathy in the elderly. Injury to the limbic system related to herpes simplex encephalitis, anoxic encephalopathy, and carbon monoxide is also associated with amotivational states.

The prefrontal cortex is instrumental in real-life decision making. Individuals with damage to the prefrontal cortex fail to act according to their understanding of the consequences of their actions and thus appear oblivious to the future (19). Apathy and amotivation may be reflections of an underactivated approach system. The left prefrontal cortex may play a role in setting positive goals; when this region is underactivated or dysfunctional, apathy is likely to occur (20). Data from position emission tomography (PET) and functional magnetic resonance imaging (fMRI) indicate lateralization of cerebral hemispheric functions of goal-directed behavior. Functional imaging demonstrates an association between positive goal attainment and activity in the left prefrontal cortex. In general, the left prefrontal cortex is associated with positive, expansive, and optimistic emotions, whereas the right prefrontal cortex is associated with more negative and withdrawn behaviors (21, 22).

Levy et al. (23) operationally define apathy as "the quantitative reduction of self-generated voluntary and purposeful behavior." They describe 3 subgroups of apathy syndromes based on different anatomic correlates and mechanisms: (a) emotional-affective deficits, (b) cognitive deficits, and (c) deficits of autoactivation. Recent studies suggest that emotional-affective apathy (inability to assimilate emotional signals to predict ongoing and future behaviors) occurs when there is a disruption of the orbital-medial prefrontal cortex. Cognitive apathy occurs when there is a lesion in the lateral prefrontal cortex or a defect in its striatal input from the dorsal portion of the head of the caudate nuclei. Cognitive apathy is a dysexecutive syndrome consisting of decreased goal-directed behaviors such as planning, rule finding, and utilizing working memory. Finally, autoactivation deficits appear with lesions in the basal ganglia, especially the associative and limbic territories, including the globus pallidus and deep frontal white matter. Autoactivation deficits are also referred to as athymhormia, a deficit in initiation and activation of behavior. Hypotheses are emerging about which of these subtypes best describes apathy in PD, but the exact mechanism remains unclear (24).

Anatomic correlates for apathy in PD have been investigated by studying outcomes of surgical procedures to treat PD. Merello et al. (25) compared neuropsychiatric symptoms that emerged after lesioning the bilateral globus pallidus (GPi) to a combination of a unilateral GPi lesion with contralateral GPi stimulation. Bilateral posteroventral pallidotomy induced both profound depression and apathy in 3 patients, resulting in discontinuation of this protocol prior to completion of the study. Although the authors did not use an apathy scale to make this assessment, they described "severe loss of initiative, motivation, and motor drive" that persisted for 3 months following the procedure. Conversely, an increase in the frequency or severity of apathy was not seen in patients with a combination of unilateral GPi lesion and contralateral stimulation. Schupbach, et al. (26) found that stimulation of the subthalamic nucleus (STN) significantly improved motor disability in PD but did not improve apathy. In contrast, when Cxernecki et al. (27) directly compared apathy scales in PD patients treated with bilateral STN stimulation with 23 patients undergoing long-term treatment with levodopa, apathy scores improved to the same degree in both groups of patients following surgical or medical treatment.

Goerendt et al. (28) used PET to compare reward processing in 9 healthy adults and 9 PD patients. Monetary rewards of varying magnitudes were offered and brain activation patterns recorded. In healthy adults, reward magnitude correlated with increased activity (by measure of regional cerebral blood flow) in the rhinal cortex, the orbital and medial prefrontal cortices, and the thalamus. However, in PD patients, increased activity was seen only in the cerebellar vermis. Two distinct motivational systems in the brain have been described: the dopamine-dependent cortico-striatal-thalamocortical circuits and the dopamine-independent brainstem pedunculopontine tegmental nucleus, which has strong interconnections to the cerebellum (29, 30). Parkinson's patients may utilize the latter circuit when the former has been damaged. These new PET findings provide evidence for a compensatory cerebellar recruitment controlling motivation in PD patients with damage to the cortico-striatal-thalamocortical circuit.

Dopamine is the principal neurotransmitter of goal-directed behavior, modulating motivation, arousal, motor response, and sensorimotor integration (10). There is abundant evidence of the impact of dopaminergic input on goal-directed behavior, including the effects of amphetamines, which initially give rise to enhanced focus and motivation; with chronic use, however, they later result in stereotyped behaviors. Chronic administration of neuroleptic drugs is often associated with apathetic behavior. Parkinson's patients frequently describe improved arousal and motivation with the use of dopaminergic medications; this is not solely explained by the antiparkinsonian motor response. A number of other neurotransmitters modify dopamine's effects on motivation including N-methyl-D-aspartate, AMPA (alpha-amino-3-hydroxy-5-methyl-4-isoxazolepropionic acid), neurotensin, and substance P as well as agonists of the nicotinic and opioid receptors. Cholinergic and serotonergic pathways also play a neuromodulatory role in the motivational circuitry. A rare dominantly inherited syndrome of apathy, central hypoventilation, and parkinsonism is characterized by deficiencies of multiple neurotransmitters including dopamine, serotonin, glutamate, and gamma-aminobutyric acid (GABA), with severe neuronal loss and gliosis of the substantia nigra (31).

APATHY AND PERSONALITY

Another approach to understanding apathy and its association with PD is derived from theories of personality. Cloninger's theory describes 3 heritable major dimensions of personality: novelty seeking, harm avoidance, and reward dependence (32). Novelty seeking is believed to be modulated by dopamine and is associated with behavioral activation, exploratory behavior, and avoidance of monotony. Harm avoidance is believed to be determined by serotonergic activity and reward dependence by norepinephrine. Scientific evidence of dopamine's role in novelty-seeking behavior includes the reduction of spontaneous investigatory behavior of animals following dopamine-depleting lesions (33), increased novelty-induced motor activity following dopamine microinjection in the ventral pallidum and nucleus accumbens (34), and the appearance of self-stimulation behavior secondary to electrode placement in the dopaminergic pathways (35, 36). When Cloninger's Tridimensional Personality Questionnaire (TPQ) was administered to patients with PD, they showed significantly reduced novelty-seeking behavior as compared with a group of age- and disability-matched rheumatologic and orthopedic patients (37, 38). There was no significant difference between patient groups on the harm-avoidance or reward-dependence ratings. These results confirm the notion of a discrete set of personality traits associated with PD patients that has been commonly described as rigid, serious, cautious, and introverted (39–41). Speculation that these personality traits precede the diagnosis of PD led Menza et al. (37) to repeat a questionnaire asking the PD patient and spouse to complete the questions as they would have 20 years ago. The PD patients persisted in scoring lower on novelty seeking based on the premorbid ratings. Novelty-seeking behaviors were negatively correlated with advanced age, in agreement with the TPQ normative data indicating that the total novelty-seeking score declined 1 point per decade (42). This finding is consistent with the common observation of increased passivity and amotivation among the elderly and may be related to the reduction of dopaminergic tone with advancing age. Two studies demonstrated an intriguing association between novelty-seeking behavior and the dopamine D4 receptor alleles (43, 44), whereas 2 follow-up studies failed to replicate these results (45, 46).

APATHY VERSUS DEPRESSION

Apathy has often been viewed as a feature of depression. Criteria for depression—including poor concentration, difficulty making decisions, low self-esteem, markedly diminished interest, and feelings of hopelessness and fatigue—overlap with loss of motivation (47). It is unclear whether apathy can be clearly differentiated from depression and whether this distinction holds clinical relevance.

Marin et al. (14, 48) explored the ability to discriminate between apathy and depression by rating 5 patient subgroups [healthy elderly adults and patients with left hemispheric stroke, right hemispheric stroke, AD, and major depression] with both the Apathy Evaluation Scale and the Hamilton Rating Scale for Depression. The results suggest that the relationship between apathy and depression varies according to diagnosis. Mean apathy scores were significantly higher in patients with right hemispheric stroke, AD, and major depression than in the healthy elderly. Elevated apathy scores were associated with low depression scores in AD, high depression scores in major depression, and intermediate depression scores in right hemispheric stroke. The prevalence of apathy ranged from 73% in AD, 53% in major depression, 32% in right hemispheric stroke, 22% in left hemispheric stroke, to 7% in normal subjects. The prevalence of an apathy syndrome, characterized by high apathy and low depression, was 55% in AD and 23% in right hemispheric stroke. Between-group differences in

education and income were not correlated with apathy scores. The authors suggest that the discriminability of apathy and depression between these 6 groups suggests possible differences in mechanisms and management.

Syndromes of high apathy with relatively low depression were also described in frontotemporal dementia and progressive supranuclear palsy using the Neuropsychiatric Inventory (NPI)(49, 50). This scale measures frequency and severity of 10 symptom subgroups: agitation, anxiety, apathy, delusions, depression, disinhibition, euphoria, hallucinations, irritability, and abnormal motor activity. Levy et al. (11) used this scale to study apathy and depression in 154 patients with 5 different neurodegenerative disorders: PD, AD, frontotemporal dementia, Huntington's disease, and progressive supranuclear palsy. The prevalence of apathy (with and without depression) was extremely high in nearly all the patient subgroups: 91% in progressive supranuclear palsy, 90% in frontotemporal dementia, 80% in AD, 59% in Huntington's disease, and 33% in PD. It should be noted that this sample of PD patients had relatively higher functional status and relatively less cognitive impairment than the other patient subgroups. In progressive supranuclear palsy, AD, and frontotemporal dementia, the severity of apathy was disproportionately high as compared with the severity of depression, whereas the severity of apathy and depression were similar in the PD and Huntington's disease patients. Apathy, but not depression, correlated with increased cognitive impairment in the patients with PD and AD but not in those with progressive supranuclear palsy or Huntington's disease. There was no correlation between the presence of apathy and depression in the total sample, and the authors concluded that apathy and depression are distinct behavioral syndromes.

Comorbidity between apathy and depression poses a conundrum: how to reconcile the presence of one disorder characterized by blunted emotion and flattening of affect (apathy) with a disorder that is often characterized by considerable emotional distress (depression). Level of insight may be one factor determining the association of apathy with depression.

Ott et al. (15) studied apathy and loss of insight in AD patients, a disorder characterized by high apathy and low depression. Apathy was measured with the Apathy Evaluation Scale and awareness of dementia with the Clinical Insight Rating Scale. The presence of problem behaviors that cause distress to the caregiver was measured with the Dementia Behavior Disturbance Scale. Increased apathy was highly correlated with loss of insight ($P < .005$) but not with general cognitive impairment. Problem behaviors were highly correlated with apathy ($P < .005$) but not with level of insight or level of cognitive impairment. These results suggest that the presence of apathy may increase the likelihood of caregiver distress. This may "ring a bell" for clinicians caring for patients with PD, who frequently hear the concerns of caregivers who are less prone to complain about motor symptoms than to report that the patient "no longer wants to do anything."

Additional studies have been performed in the past several years specifically addressing the relationship between apathy and depression in PD. Aarsland et al. (51) evaluated the distribution of neuropsychiatric symptoms present in PD patients using the NPI. The highest mean scores on the NPI were found for depression, hallucinations, and apathy. Hallucinations clustered with delusions and irritability, while apathy clustered with anxiety. Sixteen percent of the patients exhibited symptoms of apathy, and of these, 4.3% showed no evidence of depression while the remainder had positive scores on the depression subscale. However, no direct comparison between severity of depressive symptoms and apathy in these individuals was made.

Isella et al. (52) used the geriatric depression scale (GDS) (13) and the AES to assess the prevalence of apathy and depression in PD and found no correlation between the severity of apathy and depression. The overall prevalence of apathy in PD was 43%, consistent with other studies reporting a prevalence of about 42% (3, 8, 9). Kirsch-Darrow et al. (53, 54) compared severity of apathy and depression in patients with PD to those in patients with dystonia using the AES, BDI, and Centers for Epidemiologic Studies-Depression Scale. The frequency of apathy was 51% in PD patients compared to 20% in the dystonia group. In addition, 28% of PD patients had apathy without depression, while all dystonic patients with apathy also exhibited depressive symptoms. The findings of these studies indicate that apathy is a common nonmotor symptom in PD and that its severity is independent of depressive symptoms.

APATHY AND COGNITIVE DYSFUNCTION

The prevalence of dementia in PD is approximately 40% according to several population-based studies defined according to the criteria of the *Diagnostic and Statistical Manual of Mental Disorders*, fourth edition (DSM-IV), with the most prominent cognitive deficits found in visuospatial tasks and executive function (55–57). The incidence of dementia in PD increases with age, such that PD patients below age 50 have almost no chance of developing dementia, while patients above age 80 have a greater than 60% chance (58). Isella et al. (52) administered the Unified Parkinson's Disease Rating Scale (UPDRS) to a group of PD patients as well as an abridged form (14 items) of the AES and a broad neuropsychological battery. They found a direct correlation between apathy and executive dysfunction (3, 57). The severity of apathy correlated with performance on the Stroop test (51), a "willed action" test of verbal

fluency (59), the Wisconsin card sorting test, and the Cambridge Cognitive Examination CAMCOG, a brief neuropsychological battery designed to measure cognitive function (60).

Researchers have investigated whether depression or apathy correlates more closely with the level of cognitive dysfunction in PD. Kuzis et al. (61) found that AD patients with high levels of apathy but not depression had greater cognitive dysfunction. Aarsland et al. (62) compared neuropsychiatric differences between patients with AD and those with PD with dementia (PDD). They used the NPI and found that the most common psychiatric symptoms in PDD patients were depression and hallucinations, while apathy and aberrant motor behavior (repetitive activities) were most common in the AD patients. However, among the PDD patients with abnormalities in the NPI, apathy and aberrant motor behavior were greater than among those with AD. This indicates that although apathy is less common in PDD than AD, it is more severe in PD when dementia is present. A surprising finding in this study was that apathy correlated *negatively* with disease stage in PDD. Possible explanations include early frontal impairment in PD (63), a shift from early dopaminergic deficits to later cholinergic deficits (64), or difficulty in assessing the degree of apathy as parkinsonism becomes more severe. Gibb et al. (65) studied the anatomic correlates of PDD and reported that degeneration of the ventral tegmental area is often found in PDD with apathy.

APATHY IN MEDICAL, NEUROLOGIC, AND PSYCHIATRIC DISORDERS

Apathy poses a problem in many medical conditions (13, 66). Endocrinopathies including hypothyroidism (67), Cushing's syndrome (68), and Addison's disease (69) may be associated with amotivational states that can be difficult to distinguish from primary behavioral disorders. Human immunodeficiency virus (HIV) is associated with cognitive dysfunction and impaired motivation in the AIDS-dementia complex (70). Fatigue, depression, and amotivation are significant parts of chronic fatigue syndrome (71). Depression and apathy are commonly observed as components of the negative symptoms of schizophrenia (59, 72). Impaired motivation often accompanies substance abuse and is an adverse effect of many prescription drugs. Administration of sedatives, catecholamine-depleting drugs (reserpine, tetrabenazine), and dopamine receptor antagonists (neuroleptics) may result in apathy. Chronic alcoholism and long-term marijuana usage may be associated with amotivational states (73, 74).

In addition to PD, neurologic disorders associated with apathy include cerebrovascular disease, dementia, traumatic brain injury, and sleep disorder. Starkstein et al. (16) evaluated 80 patients within 10 days of cerebral infarction with a battery of tests measuring apathy, depression, anxiety, cognitive function, and physical impairment. Apathy was seen in 22.5% of the patients, half of whom had both apathy and depression. Patients with apathy were older, had more cognitive dysfunction, and experienced more disability. The subgroup with mixed apathy and depression had the greatest disability. Neither lesion size nor side correlated with the presence of apathy or depression; however, patients with apathy had a higher frequency of lesions of the posterior limb of the internal capsule.

Traumatic brain injury frequently results in damage to the prefrontal region and the deep white matter tracts. It is not surprising that amotivation is a significant component of the behavioral syndrome that follows closed head injury. Kant et al. (75) found that 71% of these patients exhibited apathy. Sleep disorders such as obstructive sleep apnea are also accompanied by amotivation, along with excessive daytime sleepiness and irritability (76).

RECOGNITION OF APATHY AND AMOTIVATION

Nonpsychiatrists require a high index of suspicion to recognize behavioral disorders during routine office visits. Depression has a much higher profile than the symptoms of apathy and amotivation, yet when the physician's recognition of depression is compared to standardized testing, the physician has a mean diagnostic accuracy of only 30% to 40% (77–80). Shulman et al. (81) studied the diagnostic accuracy of the treating neurologist for the detection of depression, anxiety, fatigue, or sleep disturbance in patients with PD. The neurologist's impression following a routine office visit was compared to the patient's performance on the Beck Depression Inventory, Beck Anxiety Inventory, Fatigue Severity Scale, and Pittsburgh Sleep Quality Inventory. The neurologist's diagnostic accuracy was 35% for depression, 42% for anxiety, 25% for fatigue, and 60% for sleep disturbance.

In the absence of clinical studies, one can speculate that physician awareness and diagnostic accuracy are likely to be lower for apathy than depression. The patient suffering from apathy is unlikely to spontaneously report this problem to a physician. Indeed, the patient's insight into the changes in his or her behavior may be impaired as well. The patient's spouse is likely to be an important source of information about changes in motivation. The training of physicians has tended to emphasize disorders of emotion over disorders of motivation (2). Recognition of behavioral symptoms is also affected by the time constraints of the office visit, preoccupation of the phy-

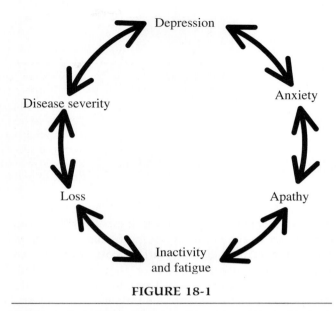

FIGURE 18-1

The interrelationships between disease severity and behavioral symptoms generate a vicious cycle of increasing symptom severity and loss of function.

sician with the medical pathology, and the physician's general level of comfort with discussion and treatment of behavioral symptoms.

Amotivation is more likely to be observed in patients with other comorbid behavioral symptoms. Covington (82) conceptualized a feedback loop in which behavioral and organic symptoms—along with inactivity, loss, and deconditioning—act synergistically to increase suffering and disability (Figure 18-1). In a study of the comorbidity of nonmotor symptoms in PD (including depression, anxiety, fatigue, sleep disturbance, and sensory symptoms), 60% of patients were found to have 2 or more nonmotor disorders and 25% had 4 or more (83). The index of suspicion for comorbid behavioral disorders such as apathy should be increased when other nonmotor symptoms are identified.

The failure to recognize the emergence of an amotivational state may lead to misattribution of the patient's behavior as lazy, uncaring, self-centered, or as evidence of cognitive impairment (84). Family members may become resentful and angry as the patient becomes increasingly withdrawn. Health professionals may find the care of the apathetic patient unrewarding, since the patient is likely to be more passive, less interested in his or her condition, and less compliant. It is common for both the health care staff and family to lose sight of the fact that behavioral symptoms including apathy, depression, and anxiety are often endogenous to the organic pathology of the disorder rather than evidence of maladjustment or "being difficult."

TABLE 18-2
Apathy and Amotivation in Parkinson's Disease

APATHY/AMOTIVATION	SIGNS/SYMPTOMS	PARKINSON'S DISEASE
Indifference	Absence of facial animation	Masked facial expression
Lack of effort	Paucity of body language	Bradykinesia
Flat affect	Monotone speech	Hypophonia
Passivity	Reduced spontaneous speech	Cognitive dysfunction
Withdrawn behavior	Reduced socialization	Bradyphrenia
	Reduced interest in hobbies	

In particular, the phenomenology of parkinsonism contributes to the nonrecognition of behavioral symptoms. How can the clinician differentiate PD signs and symptoms of masking of facial expression, akinesia, bradyphrenia, stooping of posture, hypophonia, and cognitive dysfunction from the common clinical signs of apathy and depression (Table 18-2)? Focused interviewing skills are critical in improving the detection of behavioral symptoms in all patients, especially patients with extrapyramidal disorders. Straightforward questions such as "What do you do for fun?" or "What do you enjoy doing these days?" to assess anhedonia or apathy are deceptively simple yet often neglected (85).

In some situations family members will be reassured simply to learn that facial masking is a common symptom in patients with PD or that apathy is a common behavioral manifestation. At a conference for patients with PD, when the topic of coping with PD was under discussion, a gentleman with PD volunteered that he frequently tells new acquaintances that the blankness of his face does not mean that he is not interested in what they are saying. Perhaps as clinicians we have neglected the simple approach of explaining to the patient and family the variety of motor and behavioral symptoms in PD and the manner in which they may interfere with communication and social interaction.

THE MANAGEMENT OF APATHY AND AMOTIVATION

The evidence-base for the clinical management of apathy comprises mainly case reports rather than methodologically sound clinical trials. It is important to note potential "ethical pitfalls" in the care of patients with apathy (54, 86). Such patients may be less likely to question recommendations from the physician; passive compliance is not equivalent to informed consent. Thorough discussion of the rationale and goals of therapy with the patient and family, as well as careful documentation, is important to alleviate concerns that the patient was not informed.

Early attempts to treat apathy involved the use of methylphenidate in demented or depressed elderly patients. Amphetamines are still occasionally prescribed by physicians for symptoms of amotivation and/or fatigue, with inconsistent results (87–90), and case reports continue to illustrate efficacy in PD patients. In 2002, Chatterjee et al. (91) described an 82-year-old man with PD and comorbid depression and apathy whose depression responded to paroxetine 20 mg/day, although apathy persisted. Methylphenidate 5 mg twice a day was added, and within a week, his family reported improved interest and motivation. Aureil et al. (92) studied 22 PD patients given a single daily dose of 20 mg of methylphenidate and reported a significant increase in attention but no improvement in cognitive function. Dopaminergic agents including levodopa, dopamine agonists, selegiline, and amantadine have all been reported to be effective for apathy in selected cases (84, 93, 94).

Rational pharmacotherapy for apathy rests on the traditional foundation of accurate recognition and diagnosis as well as exclusion of reversible medical, pharmacologic, or psychosocial factors. A review of case reports of pharmacologic treatment of apathy yields a number of general observations. Among the dopaminergic agents, dopamine receptor agonists are reported to be the most effective in treating apathy. The therapeutic dose range used in patients without PD is variable but has often been fairly high (bromocriptine: mean 10 mg/d, range 2.5 to 60 mg/d, pergolide mean 3 mg/d, range 1 to 5 mg/d) (84). Pramipexole has been suggested to have particular efficacy for depression and apathy (95), but this has not been adequately studied. It has been observed that apathy uncomplicated by cognitive dysfunction tends to respond better to pharmacotherapy. This may in part be related to the increased risk of drug-induced adverse effects in patients with cognitive dysfunction.

In PD, apathy should be considered along with the parkinsonian symptoms that may respond to dopaminergic therapy. If apathy persists when the motor symptoms are adequately treated, introduction of a dopamine agonist or elevation of the dosages of the dopaminergic medications should be considered. In patients with AD, apathy may contribute to poor cognitive performance; the cholinesterase inhibitor tacrine has been reported to improve motivation in these patients (96, 97). Adverse hepatic effects have limited its general use, especially with the other safer drugs currently available in that class. A study measuring treatment response to galantamine with flourodeoxyglucose ^{18}F PET in AD revealed a patient subgroup whose apathy improved in association with a change of metabolism in the right ventral putamen (98). Multiple studies also have shown that rivastigmine improves apathy in patients with dementia with Lewy bodies (DLB) and in PDD (99–105).

Memantine is an N-methyl-D-aspartate (NMDA) receptor antagonist that is now in use in treating dementia in AD, DLB and PDD. While several recent studies have shown that memantine provides no significant benefit in the treatment of depression in AD or PDD, no specific studies have addressed its efficacy in treating apathy (94, 106, 107). Patients with mixed apathy and depression may benefit from combined therapy with dopaminergic and antidepressant medication. Theoretically, antidepressants with stimulant properties (bupropion, protryptilline, venlafaxine, sertraline) are indicated, although little data is available to corroborate this recommendation.

Low testosterone levels correlate with the severity of apathy in PD patients (108). Based on these findings, Okun et al. (109) treated 10 PD patients with daily transdermal testosterone gel and found a significant improvement in libido, energy, and enjoyment after 1 and 3 months of treatment. A placeo-controlled trial, however, was negative (110).

APATHY AND LIVING WITH CHRONIC ILLNESS

Both aging and chronic illness may have profound effects on an individual's perception of control, competency, and autonomy. While self-determination depends upon the belief that outcomes are controllable, amotivation is associated with a perceived disconnection of behavior from outcomes (111). Vallerand et al. studied the relationship between level of motivation and quality of life in elderly nursing home residents. Intact intrinsic motivation was correlated with increased self-esteem, satisfaction with life, fulfillment, feelings of control, and less depression. Conversely, the presence of amotivation was correlated with reduced self-esteem, decreased satisfaction with life, the perception of loss of control, and reduced general health status. This vicious cycle of organic illness, depression, apathy, and helplessness (see Figure 18-1) is often intractable to medical intervention even when other disabling symptoms are relieved.

Patients with chronic disability from nonneurologic causes such as osteoarthritis have also been found to have high levels of apathy and depression. When osteoarthritis and PD patients with similar levels of disability were directly compared to determine whether apathy in PD is a response to disability alone (60), PD patients had higher levels of apathy that did not correlate with their level of disability.

Motivational status is an important determinant of successful adjustment to stressful life events and illness. Patients with self-determination and motivation are more likely to deal with health problems in a more constructive manner. It is instructive to observe the common behaviors of PD patients with and without apathy syndromes. Patients with intact motivation are more likely to be proactive, searching out current information about medical and surgical interventions as well as new clinical research opportunities. These patients are more likely to expect to be consulted regarding clinical decision making and will often provide more detailed historical information. They may follow instructions more reliably and will often provide better feedback regarding their response to therapy. The motivated patient is more likely to seek out specialty consultation, to practice preventive medicine, and to make lifestyle choices regarding exercise, nutrition, and stress management that are designed to enhance their feelings of well-being. Conversely, the consequences of amotivation on self-management, lifestyle, socialization, family interaction, and community involvement are likely to result in a greater loss of functional status (112). Increased scrutiny of the relationships between apathy, disease severity, and quality of life may indeed identify apathy as a "red flag" associated with a poorer prognosis.

CONCLUSION

The determinants of an individual's motivational tendencies are likely to be a combination of factors: intrinsic personality traits (heredity), experiential learning (environment), and acquired conditions such as PD. Motivational behavior is an ongoing construct, continuously being remodeled by all of these influences. Clinical research studies are needed to identify effective therapies for apathy and amotivation associated with PD. Both pharmacologic and nonpharmacologic interventions are likely to be effective.

Management styles that foster autonomy and choice may accentuate the individual's sense of personal responsibility and control, while authoritative styles may promote passivity and a sense of incompetence. The expectation of a person's active role in his or her daily management and long-range decision making preserves dignity and a sense of self. As we become increasingly aware of the factors that determine quality of life, we are likely to discover that restoration of motor function is only one facet of restoring quality of life for patients with PD.

References

1. Silva SJ, Marin RS. Apathy in neuropsychiatric disorders. *CNS Spectrums* 1999; 4:31–50.
2. Marin RS. Differential diagnosis of apathy and related disorders of diminished motivation. *Psychiatr Ann* 1997; 27:30–33.
3. Starkstein SE, Merello M. *Psychiatric and Cognitive Disorders in Parkinson's Disease,* New York: Cambridge University Press, 2002.
4. Marin RS. Apathy: A neuropsychiatric syndrome. *J Neuropsychiatry Clin Neurosci* 1991; 3:243–254.
5. Marsden CD, Parkes JD. Success and problems of long-term levodopa therapy in Parkinson's disease. *Lancet* 1977; 1:345–349.
6. Marin RS. Differential diagnosis and classification of apathy. *Am J Psychiatry* 1990; 147:22–30.
7. Marin RS, Biedrzycki RC, Firinciogullari S. Reliability and validity of the apathy evaluation scale. *Psychiatry Res* 1991; 38:143–162.
8. Starkstein SE, Mayberg HS, Preziosi TJ, et al. Reliability, validity and clinical correlates of apathy in Parkinson's disease. *J Neuropsychiatr Clin Neurosci* 1992; 4:134–139.
9. Sockeel P, Dujardin K, Devos D, et al. The Lille apathy rating scale (LARS), a new instrument for detecting and quantifying apathy: Validation in Parkinson's disease. *J Neurol Neurosurg Psychiatry* 2006; 77:579–584.
10. Duffy JD. The neural substrates of motivation. *Psychiatr Ann* 1997; 27:24–29.
11. Levy ML, Cummings JL, Fairbanks LA, et al. Apathy is not depression. *J Neuropsychiatr Clin Neurosci* 1998; 10:314–319.
12. Mayeux R, Stern Y, Sano M, et al. Clinical and biochemical correlates of bradyphrenia in Parkinson's disease. *Neurology* 1987; 37:1130–1134.
13. Duffy JD, Kant R. Apathy secondary to neurologic disease. *Psychiatr Ann* 1997; 27: 39–43.
14. Starkstein, SE, Manes F. Apathy and depression following stroke. *CNS Spectrums* 2000; 5(3):43–50.
15. Ott BR, Noto RB, Fogel BS. Apathy and loss of insight in AD: A SPECT imaging study. *J Neuropsychiatr Clin Neurosci* 1996; 8:41–46.
16. Starkstein SE, Federoff JP, Price TR, et al. Apathy following cerebrovascular lesions. *Stroke* 1993; 24:1625–1630.
17. Helgason C, Wilbur A, Weiss A, et al. Acute pseudobulbar mutism due to discrete bilateral capsular infarction in the territory of the anterior choroidal artery. *Brain* 1988; 111:507–519.
18. Salloway SP, Malloy PF, Rogg J, et al. MRI and neuropsychological differences in early- and late-life-onset geriatric depression. *Neurology* 1996; 46:1567–1574.
19. Bechara A, Tranel D, Damasio H, et al. Failure to respond autonomically to anticipated future outcomes following damage to prefrontal cortex. *Cereb Cortex* 1996; 6:215–225.
20. Davidson RJ. Internet communication: *Washington-post. com.* Live online, 11/2/99.
21. Davidson RJ, Coe CC, Dolski I, et al. Individual differences in prefrontal activation asymmetry predict natural killer cell activity at rest and in response to challenge. *Brain Behav Immun* 1999; 13:93–108.
22. Davidson RJ, Abercrombie H, Nitschke JB, et al. Regional brain function, emotion and disorders of emotion. *Curr Opin Neurobiol* 1999; 9:228–234.
23. Levy R, Dubois B. Apathy and the functional anatomy of the prefrontal cortex-basal ganglia circuits. *Cerebral Cortex*. 2006; 16:916–928.
24. Pillon B, Boller F, Levy R, Dubois B. Cognitive deficits in Parkinson's disease. In: Boller F, Grafman J (eds). *Handbook of Neuropsychology.* Amsterdam: Elsevier, 2002.
25. Merello M, Starkstein S, Nouzeilles MI, et al. Bilateral pallidotomy for treatment of Parkinson's disease induced corticobulbar syndrome and psychic akinesis avoidable by globus pallidus lesion combined with contralateral stimulation. *J Neurol Neurosurg Psychiatry* 2001; 71:611–614.
26. Schupbach WMM, Chastan N, Welter ML, et al. Stimulation of the subthalamic nucleus in Parkinson's disease: A 5 year follow up. *J Neurol Neurosurg Psychiatry* 2005; 76:1640–1644.
27. Czernecki V, Pillon B, Houeto JL, et al. Does bilateral stimulation of the subthalamic nucleus aggravate apathy in Parkinson's disease? *J Neurol Neurosurg Psychiatry* 2005; 76:775–779.
28. Goerendt IK, Lawrence AD, Brooks DJ. Reward processing in health and Parkinson's disease: Neural organization and reorganization. *Cereb Cortex* 2004; 14:73–80.
29. Nader K, Bechara A, van der Kooy D. Neurobiological constraints on behavioral models of motivation. *Annu Rev Psychol* 1997; 48:85–114.
30. Weintraub D, Potenza MN. Pathological gambling and other impulse control disorders in Parkinson's. *Pract Neurol* 2006; 5(7):23–29.
31. Perry TL, Wright JM, Berry K, et al. Dominantly inherited apathy, central hypoventilation, and Parkinson's syndrome: Clinical, biochemical, and neuropathologic studies of 2 new cases. *Neurology* 1990; 40:1882–1887.
32. Cloninger CR. A systematic method for clinical description and classification of personality variants: A proposal. *Arch Gen Psychiatry* 1987; 44:573–588.
33. Stellar JR, Stellar E. *The Neurobiology of Motivation and Reward.* New York: Springer-Verlag, 1985.
34. Hooks MS, Kalivas PW. Involvement of dopamine and excitatory amino acid transmission in novelty-induced motor activity. *J Pharmacol Exp Ther* 1994; 269:976–988.
35. Crow TJ. A map of rap mesencephalon for electrical self-stimulation. *Brain Res* 1972; 36:265–273.
36. Fray P, Dunnett S, Iverson S, et al. Nigral transplants reinnervating the dopamine-depleted neostriatum can sustain intracranial self-stimulation. *Science* 1983; 219:416–419.
37. Menza MA, Forman NE, Goldstein HS, et al. Parkinson's disease, personality and dopamine. *J Neuropsychiatr Clin Neurosci* 1990; 2:282–287.
38. Menza MA, Golbe LI, Cody RA, et al. Dopamine-related personality traits in Parkinson's disease. *Neurology* 1993; 43:505–508.
39. Todes CJ, Lees AJ. The pre-morbid personality of patients with Parkinson's disease. *J Neurol Neurosurg Psychiatry* 1985; 48:97–100.
40. Estough VM, Kempster PA, Stern GM, et al. Premorbid personality and idiopathic Parkinson's disease. In: Streifler MB, Korzyn AD, Melamed E, et al (eds). *Parkinson's Disease: Anatomy, Pathology, and Therapy. Advances in Neurology.* Vol 53. New York: Raven Press, 1990:335–337.
41. Poewe W, Karamat E, Kemmler GW, et al. The pre-morbid personality of patients with Parkinson's disease: A comparative study with healthy controls and patients with essential tremor. In: Streifler MB, Korczyn AD, Melamed E, et al. (eds). *Parkinson's Disease: Anatomy, Pathology and Therapy. Advances in Neurology.* Vol 53. New York: Raven Press, 1990:339–342.
42. Cloninger CR, Przybeck TR, Svrajuc DM. The tridimensional personality questionnaire: U.S. normative data. *Psychol Rep* 1991; 69:1047–1057.
43. Ebstein RP, Novick O, Umansky R, et al. Dopamine D4 receptor (D4DR) exon III polymorphism associated with the human personality trait of novelty seeking. *Nat Genet* 1996; 12:78–80.
44. Benjamin J, Li L, Patterson C, et al. Population and familial association between the D4 dopamine receptor gene and measures of novelty seeking. *Nat Genet* 1996; 12:81–84.
45. Jonsson EG, Nothen MM, Gustavsson P, et al. Lack of evidence for allelic association between personality traits and the dopamine D4 receptor gene polymorphisms. *Am J Psychiatry* 1997; 154:697–699.
46. Sullivan PF, Fifield WJ, Kennedy MA, et al. No association between novelty seeking and the type 4 dopamine receptor gene (DRD4) in two New Zealand samples. *Am J Psychiatry* 1998; 155:98–101.
47. American Psychiatric Association. *Diagnostic and Statistical Manual of Mental Disorders,* 4th ed. Washington, DC: American Psychiatric Association, 1994.
48. Marin RS, Firinciogullari S, Biedrzycki RC. Differences in the relationship between apathy and depression. *J Nerv Ment Dis* 1994; 182:235–239.
49. Levy ML, Miller BL, Cummings JL, et al. AD and frontotemporal dementias: Behavioral distinctions. *Arch Neurol* 1996; 53:687–690.
50. Litvan I, Mega MS, Cummings JL, et al. Neuropsychiatric aspects of progressive supranuclear palsy. *Neurology* 1996; 47:1184–1189.
51. Aarsland D, Larsen JP, Lim NG, et al. Range of neuropsychiatric disturbances in patients with Parkinson's disease. *J Neurol Neurosurg Psychiatry* 1999; 67:492–496.
52. Isella V, Melzi P, Grimaldi M, et al. Clinical, neuropsychological, and morphometric correlates of apathy in Parkinson's disease. *Mov Disord* 2002; 17:366–371.
53. Kirsch-Darrow L, Fernandez HF, Marsiske M, et al. Dissociating apathy and depression in Parkinson's disease. *Neurology* 2006; 67:33–38.
54. Richard IH. Apathy does not equal depression in Parkinson disease: Why should we care? *Neurology* 2006; 67:10–11.
55. Hobson R, Meara J. The detection of dementia and cognitive impairment in a community population of elderly people with Parkinson's disease by use of the CAMCOG neuropsychological test. *Age Ageing* 1999; 28:39–43.
56. Jankovic JJ, Tolosa E. *Parkinson's Disease and Movement Disorders,* 4th ed. Philadelphia: Lippincott Williams & Wilkins, 2002.
57. Agronin ME, Maletta GJ. *Principles and Practice of Geriatric Psychiatry.* Philadelphia: Lippincott Williams & Wilkins, 2006.
58. Mayeux R, Denaro J, Hemenegildo N. A population based investigation of Parkinson's disease with and without dementia. *Arch Neurol.* 1992; 42:1142–1146.
59. Frith CD. *The Cognitive Neuropsychology of Schizophrenia.* Philadelphia: Psychology Press, 1992.
60. Pluck GC, Brown RG. Apathy in Parkinson's disease. *J Neurol Neurosurg Psychiatry* 2002; 73:636–642.
61. Kuzis G, Sabe L, Tiberti C, et al. Neuropsychological correlates of apathy and depression in patients with dementia. *Neurology* 1999; 57(2):1403–1407.
62. Aarsland D, Cummings JL, Larsen JP. Neuropsychiatric differences between Parkinson's disease with dementia and Alzheimer's disease. *Int J Geriatr Psychiatry* 2001; 16:184–191.
63. Piccirilli M, D'Alessandro P, Finali G, Piccinin G. Early frontal impairment as a predictor of dementia in Parkinson's disease. *Neurology* 1997; 48:546–547.
64. Whitehouse PJ, Hedreen JC, White CL III, Price DL. Basal forebrain neurons in the dementia of Parkinson's disease. *Ann Neurol* 1983; 13:243–248.
65. Gibb WRG. Dementia and Parkinson's disease. *Br J Psychiatry* 1989; 154:596–614.
66. Krupp BH, Fogel BS. Motivational impairment in primary psychiatric and medical illness. *Psychiatr Ann* 1997; 27:34–38.
67. Gold MS, Pearsall HR. Hypothyroidism—Or, is it depression? *Psychosomatics* 1983; 24:646–656.
68. Starkman MN, Schteingart DE. Neuropsychiatric manifestations of patients with Cushing's syndrome. *Arch Intern Med* 1981; 141:215–219.
69. Varadaraj R, Cooper AJ. Addison's disease presenting with psychiatric symptoms. *Am J Psychiatry* 1986; 143:553–554.
70. Navia BA, Jordan BD, Price RN. The AIDS-dementia complex I: Clinical features. *Ann Neurol* 1986; 19:517–524.
71. Holmes FP, Kaplan JE, Ganz NM, et al. Chronic fatigue syndrome: A working case definition. *Ann Intern Med* 1988; 108:387–389.

72. Andraeson NC. Negative symptoms in schizophrenia. *Arch Gen Psychiatry* 1982; 39:784–788.

73. Duffy JD. The neurology of alcoholic denial: Implications for assessment and treatment. *Can J Psychiatry* 1995; 40:257–263.

74. Gersten SP. Long term adverse effects of brief marijuana use. *J Clin Psychiatry* 1980; 41:60–61.

75. Kant R, Duffy JD, Pivovarnik A. Apathy following closed head injury. *J Neuropsychiatry Clin Neurosci* 1995; 7:425.

76. Berlin RM, Litovitz GL, Diaz M, et al. Sleep disorders on a psychiatric consultation service. *Am J Psychiatry* 1984; 141:582–584.

77. Katon W, Berg A, Robins AJ, et al. Depression: Medical utilization and somatization. *West J Med* 1986; 144:564–568.

78. Perez-Estable EJ, Miranda J, Munoz RF, et al. Depression in medical patients. *Arch Intern Med* 1990; 150:1083–1088.

79. Schulberg HC, Saul M, McClelland M. Assessing depression in primary medical and psychiatric practices. *Arch Gen Psychiatry* 1985; 12:1164–1170.

80. Simon GE, Von Korff M. Recognition, management, and outcomes of depression in primary care. *Arch Fam Med* 1995; 4:99–105.

81. Shulman LM. Singer C, Leifert R, et al. The diagnostic accuracy of neurologists for anxiety, depression, fatigue and sleep disorders in Parkinson's disease. *Mov Disord* 1997; 12(Suppl 1):127.

82. Covington EC. Depression and chronic fatigue in the patient with chronic pain. *Primary Care* 1991; 18:341–358.

83. Shulman LM, Singer C, Leifert R, et al. The comorbidity of the nonmotor symptoms of Parkinson's disease. *Ann Neurol* 1996; 40:536.

84. Campbell JJ, Duffy JD. Treatment strategies in amotivated patients. *Psychiatr Ann* 1997; 27:44–49.

85. Cole S, Raju M. Making the diagnosis of depression in the primary care setting. *Am J Med* 1996; 101(Suppl 6A):10S–17S.

86. Krupp BH. Ethical considerations in apathy syndromes. *Psychiatr Ann* 1997; 27:50–54.

87. Jaffe GV. Depression in general practice: A clinical trial of a new psychomotor stimulant. *Practitioner* 1961; 186:492–495.

88. Darvill FT, Wooley S. Double-blind evaluation of methylphenidate (Ritalin) hydrochloride: Its use in the management of institutionalized geriatric patients. *JAMA* 1959; 169:1739–1741.

89. Chiarello RJ, Cole JO. The use of psychostimulants in general psychiatry: A reconsideration. *Arch Gen Psychiatry* 1987; 44:286–295.

90. Masand PS, Tesar GE. Use of stimulants in medically ill. *Psychiatr Clin North Am* 1996; 19:515–547.

91. Chatterjee A, Fahn S. Methylphenidate treats apathy in Parkinson's disease. *J Neuropsychiatry Clin Neurosci* 2002; 14:461–462.

92. Levy R, Dubois B. Apathy and the functional anatomy of the prefrontal cortex-basal ganglia circuits. *Cereb Cortex* 2006; 16:916–928.

93. Marin RS, Fogel BS, Hawkins J, et al. Apathy: A treatable syndrome. *J Neuropsychiatry Clin Neurosci* 1995; 7:23–30.

94. Moryl E, Danysz W, Quack G. Potential antidepressive properties of amantadine, memantine and bifemelane. *Pharmacol Toxicol* 1993; 72(6):394–397.

95. Szegedi A, Hilbert A, Wetzel H, et al. Pramipexole, a dopaminergic agonist in major depression: Antidepressant effects and tolerability in an open label study with multiple doses. *Clin Neuropharmacol* 1997; 20:S36–S45.

96. Kaufer DI, Cummings JL, Christine D. Effect of tacrine on the behavioral symptoms of AD: Open-label study. *J Geriatr Psychiatry Neurol* 1996; 9:1–6.

97. Cummings J. Cholinesterase inhibitors: A new class of psychotropic compounds. *Am J Psychiatry* 2000; 157(1):4–15.

98. Mega MS, Dinov ID, Porter V, et al. Metabolic patterns associated with the clinical response to galantamine therapy. *Arch Neurol* 2005; 62:721–728.

99. Poewe, W. Treatment of dementia with Lewy bodies and Parkinson's disease dementia. *Mov Disord* 2005; 20(12):S77–S82.

100. Schrag A. Psychiatric aspects of Parkinson's disease—An update. *J Neurol* 2004; 251(7):795–804.

101. Burn DJ, McKeith IG. Current treatment of dementia with Lewy bodies and dementia associated with Parkinson's disease. *Mov Disord* 2003; 18(6):S72–79.

102. Del Ser T, McKeith I, Anand R, et al. Dementia with Lewy bodies: Findings from an international multicentre study. *Int J Geriatr Psychiatry* 2000; 15(11):1034–1045.

103. McKeith IG, Grace JB, Walker Z, et al. Rivastigmine in the treatment of dementia with Lewy bodies: Preliminary findings from an open trial. *Int J Geriatr Psychiatry* 2000; 15(5):387–392.

104. Bullock R, Cameron A. Rivastigmine for the treatment of dementia and visual hallucinations associated with Parkinson's disease: A case series. *Curr Med Res Opin* 2002; 18(5):258–264.

105. Aarsland D, Mosimann UP, McKeith IG. Role of cholinesterase inhibitors in Parkinson's disease and dementia with Lewy bodies. *J Geriatr Psychiatr Neurol* 2004; 17(3):164–171.

106. Zarate CA, Singh JB, Quiroz JA, et al. A double-blind, placebo-controlled study of memantine in the treatment of major depression. *Am J Psychiatry* 2006; 163:153–155.

107. Parsons CG, Danysz W, Quack G. Memantine is a clinically well tolerated N-methyl-D-aspartate (NMDA) receptor antagonist—A review of preclinical data. *Neuropharmacology* 1999; 38(6):735–767.

108. Ready RE, Friedman J, Grace J, Fernandez H. Testosterone deficiency and apathy in Parkinson's disease: A pilot study. *J Neurol Neurosurg Psychiatry* 2004; 75:1323–1326.

109. Okun MS, Walter BJ, McDonald WM, et al. Beneficial effects of testosterone replacement for the nonmotor symptoms of Parkinson disease. *Arch Neurol* 2002; 59:1750–1753.

110. Okun MS, Fernandez HH, Rodriguez RL, Romrell J, Suelter M, Munson S, Louis E, Mulligan T, Foster P, Shenal B, Armaghani S, Jacobson C, Wu S. Testosterone therapy in men with Parkinson disease: Results of the TEST-PD Study. *Arch Neurol* 2006;63(5):729–735.

111. Vallerand RJ, O'Connor BP, Hamel M. Motivation in later life: Theory and assessment. *Int J Aging Hum Dev* 1995; 41:221–238.

112. Webster J, Grossberg G. Disinhibition, apathy, indifference, fatigability, complaining and negativism. *Int Psychogeriatr* 1996; 8(Suppl 3):403–408.

19 Impulse-control Disorders

Valerie Voon
Susan H. Fox

Neuropsychiatric symptoms are varied and common in Parkinson's disease (PD) and include depressive, psychotic, and anxiety disorders; cognitive deficits; apathy; and fluctuations in mood and anxiety. The pathophysiology may be related to the primary underlying pathology or to secondary issues such as compensatory mechanisms, treatments (medical and surgical), unrelated comorbid disorders, or underlying individual (hereditary, biological, or psychological) vulnerabilities.

A set of behaviors characterized by their repetitive and reward- or motivation-based natures—which are presumed to be related to aberrant or excessive dopaminergic stimulation—have recently been recognized in PD. These behaviors include pathologic gambling (PG) (1–7), hypersexuality (HS) (2, 8, 9), compulsive shopping (CS) (2, 8), compulsive eating (10), hobbyism, punding (11, 12), and compulsive medication use (13, 14). Hypersexuality has been described in PD patients since the 1970s (9). Although punding had been recognized with psychostimulant abuse since the 1970s, it was first reported in PD by Friedman in 1994 (11). This was followed by compulsive medication use, reported by Giovannoni et al. in 2000 (13) and pathological gambling by Molina et al. in 2000 (6). These disorders commonly occur without subjective distress, are frequently hidden or unnoticed by patients and family members, and can have potentially devastating consequences.

The literature on these behaviors in PD—including definitions, epidemiology, potential pathophysiology, and management—is reviewed.

DEFINITION AND CLASSIFICATIONS

Impulsive behaviors encompass repetitive actions, with or without urges, and with associated negative consequences. From a clinical perspective, the inclusion of consequences in the definition allows for differentiation of pathologic behavior. However, from a pathophysiologic perspective, subsyndromal inconsequential forms can also occur.

Pathologic gambling is defined as impaired control over gambling urges resulting in marked negative consequences. It is classified within the Impulse-Control Disorders in the fourth edition of the *Diagnostic and Statistical Manual of Mental Disorders* (DSM-IV) (15). The definition includes criteria central to substance use disorders including states of tolerance and withdrawal, thus suggesting a "behavioral addiction." A subsyndromal form of problem gambling that fulfills fewer criteria than PG has also been described. Hypersexuality is defined as atypical or excessive sexual behaviors resulting in negative consequences and is classified under both the

Impulse-Control Disorders (excessive) and Paraphilias (atypical) in the DSM-IV (15). A working definition of HS has been put forward by Voon et al (8). Compulsive shopping, as defined by McElroy et al., includes maladaptive shopping behaviors that result in negative consequences (16). Compulsive eating in PD was defined in a case series on PD by Nirenberg et al. as "an uncontrollable consumption of a larger amount of food than normal in excess of that necessary to alleviate hunger" (10). A more stringent definition of Binge Eating Disorder can be found in the Research Diagnostic Criteria of the DSM-IV (15).

Punding is an intense fascination with complex, excessive, repetitive, non-goal-oriented behaviors. The behaviors include less complex acts such as shuffling papers, reordering bricks, or sorting handbags and more complex acts such as hobbyism (gardening, painting), writing (17), or excessive computer use (18). Punding behaviors are often related to an individual's previous occupation or interests (i.e., prepotent habits) but can occur de novo. A video of punding can be viewed on line; the link is given in Evans et al. (12). Compulsive medication use in PD was initially known as "hedonistic homeostatic dysregulation," which was subsequently replaced with "dopamine dysregulation syndrome" (19). The diagnosis is defined as pathologic use of dopaminergic medications by levodopa-responsive PD patients in excess of that required for motor response, with resultant medication-induced motor and behavioral side effects and dopaminergic withdrawal symptoms (13).

In the definition of these disorders, the DSM emphasizes that the behavior should not occur solely in the context of hypomania or mania (15). Voon et al. found that DSM-defined medication-induced mania was robustly associated with PG (32). However, in contrast to the age of onset of bipolar disorder, the age of medication-induced mania onset in PD was much later, without the commonly observed premorbid depression. Furthermore, the onset of mania occurred after the onset of PG. The authors suggest that medication-induced mania should be considered within this spectrum of medication-induced behaviors rather than as a separate disorder or a rule-out diagnosis (32). Thus, rather than a pathophysiologic similarity to bipolar disorder, dopaminergic medication–induced mania in PD may be part of the spectrum of behaviors, with dopamine dysregulation affecting pathways involved in mood, psychomotor speed, cognition, and approach behaviors.

There is much disagreement surrounding the classification of these behaviors. The behaviors likely exist on a spectrum and may be idiosyncratic to an individual's susceptibility, hence complicating any classification by phenomenology. Classification within psychiatrically based categories—which include obsessive-compulsive behaviors, impulse control, or addiction processes—is complicated given the overlapping cognitive processes underlying these behaviors (20). Furthermore, which cognitive processes are dysregulated in these behaviors in PD is poorly understood. For instance, punding, which appears as disinhibited habitual behaviors, likely differs from but overlaps with PG, which has a more prominent reward or incentive component.

In this chapter, the terms *impulse-control disorders* and *repetitive behaviors* are used; these terms are not intended to refer to underlying pathophysiology.

PREVALENCE

The term *prevalence* intimates prevalence rates either after medication initiation or sometime during the course of disease.

The prevalence of DSM-defined PG in PD in North American clinics has been reported between 2.6% and 7.6% (1–3) and is higher than in the general North American population, where the lifetime prevalence of DSM-defined PG is 1.7% (21). In a study based in Italy, PG in PD (6.1%) was significantly more likely to occur than PG in patients attending general clinics (0.3%) (4). Similarly, in a study based in west Scotland, PG was observed in 4.4% of PD patients (5). In studies differentiating PG by medication subtype, whereas PG was observed in 2.6% to 4.4% of all PD patients, PG was observed in 7.2% to 8.0% of patients on dopamine agonists (1, 5).

The prevalence of HS in PD has been reported in two studies at approximately 2.5% (2, 8). The prevalence of CS in PD was reported at between 0.4% and 1.5% (2, 8), which is lower than the prevalence of CS in the general population, which is estimated at between 2% and 6% (22).

Determining the actual prevalence rates of impulse-control disorders in PD may vary according to the method of ascertainment. Voon et al. reported the overall prevalence of PG, HS, or CS in PD patients at 5.9%, with a point prevalence of 4.2% (1, 8). The prevalence in those on levodopa treatment alone was 0.7%, whereas it was 13.5% in those on dopamine agonists (4). In these studies, PD patients were screened using patient-rated questionnaires (the South Oaks Gambling Screen, a clinician-designed screening HS questionnaire, and Lejoyeux's compulsive shopping questionnaire) (1, 8). PG was defined using DSM-IV criteria, HS using clinician-designed working diagnostic criteria, and CS using McElroy's criteria (1, 4). Weintraub et al. reported similar prevalence rates of problem gambling, HS, and CS in patients with PD of 6.6%, with a point prevalence of 4.0% (2). The authors used systematic but unstructured clinical interview screening and diagnostic criteria based on the Minnesota Impulsive Disorders Interview (2). However, despite the screening and definitional differences, the prevalence rates of both studies were similar.

Using a structured clinician-interview, Evans et al. reported a 14% point prevalence of punding in a tertiary referral center based in the United Kingdom (12). In contrast, Miyasaki et al., using a patient-rated adaptation of Evans's questionnaire, found only a 1.4% point prevalence in a clinic with community-based referrals based in Canada (23). These differences were suggested to be related to the clinician- versus patient-rated questionnaires, the referral base, and the potential for the short-acting dopamine agonist apomorphine to accentuate these behaviors owing to the greater availability and use of apomorphine in the United Kingdom than in Canada (23).

The prevalence of compulsive dopaminergic medication use has been reported at 3.4% to 4% in movement disorder clinics (13, 24).

PATHOPHYSIOLOGY

Background: Neuroanatomy and Theories of Addiction Processes

Although differences exist in the phenomenology of impulse-control disorders in PD, they are linked by their reward- or incentive-based and repetitive natures. The rewards may be learned (PG and CS), intrinsic (HS and compulsive eating), and/or drug-related (compulsive medication use).

The neuroanatomic regions implicated include the ventral tegmental area; its ventral striatal, limbic, and prefrontal cortical dopaminergic projections; and the dorsal striatum and associated frontostriatal circuitry. These regions are thought to be involved in impulse-control disorders in the general population and may also be involved in the processes underlying addiction. There are several proposed theories on addiction that are not mutually exclusive and are relevant to these behaviors (for review, see Ref. 25). A discussion of the merits of these theories is not within the scope of this chapter. Although specific theories may have different relevance for the addictions literature, they may also be relevant for the range of behaviors observed in PD. For instance, Everitt and Robbins suggest that drug-seeking actions, similar to habits, start out as explicit but become implicit, automatic, or overlearned stimulus-response pathologic behaviors engaging the dorsal striatum. Koob et al. suggest that the negative hedonic tone secondary to neural sensitization and observed in drug withdrawal states plays a role in the compulsive drug abuse required to maintain homeostasis. Alternatively, Robinson and Berridge suggest that drugs of abuse alter nucleus accumbens–related circuitry engaged in incentive processes (i.e., the process of "wanting" rather than the process of "liking," as seen in reward or hedonic tone). Behavioral sensitization (i.e., an increase

in behavioral drug effects with repeated exposure) occurs with psychostimulants, particularly with high or escalating doses and intermittent administration; it is associated with neuronal changes in the nucleus accumbens and prefrontal cortex. The compulsive pursuit of drugs (e.g., neutral stimuli such as drug cues becoming salient out of proportion with other stimuli) is suggested to occur through Pavlovian stimulus-stimulus associations and adaptations of accumbens-related circuitry. Finally, Jentsch and Taylor have suggested that aberrant functioning of the prefrontal cortex as observed in drug abuse may also be associated with loss of cognitive inhibitory control over "prepotent tendencies," thus resulting in impulsive behaviors.

Associations with Dopaminergic Medications

In three studies systematically assessing medications associated with PG, HS, and CS in PD, there was a robust association with the use of dopamine agonists as a class but not with any specific agonists (1, 2, 8). This observation neither rules in nor rules out an association with D3 receptors.

All of these behaviors can be but are not necessarily related to total dopamine agonist dose. In other words, using the regular dose range is sufficient to trigger these behaviors in susceptible individuals, but higher doses may be more likely to do so.

Pathologic Gambling. In two studies, PG was not associated with dopamine agonist dose or total levodopa equivalent dose (LED) (1, 4), whereas in a third study, PG was associated with higher pramipexole dose but not ropinorole or levodopa dose (5). This suggests that PG is not associated with levodopa dose per se and can be but is not necessarily associated with higher dopamine agonist dose. That pramipexole is also more easily titrated to full therapeutic doses than ropinorole may also play a role in the initial observations of the association with PG in some of the earlier uncontrolled case series (26).

Hypersexuality. In contrast, HS was associated with higher total LED but not agonist dose, suggesting a role for total dopaminergic dose but not specifically for dopamine agonist dose (8). In a separate study, PG, HS, and CS assessed as a group were associated with higher LED (2).

Punding. The relationship between specific dopaminergic medications and punding is less clear. In the study by Evans et al., punding was not associated with any specific medication subtype, but an association with high LED was noted (7). In this study, only patients with LED higher than 800 mg/d were assessed for punding. In contrast, the 4 of 291 PD patients with punding identified by Miyasaki et al. were on dopamine agonists and had a mean LED of 850 mg (range 450 to 1100 mg) (23). Although the medication status of PD patients with punding was not compared to those without punding, the study results suggest a potential role for dopamine agonists. However, a simple dopaminergic dose effect cannot be excluded.

Of interest, in a case report, punding was reported with the dopamine antagonist quetiapine in 2 PD patients, suggesting either a nondopaminergic role (given the relatively high 5HT2A-receptor binding affinity of quetiapine) or that these behaviors occur outside of an optimal dopaminergic tone (27).

Compulsive Medication Use.   Compulsive medication use is associated with high LED but not with oral dopamine agonists per se (14). One case series has suggested an association with the short-acting agonist apomorphine, which is administered as intermittent subcutaneous injection (13). However, it should be noted that the associations of punding and compulsive medication use with higher LED may be secondary to the excessive medication use rather than causative of the behaviors.

How Are Dopaminergic Medications Associated with These Behaviors?

The administration of dopaminergic medications may be associated with aberrant behavior by (a) interference with the pattern of dopamine release and its normal physiologic role as an error prediction or teaching signal (28, 29) or (b) stimulation of particular dopamine receptors, thus resulting in aberrant activity of implicated regions (26).

Several lines of evidence suggest that phasic release of dopamine from the ventral tegmental area to the nucleus accumbens occurs at the time of anticipation of reward and of receiving an unanticipated reward (i.e., reward prediction error) (28). Conversely, phasic suppression occurs when a reward is expected but not received. The magnitude of dopamine release varies with the magnitude of the reward. In contrast to phasic release, tonic dopamine release occurs with anticipation of greatest reward uncertainty (i.e., when there is an equal probability or chance of either receiving or not receiving a reward) (29). This observation has been interpreted to suggest that anticipation of conditions of high uncertainty—as, for example, gambling—may itself be rewarding (29).

Treatment of PD with intermittent dopaminergic stimulation may lead to alterations or sensitization in the neural patterns due to the nonphysiologic stimulation of dopaminergic receptors. This is analogous to the pathophysiology of motor fluctuations such as levodopa-induced dyskinesias, which occur in advanced PD. The neural mechanism underlying dyskinesia has been suggested to be related to the phasic stimulation of dopaminergic receptors within the "motor" striatum (putamen-caudate)

(for review, see Ref. 57). In PD patients susceptible to impulse-control behaviors, similar changes may occur within the "limbic" or ventral striatum.

Levodopa and dopamine agonists have different pharmacologic properties that may result in differences in phasic versus tonic stimulation of dopamine receptors. Levodopa has a relatively short half-life as compared to orally acting dopamine agonists, and several pharmacokinetic and pharmacodynamic factors affect the availability of levodopa, thus potentially resulting in a phasic dopaminergic effect. In the healthy brain or early in the course of PD with still intact nigrostriatal terminals, levodopa is converted to dopamine in presynaptic dopaminergic nerve terminals. In this situation, dopamine can be normally stored in vesicles and released as required. Hence, levodopa administration may be more likely to mimic the physiologic role of dopamine. This is seen clinically in terms of the motoric effects of levodopa, with excellent benefit on disability and long-lasting effect despite its relatively short half-life (58). However, with progression of PD and loss of presynaptic dopaminergic neurons and/or with excessive doses, levodopa is converted to dopamine in nondopaminergic neurons, with subsequent loss of normal storage and normal physiologic control of dopamine release. Hence, either excessive doses, appropriate doses in the context of impaired neuronal density, or postsynaptic dopamine receptor stimulation from dopamine agonists may result in loss of the normal physiologic pattern of dopamine activity. Thus impulse-control disorders in PD may then result, as a person may anticipate a reward without the feedback teaching signal indicating the lack of reward. As such, the pathologic qualities of the behavior become apparent.

Alternatively, stimulation of specific dopamine receptor subtypes may be associated with aberrant activity, which may account for the ability of dopamine agonists to induce impulse-control behaviors. For instance, the affinities of dopamine D3 receptor binding differ between clinically available dopamine agonists in addition to the relative ratio of binding affinities of dopamine D3/D1 or D3/D2 (30). Unlike dopamine D1 or D2 receptors, D3 receptors are found predominantly in limbic regions and have been implicated in the addiction process. Dodds et al. suggest an association between pathologic gambling in PD patients and the use of the dopamine D3–preferring agonist pramipexole; however, other clinical studies have not confirmed this association (1, 2, 4).

Susceptibility

The lack of a consistent dose effect (1, 4) and occurrence of symptoms in only a subset of patients clearly suggests an underlying susceptibility. This susceptibility may be mediated by PD-related factors such as (a) the neurobiology of PD (e.g., pathology and compensatory mechanisms that may also modulate underlying temperamental traits or cognitive processes), (b) PD-specific medication practices, or (c) individual factors underlying the vulnerability to PG, addiction disorders, or impulse-control behaviors. The latter suggests that dopamine agonists used for non-PD disorders (e.g. restless legs syndrome or depression) may also trigger these symptoms.

Parkinson's Disease–Related Factors: Subgroups

Factors related to PD could result from the existence of subgroups of PD patients who have a greater risk for developing behavioral disorders. For instance, recurrent psychosis tends to occur more frequently in patients who have *parkin* gene mutations (31) and depression occurs more frequently in young-onset PD. Young onset PD may also be more likely to have a genetic cause. The susceptibility is presumably related to a different distribution and nature of pathology and, in turn, of medication response. Both PG and compulsive medication use are associated with younger PD onset (1, 14, 32) suggesting a potential role for selective vulnerability. However, this association may be confounded by the relatively greater use and higher doses of dopamine agonists used in young onset PD.

Parkinson's Disease–Related Factors: General Neurobiology

Aberrant functioning secondary to PD pathology (e.g., neurodegeneration, alpha-synuclein deposition) or compensatory upregulation of relevant neuroanatomic networks may be implicated. The effect of PD pathology and dopaminergic medications on dopaminergic tone may influence cognitive functions relevant to these behaviors. For instance, PD patients off medications have been demonstrated to be more sensitive to punishment learning, whereas those on medications are more sensitive to reward learning (33). Impairments in cognitive flexibility (e.g., reversal learning, attentional set shifting) have also been associated with PD or to medication administration (34). Which cognitive functions are relevant to these behaviors and how medications and PD affect them are not known, as medications can both enhance or impair cognitive function. In a study investigating working memory in PD patients, Mattay et al. suggested that dopamine influences working memory in a U-shaped curve (e.g., optimal dopamine tone) rather than in linear fashion. The "overdose" hypothesis suggests that in PD patients, relatively preserved functions associated with the ventral striatum and ventral prefrontal cortex (e.g., reversal learning) may be more sensitive to overstimulation and impairment from dopaminergic medications compared to the dorsal striatum and dorsolateral prefrontal cortical functions (e.g., attentional

set shifting and working memory) (34). Untreated PD is associated with impairments in dorsolateral prefrontal cortical functioning (e.g., working memory) which are improved with dopaminergic medications.

However, an exclusive relationship to general PD-related neurobiology suggests that repetitive behaviors should be more common than they seem to be or that, as the disease progresses, the onset or severity of repetitive behaviors may be mediated by disease markers such as stage, duration, or levodopa dose. We did not find an association between PG and disease markers, thus arguing that PD-related neurobiology, rather than playing a primary role, may interact with individual vulnerabilities to increase susceptibility (32). A comparison of the dose-adjusted prevalence rates of these behaviors between PD and an alternate disorder requiring dopamine agonists, such as restless legs syndrome, may help clarify the role of PD-related neurobiology.

A weak association between PG and right-sided PD onset (left hemispheric onset) was found, although this remains to be replicated (32).

Parkinson's Disease–Related Factors: Medication Practices

Although PD is not the only disorder treated with dopaminergic drugs, the strategy for their use is unique, requiring higher doses, diurnal administration of dopamine agonists, and concurrent levodopa use.

In one study, Voon et al. suggest that levodopa may play a priming role potentiating the onset of these behaviors (1). But a robust association of PG with dopamine agonists as an adjunct rather than as monotherapy was observed, although the data were limited by sample size and variation in agonist doses (1, 32). It was believed by the authors that exposure to pulsatile brain levels of dopamine due to levodopa administration prior to the initiation of dopamine agonists played a role in neuronal sensitization. However, these observations remain to be confirmed, since Grossett et al., in another study, did not find any differences in prevalence rates between PD patients who developed PG on a dopamine agonist as monotherapy or as an adjunct (5).

In keeping with the earlier discussion on dykinesias, Silveira-Moriyama et al. found that punding was associated with the need for more frequent interventions to reduce dyskinesias and with greater dyskinesia severity. These findings suggest that similarities in the underlying pathophysiology of neuronal sensitization of motor and behavioral systems (35).

Studies in normal rodents and primates suggest that pulsatile and chronic administration of psychostimulants results in psychomotor behaviors associated with functional and anatomic changes in the ventral striatum and prefrontal cortex, which are presumed to underlie the behavioral sensitization process. In MPTP (1-methyl 4-phenyl 1,2,3,6-tetrahydropyridine)-lesioned marmosets repeated treatment with levodopa results in the development of abnormal psychomimetic behaviors which have been proposed to represent psychosis (36). In this model, there is an association between dose of levodopa and production of these psychosis-like behaviors.

Preclinical studies in unilateral MPTP models of PD also suggest that levodopa administration may result in aberrant D3 receptor expression, which has been implicated in sensitization processes and in the pathophysiology of dyskinesias (37). Exposure to levodopa may thus result in increased susceptibility to the potential of D3 agonists to induce repetitive behaviors. However, studies in the MPTP-lesioned primate primed to express psychosis- and compulsive-like behaviors with chronic levodopa demonstrated that there was no significant difference between the ability of equivalent doses of levodopa, pergolide, ropinirole, and pramipexole to induce compulsive-like behaviors (38). This suggests that dopamine D3–preferring agonists may be no more likely to induce compulsive-like behaviors than levodopa. However, whether this animal model represents the full spectrum of repetitive behaviors is not known.

INDIVIDUAL SUSCEPTIBILITY

Parkinson's patients may be susceptible to the development PG or other addiction disorders through underlying heritable temperamental traits (e.g., novelty or sensation seeking, impulsivity), cognitive processes (e.g., in temporal discounting, impulse control, risk taking, sensitivity to reward or punishment, reversal learning, set shifting), developmental aberrant neural networks (e.g., ventral or dorsal striatal, prefrontal cortex, and limbic regions), age, gender, or genetic polymorphisms.

For instance, PG in the general population is associated with male gender, a history of substance abuse, higher impulsivity, and sensation-seeking traits (39). In addition, executive dysfunction focusing on impairments of response inhibition (a measure of the ability to inhibit prepotent or ongoing responses such as the Stroop interference task or stop signal task) and planning, decision making (Iowa Gambling Task), and higher delay discounting rates (a measure of the extent of loss of value of outcomes when delayed or of the preference for a small immediate reward compared to a larger delayed reward) have been consistently demonstrated (40) (for review, see Ref. 41). Pathologic gambling has been associated with aberrant frontostriatal and limbic activity in imaging studies, with decreased activity in the ventromedial prefrontal cortex during the Stroop interference task (42) and decreased activity in the ventral striatum to a forced-choice win-versus-lose task (43). The latter study was suggested to reflect a lowered baseline hedonic tone to

wins in PG patients compared to controls. Furthermore, PG in the general population has been associated with increased dopamine function as measured by reduced acoustic startle prepulse inhibition (44), increased dopamine metabolites in the cerebrospinal fluid (45), and, in one study, the ability of amphetamine to prime the motivation to gamble in PG patients (46).

Several studies have since demonstrated that a diathesis in part underlies the expression of these behaviors with dopamine agonists in PD. In case-control studies by Weintraub et al. and Marsh et al., a premorbid history of impulse-control behaviors, depressed mood, increased irritability, disinhibition, and appetite disturbances were more common in patients with either PG, HS, or CS (2, 47). Similarly, in an uncontrolled case series, Nirenberg et al. found that PD patients with compulsive eating behaviors on dopamine agonists were likely to have premorbid histories of dysregulated eating behaviors or being overweight (10).

High novelty seeking is a heritable trait that has been associated with PG and substance-use disorders; it is characterized by exploratory approach rather than avoidance behaviors, excitement with novel situations, impulsivity, and rapid decision making. Low novelty seeking has been variably but not consistently associated with PD and is characterized by a reflective, rigid, and slow-tempered temperament (48). Evans et al. found that PD subjects with lower sensation-seeking scores had lower rates of alcohol intake, smoking, and drug use. Thus the lower rates of smoking observed in epidemiologic studies of the PD population, rather than being causally related to PD, may be an effect of the PD-related lowered novelty-seeking tone.

In keeping with the addictions literature, Evans et al. found that compulsive medication use in PD was independently associated with novelty seeking, depression scores, alcohol intake, and earlier age of PD onset (14). In a PET imaging study using ^{11}C raclopride (D2/3 receptor ligand), Evans et al. demonstrated increased dopamine release in the ventral striatum in response to levodopa challenge in PD patients with compulsive medication use (49). The baseline index of ^{11}C raclopride binding was similar between the PD patients with and without compulsive medication use. The authors suggest that this finding supports Robinson and Berridge's theory of neural sensitization leading to the behavior of compulsive drug seeking. Furthermore, the subjective "wanting" but not "liking" of levodopa was positively correlated with the degree of ventral striatal dopamine release. This observation was suggested to reflect an incentive salience for levodopa use rather than a pleasurable or reward-related quality (49).

Voon et al. found PG in PD to be independently associated with elevated novelty-seeking traits, a personal or family history of alcohol use disorders, and earlier age of PD onset (32). When studied with the use of a logistic regression model, these factors accounted for 62% of the variance. Impulsivity scores, particularly planning for long-term consequences, were more weakly associated with PG. The data, albeit preliminary, suggest that novelty seeking may be more likely to be trait-related (i.e., to reflect an underlying heritable vulnerability), whereas the impulsivity scores may be more state-related (i.e., related to the presence of dopamine agonist or the state of active PG) (32). Parkinson's patients without medication-induced repetitive behaviors (the control group) had novelty-seeking scores significantly lower than those of the general population. That the PD patients with PG had scores similar to those of the general population suggests that PD may modulate the heritable trait of novelty seeking. This observation includes those with expected high scores, in keeping with epidemiologic associations of PD with lowered risk-taking behaviors.

Voon et al. also found a weak association of PG with right-sided PD onset (left hemispheric onset); however, the implications are not clear. For instance, explanatory models include either the triggering of PG by aberrant dopamine receptor stimulation of the side with greater dysregulation due to pathology or post-synaptic compensatory upregulation (left hemisphere) or excessive and imbalanced stimulation of the side with less pathology (right hemisphere). There is no clear association of PG in the general population with laterality. Alternatively, the association may be mediated through mechanisms known to have a laterality effect. High novelty seeking has been associated with greater [^{18}F]-dopa uptake in the left caudate, which correlates with presynaptic dopamine neuronal density (51), and decreased novelty seeking has been associated with left hemispheric PD onset (52). In other words, the degree of left hemispheric neuronal degeneration may correlate with novelty seeking. However, the subset of PD patients with the inherited trait of high novelty seeking who develop left hemispheric PD onset may have greater dysregulation of underlying processes and be more susceptible to the behavioral effects of dopamine agonist stimulation. With respect to response inhibition, the stop signal task has been associated with the right inferior frontal or ventrolateral prefrontal cortex, as demonstrated by lesion and imaging studies (53). However, a relationship to the findings observed is not clear.

In contrast to the studies on compulsive medication use and general PG, PG was not association with depression or male gender. However, that PG occurs at twice the rate in men compared to women in the general population (39) suggests that the negative findings may be related to sample size issues.

Hypersexuality in PD is more likely to be associated with younger-onset PD and with males (8).

SUBTHALAMIC STIMULATION

Witjas et al. reported on 2 PD patients who experienced severe compulsive medication use and underwent deep brain stimulation targeting the subthalamic nucleus (STN DBS). Both had good postoperative behavioral outcomes (54). One patient had transient postoperative episode of alcohol abuse. The latter case demonstrates the efficacy of marked decreases in medication dose immediately after surgery in well-selected patients with a younger age of PD onset, shorter PD duration, and high motivation. The mechanism was suggested to be related to the replacement of the pulsatile administration of high medication doses with continuous stimulation, with a resultant decrease in neuronal and behavioral sensitization.

Similarly, Ardouin et al. describe the results of a multicenter retrospective series of 7 PD patients with active PG prior to STN DBS (55). The PG symptoms either resolved immediately after treatment or over the course of months in parallel with the decrease in LED. The authors suggest that improvement may be related to decreased doses, the relative specificity of DBS compared to medications for motor regions, the replacement of pulsatile stimulation with chronic stimulation, and to the actions of DBS targeting the STN (55). The last point is exemplified by STN lesion studies in rodent models of psychostimulant abuse (56). However, the behaviors can worsen in the early postoperative period, which suggests that caution be applied in the selection and postoperative management of these patients. In relation to this, we found in a recent multicenter retrospective study involving more than 5000 STN DBS patients with a history of impulse-control disorders or compulsive medication use indicating that these two disorders may actually be risk factors for postoperative suicide attempts (unpublished).

MANAGEMENT

Patients should be warned of the potential risks of these behaviors prior to initiation of treatment with dopamine agonists. Identification of patients at greater risk to allow for closer follow-up would be an ideal component to the ongoing management of PD. Dopamine agonists as a class appear to be associated with PG, HS, and CS (1, 2), while higher medication dose can be but is not necessarily associated (1, 2, 4, 5, 8). With all behaviors, earlier age of PD onset is associated, although differences in medication practices may mediate this association (1, 2, 8, 14, 32). Current studies suggest that specific risk factors for PG may include a personal or family history of alcohol-use disorders and increased novelty-seeking traits (32), whereas impulsivity (32) or disinhibition (47) may be associated but is more likely state-related. Specific risk factors for compulsive medication use include increased novelty seeking, alcohol use, and higher depression scores (14). Hypersexuality is associated with the male gender (8). Nonspecific associated factors include a premorbid history of these behaviors (2), depressed mood, irritability, and appetite disturbances (24).

The management of PG has been described only in anecdotal reports. In patients with compulsive medication use or those who are taking high doses, a decrease in medication dose may be sufficient. Decreasing, discontinuing, or switching to a different dopamine agonist is not consistently effective. Antidepressants have not been found to be useful in case reports. External controls (e.g., external control of finances) and referrals for gambling treatment have been anecdotally reported to be useful in a proportion of patients. As discussed above, STN DBS may be an option for well-selected patients who are unable to tolerate medication changes (55). The patient should be warned of the risk of decompensation, and careful postoperative management should be instituted.

In subjects with compulsive medication use, management includes decreasing doses; external controls

of doses; treatment of secondary psychotic, manic, or behavioral symptoms; and management of dopaminergic depressive withdrawal symptoms. Multidisciplinary involvement may be necessary (13, 19). Relapse of pathologic dopaminergic drug use behaviors is not infrequent in these patients. Stimulation of the STN may also be an option for well-selected patients (54).

CONCLUSION

Impulse-control disorders and repetitive behaviors are not uncommon in PD and can be associated with significant psychosocial dysfunction. The study of these intriguing behaviors allows not only improved clinical management but also greater insight into a biologically mediated complex behavioral model.

ACKNOWLEDGMENTS

This chapter is an adaptation of a review for *Archives of Neurology*.

References

1. Voon V, Hassan K, Zurowski M et al. Prospective prevalence of pathological gambling and medication association in Parkinson's disease. *Neurology* 2006; 66:1750–1752.
2. Weintraub D, Siderowf AD, Potenza MN, et al. Association of dopamine agonist use with impulse control disorders in Parkinson disease. *Arch Neurol* 2006; 63:969–973.
3. Lu C, Bharmal A, Suchowersky O. Gambling and Parkinson disease. *Arch Neurol* 2006; 63:298.
4. Avanzi M, Baratti M, Cabrini S, et al. Prevalence of pathological gambling in patients with Parkinson's disease. *Mov Disord* 2006; 21:2068–2072.
5. Grosset KA, Macphee G, Pal G, et al. Problematic gambling on dopamine agonists: Not such a rarity. *Mov Disord* 2006; 21(12): 2206–2208.
6. Molina JA, Sainz-Artiga MJ, Fraile A, et al. Pathologic gambling in Parkinson's disease: A behavioral manifestation of pharmacologic treatment? *Mov Disord* 2000; 15:869–872.
7. Dodd ML, Klos KJ, Bower JH, et al. Pathological gambling caused by drugs used to treat Parkinson disease. *Arch Neurol* 2005; 62:1377–1381.
8. Voon V, Hassan K, Zurowski M, et al. Prevalence of repetitive and reward-seeking behaviors in Parkinson's disease. *Neurology* 2006; 67:1254–1257.
9. Goodwin FK. Psychiatric side effects of levodopa in man. *JAMA* 1971; 1915–1920.
10. Nirenberg MJ, Waters C. Compulsive eating and weight gain related to dopamine agonist use. *Mov Disord* 2006; 21:524–529.
11. Fernandez HH, Friedman JH. Punding on L-dopa. *Mov Disord* 1999; 14:836–838.
12. Evans A H, Katzenschlager R, Paviour DC, et al. Punding in Parkinson's disease: Its relation to the dopamine dysregulation syndrome. *Mov Disord* 2004; 19(4):397–405.
13. Giovannoni G, O'Sullivan JD, Turner K, et al. Hedonistic homeostatic dysregulation in patients with Parkinson's disease on dopamine replacement therapies. *J Neurol Neurosurg Psychiatry* 2000; 68:423–428.
14. Evans AH, Lawrence AD, Potts J, et al. Factors influencing susceptibility to compulsive dopaminergic drug use in Parkinson. *Neurology* 2005; 65:1570–1574
15. *Diagnostic and Statistical Manual of Mental Disorders*, ed IV. Washington, DC: American Psychiatric Association. 1994
16. McElroy SL, Keck PE Jr, Pope HG Jr, et al. Compulsive buying: A report of 20 cases. *J Clin Psychiatry* 1994; 55:242–248.
17. Miwa H, Kondo T. Increased writing activity in Parkinson's disease: A punding-like behavior? *Parkinsonism Relat Disord* 2005; 11:323–325.
18. Fasano A, Elia AE, Soleti F, et al. Punding and computer addiction in Parkinson's disease. *Mov Disord* 2006; 21:1217–1218.
19. Evans AH, Lees AJ. Dopamine dysregulation syndrome in Parkinson's disease. *Curr Opin Neurol* 2004; 17:393–398.
20. Potenza MN. Should addictive disorders include non-substance-related conditions? *Addiction* 2006; 101(Suppl 1):142–151.
21. Ferris J, Stirpe T, Ialomiteanu A. Gambling in Ontario: A report from a general population survey on gambling-related problems and opinions. Toronto: Addiction Research Foundation, 1996.
22. Koran LM, Faber RJ, Aboujaoude E, et al. Estimated prevalence of compulsive buying behavior in the United States *Am J Psychiatry* 2006; 163:1806–1812.
23. Miyasaki JM, Hassan K, Lang AE, Voon V. A prospective survey of punding in Parkinson's disease. *Mov Disord*. In press.
24. Pezzella FR, Colosimo C, Vanacore N, et al. Prevalence and clinical features of hedonistic homeostatic dysregulation in Parkinson's disease. *Mov Disord* 2005; 20:77–81.
25. Robinson TE, Berridge KC. Addiction. *Annu Rev Psychol* 2003; 54:23–53.
26. Dodd ML, Klos KJ, Bower JH, et al. Pathological gambling caused by drugs used to treat Parkinson disease. *Arch Neurol* 2005; 62:1377–1381.
27. Miwa H, Morita S, Nakanishi I, Kondo T. Stereotyped behaviors or punding after quetiapine administration in Parkinson's disease. *Parkinsonism Rel Disord* 2004; 10:177–180.
28. Schultz W. Predictive reward signal of dopamine neurons. *J Neurophysiol* 1998; 80:1–27.
29. Fiorillo CD, Tobler PN, Schultz W. Discrete coding of reward probability and uncertainty by dopamine neurons. *Science* 2003; 299;1898–1902.
30. Millan MJ, Maiofiss L, Cussac D, et al. Differential actions of antiparkinsonian agents at multiple classes of monoaminergic receptor. I. A multivariate analysis of the binding profiles of 14 drugs at 21 native and cloned human receptor subtypes. *J Pharmacol Exp Ther* 2002; 303;791–804.
31. Khan NL, Graham E, Critchley P, et al. Parkin disease: A phenotypic study of a large case series. *Brain* 2003; 126:1279–1292.
32. Voon V, Thomsen T, Miyasaki JM, et al. Factors associated with dopaminergic drug–related pathological gambling in Parkinson disease. *Arch Neurol*, 2007; 64: 212–216.
33. Frank MJ, Seeberger LJ, O'Reilly RC. By carrot or by stick: Cognitive reinforcement learning in parkinsonism. *Science* 2004; 306:1940–1943.
34. Cools R. Dopaminergic modulation of cognitive function: Implications for L-dopa treatment in Parkinson's disease. *Neurosci Biobehav Rev* 2006; 30:1–23.
35. Silveira-Moriyama L, Evans AH, Katzenschlager R, Lees AJ. Punding and dyskinesias. *Mov Disord* 2006; 21:2214–7.
36. Visanji NP, Gomez-Ramirez J, Johnston TH, et al. Pharmacological characterization of psychosis-like behavior in the MPTP-lesioned nonhuman primate model of Parkinson's disease. *Mov Disord* 2006; 21: 1879–1891.
37. Bezard E, Ferry S, Mach U, et al. Attenuation of levodopa-induced dyskinesia by normalizing dopamine D3 receptor function. *Nat Med* 2003; 9:762–767.
38. Fox SH, Visanji NP, Johnston TH, et al. Dopamine receptor agonists and levodopa and inducing psychosis-like behavior in the MPTP primate model of Parkinson disease. *Arch Neurol* 2006; 63:1343–1344.
39. Potenza MN, Kosten TR, Rounsaville BJ. Pathological gambling. *JAMA* 2001; 286: 141–144.
40. Goudriaan AE, Oosterlaan J, de Beurs E, van den Brink W. Neurocognitive functions in pathological gambling: A comparison with alcohol dependence, Tourette syndrome and normal controls. *Addiction* 2006; 101:534–547.

41. Goudriaan AE, Oosterlaan J, de Beurs E, van der Brink W. Pathological gambling: A comprehensive review of biobehavioral findings. *Neurosci Biobehav Rev* 2004; 28: 123–141.

42. Potenza MN, Leung HC, Blumberg HP, et al. An FMRI Stroop task study of ventro-medial prefrontal cortical function in pathological gamblers. *Am J Psychiatry* 2003; 160:1990–1994.

43. Reuter J, Raedler T, Rose M, et al. Pathological gambling is linked to reduced activation of the mesolimbic reward system. *Nat Neurosci* 2005; 8:147–148.

44. Stojanov W, Karayanidis F, Johnston P, et al. Disrupted sensory gating in pathological gambling. *Biol Psychiatry* 2003; 54:474–484.

45. Bergh C, Eklund T, Sodersten P, Nordin C. Altered dopamine function in pathological gambling. *Psychol Med* 1997; 27:473–475.

46. Zack M, Poulos CX. Amphetamine primes motivation to gamble and gambling-related semantic networks in problem gamblers. *Neuropsychopharmacology* 2004; 29: 195–207.

47. Pontone G, Williams JR, Bassett SS, Marsh L. Clinical features associated with impulse control disorders in Parkinson disease. *Neurology* 2006; 67:1258–1261.

48. Menza MA, Forman NE, Goldstein HS, Golbe LI. Parkinson's disease, personality, and dopamine. *J Neuropsychiatr Clin Neurosci* 1990; 2:282–287.

49. Evans AH, Lawrence AD, Potts J, et al. Relationship between impulsive sensation seeking traits, smoking, alcohol and caffeine intake, and Parkinson's disease. *J Neurol Neurosurg Psychiatry* 2006; 77:317–321.

50. Evans AH, Pavese N, Lawrence AD, et al. Compulsive drug use linked to sensitized ventral striatal dopamine transmission. *Ann Neurol* 2006; 59:852–858.

51. Menza MA, Mark MH, Burn DJ, Brooks DJ. Personality correlates of [18F]dopa striatal uptake: Results of positron-emission tomography in Parkinson's disease. *J Neuropsychiatry Clin Neurosci* 1995; 7:176–179.

52. Tomer R, Aharon–Peretz J. Novelty seeking and harm avoidance in Parkinson's dis-ease: Effects of asymmetric dopamine deficiency. *J Neurol Neurosurg Psychiatry* 2004; 75:972–975.

53. Aron AR, Fletcher PC, Bullmore ET, et al. Stop-signal inhibition disrupted by damage to right inferior frontal gyrus in humans. *Nat Neurosci* 2003; 6:115–116.

54. Witjas T, Baunez C, Henry JM, et al. Addiction in Parkinson's disease: Impact of subtha-lamic nucleus deep brain stimulation. *Mov Disord* 2005; 20:1052–1055.

55. Ardouin CA, Voon V, Worbe C, et al. The effects of subthalamic stimulation on patholog-ical gambling in Parkinson's disease: A retrospective multicenter case series. *Mov Disord* 2006; 21:1941–1946.

56. Baunez C, Dias C, Cador M, Amalric M. The subthalamic nucleus exerts opposite control on cocaine and "natural" rewards. *Nat Neurosci* 2005; 8:484–489.

57. Brotchie JM. Advances in understanding the neural mechanisms underlying L-DOPA–induced dyskinesia. *Adv Neurol* 1999; 80:71–85.

58. Nutt JG, Carter JH, Lea ES, Sexton GJ. Evolution of the response to levodopa during the first 4 years of therapy. *Ann Neurol* 2002; 51:686–693.

IV

PATHOLOGY AND NEUROCHEMISTRY

20 Neuropathology

Dennis W. Dickson

Parkinson's disease (PD) is characterized clinically by a motor syndrome featuring bradykinesia, tremor, rigidity and postural instability. In addition, nonmotor manifestations—including autonomic, psychiatric and cognitive dysfunction—are being increasingly recognized as part of the wider clinical syndrome. The histopathology of PD is classically characterized by a loss of dopaminergic neurons in the substantia nigra (SN) that project to the striatum. For the most part, disorders that produce clinical parkinsonism share the common feature of nigrostriatal dopaminergic deficiency even if they have different molecular pathologies. Neurons that degenerate in PD accumulate cytoplasmic inclusion bodies composed of α-synuclein (1), referred to as Lewy bodies (LBs). Other parkinsonian disorders, for the most part, are not associated with LBs. While LBs are the histologic hallmark of PD, they can be associated with a range of other clinical syndromes, such as dementia, psychosis, or dysautonomia. Moreover, their distribution in the central and peripheral nervous systems is more widespread than merely the SN. This chapter focuses on the pathology of PD and other disorders that cause clinical parkinsonism.

NEUROPATHOLOGY OF PARKINSON'S DISEASE

Macroscopic Pathology

The external appearance of the brain in PD is often unremarkable, with mild frontal atrophy in some cases (Figure 20-1). There is no significant atrophy of the brainstem, which can be useful in the differential diagnosis of other parkinsonian disorders, such as progressive supranuclear palsy (PSP) and multiple system atrophy (MSA), where there is midbrain (PSP) or pontine (MSA) atrophy. When the brain is sectioned, the cortical ribbon, white matter, and basal ganglia are unremarkable. There may be mild ventricular enlargement, particularly of the frontal horn; in some cases, rust coloration of the globus pallidus may be noted. Sections of the brainstem usually reveal loss of the normally dark black pigment in the SN and locus ceruleus (LC) (Figure 20-1), pigmentation that correlates with neuronal cytoplasmic neuromelanin pigment that accumulates in an age-related manner. Loss of pigment correlates with neuronal loss and with the duration of parkinsonism.

parkinsonian disorders. In contrast, there is evidence to suggest that dorsal tier neurons may be vulnerable to age-related neuronal loss (2), and the medial neuronal groups (e.g., ventral tegmental region or A10) may be lost in patients with dementia (3).

The mechanisms implicated in cell death in PD are not reviewed here, but they include both programmed cell death (apoptosis) and lysosome-mediated cell death (autophagy). Most of the evidence for these mechanisms is based on animal or cell culture models. There is little evidence for a particular type of neuronal death in human PD brains (4,5), and these cellular processes are pleiotropic in nature; for example, both protective and toxic effects have been attributed to autophagy (6).

In addition to the SN and LC, neuronal loss is readily apparent in the basal nucleus of Meynert (nbM) and dorsal motor nucleus of the vagus (DMN) (Figure 20-2). In all of these regions neuronal loss is accompanied by LBs as well as α-synuclein immunoreactive neuritic processes

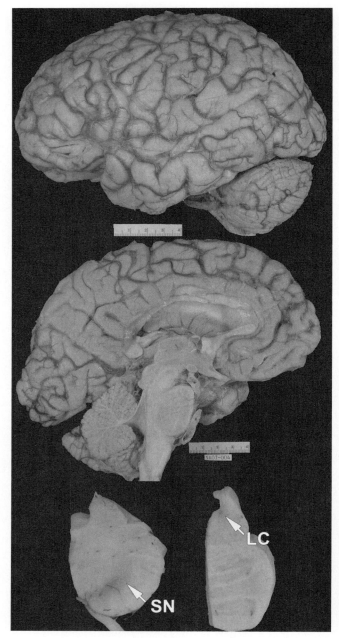

FIGURE 20-1

The external appearance of the brain in PD reveals no significant pathology on the lateral or medial surfaces. In contrast, transverse sections of the brainstem reveal pigment loss in the substantia nigra (SN, arrow) and locus ceruleus (LC, arrow). See color section following page 356.

Microscopic Pathology

The hallmark of any neurodegenerative disease is selective neuronal loss, and this is also true for PD. Neuronal loss in the SN is not uniform. The ventrolateral tier of neurons in the pars compacta (A9) is selectively vulnerable in all

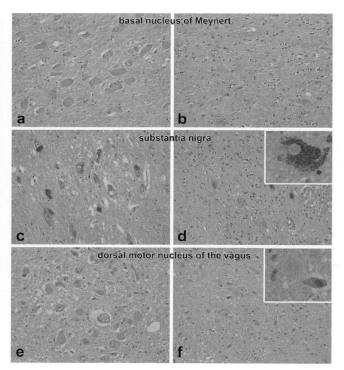

FIGURE 20-2

The appearance of select nuclei in a patent with a long history of PD (b, d, and f) and in a clinically normal subject with incidental LBs (a, c, and e). Note severe neuronal loss in the basal nucleus of Meynert (b), substantia nigra (d), and dorsal motor nucleus of the vagus (f) in PD but corresponding normal neuronal populations in the case with incidental LBs. Inset in (d) shows a typical hyaline cytoplasmic LB, while the inset in (f) shows a similar-appearing inclusion in a cell process, a so-called intraneuritic LB. See color section following page 356.

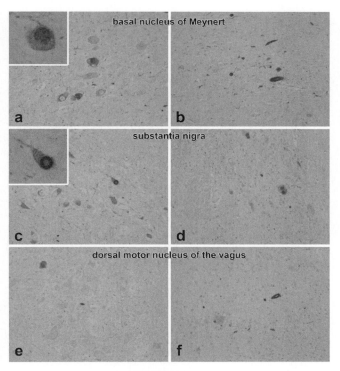

FIGURE 20-3

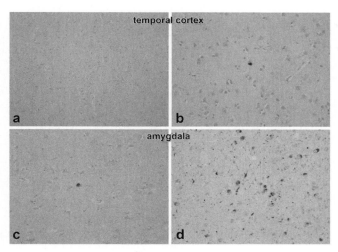

FIGURE 20-4

The same two cases from Figures 20-2 and 20-3 showing cortical-type LBs immunostained for α-synuclein. There are many LBs in the amygdala in PD (d) and sparse LBs in the case with incidental LBs (c), but in the association cortices there are sparse LBs in PD (b) but none in the case with incidental LBs (a). In DLB and in PD with dementia, the number of cortical LBs in association cortices is greatly increased. See color section following page 356.

The same two cases and anatomic regions as in Figure 20-2, but in this case immunostained for α-synuclein. In both PD (b, d, and f) and a case with incidental LBs (a, c, and e) there are LBs and intraneuritic LBs in the vulnerable brain regions. In some regions (e.g., subtantia nigra), the LB density is greater in the incidental LB case than in PD, related to severe neuronal loss in PD. Insets in (a) show a cortical-type LBs in the basal nucleus of Meynert and in (c) a classic brainstem-type LB in the substanta nigra. See color section following page 356.

(Figure 20-3). Some of these neuritic processes are apparent with routine histologic stains, such as hematoxylin and eosin (H&E). Others are essentially invisible with routine histologic methods. The former are referred to as intraneuritic LBs, while the latter are referred to as Lewy neurites (LNs). In addition to the major nuclei that show neuronal loss and LBs, LNs are also detected in areas that are not vulnerable to classical LBs, such as the amygdala (7), hippocampus (8), and neocortex (9). Classic LBs have a hyaline appearance on H&E, while α-synuclein immunoreactive inclusions in less vulnerable neuronal populations, such as those of the amygdala and cortex, are pale-staining and poorly circumscribed. These lesions are referred to as "cortical LBs" (Figure 20-4) (10). A related pale-staining neuronal cytoplasmic inclusion found in pigmented brainstem neurons of the SN and LC is the "pale body" (11, 12). Evidence suggests that cortical LBs and pale bodies may be early cytologic alterations that precede the classic LB, so-called pre-LBs. In some

cases with severe pathology, hyaline type inclusions consistent with classic LBs can be detected in the amygdala and cortex, particularly the limbic cortex. While most of the α-synuclein immunoreactive cytopathology in PD is within neurons, careful inspection often reveals small α-synuclein immunoreactive glia, particularly in the midbrain and basal ganglia (13, 14).

Composition of Lewy Bodies and the Role of α-Synuclein in Parkinson's Disease

At the ultrastructural level, LBs are composed of dense granular material and straight filaments approximately 10 to 15 nm in diameter (15–17). Similar filaments can be created in the test tube with recombinant α-synuclein, which is normally an unfolded and structureless protein (18, 19). This fact, as well as the immunolocalization of α-synuclein to the filaments in tissue sections subjected to electron microscopy, indicates that the filaments in LBs are almost certainly derived from aggregates of α-synuclein that have an abnormal conformation. The presence of α-synuclein in cytoplasmic inclusions represents aberrant cytologic localization, since it is normally a protein enriched in presynaptic terminals. The factors that give rise to the abnormal conformation remain to be determined, but several posttranslational modifications—including phosphorylation, truncation, and oxidative damage—are implicated (reviewed in Ref. 20). The composition of the dense granular material in LBs is unknown but perhaps related to other components that immuno-histochemical studies have shown to be present in LBs. Antibodies to neurofilament (21), ubiquitin (22), and the ubiquitin-binding protein p62 (23) are among the most consistently detected proteins in LBs. A subset (<50%) of LBs and LNs shows immunoreactivity with antibodies to the microtubule protein tau (24), which is the molecular determinant of neurofibrillary tangles (NFTs), inclusions found in Alzheimer's disease and other disorders ("tauopathies") (25). Many other antibodies that inconsistently label LBs have been reported (Table 20-1) (26). LNs and intraneuritic LBs have the same immunoreactivity profile as LBs. Biochemical studies of purified LBs indicate that they contain a mixture of proteins, with the most abundant being neurofilament (27, 28) and α-synuclein (29).

α-Synuclein is a 140–amino acid protein with an estimated molecular weight of 19 kDa that is highly enriched in presynaptic terminals throughout the central nervous system (20, 30). It shares homology with two other proteins,

TABLE 20-1
Lewy Body Composition

Consistent and reproducible in many studies
    α-Synuclein
    Ubiquitin
    P62 (ubiquitin-binding protein)
    Neurofilament

Inconsistent or positive in a limited number of studies
    Proteolysis and stress proteins
        Ubiquitin–C-terminal hydrolase
        Multicatalytic proteinase
        Heat-shock proteins (HSP70, HSP90)
        CHIP
        αB-Crystallin
    Protein kinases
        Lrrk2 (dardarin)
        G protein–coupled protein kinase
        Calcium-calmodulin–dependent kinase II
    Neuronal proteins
        Synphilin
        Microtubule associated protein tau
        Tubulin
        Tropomyosin
        Tyrosine hydroxylase
        Calbindin
        β-Amyloid precursor protein
        Gelsolin-related amyloid protein
        Glutathione S-transferase
    Inflammatory molecules
        Complement factors
        α2-Macroglobulin
        Immunoglobulins

Source: Adapted from Pollanen et al. (26). With permission.

β- and γ-synuclein. In the nervous system, β-synuclein but not γ-synuclein is expressed (31). Sequence analysis reveals 3 protein domains in α-synuclein; (a) a highly conserved amino-terminal region (where all known mutations that cause PD reside), which may have lipid-binding apolipoprotein-like properties and an α-helical secondary structure (32); (b) an internal hydrophobic domain that is critical for self-aggregation and fibril formation (33); and (c) a carboxyl-terminal acidic region rich in glutamate and aspartate residues and also the site of phosphorylation (34). In solution, α-synuclein is a natively unfolded protein, but it is more structured when it binds lipids (35). In LBs and LNs as well as other in glial inclusions, it assumes a β-sheet structure similar to that of amyloid (18), a structural change associated with increased propensity of α-synuclein to aggregate. In contrast to α-synuclein, β-synuclein has sequence differences in the hydrophobic domain that make it incapable of aggregating (33). In fact, when expressed simultaneously, β-synuclein may have antiaggregating effects on α-synuclein (36).

The known mutations in the coding region of the gene for α-synuclein are associated with the generation of α-synuclein species that have greater toxicity than wild-type α-synuclein (37, 38); however, there are other mutations [e.g., gene multiplications (39, 40)] that do not alter the sequence but rather lead to overexpression of α-synuclein. How excessive α-synuclein leads to toxicity remains to be determined, but protein aggregation is likely critical (41). In sporadic PD, defective protein degradation may lead to increases in the concentration of α-synuclein to critical levels that favor aggregation within the cell. Both proteasomal and nonproteasomal [e.g., calpain (42)] pathways may be involved in the proteolysis of α-synuclein, and there is evidence to suggest that proteasomal functions may be impaired in PD (43). Truncated species of α-synuclein are increased in PD compared to normals (44). The proteasomal pathway is of interest because it interfaces with protein ubiquitination, and pathologic α-synuclein is ubiquitinated. Thus, deficiencies in the ubiquitin-proteasomal processing of α-synuclein may lead to its accumulation to critical levels that lead to aggregation.

The normal function of α-synuclein is unknown, but structural analysis suggests that it may have chaperone properties. It shares sequence homology with the family of 14-3-3 chaperone molecules (45) and may modulate of the activity of tyrosine hydroxylase, the rate-limited enzyme in dopamine synthesis (46). It has also been suggested to play a role in synaptic vesicle trafficking in dopaminergic neurons (47). It undergoes phosphorylation, and phosphorylated forms are enriched in LBs (34), but whether phosphorylation is critical to lesion formation remains unknown. The physiologic function of phosphorylation and the kinases responsible are not known with certainty. While aggregated forms of α-synuclein

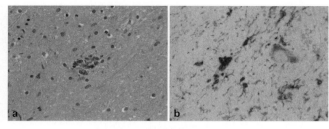

FIGURE 20-5

Neuronophagia in the substantia nigra in PD can be detected with H&E stain and with immunohistochemistry for major histocompatibility antigen HLA-DR to detect activated microglia. Note that in addition to clusters of pigment-laden macrophages (a) there is more widespread microglial activation in the substantia nigra in PD (b).

TABLE 20-2
Proposed Staging of PD

Stage 0	Peripheral autonomic nerves and ganglia
Stage 1	Olfactory nucleus, dorsal motor nucleus of the vagus
Stage 2	Locus ceruleus
Stage 3	Substantia nigra
Stage 4	Basal forebrain and amygdala
Stage 5	Limbic cortices
Stage 6	Multimodal association and primary cortices

Source: Adapted from Braak et al. (59). With permission.

may be toxic to neurons, there is evidence to suggest that normal α-synuclein may have neuroprotective properties (48). In cell culture studies, α-synuclein expression is associated with a more differentiated state and relative resistance to apoptotic stimuli (49).

Other Microscopic Features of Parkinson's Disease

Accompanying neuronal degeneration and neuronal loss in all neurodegenerative disorders are reactive changes in astrocytes and microglia. Microglia express markers of activation such as the class II major histocompatibility antigen HLA-DR (50). There may occasionally be evidence in the SN and LC of phagocytosis of neurons by microglia, a term referred to as neuronophagia (Figure 20-5). Furthermore, a hallmark of neuronal loss in the SN and LC is the presence of neuromelanin pigment in the cytoplasm of microglia. In patients with very long disease duration, even this pigment is lost as microglia migrate to blood vessels and exit the brain along with the neuromelanin pigment they carry. Additional findings that are common in the SN but not in other areas vulnerable to neurodegeneration are axonal spheroids and hemosiderin granules. Eosinophilic intranuclear inclusions, so-called Marinesco bodies, are also common in the SN. While they can be found in normal elderly brains, there is at least one study suggesting that they may be associated with dopaminergic pathology (51).

Neurochemistry of Parkinson's Disease (See Chapter 21)

Neuronal loss in PD is not limited to dopaminergic neurons of the SN but also affects cholinergic neurons in the basal nucleus of Meynert (52, 53) and the pedunculopontine nucleus (54), noradrenergic neurons in the LC (55, 56) and serotonergic neurons of the raphe nuclei (57). It is clear that neurochemical deficits in PD include not only dopamine but also noradrenalin, serotonin, and acetylcholine. Other neurotransmitter deficits, including deficits in glutamatergic neurons in the cortex and hypothalamic neuropeptides [reviewed in Ref. 58)], may also be important with respect to nonmotor manifestations of PD.

Staging Schemes for Parkinson's Disease

Braak and co-workers have recently proposed a new pathologic staging system for PD (59) (Table 20-2). In this scheme, pathology in the DMN, LC, and anterior olfactory nucleus occurs early in the course of disease, while SN involvement is at midstage (stage 3). In later stages, as pathology ascends, cortical areas are affected, with limbic regions affected before multimodal association and primary cortices. The pathology at endstage is similar to that in LB dementia (60). The Braak staging system has been derived from autopsy studies of normals and of patients with disorders associated with LBs (61). However, not all disorders associated with LBs appear to fit the scheme. In a large cross-sectional study of 904 brains, Parkkinen and coworkers used α-synuclein immunohistochemistry to study the frequency and distribution of LBs in non-PD brains (62, 63). Several patients had LBs in the SN without involvement of the DMN, a finding also noted by Jellinger (64). The stage at which autonomic ganglia are affected is unknown, but involvement of the spinal cord's intermediolateral column has been addressed in a recent study, which suggests that the spinal cord becomes involved after the DMN but before the SN (65). The stage at which the basal ganglia are affected has not been addressed systematically, but it is probably a late manifestation (66).

It is increasingly recognized that LBs are frequent in the setting of advanced Alzheimer's disease (AD) (67) and that the most common location for LBs in AD is the amygdala (68, 69). In a cross-sectional study of AD, LBs were almost completely limited to the amygdala in about 15% to 20% of the cases (70). Most of these did not have brainstem pathology, including the DMN. Thus, LBs found in the setting of advanced AD represent the most common exception to the Braak staging scheme (61). It has also been shown that brainstem involvement may be minimal in some cases of diffuse LB disease, particularly in patients who present with dementia and minimal or no parkinsonism (66). This form of LB disease also appears to have a different pattern of disease progression than that described for PD.

Clinical Features of Various Stages of Parkinson's Disease

If the staging scheme proposed by Braak is correct, non-motor, nondopaminergic symptoms should precede motor symptoms (71, 72). In particular, one might predict that early PD may be characterized by autonomic dysfunction, olfactory dysfunction, sleep disorder, and depression, given the role that lower brainstem monoaminergic nuclei as well as spinal and enteric ganglia have in these processes (71). It is of interest that epidemiologic studies indicate that autonomic symptoms may precede clinical PD by as much as 12 years (73). One might speculate that the pathology responsible for this syndrome involves LB formation in autonomic nuclei of the lower brainstem and spinal cord as well as the enteric plexus (74). Epidemiologic studies also suggest that a history of anxiety and depression or both may precede PD (75), possibly related to norepinephrine deficiencies due to involvement of the LC. Another clinical syndrome that may be a harbinger of PD is rapid-eye-movement behavior disorder (RBD), a condition that appears a number of years before PD (76). The RBD syndrome appears to have its anatomic origins within lower brainstem nuclei (77), which are consistently affected in PD. Olfactory dysfunction is common in PD (78) and may precede overt motor symptoms (79). The later stages of PD are associated with the involvement of limbic cortices and multimodal association and finally unimodal association and primary cortices. These later stages may be characterized largely by cognitive and psychiatric features similar to those found in dementia with LB (DLB) (80).

LEWY BODY DISORDERS OTHER THAN PARKINSON'S DISEASE

Incidental Lewy Bodies

LBs can be found in the brains of about 10% of normal elderly individuals over 65 years of age (15). These cases may represent the earliest stages of PD; the distribution of LBs and development of nonmotor clinical manifestations (e.g., RBD) in some cases would seem to favor this argument (63–65, 81–84). In particular, such cases have LBs, albeit in small numbers and not accompanied by neuronal loss or gliosis, in brain regions that are vulnerable

to PD pathology (Figures 20-1, 20-2, and 20-3). Given the lack of overt parkinsonism, such cases have been referred to as being "incidental" (15). It remains to be determined whether these individuals, who may or may not have nonmotor prodromal features of PD, would eventually progress to PD.

Pure Autonomic Failure

With renewed interest in the involvement of the autonomic nervous system in PD and prodromal PD (74), it is of note that some individuals with pure autonomic failure have LB pathology at autopsy (85). These cases show LBs in brain and autonomic ganglia and LNs in sympathetic nerve fibers in epicardium and periadrenal tissues (86). While adrenal medullary chromaffin cells accumulate inclusion bodies resembling LBs in PD associated with autonomic dysfunction, these inclusions are not composed of α-synuclein (87).

Dementia with Lewy Bodies

Dementia with Lewy bodies (DLB) is a clinicopathologic entity with a specific constellation of clinical features, including cognitive impairment, visual hallucinations, fluctuating cognition, and spontaneous extrapyramidal signs occurring within a year of the onset (80). Other common clinical features are RBD, severe neuroleptic sensitivity, and reduced striatal dopamine transporter activity on functional neuroimaging (80). The initial neuropathologic criteria for DLB were the presence of LBs in the brain of a patient with a clinical history of dementia (88), but these criteria were not rigorous and led to poor clinicopathologic correlations, since LBs are also common in AD, which produces a dementia syndrome that differs from the DLB syndrome. A refinement of the criteria has emphasized that the likelihood of DLB is directly related to the severity of LB accumulation and inversely related to the severity of AD pathology (Table 20-3) (88). Severity of LB pathology is based upon the the distribution of brainstem-predominant LBs, LBs in mostly limbic cortices, and LBs in multimodal association cortices. Severity of AD type pathology is assessed with widely used methods to score the density of cortical plaques and the topography of neurofibrillary degeneration incorporated in the criteria of the National Institutes on Aging (89). This revision of neuropathologic criteria was based upon prevailing evidence that the more AD type pathology, the less likely the patient would present with the DLB clinical syndrome even if there were diffuse cortical LBs (90). Validation of the new neuropathologic criteria remains to be demonstrated.

Dementia in Parkinson's Disease

Pathologic findings considered to account for dementia in PD include severe pathology in monoaminergic and

TABLE 20-3
Proposed Neuropathologic Criteria for Dementia with Lewy Bodies

		ALZHEIMER TYPE PATHOLOGY		
		NIA-REAGAN LOW	NIA-REAGAN INTERMEDIATE	NIA-REAGAN HIGH
Lewy Body-type pathology	Brainstem-predominant	Low	Low	Low
	Limbic (transitional)	High	Intermediate	Low
	Diffuse neocortical	High	High	Intermediate

The likelihood that the observed pathologic findings are associated with the DLB clinical syndrome (i.e., dementia with visual hallucinations, spontaneous parkinsonism, fluctuations, and RBD) is related to the severity of LB pathology as assessed by the distribution of LBs (152) and inversely related to the severity of the Alzheimer-type pathology as assessed by the NIA-Reagan criteria (89).
Source: From McKeith et al. (151). With permission.

cholinergic nuclei that project to the cortex, producing a "subcortical dementia" (39%), coexistent Alzheimer's disease (29%), and diffuse cortical LBs (26%) (91). The basal forebrain cholinergic system is implicated in dementia in PD. Neuronal loss occurs in the basal nucleus of Meynert in PD, but it is even worse in PD with dementia (52, 53). Cholinergic deficits are common in PD (92), and they may contribute to dementia in those patients who do not have concurrent AD or cortical LBs.

While virtually every PD brain has a few cortical LBs, they are usually neither widespread nor numerous. Several recent studies have shown, however, that cortical LBs are numerous and widespread in PD with dementia (93–95) and that the density of cortical LBs and LNs, especially in medial temporal lobe structures (96), correlates with the severity of dementia. There are exceptions to this rule, with occasional reports of patients with many LBs who were cognitively normal (62).

Neuropathology of Familial Parkinson's Disease

Mutations in the gene for α-synuclein (*SNCA*) cause autosomal dominant, early onset PD (40, 97–99). The pathology in cases with *SNCA* mutations is characterized by LBs, with many cases showing widespread diffuse LBs. Limbic system pathology is particularly severely affected and hippocampal neuritic pathology and neuronal loss in CA2 sector is often marked (Figure 20-6) (100). Glial inclusions similar to those in MSA are found in some cases (Figure 20-6) (100).

The most common genetic basis for late-onset autosomal dominant PD is a mutation in *LRRK2*, a gene on chromosome 12 (101, 102). Most cases are clinically indistinguishable from typical sporadic PD, with late age of disease onset as well as the presence of resting tremor, asymmetry, levodopa responsiveness, and potential for

motor complications (101, 103). The most common mutation is G2019S, and autopsy studies suggest that the most cases with *LRRK2* mutations and PD have LB pathology (104). There are rare individuals with PSP-like tau pathology (105) or nonspecific neurodegeneration in the SN (106).

Mutations in the gene for parkin (*PRKN*) on chromosome 6 cause autosomal recessive juvenile-onset PD (107); in most cases of this disorder the SN degeneration is not associated with LBs. However, there are only a few autopsy reports based on individuals who have had parkinsonism for decades (108). LBs have been reported in several individuals with compound heterozygous *PRKN* mutations (109, 110), but it is unclear whether these are linked to the disease or are incidental findings. There are also reports of tau pathology in some cases (111), but the significance of this finding awaits analysis of additional cases and also may be an aging-associated change.

In addition to *SNCA*, *LRRK2*, *and PRKN*, there are about 10 other genetic assignments for familial PD (112). Description of neuropathology is lacking for almost all of these familial PD disorders.

Mutations in the tau gene (*MAPT*) have been discovered in some forms of frontotemporal dementia, and some of these kindreds have prominent parkinsonism as part of the clinical syndrome, most often with features similar to those of PSP or CBD (113). The accepted term for this disorder is FTDP-17 (114). For this reason, *MAPT* is sometimes included among the genes responsible for parkinsonism. These cases do not have LBs but rather NFTs. Recently, another gene causing FTDP-17 has been found to be progranulin (*PGRN*) (115). More than half the patients with the *PGRN* mutation also have parkinsonism (116), which suggests that *PGRN* should be added to the list of PD genes. These cases have nonspecific degeneration in the SN and striatum associated with

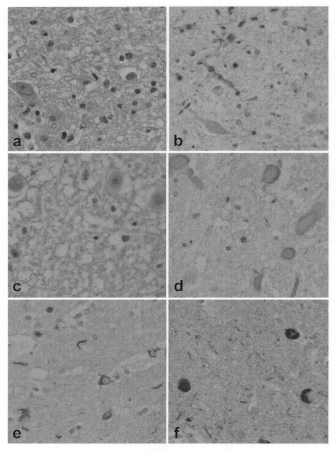

FIGURE 20-6

Familial PD due to mutations in the *SNCA* gene. In cases with A53T mutation there is often severe neuronal loss and gliosis in CA2 sector of the hippocampus (a) and many α-synuclein immunoreactive neuritic processes in the same region (b). In brainstem nuclei such as the locus ceruleus (c and d), many of the LBs are intraneuritic and readily visible with H&E stain (c) but more clearly seen with α-synuclein immunohistochemistry (d). In cases with *SCNA* gene triplication (Iowa kindred), α-synuclein immunohistochemistry reveals glial inclusions (e) and many cortical LBs (d) consistent with diffuse LB disease.

ubiquitin-immunoreactive neuronal inclusions but not LBs. There is also evidence to suggest that glucocerebrosidase mutations, which cause Gaucher's disease, may be associated with parkinsonism, and autopsy studies in these individuals show findings typical of PD, including LBs (117).

Neuropathology of Parkinson's Disease Associated with Neurotoxins

While environmental exposures almost certainly play a role as a risk factor for PD, there are few examples where the neuropathology has been described in obvi-ous environmental cases. The exception is 1-methyl-4-phenyl-1,2,3,6-tetrahydropyridine (MPTP), a byproduct of illicit synthesis of meperidine (118). Individuals who are exposed to MPTP develop parkinsonism with many features similar to those of sporadic PD. Autopsy studies reveal selective neuronal loss in the SN but no LBs (118). Systemic administration of MPTP to monkeys induces parkinsonism with neuronal loss in both SN and LC. Some neurons have eosinophilic cytoplasmic inclusions that resemble LBs (119, 120). Another environmental toxin that has been used to produce animal models of PD is rotenone; it also has been shown to be associated with neuronal inclusions that resemble LBs (121). There are no known human cases with pathologically confirmed PD due to rotenone toxicity.

OTHER PARKINSONIAN DISORDERS

Multiple System Atrophy

Multiple system atrophy (MSA) is a nonheritable neurodegenerative disease characterized by parkinsonism, cerebellar ataxia, and autonomic failure, a syndrome complex first recognized by Oppenheimer, who noted the overlapping pathology of sporadic olivopontocerebellar atrophy, Shy-Drager syndrome, and striatonigral degeneration (122). Depending upon the predominant signs and symptoms, MSA is now subdivided into MSA-C for those with predominant degeneration in cerebellar circuitry and ataxia and MSA-P for those with predominant degeneration in the basal ganglia with parkinsonism (123). Despite the different clinical presentations, there is extensive pathologic overlap in MSA-C and MSA-P, particularly at the microscopic level.

The MSA-P brain macroscopically shows atrophy and discoloration of the posterolateral putamen and loss of pigment in the ventrolateral substantia nigra (Figure 20-7). In MSA-C, there is atrophy with neuronal loss and gliosis in pontine base, inferior olive, and cerebellum (Figure 20-7). The histopathologic findings include neuronal loss, gliosis, and microvacuolation of the affected areas. In the striatum there is often prominent accumulation of brown granular pigment. Lantos and coworkers first described glial (oligodendroglial) cytoplasmic inclusions (GCIs) in MSA (124). GCIs can be detected with silver stains, in particular the Gallyas silver stain, but are best seen with antibodies to α-synuclein and ubiquitin, where they appear as flame- or sickle-shaped inclusions in oligodendrocytes (Figure 20-8). At the ultrastructural level, GCIs are non-membrane-bound cytoplasmic inclusions composed of coated filaments 10 to 20 nm in diameter similar to the filaments in LBs (125). Biochemical studies of α-synuclein in MSA reveal alterations similar to those in PD. In particular, α-synuclein has unusual

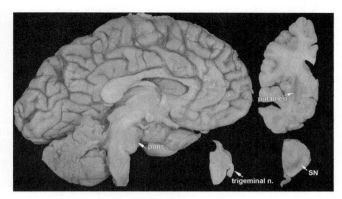

FIGURE 20-7

In MSA, the external appearance of the brain reveals atrophy of the pontine base (pons, arrow), making the trigeminal nerve (arrow) more prominent than usual on transverse sections of the pons. The midbrain has marked pigment loss in the substantia nigra (SN, arrow); the posterior putamen (arrow) is atrophic and has a brownish-red discoloration.

solubility properties and is associated with high-molecular-weight forms that may represent posttranslationally modified (e.g., ubiquitinated) or aggregated forms of α-synuclein with evidence of ubiquitination (126).

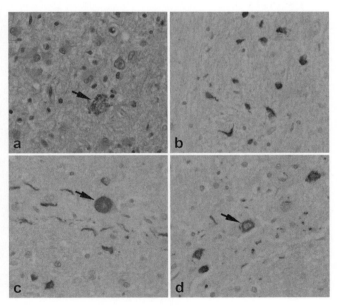

FIGURE 20-8

Microscopic findings in MSA include neuronal loss and gliosis in the putamen (a) associated with brown granular pigment (iron pigment, arrow). The fiber tracts in the putamen have numerous glial cytoplasmic inclusions (GCI) with α-synuclein immunohistochemistry (b). In the pontine base (c and d) α-synuclein immunohistochemistry reveals neuronal cytoplasmic inclusions (arrow in c) and neurons with intranuclear inclusions (arrow in d). Note also neuritic cell processes in vicinity of neurons with cytoplasmic inclusions. See color section following page 356.

While most inclusions in MSA are in oligodendroglial cells, certain neuronal populations are vulnerable to neuronal cytoplasmic and nuclear inclusions, particularly those in the pontine base, inferior olive, and putamen. A few of the neuronal inclusions in MSA resemble LBs in PD, but their anatomical distribution is distinct from neuronal populations vulnerable to LBs. Some neurons have intranuclear α-synuclein-immunoreactive inclusions (Figure 20-8) (125). Interestingly, α-synuclein-immunoreactive glial lesions have also been reported in PD, mostly in midbrain and basal ganglia (13, 14). Glial pathology may be particularly striking in early-onset familial PD (Figure 20-6) (100), suggesting that MSA and LB disease are part of a pathologic spectrum.

Progressive Supranuclear Palsy

PSP is a common cause of levodopa-nonresponsive parkinsonism. One of the earliest clinical features of PSP is unexplained falls. Eventually most patients with PSP develop postural instability, vertical gaze paresis, nuchal and axial rigidity, and dysarthria. Despite many differences in clinical presentation, it is not uncommon for an individual to carry a diagnosis of PD for years before a correct diagnosis of PSP is made (127, 128). It has been suggested that only with longitudinal evaluation is it possible to accurately differentiate PD from other parkinsonian disorders (127). It has recently been suggested that a subset of cases of pathologically confirmed PSP have parkinsonism with many similarities to PD, so-called PSP-P (129).

Macroscopically, the brain in PSP usually has mild frontal and more marked midbrain atrophy (Figure 20-9). The latter is uncommon in PD. The substantia nigra invariably shows depigmentation and the subthalamic nucleus is smaller than expected. The superior cerebellar peduncle is often atrophic (Figure 20-9) (130). This finding is useful in differential diagnosis, since it is not seen in PD or MSA. Microscopic findings include neuronal loss and fibrillary gliosis of the globus pallidus, subthalamic nucleus, and substantia nigra (Figure 20-10). Other regions that are affected include striatum, diencephalon, and brainstem. Silver stains or immunostaining for tau reveal NFTs and glial lesions. The distribution of pathology is highly characteristic and permits differentiation of PSP from other disorders associated with tau-immunoreactive neuronal inclusions (i.e., tauopathies) (131). The brainstem regions that are affected include the superior colliculus, periaqueductal gray matter, oculomotor nuclei, locus ceruleus, pontine nuclei, pontine tegmentum, vestibular nuclei, medullary tegmentum, and inferior olives. The cerebellar dentate nucleus is also frequently affected. Spinal cord involvement is common, where neuronal inclusions can be found in anterior horn and intermediolateral cells.

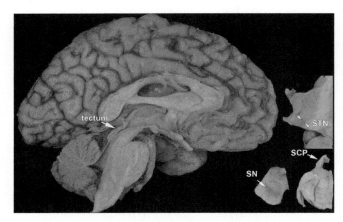

FIGURE 20-9

In PSP, the most remarkable change on gross examination is atrophy of the midbrain, with flattening of the tectal plate (tectum, arrow). The midbrain has marked pigment loss in the substantia nigra (SN, arrow), and the superior cerebellar peduncle (SCP, arrow) in the rostral pons is atrophic. The subthalamic nucleus (STN, double arrows) is atrophic and has slight brownish discoloration.

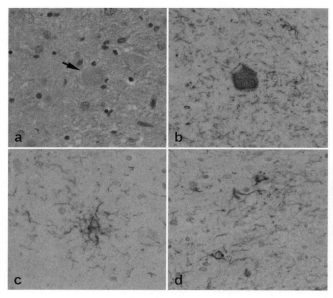

FIGURE 20-10

Microscopic examination of PSP reveals neuronal loss and gliosis in the subthalamic nucleus (a) with globose NFTs in residual neurons (arrow). The same region immunostained for tau protein reveals not only NFTs but also many neuritic processes. A characteristic tau-immunoreactive astrocytic lesion in PSP is the tufted astrocyte (c), as seen in the motor cortex and striatum. The white matter in diencephalic tracts has characteristic oligodendroglial "coiled bodies" (d). See color section following page 356.

In addition to NFTs, the pathology of PSP is also characterized by tau pathology in astrocytes ("tufted astrocytes") and oligodendroglia ("coiled bodies") (Figure 20-10). These glial lesions are distinct from the GCIs of MSA and the sparse glial lesions detected in PD not only based upon their immunoreactivity with tau but also on their morphology.

Corticobasal Degeneration

Corticobasal degeneration (CBD) is only rarely mistaken for PD due to characteristic focal cortical signs that constitute the clinical hallmark of this disorder (132, 133). Common clinical presentations include progressive asymmetric rigidity and apraxia, progressive aphasia, and progressive frontal lobe dementia (134, 135). Most cases also have some degree of parkinsonism, with bradykinesia, rigidity, dystonia, and myoclonus, which are more common than tremor. Given the prominent cortical findings on clinical evaluations, it is not surprising that gross examination of the brain often reveals focal cortical atrophy that may be asymmetric (Figure 20-11). Atrophy is often most marked in the superior frontal gyrus, parasagittal pre- and post-central gyri, and the superior parietal lobule. The brainstem does not have gross atrophy, as in PSP, but pigment loss is common in the substantia nigra. In contrast to PSP, the superior cerebellar peduncle and the subthalamic nucleus are grossly normal (136).

Microscopic examination reveals neuronal loss, spongiosis, gliosis, and usually many achromatic or ballooned neurons (Figure 20-12). Ballooned neurons are swollen and vacuolated neurons found in middle and

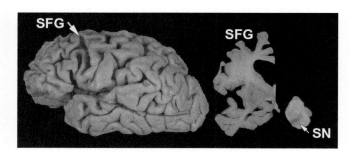

FIGURE 20-11

In CBD, the gross findings are notable for circumscribed cortical atrophy affecting the parasagittal superior frontal gyrus (SFG, arrow) as well as the superior parietal lobule. On coronal sections, the cortical ribbon in the superior frontal gyrus (SFG) is thinned, and there is enlargement of the frontal horn of the lateral ventricle. The midbrain has pigment loss in the substantia nigra (SN, arrow) as well as a rust-like pigment that is variably present in the globus pallidus.

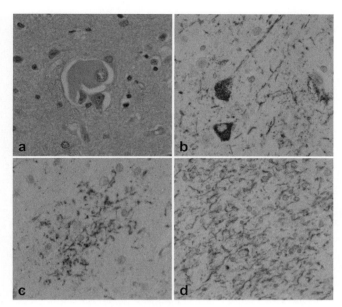

FIGURE 20-12

Microscopic examination of the cortex in CBD reveals swollen achromatic neurons, also known as "ballooned neurons" (a). The tau immunostain reveals pleomorphic neuronal inclusions in the cortex (b) and subcortical regions that only occasionally resemble well-formed NFTs. A characteristic tau-immunoreactive astrocytic lesion is the astrocytic plaque (c); such plaques are often most numerous in the cortex and striatum. The white matter in the telencephalon has numerous thread-like processes but few or no coiled bodies (d). See color section following page 356.

lower cortical layers, which are variably positive with silver stains and tau immunohistochemistry but intensely stained with immunohistochemistry for alpha-B-crystallin, a small heat-shock protein, and for neurofilaments (137). Cortical neurons in affected areas have pleomorphic tau-immunoreactive lesions. In addition, the neuropil of CBD invariably contains a large number of thread-like tau-immunoreactive processes (Figure 20-12). They are usually profuse in both gray and white matter. This latter feature is an important attribute of CBD and a useful feature in differentiating it from other disorders (137). The most characteristic tau-immunoreactive lesion in the cortex in CBD is an annular cluster of short, stubby processes with fuzzy outlines that represent tau accumulation in distal processes of astrocytes. These lesions have been referred to as "astrocytic plaques" (Figure 20-12) (138). Astrocytic plaques differ from the tufted astrocytes seen in PSP, and the two lesions do not coexist in the same brain (139).

In addition to cortical pathology, deep gray matter is consistently affected in CBD. The globus pallidus and putamen show mild neuronal loss with gliosis. Thalamic nuclei may also be affected. The SN usually shows mod-

erate to severe neuronal loss with extraneuronal neuromelanin, gliosis, and tau immunoreactive neuronal lesions ("corticobasal bodies"). In contrast to PSP, where neurons in the pontine base almost always have at least a few NFTs, the pontine base is largely free of NFTs in CBD (136).

Guamanian Parkinson-Dementia Complex

Parkinson-dementia complex (PDC) has a number of features that overlap with PSP (140,141); it is common in the native Chamorro population of Guam and in the Kii Peninsula of Japan (142). The gross findings in PDC are notable for cortical atrophy affecting especially the medial temporal lobe as well as atrophy of the hippocampus and the tegmentum of the rostral brainstem (Figure 20-13). These areas typically have neuronal loss and gliosis with many NFTs in residual neurons; extracellular NFTs are also numerous (Figure 20-14) (143). In the cortex, NFTs show a different laminar distribution from that seen in AD, with more NFTs in superficial cortical layers in Guamanian PDC and in lower cortical layers in AD (144). The SN and LC have neuronal loss and NFTs (Figure 20-14). The basal nucleus and large neurons in the striatum are also vulnerable to NFTs. Biochemically and morphologically, NFTs in Guamanian PDC, like those in postencephalitic parkinsonism, are indistinguishable from those in AD (145, 146).

Postencephalitic Parkinsonism

Parkinsonism following encephalitis lethargica during the influenza pandemic between 1916 and 1926, known

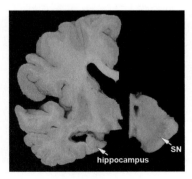

FIGURE 20-13

In Guamanian Parkinson-dementia complex, gross examination reveals medial temporal lobe atrophy due to severe hippocampal pathology (hippocampus, arrow) on coronal sections. There is also moderate ventricular enlargement. The midbrain has severe pigment loss in the substantia nigra (SN, arrow).

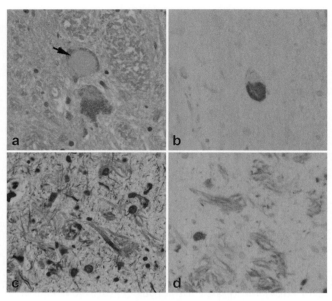

FIGURE 20-14

Microscopic examination of the SN in Guamanian Parkinson-dementia complex (a and b) reveals severe neuronal loss and gliosis with NFTs (arrow) in the few residual neurons. The tau immunostain with an antibody specific to 3R tau reveals a NFT in the SN (b). In the hippocampus (c and d) there are numerous NFTs, most of which are extracellular (c, Bielschowsky silver stain). The tau immunostain using an antibody specific to 3R tau reveals many extracellular NFTs in the hippocampus (d).

as postencephalitic parkinsonism (PEP), is almost never detected today (147). Most cases considered to have PEP on pathologic examination actually have PSP (148). The pathology in PEP is characterized by NFTs in cortex, basal ganglia, thalamus, hypothalamus, substantia nigra, brainstem tegmentum, and cerebellar dentate nucleus. The distribution of the pathology overlaps with that of PSP. PEP can be differentiated from PSP by biochemical characterization of the tau protein (149) and electron microscopy (150), which show that the NFTs are similar to those in AD and different from those in PSP.

ACKNOWLEDGMENTS

Supported by NIH grants P50-NS40256, P50-AG25711, P50-AG16574, P01-AG17216 and P01-AG03949. The histological support of Virginia Phillips, Linda Rousseau, and Monica Casey-Castanedes is greatly appreciated. Dr. John Steele is acknowledged for his efforts to provide samples from his patients on Guam for neuropathologic study. The clinicians and geneticists involved in familial PD studies, including Drs. Zbigniew Wszolek, Katerina Gwinn Hardy, and Matt Farrer are acknowledged. These studies would not be possible without the generous donation of patients and their families toward research on parkinsonism.

*R*eferences

1. Spillantini MG, Schmidt ML, Lee VM, et al. Alpha-synuclein in Lewy bodies. *Nature* 1997; 388:839–840.
2. Gibb WR, Lees AJ. Anatomy, pigmentation, ventral and dorsal subpopulations of the substantia nigra, and differential cell death in Parkinson's disease. *J Neurol Neurosurg Psychiatry* 1991; 54:388–896.
3. Rinne JO, Rummukainen J, Paljarvi L, et al. Dementia in Parkinson's disease is related to neuronal loss in the medial substantia nigra. *Ann Neurol* 1989; 26:47–50.
4. Anglade P, Vyas S, Javoy-Agid F, et al. Apoptosis and autophagy in nigral neurons of patients with Parkinson's disease. *Histol Histopathol* 1997; 12:25–31.
5. Jellinger KA, Stadelmann C. Mechanisms of cell death in neurodegenerative disorders. *J Neural Transm Suppl* 2000; 59:95–114.
6. Rubinsztein DC, DiFiglia M, Heintz N, et al. Autophagy and its possible roles in nervous system diseases, damage and repair. *Autophagy* 2006; 1:11–22.
7. Braak H, Braak E, Yilmazer D, et al. Amygdala pathology in Parkinson's disease. *Acta Neuropathol (Berl)* 1994; 88:493–500.
8. Dickson DW, Ruan D, Crystal H, et al. Hippocampal degeneration differentiates diffuse Lewy body disease (DLBD) from Alzheimer's disease: Light and electron microscopic immunocytochemistry of CA2-3 neurites specific to DLBD. *Neurology* 1991; 41:1402–1409.
9. Irizarry MC, Growdon W, Gomez-Isla T, et al. Nigral and cortical Lewy bodies and dystrophic nigral neurites in Parkinson's disease and cortical Lewy body disease contain alpha-synuclein immunoreactivity. *J Neuropathol Exp Neurol* 1998; 57:334–337.
10. Ikeda K, Ikeda S, Yoshimura T, et al. Idiopathic parkinsonism with Lewy-type inclusions in cerebral cortex. A case report. *Acta Neuropathol (Berl)* 1978; 41:165–168.
11. Dale GE, Probst A, Luthert P, et al. Relationships between Lewy bodies and pale bodies in Parkinson's disease. *Acta Neuropathol (Berl)* 1992; 83:525–529.
12. Pappolla MA, Shank DL, Alzofon J, et al. Colloid (hyaline) inclusion bodies in the central nervous system: Their presence in the substantia nigra is diagnostic of Parkinson's disease. *Hum Pathol* 1988; 19:27–31.
13. Wakabayashi K, Hayashi S, Yoshimoto M, et al. NACP/alpha-synuclein-positive filamentous inclusions in astrocytes and oligodendrocytes of Parkinson's disease brains. *Acta Neuropathol (Berl)* 2000; 99:14–20.
14. Wakabayashi K, Takahashi H. Gallyas-positive, tau-negative glial inclusions in Parkinson's disease midbrain. *Neurosci Lett* 1996; 217:133–136.

15. Forno LS. Concentric hyalin intraneuronal inclusions of Lewy type in the brains of elderly persons (50 incidental cases): Relationship to parkinsonism. *J Am Geriatr Soc* 1969; 17:557–575.
16. Tiller-Borcich JK, Forno LS. Parkinson's disease and dementia with neuronal inclusions in the cerebral cortex: Lewy bodies or Pick bodies. *J Neuropathol Exp Neurol* 1988; 47:526–535.
17. Galloway PG, Mulvihill P, Perry G. Filaments of Lewy bodies contain insoluble cytoskeletal elements. *Am J Pathol* 1992; 140:809–822.
18. Conway KA, Harper JD, Lansbury PT Jr. Fibrils formed in vitro from alpha-synuclein and two mutant forms linked to Parkinson's disease are typical amyloid. *Biochemistry* 2000; 39:2552–2563.
19. Crowther RA, Daniel SE, Goedert M. Characterisation of isolated alpha-synuclein filaments from substantia nigra of Parkinson's disease brain. *Neurosci Lett* 2000; 292:128–130.
20. Dickson DW. Alpha-synuclein and the Lewy body disorders. *Curr Opin Neurol* 2001; 14:423–432.
21. Galvin JE, Lee VM, Baba M, et al. Monoclonal antibodies to purified cortical Lewy bodies recognize the mid-size neurofilament subunit. *Ann Neurol* 1997; 42:595–603.
22. Kuzuhara S, Mori H, Izumiyama N, et al. Lewy bodies are ubiquitinated. A light and electron microscopic immunocytochemical study. *Acta Neuropathol (Berl)* 1998; 75:345–353.
23. Kuusisto E, Parkkinen L, Alafuzoff I. Morphogenesis of Lewy bodies: Dissimilar incorporation of alpha-synuclein, ubiquitin, and p62. *J Neuropathol Exp Neurol* 2003; 62:1241–1253.
24. Ishizawa T, Mattila P, Davies P, et al. Colocalization of tau and alpha-synuclein epitopes in Lewy bodies. *J Neuropathol Exp Neurol* 2003; 62:389–397.
25. Goedert M. Tau protein and neurodegeneration. *Semin Cell Dev Biol* 2004; 15:45–49.
26. Pollanen MS, Dickson DW, Bergeron C. Pathology and biology of the Lewy body. *J Neuropathol Exp Neurol* 1993; 52:183–191.
27. Pollanen MS, Bergeron C, Weyer L. Detergent-insoluble cortical Lewy body fibrils share epitopes with neurofilament and tau. *J Neurochem* 1992; 58:1953–1956.
28. Pollanen MS, Bergeron C, Weyer L. Deposition of detergent-resistant neurofilaments into Lewy body fibrils. *Brain Res* 1993; 603:121–124.

29. Baba M, Nakajo S, Tu PH, et al. Aggregation of alpha-synuclein in Lewy bodies of sporadic Parkinson's disease and dementia with Lewy bodies. *Am J Pathol* 1998; 152:879–884.
30. Beyer K. Alpha-synuclein structure, posttranslational modification and alternative splicing as aggregation enhancers. *Acta Neuropathol (Berl)* 2006; 112:237–251.
31. Galvin JE, Schuck TM, Lee VM, et al. Differential expression and distribution of alpha-, beta-, and gamma-synuclein in the developing human substantia nigra. *Exp Neurol* 2001; 168:347–355.
32. Bussell R Jr, Eliezer D. A structural and functional role for 11-mer repeats in alpha-synuclein and other exchangeable lipid binding proteins. *J Mol Biol* 2003; 329:763–778.
33. Giasson BI, Murray IV, Trojanowski JQ, et al. A hydrophobic stretch of 12 amino acid residues in the middle of alpha-synuclein is essential for filament assembly. *J Biol Chem* 2001; 276:2380–2386.
34. Saito Y, Kawashima A, Ruberu NN, et al. Accumulation of phosphorylated alpha-synuclein in aging human brain. *J Neuropathol Exp Neurol* 2003;62:644–654.
35. Perrin RJ, Woods WS, Clayton DF, et al. Interaction of human alpha-synuclein and Parkinson's disease variants with phospholipids. Structural analysis using site-directed mutagenesis. *J Biol Chem* 2000; 275:34393–34398.
36. Hashimoto M, Rockenstein E, Mante M, et al. Beta-synuclein inhibits alpha-synuclein aggregation: A possible role as an anti-parkinsonian factor. *Neuron* 2001; 32:213–223.
37. Jiang H, Wu YC, Nakamura M, et al. Parkinson's disease genetic mutations increase cell susceptibility to stress: Mutant alpha-synuclein enhances H(2)O(2)- and Sin-1-induced cell death. *Neurobiol Aging*. 2006.
38. Moussa CE, Wersinger C, Tomita Y, et al. Differential cytotoxicity of human wild type and mutant alpha-synuclein in human neuroblastoma SH-SY5Y cells in the presence of dopamine. *Biochemistry* 2004; 43:5539–5550.
39. Chartier-Harlin MC, Kachergus J, Roumier C, et al. Alpha-synuclein locus duplication as a cause of familial Parkinson's disease. *Lancet* 2004; 364:1167–1169.
40. Singleton AB, Farrer M, Johnson J, et al. Alpha-synuclein locus triplication causes Parkinson's disease. *Science* 2003; 302:841.
41. Periquet M, Fulga T, Myllykangas L, et al. Aggregated alpha-synuclein mediates dopaminergic neurotoxicity in vivo. *J Neurosci* 2007; 27:3338–3346.
42. Mishizen-Eberz AJ, Norris EH, Giasson BI, et al. Cleavage of alpha-synuclein by calpain: Potential role in degradation of fibrillized and nitrated species of alpha-synuclein. *Biochemistry* 2005; 44:7818–7829.
43. McNaught KS, Jenner P. Proteasomal function is impaired in substantia nigra in Parkinson's disease. *Neurosci Lett* 2001; 297:191–194.
44. Li W, West N, Colla E, et al. Aggregation promoting C-terminal truncation of alpha-synuclein is a normal cellular process and is enhanced by the familial Parkinson's disease-linked mutations. *Proc Natl Acad Sci USA*2005; 102:2162–2167.
45. Ostrerova N, Petrucelli L, Farrer M, et al. Alpha-synuclein shares physical and functional homology with 14-3-3 proteins. *J Neurosci* 1999; 19:5782–5791.
46. Perez RG, Waymire JC, Lin E, et al. A role for alpha-synuclein in the regulation of dopamine biosynthesis. *J Neurosci* 2002; 22:3090–3099.
47. Murphy DD, Rueter SM, Trojanowski JQ, et al. Synucleins are developmentally expressed, and alpha-synuclein regulates the size of the presynaptic vesicular pool in primary hippocampal neurons. 2000; *J Neurosci* 20:3214–3220.
48. Kim TD, Choi E, Rhim H, et al. Alpha-synuclein has structural and functional similarities to small heat shock proteins. *Biochem Biophys Res Commun* 2004 ; 324:1352–1359.
49. Sidhu A, Wersinger C, Moussa CE, et al. The role of alpha-synuclein in both neuroprotection and neurodegeneration. *Ann NY Acad Sci* 2004; 1035:250–270.
50. McGeer PL, Itagaki S, Boyes BE, et al. Reactive microglia are positive for HLA-DR in the substantia nigra of Parkinson's and Alzheimer's disease brains. *Neurology* 1988; 38:1285–1291.
51. Beach TG, Walker DG, Sue LI, et al. Substantia nigra Marinesco bodies are associated with decreased striatal expression of dopaminergic markers. *J Neuropathol Exp Neurol* 2004; 63:329–337.
52. Nakano I, Hirano A. Parkinson's disease: Neuron loss in the nucleus basalis without concomitant Alzheimer's disease. *Ann Neurol* 1984; 15:415–418.
53. Whitehouse PJ, Hedreen JC, White CL III, et al. Basal forebrain neurons in the dementia of Parkinson disease. *Ann Neurol* 1983; 13:243–248.
54. Zweig RM, Jankel WR, Hedreen JC, et al. The pedunculopontine nucleus in Parkinson's disease. *Ann Neurol* 1989; 26:41–46.
55. Mann DM, Yates PO, Hawkes J. The pathology of the human locus ceruleus. *Clin Neuropathol* 1983; 2:1–7.
56. Jellinger KA. Pathology of Parkinson's disease. Changes other than the nigrostriatal pathway. *Mol Chem Neuropathol* 1991; 14:153–197.
57. Halliday GM, Blumbergs PC, Cotton RG, et al. Loss of brainstem serotonin- and substance P-containing neurons in Parkinson's disease. *Brain Res* 1990; 510:104–107.
58. Jellinger K, Mizuno Y. Parkinson's disease. In: Dickson DW (ed). Neurodegeneration: *The Molecular Pathology of Dementia and Movement Disorders*. Basel: International Society of Neuropathology, 2003:159–187.
59. Braak H, Ghebremedhin E, Rub U, et al. Stages in the development of Parkinson's disease-related pathology. *Cell Tissue Res* 2004; 318:121–134.
60. Katsuse O, Iseki E, Marui W, et al. Developmental stages of cortical Lewy bodies and their relation to axonal transport blockage in brains of patients with dementia with Lewy bodies. *J Neurol Sci* 2003; 211:29–35.
61. Dickson DW, Uchikado H, Klos KJ, et al. A critical review of the Braak staging scheme for Parkinson's disease. *Mov Disord* 2006; 21:S559.
62. Parkkinen L, Kauppinen T, Pirttila T, et al. Alpha-synuclein pathology does not predict extrapyramidal symptoms or dementia. *Ann Neurol* 2005; 57:82–91.
63. Parkkinen L, Soininen H, Alafuzoff I. Regional distribution of alpha-synuclein pathology in unimpaired aging and Alzheimer disease. *J Neuropathol Exp Neurol* 2003; 62:363–367.
64. Jellinger KA. Alpha-synuclein pathology in Parkinson's and Alzheimer's disease brain: Incidence and topographic distribution--A pilot study. *Acta Neuropathol (Berl)* 2003; 106:191–201.
65. Klos KJ, Ahlskog JE, Josephs KA, et al. Alpha-synuclein pathology in the spinal cords of neurologically asymptomatic aged individuals. *Neurology* 66:1100–1102.
66. Tsuboi Y, Dickson DW. Dementia with Lewy bodies and Parkinson's disease with dementia: Are they different? *Parkinsonism Relat Disord* 2005; 11(Suppl 1):S47–S51.
67. Hamilton RL. Lewy bodies in Alzheimer's disease: A neuropathological review of 145 cases using alpha-synuclein immunohistochemistry. *Brain Pathol* 2000; 10:378–384.
68. Lippa CF, Fujiwara H, Mann DM, et al. Lewy bodies contain altered alpha-synuclein in brains of many familial Alzheimer's disease patients with mutations in presenilin and amyloid precursor protein genes. *Am J Pathol* 1998; 153:1365–1370.
69. Lippa CF, Schmidt ML, Lee VM, et al. Antibodies to alpha-synuclein detect Lewy bodies in many Down's syndrome brains with Alzheimer's disease. *Ann Neurol* 1999; 45:353–357.
70. Uchikado H, Lin WL, DeLucia MW, et al. Alzheimer disease with amygdala Lewy bodies: A distinct form of alpha-synucleinopathy. *J Neuropathol Exp Neurol* 2006; 65:685–697.
71. Langston JW. The Parkinson's complex: Parkinsonism is just the tip of the iceberg. *Ann Neurol* 2006; 59:591–596.
72. Lang AE. The progression of Parkinson disease: A hypothesis. *Neurology* 2007; 8:948–952.
73. Abbott RD, Petrovitch H, White LR, et al. Frequency of bowel movements and the future risk of Parkinson's disease. *Neurology* 2001; 57:456–462.
74. Braak H, de Vos RA, Bohl J, et al. Gastric alpha-synuclein immunoreactive inclusions in Meissner's and Auerbach's plexuses in cases staged for Parkinson's disease-related brain pathology. *Neurosci Lett* 2006; 396:67–72.
75. Shiba M, Bower JH, Maraganore DM, et al. Anxiety disorders and depressive disorders preceding Parkinson's disease: a case-control study. *Mov Disord* 2000; 15:669–677.
76. Schenck CH, Bundlie SR, Mahowald MW. Delayed emergence of a parkinsonian disorder in 38% of 29 older men initially diagnosed with idiopathic rapid eye movement sleep behaviour disorder. *Neurology* 1996; 46:388–393.
77. Kayama Y, Koyama Y. Control of sleep and wakefulness by brainstem monoaminergic and cholinergic neurons. *Acta Neurochir Suppl* 2003; 87:3–6.
78. Hawkes CH, Shephard BC, Daniel SE. Olfactory dysfunction in Parkinson's disease. *J Neurol Neurosurg Psychiatry* 1997; 62:436–446.
79. Berendse HW, Booij J, Francot CM, et al. Subclinical dopaminergic dysfunction in asymptomatic Parkinson's disease patients' relatives with a decreased sense of smell. *Ann Neurol* 2001; 50:34–41.
80. McKeith I, Mintzer J, Aarsland D, et al. Dementia with Lewy bodies. *Lancet Neurol* 2004; 3:19–28.
81. Bloch A, Probst A, Bissig H, et al. Alpha-synuclein pathology of the spinal and peripheral autonomic nervous system in neurologically unimpaired elderly subjects. *Neuropathol Appl Neurobiol* 2006; 32:284–295.
82. Del Tredici K, Rub U, De Vos RA, et al. Where does Parkinson disease pathology begin in the brain? *J Neuropathol Exp Neurol* 2002; 61:413–426.
83. Iwanaga K, Wakabayashi K, Yoshimoto M, et al. Lewy body-type degeneration in cardiac plexus in Parkinson's and incidental Lewy body diseases. *Neurology* 1999; 52:1269–1271.
84. Uchiyama M, Isse K, Tanaka K, et al. Incidental Lewy body disease in a patient with REM sleep behavior disorder. *Neurology* 1995; 45:709–712.
85. Arai K, Kato N, Kashiwado K, et al. Pure autonomic failure in association with human alpha-synucleinopathy. *Neurosci Lett* 2000; 296:171–173.
86. Hague K, Lento P, Morgello S, et al. The distribution of Lewy bodies in pure autonomic failure: Autopsy findings and review of the literature. *Acta Neuropathol (Berl)* 1997 ; 94:192–196.
87. Sugie M, Goto J, Kawamura M, et al. Increased norepinephrine-associated adrenomedullary inclusions in Parkinson's disease. *Pathol Int* 2005; 55:130–136.
88. McKeith IG, Galasko D, Kosaka K, et al. Consensus guidelines for the clinical and pathologic diagnosis of dementia with Lewy bodies (DLB): Report of the consortium on DLB international workshop. *Neurology* 1996; 47:1113–1124.
89. Hyman BT, Trojanowski JQ. Consensus recommendations for the postmortem diagnosis of Alzheimer disease from the National Institute on Aging and the Reagan Institute Working Group on diagnostic criteria for the neuropathological assessment of Alzheimer disease. *J Neuropathol Exp Neurol* 1997; 56:1095–1097.
90. Lopez OL, Becker JT, Kaufer DI, et al. Research evaluation and prospective diagnosis of dementia with Lewy bodies. *Arch Neurol* 2002; 59:43–46.
91. Hughes AJ, Daniel SE, Blankson S, et al. A clinicopathologic study of 100 cases of Parkinson's disease. *Arch Neurol* 1993; 50:140–148.
92. Perry EK, Marshall E, Perry RH, et al. Cholinergic and dopaminergic activities in senile dementia of Lewy body type. *Alzheimer Dis Assoc Disord* 1990; 4:87–95.
93. Hurtig HI, Trojanowski JQ, Galvin J, et al. Alpha-synuclein cortical Lewy bodies correlate with dementia in Parkinson's disease. *Neurology* 2000; 54:1916–1921.
94. Apaydin H, Ahlskog JE, Parisi JE, et al. Parkinson disease neuropathology: Later-developing dementia and loss of the levodopa response. *Arch Neurol* 2002; 59:102–112.
95. Aarsland D, Perry R, Brown A, et al. Neuropathology of dementia in Parkinson's disease: A prospective, community-based study. *Ann Neurol* 2005; 58:773–776.
96. Churchyard A, Lees AJ. The relationship between dementia and direct involvement of the hippocampus and amygdala in Parkinson's disease. *Neurology* 1997; 49:1570–1576.
97. Polymeropoulos MH, Lavedan C, Leroy E, et al. Mutation in the alpha-synuclein gene identified in families with Parkinson's disease. *Science* 1997; 276:2045–2047.

98. Kruger R, Kuhn W, Muller T, et al. Ala30Pro mutation in the gene encoding alpha-synuclein in Parkinson's disease. *Nat Genet* 1998; 18:106–108.

99. Zarranz JJ, Alegre J, Gomez-Esteban JC, et al. The new mutation, E46K, of alpha-synuclein causes Parkinson and Lewy body dementia. *Ann Neurol* 2004; 55:164–173.

100. Gwinn-Hardy K, Mehta ND, Farrer M, et al. Distinctive neuropathology revealed by alpha-synuclein antibodies in hereditary parkinsonism and dementia linked to chromosome 4p. *Acta Neuropathol (Berl)* 2000; 99:663–672.

101. Zimprich A, Biskup S, Leitner P, et al. Mutations in LRRK2 cause autosomal-dominant parkinsonism with pleomorphic pathology. *Neuron* 2004; 44:601–607.

102. Paisan-Ruiz C, Jain S, Evans EW, et al. Cloning of the gene containing mutations that cause PARK8-linked Parkinson's disease. *Neuron* 2001; 44:595–600.

103. Wszolek ZK, Pfeiffer RF, Tsuboi Y, et al. Autosomal dominant parkinsonism associated with variable synuclein and tau pathology. *Neurology* 2004; 62:1619–1622.

104. Ross OA, Toft M, Whittle AJ, et al. Lrrk2 and Lewy body disease. *Ann Neurol* 2006 ; 59:388–393.

105. Rajput A, Dickson DW, Robinson CA, et al. Parkinsonism, Lrrk2 G2019S, and tau neuropathology. *Neurology* 2006; 67:1506–1508.

106. Dachsel JC, Ross OA, Mata IF, et al. Lrrk2 G2019S substitution in frontotemporal lobar degeneration with ubiquitin-immunoreactive neuronal inclusions. *Acta Neuropathol (Berl)* 2007; 113(5):601–606.

107. Kitada T, Asakawa S, Hattori N, et al. Mutations in the parkin gene cause autosomal recessive juvenile parkinsonism. *Nature* 1998; 392:605–608.

108. Hattori N, Shimura H, Kubo S, et al. Autosomal recessive juvenile parkinsonism: A key to understanding nigral degeneration in sporadic Parkinson's disease. *Neuropathology* 2000; 20(Suppl):S85–S90.

109. Farrer M, Chan P, Chen R, et al. Lewy bodies and parkinsonism in families with parkin mutations. *Ann Neurol* 2001; 50:293–300.

110. Pramstaller PP, Schlossmacher MG, Jacques TS, et al. Lewy body Parkinson's disease in a large pedigree with 77 Parkin mutation carriers. *Ann Neurol* 2005; 58:411–422.

111. Sanchez MP, Gonzalo I, Avila J, et al. Progressive supranuclear palsy and tau hyperphosphorylation in a patient with a C212Y parkin mutation. *J Alzheimer Dis* 2002; 4:399–404.

112. Farrer MJ. Genetics of Parkinson disease: paradigm shifts and future prospects. *Nat Rev Genet* 2006; 7:306–318.

113. Wszolek ZK, Slowinski J, Golan M, et al. Frontotemporal dementia and parkinsonism linked to chromosome 17. *Folia Neuropathol* 2005; 43:258–270.

114. Foster NL, Wilhelmsen K, Sima AA, et al. Frontotemporal dementia and parkinsonism linked to chromosome 17: A consensus conference. Conference Participants. *Ann Neurol* 1997; 41:706–715.

115. Baker M, Mackenzie IR, Pickering-Brown SM, et al. Mutations in progranulin cause tau-negative frontotemporal dementia linked to chromosome 17. *Nature* 2005; 442:916–919.

116. Josephs KA, Ahmed Z, Katsuse O, et al. Neuropathologic features of frontotemporal lobar degeneration with ubiquitin-positive inclusions with progranulin gene (PGRN) mutations. *J Neuropathol Exp Neurol* 2007; 66:142–151.

117. Goker-Alpan O, Giasson BI, Eblan MJ, et al. Glucocerebrosidase mutations are an important risk factor for Lewy body disorders. *Neurology* 2006; 67:908–910.

118. Langston JW, Forno LS, Tetrud J, et al. Evidence of active nerve cell degeneration in the substantia nigra of humans years after 1-methyl-4-phenyl-1,2,3,6-tetrahydropyridine exposure. *Ann Neurol* 1999; 46:598–605.

119. Forno LS, DeLanney LE, Irwin I, et al. Ultrastructure of eosinophilic inclusion bodies in the amygdala-parahippocampal region of aged squirrel monkeys treated with 1-methyl-4-phenyl-1,2,3,6-tetrahydropyridine, a dopaminergic neurotoxin. *Neurosci Lett* 1995; 184:44–47.

120. Forno LS, Langston JW, DeLanney LE, et al. Locus ceruleus lesions and eosinophilic inclusions in MPTP-treated monkeys. *Ann Neurol* 1986; 20:449–455.

121. Betarbet R, Sherer TB, MacKenzie G, et al. Chronic systemic pesticide exposure reproduces features of Parkinson's disease. *Nat Neurosci* 2000; 3:1301–1306.

122. Oppenheimer DR. Diseases of the basal ganglia, cerebellum and motor neurons. In: Blackwood W, Corsellis JAN (eds). *Greenfield's Neuropathology.* Chicago: Year Book Medical Publishers, 1976:608–651.

123. Gilman S, Low PA, Quinn N, et al. Consensus statement on the diagnosis of multiple system atrophy. *J Neurol Sci* 1999; 163:94–98.

124. Lantos PL. The definition of multiple system atrophy: A review of recent developments. *J Neuropathol Exp Neurol* 1998; 57:1099–1111.

125. Lin WL, DeLucia MW, Dickson DW. Alpha-synuclein immunoreactivity in neuronal nuclear inclusions and neurites in multiple system atrophy. *Neurosci Lett* 2004; 354:99–102.

126. Dickson DW, Liu W, Hardy J, et al. Widespread alterations of alpha-synuclein in multiple system atrophy. *Am J Pathol* 1999; 155:1241–1251.

127. Rajput AH, Rozdilsky B, Rajput A. Accuracy of clinical diagnosis in parkinsonism: A prospective study. *Can J Neurol Sci* 1991; 18:275–278.

128. Josephs KA, Dickson DW. Diagnostic accuracy of progressive supranuclear palsy in the Society for Progressive Supranuclear Palsy brain bank. *Mov Disord* 2003; 18:1018–1026.

129. Williams DR, de Silva R, Paviour DC, et al. Characteristics of two distinct clinical phenotypes in pathologically proven progressive supranuclear palsy: Richardson's syndrome and PSP-parkinsonism. *Brain* 2005; 128:1247–1258.

130. Tsuboi Y, Slowinski J, Josephs KA, et al. Atrophy of superior cerebellar peduncle in progressive supranuclear palsy. *Neurology* 2003; 60:1766–1769.

131. Dickson DW. Sporadic tauopathies: Pick's disease, corticobasal degeneration, progressive supranuclear palsy and argyrophilic grain disease. In: Esiri MM, Lee VMY, Trojanowski JQ (eds). *The Neuropathology of Dementia.* New York: Cambridge University Press, 2005:227–256.

132. Boeve BF, Maraganore DM, Parisi JE, et al. Pathologic heterogeneity in clinically diagnosed corticobasal degeneration. *Neurology* 1999; 53:795–800.

133. Litvan I, Agid Y, Goetz C, et al. Accuracy of the clinical diagnosis of corticobasal degeneration: A clinicopathologic study. *Neurology* 1997; 48:119–125.

134. Litvan I. Recent advances in atypical parkinsonian disorders. *Curr Opin Neurol* 1999; 12:441–446.

135. Litvan I, Grimes DA, Lang AE. Phenotypes and prognosis: Clinicopathologic studies of corticobasal degeneration. *Adv Neurol* 2000; 82:183–196.

136. Dickson DW. Neuropathologic differentiation of progressive supranuclear palsy and corticobasal degeneration. *J Neurol* 1999 ; 246(Suppl 2):II6–II15.

137. Dickson DW, Bergeron C, Chin SS, et al. Office of Rare Diseases neuropathologic criteria for corticobasal degeneration. *J Neuropathol Exp Neurol* 2002; 61:935–946.

138. Feany MB, Dickson DW. Widespread cytoskeletal pathology characterizes corticobasal degeneration. *Am J Pathol* 1995; 146:1388–1396.

139. Komori T. Tau-positive glial inclusions in progressive supranuclear palsy, corticobasal degeneration and Pick's disease. *Brain Pathol* 1999; 9:663–679.

140. Steele JC. Parkinsonism-dementia complex of Guam. *Mov Disord* 2005; 20(Suppl 12): S99–S107.

141. Steele JC, Caparros-Lefebvre D, Lees AJ, et al. Progressive supranuclear palsy and its relation to pacific foci of the parkinsonism-dementia complex and Guadeloupean parkinsonism. *Parkinsonism Relat Disord* 2002; 9:39–54.

142. Kuzuhara S, Kokubo Y. Atypical parkinsonism of Japan: Amyotrophic lateral sclerosis-parkinsonism-dementia complex of the Kii peninsula of Japan (Muro disease): An update. *Mov Disord* 2005; 20(Suppl 12):S108–S113.

143. Hirano A, Kurland LT, Krooth RS, et al. Parkinsonism-dementia complex, an endemic disease on the island of Guam. I. Clinical features. *Brain* 1961; 84:642–661.

144. Hof PR, Perl DP, Loerzel AJ, et al. Neurofibrillary tangle distribution in the cerebral cortex of parkinsonism-dementia cases from Guam: Differences with Alzheimer's disease. *Brain Res* 1991; 564:306–313.

145. Buee-Scherrer V, Buee L, Hof PR, et al. Neurofibrillary degeneration in amyotrophic lateral sclerosis/parkinsonism-dementia complex of Guam. Immunochemical characterization of tau proteins. *Am J Pathol* 1995; 146:924–932.

146. Morris HR, Lees AJ, Wood NW. Neurofibrillary tangle parkinsonian disorders: Tau pathology and tau genetics. *Mov Disord* 1999; 14:731–736.

147. Reid AH, McCall S, Henry JM, et al. Experimenting on the past: The enigma of von Economo's encephalitis lethargica. *J Neuropathol Exp Neurol* 2001; 60:663–670.

148. Geddes JF, Hughes AJ, Lees AJ, et al. Pathological overlap in cases of parkinsonism associated with neurofibrillary tangles. A study of recent cases of postencephalitic parkinsonism and comparison with progressive supranuclear palsy and Guamanian parkinsonism-dementia complex. *Brain* 1993; 116(Pt 1):281–302.

149. Buee-Scherrer V, Buee L, Leveugle B, et al. Pathological tau proteins in postencephalitic parkinsonism: Comparison with Alzheimer's disease and other neurodegenerative disorders. *Ann Neurol* 1997; 42:356–359.

150. Mizukami K, Sasaki M, Shiraishi H, et al. A neuropathologic study of long-term, Economo-type postencephalitic parkinsonism with a prolonged clinical course. *Psychiatry Clin Neurosci* 1996; 50:79–83.

151. McKeith IG, Dickson DW, Lowe J, et al. Diagnosis and management of dementia with Lewy bodies: Third report of the DLB Consortium. *Neurology* 2005; 65:1863–1872.

152. Kosaka K, Yoshimura M, Ikeda K, et al. Diffuse type of Lewy body disease: Progressive dementia with abundant cortical Lewy bodies and senile changes of varying degree--A new disease? *Clin Neuropathol* 1984; 3:185–192.

21 Neurochemistry

Jose Martin Rabey
Richard Stanley Burns

ANATOMY OF THE BASAL GANGLIA AND RELATED CIRCUITS

The motor features of Parkinson's disease (PD) result from altered functions of the basal ganglia (see Chapter 22). The basal ganglia include the caudate nucleus and putamen (collectively referred to as the striatum), the globus pallidus [pars interna and pars externa (Gpi and Gpe)], the subthalamic nucleus (STN), and the substantia nigra [pars reticulata and pars compacta (SNr and SNc)] (1). Other structures that are integrated into the basal ganglia circuitry and play an important role in extrapyramidal motor function include the premotor cortex, primary motor cortex, and thalamus. A somatotopic organization of motor function exists within this circuitry (2) (Figure 21-1).

The principal afferents to the basal ganglia arising from extrinsic neuronal groups include projections from the neocortex to the caudate and putamen, from the thalamus to the striatum, from the locus ceruleus to the SN, and from the raphe nuclei to the striatum and SN. The principal efferent pathways from the basal ganglia to external neuronal groups project from the Gpi and SNr to the thalamus and from the SNr to the superior colliculus, brainstem reticular formation, and spinal cord. Intrinsic connections between basal ganglia structures include projections from the striatum to both segments of

the globus pallidus and reciprocal connections between the SN and the striatum. In addition, the STN receives afferents from the Gpe and projects to both the Gpi and the SNr (3). The principal intrinsic and extrinsic connections of the nerve cell groups that comprise the basal ganglia and their neurotransmitters are depicted in Figure 21-2.

The input to the putamen from the neocortex is excitatory, with glutamate as the neurotransmitter. The putamen, in turn, projects to the Gpi via the "direct" and "indirect" pathways. The direct pathway from the putamen to the Gpi involves the neurotransmitters gamma-aminobutyric acid (GABA)–substance P (Sub P) and is considered to be primarily inhibitory in nature. The indirect pathway is more complex and involves 2 other nuclei, the Gpe and STN. The primary projection from the putamen to the Gpe via GABA-enkephalin neurons and the secondary projection from the Gpe to the STN via GABA neurons are both inhibitory in nature. The tertiary projection from the STN to the Gpi is excitatory and involves glutamatergic neurons. The output from the Gpi to the thalamus occurs via inhibitory GABAergic neurons. The thalamus, in turn, projects to the cortex via excitatory glutamatergic neurons (4). Dopaminergic neurons from the SNc project to the putamen, leading to excitation of D1 receptors on the striatal output neurons. These are the origin of the direct pathway as well as inhibition of

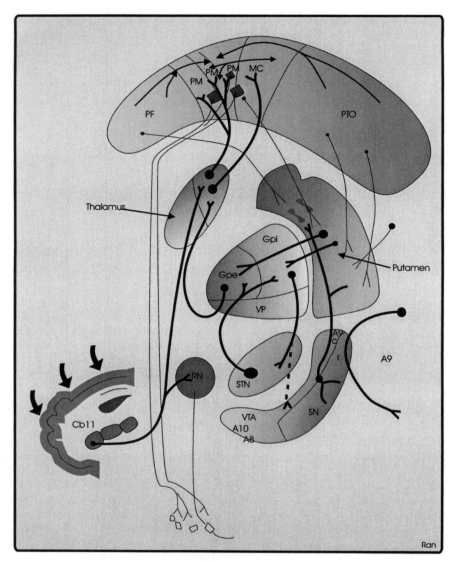

FIGURE 21-1

Schematic presentation of extrapyramidal motor system. Pallido-thalamo-cortical and cerebello-thalamo-cortical pathways in heavy lines. Also shown in heavy lines are inputs to globus pallidus from the striatum and the putamen and the pallido-subthalamo-pallidal loop. MC, motor cortex; PM, premotor cortex; PF, prefrontal cortex; PTO, parieto-temporo-occipital association cortex; GP, globus pallidus; SN, substantia nigra AQ, dopaminergic cells comprising substantia nigra compacta; STN, subthalamic nucleus; RN red nucleus; VP ventral pallidus; VTH ventral tegmental area; Cbll, cerebellum.

D2 receptors on the striatal output neurons of the indirect pathway to Gpe; thus they modulate activity in both pathways (see Figure 21-2).

DOPAMINERGIC SYSTEMS

Several dopaminergic pathways have been identified in the central nervous system. One of the most important heterogeneous populations of dopaminergic cells is located

in the midbrain (it is estimated that in humans there are about 450,000 cells on each side of the brainstem) (5–7). On the basis of retrograde tracing techniques (8), the dopaminergic systems that have been identified include the following:

1. Ultrashort systems such as the interplexiform amacrine-like neurons located in the outer plexiform layers of the retina and the periglomerular dopamine (DA) cells of the olfactory bulb

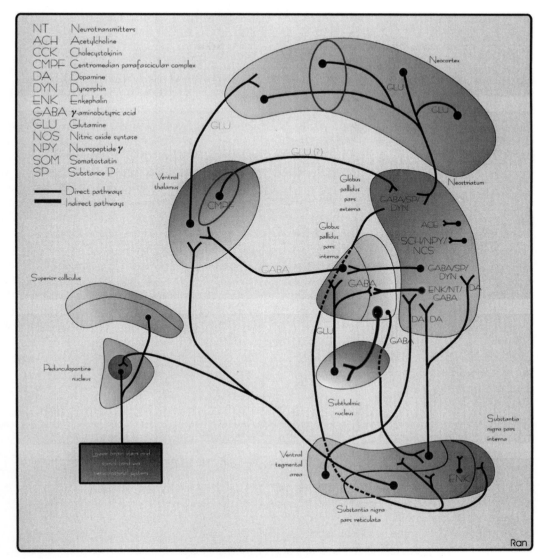

FIGURE 21-2

Neurochemical anatomy of the neostriatum.

2. Intermediate-length systems
   a. The tuberoinfundibular DA cells that project from the arcuate and periventricular nuclei to the intermediate lobe of the hypophysis and the median eminence (the tuberoinfundibular dopaminergic system)
   b. The incertohypothalamic neurons that link the dorsal and posterior hypothalamus with the dorsal anterior hypothalamus and lateral septal nuclei
   c. The medullary periventricular group, which includes those DA cells in the dorsal motor nucleus of the vagus, the nucleus tractus solitarius, and the cells dispersed in the tegmental radiation of the periaqueductal gray matter

3. Long-length systems, which include the long projections linking the ventral tegmental and SN dopaminergic cells with three principal sets of target nuclei
   a. The neostriatum (caudate nucleus and putamen)
   b. The limbic cortex (medial prefrontal, cingulate, and entorhinal areas)
   c. Other limbic structures (septum, olfactory tubercle, nucleus accumbens septi, amygdala complex, and piriform cortex)

The first of the long-length systems is referred to as the nigrostriatal dopaminergic system and the latter two are the mesocortical and mesolimbic dopaminergic systems, respectively.

DOPAMINE METABOLISM

The conversion of L-tyrosine to L-dihydroxyphenylalanine (L-dopa) by the enzyme tyrosine hydroxylase (TH) is the rate-limiting step in DA synthesis. Dopa is subsequently converted to DA by the enzyme L-aromatic amino acid decarboxylase (LAAD) (Figure 21-3).

Several endogenous mechanisms that involve modulation of the TH activity have been identified for the regulation of DA synthesis. DA and other catecholamines act as end-product inhibitors of TH by competing with the cofactor tetrahydrobiopterin (BH-4) for its binding site on the enzyme. The availability of BH-4 also plays a role in the regulation of TH activity. TH exists in 2 kinetic forms that exhibit different affinities for BH-4. The conversion of TH from the low- to high-affinity form involves phosphorylation of the enzyme. Presynaptic DA receptors also modulate TH activity. These receptors (autoreceptors) are activated by DA released from the nerve terminals, resulting in feedback inhibition of DA synthesis. DA synthesis also depends on the rate of impulse flow in the nigrostriatal pathway. During increased impulse flow, TH activity is increased primarily through kinetic activation of TH, which increases its affinity for BH-4 and decreases its affinity for the normal end-product inhibitor DA.

DOPAMINE, NEUROMELANIN, AND TYROSINE HYDROXYLASE

Once synthesized, DA is sequestered in storage vesicles. The membrane of these vesicles contains a high-affinity, energy-dependent (Na^+-pump), carrier-mediated transport system that concentrates DA within the vesicles. The release of DA from the vesicles at synaptic terminals occurs by a Ca^{2+}-dependent mechanism. DA released into the synaptic cleft can interact with specific membrane-bound, cell surface receptors (DA receptors) on a postsynaptic neuron (postsynaptic heteroreceptors) or on the same neuron from which it is released (autoreceptors). DA released into the synaptic cleft is inactivated primarily by a high-affinity, stereospecific, carrier-mediated reuptake process (dopamine transporter). The membrane carrier is capable of transporting DA in either direction, depending on the existing concentration gradient. The DA transporter plays an important physiologic role in the inactivation and recycling of DA released into the synaptic cleft.

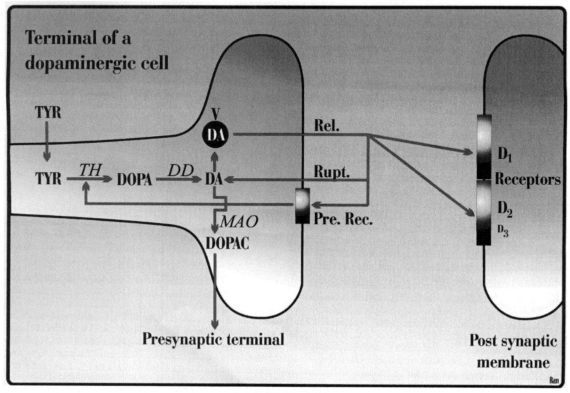

FIGURE 21-3

Diagram of a dopaminergic terminal. TYR, tyrosine; DOPA, 3, 4-dihydroxyphenylalanine; DA, dopamine; TH, tyrosine hydroxylase; DD, dopa-decarboxylase; V, vesicles; REL, release; RUPT, reuptake; PRE REC, presynaptic receptor; PFR, presynaptic feedback regulation; DOPAC, 3, 4-dihydroxphenylacetic acid; MAO, monoamine oxidase.

Considering that platelets are a relatively good peripheral model for the study of catecholaminergic cells, Rabey et al. (9) studied DA incorporation by platelet granules in PD patients. DA incorporation into the platelet granules was found to be altered in naive PD patients and partially improved after treatment with levodopa.

After its reuptake into nerve terminals, DA is inactivated by enzymatic conversion to dihydroxyphenylacetic acid (DOPAC) by the action of monoamine oxidase, type B (MAO-B), located within the mitochondria. Released DA that diffuses out of the synapse is converted to homovanillic acid (HVA) outside the neuron by the sequential action of catechol-O-methyltransferase (COMT) and MAO; both enzymes are located primarily in glial cells. The principal metabolite of DA in humans is HVA in its free form, which results from the deamination and 3-O-methylation of DA and the 3-O-methylation of DOPAC at an extraneuronal site (5).

Since the levels of L-tyrosine in the brain are relatively high (above the Km for tyrosine hydroxylase), it is not feasible to increase DA synthesis in the brain by increasing the availability of L-tyrosine. The activity of LAAD in dopaminergic neurons is very high under normal conditions and, as a result, levodopa levels in the brain are negligible. LAAD is also present in nondopaminergic neurons such as serotonergic neurons (5). Exogenous levodopa is converted to DA within dopaminergic neurons by LAAD; the activity of LAAD in DA terminals within the striatum remains relatively high in PD.

Exogenous levodopa is transported across the endothelial cells of cerebral vessels (the blood-brain barrier) into the brain by the L-transport system for neutral amino acids. The L-system is stereospecific, bidirectional, saturable, and competitively inhibited. The L-system is also involved in the transport of other L-neutral amino acids including phenylalanine, tyrosine, tryptophan, leucine, isoleucine, methionine, valine, and histadine. Blockade of the motor effects of levodopa by the ingestion of proteins containing these other amino acids is thought to occur at the blood-brain barrier by competitive inhibition (10, 11).

The existence of morphologic changes in the SN, consisting primarily of neuronal loss combined with decreased neuromelanin, had already been described in PD in the first half of the twentieth century (12, 13). In 1957, DA was discovered to be a neurotransmitter in the brain by Carlsson et al. (14, 15), who applied a newly developed histofluorescence method. This finding was important for the future isolation of DA in human postmortem brains (16) and for the identification of the loss of DA in the striatum in PD (16) (Table 21-1). Shortly

TABLE 21-1

DA and HVA Concentration in Selected Brain Regions in Parkinsonian Patients and Controls

	DA	HVA	DA/HVA
Putamen[†]			
Controls	5.06 ± 0.39 (17)	4.92 ± 0.32 (16)	1.03
PD patients	0.14 ± 0.13 (3)	0.54 ± 0.13 (3)	0.26
Caudate nucleus[†]			
Controls	4.06 ± 0.47 (18)	2.92 ± 0.37 (19)	1.39
PD patients	0.2 ± 0.19 (3)	1.19 ± 0.10 (3)	0.17
Nucleus accumbens[‡]			
Controls	3.79 ± 0.82 (8)	4.38 ± 0.64 (8)	0.86
PD patients	1.61 ± 0.28 (4)	3.13 ± 0.13 (3)	0.51
Parolfactory gyrus[‡]			
Controls	0.35 ± 0.09 (4)	0.98 (2)	0.35
PD patients	< 0.03 (2)		
Lateral hypothalamus[¶]			
Controls	0.51 ± 0.08 (4)	1.96 ± 0.28 (3)	0.26
PD patients	< 0.03 (2)	1.03 ± 0.23 (3)	
Substantia nigra[§][¶]			
Controls	0.46 ± (13)	2.32 (7)	0.20
PD patients	0.07 (10)	0.41 (9)	0.17

*Results are expressed as mean ± SEM; numbers of cases are in parentheses.
[†]Ref. 22.
[‡]Ref. 122.
[§]Ref. 121.
[¶]Ref. 123.

after that discovery, Birkmayer and Hornykiewicz (18, 19) reported that intravenous DOPA (the racemic mixture of L-and D-dopa),the amino acid precursor of DA, was able to substantially reduce the symptoms of PD. Monoamine oxidase (MAO) inhibitors intensified the effects, and later D-dopa (the dextrorotatory isomer) and 5-hydroxytryptophan (5-HTP) were found to be ineffective. Together, these findings demonstrated that DA was the primary neurotransmitter in the nigrostriatal tract, and they gave a clearer picture about the biochemical characteristics of PD as a disease of dopamine depletion.

A link between the vulnerability of nigral neurons and their prominent pigmentation, although long suspected, was not proven until Hirsch et al. (20) performed a quantitative analysis of neuromelanin-containing neurons in the midbrain in control and PD brains. He and his colleagues demonstrated that DA-containing cell groups in the normal human midbrain differ markedly from each other in the percentage of neuromelanin contained in the neurons. In addition, they showed a significant positive correlation between the cell loss in different brainstem nuclei and the percentage of neuromelanin-containing neurons normally present in those nuclei. They also demonstrated that in PD there was a relative sparing of nonpigmented neurons compared to pigmented neurons within each cell group. This evidence suggested a "selective vulnerability of the neuromelanin-pigmented subpopulation of DA-containing mesencephalic neurons in PD" (20).

The loss of dopaminergic neurons in the nigrostriatal pathway follows an identifiable topographic pattern: the decrease of DA is greater in the rostral than caudal striatum (21), and the putamen is more severely affected than the caudate nucleus (17). This finding is thought to be related to the fact that cell loss is more severe in the caudal and internal portions of the SN that preferentially project to the putamen.

The degree of neuronal loss in the SN correlates with the loss of activity of TH in the striatum (Table 21-2) (22, 23). These changes are associated with a marked decrease in the DA and its metabolites, DOPAC and HVA, in the striatum. The loss of DA is more pronounced than that of HVA (23). It is generally considered that DA loss in the striatum must be reduced by about 70% to 80% before PD motor symptoms (akinesia, rigidity, rest tremor) become apparent.

The loss of TH activity is one of the most prominent pathologic and neurochemical findings in PD. Because TH is highly localized in catecholamine neurons, it is often utilized as a specific marker for DA neurons. Biochemical

TABLE 21-2

*Enzyme Activities in Selected Brain Areas from Parkinsonian Patients and Controls**

Brain Region	Tyrosine Hydroxylase (TH)	Dopa Decarboxylase (DDC)	Catechol-O-Methyltransferase (COMT)	Monoamine Oxidase (MAO)
Putamen				
Control	17.4 ± 2.4 (3)	432 ± 109 (18)	24.1 ± 2.5 (11)	1520 ± 127 (11)
PD patients	3.1 ± 1.2 (3)†	32 ± 7 (13)‡	19.8 ± 3.7 (9)	1648 ± 128 (10)
Caudate nucleus				
Control	18.7 ± 2.0 (3)	364 ± 95 (19)	25.4 ± 2.8 (10)	1726 ± 149 (10)
PD patients	3.2 ± 0.5 (2)†	54 ± 14 (13)‡	17.8 ± 3.8 (9)	1742 ± 197 (10)
Substantia nigra				
Control	17.4 (1)	549 ± 294 (15)	26.4 ± 4.7 (5)	1828 ± 200 (5)
PD patients	6.1 ± 1.5 (3)	21 ± 6 (10)	21.7 ± 10.2 (9)	1477 ± 284 (4)
Frontal cortex				
Control	3.7 (2)	32 ± 4 (6)	24.1 ± 4.4 (9)	
PD patients	2.5 ± 0.2 (3)	10 ± 2 (3)†	28.7 ± 4.1 (7)	
Hypothalamus				
Control	4.4 (2)	149 ± 53 (9)	29.4 ± 4.5 (3)	
PD patients	2.7 (2)	63 ± 17 (5)		

TH: (nmol/CO_2/30 min/100 mg protein); DDC: (nmol/CO_2/2 hr/100 mg protein); COMT: (nmol/NMN/hr 100 mg protein); MAO: (nmol/PPA/30 min/100 mg protein).
*Results are expressed as mean ± SEM; numbers of cases shown in parentheses.
†Differs from control $P < 0.02$.
‡Differs from control $P < 0.01$.
Source: Birkmayer and Hornykiewicz (18). With permission.

analysis and immunocytochemistry with TH have shown a substantial loss of TH staining in the ventral tegmental area (VTA) and in the nucleus paranigralis as well as the SN (25–27).

PROTEIN SYNTHESIS

In PD, a disturbance in protein synthesis in the SN and locus ceruleus has been demonstrated (28) and histologic studies indicate that this may be an important component in its pathogenesis (29). The loss of TH activity seems to be due to reduced TH protein synthesis. The hypothesis suggesting a role for TH in the pathophysiology of PD is supported by the findings indicating that TH antisera stain Lewy bodies in catecholaminergic neurons (30).

Cyclic adenosine monophosphate (cAMP)–dependent protein kinase activity is reduced in the brains of patients with PD (31). Moreover, TH synthesis measured in the putamen from PD patients shows supersensitivity to stimulation by this cAMP-dependent protein kinase in vitro (32). These findings and the increase in histones H1, H2B, and H4 in the SN but not in the striatum and frontal cortex indicate disturbances in protein phosphorylation and protein synthesis in that region. It appears that degeneration of dopaminergic neurons is connected to a reduction in the transcription rate, as indicated by the increase in histones (33). It also seems likely that protein synthesis in the central nervous system is influenced by synaptic activity—that is, the stimulatory capacity of adenylate cyclase–dependent processes. Functional disturbances at the synaptic level are thought to cause changes in the conformation of chromatin and a reduction in the transcription rate and RNA content, with changes in the ratio of RNA to DNA (34). These processes show an age-dependent decline, with increased vulnerability over time.

LEVODOPA TOXICITY TO AMINERGIC NEURONS

Dopamine-replacement therapy with the precursor levodopa is highly effective in ameliorating the motor signs and symptoms in the early stages of PD and in improving the quality of life and survival of treated patients. Moreover, it provides superior benefit to all other currently available therapies. (35).

However, over recent decades a substantial literature has suggested that levodopa may be toxic to aminergic cells in vitro (36–38). The most common explanation for this phenomenon is that levodopa augments oxidative stress via the production of quinones, hydrogen peroxide, and oxyradicals. Evidence of the existence of oxidative stress in the SN includes a reduction of reduced

glutathione, increased levels of malondialdehyde and lipid hydroperoxides, oxidative DNA and protein damage, oxidative (nitrative) modifications of α-synuclein, and reduced mitochondrial complex I activity. Moreover, the rotenone and 1-methyl-4-phenyl-1,2,3,6-tetrahydropiridine (MPTP) animal models of PD appear to be derived from oxidative stress (39–41). Because the dopaminergic neurons in patients with PD are already under stressful conditions, which apparently contribute to neuronal death, enhancement of oxyradical formation through levodopa therapy would enhance the derangement of these neurons. The main criticism of these conclusions is that in a majority of these in vitro studies, investigations were conducted under conditions not typically exhibited "in vivo". For example, the concentrations of levodopa used were higher than the peak plasma or brain concentrations observed in treated PD patients (42). In addition, glial cells, whose high concentration of antioxidants and trophic factors combats the effect of reactive oxygen species, were absent from the culture system. To address these issues, in vitro experiments were repeated, using concentrations of levodopa found in vivo and in the presence of glial cells. The data reported from these studies (43–45) showed the opposite effect: levodopa was not toxic; but in the presence of glial cells, the dopaminergic neurons were actually protected by levodopa.

To further examine this issue of levodopa toxicity a recent clinical trial (ELLDOPA) made a direct comparison between the rate of PD progression in those patients treated with levodopa (150, 300, or 600 mg/day) and those given placebo (46). From a clinical perspective, this study showed that levodopa does not hasten the progression of PD. As expected, the smaller doses of levodopa provided less clinical benefit than the higher doses. However, the higher dose (600 mg/day) was associated with the onset of dyskinesias in 16% of patients, one of the fundamental limitations associated with traditional levodopa therapy. Moreover, results of neuroimaging studies [using B-CIT putaminal uptake by single photon emission computed tomography (SPECT)] indicated that levodopa treatment was associated with a greater rate of decline in dopamine binding than seen in the placebo group, a possible biomarker of nigrostriatal function. The question of this being related to levodopa toxicity or a long term pharmacological effect of the drug still needs to be elucidated.

The overall question of possible toxic effects of levodopa on the dopaminergic system remains unresolved (47). Two additional studies examining the effects of dopamine agonists versus levodopa in which functional neuroimaging techniques were utilized addressed the question further. Both pramipexole vs. levodopa (CALM-PD) and ropinirole vs. levodopa (REAL-PD) suggested that levodopa could accelerate the demise of dopaminergic neurons. In the CALM-PD (48) study, researchers used

SPECT to examine striatal dopamine transporter (DAT) activity (B-CIT uptake) as a marker for intact striatal dopaminergic nerve terminals. In this 4-year study. it was found that the groups assigned to early levodopa showed a more rapid rate of decline of beta CIT uptake compared with early pramipexole treatment. On the other hand, the results of this study also showed that levodopa was more effective than pramipexole in reducing the clinical signs of PD (49). Similar results were shown in the REAL-PET trial, which used positron emission tomography (PET) to look at putaminal ^{18}F accumulation as a marker for functional dopaminergic terminals. This study showed a more rapid rate of reduction of ^{18}F accumulation in patients who were initially treated with levodopa vs. ropinirole (50) but a better clinical response with levodopa. The main criticism raised concerning these studies is that there was no placebo group in either one. As a consequence, it can be inferred that dopamine agonists slow the progression of PD, levodopa accelerates the progression of PD, or both. Another unresolved question is whether levodopa or dopamine agonists have direct pharmacologic effects on DAT or L-aromatic amino acid (dopa) decarboxylase, which may confound the interpretation of the results. As a consequence of these criticisms, we must interpret studies that use imaging markers to document neuroprotection with caution until these issues are resolved (51, 52).

Neurologists who support using levodopa as first-line therapy argue that is inappropriate to withhold the most potent symptomatic treatment for PD in the absence of human studies supporting the toxic levodopa theory (53, 54).

DOPAMINE METABOLITES

The metabolites of DA (DOPAC and HVA) are decreased in the SN and the striatum in PD (22, 24, 55). However, they are reduced to a lesser degree than DA itself (56). This may in part be explained by two hypotheses: (a) Postmortem, DA diffuses from its storage sites and is subsequently catabolized by endogenous enzymes that are still active. MAO-A and MAO-B activity (the latter more specific for DA) and COMT activity are not affected by the disease (see Table 21-2). These enzymes are located primarily outside dopaminergic neurons. (b) There is an increase in the turnover of DA in surviving neurons (57).

Compensatory changes in dopaminergic neurotransmission in remaining Nissl cells with functional overactivity have been described. The ratio of HVA (concentration) to DA (content) (HVA/DA ratio) can be used as an index of the presynaptic activity of the surviving dopaminergic neurons. The level of HVA has been considered to be a good measure of the amount of DA released, and the density of the DA terminals is indicated by the DA content. Thus the HVA/DA ratio provides an index of the rate of DA turnover in the remaining dopaminergic nerve terminals. This has been confirmed by experimental lesions in animals. Partial nigral lesions in animals do not produce a significant change in the HVA/DA ratio; with lesions of 70% to 85%, changes in the release of DA from surviving dopaminergic nerve terminals are able to compensate functionally for the derangement. When lesions exceed 90%, surviving presynaptic DA neurons cannot compensate and DA receptors become hypersensitive and a change in behavioral response is observed (58, 59).

In PD, the HVA/DA ratio is significantly increased in the putamen, caudate nucleus, and nucleus accumbens but not in the hippocampus and frontal cortex (see Table 21-1). These findings suggest that the lesions of the mesocortical pathway are not severe enough to induce compensatory changes in DA turnover. Alternatively, DA neurons that project to the cortex and hippocampus, compared to the nigral DA neurons, lack the capability to increase their synthesis and turnover of DA (60).

LEVODOPA AND HOMOCYSTEINE

Elevated plasma homocysteine is an independent risk factor for systemic vascular diseases (including cardiac, cerebral, and peripheral vascular diseases and venous thrombosis) (61), cognitive impairment, and dementia (62, 63).

Several factors influence total homocysteine plasma levels. The most important are age, gender, caffeine intake, smoking, and poor vitamin B status.

Some drugs may also increase homocysteine concentration in the blood. Levodopa interferes with the metabolism of homocysteine as a consumer of methyl-groups in the transmethylation reaction (Figure 21-4). The enzyme COMT plays the key role, and S-adenosylmethionine serves as the methyl donor. When given with decarboxylase inhibitor, most of the levodopa is COMT-methylated to 3-OMD, thus increasing the level of homocysteine after the hydrolysis of S-adenosylhomocysteine (Figure 21-4). As a result, elevated levels of homocysteine have been found in PD patients treated with levodopa (64, 65). The clinical impact of the elevated homocysteine in PD patients is unknown. In many of these studies, the levels, though elevated when compared to controls, were still in the normal range.

It has been shown that the addition of entacapone, an effective COMT peripheral inhibitor, to levodopa, effectively reduces homocysteine levels in PD patients (66, 67).These findings may play a promising role in successfully controlling levodopa-induced hyperhomocysteinemia and in reducing the risk for diseases probably linked to it.

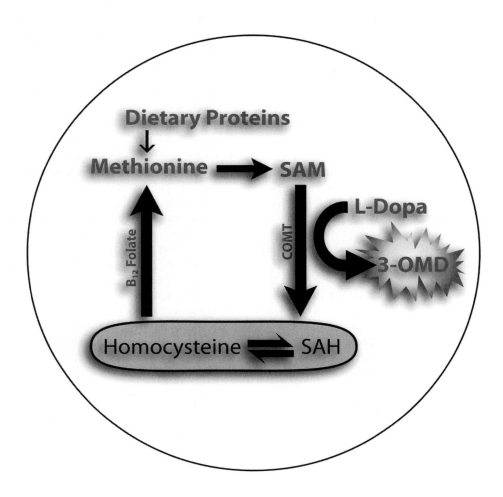

FIGURE 21-4

Pathway showing the effect of levodopa in homocysteine synthesis.

DOPAMINE RECEPTORS

Five distinct types of DA receptors (see Chapter 23) have been identified (68). They are classified into a D1-family (D1 and D5 receptors) and a D2-family (D2, D3, and D4 receptors) based on similarities in their structural and pharmacologic properties. The dopamine receptors consist of a polypeptide chain of 387 to 477 amino acids with variable carbohydrate chains and an overall size range of 90 to 120 kDa. They belong to the G protein–coupled receptor family with 7 transmembrane domains and G-protein coupling sites in the third cytoplasmic loop (see Figure 23-1). The subtypes of dopamine receptors differ in their extracellular and intracellular loops but are highly homologous in their transmembrane domains. The third cytoplasmic loop is short in the dopamine receptors, which belong to the D1-family and long in those that belong to the D2-family. The D1-family of dopamine receptors with a short third loop are coupled to stimulatory G proteins (Gs), which activate adenylate cyclase. The D2-family of dopamine receptors with a long third loop are coupled to Gi or Go proteins, which inhibit adenylate cyclase or are inactive, respectively, and to Gq proteins that couple with phospholipase C. As a general biochemical property, the D1-family of receptors stimulate adenylate cyclase, leading to an increase in the formation of cAMP, whereas the D2-family of dopamine receptors either inhibit adenylate cyclase (D2 receptor) or do not modify its activity (D3 and D4 receptors). The effects of the D2 receptor on second-messenger systems are complex and include an increase in phosphatidyl inositol metabolism, the release of arachnidonic acid, and the activation of K^+ channels in addition to the inhibition of adenylate cyclase.

The genes that code for the 5 subtypes of DA receptors are located on different chromosomes: D1 receptor at 5q34–35, D2 receptor at 11q22–23, D3 receptor at 3q13.3, and D4 and D5 receptors at 4p16. The genes that code for the D1-family of dopamine receptors have no introns, in contrast to the genes for the D2-family of receptors, which possess introns in their coding regions: the D2 receptor gene has 6 introns; the D3 receptor gene has 5 introns; and, the D4 receptor gene has 4 introns.

D1 receptors are present on striatal GABA-Sub P output neurons (which project to the Gpi and SNr—the "direct pathway") and at terminal regions of neurons in the SN. In contrast, D2 receptors are present on striatal GABA-enkephalin output neurons (which project to the Gpe—the "indirect pathway") and on DA neurons of the SNc (autoreceptors). The D1 and D2 receptors are the most abundant subtypes in the striatum; D3 receptors are expressed at low levels and D4 receptors at very low levels in the striatum (see Figure 23-2). Most of the DA receptors in the SNc are of the D2 subtype with a small number of the D3 subtype. All 5 subtypes of dopamine receptors are expressed in the cortex with a greater number of D4 and D5 receptors than of D3 receptors. The D3 receptor has the highest affinity (nM range) for the natural ligand DA.

D1 and D2 receptors are thought to play a central role in the motor disturbances in PD. The number of D2 receptors in the striatum has been found to be increased in the early stages of PD, while the number of D1 receptors remains unchanged in this disease. DA generated from exogenous levodopa acts at all of the DA receptor subtypes (69, 70).

DOPAMINE TRANSPORTER

Dopamine transporters terminate dopaminergic neurotransmission by actively pumping extracellular DA back into the presynaptic nerve terminal (Na^C and Cl-dependent) (71, 72). DA uptake is accomplished by a membrane carrier that is capable of transporting DA in either direction, depending on the concentration gradient.

A complementary DNA encoding a rat DA transporter (DAT) has been isolated with high sequence homology with the previously cloned norepinephrine and gamma-aminobutyric acid transporters. DAT is a 619–amino acid protein with 12 hydrophobic putative membrane-spanning domains and is a member of the family of Na/Cl-dependent plasma membrane transporters. Using the energy provided by the Na gradient generated by the Na/K-transporting ATPase, DAT recaptures DA soon after its release, modulating its concentration in the synapse and its time-dependent interaction with both pre-and postsynaptic DA receptors (73).

Studies of the binding of tritiated alpha-dihydrotetrabenazine ([3H] TBZOH) (a specific ligand for the vesicular monoamine transporter) in the striatum in postmortem brains from 49 controls and 57 PD patients suggested that parkinsonian symptoms appear when the degeneration of the striatal dopamine terminals is greater than 50% of normal innervation (74). The expression of the DA transporter messenger RNA (mRNA) assessed by in situ hybridization in individual pigmented neurons of the SNc in sections of the midbrain from 7 PD and 7 control brains showed that DA transporter mRNA expression in surviving SNc neurons was only 57% of normal control levels in PD (75). The authors speculate that the decrease in the level of DA transporter mRNA expression in the remaining neurons in the SNc of PD patients reflected neuronal dysfunction. They add, "conceivably it might also reflect differential vulnerability of those neurons that initially expressed higher levels of DA transporter to the insult of parkinsonism" (75).

DOPAMINE-MEDIATED REGULATION OF STRIATAL NEURONS

Although D1 and D2 receptors can have opposite effects on adenylate cyclase activity, it is clear that the physiologic significance of their interaction is more complex (5). Electrophysiologic experiments have suggested that D1 receptor activation is required for full postsynaptic expression of D2 effects. The interaction of the D1 receptor with other neurotransmitter systems is still not completely clear. The phosphoprotein DARPP-32(dopamine and cAMP–regulated phosphoprotein of 32 kDa), plays a key role in the biology of neurons under the influence of DA (Figure 21-5). By acting on the D1 receptors, DA stimulates adenylyl cyclase via a G protein to increase cAMP formation and the activity of cAMP-dependent protein kinase (protein kinase A, PKA) leads to phophorylation of DARPP-32 on a single threonin residue. Phophorylation converts this phosphoprotein into a potent inhibitor of protein phosphatase-1.

At least 2 intracellular pathways that decrease DARPP-32 phophorylation are involved in the modulation of dopamine signaling via D2 receptors. One mechanism involves inhibition of adenylyl cyclase, a decrease in cAMP, a decrease in the activity of PKA, and a decrease in DARPP32 phosphorylation. The other D2-mediated effect involves an increase in intracellular calcium and activation of calcineurin. One of the actions of calcineurin

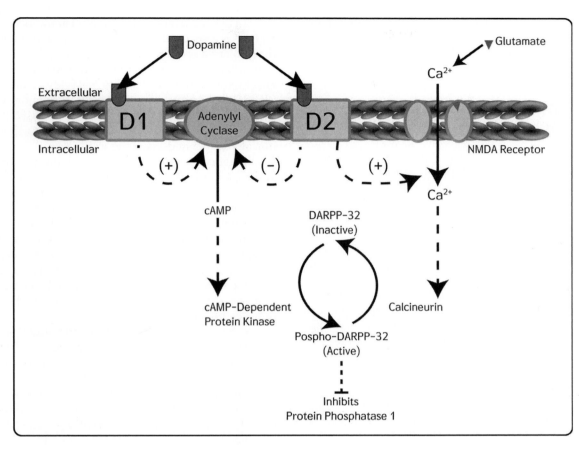

FIGURE 21-5

Proposed pathway by which dopamine and glutamate may regulate phosphorylation of the protein DARPP-32 in striatal cells.

is to dephosphorylate DARPP-32 and this relieves the inhibition of protein phosphatase-1.

Striationigral neurons receive glutamate input from the cerebral cortex as well as a rich dopamine innervation from the substantia nigra. Glutamate stimulates N-methyl-d-aspartate (NMDA) receptors, resulting in a large influx of calcium (see Figure 21-5). Thus, in this system, stimulation of NMDA receptors also results in activation of calcineurin and enhanced dephosphorylation of DARPP-32, producing an effect very similar to the stimulation of D2 receptors.

The physiologic action of DA is thought to be inhibitory in the striatum based on its effect on the firing frequency of dopamine-receptive neurons. Thus apparently DA applied iontophoretically in vivo or bath-applied DA in vitro predominantly decreases spontaneous or intracellular current, elicited firing frequency of striatal spiny neurons. This inhibition is probably mediated postsynaptically and occurs independently of membrane depolarization or hyperpolarization by D2 and D1 receptor agonists, respectively (7).

In addition, DA receptors exert a regulatory influence over glutamate-mediated "tone" in the striatum.

Thus activation of D2 receptors on cortical afferent terminals reduces cortically elicited excitatory postsynaptic potentials (ESPSs) recorded in spiny neurons (7). There is also evidence that D1-receptor agonists can attenuate glutamate-mediated transmission indirectly via the release of adenosine from postsynaptic neurons resulting in trans-synaptic feedback suppression of glutamate-mediated transmission (7).

It is known that D1- or D2-receptor agonists applied alone or simultaneously typically produce a reduction in membrane excitability of striatal spiny neurons. However, it appears that the D1 receptor-agonist–induced decrease in excitability can be reversed to a facilitation of spiking upon subsequent administration of D2 receptor agonist. Thus the response produced by the combined stimulation of D1- and D2-receptor agonists is dependent on the temporal sequence of agonist administration. This type of D1 receptor–dependent modulation of D2 receptor–mediated excitation is absent in slices taken from the DARPP-32 knockout mice, which suggests involvement of a G protein–mediated response via the cAMP-protein kinase cascade. One possible explanation to this finding might be that

D2-receptor activation can reverse the phophorylation of DARPP-32 proteins caused by D1-receptor activation, which decrease the inhibitory influence of this signaling pathway on spiny-neuron activity.(see Figure 21-5) (7).

NIGROSTRIATAL DOPAMINE SYSTEM AND PARKINSONIAN SYMPTOMS

Deficiency of DA in the striatum plays a major role in the development of motor symptoms of PD. However, it is unclear whether all of these symptoms result from DA deficiency alone or if other neurotransmitters are involved. A strong correlation has been demonstrated between the severity of akinesia, decrease in striatal DA, and degree of neuronal loss in the SN (24). Moreover, akinesia has been found to be more severe on the side of the body contralateral to the greatest degree of neuronal loss in the SN (24). Furthermore, this correlation has been demonstrated on ^{18}Fluorodopa PET (76). DA depletion may influences tremor but may not do so in isolation. Monkeys exhibiting rest tremor must have combined lesions of the nigrostriatal DA system and the rubro-olivocerebellar rubral loop (77). The role of the derangement of DA systems in the occurrence of rigidity is less clear (78). Rigidity is thought to result from hyperactive alpha motoneurons of supraspinal origin. The freezing gait appears to be, for the most part, unrelated to DA loss. It occurs randomly and does not respond to dopaminergic therapy. Later onset postural instability is another non-dopaminergic feaure that appears to be at least partially related to other transmitters.

OTHER NEUROTRANSMITTERS AND RECEPTORS

Other brainstem nuclei (locus ceruleus, raphe nuclei, nucleus basalis of Meynert) are affected in PD (79–82); these nuclei are the origin of the noradrenergic, serotonergic, and cholinergic systems, respectively.

Noradrenergic Systems

Two ascending noradrenergic pathways have been identified in the rat: a dorsal system originating in the locus ceruleus and projecting to the neocortex and the limbic forebrain (amygdala, septum, hippocampus) and a ventral system extending from the lower brainstem to the hypothalamus and the nucleus interstitialis terminalis. A descending noradrenergic pathway innervates the spinal cord (83). In human brain, the highest levels of norepinephrine (NE) are found in the nucleus accumbens and hypothalamus, with low levels in the cortex and undetectable amounts in the striatum, suggesting a similar organization in the rat and human brain (84).

In PD, the level of NE is reduced in the locus ceruleus, and this is associated with a loss of pigmented neurons and the formation of Lewy body inclusions. Moreover, NE concentrations in the neocortex, nucleus accumbens, amygdala, and hippocampus are 40% to 70% lower than normal (85, 86). In limbic regions, the level of the major metabolite of NE, 3-methoxy-4-hydroxyphenylglycol (MHPG), is also reduced (86). These changes taken together suggest that the dorsal NE system degenerates in PD.

Nagatsu et al. (87) reported a reduction in MHPG and dopamine beta-hydroxylase (DBH) activity (the enzyme that converts DA to NE in noradrenergic neurons) in the cerebrospinal fluid (CSF) of PD patients, suggesting a more general noradrenergic deficiency.

It has been hypothesized that depressive features commonly observed in PD patients may be related to a central NE deficiency (88). This is supported by the finding that administration of NE reuptake blockers (89, 90) improves depression in some of these patients. This finding requires further study.

It has been postulated that NE might impact on the motor system through a dual effect, indirectly via the modulation of the activity of dopaminergic cells (91) and directly. For example, freezing episodes have been attributed directly to a deficiency of NE. This was initially corroborated by reports that freezing was alleviated by the administration of dihydroxyphenylserine (DOPS), a specific precursor of NE (92). However, this observation has not been replicated.

Serotonergic Systems

Two major serotonergic systems exist in the central nervous system: an ascending pathway from the mesencephalic raphe nuclei to the forebrain and a descending pathway from the pontine raphe nuclei to the spinal cord (93). The highest concentrations of serotonin (5HT) and its metabolite, 5-hydroxyindole acetic acid (5-HIAA), are found in the SN, striatum, amygdala, and spinal cord. The levels are lower in the neocortex and hippocampus (94).

In PD, 5HT concentrations are reduced in the basal ganglia, hipppocampus, cerebral cortex, lumbar spinal cord, and hypothalamus (72). These biochemical changes are not uniformly distributed, reflecting selective damage to some cell groups in the raphe nuclei (72). In the caudate nucleus and frontal cortex, 5HT itself (a marker of serotonergic nerve terminals) is reduced more than 5-HIAA (a marker of 5HT metabolism). The increase in the 5-HIAA/5HT ratio probably reflects a compensatory increase in the turnover of 5HT in surviving serotonergic neurons, similar to that seen with DA.

Although DA transmission in both the SN and the striatum are known to be under the inhibitory control of ascending serotonergic systems, at the present time there is no evidence of a relationship between the motor symptoms of parkinsonism and the changes in the serotonergic systems. However, some reports suggest that low 5HT levels might play a role in the occurrence of depression in PD. Lower levels of 5-HIAA were found in the CSF of PD patients with depression compared to that seen in subjects without depression (95).

Cholinergic Systems

The cholinergic system can be divided into groups of short neurons intrinsic to particular brain regions (i.e., basal ganglia and cortex) and long fiber systems extending from the brainstem and basal forebrain to subcortical and cortical regions. In the striatum, acetylcholine (ACh) is released predominantly by the large spiny interneurons. The principal cholinergic fibers projecting to forebrain areas (olfactory bulb, hippocampus, amygdala, thalamus, cortex) emanate from large neurons with long axons from several locations. The fibers innervating the neocortex originate mainly in the substantia innominata, in particular the nucleus basalis of Meynert, but there is also input from the mesencephalic nuclei (pedunculopontine nucleus). The fibers innervating the hippocampus are located in the septum (96).

Studies in animals indicate that the nigrostriatal dopaminergic neurons make synapses with cholinergic interneurons in the striatum, inhibiting their activity (97–99). Choline acetyltransferase (CAT), a marker of cholinergic neurons, does not seem to be affected in PD (100). Therefore, it is generally accepted that the striatal cholinergic neurons are released from the inhibitory influence of dopaminergic neurons in PD and, as a consequence, are hyperactive. The effects of degeneration of the nigrostriatal dopaminergic projection neurons would be counterbalanced by the use of anticholinergic drugs. This was demonstrated long ago in clinical practice. The therapeutic effects of muscarinic receptor antagonists in PD are thought to be due to inhibition of M1 receptor–mediated excitation of striatal GABA-enkephalin neurons (which project via the indirect pathway to the Gpe) and of M4 receptor–mediated inhibition of GABA–Sub P neurons (which project via the direct pathway to the Gpi and SNr) (101).

Several studies have demonstrated severe neuronal loss and subnormal CAT activity in the substantia innominata (especially the nucleus basalis of Meynert) in PD, supporting the contention that the innominatocortical cholinergic system is deranged in PD associated with cognitive impairment (102, 103). More intriguing is the fact that a diffuse cortical cholinergic deficiency has also been found in PD patients without mental deterioration (mainly in the frontal and occipital lobes) (103, 104). This fact suggests that degeneration of subcortical cholinergic systems might precede the appearance of intellectual impairment in PD. Subnormal levels of CAT activity have also been described in the septohippocampal cholinergic system and

in the pedunculpontine nucleus (105). The significance of this diffuse degeneration of cholinergic neurons in the basal forebrain in PD is not clearly understood.

Gabaergic Systems

Long GABAergic striatopallidal, striatonigral, pallidothalamic pathways, and intrinsic striatal GABAergic neurons have been identified using an assay that measures the activity of the GABA-synthesizing enzyme glutamate decarboxylase (GAD) (106) (see Figures 21-1 and 21-2).

Although some studies have been inconclusive regarding the integrity of GABAergic systems in PD (107–109); others, using brain samples that were carefully matched for age and pre- and postmortem conditions, have found no significant changes in the content of GABA in brain of PD (110).

The critical issue concerning the GABAergic system is whether GABA turnover is altered, and if so, in which neuronal groups. It would be unlikely, however, that up- or downregulation of GABA activity might occur as a consequence of DA depletion in the striatum.

Adenosine A2A Receptor

The adenosine A2A receptor, 1 of 4 cloned adenosine receptors, is a member of the G protein–coupled receptor family; when activated, it stimulates adenylate cyclase. It is highly concentrated in the striatum; it colocalizes with D2 receptors on striatal GABA-enkephalin output neurons and is present on striatal cholinergic interneurons. The adenosine A2A receptor is thought to modulate the neuronal activity of striatal GABA-enkephalin output neurons, which project to the Gpe via the indirect pathway. Striatal GABA-enkephalin neurons are excited by inputs from cortical glutamatergic neurons and cholinergic interneurons and inhibited by inputs from nigral dopaminergic neurons via D2 receptors and recurrent neurons and collaterals via GABA receptors. Antagonism at the adenosine A2A receptor is thought to result in a decrease in the stimulation of GABA-enkephalin output neurons by striatal cholinergic interneurons and an increase in the GABA-mediated recurrent inhibition of these neurons. Antagonist activity at adenosine A2A receptors in the striatum might effectively compensate for the lack of dopamine-mediated inhibition of these neurons in PD (111).

Neuropeptides

The distribution of neuropeptides in the brain is heterogeneous. Cholecystokinin-8 (CCK-8) and vasointestinal peptide (VIP) are most abundant in cortical areas, whereas methionine (Met) and leucine (Leu) enkephalins, Substance P, and thyrotropin-releasing factor (TRH) are most abundant in the basal ganglia (112). Subnormal concentrations of various neuropeptides have been reported in various brain regions in PD using radioimmunoassay (RIA) methods. These changes have not always been confirmed by immunocytochemical techniques (113). The role of these peptides in the symptomatology of PD is not clear.

Hokfelt et al. (114) reported that CCK-8 is colocalized with DA in dopaminergic neurons in the SNc and the VTA. The level of CCK-8 in the SNc has been found to be decreased by 30% in PD subjects. However, normal levels of CCK-8 have been found (115) in the caudate nucleus, putamen, amygdala, cerebral cortex, and hippocampus using RIA methods. The decrease in CCK-8 in the SN might result from selective degeneration of CCK-8–containing neurons or of CCK8 afferent fibers of unknown origin. The functional consequences of the nigral CCK-8 deficiency are not known. This peptide apparently has an excitatory effect on nigral dopaminergic neurons (116). However, CCK-8 has also been shown to decrease DA release in the striatum (117).

Mauborgne et al. (118) reported reduced Substance P levels in the basal ganglia in PD based on the RIA method (3). Grafe et al. (119), using an immunocytochemical technique, did not confirm these findings. If confirmed, the observed decrease in Substance P concentrations might indicate a change in the turnover rate due to the loss of regulatory input from depaminergic cell loss rather than the primary loss of Substance P–containing neurons.

The highest concentration of dynorphin in the brain is found in the SN (120). Its levels are unchanged in PD (120).

Met-enkephalin levels are reduced by 70% in the SN and VTA and by 30 to 40% in the putamen and globus pallidus in PD. They are similar to controls in the nucleus accumbens, caudate nucleus, amygdala, cerebral cortex, and hippocampus (121, 122). If Met-enkephalin modulates the activity of DA neurons in the SN, changes in its levels might influence the turnover of DA at the cell body level. In PD, Leu-enkephalin levels are reduced by 30% to 40% in the putamen and the globus pallidus. However, in the SN and VTA, the concentrations of this peptide are similar to control values (122).

Somatostatin levels in the basal ganglia of PD patients are similar to those of control subjects (123). However, in demented PD subjects, somatostatin levels are reduced in the frontal cortex, entorhinal cortex, and hippocampus when compared to nondemented PD patients.

At present there are not enough data to support the hypothesis that an alteration in the concentration of neuropeptides plays a primary role in the pathogenesis of PD.

LEWY BODIES

The chemical composition of the Lewy body is complex. The classic cytoplasmic, eosinophilic inclusions found in brainstem nuclei are composed mainly of neurofilament

proteins and ubiquitin. In addition to all three molecular forms of neurofilament proteins (NF-H; NF-M; NF-L) in both the phosphorylated and nonphosphorylated state, Lewy bodies have been found to contain protein kinases (Ca^{2+}-calmodulin-dependent protein kinase II), high-molecular-weight microtubule-associated proteins and tubulin, ubiquitin carboxyl terminal hydrolase (PGP-9), gelsolin, and amyloid precursor protein. Cortical Lewy bodies are distinct in containing alpha-B-crystalline and tropomysin (124). In addition, it has been discovered that Lewy bodies also contain α-synuclein (58).

THE EFFECT OF GENES ON THE DEVELOPMENT AND SURVIVAL OF DOPAMINERGIC CELLS

The primary cause and pathogenesis of PD are still unknown, although various genetic and environmental factors have been implicated (125). Genetic factors have been discovered by the study of families with PD. Causative genes now include α-synuclein gene on 4q21-q23 (126), a parkin gene on 6q (1), and others (127, 128). Several reports have also focused on susceptibility polymorphisms of genes that influence neurotransmitter or receptor function (129, 130).

The Nurr1 gene, a member of the nuclear receptor superfamily, is of special interest because it is critical for the development and maintenance of the midbrain dopaminergic cells (131–133). The Nurr1 gene is highly expressed in dopaminergic neurons of the midbrain and can activate or enhance the transcription of tyrosine hydroxylase (134) and expression of dopamine transporter (135). The reduced Nurr1 expression resulting from a natural aging process or a genetic defect increases the vulnerability of midbrain dopaminergic neurons (135). Knockout of the gene results in agenesis of nigral dopaminergic neurons; in addition, increased MPTP-induced neurotoxicity is observed in heterogeneous knockout mice (136).

The human Nurr1 (NOT) gene maps to chromosome 2q22-23 and is approximately 8.3 kb long, consisting of 8 exons and 7 introns. The current findings based on investigation of the human Nurr1 gene suggest that a variant of the gene may be associated with PD (134). Moreover, very recently it was shown that homozygote polymorphism of 7048G7049 in intron 6 of the Nurr1 gene is associated with typical PD (137).

CONCLUSIONS

With the increasing age of the general population, the prevalence of PD is steadily rising. In fact, it is estimated that by the year 2040, neurodegenerative diseases (Parkinson's disease, dementia, and motor neuron disease) will surpass cancer as the second most common cause of death among the elderly (138).

Currently there is no consensus on the probable cause of PD. Many investigations discount the possibility that idiopathic sporadic PD has an inherited basis as the primary cause. As a contributory factor, however, it is considered that genetic factors perhaps play a key role in conjunction with other elements (multifactorial hypothesis).

Nevertheless, despite the tremendous body of information that has accumulated over the past several years as the result of advances in biochemical techniques, the pathophysiology of PD is still not understood. The selective loss of dopaminergic cells in the nigrostriatal system explains part of the motor symptomatology, but a number of features of the disease are apparently not related to the deficiency of DA in the striatum. For example, the midline symptoms of the disease (speech, postural stability, and freezing gait) are not responsive to treatment with exogenous levodopa. Moreover, other ascending neurotransmitter systems are also damaged in PD: the noradrenergic ceruleocortical, the serotonergic projections from the raphe nuclei, as well as the dopaminergic mesocorticolimbic, innominatocortical, and septohippocampal cholinergic systems. Alterations in the integrity of these systems would be expected to contribute to the disruption of circuits responsible for the motor and cognitive features of PD. The application of the new methods of molecular biology together with new biochemical (PET, SPECT, MRS) and functional (fMRI) neuroimaging techniques will undoubtedly lead to a better understanding of the pathophysiology of PD in the coming decade.

References

1. Anthoney TR. *Neuroanatomy and the Neurologic Exam*. Boca Raton, FL: Ann Arbor Press/CRC Press, 1994:106–109.
2. Cote L, Crutcher MD. The basal ganglia. In: Kandel E, Schwartz JH, Thomas MG (eds). *Principles of Neural Science*, 3rd ed. New York: Elsevier, 1991:647–659.
3. Alexander GE, Crutcher MD. Functional architecture of basal ganglia circuits: Neural substrates of parallel processing. *Trends Neurosci* 1990; 13:266–271.
4. De Long MR. Primates models of movement disorders of basal ganglia origin. *Trends Neurosci* 1990; 13:231–285.
5. Cooper JR, Bloom FE, Roth RH. Dopamine. In: Cooper JR, Bloom FE, Roth RH (eds). *The Biochemical Basis of Neuropharmacology*, 8th ed. New York: Oxford University Press, 2003:225–270.
6. Lang AE, Lozano AM. Parkinson's disease. First of two parts. *N Engl J Med* 1998; 339:1044–1053.
7. Onn SP, West AR, Grace AA. Dopamine-mediated regulation of striatal neuronal and network interactions. *Trends Neurosci* 2000; 23(10 Suppl):S48–S56.
8. Björklund A, Lindvall O. Dopamine-containing systems in the CNS. In: Björklund A, Hökfelt T (eds). *Handbook of Chemical Neuroanatomy*. Vol 2: *Clinical Transmitters in the CNS*. Amsterdam: Elsevier, 1984:55–122.
9. Rabey JM, Shabtai H, Graff E, et al. (3H) Dopamine uptake by platelet storage granules in Parkinson's disease. *Life Sci* 1993; 53:1753–1761.
10. Cancilla PA, Bready J, Berliner J. Brain endothelial–astrocyte interactions. In: Pardridge WM (eds). *The Blood-Brain Barrier; Cellular and Molecular Biology*. New York: Raven Press, 1993:25–46.
11. Eriksson R, Graneros A, Linde A, et al. "On-off" phenomenon in Parkinson's disease: Relationship between dopa and other large neutral amino acids in plasma. *Neurology* 1988; 38:1245–1248.
12. Tretiakoff C. *Contribution à l'Étude de l'Anatomie Pathologique du Locus Niger*. Thesis, University of Paris, 1919.
13. Hassler R. Zur Pathologie der Paralysis agitans und des postenzephalitischen Parkinsonism. *J Psychol Neurol (Lpz)* 1938; 48:387–476.
14. Carlsson A, Lindquist M, Magnusson T. 3-4 dihydroxyphenylalanine and 5-hydroxytryptophan as reserpine antagonists. *Nature* (Lond) 1957; 180:1200.
15. Carlsson A, Lindquist M, Magnusson T, et al. On the presence of 3-hydroxy-tyramine in brain. *Science* 1958; 127:471.
16. Sano I, Gamo T, Kakimoto Y, et al. Distribution of catechol compounds in human brain. *Biochem Biophys Acta* 1959; 32:586–587.
17. Ehringer H, Hornykiewicz O. Verteilung von Noradrenalin und Dopamin im Gehirn des Menschen und ihr Verhalten bei Erkrankungen des extrapyramidalen Systems. *Wien Klin Wschr* 1960; 38:1236–1239.
18. Birkmayer W, Hornykiewicz O. Der L-3-4-Dioxyphenylalanin (D-dopa). Effeckt bei Parkinson Akinese. *Wien Klin Wschr* 1961; 73:787–788.
19. Birkmayer W, Hornykiewicz O. Der L-Dioxyphenylalanin (L-dopa). Effekt beim Parkinson-Syndrom des Menschen. *Arch Psychiatr Nervenkr* 1962; 203:560–574.
20. Hirsch E, Graybiel AM, Javoy-Agid A. Melanized dopaminergic neurons are differentially suceptible to degeneration in Parkinson's disease. *Nature* 1988; 334:345–348.
21. Fahn S, Libsch IR, Cuttler RW. Monoamines in the human neostriatum. Topographic distribution in normals and in Parkinson's disease and their role in akinesia, rigidity, chorea and tremor. *J Neurol Sci* 1971; 14:427–455.
22. Lloyd KG, Davidson L, Hornykiewicz O. The neurochemistry of Parkinson's disease: Effect of L-dopa therapy. *J Pharmacol Exp Ther* 1975; 195:453–464.
23. Riederer P, Rausch WD, Birkmayer W, et al. CNS modulation of adrenal tyrosine hydroxylase in Parkinson's disease and metabolic encephalophathies. *J Neural Transm* (Suppl) 1978; 14:121.
24. Bernheimer H, Birkmayer W, Hornykiewicz O, et al. Brain dopamine and the syndromes of Parkinson's and Huntington's: Clinical morphological and neurochemical correlation. *J Neurol Sci* 1973; 20:415–455.
25. Riederer P, Wuketich S. Time course of nigrostriatal degeneration in Parkinson's disease. *J Neural Transm* 1976; 38:277–301.
26. Nakashima S, Kumanishi T, Ikuta F. Immunohistochemistry on tyrosine hydroxylase in the substantia nigra of human autopsied cases. *Brain Nerve* 1983; 35:1023–1029.
27. Pearson J, Goldstein M, Markey K, et al. Human brain catecholamine neuronal anatomy as indicated by immunocytochemistry with antibodies to tyrosine hydroxylase. *Neuroscience* 1983; 8:3–32.
28. Issidorides MR, Mytilineou C, Whetsell WO, et al. Protein-rich cytoplasmic bodies of substantia nigra and locus coeruleus. *Arch Neurol* 1978; 35:633–637.
29. Jacob H. Klinische Neuropathologie des Parkinsonismus. In: Ganshirt H (ed). *Pathophysiologie, Klinik und Therapie des Parkinsonismus*. Basel: Roche, 1983:5–18.
30. Nakashima S, Ikuta F. Tyrosine hydroxylase proteins in Lewy bodies of Parkinsonism and senile brain. *J Neurol Sci* 1984; 66:91–96.
31. Kato T, Nagatsu T, Iizuka R, et al. Cyclic AMP-dependent protein kinase activity in human brain: Values in parkinsonism. *Biochem Med* 1979; 21:141.
32. Rausch WD, Hirata Y, Nagatsu T, et al. Human brain tyrosine hydroxylase; In vitro effects of iron and phosphorylating agents in the CNS of controls, Parkinson's disease and schizophrenia. *J Neurochem* 1988; 50:202–208.
33. Crapper-Mc Lachlan DR, Bebon U. Models for the study of pathological neural aging. In: Terry RD, Bolis CL, Toffano G (eds). *Neural Aging and Its Implications in Human Neurological Pathology*. Vol 18: *Aging*. New York: Raven Press, 1982:61–71.
34. Ringborg U. Composition of RNA in neurons of rat hippocampus at different ages. *Brain Res* 1966; 2:296–298.
35. Miyasaki JM, Martin W, Suchowersky O, et al. Practice parameter: Initiation of treatment for Parkinson's disease: An evidence based review. *Neurology* 2002; 58:11–17.
36. Fahn S. Levodopa-induced neurotoxicity: Does it represent a problem for the treatment of Parkinson's disease? *CNS Drugs* 1997; 8:376–393.
37. Mena MA, Pardo B, Casarejos MJ, et al. Neurotoxicity of levodopa on catecholamine-rich neurons. *Mov Disord* 1992; 7:23–31.
38. Mytilineou C, Han SK, Cohen G. Toxic and protective effects of L-dopa on mesencephalic cell cultures. *J Neurochem* 1993; 61:1470–1478.
39. Dauer W, Przedborski S. Parkinson's disease: Mechanisms and models. *Neuron* 2003; 39:889–909.
40. Vila M, Przedborski S. Targeting programmed cell death in neurodegenretative disease. *Nat Rerv Neurosci* 2003; 4:365–375.
41. Fahn S, Sulzer D. Neurodegeneration and neuroprotection in Parkinson disease. *NeuronRx* 2004; 1:139–154.
42. Olanow CW, Gauger LL, Cedarbaum JM. Temporal relationships between plasma and cerebrospinal fluid phamacokinetics of levodopa and clinical effect in Parkinson's disease. *Ann Neurol* 1991; 29:556–559.
43. Desagher S, Glowinski J. Astrocytes protect neurons from hydrogen peroxide toxicity. *J Neurosci* 1996; 16:2553–2562.
44. Langeveld CH, Jongelenen CA, Schepens E, et al. Cultured rat striatal and cortical astrocytes protect mesencephalic dopaminergic neurons against hydrogen peroxide toxicity independent of their effect on neuronal development. *Neurosci Lett* 1995; 192:13–16.

45. Mena MA, Casarejos MJ, Carazo A, et al. Glia conditioned medium protects fetal rat midbrain neurons in culture from L-dopa toxicity. *Neuroreport* 1996; 7:441–445.

46. Fahn S, Oakes D, Shoulson I, et al. Levodopa and the progression of Parkinson's disease. *N Engl J Med* 2004; 351:2498–2508.

47. Schapira AH, Olanow CW. Neuroprotection in Parkinson's disease: Mysteries, myths, and misconceptions. *JAMA* 2004; 291:358–364.

48. Parkinson Study Group .Dopamine transporter brain imaging to assess the effects of pramipexole vs levodopa in Parkinson's disease progression. *JAMA* 2002; 287:1653–1661.

49. Parkinson Study Group. Pramipexole vs levodopa as initial treatment for Parkinson disease. A 4 year randomized controlled trial. *Arch Neurol* 2004; 61:1044–1053.

50. Whone AL, Watts RL, Stoessl AJ, et al. Slower progression of Parkinson's disease with ropinirole versus levodopa: The REAL-PET study. *Ann Neurol* 2003; 4:93–101.

51. Morrish PK, Sawle GV, Brooks D. An [F-18]dopa-PET and clinical study of the rate of progression in Parkinson's disease. *Brain* 1996; 119:585–591.

52. Marek K, Jennings D, Seibyl J. Do dopamine agonists or levodopa modify Parkinson's disease progression? *Eur J Neurol* 2002; 9(Suppl 3):15–22.

53. Agid Y. Levodopa: is toxicity a myth? *Neurology* 1998; 50:858–863.

54. Weiner WJ. The initial treatment of Parkinson's disease should begin with levodopa. *Mov Disord* 1999; 14:716–724.

55. Bokobza B, Ruberg M, Scatton B, et al. (³H) spiper-one binding, dopamine and HVA concentrations in Parkinson's disease and supranuclear palsy. *Europ J Pharmacol* 1984; 99:167–175.

56. Scatton B, Monfort JC, Javoy-Agid F, et al. Neurochemistry of monoaminergic neurons in Parkinson's disease. In: Alan R (ed). *Catecholamines: Neuropharmacology and Central Nervous System. Therapeutic Aspects.* New York: Liss, 1984:43– 52.

57. Hornykiewicz O. Compensatory biochemical changes at the striatal dopamine synapse in Parkinson's disease. Limitations of L-dopa therapy. *Adv Neurol* 1979; 24:275–281.

58. Melamed E, Hefti F, Wurtman RJ. Compensatory mechanism in the nigrostriatal dopaminergic system in Parkinson's disease studies in an animal model. *Israel J Med Sci* 1982; 18:159–163.

59. Creese I, Snyder SH. Nigrostriatal lesions enhance striatal (3H) apomorphine and (3H) spiroperidol binding. *Eur J Pharmacol* 1979; 56:277–281.

60. Javoy-Agid F, Ruberg M, Taquet H, et al. Biochemical neuropathology of Parkinson's disease. *Adv Neurol* 1984; 40:189–198.

61. Boushey CJ, Beresford SA, Omena GS, et al. A quantitative assessment of plasma homocysteine as a risk factor for vascular disease. *JAMA* 1995; 274:1049–1057.

62. Seshadri S, Beiser A, Selhub J, et al. Plasma homocysteine as a risk factor for dementia and Alzheimer's disease. *N Engl J Med* 2002; 346:476–483.

63. Morris MS. Homocysteine and Alzheimer's disease. *Lancet Neurol* 2003; 2:425–428.

64. Miller JW, Selhub J, Nadeau MR, et al. Effect of L-dopa on plasma homocysteine in PD patients: Relationship to B-vitamin status. *Neurology* 2003; 60:1125–1129.

65. Rogers JD, Sanchez-Suffon A, Frol AB, et al. Elevated plasma homocysteine levels in patients treated with levodopa: Association with vascular disease. *Arch Neurol* 2003; 60:59–64.

66. Valkovic P, Benetin J, Blazicek P, et al. Reduced plasma homocysteine levels in levodopa/entacapone treated Parkinson patients. *Parkinsonism Relat Disord* 2005; 11:253–256.

67. Lamberti P, Zoccolella S, Iliceto G, et al. Effects of levodopa and COMT inhibitors on plasma homocysteine in Parkinson's disease patients. *Mov Disord* 2005; 20:69–72.

68. Ogawa N. Molecular and chemical neuropharmacology of dopamine receptor subtypes. *Acta Med Okayama* 1995; 49:1–11.

69. Sokoloff P, Schwartz JC. Novel dopamine receptors half a decade later. *Trends Pharmacol Sci* 1995; 16:270–275.

70. Meador-Woodruff JH. Neuroanatomy of dopamine receptor gene expression: Potential substrates for neuropsychiatric illness. *Clin Neuropharmacol* 1995; 18(Suppl 1):S14–S24.

71. Horn AS. Dopamine uptake: A review of progress in the last decade. *Prog Neurobiol* 1990; 34:397–400.

72. Iversen LL. Role of transmitter uptake mechanisms in synaptic neurotransmission. *Br J Pharmacol* 1971; 41:571–591.

73. Giros B, Caron MG. Molecular characterization of the dopamine transporter. *TIPS* 1993; 14:43–49.

74. Scherman D, Desnos C, Darchen F, et al. Striatal dopamine deficiency in Parkinson's disease: Role of aging. *Ann Neurol* 1989; 26:551–557.

75. Uhl G, Walther D, Mash D, et al. Dopamine transporter messenger RNA in Parkinson's disease and control substantia nigra neurons. *Ann Neurol* 1994; 35:494–498.

76. Vingerhoets FJ, Schulzer M, Calne DB, Snow BJ. Which clinical sign of Parkinson's disease best reflects the nigrostriatal lesion? Ann Neurol 1997; 41:58–64.

77. Jenner P, Marsden CD. Neurochemical basis of parkinsonian tremor. In: Findley LJ, Capildeo R (eds). *Movement Disorders: Tremor.* London: Macmillan, 1984:305–319.

78. Ellenbroeck B, Schwarcz M, Sontag KH, et al. Muscular rigidity and delineation of a dopamine-specific neostriatal subregion: Tonic EMG activity in rats. *Brain Res* 1985; 345:132–140.

79. Jellinger K. Pathology of parkinsonism. In: Fahn S, Marsden CD, Jenner P, et al. (eds). *Recent Development in Parkinson's Disease.* New York: Raven Press, 1986:33–66.

80. Hornykiewicz O. Die topische Lokalization und das Verhalten von Noradrenalin und Dopamin (3-Hydroxytyramin) in der Substantia nigra des normalen und parkinsonkranken Menschen. *Wien Klin Wochenschr* 1963; 75:309–312.

81. Price KS, Farley U, Hornykiewicz O. Neurochemistry of Parkinson's disease. Relation between striatal and limbic dopamine. *Adv Biochem Psychopharmacol* 1978; 19: 293–300.

82. Bernheimer H, Hornykiewicz O. Herabgesetzte Konzentration der Homovanillinsaure im Gehirn von parkinsonkranken Menschen als Ausdruck der Storung des zentralen Dopaminestroffwechsels. *Klin Wochenschr* 1965; 43:711–715.

83. Lindvall O, Björklund A. Organization of catecholamine neurons in the rat central nervous system. In: Iversen LI, Iversen SD, Snyder SH (eds). *Handbook of Psychopharmacology.* Vol. 9. New York: Plenum Press, 1978:139–231.

84. Farley IJ, Hornykiewicz O. Noradrenaline in subcortical brain regions of patients with Parkinson's disease and control subjects. In: Birkmayer W, Hornykiewicz O, (eds). *Advances in Parkinsonism.* Basel: Roche, 1976:178–185.

85. Scatton B, Javoy-Agid F, Rouquier L, et al. Reduction of cortical dopamine, noradrenaline, serotonin and their metabolites in Parkinson's disease. *Brain Res* 1983; 275:321–328.

86. Riederer P, Birkmayer W, Seeman D, et al. Brain-noradrenaline and 3-methoxy-hydroxyphenylglycol in Parkinson's syndrome. *J Neural Transm* 1977; 41:241–251.

87. Nagatsu T, Wakui Y, Kato TJ, et al. Dopamine beta-hydroxylase activity in cerebrospinal fluid of parkinsonian patients. *Biomed Res* 1982; 3:395–398.

88. Mayeaux R, Williams JBW, Stern Y, et al. Depression and Parkinson's disease. *Adv Neurol* 1984; 40:241–250.

89. Strang RR. Imipramine in the treatment of parkinsonism: A double-blind placebo study. *Br J Med* 1965; 2:33–34.

90. Anderson J, Aabro E, Gulman N, et al. Antidepressant treatment of Parkinson's disease. *Acta Neurol Scand* 1980; 62:210–219.

91. Hornykiewicz O. Parkinson's disease. In: Crow TJ (ed). *Disorders of Neurohumoral Transmission.* London: Academic Press, 1982:121–143.

92. Narabayashi H, Kondo T, Hayashi A, et al. L-threo-3, 4-Dyhydroxyphenylserine treatment for akinesia and freezing of parkinsonism. *Proc J Acad* 1981; 3:395–398. Björklund A, Lindvall O. Dopamine-containing systems in the CNS. In: Björklund A, Hökfelt T (eds). *Handbook of Chemical Neuroanatomy.* Vol 2: *Clinical Transmitters in the CNS.* Amsterdam: Elsevier, 1984:55–122.

93. Steinbusch HWM. Serotonin-immunoreactive neurons and their projection in the CNS. In: Björklund A, Hökfelt T, Kuhar ML (eds). *Classical Transmitters and Receptors in the CNS. Part II: Handbook of Chemical Neuroanatomy.* Vol 3. Amsterdam: Elsevier, 1984:68–126.

94. Forno LS. Pathology of Parkinson's disease. In: Marsden CD, Fahn S (eds). *Movement Disorders Neurology 2.* London: Butterworth, 1982:40–85.

95. Mayeaux R, Stern Y, Cote L, et al. Altered serotonin metabolism in depressed patients with Parkinson's disease. *Neurology* 1984; 34:642–646.

96. Woolf NJ, Butcher LL. Central cholinergic systems: Synopsis of anatomy and overview of pharmacology and pathology. In: Scheibel AB, Wechsler AF (eds). *The Biological Substrates of Alzheimer's Disease,* New York: Academic Press, 1989:73–78.

97. Agid Y, Javoy F, Guyenet P, et al. Effects of surgical and pharmacological manipulation of the dopaminergic nigrostriatal neurons on the activity of the neostriatal cholinergic system in the rat. In: Boissier JR, Hippius H, Pichot P (eds). *Neuropsychopharmacology.* Amsterdam: Excerpta Medica, 1975:480–486.

98. Javoy-Agid F, Ploska A, Agid Y. Microtopography of TH, CAT and GAD activity in the substantia nigra and ventral tegmental area of control and parkinsonian human brain. *Neurochemistry* 1982; 37:1221–1227.

99. Hattori T, Singh VK, Mc Geer EG, et al. Immunohistochemical localization of choline acetyltransferase containing neostriatal neurons and their relationship with dopaminergic synapses. *Brain Res* 1976; 102:164–173.

100. Mc Geer PL, Mc Geer EG. Enzyme associated with the metabolism of catecholamines, acetylcholine and GABA in human controls and patients with Parkinson's disease and Huntington's chorea. *J Neurochem* 1976; 26:65–76.

101. Mayorga AJ, Cousins MS, Trevitt JT, et al. Characterization of the muscarinic receptor subtype mediating pilocarpine-induced tremulous jaw movements in rats. *Eur J Pharmacol* 1999; 364:7–11.

102. Candy JM, Perry RH, Perry EK, et al. Pathological changes in the nucleus of Meynert in Alzheimer's and Parkinson's disease. *J Neurol Sci* 1983; 54:277–289.

103. Dubois B, Ruberg M, Javoy-Agid F, et al. A sub- cortico-cortical cholinergic system is affected in Parkinson's disease. *Brain Res* 1983; 288:213–218.

104. Perry EK, Curtis M, Dick DJ, et al. Cholinergic correlates of cognitive impairment in Parkinson's disease: Comparison with Alzheimer's disease. *J Neurol Neurosurg Psychiatry* 1985; 48:413–421.

105. Ruberg M, Ploska A, Javoy-Agic F, et al. Muscarinic binding and choline acetyltransferase activity in parkinsonian subject with reference to dementia. *Brain Res* 1982; 232:129–139.

106. Javoy Agid F, Ruberg M, Hirsch E, et al. Recent progress in the neurochemistry of PD. In: Fahn S (ed). *Recent Developments in PD.* New York: Raven Press, 1986:67–83.

107. Lloyd KG, Hornykiewicz O. L-glutamic acid decarboxylase in Parkinson's disease. Effects of L-dopa therapy. *Nature* 1973; 243:521–523.

108. Laaksonen H, Rinne UK, Sonninen V, et al. Brain GABA neurons in Parkinson's disease. *Acta Neurol Scand* 1978; 57(Suppl 67):282–283.

109. Perry TL, Javoy-Agid F, Agid Y, et al. Striatal GABAergic neuronal activity is not reduced in Parkinson's disease. *J Neurochem* 1983; 40:1120–1123.

110. Monfort JE, Javoy-Agid F, Hauw JJ, et al. Brain glutamate decarboxylase and "premortem severity index" with a special reference to Parkinson's disease. *Brain* 1985; 108: 301–303.

111. Richardson PJ, Kase H, Jenner PG. Adenosine A2A receptor antagonists as new agents for the treatment of Parkinson's disease. *Trends Pharmacol Sci* 1997; 18:338–344.

112. Bartfai T. Presynaptic aspects of the coexistence of classical neurotransmitters and peptides. *Trends Pharmacol Sci* 1985; 6:331–334.

113. Agid Y, Javoy-Agid F. Peptides and Parkinson's disease. *Trends Neurosci* 1985; 8:30–35.

114. Hökfelt T, Skirboll l, Rehfeld JF, et al. A subpopulation of mesencephalic dopamine neurones projecting to limbic areas contains a cholesystokinin-like peptide: Evidence from immunohistochemistry combines with retrograde tracing. *Neuroscience* 1980; 5:2093–2124.

115. Studler JM, Javoy-Agid F, Cesselin F, et al. CCK-8 immunoreactivity distribution in human brain: Selective decrease in the substantia nigra from parkinsonian patients. *Brain Res* 1982; 243:176–179.

116. Skirboll LR, Grace AA, Hommer DW, et al. Peptide-monoamine coexistence: Studies of the actions of cholecystokinin-like peptide on the electrical activity of mid-brain dopamine neurons. *Neuroscience* 1981; 6:2111–2124.

117. Markstein R, Hökfelt T. Effects of cholecystokinin-octapeptide on dopamine release from slices of cat caudate nucleus. *J Neurosci* 1984; 4:570–575.

118. Mauborgne A, Javoy-Agid F, Legrand JC, et al. Decrease of substance P-like immuno-reactivity in the substantia nigra and pallidum of parkinsonian brains. *Brain Res* 1983; 268:167–170.

119. Grafe MR, Forno LS, Eng LF. Immunocytochemical studies of substance P and Metenkephalin in the basal ganglia and substantia nigra in Huntington's, Parkinson's and Alzheimer's diseases. *J Neuropathol Exp Neurol* 1985; 44:47–59.

120. Taquet H, Javoy-Agid F, Giraud P, et al. Dynorphin levels in parkinsonian patients; Leu-enkephalin production from either proenkephalin A or prodynorphin in human brain. *Brain Res* 1985; 341:390–392.

121. Taquet H, Javoy-Agid F, Cesselin F, et al. Microtopography of methionine-enkephalin dopamine and noradrenaline in the ventral mesencephalon of human control and parkinsonian brains. *Brain Res* 1982; 235:303–314.

122. Taquet H, Javoy-Agid F, Hamon M, et al. Parkinson's disease affects differently Met[5] and Leu[5]-enkephalin production in the human brain. *Brain Res* 1983; 280:379–382.

123. Epelbaum J, Ruberg M, Moyse E, et al. Somatostatin and dementia in Parkinson's disease. *Brain Res* 1983; 278:376–378.

124. Lowe J. Lewy bodies. In: Calne DB (ed). *Neurodegenerative Diseases*. Philadelphia: Saunders, 1994:51–69.

125. Kitada T, Asakawa S, Hattori N, et al. Mutations in the Parkin gene cause autosomal recessive juvenile parkinsonism. *Nature* 1998; 392:605–608.

126. Polymeropoulos MH, Lavedan C, Leroy E, et al. Mutation in the alpha synuclein gene identified in families with Parkinson's disease. *Science* 1997; 276:2045–2047.

127. Gasser T, Muller-Myhsok B, Wszolec ZK, et al. A susceptibility locus for Parkinson's disease maps to chromosome 2p13. *Nat Genet* 1998; 18:262–265.

128. Ferrer M, Gwinn-Hardy K, Muenter M, et al. A chromosome 4p haplotype segregating with Parkinson's disease and postural tremor. *Hum Mol Genet* 1999; 8:81–85.

129. Markopoulu K, Langston JW. Candidate genes and Parkinson's disease: Where to next. *Neurology* 1999; 53:1382–1383.

130. Tan EK, Khajavi M, Nagamitsu S, et al. Variability and validity of polymorphism association studies in Parkinson's disease. *Neurology* 2000; 55:533–538.

131. Lar SW, Connely OM, DeMayo FJ, et al. Identification of a new brain-specific transcription factor Nurr1. *Mol Endocrinol* 1992; 6:2129–2135.

132. Castillo SO, Baffi JS, Palkivitis M, et al. Dopamine byosinthesis is selectively abolished in substantia nigra/ventral tegmental area but not in hypothalamic neurons in mice with targeted disruption of the Nurr1 gene. *Mol Cell Neuorsci* 1998; 11:36–46.

133. Saucedo-Cardenas O, Quintana-Hau JD, Le WD, et al. Nurr1 is essential for the induction of the dopaminergic phenotype and the survival of ventral mesencephalic late dopaminergic precursor neurons. *Proc Natl Acad Sci USA* 1998; 95:4013–4018.

134. Sakurada K, Ohshima-Sakurada M, Palmer TD, et al. Nurr1, an orphan nuclear receptor, is a transcriptional activator of endogenous tyrosine hydroxylase in neuronal progenitor cells derived from the adult brain. *Development* 199; 126:4017–4026.

135. Sacchetti P, Mitchell TR, Granneman JG, et al. Nurr1 enhances transcription of the human dopamine transporter gene through a novel mechanism. *J Neurochem* 2001; 76:1565–1572.

136. Zetterstrom RH, Solomin L, Jansson L, et al. Dopamine neuron agenesis in Nurr1-deficient mice. *Science* 1997; 276:248–250.

137. Xu PY, Liang R, Jankovic J, et al. Association of homozygous 7048G7049 variant in the intron six of Nurr1 gene with Parkinson's disease. *Neurology* 2002; 58: 881–884.

138. Lilienfeld DE, Perl DP. Projected neurodegenerative disease mortality in the United States, 1990–2040. *Neuroepidemiology* 1993; 12:219–228.

22 Basal Ganglia: Anatomy and Physiology

Thomas Wichmann
Yoland Smith
Jerrold L. Vitek

Research in the past decade has led to major insights into the structure and function of the basal ganglia and, in turn, the pathophysiologic basis of basal ganglia disorders, such as Parkinson's disease (PD) (1–10). This chapter summarizes current concepts of the anatomy and physiology of the basal ganglia as well as the pathophysiology of motor features of PD.

STRUCTURE OF BASAL GANGLIA CIRCUITS

In primates, the basal ganglia (Figure 22-1) are a group of functionally related subcortical nuclei that include the dorsal striatum (comprising the caudate nucleus and putamen); the external globus pallidus (GPe); the internal globus pallidus (GPi); the substantia nigra, which comprises the dopaminergic neurons in the pars compacta (SNc) and the GABAergic neurons in the pars reticulata (SNr); and the subthalamic nucleus (STN). In rodents, the caudate nucleus and putamen are part of a single nucleus called the "caudate-putamen complex," while the globus pallidus (GP) and the entopeduncular nucleus (EPN) are the functional homologs of GPe and GPi, respectively. Anatomically and physiologically, these structures are integrally related to large portions of the cerebral cortex. The striatum and to a lesser extent, the STN are the

main entries for cortical information to the basal ganglia circuitry. From the striatum and the STN, cortical information is conveyed to the basal ganglia output nuclei, GPi and SNr. Basal ganglia outflow is directed at a variety of targets, among them frontal areas of the cerebral cortex (via the ventral motor thalamic nuclei), various brainstem structures (superior colliculus, lateral habenular nucleus, pedunculopontine nucleus (PPN), parvicellular reticular formation), and the striatum (via connections with thalamostriatal neurons in intralaminar and nonintralaminar nuclei). The ventral striatopallidal complex and related basal ganglia nuclei that play an important role in limbic and reward-related behaviors are not discussed in this review. Readers are referred to recent reviews for more information on these regions (11–21).

INTRINSIC NEURONAL ORGANIZATION OF BASAL GANGLIA NUCLEI

At the cellular level, the striatum is the most complex structure of the basal ganglia. It is made up of spiny and aspiny neurons that are easily recognized by the abundance or scarcity of dendritic spines, respectively. The spiny neurons are the output neurons of the striatum that project to both segments of the globus pallidus and the substantia nigra, while aspiny neurons are interneurons.

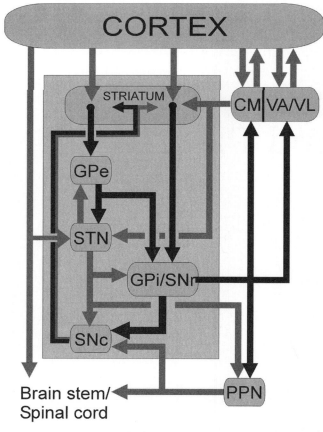

FIGURE 22-1

Schematic diagram of the basal ganglia–thalamocortical circuitry under normal conditions. Inhibitory connections are shown as black arrows, excitatory connections as gray arrows. GPe, external segment of the globus pallidus; GPi, internal segment of the globus pallidus; SNr, substantia nigra pars reticulata; SNc, substantia nigra pars compacta; STN, subthalamic nucleus; CM, centromedian nucleus of thalamus; VA/VL, ventroanterior and ventrolateral nuclei of thalamus.

In rodents, interneurons represent only 2% to 3% of the total striatal neuronal population, while in monkeys they account for as much as 23% of all striatal neurons (22, 23). All spiny neurons are GABAergic, but they can be separated into two populations based on their main projection site as well as their neuropeptide and dopamine receptor expression (see below). Some neurons contain enkephalin mRNA, project preferentially to GPe, and express D2-dopamine receptors, while another group that contains substance P/dynorphin and expresses D1 dopamine receptors projects mainly to the GPi and SNr (24). Single-cell filling studies have reported a higher degree of axon collateralization of striatofugal neurons than previously thought (25, 26). Axon collaterals of spiny neurons arborize profusely in the vicinity of their

parent cell bodies, providing GABAergic innervation to neighboring projection neurons. Although this intrinsic inhibitory connectivity between medium spiny neurons has long been thought of as the substrate for lateral inhibition in the striatum (27–29), it has been shown that these connections are weak and likely mediate subtle modulatory influence on striatal activity (30, 31). Striatal interneurons comprise 4 chemically characterized populations: (a) *cholinergic interneurons*, of which more than 50% coexpress calretinin in humans (32) and likely correspond to the "tonically active" neurons (TANs) that can be physiologically identified in the rat and monkey striatum (33, 34). These neurons play a pivotal role in reward-related learning and motivated behaviors (35, 36). (b) *GABA/parvalbumin interneurons*, also referred to as "fast spiking interneurons." They form multiple axosomatic synapses on projection neurons, are electrotonically coupled through gap junctions (23), and exert a powerful control on spike timing in projection neurons, thereby providing the substrate for fast-forward intrastriatal inhibition of projection neurons in response to cortical activation (23, 37)). (c) *GABA/nitric oxide synthase/neuropeptide Y/ somatostatin interneurons*, categorized physiologically as "persistent and low-threshold spike" neurons. These cells induce large inhibitory currents in projection neurons and release nitric oxide, which modulates plasticity at glutamatergic synapses (23). (d) *Medium-sized GABA/calretinin interneurons*, which represent the largest population of striatal interneurons in humans (32). In rats, these neurons display physiologic characteristics similar to those of the persistent- and low-threshold spike neurons and exert powerful monosynaptic inhibition of medium spiny projection neurons (23). A small population of dopaminergic neurons has also been described in the striatum of dopamine-depleted rats and monkeys and in the caudate nucleus and putamen of patients with PD (38–42). These aspiny neurons coexpress various markers of dopaminergic neurons, glutamic acid decarboxylase, and, for a small subset, calretinin (38, 39, 41). They receive very scarce synaptic inputs and are preferentially expressed in the precommissural putamen and caudate nucleus (41). Their density significantly increases following dopamine depletion in rat and monkey models of parkinsonism, suggesting that they may serve as a potential compensatory mechanism in PD (36–40). In MPTP-treated monkeys, these neurons give rise to local axon terminals containing both GABA and tyrosine hydroxylase (39).

Although medium spiny neurons are homogenously distributed throughout the striatum, they are divided into 2 neurochemically defined striatal compartments—namely, the patch (or striosome) and the matrix compartment (43, 44). Projections from sensorimotor cortices and most thalamic nuclei innervate the matrix preferentially (44–51), while corticostriatal afferents from limbic and prefrontal association cortices as well as thalamic inputs from the paraventricular (PV) and rhomboid nuclei terminate rather selectively within patches (46, 48, 49, 52, 53). Various neurochemical markers and projections have been specifically associated with the patch or matrix compartments (54). In rats, a significantly higher proportion of thalamostriatal afferents forms axodendritic terminations in the patch compartments than in the matrix compartment (55). The behavioral importance of the patch-matrix organization of the striatum is underscored by recent findings that a disturbance of the balance of activity between the patch and matrix compartments may lead to repetitive motor behaviors (56–58) and that selective neurodegeneration of patches occurs in X-linked progressive dystonia-parkinsonism (59).

The internal and external segments of the globus pallidus are largely made up of GABAergic projection neurons (60–62). In rats, two primary populations of pallidal projection neurons, characterized by the expression of parvalbumin (PV) and preproenkephalin (PPE) mRNA, have been identified. The PV+/PPE- neurons account for about 60% of the total population of pallidal neurons and project preferentially to the STN, the entopeduncular nucleus (the rodent equivalent of the GPi), and the SNr, whereas the PV-/PPE+ neurons constitute 40% of GP neurons and project mainly to the striatum (63–65). These two populations of neurons respond differently to dopamine receptor antagonists (64, 66). Pallidostriatal and pallidosubthalamic neurons also form segregated populations in the monkey GPe (67). Interneurons are rare in GPe and GPi, but GPe projection neurons have intrinsic axon collaterals that likely contribute to local inhibition in GPe and provide strong inhibitory influences to GPi (67–69). Two types of projection neurons have been identified in the monkey GPi based on single-cell filling studies (70). The most common neurons are centrally located and send axonal projections to the thalamus (ventral motor and caudal intralaminar nuclei) and brainstem pedunculopontine region, while less numerous peripherally located neurons send their axons through the stria medullaris up to the lateral habenular nucleus, one of the most densely innervated pallidal targets in monkeys (70). Almost half of these neurons have both ipsi- and contralateral projections to their thalamic or brainstem targets (70). Pallidothalamic axons travel through 2 main tracts to reach their targets, the ansa lenticularis and the lenticular fasciculus. Although these tracts have long been known as distinct anatomic and functional pathways (71), more recent findings have challenged this concept and concluded that both sensorimotor and associative pallidofugal axons originating from the caudal GPi travel predominately through the lenticular fasciculus en route to the thalamus (72). In contrast, the ansa lenticularis is largely made up of nonmotor and limbic axons from the rostral and medial GPi and incoming serotonergic and dopaminergic striatal

and pallidal inputs from the brainstem (72). Thus, proposals to target the subpallidal fibers during posterior pallidotomy or deep brain stimulation for treatment of PD seem misguided (72).

In the substantia nigra, axon collaterals of SNr neurons innervate neighboring SNr neurons and dopaminergic SNc neurons in a highly organized and topographic manner, thereby contributing to an indirect route through which the striatum can upregulate its level of dopaminergic transmission via disinhibition of nigrostriatal neurons (73). The STN mainly comprises glutamatergic projection neurons to GPi but also includes a small population (about 7% total population) of GABAergic interneurons in humans (67, 74, 75).

SOURCES OF INPUTS TO THE BASAL GANGLIA

The Corticostriatal Projection

The corticostriatal projection terminates in a strict topographic organization that imposes on the striatum a segregation of functional territories (76–79). In primates, the somatosensory, motor, and premotor cortices project somatotopically to the postcommissural region of the putamen (80–83); the associative cortical areas project to the caudate nucleus; and the precommissural putamen (84–88); whereas the limbic cortices, the amygdala, and the hippocampus terminate preferentially in the ventral striatum, which includes the nucleus accumbens and the olfactory tubercle (89–94).

Processing and integration of functionally related information in these striatal territories is likely governed by both convergence and segregation of cortical inputs. For instance, evidence that associative areas of the cerebral cortex, which have reciprocal corticocortical projections, innervate common regions of the caudate nucleus in rhesus monkeys (85, 95) is opposed by studies demonstrating that projections from linked associative cortical areas are either completely segregated or minimally overlapping in the monkey striatum (86). Somatosensory and motor cortical areas related to the same body parts tightly overlap in the ipsilateral postcommissural putamen, while contralateral projections from the primary motor cortex (M1) except those from the face area interdigitate with projections from the ipsilateral somatosensory and M1 cortices (83).

Dendritic spines of output striatal neurons are by far the main targets of corticostriatal afferents (96), although the GABA/PV-containing interneurons also receive significant cortical inputs in rats and monkeys (97). Recent in vivo electrophysiologic data demonstrate that spike responses in GABA/PV interneurons occur earlier and can be induced by a lower intensity of cortical stimulation than that required for medium spiny projection neurons (37). In general, increased cortical activity facilitates responses in GABA/PV interneurons, while opposite effects are found in projection neurons, which indicates that feed-forward inhibition of GABA/PV interneurons filters cortical information effectively transmitted to striatal output neurons (23, 37). Cortical inputs and feed-forward inhibition from GABA/PV interneurons contribute to the imbalance of activity between the 2 main populations of striatofugal neurons in the rat model of PD (see below for more details and also Ref. 98). Cortical inputs to other interneuron populations are sparse and often located on distal dendrites (99). There is also evidence for differential cortical innervation of the 2 main populations of striatofugal neurons (see below for more details).

The Thalamostriatal Projection

The intralaminar thalamic nuclei are a major source of excitatory afferents to the striatum (51, 96, 100, 101). In primates, the caudal intralaminar nuclear group, the centromedian (CM), and the parafascicular (PF) nuclei provide inputs that largely terminate in different functional territories in the striatum (51, 102, 103). The medial part of CM projects to the postcommissural sensorimotor putamen, while the lateral CM innervates M1 preferentially. On the other hand, the PF innervates predominantly the associative part of the caudate nucleus and the ventral striatum (51, 103–105) while the dorsolateral PF projects selectively to the precommissural putamen (106, 107). CM and PF inputs preferentially innervate the dendritic shafts of striatal output neurons (101, 105, 108, 109). In monkeys, striatofugal neurons that project to GPi are more frequently contacted by CM inputs than striato-GPe neurons (109). However, a PF lesion prevents upregulation of enkephalin mRNA (marker of indirect pathway neurons) but does not affect the downregulation of substance P mRNA (marker of direct pathway neurons) in 6-OHDA–treated rats (110, 111). Together, these anatomic and functional data indicate that both populations of striatofugal neurons are likely regulated by the thalamostriatal projection from CM/PF (107), albeit perhaps to different degrees in monkeys and rodents. Striatal interneurons—immunoreactive for choline acetyltransferase, parvalbumin, and somatostatin but not calretinin—also receive inputs from CM in monkeys (109). In rats, PF projections avoid parvalbumin-containing interneurons but strongly innervate cholinergic interneurons (112, 113). In line with these electron microscopic data, there is evidence that projections from CM/PF tightly regulate cholinergic neuronal activity in the rat striatum (114–116) and are required for the sensory responses of TANs (likely cholinergic) acquired through sensorimotor learning in monkeys (117).

Although the CM/PF complex is the main source of thalamostriatal afferents, most thalamic nuclei contribute a varying degree of striatal innervation (107, 118). Albeit sparse compared to those from CM/PF, these projections are topographically and functionally organized in the rat and monkey striatum (107). The synaptic connectivity of striatal projections from CM/PF is strikingly different from that of other thalamic nuclei. CM/PF terminals form synapses predominantly with dendritic shafts of medium spiny neurons, whereas projections from other nuclear groups—including rostral intralaminar, midline, and relay thalamic nuclei—target dendritic spines almost exclusively (55, 107, 119). Another main difference between striatal inputs from CM/PF and other thalamic nuclei relates to the degree of axon collateralization to the cerebral cortex. Based on data from double retrograde fluorescent studies and single-cell filling injections, projections from CM/PF in both rats and monkeys are mainly directed toward the striatum, with minimal innervation of frontal cortical areas, whereas relay and rostral intralaminar nuclei project predominantly to the cerebral cortex, with light to moderate striatal innervation (107, 120–122). In general, striatal projections from CM/PF are much more focused and give rise to a significantly larger number of terminals than individual corticostriatal axons (120–125), which underlines the importance of the thalamostriatal system in the functional scheme of basal ganglia organization (107, 126, 127).

The introduction of vesicular glutamate transporters 1 and 2 (vGluT1 and vGluT2) as selective markers of the corticostriatal and thalamostriatal glutamatergic projections, respectively, provides exciting new tools to compare these 2 pathways. Recent findings demonstrate that the synaptic microcircuitry of vGluT1- and vGluT2-immunoreactive glutamatergic terminals is strikingly different between the 2 main anatomic compartments of the striatum—that is, the patches (or striosomes) and the matrix (55). About 90% of vGluT1- and vGluT2-containing boutons form axospinous synapses in both compartments, but only half of vGluT2-positive terminals do so in the matrix, suggesting differential regulatory mechanisms of striatal outflow by the thalamostriatal system in the patch and matrix (55, 119).

The role (or roles) of the thalamostriatal system remains poorly understood and likely differs between projections that arise from CM/PF and those arising from other thalamic nuclei. Kimura and colleagues have proposed that the CM and PF supply striatal neurons with information that have attentional values, thus acting as detectors of behaviorally significant events occurring on the contralateral side (117, 128–130). Positron emission tomographic (PET) studies in humans showing that activation of the CM/PF complex changes when participants switch from a relaxed state to an attention-demanding reaction-time task are consistent with these observations in nonhuman primates (107, 131). The function of other thalamostriatal systems might be to provide a positive reinforcer of specific populations of striatal neurons involved in performing a selected cortically driven behavior (132).

Significant neuronal loss has been found in the CM/PF of patients with progressive supranuclear palsy, Huntington's disease, and PD (107, 133, 134). In parkinsonian patients, subpopulations of parvalbumin-containing neurons are mainly affected in PF; while in CM, nonparvalbumin/noncalbindin neurons are specifically targeted (133, 134). In rodents, there is controversy as to whether unilateral 6-OHDA lesion of the dopaminergic nigrostriatal pathway induces PF neurodegeneration; while some authors could not find evidence for neuronal loss in the ipsilateral PF 3 months after nigrostriatal dopaminergic lesion, another recent study demonstrated more than 50% loss of PF neurons projecting to the dopamine-depleted striatum 1 month after the lesion (135, 136). Systemic MPTP administration also induces significant loss of midline and intralaminar nuclei in mice (137).

The Cortico- and Thalamosubthalamic Projections

Anatomic evidence indicates that the corticosubthalamic projection is exclusively ipsilateral (138, 139). In contrast to the corticostriatal projection, which arises from the entire cortical mantle, the corticosubthalamic projection arises largely from the primary motor cortex (M1), with lesser contributions from prefrontal, premotor, and cingulate cortices (80, 138–141). M1 afferents are confined to the dorsolateral part of the STN (138, 140), while afferents from premotor, supplementary, and cingulate motor areas innervate mainly the medial third of the nucleus (81, 138, 140–142). The prefrontal-limbic cortices project to the medialmost tip of the STN (138, 139, 143, 144). Anatomic and physiologic evidence indicates that, like the cortical input to the striatum, the corticosubthalamic projection from M1 is somatotopically organized with the face area projecting laterally, the arm area centrally, and the leg area medially (80, 138, 140, 145, 146). A similar somatotopic organization has been reported in the STN of humans with PD undergoing microelectrode mapping during functional neurosurgical procedures (147). Input from the supplementary motor area (SMA) to the STN shows a somatotopy that is reversed to the one from M1 (140, 146). It is worth noting, however, that STN neurons in rats have long dendrites that may cross the boundaries of functional territories imposed by cortical projections (148). There is anatomic evidence that the corticostriatal and corticosubthalamic tracts originate largely from segregated populations of corticofugal neurons in monkeys (125). In rats and cats, the cortical input to the STN arises from long-range axons descending to the brainstem and spinal cord (149, 150). Single axon tracing studies devoted to the corticosubthalamic projection are needed to further characterize the sources and collateralization of corticosubthalamic neurons in primates.

A second major source of excitatory inputs to the STN arises from the caudal intralaminar thalamic nuclei (51, 151–153). The thalamosubthalamic and thalamostriatal projections arise largely from segregated sets of neurons in the rat PF (152), although neurons that project to both structures were also found (154). In a recent single axon-tracing study in monkeys, none of the 29 CM/PF axons analyzed gave rise to significant projection to the STN, suggesting the possibility that the bulk of the thalamosubthalamic projections arise, in fact, from the subparafascicular nucleus in nonhuman primates (122). Cortical and thalamic inputs are thought to be excitatory on STN neurons, resulting in faster transmission of cortical information to the basal ganglia output structures than via striatofugal pathways (144, 146, 155–158).

INTRINSIC BASAL GANGLIA CONNECTIONS

"Direct" and "Indirect" Striatofugal Projections

In the early 1990s, a model of the functional connectivity of the basal ganglia emerged that described how cortical information is conveyed from the striatum to the output nuclei of the basal ganglia (GPi and SNr). Most authors agree that the intrinsic organization of striatofugal projections impose the striatal organization into motor, limbic, associative, and oculomotor territories on the other basal ganglia structures (76). This organizational principle results in the formation of distinct motor, associative, limbic, and oculomotor corticobasal gangliathalamocortical circuits that remain segregated throughout their subcortical course (76). Within the boundaries of each of these circuits, striatofugal pathways are divided into the so-called direct and indirect striatofugal pathways (3, 159, 160). The direct pathway arises from a sub-population of medium spiny neurons that project directly to neurons of GPi and SNr, whereas the indirect pathway arises largely from a separate population of spiny neurons that project to GPe (24). In turn, GPe conveys the information either directly, or via the intercalated STN, to GPi and SNr. The direct GABAergic GPe-GPi/SNr projection terminates predominately on the proximal part of GPi and SNr neurons. In monkey, GPe terminals account for more than 50% of the total number of terminals in contact with the perikarya of GPi neurons (160-164).

Although the degree of segregation of striatofugal neurons has been a matter of debate (see, e.g., Refs. 24 to 26 and 165), it appears that the subpopulation of striatal neurons that gives rise to the direct pathway can be further characterized by the presence of the neuropeptides substance P and dynorphin and by the preferential expression of the dopamine D1 receptors, while the subpopulation that gives rise to the indirect pathway expresses enkephalin and dopamine D2 receptors preferentially (166–172). The axons of striatal output neurons tend to form distinct bands of termination (24, 25, 173–175) that are highly specific (26, 174, 175). There is anatomic and functional evidence that the glutamatergic corticostriatal system regulates the 2 main populations of striatofugal neurons differently. For instance, stimulation of sensorimotor cortices induces preferential immediate-early gene expression in enkephalin-containing neurons in rats and monkeys (176, 177), and injections of the transneuronal anterograde herpes simplex virus into monkey M1 result in selective aggregation of third-order infected neurons in GPe (178). However, rodent studies have reported that both populations of striatofugal neurons respond to cortical stimulation (e.g., Ref. 179). Potential species and technical differences must be considered to explain these discrepancies.

The two principal populations of striatal neurons may differ in the type of cortical inputs they receive. Thus, cortical intratelencephalic (IT) neurons, which project to contralateral cortices and striatum, appear to target preferentially D1-containing "direct" striatofugal neurons, while pyramidal tract (PT) neurons, which project to the brainstem and spinal cord, innervate preferentially D2-containing "indirect" striatofugal neurons (180). At the cortical level, corticostriatal IT neurons provide inputs to other IT neurons and PT neurons (181), whereas PT neuron projections to IT neurons are far less common, which suggest a high degree of specificity in the microcircuitry of different populations of corticostriatal neurons. In monkeys, most data suggest that corticostriatal neurons are segregated from long-range corticospinal neurons (182–184), but a recent single-axon-tracing study demonstrated that this segregation may not be as strict as previously thought (125).

Dopaminergic Projections

The SNc (A9), ventral tegmental area (VTA, A10) and retrorubral field (RRF, A8) are the main sources of dopamine to the basal ganglia. The striatum is the main target of midbrain dopaminergic neurons, but extrastriatal dopaminergic projection to other basal ganglia nuclei and the thalamus may also play an important role in basal ganglia functions (39). Both the caudate nucleus and putamen receive strong dopaminergic inputs from segregated populations of SNc and RRF neurons, while the VTA innervates mainly the ventral striatum (24, 165, 185). The SNc comprises 2 main populations of dopaminergic neurons, which can be differentiated by their location and relative content of calbindin D28k and dopamine transporter (186). The ventral-tier SNc (SNc-v) comprises a densocellular part located dorsomedially and a ventral part made up of cell columns and clusters that

interdigitate with the SNr. These neurons are enriched in the dopamine transporter (DAT), do not express calbindin D28k, and are most sensitive to neurodegeneration in PD. In contrast, dorsal-tier SNc neurons (SNc-d) express low DAT immunoreactivity but are riched in calbindin. These neurons and those of the VTA are relatively spared in PD (187, 188). These 2 populations of dopaminergic neurons give rise to morphologically different types of axons, which display specific patterns of distribution in the rat striatum (189–191). The SNc-v neurons innervate the patch compartment preferentially, whereas SNc-d neurons project mainly to the matrix, although this segregation is not complete (189, 192). In monkeys, 4 main features characterize the topographic organization of the nigrostriatal system: (a) the sensorimotor striatum receives its main dopaminergic innervation from cell columns in the SNc-v, (b) the associative striatum is widely innervated by neurons in the densocellular part of the SNc-v, (c) the VTA and SNc-d innervate the limbic-related ventral striatum (193), and (d) both dorsal- and ventral-tier SNc neurons innervate the ventral striatum tio varying degrees (191). Together, these findings demonstrate that the nigrostriatal system is made up of several neuronal subsystems that allow for complex multifaceted regulation of widespread striatal regions.

Dopaminergic inputs functionally regulate the activity of striatal medium spiny projection neurons through pre- and postsynaptic interactions with D1- and D2-family receptors. The D1 family of receptors comprises D1 and D5 receptors, while the D2 family of receptors consists of D2, D3, and D4 receptors. Activation of D1-family receptors is thought to exert excitatory effects, while activation of D2-family receptors is generally inhibitory. D1 and D2 receptors are largely found in dendrites and spines of "direct" and "indirect" striatofugal neurons, respectively. In addition, D2 receptors are significantly expressed in cholinergic interneurons (39) and may be involved in long-term plasticity in striatal projection neurons (172, 194).

One of the principal functions of dopamine in the striatum may be the regulation of corticostriatal transmission. In large part, this is accomplished through complex interactions between pre- and postsynaptic dopamine receptors (39, 195). The interactions between the glutamatergic cortical inputs and modulatory dopaminergic projections occur specifically at postsynaptic dendritic spines (161). The convergence of glutamatergic and dopaminergic terminals on the head and neck of dendritic spines, respectively, provides a substrate where dopaminergic inputs can filter more distal glutamatergic afferents (161, 196, 197). This interaction involves both D1 and D2 receptors. The filtering mechanism appears to target specifically subsets of less active glutamatergic terminals (198, 199). D2-receptor activation also affects glutamate release in the striatum, likely mediated via retrograde endocannabinoid signaling, induced by high-frequency stimulation of D2 receptors on dendritic spines of medium spiny neurons (200).

The other classes of dopamine receptors are found at lower levels in the striatum. The D3 receptor is mainly confined to the ventral striatum (nucleus accumbens). Lower levels of D4 and D5 receptors are found in striatal projection neurons. D5 receptors are preferentially expressed in cholinergic and parvalbumin-containing interneurons (201–204). D5 receptors may be important in long-term synaptic plasticity and in the regulation of acetylcholine release and GABA(A)-mediated currents (203–206).

Dopamine does not mediate its effects on basal ganglia functions solely through the striatum. The role of extrastriatal dopamine in regulating activity of pallidal, subthalamic, and nigral neurons has been clearly demonstrated (39). SNc neurons send axonal projections to GPe, Gpi, and STN. Tyrosine hydroxylase–positive terminals forming symmetrical synapses have been found in the pallidum and STN (39, 207). Dopamine release, albeit at levels that are substantially lower than those in the striatum, has been shown in the rat GP and STN (207, 208). In the substantia nigra, dopamine is released through dendrites of SNc neurons that extend ventrally into the SNr (39, 209). Neurons in the extrastriatal basal ganglia nuclei express pre- and postsynaptic D1- and D2-family dopamine receptors that mediate the functional effects of dopamine and dopamine-related drugs on GP, STN, and SNr neurons (39, 63, 66, 210, 211). Widespread dopamine innervation of the monkey thalamus has been demonstrated, which provides another important extrastriatal target where dopamine could regulate basal ganglia-thalamocortical systems (212, 213).

STN Projections

The main projection sites of the STN are GPi (EP in the rat) and SNr. The STN also provides a dense glutamatergic feedback projection to the GPe (148, 163, 214–218) and sends modest inputs to the striatum (104, 219, 220), the SNc (217, 221, 222), the PPN (220, 221, 223), and the spinal cord (224). STN output is highly collateralized in the rat (225, 226) but is thought to be more specific in primates (143, 218, 220, 226, 227) (but also see Refs. 175 and 185).

Several studies have demonstrated that the relationships between neurons of the GPe, STN, and GPi are highly specific (69, 64, 218, 228–230). Populations of neurons within sensorimotor, cognitive, and limbic territories in the GPe are reciprocally connected with populations of neurons in the same functional territories of the STN, and the neurons in each of these regions, in turn, innervate the same functional territory of the GPi (164, 218). It is possible, however, that additional, more divergent circuits may exist (69, 164, 218, 231).

In contrast to the previous belief that the STN is a homogeneous structure made up of a single population of output neurons, recent single-axon-tracing data demonstrate neuronal heterogeneity in the primate STN. In monkeys, 5 populations of STN neurons have been identified based on their termination sites and collateralization of their axonal projections to other basal ganglia nuclei (67). These include neurons that project to GPe and GPi (48%); neurons that project to SNr, Gpi, and GPe (21%); neurons with axons that course toward the striatum (17%); neurons that project only to GPe (11%); and neurons that target SNr and GPe (3%) (67). It remains unclear how these data can be reconciled with the above-cited work demonstrating the specificity of most STN projection neurons.

OUTPUT PROJECTIONS OF THE BASAL GANGLIA

Nigrofugal Pathways

Based on the arrangement of striatal inputs and nigral outputs, the SNr in rats can be subdivided into a dorsolateral sensorimotor and a ventromedial associative territory (232), further supporting the hypothesis of a broad organization of the basal ganglia into segregated channels (76). SNr neurons possess a rich network of local axon collaterals, which are confined to the same functional domain as the parent cell body.

The pattern of axonal arborization of SNr neurons has been the topic of many recent single axon-tracing studies in rats and monkeys (73, 233–235). These studies have shown that SNr neurons are highly heterogeneous in their degree of innervation and axonal collateralization to thalamic and other targets (233–235).

Thalamic projections from the medial part of the SNr terminate mostly in the medial magnocellular division of the ventral anterior nucleus (VAmc) and the mediodorsal nucleus (MDmc) which, in turn, innervate anterior regions of the frontal lobe including the principal sulcus (Walker's area 46) and the orbital cortex (Walker's area 11) in monkeys (236). Neurons in the lateral part of the SNr project preferentially to the lateral posterior region of the VAmc and to different parts of the MD. These areas of the thalamus are predominately related to posterior regions of the frontal lobe, including the frontal eye field and areas of the premotor cortex, respectively (236). More detailed anatomic studies using the technique of retrograde transsynaptic transport of viruses have directly visualized different nigro-thalamo-cortical channels along which basal ganglia outflow gains access to cognitive, sensory, and oculomotor cortical areas of the frontal, temporal, and parietal lobes in monkeys (237, 238).

SNr neurons also project to the superior colliculus, PPN, and the medullary reticular formation. Nigrocollicular fibers terminate mainly on tectospinal neurons in the intermediate layer of the superior colliculus and play a critical role in the control of visual saccades (239). A reciprocal tectonigral projection that terminates in the vicinity of dopaminergic SNc neurons has been described in rats and cat (240, 241). This projection is a relay for short-latency visual information to influence basal ganglia through the nigrofugal dopaminergic system (240). Nigrotegmental neurons terminate predominantly on noncholinergic neurons in the medial two-thirds of the PPN (242, 243). The nigroreticular projection terminates in the parvicellular reticular formation, which is directly connected with orofacial motor nuclei (244–246).

SNr outputs are also involved in several feedback circuits. Thus, many PPN neurons send projections back to the basal ganglia nuclei, including the SNr. SNr neurons also innervate thalamostriatal projection neurons in PF (106). Another example for a feedback circuit is a local reentrant loop, by which projections from the SNr target SNc neurons that project to the striatal sector from which the parent cell bodies in the SNr receive their afferents (73). Studies in rats suggest that SNr neurons also project directly to the striatum (247).

Pallidofugal Pathways

Two principal anatomic types of neurons have been identified in the monkey GPi. The most abundant cell type (type I neurons), located in the core of GPi, projects discretely to the PPN but arborizes profusely in the ventral motor and caudal intralaminar thalamic nuclei. In contrast, type II neurons are located in the periphery of GPi, and send massive projections to the lateral habenular nucleus. A small proportion of both type I and type II neurons project contralaterally to thalamic and brainstem targets (70, 248–250).

Primarily based on studies of striatopallidal inputs and palliothalamic projections, GPi is viewed as an anatomically and functionally largely segregated structure. The ventrolateral two-thirds of the nucleus receive afferents arising from sensorimotor cortical areas, while the dorsal third and the rostromedial pole of the GPi receive afferents arising from associative and limbic cortical areas, respectively (78). The segregation is maintained in the pallidothalamic projection (251). Sensorimotor information is conveyed almost exclusively to the posterior part of the ventrolateral nucleus (VLo in macaques), while "associative" portions of GPi project preferentially to the parvocellular part of the ventral anterior (VA) and the dorsal ventrolateral nucleus of thalamus (VLc in macaques) (251–253). Projections from "associative" and "limbic" portions of GPi innervate the same thalamic nuclei, suggesting that emotional and cognitive information from the basal ganglia may converge onto individual thalamocortical neurons.

Via the thalamus, sensorimotor output from GPi is projected toward the supplementary motor area (SMA) (254–257), M1 (256–263) and premotor (PM) cortical area (259). Virus transport studies have suggested that the pallidal projections directed at cortical areas MI, PM, and SMA arise from segregated populations of GPi neurons in monkeys (259, 264). Basal ganglia output related to associative and limbic functions may be transmitted in a less specific manner to prefrontal areas (265, 66) and frontal cortical regions (256, 267).

Most GPi neurons that project to VA/VLo also send axon collaterals to the caudal intralaminar nuclear group (CM/PF), which, in turn, projects predominately to the striatum (see above and Ref. 251). Neurons in the sensorimotor territory of GPi project exclusively to CM, while associative and limbic areas predominantly reach PF, which provides the substrate for functionally segregated pallidothalamostriatal loops in primates (106, 107).

In monkeys, a large proportion of neurons that project to the VA/VLo also send axon collaterals to the noncholinergic portion of the PPN (268–272). This projection is less specific than the pallidal projections to the thalamus. In fact, processing at the level of the PPN may serve to integrate neuronal input from different functional GPi territories (268). The PPN gives rise to descending projections to the pons, medulla, and spinal cord as well as prominent ascending projections to the basal ganglia, thalamus, and basal forebrain (see, e.g., Refs. 273 and 274). Of the basal ganglia projections, the massive projection to the dopaminergic SNc is perhaps most noteworthy (275–280).

Another important target of GPi neurons is the lateral habenular nucleus. In monkeys, neurons located in the periphery and the medial limbic-related territory of GPi mainly contribute to this projection (70), which represents a prominent interface between limbic and motor related information processed in basal ganglia.

FUNCTIONAL CONSIDERATIONS

Convergence or Segregation?

The anatomic organization of the basal ganglia suggests that the basal ganglia–thalamocortical circuits are a highly specific system in which territories related to motor and nonmotor functions remain segregated. This anatomic concept is strongly supported by evidence from electrophysiologic recording studies. Each region contains neurons that respond selectively to a narrow range of specific inputs or behaviors (at least within the experimental framework studied). For instance, the sensorimotor portion of the basal ganglia contains specific areas with neurons concerned with active or passive limb movements (145, 281–298). This region is anatomically separated from other areas, in which neuronal function is, for instance, related to eye movements (oculomotor circuit) (299, 300–303). Most physiologic studies to date have failed to demonstrate correlated discharge of neighboring striatal or pallidal cells (30, 145, 304) under normal conditions, although more subtle collateral interactions in the striatum have recently been described (37, 305, 306). Furthermore, functional neurosurgical studies have demonstrated that lesions in the sensorimotor portion of the GPi alleviate the motor signs associated with parkinsonism without affecting cognitive functions, while lesions outside of this region do not improve motor function but may affect cognition.

The evidence in favor of segregation of information in the basal ganglia contrasts with other data which suggest at least partial convergence of information. Thus it is clear that the number of striatal neurons is much smaller than that of cortical neurons that project upon them and much greater than the number of neurons in the nuclei that receive striatal inputs (see, e.g., Refs. 308 and 309), suggesting some degree of "funneling" of information, at least within the major functional territories in the basal ganglia.

The question of whether or not information in the basal ganglia remains segregated is functionally relevant. Intuitively, convergence of motor- and nonmotor information would seem advantageous from a functional point of view. Consequently, there is ongoing debate whether motor- and nonmotor information converges along the subcortical paths of these circuits (310, 311). Direct large-scale anatomic convergence between the major functional divisions within the basal ganglia appears to be unlikely, but it is clear that motor- and nonmotor circuits converge to some extent—for instance, at the level of the PPN, cortex, and STN (see above for details).

Interactions between basal ganglia circuits at a smaller scale may also occur via local axon collaterals or interactions between subchannels within the larger circuits described above. These interactions are particularly important for hypotheses regarding "center-surround" inhibitory phenomena in the basal ganglia. There is evidence for the existence of such collateral inhibition in the striatum. While some medium spiny striatal neurons are directly activated by glutamatergic inputs from the cortex, neighboring neurons may be inhibited via axon collaterals of the activated neuron or via intercalated fast-spiking interneurons (31, 37, 306), resulting in a "winner-takes-all" scenario, which favors the (locally) strongest focus of corticostriatal stimulation and reduces the excitability of neighboring areas of the striatum and related circuitry. Another well-known example of possible center-surround inhibition is the interaction between direct and indirect pathways in GPi/SNr. The direct/indirect pathway

interaction has been hypothesized to play a role in the "focusing" of movement via a selection process that favors intended over unintended movements, represented by information traveling along direct and indirect pathways, respectively (146, 230, 312–316).

It is possible that the level of dopamine or other neuromodulators dynamically influences the level of functional segregation through modulation of synaptic collateral interactions, particularly in the striatum (317–320). This could transiently affect the level of synchrony between neighboring basal ganglia neurons—for instance, during learning (308, 309) or more permanently during dopamine depletion where a greater level of interneuronal synchrony is observed throughout the basal ganglia (see below, specifically Refs. 9, 304, 321, and 322 to 327).

The Role of the Basal Ganglia in Motor Control

In functional terms, voluntary movements appear to be initiated at the cortical level of the motor circuit with simultaneous output to the brainstem and spinal cord, as well as to multiple subcortical targets, including the thalamus, putamen, and STN. According to the current models, interactions between the direct and indirect pathways are important for basal ganglia regulation of motor control. Cortical movement-related inputs may activate striatal neurons that give rise to the monosynaptic direct pathway, resulting in inhibition of basal ganglia output. In contrast, activation of indirect-pathway neurons—that is, neurons projecting to GPe, which, in turn, project to GPi and SNr either directly or via the STN—would result in activation of basal ganglia output. Current models of basal ganglia function posit that cortical activity related to an intended movement activates specific portions of the direct pathway, resulting in appropriate reduction of inhibitory basal ganglia output to the thalamus and *facilitation* of cortical activity related to the intended movement. Activation of the indirect pathway would have the opposite effects. Via activation of the indirect pathway, the basal ganglia may act to *suppress* unintended movement (146, 230, 312–316). Because the most common change in discharge in GPi output neurons during movement is an increase in activity, suppression of unintended or competing movement may, in fact, be a particularly important role of the basal ganglia. Since the functions of the direct and indirect pathways appear to be distinctly different, it is possible that selective dysfunction of one or the other pathway may result in distinct clinical disturbances (see below).

The combination of information traveling via the direct and the indirect pathways of the motor circuit has been proposed to "scale" or "focus" movements (77, 328). Based on clinical and experimental studies, basal ganglia may play a role in specifying the amplitude or velocity of movement (329). To achieve scaling and termination of movements, striatal output would first inhibit specific neuronal populations in GPi/SNr via the direct pathway, facilitating movement, followed after a delay by disinhibition of the same GPi/SNr neuron via inputs over the indirect pathway, leading to an inhibition of the ongoing movement. In the focusing model, inhibition of relevant pallidal/nigral neurons via the direct pathway would allow intended movements to proceed, whereas unintended movements would be suppressed by concomitant increased excitatory input via the indirect pathway in other GPi/SNr neurons. Similar models have been proposed for the generation of saccades in the oculomotor circuit (e.g., Ref. 301). Direct anatomic support for either of these functions is lacking, because it is uncertain whether the direct and indirect pathways (emanating from neurons that are concerned with the same movement) converge on the same or separate neurons in GPi/SNr (165, 330–332).

Although changes in discharge rate and pattern in most movement-related neurons in the basal ganglia occurs too late to influence the initiation of movement, changes in discharge could influence the amplitude or focus of ongoing movements (145, 333). Conceivably, neurons with shorter onset latencies or with "preparatory" activity may indeed play such a role (261, 334–342). PET studies have reported that basal ganglia activity is modulated in relation to low-level parameters of movement, such as force or movement speed (343, 344), thus supporting a scaling function of the basal ganglia.

Other proposed motor functions of the basal ganglia include roles in self-initiated (internally generated) movements, in motor learning and in movement sequencing (e.g., Refs. 345 and 346 to 349). For instance, both dopaminergic nigrostriatal neurons and tonically active neurons in the striatum have been shown to develop transient responses to sensory conditioning stimuli during behavioral training in classical conditioning tasks (347, 350–352). This supports a role of these cells and of basal ganglia areas whose activity they influence in motor learning. Shifts in the response properties of striatal output neurons during performance of a maze task that involved learning were recently demonstrated in the rat (353). In addition to these concepts a number of other theories have gained varying degrees of popularity, including concepts that the basal ganglia may globally act to extract cortical information through dimensionality reduction (309) or may assist in resource allocation (354).

Lesion studies have yielded conflicting evidence regarding the motor functions of the basal ganglia. Most studies have found either no or only short-lived effects on skilled fine movements or mild bradykinesia after pallidal lesions (355–365). A notable exception to this is a study by Mink and Thach (316, 328, 366) in which cocontractions were observed after lesioning or inactivation of GPi, although this may have been due to inadvertent involvement of GPe in these experiments. Given the relative paucity of motor side effects of pallidal lesions in animals and humans (as discussed later), it could be concluded that, under normal conditions, basal ganglia output may not play a significant role in movement initiation or execution (345). When output from these structures is altered (as is the case in movement disorders), however, the disruption of otherwise normal motor systems produces major abnormalities of movement.

It is also possible that the motor system may be sufficiently redundant so that loss of basal ganglia function after lesioning is compensated for by other neuronal mechanisms. The striking lack of motor side effects *immediately* after pallidal lesions, however, argues against this possibility, because it could be expected that reorganization and changes in synaptic strength in other areas would require time to develop.

PATHOPHYSIOLOGY OF PARKINSON'S DISEASE

General Characteristics of Parkinson's Disease

Parkinson's disease (PD) is a syndrome characterized by movement abnormalities such as akinesia (poverty of movement and impaired movement initiation), bradykinesia (slowness of movement), muscular rigidity, and tremor at rest. These motor disturbances are jointly called parkinsonism and are in large part related to the degeneration of neurons in the dopaminergic SNc (367–369). More recently, however, more widespread neuronal degeneration has been identified that may involve other brainstem areas, the olfactory tubercle and cortex, even in early phases of the disease (370, 371). These abnormalities may underlie some of the nonmotor problems seen in PD, such as cognitive and affective problems or autonomic disturbances. Little is known about the pathophysiologic changes that eventually lead to the development of these nonmotor features. In the following account, we therefore concentrate on the relatively well known pathophysiologic steps that lead to motor abnormalities in parkinsonism.

In the earlier stages of PD, dopamine depletion is greatest in the sensorimotor territory of the striatum—that is, the postcommissural portion of the putamen, suggesting that the motor circuit is preferentially involved in the pathophysiology underlying the motor abnormalities (372). Reduced activation of dopamine receptors on striatal projection neurons is thought to result in a cascade of activity changes throughout the basal ganglia. These are discussed below. In addition, striatal dopamine loss has recently been shown to induce substantial morphologic changes in the striatal neurons that receive dopaminergic innervation. Thus, the spine density of striatal neurons is reduced in dopamine-depleted animals (373, 374) and human PD patients (375), apparently affecting preferentially those neurons that give rise to the indirect pathway (170). The functional significance of these morphologic changes is not well understood.

Pathophysiology of Parkinson's Disease: The "Rate Model"

Most of the pathophysiologic changes in the basal ganglia resulting from striatal dopamine loss are interpreted as the result of reduced activation of striatal dopamine receptors. The study of these changes has been facilitated by the discovery that primates treated with the neurotoxin 1-methyl-4-phenyl-1,2,3,6-tetrahydropyridine (MPTP) develop behavioral and anatomic changes that closely mimic the features of PD (376–382). Physiological changes in the striatopallidal pathways were first documented in biochemical studies, which indicated that in MPTP-induced parkinsonism in primates, the metabolic activity (as measured with the 2-deoxyglucose technique) is increased in both pallidal segments (383–389). This was interpreted as evidence for increased activity of the striatum-GPe connection and the STN-GPi pathway or, alternatively, as evidence for increased activity via the projections from the STN to both pallidal segments. Later, it was shown with microelectrode recordings of neuronal activity, that MPTP-induced parkinsonism in primates is associated with reduced tonic neuronal discharge in GPe, and increased mean discharge rates in the STN and GPi, as compared to normal controls (321–323, 325, 390)(see Figure 22-2). In human parkinsonian patients undergoing pallidotomy, it has also been shown that, similar to findings in parkinsonian animals, the discharge rates in GPe are significantly lower than those in GPi (391–394), although, of course, there has been no recording in normal controls for comparison. These findings have been interpreted as indicating that striatal dopamine depletion leads to increased activity of those striatal neurons that give rise to the projection to GPe, suppressing neuronal discharge in Gpe, and resulting in disinhibition of STN and GPi via the indirect pathway. Loss of dopamine in the striatum is also postulated to lead to reduced activity via the inhibitory direct pathway (see Figure 22-3).

Reciprocal changes in the indirect and direct pathways following dopamine depletion should have the same net effect—that is, increased activity in GPi/SNr, leading to increased basal ganglia output to the thalamus and excessive inhibition of thalamocortical neurons. The 2-deoxyglucose studies mentioned above demonstrated increased (synaptic) activity in the VA and VL nucleus of the thalamus (383–385), presumably reflecting increased inhibitory basal ganglia output to these subnuclei. Consistent with this are PET studies in parkinsonian patients, which have consistently shown reduced activation of motor and premotor areas in such patients (395–397) that are at least partially reversed after neurosurgical interventions designed to reduce GPi output, such as pallidotomies

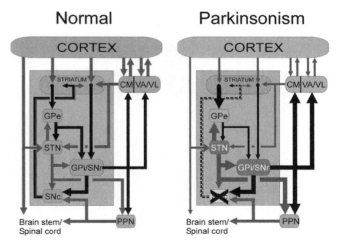

Normal   Parkinsonism

FIGURE 22-2

Schematic diagram of the basal ganglia–thalamocortical circuitry under normal and parkinsonian conditions. Parkinsonism leads to differential changes in the two stratopallidal projections, which are indicated by the thickness of the connecting arrows. Basal ganglia output to the thalamus is increased. Same abbreviations as in Figure 22-1.

(398–400). Alterations of cortical activity in M1 and SMA have also been demonstrated with single-cell recording in hemiparkinsonian primates (401, 402).

The fact that the thalamic nucleus CM is tightly linked to the basal ganglia structures (see above), renders it highly likely that abnormal GPi output to CM plays a role in parkinsonism. Increased inhibition of CM would not only lead to reduced activation of the CM-cortical pathway but also to a further reduction of activity in the direct pathway via the thalamostriatal projections arising in the CM.

The PPN may also be involved in the development of parkinsonian signs. It has been shown that lesions of this nucleus in normal monkeys can lead to a hemiparkinsonian syndrome, possibly by reducing excitation of SNc neurons by input from the PPN or through mechanisms independent of the dopaminergic system (274, 403–406). Conceivably, in PD, activity in the PPN is inhibited by increased basal ganglia output, with the detrimental consequence that SNc activity would be further reduced, leading to worsening of parkinsonian signs (407).

Strong evidence for the importance of increased basal ganglia output in the development of parkinsonian motor signs comes from lesion studies. Specifically, lesions of the STN in MPTP-treated primates have been shown to reverse all of the cardinal motor signs of parkinsonism, probably by reducing GPi activity but possibly also by normalizing the pattern of pallidal output (408–410). STN lesions in parkinsonian patients have been shown to reverse parkinsonian signs in humans as

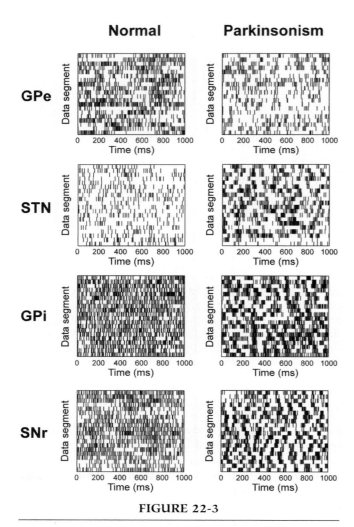

Normal   **Parkinsonism**

GPe

STN

GPi

SNr

FIGURE 22-3

Raster display of spontaneous neuronal activity from different structures within the basal ganglia circuitry in the normal and parkinsonian state. Same abbreviations as in Figure 22-1.

well (411–413). Stereotactic lesions of the motor portion of GPi have been reintroduced in patients as treatment for medically intractable parkinsonism and have been found effective against all major parkinsonian motor signs and drug-induced dyskinesias (363–365, 414, 415). PET studies in such patients have shown that frontal motor areas whose metabolic activity was reduced in the parkinsonian state were again active following pallidotomy (398–400, 414).

Pathophysiology of Parkinson's Disease: Changes in Discharge Patterns

Although they are supported by some of the lesion studies, the rate-based models of the pathophysiology of parkinsonism fail to explain all of the findings. For instance,

lesions of the motor thalamus that completely abolish thalamocortical output from the motor circuit do not result in akinesia/bradykinesia; conversely, GPi lesions do not result in excessive movement. Furthermore, electrical stimulation of STN in the MPTP monkey model of PD increases the mean discharge rates of neurons in GPi, coincident with an improvement, not a worsening, of parkinsonian motor signs (416). It is increasingly recognized that basal ganglia activity undergoes not only changes in discharge rates but also prominent changes in discharge patterns in parkinsonism. These changes are now seen to be crucial for the development of specific parkinsonian motor signs.

Neuronal responses to passive limb manipulations in STN, Gpi, and thalamus (321–323, 417) have been shown to occur more often, to be more pronounced, to have widened receptive fields, and to be more often inhibitory (315) after treatment with MPTP and the development of parkinsonian motor signs. Cross-correlation studies have also revealed that a substantial proportion of neighboring neurons in globus pallidus, STN, and cortex discharge in unison in MPTP-treated primates (303, 323, 402, 418–420). This is in contrast to the virtual absence of synchronized discharge of such neurons in normal monkeys (e.g., Refs. 145 and 333). Finally, the proportion of cells in STN, Gpi, and SNr that discharge in oscillatory or nonoscillatory bursts is greatly increased in the parkinsonian state (10, 321–323, 325, 394, 421–424), and the temporal structure of burst- and periburst discharges is altered (425).

It has recently become possible to record local field potentials in the basal ganglia of human patients with movement disorders by using implanted deep-brain-stimulation leads as recording electrodes (9, 327, 426–434). These recordings have demonstrated prominent oscillatory local field potential activity in the beta band (10 to 25 Hz) in STN and GPi in parkinsonian patients. The increased beta-band activity can be abolished by treatment with dopaminergic medications in favor of activity at higher frequencies (9, 431–433). Building on experience with cortical LFP recordings, and (limited) correlative experience with combined single-unit and LFP basal ganglia recordings (e.g., Ref. 435), LFPs are often seen as representative of neuronal ensemble activity. However, it remains uncertain which excitable elements contribute most to the oscillatory LFPs recorded in parkinsonian patients.

Pathophysiology of Parkinsonian Motor Signs

Most of the available evidence suggests that the cardinal parkinsonian motor disturbances result from abnormal basal ganglia output to cortical motor areas. The individual motor signs are discussed separately in the following paragraphs, but in reality they often occur concurrently in PD patients.

Akinesia—that is, the global impairment of movement initiation—is a hallmark sign of PD. The involvement of cortical circuits in akinesia is supported by the finding that PET studies of cortical activation in akinesia-predominant parkinsonism show that SMA and dorsal prefrontal motor areas are hypoactive in such patients (436, 437). Further evidence for abnormal activity in these areas comes from studies of the Bereitschaftspotential (readiness potential), a slow negative cortical potential that precedes self-paced movements and is thought to reflect the neural activity in SMA (438). The early portion of the Bereitschaftspotential is smaller in parkinsonian patients than in age-matched controls (439, 440), suggesting a deficit in the normal function of the SMA in the early stages of preparation for self-initiated movements. A disorganization of preparatory activity in SMA neurons was indeed identified with electrophysiologic methods in hemiparkinsonian primates (400) and is consistent with this proposal.

The increased discharge rates in the basal ganglia output nuclei which are found in PD may significantly impact the amount of movement. Conceivably, increased tonic inhibition of thalamocortical neurons may render cortical motor areas less responsive to other inputs normally involved in initiating movements or could interfere with "set" functions that may depend on the integrity of basal ganglia pathways (159). Akinesia is also often discussed in terms of the proposed "focusing" function of the basal ganglia (146, 230, 312–316). With increased activity along the indirect pathway, the "focus" provided by the direct pathway is seen to become abnormally narrow.

A problem with any hypothesis claiming underactivity of thalamocortical circuits as a significant contributor to akinesia is the fact that lesions of the basal ganglia or cerebellar receiving areas of thalamus (VLo, and VPLo, respectively) do not induce akinesia. This finding suggests that mechanisms other than increased basal ganglia output are important for the development of this motor sign. Altered discharge patterns in basal ganglia–thalamocortical activity, particularly synchronized oscillatory activity, may be more important than rate changes alone. The behavioral significance of oscillatory entrainment of the basal ganglia–thalamocortical circuitry is directly evident from studies investigating the impact of different DBS stimulation protocols on parkinsonian motor signs (441, 442). Stimulation of the STN area at 10 Hz exacerbates akinesia (441), while therapeutic high-frequency deep brain stimulation of the STN (130 Hz) (see, e.g., Ref. 443) reduces the coherent low-frequency activity in the basal ganglia (433, 434) and may impose oscillatory patterns on the basal ganglia–thalamocortical circuits that are easier to tolerate.

Some aspects of akinesia may also be related to abnormal activity along the brainstem projections of the basal ganglia output nuclei, particularly the PPN, as has been shown in primate studies (403, 404, 406). Based on these results, low-frequency stimulation of the PPN is currently being tested in animals and patients as a potential treatment for PD (444–447).

Bradykinesia—that is, slowness of movement—may be due to a more specific abnormality in processing in prefrontal cortical areas induced by altered basal ganglia output. This motor sign may be closely associated with the postulated "scaling" function of basal ganglia output. Electrophysiologic studies in normal monkeys as well as PET studies investigating cerebral blood flow in human probands have demonstrated that the velocity or amplitude of movement has a strong impact on the activity of neurons in premotor cortical areas (e.g., Refs. 291, 292–298, 343, 344, 448). Abnormally increased phasic basal ganglia output during movement may signal excessive speed and/or amplitude of ongoing movement, leading to a corrective reduction in cortical motor output. PET studies, measuring cerebral blood flow in human parkinsonian patients investigated before and during deep brain stimulation of Gpi, have revealed that stimulation which improved bradykinesia lead to an increase in blood flow in the ipsilateral premotor cortical areas (449). Other PET studies have shown a significant correlation between movement speed and basal ganglia activation (344) that is lost in PD (Turner et al., personal communication).

The pathophysiology of muscle rigidity in PD is elusive. Rigidity is abolished by both pallidal and thalamic lesions, which suggests that basal ganglia output leads to rigidity via the thalamocortical route. This contrasts with findings suggesting that that altered basal ganglia output, mediated via the PPN and its output to the pontine nucleus gigantocellularis and the dorsal longitudinal fasciculus of the reticulospinal projection, may lead to increased inhibition of Ib interneurons, which in turn may disinhibit α-motor neurons (450–452). Abnormalities of long-latency reflexes (LLRs) may also play a role in abnormal excitablilty of α-motor neurons ty (453–455), although the velocity-independence of rigidity suggests that it is not a reflex phenomenon per se.

Tremor at rest is also a cardinal parkinsonian motor sign. The effectiveness of lesions or stimulation of the ventral thalamus, particularly the thalamic nucleus ventralis intermedius (Vim), as treatment for parkinsonian tremor indicates that the integrity of this nucleus is as important for parkinsonian tremor as it is for other forms of tremor. In tremor patients, Vim contains neurons that exhibit oscillatory discharge at the tremor frequency (456–461). A possible link between oscillatory discharge in the thalamus and increased inhibitory basal ganglia output is that many thalamic cells may be induced to produce oscillatory firing patterns by hyperpolarization (462–468). Tremor may also arise from oscillatory discharge generated within the basal ganglia. Thus, oscillatory discharge patterns are demonstrated in the STN and GPi in parkinsonian patients and animals (323, 393, 422, 469–472), and intrinsic membrane properties of basal ganglia neurons are also conducive to the development of oscillatory discharge (473). Furthermore, lesions of STN or GPi reduce tremor in parkinsonian monkeys and in PD patients (160, 364, 393, 415, 474). Yet, the relationship between the oscillatory movements in parkinsonian tremor and pathologic oscillatory discharge in the basal ganglia (475, 476) is complicated. Although oscillations in LFPs in the STN and EMGs recorded in tremulous extremities have been reported in patients with PD (477), other studies of the correlation between tremor movements and oscillatory activity in the basal ganglia have not been conclusive. One of the problems is that multiple oscillators may be at work in the parkinsonian state (478), with different limbs of parkinsonian patients engaged in tremors of different frequencies (479, 480), which easily explains that tremor movement and oscillatory discharge in the basal ganglia are not always coherent and may even shift in and out of correlation (420, 481). The synchronization between basal ganglia "channels" may also be an important ingredient in the pathophysiology of tremor (481).

CONCLUSIONS

The basal ganglia represent parts of corticosubcortical circuits involved in a large variety of motor as well as nonmotor functions. Although fairly straigthforward in pathologic terms, parkinsonism emerges as a complex disorder in which striatal dopamine depletion results in an increased and disordered discharge in motor areas of basal ganglia thalamocortical loops. It is likely that individual parkinsonian motor signs are caused by distinct abnormalities in basal ganglia discharge and by involvement of specific subcircuits related to distinct cortical targets.

The current models of basal ganglia anatomy, physiology, and pathophysiology clearly need further refinement. Most pertinently, changes in the pattern, degree of synchronization, and receptive field properties of neurons in the basal ganglia and thalamus need to be better incorporated with new anatomic connections into future models of basal ganglia pathophysiology. A greater emphasis also needs to be placed on the manner in which thalamic, brainstem, and cortical neurons utilize basal ganglia output as we continue to define and develop new concepts of basal ganglia function.

References

1. DeLong MR. Primate models of movement disorders of basal ganglia origin. *Trends Neurosci* 1990; 13:281–285.
2. Wichmann T, DeLong MR. Functional and pathophysiological models of the basal ganglia. *Curr Opin Neurobiol* 1996; 6:751–758.
3. Albin RL, Young AB, Penney JB. The functional anatomy of basal ganglia disorders. *Trends Neurosci* 1989; 12:366–375.
4. Albin RL. The pathophysiology of chorea/ballism and parkinsonism. *Parkinsonism Relat Disord* 1995; 1:3–11.
5. Chesselet MF, Delfs JM. Basal ganglia and movement disorders: An update. *Trends Neurosci* 1996; 19:417–422.
6. Brooks DJ. The role of the basal ganglia in motor control: Contributions from pet. *J Neurol Sci* 1995; 128:1–13.
7. Graybiel AM. Basal ganglia: New therapeutic approaches to Parkinson's disease. *Curr Biol* 1996; 6:368–371.
8. Graybiel AM, Aosaki T, Flaherty AW, Kimura M. The basal ganglia and adaptive motor control. *Science* 1994; 265:1826–1831.
9. Brown P. Oscillatory nature of human basal ganglia activity: Relationship to the pathophysiology of parkinson's disease. *Mov Disord* 2003; 18:357–363.
10. Gatev PG, Darbin O, Wichmann T. Oscillations in the basal ganglia under normal conditions and in movement disorders. *Mov Disord* 2006. 21(10):1566–1577.
11. Heimer L, Zahm DS, Alheid GF. Basal ganglia. In: Paxinos G (ed). *The rat Nervous System,* 2nd ed. San Diego, CA: Academic Press, 1995:579–628.
12. Groenewegen HJ, Wright CI, Beijer AV. The nucleus accumbens: Gateway for limbic structures to reach the motor system? *Prog Brain Res* 1996; 107:485–511.
13. Pierce RC, Kalivas PW. A circuitry model of the expression of behavioral sensitization to amphetamine-like psychostimulants. *Brain Res Brain Res Rev* 1997; 25: 192–216.
14. Haber SN, McFarland NR. The concept of the ventral striatum in nonhuman primates. *Ann N Y Acad Sci* 1999; 877:33–48.
15. Grace AA. Gating of information flow within the limbic system and the pathophysiology of schizophrenia. *Brain Res Brain Res Rev* 2000; 31:330–341.
16. Heimer L. Basal forebrain in the context of schizophrenia. *Brain Res Brain Res Rev* 2000; 31:205–235.
17. Kalivas PW, Volkow ND. The neural basis of addiction: A pathology of motivation and choice. *Am J Psychiatry* 2005; 162:1403–1413.
18. Zahm DS. Functional-anatomical implications of the nucleus accumbens core and shell subterritories. *Ann N Y Acad Sci* 1999; 877:113–128.
19. Haber SN, Gdowski MJ. The basal ganglia. In: Paxinos G, Mai JK (eds). *The Human Nervous System,* 2nd ed. Amsterdam: Elsevier/Academic Press, 2004: 677–738.
20. Smith Y. Glutamatergic pathways: Their relevance for psychiatric diseases. In: Schmidt WJ, Reith MEA (eds). *Dopamine and Glutamate in Psychiatric Disorders.* Totowa, NJ: Humana Press, 2005:65–77.
21. Kalivas PW, McFarland K. Brain circuitry and the reinstatement of cocaine-seeking behavior. *Psychopharmacology (Berl)* 2003; 168:44–56.
22. Graveland GA, Difiglia M. The frequency and distribution of medium-sized neurons with indented nuclei in the primate and rodent neostriatum. *Brain Res* 1985; 327:307–311.
23. Tepper JM, Bolam JP. Functional diversity and specificity of neostriatal interneurons. *Curr Opin Neurobiol* 2004; 14:685–692.
24. Gerfen CR, Wilson CJ. The basal ganglia. In: Björklund A, Hökfeld T, Swanson L (eds). *Handbook of Chemical Neuroanatomy, Integrated Systems of the CNS.* Part III. Amsterdam: Elsevier, 1996:369.
25. Kawaguchi Y, Wilson CJ, Emson PC. Projection subtypes of rat neostriatal matrix cells revealed by intracellular injection of biocytin. *J Neurosci* 1990; 10:3421–3438.
26. Levesque M, Parent A. The striatofugal fiber system in primates: A reevaluation of its organization based on single-axon tracing studies. *Proc Natl Acad Sci USA* 2005; 102:11888–11893.
27. Wilson CJ, Groves PM. Fine structure and synaptic connections of the common spiny neuron of the rat neostriatum: A study employing intracellular inject of horseradish peroxidase. *J Comp Neurol* 1980; 194:599–615.
28. Bishop GA, Chang HT, Kitai ST. Morphological and physiological properties of neostriatal neurons: An intracellular horseradish peroxidase study in the rat. *Neuroscience* 1982; 7:179–191.
29. Smith AD, Bolam JP. The neural network of the basal ganglia as revealed by the study of synaptic connections of identified neurones. *Trends Neurosci* 1990; 13:259–265.
30. Jaeger D, Kita H, Wilson CJ. Surround inhibition among projection neurons is weak or nonexistent in the rat neostriatum. *J Neurophysiol* 1994; 72:2555–2558.
31. Koos T, Tepper JM, Wilson CJ. Comparison of IPSCs evoked by spiny and fast—spiking neurons in the neostriatum. *J Neurosci* 2004; 24:7916–7922.
32. Cicchetti F, Beach TG, Parent A. Chemical phenotype of calretinin interneurons in the human striatum. *Synapse* 1998; 30:284–297.
33. Kawaguchi Y, Wilson CJ, Augood SJ, Emson PC. Striatal interneurones: Chemical, physiological and morphological characterization. *Trends Neurosci* 1995; 18:527–535.
34. Bennett BD, Wilson CJ. Spontaneous activity of neostriatal cholinergic interneurons in vitro. *J Neurosci* 1999; 19:5586–5596.
35. Aosaki T, Tsubokawa H, Ishida A, et al. Responses of tonically active neurons in the primate's striatum undergo systematic changes during behavioral sensorimotor conditioning. *J Neurosc* 1994; 14:3969–3984.

36. Yamada H, Matsumoto N, Kimura M. Tonically active neurons in the primate caudate nucleus and putamen differentially encode instructed motivational outcomes of action. *J Neurosci* 2004; 24(14): 3500–3510.

37. Mallet N, Le Moine C, Charpier S, Gonon F. Feedforward inhibition of projection neurons by fast-spiking GABA interneurons in the rat striatum in vivo. *J Neurosci* 2005; 25:3857–3869.

38. Betarbet R, Turner R, Chockkan V, et al. Dopaminergic neurons intrinsic to the primate striatum. *J Neurosci* 1997; 17:6761–6768.

39. Smith Y, Kieval JZ. Anatomy of the dopamine system in the basal ganglia. *Trends Neurosci* 2000; 23:S28–S33.

40. Cossette M, Levesque D, Parent A. Neurochemical characterization of dopaminergic neurons in human striatum. *Parkinsonism Relat Disord* 2005; 11:277–286.

41. Mazloom M, Smith Y. Synaptic microcircuitry of tyrosine hydroxylase–containing neurons and terminals in the striatum of 1-methyl-4-phenyl-1,2,3,6-tetrahydropyridine–treated monkeys. *J Comp Neurol* 2006; 495:453–469.

42. Tande D, Hoglinger G, Debeir T, et al. New striatal dopamine neurons in MPTP-treated macaques result from a phenotypic shift and not neurogenesis. *Brain* 2006; 129:1194–1200.

43. Graybiel AM, Ragsdale CW Jr, Yoneoka ES, Elde RP. An immunohistochemical study of enkephalins and other neuropeptides in the striatum of the cat with evidence that the opiate peptides are arranged to form mosaic patterns in register with the striosomal compartments visible by acetylcholinesterase staining. *Neuroscience* 1981; 6:377–397.

44. Herkenham M, Pert C. Mosaic distribution of opiate receptors, parafascicular projections and acetylcholinesterase in rat striatum. *Nature (London)* 1981; 291:415–417.

45. Ragsdale CW Jr, Graybiel AM. The fronto-striatal projection in the cat and monkey and its relationship to inhomogeneities established by acetylcholinesterase histochemistry. *Brain Res* 1981; 208:259–266.

46. Gerfen CR. The neostriatal mosaic: Striatal patch-matrix organization is related to cortical lamination. *Science* 1989; 246:385–388.

47. Gerfen CR. The neostriatal mosaic: Multiple levels of compartmental organization. *Trends Neurosci* 1992; 14:133–139.

48. Gerfen CR. The neostriatal mosaic: Compartmentalization of corticostriatal input and striatonigral output systems. *Nature* 1984; 311:461–464.

49. Berendse HW, Groenewegen HJ. Organization of the thalamostriatal projections in the rat, with special emphasis on the ventral striatum. *J Comp Neurol* 1990; 299:187–228.

50. Ragsdale CW Jr, Graybiel AM. Compartmental organization of the thalamostriatal connection in the cat. *J Comp Neurol* 1991; 311:134–167.

51. Sadikot AF, Parent A, Smith Y, Bolam JP. Efferent connections of the centromedian and parafascicular thalamic nuclei in the squirrel monkey: A light and electron microscopic study of the thalamostriatal projection in relation to striatal heterogeneity. *J Comp Neurol* 1992; 320:228–242.

52. Wang H, Pickel VM. Dendritic spines containing mu-opioid receptors in rat striatal patches receive asymmetric synapses from prefrontal corticostriatal afferents. *J Comp Neurol* 1998; 396:223–237.

53. Eblen F, Graybiel AM. Highly restricted origin of prefrontal cortical inputs to striosomes in the macaque monkey. *J Neurosci* 1995; 15:5999–6013.

54. Graybiel AM. Neurotransmitters and neuromodulators in the basal ganglia. *Trends Neurosci* 1990; 13:244–254.

55. Raju DV, Shah DJ, Wright TM, Hall RA, Smith Y. Differential synaptology of vglut2-containing thalamostriatal afferents between the patch and matrix compartments in rats. *J Comp Neurol* 2006. 499(2):231–243

56. Graybiel AM, Canales JJ, Capper-Loup C. Levodopa-induced dyskinesias and dopamine-dependent stereotypies: A new hypothesis. *Trends Neurosci* 2000; 23:S71–77.

57. Canales JJ, Capper-Loup C, Hu D, et al. Shifts in striatal responsivity evoked by chronic stimulation of dopamine and glutamate systems. *Brain* 2002; 125:2353–2363.

58. Graybiel AM, Canales JJ. The neurobiology of repetitive behaviors: Clues to the neurobiology of Tourette syndrome. *Adv Neurol* 2001; 85:123–131.

59. Goto S, Lee LV, Munoz EL, et al. Functional anatomy of the basal ganglia in x-linked recessive dystonia-parkinsonism. *Ann Neurol* 2005; 58:7–17.

60. Difiglia M, Pasik P, Pasik T. A Golgi and ultrastructural study of the monkey globus pallidus. *J Comp Neurol* 1982; 212:53–75.

61. Francois C, Percheron G, Yelnik J, Heyner S. A Golgi analysis of the primate globus pallidus. I. Inconstant processes of large neurons, other neuronal types, and afferent axons. *J Comp Neurol* 1984; 227:182–199.

62. Hassler R, Chung YW. Identification of eight types of synapses in the pallidum externum and internum in squirrel monkey (*Saimiri sciureus*). *Acta Anat (Basel)* 1984; 118:65–81.

63. Hoover BR, Marshall JF. Further characterization of preproenkephalin MRNA-containing cells in the rodent globus pallidus. *Neuroscience* 2002; 111:111–125.

64. Hoover BR, Marshall JF. Population characteristics of preproenkephalin MRNA-containing neurons in the globus pallidus of the rat. *Neurosci Lett* 1999; 265:199–202.

65. Sato F, Lavallee P, Levesque M, Parent A. Single-axon tracing study of neurons of the external segment of the globus pallidus in primate. *J Comp Neurol* 2000; 417:17–31.

66. Billings LM, Marshall JF. D2 antagonist-induced c-fos in an identified subpopulation of globus pallidus neurons by a direct intrapallidal action. *Brain Res* 2003; 964:237–243.

67. Sato F, Parent M, Levesque M, Parent A. Axonal branching pattern of neurons of the subthalamic nucleus in primates. *J Comp Neurol* 2000; 424:142–152.

68. Kita H, Kitai ST. The morphology of globus pallidus projection neurons in the rat: An intracellular staining study. *Brain Res* 1994; 636:308–319.

69. Smith Y, Shink E, Sidibe M. Neuronal circuitry and synaptic connectivity of the basal ganglia. *Neurosurg Clin North Am* 1998; 9:203–222.

70. Parent M, Levesque M, Parent A. Two types of projection neurons in the internal pallidum of primates: Single-axon tracing and three-dimensional reconstruction. *J Comp Neurol* 2001; 439:162–175.

71. Kuo JS, Carpenter MB. Organization of pallidothalamic projections in the rhesus monkey. *J Comp Neurol* 1973; 151:201–236.

72. Baron MS, Sidibe M, DeLong MR, Smith Y. Course of motor and associative pallido-thalamic projections in monkeys. *J Comp Neurol* 2001; 429:490–501.

73. Mailly P, Charpier S, Menetrey A, Deniau JM. Three-dimensional organization of the recurrent axon collateral network of the substantia nigra pars reticulata neurons in the rat. *J Neurosci* 2003; 23:5247–5257.

74. Yelnik J, Percheron G. Subthalamic neurons in primates: A quantitative and comparative analysis. *Neuroscience* 1979; 4:1717–1743.

75. Levesque JC, Parent A. Gabaergic interneurons in human subthalamic nucleus. *Mov Disord* 2005; 20:574–584.

76. Alexander GE, DeLong MR, Strick PL. Parallel organization of functionally segregated circuits linking basal ganglia and cortex. *Annu Rev Neurosci* 1986; 9:357–381.

77. Alexander GE, Crutcher MD, DeLong MR. Basal ganglia–thalamocortical circuits: Parallel substrates for motor, oculomotor, "prefrontal" and "limbic" functions. *Prog Brain Res* 1990; 85:119–146.

78. Parent A. Extrinsic connections of the basal ganglia. *Trends Neurosci* 1990; 13:254–258.

79. Romanelli P, Esposito V, Schaal DW, Heit G. Somatotopy in the basal ganglia: Experimental and clinical evidence for segregated sensorimotor channels. *Brain Res Brain Res Rev* 2005; 48:112–128.

80. Kunzle H. Bilateral projections from precentral motor cortex to the putamen and other parts of the basal ganglia. An autoradiographic study in macaca fascicularis. *Brain Res* 1975; 88:195–209.

81. Kunzle H. An autoradiographic analysis of the efferent connections from premotor and adjacent prefrontal regions (areas 6 and 9) in *Macaca fascicularis*. *Brain BehavEvol* 1978; 15:185–234.

82. Flaherty AW, Graybiel AM. Corticostriatal transformations in the primate somatosensory sstem. Projections from physiologically mapped body-part representations. *J Neurophysiol* 1991; 66:1249–1263.

83. Flaherty AW, Graybiel AM. Two input systems for body representations in the primate striatal matrix: Experimental evidence in the squirrel monkey. *J Neurosci* 1993; 13:1120–1137.

84. Goldman PS, Nauta WJH. An intricately patterned prefronto-caudate projection in the rhesus monkey. *J Comp Neurol* 1977; 171:369–386.

85. Yeterian EH, VanHoesen GW. Cortico-striate projections in the rhesus monkey: The organization of certain cortico-caudate connections. *Brain Res* 1978; 139:43–63.

86. Selemon LD, Goldman-Rakic PS. Longitudinal topography and interdigitation of corticostriatal projections in the rhesus monkey. *J Neurosci* 1985; 5:776–794.

87. Yeterian EH, Pandya DN. Prefrontostriatal connections in relation to cortical architectonic organization in rhesus monkeys. *J Comp Neurol* 1991; 312:43–67.

88. Yeterian EH, Pandya DN. Corticostriatal connections of the superior temporal region in rhesus monkeys. *J Comp Neurol* 1998; 399:384–402.

89. Russchen FT, Bakst I, Amaral DG, Price JL. The amygdalostriatal projections in the monkey. An anterograde tracing study. *Brain Res* 1985; 329:241–257.

90. Alheid GF, Heimer L. New perspectives in basal forebrain organization of special relevance for neuropsychiatric disorders: The striatopallidal, amygdaloid, and corticopetal components of substantia innominata. *Neuroscience* 1988; 27:1–39.

91. Kunishio K, Haber SN. Primate cingulostriatal projection: Limbic striatal versus sensorimotor striatal input. *J Comp Neurol* 1994; 350:337–356.

92. Haber SN, Kunishio K, Mizobuchi M, Lynd-Balta E. The orbital and medial prefrontal circuit through the primate basal ganglia. *J Neurosci* 1995; 15:4851–4867.

93. Fudge JL, Haber SN. Defining the caudal ventral striatum in primates: Cellular and histochemical features. *J Neurosci* 2002; 22:10078–10082.

94. Fudge JL, Breitbart MA, McClain C. Amygdaloid inputs define a caudal component of the ventral striatum in primates. *J Comp Neurol* 2004; 476:330–347.

95. Parthasarathy HB, Schall JD, Graybiel AM. Distributed but convergent ordering of corticostriatal projections: Analysis of the frontal eye field and the supplementary eye field in the macaque monkey. *J Neurosci* 1992; 12:4468–4488.

96. Kemp JM, Powell TPS. The connections of the striatum and globus pallidus: Synthesis and speculation. *Philos Trans R Soc Lond* 1971; 262:441–457.

97. Lapper SR, Smith Y, Sadikot AF, Parent A, Bolam JP. Cortical input to parvalbumin-immunoreactive neurones in the putamen of the squirrel monkey. *Brain Res* 1992; 580:215–224.

98. Mallet N, Ballion B, Le Moine C, Gonon F. Cortical inputs and GABA interneurons imbalance projection neurons in the striatum of parkinsonian rats. *J Neurosci* 2006; 26:3875–3884.

99. Thomas TM, Smith Y, Levey AI, Hersch SM. Cortical inputs to m2-immunoreactive striatal interneurons in rat and monkey. *Synapse* 2000; 37:252–261.

100. Wilson CJ, Chang HT, Kitai ST. Origins of post synaptic potentials evoked in spiny neostriatal projection neurons by thalamic stimulation in the rat. *Exp Brain Res* 1983; 51:217–226.

101. Dube L, Smith AD, Bolam JP. Identification of synaptic terminals of thalamic or cortical origin in contact with distinct medium-size spiny neurons in the rat neostriatum. *J Comp Neurol* 1988; 267:455–471.

102. Smith Y, Parent A. Differential connections of caudate nucleus and putamen in the squirrel monkey (*Saimiri sciureus*). *Neuroscience* 1986; 18:347–371.

103. Nakano K, Hasegawa Y, Tokushige A, et al. Topographical projections from the thalamus, subthalamic nucleus and pedunculopontine tegmental nucleus to the striatum in the Japanese monkey, *Macaca fuscata*. *Brain Res* 1990; 537:54–68.

104. Smith Y, Parent A. Differential connections of caudate nucleus and putamen in the squirrel monkey (*Saimiri sciureus*). *Neuroscience* 1986; 18:347–371.
105. Sadikot AF, Parent A, Francois C. Efferent connections of the centromedian and parafascicular thalamic nuclei in the squirrel monkey: A pha-l study of subcortical projections. *J Comp Neurol* 1992; 315:137–159.
106. Sidibe M, Pare JF, Smith Y. Nigral and pallidal inputs to functionally segregated thalamostriatal neurons in the centromedian/parafascicular intralaminar nuclear complex in monkey. *J Comp Neurol* 2002; 447:286–299.
107. Smith Y, Raju DV, Pare J-F, Sidibe M. The thalamostriatal system: A highly specific network of the basal ganglia circuitry. *Trends Neurosci* 2004; 27:520–527.
108. Smith Y, Bennett BD, Bolam JP, et al. Synaptic relationships between dopaminergic afferents and cortical or thalamic input in the sensorimotor territory of the striatum in monkey. *J Comp Neurol* 1994; 344:1–19.
109. Sidibe M, Smith Y. Differential synaptic innervation of striatofugal neurones projecting to the internal or external segments of the globus pallidus by thalamic afferents in the squirrel monkey. *J Comp Neurol* 1996; 365:445–465.
110. Salin P, Kachidian P. Thalamo-striatal deafferentation affects preproenkephalin but not preprotachykinin gene expression in the rat striatum. *Brain Res Mol Brain Res* 1998; 57:257–265.
111. Bacci JJ, Kachidian P, Kerkerian-Le Goff L, Salin P. Intralaminar thalamic nuclei lesions: Widespread impact on dopamine denervation-mediated cellular defects in the rat basal ganglia. *J Neuropathol Exp Neurol* 2004; 63:20–31.
112. Meredith GE, Wouterlood FG. Hippocampal and midline thalamic fibers and terminals in relation to the choline acetyltransferase-immunoreactive neurons in nucleus accumbens of the rat: A light and electron microscopic study. *J Comp Neurol* 1990; 296:204–221.
113. Rudkin TM, Sadikot AF. Thalamic input to parvalbumin-immunoreactive gabaergic interneurons: Organization in normal striatum and effect of neonatal decortication. *Neuroscience* 1999; 88:1165–1175.
114. Consolo S, Baldi G, Giorgi S, Nannini L. The cerebral cortex and parafascicular thalamic nucleus facilitate in vivo acetylcholine release in the rat striatum through distinct glutamate receptor subtypes. *Eur J Neurosci* 1996; 8:2702–2710.
115. Consolo S, Baronio P, Guidi G, Di Chiara G. Role of the parafascicular thalamic nucleus and n-methyl-d-aspartate transmission in the d1-dependent control of in vivo acetylcholine release in rat striatum. *Neuroscience* 1996; 71:157–165.
116. Zackheim J, Abercrombie ED. Thalamic regulation of striatal acetylcholine efflux is both direct and indirect and qualitatively altered in the dopamine-depleted striatum. *Neuroscience* 2005; 131:423–436.
117. Matsumoto N, Minamimoto T, Graybiel AM, Kimura M. Neurons in the thalamic cm-pf complex supply striatal neurons with information about behaviorally significant sensory events. *J Neurophysiol* 2001; 85:960–976.
118. Berendse HW, Groenewegen HJ. Organization of the thalamostriatal projections in the rat, with special emphasis on the ventral striatum. *J Comp Neurol* 1990; 299:187–228.
119. Raju DV, Smith Y. Differential localization of vesicular glutamate transporters 1 and 2 in the rat striatum. In: Bolam JP, Ingham CA, Magill PJ (eds). *The Basal Ganglia VIII*. Singapore: Springer, 2005: 601–610.
120. Deschenes M, Bourassa J, Parent A. Striatal and cortical projections of single neurons from the central lateral thalamic nucleus in the rat. *Neuroscience* 1996; 72:679–687.
121. Deschenes M, Bourassa J, Doan VD, Parent A. A single-cell study of the axonal projections arising from the posterior intralaminar thalamic nuclei in the rat. *Eur J Neurosci* 1996; 8:329–343.
122. Parent M, Parent A. Single-axon tracing and three-dimensional reconstruction of centre median-parafascicular thalamic neurons in primates. *J Comp Neurol* 2005; 481:127–144.
123. Cowan RL, Wilson CJ. Spontaneous firing patterns and axonal projections of single corticostriatal neurons in the rat medial agranular cortex. *J Neurosci* 1994; 71:17–32.
124. Levesque M, Parent A. Axonal arborization of corticostriatal and corticothalamic fibers arising from prelimbic cortex in the rat. *Cereb Cortex* 1998; 8:602–613.
125. Parent M, Parent A. Single-axon tracing study of corticostriatal projections arising from primary motor cortex in primates. *J Comp Neurol* 2006; 496:202–213.
126. Groenewegen HJ, Berendse HW. The specificity of the "nonspecific" midline and intralaminar thalamic nuclei. *Trends Neurosci* 1994; 17:52–57.
127. Van der Werf YD, Witter MP, Groenewegen HJ. The intralaminar and midline nuclei of the thalamus. Anatomical and functional evidence for participation in processes of arousal and awareness. *Brain Res Brain Res Rev* 2002; 39:107–140.
128. Minamimoto T, Kimura M. Participation of the thalamic cm-pf complex in attentional orienting. *J Neurophysiol* 2002; 87:3090–3101.
129. Kimura M, Minamimoto T, Matsumoto N, Hori Y. Monitoring and switching of cortico-basal ganglia loop functions by the thalamo-striatal system. *Neurosci Res* 2004; 48:355–360.
130. Minamimoto T, Hori Y, Kimura M. Complementary process to response bias in the centromedian nucleus of the thalamus. *Science* 2005; 308:1798–1801.
131. Kinomura S, Larsson J, Gulyas B, Roland PE. Activation by attention of the human reticular formation and thalamic intralaminar nuclei. *Science* 1996; 271:512–515.
132. McFarland NR, Haber SN. Convergent inputs from thalamic motor nuclei and frontal cortical areas to the dorsal striatum in the primate. *J Neurosci* 2000; 20:3798–3813.
133. Henderson JM, Carpenter K, Cartwright H, Halliday GM. Degeneration of the centre median–parafascicular complex in Parkinson's disease. *Ann Neurol* 2000; 47: 345–352.
134. Henderson JM, Carpenter K, Cartwright H, Halliday GM. Loss of thalamic intralaminar nuclei in progressive supranuclear palsy and parkinson's disease: Clinical and therapeutic implications. *Brain* 2000; 123(Pt 7):1410–1421.
135. Henderson JM, Schleimer SB, Allbutt H, et al. Behavioural effects of parafascicular thalamic lesions in an animal model of parkinsonism. *Behav Brain Res* 2005; 162:222–232.
136. Aymerich MS, Barroso-Chinea P, Perez-Manso M, et al. Consequences of unilateral nigrostriatal denervation on the thalamostriatal pathway in rats. *Eur J Neurosci* 2006; 23:2099–2108.
137. Freyaldenhoven TE, Ali SF, Schmued LC. Systemic administration of mptp induces thalamic neuronal degeneration in mice. *Brain Res* 1997; 759:9–17.
138. Hartmann-von Monakow K, Akert K, Kunzle H. Projections of the precentral motor cortex and other cortical areas of the frontal lobe to the subthalamic nucleus in the monkey. *ExpBrain Res* 1978; 33:395–403.
139. Afsharpour S. Topographical projections of the cerebral cortex to the subthalamic nucleus. *J Comp Neurol* 1985; 236:14–28.
140. Nambu A, Takada M, Inase M, Tokuno H. Dual somatotopical representations in the primate subthalamic nucleus: Evidence for ordered but reversed body-map transformations from the primary motor cortex and the supplementary motor area. *J Neurosci* 1996; 16:2671–2683.
141. Takada M, Tokuno H, Hamada I, et al. Organization of inputs from cingulate motor areas to basal ganglia in macaque monkey. *Eur J Neurosci* 2001; 14:1633–1650.
142. Nambu A, Tokuno H, Inase M, Takada M. Corticosubthalamic input zones from forelimb representations of the dorsal and ventral divisions of the premotor cortex in the macaque monkey: Comparison with the input zones from the primary motor cortex and the supplementary motor area. *Neurosci Lett* 1997; 239:13–16.
143. Berendse HW, Groenewegen HJ. The connections of the medial part of the subthalamic nucleus in the rat. Evidence for a parallel organization. In: Bernardi G, Carpenter MB, Di Chiara G, et al (eds). *The Basal Ganglia II*. New York: Plenum Press, 1989:89–98.
144. Maurice N, Deniau JM, Glowinski J, Thierry AM. Relationships between the prefrontal cortex and the basal ganglia in the rat: Physiology of the corticosubthalamic circuits. *J Neurosci* 1998; 18:9539–9546.
145. Wichmann T, Bergman H, DeLong MR. The primate subthalamic nucleus: I. Functional properties in intact animals. *J Neurophysiol* 1994; 72:494–506.
146. Nambu A, Tokuno H, Takada M. Functional significance of the cortico-subthalamo-pallidal "hyperdirect" pathway. *Neurosci Res* 2002; 43:111–117.
147. Rodriguez-Oroz MC, Rodriguez M, Guridi J, et al. The subthalamic nucleus in Parkinson's disease: Somatotopic organization and physiological characteristics. *Brain* 2001; 124: 1777–1790.
148. Bevan MD, Clarke NP, Bolam JP. Synaptic integration of functionally diverse pallidal information in the entopeduncular nucleus and subthalamic nucleus in the rat. *J Neurosci* 1997; 17:308–324.
149. Kitai ST, Deniau JM. Cortical inputs to the subthalamus: Intracellular analysis. *Brain Res* 1981; 214:411–415.
150. Giuffrida R, Li Volsi G, Maugeri G, Perciavalle V. Influences of pyramidal tract on the subthalamic nucleus in the cat. *Neurosci Lett* 1985; 54:231–235.
151. Sugimoto T, Hattori T, Mizuno N, et al. Direct projections from the centre median-parafascicular complex to the subthalamic nucleus in the cat and rat. *J Comp Neurol* 1983; 214:209–216.
152. Feger J, Bevan M, Crossman AR. The projections from the parafascicular thalamic nucleus to the subthalamic nucleus and the striatum arise from separate neuronal populations: A comparison with the corticostriatal and corticosubthalamic efferents in a retrograde double-labelling study. *Neuroscience* 1994; 60:125–132.
153. Lanciego JL, Gonzalo N, Castle M, et al. Thalamic innervation of striatal and subthalamic neurons projecting to the rat entopeduncular nucleus. *Eur J Neurosci* 2004; 19:1267–1277.
154. Deschenes M, Bourassa J, Doan VD, Parent A. A single–cell study of the axonal projections arising from the posterior intralaminar thalamic nuclei in the rat. *Eur J Neurosci* 1996; 8:329–343.
155. Ryan LJ, Clark KB. The role of the subthalamic nucleus in the response of globus pallidus neurons to stimulation of the prelimbic and agranular frontal cortices in rats. *Exp Brain Res* 1991; 86:641–651.
156. Kita H. Physiology of two disynaptic pathways from the sensorimotor cortex to the basal ganglia output nuclei. In: Percheron G, McKenzie JS, Feger J (eds). *The Basal Ganglia IV: New Ideas and Data on Structure and Function*. New York and London: Plenum Press, 1994:263–276.
157. Maurice N, Deniau JM, Glowinski J, Thierry AM. Relationships between the prefrontal cortex and the basal ganglia in the rat: Physiology of the cortico-nigral circuits. *J Neurosci* 1999; 19:4674–4681.
158. Kolomiets BP, Deniau JM, Glowinski J, Thierry AM. Basal ganglia and processing of cortical information: Functional interactions between trans-striatal and trans-subthalamic circuits in the substantia nigra pars reticulata. *Neuroscience* 2003; 117:931–938.
159. Alexander GE, Crutcher MD. Functional architecture of basal ganglia circuits: Neural substrates of parallel processing. *Trends Neurosci* 1990; 13:266–271.
160. Bergman H, Wichmann T, DeLong MR. Amelioration of parkinsonian symptoms by inactivation of the subthalamic nucleus (STN) in MPTP treated green monkeys. *Mov Disord* 1990; 5(Suppl. 1):79.
161. Smith AD, Bolam JP. The neural network of the basal ganglia as revealed by the study of synaptic connections of identified neurones. *Trends Neurosci* 1990; 13:259–265.
162. Smith Y, Bolam JP. Convergence of synaptic inputs from the striatum and the globus pallidus onto identified nigrocollicular cells in the rat: A double anterograde labelling study. *Neuroscience* 1991; 44:45–73.
163. Shink E, Smith Y. Differential synaptic innervation of neurons in the internal and external segments of the globus pallidus by the GABA- and glutamate-containing terminals in the squirrel monkey. *J Comp Neurol* 1995; 358:119–141.

164. Smith Y, Bevan MD, Shink E, Bolam JP. Microcircuitry of the direct and indirect pathways of the basal ganglia. *Neuroscience* 1998; 86:353–387.

165. Parent A, Hazrati L-N. Functional anatomy of the basal ganglia. I. The cortico-basal ganglia-thalamo-cortical loop. *Brain Res Rev* 1995; 20:91–127.

166. Gerfen CR, Engber TM, Mahan LC, et al. D1 and d2 dopamine receptor–regulated gene expression of striatonigral and striatopallidal neurons. *Science* 1990; 250:1429–1432.

167. LeMoine C, Normand E, Guitteny AF, et al. Dopamine receptor gene expression by enkephalin neurons in rat forebrain. *Proc Natl Acad Sci USA* 1990; 182:611–612.

168. Surmeier DJ, Song WJ, Yan Z. Coordinated expression of dopamine receptors in neostriatal medium spiny neurons. *J Neurosci* 1996; 16:6579–6591.

169. Aubert I, Ghorayeb I, Normand E, Bloch B. Phenotypical characterization of the neurons expressing the D1 and D2 dopamine receptors in the monkey striatum. *J Comp Neurol* 2000; 418:22–32.

170. Day M, Wang Z, Ding J, et al. Selective elimination of glutamatergic synapses on striatopallidal neurons in Parkinson disease models. *Nat Neurosci* 2006; 9:251–259.

171. Gerfen CR. Indirect-pathway neurons lose their spines in Parkinson disease. *Nat Neurosci* 2006; 9:157–158.

172. Wilson CJ. Striatal D2 receptors and ltd: Yes, but not where you thought they were. *Neuron* 2006; 50:347–348.

173. Chang HT, Wilson CJ, Kitai ST. Single neostriatal efferent axons in the globus pallidus: A light and electron microscopic study. *Science* 1981; 213:915–918.

174. Gerfen CR. The neostriatal mosaic. I. Compartmental organization of projections from the striatum to the substantia nigra in the rat. *J Comp Neurol* 1985; 236:454–476.

175. Parent A, Hazrati L. Anatomical aspects of information processing in primate basal ganglia. *Trends Neurosci* 1993; 16:111–116.

176. Berretta S, Parthasarathy HB, Graybiel AM. Local release of GABAergic inhibition in the motor cortex induces immediate-early gene expression in indirect pathway neurons of the striatum. *J Neurosci* 1997; 17:4752–4763.

177. Parthasarathy HB, Graybiel AM. Cortically driven immediate-early gene expression reflects modular influence of sensorimotor cortex on identified striatal neurons in the squirrel monkey. *J Neurosci* 1997; 17:2477–2491.

178. Zemanick MC, Strick PL, Dix RD. Direction of transneuronal transport of herpes simplex virus 1 in the primate motor system is strain-dependent. *Proc Natl Acad Sci USA* 1991; 88:8048–8051.

179. Sgambato V, Abo V, Rogard M, et al. Effect of electrical stimulation of the cerebral cortex on the expression of the fos protein in the basal ganglia. *Neuroscience* 1997; 81:93–112.

180. Lei W, Jiao Y, Del Mar N, Reiner A. Evidence for differential cortical input to direct pathway versus indirect pathway striatal projection neurons in rats. *J Neurosci* 2004; 24:8289–8299.

181. Morishima M, Kawaguchi Y. Recurrent connection patterns of corticostriatal pyramidal cells in frontal cortex. *J Neurosci* 2006; 26:4394–4405.

182. Jones EG, Coulter JD, Burton H, Porter R. Cells of origin and terminal distribution of corticostriatal fibers arising in the sensory-motor cortex of monkeys. *J Comp Neurol* 1977; 173:53–80.

183. Turner RS, DeLong MR. Corticostriatal activity in primary motor cortex of the macaque. *J Neurosci* 2000; 20:7096–7108.

184. Bauswein E, Fromm C, Preuss A. Corticostriatal cells in comparison with pyramidal tract neurons: Contrasting properties in the behaving monkey. *Brain Res* 1989; 493:198–203.

185. Parent A, Hazrati L-N. Functional anatomy of the basal ganglia: II. The place of subthalamic nucleus and external pallidum in basal ganglia circuitry. *Brain Res Rev* 1995; 20:128–154.

186. Gerfen CR, Baimbridge KG, Miller JJ. The neostriatal mosaic: Compartmental distribution of calcium-binding protein and parvalbumin in the basal ganglia of the rat and monkey. *Proc Natl Acad Sci USA* 1985; 82:8780–8784.

187. Iacopino A, Christakos S, German D, et al. Calbindin-d28k-containing neurons in animal models of neurodegeneration: Possible protection from excitotoxicity. *Brain Res Mol Brain Res* 1992; 13:251–261.

188. Haber SN, Ryoo H, Cox C, Lu W. Subsets of midbrain dopaminergic neurons in monkeys are distinguished by different levels of MRNA for the dopamine transporter: Comparison with the mrna for the D2 receptor, tyrosine hydroxylase and calbindin immunoreactivity. *J Comp Neurol* 1995; 362:400–410.

189. Gerfen CR, Herkenham M, Thibault J. The neostriatal mosaic: II. Patch- and matrix-directed mesostriatal dopaminergic and non-dopaminergic systems. *J Neurosci* 1987; 7:3915–3934.

190. Lynd-Balta E, Haber SN. Primate striatonigral projections: A comparison of the sensorimotor-related striatum and the ventral striatum. *J Comp Neurol* 1994; 345:562–578.

191. Lynd-Balta E, Haber SN. The organization of midbrain projections to the ventral striatum in the primate. *Neuroscience* 1994; 59:609–623.

192. Prensa L, Parent A. The nigrostriatal pathway in the rat: A single-axon study of the relationship between dorsal and ventral tier nigral neurons and the striosome/matrix striatal compartments. *J Neurosci* 2001; 21:7247–7260.

193. Haber SN, Fudge JL. The primate substantia nigra and VTA: Integrative circuitry and function. *Crit Rev Neurobiol* 1997; 11:323–342.

194. Wang Z, Kai L, Day M, et al. Dopaminergic control of corticostriatal long-term synaptic depression in medium spiny neurons is mediated by cholinergic interneurons. *Neuron* 2006; 50:443–452.

195. Nicola SM, Surmeier J, Malenka RC. Dopaminergic modulation of neuronal excitability in the striatum and nucleus accumbens. *Annu Rev Neurosci* 2000; 23:185–215.

196. Bouyer JJ, Park DH, Joh TH, Pickel VM. Chemical and structural analysis of the relation between cortical inputs and tyrosine hydroxylase–containing terminalsin rat neostriatum. *Brain Res* 1984; 302:267–275.

197. Freund TF, Powell JF, Smith AD. Tyrosine hydroxylase–immunoreactive boutons in synaptic contact with identified striatonigral neurons, with particular reference to dendritic spines. *Neuroscience* 1984; 13:1189–1215.

198. Bamford NS, Zhang H, Schmitz Y, et al. Heterosynaptic dopamine neurotransmission selects sets of corticostriatal terminals. *Neuron* 2004; 42:653–663.

199. Bamford NS, Robinson S, Palmiter RD, et al. Dopamine modulates release from corticostriatal terminals. *J Neurosci* 2004; 24:9541–9552.

200. Yin HH, Lovinger DM. Frequency-specific and D2 receptor–mediated inhibition of glutamate release by retrograde endocannabinoid signaling. *Proc Natl Acad Sci USA* 2006; 103:8251–8256.

201. Khan ZU, Gutierrez A, Martin R, et al. Dopamine d5 receptors of rat and human brain. *Neuroscience* 2000; 100:689–699.

202. Rivera A, Alberti I, Martin AB, et al. Molecular phenotype of rat striatal neurons expressing the dopamine D5 receptor subtype. *Eur J Neurosci* 2002; 16:2049–2058.

203. Centonze D, Grande C, Usiello A, et al. Receptor subtypes involved in the presynaptic and postsynaptic actions of dopamine on striatal interneurons. *J Neurosci* 2003; 23:6245–6254.

204. Berlanga ML, Simpson TK, Alcantara AA. Dopamine D5 receptor localization on cholinergic neurons of the rat forebrain and diencephalon: A potential neuroanatomical substrate involved in mediating dopaminergic influences on acetylcholine release. *J Comp Neurol* 2005; 492:34–49.

205. Yan Z, Surmeier DJ. D5 dopamine receptors enhance zn2+-sensitive gaba(a) currents in striatal cholinergic interneurons through a pka/pp1 cascade. *Neuron* 1997; 19: 1115–1126.

206. Suzuki T, Miura M, Nishimura K, Aosaki T. Dopamine-dependent synaptic plasticity in the striatal cholinergic interneurons. *J Neurosci* 2001; 21:6492–6501.

207. Cragg SJ. Singing to the tune of dopamine. Focus on "Properties of dopamine release and uptake in the songbird basal ganglia". *J Neurophysiol* 2005; 93:1827–1828.

208. Fuchs H, Nagel J, Hauber W. Effects of physiological and pharmacological stimuli on dopamine release in the rat globus pallidus. *Neurochem Int* 2005; 47:474–481.

209. Cheramy A, Leviel V, Glowinski J. Dendritic release of dopamine in the substantia nigra. *Nature* 1981; 289:537–542.

210. Waszczak BL. Differential effects of D1 and D2 dopamine receptor agonists on substantia nigra pars reticulata neurons. *Brain Res* 1990; 513:125–135.

211. Galvan A, Kliem MA, Smith Y, Wichmann T. Gabaergic and dopaminergic modulation of basal ganglia output in primates. In: Bolam JP, Magill PJ (eds). *The Basal Ganglia*, 2005. VII edition, Springer, New York, London. 575–584.

212. Freeman A, Ciliax B, Bakay R, et al. Nigrostriatal collaterals to thalamus degenerate in parkinsonian animal models. *Annals of Neurology* 2001; 50:321–329.

213. Sanchez-Gonzalez MA, Garcia-Cabezas MA, Rico B, Cavada C. The primate thalamus is a key target for brain dopamine. *J Neurosci* 2005; 25:6076–6083.

214. Nauta HJ, Cole M. Efferent projections of the subthalamic nucleus: An autoradiographic study in monkey and cat. *J Comp Neurol* 1978; 180:1–16.

215. Carpenter MB, Batton RRI, Carleton SC, Keller JT. Interconnections and organization of pallidal and subthalamic nucleus neurons in the monkey. *J Comp Neurol* 1981; 197:579–603.

216. Moriizumi T, Nakamura Y, Kitao Y, Kudo M. Ultrastructural analyses of afferent terminals in the subthalamic nucleus of the cat with a combined degeneration and horseradish peroxidase tracing method. *J Comp Neurol* 1987; 265:159–174.

217. Smith Y, Hazrati LN, Parent A. Efferent projections of the subthalamic nucleus in the squirrel monkey as studied by pha-l anterograde tracing method. *J Comp Neurol* 1990; 294:306–323.

218. Shink E, Bevan MD, Bolam JP, Smith Y. The subthalamic nucleus and the external pallidum: Two tightly interconnected structures that control the output of the basal ganglia in the monkey. *Neuroscience* 1996. 73(2):335–357.

219. Beckstead RM. A reciprocal axonal connection between the subthalamic nucleus and the neostriatum in the cat. *Brain Res* 1983; 275:137–142.

220. Parent A, Smith Y. Organization of efferent projections of the subthalamic nucleus in the squirrel monkey as revealed by retrograde labeling methods. *Brain Res* 1987; 436:296–310.

221. Kita H, Kitai ST. Efferent projections of the subthalamic nucleus in the rat: Light and electron microscope analysis with the pha-l method. *J Comp Neurol* 1987; 260:435–452.

222. Smith ID, Grace AA. Role of the subthalamic nucleus in the regulation of nigral dopamine neuron activity. *Synapse* 1992; 12:287–303.

223. Hammond C, Rouzaire-Dubois B, Feger J, et al. Anatomical and electrophysiological studies on the reciprocal projections between the subthalamic nucleus and nucleus tegmenti pedunculopontinus in the rat. *Neuroscience* 1983; 9:41–52.

224. Takada M, Li ZK, Hattori T. Long descending direct projection from the basal ganglia to the spinal cord: A revival of the extrapyramidal concept. *Brain Res* 1987; 436:129–135.

225. Deniau JM, Hammond C, Riszk A, Feger J. Electrophysiological properties of identified output neurons of the rat substantia nigra (pars compacta and pars reticulata): Evidences for the existence of branched neurons. *Exp Brain Res* 1978; 32:409–422.

226. Van Der Kooy D, Hattori T. Single subthalamic nucleus neurons project to both the globus pallidus and substantia nigra in rat. *J Comp Neurol* 1980; 192:751–768.

227. Haber SN, Lynd-Balta E, Mitchell SJ. The organization of the descending ventral pallidal projections in the monkey. *J Comp Neurol* 1993; 329:111–128.

228. Hamani C, Saint-Cyr JA, Fraser J, Kaplitt M, Lozano AM. The subthalamic nucleus in the context of movement disorders. *Brain* 2004; 127:4–20.

229. Karachi C, Yelnik J, Tande D, et al. The pallidosubthalamic projection: An anatomical substrate for nonmotor functions of the subthalamic nucleus in primates. *Mov Disord* 2005; 20:172–180.

230. Kita H, Tachibana Y, Nambu A, Chiken S. Balance of monosynaptic excitatory and disynaptic inhibitory responses of the globus pallidus induced after stimulation of the subthalamic nucleus in the monkey. *J Neurosci* 2005; 25:8611–8619.
231. Joel D, Weiner I. The connections of the primate subthalamic nucleus: Indirect pathways and the open-interconnected scheme of basal ganglia-thalamocortical circuitry. *Brain Res Rev* 1997; 23:62–78.
232. Deniau JM, Thierry AM. Anatomical segregation of information processing in the rat substantia nigra pars reticulata. *Adv Neurol* 1997; 74:83–96.
233. Kha HT, Finkelstein DI, Tomas D, et al. Projections from the substantia nigra pars reticulata to the motor thalamus of the rat: Single axon reconstructions and immunohistochemical study. *J Comp Neurol* 2001; 440:20–30.
234. Francois C, Tande D, Yelnik J, Hirsch EC. Distribution and morphology of nigral axons projecting to the thalamus in primates. *J Comp Neurol* 2002; 447:249–260.
235. Cebrian C, Parent A, Prensa L. Patterns of axonal branching of neurons of the substantia nigra pars reticulata and pars lateralis in the rat. *J Comp Neurol* 2005; 492:349–369.
236. Ilinsky IA, Jouandet ML, Goldman-Rakic PS. Organization of the nigrothalamocortical system in the rhesus monkey. *J Comp Neurol* 1985; 236:315–330.
237. Middleton FA, Strick PL. Basal ganglia and cerebellar loops: Motor and cognitive circuits. *Brain Res Brain Res Rev* 2000; 31:236–250.
238. Clower DM, Dum RP, Strick PL. Basal ganglia and cerebellar inputs to "aip." *Cereb Cortex* 2005; 15:913–920.
239. Wurtz RH, Hikosaka O. Role of the basal ganglia in the initiation of saccadic eye movements. *Prog Brain Res* 1986; 64:175–190.
240. Comoli E, Coizet V, Boyes J, et al. A direct projection from superior colliculus to substantia nigra for detecting salient visual events. *Nature Neurosci* 2003; 6:974–980.
241. McHaffie JG, Jiang H, May PJ, et al. A direct projection from superior colliculus to substantia nigra pars compacta in the cat. *Neuroscience* 2006; 138:221–234.
242. Spann BM, Grofova I. Origin of ascending and spinal pathways from the nucleus tegmenti pedunculopontinus in the rat. *J Comp Neurol* 1989; 283:13–27.
243. Grofova I, Zhou M. Nigral innervation of cholinergic and glutamatergic cells in the rat mesopontine tegmentum: Light and electron microscopic anterograde tracing and immunohistochemical studies. *J Comp Neurol* 1998; 395:359–379.
244. Chandler SH, Turman J Jr, Salem L, Goldberg LJ. The effects of nanoliter ejections of lidocaine into the pontomedullary reticular formation on cortically induced rhythmical jaw movements in the guinea pig. *Brain Res* 1990; 526:54–64.
245. von Krosigk M, Smith Y, Bolam JP, Smith AD. Synaptic organization of gabaergic inputs from the striatum and the globus pallidus onto neurons in the substantia nigra and retrorubral field which project to the medullary reticular formation. *Neuroscience* 1993; 50:531–549.
246. Mogoseanu D, Smith AD, Bolam JP. Monosynaptic innervation of facial motoneurones by neurones of the parvicellular reticular formation. *Exp Brain Res* 1994; 101: 427–438.
247. Rodriguez M, Gonzalez-Hernandez T. Electrophysiological and morphological evidence for a gabaergic nigrostriatal pathway. *J Neurosci* 1999; 19:4682–4694.
248. Arecchi-Bouchhioua P, Yelnik J, et al. Three-dimensional morphology and distribution of pallidal axons projecting to both the lateral region of the thalamus and the central complex in primates. *Brain Res* 1997; 754:311–314.
249. Hazrati LN, Parent A. Contralateral pallidothalamic and pallidotegmental projections in primates: An anterograde and retrograde labeling study. *Brain Res* 1991; 567:212–223.
250. Parent M, Levesque M, Parent A. The pallidofugal projection system in primates: Evidence for neurons branching ipsilaterally and contralaterally to the thalamus and brainstem. *J Chem Neuroanat* 1999; 16:153–165.
251. Sidibe M, Bevan MD, Bolam JP, Smith Y. Efferent connections of the internal globus pallidus in the squirrel monkey: I. Topography and synaptic organization of the pallidothalamic projection. *J Comp Neurol* 1997; 382:323–347.
252. Kim R, Nakano K, Jayaraman A, Carpenter MB. Projections of the globus pallidus and adjacent structures: An autoradiographic study in the monkey. *J Comp Neurol* 1976; 169:263–290.
253. DeVito JL, Anderson ME. An autoradiographic study of efferent connections of the globus pallidus in macaca mulatta. *Exp Brain Res* 1982; 46:107–117.
254. Schell GR, Strick PL. The origin of thalamic inputs to the arcuate premotor and supplementary motor areas. *J Neurosci* 1984; 4:539–560.
255. Strick PL. How do the basal ganglia and cerebellum gain access to the cortical motor areas? *Behav Brain Res* 1985; 18:107–123.
256. Inase M, Tanji J. Thalamic distribution of projection neurons to the primary motor cortex relative to afferent terminal fields from the globus pallidus in the macaque monkey. *J Comp Neurol* 1995; 353:415–426.
257. Sakai ST, Inase M, Tanji J. The relationship between mi and sma afferents and cerebellar and pallidal efferents in the macaque monkey. *Somatosens Motor Res* 2002; 19:139–148.
258. Nambu A, Yoshida S, Jinnai K. Projection on the motor cortex of thalamic neurons with pallidal input in the monkey. *Exp Brain Res* 1988; 71:658–662.
259. Hoover JE, Strick PL. Multiple output channels in the basal ganglia. *Science* 1993; 259:819–821.
260. Hoover JE, Strick PL. The organization of cerebellar and basal ganglia outputs to primary motor cortex as revealed by retrograde transneuronal transport of herpes simplex virus type 1. *J Neurosci* 1999; 19:1446–1463.
261. Jinnai K, Nambu A, Yoshida S, Tanibuchi I. The two separate neuron circuits through the basal ganglia concerning the preparatory or execution proceses of motor control. In: Mamo N, Hamada I, DeLong MR (eds). *Role of the Cerebellum and Basal Ganglia in Voluntary Movement.* Elsevier Science, Amsterdam, New York: Excerpta Medica,1993: 153–161.
262. Rouiller EM, Liang F, Babalian A, et al. Cerebellothalamocortical and pallidothalamocortical projections to the primary and supplementary motor cortical areas: A multiple tracing study in macaque monkeys. *J Comp Neurol* 1994; 345:185–213.
263. Kayahara T, Nakano K. Pallido-thalamo-motor cortical connections: An electron microscopic study in the macaque monkey. *Brain Res* 1996; 706:337–342.
264. Middleton FA, Strick PL. Basal ganglia output and cognition: Evidence from anatomical, behavioral, and clinical studies. *Brain Cogn* 2000; 42:183–200.
265. Goldman-Rakic PS, Porrino LJ. The primate mediodorsal (md) nucleus and its projection to the frontal lobe. *J Comp Neurol* 1985; 242:535–560.
266. Middleton FA, Strick PL. Anatomical evidence for cerebellar and basal ganglia involvement in higher cognitive function. *Science* 1994; 266:458–461.
267. Darian-Smith C, Darian-Smith I, Cheema SS. Thalamic projections to sensorimotor cortex in the macaque monkey: Use of multiple retrograde fluorescent tracers. *J Comp Neurol* 1990; 299:17–46.
268. Shink E, Sidibe M, Smith Y. Efferent connections of the internal globus pallidus in the squirrel monkey: II. Topography and synaptic organization of pallidal efferents to the pedunculopontine nucleus. *J Comp Neurol* 1997; 382:348–363.
269. Harnois C, Filion M. Pallidofugal projections to thalamus and midbrain: A quantitative antidromic activation study in monkeys and cats. *Exp Brain Res* 1982; 47:277–285.
270. Parent A, DeBellefeuille L. Organization of efferent projections from the internal segment of globus pallidus in primate as revealed by fluorescence retrograde labeling method. *Brain Res* 1982; 245:201–213.
271. Rye DB, Lee HJ, Saper CB, Wainer BH. Medullary and spinal efferents of the pedunculopontine tegmental nucleus and adjacent mesopontine tegmentum in the rat. *J Comp Neurol* 1988; 269:315–341.
272. Steininger TL, Rye DB, Wainer BH. Afferent projections to the cholinergic pedunculopontine tegmental nucleus and adjacent midbrain extrapyramidal area in the albino rat. I. Retrograde tracing studies. *J Comp Neurol* 1992; 321:515–543.
273. Inglis WL, Winn P. The pedunculopontine tegmental nucleus: Where the striatum meets the reticular formation. *Prog Neurobiol* 1995; 47:1–29.
274. Mena-Segovia J, Bolam JP, Magill PJ. Pedunculopontine nucleus and basal ganglia: Distant relatives or part of the same family? *Trends Neurosci* 2004; 27:585–588.
275. Jackson A, Crossman AR. Nucleus tegmenti pedunculopontinus: Efferent connections with special reference to the basal ganglia, studied in the rat by anterograde and retrograde transport of horseradish peroxidase. *Neuroscience* 1983; 10:725–765.
276. Moon-Edley S, Graybiel AM. The afferent and efferent connections of the feline nucleus tegmenti pedunculopontinus, pars compacta. *J Comp Neurol* 1983; 217:187–215.
277. Lee HJ, Rye DB, Hallanger AE, Levey AI, Wainer BH. Cholinergic vs Noncholinergic efferents from the mesopontine tegmentum to the extrapyramidal motor system nuclei. *J Comp Neurol* 1988; 275:469–492.
278. Lavoie B, Parent A. Pedunculopontine nucleus in the squirrel monkey: Projections to the basal ganglia as revealed by anterograde tract-tracing methods. *J Comp Neurol* 1994; 344:210–231.
279. Oakman SA, Faris PL, Kerr PE, et al. Distribution of pontomesencephalic cholinergic neurons projecting to substantia nigra differs significantly from those projecting to ventral tegmental area. *J Neurosci* 1995; 15:5859–5869.
280. Charara A, Smith Y, Parent A. Glutamatergic inputs from the pedunculopontine nucleus to midbrain dopaminergic neurons in primates: *Phaseolus vulgaris*–leucoagglutinin anterograde labeling combined with postembedding glutamate and gaba immunohistochemistry. *J Comp Neurol* 1996; 364:254–266.
281. DeLong MR. Activity of pallidal neurons during movement. *J Neurophysiol* 1971; 34:414–427.
282. DeLong MR, Strick PL. Relation of basal ganglia, cerebellum, and motor cortex units to ramp and ballistic limb movements. *Brain Res* 1974; 71:327–335.
283. DeLong MR, Crutcher MD, Georgopoulos AP. Relations between movement and single cell discharge in the substantia nigra of the behaving monkey. *J Neurosci* 1983; 3:1599–1606.
284. Crutcher MD, DeLong MR. Single cell studies of the primate putamen. I. Functional organization. *Exp Brain Res* 1984; 53:233–243.
285. Crutcher MD, DeLong MR. Single cell studies of the primate putamen. II. Relations to direction of movement and pattern of muscular activity. *Exp Brain Res* 1984; 53:244–258.
286. DeLong MR, Crutcher MD, Georgopoulos AP. Primate globus pallidus and subthalamic nucleus: Functional organization. *J Neurophysiol* 1985; 53:530–543.
287. Magarinos-Ascone C, Buno W, Garcia-Austt E. Activity in monkey substantial nigra neurons related to a simple learned movement. *ExpBrain Res* 1992; 88:283–291.
288. Allum JHJ, Anner-Baratti REC, Hepp-Raymond MC. Activity of neurons in the motor thalamus and globus pallidus during the control of isometric finger force in the monkey. In: Paillard MJ, Schultz W, Wiesendanger M (eds). *Neural Coding of Motor Performance.* Exp Brain Res Suppl 7. New York: Springer, 1983:194–203.
289. Apicella P, Scarnati E, Ljungberg T, Schultz W. Neuronal activity in monkey striatum related to the expectation of predictable environmental events. *J Neurophysiol* 1992; 68:945–960.
290. Schultz W. Activity of pars reticulata neurons of monkey substantia nigra in relation to motor, sensory, and complex events. *J Neurophysiol* 1986; 4:660–677.
291. Ashe J, Georgopoulos AP. Movement parameters and neural activity in motor cortex and area 5. *Cerebr Cortex* 1994; 4:590–600.
292. Bauswein E, Fromm C, Werner W, Ziemann U. Phasic and tonic responses of premotor and primary motor cortex neurons to torque changes. *Exp Brain Res* 1991; 86: 303–310.
293. Crutcher MD, Alexander GE. Movement-related neuronal activity selectively coding either direction or muscle pattern in three motor areas of the monkey. *J Neurophysiol* 1990; 64:151–163.

294. Fu QG, Suarez JI, Ebner TJ. Neuronal specification of direction and distance during reaching movements in the superior precentral premotor area and primary motor cortex of monkeys. *J Neurophysiol* 1993; 70:2097–2116.

295. Hepp-Reymond MC, Husler EJ, Maier MA, Ql HX. Force-related neuronal activity in two regions of the primate ventral premotor cortex. *Can J Physiol Pharmacol* 1994; 72:571–579.

296. Kurata K. Premotor cortex of monkeys: Set- and movement-related activity reflecting amplitude and direction of wrist movements. *J Neurophysiol* 1993; 69:187–200.

297. Smith AM. The activity of supplementary motor area neurons during a maintained precision grip. *Brain Res* 1979; 172:315–327.

298. Werner W, Bauswein E, Fromm C. Static firing rates of premotor and primary motor cortical neurons associated with torque and joint position. *Exp Brain Res* 1991; 86:293–302.

299. Hikosaka O, Wurtz RH. Visual and oculomotor functions of monkey substantia nigra pars reticulata. I. Relation of visual and auditory responses to saccades. *J Neurophysiol* 1983; 49:1230–1253.

300. Hikosaka O, Sakamoto M, Usui S. Functional properties of monkey caudate neurons. I. Activities related to saccadic eye movements. *J Neurophysiol* 1989; 61:780–798.

301. Hikosaka O, Matsumara M, Kojima J, Gardiner TW. Role of basal ganglia in initiation and suppression of saccadic eye movements. In: Mano N, Hamada I, DeLong MR, eds. *Role of the Cerebellum and Basal Ganglia in Voluntary Movement*. Excerpta Medica ed. Amsterdam: Elsevier, 1993: 213–220.

302. Kato M, Miyashita N, Hikosaka O, et al. Eye movements in monkeys with local dopamine depletion in the caudate nucleus. I. Deficits in spontaneous saccades. *J Neurosci* 1995; 15:912–927.

303. Kori A, Miyashita N, Kato M, et al. Eye movements in monkeys with local dopamine depletion in the caudate nucleus. II. Deficits in voluntary saccades. *J Neurosci* 1995; 15:928–941.

304. Nini A, Feingold A, Slovin H, Bergman H. Neurons in the globus pallidus do not show correlated activity in the normal monkey, but phase—locked oscillations appear in the MPTP model of parkinsonism. *J Neurophysiol* 1995; 74:1800–1805.

305. Nicola SM, Woodward Hopf F, Hjelmstad GO. Contrast enhancement: A physiological effect of striatal dopamine? *Cell Tissue Res* 2004; 318:93–106.

306. Tepper JM, Koos T, Wilson CJ. Gabaergic microcircuits in the neostriatum. *Trends Neurosci* 2004; 27:662–669.

307. Gross RE, Lombardi WD, Hutchison WD, et al. Lesion location and outcome following pallidotomy: Support for multiple output channels in the human pallidum. *Mov Disord* 1998; 13(Suppl 2):262.

308. Bar-Gad I, Bergman H. Stepping out of the box: Information processing in the neural networks of the basal ganglia. *Curr Opin Neurobiol* 2001; 11:689–695.

309. Bar-Gad I, Morris G, Bergman H. Information processing, dimensionality reduction and reinforcement learning in the basal ganglia. *Prog Neurobiol* 2003; 71:439–473.

310. Spooren WP, Lynd-Balta E, Mitchell S, Haber SN. Ventral pallidostriatal pathway in the monkey: Evidence for modulation of basal ganglia circuits. *J Comp Neurol* 1996; 370:295–312.

311. Haber SN. The primate basal ganglia: Parallel and integrative networks. *J Chem Neuroanat* 2003; 26:317–330.

312. Kaji R. Basal ganglia as a sensory gating devise for motor control. *J Med Invest* 2001; 48:142–146.

313. Nambu A. A new approach to understand the pathophysiology of parkinson's disease. *J Neurol* 2005; 252(Suppl 4):iv1–iv4.

314. Nambu A, Tokuno H, Hamada I, et al. Excitatory cortical inputs to pallidal neurons via the subthalamic nucleus in the monkey. *J Neurophysiol* 2000; 84:289–300.

315. Boraud T, Bezard E, Bioulac B, Gross CE. Ratio of inhibited-to-activated pallidal neurons decreases dramatically during passive limb movement in the MPTP-treated monkey. *J Neurophysiol* 2000; 83:1760–1763.

316. Mink JW. The basal ganglia: Focused selection and inhibition of competing motor programs. *Prog Neurobiol* 1996; 50:381–425.

317. Guzman JN, Hernandez A, Galarraga E, et al. Dopaminergic modulation of axon collaterals interconnecting spiny neurons of the rat striatum. *J Neurosci* 2003; 23:8931–8940.

318. Onn SP, Grace AA. Repeated treatment with haloperidol and clozapine exerts differential effects on dye coupling between neurons in subregions of striatum and nucleus accumbens. *J Neurosci* 1995; 15:7024–7036.

319. Onn SP, Grace AA. Dye coupling between rat striatal neurons recorded in vivo: Compartmental organization and modulation by dopamine. *J Neurophysiol* 1994; 71:1917–1934.

320. O'Donnell P, Grace AA. Different effects of subchronic clozapine and haloperidol on dye-coupling between neurons in the rat striatal complex. *Neuroscience* 1995; 66:763–767.

321. Filion M, Tremblay L, Bedard PJ. Abnormal influences of passive limb movement on the activity of globus pallidus neurons in parkinsonian monkeys. *Brain Res* 1988; 444:165–176.

322. Miller WC, DeLong MR. Altered tonic activity of neurons in the globus pallidus and subthalamic nucleus in the primate mptp model of parkinsonism. In: Carpenter MB, Jayaraman A (eds). *The Basal Ganglia II*. New York: Plenum Press, 1987: 415–427.

323. Bergman H, Wichmann T, Karmon B, DeLong MR. The primate subthalamic nucleus. II. Neuronal activity in the MPTP model of parkinsonism. *J Neurophysiol* 1994; 72:507–520.

324. Raz A, Feingold A, Zelanskaya V, et al. Neuronal synchronization of tonically active neurons in the striatum of normal and parkinsonian primates. *J Neurophysiol* 1996; 76:2083–2088.

325. Filion M, Tremblay L. Abnormal spontaneous activity of globus-pallidus neurons in monkeys with MPTP-induced parkinsonism. *Brain Res* 1991; 547:142–151.

326. Tremblay L, Filion M, Bedard PJ. Responses of pallidal neurons to striatal stimulation in monkeys with MPTP-induced parkinsonism. *Brain Res* 1989; 498:17–33.

327. Williams D, Kuhn A, Kupsch A, et al. The relationship between oscillatory activity and motor reaction time in the parkinsonian subthalamic nucleus. *Eur J Neurosci* 2005; 21:249–258.

328. Mink JW, Thach WT. Basal ganglia motor control. III. Pallidal ablation: Normal reaction time, muscle cocontraction, and slow movement. *J Neurophysiol* 1991; 65:330–351.

329. Georgopoulos AP, DeLong MR, Crutcher MD. Relations between parameters of step-tracking movements and single cell discharge in the globus pallidus and subthalamic nucleus of the behaving monkey. *J Neurosci* 1983; 3:1586–1598.

330. Bevan MD, Bolam JP, Crossman AR. Convergent synaptic input from the neostriatum and the subthalamus onto identified nigrothalamic neurons in the rat. *Eur J Neurosci* 1994; 6:320–334.

331. Bolam JP, Smith Y. The striatum and the globus pallidus send convergent synaptic inputs onto single cells in the entopeduncular nucleus of the rat: A double anterograde labelling study combined with postembedding immunocytochemistry for GABA. *J Comp Neurol* 1992; 321:456–476.

332. Hazrati L, Parent A. Convergence of subthalamic and striatal efferents at pallidal level in primates: An anterograde double-labeling study with biocytin and pha-l. *Brain Res* 1992; 569:336–340.

333. Jaeger D, Gilman S, Aldridge JW. Neuronal activity in the striatum and pallidum of primates related to the execution of externally cued reaching movements. *Brain Res* 1995; 694:111–127.

334. Jaeger D, Gilman S, Aldridge JW. Primate basal ganglia activity in a precued reaching task: Preparation for movement. *Exp Brain Res* 1993; 95:51–64.

335. Alexander GE, Crutcher MD. Preparatory activity in primate motor cortex and putamen coded in spatial rather than limb coordinates. *Soc Neurosci Abstr* 1987; 13:245.

336. Alexander GE, Crutcher MD. Coding in spatial rather than joint coordinates of putamen and motor cortex preparatory activity preceding planned limb movements. In: Sambrook MA, Crossman AR (eds). *Neural Mechanisms in Disorders of Movement*. London: Blackwell, 1989:55–62.

337. Anderson M, Inase M, Buford J, Turner R. Movement and preparatory activity of neurons in pallidal-receiving areas of the monkey thalamus. In: Mano N, Hamada I, DeLong MR (eds). *Role of Cerebellum and Basal Ganglia in Voluntary Movement*. Amsterdam: Elsevier, 1992:163–170.

338. Apicella P, Scarnati E, Schultz W. Tonically discharging neurons of monkey striatum respond to preparatory and rewarding stimuli. *Exp Brain Res* 1991; 84:672–675.

339. Boussaoud D, Kermadi I. The primate striatum: Neuronal activity in relation to spatial attention versus motor preparation. *Eur J Neurosci* 1997; 9:2152–2168.

340. Crutcher MD, Alexander GE. Supplementary motor area (SMA): Coding of both preparatory and movement-related neural activity in spatial rather than joint coordinates. *Soc Neurosci Abstr* 1988; 14:342.

341. Kubota K, Hamada I. Preparatory activity of monkey pyramidal tract neurons related to quick movement onset during visual tracking performance. *Brain Res* 1979; 168:435–439.

342. Schultz W, Romo R. Role of primate basal ganglia and frontal cortex in the internal generation of movement. I. Preparatory activity in the anterior striatum. *ExpBrain Res* 1992; 91:363–384.

343. Dettmers C, Fink GR, Lemon RN, et al. Relation between cerebral activity and force in the motor areas of the human brain. *J Neurophysiol* 1995; 74:802–815.

344. Turner RS, Grafton ST, Votaw JR, et al. Motor subcircuits mediating the control of movement velocity: A pet study. *J Neurophysiol* 1998; 80:2162–2176.

345. Marsden CD, Obeso JA. The functions of the basal ganglia and the paradox of stereotaxic surgery in Parkinson's disease. *Brain* 1994; 117:877–897.

346. Joel D, Weiner I. The organization of the basal ganglia–thalamocortical circuits: Open interconnected rather than closed segregated. *Neuroscience* 1994; 63:363–379.

347. Graybiel AM. Building action repertoires: Memory and learning functions of the basal ganglia. *Curr Opin Neurobiol* 1995; 5:733–741.

348. Beiser DG, Hua SE, Houk JC. Network models of the basal ganglia. *Curr Opin Neurobiol* 1997; 7:185–190.

349. Beiser DG, Houk JC. Model of cortical-basal ganglionic processing: Encoding the serial order of sensory events. *J Neurophysiol* 1998; 79:3168–3188.

350. Schultz W. The phasic reward signal of primate dopamine neurons. *Adv Pharmacol* 1998; 42:686–690.

351. Aosaki T, Kimura M, Graybiel AM. Temporal and spatial characteristics of tonically active neurons of the primate striatum. *J Neurophysiol* 1995; 73:1234–1252.

352. Aosaki T, Tsubokawa H, Watanabe K, et al. Responses of tonically active neurons in the primate's striatum undergo systematic changes during behavioral sensory-motor conditioning. *J Neurosci* 1994; 14:3969–3984.

353. Jog MS, Kubota Y, Connolly CI, et al. Building neural representations of habits. *Science* 1999; 286:1745–1749.

354. McHaffie JG, Stanford TR, Stein BE, et al. Subcortical loops through the basal ganglia. *Trends Neurosci* 2005; 28:401–407.

355. Hore J, Villis T. Arm movement performance during reversible basal ganglia lesions in the monkey. *Exp Brain Res* 1980; 39:217–228.

356. Inase M, Buford JA, Anderson ME. Changes in the control of arm position, movement, and thalamic discharge during local inactivation in the globus pallidus of the monkey. *J Neurophysiol* 1996; 75:1087–1104.

357. Kato M, Kimura M. Effects of reversible blockade of basal ganglia on a voluntary arm movement. *J Neurophysiol* 1992; 68:1516–1534.

358. Horak FB, Anderson ME. Influence of globus pallidus on arm movements in monkeys. II. Effects of stimulation. *J Neurophysiol* 1984; 52:305–322.

359. Horak FB, Anderson ME. Influence of globus pallidus on arm movements in monkeys. I. Effects of kainic-induced lesions. *J Neurophysiol* 1984; 52:290–304.

360. Alamy M, Pons JC, Gambarelli D, Trouche E. A defective control of small-amplitude movements in monkeys with globus pallidus lesions: An experimental study on one component of pallidal bradykinesia. *Behav Brain Res* 1995; 72:57–62.

361. Alamy M, Trouche E, Nieoullon A, Legallet E. Globus pallidus and motor initiation: The bilateral effects of unilateral quisqualic acid–induced lesion on reaction times in monkeys. *Exp Brain Res* 1994; 99:247–258.

362. DeLong MR, Georgopoulos AP. Motor functions of the basal ganglia. In: Brookhart JM, Mountcastle VB, Brooks VB, Geiger SR (eds). *Handbook of Physiology the Nervous System Motor Control.* Sec 1, Vol II, Pt 2. Bethesda, MD: American Physiological Society, 1981:1017–1061.

363. Laitinen LV. Pallidotomy for Parkinson's disease. *Neurosurg Clin North Am* 1995; 6:105–112.

364. Baron MS, Vitek JL, Bakay RAE, et al. Treatment of advanced Parkinson's disease by GPi pallidotomy: 1 year pilot-study results. *Ann Neurol* 1996; 40:355–366.

365. Lozano AM, Lang AE, Galvez-Jimenez N, et al. Effect of GPi pallidotomy on motor function in Parkinson's disease. *Lancet* 1995; 346:1383–1387.

366. Mink JW, Thach WT. Basal ganglia intrinsic circuits and their role in behavior. *Curr Opin Neurobiol* 1993; 3:950–957.

367. Ehringer H, Hornykiewicz O. Verteilung von Noradrenalin und Dopamin (3-Hydroxytyramin) im Gehirn des Menschen und ihr Verhalten bei Erkrankungen des extrapyramidalen Systems. *Klin Wochenschr* 1960; 38:1236–1239.

368. Bernheimer H, Birkmayer W, Hornykiewicz O, et al. Brain dopamine and the syndromes of Parkinson and Huntington. *J Neurol Sci* 1973; 20:415–455.

369. Hornykiewicz O, Kish SJ. Biochemical pathophysiology of Parkinson's disease. *Adv Neurol* 1987; 45:19–34.

370. Braak H, Del Tredici K, Rub U, et al. Staging of brain pathology related to sporadic Parkinson's disease. *Neurobiol Aging* 2003; 24:197–211.

371. Braak H, Rub U, Gai WP, Del Tredici K. Idiopathic Parkinson's disease: Possible routes by which vulnerable neuronal types may be subject to neuroinvasion by an unknown pathogen. *J Neural Transm* 2003; 110:517–536.

372. Kish SJ, Shannak K, Hornykiewicz O. Uneven pattern of dopamine loss in the striatum of patients with idiopathic Parkinson's disease. *N Engl J Med* 1988; 318: 876–880.

373. Ingham CA, Hood SH, van Maldegem B, et al. Morphological changes in the rat neostriatum after unilateral 6-hydroxydopamine injections into the nigrostriatal pathway. *Exp Brain Res* 1993; 93:17–27.

374. Ingham CA, Hood SH, Arbuthnott GW. Spine density on neostriatal neurones changes with 6-hydroxydopamine lesions and with age. *Brain Res* 1989; 503:334–338.

375. Stephens B, Mueller AJ, Shering AF, et al. Evidence of a breakdown of corticostriatal connections in Parkinson's disease. *Neuroscience* 2005; 132:741–754.

376. Burns RS, Chiueh CC, Markey SP, et al. A primate model of parkinsonism: Selective destruction of dopaminergic neurons in the pars compacta of the substantia nigra by n-methyl-4-phenyl-1,2,3,6-tetrahydropyridine. *Proc Natl Acad Sci USA* 1983; 80:4546–4550.

377. Burns RS, LeWitt PA, Ebert MH, et al. The clinical syndrome of striatal dopamine deficiency. *N Engl J Med* 1985; 312(22):1418–1421.

378. Bankiewicz KS, Oldfield EH, Chiueh CC, et alJ. Hemiparkinsonism in monkeys after unilateral internal carotid artery infusion of 1-methyl-4-phenyl-1,2,3,6-tetrahydropyridine (MPTP). *Life Sci* 1986; 39:7–16.

379. Forno LS, Langston JW, DeLanney LE, et al. Locus ceruleus lesions and eosinophilic inclusions in MPTP-treated monkeys. *Ann Neurol* 1986; 20:449–455.

380. Forno LS, DeLanney LE, Irwin I, Langston JW. Similarities and differences between MPTP-induced parkinsonism and Parkinson's disease. *Adv Neurol* 1993; 60:600–608.

381. Irwin I, DeLanney LE, Forno LS, et al. The evolution of nigrostriatal neurochemical changes in the MPTP-treated squirrel monkey. *Brain Res* 1990; 531:242–252.

382. Langston JW. MPTP: The promise of a new neurotoxin. In: Marsden CD, Fahn S (eds). *Movement Disorders 2.* London: Butterworth, 1987:73–90.

383. Crossman AR, Mitchell IJ, Sambrook MA. Regional brain uptake of 2-deoxyglucose in n-methyl-4-phenyl-1,2,3,6-tetrahydropyridine (MPTP)-induced parkinsonism in the macaque monkey. *Neuropharmacology* 1985; 24:587–591.

384. Mitchell IJ, Cross AJ, Sambrook MA, Crossman AR. Neural mechanisms mediating 1-methyl-4-phenyl-1,2,3,6-tetrahydropyridine-induced parkinsonism in the monkey: Relative contributions of the striatopallidal and striatonigral pathways as suggested by 2-deoxyglucose uptake. *Neurosci Lett* 1986; 63:61–65.

385. Mitchell IJ, Clarke CE, Boyce S, et al. Neural mechanisms underlying parkinsonian symptoms based upon regional uptake of 2-deoxyglucose in monkeys exposed to 1-methyl-4-phenyl-1,2,3,6-tetrahydropyridine. *Neuroscience* 1989; 32:213–226.

386. Schwartzman RJ, Alexander GM. Changes in the local cerebral metabolic rate for glucose in the 1-methyl-4-phenyl-1,2,3,6-tetrahydropyridine (MPTP) primate model of Parkinson's disease. *Brain Res* 1985; 358:137–143.

387. Schwartzman RJ, Alexander GM, Ferraro TN, et al. Cerebral metabolism of parkinsonian primates 21 days after mptp. *Exp Neurol* 1988; 102:307–313.

388. Palombo E, Porrino LJ, Bankiewicz KS, et al. Local cerebral glucose utilization in monkeys with hemiparkinsonism induced by intracarotid infusion of the neurotoxin MPTP. *J Neurosci* 1990; 10:860–869.

389. Porrino LJ, Burns RS, Crane AM, et al. Changes in local cerebral glucose utilization associated with Parkinson's syndrome induced by 1-methyl-4-phenyl-1,2,3,6-tetrahydropyridine (MPTP) in the primate. *Life Sciences* 1987; 40:1657–1664.

390. Boraud T, Bezard E, Guehl D, et al. Effects of L-dopa on neuronal activity of the globus pallidus externalis (GPE) and globus pallidus internalis (GPi) in the MPTP-treated monkey. *Brain Res* 1998; 787:157–160.

391. Dogali M, Beric A, Sterio D, et al. Anatomic and physiological considerations in pallidotomy for parkinson's disease. *Stereotact Funct Neurosurg* 1994; 62:53–60.

392. Lozano A, Hutchison W, Kiss Z, et al. Methods for microelectrode-guided posteroventral pallidotomy. *J Neurosurg* 1996; 84:194–202.

393. Taha JM, Favre J, Baumann TK, Burchiel KJ. Tremor control after pallidotomy in patients with parkinson's disease: Correlation with microrecording findings. *J Neurosurg* 1997; 86:642–647.

394. Vitek JL, Kaneoke Y, Turner R, et al. Neuronal activity in the internal (GPi) and external (GPe) segments of the globus pallidus (GP) of parkinsonian patients is similar to that in the MPTP-treated primate model of parkinsonism. *Soc Neurosci Abstr* 1993; 19:1584.

395. Brooks DJ. Detection of preclinical parkinson's disease with pet. *Neurology* 1991; 41(Suppl 2):24–27.

396. Calne D, Snow BJ. Pet imaging in parkinsonism. *Adv Neurol* 1993; 60:484.

397. Eidelberg D, Moeller JR, Dhawan V, et al. The metabolic topography of parkinsonism. *J Cereb Blood Flow Metab* 1994; 14:783–801.

398. Ceballos-Bauman AO, Obeso JA, Vitek JL, et al. Restoration of thalamocortical activity after posteroventrolateral pallidotomy in Parkinson's disease. *Lancet* 1994; 344:814.

399. Grafton S, Waters C, Sutton J, et al. Pallidotomy increases activity of motor association cortex in Parkinson's disease: A positron emission tomographic study. *Ann Neurol* 1995; 37:776–783.

400. Samuel M, Ceballos-Baumann AO, Turjanski N, et al. Pallidotomy in Parkinson's disease increases supplementary motor area and prefrontal activation during performance of volitional movements an h2(15)o PET study. *Brain* 1997; 120:1301–1313.

401. Watts RL, Mandir AS. The role of motor cortex in the pathophysiology of voluntary movement deficits associated with parkinsonism. *Neurol Clin* 1992; 10:451–469.

402. Goldberg JA, Boraud T, Maraton S, et al. Enhanced synchrony among primary motor cortex neurons in the 1-methyl-4-phenyl-1,2,3,6-tetrahydropyridine primate model of Parkinson's disease. *J Neurosci* 2002; 22:4639–4653.

403. Kojima J, Yamaji Y, Matsumura M, et al. Excitotoxic lesions of the pedunculopontine tegmental nucleus produce contralateral hemiparkinsonism in the monkey. *Neurosci Lett* 1997; 226:111–114.

404. Munro-Davies LE, Winter J, Aziz TZ, Stein JF. The role of the pedunculopontine region in basal-ganglia mechanisms of akinesia. *Exp Brain Res* 1999; 129:511–517.

405. Carlson JD, Pearlstein RD, Buchholz J, et al. Regional metabolic changes in the pedunculopontine nucleus of unilateral 6-hydroxydopamine Parkinson's model rats. *Brain Res* 1999; 828:12–19.

406. Nandi D, Aziz TZ, Giladi N, et al. Reversal of akinesia in experimental parkinsonism by gaba antagonist microinjections in the pedunculopontine nucleus. *Brain* 2002; 125:2418–2430.

407. Pahapill PA, Lozano AM. The pedunculopontine nucleus and parkinson's disease. *Brain* 2000; 123 (Pt 9):1767–1783.

408. Bergman H, Wichmann T, DeLong MR. Reversal of experimental parkinsonism by lesions of the subthalamic nucleus. *Science* 1990; 249:1436–1438.

409. Aziz TZ, Peggs D, Sambrook MA, Crossman AR. Lesion of the subthalamic nucleus for the alleviation of 1-methyl-4-phenyl-,2,3,6-tetrahydropyridine (MPTP)–induced parkinsonism in the primate. *Mov Disord* 1991; 6:288–292.

410. Guridi J, Herrero MT, Luquin R, et al. Subthalamotomy improves MPTP–induced parkinsonism in monkeys. *Stereotact Funct Neurosurg* 1994; 62:98–102.

411. Gill SS, Heywood P. Bilateral dorsolateral subthalamotomy for advanced parkinson's disease (letter). *Lancet* 1997; 350:1224.

412. Gill SS, Heywood P. Bilateral subthalamic nucleotomy can be accomplished safely. *Mov Disord* 1998; 13:201.

413. Alvarez L, Macias R, Lopez G, et al. Bilateral subthalamotomy in Parkinson's disease: Initial and long-term response. *Brain* 2005; 128:570–583.

414. Dogali M, Fazzini E, Kolodny E, et al. Stereotactic ventral pallidotomy for Parkinson's disease. *Neurology* 1995; 45:753–761.

415. Vitek JL, Bakay RAE, Freeman A, et al. Randomized clinical trial of GPi pallidotomy versus best medical therapy for parkinson's disease. *Ann Neurol* 2003; 53-668-569.

416. Hashimoto T, Elder CM, Okun MS, et al. Stimulation of the subthalamic nucleus changes the firing pattern of pallidal neurons. *J Neurosci* 2003; 23:1916–1923.

417. Vitek JL, Ashe J, DeLong MR, Alexander GE. Altered somatosensory response properties of neurons in the "motor" thalamus of MPTP treated parkinsonian monkeys. *Soc Neurosci Abstr* 1990; 16:425.

418. Heimer G, Bar-Gad I, Goldberg JA, Bergman H. Dopamine replacement therapy reverses abnormal synchronization of pallidal neurons in the 1-methyl-4-phenyl-1,2,3,6-tetrahydropyridine primate model of parkinsonism. *J Neurosci* 2002; 22:7850–7855.

419. Raz A, Frechter-Mazar V, Feingold A, et al. Activity of pallidal and striatal tonically active neurons is correlated in MPTP-treated monkeys but not in normal monkeys. *J Neurosci* 2001; 21:RC128.

420. Raz A, Vaadia E, Bergman H. Firing patterns and correlations of spontaneous discharge of pallidal neurons in the normal and the tremulous 1-methyl-4-phenyl-1,2,3,6-tetrahydropyridine vervet model of parkinsonism. *J Neurosci* 2000; 20:8559–8571.

421. Vitek JL, Ashe J, DeLong MR, Alexander GE. Physiologic properties and somatotopic organization of the primate motor thalamus. *J Neurophysiol* 1994; 71:1498–1513.

422. Wichmann T, Bergman H, DeLong MR. Comparison of the effects of experimental parkinsonism on neuronal discharge in motor and non-motor portions of the basal ganglia output nuclei in primates. *Soc Neurosci Abstr* 1996; 22:415.

423. Filion M, Boucher R, Bedard P. Globus pallidus unit activity in the monkey during the induction of parkinsonism by 1-methyl-4-phenyl-1,2,3,6,-tetrahydropyridine (MPTP). *Soc Neurosci Abstr* 1985; 11:1160.

424. Soares J, Kliem MA, Betarbet R, et al. Role of external pallidal segment in primate parkinsonism: Comparison of the effects of MPTP-induced parkinsonism and lesions of the external pallidal segment. *J Neurosci* 2004; 24:6417–6426.

425. Wichmann T, Soares J. Neuronal firing before and after burst discharges in the monkey basal ganglia is predictably patterned in the normal state and altered in parkinsonism. *J Neurophysiol* 2006; 95:2120–2133.

426. Silberstein P, Kuhn AA, Kupsch A, et al. Patterning of globus pallidus local field potentials differs between Parkinson's disease and dystonia. *Brain* 2003; 126:2597–2608.

427. Kuhn AA, Doyle L, Pogosyan A, et al. Modulation of beta oscillations in the subthalamic area during motor imagery in Parkinson's disease. *Brain* 2006; 129:695–706.

428. Silberstein P, Oliviero A, Di Lazzaro V, et al. Oscillatory pallidal local field potential activity inversely correlates with limb dyskinesias in Parkinson's disease. *Exp Neurol* 2005; 194:523–529.

429. Fogelson N, Williams D, Tijssen M, et al. Different functional loops between cerebral cortex and the subthalmic area in Parkinson's disease. *Cereb Cortex* 2006; 16(1): 64–75

430. Brown P, Williams D. Basal ganglia local field potential activity: Character and functional significance in the human. *Clin Neurophysiol* 2005; 116:2510–2519.

431. Foffani G, Priori A, Egidi M, et al. 300–hz subthalamic oscillations in parkinson's disease. *Brain* 2003; 126:2153–2163.

432. Foffani G, Ardolino G, Meda B, et al. Altered subthalamo-pallidal synchronisation in parkinsonian dyskinesias. *J Neurol Neurosurg Psychiatry* 2005; 76:426–428.

433. Brown P, Oliviero A, Mazzone P, et al. Dopamine dependency of oscillations between subthalamic nucleus and pallidum in Parkinson's disease. *J Neurosci* 2001; 21:1033–1038.

434. Brown P, Mazzone P, Oliviero A, et al. Effects of stimulation of the subthalamic area on oscillatory pallidal activity in Parkinson's disease. *Exp Neurol* 2004; 188:480–490.

435. Goldberg JA, Rokni U, Boraud T, et al. Spike synchronization in the cortex/basal–ganglia networks of parkinsonian primates reflects global dynamics of the local field potentials. *J Neurosci* 2004; 24:6003–6010.

436. Brooks DJ. Pet and spect studies in Parkinson's disease. *Baillieres Clinic Neurol* 1997; 6:69–87.

437. Jenkins IH, Fernandez W, Playford ED, et al. Impaired activation of the supplementary motor area in Parkinson's disease is reversed when akinesia is treated with apomorphine. *Ann Neurol* 1992; 32:749–757.

438. Deecke L. Cerebral potentials related to voluntary actions: Parkinsonism and normal subjects. In: Delwaide PJ, Agnoli A (eds). *Clinical Neurophysiology in Parkinsonism.* Amsterdam and Oxford: Elsevier, 1985: 91–105.

439. Dick JPR, Rothwell JC, Day BL, et al. The bereitschaftspotential is abnormal in Parkinson's disease. *Brain* 1989; 112:233–244.

440. Obeso JA, Rothwell JC, Ceballos-Bauman A, et al. The mechanism of action of pallidotomy in Parkinson's disease (PD): Physiological and imaging studies. *Soc Neurosci Abstr* 1995; 21:1982.

441. Timmermann L, Wojtecki L, Gross J, et al. Ten-hertz stimulation of subthalamic nucleus deteriorates motor symptoms in Parkinson's disease. *Mov Disord* 2004; 19:1328–1333.

442. Moro E, Esselink RJ, Xie J, et al. The impact on Parkinson's disease of electrical parameter settings in STN stimulation. *Neurology* 2002; 59:706–713.

443. Kleiner-Fisman G, Fisman DN, et al. Long-term follow up of bilateral deep brain stimulation of the subthalamic nucleus in patients with advanced Parkinson disease. *J Neurosurg* 2003; 99:489–495.

444. Plaha P, Gill SS. Bilateral deep brain stimulation of the pedunculopontine nucleus for Parkinson's disease. *Neuroreport* 2005; 16:1883–1887.

445. Mazzone P, Lozano A, Stanzione P, et al. Implantation of human pedunculopontine nucleus: A safe and clinically relevant target in Parkinson's disease. *Neuroreport* 2005; 16:1877–1881.

446. Jenkinson N, Nandi D, Aziz TZ, Stein JF. Pedunculopontine nucleus: A new target for deep brain stimulation for akinesia. *Neuroreport* 2005; 16:1875–1876.

447. Jenkinson N, Nandi D, Miall RC, et al. Pedunculopontine nucleus stimulation improves akinesia in a parkinsonian monkey. *Neuroreport* 2004; 15:2621–2624.

448. Winstein CJ, Grafton ST, Pohl PS. Motor task difficulty and brain activity: Investigation of goal-directed reciprocal aiming using positron emission tomography. *J Neurophysiol* 1997; 77:1581–1594.

449. Davis KD, Taub E, Houle S, et al. Globus pallidus stimulation activates the cortical motor system during alleviation of parkinsonian symptoms. *Nat Med* 1997; 3:671–674.

450. Delwaide PJ, Pepin JL, Maertens de Noordhout A. Short-latency autogenic inhibition in patients with parkinsonian rigidity. *AnnNeurol* 1991; 30:83–89.

451. Hyland B, Chen DF, Maier V, et al. What is the role of the supplementary motor area in movement initiation? *Prog Brain Res* 1989; 80:431–436; discussion 427–430.

452. Delwaide PJ, Pepin JL, Maertens de Noordhout A. Contribution of reticular nuclei to the pathophysiology of parkinsonian rigidity. *Adv Neurol* 1993; 60:381–385.

453. Lee RG, Murphy JT, Tatton WG. Long-latency myotatic reflexes in man: Mechanisms, functional significance, and changes in patients with parkinson's disease or hemiplegia. In: Desmedt JE (ed). *Motor Control Mechanisms in Health and Disease.* New York: Raven Press, 1983: 489–507.

454. Berardelli A, Sabra A, Hallett M. Physiological mechanisms of rigidity in Parkinson's disease. *J Neurol Neurosurg Psychiatry* 1983; 46:45–53.

455. Tsai CH, Chen RS, Lu CS. Reciprocal inhibition in Parkinson's disease. *Acta Neuro lScand* 1997; 95:13–18.

456. Lenz FA, Tasker RR, Kwan HC, et al. Cross-correlation analysis of thalamic neurons and emg activity in parkinsonian tremor. *Appl Neurophysiol* 1985; 48:305–308.

457. Lenz FA, Tasker RR, Kwan HC, et al. Single unit analysis of the human thalamic ventral nuclear group: Correlation of thalamic "tremor cells" With the 3–6 Hz component of parkinsonian tremor. *J Neurosci* 1988; 8:754–764.

458. Lenz FA, Tasker RR, Kwan HC, et al. Functional classes of "tremor cells" In the ventral tier of lateral thalamic nuclei of patients with parkinsonian tremor. In: Brock M (ed). *Modern Neurosurgery.* Berlin: Springer-Verlag, 1989:205–217.

459. Ohye C, Nakamura R, Fukamachi A, Narabayashi H. Recording and stimulation of the ventralis intermedius nucleus of the human thalamus. *Conf Neurol* 1975;37:258.

460. Narabayashi H, Ohye C. Parkinsonian tremor in nucleus ventralis intermedius of the human thalamus. In: Desmedt JE (ed). *Progress in Clinical Neurophysiology: Physiological Tremor, Pathological Tremors and Clonus.* New York: Karger, 1978:165–172.

461. Ohye C, Narabayashi H. Physiological study of presumed ventralis intermedius neurons in the human thalamus. *J Neurosurg* 1979; 50:290–297.

462. Pare D, Curro'Dossi R, Steriade M. Neuronal basis of the parkinsonian resting tremor: A hypothesis and its implications for treatment. *Neuroscience* 1990; 35:217–226.

463. Steriade M, Jones EG, Llinas RR. Thalamic oscillations and signaling. New York: Wiley-Interscience, 1990.

464. Steriade M, McCormick DA, Sejnowski TJ. Thalamocortical oscillations in the sleeping and aroused brain. *Science* 1993; 262:679–685.

465. Llinas R, Jahnsen H. Electrophysiology of mammalian thalamic neurones in vitro. *Nature* 1982; 29:406–408.

466. Jahnsen H, Llinas R. Ionic basis for the electro-responsiveness and oscillatory properties of guinea-pig thalamic neurones in vitro. *J Physiol (Lond)* 1984; 349:227–247.

467. Jahnsen H, Llinas R. Electrophysiological properties of guinea-pig thalamic neurones: An in vitro study. *JPhysiol* 1984; 349:205–226.

468. Kim U, Sanchez-Vives MV, McCormick DA. Functional dynamics of gabaergic inhibition in the thalamus. *Science* 1997; 278:130–134.

469. Lenz FA, Vitek JL, DeLong MR. Role of the thalamus in parkinsonian tremor: Evidence from studies in patients and primate models. *Stereotact Funct Neurosurg* 1993; 60: 94–103.

470. Dogali M, Beric A, Sterio D, et al. Anatomic and physiological considerations in pallidotomy for Parkinson's disease. *Acta Neurochir Suppl (Wien)* 1995; 64:9–12.

471. Karmon B, Bergman H. Detection of neuronal periodic oscillations in the basal ganglia of normal and parkinsonian monkeys. *Isr J Med Sci* 1993; 29:570–579.

472. Chockkan V, Mewes K, Zhang J, et al. A comparison of discharge pattern of internal segment neurons of the globus pallidus (GPi) in akinetic and tremor parkinsonian patients (PD). *Soc Neurosci Abstr* 1997; 23:470.

473. Nambu A, Llinas R. Electrophysiology of the globus pallidus neurons: An in vitro study in guinea pig brain slices. *Soc Neurosci Abstr* 1990; 16:428.

474. Wichmann T, Bergman H, DeLong MR. The primate subthalamic nucleus. III. Changes in motor behavior and neuronal activity in the internal pallidum induced by subthalamic inactivation in the MPTP model of parkinsonism. *J Neurophysiol* 1994; 72:521–530.

475. Bergman H, Deuschl G. Pathophysiology of Parkinson's disease: From clinical neurology to basic neuroscience and back. *Mov Disord* 2002; 17(Suppl 3):S28–S40.

476. Deuschl G, Raethjen J, Baron R, et al. The pathophysiology of parkinsonian tremor: A review. *J Neurol* 2000; 247(Suppl 5):V33–V48.

477. Wang SY, Aziz TZ, Stein JF, Liu X. Time-frequency analysis of transient neuromuscular events: Dynamic changes in activity of the subthalamic nucleus and forearm muscles related to the intermittent resting tremor. *J Neurosci Meth* 2005; 145:151–158.

478. Priori A, Foffani G, Pesenti A, et al. Rhythm-specific pharmacological modulation of subthalamic activity in parkinson's disease. *Exp Neurol* 2004; 189:369–379.

479. Ben-Pazi H, Bergman H, Goldberg JA, et al. Synchrony of rest tremor in multiple limbs in Parkinson's disease: Evidence for multiple oscillators. *J Neural Transm* 2001; 108:287–296.

480. Bergman H, Raz A, Feingold A, et al. Physiology of MPTP tremor. *Mov Disord* 1998; 13(Suppl 3):29–34.

481. Levy R, Hutchison WD, Lozano AM, Dostrovsky JO. Synchronized neuronal discharge in the basal ganglia of parkinsonian patients is limited to oscillatory activity. *J Neurosci* 2002; 22:2855–2861.

23 Dopamine Receptor Diversity

Deborah C. Mash

opamine plays a role not only in the execution of movement but also in higher-order cognitive processes, including motor planning and sequencing, motor learning, and motivational drives and affect. Of the many slow-acting neurotransmitters in the central nervous system (CNS), dopamine has been the best studied. The actions of dopamine are segregated into specific neuronal circuits within a diffuse axonal projection system. For example, dopamine in the nigrostriatal pathway is involved in the generation and execution of voluntary movement. In this function, dopamine is a prime modulator of various other basal ganglial neurotransmitters implicated in motor control, including gamma-aminobutyric acid (GABA), acetylcholine, glutamate, enkephalin, and substance P. Dopamine in the mesolimbic pathway plays a role in the control of various cognitive functions, including reinforcement, attention, instrumental avoidance, and addiction to psychostimulant drugs. Dopaminergic receptor genes are likely candidates for genetic effects on cognition because of the importance of dopaminergic innveration on memory and attention.

The central effects of dopamine are mediated by 5 different molecular receptor subtypes, which are members of the large G protein–coupled receptor superfamily. Dopamine receptors are divided into 2 major subclasses,

D1-like and D2-like receptors, which differ in their pharmacology, messenger transduction systems, and anatomic locations. The cloning of these receptors and their genes in the last decade has led to the identification of multiple molecular receptor subtypes termed D1, D2, D3, D4, and D5. The molecular D1 and D5 subtypes of dopamine receptors exhibit overlapping functional and pharmacologic properties related to the D1 receptor (D1-like), whereas the remaining members of this receptor family share pharmacologic characteristics in keeping with the D2 receptor subtype (D2-like). The two receptor subclasses have overlapping but distinct neuroanatomic distributions as determined by radioligand binding autoradiography. The gene controlling the D4 receptor (DRD4 on chromosome 11) has very high variability. Thus, the various functions of dopaminergic neurotransmission appear to be mediated by the expression of different receptor proteins.

Studies of dopamine neurotransmission have been an important research focus for decades, because it is known that alterations in dopamine function are involved in many different neurodegenerative and psychiatric brain disorders. Degeneration of the nigral dopamine-containing neurons contributes to the pathogenesis of Parkinson's disease (PD) (1). Dopamine receptor agonists acting at multiple receptors, but primarily D2, are used to treat the dopamine deficiency of this disease (2). Drugs acting at dopamine D2 receptors are commonly used to alleviate symptoms produced by diseases such as schizophrenia and depression (3). The chorea of Huntington's disease is related to a deterioration of the dopaminoceptive cells localized in the striatum. Schizophrenia and other psychotic disorders are thought to be due to an imbalance in corticolimbic dopamine signaling (4). Dopamine receptor antagonists are used for the clinical management of these disorders (4–6). Chronic dopamine receptor blockade leads to a dysregulation of dopaminergic tone and the development of extrapyramidal syndromes including parkinsonism and chorea, whereas involuntary movements and psychosis are observed with chronic administration of the indirect-acting agonist levodopa in PD (2). Although none of the dopamine receptor subtypes have been linked to the etiology of schizophrenia, the distinct regional locations of D3 and D4 receptors in cerebrocortical and associated subcortical limbic brain areas have led to the suggestion that subtype-selective neuroleptics that lack extrapyramidal side effects can be developed. Clozapine, an antipsychotic that antagonizes the D4 receptor, is a perfect example of this possibility (for review, see ref. 7) .

MOLECULAR CHARACTERIZATION OF DOPAMINE RECEPTORS

The molecular characterization of dopamine receptor heterogeneity was advanced by the recognition line SK-N-MC (8). The D4 glycoprotein is 387 amino acid residues in length, with the characteristic 7 transmembrane-spanning domains, a large third intracellular loop, and a short C-terminus. The dopamine D1 (or D1a) receptor was independently cloned by 4 separate groups of investigators (9–12). The isolation of cDNAs or genes from rat or human DNA libraries was done by either homology screening with a D2 receptor probe or by polymerase chain reaction (PCR) with degenerate primers. Both the rat and human D1 receptor genes encode a protein that is 91% homologous for amino acid sequence. The second member of the D1-like receptor family, D5, was isolated using the sequence of the D1 receptor (13). The coding region for the carboxy terminal of the protein is about 7 times longer for D1-like than for D2-like receptors (14). The cloned D1 and D5 receptors are 446 residues in length and exhibit 91% amino acid sequence homology within the highly conserved 7-transmembrane-spanning region (Figure 23-1).

Analysis of the gene structure of D2 receptors demonstrated that the coding region contains 6 introns, the D3 receptor contains 5, and the D4 contains 3 (14, 15). The presence of introns within the coding region of the D2 receptor family allows the generation of receptor variants. For example, alternative splicing of the D2 receptor at the exon between introns 4 and 5 results in functional

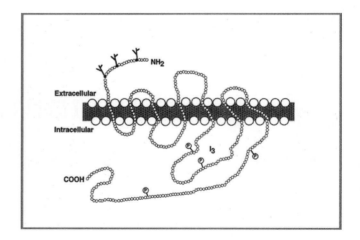

FIGURE 23-1

Dopamine receptor structure. Proposed structure of D_1-like dopamine receptor. The seven transmembrane domains have highly conserved amino acid sequences. Potential glycosylation sites are shown on the NH_2 terminal. The intracellular loop 3 and the carboxy terminus have multiple phosphorylation sites. The coupling of the receptor to G proteins occurs through the interactions of the proteins at sites on the carboxy-terminus and the third cytoplasmic loop (l_3) to activate second messenger signaling pathways.

D2S and D2L isoforms (16, 17). Nonfunctional proteins encoded by alternative splice variants of the D3 receptor have been demonstrated (18–20). The human D4 receptor gene, located on the short arm of chromosome 11, has 8 different polymorphic variants. The existence of polymorphic variations within the coding sequence of the D4 receptor demonstrated a 48-base-pair sequence in the third cytoplasmic loop, which exists with multiple repeated sequences (21). The number of repeated sequences is related to ethnicity, with most humans (70%) having 4 repeats. The 7-repeat allele of the DRD4 gene has been associated with the personality trait of "novelty seeking" (22, 23). Nonfunctional, truncated isoforms of the D5 receptor have been reported on human chromosomes 1 and 2 (15, 21).

NEUROANATOMIC LOCALIZATION OF DOPAMINE RECEPTOR PROTEIN AND mRNA

The dopaminergic systems in brain comprise 3 distinct pathways, including the nigrostriatal, mesocortical, and mesolimbic projections (24). The nigrostriatal pathway originates in the substantia nigra pars compacta and terminates in the striatum. The mesolimbic pathway originates in the ventral tegmental area (VTA) and projects to the limbic sectors of the striatum, amygdala, and olfactory tubercle. The mesocortical pathway originates in the VTA and terminates within particular sectors of the cerebrocortical mantle, including the prefrontal, cingulate, and entorhinal cortices.

D1-like and D2-like receptors and their mRNAs are abundant in the CNS, having a widespread distribution within the different dopaminergic systems (15). The neuroanatomic localization of D1 receptors correlates with DA-stimulated adenylyl cyclase activities and radioligand binding. High densities of radioligand binding sites are found within the caudate, putamen, and nucleus accumbens, with lower levels in the thalamus and cerebrocortical sectors (A in Figure 23-2). D1-receptor mRNA has been localized to medium-sized neurons of the striatonigral projection, which also express substance P (25). D5 mRNA is distributed in a more restricted pattern than D1 mRNA, with the highest expression seen in limbic and cortical brain areas Very low levels of D5 mRNA are found within the striatum (15).

Radioligand binding and mRNA studies have confirmed a good correlation for the D2-like receptors. D2 receptors and message are found in the striatum and substantia nigra of the rat and human brain (B in Figure 23-2). The globus pallidus, a major efferent projection system of the striatum, has high densities of D2 receptors (26). However, neurons expressing D2-receptor mRNA are lower in the globus pallidus than in the caudate and putamen. D2-receptor mRNA is colocalized with enkephalin in many brain areas, including the periaquaductal gray, suggesting a role for these sites in the modulation of analgesia (25). Radioligand binding to D3 receptors in human brain demonstrates a distinct localization pattern and a less widespread distribution than D2-binding sites (Figure 23-2). The highest densities are seen over limbic brain regions, with very low levels over the ventromedial sectors of the striatum (26). The highest levels of message expression are found within the telencephalic areas receiving mesocortical dopaminergic inputs, including the islands of Calleja, bed nucleus of the stria terminalis, hippocampus, and hypothalamus. In the cerebellum, Purkinje cells in lobules IX and X express abundant D3 mRNA, whereas binding sites are found only in the molecular layer (26, 27). Since no dopaminergic projections are known to exist in these areas, it has been suggested that the D3 receptor may mediate the nonsynaptic (paracrine) actions of dopamine (27). D4 receptor message is localized to dopamine cell body

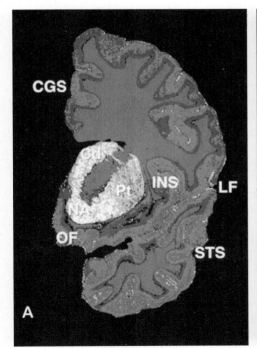
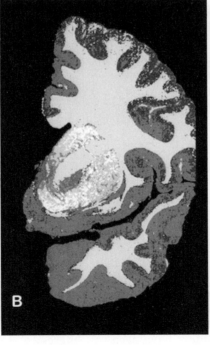
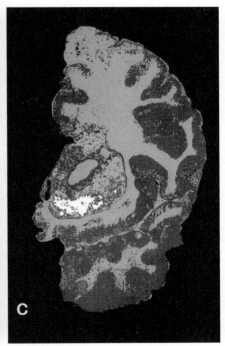

FIGURE 23-2

Autoradiographic localization of the distribution of D1 and D2 receptors in representative coronal half-hemisphere sections of the human brain. Panels show pseudocolor autoradiograms (red D, high densities; green D, intermediate densities; purple D, low densities) for a control subject (male, age 28 years). Panel A illustrates the distribution of D1 receptors with 1 nM [³H]SCH 23390 in the presence of 10 nM mianserin to occlude labeling of the 5-HT2 receptor. Panel B shows the distribution of D2 receptors labeled with 2 nM [³H] raclopride. Panel C illustrates the distribution of D3 receptors labeled with [³H]7OH DPAT. Cd, caudate; CGS, cingulate sulcus; INS, insular cortex; LF, lateral fissure; NA, nucleus accumbens; Pt, putamen; STS, superior temporal sulcus.

fields of the substantia nigra and VTA. This pattern suggests that the D4 receptor protein may function as a presynaptic autoreceptor in dendrites and/or presynaptic terminals (8). The highest areas of D4 expression are found in the frontal cortex, amygdala, and brainstem areas. The expression of D4 receptors in the prefrontal cortex suggests a role for these receptors in the aspect of cognition considered to be a component process of attention: that of executive control. In contrast, the very low levels of D4 receptor message in the striatum are in keeping with the lack of extrapyramidal side effects observed following treatment with putative D4-selective atypical antipsychotic drugs (28).

Previous studies suggested that D1- and D2-like receptors may be colocalized in a subpopulation of the same neostriatal cells (29). This hypothesis has been questioned by recent data from Gerfen and Keefe (30), which suggest that the interactions may occur at an intercellular level as opposed to an intracellular level with second-messenger integration. This hypothesis suggests that the D1- and D2-like receptor proteins are on distinct populations of neurons with extensive axon collateral systems subserving the integration across neural subfields. However, evidence indicating that direct cointegration may occur at the single cell level from anatomic and electrophysiologic studies, is considerable (29). This anatomic arrangement would afford D1-mediated cooperative-synergistic control of D2-mediated motor activity and other psychomotor behaviors. Most studies have demonstrated opposing roles of D1 and D2 receptor–mediated actions in the striatum, resulting from the stimulation and inhibition of adenylyl cyclase, respectively (31). Although more studies are needed to clarify the precise nature and extent of these functional interactions on cAMP second-messenger systems, species-specific differences may limit the extrapolation of rodent studies to monkeys and humans (32).

Second-Messenger Pathways

Dopamine receptors transduce their effects by coupling to specific heterotrimeric GTP binding proteins (i.e., G proteins) consisting of alpha, beta, and gamma subunits (33). Within the dopamine receptor family, the adenylyl cyclase stimulatory receptors include the D1 and D5 subtypes. Although the D1 and D5 share greater than 80% sequence homology, the receptors display 50% overall homology at the amino acid level (14). D5 receptors have been suggested to have higher affinity toward dopamine and lower affinity for the antagonists positive for butaclamol (15, 34). However, when the D1 and D5 subtypes are expressed in transfected cell lines derived from the rat pituitary, both D1 and D5 receptors stimulate adenylyl cyclase and have identical affinities for agonists and antagonists (35). Studies done in transfected cell lines are complicated by the fact that transfection systems may not

express the relevant complement of G proteins as in the native tissue environment. In the primate brain, there is an overlap in the regional brain expression of D1 and D5 receptors. Thus, because of the identical affinities of D1 and D5 receptors for agonists and antagonists and the lack of subtype-selective drugs that fully discriminate between these receptor subtypes, it is not yet possible to assign with certainty specific functions to D1 vs. D5 receptor activation.

Although G protein–coupled receptors were initially believed to selectively activate a single effector, they are now known to have an intrinsic ability to generate multiple signals through an interaction with different α subunits (36). D1 and D5 receptors have been shown by a variety of methodologies to couple to the Gsα subunit of G proteins. The Gsα subunit has been linked to the regulation of Na$^+$, Ca$^+$, and K$^+$ channels, suggesting that D1 receptor activation affects the functional activity of these ion channels. To complicate this picture, D1 receptors inactivate a slow K$^+$ current in the resting state of medium spiny neurons in the striatum (37) through an activation of Goα in the absence of D1 receptor Gsα coupling (35, 38). These studies provide evidence for the involvement of this G-protein subunit in the D1-mediated regulation of diverse ion channels.

The ability of the D5 receptor to stimulate adenyl-cyclase predicts that this subtype couples to Gsα. D5 receptors inhibit catecholamine secretion in bovine chromaffin cells (39). The negligible dopamine stimulation of adenyl cyclase demonstrated in these cells suggests the possibility that this activity of D5 receptor is mediated by a different G protein. Studies have demonstrated that the D5 receptor can couple to a novel G protein termed Gzα (40), which is abundantly expressed in neurons. Thus, despite similar pharmacologic properties, differential coupling of D1 and D5 receptors to distinct G proteins can transduce varied signaling responses by dopamine stimulation. However, since the precise function of Gzα has not been established, the molecular implications of D5/Gzα coupling is not yet known. Activation of Gzα has been shown to inhibit adenyl-cyclase activity in certain cell types (44). Although it is not clear which signaling pathways are linked to D5/Gzα coupling, the colocalization of D5, Gzα, and specific cyclase subtypes may provide a clue to the physiologic relevance. For example, Gzα inhibits adenyl cyclase types I and V (41). Both type V cyclase and D1 receptors are expressed in very high amounts in striatum, which has dense dopaminergic input (42). D1-receptor activation in the striatum is known to stimulate the activity of adenyl cyclase type V (43). In contrast, the hippocampus is rich in D5 but not D1 receptors, and type I cyclase is abundantly expressed in this brain region (44). Taken together, these studies suggest the functional relevance of colocalization of specific cyclases with a particular member of the D1-like receptor family.

D2, D3, and D4 receptors have introns in their coding region and exist in various forms by alternate splicing in the region of the third cytoplasmic loop. These receptors produce rapid physiologic actions by two major mechanisms, involving the activation of inward K^+ channels, the inhibition of a voltage-dependent Ca^+ channels, oractivation of Gi/Go proteins to inhibit adenyl-cyclase activity (15). D2 and D4 receptors inhibit adenyl cyclase by coupling to inhibitory G proteins of the Gi/Go family (14, 15), whereas D3 receptors demonstrate weak inhibition of adenyl-cyclase activity (45). This weak effect on inhibiting cAMP production led to the conclusion that the D3 receptor does not couple to G proteins (15, 45). Both isoforms of the D2 receptor inhibit adenyl-cyclase activity, although the short isoform requires lower concentrations of agonist to cause half maximal inhibition than the long isoform expressed in transfected cell lines (46, 47). The short D2-receptor isoform couples to K^+ currents via a pertussis toxin–insensitive mechanism (48), whereas the long isoform couples to the same current via a pertussis toxin–sensitive mechanism (49). Thus D2 receptors, if expressed by the same cells, can influence transmembrane currents in similar ways but through independent transduction pathways. D2-like receptors that couple to G proteins modulate a variety of other second-messenger pathways, including ion channels, Ca^+ levels, K^+ currents, arachidonic acid release, phosphoinositide hydrolysis, and cell growth and differentiation (50).

Although some neurons have only D1 or D2 receptors, most exhibit D2/D1 antagonism. In striatal neurons, D2 receptors prevent activation of DARPP-32, a primary target of protein kinase A (PKA) (51). Thus, dopamine normally activates neurons through D1 receptors, an action that is limited by the concurrent D2 receptor agonism. The activity of D2 receptors is regulated by desensitization, leading to uncoupling of the receptor from its G proteins and receptor internalization. D2 receptors do not act in isolation, but exist in a complex with other regulatory and scaffolding proteins that traffic receptors to parts of the neuron (52, 53). These studies suggest further that D2 receptors activate other novel second-messenger pathways that are cAMP-independent, involving beta-arrestin and serine threonine kinase Akt signaling complex. Elucidation of the downstream mechanisms may afford more selective D2-receptor targets that are free of side effects.

PHARMACOLOGIC SELECTIVITY

Central dopamine systems have properties that make them unique in comparison to other neurotransmitter systems. For example, dopaminergic projections are mainly associated with diffuse neural pathways. This anatomic arrangement argues for dopamine to act as a neuromodulatory molecule in addition to its role as a neurotransmitter in brain. Dopamine neurons are highly branched, with elongated axons capable of releasing neurotransmitter from many points along their terminal networks en route to the striatum (54). This mode of volumetric transmission of action potentials suggests that dopamine release mediates paracrine (i.e., neurohumoral) signals across the network. This view is supported by the observation that dopamine is released by axon terminals and dendrites, providing a double polarity for regulating basal ganglial function, simultaneously gating signaling at nigral, striatal, and pallidal levels. These properties have important implications in the clinical expression of human disorders involving dopamine neuron dysfunction. Drugs acting primarily at dopamine D2 receptors are commonly used to alleviate symptoms produced by diseases such as PD, schizophrenia, and depression.

The members of the D1-receptor subfamily have several characteristics that distinguish them from the D2 subfamily. All members of the D1 subfamily bind benzazepines with high affinity and butyrophenones and benzamides with low affinity (13). Subtypes in the D1 family have approximately 50% homology overall and 80% homology in the highly conserved transmembrane region. All of the receptors in this family have short third intracellular loops and a long carboxy terminus. These regions are important for the generation of second-messenger signals, as explained earlier. D5 and the rat D1b are species homologs because they map to the same chromosomal locus (55). D5 and D1b have a 10-fold higher affinity for dopamine, suggesting that D5 receptors are activated at neurotransmitter concentrations that are subthreshold for the D1 receptor (15, 56). The D2-like receptors bind butyrophenones and benzamides with high affinity and bind benzazepines with low affinity (57).

The pharmacologic distinction of dopamine receptor subtypes holds tremendous potential for treatment of nervous system dysfunction. Dopamine receptors are the primary targets for the pharmacologic treatment of PD, schizophrenia, and several other nervous system disorders. Presently used drugs have significant limitations that are in part due to their nonselective binding to many receptor subtypes. For example, drug-related side effects, including dyskinesias and psychosis, are frequent and important problems in parkinsonian patients receiving levodopa or dopamine agonist therapy. These adverse effects result from stimulation of dopamine receptors in motor and cognitive circuits, respectively (58). Conversely, treatment of schizophrenia with dopaminergic antagonists, although intended to selectively block receptors in cortical and limbic circuits, may induce parkinsonian symptoms or even permanent dyskinesias by interaction with dopamine receptor subtypes in motor pathways. Clearly, drugs aimed at molecular subtypes of dopamine receptors offer the potential for specific

TABLE 23-1
Properties of Dopamine Receptor Subtypes

RECEPTOR SUBTYPE	D_1-LIKE D_1	D_5	D_2-LIKE D_2	D_3	D_4
Amino acids	446	477	443	400	387
Chromosome	5q35.1	4p15.1-16.1	11q22-23	3p13.3	11p15.5
Second messenger	↑cAMP	↑cAMP	↓cAMP K^+ channel Ca^+ channel	K^+ channel Ca^+ channel	↓ cAMP K^+ channel
mRNA	Striatum	Hippocampus Kidney	Striatum	Nucleus Accumbens	Cerebral Cortex
Selective agonists	SKF38393	SKF38393	Bromocriptine Butaclamol Pergolide Ropinirole	7-OH-DPAT Pramipexole Ropinirole	–
Selective antagonists	SCH23390	SCH23390	Spiperone Raclopride Sulpiride	Spiperone Raclopride Sulpiride	Spiperone Clozapine

therapeutic interventions for motor and psychiatric disorders of the nervous system.

Although there are agonists and antagonists which are selective and can discriminate between D1- and D2-like receptor subfamilies, there are few agents that are highly selective for any of the individual receptor subtypes (Table 23-1). Some progress has been made in the development of antagonists for the D2-receptor family. For the D1/D5 receptor subtypes, there are currently no compounds that exhibit high selectivity. Thus, the high overall sequence homology between dopamine receptors of the same subfamily have made it difficult to develop specific ligands that do not interact with related receptors. The high affinity of the "atypical" antipsychotic agent clozapine for D4 receptors and the low level of D4 receptor expression in the striatum and high levels in the cerebral cortex and certain limbic brain areas led to the suggestion that the antipsychotic properties of the neuroleptics may be mediated through blockade of D4 receptors, whereas the side effects may be mediated through blockade of D2 receptors (58, 59). This hypothesis was strengthened by the low incidence of extrapyramidal side effects for clozapine. However, clozapine at therapeutic doses also blocks many other types of receptors in addition to D4 receptors, making it difficult to draw definitive conclusions. For example, clozapine binds to muscarinic acetylcholine receptors and is 20- to 50-fold more potent at these sites than at D2 receptors (60).

It has been suggested that clozapine and quetiapine, drugs that elicit little or no parkinsonism, bind more loosely than dopamine to brain D2 receptors yet have high occupancy of these receptors (61). By determining fractional occupancies of receptors bound at therapeutic drug levels, these authors demonstrate that the dominant factor for deciding if a particular antipsychotic drug will elicit parkinsonism is whether it binds more tightly or more loosely than dopamine at the D2 receptor subtype. Thus, for those antipsychotic drugs that elicit little or no parkinsonism, it appears that the high endogenous dopamine in the human striatum displaces the more loosely bound neuroleptic at the striatal D2-receptor subtype. Dopamine less readily displaces the more hydrophobic radioligands of the haloperidol type, providing an additional correlate between the magnitude of in vivo competition with endogenous agonist and the development of parkinsonism. The separation of antipsychotic drugs into those that bind "loosely" and "tightly" to D2 receptors is consistent with the observation that catalepsy induced by olanzepine and loxapine (more loosely bound than dopamine) but not haloperidol (more tightly bound than dopamine to D2 receptors) is fully reversible (61). Taken together, these observations suggest that D2 blockade may be necessary for achieving antipsychotic action. This suggestion is in keeping with the observation that many patients will suddenly relapse when stopping clozapine, perhaps due to a sudden pulse of endogenous dopamine arising from emotional or physical activity that displaces the loosely bound drug from the receptor. Clinical dosing schedules can be adjusted to obtain sufficient but low occupancies of D2 receptors to minimize the development of parkinsonism. The psychosis caused by levodopa or bromocriptine can be readily treated by low doses of either clozapine (62), remoxipride (63), or quetiapine (64), as there is very little endogenous dopamine to compete with the antagonist. Further studies are needed to determine whether newer antipsychotic drugs with low affinity for D2 receptors and with low risk for parkinsonism will also cause less tardive dyskinesia.

The success in treating parkinsonian symptoms with the dopamine precursor levodopa relates to its ability to reverse the dopamine deficiency. Unfortunately, treatment complications emerge shortly after levodopa therapy is begun. In the DATATOP study (65), almost half of the patients developed wearing off (loss of efficacy toward the end of a dosing interval), about one-third showed dyskinesias, and about one-fourth showed early signs of freezing (sudden loss of the capacity to ambulate) with a mean duration of treatment of only 18 months. Modern pharmacologic treatment of PD has been advanced by the increased understanding of the complexity of dopamine receptor pharmacology and the ability to screen drug candidates in vitro against cloned and expressed human dopamine receptor subtypes. New treatment approaches are aimed at developing subtype-selective, direct-acting agonists to restore dopaminergic function (2).

Symptoms of parkinsonism in primate models are treated with agonists that activate the D2-like receptor subfamily. D2 agonists with long half-lives can relieve parkinsonism in these animals with little risk of motor complications, whereas repetitive levodopa doses will induce motor fluctuations and dyskinesias (66). In dyskinetic animals that had received levodopa doses, D2 agonists that had few side effects on their own elicit dyskinesias. These observations suggest that repetitive coactivation of denervated striatal dopamine receptor subtypes initiates the development of these movements by nonselective activation of postsynaptic D1 and D2/D3 receptors.

Pramipexole is a novel dopamine agonist with preferential affinity for D3 receptors (see Table 23-1). It has little affinity for the D1-like receptors; within the D2 receptor subfamily, it exhibits its highest affinity at the D3-receptor subtype distinguishing it from all other dopamine agonists currently used for the treatment of PD (67). Dopamine normally inhibits striatal GABAergic cells of the indirect pathway by acting on D2 receptors and stimulates GABAergic cells of the direct pathway by stimulating D1 and D3 receptors (68). These effects result in the inhibition of the globus pallidus (GPi, internal segment). In PD, when dopamine innervation has been lost, the GPi fires at very high rates to inhibit thalamic relay neurons, resulting in bradykinesia (67). Pramipexole stimulates D3 receptors, which directly inhibit GPi neurons, removing an inhibitory gate on thalamocortical motor pathways and stimulating D2 receptors to indirectly inhibit GPi neurons (69). Thus pramipexole has two synergistic mechanisms to mimic dopamine and restore function in PD. Although D3 receptors have a lower density in the striatum as compared with D2 receptors (see Figure 23-2), chronic administration of indirect-acting agonists may cause an upregulation in the number of D3 binding sites in this region. In keeping with this suggestion, chronic cocaine abusers have elevated densities of D3 receptor sites in limbic sectors of the striatum and nucleus accumbens (70). It is not known whether this regulatory change occurs in the denervated striatum, early in the course of agonist replacement for PD. Pramipexole has also shown efficacy for the treatment of depression in PD, in keeping with its postsynaptic effects on limbic targets (69). Thus the antidepressant activity of pramipexole for treating moderate depression may possibly be tied to its preferential binding to the D3-receptor subtype (67).

Whether other subtypes of dopamine receptors exist is not known. However, rapid advances in molecular cloning may reveal additional heterogeneity in the expression of synaptic proteins involved in dopaminergic neurotransmission. At this time, 5 cloned and expressed dopaminergic receptor proteins provide a complex molecular basis for a variety of neural signals mediated by a single neurotransmitter. Evidence for several proteins, which represent novel mediators of the downstream consequences of D2 receptor activation, suggests the possibility of targeting signaling pathways as improved treatment for PD.

References

1. Hornykiewicz O. Dopamine and brain function *Pharmacol Res* 1966; 18:925–964.
2. Factor SA. Dopamine agonists. *Med Clin NorthAm* 1999; 83(2):415–443.
3. Dailly E, Chenu F, Renard CE, Bourin M. Dopamine, depression, and antidepressants. *Fundam Clin Pharmacol* 2004; 18:601–607
4. Carlsson A. The current status of the dopamine hypothesis of schizophrenia. *Neuropsychopharm* 1988; 1:179–186.
5. Creese I, Burt DR, Snyder SH. Dopamine receptor binding predicts clinical and pharmacologic potencies of antischizophrenic drugs. *Science* 1976; 192:481–483.
6. Seeman P, Lee T, Chan-Wong M, et al. Antipsychotic drug doses and neuroleptic/dopamine receptors. *Nature* 1976; 261:717–719.
7. Miyamoto S, Duncan GE, Marx CE, Lieberman JA, Treatments for schizophrenia: A critical review of pharmacology and mechanisms of action of antipsychotic drugs. *Mol Psychiatry* 2005; 10(1):79–104.
8. Van Tol HHM, Bunzow JR, Guan H-C, et al. Cloning of the gene for a human dopamine D4 receptor with high affinity for the antipsychotic clozapine. *Nature* 1991; 350:610–614.
9. Dearry A, Gingrich JA, Falardeau P, et al. Molecular cloning and expression of the gene for a human D1 dopamine receptor. *Nature* 1990; 347:72–76.
10. Monsma FJ Jr, Mahan LC, McVittie LD, et al. Molecular cloning and expression of a D1 dopamine receptor linked to adenylyl cyclase activation. *Proc Natl Acad Sci USA* 1990; 87(17):6723–6727.

11. Sunahara RK, Niznik HB, Weiner DM, et al. Human dopamine D1 receptor encoded by an intronless gene on chromosome 5. *Nature* 1990; 347:80–83.

12. Zhou QY, Grandy DK, Thambi L, et al. Cloning and expression of human and rat D1 dopamine receptors. *Nature* 1990; 347:76–80.

13. Sunhara RK, Guan H-C, O'Dowd BF, et al. Cloning of the gene for a human dopamine D5 receptor with higher affinity for dopamine than D1. *Nature* 1991; 350:614–619.

14. O'Dowd BF. Structures of dopamine receptors. *J Neurochem* 1993; 60:804–816.

15. Lachowicz J, Sibley DR. Molecular characteristics of mammalian dopamine receptors. *Pharmacol Toxicol* (Mini Review) 1997; 81:105–113.

16. Dal Tosos R, Sommer B, Ewart M, et al. The dopamine receptor: Two molecular forms generated by alternative splicing. *EMBO J* 1989; 8:4025–4034.

17. Monsuma FJ, McVittie LD, Gerfen CR, et al. Multiple D2 dopamine receptors produced by alternative RNA splicing. *Nature* 1989; 324:926–929.

18. Snyder LA, Roberts JL, Sealfon SC. Alternative transcripts of the rat and human dopamine D3 receptor. *Biochem Biophys Res Commun* 1991; 180(2):1031–1035.

19. Fishburn CS, Belleli D, David C, et al. A novel short isoform of the D3 dopamine receptor generated by alternative splicing in the third cytoplasmic loop. *J Biol Chem* 1993; 268(8):5872–5878.

20. Giros B, Martres MP, Pilon C, et al. Shorter variants of the D3 dopamine receptor produced through various patterns of alternative splicing. *Biochem Biophys Res Commun* 1991; 176(3):1584–1592.

21. Van Tol HH, Wu CM, Guan HC, et al. Multiple dopamine D4 receptor variants in the human population. *Nature* 1992; 358(6382):149–152.

22. Fosella J, Sommer T, Fan J, et al. Assessing the molecular genetics of attention networks. *BMC Neurosci* 2002; 3(1):14.

23. Swanson J, Oosterlaan J, Murias M, et al. Attention deficit/hyperactivity disorder children with a 7-repeat allele of the dopamine receptor D4 gene have extreme behavior but normal performance on critical neuropsychological tests of attention. *Proc Natl Acad Sci U S A.* 2000; 97(9):4754-4759.

24. Bjorklund A, Lindvall O. Dopamine-containing systems in the CNS. In: Bjorklund A, Hokfelt T (eds). *Handbook of Chemical Neuroanatomy.* Vol 2: *Classical Transmitters in the CNS, Part I.* Amsterdam: Elsevier, 1994:55–122.

25. Le Moine C, Normand E, Guitteny AF, et al. Dopamine receptor gene expression by enkephalin neurons in rat forebrain. *Proc Natl Acad Sci USA* 1990; 87(1):230–234.

26. Diaz J, Levesque D, Griffon N, et al. Opposing roles for dopamine D2 and D3 receptors on neurotensin mRNA expression in nucleus accumbens. *Eur J Neurosci* 1994; 6(8):1384–1387.

27. Bouthenet ML, Souil MP, Martes P, et al. Localization of dopamine D3 mRNA in the rat brain using in situ hybridization histochemistry: Comparision with D2 dopamine receptor. *Brain Res* 1991; 564:203–219.

28. Le Moine C, Bloch B. Anatomical and cellular analysis of dopamine receptor gene expression. In: Ariano MA, Surmeir DJ (eds). *Molecular and Cellular Mechanisms of Neostriatal Function.* New York: Springer-Verlag, 1995:45–58.

29. Surmier DJ, Eberwine J, Wilson CJ, et al. Dopamine receptor subtypes colocalize in rat striatonigral neurons. *Proc Natl Acad Sci USA* 1992; 89:10178–10182.

30. Gerfen CR, Keefe KA, Steiner H. Dopamine-mediated gene regulation in the striatum. *Adv Pharmacol* 1998; 42:670–673.

31. Waddington JL, O'Boyle KM, Drugs acting on brain dopamine receptors: A conceptual reevaluation five years afer the first selective D1 antagonist. *Pharmacol Ther* 1989; 43:1–52.

32. Loschmann PA, Smith LA, Lange KW, et al. Motor activity following the administration of selective D-1 and D-2 dopaminergic drugs to normal common marmosets. *Psychopharmacology* 1991; 105(3):303–309.

33. Hepler JR, Gilman AG. G proteins. *Trends Biochem Sci* 1992; 17(10):383–387.

34. Grandy DK, Zhang Y, Bouvier C, et al. Multiple human D5 dopamine receptor genes, a functional receptor and two pseudogenes. *Proc Natl Acad Sci USA* 1991; 88:9175–9179.

35. Sidhu A. Coupling of D1 and D5 dopamine receptors to multiple G proteins: Implications for understanding the diversity in receptor-G protein coupling. *Mol Neurobiol* 1998; 16(2):125–134.

36. Birnbaumer L, Abramowitz J, Brown AM. Receptor-effector coupling by G proteins. *Biochim Biophys Acta* 1990; 1031(2):163–224.

37. Kitai ST, Surmeier DJ. Cholinergic and dopaminergic modulation of potassium conductances in neostriatal neurons. *Adv Neurol* 1993; 60:40–52.

38. Kimura K, White BH, Sidhu A. Coupling of human D1 dopamine receptors to different guanine nucleotide binding proteins. Evidence that D1 dopamine receptors can couple to both Gs and G(o). *J Biol Chem* 1995; 270:14672–14678.

39. Dahmer MK, Senolges SE. Dopaminergic inhibition of catecholamine secretion from chromaffin cells: Evidence that inhibition is mediated by D4 and D5 dopamine receptors. *J Neurochem* 1996; 66:222–232.

40. Sidhu A. Regulation and expression of D-1, but not D-5, dopamine receptors in human SK-N-MC neuroblastoma cells. *J Recep Res/Sig Trans* 1997; 17:777–784.

41. Kozasa T Gilman AG. Purification of recombinant G proteins from Sf9 cells by hexahistidine tagging of associated subunits: Characterization of 12 and inhibition of adenylyl cyclase by Gz. *J Biol Chem* 1995; 270:1734–1741.

42. Glatt CE, Snyder SH. Cloning and expression of an adenylyl cyclase localized to the corpus striatum. *Nature* 1993; 361:536–538.

43. Yoshimurea M, Ikeda H, Tabakoff B. Opioid receptors inhibit dopamine-stimulated activity of type V adenylyl cyclase and enhance dopamine-stimulated activity of type VII adenylyl cyclase. *Mol Pharmacol* 1996; 50:43–51.

44. Cooper DMF, Mons N, Karpen JW. Adenylyl cyclases and the interaction between calcium and cAMP signalling. *Nature* 1995; 374:421–424.

45. McAllister G, Knowles MR, Ward-Booth SM, et al. Functional coupling of human D2, D3, and D4 dopamine receptors in HEK293 cells. *J Recept Signal Trans Res* 1995; 15:267–281.

46. Hayes G, Biden TJ, Selbie LA, et al. Structural subtypes of the dopamine D2 receptor are functionally distinct: Expression of the cloned D2Aand D2B subtypes in a heterologous cell line. *Mol Endocrinol* 1992; 6:920–926.

47. Montmaueur J-P , Borelli E. Transcription mediated by a cAMP-responsive promoter element is reduced upon activation of dopamine D2 receptors. *Proc Natl Acad Sci USA* 1991; 7:161–170.

48. Castellano MA, Liu LX, Monsma FJ Jr, et al. Transfected D2 short dopamine receptors inhibit voltage-dependent potassium current in neuroblastoma x glioma hybrid (NG108-15) cells. *Mol Pharmacol* 1993; 44(3):649–656.

49. Liu L-X, Monsma FJ Jr, Sibley DR, et al. Coupling of D2-long receptor isoform to KC currents in neuroblastoma x glioma (NG108-15) cells. *Soc Neurosci* 1993; 19:79.

50. Jaber M, Robinson SW, Missale C, et al. Dopamine receptors and brain function. *Neuropharmacology* 1996; 35(11):1503–1519.

51. Neve KA, Seamans JK, Trantham-Davidson H J. Dopamine receptor signaling. *Recept Signal Transduct Res* 2004; 23:626–637

52. Beaulieu JM, Sotnikova TD, Yao WD, et al. Lithium antagonizes dopamine-dependent behaviors mediated by an AKT/glycogen synthase kinase 3 signaling cascade. *Proc Natl Acad Sci USA* 2005; 101:5099–5104.

53. Park SK, Nguyen MK, Fischer A, et al. Par-4 links dopamine signaling and depression. *Cell* 2005; 122:275–287.

54. Levey AI, Hersch SM, Rye DM, et al. Localization of D1 and D2 receptors in brain with subtype-specific antibodies. *Proc Nat Acad Sci USA* 1993; 90:8861–8865.

55. Tiberi M, Jarvie KR, Silvia C, et al. Cloning, molecular characterization and chromosomal assignment of a gene endocing a second D1 dopamine receptor subtype: Differential expression pattern in rat brain compared with the D1 receptor. *Proc Natl Acad Sci USA* 1991; 88:7491–7495.

56. Jarvie KR, Tiberi M, Silvia C, et al. Molecular cloning, stable expression and desensitization of the human dopamine D1b/D5 receptor. *J Recept Res* 1993; 13: 573–590.

57. Bunzow JR, Van Tol HH, Grandy DK, et al. Cloning and expression of a rat D2 dopamine receptor cDNA. *Nature* 1989; 336(6201):783–787.

58. Van Tol HH, Bunzow JR, Guan HC, et al. Cloning of the gene for a human dopamine D4 receptor with high affinity for the antipsychotic clozapine. *Nature* 1991; 350(6319):610–614.

59. Sokoloff P, Giros B, Martress M-P, et al. Molecular cloning and characterization of a novel dopamine receptor (D3) as a target for neuroleptics. *Nature* 1990; 347:146–151.

60. Gerlach J, Behnkek K, Heltberg J, et al. Sulpiride and haloperidol in schizophrenia: A double-blind cross-over study of therapeutic effect, side effects and plasma concentrations. *Br J Psychiatry* 1985; 147:283–288.

61. Seeman P, Tallerico T. Antipsychotic drugs which elicit little or no parkinsonism bind more loosely to brain D2 receptors, yet occupy high levels of these receptors. *Mol Psychiatry* 1998; 3:123–134.

62. Rabey JM, Reves TA, Nuefeld MY, et al. Low dose clozapine in the treatment of levodopa-induced mental disorders in Parkinson's disease. *Neurology* 1995; 48:432–434.

63. Sandor P, Lang AE, Singal S, et al. Remoxipride in the treatment of levodopa-induced psychosis. *J Clin Psychopharmacol* 1996; 18:395–399.

64. Reddy S, Factor SA, Molho ES, Feustel PJ. The effect of quetiapine on psychosis and motor function in parkinsonian patients with and without dementia. *Mov Disord* 2002; 17:676–681.

65. Parkinson Study Group. Impact of deprenyl and tocopherol treatment in progression of disability in early Parkinson's disease. *N Engl J Med* 1993; 328:176–183.

66. Blanchet PJ, Calon F, Martel JC, et al. Continuous administration decreases and pulsatile administration increases behavioral sensitivity to a novel dopamine D2 agonist (U-91356A) in MPTP-exposed monkeys. *J Pharmacol Exp Ther* 1995; 272:854–859.

67. Bennett JP Jr, Piercey MF. Pramipexole: A new dopamine agonist for the treatment of Parkinson's disease. *J Neurol Sci* 1999; 163:25–31.

68. Piercey MF, Hyslop DK, Hoffman WE. Excitation of type II anterior caudate neurons by stimulation of D3 receptors. *Brain Res* 1997; 762:19–28.

69. Szegedi A, Wetzel J, Hillert A, et al. Pramipexole, a novel selective dopamine agonist in major depression. *Mov Disord* 1996; 11(Suppl 1):266.

70. Staley JK, Mash DC. Adaptive increase in D3 dopamine receptors in the brain reward circuits of human cocaine fatalities. *J Neurosci* 1996; 16(19):6100–6106.

V

BIOMARKERS

24 Status of Biological Markers

E. Ray Dorsey
Robert G. Holloway
Bernard M. Ravina

According to the Biomarkers Definitions Working Group, a biomarker is a "characteristic that is objectively measured and evaluated as an indicator of normal biological processes, pathogenic processes, or pharmacological responses to a therapeutic intervention" (1). Biomarkers can be used to elucidate the pathophysiology of a disease, screen for a therapeutic response, assist in the diagnosis of a condition, or monitor response to therapy (Figure 24-1).

A surrogate endpoint is a "biomarker that is intended to substitute for a clinical endpoint. A surrogate endpoint is expected to predict clinical benefit (or harm or lack of benefit or harm) based on epidemiologic, therapeutic, pathophysiologic, or other scientific evidence" (1). Surrogate endpoints are used in clinical trials as an earlier outcome than the true clinical endpoint. However, in order to be considered a valid surrogate endpoint, a biomarker faces many hurdles. Among them is the need for large clinical trials that consistently demonstrate that the biomarker and the true clinical endpoint respond in the same manner to an intervention. In addition, the response of the biomarker and the true clinical endpoint to the intervention must occur through the same biological pathway. For these reasons, surrogate endpoints in PD are difficult to identify.

Biomarkers for Parkinson's disease (PD) include clinical tests, imaging studies, blood tests, cerebrospinal fluid tests, and genetic tests. Some of these biomarkers have been evaluated as surrogate endpoints in PD. This chapter highlights many of the most promising and widely studied biomarkers.

CLINICAL TESTS

Motor Tests

Clinical tests for PD are numerous; three classes of tests—motor tests, pharmacologic challenges, and tests of olfaction—are summarized in Table 24-1. Motor tests are in many respects an extension of the clinical examination (2). Investigators have evaluated multiple motor tasks, including wrist flexion/extension (3), speech (4, 5), eye movements (6), and visuomotor coordination (7). The principal benefit has been the ability to quantify deficits (8) and monitor response to medical and surgical interventions (4, 5). Motor tests have not been able to differentiate PD from other parkinsonian syndromes (2). Motor tests combined with a battery of other tests have shown some ability to distinguish asymptomatic first-degree relatives of individuals with PD from by normal controls (3). These studies hold promise for identifying a cohort of individuals at high risk for developing PD.

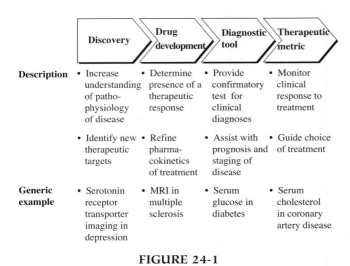

FIGURE 24-1

Potential applications of biomarkers.

Pharmacologic Challenges

Because PD responds to dopaminergic treatment, these treatments have been used to identify individuals with PD in whom there was diagnostic uncertainty. Investigators have studied the therapeutic response to levodopa and apomorphine, a dopamine agonist.

In one study (9), 82 patients with a parkinsonian syndrome without a specific diagnosis were given 250/25 mg of levodopa/carbidopa. A positive response [greater than 30% improvement on the Unified Parkinson's Disease Rating Scale (UPDRS)] had a sensitivity of 71% and a specificity of 81% for predicting the diagnosis of PD on clinical follow-up 2 years later (9). Based on this study and others, the American Academy of Neurology concluded in a practice parameter that "Levodopa and

apormphine challenge tests are probably useful in distinguishing PD from other parkinsonian syndromes" (10).

Olfaction

In PD, the loss of smell detection, identification, or discrimination may precede the development of motor disability (2). This loss may be due to neurodegeneration within the olfactory bulb (2). The ability of olfactory loss to differentiate idiopathic PD from other parkinsonian syndromes has been evaluated, with good results.

In one large study of 118 patients with PD—29 with multiple system atrophy, 15 with progressive supranuclear palsy, 7 with corticobasal degeneration—and 123 healthy controls, olfactory function was found to differentiate PD from other parkinsonian syndromes (11). Olfactory function was measured using the University of Pennsylvania Smell Identification test (UPSIT), which is available commercially for $27. On the UPSIT, individuals with PD had marked impairment compared to mild impairment in multiple system atrophy and normal results in progressive supranuclear palsy and corticobasal degeneration (11). A score of 25 odorants identified out of a possible 40 on the UPSIT was associated with a sensitivity of 77% and a specificity of 85% in differentiating PD from other parkinsonian syndromes (11). More broadly, severe olfactory deficits in odor identification, recognition, and detection have consistently been found in PD and Alzheimer's disease; however, discrimination between these two neurodegenerative disorders based on olfactory function is more difficult (12).

One study evaluated the ability of olfactory testing combined with imaging using the radiotracer [^{123}I]β-CIT with single photon emission computed tomography (SPECT) to identify, before symptoms developed,

TABLE 24-1
Clinical Biomarkers of Parkinson's Disease

TEST	DESCRIPTION	BENEFITS	LIMITATIONS
Motor tests	Evaluate performance on motor tasks to quantify disability	Can be relatively easy to perform Quantify response to treatment	Have limited trial data to support diagnostic use Add little understanding to underlying pathophysiology
Pharmacologic challenges	Examine response to levodopa or dopamine agonists to differentiate PD from other parkinsonian syndromes	Are readily and routinely performed clinically Have fair sensitivity (~70%) and specificity (~70%)	Provides primarily only diagnostic information
Olfaction	Assesses sense of smell, which is lost early in the course of PD	Is easy and inexpensive to perform Appears able to differentiate PD from other parkinsonian syndromes	Has limited application beyond diagnosis

individuals with PD in a cohort of at-risk individuals (13). Ponsen and colleagues screened 361 asymptomatic first-degree relatives of individuals with PD, first with an olfactory test (odor detection, discrimination, and identification) and then with SPECT scans. The individuals performing in the bottom 10% of the cohort on the smell test underwent imaging. Of the 39 hyposmic individuals, 7 had one or more significantly reduced [123I]β-CIT binding ratios, and—after 2 years—4 of those developed PD. None of the other first-degree relatives in the cohort developed PD as determined by clinical exam or questionnaire (13). This study offers promise that olfactory testing in combination with other biomarkers can identify a segment of individuals at high risk for PD.

IMAGING STUDIES

Cerebral Radiotracer Imaging

Radiotracer imaging of the brain is the most extensively studied imaging modality for PD. Based on the understanding of dopaminergic cell loss in PD, 4 major classes of imaging biomarkers have been developed. These assess the activity of the enzyme aromatic acid decarboxylase, the vesicular monoamine transporter type 2, the dopamine transporter, and glucose utilization patterns in the basal ganglia (14, 15). Table 24-2 provides a summary of the principal radiotracers used in PD, their benefits, and their limitations.

TABLE 24-2
Principal Radiotracer Imaging Biomarkers in Parkinson's Disease

RADIOTRACER	IMAGING MODALITY	DESCRIPTION	BENEFITS	LIMITATIONS
[18F]Fluorodopa	PET	Measures uptake and conversion of fluorodopa to fluorodopamine	Correlates well with declining motor function and with disease progression in longitudinal studies	Demonstrates an unclear relationship between clinical and possible pathologic progression
[11C]Dihydrotetrabenazine	PET	Measures intraneuronal vesicular transport activity of monoamines	Has shown ability to distinguish typical PD from normal controls	Has less robust evidence to date for correlation with declining motor function
[123I]β-CIT	SPECT	Measures presynaptic dopamine transporter expression in dopaminergic neurons	Has high target:background tissue ratio Correlates well with declining motor function and with disease progression in longitudinal studies May be useful diagnostic tool for patients with uncertain parkinsonism	Has long time to peak specific uptake (8–18 hours) Is less selective for dopamine transporter than other agents
[123I]FP-CIT	SPECT	Measures presynaptic dopamine transporter expression in dopaminergic neurons	Available commercially in Europe to differentiate PD from essential tremor Has high target:background tissue ratio Has rapid time to peak uptake (2–3 hours)	Like other radiotracers, cannot differentiate among parkinsonian syndromes
99mTc-TRODAT	SPECT	Measures presynaptic dopamine transporter expression in dopaminergic neurons	Is highly selective for dopamine transporter Has rapid time to peak uptake (2–3 hours)	Has low target:background tissue ratio
[18F]Fluorodeoxyglucose	PET	Measures glucose utilization pattern	Can assess network activity rather than specific aspects of dopaminergic neurons	Has been less well studied in clinical trials than other radiotracers in PD

Sources: Ravina et al.(14) and Seibyl et al.(15). With permission.

The first class is represented by [18F]fluorodopa (F-dopa). After intravenous administration, F-dopa crosses the blood-brain barrier via a large neutral amino acid transporter. F-dopa is taken up into neurons by an active transport system and subsequently converted to fluorodopamine by the enzyme aromatic acid decarboxylase (14). Once dopamine is produced in neuronal cells, it is pumped into synaptic vesicles by the type 2 vesicular monoamine transporter (VMAT2). In the striatum (caudate and putamen), more than 95% of VMAT2 is associated with dopaminergic nerve terminals. Dihydrotetrabenazine binds to VMAT2. [11C]Dihydrotetrabenazine is an example of the second class of radiotracer agents for PD (14).

After dopamine is released from synaptic vesicles into the synaptic cleft, dopamine is removed from the cleft primarily through the action of presynaptic dopamine transporters, which are the targets of the third class of radiotracer agents (14). The dopamine transporter is specific to dopaminergic neurons. Several radiotracers target the dopamine transporter—e.g., [123I]β-CIT, [123I]FP-CIT, and 99mTc-TRODAT; these, most notably [123I]β-CIT, have been used in multiple large-scale clinical trials.

The fourth class of radiotracer agents for PD is [18F]fluorodeoxyglucose (FDG), which is a marker of resting glucose utilization (14). Rather than imaging a particular protein or ligand, FDG positron emission tomography (PET) can identify specific metabolic brain networks associated with PD (1, 4).

The various radiotracers for PD are designed for use with PET or SPECT (Table 24-2). Both are sensitive methods. The choice of imaging modality is usually determined by the specific study questions and study design (16). PET generally provides better resolution than SPECT, but SPECT studies may be technologically and clinically more feasible (16).

Radiotracers have helped increase our understanding of the pathology of PD. For example, the 3 dopaminergic ligands have shown negative correlations between striatal uptake and disease progression (14). In one study, investigators used F-dopa PET to estimate the duration of the preclinical period of PD, assuming a linear progression in the disease course; they concluded that the average preclinical period was unlikely to be more than 7 years (17).

Radiotracers for PD have also been evaluated as a diagnostic tool. One dopamine transporter ligand, [123I]FP-CIT, is commercially available in Europe as DaTSCAN; it is used to differentiate parkinsonian syndromes from essential tremor. Investigators have also evaluated imaging with [123I]β-CIT SPECT in individuals with parkinsonian syndromes (e.g., PD, multiple system atrophy, progressive supranuclear palsy) in whom there was initial diagnostic uncertainty on the part of the referring neurologist (18). Compared with a movement disorder expert's "gold standard" diagnosis at 6 months, imaging showed 92% sensitivity and 100% specificity for parkinsonian syndromes in 35 subjects (18). The main limitation of imaging has been the ability to differentiate among parkinsonian syndromes, such as PD, multiple system atrophy, progressive supranuclear palsy, and corticobasal ganglionic degeneration.

Radiotracer imaging has played a large role in the evaluation of therapeutics for PD (Table 24-3). However, radiotracer imaging has shown results that are inconsistent with clinical measures. One of the largest studies involving [123I]β-CIT SPECT was the Elldopa trial (19), which randomized 361 individuals to placebo or to 3 different doses of carbidopa/levodopa to assess the impact of treatment on clinical function as measured by the change in the UPDRS "off" motor scores. The 3 levodopa-treated arms all showed significantly better clinical outcomes than the placebo arms even after a 2-week washout period. However, the imaging results showed the opposite: levodopa use was associated with a more rapid decline in binding of the dopamine transporter as measured by [123I]β-CIT SPECT (19).

The REAL-PET study evaluated the rate of loss of dopamine-terminal function in individuals with PD who were randomized to receive either levodopa or ropinirole (20). The primary outcome measure of the study was the mean percentage reduction in side-to-side average putamen [18F]fluorodopa uptake (20). As assessed by F-dopa, ropinirole was associated with a slower progression of PD (20). However, levodopa-treated individuals had a better clinical response as measured by "on" scores of the UPDRS motor section but similar Global Clinical Impressions scale scores (14). Other studies evaluating therapeutic interventions have shown similarly discordant results (see Table 24-3).

The reason for the discordant results is not clear. One distinct possibility is the direct pharmacologic regulation of the targets of the radiotracers. Levodopa and dopamine agonists can change the uptake or metabolism of fluorodopa and alter the number, occupancy, or affinity of receptors that bind the radiolabeled ligands. Owing to the discordant results and uncertain pharmacologic response, no radiotracer image should be considered as a surrogate endpoint in PD at present, and the use of radiotracers in drug development depends on the specific question and suitability of the tracer (14).

Cardiac Radiotracer Imaging

Cardiac radiotracer imaging permits an assessment of the autonomic dysfunction that often accompanies PD and may help diagnose PD and differentiate PD from other parkinsonian syndromes, such as multiple system atrophy and progressive supranuclear palsy (21). Research using [123I]metaiodobenzylguanidine (MIBG), a radiolabeled

TABLE 24-3
Key Phase III and IV Trials Using Imaging in Parkinson's Disease

Radiotracer	Study	Duration	Number in Study (Number imaged)	Population Studied	Primary Clinical Endpoint	Correlation Between Clinical Endpoint and Imaging Results
[¹⁸F]fluorodopa PET	Fetal cell transplantion vs. sham	12 months 24 months	40 (39) 34 (34)	Advanced PD Advanced PD	Global change UPDRS motor "off"	Discordant Discordant
[¹⁸F]fluorodopa PET	Ropinirole v. levodopa (REAL-PET)	24 months	186 (162)	Early PD, requiring therapy	None specified	Discordant for UPDRS "off"; concordant for motor fluctuations
[¹²³I]β-CIT SPECT	Pramipexole vs. levodopa (CALM-PD)	24 months 48 months	301 (82) 82 (82)	Early PD, requiring therapy	Motor fluctuations	Concordant for motor fluctuations Discordant for UPDRS "on"
[¹²³I]β-CIT SPECT	Levodopa vs. placebo (Elldopa)	42 weeks	361 (135)	Early PD not requiring therapy	UPDRS "off"	Discordant

UPDRS = Unified Parkinson's Disease Rating Scale
Source: Adapted from Ravina et al.(14). With permission.

norepinephrine analog that is taken up and stored in sympathetic nerve endings, has demonstrated myocardial postganglionic sympathetic dysfunction in individuals with PD. In contrast, postganglionic sympathetic nerve fibers remain intact in individuals with multiple system atrophy. At least one study has suggested that MIBG may be a more sensitive test of autonomic function in PD than traditional autonomic testing, such as heart rate and blood pressure (22).

Transcranial Sonography

Transcranial sonography (TCS) has been primarily evaluated as a diagnostic aid in PD. It utilizes color-coded duplex ultrasound systems to image the substantia nigra (23). To date, most transcranial sonography has been used as a relatively inexpensive, noninvasive diagnostic tool for patients with cerebrovascular disorders. However, investigators have been examining its use in PD. The majority of individuals with PD are reported to have increased echogenicity of the substantia nigra on TCS. The mechanisms underlying the increased echogenicity are not clear and may be related to iron and ferritin levels (2, 24).

In one study, 157 patients with a degenerative parkinsonian syndrome (either PD, multiple system atrophy, or progressive supranuclear palsy) underwent TCS. Of those who could be imaged, 89% with PD had marked hyperechogenicity of the substantia nigra on one or both sides, compared with 25% of those with multiple system atrophy and 39% of those with progressive supranuclear palsy (25).

Investigators are also examining the role of TCS in the detection of presymptomatic PD. In one study, 30 individuals with loss of smell (which is associated with PD) underwent TCS. Of these, 11 had increased echogenicity of the substantia nigra and 10 of the 11 subsequently had [¹²³I]FP-CIT performed. Uptake was pathologic in 5 of the individuals and borderline in 2. Longitudinal follow-up is needed to determine whether any of them subsequently developed PD (26).

TCS has shortcomings. In addition to the unclear mechanisms underlying the hyperechogenicity of the substantia nigra in PD, the test has technical limitations. For example, in the study of 157 patients with parkinsonian syndrome, the investigators could not obtain a temporal bone window (skull location through which

Doppler images are obtained) sufficient for adequate sonographic analysis in 13% of the individuals examined (25). Diagnostic studies using TCS have varied widely in their results even in those with established parkinsonian syndromes. For example, sensitivities have varied from 40% to 100% (27, 28) and specificities from 55% to 100% (27, 29). Finally, hyperechogenicity of the substantia nigra has been identified in approximately 9% of healthy adults (24).

BLOOD AND CEREBROSPINAL FLUID TESTS

Biomarkers in the cerebrospinal fluid (CSF), especially blood, offer promise for increasing our understanding of PD; to date, however, these have had little impact as a diagnostic tool or therapeutic metric. Much of the focus on serum and CSF biomarkers (Table 24-4) has been on markers of oxidative stress, which is thought to contribute to the pathophysiology of PD (2). Levels of mitochondrial complex I are

reduced in the substantia nigra (2). To identify a peripheral marker, investigators have studied levels of mitochondrial complex I in platelets and 8-hydroxy-2'-deoxyguanosine as signs of oxidative stress. However, platelets showed no difference in complex I levels in one study (30), and the increased levels of 8-hydroxy-2'-deoxyguanosine in another study (31) were not robust enough to serve as a biomarker in clinical practice (2). Other investigators found low platelet mitochondrial complex I and II/III activities, which appear to be related to the etiology of PD (32). Another study has shown a difference in platelet morphology by electron microscopy (33), but the significance of this finding is unclear.

In addition to oxidative stress, investigators examined other proteins and processes implicated in the pathogenesis of PD. Lewy bodies and Lewy neurites, pathologic hallmarks of PD, contain insoluble α-synuclein fibrils. Investigators found significantly elevated levels of soluble aggregates of α-synuclein protein in individuals with PD compared with controls (34). Defects in

TABLE 24-4
Select Possible PD Biomarkers in the Blood and Cerebrospinal Fluid

POTENTIAL BIOMARKER	LOCATION	DESCRIPTION	EVIDENCE TO DATE AND SOURCE
Mitochondrial complex I level	Blood	May be a biomarker of oxidative stress in platelets that is seen within the substantia nigra.	No difference in complex I levels between individuals with PD and controls (30). Other investigators have found low levels that appear to be related to the etiology of PD (32).
Monoamine oxidase B activity	Blood	Contributes to the metabolism of dopamine.	Level is increased in PD and reversed by selegiline, a monoamine oxidase B inhibitor (36).
Dopamine transporter	Blood	Present on peripheral lymphocytes and is a marker of the peripheral dopamine system.	Immunoreactivity is decreased in the early clinical stages of PD (42).
Proteasome	Blood	Degrades polyubiquinated proteins.	Proteasome 20S activity is decreased in individuals with PD (35).
α-Synuclein	Blood and CSF	Present in platelets and CSF and protein; implicated in the pathophysiology of PD.	Level of soluble aggregates of α-synuclein increased in individuals with PD relative to controls (34).
8-hydroxy-2'-deoxyguanosine	Blood and CSF	May be a marker of oxidative stress from oxidized DNA.	Level tends to be increased in both blood and CSF in PD and other neurodegenerative diseases (31).
Orexin	CSF	May be a biomarker of sleepiness, which is present in PD.	Orexin levels were lower in PD and decreased with the severity of the disease (43).

CSF = cerebrospinal fluid.

TABLE 24-5
Genes Linked to Parkinson's Disease

Locus	Gene/Protein	Inheritance Pattern	Clinical Phenotype
PARK1	SNCA/α-synuclein	Autosomal dominant	Mid-age onset (45-60 years old) with typical PD +/− dementia
PARK2	PARK2/parkin	Autosomal recessive	Juvenile (<20) onset with atypical features
PARK3	Unknown	Autosomal dominant	Typical PD
PARK5	UCH-L1	Autosomal dominant	Mid-age onset with typical PD
PARK6	PINK1	Autosomal recessive	Early onset (20-45) PD with slow progression
PARK7	PARK7/DJ-1	Autosomal recessive	Early onset PD with slow progression
PARK8	LRRK2/dardarin	Autosomal dominant	Mid-age onset with typical PD +/− dementia & amyotrophy
PARK10	Unknown	Genetic susceptibility	Typical PD
PARK11	Unknown	Genetic susceptibility	Typical PD
FTDP-17	MAPT/tau	Autosomal dominant	Parkinsonism associated with frontotemporal dementia
SCA2	ATXN2/ataxin-2	Autosomal dominant	Typical PD
SCA3	ATXN3/ataxin-3	Autosomal dominant	Typical PD
Nurr1	NR4A2/NURR1	Likely autosomal dominant	Typical PD
Synphilin-1	SNCAIP/synphilin-1	Likely autosomal dominant	Typical PD
Mitochondria	NADH complex I	Mitochondrial	Typical PD

Source: Adapted from Forman et al.(44) and Pankratz et al.(45). With permission.

the ubiquitin-proteasome system, which is responsible for degrading polyubiquinated proteins, may contribute to the pathogenesis of PD, and proteasome activity in peripheral blood lymphocytes is decreased in individuals with PD compared with healthy controls (35).

One study has shown the potential of a platelet biomarker to respond to treatment. The increased monoamine oxidase B activity seen in platelets of individuals with PD can be reversed with the addition of selegiline, an inhibitor of monoamine oxidase B (36).

GENETIC TESTING

Genes, as indicators of pathogenic processes, can be considered biomarkers of PD. For the majority of individuals with PD, genetic factors do not clearly play a role (2). However, individuals with a family history of PD are at about a 2- to 4-fold increased risk for PD (37), and the incidence of PD is increased in identical twins of individuals with PD who have onset before age 50 (38).

In 1997, Polymeropoulos identified a mutation in the α-synuclein gene, which was responsible for PD

in a large Italian kindred (39). Since that time, investigators have identified many genes associated with PD (Table 24-5). The inheritance pattern of the genes varies from autosomal dominant (e.g., PARK1) to autosomal recessive (e.g., PARK7/DJ-1) to conferring genetic susceptibility (e.g., PARK10). For cases of early onset with a family history, genetics is helpful in diagnosis and in patient education, as many patients with PD due to genetic causes have a different clinical course than those with sporadic PD (see Table 24-5) (2). In sporadic PD occurring above age 50, the use of genetic markers is less clear, but progress is slowly being made. Researchers have found a mutation in LRRK2 in 1% to 8% of sporadic PD in populations of European descent (40), and the same mutation has been found in higher proportions of specific subpopulations (41).

SUMMARY

PD is managed clinically without the use of biomarkers or ancillary tests. Biomarkers are indicators of biological processes and have increasingly been studied in PD to increase our understanding of the disease, evaluate potential therapies, assist in diagnosis, and monitor treatment response. The most extensively studied biomarkers are those found through radiotracer imaging studies, which combine radiolabeled ligands with PET or SPECT modalities. Radiotracers can assist in the diagnosis of PD but currently are not widely available or used clinically.

Other biomarkers—including clinical, imaging, blood, cerebrospinal fluid, and genetic tests—all offer different advantages but have not yet gained widespread application. Collectively, they have increased our understanding of PD and can assist in diagnosis and prognosis, but they have not yet performed well as surrogate endpoints in clinical trials.

*R*eferences

1. Atkinson AJ, Colburn WA, DeGruttola VG, et al. Biomarkers and surrogate endpoints: Preferred definitions and conceptual framework. *Clin Pharmacol Ther* 2001; 69(3):89–95.
2. Michell AW, Lewis SJG, Foltynie T, Barker RA. Biomarkers and Parkinson's disease. *Brain* 2004; 127:1693–1705.
3. Montgomery EB, Baker KB, Lyons K, Koller WC. Abnormal performance on the PD test battery by asymptomatic first-degree relatives. *Neurology* 1999; 52(4):757–762.
4. Mourao LF, Aguiar PMD, Ferraz FAP, et al. Acoustic voice assessment in Parkinson's disease patients submitted to posteroventral pallidotomy. *Arq Neuro-Psiquiatria* 2005; 63(1):20–25.
5. Nagulic M, Davidovic J, Nagulic I. Parkinsonian voice acoustic analysis in real-time after stereotactic thalamotomy. *Stereotac Funct Neurosurg* 2005; 83(2–3):115–121.
6. Rascol O, Sabatini U, Simonettamoreau M, et al. Square-wave jerks in parkinsonian syndromes. *J Neurol Neurosurg Psychiatry* 1991; 54(7):599–602.
7. Hocherman S, Giladi N. Visuomotor control abnormalities in patients with unilateral parkinsonism. *Neurology* 1998; 50(6):1648–1654.
8. Pinter MM, Helscher RJ, Nasel COJ, et al. Quantification of motor deficit in Parkinson's disease with a motor performance test series. *J Neural Transm* [Parkinson's Disease and Dementia Section] 1992; 4(2):131–141.
9. Merello M, Nouzeilles MI, Arce GP, Leiguarda R. Accuracy of acute levodopa challenge for clinical prediction of sustained long-term levodopa response as a major criterion for idiopathic Parkinson's disease diagnosis. *Mov Disord* 2002; 17(4):795–798.
10. Suchowersky O, Reich S, Perlmutter J, et al. Practice parameter: Diagnosis and prognosis of new onset Parkinson disease (an evidence-based review). Report of the Quality Standards Subcommittee of the American Academy of Neurology. *Neurology* 2006; 66(7):968–975.
11. Wenning GK, Shephard B, Hawkes C, et al. Olfactory function in atypical parkinsonian syndromes. *Acta Neurol Scand* 1995; 91(4):247–250.
12. Mesholam RI, Moberg PJ, Mahr RN, Doty RL. Olfaction in neurodegenerative disease:- A meta-analysis of olfactory functioning in Alzheimer's and Parkinson's diseases. *Arch Neurol* 1998; 55(1):84–90.
13. Ponsen MM, Stoffers D, Booij J, et al. Idiopathic hyposmia as a preclinical sign of Parkinson's disease. *Ann Neurol* 2004; 56(2):173–181.
14. Ravina B, Eidelberg D, Ahlskog JE, et al. The role of radiotracer imaging in Parkinson disease. *Neurology* 2005; 64(2):208–215.
15. Seibyl J, Jennings D, Tabamo R, Marek K. Neuroimaging trials of Parkinson's disease progression. *J Neurol* 2004; 251:9–13.
16. Marek K, Jennings D, Seibyl J. Imaging the dopamine system to assess disease-modifying drugs: Studies comparing dopamine agonists and levodopa. *Neurology* 2003; 61(6): S43–S48.
17. Morrish PK, Rakshi JS, Bailey DL, et al. Measuring the rate of progression and estimating the preclinical period of Parkinson's disease with [F-18] dopa PET. *J Neurol Neurosurg Psychiatry* 1998; 64(3):314–319.
18. Jennings DL, Seibyl JP, Oakes D, et al. (I-123) beta-CIT and single-photon emission computed tomographic imaging vs clinical evaluation in Parkinsonian syndrome: Unmasking an early diagnosis. *Arch Neurol* 2004; 61(8):1224–1229.
19. Fahn S. Does levodopa slow or hasten the rate of progression of Parkinson's disease? *J Neurol* 2005; 252:37–42.
20. Whone AL, Watts RL, Stoessl AJ, et al. Slower progression of Parkinson's disease with ropinirole versus levodopa: The REAL-PET study. *Ann Neurol* 2003; 54(1):93–101.
21. Spiegel J, Mollers MO, Jost WH, et al. FP-CIT and MIBG scintigraphy in early Parkinson's disease. *Mov Disord* 2005; 20(5):552–561.
22. Courbon F, Brefel-Courbon C, Thalamas C, et al. Cardiac MIBG scintigraphy is a sensitive tool for detecting cardiac sympathetic denervation in Parkinson's disease. *Mov Disord* 2003; 18(8):890–897.
23. Becker G, Berg D. Neuroimaging in basal ganglia disorders: Perspectives for transcranial ultrasound. *Mov Disord* 2001; 16(1):23–32.
24. Berg D, Siefker C, Ruprecht-Dorfler P, Becker G. Relationship of substantia nigra echogenicity and motor function in elderly subjects. *Neurology* 2001; 56(1):13–17.
25. Behnke S, Berg D, Naumann M, Becker G. Differentiation of Parkinson's disease and atypical parkinsonian syndromes by transcranial ultrasound. *J Neurol Neurosurg Psychiatry* 2005; 76(3):423–425.
26. Sommer U, Hummel T, Cormann K, et al. Detection of presymptomatic Parkinson's disease: Combining smell tests, transcranial sonography, and SPECT. *Mov Disord* 2004; 19(10):1196–1202.
27. Becker G, Seufert J, Bogdahn U, et al. Degeneration of substantia nigra in chronic Parkinson's disease visualized by transcranial color-coded real-time sonography. *Neurology* 1995; 45(1):182–184.
28. Walter U, Wittstock M, Benecke R, Dressler D. Substantia nigra echogenicity is normal in non-extrapyramidal cerebral disorders but increased in Parkinson's disease. *J Neural Transm* 2002; 109(2):191–196.
29. Ruprecht-Dorfler P, Berg D, Tucha O, et al. Echogenicity of the substantia nigra in relatives of patients with sporadic Parkinson's disease. *Neuroimage* 2003; 18(2):416–422.
30. Mann VM, Cooper JM, Krige D, et al. Brain, Skeletal muscle and platelet homogenate mitochondrial function in Parkinson's disease. *Brain* 1992; 115:333–342.
31. Kikuchi A, Takeda A, Onodera H, et al. Systemic increase of oxidative nucleic acid damage in Parkinson's disease and multiple system atrophy. *Neurobiol Dis* 2002; 9(2): 244–248.
32. Haas RH, Nasirian F, Nakano K, et al. Low platelet mitochondrial complex-i and complex-Ii/Iii activity in early untreated Parkinson's disease. *Ann Neurol* 1995; 37(6): 714–722.
33. Factor SA, Ortof E, Dentinger MP, Mankes R, Barron KD. Platelet morphology in Parkinsons disease: An electron-microscopic study. *J Neurol Sci* 1994; 122(1):84–89.
34. El-Agnaf OMA, Salem SA, Paleologou KE, et al. Detection of oligomeric forms of alpha-synuclein protein in human plasma as a potential biomarker for Parkinson's disease. *FASEB J* 2006; 20:419–425.
35. Blandini F, Sinforiani E, Pacchetti C, et al. Peripheral proteasome and caspase activity in Parkinson disease and Alzheimer disease. *Neurology* 2006; 66(4):529–534.
36. Zhou G, Miura Y, Shoji H, Yamada S, Matsuishi T. Platelet monoamine oxidase B and plasma beta-phenylethylamine in Parkinson's disease. *J Neurol Neurosurg Psychiatry* 2001; 70(2):229–231.
37. Marder K, Tang MX, Mejia H, et al. Risk of Parkinson's disease among first-degree relatives: A community-based study. *Neurology* 1996; 47(1):155–160.
38. Tanner CM, Ottman R, Goldman SM, et al. Parkinson disease in twins: An etiologic study. *JAMA* 1999; 281(4):341–346.
39. Polymeropoulos MH, Lavedan C, Leroy E, et al. Mutation in the alpha-synuclein gene identified in families with Parkinson's disease. *Science* 1997; 276(5321):2045–2047.
40. Hernandez D, Ruiz CP, Crawley A, et al. The dardarin G2019S mutation is a common cause of Parkinson's disease but not other neurodegenerative diseases. *Neurosci Lett* 2005; 389(3):137–139.
41. Lesage S, Durr A, Tazir M, et al. LRRK2 G2019S as a cause of Parkinson's disease in North African Arabs. *N Engl J Med* 2006; 354(4):422–423.
42. Caronti B, Antonini G, Calderaro C, et al. Dopamine transporter immunoreactivity in peripheral blood lymphocytes in Parkinson's disease. *J Neural Transm* 2001; 108(7): 803–807.
43. Drouot X, Moutereau S, Nguyen JP, et al. Low levels of ventricular CSF orexin/hypocretin in advanced PD. *Neurology* 2003; 61(4):540–543.
44. Forman MS, Lee VMY, Trojanowski JQ. Nosology of Parkinson's disease: Looking for the way out of a quackmire. *Neuron* 2005; 47(4):479–482.
45. Pankratz N, Foroud T. Genetics of Parkinson disease. *NeuroRx* 2004; 1:235–242.

25

Positron Emission Tomography

Joel S. Perlmutter

his chapter reviews the potentials and the pitfalls of using positron emission tomography (PET) or single photon emission computed tomography (SPECT) to diagnose Parkinson's disease (PD) or monitor its progression, which is important for assessing the efficacy of interventions. Initially some historical perspective is provided on how this methodology developed; then the notion of biomarkers and surrogate endpoints is introduced. Finally, evidence supporting the use of PET in the diagnosis and monitoring of PD is reviewed.

HISTORICAL BACKGROUND

Since degeneration of nigrostriatal neurons underlies PD, the measurement of these presynaptic neurons has been a key goal of many PET studies. Garnett and coworkers (1) first reported the preferential striatal accumulation of radioactivity in normal humans after intravenous injection of the dopa analog [18F]fluorodopa (FD), which crosses the blood-brain barrier (BBB) and is decarboxylated to [18F]fluorodopamine, a charged molecule that is trapped within the BBB. Presynaptic terminals of nigrostriatal dopaminergic neurons contain most of the striatal decarboxylase activity; therefore FD PET reflects dopaminergic innervation under normal conditions.

However, as presynaptic neurons degenerate, a greater portion of residual decarboxylase activity resides in other compartments (2) Nevertheless, the accumulation of [18F]fluorodopamine may to some degree indirectly reflect residual nigrostriatal neurons (3,4).

Initial FD PET studies revealed decreased striatal radioactivity accumulation in people with PD (5–8). Other radiotracers label other components of presynaptic nigrostriatal neurons. These other tracers can be divided into those that bind to presynaptic dopamine transporter (DAT) sites (9) or vesicular monoamine transport sites (VMAT2). Radiotracers with high affinity for DAT sites include analogs of amphetamine-like compounds (9). The most commonly used is the SPECT tracer beta-carbomethoxy-3beta-(4-iodophenyl)tropane (β-CIT), which demonstrates reduced uptake with PD progression (10). A variety of other tropane analogs have been developed for use with PET or SPECT. Alternatively, [11C]dihydro tetrabenazine (DTBZ) is a PET tracer that has high affinity for VMAT2 located exclusively on presynaptic vesicles of monoaminergic neurons (11). Striatal uptake of DTBZ represents mainly dopaminergic terminals, since they represent more than 95% of the striatal monoaminergic terminals. Like that of FD or β-CIT, DTBZ uptake is decreased in humans with PD (12).

Regional PET measurements of blood flow, oxygen, or glucose metabolism have been used to identify sites of abnormal function that occur in diseases such as PD. For example, abnormalities of local flow or metabolism found in basal ganglia in patients with PD reflect the known striatal dopamine deficiency as well as other functional abnormalities associated with motor control and cognitive function (13–19). These measurements of flow and metabolism have also been used for studies of diagnosis and disease progression.

BIOMARKERS AND SURROGATE ENDPOINTS

Prior to discussing the application of these neuroimaging methods to PD, it is important to review the notions of biomarkers and surrogate endpoints. A biomarker is an objectively measured indicator of normal biological processes, pathogenic processes, or pharmacologic responses to a therapeutic intervention (20). For example, the number of triplet repeats of the base sequence CAG for the huntingtin gene is a biomarker for Huntington's disease. The finding of 40 or more triplet repeats of this sequence indicates that an individual has or will develop the disease (21). There is no analogous straightforward biomarker for PD. No measurement of a biological process in living humans predicts with great accuracy the diagnosis of idiopathic PD or progression of disease. Several biomarkers have been proposed that provide evidence of early PD, such as deficiencies of smell acuity (22–24). However, clear distinction from other parkinsonian conditions may be problematic. Further and more importantly, smell acuity does not provide a reliable measure of disease progression. How such limitations apply to the neuroimaging measures that have been proposed for PD is discussed below. Some may provide greater sensitivity for reduced nigrostriatal neurons than clinical examination, but they suffer from limited specificity; the biomarker does not distinguish PD from progressive supranuclear palsy or multisystems atrophy. Nevertheless, can one of these biomarkers provide a good measure of disease severity or progression, and what role could that play in clinical trials?

To answer this question, it is important to clarify the definition of a surrogate endpoint and distinguish that from the more general term *biomarker*. A biomarker that could measure PD progression would be valuable for measuring the effect of an intervention on the underlying pathologic process—loss of dopaminergic neurons. Some proposed interventions, such as orally administered creatine, could conceivably improve a clinically meaningful endpoint such as the ability to live independently or reduce fall risk by improving muscle strength rather than necessarily reducing rate of disease progression. In this situation, a neuroimaging biomarker reflecting disease progression could provide valuable insight into the key action of the intervention. That use of a biomarker is different from its use as a surrogate endpoint, where the biomarker can substitute for a clinically meaningful endpoint (20). This more limited use of the biomarker has value for understanding the effects of an intervention but does not substitute for the clinically meaningful endpoint, since it may not predict toxicity or mediate all the effects of the intervention on the clinical outcome. In other words, a surrogate endpoint must meet much more stringent criteria before it can substitute for a clinically meaningful endpoint. A biomarker of disease progression, on the other hand, only needs to be a reliable measure of disease progression. Several neuroimaging methods have a potential role for this more restricted application—that is, as a reliable measure of the nigrostriatal neuronal pathway.

DIAGNOSIS OF PARKINSON'S DISEASE

One key question is whether PET imaging can be used as a diagnostic test to supplement clinical diagnosis of PD "(a related issue, of course, is the definition of PD." For this review, PD is defined as the clinical syndrome associated with progressive nigrostriatal neuronal loss with Lewy bodies found on pathologic examination). A diagnostic test requires high specificity and high sensitivity with a high positive predictive value. Several studies have begun to address these issues. Low striatal FD uptake may distinguish individuals with PD from normals (25–28) or those with dopa-responsive dystonia (29), and other presynaptic tracers may provide similar information (30–32) or distinguish PD from essential tremor (33). However, a more stringent question is whether PET can distinguish PD from other parkinsonian syndromes. FD uptake alone does not separate persons with PD from those with multiple system atrophy (MSA) (19, 34), Machado-Joseph disease (35), or spinocerebellar ataxia with parkinsonism (36). However, relatively small studies suggest that combining FD with other tracers, such as measures of dopamine receptors or [^{18}F]fluorodeoxyglucose (FDG), may improve the ability to distinguish PD from MSA or progressive supranuclear palsy (PSP) (37, 38). Markers of the dopamine transporter system also provide some distinction between these different parkinsonian groups (39–41), but there is substantial controversy as to whether this distinction is sufficient to be clinically useful (42, 43). A linear combination of regional FDG uptake in caudate, lentiform nuclei, and thalamus may distinguish PD from atypical parkinsonism (44). Application of sophisticated statistical techniques to determine the pattern of regional FDG uptake permits differentiation of PD patients from normals and those with clinically defined striatonigral degeneration (45). Potentially, PET may be able to distinguish underlying PD in people with exposure to dopamine receptor–blocking drugs, since patients with low FD uptake may be more likely to have long-lasting or progressive parkinsonism after cessation of the offending drug compared with those with normal FD uptake (46).

PET or SPECT may also reveal a normal-appearing scan in some individuals who appear to have a clinical diagnosis of PD (47, 48). Does this mean that these people have an atypical parkinsonian syndrome or other conditions that mimic PD, like essential tremor or drug-induced parkinsonism? Alternatively, could some of these people have less severe pathologic changes associated with relatively mild PD manifestations? Will they progress more slowly? Are there other clinical features that distinguished these people from those with more typically abnormal scans? Also, some with normal-appearing scans could represent a limitation in sensitivity of the imaging modality, as revealed by 1 person in 56 with typical early PD (asymmetric resting tremor, bradykinesia, rigidity and dopa responsive) who had a normal FD PET (49). Ongoing research will hopefully address some of these questions. Nevertheless, it seems reasonable that either PET or SPECT could be used to identify a more homogenous group of participants for a clinical trial. Of course, the limitation of this approach would be the lack of generalizability of findings from such a trial to clinical practice, unless of course that clinical practice also included the imaging modality implemented with the same expertise as used in the clinical trial.

Despite the limited specificity of PET or SPECT measures to distinguish PD from other parkinsonian conditions, there are still several potential uses of these PET markers. Clearly, presymptomatic diagnosis of PD could be an important clinical tool once protective therapies have been proven. Much of this is based on the higher sensitivity of these measures to detect defects in nigrostriatal pathways compared with clinical examination. For example, asymptomatic patients exposed to MPTP had intermediate values of striatal FD uptake compared with PD patients and normals (5). Monkeys treated with low doses of MPTP that did not produce parkinsonian signs had decreased striatal uptake (50, 51). Some unaffected monozygotic twins and nontwin relatives of PD patients had abnormally low striatal FD uptake (52–55), as has been found in some asymptomatic family members with a parkin gene mutation (56). These latter studies emphasize the importance of the ability to potentially identify an endophenotype for genetics research. PET potentially could "convert" a normal to an "affected" person for genetic investigations of pedigrees with familial parkinsonism (49).

In summary, each of the three classes of nigrostriatal neuronal markers has been demonstrated to have reduced striatal uptake in either people with PD or animal models of parkinsonism (57–60), with differing degrees of correlation to various motor manifestations or in vitro measures of nigrostriatal function (61–63). It is also clear that PET or SPECT methods usually provide greater sensitivity for the detection of a nigrostriatal defect than clinical examination. However, there are inadequate data to demonstrate that PET or SPECT can provide helpful information to distinguish among the different parkinsonian conditions—in a way that would provide meaningful clinical information—to either help with counseling or guide treatment for individual patients.

MONITORING DISEASE PROGRESSION OR EFFICACY OF TREATMENT

Development of therapies to slow or reverse progression of PD requires an endpoint to determine the effectiveness of the intervention (64). Currently, a clinical endpoint such as quality of life, lifespan, or other measure of clinical disease progression may be the most appropriate one. Alternatively, change on a clinical rating scale such as the Unified Parkinson Disease Rating Scale (UPDRS) has been used (47), but it is important to connect a change in UPDRS with an endpoint that is meaningful to patients, such as quality of life. However, even a clinically meaningful endpoint has limitations for interpretation of the effects of an intervention. An intervention may alter an endpoint without retarding the pathophysiologic progression of disease. For example, a drug could directly increase muscle strength in patients with PD, improve quality of life, or perhaps even reduce progression on a UPDRS rating but still do nothing for progression of disease. In this situation, a biomarker would be invaluable to determine the effect of the intervention on pathology. Neuroimaging could potentially provide such a biomarker if it could objectively measure the loss of nigrostriatal neurons that occurs in PD and assess changes in dopaminergic cell numbers.

Unfortunately, neuroimaging biomarkers have not achieved this potential for PD (65). Multiple issues complicate interpretation of currently available SPECT- or PET-based biomarkers. Large multicenter trials have revealed marked discrepancies between neuroimaging biomarkers and clinical endpoints(47, 64, 65). In fact, a panel sponsored by the National Institute Of Neurological Disorders and Stroke reviewed this issue and concluded that "current evidence does not support the use of imaging . . . in clinical trials." A valid biomarker must reflect the natural history of disease and accurately reflect alterations produced by an intervention (66).

For PD, this requires an imaging biomarker to maintain a consistent amount of tracer uptake per individual nigrostriatal neuron despite changes in the numbers of residual nigrostriatal neurons or the nature of the intervention. The specific binding site or enzyme activity responsible for radiotracer uptake may change owing to an attempt to compensate for the loss of neurons. This process, called regulation, may alter the quantitative relationship between tracer uptake and number of residual neurons. Although it is known that several neuroimaging markers detect a reduction in nigrostriatal neurons as seen in PD, uptake of these radiotracers may be affected by regulation, thus confounding interpretation of the endpoint.

Evidence Supporting [¹⁸F]Fluorodopa as a Biomarker

The following data support the use of FD, a DAT marker (e.g., β-CIT), or a VMAT2 tracer (e.g., DTBZ) as a valid biomarker of disease progression (67). FD PET primarily reflects neuronal decarboxylase activity that converts FD into (¹⁸F]dopamine (2). Since [¹⁸F]dopamine is a charged molecule, it is trapped in the brain and its uptake provides an index of decarboxylase activity. Multiple studies in humans and nonhuman primates suggest that FD uptake reflects nigrostriatal function. These studies fall into two categories: those that directly attempt to determine whether FD uptake correlates with the number of nigrostriatal neurons and those that demonstrate changes in striatal uptake of FD with disease state or progression of disease. Studies in humans have found that FD uptake is decreased in PD compared with normals (68, 69) and that striatal uptake modestly correlates with parkinsonian signs (70). Longitudinal studies demonstrate a reduction of FD uptake in people with PD (71–73). However, a trial of levodopa vs. ropinirole treatment for early PD where FD PET was used as the primary endpoint revealed greater loss over 2 years in the levodopa-treated group despite greater functional improvement on motor ratings (UPDRS). If, on the other hand, one interprets development of dopa-induced dyskinesias as a sign of disease progression, it would be concordant with the PET findings (48). In a trial of sham surgery vs. midbrain fetal cell transplant, striatal FD uptake increased in those over and under 60 years of age despite clinical benefit only in the younger group (74). Similarly, a recent study of an intraputamenal glial cell line–derived neurotrophic factor (GDNF) infusion in people with PD demonstrated no clinical benefit with motor scales but increased uptake of FD (75). These studies demonstrate discordance between FD PET and clinical endpoints (67).

Several studies have attempted to correlate striatal uptake of FD with postmortem measures of striatal dopamine or numbers of substantia nigra pars compacta (SNpc) dopaminergic cells (3, 4, 76). Only one study has been done in humans (4). The density of dopaminergic neurons in SNpc was measured postmortem on a single midbrain slice in 2 people with PD, 2 with Alzheimer's disease, and 1 with PSP. The patients died several years after the last PET measurement, and there are likely differences in drug exposures and other factors that may have altered dopaminergic neurons. These findings have 3 main limitations. First, dopaminergic cell counts were not done with an unbiased technique, such as stereology. Rather, a more limited sample of the nigra was used, and that may have biased the results. Second, only 5 subjects

were included, which is far too small a sample to produce meaningful conclusions. Third, with such a small number of subjects, it is not possible to accurately determine whether the data are normally distributed—a necessary condition for the correlation analysis to be valid. These data do not provide convincing support of a relationship between cell counts and FD uptake. Interestingly, 3 more subjects have been added to this curve (67), but these new findings have been described only sparsely, without any information about appropriately unbiased cell counts. This is a difficult task to execute with human subjects.

There have been two studies in nonhuman primates, and these provide greater potential to control variables. The first included 8 monkeys, and the authors reported a high correlation between the right/left striatal ratio of FD uptake with the right/left ratio of tyrosine hydroxylase staining density used as an index of dopaminergic nigral cell counts (3). There are 3e major limitations of this study. First, the investigators used only optical density on one slice through the midbrain rather than a more precise measure, such as stereologic counts of TH-staining neurons, possibly introducing bias. Second, the number of animals was too small for a correlation analysis. Third, the variation across the spectrum of reduced cell counts is too limited for a proper correlation analysis. In particular, the data from the monkeys with abnormally low striatal neurons tend to cluster in the lower left of the graph provided in the publication, whereas the normal striatal measures cluster in the upper right. These are not the normally distributed data required for a valid correlation analysis, and there is no indication that there is a correlation within either of the clusters individually.

A larger study was done in 17 monkeys using graded MPTP-induced lesions of the SNpc, but the MPTP-induced lesions were restricted to only modest loss of neurons, up to a 35% loss. These investigators did use stereologic counts with appropriate tissue sampling as required by an unbiased counting technique (77). Interestingly, the published figure comparing nigral cell counts with striatal FD uptake reveals no correlation between the 2 measures. These data contradict the reported findings of the previous 2 publications, yet this paper is often incorrectly cited as supporting the relationship between FD uptake and SNpc cell counts. The explanation for that lies in the P value shown in the figure in the upper left of the graph. This P value refers to the difference between two different methods for estimating FD uptake and not to a significant relationship between cell counts and FD uptake. Therefore there are no clear data to support the notion that striatal FD uptake reflects SNpc dopaminergic cell counts. Interestingly, striatal FD uptake does appear to correlate with striatal dopamine content (as found by this study and the previously discussed monkey paper (3), but that is different from cell counts.

Evidence Supporting a DAT Tracer as a Biomarker

What are the data that DAT tracers can measure PD progression? The most commonly used DAT marker is the SPECT radiopharmaceutical β-CIT, and striatal uptake of β-CIT decreases with PD progression (10). However, in a large 9-month human trial of testing different doses of L-dopa for treatment of early PD, β-CIT SPECT revealed no significant change across treatment groups despite reduced progression of motor ratings in the group treated with the highest dose (done after a 2-week washout with no change found between 1 and 2 weeks of washout, as would be expected if there were an inadequate washout time—although the number of subjects in this part of the study was relatively low) (47). After retrospective censoring of data in people with normal baseline SPECT scans, striatal β-CIT reduction was greater in the group treated with the highest dose of L-dopa. This post hoc analysis provides an even greater contradiction between the clinical endpoint and the SPECT findings. In any event, both analyses demonstrate that β-CIT SPECT findings contradict the primary clinical endpoint. Therefore the ability of this class of imaging markers accurately to reflect underlying pathologic progression studies remains unclear.

Evidence Supporting DTBZ as a Biomarker

PET measurement of DTBZ binding to VMAT2 (vesicular monoamine transporter type 2) is another alternative. VMAT2 is located exclusively in the membranes of presynaptic vesicles of monoaminergic neurons (11). Validation of DTBZ as a measure of striatal dopamine innervation has been attempted in several ways. Studies have shown that in vivo regional binding of DTBZ correlates with the known distribution of VMAT2 in rodent brain (78). There is a linear relationship between the level of in vitro striatal radioligand binding to VMAT2 and the extent of nigral injury in 6OHDA-lesioned rats (79), suggesting that there is no regulation of this binding site, at least in rats. DTBZ exhibits high-affinity binding only to VMAT2 and a lack of regulation of VMAT2 by repeated or chronic dopaminergic or cholinergic drug treatments in rodents (80,81). Striatal uptake represents mainly dopaminergic terminals, since they constitute more than 95% of the striatal monoaminergic terminals. DTBZ uptake is decreased in humans with PD, and this decrease may correlate with severity of parkinsonian signs (12). However, a larger study recently found that striatal uptake correlated with PD duration and activities of daily living, not with UPDRS motor scales (82). Finally, human DTBZ uptake is highly reproducible (83).

The critical point is that VMAT2 sites on presynaptic vesicles may be less likely to be regulated than either decarboxylase or DAT. The [+]enantiomer of DTBZ has greater specificity, selective uptake, and improved imaging characteristics compared with the racemic form (84). These features, together with the lower potential for regulation, make DTBZ the currently available radioligand with the greatest potential to accurately reflect changes in presynaptic nigrostriatal neurons.

Once a standard curve has been established for one of the radiotracers, the next step before its application in an interventional study is to demonstrate that the intervention to be tested does not alter the relationship between tracer uptake and residual dopaminergic neurons. For example, there might be differential alteration by levodopa compared to a dopamine agonist for the uptake of PET tracer that marks DAT sites (65, 67, 85). Other interventions, like fetal transplant surgery, may directly alter some assumptions underlying tracer kinetic analysis, which may confound interpretation of longitudinal changes to tracer uptake (2, 86). Frequently, relatively small studies regarding the lack of effects of an intervention are used to indicate a lack of an effect on an imaging biomarker, but this may not be relevant for a much larger study in which small effect sizes can be statistically significant. This important issue has become the focus of ongoing studies.

There are no convincing data demonstrating that one of these potential neuroimaging biomarkers faithfully reflects reduction of nigrostriatal neuron number—a measure of disease progression. In other words, no standard curve has convincingly provided proof that one of these radiotracers accurately reflects a reduction in nigrostriatal neurons. Thus, there are currently inadequate data to support the use of any of these markers as biomarkers of disease progression. Furthermore, there is no justification for the use of one of these as a surrogate endpoint—supplanting a clinically based endpoint—for a clinical study, since the imaging biomarkers could miss important untoward effects of an intervention.

CONCLUSIONS

Neuroimaging with PET or SPECT may provide confirmation of a defect in the nigrostriatal pathways in someone with parkinsonism. These neuroimaging methods may provide greater sensitivity than clinical examination for identifying the effects of such defects. There are inadequate data to justify clinical use of these methods for differential diagnosis of the type that would be useful clinically to distinguish among the various parkinsonian syndromes. Although the sensitivity of the PET or SPECT methods may play a role in subject identification for clinical trials or research studies, this application comes at a cost of limited generalizability of the findings from such a study. Finally, current evidence does not support the use of any of these radiotracers as biomarkers of disease progression or surrogate endpoints for a clinical trial testing a new intervention.

ACKNOWLEDGMENTS

Joel S. Perlmutter has received support from NIH grants NS050425, NS41509, NS041771, RR020092, and the Greater St. Louis chapter of the American Parkinson Disease Association (APDA), the APDA Center for Advanced PD Research at Washington University, the Barnes-Jewish Hospital Foundation (the Jack Buck Fund and the Elliot H. Stein Family Fund), the Missouri chapter of the Dystonia Medical Research Foundation, the Ruth Kopolow Fund, and the Sam and Barbara Murphy Fund.

References

1. Garnett ES, Firnau G, Nahmias C. Dopamine visualised in the basal ganglia of living man. *Nature* 1983; 305:137–138.
2. Martin WRW, Perlmutter JS. Assessment of fetal tissue transplantation in Parkinson's disease: Does PET play a role? *Neurology* 1994; 44:1777–1780.
3. Pate BD, Kawamata T, Yamada T, et al. Correlation of striatal fluorodopa uptake in the MPTP monkey with dopaminergic indices. *Ann Neurol* 1993; 34:331–338.
4. Snow BJ, Tooyama I, McGeer EG, et al. Human positron emission tomographic [18F]fluorodopa studies correlate with dopamine cell counts and levels. *Ann Neurol* 1993; 34:324–330.
5. Calne DB, Langston JW, Martin WRW, et al. Positron emission tomography after MPTP: Observations relating to the cause of Parkinson's disease. *Nature* 317:246–248.
6. Hoshi H, Kuwabara H, Léger G, et al. 6-[18F] fluoro-L-dopa metabolism in living human brain: a comparison of six analytical methods. *J Cereb Blood Flow Metab* 1993; 13:57–69.
7. Leenders KL, Salmon EP, Tyrrell P, et al. The nigrostriatal dopaminergic system assessed in vivo by positron emission tomography in healthy volunteer subjects and patients with Parkinson's disease. *Arch Neurol* 1990; 47:1290–1298.
8. Eidelberg D, Moeller JR, Dhawan V, et al. The metabolic anatomy of Parkinson's disease: Complementary [18F]fluorodeoxyglucose and [18F]fluorodopa positron emission tomographic studies. *Mov Disord* 1990; 5:203–213.
9. Winogrodzka A, Bergmans P, Booij J, et al. [123I]FP-CIT SPECT is a useful method to monitor the rate of dopaminergic degeneration in early-stage Parkinson's disease. *J Neural Transm* 2001; 108:1011–1019.
10. Marek K, Innis R, van Dyck C, et al. [123I]beta-CIT SPECT imaging assessment of the rate of Parkinson's disease progression. *Neurology* 2001; 57:2089–2094.
11. Henry JP, Scherman D. Radioligands of the vesicular monoamine transporter and their use as markers of monoamine storage vesicles. Biochem Pharmacol 1989; 38:2395–2404.
12. Kumar A, Mann S, Sossi V, et al. [11C]DTBZ-PET correlates of levodopa responses in asymmetric Parkinson's disease. *Brain* 2003; 126:2648–2655.
13. Leenders KL, Wolfson LI, Gibbs JM, et al. The effects of L-dopa on regional cerebral blood flow and oxygen metabolism in patients with Parkinson's disease. *Brain* 1985; 108:171–191.
14. Martin WR, Stoessl AJ, Adam MJ, et al. Positron emission tomography in Parkinson's disease: Glucose and DOPA metabolism. *Adv Neurol* 1989; 45:95–98.
15. Perlmutter JS, Raichle ME. Regional blood flow in hemiparkinsonism. *Neurology* 1985; 35:1127–1134.
16. Wolfson L, Leenders KL, Brown L, Jones T. Alterations of regional cerebral blood flow and oxygen metabolism in Parkinson's disease. *Neurology* 1985; 35:1399–1405.
17. Lozza C, Marie R, Baron J. The metabolic substrates of bradykinesia and tremor in uncomplicated Parkinson's disease. *Neuroimage* 2002; 17:688.
18. Mentis MJ, McIntosh AR, Perrine K, et al. Relationships among the metabolic patterns that correlate with mnemonic, visuospatial, and mood symptoms in Parkinson's disease. *Am J Psychiatry* 2002; 159:746–754.
19. Antonini A, Leenders KL, Vontobel P, et al. Complementary PET studies of striatal neuronal function in the differential diagnosis between multiple system atrophy and Parkinson's disease. *Brain* 1997; 120:2187–2195.
20. Fleming TR, DeMets DL. Surrogate end points in clinical trials: are we being misled? *Ann Intern Med* 1996; 125:605–613.
21. Beilby J, Chin CY, Porter I, et al. Improving diagnosis of Huntington's disease by analysis of an intragenic trinucleotide repeat expansion. *Med J Aust* 1994; 161:356–360.
22. Bohnen NI, Albin RL, Koeppe RA, et al. Positron emission tomography of monoaminergic vesicular binding in aging and Parkinson disease. *J Cereb Blood Flow Metab* 2006; 26:1198–1212.
23. Montgomery EB Jr, Koller WC, LaMantia TJ, et al. Early detection of probable idiopathic Parkinson's disease: I. Development of a diagnostic test battery. *Mov Disord* 2000; 15:467–473.
24. Double KL, Rowe DB, Hayes M, et al. Identifying the pattern of olfactory deficits in Parkinson disease using the brief smell identification test. *Arch Neurol* 2003; 60:545–549.
25. Morrish PK, Rakshi JS, Bailey DL, et al. Measuring the rate of progression and estimating the preclinical period of Parkinson's disease with [18F]dopa PET. *J Neurol Neurosurg Psychiatry* 1998; 64:314–319.
26. Ishikawa T, Dhawan V, Kazumata K, et al. Comparative nigrostriatal dopaminergic imaging with iodine-123-beta CIT-FP/SPECT and fluorine-18-FDOPA/PET. *J Nucl Med* 1996; 37:1760–1765.
27. Morrish PK, Sawle GV, Brooks DJ. An [18F]dopa-PET and clinical study of the rate of the progresssion in Parkinson's disease. *Brain* 1996; 119: 585–591.
28. Sossi V, Fuente-Fernandez R, Holden JE, et al. Increase in dopamine turnover occurs early in Parkinson's disease: evidence from a new modeling approach to PET 18 F-fluorodopa data. *J Cereb Blood Flow Metab* 2002; 22:232–239.
29. Snow BJ, Nygaard TG, Takahashi H, Calne DB. Positron emission tomographic studies of dopa-responsive dystonia and early-onset idiopathic parkinsonism. *Ann Neurol* 1993; 34:733–738.
30. Ma Y, Dhawan V, Mentis M, et al. Parametric mapping of [18F]FPCIT binding in early stage Parkinson's disease: A PET study. *Synapse* 2002; 45:125–133.
31. Frey KA, Koeppe RA, Kilbourn MR, et al. Presynaptic monoaminergic vesicles in Parkinson's disease and normal aging. *Ann Neurol* 1996; 40:873–884.
32. Rinne JO, Ruottinen H, Bergman J, et al. Usefulness of a dopamine transporter PET ligand [(18)F]beta-CFT in assessing disability in Parkinson's disease. *J Neurol Neurosurg Psychiatry* 1999; 67:737–741.
33. Antonini A, Moresco RM, Gobbo C, et al. The status of dopamine nerve terminals in Parkinson's disease and essential tremor: a PET study with the tracer [11-C]FE-CIT. *Neurol Sci* 2001; 22:47–48.
34. Burn DJ, Sawle GV, Brooks DJ. Differential diagnosis of Parkinson's disease, multiple system atrophy, and Steele-Richardson-Olszewski syndrome: discriminant analysis of striatal 18F-dopa PET data. *J Neurol Neurosurg Psychiatry* 1994; 57:278–284.
35. Shinotoh H, Thiessen B, Snow BJ, et al. Fluorodopa and raclopride PET analysis of patients with Machado-Joseph disease. *Neurology* 1997; 49:1133–1136.
36. Furtado S, Farrer M, Tsuboi Y, et al. SCA-2 presenting as parkinsonism in an Alberta family: clinical, genetic, and PET findings. *Neurology* 2002; 59:1625–1627.
37. Kim YJ, Ichise M, Ballinger JR, et al. Combination of dopamine transporter and D2 receptor SPECT in the diagnostic evaluation of PD, MSA, and PSP. *Mov Disord* 2002; 17:303–312.
38. Ghaemi M, Hilker R, Rudolf J, et al. Differentiating multiple system atrophy from Parkinson's disease: Contribution of striatal and midbrain MRI volumetry and multi-tracer PET imaging. *J Neurol Neurosurg Psychiatry* 2002; 73:517–523.
39. Booij J, Speelman JD, Horstink MW, Wolters EC. The clinical benefit of imaging striatal dopamine transporters with [123I]FP-CIT SPET in differentiating patients with presynaptic parkinsonism from those with other forms of parkinsonism. *Eur J Nucl Med* 2001; 28:266–272.
40. Scherfler C, Seppi K, Donnemiller E, et al. Voxel-wise analysis of [123I]beta-CIT SPECT differentiates the Parkinson variant of multiple system atrophy from idiopathic Parkinson's disease. *Brain* 2005; 128:1605–1612.
41. Jennings DL, Seibyl JP, Oakes D, et al. (123I) beta-CIT and single-photon emission computed tomographic imaging vs clinical evaluation in parkinsonian syndrome: Unmasking an early diagnosis. *Arch Neurol* 2004; 61:1224–1229.
42. Eerola J, Tienari PJ, Kaakkola S, et al. How useful is [123I]beta-CIT SPECT in clinical practice? *J Neurol Neurosurg Psychiatry* 2005; 76:1211–1216.
43. Stoffers D, Booij J, Bosscher L, et al. Early-stage [123I]beta-CIT SPECT and long-term clinical follow-up in patients with an initial diagnosis of Parkinson's disease. *Eur J Nucl Med Mol Imaging* 2005; 32:689–695.
44. Antonini A, Kazumata K, Feigin A, et al. Differential diagnosis of parkinsonism with [18F]fluorodeoxyglucose and PET. *Mov Disord* 1998; 13:268–274.
45. Eidelberg D, Moeller JR, Dhawan V, et al. The metabolic topography of Parkinsonism. *J Cereb Blood Flow Metab* 1994; 14:783–801.
46. Burn DJ, Brooks DJ. Nigral dysfunction in drug-induced parkinsonism: An 18F-dopa PET study. *Neurology* 1993; 43:552–556.
47. Fahn S, Oakes D, Shoulson I, et al. Levodopa and the progression of Parkinson's disease. *N Engl J Med* 2004; 351:2498–2508.
48. Whone AL, Watts RL, Stoessl AJ, et al. Slower progression of Parkinson's disease with ropinirole versus levodopa: The REAL-PET study. *Ann Neurol* 2003; 54:93–101.
49. Racette BA, Good L, Antenor JA, et al. [18F]FDOPA PET as an endophenotype for Parkinson's Disease linkage studies. *Am J Med Genet B Neuropsychiatr Genet* 2006; 141:245–249.

50. Guttman M, Yong VW, Kim SU, et al. Asymptomatic striatal dopamine depletion: PET scans in unilateral MPTP monkeys. *Synapse* 1988; 2:469–473.

51. Tabbal SD, Mink JW, Antenor JV, et al. MPTP-induced acute transient dystonia in monkeys associated with low striatal dopamine. *Neuroscience* 2006. 141:1281–1287.

52. Piccini P, Morrish PK, Turjanski N, et al. Dopaminergic function in familial Parkinson's disease: a clinical and 18F-dopa positron emission tomography study. *Ann Neurol* 1997; 41:222–229.

53. Burn DJ, Mark MH, Playford ED, et Parkinson's disease in twins studied with 18F-dopa and positron emission tomography. *Neurology* 1992; 42:1894–1900.

54. Holthoff VA, Vieregge P, Kessler J, et al. Discordant twins with Parkinson's disease: Positron emission tomography and early signs of impaired cognitive circuits. *Ann Neurol* 1994; 36:176–182.

55. Laihinen A, Ruottinen H, Rinne JO, et al. Risk for Parkinson's disease: twin studies for the detection of asymptomatic subjects using [18F]6-fluorodopa PET. *J Neurol* 2000; 247(Suppl 2):II110–II113.

56. Khan NL, Valente EM, Bentivoglio AR, et al. Clinical and subclinical dopaminergic dysfunction in PARK6-linked parkinsonism: an 18F-dopa PET study. *Ann Neurol* 2002; 52:849–853.

57. Fuente-Fernandez R, Lim AS, et al. Age and severity of nigrostriatal damage at onset of Parkinson's disease. *Synapse* 2003; 47:152–158.

58. Ribeiro MJ, Vidailhet M, Loc'h C, et al. Dopaminergic function and dopamine transporter binding assessed with positron emission tomography in Parkinson disease. *Arch Neurol* 2002; 59:580–586.

59. Kazumata K, Dhawan V, Chaly T, et al. Dopamine transporter imaging with fluorine-18-FPCIT and PET. *J Nucl Med* 1988; 39:1521–1530.

60. Huang WS, Ma KH, Chou YH, et al. 99mTc-TRODAT-1 SPECT in healthy and 6-OHDA lesioned parkinsonian monkeys: Comparison with 18F-FDOPA PET. *Nucl Med Commun* 2003; 24:77–83.

61. Eberling JL, Pivirotto P, Bringas J, Bankiewicz KS. Tremor is associated with PET measures of nigrostriatal dopamine function in MPTP-lesioned monkeys. *Exp Neurol* 2000; 165:342–346.

62. Yee RE, Huang SC, Stout DB, et al. Nigrostriatal reduction of aromatic L-amino acid decarboxylase activity in MPTP-treated squirrel monkeys: In vivo and in vitro investigations. *J Neurochem* 2000; 74:1147–1157.

63. Broussolle E, Dentresangle C, Landais P, et al. The relation of putamen and caudate nucleus 18F-dopa uptake to motor and cognitive performances in Parkinson's disease. *J Neurol Sci* 1999; 166:141–151.

64. Biglan KM, Holloway RG. Surrogate endpoints in Parkinson's disease research. *Curr Neurol Neurosci Rep* 2003; 3:314–320.

65. Ravina B, Eidelberg D, Ahlskog JE, et al. The role of radiotracer imaging in Parkinson disease. *Neurology* 2005; 64:208–215.

66. Prentice RL. Surrogate endpoints in clinical trials: Definitions and operational criteria (abstract). *Stat Med* 2005; 8:431–440.

67. Brooks DJ, Frey KA, Marek KL, et al. Assessment of neuroimaging techniques as biomarkers of the progression of Parkinson's disease. *Exp Neurol* 2003; 184(Suppl 1):S68–S79.

68. Martin WR, Palmer MR, Patlak CS, Calne DB. Nigrostriatal function in humans studies with positron emission tomography. *Ann Neurol* 1989; 26:535–542.

69. Heiss WD, Hilker R. The sensitivity of 18-fluorodopa positron emission tomography and magnetic resonance imaging in Parkinson's disease. *Eur J Neurol* 2004; 11:5–12.

70. Ishikawa T, Dhawan V, Chaly T, et al. Clinical significance of striatal dopa decarboxylase activity in Parkinson's disease. *J Nucl Med* 1996; 37:216–222.

71. Vingerhoets FJG, Snow BJ, Lee CS, et al. Longitudinal fluorodopa positron emission tomographic studies of the evolution of idiopathic parkinsonism. *Ann Neurol* 1994; 36:759–764.

72. Au WL, Adams JR, Troiano AR, Stoessl AJ. Parkinson's disease: In vivo assessment of disease progression using positron emission tomography. *Brain Res Mol Brain Res* 2005; 134:24–33.

73. Hilker R, Schweitzer K, Coburger S, et al. Nonlinear progression of Parkinson disease as determined by serial positron emission tomographic imaging of striatal fluorodopa F 18 activity. *Arch Neurol* 2005; 62:378–382.

74. Freed CR, Greene PE, Breeze RE, et al. Transplantation of embryonic dopamine neurons for severe Parkinson's disease. *N Engl J Med* 2001; 344:710–718.

75. Lang AE, Gill S, Patel NK, et al. Randomized controlled trial of intraputamenal glial cell line–derived neurotrophic factor infusion in Parkinson disease. *Ann Neurol* 2006; 59:459–466.

76. Yee RE, Irwin I, Milonas C, et al. Novel observations with FDOPA-PET imaging after early nigrostriatal damage. *Mov Disord* 2001; 16:838–848.

77. Gundersen HJ, Jensen EB. The efficiency of systematic sampling in stereology and its prediction. *J Microsc* 1987; 147(Pt 3):229–263.

78. Kilbourn M, Lee L, Vander BT, et al. Binding of alpha-dihydrotetrabenazine to the vesicular monoamine transporter is stereospecific. *Eur J Pharmacol* 1995; 278:249–252.

79. Vander Borght TM, Sima AA, Kilbourn MR, et al. [3H]methoxytetrabenazine: A high specific activity ligand for estimating monoaminergic neuronal integrity. *Neuroscience* 1995; 68:955–962.

80. Wilson JM, Kish SJ. The vesicular monoamine transporter, in contrast to the dopamine transporter, is not altered by chronic cocaine self-administration in the rat. *J Neurosci* 1996; 16:3507–3510.

81. Kilbourn MR, Sherman PS, Kuszpit K. In vivo measures of dopaminergic radioligands in the rat brain: Equilibrium infusion studies. *Synapse* 2002; 43:188–194.

82. Doty RL, Bromley SM, Stern MB. Olfactory testing as an aid in the diagnosis of Parkinson's disease: Development of optimal discrimination criteria. *Neurodegeneration* 1995; 4:93–97.

83. Sossi V, Holden JE, Chan G, et al. Analysis of four dopaminergic tracers kinetics using two different tissue input function methods. *J Cereb Blood Flow Metab* 2000; 20:653–660.

84. Frey KA, Koeppe RA, Kilbourn MR. Imaging the vesicular monoamine transporter. *Adv Neurol* 2001; 86:237–247.

85. Guttman M, Stewart D, Hussey D, et al. Influence of L-dopa and pramipexole on striatal dopamine transporter in early PD. *Neurology* 2001; 56:1559–1564.

86. Perlmutter JS, Martin WRW (2004) MRI and PET Investigations of Parkinson disease. In: Pahwa RKW (ed). *Therapy of Parkinson Disease*. New York: Marcel Dekker, 2004:53–70.

26 Single Photon Emission Computed Tomography

Andrew B. Newberg
Paul D. Acton

Parkinson's disease (PD) (also known as paralysis agitans)—a neurodegenerative disorder that affects over a million people in North America—leads to clinical symptoms of motor deficit such as tremor, rigidity, hypokinesia, and bradykinesia (1). It is one of a family of such diseases associated with the loss of central nervous system neurons, such as progressive supranuclear palsy (PSP) and multiple system atrophy (MSA). Discrimination between these diseases is important early in the course since each has a different prognosis and requires a distinct treatment regimen (2).

Postmortem studies indicate that these parkinsonian disorders exhibit dramatic losses of various neurons, particularly the dopaminergic neurotransmitter system in the nigrostriatum (3, 4). The predominant cause of parkinsonism is PD, accounting for up to 85% of all reported cases. Pathologic findings show that most of the neuronal loss in early in PD takes place in the ventro-lateral tier of the substantia nigra, which projects to the posterior putamen (5). This leaves the ventral putamen and caudate relatively spared in the early stages. In addition, PD is characterized by the formation of neuronal Lewy bodies.

Multiple system atrophy, also called Shy-Drager syndrome, can include syndromes of olivopontocerebellar atrophy, striatonigral degeneration, pallidopyramidal

degeneration, and pure autonomic failure. Although rare, this entity is believed to account for 5% to 11% of patients diagnosed with PD (6, 7). MSA accounts for up to 10% of patients presenting with parkinsonian symptoms. It gives rise to much more widespread disruptions in the brain—with symptoms associated with extrapyramidal, pyramidal, autonomic, and cerebellar involvement—and is characterized by degeneration and gliosis in the brainstem, spinal cord, striatum, globus pallidus, and cerebellum (8, 9). Although most MSA patients do not respond to dopaminergic therapy, the disease exhibits neurodegeneration in the nigrostriatum similar to that observed in PD. Progressive supranuclear palsy causes a a supranuclear gaze palsy, dystonia, axial rigidity, and eventually dementia. The neuronal loss in PSP is comparable to that in PD, but without the formation of Lewy bodies. Degeneration occurs primarily in the brainstem and striatum, with the formation of neurofibrillary tangles (10).

Other important confounds in the differential diagnosis of PD include dopa-responsive dystonia and essential tremor. Dopa-responsive dystonia is an inherited disorder that presents with clinical symptoms very similar to those of early-onset PD (11). A fluorodeoxyglucose (FDG) positron emission tomography (PET) study of patients with dopa-responsive dystonia showed increases in the dorsal midbrain, cerebellum, and supplementary motor area as well as reductions in the motor and lateral premotor cortex and the basal ganglia (12). However, SPECT and PET studies have shown either normal or only slight reductions in dopaminergic function, which is in marked contrast to PD (13–16). Essential tremor presents with clinical symptoms of postural tremor, usually involving the hands or forearms. Similarities between the clinical symptoms of PD and essential tremor can lead to misdiagnosis, although SPECT and PET studies show clearly that there is no loss of dopaminergic neurons in patients with essential tremor (17–19).

Until recently, SPECT and PET imaging in neurodegenerative disorders primarily focused on differentiating patients from healthy control subjects. Indeed, it may be that the differential diagnosis of neurodegenerative diseases will provide the first routine clinical application for studies of neuroreceptor and transporter binding. However, imaging studies are becoming increasingly important in elucidating the pathogenesis of neurodegenerative disease and deciphering any genetic contribution to these disorders. In addition, they are being utilized in longitudinal studies to assess the efficacy of surgical and neuroprotective therapies.

This chapter discusses the contributions of single photon emission computed tomography (SPECT) and PET imaging in the diagnosis, understanding, and management of parkinsonian disorders, with particular emphasis on SPECT. Although PET is generally regarded as having higher spatial resolution, the use SPECT is beginning to produce important advances in the field. This is partially owing to the development of excellent SPECT tracers but also because of the lower cost and wider availability of SPECT tracers versus those used in PET.

IMAGING IN THE DIFFERENTIAL DIAGNOSIS OF PARKINSONIAN DISORDERS

The differential diagnosis of the various parkinsonian disorders based on clinical symptoms alone is difficult, especially early in their course (20, 21). Tremor is a classic feature of PD, although this can also be found in patients with PSP and MSA. Similarly, a criterion for diagnosing PD is a good, sustained response to levodopa (L-dopa) therapy, although this is also found in some patients with MSA and dopa-responsive dystonia. Postmortem studies show that the clinical diagnosis of PD is incorrect in almost half the cases diagnosed by general neurologists. The error rate is still thought to exceed 25% when the diagnosis is made by a subspecialist in movement disorders. These observations have contributed to the motivation for developing functional neuroimaging techniques that can help to tell these disorders apart.

Structural changes induced by parkinsonian diseases are generally small and often evident only when the disease is in its advanced stages. Consequently, the diagnostic accuracy of anatomic imaging modalities (e.g., magnetic resonance imaging, or MRI) in neurodegenerative disorders is poor (22). In general, SPECT and PET imaging have the potential to provide more physiologic information that might help to diagnose patients before anatomic changes occur. Functional imaging of neurodegenerative disease with SPECT and PET has followed 2 main paths; studies of blood flow and cerebral metabolism to detect abnormal tissue function and imaging of the dopaminergic neurotransmitter system to study the loss of dopamine neurons.

PET studies of cerebral glucose metabolism have used the glucose analog fluorodeoxyglucose (^{18}F FDG), whereas the SPECT tracers ^{99m}Tc hexamethylpropylene amine oxime (^{99m}Tc HMPAO) and ^{99m}Tc ethylcysteinate dimer (^{99m}Tc ECD) are markers of cerebral perfusion. Striatal glucose metabolism and perfusion are normal in PD (23–27), although some studies have demonstrated an asymmetry of striatal metabolism (23). Many studies have shown global cortical hypometabolism or hypoperfusion or a loss of posterior parietal metabolism with a pattern similar to that observed in Alzheimer's disease (29–32). Other investigators have used the differences in regional metabolism or cerebral blood flow to discriminate between PD and MSA (33, 34) or PSP (35). However, the diagnostic accuracy of cerebral blood flow and glucose metabolism in differentiating neurodegenerative disorders is relatively poor in comparison with direct imaging of the dopaminergic nigrostriatal pathway. Thus, general brain function is not nearly as affected by the disease process as are specific neurotransmitter systems. This may be particularly true in PD patients with dementia. Studies of blood flow and glucose metabolism in patients with pure Lewy body disease with no features of Alzheimer's disease have consistently shown biparietal, bitemporal hypometabolism—a pattern that was once thought to represent the signature of Alzheimer's.

A variety of tracers exist for the study of the dopaminergic neurotransmitter system using both SPECT and PET (Table 26-1). Early PET studies of the nigrostriatal pathway used the uptake of 6-[^{18}F]fluoro-L-3, 4-dihydroxyphenylalanine (^{18}F-dopa) as a measure of the integrity of dopamine neurons (36, 37). ^{18}F-dopa measures changes in striatal dopa decarboxylase activity, which is dependent on the availability of striatal dopaminergic nerve terminals and is proportional to the number of dopamine neurons in the substantia nigra (38).

Direct measurements of dopamine transporter binding sites are possible with ^{11}C cocaine (39), or the cocaine analogs 2β-carbomethoxy-3β-[4-iodophenyl] tropane (β-CIT) and N-ω-fluoropropyl-2β-carbomethoxy-3β-[4-iodophenyl] tropane (FP-CIT), labeled with either ^{18}F or ^{11}C for PET or ^{123}I for SPECT (40, 41). Other dopamine transporter ligands include N-[3-iodopropen-2-yl]-2β-carbomethoxy-3β-[4-chlorophenyl] tropane (^{123}I IPT)

TABLE 26-1

Selected SPECT and PET Tracers for Imaging the Dopaminergic Neurotransmitter System

BINDING SITE	TRACER	PET OR SPECT	REFERENCES
Dopamine synthesis	^{18}F-dopa	PET	36, 37
Dopamine transporters	^{11}C cocaine	PET	39
	[^{11}C] [^{18}F] [^{123}I]β-CIT	Both	40, 41
	[^{11}C] [^{18}F] [^{123}I]FP-CIT	Both	40, 41
	^{123}I IPT	SPECT	42
	^{123}I altropane	SPECT	43
	^{11}C methylphenidate	PET	44
	^{99m}Tc TRODAT-1	SPECT	45, 46
Dopamine	^{123}I IBZM	SPECT	48, 49
D2 receptors	^{123}I epidepride	SPECT	50, 51
	^{11}C raclopride	PET	52
	[^{11}C] [^{18}F]N-methylspiroperidol	PET	53, 54

(42), its 4-fluorophenyl analog ^{123}I altropane (43), 2β-carbomethoxy-3β-[4-fluorophenyl] tropane (^{11}C CFT) (34), and ^{11}C *d-threo*-methylphenidate (44).

Of particular importance is the development of the first successful ^{99m}Tc-labeled dopamine transporter ligand ^{99m}Tc [2-[[2-[[[3-(4-chlorophenyl)-8-methyl-8-azabicyclo[3.2.1] oct-2-yl]-methyl](2-mercaptoethyl) amino]-ethyl] amino] ethane-thiolato(3-)-N2,N2',S2,S2'] oxo-[1R-(exo-exo)] (^{99m}Tc TRODAT-1) (45, 46). Since ^{99m}Tc is much more widely available and less expensive than ^{123}I, this new tracer may move imaging of the dopaminergic system from a research environment into routine clinical practice, particularly with simplified imaging protocols (47).

There are several tracers for imaging postsynaptic dopamine D2 receptors using radioactively labeled dopamine receptor antagonists. The most widely used for SPECT include S-(-)-3-iodo-2-hydroxy-6-methoxy-N-[(1-ethyl-2-pyrrolidinyl) methyl] benzamide (^{123}I IBZM) (48, 49), S-5-iodo-7-N-[(1-ethyl-2-pyrrolidinyl) methyl] carboxamido-2, 3-dihydrobenzofuran (^{123}I IBF) (14), S-N-[(1-ethyl-2-pyrrolidinyl) methyl]-5-iodo-2, 3-dimethoxybenzamide (^{123}I epidepride) (50, 51); for PET, they include S-(-)-3, 5-dichloro-N-[(1-ethyl-2-pyrrolidinyl)] methyl-2-hydroxy-6-methoxybenzamide (^{11}C raclopride) (52) and ^{11}C or ^{18}F N-methylspiroperidol (53, 54).

SPECT and PET used in studies of radiotracer binding to postsynaptic dopamine receptors and presynaptic dopamine transporters and neurons have proved to be powerful techniques for quantifying the loss of dopaminergic neurons in normal aging, PD, and other neurodegenerative disorders (Table 26-2). Studies of neuronal degeneration associated with the effects of normal aging indicate that, although the concentrations of dopamine transporters decrease as a natural consequence of aging,

these changes are small compared with the effects of disease (Figure 26-1) (55). SPECT and PET studies indicate a consistent pattern of dopaminergic neuronal loss in PD, usually with a more pronounced decrease in the putamen than in the caudate (Figures 26-2 and 26-3). In addition, there is often a marked asymmetry of uptake in the striatum, particularly in the early stages of the disease. This asymmetry usually has a good correlation with symptom severity (56) and illness duration (57). Most importantly, imaging studies may be sensitive enough to detect very early PD (58–60), perhaps even before clinical symptoms become apparent.

Characteristically, PD begins with unilateral symptoms of motor deficit, which gradually progress to become bilateral. Studies of patients with early hemi-PD, in which they have symptoms only on one side for an extended period, have produced SPECT and PET findings demonstrating bilateral decreases in tracer binding, with a greater reduction in the side contralateral to the clinical signs (61–63). The ability of SPECT and PET to detect presymptomatic PD may have important implications for the screening of familial PD and also for the evaluation of neuroprotective therapies.

Although most of the SPECT and PET imaging studies have shown highly significant differences between groups of Parkinson's patients and age-matched normal controls, the differential diagnosis of an individual subject is more problematic. Patients with severe PD are easily separated from healthy controls even from a simple visual inspection of striatal images, which can be quantified using some form of discriminant analysis (64, 65); this has a sensitivity and specificity from 90% to 100% in the proper clinical setting (66, 67). However, disease in patients presenting much earlier in the course is more difficult to detect, since there can be a substantial overlap

TABLE 26-2

Summary of SPECT and PET Measurements of Neurodegenerative and Parkinsonian Disorders

	INTEGRITY OF THE DOPAMINERGIC NIGROSTRIATAL PATHWAY DETERMINED BY PET OR SPECT			
SYNDROMES	DOPAMINE TRANSPORTERS IN CAUDATE	DOPAMINE TRANSPORTERS IN PUTAMEN	POSTSYNAPTIC DOPAMINE RECEPTORS	BLOOD FLOW AND METABOLISM
Parkinson's disease	Normal or slight loss	Loss	Normal or upregulated	General reduction; striatum normal
Multiple system atrophy	Normal or slight loss	Loss	Loss	Reduced in contralateral putamen
Progressive supranuclear palsy	Loss	Loss	Normal or slight loss	Reduced in cortex and striatum
Dopa-responsive dystonia	Normal	Normal	Increase	Increased in midbrain, cerebellum, and supplementary motor area; Reduced in motor, premotor, and basal ganglia
MPTP exposure/	Loss	Loss	Loss in caudate?	Increased in the globus pallidus; Reduced in the caudate, putamen, thalamus, and primary motor cortex?
Essential tremor	Normal	Normal	?	Increased in the medulla and thalamus?

The question mark (?) Implies that there are either controversial or insufficient data to demonstrate a clear pattern but that these are the changes that have been reported.

with an age-matched control group (60, 63, 68) and consequently a loss of diagnostic accuracy. The situation may be further complicated if an early differential diagnosis between several different neurodegenerative disorders is required. Many of the symptoms associated with parkinsonian disorders are nonspecific, which is why the accurate clinical diagnosis of these diseases is difficult. Indeed, some histopathologic studies have shown that as many as 25% of all patients who were diagnosed with PD before death had been misdiagnosed (69, 70). Studies measuring dopamine transporter activity have had more difficulty in separating PD from MSA or PSP (64, 71).

There have been only limited studies of the dopaminergic system in patients with MSA, with most reports including fewer than 15 subjects in any patient category (Figure 26-4). Several SPECT studies utilizing ^{123}I β-CIT demonstrated significantly decreased binding in MSA patients compared with controls but did not help in differentiating MSA from PSP (72–74). Other studies have revealed controversial findings regarding dopamine transporter activity in the striatum (75–77). Part of the reason for the discrepancies in these studies is the method for diagnosing them, the disease severity of the patients studied, and the duration of illness. However, the results have been encouraging, including one

F-dopa PET study demonstrating that according to the caudate-putamen index (calculated by the difference in the uptakes in the caudate and putamen divided by the caudate uptake), MSA patients have values lower than those of patients with PD (78). PET studies of patients with MSA compared with controls report decreased F-dopa uptake in the putamen and caudate. Another study demonstrated that the severity of extrapyramidal signs correlated with the decline of F-dopa uptake within the striatum (79). However, another study demonstrated decreased F-dopa uptake in both MSA and PD patients (80).

In PSP patients, Leenders and colleagues (91) found decreased dopamine formation and storage in the striatum. This decrease correlated with the degree of reduced frontal blood flow. A SPECT study with ^{123}I β-CIT demonstrated decreased binding in 8 PSP patients compared with controls but did not differentiate these individuals from patients with other parkinsonian syndromes (4). Other studies with ^{123}I β-CIT SPECT have yielded similar results but still included very small numbers (3). A study using ^{123}I -IPT SPECT in imaging 9 patients with PSP showed much greater reductions in the caudate and putamen compared with PD (82). In addition, PD patients showed a significantly higher posterior putamen/caudate ratio of reduced ^{123}I-IPT uptake than the anterior putamen/caudate ratio.

Essential tremor (ET) is another possible diagnostic consideration in evaluating a patient for PD. A recent TRODAT SPECT study of 27 patients with idiopathic PD, 12 patients with ET, and 10 controls demonstrated sensitivity and specificity of differentiating early PD from ET at 96.4% and 91.7%, respectively (83). In particular, PD patients had much lower binding than those with ET, which may be easier to distinguish from PD, since the former does not typically involve the dopaminergic pathways.

Imaging studies with dopamine transporter tracers suggest that these patient groups can be differentiated, even if it is more difficult to distinguish diseases within an individual patient. Thus, based on current methods of analysis, it appears that the detection of early PD, or the differential diagnosis between various neurodegenerative disorders, may not be possible in individual cases based on imaging of a single neurotransmitter system (84). However, developments in the automated, pixel-based analysis of PD may improve the sensitivity of imaging techniques (85).

The relative merits of anatomic and functional imaging have been combined in some studies, which utilize either several different radiotracers or data from both MRI and SPECT or PET. Regional glucose metabolism has been studied in parkinsonian disorders with ^{18}F FDG and PET; the resulting data were combined with striatal ^{18}F fluorodopa uptake measurements to provide an improved diagnostic indicator and a better understanding of the underlying disease processes (86, 87). However, it should be noted that in these patient groups, the improvement was small over the good predictive capabilities of ^{18}F fluorodopa by itself. Another study investigated whether combining perfusion and dopamine transporter (DAT) imaging could help discriminate different parkinsonian disorders (88). One hundred twenty-nine patients were studied retrospectively and characteristic patterns for perfusion and DAT were found for all pathologies. For example, in the Parkinson-plus group, MSA, PSP, and LBD could be discriminated in 100% of the cases. When PD was included, discrimination accuracy was 82.4%. As a single technique, 2β-carbomethoxy-3beta-(4-iodophenyl) nortropane imaging was able to discriminate between ET and neurodegenerative forms with an accuracy of 93.0%; the inclusion of perfusion information augmented this slightly to 97%. The results of this study suggest that dual-tracer DAT and perfusion SPECT in combination with discrimination analysis can provide accurate differentiation between the most common parkinsonian disorders.

Some studies utilized the complementary information coming from structural MRI and functional ^{18}F FDG PET in distinguishing between patients with MSA and control subjects (89, 90), where both focal MRI hypointensities and reduced glucose metabolism occurred on the side contralateral to clinical symptoms. Other studies combined data from MRI and postsynaptic dopamine receptor concentrations using ^{123}I IBZM and SPECT, giving useful information on the involvement of multiple brain regions in PSP (91) and MSA (92).

However, the greatest discrimination between various neurodegenerative disorders may be found using SPECT or PET imaging of both pre- and postsynaptic dopamine binding sites. A study of ^{123}I β-CIT and ^{123}I IBZM binding in patients with early PD showed marked unilateral reductions in dopamine transporters measured by ^{123}I β-CIT concomitant with elevated dopamine D2 receptor binding of ^{123}I IBZM (93). SPECT studies investigating pre- and postsynaptic dopamine binding sites in the differential diagnosis of PD, MSA, and PSP have shown promising results, with a reduction in dopamine transporter availability in all diseases and some discrimination between disorders in the pattern of dopamine D2 receptor concentrations (94) (Figure 26-5).

SPECT imaging of both pre- and postsynaptic dopamine binding sites simultaneously has now been performed in nonhuman primates, using ^{99m}Tc TRODAT-1 and ^{123}I IBZM and separating the 2 radiotracers based on their different photon energy of the isotopes (95). The possibility of simultaneously imaging both dopamine transporters and D2 receptors in neurodegenerative disorders is an exciting prospect, providing a unique probe in the investigation and diagnosis of these diseases. One SPECT study utilized ^{123}I β-CIT to measure the dopamine transporters and ^{123}I IBF to measure the D2 postsynaptic receptors in 18 patients with PD (12 dopa-naive and 6 on levodopa and/or dopamine agonists), 7 with MSA of the striatonigral degeneration type, 6 with PSP, and 29 normal controls (96). DAT binding in the posterior putamen was markedly reduced in all patients. However, D2 binding in the posterior putamen was significantly increased in dopa-untreated PD, being greater than the normal range in 33% of the patients. D2 binding was significantly reduced in MSA patients. None of the patients with PD showed reduced D2 binding below the normal range in the posterior putamen. DAT binding did not discriminate between the patient groups. Overall, the findings suggested that SPECT of the DAT may be useful in differentiating parkinsonism from controls and SPECT of postsynaptic receptor binding may be useful in further differentiating MSA from PD and possibly PSP.

LONGITUDINAL IMAGING STUDIES IN PARKINSONIAN DISORDERS

The majority of SPECT and PET imaging studies in parkinsonian disorders have concentrated on differentiating between the various diseases. However, follow-up longitudinal studies of patient groups have been undertaken, providing important insights into the rate of progression of disease and also enabling estimates of the duration of the preclinical phase. Both SPECT and PET imaging provide reproducible results that are also sensitive to the measurement changes in dopaminergic function associated with the progression of neurodegenerative disease.

Longitudinal SPECT and PET studies have been performed on patients with PD (97–99) and MPTP-induced parkinsonian disorder (100). Most longitudinal studies have shown that the rate of deterioration of dopaminergic neurons is much greater in PD than that associated with the effects of normal aging. Recent SPECT studies have demonstrated relatively consistent reductions in dopamine transporter binding between 7% and 11% per year (55, 101), although these data are still preliminary. Extrapolating back to the time of onset of clinical symptoms, the magnitude of neuronal loss required before external clinical signs become apparent has been estimated to be approximately 75% of normal in the putamen and 91% of normal in the caudate (29). This agrees to some extent with studies of the asymptomatic side in patients with hemi-PD (92). Extrapolating beyond the threshold for clinical symptom onset, the same study estimated that the mean preclinical period (the time between disease onset and symptom onset) was less than 7 years (29). These results have important implications for models of disease pathogenesis and progression.

IMAGING IN THE PATHOGENESIS OF PARKINSON'S DISEASE

Many neurotoxins and neurologic traumas which lead to damage of the basal ganglia or substantia nigra produce parkinsonism. One well-known toxin, 1-methyl-4-phenyl-1, 2, 3, 6-tetrahydropyridine (MPTP), targets with high specificity neurons involved in PD and has been very useful for developing animal models of the disease. The mechanism of MPTP neurotoxicity may shed some light on the pathogenesis of PD and other neurodegenerative disorders (103). MPTP is highly lipophilic and crosses the blood-brain barrier, where it is oxidized to MPP+. Although MPTP itself does not appear to be toxic, the oxidized product MPP+ is taken up by the dopamine transporter protein, where it is actively transported into the dopaminergic nerve terminals (104). Once inside the presynaptic neuron, MPP+ is a potent toxin that causes neuronal cell death. A PET study of cerebral blood flow and metabolism in macaques showed increased activity in the globus pallidus but decreased activity in the caudate, putamen, thalamus, and primary motor cortex (105).

This mechanism for MPTP neurotoxicity has led to the suggestion that parkinsonian disorders may be caused by other toxins, whether endogenous or acquired from the environment, that ultimately cause cell death of dopaminergic neurons (106). Further, there may be a predisposition to producing endogenous toxins, which introduces a genetic aspect to PD. A prime candidate for these neurotoxins are free radicals, which may cause neuronal injury through a number of mechanisms, including excitotoxicity, metabolic dysfunction, and interference with intracellular calcium physiology (107–109).

The central role of dopamine reuptake sites in the transport of the toxin into the neuron has been investigated using SPECT imaging of ^{123}I β-CIT binding in normal controls and patients with PD (101). It is hypothesized that if the transport of endogenous toxins by dopamine transporters into the neuron causes cell death, a patient with a greater initial concentration of functioning transporters should degenerate faster owing to the increased uptake of neurotoxins. Consequently, an initial SPECT scan of the concentration of available dopamine reuptake sites should be a good marker for the rate of progression of the disease, monitored by a follow-up scan some time later. This was found to be the case, where among PD patients the reduction in ^{123}I β-CIT binding in sequential scans was highly correlated with the initial scan ^{123}I β-CIT uptake. This is the first evidence from in vivo imaging that neurotoxin uptake may be implicated in the pathogenesis of PD.

The genetic contribution to the etiology of neurodegenerative parkinsonian disorders is still unclear, although it is now believed that heredity plays some role in PD. Early twin studies did not suggest a genetic contribution (110, 111). However, it now appears that genetic factors may confer some degree of susceptibility for acquiring PD (112–114), particularly in light of PET studies in twins (115, 116) and in families in which clinically asymptomatic relatives of PD patients exhibited signs of striatal degeneration on their scans (117, 118). These studies have shown very effectively the potential for SPECT and PET screening of subjects at risk from familial PD. However, given the range of normal, it may be difficult to know how best to manage at-risk patients who show slightly low dopamine transporter activity on SPECT scans.

IMAGING THE EFFECTS OF DRUG TREATMENT IN PARKINSON'S DISEASE

The management and treatment of PD with dopamine replacement therapies has been very successful. L-dopa and dopamine receptor agonists are highly efficacious in reducing the clinical symptoms associated with PD. However, these medications do not reverse or slow the actual course of the disease. Their effectiveness can decrease over time, and patients can also develop some side effects and the characteristic "on-off" periods (119, 120). Medication-refractory periods of severe bradykinesia and rigidity tend to increase in frequency and severity with time (121) and can alternate with disabling dyskinesias and dystonias. Although a number of promising neuroprotective drugs, currently in development, may delay the onset of these symptoms, about half of all patients begin to suffer from these sequelae in less than 5 years.

It is the deficit of striatal dopamine that induces the motor symptoms in PD, hence several treatment mechanisms operate by increasing the quantity of endogenous dopamine. For example, L-dopa is the amino acid precursor which is decarboxylated in the synthesis of dopamine in the brain. It has been used for many years to treat PD in the form of dopamine replacement therapy. Newer drugs for PD target 2 important enzymes in the metabolism of dopamine: monoamine oxidase-B (MAO-B) and catechol-O-methyltransferase (COMT) (122). The inhibition of MAO-B or COMT enhances the availability of dopamine at postsynaptic receptor sites. MAO-B and COMT inhibitors have been shown to reduce motor fluctuations and enhance levodopa efficacy (2, 123). Other neuroprotective agents have been proposed that scavenge free radicals and reduce or even reverse the effects of neuronal degeneration (124–126).

It is unclear whether these drugs operate solely by enhancing the levels of endogenous dopamine or by a true neuroprotective quality in slowing down or reversing the degeneration of dopamine neurons (127). Clinical studies alone cannot determine whether these drugs exhibit genuine neuroprotective properties or simply increase available dopamine.

A quantitative method for measuring in vivo dopaminergic neurons would provide a vital probe to examine the mode of action and efficacy of various drugs in the treatment of PD. SPECT and PET could be used to determine whether neuroprotective therapies are genuinely slowing the degeneration of dopaminergic neurons or simply altering levels of endogenous neurotransmitter (128). Both SPECT and PET imaging of the dopaminergic system have exquisite sensitivity to detect and measure subtle changes in neuronal integrity and have been used in longitudinal studies to monitor the progression of disease in PD (20, 107) and other parkinsonian disorders (129). For example, comparisons between dopamine D2 receptor availability, measured with ^{123}I IBZM SPECT, and long-term clinical follow-up showed a strong correlation between initial ^{123}I IBZM binding and the response to L-dopa therapy as well as the likelihood of developing non-PD clinical symptoms (130). The ability of SPECT imaging to predict those subjects who will respond to certain therapies is a vital tool in the clinical management of patients with PD and other parkinsonian diseases.

In the Ropinirole in Early Parkinson's Disease versus L-dopa (REAL) PET 2-year double-blind multinational trial, 186 de novo PD patients were randomized to either ropinirole or L-dopa (131). The primary endpoint was relative loss of putamen ^{18}F-dopa uptake. Analysis of the PET scans found that in subjects with both clinical and imaging evidence of PD, loss of putamen uptake was significantly slower over 2 years with ropinirole (–13.4%) than with L-dopa (–20.3%). This matched clinical progression, with the incidence of dyskinesia over 2 years at 27% with L-dopa but only 3% with ropinirole. The CALM-CIT trial involved a subgroup of 82 early-PD patients from the CALM-PD study (132). This cohort was randomized to the dopamine agonist pramipexole or levodopa and had serial [123]I β-CIT SPECT scans performed over a 4-year period. Patients treated initially with pramipexole showed a significantly slower decline of striatal [123]I β-CIT uptake compared with subjects treated initially with levodopa at 2, 3, and 4 years. The results of these 2 trials have become controversial, since the imaging results did not correlate with the clinical results.

IMAGING IN THE SURGICAL TREATMENT OF PARKINSON'S DISEASE

Several neurosurgical procedures have developed over a number of years to treat patients with PD, particularly those who exhibit a poor or declining response to conventional L-dopa drug therapy. Initially, the primary surgical intervention for palliation of tremor was thallidotomy, whereas for the palliation of dyskinesias and "off" periods it was pallidotomy (133). Pallidotomy theoretically reduces the hyperactivity in the internal segment of the globus pallidus caused by excessive input from the subthalamic nuclei (104). This improves motor function in PD, since it is postulated that striatal dopamine deficiency produces an overactive medial globus pallidus. Initial studies indicated promising results in the capability of functional imaging to predict the outcome of pallidotomy (134, 135) and correlated with the improvements in functional ability (136).

An alternative to pallidotomy has been electrical stimulation of the subthalamus through implantable electrodes (137–142). Its advantages include reversibility and a lesser degree of invasiveness. If external pulsing does not produce benefits, the electrodes can be removed with little morbidity, obviating the need to perform the more invasive procedure of implanting an indwelling power source. The frequency and duration of the pulses can be modulated individually to maximize benefit and minimize untoward effects. Although the mechanism of action of subthalamic stimulation is not fully understood, it is believed to be conceptually related to pallidotomy, in that the source of overstimulation to the globus pallidus is removed by electrical pulses. This technique is less invasive than pallidotomy and is also reversible. However, like any neurosurgical procedure, it involves some degree of risk, such as hemorrhage and even cognitive degradation in a few patients (143). Favorable assessments have been based primarily on subjective descriptions of symptom severity tracked with patient diaries and clinical rating scales. As compelling as these descriptions are and as useful as these subjective measures have been in assessing changes within patients, there have not been many objective ways of comparing results between groups of patients treated with different operations and protocols. Initial imaging studies evaluated both general brain function and changes in the dopaminergic system. For example, one study evaluated cerebral blood flow with SPECT in 10 patients who underwent STN therapy (144). The results suggested that long-term STN stimulation leads to improvement in neural activity in the frontal motor/associative areas. Another study utilizing F-dopa PET revealed that STN patients still had the same progression of dopamine loss as those treated with medication, even though the STN patients had substantial improvements in their symptoms (145).

A third surgical methodology involves the transplantation of fetal tissue into the nigrostriatal dopaminergic pathway, either using tissue from aborted human fetuses (146) or from animals (147). The concept behind this technique is that the grafted fetal nigral cells will survive and reinnervate the striatum, replacing the dopaminergic striatal neurons lost in PD. To assess the efficacy of fetal grafts in PD, several studies have used ^{18}F-dopa PET to measure any increases in dopaminergic function following surgery (148–150). Fetal cell transplantation for the treatment of PD and Huntington's disease has been developed over the past 2 decades and is now in the early phase of clinical testing (151). Direct assessment of the graft's survival, integration into the host brain, and impact on neuronal function requires advanced in vivo neuroimaging techniques. Two major double-blind controlled trials on the efficacy of implantation of human fetal cells in PD have been performed. In the first, 40 patients who had severe PD were randomized to receive either an implant of human fetal mesencephalic tissue or to undergo sham surgery and were followed for 1 year with a subsequent extension to 3 years (152). The transplanted patients showed no significant improvement in the primary endpoint, clinical global impression, at 1 year, but there was a significant mean improvement in the mean Unified Parkinson's Disease Rating Scale (UPDRS) motor score. From an imaging perspective, 16 of 19 transplanted patients showed an increase in putamen ^{18}F-dopa uptake (group mean increase of 40%), and increases were similar in the younger and older cohorts. In the second NIH trial, 34 patients were randomized to receive bilateral implants of fetal mesencephalic tissue or had sham surgery (153). Mean putamen:occipital ^{18}F-dopa uptake ratios were unchanged in the control patients but showed 20% and

30% increases in patients receiving tissue from 1 and 4 fetuses, respectively. Although ^{18}F-dopa PET showed evidence of graft function, neither of these controlled trials demonstrated clinical efficacy. Thus, future studies will be necessary to determine whether fetal transplantation will be useful in more specific patient populations.

Clinical measures of the outcome of these surgical techniques indicated that pallidotomy may produce the best results, but some investigators conclude that "the role of surgery in managing other levodopa-resistant problems is controversial, and to date there are no convincing reports demonstrating a benefit" (lii). The potential morbidity as well as the costs of these operations require systematic and longitudinal assessments of their efficacy, a role for which SPECT and PET imaging of the dopaminergic system is uniquely suited (154).

IMAGING OF NONDOPAMINERGIC NEURONS IN PARKINSON'S DISEASE

Although the majority of studies investigating neuronal changes caused by parkinsonian diseases have focused on the dopaminergic system, other neurotransmitters may also be involved or affected by the disease process. Another neurotransmitter believed to be intimately linked to the pathogenesis of PD is glutamate (NMDA). NMDA is an excitatory amino acid and has been implicated as the neurotransmitter causing excitotoxicity in the pathophysiology of PD (155–157). NMDA induces excitotoxicity in the presence of impaired cellular energy metabolism, which may be just the environment produced in dopaminergic neurons in the substantia nigra pars compacta by PD. Dopamine deficiency in PD causes disinhibition and overactivity of the subthalamic nuclei, which project to the external and internal segments of the globus pallidus and the substantia nigra. Neurons from the subthalamus are excitatory, using NMDA as a neurotransmitter, and innervate dopaminergic neurons in the substantia nigra pars compacta containing NMDA receptors. Hence, disinhibition of the neurons of the subthalamic nuclei caused by PD may induce NMDA excitotoxic damage in target structures, such as the substantia nigra pars compacta. This scenario of dopamine loss augmenting subthalamic activity, which, in turn, causes further NMDA-induced damage to dopamine neurons creates the ideal environment for an increasing cycle of neuronal cell death.

The role of NMDA and a possible dysfunction of the NMDA receptor in PD makes it an important target for new neuroprotective treatments. In particular, the modulation of NMDA receptor-mediated neurotransmission may provide an exciting alternative to dopaminergic drug therapies (155, 156). However, the role of NMDA receptors in PD requires investigation with imaging techniques to measure any changes in NMDA function as a result of disease and to study NMDA excitotoxicity as a mechanism in the initial onset of PD.

The development of specific agents for imaging the NMDA receptor is still in its infancy, with just a small number of potential ligands under development for SPECT and PET. [11]C ketamine exhibited relatively poor brain uptake in animal studies, probably due to its rapid metabolism (158). Preliminary results for a recently developed tracer [^{18}F]1-amino-3-fluoromethyl-5-methyl-adamantane (^{18}F AFA) are much more promising, with high brain uptake in mice and a cerebral distribution consistent with the known concentrations of NMDA receptors (159).

Another neurotransmitter, gamma-aminobutyric acid (GABA), is a major component of the neural pathways involved in motor function. GABA is an inhibitory neurotransmitter and is involved in the transmission of signals from the striatum to the globus pallidus and into the subthalamic nuclei. It also provides control over the thalamic nuclei and brainstem from the internal globus pallidus and substantia nigra reticulata. Because these structures use the inhibitory neurotransmitter GABA, the increased glutamatergic-driven input resulting from PD causes excessive GABAergic inhibition, which leads to an effective shutdown of the thalamic and brainstem nuclei (lii). This inhibition leads to suppression of the motor cortex and brainstem locomotor areas, which may cause many of the motor deficits inherent in PD.

Despite the widespread and vital role of the GABAergic system in PD, very few imaging studies of the GABA system have been performed. However, a Japanese study, using the SPECT ligand ^{123}I iomazenil, demonstrated a pronounced impairment of cortical GABAergic function in PD, with the reduction in ^{123}I iomazenil binding directly correlated with motor disability (160, 161).

Another neurotransmitter that may be affected in PD is serotonin, especially because of its reciprocal interaction with dopaminergic neurons. Studies have suggested that the serotonergic system appears to be involved in PD. One postmortem study demonstrated a reduction of 40% to 50% in serotonergic uptake sites in PD (162, 163). The relationship between serotonin and PD has been observed with regard to genetic studies linking the serotonin transporter gene–linked polymorphic region to depression in PD (164). Early imaging studies of the serotonin transporter in PD suggest that there is a decrease compared with controls. One PET study utilizing the [^{11}C](+)McN5652 compound in 13 PD patients demonstrated significantly decreased serotonin transporter binding in the striatum, which appeared similar to the loss of dopamine transporters (165). Several SPECT studies utilizing [123]I β-CIT in a limited number of PD patients demonstrated significantly decreased uptake compared with controls (166, 167). Seven PD patients with depression did not demonstrate

any further abnormalities in the serotonin transporter compared with controls or with PD patients who were not depressed. However, the limited number of subjects makes interpretation of these findings difficult. The relationship between the serotonin system and PD is yet to be adequately determined.

It is unclear how the serotonin system contributes to neuropsychological dysfunction in PD, both with and without depressive symptoms. It would seem that the serotonin system, or more likely some combination of serotonin and dopamine abnormalities, contributes to depressive symptoms in PD. That such symptoms result from the combined involvement of these two systems is suggested by data indicating that neither the dopaminergic or serotonergic system alone completely explains the prevalence and severity of depressive symptoms in PD patients. A combination of serotonin and dopamine transporter imaging should help elucidate the reciprocal relationship between these two systems and also clarify the role of each in cognitive, emotional, and motor abnormalities.

FUTURE DIRECTIONS

A large number of imaging techniques can be used to attempt to differentiate between the various neurodegenerative disorders. Taken in isolation, many of them can diagnose PD, MSA, and PSP with some success. However, the diagnosis at an early stage in the progression of each disease, possibly even before clinical symptoms have become apparent, is much more difficult and may require multiple imaging modalities or combinations of tracers. The widespread availability of SPECT imaging, perhaps combined with newer and less expensive tracers, may lead to the routine implementation of SPECT scanning in the diagnosis of parkinsonian disorders.

Early diagnosis may become increasingly important once the genetic contribution to parkinsonian disorders is fully understood. SPECT imaging is beginning to make important contributions to the understanding of the pathogenesis of PD and may be able to elucidate the role of other neurotransmitter systems, such as NMDA and GABA, in the onset and progression of PD. The screening of "at risk" subjects before they present with clinical symptoms may be an effective preventive measure, particularly as neuroprotective therapies become available. Longitudinal studies of patients undergoing treatment will become increasingly important in the assessment of treatment efficacy and also to determine the exact mode of action of each therapy.

The next few years should provide important and exciting advances in the understanding and treatment of parkinsonian disorders, and SPECT imaging will play a key role in these investigations.

Acknowledgments

The work of these authors is supported by NIH grants R01-EB002774 and R01-AG17524. The authors also would like to thank Dr. Jim Patterson of the Institute of Neurological Sciences, Glasgow, Scotland, for kindly providing several SPECT images for this chapter.

References

1. Marsden CD. Parkinson's disease. *J Neurology Neurosurg Psychiatry* 1994; 57: 672–681.
2. Parkinson Study Group. Effects of tocopherol and deprenyl on the progression of disability in early Parkinson's disease, *N Eng J Med* 1993; 328:176–183.
3. Kaufman MJ, Madras BK. Severe depletion of cocaine recognition sites associated with the dopamine transporter in Parkinson's diseased striatum. *Synapse* 1991; 49: 43–49.
4. Kish SJ, Shannak K, Hornykiewicz O. Uneven pattern of dopamine loss in the striatum of patients with idiopathic Parkinson's disease. *N Engl J Med* 1988; 318:876–880.
5. Fearnley JM, Less AJ. Aging and Parkinson's disease: Substantia nigra regional selectivity, *Brain* 1991; 114:2283–2301.
6. Takei T, Mirra SS. Striatonigral degeneration: A form of multiple system atrophy with clinical Parkinsonism. In: Zimmerman HM (ed). *Progress in Neuropathology*. Vol. 2. New York: Grune & Stratton, 1973.
7. Duvoisin RC. An apology and an introduction to the olivopontocerebellar atrophies. *Adv Neurol* 1984; 41:5–12.
8. Papp MI, Lantos PL. The distribution of oligodendroglial inclusions in multiple system atrophy and its relevance to the rate of clinical symptomatology. *Brain* 1996; 119:235–243.
9. Quinn N. Multiple system atrophy: The nature of the beast. *J Neurology Neurosurg Psychiatry* 1989; 52:78–89.
10. Pahwa R. Progressive supranuclear palsy. *Med Clin North Am* 1999; 83:369–379.
11. Nygaard TG. Dopa-responsive dystonia: Delineation of the clinical syndrome and clues to the pathogenesis. *Adv Neurology* 1993; 60:577–585.
12. Asanuma K, Ma Y, Huang C, Carbon-Correll M, et al. The metabolic pathology of dopa-responsive dystonia. *Ann Neurol* 2005; 57(4):596–600.
13. Calne DB, de la Fuente-Fernandez R, Kishore A. Contributions of positron emission tomography to elucidating the pathogenesis of idiopathic parkinsonism and dopa responsive dystonia. *J Neural Transm* 1997; 50:47–52.
14. Jeon BS, Jeong JM, Park SS, et al. Dopamine transporter density measured by 123I beta-CIT single photon emission computed tomography is normal in dopa-responsive dystonia. *Ann Neurology* 1998; 43:792–800.
15. Naumann M, Pirker W, Reiners K, et al. 123I beta-CIT single-photon emission tomography in DOPA-responsive dystonia. *Mov Disord* 1997; 12:448–451.
16. Nygaard TG, Takahashi H, Heiman GA, et al. Long-term treatment response and fluorodopa positron emission tomographic scanning of parkinsonism in a family with dopa-responsive dystonia. *Ann Neurol* 1992; 32:603–608.
17. Asenbaum S, Pirker W, Angelberger P, et al. 123I beta-CIT and SPECT in essential tremor and Parkinson's disease. *J Neural Transm* 1998; 105:1213–1228.
18. Brooks DJ, Playford ED, Ibanez V, et al. Isolated tremor and disruption of the nigrostriatal dopaminergic system: An 18F-dopa PET study. *Neurology* 1992; 42:1554–1560.
19. Lee MS, Kim YD, Im JH, et al. 123I-IPT brain SPECT study in essential tremor and Parkinson's disease. *Neurology* 1999; 52:1422–1426.
20. Hughes AJ, Daniel SE, Blankson S, Lees AJ. A clinicopathologic study of 100 cases of Parkinson's disease. *Arch Neurol* 1993; 50:140–148.
21. Raiput AH, Rozdilsky B, Raiput A. Accuracy of clinical diagnosis in parkinsonism: A prospective study. *Can J Neurol Sci* 1991; 12:219–228.
22. Schrag A, Kingsley D, Phatouros C, et al. Clinical usefulness of magnetic resonance imaging in multiple system atrophy. *J Neurology Neurosurg Psychiatry* 1998; 65:65–71.
23. Kuhl DE, Metter EJ, Riege WH, Markham CH. Patterns of cerebral glucose utilisation in Parkinson's disease and Huntington's disease. *Ann Neurol* 1984; 15:119–125.
24. Markus HS, Lees AJ, Lennox G, et al. Patterns of regional cerebral blood flow in corticobasal degeneration studied using HMPAO SPECT: Comparison with Parkinson's disease and normal controls. *Mov Disord* 1995; 10:179–187.
25. Otsuka M, Ichiya Y, Kuwabara Y, et al. Glucose metabolism in the cortical and subcortical brain structures in multiple system atrophy and Parkinson's disease: A positron emission tomography study. *J Neurol Sci* 1996; 144:77–83.
26. Smith FW, Gemmell HG, Sharp PF, Besson JA. Technetium-99m HMPAO imaging in patients with basal ganglia disease. *Br J Radiol* 1988; 61:914–920.
27. Wang SJ, RS Liu, Liu HC, et al. Technetium-99m hexamethylpropylene amine oxime single photon emission tomography of the brain in early Parkinson's disease: Correlation with dementia and lateralization. *Eur J Nucl Med* 1993; 20:339–344.
28. Dethy S, Van Blercom N, Damhaut P, et al. Asymmetry of basal ganglia glucose metabolism and dopa responsiveness in parkinsonism. *Mov Disord* 1998; 13:275–280.
29. Eberling JL, Richardson BC, Reed BR, et al. Cortical glucose metabolism in Parkinson's disease without dementia. *Neurobiol Aging* 1994; 15:329–335.
30. Liu RS, Lin KN, Wang SJ, et al. Cognition and 99mTc-HMPAO SPECT in Parkinson's disease, *Nucl Med Commun* 1992; 13:744–748.
31. Piert M, Koeppe RA, Giordani B, et al. Determination of regional rate constants from dynamic FDG-PET studies in Parkinson's disease. *J Nucl Med* 1996; 37:1115–1122.
32. Wang SJ, Liu RS, Liu HC, et al. Technetium-99m hexamethylpropylene amine oxime single photon emission tomography of the brain in early Parkinson's disease: Correlation with dementia and lateralization. *Eur J Nucl Med* 1993; 20:339–344.
33. Otsuka M, Ichiya Y, Kuwabara Y, et al. Glucose metabolism in the cortical and subcortical brain structures in multiple system atrophy and Parkinson's disease: A positron emission tomography study. *J Neurol Sci* 1996; 144:77–83.
34. Otsuka M, Kuwabara Y, Ichiya Y, et al. Differentiating between multiple system atrophy and Parkinson's disease by positron emission tomography with 18F-dopa and 18F-FDG. *Ann Nucl Med* 1997; 11:251–257.
35. Defebvre L, Lecouffe P, Destee A, et al. Tomographic measurements of regional cerebral blood flow in progressive supranuclear palsy and Parkinson's disease. *Acta Neurol Scand* 1995; 92:235–241.
36. Garnett ES, Firnau G, Chan PKH, et al. [18F]-Fluoro-dopa, an analogue of dopa, and its use in direct external measurements of storage, degradation, and turnover of intracerebral dopamine. *Proc Natl Acad Sci USA* 1978; 75:464.
37. Garnett ES, Firnau G, Nahmias C. Dopamine visualised in the basal ganglia of living man. *Nature* 1983; 305:137.
38. Snow BJ, Tooyama I, McGeer EG. Human positron emission tomographic (fluorine-18) fluorodopa studies correlate with dopamine cell counts and levels. *Ann Neur* 1993; 34:324–330.
39. Fowler JS, Volkow ND, Wolf AP, et al. Mapping cocaine binding sites in human and baboon brain in vivo. *Synapse* 1989; 4:371–377.
40. Madras BK, Spealman RD, Fahey MA, et al. Cocaine receptors labeled by [3H]2β-carbomethoxy-3β-(4-fluorophenyl)tropane. *Mol Pharmacol* 1989; 36:518–524.
41. Neumeyer JL, Wang S-Y, Milius RA, et al. 123I-2β-Carbomethoxy-3β-(4-iodophenyl)tropane: High-affinity SPECT radiotracer of monoamine reuptake sites in brain. *J Med Chem* 1991; 34:3144–3146.
42. Kung M-P, Essman WD, Frederick D, et al. IPT: A novel iodinated ligand for the CNS dopamine transporter *Synapse* 1995; 20:316–324.
43. Madras BK, Gracz LM, Meltzer PC, et al. Altropane, a SPECT or PET imaging probe for dopamine neurons: II. Distribution to dopamine-rich regions of primate brain. *Synapse* 1998; 29:105–115.
44. Volkow ND, Ding YS, Fowler JS, et al. A new PET ligand for the dopamine transporter: Studies in the human brain. *J Nucl Med* 1995; 36:2162–2168.
45. Kung HF, Kim H-J, Kung M-P, et al. Imaging of dopamine transporters in humans with technetium-99m TRODAT-1. *Eur J Nucl Med* 1996; 23:1527–1530.
46. Kung M-P, Stevenson DA, Plössl K, et al. [99mTc]TRODAT-1: a novel technetium-99m complex as a dopamine transporter imaging agent. *Eur J Nucl Med* 1997; 24:37–380.
47. Acton PD, Kushner SA, Kung MP, et al. Simplified reference region model for the kinetic analysis of [99mTc]TRODAT-1 binding to dopamine transporters in non-human primates using SPET. *Eur J Nucl Med* 1999; 26:518–526.
48. Kung HF, Alavi A, Chang W, et al. In vivo SPECT imaging of CNS D2 dopamine receptors: Initial studies with iodine-123-IBZM in humans. *J Nucl Med* 1990; 31:573–579.
49. Kung HF, Billings JJ, Guo Y-Z, et al. Preparation and biodistribution of 125I IBZM: A potential CNS D2 dopamine receptor imaging agent. *Nucl Med Biol* 1988; 15:195–201.
50. Kessler RM, Ansari MS, Schmidt DE, et al. High affinity dopamine D2 receptor radioligands. 2. 125I Epipride: A potent and specific radioligand for the characterization of striatal and extrastriatal dopamine D2 receptors. *Life Sci* 1991; 49:617–628.
51. Kessler RM, Mason NS, Votaw JR, et al. Visualization of extrastriatal dopamine D2 receptors in the human brain. *Eur J Pharmacol* 1992; 223:105–107.
52. Ehrin E, Farde L, de Paulis T. Preparation of 11C-labelled raclopride, a new potent dopamine receptor antagonist: Preliminary PET studies of cerebral dopamine receptors in the monkey. *Int J App Radiat Isotopes* 1985; 36:269–273.
53. Arnett CD, Wolf AP, Shiue C-Y, et al. Improved delineation of human dopamine receptors using 18F-N-methylspiroperidol and PET. *J Nucl Med* 1986; 27:1878–1882.
54. Shiue C-Y, Fowler JS, Wolf AP, et al. No-carrier-added fluorine-18-labeled N-methylspiroperidol: Synthesis and distribution in mice. *J Nucl Med* 1986; 27:226–234.
55. Mozley PD, Acton PD, Barraclough ED, et al. Effects of age on dopamine transporters in healthy humans. *J Nucl Med* 1999; 40(11):1812–1817.
56. Tatsch K, Schwarz J, Mozley PD, et al. Relationship between clinical features of Parkinson's disease and presynaptic dopamine transporter binding assessed with 123I IPT and single-photon emission tomography. *Eur J Nucl Med* 1997; 24:415–421.
57. Mozley PD, Schneider JS, Acton PD, et al. Binding of [99mTc]TRODAT-1 to dopamine transporters in patients with Parkinson's disease and in healthy volunteers. *J Nucl Med* 2000; 41(4):584–589.
58. Chow KL, Colcher A, Hurtig HI, et al. Diagnostic accuracy of [99mTc]TRODAT-1 SPECT imaging in early Parkinson's disease. *Parkinsonism Relat Dis* 2004; 10(6):375–379.
59. Tissingh G, Bergmans P, Booij J, et al. Drug-naive patients with Parkinson's disease in Hoehn and Yahr stages I and II show a bilateral decrease in striatal dopamine transporters as revealed by 123I beta-CIT SPECT. *J Neurol* 1998; 245:14–20.

60. Morrish PK, Sawle GV, Brooks DJ. Clinical and [18F]dopa PET findings in early Parkinson's disease. *J Neurol Neurosurg Psychiatry* 1995; 59:597–600.

61. Booij J, Tissingh G, Boer GJ, et al. 123I FP-CIT SPECT shows a pronounced decline of striatal dopamine transporter labelling in early and advanced Parkinson's disease. *J Neurol Neurosurg Psychiatry* 1997; 62:133–140.

62. Acton PD, Mozley PD, Kung HF. Logistic discriminant parametric mapping: A novel method for the pixel-based differential diagnosis of Parkinson's disease. *Eur J Nucl Med* 1999; 26(11): 1413–1423.

63. Marek KL, Seibyl JP, Zoghbi SS, et al. 123I beta-CIT/SPECT imaging demonstrates bilateral loss of dopamine transporters in hemi-Parkinson's disease. *Neurology* 1996; 46(1):231–237.

64. Burn DJ, Sawle GV, Brooks DJ. Differential diagnosis of Parkinson's disease, multiple system atrophy, and Steele-Richardson Olszewski syndrome: Discriminant analysis of striatal 18F-dopa PET data. *J Neurol Neurosurg Psychiatry* 1994; 57(3):278–284.

65. Sawle GV, Playford ED, Burn DJ, et al. Separating Parkinson's disease from normality. Discriminant function analysis of fluorodopa F18 positron emission tomography data. *Arch Neurol* 1994; 51(3):237–243.

66. Van Laere K, De Ceuninck L, Dom R, et al. Dopamine transporter SPECT using fast kinetic ligands: 123I-FP-beta-CIT versus 99mTc-TRODAT-1. *Eur J Nucl Med Mol Imaging* 2004; 31(8):1119–1127.

67. Weng YH, Yen TC, Chen MC, et al. Sensitivity and specificity of 99mTc-TRODAT-1 SPECT imaging in differentiating patients with idiopathic Parkinson's disease from healthy subjects. *J Nucl Med* 2004; 45(3):393–401.

68. Rinne JO, Laihinen A, Nagren K, et al. PET examination of the monoamine transporter with [11C]beta-CIT and [11C]beta-CFT in early Parkinson's disease. *Synapse* 1995; 21(2):97–103.

69. Hughes AJ, Daniel SE, Blankson S, Lees AJ. A clinicopathologic study of 100 cases of Parkinson's disease. *Arch Neurol* 1993; 50(2):140–148.

70. Rajput AH, Rozdilsky B, Rajput A. Accuracy of clinical diagnosis in parkinsonism: A prospective study. *Can J Neurol Sci* 1991; 12:219–228.

71. Brucke T, Asenbaum S, Pirker W, et al. Measurement of the dopaminergic degeneration in Parkinson's disease with 123I beta-CIT and SPECT. Correlation with clinical findings and comparison with multiple system atrophy and progressive supranuclear palsy. *J Neural Transm Suppl* 1997; 50:9–24.

72. Pirker W, Asenbaum S, Bencsits G, et al. 123I β-CIT SPECT in multiple system atrophy, progressive supranuclear palsy, and corticobasal degeneration. Mov Disord 2000; 15:1158–1167.

73. Booij J, Speelman JD, Horstink MW, Wolters EC. The clinical benefits of imaging striatal dopamine transporter with I-123 FP-CIT SPECT in differentiating patients with presynaptic parkinsonism from those with other forms of parkinsonism. *Eur J Nucl Med* 2001; 28:266–272.

74. Varrone A, Marek KL, Jennings D, et al. I-123 β-CIT SPECT imaging demonstrates reduced density of striatal dopamine transporters in Parkinson's disease and multiple system atrophy. Mov Disord 2001; 16:1023–1032.

75. El Fakhri G, Habert MO, Maksud P, et al. Quantitative simultaneous (99m)Tc-ECD/123I-FP-CIT SPECT in Parkinson's disease and multiple system atrophy. *Eur J Nucl Med Mol Imaging* 2006; 33(1):87–92.

76. Swanson RL, Newberg AB, Acton PD, et al. Differences in [99mTc]TRODAT-1 SPECT binding to dopamine transporters in patients with multiple system atrophy and Parkinson's disease. *Eur J Nucl Med Mol Imaging* 2005; 32(3):302–307.

77. Scherfler C, Seppi K, Donnemiller E, et al. Voxel-wise analysis of 123I beta-CIT SPECT differentiates the Parkinson variant of multiple system atrophy from idiopathic Parkinson's disease. *Brain* 2005; 128(Pt 7):1605–1612.

78. Otsuka M, Kuwabara Y, Ichiya Y, et al. Differentiating between multiple system atrophy and Parkinson's disease by positron emission tomography with 18F-dopa and 18F-FDG. *Ann Nucl Med* 1997; 11:251–257.

79. Taniwaki T, Nakagawa M, Yamada T, et al. Cerebral metabolic changes in early multiple system atrophy: A PET study. *J Neurol Sci* 2002; 200(1–2):79–84.

80. Ghaemi M, Hilker R, Rudolf J, et al. Differentiating multiple system atrophy from Parkinson's disease: Contribution of striatal and midbrain MRI volumetry and multitracer PET imaging. *J Neurol Neurosurg Psychiatry* 2002; 73(5):517–523.

81. Leenders KL, Frackowiak RS, Lees AJ. Steele-Richardson-Olszewski syndrome. Brain energy metabolism, blood flow and fluorodopa uptake measured by positron emission tomography. *Brain* 1988; 111(Pt 3):615–630.

82. Im JH, Chung SJ, Kim JS, Lee MC. Differential patterns of dopamine transporter loss in the basal ganglia of progressive supranuclear palsy and Parkinson's disease: analysis with 123I IPT single photon emission computed tomography. *J Neurol Sci* 2006; 15;244(1–2):103–109.

83. Wang J, Jiang YP, Liu XD, et al. 99mTc-TRODAT-1 SPECT study in early Parkinson's disease and essential tremor. *Acta Neurol Scand* 2005; 112(6):380–385.

84. Booij J, Tissingh G, Winogrodzka A, van Royen EA. Imaging of the dopaminergic neurotransmission system using single-photon emission tomography and positron emission tomography in patients with parkinsonism. *Eur J Nucl Med* 1999; 26(2):171–182.

85. Habraken JB, Booij J, Slomka P, et al. Quantification and visualization of defects of the functional dopaminergic system using an automatic algorithm. *J Nucl Med* 1999; 40(7):1091–1097.

86. Boecker H, Weindl A, Leenders K, et al. Secondary parkinsonism due to focal substantia nigra lesions: A PET study with [18F]FDG and [18F]fluorodopa. *Acta Neurol Scand* 1996; 93(6):387–392.

87. Eidelberg D, Moeller JR, Dhawan V, et al. The metabolic anatomy of Parkinson's disease: Complementary [18F]fluorodeoxyglucose and [18F]fluorodopa positron emission tomographic studies. *Mov Disord* 1990; 5(3):203–213.

88. Van Laere K, Casteels C, De Ceuninck L, et al. Dual-tracer dopamine transporter and perfusion SPECT in differential diagnosis of parkinsonism using template-based discriminant analysis. *J Nucl Med* 2006; 47(3):384–392.

89. Kato T, Kume A, Ito K, et al. Asymmetrical FDG-PET and MRI findings of striatonigral system in multiple system atrophy with hemiparkinsonism. *Radiat Med* 1992; 10(3):87–93.

90. Kume A, Shiratori M, Takahashi A, et al. Hemi-parkinsonism in multiple system atrophy: A PET and MRI study. *J Neurol Sci* 1992; 110: 37–45.

91. Arnold G, Tatsch K, Oertel WH, et al. Clinical progressive supranuclear palsy: Differential diagnosis by IBZM-SPECT and MRI. *J Neural Transm Suppl* 1994; 42:111–118.

92. Schulz JB, Klockgether T, Petersen D, et al. Multiple system atrophy: Natural history, MRI morphology, and dopamine receptor imaging with 123IBZM-SPECT. *J Neurol Neurosurg Psychiatry* 1994; 57(9):1047–1056.

93. Wenning GK, Donnemiller E, Granata R, et al. 123I-beta-CIT and 123I-IBZM-SPECT scanning in levodopa-naive Parkinson's disease. *Mov Disord* 1998; 13(3):438–445.

94. Kim YJ, Ichise M, Tatschida T, et al. Differential diagnosis of parkinsonism using dopamine transporter and D2 receptor SPECT. *J Nucl Med* 1999; 5(Suppl):68P.

95. Dresel SHJ, Kung MP, Huang XF, et al. Simultaneous SPECT studies of pre- and postsynaptic dopamine binding sites in baboons. *J Nucl Med* 1999; 40:660–666.

96. Kim YJ, Ichise M, Ballinger JR, et al. Combination of dopamine transporter and D2 receptor SPECT in the diagnostic evaluation of PD, MSA, and PSP. *Mov Disord* 2002; 17(2):303–312.

97. Morrish PK, Rakshi JS, Bailey DL, et al. Measuring the rate of progression and estimating the preclinical period of Parkinson's disease with [18F]dopa PET. *J Neurol Neurosurg Psychiatry* 1998; 64(3):314–319.

98. Morrish PK, Sawle GV, Brooks DJ. An [18F]dopa-PET and clinical study of the rate of progression in Parkinson's disease. *Brain* 1996; 119 (Pt 2):585–591.

99. Morrish PK, Sawle GV, Brooks DJ. The rate of progression of Parkinson's disease. A longitudinal [18F]DOPA PET study. *Adv Neurol* 1996; 69:427–431.

100. Vingerhoets FJ, Snow BJ, Tetrud JW, et al. Positron emission tomographic evidence for progression of human MPTP-induced dopaminergic lesions. *Ann Neurol* 1994; 36(5):765–770.

101. Seibyl JP, Innis RB, Early ML, et al. Baseline striatal dopamine transporter uptake measured with I-123 beta-CIT may predict the rate of disease progression in idiopathic Parkinson's disease *J Nucl Med* 1999; 5(Suppl):27P.

102. Brooks DJ. Detection of preclinical Parkinson's disease with PET. *Geriatrics* 1991; 46(Suppl 1):25–30.

103. Kopin IJ. Features of the dopaminergic neurotoxin MPTP. *Ann NY Acad Sci* 1992; 648:96–104.

104. Siegel GJ, Agranoff BW, Albers RW, et al. *Basic Neurochemistry*, 6th ed. Philadelphia: Lippincott Williams & Wilkins, 1998.

105. Brownell AL, Canales K, Chen YI, et al. Mapping of brain function after MPTP-induced neurotoxicity in a primate Parkinson's disease model. *Neuroimage* 2003; 20(2):1064–1075.

106. McNaught KS, Carrupt PA, Altomare C, et al. Isoquinoline derivatives as endogenous neurotoxins in the aetiology of Parkinson's disease. *Biochem Pharmacol* 1998; 56(8):921–933.

107. Facchinetti F, Dawson VL, Dawson TM. Free radicals as mediators of neuronal injury, *Cell Mol Neurobiol* 1998; 18:667–682.

108. Jenner P Oxidative mechanisms in nigral cell death in Parkinson's disease. *Mov Disord* 1998; 13(Suppl 1):24–34.

109. Selley ML. (E)-4-hydroxy-2-nonenal may be involved in the pathogenesis of Parkinson's disease. *Free Radic Biol Med* 1998; 25:169–174.

110. Duvoisin RC. On heredity, twins and Parkinson's disease. *Ann Neurol* 1986; 19: 409–411.

111. Ward CD, Duvoisin RC, Ince SE, et al. Parkinson's disease in 65 pairs of twins and in a set of quadruplets. *Neurology* 1983; 33(7):815–824.

112. Foltynie T, Sawcer S, Brayne C, Barker RA. The genetic basis of Parkinson's disease. *J Neurol Neurosurg Psychiatry* 2002; 73(4):363–370.

113. Riess O, Kruger R, Schulz JB. Spectrum of phenotypes and genotypes in Parkinson's disease. *J Neurol* 2002; 249(Suppl 3):III/15–III/20.

114. West AB, Maidment NT. Genetics of parkin-linked disease. *Hum Genet* 2004; 114(4):327–336.

115. Burn DJ, Mark MH, Playford ED, et al. Parkinson's disease in twins studied with 18F-dopa and positron emission tomography. *Neurology* 1992; 42(10):1894–1900.

116. Piccini P, Burn DJ, Ceravolo R, et al. The role of inheritance in sporadic Parkinson's disease: Evidence from a longitudinal study of dopaminergic function in twins. *Ann Neurol* 1999; 45(5):577–582.

117. Sawle GV, Wroe SJ, Lees AJ, et al. The identification of presymptomatic parkinsonism: Clinical and [18F]dopa positron emission tomography studies in an Irish kindred. *Ann Neurol* 1992; 32(5):609–617.

118. Piccini P, Morrish PK, Turjanski N, et al. Dopaminergic function in familial Parkinson's disease: A clinical and 18F-dopa positron emission tomography study. *Ann Neurol* 1997; 41(2):222–229.

119. Lang AE, Lozano AM. Parkinson's disease. First of two parts. *N Engl J Med* 1998; 339:1044–1053.

120. Lang AE, Lozano AM. Parkinson's disease. Second of two parts. *N Engl J Med* 1998; 339:1130–1143.

121. Miyawaki E, Lyons K, Pahwa R, et al. Motor complications of chronic levodopa therapy in Parkinson's disease. *Clin Neuropharmacol* 1997; 20(6):523–530.

122. Birkmayer W, Riederer P, Youdim MBH, Linauer W. Potentiation of antikinetic effect after L-dopa treatment by an inhibitor of MAO B, L-deprenyl. *J Neural Transm* 1975; 36:303–323.

123. Tetrud JW, Langston JW. The effect of deprenyl (selegiline) on the natural history of Parkinson's disease. *Science* 1989; 245:519–522.

124. Iacovitti L, Stull ND, Johnston K. Melatonin rescues dopamine neurons from cell death in tissue culture models of oxidative stress. *Brain Res* 1997; 768:317–326.

125. Reiter RJ. Oxidative damage in the central nervous system: Protection by melatonin. *Prog Neurobiol* 1998; 56:359–384.

126. Zou L, Jankovic J, Rowe DB, et al. Neuroprotection by pramipexole against dopamine- and levodopa-induced cytotoxicity. *Life Sci* 1999; 64(15):1275–1285.

127. Koller WC. Neuroprotective therapy for Parkinson's disease. Exp Neurol 1997; 144:24–28.

128. Morrish PK, Rakshi JS, Brooks JD. Can the neuroprotective efficacy of an agent ever be conclusively proven? *Eur J Neurol* 1997; 4(Suppl 3):S19–S24.

129. Hierholzer J, Cordes M, Venz S, et al. Loss of dopamine-D2 receptor binding sites in parkinsonian plus syndromes. *J Nucl Med* 1998; 39(6):954–960.

130. Schwarz J, Tatsch K, Gasser T, et al. ^{123}I-IBZM binding compared with long-term clinical follow up in patients with de novo parkinsonism. *Mov Disord* 1998; 13(1):16–19.

131. Whone AL, Watts RL, Stoessl J, et al. Slower progression of PD with ropinirol versus L-dopa: the REAL-PET study. *Ann Neurol* 2003; 54:93–101.

132. Parkinson Study Group. Dopamine transporter brain imaging to assess the effects of pramipexole vs levodopa Parkinson disease progression. *JAMA* 2002; 287:1653–1661.

133. Laiten LV, Bergenheim AT, Hariz MI. Leksell's postero-ventral pallidotomy in the treatment of Parkinson's disease. *J Neurosurg* 1992; 76:53–61.

134. Alterman RL, Kelly P, Sterio D, et al. Selection criteria for unilateral posteroventral pallidotomy. *Acta Neurochir Suppl* 1997; 68:18–23.

135. Kazumata K, Antonini A, Dhawan V, et al. Preoperative indicators of clinical outcome following stereotaxic pallidotomy. *Neurology* 1997; 49(4):1083–1090.

136. Eidelberg D, Moeller JR, Ishikawa T, et al. Regional metabolic correlates of surgical outcome following unilateral pallidotomy for Parkinson's disease. *Ann Neurol* 1996; 39(4):450–459.

137. Limousin P, Pollak P, Benazzouz A, et al. Bilateral subthalamic nucleus stimulation for severe Parkinson's disease. *Mov Disord* 1995; 10:672–674.

138. Benjjani B, Damier P, Arnulf I, et al. Pallidal stimulation for Parkinson's disease. Two targets?. *Neurology* 1997; 49:1564–1569.

139. Pollak P, Benabid AL, Limousin P, et al. Subthalamic nucleus stimulation alleviates akinesia and rigidity in parkinsonian patients. *Adv Neurol* 1996; 69:591–594.

140. Limousin P, Greene J, Pollak P, et al. Changes in cerebral activity pattern due to subthalamic nucleus or internal pallidum stimulation in Parkinson's disease. *Ann Neurol* 1997; 42:283–291.

141. Limousin P, Krack P, Pollak P, et al. Electrical stimulation of the subthalamic nucleus in advanced Parkinson's disease. *N Eng J Med* 1998; 339:1105–1111.

142. Benabid AL, Pollak P, Seigneuret E, et al. Chronic VtM thalamic stimulation in Parkinson's disease, essential tremor and extrapyramidal dyskinesias. *Acta Neurochir* 1993; 58(Suppl):39–44.

143. Kumar R, Lozano AM, Kim YJ, et al. Double blind evaluation of subthalamic nucleus deep brain stimulation in advanced Parkinson's disease. *Neurology* 1998; 51:850–855.

144. Sestini S, Ramat S, Formiconi AR, et al. Brain networks underlying the clinical effects of long-term subthalamic stimulation for Parkinson's disease: A 4-year follow-up study with rCBF SPECT. *J Nucl Med* 2005; 46(9):1444–1454.

145. Hilker R, Voges J, Thiel A, et al. Deep brain stimulation of the subthalamic nucleus versus levodopa challenge in Parkinson's disease: Measuring the on- and off-conditions with FDG-PET. *J Neural Transm* 2002; 109(10):1257–1264.

146. Lindvall O, Rehncrona S, Brundin P, et al. Human fetal dopamine neurons grafted into the striatum in two patients with severe Parkinson's disease. A detailed account of methodology and a 6-month follow-up. *Arch Neurol* 1989; 46(6):615–631.

147. Deacon T, Schumacher J, Dinsmore J, et al. Histological evidence of fetal pig neural cell survival after transplantation into a patient with Parkinson's disease. *Nat Med* 1997; 3(3):350–353.

148. Kordower JH, Freeman TB, Chen EY, et al. Fetal nigral grafts survive and mediate clinical benefit in a patient with Parkinson's disease. *Mov Disord* 1998; 13(3):383–393.

149. Remy P, Samson Y, Hantraye P, et al. Clinical correlates of [^{18}F]fluorodopa uptake in five grafted parkinsonian patients. *Ann Neurol* 1995; 38(4):580–588.

150. Sawle GV, Bloomfield PM, Bjorklund A, et al. Transplantation of fetal dopamine neurons in Parkinson's disease: PET [^{18}F]6-L-fluorodopa studies in two patients with putaminal implants. *Ann Neurol* 1989; 31:166–173.

151. Kirik D, Breysse N, Bjorklund T, et al. Imaging in cell-based therapy for neurodegenerative diseases. *Eur J Nucl Med Mol Imaging* 2005; 32(Suppl 2):S417–S434.

152. Freed CR, Greene PE, Breeze RE, et al. Transplantation of embryonic dopamine neurons for severe Parkinson's disease. *N Engl J Med* 2001; 344:710–719.

153. Olanow CW, Goetz CG, Kordower JH, et al. A double-blind controlled trial of bilateral fetal nigral transplantation in Parkinson's disease. *Ann Neurol* 2003; 54:403–414.

154. Brooks DJ. Positron emission tomography studies in movement disorders, *Neurosurg Clin North Am* 1998; 9:263–282.

155. Blandini F, Greenamyre JT. Prospects of glutamate antagonists in the therapy of Parkinson's disease. *Fundam Clin Pharmacol* 1998; 12(1):4–12.

156. Loopuijt LD, Schmidt WJ. The role of NMDA receptors in the slow neuronal degeneration of Parkinson's disease. *Amino Acids* 1998; 14:17–23.

157. Sonsalla PK, Albers DS, Zeevalk GD. Role of glutamate in neurodegeneration of dopamine neurons in several animal models of parkinsonism. *Amino Acids* 1998; 14 (1–3):69–74.

158. Shiue CY, Vallabhahosula S, Wolf AP, et al. Carbon-11 labelled ketamine-synthesis, distribution in mice and PET studies in baboons. *Nucl Med Biol* 1997; 24(2):145–150.

159. Ametamey SM, Samnick S, Leenders KL, et al. Fluorine-18 radiolabelling, biodistribution studies and preliminary PET evaluation of a new memantine derivative for imaging the NMDA receptor. *J Recept Signal Transduct Res* 1999; 19(1–4):129–141.

160. Kawabata K, Tachibana H. Evaluation of benzodiazepine receptor in the cerebral cortex of Parkinson's disease using ^{123}I-iomazenil SPECT. *Nippon Rinsho* 1997; 55(1)244–248.

161. Kawabata K, Tachibana H, Sugita M, Fukuchi M. [Impairment of benzodiazepine receptor in Parkinson's disease evaluaged by ^{123}I-iomazenil SPECT.] Kaku Igaku 1996; 33(4):391–397.

162. D'Amato RJ, Zweig RM, Whitehouse PJ, et al. Aminergic systems in Alzheimer's disease and Parkinson's disease. *Ann Neurol* 1987; 22:229–236.

163. Chinaglia G, Landwehrmeyer B, Probst A, Palacios JM. Serotoninergic terminal transporters are differentially affected in Parkinson's disease and progressive supranuclear palsy: An autoradiographic study with [3H]citalopram. *Neuroscience* 1993; 54:691–699.

164. Mossner R, Schmitt A, Syagailo Y, et al. The serotonin transporter in Alzheimer's and Parkinson's disease. *J Neural Transm Suppl* 2000; 60:345–350.

165. Kerenyi L, Ricaurte GA, Schretlen DJ, et al. Positron emission tomography of striatal serotonin transporters in Parkinson disease. *Arch Neurol* 2003; 60:1223–1229.

166. Kim SE, Choi JY, Choe YS, et al. Serotonin transporters in the midbrain of Parkinson's disease patients: A study with ^{123}I-beta-CIT SPECT. *J Nucl Med* 2003; 44:870–876.

167. Berding G, Brucke T, Odin P, et al. ^{123}I beta-CIT SPECT imaging of dopamine and serotonin transporters in Parkinson's disease and multiple system atrophy. *Nuklearmedizin* 2003; 42:31–38.

27 Magnetic Resonance Imaging

Tao Wu
Mark Hallett

The development of magnetic resonance imaging (MRI) in the early 1980s significantly improved image resolution. It is a relatively simple and safe technique that has been proven to play an important role in the diagnosis of neurologic disorders. The value of structural MRI is limited in the diagnosis of Parkinson's disease (PD) because no convincing specific structural change has been found. However, structural MRI may be helpful in distinguishing PD from other parkinsonian syndromes. In addition to structural MRI, several techniques have been developed, such as magnetic resonance spectroscopy, magnetic resonance imaging-based volumetry, diffusion-weighted imaging, magnetic transfer imaging, and functional magnetic resonance imaging. The value of these methods in investigating PD is also discussed.

STRUCTURAL MRI

The structural MRI is not usually normal in patients with PD, especially in advanced cases. PD is associated with an increased incidence of brain atrophy, which is usually general or frontally predominant. The pattern of atrophy is not specific enough to help to distinguish PD from other neurologic degenerative disorders (1). Atrophy of the substantia nigra can be detected as a decrease in the width of the relatively hyperintense band seen in T2-weighted images of high-field-intensity MRI in some PD patients (2). A low-signal area in the red nucleus and the substantia nigra pars reticulata can be observed in T2-weighted images (3). A narrowing or smudging of this high-signal zone separating the red nucleus and the pars reticulata has been reported in PD, consistent with the well-established prominent pathologic involvement in this area (4, 5). Although these studies demonstrate some changes in PD, conventional structural MRI techniques are not sensitive enough to consistently detect these changes. It is still difficult to detect abnormalities in the substantia nigra in individual patients in routine clinical scans.

The most important role of structural MRI is in helping to differentiate PD from other parkinsonian disorders, such as multiple system atrophy (MSA), progressive supranuclear palsy (PSP), corticobasal degeneration (CBD), and parkinsonism secondary to other brain lesions. MSA is subcategorized into three syndromes by predominant automatic dysfunction (MSA-A), predominant parkinsonism (MSA-P), and predominant cerebellar ataxia (MSA-C) (6). The pathologic substrate of these three syndromes is mainly located in the spinal cord, putamen, and brainstem and cerebellum, respectively. Because MRI is not able to detect changes in the intermediolateral columns of the spinal cord, most studies

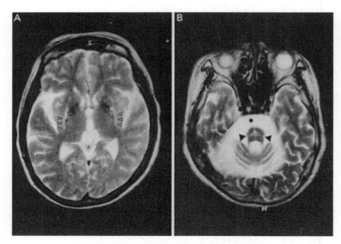

FIGURE 27-1

MRI signal abnormalities in patients with multiple system atrophy. (A) "Slit-like" hyperintense putaminal rim on T2-weighted images (1.5 T; 4000-ms repetition time (TR), 120-ms echo time (TE)) in the axial plane (arrowheads). (B) Signal change in the pons on T2-weighted images ("hot cross bun"; 1.5 T; TR, 4000 ms; TE, 120 ms) in the axial plane (arrowheads). (Modified from reference 10 with permission from Oxford University Press.)

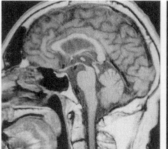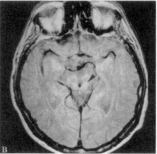

FIGURE 27-2

MRI of a patient with progressive supranuclear palsy. T1-weighted midline sagittal section (A) shows midbrain atrophy. Axial proton-density image (B) shows slight hyperintensity in dorsal midbrain (arrowhead). (Modified from reference 18 with permission from Lippincott Williams & Wilkins.)

have focused on the changes of MSA-P and MSA-C. In some MSA-A patients, MRI reveals decreased signal in the posterolateral putamen on T2-weighted images (7). In MSA-P, patients have mostly parkinsonism (8). Clinically, differentiation of MSA-P and PD is often difficult. MRI has the potential to be helpful in the differential diagnosis of MSA-P. A characteristic finding in MSA-P is the "slit-like" hyperintensity in the lateral margin of the putamen (9), which is quite specific for MSA. Other abnormalities of the putamen include atrophy and hypointensity in T2-weighted images. In addition, a "hot cross bun" sign may be seen in the pons in 63.3% of MSA patients (10) (Figure 27-1). This appearance is due to atrophy of the corticopontine fibers. A diagnostic algorithm based MRI findings has been proposed to help distinguish MSA-P patients from PD patients (11). However, some patients fulfilling diagnostic criteria for clinically probable MSA-P had normal findings with these routine MRI methods (12). Some modified methods may help to differentiate MSA and PD, as with T2*-weighted MRI, in which hypointense putaminal signal changes are more often observed in MSA than in PD (13). Using thin slice thickness substantially increases MR sensitivity in detecting abnormal putaminal T2 hypointensity in MSA patients (14). MSA-C typically shows atrophy of the pons, middle cerebellar peduncles, and cerebellum, enlargement of the fourth ventricle, and cerebellopontine angle cisterns. Abnormalities of the transverse pontine fibers,

middle cerebellar peduncles, and cerebellum (claimed to be demyelination) may be detected on T2-weighted MR images (15). The inferior olives may also be slightly hyperintense. The specificity and sensitivity of MRI findings of MSA-C are high (12). The combination of clinical features and MRI results makes the differential diagnosis of PD from MSA-C not difficult.

In PSP, the typical finding on MRI is atrophy of the midbrain, accompanied by an enlarged cerebral aqueduct and perimesencephalic cisterns (9, 16–18) (Figure 27-2). The presentation of this atrophy suggests a radiological diagnosis of PSP in 80% to 90% of patients (18, 19). Warmuth-Metz and colleagues (20) found that the anteroposterior diameter of the midbrain measured on axial T2-weighted MRI in PSP patients is significantly lower than that in PD patients and suggested that this difference is helpful in distinguishing PD and PSP. Other atrophic features include the thinning of the superior quadrigeminal plate, enlargement of the third ventricle, and a superior concave profile of the midbrain forming the floor of the third ventricle (9, 18). The presence of marked atrophy and hyperintensity of the midbrain and atrophy of the frontal and temporal lobes may help to differentiate PSP from MSA (19). Putaminal hypointensity on T2-weighted MRI may be observed in patients with PSP, but this finding is less consistently detected in PSP than in the other parkinsonism-plus syndromes (17, 21). The "eye of the tiger" sign on brain MRI, which appears as bilaterally symmetric hyperintense signal changes in the anterior medial globus pallidus with surrounding hypointensity in the globus pallidus on T2-weighted images and is typically associated with Hallervorden-Spatz disease, has also been reported in PSP (22). Oba and colleagues (23) measured the area of the midbrain and pons on midsagittal MRI and found that the average midbrain area of patients with PSP (56.0 mm²) was significantly smaller than that of those with PD (103.0 mm²) and MSA-P (97.2 mm²) and that of the age-matched control group (117.7 mm²). Although there were some overlap between PSP patients and MSA-P patients, the ratio of the area of the midbrain to the area of the pons in the patients with PSP (0.124) was significantly smaller than that in those with PD (0.208) and MSA-P (0.266) and could be used to differentiate PSP patients from MSA-P patients. The authors suggested that the area of the midbrain on midsagittal MRI is helpful in differentiating PSP from PD and MSA-P. Another study suggested that an abnormal superior midbrain profile (flat or concave aspect) is helpful in the distinction of PSP from PD (24).

Only a few studies have investigated the role of MRI in patients with corticobasal degeneration (CBD). CBD is characterized by asymmetric frontoparietal atrophy mostly involving the contralateral side of the more clinically affected body side. Other features include putaminal hypointensity and hyperintense signal changes in the motor cortex or subcortical white matter on T2-weighted images (18, 25–27) (Figure 27-3). Occasionally, the "eye of the tiger" sign on brain MRI could be observed in CBD (28). Asymmetric frontoparietal atrophy helps to differentiate CBD from PSP (18). However, no specific abnormality has been found to aid in the diagnosis of CBD (19, 29).

Structural MRI also plays an important role in the differential diagnosis of parkinsonism secondary to other structural brain lesions, such as brain tumors, multiple sclerosis, normal-pressure or obstructive hydrocephalus, subdural hematoma, multiple infarcts, or other causes (30–36).

In recent years, together with improved MRI technique, subtle changes in the substantia nigra have been

identified using special methods. Hutchinson and Raff (37) developed a technique that uses a combination of 2 distinct inversion-recovery pulse sequences. This technique is based on calculating the ratio between images acquired by the 2 sequences. By dividing the signal intensity of a white matter suppressed inversion-recovery sequence of the substantia nigra by that of a gray matter suppressed sequence, an image is obtained that clearly demonstrates the gray matter of the substantia nigra. These investigators found a loss of signal in a lateral-to-medial gradient in PD, even in early cases (37, 38). This is not demonstrated by routine MRI methods (39, 40). Because this method is not necessarily specific for PD, a semiautomated segmentation analysis (segmented inversion-recovery ratio imaging, or SIRRIM) was developed (41). SIRRIM includes a segmentation analysis that allows the substantia nigra to be displayed as an isolated structure. The preliminary work found a gradient of radiologic change in the substantia nigra, indicating that the areas of highest signal are thinned in PD patients compared to normal controls. Additionally, the substantia nigra is broadened in a ventrodorsal direction in PD compared with normal controls (Figure 27-4). It has been reported that the structural changes within the substantia nigra in PD detected by using inversion-recovery MRI correlate with the striatal dopaminergic function measured by (18)F-dopa positron emission tomography (PET) (42). These studies point to the possibility, with refinement of this technique, of detecting early or even presymptomatic PD.

MAGNETIC RESONANCE SPECTROSCOPY

Magnetic resonance spectroscopy (MRS) offers a noninvasive method of quantifying metabolite concentrations of human brain in vivo. MRS studies have primarily concentrated on the metabolites that could be visible with proton (¹H) spectroscopy. Principal metabolites detected by ¹H-MRS include N-acetylaspartate (NAA), creatine (Cr), choline (Cho), and lactate (43, 44). An early single-voxel ¹H MRS study found no significant difference of brain metabolism in the striatum between PD patients (27 to 83 years old) and controls. However, in an elderly subset of patients (51 to 70 years old), a significant decrease in striatal NAA/Cho was observed (45). Other early ¹H-MRS studies found a reduction of NAA/Cr or NAA/Cho ratio in the lentiform nucleus in MSA and PSP patients but not in those with PD (46, 47). In contrast, later studies found that the ratio of NAA/Cr or NAA/Cho in the lentiform nucleus is also decreased in PD patients (43, 48, 49). The different techniques used in these studies may be responsible for some of the difference in reported results (43). O'Neill and colleagues (50) used ¹H MRS of the substantia nigra, basal ganglia, and cerebral cortex in PD patients and healthy control subjects. Compared

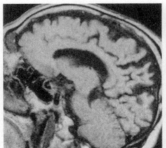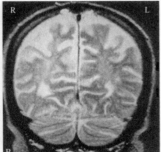

FIGURE 27-3

MRI of a patient with corticobasal degeneration signs more prominent on left. T1-weighted sagittal section of right hemisphere (A) shows atrophy in posterior frontal and parietal regions. T2-weighted coronal section (B) shows cerebral atrophy, more severe on the right. R: right; L: left. (Modified from reference 18 with permission from Lippincott Williams & Wilkins.)

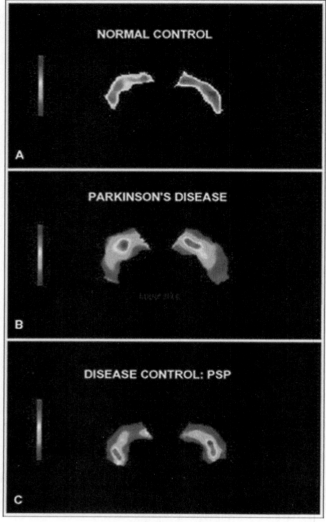

FIGURE 27-4

Segmented inversion-recovery ratio image of the substantia nigra pars compacta (SNC) in a normal control subject (A); a patient with Parkinson's disease (PD) (B); and a patient with progressive supranuclear palsy (PSP) (C). (Modified from reference 41 with permission from Elsevier.) See color section following page 356.

to controls, PD patients had approximately 24% lower creatine in the region of the substantia nigra, but no other significant between-group differences were found in the other nine regions examined. These findings indicate that PD-linked extranigral metabolic abnormalities may be difficult to detect with ¹H MRS.

MRS may be useful in the differentiation of various types of parkinsonism. A study of 82 patients with various parkinsonian disorders using ¹H-MRS found that patients with PD, PSP, CBD, MSA, and vascular parkinsonism (VP) all had significant reduction of the NAA/creatine/phosphocreatine (CRE) ratio in the putamen.

Patients with PSP, CBD, MSA and VP, but not PD had significant reductions of the NAA/CRE ratio in the frontal cortex. Patients with CBD and PSP had significant reductions of the NAA/CRE ratio in the putamen compared to patients with PD. The reduction of the NAA/CRE ratio in the putamen correlated with the severity of parkinsonism (51). Using multiple regional single-voxel ¹H-MRS at a magnetic field strength of 3.0 T, significant NAA/Cr reductions could be detected in the pontine basis or putamen in patients with MSA, which may help to differentiate MSA from PD (52). These research studies with MRS have revealed abnormalities in brain energy metabolism in patients with PD and prove that MRS may provide useful information in distinguishing PD from other parkinsonian disorders. However, the clinical role of MRS is still inconclusive.

A 31 phosphorus MRS (31)P MRS) technique with high temporal and spatial resolution has been developed to show mitochondrial function in PD patients by observing high-energy phosphates (HEPs) and intracellular pH (pH) in the visual cortex at rest, during, and after visual activation. In normal controls, HEPs remained unchanged during visual activation, but they rose significantly (by 16%) following visual stimulation; pH also increased during visual activation, with a slow return to rest values. In PD patients, HEPs were normal at rest and did not change during visual activation, but they fell significantly (by 36%) in the recovery period; pH did not reveal a homogeneous pattern, with a wide spread of values. Energy imbalance under increased oxidative metabolism requirements discloses a mitochondrial dysfunction present in the brain of patients with PD even in the absence of overt clinical manifestations. The heterogeneity of the physicochemical environment (i.e., pH) points to various degrees of subclinical brain involvement in PD. This study suggests that the combined use of MRS and brain activation is fundamental for the study of brain energetics in PD (53).

MAGNETIC RESONANCE IMAGING-BASED VOLUMETRY

Using MRI-based volumetry (MRV) with automated segmentation techniques, volume loss of brain can be detected. In recent years, voxel-based morphometry (VBM) has been increasingly used in neuroscientific and neurologic studies. The advantage of VBM is that it can determine in vivo volumetric changes in gray matter, white matter, and cerebrospinal fluid and is independent of the observer and region of interest (ROI) (54).

Studies using ROI-based MRV did not find any difference between PD patients and controls (55–57). But changes in several structures have been reported, such as a decrease in striatal and brainstem volumes in MSA and PSP patients and a reduction in cerebellar volume in MSA patients (55); a decreased putaminal volume in MSA patients (57); a whole brain volume loss, disproportionate atrophy of the frontal cortex, and caudate nucleus volume loss in PSP patients (56); and a reduction in average brain, brainstem, midbrain, and frontal gray matter volumes in PSP patients as well as an atrophy of parietal cortex and corpus callosum in CBD patients (58).

In contrast to these MRV studies, use of the VBM method did reveal gray-matter loss in PD patients. In PD with dementia, reduced gray matter volume compared to controls has been shown in extensive brain regions, including the temporal lobe, occipital lobe, hippocampus, parahippocampal gyrus, frontal lobe and left parietal lobe, anterior cingulate gyrus, thalamus, caudate nucleus, bilateral putamen, and accumbens nuclei (59–61). PD patients without dementia have reduced gray matter volume in the frontal lobe, limbic/paralimbic areas, hippocampus, left anterior cingulate gyrus, caudate nucleus, and left superior temporal gyrus (59–62) (Figure 27-5). A recent report found that a significant volume reduction of the putamen could be detected in early PD (63).

Some VBM studies have investigated volume loss in parkinsonian patients and compared the results with PD. There is extensive cortical and subcortical volume loss in MSA-P patients compared to PD patients and controls (62) as well as atrophy in the cerebellar hemispheres, vermis, mesencephalon, pons, orbitofrontal and midfrontal regions, and the temporomesial and insular areas of MSA-C patients compared to controls (64). In PSP patients, loss of gray matter has been shown in the prefrontal cortex, the insular region including the frontal opercula, both supplementary motor areas (SMA), and the left mediotemporal area compared to controls. White matter volume loss has been found in both frontotemporal regions and the mesencephalon (65). There is also significant tissue reduction in the cerebral peduncles and midbrain in PSP compared to PD and controls. Using VBM differences as a guide for the differential diagnosis of PSP from PD achieved a sensitivity of 83% and a specificity of 79% (66). PSP could be distinguished from PD by symmetric tissue loss in the frontal cortex (maximal in the orbitofrontal and medial frontal cortices), subcortical nuclei (midbrain, caudate and thalamic), and periventricular white matter. The intrinsic neurodegeneration of specific subcortical nuclei and frontal cortical subregions together may contribute to motor and behavioral disturbances in PSP and differentiate this disorder from PD within 2 to 4 years of symptom onset (67). The mean volume of the superior cerebellar peduncle is lower in patients with PSP than in those with PD or MSA, with a sensitivity of 74% and a specificity of 94%. These results suggest that visual assessment of the superior cerebellar peduncle may help to increase the clinical diagnostic accuracy in PSP as well as differentiating it from PD (68).

(A) TIV: Loss in PD

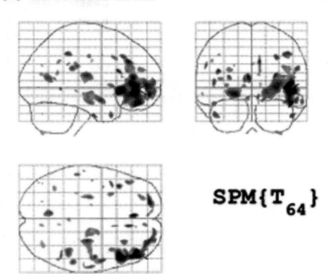

$$SPM\{T_{64}\}$$

(B) Global grey matter: Loss in PD

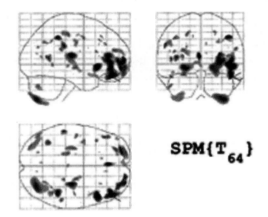

$$SPM\{T_{64}\}$$

FIGURE 27-5

Atrophy in Parkinson's disease patients shown (A) compensated for differences in head size, with significant gray matter loss observed in the right frontal lobe at $P < .001$ uncorrected, and (B) as regional changes in gray matter, above that occurring globally, with less significant changes in the right frontal lobe at $P < .01$ uncorrected. TIV: total intracranial volume. (Modified from reference 59 with permission from Oxford University Press.)

MRV may also help to predict the outcome of deep brain stimulation (DBS) of the subthalamic nucleus (STN). In an investigation of PD patients receiving bilateral STN stimulation, the volumes of the brain parenchyma, caudate nucleus, putamen, pallidum, and red nucleus and the surface of the mesencephalon were measured and normalized as percentages of the intracranial volume. The normalized brain parenchymal volume was lower in patients who were older and had a longer disease duration or a lower frontal score and was not predictive of the postoperative outcome. The residual scores for activities of daily living and parkinsonian motor disability were higher in patients with a smaller normalized mesencephalon. The normalized volume of the caudate nucleus was predictive of the pre- and postoperative levodopa-equivalent dosage. A smaller normalized mesencephalic surface was associated with a lower beneficial effect of subthalamic nucleus stimulation on parkinsonian motor disability, suggesting that the normalized mesencephalic surface is predictive of the postoperative outcome (69).

A novel morphometric method, voxel-based relaxometry (VBR), which analyzes the relaxation rate (R2) derived from multiecho T2-weighted images on a voxel-by-voxel basis, has been used to study the brain morphology of patients with MSA-C (70); the results were compared to those obtained by VBM (71). VBR analysis revealed a reduction in the R2 in the cerebellum and brainstem, reflecting infratentorial brain atrophy. The affected regions largely corresponded to those regions in which VBM showed reductions of gray and white matter. In addition, VBR analysis found increased R2 in the putamen, which did not display abnormalities in VBM study. These findings suggest that the combination of VBR and VBM may provide convergent and complementary information about brain morphology.

DIFFUSION-WEIGHTED IMAGING

Diffusion-weighted imaging (DWI) can detect fiber tracts in humans in vivo (72–76). It is sensitive to the random translational motion of water molecules in tissue and restricted by the highly organized architecture of fiber tracts. Diffusion in the white matter strongly follows the direction of fiber bundles. By varying the strength of the diffusion gradient, an apparent diffusion coefficient (ADC) in the direction of the gradient can be measured for each voxel. Neuronal loss and astrogliosis can increase the mobility of water molecules within the tissue architecture and result in an increased ADC. The diffusion tensor imaging (DTI) method allows quantitative analysis of DWI. In DTI, a tensor that describes diffusion in all spatial directions is calculated for each voxel. The diffusion tensor (DT) has 6 parameters, which express the magnitude of the directional components in 3 orthogonal directions (75, 77–79). Scalar measures include mean diffusivity (MD) and fractional anisotropy (FA). MD is the average of the ADCs estimated along any 3 orthogonal directions. FA expresses the extent to which diffusion varies in different directions and shows good contrast between gray and white matter. The most general method

to analyze data from DTI is to characterize the overall displacement of the molecules (average ellipsoid size) by calculating the mean diffusivity. For this purpose, the trace of the diffusion tensor (trace (D), calculated as the sum of the eigenvalues of the tensor, has been introduced. The mean diffusivity is then calculated by trace(D)/3.

DTI can demonstrate the distinct corticostriatal circuits in humans (80) and is increasingly used in PD studies. It has been observed that PD patients have a significantly decreased FA between the substantia nigra and the lower part of the putamen/caudate complex, which is obvious even in the early stages of PD (81). In a recent study with DWI of 12 PD patients with disease duration of 3.5 ± 1.5 years, significant increases in diffusivity in the region of both olfactory tracts was found among those with PD compared to normal controls. The trace (D) cutoff values for the voxel cluster of the olfactory tracts have been calculated from 9 patients with PD, disease duration 3.1 ± 1.3 years and 8 healthy subjects; 94% of the subjects were correctly discriminated with a sensitivity of 100% and a specificity of 88%. All PD patients were correctly classified and only 1 normal subject was classified as having the disease. Increased diffusivity in the olfactory tract is consonant with the well-established clinical finding of hyposmia in PD. These findings indicate the potential of this method in helping to diagnose PD (82).

This method also has the potential to be useful in differentiating PD from other parkinsonian syndromes. Schocke and colleagues (83) found that MSA-P patients have higher putaminal regional ADC (rADC) than PD patients, and suggest this method may provide additional support for the diagnosis of MSA-P (Figure 27-6). Because rADCs measured in one direction may underestimate diffusion-related pathologic processes, these authors later investigated the diffusivity in different brain areas by trace (D). They found that MSA-P patients had significantly higher putaminal and pallidal trace (D) values as well as rADCs in the y- and z-directions than PD patients. Putaminal trace (D) discriminated MSA-P from PD completely. Trace (D) imaging appears to be more accurate in the differentiation of MSA-P from PD (84). Another study found that striatal rADCs have a higher overall predictive accuracy than D2 receptor binding single-photon emission computed tomography (SPECT) with (123I) iodobenzamide (IBZM), suggesting that DWI may be more accurate than IBZM-SPECT in the differential diagnosis of PD and MSA-P (85).

MAGNETIZATION TRANSFER IMAGING

Magnetization transfer imaging (MTI) is based on the interactions between highly bound protons within structures such as myelin or cell membranes and the very mobile protons of free water (86, 87). By application of irradiation that

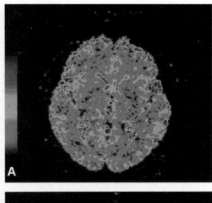

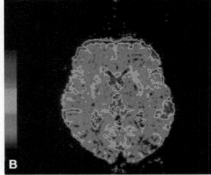

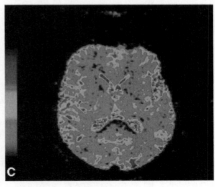

FIGURE 27-6

Apparent diffusion coefficient (ADC) maps (diffusion gradient switched in slice direction) were calculated by fitting the logarithm of the signal intensity as a function of the gradient factor "b" over 3 different b values for each pixel in patients with Parkinson's disease (A), patients with the Parkinson variant of multiple system atrophy (MSA-P) (B), and controls (C). Blue, green, red, and black represent descending regional ADC values. (Modified from reference 83 with permission from Lippincott Williams & Wilkins.) See color section following page 356.

selectively saturates the energy level of bound protons, exchange of magnetization between bound and free protons is induced and the signal intensity of bound protons reduced. The difference between signal intensities with and without application of the MT is measured by calculating the magnetization transfer ratios (MTRs), which correlate with the degree of myelination and axonal density. MT can be used to detect changes in the structural status of brain parenchyma that may or may not be visible with standard MR techniques (86, 88).

MTI has been used in PD investigations. One study found no differences in MTRs in any region between nondemented PD patients and controls. However, PD patients with dementia had significantly lower MTRs in the subcortical white matter—including the frontal white matter and the genu of the corpus callosum—compared to controls, whereas patients with PSP had lower MTRs in the subcortical gray matter, including the putamen, globus pallidus, and thalamus in addition to the subcortical white matter (89). In a later study, MTR differences between PD patients and controls were found in the supratentorial white matter and brainstem, including the substantia nigra, red nucleus, and pons. In particular, lower MTR values were found in the paraventricular white matter of PD patients. The authors proposed that MTR measurements in the paraventricular white matter and brainstem may be a marker for probable PD (90).

Another study comprising 15 PD patients, 12 MSA patients, 10 PSP patients, and 20 aged-matched healthy control subjects, Eckert and colleagues (91) found a change in the MTR in the globus pallidus, putamen, caudate nucleus, substantia nigra, and white matter in PD, MSA, and PSP patients. A stepwise linear discriminate analysis provided a good classification of the individual patients into the different disease groups. There was also a good discrimination of PD patients from control subjects and of MSA from PSP patients. These findings indicate the potential of MTI in helping to distinguish various types of parkinsonism.

FUNCTIONAL MAGNETIC RESONANCE IMAGING

Most early functional neuroimaging studies in PD used positron emission tomography (PET); however, the limitation of this technique, including limited temporal and spatial resolution and especially the exposure of human subjects to radioactivity, restricts its popular use. In the last decade, an exciting development has been functional MRI (fMRI). The most commonly used method is the blood oxygen level–dependent (BOLD) technique (92). This method detects changes of blood levels of oxygen saturation (because of the concentration of deoxyhemoglobin), and an area with more oxygenated blood is more intense on T2*-weighted images. Advantages of fMRI compared to PET include the fact that scanners are widely available (a commercial 1.5 T MR scanner is usually enough), much better temporal and spatial resolution, and avoidance of ionizing radiation. This last allows a single subject to be scanned repeatedly and makes it possible to recruit more subjects, thus increasing statistical power. Although some drawbacks exist, including the inability to directly detect dysfunction of nigrostriatal dopamine system and the fact that tremor may induce motion artifact, extensive fMRI studies have been performed and have provided important information on our understanding of PD.

PD is primarily a movement disorder. Therefore a number of fMRI studies have investigated brain activity during movement in PD. The common and perhaps most important findings of these studies are the hypoactivation of the rostral SMA (pre-SMA), and hyperactivation of other cortical motor regions, such as the lateral premotor cortex and parietal cortex in PD patients compared to normal subjects during the performance of different self-initiated movements (93–96)(Figure 27-7). These findings are consistent with previous PET studies (97–99). In contrast, the reported PD modulations of the primary motor cortex (M1) have been controversial. Both increased (93, 94) and decreased (95) activity of M1 has been observed. Levodopa administration could relatively normalize the dysfunction of the pre-SMA (94, 95) and decrease overactivation of other motor areas (94). The increased activity in the pre-SMA is highly correlated with improved motor performance. The pre-SMA is suggested to be critical in planning and initiating of movements and might play a primary role in the preparation of self-initiated movements (100–102). This region is one of the main receiving regions of the basal ganglia motor circuit (103). These results indicate that the dysfunction of the pre-SMA due to the deficit of nigrostriatal dopamine system is an important contributor to the akinesia in PD. Meanwhile, PD patients need compensatory activity of other motor circuits to overcome their difficulty in performing movements. The inconsistent findings on the activity of M1 may due to different motor tasks being employed.

Functional MRI also has been used to investigate the difficulty PD patients have in motor learning. In an implicit rule learning study, imaging results revealed highly similar frontomedian and posterior cingulate activations in early PD patients and controls in the absence of significant striatal and inferior frontal activations in patients. These findings suggest that in early PD, with the lateral striatofrontal dopaminergic projections being affected, medial dopaminergic projections involved in the application of previously learned rules may still be spared (104). A recent study investigated the underlying neural mechanisms of difficulty in performing automatic movements. PD patients showed significantly more difficulty in achieving automaticity compared to controls. They had greater activity in the cerebellum, premotor area, parietal cortex, precuneus, and prefrontal cortex compared with normal subjects while performing automatic movements. The results indicate that PD patients can

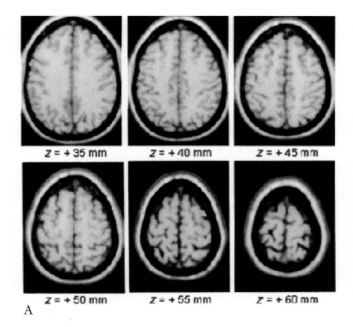

A

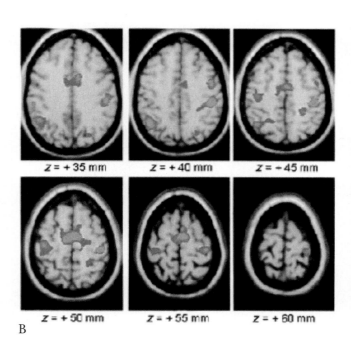

B

FIGURE 27-7

(A) Areas of relative overactivity in normal controls compared with patients with Parkinson's disease during a complex sequential right hand movement (z = location of area of activation above commissural plane; threshold = P < .01). (B) Areas of relative overactivity in patients with Parkinson's disease compared with normal controls during a complex sequential right hand movement, superimposed onto a stereotaxically normalized MRI brain scan (z = location of area of activation above commissural plane; threshold = P < .001). (Modified from reference 93 with permission from Oxford University Press.) See color section following page 356.

achieve automaticity after proper training, but with more difficulty. They require more brain activity to compensate for basal ganglia dysfunction in order to perform automatic movements (96).

Functional connectivity has been increasingly used to evaluate the interaction of neural networks. Rowe et al. (105) studied functional connectivity during a simple overlearned motor sequence task with and without an additional attentional (visual) task in PD patients. Patients had greater activation of the SMA during execution of the simple overlearned motor sequence but less increase when attending to their actions compared to normal subjects. In normal subjects, attention to action, but not attention to the visual task, increased the effective connectivity between prefrontal cortex and the lateral premotor cortex and the SMA. In patients, attention did not modulate the effective connectivity between the prefrontal, premotor cortex and SMA. These results suggest that there is a context-specific functional disconnection between the prefrontal cortex and the SMA and premotor cortex in PD.

PD patients suffer not only motor symptoms but also impaired in cognitive function. The mechanisms underlying cognitive deficits in PD are not understood. fMRI has been helpful in investigating cognitive dysfunction in PD. Comparison between cognitively impaired and unimpaired PD patients found that impaired PD patients had less activation in the prefrontal cortex and striatum during a working-memory task (106). During performing distinct phases of the Wisconsin Card Sorting Task, PD patients had decreased activation compared with controls in the ventrolateral prefrontal cortex when receiving negative feedback and in the posterior prefrontal cortex when matching after negative feedback. In controls, these prefrontal regions specifically coactivated with the striatum during those stages of task performance. In contrast, greater activation was found in the PD group compared with the control group in prefrontal regions, such as the posterior and the dorsolateral prefrontal cortex when receiving positive or negative feedback, that were not coactivated with the striatum in controls (107). When a sentence comprehension task was used, less activation in the prefrontal cortex as well as in the striatal and right temporal regions was also found in PD patients. In addition, the study also explored compensatory activation of the right inferior frontal and left posterolateral temporoparietal areas in PD patients similar to that observed during motor tasks (108).

Mattay et al. (109) studied the effects of dopaminergic deficit on working memory and the motor system in PD patients. Dopamine administration increased activation in the cortical motor regions; in contrast, the cortical regions subserving working memory displayed greater activation during the hypodopaminergic state. The increase in cortical activation during the work-

ing memory task in the hypodopaminergic state correlated positively with errors in task performance. The increased activation in the cortical motor regions during the dopamine-replete state correlated positively with improvement in motor function. These results support the idea that dopamine modulates cortical networks subserving working memory and motor function via two distinct mechanisms: nigrostriatal projections facilitate motor function indirectly via thalamic projections to motor cortices, whereas the mesocortical dopaminergic system facilitates working memory function via direct inputs to prefrontal cortex. This study suggests that the hypodopaminergic state is associated with decreased efficiency of prefrontal cortical information processing and that dopaminergic therapy improves the physiologic efficiency of this region.

Hallucinations occur in some PD patients, and this problem has been investigated with fMRI. PD patients with visual hallucinations showed greater activation in the inferior frontal gyrus and the caudate nucleus, and less activation in the parietal lobe and cingulate gyrus compared to PD patients without hallucination during stroboscopic (flashing) visual stimulation. During kinematic (apparent motion) stimulation, hallucinating PD subjects showed greater activation in the superior frontal gyrus and less activation in area V5/MT, parietal lobe, and cingulate gyrus compared to nonhallucinating PD subjects. These results suggest that PD patients with chronic visual hallucinations respond to visual stimuli with greater frontal and subcortical activation and less visual cortical activation than nonhallucinating PD subjects. Shifting visual circuitry from posterior to anterior regions associated primarily with attention processes suggests altered network organization may play a role in the pathophysiology of visual hallucinations in PD (110).

Modulation of brain activity can be detected in Parkin mutation carriers even without clinical symptoms. While performing internally selected or externally determined movements, asymptomatic carriers showed greater activity in the right rostral cingulate motor area (rCMA) and left dorsal premotor cortex specifically during internally selected movement compared to controls. In addition, synaptic activity in the rCMA had a stronger influence on activity in the basal ganglia in the context of internally selected movements in asymptomatic carriers. These results suggest that a subclinical nigrostriatal dysfunction exists even in asymptomatic Parkin mutation carriers. This deficit can be compensated by reorganization of striatocortical motor loops (111).

Treatment of PD with DBS of the thalamus, STN, or globus pallidus is common. However, the mechanism of DBS and its effects on the central nervous system is unclear. DBS of STN or thalamus is accompanied by increased activity of the subcortical regions ipsilateral to the stimulated nucleus, such as the thalamus, globus pallidus, substantia nigra, and superior colliculus and in prefrontal cortex and lateral premotor cortex (112) or decreased activation in the contralateral M1 and the ipsilateral cerebellum. Increased activation in the contralateral basal ganglia and insula region was also detected (113). Left-sided STN DBS, high-frequency stimulation improved motor symptoms, while stimulation of the right DBS alone elicited several reproducible episodes of acute depressive dysphoria. The electrode on the left was within the inferior STN, whereas the right electrode was marginally superior and lateral to the intended STN target within the fields of Forel/zona incerta. Comparing stimulation "off" versus "on" found that the left DBS was followed by increased activity in the M1, premotor cortex, ventrolateral thalamus, putamen, and cerebellum as well as decreased activity in the sensorimotor cortex and SMA. Right DBS showed increased activity in the superior prefrontal cortex, anterior cingulate, anterior thalamus, caudate, and brainstem and decreased activity in medial prefrontal cortex (114). These studies suggest that fMRI during DBS is safe, with considerable potential for investigating the functional connectivity of the stimulated nuclei.

SUMMARY

Conventional structural MRI shows no convincing structural changes in PD but may provide a useful tool in distinguishing PD from other neurodegenerative parkinsonian syndromes. However, the sensitivity and specificity of structural MRI on an individual basis is not sufficient for differential diagnosis of parkinsonian disorders, and further technical and methodological improvements are necessary. Other methods such as MRS, DWI, MRV, and MTI may help to differentiate between parkinsonian syndromes and PD and probably have superior sensitivity compared to structural MRI. Although some findings related to these techniques are promising and might even detect abnormalities in the early PD, they are still far from being standard methods in the routine clinical investigation of patients with parkinsonism and require additional extensive studies. Functional MRI is increasingly used in investigating PD and may be helpful in exploring PD related functional and pathologic changes.

References

1. Rutledge JN. Magnetic resonance imaging of movement disorders. In: Jankovic J, Tolosa E (eds). Parkinson's Disease and Movement Disorders, 2nd ed. Philadelphia: Lippincott Williams & Wilkins, 1993:511–530.
2. Savoiardo M, Grisoli M. Magnetic resonance imaging of movement disorders. In: Jankovic J, Tolosa E (eds). Parkinson's Disease and Movement Disorders, 4th ed. Philadelphia: Lippincott Williams & Wilkins, 2002:596–609.
3. Olanow CW. Magnetic resonance imaging in parkinsonism. Neurol Clin 1992; 10:405–420.
4. Duguid JR, De La Paz R, DeGroot J. Magnetic resonance imaging of the midbrain in Parkinson's disease. Ann Neurol 1986; 20:744–747.
5. Braffman BH, Grossman RI, Goldberg HI, et al. MR imaging of Parkinson disease with spin-echo and gradient-echo sequences. AJR Am J Roentgenol 1989; 152:159–165.
6. American Academy of Neurology. Assessment. Clinical autonomic testing report of the therapeutics and technology assessment subcommittee of the American Academy of Neurology. Neurology 1996; 46:873–880.
7. Pastakia B, Polinsky R, Di Chiro G, et al. Multiple system atrophy (Shy-Drager syndrome): MR imaging. Radiology 1986; 159:499–502.
8. Gilman S, Low P, Quinn N, et al. Consensus statement on the diagnosis of multiple system atrophy: American Society and American Academy of Neurology. Clin Auton Res 1998; 8:359–362.
9. Savoiardo M, Girotti F, Strada L, et al. Magnetic resonance imaging in progressive supranuclear palsy and other parkinsonian disorders. J Neurol Transm 1994; 42 (Suppl):93–110.
10. Watanabe H, Saito Y, Terao S, et al. Progression and prognosis in multiple system atrophy: An analysis of 230 Japanese patients. Brain 2002; 125:1070–1083.
11. Bhattacharya K, Saadia D, Eisenkraft B, et al. Brain magnetic resonance imaging in multiple-system atrophy and Parkinson disease: A diagnostic algorithm. Arch Neurol 2002; 59:835–842.
12. Schrag A, Kingsley D, Phatouros C, et al. Clinical usefulness of magnetic resonance imaging in multiple system atrophy. J Neurol Neurosurg Psychiatry 1998; 65:65–71.
13. Kraft E, Trenkwalder C, Auer DP. T2ʹ-weighted MRI differentiates multiple system atrophy from Parkinson's disease. Neurology 2002; 59:1265–1267.
14. Righini A, Antonini A, Ferrarini M, et al. Thin section MR study of the basal ganglia in the differential diagnosis between striatonigral degeneration and Parkinson disease. J Comput Assist Tomogr 2002; 26:266–271.
15. Savoiardo M, Strada L, Girotti F, et al. Olivopontocerebellar atrophy: MR diagnosis and relationship to multisystem atrophy. Radiology 1990; 174:693–696.
16. Savoiardo M, Strada L, Girotti F, et al. MR imaging in progressive supranuclear palsy and Shy-Drager syndrome. J Comput Assist Tomogr 1989; 13:555–560.
17. Stern MB, Braffman BH, Skolnick BE, et al. Magnetic resonance imaging in Parkinson's disease and parkinsonian syndromes. Neurology 1989; 39:1524–1526.
18. Soliveri P, Monza D, Paridi D, et al. Cognitive and magnetic resonance imaging aspects of corticobasal degeneration and progressive supranuclear palsy. Neurology 1999; 53:502–507.
19. Schrag A, Good CD, Miszkiel K, et al. Differentiation of atypical parkinsonian syndromes with routine MRI. Neurology 2000; 54:697–702.
20. Warmuth-Metz M, Naumann M, Csoti I, Solymosi L. Measurement of the midbrain diameter on routine magnetic resonance imaging: A simple and accurate method of differentiating between Parkinson disease and progressive supranuclear palsy. Arch Neurol 2001; 58:1076–1079.
21. Drayer BP, Olanow W, Burger P, et al. Parkinson plus syndrome: Diagnosis using high field MR imaging of brain iron. Radiology 1989; 159:493–498.
22. Davie CA, Wenning GK, Barker GJ, et al. Proton magnetic resonance spectroscopy in Steele-Richardson-Olszewski syndrome. Mov Disord 1997; 12:767–771.
23. Oba H, Yagishita A, Terada H, et al. New and reliable MRI diagnosis for progressive supranuclear palsy. Neurology 2005; 64:2050–2055.
24. Righini A, Antonini A, De Notaris R, et al. MR imaging of the superior profile of the midbrain: Differential diagnosis between progressive supranuclear palsy and Parkinson disease. AJNR Am J Neuroradiol 2004; 25:927–932.
25. Hauser RA, Murtaugh FR, Akhter K, et al. Magnetic resonance imaging of corticobasal degeneration. J Neuroimaging 1996; 6:222–226.
26. Winkelmann J, Auer DP, Lechner C, et al. Magnetic resonance imaging findings in corticobasal degeneration. Mov Disord 1999; 14:669–673.
27. Savoiardo M. Differential diagnosis of Parkinson's disease and atypical parkinsonian disorders by magnetic resonance imaging. Neurol Sci 2003; 24(Suppl 1):S35–S37.
28. Molinuevo J, Munoz E, Valldeoriola F, et al. The eye of the tiger sign in cortico-basal ganglionic degeneration. Mov Disord 1999; 14:169–171.
29. Josephs KA, Tang-Wai DF, Edland SD, et al. Correlation between antemortem magnetic resonance imaging findings and pathologically confirmed corticobasal degeneration. Arch Neurol 2004; 61:1881–1884.
30. Manyam BV, Bhatt MH, Moore WD, et al. Bilateral striopallidodentate calcinosis: Cerebrospinal fluid, imaging, and electrophysiological studies. Ann Neurol 1992; 31:379–384.
31. Waters CH. Structural lesions and parkinsonism. In: Stern MB, Koller WC (eds). Parkinsonian Syndromes. New York: Marcel Dekker, 1993:483–501.
32. Krauss JK, Paduch T, Mundinger F, et al. Parkinsonism and rest tremor secondary to supratentorial tumours sparing the basal ganglia. Acta Neurochir (Wien) 1995; 133:22–29.
33. Tranchant C, Bhatia KP, Marsden CD. Movement disorders in multiple sclerosis. Mov Disord 1995; 10:418–424.
34. Saatci I, Topcu M, Baltaoglu FF, et al. Cranial MR findings in Wilson's disease. Acta Radiol 1997; 38:250–258.
35. Heiss WD, Hilker R. The sensitivity of 18-fluorodopa positron emission tomography and magnetic resonance imaging in Parkinson's disease. Eur J Neurol 2004; 11:5–12.
36. Sibon I, Tison F. Vascular parkinsonism. Curr Opin Neurol 2004; 17:49–54.
37. Hutchinson M, Raff U. Parkinson's disease: A novel MRI method for determining structural changes in the substantia nigra. J Neurol Neurosurg Psychiatry 1999; 67:815–818.
38. Hutchinson M, Raff U. Structural changes of the substantia nigra in Parkinson's disease as revealed by MR imaging. Am J Neuroradiol 2000; 21:697–701.
39. Adachi M, Hosoya T, Haku T, et al. Evaluation of the substantia nigra in patients with Parkinson's syndrome accomplished using multishot diffusion-weighted MR imaging. Am J Neuroradiol 1999; 20:1500–1506.

40. Oikawa H, Sasaki M, Tamakawa Y, et al. The substantia nigra in Parkinson's disease: Proton density-weighted spin-echo and fast short inversion time inversion-recovery MR findings. *Am J Neuroradiol* 2002; 23:1747–1756.
41. Hutchinson M, Raff U, Lebedev S. MRI correlates of pathology in parkinsonism: Segmented inversion recovery ratio imaging (SIRRIM). *Neuroimage* 2003; 20:1899–1902.
42. Hu MT, White SJ, Herlihy AH, et al. A comparison of (18)F-dopa PET and inversion recovery MRI in the diagnosis of Parkinson's disease. *Neurology* 2001; 56:1195–1200.
43. Firbank MJ, Harrison RM, O'Brien JT. A comprehensive review of proton magnetic resonance spectroscopy studies in dementia and Parkinson's disease. *Dement Geriatr Cogn Disord* 2002; 14:64–76.
44. Schocke MF, Berger T, Felber SR, et al. Serial contrast-enhanced magnetic resonance imaging and spectroscopic imaging of acute multiple sclerosis lesions under high-dose methylprednisolone therapy. Neuroimage 2003; 20:1253–1263.
45. Holshouser BA, Komu M, Moller HE, et al. Localized proton NMR spectroscopy in the striatum of patients with idiopathic Parkinson's disease: A multicenter pilot study. *Magn Reson Med* 1995; 33:589–594.
46. Davie CA, Wenning GK, Barker GJ, et al. Differentiation of multiple system atrophy from idiopathic Parkinson's disease using proton magnetic resonance spectroscopy. *Ann Neurol* 1995; 37:204–210.
47. Federico F, Simone IL, Lucivero V, et al. Proton magnetic resonance spectroscopy in Parkinson's disease and atypical parkinsonian disorders. *Mov Disord* 1997; 12:903–909.
48. Clarke CE, Lowry M. Basal ganglia metabolite concentrations in idiopathic Parkinson's disease and multiple system atrophy measured by proton magnetic resonance spectroscopy. *Eur J Neurol* 2000; 7:661–665.
49. Clarke CE, Lowry M. Systematic review of proton magnetic resonance spectroscopy of the striatum in parkinsonian syndromes. *Eur J Neurol* 2001; 8:573–577.
50. O'Neill J, Schuff N, Marks WJ Jr, et al. Quantitative 1H magnetic resonance spectroscopy and MRI of Parkinson's disease. *Mov Disord* 2002; 17:917–927.
51. Abe K, Terakawa H, Takanashi M, et al. Proton magnetic resonance spectroscopy of patients with parkinsonism. *Brain Res Bull* 2000; 52:589–595.
52. Watanabe H, Fukatsu H, Katsuno M, et al. Multiple regional 1H-MR spectroscopy in multiple system atrophy: NAA/Cr reduction in pontine base as a valuable diagnostic marker. *J Neurol Neurosurg Psychiatry* 2004; 75:103–109.
53. Rango M, Bonifati C, Bresolin N. Parkinson's disease and brain mitochondrial dysfunction: A functional phosphorus magnetic resonance spectroscopy study. *J Cereb Blood Flow Metab* 2006; 26:283–290.
54. Ashburner J, Friston KJ. Voxel-based morphometry: The methods. *Neuroimage* 2000; 11:805–821.
55. Schulz JB, Skalej M, Wedekind D, et al. Magnetic resonance imaging-based volumetry differentiates idiopathic Parkinson's syndrome from multiple system atrophy and progressive supranuclear palsy. *Ann Neurol* 1999; 45:65–74.
56. Cordato NJ, Pantelis C, Halliday GM, et al. Frontal atrophy correlates with behavioural changes in progressive supranuclear palsy. *Brain* 2002; 125:789–800.
57. Ghaemi M, Hilker R, Rudolf J, et al. Differentiating multiple system atrophy from Parkinson's disease: Contribution of striatal and midbrain MRI volumetry and multi-tracer PET imaging. *J Neurol Neurosurg Psychiatry* 2002; 73:517–523.
58. Groschel K, Hauser TK, Luft A, et al. Magnetic resonance imaging-based volumetry differentiates progressive supranuclear palsy from corticobasal degeneration. *Neuroimage* 2004; 21:714–724.
59. Burton EJ, McKeith IG, Burn DJ, et al. Cerebral atrophy in Parkinson's disease with and without dementia: A comparison with Alzheimer's disease, dementia with Lewy bodies and controls. *Brain* 2004; 127:791–800.
60. Nagano-Saito A, Washimi Y, Arahata Y, et al. Cerebral atrophy and its relation to cognitive impairment in Parkinson disease. *Neurology* 2005; 64:224–229.
61. Summerfield C, Junque C, Tolosa E, et al. Structural brain changes in Parkinson disease with dementia: A voxel-based morphometry study. *Arch Neurol* 2005; 62:281–285.
62. Brenneis C, Seppi K, Schocke MF, et al. Voxel-based morphometry detects cortical atrophy in the Parkinson variant of multiple system atrophy. *Mov Disord* 2003; 18:1132–1138.
63. Geng D, Li Y, Zee C. Magnetic resonance imaging-based volumetric analysis of basal ganglia nuclei and substantia nigra in patients with Parkinson's disease. *Neurosurgery* 2006; 58:256–262.
64. Brenneis C, Boesch SM, Egger KE, et al. Cortical atrophy in the cerebellar variant of multiple system atrophy: A voxel-based morphometry study. *Mov Disord* 2006; 21:159–165.
65. Brenneis C, Seppi K, Schocke M, et al. Voxel based morphometry reveals a distinct pattern of frontal atrophy in progressive supranuclear palsy. *J Neurol Neurosurg Psychiatry* 2004; 75:246–249.
66. Price S, Paviour D, Scahill R, et al. Voxel-based morphometry detects patterns of atrophy that help differentiate progressive supranuclear palsy and Parkinson's disease. *Neuroimage* 2004; 23:663–669.
67. Cordato NJ, Duggins AJ, Halliday GM, et al. Clinical deficits correlate with regional cerebral atrophy in progressive supranuclear palsy. *Brain* 2005; 128:1259–1266.
68. Paviour DC, Price SL, Stevens JM, et al. Quantitative MRI measurement of superior cerebellar peduncle in progressive supranuclear palsy. *Neurology* 2005; 64:675–679.
69. Bonneville F, Welter ML, Elie C, et al. Parkinson disease, brain volumes, and subthalamic nucleus stimulation. *Neurology* 2005; 64:1598–1604.
70. Specht K, Minnerop M, Muller-Hubenthal J, et al. Voxel-based analysis of multiple-system atrophy of cerebellar type: Complementary results by combining voxel-based morphometry and voxel-based relaxometry. *Neuroimage* 2005; 25:287–293.
71. Specht K, Minnerop M, Abele M, et al. In vivo voxel-based morphometry in multiple system atrophy of the cerebellar type. *Arch Neurol* 2003; 60:1431–1435.
72. Basser PJ. Inferring microstructural features and the physiological state of tissues from diffusion-weighted images. *NMR Biomed* 1995; 8:333–344.
73. Conturo TE, Lori NF, Cull TS, et al. Tracking neuronal fiber pathways in the living human brain. *Proc Natl Acad Sci USA* 1999; 96:10422–10427.
74. Mori S, Crain BJ, Chacko VP, et al. Three-dimensional tracking of axonal projections in the brain by magnetic resonance imaging. *Ann Neurol* 1999; 45:265–269.
75. Basser PJ, Pajevic S, Pierpaoli C, et al. In vivo fiber tractography using DT-MRI data. *Magn Reson Med* 2000; 44:625–632.
76. Poupon C, Clark CA, Frouin V, et al. Regularization of diffusion-based direction maps for the tracking of brain white matter fascicles. *Neuroimage* 2000; 12:184–195.
77. Basser PJ, Mattiello J, LeBihan D. MR diffusion tensor spectroscopy and imaging. *Biophys J* 1994; 66:259–267.
78. Pierpaoli C, Jezzard P, Basser PJ, et al. Diffusion tensor MR imaging of the human brain. *Radiology* 1996; 201:637–648.
79. Le Bihan D, Mangin JF, Poupon C, et al. Diffusion tensor imaging: Concepts and applications. *J Magn Reson Imaging* 2001; 13:534–546.
80. Lehericy S, Ducros M, Van de Moortele PF, et al. Diffusion tensor fiber tracking shows distinct corticostriatal circuits in humans. *Ann Neurol* 2004; 55:522–529.
81. Yoshikawa K, Nakata Y, Yamada K, et al. Early pathological changes in the parkinsonian brain demonstrated by diffusion tensor MRI. *J Neurol Neurosurg Psychiatry* 2004; 75:481–484.
82. Scherfler C, Schocke MF, Seppi K, et al. Voxel-wise analysis of diffusion weighted imaging reveals disruption of the olfactory tract in Parkinson's disease. *Brain* 2006; 129:538–542.
83. Schocke MF, Seppi K, Esterhammer R, et al. Diffusion-weighted MRI differentiates the Parkinson variant of multiple system atrophy from PD. *Neurology* 2002; 58:575–580.
84. Schocke MF, Seppi K, Esterhammer R, et al. Trace of diffusion tensor differentiates the Parkinson variant of multiple system atrophy and Parkinson's disease. *Neuroimage* 2004; 21:1443–1451.
85. Seppi K, Schocke MF, Donnemiller E, et al. Comparison of diffusion-weighted imaging and (^{123}I)IBZM-SPECT for the differentiation of patients with the Parkinson variant of multiple system atrophy from those with Parkinson's disease. *Mov Disord* 2004; 19:1438–1445.
86. Wolff SD, Balaban RS. Magnetization transfer contrast (MTC) and tissue water proton relaxation in vivo. *Magn Reson Med* 1989; 10:135–144.
87. van Buchem MA, Tofts PS. Magnetization transfer imaging. *Neuroimaging Clin North Am* 2000; 10:771–788.
88. Meyer JR, Androux RW, Salamon N, et al. Contrast-enhanced magnetization transfer MR of the brain: Importance of precontrast images. *AJNR Am J Neuroradiol* 1997; 18:1515–1521.
89. Hanyu H, Asano T, Sakurai H, et al. Magnetisation transfer measurements of the subcortical grey and white matter in Parkinson's disease with and without dementia and in progressive supranuclear palsy. *Neuroradiology* 2001; 43:542–546.
90. Tambasco N, Pelliccioli GP, Chiarini P, et al. Magnetization transfer changes of grey and white matter in Parkinson's disease. *Neuroradiology* 2003; 45:224–230.
91. Eckert T, Sailer M, Kaufmann J, et al. Differentiation of idiopathic Parkinson's disease, multiple system atrophy, progressive supranuclear palsy, and healthy controls using magnetization transfer imaging. *Neuroimage* 2004; 21:229–235.
92. Ogawa S, Lee TM, Kay AR, et al. Brain magnetic resonance imaging with contrast dependent on blood oxygenation. *Proc Natl Acad Sci USA* 1990; 87:9868–9872.
93. Sabatini U, Boulanouar K, Fabre N, et al. Cortical motor reorganization in akinetic patients with Parkinson's disease: A functional MRI study. *Brain* 2000; 123:394–403.
94. Haslinger B, Erhard P, Kampfe N, et al. Event-related functional magnetic resonance imaging in Parkinson's disease before and after levodopa. *Brain* 2001; 124:558–570.
95. Buhmann C, Glauche V, Sturenburg HJ, et al. Pharmacologically modulated fMRI—cortical responsiveness to levodopa in drug-naïve hemiparkinsonian patients. *Brain* 2003; 126:451–461.
96. Wu T, Hallett M. A functional MRI study of automatic movements in patients with Parkinson's disease. *Brain* 2005; 128:2250–2259.
97. Playford ED, Jenkins IH, Passingham RE, et al. Impaired mesial frontal and putamen activation in Parkinson's disease: A positron emission tomography study. *Ann Neurol* 1992; 32:151–161.
98. Jahanshani M, Jenkins H, Brown RG, et al. Self-initiated versus externally triggered movements. I. An investigation using measurement of regional cerebral blood flow with PET and movement-related potentials in normal and Parkinson's disease subjects. *Brain* 1995; 118:913–933.
99. Samuel M, Ceballos-Baumann AD, Blin J, et al. Evidence for lateral premotor and parietal overactivity in Parkinson's disease during sequential and bimanual movements: A PET study. *Brain* 1997; 120: 963–976.
100. Deiber MP, Passingham RE, Colebatch JG, et al. Cortical areas and the selection of movement: A study with positron emission tomography. *Exp Brain Res* 1991; 84:393–402.
101. Jenkins IH, Jahanshahi M, Jueptner M, et al. Self-initiated versus externally triggered movements. II. The effect of movement predictability on regional cerebral blood flow. *Brain* 2000; 123:1216–1228.
102. Cunnington R, Windischberger C, Deecke L, et al. The preparation and execution of self-initiated and externally triggered movement: A study of event-related fMRI. *Neuroimage* 2002; 15:373–385.
103. Schell GR, Strick PL. The origin of thalamic inputs to the arcuate premotor and supplementary motor areas. *J Neurosci* 1984; 4:539–560.
104. Werheid K, Zysset S, Muller A, et al. Rule learning in a serial reaction time task: An fMRI study on patients with early Parkinson's disease. *Brain Res Cogn Brain Res* 2003: 16:273–284.
105. Rowe J, Stephan KE, Friston K, et al. Attention to action in Parkinson's disease: Impaired effective connectivity among frontal cortical regions. *Brain* 2002; 125:276–289.

106. Lewis SJ, Dove A, Robbins TW, et al. Cognitive impairments in early Parkinson's disease are accompanied by reductions in activity in frontostriatal neural circuitry. *J Neurosci* 2003; 23:6351–6356.

107. Monchi O, Petrides M, Doyon J, et al. Neural bases of set-shifting deficits in Parkinson's disease. *J Neurosci* 2004; 24:702–710.

108. Grossman M, Cooke A, DeVita C, et al. Grammatical and resource components of sentence processing in Parkinson's disease: An fMRI study. *Neurology* 2003; 60:775–781.

109. Mattay VS, Tessitore A, Callicott JH, et al. Dopaminergic modulation of cortical function in patients with Parkinson's disease. *Ann Neurol* 2002; 51:156–164.

110. Stebbins GT, Goetz CG, Carrillo MC, et al. Altered cortical visual processing in PD with hallucinations: an fMRI study. *Neurology* 2004; 63:1409–1416.

111. Buhmann C, Binkofski F, Klein C, et al. Motor reorganization in asymptomatic carriers of a single mutant Parkin allele: A human model for presymptomatic parkinsonism. *Brain* 2005; 128:2281–2290.

112. Jech R, Urgosik D, Tintera J, et al. Functional magnetic resonance imaging during deep brain stimulation: A pilot study in four patients with Parkinson's disease. *Mov Disord* 2001; 16:1126–1132.

113. Hesselmann V, Sorger B, Girnus R, et al. Intraoperative functional MRI as a new approach to monitor deep brain stimulation in Parkinson's disease. *Eur Radiol* 2004; 14:686–690.

114. Stefurak T, Mikulis D, Mayberg H, et al. Deep brain stimulation for Parkinson's disease dissociates mood and motor circuits: A functional MRI case study. *Mov Disord* 2003; 18:1508–1516.

28 Controversies in Neuroimaging

Paul Morrish

If a man is offered a fact which goes against his instincts he will scrutinize it closely and, unless the evidence is overwhelming, he will refuse to believe it. If, on the other hand, he is offered something which affords a reason for acting in accordance to his instincts he will accept it even on the slightest evidence. The origin of myths is explained in this way.

Bertrand Russell

There is a series of speculative statements that, when coupled to persuasive images, may explain the appeal of functional imaging studies to learned publications and scientific meetings concerning Parkinson's disease (PD).

The argument runs as follows: In PD, postmortem data tell us that symptoms begin when 70% of nigrostriatal dopaminergic neurons have been lost (1). [18F]dopa positron emission tomography (dopa-PET) and dopamine presynaptic transporter ligand single photon emission computed tomography (DAT-SPECT) provide a measurement of the integrity of these dopaminergic neurons in the living human brain. These techniques can therefore be used to confirm the diagnosis in patients with PD (those that are symptomatic and have less than 70% dopaminergic neurons) and to identify asymptomatic individuals with preclinical disease (those with no symptoms but fewer than normal dopaminergic neurons). The tech-niques also allow objective measurement of progression in the dopaminergic pathology that characterizes the disease. In contradiction to the "long latency" theory (2), the majority of dopa-PET and DAT-SPECT studies (3, 4) have shown the illness to have a short preclinical period and a rapid rate of progression; thus these indices can be used as biomarkers in neuroprotection studies. Two studies, CALM (5) and REAL (6), which used imaging endpoints, have shown that agonist drugs have a neuroprotective effect, while a third (ELLDOPA) (7) has shown levodopa to be toxic. These studies have also demonstrated that some recruited patients, clinically diagnosed as having PD, have normal scans. The patients in this group have been labeled as SWEDDs (symptomatic without evidence of dopaminergic deficit) and are likely to represent misdiagnoses. Because of its cost advantage and ease of use, DAT-SPECT is more likely than dopa-PET to become the invaluable aid to diagnosis and disease monitoring that has long been needed. Ultimately, and with further investment, dopa-PET and DAT-SPECT could be used to screen the population to identify those at risk of developing PD. Neuroprotective treatment might then be introduced for the vulnerable.

Controversy has arisen whenever this series or its component statements have been questioned. This chapter considers this set of statements and the arguments that have been used for evidence in support and in opposition. It also offers an alternative view of the contribution of dopa-PET and DAT-SPECT to knowledge about PD. The chapter is confined to dopa-PET and DAT-SPECT because these are the techniques and ligands that are most readily available and for which most has been claimed and disputed.

THE CONTROVERSIES AND THE EVIDENCE

In Parkinson's Disease, Symptoms Begin When 70% of Nigrostriatal Dopaminergic Neurons Have Been Lost

Though not the basis of an imaging controversy, this statement has provided the supporting evidence for the results of many imaging studies (8). The understanding that the nigrostriatal dopamine system is massively damaged at symptom onset began 46 years ago with the pioneering work of Ehringer and Hornykiewicz (9) and their recognition of the key role of dopamine in PD. In 1973, Bernheimer (1) and colleagues published a postmortem study of 69 cases of parkinsonism and 28 controls showing severe depletion of dopamine in the striatum (greater than 80%) in PD and demonstrating a correlation between striatal dopamine and nigral cell count. Other authors (10) subsequently interpreted these data to imply that nigral cell loss was advanced by at least 50% at the onset of symptoms. Calne and Langston (2) assembled this and other evidence to argue that progression in PD was likely to be the consequence of the normal aging process superimposed on a previous insult to the striatum. Studying postmortem specimens from patients with a wide range of disease severity and duration, Fearnley and Lees (11) predicted, in contrast, an exponentially progressing disease course, a short preclinical period (4.7 years), and symptom onset when the nigral dopaminergic cell count was 69% of normal. The difficulties with all such postmortem studies include argument over the choice of cell counting method, the effects on biochemistry of delay between death and analysis, and extrapolating back from patients with unavoidably prolonged duration and clinically advanced disease. Braak and colleagues (12) have provided a reevaluation of the relationship between pathology and symptoms. These authors hypothesize a pathologic progression before and during symptom progression, emphasizing that the nigral melanoneurons are not the first brain structures to develop PD-related lesions. With regard to this chapter, the most important point may be that Braak's studies (12) do not necessarily imply massive nigral cell loss (or dopamine loss) at symptom presentation or that loss of dopaminergic nigrostriatal neurons is the most important pathologic or biochemical marker of preclinical PD.

The conclusion, pending further pathologic studies around symptom onset, has to be that assumptions about nigral cell loss at symptom onset may not be correct and do not give validity to matching imaging results.

Dopa-PET and DAT-SPECT Measure the Integrity of Nigrostriatal Dopaminergic Neurons

The meaning of dopa-PET and DAT-SPECT, in terms of dopaminergic pathology, is unknown. The crucial (and frequently overlooked) understanding is that they provide biochemical rather than pathologic or anatomic measurements. A recent multiauthor review (13) has looked for evidence that might validate them as markers of pathology but found it to be lacking. It is likely that dopa-PET makes a measurement of stored [18F]dopa or of aromatic acid decarboxylase (AADC) in whichever structure is being observed, but its relationship to actual cell or terminal count is unknown. Certainly dopa-PET results have been correlated with nigral neuron count in MPTP monkeys (14), but the single study (15) that describes a correlation in humans (and is invariably quoted in dopa-PET papers) examined only 5 subjects, 4 of whom did not have PD. DAT-SPECT provides a measurement of the availability of the presynaptic dopamine reuptake transporter, the concentration of which declines in human PD (16), but its relationship to pathology is also unclear. The biochemical measurements that arise from dopa-PET and DAT-SPECT may be vulnerable to up- or downregulation (17, 18) with disease progression or medication. They are certainly a product of complicated biochemical and mathematical analyses, and different machines and methods give different results (3). There is also significant error in the measurement of whatever they are measuring—a subject considered further on.

We cannot be confident that dopa-PET and DAT-SPECT measure cell count, but we can be confident that their results relate to clinical progression in PD. Despite the theoretical use of these techniques in identifying preclinical disease (i.e., where result is unrelated to symptom severity), one of the consistent findings in dopa-PET and DAT-SPECT studies has been a correlation between their indices and clinical severity (19, 20). The relationship between any aspect of disease severity measured clinically and that measured by these biochemical tools is likely to be imperfect. The changing pathology and neurochemistry that underlies the heterogeneous symptom progression of PD (21) is certainly likely to be a great deal more complex than a change in the single biochemical and anatomic group of neurons examined. Dopa-PET and DAT-SPECT and clinical measurements also have error, and both may be affected by medication in different ways at different stages of disease. The advantages that biomarker measurements might offer over clinical measurements have been comprehensively considered (22–24). In brief they offer (in theory) a single objective (and possibly linear) continuous measurement free of mood and medication effect. Against that lie the expense, radiation exposure, and lack of availability.

Thus the answer to the question of what dopa-PET and DAT-SPECT results mean is that they measure something that deteriorates with clinical progression and are likely to be related in some as yet unknown way to the biochemical and pathologic processes underlying progression. It is overly simplistic (and perhaps incorrect) to conclude that they measure the integrity of nigrostriatal dopamine neurons.

What Happens to Dopa-PET and DAT-SPECT Results With Normal Aging?

This is an important question; yet, although it has been considered, it has not been well answered. It seems fair to remark here that the pathology of the aging nigrostriatal dopaminergic system seems equally unclear. One study (25) suggests an age-dependent decline (5.8% per 10 years) in pigmented nigral neurons, whereas another (26) did not detect any loss in aged subjects. The question is crucial to the interpretation of imaging results; if there is no change in biomarker yet there is change in pathology with aging, then human biochemistry must be capable of compensation to provide continuing normal dopaminergic function (and presumably therefore normal dopa-PET and DAT-SPECT results). If the pathologists' estimates of 70% loss before symptom onset are correct, then there must be upregulation (or inbuilt redundancy) to permit continuing (until this point) normal function. If the system does indeed upregulate, how can the techniques be used to measure dopaminergic cell count? The question also seems apposite in assessing the validity of the technique in discriminating PD from normal. Should the results in the normal population be adjusted for age or should they not?

An early PET controversy considered the change in dopa-PET results with normal aging. The earliest study (27) identified deterioration in striatal Ki of 53% in 10 subjects between the ages of 22 and 80 years. The second published study (28), of 26 healthy individuals, showed no decline in caudate and putamenal Ki with aging. This led the author, Sawle (28), to make a direct and then controversial challenge to the long-latency theory of Calne and Langston (2), stating that the progression seen in PD (and potentially measurable by dopa-PET) was not a consequence of aging. A later study of 19 individuals by Eidelberg and colleagues (29) supported the findings of Sawle. The subject has, however, been revisited by Kumakura and colleagues (30), who, with a new analytic method, identified a 58% reduction in [18F]dopa storage in the elderly human brain.

This confusion and controversy (31, 32) regarding a group as apparently uncomplicated as the aging normal population demonstrates many problems that recur in functional imaging studies; small samples, technical differences, and defensive argument.

There appears to be more unity in DAT-SPECT studies of aging. Striatal DAT binding has been demonstrated, in cross-sectional studies, to decrease by 6.6% (n = 126) (33), 5% (n = 13) (34), and 7% (n = 36) (35) per decade. Sadly, without unity (or at least a firm majority) in pathologic studies, it cannot be concluded that DAT-SPECT is a better marker (assuming that all other things such as reproducibility, sensitivity, resistance to confounders are equal) of neuronal integrity than dopa-PET. If these aging studies are correct and dopamine reuptake transporter does not upregulate with age, then all DAT-SPECT studies (whether diagnostic or measuring progression) must be adjusted to compensate.

Can DAT-SPECT and Dopa-PET Reliably Discriminate Normal From PD at Symptom Onset and Can They Usefully Detect Preclinical PD?

It might be assumed that symptomatic individuals with dopa-PET and DAT-SPECT scan results in the normal range (SWEDDs) are misdiagnoses (36), while healthy individuals with results outside the normal range have preclinical disease (37). To answer these questions, it is necessary to consider the discriminating ability (the accurate separation of normal from abnormal) of any test in a population—a subject considered (and explained with more clarity) in many statistics textbooks but included in brief here to assist the arguments.

In any measurement in a healthy population, there is a spread of results (following a normal distribution) around the mean. The extent of spread, or standard deviation, around the mean depends on many factors. For imaging, it depends on the biochemical, physiologic, or anatomic differences within the population and also the reliability of the technique. An unreliable technique has the effect of scattering results (whether from healthy or unhealthy populations) around a mean. Some published mean and standard deviations (expressed as a percentage of the mean) from healthy individuals examined by dopa-PET and DAT-SPECT are given in Table 28-1. The assumption here is that the healthy normal is not age-dependent.

In order to estimate the ability of the technique to detect abnormality, either in healthy or unhealthy populations, it is necessary to know or to estimate the threshold for symptom onset. This can be estimated by:

1. Examining either side in patients with a pure hemiparkinsonian syndrome (i.e., one striatum is connected

TABLE 28-1
Means and SDs in Studied Healthy Populations. Method of Analysis, Structure, and Units Are not Given*

STUDY	LIGAND	N	NORMAL MEAN	SD	SD (AS % NORMAL MEAN)
Morrish (20)	Dopa-PET	16	.0123	.0023	19%
Khan (38)	Dopa-PET	16	.0169	.0031	18%
Hilker (39)	Dopa-PET	16	.0126	.0013	10%
Haapaniemi (40)	[123I]β-CIT DAT-SPECT	21	6.8	1.1	16%
Seibyl (41)	[123I]β -CIT DAT-SPECT	27	8.4	2.52	30%
Tissingh (42)	[123I]FP-CIT DAT-SPECT	14	2.38–2.48	0.7–0.8	29%–32%

*For ease of presentation.

to an asymptomatic side, the other to a symptomatic side, so the threshold lies somewhere between).

2. Correlation in a cross-sectional study. The threshold is assumed to be the value of the imaging marker when the clinical measurement is zero. The flaw in this approach is the assumption of a linear relationship between a multicomponent ordinal scale such as the Unified Parkinson Disease Rating Scale (UPDRS) and the imaging measurement.

3. Extrapolating back from a longitudinal study, where the imaging measurement at symptom onset can be estimated. An assumption must be made here of either linearity or nonlinearity in index progression over time.

Some estimated thresholds (and the method used) for symptom development are given in Table 28-2.

Taking the study (41) with the widest range in the normal population, a healthy individual could have a result up to 60% (two SDs) below or above the mean, with an inevitable overlap between the lower limit of normal and the estimated symptom threshold (of 47% to 72%) (43). A passing comment is that no

one (yet, perhaps) has referred to the group above the normal mean as having dopaminergic superiority, or PD resistance, despite the desire to label those below it as "preclinical." If everyone within that broad but normal population lost sufficient dopaminergic metabolism to reach their personal threshold for disease, those starting at the normal mean would now be at 47% to 72% of normal, but those who started out at 160% of the normal mean might still have a result above the normal mean. These latter individuals would be SWEDDs, with results within the normal range but still having PD. In a similar fashion, a population thought to be healthy will contain some individuals (those that start 50% to 60% below the mean) falling into the area expected to be parkinsonian. This group will contain healthy individuals with a low PET/SPECT index, perhaps as a consequence of their personal biochemistry or anatomy (or measurement error); it is unnecessary to invoke or assume pathology. If there are "preclinical" individuals in such a broadly spread population, most will be hidden within the normal range.

Knowledge of the threshold and the spread around the normal mean allows a calculation of the sensitivity and specificity of the technique. False negatives are those from a population at threshold (i.e., mean = threshold) whose result lies in the normal range (more than 2 SDs below the normal mean). False positives are that group of the normal population whose results lie more than 2 SDs below the normal mean. Table 28-3 gives sensitivities and specificities with arbitrarily chosen (though similar to those from the studies in Tables 28-1 and 28-2) values of threshold and standard deviation around population means.

Armed with these estimates of sensitivity and specificity, it is possible to estimate the positive and negative predictive values (using Bayes' theorem) of the techniques when they are used to examine populations in which we can give an arbitrary prevalence of abnormality (Table 28-4). The positive predictive value is the likelihood of an indi-

TABLE 28-2
Estimates of Threshold of Symptom Onset

PAPER		N	METHOD	THRESHOLD
Morrish (3)	Dopa PET	32	Longitudinal	75%
Hilker (39)	Dopa PET	31	Longitudinal	69%
Haapaniemi (40)	[123I]β-DAT-SPECT	21	X-sectional	66–72%
Tissingh (42)	[123I]FP-CIT SPECT	8	X-sectional	47–62%
Marek (43)	[123I]β-DAT-SPECT	8	Hemi-PDs	47%–72%

TABLE 28-3
Thresholds, Sensitivities, and Specificities

SD	THRESHOLD	FALSE NEGATIVES	TRUE POSITIVES	SENSITIVITY	FALSE POSITIVES	TRUE NEGATIVES	SPECIFICITY
20	75	77%	23%	23%	2%	98%	98%
10	75	31%	69%	69%	2%	98%	98%
30	60	75%	25%	25%	2%	98%	98%
20	60	50%	50%	50%	2%	98%	98%
10	60	2%	98%	98%	2%	98%	98%

vidual having parkinsonism or preclinical disease after an abnormal scan. The term *preclinical* is used here to mean "abnormal," although it does not imply that the individual will necessarily go on to develop clinical PD.

Column 3 of Table 28-4 shows the chance of an abnormal scan representing an abnormal patient, from a population in which 1% are abnormal (for example if 1% of the population assumed to be healthy had preclinical disease). It can be seen that with even the smallest SD and lowest threshold, only one-third of those identified as such are likely to be "preclinical." The other two-thirds are those healthy individuals who happen to be at the lower end of the normal range. Comparison between these arbitrary SDs and thresholds and the technique's published SDs and thresholds (Tables 28-1 and 28-2) gives us the confidence to doubt that any currently available dopa-PET or DAT-SPECT technique can reliably identify an individual who is truly preclinical (at this prevalence within a population). The situation is different where, perhaps through genetic susceptibility, 50% of the healthy individuals may be "preclinical." Column 4 of Table 28-4 shows that for every SD and threshold, an identified abnormal will have a >90% chance of being abnormal/preclinical. These techniques may therefore be useful in examining individuals in families with autosomal dominant parkinsonism.

What Are SWEDDs (Other Than Symptomatic Without Evidence of Dopaminergic Deficit)?

These calculations throw light on the examination of a group of patients with symptoms of recent onset, such those recruited for the CALM (5), REAL (6), and ELLDOPA (7) studies. Here we might anticipate [from knowledge of clinical accuracy (44) and can put into the calculation] that 10% of those recruited are healthy or have essential tremor (in which case they might also be expected to have normal dopa-PET and DAT-SPECT scans). The negative predictive value is the probability of being disease-free after a normal scan. Columns 5 and 6 of Table 28-4 demonstrate that, for the first 4 examples, the SWEDDs are more likely to be abnormal than normal. It is only if the SD and threshold are as in example 5 (which seems unlikely in the light of the published figures in Tables 28-1 and 28-2) that the SWEDDs are more likely to have a normal than an abnormal dopaminergic system. Sadly, the approximately 10% of recruits identified as SWEDDs in CALM, REAL, and ELLDOPA are unlikely to be the same 10% as the misdiagnoses. SWEDDs therefore exist not because of a failure in diagnosis but because of a failure in the techniques (45), which have the unfortunate combination of too wide a range of

TABLE 28-4
Positive and Negative Predictive Values with Arbitrary SDs and Thresholds

SD	THRESHOLD	NEGATIVE PREDICTIVE VALUE IF 1% OF POPULATION IS AFFECTED	POSITIVE PREDICTIVE VALUE IF 50% OF POPULATION IS AFFECTED	NEGATIVE PREDICTIVE VALUE IF 90% OF PD POPULATION IS AFFECTED (E.G., DE NOVO PD)	% OF SWEDDs WHO WILL HAVE PD (IN 90% OF THE POPULATION)
20	75	10%	92%	12%	88%
10	75	26%	97%	26%	74%
30	60	11%	93%	13%	87%
20	60	20%	96%	18%	82%
10	60	33%	98%	84%	16%

results in the healthy population and too high a threshold at symptom onset.

The other consideration, when the technique is used in this way, is reproducibility. The scan-to-scan errors (see below) may be sufficient to take any individual's result from unhealthy to healthy and vice versa.

Should Suspected New PD Patients Have a DAT-SPECT or Dopa-PET Scan?

Should a clinician therefore request a DAT-SPECT scan when he or she is unsure whether the diagnosis is PD or ET? Taking figures for SD (30) and threshold (60) from studies using these ligands by Tissingh (42) and Marek (43), positive and negative predictive values can be estimated in a similar way. If we assume the chance of the patient being normal (or having ET) or having PD is 50/50, then 93% of those with abnormal scans will have parkinsonism (an abnormal result cannot distinguish idiopathic PD from other akinetic-rigid disorders). If, on the other hand, the scan is normal, the chance of the patient not having PD (the negative predictive value) is 57%. So an abnormal scan in an abnormal patient may be helpful, but a normal scan in an abnormal patient will not be (because it is only marginally more likely that the patient is normal than abnormal). The clinician must then ask how much is likely to be gained by this technique in comparison with a colleague's opinion or reassessment 3 months later. My feeling, on the basis of this evidence, is that the techniques are rarely diagnostically helpful, nor are the radiation exposure and expense justifiable. The clinician must also remember the reliability of the technique (see below); today's scan result might be significantly different from tomorrow's.

What Is the Latency of PD? What Is the Rate of Progression? What Is the Pattern of Progression?

In the absence of evidence to demonstrate the relationship of dopa-PET and DAT-SPECT to cell count, speculation must be confined to considering the latency of the biochemical change leading to PD. The majority of evidence from both techniques suggests an average biochemical latency of between 5 and 12 (3, 39, 46, 47) years. Such estimates of latency and the average rate of progression in PD must be approached with a degree of caution. Most make an assumption of linearity, though not always (39), and frequently a jump is made from the biochemical data to speculation on pathology (39).

Commentators on the latency of PD and the temporal pattern of progression may also be guilty of a failure of logic in assigning a single latency or pattern of progression. We know that dopa-PET and DAT-SPECT give surrogate measurements of clinical severity, and we know that rate of progression varies widely between individuals. The logical assumption, therefore, is that latency and rate of progression measured by PET and SPECT must also have a wide range, and that there may even be a multitude of patterns of progression. The long-latency theory of PD appears to have many commentators to hold the unnecessary idea of a slow, uniform, linear progression, even if this was not its author's intent.

Should and Can Dopa-PET and DAT-SPECT Be Used in Longitudinal Studies of Disease Progression and Neuroprotection?

There are two contentious issues here. First comes the question of whether whatever is measured by imaging is sufficiently representative of the clinical or pathologic state of the illness to be useful in clinical trials. This chapter and previous comment (13, 22) have already considered the difficulty in the assumption that dopa-PET or DAT-SPECT measure dopaminergic pathology and have pointed out that parkinsonian deterioration is heterogeneous and much more widespread than striatal dopaminergic function alone. The indices do, however, show, in most studies (19, 20), a correlation with global clinical scores. If one can accept them solely as an index of something that reduces with deterioration in clinical function, they have a value in progression studies. The possibility of an objective measurement of a single variable that appears to be both continuous and linear, that may be unaffected by medication or mood, and that correlates with progression is hugely attractive. Yet whether scoring illness severity with a functional imaging index is of greater value than scoring an illness with a clinical or quality-of-life scale is debatable (22). There is an important point that appears to be forgotten in trial design but which can be made here. The question of how one would like one's illness to be measured, in a society that places value on democracy and personal freedom, is a personal decision. In clinical practice we ask whose life and whose illness it is; but when we design and recruit for medical trials, we do not yet ask whose endpoint it is. Some individuals might choose the more objective measurement of a dopa-PET or DAT-SPECT scan, but others might attach more importance to the point at which disability causes loss of employment, the point at which dyskinesia causes embarrassment, or the point at which they can no longer walk unaided to the coffee shop. A patient-oriented decision on therapy needs evidence from trials with patient-oriented measures and perhaps patient-chosen endpoints.

If we do assume that dopa-PET and DAT-SPECT provide a useful measurement, the second bone of contention is whether the techniques, at their existing level of development, can perform that role (3, 22, 48).

The first published longitudinal dopa-PET study of PD (49) measured a rate of decline in PET index of 0.78% of the normal mean per year, while the second (50) gave a rate 10 times that. The patients and PET machines were essentially similar; therefore, in order to understand the disparity, both the previous method of analysis (Ki in putamen) and the method used in the Vancouver study (total striatal ratios) were applied to a single group of patients (3). This demonstrated that the measured rate of progression depends on the method of analysis; the corollary being that some methods might not have sufficient reproducibility or sensitivity to make a measurement.

To understand this it is necessary to make a paradigm shift, from the simplistic or instinctive belief that the techniques measure something as concrete as cell count to the concept that the measurement of rate is determined more by method than by pathology. The key features of a technique (whether imaging or other) in measuring progression are sensitivity to clinical change and reproducibility. Other features, such as resistance to confounders and linearity of scale (51), are also important. Many cross-sectional studies show a relationship between dopa-PET and DAT-SPECT index and clinical state. The difficulty seems to be the idea (and evidence (3)] that, with a given amount of clinical deterioration, some techniques measure a greater change in imaging index than others. Without this consideration, there is the danger of using a technique and method that is incapable of accurately measuring the small difference in striatal dopaminergic biochemistry that accompanies the small degree of clinical progression which may be occurring in, for example, the single year of a progression study. Different dopa-PET indices, for example, might measure from 3% to 7% of the normal mean (3) with a clinical change of 10 total UPDRS points. There are no published studies of sensitivity in DAT-SPECT, although some estimates (making many assumptions) from published data have been made (48). If the technique is insensitive to clinical progression and the index changes only by tiny amounts (for example, 1.5% of normal mean for 8 total UPDRS points—see consideration of ELLDOPA below), its usefulness as a measuring tool is limited.

Although sensitivity is vital, its importance is best appreciated alongside reproducibility (3); one would wish the change in imaging index as a consequence of progression to be significantly greater than the change in index due to error. Reproducibility is the Achilles' heel in PD imaging studies (whether measuring progression, identifying PD or preclinical disease, or gauging medication effect), yet this frequently escapes attention, even in the most comprehensive reviews (13). Would it be too controversial to ask that reproducibility data (in that specific machine with that ligand and method of analysis) be published to accompany every dopa-PET or DAT-SPECT

TABLE 28-5
*Reproducibility Studies**

STUDY	METHOD	N	SUBJECTS	MEAN VARIABILITY (SD) AS % OF BASELINE
Seibyl (53)	[123I]β-CIT DAT-SPECT	7	Healthy	12.8 (8.9)
Seibyl (53)	[123I]β-CIT DAT SPECT	7	PD	16.8 (13.3)
Booij (54)	(123I)FP-CIT DAT SPECT	6	Healthy	7.2 (3.2)
Booij (54)	(123I)FP-CIT DAT SPECT	10	PD	7.9 (6.9)
Morrish (3)	Dopa-PET	8	Healthy	12 (7)%

*Variability = difference between scans 1 and 2 divided by mean of scans 1 and 2.

study? Studies have addressed the issue, but rarely in a manner sufficiently critical for the claims being made for the techniques (52). Table 28-5 shows the results of some reproducibility studies.

The challenge is for techniques with such potential to scan error so as to measure something that might change—for example in a year's progression—by as little as 1% to 2% (a figure determined both by the sensitivity of the technique to clinical progression and by the actual clinical progression). It is possible, but only if the numbers scanned are so great that positive error inevitably cancels negative error. The great difficulty for progression studies is that greater sensitivity to progression unfortunately appears to come only with reduced reproducibility (3); sensitivity is gained and reproducibility lost by analysis of data taken from smaller and smaller components of the striatum (46). Comment on data from CALM and ELLDOPA has concentrated on the possible confounding effects of the study medication (36, 55). It should be possible, in study design (and was achieved in REAL), to eliminate an effect of medication, but studies of medication effect are also vulnerable to poor reproducibility, and sample sizes thus far have probably not been large enough to permit conclusive results.

If PET/SPECT indices are surrogate measures, the range of rate of progression measured by these techniques is likely to be similar to that seen clinically; it is inevitable that groups comparable in size to those of studies using clinical indices will be needed.

In conclusion, dopa PET and DAT-SPECT may be useful in progression studies if it is acknowledged that they provide a surrogate measure and if the study design takes sufficient account of reproducibility, sensitivity, resistance to confounders, and the likely wide range in rate of progression within each cohort.

How Do We Interpret the 3 Longitudinal Neuroprotection Imaging Studies?

The CALM (5), REAL (6), and ELLDOPA (7) studies have generated a great deal of correspondence (55, 56), and the debate around each can be viewed as instructive for future imaging trials.

REAL recruited 186 new-onset patients who were treated either with L-dopa or agonist; they were assessed by [18F]dopa PET upon starting medication and again at 2 years. Patients were recruited at 34 sites and scanned twice, on any of 6 different PET machines, with data sent to one central unit for subsequent analysis. Centrally, data were normalized to a standard brain volume; the primary outcome measure was a change in mean putamen Ki between the first and second scans. A nonsignificant trend in favor of the dopamine agonist was reported first, in abstract (57). The data were published formally in 2003 (6), achieving significance in favor of the agonist after central analysis and the removal of SWEDDs. Putamen Ki dropped by 13.4 (2.14%) from baseline in the ropinirole group and by 20.3 (2.35%) in the L-dopa group, a rate of progression broadly in keeping with other dopa-PET estimates. The study concluded that either ropinirole was neuroprotective or that L-dopa was neurotoxic. Another possibility (if one accepts the adjustment as legitimate) is that L-dopa has a greater biochemical (rather than pathologic) effect on the outcome measure than ropinirole. The removal of SWEDDs was a belated addition to the trial protocol, and the author's reply to criticism of study design (58) confirmed that 2 datasets (with and without removal of SWEDDs) were available at study completion. To formally publish only the results that favored the sponsor's product was ill judged at best. In the trial's favor were the large number of patients scanned and the fact that such a complicated trial and analysis could be accomplished at all. Its failure and its expense make it unlikely to be repeated.

CALM examined 82 new-onset patients by DAT-SPECT over a 4-year period. At 46 months, the agonist group had shown a decline in striatal B-CIT uptake of 16 (13.3%) from baseline compared to 25.5 (14.1%) in the L-dopa group. The patients, in the "defined off" state deteriorated to an identical degree, by 4.1 (9.9) total UPDRS points in the agonist group and by 4.0 (8.7) total UPDRS points in the L-dopa group. The principal criticism [which Ahlskog (59) has argued well] is that this study could simply be demonstrating a biochemical effect. Another counterargument (56) is that it is hard to understand how a technique could demonstrate such large changes in dopaminergic function with such small changes in clinical function when we know that the imaging technique is likely to be relatively insensitive to clinical progression (see below). Add into the argument of limited reproducibility and we are left to wonder whether the study measured progression, pharmacologic effect, or error.

ELLDOPA sought to establish whether L-dopa was likely to be neurotoxic. Here 142 new-onset patients were scanned twice (with a 1-year interval) off medication at the start and then either off medication or on varying doses of levodopa at the end. Striatal B-CIT uptake decreased by 2.6% of baseline in the placebo group and by between 4% and 7% of baseline in the L-dopa groups in that time. The placebo arm of ELLDOPA provides evidence of a lack of sensitivity of the technique to clinical progression. This untreated group deteriorated (typically for PD) by an average of 7.8 total UPDRS points, yet the SPECT index in the subgroup of 29 who underwent scanning changed by only 2.6% of baseline (or only 1.3% of normal if baseline is assumed to be 50% normal mean). This suggests that the technique has not adequately detected the deterioration in dopaminergic biochemistry that one might have expected to accompany the clinical progression in this group. The result seems particularly inexplicable compared with CALM (which used a similar technique), where changes of 16% (in the L-dopa group) and 25% (in the agonist group) in SPECT index (from baseline) were accompanied by a clinical (total UPDRS off medication) change of 4 points in each group. Possibly the UPDRS change was undervalued (if the patients were not assessed truly off medication) in CALM. Possibly the apparent huge changes in SPECT index (for such a small clinical deterioration) measured in CALM were phamacologic, and the greater change in the L-dopa group than in the placebo group in ELLDOPA was also a pharmacologic effect. Possibly instead, the subgroups in each study were too small for negative error to cancel positive error and, because of the poor sensitivity of the technique to progression, the only thing the studies are demonstrating is the balance of error. I would not have enough faith in the technique (particularly the balance between sensitivity and reproducibility) to draw any conclusion from the data.

Perhaps the lesson from all 3 studies is to understand the abilities and limitations of a technique and to expose the sponsorship agreement, trial design, and assumptions to a critical audience before starting.

CONCLUSIONS: AN ALTERNATIVE VIEW OF THE CONTRIBUTION OF DOPA-PET AND DAT-SPECT DATA

In conclusion, I have argued for and present here an alternative interpretation of dopa-PET and DAT-SPECT studies in PD. In PD we know that the loss of nigral dopaminergic cells is one of many components of the neurodegenerative pathology of PD. We do not know the extent of this deficit at presentation nor the extent to which dopaminergic loss in the basal ganglia contributes to the symptom complex and progressive disability of PD. Imaging of the dopaminergic system is therefore, at best, a marker of one biochemical component of the complex clinical picture that makes up PD.

Scrutiny of assumptions and available data suggests that the techniques, in their current state of development, do not completely discriminate PD from normality, nor can they reliably identify true preclinical disease. As a diagnostic tool in the new-onset parkinsonian patient, they can confirm an abnormality, but a negative scan is no assurance of normality. In measuring progression and assessing neuroprotection, it may be naive to believe that the measurements made by the techniques hold great relevance to the multifaceted progression of PD or that they are capable of doing so sensitively, accurately, reproducibly, and without being affected by other factors. With further technical developments and large sample numbers, it remains a possibility that they will have a value in progression studies, but only if the lessons from CALM, REAL, and ELLDOPA are heeded.

This appraisal of the merits of the techniques might be viewed as unreasonably negative and that the pros and the cons must be viewed in balance. Yet it is striking to note how much has been claimed for these techniques over so many years when so little has been known about them. We do not know precisely what they measure, how useful that measurement is (compared with the clinical picture of PD), how well each separates PD from normality, how predictive the claimed identification of preclinical disease is, how reliable the measurements are, whether results change with age in the healthy, and what factors might confound results. Yet in the design and publication of imaging studies, particularly the longitudinal neuroprotection studies, enthusiasm has been allowed to take precedence over intellectual and scientific rigor. The most important thing that must emerge from the "imaging and neuroprotection" debacle (no other word will fit the radioisotope scanning of several hundred patients with little useful conclusion) is that the PD scientific community should not be dazzled by pictures or seduced by new techniques and ligands. Instead we should be healthily skeptical about the studies, consider the science behind them as we would with regard to any new technique, and reject the study designs and their findings if they do not have credibility.

References

1. Bernheimer H, Birkmayer W, Hornykiewicz O, et al. Brain dopamine and the syndromes of Parkinson and Huntington: Clinical, morphological and neurochemical correlations. *J Neurol Sci* 1973; 29:415–455.
2. Calne DB, Langston JW. Aetiology of Parkinson's disease. *Lancet* 1983; 2:1457–1459.
3. Morrish PK, Rakshi JS, Bailey DL, et al. Measuring the rate of progression and estimating the preclinical period of Parkinson's disease with [18F]dopa PET. *J Neurol Neurosurg Psychiatry* 1998; 64:314–319.
4. Pirker W, Djamshidian S, Asenbaum S, et al. Progression of dopaminergic degeneration in Parkinson's disease and atypical parkinsonism: A longitudinal beta-CIT SPECT study. *Mov Disord* 2002; 17(1):45–53.
5. Parkinson Study Group. Dopamine transporter brain imaging to assess the effects of pramipexole vs levodopa on Parkinson disease progression. *JAMA* 2002; 287:1653–1661.
6. Whone AL, Watts RL, Stoessl AJ, et al. Slower progression of Parkinson's disease with ropinirole versus levodopa: The REAL-PET study. *Ann Neurol* 2003; 54:93–101.
7. Parkinson Study Group. Levodopa and the progression of Parkinson's disease. *N Engl J Med* 2004; 351(24):2498–2508.
8. Calne DB, Langston JW, Wayne Martin WR, et al. Positron emission tomography after MPTP: Observations relating to the cause of Parkinson's disease. *Nature* 1985; 317:246–248.
9. Ehringer H, Hornykiewicz O. Verteilung von Noradrenalin und Dopamine (3-hydroxy-tyramin) im Gehirn des Menschen und ihr verhalten bei Erkrankungen des extrapyramidalen Systems. *Klin Wochenschr* 1960; 38:1236–1239.
10. Agid Y, Cervera P, Hirsch E, et al. Biochemistry of Parkinson's disease 28 years later: A critical review. *Mov Disord* 1989; 4(Suppl 1):126–144.
11. Fearnley JM, Lees AJ. Ageing and Parkinson's disease: Substantia nigra regional selectivity. *Brain* 1991; 114:2283–2301.
12. Braak H, Del Tredici K, Rub U, et al. Staging of brain pathology related to sporadic Parkinson's disease. *Neurobiol Aging* 2003; 24:197–211.
13. Ravina B, Eidelberg D, Ahlskog JE, et al. The role of radiotracer imaging in Parkinson's disease. *Neurology* 2005; 64:208–215.
14. Pate BD, Kawamata T, Yamada T, et al. Correlation of striatal fluorodopa uptake in the MPTP monkey with dopaminergic indices. *Ann Neurol* 1993; 34:331–338.
15. Snow BJ, Tooyama I, McGeer EG, et al. Human positron emission tomographic [18F]fluorodopa studies correlate with dopamine cell counts and levels. *Ann Neurol* 1993; 34:324–330.
16. Counihan TJ, Penny JB Jr. Regional dopamine transporter gene expression in the substantia nigra fro control and Parkinson's disease brains. *J Neurol Neurosurg Psychiatry* 1998; 65:164–169.
17. Rakshi JS, Uema T, Ito K, et al. Frontal, midbrain and striatal dopaminergic function in early and advanced Parkinson's disease. A 3D [18F]dopa-PET study. *Brain* 1999; 12:1637–1650.
18. Ahlskog JE, Uitti RJ, O'Connor MK, et al. The effect of dopamine agonist therapy on dopamine transporter imaging in Parkinson's disease. *Mov Disord* 1999; 14(6):940–946.
19. Benamer HT, Patterson J, Wyper DJ, et al. Correlation of Parkinson's disease severity and duration with 123I-FP-CIT SPECT striatal uptake. *Mov Disord* 2000; 15(4):692–698.
20. Morrish PK, Sawle GV, Brooks DJ. Clinical and [18F]dopa PET findings in early Parkinson's disease. *J Neurol Neurosurg Psychiatry* 1995; 59:597–600.
21. Hely MA, Morris JG, Reid WG, Trafficante R. Sydney Multicenter study of Parkinson's disease: Non-L-dopa responsive problems dominate at 15 years. *Mov Disord* 2005; 20(2):190–199.
22. Morrish P. Is it time to abandon functional imaging in the study of neuroprotection? *Mov Disord* 2002; 17(2):229–232.
23. Holloway RG, Dick AW. Clinical trial end points: On the road to nowhere? *Neurology* 2002; 58(5):679–686.
24. Michell AW, Lewis SJG, Foltynie T, Barker RA. Biomarkers and Parkinson's disease. *Brain* 2004; 127:1693–1705.
25. Ma SY, Roytt M, Collan Y et al. Unbiased morphometrical measurements show loss of pigmented nigral neurones with ageing. *Neuropathol Appl Neurobiol* 1999; 25:394–399.
26. Kubis N, Faucheux BA, Ransmayr G, et al. Preservation of midbrain catecholaminergic neurons in very old subjects. *Brain* 2000; 123:366–373.
27. Martin WRW, Palmer MR, Patlak CS, Calne DB. Nigrostriatal function in humans studied with positron emission tomography. *Ann Neurol* 1989; 26:535–542.
28. Sawle GV, Colebatch JG, Shah A, et al. Striatal function in normal aging: Implications for Parkinson's disease. *Ann Neurol* 1990; 28:799–804.
29. Eidelberg D, Takikawa S, Dhawan V, et al. *J Cereb Blood Flow Metab* 1991; 13:881–888.
30. Kumakura Y, Vernaleken I, Grunder G, et al. PET studies of net blood-brain clearance of F-dopa to human brain: age-dependent decline of [18F]fluorodopamine storage capacity. *J Cereb Blood Flow Metab* 2005; 25(7):807–819.
31. Sawle GV, Brooks DJ. Normal aging of the central nervous system. *Ann Neurol* 1992; 31(5); 575–576.
32. Calne DB, Eisen A, Meneilly G. Reply. *Ann Neurol* 1992; 31(5);576.
33. Van Dyck CH, Seibyl JP, Malison RT, et al. Age-related decline in dopamine transporters. *Am J Geriatr Psychiatry* 2002; 10:36–43.

34. Asenbaum S, Brucke T, Pirker W, et al. Imaging of dopamine transporters with iodine-123-beta-CIT and SPECT in Parkinson's disease. *J Nucl Med* 1997; 38(1):1–6.

35. Booij J, Bergmans P, Winogrodzka A, et al. Imaging of dopamine transporters with [123I] FP-CIT SPECT does not suggest a significant effect of age on the symptomatic threshold of disease in Parkinson's disease. *Synapse* 2001; 39(2):101–108.

36. Schapira AHV, Olanow CW. Neuroprotection in Parkinson's disease. Mysteries, myths and misconceptions. *JAMA* 2004;m291:358–364.

37. Brooks DJ. Detection of preclinical Parkinson's disease with PET. *Neurology* 1991; 41(Suppl 2):24–27.

38. Khan NL, Scherfler C, Graham E, et al. Dopaminergic dysfunction in unrelated, asymptomatic carriers of a single parkin mutation. *Neurology* 2005; 64:134–136.

39. Hilker R, Schweitzer K, Coburger S, et al. Nonlinear progression of Parkinson disease as determined by serial positron emission tomographic imaging of striatal fluorodopa F 18 activity. *Arch Neurol* 2005; 62(3):378–382.

40. Haapaniemi TH, Ahonen A, Torniainen P, et al. [123I]beta-CIT SPECT demonstrates decreased brain dopamine and serotonin transporter levels in untreated parkinsonian patients. *Mov Disord* 2001; 16(1):124–130.

41. Seibyl JP, Marek KL, Quinlan D, et al. Decreased single-photon emission computed tomographic [123I]beta-CIT striatal uptake correlates with symptom severity in Parkinson's disease. *Ann Neurol.* 1995; 38(4):589–598.

42. Tissingh G, Booij J, Bergmans P, et al. Iodine-123-N-omega-fluoropropyl-2beta-carbomethoxy-3beta-(4-iod ophenyl)tropane SPECT in healthy controls and early-stage, drug-naive Parkinson's disease. *J Nucl Med* 1998; 39(7):1143–1148.

43. Marek KL, Seibyl JP, Zoghbi SS, et al. [123I] beta-CIT/SPECT imaging demonstrates bilateral loss of dopamine transporters in hemi-Parkinson's disease. *Neurology* 1996; 46(1):231–237.

44. Hughes AJ, Daniel SE, Ben-Shlomo Y, Lees AJ. The accuracy of diagnosis of parkinsonian syndromes in a specialist movement disorder service. *Brain* 2002; 125(4);861–870.

45. Morrish P. The meaning of negative DAT SPECT and F-dopa PET scans in patients with clinical Parkinson's disease. *Mov Disord* 2005; 20(1):117.

46. Winogrodzka A, Bergmans P, Booij J, et al. [123I]FP-CIT SPECT is a useful method to monitor the rate of dopaminergic degeneration in early-stage Parkinson's disease. *J Neural Transm* 2001; 108(8–9):1011–1019.

47. Marek K, Innis R, van Dyck C, et al. 123IB-SPECT imaging assessment of the rate of Parkinson's disease progression. *Neurology* 2001; 57:2089–2094.

48. Morrish PK. How valid is dopamine transporter imaging as a surrogate marker in research trials in Parkinson's disease? *Mov Disord* 2003; 18(Suppl 7):S63–S70.

49. Vingerhoets FJG, Snow BJ, Lee CS, et al. Longitudinal fluorodopa positron emission tomographic studies of the evolution of idiopathic parkinsonism. *Ann Neurol* 1994; 36:759–764.

50. Morrish PK, Sawle GV, Brooks DJ. An [18F]dopa-PET and clinical study of the rate of progression in Parkinson's disease. *Brain* 1996; 119(Pt 2):585–591.

51. Hobart J. Rating scales for neurologists. *J Neurol Neurosurg Psychiatry* 2003; 74(S4):22–26.

52. Morrish PK. The harsh realities facing the use of SPECT imaging in monitoring disease progression in Parkinson's disease. *J Neurol Neurosurg Psychiatry* 2003; 74:1447.

53. Seibyl JP, Marek K, Sheff K, et al. Test/retest reproducibility of iodine-123-betaCIT SPECT brain measurement of dopamine transporters in Parkinson's patients. *J Nucl Med* 1997; 38(9):1453–1459.

54. Booij J, Habraken JBA, Bergmans P, et al. Imaging of dopamine transporters with iodine-123-FP-CIT SPECT in healthy controls and patients with Parkinson's disease. *J Nucl Med* 1998; 39(11):1879–1884.

55. Ahlskog JE, Uitti RJ, Uhl GR. Brain imaging to assess the effects of dopamine agonists on progression of Parkinson disease. *JAMA* 2002; 288(3):31.

56. Morrish PK. REAL and CALM. What have we learned? *Mov Disord* 2003; 18(7):839–840.

57. Whone AL, Remy P, Davis MR, et al. The REAL-PET study: Slower progression in early Parkinson's disease treated with ropinirole compared with L-dopa. *Neurology* 2002; 58:7(S3):A83.

58. Whone AL, Brooks DJ. Author's reply. *Ann Neurol* 2003; 54(5):692–693.

59. Ahlskog E. J. Slowing Parkinson's disease progression: Recent dopamine agonist trials. *Neurology* 2003; 60:381–389.

VI

PATHOGENESIS AND ETIOLOGY

29 Animal Models

Paul S. Fishman

A nimal models of neurologic disease are of increasing importance but have also come under increasing scrutiny. Basic research involving these models is expanding, while concerns over the difficulty in translational therapeutic research also rise. Animal models of Parkinson's disease (PD) are particularly notable for their diversity as well as their varied utility. These models in general cannot be viewed as replicates of human disease occurring in animals. Beal has summarized the desirable characteristics of a model system, which include gradual loss of dopamine neurons, presence of Lewy bodies, easily detectable motor deficits with similarity to PD signs, and a relatively short disease course (1). It is not surprising that no existing animal model fulfills these criteria. Each model has particular strengths in addressing specific questions about the disease, ranging from pathogenesis to therapeutic efficacy. Each model provides insight to different aspects of the molecular biology, pathology, pathogenesis, and clinical phenotype. It is not sufficient simply to raise the question of the validity of each model; we must evaluate the specific research studies using these models, examining how they employ them to address and interpret particular scientific questions. This chapter reviews two different forms of models, those generated by toxin administration and those carrying mutant genes associated with familial PD. These animal models range in focus from pathologic and clinical model systems for therapeutic assessment to proof-of-principle experiments addressing fundamental questions of the underlying cause of PD.

TOXIN MODELS OF PARKINSON'S DISEASE

Six Hydroxy Dopamine (6-OHDA)

The first widely used toxicant-induced animal model still plays a large role in PD research. Intracerebral injection of the toxin became a form of dopaminergic chemodenervation; it replaced previous older stereotactic physical or electrical lesioning methods for studying dopaminergic deficits and evaluating dopaminergic therapy.

Unilateral injection of this chemical results in local dopaminergic denervation of the nigrostriatal pathway and a reproducible clinical syndrome (2). Rodents injected intracerebrally show circling behavior toward the injected side, representing reduced motor activity of the affected nigrostriatal pathway (3, 4). This circling behavior is exaggerated with systemic administration of amphetamine, which stimulates catecholamine release. Within a few weeks after 6-OHDA treatment, striatal denervation hypersensitivity to dopamine develops; it is demonstrated by circling behavior in the opposite (away from the side of the injection site) direction with administration of the dopamine agonist apomorphine.

This hypersensitivity response in general requires substantial loss of dopaminergic innervation, but it can be proportional to the degree of dopamineric denervation (4–7). Although such circling behavior has no analogous symptom in humans, abnormalities of forepaw movement resembling parkinsonian bradykinesia have also been described in rats (8). Such behavior, although not reminiscent of PD, is quantitatively related to the degree of unilateral dopaminergic denervation. This model also shows a reproducible and quantitative corrective response to antiparkinsonian agents such as L-dopa and dopamine agonists (9, 10). The quantitative behavioral relationship of unilateral intracerebral 6-OHDA injection to dopaminergic denervation has driven its continued use to assess novel dopaminergic-based therapeutics such trophic factors, gene therapy, and cell transplantation (11–19). 6-OHDA is selectively taken up by all catecholaminergic terminals but does not cross the blood-brain barrier, so that it produces sympathetic chemodenervation rather than parkinsonian signs when given systemically (20). Although animals given bilateral intracerebral injections of 6-OHDA show symptoms more analogous to PD, such as akinesia, affected animals show such depressed feeding behavior, so that considerable support is needed for them to survive (21, 22). Such global decreases in behavior are also less specific for a dopaminergic deficit and are more difficult to quantify. In rodents, three different anatomic sites can be utilized for stereotactic injection. 6-OHDA injections into the nigra or median forebrain bundle cause the most rapid and complete loss of nigral dopaminergic neurons, while injections into the striatum result in a dying back form of dopaminergic axonal loss, followed by nigral cell degeneration (23–26). The majority of 6-OHDA use has been in rodents, likely due to the necessity of intracerebral injection of the toxin and the preference of many investigators to employ the MPTP (1-methyl 4-phenyl 1,2,3,6-tetrahydropyridine) model in primates.

Like most of the dopaminergic toxins, 6-OHDA causes cell death through the inhibition of oxidative metabolism (27, 28). After selective uptake by catecholaminergic terminals, 6-OHDA accumulates in mitochondria and inhibits complex I of the electron transport chain (29). Complex I inhibition not only interferes with mitochondrial ATP and energy generation but also results in an accumulation of free electrons and increased production of reactive oxygen. However 6-OHDA also undergoes auto-oxidation, particularly in the presence of iron, generating reactive oxygen species (30). 6-OHDA also oxidizes to paraquinone, a molecule capable of amplifying oxidative injury (31). Oxidative injury appears to be the major source of dopaminergic

cell death after 6-OHDA exposure, as evidenced by its enhancement by iron and prevention by iron chelation or antioxidant therapy with agents such as vitamin E (32–34). The response of 6-OHDA–treated animals to both oxidative stress and antioxidant strategies makes it a useful model in assessing the role of these processes in dopaminergic injury. To what extent these processes resemble those involved in PD continues to be debated. Although the major pathologic feature of PD, the Lewy body, is not seen in 6-OHDA–treated animals, there are pathologic similarities (35–37). The initial loss of dopaminergic terminals with striatal injection of 6-OHDA resembles the dying back axonal terminal loss seen in early PD (38–40). Although onset of dopaminergic injury with 6-OHDA is usually rapid and acute, over days, intrastriatal 6-OHDA has been used to create a more chronically progressive model of PD, with continuing loss of nigral dopaminergic cells over many weeks (38). 6-OHDA–treated rats remain the most popular animal model of PD, probably due to its reliable and quantitative relationship of symptoms to dopaminergic activity in the nigrostriatal pathway.

MPTP

Few events have revolutionized the understanding of PD as much as the initial human experience with MPTP. This meperidine analog was unintentionally generated in the process of attempting to create a synthetic narcotic and was self-administered by a group of narcotic abusers. These patients were initially identified in northern California with a profound irreversible parkinsonian syndrome (41). Although the syndrome was of acute onset, it was remarkable for its clinical similarity to PD and its degree of specificity for the nigrostriatal dopaminergic system (42). This syndrome—and its dopaminergic specificity—was subsequently reproduced by systemic injection of MPTP in nonhuman primates (43, 44). Over the next decade, the mechanism by which MPTP showed its nigral/dopaminergic-specific toxicity would be elucidated. The multiple mechanisms underlying toxicity can be viewed as a perfect storm for nigral dopaminergic toxicity. After systemic uptake, MPTP requires bioconversion to an active metabolite, MPP+, to be toxic (45). Within the brain, this bioconversion is performed by monoamine oxidase (MAO) type B, which is localized primarily to astrocytes (46). Unlike MPTP, MPP+ generated in the perineuronal environment is internalized by dopaminergic neurons via the high-affinity dopamine transporters (DAT) localized on the membranes of dopaminergic terminals and cell bodies (47). After internalization, MPP+, like 6-OHDA, acts as a mitochondrial inhibitor of complex I (48). In both primates and rodents, MPTP-induced neuronal loss shows a level of specificity for the nigral dopaminergic pathways that highly resembles that seen in PD (49–52). Not only are mesencephalic neurons preferentially affected compared to dopaminergic neurons in other locations, such as the limbic system, but nigral neurons are more affected than dopaminergic neurons of the adjacent ventral tegmental area (53–56). The specificity of MPTP among dopaminergic neurons is less well understood. Initial hypotheses regarding the role of neuromelanin have not been supported with more current studies pointing to DAT density, calabindin levels, α-synuclein expression, and trophic factors (57, 58).

Primate Models. MPTP is the most common toxin used in primate models of PD. Responses to MPTP vary among species of nonhuman primates, with African green monkeys showing a clinical syndrome that has striking similarity to PD, including resting tremor (59–61). Although systemic administration of MPTP can result in a model of PD in both rodents and primates, some of the primate studies utilize a hemiparkinsonian model. This is usually accomplished by unilateral intracarotid injection of MPTP rather than unilateral intracerebral injection, as performed with 6-OHDA (62). Although intracarotid injection is also technically difficult, the unilateral nature of symptoms allows even severely affected monkeys to use their unaffected limbs in grooming and feeding, thus reducing overall morbidity (63). For the majority of primate studies, MPTP is administered via one of several systemic means—intravenously, intramuscularly, or subcutaneously. Although resulting symptoms can be severe, they are significantly improved with L-dopa, as in PD (64). The response to antiparkinsonian therapies is one of several strengths of the MPTP model. Animals respond not only to L-dopa and dopamine agonists but, as a result of chronic L-dopa treatment, also develop drug-induced dyskinesias (65–67). There are other similarities between MPTP-exposed humans and primates. Although intracellular inclusions have been described, typical Lewy bodies are not seen in either setting (68–70). While acute administration of large doses of MPTP produces an acute syndrome with massive nigral cell loss, chronic exposure to lower doses results in a progressive cell loss of more gradual onset, with similarity to cases of delayed onset of parkinsonian symptoms in some patients exposed to MPTP (71–73). However, in some species of nonhuman primates, low-level chronic administration results in a syndrome that is eventually reversible (74, 75).

Chronic compared to acute use of MPTP in primates illustrates two distinct goals of the MPTP model: (a) elucidation of the mechanisms of MPTP parkinsonism to further clarify possible pathogenetic mechanisms of PD and (b) assessment of potential therapeutics for PD. Although the chronic progressive models have use in assessing therapeutics that have potential neuroprotective

properties, they remain based on the assumption that the mechanisms underlying cell death following MPTP administration are the same as those underlying the pathogenesis of PD. Assessment of therapeutics with a goal of correcting symptoms or restoring function in PD does not require mechanistic assumptions, so that primates with severe irreversible MPTP-induced parkinsonism have been viewed as the most valid model. Because primates treated with MPTP clearly respond to conventional dopaminegeric therapy, they have been employed as preclinical models of more novel therapies. The validity of resemblance of MPTP primates to PD has been established with regard to nigrostriatal circuitry by electrophysiologic studies in both settings (76–78). The response of MPTP-treated primates to stereotactic lesions led to the successful development of new targets for surgical approaches in PD, particularly the subthalamic nucleus (79–81). The primate MPTP model has also provided pivotal preclinical data for experimental forms of restorative therapies—such as trophic factor infusion, gene therapy, and tissue transplantation—which have led to clinical trials in patients (82–84). Some of these clinical studies are in progress, so that they have not yet fully validated the MPTP primate model for such forms of therapy.

Although several primate studies support the efficacy of fetal tissue transplant in MPTP-treated primates, these results were not predictive of later human trials. Although fetal tissue does survive and show signs of dopaminergic differentiation in both settings, relief of clinical symptoms has been, in general, more robust in treated primates (85–91). Some patients with fetal mesencephalic transplants developed dyskinesias even off treatment with dopaminergic drugs, while these "runaway dyskinesias" have not been described in MPTP/transplant–treated primates.

The current experience with MPTP–treated primates as preclinical models for the assessment of infusion of the trophic factor GDNF is also worrisome. Intraventricular infusion of GDNF produced significant relief of symptoms and enhanced striatal innervation in MPTP-treated primates (92–95). Subsequent human trials of intraventricular infusion of GDNF, however, did not demonstrate significant improvement of PD (96). Because of the concern that tissue penetration of GDNF into the larger human brain may have accounted for the lack of translation of the clinical benefit of GDNF, subsequent primate and human trials were performed with infusion of this tropic factor directly into the parenchyma of the striatum (97–100). It is unclear if the benefit of GDNF intracerebral infusion in the MPTP primate can be replicated in humans. There has been an unsuccessful blinded multicenter trial; however, 2 smaller but technically different open-label trials have shown benefit of GDNF treatment. This experience supports a conclusion that the MPTP primate has not yet been fully validated as a preclinical model for novel (nondopaminergic) treatments of PD.

Rodent Models.   Although rodents, particularly mice, are significantly more resistant to MPTP toxicity than primates, they are also a useful model (101–103). Transgenic mice have been particularly enlightening in unraveling the molecular mechanisms of MPTP toxicity, with implications for the pathogenesis of PD. By evaluating mice that overexpress or lack specific genes for MPTP susceptibility or resistance, several proteins and pathways have been implicated. For example, resistance to MPTP of mice overexpressing the Cu/Zn form of superoxide dismutase demonstrates the importance of oxidative injury, while the resistance of mice that lack the enzyme nitric oxide synthetase (NOS) emphasizes the role of reactive nitrogen species such as peroxynitrate in MPTP toxicity (104, 105). Several compounds have been proposed as potential neuroprotectants on the basis of their ability to prevent MPTP toxicity in rodents and primates. Although it is clear that MPTP is a highly nigral-specific dopaminergic neurotoxin, it is not clear to what extent the underlying mechanisms of PD and MPTP-induced parkinsonism resemble each other. The initial experience with MPTP-induced parkinsonism led to the first large-scale evaluation of putative neuroprotectants—selegiline and vitamin E—with the initial interpretation of neuroprotection by selegiline now viewed as an artifact of the study's design (106, 107). Two decades later, there are several other putative but still unproven neuroprotectants in clinical trials, all of which have shown protection from MPTP (CoQ10, creatine, minocycline, CEP-1347, and rasagiline) (108–112). The results of these ongoing clinical trials will either validate or refute MPTP treated animals as a preclinical model for the assessment of clinical neuroprotectants for PD (113). The current status, however, is of concern with the recent failure of CEP-1347 to slow the clinical progression of PD(114).

Rotenone

Rodents treated with the insecticide and piscicine rotenone should be viewed as a proof-of-concept model for the role of oxidative injury, rather than a preclinical model of PD. The critical studies of Greenamyre and colleagues demonstrated that some rats chronically exposed to intravenous or subcutaneous infusion of rotenone developed massive and selective nigrostriatal degeneration (114). Although subsequent studies have focused on the narrow parameters within which this phenomenon occurs, it remains remarkable. Both MPTP and rotenone act primarily through mitochondrial complex I inhibition. However, unlike MPTP, rotenone shows no selective uptake for dopaminergic neurons (115).

Rotenone-induced parkinsonism is a direct demonstration and extension from cell and explant culture studies showing that dopaminergic nigral neurons are particularly susceptible to oxidative injury (116, 117). Unlike the much more predictable MPTP and 6-OHDA models, rotenone-infused rats are more likely to show α-synuclein–positive protein aggregates suggestive of Lewy bodies (114). This phenomenon may relate to another action of rotenone besides its complex I inhibition. Rotenone inhibits the polymerization of tubulin into microtubles, which may interfere with the elimination of other aggregation-prone proteins such as α-synuclein (118, 119). Rotenone is not the only toxin in widespread use that causes parkinsonism in animals. The herbicide paraquat, which has a great deal of structural similarity to MPTP, has been a reported cause of nigrostriatal degeneration in mice, but studies have given disparate results (120, 121). A fungicide termed Maneb has also been shown to cause locomotor abnormalities in mice, along with dopaminergic nigral degeneration, but with uncertain specificity (122, 123).

Proteasomal Inhibitors

A recently reported proof- of-concept model was the development of progressive parkinsonian symptoms in animals treated with proteosomal inhibitors (124). In a manner similar to the previous experience with rotenone, the demonstration that repeated systemic injections of such compounds can cause a parkinsonian syndrome in rats with associated nigrostriatal denervation is the culmination of new concepts and in vitro studies. The initial discoveries of genes underlying familial PD (in particular parkin) emphasized the potential role of proteasomal dysfunction in both sporadic and familial PD (125, 126). The proteasomal inhibitor lactacystin causes acute degeneration of dopaminergic neurons when injected stereotacticly into the nigra. This degeneration was associated with α-synuclein–positive aggregates and changes in motor behavior typical of a hemiparkinsonian rodent (127). Lactacystin and another proteasomal inhibitor, epoxomycin, cause selective dopaminergic neurotoxicity when injected into the striatum, with retrograde degeneration of the nigrostriatal projection and apoptotic death of nigral neurons (128).

These proteasomal inhibitors have no obvious means of selective neurotoxicity in dopaminergic neurons, as they inhibit the catalytic activity of the proteolytic core of all cellular proteasomes. Systemic administration of proteasomal inhibitors including the synthetic peptide inhibitor PSI causes selective dopaminergic nigral toxicity without signs of systemic toxicity or neurotoxicity of other brain regions. The reasons for such selective toxicity appear to be twofold. Most brain regions except for ventral mesencephalon respond to these inhibitors with a compensatory upregulation of proteosomal function. Dopaminergic nigral neurons appear to have a naturally high burden of proteins that must be degraded, including oxidatively modified forms of α-synuclein. (129–133). The proteasome inhibition model shares some features with chronic MPTP administration in that a brief course (2 weeks) of exposure leads to a delayed, progressive, and apparently irreversible severe parkinsonism syndrome. As with the rotenone model, the initial publication of the proteasomal model resulted in attempts by several independent laboratories to replicate the original observations, but with mixed results Follow-up studies by the original group found that although they were able to replicate their core observations, the effect of the inhibitor PSI on motor behavior had a narrow dose window and raised questions about both the solubility and bioavailability of this compound (133a). Two other laboratories have reported nigral dopaminergic cell loss after systemic treatment with PSI. However, in only one of these studies were behavioral changes and synuclein-positive inclusion bodies seen (133b, 133c.) Three other groups failed to reproduce either the original pathologic or behavioral observations in spite of attempts to both follow the reported protocol or improve the bioavailability of the compound. At this point there is no clear explanation for the failures of proteasomal inhibitors to reproduce nigral loss, which also includes a study in monkeys (133d, 133e, 133f, 133g).

The proteasomal inhibition model adds a new tool to the study of potential mechanisms of PD. Current hypotheses of the underlying basis of PD emphasize the interaction of multiple factors. The availability of this new model will allow investigators to study the interaction of proteosomal inhibition with oxidative injury in dopaminergic cell degeneration. Both forms of toxic models (mitochondrial and proteasomal inhibition) can be used in combination with the genetic models to develop an overall working model of neuronal degeneration in PD.

GENETIC MODELS

Genetic animal models of PD usually have very different goals and uses than the toxin-induced models. No genetic model can approach the degree of nigral cell loss or motor symptoms seen with 6-OHDA or MPTP. In the investigation of mechanisms underlying cell loss in PD, several genetic models have equal or greater validity than these well-described toxin models. Most of the genetic models are animals that harbor gene alterations causing familial forms of PD. In this manner, they may reproduce and help elucidate cellular pathways that are clearly causative of PD, albeit in a minority of cases.

Genetic models of degenerative diseases utilize several different forms of manipulation. Where genes cause inherited disease with an autosomal dominant pattern, a common working assumption is that the mutation creates an aberrant protein with new toxic properties. This assumption has been very useful in earlier genetic models of Huntington's disease and familial amyotrophic lateral sclerosis (ALS) and was in part the rationale for the creation of transgenic animals that overexpress human α-synuclein genes containing mutations associated with inherited PD. Such animals usually carry multiple copies of this gene and produce the related protein at a much higher rate than PD patients, in the hope that signs of disease (phenotype) will occur within the much shorter animal lifetime. Overexpression can occur throughout all cells in the animal or can be directed to restricted groups of cells by having the mutant human gene under the control of a cell type–specific gene promoter. Although gene promoters can be nonspecific, neuron-specific or dopaminergic cell type–specific, the difference in gene regulation between humans and other species usually does not allow the use of the gene's normal promoter.

In the case of genes that cause disease with an autosomal recessive pattern of inheritance such as parkin, the assumption is that lack of the protein's normal function causes disease. This is commonly seen in inherited enzyme deficiency diseases, and the initial prediction that parkin would be proven to be an enzyme was accurate. Animal models of genes like parkin are commonly "knockout" or null mutations that render the homologous gene in the animal nonfunctional. Overexpression of parkin and other autosomal recessive disease genes is useful to test the assumption that an overabundance of the normal protein confers resistance to abnormal genes or toxins.

The current identification of 6 genes associated with familial PD with either autosomal dominant or recessive inheritance has allowed for the creation of several overexpression and knockout animal models (143, 144). These transgenic animal lines can also be mated to produce progeny carrying 2 or more genetic manipulations for the study of interactions between disease-causing and potentially disease-mitigating genes (145).

Drosophila

With a short reproductive cycle, methods for rapid screening, and ease of manipulation of genetic material, few animals rival the wealth of genetic studies as *Drosophila*. Several transgenic lines of *Drosophila* have been developed that carry genes associated with familial PD. The first PD model in *Drosophila*, human α-synuclein, is illustrative of both the strengths and difficulties of this approach. Although *Drosophila* has a small number of dopaminergic neurons (209) it does not have a homologous protein to human α-synuclein (146). However, when the normal human α-synuclein gene is overexpressed in *Drosophila*, loss of dopaminergic neurons is observed (147). This observation is consistent with the discovery that PARK 4 is actually a duplication of the normal α-synuclein gene (149–154). The neuronal motor system of insects, however, has little homology to that of any vertebrate, and there has been disagreement between laboratories over the nature of the abnormal movements (climbing defects or overactive startle) seen in flies (147, 155–157). Overexpression of α-synuclein does appear to be somewhat selectively toxic to *Drosophila* dopaminergic neurons, since serotonergic neurons do not appear to be affected (147). There is not a uniform correspondence of toxicity of a particular protein in humans and animal models. The mutation of α-synuclein initially identified to cause familial PD (A3OP) is not particularly toxic in *Drosophila*. Overall, α-synuclein overexpressing *Drosophila* has been very useful in assessing hypotheses concerning the protein's toxicity. Wild-type human α-synuclein–overexpressing flies show protein aggregates reminiscent of Lewy bodies (143, 156). *Drosophila* with mutations in α-synuclein has been created to evaluate the relationship of synuclein aggregation to cytotoxicity. A mutation (S129A) that prevents phosphorylation—a necessary step in aggregation—shows enhanced cytotoxicity, supporting the concept that sequestration of alpha-synuclein into large visible aggregates reduces its toxicity (158, 159). This observation in *Drosophila* is consistent with a view of Lewy body formation as a potentially beneficial process. In a manner similar to findings with Huntington's disease model flies, α-synuclein-overexpressing *Drosophila* shows improvement when crossed with flies overexpressing the molecular chaperone heat-shock protein (HSP) 70 (156, 160, 161). The role of molecules that assist in proper protein folding is reaffirmed by similar improvement in α-synuclein toxicity with treatment with the small molecule chaperone geldenamycin (157).

Drosophila possesses a gene with significant sequence homology to the human parkin gene (162, 163). Young-onset PD has been associated with mutations that result in a loss of parkin function (164, 165). This protein is an E3 class ubiquitin ligase that is involved in facilitating the degradation of several potentially harmful proteins by the proteasome (166, 167). In spite of this potentially vital function, *Drosophila* with null mutations of the parkin homolog shows relatively subtle abnormalities, such as reduced life span and male sterility (168, 169). Although these flies also show motor abnormalities, this is a result of muscle abnormalities rather than the degeneration of a subset of dopaminergic neurons. Parkin-null *Drosophila* has disease susceptibility features of potential relevance to PD, such as enhanced lethality to paraquat, along with signs of oxidative stress, including mitochondrial abnormalities in muscle with apoptosis (168, 170). The role of oxidative injury in parkin-deficient flies is supported when the flies are crossed with *Drosophila* transgenic for glutathione S-transferase (GST), an antioxidant enzyme. In a study that also illustrates the value of *Drosophila* for rapid screening of gene-gene interactions, GST-overexpressing flies improved parkin-deficient pathology, while GST-deficient/parkin deficient flies had enhanced dopaminergic neurodegeneration (171). The human parkin substrate PAEL-R (a transmembrane endoplasmic reticulum protein of unknown function) causes dopaminergic neuronal degeneration when overexpressed in *Drosophila*; this degeneration is suppressed by co-overexpression of human parkin (172). Overexpression of parkin also suppresses the toxic effects of human α-synuclein overexpression in *Drosophila* (173, 174).

A transgenic type of *Drosophila* has also been created, which carries either null mutations or overexpresses the DJ-1 gene. Autosomal recessive mutations of this gene, the function of which is unclear, have also been associated with young-onset familial PD (175). *Drosophila* has 2 genes that are homologous with human DJ-1, but only 1 is expressed within the nervous system. Double-knockout mutations of both *Drosophila* DJ-1 genes produce no overt abnormalities or dopaminergic neurodegeneration, but, in a manner analogous to parkin-null mutations, they enhance susceptibility to oxidative injury. These mutant flies showed strikingly enhanced lethality, locomotor dysfunction, and dopaminergic degeneration when exposed to rotenone or paraquat, with evidence of oxidative modification similar to that seen with mammalian DJ-1 (176, 177). Neuronal and dopaminergic hypersensitivity to oxidative injury has been demonstrated in transgenic *Drosophila* that overexpresses interfering RNA to inhibit expression of the normal DJ-1 gene (178).

Recently transgenic flies have been created that manipulate PINK1, another gene responsible for recessive young onset PD. PINK1 (PTEN-induced kinase-1) is a mitochondrial associated protein of unclear function (179). *Drosophila* with homozygous loss of function mutations of PINK1 shows motor abnormalities that appear to be related to both muscular and dopaminergic deficits (180). These abnormalities along with mitochondrial dysfunction and male sterility are reminiscent of flies with parkin mutations (181). Overexpression of parkin significantly ameliorates these PINK1 knockout abnormalities (but not the converse), suggesting that PINK1 and parkin function in the same pathways (182).

Transgenic Mice

Although mice have a nervous system more homologous to humans than insects do, transgenic mice carrying mutations of human PD– associated genes demonstrate many of the same successes and difficulties described with *Drosophila* (183).

Transgenic mice overexpressing human wild-type α-synuclein also show intraneuronal protein inclusions in several brain areas, including the substantia nigra (184). Transgenic lines with the highest levels of expression showed significant loss of TH-positive cells and terminals along with motor abnormalities, but not to the extent seen in toxin models of PD. Although α-synuclein-null mice have also been created, they have modest reductions in striatal dopamine; they are also notable for their resistance to MPTP toxicity, further reinforcing concepts of interaction between oxidative injury and potentially toxic proteins (185, 186). Transgenic mice overexpressing human α-synuclein with PD-associated mutations have also been created. When the A53T and A30P mutant genes are overexpressed using a neuron-specific promoter (Thy1), animals showed α-synuclein–related pathology, including synaptic degeneration and motor abnormalities, but were without dopaminergic degeneration due to poor transgene expression in the nigra (187). However, even when overexpression of the same α-synuclein mutations is targeted to nigral cells using the TH promoter, neither Lewy body–like inclusions nor dopaminergic degeneration was observed (188). The lack of striking dopaminergic or nigral degeneration in any of the human mutant α-synuclein transgenic mouse lines illustrates that level of expression or promoter qualities cannot completely account for the inability of these animals to closely reproduce a PD phenotype. However several of these lines show motor abnormalities as well as enhanced toxicity to MPTP (183, 189, 190). High levels of expression of human mutant α-synuclein (driven by the murine PrP promoter) appear to be capable of producing Lewy body and Lewy dendrite pathology. But although these animals have more widespread neuronal loss, their preservation of nigral neurons remains unexplained (191, 192). Transgenic mice overexpressing human mutant α-synuclein do show some useful PD-like abnormalities such as reduced DAT expression and abnormal motor responses to apomorphine and amphetamine (193, 194). The widespread pathology and neurodegeneration of the most severely affected lines of α-synuclein mice also make them appropriate models for studying α-synuclein toxicity in vivo. Identified factors that can reduce α-synuclein pathology include overexpression of beta-synuclein and vaccination for α-synuclein (195, 196).

Transgenic mice that are parkin-deficient have been created and also show modest nigrostriatal abnormalities. Parkin mice with null mutations do show abnormal dopamine release and metabolism, reduced DAT content, and reduced neuronal numbers in the locus ceruleus (exon 7 deletion only), but normal nigral cell numbers (197, 198). Unlike *Drosophila* models, crossing parkin-deficient mice with mutant α-synuclein overexpressers does not result in enhanced pathology (200). Parkin does appear to have a role in abnormal protein degradation in mice, since parkin null crosses with mice overexpressing mutant human tau show enhanced nigral and motor neuron abnormalities (201). In a manner similar to results in flies, mice with either α-synuclein overexpression or parkin-null mice show mitochondrial stress and enhanced susceptibility to rotenone (202, 203).

DJ-1 null mice have recently been created and show interesting abnormalities. As with virtually all of the transgenic mouse lines mentioned earlier, DJ-1 null mice have normal numbers of nigral dopaminergic neurons. However, striatal dopamine reuptake and release is substantially reduced in these animals (204). DJ-1 null transgenic mice also share an enhanced susceptibility to MPTP (205).

Viral Vector Gene Delivery

Another method for introducing PD-associated genes into animal models is through the use of a viral vector carrying the gene. This is an invasive and labor-intensive procedure where pathogenic human genes such as α-synuclein are packaged into replication-deficient viruses and stereotacticly injected into brain. This method has been useful in causing significant nigral pathology in rodents, where transgenic mice show little nigral cell loss. Targeted overexpression of human α-synuclein to nigra has been accomplished with adeno-associated or lentiviral vectors, and animals show accumulation and aggregation of the human protein, nigral cell loss, and evidence of apoptosis (206–209). In a manner analogous to toxin injections in animals where cell loss was moderate (50%), motor abnormalities were not observed. Viral delivery of mutant PD genes also allows assessment of their effects in vivo in primates, where creation of transgenic lines is not practical. Adeno-associated viral (AAV) vectors expressing human mutant α-synuclein cause substantial loss of TH-positive neurons with synuclein-related cellular changes in adult marmosets (210). In this model, coexpression of a parkin-expressing vector reduced synuclein-related cell loss; with a lentiviral vector, an increase in Lewy body–like inclusions was observed (211–213).

It is likely that there will be an increasing diversity and number of animal models of PD. These models will continue to vary in their respective applicability to assessment of pathogenetic mechanism underlying PD and identification and evaluation of potential therapeutics. Although the vast majority of PD patients have no evidence of a clearly inherited or environmental cause, there is increasing evidence for a role for both environmental and genetic factors. The diversity of these models and their increasing use in combination will contribute to 2 important goals: (a) elucidation of how genetic and environmental factors interact to cause disease and (b) improved validation of potential therapeutics prior to their entry into clinical trials.

References

1. Beal MF. Experimental models of Parkinson's disease. *Nat Rev Neurosci* 2001; 2(5): 325–334.
2. Ungerstedt U. 6-Hydroxy-dopamine induced degeneration of central monoamine neurons. *Eur J Pharmacol* 1968; 5(1):107–110.
3. Ungerstedt U. Striatal dopamine release after amphetamine or nerve degeneration revealed by rotational behaviour. *Acta Physiol Scand Suppl* 1971; 367:49–68.
4. Sauer H, Oertel WH. Progressive degeneration of nigrostriatal dopamine neurons following intrastriatal terminal lesions with 6–hydroxydopamine: A combined retrograde tracing and immunocytochemical study in the rat. *Neuroscience* 1994; 59(2):401–415.
5. Przedborski S, Levivier M, Jiang H, et al. Dose-dependent lesions of the dopaminergic nigrostriatal pathway induced by intrastriatal injection of 6-hydroxydopamine. *Neuroscience* 1995; 67(3):631–647.
6. Perese DA, Ulman J, Viola J, et al. A 6-hydroxydopamine-induced selective parkinsonian rat model. *Brain Res* 1989; 494(2):285–293.
7. Schwarting RK, Huston JP. The unilateral 6-hydroxydopamine lesion model in behavioral brain research. Analysis of functional deficits, recovery and treatments. *Prog Neurobiol* 1996; 50(2–3):275–331.
8. Olsson M, Nikkhah G, Bentlage C, Bjorklund A. Forelimb akinesia in the rat Parkinson model: Differential effects of dopamine agonists and nigral transplants as assessed by a new stepping test. *J Neurosci* 1995; 15(5 Pt 2):3863–3875.
9. Hefti F, Melamed E, Wurtman RJ. Partial lesions of the dopaminergic nigrostriatal system in rat brain: Biochemical characterization. *Brain Res* 1980; 195(1):123–137.
10. Lundblad M, Andersson M, Winkler C, et al. Pharmacological validation of behavioural measures of akinesia and dyskinesia in a rat model of Parkinson's disease. *Eur J Neurosci* 2002; 15(1):120–132.
11. Azzouz M, Martin-Rendon E, Barber RD, et al. Multicistronic lentiviral vector–mediated striatal gene transfer of aromatic L-amino acid decarboxylase, tyrosine hydroxylase, and GTP cyclohydrolase I induces sustained transgene expression, dopamine production, and functional improvement in a rat model of Parkinson's disease. *J Neurosci* 2002; 22(23):10302–10312.
12. Fan DS, Ogawa M, Fujimoto KI, et al. Behavioral recovery in 6-hydroxydopamine-lesioned rats by co-transduction of striatum with tyrosine hydroxylase and aromatic L–amino acid decarboxylase genes using two separate adeno-associated virus vectors. Hum *Gene Ther* 1998; 9(17):2527–2535.
13. Kearns CM, Gash DM. GDNF protects nigral dopamine neurons against 6-hydroxydopamine in vivo. *Brain Res* 1995; 672(1–2):104–111.
14. Horger BA, Nishimura MC, Armanini MP et al. Neurturin exerts potent actions on survival and function of midbrain dopaminergic neurons. *J Neurosci* 1998; 18(13): 4929–4937.
15. Torres EM, Monville C, Lowenstein PR, et al. Delivery of sonic hedgehog or glial derived neurotrophic factor to dopamine-rich grafts in a rat model of Parkinson's disease using adenoviral vectors Increased yield of dopamine cells is dependent on embryonic donor age. *Brain Res Bull* 2005; 68(1–2):31–41.
16. Brederlau A, Correia AS, Anisimov SV, et al. Transplantation of human embryonic stem cell–derived cells to a rat model of Parkinson's disease: Effect of in vitro differentiation on graft survival and teratoma formation. *Stem Cells* 2006; 24(6):1433–1440.
17. Harrower TP, Tyers P, Hooks Y, Barker RA. Long-term survival and integration of porcine expanded neural precursor cell grafts in a rat model of Parkinson's disease. *Exp Neurol* 2006; 197(1):56–69. Epub Oct 24, 2005.
18. Luo J, Kaplitt MG, Fitzsimons HL, et al. Subthalamic GAD gene therapy in a Parkinson's disease rat model. *Science* 2002; 298(5592):425–429.
19. Bjorklund LM, Sanchez-Pernaute R, Chung S, et al. Embryonic stem cells develop into functional dopaminergic neurons after transplantation in a Parkinson rat model. *Proc Natl Acad Sci USA* 2002; 99(4):2344–2349.
20. Soares-da-Silva P, Azevedo I. Differential effects of 6-hydroxydopamine on the two types of nerve vesicles and dopamine and noradrenaline content in mesenteric arterial vessels. *J Auton Pharmacol* 1988; 8(1):1–10.
21. Ungerstedt U. Adipsia and aphagia after 6-hydroxydopamine induced degeneration of the nigro-striatal dopamine system. *Acta Physiol Scand Suppl* 1971; 367:95–122.
22. Cenci MA, Whishaw IQ, Schallert T. Animal models of neurological deficits: How relevant is the rat? *Nat Rev Neurosci* 2002; 3(7):574–579.
23. Jeon BS, Jackson-Lewis V, Burke RE. 6-Hydroxydopamine lesion of the rat substantia nigra: Time course and morphology of cell death. *Neurodegeneration* 1995; 4(2): 131–137.
24. Javoy F, Sotelo C, Herbet A, Agid Y. Specificity of dopaminergic neuronal degeneration induced by intracerebral injection of 6-hydroxydopamine in the nigrostriatal dopamine system. *Brain Res* 1976; 102(2):201–215.
25. Yuan H, Sarre S, Ebinger G, Michotte Y. Histological, behavioural and neurochemical evaluation of medial forebrain bundle and striatal 6-OHDA lesions as rat models of Parkinson's disease. *J Neurosci Methods* 2005; 144(1):35–45.
26. Przedborski S, Levivier M, Jiang H, et al. Dose-dependent lesions of the dopaminergic nigrostriatal pathway induced by intrastriatal injection of 6-hydroxydopamine. *Neuroscience* 1995; 67(3):631–647.
27. Jonsson G, Sachs C. Actions of 6-hydroxydopamine quinones on catecholamine neurons. *J Neurochem* 1975; 25(4):509–516.
28. Sachs C, Jonsson G. Effects of 6-hydroxydopamine on central noradrenaline neurons during ontogeny. *Brain Res* 1975; 99(2):277–291.
29. Glinka YY, Youdim MB. Inhibition of mitochondrial complexes I and IV by 6-hydroxydopamine. *Eur J Pharmacol* 1995; 292(3–4):329–332.
30. Linert W, Herlinger E, Jameson RF, et al. Dopamine, 6-hydroxydopamine, iron, and dioxygen—Their mutual interactions and possible implication in the development of Parkinson's disease. *Biochim Biophys Acta* 1996; 1316(3):160–168.
31. Heikkila R, Cohen G. Inhibition of biogenic amine uptake by hydrogen peroxide: A mechanism for toxic effects of 6-hydroxydopamine. *Science* 1971; 172(989):1257–1258.
32. Ben–Shachar D, Eshel G, Finberg JP, Youdim MB. The iron chelator desferrioxamine (Desferal) retards 6-hydroxydopamine-induced degeneration of nigrostriatal dopamine neurons. *J Neurochem* 1991; 56(4):1441–1444.
33. Cadet JL, Katz M, Jackson-Lewis V, Fahn S. Vitamin E attenuates the toxic effects of intrastriatal injection of 6-hydroxydopamine (6-OHDA) in rats: Behavioral and biochemical evidence. *Brain Res* 1989; 476(1):10–15.
34. Wang J, Jiang H, Xie JX. Time dependent effects of 6-OHDA lesions on iron level and neuronal loss in rat nigrostriatal system. *Neurochem Res* 2004; 29(12):2239–2243.
35. Rodrigues RW, Gomide VC, Chadi G. Astroglial and microglial reaction after a partial nigrostriatal degeneration induced by the striatal injection of different doses of 6—hydroxydopamine. *Int J Neurosci* 2001; 109(1–2):91–126.
36. Truong L, Allbutt H, Kassiou M, Henderson JM. Developing a preclinical model of Parkinson's disease: A study of behaviour in rats with graded 6-OHDA lesions. *Behav Brain Res* 2006; 169(1):1–9.
37. Stromberg I, Bjorklund H, Dahl D, et al. Astrocyte responses to dopaminergic denervations by 6-hydroxydopamine and 1-methyl-4-phenyl-1,2,3,6-tetrahydropyridine as evidenced by glial fibrillary acidic protein immunohistochemistry. *Brain Res Bull* 1986; 17(2):225–236.
38. Sauer H, Oertel WH. Progressive degeneration of nigrostriatal dopamine neurons following intrastriatal terminal lesions with 6-hydroxydopamine: A combined retrograde tracing and immunocytochemical study in the rat. *Neuroscience* 1994; 59(2):401–415.
39. Lee CS, Sauer H, Bjorklund A. Dopaminergic neuronal degeneration and motor impairments following axon terminal lesion by instrastriatal 6-hydroxydopamine in the rat. *Neuroscience* 1996; 72(3):641–653.
40. Damier P, Hirsch EC, Agid Y, Graybiel AM. The substantia nigra of the human brain. II. Patterns of loss of dopamine-containing neurons in Parkinson's disease. *Brain* 1999; 122(Pt 8):1437–1448.
41. Langston JW, Ballard P, Tetrud JW, Irwin I. Chronic parkinsonism in humans due to a product of meperidine-analog synthesis. *Science* 1983; 219(4587):979–980.
42. Ballard PA, Tetrud JW, Langston JW. Permanent human parkinsonism due to 1-methyl-4-phenyl-1,2,3,6-etrahydropyridine (MPTP): Seven cases. *Neurology* 1985; 35(7): 949–956.
43. Burns RS, Chiueh CC, Markey SP, et al. A primate model of parkinsonism: Selective destruction of dopaminergic neurons in the pars compacta of the substantia nigra by N-methyl-4-phenyl-1,2,3,6-tetrahydropyridine. *Proc Natl Acad Sci USA* 1983; 80(7):4546–4550.
44. Langston JW, Forno LS, Rebert CS, Irwin I. Selective nigral toxicity after systemic administration of 1-methyl-4-phenyl-1,2,5,6-tetrahydropyridine (MPTP) in the squirrel monkey. *Brain Res* 1984; 292(2):390–394.
45. Langston JW, Irwin I, Langston EB, Forno LS. 1-Methyl-4-phenylpyridinium ion (MPP+): Identification of a metabolite of MPTP, a toxin selective to the substantia nigra. *Neurosci Lett* 1984; 48(1):87–92.
46. Heikkila RE, Manzino L, Cabbat FS, Duvoisin RC. Protection against the dopaminergic neurotoxicity of 1-methyl-4-phenyl-1,2,5,6-tetrahydropyridine by monoamine oxidase inhibitors. *Nature* 1984; 311(5985):467–469.
47. Javitch JA, Snyder SH. Uptake of MPP(+) by dopamine neurons explains selectivity of parkinsonism-inducing neurotoxin, MPTP. *Eur J Pharmacol* 1984; 106(2):455–456.
48. Nicklas WJ, Youngster SK, Kindt MV, Heikkila RE. MPTP, MPP+ and mitochondrial function. *Life Sci* 1987; 40(8):721–729.
49. Bove J, Prou D, Perier C, Przedborski S. Toxin-induced models of Parkinson's disease. *NeuroRx* 2005; 2(3):484–494.
50. Eslamboli A. Marmoset monkey models of Parkinson's disease: Which model, when and why? *Brain Res Bull* 2005; 68(3):140–149.
51. Smeyne RJ, Jackson-Lewis V. The MPTP model of Parkinson's disease. *Brain Res Mol Brain Res* 2005; 134(1):57–66.
52. Jakowec MW, Petzinger GM. 1-methyl-4-phenyl-1,2,3,6-tetrahydropyridine-lesioned model of parkinson's disease, with emphasis on mice and nonhuman primates. *Comp Med* 2004; 54(5):497–513.
53. Hung HC, Lee EH. The mesolimbic dopaminergic pathway is more resistant than the nigrostriatal dopaminergic pathway to MPTP and MPP+ toxicity: Role of BDNF gene expression. *Brain Res Mol Brain Res* 1996; 41(1–2):14–26.
54. Hung HC, Tao PL, Lee EH. 1-Methyl-4-phenyl-pyridinium (MPP+) uptake does not explain the differential toxicity of MPP+ in the nigrostriatal and mesolimbic dopaminergic pathways. *Neurosci Lett* 1995; 196(1–2):93–96.
55. Lavoie B, Parent A. Dopaminergic neurons expressing calbindin in normal and parkinsonian monkeys. *Neuroreport* 1991; 2(10):601–604.
56. Donovan DM, Miner LL, Perry MP, et al. Cocaine reward and MPTP toxicity: alteration by regional variant dopamine transporter overexpression. *Brain Res Mol Brain Res* 1999; 73(1–2):37–49.
57. Blanchard V, Raisman-Vozari R, Vyas S, et al. Differential expression of tyrosine hydroxylase and membrane dopamine transporter genes in subpopulations of dopaminergic neurons of the rat mesencephalon. *Brain Res Mol Brain Res* 1994; 22(1–4):29–38.
58. Dauer W, Kholodilov N, Vila M, et al. Resistance of alpha-synuclein null mice to the parkinsonian neurotoxin MPTP. *Proc Natl Acad Sci USA* 2002; 99 (22):14524–14529.

59. Tetrud JW, Langston JW. Tremor in MPTP-induced parkinsonism. *Neurology* 1992; 42(2):407–410.

60. Meissner W, Prunier C, Guilloteau D, et al. Time-course of nigrostriatal degeneration in a progressive MPTP-lesioned macaque model of Parkinson's disease. *Mol Neurobiol* 2003; 28(3):209–18.

61. Emborg ME, Tetrud JW, Moirano J, et al. Rest tremor in rhesus monkeys with MPTP-induced parkinsonism. *Front Biosci* 2003 8:a148–154.

62. Bankiewicz KS, Oldfield EH, Chiueh CC, et al. Hemiparkinsonism in monkeys after unilateral internal carotid artery infusion of 1-methyl-4-phenyl-1,2,3,6-tetrahydropyridine (MPTP). *Life Sci* 1986; 39(1):7–16.

63. Przedborski S, Jackson-Lewis V, Popilskis S, et al. Unilateral MPTP-induced parkinsonism in monkeys. A quantitative utoradiographic study of dopamine D1 and D2 receptors and re-uptake sites. *Neurochirurgie* 1991; 37(6):377–382.

64. Jenner P, Rupniak NM, Rose S, et al. 1-Methyl-4-phenyl-1,2,3,6-tetrahydropyridine–induced parkinsonism in the common marmoset. *Neurosci Lett* 1984; 50(1–3):85–90.

65. Bedard PJ, Di Paolo T, Falardeau P, Boucher R. Chronic treatment with L-DOPA, but not bromocriptine induces dyskinesia in MPTP-parkinsonian monkeys. Correlation with [3H]spiperone binding. *Brain Res* 1986; 379(2):294–299.

66. Clarke CE, Boyce S, Robertson RG, et al. Drug-induced dyskinesia in primates rendered hemiparkinsonian by intracarotid administration of 1-methyl-4-phenyl-1,2,3,6-tetrahydropyridine (MPTP). *J Neurol Sci* 1989; 90(3):307–314.

67. Jenner P. Avoidance of dyskinesia: Preclinical evidence for continuous dopaminergic stimulation. *Neurology* 2004; 62(1 Suppl 1):S47–S55.

68. Gibb WR, Lees AJ, Wells FR, et al. Pathology of MPTP in the marmoset. *Adv Neurol* 1987; 45:187–190.

69. Forno LS, Langston JW, DeLanney LE, et al. Locus ceruleus lesions and eosinophilic inclusions in MPTP-treated monkeys. *Ann Neurol* 1986; 20(4):449–455.

70. Kowall NW, Hantraye P, Brouillet E, et al. MPTP induces alpha-synuclein aggregation in the substantia nigra of baboons. *Neuroreport* 2000; 11(1):211–213.

71. Langston JW, Ballard PA Jr. Parkinson's disease in a chemist working with 1-methyl-4-phenyl-1,2,5,6-tetrahydropyridine. *N Engl J Med* 1983; 309(5):310.

72. Wright JM, Wall RA, Perry TL, Paty DW. Chronic parkinsonism secondary to intranasal administration of a product of meperidine-analogue synthesis. *N Engl J Med* 1984; 310(5):325.

73. Vingerhoets FJ, Snow BJ, Tetrud JW, et al. Positron emission tomographic evidence for progression of human MPTP-induced dopaminergic lesions. *Ann Neurol* 1994; 36(5):765–770.

74. Russ H, Mihatsch W, Gerlach M, et al. Neurochemical and behavioural features induced by chronic low dose treatment with 1-methyl-4-phenyl-1,2,3,6-tetrahydropyridine (MPTP) in the common marmoset: Implications for Parkinson's disease? *Neurosci Lett* 1991; 123(1):115–118.

75. Bezard E, Imbert C, Deloire X, et al. A chronic MPTP model reproducing the slow evolution of Parkinson's disease: Evolution of motor symptoms in the monkey. *Brain Res* 1997; 766(1–2):107–112.

76. Bergman H, Wichmann T, Karmon B, DeLong MR. The primate subthalamic nucleus. II. Neuronal activity in the MPTP model of parkinsonism. *J Neurophysiol* 1994; 72(2):507–520.

77. Wichmann T, Bergman H, DeLong MR. The primate subthalamic nucleus. III. Changes in motor behavior and neuronal activity in the internal pallidum induced by subthalamic inactivation in the MPTP model of parkinsonism. *J Neurophysiol* 1994; 72(2):521–530.

78. Brownell AL, Canales K, Chen YI, et al. Mapping brain function after MPTP-induced neurotoxicity in a primate Parkinson's disease model. *Neuroimage* 2003; 20(2):1064–1075.

79. Ceballos-Baumann AO, Obeso JA, Vitek JL, et al. Restoration of thalamocortical activity after posteroventral pallidotomy in Parkinson's disease. *Lancet* 1994; 344 (8925):814.

80. Bergman H, Wichmann T, DeLong MR. Reversal of experimental parkinsonism by lesions of the subthalamic nucleus. *Science* 1990; 249(4975):1436–1438.

81. Limousin P, Krack P, Pollak P, et al. Electrical stimulation of the subthalamic nucleus in advanced Parkinson's disease. *N Engl J Med* 1998; 339(16):1105–1111.

82. Eslamboli A, Georgievska B, Ridley RM, et al. Continuous low-level glial cell line–derived neurotrophic factor delivery using recombinant adeno-associated viral vectors provides neuroprotection and induces behavioral recovery in a primate model of Parkinson's disease. *J Neurosci* 2005; 25(4):769–777.

83. Forsayeth JR, Eberling JL, Sanftner LM, et al. A dose-ranging study of AAV-hAADC therapy in parkinsonian monkeys. *Mol Ther* 2006; [Epub ahead of print]

84. Takagi Y, Takahashi J, Saiki H, et al. Dopaminergic neurons generated from monkey embryonic stem cells function in a Parkinson primate model. *J Clin Invest* 2005; 115(1):102–109.

85. Sladek JR Jr, Collier TJ, Haber SN, et al. Survival and growth of fetal catecholamine neurons transplanted into primate brain. *Brain Res Bull* 1986; 17(6):809–818.

86. Redmond DE, Sladek JR Jr, Roth RH, et al. Fetal neuronal grafts in monkeys given methylphenyltetrahydropyridine. *Lancet* 1986; 1(8490):1125–1127.

87. Bankiewicz KS, Plunkett RJ, Jacobowitz DM, et al. The effect of fetal mesencephalon implants on primate MPTP-induced parkinsonism. Histochemical and behavioral studies. *J Neurosurg* 1990; 72(2):231–244.

88. Widner H, Tetrud J, Rehncrona S, et al. Bilateral fetal mesencephalic grafting in two patients with parkinsonism induced by 1-methyl-4-phenyl-1,2,3,6-tetrahydropyridine (MPTP) *N Engl J Med* 1992; 327(22):1556–1563.

89. Linazasoro G. Recent failures of new potential symptomatic treatments for Parkinson's disease: Causes and solutions. *Mov Disord* 2004; 19(7):743–754.

90. Olanow CW, Goetz CG, Kordower JH, et al. A double-blind controlled trial of bilateral fetal nigral transplantation in Parkinson's disease. *Ann Neurol* 2003; 54(3):403–414.

91. Freed CR, Greene PE, Breeze RE, et al. Transplantation of embryonic dopamine neurons for severe Parkinson's disease. *N Engl J Med* 2001; 344(10):710–719.

92. Eslamboli A. Assessment of GDNF in primate models of Parkinson's disease: Comparison with human studies. *Rev Neurosci* 2005; 16(4):303–310.

93. Grondin R, Zhang Z, Yi A, et al. Chronic, controlled GDNF infusion promotes structural and functional recovery in advanced parkinsonian monkeys. *Brain* 2002; 125 (Pt 10):2191–2201.

94. Zhang Z, Miyoshi Y, Lapchak PA, et al. Dose response to intraventricular glial cell line–derived neurotrophic factor administration in parkinsonian monkeys. *J Pharmacol Exp Ther* 1997; 282(3):1396–1401.

95. Gash DM, Zhang Z, Ovadia A, et al. Functional recovery in parkinsonian monkeys treated with GDNF. Nature 1996; 380(6571):252–255.

96. Nutt JG, Burchiel KJ, Comella CL, et al. Implanted intracerebroventricular. Glial cell line–derived neurotrophic factor (GDNF) in PD. *Neurology* 2003; 60(1):69–73.

97. Kordower JH, Palfi S, Chen EY, et al. Clinicopathological findings following intraventricular glial-derived neurotrophic factor treatment in a patient with Parkinson's disease. *Ann Neurol* 1999; 46(3):419–424.

98. Slevin JT, Gerhardt GA, Smith CD, et al. Improvement of bilateral motor functions in patients with Parkinson disease through the unilateral intraputaminal infusion of glial cell line–derived neurotrophic factor. *J Neurosurg* 2005; 102(2):216–222.

99. Lang AE, Gill S, Patel NK, et al. Randomized controlled trial of intraputamenal glial cell line–derived neurotrophic factor infusion in Parkinson disease. *Ann Neurol* 2006; 59(3):459–466.

100. Patel NK, Bunnage M, Plaha P, et al. Intraputamenal infusion of glial cell line–derived neurotrophic factor in PD: A two-year outcome study. *Ann Neurol* 2005; 57(2):298–302.

101. Heikkila RE, Hess A, Duvoisin RC. Dopaminergic neurotoxicity of 1-methyl-4-phenyl-1,2,5,6-tetrahydropyridine in mice. *Science* 1984; 224(4656):1451–1453.

102. Heikkila RE, Sonsalla PK. The use of the MPTP-treated mouse as an animal model of parkinsonism. *Can J Neurol Sci* 1987; 14(3 Suppl):436–440.

103. Sedelis M, Hofele K, Auburger GW, et al. MPTP susceptibility in the mouse: Behavioral, neurochemical, and histological analysis of gender and strain differences. *Behav Genet* 2000; 30(3):171–182.

104. Przedborski S, Kostic V, Jackson-Lewis V, Naini AB, Simonetti S, Fahn S, Carlson E, Epstein CJ, Cadet JL. Transgenic mice with increased Cu/Znsuperoxide dismutase activity are resistant to N-methyl-4-phenyl-1,2,3,6-tetrahydropyridine–induced neurotoxicity. *J Neurosci* 1992; 12(5):1658–1667.

105. Przedborski S, Jackson-Lewis V, Yokoyama R, et al. Role of neuronal nitric oxide in 1-methyl-4-phenyl-1,2,3,6-tetrahydropyridine (MPTP)-induced dopaminergic neurotoxicity. *Proc Natl Acad Sci USA* 1996; 93(10):4565–4571.

106. Heikkila RE, Terleckyj I, Sieber BA. Monoamine oxidase and the bioactivation of MPTP and related neurotoxins: Relevance to DATATOP. *J Neural Transm Suppl* 1990; 32:217–227.

107. Effect of deprenyl on the progression of disability in early Parkinson's disease. The Parkinson Study Group. *N Engl J Med* 1989; 321(20):1364–1371.

108. Beal MF, Matthews RT, Tieleman A, Shults CW. Coenzyme Q10 attenuates the 1-methyl-4-phenyl-1,2,3,tetrahydropyridine (MPTP) induced loss of striatal dopamine and dopaminergic axons in aged mice. *Brain Res* 1998; 783(1):109–114.

109. Matthews RT, Ferrante RJ, Klivenyi P, et al. Creatine and cyclocreatine attenuate MPTP neurotoxicity. *Exp Neurol* 1999; 157(1):142–149.

110. Du Y, Ma Z, Lin S, et al. Minocycline prevents nigrostriatal dopaminergic neurodegeneration in the MPTP model of Parkinson's disease. *Proc Natl Acad Sci USA* 2001; 98(25):14669–14674.

111. Saporito MS, Brown EM, Miller MS, Carswell S. CEP-1347/KT-7515, an inhibitor of c-jun N-terminal kinase activation, attenuates the 1-methyl4-phenyl tetrahydropyridine-mediated loss of nigrostriatal dopaminergic neurons In vivo. *J Pharmacol Exp Ther* 1999; 288(2):421–427.

112. Kupsch A, Sautter J, Gotz ME, et al. Monoamine oxidase-inhibition and MPTP-induced neurotoxicity in the non-human primate: Comparison of rasagiline (TVP 1012) with selegiline. *J Neural Transm* 2001; 108(8–9):985–1009.

113. Shults CW. Therapeutic role of coenzyme Q(10) in Parkinson's disease. Pharmacol Ther 2005; 107(1):120–130.

114. Waldmeier P, Bozyczko-Coyne D, Williams M, Vaught JL. Recent clinical failures in Parkinson's disease with apoptosis inhibitors underline the need for a paradigm shift in drug discovery for neurodegenerative diseases. *Biochem Pharmacol* 2006; 72(10):1197–1206.

115. Betarbet R, Sherer TB, MacKenzie G, et al. Chronic systemic pesticide exposure reproduces features of Parkinson's disease. *Nat Neurosci* 2000; 3(12):1301–1306.

116. Talpade DJ, Greene JG, Higgins DS Jr, Greenamyre JT. In vivo labeling of mitochondrial complex I (NADH:ubiquinone oxidoreductase) in rat brain using [(3)H]dihydrorotenone. *J Neurochem* 2000; 75(6):2611–2621.

117. Testa CM, Sherer TB, Greenamyre JT. Rotenone induces oxidative stress and dopaminergic neuron damage in organotypic substantia nigra cultures. *Brain Res Mol Brain Res* 2005; 134(1):109–118.

118. Sherer TB, Betarbet R, Stout AK, et al. An in vitro model of Parkinson's disease: Linking mitochondrial impairment to altered alpha-synuclein metabolism and oxidative damage. *J Neurosci* 2002; 22(16):7006–7015.

119. Lee HJ, Shin SY, Choi C, et al. Formation and removal of alpha-synuclein aggregates in cells exposed to mitochondrial inhibitors. *J Biol Chem* 2002; 277(7):5411–5417.

120. Marshall LE, Himes RH. Rotenone inhibition of tubulin self-assembly. *Biochim Biophys Acta* 1978; 543(4):590–594.

121. Brooks AI, Chadwick CA, Gelbard HA, et al. Paraquat elicited neurobehavioral syndrome caused by dopaminergic neuron loss. *Brain Res* 1999; 823(1–2):1–10.
122. McCormack AL, Thiruchelvam M, Manning-Bog AB, et al. Environmental risk factors and Parkinson's disease: Selective degeneration of nigral dopaminergic neurons caused by the herbicide paraquat. *Neurobiol Dis* 2002; 10(2):119–127.
123. Thiruchelvam M, McCormack A, Richfield EK, et al. Age-related irreversible progressive nigrostriatal dopaminergic neurotoxicity in the paraquat and maneb model of the Parkinson's disease phenotype. *Eur J Neurosci* 2003; 18(3):589–600.
124. Thiruchelvam M, Brockel BJ, Richfield EK, et al. Potentiated and preferential effects of combined paraquat and maneb on nigrostriatal dopamine systems: Environmental risk factors for Parkinson's disease? Brain Res 2000; 873(2):225–234.
125. McNaught KS, Perl DP, Brownell AL, Olanow CW. Systemic exposure to proteasome inhibitors causes a progressive model of Parkinson's disease. *Ann Neurol* 2004; 56(1):149–162.
126. McNaught KS, Jackson T, JnoBaptiste R, et al. Proteasomal dysfunction in sporadic Parkinson's disease. *Neurology* 2006; 66(10 Suppl 4):S37–S49.
127. Snyder H, Wolozin B. Pathological proteins in Parkinson's disease: focus on the proteasome. *J Mol Neurosci* 2004; 24(3):425–442.
128. McNaught KS, Bjorklund LM, Belizaire R, et al. Proteasome inhibition causes nigral degeneration with inclusion bodies in rats. *Neuroreport* 2002; 13(11):1437–1441.
129. Miwa H, Kubo T, Suzuki A, et al. Retrograde dopaminergic neuron degeneration following intrastriatal proteasome inhibition. *Neurosci Lett* 2005; 380(1–2):93–98.
130. Mytilineou C, McNaught KS, Shashidharan P, et al. Inhibition of proteasome activity sensitizes dopamine neurons to protein alterations and oxidative stress. *J Neural Transm* 2004; 111(10–11):1237–1251.
131. Holtz WA, O'Malley KL. Parkinsonian mimetics induce aspects of unfolded protein response in death of dopaminergic neurons. *J Biol Chem* 2003; 278(21):19367–19377.
132. Chen L, Thiruchelvam MJ, Madura K, Richfield EK. Proteaosome dysfunction in aged human alpha-synuclein transgenic mice. *Neurobiol Dis* 2006; 23(1):120–126.
133. Rideout HJ, Lang-Rollin IC, Savalle M, Stefanis L. Dopaminergic neurons in rat ventral midbrain cultures undergo selective apoptosis and form inclusions, but do not up-regulate iHSP70, following proteasomal inhibition. *J Neurochem* 2005; 93(5):1304–1313.
134. Tanaka Y, Engelender S, Igarashi S, et al. Inducible expression of mutant alpha-synuclein decreases proteasome activity and increases sensitivity to mitochondria-dependent apoptosis. *Hum Mol Genet* 2001; 10(9):919–926.
135. McNaught KS, Olanow CW. Proteasome inhibitor–induced model of Parkinson's disease. *Ann Neurol* 2006; 60(2):243–247.
136. Zeng BY, Bukhatwa S, Hikima A, et al. Reproducible nigral cell loss after systemic proteasomal inhibitor administration to rats. *Ann Neurol* 2006; 60(2):248–252.
137. Schapira AH, Cleeter MW, Muddle JR, et al. Proteasomal inhibition causes loss of nigral tyrosine hydroxylase neurons. *Ann Neurol* 2006; 60(2):253–255.
138. Kordower JH, Kanaan NM, Chu Y, et al. Failure of proteasome inhibitor administration to provide a model of Parkinson's disease in rats and monkeys. *Ann Neurol* 2006; 60(2):264–268.
139. Manning-Bog AB, Reaney SH, Chou VP, et al. Lack of nigrostriatal pathology in a rat model of proteasome inhibition. *Ann Neurol* 2006; 60(2):256–260
140. Bove J, Zhou C, Jackson-Lewis V, et al. Proteasome inhibition and Parkinson's disease modeling. *Ann Neurol* 2006; 60(2):260–264.
141. Beal F, Lang A. The proteasomal inhibition model of Parkinson's disease: "Boon or bust"? *Ann Neurol* 2006; 60(2):158–161.
142. Farrer MJ. Genetics of Parkinson disease: Paradigm shifts and future prospects. *Nat Rev Genet* 2006; 7(4):306–318.
143. Morris HR. Genetics of Parkinson's disease. *Ann Med* 2005; 37(2):86–96.
144. Shulman JM, Shulman LM, Weiner WJ, Feany MB. From fruit fly to bedside: Translating lessons from Drosophila models of neurodegenerative disease. *Curr Opin Neurol* 2003; 16(4):443–449.
145. Whitworth AJ, Wes PD, Pallanck LJ. Drosophila models pioneer a new approach to drug discovery for Parkinson's disease. *Drug Discov Today* 2006; 11(3–4):119–126.
146. Feany MB, Bender WW. A Drosophila model of Parkinson's disease. *Nature* 2000; 404(6776):394–398.
147. Polymeropoulos MH, Lavedan C, Leroy E, et al. Mutation in the alpha-synuclein gene identified in families with Parkinson's disease. *Science* 1997; 276 (5321):2045–2047.
148. El-Agnaf OM, Jakes R, Curran MD, et al. Aggregates from mutant and wild-type alpha-synuclein proteins and NAC peptide induce apoptotic cell death in human neuroblastoma cells by formation of beta-sheet and amyloid-like filaments. *FEBS Lett* 1998; 440(1–2):71–75.
149. Zhou W, Hurlbert MS, Schaack J, et al. Overexpression of human alpha-synuclein causes dopamine neuron death in rat primary culture and immortalized mesencephalon-derived cells. *Brain Res* 2000; 866(1–2):33–43.
150. Forloni G, Bertani I, Calella AM, et al. Alpha-synuclein and Parkinson's disease: Selective neurodegenerative effect of alpha-synuclein fragment on dopaminergic neurons in vitro and in vivo. *Ann Neurol* 2000; 47(5):632–640.
151. Rochet JC, Outeiro TF, Conway KA, et al. Interactions among alpha-synuclein, dopamine, and biomembranes: Some clues for understanding neurodegeneration in Parkinson's disease. *J Mol Neurosci* 2004; 23(1–2):23–34.
152. Chartier-Harlin MC, Kachergus J, Roumier C, et al. Alpha-synuclein locus duplication as a cause of familial Parkinson's disease. *Lancet* 2004; 364(9440):1167–1169.
153. Singleton AB, Farrer M, Johnson J, et al. Alpha-synuclein locus triplication causes Parkinson's disease. *Science* 2003; 302(5646):841.
154. Pendleton RG, Parvez F, Sayed M, Hillman R. Effects of pharmacological agents upon a transgenic model of Parkinson's disease in Drosophila melanogaster. *J Pharmacol Exp Ther* 2002; 300(1):91–96. Erratum in *J Pharmacol Exp Ther* 2002; 300(3):1131.
155. Auluck PK, Chan HY, Trojanowski JQ, et al. Chaperone suppression of alpha-synuclein toxicity in a Drosophila model for Parkinson's disease. *Science* 2002; 295(5556): 865–868.
156. Auluck PK, Meulener MC, Bonini NM. Mechanisms of suppression of α-synuclein neurotoxicity by geldanamycin in Drosophila. *J Biol Chem* 2005; 280(4):2873–2878.
157. Chen L, Feany MB. Alpha-synuclein phosphorylation controls neurotoxicity and inclusion formation in a Drosophila model of Parkinson disease. *Nat Neurosci* 2005; 8(5):657–663.
158. Takahashi M, Kanuka H, Fujiwara H, et al. Phosphorylation of alpha-synuclein characteristic of synucleinopathy lesions is recapitulated in alpha-synuclein transgenic Drosophila. *Neurosci Lett* 2003; 336(3):155–158.
159. Bonini NM. Chaperoning brain degeneration. *Proc Natl Acad Sci USA* 2002; 99(Suppl 4):16407–16411.
160. Warrick JM, Chan HY, Gray-Board GL, et al. Suppression of polyglutamine-mediated neurodegeneration in Drosophila by the molecular chaperone HSP70. *Nat Genet* 1999; 23(4):425–428.
161. Horowitz JM, Vernace VA, Myers J, et al. Immunodetection of Parkin protein in vertebrate and invertebrate brains: A comparative study using specific antibodies. *J Chem Neuroanat* 2001; 21(1):75–93.
162. Marin I, Ferrus A. Comparative genomics of the RBR family, including the Parkinson's disease–related gene parkin and the genes of the ariadne subfamily. *Mol Biol Evol* 2002; 19(12):2039–2050.
163. Kitada T, Asakawa S, Hattori N, et al. Mutations in the parkin gene cause autosomal recessive juvenile parkinsonism. Nature 1998; 392(6676):605–608.
164. Abbas N, Lucking CB, Ricard S, et al. A wide variety of mutations in the parkin gene are responsible for autosomal recessive parkinsonism in Europe. French Parkinson's Disease Genetics Study Group and the European Consortium on Genetic Susceptibility in Parkinson's Disease. *Hum Mol Genet* 1999; 8(4):567–574.
165. Tanaka K, Suzuki T, Hattori N, Mizuno Y. Ubiquitin, proteasome and parkin. *Biochim Biophys Acta* 2004; 1695(1–3):235–247.
166. Fishman PS, Oyler GA. Significance of the parkin gene and protein in understanding Parkinson's disease. *Curr Neurol Neurosci Rep* 2002; 2(4):296–302.
167. Pesah Y, Pham T, Burgess H, et al. Drosophila parkin mutants have decreased mass and cell size and increased sensitivity to oxygen radical stress. *Development* 2004; 131(9):2183–2194.
168. Greene JC, Whitworth AJ, Kuo I, et al. Mitochondrial pathology and apoptotic muscle degeneration in Drosophila parkin mutants. *Proc Natl Acad Sci USA* 2003; 100(7): 4078–4083.
169. Greene JC, Whitworth AJ, Andrews LA, et al. Genetic and genomic studies of Drosophila parkin mutants implicate oxidative stress and innate immune responses in pathogenesis. *Hum Mol Genet* 2005; 14(6):799–811.
170. Whitworth AJ, Theodore DA, Greene JC, et al. Increased glutathione S-transferase activity rescues dopaminergic neuron loss in a Drosophila model of Parkinson's disease. *Proc Natl Acad Sci USA* 2005; 102(22):8024–8029.
171. Yang Y, Nishimura I, Imai Y, et al. Parkin suppresses dopaminergic neuron–selective neurotoxicity induced by Pael-R in Drosophila. *Neuron* 2003; 37(6):911–924.
172. Haywood AF, Staveley BE. Parkin counteracts symptoms in a Drosophila model of Parkinson's disease. *BMC Neurosci* 2004; 5:14.
173. Haywood AF, Staveley BE. Mutant & alpha-synuclein-induced degeneration is reduced by parkin in a fly model of Parkinson's disease. *Genome* 2006; 49(5):505–510.
174. Bonifati V, Rizzu P, van Baren MJ, et al. Mutations in the J-1 gene associated with autosomal recessive early-onset parkinsonism. *Science* 2003; 299(5604):256–259.
175. Park J, Kim SY, Cha GH, et al. Drosophila DJ-1 mutants show oxidative stress-sensitive locomotive dysfunction. *Gene* 2005; 361:133–139.
176. Meulener M, Whitworth AJ, Armstrong-Gold CE, et al. Drosophila DJ-1 mutants are selectively sensitive to environmental toxins associated with Parkinson's disease. *Curr Biol* 2005; 15(17):1572–1577.
177. Yang Y, Nishimura I, Imai Y, et al. Parkin suppresses dopaminergic neuron–selective neurotoxicity induced by Pael-R in Drosophila. *Neuron* 2003; 37(6):911–924.
178. Yang Y, Gehrke S, Haque ME, et al. Inactivation of Drosophila DJ-1 leads to impairments of oxidative stressresponse and phosphatidylinositol 3-kinase/Akt signaling. *Proc Natl Acad Sci USA* 2005; 102(38):13670–13675.
179. Valente EM, Abou-Sleiman PM, Caputo V, et al. Hereditary early-onset Parkinson's disease caused by mutations in PINK1. *Science* 2004; 304(5674):1158–1160.
180. Park J, Lee SB, Lee S, et al. Mitochondrial dysfunction in Drosophila PINK1 mutants is complemented by parkin. *Nature* 2006; 441(7097):1157–1161.
181. Clark IE, Dodson MW, Jiang C, et al. Drosophila pink1 is required for mitochondrial function and interacts genetically with parkin. *Nature* 2006;441(7097):1162–1166.
182. Tan JM, Dawson TM. Parkin blushed by PINK1. *Neuron* 2006; 50(4):527–529.
183. Fleming SM, Fernagut PO, Chesselet MF. Genetic mouse models of parkinsonism: Strengths and limitations. NeuroRx 2005; 2(3):495–503.
184. Masliah E, Rockenstein E, Veinbergs I, et al. Dopaminergic loss and inclusion body formation in alpha-synuclein mice: Implications for neurodegenerative disorders. *Science* 2000; 287(5456):1265–1269.
185. Abeliovich A, Schmitz Y, Farinas I et al. Mice lacking alpha-synuclein display functional deficits in the nigrostriatal dopamine system. *Neuron* 2000; 25(1):239–252.
186. Dauer W, Kholodilov N, Vila M, et al. Resistance of alpha-synuclein null mice to the parkinsonian neurotoxin MPTP. *Proc Natl Acad Sci USA* 2002; 99(22):14524–14529.
187. van der Putten H, Wiederhold KH, Probst A, et al. Neuropathology in mice expressing human alpha-synuclein. *J Neurosci* 2000; 20(16):6021–6029.
188. Matsuoka Y, Vila M, Lincoln S, et al. Lack of nigral pathology in transgenic mice expressing human alpha synuclein driven by the tyrosine hydroxylase promoter. *Neurobiol Dis* 2001; 8(3):535–539.

189. Richfield EK, Thiruchelvam MJ, Cory-Slechta DA, et al. Behavioral and neurochemical effects of wild-type and mutated human alpha-synuclein in transgenic mice. *Exp Neurol* 2002; 175(1):35–48.

190. Song DD, Shults CW, Sisk A, et al. Enhanced substantia nigra mitochondrial pathology in human alpha-synuclein transgenic mice after treatment with MPTP. *Exp Neurol* 2004; 186(2):158–172.

191. Giasson BI, Duda JE, Quinn SM, et al. Neuronal alpha—synucleinopathy with severe movement disorder in mice expressing A53T human alpha-synuclein. *Neuron* 2002; 34(4):521–533.

192. Lee MK, Stirling W, Xu Y, et al. Human alpha-synuclein–harboring familial Parkinson's disease–linked Ala–53—>Thr mutation causes neurodegenerative disease with alpha-synuclein aggregation in transgenic mice. *Proc Natl Acad Sci USA* 2002; 99(13): 8968–8973.

193. Fleming SM, Salcedo J, Fernagut PO, et al. Early and progressive sensorimotor anomalies in mice overexpressing wild-type human alpha-synuclein. *J Neurosci* 2004; 24(42): 9434–9440.

194. Gispert S, Del Turco D, Garrett L, et al. Transgenic mice expressing mutant A53T human alpha-synuclein show neuronal dysfunction in the absence of aggregate formation. *Mol Cell Neurosci* 2003; 24(2):419–429.

195. Hashimoto M, Rockenstein E, Mante M, Mallory M, Masliah E. Beta-synuclein inhibits alpha-synuclein aggregation: A possible role as an anti-parkinsonian factor. *Neuron* 2001; 32(2):213–223.

196. Masliah E, Rockenstein E, Adame A, et al. Effects of alpha-synuclein immunization in a mouse model of Parkinson's disease. *Neuron* 2005; 46(6):857–868.

197. Itier JM, Ibanez P, Mena MA, et al. Parkin gene inactivation alters behaviour and dopamine neurotransmission in the mouse. *Hum Mol Genet* 2003; 12(18):2277–2291.

198. Goldberg MS, Fleming SM, Palacino JJ, et al. Parkin-deficient mice exhibit nigrostriatal deficits but not loss of dopaminergic neurons. *J Biol Chem* 2003; 278(44): 43628–43635.

199. Von Coelln R, Thomas B, Savitt JM, et al. Loss of locus coeruleus neurons and reduced startle in parkin null mice. *Proc Natl Acad Sci USA* 2004; 101(29):10744–10749.

200. Von Coelln R, Thomas B, Andrabi SA, et al. Inclusion body formation and neurodegeneration are parkin independent in a mouse model of alpha-synucleinopathy. *J Neurosci* 2006; 26(14):3685–3696.

201. Menendez J, Rodriguez-Navarro JA, et al. Suppression of Parkin enhances nigrostriatal and motor neuron lesion in mice over-expressing human-mutated tau protein. *Hum Mol Genet* 2006; 15(13):2045–2058.

202. Palacino JJ, Sagi D, Goldberg MS, et al. Mitochondrial dysfunction and oxidative damage in parkin-deficient mice. *J Biol Chem* 2004: 279(18):18614–18622.

203. Casarejos MJ, Menendez J, Solano RM, et al. Susceptibility to rotenone is increased in neurons from parkin null mice and is reduced by minocycline. *J Neurochem* 2006; 97(4):934–946.

204. Goldberg MS, Pisani A, Haburcak M, et al. Nigrostriatal dopaminergic deficits and hypokinesia caused by inactivation of the familial Parkinsonism-linked gene DJ-1. *Neuron* 2005; 45(4):489–496.

205. Kim RH, Smith PD, Aleyasin H, et al. Hypersensitivity of DJ-1-deficient mice to 1-methyl-4-phenyl-1,2,3,6-tetrahydropyrindine (MPTP) and oxidative stress. *Proc Natl Acad Sci USA* 2005; 102(14):5215–5220.

206. Kirik D, Rosenblad C, Burger C, et al. Parkinson-like neurodegeneration induced by targeted overexpression of alpha-synuclein in the nigrostriatal system. *J Neurosci* 2002; 22(7):2780–2791.

207. Yamada M, Iwatsubo T, Mizuno Y, Mochizuki H. Overexpression of alpha-synuclein in rat substantia nigra results in loss of dopaminergic neurons, phosphorylation of alpha-synuclein and activation of caspase-9: Resemblance to pathogenetic changes in Parkinson's disease. *J Neurochem* 2004; 91(2):451–461.

208. auwers E, Debyser Z, Van Dorpe J, et al. Neuropathology and neurodegeneration in rodent brain induced by lentiviral vector–mediated overexpression of alpha-synuclein. *Brain Pathol* 2003; 13(3):364–372.

209. Lo Bianco C, Ridet JL, Schneider BL, et al. Alpha-synucleinopathy and selective dopaminergic neuron loss in a rat lentiviral-based model of Parkinson's disease. *Proc Natl Acad Sci USA* 2002; 99(16):10813–10818.

210. Kirik D, Annett LE, Burger C, et al. Nigrostriatal alpha-synucleinopathy induced by viral vector–mediated overexpression of human alpha-synuclein: A new primate model of Parkinson's disease. *Proc Natl Acad Sci USA* 2003; 100(5):2884–2889.

211. Yamada M, Mizuno Y, Mochizuki H. Parkin gene therapy for alpha-synucleinopathy: A rat model of Parkinson's disease. *Hum Gene Ther* 2005; 16(2):262–270. Erratum in: *Hum Gene Ther* 2005; 16(3):400.

212. Lo Bianco C, Schneider BL, Bauer M, et al. Lentiviral vector delivery of parkin prevents dopaminergic degeneration in an alpha-synuclein rat model of Parkinson's disease. *Proc Natl Acad Sci USA* 2004; 101(50):17510–17515.

213. Klein RL, King MA, Hamby ME, Meyer EM. Dopaminergic cell loss induced by human A30P alpha-synuclein gene transfer to the rat substantia nigra. *Hum Gene Ther* 2002; 13(5):605–612.

30

Pathogenesis: Oxidative Stress, Mitochondrial Dysfunction, and Excitotoxicity

Claire Henchcliffe
M. Flint Beal

Parkinson's disease (PD) is associated with progressive loss of dopaminergic neurons in the substantia nigra (SN), which leads to characteristic motor features of the disease as well as more widespread neuronal changes causing complex and variable nonmotor symptoms. Recent major advances in PD genetics have emphasized that mitochondrial dysfunction plays a significant role in PD pathogenesis. Impaired mitochondrial function likely increases oxidative stress and may render cells more vulnerable to this and other interrelated processes, including excitotoxicity. This process is therefore a highly promising target for therapeutic intervention. While numerous agents are effective in treating the symptoms of PD, a more informed understanding of underlying pathophysiological mechanisms is imperative in order to guide development of novel neuroprotective therapies. In this chapter we review evidence for the roles of the interrelated mechanisms of mitochondrial dysfunction, oxidative stress, and excitotoxicity in neuronal loss leading to PD.

MITOCHONDRIAL DYSFUNCTION IN PARKINSON'S DISEASE

Mitochondria play a crucial role in energy metabolism and are abundant in tissues with high metabolic demands, such as brain and muscle. There is now strong evidence supporting mitochondrial dysfunction, either primarily or secondarily, in the PD pathogenetic process (1–5). The substantia nigra (SN) may be particularly vulnerable to such conditions, and sophisticated microarray analysis demonstrates intriguing differences in expression of genes involved in energy metabolism in dopamine neurons of the SN compared to other dopamine neurons (6).

Mitochondria are central to a number of processes thought to be integral to PD pathophysiology (Figure 30-1). These complex organelles are bounded by an inner and outer membrane and are crucial in cellular processes, including energy production, the oxidative stress response, apoptosis, calcium homeostasis, fatty acid metabolism, and pyrimidine biosynthesis. Five multisubunit complexes (I to V) function in electron transport and oxidative phosphorylation. Adenosine triphosphate (ATP) is generated during electron transfer to oxygen via the electron transport chain (ETC) of the inner mitochondrial membrane.

Oxidative stress, thought to play a significant role in PD pathogenesis (7, 8), may occur either by increased exposure to free radicals or by heightened susceptibility and impairment of the oxidative stress response. Mitochondrial dysfunction may affect either of these pathways. First, the ETC is a major source of free radicals (9)—molecules containing one or more unpaired electrons, such as superoxide

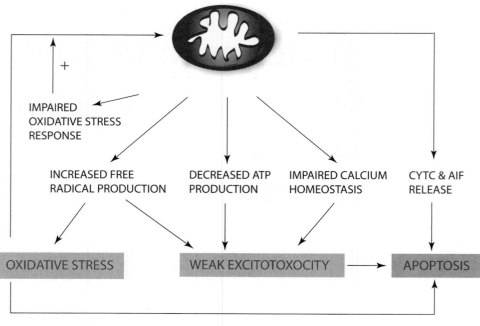

FIGURE 30-1

Mitochondrial dysfunction affects a number of cellular pathways leading to damage of intracellular components and to cell death. Mitochondria are not only a major source of free radicals resulting in oxidative stress but also integral to the oxidative stress response itself. Mitochondria sequester calcium when intracellular levels rise during the excitotoxic process. A decreased threshold for excitotoxicity may occur if mitochondrial ATP production is impaired. Mitochondria also have a pivotal role in apoptotic cell death. Mitochondrial release of cytochrome c and other "pro-apoptotic factors" such as apoptosis-initiating factor (AIF) into the cytoplasm triggers a cascade of events culminating in cell death.

and hydroxyl radicals. These are highly reactive and induce oxidative damage to neighboring molecules by extracting electrons. Impaired ETC function results in increased generation of free radicals (10–15), to which mitochondrial proteins and DNA may be particularly susceptible. Second, impaired mitochondrial function leads to increased susceptibility to oxidative stress.

Impaired energy metabolism resulting from mitochondrial dysfunction has been proposed to render cells vulnerable to excitotoxicity. In contrast to acute excitotoxic injury, "weak excitotoxicity" has been proposed to occur as a result of changes in the energy-dependent cell membrane potential due to impaired energy metabolism in PD. Mitochondrial dysfunction could therefore potentially result in a lowering in the threshold for excitotoxic injury. This excitotoxic injury may increase free radical generation and add to cellular injury (8, 16).

Mitochondria also play an integral role in the apoptotic cell death pathway. When the outer mitochondrial membrane is permeabilized by action of "death agonists" such as Bax, cytochrome c is released into the cytosol, leading to caspase activation and apoptosis (17). Similar pathways are also activated by opening of the mitochondrial

permeability transition pore, which may occur under conditions of oxidative stress or electron transport chain inhibition (18), with subsequent collapse of the mitochondrial membrane potential (19). This is associated with release of apoptosis activators, including apoptosis-inducing factor (AIF) and cytochrome c (20). Mitochondrial dysfunction and oxidative stress may therefore "reset" the threshold for activation of apoptotic pathways in response to Bax and similar signals.

Studying mitochondrial function directly in vivo in individuals with PD is technically challenging, but results of several studies support the existence of impaired oxidative phosphorylation in PD. A decrease in high-energy phosphates as examined by phosphorus magnetic resonance spectroscopy (MRS) was found in the temporoparietal regions of a small series of nondemented PD patients (21). Abnormal occipital lobe metabolism has also been observed in subjects with PD (22). Bowen and colleagues have reported high occipital lobe lactate/N-acetyl aspartate ratios in PD (23) detected by proton MRS, although other investigators have failed to detect increased lactate in basal ganglia in PD (24, 25).

Mitochondrial Complex I Impairment in Parkinson's Disease

Complex I is the largest of the ETC complexes, with 46 subunits, 7 of which are encoded by mitochondrial DNA (mtDNA). It is the major site of superoxide production in the ETC (26, 27). In PD patients, complex I activity is decreased in the brain to a greater extent than that accounted for by normal aging (28–31). Complex I impairment has been detected in the SN (29, 31) and other brain regions in individuals with PD. Using immunocapture to detect catalytically active protein, Keeney and colleagues found a differential decrease in an 8-kDa subunit of complex I in PD brain, with increased oxidative damage to complex I subunits and reduced electron transfer rates through the complex I (32). The authors suggested, therefore, that elements of complex I might be labile or misassembled in PD. Such ETC impairment may be systemic: decreased complex I activity has been demonstrated in platelets in multiple independent studies (33–37), although not by all authors (31, 38). Reports of complex I activity in muscle (39, 40) and lymphocytes (34, 41, 42) of PD patients have been variable. One question is whether impaired complex I activity represents a primary defect contributing to PD pathogenesis or whether it is secondary to the disease or associated processes, such as medication administration. Several findings argue that complex I deficiency is a primary defect in PD. Complex I activity is normal in other neurodegenerative diseases, such as multiple system atrophy (MSA), suggesting that its dysfunction is not a nonspecific consequence of neurodegeneration (29, 36). In addition, complex I activity does not correlate with levodopa dosage, is normal in MSA patients taking levodopa (29, 36), and is abnormal in platelets of individuals with PD who are levodopa-naive (37).

Complex I deficiency is known to have multiple consequences for cell viability but may directly lead to activation of apoptotic pathways due to impaired mitochondrial respiration and release of mitochondrial cytochrome c (17, 18, 43, 44). In rodents, experimental inhibition of complex I results in apoptosis of dopaminergic neurons (45, 46) in a Bax-dependent manner (47). Careful study of isolated complex I–deficient mitochondria reveals evidence of heightened oxidative stress, increased releasable soluble cytochrome c pool in the intermembrane space, with Bax-dependent permeabilization leading to release of more cytochrome c (48). It is therefore possible that mitochondrial function and oxidative stress, stemming in part from complex I deficiency, are important triggers and modulators of apoptosis in PD (49).

The Origin of Complex I Deficiency in Parkinson's Disease

While the reasons for complex I deficiency and mitochondrial dysfunction in PD are not yet well understood, it is thought that both environmental and genetic factors may contribute to the complex I defect in PD.

Complex I Inhibitors and Parkinsonism: Evidence for an Environmental Influence. Three different complex I inhibitors recapitulate many motor and pathologic features of PD and lead to the demise of dopamine neurons (50–52). Langston provided a groundbreaking description of parkinsonism resulting from unintentional exposure of humans to 1-methyl-4-phenyl-1, 2, 3, 6-tetrahydropyridine (MPTP) (53). MPTP is a complex I inhibitor that leads to dopamine neuron cell death through its active metabolite MPP+. This compound has been extensively used in animal models of PD to understand the cellular mechanisms that go awry in nigral dopaminergic neuronal cell death (50, 54–57). Moreover, when chronically infused in animals, it leads to the formation of inclusions that contain α-synuclein (58). Rotenone, a naturally occurring compound found in many pesticides, is a specific inhibitor of mitochondrial complex I. Chronic infusion of rotenone at low doses can reproduce a PD-like syndrome in rats, with selective loss of dopaminergic neurons, Lewy body–like fibrillar cytoplasmic inclusions containing ubiquitin and α-synuclein, and motor dysfunction including hypokinesia and rigidity (51). In addition, chronic rotenone administration in *Drosophila* results in levodopa-responsive locomotor deficits and loss of dopamine neurons (59). Another naturally occurring complex I inhibitor, isolated from the plant species *Annona*, is annonacin. It causes dopaminergic neuronal cell death in mesencephalic cell cultures (60) and nigral and striatal degeneration in rats (61). Annonacin ingestion by humans has been suggested to lead to atypical parkinsonism in Guadeloupe (62).

The effects of these compounds demonstrate the principle that complex I inhibition can lead to parkinsonism, supporting the hypothesis that dysfunction of the ETC could play a causal role in PD. There is also the question of whether endogenous or exogenous compounds might exert similar effects leading to PD. Several epidemiologic studies have suggested an association between certain environmental factors and the risk of PD (63–65). In addition, endogenous MPP+ analogs are capable of inducing parkinsonism in nonprimate animals (66) and have been identified in the cerebrospinal fluid of PD patients (63, 64, 67–69). The origin of such endogenous toxins is unclear, but nicotinamide N-methyltransferase has been detected in brain and is capable of converting pyridines to MPP+ analogs (70).

Genetic Effects upon Complex I Function in PD: Mitochondrial Genetics and Parkinsonism. The mitochondrial genome (mtDNA), a 16.5-kb circular molecule, encodes 13 critical components of the electron transfer chain. Mitochondrial genetic inheritance is maternal. Heteroplasmy and expansion of acquired somatic mutations complicate study interpretation (mitochondrial genetics are well reviewed in Ref. 71). Nonetheless, there is accumulating evidence that alterations in mtDNA play a role in PD.

Fusion of platelets of PD patients in which complex I deficiency has been demonstrated, with cell lines deficient in mitochondria (Rho0), produces cell cybrids that have a corresponding complex I deficiency (72, 73). This suggests that complex I deficiency results from mtDNA in at least some instances. Two studies have now demonstrated high levels of acquired mtDNA deletions leading to mitochondrial dysfunction in PD (74) and in aging substantia nigra tissue (75) that cause mitochondrial dysfunction. Bender and colleagues pooled laser microdissected neurons obtained from autopsy tissue of PD-dementia patients. Using long-range polymerase chain reaction (PCR), these investigators demonstrated higher levels of mtDNA deletions in PD compared with age-matched controls (74). Importantly, higher levels of deletions were associated with cytochrome c oxidase (COX) deficiency. It is unclear how these mtDNA deletions arise or why they should clonally expand to a degree that impairs COX activity. Additionally, regional predisposition to such a process is poorly understood, although it seems that the substantia nigra has particularly high levels of mtDNA deletions (76). Evidence from a mouse model suggests that oxidative damage could lead to mtDNA double strand DNA breaks and hence to deletions (77). Impaired mtDNA replication might also be responsible for generating deletions: a mutation in the mitochondrial-encoded mitochondrial DNA polymerase subunit γ (POLG) leads to a phenotype of clinical parkinsonism, associated with multiple mtDNA deletions (78).

Maternally inherited mitochondrial mutations have rarely been linked to parkinsonism, suggesting that acquired mutations may be more important; 1 kindred has been reported with maternally inherited PD and complex I deficiency (79), and 5 families with likely maternal inheritance have been reported by Wooten and colleagues (80). A missense mutation in subunit ND4 of complex I (position 11778) is responsible for atypical parkinsonism accompanied by nigral neuron loss in 1 kindred (81), but this mutation is better characterized as a cause of Leber's hereditary optic neuropathy (82). Several studies have suggested that specific clusters of polymorphisms, termed haplogroups, may decrease the risk of PD. The presence of haplogroups UJKT in Europeans is associated with a decreased risk of PD compared with haplogroup H (83–86) through a hypothesized reduction in free radical generation (87).

OXIDATIVE STRESS IN PARKINSON'S DISEASE

Oxidative stress is thought to contribute to PD pathogenesis through multiple pathways, and increased susceptibility to oxidative stress may render certain cell populations more vulnerable to damage in PD. Overproduction of reactive oxygen and nitrogen species can result in protein oxidation, lipid peroxidation, and DNA damage (88). This places undue stress upon the cellular system required for degradation of damaged proteins, which is itself involved in PD pathogenesis. Several factors may contribute to an increase in oxidative damage in PD: dysfunction of the mitochondrial ETC, impaired antioxidant mechanisms, increased exposure to environmental or endogenous sources of oxidative stress, and excitotoxicity. The potential health policy ramifications are profound. For example, the herbicide paraquat causes oxidative stress (89–91), leading to loss of dopamine neurons and motor deficits in rodents (92). This compound has been linked via epidemiologic studies to an increased risk of PD. Moreover, it has been suggested that a diet high in animal fat may be linked to PD risk, possibly by affecting redox balance (93–95).

Markers of Oxidative Damage in Parkinson's Disease

Direct evidence of oxidative stress in PD patients comes from analyses of levels of biochemical markers for oxidative damage in postmortem brains. Postmortem analyses of PD SN reveal increased levels of malondialdehyde and cholesterol lipid hydroperoxides markers of lipid peroxidation and other markers of oxidative stress (96–100). The increase in oxidative damage to lipids in the SN occurs within pigmented neurons, based on increased immunostaining for 4-hydroxynonenal, a marker of membrane lipid peroxidation (101). Oxidative damage to DNA has also been identified in postmortem SN of PD patients (102–104). Based upon a diffusely distributed increase in protein carbonyls, PD brain tissue has elevated levels of oxidative damage to proteins as well (102, 105). In addition, increased 3-nitrotyrosine and nitrated α-synuclein immunoreactivity has been reported in Lewy bodies in PD (106, 107). Intracellular production of peroxynitrite actually induces α-synuclein aggregation (108), and oxidative damage impairs ubiquitination and degradation of proteins by the proteasome (109). These findings thus provide a plausible link between oxidative damage and formation of protein aggregates characteristic of PD.

In vivo studies of PD patients have yielded variable results. Elevation of both cerebrospinal fluid and blood concentrations of malondialdehyde in PD patients has been demonstrated by Ilic and colleagues, coupled with increased activity of gluthathione reductase and Cu, Zn-superoxide-dismutase (110). An increase in oxidative damage to DNA has also been reported in leukocytes, serum, and cerebrospinal fluid (CSF) of PD patients (111, 112). However, other investigators have not reproduced these results, and Ahlskog and colleagues found no significant increase in malondialdehyde levels in plasma of PD patients compared to controls (113).

Oxidative Stress as a Consequence of Mitochondrial Complex I Dysfunction. Oxidative stress due to complex I deficiency may play a key role in PD. Cell cybrids expressing mtDNA from PD patients may exhibit complex I deficiency. These demonstrate increased susceptibility to MPP+, the active metabolite of MPTP, associated with free radical production (72). Increased production of superoxide radicals is also seen in patients with syndromes resulting from complex I deficiency, such as Leigh's disease and fatal infantile lactic acidosis (114). Much of our understanding of the downstream molecular pathways derives from studies of complex I inhibitors, such as MPTP (50, 52, 55). Systemic administration of MPTP or intrastriatal injection of MPP+ results in depletion of striatal ATP (115, 116) and increased free radical production (10–13) and nitrotyrosine levels (117). MPTP-induced neuron cell death is modulated by cellular anti-oxidants. For example, MPTP induces neuronal cell death in mice deficient in the antioxidant mitochondrial superoxide dismutase (MnSOD) at greater levels than in normal mice (14). Mice overexpressing MnSOD, conversely, display attenuated levels of MPTP-induced neuronal cell death (118, 119).

Other Sources of Oxidative Stress

Dopamine and Other Monoamine Oxidase-B Substrates. Central dopamine metabolism by monoamine oxidase B (MAO-B) is associated with the generation of hydrogen peroxide (H_2O_2), normally inactivated by reaction with glutathione. However, if excess H_2O_2 reacts with ferrous iron (the "Fenton reaction"), a highly reactive hydroxyl radical is produced, potentially causing lipid peroxidation (7). This raises a much debated question of whether dopamine, either endogenous or from levodopa metabolism, might lead to toxicity by increasing oxidative stress (120). There is no evidence to support this, however, in individuals with PD. In addition, MAO-B converts MPTP to its active metabolite MPP+ (121), and it has also been suggested to activate putative endogenous or environmental MPTP-like compounds (67–69). It has therefore been hypothesized that inhibition of MAO-B might prevent oxidative stress and slow neuronal loss in PD. Whether MAO-B gene polymorphisms alter PD risk is controversial (122–126). However, two MAO-B inhibitors, selegiline (deprenyl) and rasagiline, provide neuroprotection against MPTP, or other toxins, in vitro and in animal models of PD (127–129). Whether these activities extend to the clinical realm remains controversial. A large multicenter placebo-controlled clinical trial (Deprenyl and Tocopherol Antioxidant Therapy of

Parkinsonism: DATATOP) was conducted to determine if deprenyl could slow disease progression in early PD patients (21, 130–132): however, a clear neuroprotective effect could not be demonstrated. A smaller study reported sustained benefits from deprenyl even after a 2-month washout period (133), and Palhagen and colleagues recently suggested slower disease progression in PD subjects taking selegiline over a 7-year study period (134). There is also suggestive evidence from a delayed-start clinical trial of rasagiline in early PD that this MAO-B inhibitor may have a disease-modifying effect(135), but further studies are required to support such a conclusion. Whether these drugs are neuroprotective or not, it is currently difficult to argue their implications regarding oxidative stress, as many of their activities may not result from MAO inhibition but rather from other properties of these compounds (136).

Iron. Iron can act as a catalyst in the formation of hydroxyl radicals from hydrogen peroxide (137). Neuromelanin, which chelates iron, is present in some dopamine neurons, but its level is decreased in PD SN (138–140). Several studies have demonstrated increased iron levels in the brain of PD patients (100, 141, 142) as well as decreased amounts of ferritin, which inhibits iron's catalytic properties (143). However, it is unclear whether iron accumulation is a primary or secondary event in PD pathogenesis. The finding of increased iron accumulation in the substantia nigra of 6-hydroxydopamine (6-OHDA) –treated rats (144) and in MPTP-treated monkeys (145) indicates that it may accumulate secondarily. This does not rule out the possibility that increased iron content in the substantia nigra of PD patients can contribute to disease progression secondarily by increasing oxidative stress. Therefore the potential use of iron chelators, combined with MAO inhibition, is being pursued (146).

Impaired Antioxidant Mechanisms. In addition to increased exposure to free radicals, the substantia nigra may have increased susceptibility to oxidative stress. This concept is now supported by genetic studies, particularly that of DJ-1 (see below and Table 30-1). There is also substantial evidence that normal function of glutathione, an important antioxidant that can prevent formation of hydroxyl radicals from hydrogen peroxide, is disrupted in PD. Levels of the reduced form of glutathione are decreased in the substantia nigra of PD patients by approximately 50% (141, 147–149), and by 35% in individuals with "incidental" Lewy bodies (99). This may be secondary to excess mitochondrial production of hydrogen peroxide, and may result in a predisposition to further oxidative damage (150). Glutathione depletion results in abnormal mitochondrial ultrastructure and decreased activity of mitochondrial enzymes in newborn rats (151) and leads to impaired complex I activity in PC12 cells.

Parkinson's Disease Genes Affecting Mitochondrial Function and the Oxidative Stress Response

Mounting evidence points to important roles of PD gene products in mitochondrial function and oxidative stress (see Table 30-1). Although our understanding of their exact functions is in its infancy (Chapter 37), several of these gene products localize at least partially to mitochondria (Figure 30-2).

α-Synuclein (PARK1, 4).   There is no direct link between α-synuclein and mitochondria, but a number of lines of evidence point to important and reciprocal effects between them. Manipulating α-synuclein in *Caenorhabditis* results in abnormal mitochondrial function (152). Overexpression of α-synuclein in vitro impairs mitochondrial function

and α-synuclein itself leads to increased oxidative damage (153–156). MPTP administered to mice overexpressing α-synuclein results in enlarged and morphologically abnormal mitochondria (157). Consistent with this finding, Dauer and colleagues demonstrated increased resistance, at the level of complex I activity, to MPTP in α-synuclein knockout mice (158, 159). Mice overexpressing the human mutant α-synuclein A53T gene develop a severe movement disorder, with electron microscopy revealing degenerating mitochondria; interestingly, neuronal mitochondria had evidence of DNA damage (160). The same mutation expressed in PC12 cells results in mitochondrial cytochrome c release (161), again suggesting that at least some of the effects of α-synuclein in PD may be mediated by mitochondrial processes. α-Synuclein

TABLE 30-1
Genetics: Implication of Mitochondrial Dysfunction and Oxidative Stress in Parkinson's Disease

Gene	Function	Observation	Ref.
α–Synuclein (PARK1, 4)	?	Wild type: ↓mitochondrial function, ↑oxidative stress; overexpression + MPTP leads to abnormal mitochondria	153–156
			157
		Knockout mutant: ↑resistance to MPTP (mice)	158–159
		Mutation: A53T overexpression: abnormal mitochondria, mtDNA damage (mice); ↑cytochrome c release (PC12 cells)	160
			161
Parkin (PARK2)	Ubiquitin E3 ligase	Mitochondrial outer membrane association (partial), mitochondrial localization in proliferating cells	171, 173
		Mutation: abnormal mitochondria, ↑sensitivity to oxidative stress (*Drosophila*); ↓complex I/IV (mouse, human); increased oxidative stress (mouse)	166, 167
			168, 169
		Wild type: mitochondrial biogenesis/mtDNA replication	173
PINK1 (PARK6)	Serine– threonine kinase	Mitochondrial membrane localization	174–176
		siRNA: ↑sensitivity to MPP+, rotenone	178
		Mutation: abnormal mitochondria, ↑sensitivity to oxidative stress (*Drosophila*)	179, 180
		Wild type: ↓mitochondrial cytochrome c release, ↓apoptosis (cell culture)	178
DJ–1 (PARK7)	Oxidative stress sensor, chaperone	Oxidative stress causes relocalization to mitochondria (matrix/intermembrane space)	185, 186
		Protects against oxidative stress	182, 183
		siRNA: ↑sensitivity to oxidative stress (*Drosophila*)	191
		Mutation: ↑sensitivity to rotenone, paraquat, hydrogen peroxide (*Drosophila*); ↑sensitivity to oxidative stress (mice)	188, 189
			192
LRRK2 (PARK8)	Serine–threonine kinase	~10% located in outer mitochondrial membrane	198
Omi/HtrA2 (no PARK locus)	Serine protease	Mitochondrial localization	200
		Mutation: mitochondrial swelling, ↓membrane potential, ↓neuroprotection	201

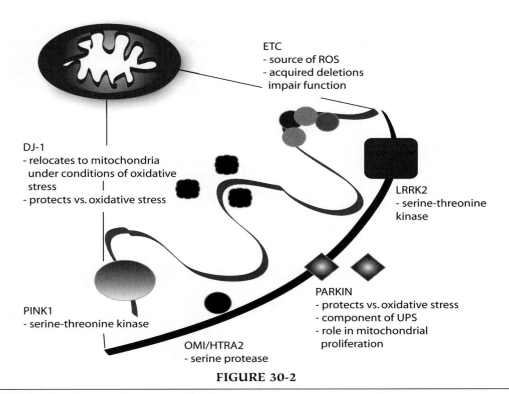

ETC
- source of ROS
- acquired deletions
  impair function

DJ-1
- relocates to mitochondria
  under conditions of oxidative
  stress
- protects vs. oxidative stress

LRRK2
- serine-threonine
  kinase

PINK1
- serine-threonine kinase

PARKIN
- protects vs. oxidative stress
- component of UPS
- role in mitochondrial
  proliferation

OMI/HTRA2
- serine protease

FIGURE 30-2

Expansion of acquired somatic mutations may affect mitochondrial electron transport chain (ETC) function and are increased in the SN in PD. Rare inherited mutations in ETC components have been associated with parkinsonism. Of the nuclear-encoded genes that can lead to PD, gene products of parkin, PINK1, DJ-1, LRRK2, and Omi/Htr2A all show a degree of localization to the mitochondria. Parkin, although better characterized as a component of the ubiquitin proteasomal system (UPS), has been localized to the outer mitochondrial membrane, and has been hypothesized to play a role in mitochondrial biogenesis. LRRK2 possesses a conserved serine-threonine MAPKKK domain and Ras ATPase domain: LRRK2 protein has recently been found to associate in part with the outer mitochondrial membrane, but its function in that location is unclear. Omi/HtrA2 is a mitochondrial serine protease, whose release may be involved in apoptotic cell death. PINK1 is a mitochondrial serine-threonine kinase, although its consequences for mitochondrial function are not yet well understood. DJ-1 is relocated to mitochondria under conditions of oxidative stress, and is thought to be neuroprotective under such conditions.

itself increases oxidative damage in vitro, as well as cellular susceptibility to oxidative insults. Finally, oxidative damage to α-synuclein may occur, affecting aggregation (108, 162, 163), which is linked to its toxicity (162, 164, 165). Lewy bodies in PD are nitrated, suggesting a role for peroxynitrite-mediated oxidative damage (107). Oxidative damage induced by rotenone and chronic MPTP administration produces α-synuclein aggregates that resemble Lewy bodies (51, 58).

Parkin (PARK2). Mutations in parkin, a ubiquitin E3 ligase, support an important role for the ubiquitin proteosomal system (UPS) for protein degradation in PD pathogenesis. However, the consequences of parkin mutation are likely broad-ranging and appear to include effects upon mitochondria. Parkin-null *Drosophila* develops prominent apoptotic muscle degeneration with mitochondrial pathol-

ogy and decreased resistance to oxidative stress (166, 167). Similarly, mice deficient in parkin show reduced striatal mitochondrial respiratory capacity with a decrease in the level of subunits of mitochondrial electron transport complexes I and IV (168). Interestingly, mitochondrial complexes I and IV activities are reduced in parkin patients' leukocytes (169). Parkin-null mice also manifest increased protein and lipid peroxidation (168). A further link between parkin and oxidative stress is provided by the finding that loss-of-function mutations in the glutathione s-transferase S1 (Gst-S1) gene are enhancers of the neurodegenerative parkin-null phenotype in *Drosophila*, whereas overexpression of the Gst-SI gene suppresses neurodegeneration in parkin *Drosophila* mutants (170). Although not primarily located in mitochondria, parkin associates with the outer mitochondrial membrane and prevents ceramide-induced mitochondrial swelling and cytochrome c release in mitochondria-dependent cell death (171). This localization raises the question of whether parkin has a critical role in degrading mitochondrial proteins, which are vulnerable to oxidative stress. In addition to being important in the degradation of oxidatively damaged proteins, oxidative damage to parkin itself may occur: S-nitrosylation of parkin reduces its ubiquitin ligase function (172). Finally, parkin may have an effect upon mitochondrial biogenesis. In proliferating cells, parkin is located within mitochondria, while rotenone and agents that block progression of the cell cycle result in release of parkin to the cytosol, opening the mitochondrial permeability transition pore (173). Moreover, in proliferating cells, transcription and replication of mitochondrial DNA is enhanced by parkin overexpression but attenuated by a parkin siRNA.

PTEN-Induced Kinase 1/PINK1 (PARK6). PINK1 is a serine threonine kinase localized to the mitochondrial membrane (174–176). The exact function of PINK1 and its consequences for cellular energetics are not well understood, but the G309D mutation that leads to autosomal recessive PD has reduced kinase activity, suggesting that phosphorylation of as yet unknown substrates is important (177). When wild-type but not mutant PINK1 is overexpressed in SH-SY5Y cells, staurosporine-induced apoptosis is attenuated and mitochondrial cytochrome c release reduced (178). Expression of siRNA for PINK1 increases susceptibility to MPP+ or rotenone (178). PINK1 deficiency results in abnormal mitochondrial morphology and enhanced susceptibility to oxidative stress in *Drosophila* (179, 180). Intriguingly, parkin overexpression can rescue some features of the PINK1–deficient phenotypes (179, 180), suggesting that they may function in a common pathway (181).

DJ-1 (PARK7). DJ-1 has multiple functions, including putative chaperone activity, but its overall wild-type function appears to be protection from oxidative stress–related cell death (182, 183). DJ-1 itself is oxidatively damaged at cysteine and methionine residues in brain tissue in PD (184). Oxidative stress leads to a change in DJ-1 isoforms, detected on the basis of their isoelectric points (185), leading to relocalization of DJ-1 from nuclei to mitochondria, where it is found in the matrix and intermembrane space (186). Mutation at cysteine 106 prevents mitochondrial relocalization and attenuates protection afforded by DJ-1 against oxidative stress and mitochondrial damage (187). In *Drosophila*, double-knockout mutations of the DJ-1 homologs DJ-1α and DJ-1β are exquisitely sensitive to the complex I inhibitor rotenone and to the environmental toxin paraquat (188). DJ-1β deficient flies have heightened susceptibility to hydrogen peroxide (189) and display a marked locomotor deficit, which is exacerbated by oxidative stress (190). Furthermore, introduction of siRNA for DJ-1α increases levels of reactive oxygen species and sensitivity to oxidative stress and results in degeneration of dopaminergic neurons (191): alterations in the phosphatidyl-inositol 3-kinase (PI3K)/Akt signaling pathway modulate these phenotypes. DJ-1 knockout mice have enhanced sensitivity to MPTP, and mutant embryonic cortical neurons are more susceptible than the wild type to oxidative stress (192).

Leucine-Rich Repeat Kinase 2/LRRK2/Dardarin (PARK7). Mutations in LRRK2 represent the most common known cause of familial PD and also account for cases of sporadic, late-onset PD (193–197). LRRK2 has a conserved serine-threonine kinase mitogen–associated protein kinase kinase kinase (MAPKKK) domain and is a member of the Roc (Ras of complex proteins) family, with a GTPase domain. The common G2019S mutation occurs in the MAPKKK domain and augments kinase activity (198). Although the majority of LRRK2 is present in the cytoplasm, West and colleagues demonstrated that approximately 10% is associated with the outer mitochondrial membrane (198). This raises the question of whether mutant LRRK2 kinase hyperactivity might directly affect mitochondrial function in those affected by this gain-of-function mutation (199).

Omi/HtrA2. Omi/HtrA2 is a serine protease localized to the mitochondria. Homozygous Omi/HtrA2 knockout mice develop striatal degeneration and parkinsonism (200), and mutations in this gene have been detected in rare PD subjects but not controls (201). Expression of the G399S mutation and the A141S Omi/HtrA2 polymorphism found in PD subjects impairs normal activation of Omi/HtrA2, causes mitochondrial swelling, decreases mitochondrial membrane potential, and increases staurosporine-induced cell death (201). It is thought that permeabilization of the mitochondrial membrane by pro-apoptotic molecules may result in release of Omi/HtrA2, as part of the programmed cell death pathway (202).

Some of these gene products appear to influence each other either directly or indirectly. DJ-1 interacts with PINK1 in transfected cells, affecting PINK1 steady-state levels (203), and one PD kindred has been reported to harbor heterozygous missense mutations in both PINK1 and DJ-1. A further link to PINK1 function is suggested by identification of DJ-1 as a PTEN suppressor in *Drosophila* (204). DJ-1 is detected in Lewy bodies (205), and forms part of a large molecular complex in association with α-synuclein (206). While Zhou and colleagues found no evidence for α-synuclein and native DJ-1 association, their connection may be modulated by DJ-1 oxidation status, suggesting that the putative chaperone activity of DJ-1 could be altered by oxidative stress (207). DJ-1 may also interact with parkin in a manner influenced by both DJ-1 mutations and oxidative stress (208). LRRK2 physically interacts with parkin; coexpression of parkin results in the presence of more protein aggregates in cell cultures overexpressing LRRK2 and higher levels of ubiquitination of these protein aggregates (209).

Clearly there is more to learn regarding the functions of the PD genes identified so far. However, the data described above supports a role for several of these genes either directly or secondarily in mitochondrial function and cellular response to oxidative stress. Identification of these genes has opened the door to a better understanding of these processes and their interplay in PD.

EXCITOTOXICITY

A large body of evidence implicates excitotoxic cell death in acute neurologic injury, and a form of "weak excitotoxicity" has been suggested to contribute to neurodegeneration in PD (8, 16). Excitotoxicity, a term coined by Olney in 1969 (210), is neuronal cell death resulting from excitatory amino acid receptor activation. The most prominent brain excitatory neurotransmitter is glutamate (211, 212), which plays a key role in neural circuits that are disrupted in PD. Its excitotoxic effects are mediated via the ionotropic NMDA receptor present on neurons and glia, although a role for AMPA and metabotropic receptors has also been proposed (213–215).

Excitotoxic processes are closely linked to mitochondrial function and oxidative stress. Calcium influx, triggered by NMDA receptor activation, is required for glutamate-induced excitotoxic cell death (216). Calcium is sequestered in mitochondria (217–219), but cell cybrid studies suggest that buffering capacity may be impaired in PD (220). Mitochondrial calcium sequestration results in the opening of the permeability transition pore complex and the release of cytochrome c and other proapoptotic factors (Figure 30-3). The PI3K/Akt pathway plays a central role in signaling (221), but multiple pathways are involved (222), including activation of proteases and endonucleases, inhibition of protein synthesis, mitochondrial damage (223), and free radical generation (224, 225), particularly through NOS activation (226–229). Activation of NOS is thought to occur by coupling of the NMDA receptor to NOS by PSD-95 (postsynaptic density-95) (230–232). The resulting elevated NO and superoxide radicals lead directly to neurotoxicity but also to inhibition of mitochondrial respiration (223, 233–235). Excitotoxic injury can be attenuated by free radical scavengers such as ubiquinone and ascorbic acid (236, 237), and by superoxide dismutase (SOD) (238, 239) as well as hydroxy radical scavengers such as mannitol (239). Interestingly, there may also exist an inbuilt feedback mechanism: redox-related forms of NO react with the NMDA receptor-ion channel complex by S-nitrosylation, resulting in blockade of the ion channel, and therefore protection against excitotoxic damage (240, 241).

The "Weak Excitotoxicity" Hypothesis

A modified form of acute excitotoxic injury, that is, "weak excitotoxicity," has been proposed as a potential mechanism of cell injury and loss in PD (8, 16). At the normal resting membrane potential, calcium influx through NMDA receptor channels is blocked by magnesium. Maintenance of the resting potential, however, is energy-dependent. Therefore impaired energy metabolism resulting from mitochondrial dysfunction may lead to a reduction in membrane potential, resulting in calcium influx (see Figure 30-3). This may, in turn, induce mitochondrial generation of free radicals (242) and activate NOS (232), as described above. Mitochondrial dysfunction may also result in an increased susceptibility to excitotoxicity. Inhibition of oxidative phosphorylation in cultured rat cerebellar neurons results in an increased sensitivity to excitotoxic damage from glutamate exposure (243). Inhibition of complex IV by cyanide also increases susceptibility of cultured hippocampal or cortical cells to excitotoxicity (244). A cycle of mitochondrial dysfunction resulting in increased susceptibility to excitotoxicity, which then induces further mitochondrial damage, may therefore be active in a vulnerable neuronal population in PD.

There is no direct evidence of a role for excitotoxicity in PD, but there are several lines of evidence suggesting a toxic effect of glutamate in neurodegeneration of dopaminergic neurons in the SN pars compacta (SNpc) (228, 245–247). In animal models of PD, antiexcitotoxic agents and NMDA antagonists protect dopaminergic neurons against excitotoxic cell death. The selective NMDA antagonists AP7, CPP, and MK-801 attenuate dopamine neuron loss induced by intranigral injection of MPP+ (248) or by systemic MPTP administration (249–253). Infusion of MK-801 into rat STN over a 4-week period reduced SNpc cell loss and behavioral changes measured by amphetamine-induced turning after unilateral 6-OHDA lesions (254). However, other groups have not reproduced these results (255–257). While the significance of these results from animal models is unclear in PD itself, it is intriguing that overexpression of parkin protects cultured midbrain dopamine neurons from kainate-induced excitotoxicity (258).

Changes in neuronal network activity in PD result in the subthalamic nucleus (STN), a source of glutamate, developing more synchronous and rhythmic neuronal firing (259, 260). This raises the question of whether its targets—which include the SN, globus pallidus, and pedunculopontine nucleus (PPN)—are at risk for excitotoxic damage. Furthermore, with progressive loss of nigral neurons, there is increased disinhibition of the STN, thus potentially leading to more

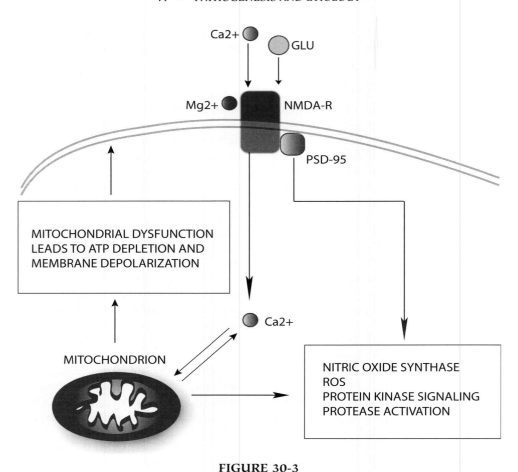

FIGURE 30-3

In PD, "weak excitotoxicity" is hypothesized to result from impaired mitochondrial metabolism leading to depletion of intracellular ATP stores, with subsequent membrane depolarization lowering the threshold for excitotoxicity. The NMDA receptor (NMDA-R), an ionotropic glutamate (GLU) receptor, has been best studied in excitotoxic processes. The AMPA and kainate glutamate receptors are not shown, but these and the metabotropic glutamate receptors may also play a role, albeit less well defined. NMDA-R regulates a channel allowing Ca^{2+} influx, gated in a voltage-dependent fashion by Mg^{2+}, with glycine as coagonist. Mitochondria buffer the calcium influx, but mitochondrial Ca^{2+} uptake can be associated with neuronal cell loss. Ligand binding at the NMDA-R leads to activation of multiple pathways including a protein kinase signaling cascade proteases, and nitric oxide synthase, this last mediated by a link to postsynaptic density protein PSD-95. This results in formation of reactive oxygen species (ROS), which inhibit mitochondrial respiration and contribute to neuronal cell death.

nigral damage (261, 262). Animal models of PD have been used to address whether altering STN activity could protect dopamine neurons in response to various insults. STN ablation (263–265) and microelectrode stimulation (266) attenuate nigral neuron loss. In primates chronically administered MPTP, lesions of the PPN reduced nigral cell loss and motor deficits (267). Luo and colleagues (268) used adeno-associated viral vector–mediated gene transfer to express the glutamic acid decarboxylase (GAD) gene in glutamatergic neurons of rat STN, resulting in increased GABA levels in the SN pars reticulate (SNpr), as predicted. Interestingly, this intervention provided protection against

dopamine neuron loss after 6-OHDA injection, raising the possibility that increasing inhibitory (GABAergic) output from the STN at the expense of excitatory (glutamatergic) output may be neuroprotective in certain conditions. The relevance of these animal studies remains to be determined in humans. Unilateral STN GAD gene therapy was safe and well-tolerated in 12 PD patients in an open label phase I trial, offering the possibility of a novel approach to investigate how glutamate affects long term disease course (269). Unfortunately, there is no evidence supporting neuroprotection from STN deep brain stimulation (DBS) or lesion therapy in PD. Most likely, however, DBS has complex effects upon glutamate release from the STN that remain far from clear (270, 271).

THERAPEUTIC IMPLICATIONS

Anti-PD treatment over the past decades has focused overwhelmingly on dopamine replacement. However, a greater understanding of the molecular processes involved in this disease now suggests a number of novel targets for drug development. The concept of "mitochondrial therapy," either pharmacologic (272) or genetic (273), may help to develop new approaches to PD as well as other neurodegenerative diseases and aging. Based on evidence discussed in this chapter, desirable drug activities include reducing oxidative stress, stabilizing the mitochondrial outer membrane against permeabilization, enhancing function of the mitochondrial electron transport chain, and modulating downstream steps in the apoptotic pathway. As noted earlier, certain drugs in use for PD, such as selegiline and rasagiline, may actually possess some of these properties. Dopamine agonists possess antioxidant activity: for example, cabergoline decreases lipid peroxidation and protects against oxidative stress in cell culture (274), pergolide enhances serum catalase activity (275), and pramipexole protects against MPTP-mediated neuron loss in primates as well as inhibiting mitochondrial membrane depolarization and cytochrome c release in cells. Unfortunately, separating symptomatic dopaminergic effects from other activities has been hampered by a lack of adequate disease biomarkers. Although nuclear imaging techniques have been used to investigate dopamine agonist effects on disease progression, it is not yet clear how to interpret those findings (276, 277). There are at present no clinical data to support the use of antiexcitotoxic agents for the purpose of neuroprotection in PD. Despite promising findings from preclinical studies of riluzole (278–284), a 2-year placebo-controlled double-blind multicenter trial of 1084 PD patients was terminated early after meeting predefined criteria for futility (285).

With increasing interest in "mitochondrial therapy," several compounds have come to the fore. Coenzyme Q10 (CoQ10) is an antioxidant that has effects upon mitochondrial depolarization and acts as an electron transporter for mitochondrial complexes I and II (286, 287). Interestingly, CoQ10 is contained in mucuna extract, an Ayurvedic treatment for PD (288). CoQ10 levels are low in mitochondria isolated from individuals with PD (289) and are present more in the oxidized form than in controls, suggestive of increased oxidative stress affecting this compound (290). CoQ10 protects against paraquat-induced oxidative stress (291), dopamine neuron loss from rotenone (292), and MPTP-induced dopamine cell death in mice (293) and primates (294). CoQ10 can cross the blood-brain barrier when orally administered, resulting in increased mitochondrial CoQ10 content measured in the frontal cortex in rats (295). It has been well tolerated in clinical trials of PD for example at doses of 2400 mg daily in early PD as part of the Neuroprotection Exploratory Trials for Parkinson Disease (NET PD) program (296) as well as in other nevrodegenerative diseases. In a small randomized double-blind placebo-controlled study in untreated individuals with early PD, high-dose supplementation with CoQ10 up to 1200 mg daily in conjunction with α-tocopherol appeared to slow progression of disease in the absence of symptomatic benefit (297). A large phase III trial, nicknamed "QE3," is underway to confirm this effect.

Creatine has multiple modes of action, and phosphocreatine buffers cellular ATP and prevents opening of the mitochondrial permeability transition pore. Creatine attenuates MPP+-mediated toxicity in ventral embryonic mesencephalic neurons and is protective against MPTP (298). In individuals with PD participating in the NET PD investigation (296), creatine was well tolerated and could not be rejected as futile (299). Minocycline, which has anti-inflammatory activity and reduces mitochondrial membrane permeabilization, was included in the same analysis; like creatine, it was not demonstrated to be futile. However, minocycline may increase neuronal cell loss from MPTP (300).

CONCLUSIONS

A growing body of evidence indicates a central role for mitochondrial dysfunction and the related mechanism of oxidative stress in the pathogenesis of PD. Although PD is unlikely to result from excitotoxicity as classically described, "weak excitotoxicity" acting chronically due to mitochondrial impairment may contribute secondarily to cell dysfunction and may itself result in increased oxidative stress. More detailed study of these pathways, and how they interconnect, is now possible due to major advances in identifying genes that lead to PD. Strategies to block oxidative stress and excitotoxicity are effective in animal models of PD, and there are encouraging, though preliminary, data suggesting that agents affecting mitochondrial function may be effective in slowing down PD progression. Such agents will likely have a place as part of a multidrug regimen, addressing the complex interconnecting cellular processes important in neurodegeneration. Finally, PD is clearly a multifactorial disorder. An individual's susceptibility to developing PD probably involves a combination of nuclear genetic, mitochondrial genetic, and environmental factors. Developing better measures of how a variety of cellular processes may contribute differently to PD in certain individuals will offer the potential to tailor and individualize patients' therapies.

References

1. Beal MF. Mitochondria take center stage in aging and neurodegeneration. *Ann Neurol* 2005; 58:495–505.

2. Beal MF. Mitochondria, oxidative damage, and inflammation in Parkinson's disease. *Ann N Y Acad Sci* 2003; 991:120–131.

3. Abou–Sleiman PM, Muqit MM, Wood NW. Expanding insights of mitochondrial dysfunction in Parkinson's disease. *Nat Rev Neurosci* 2006; 7:207–219.

4. Muqit MM, Gandhi S Wood NW. Mitochondria in Parkinson disease: Back in fashion with a little help from genetics. *Arch Neurol* 2006; 63:649–654.

5. Schapira AH, Gu M, Taanman JW, et al. Mitochondria in the etiology and pathogenesis of Parkinson's disease. *Ann Neurol* 1998; 44:S89–S98.

6. Greene JG, Dingledine R, Greenamyre JT. Gene expression profiling of rat midbrain dopamine neurons: Implications for selective vulnerability in parkinsonism. *Neurobiol Dis* 2005; 18:19–31.

7. Jenner P, Olanow CW. Oxidative stress and the pathogenesis of Parkinson's disease. *Neurology* 1996; 47:S161–S170.

8. Beal MF, Hyman BT, Koroshetz W. Do defects in mitochondrial energy metabolism underlie the pathology of neurodegenerative diseases? *Trends Neurosci* 1993; 16:125–131.

9. Guidot DM, McCord JM, Wright RM, et al. Absence of electron transport (Rho 0 state) restores growth of a manganese-superoxide dismutase-deficient Saccharomyces cerevisiae in hyperoxia. Evidence for electron transport as a major source of superoxide generation in vivo. *J Biol Chem* 1993; 268:26699–26703..

10. Zang LY Misra HP. Superoxide radical production during the autoxidation of 1-methyl-4-phenyl-2, 3-dihydropyridinium perchlorate. *J Biol Chem* 1992; 267:17547–17552.

11. Sinha BK, Singh Y Krishna G. Formation of superoxide and hydroxyl radicals from 1-methyl-4-phenylpyridinium ion (MPP+): Reductive activation by NADPH cytochrome P-450 reductase. *Biochem Biophys Res Commun* 1986; 135:583–588..

12. Poirier J, Barbeau A. A catalyst function for MPTP in superoxide formation. *Biochem Biophys Res Commun* 1985; 131:1284–1289.

13. Hasegawa E, Takeshige K, Oishi T, et al. 1-Methyl-4-phenylpyridinium (MPP+) induces NADH-dependent superoxide formation and enhances NADH-dependent lipid peroxidation in bovine heart submitochondrial particles. *Biochem Biophys Res Commun* 1990; 170:1049–1055.

14. Cortopassi G, Wang E. Modelling the effects of age-related mtDNA mutation accumulation: Complex I deficiency, superoxide and cell death. *Biochim Biophys Acta* 1995; 1271:171–176.

15. Cleeter MW, Cooper JM, Schapira AH. Irreversible inhibition of mitochondrial complex I by 1-methyl-4-phenylpyridinium: Evidence for free radical involvement. *J Neurochem* 1992; 58:786–789.

16. Albin RL, Greenamyre JT. Alternative excitotoxic hypotheses. *Neurology* 1992; 42:733–738.

17. Green DR, Kroemer G. The pathophysiology of mitochondrial cell death. *Science* 2004; 305:626–629.

18. Clayton R, Clark JB, Sharpe M. Cytochrome c release from rat brain mitochondria is proportional to the mitochondrial functional deficit: Implications for apoptosis and neurodegenerative disease. *J Neurochem* 2005; 92:840–849.

19. Zamzami N, Marchetti P, Castedo M, et al. Reduction in mitochondrial potential constitutes an early irreversible step of programmed lymphocyte death in vivo. *J Exp Med* 1995; 181:1661–1672.

20. Bras M, Queenan B, Susin SA. Programmed cell death via mitochondria: Different modes of dying. *Biochemistry (Mosc)* 2005; 70:231–239.

21. Effects of tocopherol and deprenyl on the progression of disability in early Parkinson's disease. The Parkinson Study Group. *N Engl J Med* 1993; 328:176–183.

22. Barbiroli B, Montagna P, Martinelli P, et al. Defective brain energy metabolism shown by in vivo 31P MR spectroscopy in 28 patients with mitochondrial cytopathies. *J Cereb Blood Flow Metab* 1993; 13:469–474.

23. Bowen BC, Block RE, Sanchez-Ramos J, et al. Proton MR spectroscopy of the brain in 14 patients with Parkinson disease. *AJNR* 1995; 16:61–68.

24. Tedeschi G, Litvan I, Bonavita S, et al. Proton magnetic resonance spectroscopic imaging in progressive supranuclear palsy, Parkinson's disease and corticobasal degeneration. *Brain* 1997; 120(Pt 9):1541–1552.

25. Holshouser BA, Komu M, Moller HE, et al. Localized proton NMR spectroscopy in the striatum of patients with idiopathic Parkinson's disease: A multicenter pilot study. *Magn Reson Med* 1995; 33:589–594.

26. Kudin AP, Bimpong-Buta NY, Vielhaber S, et al. Characterization of superoxide-producing sites in isolated brain mitochondria. *J Biol Chem* 2004; 279:4127–4135.

27. Lambert AJ, Brand MD. Inhibitors of the quinone-binding site allow rapid superoxide production from mitochondrial NADH:ubiquinone oxidoreductase (complex I). *J Biol Chem* 2004; 279:39414–39420.

28. Janetzky B, Hauck S, Youdim MB, et al. Unaltered aconitase activity, but decreased complex I activity in substantia nigra pars compacta of patients with Parkinson's disease. *Neurosci Lett* 1994; 169:126–128.

29. Schapira AH, Cooper JM, Dexter D, et al. Mitochondrial complex I deficiency in Parkinson's disease. *J Neurochem* 1990; 54:823–827.

30. Schapira AH, Cooper JM, Dexter D, et al. Mitochondrial complex I deficiency in Parkinson's disease. *Lancet* 1989; 1:1269.

31. Mann VM, Cooper JM, Krige D, et al. Brain, skeletal muscle and platelet homogenate mitochondrial function in Parkinson's disease. *Brain* 1992; 115(Pt 2):333–242.

32. Keeney PM, Xie J, Capaldi RA, et al. Parkinson's disease brain mitochondrial complex I has oxidatively damaged subunits and is functionally impaired and misassembled. *J Neurosci* 2006; 26:5256–5264.

33. Parker WD Jr, Boyson SJ Parks JK. Abnormalities of the electron transport chain in idiopathic Parkinson's disease. *Ann Neurol* 1989; 26:719–723.

34. Yoshino H, Nakagawa-Hattori Y, Kondo T, et al. Mitochondrial complex I and II activities of lymphocytes and platelets in Parkinson's disease. *J Neural Transm Park Dis Dement Sect* 1992; 4:27–34.

35. Krige D, Carroll MT, Cooper JM, et al. Platelet mitochondrial function in Parkinson's disease. The Royal Kings and Queens Parkinson Disease Research Group. *Ann Neurol* 1992; 32:782–788.

36. Benecke R, Strumper P, Weiss H. Electron transfer complexes I and IV of platelets are abnormal in Parkinson's disease but normal in Parkinson-plus syndromes. *Brain* 1993; 116 (Pt 6):1451–1463.

37. Haas RH, Nasirian F, Nakano K, et al. Low platelet mitochondrial complex I and complex II/III activity in early untreated Parkinson's disease. *Ann Neurol* 1995; 37:714–722.

38. Bravi D, Anderson JJ, Dagani F, et al. Effect of aging and dopaminomimetic therapy on mitochondrial respiratory function in Parkinson's disease. *Mov Disord* 1992; 7:228–231.

39. Schapira AH. Evidence for mitochondrial dysfunction in Parkinson's disease: A critical appraisal. *Mov Disord* 1994; 9:125–138.

40. Bindoff LA, Birch-Machin MA, Cartlidge NE, et al. Respiratory chain abnormalities in skeletal muscle from patients with Parkinson's disease. *J Neurol Sci* 1991; 104:203–208.

41. Martin MA, Molina JA, Jimenez-Jimenez FJ, et al. Respiratory-chain enzyme activities in isolated mitochondria of lymphocytes from untreated Parkinson's disease patients. Grupo-Centro de Trastornos del Movimiento. *Neurology* 1996; 46:1343–1346.

42. Barroso N, Campos Y, Huertas R, et al. Respiratory chain enzyme activities in lymphocytes from untreated patients with Parkinson disease. *Clin Chem* 1993; 39:667–669.

43. Kroemer G, Reed JC. Mitochondrial control of cell death. *Nat Med* 2000; 6:513–519.

44. Cassarino DS, Parks JK, Parker WD Jr, et al. The parkinsonian neurotoxin MPP+ opens the mitochondrial permeability transition pore and releases cytochrome c in isolated mitochondria via an oxidative mechanism. *Biochim Biophys Acta* 1999; 1453:49–62.

45. Vila M Przedborski S. Targeting programmed cell death in neurodegenerative diseases. *Nat Rev Neurosci* 2003; 4:365–375.

46. Tatton NA Kish SJ. In situ detection of apoptotic nuclei in the substantia nigra compacta of 1-methyl-4-phenyl-1, 2, 3, 6-tetrahydropyridine–treated mice using terminal deoxynucleotidyl transferase labelling and acridine orange staining. *Neuroscience* 1997; 77:1037–1048.

47. Vila M, Jackson-Lewis V, Vukosavic S, et al. Bax ablation prevents dopaminergic neurodegeneration in the 1-methyl- 4-phenyl-1, 2, 3, 6-tetrahydropyridine mouse model of Parkinson's disease. *Proc Natl Acad Sci USA* 2001; 98:2837–1842.

48. Perier C, Tieu K, Guegan C, et al. Complex I deficiency primes Bax-dependent neuronal apoptosis through mitochondrial oxidative damage. *Proc Natl Acad Sci USA* 2005; 102:19126–19231.

49. Ziv I, Melamed E. Role of apoptosis in the pathogenesis of Parkinson's disease: A novel therapeutic opportunity? *Mov Disord* 1998; 13:865–870.

50. Dauer W Przedborski S. Parkinson's disease: Mechanisms and models. *Neuron* 2003; 39:889–909.

51. Betarbet R, Sherer TB, MacKenzie G, et al. Chronic systemic pesticide exposure reproduces features of Parkinson's disease. *Nat Neurosci* 2000; 3:1301–1306.

52. Bove J, Prou D, Perier C, et al. Toxin-induced models of Parkinson's disease. *NeuroRx* 2005; 2:484–494.

53. Langston JW, Ballard P, Tetrud JW, et al. Chronic parkinsonism in humans due to a product of meperidine-analog synthesis. *Science* 1983; 219:979–980.

54. Smeyne RJ, Jackson-Lewis V. The MPTP model of Parkinson's disease. *Brain Res Mol Brain Res* 2005; 134:57–66.

55. Langston JW. The etiology of Parkinson's disease with emphasis on the MPTP story. *Neurology* 1996; 47:S153–S160.

56. Jackson-Lewis V Smeyne RJ. MPTP and SNpc DA neuronal vulnerability: Role of dopamine, superoxide and nitric oxide in neurotoxicity. Minireview. *Neurotox Res* 2005; 7:193–202.

57. Jakowec MW, Petzinger GM. 1-methyl-4-phenyl-1, 2, 3, 6-tetrahydropyridine–lesioned model of parkinson's disease, with emphasis on mice and nonhuman primates. *Comp Med* 2004; 54:497–513.

58. Fornai F, Schluter OM, Lenzi P, et al. Parkinson-like syndrome induced by continuous MPTP infusion: Convergent roles of the ubiquitin-proteasome system and alpha-synuclein. *Proc Natl Acad Sci USA* 2005; 102:3413–3418.

59. Coulom H, Birman S. Chronic exposure to rotenone models sporadic Parkinson's disease in Drosophila melanogaster. *J Neurosci* 2004; 24:10993–10998.

60. Lannuzel A, Michel PP, Hoglinger GU, et al. The mitochondrial complex I inhibitor annonacin is toxic to mesencephalic dopaminergic neurons by impairment of energy metabolism. *Neuroscience* 2003; 121:287–296.

61. Champy P, Hoglinger GU, Feger J, et al. Annonacin, a lipophilic inhibitor of mitochondrial complex I, induces nigral and striatal neurodegeneration in rats: Possible relevance for atypical parkinsonism in Guadeloupe. *J Neurochem* 2004; 88:63–69.

62. Champy P, Melot A, Guerineau Eng V, et al. Quantification of acetogenins in Annona muricata linked to atypical parkinsonism in guadeloupe. *Mov Disord* 2005; 20:1629–1633.

63. Tanner CM Langston JW. Do environmental toxins cause Parkinson's disease? A critical review. *Neurology* 1990; 40(Suppl):17–30; discussion 30–31.

64. Rajput AH. Environmental causation of Parkinson's disease. *Arch Neurol* 1993; 50:651–652.

65. Petrovitch H, Ross GW, Abbott RD, et al. Plantation work and risk of Parkinson disease in a population-based longitudinal study. *Arch Neurol* 2002; 59:1787–1792.

66. Matsubara K, Gonda T, Sawada H, et al. Endogenously occurring beta-carboline induces parkinsonism in nonprimate animals: A possible causative protoxin in idiopathic Parkinson's disease. J Neurochem 1998; 70:727–735.

67. Moser A Kompf D. Presence of methyl-6, 7-dihydroxy-1, 2, 3, 4-tetrahydroisoquinolines, derivatives of the neurotoxin isoquinoline, in parkinsonian lumbar CSF. Life Sci 1992; 50:1885–1891.

68. Matsubara K, Kobayashi S, Kobayashi Y, et al. Beta-carbolinium cations, endogenous MPP+ analogs, in the lumbar cerebrospinal fluid of patients with Parkinson's disease. Neurology 1995; 45:2240–2245.

69. Hao R, Norgren RB Jr, Lau YS, et al. Cerebrospinal fluid of Parkinson's disease patients inhibits the growth and function of dopaminergic neurons in culture. Neurology 1995; 45:138–142.

70. Williams AC, Ramsden DB. Autotoxicity, methylation and a road to the prevention of Parkinson's disease. J Clin Neurosci 2005; 12:6–11.

71. Dimauro S, Davidzon G. Mitochondrial DNA and disease. Ann Med 2005; 37: 222–232.

72. Swerdlow RH, Parks JK, Miller SW, et al. Origin and functional consequences of the complex I defect in Parkinson's disease. Ann Neurol 1996; 40:663–671.

73. Gu M, Cooper JM, Taanman JW, et al. Mitochondrial DNA transmission of the mitochondrial defect in Parkinson's disease. Ann Neurol 1998; 44:177–186.

74. Bender A, Krishnan KJ, Morris CM, et al. High levels of mitochondrial DNA deletions in substantia nigra neurons in aging and Parkinson disease. Nat Genet 2006; 38:515–517.

75. Kraytsberg Y, Kudryavtseva E, McKee AC, et al. Mitochondrial DNA deletions are abundant and cause functional impairment in aged human substantia nigra neurons. Nat Genet 2006; 38:518–520.

76. Soong NW, Hinton DR, Cortopassi G, et al. Mosaicism for a specific somatic mitochondrial DNA mutation in adult human brain. Nat Genet 1992; 2:318–323.

77. Srivastava S Moraes CT. Double-strand breaks of mouse muscle mtDNA promote large deletions similar to multiple mtDNA deletions in humans. Hum Mol Genet 2005; 14:893–902.

78. Luoma P, Melberg A, Rinne JO, et al. Parkinsonism, premature menopause, and mitochondrial DNA polymerase gamma mutations: Clinical and molecular genetic study. Lancet 2004; 364:875–882.

79. Swerdlow RH, Parks JK, Davis JN II, et al. Matrilineal inheritance of complex I dysfunction in a multigenerational Parkinson's disease family. Ann Neurol 1998; 44:873–881.

80. Wooten GF, Currie LJ, Bennett JP, et al. Maternal inheritance in Parkinson's disease. Ann Neurol 1997; 41:265–268.

81. Simon DK, Pulst SM, Sutton JP, et al. Familial multisystem degeneration with parkinsonism associated with the 11778 mitochondrial DNA mutation. Neurology 1999; 53:1787–1793.

82. Wallace DC, Singh G, Lott MT, et al. Mitochondrial DNA mutation associated with Leber's hereditary optic neuropathy. Science 1988; 242:1427–1430.

83. Ghezzi D, Marelli C, Achilli A, et al. Mitochondrial DNA haplogroup K is associated with a lower risk of Parkinson's disease in Italians. Eur J Hum Genet 2005; 13:748–752.

84. Huerta C, Castro MG, Coto E, et al. Mitochondrial DNA polymorphisms and risk of Parkinson's disease in Spanish population. J Neurol Sci 2005; 236:49–54.

85. Pyle A, Foltynie T, Tiangyou W, et al. Mitochondrial DNA haplogroup cluster UKJT reduces the risk of PD. Ann Neurol 2005; 57:564–567.

86. van der Walt JM, Nicodemus KK, Martin ER, et al. Mitochondrial polymorphisms significantly reduce the risk of Parkinson disease. Am J Hum Genet 2003; 72:804–811.

87. Wallace DC. A mitochondrial paradigm of metabolic and degenerative diseases, aging, and cancer: A dawn for evolutionary medicine. Annu Rev Genet 2005; 39:359–407.

88. Berg D, Youdim MB, Riederer P. Redox imbalance. Cell Tissue Res 2004; 318:201–213.

89. McCormack AL, Atienza JG, Johnston LC, et al. Role of oxidative stress in paraquat-induced dopaminergic cell degeneration. J Neurochem 2005; 93:1030–1037.

90. Yang W, Tiffany-Castiglioni E. The bipyridyl herbicide paraquat produces oxidative stress–mediated toxicity in human neuroblastoma SH-SY5Y cells: Relevance to the dopaminergic pathogenesis. J Toxicol Environ Health A 2005; 68:1939–1961.

91. Patel S, Singh V, Kumar A, et al. Status of antioxidant defense system and expression of toxicant responsive genes in striatum of maneb- and paraquat-induced Parkinson's disease phenotype in mouse: Mechanism of neurodegeneration. Brain Res 2006; 1081:9–18.

92. Cicchetti F, Lapointe N, Roberge-Tremblay A, et al. Systemic exposure to paraquat and maneb models early Parkinson's disease in young adult rats. Neurobiol Dis 2005; 20:360–371.

93. Choi JY, Jang EH, Park CS, et al. Enhanced susceptibility to 1-methyl-4-phenyl-1, 2, 3, 6-tetrahydropyridine neurotoxicity in high-fat diet-induced obesity. Free Radic Biol Med 2005; 38:806–816.

94. Logroscino G, Marder K, Graziano J, et al. Dietary iron, animal fats, and risk of Parkinson's disease. Mov Disord 1998; 13(Suppl 1):13–16.

95. Logroscino G, Marder K, Cote L, et al. Dietary lipids and antioxidants in Parkinson's disease: A population-based, case-control study. Ann Neurol 1996; 39:89–94.

96. Yoritaka A, Hattori N, Uchida K, et al. Immunohistochemical detection of 4-hydroxynonenal protein adducts in Parkinson disease. Proc Natl Acad Sci USA 1996; 93:2696–2701.

97. Dexter DT, Carter CJ, Wells FR, et al. Basal lipid peroxidation in substantia nigra is increased in Parkinson's disease. J Neurochem 1989; 52:381–389.

98. Dexter DT, Holley AE, Flitter WD, et al. Increased levels of lipid hydroperoxides in the parkinsonian substantia nigra: An HPLC and ESR study. Mov Disord 1994; 9:92–97.

99. Dexter DT, Sian J, Rose S, et al. Indices of oxidative stress and mitochondrial function in individuals with incidental Lewy body disease. Ann Neurol 1994; 35:38–44.

100. Dexter DT, Wells FR, Lees AJ, et al. Increased nigral iron content and alterations in other metal ions occurring in brain in Parkinson's disease. J Neurochem 1989; 52:1830–1836.

101. Esterbauer H, Schaur RJ Zollner H. Chemistry and biochemistry of 4-hydroxynonenal, malonaldehyde and related aldehydes. Free Radic Biol Med 1991; 11:81–128.

102. Alam ZI, Jenner A, Daniel SE, et al. Oxidative DNA damage in the parkinsonian brain: An apparent selective increase in 8-hydroxyguanine levels in substantia nigra. J Neurochem 1997; 69:1196–203.

103. Zhang J, Perry G, Smith MA, et al. Parkinson's disease is associated with oxidative damage to cytoplasmic DNA and RNA in substantia nigra neurons. Am J Pathol 1999; 154:1423–1429.

104. Montine KS, Quinn JF, Zhang J, et al. Isoprostanes and related products of lipid peroxidation in neurodegenerative diseases. Chem Phys Lipids 2004; 128:117–124.

105. Alam ZI, Daniel SE, Lees AJ, et al. A generalised increase in protein carbonyls in the brain in Parkinson's but not incidental Lewy body disease. J Neurochem 1997; 69:1326–1329.

106. Good PF, Hsu A, Werner P, et al. Protein nitration in Parkinson's disease. J Neuropathol Exp Neurol 1998; 57:338–342.

107. Giasson BI, Duda JE, Murray IV, et al. Oxidative damage linked to neurodegeneration by selective alpha-synuclein nitration in synucleinopathy lesions. Science 2000; 290:985–989.

108. Paxinou E, Chen Q, Weisse M, et al. Induction of alpha-synuclein aggregation by intracellular nitrative insult. J Neurosci 2001; 21:8053–8061.

109. Jenner P. Oxidative stress in Parkinson's disease. Ann Neurol 2003; 53(Suppl 3):S26–S36; discussion S36–S38.

110. Ilic T, Jovanovic M, Jovicic A, et al. Oxidative stress and Parkinson's disease. Vojnosanit Pregl 1998; 55:463–468.

111. Kikuchi A, Takeda A, Onodera H, et al. Systemic increase of oxidative nucleic acid damage in Parkinson's disease and multiple system atrophy. Neurobiol Dis 2002; 9:244–248.

112. Migliore L, Petrozzi L, Lucetti C, et al. Oxidative damage and cytogenetic analysis in leukocytes of Parkinson's disease patients. Neurology 2002; 58:1809–1815.

113. Ahlskog JE, Uitti RJ, Low PA, et al. No evidence for systemic oxidant stress in Parkinson's or Alzheimer's disease. Mov Disord 1995; 10:566–573.

114. Pitkanen S Robinson BH. Mitochondrial complex I deficiency leads to increased production of superoxide radicals and induction of superoxide dismutase. J Clin Invest 1996; 98:345–351.

115. Chan P, DeLanney LE, Irwin I, et al. Rapid ATP loss caused by 1-methyl-4-phenyl-1, 2, 3, 6-tetrahydropyridine in mouse brain. J Neurochem 1991; 57:348–351.

116. Storey E, Hyman BT, Jenkins B, et al. 1-Methyl-4-phenylpyridinium produces excitotoxic lesions in rat striatum as a result of impairment of oxidative metabolism. J Neurochem 1992; 58:1975–1978.

117. Przedborski S Jackson-Lewis V. Mechanisms of MPTP toxicity. Mov Disord 1998; 13(Suppl 1):35–38.

118. Przedborski S, Kostic V, Jackson_Lewis V, et al. Transgenic mice with increased Cu/Zn-superoxide dismutase activity are resistant to N-methyl-4-phenyl-1, 2, 3, 6-tetrahydropyridine-induced neurotoxicity. J Neurosci 1992; 12:1658–1667.

119. Andrews AM, Ladenheim B, Epstein CJ, et al. Transgenic mice with high levels of superoxide dismutase activity are protected from the neurotoxic effects of 2'-NH2-MPTP on serotonergic and noradrenergic nerve terminals. Mol Pharmacol 1996; 50:1511–1529.

120. Muller T, Hefter H, Hueber R, et al. Is levodopa toxic? J Neurol 2004; 251 (Suppl 6): VI/44–VI/46.

121. Singer TP, Castagnoli N Jr, Ramsay RR, et al. Biochemical events in the development of parkinsonism induced by 1-methyl-4-phenyl-1, 2, 3, 6-tetrahydropyridine. J Neurochem 1987; 49:1–8.

122. Kurth JH, Kurth MC, Poduslo SE, et al. Association of a monoamine oxidase B allele with Parkinson's disease. Ann Neurol 1993; 33:368–372.

123. Hotamisligil GS, Girmen AS, Fink JS, et al. Hereditary variations in monoamine oxidase as a risk factor for Parkinson's disease. Mov Disord 1994; 9:305–310.

124. Costa P, Checkoway H, Levy D, et al. Association of a polymorphism in intron 13 of the monoamine oxidase B gene with Parkinson disease. Am J Med Genet 1997; 74:154–156.

125. Ho SL, Kapadi AL, Ramsden DB, et al. An allelic association study of monoamine oxidase B in Parkinson's disease. Ann Neurol 1995; 37:403–405.

126. Plante-Bordeneuve V, Taussig D, Thomas F, et al. Evaluation of four candidate genes encoding proteins of the dopamine pathway in familial and sporadic Parkinson's disease: Evidence for association of a DRD2 allele. Neurology 1997; 48:1589–1593.

127. Gerlach M, Youdim MB, Riederer P. Pharmacology of selegiline. Neurology 1996; 47: S137–S145.

128. Finberg JP, Takeshima T, Johnston JM, et al. Increased survival of dopaminergic neurons by rasagiline, a monoamine oxidase B inhibitor. Neuroreport 1998; 9:703–707.

129. Heikkila RE, Duvoisin RC, Finberg JP, et al. Prevention of MPTP-induced neurotoxicity by AGN-1133 and AGN-1135, selective inhibitors of monoamine oxidase-B. Eur J Pharmacol 1985; 116:313–317.

130. Impact of deprenyl and tocopherol treatment on Parkinson's disease in DATATOP subjects not requiring levodopa. Parkinson Study Group. Ann Neurol 1996; 39:29–36.

131. Effect of deprenyl on the progression of disability in early Parkinson's disease. The Parkinson Study Group. N Engl J Med 1989; 321:1364–1371.

132. DATATOP: A multicenter controlled clinical trial in early Parkinson's disease. Parkinson Study Group. Arch Neurol 1989; 46:1052–1060.

133. Olanow CW, Hauser RA, Gauger L, et al. The effect of deprenyl and levodopa on the progression of Parkinson's disease. Ann Neurol 1995; 38:771–777.

134. Palhagen S, Heinonen E, Hagglund J, et al. Selegiline slows the progression of the symptoms of Parkinson disease. Neurology 2006; 66:1200–1206.

135. A controlled, randomized, delayed-start study of rasagiline in early Parkinson disease. Arch Neurol 2004; 61:561–566.

136. Olanow CW. Rationale for considering that propargylamines might be neuroprotective in Parkinson's disease. Neurology 2006; 66:S69–S79.

137. Olanow CW. An introduction to the free radical hypothesis in Parkinson's disease. *Ann Neurol* 1992; 32(Suppl):S2–S9.
138. Zecca L, Gallorini M, Schunemann V, et al. Iron, neuromelanin and ferritin content in the substantia nigra of normal subjects at different ages: Consequences for iron storage and neurodegenerative processes. *J Neurochem* 2001; 76:1766–1773.
139. Ben-Shachar D, Riederer P Youdim MB. Iron-melanin interaction and lipid peroxidation: Implications for Parkinson's disease. *J Neurochem* 1991; 57:1609–1614.
140. Double KL, Gerlach M, Schunemann V, et al. Iron-binding characteristics of neuromelanin of the human substantia nigra. *Biochem Pharmacol* 2003; 66:489–494.
141. Riederer P, Sofic E, Rausch WD, et al. Transition metals, ferritin, glutathione, and ascorbic acid in parkinsonian brains. *J Neurochem* 1989; 52:515–520.
142. Sofic E, Riederer P, Heinsen H, et al. Increased iron (III) and total iron content in post mortem substantia nigra of parkinsonian brain. *J Neural Transm* 1988; 74:199–205.
143. Dexter DT, Carayon A, Vidailhet M, et al. Decreased ferritin levels in brain in Parkinson's disease. *J Neurochem* 1990; 55:16–20.
144. Oestreicher E, Sengstock GJ, Riederer P, et al. Degeneration of nigrostriatal dopaminergic neurons increases iron within the substantia nigra: A histochemical and neurochemical study. *Brain Res* 1994; 660:8–18.
145. Mochizuki H, Imai H, Endo K, et al. Iron accumulation in the substantia nigra of 1-methyl-4-phenyl-1, 2, 3, 6-tetrahydropyridine (MPTP)–induced hemiparkinsonian monkeys. *Neurosci Lett* 1994; 168:251–253.
146. Zheng H, Gal S, Weiner LM, et al. Novel multifunctional neuroprotective iron chelator–monoamine oxidase inhibitor drugs for neurodegenerative diseases: In vitro studies on antioxidant activity, prevention of lipid peroxide formation and monoamine oxidase inhibition. *J Neurochem* 2005; 95:68–78.
147. Perry TL, Godin DV Hansen S. Parkinson's disease: A disorder due to nigral glutathione deficiency? *Neurosci Lett* 1982; 33:305310.
148. Perry TL, Yong VW. Idiopathic Parkinson's disease, progressive supranuclear palsy and glutathione metabolism in the substantia nigra of patients. *Neurosci Lett* 1986; 67:269–274.
149. Sofic E, Lange KW, Jellinger K, et al. Reduced and oxidized glutathione in the substantia nigra of patients with Parkinson's disease. *Neurosci Lett* 1992; 142:128–130.
150. Di Monte DA, Chan P, Sandy MS. Glutathione in Parkinson's disease: A link between oxidative stress and mitochondrial damage? *Ann Neurol* 1992; 32(Suppl):S111–S115.
151. Jain A, Martensson J, Stole E, et al. Glutathione deficiency leads to mitochondrial damage in brain. *Proc Natl Acad Sci USA* 1991; 88:1913–1917.
152. Ved R, Saha S, Westlund B, et al. Similar patterns of mitochondrial vulnerability and rescue induced by genetic modification of alpha-synuclein, parkin, and DJ-1 in Caenorhabditis elegans. *J Biol Chem* 2005; 280:42655–42668.
153. Hsu LJ, Sagara Y, Arroyo A, et al. alpha-synuclein promotes mitochondrial deficit and oxidative stress. *Am J Pathol* 2000; 157:401–410.
154. Ko L, Mehta ND, Farrer M, et al. Sensitization of neuronal cells to oxidative stress with mutated human alpha-synuclein. *J Neurochem* 2000; 75:2546–2554.
155. Ostrerova-Golts N, Petrucelli L, Hardy J, et al. The A53T alpha-synuclein mutation increases iron-dependent aggregation and toxicity. *J Neurosci* 2000; 20:6048–6054.
156. Lee M, Hyun D, Halliwell B, et al. Effect of the overexpression of wild-type or mutant alpha-synuclein on cell susceptibility to insult. *J Neurochem* 2001; 76:998–1009.
157. Song DD, Shults CW, Sisk A, et al. Enhanced substantia nigra mitochondrial pathology in human alpha-synuclein transgenic mice after treatment with MPTP. *Exp Neurol* 2004; 186:158–172.
158. Dauer W, Kholodilov N, Vila M, et al. Resistance of alpha-synuclein null mice to the parkinsonian neurotoxin MPTP. *Proc Natl Acad Sci USA* 2002; 99:14524–14529.
159. Klivenyi P, Siwek D, Gardian G, et al. Mice lacking alpha-synuclein are resistant to mitochondrial toxins. *Neurobiol Dis* 2006; 21:541–548.
160. Martin LJ, Pan Y, Price AC, et al. Parkinson's disease alpha-synuclein transgenic mice develop neuronal mitochondrial degeneration and cell death. *J Neurosci* 2006; 26:41–50.
161. Smith WW, Jiang H, Pei Z, et al. Endoplasmic reticulum stress and mitochondrial cell death pathways mediate A53T mutant alpha-synuclein–induced toxicity. *Hum Mol Genet* 2005; 14:3801–3811.
162. Conway KA, Lee SJ, Rochet JC, et al. Accelerated oligomerization by Parkinson's disease linked alpha-synuclein mutants. *Ann N Y Acad Sci* 2000; 920:42–45.
163. Souza JM, Giasson BI, Chen Q, et al. Dityrosine cross-linking promotes formation of stable alpha-synuclein polymers. Implication of nitrative and oxidative stress in the pathogenesis of neurodegenerative synucleinopathies. *J Biol Chem* 2000; 275:18344–18349.
164. Choi W, Zibaee S, Jakes R, et al. Mutation E46K increases phospholipid binding and assembly into filaments of human alpha-synuclein. *FEBS Lett* 2004; 576:363–368.
165. Greenbaum EA, Graves CL, Mishizen-Eberz AJ, et al. The E46K mutation in alpha-synuclein increases amyloid fibril formation. *J Biol Chem* 2005; 280:7800–7807.
166. Greene JC, Whitworth AJ, Kuo I, et al. Mitochondrial pathology and apoptotic muscle degeneration in Drosophila parkin mutants. *Proc Natl Acad Sci USA* 2003; 100:4078–4083.
167. Pesah Y, Pham T, Burgess H, et al. Drosophila parkin mutants have decreased mass and cell size and increased sensitivity to oxygen radical stress. *Development* 2004; 131:2183–2194.
168. Palacino JJ, Sagi D, Goldberg MS, et al. Mitochondrial dysfunction and oxidative damage in parkin-deficient mice. *J Biol Chem* 2004; 279:18614–18622.
169. Muftuoglu M, Elibol B, Dalmizrak O, et al. Mitochondrial complex I and IV activities in leukocytes from patients with parkin mutations. *Mov Disord* 2004; 19:544–548.
170. Whitworth AJ, Theodore DA, Greene JC, et al. Increased glutathione S-transferase activity rescues dopaminergic neuron loss in a Drosophila model of Parkinson's disease. *Proc Natl Acad Sci USA* 2005; 102:8024–8029.
171. Darios F, Corti O, Lucking CB, et al. Parkin prevents mitochondrial swelling and cytochrome c release in mitochondria-dependent cell death. *Hum Mol Genet* 2003; 12:517–526.
172. Chung KK, Thomas B, Li X, et al. S-nitrosylation of parkin regulates ubiquitination and compromises parkin's protective function. *Science* 2004; 304:1328–1331.
173. Kuroda Y, Mitsui T, Kunishige M, et al. Parkin enhances mitochondrial biogenesis in proliferating cells. *Hum Mol Genet* 2006; 15:883–995.
174. Valente EM, Abou-Sleiman PM, Caputo V, et al. Hereditary early-onset Parkinson's disease caused by mutations in PINK1. *Science* 2004; 304:1158–1160.
175. Silvestri L, Caputo V, Bellacchio E, et al. Mitochondrial import and enzymatic activity of PINK1 mutants associated to recessive parkinsonism. *Hum Mol Genet* 2005; 14:3477–3492.
176. Gandhi S, Muqit MM, Stanyer L, et al. PINK1 protein in normal human brain and Parkinson's disease. *Brain* 2006; 129:1720–1731.
177. Beilina A, Van Der Brug M, Ahmad R, et al. Mutations in PTEN-induced putative kinase 1 associated with recessive parkinsonism have differential effects on protein stability. *Proc Natl Acad Sci USA* 2005; 102:5703–5708.
178. Petit A, Kawarai T, Paitel E, et al. Wild-type PINK1 prevents basal and induced neuronal apoptosis, a protective effect abrogated by Parkinson's disease–related mutations. *J Biol Chem* 2005; 280:34025–34032.
179. Clark IE, Dodson MW, Jiang C, et al. Drosophila pink1 is required for mitochondrial function and interacts genetically with parkin. *Nature* 2006; 441:1162–1166.
180. Park J, Lee SB, Lee S, et al. Mitochondrial dysfunction in Drosophila PINK1 mutants is complemented by parkin. *Nature* 2006; 441:1157–1161.
181. Tan JM Dawson TM. Parkin Blushed by PINK1. *Neuron* 2006; 50:527–529.
182. Bonifati V, Rizzu P, van Baren MJ, et al. Mutations in the DJ-1 gene associated with autosomal recessive early-onset parkinsonism. *Science* 2003; 299:256–259.
183. Yokota T, Sugawara K, Ito K, et al. Down regulation of DJ-1 enhances cell death by oxidative stress, ER stress, and proteasome inhibition. *Biochem Biophys Res Commun* 2003; 312:1342–1348.
184. Choi J, Sullards MC, Olzmann JA, et al. Oxidative damage of DJ-1 is linked to sporadic Parkinson and Alzheimer diseases. *J Biol Chem* 2006; 281:10816–10824.
185. Taira T, Saito Y, Niki T, et al. DJ-1 has a role in antioxidative stress to prevent cell death. *EMBO Rep* 2004; 5:213–218.
186. Zhang L, Shimoji M, Thomas B, et al. Mitochondrial localization of the Parkinson's disease related protein DJ-1: Implications for pathogenesis. *Hum Mol Genet* 2005; 14:2063–2073.
187. Canet-Aviles RM, Wilson MA, Miller DW, et al. The Parkinson's disease protein DJ-1 is neuroprotective due to cysteine-sulfinic acid-driven mitochondrial localization. *Proc Natl Acad Sci USA* 2004; 101:9103–9108.
188. Meulener M, Whitworth AJ, Armstrong-Gold CE, et al. Drosophila DJ-1 mutants are selectively sensitive to environmental toxins associated with Parkinson's disease. *Curr Biol* 2005; 15:1572–1577.
189. Menzies FM, Yenisetti SC, Min KT. Roles of Drosophila DJ-1 in survival of dopaminergic neurons and oxidative stress. *Curr Biol* 2005; 15:1578–1582.
190. Park J, Kim SY, Cha GH, et al. Drosophila DJ-1 mutants show oxidative stress-sensitive locomotive dysfunction. *Gene* 2005; 361:133–139.
191. Yang Y, Gehrke S, Haque ME, et al. Inactivation of Drosophila DJ-1 leads to impairments of oxidative stress response and phosphatidylinositol 3-kinase/Akt signaling. *Proc Natl Acad Sci USA* 2005; 102:13670–13675.
192. Kim RH, Smith PD, Aleyasin H, et al. Hypersensitivity of DJ-1-deficient mice to 1-methyl-4-phenyl-1, 2, 3, 6-tetrahydropyrindine (MPTP) and oxidative stress. *Proc Natl Acad Sci USA* 2005; 102:5215–5220.
193. Zimprich A, Biskup S, Leitner P, et al. Mutations in LRRK2 cause autosomal-dominant parkinsonism with pleomorphic pathology. *Neuron* 2004; 44:601–607.
194. Paisan-Ruiz C, Jain S, Evans EW, et al. Cloning of the gene containing mutations that cause PARK8-linked Parkinson's disease. *Neuron* 2004; 44:595–600.
195. Ozelius LJ, Senthil G, Saunders-Pullman R, et al. LRRK2 G2019S as a cause of Parkinson's disease in Ashkenazi Jews. *N Engl J Med* 2006; 354:424–425.
196. Lesage S, Durr A, Tazir M, et al. LRRK2 G2019S as a cause of Parkinson's disease in North African Arabs. *N Engl J Med* 2006; 354:422–423.
197. Gilks WP, Abou-Sleiman PM, Gandhi S, et al. A common LRRK2 mutation in idiopathic Parkinson's disease. *Lancet* 2005; 365:415–416.
198. West AB, Moore DJ, Biskup S, et al. Parkinson's disease–associated mutations in leucine-rich repeat kinase 2 augment kinase activity. *Proc Natl Acad Sci USA* 2005; 102:16842–16847.
199. Li C Beal MF. Leucine-rich repeat kinase 2: A new player with a familiar theme for Parkinson's disease pathogenesis. *Proc Natl Acad Sci USA* 2005; 102:16535–16536.
200. Martins LM, Morrison A, Klupsch K, et al. Neuroprotective role of the Reaper-related serine protease HtrA2/Omi revealed by targeted deletion in mice. *Mol Cell Biol* 2004; 24:9848–9862.
201. Strauss KM, Martins LM, Plun-Favreau H, et al. Loss of function mutations in the gene encoding Omi/HtrA2 in Parkinson's disease. *Hum Mol Genet* 2005; 14:2099–2111.
202. Ravagnan L, Roumier T, Kroemer G. Mitochondria, the killer organelles and their weapons. *J Cell Physiol* 2002; 192:131–137.
203. Tang B, Xiong H, Sun P, et al. Association of PINK1 and DJ-1 confers digenic inheritance of early-onset Parkinson's disease. *Hum Mol Genet* 2006; 15:1816–1825.
204. Kim RH, Peters M, Jang Y, et al. DJ-1, a novel regulator of the tumor suppressor PTEN. *Cancer Cell* 2005; 7:263–273.
205. Jin J, Meredith GE, Chen L, et al. Quantitative proteomic analysis of mitochondrial proteins: Relevance to Lewy body formation and Parkinson's disease. *Brain Res Mol Brain Res* 2005; 134:119–138.
206. Meulener MC, Graves CL, Sampathu DM, et al. DJ-1 is present in a large molecular complex in human brain tissue and interacts with alpha-synuclein. *J Neurochem* 2005; 93:1524–1532.

207. Zhou W, Zhu M, Wilson MA, et al. The oxidation state of DJ-1 regulates its chaperone activity toward alpha-synuclein. *J Mol Biol* 2006; 356:1036–1048.
208. Moore DJ, Zhang L, Troncoso J, et al. Association of DJ-1 and parkin mediated by pathogenic DJ-1 mutations and oxidative stress. *Hum Mol Genet* 2005; 14:71–84.
209. Smith WW, Pei Z, Jiang H, et al. Leucine-rich repeat kinase 2 (LRRK2) interacts with parkin, and mutant LRRK2 induces neuronal degeneration. *Proc Natl Acad Sci USA* 2005; 102:18676–18681.
210. Olney JW. Brain lesions, obesity, and other disturbances in mice treated with monosodium glutamate. *Science* 1969; 164:719–721.
211. Schwartz M, Shaked I, Fisher J, et al. Protective autoimmunity against the enemy within: Fighting glutamate toxicity. *Trends Neurosci* 2003; 26:297–302.
212. Bruijn LI, Miller TM, Cleveland DW. Unraveling the mechanisms involved in motor neuron degeneration in ALS. *Annu Rev Neurosci* 2004; 27:723–749.
213. Pintor A, Pezzola A, Reggio R, et al. The mGlu5 receptor agonist CHPG stimulates striatal glutamate release: Possible involvement of A2A receptors. *Neuroreport* 2000; 11:3611–3614.
214. Bruno V, Ksiazek I, Battaglia G, et al. Selective blockade of metabotropic glutamate receptor subtype 5 is neuroprotective. *Neuropharmacology* 2000; 39:2223–2230.
215. Battaglia G, Fornai F, Busceti CL, et al. Selective blockade of mGlu5 metabotropic glutamate receptors is protective against methamphetamine neurotoxicity. *J Neurosci* 2002; 22:2135–2141.
216. Choi DW. Ionic dependence of glutamate neurotoxicity. *J Neurosci* 1987; 7:369–379.
217. Tymianski M, Wallace MC, Spigelman I, et al. Cell-permeant Ca2+ chelators reduce early excitotoxic and ischemic neuronal injury in vitro and in vivo. *Neuron* 1993; 11:221–235.
218. Wang GJ, Randall RD, Thayer SA. Glutamate-induced intracellular acidification of cultured hippocampal neurons demonstrates altered energy metabolism resulting from Ca2+ loads. *J Neurophysiol* 1994; 72:2563–2569.
219. White RJ, Reynolds IJ. Mitochondria and Na+/Ca2+ exchange buffer glutamate-induced calcium loads in cultured cortical neurons. *J Neurosci* 1995; 15:1318–1328.
220. Sheehan JP, Swerdlow RH, Parker WD, et al. Altered calcium homeostasis in cells transformed by mitochondria from individuals with Parkinson's disease. *J Neurochem* 1997; 68:1221–1233.
221. Perkinton MS, Ip JK, Wood GL, et al. Phosphatidylinositol 3-kinase is a central mediator of NMDA receptor signalling to MAP kinase (Erk1/2), Akt/PKB and CREB in striatal neurones. *J Neurochem* 2002; 80:239–254.
222. Crossthwaite AJ, Valli H Williams RJ. Inhibiting Src family tyrosine kinase activity blocks glutamate signalling to ERK1/2 and Akt/PKB but not JNK in cultured striatal neurones. *J Neurochem* 2004; 88:1127–1139.
223. Nicholls DG. Mitochondrial dysfunction and glutamate excitotoxicity studied in primary neuronal cultures. *Curr Mol Med* 2004; 4:149–177.
224. Dugan LL, Sensi SL, Canzoniero LM, et al. Mitochondrial production of reactive oxygen species in cortical neurons following exposure to N-methyl-D-aspartate. *J Neurosci* 1995; 15:6377–6388.
225. Reynolds IJ, Hastings TG. Glutamate induces the production of reactive oxygen species in cultured forebrain neurons following NMDA receptor activation. *J Neurosci* 1995; 15:3318–3327.
226. Dawson VL, Dawson TM, London ED, et al. Nitric oxide mediates glutamate neurotoxicity in primary cortical cultures. *Proc Natl Acad Sci USA* 1991; 88:6368–6371.
227. Lafon-Cazal M, Pietri S, Culcasi M, et al. NMDA-dependent superoxide production and neurotoxicity. *Nature* 1993; 364:535–537.
228. Beal MF. Excitotoxicity and nitric oxide in Parkinson's disease pathogenesis. *Ann Neurol* 1998; 44:S110–S114.
229. Mungrue IN Bredt DS. nNOS at a glance: Implications for brain and brawn. *J Cell Sci* 2004; 117:2627–2629.
230. Sattler R, Xiong Z, Lu WY, et al. Specific coupling of NMDA receptor activation to nitric oxide neurotoxicity by PSD-95 protein. *Science* 1999; 284:1845–1848.
231. Aarts MM, Tymianski M. Molecular mechanisms underlying specificity of excitotoxic signaling in neurons. *Curr Mol Med* 2004; 4:137–147.
232. Garthwaite J. Neural nitric oxide signalling. *Trends Neurosci* 1995; 18:51–52.
233. Dawson VL, Dawson TM, Bartley DA, et al. Mechanisms of nitric oxide-mediated neurotoxicity in primary brain cultures. *J Neurosci* 1993; 13:2651–2661.
234. Beckman JS, Crow JP. Pathological implications of nitric oxide, superoxide and peroxynitrite formation. *Biochem Soc Trans* 1993; 21:330–334.
235. Ciccone CD. Free-radical toxicity and antioxidant medications in Parkinson's disease. *Phys Ther* 1998; 78:313–319.
236. Favit A, Nicoletti F, Scapagnini U, et al. Ubiquinone protects cultured neurons against spontaneous and excitotoxin-induced degeneration. *J Cereb Blood Flow Metab* 1992; 12:638–645.
237. Majewska MD, Bell JA. Ascorbic acid protects neurons from injury induced by glutamate and NMDA. *Neuroreport* 1990; 1:194–196.
238. Chan PH, Chu L, Chen SF, et al. Reduced neurotoxicity in transgenic mice overexpressing human copper-zinc-superoxide dismutase. *Stroke* 1990; 21:III80–III82.
239. Dykens JA, Stern A, Trenkner E. Mechanism of kainate toxicity to cerebellar neurons in vitro is analogous to reperfusion tissue injury. *J Neurochem* 1987; 49:1222–1228.
240. Kim WK, Choi YB, Rayudu PV, et al. Attenuation of NMDA receptor activity and neurotoxicity by nitroxyl anion, NO. *Neuron* 1999; 24:461–469.
241. Choi YB, Tenneti L, Le DA, et al. Molecular basis of NMDA receptor–coupled ion channel modulation by S-nitrosylation. *Nat Neurosci* 2000; 3:15–21.
242. Dykens JA. Isolated cerebral and cerebellar mitochondria produce free radicals when exposed to elevated CA2+ and Na+: Implications for neurodegeneration. *J Neurochem* 1994; 63:584–591.

243. Novelli A, Reilly JA, Lysko PG, et al. Glutamate becomes neurotoxic via the N-methyl-D-aspartate receptor when intracellular energy levels are reduced. *Brain Res* 1988; 451:205–212.
244. Dubinsky JM Rothman SM. Intracellular calcium concentrations during "chemical hypoxia" and excitotoxic neuronal injury. *J Neurosci* 1991; 11:2545–2551.
245. Klockgether T, Turski L. Toward an understanding of the role of glutamate in experimental parkinsonism: Agonist-sensitive sites in the basal ganglia. *Ann Neurol* 1993; 34:585–593.
246. Greene JG, Greenamyre JT. Bioenergetics and glutamate excitotoxicity. *Prog Neurobiol* 1996; 48:613–634.
247. Greenamyre JT. Glutamatergic influences on the basal ganglia. *Clin Neuropharmacol* 2001; 24:65–70.
248. Turski L, Bressler K, Rettig KJ, et al. Protection of substantia nigra from MPP+ neurotoxicity by N-methyl-D-aspartate antagonists. *Nature* 1991; 349:414–418.
249. Zuddas A, Oberto G, Vaglini F, et al. MK-801 prevents 1-methyl-4-phenyl-1, 2, 3, 6-tetrahydropyridine–induced parkinsonism in primates. *J Neurochem* 1992; 59:733–739.
250. Zuddas A, Vaglini F, Fornai F, et al. Pharmacologic modulation of MPTP toxicity: MK 801 in prevention of dopaminergic cell death in monkeys and mice. *Ann N Y Acad Sci* 1992; 648:268–271.
251. Tabatabaei A, Perry TL, Hansen S, et al. Partial protective effect of MK-801 on MPTP-induced reduction of striatal dopamine in mice. *Neurosci Lett* 1992; 141:192–194.
252. Brouillet E, Beal MF. NMDA antagonists partially protect against MPTP induced neurotoxicity in mice. *Neuroreport* 1993; 4:387–390.
253. Lange KW, Loschmann PA, Sofic E, et al. The competitive NMDA antagonist CPP protects substantia nigra neurons from MPTP-induced degeneration in primates. *Naunyn Schmiedebergs Arch Pharmacol* 1993; 348:586–592.
254. Blandini F, Nappi G, Greenamyre JT. Subthalamic infusion of an NMDA antagonist prevents basal ganglia metabolic changes and nigral degeneration in a rodent model of Parkinson's disease. *Ann Neurol* 2001; 49:525–529.
255. Kupsch A, Loschmann PA, Sauer H, et al. Do NMDA receptor antagonists protect against MPTP toxicity? Biochemical and immunocytochemical analyses in black mice. *Brain Res* 1992; 592:74–83.
256. Sonsalla PK, Zeevalk GD, Manzino L, et al. MK-801 fails to protect against the dopaminergic neuropathology produced by systemic 1-methyl-4-phenyl-1, 2, 3, 6-tetrahydropyridine in mice or intranigral 1-methyl-4-phenylpyridinium in rats. *J Neurochem* 1992; 58:1979–1982.
257. Michel PP, Agid Y. The glutamate antagonist, MK-801, does not prevent dopaminergic cell death induced by the 1-methyl-4-phenylpyridinium ion (MPP+) in rat dissociated mesencephalic cultures. *Brain Res* 1992; 597:233–240.
258. Staropoli JF, McDermott C, Martinat C, et al. Parkin is a component of an SCF-like ubiquitin ligase complex and protects postmitotic neurons from kainate excitotoxicity. *Neuron* 2003; 37:735–749.
259. Obeso JA, Rodriguez–Oroz MC, Rodriguez M, et al. Pathophysiology of the basal ganglia in Parkinson's disease. *Trends Neurosci* 2000; 23:S8–S19.
260. Bevan MD, Magill PJ, Terman D, et al. Move to the rhythm: Oscillations in the subthalamic nucleus–external globus pallidus network. *Trends Neurosci* 2002; 25:525–531.
261. Yelnik J. Functional anatomy of the basal ganglia. *Mov Disord* 2002; 17(Suppl 3): S15–S21.
262. Rodriguez MC, Obeso JA, Olanow CW. Subthalamic nucleus–mediated excitotoxicity in Parkinson's disease: A target for neuroprotection. *Ann Neurol* 1998; 44:S175–S188.
263. Nakao N, Nakai E, Nakai K, et al. Ablation of the subthalamic nucleus supports the survival of nigral dopaminergic neurons after nigrostriatal lesions induced by the mitochondrial toxin 3-nitropropionic acid. *Ann Neurol* 1999; 45:640–651.
264. Chen L, Liu Z, Tian Z, et al. Prevention of neurotoxin damage of 6-OHDA to dopaminergic nigral neuron by subthalamic nucleus lesions. *Stereotact Funct Neurosurg* 2000; 75:66–75.
265. Carvalho GA, Nikkhah G. Subthalamic nucleus lesions are neuroprotective against terminal 6-OHDA–induced striatal lesions and restore postural balancing reactions. *Exp Neurol* 2001; 171:405–417.
266. Maesawa S, Kaneoke Y, Kajita Y, et al. Long-term stimulation of the subthalamic nucleus in hemiparkinsonian rats: Neuroprotection of dopaminergic neurons. *J Neurosurg* 2004; 100:679–687.
267. Takada M, Matsumura M, Kojima J, et al. Protection against dopaminergic nigrostriatal cell death by excitatory input ablation. *Eur J Neurosci* 2000; 12:1771–1780.
268. Luo J, Kaplitt MG, Fitzsimons HL, et al. Subthalamic GAD gene therapy in a Parkinson's disease rat model. *Science* 2002; 298:425–429.
269. Kaplitt MG, Feigin A, Tang C, et al. Safety and tolerability of gene therapy with an adeno-associated virus (AAV) borne GAD gene for Parkinson's disease: an open label, phase I trial. *Lancet* 2007; 369:2097–2105.
270. Stefani A, Fedele E, Galati S, et al. Subthalamic stimulation activates internal pallidus: Evidence from cGMP microdialysis in PD patients. *Ann Neurol* 2005; 57:448–452.
271. Windels F, Bruet N, Poupard A, et al. Effects of high frequency stimulation of subthalamic nucleus on extracellular glutamate and GABA in substantia nigra and globus pallidus in the normal rat. *Eur J Neurosci* 2000; 12:4141–4146.
272. Shults CW. Mitochondrial dysfunction and possible treatments in Parkinson's disease: A review. *Mitochondrion* 2004; 4:641–648.
273. Khrapko K. Mitochondrial DNA gene therapy: A gene therapy for aging? *Rejuv Res* 2005; 8:6–8.
274. Lombardi G, Varsaldi F, Miglio G, et al. Cabergoline prevents necrotic neuronal death in an in vitro model of oxidative stress. *Eur J Pharmacol* 2002; 457:95–98.
275. Chalimoniuk M, Stepien A, Strosznajder JB. Pergolide mesylate, a dopaminergic receptor agonist, applied with L-DOPA enhances serum antioxidant enzyme activity in Parkinson disease. *Clin Neuropharmacol* 2004; 27:223–229.

276. A randomized controlled trial comparing pramipexole with levodopa in early Parkinson's disease: Design and methods of the CALM-PD Study. Parkinson Study Group. *Clin Neuropharmacol* 2000; 23:34–44.

277. Marek K, Jennings D, Seibyl J. Do dopamine agonists or levodopa modify Parkinson's disease progression? *Eur J Neurol* 2002; 9(Suppl 3):15–22.

278. Storch A, Burkhardt K, Ludolph AC, et al. Protective effects of riluzole on dopamine neurons: Involvement of oxidative stress and cellular energy metabolism. *J Neurochem* 2000; 75:2259–2269.

279. Boireau A, Dubedat P, Bordier F, et al. Riluzole and experimental parkinsonism: Antagonism of MPTP-induced decrease in central dopamine levels in mice. *Neuroreport* 1994; 5:2657–2660.

280. Boireau A, Miquet JM, Dubedat P, et al. Riluzole and experimental parkinsonism: Partial antagonism of MPP(+)-induced increase in striatal extracellular dopamine in rats in vivo. *Neuroreport* 1994; 5:2157–2160.

281. Bezard E, Stutzmann JM, Imbert C, et al. Riluzole delayed appearance of parkinsonian motor abnormalities in a chronic MPTP monkey model. *Eur J Pharmacol* 1998; 356:101–104.

282. Araki T, Kumagai T, Tanaka K, et al. Neuroprotective effect of riluzole in MPTP-treated mice. *Brain Res* 2001; 918:176–181.

283. Obinu MC, Reibaud M, Blanchard V, et al. Neuroprotective effect of riluzole in a primate model of Parkinson's disease: Behavioral and histological evidence. *Mov Disord* 2002; 17:13–19.

284. Benazzouz A, Boraud T, Dubedat P, et al. Riluzole prevents MPTP-induced parkinsonism in the rhesus monkey: A pilot study. *Eur J Pharmacol* 1995; 284:299–307.

285. Rascol OO, Brooks W, Koch D, et a;. A 2-year, multicenter, placebo-controlled, double-blind, parallel-group study of the effect of riluzole on Parkinson's disease progression. *Mov Disord* 2002; 17:539.

286. Shults CW. Therapeutic role of coenzyme Q(10) in Parkinson's disease. *Pharmacol Ther* 2005; 107:120–30.

287. Beal MF. Mitochondrial dysfunction and oxidative damage in Alzheimer's and Parkinson's diseases and coenzyme Q10 as a potential treatment. *J Bioenerg Biomembr* 2004; 36:381–386.

288. Manyam BV, Dhanasekaran M, Hare TA. Neuroprotective effects of the antiparkinson drug Mucuna pruriens. *Phytother Res* 2004; 18:706–712.

289. Shults CW, Haas RH, Passov D, et al. Coenzyme Q10 levels correlate with the activities of complexes I and II/III in mitochondria from parkinsonian and nonparkinsonian subjects. *Ann Neurol* 1997; 42:261–264.

290. Sohmiya M, Tanaka M, Tak NW, et al. Redox status of plasma coenzyme Q10 indicates elevated systemic oxidative stress in Parkinson's disease. *J Neurol Sci* 2004; 223:161–166.

291. McCarthy S, Somayajulu M, Sikorska M, et al. Paraquat induces oxidative stress and neuronal cell death; Neuroprotection by water-soluble coenzyme Q10. *Toxicol Appl Pharmacol* 2004; 201:21–31.

292. Menke T, Gille G, Reber F, et al. Coenzyme Q10 reduces the toxicity of rotenone in neuronal cultures by preserving the mitochondrial membrane potential. *Biofactors* 2003; 18:65–72.

293. Beal MF, Matthews RT, Tieleman A, et al. Coenzyme Q10 attenuates the 1-methyl-4-phenyl-1, 2, 3, tetrahydropyridine (MPTP) induced loss of striatal dopamine and dopaminergic axons in aged mice. *Brain Res* 1998; 783:109–114.

294. Horvath TL, Diano S, Leranth C, et al. Coenzyme Q induces nigral mitochondrial uncoupling and prevents dopamine cell loss in a primate model of Parkinson's disease. *Endocrinology* 2003; 144:2757–2760.

295. Matthews RT, Yang L, Browne S, et al. Coenzyme Q10 administration increases brain mitochondrial concentrations and exerts neuroprotective effects. *Proc Natl Acad Sci USA* 1998; 95:8892–8897.

296. Elm JJ, Goetz CG, Ravina B, et al. The NINDS NET-PD Investigators. A randomized clinical trial of coenzyme Q10 and GPI-1485 in early Parkinson disease. *Neurology* 2007; 68:20–28.

297. Shults CW, Oakes D, Kieburtz K, et al. Effects of coenzyme Q10 in early Parkinson disease: Evidence of slowing of the functional decline. *Arch Neurol* 2002; 59:1541–1550.

298. Matthews RT, Ferrante RJ, Klivenyi P, et al. Creatine and cyclocreatine attenuate MPTP neurotoxicity. *Exp Neurol* 1999; 157:142–149.

299. A randomized, double-blind, futility clinical trial of creatine and minocycline in early Parkinson disease. *Neurology* 2006; 66:664–671.

300. Yang L, Sugama S, Chirichigno JW, et al. Minocycline enhances MPTP toxicity to dopaminergic neurons. *J Neurosci Res* 2003; 74:278–285.

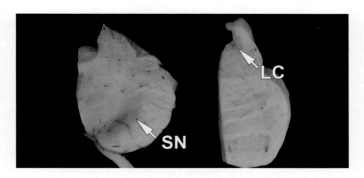

FIGURE 20-1

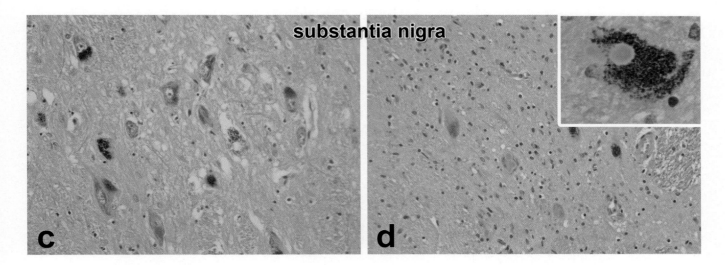

FIGURE 20-2

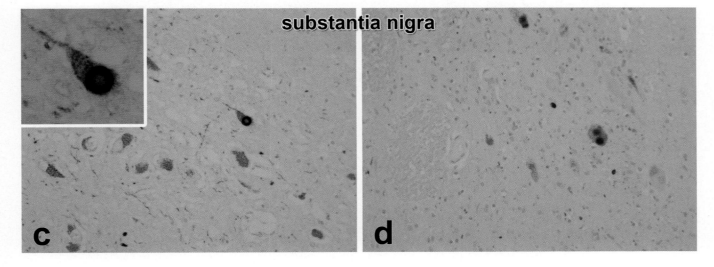

FIGURE 20-3

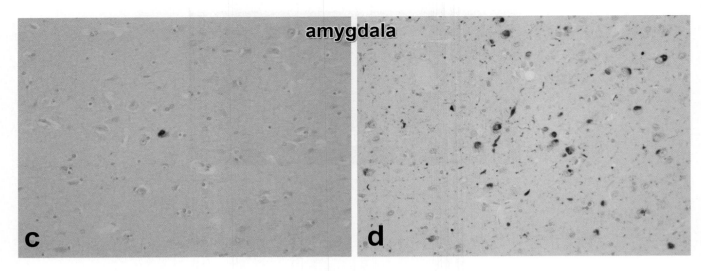

amygdala

FIGURE 20-4

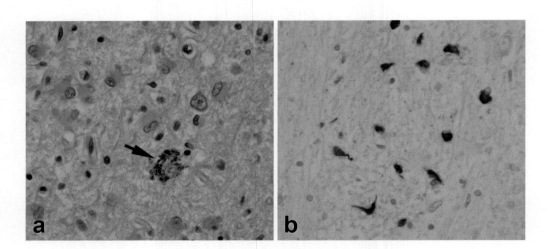

FIGURE 20-8

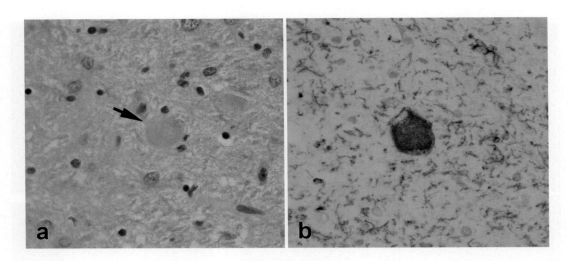

FIGURE 20-10

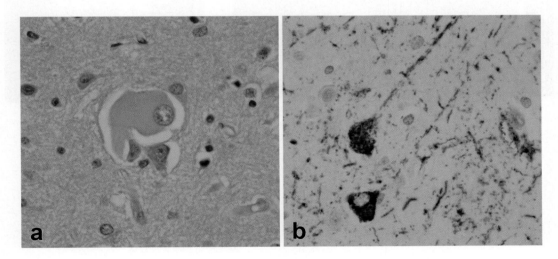

FIGURE 20-12

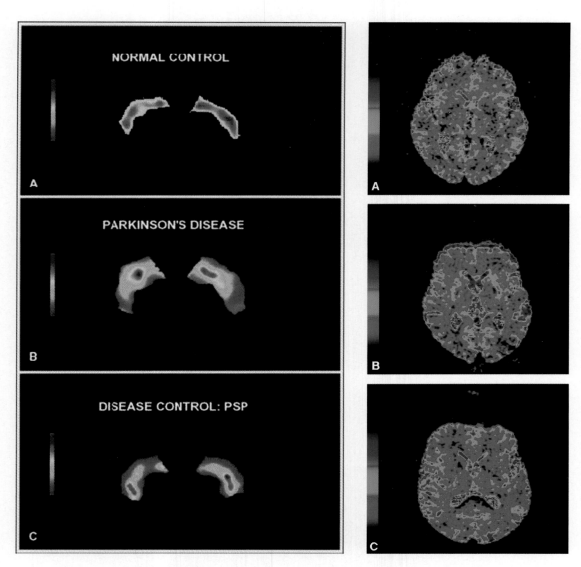

FIGURE 27-4

FIGURE 27-6

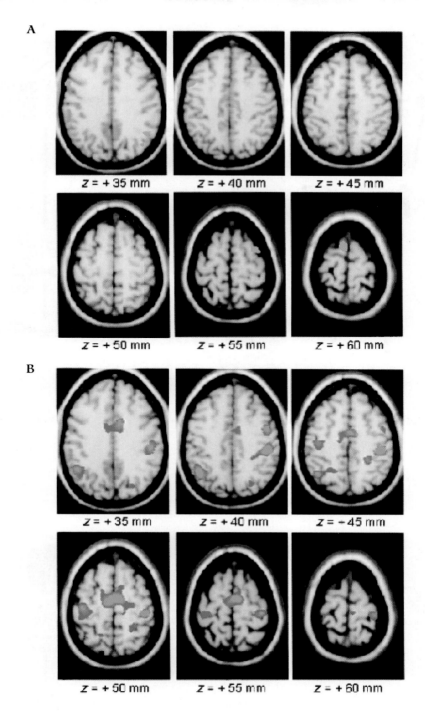

FIGURE 27-7

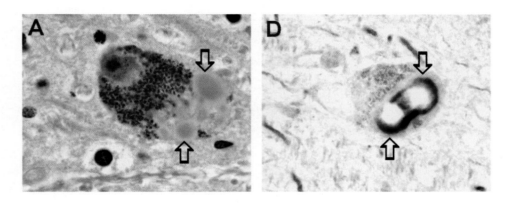

FIGURE 32-1

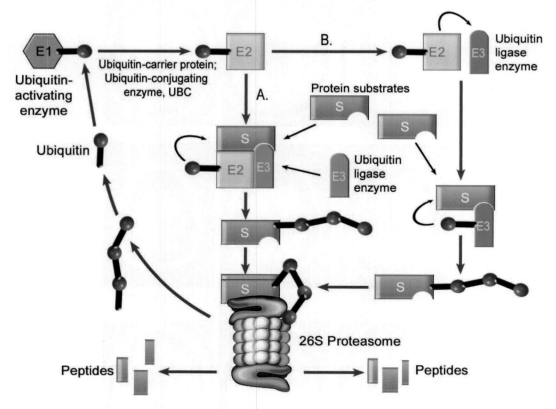

FIGURE 32-2

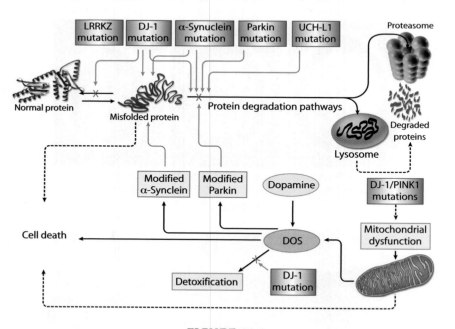

FIGURE 32-5

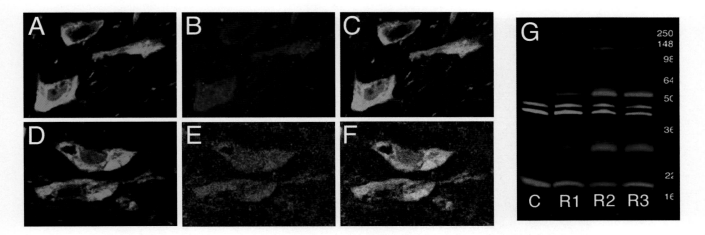

FIGURE 35-3

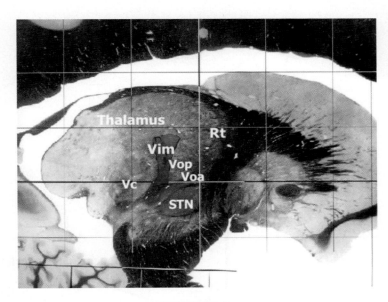

FIGURE 54-4

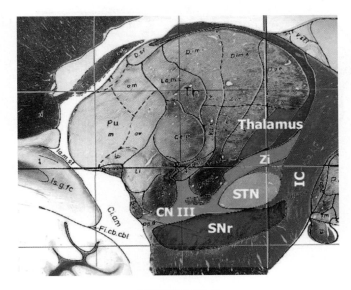

FIGURE 54-5

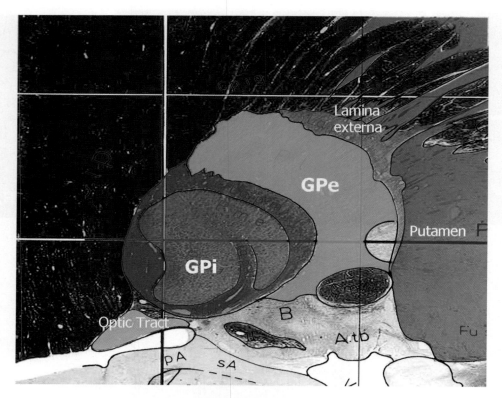

FIGURE 54-6

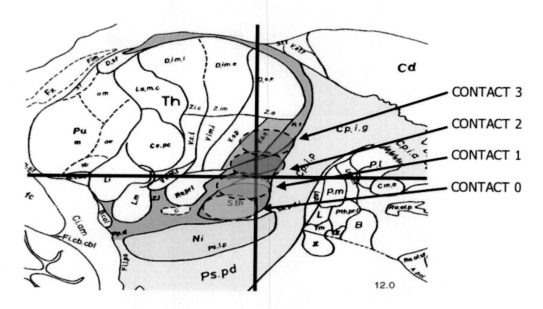

CONTACT 3
CONTACT 2
CONTACT 1
CONTACT 0

FIGURE 54-7

31 The Concept and Mechanisms of Programmed Cell Death

Robert E. Burke

HISTORY OF THE CONCEPT

Programmed cell death (PCD) is a form of death in which genetic programs intrinsic to the cell bring about its demise through orderly molecular pathways. It is to be distinguished from necrotic cell death, in which a harsh physical or biological injury destroys the cell in the absence of any mechanistic participation by the cell. Generally, necrotic cell death is characterized morphologically by the disruption of cellular and nuclear membranes and intracellular organelles. The molecular pathways of PCD are highly conserved evolutionarily, and they can be universally identified in diverse contexts of cell death. In addition, common morphologies of PCD are identified in diverse contexts as well, the most common being that of apoptosis, as described below. Historically this universal and molecularly ordered nature of PCD brought a new outlook for approaches to neuroprotection when the concept was first introduced for the pathogenesis of Parkinson's disease (PD). Prior to the introduction of the PCD concept, it was generally believed that, in order to forestall neuronal death in the disease, it would be necessary to identify its specific proximate cause(s), whether they be environmental toxins or other agents, and to block the specific paths by which these causes led to neuronal death. However, with the introduction of the concept of PCD, it became apparent that without

knowing the proximate causes or even in the presence of diverse possible proximate causes, it would still be possible to abrogate neuronal death by inhibiting of the common pathways of PCD. As reviewed herein, this approach to neuroprotection has proven to be widely effective in numerous animal models of parkinsonism, and these studies provide a firm scientific basis for the hope that similar approaches may in the future prove effective for the human disease.

The concept of PCD had its origins in the field of developmental biology, when it was demonstrated that cell death is a normal and important feature of the ontogeny of the organism (1, 2). In developmental neurobiology, the first demonstration of PCD was made by Victor Hamburger and Rita Levi-Montalcini when they observed naturally occurring cell death in dorsal root ganglia during normal development of the chick embryo (3) (reviewed by Hamburger, Ref. 4). These investigators also made the critical observation in this and related studies that the magnitude of the naturally occurring cell death event was regulated by the targets of the developing structures. They proposed that targets provide limiting amounts of trophic molecules, for which the developing neurons must compete. Their observations thus provided the basis for neurotrophic theory (5, 6), and ultimately led to the discovery of nerve growth factor (7) and other neurotrophic factors.

Another key milestone in the evolution of the PCD concept was the first description and definition of apoptosis, the most widely observed morphologic form of PCD, by Kerr and colleagues in 1972 (8). These investigators recognized that the morphology of apoptosis is widely observed in naturally occurring cell death during development as originally reported by Glucksmann (1), including that which occurs during the development of the central nervous system. Thus, these investigators were the first to recognize apoptosis as the most prevalent morphology of naturally occurring cell death in the nervous system. Since apoptosis is the most common morphology of PCD, many authors use the term as a synonym for PCD; in reviewing the work of others herein, we retain their original usage of the term. However, for this chapter, our own preference is to use the term "apoptosis" in its stricter morphologic sense, because there are alternative morphologic forms of PCD, as described below.

The field of PCD entered the molecular era with the ground-breaking studies of H. Robert Horvitz in the nematode *Caenorhabtidis elegans*, for which he was the corecipient of the Nobel Prize in Physiology or Medicine in 2002. In *C. elegans*, 131 cells undergo developmental cell death; of these, 105 are neurons. By characterizing the nature of mutations affecting the loss of these cells, Horvitz and colleagues identified critical molecular mediators of PCD, many of which were the founding members of gene families that play critical roles in PCD in higher organisms (9, 10). A critical additional milestone in the evolution of the PCD concept as a genetically regulated, orderly process was the direct demonstration in several models that gene transcription is required in order for death to occur (11–13). While this requirement depends on the cellular context (14), it nevertheless supports the mechanistic nature of PCD.

APOPTOSIS AND OTHER MORPHOLOGIES OF PROGRAMMED CELL DEATH

The initial and complete morphologic characterization of apoptosis was achieved by Kerr and colleagues (8) by ultrastructural examination of a variety of tissues. They identified what is perhaps the best-known feature because it can also be observed at the light-microscopic level—that of condensation of the nuclear chromatin. The condensed chromatin may appear as masses subjacent to the nuclear membrane (15) or as distinct rounded masses (which can be multiple) within the nucleus. On electron microscopy, the condensed chromatin is markedly electron-dense; it is homogeneous in appearance and has very distinct, well-demarcated boundaries. Some of these features can also be observed in brain tissue by the light microscope; they are so characteristic as to permit identification of apoptosis at that level. Additional features observed by

Kerr and colleagues at the ultrastructural level include preservation of cellular organelles, such as mitochondria, and both nuclear and plasma membranes. As the cells die, they form membrane blebs, which break off, forming apoptotic bodies. These may encompass cytoplasm, cellular organelles, and chromatin fragments. The apoptotic bodies are phagocytized by adjacent, intact cells. In their initial description of apoptosis, Kerr et al. made the additional important observations that apoptosis occurs rapidly, usually within 24 hours for a given cell, and that it does not elicit an inflammatory response.

While apoptosis is clearly the most prevalent morphology of PCD, it is important to recognize that other morphologies exist. Clark (16) has identified 3 other forms. Here we comment on only that of autophagy (Clark's type 2). In his review, Clark confined his description of autophagy to what is now termed "macroautophagy," to be distinguished from the related processes of microautophagy and chaperone-mediated autophagy (17). Macroautophagy is a process in which intracellular contents are enveloped by an intracellular isolation membrane. This enclosed structure, an autophagosome, subsequently merges with a lysosome, forming an autophagolysosome (18). Its contents are proteolyzed and the constituents are recycled by the cell. It is important to recognize that autophagy does not always lead to the destruction of the cell; on the contrary, in some contexts, by recycling essential molecules, it can sustain the life of the cell and the organism (19, 20). Nevertheless, autophagy has also been identified as a mediator of cellular degeneration, and in that context, it is reasonably considered as a form of PCD for two reasons. First, it leads to the elimination of cells in normal, developmental processes (16). In fact, autophagy has been identified within the cells that degenerate in *C. elegans* (9). Second, autophagy is mediated by orderly molecular pathways (17, 21). Far less is known about the molecular pathways mediating autophagy as opposed to apoptotic PCD, and they are not discussed further here. Ultimately, however, these pathways may prove to relevant to human PD, because autophagy has been identified in vitro in models of dopamine neuron degeneration (22, 23), and features suggestive of autophagy have been reported in postmortem PD substantia nigra (SN) (24).

A practical implication of the point that diverse cellular morphologies may accompany PCD is that the absence of classic apoptotic morphology in a particular setting of neuronal death does not exclude the possibility that PCD, in some other morphologic form, may be present.

The Molecular Pathways of Programmed Cell Death: A Primer

There are 3 principal pathways by which the molecular events of PCD can be initiated: by the intrinsic and extrinsic pathways and by endoplasmic reticulum (ER) stress

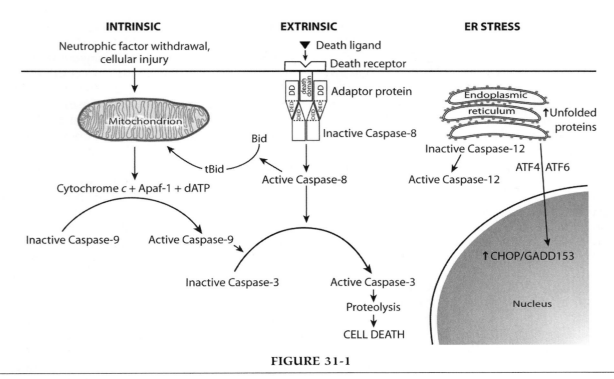

FIGURE 31-1

The three principal pathways for the activation of programmed cell death. DD = death domain; DED = death effector domain. Reprinted from Burke RE. Programmed cell death in Parkinson's disease. In: W Koller and E Melamed (eds). *The Handbook of Clinical Neurology*, 3rd ed. Philadelphia: Elsevier, 2006.

(Figure 31-1). The schematic depicted in this figure is an oversimplification as many possible interactions between these 3 pathways are not shown, but it serves as a useful organizational framework. The main focus of attention in this review is on the intrinsic pathway, which has been more extensively investigated in PD and models thereof, but some observations relevant to the extrinsic pathway and ER stress are touched upon briefly.

The extrinsic pathway of cell death has an important role in killing lymphocytes, cancer cells, and virus-infected cells (25). In the extrinsic pathway, PCD is initiated by the binding of an extracellular ligand to a cell surface receptor (a "death receptor"). An example is the binding of Fas ligand (FasL or CD95L) to the Fas (or CD95) receptor. These death receptors all contain cytoplasmic death domains (DD). Following ligand binding, these intracellular DDs interact with homologous DDs on adapter proteins, which also contain death effector domains (DED). The inactive, zymogen form of caspase-8 also contains a homologous DED, which, upon interaction with the DEDs of the adaptor proteins, permits close association ("induced proximity") of several pro–caspase-8 molecules (see Figure 31-1). The low intrinsic proteolytic activity of the pro–caspase-8 molecules then achieves autocleavage, resulting in the fully active, cleaved form of caspase-8.

Caspase-8 then mediates cleavage and activation of caspase-3, which, as an effector caspase (see below), cleaves numerous cellular proteins. Caspase-8 also cleaves and activates Bid, a proapoptotic member of the Bcl-2 family. Another protein capable of interacting with the Fas receptor is Daxx (26), which mediates apoptosis by activating c-jun kinase (JNK) (see below) (27). Daxx has been demonstrated to interact with DJ-1, which is mutated in some autosomal recessive forms of PD.

Another pathway for the activation of PCD is the stress pathway of the endoplasmic reticulum (ER) (see Figure 31-1). The ER provides a cellular compartment for the posttranslational modification and folding of membrane and secretory proteins. If the ER becomes unable to achieve prompt protein folding—due to protein mutations, or cellular stresses (such as ER Ca^{2+} depletion or inhibition of glycosylation) or protein overload—it will result in the prolonged exposure of internal protein hydrophobic domains, with potential toxicity to the cell. The cell has developed multiple mechanisms to deal with this problem, including increased production of protein-folding chaperones, suppression of protein translation, and ER-associated protein degeneration (ERAD) by the proteasome (28). If, however, these efforts to maintain cellular homeostasis fail, the ER transmits molecular signals to initiate PCD. Two transcription factors, ATF4 and

ATF6, induce expression of another transcription factor, CHOP/GADD153, which in turn mediates PCD (29), in part by increasing oxidation within the ER (30).

A possible role for ER stress has been suggested for inherited PD due to loss of function mutations in the *parkin* gene (31, 32), as reviewed below. These mutations indicate that protein processing may play an important pathogenetic role, because parkin is an E3 ubiquitin ligase (33) and as such it plays a role in targeting proteins for degradation by the proteasome (34). One target of parkin is Pael-R, a difficult-to-fold protein (35, 36). It has been postulated that loss of parkin function results in Pael-R accumulation, ER stress, and neuronal death (36). Thus, PCD due to ER stress will be an important avenue for future investigations into the pathogenesis of PD.

THE INTRINSIC PATHWAY OF PROGRAMMED CELL DEATH

In the intrinsic pathway of PCD, the pivotal event that commits the cell to death is the release of cytochrome c and other protein mediators of PCD from the mitochondrion (Figures 31-1 and 31-2). This event is controlled by members of the Bcl-2 family, of which over 20 members have now been identified (37). Among the members of

the Bcl-2 family, there are competing relationships among anti- and pro-apoptotic members, and the fate of the cell is determined by which is predominant. All members of the Bcl-2 family contain at least 1 of 4 conserved domains called Bcl-2 homology (BH) domains (38). Most anti-apoptotic Bcl-2 proteins contain at least BH1 and BH2; the 2 prototypic examples, Bcl-2 and Bcl-X_L, contain all 4. There are 2 classes of proapoptotic Bcl-2 family members. The "multidomain" members, such as Bax and Bak, contain BH1, 2, and 3 domains. The "BH3 only" members—such as Bid, Bim and Bad—contain only BH3. The antiapoptotic proteins Bcl-2 and Bcl-X_L both contain C-terminal membrane anchor domains, which localize them to the outer mitochondrial membrane as well as the ER and the nuclear membrane. At the mitochondrial outer membrane, these proteins protect against cytochrome c release and the initiation of the downstream cell death cascade.

This protective effect of the antiapoptotic Bcl-2 proteins is antagonized by interaction with Bax or Bak (Figure 31-2), an interaction that allows the release of cytochrome c and other proapoptotic proteins from the mitochondrion and initiation of the cell death cascade. Bax is normally located in the cytoplasm; with the onset of apoptotic stimulation, it translocates to the mitochondrion to initiate cytochrome c release. Bak is normally

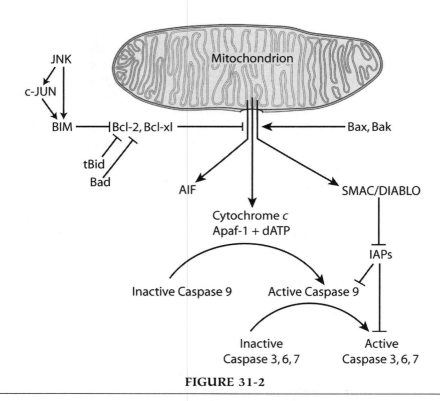

FIGURE 31-2

The intrinsic pathway of programmed cell death. Reprinted from Burke RE. Programmed cell death in Parkinson's disease. In: W Koller and E Melamed (eds). *The Handbook of Clinical Neurology*, 3rd ed. Philadelphia: Elsevier, 2006.

expressed on the outer membrane of the mitochondrion. Activation of Bax or Bak is absolutely required for apoptosis to occur, because cells that carry a double homozygous deletion of both are resistant to a wide variety of inducers of apoptosis (39). Bax and Bak are activated by BH3-only proapoptotic members of the Bcl-2 family. These proteins are, in turn, activated by death-inducing signals by a variety of posttranslational modifications. Bid, for example, is activated by cleavage by caspase-8, as previously described. Bad is activated by alteration of its phosphorylation status (40). Activation of Bax or Bak by BH3-only proteins results in their homooligomerization and, by mechanisms that are not completely understood, permeabilization of the outer mitochondrial membrane (37).

In the intrinsic pathway, the release of cytochrome c results in the activation of a caspase cascade (see Figure 31-2). In mammalian cells, there are now 14 identified caspases (41). All of these proteases contain a cysteine at their active site, and they all cleave on the carboxyl side of an aspartate (thus, "caspases"). There are 2 groups among the caspases that play a role in PCD: "initiator" caspases (-2, -8, -9, and -10) and "effector" caspases (-3, -6, and -7). These two groups are distinguished by their N-terminals. Initiator caspases contain long N-terminal regions that are involved in the regulation of their activation—for example, the DED domain in caspase-8 (see Figure 31-1). The effector caspases contain only short (20 to 30 amino acids) N-terminal prodomains. All caspases are produced by cells as inactive zymogens. All caspases are activated by proteolytic cleavage (by an initiator caspase) to produce a large (~20-kDa) and a small (~10-kDa) subunit, which then associate to form a heterodimer. These heterodimers, in turn, associate to form a heterotetramer consisting of 2 p20/p10 heterodimers, which constitute the active form of the enzyme.

Following the release of cytochrome c from mitochondria, caspase-9 becomes activated upon association with a cytoplasmic protein Apaf-1 (apoptosis-protease-activating factor-1), in the presence of dATP, to form a ~1.4 MDa complex called "the apoptosome" (42) (see Figure 31-2). Activated caspase-9 then cleaves and activates caspase-3 and other effector caspases. Effector caspases then systematically cleave select cellular proteins to either eliminate their function or, alternatively, to activate proteins which then become proapoptotic.

The activity of caspases is regulated by inhibitor-of-apoptosis proteins (IAPs), of which there are 8 known in mammalian cells (42) (see Figure 31-2). These proteins all contain regions (baculoviral IAP repeat or BIR) that bind to and inhibit select caspases. In mammalian cells, caspases-3, -7, and -9 are all subject to IAP inhibition. This inhibition by IAPs can, in turn, be blocked by a family of proteins that contain a tetrapeptide motif, which binds to and blocks the BIRs of IAPs. In mammals, the

founding member of this family was found to be released by mitochondria and termed the "second mitochondria-derived activator of caspases" (SMAC), or DIABLO (direct IAP-binding protein) (43, 44) (see Figure 31-2).

In addition to cytochrome c and SMAC/DIABLO, mitochondria release a protein apoptosis-inducing factor (AIF) in response to cell death stimuli (45). When first identified, it was shown that this protein is capable of causing nuclear condensation and DNA fragmentation, as occurs in apoptosis, and that none of these effects are blocked by caspase inhibitors (45). More recently, it has been shown that, by a mechanism not yet understood, AIF release from the mitochondrion is mediated by the DNA repair enzyme poly (ADP-ribose) polymerase I (PARP-1); PARP inhibition or genetic deletion prevents mitochondrial AIF release, translocation to the nucleus, and cell death (46). The demonstration of this pathway indicates that there are important non-caspase-dependent pathways to cell death.

While there are likely to be multiple upstream pathways acting upon the proapoptotic BH3-only proteins to initiate mitochondrial release of death mediators, one such pathway, which has been the focus of extensive investigation, involves the activation of the transcription factor c-jun by phosphorylation (reviewed in Ref. 47). Phosphorylation and activation of c-jun is mediated by c-jun N-terminal kinase (JNK), which, in turn, is activated by phosphorylation by a complex kinase cascade that includes the mixed-lineage kinases (47). There is abundant evidence from studies in tissue culture and animal models that this kinase cascade plays an important role in initiating PCD (48). In relation to PD specifically, there are now numerous experiments utilizing either pharmacologic or genetic approaches to blocking the JNK/c-jun kinase cascade that have demonstrated efficacy in preventing dopamine neuron death in animal models of parkinsonism (47). This signaling pathway acts upon BH3-only mediators in multiple ways to initiate death. There is evidence that c-jun induces the expression of Bim (49, 50) (see Figure 31-2). In addition, JNK not only phosphorylates and activates c-jun but also phosphorylates and activates Bim directly (51) (see Figure 31-2). In addition, JNK phosphorylates and directly activates Bad (52).

PROGRAMMED CELL DEATH IN DOPAMINE NEURONS OF THE SUBSTANTIA NIGRA DURING DEVELOPMENT

Before considering the possible relevance of PCD to PD, it is important to observe that dopamine neurons of the substantia nigra (SN), like most developing neural systems, undergo a naturally occurring PCD event (53, 54), which is characterized morphologically by the exclusive appearance of apoptosis. In rodents, the cell death event is largely postnatal, ending by the fourth postnatal week. As envisioned by classic neurotrophic theory, the magnitude of this death event is regulated by interactions with the striatal target, because experimental manipulations which disrupt such interactions result in increased cell death (reviewed in Ref. 55). This cell death is mediated, at least in part, by the caspases. The activated forms of caspases-9 (56) and -3 (57) can be demonstrated by immunohistochemistry with specific antibodies, as can specific caspase-3 protein cleavage products (58). This activation of caspases is likely to be mediated by the intrinsic pathway of PCD. Overexpression of Bcl-2 within dopaminergic neurons, under the control of the tyrosine hydroxylase promoter, results in suppression of natural cell death and a 30% increase in the surviving number of SN dopamine neurons (59). Thus the molecular pathways of PCD are normally activated in some dopamine neurons during development. The question then becomes: Is there evidence that these or related molecular pathways are abnormally activated in adult-onset human PD and are thereby playing a role in the neurodegenerative process?

PROGRAMMED CELL DEATH: RELEVANCE TO HUMAN PARKINSON'S DISEASE

There are 3 forms of evidence that the molecular pathways of PCD are relevant to the degeneration of dopaminergic and other neurons in human PD: (a) In current animal models of PD, in which dopamine neuron death occurs, the mechanisms of PCD have been shown to play a role; (b) for a number of the gene mutations now known to cause familial PD, evidence suggests that they may act by either inducing PCD or augmenting sensitivity to it; and (c) There is increasing evidence from studies of human PD postmortem brains that the pathways of PCD play a role. Each of these forms of evidence is reviewed below.

Programmed Cell Death in Animal Models of Parkinsonism

An important step forward in establishing the possible relevance of PCD to neurodegeneration in human PD was the demonstration that PCD occurs in dopamine neurons of the SN not only during normal naturally occurring cell death in the developmental period but also in settings of pathologic death—for example, that induced by toxins and in the adult brain. There is now evidence that the processes of PCD occur in SN dopamine neurons in the major current animal models of parkinsonism—including in adulthood—depending on the dose, timing, and route of administration of the neurotoxin. The evidence in these models is both correlative, in which activation of PCD

mediators has been demonstrated in conjunction with the occurrence of death, and functional, in which disruption of cell death pathways by pharmacologic or genetic means has led to improved survival of dopamine neurons in the model. For the purposes of this review, primarily studies that have been conducted in living animals are considered.

6-Hydroxydopamine. One of the first established models of parkinsonism utilized the selective catecholaminergic neurotoxin 6-hydroxydopamine (6-OHDA) to destroy SN dopamine neurons (60, 61). This model is considered to be potentially relevant to human PD because 6-OHDA is an endogenous oxidative metabolite of dopamine (60) and has been demonstrated in human caudate (62). We demonstrated that during the naturally occurring cell death period, intrastriatal injection of 6-OHDA induces apoptosis in SN dopamine neurons (63). While we initially attributed this induction of apoptosis to a destruction of intrastriatal dopaminergic terminals by the toxin and a resulting loss of developmental target-derived trophic support, more recent studies have suggested that this is likely to be true only in part; some of the death is likely to be due to a direct effect of the toxin. In dopamine neuron apoptosis due to naturally occurring cell death or its augmentation by axotomy, there is a characteristic pattern of immunostaining for activated caspase-3 and its cleavage products that is strictly perinuclear (57, 58). In the developmental intrastriatal 6-OHDA model, however, in addition to this pattern, a pattern of cytoplasmic staining is observed in the immunostaining for activated caspase-3 and its cleavage products (57, 58). Apoptosis occurs in SN dopamine neurons following intrastriatal 6-OHDA not only in immature animals but in adults as well, as confirmed by electron microscopy and light microscope morphologic criteria (64).

The activation of caspase-3 in the intrastriatal 6-OHDA model is likely to be mediated, at least in part, by activation of the intrinsic pathway of PCD, because it is accompanied by activation of caspase-9, as indicated by immunostaining with antibodies specific for the activated form (56). The ER stress pathway is also involved in this model, because CHOP/GADD153 expression is induced, and, in the adult model, a homozygous CHOP null mutation is protective (65).

The ability of 6-OHDA to induce apoptosis in SN in animal models depends on the site of injection and the dose. We observed that direct injection of 6-OHDA into the SN, as in the classic Ungerstedt model, did not induce apoptotic morphology (66). Other investigators have found, however, that injection of a similar or lower dose into the adjacent medial forebrain bundle does induce morphologic and DNA nick-end-labeling evidence of apoptosis (67, 68).

MPTP Models of Parkinson's Disease. As for 6-OHDA models, the occurrence of apoptosis and the participation of pathways of PCD in MPTP (1-methyl 4-phenyl 1,2,3, 6-tetrahydropyridine) models depend on how the toxin is administered. In the most widely used regimen, the acute model of MPTP toxicity, multiple doses of the toxin are administered to mice every 2 hours. In a morphologic assessment of 3 different doses of MPTP administered according to this regimen, Jackson-Lewis and colleagues were unable to detect apoptotic morphology or DNA in situ end-labeling in the SN at any of 3 time points following injection (69). Even in the absence of apoptotic morphology, some investigations have suggested a possible role for the molecular mediators of PCD. Hassouna et al. noted increased Bax mRNA and protein expression following acute MPTP, but this was not a quantitative analysis (70). Yang and collaborators clearly demonstrated the ability of Bcl-2, overexpressed in transgenic mice, to protect from loss of striatal dopamine and dopamine transporter in the acute MPTP model; in fact, the transgene was more effective in the acute model, where apoptosis is not observed, than in the chronic model, where it is (see below) (71). As these investigators pointed out, however, Bcl-2 can protect not only from apoptotic death but also necrotic death (for example, see Ref.72); therefore protection from neural death by Bcl-2 cannot be taken as direct evidence that the pathways of PCD as delineated above are involved.

In the acute MPTP model, Viswanath and colleagues demonstrated the ability of the general caspase inhibitor protein p35, expressed as a transgene, to protect from dopamine neuron loss (73). However, the protection was slight and inhibition of cell death was not directly shown. They also demonstrated, by tissue assays, increases in the activity of caspases in the SN after MPTP injection. However, these assays were performed at the tissue level, not the cellular level, so it is not known that the changes occurred in dopamine neurons; they may instead have occurred in nonneural cells. Indeed, Furuya et al. clearly demonstrated a role for caspase-11, an inflammatory caspase (41, 74), in the acute MPTP model in nondopaminergic, inflammatory cells (75). A caspase-11 null mutation protected from acute MPTP-induced SN neuron loss. However, most of the caspase-11 was expressed in microglia, not dopamine neurons. The caspase-11 null mutation was not protective in the chronic MPTP model, in which apoptosis is observed; on the other hand, a dominant negative form of Apaf-1 was protective in the chronic model (see below) but not in the acute model (75). These authors concluded that the acute model is characterized by an inflammatory process in which the role for caspase-11 is not cell autonomous to dopamine neurons. We conclude that there is little evidence to date for apoptosis or the activation of PCD pathways intrinsic to dopamine neurons in the acute MPTP model.

The chronic model of MPTP toxicity is induced by administering a single dose each day (30 mg/kg) for 5 days (76). In their original description of this model, Tatton and Kish clearly identified apoptotic nuclear chromatin clumps within phenotypically defined SN dopamine neurons and DNA nick-end labeling (76). Like Yang et al., Offen and colleagues demonstrated that overexpression of Bcl-2 in transgenic mice protects from loss of striatal dopamine in this model (77). As discussed above, given the spectrum of Bcl-2 effects, this finding does not provide direct evidence for a role of the intrinsic pathway of PCD. More convincing evidence for a role for this pathway comes from the demonstration by Vila and colleagues that mice deficient in Bax are protected from the induction of apoptosis and loss of SN dopamine neurons in the chronic model (78). In keeping with a role for the intrinsic pathway of PCD, Mochizuki et al. have demonstrated that transduction of SN dopamine neurons with a dominant negative form of Apaf-1 also protects from the loss of dopamine neurons (79). These authors conclude that the intrinsic pathway is likely to be activated in the chronic MPTP model. This activation is likely to be responsible for the activation of caspase-3, as reported by Turmel et al. (80).

The Rotenone Model of Parkinson's Disease. Chronic intravenous administration of the mitochondrial complex I inhibitor rotenone to rats has been shown to induce selective degeneration of nigral dopaminergic neurons, synuclein inclusions, and behavioral signs of parkinsonism, thus modeling human PD (81). Although information for the in vivo context is lacking, chronic rotenone exposure induces apoptosis and increases susceptibility to H_2O_2-induced apoptosis in the in vitro setting (82).

The C-Jun Signaling Cascade in Animal Models of Parkinsonism. In targeting PCD pathways in the development of neuroprotective approaches to PD, the most effective strategy would be to attempt to block upstream mediators before extensive cellular damage is done. One of the most widely studied upstream signaling pathways in PCD is the kinase cascade that leads to the activation of the transcription factor c-jun (see Figure 31-2). There are now numerous studies indicating a role for this signaling cascade in the mediation of dopamine neuron death in parkinsonian animal models (reviewed in Ref. 47). Initial studies of c-jun expression in the central nervous system of living animals in models of injury were difficult to interpret in relation to cell death because early studies in peripheral systems had shown that expression could be upregulated by regenerative processes (83). The earliest studies specifically within the substantia nigra (SN) in models of death induced by 6-OHDA (84) and axotomy (85) noted substantial and sustained increases in c-jun expression, but these changes were interpreted largely as a possible regenerative response. In the 6-OHDA model, however, other investigators subsequently showed that cell death is greatest (86) at 4 to 8 days after lesioning, when the expression of c-jun is maximal.

With increased awareness of apoptosis as a distinct morphology of programmed cell death (15) and the ability to detect it by nuclear staining, it became clear that c-jun expression could be correlated at the cellular level with this form of cell death in living animals. This was true in the context of natural cell death in the peripheral (87) and central (88) nervous systems and in models of induced natural cell death (89). Similarly, in the SN, close correlations could be made between c-jun expression and markers of apoptosis. Herdegen et al. (90) demonstrated, in the adult axotomy model, a close regional and temporal association between prolonged c-jun expression and DNA nick-end labeling for apoptosis (91). Oo et al. (92) demonstrated, in a postnatal model of apoptosis in the SNpc induced by early target deprivation, that c-jun and JNK expression could be correlated at a cellular level with apoptotic morphology. Thus, these early morphologic studies of apoptotic cell death suggested a clear correlation with c-jun expression.

A functional role for c-jun in mediating death specifically within dopamine neurons has been supported by studies using viral vector gene transfer approaches. Crocker et al. (93) demonstrated in an axotomy model that adenovirus-mediated expression of a c-jun dominant-negative construct prevents the loss of dopamine neurons in the SN and the loss of dopaminergic fibers in the striatum. A functional role for JNK/c-jun signaling in dopamine neuron death is also supported by the demonstration that gene transfer of the JNK binding domain of JIP-1 (which inhibits JNK activation) protects dopamine neurons from chronic MPTP toxicity (94). Again, this approach prevented the loss not only of SN dopamine neurons but also of their striatal terminals as assessed by catecholamine levels.

In view of this evidence that phosphorylation of c-jun plays a role in the mediation of cell death in dopamine neurons and given that JNK is the dominant kinase for c-jun (95), it would be predicted that JNK isoforms also play a role in the death of these neurons. Hunot and coinvestigators have shown, in the acute model of MPTP toxicity, that both JNK2 and JNK3 homozygous null animals are resistant (96). JNK1 null animals were not protected. Compound mutant JNK2 and JNK3 homozygous nulls were even more protected; they showed only a 15% loss of neurons. Thus both JNK2 and JNK3 play a role in cell death in this model. The compound null mutation also protected dopaminergic fibers in the striatum. These investigators postulated that increased transcriptional activity mediated by JNK phosphorylation of c-jun may mediate cell death, and they found that the immune mediator cyclooxygenase-2 is upregulated. JNK was shown to be necessary for this upregulation, as it was abolished in the compound JNK mutants. Thus, JNK may ultimately act, at least in part, in the inflammation of the acute MPTP model by upregulating cycloogenase-2, which has been implicated as a death mediator in this model (97).

These studies, based on genetic techniques using either gene transfer or transgenesis in mice, which indicate a functional role for c-jun signaling in the mediation of neuron death in living animals, have received much support from pharmacologic studies using the specific mixed lineage kinase (MLK) inhibitors CEP1347 and its analog CEP11004 (98). These MLK inhibitors have also been shown to be protective in animal models of parkinsonism. In a single-dose model of MPTP toxicity, Saporito and coinvestigators demonstrated that CEP1347 attenuated the loss of dopaminergic terminal markers and cell bodies in SN as demonstrated by immunostaining (99). In the MPTP single-dose model, there is increased phosphorylation of JNK, and this increase is attenuated by CEP1347 (100). In the intrastriatal injection of 6-OHDA model in postnatal rats, CEP11004 diminished the number of dopaminergic apoptotic profiles (56) and the number of activated caspase-9–positive profiles in proportion to overall protection from cell death (56). In this study there was almost complete protection of striatal TH-positive fibers; this is especially remarkable considering that the toxin was injected directly into striatum. Overall, these genetic and pharmacologic studies demonstrate a clear role for the JNK/c-jun signaling pathway in initiating PCD in a variety of living animal models of parkinsonism.

Programmed Cell Death and Genetic Causes of Parkinson's Disease

A number of genetic mutations are now known to cause familial PD (reviewed in Ref. 101). Although the cellular functions of the affected proteins and the mechanisms whereby the mutations result in dopamine neuron death are largely unknown, the possibility that these genes may play a role in regulating PCD has been suggested by a number of studies.

Synuclein. The first mutation identified to cause human PD is an A53T substitution in the protein α-synuclein (102). Other substitution mutations, A30P (103) and E46K (104), were also subsequently associated with autosomal dominant familial PD. In addition, a triplication mutation of the synuclein locus, in the absence of modification of the wild-type sequence, has also been identified (105). Even prior to the discovery of the PD-causing mutations in synuclein, it had been known that α-synuclein, or fragments of it, are capable of forming protein aggregates spontaneously (106, 107). With the discovery of the mutations, it was found that they tend to increase this tendency to self-aggregate (108, 109). These observations, in conjunction with the discovery that synuclein is a major component of Lewy bodies (110), have led to the prevailing concept that the synuclein mutations cause a "toxic gain of function" that results in an increased tendency to aggregate, and, by mechanisms not yet known, increased dopamine neuron death (reviewed in Ref. 111). This concept is supported by a number of studies in animal models in which overexpression of human synuclein has been associated with dopaminergic neuron dysfunction or death (112, 113).

However, the normal function of α-synuclein is still unknown, and it remains possible that a loss of its normal function, due either to the disease-causing mutations or sequestration of normal protein in disease-associated aggregates, plays a role in PD pathogenesis. Such a possibility has received support from a number of studies in diverse tissue culture contexts indicating that α-synuclein has an antiapoptotic function. Studies by da Costa and coinvestigators have shown that human wild-type α-synuclein protects cells of neocortical origin from diverse inducers of apoptosis and that the A53T mutation abrogates this protective effect (114). This protective effect of synuclein is associated with diminished expression of p53, a known transcriptional mediator of apoptosis (115). Hashimoto and colleagues made comparable observations in a neuronal cell line derived from murine hypothalamic tumor cells; when transfected with α-synuclein, these cells show increased survival and diminished activation of JNK, an apoptotic mediator, following exposure to hydrogen peroxide (116). Li and Lee have also demonstrated that human wild-type α-synuclein but not the A53T mutant protects a variety of neuronal cell lines but not nonneuronal cells from several agents that induce apoptosis (117). The protective effect was demonstrated to depend on the 20 C-terminal amino acids of α-synuclein. The effect was mediated by an attenuation of caspase-3 activity (117). Perhaps of greater direct relevance to human PD, Machida and colleagues demonstrated that antisense "knockdown" of parkin (see below) in human dopaminergic SH-SY5Y cells resulted in apoptosis, but this effect was blocked by overexpression of wild-type synuclein (118). These in vitro observations of an antiapoptotic effect of wild-type synuclein are in keeping with an earlier in vivo observation made by our own group that, upon induction of apoptosis in dopamine neurons of the SN by a lesion to their target, the striatum, during development, synuclein expression was induced only in surviving nonapoptotic neurons, suggesting the possibility of a protective effect (119).

However, these in vitro observations are far from universal. In stably transfected PC12 cells, lines expressing human wild-type α-synuclein showed no decreased sensitivity to the induction of apoptosis by serum withdrawal (120). Some investigators have in fact reported a proapoptotic effect of α-synuclein. Zhou et al., for example, reported an increased sensitivity to 6-OHDA–induced apoptosis following overexpression of human wild-type α-synuclein (121). These disparate results in tissue culture are likely to be due to differences among these studies in cells, methods of expressing α-synuclein, and methods of inducing cellular injury. Studies performed in vivo may be expected to provide better insight into the normal function of synuclein and a protective role if it exists, but such studies also do not lend themselves to simple interpretation. In line with a protective role, Manning-Bog and coworkers demonstrated a neuroprotective effect against paraquat-induced degeneration of nigral dopamine neurons in α-synuclein–overexpressing transgenic mice (122). On the other hand, Dauer et al. have shown that a synuclein homozygous null mutation in mice does not augment sensitivity to MPTP treatment; on the contrary, it completely protects from SN dopamine neuron loss (123). Similar observations have been made by other investigators (124, 125).

In conclusion, while many independent in vitro studies support an antiapoptotic role for synuclein, it remains unclear whether these observations are physiologically relevant and whether they have implications for the pathogenesis of PD.

Parkin. A second cause of familial PD and more common than mutations in the gene for α-synuclein (PARK1), are mutations in the gene *parkin* (PARK2). Mutations in *parkin* were first identified in Japanese families with an autosomal recessive juvenile onset form of PD (ARJP). These patients show all the motor features of parkinsonism, and they respond to treatment with levodopa. At postmortem, there is loss of dopamine neurons of the SN and of noradrenergic neurons of the locus ceruleus. The first mutations identified were deletion mutations (32), but subsequently a large variety of mutations were discovered in other families, including frameshift and point mutations. These various mutations result in loss of parkin function, which has been shown to be that of an E3 ubiquitin ligase (33). Thus, parkin participates in the ubiquitination and subsequent degradation by the proteasome of specific protein substrates. A number of these substrates have been identified, including CDCrel-1 (126), Pael-R (36), a glycosylated form of synuclein (127), synphilin (128), cyclin E (129), α/β tubulin (130), and the p38 subunit of aminoacyl-tRNA synthetase complex (131). It is hypothesized that the accumulation or loss of regulation of such substrates is responsible for dopamine neuron death. Unlike studies of synuclein, where both in vitro and in vivo approaches have yielded mixed results insofar as regulation of apoptosis is concerned, studies of parkin have universally demonstrated protection from apoptotic death. However, the nature of the toxic stimulus to which parkin affords protection and the means by which it does so has varied among investigations.

Imai and coworkers observed that unfolded protein stress within the ER, such as that induced by tunicamycin, resulted in upregulation of *parkin*, and that *parkin* could protect cells from this death stimulus in tissue culture (35). This protective ability was abrogated by ARJP-causing mutations. ER stress is one of the principal pathways leading to apoptosis in cells (132). These investigators further showed that one *parkin* substrate, Pael-R (Parkin-associated endothelin receptor–like receptor) is a difficult-to-fold protein, and its overexpression results in the formation of aggregates and cell death. Parkin ubiquitinates Pael-R, suppresses the formation of Pael-R aggregates, and protects from cell death (36). Thus, one hypothesis of *parkin* function is that it protects dopamine neurons from ER stress–mediated apoptosis. The possible role of ER stress–mediated cell death in dopamine neurons has received independent support from both in vitro (133, 134) and in vivo studies (65), indicating that dopamine neuron death induced by 6-OHDA is due at least in part to the activity of the transcription factor CHOP/GADD153, a mediator of apoptosis in ER stress (29).

Another pathway in which *parkin* may protect from apoptosis is that mediated by cell cycle regulators. There is now abundant evidence that proteins which mediate passage through the cell cycle can be reexpressed in postmitotic neurons and induce apoptosis (reviewed in Ref. 135). Staropoli and coinvestigators have demonstrated that parkin functions in a protein complex, which includes proteins hSel-10 and Cullin-1, to ubiquitinate and degrade the cell cycle regulator cyclin E (129). Cyclin E, like other cyclins, serves to regulate a kinase that participates in coordination of the cell cycle. It regulates cdk2, which participates in the G1-to-S cell cycle transition. Staropoli et al. have found that downregulation of *parkin* by use of short interfering RNAs (siRNAs) resulted in an accumulation of cyclin E in both embryonic cortical and dopaminergic mesencephalic neurons and an increased susceptibility to apoptosis induced by excitotoxicity. Conversely, increased parkin expression in cerebellar granule cells attenuated cyclin E accumulation and protected cells from kainic acid–induced apoptosis. The potential clinical relevance of their observations was supported by their finding that abnormal accumulation of cyclin E is detectable in human ARJP brains (129).

In addition to these contexts, in which parkin has been proposed to play an antiapoptotic role based on identification of its substrates, it has also been shown to provide protection from apoptosis in a number of in vitro studies utilizing cellular toxins. Darios and colleagues have demonstrated that PC12 cells stably transfected with parkin are resistant to apoptosis induced by ceramide (136). This protective ability was dependent on the E3 ubiquitin ligase activity of parkin. Jiang and coinvestigators showed that human neuroblastoma cells (SH-SY5Y) stably overexpressing parkin were resistant to apoptosis induced by either dopamine or 6-OHDA (137). This protective effect was accompanied by an attenuated induction of JNK and caspase-3, two apoptotic mediators. As in the study by Darios et al., the antiapoptotic effect was abrogated by mutations that disrupt the E3 ubiquitin ligase activity of parkin. Even in the absence of neurotoxin exposure, Machida and colleagues demonstrated that antisense knockdown of parkin in SH-SY5Y cells resulted in apoptotic death, with characteristic morphologic changes and activation of the caspases (118). The potential clinical relevance of these studies is suggested by the investigations of Del Rio and colleagues, who showed that lymphocytes derived from patients homozygous for loss-of-function parkin mutations have increased sensitivity to dopamine, 6-OHDA, and iron-mediated apoptosis (138).

These in vitro observations, indicating an antiapoptotic function of parkin, have been largely supported by in vivo observations made in *Drosophila*. *Drosophila* which are null for the parkin homologue demonstrate a diminished life span and locomotor deficits that are due to the apoptotic death of select muscle groups (139). This death by apoptosis has been confirmed by others (140). In addition, Pesah and coinvestigators noted an increased sensitivity of the *parkin* homologue–null flies to the herbicide paraquat (140). A possible mechanism for this increased susceptibility to apoptosis has been suggested by studies of Cha and colleagues, who determined that, in the absence of the *parkin* homolog, there is an upregulation of JNK. In these flies, dopamine neurons are shrunken; they show decreased tyrosine hydroxylase expression and increased expression of phosphorylated JNK. The reduced size of the dopamine neurons could be reversed by expression of the dominant negative form of JNK. Further experiments demonstrated that *parkin* negatively regulated the JNK signaling pathway in an E3 ligase–dependent manner (141).

In summary, multiple lines of evidence, from studies in vitro in mammalian cell lines and in vivo in *Drosophila* support the concept of an antiapoptotic function of parkin. However, disappointingly, homozygous null mutations in mice do not result in the spontaneous loss of dopamine neurons (142, 143) as loss-of-function mutations do in humans. The reason for this inability to produce dopamine neuron pathology in mice is unclear. Nevertheless, there is solid evidence that parkin may play an antiapoptotic role in dopamine neurons.

DJ-1. Mutations in the gene for *DJ-1* (PARK7) also cause autosomal recessive early-onset familial PD. Bonifati and colleagues first localized the gene for PARK7 in families from Italy and the Netherlands to chromosome 1p36

(144). They subsequently determined, in the Dutch family, that a deletion mutation affects the coding region of *DJ-1*; in the Italian family, they found that a L166P mutation is present and likely to result in loss of function (144). Human *DJ-1* was first identified as an oncogene (145) and later determined to be H_2O_2-responsive, suggesting that it may function as an antioxidant protein (146).

Consistent with the possibility that *DJ-1* may play a protective role in neurons, a number of investigators have demonstrated antiapoptotic effects in tissue culture. Yokota and coworkers demonstrated, in mouse Neuro2a cells and human embryonic kidney cells, that downregulation of *DJ-1* by siRNA increased the susceptibility to H_2O_2-induced apoptosis (147). Downregulation of *DJ-1* also increased susceptibility to death by ER stress. Using an affinity purification approach to identify proteins that interact with *DJ-1*, Xu and colleagues demonstrated that *DJ-1* interacts with nuclear RNA–binding protein p54nrb and pyrimidine tract—binding protein-associated splicing factor (PSF) (148). These proteins are both regulators of transcription and RNA metabolism. These investigators demonstrated that overexpression of PSF induces apoptosis, which can be blocked by coexpression of wild-type *DJ-1* but to a lesser extent by mutant forms. Conversely, downregulation of *DJ-1* made cells more susceptible to PSF-induced apoptosis. Like Yokota et al., Xu and colleagues demonstrated that *DJ-1* protected cells from H_2O_2-induced apoptosis; furthermore, they showed that its protein interactor p54nrb did so as well (148).

An antiapoptotic role for *DJ-1* was also demonstrated by Junn and coinvestigators, but by a different mechanism (149). Like the other investigators, they demonstrated that *DJ-1* protects cells (SH-SY5Y cells in this case) from H_2O_2. They demonstrated also that *DJ-1* is protective against cell death induced by dopamine and MPP$^+$. The protective effect against H_2O_2 was abrogated by the L166P mutation. However, they noted that the modest reduction in intracellular levels of H_2O_2 achieved by *DJ-1* overexpression did not appear to account for its marked cytoprotective effect. Using a yeast 2-hybrid screen approach, they identified an interaction between *DJ-1* and the protein Daxx. Daxx had previously been identified a protein interactor for the Fas death receptor (26), which mediates Fas-induced apoptosis by activating the kinase ASK1, which, in turn, activates JNK (27) (reviewed in Ref. 150). Junn and colleagues demonstrated that *DJ-1* sequesters Daxx in the nucleus, preventing it from activating ASK1 and thereby inhibiting apoptosis (149). This ability to block apoptosis is lost in the L166P mutant.

Studies in vivo in *Drosophila* have provided support for these observations made in vitro of an antiapoptotic function for *DJ-1*. Yang and colleagues have shown that knockdown of the *Drosophila DJ-1* homolog

in dopaminergic neurons by a transgenic RNAi approach resulted in progressive decline in their number, and in diminished dopamine content (151). As would be predicted from the in vitro studies, *DJ-1* knockdown in neurons resulted in increased sensitivity to oxidative stress due to H_2O_2 exposure. These investigators determined that the neurodegeneration phenotype induced by RNAi knockdown of *DJ-1* could by suppressed by coexpression of phosphatidylinositol-3-kinase (PI3K), an upstream activator of the antiapoptotic kinase Akt (for reviews, see Refs. 152 to 154). Conversely, the degenerative phenotype was exacerbated by coexpression of PTEN, a phosphatase that reverses the production of phosphorylated phosphoinositides by PI3K and consequently decreases the activity of Akt (see reviews). These results are complemented by those of Kim et al. (155), who demonstrated in *Drosophila* that *DJ-1* serves as a suppressor of PTEN. In addition, they demonstrated in mammalian cells that increased expression of *DJ-1* results in increased phosphorylation and activation of Akt, with enhanced cell survival (155). Thus, converging lines of evidence suggest that *DJ-1* positively regulates the antiapoptotic Akt kinase pathway.

Unfortunately, as has been the case for parkin null mutations, homozygous null mutations of *DJ-1* in mice have not led to a degenerative loss of SN dopamine neurons, as the loss of function mutations do in human patients (156, 157). However, as would be predicted based on the tissue culture and *Drosophila* studies, null mice do show a greater sensitivity to oxidative insults (158). In addition, they show a greater sensitivity to MPTP administered in a chronic regimen that induces apoptosis (76). Thus, in the mammalian in vivo context, *DJ-1* is likely to have an antiapoptotic function that protects dopamine neurons.

PINK1.   A third autosomal recessive form of PD is that due to mutations in *PINK1* (PTEN-induced kinase) (PARK6) (159). Valente and colleagues first mapped PARK6 in a Sicilian family to chromosome 1p35-p36 (160). Sequence analysis of candidate genes led to the identification of a G309D substitution mutation at a highly conserved position in a putative kinase domain in a Spanish family and another substitution resulting in truncation of 145 C-terminal amino acids in two Italian families (159). These investigators showed that the putative kinase is localized to mitochondria and protects SH-SY5Y cells from proteasome inhibitor–induced apoptosis (159). This protective effect was abrogated by the G309D mutation. The ability of wild-type PINK1 to protect from apoptotic stimulus has been confirmed by Petit and colleagues, who showed that both basal and staurosporine-induced apoptosis in SH-SY5Y cells was reduced by wild-type PINK1 (161). In addition, overexpression of PINK1 diminished both basal and staurosporine-induced activation of caspase-3. These antiapoptotic effects of

PINK1 were abrogated by disease-causing mutations (161). Deng et al. used the converse approach to downregulate PINK1 expression by siRNA, demonstrating that diminished expression of PINK1 in SH-SY5Y cells decreased their viability due to increased apoptosis (162). Thus, this preliminary evidence would suggest that PINK1, like parkin and DJ-1, is able to play an antiapoptotic role.

Evidence for Programmed Cell Death in Human Postmortem Parkinson's Disease Brain

Initial reports of apoptotic morphology or positive DNA nick-end labeling in human PD brains generated controversy, which remains unresolved. Mochizuki and colleagues (163) reported the presence of DNA nick-end labeling in the SN of PD brains and suggested that it was due to apoptosis. However, it was subsequently realized that positive DNA nick-end labeling alone (in the absence of apoptotic morphology) cannot be taken as specific evidence for apoptosis because such labeling can also be observed in necrotic cell death (164). Anglade et al. reported ultrastructural evidence for both autophagy and apoptosis in the brains of a few PD patients (24). The apoptotic features, however, were not well defined, and the phenotype of the cells as dopaminergic was not certain. Additional investigations, however, have provided more support for the possibility of apoptotic death in dopamine neurons of the PD brain. Tompkins and coworkers used a nuclear dye (propidium iodide) to demonstrate clear examples of apoptotic chromatin clumps with colabeling for DNA nick-end labeling in neuromelanin-containing SN neurons of patients with PD and diffuse Lewy body disease (165). Additional examples of such colabeling of apoptotic nuclear chromatin clumps for DNA nick-end labeling in neuromelanin-containing neurons in the SN of PD patients were provided by Tatton (166, 167). Other investigators, however, have been unable to confirm these observations (168, 169).

There are many possible reasons for these mixed results. Apoptosis is a short-lived process, and it is likely to be exceedingly difficult to identify in chronic neurologic diseases in which neuron death occurs gradually over years. In addition, as discussed earlier, apoptosis is only one of the known morphologies of PCD (16) and its absence in tissue does not exclude a possible role for PCD mechanisms. Ultrastructural analysis is required to identify these cell death morphologies, and it is exceedingly difficult to achieve a high-quality analysis in postmortem material. Thus, controversies and mixed results from studies of human postmortem material, based on purely morphologic assessment, are not unexpected.

Assessment of the possible role of PCD in human PD has been assisted by the development of antibodies for immunohistochemical demonstration of the components of PCD pathways in postmortem tissue sections, particularly

the activated forms of the caspases. Using an antibody specific for the activated form of caspase-3, Hartmann et al. demonstrated staining in the neuromelanin-containing neurons of the SN in PD brain (170). Interpretation of this result was somewhat complicated, however, by the appearance of similar staining in nondiseased controls, which was attributed to premortem agonal hypoxia. These investigators noted, however, a higher percentage of activated caspase-3–positive profiles in the PD brain when normalized for the number of remaining melanized (i.e., dopaminergic) neurons. These observations receive support from those of Tatton (167), who identified activated caspase-3 staining in neuromelanin-containing cells in PD SN and virtually none in controls.

There is also evidence for a role for activators of the extrinsic pathway of PCD in postmortem studies of PD brain. Mogi and coworkers demonstrated by immunoassay an approximately 4-fold increase in tumor necrosis factor alpha (TNF-α) in the caudate/putamen of PD patients in comparison to age-matched controls (171). They observed a similar degree of increase in lumbar cerebrospinal fluid. At a cellular level, Boka and colleagues observed TNF-α–positive glia in the SN of PD patients but not in controls (172). In keeping with a possible functional role for TNF-α signaling in human brain, they observed positive immunostaining for tumor necrosis factor receptor (TNFR) in neuromelanized neurons of the SNpc in both PD patients and controls. Studies by Mogi and colleagues have also suggested a role for Fas in PD pathogenesis. These investigators have demonstrated increases in the soluble form of Fas in the PD caudate/putamen (173). In relation to Fas signaling, Hartmann et al. have observed that the adaptor protein for the Fas receptor (Fas-associated death domain, or FADD) is expressed in melanized dopaminergic neurons of the midbrain, and its relative abundance of expression correlates with greater degree of vulnerability among dopamine neurons to degeneration in PD (174). The SNpc, the most vulnerable region, showed a higher percentage of FADD-positive profiles than the ventral tegmental area and central gray substance, which showed few. These observations suggesting that TNF-α and Fas may play roles in the neurodegeneration of PD are supported by the finding that there is an increase in the number of melanized SN neurons expressing the activated form of caspase-8, demonstrated with an antibody specific for the cleaved form, in PD brains as compared to age-matched controls (175). Viswanath et al. (73) made a similar observation. In conclusion, there are many observations in human postmortem material to suggest a role for the extrinsic PCD pathway in the pathogenesis of PD.

In addition to observations on the activated forms of the caspases, investigators have demonstrated alterations in the cellular expression of the proapoptotic protein Bax in PD brains. Hartmann and colleagues demonstrated that while there was no change in the percentage of Bax-positive profiles among neuromelanin-containing SN neurons of PD patients in comparison to controls, there was about a 3.5-fold increase in the percent of Bax-positive profiles among Lewy body–containing neurons in comparison to non-Lewy body–containing neuromelanin pigmented neurons (176). These observations suggest that Bax may be more highly expressed in "sick" Lewy body–positive dopamine neurons. Unlike Hartmann et al, Tatton observed a greater number of Bax-positive profiles in PD SN (167).

An observation supporting a possible role for JNK/c-jun signaling in human PD was made by Hunot et al., who noted that nuclear translocation of c-jun could be identified in neuromelanin-containing SN neurons of PD patients and not in controls (96).

CONCLUSIONS

In summary, there is much evidence from neurotoxin models of dopamine neuronal death, genetic studies, and human postmortem studies to suggest that the molecular pathways of PCD play a role in human PD. Nevertheless, the evidence cannot be considered definitive or complete. The case for a role for PCD pathways in human PD will be strengthened by the development of animal models that are firmly based on known causes of the disease in humans, such as genetic causes, and in which dopamine neuronal death occurs. While neurotoxin models have been highly useful in identifying the PCD pathways that may play a role in the disease, they remain of uncertain direct relevance to the human condition. In addition, the case for PCD in human PD will be strengthened by broader studies by additional investigators with reagents for known upstream mediators of PCD. And finally, perhaps the most compelling and gratifying support for the PCD hypothesis in PD will derive from clinical therapeutic trials with specific inhibitors of PCD pathways, should they prove to be neuroprotective and prevent the progression of the disease.

Acknowledgments

The author is supported by the NIH (NS26836, NS38370), DAMD17-03-1-0492, and The Parkinson's Disease Foundation.

References

1. Glucksmann A. Cell deaths in normal vertebrate ontogeny. *Biol Rev* 1951; 26:59–86.
2. Ernst M. Ueber Untergang von Zellen wahrend der normalen Entwicklung bei Wirbeltieren. *Zeitschr Anat Entw Gesch* 1926; 79:228–262.
3. Hamburger V, Levi-Montalcini R. Proliferation, differentiation and degeneration in the spinal ganglia of the chick embryo under normal and experimental conditions. *J Exp Zool* 1949; 111:457–502.
4. Hamburger V. History of the discovery of neuronal death in embryos. *J Neurobiol* 1992; 23:1116–1123.
5. Clarke PGH. Neuronal death in the development of the vertebrate nervous system. *Trends Neurosci* 1985; 8:345–349.
6. Barde YA. Trophic factors and neuronal survival. *Neuron* 1989; 2:1525–1534.
7. Levi-Montalcini R. The nerve growth factor 35 years later. *Science* 1987; 237:1154–1162.
8. Kerr JFR, Wyllie AH, Currie AR. Apoptosis: A basic biological phenomenon with wide-ranging implications in tissue kinetics. *Br J Cancer* 1972; 26:239–257.
9. Ellis RE, Yuan J, Horvitz HR. Mechanisms and functions of cell death. *Annu Rev Cell Biol* 1991; 7:663–698.
10. Putcha GV, Johnson EM Jr. Men are but worms: Neuronal cell death in *C elegans* and vertebrates. *Cell Death Diff* 2004; 11:38–48.
11. Martin DP, Schmidt RE, DiStefano P, et al. Inhibitors of protein synthesis and RNA synthesis prevent neuronal death caused by nerve growth factor deprivation. *J Cell Biol* 1988; 106:829–844.
12. Oppenheim RW, Prevette D, Tytell M, Homma S. Naturally occurring and induced neuronal death in the chick embryo in vivo requires protein and RNA synthesis: Evidence for the role of cell death genes. *Dev Biol* 1990; 138:104–113.
13. White K, Grether ME, Abrams JM, et al. Genetic control of programmed cell death in *Drosophila. Science* 1994; 264:677–683.
14. Rukenstein A, Rydel RE, Greene LA. Multiple agents rescue PC12 cells from serum-free cell death by translation- and transcription-independent mechanisms. *J Neurosci* 1991; 11:2552–2563.
15. Kerr JFR, Gobe GC, Winterford CM, Harmon BV. Anatomical methods in cell death. In: Schwartz LM, Osborne BA (eds). *Methods in Cell Biology: Cell Death*. New York: Academic Press, 1995:1–27.
16. Clarke PGH. Developmental cell death: morphological diversity and multiple mechanisms. *Anat Embryol* 1990; 181:195–213.
17. Klionsky DJ, Emr SD. Autophagy as a regulated pathway of cellular degradation. *Science* 2000; 290:1717–1721.
18. Shintani T, Klionsky DJ. Autophagy in health and disease: A double-edged sword. *Science* 2004; 306:990–995.
19. Lum JJ, Bauer DE, Kong M, et al. Growth factor regulation of autophagy and cell survival in the absence of apoptosis. *Cell* 2005; 120:237–248.
20. Kuma A, Hatano M, Matsui M, et al. The role of autophagy during the early neonatal starvation period. *Nature* 2004; 432:1032–1036.
21. Mizushima N, Yoshimori T, Ohsumi Y. Role of the Apg12 conjugation system in mammalian autophagy. *Int J Biochem Cell Biol* 2003; 35:553–561.
22. Larsen KE, Fon EA, Hastings TG, et al. Methamphetamine-induced degeneration of dopaminergic neurons involves autophagy and upregulation of dopamine synthesis. *J Neurosci* 2002; 22:8951–8960.
23. Stefanis L, Larsen KE, Rideout HJ, et al. Expression of A53T mutant but not wild-type alpha-synuclein in PC12 cells induces alterations of the ubiquitin-dependent degradation system, loss of dopamine release, and autophagic cell death. *J Neurosci* 2001; 21:9549–9560.
24. Anglade P, Vyas S, Javoy-Agid F, et al. Apoptosis and autophagy in nigral neurons of patients with Parkinson's disease. *Histol Histopathol* 1997; 12:25–31.
25. Ashkenazi A, Dixit VM. Death receptors: Signaling and modulation. *Science* 1998; 281:1305–1308.
26. Yang X, Khosravi-Far R, Chang HY, Baltimore D. Daxx, a novel Fas-binding protein that activates JNK and apoptosis. *Cell* 1997; 89:1067–1076.
27. Chang HY, Nishitoh H, Yang X, Ichijo H, Baltimore D. Activation of apoptosis signal-regulating kinase 1 (ASK1) by the adapter protein Daxx. *Science* 1998; 281:1860–1863.
28. Mori K. Tripartite management of unfolded proteins in the endoplasmic reticulum. *Cell* 2000; 101:451–454.
29. Zinszner H, Kuroda M, Wang X, et al. CHOP is implicated in programmed cell death in response to impaired function of the endoplasmic reticulum. *Genes Dev* 1998; 12:982–995.
30. Marciniak SJ, Yun CY, Oyadomari S, et al. CHOP induces death by promoting protein synthesis and oxidation in the stressed endoplasmic reticulum. *Genes Dev* 2004; 18:3066–3077.
31. Ishikawa A, Tsuji S. Clinical analysis of 17 patients in 12 Japanese families with autosomal-recessive type juvenile parkinsonism. *Neurology* 1996; 47:160–166.
32. Kitada T, Asakawa S, Hattori N, et al. Mutations in the parkin gene cause autosomal recessive juvenile parkinsonism. *Nature* 1998; 392:605–608.
33. Shimura H, Hattori N, Kubo S, et al. Familial Parkinson disease gene product, parkin, is a ubiquitin-protein ligase. *Nat Genet* 2000; 25:302–305.
34. Ciechanover A. The ubiquitin-proteasome pathway: On protein death and cell life. *EMBO J* 1998; 17:7151–7160.
35. Imai Y, Soda M, Takahashi R. Parkin suppresses unfolded protein stress-induced cell death through its E3 ubiquitin-protein ligase activity. *J Biol Chem* 2000; 275:35661–35664.
36. Imai Y, Soda M, Inoue H, et al. An unfolded putative transmembrane polypeptide, which can lead to endoplasmic reticulum stress, is a substrate of Parkin. *Cell* 2001; 105:891–902.

37. Scorrano L, Korsmeyer SJ. Mechanisms of cytochrome c release by proapoptotic BCL-2 family members. *Biochem Biophys Res Commun* 2003; 304:437–444.

38. Adams JM, Cory S. The Bcl-2 protein family: Arbiters of cell survival. *Science* 1998; 281:1322–1326.

39. Wei MC, Zong WX, Cheng EH, et al. Proapoptotic BAX and BAK: A requisite gateway to mitochondrial dysfunction and death. *Science* 2001; 292:727–730.

40. Datta SR, Katsov A, Hu L, et al. 14-3-3 proteins and survival kinases cooperate to inactivate BAD by BH3 domain phosphorylation. *Mol Cell* 2000; 6:41–51.

41. Thornberry NA, Lazebnik Y. Caspases: Enemies within. *Science* 1998; 281:1312–1316.

42. Riedl SJ, Shi Y. Molecular mechanisms of caspase regulation during apoptosis. *Nat Rev Mol Cell Biol* 2004; 5:897–907.

43. Shi Y. Mechanisms of caspase activation and inhibition during apoptosis. *Mol Cell* 2002; 9:459–470.

44. Chai J, Du C, Wu JW, et al. Structural and biochemical basis of apoptotic activation by Smac/DIABLO. *Nature* 2000; 406:855–862.

45. Susin SA, Lorenzo HK, Zamzami N, et al. Molecular characterization of mitochondrial apoptosis-inducing factor. *Nature* 1999; 397:441–446.

46. Yu SW, Wang H, Poitras MF, et al. Mediation of poly(ADP-ribose) polymerase-1-dependent cell death by apoptosis-inducing factor. *Science* 2002; 297:259–263.

47. Silva RM, Kuan CY, Rakic P, Burke RE. Mixed lineage kinase-c-jun N-terminal kinase signaling pathway: A new therapeutic target in Parkinson's disease. *Mov Disord* 2005; 20:653–664.

48. Wang LH, Besirli CG, Johnson EM Jr. Mixed-lineage kinases: A target for the prevention of neurodegeneration. *Annu Rev Pharmacol Toxicol* 2004; 44:451–474.

49. Whitfield J, Neame SJ, Paquet L, Bernard O, Ham J. Dominant-negative c-Jun promotes neuronal survival by reducing BIM expression and inhibiting mitochondrial cytochrome c release. *Neuron* 2001; 29:629–643.

50. Putcha GV, Moulder KL, Golden JP, et al. Induction of BIM, a proapoptotic BH3-only BCL-2 family member, is critical for neuronal apoptosis. *Neuron* 2001; 29:615–628.

51. Lei K, Davis RJ. JNK phosphorylation of Bim-related members of the Bcl2 family induces Bax-dependent apoptosis. *Proc Natl Acad Sci USA* 2003; 100:2432–2437.

52. Donovan N, Becker EB, Konishi Y, Bonni A. JNK phosphorylation and activation of BAD couples the stress-activated signaling pathway to the cell death machinery. *J Biol Chem* 2002; 277:40944–40949.

53. Janec E, Burke RE. Naturally occurring cell death during postnatal development of the substantia nigra of the rat. *Mol Cell Neurosci* 1993; 4:30–35.

54. Oo TF, Burke RE. The time course of developmental cell death in phenotypically defined dopaminergic neurons of the substantia nigra. *Dev Brain Res* 1997; 98:191–196.

55. Burke RE. Ontogenic cell death in the nigrostriatal system. *Cell Tissue Res* 2004; 318:63–72.

56. Ganguly A, Oo TF, Rzhetskaya M, et al. CEP11004, a novel inhibitor of the mixed lineage kinases, suppresses apoptotic death in dopamine neurons of the substantia nigra induced by 6-hydroxydopamine. *J Neurochem* 2004; 88:469–480.

57. Jeon BS, Kholodilov NG, Oo TF, et al. Activation of caspase-3 in developmental models of programmed cell death in neurons of the substantia nigra. *J Neurochem* 1999; 73:322–333.

58. Oo TF, Siman R, Burke RE. Distinct nuclear and cytoplasmic localization of caspase cleavage products in two models of induced apoptotic death in dopamine neurons of the substantia nigra. *Exp Neurol* 2002; 175:1–9.

59. Jackson-Lewis V, Vila M, Djaldetti R, et al. Developmental cell death in dopaminergic neurons of the substantia nigra of mice. *J Comp Neurol* 2000; 424:476–488.

60. Kostrzewa RM, Jacobowitz DM. Pharmacological actions of 6-hydroxydopamine. *Pharmacol Rev* 1974; 26:199–288.

61. Ungerstedt U. 6-Hydroxy-dopamine induced degeneration of central monoamine neurons. *Eur J Pharmacol* 1968; 5:107–110.

62. Curtius HC, Wolfensberger M, Steinmann B, et al. Mass fragmentography of dopamine and 6-hydroxydopamine. Application to the determination of dopamine in human brain biopsies from the caudate nucleus. *J Chromatogr* 1974; 99:529–540.

63. Marti MJ, James CJ, Oo TF, et al. Early developmental destruction of terminals in the striatal target induces apoptosis in dopamine neurons of the substantia nigra. *J Neurosci* 1997; 17:2030–2039.

64. Marti MJ, Saura J, Burke RE, et al. Striatal 6-hydroxydopamine induces apoptosis of nigral neurons in the adult rat. *Brain Res* 2002; 958:185–191.

65. Silva RM, Ries V, Oo TF, et al. CHOP/GADD153 is a mediator of apoptotic death in substantia nigra dopamine neurons in an in vivo neurotoxin model of parkinsonism. *J Neurochem* 2005; 95:974–986.

66. Jeon BS, Jackson-Lewis V, Burke RE. 6-Hydroxydopamine lesion of the rat substantia nigra: Time course and morphology of cell death. *Neurodegeneration* 1995; 4:131–137.

67. Zuch CL, Nordstroem VK, Briedrick LA, et al. Time course of degenerative alterations in nigral dopaminergic neurons following a 6-hydroxydopamine lesion. *J Comp Neurol* 2000; 427:440–454.

68. He Y, Lee T, Leong SK. 6-Hydroxydopamine induced apoptosis of dopaminergic cells in the rat substantia nigra. *Brain Res* 2000; 858:163–166.

69. Jackson-Lewis V, Jakowec M, Burke RE, Przedborski S. Time course and morphology of dopaminergic neuronal death caused by the neurotoxin 1-methyl-4-phenyl-1,2,3,6, -tetrahydropyridine. *Neurodegeneration* 1995; 4:257–269.

70. Hassouna I, Wickert H, Zimmermann M, Gillardon F. Increase in bax expression in substantia-nigra following 1- methyl-4-phenyl-1,2,3,6- tetrahydropyridine (MPTP) treatment of mice. *Neurosci Lett* 1996; 204:85–88.

71. Yang L, Matthews RT, Schulz JB, et al. 1-Methyl-4-phenyl-1,2,3,6-tetrahydropyride neurotoxicity is attenuated in mice overexpressing Bcl-2. *J Neurosci* 1998; 18: 8145–8152.

72. Kane DJ, Sarafian TA, Anton R, et al. Bcl 2 inhibition of neural death: Decreased generation of reactive oxygen species. *Science* 1993; 262:1274–1277.

73. Viswanath V, Wu Y, Boonplueang R, et al. Caspase-9 activation results in downstream caspase-8 activation and bid cleavage in 1-methyl-4-phenyl-1,2,3,6-tetrahydropyridine-induced Parkinson's disease. *J Neurosci* 2001; 21:9519–9528.

74. Strasser A, O'Connor L, Dixit VM. Apoptosis signaling. *Annu Rev Biochem* 2000; 69:217–245.

75. Furuya T, Hayakawa H, Yamada M, et al. Caspase-11 mediates inflammatory dopaminergic cell death in the 1-methyl-4-phenyl-1,2,3,6-tetrahydropyridine mouse model of Parkinson's disease. *J Neurosci* 2004; 24:1865–1872.

76. Tatton NA, Kish SJ. In situ detection of apoptotic nuclei in the substantia nigra compacta of 1-methyl-4-phenyl-1,2,3,6-tetrahydropyridine-treated mice using terminal deoxynucleotidyl transferase labelling and acridine orange. *Neuroscience* 1997; 77:1037–1048.

77. Offen D, Beart PM, Cheung NS, et al. Transgenic mice expressing human Bcl-2 in their neurons are resistant to 6-hydroxydopamine and 1-methyl-4-phenyl-1,2,3, 6-tetrahydropyridine neurotoxicity. *Proc Natl Acad Sci USA* 1998; 95:5789–5794.

78. Vila M, Jackson-Lewis V, Vukosavic S, et al. Bax ablation prevents dopaminergic neurodegeneration in the 1-methyl- 4-phenyl-1,2,3,6-tetrahydropyridine mouse model of Parkinson's disease. *Proc Natl Acad Sci USA* 2001; 98:2837–2842.

79. Mochizuki H, Hayakawa H, Migita M, et al. An AAV-derived Apaf-1 dominant negative inhibitor prevents MPTP toxicity as antiapoptotic gene therapy for Parkinson's disease. *Proc Natl Acad Sci USA* 2001; 98:10918–10923.

80. Turmel H, Hartmann A, Parain K, et al. Caspase-3 activation in 1-methyl-4-phenyl-1,2,3,6-tetrahydropyridine (MPTP)-treated mice. *Mov Disord* 2001; 16:185–189.

81. Betarbet R, Sherer TB, MacKenzie G, et al. Chronic systemic pesticide exposure reproduces features of Parkinson's disease. *Nat Neurosci* 2000; 3:1301–1306.

82. Sherer TB, Betarbet R, Stout AK, et al. An in vitro model of Parkinson's disease: Linking mitochondrial impairment to altered alpha-synuclein metabolism and oxidative damage. *J Neurosci* 2002; 22:7006–7015.

83. Jenkins R, Hunt SP. Long-term increase in the levels of c-jun mRNA and jun protein-like immunoreactivity in motor and sensory neurons following axon damage. *Neurosci Lett* 1991; 129:107–110.

84. Jenkins R, O'Shea R, Thomas KL, Hunt SP. c-jun expression in substantia nigra neurons following striatal 6-hydroxydopamine lesions in the rat. *Neuroscience* 1993; 53: 447–455.

85. Leah JD, Herdegen T, Murashov A, et al. Expression of immediate early gene proteins following axotomy and inhibition of axonal transport in the rat central nervous system. *Neuroscience* 1993; 57:53–66.

86. Sauer H, Oertel WH. Progressive degeneration of nigrostriatal dopamine neurons following intrastriatal terminal lesions with 6 hydroxydopamine: A combined retrograde tracing and immunocytochemical study in the rat. *Neuroscience* 1994; 59:401–415.

87. Messina A, Jaworowski A, Bell C. Detection of jun but not fos protein during developmental cell death in sympathetic neurons. *J Comp Neurol* 1996; 372:544–550.

88. Ferrer I, Olive M, Ribera J, Planas AM. Naturally occurring (programmed) and radiation-induced apoptosis are associated with selective c-jun expression in the developing rat brain. *Eur J Neurosci* 1996; 8:1286–1298.

89. Ferrer I, Olive M, Blanco R, Cinos C, Planas AM. Selective c-Jun overexpression is associated with ionizing radiation-induced apoptosis in the developing cerebellum of the rat. *Mol Brain Res* 1996; 38:91–100.

90. Herdegen T, Claret FX, Kallunki T, et al. Lasting N-terminal phosphorylation of c-Jun and activation of c-Jun N- terminal kinases after neuronal injury. *J Neurosci* 1998; 18:5124–5135.

91. Gavrieli Y, Sherman Y, Ben-Sasson SA. Identification of programmed cell death in situ via specific labeling of nuclear DNA fragmentation. *J Cell Biol* 1992; 119:493–501.

92. Oo TF, Henchcliffe C, James D, Burke RE. Expression of c-fos, c-jun, and c-jun N-terminal kinase (JNK) in a developmental model of induced apoptotic death in neurons of the substantia nigra. *J Neurochem* 1999; 72:557–564.

93. Crocker SJ, Lamba WR, Smith PD, et al. c-Jun mediates axotomy-induced dopamine neuron death in vivo. *Proc Natl Acad Sci USA* 2001; 98:13385–13390.

94. Xia XG, Harding T, Weller M, et al. Gene transfer of the JNK interacting protein-1 protects dopaminergic neurons in the MPTP model of Parkinson's disease. *Proc Natl Acad Sci USA* 2001; 98:10433–10438.

95. Kyriakis JM, Avruch J. Mammalian mitogen-activated protein kinase signal transduction pathways activated by stress and inflammation. *Physiol Rev* 2001; 81:807–869.

96. Hunot S, Vila M, Teismann P, et al. JNK-mediated induction of cyclooxygenase 2 is required for neurodegeneration in a mouse model of Parkinson's disease. *Proc Natl Acad Sci USA* 2004; 101:665–670.

97. Teismann P, Tieu K, Choi DK, et al. Cyclooxygenase-2 is instrumental in Parkinson's disease neurodegeneration. *Proc Natl Acad Sci USA* 2003; 100:5473–5478.

98. Murakata C, Kaneko M, Gessner G, et al. Mixed lineage kinase activity of indolocarbazole analogues. *Bioorg Med Chem Lett* 2002; 12:147–150.

99. Saporito MS, Brown EM, Miller MS, Carswell S. CEP-1347/KT-7515, an inhibitor of c-jun N-terminal kinase activation, attenuates the 1-methyl-4-phenyl tetrahydropyridine-mediated loss of nigrostriatal dopaminergic neurons In vivo. *J Pharmacol Exp Ther* 1999; 288:421–427.

100. Saporito MS, Thomas BA, Scott RW. MPTP activates c-Jun NH(2)-terminal kinase (JNK) and its upstream regulatory kinase MKK4 in nigrostriatal neurons in vivo. *J Neurochem* 2000; 75:1200–1208.

101. Shen J. Protein kinases linked to the pathogenesis of Parkinson's disease. *Neuron* 2004; 44:575–577.

102. Polymeropoulos MH, Lavedan C, Leroy E, et al. Mutation in the α-synuclein gene identified in families with Parkinson's disease. *Science* 1997; 276:2045–2047.

103. Kruger R, Kuhn W, Muller T, et al. Ala30Pro mutation in the gene encoding alpha-synuclein in Parkinson's disease (letter). *Nat Genet* 1998; 18:106–108.

104. Zarranz JJ, Alegre J, Gomez-Esteban JC, et al. The new mutation, E46K, of alpha-synuclein causes Parkinson and Lewy body dementia. *Ann Neurol* 2004; 55:164–173.

105. Singleton AB, Farrer M, Johnson J, et al. Alpha-synuclein locus triplication causes Parkinson's disease. *Science* 2003; 302:841.

106. Iwai A, Yoshimoto M, Masliah E, Saitoh T. Non-Aβ component of Alzheimer's disease amyloid (NAC) is amyloidogenic. *Biochemistry* 1995; 34:10139–10145.

107. Han H, Weinreb PH, Lansbury PTJ. The core Alzheimer's peptide NAC forms amyloid fibrils which seed and are seeded by beta-amyloid: Is NAC a common trigger or target in neurodegenerative disease? *Chem Biol* 1995; 2:163–169.

108. El-Agnaf OM, Jakes R, Curran MD, Wallace A. Effects of the mutations Ala30 to Pro and Ala53 to Thr on the physical and morphological properties of alpha-synuclein protein implicated in Parkinson's disease. *FEBS Lett* 1998; 440:67–70.

109. Conway KA, Harper JD, Lansbury PT. Accelerated in vitro fibril formation by a mutant alpha-synuclein linked to early-onset Parkinson disease. *Nat Med* 1998; 4:1318–1320.

110. Spillantini MG, Schmidt ML, Lee VMY, et al. α-Synuclein in Lewy bodies. *Nature* 1997; 388:839–840.

111. Cookson MR. The biochemistry of Parkinson's disease. *Annu Rev Biochem* 2005; 74:29–52.

112. Masliah E, Rockenstein E, Veinbergs I, et al. Dopaminergic loss and inclusion body formation in alpha-synuclein mice: Implications for neurodegenerative disorders. *Science* 2000; 287:1265–1269.

113. Feany MB, Bender WW. A *Drosophila* model of Parkinson's disease. *Nature* 2000; 404:394–398.

114. da Costa CA, Ancolio K, Checler F. Wild-type but not Parkinson's disease-related ala-53—Thr mutant alpha-synuclein protects neuronal cells from apoptotic stimuli. *J Biol Chem* 2000; 275:24065–24069.

115. da Costa CA, Paitel E, Vincent B, Checler F. Alpha-synuclein lowers p53-dependent apoptotic response of neuronal cells. Abolishment by 6-hydroxydopamine and implication for Parkinson's disease. *J Biol Chem* 2002; 277:50980–50984.

116. Hashimoto M, Hsu LJ, Rockenstein E, et al. Alpha-synuclein protects against oxidative stress via inactivation of the c-Jun N-terminal kinase stress-signaling pathway in neuronal cells. *J Biol Chem* 2002; 277:11465–11472.

117. Li W, Lee MK. Antiapoptotic property of human alpha-synuclein in neuronal cell lines is associated with the inhibition of caspase-3 but not caspase-9 activity. *J Neurochem* 2005; 93:1542–1550.

118. Machida Y, Chiba T, Takayanagi A, et al. Common anti-apoptotic roles of parkin and alpha-synuclein in human dopaminergic cells. *Biochem Biophys Res Commun* 2005; 332:233–240.

119. Kholodilov NG, Neystat M, Oo TF, et al. Increased expression of rat synuclein1 in the substantia nigra pars compacta identified by differential display in a model of developmental target injury. *J Neurochem* 1999; 73:2586–2599.

120. Stefanis L, Kholodilov N, Rideout HJ, et al. Synuclein-1 is selectively up-regulated in response to nerve growth factor treatment in PC12 cells. *J Neurochem* 2001; 76: 1165–1176.

121. Zhou W, Hurlbert MS, Schaack J, et al. Overexpression of human alpha-synuclein causes dopamine neuron death in rat primary culture and immortalized mesencephalon-derived cells. *Brain Res* 2000; 866:33–43.

122. Manning-Bog AB, McCormack AL, Purisai MG, et al. Alpha-synuclein overexpression protects against paraquat-induced neurodegeneration. *J Neurosci* 2003; 23: 3095–3099.

123. Dauer WT, Kholodilov N, Vila M, et al. Resistance of α-synuclein null mice to the parkinsonian neurotoxin MPTP. *Proc Natl Acad Sci USA* 2002; 99:14524–14529.

124. Robertson DC, Schmidt O, Ninkina N, et al. Developmental loss and resistance to MPTP toxicity of dopaminergic neurones in substantia nigra pars compacta of gamma-synuclein, alpha-synuclein and double alpha/gamma-synuclein null mutant mice. *J Neurochem* 2004; 89:1126–1136.

125. Drolet RE, Behrouz B, Lookingland KJ, Goudreau JL. Mice lacking alpha-synuclein have an attenuated loss of striatal dopamine following prolonged chronic MPTP administration. *Neurotoxicology* 2004; 25:761–769.

126. Zhang Y, Gao J, Chung KK, et al. Parkin functions as an E2-dependent ubiquitin- protein ligase and promotes the degradation of the synaptic vesicle-associated protein, CDCrel-1. *Proc Natl Acad Sci USA* 2000; 97:13354–13359.

127. Shimura H, Schlossmacher MG, Hattori N, et al. Ubiquitination of a new form of alpha-synuclein by parkin from human brain: Implications for Parkinson's disease. *Science* 2001; 293:263–269.

128. Chung KKK, Zhang Y, Lim KL, et al. Parkin ubiquitinates the α-synuclein-interacting protein, synphilin-1: Implications for Lewy-body formation in Parkinson disease. *Nat Med* 2001; 7:1144–1150.

129. Staropoli JF, McDermott C, Martinat C, et al. Parkin is a component of an SCF-like ubiquitin ligase complex and protects postmitotic neurons from kainate excitotoxicity. *Neuron* 2003; 37:735–749.

130. Ren Y, Zhao J, Feng J. Parkin binds to alpha/beta tubulin and increases their ubiquitination and degradation. *J Neurosci* 2003; 23:3316–3324.

131. Ko HS, von Coelln R, Sriram SR, et al. Accumulation of the authentic parkin substrate aminoacyl-tRNA synthetase cofactor, p38/JTV-1, leads to catecholaminergic cell death. *J Neurosci* 2005; 25:7968–7978.

132. Mehmet H. Caspases find a new place to hide. *Nature* 2000; 403:29–30.

133. Ryu EJ, Harding HP, Angelastro JM, et al. Endoplasmic reticulum stress and the unfolded protein response in cellular models of Parkinson's disease. *J Neurosci* 2002; 22:10690–10698.

134. Holtz WA, O'Malley KL. Parkinsonian mimetics induce aspects of unfolded protein response in death of dopaminergic neurons. *J Biol Chem* 2003; 278:19367–19377.

135. Greene LA, Biswas SC, Liu DX. Cell cycle molecules and vertebrate neuron death: E2F at the hub. *Cell Death Differ* 2004; 11:49–60.

136. Darios F, Corti O, Lucking CB, et al. Parkin prevents mitochondrial swelling and cytochrome c release in mitochondria-dependent cell death. *Hum Mol Genet* 2003; 12:517–526.

137. Jiang H, Ren Y, Zhao J, Feng J. Parkin protects human dopaminergic neuroblastoma cells against dopamine-induced apoptosis. *Hum Mol Genet* 2004; 13:1745–1754.

138. Jimenez DR, Moreno S, Garcia-Ospina G, et al. Autosomal recessive juvenile parkinsonism Cys212Tyr mutation in parkin renders lymphocytes susceptible to dopamine- and iron-mediated apoptosis. *Mov Disord* 2004; 19:324–330.

139. Greene JC, Whitworth AJ, Kuo I, et al. Mitochondrial pathology and apoptotic muscle degeneration in *Drosophila* parkin mutants. *Proc Natl Acad Sci USA* 2003; 100:4078–4083.

140. Pesah Y, Pham T, Burgess H, et al. *Drosophila* parkin mutants have decreased mass and cell size and increased sensitivity to oxygen radical stress. *Development* 2004; 131:2183–2194.

141. Cha GH, Kim S, Park J, et al. Parkin negatively regulates JNK pathway in the dopaminergic neurons of *Drosophila*. *Proc Natl Acad Sci USA* 2005; 102:10345–10350.

142. Goldberg MS, Fleming SM, Palacino JJ, et al. Parkin-deficient mice exhibit nigrostriatal deficits but not loss of dopaminergic neurons. *J Biol Chem* 2003; 278:43628–43635.

143. von Coelln R, Thomas B, Savitt JM, et al. Loss of locus coeruleus neurons and reduced startle in parkin null mice. *Proc Natl Acad Sci USA* 2004; 101:10744–10749.

144. Bonifati V, Rizzu P, van Baren MJ, et al. Mutations in the DJ-1 gene associated with autosomal recessive early-onset parkinsonism. *Science* 2003; 299:256–259.

145. Nagakubo D, Taira T, Kitaura H, et al. DJ-1, a novel oncogene which transforms mouse NIH3T3 cells in cooperation with *ras*. *Biochem Biophys Res Commun* 1997; 231:509–513.

146. Mitsumoto A, Nakagawa Y. DJ-1 is an indicator for endogenous reactive oxygen species elicited by endotoxin. *Free Radic Res* 2001; 35:885–893.

147. Yokota T, Sugawara K, Ito K, et al. Down regulation of DJ-1 enhances cell death by oxidative stress, ER stress, and proteasome inhibition. *Biochem Biophys Res Commun* 2003; 312:1342–1348.

148. Xu J, Zhong N, Wang H, et al. The Parkinson's disease-associated DJ-1 protein is a transcriptional co-activator that protects against neuronal apoptosis. *Hum Mol Genet* 2005; 14:1231–1241.

149. Junn E, Taniguchi H, Jeong BS, et al. Interaction of DJ-1 with Daxx inhibits apoptosis signal-regulating kinase 1 activity and cell death. *Proc Natl Acad Sci USA* 2005; 102:9691–9696.

150. Choi C, Benveniste EN. Fas ligand/Fas system in the brain: Regulator of immune and apoptotic responses. *Brain Res Brain Res Rev* 2004; 44:65–81.

151. Yang Y, Gehrke S, Haque ME, et al. Inactivation of *Drosophila* DJ-1 leads to impairments of oxidative stress response and phosphatidylinositol 3-kinase/Akt signaling. *Proc Natl Acad Sci USA* 2005; 102:13670–13675.

152. Datta SR, Brunet A, Greenberg ME. Cellular survival: A play in three Akts. *Genes Dev* 1999; 13:2905–2927.

153. Downward J. PI 3-kinase, Akt and cell survival. *Semin Cell Dev Biol* 2004; 15:177–182.

154. Hanada M, Feng J, Hemmings BA. Structure, regulation and function of PKB/AKT: A major therapeutic target. *Biochim Biophys Acta* 2004; 1697:3–16.

155. Kim RH, Peters M, Jang Y, et al. DJ-1, a novel regulator of the tumor suppressor PTEN. *Cancer Cell* 2005; 7:263–273.

156. Goldberg MS, Pisani A, Haburcak M, et al. Nigrostriatal dopaminergic deficits and hypokinesia caused by inactivation of the familial Parkinsonism-linked gene DJ-1. *Neuron* 2005; 45:489–496.

157. Chen L, Cagniard B, Mathews T, et al. Age-dependent motor deficits and dopaminergic dysfunction in DJ-1 null mice. *J Biol Chem* 2005; 280:21418–21426.

158. Kim RH, Smith PD, Aleyasin H, et al. Hypersensitivity of DJ-1-deficient mice to 1-methyl-4-phenyl-1,2,3,6-tetrahydropyridine (MPTP) and oxidative stress. *Proc Natl Acad Sci USA* 2005; 102:5215–5220.

159. Valente EM, Abou-Sleiman PM, Caputo V, et al. Hereditary early-onset Parkinson's disease caused by mutations in PINK1. *Science* 2004; 304:1158–1160.

160. Valente EM, Bentivoglio AR, Dixon PH, et al. Localization of a novel locus for autosomal recessive early-onset parkinsonism, PARK6, on human chromosome 1p35-p36. *Am J Hum Genet* 2001; 68:895–900.

161. Petit A, Kawarai T, Paitel E, et al. Wild-type PINK1 prevents basal and induced neuronal apoptosis, a protective effect abrogated by Parkinson disease-related mutations. *J Biol Chem* 2005; 280:34025–34032.

162. Deng H, Jankovic J, Guo Y, et al. Small interfering RNA targeting the PINK1 induces apoptosis in dopaminergic cells SH-SY5Y. *Biochem Biophys Res Commun* 2005; 337:1133–1138.

163. Mochizuki H, Goto K, Mori H, Mizuno Y. Histochemical detection of apoptosis in Parkinson's disease. *J Neurol Sci* 1996; 137:120–123.

164. Grasl-Kraupp B, Ruttkay-Nedecky B, Koudelka H, et al. In situ detection of fragmented DNA (TUNEL assay) fails to discriminate among apoptosis, necrosis, and autolytic cell death: A cautionary note. *Hepatology* 1995; 21:1465–1468.

165. Tompkins MM, Basgall EJ, Zamrini E, Hill WD. Apoptotic-like changes in Lewy-body-associated disorders and normal aging in substantia nigral neurons. *Am J Pathol* 1997; 150:119–131.

166. Tatton NA, Maclean-Fraser A, Tatton WG, et al. A fluorescent double-labeling method to detect and confirm apoptotic nuclei in Parkinson's disease. *Ann Neurol* 1998; 44: S142–S148.

167. Tatton NA. Increased caspase 3 and Bax immunoreactivity accompany nuclear GAPDH translocation and neuronal apoptosis in Parkinson's disease. *Exp Neurol* 2000; 166:29–43.

168. Kosel S, Egensperger R, von Eitzen U, et al. On the question of apoptosis in the parkinsonian substantia nigra. *Acta Neuropathol* 1997; 93:105–108.

169. Wullner U, Kornhuber J, Weller M, et al. Cell death and apoptosis regulating proteins in Parkinson's disease—A cautionary note. *Acta Neuropathol (Berl)* 1999; 97: 408–412.

170. Hartmann A, Hunot S, Michel PP, et al. Caspase-3: A vulnerability factor and final effector in apoptotic death of dopaminergic neurons in Parkinson's disease. *Proc Natl Acad Sci USA* 2000; 97:2875–2880.

171. Mogi M, Harada M, Riederer P, et al. Tumor necrosis factor-alpha (TNF-alpha) increases both in the brain and in the cerebrospinal fluid from parkinsonian patients. *Neurosci Lett* 1994; 165:208–210.

172. Boka G, Anglade P, Wallach D, et al. Immunocytochemical analysis of tumor necrosis factor and its receptors in Parkinson's disease. *Neurosci Lett* 1994; 172:151–154.

173. Mogi M, Harada M, Kondo T, et al. The soluble form of Fas molecule is elevated in parkinsonian brain tissues. *Neurosci Lett* 1996; 220:195–198.

174. Hartmann A, Mouatt-Prigent A, Faucheux BA, et al. FADD: A link between TNF family receptors and caspases in Parkinson's disease. *Neurology* 2002; 58:308–310.

175. Hartmann A, Troadec JD, Hunot S, et al. Caspase-8 is an effector in apoptotic death of dopaminergic neurons in Parkinson's disease, but pathway inhibition results in neuronal necrosis. *J Neurosci* 2001; 21:2247–2255.

176. Hartmann A, Michel PP, Troadec JD, et al. Is Bax a mitochondrial mediator in apoptotic death of dopaminergic neurons in Parkinson's disease? *J Neurochem* 2001; 76:1785–1793.

32 Protein Aggregation

Leonard Petrucelli
Ana Maria Cuervo
Serge Przedborski

arkinson's disease (PD) is one of the most common neurodegenerative disorders of the aging brain (1) whose cardinal clinical features include resting tremor, muscle rigidity, slowness of voluntary movement, and postural instability (1). Although traditionally neuropathology of PD is characterized by the degeneration of the nigrostriatal dopaminergic pathway, it is far from being restricted to a single neurotransmitter system; histologic changes can also be detected in almost every dopaminergic as well as many nondopaminergic neuronal nuclei of the brain (2). Since more than 40 different neurologic diseases can show signs of *parkinsonism* (i.e., clinical features of PD), a definitive diagnosis of PD can be made only at autopsy, and it has customarily been based not only on the loss of nigrostriatal dopaminergic neurons but also on the presence of intraneuronal eosinophilic inclusions called *Lewy bodies* (LBs).

The cause of almost all PD occurrences remains unknown and, in more than 90% of the cases, PD arises as a sporadic disorder of the brain (i.e., it occurs in absence of any evidence of genetic linkage). However, in some rare instances, PD may be inherited as a simple Mendelian trait; despite the rarity of such patients, intense research activity has revolved around these uncommon familial forms of PD (3). This research has been fueled by the expectation that the clinical similarity between the familial and sporadic forms of PD indicates that they share important pathogenic mechanisms and that, consequently, information generated by the study of these genetic cases will help focus research on key biochemical pathways (3).

Until recently, all the hypotheses regarding the mechanisms of neurodegeneration in PD have derived from investigations carried out on autopsy tissues from individuals with sporadic PD or in neurotoxic animal models such as that produced by the mitochondrial poison 1-methyl-4-phenyl-1, 2, 3, 6-tetrahydropyridine (MPTP). These studies have led to the popular but highly speculative idea that two distinct and not mutually exclusive pathogenetic events—namely, mitochondrial respiration defect and oxidative stress—may underlie the demise of the nigrostriatal dopaminergic neurons in PD (1). However, finding that PD can be caused by genetic mutations in α-synuclein (4–6), parkin (7), ubiquitin C-terminal hydrolase-L1 (UCH-L1) (8), DJ-1 (9), PINK1 (10), and leucine-rich repeat kinase-2 (LRRK2) (11, 12) has triggered a dramatic paradigm shift in the way researchers consider the question of PD pathogenesis. The discovery of PD-related genes has led to a new hypothesis, that the misfolding of proteins and dysfunction in the protein degradation systems may be pivotal in the cascade of deleterious events implicated in the neurodegenerative process of PD. These novel directions have also renewed interest among researchers in LBs and other types of proteinaceous deposits found in PD brains, not as neuropathologic hallmarks but rather as putative effectors in PD pathogenesis.

PROTEINACEOUS DEPOSITS IN PARKINSON'S DISEASE

As emphasized at the beginning of this chapter, the diagnosis of PD can be made only at autopsy, and it has customarily been based on the association of a loss of nigrostriatal dopaminergic neurons and the presence of LBs (1). However, with the development of more modern histologic techniques, pathologists have recognized that intraneuronal proteinaceous deposits in PD brains encompass more than cytoplasmic LBs alone. It is now well accepted that compromised neurons may also exhibit polymorphic LB-like structures in neuronal processes, which are sometimes referred to as intraneuritic LBs, as well as dystrophic neurites, which contain thread-like amorphous material exhibiting immunohistochemical properties comparable to LBs (13). That being said, interest in proteinaceous deposits other than LBs is recent and information about their anatomic distribution or structural composition remains limited. The current consensus is that all forms of protein deposits in PD brains likely result from the same molecular and cellular process and all of the data relevant to cytoplasmic LBs may turn out to be relevant to other types of proteinaceous deposits, such as those seen in dystrophic neurites.

Distribution of LBs in Parkinson's Disease

Parkinson's disease represents 66% to 85% of all pathologically confirmed cases of parkinsonism, 82% to 100% of which show LBs (14). From the very first descriptions of LBs, it was claimed that those inclusions could be seen in all affected regions of the central nervous system (CNS) of PD patients. Although this conclusion is correct from a *qualitative* point of view, it must be stressed that, from a *quantitative* point of view, the numbers of LBs among the different regions of the CNS are not even. LBs are preferentially found in brain nuclei composed of neurons containing a dark pigment called neuromelanin that includes substantia nigra pars compacta, locus ceruleus, and dorsal motor nucleus of the vagus (14). Less often, they can be found in other subcortical nuclei, such as the nucleus basalis of Meynert, thalamus, hypothalamus, and substantia innominata (13, 14); they have even been found in some regions of the cerebral cortex, especially in the insular cortex and the parahippocampal and cingular gyri (13). The diversity of neuronal pathways associated with LBs in PD brains argues against the idea that LB formation is specific to dopaminergic neurons (14, 15).

Another remarkable aspect of LBs in PD is the fact that, contrary to popular belief, these proteinaceous inclusions are not restricted to the CNS. They can also be detected at autopsy in the sympathetic ganglia and visceral autonomic nervous systems of PD patients (14, 16).

Two tenets have traditionally been embraced by the PD research community. First, dopaminergic neurons in the substantia nigra are among the most susceptible cell subpopulations to the PD disease process. Second, LBs are faithful markers of neuronal damage, even if uncertainties persist about their actual role in the demise of the neurons they occupy. These two beliefs have led many to assume that the prevalence of LBs parallels the topography and magnitude of neuronal degeneration in the brain of PD patients. Opposing this view is the work of Braak and collaborators (17). In their study of a series of brains that presumably reflected different stages of PD, they showed that LBs and related pathologic features might have occurred in neurons from the raphe or reticular nuclei or the locus ceruleus before they occurred in neurons from the substantia nigra and prior to any overt neurodegeneration. This study suggests that the mechanisms underlying LB formation and neurodegeneration may be distinct and happen to converge in only a few cell groups and only in advanced cases. It also supports the idea that the pathogenesis of PD may simultaneously affect all neurons but that different neuron subtypes may have different pathologic thresholds for LB formation and death.

Structural Description and Composition of Lewy Bodies

Lewy bodies can harbor two main morphologies under light microscopy: the classic LB type, which conform to the original description of such intraneuronal inclusions (see below), and the subsequently recognized cortical LB type. Classic LBs are primarily found in the cytoplasm of brainstem neuromelanized neurons. They are composed of proteins, free fatty acids, sphingomyelin, and polysaccharides (18, 19). By hematoxylin and eosin (H&E) staining, classic LBs appear round with an eosinophilic, hyaline core surrounded by a narrow, almost unstained halo (Figure 32-1). They are typically 8 to 30 μm in diameter, and there may be many in one neuron. Under electron microscopy, classic LBs are not surrounded by any bilayer membrane structure. They consist of a peripheral zone (corresponding to the halo) comprising radially arranged filaments of 7 to 20 nm and a central zone (corresponding to the core) of densely packed vesicular and granular material (20). As emphasized by Lowe (21), in the substantia nigra and the locus ceruleus, classic LBs generally conform to this description. However, in other areas—such as the nucleus basalis of Meynert, thalamus, and dorsal motor nucleus of the vagus—classic LBs are more pleomorphic. As for the cortical LBs, in H&E stain-

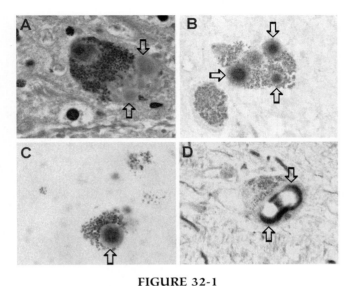

FIGURE 32-1

Illustrations of classic Lewy bodies (arrows) in nigral neuromelanized dopaminergic neurons revealed by staining for hematoxilin and eosin (A), and by immunostaining for ubiquitin (B), α-synuclein (C), and neurofilament (D). See color section following page 356.

ing they appear as round, triangular, or reniform with or without a halo. Ultrastructurally, cortical LBs, which are sometimes called pale LBs, are composed of random arranged filaments of 9 to 20 nm. As in classic LBs, the density of filaments in cortical LBs appears greatest at the center of the aggregates. However, at the periphery, the filaments do not assume the radial organization seen in classic LBs (22, 23). Whether the structural differences between classic and cortical LBs reflect distinct formation mechanisms, distinct degrees of maturation of the aggregates, or distinct cellular environments is unknown.

As pointed out by Shults (24), immunostaining for ubiquitin and α-synuclein (see Figure 32-1), the major protein constituents of the LB (25), has become the "gold standard" for revealing both classic and cortical LBs. These new histologic approaches have affected our understanding of the description and prevalence of LBs and related proteinaceous deposits in PD (24). Aside from serving to refine the neuropathologic diagnostic methods, immunohistochemical studies of LBs are also used in combination with antibodies raised against a variety of cellular proteins—including structural proteins, kinases, and immune factors—to better define the actual composition of these aggregates (13, 26). Consistently, classic LBs were found immunoreactive for α-synuclein, ubiquitin, and neurofilaments (26). They were only occasionally reported to be immunopositive for structural proteins such as chromogranin-A (27), ubiquitin-proteasome components such as ubiquitin C-terminal hydrolase (28),

for cell-cycle proteins such as cyclin-dependent kinase 5 (29), and many others (13, 26). How many of these proteins may be active contributors in the pathobiology of LBs or represent passively sequestered macromolecules is the subject of an ongoing debate.

Association of Lewy Bodies with Brain Diseases Other Than Parkinson's Disease

Although LBs are presented as pathognomonic of PD, they can also be detected in a number of familial forms of PD (3). They may also occur in a number of parkinsonian syndromes including multisystem atrophy (30), diffuse LB disease (21), and neurodegeneration with brain iron accumulation type 1 (31). More surprising is the fact that LBs have also been described in a number of neurologic disorders not thought to be related to PD, such as Alzheimer's disease (AD), Down's syndrome, progressive autonomic failure, rapid-eye-movement sleep disorder, Gaucher's disease, and Pick's disease (24). However, the number of LBs present in the brains of patients afflicted by these alternative conditions is markedly smaller than that in those with PD. Nevertheless, the range of conditions in which LBs have been identified raises the question of whether the identification of LBs should still be considered necessary for the diagnosis of PD. This interrogation is echoed by the demonstration that some individuals with inherited PD linked to mutations in the gene encoding parkin or LRRK2 exhibit nigrostriatal neurodegeneration without LBs (11, 32).

The Case of Incidental Lewy Bodies: Insights and Interrogations

In addition to the various neurologic diseases cited above, LBs can also be found in 4% to 10% of routine autopsied brains from individuals above age 60 who did not have any evidence of parkinsonism at the time of death. This neuropathologic situation has been termed "incidental LB" to reflect the serendipitous nature of the finding. In one of the largest studies of such cases, the results of 1199 autopsies were reviewed (33). This work revealed that at least 2 LBs were noted in known predilection sites of the brainstem of 98 brains, 48 of which came from individuals who did not exhibit any clinical features of PD or AD before death. In this study, only the presence of classic LBs in the substantia nigra and locus ceruleus were surveyed. Therefore one may wonder whether the same conclusions would have been reached if, instead of counting only classic LBs revealed by H&E, all α-synuclein–positive intraneuronal aggregates were counted and that, instead of surveying the brainstem only, more brain regions were analyzed. In two such studies (34, 35), data from neurologically asymptomatic subjects with a mean age of around 80 showed that incidental α-synuclein–positive brain deposits were found in 12% to 31% of the cases analyzed. As expected, these percentages are higher than the 10% found for this age group in the more *conservative* study cited above (33). The importance of analyzing a range of brain regions for the presence of LBs to avoid missing any case of incidental LB is demonstrated by Jellinger (34), who found that α-synuclein–positive deposits involved either a single brain region (e.g., nucleus basalis of Meynert or SNpc); two regions (e.g., SNpc and limbic cortex); or many regions (e.g., medullary nuclei, SNpc, and locus ceruleus) both inside and outside the brainstem.

Another important aspect of the study by Forno and Langston (33) is the demonstration that the prevalence of incidental LBs in the substantia nigra rose with age up to the ninth decade. Interestingly, these authors also found a relationship between age and LB prevalence in PD and AD cases (33). These findings raise the possibility that the occurrence of LBs in the brains of normal elderly individuals–assuming that they are normal and not asymptomatic–may reflect a generic response of neurons, which are postmitotic cells, to aging rather than to a disease. The increase in neuromelanin content in dopaminergic neurons with time could be another example of such an age-related change in this dopaminergic pathway (36). As indicated before, in definite cases of PD, the prevalence of LBs in the substantia nigra is close to 100%. Given the above hypothesis, would this fact suggest that PD represents a pathologic acceleration of the normal aging process? Functional brain imaging studies have found that the time-course of changes in the brain topography of glucose metabolism in PD diverges from that seen in normal aging (37). Furthermore, in PD, neuronal loss in the substantia nigra predominates in ventrolateral and caudal regions, whereas during normal aging the dorsomedial aspect is most affected (38). These results suggest that the processes that produce age-related dopaminergic neuronal alterations are likely distinct from those in PD; consequently, these LBs may not represent an expression of normal aging. Correlatively, LBs in the brain of apparently normal elderly individuals may in fact reflect a specific response of neurons to a disease process; therefore incidental LBs might represent presymptomatic cases of PD. Consistent with this view is the demonstration that incidental LBs were associated with a 17% lower density of dopaminergic neurons in the ventrolateral aspect of the substantia nigra compared to age-matched controls without LBs in the substantia nigra (39).

THE PATHOGENIC CONCEPT OF PROTEIN MISFOLDING AND AGGREGATION

By now it is well recognized that the development of protein aggregates in brain tissue is a feature shared by a number of prominent, age-related neurodegenerative diseases (40). Although the composition and location (i.e., intra- or extracellular) of protein aggregates differ from disease to disease, this common feature suggests that protein deposition per se, or some related event, might be toxic to neurons.

Aggregated or soluble misfolded proteins could be neurotoxic through a variety of mechanisms. Protein aggregates could directly cause damage, perhaps by a *crowding effect,* leading to deformation of the cell or interference with the trafficking systems inside the neurons. These aggregates might also sequester proteins that are important for cell survival, like the antiapoptotic protein Bcl-2; such a scenario has been proposed previously in the setting of a familial form of amyotrophic lateral sclerosis (41). If any of the above mechanisms operate herein, it might be expected that the frequency of aggregates such as LBs would correlate with the magnitude of neurodegeneration. This relationship has not yet been convincingly demonstrated in postmortem tissue samples from patients with sporadic PD. In cell models in which the development of α-synuclein positive aggregates are stimulated by combining α-synuclein overexpression and mitochondrial poisoning with rotenone (42, 43), the results support the notion that the formation of aggregates reflects a state of cellular distress. However, studies in models of Huntington's disease (HD) and other polyglutamine diseases (44, 45), also suggest that there is no correlation between inclusion formation and cell death. It is possible that cytoplasmic protein inclusions may not result from precipitated misfolded proteins but rather from an active process meant to sequester soluble misfolded proteins from the cellular milieu (46). This suggests that aggregate formation, while possibly indicative of a "cell under attack," may be a defensive measure aimed at removing toxic soluble misfolded proteins (47–50). The ability of chaperones, such as Hsp-70, to protect against neurodegeneration provoked by disease-related proteins, including α-synuclein–mediated dopaminergic neuronal loss, is consistent with the view that soluble misfolded proteins and not aggregates are neurotoxic (50, 51).

In PD patients with either α-synuclein point mutations (4–6) or gene multiplication (52), dopaminergic neurodegeneration is thought to be caused by mutant or excess of normal α-synuclein adopting toxic conformations (53) or interfering with the cellular handling of misfolded proteins. In sporadic PD, there is a similar focus on both protein-damaging modifications and dysfunction of protein degradation systems (see below). The trigger for impaired protein homeostasis in sporadic PD may be oxidative stress. Relevant to this view is the demonstration by Giasson and collaborators that LBs in PD contain oxidatively modified α-synuclein, which exhibits a greater propensity to aggregate compared to nonoxidized α-synuclein (54). Several environmental toxins, such as herbicides and pesticides, can also induce misfolding or aggregation of α-synuclein (55, 56). From the above, it is clear that a definite demonstration of the toxicity of misfolded proteins and related aggregates on dopaminergic neurons is still lacking. However, even in absence of such evidence, it is crucial to elucidate the basis for the excess of misfolding and aggregation of proteins in dopaminergic neurons as seen in PD. It can be theorized that increased misfolding and aggregation of proteins may result not only from an increased formation but also from a decreased clearance due to a dysfunction in either or both of the ubiquitin-proteasome and autophagy systems. It is in this context that these 2 major protein degradation systems are now discussed.

THE UBIQUITIN PROTEASOME SYSTEM

The ubiquitin-proteasome system (UPS) is one of the pivotal means by which proteins, and especially short-lived ones, are degraded in eukaryotic cells (57–59). Over the past decade, the possibility that dysfunction of the UPS contributes to the neurodegenerative process in PD has received major attention. The UPS can degrade proteins that misfold or misassemble as a consequence of mutation, environmental stress, or intrinsic folding inefficiency (57–59). While this property is quite relevant to pathologic situations like PD, the UPS is also responsible for the turnover of a wide variety of normal proteins, including many cell regulators such as kinases and transcription factors, whose expressions are controlled by the balance between synthesis and proteolysis (57–59). Thus, failure of the UPS in PD may potentially have disastrous consequences on neuronal homeostasis, independent of any deleterious effects that accumulation of misfolded proteins may have on cell survival.

Protein Degradation Mediated by the Ubiquitin-Proteasome System

The degradation of protein mediated by the UPS is a complex multistep process that starts with the tagging of proteins by covalent attachment of the polypeptide ubiquitin and ends by the actual degradation of the tagged protein by the 26S proteasome complex (Figure 32-2). Ubiquitin is a highly conserved 76-residue polypeptide which, as a monomer, is attached sequentially to target proteins through the cascade of E1 ubiquitin activating, E2 ubiquitin conjugating, and E3 ubiquitin ligase enzymes (see Figure 32-2). The ubiquitin-activating enzyme E1 catalyzes the formation of a thiol ester bond between the E1 cysteine residues and the carboxy-terminal glycine in ubiquitin via an ATP-dependent reaction. Then, one of several ubiquitin-carrier proteins

or ubiquitin-conjugating E2 enzymes transfer ubiquitin from E1 to the protein substrate that is specifically bound to an ubiquitin-protein ligase E3 enzyme (see Figure 32-2). During this reaction, ubiquitin is ligated to the lysine residue of the protein substrate. Once the first ubiquitin molecule has been conjugated to the protein substrate, additional ubiquitin molecules can be added to the internal lysine residues of ubiquitin to form polyubiquitin chains, which is an essential event, since a minimum of 4 ubiquitin molecules is required for efficient targeting to the proteasome. As illustrated in Figure 32-2, both E1 and E2 enzymes cooperate to nonspecifically tag proteins with ubiquitin, while E3 enzymes confer target specificity to the UPS proteolysis by binding to specific proteins. Thus, protein ubiquitination, while epitomizing a generic cellular mechanism, is in fact quite a selective process, with only specific proteins being degraded by this pathway at a precise moment in response to precise cellular events.

Degradation of polyubiquitinated proteins is carried out by a large protease complex called the 26S proteasome (57–59). It is a hollow structure composed of a 20S core particle which carries out the catalytic activity and 2 regulatory 19S regulatory particles flanking the 20S catalytic core (see Figure 32-2). The main role of the 19S particles is to recognize ubiquitinated proteins and to open an orifice in the 26S proteasome, allowing entry of the substrate into the proteolytic chamber. Because folded proteins do not fit through the narrow proteasomal channel, it is also believed that the 19S particle unfolds substrates and inserts them into the 20S catalytic core. The channel opening function and the unfolding of the substrate is dependent on energy generated by ATPase subunits contained in the 19S particles. Following degradation of a polyubiquitinated protein by the 26S proteasome, short peptides are released, along with free and reusable ubiquitin (see Figure 32-2).

Alterations in Familial Parkinsonian Syndromes Due to the Ubiquitin-Proteasome System

As discussed in the introduction, mutations in enzymes related to the UPS pathway have been linked to familial forms of PD, including mutations in the E3 ubiquitin ligase parkin (7) and the deubiquitinating enzyme UCH-L1 (8). Although to date there is a plethora of studies reporting various kinds of UPS alterations in PD postmortem tissues and in experimental models of PD, these genetic findings are what provide the most compelling arguments in favor of the idea that UPS dysfunction may play a pathogenic role in PD. Thus, while the genetics of PD is reviewed in detail by Payami in Chapter 37 of this book, the relevance of parkin and UCH-L1 mutations to PD pathogenesis are discussed here.

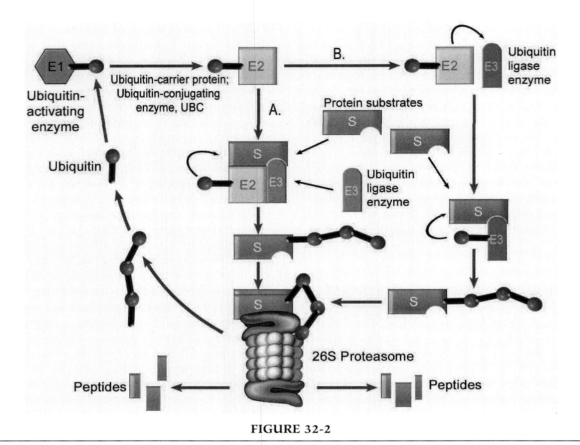

FIGURE 32-2

Representation of ubiquitin-proteasome proteolysis. This process starts with the activation of ubiquitin by the ubiquitin-activating enzyme E1, an ubiquitin-carrier protein, E2 (ubiquitin-conjugating enzyme; UBC), and ATP. The product of this reaction is a high-energy E2~ubiquitin thiol ester intermediate. Then, the protein substrate is ubiquitinated and this key step may occur by two different pathways. In pathway A, the protein substrate binds to a specific ubiquitin-protein ligase, E3 and only then is the E2-bound activated ubiquitin transferred to the E3-bound protein substrate. Multiple cycles of conjugation of ubiquitin to the target substrate yield a polyubiquitin chain. Pathway B is similar to pathway A, except that here, the activated ubiquitin is transferred from E2 to E3 before its conjugation to the E3-bound protein substrate. Then, the ubiquitin-tagged protein substrate is degraded by the 26S proteasome complex with the release of short peptides. Finally, ubiquitin is recycled via the activity of deubiquitinating enzymes. See color section following page 356.

Loss-of-function mutations in the parkin gene cause a recessively inherited form of parkinsonism (7), which usually but not exclusively emerges clinically before the age of 30 (1). Pathologically, parkin-related parkinsonism is associated with a loss of dopaminergic neurons but not typically with LBs (60). This striking departure from the neuropathology of sporadic PD (see above) supports a key role of parkin in LB formation. Parkin function has been identified as an E3 ubiquitin ligase (32, 61), and many parkin mutations abolish this UPS-related activity. Remarkably, the E3 ubiquitin ligase activity of normal parkin can also be impaired by the posttranslational modification S-nitrosylation (62); hence parkin dysfunction may participate in the pathogenesis of both familial and sporadic PD. Like the loss of any E3, the loss of parkin function is thought to compromise the polyubiquitination and thus

degradation of specific proteins. Relevant to this view are the demonstrations that mutant mice deficient of parkin exhibit increased brain levels of the aminoacyl-tRNA synthetase-interacting multifunctional protein type 2 and the far upstream element-binding protein-1, both putative parkin substrates (63, 64). Although several studies have stressed the multiplicity of parkin substrates (1, 59), how their accumulation in the brain, in response to a loss of parkin activity, might provoke neurodegeneration remains unclear. Other investigations have suggested that a loss of parkin may trigger cell death by sensitizing neurons to cytotoxic insults, like those caused by proteasome inhibition or mutant α-synuclein (42, 65, 66), but here again the mechanisms that underlie this effect remain to be elucidated.

As for UCH-L1, it is mainly expressed in the brain, where it catalyzes the hydrolysis of C-terminal ubiquityl esters (67). As discussed in more detail in Dauer and Przedborski 1 (1), UCH-L1 is at the center of a complex genetic situation and dispute with respect to PD. On the one hand, a coding substitution (I93M), which is presented as a dominant mutation in UCH-L1, has been associated with the development of an inherited form of PD in a single family (8), while, on the other hand, a polymorphism (S18Y) of UCH-L1 has been linked to a reduced risk of developing PD (68). Although the I93M mutation has been shown to decrease the activity of this deubiquitinating enzyme, there is still no evidence that this loss of function is responsible for triggering neurodegeneration, since mice carrying a UCH-L1 null mutation do not display dopaminergic neuronal loss (69). Alternatively, UCH-L1 can also operate as an ubiquitin ligase, an activity that is decreased by the pathogenic I93M mutation and increased by the protective S18Y polymorphism (70). UCH-L1 was also identified as a protease with specificity for Nedd8 (71), a small ubiquitin-like protein implicated in the regulation of the cell cycle. Although all of the aforementioned findings are consistent with the idea that dysfunction in the UPS might be neurotoxic, further studies are required to explain how parkin and UCH-L1 mutations contribute to the death of dopaminergic neurons in their respective familial forms of PD.

The Status of the Ubiquitin-Proteasome System in Sporadic Parkinson's Disease

Both protein misfolding and UPS dysfunction are believed to contribute to neurodegeneration in sporadic PD. However, the situation here is even murkier, as the triggers of dysfunctional protein degradation in this predominant form of the illness is only just beginning to be addressed. At this point, we know that several studies (72–74) suggest that inhibition of proteasomal activity leads to accumulation of α-synuclein or the formation of ubiquitinated α-synuclein–containing aggregates. Because degradation, not ubiquitination, is rate-limiting for most UPS substrates (75), the presence of undegraded, stable ubiquitin conjugates such as LBs in the brains of PD patients and of genetic and toxic models of PD suggests that unwanted proteins in sporadic PD are properly recognized and ubiquitinated but not efficiently cleared. Such inefficient degradation may be the result of intrinsic resistance to proteasomal degradation of α-synuclein–containing aggregates (76, 77) or a reflection of the difficulty in unfolding stable proteinaceous aggregates by the 19S subunits of the proteasome complex (78). Moreover, the accumulation of α-synuclein and other aggregation-prone proteins potently impairs the activity of the UPS (79–81), possibly at the level of the proteasome. Ultimately, this would set up a feed-forward effect by which accumulation of aggregated α-synuclein, in response to, for example, oxidative stress or environmental toxic factors, would impair UPS

function, leading to a further accumulation of α-synuclein and other toxic proteins. Despite the growing number of studies supporting UPS dysfunction and protein misfolding in cell culture and animal models and even in brain tissue from PD patients, it must be stressed that all of these observations remain at this point correlational in nature and many could not be reproduced. At this time it is our opinion that there is no study that convincingly links a *primary* abnormality of the UPS with sporadic PD, and many of the reported abnormalities, if real, may merely be nonspecific molecular perturbations in dying neurons.

AUTOPHAGY AS A CELLULAR CLEANING MECHANISM

In addition to the UPS, a whole organelle, the lysosome, is devoted to continuous cellular cleaning. The degradation of intracellular components inside lysosomes is known as autophagy, which means "eating oneself" (82–85). Autophagy plays a major role in the maintenance of cellular homeostasis, the defense of cells against intracellular and extracellular aggressors, and all processes requiring major cellular remodeling, as in embryogenesis and tissue differentiation (86). Autophagy also contributes to the removal of proteinaceous aggregates seen in neurodegenerative diseases (87, 88). Hence failure of the autophagic system may be responsible for the accumulation of misfolded proteins in some of these disorders, including PD.

Types of Autophagy

Although the terminal intracellular compartment in autophagy is always the lysosome, the substrates are delivered to this organelle by different mechanisms, giving rise to three different types of autophagy in mammalian cells: macroautophagy, microautophagy, and chaperone-mediated autophagy (CMA).

Macroautophagy, the best-characterized form of autophagy, involves the sequestration of a complete region of the cytosol, including whole organelles, by a double-membrane vesicle known as an autophagosome (Figure 32-3). The latter acquires the enzymes required for the degradation of its content after fusion with a lysosome. Macroautophagy is activated in response to nutrient deprivation, where degradation of intracellular components by this pathway provides cells with the amino acids, no longer obtained by the diet but required for the synthesis of proteins essential for survival (89). Stressors such as physical and chemical aggressors as well as infectious agents also activate macroautophagy (84). Activation of autophagy under these conditions is aimed at the removal of the aggressor itself (i.e., invading

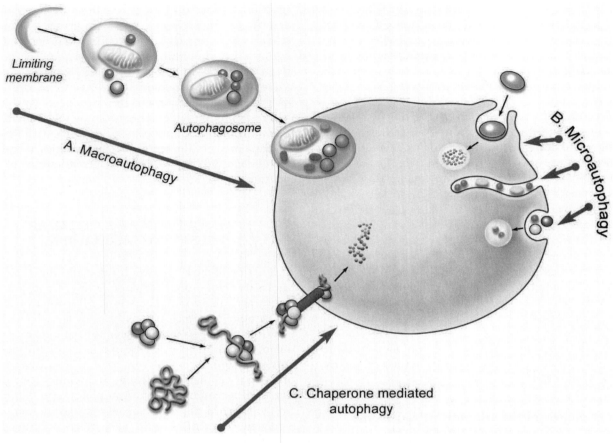

FIGURE 32-3

Types of autophagy in mammalian cells. Intracellular components can be delivered to lysosomes for degradation via three different types of autophagy. A. *Macroautophagy:* complete regions of the cytosol are sequestered by a limiting membrane to form a double-membraned vesicle (autophagosome), which fuses to lysosomes. Once the lysosomal hydrolases are transferred to autophagosomes, the sequestered material is rapidly degraded. B. *Microautophagy:* lysosomes invaginate or tubulate to trap cytosolic portions that are internalized inside of single-membraned vesicles. Lysosomal hydrolases digest the limiting membrane of these vesicles to gain access to the trapped components and degrade them. C. *Chaperone-mediated autophagy:* particular cytosolic proteins bearing a targeting motif in their sequence are recognized by a chaperone which takes them to the lysosomal membrane where they interact with a receptor protein. Once in the membrane, the substrate protein is unfolded and translocated across the membrane with the assistance of a lysosomal resident chaperone.

microorganisms) or of the intracellular components damaged during the stress. Furthermore, studies in genetically altered mice lacking one of the essential genes for macroautophagy have revealed that some level of macroautophagy is almost always present in all tissues and that this basal activity plays an important role in the continuous turnover of organelles and clearance of altered proteins (90–92).

Complete cytosolic regions can also be delivered to lysosomes for degradation via microautophagy. In this case, the lysosomal membrane invaginates or generates protrusions and tubulations to sequester the cytosolic content "in bulk" (see Figure 32-3). Microautophagy is a constitutively active pathway that contributes to continuous slow turnover of cytosolic proteins (93).

In contrast to the "in bulk" degradation, cytosolic proteins can be taken one-by-one to lysosomes for their degradation through CMA. The interaction of the chaperone with the substrate protein brings it to the lysosomal membrane, where it binds to a receptor protein; after unfolding, the substrate protein crosses the lysosomal membrane assisted by a second chaperone present in the lysosomal lumen (94). As in any other type of autophagy, once the substrate protein reaches the inside of the lysosome, it is rapidly degraded by potent hydrolases. Although some level of basal CMA activity is detectable in almost all cell types, this pathway is maximally activated under conditions of stress. Stressors known to activate this pathway include prolonged starvation, mild oxidative stress, and exposure to different toxic compounds that alter the conformation of particular proteins (95). The intrinsic selectivity associated with this pathway allows the removal of altered proteins without affecting normal proteins nearby.

AUTOPHAGY AND PROTEIN MISFOLDING

As described in previous sections, the UPS plays a critical role in the removal of misfolded proteins, which otherwise may form aggregates. For a long time, lysosomes were not considered suitable for this task because of the nonselective nature of their degradation. However, as CMA was identified, it became evident that lysosomes could also play a role in the clearance of specifically misfolded proteins. As in the case of the proteasome, CMA is able to degrade only those misfolded proteins that have not yet formed aggregates, as these cannot translocate across the lysosomal membrane and consequently cannot be cleared through CMA (Figure 32-4).

Once misfolded proteins form aggregates, macroautophagy is the only mechanism able to efficiently remove them from inside the cells. In fact, pharmacologic activation of macroautophagy decreases levels of intracellular aggregates and protects against the neurodegeneration induced by certain prone-to-aggregate proteins, such as polyglutamine huntingtin or mutant forms of α-synuclein (87). Activation of macroautophagy has been described in different conditions that induce presence of intracellular protein aggregates (96, 97). Abundant autophagic vacuoles, the morphologic expression for the activation of macroautophagy, have been described in the brains of patients affected by different neurodegenerative disorders (98–100). As dying neurons contain higher amounts of these structures, it was erroneously hypothesized that macroautophagy was activated as a mechanism of cell death. However, the beneficial effect in cell survival observed in different experimental models of neurodegenerative disorders when macroautophagy was enhanced supports a defensive role for macroautophagy in these disorders.

The notion of cellular death by autophagy has not been completely abandoned, as recent experimental evidence supports that excessive upregulation of macroautophagy, at least in cultured cells, dramatically reduces cell viability; under these conditions, blockage of macroautophagy protects from cellular death (101). It is thus plausible that macroautophagy is initially activated in conditions with increased amounts of misfolded proteins as a protective mechanism aimed at getting rid of the altered proteins. But if the harmful situation persists, macroautophagy is instead used to completely eliminate the affected cell (see Figure 32-4). The presence of aggregate proteins seems sufficient to upregulate this pathway in most of these conditions. As described before, some

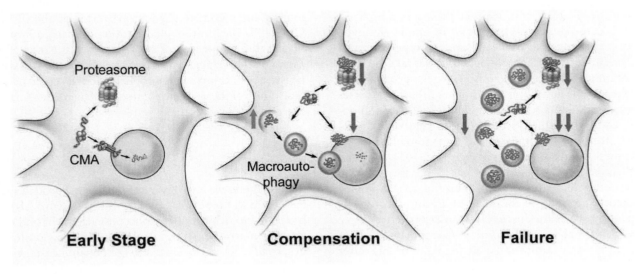

FIGURE 32-4

Autophagic changes in PD. Based in the recent findings in the field, three stages are proposed in the pathogenesis of PD with respect to autophagy. (1). *Early stage*: Misfolded proteins are recognized by the UPS or by the CMA-related chaperones and are degraded by these two pathways. (2). *Compensation stage*: Misfolded proteins organize into complex structures (aggregates), which impair the activity of the ubiquitin-proteasome system and block CMA. Macroautophagy is upregulated as a compensatory mechanism to eliminate the aggregated proteins. (3). *Failure stage*: Aggravating factors such as oxidative stress, aging, or unidentified agents further block the activity of the already altered proteolytic systems and also impair macroautophagy, resulting in the accumulation of autophagic vacuoles and eventually cell death.

of these altered proteins block the proteasome system, and this blockage has been shown experimentally to induce macroautophagy (97). In addition, blockage of CMA, shown to occur in the presence of some of these abnormal proteins (see below), has a similar outcome on macroautophagy activity (102). Thus, blockage of the pathways that would normally take care of the removal of these soluble proteins is compensated for by activation of macroautophagic "in bulk" degradation.

How can cells deal with the random destruction of whole regions of their cytosol? In the case of aggregate removal, the process is not as indiscriminate as initially proposed. Essential macroautophagy components and lysosomes are mobilized in a microtubule-dependent manner to the perinuclear region of the cells, where inclusion bodies normally accumulate, thus increasing the chances for engulfment of these proteinaceous deposits against other cytosolic components (88). The critical role of macroautophagy in the removal of aggregated proteins has been convincingly confirmed by showing that the selective blockage of macroautophagy in mouse neurons results in accumulation of proteinaceous inclusions and neuronal death (91, 92).

With macroautophagy left as the only remaining pathway for the turnover of intracellular components in the compensatory stage of these neurodegenerative disorders, it can be inferred that small alterations in this system may have major impacts on neuron survival. Oxidative stress and aging are probably the main aggravating factors that precipitate the failure of macroautophagy. Conditions promoting oxidative stress overload the macroautophagic system because the two systems that normally eliminate oxidized proteins are no longer capable to perform this task. Engulfed oxidized products and damaged organelles become a source of reactive oxygen species inside autophagosomes and lysosomes. These reactive species can eventually damage lysosomal hydrolases and components required for the lysosome/autophagosome fusion and result in the accumulation of undegraded products inside these compartments (see Figure 32-4). Unspecific protein cross linking induced by free radicals increases the indigestibility of the substrates which end up accumulating inside lysosomes in the form of an autofluorescent pigment known as lipofuscin (103). Age-related changes in the lysosomal system also play an important role in macroautophagic failure and could explain the late onset of many of these neurodegenerative disorders. Both macroautophagy and CMA activity decrease with age (104). The main defect in macroautophagy is the diminished ability of lysosomes to clear up autophagic vacuoles. Autophagic vacuoles form to trap the intracellular components that need to be removed, but a combination of defective lysosomal fusion and impaired activity of the lysosomal hydrolases with age results in the accumulation of undigested materials inside old cells.

IMPAIRED AUTOPHAGY AND PARKINSON'S DISEASE

Normal α-synuclein is degraded by the UPS and also by autophagy. α-Synuclein can be delivered to lysosomes through the CMA pathway for degradation (105). Pathogenic mutant forms of α-synuclein are still delivered to lysosomes by the cytosolic chaperone and bind to the lysosomal membrane receptor, but they cannot be degraded in this compartment as they are unable to cross the lysosomal membrane. Instead, α-synuclein mutants remain tightly bound to the lysosomal membrane, interfering with the degradation of other CMA substrates (105). The similar ability to block CMA has been observed for wild-type α-synuclein when exposed to dopamine (Martinez-Vicente and Cuervo, unpublished observation). Cells respond to this blockage of CMA by upregulating macroautophagy to guarantee normal rates of protein degradation (102). However, the absence of CMA leaves the cells more vulnerable to stress, and apoptotic cell death is readily activated in these cells after exposure to different stressors.

As suggested above once α-synuclein aggregates, it can no longer be degraded by either the UPS or CMA; hence macroautophagy becomes the only proteolytic pathway able to remove these proteinaceous deposits from the neuronal cytosol. This view is consistent with the demonstration that aggregates of mutant α-synuclein can be cleared by macroautophagy (106), and activation of the latter under this condition is likely a result of the inhibition that mutant and modified α-synuclein exerted on the UPS and CMA (97, 102). Although activation of macroautophagy during this compensatory stage prevents the intracellular accumulation of aggregated α-synuclein, conditions with a negative impact on macroautophagic activity could precipitate failure of the clearance of toxic and aggregate forms of α-synuclein and eventually result in cell death.

CONCLUSION

In this chapter we have reviewed the issue of protein aggregations in PD brains, especially with respect to LBs. We have tried to dispel the misconception that LBs and other types of α-synuclein–positive deposits, if most prominent in sporadic PD, are restricted to the dopaminergic systems or sporadic PD. It is clear from the above discussion that their role, as far as cell toxicity is concerned, remains highly speculative and, since dopaminergic neurodegeneration and parkinsonism may emerge in absence of LBs, the idea that these protein deposits are a necessary part of the disease process in PD is even questionable. By now, all of the identified PD-related genes have been studied in some detail, and the fruits of these investigations have led to the concept that abnormal protein degradation and accumulation might

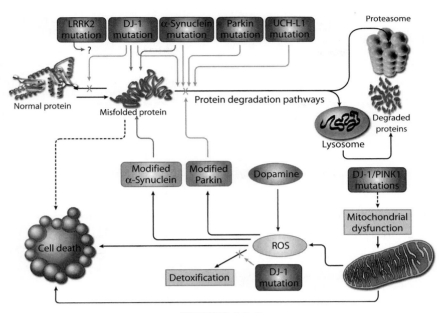

FIGURE 32-5

Hypothetical unifying pathogenic scenario in PD revolving around the theme of protein misfolding. Mutant α-synuclein and DJ-1 may be misfolded (blue arrows), thus overwhelming the UPS and lysosomal degradation pathways. Other mutant proteins, such as parkin and UCH-L1, may lack their wild-type function. Both of these proteins, which belong to the ubiquitin-proteasome system, upon mutation may no longer exert their ubiquitin ligase activity, thus damaging the ability of the cellular machinery to detect and degrade misfolded proteins (red arrows). Mutations in DJ-1 may also alter its supposed chaperone activity, disrupting the refolding of damaged proteins or the targeting and delivery of damaged proteins for degradation (red arrows). These different alterations may lead to the accumulation of unwanted proteins, which, by unknown mechanisms (dashed arrows), may lead to neurodegeneration. Oxidative stress generated by mitochondrial dysfunction and dopamine metabolism may also promote protein misfolding as a result of posttranslational modifications, especially of alpha-synuclein and parkin. Oxidative stress in PD may also originate from a defect in the reduced capacity of DJ-1 to detoxify reactive oxygen species, whereas the mitochondrial dysfunction may, at least in part, derive from defective activity and mislocation of DJ-1 and PINK1. Mitochondrial dysfunction, oxidative stress, and protein mishandling are thus tightly interconnected in this hypothesized pathogenic cascade. LRRK2 function is unknown. Additional possible interactions have been omitted for clarity. (Adapted from Vila M, Przedborski S. Genetic clues to the pathogenesis of Parkinson's disease. Nat Med 2004;10 Suppl:S58–62). See color section following page 356.

be a critical factor in dopaminergic neurodegeneration in familial PD (Figure 32-5). According to this reasoning, α-synuclein and DJ-1 mutations could be envisioned to cause abnormal protein conformations, overwhelming the main cellular protein degradation systems—the UPS and lysosomal autophagic pathways—whereas parkin and UCH-L1 mutations would undermine the cell's ability to detect and degrade misfolded proteins (see Figure 32-5). The common end result of these different perturbations is thus expected to be a cellular buildup of unwanted proteins that should have been eliminated (see Figure 32-5). A similar pathogenic scenario has been proposed for sporadic PD, but here the data used to support such a concept are, up to now, mostly indirect and too often unsound.

ACKNOWLEDGMENTS

The authors wish to acknowledge the support of NIH/NINDS grants NS38586, NS42269, and NS38370, NIH/NIA grants AG21617, AG19834 and AG021904, the US Department of Defense grant DAMD 17–03–1, the Parkinson Disease Foundation (New York, USA), the MDA/Wings Over Wall Street, Michael J. Fox and the Mayo Clinic Foundation and the Ellison Medical Foundation.

References

1. Dauer W, Przedborski S. Parkinson's disease: Mechanisms and models. *Neuron* 2003; 39:889–909.
2. Braak H, Braak E, Yilmazer D, et al. Nigral and extranigral pathology in Parkinson's disease. *J Neural Transm Suppl* 1995; 46:15–31.
3. Vila M, Przedborski S. Genetic clues to the pathogenesis of Parkinson's disease. *Nat Med* 2004; 10(Suppl):S58–S62.
4. Polymeropoulos MH, Lavedan C, Leroy E, et al. Mutation in the alpha-synuclein gene identified in families with Parkinson's disease. *Science* 1997; 276:2045–2047.
5. Kruger R, Kuhn W, Muller T, et al. Ala30Pro mutation in the gene encoding alpha-synuclein in Parkinson's disease. *Nat Genet* 1998; 18:107–108.
6. Zarranz JJ, Alegre J, Gomez-Esteban JC, et al. The new mutation, E46K, of alpha-synuclein causes Parkinson and Lewy body dementia. *Ann Neurol* 2004; 55:164–173.

7. Kitada T, Asakawa S, Hattori N, et al. Mutations in the parkin gene cause autosomal recessive juvenile parkinsonism. *Nature* 1998; 392:605–608.

8. Leroy E, Boyer R, Auburger G, et al. The ubiquitin pathway in Parkinson's disease. *Nature* 1998; 395:451–452.

9. Bonifati V, Rizzu P, Van Baren MJ, et al. Mutations in the DJ-1 gene associated with autosomal recessive early-onset parkinsonism. *Science* 2003; 299:256–259.

10. Valente EM, Abou-Sleiman PM, Caputo V, et al. Hereditary early-onset Parkinson's disease caused by mutations in PINK1. *Science* 2004; 304:1158–1160.

11. Zimprich A, Biskup S, Leitner P, et al. Mutations in LRRK2 cause autosomal-dominant parkinsonism with pleomorphic pathology. *Neuron* 2004; 44:601–607.

12. Paisan-Ruiz C, Jain S, Evans EW, et al. Cloning of the gene containing mutations that cause PARK8-linked Parkinson's disease. *Neuron* 2004; 44:595–600.

13. Dickson DW. Neuropathology of Parkinson's disease. In: Beal MF, Lang AE, Ludolph A (eds). *Neurodegenerative DIseases. Neurobiology, Pathogenesis and Therapeutics.* New York: Cambridge University Press, 2005:575–585.

14. Jellinger K. The pathology of parkinsonism. In: Marsden CD, Fahn S (eds). *Movement Disorders 2.* Boston: Butterworth, 1987:124–165.

15. Ohama E, Ikuta F. Parkinson's disease: Distribution of Lewy bodies and monoamine neuron system. *Acta Neuropathol (Berl)* 1976; 34:311–319.

16. Wakabayashi K, Takahashi H, Takeda S, et al. Parkinson's disease: The presence of Lewy bodies in Auerbach's and Meissner's plexuses. *Acta Neuropathol (Berl)* 1988; 76:217–221.

17. Braak H, Del Tredici K, Rub U, et al. Staging of brain pathology related to sporadic Parkinson's disease. *Neurobiol Aging* 2003; 24:197–211.

18. den Jager WA. Sphingomyelin in Lewy inclusion bodies in Parkinson's disease. *Arch Neurol* 1969; 21:615–619.

19. Gai WP, Yuan HX, Li XQ, et al. In situ and in vitro study of colocalization and segregation of alpha-synuclein, ubiquitin, and lipids in Lewy bodies. *Exp Neurol* 2000; 166:324–333.

20. Duffy PE, Tennyson VM. Phase and electron microscopic observations of Lewy bodies and melanin granules in the substantia nigra and locus coeruleus in Parkinson's disease. *J Neuropathol Exp Neurol* 1965; 24:398–414.

21. Lowe J. Lewy bodies. In: Calne DB (ed). *Neurodegenerative Diseases.* Phialdelphia: Sanders, 1994:51–69.

22. Kosaka K. Lewy bodies in cerebral cortex: Report of three cases. *Acta Neuropathol (Berl)* 1978; 42:127–134.

23. Yoshimura M. Cortical changes in the parkinsonian brain: A contribution to the delineation of "diffuse Lewy body disease." *J Neurol* 1983; 229:17–32.

24. Shults CW. Lewy bodies. *Proc Natl Acad Sci USA* 2006; 103:1661–1668.

25. Spillantini MG, Schmidt ML, Lee VMY, et al. α-Synuclein in Lewy bodies. *Nature* 1997; 388:839–840.

26. Galvin JE, Lee VM, Schmidt ML, et al. Pathobiology of the Lewy body. *Adv Neurol* 1999; 80:313–324.

27. Nishimura M, Tomimoto H, Suenaga T, et al. Synaptophysin and chromogranin A immunoreactivities of Lewy bodies in Parkinson's disease brains. *Brain Res* 1994; 634:339–344.

28. Lowe J, McDermott H, Landon M, et al. Ubiquitin carboxyl-terminal hydrolase (PGP 9.5) is selectively present in ubiquitinated inclusion bodies characteristic of human neurodegenerative diseases. *J Pathol* 1990; 161:153–160.

29. Takahashi M, Iseki E, Kosaka K. Cyclin-dependent kinase 5 (Cdk5) associated with Lewy bodies in diffuse Lewy body disease. *Brain Res* 2000; 862:253–256.

30. Gibb WR, Lees AJ. The significance of the Lewy body in the diagnosis of idiopathic Parkinson's disease. *Neuropathol Appl Neurobiol* 1989; 15:27–44.

31. Arawaka S, Saito Y, Murayama S, et al. Lewy body in neurodegeneration with brain iron accumulation type 1 is immunoreactive for alpha-synuclein. *Neurology* 1998; 51:887–889.

32. Shimura H, Hattori N, Kubo S, et al. Familial Parkinson disease gene product, parkin, is a ubiquitin-protein ligase. *Nat Genet* 2000; 25:302–305.

33. Forno LS, Langston JW. Lewy bodies and aging: Relation to Alzheimer's and Parkinson's diseases. *Neurodegeneration* 1993; 2:19–24.

34. Jellinger KA. Lewy body–related alpha-synucleinopathy in the aged human brain. *J Neural Transm* 2004; 111:1219–1235.

35. Parkkinen L, Soininen H, Alafuzoff I. Regional distribution of alpha-synuclein pathology in unimpaired aging and Alzheimer disease. *J Neuropathol Exp Neurol* 2003; 62:363–367.

36. Zecca L, Tampellini D, Gerlach M, et al. Substantia nigra neuromelanin: Structure, synthesis, and molecular behaviour. *Mol Pathol* 2001; 54:414–418.

37. Moeller JR, Ishikawa T, Dhawan V, et al. The metabolic topography of normal aging. *J Cereb Blood Flow Metab* 1996; 16:385–398.

38. Fearnley JM, Lees AJ. Ageing and Parkinson's disease: Substantia nigra regional selectivity. *Brain* 1991; 114:2283–2301.

39. Ross GW, Petrovitch H, Abbott RD, et al. Parkinsonian signs and substantia nigra neuron density in descendants of elders without PD. *Ann Neurol* 2004; 56:532–539.

40. Ross CA, Poirier MA. Protein aggregation and neurodegenerative disease. *Nat Med* 2004; 10(Suppl):S10–S17.

41. Pasinelli P, Belford ME, Lennon N, et al. Amyotrophic lateral sclerosis–associated SOD1 mutant proteins bind and aggregate with Bcl-2 in spinal cord mitochondria. *Neuron* 2004; 43:19–30.

42. Petrucelli L, O'Farrell C, Lockhart PJ, et al. Parkin protects against the toxicity associated with mutant alpha-synuclein: Proteasome dysfunction selectively affects catecholaminergic neurons. *Neuron* 2002; 36:1007–1019.

43. Lee HJ, Shin SY, Choi C, et al. Formation and removal of alpha-synuclein aggregates in cells exposed to mitochondrial inhibitors. *J Biol Chem* 2002; 277:5411–5417.

44. Saudou F, Finkbeiner S, Devys D, et al. Huntingtin acts in the nucleus to induce apoptosis but death does not correlate with the formation of intranuclear inclusions. *Cell* 1998; 95:55–66.

45. Cummings CJ, Zoghbi HY. Trinucleotide repeats: Mechanisms and pathophysiology. *Annu Rev Genomics Hum Genet* 2000; 1:281–328.

46. Kopito RR. Aggresomes, inclusion bodies and protein aggregation. *Trends Cell Biol* 2000; 10:524–530.

47. Cummings CJ, Reinstein E, Sun Y, et al. Mutation of the E6-AP ubiquitin ligase reduces nuclear inclusion frequency while accelerating polyglutamine-induced pathology in SCA1 mice. *Neuron* 1999; 24:879–892.

48. Warrick JM, Chan HY, Gray-Board GL, et al. Suppression of polyglutamine-mediated neurodegeneration in Drosophila by the molecular chaperone HSP70. *Nat Genet* 1999; 23:425–428.

49. Cummings CJ, Sun Y, Opal P, et al. Over-expression of inducible HSP70 chaperone suppresses neuropathology and improves motor function in SCA1 mice. *Hum Mol Genet* 2001; 10:1511–1518.

50. Auluck PK, Chan HY, Trojanowski JQ, et al. Chaperone suppression of alpha-synuclein toxicity in a Drosophila model for Parkinson's disease. *Science* 2002; 295:865–868.

51. Muchowski PJ. Protein misfolding, amyloid formation, and neurodegeneration: a critical role for molecular chaperones. *Neuron* 2002; 35:9–12.

52. Singleton AB, Farrer M, Johnson J, et al. Alpha-synuclein locus triplication causes Parkinson's disease. *Science* 2003; 302:841.

53. Bussell R Jr, Eliezer D. Residual structure and dynamics in Parkinson's disease–associated mutants of alpha-synuclein. *J Biol Chem* 2001; 276:45996–46003.

54. Giasson BI, Duda JE, Murray IV, et al. Oxidative damage linked to neurodegeneration by selective alpha-synuclein nitration in synucleinopathy lesions. *Science* 2000; 290:985–989.

55. Uversky VN, Li J, Fink AL. Pesticides directly accelerate the rate of alpha-synuclein fibril formation: A possible factor in Parkinson's disease. *FEBS Lett* 2001; 500:105–108.

56. Manning-Bog AB, McCormack AL, Li J, et al. The herbicide paraquat causes up-regulation and aggregation of alpha-synuclein in mice: Paraquat and alpha-synuclein. *J Biol Chem* 2002; 277:1641–1644.

57. Hershko A, Ciechanover A. The ubiquitin system. *Annu Rev Biochem* 1998; 67: 425–479.

58. Ciechanover A, Orian A, Schwartz AL. Ubiquitin-mediated proteolysis: Biological regulation via destruction. *Bioessays* 2000; 22:442–451.

59. Ciechanover A, Brundin P. The ubiquitin proteasome system in neurodegenerative diseases: Sometimes the chicken, sometimes the egg. *Neuron* 2003; 40:427–446.

60. Mizuno Y, Hattori N, Mori H, et al. Parkin and Parkinson's disease. *Curr Opin Neurol* 2001; 14:477–482.

61. Zhang Y, Gao J, Chung KK, et al. Parkin functions as an E2-dependent ubiquitin-protein ligase and promotes the degradation of the synaptic vesicle-associated protein, CDCrel-1. *Proc Natl Acad Sci USA* 2000; 97:13354–13359.

62. Chung KK, Thomas B, Li X, et al. S-Nitrosylation of Parkin regulates ubiquitination and compromises Parkin's protective function. *Science* 2004; 304:1328–1331.

63. Ko HS, Kim SW, Sriram SR, et al. Identification of far upstream element-binding protein-1 as an authentic Parkin substrate. *J Biol Chem* 2006; 281:16193–16196.

64. Corti O, Hampe C, Koutnikova H, et al. The p38 subunit of the aminoacyl-tRNA synthetase complex is a Parkin substrate: Linking protein biosynthesis and neurodegeneration. *Hum Mol Genet* 2003; 12:1427–1437.

65. Stefanis L, Larsen KE, Rideout HJ, et al. Expression of A53T mutant but not wild-type alpha-synuclein in PC12 cells induces alterations of the ubiquitin-dependent degradation system, loss of dopamine release, and autophagic cell death. *J Neurosci* 2001; 21:9549–9560.

66. Lee EN, Cho HJ, Lee CH, et al. Phthalocyanine tetrasulfonates affect the amyloid formation and cytotoxicity of alpha-synuclein. *Biochemistry* 2004; 43:3704–3715.

67. Wilkinson KD, Lee KM, Deshpande S, et al. The neuron-specific protein PGP 9.5 is a ubiquitin carboxyl-terminal hydrolase. *Science* 1989; 246:670–673.

68. Levecque C, Destee A, Mouroux V, et al. No genetic association of the ubiquitin carboxy-terminal hydrolase-L1 gene S18Y polymorphism with familial Parkinson's disease. *J Neural Transm* 2001; 108:979–984.

69. Saigoh K, Wang YL, Suh JG, et al. Intragenic deletion in the gene encoding ubiquitin carboxy-terminal hydrolase in gad mice. *Nat Genet* 1999; 23:47–51.

70. Liu Y, Fallon L, Lashuel HA, et al. The UCH-L1 gene encodes two opposing enzymatic activities that affect alpha-synuclein degradation and Parkinson's disease susceptibility. *Cell* 2002; 111:209–218.

71. Hemelaar J, Borodovsky A, Kessler BM, et al. Specific and covalent targeting of conjugating and deconjugating enzymes of ubiquitin-like proteins. *Mol Cell Biol* 2004; 24:84–95.

72. Rideout HJ, Larsen KE, Sulzer D, et al. Proteasomal inhibition leads to formation of ubiquitin/alpha-synuclein-immunoreactive inclusions in PC12 cells. *J Neurochem* 2001; 78:899–908.

73. Snyder H, Mensah K, Theisler C, et al. Aggregated and monomeric alpha-synuclein bind to the S6' proteasomal protein and inhibit proteasomal function. *J Biol Chem* 2003; 278:11753–11759.

74. Tofaris GK, Layfield R, Spillantini MG. alpha-synuclein metabolism and aggregation is linked to ubiquitin-independent degradation by the proteasome. *FEBS Lett* 2001; 509:22–26.

75. Pickart CM. Mechanisms underlying ubiquitination. *Annu Rev Biochem* 2001; 70:503–533.

76. Holmberg CI, Staniszewski KE, Mensah KN, et al. Inefficient degradation of truncated polyglutamine proteins by the proteasome. *EMBO J* 2004; 23:4307–4318.

77. Venkatraman P, Wetzel R, Tanaka M, et al. Eukaryotic proteasomes cannot digest polyglutamine sequences and release them during degradation of polyglutamine-containing proteins. *Mol Cell* 2004; 14:95–104.

78. Voges D, Zwickl P, Baumeister W. The 26S proteasome: A molecular machine designed for controlled proteolysis. *Annu Rev Biochem* 1999; 68:1015–1068.

79. Bence NF, Sampat RM, Kopito RR. Impairment of the ubiquitin-proteasome system by protein aggregation. *Science* 2001; 292:1552–1555.

80. Jana NR, Zemskov EA, Wang G, et al. Altered proteasomal function due to the expression of polyglutamine-expanded truncated N-terminal huntingtin induces apoptosis by caspase activation through mitochondrial cytochrome c release. *Hum Mol Genet* 2001; 10:1049–1059.

81. Bennett EJ, Bence NF, Jayakumar R, et al. Global impairment of the ubiquitin-proteasome system by nuclear or cytoplasmic protein aggregates precedes inclusion body formation. *Mol Cell* 2005; 17:351–365.

82. Cuervo A. Autophagy: In sickness and in health. *Trends Cell Biol* 2004; 14:70–77.

83. Klionsky DJ. Autophagy. *Curr Biol* 2005; 15:282–283.

84. Levine B, Klionsky DJ. Development by self-digestion: Molecular mechanisms and biological functions of autophagy. *Dev Cell* 2004; 6:463–477.

85. Yorimitsu T, Klionsky DJ. Autophagy: Molecular machinery for self-eating. *Cell Death Differ* 2005; 12(Suppl 2):1542–1552.

86. Mizushima N. The pleiotropic role of autophagy: From protein metabolism to bactericide. *Cell Death Differ* 2005; 12:1535–1541.

87. Ravikumar B, Vacher C, Berger Z, et al. Inhibition of mTOR induces autophagy and reduces toxicity of polyglutamine expansions in fly and mouse models of Huntington disease. *Nat Genet* 2004; 36:585–595.

88. Iwata A, Riley BE, Johnston JA, et al. HDAC6 and microtubules are required for autophagic degradation of aggregated huntingtin. *J Biol Chem* 2005; 280:40282–40292.

89. Mizushima N, Yamamoto A, Matsui M, et al. In vivo analysis of autophagy in response to nutrient starvation using transgenic mice expressing a fluorescent autophagosome marker. *Mol Biol Cell* 2004; 15:1101–1111.

90. Komatsu M, Waguri S, Ueno T, et al. Impairment of starvation-induced and constitutive autophagy in Atg7-deficient mice. *J Cell Biol* 2005; 169:425–434.

91. Hara T, Nakamura K, Matsui M, et al. Suppression of basal autophagy in neural cells causes neurodegenerative disease in mice. *Nature* 2006; 441:885–889.

92. Komatsu M, Waguri S, Chiba T, et al. Loss of autophagy in the central nervous system causes neurodegeneration in mice. *Nature* 2006; 441:880–884.

93. Mortimore GE, Lardeux BR, Adams CE. Regulation of microautophagy and basal protein turnover in rat liver. Effects of short-term starvation. *J Biol Chem* 1988; 263:2506–2512.

94. Cuervo A, Dice J. A receptor for the selective uptake and degradation of proteins by lysosomes. *Science* 1996; 273:501–503.

95. Massey A, Kiffin R, Cuervo AM. Pathophysiology of chaperone-mediated autophagy. *Int J Biochem Cell Biol* 2004; 36:2420–2434.

96. Kamimoto T, Shoji S, Hidvegi T, et al. Intracellular inclusions containing mutant alpha1-antitrypsin Z are propagated in the absence of autophagic activity. *J Biol Chem* 2006; 28:4467–4476.

97. Iwata A, Christianson JC, Bucci M, et al. Increased susceptibility of cytoplasmic over nuclear polyglutamine aggregates to autophagic degradation. *Proc Natl Acad Sci USA* 2005; 102:13135–13140.

98. Nixon RA, Wegiel J, Kumar A, et al. Extensive involvement of autophagy in Alzheimer disease: An immuno-electron microscopy study. *J Neuropathol Exp Neurol* 2005; 64:113–122.

99. Kegel KB, Kim M, Sapp E, et al. Huntingtin expression stimulates endosomal-lysosomal activity, endosome tubulation, and autophagy. *J Neurosci* 2000; 20:7268–7278.

100. Larsen K, Fon E, Hastings T, et al. Methamphetamine-induced degeneration of dopaminergic neurons involves autophagy and upregulation of dopamine synthesis. *J Neurosci* 2002; 22:8951–8960.

101. Pattingre S, Tassa A, Qu X, et al. Bcl-2 antiapoptotic proteins inhibit Beclin 1-dependent autophagy. *Cell* 2005; 122:927–939.

102. Massey AC, Kaushik S, Sovak G, et al. Consequences of the selective blockage of chaperone-mediated autophagy. *Proc Natl Acad Sci USA* 2006; 103:5905–5910.

103. Terman A, Brunk UT. Lipofuscin. *Int J Biochem Cell Biol* 2004; 36:1400–1404.

104. Cuervo AM, Bergamini E, Brunk UT. Autophagy and aging: the importance of maintaining "clean" cells. *Autophagy* 2005; 1:131–140.

105. Cuervo AM, Stefanis L, Fredenburg R, et al. Impaired degradation of mutant alpha-synuclein by chaperone-mediated autophagy. *Science* 2004; 305:1292–1295.

106. Webb JL, Ravikumar B, Atkins J, et al. Alpha-synuclein is degraded by both autophagy and the proteasome. *J Biol Chem* 2003; 278:25009–25013.

33 Etiology: The Role of Environment and Genetics

Caroline M. Tanner

During the last century, theories regarding the causes of Parkinson's disease (PD) regularly cycled between heredity and environment. More recently, multifactorial theories of gene–environment interaction have emerged (1, 2). Whatever the prevailing theory, epidemiologic observations—that is, the distribution of PD in human populations and associated risk factors identified in these groups—were cited as providing, supporting, or detracting evidence. Yet only a few distinct forms of parkinsonism have been described. The causes of the majority of cases remain unexplained.

This chapter provides an intellectual framework for the clinical investigation of the determinants of PD. First, the challenges particular to the investigation of the cause(s) of PD are reviewed. Second, parkinsonisms of known cause are discussed briefly, with particular attention being given to the degree to which investigation of these unique and, so far, rare disorders can guide the study of typical PD. Third, etiologic clues for common forms of PD provided by epidemiologic studies are presented. Finally, some speculation regarding what the most fruitful next steps might be is provided.

CHALLENGES IN INVESTIGATING PARKINSON'S DISEASE

The interpretation of the epidemiologic studies discussed in this chapter must be tempered by the limitations imposed by the current state of knowledge regarding the clinical entity known as Parkinson's disease. The first step in understanding the cause of PD is to define the disorder. Although on the surface this appears to be a straightforward task, there are many potential difficulties.

First, the clinical definition of PD has evolved over the past 50 years. Thus, knowledge of the diagnostic criteria used in a given study is critical to interpretation of its results. In the middle of the twentieth century, the term *Parkinson's disease* was often applied to the syndrome of parkinsonism without distinguishing etiology. Thus postencephalitic parkinsonism, parkinsonism secondary to dopamine receptor–blocking drugs, or neurodegenerative parkinsonism of any type would not be distinguished in epidemiologic or clinical reports. Over the last 3 or 4 decades, distinct causes of parkinsonism have increasingly been identified. As the causes of different parkinsonian syndromes have been understood, studies have incorporated more precise diagnostic criteria, excluding parkinsonism of known etiology, such as drug-induced disease, and clinical syndromes thought to reflect a different pathologic substrate than "idiopathic" parkinsonism (such as progressive supranuclear palsy or multiple system atrophy). Most recently, two rare genetic forms of parkinsonism have been identified. To date, no epidemiologic study published has distinguished these genetic parkinsonisms from "idiopathic" disease. Over time, more causes of the syndrome will surely be identified. To be most useful, descriptive epidemiologic studies should enumerate these different forms of parkinsonism separately. In analytic studies, failure to study parkinsonism of known cause separately from the "idiopathic" disorder lessens the ability to identify potential causative factors unless all cases have the same cause. In this chapter, the term *Parkinson's disease* is reserved for that component of parkinsonism that as yet has no known cause. This includes those cases with the syndrome of bradykinesia, muscle rigidity, resting tremor, and postural instability, reflecting underlying degeneration of pigmented brainstem neurons and where characteristic neuronal intracytoplasmic inclusions (Lewy bodies) staining for alpha-synuclein are observed.

Improved methods of investigating neuropathology have led to the proposal that neuropathologic injury in PD begins in lower brainstem and olfactory nuclei and progresses through predictable stages over time, involving the substantia nigra and producing classical parkinsonism only relatively late, at stages 3 and 4 (3, 4). Lewy neurite pathology can also be seen in autonomic ganglia outside of the CNS, leading to the further hypothesis that PD may begin outside of the CNS well before the classic signs of parkinsonism develop (5). If this is correct, the onset of the disease process may begin long before the neurologic syndrome is diagnosed. While new approaches are promising, their abilities to distinguish normal from abnormal and to distinguish PD from other forms of parkinsonism have not yet been developed to the extent that any of these techniques can be used outside the research setting. In epidemiologic research, broad application of these techniques remains difficult, as they are not widely available.

Variations in diagnostic criteria also make it difficult to compare studies performed at different times or in different areas. In reports from earlier in this century, cases that today might be considered typical PD were classified as "arteriosclerotic parkinsonism" (6, 7). Other reports grouped secondary parkinsonism, such as drug-induced parkinsonism and postencephalitic parkinsonism, along with PD in determining incidence or prevalence rates, although these disorders are etiologically and pathologically distinct (6, 8). And many of the currently recognized "atypical" parkinsonian syndromes were described only in the last several decades and, in all likelihood, were included with idiopathic PD. More recently, genetic causes of parkinsonism have been identified. These disorders probably would have been classified as PD in earlier and even in more recent reports and likely represent just a fraction of all parkinsonism. However, the clinical characteristics, particularly in younger-onset forms, make them likely to be disproportionately included in clinical studies. Mitochondrial mechanisms, oxidative stress, and protein clearance appear to be pathogenic in animal models derived both from toxicant and genetic forms of parkinsonism (9, 10)

A further challenge in investigating PD is the lack of a diagnostic test. Diagnosis is entirely dependent on the neurologic history and examination. This forced reliance on clinical diagnostic methods is a potential source of error. Variations in the experience of diagnosticians can affect diagnostic accuracy. For example, a different neurologic disorder, essential tremor, may be confused with PD. Up to 40% of the diagnoses of PD gleaned from public health registries were false-positives, largely comprising cases of essential tremor (11). Conversely, bona fide PD may be misdiagnosed, particularly in the very elderly, thus underestimating the pattern of disease in these age groups. In the older age groups, slowness and tremor may be considered "normal" by some. Other common disorders—including Alzheimer's disease (AD), hypothyroidism, depression, arthritis, and stroke—may not always be easily distinguished from PD. A further difficulty is presented by people with both parkinsonism and dementia, whose condition may be classified as either primary disorder in different epidemiologic surveys. The common use of neuroleptics in institutionalized elderly, especially those with cognitive impairment, can further confound diagnosis in this age group, because these drugs can cause parkinsonism.

There is no clinical criterion that predicts with absolute certainty the pathologic changes typical of PD. In postmortem studies, only 80% of cases clinically diagnosed as PD were found to have typical Lewy body neuropathology (12, 13). These results probably overestimate the actual misdiagnosis rate, however, because autopsy most likely is performed when clinical diagnosis is questioned (14). The identification of individuals with very early disease presents additional uncertainties, because at least 50% of substantia nigra pars compacta (SNPC) cells are believed to be lost before the symptoms prompt medical attention (15). Furthermore, in autopsy series, the pathologic changes of PD are identified in the brains of people who were not diagnosed during life; these "incidental Lewy body" cases increase with increasing age of the population surveyed and may represent clinically presymptomatic PD (16). Postmortem validation of clinical diagnosis, in the few settings where it is possible, offers valuable insights (17).

The uncertainty of clinical diagnosis is an important factor in the design and critical analysis of studies of the etiology of PD. Inclusion of patients who do not have typical disease serves to increase estimates of disease frequency, whereas excluding early disease has the opposite effect. Either type of misclassification can alter demographic patterns. In case-control studies, the inclusion of people who do not actually have PD usually lowers the precision of the study, decreasing the ability to find a risk factor for disease. If many such patients were included in a study, however, it is possible that a risk factor identified with the non-PD cases might erroneously be associated with PD. In genetic studies, inclusion of such cases would usually lower the likelihood of finding an association of a gene or chromosome marker with PD. Moreover, the mode of inheritance of a genetic defect could be misinterpreted, particularly if a disorder frequently misclassified as PD were inherited.

Finally, PD is a relatively rare disorder. As a result, even studies of large populations will find relatively few cases, and the potential error in any single study may be significant. In analytic studies, this can be particularly problematic if the cause or causes of disease differ across populations.

PARKINSONISM OF KNOWN CAUSE

Current theories on the pathogenic mechanisms underlying PD are derived largely from investigations of the forms of parkinsonism with identifiable causes (both genetic and environmental) and the pursuit of the mechanisms of these disorders. Although it is popular to pose debates supporting a purely genetic or environmental causes of disease, this formulation is probably a gross oversimplification. More likely, PD is a complex disorder resulting from the interaction of both genetic and environmental factors. Regardless of triggering factors, if the final mechanisms of neuronal injury and death discovered in these forms of parkinsonism with known causes are relevant to idiopathic Parkinsonian cases, delineation of these mechanisms will help to shed light on the determinants of the larger proportion of patients with this disease. For this reason, this chapter begins with a discussion of the clinical and laboratory knowledge gleaned from several forms of parkinsonism very closely resembling PD, but with known causes. Investigation of the mechanisms of neurodegeneration underlying these may provide insights into the determinants of PD in general. For example, the final common pathway or pathways of injury produced by both genetic and environmental risk factors for PD may be similar, even if initiating factors differ. Elucidation of the pathophysiologic mechanisms of neuronal death in these rare disorders may eventually lead to an understanding of the cause(s) of all forms of parkinsonism.

Parkinsonism can be a manifestation of many neurologic disorders and may be caused by toxicants or infectious brain injury (18, 19). In general, however, these disorders have not been informative in the investigation of typical PD, as their neurologic injury is more extensive and the resultant clinical features distinct. However, some forms of parkinsonism in humans are clinically very similar to PD. One is caused by toxicant exposure and the others result from mutations in specific genes. Each differs from PD in some regards, but all have significant clinical or pathologic overlap with the "typical" disease of unknown etiology. Each is considered here in terms of the possible clues to the cause of typical PD.

MPTP-Induced Parkinsonism

Parkinsonism seen in a cluster of narcotics addicts was caused by the intravenous injection of the compound 1-methyl-4-phenyl, 1, 2, 3, 6-tetrahydropyridine (MPTP) (see Chapter 34) (20). Before this discovery, parkinsonism was known to result from numerous other chemical injuries, such as carbon disulfide, manganese, and hydrocarbon solvents (18, 19). However, the clinical syndromes and patterns of pathologic injury resulting from these compounds are more widely distributed than those of PD. In contrast, MPTP-induced parkinsonism is remarkable in that, with the exception of its rapid onset, it closely mimics the clinical and anatomic features of PD. In addition, animal studies have found that susceptibility to MPTP toxicity increases with age (21). These observations led to the proposal that exposure to an exogenous agent might cause PD. Many studies seeking an environmental cause of PD were launched (see subsequent section). Thus far, no other exposure has been proven to cause a pure parkinsonian syndrome in humans. Because PD onset is insidious, in contrast to the abrupt or subacute onset of symptoms after a large toxic exposure, chronic low-dose exposure to a single agent or multiple low-dose exposures to different agents may be involved. Substances that are mildly toxic or that slowly ingress or accumulate in the brain are difficult to evaluate, and their significance could be missed (22). To narrow this search, the MPTP observation has been used as a paradigm, and research focuses on compounds that are toxicologically or structurally similar to MPTP. This approach serves as a model for the interaction of clinical scientists and basic scientists in seeking the cause of PD.

The toxicology of MPTP is well characterized. Parenterally administered MPTP readily crosses the blood-brain barrier because of its lipophilicity (23). In the central nervous system (CNS), it is oxidized, primarily by glial monoamine oxidase B (MAO-B), into the charged molecule 1-methyl-4-phenylpyridinium ion (MPP+), the active neurotoxin (24). MPP+ is actively taken up into nerve terminals by the dopamine transporter (25) and is further concentrated in mitochondria because of the electrochemical membrane potential gradient (26). In mitochondria it binds to and inhibits reduced nicotinamide-adenine-dinucleotide (NADH) complex I (the rotenone-sensitive site), thereby blocking oxidative phosphorylation and adenosine-triphosphate (ATP) production (27–29).

If inhibition of mitochondrial complex I is the key toxic action of MPP$^+$, then other compounds with similar actions may also be suspected as parkinsonism-causing agents, such as mitochondrial poisons (30, 31), including cyanide, carbon monoxide, hydrogen sulfide, diphenylether herbicides, and nitric oxide. Mitochondrial ATP synthesis is also impaired by fluorinated hydrocarbons, DDT and other organochlorine insecticides, dinitrophenol, thiadiazole herbicides, and crotonalide fungicides, among others. Furthermore, mitochondrial defects and oxidative stress are intertwined phenomena, both resulting from and inducing the other (32, 33), and a growing body of evidence suggests that oxidative damage also contributes to the pathogenesis of PD (34–37) (see also Chapter 30). This adds an additional list of compounds that could potentially contribute to nigral nerve cell injury, including heavy metals, compounds metabolized to reactive intermediates (e.g., quinones), and compounds interfering with endogenous protective mechanisms, such as sulfhydryl-depleting agents (with consequent loss of glutathione) (38). Also, diets deficient in antioxidant vitamins could represent a risk factor for nigral cell degeneration. Finally, structural analogs of MPTP with different chemical mechanisms, such as paraquat (39) and diquat, have been associated with parkinsonism in humans. Other structurally similar compounds, such as isoquinolines (31, 40, 41) and 4-substituted pyridines (42, 43) may be nigral toxins in animals or in human brain (44, 45) and have been found in postmortem parkinsonian substantia nigra (31, 46).

Consistent with the possibility that environmental agents acting as mitochondrial toxins may contribute to PD risk (47), one small study (48) reported finding the organochlorine insecticide dieldrin in brain samples from 6 of 20 PD patients compared with none of 14 control brains. Most interesting is the recent demonstration (49) of a progressive nigral lesion in animals resulting from exposure to rotenone, a common pesticide that specifically blocks mitochondrial complex I. As with the MPP$^+$-induced lesions, rotenone-induced injury is selective and specific to the areas damaged in PD. To date, no case of human parkinsonism has been associated with rotenone exposure. However, the demonstration of parkinsonism in association with a second specific inhibitor of mitochondrial complex I supports the hypothesis that agents with this chemical mechanism may cause PD.

Parkinsonism Resulting from Genetic Mutations

At present, mutations in at least 5 genes have been firmly associated with parkinsonism: (a) α-synuclein [SNCA or PARK1] (50), (b) parkin [PRKN or PARK2] (51), (c) DJ-1 [DJ1 or PARK7] (52), (d) PTEN-induced putative kinase I [PINK1 or PARK6] (50), and (e) leucine-rich repeat kinase 2 or dardarin [LRRK2 or PARK8] (53, 54). A sixth, the UCH-L1 [PARK5] gene, was identified in 2 German siblings with PD and thought to represent a causative single missense mutation (55), but further analysis has not been definitive.

Parkinsonism Resulting from Mutations in the α-Synuclein Gene (PARK1). The first mutation linked to familial parkinsonism was found in the coding region of the gene on chromosome 4 encoding for the α-synuclein protein (SNCA) (56, 57). The mutation caused parkinsonism in a large Italian-Greek family (known as the Contursi kindred). Inheritance is in an autosomal dominant pattern. The clinical features are not entirely typical of PD, as onset is earlier than usual, the course is more rapid, response to levodopa therapy is poor, rest tremor is uncommon, dementia appears to be more common, and signs not usually seen in PD, such as fluent aphasia, are seen in some patients (58). A second mutation in this gene was associated with dominantly inherited parkinsonism in a German family (59). However, parkinsonism resulting from an α-synuclein mutation appears to be limited so far to fewer than 70 cases worldwide. This mutation has never been associated with sporadic PD, and no additional affected kindreds have been reported (60, 61). Recently, SNCA genomic multiplications in familial parkinsonism have been reported in 2 families, with duplications and triplications; these are associated with early-onset parkinsonism (62–65).

Although parkinsonism associated with α-synuclein mutations is rare, investigation of the mechanisms underlying that disease may provide useful clues to understanding the cause of sporadic PD. Several lines of evidence have been uncovered. α-Synuclein protein is normally abundant in nerve terminals. In the laboratory, mutated protein promotes aggregation into filaments (66). A fragment of α-synuclein is found in plaques of AD (67). In transgenic animal models, abnormalities of dopamine systems and inclusions are seen. Most remarkably, in fruit flies, which normally have no α-synuclein, expression of the α-synuclein gene or of either mutant caused dopamine neuron loss, Lewy-like inclusions, and mobility problems (68). Furthermore, aggregates of α-synuclein are present in the intracytoplasmic inclusions of PD and Lewy body dementia and in the glial cytoplasmic inclusions in multiple system atrophy (69). Aggregates of α-synuclein may promote further protein aggregation, but whether this is a cause of disease or merely one feature of disease-causing pathology is not known. Intriguingly, abnormal protein aggregation is seen in other neurodegenerative disorders, suggesting similarities in the pathogenetic mechanisms of these conditions. If this is true, identifying factors promoting and preventing this protein aggregation may be a fruitful direction of research.

Parkinsonism Resulting from Mutations in the Parkin Gene (PARK2).   Recessively inherited parkinsonism is most commonly caused by either point mutations or large deletions in the "*parkin*" gene (chromosome 6q25.2–27) (51, 70–72). Patients typically have disease onset before the age of 40 and a family history of PD. Clinically, they have a high incidence of foot dystonia, levodopa-induced dyskinesias, diurnal variation of symptoms with prominent sleep benefit, and early motor fluctuations in response to levodopa therapy. A critical difference between *parkin*-associated parkinsonism and sporadic PD is at the absence of Lewy bodies on postmortem exam (73, 74).

PARK2 mutations are more common than PARK1 mutations but still cause only a fraction of all parkinsonism. In a European study, PARK2 mutations were found in 77% of people with parkinsonism beginning before age 20 but in only 3% of those with symptoms starting after age 30 (75). Because at least 95% of parkinsonism in the community has onset after age 50 (76), PARK2 remains a rare cause of parkinsonism.

As with α-synuclein, investigation of the disease-causing mechanisms associated with this gene may provide insight into the pathogenesis of sporadic PD. The function of parkin protein is not known although it is thought to be an ε3 ubiquitin ligase playing a role in protein aggregation. It is normally expressed in substantia nigra in a pattern similar to the expression of α-synuclein. PARK2 protein is associated with Golgi complexes and may assist in protein processing. In addition, it is found in Lewy bodies in nonfamilial PD. Unlike α-synuclein, however, the protein product is not expressed in PARK 2–associated parkinsonism.

Parkinsonism Resulting from Mutations in PTEN-Induced Putative Kinase I (PARK6 PINK1).   PINK1 is a rare form of recessive parkinsonism. The first mutations in the PINK1 gene were described in three consanguineous families of Italian and Spanish origin (77, 78). The PINK1 gene on chromosome 1 has been shown to encode a putative protein kinase, and PINK1 proteins appear to be located on the mitochondrion. PINK1 may exert a protective effect on the cell, and it is hypothesized that mutations in the PINK1 gene may increase susceptibility to cellular stress (79). PINK1 mutations cause symptoms resembling *parkin*-associated disease. Age of onset is usually in the third or fourth decade, the disease progresses slowly, and there is good response to levodopa. Since the original reports, PINK1 mutations have been found in European (80) and Asian populations (81) but are thought to be less common than *parkin* mutations (82, 83). It has been suggested that haploinsufficiency of PINK1 is a susceptibility factor for parkinsonism (82).

Parkinsonism Resulting from Mutations in DJ-1(PARK7).   DJ-1 is another rare recessive form of parkinsonism. The first mutations in the DJ-1 gene were described in a Dutch kindred carrying a homozygous deletion (52). Different DJ-1 mutations in other ethnic groups have also been identified (52, 84–87). In the original Dutch kindred there is a homozygous deletion (52) and complete absence of the protein product, which suggests the pathogenesis results from loss of DJ-1 function. The function of the DJ-1 protein, however, is not yet known. Symptoms appear to be similar to those of *parkin*- and PINK1-associated parkinsonism, including early age of onset (17 to about 40 years), good response to levodopa, slow progression, and levodopa-induced dyskinesias (84, 85, 87–90). Psychological symptoms at onset or in the early stages in the disease course and focal dystonias have been reported (88, 89). The frequency of the mutations appears to be low (87, 91); in one study, only 2% of those with early-onset PD had DJ-1 mutations (87).

Parkinsonism Resulting from Mutations In Leucine-Rich Repeat Kinase 2 (LRRK2) or Dardarin (PARK8).   LRRK2-related parkinsonism is the most common autosomal dominant form. Mutations in the LRRK2 gene are the most common cause of genetic parkinsonism, accounting for up to 5% to 6% of familial and 1% to 2% of sporadic parkinsonism cases (53, 54, 92–95). In persons of Ashkenazi Jewish and North African origin, as many as 15% to 20% have mutations in the LRRK2 gene (96, 97). LRRK2 clinical features include early- and late-onset disease, and there is a wide range of pathology, including LB pathology and neurofibrillary tangles as well as pure nigral degeneration without LBs (54, 98). Patients with LRRK2 mutations typically have clinical features resembling those of idiopathic PD (54, 99–101). In one study (101), age at onset was variable, ranging from 33 to 78 years, with mean age at onset of 57.1 ± 13.2 years, which is similar to that of idiopathic PD. Onset was frequently asymmetrical, with rest tremor or motor slowness, and the majority patients had minimal or no rest tremor even with long disease duration. All of the patients were taking levodopa. Although most reports indicate low rates of associated psychiatric or cognitive dysfunction (54, 100, 102), more recently some patients with LRRK2 mutations have been noted to have severe hallucinations, moderate dementia, delusions, and depression with early-stage disease (103). Penetrance has been reported to be between 30% and 100% in different families with LRRK2 mutations (53, 104), and Gaig et al., in their publication (101), note an unaffected 91-year-old carrying the G2019S mutation.

Parkinsonism Resulting from Other Mutations and Polymorphisms. Other candidate PD loci have been proposed, including putative disease-causing mutations in the ubiquitin carboxy-terminal hydrolase L1 (*UCHL1*) (55) and in a nuclear receptor of subfamily 4 (*NR4A2* or *NURRI*) (105). These candidates do not map to known parkinsonism linkage regions, but polymorphisms in both genes have been associated with parkinsonism in some case-control studies (106). From an epidemiologic perspective, the monogenic causes of parkinsonism appear to constitute a small proportion of cases worldwide. However, investigation of the protein products of these genes can provide further understanding of the process of neuronal death in parkinsonism. Investigation of these forms has emphasized the role of key proteins (like α-synuclein) and molecular pathways leading to neurodegeneration. Intriguingly, mitochondrial mechanisms, oxidative stress, and protein clearance appear to be pathogenic in animal models derived both from toxicant and genetic forms of parkinsonism (9, 10).

CLUES TO THE CAUSE OF PARKINSON'S DISEASE FROM EPIDEMIOLOGIC STUDIES

Epidemiologists study the frequencies and determinants of disease in populations. By comparing disease frequencies between populations with differing characteristics, putative risk factors can be identified. Epidemiologic investigations cannot "prove" a specific cause of the disease. In the end, the determination of causality must be demonstrated in the laboratory. However, descriptive epidemiologic studies reporting the distribution of disease within populations may lead to theories that can in turn be tested in the laboratory or in analytical investigations. Analytical epidemiologic studies focused on the identification of the determinants of disease can provide strong clues for laboratory scientists. For example, in most cases a genetic cause of disease is first suspected because of a characteristic familial pattern. An environmental cause, such as infection or toxicant exposure, would classically be associated with clustering of cases in time or space. As described previously, for parkinsonism, each pattern is seen in only a small percentage of cases but not in most. The following section briefly reviews potential risk factors identified through epidemiologic studies.

Risk Factors Proposed from Studies of Disease Frequency

Increasing Age. In any population studied, regardless of geographic location, an increase in PD frequency is associated with increasing age (6, 11, 107–111). Parkinson's disease incidence increases dramatically from less than 10 new cases per 100, 000 at age 50 to at least 200 new cases per 100, 000 at age 80 (112–114). Indeed, in all populations studied, PD is very rare before age 50 (6, 10, 112, 115–123) and increases steadily in the sixth through the eighth decades in most populations. A decrease in late life is seen in some studies; whether this apparent decline in PD incidence is the result of methodologic challenges, such as the greater difficulty identifying and diagnosing PD in the very old (124) rather than an actual decline in disease frequency, is not certain. If the decline is real, a biological "window of vulnerability" for PD may exist.

Investigation of the determinants of age-related incidence could provide important insights into the causes of PD, as this pattern could reflect an age-determined process, such as an acquired defect in cellular metabolism. Alternatively, a process requiring a long period to manifest, as might result from prolonged toxicant exposure or the cumulative effects of many individual injuries to nerve cells, might cause a similar pattern. Or, both age-related vulnerability and time-dependent processes could explain the late-life preponderance of PD.

Male Gender. Parkinson's disease is typically approximately 1.2 to 1.5 times more common in men than in women, although age-adjusted gender-specific differences show some variability worldwide (107, 108, 110–112, 118, 125–135). The greater disease frequency in men may reflect a biologic phenomenon, such as might result, for example, from the influence of sex hormones, or a male-associated exposure, such as an occupational toxicant exposure or other behavioral factors. In a large study in northern California, PD incidence in men was 91% higher than for women (19 per 100, 000 for men vs. 9.9 per 100, 000 for women, age-adjusted) (122).

Caucasian Race. Most prevalence studies have shown a similar pattern of greater frequency of PD in Caucasians (2). Whether this reflects biased ascertainment, differences in survival, or a true risk remains unknown. Studies of incidence can address the question of different survival, but the incidence of PD in non-Caucasians has been estimated in only a few studies. Two multiracial population-based studies estimating the incidence of PD in the Upper West Side of Manhattan (112) and in Northern California (122) suggest racial differences in PD incidence. In the Manhattan study, African-American women had lower rates, but African-American men had higher rates than whites (112). The Northern California study, a much larger evaluation of PD incidence, showed a lower frequency of PD in both men and women of African or Asian descent than in non-Hispanic whites (122). Results remain equivocal in both studies, however, as even in this large study the numbers of nonwhites were low and between-group confidence intervals for race-specific PD incidence overlapped.

If there are true differences in PD risk among groups defined by race or ethnicity, this may reflect either differences in biologic susceptibility or in nongenetic risk factors. For example, mutations in the LRRK2 gene account for about 2% of parkinsonism in northern European populations but are 15% to 20% in persons of Ashkenazi Jewish and North African origin (96, 97). Others have suggested that dermal melanin may protect against PD by trapping potential neurotoxins before they reach the brain (136). Because dermal melanin is regularly sloughed with keratinized skin, persons with more dermal melanin might be protected from the passage of toxicant compounds into the CNS. Alternatively, differences in nongenetic risk factors may explain differences in among populations. For example, PD prevalence is high in the Inuit population of Greenland (137). This population is at risk for dietary and other exposures to persistent organic pollutants (138), agents suggested to be risk factors for PD. More studies are needed to determine whether people of different ethnicities have differing risks of PD. If present, this difference could provide clues to ethnicity-specific genetic or environmental etiologic factors.

More Recent Calendar Time. In only a few populations worldwide has the incidence of PD been determined at more than one point of time. Reviews of the Mayo Clinic database from Olmsted County, Minnesota, found no change in age-specific Parkinson's disease incidence between 1935 and 1990 (128, 139). One limitation to this work is the small population size. Only 154 PD cases were incident in 15 years, resulting in poor precision of these estimates. In contrast, in southwestern Finland, based on a larger number of cases, estimated incidence of PD was increased in men, particularly those aged 60 and older, in 1992 as compared to 1971 (140). While it is possible that these differences may reflect temporal changes in environmental exposures in Finland but not in Minnesota, this cannot be determined from the published studies. In China, prevalence estimated from population surveys in the 1980s was low, but more recent rates have been similar to those in western countries (141). The increased frequency of PD in these studies may reflect real increases in the disease, possibly as the result of increased exposure to disease-causing toxicants, or could have no relationship to the cause of PD but instead reflect factors such as improved diagnosis, improved record keeping, or relative changes in mortality as a result of better treatment of competing diseases (142).

RISK FACTORS FROM ANALYTIC STUDIES

Genetic and Hereditary Risk Factors

Although early observers did not believe that PD was inherited (143, 144), approximately 11% of patients in Gowers' London clinic reported an affected relative (145).

Familial clusters generally are interpreted to indicate a genetic cause for disease, but certain patterns within families, such as temporal clustering of disease, may be more suggestive of shared environmental risks. A number of case-control studies have found increased PD risk if a first degree relative has PD (1, 146–150). Because persons with disease may be more aware of disease in relatives, these studies in part may reflect reporting bias. Elbaz et al. (151) showed evidence for family information bias, whereby individuals with PD are more likely to report a relative with PD than are control subjects, increasing the risk estimate 133%. Additionally, studies in twins do not support a genetic cause for typical age at PD onset, although genetic factors appear to be increased in those with younger age at onset (152–157).

This section briefly reviews studies investigating heritable causes of PD. Much of this work is detailed in other chapters (see Chapter 37). Although a familial disease pattern is often the result of a specific genotype, nongenetic factors such as common exposures to infection or toxicants and lifestyle factors are also commonly shared among family members and can cause similar patterns of disease (158). Familial risk factors for PD have been sought using three general approaches: family studies and genetic linkage analysis; studies in relative pairs (twins, sibling pairs); and case-control comparisons of family history of PD or single genes proposed to be associated with it.

Studies in Families. Genetic defects responsible for parkinsonism have been identified in families as discussed above (50, 51–54, 56, 71, 77, 78, 147, 159, 160). In many cases, the clinical features resemble typical PD. However, within affected families there are often clinical features that are unusual for PD. Most of these families have had patterns consistent with Mendelian inheritance. In other families, specific genetic defects have not been associated with disease.

In the small number of cases in which autopsy has been performed, neuropathology was rarely identical to that of typical PD (161, 162). Reports of PD in familial patterns suggest that additional genes causing parkinsonism will probably be identified. Whether these new genes, as with the genes identified so far, will be linked to just a few individuals with parkinsonism or will contribute to the cause of most patients with the disease remains to be deciphered. Nevertheless, investigations of their gene products can potentially provide important clues to investigations of the etiology of PD.

Studies in Twins and Sibling Pairs. Studies of twins or siblings are another approach used to investigate the determinants of PD. In twin studies, the relative contribution of genetics and environment is determined by comparing concordance in monozygotic (MZ) twins (who share all autosomal genes) and dizygotic (DZ) twins (who share, on average, 50% of autosomal genes). If genetic factors are primary to the cause of PD, concordance in MZ pairs will be high, whereas that in DZ pairs will be similar to disease rates in other siblings (sharing, on average, 50% of genes). Monozygotic twin pairs discordant for PD were reported by Gudmundsson (7) and Pembrey (163). In 1977, Duvoisin and coworkers (152) initiated a collaborative study of PD in twins. They collected 43 MZ and 19 DZ twins by 1983 and found that concordance for parkinsonism is no more frequent in twins than would be expected from the age-specific incidence of the disease. Thus, they concluded that the main factors in the etiology of PD must be nongenetic. However, in a follow-up review of the data, they have suggested that these results neither exclude nor prove a genetic role (164). Imaging studies found that 4 of 15 MZ and 2 of 8 DZ asymptomatic co-twins had reduced putamen ^{18}F-dopa uptake (102). Those co-twins with impaired function had isolated postural tremor and/or possible bradykinesia. Concordance for reduced ^{18}F-dopa uptake (27% for MZ and 25% for DZ co-twins) was higher than was clinical concordance but not different between MZ and DZ pairs.

These studies suggested that genetic factors are not important in PD. However, the groups were small and highly selected. In most cases, diagnosis was derived only from medical databases, potentially causing an underestimate of concordance. To address these concerns, Tanner and colleagues compared concordance for PD in MZ and DZ twins in a long-established cohort of elderly male twins, unselected for diseases of late life, using direct assessment by a movement disorders specialist (165). Overall, concordance for PD in MZ and DZ pairs was similar. This finding is not consistent with a significant genetic cause of PD. The exception to this conclusion was those few pairs with age of onset under age 50, in whom concordance was much higher in MZ twins, suggesting strong genetic determinants in younger-onset disease.

Although these results appear clear-cut, twins were evaluated at a single point in time, and new cases occurring after this examination may have been missed. Two small follow-up studies highlighted this concern. In the first, a study of 34 twin pairs, concordance for decreased putamenal ^{18}F-dopa uptake was higher in MZ twins than in DZ twin pairs. Higher MZ concordance was most evident in the 19 pairs in whom longitudinal follow-up was possible, particularly when concordance was further defined to include an increased rate of loss of putamenal ^{18}F-dopa (166). These findings were interpreted to strongly support a genetic cause of PD. In contrast, follow-up of 23 twin pairs for 8 years did not find differences in clinical concordance when comparing MZ twins and DZ twins (167). In this study, twins with prior decreased ^{18}F-dopa uptake on PET had not developed clinical PD. Because both studies are small in number and subject to selection and other possible biases, a final interpretation of these different findings awaits confirmation in a larger, unselected population. Moreover, the radiographic finding itself is of uncertain clinical and prognostic significance and will require further investigation. To address these concerns, a second evaluation of the National Academy of Sciences/National Research Council (NAS/NRC) World War II veteran twins cohort is underway, using both clinical examination and B-CIT SPECT (single photon emission computed tomography) imaging. Other researchers are using a different research strategy to investigate a genetic determinant of PD, the investigation of affected sibling pairs (168–174). To date, these studies have shown inconsistent findings, suggesting that complex gene-gene and gene-environment interactions may be important causes of PD. An evaluation of the heritability of PD in same-sexed and opposite-sexed twin pairs in the Swedish Twin Registry identified 247 twins with self-reported PD or a PD diagnosis ("possible PD"), and 517 twins who reported parkinsonian symptoms or use of antiparkinsonian medication ("suspected parkinsonism or movement disorder") (157). In the "possible PD" group, there were only two concordant pairs, both female dizygotic, and concordances were low in all zygosity groups, even when the definition of affected was expanded to include twins with suspected parkinsonism or movement disorder in addition to possible PD. Overall, the authors concluded these results suggested environmental factors were most important in the etiology of PD.

Case-Control Studies of Genetic Risk Factors. Case-control studies compare the rates of a proposed risk proposed risk (or protective) factor between people with the disease and people in the general population without the disease. Genetic risk factors for PD that have been studied using this method include family history of PD, specific genetic polymorphisms, and interaction of genes and other exposures. Case-control studies can demonstrate an association between a specific factor and disease. However, association does not prove causation. The significance of any association observed must be determined using other methods.

Case-control studies that compared the rate of PD in family members of cases and controls have also implicated a genetic contribution to the cause of the disease. On an average, reported rates reflect those first described by Gowers (145): approximately 10% to 15% of cases selected from clinics report a first-degree relative with PD. In some studies based in specialty clinics, much higher rates of PD and isolated tremor in relatives are reported (149, 150, 175). Because attendance at such clinics may be more likely if there are unusual characteristics to the illness, such as a familial pattern, these findings may not be generalizable to the population at large.

A community-based study (148) also found a significantly increased risk of PD in first-degree relatives of PD patients, but the magnitude of risk was considerably less. After controlling for sex, ethnicity, and relationship to proband, first-degree relatives of cases were 2.3 times more likely to develop PD than relatives of controls, and male relatives were at twice the risk as female relatives. The lifetime incidence (to age 75) in first-degree relatives of patients was only 2% versus 1% in control families, suggesting that, although there is a significant familial component, PD is probably not due to simple Mendelian inheritance. A similar 2.5-fold increased risk was also found in a recent, prospective, community-based study among people reporting a family history of PD (176). A historical cohort study (177) of 1001 first-degree relatives of 162 probands with PD and of 851 relatives of 147 control probands representative of the population of Olmsted County, Minnesota (from 1976 through 1995), was performed; 2713 first-degree relatives of 411 probands with PD referred to the Mayo Clinic from 1996 through 2000 and 625 spouses of PD or control probands were also interviewed and screened. Relatives of probands with younger onset (at or below age 66; first tertile) had a more significantly increased risk (relative risk, 2.62; 95% confidence interval, 1.66 to 4.15), whereas relatives of probands with later onset had no increased risk.

Others have used a case-control method to investigate whether specific genetic polymorphisms alter the risk of PD. So far, polymorphisms of several genes have been associated with PD in some studies, but no finding is consistent across populations. These associations have been proposed to be directly or indirectly related to disease etiology. Many of the genes associated with PD encode enzymes involved in xenobiotic metabolism. If PD is multifactorial, resulting from both genetic factors and environmental factors, risk from various environmental factors could be influenced by metabolizing enzymes. An interaction of genetic factors with these exposures could result in a high level of disease risk. Differences in the activity of enzymes metabolizing xenobiotics might result in toxicity in one person (i.e., low metabolizer) but not affect another (i.e., normal or high metabolizer.) Polymorphisms of several genes involved in xenobiotic metabolism have been associated with increased PD risk, including cytochrome P 450 2D6, cytochrome P 450 1A1, glutathione transferase, N-acetyl transferase, the dopamine transporter, MAO-B, paraoxonase, alpha-1 antichymotrypsin, and ubiquitin carboxy-terminal hydrolase L1, but results are not consistent (178–194).

The inconsistent nature of these associations with PD risk could represent spurious findings. Factors such as differences in ethnicity, presence of other diseases, or survival could cause control populations to differ from case populations in genetic makeup independent of disease-specific factors. However, inconsistent results may also be observed if gene-environment interactions are the determinant of PD (195); that is, these variants might only result in an increased risk if an individual were exposed to certain environmental factors, resulting in toxic effects from levels of compounds that might not otherwise be toxic. Enzymatic variability could result in decreased detoxification of toxic compounds or increased bioactivation of otherwise nontoxic compounds. Interactions of genetic polymorphisms and exposures have only rarely been studied (196–199). The combined effects of multiple genes, alone or in combination with exposures, may also be important (200). Whether the inconsistent results of studies to date are because of design differences or reflect a true absence of an important gene environment or gene-gene interaction in PD cannot be determined. Most investigators agree that further investigation in this area is clearly warranted.

Indeed, the search for PD susceptibility genes has been largely limited to the candidate-gene approach. Although mutations in the identified genes only rarely cause PD, common variations in some of these genes may be related to increased susceptibility to PD (201, 202). In a report of results drawing the first genomic map of PD, a 2-tiered, whole-genome association study identified 11 single-nucleotide polymorphisms (SNPs) associated with PD in both tier 1 and tier 2 samples (203). In addition, several new susceptibility genes for PD were nominated, with the SEMA5A gene being particularly notable. However, replication and cautious interpretation is essential (204). Such findings may ultimately identify biomarkers for early disease detection and suggest new molecular targets for therapy.

Environmental Risk Factors

More than 20 case-control studies have evaluated the role of environmental factors in the etiology of PD (2, 205). Many of these have implicated agricultural or industrial chemical exposures but have focused on broad groupings of agents or classes of chemicals rather than on specific exposures. Although these categories provide important leads, they have been too broad to pinpoint causal agents. The major findings are summarized in the following sections.

Agriculture and Related Factors. Rural living, farming, gardening, pesticide use, or well-water drinking have been associated with PD in almost every study (2, 123, 205–209). Overall, risk of PD appears to be increased in rural dwellers—especially in the United States. Meta-analysis results of 19 published studies (210) also support that risk factors include farm living and use of well water and pesticides. Although the specific associations are varied, the consistency of these general findings is remarkable and has contributed to interest in the relationship between farming and PD. Pesticide exposure (defined as including herbicides and fungicides) was associated with an increased PD risk in numerous studies (211–214). The risk was increased from 1.6 to 7 times in those exposed. In the meta-analysis of 19 studies, a combined odds ratio (OR) of 1.94 (95% C.I. 1.49 to 2.53) was seen for pesticide exposure (210). The structural and mechanistic resemblance of some common agricultural chemicals to MPTP and the potential of others to cause oxidative stress make this association particularly intriguing.

The category of pesticides is very broad and includes chemicals with many different mechanisms of action. Only a few studies have identified specific compounds or compound classes, including herbicides, insecticides, alkylated phosphates, organochlorines, wood preservatives, dieldrin, and paraquat (211–214). In Taiwan, PD risk was more than 6 times greater in people using paraquat for 20 years or more (215). Paraquat use was also associated with an increased risk in univariate but not multivariate analyses in two Canadian studies (216, 217). In Germany, organochlorines were associated with a 5.8-fold increased risk of PD, and using alkylated phosphates or carbamates had a 2.5-fold increase if cases were compared with regional controls but not if neighborhood controls were used (218). In other studies, chlorphenoxy and thiocarbamate herbicides and organophosphates are associated with increased PD risk in univariate but not multivariate analyses (215, 216). In a postmortem comparison of organochlorine pesticide concentrations in the brains of PD patients, people with AD, and controls, the organochlorine insecticide dieldrin was associated with an elevated risk of PD (219). So far, no study in humans has investigated the combined effects of several agents, although combined exposure is the norm in an agricultural setting. In support of the importance of pursuing such questions, in an animal model, combined exposure to the herbicide paraquat and the fumigant maneb caused greater damage to dopamine systems than exposure to either agent alone (220). Most of these studies have been limited by very broad measures of exposure. In many studies, the proportion of exposed persons was low, little was known about specific exposures, and validation of exposure was not possible.

Gene-environment interaction may also be important, and those with impaired pesticide metabolism may be most vulnerable. A recent report (197) indicates an increased of risk of PD with pesticide exposure in normal metabolizers, and about 2-fold further increase in risk with pesticide exposure for CYP2D6 poor metabolizers, and effect of the metabolizing status on risk for PD without pesticide exposure. Although none of this evidence is conclusive regarding possible causative agents in PD, these investigations certainly point to specific compounds that should be included in future studies.

Other Occupational Risk Factors. Several other occupational exposures have been associated with an increased risk of PD. Gorell and coworkers (221) reported significant associations with prolonged occupational exposure to copper and manganese and from combined exposures to lead-copper, lead-iron, and iron-copper. Odds ratios rose with duration of exposure to 2.5 for copper and to over 10 for manganese among workers with 20 or more years of employment. Interestingly, at least 1 group has reported that manganese can result in progressive parkinsonism (222). Ecological studies have reported increased parkinsonism in proximity to areas in which iron ore mining and wood pulp and paper manufacture have occurred (19). In addition to these specific agents, some very broad categories of chemicals or specific occupations have been associated with PD in case-control studies, including organic solvent exposure, chemical manufacturing, metal working, teaching and health professions, carpentry (men only), and cleaning (women only) (2, 205–207, 223, 224). For example, case-control studies suggest that occupational exposure to metals (225, 226), may increase risk of PD, although cohort studies have not replicated this (227, 228). Although these studies have not identified specific compounds that may contribute to PD, they add support to the proposition that environmental factors are at play in the disease. It has been suggested that an infectious etiology could explain the increased risk in occupational groups such as teachers and health care professionals (224).

Lifestyle-Associated Risk Factors. Lifestyle-associated factors such as habits and diet have also been investigated as risk factors for PD (229). The most consistent association in this category is the inverse association between cigarette smoking and PD. Cigarette smoking has been associated with a lower risk of PD in numerous prevalent case-control studies in a wide variety of populations, but whether this association is due to a biologic effect of tobacco or is the result of some other factor remains controversial (2, 205). Alternative explanations for the association have been put forth, including a higher mortality in smokers with PD (230) and that nonsmoking behavior in people fated to develop PD may be the result of a lower reward of smoking due to low dopaminergic tone, a genetically conferred decreased propensity to smoke, or a premorbid personality (231). Evidence against this theory derives from a study in twin pairs discordant for PD (232) in which twins without PD had smoked more than their brothers. Despite high correlation for smoking in MZ twin pairs, this difference was more marked in the MZ pairs, known to be remarkably similar in personality. Similar results have been reported in other studies of twins (233) and siblings (234) discordant for PD.

Interestingly, there is persuasive support for a biologic effect of tobacco based on a number of studies that used rigorous methodology. For example, an inverse dose-response relationship between cigarette smoking and PD has been found in both prevalent and incident case-control investigations as well as in a prospective cohort study (221, 235). A meta-analysis (236) indicated a 40% reduced risk of PD in smokers. Three basic categories of smoking were evaluated: ever smoking, past smoking, and current smoking behavior. Long duration (highest pack/year) correlated with dose, and smoking more than 5 years prior to PD onset was not protective; recent smoking appeared more protective. Other research suggests cigarette smoking, on average, appears to lower the risk of developing PD by about half (237). A recent study in a population characterized by a high prevalence of occupational pesticide exposure confirms an inverse correlation between cigarette smoking and PD in potentially "high-risk" group as well (238). One report suggests the inverse association of smoking and PD is present only in those with a specific MAOB allele (239), although this was not replicated (240); other single observations suggest other interactions of genes and smoking (241). Furthermore, laboratory studies support a direct effect of nicotine, the major bioactive component of cigarette smoke. For example, nicotine has been found to protect against transection-induced and MPTP-induced dopaminergic neuronal cell loss in rodent substantia nigra (242–245). Indirect evidence supporting a role for nicotine is also provided by the observation that PD was less commonly reported among users of smokeless tobacco in a large prospective cohort (246). A pooled analysis also indicates a dose-dependent reduction of PD risk associated with cigarette smoking and potentially with other types of tobacco (247).

Assuming smoking is neuroprotective, one might expect it to delay the onset of PD and improve the course of the disease in people already affected. Neither hypothesis has yet been proven. Two studies compared clinical features and did not find differences between smokers and nonsmokers (248, 249). Although a study by Kuopio et al. reported the mean age at onset in ever-smoking men was significantly higher than in never-smoking men (249), results of other studies assessing age at onset of PD in relation to smoking status (250–253) revealed the same or a younger age of onset in smokers. Interestingly, however, in several prospective cohort studies, survival of those persons with PD who continue to smoke cigarettes appears to be similar to or even somewhat better than survival of nonsmokers with PD (235, 254, 255), in contrast to the typically increased mortality observed in cigarette smokers. This preliminary information suggests that some aspect of smoking may not only modify disease risk but also improve survival once PD is manifest.

Although the evidence supporting a neuroprotective effect of nicotine is compelling, it is possible that drinking coffee or alcohol, behaviors that are commonly associated with cigarette smoking, might actually be the factor or factors responsible for the observed inverse association between cigarette smoking and PD risk. Nevertheless an inverse association of both coffee and caffeine consumption and PD have been reported in case-control and cohort studies (206, 256–258). In a longitudinal study of Japanese-American men, greater consumption of coffee was inversely associated with PD risk in a dose-dependent fashion (259). A very provocative finding in the same cohort was that greater intake of coffee was inversely associated with incidental Lewy bodies at postmortem (260). A similar dose-dependent inverse association between coffee drinking and PD was observed in two prospective studies (256, 261). In each case, the inverse association between PD and coffee drinking continued to be observed in multivariate analyses adjusting for cigarette smoking, alcohol use, and other potential confounders. Similar associations had previously been reported in a few case-control studies of prevalent cases, but these results were inconsistent and a dose-response gradient was not described (2, 205).

The effect of coffee appears to differ between men and women, with a direct dose-response association in men (higher consumption associated with lower risk) but a U-shaped pattern in women, although fewer women have been studied. It has been suggested a potential interaction between hormone exposure, primarily estrogen, and caffeine consumption may mediate PD. In participants of the Cancer Prevention Study II, caffeine intake was associated with a significantly lower mortality by PD in men but not in women (262). In women, the association depended on estrogen use, with a RR for PD of 0.47 (95% CI 0.27 to 0.8) in caffeine consumers not using hormones and of 1.31 (95% CI 0.75 to 2.3) in hormone users.

Caffeine may be neuroprotective through its antagonist action on the adenosine A_{2A} receptor (263), which, in laboratory studies, modulates dopaminergic neurotransmission (264, 265) and protects against striatal dopamine loss caused be MPTP (266, 267). A_{2A} receptor antagonists are receiving increasing attention as potential treatments, in particular for on/off fluctuations and dyskinesia in combination with levodopa therapy (268) but also as a possible monotherapy in early-stage PD because of positive results from animal studies and a small clinical trial (269, 270) (see also Chapter 44).

Alcohol use has been found by some to be inversely associated with PD even after controlling for possible confounding by smoking (206, 258, 271). A biological explanation for this observation has not been articulated. One study found that fewer cases with PD had a diagnosis of alcoholism than controls (254). The variability across studies is great and, overall, the current evidence for an association between alcohol intake and risk of PD is weak. In the Nurses' Health and the Health Professionals' cohorts, no association between incidence of PD and overall alcohol consumption was observed (272); however, an inverse association of beer (but not wine or liquor) consumption was seen. Comparison of alcoholics and nonalcoholics in a large database found comparable PD incidence in both groups (273). Interestingly, in a stratified analysis for men and women separately, male alcoholics had a significantly lower incidence of PD while female alcoholics had a 2-fold increased incidence. Low consumption of alcohol in PD has commonly been attributed to the reserved personality that has been observed prior to PD manifestation (231). In most studies to date, however, the possible confounding effects of cigarette smoking or coffee drinking cannot be assessed definitively.

Diet is a very difficult exposure to measure both because of its complexity and the fact that most individuals have diets that are qualitatively relatively similar (274). Despite these challenges, several dietary factors have been associated with PD. A diet that is high in antioxidants has been proposed to lower the risk of PD, but to date such a diet has not been consistently associated with this lower risk (206, 134, 271, 275–277). On the other hand, positive associations of PD with animal fat consumption and with a diet that is high in iron have been reported (221, 275, 276, 278). Excess intake of dairy products has been associated with increased risk of PD in two large prospective cohorts (279, 280). In a study of health professionals (279), it could not be determined whether the effect was due to calcium or milk. Moreover, the risk was most marked in men and not clearly observed in women. In the second study, PD incidence was more than twice as high in men drinking more than 16 oz daily in midlife compared to those who consumed no milk. This effect was independent of calcium. No women were included in this cohort. The reason for this association is unclear. One explanation is that milk may be a vehicle for potential neurotoxicants such as organochlorine pesticides or tetrahydroisoquinolines.

Multiple lines of evidence indicate that oxidative stress plays a major role in the pathogenesis of PD. In animal models of the disease, administration of toxic agents known to reproduce the pathologic features of PD cause formation of reactive oxidizing species which attack essential cellular constituents such as lipids and proteins; this toxic effect can be mitigated by enhancing cellular antioxidant capability (281, 282). Uric acid (UA) binds pro-oxidant ferric iron and scavenges free radicals (283). Men with baseline UA levels above the median had a 40% reduction in PD incidence adjusted for age and smoking (284); another study showed the hazard ratio of developing PD was inversely associated with UA levels in a dose-related fashion [overall hazard ratio 0.71 after adjustment for age, sex, smoking, alcohol intake, dairy product consumption and body-mass index (BMI)] (285).

Conversely, oxidative stress may be increased by lipid consumption and higher caloric intake, and eating foods high in animal fat has been associated with

increased risk of PD in several studies (123). The link between measures of body composition and obesity and risk of PD, however, is unclear. A large study in Japanese-American men in Hawaii observed higher prevalence of PD with higher triceps skinfold thickness, subscapular skinfold thickness, and BMI (286). A similar analysis in the Nurses' Health and the Heath Professionals' study did not find an association between BMI and risk of PD but, among never smokers, both waist circumference and waist-hip ratio showed significantly positive associations with PD risk as compared to smokers (287).

Other studies suggested different dietary risk factors for PD. The risk was mildly increased in association with high dietary iron intake, but risk was markedly increased with high intake of both iron and manganese (288). Another study (289) indicated increased risk with intake high vitamin C, carotenoids, and sweet food including fruit, but the number of cases studied was small (n= 57). Among those with PD, homocysteinemia has been indicated as a potentially reversible risk factor for depression or cognitive decline (290). Protective effects were proposed for B vitamins and folate because of their shared pathways with homocysteine and ability to lessen oxidative stress (291). Comparison of 2 large prospective cohorts (292) with 415 cases indicated that PD risks did not differ in relation to dietary intakes of B vitamins and folate [RR 1.0 (95% CI 0.7 to 1.5) comparing the lowest to the highest intake quintile in men and 1.3 (95% CI 0.8 to 2.3) in women]. Certain exotic dietary exposures have been proposed to cause atypical forms of parkinsonism, including ingestion of indigenous species from Guam (293, 294), or the British West Indies (295), although these reports are controversial.

Nonsteroidal Anti-Inflammatory Drugs. Inflammatory mechanisms appear to contribute to neurodegeneration in PD, and animal studies suggest that nonsteroidal anti-inflammatory drugs (NSAIDs) have neuroprotective properties (296) by reducing general inflammation. Studies of AD have shown that the regular use of NSAIDs may reduce the risk of AD in humans (296–298). That similarities exist in the pathogenetic background of PD and AD and animal data suggesting that anti-inflammatory drugs may protect against PD (299) have encouraged investigation of the association between NSAID use and PD risk in humans. An inverse association of NSAID use with risk of PD has been observed in 2 prospective studies for nonaspirin NSAIDs, as well as for aspirin (300, 301). Interestingly, in a cross-sectional study of 1258 PD cases and 6638 controls from the General Practice Research Database, this inverse association was again observed for men but not women, in whom nonaspirin NSAID use was associated with a higher risk of PD (302). Whether this reflects a characteristic of the study population or method or a true gender difference in risk will require studies in other populations.

Infectious Risk Factors.   The observation that encephalitis lethargica often resulted in parkinsonism during the influenza pandemic of the early 1900s suggested a possible infectious etiology for PD. Since that time, however, clinical and neuropathologic criteria have clearly differentiated postencephalitic parkinsonism from typical idiopathic PD. Although many subsequent studies have been unable to identify an infectious agent in PD (116, 303–305), a number of studies have continued to suggest that infection may play a role in the cause of PD. Also, rather than reflecting exposure to a chemical, the increased risk of developing PD associated with rural residence may reflect exposure to an infectious agent.

Mattock and coworkers (306) suggested that exposure to influenza virus in utero may result in damage to fetal substantia nigra, predisposing to the occurrence of PD in adulthood, but this observation was not confirmed (307). Fazzini and coworkers (308) found increased cerebrospinal fluid antibody titers to coronaviruses in PD patients, whereas Hubble and colleagues (309) and Kohbata and Shimokawa (310) found increased *Nocardia* antibody titers. Although elevated *Nocardia* titers were not found in a subsequent case-control study (305), *Nocardia* has a specific affinity for substantia nigral neurons and has been shown to cause a levodopa-responsive movement disorder in mice (311, 312). Martyn and Osmond (313) found that PD patients were more likely to report childhood infection with diphtheria and croup than controls, but there were no reported differences in the frequency of other lifetime infections. Conversely, Sasco and Paffenbarger (314) found an inverse association between most childhood viral infections and PD, and a significant inverse association with childhood measles was reported. Rather than a protective effect, this may reflect a relatively greater risk associated with subclinical or adult measles infection.

Trauma.   Several case-control studies have reported that head trauma is associated with an increased risk for PD (1, 132, 315–318), including a recent report showing a dose-dependent increase associated with more frequent or more severe injuries (319). Because parkinsonism and dementia can follow repeated head injury, as experienced by boxers, this result is interesting. However, an equally plausible explanation for this association is that of recall bias; that is, those with the disease are more likely to remember past injuries than nondiseased controls, and those with brain disease are more likely to remember head injuries in particular. In a prospective study, recall is not a factor. In the only study reported to date using prospectively collected information on head trauma, no association between head trauma and PD was observed (320).

There are several explanations for the association between head trauma and PD. It could be a recall bias, because subjects with PD are more likely to remember some significant events, especially when they occur to the head. On the other hand, laboratory studies have suggested that chronic head injuries could affect the delivery of oxygen and cause defective energy metabolism and subsequently excitotoxicity in certain susceptible areas of the brain, including the nigrostriatal system. Head injury can trigger an inflammatory cascade or conceivably disrupt the blood-brain barrier, increasing risk of exposure to toxicants or infectious agents. In a sibpair study (321) and a study of twin pairs concordant for PD (322), the sibling with younger-onset PD was more likely to have sustained a head injury. Additional well-designed studies (particularly prospective studies) are needed to clarify this association.

Emotional Stress.   There are reports indicating that people experiencing the extreme emotional and physical hardships of concentration camp imprisonment during the Holocaust or a war have been shown to have an increased risk for developing PD (323–325). Whether these observations reflect an accelerated nigral injury as the result of stress-related increase in dopamine turnover with resultant increased oxidative injury (326), nutritional deficiencies of dietary protective agents, or other factors cannot be determined. Evaluation of the relationship of less severe emotional or physical stress to the development of PD poses significant methodologic challenges.

Personality.   It has been reported that certain premorbid personality traits may predispose individuals to PD. Several studies suggest that people who are characterized as introverted, shy, timid, subordinate, less outgoing, nervous, responsible, morally rigid, and law-abiding have a higher risk of developing PD (327–330). This finding was explained by a potential illness-related distortion of recall bias. However, it could also reflect genetically determined endogenous individual differences in dopamine metabolism and in biochemical capacity to detoxify certain xenobiotics.

Emerging Research.   A variety of symptoms or disorders may precede formal diagnosis of PD, including olfactory dysfunction, rapid-eye-movement sleep behavior disorders (RBD), QT or rate-corrected QT (QTc) interval prolongation on the electrocardiogram, adiposity, and constipation. In vivo imaging of the dopamine transporter in the striatum with [99mTc]TRODAT-1 (TRODAT) and olfactory testing have both been proposed as potential biomarkers in PD, and impaired smell recognition correlated with lower TRODAT uptake (331). RBD is strongly predictive of PD, and RBD patients have been shown to have impaired olfactory function compared to controls (332). In addition to olfactory dysfunction and RBD, a number of patients with PD and multiple system atrophy (MSA) have QT or QTc interval prolongation on the electrocardiogram. In one prospective cohort, these findings were highly predictive of PD incidence (L. R. White, personal communication). Although these QT or QTc interval abnormalities are likely related to autonomic dysfunction, the pathophysiology remains unknown (333). Other characteristics in midlife associated with increased PD risk include increased triceps skinfold thickness and constipation (334). Men with less than 1 bowel movement/ day at midlife had a 4.1-fold excess incidence of PD when compared with men with more frequent bowel movements. Taken together, these observations suggest that PD may begin decades before nervous system symptoms are observed. That is, PD may be first a disorder of the peripheral autonomic nervous system. If an environmental trigger is involved, the GI tract or the olfactory epithelium may be portals of entry. This hypothesis is indirectly supported by neuropathologic findings, suggesting that nigral pathology is a relatively late event in the pathogenesis of PD (4). Further studies to identify those at risk will be essential in determining the causes of PD and methods for its prevention.

together account for only a small fraction of patients with the disease. In the next half century, the average age of individuals in both developed and developing countries is expected to show a progressive increase. In the United States alone, this phenomenon of population aging is predicted to result in a 3- to 4-fold increase in PD frequency, or several million persons with the disease. The impact of PD can also be expected to affect disease-associated health expenditures, lost income, and personal suffering. As described in this chapter, despite intensive research efforts during the past several decades, the cause (or causes) of typical PD remains unknown. Likely, PD will be understood to be multifactorial, and both genetic and environmental determinants will be important. Sophisticated methods of investigation are needed to arrive at an answer. These will include prospective investigations of large populations, use of incident cases in case-control studies, and the study of populations with known exposures in addition to the studies described in this chapter. In each case, close collaboration with basic scientists involved in laboratory investigations of disease mechanisms will be critical in guiding the questions addressed in these populations.

CONCLUSION

Although both genetic and environmental causes of parkinsonism have been identified, these causes taken

ACKNOWLEDGMENT

Thanks to Jennifer Wright for editorial assistance.

References

1. Semchuk K, Love EG, Lee RG. et al. Parkinson's disease: A test of the multifactorial etiologic hypothesis. *Neurology* 1993; 43:1173–1180.
2. Tanner C, Goldman S. Epidemiology of Parkinson's disease. *Neurol Clin* 1996; 14:317–335.
3. Braak H, Rub U, Gai WP, Del Tredici K. et al. Idiopathic Parkinson's disease: Possible routes by which vulnerable neuronal types may be subject to neuroinvasion by an unknown pathogen. *J Neural Transm* 2003; 110: 517–536.
4. Braak H, Ghebremedhin E, Rub U, Bratzke H, Del Tredici K. et al. Stages in the development of Parkinson's disease-related pathology. *Cell Tissue Res* 2004; 318:121–134.
5. Braak H, Del Tredici K, et al. Staging of brain pathology related to sporadic Parkinson's disease. *Neurobiol Aging* 2003; 24:197–211.
6. Kurland LT. Descriptive epidemiology of selected neurologic and myopathic disorders with particular reference to a survey in Rochester, Minnesota. *J Chronic Dis* 1958; 8(4):378–418.
7. Gudmundsson KR. A clinical survey of parkinsonism in Iceland. *Acta Neurol Scand* 1967; 33:9–61.
8. Schoenberg BS, Anderson DW, Haerer AF. et al. Prevalence of Parkinson's disease in the biracial population of Copiah County, Mississippi. *Neurology* 1985; 35:841–845.
9. Dawson TM, Dawson VL. Molecular pathways of neurodegeneration in Parkinson's disease. *Science* 2003; 302: 819–822.
10. DiMonte DA. The environment and Parkinson's disease: Is the nigrostriatal system preferentially targeted by neurotoxins? *Lancet Neurol* 2003; 2: 531–538.
11. Mutch WJ, Dingwall-Fordyce I, Downie AW, et al. Parkinson's disease in a Scottish city. *Br Med J* 1986; 292(6519):534–536.
12. Rajput AH, Calne D, Lang AE. et al. National conference on Parkinson's disease. *Can J Neurol Sci* 1991; 18:87–92.
13. Hughes AJ, Daniel SE, Blankson S, Lees AJ. et al. A clinicopathologic study of 100 cases of Parkinson's disease. *Arch Neurol* 1993; 50:140–148.
14. Maraganore DM, Anderson DW, Bower JH, et al. Autopsy patterns for Parkinson's disease and related disorders in Olmsted County, Minnesota. *Neurology* 1999; 53(6):1342–1344.
15. Bernheimer H, Birkmayer W, Hornykiewicz O, et al. Brain dopamine and the syndromes of Parkinson and Huntington: Clinical, morphological, and neurochemical correlations. *J Neurol Sci.* 1973; 20:415–455.
16. Gibb WR, Lees AJ. Anatomy, pigmentation, ventral, and dorsal subpopulations of the substantia nigra, and differential cell death in Parkinson's disease. *J Neurol Neurosurg Psychiatry* 1991; 54(5):388–396.
17. Ross GW, Petrovitch H, Abbott RD, et al. Parkinsonian signs and substantia nigra neuron density in decendants elders without PD. *Ann Neurol* 2004; 56:532–539.
18. Goetz C. *Neurotoxins in Clinical Practice.* New York: Spectrum Publications, 1985.
19. Tanner CM. Occupational and environmental causes of parkinsonism. In: Shusterman D, Blanc P (eds). *Occupational Medicine: State of the Art Reviews.* Philadelphia: Hanley & Belfus, 1992:503–513.
20. Langston JW, Ballard P, Tetrud JW, Irwin I. et al. Chronic parkinsonism in humans due to a product of meperidine analog synthesis. *Science* 1983; 219:979–980.
21. Irwin I, DeLanney LE, Langston JW. et al. MPTP and aging: Studies in the C57BL/6 Mouse. *Adv Neurol* 1993; 60:197–206.
22. Tipton K, Singer T. Advances in our understanding of the mechanisms of the neurotoxicity of MPTP and related compounds. *J Neurochem* 1993; 61:1191–1206.
23. McCrodden JM, Tipton KF, Sullivan JP. et al. The neurotoxicity of MPTP and the relevance to Parkinson's disease. *Pharmacol Toxicol* 1990; 67(1):8–13.
24. Salach JI, Singer TP, Castagnoli N Jr, Trevor A et al. Oxidation of the neurotoxic amine 1-methyl-4-phenyl-1, 2, 3, 6-tetrahydropyridine (MPTP) by monoamine oxidases A and B and suicide inactivation of the enzymes by MPTP. *Biochem Biophys Res Commun* 1984; 125:831–835.
25. Javitch JA, Snyder SH. Uptake of MPP(C) by dopamine neurons explains selectivity of Parkinsonism-inducing neurotoxin, MPTP. *Eur J Pharmacol* 1985; 106:455–456.
26. Ramsay RR, Dadgar J, Trevor A, Singer TP. et al. Energy driven uptake of MPP$^+$ by brain mitochondria mediates the neurotoxicity of MPTP. *Life Sci* 1986; 39:581–588.
27. Nicklas WJ, Vyas I, Heikkila RE. et al. Inhibition of NADH-linked oxidation in brain mitochondria by 1-methyl-4-phenyl-pyridine, a metabolite of the neurotoxin, 1-methyl-4-phenyl-1, 2, 5, 6-tetrahydropyridine. *Life Sci* 1985; 36(26):2503–2508.
28. Di Monte DA, Smith MT. Free radicals, lipid peroxidation and 1-methyl-4-phenyl-1, 2, 3, 6tetrahydropyridine (MPTP)-induced Parkinsonism. *Rev Neurosci* 1988; 2(1):67–81.
29. Singer TP, Castagnoli N, Ramsay RR, Trevor AJ. et al. Biochemical events in the development of Parkinsonism induced by MPTP. *J Neurochem* 1987; 49(1):1–8.
30. Klaassen CD, Amdur MO, and Doull J. Casarett & Doull's Toxicology: The Basic Science of Poisons, 5th edition, 1996, McGraw-Hill, New York, NY.

31. McNaught KS, Carrupt PA, Altomare C, et al. Isoquinoline derivatives as endogenous neurotoxins in the aetiology of Parkinson's disease. *Biochem Pharmacol* 1998; 56(8):921–933.

32. Di Monte DA, Chan P, Sandy MS. et al. Glutathione in Parkinson's disease: A link between oxidative stress and mitochondrial damage. *Ann Neurol* 1992; 32(Suppl): S111–S115.

33. Ames BN, Shigenaga MK, Hagen TM. et al. Mitochondrial decay in aging. *Biochim Biophys Acta* 1995; 1271(1):165–170.

34. Ames BN, Shigenaga MK, Hagen TM. et al. Oxidants, antioxidants, and the degenerative diseases of aging. *Proc Natl Acad Sci USA* 1993; 90:7915–7922.

35. Olanow CW, Arendash GW. Metals and free radicals in neurodegeneration. *Curr Opin Neurol* 1994; 7(6):548–558.

36. Simonian NA, Coyle JT. Oxidative stress in neurodegenerative diseases. *Annu Rev Pharmacol Toxicol* 1996; 36:83–106.

37. Facchinetti F, Dawson VL, Dawson TM. et al. Free radicals as mediators of neuronal injury. *Cell Mol Neurobiol* 1998; 18(6):667–682.

38. Amdur M, Doull J, Klaassen C. Casarett and Doull's Toxicology: *The Basic Science of Poisons.* 4th ed. New York: Pergamon Press, 1991.

39. Sanchez-Ramos JR, Hefti F, Weiner WJ. et al. Paraquat and Parkinson's disease. *Neurology* 1987; 37:728.

40. Makino Y, Ohta S, Tachikawa O, Hirobe M. et al. Presence of tetrahydroisoquinoline and 1-methyl-tetrahydroisoquinoline in foods: Compounds related to Parkinson's disease. *Life Sci* 1988; 43:373–378.

41. Niwa T, Yoshizumi H, Tatematsu A, et al. et al. Presence of tetrahydroisoquinoline, a parkinsonism-related compound, in foods. *J Chromatogr* 1989; 493:347–352.

42. Williams AC, Pall HS, Steventon GB, et al. N-methylation of pyridines and Parkinson's disease. *Adv Neurol* 1993; 60:194–196.

43. Tipton KF, McCrodden JM, Sullivan JP. et al. Metabolic aspects of the behavior of MPTP and some analogues. *Adv Neurol* 1993; 60:186–193.

44. Naoi M, Dostert P, Yoshida M, Nagatsu T. et al. N-methylated tetrahydroisoquinolines as dopaminergic neurotoxins. *Adv Neurol* 1993; 60:212–217.

45. Ansher SS, Cadet JL, Jakoby WB, Baker JK. et al. Role of N-methyltransferases in the neurotoxicity associated with the metabolites of 1-methyl-4-phenyl-1, 2, 3, 6-tetrahydropyridine (MPTP) and other 4-substituted pyridines present in the environment. *Biochem Pharmacol* 1986; 35:3359–3363.

46. Niwa T, Takeda N, Yoshizumi H, et al. Presence of tetrahydroisoquinoline-related compounds, possible MPTP-like neurotoxins, in Parkinsonian brain. *Adv Neurol* 1993; 60:234–237.

47. Di Monte DA, Lavasani M, Manning-Bog AB. et al. Environmental factors in Parkinson's disease. *Neurotoxicology* 2002; 23(4–5):487–502.

48. Fleming L, Mann JB, Bean J, et al. Parkinson's disease and brain levels of organochlorine pesticides. *Ann Neurol* 1994; 36:100–103.

49. Friedrich M. Pesticide study aids Parkinson research. *JAMA* 1999; 282:2200.

50. Polymeropoulos MH, Lavedan C, Leroy E, et al. Mutation in tha alpha-synuclein gene identified in families with Parkinson's disease. *Science* 1997; 276:2045–2047.

51. Kitada T, Asakawa S, Hattori N, et al. Mutations in the parkin gene cause autosomal recessive juvenile parkinsonism. *Nature* 1998; 392:605–608.

52. Bonifati V, Rizzu P, van Baren MJ, et al. Mutations in the DJ-1 gene associated with autosomal recessive early-onset parkinsonism. *Science* 2003; 299:256–259.

53. Paisán-Ruíz C, Jain S, Evans EW, et al. Cloning of the gene containing mutations that cause PARK8-linked Parkinson's disease. *Neuron* 2004; 44:595–600.

54. Zimprich A, Biskup S, Leitner P, et al. Mutations in LRRK2 cause autosomal-dominant parkinsonism with pleomorphic pathology. *Neuron* 2004; 44:601–607.

55. Leroy E, Boyer R, Auburger G, et al. The ubiquitin pathway in Parkinson's disease. *Nature.* 1998; 395: 451–2.

56. Polymeropoulos MH, Higgins JJ, Golbe LI, et al. Mapping of a gene for Parkinson's disease to chromosome 4q–21.q23. *Science.* 1996; 274:1197–1199.

57. Papadimitriou A, Veletza V, Hadjigeorgiou GM, et al. Mutated alpha-synuclein gene in two Greek kindreds with familial PD: Incomplete penetrance? *Neurology.* 1999; 52(3):651–654.

58. Golbe LI, Di Iorio G, Sanges G, et al. Clinical genetic analysis of Parkinson's disease in the Contursi kindred. *Ann Neurol.* 1996; 40:767–775.

59. Kruger R, Kuhn W, Muller T, et al. Ala30Pro mutation in the gene encoding alpha-synuclein in Parkinson's disease [letter]. *Nat Genet.* 1998; 18(2):106–108.

60. Chan DK, Woo J, Ho SC, et al. Genetic and environmental risk factors for Parkin-son's disease in a Chinese population. *J Neurol Neurosurg Psychiatry.* 1998; 65(5):781–784.

61. Vaughan J, Durr A, Tassin J, et al. The alpha-synuclein Ala53Thr mutation is not a common cause of familial Parkinson's disease: A study of 230 European cases. European Consortium on Genetic Susceptibility in Parkinson's Disease. *Ann Neurol.* 1998; 44(2):270–273.

62. Singleton AB, Farrer M, Johnson J, et al. α-Synuclein locus triplication causes Parkinson's disease. *Science.* 2003; 302:841.

63. Chartier-Harlin MC, Kachergus J, Roumier C, et al. α-Synuclein locus duplication as a cause of familial Parkinson's disease. *Lancet.* 2004; 364:1167–1169.

64. Ibanez P, Bonnet AM, Debarges B, et al. Causal relation between alpha-synuclein gene duplication and familial Parkinson's disease. *Lancet* 2004; 25:1169–1171.

65. Farrer M, Kachergus J, Forno L, et al. Comparison of kindreds with parkinsonism and α-synuclein genomic multiplications. *Ann Neurol.* 2004; 55:174–179.

66. Conway KA, Lee SJ, Rochet JC, et al. Accelerated in vitro fibril formation by a mutant alpha-synuclein linked to early-onset Parkinson disease. *Nat Med* 1998; 4:1318–1320.

67. Irizarry MC, Kim TW, McNamara M, et al. Characterization of the precursor protein of the non-A beta component of senile plaques (NACP) in the human central nervous system. *J Neuropathol Exp Neurol* 1996; 55:889–895.

68. Feany M, Bender W. A drosophila model of Parkinson's disease. *Nature* 2000; 404:394–400.

69. Spillantini MG, Crowther RA, Jakes R, et al. Alpha-synuclein in filamentous inclusions of Lewy bodies from Parkinson's disease and dementia with Lewy bodies. *Proc Natl Acad Sci USA* 1998; 95:6469–6473.

70. Matsumine H, Saito M, Shimoda-Matsubayashi S, et al. Localisation of a gene for autosomal recessive form of juvenile parkinsonism to chromosome 6q–25.2-27. *Am J Hum Genet* 1997; 60:588–596.

71. Hattori N, Matsumine H, Asakawa S, et al. Point mutations (Thr240Arg and Ala-311Stop) in the Parkin gene. *Biochem Biophys Res Commun* 1998; 249:754–758.

72. Abbas N, Lucking CB, Ricard S, et al. A wide variety of mutations in the Parkin gene are responsible for autosomal recessive Parkinsonism in Europe. *Hum Mol Genet* 1999; 8(4):567–574.

73. Yamamura Y, Sobue I, Ando K, Iida M, Yanagi T. et al. Paralysis agitans of early onset with marked diurnal fluctuations of symptoms. *Neurology* 1973; 23:239–244.

74. Takahashi H, Ohama E, Suzuki S, et al. Familial juvenile Parkinsonism: Clinical and pathologic study in a family. *Neurology* 1994; 44:437–441.

75. Lucking CB, Durr A, Bonifati V, et al. Association between early-onset Parkinson's disease and mutations in the Parkin gene. *N Engl J Med* 2000; 342(21):1560–1567.

76. Nelson LM, Van Den Eeden SK, Tanner CM, et al. Incidence of idiopathic Parkinson's disease (PD) in a health maintenance organization (HMO): Variations by age, gender, and race/ethnicity. *Neurology* 1997; 48(suppl 2):A334.

77. Valente EM, Bentivoglio AR, Dixon PH, et al. Localization of a novel locus for autosomal recessive early-onset parkinsonism, PARK6, on human chromosome 1p35-p36. *Am J Hum Genet* 2001; 68:895–900.

78. Bentivoglio AR, Cortelli P, Valente EM, et al. Phenotypic characterisation of autosomal recessive PARK6-linked parkinsonism in three unrelated Italian families. *Mov Disord* 2001; 16:999–1006.

79. Valente EM, Abou-Sleiman PM, Caputo V, et al. Hereditary early onset Parkinson's disease is caused by mutations in PINK1. *Science* 2004; 304:1158–1160.

80. Rohe CF, Montagna P, Breedveld G, et al. Homozygous PINK1 C-terminus mutation causing early-onset parkinsonism. *Ann Neurol* 2004; 56:427–431.

81. Hatano Y, Li Y, Sato K, Asakawa S, et al. Novel PINK1 mutations in early-onset parkinsonism. *Ann Neurol* 2004; 56:424–427.

82. Valente EM, Salvi S, Ialongo T, et al. PINK1 mutations are associated with sporadic early-onset parkinsonism. *Ann Neurol* 2004; 56:336–341.

83. Healy DG, Abou-Sleiman PM, Gibson JM, et al. PINK1 (PARK6) associated Parkinson's disease in Ireland. *Neurology* 2004; 63:1486–1488.

84. Hague S, Rogaeva E, Hernandez D, et al. Early-onset Parkinson's disease caused by a compound heterozygous DJ-1 mutation. *Ann Neurol* 2003; 54:271–274.

85. Abou-Sleiman PM, Healy DG, Quinn N, et al. The role of pathogenic DJ-1 mutations in Parkinson's disease. *Ann Neurol* 2003; 54:283–286.

86. Bonifati V, Oostra BA, Heutink P. Linking DJ-1 to neurodegeneration offers novel insights for understanding the pathogenesis of Parkinson's disease. *J Mol Med.* 2004; 82:163–174.

87. Hedrich K, Djarmati A, Schafer N, et al. DJ-1 mutations are less frequent than parkin mutations in early-onset Parkinson's disease. *Neurology* 2004; 62:389–394.

88. van Duijn CM, Dekker MC, Bonifati V, et al. Park7, a novel locus for autosomal recessive early-onset parkinsonism, on chromosome 1p36. *Am J Hum Genet* 2001; 69:629–634.

89. Bonifati V, Breedveld GJ, Squitieri F, et al. Localization of autosomal recessive early-onset parkinsonism to chromosome 1p36 (PARK7) in an independent dataset. *Ann Neurol* 2002; 51:253–256.

90. Hering R, Strauss KM, Tao X, et al. Novel homozygous p.E64D mutation in DJ1 in early onset Parkinson disease (PARK7). *Hum Mutat* 2004; 24:321–329.

91. Klein C, Djarmati A, Hedrich K, et al. PINK1, Parkin, and DJ-1 mutations in Italian patients with early-onset parkinsonism. *Eur J Hum Genet* 2005; 13:1086–1093.

92. Paisan-Ruiz C, Saenz A, Lopez de Munain A, et al. Familial Parkinson's disease: Clinical and genetic analysis of four Basque families. *Ann Neurol* 2005, 57:365–372.

93. Nichols WC, Pankratz N, Hernandez D, et al. Genetic screening for a single common LRRK2 mutation in familial Parkinson's disease. *Lancet* 2005; 365:410–411.

94. Di Fonzo A, Rohe CF, Ferreira J, et al. A frequent LRRK2 gene mutation associated with autosomal dominant Parkinson's disease. *Lancet* 2005; 365:412–415.

95. Gilks WP, Abou-Sleiman PM, Gandhi S, et al. A common LRRK2 mutation in idiopathic Parkinson's disease. *Lancet* 2005; 365:415–416.

96. Lesage S, Ibanez P, Lohmann E, et al. G2019S LRRK2 mutation in French and North African families with Parkinson's disease. *Ann Neurol* 2005; 58:784–787.

97. Ozelius LJ, Senthil G, Saunders-Pullman R, et al. LRRK2 G2019S as a cause of Parkinson's disease in Ashkenazi Jews (letter). *N Engl J Med* 2006; 354:424–425.

98. Wszolek ZK, Pfeiffer RF, Tsuboi Y, et al. Autosomal dominant parkinsonism associated with variable synuclein and tau pathology. *Neurology* 2004; 62:1619–1622.

99. Kachergus J, Mata IF, Hulihan M, et al. Identification of a novel LRRK2 mutation linked to autosomal dominant parkinsonism: Evidence of a common founder across European populations. *Am J Hum Genet* 2005; 76:672–680.

100. Aasly JO, Toft M, Fernandez-Mata I, et al. Clinical features of LRRK2-associated Parkinson's disease in central Norway. *Ann Neurol* 2005; 57:762–765.

101. Gaig C, Ezquerra M, Marti MJ, et al. LRRK2 mutations in Spanish patients with Parkinson disease: Frequency, clinical features, and incomplete penetrance. *Arch Neurol* 2006; 63(3):377–382.

102. Funayama M, Hasegawa K, Ohta E, et al. An LRRK2 mutation as a cause for the parkinsonism in the original PARK8 family. *Ann Neurol* 2005; 57:918–921.

103. Tomiyama H, Li Y, Funayama M, et al. Clinicogenetic study of mutations in LRRK2 exon 41 in Parkinson's disease patients from 18 countries. *Mov Disord* 2006; 21:1102–8.

104. Funayama M, Hasegawa K, Kowa H, et al. A new locus for Parkinson's disease (PARK8) maps to chromosome 12p11.2-q13.1. *Ann Neurol* 2002; 51:296–301.

105. Le WD, Xu P, Jankovic J, et al. Mutations in NR4A2 associated with familial Parkinson's disease. *Nat Genet* 2003; 33:85–89.

106. Bertram L, Tanzi RE. The genetic epidemiology of neurodegenerative disease. *J Clin Invest* 2005; 115:1449–1457.

107. Harada H, Nishikawa S, Takahashi K. et al. Epidemiology of Parkinson's disease in a Japanese city. *Arch Neurol* 1983; 40:151–154.

108. Mayeux R, Denaro J, Hemenegildo N, et al. A population-based investigation of Parkinson's disease with and without dementia: Relationship to age and gender. *Arch Neurol* 1992; 49:492–497.

109. Morgante L, Rocca WA, Di Rosa AE, et al. Prevalence of Parkinson's disease and other types of parkinsonism: A door-to-door survey in three Sicilian municipalities. *Neurology* 1992; 42:1901–1907.

110. Rosati G, Granieri E, Pinna L, et al. The risk of Parkinson disease in Mediterranean people. *Neurology* 1980; 30:250–255.

111. Sutcliffe RL, Prior R, Mawby B, McQuillan WJ. et al. Parkinson's disease in the district of Northampton Health Authority, United Kingdom. A study of prevalence and disability. *Acta Neurol Scand* 1985; 72:363–379.

112. Mayeux R, Marder K, Cote LJ, et al. The frequency of idiopathic Parkinson's disease by age, ethnic group, and sex in northern Manhattan, 1988–1993. *Am J Epidemiol* 1995; 142:820–827.

113. Granieri E, Carreras M, Casetta I, et al. Parkinson's disease in Ferrara, Italy, 1967 through 1987. *Arch Neurol* 1991; 48:854–857.

114. Morens DM, White LR, Davis JW. Re: The frequency of idiopathic Parkinson's disease by age, ethnic group, and sex in northern Manhattan, 1988–1993 (comment). *Am J Epidemiol* 1996; 144(2):198–199.

115. Brewis M, Poskanzer DC, Rolland C, Miller H. et al. Neurological disease in an English city. *Acta Neurol Scand* 1966; 42(Suppl 24):9–89.

116. Wang WZ, Fang XH, Cheng XM, et al. A case-control study on the environmental risk factors of Parkinson's disease in Tianjin, China. *Neuroepidemiology* 1993; 12:209–218.

117. Tanner CM, Thelen JA, Offord KP, et al. Parkinson's disease incidence in Olmsted County, MN: 1935–1988. *Neurology* 1992; 42(Suppl 3):194.

118. Ashok PP, Radhakrishnan K, Sridharan R, Mousa ME. et al. Parkinsonism in Benghazi, East Libya. *Clin Neurol Neurosurg* 1986; 88:109–113.

119. Schrag A, Schott JM. Epidemiological, clinical, and genetic characteristics of early-onset parkinsonism. *Lancet Neurol* 2006; 5(4):355–363.

120. Morens DM, Davis JW, Grandinetti A, et al. Epidemiologic observations on Parkinson's disease: Incidence and mortality in a prospective study of middle-aged men. *Neurology* 1996; 46:1044–1050.

121. Marras C, Tanner CM. Epidemiology of Parkinson's disease. In: Watts RL, Koller WC (eds). *Movement Disorders, Neurologic Principles and Practice*. New York: McGraw-Hill, 2002:177–195.

122. Van Den Eeden SK, Tanner CM, Bernstein AL, et al. Incidence of Parkinson's disease: Variation by age, gender, and race/ethnicity. *Am J Epidemiol* 2003; 157:1015–1022.

123. Korell M, Tanner CM. Epidemiology of Parkinson's disease: An overview. In: Ebadi M, Pfeiffer RF (eds). *Parkinson's Disease*. New York: CRC Press, 2005:39–50.

124. Bower JH, Maraganore DM, McDonnell SK, Rocca WA. et al. Influence of strict, intermediate, and broad diagnostic criteria on the age and sex-specific incidence of Parkinson's disease. *Mov Disord* 2000; 15:819–825.

125. D'Alessandro R, Gamberini G, Granieri E, et al. Prevalence of Parkinson's disease in the republic of San Marino. *Neurology* 1987; 37:1679–1682.

126. Jenkins AC. Epidemiology of parkinsonism in Victoria. *Med J Aust* 1966; 2:496–502.

127. Kessler II. Epidemiologic study of Parkinson's disease. *Am J Epidemiol* 1972; 96:242–254.

128. Rajput AH, Offord KP, Beard CM, Kurland LT. et al. Epidemiology of parkinsonism: Incidence, classification, and mortality. *Ann Neurol* 1984; 16:278–282.

129. Svenson LW, Platt GH, Woodhead SE. et al. Geographic variations in the prevalence rates of Parkinson's disease in Alberta. *Can J Neurol Sci* 1993; 20:307–311.

130. Imaizumi Y. Geographical variations in mortality from Parkinson's disease in Japan, 1977–1985. *Acta Neurol Scand* 1995; 91:311–316.

131. Kurtzke JF, Murphy FM. The changing patterns of death rates in Parkinsonism. *Neurology* 1990; 40:42–49.

132. Chia LG, Liu LH. et al. Parkinson's disease in Taiwan: An analysis of 215 patients. *Neuroepidemiology* 1992; 11:113–120.

133. Li SC, Schoenberg BS, Wang CC, et al. A prevalence survey of Parkinson's disease and other movement disorders in the People's Republic of China. *Arch Neurol* 1985; 42:655–657.

134. Tanner CM, Chen B, Wang W, et al. Environmental factors and Parkinson's disease: A case-control study in China. *Neurology* 1989; 39:660–664.

135. Wang SJ, Fuh JL, Liu CY, et al. Parkinson's disease in Kin-Hu, Kinmen: A community survey by neurologists. *Neuroepidemiology* 1994; 13:69–74.

136. Mars U, Larsson BS. Pheomelanin as a binding site for drugs and chemicals. *Pigment Cell Res* 1999; 12:266–274.

137. Wermuth L, Bunger N, von Weitzel-Mudersback P, et al. Clinical characteristics of Parkinson's disease among Inuit in Greenland and inhabitants of the Faroe Islands and Als (Denmark). *Mov Disord* 2004; 19: 821–824.

138. Dewailly E, Mulvad G, Pedersen HS, et al. Concentration of organochlorines in human brain, liver, and adipose tissue autopsy samples from Greenland. *Environ Health Perspect* 1999; 107:823–828.

139. Rocca WA, Bower JH, McDonnell SK, et al. Time trends in the incidence of parkinsonism in Olmsted County, Minnesota. *Neurology* 2001; 57:462–467.

140. Kuopio AM, Marttila RJ, Helenius H, Rinne UK. et al. Changing epidemiology of Parkinson's disease in southwestern Finland. *Neurology* 1999; 52:302–308.

141. Wang F, Feng X, Ma J, Zou H, Chan P. et al. Prevalence of Parkinson's disease in Beijing, China. *Neurology* 2000; 54(7 Suppl 3):A348.

142. Riggs J. The environmental basis for rising mortality from Parkinson's disease. *Arch Neurol* 1993; 50:653–656.

143. Parkinson J. An essay on the shaking palsy. London: Sherwood, Neely and Jones; 1817. Reprinted in: Neuropsychiatric classics. *J Neuropsychiatry Clin Neurosci* 2002; 14:223–236.

144. Charcot J. *Lectures on the Diseases of the Nervous System*. Delivered at La Salpêtrière. Tr. by George Sigerson. London, The New Sydenham Society, 1877–89.

145. Gowers WR. A manual of diseases of the nervous system. Vol 1, 1886; Vol 2, 1888, J & A Churchill (publisher), London.

146. Morano A, Jimenez-Jimenez FJ, Molina JA, Antolin MA. et al. Risk-factors for Parkinson's disease: Case-control study in the province of Caceres, Spain. *Acta Neurol Scand* 1994; 89:164–170.

147. Bonifati V, Fabrizio E, Vanacore N, et al. Familial Parkinson's disease: A clinical genetic analysis. *Can J Neurol Sci* 1995; 22:272–279.

148. Marder K, Tang MX, Mejia H, et al. Risk of Parkinson's disease among first-degree relatives: A community-based study. *Neurology* 1996; 47:155–160.

149. De Michele G, Filla A, Volpe G, et al. Environmental and genetic risk factors in Parkinson's disease: A case-control study in Southern Italy. *Mov Disord* 1996; 11(1):17–23.

150. Payami H, Larsen K, Bernard S, Nutt J. et al. Increased risk of Parkinson's disease in parents and siblings of patients. *Ann Neurol* 1994; 36:659–661.

151. Elbaz A, McDonnell SK, Maraganore DM, et al. Validity of family history data on PD: Evidence for a family information bias. *Neurology* 2003; 61:11–17.

152. Duvoisin RC, Eldridge R, Williams A, et al. Twin study of Parkinson's disease. *Neurology* 1981; 31:77–80.

153. Marsden CD. Twins and Parkinson's disease. *J Neurology Neurosurg Psychiatry* 1987; 50:105–106.

154. Marttila RJ, Kaprio J, Koskenvuo M, Rinne UK. et al. Parkinson's disease in a nationwide twin cohort. *Neurology* 1988; 38:1217–1219.

155. Vieregge P, Schiffke KA, Friedrich HJ, et al. Parkinson's disease in twins. *Neurology* 1992; 42:1453–1461.

156. Tanner CM, Goldman SM. Epidemiology of movement disorders. *Curr Opin Neurol* 1994; 7:340–345.

157. Wirdefeldt K, Gatz M, Schalling M, Pedersen NL. et al. No evidence for heritability of Parkinson disease in Swedish twins. *Neurology* 2004; 63:305–311.

158. Calne S, Schoenberg B, Martin W, et al. Familial Parkinson's disease: Possible role of environmental factors. *Can J Neurol Sci* 1987; 14:303–305.

159. Kubo S, Hattori N, Mizuno Y. Recessive Parkinson's disease. *Mov Disord*. 2006; 21:885–93.

160. Marongiu R, Ghezzi D, Ialongo T, et al. Frequency and phenotypes of LRRK2 G2019S mutation in Italian patients with Parkinson's disease. *Mov Disord* 2006; 21:1232–5.

161. Wszolek ZK, Pfeiffer RF, Denson MA, McComb RD. et al. Danish-American family (family E) with "Parkinson's disease": Pitfalls of genetic studies. *Parkinsonism Relat Disord* 1996; 2(1):47–49.

162. Denson MA, Wszolek ZK. Familial Parkinsonism: Our experience and review. *Parkinsonism Relat Disord* 1995; 1(1):35–46.

163. Pembrey ME. Discordant identical twins. II. *Parkinsonism Practitioner* 1972; 209:240–242.

164. Johnson WG, Hodge SE, Duvoisin R. et al. Twin studies and the genetics of Parkinson's disease. *Mov Disord* 1990; 5(3):187–194.

165. Tanner CM, Ottman R, Goldman SM, et al. Parkinson disease in twins: An etiologic study. *JAMA* 1999; 281:341–346.

166. Piccini P, Brooks D. Etiology of Parkinson's disease: Contributions from 18F-DOPA positron emission tomography. *Adv Neurol* 1999; 80:227–231.

167. Vieregge P, Hagenah J, Heberlein I, et al. Parkinson's disease in twins: A follow-up study. *Neurology* 1999; 53(3):566–572.

168. DeStefano AL, Golbe LI, Mark MH, et al. Genome-wide scan for Parkinson's disease: The GenePD Study. *Neurology*. 2001; 57(6):1124–1126.

169. DeStefano AL, Lew MF, Golbe LI, et al. PARK3 influences age at onset in Parkinson disease: A genome scan in the GenePD study. *Am J Hum Genet* 2002; 70(5):1089–1095.

170. Pankratz N, Nichols WC, Uniacke SK, et al. Genome screen to identify susceptibility genes for Parkinson disease in a sample without parkin mutations. *Am J Hum Genet* 2002; 71(1):124–135.

171. Pankratz N, Nichols WC, Uniacke SK, et al. Genome-wide linkage analysis and evidence of gene-by-gene interactions in a sample of 362 multiplex Parkinson disease families. *Hum Mol Genet* 2003; 12(20):2599–2608.

172. Pankratz N, Nichols WC, Uniacke SK, et al. Significant linkage of Parkinson disease to chromosome 2q36-37. *Am J Hum Genet* 2003; 72(4):1053–1057.

173. Sun M, Latourelle JC, Wooten GF, et al. Influence of heterozygosity for parkin mutation on onset age in familial Parkinson disease: The GenePD study. *Arch Neurol* 2006; 63(6):826–832.

174. Hubble JP, Weeks CC, Nance M, et al. Parkinson's disease: Clinical features in sibships. *Neurology* 1999; 52(Suppl 2):A13.

175. Vieregge P, Heberlein I. Increased risk of Parkinson's disease in relatives of patients. *Ann Neurol* 1995; 37:685.

176. de Rijk MC, Tzourio C, Breteler MM, et al. Prevalence of parkinsonism and Parkinson's disease in Europe: The EUROPARKINSON collaborative study. *J Neurol Neurosurg Psychiatry* 1997; 62:10–15.

177. Rocca WA, McDonnell SK, Strain KJ, et al. Familial aggregation of Parkinson's disease: The Mayo Clinic Family Study. *Ann Neurol* 2004; 56:495–502.

178. Smith CA, Gough AC, Leigh PN, et al. Debrisoquine hydroxylase gene polymorphism and susceptibility to Parkinson's disease. *Lancet* 1992; 339:1375–1377

179. Armstrong M, Daly AK, Cholerton S, et al. Mutant debrisoquine hydroxylase genes in Parkinson's disease. *Lancet* 1992; 339:1017–1018.

180. Tsuneoka Y, Matsuo Y, Iwahashi K, et al. A novel cytochrome P450IID6 mutant gene associated with Parkinson's disease. *J Biochem* 1993; 114:263–266.

181. Akhmedova SN, Pushnova EA, Yakimovsky AF, et al. Frequency of a specific cytochrome P4502–6. (CYP2–6.) mutant allele in clinically differentiated groups of patients with Parkinson's disease. *Biochem Mol Med* 1995; 54:88–90.

182. Lucotte G, Turpin JC, Gerard N, Panserat S, Krishnamoorthy R. et al. Mutation frequencies of the cytochrome CYP2–6.gene in Parkinson's disease patients and in families. *Am J Med Genet* 1996; 67:361–365.

183. Sandy MS, Armstrong M, Tanner CM, et al. CYP2–6. allelic frequencies in young onset Parkinson's disease. *Neurology* 1996; 47:225–230.

184. Bordet R, Broly F, Destee A, Libersa C. et al. Debrisoquine hydroxylation genotype in familial forms of idiopathic Parkinson's disease. *Adv Neurol* 1996; 69:97–100.

185. Kurth MC, Koller WC, Lieberman AN. et al. Lack of association of CYP3–6. and MAO-B alleles with Parkinson's disease in a Kansas cohort. *Neurology* 1995; 45(Suppl 4):A429.

186. Diederich N, Hilger C, Goetz CG, et al. Genetic variability of the *CYP 2D6* gene is not a risk factor for sporadic Parkinson's disease. *Ann Neurol* 1996; 40:463–465.

187. Bandmann O, Davis MB, Marsden CD, Harding AE. et al. Sequence of the superoxide dismutase 1(SOD1) gene in familial Parkinson's disease. *J Neurol Neurosurg Psychiatry* 1995; 59:90–91.

188. Stroombergen MC, Waring RH. et al. Determination of the *GSTM1* gene deletion frequency in Parkinson's disease by allele specific PCR. *Parkinsonism Relat Disord* 1996; 2(3):151–154.

189. Kurth JH, Kurth MC, Poduslo SE, Schwankhaus JD. et al. Association of a monoamine oxidase B allele with Parkinson's disease. *Ann Neurol* 1993; 33:368–372.

190. Hotamisligil GS, Girmen AS, Fink JS, et al. Hereditary variations in monoamine oxidase as a risk factor for Parkinson's disease. *Mov Disord* 1994; 9(3):305–310.

191. Nicholl DJ, Bennett P, Hiller L, et al. A study of five candidate genes in Parkinson's disease and related neurodegenerative disorders. *Neurology* 1999:1415–1421.

192. Munoz E, Obach V, Oliva R, et al. Alphal-antichymotryspin gene polymorphism and susceptibility to Parkinson's disease. *Neurology* 1999; 52(2):297–301.

193. Maraganore DM, Farrer MJ, Hardy JA, et al. Case-control study of the ubiquitin carboxy-terminal hydrolase *L1* gene in Parkinson's disease. *Neurology* 1999; 53(8):1858–1860.

194. Lincoln S, Vaughan J, Wood N, et al. Low frequency of pathogenic mutations in the ubiquitin carboxyterminal hydrolase gene in familial Parkinson's disease. *NeuroReport* 1999; 10(2):427–429.

195. Landi MT, Ceroni M, Martignoni E, et al. Gene–environment interaction in Parkinson's disease: The case of *CYP2D6* gene polymorphisms. *Adv Neurol* 1996; 69:61–72.

196. Checkoway H, Franklin GM, Costa-Mallen P, et al. A genetic polymorphism of MAO-B modifies the association of cigarette smoking and Parkinson's disease. *Neurology* 1998; 50:1458–1461.

197. Elbaz A, Levecque C, Clavel J, et al. CYP2D6 polymorphism, pesticide exposure, and Parkinson's disease. *Ann Neurol* 2004; 55:430–434.

198. Agundez JA, Jimenez-Jimenez FJ, Luengo A, et al. Association between the oxidative polymorphism and early onset of Parkinson's disease. *Clin Pharmacol Ther* 1995; 57(3):291–298.

199. Kitada M. Genetic polymorphism of cytochrome P450 enzymes in Asian populations: Focus on CYP2D6. *Int J Clin Pharmacol Res* 2003; 23(1):31–35.

200. Bon MA, Jansen Steur EN, de Vos RA, Vermes I. et al. Neurogenetic correlates of Parkinson's disease: Apolipoprotein-E and cytochrome P450 2–6. genetic polymorphism. *Neurosci Lett* 1999; 266(2):149–151.

201. Farrer M, Maraganore DM, Lockhart P, et al. α-Synuclein gene haplotypes are associated with Parkinson's disease. *Hum Mol Genet* 2001; 10:1847–1851.

202. Maraganore DM, Lesnick TG, Elbaz A, et al. UCHL1 is a Parkinson's disease susceptibility locus. *Ann Neurol* 2004; 55:512–521.

203. Maraganore DM, de Andrade M, Lesnick TG, et al. High-resolution whole-genome association study of Parkinson disease. *Am J Hum Genet*. 2005; 77(5):685–693.

204. Elbaz A, Nelson LM, Payami H, et al. Lack of replication of thirteen single-nucleotide polymorphisms implicated in Parkinson's disease: A large-scale international study. *Lancet Neurol* 2006; 5:917–923.

205. Checkoway H, Nelson L. Epidemiologic approaches to the study of Parkinson's disease etiology. *Epidemiology* 1999; 10(3):327–336.

206. Fall PA, Fredrikson M, Axelson O, Granerus AK. et al. Nutritional and occupational factors influencing the risk of Parkinson's disease: A case-control study in southeastern Sweden. *Mov Disord* 1999; 14(1):28–37.

207. Smargiassi A, Mutti A, De Rosa A, et al. A case-control study of occupational and environmental risk factors for Parkinson's disease in the Emilia-Romagna region of Italy. *Neurotoxicology* 1998; 19(4–5):709–712.

208. Tuchsen F, Jensen A. Agricultural work and the risk of Parkinson's disease in Denmark, 1981–1993. *Scand J Work Environ Health* 2000; 26(4):359–362.

209. Zorzon M, Capus L, Pellegrino A, et al. Familial and environmental risk factors in Parkinson's disease: A case-control study in north-east Italy. *Acta Neurol Scand* 2002; 105:77–82.

210. Priyadarshi A, Khuder SA, Schaub EA, Shrivastava S. et al. A meta-analysis of Parkinson's disease and exposure to pesticides. *Neurotoxicology* 2000; 21:435–440.

211. Firestone JA, Smith-Weller T, Franklin G, et al. Pesticides and risk of Parkinson disease: A population-based case-control study. *Arch Neurol* 2005; 62(1):91–95.

212. Frigerio R, Sanft KR, Grossardt BR, et al. Chemical exposures and Parkinson's disease: A population-based, case-control study. *Mov Disord* 2006; 21:1688–92.

213. Ascherio A, Chen H, Weisskopf MG, et al. Pesticide exposure and risk for Parkinson's disease. *Ann Neurol* 2006; 60:197–203.

214. Kamel F, Tanner C, Umbach D, et al. Pesticide exposure and self-reported parkinson's disease in the Agricultural Health Study. *Am J Epidemiol* 2007; 15;165:364–74.

215. Liou HH, Tsai MC, Chen CJ, et al. Environmental risk factors and Parkinson's disease: A case-control study in Taiwan. *Neurology* 1997; 48(6):1583–1588.

216. Semchuk KM, Love EJ, Lee RG. et al. Etiology of Parkinson's disease: A test of the multifactorial hypothesis. *Can J Neurol Sci* 1992; 19(2):251.

217. Hertzman C, Wiens M, Snow B, et al. A case-control study of Parkinson's disease in a horticultural region of British Columbia. *Mov Disord* 1994; 9(1):69–75.

218. Seidler A, Hellenbrand W, Robra BP, et al. Possible environmental, occupational, and other etiologic factors for Parkinson's disease: A case-control study in Germany. *Neurology* 1996; 46:1275–1284.

219. Fleming L, Mann JB, Bean J, et al. Parkinson's disease and brain levels of organochlorine pesticides. *Ann Neurol* 1994; 36:100–103.

220. Thiruchelvam M, Brockel BJ, Richfield EK, et al. Potentiated and preferential effects of combined paraquat and maneb on nigrostriatal dopamine systems: Environmental risk factors for Parkinson's disease. *Brain Res* 2000; 873(2):225–234.

221. Gorell JM, Peterson EL, Rybicki BA, Johnson CC. et al. Multiple risk factors for Parkinson's disease. *J Neurol Sci* 2004; 217:169–174.

222. Huang CC, Chu NS, Lu CS, et al. Long-term progression in chronic manganism: Ten years of follow-up. *Neurology* 1998; 50(3):698–700.

223. Tsui JK, Calne DB, Wang Y, et al. Occupational risk factors in Parkinson's disease. *Can J Public Health* 1999; 90:334–337.

224. Goldman SM, Tanner CM, Olanow CW, et al. Occupation and parkinsonism in three movement disorders clinics. *Neurology* 2005; 65(9):1430–1435.

225. Coon S, Stark A, Peterson E, et al. Whole-body lifetime occupational lead exposure and risk of Parkinson's disease. *Environ Health Perspect* 2006; 114(12); 1872–1876.

226. Racette BA, Tabbal SD, Jennings D, et al. Prevalence of parkinsonism and relationship to exposure in a large sample of Alabama welders. *Neurology* 2005; 64:230–235.

227. Fryzek JP, Hansen J, Cohen S, et al. A cohort study of Parkinson's disease and other neurodegenerative disorders in Danish welders. *J Occup Environ Med* 2005; 47:466–472.

228. Fored CM, Fryzek JP, Brandt L, et al. Parkinson's disease and other basal ganglia or movement disorders in a large nationwide cohort of Swedish welders. *Occup Environ Med* 2006; 63:135–140.

229. Tanner CM, Ben-Shlomo Y. Epidemiology of Parkinson's disease. *Adv Neurol* 1999; 80:153–159.

230. Ellenberg JH. Differential postmorbidity mortality in observational studies of risk factors for neurologic disorders. *Neuroepidemiology* 1994; 13:187–194.

231. Menza M. The personality associated with Parkinson's disease. *Curr Psychiatry Rep* 2000; 2:421–426.

232. Tanner CM, Goldman SM, Aston DA, et al. Smoking and Parkinson's disease in twins. *Neurology* 2002; 58:581–588.

233. Bharucha NE, Stokes L, Schoenberg BS, et al. A case-control study of twin pairs discordant for Parkinson's disease: A search for environmental risk factors. *Neurology* 1986; 36:284–288.

234. Scott WK, Zhang F, Stajich JM, et al. Family-based case-control study of cigarette smoking and Parkinson disease. *Neurology* 2005; 64:442–447.

235. Grandinetti A, Morens DM, Reed D, MacEachern D. et al. Prospective study of cigarette smoking and the risk of developing idiopathic Parkinson's disease. *Am J Epidemiol* 1994; 139:1129–1138.

236. Hernan MA, Takkouche B, Caamano-Isorna F, Gestal-Otero JJ, et al. A meta-analysis of coffee drinking, cigarette smoking, and the risk of Parkinson's disease. *Ann Neurol* 2002; 52:276–284.

237. Sugita M, Izuno T, Tatemichi M, Otahara Y. et al. Meta-analysis for epidemiologic studies on the relationship between smoking and Parkinson's disease. *J Epidemiol* 2001; 11:87–94.

238. Galanaud JP, Elbaz A, Clavel J, et al. Cigarette smoking and Parkinson's disease: A case-control study in a population characterized by a high prevalence of pesticide exposure. *Mov Disord* 2005; 20:181–189.

239. Checkoway H, Farin FM, Costa-Mallen P, et al. Genetic polymorphisms in Parkinson's disease. *Neurotoxicology* 1998; 19(4–5):635–643.

240. Hernan MA, Checkoway H, O'Brien R, et al. MAOB intron 13 and COMT codon 158 polymorphisms, cigarette smoking, and the risk of PD. *Neurology* 2002; 58:1381–1387.

241. Tan EK, Chai A, Zhao Y, et al. Mitochondrial complex I polymorphism and cigarette smoking in Parkinson's disease. *Neurology* 2002; 59:1288–1289.

242. Janson AM, Fuxe K, Goldstein M. et al. Differential effects of acute and chronic nicotine treatment on MPTP-(1-methyl-4-phenyl-1, 2, 3, 6tetrahydropyridine) induced degeneration of nigrostriatal dopamine neurons in the black mouse. *Klin Wochenschr* 1992; 70:232–238.

243. Janson AM, Moller A. Chronic nicotine treatment counteracts nigral cell loss induced by a partial mesodiencephalic hemitransection: An analysis of the total number and mean volume of neurons and glia in substantia nigra of the male rat. *Neuroscience*. 1993; 57:931–941.

244. Janson AM, Hedlund PB, Fuxe K, von Euler G. et al. Chronic nicotine treatment counteracts dopamine D2 receptor upregulation induced by a partial meso-diencephalic hemitransection in the rat. *Brain Res* 1994; 655(1–2):25–32.

245. Prasad C, Ikegami H, Shimizu I, Onaivi ES. et al. Chronic nicotine intake decelerates aging of nigrostriatal dopaminergic neurons. *Life Sci* 1994; 54:1169–1184.

246. O'Reilly EJ, McCullough ML, Chao A, et al. Smokeless tobacco use and the risk of Parkinson's disease mortality. *Mov Disord* 2005; 20:1383–1384.

247. Ritz B, Ascherio A, Checkoway H, et al. Pooled analysis of tobacco use and risk of Parkinson disease. *Arch Neurol* 2007; 64(7):990–997.

248. Papapetropoulos S, Singer C, Villar JM, et al. Does cigarette smoking provide clinically significant neuroprotection among patients diagnosed with Parkinson's disease? *Mov Disord* 2005; 20:641–642.

249. Kuopio AM, Marttila RJ, Helenius H, Rinne UK. Environmental risk factors in Parkinson's disease. *Mov Disord* 1999; 14:928–939.

250. Rajput AH, Offord KP, Beard CM, Kurland LT. et al. A case-control study of smoking habits, dementia, and other illnesses in idiopathic Parkinson's disease. *Neurology.* 1987; 37:226–232.

251. Morens DM, Grandinetti A, Davis JW, et al. Evidence against the operation of selective mortality in explaining the association between cigarette smoking and reduced occurrence of idiopathic Parkinson disease. *Am J Epidemiol* 1996; 144:400–404.

252. Levy G, Tang MX, Cote LJ, et al. Do risk factors for Alzheimer's disease predict dementia in Parkinson's disease? An exploratory study. *Mov Disord* 2002; 17:250–257.

253. De Reuck J, De Weweire M, Van Maele G, Santens P, et al. Comparison of age of onset and development of motor complications between smokers and non-smokers in Parkinson's disease. *J Neurol Sci* 2005; 231:35–39.

254. Elbaz A, Bower JH, Peterson BJ, et al. Survival study of Parkinson disease in Olmsted County, Minnesota. *Arch Neurol* 2003; 60:91–96.

255. Chen H, Zhang SM, Schwarzschild MA, et al. Survival of Parkinson's disease patients in a large prospective cohort of male health professionals. *Mov Disord* 2006;21:1002–7.

256. Benedetti MD, Bower JH, Maraganore DM, et al. Smoking, alcohol, and coffee consumption preceding Parkinson's disease: A case-control study. *Neurology* 2000; 55:1350–1358.

257. Ascherio A, Zhang SM, Hernan MA, et al. Prospective study of caffeine consumption and risk of Parkinson's disease in men and women. *Ann Neurol* 2001; 50:56–63.

258. Paganini-Hill A. Risk factors for Parkinson's disease: The leisure world cohort study. *Neuroepidemiology.* 2001; 20:118–124.

259. Ross GW, Abbott RD, Petrovitch H, et al. Association of coffee and caffeine intake with the risk of Parkinson disease. *JAMA* 2000; 283:2674–2679.

260. Ross GW, Abbott RD, Petrovitch H, et al. Lack of association to midlife smoking or coffee consumption with presence of Lewy bodies in the locus ceruleus or substantia nigra at autopsy. *Neurology* 1999; 52(Suppl 2):A539.

261. Willems-Giesbergen P, de Rijk M, van Swieten J, et al. Smoking, alcohol, and coffee consumption and the risk of Parkinson's disease: Results from the Rotterdam Study. *Neurology* 2000; 54:A347.

262. Ascherio A, Weisskopf MG, O'Reilly EJ, et al. Coffee consumption, gender, and Parkinson's disease mortality in the cancer prevention study II cohort: The modifying effects of estrogen. *Am J Epidemiol* 2004; 160:977–984.

263. Chen JF, Fredduzzi S, Bastia E, et al. Adenosine A2A receptors in neuroadaptation to repeated dopaminergic stimulation: Implications for the treatment of dyskinesias in Parkinson's disease. *Neurology* 2003; 61(11 Suppl 6):S74–S81.

264. Popoli P, Caporali MG, Scotti de Carolis A. et al. Akinesia due to catecholamine depletion in mice is prevented by caffeine. Further evidence for an involvement of adenosinergic system in the control of motility. *J Pharm Pharmacol* 1991; 43:280–281.

265. Nehlig A, Daval JL, Debry G. et al. Caffeine and the central nervous system: Mechanisms of action, biochemical, metabolic and psychostimulant effects. *Brain Res Rev* 1992; 17:139–170.

266. Richardson PJ, Kase H, Jenner PG. et al. Adenosine A2A receptor antagonists as new agents for the treatment of Parkinson's disease. *Trends Pharmacol Sci* 1997; 18:338–344.

267. Kanda T, Tashiro T, Kuwana Y, Jenner P. et al. Adenosine A2A receptors modify motor function in MPTP-treated common marmosets. *Neuroreport* 1998; 9:2857–2860.

268. Xu K, Bastia E, Schwarzschild M. et al. Therapeutic potential of adenosine A(2A) receptor antagonists in Parkinson's disease. *Pharmacol Ther* 2005; 105:267–310.

269. Hauser RA, Zesiewicz TA, Rosemurgy AS, et al. Manganese intoxication and chronic liver failure. *Ann Neurol* 1994; 36: 871–875.

270. Jenner P. A2A antagonists as novel non-dopaminergic therapy for motor dysfunction in PD. *Neurology* 2003; 61(11 Suppl 6):S32–S38.

271. Hellenbrand W, Boeing H, Robra BP, et al. Diet and Parkinson's disease. II: A possible role for the past intake of specific nutrients. Results from a self-administered food-frequency questionnaire in a case-control study. *Neurology* 1996; 47:644–650.

272. Hernan MA, Chen H, Schwarzschild MA, Ascherio A. et al. Alcohol consumption and the incidence of Parkinson's disease. *Ann Neurol* 2003; 54:170–175.

273. Hernan MA, Logroscino G, Rodriguez LA. et al. A prospective study of alcoholism and the risk of Parkinson's disease. *J Neurol* 2004; 251(Suppl 7):vii14–vii17.

274. Willett W. Overview of Nutritional Epidemiology. In: Willett W (ed). *Nutritional Epidemiology.* New York: Oxford University Press, 1990:3–19.

275. Logroscino G, Marder K, Cote L, et al. Dietary lipids and antioxidants in Parkinson's disease: A population-based, case-control study. *Ann Neurol* 1996; 39:89–94.

276. Anderson C, Checkoway H, Franklin GM, et al. Dietary factors in Parkinson's disease: The role of food groups and specific foods. *Mov Disord* 1999; 14(1):21–27.

277. Morens DM, Grandinetti A, Waslien CI, et al. Case-control study of idiopathic Parkinson's disease and dietary vitamin E intake. *Neurology* 1996; 46:1270–1274.

278. Logroscino G, Mayeux R. Diet and Parkinson's disease (letter; comment). *Neurology* 1997; 49(1):310–311.

279. Chen H, Zhang SM, Hernan MA, et al. Diet and Parkinson's disease: A potential role of dairy products in men. *Ann Neurol* 2002; 52:793–801.

280. Park M, Ross GW, Petrovitch H, et al. Consumption of milk and calcium in midlife and the future risk of Parkinson disease. *Neurology* 2005; 64:1047–1051.

281. Przedborski S, Ischiropoulos H. Reactive oxygen and nitrogen species: Weapons of neuronal destruction in models of Parkinson's disease. *Antiox Redox Signal* 2005; 7(5–6):685–693.

282. Peng J, Stevenson FF, Doctrow SR, Andersen JK. et al. Superoxide dismutase/catalase mimetics are neuroprotective against selective paraquat-mediated dopaminergic neuron death in the substantia nigra: Implications for Parkinson's disease. *J Biol Chem* 2005; 280(32):29194–29198.

283. Glantzounis GK, Tsimoyiannis EC, Kappas AM, Galaris DA. et al. Uric acid and oxidative stress. *Curr Pharm Des* 2005; 11(32):4145–4151.

284. Davis JW, Grandinetti A, Waslien CI, et al. Observations on serum uric acid levels and the risk of idiopathic Parkinson's disease. *Am J Epidemiol* 1996; 144(5):480–484.

285. de Lau LM, Giesbergen PC, de Rijk MC, et al. Incidence of parkinsonism and Parkinson disease in a general population. The Rotterdam Study. *Neurology* 2004; 63:1240–1244.

286. Abbott RD, Ross GW, White LR, et al. Midlife adiposity and the future risk of Parkinson's disease. *Neurology* 2002; 59:1051–1057.

287. Chen H, Zhang SM, Schwarzschild MA, et al. Obesity and the risk of Parkinson's disease. *Am J Epidemiol* 2004; 159:547–555.

288. Powers KM, Smith-Weller T, Franklin GM, et al. Parkinson's disease risks associated with dietary iron, manganese, and other nutrient intakes. *Neurology* 2003; 60:1761–1766.

289. Scheider WL, Hershey LA, Vena JE, et al. Dietary antioxidants and other dietary factors in the etiology of Parkinson's disease. *Mov Disord* 1997; 12:190–196.

290. O'Suilleabhain PE, Sung V, Hernandez C, et al. Elevated plasma homocysteine level in patients with Parkinson disease: Motor, affective, and cognitive associations. *Arch Neurol* 2004; 61:865–868.

291. Duan W, Ladenheim B, Cutler RG, et al. Dietary folate deficiency and elevated homocysteine levels endanger dopaminergic neurons in models of Parkinson's disease. *J Neurochem* 2002; 80:101–110.

292. Chen H, Zhang SM, Schwarzschild MA, et al. Folate intake and risk of Parkinson's disease. *Am J Epidemiol.* 2004; 160:368–375.

293. Spencer P. Guam ALS/parkinsonism-dementia: A long-latency neurotoxic disorder caused by "slow toxin(s)" in food? *Can J Neurol Sci* 1987; 14:347–357.

294. Murch SJ, Cox PA, Banack SA. et al. A mechanism for slow release of biomagnified cyanobacterial neurotoxins and neurodegenerative disease in Guam. *Proc Natl Acad Sci USA.* 2004; 101:12228–122231.

295. Champy P, Melot A, Guerineau Eng V, et al. Quantification of acetogenins in *Annona muricata* linked to atypical parkinsonism in Guadeloupe. *Mov Disord* 2005; 20:1629–1633.

296. McGeer PL, McGeer EG. Inflammation and the degenerative diseases of aging. *Ann NY Acad Sci.* 2004; 1035:104–116.

297. Breitner JC, Zandi PP. Do nonsteroidal antiinflammatory drugs reduce the risk of Alzheimer's disease? *N Engl J Med* 2001; 345:1567–1568.

298. in t' Veld BA, Ruitenberg A, Hofman A, et al. Nonsteroidal anti-inflammatory drugs and the risk of Alzheimer's disease. *N Engl J Med.* 2001; 345:1515–1521.

299. Ferger B, Spratt C, Earl CD, et al. Effects of nicotine on hydroxyl free radical formation in vitro and on MPTP-induced neurotoxicity in vivo. *Naunyn Schmiedebergs Arch Pharmacol* 1998; 358:351–359.

300. Abbott RD, Ross GW, White LR, et al. Environmental, life-style, and physical precursors of clinical Parkinson's disease: Recent findings from the Honolulu-Asia Aging Study. *J Neurol* 2003; 250:(Suppl 3):30–39.

301. Chen H, Zhang SM, Hernan MA, et al. Nonsteroidal anti-inflammatory drugs and the risk of Parkinson disease. *Arch Neurol* 2003; 60:1059–1064.

302. Hernan MA, Logroscino G, Garcia Rodriguez LA. et al. Nonsteroidal anti-inflammatory drugs and the incidence of Parkinson disease. *Neurology* 2006; 66(7):1097–1099.

303. Elizan TS, Casals J. The viral hypothesis in parkinsonism. *J Neural Transm Suppl* 1983; 19:75–88.

304. Marttila RJ, Arstila P, Nikoskelainen J, et al. Viral antibodies in the sera from patients with Parkinson's disease. *Eur Neurol* 1977; 15:25–33.

305. Hubble JP, Cao T, Kjelstrom JA, et al. *Nocardia* species as an etiologic agent in Parkinson's disease: Serological testing in a case-control study. *J Clin Microbiol* 1995; 33(10):2768–2769.

306. Mattock C, Marmot M, Stern G. et al. Could Parkinson's disease follow intrauterine influenza: A speculative hypothesis. *J Neurol Neurosurg Psychiatry* 1988; 51:753–756.

307. Ebmeier KP, Mutch WJ, Calder SA, et al. Does idiopathic Parkinsonism in Aberdeen follow intrauterine influenza? *JNeurol Neurosurg Psychiatry* 1989; 52:911–913.

308. Fazzini E, Fleming J, Fahn S. et al. Cerebrospinal fluid antibodies to coronaviruses in patients with Parkinson's disease. *Neurology.* 1990; 40(Suppl 1):169.

309. Hubble J, Kjelstrom J, Beamann B, Koller W, et al. *Nocardia* serology in Parkinson's disease. *Mov Disord* 1992; 7:292.

310. Kohbata S, Shimokawa K. Circulating antibody to *Nocardia* in the serum of patients with Parkinson's disease. *Adv Neurol* 1993; 60:355–357.

311. Kohbata S, Beaman BL. L-dopa–responsive movement disorder caused by *Nocardia* asteroids localized in the brains of mice. *Infect Immun* 1991; 59:181–191.

312. Beaman BL. *Nocardia* as a pathogen of the brain: Mechanisms of interactions in the murine brain: A review. *Gene* 1992; 115:213–217.

313. Martyn C, Osmond C. Parkinson's disease and the environment in early life. *J Neurol Sci* 1995; 132:201–206.

314. Sasco AJ, Paffenbarger JRS. Measles infection and Parkinson's disease. *Am J Epidemiol* 1985; 122:1017–1031.

315. Tanner CM, Chen B, Wang WZ, et al. Environmental factors in the etiology of Parkinson's disease. *Can J Neurol Sci* 1987; 14:419–423.

316. Stern MB. Head trauma as a risk factor for Parkinson's disease. *Mov Disord* 1991; 6(2):95–97.

317. Factor SA, Weiner WJ. Prior history of head trauma in Parkinson's disease. *Mov Disord* 1991; 6:225–229.

318. Bower JH, Maraganore DM, Peterson BJ, et al. Head trauma preceding PD: A case-control study. *Neurology* 2003; 60:1610–1615.

319. Van den Eeden S, Tanner CM, Popat R, et al. The risk of Parkinson's disease associated with head injury and depression: A population-based case-control study. *Neurology* 2000; 54(7)(Suppl 3):A347.

320. Rajput AH, Offord KP, Beard CM, Kurland LT. et al. Epidemiology of parkinsonism: Incidence, classification and mortality. *Ann Neurol* 1984; 16:278–282.

321. Maher NE, Golbe LI, Lazzarini AM, et al. Epidemiologic study of 203 sibling pairs with Parkinson's disease: The GenePD study. *Neurology* 2002; 58:79–84.

322. Goldman SM, Tanner CM, Oakes D, et al. Head injury and Parkinson's disease risk in twins. *Ann Neurol* 2006; 60:65–72.

323. Gibberd FB, Simmonds JP. Neurological disease in ex-Far East prisoners of war. *Lancet* 1980; 2:135–137.

324. Treves TA. Parkinson's disease mortality: Preliminary report. *Adv Neurol* 1990; 53:411–415.

325. Page W, Tanner C. Parkinson's disease and motor-neuron disease in former prisoners-of-war. *Lancet* 2000; 355(9206):843.

326. Spina MB, Cohen G. Dopamine turnover and glutathione oxidation: Implications for Parkinson disease. *Proc Nat Acad Sci USA.* 1989; 86:1398–1400.

327. Todes CJ, Lees AJ. The pre-morbid personality of patients with Parkinson's disease. *J Neurol Neurosurg Psychiatry.* 1985; 48:97–100.

328. Paulson G, Dadmehr N. Is there a premorbid personality typical for Parkinson's disease? *Neurology* 1991; 41(Suppl 2):73–76.

329. Menza MA, Robertson-Hoffman DE, Bonapace AS. et al. Parkinson's disease and anxiety: Comorbidity with depression. *Biol Psychiatry.* 1993; 34:465–470.

330. Hubble JP, Venkatesh R, Hassanein RE, et al. Personality and depression in Parkinson's disease. *J Nerv Ment Dis* 1993; 181:657–662.

331. Siderowf A, Newberg A, Chou KL, et al. [99mTc]TRODAT-1 SPECT imaging correlates with odor identification in early Parkinson disease. *Neurology* 2005; 64:1716–1720.

332. Stiasny-Kolster K, Doerr Y, Moller JC, et al. Combination of "idiopathic" REM sleep behaviour disorder and olfactory dysfunction as possible indicator for alpha-synucleinopathy demonstrated by dopamine transporter FP-CIT-SPECT. *Brain* 2005; 128(Pt 1):126–137.

333. Deguchi K, Sasaki I, Tsukaguchi M, et al. Abnormalities of rate-corrected QT intervals in Parkinson's disease: A comparison with multiple system atrophy and progressive supranuclear palsy. *J Neurol Sci* 2002; 199:31–37.

334. Abbott RD, Petrovitch H, White LR, et al. Frequency of bowel movements and the future risk of Parkinson's disease. *Neurology* 2001; 57:456–462.

34 The Impact of MPTP on Parkinson's Disease Research: Past, Present, and Future

J. William Langston

Recognition of the biologic effects of MPTP (1-methyl-4-phenyl-1,2, 3,6-tetrahydropyridine), an event that occurred in 1983, has proved to be a fertile step in the history of Parkinson's disease (PD) research. This observation applies to many levels of work and thought, ranging from its influence on etiologic concepts to the creation of a new animal model of the disease. This chapter reviews the discovery of this fascinating compound and summarizes current knowledge regarding its mechanism of action. The major focus is on areas where MPTP has had a significant impact on PD research, with an emphasis on its use as a tool to investigate the cause and treatment of the disease. Wherever possible, future directions of research are highlighted with a goal of furthering the already prolific scientific career of this novel and interesting compound.

THE DISCOVERY OF THE BIOLOGIC EFFECTS OF MPTP

MPTP was not discovered in the environment but rather emerged from a pharmaceutical laboratory in 1947 (1), where it was first synthesized as part of a search for novel narcotic analgesics. In a remarkable harbinger of things to come, the compound was actually tested in rodents and primates as a possible therapeutic agent for PD (2). These studies were abandoned, at least in part because of the compound's toxic profile, but it remains a mystery to this day why its potential as a tool for the study of PD was not recognized at the time.

Over the next 35 years, MPTP continued to have some use in the chemical industry, primarily as a chemical building block for other compounds. In fact, in 1983, when its parkinsonogenic effects were finally recognized, MPTP was commercially available through a specialty supplier of chemical products (3). Unfortunately, it probably first caused parkinsonism in humans well before this time in a number of chemists who were using MPTP for legitimate purposes. Exposure in these cases probably occurred either through cutaneous absorption or vapor inhalation (4–6). At least one case of MPTP-induced neurotoxicity through self-administration (by an individual who made a tainted batch of a "synthetic narcotic") was published in 1979, but the identity of the offending agent was not clearly determined at the time (7).

Final recognition that MPTP induces parkinsonism would have to await a dramatic outbreak of parkinsonism among relatively young drug abusers in northern California in 1982 (3). This occurred after a clandestine chemist in Morgan Hill, California, began making and selling a meperidine analog known as 1-methyl-4-phenyl-4-proprionoxy-piperidine (MPPP). This synthetic narcotic was sold under the name of "China White" and was selling quite well until the chemist used either too much heat or acid and made a bad batch. When this "tainted heroin" reached the streets, its users began experiencing a myriad of untoward effects (8), the worst of which was enduring and profoundly disabling parkinsonism. On the basis of the analysis of heroin bindles used by these patients, their clinical picture, and an autopsy study of the earlier reported case, we concluded that MPTP was the culprit and that it was selectively toxic to the substantia nigra (SN) (3), something which has since been confirmed in both humans (9) and nonhuman primates (10–16) as well as in other species, including mice (17). As this chapter shows, this discovery opened up an entirely new research era in PD. Yet it did not emerge from bench research but rather clinical observation, reminding us yet again that, when it comes to advancing medical research, pursuing leads in the clinic can be just as powerful as high-technology research in the laboratory.

WHAT HAVE WE LEARNED FROM MPTP-INDUCED PARKINSONISM IN HUMANS?

Since the first observations that MPTP had caused parkinsonism in a number of young addicts, a great deal has been learned that has expanded our understanding of the idiopathic form of the disease. First, observations in these patients have made it quite clear that the key motor features (bradykinesa, rigidity, and tremor) can result solely from a lesion of the SN (18). This conclusion is based on two findings: (a) our patients with MPTP-induced parkinsonism exhibited these cardinal features of PD, including rest tremor, and (b) we now have clear-cut pathologic evidence that MPTP induces a selective lesion of the zona compacta of the SN in humans (9). The observation regarding tremor is particularly important, because there has been substantial controversy over the years regarding the neuroanatomic origins of rest tremor and whether a purely nigral lesion can induce it (19). Observations in these patients also allow us to draw that same conclusion regarding at least two nonmotor features of PD; the mild cognitive deficits seen in nondemented patients with the disease (20, 21) and facial seborrhea (18), which can be the results of a pure nigral lesion. The fact that a primary nigrostriatal dopaminergic deficit can cause these central motor features of PD has enormous therapeutic consequences for those attempting to restore dopaminergic function using cellular replacement techniques.

A second observation in patients with MPTP-induced parkinsonism relates to the side effects of therapy. The parkinsonism in the drug-addicted patients mentioned above was not only dramatically responsive to dopaminergic therapy, as might be expected (18), but these patients also experienced all of the side effects typically

encountered with chronic levodopa treatment (13). Furthermore, complications of levodopa therapy were seen surprisingly early in the course of treatment. For example, in several cases, a short-duration response was seen almost immediately after starting treatment, and dyskinesias were encountered within days, which suggests that severity of disease may be more important than duration of treatment, at least for these particular complications of levodopa. As a qualifier to this statement, however, it must be pointed out that a second variable cannot be controlled in this group, and that is age of onset. Dyskinesias are well known to begin earlier in younger patients (22), and the MPTP patients were much younger than is typical for PD. However, the short duration response is not known to be age-dependent; therefore it can be concluded that it is related to disease severity—an observation that is consistent with the hypothesis that diminishing storage at the level of the synaptic vesicles may be a key feature underlying this phenomenon.

Although the forgoing observations have been available to the scientific community for some time, a more recent observation has emerged from neuropathologic studies in two of the original MPTP patients who died and a third more recent one from New Hampshire (9). The time from exposure to MPTP until death in these three cases ranged from 3 to 14 years. Surprisingly, in each of these individuals there was neuropathologic evidence of active, ongoing nerve cell death. Specific findings included microglial proliferation and clustering with clear-cut neuronophagias; in two of these cases, there was abundant extraneuronal melanin. The mechanism of this active neuropathologic process is not clear at present but could include enhanced oxidative stress from increased dopamine turnover in remaining dopaminergic neurons or an active inflammatory process that has become self-sustaining. The latter possibility is supported by the surprising degree of microglial proliferation. One hypothesis is that neuromelanin is playing a role in triggering an ongoing autoimmune phenomenon (23). In any case, these observations may be precedent-setting, as they provide compelling evidence that a time-limited exposure to an exogenous toxin can induce an active neurodegenerative process that can persist for many years. The working hypothesis is that this process may be due to chronic inflammation, perhaps through an autoendocrine inflammatory loop. A number of groups have explored this hypothesis experimentally. For example, in the MPTP mouse model, it has been shown that there is a inflammatory response accompanying nigral cell degeneration after MPTP and that the cell loss can be partially or fully prevented with a variety of anti-inflammatory agents including dexamethasone (24), vasoactive intestinal peptide (25), and simvastatin (26). Interestingly an adenosine A2A antagonist now in clinical trials has been reported to protect against MPTP neurotoxicity, possibly through an anti-inflammatory effect (27). In another study, intercellular adhesion molecule-1 (ICAM-1), which plays a key role in inflammation, was found to be increased in astrocytes in the SN of patients with PD compared to controls and similarly in MPTP treated monkeys up to 14 years after MPTP exposure (28). Finally, at least one anti-inflammatory agent, minocycline, has been tested in a preliminary clinical trial to slow disease progression and found to be promising enough to warrant testing in a phase III trial. The further development of such models to explore the inflammatory hypothesis of PD could have important therapeutic implications by raising the possibility that anti-inflammatory agents slow or halt the process of disease progression (see Chapter 37).

An Animal Model for Parkinson's Disease

When viewed from a broad perspective, the discovery of MPTP opened at least three new research avenues: (a) knowledge of its effects in humans gave immediate promise for the development of a new animal model for PD, (b) it provided an entirely new tool to investigate mechanisms of nigral cell degeneration and to test new protective strategies to block that degeneration, and (c) the discovery focused attention on the hypothesis that environmental toxins might play a causative role in the disease. This section reviews the first of these new research avenues.

MPTP remains unusual among experimental compounds in that its toxic effects were serendipitously discovered in humans who self-administered the compound, but this has had some powerful scientific consequences. For example, because its effects were first observed in humans, we have a remarkably clear picture of just how faithfully MPTP intoxication replicates the motor aspects of PD—an observation that gave birth to the immediate development of new animal models. And indeed, the drug has been given to animals ranging from monkeys (14, 29) to goldfish (30). However, the models that have found most favor over the years are those of the mouse and the nonhuman primate. But these two species have proved to be quite different. In spite of inducing substantial nigrostriatal damage in mice, they fail to develop behaviorally evident parkinsonism (31, 32), although a variety of motor effects have been reported. Surprisingly, rats were found to be almost impervious to the toxic effects of the compound after systemic administration (33). Indeed, only human and nonhuman primates develop full-blown, characteristic parkinsonism after MPTP exposure. Therefore, when it comes to investigating the therapeutic benefit of antiparkinsonian agents or exploring the aspects of nigrostriatal circuitry that are deranged in the parkinsonian state, the primate model has proved not only invaluable but also a necessity, because only in this model can one directly

observe the effects of any manipulations on clinically overt parkinsonism. And indeed this model has been used intensively to investigate new pharmacologic and surgical approaches to the treatment of PD. As this chapter shows, if there is one consistent theme that has emerged from MPTP-related research, it is that the primate model has been highly predictive and reflective of human parkinsonism, its physiology, and symptomatic responses to therapy (including side effects). On the other hand, it still is not clear how useful the model is for predicting agents that could modify disease progression.

The Role of the Subthalamic Nucleus (STN). One of the most important critical advances came from the work of DeLong and colleagues (34–39), who carefully investigated the neurophysiologic changes in basal ganglia circuitry in primates with MPTP-induced parkinsonism. In 1990, they made the seminal observation that lesioning of the subthalamic nucleus results in a reversal of motor deficits, including akinesia, rigidity, and tremor, on the contralateral side in primates rendered parkinsonian by MPTP (35). This experiment came after painstaking neurophysiologic work indicating that the lesioning of the STN with MPTP resulted in a decrease in striatal inhibitory output, with subsequent disinhibition of the STN. Because the output of the STN to the internal segment of the pallidum is excitatory, this appears to cause overstimulation of the globus pallidus, thus altering outflow to the thalamus and cortex. Blocking this pallidal overstimulation appears to correct many of the features of PD.

The impact of these experimental observations has been enormous. The immediate effect was to renew interest in pallidotomy, a procedure that was first attempted half a century ago (see Chapter 56). However, with the advent of deep brain stimulation, which can be done bilaterally and implanted directly into the STN, interest has increasingly turned to this procedure (see Chapter 54). And indeed, high-frequency stimulation of the STN in MPTP-lesioned parkinsonian monkeys has been shown to reverse parkinsonism (40, 41), and the procedure is now FDA-approved and widely used to treat patients with PD, offering what perhaps is the most immediate hope for patients no longer enjoying satisfactory control from current forms of medical therapy (42).

Neurotransplantation. The other surgical approach to the treatment of PD for which the MPTP model has been very helpful is neural transplantation. Although a huge amount of the original work laying the foundation for this approach was carried out in rodents (43), the lack of clinically identifiable parkinsonism in this species kept it a step short of being an ideal model to transition to patients with PD. The MPTP-lesioned primate, however, with its full array of parkinsonian features, has proved an excellent testing ground for the effectiveness of this approach. Indeed, many groups have been able to demonstrate clear-cut therapeutic benefits of neural grafting in this model (44–47). It has also been used for a wide variety of related investigations, which include autologous superior cervical ganglion grafting (48), intracerebral adrenomedullary grafting (49), polymer-encapsulated PC12 cells (50), and the use of ex vivo and in vivo gene therapy (51). Furthermore, using this model, it has been possible to show the effects of grafts at the neuropharmacologic level. For example, Elsworth and colleagues (52) have shown that D2 receptors (which are upregulated after MPTP-induced nigrostriatal denervation) are downregulated after neural grafting, suggesting a return to normal synaptic function, and others have shown that there is extensive graft reinnervation and interaction with surrounding tissue in primates with MPTP-induced parkinsonism (53). Such studies have been invaluable in translating this therapeutic approach to humans in terms of showing feasibility, potential efficacy, and safety.

In the late 1980s this fetal grafting procedure was extended to 3 human subjects with MPTP-induced parkinsonism. All 3 traveled to Lund, Sweden, where they underwent neural grafting, and all experienced substantial improvement. Of these patients, 2 have been reported in detail (54). Interestingly, they seem to have done slightly better than patients with the idiopathic disease, possibly because of their age, the amount of tissue transplanted, or because they have more selective lesions of the SN. On the other hand, placebo-controlled, randomized clinical trials in humans with PD have not produced the hoped for results (see Chapter 55), prompting a critical reappraisal of the models and clinical approaches used (55). However, using models such as that provided by MPTP-induced parkinsonism in primates seems to be the main hope for sorting these issues out in the future (56). One example of such a study was an investigation by Collier and colleagues in which the fetal cell transplants where placed in the SN of monkeys, indicating the feasibility of such an approach (57). In summary, neurotransplantation remains an important direction in the long-term search for a cure for this disease, which may ultimately depend on elucidating why the human trials were not more successful as well as finding alternative tissue sources for transplantation. Takagi and colleagues (58) were able to show behavioral and imaging evidence of improvement in monkeys with MPTP-induced parkinsonism after neural grafting with stem cell–derived dopaminergic neurons. A review of the current status of neural transplantation can be found in Chapter 55.

Dopamine Receptors.   The MPTP-lesioned monkey has provided an excellent opportunity to better understand the dopamine receptor system in the presence of nigrostriatal denervation and behaviorally overt parkinsonism. After lesioning with MPTP, dopamine receptor studies (using D1- and D2-specific radioligands) have typically shown that D2 receptors are upregulated (denervation supersensitivity). On the other hand, D1 receptors have been reported to be either unchanged, increased, or decreased after denervation (59–63). The parkinsonian primate has been used for a wide variety of approaches to pharmacologic therapy, which includes the study of D1 and D2 agonists and their value in the treatment of PD. The antiparkinsonian effects of D2 agonists have been consistently demonstrated as predicted from both clinical experience and the dopamine receptor studies in MPTP-lesioned monkeys (64, 65). However, results of studies using D1 agonists have not always been consistent (possibly reflecting the variable results of studies on D1 receptors after MPTP lesioning), with some groups demonstrating antiparkinsonian effects (66–68) but others failing to show any benefit (69–71). At least one group has reported that D1 agonists may exhibit fairly rapid desensitization with a shorten duration of response (72). Interestingly, another selective D1 agonist has been shown to improve cognition in a chronic model of MPTP intoxication (73) and, in at least one primate study, to be more effective in more severe parkinsonism compared to milder stages (74). The MPTP-induced primate model of parkinsonism has been used to evaluate the effects of the D1-3 dopamine agonist rotigotine (75), which has been developed for transdermal delivery in PD patients as a patch, as well as another promising selective D2 agonist known as sumanirole (76).

Dopa Dyskinesias.   Perhaps one of the more intensive areas of investigation utilizing the MPTP-induced primate model relates the side effects of dopaminergic therapy, particularly levodopa. As expected from the experience with PD patients, monkeys with MPTP-induced parkinsonism were quickly found to develop classic dopa dyskinesias (77–79), something that to date seems to be unique to primates. Thus this model has found increasing use and indeed has become the "gold standard" for investigating this troubling and dose-limiting side effect of levodopa therapy. Several studies have suggested that the more severe the lesion, the more likely animals are to develop dyskinesias (80–82). Somewhat surprisingly, it is often difficult to obtain a therapeutic response without also encountering dyskinesias (80). The reason for this is not clear, but it may be related to the high-dose acute regimens of levodopa that most investigators use. Another potentially important observation is that these animals never develop dyskinesias on their first dose of levodopa, thus confirming the need for "priming"—something that may hold a clue as to their cause but for which there has not previously been an adequate model (83).

There is no doubt that DA receptors play a role in dyskinesias, since D1, D2, and D3 dopamine receptor subtype-selective agonists have all been shown to induce dyskinetic movements in MPTP-lesioned monkeys (67, 71, 84–90). When given in combination, D1 and D2 agonists cause dyskinesias more prominently than either agent does alone, perhaps because they simulate the effect of levodopa more completely (91). However, dopamine agonists given individually seem less likely to induce dyskinesias than levodopa, even when given at an apparently equivalent therapeutic dose (92). Indeed, the MPTP primate model was successfully used to predict that dopamine agonists are far less likely to induced dyskinesias in previously untreated animals than levodopa (93), an observation that has now been validate in several large clinical trials in PD (94, 95), and which subsequently led to the widespread practice of initiating agonist therapy to forestall the onset of dyskinesias and motor fluctuations. In a head-to-head match, D1 agonists were less likely to cause dyskinesias than either levodopa or a D2 agonist in levodopa-primed animals (96). Not surprisingly, apomorphine has also been found to induce dyskinesias in this model (97).

It has been reported that pulsatile administration of D1 and D2 agonists is more likely to cause dyskinesias than constant administration (98, 99). Despite these compelling observations on the importance of dopamine receptors in the generation of dyskinesias, neither D1 nor D2 receptor changes in the striatopallidal complex have been found to correlate with their occurrence (98, 100–102). Furthermore, we have demonstrated that D3 receptors decline after MPTP lesioning only in the caudate and that, in levodopa-treated dyskinetic animals, D3 receptors return to normal (103). Thus we have not been able to establish that an abnormality of this receptor population is related to dyskinesias. More recently, this model has been used to provide even more compelling evidence that continuous dopaminergic stimulation may reduce the incidence of dyskinesias. In one study, it was shown that multiple small doses of levodopa plus the catechol-O-methyltransferase inhibitor entacapone, which would be expected to provide a more continuous exposure of the receptors to dopamine, clearly reduced the incidence of dyskinesias when compared to levodopa alone (104).

There has been increasing interest in the possibility that NMDA receptors mediate dopa dyskinesias; indeed, similar to observations in humans with PD, the administration of NMDA receptor antagonists attenuates dopa-dyskinesias in the MPTP-lesioned monkey (105–110). This suggests that excessive activity at NMDA glutamatergic receptors may be playing a role. However, the molecular mechanisms by which glutamate receptors are activated and in turn contribute to dopa dyskinesias remains unknown, although rodent studies have suggested that alterations in certain levodopa-induced motor responses may be linked to modifications in the phosphorylation state of the NR2A and NR2B subunits of the NMDA receptor (111, 112). More recently, primate studies have highlighted the potential importance of alterations in the NR2A subunit in the genesis of dyskinesias (113).

Preproenkephalin (PPE) has also been investigated as a link in the sequence of events that could lead to dyskinesias. Nigral dopaminergic neurons are thought to tonically inhibit striatopallidal output through activation of D2 receptors located on enkephalin-containing GABAergic striatal neurons in the striatum. Lesioning of the nigrostriatal system in rodents has been shown to increase in PPE mRNA in these neurons (114–115). Striatal PPE mRNA levels are also known to increase in MPTP-lesioned monkeys (116–121). However, these elevations do not appear to be appreciably changed in MPTP-lesioned monkeys with dopa dyskinesias (119, 120, 122). On the other hand, Morissette et al. (121) found that these elevations were corrected in animals treated with a D2 agonist at a dose that corrected the parkinsonism but did not cause dyskinesias, whereas D1 agonist treatment at a level that induced dyskinesias further elevated PPE mRNA. They subsequently reported that chronic blockade of NR1A/2B NMDA receptors with CI-1041 normalizes PPE-A mRNA expression and prevents the development of levodopa-induced dyskinesias in MPTP-lesioned primates (123). Further studies are needed to see whether this peptide is marking one or more important cellular changes in the sequence of events that lead to dopa dyskinesias.

This model has also been employed in the search for pharmacologic agents that might block or lessen dopa dyskinesias. Among those that have been reported to ameliorate dyskinesias in parkinsonian primates are CCK (124), (-)-OSU 6160 (a D2-receptor selective compound) (125), 17 beta-estradiol (126), the alpha-2-adrenergic receptor antagonist idazoxan (117, 127), the clozapine analog JL-18 (128), the noncompetitive AMPA antagonist LY300164 (129), Mu- and delta-opioid receptor antagonists (130), naloxone (131), quetiapine (an atypical antipsychotic with 5HT2A/C and D2/3 antagonistic activity) (132), the selective adenosine A(2A) receptor antagonist KW-6002 (133), magnesium sulfate (presumably through NMDA receptor antagnosism) (134), the antiepileptic drug levetiracetam (135), 3,4-methylenedioxymethamphetamine (ecstasy) (136), fipamezole (JP-1730) (an alpha-2-adrenergic receptor antagonist) (137), topiramate (which attenuations AMPA receptor-mediated transmission) (138), the histamine H3 receptor agonists immepip and imetit (139), and docosahexaenoic acid (140). Although many of these studies have yet to be replicated, Fox and colleagues (141), in a review of the literature, found that for all 6 nondopaminergic transmitter systems reviewed, the MPTP-lesioned primate correctly predicted phase II efficacy of at least one drug in each class of compounds. Thus, exploring new pharmacologic approaches to minimize or even prevent dyskinesias may be one of the more fruitful ways to learn more about their underlying pathophysiology and, at a more practical level, may be the quickest way to find approaches for their prevention. Given the number of compounds tested to date, we are already off to a good start; indeed, there are few advances that could have more of an immediate impact on the successful long-term treatment of PD.

Before leaving the subject of dyskinesias, two interesting observations warrant note. The first relates to the neurophysiology of the internal segment of the globus pallidus (GPi). Quite early after the MPTP model was developed, Crossman and colleagues (142) observed that 2-deoxyglucose use was markedly increased in the GPi of MPTP-lesioned parkinsonian animals but markedly decreased when the animals were experiencing dopa dyskinesias. Their observations were subsequently confirmed physiologically by Papa and colleagues (143), who found that cellular firing in the internal segment of the globus pallidus is almost completely suppressed in animals with dopa dyskinesias. This may be a key change in the cascade of events that leads to dyskinesias and certainly warrants further study. However, one of the first tasks ahead is to explain the paradox of why pallidotomy, which might be expected to have the same effect, clearly has an anti-dyskinetic effect.

The other, and perhaps one of the most provocative observations to emerge from work using primates to study dopa dyskinesias, relates to the conventional wisdom that a loss of nigrostriatal terminals is required for their development. This generally accepted convention is based not only on clinical observation but also a substantial body of experimental literature. For example, using a dose of 40 mg/kg of levodopa, Boyce et al. (81) reported that animals with an intact nigrostriatal system became hyperactive but did not show typical dopa-dyskinesias, whereas animals with a lesioned nigrostriatal system developed peak-dose dyskinesias that were choreoathetoid in nature. Alexander et al. (61, 144) were also unable to induce dyskinesias in animals with an intact nigrostriatal system. However, R. K. Pearce et al. (145) challenged this view by reporting that normal monkeys that received extremely high doses of levodopa (80 mg/kg) over many months did exhibit dyskinesias. Recent observations have revealed dyskinesias in normal monkeys receiving short-term levodopa. Because of the importance of this issue, we carried out a prospective, blinded study using the Global Primate Dyskinesia Scale, which has been tested for both reliability and validity (146, 147). The results of this experiment were clear-cut, as all of the nonlesioned levodopa-treated animals developed dyskinesias that were indistinguishable from dyskinesias in animals with MPTP-induced parkinsonism (148). A careful review

of the literature revealed that, in one of the original experimental studies of levodopa in monkeys in 1973, Mones (149) reported that normal animals developed involuntary choreiform movements of the limbs along with hyperactivity and orofacial movements when very high doses of levodopa were given (200 to 400 mg/kg). What is different about the recent prospective study is that far lower doses of levodopa were given (15 mg/kg), which are much closer to the range used in humans with PD.

Variations on the MPTP Model in Primates. A number of variations of the MPTP model have been developed. These include the hemilesioned model, which uses unilateral MPTP intracarotid injection (150); the bilateral intracarotid model (151); the so-called overlesioned model (unilateral intracarotid lesioning followed by low-dose systemic injection); and a low-dose chronic model (152). The advantages and disadvantages of each of these have been reviewed in detail elsewhere (153).

Summary. The MPTP model continues to be used for the testing of new therapeutic strategies in PD and to better understand the complications of therapy, because monkeys lesioned with MPTP exhibit not only the clinical consequences of a nigrostriatal dopaminergic deficit—that is, clinically overt parkinsonism—but almost all of the underlying neurophysiologic changes in the basal ganglia that seem to occur in the idiopathic disease. For these reasons, it is clear that one can expect this model to be highly predictive of the symptomatic responses that will be observed in humans with the disease and that it will continue to provide invaluable opportunities for transitioning new therapies from the laboratory to patients. On the other hand, as noted earlier, the usefulness of this model for the study of disease-modifying therapies has yet to be determined This is discussed further in the next section.

Mechanism of Action of MPTP: The Beginning of the Age of Neuroprotection

The observation that MPTP was capable of inducing parkinsonism in humans by virtue of selectively killing nigral neurons (3) led to a tremendous surge in research activity directed toward unraveling its mechanism of action (154). Perhaps the most fascinating puzzle was understanding exactly how a compound could be so selectively toxic to the neurons of the SN. This research has also led to a myriad of new strategies to protect against MPTP toxicity; these have been tested at almost every level of biologic complexity, ranging from tissue culture to patients with PD. Indeed, it would not be an overstatement to say that these studies ushered in a new age of research on neuroprotective strategies aimed at slowing the progress of PD.

The Biotransformation of MPTP: The Monoamine Oxidase Story. The first major step in unraveling the mechanism of action of MPTP was the discovery that MPTP itself is not toxic. Rather, it requires biotransformation to a toxic metabolite, the 1-methyl-4-phenylpyridinium ion, or MPP+ (15, 28). A clue that monoamine oxidase might be responsible for this biotransformation came from Parsons and Rainbow (155), who astutely observed that the distribution of MPP+ binding in the rodent brain corresponded closely to the known distribution of MAO. However, definitive evidence that MAO (and specifically MAO B) was the enzyme mediating the bioactivation of MPTP came from Chiba and colleagues (156), who demonstrated that the MAO B inhibitors deprenyl and pargyline blocked the conversion of MPTP to its toxic metabolite. It was quickly shown that blocking MAO B prevented dopamine depletion in mice (27, 28) and nigral cell degeneration in primates (11). This transition almost certainly is taking place in glia, not intraneuronally (157–160).

These observations had several interesting implications, both practical and theoretical. First, they triggered a renaissance of interest in MAO and its role in the human nervous system (161). Although MAO was generally thought to be a housekeeping enzyme, these new data raised the possibility that it might have other less well known biologic functions. Second, the potential therapeutic implications were immediately obvious. If deprenyl could be used to block the neurodegenerative effects of MPTP, might this drug be used to slow or halt the progression of PD? For this reason, we initiated a prospective controlled trial in patients with PD to assess the effect of selegiline (deprenyl) on disease progression (162). Shortly thereafter, planning for a much larger trial (DATATOP) was initiated, which was also designed to assess alpha tocopherol in addition to selegiline. In 1988 the results of both of these studies were published (162, 163), and both showed that levodopa therapy could be substantially delayed with the initiation of early selegiline therapy in de novo patients. Furthermore, based on clinical evaluation, the drug appeared to slow disease progression by about 50%. However, these findings became controversial when the larger study showed that a small but definite and statistically significant symptomatic benefit was derived from selegiline. Many argued that this small symptomatic benefit confounded the results of the study in that it could mimic the slowing of disease progression. Although this debate can never be unequivocally resolved until there is a way to monitor nigral cell degeneration in patients, selegiline has continued to enjoy substantial use in clinical practice. Furthermore, this compound seems to have had a second life as a neuroprotective agent after the discovery that it may also have a "rescue effect" independent of MAO B inhibition (discussed below in the section on apoptosis).

The MAO-inhibitor approach has recently received even more attention with the introduction a second-generation irreversible MAO-B inhibitor for PD known as rasagiline (164, 165). Although rasagiline was approved for both the early and late treatment of PD, perhaps the most interesting part of this story comes from studies attempting to evaluate its neuroprotective properties. This investigation was the first to address a new trial approach known as the delayed-start design (166). As noted above, previous trials were confounded by a symptomatic effect of MAO B inhibition, leading to the argument that the day-to-day improvement evoked by MAO B-inhibitor therapy would have mimicked a disease-modifying effect by making patients appear better than their underlying disease process. A simple solution to this problem was to stop the MAO inhibitor for a month (the "washout" period") to assess what each patient's underlying condition really was. However, it was argued that a 1-month (and later even a 2-month washout) was not long enough. The delayed-start design obviates the need for a washout. Rather, this design delays the start of a putative neuroprotective agent in one group of patients and then determines whether they can "catch up" with the group that got the drug from the beginning. If a drug is just symptomatic, they should quickly catch up. But if it is neuroprotective, then the delayed group should never completely catch up. And this in fact appeared to be the case in the study with rasagiline (166). Importantly, a much larger study is in progress to see if these results can be replicated.

It is worth noting that the MAO-mediated biotransformation of MPTP to MPP+ could have broader implications for neurodegenerative disease. This is because it provides an example of a nontoxic compound being converted to a neurotoxin by the brain's own enzymatic machinery. This is precedent-setting and could represent a metabolic "Achilles' heel" of the brain. Xenobiotics are frequently metabolized into reactive compounds that can then be conjugated and excreted. However, in this instance, MPP+ cannot be further metabolized and is toxic. This failure of the xenobiotic metabolic pathway could have implications for PD and other neurodegenerative processes and has generated an entire field of research on genetically determined abnormalities of xenobiotic metabolism as potential risk factors for neurodegenerative disease.

Uptake of MPP+. The mystery of the remarkable selectivity of MPTP was at least partially solved when it was found that MPP+ (but not MPTP) is selectively taken up via the dopamine transporter, thus accounting for its selective accumulation in dopaminergic neurons (167). Uptake inhibitors were quickly shown to protect against MPTP toxicity in rodents (168–170), but protection in primates was more difficult to achieve (171), probably because of the long half-life of MPP+ in this species and difficulties in maintaining constant uptake inhibition with currently available agents. Perhaps for this reason there has yet to be serious consideration of a neuroprotective trial in PD using dopamine uptake inhibitors. More recently, in an elegant study using transgenic mice, Bezard and colleagues (172) showed that animals that lack the dopamine transporter were completely protected from MPTP-induced cell loss.

If one considers this aspect of MPTP toxicity, it could be argued that it exemplifies a remarkable sequence of events. First, the brain (more specifically glia) converts a nontoxic substance into a toxin that cannot be further metabolized or conjugated. Next, the dopaminergic uptake system recognizes this potentially toxic compound as a friendly substance (i.e., dopamine or a dopamine-like compound) and transports it intracellularly, where it can cause cell death. The vast abundance of uptake systems in the brain accounts for the need for a tight barrier between the blood and the brain, but in this instance the blood-brain barrier is circumvented in the form of MPTP, a nontoxic and lipophilic compound. The system is then undone from within by the creation of MPP+, representing what could be considered a biologic "Trojan horse" phenomenon. Certainly one of the more interesting questions to address is whether this remarkable sequence of events is a rare aberration or a much more common scenario that plays a role in one or more human neurodegenerative diseases.

MPP+ was used in an elegant series of experiments to clone the dopamine vesicular transporter (173). Additional work since that time has shown that accumulation of toxins such MPP+ in the vesicular transporter may actually protect cells from the harmful effects of such compounds (174)—an observation that could have implications for other neurodegenerative diseases as well.

MPP+: A Mitochondrial Toxin.   Once in nigral neurons, MPP+ accumulates as much as 40-fold in mitochondria (175, 176). This is apparently due to the energy-dependent electrical gradient that is maintained across the mitochondrial membrane. Once accumulated in mitochondria, MPP+ inhibits complex I of the electron transport chain (177, 178) at or near the rotenone-sensitive site. Di Monte and colleagues (179) demonstrated the functional consequences of this effect when they showed that MPTP induced a dramatic depletion of ATP in isolated hepatocytes. These observations led to the search for similar deficits in PD, and a complex I deficiency was found (180–182). Indeed, the mitochondrial hypothesis of PD, which was largely precipitated by MPTP-related discoveries, continues to be one of the most viable hypotheses regarding potential mechanisms that may underlie cell death. However, there is still much that is not known. Whereas there is near universal agreement that a complex I deficit is present in the SN of patients with PD (183),

whether a similar deficit is present in other tissues, such as muscle, remains controversial, although the data from platelets appears to be the compelling (184–189). Nor do we know if the mitochondrial deficit is primary or secondary. If primary, what causes the deficit in the first place? Perhaps the strongest argument against mitochondrial DNA playing a major role in PD is the paucity of evidence for maternal inheritance (190), as would be expected if mitochondrial DNA were involved. On the other hand, Shapira and colleagues (183) have shown that, at least in a subset of patients, this deficit in complex I activity does appear to be determined by mitochondrial DNA—a conclusion based on experiments using rho cybrid cells that carried mitochondrial DNA from patients with PD (191). More recently, Parker and Parks (192), using brain tissues from PD patients and controls, evaluated low-frequency amino acid–changing mutations in a narrow region of the mitochondrial gene encoding the complex I subunit know as ND5 in brain tissue from PD and controls; they found that the presence or absence of these mutations correctly classified 15 of 16 PD samples. If these impressive results are replicated, it would certainly support a contributing role for mitochondrial DNA.

Regardless of the answers to these questions, interest in the energy-depleting effects of MPTP, which have now been confirmed in vivo experimentally (193), has led to intensive investigations that focus on blocking these effects using a variety of approaches. Fructose was shown to be neuroprotective in isolated hepatocytes (194) In models of mild MPTP toxicity (i.e., modest MPTP-induced striatal dopamine depletions in the mouse), a combination of coenzyme Q10 and nicotinamide (both thought to improve mitochondrial function) protected against toxicity (195). Oral administration of creatine or cyclocreatine, which may increase phosphocreatine or cyclophosphocreatine buffering against ATP depletion, also protects against MPTP-induced striatal dopamine depletion in mice. Creatine has also been shown to be protective in an in vitro model (196). Another strategy aimed at compensating for bioenergetic defects is to administer triacetyluridine (TAU) as a means of delivering exogenous pyrimidines (197). TAU has previously been shown to be neuroprotective in animal models of Huntington's and Alzheimer's diseases and has recently been shown to significantly attenuate MPTP-induced depletion of striatal dopamine and loss of tyrosine-hydroxylase–positive neurons in the STN. This suggests that TAU might provide a novel approach for treating neurodegenerative diseases associated with impaired mitochondrial function (197). Promethazine (PMZ), an FDA-approved antihistaminergic drug that accumulates in brain mitochondria in vivo and inhibits Ca^{2+}-induced mitochondrial permeability transition pore (PTP) in rat liver mitochondria in vitro, has also been found to protect against MPTP toxicity in the mouse without affecting its effects on complex 1, suggesting that there may be multiple ways MPTP causes neurodegeneration.

Finally, in an interesting set of experiments by Richards and colleagues (198) it was shown that overexpression the yeast single-subunit NADH dehydrogenase (NDI1) (thereby bypassing the need for complex 1) in cell culture abolished the toxicity of MPP(+). Furthermore, overexpression of NDI1 through stereotactic administration of a viral vector harboring the NDI1 gene into the SN protected mice from both the neurochemical and behavioral deficits elicited by MPTP. These data not only verified the importance of complex I in the process leading to MPTP-induced parkinsonism but adds weight to the role of complex 1 in PD and the utility of using the MPTP model to study. They also further support strategies to improve complex 1 function (or even bypass it) as a therapeutic role in PD.

The mitochondrial story has once again provided examples of basic science having direct implications for PD. First, a controlled clinical trial is has now been completed which was designed to determine whether coenzyme Q, a promoter of mitochondrial function, could be used to slow or halt the progression of the disease (199, 200). This trial met prespecific criteria showing a trend toward a slowing of disability in those receiving coenzyme Q10 at 1200 mg/kg per day. A larger trial is now planned that should be more conclusive and will utilize an even higher dose (2400 mg/kg). Second, creatine has been tested for neuroprotective effects in a futility trial in patients with Parkinson's disease (201) and is now under consideration for a much larger clinical trial for its potentially neuroprotective effects.

Oxidative Stress. Although evidence that MPP+ is a mitochondrial toxin is incontrovertible, it is certainly not the only mechanism that has been proposed to explain how MPTP/MPP+ kills cells. The foremost of the other theories relates to oxidative stress. Although it was originally proposed that MPP+ undergoes redox cycling in a manner similar to paraquat, this concept has long since been abandoned (202, 203). On the other hand, there is now good evidence that paraquat, which has been shown to be selectively toxic to dopaminergic neurons as well (204), generates oxygen free radicals through a process or redox-cycling (205) and acts in a manner that is very different from MPP+ and rotenone, another complex 1 inhibitor (206). However, there are a myriad of other ways that this compound could induce oxidative stress, including disruption of the electron transport chain (207).

One of the most common approaches used to investigate the "free radical hypothesis" is to use antioxidants to protect against MPTP toxicity, but these studies have been frustratingly contradictory. Alpha tocopherol (208), beta carotene (157), melatonin (209–211), and ascorbic acid (208, 212) have been reported to protect against MPTP-induced striatal dopamine depletion in the mouse, but not all investigators have seen these effects (213–216). Furthermore, investigations in the nonhuman primate using alpha tocopherol and beta carotene (217) as well as ascorbic acid (218) have failed to show a neuroprotective effect. Blanchet and colleagues (219) used OPC-14117, a potent antioxidant, to block MPTP-induced parkinsonism in a chronic model of MPTP intoxication (a model that attempts to closely mimic the slow progression of PD), but this effort failed. On the other hand, AD4, a novel low-molecular-weight thiol antioxidant, has been reported to be neuroprotective in the MPTP model (220). Spin-trapping agents such as alpha-phenyl-ter-butyl-nitrone (PBN) (221), azulenyl nitrone (222), MDL 101, 002 (223), and stilbazulenyl nitrone (224) have also been reported to be at least partially neuroprotective in the mouse model of MPTP toxicity, but Ferger and colleagues (225) were unable to make an association between the hydroxyl radical–savaging effect of PBN and MPTP neurotoxicity. In yet another study, bromocriptine was found to block MPTP toxicity in the mouse (226). Because this drug was also effective in blocking striatal glutathione depletion, the possibility was raised that this dopamine agonist was acting by stimulating antioxidant activity in the brain. Melatonin, an endogenous antioxidant, has been shown to inhibit a loss of tyrosine hydroxylase (TH) immunoreactivity in the mouse striatum, presumably through a similar mechanism (227). Another interesting agent that has been found to ameliorate the effects of MPTP is apomorphine, which could be working as a radical scavenger (228). Finally, the angiotensin converting enzyme (ACE) inhibitor captopril, which appears to have antioxidant properties, has been shown to attenuate MPTP toxicity in mice while at the same time decreasing markers of oxidative stress (229). Similar findings have also been reported with the antituberculosis drug rifampicin (230, 231).

Metallothioneins, free radical scavengers, have also been used to investigate the free radical hypothesis of MPTP neurotoxicity. In 1997, Rojas and Rios (232) reported that inducers of metallothionein provided significant protection against MPTP-induced striatal dopamine depletions in the mouse. MPTP alone produced a 50% reduction in striatal metallothionein, and in another set of experiments induced a 30% to 39% reduction in metallothionein mRNA. However, in a later study, metallothionein I and metallothionein II knockout mice were not found to be more sensitive to MPTP, which suggests that these proteins are not directly involved in blocking the effects of MPTP (233). Because iron may be involved in the process of free radical generation, chelators of iron have been examined. Ferger and colleagues (234) showed that cytosine is an effective chelator of iron and that it significantly protected against MPTP-induced striatal dopamine depletion in the mouse.

In a study by Aubin and colleagues (235), salicylate, aspirin, and aspergic (acetylsalicylate of DL lysine) were all found to prevent MPTP neurotoxicity. These investigators also demonstrated that cyclo-oxygenase inhibitors or agents that inhibited NF-kappB did not have this effect and that this effect of salicylates was not due to either inhibition of MAO B or dopamine uptake. In a separate study, this same group reported that hydroxylated salicylate metabolites were present in the brains of MPTP- and salicylate-treated mice, suggesting that hydroxyl radical savaging may be the mechanism underlying this neuroprotective effect. Subsequently, Ferger and colleagues (236) showed that salicylate blocks the MPTP-induced decline in TH-positive cells in the mouse SN, further suggesting that salicylate is neuroprotective. Interestingly, green tea polyphenols have been found to prevent MPTP neurotoxicity in mice (237); they are now being tested for neuroprotective effects in a clinical trial that is being conducted in China in conjunction with our Institute, representing yet another translational event to emerge from studies in laboratory animals, which have now reach the clinical trials stage.

Another way to investigate the role of oxidative stress is to search for evidence of reactive oxygen species in the brain of animals exposed to MPTP. For example, Sriram and colleagues (238) used both sagittal slices of mouse brain exposed directly to MPTP and mice exposed via systemic administration of MPTP and found that there were significant increases in both reactive oxygen species and lipid peroxidation products and declines in glutathione. Because these changes preceded complex I inhibition, they suggested that free radical generation was the primary event leading to toxicity. Ali and colleagues (239) identified the generation of reactive oxygen species in older but not young mice given MPTP, and a number of investigators have reported evidence that MPTP alone induces hydroxyl radical formation (240–242). In cell culture systems, it has been shown that cell lines deficient in catalase activity are more sensitive to the effects of MPP+ than those with higher levels (243). On the other hand, in a series of experiments using a murine dopaminergic cell line comparing 6-hydroxydopamine and MPTP, Choi and colleagues (244) found that reactive oxygen radicals seemed to play an essential role in 6-OHDA–mediated apoptosis, but there was no evidence of this in the setting of MPP+-induced necrosis.

Transgenic mice have also been used to investigate the possible role of oxidative stress in MPTP toxicity. For example, mice overexpressing the mitochondrial form of dismutase superoxide seem to be at least partially protected from MPTP (245, 246), and mice overexpressing Bcl-2, which may protect against free radicals, were found to be partially protected against MPTP toxicity (247, 248). Conversely, administration of MPTP to glutathione peroxidase (a critical intracellular enzyme involved in

detoxification of hydrogen peroxide to water) knockout mice resulted in significantly greater depletions of dopamine, 3, 4-dihydroxybenzoic acid, and homovanillic acid when compared to wild-type control mice (249–250). Similarly, Zn CuZn-superoxide dismutase (SOD) knockout mice have been found to be similarly affected by MPTP and mice overexpressing mitochondrial SOD2 are at least partially protected from the effects of MPTP, possibly by preventing aconitase inactivation and iron accumulation (251).

In summary, there is a diverse literature on the possible role of free radicals in MPTP neurotoxicity, but this literature is conflicting, much as it is in PD. At least part of the problem relates to the use of different models, animal strains, and experimental paradigms. Also contributing to the confusion may be the fact that other actions of putative antioxidants, such as inhibition of MAO B or blocking the dopamine transporter, were not ruled out as contributing to their possible "neuroprotective" effects. Finally, many of these studies relied on striatal dopamine concentrations as the primary measure of nigrostriatal integrity and therefore may not have actually been assessing the process of neuronal degeneration. Adding to the complexity of this problem is that any process that affects the mitochondrial respiratory chain and energy production will probably cause leakage or generation of oxyradicals and subsequent oxidative stress, so that the two processes are probably inexorably linked (252) (see Chapter 30). A role for oxidative stress in the cascade of events that lead to toxicity seems to be established and will probably continue to be an important and challenging area of investigation—one that continues to have implications for the cause and treatment of PD.

MPTP-related research continues to be surprisingly translational. Although interest in the "free-radical" hypothesis of PD long antedates the discovery of MPTP (253), it took the MAO B inhibitor trial to precipitate an antioxidant trial in PD, as alpha tocopherol was added as an additional component to the DATATOP trial that tested deprenyl (163). This arm of the trial showed no evidence of neuroprotection, somewhat dampening hopes that antioxidants might be able to slow disease progression in PD. However, it is not known if adequate levels of alpha tocopherol were ever achieved in the central nervous system (CNS), so it is difficult to know how much weight to place on a negative result. Successful neuroprotection against MPTP neurotoxicity in experimental models, particularly in the primate, could well lead to a second attempt for forestall progression of PD in patients by using effective antioxidant therapy.

Nitric Oxide. During the last few decades, nitric oxide (NO) has come to the forefront as a possible endogenous toxin that could play a role in the process of neurodegeneration in a variety of diseases including PD (254).

To some degree this interest is a result of studies using the MPTP model. This began when several investigators reported that inhibiting NO synthetase (NOS) was partially protective against MPTP neurotoxicity in mice (255–258) and the baboon (259). It was also shown in the baboon that MPTP-induced increase in nigral perxoynitrite was prevented by inhibiting NOS (260). Furthermore, MPTP administration causes upregulation of iNOS in the STN. NO production has been shown to be increased by around 50% after MPTP administration (261). Increases in iNOS after MPTP can be partially prevented by nNOS and iNOS inhibitors (262), and iNOS knockouts have been reported to be less sensitive to the effects of MPTP by one group (263) but not another (264). In one study using iNOS knockout mice, MPTP induced microglial activation as expected in the nigra, but cells were nearly completely preserved. Oddly, however, MPTP-induce loss of dopaminergic terminals was not ameliorated in the knockout mice, suggesting a different mechanism of terminal damage (265).

The importance of NO in MPTP toxicity was questioned when several groups found that the most commonly used NOS inhibitor, 7-nitroindazole (7-NI), also inhibited MAO B (266–268), raising the possibility that, rather than by blocking the synthesis of NO, inhibition of MAO might explain at least some of the effects of 7-NI in protecting against MPTP toxicity (269). The next step was to examine other NOS inhibitors to see if they blocked MPTP toxicity as well. Although Matthews et al. (270) reported that S-methylthiocitrulline, a relatively selective inhibitor of NOS, protected mice against MPTP-induced striatal dopamine depletion, MacKenzie and colleagues (271) were unable to inhibit MPTP toxicity in the monkey using another NOS inhibitor (L-NGnitro-arginine methyl ester, or LNAME).

The reasons for these disparate results regarding a role for NO in MPTP toxicity are not clear. However, it seems likely that the effects of 7-NI on MAO B have confounded at least some of the studies. Other investigators have suggested that iNOS inhibitors are actually acting as antioxidants (272). In a study by Tsai and Lee (273), NO donors actually appeared to protect astrocytes from MPP+-induced damage. More recently, Rose and colleagues (274), using intracerebral microdialysis in rats, found that NO appeared to be involved in the MPP+-induced production of hydroxyl radical but not MPP+-induced dopamine release. A number of other interesting studies bear mentioning. In a study on the neuroprotective effects of minocycline, the authors found evidence that minocycline blocks MPTP neurotoxicity in vivo by indirectly inhibiting MPTP/MPP(+)-induced glial iNOS expression and/or directly inhibiting NO-induced neurotoxicity, most likely by inhibiting the phosphorylation of p38 MAPK (275). The neuroprotective effects of pioglitazone may also be mediated, at least partially, by

moderating NO production (276). Green tea polynoles have also been shown to decrease nitric oxide–mediated MPTP toxicity in mice (237). Somewhat paradoxically, Genc and colleagues (277) reported that neuroprotective effects of erythropoietin against MPTP-induced neurotoxicity in the mouse seem to be mediated by increasing nitric oxide production. Similar observations have been reported with the ACE inhibitor perindopril (278). In contrast to these two studies, increase NO production has also been implicated in another model of increased susceptiblity to MPTP that occurs after development of obesity induced by a high-fat diet (279).

At the moment one can only say that the transition of experimental studies with NO and NOS inhibitors to PD is a work in progress. The only primate study done to date, which used a NOS inhibitor other than 7-NI, failed to show a neuroprotective effect. Although there have been some hints of a role for NO in PD (280, 281), the exact role is far from established (254). Interestingly, an association between polymorphisms in the genes for iNOS and nNOS has been reported by at least one group (282), suggesting that some relationship of NO and PD in a human population exists. Another problem is that the clinical effects of NOS inhibitors remain unknown (283). Should new evidence of the importance of NO in MPTP toxicity be forthcoming in primates, there might well be a revitalization of research interest in NOS inhibitors as neuroprotective agents for PD.

Excitotoxicity. Unraveling the importance of excitotoxicity as a mechanism that underlies neurotoxicity of MPTP has proved to be a challenging. Whereas NMDA antagonists were first used in an attempt to induce symptomatic improvement in the MPTP-lesioned monkey with variable results (284–286), these agents were also used as potentially protective therapies. In a study by Turski and colleagues (287) and several others that followed (288, 289), NMDA antagonists were shown to protect against MPTP/MPP+ toxicity, including actual nigral cell degeneration. However, the waters were clouded by a rapid succession of reports that NMDA antagonists provided only partial (290, 291) or no protection (292–294) in mice. Similar results were reported using rat mesencephalic cell cultures (295). On the other hand, Srivastava and colleagues (296) found that decortication (a procedure that removes glutameric input to the striatum) or MK-801, a prototype NMDA antagonist, blocked MPP+-induced cell loss in the rat using direct intrastriatal injections of MPP+. Clonidine, an alpha-2 agonist that is thought to block glutamate overflow, has been shown to partially protect mice against MPTP-induced dopamine depletion (297).

We found that MK-801 did protect against MPTP-induced striatal dopamine depletion in the mouse, but this protection was only transient, lasting less than 12 hours. The drug did not block degeneration of dopaminergic neurons (294). However, MK-801 was also found to delay elimination of MPP+ from the brain. Since sequestration of MPP+ in synaptic vesicles has been shown to protect neurons from its toxic effects (298), one possibility is MK-801 is at least temporarily promoting vesicular storage. In support of this possibility is the observation that MK-801 inhibits MPP+-induced striatal dopamine release (299), although whether this is related to an effect on vesicular release is not known.

Although the mixed results described may have tempered enthusiasm, there continues to be abundant interest in exploring the possibility that NMDA receptor antagonists might be neuroprotective in PD (see Chapter 43). One agent that has come under close scrutiny is the NMDA inhibitor riluzole. Although there has been great interest in this drug as a potential neuroprotective agent in amyotrophic lateral sclerosis (ALS), it has also been found to block MPTP-induced striatal dopamine depletion in mice (300) and monkeys (301, 302). Because of its potential as a neuroprotective agent in PD, a pilot study has now been carried out with riluzole in patients with PD (303). Although the observed deterioration in scores on the United Parkinson's Disease Rating Scale (UPDRS) appeared to slightly more pronounced in the placebo group, the difference between this group and the riluzole group did not reach statistical significance and there was no statistically significant difference in the time between enrollment and start of symptomatic therapy when patients initially treated with riluzole were compared to those initially treated with placebo. The authors concluded that riluzole (100 mg/day) was well tolerated but that because the trial was only a pilot, larger longitudinal studies were still warranted.

Clinical trials have also been completed with remacemide, another glutamate antagonist (304–306), but none of these trials have been designed specifically to assess potential neuroprotective effects.

Growth Factors. The use of trophic factors to treat PD has been considered a very attractive approach because they could theoretically achieve the same goals as surgery. Current evidence suggests that, although dopamine depletion in the disease exceeds 80%, cell loss is more in the range of 60%. This suggests that there may be a substantial number of "dormant" or nonfunctional neurons still present. If these could be reactivated, it is theoretically possible that trophic factors could be used not only to slow or halt disease progression but actually reverse signs and symptoms if enough of these cells could be rejuvenated. This represents one of the potentially most exciting options for the future, but it may well prove to be one of the most challenging.

MPTP models have provided a vigorous testing ground for trophic factors in PD. Indeed, fibroblast growth factor (FGF) (307–310), glial-derived neurotrophic factor (GDNF) (311, 312), epidermal growth factor (EGF) (313), brain-derived neurotrophic factor (BDNF) (314–316), and even nerve growth factor (NGF) (315) have all been tested in the MPTP model. However, the results of these studies have not always been consistent. For example, although FGF was effective in the mouse model, it was not found to be neuroprotective in tissue culture (317). When studies with this trophic factor were extended to primates, no effect was seen on the nigrostriatal system in one study (318), but positive results were seen in another (319). With higher intraventricular doses used in the former of these two studies, ependymal and choroids plexus overgrowth was observed. In some instances this led to hydrocephalus, reminding us that this approach is not without hazard.

It is important to note that at least two strategies have been employed in the testing of growth factors. The first can be described as a neuroprotective strategy, in which the trophic factor is given before or around the time of MPTP administration to block or ameliorate toxicity. The other strategy, which is typically carried out in vivo, is to give the trophic factor after an animal has been lesioned in an attempt to induce recovery. Studies on GDNF illustrate these two approaches. This neurotrophic factor was first studied in 1995, when it was shown to both protect against MPTP-induced striatal dopamine depletion and nigral cell loss in the mouse as well as to at least partially restore nerve fiber densities and dopamine levels when given after MPTP administration (311). Investigations were quickly extended to primates, where GDNF was found to improve bradykinesia, rigidity, and postural instability and also to increase nigral dopamine levels after direct intrastriatal injection (312, 319). This restorative effect of GDNF has been shown to be effective in old as well as young mice (320), an important observation if this approach is to be used in PD. One puzzling but fascinating feature about GDNF is its apparent ability to improve dopaminergic function at the level of the SN but not at the level of nigrostriatal terminals (321). This is a unique effect and suggests that, because these animals improve, the events occurring at the level of the SN deserve more attention in regard to their neurophysiologic role in movement. Importantly, GDNF has now been shown to improve MPTP-induced parkinsonism in monkeys after intraventricular delivery (322, 323), using viral vectors for delivery (324, 325), and the placement of encapsulated GDNF-producing C2C12 cells into the ventricles of chronic MPTP-treated baboons (326).

Glial cells may also be mediators of neurotrophic effects in response to nigrostriatal injury. For example, Chen and colleagues (327), having observed the proliferation of nestin-expressing astroglial cells in MPTP-treated C57/BL mice, have suggested that these nestin-expressing activated astroglial cells may play important roles in protection of nigrostriatal dopamine neurons and in the pathogenesis of PD, possibly by virtue of synthesizing and releasing neurotrophic factors. This group subsequently showed that these cells expressed a variety of trophic factors, including nerve growth factor (NGF), neurotrophin-3 (NT3), and GDNF (328).

In 1996 the first human trial using GDNF for the treatment of PD began. One problem was the fact that, because trophic factors are large molecules, delivery to the CNS represents a major challenge. Because animal studies have shown that GDNF reaches the SN after intraventricular administration (329), this offered one route by which to administer the drug, although this approach required the use of an intraventicular cannula. In all, 12 subjects received placebo and 7 or 8 were assigned to each of several different dosage groups. Parkinson disability scores did not improve at any dose. Unfortunately a number of side effects were seen, including nausea and vomiting hours to days after dosing, weight loss, asymptomatic hyponatremia, and bothersome paresthesias, often described as electric shocks (Lhermitte's sign). For these reasons, the intracerebroventricular route of administration has been largely abandoned. Several other approaches, including direct intraputamenal delivery, were considered. The first such trial in humans, which was open-label, was encouraging (330, 331), but a subsequent controlled trial using a similar approach failed to reach significance using the designated primary outcome variable (332). This plus concerns over potential side effects (the development of neutralizing antibodies in some patients and the development cerebellar lesions in a few nonhuman primates) led to discontinuation of studies using this approach. However a number of technical concerns regarding the way GDNF was delivered confound interpretation of the double-blind study and suggest that we still cannot conclude whether this approach will be effective in patients with PD (333). In the meantime, several alternative approaches are being pursued, including in vivo gene therapy and the use of encapsulated GDNF factors, an approach that has been shown to have promise in experimental animals (334, 335).

An alternative approach is to search for small molecules that can cross the blood-brain barrier and that have trophic activity. One class of compounds thought to have had such activity are the neuroimmunophilins. In 1997, one of these compounds, GPI-1046, was shown to induce regenerative sprouting of surviving dopaminergic neurons after MPTP lesioning in mice (336). Subsequently, another immunophilin, V-10, 367, was reported to completely protect against MPTP-induced loss of TH staining in the mouse striatum (337), again suggesting that this class of compounds may be effective in protecting and possibly even restoring dopaminergic neurons. Primate studies have yet to be reported; but given the potential of this class of drugs to treat PD, ease of administration, and the impressive data in the MPTP-treated mouse, clinical trials seemed a logical next step. However, the limited trials carried out to date have been disappointing (338).

Does MPTP Cause Apoptosis and/or Necrosis? Many of the theories on the mechanism of action of MPTP are not only highly reflective of current theories on PD pathogenesis but some are also controversial. Nowhere has this been more evident than when it comes to determining the role of apoptosis in MPTP-induced cell death (339). This possibility was raised by Mochizuki and colleagues (340) when they reported morphologic and histochemical evidence of apoptotic cell death in mesencephalic–striatal cocultures exposed to MPTP. However, a year later, using an acute dose paradigm in mice, Jackson-Lewis and colleagues (341) failed to find any evidence of apoptosis (although, interestingly, they did note that MPTP can induce a loss of TH immunoreactivity without causing neuronal degeneration). Subsequent studies, however, have found evidence of apoptosis in vitro, including experiments involving the exposure of PC12 cells in tissue culture to the 2-ethylphenyl analog of MPTP (342), SH-SY5Y human neuroblastoma cells to MPP+ (343), and GH3 cells (a clonal strain from the rat anterior pituitary) treated with MPP+, which was inhibited by a pancaspase inhibitor (344). Similar results have been reported in SN4741 cells (345), ventral mesencephalic cells (where MPP+ activates phosporylation of c-Jun, a pro-apoptotic factor) (346), and in human SH-SY5Y neuroblastoma cells using low concentrations of MPP+ (347). On the other hand, another investigation using PC12 cells failed to find evidence apoptosis (348), and Choi et al. (244), using a murine dopaminergic cell line, found that MPP+ (in contrast to 6-OHDA) caused non-caspase-dependent necrosis rather than apoptosis.

Favoring a role for apoptosis is the fact that a number of compounds have been found to inhibit apoptosis induced by MPP+ in cellular models, including epidermal growth factor (344), selegiline (see below) (349), certain caspase inhibitors (347), and CEP-1347 (a mixed-lineage kinase inhibitor) (350).

Several groups have reported evidence of apoptosis in mice given systemically administered MPTP (351, 352). However, Usha and colleagues (353) failed to find evidence of typical apoptotic-like DNA cleavage in the SN or caudate-putamen after a robust two-dose regimen of MPTP that caused a 75% dopamine depletion; caspase 3 levels were elevated in this model, but caspase 1 was unchanged. It has been reported that delivery of Apaf-1-DN, which blocks apoptosis, by using an AAV vector system prevents nigrostriatal degeneration in MPTP mice (354). Turmel and colleagues (355) have also shown that MPTP elevates caspase 3 levels mice, which would be expected to promote apoptosis. Also favoring a role for apoptosis is the observation that mutant mice lacking the proapoptotic protein Bax are significantly more resistant to MPTP than their wild-type littermates. In summary, while there are an increasing number of studies incriminating apoptosis, there continues to be a lack of consensus on the role apoptosis in MPTP-induced neurotoxicity. Much the same controversy continues to brew in regard to apoptosis in PD (356, 357).

Selegiline has resurfaced as part of the evolving body of work on apoptotic pathways and cell death related to MPTP toxicity. The original deprenyl story seemed straightforward enough in that the drug appeared to prevent MPTP toxicity simply by blocking the conversion of MPTP to its toxic metabolite MPP+ by inhibiting MAO B. However, there was one loose end that appeared quite early. In 1985. Mytilineou and colleagues (358) reported the curious observation that selegiline prevented neurotoxicity of MPP+ in rat mesencephalic cultures, an observation that was later replicated in another cell system (and linked to apoptosis) (359). This early finding hinted that selegiline might have other neuroprotective actions besides simply inhibiting MAO B. In 1991, Tatton et al. (360) reported that selegiline could at least partially protect against the neurodegenerative effects of MPTP in mice, even when given for up to 5 days after MPTP administration, apparently "rescuing" neurons that were destined for destruction. Further evidence that the drug had other actions besides its effect on MAO came from a study by Wu and colleagues (361). These investigators found that dopamine release and hydroxyl radical formation produced by the infusion of MPP+ into the striatum of rats declined significantly when selegiline was added to the perfusate. Later, this same group also provided evidence of a rescue effect using a very different paradigm, one that involved lesioning the nigrostriatal system by infusing MPP+ directly into the SN (362). When selegiline was given for 4 days following the infusion, it partially protected against even high doses of MPP+. These investigators suggested that selegiline was acting as an antioxidant, because similar results were obtained when 2-methylaminochromans (an inhibitor of iron-catalyzed lipid peroxidation) and DSMO (a hydroxyl radical scavenger) were used (363).

In 1996, Magyar and colleagues (364) reported that selegiline was a potent inhibitor of MPTP-induced apoptosis in PC12 cells, and Hassouna et al. (365) demonstrated that bax expression was increased in the SN of MPTP lesioned mice. Tatton and colleagues (351, 366) have shown that one of the metabolites of selegiline, desmethyldeprenyl, appears to mediate an antiapoptotic action and that it alters expression of SOD 1 and 2, BCL-, BCL-XL, NOS, c-JUN, and nicotinamides in a variety of cell systems. This antiapoptotic effect appears to be associated with reduction of the mitochondrial membrane potential, an early stage in the evolution of apoptosis, possibly by binding to

glyceraldehyde-3-phosphate dehydrogenase (GAPDH). At least one in vivo study appears to support this mechanism of action, as Guo and colleagues (367) have reported that selegiline blocks MPTP-induced apoptosis in mice. Although apoptosis is still controversial in regard to MPTP toxicity, these findings certainly suggest there are properties of the drug that have yet to be fully elucidated in spite of the fact that it has been almost 25 years since it was first introduced as a treatment for PD (368). Interestingly, there is now increasing evidence that the novel second-generation MAO inhibitor rasagiline, which is now approved for the treatment of early and late-stage PD, may have similar properties. Rasagline is a selegiline-related propargylamine, which also appears to block apoptosis in a variety of models including that induced by MPTP (369).

Poly(ADF-ribose) Polymerase (PARP). One of the most interesting and perplexing observations regarding the mechanism of action of MPTP relates to the role of poly(ADF-ribose) polymerase (PARP) in the cascade of events that lead to MPTP neurotoxicity. PARP is an enzyme repair system for DNA that catalyzes the attachment of ADP ribose units (from NAD) to nuclear proteins after DNA damage occurs, a process that consumes considerable energy. In 1996, Cosi et al. (370) reported that a variety of PARP inhibitors partially protected against MPTP-induced striatal dopamine depletion (and cortical noradrenaline depletion as well) in the mouse. PARP inhibitors were subsequently found to block MPTP-induced ATP depletion (371). In accordance with this observation, these investigators reported that MPTP reduced NAD+ levels, which could also be blocked with PARP inhibition (372). More recently a novel and more potent PARP inhibitor known as FR255595 was found to be partially protective against the effects of MPTP in mice as well (373). One of the most compelling pieces of evidence to date is the observation that PARP knockout mice are almost completely resistant to MPTP (374). However, at least one study failed to support a role for PARP; in this investigation inhibition of PARP with 3-aminobenzamide failed to protect against striatal DAT loss after intranigral injection of MPP+ (375).

Overall, the evidence that PARP plays a role in MPTP toxicity is fairly compelling but far from understood. Mandir and colleagues (376) have reported that the tumor suppressor protein p53, which, when activated, can lead to death in a variety of cells including neurons, is heavily poly(ADP-ribosyl)ated by PARP-1 following MPTP intoxication. The p53 protein typically has a fleeting half-life, but this posttranslational modification appears to stabilize p53. The authors suggest that this effect of PARP-1 on p53 could provide a mechanism underlying MPTP toxicity and even other models of neuronal death. Another possible explanation relates to energy perturbation. In view of the evidence that an energy deficit may be important in PD, this "energy perturbation hypothesis" could have implications for the idiopathic disease itself. In the MPTP model, it may be that the energy deficit induced by this mitochondrial toxin is simply not enough to kill the cell but rather that an additional oxygen-depleting event is necessary to administer the coup de grâce to the cell, that event being PARP activation in response to free radical–induced DNA damage. Studies in primates represent a logical next step in the evaluation of the importance of PARP activation in MPTP toxicity and perhaps PD.

GM$_1$ as a Neuroprotective Agent. Interest in GM$_1$ was first sparked by Hadji Constantinou and colleagues (377) in 1986 when they reported that its administration largely restored striatal dopamine levels in mice with MPTP-induced dopamine depletion. They later showed that GM$_1$ also restored normal morphology to remaining dopaminergic neurons (378) and corrected MPTP-induced D2 receptor supersensitivity (379). Although concerns were originally expressed that systemically administered GM$_1$ would be unlikely to reach the target areas in the CNS, it has since been shown to at least reach the CSF (380). Date et al. (381) reported similar reversal of dopamine depletion in young but not older mice, but others have observed at least some recovery in older mice as well (382). On the other hand, Fazzini et al. (383) found that the effects of GM$_1$ were only transient in the MPTP model.

Schneider and colleagues (384) have shown that there is a return of TH immunoreactivity in MPTP-lesioned GM$_1$-treated mice and suggested that the compound could cause regenerative sprouting in the damaged nigrostriatal system, an observation that was supported by later studies indicating that both mazindole-binding and KCL-induced striatal dopamine release are improved in MPTP-lesioned mice after GM$_1$ administration (385). GM$_1$ treatment may also improve the ability of remaining dopaminergic neurons to convert levodopa to dopamine (386), which of course could have implications for treating PD. Recently, it has been shown that a synthetic form of GM$_1$ is more effective in aged mice and actually works in mice with very extensive MPTP-induced lesions not responsive to GM$_1$ itself (387).

Finally, GM$_1$ has been reported to facilitate behavioral and neurochemical recovery after MPTP exposure in both cats (388) and monkeys (*Macaca fascicularis*) (389, 390), including effects on cognition (391). On the other hand, Herrero and colleagues (392) reported that GM$_1$ did not protect against either striatal neurochemical changes or nigral cell loss in cynomolgus monkeys, although it did seem to enhance TH cellular content in the SN. They suggested that this compound might be a "palliative" approach to PD.

The GM$_1$ story represents yet another example of basic research with MPTP stimulating clinical trials in PD. On the basis of the promising work in mice and their own studies in primates, Schneider and colleagues initiated an open-label trial in parkinsonian patients and reported promising if not dramatic results in 1995 (393). The results of a double-blind, controlled study were subsequently reported in 1998, and a significant difference in UPDRS motor scores was found at 16 weeks (394). The activities of daily living (ADL) scores in "off" periods were also improved, as were timed motor tests of arm, hand, and foot movements as well as walking. These encouraging results led to a 5-year double-blind, placebo-controlled trial using 100 patients to examine symptomatic improvement with GM$_1$ treatment over a 6-month period as well as long-term effects on disease and symptom progression (Jay Schneider, personal communication).

Other Neuroprotective Agents to Emerge from the Study of MPTP. A variety of other agents have been identified as possible inhibitors of MPTP toxicity. Pai et al. (395), using lactic acid release in striatal tissue slices as a marker of toxicity, reported that inhibitors of cytochrome P450 at least partially protect against MPTP toxicity. Bodis-Wollner and colleagues (396) observed that neither parkinsonism nor electroretinograph features of MPTP toxicity were seen in primates pretreated with acetyl-levo-carnitine. The very robust epidemiologic finding that cigarette smoking protects against PD has also been pursued in the MPTP model. In fact, one group actually tested cigarette smoke directly and found that it partially protected against MPTP-induced striatal dopamine depletion (397), an effect that was associated with inhibition of MAO. Nicotine, when given in an acute intermittent but not a chronic continuous fashion, partially protects against MPTP-induced striatal dopamine depletion in the mouse (398). Our own group, using a primate model that closely mimics the continuous exposure to nicotine experienced by cigarette smokers, found partial protection from the effects of MPTP (399). Thalidomide has also been shown to protect again MPTP-induced striatal dopamine depletion in the mouse, presumably by blocking the inflammatory component of the response (400). Agents that stimulate dopamine receptor activity may be neuroprotective in the mouse model (401), and adenosine A1 agonists prevent MPTP-induced striatal dopamine depletion in mice both when given before and up to 5 hours after MPTP administration (402). Coadministration of the vigilance-promoting drug modafinil has been reported to block MPTP-induced loss of both TH-positive and TH-negative neurons using stereologic counting techniques in the mouse (403), but the mechanism by which this occurs has yet to be determined. Other agents that have been reported to be neuroprotective include estrogen (404, 405), 17 beta-estradiol (406–411), progesterone and raloxifene (412), the spin-trapping agent PBN (413), copper sulfate (414), other compounds related to tobacco (415, 416), caffeine and related compounds (417–419), the ginsenosides Rb(1) and Rg(1) (420), inhibitors of cyclooxygenase isoenzymes COX-1 and COX-2 (421), other adenosine A2A receptor antagonists (422, 423), nicotinic acetylcholine receptor agonists (424), parasite-derived counterpart of neurotrophic factors (PDNF) (425), calpain inhibitors (426, 427), the astrocyte-modulating agent arundic acid (428), green tea polyphenols (429), environmental enrichment (430), a synthetic new derivative of squamosamide known as FLZ (431), immunization with myelin oligodendrocyte glycoprotein and complete Freund adjuvant (432), geldanamycin, which induces heat shock protein 70 (433), an azulenyl nitrone antioxidant (224), dextromethorphan and a series of its analogues (434), the 5-HT1A agonists BAY 639044 and repinotan (in primates) (435), gamma-glutamylcysteine ethyl ester (436), low dose whole-body gamma-irradiation (437), curcumin (a polyphenolic antioxidant) (231), and cystamine (438). These studies provide an almost bewildering array of potentially tantalizing leads in the search for neuroprotective agents for PD. Which ones, if any, will prove to be key remains to be determined, but looking for commonality of mechanism or biochemical pathways may be good starting points for teasing out the most promising starting point for research.

Exacerbation of MPTP Toxicity

Although the preceding section focused almost exclusively on ways to prevent toxicity, there has been a parallel, though perhaps less vigorous, effort focusing on ways to enhance toxicity. Such studies are important because of their obvious implications regarding environmental toxicants that might play a causative role in PD. In 1985 Corsini and colleagues (439) reported what was probably the first example of a compound that actually exacerbated MPTP toxicity. The compound was diethyldithiocarbamate (DDC), and it exacerbated MPTP-induced dopamine depletion in the mouse. This was at first thought to be due to an enhancement of oxidative stress; however, Irwin and colleagues (440) subsequently showed that DDC administration led to a marked increase in MPP+ concentrations in the rodent brain, possibly through enhanced delivery of MPTP to the CNS and its biotransformation to MPP+. Miller and colleagues (441) reported that DDC, when given with MPTP, enhanced gliosis as measured by GFAP and resulted in more extended toxicity, with norepinephrine depletion and gliosis in the hippocampus. Walters and colleagues (442) demonstrated that DDC can "unmask" MPTP toxicity by virtue of converting a nontoxic dose of MPTP into one that causes toxicity. An important aspect of this study was that stereologic cell-counting techniques were used, so the neurodegenerative effects of MPTP were being studied, not just its ability to deplete striatal dopamine. These findings have

implications for PD in that they raise the possibility that multiple environmental "hits" may be required to cause the disease. This might explain why no single agent has been identified to date as "the cause" of PD.

A variety of other compounds have been identified that enhance the dopamine-depleting effects of MPTP in mice, including N-methylmercaptoimidazole (443), tetraphenylboron, ethanol and acetaldehyde (444), DSP-4 (445), DFP and nicotine (446), and magnesium sulfate (447). N-methylmercaptoimidazole probably enhances toxicity by inhibition MPTP N-oxygenation in the liver (by virtue of blocking flavin-containing monoxygenase), and tetraphenylboron is thought to potentiate inhibition of mitochondrial respiration. The mechanisms by which these other compounds are working are less clear. In an observation that could have more direct implications for environmental causes of nigrostriatal degeneration, Takahashi et al. (448) reported that the agricultural fumigant Maneb (a dithiocarbamate) enhanced locomotor effects and cataplexy induced by MPTP; however, neurochemical measurements were not done. We tested two other widely used dithiocarbamates and found that one (ethylene bis dithiocarbamate) enhanced MPTP-induced striatal dopamine depletion in the mouse (449). Ironically, minocycline, which has been reported to protect against the effects of MPTP and was tested as a potential "neuroprotect agent" in a futility trial, has also been found to exacerbate MPTP toxicity (450, 451).

Several other approaches have been taken to exacerbate MPTP toxicity. Duan and colleagues (452) found that dietary folate deficiency and elevated homocysteine levels increased sensitivity to MPTP in mice. In another study, fas-deficient lymphoproliferative mice were unexpectedly found to be highly susceptible to the neurotoxic effects of MPTP (453). Fas (CD95) is a member of the tumor necrosis factor receptor superfamily, but the mechanism of this effect is not clear. Another interesting approach involved administering iron to neonatal mice, and then exposing them to MPTP at 2 months (454). Iron-exposed mice were much more sensitive to the effects of MPTP, although this conclusion was based on behavioral studies only. In somewhat similar paradigm. Richardson and colleagues exposed mice to dieldrin during the perinatal period and found and enhanced sensitivity to MPTP at 3 months. This study is of particular interest since dieldrin has been implicated as a possible causative agent in PD. Given the current interest in PD as a protein misfolding disorder, a number of investigators have explored the possibility that overexpression of alpha synuclein enhances susceptibility to MPTP, and several have found that this is indeed the case (455–457), indicating that alpha synuclein overexpression enhances MPTP. However, other investigators have not seen this effect (458, 459).

AGING AND MPTP

In what seemed to be more than coincidence, the effects of MPTP were quickly found to increase with age, making it an even more compelling compound for modeling an age-related neurodegenerative disease. The first indication that this was the case came from Jarvis and Wagner (460), who found that effects of MPTP on striatal dopamine concentrations were more pronounced in older rats, compared with very young ones. Shortly thereafter, similar results were reported in the mouse, with a shift to the left of the dose/effect curve for MPTP-induced dopamine depletion in older animals (461), and Gupta et al. demonstrated that a loss of catecholamine fluorescence in the locus ceruleus and ventral tegmental area in old but not young mice lesioned with MPTP (462). Further highlighting the importance of aging was the observation that older mice do not recover from the effects of MPTP, whereas young mice do (463), and the clear-cut demonstration that MPTP induced greater cell loss in older animals compared with younger ones (464). In addition, a much more robust microglial activation is seen in older mice after MPTP administration (465).

The likelihood that this was due to pharmacokinetic effects (at least in the mouse) was suggested by the fact that much higher levels of MPP+ were observed in older versus younger mice after equivalent doses of MPTP were given (461, 466). Furthermore, intraventricular administration of MPP+, which circumvents pharmacokinetic factors, showed no difference between age groups, which again suggests that it was the amount of MPTP/MPP+ delivered to the nigrostriatal system that was the key rather than an increased sensitivity of the neurons themselves with aging (a pharmacodynamic effect). The relationship between MPTP toxicity, aging, and brain MAO levels was further teased out by Irwin and colleagues (467), who showed that the dopamine-depleting effects of MPTP increased through 16 months of age and then decreased slightly in very old animals (20 months). These changes were closely mirrored by age-dependent changes in MAO B, suggesting that this enzyme is responsible for changes in MPTP toxicity that occur during the aging process in the mouse. Similar age-related changes in MAO B (but not MAO A) have been demonstrated by others as well (468), and inhibition of MAO B but not MAO A has been shown to block the age-related effects of an analog of MPTP that is activated by both forms of this enzyme (469).

Work in primates has had a somewhat different evolution. One of the earliest observations related to aging was the novel finding that MPTP induced eosinophilic inclusion bodies and cell loss in the locus ceruleus in very old squirrel monkeys (470). Neither of these findings had been seen in younger animals. The inclusion bodies were of particular interest in that they were reminiscent of Lewy bodies in humans, both in regard to their distribution and the fact that they were seen only in older animals. Rose and colleagues (471) have reported that larger doses of MPTP were required to induce parkinsonism in younger animals, which suggests that older animals were more sensitive to MPTP. However, neither of these investigations was a prospective or systematic investigation in terms of its approach to aging. Using an intracarotid infusion paradigm of MPTP, Ovadia (472) found that older animals required less MPTP to become parkinsonian, and that their parkinsonism tended to be less severe. We carried out a careful prospective study of aging in the primate and found unexpectedly that neither MAO B nor MAO A changed with aging (473). Thus, in monkeys at least, there may be different reasons for increased sensitivity to age, which may relate more to changes in neuronal vulnerability.

Because aging remains the only unequivocal risk factor for PD to this day, this would appear to be a valuable experimental model in which to pursue the underlying mechanisms that make us more susceptible to the disease as we age. One interesting example of the potential relevance of such studies comes from recent work in young (3 months) and old (18 months) Fischer F344 rats (474). In this investigation livers were perfused with either MPTP, DDT, or malathion. The recovery of all 3 compounds was increased in older rats (by 258%, 253% and 134% respectively) compared to young rats. The transport of DDT and malathion into hepatocytes was reduced with age, and the authors suggested age-related impairment of hepatic detoxification would increase the bioavailability of potentially toxic xenobiotics which could, in turn, increase the risk for developing PD with aging. It is also worth noting that enhanced sensitivity of the aging nigrostriatal dopamine pathway to other pesticides, particularly paraquat and maneb in combination, have also been reported (475).

In summary, research on the relationship between aging and susceptibility to PD seems to have been by and large understudied. In part this may have been because of inadequate models or lack of good hypotheses. The MPTP model continues to provide a remarkable opportunity to explore this relationship, and it can only be hoped that there will be an acceleration of research in this area.

SPECIES SUSCEPTIBILITY

One of the earliest and perhaps most surprising findings regarding the biologic effects of MPTP was that although human and nonhuman primates are exquisitely sensitive to its effects, rodents are much less sensitive, and rats are nearly refractory to systemically administered toxin (33). One dramatic difference, which to this day defies explanation, is that MPP+ is rapidly removed from the mouse brain (in a matter of hours), whereas it persists for weeks or longer in the primate brain (476). Obviously the inability to remove potentially noxious xenobiotics from the brain could represent a major risk factor for neurodegeneration in the primate, but this research lead has been by and large ignored. This is unfortunate, because it might provide clues as to risk factors for PD. Although differences between primates and rodents may not be surprising, it is now clear that substantial differences in sensitivity to MPTP may be seen even with different strains of mice (477), with C57Bl/6 mice being the most vulnerable (478, 479). Because of their sensitivity, this species is widely used for studies with MPTP. Remarkably, sensitivity to MPTP may vary within the same strain of mouse. Heikkila et al. (480) found, for example, that the same strain of mouse from different commercial suppliers differed in sensitivity to MPTP, suggesting that very subtle biologic variations can affect vulnerability. This observation also has practical implications in the laboratory, because changing commercial supplier can seriously alter the experimental conditions. In a novel study using 7 strains of mice, Hamre and Tharp (481) presented fascinating evidence that susceptibility to MPTP-induced cell loss may be autosomal dominant and is due to a polymorphism carried on C57BL/6J allele. Differences in susceptibility have even been observed between different species of snakes (482).

Differing levels of MAO B in the CNS appears to be one of the factors that affect species sensitivity (483). Kalaria and colleagues (484, 485) pointed out the importance of MAO B levels in the blood-brain barrier, and indeed this factor may be a key to explaining the refractoriness of rats to the effects of systemically administered MPTP. This was clearly illustrated in a study of 5 different strains of rats using intracarotid injection of MPTP, in which the degree of toxicity best correlated with levels of MAO B in the capillary endothelia of the brain (486). A similar phenomenon may explain differences between mouse strains (487). On the other hand, Mushiroda and colleagues (488) have provided evidence that flavin-containing mono-oxygenases (FMOs) may also play a significant role in the detoxification of MPTP in cerebral endothelial cells and thereby account for variations between species. Furthermore, striking strain differences have been found in the ability of glia to convert MPTP to MPP+ (489), and considerable variations between species in levels and ratios of MAO A and B have been found in both brain and liver as well (490). Another factor that may account for differences between mouse and rat relates to the transport system of synaptic vesicles,

VMAT2, as it is generally thought that uptake of cytosolic MPP+ (and dopamine) may protect cells for toxicity (see earlier discussion on VMAT2). Staal and colleagues (491) investigated this hypothesis and found that the maximal transport rate (V_{max}) was 2-fold greater in vesicles from rats than in those from mice.

In conclusion, it seems quite possible that further exploration of these species and strain differences could provide clues regarding susceptibility to PD and may therefore represent a potentially important and fertile area for future research, as exemplified by the provocative study of Hamre and Tharp (481) or searching for chromosomal loci that might be determinants of genetic susceptibility to MPTP (492) or other potentially toxic xenobiotics.

INTRANIGRAL SELECTIVE VULNERABILITY

The selective vulnerability of subsets of nigral neurons in response to MPTP has been a subject of interest for some time, just as it is in PD. A very interesting observation, first published in 1991, was that calbindin-containing nigral neurons appeared to be spared in mice (493) and primates (494) exposed to MPTP, an observation subsequently confirmed by German and colleagues (495) in both species. Importantly, these investigators subsequently extended these observation to PD (495). Parent et al. (496) also confirmed this finding in monkeys. However, this story has undergone an interesting twist with the findings of Sanghera and colleagues (497). Using in situ hybridization and immunocytochemistry in rat and mouse, these investigators reported that DAT mRNA was much lower (approximately 10-fold) in regions with calbindin-containing neurons and that subpopulations of neurons higher in DAT were actually more sensitive to MPTP (498). Their observations raise the possibility that the lack of a dopamine transporter might explain why these neurons are less vulnerable to MPTP/MPP+. Similarly, there is now evidence that low levels of DAT in the ventral tegmental area may explain the long-standing mystery as to why this dopaminergic area is less sensitive to the effects of MPTP than the zona compacta of the SN (499). These observations are supported by the work of Airaksinen and colleagues (500), who found that calbindin null-mutant mice exposed to MPTP were not more sensitive to its effects, as would have been predicted if calbindin itself was neuroprotective in some manner. This refocusing on the dopamine transporter as a key to selective vulnerability within the nigra could also be quite relevant to the etiopathogenesis of PD. This is because a similar pattern of intranigral vulnerability has been seen in patients with the disorder, possibly representing a clue that selective uptake of an exogenous or endogenous toxin may be important. On the other hand, Liss and colleagues (501) have provided evidence that K-ATP channels promote the differential degeneration of dopaminergic midbrain neurons after exposure to MPTP. Others have provided evidence for the expression pattern of metabotropic glutamate receptor 1alpha in the nigra playing a role in differential susceptibility of nigral neurons (502). So it is probably safe to say that we have much more to learn about this phenomenon both in toxicant-induced parkinsonism and in PD.

EPIDEMIOLOGIC INVESTIGATIONS

The discovery of the biologic effects of MPTP had at least 3 major scientific implications, the third of which is its impact on thinking regarding the environmental hypothesis of PD. The fact that such a simple compound could induce the classic motor (and even some nonmotor) features of PD raised the possibility that one or more environmental agents might play a role in the causing or triggering the idiopathic disease. This possibility was further stimulated by the similarities between MPP+ and the herbicide paraquat, although their basic mechanisms action were quickly shown to be different (202, 203). Although earlier studies failed to show that paraquat was toxic to the dopaminergic system in mice (503, 504), subsequent investigation have clearly shown that this herbicide causes dopamine depletion and actual degeneration of nigrostriatal neurons after systemic injection (203, 505).

Armed with knowledge of the biologic effects MPTP and the results of a twin study also published in 1983 (506) that failed to show a genetic influence on PD, investigators initiated a wide variety of epidemiologic studies aimed at finding environmental risk factors in PD; indeed, many such factors, including rural living, pesticide exposure, well-water consumption, and excessive exposure to metals have all been reported to apparently increase risk.

Another line of research enhanced by MPTP relates to the metabolism of xenobiotics and the risk for PD. Simply put, the hypothesis indicates that inherited defects in xenobiotic metabolism could enhance the susceptibility to toxicity from exogenous agents and thereby increase the risk for PD. This concept was fostered by earlier observations suggesting that inherited abnormalities in the cytochrome P450 system could enhance the risk for PD. This has since led to a fascinating and complex literature (507). Finally, it should be pointed out that two large twin studies have failed to show a significant genetic influence in typical PD (508, 509), particularly when beginning over the age of 50 years, thus strongly pointing to the importance of environment. Furthermore, an in-depth genomewide screen showed no evidence of a major genetic determinant in the disease, again suggesting the need to search the environment for causative trigger factors (510). Thus is seems fitting that a line of research

that was spurred nearly 25 years ago after the discovery of a relatively simple molecule is now not only alive and well but thriving. It will be interesting to see which next steps will prove to be the most revealing as we search for the environmental determinants of PD.

PROTEIN MISFOLDING, PARKINSON'S DISEASE, AND MPTP

As noted above, environmental influences appear to play an important role in PD, but at the same time it would be very difficult to overestimate the impact of genetics. To date, at least 5 monogenetic forms of parkinsonism have been identified, but the one that has had the greatest impact is known as PARK 1. This form of genetic parkinsonism is due to a mutation in the gene that encodes for the protein alpha synuclein (511). While families with mutations in this gene are exceeding rare, alpha synuclein was quickly found to be a major constituent of Lewy bodies (a cardinal pathologic feature of PD) (512). However, the exact relevance of this protein to PD remained unclear, since the vast majority of patients with the disease do not have mutations in this gene. This view changed with what many considered to be a series of seminal observations reporting that either triplication (513) or duplication (514, 515) of the normal alpha-synuclein gene can cause parkinsonism, probably as the result of a lifetime of exposure to increased concentrations of the endogenous protein (516). These observations are important because they showed for the first time a direct connection between normal synuclein and parkinsonism. Furthermore, autopsied cases have revealed a distribution of cell loss, Lewy bodies, and Lewy neuritic pathology (513, 517) that is highly reminiscent of that which is seen in PD. These observations suggest that when overexpressed in humans, normal synclein can be neurotoxic, induce Lewy body formation, and recapitulate the pattern of selective vulnerability seen in PD. These observations have had a profound influence on the thinking of many researchers in the field and have given birth to a whole new generation of research on PD as a protein misfolding or aggregation disorder.

Although at first glance the relationship between an exogenous neurotoxicant such as MPTP and an endogenously produce protein discovered though genetics might not be apparent, there have been a series of fascinating observations on the relationship between the two. One of the earliest clues that there might be a connection came from a study in baboons demonstrating an aggregation of alpha synuclein in cell bodies in the SN of MPTP-exposed animals (519). We found that 1 week after squirrel monkeys are exposed to MPTP (at a time when only 10% of dopaminergic neurons a lost), there is a marked increase in alpha-synuclein mRNA and protein in the neuronal network of the SN only but not in the nigral cell bodies themselves. However, 1 month after MPTP exposure (when the neuronal loss had reached around 40%), robust immunoreactivity was present in the cell bodies, the vast majority of which contained neuromelanin. Approximately 80% of the dopaminergic cell bodies that survived MPTP toxicity stained positive for alpha synuclein. The results indicate that a single toxic insult is capable of inducing a sustained alpha-synuclein upregulation in the primate brain and that this occurs primarily in dopaminergic neurons. Vila and colleagues have also shown an upregulation of alpha-synuclein mRNA and protein in ventral midbrain in mice after MPTP administration (519). Similar to studies in primates, immunohistochemistry revealed a marked increase in the number of alpha synuclein–positive neurons that occurred only in TH-positive neurons. These investigators have also reported that tyrosine nitration of alpha synuclein occurs in the striatum and ventral midbrain of MPTP-exposed mice (520), which would likely disrupt the physical properties of the protein. On the other hand, other gene expression studies in mice have been mixed, with some studies showing upregulation of gene expression but others reporting that there is a downregulation of alpha-synuclein gene expression after MPTP exposure in mice (521).

Meredith and colleagues (522) have observed alpha synuclein–positive granular and filamentous inclusions in dopaminergic and cortical neurons from C57/black mice treated chronically with MPTP and probenecid. Interestingly, lipofuscin granules were also seen in nigral and limbic cortical neurons. The inclusions appeared to be present the neurons that survived the initial toxic MPTP insult. However, in their study, alpha-synuclein mRNA was actually downregulated at the time point studied. Therefore the authors concluded that defective protein degradation rather than altered gene expression leads to alpha-synuclein deposition and raised the possibility that lysosomal compartments could be activated to seal off the potentially toxic material.

Fornai and colleagues (523) have reported a potentially important new MPTP model using chronic infusion of MPTP with an osmotic minipump. In addition to nigral cell damage, synuclein- and ubiquitin-positive inclusions were seen in the SN (523). However, Shimoji and colleagues (524) were unable to induce inclusions using a chronic model involving daily injections rather than continuous infusion. Because of its potential usefulness for the study of neuroprotective agents in PD, it will be important to see whether others can replicate the continuous infusion model.

The relationship between MPTP toxicity and alpha synuclein took a fascinating turn when Dauer and colleagues reported that alpha-synuclein knockout mice were resistant to the effects of MPTP (525). In their study it appeared that MPTP administration did not cause mitochondrial complex I inhibition in the null mice. At least 4 other groups have also observed that an absence of alpha synuclein protects against MPTP toxicity (523, 526–528). Interestingly, several of these studies also noted that alpha-synuclein knockout mice have few dopaminergic neurons to begin with. The mechanism underlying this phenomenon is far from clear, but these observations almost certainly represent one more piece of the puzzle regarding neurodegeneration in the subtantia nigra in both MPTP-induced parkinsonism and the idiopathic disease.

Finally, there have been a number of interesting in vivo studies on the mechanisms of interaction between MPTP and alpha synuclein. Gomez-Santos and colleagues (529) found that MPP+ increases alpha-synuclein expression and ERK/MAP-kinase phosphorylation in human neuroblastoma SH-SY5Y cells. They suggested that increases in synuclein after injury may actually be protective but that ERK/MAP activation may play direct role in the toxic effects of MPTP. In another study, heat-shock proteins were found to reduce alpha-synuclein aggregation induced by MPP+ in SK-N-SH cells (530), suggesting that such proteins may play an important neuroprotective role.

At this point it time, it seems clear that there is a relationship between MPTP neurotoxicity and changes in alpha-synuclein regulation, but it is far from clear what the underlying mechanisms are. It does appear that under some circumstances, alpha synuclein may be protective, but clearly it plays a role in neurotoxicity under other conditions. One of the great challenges for the future will be in further defining each of these and the roles they play in heath and disease.

Before concluding this section, it is worth highlighting the fascinating ways in which these different areas of inquiry can come together. Braak and colleagues (531, 532), using synuclein immunohistochemistry to stage Parkinson's disease, have suggested that Parkinson's disease actually begins in the lower brainstem and olfactory bulb, with nigral involvement coming only in mid-stage disease. This evolution has been given additional credibility as the clinical syndromes that go with these other stages have been identified and better defined (533). In a novel study, Rojo and colleagues (534) administered MPTP daily via intranasal inoculation to C57BL/6 mice for 30 days. These animals developed progressive motor deficits that correlated with a severe depletion of striatal dopamine levels and loss of tyrosine hydroxylase and dopamine transporter in SN and striatum; these changes were accompanied by gliosis in the in SN and striatum. This work represents the kind of creative approach that can be carried out to merge clinical, pathologic, and experimental observations, and, as the authors suggest, represents yet another way to assess the risk from environmental neurotoxins.

CONCLUSIONS

The discovery of the biologic effects of MPTP has had a richly diverse impact on research in PD. Indeed, knowledge of the very existence of such a compound ushered in a research renaissance on the disease, with new initiatives ranging from those focused on basic mechanisms of cell death to large epidemiologic studies. In regard to mechanisms of neurodegeneration, it is striking to see how each step in the cascade of events that lead to MPTP toxicity have in some way or another been implicated in PD. Perhaps the most impressive outcome of this research is the number of clinical trials that have been generated from basic science on MPTP and its mechanisms. However, this impact has undoubtedly been equaled by its usefulness in the primate model in unraveling basal ganglia circuitry. It is now possible to say that this model has stood the test of time in terms of relevance to the idiopathic disease, at least when it comes to neuropharmacologic and neurophysiologic changes in the basal ganglia that occur in parkinsonism. The model has therefore proved to be a widely used testing ground, even a gold standard, for investigating new pharmacologic and surgical forms of therapy. Finally, almost all aspects of research on MPTP have fostered new investigations directed at finding the cause or causes of PD. Caveats are that it remains unclear how useful the model is for identifying disease-modifying therapies and that it does not model the widespread symptomatology and neuropathology of the idiopathic disease (533). What can we expect in the coming years from MPTP-related research? Undoubtedly new compounds will continue to be tested for their symptomatic and/or neuroprotective effects in MPTP-induced models of the disease. Although neuroprotective studies will be performed in a variety of settings and models, symptomatic forms of therapy will ultimately rely on primate studies, as they are the only species to manifest full-blown and behaviorally typical parkinsonism. This model is proving equally valuable in the investigation of side effects of therapy, particularly dopa dyskinesias.

From a basic research standpoint, there remain an abundance of controversies to be resolved regarding various aspects of the mechanism of action of MPTP. Furthermore, there are many unsolved mysteries, such as the question of why the primate brain has such difficulty eliminating MPP+ while the rodent brain can do it in a matter of hours. Also, it seems almost certain that, as new theories regarding cell death in PD emerge, they will probably be explored using MPTP. The evolving investigations on the relationship between alpha synuclein and MPTP represents an excellent example of this, and it seems safe to predict that there will be many more studies investigating the interaction between MPTP (and other putative environmental agents) and alpha synuclein.

In closing, it seems reasonable to ask the rhetorical question: Will MPTP-related research eventually solve the complex riddle that we call PD? Certainly it has had an enormous impact on research and will likely do so in the future. There is little doubt that it will continue to be used as a readily accessible tool to explore new hypotheses on the cause and treatments of the disease. The good news is research on this disease has never been at a higher level, and there is reason for optimism. But science must continue at its own pace. If and when the disease is solved, it seems MPTP will likely be allowed to take a bow as a member of the cast, regardless of whether or not it plays the leading role.

References

1. Ziering ABL, Heineman SD, Lee J. Piperidine derivatives: III 4-Arylpiperidines. *J Org Chem* 1947; 12:894–903.
2. Langston J, Palfremann J. *The Case of the Frozen Addicts.* New York: Random House, 1995.
3. Langston JW, Ballard P, Tetrud JW, et al. Chronic parkinsonism in humans due to a product of meperidine-analog synthesis *Science* 1983; 219(4587):979–980 .
4. Langston JW, Ballard PA Jr. Parkinson's disease in a chemist working with 1-methyl-4-phenyl-1,2,5,6-tetrahydropyridine (letter). *N Engl J Med* 1983; 309(5):310.
5. Barbeau A, Roy M, Langston JW. Neurological consequence of industrial exposure to 1-methyl-4-phenyl-1,2,3,6-tetrahydropyridine. *Lancet* 1985; 1(8431):747.
6. Burns RS, LeWitt PA, Ebert MH, et al. The clinical syndrome of striatal dopamine deficiency: Parkinsonism induced by 1-methyl-4-phenyl-1,2,3,6-tetrahydropyridine (MPTP). *N Engl J Med* 1985; 312(22):1418–1421.
7. Davis GC, Williams AC, Markey SP, et al. Chronic parkinsonism secondary to intravenous injection of meperidine analogues. *Psychiatr Res* 1979; 1(3):249–254.
8. Langston JW. MPTP neurotoxicity: An overview and characterization of phases of toxicity. *Life Sci* 1985; 36(3):201–206.
9. Langston JW, Forno LS, Tetrud J, et al. Evidence of active nerve cell degeneration in the substantia nigra of humans years after 1-methyl-4-phenyl-1,2,3,6-tetrahydropyridine exposure. *Ann Neurol* 1999; 46(4):598–605.
10. Burns RS, Chiueh CC, Markey SP, et al. A primate model of parkinsonism: Selective destruction of dopaminergic neurons in the pars compacta of the substantia nigra by N-methyl-4-phenyl-1,2,3,6-tetrahydropyridine. *Proc Natl Acad Sci USA* 1983; 80(14):4546–4550.
11. Langston JW, Irwin I, Langston EB, et al. Pargyline prevents MPTP-induced parkinsonism in primates. *Science* 1984; 225(4669):1480–1482.
12. Langston JW, Langston EB, Irwin I. MPTP-induced parkinsonism in human and non-human primates:Clinical and experimental aspects. *Acta Neurol Scand Suppl* 1984; 100:49–54.
13. Langston JW, Ballard P Parkinsonism induced by 1-methyl-4-phenyl-1,2,3,6-tetrahydropyridine (MPTP):Implications for treatment and the pathogenesis of Parkinson's disease *Can J Neurol Sci* 1984; 11(Suppl 1):160–165.
14. Langston JW, Forno LS, Rebert CS, et al. Selective nigral toxicity after systemic administration of 1-methyl-4-phenyl-1,2,3,6-tetrahydropyridine (MPTP) in the squirrel monkey *Brain Res* 1984; 292(2):390–394.
15. Langston JW, Irwin I, Langston EB, et al. 1-Methyl-4-phenylpyridinium ion (MPPC): Identification of a metabolite of MPTP, a toxin selective to the substantia nigra. *Neurosci Lett* 1984; 48(1):87–92.
16. Jenner P, Rupniak NM, Rose S, et al. 1-Methyl-4-phenyl-1,2,3,6-tetrahydropyridine-induced parkin sonism in the common marmoset. *Neurosci Lett* 1984; 50(1–3):85–90.
17. Gerlach M, Riederer P, Przuntek H, et al. MPTP mechanisms of neurotoxicity and their implications for Parkinson's disease. *Eur J Pharmacol* 1991; 208(4):273–286.
18. Ballard PA, Tetrud JW, Langston JW. Permanent human parkinsonism due to 1-methyl-4-phenyl-1,2,3,6-tetrahydropyridine (MPTP):Seven cases. *Neurology* 1985; 35(7):949–956.
19. Tetrud JW, Langston JW. Tremor in MPTP-induced parkinsonism. *Neurology* 1992; 42(2):407–410.
20. Stern Y, Langston JW. Intellectual changes in patients with MPTP-induced parkinsonism. *Neurology* 1985; 35(10):1506–1509.
21. Stern Y, Tetrud JW, Martin WR, et al. Cognitive change following MPTP exposure. *Neurology* 1990; 40(2):261–264.
22. Quinn N, Critchley P, Marsden CD. Young onset Parkinson's disease *Mov Disord* 1987; 2(2):73–91.

23. D'Amato RJ, Alexander GM, Schwartzman RJ, et al. Evidence for neuromelanin involvement in MPTP-induced neurotoxicity. *Nature* 1987; 327(6120):324–326.

24. Kurkowska-Jastrzebska I, Wronska A, Kohutnicka M, et al. The inflammatory reaction following 1-methyl-4-phenyl-1,2,3,6-tetrahydropyridine intoxication in mouse. *Exp Neurol* 1999; 156(1):50–61.

25. Delgado M, Ganea D. Neuroprotective effect of vasoactive intestinal peptide (VIP) in a mouse model of Parkinson's disease by blocking microglial activation. *FASEB J* 2003; 17(8):944–946.

26. Selley ML. Simvastatin prevents 1-methyl-4-phenyl-1,2,3,6-tetrahydropyridine-induced striatal dopamine depletion and protein tyrosine nitration in mice *Brain Res* 2005; 1037(1–2):1–6.

27. Pierri M, Vaudano E, et al. KW-6002 protects from MPTP induced dopaminergic toxicity in the mouse. *Neuropharmacology* 2005; 48(4):517–524.

28. Miklossy J, Doudet DD, et al. Role of ICAM-1 in persisting inflammation in Parkinson disease and MPTP monkeys. *Exp Neurol* 2006; 197(2):275–283.

29. Burns RS, Markey SP, Phillips JM, et al. The neurotoxicity of 1-methyl-4-phenyl-1,2,3,6-tetrahydropyridine in the monkey and man. *Can J Neurol Sci* 1984; 11 (Suppl 1):166–168.

30. Poli A, Gandolfi O, Lucchi R, et al. Spontaneous recovery of MPTP-damaged catecholamine systems in goldfish brain areas. *Brain Res* 1992; 585(1–2):128–134.

31. Heikkila RE, Hess A, Duvoisin RC. Dopaminergic neurotoxicity of 1-methyl-4-phenyl-1,2,3,6-tetra-hydropyridine in mice. *Science* 1984; 224(4656):1451–1453.

32. Markey SP, Johannessen JN, Chiueh CC, et al. Intraneuronal generation of a pyridinium metabolite may cause drug-induced parkinsonism. *Nature* 1984; 311(5985):464–467.

33. Boyce S, Kelly E, Reavill C, et al. Repeated administration of N-methyl-4-phenyl 1,2,5,6-tetrahydropyridine to rats is not toxic to striatal dopamine neurones. *Biochem Pharmacol* 1984; 33(11):1747–1752.

34. DeLong MR. Primate models of movement disorders of basal ganglia origin. *Trends Neurosci* 1990; 13(7):281–285.

35. Bergman H, Wichmann T, DeLong MR. Reversal of experimental parkinsonism by lesions of the subthalamic nucleus. *Science* 1990; 249(4975): 1436–1438.

36. Wichmann T, DeLong MR. Pathophysiology of parkinsonian motor abnormalities. *Adv Neurol* 1993; 60:53–61.

37. Wichmann T, Bergman H, DeLong MR. The primate subthalamic nucleus: I. Functional properties in intact animals. *J Neurophysiol* 1994; 72(2):494–506.

38. Bergman H, Wichmann T, Karmon B, et al. The primate subthalamic nucleus: II Neuronal activity in the MPTP model of parkinsonism. *J Neurophysiol* 1994; 72(2):507–520.

39. Wichmann T, Bergman H, DeLong MR. The primate subthalamic nucleus: III. Changes in motor behavior and neuronal activity in the internal pallidum induced by subthalamic inactivation in the MPTP model of parkinsonism. *J Neurophysiol* 1994; 72(2):521–530.

40. Benazzouz A, Gross C, Feger J, et al. Reversal of rigidity and improvement in motor performance by subthalamic high-frequency stimulation in MPTP-treated monkeys. *Eur J Neurosci* 1993; 5(4):382–389.

41. Benazzouz A, Boraud T, Feger J, et al. Alleviation of experimental hemiparkinsonism by high-frequency stimulation of the subthalamic nucleus in primates: A comparison with L-Dopa treatment. *Mov Disord* 1996; 11(6):627–632.

42. Kleiner-Fisman G, Herzog J, et al. Subthalamic nucleus deep brain stimulation: Summary and meta-analysis of outcomes. *Mov Disord* 2006; 21(Suppl 14):S290–S304.

43. Bjorklund A. Neural transplantation < – an experimental tool with clinical possibilities. *Trends Neurosci* 1991; 14(8):319–322.

44. Bakay RA, Barrow DL, Fiandaca MS, et al. Biochemical and behavioral correction of MPTP Parkinson-like syndrome by fetal cell transplantation. *Ann NY Acad Sci* 1987; 495: 623– 640.

45. Bankiewicz KS, Plunkett RJ, Jacobowitz DM, et al. The effect of fetal mesencephalon implants on primate MPTP-induced parkinsonism Histochemical and behavioral studies. *J Neurosurg* 1990; 72(2):231–244.

46. Elsworth JD, Sladek JR Jr, Taylor JR, et al. Early gestational mesencephalon grafts, but not later gestational mesencephalon, cerebellum or sham grafts, increase dopamine in caudate nucleus of MPTP-treated monkeys. *Neuroscience* 1996; 72(2):477–484.

47. Sladek JR Jr, Redmond DE Jr, Collier TJ, et al. Transplantation of fetal dopamine neurons in primate brain reverses MPTP induced parkinsonism. *Prog Brain Res* 1987; 71:309–323.

48. Nakai M, Itakura T, Kamei I, et al. Autologous transplantation of the superior cervical ganglion into the brain of parkinsonian monkeys. *J Neurosurg* 1990; 72(1):91–95.

49. Freed WJ, Poltorak M, Becker JB. Intracerebral adrenal medulla grafts: A review. *Exp Neurol* 1990; 110(2):139–166.

50. Aebischer P, Goddard M, Signore AP, et al. Functional recovery in hemiparkinsonian primates transplanted with polymer-encapsulated PC12 cells. *Exp Neurol* 1994; 126(2):151–158.

51. Bankiewicz KS, Bringas JR, McLaughlin W, et al. Application of gene therapy for Parkinson's disease: Nonhuman primate experience. *Adv Pharmacol* 1998; 42:801–806.

52. Elsworth JD, Brittan MS, Taylor JR, et al. Upregulation of striatal D2 receptors in the MPTP-treated vervet monkey is reversed by grafts of fetal ventral mesencephalon: An autoradiographic study. *Brain Res* 1998; 795(1–2):55–62.

53. Sortwell CE, Blanchard BC, Collier TJ, et al. Pattern of synaptophysin immunoreactivity within mesencephalic grafts following transplantation in a parkinsonian primate model. *Brain Res* 1998; 791(1–2):117–124.

54. Widner H, Tetrud J, Rehncrona S, et al. Bilateral fetal mesencephalic grafting in two patients with parkinsonism induced by 1-methyl-4-phenyl-1,2,3,6-tetrahydropyridine (MPTP). *N Engl J Med* 1992; 327(22):1556–1563.

55. Linazasoro G. Recent failures of new potential symptomatic treatments for Parkinson's disease: causes and solutions. *Mov Disord* 2004; 19(7):743–754.

56. Redmond DE, Vinuela A, Kordower JH, and Isacson O. Influence of cell preparation and target location on the behavioral recovery after striatal transplantation of fetal dopaminergic neurons in a primate model of Parkinson's disease. Neurobiology of Disease, in press.

57. Collier TJ, Sortwell CE, et al. Embryonic ventral mesencephalic grafts to the substantia nigra of MPTP-treated monkeys: Feasibility relevant to multiple-target grafting as a therapy for Parkinson's disease. *J Comp Neurol* 2002; 442(4):320–330.

58. Takagi Y, Takahashi J, et al. Dopaminergic neurons generated from monkey embryonic stem cells function in a Parkinson primate model. *J Clin Invest* 2005; 115(1):102–109.

59. Falardeau P, Bouchard S, Bedard PJ. Behavioral and biochemical effect of chronic treatment with D-1 and/or D-2 dopamine agonists in MPTP monkeys. *Eur J Pharmacol* 1988; 150(1–2):59–66.

60. Gagnon C, Bedard PJ, Di Paolo T. Effect of chronic treatment of MPTP monkeys with dopamine D-1 and/or D-2 receptor agonists. *Eur J Pharmacol* 1990; 178(1):115–120.

61. Alexander GM, Brainard DL, Gordon SW, et al. Dopamine receptor changes in untreated and (C)-PHNO-treated MPTP parkinsonian primates. *Brain Res* 1991; 547(2): 181–189.

62. Alexander GM, Schwartzman RJ, Grothusen JR, et al. Changes in brain dopamine receptors in MPTP parkinsonian monkeys following L-dopa treatment. *Brain Res* 1993; 625(2):276–282.

63. Graham WC, Sambrook MA, Crossman AR. Differential effect of chronic dopaminergic treatment on dopamine D1 and D2 receptors in the monkey brain in MPTP-induced parkinsonism. *Brain Res* 1993; 602(2):290–303.

64. Mierau J, Schingnitz G. Biochemical and pharmacological studies on pramipexole, a potent and selective dopamine D2 receptor agonist. *Eur J Pharmacol* 1992; 215(2–3):161–170.

65. Vermeulen RJ, Drukarch B, Sahadat MC, et al. The dopamine D1 agonist SKF 81297 and the dopamine D2 agonist LY 171555 act synergistically to stimulate motor behavior of 1-methyl-4-phenyl-1,2,3,6-tetrahydropyridine-lesioned parkinsonian rhesus monkeys. *Mov Disord* 1994; 9(6):664–672.

66. Kebabian JW, Britton DR, DeNinno MP, et al. A77636: A potent and selective dopamine D1 receptor agonist with anti-parkinsonian activity in marmosets. *Eur J Pharmacol* 1992; 229(2–3):203–209.

67. Blanchet P, Bedard PJ, Britton DR, et al. Differential effect of selective D-1 and D-2 dopamine receptor agonists on levodopa-induced dyskinesia in 1-methyl-4-phenyl-1,2,3,6-tetrahydropyridine–exposed monkeys. *J Pharmacol Exp Ther* 1993; 267(1):275–279.

68. Shiosaki K, Jenner P, Asin KE, et al. ABT-431: The diacetyl prodrug of A-86929, a potent and selective dopamine D1 receptor agonist: in vitro characterization and effects in animal models of Parkinson's disease. *J Pharmacol Exp Ther* 1996; 276(1):150–160.

69. Nomoto M, Jenner P, Marsden CD. The D1 agonist SKF 38393 inhibits the anti-parkinsonian activity of the D2 agonist LY 171555 in the MPTP-treated marmoset. *Neurosci Lett* 1988; 93(2–3):275–280.

70. Close SP, Elliott PJ, Hayes AG, et al. Effects of classical and novel agents in a MPTP-induced reversible model of Parkinson's disease. *Psychopharmacology* 1990; 102(3):295–300.

71. Boyce S, Rupniak NM, Steventon MJ, et al. Differential effects of D1 and D2 agonists in MPTP-treated primates: Functional implications for Parkinson's disease. *Neurology* 1990; 40(6):927–933.

72. Blanchet PJ, Grondin R, Bedard PJ, et al. Dopamine D1 receptor desensitization profile in MPTP-lesioned primates. *Eur J Pharmacol* 1996; 309(1):13–20.

73. Schneider JS, Sun ZQ, Roeltgen DP. Effects of dihydrexine, a full dopamine D-1 receptor agonist, on delayed response performance in chronic low dose MPTP-treated monkeys. *Brain Res* 1994; 663(1):140–144.

74. Goulet M, Madras BK. D(1) dopamine receptor agonists are more effective in alleviating advanced than mild parkinsonism in 1-methyl-4-phenyl-1,2,3,6-tetrahydropyridine-treated monkeys. *J Pharmacol Exp Ther* 2000; 292(2):714–724.

75. Jenner P. A novel dopamine agonist for the transdermal treatment of Parkinson's disease. *Neurology* 2005; 65(2 Suppl 1):S3–S5.

76. McCall RB, Lookingland KJ, et al. Sumanirole, a highly dopamine D2-selective receptor agonist: In vitro and in vivo pharmacological characterization and efficacy in animal models of Parkinson's disease. *J Pharmacol Exp Ther* 2005; 314(3):1248–1256.

77. Crossman AR, Clarke CE, Boyce S, et al. MPTP-induced parkinsonism in the monkey: Neurochemical pathology, complications of treatment and pathophysiological mechanisms. *Can J Neurol Sci* 1987; 14(Suppl 3):428–435.

78. Clarke CE, Sambrook MA, Mitchell IJ, et al. Levodopa-induced dyskinesia and response fluctuations in primates rendered parkinsonian with 1-methyl-4-phenyl-1,2,3,6-tetrahydropyridine (MPTP). *J Neurol Sci* 1987; 78(3):273–280.

79. Boyce S, Rupniak NM, Steventon MJ, et al. Characterization of dyskinesias induced by L-dopa in MPTP treated squirrel monkeys. *Psychopharmacology* 1990; 102(1):21–27.

80. Schneider JS. levodopa-induced dyskinesias in parkinsonian monkeys: Relationship to extent of nigrostriatal damage. *Pharmacol Biochem Behav* 1989; 34(1):193–196.

81. Boyce S, Rupniak NM, Steventon MJ, et al. Nigrostriatal damage is required for induction of dyskinesias by L-DOPA in squirrel monkeys. *Clin Neuropharmacol* 1990; 13(5):448–458.

82. Di Monte DA, McCormack A, et al. Relationship among nigrostriatal denervation, parkinsonism, and dyskinesias in the MPTP primate model. *Mov Disord* 2000; 5(3):459–466.

83. Blanchet PJ, Calon F, et al. Relevance of the MPTP primate model in the study of dyskinesia priming mechanisms. *Parkinsonism Relat Disord* 2004; 10(5):297–304.

84. Clarke CE, Boyce S, Sambrook MA, et al. Behavioral effects of (C)-4-propyl-9-hydroxynaphthoxazine in primates rendered parkinsonian with 1-methyl-4-phenyl-1, 2, 3, 6-tetrahydropyridine. *Naunyn Schmiedebergs Arch Pharmacol* 1988; 338(1):35–38.

85. Gomez-Mancilla B, Bedard PJ. Effect of D1 and D2 agonists and antagonists on dyskinesia produced by L-dopa in 1-methyl-4-phenyl-1,2,3,6-tetrahydropyridine–treated monkeys. *J Pharmacol Exp Ther* 1991; 259(1):409–413.

86. Nomoto M, Fukuda T. The effects of D1 and D2 dopamine receptor agonist and antagonist on parkinsonism in chronic MPTP-treated monkeys. *Adv Neurol* 1993; 60:119–122.

87. Blanchet PJ, Gomez-Mancilla B, Bedard PJ. DOPA-induced "peak dose" dyskinesia: Clues implicating D2 receptor–mediated mechanisms using dopaminergic agonists in MPTP monkeys. *J Neural Transm Suppl* 1995; 45:103–112.

88. Blanchet PJ, Konitsiotis S, Chase TN. Motor response to a dopamine D3 receptor preferring agonist compared to apomorphine in levodopa-primed 1-methyl-4-phenyl-1,2,3,6-tetrahydropyridine mon-keys. *J Pharmacol Exp Ther* 1997; 283(2):794–799.

89. Pearce RK, Jackson M, Smith L, et al. Chronic L-DOPA administration induces dyskinesias in the 1-methyl-4-phenyl-1,2,3,6-tetrahydropyridine-treated common marmoset (*Callithrix jacchus*). *Mov Disord* 1995; 10(6):731–740.

90. Grondin R, Doan VD, Gregoire L, et al. D1 receptor blockade improves L-dopa-induced dyskinesia but worsens parkinsonism in MPTP monkeys. *Neurology* 1999; 52(4):771–776.

91. Akai T, Ozawa M, Yamaguchi M, et al. Combination treatment of the partial D2 agonist terguide with the D1 agonist SKF 82958 in 1-methyl-4-phenyl-1,2,3,6-tetrahydropyridine-lesioned parkinsonian cynomolgus monkeys. *J Pharmacol Exp Ther* 1995; 273(1):309–314.

92. Pearce RK, Banerji T, Jenner P, et al. De novo administration of ropinirole and bromocriptine induces less dyskinesia than L-dopa in the MPTP-treated marmoset. *Mov Disord* 1998; 13(2):234–241.

93. Langston James W, Maratos EC, Jackson MJ, et al. (2001). "Antiparkinsonian activity and dyskinesia risk of ropinirole and L-DOPA combination therapy in drug naive MPTP-lesioned common marmosets (Callithrix jacchus)." *Mov Disord* 16(4): 631–641.

94. Parkinson Study Group. Pramipexole vs levodopa as initial treatment for Parkinson disease: A randomized controlled trial. Parkinson Study Group *JAMA* 2000; 284(15):1931–1938.

95. Rascol O, Brooks DJ, et al. A five-year study of the incidence of dyskinesia in patients with early Parkinson's disease who were treated with ropinirole or levodopa. 056 Study Group. *N Engl J Med* 2000; 342(20):1484–1491.

96. Grondin R, Bedard PJ, Britton DR, et al. Potential therapeutic use of the selective dopamine D1 receptor agonist, A-86929: An acute study in parkinsonian levodopa-primed monkeys. *Neurology* 1997; 49(2):421–426.

97. Filion M, Tremblay L, Bedard PJ. Effects of dopamine agonists on the spontaneous activity of globus pallidus neurons in monkeys with MPTP-induced parkinsonism. *Brain Res* 1991; 547(1):152–161.

98. Blanchet PJ, Calon F, Martel JC, et al. Continuous administration decreases and pulsatile administration increases behavioral sensitivity to a novel dopamine D2 agonist (U-91356A) in MPTP-exposed monkeys. *J Pharmacol Exp Ther* 1995; 272(2):854–859.

99. Goulet M, Morissette M, Calon F, et al. Continuous or pulsatile chronic D2 dopamine receptor agonist (U91356A) treatment of drug-naive 4-phenyl-1,2,3,6-tetrahydropyridine monkeys differentially regulates brain D1 and D2 receptor expression: in situ hybridization histochemical analysis. *Neuroscience* 1997; 79(2):497–507.

100. Blanchet PJ, Grondin R, Bedard PJ. Dyskinesia and wearing-off following dopamine D1 agonist treatment in drug-naive 1-methyl-4-phenyl-1,2,3,6-tetrahydropyridine-lesioned primates. *Mov Disord* 1996; 11(1):91–94.

101. Calon F, Goulet M, Blanchet PJ, et al. levodopa or D2 agonist induced dyskinesia in MPTP monkeys: correlation with changes in dopamine and GABAA receptors in the striatopallidal complex. *Brain Res* 1995; 680(1–2):43–52.

102. Goulet M, Grondin R, Blanchet PJ, et al. Dyskinesias and tolerance induced by chronic treatment with a D1 agonist administered in pulsatile or continuous mode do not correlate with changes of putamenal D1 receptors in drug-naive MPTP monkeys. *Brain Res* 1996; 719(1–2):129–137.

103. Quik M, Police S, He L, et al. Expression of D(3) receptor messenger RNA and binding sites in monkey striatum and substantia nigra after nigrostriatal degeneration: Effect of levodopa treatment *Neuroscience* 2000; 98(2):263–273.

104. Smith LA, Jackson MJ, et al. Multiple small doses of levodopa plus entacapone produce continuous dopaminergic stimulation and reduce dyskinesia induction in MPTP-treated drug-naive primates. *Mov Disord* 2005; 20(3):306–314.

105. Blanchet PJ, Metman LV, Mouradian MM, et al. Acute pharmacologic blockade of dyskinesias in Parkinson's disease. *Mov Disord* 1996; 11(5):580–581.

106. Blanchet PJ, Konitsiotis S, Chase TN. Amantadine reduces levodopa-induced dyskinesias in parkinsonian monkeys. *Mov Disord* 1998; 13(5):798–802.

107. Papa SM BR, Engber TM, Kask AM, et al. Reversal of levodopa-induced motor fluctuations in experimental parkinsonism by NMDA receptor blockade. *Brain Res* 1995; 701:13–18.

108. Papa S, Chase T. levodopa-induced dyskinesias improved by a glutamate antagonist in parkinsonian monkeys. *Ann Neurol* 1996; 39(5):574–578.

109. Verhagen ML BP, van den Munckhof P, Del Dotto P, et al. A trial of dextromethorphan in parkinsonian patients with motor response complications. *Mov Disord* 1998; 13:414–417.

110. Morissette M, Dridi M, et al. Prevention of dyskinesia by an NMDA receptor antagonist in MPTP monkeys: Effect on adenosine A2A receptors. *Synapse* 2006; 60(3):239–250.

111. Oh JD, Russell DS, Vaughan CL, et al. Enhanced tyrosine phosphorylation of striatal NMDA receptor subunits: effect of dopaminergic denervation and LDOPA administration. [Published erratum appears in Brain Res 1999 Feb 27; 820(1– 2):117.] *Brain Res* 1998; 813(1):150–159.

112. Oh JD, Vaughan CL, Chase TN. Effect of dopamine denervation and dopamine agonist administration on serine phosphorylation of striatal NMDA receptor subunits. *Brain Res* 1999; 821(2):433–442.

113. Langston James W, Hallett PJ, Dunah AW, et al. (2005). "Alterations of striatal NMDA receptor subunits associated with the development of dyskinesia in the MPTP-lesioned primate model of Parkinson's disease." *Neuropharmacology* 48(4): 503-16.

114. Normand E, Popovici T, Onteniente B, et al. Dopaminergic neurons of the substantia nigra modulate preproenkephalin A gene expression in rat striatal neurons. *Brain Res* 1988; 439(1– 2):39–46

115. Gudehithlu KP, Duchemin AM, Tejwani GA, et al. Preproenkephalin mRNA and methionine-enkephalin increase in mouse striatum after 1-methyl-4-phenyl-1,2,3,6-tetrahydropyridine treatment. *J Neurochem* 1991; 56(3):1043–1048.

116. Campbell K, Bjorklund A. Prefrontal corticostriatal afferents maintain increased enkephalin gene locomotion and dyskinesia in MPTP-treated L-dopa-primed common marmosets. *Psychopharmacology* (Berl) 1999; 142(1)51–60.

117. Henry B, Fox SH, Peggs D, et al. The alpha2adrenergic receptor antagonist idazoxan reduces dyskinesia and enhances anti-parkinsonian actions of L-dopa in the MPTP-lesioned primate model of Parkinson's disease. *Mov Disord* 1999; 14(5):744–753.

118. Augood SJ, Emson PC, Mitchell IJ, et al. Cellular localization of enkephalin gene expression in MPTP-treated cynomolgus monkeys. *Brain Res Mol Brain Res* 1989; 6(1):85–92.

119. Herrero MT, Augood SJ, Hirsch EC, et al. Effects of L-DOPA on preproenkephalin and preprotachykinin gene expression in the MPTP-treated monkey striatum. *Neuroscience* 1995; 68(4):1189– 1198.

120. Jolkkonen J, Jenner P, Marsden CD L-DOPA reverses altered gene expression of substance P but not enkephalin in the caudate-putamen of common marmosets treated with MPTP. *Brain Res Mol Brain Res* 1995; 32(2):297–307.

121. Morissette M, Grondin R, Goulet M, et al. Differential regulation of striatal preproenkephalin and preprotachykinin mRNA levels in MPTP-lesioned monkeys chronically treated with dopamine D1 or D2 receptor agonists. *J Neurochem* 1999; 72(2):682–692.

122. Quik M, Police S, et al. Increases in striatal preproenkephalin gene expression are associated with nigrostriatal damage but not L-DOPA–induced dyskinesias in the squirrel monkey. *Neuroscience* 2002; 113(1):213–220.

123. Morissette M, Dridi M, et al. Prevention of levodopa-induced dyskinesias by a selective NR1A/2B N-methyl-D-aspartate receptor antagonist in parkinsonian monkeys: Implication of preproenkephalin. *Mov Disord* 2006; 21(1):9–17.

124. Boyce S, Rupniak NM, Steventon M, et al. CCK-8S inhibits L-dopa-induced dyskinesias in parkinsonian squirrel monkeys. *Neurology* 1990; 40(4):717–718.

125. Ekesbo A, Andren PE, Gunne LM, et al. (-)-OSU 6162 inhibits levodopa-induced dyskinesias in a monkey model of Parkinson's disease. *Neuroreport* 1997; 8(11): 2567–2570.

126. Gomez-Mancilla B, Bedard PJ Effect of estrogen and progesterone on L-dopa induced dyskinesia in MPTP-treated monkeys. *Neurosci Lett* 1992; 135(1):129–132.

127. Grondin R, Tahar AH, Doan VD, et al. Noradrenoceptor antagonism with idazoxan improves L-dopa-induced dyskinesias in MPTP monkeys. *Naunyn Schmiedebergs Arch Pharmacol* 2000; 361(2):181–186.

128. Hadj Tahar A, Belanger N, et al. Antidyskinetic effect of JL-18, a clozapine analog, in parkinsonian monkeys. *Eur J Pharmacol* 2000; 399(2-3):183–186.

129. Konitsiotis S, Blanchet PJ, et al. AMPA receptor blockade improves levodopa-induced dyskinesia in MPTP monkeys. *Neurology* 2000; 54(8):1589–1595.

130. Henry B, Fox SH, et al. Mu- and delta-opioid receptor antagonists reduce levodopa-induced dyskinesia in the MPTP-lesioned primate model of Parkinson's disease. *Exp Neurol* 2001; 171(1):139–146.

131. Klintenberg R, Svenningsson P, et al. Naloxone reduces levodopa-induced dyskinesias and apomorphine-induced rotations in primate models of parkinsonism. *J Neural Transm* 2002; 109(10):1295–1307.

132. Oh JD, Bibbiani F, et al. Quetiapine attenuates levodopa-induced motor complications in rodent and primate parkinsonian models. *Exp Neurol* 2002; 177(2):557–564.

133. Bibbiani F, Oh JD, et al. A2A antagonist prevents dopamine agonist-induced motor complications in animal models of Parkinson's disease. *Exp Neurol* 2003; 184(1):285–294.

134. Chassain C, Eschalier A, et al. Antidyskinetic effect of magnesium sulfate in MPTP-lesioned monkeys. *Exp Neurol* 2003; 182(2):490–496.

135. Hill MP, Bezard E, et al. Novel antiepileptic drug levetiracetam decreases dyskinesia elicited by L-dopa and ropinirole in the MPTP-lesioned marmoset. *Mov Disord* 2003; 18(11):1301–1305.

136. Iravani MM, Jackson MJ, et al. 3,4-methylenedioxymethamphetamine (ecstasy) inhibits dyskinesia expression and normalizes motor activity in 1-methyl-4-phenyl-1,2,3,6-tetrahydropyridine-treated primates. *J Neurosci* 2003; 23(27):9107–9115.

137. Savola JM, Hill M, et al. Fipamezole (JP-1730) is a potent alpha2 adrenergic receptor antagonist that reduces levodopa-induced dyskinesia in the MPTP-lesioned primate model of Parkinson's disease. *Mov Disord* 2003; 18(8):872–883.

138. Silverdale MA, Nicholson SL, et al. Topiramate reduces levodopa-induced dyskinesia in the MPTP-lesioned marmoset model of Parkinson's disease. *Mov Disord* 2005; 20(4):403–409.

139. Gomez-Ramirez J, Johnston TH, et al. Histamine H3 receptor agonists reduce L-dopa–induced chorea, but not dystonia, in the MPTP-lesioned nonhuman primate model of Parkinson's disease. *Mov Disord* 2006; 21(6):839–846.

140. Samadi P, Gregoire L, et al. Docosahexaenoic acid reduces levodopa-induced dyskinesias in 1-methyl-4-phenyl-1,2,3,6-tetrahydropyridine monkeys. *Ann Neurol* 2006; 59(2):282–288.

141. Fox SH, Lang, et al. Translation of nondopaminergic treatments for levodopa-induced dyskinesia from MPTP-lesioned nonhuman primates to phase IIa clinical studies: Keys to success and roads to failure. *Mov Disord* 2006 Oct;21(10):1578-94.

142. Crossman AR, Mitchell IJ, Sambrook MA. Regional brain uptake of 2-deoxyglucose in N-methyl-4-phenyl-1,2,3,6-tetrahydropyridine (MPTP)-induced parkinsonism in the macaque monkey. *Neuropharmacology* 1985; 24(6):587–591.

143. Papa SM, Desimone R, Fiorani M, et al. Internal globus pallidus discharge is nearly suppressed during levodopa-induced dyskinesias. *Ann Neurol* 1999; 46(5):732– 738.

144. Alexander GM, Schwartzman RJ, Brainard L, et al. Changes in brain catecholamines and dopamine uptake sites at different stages of MPTP parkinsonism in monkeys. *Brain Res* 1992; 588(2):261–269.

145. Pearce RK, Heikkila M, Linden IB, Jenner P. L-dopa induces dyskinesia in normal monkeys: behavioural and pharmacokinetic observations. *Psychopharmacology* (Berl). 2001 Aug;156(4):402–409.

146. Langston J, Quik M, Petzinger G, et al. Investigating levodopa-induced dyskinesias in the parkinsonian primate. *Ann Neurol* 2000; 47(Suppl 1):S79–S89.

147. Petzinger G, Quik M, Ivashina E, et al. Reliability and validity of a new global dyskinesia rating scale in the MPTP-lesioned non-human primate. *Mov Disord* 2001 Mar;16(2):202–207.

148. Togasaki DM, Tan L, et al. Levodopa induces dyskinesias in normal squirrel monkeys. *Ann Neurol* 2001; 50(2):254–257.

149. Mones R Experimental dyskinesias in normal rhesus monkey. *Adv Neurol* 1973; 1:665–669.

150. Bankiewicz KS, Oldfield EH, Chiueh CC, et al. Hemi-parkinsonism in monkeys after unilateral internal carotid artery infusion of 1-methyl-4-phenyl-1,2,3,6-tetrahydropyridine (MPTP) *Life Sci* 1986; 39(1):7–16.

151. Smith RD, Zhang Z, Kurlan R, et al. Developing a stable bilateral model of parkinsonism in rhesus monkeys. *Neuroscience* 1993; 52(1):7–16.

152. Bezard E, Imbert C, Deloire X, et al. A chronic MPTP model reproducing the slow evolution of Parkinson's disease: evolution of motor symptoms in the monkey. *Brain Res* 1997; 766(1–2):107–112.

153. Tolwani RJ, Jakowec MW, Petzinger GM, et al. Experimental models of Parkinson's disease: Insights from many models. *Lab Anim Sci* 1999; 49(4):363– 371.

154. Lewin R. Brain enzyme is the target of drug toxin [news] *Science* 1984; 225(4669):1460–1462.

155. Parsons B, Rainbow TC. High-affinity binding sites for [3H]MPTP may correspond to monamine oxidase. *Eur J Pharmacol* 1984; 102(2):375– 377.

156. Chiba K, Trevor A, Castagnoli N, Jr. Metabolism of the neurotoxic tertiary amine, MPTP, by brain monoamine oxidase. *Biochem Biophys Res Commun* 1984; 120(2):574–578.

157. Di Monte DA, Wu EY, Irwin I, et al. Production and disposition of 1-methyl-4-phenylpyridinium in primary cultures of mouse astrocytes. *Glia* 1992; 5(1):48–55.

158. Di Monte DA, Wu EY, DeLanney LE, et al. Toxicity of 1-methyl-4-phenyl-1,2,3,6-tetrahydropyridine in primary cultures of mouse astrocytes. *J Pharmacol Exp Ther* 1992; 261(1):44–49.

159. Di Monte DA, Schipper HM, Hetts S, et al. Iron-mediated bioactivation of 1-methyl-4-phenyl-1, 2, 3, 6-tetrahydropyridine (MPTP) in glial cultures. *Glia* 1995; 15(2):203–206.

160. Di Monte DA, Royland JE, Irwin I, et al. Astrocytes as the site for bioactivation of neurotoxins. *Neurotoxicology* 1996; 17(3–4):697–703.

161. Westlund KN, Denney RM, Rose RM, et al. Localization of distinct monoamine oxidase A and monoamine oxidase B cell populations in human brainstem. *Neuroscience* 1988; 25(2):439–456.

162. Tetrud JW, Langston JW. The effect of deprenyl (selegiline) on the natural history of Parkinson's disease. *Science* 1989; 245(4917):519–522.

163. Parkinson's Study Group. Effect of deprenyl on the progression of disability in early Parkinson's disease. *N Engl J Med* 1989; 321:1364–1371.

164. Rascol O. Rasagiline in the pharmacotherapy of Parkinson's disease—A review. *Expert Opin Pharmacother* 2005; 6(12):2061–2075.

165. Chen JJ, Ly AV. Rasagiline: A second-generation monoamine oxidase type-B inhibitor for the treatment of Parkinson's disease. *Am J Health Syst Pharm* 2006; 63(10):915–928.

166. Parkinson Study Group. A controlled, randomized, delayed-start study of rasagiline in early Parkinson disease. *Arch Neurol* 2004; 61(4):561–566.

167. Javitch JA, Snyder SH. Uptake of MPP(C)by dopamine neurons explains selectivity of parkin-sonism-inducing neurotoxin, MPTP. *Eur J Pharmacol* 1984; 106(2):455–456.

168. Ricaurte GA, Langston JW, DeLanney LE, et al. Dopamine uptake blockers protect against the dopamine depleting effect of 1-methyl-4-phenyl-1,2,3,6-tetrahydropyridine (MPTP) in the mouse striatum. *Neurosci Lett* 1985; 59(3):259–264.

169. Mayer RA, Jarvis MF, Wagner GC. Cocaine blocks the dopamine depletion induced by MPTP. *Res Commun Chem Pathol Pharmacol* 1985; 49(1):145–148.

170. Sundstrom E, Jonsson G. Differential time course of protection by monoamine oxidase inhibition and uptake inhibition against MPTP neurotoxicity on central catecholamine neurons in mice. *Eur J Pharmacol* 1986; 122(2):275–278.

171. Schultz W, Scarnati E, Sundstrom E, et al. The catecholamine uptake blocker nomifensine protects against MPTP-induced parkinsonism in monkeys. *Exp Brain Res* 1986; 63(1):216–220.

172. Bezard E, Gross CE, Fournier MC, et al. Absence of MPTP-induced neuronal death in mice lacking the dopamine transporter. *Exp Neurol* 1999; 155(2):268–273.

173. Liu Y, Peter D, et al. A cDNA that suppresses MPP+ toxicity encodes a vesicular amine transporter. *Cell* 1992; 70(4):539–551.

174. Speciale SG, Liang CL, et al. The neurotoxin 1-methyl-4-phenylpyridinium is sequestered within neurons that contain the vesicular monoamine transporter. *Neuroscience* 1998; 84(4):1177–1185.

175. Ramsay RR, Salach JI, Dadgar J, et al. Inhibition of mitochondrial NADH dehydrogenase by pyridine derivatives and its possible relation to experimental and idiopathic parkinsonism. *Biochem Biophys Res Commun* 1986; 135(1):269–275.

176. Ramsay RR, Salach JI, Singer TP. Uptake of the neurotoxin 1-methyl-4-phenylpyridine (MPPC)by mitochondria and its relation to the inhibition of the mitochondrial oxidation of ANDC-linked substrates by MPPC. *Biochem Biophys Res Commun* 1986; 134(2):743–748.

177. Nicklas WJ, Vyas I, Heikkila RE. Inhibition of NADH-linked oxidation in brain mitochondria by 1-methyl-4-phenyl-pyridine, a metabolite of the neurotoxin, 1-methyl-4-phenyl-1, 2, 5, 6-tetrahydropyridine. *Life Sci* 1985; 36(26):2503–2508.

178. Vyas I, Heikkila RE, Nicklas WJ. Studies on the neurotoxicity of 1-methyl-4-phenyl-1, 2, 3, 6-tetra-hydropyridine: Inhibition of AND-linked substrate oxidation by its metabolite, 1-methyl-4-phenyl-pyridinium. *J Neurochem* 1986; 46(5):1501–1507.

179. Di Monte D, Jewell SA, Ekstrom G, et al. 1-Methyl-4-phenyl-1, 2, 3, 6-tetrahydro-pyridine (MPTP) and 1-methyl-4-phenylpyridine (MPPC) cause rapid ATP depletion in isolated hepatocytes. *Biochem Biophys Res Commun* 1986; 137(1):310–315.

180. Schapira AH, Cooper JM, Dexter D, et al. Mitochondrial complex I deficiency in Parkinson's disease. *Lancet* 1989; 1(8649):1269.

181. Parker W, Boyson S, Parks J. Abnormalities of the electron transport chain in idiopathic Parkinson's disease. *Ann Neurol* 1989; 26:719–723.

182. Mizuno Y. [Contribution of MPTP to studies on the pathogenesis of Parkinson's disease]. *Rinsho Shinkeigaku* 1989; 29(12):1494–1496.

183. Schapira AH. Human complex I defects in neurodegenerative diseases. *Biochem Biophys Acta* 1998; 1364(2):261–270.

184. Anderson WM, Wood JM, Anderson AC. Inhibition of mitochondrial and *Paracoccus denitrificans* NADH-ubiquinone reductase by oxacarbocyanine dyes A structure-activity study. *Biochem Pharmacol* 1993; 45(10):2115–2122.

185. Bindoff LA, Howell N, Poulton J, et al. Abnormal RNA processing associated with a novel tRNA mutation in mitochondrial DNA A potential disease mechanism. *J Biol Chem* 1993; 268(26):19559–19564.

186. Blin O, Desnuelle C, Rascol O, et al. Mitochondrial respiratory failure in skeletal muscle from patients with Parkinson's disease and multiple system atrophy. *J Neurol Sci* 1994; 125(1):95–101.

187. Mann V, Cooper J, Krige D, et al. Brain, skeletal muscle and platelet homogenate mitochondrial function in Parkinson's disease. *Brain* 1992; 115:333–342.

188. Cardellach F, Marti MJ, Fernandez-Sola J, et al. Mitochondrial respiratory chain activity in skeletal muscle from patients with Parkinson's disease. *Neurology* 1993; 43(11):2258–2262.

189. Di Monte D, Sandy M, Jewell S, et al. Oxidative phosphorylation by intact muscle mitochondria in Parkinson's disease. *Neurodegeneration* 1993; 2(4):275–281.

190. Zweig RM, Singh A, Cardillo JE, et al. The familial occurrence of Parkinson's disease. Lack of evidence for maternal inheritance [Published erratum appears in Arch Neurol 1993 Feb;50(2):153.] *Arch Neurol* 1992; 49(11):1205–1207.

191. Gu M, Owen A, Toffa S, et al. Mitochondrial function, GSH and iron in neurodegeneration and Lewy body diseases. *J Neurol Sci* 1998; 158:24–29.

192. Parker WD Jr, Parks JK. Mitochondrial ND5 mutations in idiopathic Parkinson's disease. *Biochem Biophys Res Commun* 2005; 326(3):667–669.

193. Chan P, DeLanney LE, Irwin I, et al. Rapid ATP loss caused by 1-methyl-4-phenyl-1,2,3,6-tetrahydropyridine in mouse brain. *J Neurochem* 1991; 57(1):348–351.

194. Di Monte D, Sandy MS, Blank L, et al. Fructose prevents 1-methyl-4-phenyl-1,2,3,6-tetrahydropyridine (MPTP)-induced ATP depletion and toxicity in isolated hepatocytes. *Biochem Biophys Res Commun* 1988; 153(2):734–740.

195. Schulz JB, Henshaw DR, Matthews RT, et al. Coenzyme Q10 and nicotinamide and a free radical spin trap protect against MPTP neurotoxicity. *Exp Neurol* 1995; 132(2):279–283.

196. Klivenyi P, Gardian G, et al. Additive neuroprotective effects of creatine and a cyclo-oxygenase 2 inhibitor against dopamine depletion in the 1-methyl-4-phenyl-1,2,3,6-tetrahydropyridine (MPTP) mouse model of Parkinson's disease. *J Mol Neurosci* 2003; 21(3):191–198.

197. Klivenyi P, Gardian G, et al. Neuroprotective effects of oral administration of triacetyluridine against MPTP neurotoxicity. *Neuromolecular Med* 2004; 6(2–3):87–92.

198. Richardson JR, Caudle WW, et al. Obligatory role for complex I inhibition in the dopaminergic neurotoxicity of 1-methyl-4-phenyl-1,2,3,6-tetrahydropyridine (MPTP). *Toxicol Sci* 2007 Jan;95(1):196-204.

199. Shults CW, Haas RH, Beal MF. A possible role of coenzyme Q10 in the etiology and treatment of Parkinson's disease. *Biofactors* 1999; 9(2–4):267–272.

200. Shults CW, Oakes D, et al. Effects of coenzyme Q10 in early Parkinson disease: Evidence of slowing of the functional decline. *Arch Neurol* 2002; 59(10):1541–1550.

201. NINDS NET-PD. A randomized, double-blind, futility clinical trial of creatine and minocycline in early Parkinson disease. *Neurology* 2006; 66(5):664–671.

202. Frank DM, Arora PK, Blumer JL, et al. Model study on the bioreduction of paraquat, MPPC, and analogs: Evidence against a "redox cycling" mechanism in MPTP neurotoxicity *Biochem Biophys Res Commun* 1987; 147(3):1095–1104.

203. Di Monte D, Sandy MS, Ekstrom G, et al. Comparative studies on the mechanisms of paraquat and 1-methyl-4-phenylpyridine (MPPC) cytotoxicity. *Biochem Biophys Res Commun* 1986; 137(1):303–309.

204. McCormack AL, Thiruchelvam M, et al. Environmental risk factors and Parkinson's disease: Selective degeneration of nigral dopaminergic neurons caused by the herbicide paraquat. *Neurobiol Dis* 2002; 10(2):119–127.

205. Bonneh-Barkay D, Langston WJ, et al. Toxicity of redox cycling pesticides in primary mesencephalic cultures. *Antioxid Redox Signal* 2005; 7(5–6):649–653.

206. Richardson JR, Quan Y, et al. Paraquat neurotoxicity is distinct from that of MPTP and rotenone. *Toxicol Sci* 2005; 88(1):193–201.

207. Adams JD, Jr., Klaidman LK, Leung AC. MPPC and MPDPC induced oxygen radical formation with mitochondrial enzymes. *Free Radic Biol Med* 1993; 15(2):181–186.

208. Perry TL, Yong VW, Clavier RM, et al. Partial protection from the dopaminergic neurotoxin N-methyl-4-phenyl-1, 2, 3, 6-tetrahydropyridine by four different antioxidants in the mouse. *Neurosci Lett* 1985; 60(2):109–114.

209. Antolin I, Mayo JC, et al. Protective effect of melatonin in a chronic experimental model of Parkinson's disease. *Brain Res* 2002; 943(2):163–173.

210. Thomas B, Mohanakumar KP. Melatonin protects against oxidative stress caused by 1-methyl-4-phenyl-1,2,3,6-tetrahydropyridine in the mouse nigrostriatum. *J Pineal Res* 2004; 36(1):25–32.

211. Chen LJ, Gao YQ, et al. Melatonin protects against MPTP/MPP+ -induced mitochondrial DNA oxidative damage in vivo and in vitro. *J Pineal Res* 2005; 39(1):34–42.

212. Sershen H, Reith ME, Hashim A, et al. Protection against 1-methyl-4-phenyl-1,2,3,6-tetrahydropyridine neurotoxicity by the antioxidant ascorbic acid. *Neuropharmacology* 1985; 24(12):1257–1259.

213. Baldessarini RJ, Kula NS, Francoeur D, et al. Antioxidants fail to inhibit depletion of striatal dopamine by MPTP. *Neurology* 1986; 36(5):735.

214. Martinovits G, Melamed E, Cohen O, et al. Systemic administration of antioxidants does not protect mice against the dopaminergic neurotoxicity of 1-methyl-4-phenyl-1,2,5,6-tetrahydropyridine (MPTP). *Neurosci Lett* 1986; 69(2):192–197.

215. van der Schyf CJ, Castagnoli K, et al. Melatonin fails to protect against long-term MPTP-induced dopamine depletion in mouse striatum. *Neurotox Res* 2000; 1(4):261–269.

216. Morgan WW, Nelson JF. Chronic administration of pharmacological levels of melatonin does not ameliorate the MPTP-induced degeneration of the nigrostriatal pathway. *Brain Res* 2001; 921(1–2):115–121.

217. Perry TL, Yong VW, Hansen S, et al. Alpha-tocopherol and beta-carotene do not protect marmosets against the dopaminergic neurotoxicity of N-methyl-4-phenyl-1,2,3,6-tetrahydropyridine. *J Neurol Sci* 1987; 81(2–3):321–331.

218. Mihatsch W, Russ H, Gerlach M, et al. Treatment with antioxidants does not prevent loss of dopamine in the striatum of MPTP-treated common marmosets: Preliminary observations. *J Neural Transm Park Dis Dement Sect* 1991; 3(1):73–78.

219. Blanchet PJ, Konitsiotis S, Hyland K, et al. Chronic exposure to MPTP as a primate model of progressive parkinsonism: A pilot study with a free radical scavenger. *Exp Neurol* 1998; 153(2):214–222.

220. Bahat-Stroomza M, Gilgun-Sherki Y, et al. A novel thiol antioxidant that crosses the blood brain barrier protects dopaminergic neurons in experimental models of Parkinson's disease. *Eur J Neurosci* 2005; 21(3):637–646.

221. Fredriksson A, Eriksson P, Archer T. MPTP-induced deficits in motor activity: Neuroprotective effects of the spintrapping agent, alpha-phenyl-tert-butyl-nitrone (PBN). *J Neural Transm* 1997; 104(6–7):579–592.

222. Klivenyi P, Matthews RT, Wermer M, et al. Azulenyl nitrone spin traps protect against MPTP neurotoxicity. *Exp Neurol* 1998; 152(1):163–166.

223. Matthews RT, Klivenyi P, Mueller G, et al. Novel free radical spin traps protect against malonate and MPTP neurotoxicity. *Exp Neurol* 1999; 157(1):120–126.

224. Yang L, Calingasan NY, et al. A novel azulenyl nitrone antioxidant protects against MPTP and 3-nitropropionic acid neurotoxicities. *Exp Neurol* 2005; 191(1):86–93.

225. Ferger B, Teismann P, Earl CD, et al. The protective effects of PBN against MPTP toxicity are independent of hydroxyl radical trapping. *Pharmacol Biochem Behav* 2000; 65(3):425–431.

226. Muralikrishnan D, Mohanakumar KP. Neuroprotection by bromocriptine against 1-methyl-4-phenyl-1,2,3,6-tetrahydropyridine-induced neurotoxicity in mice. *FASEB J* 1998; 12(10):905–912.

227. Acuna-Castroviejo D, Coto-Montes A, Gaia Monti M, et al. Melatonin is protective against MPTP-induced striatal and hippocampal lesions. *Life Sci* 1997; 60(2):L23–L29.

228. Grunblatt E, Mandel S, Gassen M, et al. Potent neuroprotective and antioxidant activity of apomorphine in MPTP and 6-hydroxydopamine induced neurotoxicity. *J Neural Transm Suppl* 1999; 55:57–70.

229. Munoz A, Rey P, et al. Reduction of dopaminergic degeneration and oxidative stress by inhibition of angiotensin converting enzyme in a MPTP model of parkinsonism. *Neuropharmacology* 2006; 51(1):112–120.

230. Oida Y, Kitaichi K, et al. Rifampicin attenuates the MPTP-induced neurotoxicity in mouse brain. *Brain Res* 2006; 1082(1):196–204.

231. Rajeswari A. Curcumin protects mouse brain from oxidative stress caused by 1-methyl-4-phenyl-1,2,3,6-tetrahydropyridine. *Eur Rev Med Pharmacol Sci* 2006; 10(4):157–161.

232. Rojas P, Rios C. Metallothionein inducers protect against 1-methyl-4-phenyl-1,2,3,6-tetrahydropyridine neurotoxicity in mice. *Neurochem Res* 1997; 22(1):17–22.

233. Rojas P, Klaassen CD. Metallothionein-I and -II knock-out mice are not more sensitive than control mice to 1-methyl-4-phenyl-1,2,3,6-tetrahydropyridine neurotoxicity. *Neurosci Lett* 1999; 273(2):113–116.

234. Ferger B, Spratt C, Teismann P, et al. Effects of cytisine on hydroxyl radicals in vitro and MPTP-induced dopamine depletion in vivo. *Eur J Pharmacol* 1998; 360(2–3):155–163.

235. Aubin N, Curet O, Deffois A, et al. Aspirin and salicylate protect against MPTP-induced dopamine depletion in mice. *J Neurochem* 1998; 71(4):1635–1642.

236. Ferger B, Teismann P, Earl CD, et al. Salicylate protects against MPTP-induced impairments in dopaminergic neurotransmission at the striatal and nigral level in mice. *Naunyn Schmiedebergs Arch Pharmacol* 1999; 360(3):256–261.

237. Choi JY, Park CS, et al. Prevention of nitric oxide-mediated 1-methyl-4-phenyl-1,2,3,6-tetrahydropyridine–induced Parkinson's disease in mice by tea phenolic epigallocatechin 3-gallate *Neurotoxicology* 2002; 23(3):367–374.

238. Sriram K, Pai KS, Boyd MR, et al. Evidence for generation of oxidative stress in brain by MPTP: In vitro and in vivo studies in mice. *Brain Res* 1997; 749(1):44–52.

239. Ali SF, David SN, Newport GD, et al. MPTP-induced oxidative stress and neurotoxicity are age-dependent: Evidence from measures of reactive oxygen species and striatal dopamine levels. *Synapse* 1994; 18(1):27–34.

240. Chiueh CC, Wu RM, Mohanakumar KP, et al. In vivo generation of hydroxyl radicals and MPTP-induced dopaminergic toxicity in the basal ganglia. *Ann NY Acad Sci* 1994; 738:25–36.

241. Smith TS, Bennett JP, Jr. Mitochondrial toxins in models of neurodegenerative diseases: I. In vivo brain hydroxyl radical production during systemic MPTP treatment or following microdialysis infusion of methylpyridinium or azide ions. *Brain Res* 1997; 765(2):183–188.

242. Thomas B, Muralikrishnan D, Mohanakumar KP. In vivo hydroxyl radical generation in the striatum following systemic administration of 1-methyl-4-phenyl-1,2,3,6-tetrahydropyridine in mice. *Brain Res* 2000; 852(1):221–224.

243. Hussain S, Hass BS, Slikker W, Jr, et al. Reduced levels of catalase activity potentiate MPPC induced toxicity: Comparison between MN9D cells and CHO cells. *Toxicol Lett* 1999; 104(1–2):49–56.

244. Choi WS, Yoon SY, Oh TH, et al. Two distinct mechanisms are involved in 6-hydroxy-dopamine-and MPPC-induced dopaminergic neuronal cell death: Role of caspases, ROS, and JNK. *J Neurosci Res* 1999; 57(1):86–94.

245. Przedborski S, Kostic V, Jackson-Lewis V, et al. Transgenic mice with increased Cu/Zn-superoxide dismutase activity are resistant to N-methyl-4-phenyl-1,2,3,6-tetrahydropyridine-induced neurotoxicity. *J Neurosci* 1992; 12(5):1658–1667.

246. Klivenyi P, St Clair D, Wermer M, et al. Manganese superoxide dismutase overexpression attenuates MPTP toxicity. *Neurobiol Dis* 1998; 5(4):253–258.

247. Offen D, Beart PM, Cheung NS, et al. Transgenic mice expressing human Bcl-2 in their neurons are resistant to 6-hydroxydopamine and 1-methyl-4-phenyl-1,2,3,6-tetrahydropyridine neurotoxicity. *Proc Natl Acad Sci USA* 1998; 95(10):5789–5794.

248. Yang L, Matthews RT, Schulz JB, et al. 1-Methyl-4-phenyl-1, 2, 3, 6-tetrahydropyride neurotoxicity is attenuated in mice overexpressing Bcl-2. *J Neurosci* 1998; 18(20):8145–8152.

249. Klivenyi, P, Andreassen OA, et al. Mice deficient in cellular glutathione peroxidase show increased vulnerability to malonate, 3-nitropropionic acid, and 1-methyl-4-phenyl-1,2,5,6-tetrahydropyridine. *J Neurosci* 2000; 20(1):1–7.

250. Zhang J, Graham DG, et al. Enhanced N-methyl-4-phenyl-1,2,3,6-tetrahydropyridine toxicity in mice deficient in or glutathione peroxidase. *J Neuropathol Exp Neurol* 2000; 59(1):53–61.

251. Liang LP, Patel M. Iron-sulfur enzyme mediated mitochondrial superoxide toxicity in experimental Parkinson's disease. *J Neurochem* 2004; 90(5):1076–1084.

252. Di Monte D, Chan P, Sandy M. Glutathione in Parkinson's disease: A link between oxidative stress and mitochondrial damage? *Ann Neurol* 1992; 32:S111–S115.

253. Graham D. On the origin and significance of neuromelanin. *Arch Pathol Lab Med* 1979; 103:359–362.

254. Chabrier PE, Demerle-Pallardy C, Auguet M. Nitric oxide synthases: Targets for therapeutic strategies in neurological diseases. *Cell Mol Life Sci* 1999; 55(8–9):1029–1035.

255. Schulz JB, Matthews RT, Muqit MM, et al. Inhibition of neuronal nitric oxide synthase by 7-nitroindazole protects against MPTP-induced neurotoxicity in mice. *J Neurochem* 1995; 64(2):936–939.

256. Przedborski S, Jackson-Lewis V, Yokoyama R, et al. Role of neuronal nitric oxide in 1-methyl-4-phenyl-1, 2, 3, 6-tetrahydropyridine (MPTP)-induced dopaminergic neurotoxicity. *Proc Natl Acad Sci USA* 1996; 93(10):4565–4571.

257. Klivenyi P, Andreassen OA, et al. Inhibition of neuronal nitric oxide synthase protects against MPTP toxicity. *Neuroreport* 2000; 11(6):1265–1268.

258. Watanabe H, Muramatsu Y, et al. Protective effects of neuronal nitric oxide synthase inhibitor in mouse brain against MPTP neurotoxicity: an immunohistological study. *Eur Neuropsychopharmacol* 2004; 14(2):93–104.

259. Hantraye P, Brouillet E, Ferrante R, et al. Inhibition of neuronal nitric oxide synthase prevents MPTP-induced parkinsonism in baboons (see comments). *Nat Med* 1996; 2(9):1017–1021.

260. Ferrante RJ, Hantraye P, Brouillet E, et al. Increased nitrotyrosine immunoreactivity in substantia nigra neurons in MPTP treated baboons is blocked by inhibition of neuronal nitric oxide synthase. *Brain Res* 1999; 823(1–2):177–182.

261. Halasz AS, Palfi M, et al. Altered nitric oxide production in mouse brain after administration of 1-methyl-4-phenyl-1,2,3,6-tetrahydro-pyridin or methamphetamine. *Neurochem Int* 2004;44(8):641–646.

262. Chalimoniuk M, Lukacova N, et al. Alterations of the expression and activity of midbrain nitric oxide synthase and soluble guanylyl cyclase in 1-methyl-4-phenyl-1,2,3,6-tetrahydropyridine-induced parkinsonism in mice. *Neuroscience* 2006; 141(2):1033–1046.

263. Liberatore GT, Jackson-Lewis V, Vukosavic S, et al. Inducible nitric oxide synthase stimulates dopaminergic neurodegeneration in the MPTP model of Parkinson disease. *Nat Med* 1999; 5(12):1403–1409.

264. Itzhak Y, Martin JL, Ali SF. Methamphetamine-and 1-methyl-4-phenyl-1,2,3,6-tetrahydropyridine-induced dopaminergic neurotoxicity in inducible nitric oxide synthase-deficient mice [In Process Citation] *Synapse* 1999; 34(4):305–312.

265. Langston, James W. Dehmer, T., J. Lindenau, et al. (2000). "Deficiency of inducible nitric oxide synthase protects against MPTP toxicity in vivo." *J Neurochem* 74(5):2213–2216.

266. Castagnoli K, Palmer S, Anderson A, et al. The neuronal nitric oxide synthase inhibitor 7nitroindazole also inhibits the monoamine oxidase-B-catalyzed oxidation of 1-methyl-4-phenyl-1, 2, 3, 6-tetrahydropyridine. *Chem Res Toxicol* 1997; 10(4):364–368.

267. Di Monte DA, Royland JE, Anderson A, et al. Inhibition of monoamine oxidase contributes to the protective effect of 7-nitroindazole against MPTP neurotoxicity. *J Neurochem* 1997; 69(4):1771–1773.
268. Castagnoli K, Palmer S, Castagnoli N, Jr. Neuroprotection by (R)-deprenyl and 7-nitroindazole in the MPTP C57BL/6 mouse model of neurotoxicity. *Neurobiology* 1999; 7(2):135–149.
269. Muramatsu Y, Kurosaki R, et al. Therapeutic effect of neuronal nitric oxide synthase inhibitor (7-nitroindazole) against MPTP neurotoxicity in mice. *Metab Brain Dis* 2002; 17(3):169–182.
270. Matthews RT, Yang L, Beal MF. S-Methylthiocitrulline, a neuronal nitric oxide synthase inhibitor, protects against malonate and MPTP neurotoxicity. *Exp Neurol* 1997; 143(2):282–286.
271. Mackenzie GM, Jackson MJ, Jenner P, et al. Nitric oxide synthase inhibition and MPTP-induced toxicity in the common marmoset. *Synapse* 1997; 26(3):301–316.
272. Mohanakumar KP, Thomas B, et al. Nitric oxide: An antioxidant and neuroprotector. *Ann N Y Acad Sci* 2002; 962:389–401.
273. Tsai MJ, Lee EH. Nitric oxide donors protect cultured rat astrocytes from 1-methyl-4-phenylpyridinium-induced toxicity. *Free Radic Biol Med* 1998; 24(5):705–713.
274. Rose S, Hindmarsh JG, Jenner P. Neuronal nitric oxide synthase inhibition reduces MPP+-evoked hydroxyl radical formation but not dopamine efflux in rat striatum. *J Neural Transm* 1999; 106(5–6):477–486.
275. Du Y, Ma Z, et al. Minocycline prevents nigrostriatal dopaminergic neurodegeneration in the MPTP model of Parkinson's disease. *Proc Natl Acad Sci USA* 2001; 98(25):14669–14674.
276. Dehmer T, Lindenau J, et al. Deficiency of inducible nitric oxide synthase protects against MPTP toxicity in vivo. *J Neurochem* 2000; 74(5):2213–2216.
277. Genc S, Kuralay K, et al. Erythropoietin exerts neuroprotection in 1-methyl-4-phenyl-1,2,3,6-tetrahydropyridine-treated C57/BL mice via increasing nitric oxide production. *Neurosci Lett* 2001; 298(2):139–141.
278. Kurosaki R, Muramatsu Y, et al. Effect of angiotensin-converting enzyme inhibitor perindopril on interneurons in MPTP-treated mice. *Eur Neuropsychopharmacol* 2005; 15(1):57–67.
279. Choi JY, Jang EH, et al. Enhanced susceptibility to 1-methyl-4-phenyl-1,2,3,6-tetrahydropyridine neurotoxicity in high-fat diet-induced obesity. *Free Radic Biol Med* 2005; 38(6):806–816.
280. Youdim MB, Lavie L, Riederer P. Oxygen free radicals and neurodegeneration in Parkinson's disease: A role for nitric oxide. *Ann NY Acad Sci* 1994; 738:64–68.
281. Hunot S, Boissiere F, Faucheux B, et al. Nitric oxide synthase and neuronal vulnerability in Parkinson's disease. *Neuroscience* 1996; 72(2):355–363.
282. Levecque C, Elbaz A, et al. Association between Parkinson's disease and polymorphisms in the nNOS and iNOS genes in a community-based case-control study. *Hum Mol Genet* 2003; 12(1):79–86.
283. Molina JA, Jimenez-Jimenez FJ, Orti-Pareja M. The role of nitric oxide in neurodegeneration Potential for pharmacological intervention. *Drugs Aging* 1998; 12(4):251–259.
284. Crossman AR, Peggs D, Boyce S. Effect of the NMDA antagonist MK-801 on MPT+-induced parkinsonism in the monkey. *Neuropharmacology* 1989; 28(11):1271–1273.
285. Graham WC, Robertson RG, Sambrook MA, et al. Injection of excitatory amino acid antagonists into the medial pallidal segment of a 1-methyl-4-phenyl-1,2,3,6-tetrahydropyridine (MPTP) treated primate reverses motor symptoms of parkinsonism. *Life Sci* 1990; 47(18):L91–97.
286. Loschmann PA, Lange KW, Kunow M, et al. Synergism of the AMPA-antagonist NBQX and the NMDA-antagonist CPP with L-dopa in models of Parkinson's disease. *J Neural Transm Park Dis Dement Sect* 1991; 3(3):203–213.
287. Turski L, Bressler K, Rettig KJ, et al. Protection of substantia nigra from MPP+ neurotoxicity by N-methyl-D-aspartate antagonists (see comments). *Nature* 1991; 349(6308):414–418.
288. Zuddas A, Oberto G, Vaglini F, et al. MK-801 prevents 1-methyl-4-phenyl-1, 2, 3, 6-tetrahydropyridine-induced parkinsonism in primates. *J Neurochem* 1992; 59(2):733–739.
289. Lange KW, Loschmann PA, Sofic E, et al. The competitive NMDA antagonist CPP protects substantia nigra neurons from MPTP-induced degeneration in primates. *Naunyn Schmiedebergs Arch Pharmacol* 1993; 348(6):586–592.
290. Tabatabaei A, Perry TL, Hansen S, et al. Partial protective effect of MK-801 on MPTP-induced reduction of striatal dopamine in mice. *Neurosci Lett* 1992; 141(2):192–194.
291. Brouillet E, Beal MF. NMDA antagonists partially protect against MPTP induced neurotoxicity in mice. *Neuroreport* 1993; 4(4):387–390.
292. Sonsalla PK, Zeevalk GD, Manzino L, et al. MK-801 fails to protect against the dopaminergic neuropathology produced by systemic 1-methyl-4-phenyl-1,2,3,6-tetrahydropyridine in mice or intranigral 1-methyl-4-phenylpyridinium in rats. *J Neurochem* 1992; 58(5):1979–1982.
293. Kupsch A, Loschmann PA, Sauer H, et al. Do NMDA receptor antagonists protect against MPTP-toxicity? Biochemical and immunocytochemical analyses in black mice. *Brain Res* 1992; 592(1–2):74–83.
294. Chan P, Di Monte DA, Langston JW, et al. (C)MK-801 does not prevent MPTP-induced loss of nigral neurons in mice. *J Pharmacol Exp Ther* 1997; 280(1):439–446.
295. Michel PP, Agid Y. The glutamate antagonist, MK801, does not prevent dopaminergic cell death induced by the 1-methyl-4-phenylpyridinium ion (MPPC) in rat dissociated mesencephalic cultures. *Brain Res* 1992; 597(2):233–240.
296. Srivastava R, Brouillet E, Beal MF, et al. Blockade of 1-methyl-4-phenylpyridinium ion (MPPC)nigral toxicity in the rat by prior decortication or MK-801 treatment: a stereological estimate of neuronal loss. *Neurobiol Aging* 1993; 14(4):295–301.
297. Fornai F, Alessandri MG, Fascetti F, et al. Clonidine suppresses 1-methyl-4-phenyl-1, 2, 3, 6-tetrahydropyri-dine-induced reductions of striatal dopamine and tyrosine hydroxylase activity in mice. *J Neurochem* 1995; 65(2):704–709.
298. Reinhard JF Jr, Miller DB, O'Callaghan JP. The neurotoxicant MPTP (1-methyl-4-phenyl-1,2,3,6-tetrahydropyridine) increases glial fibrillary acidic protein and decreases dopamine levels of the mouse striatum: Evidence for glial response to injury. *Neurosci Lett* 1988; 95(1–3):246–251.
299. Clarke PB, Reuben M. Inhibition by dizocilpine (MK-801) of striatal dopamine release induced by MPTP and MPP+: Possible action at the dopamine transporter. *Br J Pharmacol* 1995; 114(2):315–322.
300. Boireau A, Dubedat P, Bordier F, et al. Riluzole and experimental parkinsonism: Antagonism of MPTP-induced decrease in central dopamine levels in mice. *Neuroreport* 1994; 5(18):2657–2660.
301. Benazzouz A, Boraud T, Dubedat P, et al. Riluzole prevents MPTP-induced parkinsonism in the rhesus monkey: A pilot study. *Eur J Pharmacol* 1995; 284(3):299–307.
302. Bezard E, Stutzmann JM, Imbert C, et al. Riluzole delayed appearance of parkinsonian motor abnormalities in a chronic MPTP monkey model. *Eur J Pharmacol* 1998; 356(2–3):101–104.
303. Jankovic J, Hunter C. A double-blind, placebo-controlled and longitudinal study of riluzole in early Parkinson's disease. *Parkinsonism Relat Disord* 2002; 8(4):271–276.
304. Parkinson's Study Group. A multicenter randomized controlled trial of remacemide hydrochloride as monotherapy for Parkinson's disease. *Neurology* 2000; 54:1583–1588.
305. Clarke CE, Cooper JA, et al. A randomized, double-blind, placebo-controlled, ascending-dose tolerability and safety study of remacemide as adjuvant therapy in Parkinson's disease with response fluctuations. *Clin Neuropharmacol* 2001; 24(3):133–138.
306. Shoulson I, Penney J, et al. A randomized, controlled trial of remacemide for motor fluctuations in Parkinson's disease. *Neurology* 2001; 56(4):455–462.
307. Otto D, Unsicker K. Basic FGF reverses chemical and morphological deficits in the nigrostriatal system of MPTP-treated mice. *J Neurosci* 1990; 10(6):1912–1921.
308. Date I, Yoshimoto Y, Imaoka T, et al. Enhanced recovery of the nigrostriatal dopaminergic system in MPTP-treated mice following intrastriatal injection of basic fibroblast growth factor in relation to aging. *Brain Res* 1993; 621(1):150–154.
309. Otto D, Unsicker K. FGF-2-mediated protection of cultured mesencephalic dopaminergic neurons against MPTP and MPPC: Specificity and impact of culture conditions, non-dopaminergic neurons, and astroglial cells. *J Neurosci Res* 1993; 34(4):382–393.
310. Chadi G, Moller A, Rosen L, et al. Protective actions of human recombinant basic fibroblast growth factor on MPTP-lesioned nigrostriatal dopamine neurons after intraventricular infusion. *Exp Brain Res* 1993; 97(1):145–158.
311. Tomac A, Lindqvist E, Lin LF, et al. Protection and repair of the nigrostriatal dopaminergic system by GDNF in vivo. *Nature* 1995; 373(6512):335–339.
312. Gash DM, Zhang Z, Ovadia A, et al. Functional recovery in parkinsonian monkeys treated with GDNF. *Nature* 1996; 380(6571):252–255.
313. Hadjiconstantinou M, Fitkin JG, Dalia A. Epidermal growth factor enhances striatal dopaminergic parameters in the 1-methyl-4-phenyl-1,2,3,6-tetrahydropyridine-treated mouse. *J Neurochem* 1991; 57(2):479–482.
314. Spina MB, Squinto SP, Miller J, et al. Brain-derived neurotrophic factor protects dopamine neurons against 6-hydroxydopamine and N-methyl-4-phenyl-pyridinium ion toxicity: involvement of the glutathione system (see comments). *J Neurochem* 1992; 59(1):99–106.
315. Garcia E, Rios C, Sotelo J. Ventricular injection of nerve growth factor increases dopamine content in the striata of MPTP-treated mice. *Neurochem Res* 1992; 17(10):979–982.
316. Tsukahara T, Takeda M, Shimohama S, et al. Effects of brain-derived neurotrophic factor on 1-methyl-4-phenyl-1,2,3,6-tetrahydropyridine-induced parkinsonism in monkeys. *Neurosurgery* 1995; 37(4):733–739; discussion 739–741.
317. Hartikka J, Staufenbiel M, Lubbert H. Cyclic AMP, but not basic FGF, increases the in vitro survival of mesencephalic dopaminergic neurons and protects them from MPP(C)-induced degeneration. *J Neurosci Res* 1992; 32(2):190–201.
318. Pearce RK, Collins P, Jenner P, et al. Intraventricular infusion of basic fibroblast growth factor (bFGF) in the MPTP-treated common marmoset. *Synapse* 1996; 23(3):192–200.
319. Fontan A, Rojo A, et al. Effects of fibroblast growth factor and glial-derived neurotrophic factor on akinesia, F-DOPA uptake and dopamine cells in parkinsonian primates. *Parkinsonism Relat Disord* 2002; 8(5):311–323.
320. Date I, Aoi M, Tomita S, et al. GDNF administration induces recovery of the nigrostriatal dopaminergic system both in young and aged parkinsonian mice. *Neuroreport* 1998; 9(10):2365–2369.
321. Gerhardt GA, Cass WA, Huettl P, et al. GDNF improves dopamine function in the substantia nigra but not the putamen of unilateral MPTP-lesioned rhesus monkeys. *Brain Res* 1999; 817(1–2):163–171.
322. Zhang Z, Miyoshi Y, et al. Dose response to intraventricular glial cell line–derived neurotrophic factor administration in parkinsonian monkeys. *J Pharmacol Exp Ther* 1997; 282(3):1396–1401.
323. Costa S, Iravani MM, et al. Glial cell line–derived neurotrophic factor concentration dependently improves disability and motor activity in MPTP-treated common marmosets. *Eur J Pharmacol* 2001; 412(1):45–50.
324. Kordower JH, Emborg ME, et al. Neurodegeneration prevented by lentiviral vector delivery of GDNF in primate models of Parkinson's disease. *Science* 2000; 290(5492):767–773.
325. Kojima H, Abiru Y, Sakajiri K, et al. Adenovirus-mediated transduction with human glial cell line-derived neurotrophic factor gene prevents 1-methyl-4-phenyl-1,2,3,6-tetrahydropyridine-induced dopamine depletion in striatum of mouse brain. *Biochem Biophys Res Commun* 1997; 238(2):569–573.
326. Kishima H, Poyot T, et al. Encapsulated GDNF-producing C2C12 cells for Parkinson's disease: A pre-clinical study in chronic MPTP-treated baboons. *Neurobiol Dis* 2004; 16(2):428–439.
327. Chen LW, Hu HJ, et al. Identification of brain-derived neurotrophic factor in nestin-expressing astroglial cells in the neostriatum of 1-methyl-4-phenyl-1,2,3,6-tetrahydropyridine-treated mice. *Neuroscience* 2004; 126(4):941–953.

328. Chen LW, Zhang JP, et al. Localization of nerve growth factor, neurotrophin-3, and glial cell line–derived neurotrophic factor in nestin-expressing reactive astrocytes in the caudate-putamen of 1-methyl-4-phenyl-1,2,3,6-tetrahydropyridine-treated C57/Bl mice. *J Comp Neurol* 2006; 497(6):898–909.
329. Lapchak PA, Araujo DM, et al. Topographical distribution of [125I]-glial cell line-derived neurotrophic factor in unlesioned and MPTP-lesioned rhesus monkey brain following a bolus intraventricular injection. *Brain Res* 1998; 789(1):9–22.
330. Gill SS, Patel NK, et al. Direct brain infusion of glial cell line–derived neurotrophic factor in Parkinson disease. *Nat Med* 2003; 9(5):589–595.
331. Patel NK, Bunnage M, et al. Intraputamenal infusion of glial cell line–derived neurotrophic factor in PD: A two-year outcome study. *Ann Neurol* 2005; 57(2):298–302.
332. Lang AE, Gill S, et al. Randomized controlled trial of intraputamenal glial cell line–derived neurotrophic factor infusion in Parkinson disease. *Ann Neurol* 2006; 59(3):459–466.
333. Sherer TB, Fiske BK, et al. Crossroads in GDNF therapy for Parkinson's disease. Mov Disord 2006; 21(2):136–141.
334. Yasuhara T, Shingo T, et al. Early transplantation of an encapsulated glial cell line-derived neurotrophic factor-producing cell demonstrating strong neuroprotective effects in a rat model of Parkinson disease. *J Neurosurg* 2005; 102(1):80–89.
335. Sajadi A, Bensadoun JC, et al. Transient striatal delivery of GDNF via encapsulated cells leads to sustained behavioral improvement in a bilateral model of Parkinson disease. *Neurobiol Dis* 2006; 22(1):119–129.
336. Steiner JP, Hamilton GS, Ross DT, et al. Neurotrophic immunophilin ligands stimulate structural and functional recovery in neurodegenerative animal models. *Proc Natl Acad Sci USA* 1997; 94(5):2019–2024.
337. Costantini LC, Chaturvedi P, Armistead DM, et al. A novel immunophilin ligand: distinct branching effects on dopaminergic neurons in culture and neurotrophic actions after oral administration in an animal model of Parkinson's disease. *Neurobiol Dis* 1998; 5(2):97–106.
338. Gold BG, Nutt JG. Neuroimmunophilin ligands in the treatment of Parkinson's disease. *Curr Opin Pharmacol* 2002; 2(1):82–86.
339. Nicotra A, Parvez SH. Cell death induced by MPTP, a substrate for monoamine oxidase B. *Toxicology* 2000; 153(1–3):157–166.
340. Mochizuki H, Nakamura N, Nishi K, et al. Apoptosis is induced by 1-methyl-4-phenylpyridinium ion (MPPC) in ventral mesencephalic-striatal co-culture in rat. *Neurosci Lett* 1994; 170(1):191–194.
341. Jackson-Lewis V, Jakowec M, Burke RE, et al. Time course and morphology of dopaminergic neuronal death caused by the neurotoxin 1-methyl-4-phenyl-1,2,3,6-tetrahydropyridine. *Neurodegeneration* 1995; 4(3):257–269.
342. Desole MS, Sciola L, Delogu MR, et al. Manganese and 1-methyl-4-(2°-ethylpheny1)-1,2,3,6-tetrahydro-pyridine induce apoptosis in PC12 cells. *Neurosci Lett* 1996; 209(3):193–196.
343. Sheehan JP, Palmer PE, Helm GA, et al. MPP+ induced apoptotic cell death in SH-SY5Y neuroblastoma cells: An electron microscope study. *J Neurosci Res* 1997; 48(3):226–237.
344. Yoshinaga, N, Murayama T, et al. Apoptosis induction by a dopaminergic neurotoxin, 1-methyl-4-phenylpyridinium ion (MPP+), and inhibition by epidermal growth factor in GH3 cells. *Biochem Pharmacol* 2000; 60(1):111–120.
345. Chun HS, Gibson GE, et al. Dopaminergic cell death induced by MPP(+), oxidant and specific neurotoxicants shares the common molecular mechanism. *J Neurochem* 76(4):1010–1021.
346. Gearan T, Castillo OA, et al. The parkinsonian neurotoxin MPP+ induces phosphorylated c-Jun in dopaminergic neurons of mesencephalic cultures. *Parkinsonism Relat Disord* 2001; 8(1):19–22.
347. Gomez C, Reiriz J, et al. Low concentrations of 1-methyl-4-phenylpyridinium ion induce caspase-mediated apoptosis in human SH-SY5Y neuroblastoma cells. *J Neurosci Res* 2001; 63(5):421–428.
348. Soldner F, Weller M, Haid S, et al. MPP+ inhibits proliferation of PC12 cells by a p21(WAF1/Cip1)-dependent pathway and induces cell death in cells lacking p21(WAF1/Cip1). *Exp Cell Res* 1999; 250(1):75–85.
349. Andoh T, Chock PB, et al. Role of the redox protein thioredoxin in cytoprotective mechanism evoked by (−)-deprenyl. *Mol Pharmacol* 2005; 68(5):1408–1414.
350. Mathiasen JR, McKenna BA, et al. Inhibition of mixed lineage kinase 3 attenuates MPP+-induced neurotoxicity in SH-SY5Y cells. *Brain Res* 2004; 1003(1–2):86–97.
351. Tatton N, Kish S. In situ detection of apoptotic nuclei in the substantia nigra compacta of 1-methyl-4-phenyl-1,2,3,6-tetrahydropyridine-treated mice using terminal deoxynucleotidyl transferase labelling and acridine orange staining. *Neuroscience* 1997; 77(4):1037–1048.
352. Spooren WP, Gentsch C, Wiessner C. TUNEL-positive cells in the substantia nigra of C57BL/6 mice after a single bolus of 1-methyl-4-phenyl-1,2,3,6-tetrahydropyridine. *Neuroscience* 1998; 85(2):649–651; discussion 653.
353. Usha R, Muralikrishnan D, et al. Region-specific attenuation of a trypsin-like protease in substantia nigra following dopaminergic neurotoxicity by 1-methyl-4-phenyl-1,2,3,6-tetrahydropyridine. *Brain Res* 2000; 882(1–2):191–195.
354. Mochizuki H, Hayakawa H, et al. An AAV-derived Apaf-1 dominant negative inhibitor prevents MPTP toxicity as antiapoptotic gene therapy for Parkinson's disease. *Proc Natl Acad Sci USA* 2001; 98(19):10918–10923.
355. Turmel H, Hartmann A, et al. Caspase-3 activation in 1-methyl-4-phenyl-1,2,3,6-tetrahydropyridine (MPTP)-treated mice. *Mov Disord* 2001; 16(2):185–189.
356. Hirsch EC, Hunot S, Faucheux B, et al. Dopaminergic neurons degenerate by apoptosis in Parkinson's disease (letter; comment). *Mov Disord* 1999; 14(2):383–385.
357. Jellinger KA. Is there apoptosis in Lewy body disease? *Acta Neuropathol* (Berl) 1999; 97(4):413–415.
358. Mytilineou C, Cohen G. Deprenyl protects dopamine neurons from the neurotoxic effect of 1-methyl-4-phenylpyridinium ion. *J Neurochem* 1985; 45(6):1951–1953.
359. Le W, Jankovic J, Xie W, et al. (−)-Deprenyl protection of 1-methyl-4 phenylpyridium ion (MPPC)-induced apoptosis independent of MAO-B inhibition. [Published erratum appears in *Neurosci Lett* 1997 May 30; 228(1):67.] *Neurosci Lett* 1997; 224(3):197–200.
360. Tatton WG, Greenwood CE. Rescue of dying neurons: a new action for deprenyl in MPTP parkinsonism. *J Neurosci Res* 1991; 30(4):666–672.
361. Wu RM, Chiueh CC, Pert A, et al. Apparent antioxidant effect of l-deprenyl on hydroxyl radical formation and nigral injury elicited by MPP+ in vivo. *Eur J Pharmacol* 1993; 243(3):241–247.
362. Wu RM, Murphy DL, Chiueh CC. Neuronal protective and rescue effects of deprenyl against MPP+ dopaminergic toxicity. *J Neural Transm Gen Sect* 1995; 100(1):53–61.
363. Wu RM, Murphy DL, Chiueh CC. Suppression of hydroxyl radical formation and protection of nigral neurons by l-deprenyl (selegiline). *Ann NY Acad Sci* 1996; 786:379–390.
364. Magyar K, Szende B, Lengyel J, et al. The pharmacology of B-type selective monoamine oxidase inhibitors: Milestones in (-)-deprenyl research. *J Neural Transm Suppl* 1996; 48:29–43.
365. Hassouna I, Wickert H, Zimmermann M, et al. Increase in bax expression in substantia nigra following 1-methyl-4-phenyl-1,2,3,6-tetrahydropyridine (MPTP) treatment of mice. *Neurosci Lett* 1996; 204(1–2):85–88.
366. Tatton WG, Wadia JS, Ju WY, et al. (-)-Deprenyl reduces neuronal apoptosis and facilitates neuronal outgrowth by altering protein synthesis without inhibiting monoamine oxidase. *J Neural Transm Suppl* 1996; 48:45–59.
367. Guo M, Chen S, et al. Eldepryl prevents 1-methyl-4-phenyl-1,2,3,6-tetrahydropyridine-induced nigral neuronal apoptosis in mice. *Chin Med J (Engl)* 2001; 114(3):240–243.
368. Birkmayer W. (−)-Deprenyl leads to prolongation of L-dopa efficacy in Parkinson's disease. *Mod Probl Pharmacopsychiatry* 1983; 19:170–176.
369. Mandel S, Weinreb O, et al. Mechanism of neuroprotective action of the anti-Parkinson drug rasagiline and its derivatives. *Brain Res Rev* 2005; 48(2):379–387.
370. Cosi C, Colpaert F, Koek W, et al. Poly(ADP-ribose) polymerase inhibitors protect against MPTP-induced depletions of striatal dopamine and cortical noradrenaline in C57B1/6 mice. *Brain Res* 1996; 729(2):264–269.
371. Cosi C, Marien M. Decreases in mouse brain ANDC and ATP induced by 1-methyl-4-phenyl-1,2,3,6-tetrahydropyridine (MPTP): Prevention by the poly(ADP-ribose) polymerase inhibitor, benzamide. *Brain Res* 1998; 809(1):58–67.
372. Cosi C, Marien M. Implication of poly (ADP-ribose) polymerase (PARP) in neurodegeneration and brain energy metabolism Decreases in mouse brain NAD+ and ATP caused by MPTP are prevented by the PARP inhibitor benzamide [In Process Citation]. *Ann NY Acad Sci* 1999; 890:227–239.
373. Iwashita, A, Yamazaki S, et al. Neuroprotective effects of a novel poly(ADP-ribose) polymerase-1 inhibitor, 2-[3-[4-(4-chlorophenyl)-1-piperazinyl] propyl]-4(3H)-quinazolinone (FR255595), in an in vitro model of cell death and in mouse 1-methyl-4-phenyl-1,2,3,6-tetrahydropyridine model of Parkinson's disease. *J Pharmacol Exp Ther* 2004; 309(3):1067–1078.
374. Mandir AS, Przedborski S, Jackson-Lewis V, et al. Poly(ADP-ribose) polymerase activation mediates 1-methyl-4-phenyl-1,2,3,6-tetrahydropyridine (MPTP)-induced parkinsonism. *Proc Natl Acad Sci USA* 1999; 96(10):5774–5779.
375. Barc S, Page G, et al. Impairment of the neuronal dopamine transporter activity in MPP(+)-treated rat was not prevented by treatments with nitric oxide synthase or poly(ADP-ribose) polymerase inhibitors. *Neurosci Lett* 2001; 314(1–2):82–86.
376. Mandir AS, Simbulan-Rosenthal CM, et al. A novel in vivo post-translational modification of p53 by PARP-1 in MPTP-induced parkinsonism. *J Neurochem* 2002; 83(1):186–192.
377. Hadjiconstantinou M, Rossetti ZL, Paxton RC, et al. Administration of GM1 ganglioside restores the dopamine content in striatum after chronic treatment with MPTP. *Neuropharmacology* 1986; 25(9):1075–1077.
378. Hadjiconstantinou M, Mariani AP, Neff NH. GM1 ganglioside-induced recovery of nigrostriatal dopaminergic neurons after MPTP: An immunohistochemical study. *Brain Res* 1989; 484(1–2):297–303.
379. Hadjiconstantinou M, Weihmuller F, Neff NH. Treatment with GM1 ganglioside reverses dopamine D-2 receptor supersensitivity induced by the neurotoxin MPTP. *Eur J Pharmacol* 1989; 168(2):261–264.
380. Saulino MF, Schengrund CL. Differential accumulation of gangliosides by the brains of MPTP-lesioned mice. *J Neurosci Res* 1994; 37(3):384–391.
381. Date I, Felten SY, Felten DL. Exogenous GM1 gangliosides induce partial recovery of the nigrostriatal dopaminergic system in MPTP-treated young mice but not in aging mice. *Neurosci Lett* 1989; 106(3):282–286.
382. Schneider JS. Effects of age on GM1 ganglioside-induced recovery of concentrations of dopamine in the striatum in 1-methyl-4-phenyl-1,2,3,6-tetrahydro-pyridine-treated mice. *Neuropharmacology* 1992; 31(2):185–192.
383. Fazzini E, Durso R, Davoudi H, et al. GM1 gangliosides alter acute MPTP-induced behavioral and neurochemical toxicity in mice. *J Neurol Sci* 1990; 99(1):59–68.
384. Schneider JS, Yuwiler A. GM1 ganglioside treatment promotes recovery of striatal dopamine concentrations in the mouse model of MPTP-induced parkinsonism. *Exp Neurol* 1989; 105(2):177–183.
385. Rothblat DS, Schneider JS. Effects of GM1 ganglioside treatment on dopamine innervation of the striatum of MPTP-treated mice. *Ann NY Acad Sci* 1998; 845:274–277.
386. Schneider JS, Kean A, DiStefano L. GM1 ganglioside rescues substantia nigra pars compacta neurons and increases dopamine synthesis in residual nigrostriatal dopaminergic neurons in MPTP-treated mice. *J Neurosci Res* 1995; 42(1):117–123.
387. Schneider JS, Distefano L. Response of the damaged dopamine system to GM1 and semisynthetic gangliosides: Effects of dose and extent of lesion. *Neuropharmacology* 1995; 34(5):489–493.

388. Schneider JS. MPTP-induced parkinsonism: acceleration of biochemical and behavioral recovery by GM1 ganglioside treatment. *J Neurosci Res* 1992; 31(1):112–119.

389. Schneider JS, Pope A, Simpson K, et al. Recovery from experimental parkinsonism in primates with GM1 ganglioside treatment. *Science* 1992; 256(5058):843–846.

390. Pope-Coleman A, Tinker JP, et al. Effects of GM1 ganglioside treatment on pre- and postsynaptic dopaminergic markers in the striatum of parkinsonian monkeys. *Synapse* 2000; 36(2):120–128.

391. Pope-Coleman A, Schneider JS. Effects of chronic GM1 ganglioside treatment on cognitieve and motor deficits in a slowly progressing model of parkinsonism in non-human primates. *Restor Neurol Neurosci* 1998; 12(4):255–266.

392. Herrero MT, Kastner A, Perez-Otano I, et al. Gangliosides and parkinsonism. *Neurology* 1993; 43(10):2132–2134.

393. Schneider JS, Roeltgen DP, Rothblat DS. GM1 ganglioside treatment of Parkinson's disease: An open pilot study of safety and efficacy. *Neurology* 1995; 45(6):1149–1154.

394. Schneider JS. GM1 ganglioside in the treatment of Parkinson's disease. *Ann N Y Acad Sci* 1998; 845: 363–373.

395. Pai KS, Ravindranath V. Protection and potentiation of MPTP-induced toxicity by cytochrome P-450 inhibitors and inducer: In vitro studies with brain slices. *Brain Res* 1991; 555(2):239–244.

396. Bodis-Wollner I, Chung E, Ghilardi MF, et al. Acetyl-levo-carnitine protects against MPTP-induced parkinsonism in primates. *J Neural Transm Park Dis Dement Sect* 1991; 3(1):63–72.

397. Shahi GS, Das NP, Moochhala SM. 1-Methyl-4-phenyl-1,2,3,6-tetrahydropyridine-induced neurotoxicity: Partial protection against striato-nigral dopamine depletion in C57BL/6J mice by cigarette smoke exposure and by beta-naphthoflavone-pretreatment. *Neurosci Lett* 1991; 127(2):247–250.

398. Janson AM, Fuxe K, Goldstein M. Differential effects of acute and chronic nicotine treatment on MPTP-(1-methyl-4-phenyl-1,2,3,6-tetrahydropyridine) induced degeneration of nigrostriatal dopamine neurons in the black mouse. *Clin Invest* 1992; 70(3–4):232–238.

399. Quik M, Parameswaran N, et al. Chronic oral nicotine treatment protects against striatal degeneration in MPTP-treated primates. *J Neurochem* 2006; 98(6):1866–1875.

400. Boireau A, Bordier F, Dubedat P, et al. Thalidomide reduces MPTP-induced decrease in striatal dopamine levels in mice. *Neurosci Lett* 1997; 234(2–3):123–126.

401. Marcotte ER, Chugh A, Mishra RK, et al. Protection against MPTP treatment by an analog of Pro-Leu-Gly-NH2 (PLG, MIF-1). *Peptides* 1998; 19(2):403–406.

402. Lau YS, Mouradian MM. Protection against acute MPTP-induced dopamine depletion in mice by adenosine A1 agonist. *J Neurochem* 1993; 60(2):768–771.

403. Aguirre JA, Cintra A, Hillion J, et al. A stereological study on the neuroprotective actions of acute modafinil treatment on 1-methyl-4-phenyl-1,2,3,6-tetrahydropyridine-induced nigral lesions of the male black mouse. *Neurosci Lett* 1999; 275(3):215–218.

404. Dluzen DE. Neuroprotective effects of estrogen upon the nigrostriatal dopaminergic system. *J Neurocytol* 2000; 29(5–6):387–399.

405. Tripanichkul W, Sripanichkulchai K, et al. Estrogen down-regulates glial activation in male mice following 1-methyl-4-phenyl-1,2,3,6-tetrahydropyridine intoxication. *Brain Res* 2006; 1084(1):28–37.

406. Gelinas S, Martinoli MG. Neuroprotective effect of estradiol and phytoestrogens on MPP+-induced cytotoxicity in neuronal PC12 cells. *J Neurosci Res* 2002; 70(1):90–6.

407. D'Astous M, Morissette M, et al. Dehydroepiandrosterone (DHEA) such as 17beta-estradiol prevents MPTP-induced dopamine depletion in mice. *Synapse* 2003; 47(1):10–14.

408. Ramirez AD, Liu X, et al. Repeated estradiol treatment prevents MPTP-induced dopamine depletion in male mice. *Neuroendocrinology* 2003; 77(4):223–231.

409. D'Astous, M, Morissette M, et al. Effect of estrogen receptor agonists treatment in MPTP mice: Evidence of neuroprotection by an ER alpha agonist. *Neuropharmacology* 2004; 47(8):1180–1188.

410. Kenchappa RS, Diwakar L, et al. Estrogen and neuroprotection: Higher constitutive expression of glutaredoxin in female mice offers protection against MPTP-mediated neurodegeneration. *FASEB J* 2004; 18(10):1102–1104.

411. D'Astous M, Mendez P, et al. Implication of the phosphatidylinositol-3 kinase/protein kinase B signaling pathway in the neuroprotective effect of estradiol in the striatum of 1-methyl-4-phenyl-1,2,3,6-tetrahydropyridine mice. *Mol Pharmacol* 2006; 69(4):1492–1498.

412. Callier S, Morissette S, et al. Neuroprotective properties of 17beta-estradiol, progesterone, and raloxifene in MPTP C57Bl/6 mice. *Synapse* 2001; 41(2):131–138.

413. Ferger B, Teismann P, et al. The protective effects of PBN against MPTP toxicity are independent of hydroxyl radical trapping. *Pharmacol Biochem Behav* 2000; 65(3):425–431.

414. Alcaraz-Zubeldia M, Montes S, et al. Participation of manganese-superoxide dismutase in the neuroprotection exerted by copper sulfate against 1-methyl 4-phenylpyridinium neurotoxicity. *Brain Res Bull* 2001; 55(2):277–229.

415. Castagnoli KP, Steyn SJ, et al. Neuroprotection in the MPTP parkinsonian C57BL/6 mouse model by a compound isolated from tobacco. *Chem Res Toxicol* 2001; 14(5):523–527.

416. Castagnoli K, Petzer JB, et al. Inhibition of human MAO-A and MAO-B by a compound isolated from flue-cured tobacco leaves and its neuroprotective properties in the MPTP mouse model of neurodegeneration. *Inflammopharmacology* 2003; 11(2):183–188.

417. Chen, JF, Xu K, et al. Neuroprotection by caffeine and A(2A) adenosine receptor inactivation in a model of Parkinson's disease. *J Neurosci* 2001; 21(10):RC143.

418. Xu K, Xu YH, et al. Caffeine's neuroprotection against 1-methyl-4-phenyl-1,2,3,6-tetrahydropyridine toxicity shows no tolerance to chronic caffeine administration in mice. *Neurosci Lett* 2002;322(1):13–16.

419. Schwarzschild MA, Xu K, et al. Neuroprotection by caffeine and more specific A2A receptor antagonists in animal models of Parkinson's disease. *Neurology* 2003; 61(11 Suppl 6):S55–S61.

420. Rudakewich M, Ba F, et al. Neurotrophic and neuroprotective actions of ginsenosides Rb(1) and Rg(1). *Planta Med* 2001; 67(6):533–537.

421. Teismann P, Ferger B. Inhibition of the cyclooxygenase isoenzymes COX-1 and COX-2 provide neuroprotection in the MPTP-mouse model of Parkinson's disease. *Synapse* 2001; 39(2):167–174.

422. Ikeda K, Kurokawa M, et al. Neuroprotection by adenosine A2A receptor blockade in experimental models of Parkinson's disease. *J Neurochem* 2002; 80(2):262–270.

423. Castagnoli N Jr, Petzer JP, et al. Monoamine oxidase B inhibition and neuroprotection: Studies on selective adenosine A2A receptor antagonists. *Neurology* 2003; 61(11 Suppl 6):S62–S68.

424. O'Neil MJ, Murray TK, et al. The role of neuronal nicotinic acetylcholine receptors in acute and chronic neurodegeneration. *Curr Drug Targets CNS Neurol Disord* 2002; 1(4):399–411.

425. Chuenkova MV, Pereira MA. PDNF, a human parasite–derived mimic of neurotrophic factors, prevents caspase activation, free radical formation, and death of dopaminergic cells exposed to the parkinsonism-inducing neurotoxin MPP+. *Brain Res Mol Brain Res* 2003; 119(1):50–61.

426. Crocker SJ, Smith PD, et al. Inhibition of calpains prevents neuronal and behavioral deficits in an MPTP mouse model of Parkinson's disease. 2003; *J Neurosci* 23(10):4081–4091.

427. Smith PD, Mount MP, et al. Calpain-regulated p35/cdk5 plays a central role in dopaminergic neuron death through modulation of the transcription factor myocyte enhancer factor 2. *J Neurosci* 2006; 26(2):440–447.

428. Kato H, Kurosaki R, et al. Arundic acid, an astrocyte-modulating agent, protects dopaminergic neurons against MPTP neurotoxicity in mice. *Brain Res* 2004; 1030(1):66–73.

429. Mandel S, Maor G, et al. Iron and alpha-synuclein in the substantia nigra of MPTP-treated mice: Effect of neuroprotective drugs R-apomorphine and green tea polyphenol (−)-epigallocatechin-3-gallate. *J Mol Neurosci* 2004; 24(3):401–416.

430. Faherty CJ, Raviie Shepherd K, et al. Environmental enrichment in adulthood eliminates neuronal death in experimental. *Parkinsonism Brain Res Mol Brain Res* 2005; 134(1):170–179.

431. Feng W, Wei H, et al. Pharmacological study of the novel compound FLZ against experimental Parkinson's models and its active mechanism. *Mol Neurobiol* 2005; 31(1–3):295–300.

432. Kurkowska-Jastrzebska I, Balkowiec-Iskra E, et al. Immunization with myelin oligodendrocyte glycoprotein and complete Freund adjuvant partially protects dopaminergic neurons from 1-methyl-4-phenyl-1,2,3,6-tetrahydropyridine-induced damage in mouse model of Parkinson's disease. *Neuroscience* 2005; 131(1):247–254.

433. Shen HY, He JC, et al. Geldanamycin induces heat shock protein 70 and protects against MPTP-induced dopaminergic neurotoxicity in mice. *J Biol Chem* 2005; 280(48):39962–39969.

434. Zhang W, Qin L, et al. 3-Hydroxymorphinan is neurotrophic to dopaminergic neurons and is also neuroprotective against LPS-induced neurotoxicity. *FASEB J* 2005; 19(3):395–397.

435. Bezard E, Gerlach I, et al. 5-HT1A receptor agonist-mediated protection from MPTP toxicity in mouse and macaque models of Parkinson's disease. *Neurobiol Dis* 2006; 23(1):77–86.

436. Chinta SJ, Rajagopalan S, et al. In vitro and in vivo neuroprotection by gamma-glutamylcysteine ethyl ester against MPTP: Relevance to the role of glutathione in Parkinson's disease. *Neurosci Lett* 2006; 402(1–2):137–141.

437. Liang Y, Li S, et al. Potential neuroprotective effect of low dose whole-body gamma-irradiation against 1-methyl-4-phenyl-1,2,3,6-tetrahydropyridine (MPTP)–induced dopaminergic toxicity in C57 mice Neurosci Lett. 2006; 400(3):213–217.

438. Tremblay ME, Saint-Pierre M, et al. Neuroprotective effects of cystamine in aged parkinsonian mice. *Neurobiol Aging* 2006; 27(6):862–870.

439. Corsini GU, Pintus S, Chiueh CC, et al. 1-Methyl-4-phenyl-1,2,3,6-tetrahydropyridine (MPTP) neurotoxicity in mice is enhanced by pretreatment with diethyldithiocarbamate. *Eur J Pharmacol* 1985; 119(1–2):127–128.

440. Irwin I, Wu EY, DeLanney LE, et al. The effect of diethyldithiocarbamate on the biodisposition of MPTP: An explanation for enhanced neurotoxicity. *Eur J Pharmacol* 1987; 141(2):209–217.

441. Miller DB, Reinhard JF Jr, Daniels AJ, et al. Diethyldithiocarbamate potentiates the neurotoxicity of in vivo 1-methyl-4-phenyl-1,2,3,6-tetrahydropyridine and of in vitro 1-methyl-4-phenylpyridinium. *J Neurochem* 1991; 57(2):541–549.

442. Walters TL, Irwin I, Delfani K, et al. Diethyldithiocarbamate causes nigral cell loss and dopamine depletion with nontoxic doses of MPTP. *Exp Neurol* 1999; 156(1):62–70.

443. Chiba K, Horii H, Kubota E, et al. Effects of N-methyl-mercaptoimidazole on the disposition of MPTP and its metabolites in mice. *Eur J Pharmacol* 1990; 180(1):59–67.

444. Corsini GU, Zuddas A, Bonuccelli U, et al. 1-Methyl-4-phenyl-1,2,3,6-tetrahydropyridine (MPTP) neurotoxicity in mice is enhanced by ethanol or acetaldehyde. *Life Sci* 1987; 40(9):827–832.

445. Marien M, Briley M, Colpaert F. Noradrenaline depletion exacerbates MPTP-induced striatal dopamine loss in mice. *Eur J Pharmacol* 1993; 236(3):487–489.

446. Hadjiconstantinou M, Hubble JP, Wemlinger TA, et al. Enhanced MPTP neurotoxicity after treatment with isoflurophate or cholinergic agonists. *J Pharmacol Exp Ther* 1994; 270(2):639–644.

447. Tariq M, Khan HA, al Moutaery K, et al. Effect of chronic administration of magnesium sulfate on 1-methyl-4-phenyl-1,2,3,6-tetrahydropyridine–induced neurotoxicity in mice. *Pharmacol Toxicol* 1998; 82(5):218–222.

448. Takahashi RN, Rogerio R, Zanin M. Maneb enhances MPTP neurotoxicity in mice. *Res Commun Chem Pathol Pharmacol* 1989; 66(1):167–170.

449. McGrew D, Irwin I, Langston J. Ethylenebis but not methyldithiocarbamate enhances MPTP-induced striatal dopamine depletion in mice *NeuroToxicology* 2000; 21(3):309–312.

450. Yang L, Sugama S, et al. Minocycline enhances MPTP toxicity to dopaminergic neurons. *J Neurosci Res* 2003; 74(2):278–285.

451. Diguet E, Fernagut PO, et al. Deleterious effects of minocycline in animal models of Parkinson's disease and Huntington's disease. *Eur J Neurosci* 2004; 19(12):3266–3276.

452. Duan W, Ladenheim B, et al. Dietary folate deficiency and elevated homocysteine levels endanger dopaminergic neurons in models of Parkinson's disease. *J Neurochem* 2002; 80(1):101–110.

453. Langston, James W. Landau, A. M., K. C. Luk, et al. (2005). "Defective Fas expression exacerbates neurotoxicity in a model of Parkinson's disease." *J Exp Med* 202(5): 575–581.

454. Fredriksson, A. and T. Archer. "Postnatal iron overload destroys NA-DA functional interactions." *J Neural Transm* 2007 Feb;114(2):195-203.

455. Richfield EK, Thiruchelvam MJ, et al. Behavioral and neurochemical effects of wild-type and mutated human alpha-synuclein in transgenic mice. *Exp Neurol* 2002; 175(1):35–48.

456. Song DD, Shults CW, et al. Enhanced substantia nigra mitochondrial pathology in human alpha-synuclein transgenic mice after treatment with MPTP. *Exp Neurol* 2004; 186(2):158–172.

457. Nieto M, Gil-Bea FJ, et al. Increased sensitivity to MPTP in human alpha-synuclein A30P transgenic mice. *Neurobiol Aging* 2006; 27(6):848–856.

458. Rathke-Hartlieb S, Kahle PJ, et al. Sensitivity to MPTP is not increased in Parkinson's disease–associated mutant alpha-synuclein transgenic mice. *J Neurochem* 2001; 77(4):1181–1184.

459. Dong Z, Ferger B, et al. Overexpression of Parkinson's disease–associated alpha-synuclein A53T by recombinant adeno-associated virus in mice does not increase the vulnerability of dopaminergic neurons to MPTP. *J Neurobiol* 2000; 53(1):1–10.

460. Jarvis MF, Wagner GC. Age-dependent effects of 1-methyl-4-phenyl-1,2,5,6-tetrahydropyridine (MPTP). *Neuropharmacology* 1985; 24(6):581–583.

461. Langston JW, Irwin I, DeLanney LE. The biotransformation of MPTP and disposition of MPPC: the effects of aging. *Life Sci* 1987; 40(8):749–754.

462. Gupta M, Gupta BK, Thomas R, et al. Aged mice are more sensitive to 1-methyl-4-phenyl-1,2,3,6-tetra-hydropyridine treatment than young adults. *Neurosci Lett* 1986; 70(3):326–331

463. Ricaurte GA, DeLanney LE, Irwin I, et al. Older dopaminergic neurons do not recover from the effects of MPTP. *Neuropharmacology* 1987; 26(1):97–99.

464. Ricaurte GA, Irwin I, Forno LS, et al. Aging and 1-methyl-4-phenyl-1,2,3,6-tetrahydropyridine–induced degeneration of dopaminergic neurons in the substantia nigra. *Brain Res* 1987; 403(1):43–51.

465. Sugama S, Yang L, et al. Age-related microglial activation in 1-methyl-4-phenyl-1,2,3,6-tetrahydropyridine (MPTP)-induced dopaminergic neurodegeneration in C57BL/6 mice. *Brain Res* 2003; 964(2):288–294.

466. Desole MS, Esposito G, Enrico P, et al. Effects of ageing on 1-methyl-4-phenyl-1,2,3,6-tetrahydropyridine (MPTP) neurotoxic effects on striatum and brainstem in the rat. *Neurosci Lett* 1993; 159(1–2):143–146.

467. Irwin I, Finnegan KT, Delanney LE, et al. The relationships between aging, monoamine oxidase, striatal dopamine and the effects of MPTP in C57BL/6 mice: A critical reassessment. *Brain Res* 1992; 572(1–2):224–231.

468. Saura J, Richards JG, Mahy N. Age-related changes on MAO in Bl/C57 mouse tissues: a quantitative radioautographic study. *J Neural Transm Suppl* 1994; 41:89–94.

469. Finnegan KT, Irwin I, Delanney LE, et al. Age-dependent effects of the 2°-methyl analog of 1-methyl-4-phenyl-1,2,3,6-tetrahydropyridine: prevention by inhibitors of monoamine oxidase B. *J Pharmacol Exp Ther* 1995; 273(2):716–720.

470. Forno LS, Langston JW, DeLanney LE, et al. Locus ceruleus lesions and eosinophilic inclusions in MPTP-treated monkeys. *Ann Neurol* 1986; 20(4):449–455.

471. Rose S, Nomoto M, Jackson EA, et al. Age-related effects of 1-methyl-4-phenyl-1,2,3,6-tetra-hydropyri-dine treatment of common marmosets. *Eur J Pharmacol* 1993; 230(2):177–185.

472. Ovadia A, Zhang Z, Gash DM. Increased susceptibility to MPTP toxicity in middle-aged rhesus monkeys. *Neurobiol Aging* 1995; 16(6):931–937.

473. Irwin I, Delanney L, Chan P, et al. Nigrostriatal monoamine oxidase A and B in aging squirrel monkeys and C57BL/6 mice. *Neurobiol Aging* 1997; 18(2):235–241.

474. Yang MC, McLean AJ, et al. Age-related alteration in hepatic disposition of the neurotoxin 1-methyl-4-phenyl-1,2,3,6-tetrahydropyridine and pesticides. *Pharmacol Toxicol* 2002; 90(4):203–207.

475. Thiruchelvam M, McCormack A, et al. Age-related irreversible progressive nigrostriatal dopaminergic neurotoxicity in the paraquat and maneb model of the Parkinson's disease phenotype. *Eur J Neurosci* 2003; 18(3):589–600.

476. Johannessen JN, Chiueh CC, Burns RS, et al. Differences in the metabolism of MPTP in the rodent and primate parallel differences in sensitivity to its neurotoxic effects. *Life Sci* 1985; 36(3):219–224.

477. Hoskins JA, Davis LJ. The acute effect on levels of catecholamines and metabolites in brain, of a single dose of MPTP in 8 strains of mice. *Neuropharmacology* 1989; 28(12):1389–1397.

478. Donnan GA, Kaczmarczyk SJ, Solopotias T, et al. The neurochemical and clinical effects of 1-methyl-4-phenyl-1,2,3,6-tetrahydropyridine in small animals. *Clin Exp Neurol* 1986; 22:155–164.

479. Sedelis M, Hofele K, et al. MPTP susceptibility in the mouse: Behavioral, neurochemical, and histological analysis of gender and strain differences. *Behav Genet* 2000; 30(3):171–182.

480. Heikkila RE. Differential neurotoxicity of 1-methyl-4-phenyl-1,2,3,6-tetrahydropyridine (MPTP) in Swiss-Webster mice from different sources. *Eur J Pharmacol* 1985; 117(1):131–134.

481. Hamre K, Tharp R, Poon K, et al. Differential strain susceptibility following 1-methyl-4-phenyl-1,2,3,6-tetrahydropyridine (MPTP) administration acts in an autosomal dominant fashion: Quantitative analysis in seven strains of Mus musculus. *Brain Res* 1999; 828(1–2):91–103.

482. Temple JG, Miller DB, et al. Differential vulnerability of snake species to MPTP: A behavioral and biochemical comparison in ratsnakes (*Elaphe*) and watersnakes (*Nerodia*). *Neurotoxicol Teratol* 2002; 24(2):227–233.

483. Zimmer J, Geneser FA. Difference in monoamine oxidase B activity between C57 black and albino NMRI mouse strains may explain differential effects of the neurotoxin MPTP. *Neurosci Lett* 1987; 78(3):253–258.

484. Kalaria RN, Harik SI. Blood-brain barrier monoamine oxidase: Enzyme characterization in cerebral microvessels and other tissues from six mammalian species, including human. *J Neurochem* 1987; 49(3):856–864.

485. Kalaria RN, Mitchell MJ, Harik SI. Correlation of 1-methyl-4-phenyl-1,2,3,6-tetrahydropyridine neurotoxicity with blood-brain barrier monoamine oxidase activity. *Proc Natl Acad Sci USA* 1987; 84(10):3521–3525.

486. Riachi NJ, Behmand RA, Harik SI. Correlation of MPTP neurotoxicity in vivo with oxidation of MPTP by the brain and blood-brain barrier in vitro in five rat strains. *Brain Res* 1991; 555(1):19–24.

487. Riachi NJ, Harik SI. Strain differences in systemic 1-methyl-4-phenyl-1,2,3,6-tetrahydropyridine neurotoxicity in mice correlate best with monoamine oxidase activity at the blood-brain barrier. *Life Sci* 1988; 42(23):2359–2363.

488. Mushiroda T, Ariyoshi N, et al. Accumulation of the 1-methyl-4-phenylpyridinium ion in suncus (*Suncus murinus*) brain: Implication for flavin-containing monooxygenase activity in brain microvessels. *Chem Res Toxicol* 2001; 14(2):228–232.

489. Smeyne M, Goloubeva O, et al. Strain-dependent susceptibility to MPTP and MPP(+)-induced parkinsonism is determined by glia. *Glia* 2001; 34(2):73–80.

490. Inoue H, Castagnoli K, et al. Species-dependent differences in monoamine oxidase A and B-catalyzed oxidation of various C4 substituted 1-methyl-4-phenyl-1,2,3, 6-tetrahydropyridinyl derivatives. *J Pharmacol Exp Ther* 1999; 291(2):856–864.

491. Staal RG, Hogan KA, et al. In vitro studies of striatal vesicles containing the vesicular monoamine transporter (VMAT2): Rat versus mouse differences in sequestration of 1-methyl-4-phenylpyridinium. *J Pharmacol Exp Ther* 2000; 293(2):329–335.

492. Sedelis, M, Hofele K, et al. Chromosomal loci influencing the susceptibility to the parkinsonian neurotoxin 1-methyl-4-phenyl-1,2,3,6-tetrahydropyridine. *J Neurosci* 2003; 23(23):8247–8253.

493. Iacopino A, Christakos S, German D, et al. Calbind-in-D28K-containing neurons in animal models of neurodegeneration: Possible protection from excitotoxicity. *Brain Res Mol Brain Res* 1992; 13(3):251–261.

494. Lavoie B, Parent A, Bedard PJ. Effects of dopamine denervation on striatal peptide expression in parkinsonian monkeys. *Can J Neurol Sci* 1991; 18(Suppl 3):373–375.

495. German DC, Manaye KF, Sonsalla PK, et al. Midbrain dopaminergic cell loss in Parkinson's disease and MPTP-induced parkinsonism: Sparing of calbindin-D28k-containing cells. *Ann NY Acad Sci* 1992; 648:42–62.

496. Parent A, Lavoie B. The heterogeneity of the mesostriatal dopaminergic system as revealed in normal and parkinsonian monkeys. *Adv Neurol* 1993; 60:25–33.

497. Sanghera MK, Manaye KF, Liang CL, et al. Low dopamine transporter mRNA levels in midbrain regions containing calbindin. *Neuroreport* 1994; 5(13):1641–1644.

498. Sanghera MK, Manaye K, McMahon A, et al. Dopamine transporter mRNA levels are high in midbrain neurons vulnerable to MPTP. *Neuroreport* 1997; 8(15):3327–3331.

499. Haber SN, Ryoo H, Cox C, et al. Subsets of midbrain dopaminergic neurons in monkeys are distinguished by different levels of mRNA for the dopamine transporter: Comparison with the mRNA for the D2 receptor, tyrosine hydroxylase and calbindin immunoreactivity. *J Comp Neurol* 1995; 362(3):400–410.

500. Airaksinen MS, Thoenen H, Meyer M. Vulnerability of midbrain dopaminergic neurons in calbindin-D28k-deficient mice: Lack of evidence for a neuroprotective role of endogenous calbindin in MPTP-treated and weaver mice. *Eur J Neurosci* 1997; 9(1):120–127.

501. Liss B, Haeckel O, et al. K-ATP channels promote the differential degeneration of dopaminergic midbrain neurons. *Nat Neurosci* 2005; 8(12):1742–1751.

502. Kaneda, K, Imanishi M, et al. Differential expression patterns of mGluR1 alpha in monkey nigral dopamine neurons. *Neuroreport* 2003; 14(7):947–950.

503. Perry TL, Yong VW, Wall RA, et al. Paraquat and two endogenous analogues of the neurotoxic substance N-methyl-4-phenyl-1,2,3,6-tetrahydropyridine do not damage dopaminergic nigrostriatal neurons in the mouse. *Neurosci Lett* 1986; 69(3):285–289.

504. Markey SP, Weisz A, Bacon JP. Reduced paraquat does not exhibit MPTP-like neurotoxicity (letter). *J Anal Toxicol* 1986; 10(6):257.

505. Brooks AI, Chadwick CA, Gelbard HA, et al. Paraquat elicited neurobehavioral syndrome caused by dopaminergic neuron loss. *Brain Res* 1999; 823(1–2):1–10.

506. Ward C, Duvoisin R, Ince S, et al. Parkinson's disease in 65 pairs of twins and in a set of quadruplets. *Neurology* 1983; 33:815–824.

507. Markopoulou K, Langston JW. Candidate genes and Parkinson's disease: Where to next? *Neurology* 1999; 53(7):1382–1383.

508. Tanner CM, Ottman R, Goldman SM, et al. Parkin-son disease in twins: an etiologic study. *Jama* 1999; 281(4):341-346.

509. Pedersen NL, Lichtenstein P, et al. The Swedish Twin Registry in the third millennium. *Twin Res* 2002; 5(5):427–432.

510. Fung HC, Scholz S, et al. Genome-wide genotyping in Parkinson's disease and neurologically normal controls: First stage analysis and public release of data. *Lancet Neurol* 2006; 5(11):911–916.

511. Polymeropoulos MH, Lavedan C, et al. Mutation in the alpha-synuclein gene identified in families with Parkinson's disease. *Science* 1997; 276(5321):2045–2047.

512. Spillantini MG, Schmidt ML, et al. Alpha-synuclein in Lewy bodies. *Nature* 1997; 388(6645):839–840.

513. Hallett PJ, Dunah AW, et al. Alterations of striatal NMDA receptor subunits associated with the development of dyskinesia in the MPTP-lesioned primate model of Parkinson's disease. *Neuropharmacology* 2005; 48(4):503–516.

514. Farrer M, Kachergus J, et al. Comparison of kindreds with parkinsonism and alpha-synuclein genomic multiplications. *Ann Neurol* 2004; 55(2):174–179.

515. Chartier-Harlin MC, Kachergus J, et al. Alpha-synuclein locus duplication as a cause of familial Parkinson's disease. *Lancet* 2004; 364(9440):1167–1169.

516. Ibanez P, Bonnet AM, et al. Causal relation between alpha-synuclein gene duplication and familial Parkinson's disease. *Lancet* 2004; 364(9440):1169–1171.

517. Miller DW, Hague SM, et al. Alpha-synuclein in blood and brain from familial Parkinson disease with SNCA locus triplication. *Neurology* 2004; 62(10):1835–1838.

518. Muenter MD, Forno LS, et al. Hereditary form of parkinsonism-dementia. *Ann Neurol* 1998; 43(6):768–81

519. Kowall NW, Hantraye P, et al. MPTP induces alpha-synuclein aggregation in the substantia nigra of baboons. *Neuroreport* 2000; 11(1):211–213.

520. Vila M, Vukosavic S, et al. Alpha-synuclein up-regulation in substantia nigra dopaminergic neurons following administration of the parkinsonian toxin MPTP. *J Neurochem* 2000; 74(2):721–729.

521. Przedborski S, Chen Q, et al. Oxidative post-translational modifications of alpha-synuclein in the 1-methyl-4-phenyl-1,2,3,6-tetrahydropyridine (MPTP) mouse model of Parkinson's disease. *J Neurochem* 2001; 76(2):637–640.

522. Xu Z, Cawthon D, et al. Selective alterations of gene expression in mice induced by MPTP. *Synapse* 2005; 55(1):45–51.

523. Meredith GE, Totterdell S, et al. Lysosomal malfunction accompanies alpha-synuclein aggregation in a progressive mouse model of Parkinson's disease. *Brain Res* 2002; 956(1):156–165.

524. Fornai F, Schluter OM, et al. Parkinson-like syndrome induced by continuous MPTP infusion: Convergent roles of the ubiquitin-proteasome system and alpha-synuclein. *Proc Natl Acad Sci USA* 2005; 102(9):3413–3418.

525. Shimoji M, Zhang L, et al. Absence of inclusion body formation in the MPTP mouse model of Parkinson's disease. *Brain Res Mol Brain Res* 2005; 134(1):103–108.

526. Dauer W, Kholodilov N, et al. Resistance of alpha-synuclein null mice to the parkinsonian neurotoxin MPTP. *Proc Natl Acad Sci USA* 2002; 99(22):14524–14529.

527. Drolet, R E, B Behrouz, et al. Mice lacking alpha-synuclein have an attenuated loss of striatal dopamine following prolonged chronic MPTP administration. *Neurotoxicology* 2004; 25(5):761–769.

528. Robertson DC, Schmidt O, et al. Developmental loss and resistance to MPTP toxicity of dopaminergic neurones in substantia nigra pars compacta of gamma-synuclein, alpha-synuclein and double alpha/gamma-synuclein null mutant mice. *J Neurochem* 2004; 89(5):1126–1136.

530. Klivenyi P, Siwek D, et al. Mice lacking alpha-synuclein are resistant to mitochondrial toxins. *Neurobiol Dis* 2006; 21(3):541–548.

531. Gomez-Santos C, Ferrer I, et al. MPP+ increases alpha-synuclein expression and ERK/MAP-kinase phosphorylation in human neuroblastoma SH-SY5Y cells. *Brain Res* 2002; 935(1–2):32–39.

532. Fan GH, Zhou HY, et al. Heat shock proteins reduce alpha-synuclein aggregation induced by MPP+ in SK-N-SH cells. *FEBS Lett* 2006; 580(13):3091–3098.

533. Braak H, Del Tredici K, et al. Staging of the intracerebral inclusion body pathology associated with idiopathic Parkinson's disease (preclinical and clinical stages). *J Neurol* 2002; 249(Suppl 3): III/1–5.

534. Braak, H, Del Tredici K, et al. Staging of brain pathology related to sporadic Parkinson's disease. *Neurobiol Aging* 2003; 24(2):197–211.

535. Langston J W. The Parkinson's complex: Parkinsonism is just the tip of the iceberg. *Ann Neurol* 2006; 59(4):591–596.

536. Rojo AI, Montero C, et al. Persistent penetration of MPTP through the nasal route induces Parkinson's disease in mice. *Eur J Neurosci* 2006; 24(7):1874–1884.

35 Rotenone and Other Toxins

Ranjita Betarbet
J. Timothy Greenamyre

NATURE AND COURSE OF PARKINSON'S DISEASE

Parkinson's disease (PD) is a late-onset, progressive neurodegenerative disorder affecting approximately 2% of the population over the age of 65. Clinical symptoms consist of resting tremor, muscular rigidity, bradykinesia, and abnormal postural reflexes (1). The pathologic hallmark of PD is the progressive degeneration of the nigrostriatal pathway and dopaminergic cells of the substantia nigra (2), although recent neuropathologic studies suggest a more extended neuronal degeneration starting in the medulla oblongata that later spreads to the midbrain and finally the cerebral cortex (3). Nevertheless, it is the degeneration of the nigrostriatal pathway and subsequent dopamine deficiency in striatum that is believed to underlie many of the motor manifestations of PD (4–8).

Another important pathologic feature of PD is the presence of fibrillar cytoplasmic inclusions known as Lewy bodies. Lewy bodies contain aggregates of many different proteins, including ubiquitin and α-synuclein (9), and are present in the surviving dopaminergic neurons of substantia nigra and in brain regions, such as the cerebral cortex and magnocellular basal forebrain nuclei (10).

The etiopathogenesis of sporadic PD, the more common form, is not fully understood, although the general consensus today is that it is multifactorial, as evident from genetic analyses of the few familial PD cases, epidemiologic studies suggesting environmental associations, neuropathologic investigations, and new experimental models of PD (11–13).

Genetics and Parkinson's Disease (See Also Chapter 37)

Mutations in the α-synuclein gene have been associated with rare familial cases of PD (14). Furthermore, Lewy bodies contain α-synuclein in the majority of idiopathic PD cases that actually lack α-synuclein mutations, suggesting a central role for α-synuclein protein aggregation in PD pathogenesis (9, 15). Additional mutations in 2 other genes, parkin (16–18) and ubiquitin carboxy-terminal hydrolase L1 (UCH-L1) (19), have been associated with familial PD and have added to data supporting the belief that dysfunctional protein degradation might be an important factor in the etiology of PD. While proteasomal dysfunction has been reported in sporadic cases of PD (20), mitochondrial dysfunction (21–25) and oxidative stress (26) have been the pathogenic mechanisms most strongly implicated in PD. Evidence linking recessively inherited mutations in PINK1 (PTEN-induced kinase 1), a putative mitochondrial protein kinase (27) and DJ-1, a protein allegedly associated with oxidative stress (28–30), to familial forms of PD further augment the role of mitochondrial dysfunction and oxidative stress in PD pathogenesis. More recently, mutations of LRRK2 or leucine-rich repeat kinase 2 (PARK 8) have been shown to cause autosomal dominant PD (31,32). It is estimated that LRRK2 mutations account for 5% to 6% of cases with positive family history and of up to 1.6% of apparently sporadic cases of PD (33). At present, little is known about LRRK2 function, and preliminary data regarding its association with the outer mitochondrial membrane (34, 35) and parkin (36) requires further validation.

Environment and Parkinson's Disease

Environmental toxins (11) have also been determined to be risk factors for PD, based on numerous epidemiologic observations. Living in rural areas, farming, and drinking well water have been associated with increased exposure to agricultural chemicals (i.e., pesticides, herbicides, and insecticides, which in turn are associated with increased risk for PD) (37, 38). High doses and long duration (>20 years) of exposure of these chemicals are particularly important risks for developing PD (11, 39). Among individual pesticides, paraquat exposure has been shown to be either significantly associated with PD (40, 41), especially with more than 20 years of exposure or to demonstrate a statistical trend in association with PD risk (40, 42).

Analyses of genetic and environmental factors suggest that diverse pathways converging on mitochondrial defects, oxidative stress, and aberrant protein aggregation account for most cases of PD (12, 43). This chapter discusses the toxin models—including the rotenone, paraquat, and paraquat/maneb models—that give credence to "gene-environment interactions" in PD pathogenesis and emphasizes the role of mitochondrial dysfunction, systemic complex I inhibition, and oxidative stress in parkinsonian-like pathology and neurodegeneration.

Mitochondria and Parkinson's Disease

Both genes (30, 44–46) and environmental toxins (47–49) associated with the development of PD have implicated mitochondrial dysfunction and oxidative stress in the pathogenesis of neuronal degeneration. Prior to these studies, however, biochemical analysis had associated PD with a systemic but modest complex I deficiency (22–24, 50–54). In addition, the observation that MPP+, the active metabolite of 1-methyl-4-phenyl-1,2,3,6-tetrahydropyridine (MPTP) and an inhibitor of complex I of the mitochondrial electron transport chain, causes an acute parkinsonian syndrome (55–57) further accentuated the potential role of mitochondria in PD.

Mitochondrial Complex I Mitochondria are cellular organelles that are present in virtually every eukaryotic cell, though they differ in shape, size, and number.

The central role of mitochondria lies in the production of energy in the form of adenosine triphosphate (ATP) acquired by the cell via two interrelated sets of reactions: the Krebs or the tricarboxylic acid (TCA) cycle and oxidative phosphorylation (58). The TCA cycle takes place in the mitochondrial matrix and generates reduced nicotinamide adenine dinucleotide (NADH) and flavin adenine dinucleotide ($FADH_2$). NADH and $FADH_2$ undergo oxidative phosphorylation (oxphos) by donating electrons to the electron transport chain (ETC) and its constituent complex array of enzymes located on the inner mitochondrial membrane (Figure 35-1). This membrane is selectively permeable to ions, and the control of its permeability is the key to most mitochondrial functions, including oxphos, intracellular calcium regulation, apoptosis, and cell death. Oxphos consists of 2 closely coupled processes: electron transport to oxygen and phosphorylation of adenosine diphosphate (ADP). Electrons from NADH enter the ETC via complex I (NADH dehydrogenase or NADH- ubiquinone oxidoreductase). Complex I is composed of 46 subunits, 7 of which are mitochondrially encoded. Rotenone and MPP+ are known inhibitors (see Figure 35-1) of this enzyme (56, 59). Electrons from complex I are transferred to complex III (ubiquinol–cytochrome *c* oxidoreductase) via ubiquinone. Ubiquinone also receives electrons from $FADH_2$ most of which is generated by the TCA cycle. From complex III the electrons are donated to cytochrome *c*, which transfer them to complex IV. Complex IV transfers electrons to molecular oxygen, the final electron acceptor. Complexes I, III, and IV pump protons from the inner mitochondrial matrix to the outer mitochondrial matrix, creating potential energy that is stored in the form of an electrochemical gradient. These protons flow back into the matrix through complex V or ATP synthase and provide the energy needed for ATP production (60). The knowledge that human brain contributes 2% of the body weight but produces 20% of ATP confirms the importance of oxphos (61).

Mitochondria and Oxidative Stress Mitochondrial respiration is also a source of reactive oxygen species (ROS). At several locations along the mitochondrial ETC, there are sites of "electron leaks" (see Figure 35-1). These electrons can combine with molecular oxygen and form reactive oxygen species (62,63), such as superoxide (O_2-) and hydrogen peroxide (H_2O_2). The ROS can readily react with DNA, lipids, and proteins and cause oxidative damage. Partial complex I inhibition is known to enhance ROS production (63–65).

Biochemical analysis has provided evidence for the involvement of oxidative stress in PD. Increased lipid peroxidation and oxidative damage to DNA and proteins have been observed in the substantia nigra of PD patients (26, 66–68). Decreased levels of glutathione in this region have also been found, further implicating oxidative stress (69).

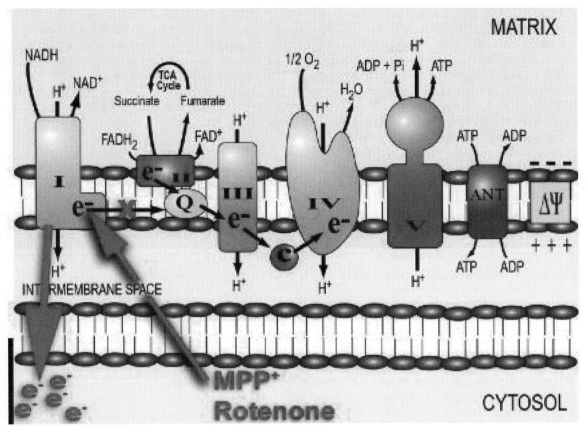

FIGURE 35-1

Schematic diagram of the mitochondrial ETC. Note the site of complex I inhibition by rotenone and MPP$^+$, electron leakage, and ROS production.

Keeping with the concept that mitochondrial dysfunction and, more specifically, "systemic complex I inhibition" has a central role in PD pathogenesis, we hypothesized that systemic low levels of chronic complex I inhibition would induce selective degeneration of the nigrostriatal pathway. Indeed, continuous low levels of rotenone (a selective complex I inhibitor) exposure in rats resulted in selective degeneration of the nigrostriatal pathway.

THE ROTENONE MODEL IN RATS

A naturally occurring compound derived from the roots of *Lonchocarpus*, a plant, rotenone is commonly used as an "organic" insecticide and to kill nuisance fish in lakes. Rotenone is also a classic high-affinity complex I inhibitor and is typically used to define the specific activity of complex I (70, 71). Additionally, rotenone is a lipophilic compound that easily crosses the blood-brain barrier. Unlike MPP$^+$, rotenone does not require the help

of transporters (72) to cross cellular membranes. Once inside the cell, rotenone accumulates in the mitochondria (73), where it impairs oxidative phosphorylation by inhibiting complex I (71).

Rotenone Administration

To simulate low levels of exposure of a complex I inhibitor during a normal life span, Sprague-Dawley and Lewis rats were systemically and chronically exposed to low levels of rotenone via an intrajugular cannula attached to a subcutaneous osmotic minipump (74). Lewis rats developed more consistent lesions and were therefore used exclusively for further studies. At first the doses of rotenone used ranged from 1 to 12 mg/kg/day. At high doses, rotenone produced systemic cardiovascular toxicity and nonspecific brain lesions similar to those observed by others (75, 76). Downward titration of rotenone dosing resulted in less systemic toxicity and more specific nigrostriatal dopaminergic degeneration. The optimal dose for inducing PD-like pathology was determined to be 2 to 3 mg/kg/day. It is important to note at this point that even at the "optimal dose," only 30% to 50% of Lewis rats demonstrated PD-like pathology. Nonetheless, low levels of systemic rotenone administration produced pathologic features characteristic of PD (74). Intrajugular cannulation surgeries are, however, labor-intensive and increase the risk of postsurgical complications. Therefore an alternative route was developed to administer rotenone. Instead of cannulation and vascular administration, rotenone was administered by subcutaneously placed osmotic minipumps that released rotenone into the body cavity (74, 77). Subcutaneous administration of rotenone, at 2 to 3 mg/kg/day in Lewis rats also produced selective nigrostriatal dopaminergic lesions, as previously reported (74).

Rotenone emulsified in sunflower oil and administered daily by intraperitoneal injection was also able to induce parkinsonian symptoms and degeneration of nigral dopaminergic neurons in Sprague-Dawley rats (78).

Characteristics of Rotenone-Induced Toxicity

Systemic Complex I Inhibition Consistent with its ability to cross biological membranes easily, chronic low doses of systemic rotenone infusion resulted in uniform inhibition of complex I throughout the rat brain. (^{3}H) dihydrorotenone binding to complex I in brain was reduced by approximately 75%. This inhibition of specific binding translated to be 20 to 30 nM of free rotenone in the brain. Rotenone infusion did not have any effect on the enzymatic activities of complex II and complex IV, analyzed histochemically (74). This uniform complex I inhibition induced by rotenone was unlike the effects of MPTP, which selectively inhibits complex I in dopaminergic neurons due to the dependence of MPP$^+$, the active metabolite of MPTP, on the dopamine transporter (79).

Selective Nigrostriatal Dopaminergic Degeneration Interestingly, despite this uniform complex I inhibition, rotenone caused selective degeneration of the nigrostriatal dopaminergic pathway (74, 77, 78, 80). Immunocytochemistry for tyrosine hydroxylase (TH), a rate-limiting enzyme involved in the production of dopamine and a phenotypic marker for dopaminergic neurons, demonstrated absence of dopaminergic innervation in the striatum (Figure 35-2). Other dopaminergic markers, including dopamine transporter (DAT) and vesicular monoamine transporter type 2 (VMAT2), confirmed the striatal lesions (80). Staining for neurodegeneration such as silver and fluoro-jade B unambiguously verified that the absence of dopaminergic phenotypic markers in the striatum was due to degeneration of dopaminergic terminals. The striatal dopaminergic lesions were either partial or focal, located in the central or dorsolateral region of the anterior striatum, or were diffused and spread out to involve most of the motor striatum (see Figure 35-2). Interestingly, even when the lesion was severe, there was relative sparing of

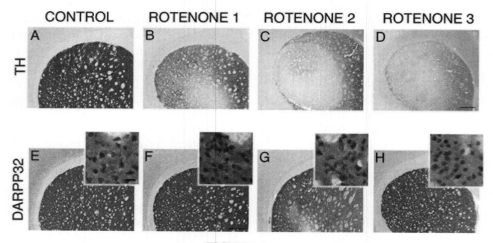

FIGURE 35-2

Selective degeneration of dopaminergic terminals in the striatum of rotenone-infused rats (2.5–3.0 mg/kg/day). Striatal sections from control (A, E) and rotenone-infused rats (B, C, D, F, G, H) were stained for TH (A, B, C, D) and DARPP32 (E, F, G, H) ICC. B, C, and D represent 3 different patterns of striatal lesions following rotenone exposure (3–21 days of rotenone exposure) as determined by TH-ir. Striatal DARPP32-positive neurons were mostly intact following rotenone infusion (F, H), despite extensive TH loss, except for a small necrotic focal area (G) devoid of DARPP32-ir.

dopaminergic fibers in the medial aspects of the striatum, nucleus accumbens and olfactory tubercle, areas that are relatively spared in idiopathic PD (74).

Neurodegeneration of various extents was also evident in the dopaminergic neurons of the substantia nigra. Animals with partial striatal lesions had dopaminergic neurons in the substantia nigra that looked relatively normal, while animals with extensive striatal lesions had obvious reductions in nigral TH-positive neurons. Silver staining demonstrated clear signs of degenerating nigral neurons with silver deposits in their cell bodies and processes; this was found even in animals that had normal-looking TH-positive cells and partial striatal lesions. Rats with severe striatal lesions exhibited more extensive signs of degeneration in the nigral neurons.

Both TH immunocytochemistry and silver staining demonstrated retrograde degeneration of nigral dopaminergic neurons following rotenone exposure; degeneration began at the terminals in the striatum, where the effects were more severe compared to the nigral neurons (74, 80, 81). Quantitative analysis of dopamine levels has also shown extensive deficiency in the striatum (78), similar to postmortem analysis of brains from PD patients, which have shown more extensive loss of striatal dopamine compared to substantia nigra (82). Furthermore, neurons in the lateral and ventral tiers of the substantia nigra appeared to be more vulnerable to systemic rotenone infusion, very similar to the pattern of neuronal vulnerability observed in PD. Despite the loss of TH-immunoreactivity in the substantia nigra, dopaminergic neurons of the ventral tegmental area (VTA) were spared, as is also seen in PD. In addition, similar to PD, noradrenergic neurons of the locus ceruleus were susceptible to rotenone toxicity (74, 80, 81).

Despite profound loss of presynaptic dopaminergic terminals in the striatum, the postsynaptic striatal neurons remained intact. In the majority of the rotenone-infused rats, striatal neurons were minimally affected (see Figure 35-2), as observed with Nissl stain and NeuN and with immunocytochemistry for various striatal phenotypic markers such as (dopamine and cAMP-regulated phosphoprotein (DARPP32), glutamic acid decarboxylase (GAD), neuronal nitric oxide synthase (nNOS), and histochemistry for acetylcholinesterase (AchE). There was an exception to this rule, however. One or two rats with acute focal lesions had a necrotic core (see Figure 35-2) and showed evidence of striatal cell loss (80, 83). Rotenone toxicity also had minimal effects on neurons of other brain regions, including globus pallidus and subthalamic nucleus, as confirmed with silver staining (77). These data further support the nigrostriatal dopaminergic selectivity of rotenone-induced neurodegeneration.

Microglial Activation PD is characterized by selective activation of a nigrostriatal microglial response, while astrocytosis is rarely observed. Selective microglial activation in the striatum and nigral brain regions was detected in rotenone-infused rats (80, 84). Enlarged microglia with short, stubby processes were detected prior to dopaminergic lesions. Rotenone-induced microglial activation was less pronounced in the cortex and in rats that did not develop a striatal lesion. Microglia are the brain's resident immune cells and are activated in response to immunological stimuli and/or neuronal injuries. They are known to produce potentially neurotoxic reactive oxygen species, which probably add to the oxidative stress reported in PD (85, 86).

Oxidative Stress Rotenone-induced complex I inhibition resulted in increased oxidative stress, both in vitro in neuroblastoma cells (87) and in vivo in rats (88), as implicated by increased levels of protein carbonyls, a marker for oxidative stress. It was observed that the toxicity in neuroblastoma cells chronically exposed to low levels of rotenone was mainly due to increased levels of oxidative stress and minimally due to ATP depletion. Furthermore, rotenone-induced toxicity in cells was attenuated by prior treatment with α-tocopherol, a known antioxidant, confirming that the toxic action of rotenone was via oxidative stress (88). Rotenone-infused rats also demonstrated increased levels of oxidative stress, most notably in dopaminergic regions, including the striatum, ventral midbrain, and olfactory bulb.

DJ-1 mutations are associated with an early-onset, recessive form of parkinsonism in patients (28). The function of DJ-1 appears to relate to oxidative stress. Interestingly, chronic rotenone exposure, both in vitro and in vivo, resulted in oxidative modifications of DJ-1 protein by a shift in pI toward a more acidic form and translocating it to the outer mitochondrial membrane from the cytoplasm (47). It is suggested that DJ-1 is normally neuroprotective, while mutations or oxidative modifications can reduce these effects (89, 90). Thus rotenone-induced toxicity appears to be strongly associated with oxidative stress, which in turn has been strongly implicated in PD pathogenesis (26),

α-Synuclein–Positive Cytoplasmic Inclusions α-Synuclein–positive cytoplasmic inclusions, called Lewy bodies, are characteristic hallmarks of PD pathology. Such inclusions in nigral cells were also detected in rotenone-infused rats (74, 77, 81). They also stained positively for ubiquitin and appeared as "pale eosinophilic" inclusions with hematoxylin and eosin (H&E) staining. These inclusions were ultrastructurally similar to the Lewy bodies of PD in that they had a homogenous dense core surrounded by fibrillar elements (74). Biochemical analysis confirmed the accumulation and aggregation of α-synuclein in rotenone-infused rats (Figure 35-3). Western immunoblotting demonstrated significant and selective increases in

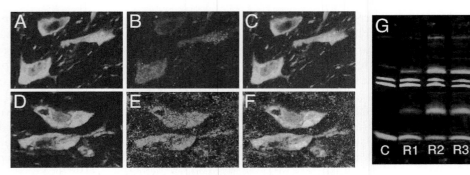

FIGURE 35-3

α-Synuclein accumulation in dopaminergic nigral neurons. Coronal sections through the substantia nigra from control (A, B, C) and rotenone-infused (D, E, F) rats were double labeled for TH (A, D) and α-synuclein (B, E). Note the increased α-synuclein expression in dopaminergic neurons following rotenone exposure. Western immunoblotting (G) confirmed the increase in α-synuclein levels (red bands) and accumulation in the ventral midbrain. Note the increased expression and presence of higher-molecular-weight bands in rotenone-exposed rats (R1, R2, R3) as compared to a control rat (C). MAPk (green bands) was used as a loading control. See color section following page 356.

α-synuclein levels in the ventral midbrain regions. Higher-molecular-weight bands (~30 and ~52 kDa) were also seen in addition to the 19 kDa α-synuclein band (47). In the striatum, punctate α-synuclein accumulation was detected in regions that were devoid of TH immunoreactivity (47), very similar to that observed patients with Alzheimer's/Lewy body disease (AD/LBD) (91).

Proteasomal Dysfunction   A dysfunctional ubiquitin proteasomal system (UPS) was also found to be a consequence of rotenone-induced complex I inhibition. Ubiquitin-independent proteasomal enzymatic activities were significantly and selectively reduced in the ventral midbrain regions (VMB) of rotenone-infused rats with striatal lesions. Furthermore, ubiquitin conjugated proteins, an indicator of proteins marked for degradation, were markedly increased in VMB, suggesting impairment of the ubiquitin-dependent proteasome degradation pathway (47).

Impairment of proteasomal function could be due to complex I inhibition–induced changes in bioenergetics, such as ATP production and/or complex I inhibition–induced increase in free radicals production resulting in oxidatively damaged proteins. An acute in vitro design using ventral mesencephalic primary cultures indicated that rotenone-induced impairment of proteasomal function is primarily due to ATP depletion and not free radical production (92). However, chronic exposure to low levels of rotenone, while minimally affecting bioenergetics, significantly increases the levels of oxidative stress, which—under these circumstances—may play a greater role in neuronal degeneration (47, 87, 88). It is possible that the increased levels of oxidatively damaged proteins observed following rotenone-infusion/treatment could

impair the proteasomal pathway by either "clogging-up" the UPS or by oxidatively modifying the proteasomal subunits themselves. In fact Shamoto-Nagai et al. (93) have shown that complex I inhibition with rotenone in neuroblastoma SH-SY5Y cells reduced proteasomal activity through increased production of oxidatively modified proteins, including oxidative modification of the proteasome itself. Thus it appears that increased oxidative stress could inhibit proteasomal function and eventually lead to neuronal degeneration.

Behavior   Reduced striatal dopaminergic activity is known to cause parkinsonian symptoms in humans (1). In rats, rigidity and akinetic behavior are referred to as catalepsy. Catalepsy tests revealed a significant increase in cataleptic behavior in rotenone-treated rats as compared to control, vehicle-treated rats (78). In addition, rotenone-treated rats displayed a significant decline in locomotor activities, including active sitting, rearing, and line-crossing behavior (78). Rigidity and hypokinetic behavior as well as flexed posture, similar to the stooped posture of PD patients, were previously reported in rotenone-exposed rats (74, 77). Some of the rotenone-infused rats also developed severe rigidity and a few had spontaneously shaking paws, reminiscent of resting tremor in PD.

Variability in the Rotenone Model

Since the initial studies with rotenone, numerous reports have either confirmed (78, 80) or questioned (76, 81) the selectivity of rotenone-induced degeneration of the nigrostriatal dopaminergic pathway. These differences could be due to a "small window" for rotenone's action that results in selective neurodegeneration. There is a threshold for every drug beyond which it has nonspecific or "side effects." For rotenone, this threshold appears to be very small—some animals have an acute response while some are not affected by rotenone at all, and yet there are some rats that develop very characteristic features of PD. At high doses, as shown by Ferrante et al. (75), rotenone can have nonspecific effects.

That the variability observed in the effect of rotenone-induced toxicity ranges from none to nearly complete striatal dopaminergic lesions (74, 76, 77, 80, 81) is interesting. This variability clearly demonstrates the individual susceptibility to complex I inhibition in rats, which could be due to genetic differences and/or differences in the ability to metabolize environmental toxins (72). Similar individual differences in humans may determine one's susceptibility to the development of PD.

THE ROTENONE MODEL IN FLIES

Interestingly, many PD features have been recapitulated in *Drosophila melanogaster* (94). Following several days of sublethal doses of rotenone exposure, these flies developed locomotor impairments that increased with dose. Immunocytochemistry studies demonstrated a significant and selective loss of dopaminergic neurons in the brain clusters. Placing L-dopa into the feeding medium rescued the behavioral deficits but not neuronal loss, implying that locomotor deficits are due to loss of dopaminergic neurons. In contrast, the antioxidant melatonin alleviated both behavioral deficits and neuronal loss, suggesting a major role for oxidative stress in neuronal degeneration in *Drosophila*. These studies provide a new model from which to study PD pathogenesis and to screen therapeutic drugs.

OTHER TOXINS

The Paraquat Model in Mice

Paraquat (PQ), or 1, 1′-dimethyl-4,4α-bi-pyridinium, is an herbicide and an environmental toxin that is structurally similar to MPP+ (95). The proposal that PQ may be toxic to the nigrostriatal dopaminergic system and may contribute to PD pathogenesis was also based on epidemiologic studies that have shown a positive correlation between PQ exposure and incidence of PD in some rural areas (40, 41). In addition, PQ is the only herbicide for which a dose-dependent relationship has been reported between lifetime cumulative exposure and increased PD risk (41). In an investigation based in Taiwan, where paraquat is commonly sprayed on rice fields, the odds ratio for PD incidence was as high as 6.4 among subjects who had been exposed to the herbicide for more than 20 years.

Despite the fact that PQ does not readily cross the blood-brain barrier (96), significant brain damage (not specific to the nigrostriatal dopaminergic system) has been reported in individuals who have died from high PQ exposure (97, 98). To test the role for PQ in PD pathogenesis and its potential use as a model for toxicant-induced nigrostriatal injury, PQ has been administered in animals via different routes, including intracerebral injections in rats (41) as well as systemic injections in mice (49, 99); however, not all studies have reported dopaminergic toxicity or, more specifically, striatal dopamine depletion and loss of nigral neurons (49, 99, 100). McCormack et al., for the first time, correlated stereologic cell counts with pathologic observations in substantia nigra and neurochemical evaluations in the striatum (48). Mice at different ages received three intraperitoneal injections of PQ once a week for 3 weeks; brains were then harvested at different time points after the last injection. Systemic PQ administration resulted in a dose- and age-dependent loss of dopaminergic neurons (25% to 33%) in the substantia nigra. Furthermore, PQ toxicity was specific to the dopaminergic nigral neurons and did not affect the GABAergic nigral neurons or neurons of the hippocampus. However, nigral dopaminergic cell loss did not accompany any significant depletion in striatal dopamine levels, although enhanced dopamine synthesis was suggested by an increase in striatal TH activity. Interestingly, α-synuclein levels were elevated in both the frontal cortex as well as the ventral midbrain, and α-synuclein-positive inclusions were present in the substantia nigra neurons (101). PQ-induced dopaminergic cell death and α-synuclein aggregation, features characteristic of PD pathology, suggests that paraquat could be used to model PD in animals.

The Paraquat-Maneb Model in Mice

The fungicide manganese ethylenebisdithiocarbamate, or maneb, is used in overlapping geographic areas with PQ; it has been shown to decrease locomotor activity and potentiate MPTP toxicity in animals (102, 103), suggesting that exposure to a mixture of chemicals may also be relevant to PD etiology. Maneb itself has been directly implicated in at least 2 cases of parkinsonism in humans (104, 105), further implicating environmental toxins in PD pathogenesis.

The use of the combination of PQ and diethydithiocarbamates such as maneb is practiced along the Pacific Coast, in the Northeast, the plains states, the mid-Atlantic, the Southeast, and Texas (49). PQ and diethydithiocarbamates are used on many of the same crops, including tomatoes (49). The geographical overlap in use of pesticides and the fact that multiple pesticide residues can be detected in foods suggest the possibility of multitoxin human exposure underlying PD pathogenesis and therefore a possible multihit toxin exposure as a model for PD.

On the basis of this premise, Thiruchelvam et al. (49) have examined and compared individual effects and the combined effects of PQ and maneb exposures on the nigrostriatal dopaminergic systems. Male C57 BL/6 mice were treated twice a week for 6 weeks with intraperitoneal saline, 10 mg/kg PQ, 30 mg/kg maneb, or a combination of PQ and maneb. The mice were killed at varying time points ranging from 1 hour to 7 days after treatment. No treatment-related changes in body weight or lung pathology were observed at any point during the experiments. Behavioral changes, in terms of failure of motor activity to recover within 24 hours, were evident only in combined PQ and maneb-treated mice. Tyrosine hydroxylase (TH) and dopamine transporter (DAT) immunoreactivity as well as TH protein levels were also reduced in PQ/maneb-treated mice. TH and DAT related changes were evident only in the dorsal striatum and not the nucleus accumbens. In addition, TH-positive cell counts were reduced in the substantia nigra but not the ventral tegmental region in PQ/maneb-treated mice, suggesting the involvement of only the dopaminergic nigrostriatal pathway. In this study, exposure to PQ or maneb alone did not produce any significant changes. Interestingly, however, all three groups showed an increase in locomotor deficits when challenged with an acute exposure to MPTP. These studies, demonstrating the effects of a multitoxin exposure on the dopaminergic nigrostriatal pathway, suggest a possible role of multiple-toxin exposure in the etiology of PD. Furthermore, such exposures could act in conjunction with a genetic predisposition, resulting in gene-environment interactions; this is the current basis for PD pathogenesis.

A word of caution before using these models to study PD is that the selectivity and specificity of PQ and maneb are not documented. To date, no data are available pertaining to the effects of PQ and maneb on GABAergic or cholinergic systems in addition to dopaminergic neurons (106).

MECHANISMS OF TOXICITY

Rotenone-Induced Toxicity

Rotenone is a specific inhibitor of complex I of the mitochondrial electron transport chain (73). In rats, chronic and systemic infusion of rotenone resulted in selective and uniform inhibition of complex I. Based on (3H)dihydrorotenone binding studies (74, 107), it was deduced that the free rotenone in the brain of rotenone-infused rats was approximately 20 to 30 nM. This concentration of rotenone is known to partially inhibit complex I activity. Oximetry analysis of brain mitochondria indicated that this level of complex I inhibition was inadequate to inhibit glutamate-supported respiration, suggesting that defective ATP production may not be responsible for neurodegeneration. Partial complex I inhibition also stimulates the production of reactive oxygen species (62), as also confirmed in the rotenone-infused rats and in neuroblastoma cells exposed to rotenone; increased levels of carbonyls, a marker for oxidative stress, were detected in dopaminergic brain regions and in cells (88). DJ-1, an oxidative stress–associated protein, underwent oxidative modifications in the same brain regions in rotenone-infused rats (47, 108). Furthermore α-tocopherol, a known antioxidant, attenuated rotenone-induced toxicity in cells and organotypic slice cultures (88). Thus studies to elucidate the mechanisms of rotenone toxicity have indicated that free radical production and subsequent oxidative stress has a pivotal role in rotenone-induced neurodegeneration.

Oxidative damage can also provide a partial explanation for the rotenone-induced elevations and aggregation of α-synuclein observed selectively in nigral neurons. α-Synuclein is known to undergo oxidative modifications in PD brains. which can render the protein insoluble, leading to aggregation (109). Both in vivo and in vitro studies have demonstrated that rotenone accumulation correlates with upregulation in protein carbonyls, suggesting that rotenone can cause oxidative modifications to α-synuclein and its aggregation (109, 110). Furthermore, prior treatment with α-tocopherol attenuated rotenone-induced increases in α-synuclein in vitro, confirming the association between α-synuclein and oxidative stress (47).

Rotenone exposure also resulted in selective proteasomal inhibition in the ventral midbrain regions of rotenone-infused rats with striatal lesions (47, 111). Proteasomal dysfunction can be attributed to both increased oxidative stress and an increase in α-synuclein levels. Increased oxidative stress can result in the generation of oxidatively modified proteins. which can ultimately clog the protein degradation pathway (112, 113) or oxidatively modify the proteasomal subunits, rendering them dysfunctional (93). Although it is not clear whether α-synuclein is degraded by the ubiquitin proteasomal pathway (114), increased levels of α-synuclein can inhibit the UPS by interacting with the proteasomal subunits (115). Thus rotenone-induced oxidative stress and α-synuclein accumulation can inhibit the UPS.

Interestingly, the effects of chronic and systemic rotenone infusion such as uniform complex I inhibition, oxidative stress, α-synuclein aggregation, and proteasomal dysfunction became regionally restricted, finally resulting in highly selective nigrostriatal dopaminergic degeneration.

Paraquat-Maneb–Induced Toxicity

Paraquat is known to exert its toxic effects through oxidative stress mediated by redox cycling with cellular diaphorase, such as nitric oxide synthase (116,117), yielding reactive oxygen species (ROS). The mechanism of maneb-induced toxicity is not well known; however. indirect evidence suggests the involvement of oxidative stress as well (118). Furthermore, the association of oxidative stress with combined PQ- and maneb-induced toxicity is evident from the significant increase in striatal catalase, glutathione S-transferase, and lipid peroxidation following 3, 6, and 9 weeks of cotreatment as compared with individual treatments or controls. Furthermore, antioxidant pathways involving cytochrome P4502E1(CYP2E1) and glutathione-S-transferases A4-4 (GSTA4-4) in the detoxification of several pesticides including PQ and maneb have been previously documented (118). Combined treatment with PQ (10 mg/kg IP) and maneb (30 mg/kg IP) augmented the gene expression levels of CYP2E1 and GSTA4-4. CYP2E1 is associated with free radical production, contributing to lipid peroxidation and oxidative stress.

CONCLUSIONS

The rotenone model appears to be an accurate model in that systemic complex I inhibition results in specific, progressive, and chronic degeneration of the nigrostriatal pathway similar to that observed in PD. It also reproduces oxidative damage, neuronal inclusions, and α-synuclein aggregation as well as the proteasomal dysfunction seen in PD. Thus, the rotenone model recapitulates most of the mechanisms apparently associated with PD pathogenesis. For this reason, neuroprotective drug treatment trials in this model may be more relevant to PD than other, more acute model systems. The major disadvantage of this model is the variability, with some animals showing lesions while others do not. However, the variability in individual responses to rotenone toxicity provides an opportunity to identify mechanisms involved in selective susceptibility/protection of dopaminergic neurons to complex I inhibition.

The paraquat model in mice demonstrates characteristic features of PD, including nigral dopaminergic cell death and α-synuclein aggregation, while the PQ-maneb model displays degeneration of nigral dopaminergic neurons. However, the selectivity and specificity of PQ- or PQ-maneb–induced toxicity remain to be elucidated. Furthermore, the changes observed in the striatum are subtle. Future studies, including the exposure of animals with a PD-related genetic predisposition to PQ and maneb, could be of interest.

ACKNOWLEDGMENTS

This work was supported by NIH grants NS38899 and ES012068 to JTG.

References

1. Klockgether T. Parkinson's disease: Clinical aspects. *Cell Tissue Res* 2004; 318(1):115–120.
2. Wooten GF. Neurochemistry and neuropharmacology of Parkinson's disease. In: Watts RL, Koller W. (eds). *Movement Disorders: Neurologic Principles and Practice* New York: McGraw-Hill, 1997:153–160.
3. Braak H Ghebrenedhin E, Rub U, et al. Stages in the development of Parkinson's disease–related pathology. *Cell Tissue Res* 2004; 318(1):121–134.
4. Albin RL, Young AB, Penney JB. The functional anatomy of basal ganglia disorders. *Trends Neurosci* 1989; 12(10):366–375.
5. Crossman AR. Neural mechanisms in disorders of movement. *Comp Biochem Physiol A* 1989; 93(1):141–149.
6. DeLong MR. Primate models of movement disorders of basal ganglia origin. *Trends Neurosci* 1990; 13(7)281–285.
7. Greenamyre JT. Glutamate-dopamine interactions in the basal ganglia: Relationship to Parkinson's disease. *J Neural Transm Genet Sect* 1993; 91(2–3):255–269.
8. Klockgether T, Turski L. Excitatory amino acids and the basal ganglia: Implications for the therapy of Parkinson's disease. *Trends Neurosci* 1989; 12(8):285–286.
9. Spillantini MG, Schmidt, ML, Lee VM, et al. Alpha-synuclein in Lewy bodies (letter). *Nature* 1997; 388(6645):839–840.
10. Braak H Braak E, Yilmazer D, et al. Nigral and extranigral pathology in Parkinson's disease. *J Neural Transm Suppl* 1995; 46:15–31.
11. Brown, TP Rumsby, PC, Capleton AC, et al. Pesticides and Parkinson's disease—Is there a link? *Environ Health Perspect* 2006; 114(2):156–164.
12. Dawson TM, Dawson VL. Molecular pathways of neurodegeneration in Parkinson's disease. *Science* 2003; 302(5646):819–822.
13. Logroscino G. The role of early life environmental risk factors in Parkinson disease: What is the evidence? *Environ Health Perspect* 2005; 113(9):1234–1238.
14. Polymeropoulos MH Lavedan C, Leroy E, et al. Mutation in the alpha-synuclein gene identified in families with parkinson's disease (see comments). *Science* 1997; 276(5321):2045–2047.
15. Irizarry MC Growden, W, Gomez-Isla T, et al. Nigral and cortical Lewy bodies and dystrophic nigral neurites in Parkinson's disease and cortical Lewy body disease contain alpha-synuclein immunoreactivity. *J Neuropathol Exp Neurol* 1998; 57(4):334–337.
16. Hattori N Matsumine, H, Asakawa S, et al. Point mutations (thr240arg and gln311stop) [correction of thr240arg and ala311stop] in the parkin gene [published erratum appears in *Biochem Biophys Res Commun* 1998 Oct 20;251(2):666]. *Biochem Biophys Res Commun* 1998; 249(3):754–758.
17. Kitada T Asakawa S, Hattori N, et al., Mutations in the parkin gene cause autosomal recessive juvenile parkinsonism (see comments). *Nature* 1998; 392(6676):605–608.
18. Lucking CB Abbas N, Durr A, et al. Homozygous deletions in parkin gene in European and North African families with autosomal recessive juvenile parkinsonism. The European Consortium on Genetic Susceptibility in Parkinson's Disease and the French Parkinson's Disease Genetics Study Group (letter). *Lancet* 1998; 352(9137):1355–1356.
19. Leroy E Boyer R, Auburger G, et al. The ubiquitin pathway in Parkinson's disease (letter). *Nature* 1998; 395(6701): 451–452.
20. McNaught KS Olanow CW, Halliwell B, et al. Failure of the ubiquitin-proteasome system in Parkinson's disease. *Nat Rev Neurosci* 2001; 2(8):589–594.
21. Mizuno Y Ohta S, Tanaka M, et al. Deficiencies in complex I subunits of the respiratory chain in Parkinson's disease. *Biochem Biophys Res Commun* 1989; 163(3):1450–1455.
22. Parker WD Jr, Boyson SJ, Parks JK. Abnormalities of the electron transport chain in idiopathic Parkinson's disease. *Ann Neurol* 1989: 26(6):719–723.
23. Schapira AH Cooper JM, Dexter D, et al. Mitochondrial complex I deficiency in Parkinson's disease (letter) (see comments). *Lancet* 1989: 1(8649):1269.
24. Cardellach F Marti MJ, Fernandez-Sola J, et al. Mitochondrial respiratory chain activity in skeletal muscle from patients with Parkinson's disease (see comments). *Neurology* 1993: 43(11):2258–2262.
25. Haas RH Nasirian F, Nakano K, et al. Low platelet mitochondrial complex I and complex II/III activity in early untreated Parkinson's disease. *Ann Neurol* 1995; 37(6):714–722.
26. Jenner P. Oxidative mechanisms in nigral cell death in parkinson's disease. *Mov Disord* 1998; 13(Suppl 1):24–34.
27. Valente EM Abou-Sleiman PM, Caputo V, et al. Hereditary early-onset Parkinson's disease caused by mutations in pink1. *Science* 2004; 304(5674):1158–1160.
28. Bonifati V Rizzu P, van Baren MJ, et al. Mutations in the DJ-1 gene associated with autosomal recessive early-onset parkinsonism. *Science* 2003; 299(5604): 256–259.
29. Yokata T Sugawara K, Ito, K, et al. Down regulation of DJ-1 enhances cell death by oxidative stress, ER stress and proteasome inhibition. *Biochem Biophys Res Commun* 2003; 312:1342–1348.
30. Canet-Aviles RM Wilson MA, Miller DW, et al. The Parkinson's disease protein DJ-1 is neuroprotective due to cysteine-sulfinic acid–driven mitochondrial localization. *Proc Natl Acad Sci USA* 2004; 101(24):9103–9108.

31. Paisan-Ruiz C Jain S, Evans EW, et al. Cloning of the gene containing mutations that cause park8-linked Parkinson's disease. *Neuron* 2004; 44(4):595–600.
32. Zimprich A Biskup S, Leitner P, et al. Mutations in LRRK2 cause autosomal-dominant parkinsonism with pleomorphic pathology. *Neuron* 2004; 44(4):601–607.
33. Gilks WP Abou-Sleiman PM, Gandhi S, et al. A common LRRK2 mutation in idiopathic parkinson's disease. *Lancet* 2005; 365(9457):415–416.
34. Gloeckner CJ Kinkl N, Schumacher A, et al. The Parkinson disease causing LRRK2 mutation i2020t is associated with increased kinase activity. *Hum Mol Genet* 2006; 15(2):223–232.
35. West AB Moore DJ, Biskup S, et al. Parkinson's disease–associated mutations in leucine-rich repeat kinase 2 augment kinase activity. *Proc Natl Acad Sci USA* 2005; 102(46):16842–16847.
36. Smith WW Pei Z, Jiang H, et al. Leucine-rich repeat kinase 2 (lrrk2) interacts with parkin, and mutant lrrk2 induces neuronal degeneration. *Proc Natl Acad Sci USA* 2005; 102(51):18676–18681.
37. Priyadarshi A Khuder SA, Schaub EA, et al. Environmental risk factors and Parkinson's disease: A metaanalysis. *Environ Res* 2001; 86(2):122–127.
38. Priyadarshi A Khuder SA, Schaub EA, et al. A meta-analysis of Parkinson's disease and exposure to pesticides. *Neurotoxicology* 2000; 21(4):435–440.
39. Seidler A Hellenbrand W, Robra BP, et al. Possible environmental, occupational, and other etiologic factors for Parkinson's disease: A case-control study in Germany. *Neurology* 1996; 46(5):1275–1284.
40. Hertzman C Wiens M, Snow B, et al. A case-control study of Parkinson's disease in a horticultural region of British Columbia. *Mov Disord* 1994; 9(1):69–75.
41. Liou HH Tsai MC, Chen CJ, et al. Environmental risk factors and Parkinson's disease: A case-control study in Taiwan. *Neurology* 1997; 48(6):1583–1588.
42. Firestone, JA Smith-Weller T, Franklin G, et al. Pesticides and risk of Parkinson disease: A population-based case-control study. *Arch Neurol* 2005; 62(1):91–95.
43. Abou-Sleiman PM, Muqit MM, Wood NW. Expanding insights of mitochondrial dysfunction in Parkinson's disease. *Nat Rev Neurosci* 2006; 7(3):207–219.
44. Greene JC Whitworth AJ, Kuo I, et al. Mitochondrial pathology and apoptotic muscle degeneration in *Drosophila* parkin mutants. *Proc Natl Acad Sci USA* 2003; 100(7):4078–4083.
45. Valente EM Bentivoglio AR, Dixon PH, et al. Localization of a novel locus for autosomal recessive early-onset parkinsonism, park6, on human chromosome 1p35-p36. *Am J Hum Genet* 2001; 68(4):895–900.
46. Zhang L Shimoji M, Thomas B, et al. Mitochondrial localization of the Parkinson's disease related protein DJ-1: Implications for pathogenesis. *Hum Mol Genet* 2005; 14(14):2063–2073.
47. Betarbet R Canet-Aviles RM, Sherer TB, et al. Intersecting pathways to neurodegeneration in Parkinson's disease: Effects of the pesticide rotenone on DJ-1, alpha-synuclein, and the ubiquitin-proteasome system. *Neurobiol Dis* 2006; 22(2):404–420.
48. McCormack AL Thiruchelvam M, Manning-Bog AB, et al. Environmental risk factors and Parkinson's disease: Selective degeneration of nigral dopaminergic neurons caused by the herbicide paraquat. *Neurobiol Dis* 2002; 10(2):119–127.
49. Thiruchelvam M Richfield EK, Baggs, RB, et al. The nigrostriatal dopaminergic system as a preferential target of repeated exposures to combined paraquat and maneb: Implications for parkinson's disease. *J Neurosci* 2000; 20(24):9207–9214.
50. Bindoff LA Birch-Machin M, Cartlidge NE, et al. Mitochondrial function in parkinson's disease (letter; comment). *Lancet* 1989; 2(8653):49.
51. Blin O Desnuelle C, Rascol O, et al. Mitochondrial respiratory failure in skeletal muscle from patients with Parkinson's disease and multiple system atrophy. *J Neurol Sci* 1994; 125(1):95–101.
52. Mann VM Cooper JM, Krige D, et al. Brain, skeletal muscle and platelet homogenate mitochondrial function in Parkinson's disease. *Brain* 1992: 115(Pt 2):333–342.
53. Mizuno Y Yoshino H, Ikebe S, et al. Mitochondrial dysfunction in Parkinson's disease. *Ann Neurol* 1998; 44(3 Suppl 1):S99–S109.
54. Shoffner Watts RL, Juncos JL, JM et al. Mitochondrial oxidative phosphorylation defects in Parkinson's disease (see comments). *Ann Neurol* 1991; 30(3):332–339.
55. Javitch JA D'Amato RJ, Strittmatter SM, et al. Parkinsonism-inducing neurotoxin, n-methyl-4-phenyl-1,2,3,6 -tetrahydropyridine: Uptake of the metabolite n-methyl-4-phenylpyridine by dopamine neurons explains selective toxicity. *Proc Natl Acad Sci USA* 1985; 82(7):2173–2177.
56. Nicklas WJ, Vyas I, Heikkila RE. Inhibition of NADH-linked oxidation in brain mitochondria by 1-methyl-4- phenyl-pyridine, a metabolite of the neurotoxin, 1-methyl-4-phenyl- 1,2,5,6-tetrahydropyridine. *Life Sci* 1985; 36(26):2503–2508.
57. Tipton KF, Singer TP. Advances in our understanding of the mechanisms of the neurotoxicity of MPTP and related compounds. *J Neurochem* 1993; 61(4):1191–1206.
58. Wallace DC. Diseases of the mitochondrial DNA. *Annu Rev Biochem* 1992; 61:1175–1212.
59. Ramsay RR Krueger MJ, Youngster SK, et al. Interaction of 1-methyl-4-phenylpyridinium ion (MPP+) and its analogs with the rotenone/piericidin binding site of NADH dehydrogenase. *J Neurochem* 1991; 56(4):1184–1190.
60. Hatefi Y. The mitochondrial electron transport and oxidative phosphorylation system. *Annu Rev Biochem* 1985; 54:1015–1069.
61. Greene JG, Greenamyre JT. Bioenergetics and glutamate excitotoxicity. *Prog Neurobiol* 1996; 48(6):613–634.
62. Hensley K Pye QN, Maidt ML, et al. Interaction of alpha-phenyl-n-tert-butyl nitrone and alternative electron acceptors with complex I indicates a substrate reduction site upstream from the rotenone binding site. *J Neurochem* 1998; 71(6):2549–2557.
63. Kushnareva Y, Murphy AN, Andreyev A. Complex I–mediated reactive oxygen species generation: Modulation by cytochrome c and NAD(P)+ oxidation-reduction state. Biochem J 2002; 368(Pt 2):545–553.
64. Cassarino DS Fall CP, Swerdlow RH, et al., Elevated reactive oxygen species and antioxidant enzyme activities in animal and cellular models of Parkinson's disease. *Biochim Biophys Acta* 1997; 1362(1):77–86.
65. Barrientos A, Moraes CT. Titrating the effects of mitochondrial complex I impairment in the cell physiology. *J Biol Chem* 1999; 274(23):16188–16197.
66. Dexter, DT Carter CJ, Wells FR, et al. Basal lipid peroxidation in substantia nigra is increased in Parkinson's disease. *J Neurochem* 1989; 52(2):381–389.
67. Yoritaka A Hattori N, Uchida K, et al. Immunohistochemical detection of 4-hydroxynonenal protein adducts in Parkinson disease. *Proc Natl Acad Sci USA* 1996; 93(7):2696–2701.
68. Floor E, Wetzel MG. Increased protein oxidation in human substantia nigra pars compacta in comparison with basal ganglia and prefrontal cortex measured with an improved dinitrophenylhydrazine assay. *J Neurochem* 1998; 70:268–275.
69. Sian J Dexter DT, Lees AJ, et al. Alterations in glutathione levels in Parkinson's disease and other neurodegenerative disorders affecting basal ganglia. *Ann Neurol* 1994; 36(3):348–355.
70. Nicolaou K Pfefferkorn J, Schuler F, et al. Combinatorial synthesis of novel and potent inhibitors of NADH:ubiquinone oxidoreductase. *Chem Biol* 2000; 7(12):979–992.
71. Schuler F, Casida JE. Functional coupling of PSST and ND1 subunits in NADH:ubiquinone oxidoreductase established by photoaffinity labeling. *Biochim Biophys Acta* 2001; 1506(1):79–87.
72. Uversky VN. Neurotoxicant-induced animal models of Parkinson's disease: Understanding the role of rotenone, maneb and paraquat in neurodegeneration. *Cell Tissue Res* 2004; 318(1):225–241.
73. Talpade DJ GreeneJG, Higgins DS.Jr et al. In vivo labeling of mitochondrial complex i (NADH:ubiquinone oxidoreductase) in rat brain using [(3)h]dihydrorotenone. *J Neurochem* 2000; 75(6):2611–2621.
74. Betarbet R Sherer TB, Mackenzie G, et al. Chronic systemic pesticide exposure reproduces features of Parkinson's disease *Nat Neurosci* 2000; 3(12):1301–1306.
75. Ferrante RJ Schulz JB, Kowall NW, et al. Systemic administration of rotenone produces selective damage in the striatum and globus pallidus, but not in the substantia nigra. *Brain Res* 1997; 753(1):157–162.
76. Lapointe N St-Hilaire M, Martinoli MG, et al. Rotenone induces non-specific central nervous system and systemic toxicity. *FASEB J* 2004; 18(6):717–719.
77. Sherer TB Kim JH, Betarbet R, et al. Subcutaneous rotenone exposure causes highly selective dopaminergic degeneration and alpha-synuclein aggregation. *Exp Neurol* 2003; 179(1):9–16.
78. Alam M, Schmidt WJ. Rotenone destroys dopaminergic neurons and induces parkinsonian symptoms in rats. *Behav Brain Res* 2002; 136(1):317–324.
79. Storch A, Ludolph AC, Schwarz J. Dopamine transporter: Involvement in selective dopaminergic neurotoxicity and degeneration. *J Neural Transm* 2004; 111(10–11):1267–1286.
80. Zhu C Vourc'h P, Fernagut PO, et al. Variable effects of chronic subcutaneous administration of rotenone on striatal histology. *J Comp Neurol* 2004; 478(4):418–426.
81. Hoglinger GU Feget J, Prigent A, et al. Chronic systemic complex I inhibition induces a hypokinetic multisystem degeneration in rats. *J Neurochem* 2003; 84(3):491–502.
82. Hornykiewicz O. Dopamine (3-hydroxytyramine) and brain function. *Pharmacol Rev* 1966; 18(2):925–964.
83. Na HM Betarbet R, Jim JH, et al. Rotenone models of Parkinson's disease selectively destroy striatal dopaminergic terminals and spare postsynaptic striatal neurons. *Soc Neurosci Abstr* 2003.
84. Sherer TB Betarbet R, Kim JH, et al. Selective microglial activation in the rat rotenone model of Parkinson's disease. *Neurosci Lett* 2003; 341(2):87–90.
85. Liberatore GT Jackson-Lewis V, Vukosavic S, et al. Inducible nitric oxide synthase stimulates dopaminergic neurodegeneration in the MPTP model of Parkinson disease. *Nat Med* 1999; 5(12):1403–1409.
86. Gao HM Jiang J, Wilson B, et al. Microglial activation–mediated delayed and progressive degeneration of rat nigral dopaminergic neurons: Relevance to Parkinson's disease. *J Neurochem* 2002; 81(6):1285–1297.
87. Sherer TB Betarbet R, Lund S, et al. An in vitro model of Parkinson's disease: Linking mitochondrial impairment to altered alpha-synuclein metabolism and oxidative damage. *J Neurosci* 2002; 22(16): p. 7006–7015.
88. Sherer TB Betarbet R, Testa CM, et al. Mechanism of toxicity in rotenone models of Parkinson's disease. *J Neurosci* 2003; 23(34):10756–10764.
89. Mitsumoto A Nakagawa Y. DJ-1 is an indicator for endogenous reactive oxygen species elicited by endotoxin. *Free Radic Res* 2001; 35(6):885–893.
90. Mitsumoto A Nakagawa Y, Takeuchi A, et al. Oxidized forms of peroxiredoxins and DJ-1 on two-dimensional gels increased in response to sublethal levels of paraquat. *Free Radic Res* 2001; 35(3):301–310.
91. Duda JE Giasson BI, Mabon ME, et al. Novel antibodies to synuclein show abundant striatal pathology in Lewy body diseases. *Ann Neurol* 2002; 52(2): 205–210.
92. Hoglinger GU Carrard G, Michel PP, et al. Dysfunction of mitochondrial complex I and the proteasome: Interactions between two biochemical deficits in a cellular model of Parkinson's disease. *J Neurochem* 2003; 86(5):1297–1307.
93. Shamoto-Nagai M Maruyama W, Kato Y, et al. An inhibitor of mitochondrial complex I, rotenone, inactivates proteasome by oxidative modification and induces aggregation of oxidized proteins in sh-sy5y cells. *J Neurosci Res* 2003; 74(4):589–597.
94. Coulom H, Birman S. Chronic exposure to rotenone models sporadic Parkinson's disease in *Drosophila melanogaster*. *J Neurosci* 2004; 24(48):10993–10998.
95. Snyder SH, D'Amato RJ. Predicting parkinson's disease. *Nature* 1985; 317(6034):198–199.
96. Shimizu K Ohtaki K, Matsubara K, et al. Carrier-mediated processes in blood–brain barrier penetration and neural uptake of paraquat. *Brain Res* 2001; 906(1–2):135–142.
97. Grant H, Lantos PL, Parkinson C. Cerebral damage in paraquat poisoning. *Histopathology* 1980; 4(2):185–195.

98. Hughes, J.T., Brain damage due to paraquat poisoning: A fatal case with neuropathological examination of the brain. Neurotoxicology 1988; 9(2):243–248.

99. Perry TL Yog VW, Wall RA, et al. Paraquat and two endogenous analogues of the neurotoxic substance n-methyl-4-phenyl-1,2,3,6-tetrahydropyridine do not damage dopaminergic nigrostriatal neurons in the mouse. *Neurosci Lett* 1986; 69(3): 285–289.

100. Brooks AI Chadwick CA, Gelbard HA, et al. Paraquat elicited neurobehavioral syndrome caused by dopaminergic neuron loss. Brain Res 1999; 823(1–2):1–10.

101. Manning-Bog AB McCormack AL, Li J, et al. The herbicide paraquat causes up-regulation and aggregation of alpha-synuclein in mice: Paraquat and alpha-synuclein. *J Biol Chem* 2002; 277(3):1641–1644.

102. Miller DB Reinhard JF, Daniels AJ, et al. Diethyldithiocarbamate potentiates the neurotoxicity of in vivo 1-methyl-4-phenyl-1,2,3,6-tetrahydropyridine and of in vitro 1-methyl-4-phenylpyridinium. *J Neurochem* 1991; 57(2):541–549.

103. Walters TL Irwin I, Delfani K, et al. Diethyldithiocarbamate causes nigral cell loss and dopamine depletion with nontoxic doses of MPTP. *Exp Neurol* 1999; 156(1):62–70.

104. Ferraz HB Bertolucci PK, Pereira JS, et al. Chronic exposure to the fungicide maneb may produce symptoms and signs of CNS manganese intoxication. *Neurology* 1988; 38(4):550–553.

105. Meco G Bonifati V, Vanacore N, et al. Parkinsonism after chronic exposure to the fungicide maneb (manganese ethylene-bis-dithiocarbamate). *Scand J Work Environ Health* 1994; 20(4):301–305.

106. Bove J Prou D, Perier C, et al. Toxin-induced models of Parkinson's disease. *NeuroRx* 2005; 2(3):484–494.

107. Higgins DS Jr, Greenamyre JT. [3h]dihydrorotenone binding to Nadh: Ubiquinone reductase (complex I) of the electron transport chain: An autoradiographic study. *J Neurosci* 1996; 16(12):3807–3816.

108. Cookson MR. Canet-Aviles R, Miller D, et al. DJ-I controls neuronal viability in response to mitochondrial damage. *Soc Neurosci Abstr* 2004.

109. Giasson BI Duda JE, Murray IV, et al. Oxidative damage linked to neurodegeneration by selective alpha-synuclein nitration in synucleinopathy lesions [in process citation]. *Science* 2000; 290(5493):985–989.

110. Krishnan S Chi EY, Wood SJ, et al. Oxidative dimer formation is the critical rate-limiting step for Parkinson's disease alpha-synuclein fibrillogenesis. *Biochemistry* 2003; 42(3):829–837.

111. Betarbet R Sherer TB, Lund S, et al. Rotenone models of Parkinson's disease: Altered proteasomal activity following sustained inhibition of complex i. *Soc Neurosci Abstr* 2003.

112. Reinheckel T Sitte N, Ullrich O, et al. Comparative resistance of the 20s and 26s proteasome to oxidative stress. *Biochem J* 1998; 335(Pt 3):637–642.

113. Keller JN Huang FF, Dimayuga ER, et al. Dopamine induces proteasome inhibition in neural pc12 cell line. *Free Radic Biol Med* 2000; 29(10):1037–1042.

114. Ciechanover A, Brundin P. The ubiquitin proteasome system in neurodegenerative diseases: Sometimes the chicken, sometimes the egg. *Neuron* 2003; 40(2):427–446.

115. Snyder H Mensah K, Theisler C, et al. Aggregated and monomeric alpha-synuclein bind to the s6' proteasomal protein and inhibit proteasomal function. *J Biol Chem* 2003; 278(14):11753–11759.

116. Day BJ Patel M, Calavetta L, et al. A mechanism of paraquat toxicity involving nitric oxide synthase. *Proc Natl Acad Sci USA* 1999; 96(22):12760–12765.

117. Przedborski S, Ischiropoulos H. Reactive oxygen and nitrogen species: Weapons of neuronal destruction in models of parkinson's disease. *Antioxid Redox Signal* 2005; 7(5–6):685–693.

118. Patel S Singh V, Kumar A, et al. Status of antioxidant defense system and expression of toxicant responsive genes in striatum of maneb- and paraquat-induced parkinson's disease phenotype in mouse: Mechanism of neurodegeneration. *Brain Res* 2006; 1081(1):9–18.

36 Inflammation

Ronald F. Pfeiffer

lthough much has been learned about Parkinson's disease (PD) since James Parkinson penned its first distinctive description, the events that trigger neuronal destruction and the processes that fuel its relentless progression remain uncertain.

Numerous theories regarding the possible etiology of PD, including both genetic and environmental causes, have been postulated. Epidemiologic studies have associated increased risk for the development of PD with a diverse array of occupations, including teaching and the medical professions (1, 2). A common thread connecting all occupations singled out for increased risk of PD has not been identified, but it has been suggested that repeated exposure to viral or other infections might link teachers and medical professionals (1). Although it is known that victims of von Economo's encephalitis could, sometimes decades later, develop postencephalitic parkinsonism, no specific infectious agent, viral or otherwise, has ever been clearly linked with the development of PD (3).

The pathology of PD has received exhaustive investigative attention, and progressive loss of nigrostriatal dopaminergic neurons with consequent striatal dopamine deficiency has been identified as the core abnormality accountable for the development of the primary motor features. It has been demonstrated that the neuronal damage in PD is not limited to the nigrostriatal dopaminergic

system but also engulfs other dopaminergic systems within the brain, other neurotransmitter systems, and even systems outside the central nervous system (CNS) such as the enteric nervous system; however, an explanation of what drives the relentless neuronal destruction has eluded firm identification. A number of theories have been advanced, including oxidative stress, excitotoxicity, proteasomal dysfunction, and others. Inflammatory mechanisms within the CNS have also been proposed. This chapter focuses on neuroinflammation and its potential role in the pathogenesis of PD.

INFLAMMATION IN THE BRAIN

It has traditionally been taught that the brain is an immunologically privileged organ, protected from systemic pathogens by the blood-brain barrier and unable to mount a significant immune response of its own. However, this is not true. The CNS is fully capable of generating a well-organized innate, or early-response immune reaction, as when faced with bacterial infection or other insults. This response originates in structures within the brain (median eminence, area postrema, subfornical organ and others) that lack a blood-brain barrier and act as immune sentinels for the brain. This response spreads from these regions to involve microglia within

449

the brain parenchyma (4). This initial immune response may evolve into an adaptive immune response designed to lead to long-term immune protection. In the periphery, the primary mediators of the innate immune response are macrophages, neutrophils, dendritic cells, and natural killer cells, while the adaptive immune response is marshaled by lymphocytes, divided into B cells, which generate the humoral immune response, and T cells, which are responsible for cell-mediated immune responses (4, 5). Within the CNS, the glial cells—specifically astrocytes and microglia—play a dominant though probably not exclusive role (6). Despite these differences, the CNS is capable of generating an active immune response, not only against acute attacks from foreign sources but also in response to processes that appear to originate from within the CNS itself.

An important aspect of the glial-based immune response within the CNS is the ability of glial cells to produce both destructive and protective mediators (7–10). In recent years, it has been recognized that disturbances in this delicate balance between neuronal nurturing and neuronal destruction may be the genesis of neurodegenerative diseases such as PD.

Astrocytes in Neuroinflammation

In the normal brain, astrocytes participate in the homeostatic control of the neuronal extracellular environment (11, 12). They are instrumental in maintaining extracellular potassium concentration and also play a role in uptake of synaptic transmitters and in maintenance of the blood-brain barrier (12, 13). When activated by injury or other insult, astrocytes take on additional duties that may protect surviving neighboring neurons by detoxifying (via the action of glutathione peroxidase) oxygen free radicals released by dying neurons, by removing excessive extracellular glutamate and by producing neurotrophic factors (8, 14, 15).

Microglia in Neuroinflammation

Approximately 10% to 13% of glial cells within the CNS are microglia (16–18). Microglia are not evenly distributed throughout the brain; their density is particularly high in the substantia nigra (19, 20). Under normal conditions, microglia are in a resting state and display a ramified, extensively branched morphology (21). Like astrocytes, microglia become activated by disturbances in their microenvironment and when activated assume an ameboid, macrophage-like appearance (22). They then express marker molecules, such as major histocompatibility complex (MHC) antigens and complement receptors, and they release proinflammatory molecules whose ingredients include reactive oxygen species, reactive nitrogen species, proinflammatory

prostaglandins, and cytokines such as tumor necrosis factor alpha (TNF-α) and interleukin-1beta (IL-1β) (13, 21, 23). In assuming these characteristics, microglia become phagocytic cells (24) and their actions promote the removal of dying cells and other cellular debris following injury, which are necessary functions in damage repair. In carrying out their phagocytotic mission, activated microglia also make use of the complement system (25) and develop the ability to present antigen to T cells (26). Products of activation of the complement system have been noted to be present in the setting of inflammation within the CNS, where the complement system can apparently be activated by molecules other than antibodies (17, 25, 27, 28).

NEUROINFLAMMATION IN PARKINSON'S DISEASE

Innate inflammatory responses are usually self-limited events, subsiding as the immunologic threat recedes and damage control and repair are completed. In certain situations within the CNS, however, the neuroinflammatory process appears to take on a life of its own and sustained activation of astrocytes and microglia is perpetuated, apparently indefinitely and with disastrous consequences, as presumably healthy neurons, which might be viewed as innocent bystanders in the vicinity of the activation, are ultimately attacked and destroyed in what in military terms would be called "collateral damage." Sustained glial activation has been documented in neurodegenerative disorders such as Alzheimer's disease (29) and PD (30) and also in individuals with parkinsonism induced by the toxin 1-methyl-4-phenyl-1, 2, 3, 6-tetrahydropyridine (MPTP) (31). It is uncertain whether this is the result of a sustained assault from an as yet unidentified pathogenic source or whether it reflects a smoldering, self-perpetuating immunologic reaction that, once kindled, feeds upon itself long after the primary insult has passed.

In PD, there is no indication that oligodendroglial cells participate in the pathologic process. It also appears that astrocytes play only a minor role. There is little evidence of prominent astrocytic activation in the substantia nigra of individuals with PD (8, 11, 32), although it has been suggested that astrocytes may mediate microglial proliferation, perhaps via release of the cytokine, granulocyte macrophage colony-stimulating factor (GM-CSF) (33), and that they release myeloperoxidase, an oxidant-producing enzyme that may produce dopamine neuronal damage (34). In contrast, a striking and robust increase in microglial activation has been consistently recognized, both in animal models of PD (35–37) and in autopsy studies of PD (30) or parkinsonism induced by MPTP (31). It is this microglial activation and proliferation that is recognized as the neuroinflammatory hallmark of PD.

Microglia in Parkinson's Disease

The recognition that microglial activation might be playing a role in PD is credited to McGeer and colleagues (30), who described prominent proliferation of HLA-DR-positive reactive microglia in the substantia nigra of 5 autopsy cases of PD and then expanded their observations in a string of reports and reviews (17, 23, 25, 38). Other investigators have further illuminated and expanded the picture of neuroinflammation in PD. Increased levels of a number of cytokines and other proteins—including TNF-α, IL-1β, IL-2, IL-4, IL-6, epidermal growth factor (EGF), transforming growth factor alpha (TGF-α), TGF-β1, and TGF-β2—have been identified in nigrostriatal regions of the brain and in the ventricular cerebrospinal fluid of individuals with PD, presumably erupting from activated microglia (39–45). It has been suggested that prolonged exposure to proinflammatory cytokines, such as IL-1β, may be necessary to trigger neuronal damage (46). Receptors for proinflammatory cytokines, such as TNF-α, are present on the cell bodies and processes of nigrostriatal neurons, which presumably render the neurons vulnerable to the cytotoxic effects of the cytokines released by the activated microglia (14, 21). Stimulation of these receptors may trigger or activate a caspase cascade that results in apoptotic death of the targeted neuron (47).

In addition to cytokines that attack the nigrostriatal neurons, microglial activation may also damage and destroy neurons by other mechanisms. Evidence of oxidative stress has been documented in postmortem examination of PD brains. Activated microglia produce both nitric oxide (NO) and superoxide, which can combine to form peroxynitrite, a highly reactive and destructive oxidant that reacts with DNA, proteins, and lipids to produce cellular damage and death (48). Perhaps more importantly, NO released from activated microglia can cross cell membranes and penetrate dopaminergic neurons, where it can react with superoxide produced within the neuron itself and inflict oxidative damage that eventually leads to neuronal destruction (11, 49). This has been demonstrated in MPTP-induced animal models of PD and has been hypothesized to occur in PD (48).

Other processes amplify and perpetuate the microglial onslaught against dopaminergic neurons in experimental models of PD. Cyclo-oxygenase (COX), which occurs in two isoforms (COX-1 and COX-2), is the rate-limiting enzyme in arachidonic acid–derived prostaglandin production (50, 51). Inflammation triggers increased COX-2 expression, with consequent increased production of prostaglandin-E2 (PGE2). Postmortem examination of the substantia nigra in PD demonstrates increased PGE2 content (52, 53). Reactive oxygen radicals are formed by this process (54) and could further fuel microglia-induced cellular damage. It has been suggested that PGE2 itself, via receptors located on microglia, may play a role in fomenting and perpetuating microglial activation (55).

Some investigators have suggested that the neuroinflammatory process in PD may actually not be entirely generated by neuronal and glial processes but also involve peripheral immune cells and even brain capillaries (15). The presence of T cells, presumably infiltrating the brain parenchyma from the circulatory system, has been conjectured on the basis of the identification of interferon-γ–positive cells within the substantia nigra of PD patients (56). The significance of the presence of these cells is uncertain, but it may indicate that the blood-brain barrier is actually modified or altered in some way in PD (56).

POTENTIAL THERAPEUTIC IMPLICATIONS

Contemporary treatment of PD is quite effective in ameliorating disease symptoms but does not alter the progression of the disease process. However, recognition of the role that neuroinflammation may be playing in PD has focused attention on the possibility that anti-inflammatory therapeutic approaches may offer a means to slow disease progression.

Anti-inflammatory drugs have been shown to protect against MPTP toxicity in animal models of PD. The tetracycline derivative minocycline possesses anti-inflammatory qualities distinct from its antibiotic actions. In MPTP-treated mice, investigators have reported that minocycline increased the survival of tyrosine hydroxylase–positive neurons in the substantia nigra in a dose-related fashion, decreased MPTP-mediated nitrotyrosine formation, inhibited MPTP-induced microglial activation, and reduced production of microglia-derived toxic mediators such as IL-1β (35). Others report that minocycline attenuates microglial activation but does not provide neuroprotection against MPTP insult (57). A possible explanation for these disparate results resides in differences in the MPTP dosing utilized by the two groups of investigators. Dexamethasone has also been shown to diminish glial reaction and reduce dopaminergic neuronal loss in MPTP-treated mice (58, 59).

Inhibition of COX has also provided neuroprotection in MPTP-exposed mice. Indomethacin, a nonspecific COX inhibitor, protects against MPTP-induced toxicity in mice by reducing microglial activation (60). Both meloxicam, a preferential COX-2 inhibitor, and acetylsalicylic acid, a nonspecific inhibitor, prevent nigral neuronal loss and preserve locomotor activity in this paradigm (61). The selective COX-2 inhibitor valdecoxib also attenuates MPTP-induced loss of both nigral dopaminergic neurons and striatal dopaminergic fibers and reduces microglial activation (51). Other investigators, however, have not been able to demonstrate an effect of COX-2 inhibition on microglial activation (53).

Valproic acid (VPA), a short-chain fatty acid used extensively in a number of neurologic and psychiatric disorders, has also been reported to possess anti-inflammatory and neuroprotective properties. In rat midbrain primary neuron-glial cell cultures exposed to lipopolysaccharide, VPA protected dopaminergic neurons by suppressing microglial activation and downregulating expression of proinflammatory factors, including TNF-α, NO, and reactive oxygen species (62). Other investigators have reported that VPA induces caspase-dependent microglial apoptosis (63). Valproic acid has also been demonstrated to upregulate expression of neurotrophic factors, such as brain-derived neurotrophic factor (BDNF) and glial cell line–derived neurotrophic factor (GDNF) in astrocytes and thus may actually possess a dual mechanism for protecting dopaminergic neurons, stimulating the neuroprotective properties of astrocytes while inhibiting the neurodestructive actions of microglia (64). It is worth noting, however, that there are anecdotal reports of VPA producing reversible parkinsonism in humans (65).

Information regarding the effects of anti-inflammatory drugs in PD is beginning to surface. Utilizing data from two large prospective cohorts—the Health Professionals Follow-Up Study involving 44,057 men and the Nurses' Health Study involving 98,845 women—Chen and colleagues documented that self-reported regular users of nonsteroidal anti-inflammatory drugs (NSAIDs) had a reduced risk of developing PD compared to nonregular users, with a relative risk of 0.55 (95% confidence interval, 0.32 to 0.96, $P = .04$) (66). In those who took 2 or more aspirin tablets daily, a non–statistically significant reduction in risk was also catalogued, with a relative risk of 0.56 but a 95% confidence interval of 0.26 to 1.21. In a population-based case-control study in which an automated pharmacy database was employed to document use of NSAIDs and aspirin or aspirin combination drugs, however, no correlation between the use of nonaspirin NSAIDs and PD was evident; only a nonsignificant reduction in risk among regular aspirin users was noted (67).

The frequent use of over-the-counter aspirin and other NSAIDs, however, complicates and potentially compromises interpretation of the results of this study. In another case-control study involving 196 individuals with PD and 196 matched controls, the use of NSAIDs was less in the PD group than in controls, but the difference did not reach statistical significance (68). Prospective controlled clinical trials of NSAIDs in PD have not yet been initiated.

Other drugs have also demonstrated efficacy in reducing microglial activation and providing protection to dopaminergic neurons in animal models of PD. Dextromethorphan, a dextrorotatory morphinan compound, protects against lipopolysaccharide-induced mesencephalic dopaminergic toxicity (69). Similar effects have been demonstrated with naloxone (70, 71). Formal clinical trials of these drugs as potential disease-modifying agents in humans have not yet been initiated, although dextromethorphan has been reported to ameliorate levodopa-induced dyskinesia via its activity as a glutamate antagonist (72, 73) and naloxone has been shown to reduce end-of-dose wearing off of levodopa efficacy but not to reduce dyskinesia (74).

Minocycline has been evaluated in a phase II randomized double-blind futility trial (75). Minocycline could not be rejected as futile in this trial and thus is considered a suitable candidate drug for further study in phase III clinical trials.

CONCLUSION

The recognition that a neuroinflammatory response is present in the substantia nigra of patients with PD and can be demonstrated in some animal models of PD has provided impetus for investigation into possible mechanisms of neuronal injury and death in PD. It has also opened up new vistas for potential treatment approaches that might alter progression of the disease process. The concept of neuroinflammation as part of PD has been an advance in our understanding of this neurodegenerative disorder.

References

1. Tsui JK, Calne DB, Wang Y, et al. Occupational risk factors in Parkinson's disease. Can J Public Health 1999; 90:334–337.
2. Goldman SM, Tanner CM, Olanow CW, et al. Occupation and parkinsonism in three movement disorders clinics. Neurology 2005; 65:1430–1435.
3. Arai H, Furuya T, Mizuno Y, et al. Inflammation and infection in Parkinson's disease. Histol Histopathol 2006; 21:673–678.
4. Nguyen MD, Julien J-P, Rivest S. Innate immunity: The missing link in neuroprotection and neurodegeneration? Nat Rev Neurosci 2002; 3:216–227.
5. Town T, Nikolic V, Tan J. The microglial "activation" continuum: From innate to adaptive responses. J Neuroinflam 2005; 2:24.
6. Streit WJ, Mrak RE, Griffin WST. Microglia and neuroinflammation: A pathological perspective. J Neuroinflam 2004; 1:14.
7. Morale MC, Serra PA, L'Episcopo F, et al. Estrogen, neuroinflammation and neuroprotection in Parkinson's disease: Glia dictates resistance versus vulnerability to neurodegeneration. Neuroscience 2006; 138:869–878.
8. Vila M, Jackson-Lewis V, Guégan C, et al. The role of glial cells in Parkinson's disease. Curr Opin Neurol 2001; 14:483–489.
9. Gao H-M, Liu B, Zhang W, et al. Novel anti-inflammatory therapy for Parkinson's disease. Trends Pharmacol Sci 2003; 24:395–401.
10. Liu B, Hong J-S. Role of microglia in inflammation-mediated neurodegenerative diseases: Mechanisms and strategies for therapeutic intervention. J Pharmacol Exp Ther 2003; 304:1–7.
11. Teismann P, Tieu K, Cohen O, et al. Pathogenic role of glial cells in Parkinson's disease. Mov Disord 2003; 18:121–129.
12. Wilkin GP, Knott C. Glia: A curtain raiser. Adv Neurol 1999; 80:3–7.
13. Teismann P, Schulz JB. Cellular pathology of Parkinson's disease: Astrocytes, microglia and inflammation. Cell Tissue Res 2004; 318:149–161.
14. Hirsch EC, Hunot S, Damier P, et al. Glial cell participation in the degeneration of dopaminergic neurons in Parkinson's disease. Adv Neurol 1999; 80:9–18.
15. Hirsch EC, Hunoy S, Hartmann A. Neuroinflammatory processes in Parkinson's disease. Parkinsonism Relat Disord 2005; 11:S9–S15.

16. Hayes GM, Woodroofe MN, Cuzner ML. Microglia are the major cell type expressing MHC class II in human white matter. *J Neurol Sci* 1987; 80:25–37.

17. McGeer PL, McGeer EG. Inflammation and neurodegeneration in Parkinson's disease. *Parkinsonism Relat Disord* 2004; 10:S3–S7.

18. Kim YS, Joh TH. Microglia, major player in the brain inflammation: Their roles in the pathogenesis of Parkinson's disease. *Exp Mol Med* 2006; 38:333–347.

19. Lawson LJ, Perry VH, Dri P, et al. Heterogeneity in the distribution and morphology of microglia in the normal adult mouse brain. *Neuroscience* 1990; 39:151–170.

20. Kim W-G, Mohney RP, Wilson B, et al. Regional difference in susceptibility to lipopolysaccharide-induced neurotoxicity in the rat brain: Role of microglia. *J Neurosci* 2000; 20:6309–6316.

21. Hald A, Lotharius J. Oxidative stress and inflammation in Parkinson's disease: Is there a causal link? *Exp Neurol* 2005; 193:279–290.

22. Kreutzberg GW. Microglia: A sensor for pathological events in the CNS. *Trends Neurosci* 1996; 19:312–318.

23. McGeer EG, Klegeris A, McGeer PL. Inflammation, the complement system and the diseases of aging. *Neurobiol Aging* 2005; 26S:S94–S97.

24. Hayes GM, Woodroofe MN, Cuzner ML. Characterization of microglia isolated from adult human and rat brain. *J Neuroimmunol* 1988; 19:177–189.

25. McGeer PL, Yasojima K, McGeer EG. Inflammation in Parkinson's disease. *Adv Neurol* 2001; 86:83–89.

26. Cross AK, Woodroofe MN. Immunoregulation of microglial functional properties. *Microsc Res Tech* 2001; 54:10–17.

27. Loeffler DA, Camp DM, Conant SB. Complement activation in the Parkinson's disease substantia nigra: An immunocytochemical study. *J Neuroinflam* 2006; 3:29.

28. Bonifati DM, Kishore U. Role of complement in neurodegeneration and neuroinflammation. *Mol Immunol* 2007; 44:999–1010.

29. McGeer EG, McGeer PL. Inflammatory processes in Alzheimer's disease. *Prog Neuropsychopharmacol Biol Psychiatry* 2003; 27:741–749.

30. McGeer PL, Itagaki S, Boyes BE, et al. Reactive microglia are positive for HLA-DR in the substantia nigra of Parkinson's and Alzheimer's disease brains. *Neurology* 1988; 38:1285–1291.

31. Langston JW, Forno LS, Tetrud J, et al. Evidence of active nerve cell degeneration in the substantia nigra of humans years after 1-methyl-4-phenyl-1,2,3,6-tetrahydropyridine exposure. *Ann Neurol* 1999; 46:598–605.

32. Mirza B, Hadberg H, Thomsen P, et al. The absence of reactive astrocytosis is indicative of a unique inflammatory process in Parkinson's disease. *Neuroscience* 2000; 95:425–432

33. Henze C, Hartmann A, Lescot T, et al. Proliferation of microglial cells induced by 1-methyl-4-phenylpyridinium in mesencephalic cultures results from an astrocyte-dependent mechanism: Role of granulocyte macrophage colony-stimulating factor. *J Neurochem* 2005; 95:1069–1077.

34. Choi D-K, Pennathur S, Perier C, et al. Ablation of the inflammatory enzyme myeloperoxidase mitigates features of Parkinson's disease in mice. *J Neurosci* 2005; 28:6594–6600.

35. Wu DC, Jackson-Lewis V, Vila M, et al. Blockade of microglial activation is neuroprotective in the 1-methyl-4-phenyl-1,2,3,6-tetrahydropyridine mouse model of Parkinson disease. *J Neurosci* 2002; 22:1763–1771.

36. McGeer PL, Schwab C, Parent A, Doudet D. Presence of reactive microglia in monkey substantia nigra years after 1-methyl-4-phenyl-1,2,3,6-tetrahydropyridine administration. *Ann Neurol* 2003; 54:599–604.

37. Sherer TB, Betarbet R, Kim JH, et al. Selective microglial activation in the rat rotenone model of Parkinson's disease. *Neurosci Lett* 2003; 341:87–90.

38. McGeer PL, Itagaki S, Akiyama H, McGeer EG. Rate of cell death in parkinsonism indicates active neuropathological process. *Ann Neurol* 1988; 24:574–576.

39. Mogi M, Harada M, Riederer P, et al. Tumor necrosis factor-alpha (TNF-alpha) increases both in the brain and in the cerebrospinal fluid from parkinsonian patients. *Neurosci Lett* 1994; 165:208–210.

40. Mogi M, Harada M, Kondo T, et al. Interleukin-1 beta, interleukin-6, epidermal growth factor and transforming growth factor-alpha are elevated in the brain from parkinsonian patients. *Neurosci Lett* 1994; 180:147–150.

41. Mogi M, Harada M, Narabayashi H, et al. Interleukin (IL)-1β, IL-2, IL-4, IL-6 and transforming growth factor-α levels are elevated in ventricular cerebrospinal fluid in juvenile parkinsonism and Parkinson's disease. *Neurosci Lett* 1996; 211:13–16.

42. Nagatsu T, Mogi M, Ichinose H, et al. Cytokines in Parkinson's disease. *J Neural Transm Suppl* 2000; (58):143–151.

43. Nagatsu T, Mogi M, Ichinose H, et al. Changes in cytokines and neurotrophins in Parkinson's disease. *J Neural Transm Suppl* 2000; (70):277–290.

44. Nagatsu T, Sawada M. Inflammatory process in Parkinson's disease: Role for cytokines. *Curr Pharm Des* 2005; 11:999–1016.

45. Sawada M, Imamura K, Nagatsu T. Role of cytokines in inflammatory process in Parkinson's disease. *J Neural Transm Suppl* 2006; (70):373–381.

46. Ferrari CC, Pott Godoy MC, Tarelli R, et al. Progressive neurodegeneration and motor disabilities induced by chronic expression of IL-1β in the substantia nigra. *Neurobiol Dis* 2006; 24:183–193.

47. Kaufmann SH, Hengartner MO. Programmed cell death: Alive and well in the new millennium. *Trends Cell Biol* 2001; 11:526–534.

48. Przedborski S, Jackson-Lewis V, Vila M, et al. Free radical and nitric oxide toxicity in Parkinson's disease. *Adv Neurol* 2003; 91:83–94.

49. Przedborski S, Jackson-Lewis V, Yokoyama R, et al. Role of neuronal nitric oxide in 1-methyl-4phenyl-1,2,3,6-tetrahydropyridine (MPTP)–induced dopaminergic neurotoxicity. *Proc Natl Acad Sci USA* 1996; 93:4565–4571.

50. Samuelsson B. Arachidonic acid metabolism: Role in inflammation. *Z Zeitschrifte Für Rheumatol* 1991; 50(Suppl 1):3–6.

51. Vijitruth R, Liu M, Choi D-Y, et al. Cyclooxygenase-2 mediates microglial activation and secondary dopaminergic cell death in the mouse MPTP model of Parkinson's disease. *J Neuroinflammation* 2006; 3:6.

52. Mattammal MB, Strong R, Lakshmi VM, et al. Prostaglandin H synthetase-mediated metabolism of dopamine: Implication for Parkinson's disease. *J Neurochem* 1995; 64:1645–1654.

53. Teismann P, Tieu K, Choi D-K, et al. Cyclooxygenase-2 is instrumental in Parkinson's disease neurodegeneration. *Proc Natl Acad Sci* 2003; 100:5473–5478.

54. Nikolic D, van Breemen RB. DNA oxidation induced by cyclooxygenase-2. *Chem Res Toxicol* 2001; 14:351–354.

55. Jin J, Shie F-S, Liu J, et al. Prostaglandin E₂ receptor subtype 2 (EP2) regulates microglial activation and associated neurotoxicity induced by aggregated α-synuclein. *J Neuroinflam* 2007; 4:2.

56. Hunot S, Hirsch EC. Neuroinflammatory processes in Parkinson's disease. *Ann Neurol* 2003; 53(Suppl 3):S49–S60.

57. Sriram K, Miller DB, O'Callaghan JP. Minocycline attenuates microglial activation but fails to mitigate striatal dopaminergic neurotoxicity: Role of tumor necrosis factor-α. *J Neurochem* 2006; 96:706–718.

58. Kurkowska-Jastrzebska I, Litwin T, Joniec I, et al. Dexamethasone protects against dopaminergic neurons damage in a mouse model of Parkinson's disease. *Int Immunopharmacol* 2004; 4:1307–1318.

59. Kurkowska-Jastrzebska I, Wronska A, Kohutnicka M, et al. The inflammatory reaction following 1-methyl-4-phenyl-1,2,3,6-tetrahydropyridine intoxication in mouse. *Exp Neurol* 1999; 156:50–61.

60. Kurkowska-Jastrzebska I, Babiuch M, Joniec I, et al. Indomethacin protects against neurodegeneration caused by MPTP intoxication in mice. *Int Immunopharmacol* 2002; 2:1213–1218.

61. Teismann P, Ferger B. Inhibition of the cyclooxygenase isoenzymes COX-1 and COX-2 provides neuroprotection in the MPTP-mouse model of Parkinson's disease. *Synapse* 2001; 39:167–174.

62. Peng GS, Li G, Tzeng NS, et al. Valproate pretreatment protects dopaminergic neurons from LPS-induced neurotoxicity in rat primary midbrain cultures: Role of microglia. *Brain Res Mol Brain Res* 2005; 134:162–169.

63. Dragunow M, Greenwood JM, Cameron RE, et al. Valproic acid induces caspase 3-mediated apoptosis in microglial cells. *Neuroscience* 2006; 140:1149–1156.

64. Chen P-S, Peng G-S, Li G, et al. Valproate protects dopaminergic neurons in midbrain neuron/glia cultures by stimulating the release of neurotrophic factors from astrocytes. *Mol Psychiatry* 2006; 11:1116–1125.

65. Armon C, Shin C, Miler P, et al. Reversible parkinsonism and cognitive impairment with chronic valproate use. *Neurology* 1996; 47:626–635.

66. Chen H, Zhang SM, Hernan MA, et al. Nonsteroidal anti-inflammatory drugs and the risk of Parkinson disease. *Arch Neurol* 2003; 60:1059–1064.

67. Ton TG, Heckbert SR, Longstreth WT, et al. Nonsteroidal anti-inflammatory drugs and risk of Parkinson's disease. *Mov Disord* 2006; 21:964–969.

68. Bower JH, Maraganore DM, Peterson BJ, et al. Immunologic diseases, anti-inflammatory drugs, and Parkinson disease: A case-control study. *Neurology* 2006; 67:494–496.

69. Liu Y, Qin L, Li G, et al. Dextromethorphan protects dopaminergic neurons against inflammation-mediated degeneration through inhibition of microglial activation. *J Pharmacol Exp Ther* 2003; 305:212–218.

70. Lu X, Bing G, Hagg T. Naloxone prevents microglia-induced degeneration of dopaminergic substantia nigra neurons in adult rats. *Neuroscience* 2000; 97:285–291.

71. Liu B, Du L, Hong J-S. Naloxone protects rat dopaminergic neurons against inflammatory damage through inhibition of microglial activation and superoxide generation. *J Pharmacol Exp Ther* 2000; 293:607–617.

72. Verhagen Metman L, Blanchet PJ, van den Munckhof P, et al. A trial of dextromethorphan in parkinsonian patients with motor response complications. *Mov Disord* 1998; 13:414–417.

73. Verhagen Metman L, Del Dotto P, Natte R, et al. Dextromethorphan improves levodopa-induced dyskinesias in Parkinson's disease. *Neurology* 1998; 51:203–206.

74. Fox S, Silverdale M, Kellett M, et al. Non-subtype-selective opioid receptor antagonism in treatment of levodopa-induced motor complications in Parkinson's disease. *Mov Disord* 2004; 19:554–560.

75. NINDS NET-PD Investigators. A randomized, double-blind, futility clinical trial of creatine and minocycline in early Parkinson disease. *Neurology* 2006; 66:664–671.

37 Genetics

Denise M. Kay
Jennifer S. Montimurro
Haydeh Payami

PARADIGM SHIFT: ENVIRONMENT VERSUS GENES

In 1817, James Parkinson theorized that "shaking palsy" might be a result of stress (1); 50 years later, this was reiterated by Charcot (see Chapter 3). A familial component to Parkinson's disease (PD) was proposed by Gowers more than 70 years later (2). In the century that followed, many studies reported familial clustering of PD, but they were later dismissed because of confounding by selection bias, diagnostic uncertainties, and methodologic limitations. Up until the last decade, PD was believed to be an environmentally caused disorder with little or no genetic component. The nongenetic dogma was challenged in the 1990s by a series of sophisticated family studies that approached PD genetics from two angles: the identification of families with inherited Mendelian forms of PD and case-control familial aggregation studies designed to assess the genetic contribution to typical forms of PD.

Mendelian Parkinson's Disease

Both autosomal dominant and autosomal recessive forms of PD have been described (Table 37-1). The significance of identifying such families is 2-fold: they provide the most convincing evidence for the existence of a disease gene and they lend themselves to linkage analysis, which is the most powerful method of gene discovery. The best-known example of autosomal dominant PD is the Contursi kindred, a well-characterized family with 60 affected individuals spanning several consecutive generations (3). One glance at this pedigree and there is little doubt that an autosomal dominant gene is at play. The Contursi kindred took decades to characterize, but the gene responsible for disease, α-synuclein (*SNCA*), took only a few months to find. Continued work on additional autosomal dominant pedigrees has led to the discovery of genetic linkage to *UCH-L1, LRRK2, NR4A2,* and *SNCAIP*. Autosomal recessive disease is less obvious because it does not show a vertical transmission pattern, and each family may have only one or few affected individuals. Autosomal recessive juvenile parkinsonism (AR-JP) was best illustrated by consanguineous families with multiple occurrences of juvenile-onset parkinsonism, in which the affected individuals are identical by descent and homozygous for an ancestral mutation (4). The proof of principle for autosomal recessive genes was the discovery of *parkin*, followed by *PINK1* and *DJ-1*.

Evidence for a Genetic Component in Typical Parkinson's Disease

More than 70% of PD patients report no prior family history of PD. It is generally believed that nonfamilial

TABLE 37-1
Parkinson's Disease Genes and Loci

LOCUS (GENE)	CHROMOSOMAL LOCUS	ENCODED PROTEIN	PUTATIVE FUNCTION	MODE OF INHERITANCE	AGE AT ONSET	PATHOGENIC MUTATIONS
PARK1, PARK4 (SNCA)	4q21-23	α-synuclein	Unknown; major component of LB	AD	Middle	Point mutations, whole-gene multiplications
PARK2 (parkin)	6q25.2-27	Parkin	Ubiquitin E3 ligase in the UPS	AR	Juvenile, early	Point mutations, exon deletions and multiplications
PARK3	2p13	Not identified	NA	AD	Late	NA
PARK5 (UCH-L1)	4p14	UCH-L1 (ubiquitin carboxy-terminal hydrolase L1)	Ubiquitin hydrolase in the UPS	AD	Middle	Point mutation
PARK6 (PINK1)	1p35-36	PINK1 (PTEN-induced kinase 1)	mitochondrial kinase	AR	Early	Point mutations, exon deletions, multiplications
PARK7 (DJ-1)	1p36	DJ-1	Redox sensor; protection against oxidative stress	AR	Early	Point mutation, deletion
PARK8 (LRRK2)	12q12	LRRK2 (leucine-rich repeat kinase 2/Dardarin)	protein kinase	AD	Early, middle, late	Point mutations
NR4A2	2q22-23	Nurr1 (nuclear-related receptor 1)	Important in differentiation/ maintenance of dopaminergic neurons; transcription activation	AD	Late	Point mutation, deletion
PARK10	1p32	Not identified	NA	Susceptibility locus	Late	NA
PARK11	2q36-37	Not identified	NA	Susceptibility locus	Late	NA

AD, autosomal dominant; AR, autosomal recessive; NA, not applicable/unknown.

PD is the result of small but cumulative effects of genes and environment. However, as was shown recently, with the discovery of the *LRRK2* G2019S mutation, that even sporadic PD could be due to a highly penetrant Mendelian mutation.

A twin study conducted in 1999 showed an increased monozygotic (MZ) concordance rate for early- but not late-onset PD, suggesting that genetic factors play a major role in early- but not late-onset disease (5). However [18F]-dopa PET studies in twins discordant for PD find substantially higher concordance in subclinical disease in MZ twins than in dizygotic (DZ) twins even in later-onset disease (6). Hence, estimation of disease concordance by clinical examination in twins may not be optimal for studies of complex disease, in which environmental triggers may be required to push subclinical disease to symptom manifestation; this may not occur until very late in life. Thus the lack of evidence from twin studies should not be taken as an absence of a genetic component in late-onset PD. In fact, all other lines of evidence appear to point to a significant genetic contribution.

A study performed in the Icelandic population traced the genealogical information on 600,000 people over 11 centuries and found that individuals who developed late-onset PD were significantly more related to each other than were subjects in matched groups of controls (7). The estimated risk ratio was 6.7 for siblings and 3.2 for the offspring of patients. Furthermore, 12 case-control familial aggregation studies have been conducted in the United States and Europe; 11 of 12 showed a significantly higher risk for relatives of patients, suggesting a genetic component (8–18). The relative risk ranges from 2.3-fold for an ethnically mixed community in New York (12) to 41-fold for an Italian population (15). The variation among studies may partly reflect genetic differences among ethnic groups and/or geographic differences in exposure to environmental factors. If a patient has early-onset PD, the risk to relatives is elevated 8-fold and 3-fold if a patient has late-onset PD (16). The increased risk to relatives is too high, even for late-onset PD, to be attributed solely to nongenetic familial factors, such as shared environment. Four complex segregation analyses have been performed to test various genetic and environmental models in PD (19–22). All have rejected the purely environmental model in favor of a genetic model. Two studies that examined age at onset found stronger evidence for genes that affect age at onset than genes that affect disease susceptibility (21, 22).

PARKINSON'S DISEASE GENES

PARK1: α-Synuclein (SNCA)

The first major breakthrough in PD genetics came in 1996–1997: the mapping and subsequent identification of the PD-causing mutation in the Contursi kindred. The locus, PARK1, was localized to chromosome 4q21-23 by means of a genome scan in late 1996 (23). Shortly after, a G209A mutation in the SNCA gene (encoding α-synuclein) was shown to be responsible for the PD phenotype in the Contursi kindred and 3 other Greek families (24). The G209A mutation, which results in an Ala to Thr substitution at amino acid 53 (A53T), segregated with disease in the families and was not detected in unrelated control subjects or in patients with sporadic PD. These data provided the first evidence that α-synuclein must somehow be important in PD pathogenesis. The G209A mutation has since been identified in additional Greek families (25–29) and a Greek-American pedigree with apparent anticipation (30). Because families with the

A53T mutation are descendants of individuals born in Greece or southern Italy, a common founder has been suggested (25).

Soon after the discovery of the A53T mutation, a G88C transversion (encoding A30P) was identified in a 52-year-old patient and shown to cosegregate with disease in a small autosomal dominant German kindred with apparently reduced penetrance (31). The mutation was not present in several hundred screened controls, so it could be concluded that the mutation was likely pathogenic. Only one other SNCA point mutation (G188A, resulting in E46K) has been described that segregates with disease and is absent in controls (32). The search for SNCA mutations in various PD subtypes (i.e., early- and late-onset, familial and sporadic PD) has continued since its identification as a PD gene. However, pathogenic SNCA mutations are rare, and even studies using large cohorts or studies enriched with early-onset autosomal dominant families with phenotypes resembling those in the Contursi kindred rarely find mutations.

Triplication of the entire SNCA gene can also cause PD, as was shown in the Spellman-Muenter Iowa kindred (33). SNCA triplication and duplication mutations were subsequently found in families exhibiting autosomal dominant inheritance from diverse origins [Swedish-American (34), French, Italian, and Japanese (35–37)]. The sizes of the duplicated and triplicated regions are variable, indicating de novo rearrangements (35, 37). The triplication/duplication mutations were originally thought to represent a novel locus on the short arm of chromosome 4 and thus were assigned PARK4, but they turned out to be mutations in the same gene as PARK1.

The clinical picture of SNCA mutation carriers can vary but in general, resembles idiopathic PD. The clinical phenotype in the Contursi kindred is consistent with idiopathic PD, although tremor is often absent. Most affected individuals had an early onset of disease (average 46 years), good response to levodopa therapy, and a rapid and aggressive course. Parkinson's disease was pathologically confirmed for several affected family members in the Contursi kindred. The Iowa kindred, which has a triplication mutation, had early-onset (average 34 years) levodopa-responsive disease. In general, the onset age of SNCA mutation carriers is relatively early, but tremor is often not a predominant characteristic (28). Additional clinical features have been described, including myoclonus, progressive cognitive decline, variation in symptom onset, severity, and duration, and severity of brainstem pathologic features (38). The phenotype of A30P mutation carriers is also similar to that of sporadic idiopathic PD (39). Studies with positron emission tomography (PET) have shown that nigrostriatal dysfunction in carriers of the SNCA A53T (40) and A30P (39) mutation is similar to that of idiopathic PD patients. E46K has been identified in only one autosomal dominant Spanish family with typical age at onset (range 50 to 65), severe parkinsonism, and pathology consistent with Lewy body dementia (DLB) (32).

Disease caused by *SNCA* multiplication can present as idiopathic PD, PD with dementia, or DLB (34–37, 41). Duplication of *SNCA* has been reported to cause disease in families with autosomal dominant PD, all with clinical phenotypes resembling typical later-onset PD without prominent or early cognitive decline or dementia (35–37). *SNCA* triplication has a clinical and pathologic phenotype ranging from typical PD to dementia with psychosis (34, 41). Thus it is thought that the severity of PD could be correlated with *SNCA* copy number.

The *SNCA* gene consists of 6 exons spanning about 112 kb on the long arm of chromosome 4. It encodes α-synuclein, a 140–amino acid heat-stable protein (42) whose function is largely unknown. α-synuclein is the major component of Lewy bodies (LB) and Lewy neurites (LN) (43, 44). The N-terminal region of the protein contains a well-conserved imperfect repeat motif through which it may bind phospholipid membranes (45). α-synuclein is natively unfolded (46) but can polymerize into amyloid fibrils and protofibrils (nonfibrillary oligomers). This presynaptic nerve terminal protein was originally identified as a precursor for the non-Aβ-amyloid component (*NACP*) of amyloid plaques characteristic of Alzheimer's disease (AD) (47). *NACP* was later renamed *SNCA* due to its resemblance to brain synucleins in other organisms (48). *SNCA* point mutations have been shown to have altered protein activity, which can lead to increased α-synuclein accumulation in vitro (49, 50). The fact that triplication and duplication of a normal gene can cause disease also suggests that overexpression of α-synuclein and abnormal protein accumulation and aggregation may be at the root of dopaminergic neuronal loss leading to PD.

PARK2: Parkin (*parkin*)

A gene responsible for AR-JP was localized to chromosome 6q25.2-27 (*PARK2*) in 1997 (51). Homozygous deletions in *parkin*, a novel gene, were identified in a Japanese consanguineous family with AR-JP (4). Many types of mutations (more than 90) have since been identified, ranging in size from single-bp substitutions to small insertions and deletions and large exonic deletions or multiplications (4, 52, 53). A recent study of recessive early-onset (at or below 45 years) and sporadic early-onset (at or below 40 years) PD found *parkin* mutations in 21% of sporadic cases and in 53% of recessive cases (54), which is in line with other reports.

Since its discovery as a cause of AR-JP, the *parkin* gene has been analyzed in patients with typical PD, and variants have been found in virtually every disease subtype [early- and late-onset, familial and sporadic PD (55–57)].

The frequency of mutations decreases with increasing age at onset (54, 58). Whether a single heterozygous mutation can cause or increase the risk of typical late-onset PD (i.e., fully or partially dominant) remains an issue of debate (56, 59–62). The true population-attributable risk due to mutation of the *parkin* gene will remain largely unknown until the pathogenicity of heterozygous mutations is resolved.

The *parkin* gene is one of the largest known human genes with 12 exons spanning more than 500 kb (4). The gene is contained within *FRA6E*, one of the most common fragile sites in the human genome (63), and encodes a 465–amino acid protein. In AR-JP, mutations are either homozygous or heterozygous for 2 different mutant alleles (compound heterozygous), suggesting that loss of Parkin function results in disease. The Parkin protein contains several domains, including an N-terminal ubiquitin-like domain followed by a unique Parkin domain and a RING motif thought to be important for substrate interactions. Transcripts of *parkin* are expressed throughout the human brain, including the substantia nigra (4). Parkin functions as an E3-ubiquitin ligase, which specifically catalyzes the addition of ubiquitin to proteins, targeting them for degradation by the 26S proteasome (64, 65). Thus, *parkin*-disease may result from a defect in the ubiquitin-proteasome protein degradation pathway (UPS), in which toxic accumulation of Parkin substrates may contribute to dopaminergic cell death. Many proteins that interact with and are ubiquitinated by Parkin in vitro have been identified (66, 67), and some *parkin* mutations result in a decrease in such ubiquitin ligase activity (64, 65, 68). Parkin also appears to play a role in oxidative stress and mitochondrial function (see Chapter 29).

Patients with *parkin*-PD are most often levodopa-responsive; they have an early disease onset and relatively slow disease progression. Additional clinical features are often present, including dystonia, hyperreflexia, diurnal fluctuations, sleep benefit, and levodopa-induced dyskinesias (4, 69–71). Brains of AR-JP patients show neuronal degeneration in the substantia nigra and locus ceruleus and gliosis, but LBs are often absent (72). However, patients with compound heterozygous *parkin* mutations and LBs or tau pathology have been reported (62, 73, 74).

PARK3

PARK3 was mapped to chromosome 2p13 in European families with autosomal dominant PD (75). The phenotype resembled typical late-onset PD (average 59 years). The penetrance was below 40%; therefore *PARK3* was suggested to be a susceptibility locus. Four genome-wide linkage studies have provided further evidence for *PARK3*: 2 studies showed evidence for association with age at onset (76, 77), 1 showed association with risk (78), and 1 showed evidence for association with both risk and age at onset (79). The gene has not yet been identified.

PARK4: α-synuclein (SNCA)

A genome-wide screen in a large, well-characterized kindred (Spellman-Muenter Iowa kindred) with early-onset levodopa-responsive autosomal dominant parkinsonism revealed a common haplotype on chromosome 4p15 (PARK4), which segregated with PD and postural tremor (80–83). Since the locus was near SNCA, the authors screened for SNCA point mutations; however, none were found and PARK4 was considered a novel PD locus. It was later determined that triplication of SNCA (along with 16 other flanking putative genes) was in fact the cause of disease in this family (33). therefore the PARK4 locus is not different from PARK1 (SNCA).

PARK5: Ubiquitin C-Terminal Hydrolase L1 (UCH-L1)

The UPS pathway was implicated in PD pathogenesis after the identification of parkin. Consequently, UCH-L1 became a candidate gene for PD because of its central function in the UPS system. The UCH-L1 gene, on chromosome 4p14 (84), contains 9 exons encoding the ubiquitin carboxy-terminal hydrolase L1 (UCH-L1) protein. UCH-L1 is an ε1 enzyme that catalyzes the disassembly of ubiquitin-protein conjugates (deubiquitylation) formed during normal protein metabolism (85) and also possesses ubiquityl ligase (ε3) activity (86). A defect or alteration in UCH-L1 could therefore result in an overall defect in the UPS, leading to abnormal clearance of misfolded or damaged proteins and protein aggregate formation. UCH-L1 is prone to aggregation, particularly when proteasomal activity is reduced, and colocalizes with both Parkin and α-synuclein in some protein inclusions (87). It has been shown that UCH-L1 undergoes extensive oxidative modifications, in support of the theory that PD pathogenesis can result from oxidative damage (88). The gad (gracile axonal dystrophy) mouse (89), which has sensory and motor neuron degeneration and ubiquitin-positive neuronal inclusions, is a result of UCH-L1 truncation (90). The abundance of UCH-L1 protein in human brain (about 2% of all soluble brain protein) (85, 91), its presence in LBs along with abnormally aggregated α-synuclein protein (92), and its role in the ubiquitin-dependent proteolytic pathway support its theoretical role in the pathogenesis of PD (93). Genetic linkage, however, has been equivocal. Sequencing of the coding regions of UCH-L1 led to the identification of one mutation (I93M) in one family in which 2 mutation carriers had developed typical idiopathic PD with a good levodopa response at ages 49 and 51 years (93). The I93M mutation affects

an evolutionarily conserved amino acid and may alter structure and function of the catalytic site. Despite the biological rationale, the pathogenicity of the UCH-L1 mutation is not proven because only 1 mutation has thus far been found in 2 members of a single family; no other families or mutations have been described, and in the original family the mutation did not segregate well with disease.

PARK6: Phosphatase and Tensin-Induced Putative Kinase 1 (PINK1)

PARK6 was localized to chromosome 1p35-36 in a large consanguineous Sicilian family (the Marsala kindred) with early-onset autosomal recessive parkinsonism (94). Seventeen additional families were subsequently linked to PARK6, including 9 of Dutch, German, British, Italian, and Spanish origin (95, 96) and 8 of Japanese, Taiwanese, Turkish, Israeli, and Philippine origin (97). Mutations in the PINK1 gene were subsequently identified as the cause of PARK6-parkinsonism (95). A homozygous G309D missense mutation was found in a consanguineous Spanish family, and a truncation mutation, W437*, was identified in 2 consanguineous Italian families sharing a common haplotype. Both mutations segregated with disease in families and were absent in control subjects. Numerous missense, nonsense, insertion, and deletion mutations have since been identified (98–103). PINK1 exon copy number variants are rare compared to parkin and DJ-1 (98, 102). A kindred with autosomal recessive parkinsonism has been described, with compound heterozygous DJ-1 and PINK1 mutations likely causing disease (104).

The PINK1 phenotype is consistent with that of other autosomal recessive parkinsonisms including parkin and DJ-1. Typically, patients have an early disease onset and good levodopa response; they often have early dyskinesias and a slow disease progression. Atypical features are not common but have been reported (99, 105). It was originally suspected that features common to AR-JP, such as dystonia at onset and sleep benefit, may not be observed in PARK6 families (96, 99, 105); however, subjects with these characteristics have since been observed (98, 100). Families with proven PINK1 parkinsonism have 2 mutations affecting both chromosomes. However, heterozygous PINK1 mutation carriers have also been identified, suggesting that, as with parkin, having a single mutation predisposes to typical late-onset PD (102, 106, 107). A PET study showed reduced striatal [18F]-dopa uptake in homozygotes and a less dramatic decrease in heterozygous carriers compared with controls (108). The prevalence of PINK1-linked parkinsonism falls between that of parkin and DJ-1 (100–103, 106, 107, 109) and may be ethnicity-dependent (98).

PINK1 comprises 8 exons that span about 1.8 kb and encode the ubiquitously expressed 581–amino acid protein phosphatase and tensin (PTEN)–induced putative kinase 1. The protein contains a short N-terminal mitochondrial targeting domain, a highly conserved kinase domain (similar to serine/threonine kinases), and a C-terminal autoregulatory domain (95, 110). Since PINK1 is a mitochondrial protein, it may function in part to protect cells from mitochondrial dysfunction or oxidative stress. PINK1 may protect neurons from apoptosis when exposed to stress, and some missense mutations may alter this function (111, 112). PINK1 kinase activity has been confirmed in vitro, with previously identified mutations having decreased kinase activity and/or altered autophosphorylation (110, 113). The identification of *PINK1* as a PD gene provided new evidence that mitochondrial dysfunction, as long suspected, contributes to PD pathogenesis.

PARK7: DJ-1

Homozygosity mapping in a consanguineous family with early-onset recessive parkinsonism led to the localization of *PARK7* to chromosome 1p36 (114). Mutations in the *DJ-1* gene were subsequently identified as the cause of *PARK7*-linked parkinsonism. A family from a genetically isolated region of the Netherlands was described with a large deletion of the first *5 DJ-1* exons that cosegregated with disease (115). In this region of the Netherlands, 0.9% of the residents were heterozygous carriers of the deletion, but the mutant allele was not detected in the general population in the surrounding areas, the general Dutch population, or patients with late-onset PD. Therefore this pathogenic mutation is likely confined to this isolated community. A homozygous *DJ-1* missense mutation affecting a highly conserved amino acid (L166P) that cosegregated with disease was also identified in an Italian family and was absent in healthy controls. L166P and the exons 1–5 deletion are the only pathogenic mutations identified in *DJ-1*, which account for 1% or less of early-onset parkinsonism (116–118).

Although the clinical phenotype of *DJ-1*-linked PD is not well characterized due to its rarity, it appears to be similar to that of *parkin*- and *PINK1*-linked autosomal recessive parkinsonism. In the family where the original mutation was described, at least 3 of the 4 affected individuals had onset at or below 40 years of age; all had a good response to levodopa (or dopamine agonists) and a slow disease progression without atypical features (115). Imaging studies have shown reduced [18F]-dopa uptake in homozygous, but not heterozygous *DJ-1* mutation carriers (119), consistent with a recessive mode of inheritance. Homozygous *DJ-1* mutations have recently been found to segregate with disease in a family with early-onset parkinsonism–dementia–amyotrophic lateral sclerosis complex (120), further expanding the scope of clinical disease.

DJ-1, which has 8 exons spanning 24 kb, was originally identified as a *ras* oncogene (121). It codes for a 189–amino acid protein that is ubiquitously expressed and present in mitochondria in brain tissue (122). DJ-1 forms high-molecular-weight aggregates with α-synuclein (123) and Parkin (124) and is present but not abundant in LBs, LNs (125), and tau inclusions (126). DJ-1 has multiple functions. It is involved in regulation of RNA-binding protein complexes (127); protection against oxidative stress (128); and redox-dependent molecular chaperoning and prevention of heat-induced aggregation of substrates, including α-synuclein (129, 130). DJ-1 interacts with PINK1 in cell culture, and coexpression of wild-type but not mutant PINK1 can protect cells against MPP+-induced oxidative stress (104). The L166P mutation renders DJ-1 more susceptible to degradation via the UPS (131), resulting in low steady-state levels of mutant protein. L166P also disrupts proper folding of DJ-1, resulting in loss of catalytic function and subsequent degradation by the proteasome (132, 133).

PARK8: Leucine-Rich Repeat Kinase-2 (*LRRK2*)

Linkage of a PD locus (*PARK8*) to chromosome 12q12 was first demonstrated in a Japanese family (Sagamihara kindred) with autosomal dominant parkinsonism (134). In 2004, two independent groups studying unrelated *PARK8*-linked families identified 2 highly penetrant missense mutations (R1441C and Y1699C) in a gene coding for a protein that was named Dardarin by one group and LRRK2 (leucine-rich repeat kinase 2) by the other (135, 136). Over 20 missense mutations have since been described in *LRRK2*, several of which (I1122V, R1441H, I2012T, I2020T, and G2019S) are thought to be pathogenic in that they segregate with PD in families and are absent in controls (136–142). Mutations in *LRRK2* are autosomal dominant and highly penetrant (143).

The most common *LRRK2* mutation is G2019S, which is encoded by a G6055A transition in exon 41. The frequency of G2019S mutation in PD ranges from 1% to over 30%, depending primarily on the ethnic background and family history. Studies performed in the United States and Europe have consistently found a mutation frequency between 1% and 6.6% in Caucasian PD patients (139–142). This mutation is infrequent in Asian populations (144, 145). However, in Ashkenazi Jews and North African Arabs, the mutation frequency of unselected patients is as high as 18% (146) and 30% (147), respectively. G2019S mutation frequency is highest in autosomal dominant pedigrees, although many patients with this mutation have no known family history of PD (139,140), and it is equally frequent in early- and late-onset PD (148, 149). G2019S is absent in patients with other parkinsonisms and neurodegenerative diseases, including DLB and AD (150–154).

Early studies estimated G2019S penetrance as 15% at age 40, 85% by age 70, and nearly 100% by age 80 (141, 155, 156). More recent evidence suggests that penetrance is not 100% by age 80. G2019S carriers have been identified who have remained unaffected to advanced ages (141, 152, 156–159). G2019S-positive families from the United States, Europe, North Africa, and the Middle East have been shown to share one of few ancestral haplotypes (141, 160), one of which dates back to 2250 years ago (161).

LRRK2-linked PD often presents as late-onset levodopa-responsive disease, indistinguishable from typical idiopathic PD (149, 162, 163). Clinical features can vary between and within families who carry the same mutation. G2019S homozygotes are clinically indistinguishable from heterozygotes, and no obvious dose effects have been found (142, 147, 149, 156). Reduced [^{18}F]-dopa uptake, indistinguishable from that of idiopathic PD, has been noted in carriers of Y1699C, R1441C, and G2019S (164, 165). LRRK2 mutation carriers have pleomorphic pathology, including classic nigral degeneration and the presence of LBs and LNs but also tau-positive neurofibrillary tangles and ubiquitin-positive inclusions (135, 136, 166). Some groups have suggested that G2019S carriers have more severe progression and more cognitive changes (138, 147).

The LRRK2 gene, spanning 144 kb, contains 51 exons and encodes a large (2527–amino acid) member of the ROCO [Roc-GTPase, COR (C-terminal of Roc)] protein family (135, 136). LRRK2 is a multidomain protein consisting of a leucine-rich repeat, a kinase-like domain, a RAS domain, and a WD40 domain. LRRK2 is predominantly a cytoplasmic protein that can associate with the mitochondrial outer membrane and is found throughout the brain (135, 167–169). LRRK2 interacts with Parkin but not α-synuclein, DJ-1, or Tau. LRRK2 likely functions as a protein kinase, but the native biological function is unknown and its role in PD pathogenesis remains unclear. Mutations in LRRK2 are associated with a dominant effect; it is therefore likely that mutations result in a toxic gain of function, such as increased or abnormal phosphorylation. LRRK2 kinase activity has recently been confirmed (170), and G2019S, R1441C (170), and I2020T (171) mutations have been shown to promote increased kinase activity. The G2019S mutation affects a conserved region of the activation loop of the kinase domain. Additionally, the R1441C, Y1699C, and G2019S mutations have been linked to cellular toxicity in vitro (167).

PARK9

A locus on chromosome 1p36, which is responsible for Kufor-Rakeb syndrome (172), has been designated PARK9; however, there is no evidence that this locus is associated with PD.

PARK10

Using a population-based cohort of PD patients and their extended families in Iceland (7, 173), PARK10 was identified as a locus for late-onset PD on chromosome 1p32. Other genomewide studies have associated PARK10 with age at disease onset (174) and risk (175). Candidate genes in or near the PARK10 interval—including EIF2B3 (a translation initiation factor) and USP24 (a member of the ubiquitin-specific protease family) contributing to age at disease onset, HIVEP3 (a transcription regulator of viral genes) contributing to risk (176), and ELAVL4 (a neuron-specific RNA-binding protein) contributing to age at onset (177)— have been examined as possible candidates, but the gene remains unknown.

PARK11

PARK11 was mapped to chromosome 2q36-37 via a whole-genome screen in 160 North American sibling pairs with PD (178–180). The gene responsible for PARK11 has not been identified.

Nurr1: Nuclear-Related Receptor 1 (NR4A2 or NOT)

Nurr1 is a 598–amino acid protein encoded by 8 exons spanning 8.3 kb (181) on chromosome 2q22-23 (182). This orphan nuclear receptor, expressed predominantly in the substantia nigra and ventral tegmental area of the brain, is critical for midbrain dopaminergic cell development and survival (183–187). Nurr1 functions as a transcription factor and can enhance expression of the dopamine transporter in cell lines (188) through transcriptional activation of tyrosine hydroxylase (189). These data, coupled with the dysfunction of dopaminergic neurons in Nurr1-deficient mice, implicated Nurr1 as a candidate gene for neurologic disorders such as schizophrenia and PD.

In 2000, a study of Nurr1 sequence variation in schizophrenic, bipolar, and PD patients revealed a 3-bp deletion in one childhood-onset schizophrenic patient, a missense mutation in another schizophrenic patient, and a different missense mutation in a bipolar patient with psychotic features (190). Although family studies were not carried out, none of the mutations was found in healthy controls or other patients, and functional studies of the mutations demonstrated significantly reduced transcriptional activity, suggesting that these were pathogenic mutations. Mutations were not detected in PD patients, but the authors concluded that further studies of Nurr1 in patients with disorders involving the dopamine system were warranted.

Two heterozygous *Nurr1* mutations associated with familial PD were identified in 2003 (-291Tdel and -245 t>g, both in exon 1) (191). The mutations cosegregated with PD in families, and both were absent in sporadic PD patients and controls. Both cases were heterozygous, consistent with a dominant mode of inheritance. The mutations resulted in decreased mRNA and altered tyrosine hydroxylase transcription, and a dominant negative effect was suggested. Patients with these mutations had a clinical phenotype similar to idiopathic PD (mean age at onset 54 years). Neuropathologic data were not available, and to date no known *Nurr1* mutation carriers have come to autopsy.

Only 3 other potentially pathogenic *Nurr1* mutations have been identified: S125C in a sporadic patient (192), −253 c>t in a sporadic PD patient from Ghana, and −223 c>t in a patient from southern Germany. Although Nurr1 is critical for the development and maintenance of the dopaminergic system and thus a good candidate PD gene, mutations in *Nurr1* are clearly rare and account for disease in only a few documented patients.

Synphilin-1 (*SNCAIP*)

Synphilin-1, encoded by *SNCAIP* (synuclein-α-interacting protein) on chromosome 5q23.1-q23.3, was isolated as a protein present in human brain that interacts with *SNCA* in neurons (193). A component of LBs (194, 195), Synphilin-1 can be degraded by the proteasome (196). This protein also interacts with and can be ubiquitinated by Parkin (197). Some *parkin* mutations can alter Parkin-mediated Synphilin-1 ubiquitination (197, 198). The identification of Synphilin-1 as an α-synuclein interacting protein prompted the search for Synphilin-1 mutations in PD patients (199, 200). One study found a variant (R621C) that was present in 2 patients and absent in controls. It is unknown if the mutation is pathogenic.

SUSCEPTIBILITY GENES AND MODIFIERS

The current theory is that a large proportion of PD results from cumulative and interactive effects of genes and environment. In fact, over 70% of PD patients have no prior family history and the vast majority of cases are not caused by mutation of any of the known PD genes. Yet, as outlined above, genetic-epidemiologic studies strongly support the existence of a genetic component, even in sporadic late-onset disease. In pursuit of susceptibility genes, several hundred genetic association studies have been performed and published, but none of the findings have been consistently replicated. The standards for the conduct of association studies have been raised dramatically in recent years; therefore we should expect future studies to be far more rigorous and robust. In the

following, we will highlight a few of the more promising association findings reported to date.

NACP-Rep1

A mixed dinucleotide repeat polymorphism located in the promoter region of *SNCA* (*NACP-Rep1*) has been associated with susceptibility to common late-onset PD. Although the findings are inconsistent across studies (201–211), a meta-analysis revealed a modest but statistically significant effect in populations of European descent (212). This polymorphism (i.e., allele size variability within the *Rep1* region) has been shown to influence expression levels of *SNCA* in vitro (213, 214). Thus, *Rep1* may be associated with PD via modulation of α-synuclein expression to varying degrees, depending on the allele size.

UCH-L1 S18Y

One *UCH-L1* polymorphism (S18Y) was reported to be associated with PD in a Caucasian population (215). Subsequent replication studies were inconsistent (216–218). Two meta-analyses were performed, neither of which supported an association in Caucasians, but one confirmed an association in an Asian population (219, 220).

Nurr1 7048g7049

An insertion polymorphism (7048g7049) in intron 6 of *Nurr1* was shown to be more prevalent in both familial and sporadic PD patients when compared with controls (221). Since this polymorphism is located near the exon/intron 6 junction, it was thought that the homozygote may alter *Nurr1* splicing, thereby altering part of the ligand binding domain in exon 6, but this has not been demonstrated in vivo or in vitro. One study has replicated the association of 7048g7049 with PD and found a borderline association with diffuse Lewy body disease (222).

Other Associations

The original reports of association of PD susceptibility with *parkin* polymorphisms (55, 223–229), *LRRK2* haplotypes (230, 231), and *DJ-1* (232) have not been confirmed. No association has been found with *PINK1* polymorphisms. Numerous functionally relevant candidate genes have been studied for possible association with PD risk, age at onset, disease outcomes (dementia, dyskinesia, severity), and response to treatment. The candidate genes were chosen from various pathways (oxidative stress response, apoptosis, mitochondria, iron metabolism, inflammation, and metabolite detoxification) and included apolipoprotein E (*APOE*) (233, 234), brain-derived neurotrophic factor (*BDNF*) (235,

236), paraoxonase 1 (*PON1*) (237, 238), *N*-acetyltransferase 2 (*NAT2*) (239, 240), monoamine oxidase A and B (*MAO-A* and *MAO-B*) (241–243), catechol-O-methyltransferase (*COMT*) (244, 245), mitochondrial complex I genes (246, 247), and cytochrome P450 2D6 (*CYP2D6*) (248, 249). There have also been reports of association of age at onset of PD with *APOE* (see below), *NACP-Rep1* (204), *BDNF* (250), *ER* (estrogen receptor) (251), *GSTO1* and *GSTO2* (glutathione S-transferase omega 1 and 2, respectively) (252), *GSTM1* (glutathione S-transferase M1) (253), *IL-1β* (interleukin 1 beta) (254), and *IFNγ* (interferon gamma) (254).

Whole-Genome Association Study

A whole-genome association study tested about 200,000 SNPs, spanning the human genome, for association with PD risk. Thirteen SNPs were identified and reported as risk factors for PD, including SNPs that tagged *PARK10*, *PARK11*, an X-linked locus involved in signal transduction, and the *SEMA5A* gene, which may be involved in dopamine-induced apoptosis. Early follow-up replication studies were either negative (255–258) or inconclusive (259). A large international collaborative study with over 12,000 subjects clearly demonstrated a lack of association with PD and any of the 13 SNPs (260). However, the failure of one whole-genome association study does not negate the existence of a strong genetic component; rather, it emphasizes key areas in study design that are crucial for the success of such studies.

GENETIC LINKS WITH OTHER DISORDERS

A pathophysiologic link between PD and dementias, particularly AD, has long been suspected. In recent years, with the discovery of genetic factors in dementias and parkinsonism, the exploration of genetic links between these related disorders has been of great interest.

SNCA

The *SNCA* gene, which codes for α-synuclein, was originally known as *NACP* (nonamyloid component of amyloid plaques). α-synuclein, the most abundant protein in LBs found in PD pathogenesis, is also the second most abundant protein in senile plaques characteristic of AD. While mutations of the *SNCA* gene have been unequivocally linked to PD, a genetic connection between *SNCA* and AD has not been clearly defined.

APOE

APOE, a well characterized gene on chromosome 19q13.2, is well established as a risk factor for AD. Carriers of the ε4 allele have significantly earlier onset and the highest age-specific risk of developing AD, while ε2 carriers have delayed onset and the lowest age-specific risk (261–263). Although early studies with PD were controversial, more recent studies with substantially larger sample sizes have consistently detected a significant effect, linking ε4 with an earlier onset of PD (264–266), and both ε4 and ε2 have been reported as risk factors for development of dementia in PD patients (267–269).

Tau

Microtubule-associated protein Tau, encoded by *MAPT* on chromosome 17q21, is the main component of neurofibrillary tangles. Pathogenic mutations in *MAPT* cause frontotemporal dementia (FTD). Polymorphisms in or spanning *MAPT* were shown to be associated with progressive supranuclear palsy (270) and later with PD (271). Additionally, a genome screen revealed linkage to the FTD region on 17q in multiplex PD families (272). Two meta-analyses in 2001 (273) and 2004 (274) have confirmed the association of *MAPT* polymorphisms with PD.

Spinocerebellar Ataxias

Spinocerebellar ataxias (SCAs) are a group of neurodegenerative disorders characterized by cerebellar dysfunction alone or in combination with other abnormalities. Triplet repeat expansions in the *SCA* loci typically result in an ataxia phenotype; however, expansions of *SCA2* (275–280), *SCA3* (281, 282), *SCA8* and *SCA17* (283), and *SCA6* (284) have been linked to phenotypes including parkinsonism and classic levodopa-responsive PD. It has been estimated that 2% of Caucasian (277) and up to 10% of Chinese patients with PD (285) have a pathogenic expansion mutation in *SCA2*.

Glucocerebrosidase

Gaucher disease is an inherited metabolic deficiency due to recessive mutations in the glucocerebrosidase (*GBA*) gene on chromosome 1q21. One of the rare manifestations of Gaucher's is early-onset parkinsonism; *SNCA*-reactive LBs have been noted in brain regions associated with Gaucher disease; family studies suggest that the incidence of parkinsonism is more frequent in obligate heterozygotes, and one study reported increased frequency of DNA sequence variations in *GBA* in brains of sporadic PD patients (286). One study showed an increased risk of PD among Ashkenazi Jews who were carriers of a *GBA* N370S mutation (287); this remains to be replicated.

MITOCHONDRIA

Deletions in mtDNA are known to accumulate with age, specifically in substantia nigra dopaminergic neurons (288). Several groups have identified mutations in mtDNA that may cause (289) or modulate risk for PD (290, 291); however, to date, mutations/polymorphisms in mitochondrial genes are not well established as a cause/risk factor for PD. Nevertheless, mitochondrial dysfunction appears to be central to PD pathogenesis. MPTP, for example, confers toxicity and neuronal death through mitochondrial complex I inhibition (292). Loss of complex I activity has been shown in the substantia nigra of PD patients (293). Mitochondrial dysfunction, caused by either environmental or genetic factors, can result in excessive production of reactive oxygen species, triggering the apoptotic death of dopaminergic cells (294). Several of the nuclear-encoded PD genes have functional roles that involve mitochondria. PINK1 is localized to the mitochondria via a short N-terminal mitochondrial targeting domain and may function in part to protect cells from mitochondrial dysfunction or oxidative stress (95, 110). *PINK1* may protect neurons from stress-induced apoptosis, and mutations in *PINK1* may compromise this protective function (111, 112). The LRRK2 protein, although predominantly cytoplasmic, interacts with the mitochondrial outer membrane (170). DJ-1 overexpression in cell culture has been shown to protect cells from oxidative stress, while *DJ-1*

knockdown mutants are more susceptible to oxidative damage (128). DJ-1 functions as a redox-dependent molecular chaperone preventing heat-induced aggregation of substrates, including α-synuclein (129, 130); it can protect cells against MPP$^+$-induced oxidative stress (104). Although mitochondrial involvement in PD is clear, it is yet to be determined whether it is a cause or a consequence of disease.

CONCLUSION

The progress made in the study of PD over the past decade is unprecedented in human genetics research. In the span of 15 years, PD was transformed from what was thought to be a purely environmental disorder to one with strong genetic influences. The number of publications on genetics of PD has multiplied 66-fold in the last decade. Mendelian forms of PD have been identified, disease-causing genes have been characterized, transgenic animal models have been created, and commercial gene tests are now available. Genetic discoveries have given us the first glimpses of disease pathophysiology, with each gene discovered contributing another piece to the puzzle. The progress so far has been primarily in Mendelian forms of PD. The task ahead is to tease out genetic and environmental contributions to the multifactorial forms of PD. The key is to keep an open mind about the unknown nature of the problem at hand. We have been wrong before.

References

1. Parkinson J. *An Essay on the Shaking Palsy.* London: Sherwood, Neely and Jones. 1817.
2. Gowers W. *Diseases of the Nervous System.* Philadelphia: P. Blakiston, Son and Company. 1888.
3. Golbe LI, Di Iorio G, Bonavita V, et al. A large kindred with autosomal dominant Parkinson's disease. *Ann Neurol* 1990; 27:276–282.
4. Kitada T, Asakawa S, Hattori N, et al. Mutations in the *parkin* gene cause autosomal recessive juvenile parkinsonism. *Nature* 1998; 392:605–608.
5. Tanner CM, Ottman R, Goldman SM, et al. Parkinson disease in twins: An etiologic study. *JAMA* 1999; 281:341–346.
6. Piccini P, Burn DJ, Ceravolo R, et al. The role of inheritance in sporadic Parkinson's disease: Evidence from a longitudinal study of dopaminergic function in twins. *Ann Neurol* 1999; 45:577–582.
7. Sveinbjornsdottir S, Hicks AA, Jonsson T, et al. Familial aggregation of Parkinson's disease in Iceland. *N Engl J Med* 2000; 343:1765–1770.
8. Payami H, Larsen K, Bernard S, et al. Increased Risk of Parkinson's disease in parents and siblings of patients. *Ann Neurol* 1994; 36:659–661.
9. Bonifati V, Fabrizio E, Vanacore N, et al. Familial Parkinson's disease: A clinical genetic analysis. *Can J Neurol Sci* 1995; 22:272–279.
10. Vieregge P, Heberlein I. Increased risk of Parkinson's disease in relatives of patients. *Ann Neurol* 1995; 37:685.
11. De Michele G, Filla A, Volpe G, et al. Environmental and genetic risk factors in Parkinson's disease: A case-control study in southern Italy. *Mov Disord* 1996; 11:17–23.
12. Marder K, Tang MX, Mejia H, et al. Risk of Parkinson's disease among first-degree relatives: A community-based study. *Neurology* 1996; 47:155–160.
13. Uitti RJ, Shinotoh H, Hayward M, et al. "Familial Parkinson's disease": A case-control study of families. *Can J Neurol Sci* 1997; 24:127–132.
14. Autere JM, Moilanen JS, Myllyla VV, et al. Familial aggregation of Parkinson's disease in a Finnish population. *J Neurol Neurosurg Psychiatry* 2000; 69:107–109.
15. Zorzon M, Capus L, Pellegrino A, et al. Familial and environmental risk factors in Parkinson's disease: A case-control study in north-east Italy. *Acta Neurol Scand* 2002; 105:77–82.
16. Payami H, Zareparsi S, James D, et al. Familial aggregation of Parkinson disease: A comparative study of early-onset and late-onset disease. *Arch Neurol* 2002; 59:848–850.

17. Marder K, Levy G, Louis ED, et al. Familial aggregation of early- and late-onset Parkinson's disease. *Ann Neurol* 2003; 54:507–513.
18. Kurz M, Alves G, Aarsland D, et al. Familial Parkinson's disease: A community-based study. *Eur J Neurol* 2003; 10:159–163.
19. McDonnell SK, Schaid DJ, Elbaz A, et al. Complex segregation analysis of Parkinson's disease: The Mayo Clinic Family Study. *Ann Neurol* 2006; 59:788–795.
20. Moilanen JS, Autere JM, Myllyla VV, et al. Complex segregation analysis of Parkinson's disease in the Finnish population. *Hum Genet* 2001; 108:184–189.
21. Maher NE, Currie LJ, Lazzarini AM, et al. Segregation analysis of Parkinson disease revealing evidence for a major causative gene. *Am J Med Genet* 2002; 109:191–197.
22. Zareparsi S, Taylor TD, Harris EL, et al. Segregation analysis of Parkinson disease. *Am J Med Genet* 1998; 80:410–417.
23. Polymeropoulos MH. Mapping of a gene for Parkinson's disease to chromosome 4q21-q23. *Science* 1996; 274:1197–1199.
24. Polymeropoulos M, Lavedan C, Leroy E, et al. Mutation in the alpha-synuclein gene identified in families with Parkinson's disease. *Science* 1997; 276:2045–2047.
25. Athanassiadou A, Voutsinas G, Psiouri L, et al. Genetic analysis of families with Parkinson disease that carry the Ala53Thr mutation in the gene encoding alpha-synuclein. *Am J Hum Genet* 1999; 65:555–558.
26. Papapetropoulos S, Ellul J, Paschalis C, et al. Clinical characteristics of the alpha-synuclein mutation (G209A)-associated Parkinson's disease in comparison with other forms of familial Parkinson's disease in Greece. *Eur J Neurol* 2003; 10:281–286.
27. Papadimitriou A, Veletza V, Hadjigeorgiou GM, et al. Mutated alpha-synuclein gene in two Greek kindreds with familial PD: Incomplete penetrance? *Neurology* 1999; 52:651–654.
28. Bostantjopoulou S, Katsarou Z, Papadimitriou A, et al. Clinical features of parkinsonian patients with the alpha-synuclein (G209A) mutation. *Mov Disord* 2001; 16:1007–1013.
29. Scott WK, Yamaoka LH, Stajich JM, et al. The alpha-synuclein gene is not a major risk factor in familial Parkinson disease. *Neurogenetics* 1999; 2:191–192.
30. Markopoulou K, Wszolek ZK, Pfeiffer RF, et al. Reduced expression of the G209A alpha-synuclein allele in familial parkinsonism. *Ann Neurol* 1999; 46:374–381.
31. Kruger R, Kuhn W, Muller T, et al. Ala30Pro mutation in the gene encoding alpha-synuclein in Parkinson's disease. *Nat Genet* 1998; 18:106–108.

32. Zarranz JJ, Alegre J, Gomez-Esteban JC, et al. The new mutation, E46K, of alpha-synuclein causes Parkinson and Lewy body dementia. *Ann Neurol* 2004; 55:164–173.

33. Singleton AB, Farrer M, Johnson J, et al. Alpha-synuclein locus triplication causes Parkinson's disease. *Science* 2003; 302:841.

34. Farrer M, Kachergus J, Forno L, et al. Comparison of kindreds with parkinsonism and alpha-synuclein genomic multiplications. *Ann Neurol* 2004; 55:174–179.

35. Chartier-Harlin MC, Kachergus J, Roumier C, et al. Alpha-synuclein locus duplication as a cause of familial Parkinson's disease. *Lancet* 2004; 364:1167–1169.

36. Nishioka K, Hayashi S, Farrer MJ, et al. Clinical heterogeneity of alpha-synuclein gene duplication in Parkinson's disease. *Ann Neurol* 2006; 59:298–309.

37. Ibanez P, Bonnet AM, Debarges B, et al. Causal relation between alpha-synuclein gene duplication and familial Parkinson's disease. *Lancet* 2004; 364:1169–1171.

38. Spira PJ, Sharpe DM, Halliday G, et al. Clinical and pathological features of a parkinsonian syndrome in a family with an Ala53Thr alpha-synuclein mutation. *Ann Neurol* 2001; 49:313–319.

39. Kruger R, Kuhn W, Leenders KL, et al. Familial parkinsonism with synuclein pathology: Clinical and PET studies of A30P mutation carriers. *Neurology* 2001; 56:1355–1362.

40. Samii A, Markopoulou K, Wszolek ZK, et al. PET studies of parkinsonism associated with mutation in the alpha-synuclein gene. *Neurology* 1999; 53:2097–2102.

41. Gwinn-Hardy K, Mehta ND, Farrer M, et al. Distinctive neuropathology revealed by alpha-synuclein antibodies in hereditary parkinsonism and dementia linked to chromosome 4p. *Acta Neuropathol (Berl)* 2000; 99:663–672.

42. Touchman JW, Dehejia A, Chiba-Falek O, et al. Human and mouse alpha-synuclein genes: Comparative genomic sequence analysis and identification of a novel gene regulatory element. *Genome Res* 2001; 11:78–86.

43. Spillantini MG, Crowther RA, Jakes R, et al. Alpha-synuclein in filamentous inclusions of Lewy bodies from Parkinson's disease and dementia with Lewy bodies. *Proc Natl Acad Sci USA* 1998; 95:6469–6473.

44. Spillantini MG, Schmidt ML, Lee VM, et al. Alpha-synuclein in Lewy bodies. *Nature* 1997; 388:839–840.

45. Davidson WS, Jonas A, Clayton DF, et al. Stabilization of alpha-synuclein secondary structure upon binding to synthetic membranes. *J Biol Chem* 1998; 273:9443–9449.

46. Weinreb PH, Zhen W, Poon AW, et al. NACP, a protein implicated in Alzheimer's disease and learning, is natively unfolded. *Biochemistry* 1996; 35:13709–13715.

47. Ueda K, Fukushima H, Masliah E, et al. Molecular cloning of cDNA encoding an unrecognized component of amyloid in Alzheimer disease. *Proc Natl Acad Sci USA* 1993; 90:11282–11286.

48. Jakes R, Spillantini MG and Goedert M. Identification of two distinct synucleins from human brain. *FEBS Lett* 1994; 345:27–32.

49. Narhi L, Wood SJ, Steavenson S, et al. Both familial Parkinson's disease mutations accelerate alpha-synuclein aggregation. *J Biol Chem* 1999; 274:9843–9846.

50. Li J, Uversky VN, Fink AL. Effect of familial Parkinson's disease point mutations A30P and A53T on the structural properties, aggregation, and fibrillation of human alpha-synuclein. *Biochemistry* 2001; 40:11604–11613.

51. Matsumine H, Saito M, Shimoda-Matsubayashi S, et al. Localization of a gene for an autosomal recessive form of juvenile Parkinsonism to chromosome 6q25.2-27. *Am J Hum Genet* 1997; 60:588–596.

52. Lucking CB, Abbas N, Durr A, et al. Homozygous deletions in *parkin* gene in European and North African families with autosomal recessive juvenile parkinsonism. *Lancet* 1998; 352:1355–1356.

53. Leroy E, Anastasopoulos D, Konitsiotis S, et al. Deletions in the *parkin* gene and genetic heterogeneity in a Greek family with early onset Parkinson's disease. *Hum Genet* 1998; 103:424–427.

54. Bertoli-Avella AM, Giroud-Benitez JL, Akyol A, et al. Novel *parkin* mutations detected in patients with early-onset Parkinson's disease. *Mov Disord* 2005; 20:424–431.

55. Lucking C-B, Chesneau V, Lohmann E, et al. Coding Polymorphisms in the *parkin* gene and susceptibility to Parkinson disease. *Arch Neurol* 2003; 60:1253–1256.

56. Oliveira SA, Scott WK, Martin ER, et al. *Parkin* mutations and susceptibility alleles in late-onset Parkinson's disease. *Ann Neurol* 2003; 53:624–629.

57. Hedrich K, Eskelson C, Wilmot B, et al. Distribution, type and origin of *parkin* mutations: Review and case studies. *Mov Disord* 2004; 19:1146–1157.

58. Lucking CB, Durr A, Bonifati V, et al. Association between early-onset Parkinson's disease and mutations in the *parkin* gene. French Parkinson's Disease Genetics Study Group. *N Engl J Med* 2000; 342:1560–1567.

59. Foroud T, Uniacke SK, Liu L, et al. Heterozygosity for a mutation in the *parkin* gene leads to later onset Parkinson disease. *Neurology* 2003; 60:796–801.

60. Klein C, Pramstaller P, Kis B, et al. *Parkin* deletions in a family with adult-onset, tremor-dominant parkinsonism: Expanding the phenotype. *Ann Neurol* 2000; 48:65.

61. Hoenicka J, Vidal L, Morales B, et al. Molecular findings in familial Parkinson disease in Spain. *Arch Neurol* 2002; 59:966–970.

62. Farrer M, Chan P, Chen R, et al. Lewy bodies and parkinsonism in families with *parkin* mutations. *Ann Neurol* 2001; 50:293–300.

63. Denison SR, Callahan G, Phillips LA, Smith DI. Characterization of *FRA6E* and its potential role in autosomal recessive juvenile parkinsonism and ovarian cancer. *Genes Chromosomes Cancer* 2003; 38:40–52.

64. Shimura H, Hattori N, Kubo S, et al. Familial Parkinson disease gene product, *parkin*, is a ubiquitin-protein ligase. *Nat Genet* 2000; 25:302–305.

65. Imai Y, Soda M, Takahashi R. *Parkin* suppresses unfolded protein stress-induced cell death through its E3 ubiquitin-protein ligase activity. *J Biol Chem* 2000; 275:35661–35664.

66. Imai Y, Takahashi R. How do *parkin* mutations result in neurodegeneration? *Curr Opin Neurobiol* 2004; 14:384–389.

67. Kahle PJ, Haass C. How does *parkin* ligate ubiquitin to Parkinson's disease? First in Molecular Medicine Review Series. *EMBO Rep* 2004; 5:681–685.

68. Zhang Y, Gao J, Chung KKK, et al. *Parkin* functions as an E2-dependent ubiquitin-protein ligase and promotes the degradation of the synaptic vesicle-associated protein, CDCrel-1. *Proc Natl Acad Sci* 2000; 97:13354–13359.

69. Hattori N, Mizuno Y. Pathogenetic mechanisms of *parkin* in Parkinson's disease. *Lancet* 2004; 364:722–724.

70. Hattori N, Matsumine H, Asakawa S, et al. Point mutations (Thr240Arg and Ala-311Stop) in the *parkin* gene. *Biochem Biophys Res Commun* 1998; 249:754–758.

71. Yamamura Y, Hattori N, Matsumine H, et al. Autosomal recessive early-onset parkinsonism with diurnal fluctuation: clinicopathologic characteristics and molecular genetic identification. *Brain Dev* 2000; 22(Suppl 1):S87–S91.

72. Takahashi H, Ohama E, Suzuki S, et al. Familial juvenile parkinsonism: Clinical and pathologic study in a family. *Neurology* 1994; 44:437–441.

73. Pramstaller PP, Schlossmacher MG, Jacques TS, et al. Lewy body Parkinson's disease in a large pedigree with 77 *parkin* mutation carriers. *Ann Neurol* 2005; 58:411–422.

74. van de Warrenburg B, Lammens M, Lucking M, et al. Clinical and pathologic abnormalities in a family with parkinsonism and *parkin* gene mutations. *Neurology* 2001; 56:555–557.

75. Gasser T, Muller-Myhsok B, Wszolek Z, et al. A susceptibility locus for Parkinson's disease maps to chromosome 2p13. *Nat Genet* 1998; 18:262–265.

76. DeStefano AL, Lew MF, Golbe LI, et al. *PARK3* influences age at onset in Parkinson disease: A genome scan in the GenePD study. *Am J Hum Genet* 2002; 70:1089–1095.

77. Pankratz N, Uniacke SK, Halter CA, et al. Genes influencing Parkinson disease onset: Replication of *PARK3* and identification of novel loci. *Neurology* 2004; 62:1616–1618.

78. Martinez M, Brice A, Vaughan JR, et al. Genome-wide scan linkage analysis for Parkinson's disease: The European genetic study of Parkinson's disease. *J Med Genet* 2004; 41:900–907.

79. Sharma M, Mueller JC, Zimprich A, et al. The sepiapterin reductase gene region reveals association in the *PARK3* locus: Analysis of familial and sporadic Parkinson disease in European populations. *J Med Genet* 2006; 43:557–562.

80. Farrer M, Gwinn-Hardy K, Muenter M, et al. A chromosome 4p haplotype segregating with Parkinson's disease and postural tremor. *Hum Mol Genet* 1999; 8:81–85.

81. Waters CH and Miller CA. Autosomal dominant Lewy body parkinsonism in a four-generation family. *Ann Neurol* 1994; 35:59–64.

82. Muenter MD, Forno LS, Hornykiewicz O, et al. Hereditary form of parkinsonism-dementia. *Ann Neurol* 1998; 43:768–781.

83. Spellman GG. Report of familial cases of parkinsonism. Evidence of a dominant trait in a patient's family. *JAMA* 1962; 179:372–374.

84. Edwards YH, Fox MF, Povey S, et al. The gene for human neurone specific ubiquitin C-terminal hydrolase (*UCHL1*, *PGP9.5*) maps to chromosome 4p14. *Ann Hum Genet* 1991; 55(Pt 4):273–278.

85. Wilkinson KD, Lee KM, Deshpande S, et al. The neuron-specific protein *PGP 9.5* is a ubiquitin carboxyl-terminal hydrolase. *Science* 1989; 246:670–673.

86. Liu Y, Fallon L, Lashuel HA, et al. The *UCH-L1* gene encodes two opposing enzymatic activities that affect alpha-synuclein degradation and Parkinson's disease susceptibility. *Cell* 2002; 111:209–218.

87. Ardley HC, Scott GB, Rose SA, et al. *UCH-L1* aggresome formation in response to proteasome impairment indicates a role in inclusion formation in Parkinson's disease. *J Neurochem* 2004; 90:379–391.

88. Choi J, Levey AI, Weintraub ST, et al. Oxidative modifications and down-regulation of ubiquitin carboxyl-terminal hydrolase L1 associated with idiopathic Parkinson's and Alzheimer's diseases. *J Biol Chem* 2004; 279:13256–13264.

89. Yamazaki K, Wakasugi N, Tomita T, et al. Gracile axonal dystrophy (*GAD*), a new neurological mutant in the mouse. *Proc Soc Exp Biol Med* 1988; 187:209–215.

90. Saigoh K, Wang YL, Suh JG, et al. Intragenic deletion in the gene encoding ubiquitin carboxy-terminal hydrolase in gad mice. *Nat Genet* 1999; 23:47–51.

91. Doran JF, Jackson P, Kynoch PA, et al. Isolation of *PGP 9.5*, a new human neurone-specific protein detected by high-resolution two-dimensional electrophoresis. *J Neurochem* 1983; 40:1542–1547.

92. Lowe J, McDermott H, Landon M, et al. Ubiquitin carboxyl-terminal hydrolase (*PGP 9.5*) is selectively present in ubiquitinated inclusion bodies characteristic of human neurodegenerative diseases. *J Pathol* 1990; 161:153–160.

93. Leroy E, Boyer R, Auburger G, et al. The ubiquitin pathway in Parkinson's disease. *Nature* 1998; 395:451–452.

94. Valente EM, Bentivoglio AR, Dixon PH, et al. Localization of a novel locus for autosomal recessive early-onset parkinsonism, *PARK6*, on human chromosome 1p35-p36. *Am J Hum Genet* 2001; 68:895–900.

95. Valente EM, Abou-Sleiman PM, Caputo V, et al. Hereditary early-onset Parkinson's disease caused by mutations in *PINK1*. *Science* 2004; 304:1158–1160.

96. Valente EM, Brancati F, Ferraris A, et al. *PARK6*-linked parkinsonism occurs in several European families. *Ann Neurol* 2002; 51:14–18.

97. Hatano Y, Sato K, Elibol B, et al. *PARK6*-linked autosomal recessive early-onset parkinsonism in Asian populations. *Neurology* 2004; 63:1482–1485.

98. Bonifati V, Rohe CF, Breedveld GJ, et al. Early-onset parkinsonism associated with *PINK1* mutations: Frequency, genotypes, and phenotypes. *Neurology* 2005; 65:87–95.

99. Hatano Y, Li Y, Sato K, et al. Novel *PINK1* mutations in early-onset parkinsonism. *Ann Neurol* 2004; 56:424–427.

100. Ibanez P, Lesage S, Lohmann E, et al. Mutational analysis of the *PINK1* gene in early-onset parkinsonism in Europe and North Africa. *Brain* 2006; 129:686–694.

101. Rogaeva E, Johnson J, Lang A, et al. Analysis of the *PINK1* gene in a large cohort of cases with Parkinson disease. *Arch Neurol* 2004; 61:1898–1904.

102. Valente EM, Salvi S, Ialongo T, et al. *PINK1* mutations are associated with sporadic early-onset parkinsonism. *Ann Neurol* 2004; 56:336–341.
103. Rohe CF, Montagna P, Breedveld G, et al. Homozygous *PINK1* C-terminus mutation causing early-onset parkinsonism. *Ann Neurol* 2004; 56:427–431.
104. Tang B, Xiong H, Sun P, et al. Association of *PINK1* and *DJ-1* confers digenic inheritance of early onset Parkinson's disease. *Hum Mol Genet* 2006; 15:1816–1825.
105. Li Y, Tomiyama H, Sato K, et al. Clinicogenetic study of *PINK1* mutations in autosomal recessive early-onset parkinsonism. *Neurology* 2005; 64:1955–1957.
106. Healy DG, Abou-Sleiman PM, Gibson JM, et al. *PINK1 (PARK6)* associated Parkinson disease in Ireland. *Neurology* 2004; 63:1486–1488.
107. Tan EK, Yew K, Chua E, et al. *PINK1* mutations in sporadic early-onset Parkinson's disease. *Mov Disord* 2006; 21:789–793.
108. Khan NL, Valente EM, Bentivoglio AR, et al. Clinical and subclinical dopaminergic dysfunction in *PARK6*-linked parkinsonism: an 18F-dopa PET study. *Ann Neurol* 2002; 52:849–853.
109. Tan EK, Yew K, Chua E, et al. Analysis of *PINK1* in Asian patients with familial parkinsonism. *Clin Genet* 2005; 68:468–470.
110. Silvestri L, Caputo V, Bellacchio E, et al. Mitochondrial import and enzymatic activity of *PINK1* mutants associated to recessive parkinsonism. *Hum Mol Genet* 2005; 14:3477–3492.
111. Deng H, Jankovic J, Guo Y, et al. Small interfering RNA targeting the *PINK1* induces apoptosis in dopaminergic cells SH-SY5Y. *Biochem Biophys Res Commun* 2005; 337:1133–1138.
112. Petit A, Kawarai T, Paitel E, et al. Wild-type *PINK1* prevents basal and induced neuronal apoptosis, a protective effect abrogated by Parkinson disease–related mutations. *J Biol Chem* 2005; 280:34025–34032.
113. Beilina A, Van Der Brug M, Ahmad R, et al. Mutations in PTEN-induced putative kinase 1 associated with recessive parkinsonism have differential effects on protein stability. *Proc Natl Acad Sci USA* 2005; 102:5703–5708.
114. van Duijn CM, Dekker MC, Bonifati V, et al. *PARK7*, a novel locus for autosomal recessive early-onset parkinsonism, on chromosome 1p36. *Am J Hum Genet* 2001; 69:629–634.
115. Bonifati V, Rizzu P, van Baren M, et al. Mutations in the *DJ-1* gene associated with autosomal recessive early-onset parkinsonism. *Science* 2003; 299:256–259.
116. Hague S, Rogaeva E, Hernandez D, et al. Early-onset Parkinson's disease caused by a compound heterozygous *DJ-1* mutation. *Ann Neurol* 2003; 54:271–274.
117. Abou-Sleiman PM, Healy DG, Quinn N, et al. The role of pathogenic *DJ-1* mutations in Parkinson's disease. *Ann Neurol* 2003; 54:283–286.
118. Hedrich K, Djarmati A, Schafer N, et al. *DJ-1* (*PARK7*) mutations are less frequent than *parkin* (*PARK2*) mutations in early-onset Parkinson disease. *Neurology* 2004; 62:389–394.
119. Dekker MC, Eshuis SA, Maguire RP, et al. PET neuroimaging and mutations in the *DJ-1* gene. *J Neural Transm* 2004; 111:1575–1581.
120. Annesi G, Savettieri G, Pugliese P, et al. *DJ-1* mutations and parkinsonism-dementia-amyotrophic lateral sclerosis complex. *Ann Neurol* 2005; 58:803–807.
121. Nagakubo D, Taira T, Kitaura H, et al. *DJ-1*, a novel oncogene which transforms mouse NIH3T3 cells in cooperation with *ras*. *Biochem Biophys Res Commun* 1997; 231:509–513.
122. Zhang L, Shimoji M, Thomas B, et al. Mitochondrial localization of the Parkinson's disease related protein *DJ-1*: Implications for pathogenesis. *Hum Mol Genet* 2005; 14:2063–2073.
123. Meulener MC, Graves CL, Sampathu DM, et al. *DJ-1* is present in a large molecular complex in human brain tissue and interacts with alpha-synuclein. *J Neurochem* 2005; 93:1524–1532.
124. Baulac S, LaVoie MJ, Strahle J, et al. Dimerization of Parkinson's disease–causing *DJ-1* and formation of high molecular weight complexes in human brain. *Mol Cell Neurosci* 2004; 27:236–246.
125. Bandopadhyay R, Kingsbury AE, Cookson MR, et al. The expression of *DJ-1* (*PARK7*) in normal human CNS and idiopathic Parkinson's disease. *Brain* 2004; 127:420–430.
126. Rizzu P, Hinkle DA, Zhukareva V, et al. *DJ-1* colocalizes with tau inclusions: A link between parkinsonism and dementia. *Ann Neurol* 2004; 55:113–118.
127. Hod Y, Pentyala SN, Whyard TC, et al. Identification and characterization of a novel protein that regulates RNA-protein interaction. *J Cell Biochem* 1999; 72:435–444.
128. Zhou W, Freed CR. *DJ-1* up-regulates glutathione synthesis during oxidative stress and inhibits A53T alpha-synuclein toxicity. *J Biol Chem* 2005; 280:43150–43158.
129. Shendelman S, Jonason A, Martinat C, et al. *DJ-1* Is a redox-dependent molecular chaperone that inhibits alpha-synuclein aggregate formation. *PLoS Biology* 2004; 2:e362.
130. Zhou W, Zhu M, Wilson MA, et al. The oxidation state of *DJ-1* regulates its chaperone activity toward alpha-synuclein. *J Mol Biol* 2006; 356:1036–1048.
131. Miller DW, Ahmad R, Hague S, et al. L166P mutant *DJ-1*, causative for recessive Parkinson's disease, is degraded through the ubiquitin-proteasome system. *J Biol Chem* 2003; 278:36588–36595.
132. Olzmann JA, Brown K, Wilkinson KD, et al. Familial Parkinson's disease–associated L166P mutation disrupts *DJ-1* protein folding and function. *J Biol Chem* 2004; 279:8506–8515.
133. Moore DJ, Zhang L, Dawson TM, et al. A missense mutation (L166P) in *DJ-1*, linked to familial Parkinson's disease, confers reduced protein stability and impairs homo-oligomerization. *J Neurochem* 2003; 87:1558–1567.
134. Funayama M, Hasegawa K, Kowa H, et al. A new locus for Parkinson's disease (*PARK8*) maps to chromosome 12p11.2-q13.1. *Ann Neurol* 2002; 51:296–301.
135. Paisan-Ruiz C, Jain S, Evans EW, et al. Cloning of the gene containing mutations that cause *PARK8*-linked Parkinson's disease. *Neuron* 2004; 44:1–12.
136. Zimprich A, Biskup S, Leitner P, et al. Mutations in *LRRK2* cause autosomal dominant parkinsonism with pleomorphic pathology. *Neuron* 2004; 44:601–607.
137. Zabetian CP, Samii A, Mosley AD, et al. A clinic-based study of the *LRRK2* gene in Parkinson disease yields new mutations. *Neurology* 2005; 65:741–744.
138. Tomiyama H, Li Y, Funayama M, et al. Clinicogenetic study of mutations in *LRRK2* exon 41 in Parkinson's disease patients from 18 countries. *Mov Disord* 2006; 21:1102–1108.
139. Di Fonzo A, Rohe CF, Ferreira J, et al. A frequent *LRRK2* gene mutation associated with autosomal dominant Parkinson's disease. *Lancet* 2005; 365:412–415.
140. Gilks WP, Abou-Sleiman PM, Gandhi S, et al. A common *LRRK2* mutation in idiopathic Parkinson's disease. *Lancet* 2005; 365:415–416.
141. Kachergus J, Mata IF, Hulihan M, et al. Identification of a novel *LRRK2* mutation linked to autosomal dominant parkinsonism: Evidence of a common founder across European populations. *Am J Hum Genet* 2005; 76:672–680.
142. Nichols WC, Pankratz N, Hernandez D, et al. Genetic screening for a single common *LRRK2* mutation in familial Parkinson's disease. *Lancet* 2005; 365:410–412.
143. Berg D, Schweitzer KJ, Leitner P, et al. Type and frequency of mutations in the *LRRK2* gene in familiar and sporadic Parkinson's disease. *Brain* 2005; 128:3000–3011.
144. Tan EK, Shen H, Tan LC, et al. The *G2019S LRRK2* mutation is uncommon in an Asian cohort of Parkinson's disease patients. *Neurosci Lett* 2005; 384:327–329.
145. Lu CS, Simons EJ, Wu-Chou YH, et al. The *LRRK2 I2012T, G2019S*, and *I2020T* mutations are rare in Taiwanese patients with sporadic Parkinson's disease. *Parkinsonism Relat Disord* 2005; 11:521–522.
146. Ozelius LJ, Senthil G, Saunders-Pullman R, et al. *LRRK2 G2019S* as a cause of Parkinson's disease in Ashkenazi Jews. *N Engl J Med* 2006; 354:424–425.
147. Lesage S, Durr A, Tazir M, et al. *LRRK2 G2019S* as a cause of Parkinson's disease in North African Arabs. *N Engl J Med* 2006; 354:422–423.
148. Goldwurm S, Di Fonzo A, Simons EJ, et al. The *G6055A* (*G2019S*) mutation in *LRRK2* is frequent in both early and late onset Parkinson's disease and originates from a common ancestor. *J Med Genet* 2005; 42:e65.
149. Kay DM, Zabetian CP, Factor SA, et al. Parkinson's disease and *LRRK2*: Frequency of a common mutation in U.S. movement disorder clinics. *Mov Disord* 2006; 21:519–523.
150. Zabetian CP, Lauricella CJ, Tsuang DW, et al. Analysis of the *LRRK2 G2019S mutation* in Alzheimer disease. *Arch Neurol* 2006; 63:156–157.
151. Toft M, Sando SB, Melquist S, et al. *LRRK2* mutations are not common in Alzheimer's disease. *Mech Ageing Dev* 2005; 126:1201–1205.
152. Saunders-Pullman R, Lipton RB, Senthil G, et al. Increased frequency of the *LRRK2 G2019S* mutation in an elderly Ashkenazi Jewish population is not associated with dementia. *Neurosci Lett* 2006; 402:92–96.
153. Ross OA, Whittle AJ, Cobb SA, et al. *LRRK2 R1441* substitution and progressive supranuclear palsy. *Neuropathol Appl Neurobiol* 2006; 32:23–25.
154. Hernandez D, Paisan Ruiz C, Crawley A, et al. The dardarin *G2019S* mutation is a common cause of Parkinson's disease but not other neurodegenerative diseases. *Neurosci Lett* 2005; 389:137–139.
155. Di Fonzo A, Tassorelli C, De Mari M, et al. Comprehensive analysis of the *LRRK2* gene in sixty families with Parkinson's disease. *Eur J Hum Genet* 2006; 14:322–331.
156. Lesage S, Ibanez P, Lohmann E, et al. *G2019S LRRK2* mutation in French and North African families with Parkinson's disease. *Ann Neurol* 2005; 58:784–787.
157. Paisan-Ruiz C, Lang AE, Kawarai T, et al. *LRRK2* gene in Parkinson disease: Mutation analysis and case control association study. *Neurology* 2005; 65:696–700.
158. Gaig C, Ezquerra M, Marti MJ, et al. *LRRK2* mutations in Spanish patients with Parkinson disease: Frequency, clinical features, and incomplete penetrance. *Arch Neurol* 2006; 63:377–382.
159. Kay DM, Kramer P, Higgins D, et al. Escaping Parkinson's disease: A neurologically healthy octogenarian with the *LRRK2 G2019S* mutation. *Mov Disord* 2005; 20:1077–1078.
160. Lesage S, Leutenegger AL, Ibanez P, et al. *LRRK2* haplotype analyses in European and North African families with Parkinson disease: A common founder for the *G2019S* mutation dating from the 13th century. *Am J Hum Genet* 2005; 77:330–332.
161. Zabetian CP, Hutter CM, Yearout D, et al. *LRRK2 G2019S* in families with Parkinson disease who originated from Europe and the Middle East: Evidence of two distinct founding events beginning two millennia ago. *Am J Hum Genet* 2006; 79:752–758.
162. Ross OA, Toft M, Whittle AJ, et al. *LRRK2* and Lewy body disease. *Ann Neurol* 2006; 59:388–393.
163. Aasly JO, Toft M, Fernandez-Mata I, et al. Clinical features of *LRRK2*-associated Parkinson's disease in central Norway. *Ann Neurol* 2005; 57:762–765.
164. Adams JR, van Netten H, Schulzer M, et al. PET in *LRRK2* mutations: comparison to sporadic Parkinson's disease and evidence for presymptomatic compensation. *Brain* 2005; 128:2777–2785.
165. Hernandez DG, Paisan-Ruiz C, McInerney-Leo A, et al. Clinical and positron emission tomography of Parkinson's disease caused by *LRRK2*. *Ann Neurol* 2005; 57:453–456.
166. Zimprich A, Muller-Myhsok B, Farrer M, et al. The *PARK8* locus in autosomal dominant parkinsonism: Confirmation of linkage and further delineation of the disease-containing interval. *Am J Hum Genet* 2004; 74:11–19.
167. Smith WW, Pei Z, Jiang H, et al. Leucine-rich repeat kinase 2 (*LRRK2*) interacts with *parkin* and mutant *LRRK2* induces neuronal degeneration. *Proc Natl Acad Sci* 2005; 102:18676–18681.
168. Giasson BI, Covy JP, Bonini NM, et al. Biochemical and pathological characterization of *Lrrk2*. *Ann Neurol* 2006; 59:315–322.
169. Galter D, Westerlund M, Carmine A, et al. *LRRK2* expression linked to dopamine-innervated areas. *Ann Neurol* 2006; 59:714–719.
170. West AB, Moore DJ, Biskup S, et al. From The cover: Parkinson's disease–associated mutations in leucine-rich repeat kinase 2 augment kinase activity. *Proc Natl Acad Sci USA* 2005; 102:16842–16847.

171. Gloeckner CJ, Kinkl N, Schumacher A, et al. The Parkinson disease causing *LRRK2* mutation *I2020T* is associated with increased kinase activity. *Hum Mol Genet* 2006; 15:223–232.
172. Najim al-Din AS, Wriekat A, Mubaidin A, et al. Pallido-pyramidal degeneration, supranuclear upgaze paresis and dementia: Kufor-Rakeb syndrome. *Acta Neurol Scand* 1994; 89:347–352.
173. Hicks AA, Pétursson H, Jónsson T, et al. A susceptibility gene for late-onset idiopathic Parkinson's disease. *Annals of Neurology* 2002; 52:549–555.
174. Li YJ, Scott WK, Hedges DJ, et al. Age at onset in two common neurodegenerative diseases is genetically controlled. *Am J Hum Genet* 2002; 70:985–993.
175. Maraganore DM, de Andrade M, Lesnick TG, et al. High-resolution whole-genome association study of Parkinson disease. *Am J Hum Genet* 2005; 77:685–693.
176. Oliveira SA, Li YJ, Noureddine MA, et al. Identification of risk and age-at-onset genes on chromosome 1p in Parkinson disease. *Am J Hum Genet* 2005; 77:252–264.
177. Noureddine MA, Qin XJ, Oliveira SA, et al. Association between the neuron-specific RNA-binding protein *ELAVL4* and Parkinson disease. *Hum Genet* 2005; 117:27–33.
178. Pankratz N, Nichols WC, Uniacke SK, et al. Genome screen to identify susceptibilty genes for Parkinson's disease in a sample without *parkin* mutations. *Am J Hum Genet* 2002; 71:124–135.
179. Pankratz N, Nichols WC, Uniacke SK, et al. Genome-wide linkage analysis and evidence of gene-by-gene interactions in a sample of 362 multiplex Parkinson disease families. *Hum Mol Genet* 2003; 12:2599–2608.
180. Pankratz N, Nichols WC, Uniacke SK, et al. Significant linkage of Parkinson disease to chromosome 2q36-37. *Am J Hum Genet* 2003; 72:1053–1057.
181. Ichinose H, Ohye T, Suzuki T, et al. Molecular cloning of the human *Nurr1* gene: Characterization of the human gene and cDNAs. *Gene* 1999; 230:233–239.
182. Mages HW, Rilke O, Bravo R, et al. *NOT*, a human immediate-early response gene closely related to the steroid/thyroid hormone receptor NAK1/TR3. *Mol Endocrinol* 1994; 8:1583–1591.
183. Saucedo-Cardenas O, Kardon R, Ediger TR, et al. Cloning and structural organization of the gene encoding the murine nuclear receptor transcription factor, *NURR1*. *Gene* 1997; 187:135–139.
184. Zetterstrom RH, Williams R, Perlmann T, et al. Cellular expression of the immediate early transcription factors *Nurr1* and *NGFI-B* suggests a gene regulatory role in several brain regions including the nigrostriatal dopamine system. *Brain Res Mol Brain Res* 1996; 41:111–120.
185. Zetterstrom RH, Solomin L, Jansson L, et al. Dopamine neuron agenesis in *Nurr1*-deficient mice. *Science* 1997; 276:248–250.
186. Law SW, Conneely OM, DeMayo FJ, et al. Identification of a new brain-specific transcription factor, *NURR1*. *Mol Endocrinol* 1992; 6:2129–2135.
187. Castillo SO, Baffi JS, Palkovits M, et al. Dopamine biosynthesis is selectively abolished in substantia nigra/ventral tegmental area but not in hypothalamic neurons in mice with targeted disruption of the *Nurr1* gene. *Mol Cell Neurosci* 1998; 11:36–46.
188. Sacchetti P, Mitchell TR, Granneman JG, et al. *Nurr1* enhances transcription of the human dopamine transporter gene through a novel mechanism. *J Neurochem* 2001; 76:1565–1572.
189. Sakurada K, Ohshima-Sakurada M, Palmer TD, et al. *Nurr1*, an orphan nuclear receptor, is a transcriptional activator of endogenous tyrosine hydroxylase in neural progenitor cells derived from the adult brain. *Development* 1999; 126:4017–4026.
190. Buervenich S, Carmine A, Arvidsson M, et al. *NURR1* mutations in cases of schizophrenia and manic-depressive disorder. *Am J Med Genet* 2000; 96:808–813.
191. Le WD, Xu P, Jankovic J, et al. Mutations in *NR4A2* associated with familial Parkinson disease. *Nat Genet* 2003; 33:85–89.
192. Grimes DA, Han F, Panisset M, et al. Translated mutation in the *Nurr1* gene as a cause for Parkinson's disease. *Mov Disord* 2006; 21: 906-909.
193. Engelender S, Kaminsky Z, Guo X, et al. Synphilin-1 associates with alpha-synuclein and promotes the formation of cytosolic inclusions. *Nat Genet* 1999; 22:110–114.
194. Wakabayashi K, Engelender S, Yoshimoto M, et al. Synphilin-1 is present in Lewy bodies in Parkinson's disease. *Ann Neurol* 2000; 47:521–523.
195. Wakabayashi K, Engelender S, Tanaka Y, et al. Immunocytochemical localization of synphilin-1, an alpha-synuclein-associated protein, in neurodegenerative disorders. *Acta Neuropathol (Berl)* 2002; 103:209–214.
196. Lee G, Junn E, Tanaka M, et al. Synphilin-1 degradation by the ubiquitin-proteasome pathway and effects on cell survival. *J Neurochem* 2002; 83:346–352.
197. Chung KK, Zhang Y, Lim KL, et al. *Parkin* ubiquitinates the alpha-synuclein-interacting protein, synphilin-1: Implications for Lewy-body formation in Parkinson disease. *Nat Med* 2001; 7:1144–1150.
198. Sriram SR, Li X, Ko HS, et al. Familial-associated mutations differentially disrupt the solubility, localization, binding and ubiquitination properties of *parkin*. *Hum Mol Genet* 2005; 14:2571–2586.
199. Farrer M, Destee A, Levecque C, et al. Genetic analysis of synphilin-1 in familial Parkinson's disease. *Neurobiol Dis* 2001; 8:317–323.
200. Bandopadhyay R, de Silva R, Khan N, et al. No pathogenic mutations in the synphilin-1 gene in Parkinson's disease. *Neurosci Lett* 2001; 307:125–127.
201. Tan E, Matsuura T, Nagamitsu S, et al. Polymorphism of *NACP-Rep1* in Parkinson's disease: An etiologic link with essential tremor? *Neurology* 2000; 54:1195–1198.
202. Tan EK, Tan C, Shen H, et al. Alpha synuclein promoter and risk of Parkinson's disease: Microsatellite and allelic size variability. *Neurosci Lett* 2003; 336:70–72.
203. Tan E, Chai A, Teo Y, et al. Alpha-synuclein haplotypes implicated in risk of Parkinson's disease. *Neurology* 2004; 62:128–131.
204. Hadjigeorgiou GM, Xiromerisiou G, Gourbali V, et al. Association of alpha-synuclein *Rep1* polymorphism and Parkinson's disease: Influence of *Rep1* on age at onset. *Mov Disord* 2005; 21:534–539.
205. Farrer M, Maraganore DM, Lockhart P, et al. alpha-synuclein gene haplotypes are associated with Parkinson's disease. *Hum Mol Genet* 2001; 10:1847–1851.
206. Mamah CE, Lesnick TG, Lincoln SJ, et al. Interaction of alpha-synuclein and *tau* genotypes in Parkinson's disease. *Ann Neurol* 2005; 57:439–443.
207. Xia Y, Saitoh T, Ueda K, et al. Characterization of the human alpha-synuclein gene: Genomic structure, transcription start site, promoter region and polymorphisms. *J Alzheimers Dis* 2001; 3:485–494.
208. Kruger R, Vieira-Saecker AMM, Kuhn W, et al. Increased susceptibility to sporadic parkinson's disease by a certain combined alpha-synuclein/apolipoprotein E genotype. *Ann Neurol* 1999; 45:611–617.
209. Izumi Y, Morino H, Oda M, et al. Genetic studies in Parkinson's disease with an alpha-synuclein/*NACP* gene polymorphism in Japan. *Neurosci Lett* 2001; 300:125–127.
210. Khan N, Graham E, Dixon P, et al. Parkinson's disease is not associated with the combined alpha-synuclein/apolipoprotein E susceptibility genotype. *Ann Neurol* 2001; 49:665–668.
211. Mueller JC, Fuchs J, Hofer A, et al. Multiple regions of alpha-synuclein are associated with Parkinson's disease. *Ann Neurol* 2005; 57:535–541.
212. Mellick GD, Maraganore DM and Silburn PA. Australian data and meta-analysis lend support for alpha-synuclein (*NACP-Rep1*) as a risk factor for Parkinson's disease. *Neurosci Lett* 2005; 375:112–116.
213. Chiba-Falek O, Nussbaum RL. Effect of allelic variation at the *NACP-Rep1* repeat upstream of the alpha-synuclein gene (*SNCA)* on transcription in a cell culture luciferase reporter system. *Hum Mol Genet* 2001; 10:3101–3109.
214. Chiba-Falek O, Touchman JW, Nussbaum RL. Functional analysis of intra-allelic variation at *NACP-Rep1* in the alpha-synuclein gene. *Hum Genet* 2003; 113:426–431.
215. Maraganore DM, Farrer MJ, Hardy JA, et al. Case-control study of the ubiquitin carboxy-terminal hydrolase L1 gene in Parkinson's disease. *Neurology* 1999; 53:1858–1860.
216. Wintermeyer P, Kruger R, Kuhn W, et al. Mutation analysis and association studies of the *UCHL1* gene in German Parkinson's disease patients. *Neuroreport* 2000; 11:2079–2082.
217. Wang J, Zhao CY, Si YM, et al. *ACT* and *UCH-L1* polymorphisms in Parkinson's disease and age of onset. *Mov Disord* 2002; 17:767–771.
218. Elbaz A, Levecque C, Clavel J, et al. *S18Y* polymorphism in the *UCH-L1* gene and Parkinson's disease: Evidence for an age-dependent relationship. *Mov Disord* 2003; 18:130–137.
219. Healy DG, Abou-Sleiman PM, Casas JP, et al. *UCHL-1* is not a Parkinson's disease susceptibility gene. *Ann Neurol* 2006; 59:627–633.
220. Maraganore DM, Lesnick TG, Elbaz A, et al. *UCHL1* is a Parkinson's disease susceptibility gene. *Ann Neurol* 2004; 55:512–521.
221. Xu PY, Liang R, Jankovic J, et al. Association of homozygous *7048G7049* variant in the intron six of *Nurr1* gene with Parkinson's disease. *Neurology* 2002; 58:881–884.
222. Zheng K, Heydari B, Simon DK. A common *NURR1* polymorphism associated with Parkinson disease and diffuse Lewy body disease. *Arch Neurol* 2003; 60:722–725.
223. Peng R, Gou Y, Yuan Q, et al. Mutation screening and association analysis of the *parkin* gene in Parkinson's disease patients from south-west China. *Eur Neurol* 2003; 49:85–89.
224. Satoh J, Kuroda Y. Association of codon 167 Ser/Asn heterozygosity in the *parkin* gene with sporadic Parkinson's disease. *Neuroreport* 1999; 10:2735–2739.
225. Wang M, Hattori N, Matsumine H, et al. Polymorphism in the *parkin* gene in sporadic Parkinson's disease. *Ann Neurol* 1999; 45:655–658.
226. Lincoln S, Maraganore D, Lesnick T, et al. *Parkin* variants in North American Parkinson's disease: Cases and controls. *Mov Disord* 2003; 18:1306–1311.
227. West AB, Maraganore D, Crook J, et al. Functional association of the *parkin* gene promoter with idiopathic Parkinson's disease. *Hum Mol Genet* 2002; 11:2787–2792.
228. Klein C, Schumacher K, Jacobs H, et al. Association studies of Parkinson's disease and *parkin* polymorphisms. *Ann Neurol* 2000; 48:126–127.
229. Mellick G, Buchanan D, Hattori N, et al. The *parkin* gene S/N167 polymorphism in Australian Parkinson's disease patients and controls. *Parkinsonism Relat Disord* 2001; 7:89–91.
230. Skipper L, Li Y, Bonnard C, et al. Comprehensive evaluation of common genetic variation within *LRRK2* reveals evidence for association with sporadic Parkinson's disease. *Hum Mol Genet* 2005; 14:3549–3556.
231. Di Fonzo A, Wu-Chou YH, Lu CS, et al. A common missense variant in the *LRRK2* gene, *Gly2385Arg*, associated with Parkinson's disease risk in Taiwan. *Neurogenetics* 2006; 7:133–138.
232. Maraganore DM, Wilkes K, Lesnick TG, et al. A limited role for *DJ1* in Parkinson disease susceptibility. *Neurology* 2004; 63:550–553.
233. Benjamin R, Leake A, Edwardson JA, et al. Apolipoprotein E genes in Lewy body and Parkinson's disease. *Lancet* 1994; 343:1565.
234. Huang X, Chen PC., Poole C. *APOE-[epsilon]2* allele associated with higher prevalence of sporadic Parkinson disease. *Neurology* 2004; 62:2198–2202.
235. Momose Y, Murata M, Kobayashi K, et al. Association studies of multiple candidate genes for Parkinson's disease using single nucleotide polymorphisms. *Ann Neurol* 2002; 51:133–136.
236. Zintzaras E and Hadjigeorgiou GM. The role of *G196A* polymorphism in the brain-derived neurotrophic factor gene in the cause of Parkinson's disease: A meta-analysis. *J Hum Genet* 2005; 50:560–566.
237. Kondo I and Yamamoto M. Genetic polymorphism of paraoxonase 1 (*PON1*) and susceptibility to Parkinson's disease. *Brain Res* 1998; 806:271–273.
238. Zintzaras E, Hadjigeorgiou GM. Association of paraoxonase 1 gene polymorphisms with risk of Parkinson's disease: A meta-analysis. *J Hum Genet* 2004; 49:474–481.
239. Bandmann O, Vaughan J, Holmans P, et al. Association of slow acetylator genotype for N-acetyltransferase 2 with familial Parkinson's disease. *Lancet* 1997; 350:1136–1139.

240. Borlak J, Reamon-Buettner SM. N-acetyltransferase 2 (NAT2) gene polymorphisms in Parkinson's disease. BMC Med Genet 2006; 7:30.

241. Kurth JH, Kurth MC, Poduslo SE, et al. Association of a monoamine oxidase B allele with Parkinson's disease. Ann Neurol 1993; 33:368–372.

242. Hotamisligil GS, Girmen AS, Fink JS, et al. Hereditary variations in monoamine oxidase as a risk factor for Parkinson's disease. Mov Disord 1994; 9:305–310.

243. Parsian A, Racette B, Zhang ZH, et al. Association of variations in monoamine oxidases A and B with Parkinson's disease subgroups. Genomics 2004; 83:454–460.

244. Hoda F, Nicholl D, Bennett P, et al. No association between Parkinson's disease and low-activity alleles of catechol O-methyltransferase. Biochem Biophys Res Commun 1996; 228:780–784.

245. Bialecka M, Drozdzik M, Honczarenko K, et al. Catechol-O-methyltransferase and monoamine oxidase B genes and susceptibility to sporadic Parkinson's disease in a Polish population. Eur Neurol 2005; 53:68–73.

246. Kosel S, Lucking CB, Egensperger R, et al. Mitochondrial NADH dehydrogenase and CYP2D6 genotypes in Lewy-body parkinsonism. J Neurosci Res 1996; 44:174–183.

247. Huerta C, Castro MG, Coto E, et al. Mitochondrial DNA polymorphisms and risk of Parkinson's disease in Spanish population. J Neurol Sci 2005; 236:49–54.

248. Maraganore DM, Farrer MJ, Hardy JA, et al. Case-control study of debrisoquine 4-hydroxylase, N-acetyltransferase 2, and apolipoprotein E gene polymorphisms in Parkinson's disease. Mov Disord 2000; 15:714–719.

249. Harhangi BS, Oostra BA, Heutink P, et al. CYP2D6 polymorphism in Parkinson's disease: The Rotterdam Study. Mov Disord 2001; 16:290–293.

250. Karamohamed S, Latourelle JC, Racette BA, et al. BDNF genetic variants are associated with onset age of familial Parkinson disease: GenePD Study. Neurology 2005; 65:1823–1825.

251. Westberg L, Hakansson A, Melke J, et al. Association between the estrogen receptor beta gene and age of onset of Parkinson's disease. Psychoneuroendocrinology 2004; 29:993–998.

252. Li YJ, Scott WK, Zhang L, et al. Revealing the role of glutathione S-transferase omega in age-at-onset of Alzheimer and Parkinson diseases. Neurobiol Aging 2005;

253. Ahmadi A, Fredrikson M, Jerregard H, et al. GSTM1 and mEPHX polymorphisms in Parkinson's disease and age of onset. Biochem Biophys Res Commun 2000; 269:676–680.

254. Nishimura M, Mizuta I, Mizuta E, et al. Influence of interleukin-1 beta gene polymorphisms on age-at-onset of sporadic Parkinson's disease. Neurosci Lett 2000; 284:73–76.

255. Farrer MJ, Haugarvoll K, Ross OA, et al. Genomewide association, Parkinson disease, and PARK10. Am J Hum Genet 2006; 78:1084–1088.

256. Goris A, Williams-Gray CH, Foltynie T, et al. No evidence for association with Parkinson disease for 13 single-nucleotide polymorphisms identified by whole-genome association screening. Am J Hum Genet 2006; 78:1088–1090.

257. Bialecka M, Kurzawski M, Klodowska-Duda G, et al. Polymorphism in semaphorin 5A (Sema5A) gene is not a marker of Parkinson's disease risk. Neurosci Lett 2006; 399:121–123.

258. Clarimon J, Scholz S, Fung HC, et al. Conflicting results regarding the semaphorin gene (SEMA5A) and the risk for Parkinson disease. Am J Hum Genet 2006; 78:1082–1084.

259. Li Y, Rowland C, Schrodi S, et al. A case-control association study of the 12 single-nucleotide polymorphisms implicated in Parkinson disease by a recent genome scan. Am J Hum Genet 2006; 78:1090–1092.

260. Elbaz A, Nelson LM, Payami H, et al. Lack of replication of thirteen single-nucleotide polymorphisms in Parkinson's disease: Aa large-scale international study. Lancet Neurol 2006; 5:917–923.

261. Corder EH, Saunders AM, Strittmatter WJ, et al. Gene dose of apolipoprotein E type 4 allele and the risk of Alzheimer's disease in late onset families. Science 1993; 261:921–923.

262. Schellenberg GD. Genetic dissection of Alzheimer disease, a heterogeneous disorder. Proc Natl Acad Sci USA 1995; 92:8552–8559.

263. Corder EH, Saunders AM, Risch NJ, et al. Protective effect of apolipoprotein E type 2 allele for late onset Alzheimer disease. Nat Genet 1994; 7:180–184.

264. Zareparsi S, Kaye J, Camicioli R, et al. Modulation of the age at onset of Parkinson's disease by apolipoprotein E genotypes. Ann Neurol 1997; 42:655–658.

265. Zareparsi S, Camicioli R, Sexton G, et al. Age at onset of Parkinson disease and apolipoprotein E genotypes. Am J Med Genet 2002; 107:156–161.

266. Li YJ, Hauser MA, Scott WK, et al. Apolipoprotein E controls the risk and age at onset of Parkinson disease. Neurology 2004; 62:2005–2009.

267. Huang X, Chen P, Kaufer DI, et al. Apolipoprotein E and dementia in Parkinson disease: A meta-analysis. Arch Neurol 2006; 63:189–193.

268. Pankratz N, Byder L, Halter C, et al. Presence of an APOE4 allele results in significantly earlier onset of Parkinson's disease and a higher risk with dementia. Mov Disord 2006; 21:45–49.

269. de Lau LM, Schipper CM, Hofman A, et al. Prognosis of Parkinson disease: Risk of dementia and mortality: The Rotterdam Study. Arch Neurol 2005; 62:1265–1269.

270. Conrad C, Andreadis A, Trojanowski JQ, et al. Genetic evidence for the involvement of tau in progressive supranuclear palsy. Ann Neurol 1997; 41:277–281.

271. Pastor P, Ezquerra M, Munoz E, et al. Significant association between the tau gene A0/A0 genotype and Parkinson's disease. Ann Neurol 2000; 47:242–245.

272. Scott WK, Nance MA, Watts RL, et al. Complete genomic screen in Parkinson disease: Evidence for multiple genes. JAMA 2001; 286:2239–2244.

273. Golbe LI, Lazzarini AM, Spychala JR, et al. The tau A0 allele in Parkinson's disease. Mov Disord 2001; 16:442–447.

274. Healy DG, Abou-Sleiman PM, Lees AJ, et al. Tau gene and Parkinson's disease: A case-control study and meta-analysis. J Neurol Neurosurg Psychiatry 2004; 75:962–965.

275. Sasaki H, Wakisaka A, Sanpei K, et al. Phenotype variation correlates with CAG repeat length in SCA2: A study of 28 Japanese patients. J Neurol Sci 1998; 159:202–208.

276. Gwinn-Hardy K, Chen JY, Liu HC, et al. Spinocerebellar ataxia type 2 with parkinsonism in ethnic Chinese. Neurology 2000; 55:800–805.

277. Simon-Sanchez J, Hanson M, Singleton A, et al. Analysis of SCA-2 and SCA-3 repeats in Parkinsonism: evidence of SCA-2 expansion in a family with autosomal dominant Parkinson's disease. Neurosci Lett 2005; 382:191–194.

278. Payami H, Nutt J, Gancher S, et al. SCA2 may present as levodopa-responsive parkinsonism. Mov Disord 2003; 18:425–429.

279. Shan DE, Liu RS, Sun CM, et al. Presence of spinocerebellar ataxia type 2 gene mutation in a patient with apparently sporadic Parkinson's disease: Clinical implications. Mov Disord 2004; 19:1357–1360.

280. Lu CS, Wu Chou YH, Kuo PC, et al. The parkinsonian phenotype of spinocerebellar ataxia type 2. Arch Neurol 2004; 61:35–38.

281. Gwinn-Hardy K, Singleton A, O'Suilleabhain P, et al. Spinocerebellar ataxia type 3 phenotypically resembling Parkinson disease in a black family. Arch Neurol 2001; 58:296–299.

282. Lu CS, Chang HC, Kuo PC, et al. The parkinsonian phenotype of spinocerebellar ataxia type 3 in a Taiwanese family. Parkinsonism Relat Disord 2004; 10:369–373.

283. Wu YR, Lin HY, Chen CM, et al. Genetic testing in spinocerebellar ataxia in Taiwan: Expansions of trinucleotide repeats in SCA8 and SCA17 are associated with typical Parkinson's disease. Clin Genet 2004; 65:209–214.

284. Khan NL, Giunti P, Sweeney MG, et al. Parkinsonism and nigrostriatal dysfunction are associated with spinocerebellar ataxia type 6 (SCA6). Mov Disord 2005; 20:1115–1119.

285. Shan DE, Soong BW, Sun CM, et al. Spinocerebellar ataxia type 2 presenting as familial levodopa-responsive parkinsonism. Ann Neurol 2001; 50:812–815.

286. Sidransky E. Gaucher disease and parkinsonism. Mol Genet Metab 2005; 84:302–304.

287. Aharon-Peretz J, Rosenbaum H, Gershoni-Baruch R. Mutations in the glucocerebrosidase gene and Parkinson's disease in Ashkenazi Jews. N Engl J Med 2004; 351:1972–1977.

288. Manfredi G. mtDNA clock runs out for dopaminergic neurons. Nat Genet 2006; 38:507–508.

289. Davidzon G, Greene P, Mancuso M, et al. Early-onset familial parkinsonism due to POLG1 mutations. Ann Neurol 2006; 59:859–862.

290. Hattori N, Yoshino H, Tanaka M, et al. Genotype in the 24-kDa subunit gene (NDUFV2) of mitochondrial complex I and susceptibility to Parkinson disease. Genomics 1998; 49:52–58.

291. van der Walt JM, Nicodemus KK, Martin ER, et al. Mitochondrial polymorphisms significantly reduce the risk of Parkinson disease. Am J Hum Genet 2003; 72:804–811.

292. Nicklas WJ, Vyas I and Heikkila RE. Inhibition of NADH-linked oxidation in brain mitochondria by 1-methyl-4-phenyl-pyridine, a metabolite of the neurotoxin, 1-methyl-4-phenyl-1,2,5,6-tetrahydropyridine. Life Sci 1985; 36:2503–2508.

293. Schapira AH, Cooper JM, Dexter D, et al. Mitochondrial complex I deficiency in Parkinson's disease. Lancet 1989; 1:1269.

294. Fiskum G, Starkov A, Polster BM, et al. Mitochondrial mechanisms of neural cell death and neuroprotective interventions in Parkinson's disease. Ann N Y Acad Sci 2003; 991:111–119.

VII

DRUGS

38 Levodopa: A Pharmacologic Miracle Four Decades Later

Tanya Simuni
Howard Hurtig

The designation of levodopa as a miracle drug is no exaggeration. It was first used to treat Parkinson's disease (PD) in the early 1960s, and by the time it was approved by the U.S. FDA in 1967, it was hailed as one of the most important advances in the pharmacotherapy of neurologic diseases of the first half of the twentieth century. Its development was based on a series of major advances in the understanding of the neurochemical mechanisms underlying the disease. Now, almost 40 years later and despite significant advances in the pharmacotherapy of PD, levodopa remains the "gold standard" of treatment. The gold, however, has been tarnished by a variety of intrinsic problems and complications of long-term use, such as motor fluctuations (the "on-off" phenomenon) and dyskinesia, which can be no less disabling than the parkinsonian symptoms it suppresses. Moreover, the early and unrealistic belief that levodopa could actually cure or at least slow the process of neurodegeneration by the simple replacement of a depleted neurotransmitter was quickly undercut by the harsh truth of practical experience and scientific discovery. In fact, one of the most active controversies swirling around levodopa today centers on whether it might *increase* the pace of neuronal degeneration by promoting oxidative neurotoxicity.

In this chapter we review the history of levodopa's development and the major milestones that punctuate its maturation as the mainstay of treatment for PD. We also cover the impact of levodopa on the mortality and morbidity of PD, the proposed mechanism of levodopa-induced complications (fluctuations and dyskinesia), and the data regarding levodopa toxicity.

HISTORICAL REVIEW

In his classic 1817 monograph *An Essay on the Shaking Palsy*, James Parkinson (1) described a series of 6 patients afflicted by the highly visible malady that now bears his name. The precision of much of the description is remarkable considering that Parkinson examined only 3 of the patients directly, whereas the others were observed by him as a vigilant spectator on the streets of London. His language has forever captured the cardinal manifestations of the disease, although the accuracy of some of his observations (i.e., the italicized segments, italics added) has been refuted by modern experience: "Involuntary tremulous motion, with *lessened muscular power*, in parts not in action and even when supported: with the propensity to bend the trunk forward and to pass from a walking to a running pace: the senses and the *intellect being unimpaired*." Parkinson himself did not comment on how to treat this new condition. Instead, he concluded his essay with an appeal "to those who humanely employ anatomical examination in detecting the courses and nature of diseases" to study the brain and find the cause. Later in the nineteenth century, Jean-Martin Charcot (2) described a "pill rolling" tremor and masked face as particular features of PD. As a corrective revision, he commented on the absence of weakness and the occasional impairment of intellect. By the beginning of the twentieth century, the clinical picture of the disease was well defined but the pathologic substrate remained unknown. In 1913, Lewy (3) first described the characteristic eosinophilic intracytoplasmic inclusion bodies in various regions of the brainstem but mistakenly reported that the substantia nigra (SN) was not affected. It was only a few years later, in 1919, that Tretiakoff (4) discovered that neuronal degeneration of the SN was a consistent pathologic signature in the brains of patients with clinical parkinsonism.

The anticholinergic belladona was the first pharmacologic agent used to treat PD. Ordenstein (5) observed, in 1867, that stiffness and tremor improved in addition to the drooling that belladonna was intended to treat. Antiparkinsonian drug development was slow to evolve, but by the early 1950s, synthetic anticholinergic drugs, such as benztropine mesylate and trihexyphenidyl, had been introduced. Although benefit was modest and inconsistent, anticholinergics remained the cornerstone of therapy for nearly 100 years. How anticholinergics ameliorate symptoms in PD is not clear. It is believed that they block muscarinic receptors in the striatum and thereby restore balance to the biochemical polarity that normally characterizes the relationship between dopamine and acetylcholine (6).

Because limited pharmacologic therapy in the early twentieth century was largely ineffective (except in dampening tremor and modestly reducing rigidity), neurosurgical ablation of a variety of sites in the brain and spinal cord became a popular alternative. The clinical finding that parkinsonian tremor was abolished by a stroke in the contralateral brain—an observation first made by James Parkinson in his essay—led to the conclusion that well-placed surgical lesions in particular motor centers might be useful in suppressing symptoms (7). Early surgical trials showed that lesions in the cortex or descending pyramidal tracts could truly arrest tremor, but often at the expense of paralysis. In 1952, Cooper (8) serendipitously discovered that accidental ligation of the anterior choroidal artery abolished parkinsonian tremor and rigidity (without causing paralysis) by producing a lesion in the globus pallidus. A variety of stereotactic surgical approaches were subsequently used to target the globus pallidus (9) and later the thalamus (10), specifically for tremor suppression but at considerable risk to the patient of major adverse effects and little chance that the underlying progressive disability could be favorably modified. The advent and widespread use of levodopa

rapidly eclipsed the application of surgical treatment in the management of PD, until the gradual appearance of motor complications associated with long-term levodopa therapy brought about the revival of a more sophisticated version of targeted lesioning. The evolution of both thinking and technology eventually led to electrical stimulation of key anatomic sites in the basal ganglia, today's standard of care in the surgical management of the symptoms of PD in selected patients.

Dopamine and the Rational Treatment of Parkinson's Disease

The development of levodopa as effective pharmacotherapy for PD was a logical outcome of advances in understanding the pathophysiology of parkinsonism. In the early 1950s, Brodie et al. (11) discovered that reserpine depleted serotonin in the brains of rats by altering storage in synaptic vesicles, following which Carlsson et al. (12) demonstrated that reserpine had the same effect on dopamine. Brodie (11) further showed that the motor slowing, or bradykinesia, induced by administration of reserpine to rabbits could be reversed by administration of levodopa, an inert precursor of dopamine. Subsequent investigations by Carlsson et al. (13) and by Bertler and Rosengren (14) showed that dopamine was highly concentrated in the caudate and putamen of the basal ganglia (the striatum), compared with other biogenic amines such as noradrenaline, which accumulated in the brainstem. By the end of the 1950s, these findings had led to the hypothesis that dopamine deficiency was the biochemical link to the pathophysiology of PD. Hornykiewiecz (15), whose seminal work and landmark publication in 1960 proved the hypothesis correct, subsequently wrote, "On the basis of these findings (in animals), it was to my mind a very simple and very logical step to go from animal to human brain to see whether it was possible to discover any abnormalities of dopamine metabolism in certain neurological disorders involving the basal ganglia." Ehringer and Hornykiewicz (16) studied the brains of patients dying of PD and consistently demonstrated a 90% reduction in the concentration of dopamine in the striatum and substantia nigra. They also showed that the content of striatal homovanillic acid (HVA), a stable by-product of dopamine metabolism, directly correlated with the degree of dopamine deficiency and of cell loss in the SN (17). They further observed that parkinsonism associated with chronic manganese poisoning was also characterized by degeneration of nigral neurons and a decrease in dopamine and HVA in the striatum and SN (18). However, authors of a recent review (Perl D, Olanow CW. The neuropathology of manganese-induced parkinsonism. J Neuropath Exp Neurol 2007; 66:675–682) of the subject of manganism have disputed Ehringer and Hornykiewicz's conclusion in this single case of presumed manganese induced parkinsonism, since the patient developed symptoms of parkinsonism ten years after exposure to manganese had ceased and had Lewy bodies in the SN, thereby strongly suggesting that the patient, despite the remote history of exposure to manganese, actually had PD as the basis for the neurologic illness and not manganism. Moreover, it is now generally accepted, as described in the recent review, that the pathology of manganism is confined to the medial globus pallidus. The SN in manganism is unaffected.

By the mid-1960s, sophisticated histofluorescence techniques had been developed and new knowledge quickly accumulated. Anden et al. (19), using this new methodology, demonstrated that dopamine was concentrated in neurons of the SN pars compacta (pc) and that axonal terminals projected cephalad to the striatum. Poirier and Sourkes (20), by showing that a unilateral nigral lesion in the monkey could cause ipsilateral depletion of striatal dopamine, mapped the previously unknown nigrostriatal pathway and thus explained the relationship between neuronal loss in the SNpc and dopamine depletion downstream in the striatum.

These pivotal discoveries provided the foundation for the logical and imaginative next step: treatment of PD by replacing the depleted neurotransmitter dopamine. The simplicity of the concept had to be a siren signal that implementation would not be easy.

Levodopa Therapy

One of the early findings of research into the pharmacologic properties of dopamine was that it did not penetrate the blood–brain barrier (BBB). Its immediate amino acid precursor, dihydroxyphenylalanine (dopa), could, however, cross the barrier and enter the brain, where it was enzymatically converted to dopamine. Proof of access to the central nervous system lay in levodopa's ability to reverse the behavioral effects of reserpine in experimental animals and elevate brain dopamine levels when administered systemically. In 1961, two independent research groups launched clinical trials of dopa in patients with advanced PD. Birkmayer and Hornykiewicz (21) administered dopa intravenously to parkinsonian patients in doses up to 150 mg. They observed "complete abolition or substantial reduction" of parkinsonian akinesia. Barbeau et al. (22) reported similar results following oral doses up to 300 mg of dopa daily (22). These early therapeutic experiments were soon repeated by many other investigators, with conflicting and frequently unimpressive results. Birkmayer and Hornykiewicz (23) later reported a positive response to dopa in only half of the patients and saw no recognizable effect if the patient's previous anticholinergic medication had been withdrawn. In 1964, McGeer and Zeldowitz (24) treated 10 patients with an oral dose of dopa ranging from 1 to 3 g daily. Only 2 of 10 patients improved at the highest dose, and the investigators concluded that dopa was not useful. In their experiment, dopa was combined with pyridoxine because of the erroneous belief that pyridoxine, a cofactor for dopa decarboxylase in the dopa-to-dopamine conversion reaction, would enhance the therapeutic impact. The fact that pyridoxine actually diminishes the effect of dopa by potentiating peripheral decarboxylation was not appreciated until 5 years later, when it was described by Duvoisin and coworkers (25).

Challenged by the inconsistent and even disappointing early experience with dopa therapy, Cotzias achieved what others could not by bringing dedication and an unswerving vision to the goal of proving that dopa really works. After years of deliberative trial and error, he and his colleagues reported in 1967 (26) that high doses (4 to 16 g) of oral racemic (D, L) dopa brought about "either complete, sustained disappearance or marked amelioration of parkinsonism" in 8 of 16 patients. There was a clear dose–response relationship, with only the patients on the highest dose responding. However, 25% of the patients developed granulocytopenia attributable to the drug and withdrew from the trial. In the same study the patients were exposed to melanocyte-stimulating hormone and phenylalanine, a dopa precursor, both of which aggravated the parkinsonian symptoms. The authors concluded that D, L dopa was effective in certain cases of parkinsonism but that the significant risk of granulocytopenia nullified its potential as a useful antiparkinsonian drug.

Two years later, Cotzias et al. (27) published the results of a study of levodopa (L-dopa) in 28 patients with PD, of whom 20 experienced marked and sustained improvement for up to 20 years. The daily dose of levodopa ranged from 4.5 to 8 g. None of the patients experienced the granulocytopenia observed with the use of D, L dopa. Nausea and vomiting—adverse drug effects common to other studies of dopa in PD—were overcome by the use of low-doses at the initiation of treatment followed by slow dose escalation. In the same study, the authors observed involuntary choreiform movements in 14 of 28 patients, ranging from mild to severe and correlating in severity with theduration of disease. Within the next few years similar studies using large oral doses of levodopa were reported by Yahr et al. (28), McDowell et al. (29), Markham (30), Godwin-Austen (31), and others, confirming the dramatic findings reported by Cotzias. A major breakthrough in the treatment of PD was duly recognized—Cotzias received the Lasker award in 1970—but just as important was the idea that replacement pharmacotherapy could be successful and might be applicable to other neurodegenerative disorders involving specific biochemical defects.

The next 5 years were marked by a number of studies that supported pronounced and sustained response of all parkinsonian symptoms to treatment with levodopa. Markham (30) demonstrated that the overall response to medication achieved at 1 year was sustained at 2 1/2 years.

Similar results were published by Yahr (32) and Cotzias et al. (33) as well as Godwin-Austen (31). At the same time, clinicians observed that despite levodopa's broad efficacy, tremor tended to respond less predictably than rigidity or bradykinesia (34).

The complete or near complete reversal of the physical signs and symptoms of a chronic progressive neurodegenerative disorder had not been previously seen or reported. The spectacle of patients being able to get out of bed and wheelchair to resume long lost daily and athletic activities was truly incredible to professional and lay witnesses alike. Furthermore, the evidence that levodopa was having a long-term impact on the natural history of PD began to accumulate. When progression of parkinsonian disability was compared in 182 patients receiving levodopa treatment with a cohort of patients from the prelevodopa era, Hoehn (35,36) found that patients on levodopa remained stable in each Hoehn and Yahr stage of the disease 3 to 5 years longer than was the case in the prelevodopa era. Also, the number of patients classified as disabled or dead at each stage was reduced by 30% to 50%. Yet there was no detectable difference in the severity of the parkinsonian symptoms between treated and untreated patients evaluated in the setting of withdrawal from levodopa, suggesting that the benefit derived from using levodopa was purely symptomatic, quickly reversible, and not in any way disease-modifying.

Levodopa's success was shadowed from the beginning by the emergence of a unique set of drug-related complications not seen by previous observers of the phenomenology of PD. Cotzias (26) was among the first to report that abnormal involuntary movements (called dyskinesia) became increasingly common and problematic with chronic use of levodopa. As early as 1968, the issue of levodopa-induced dyskinesia was the subject of a symposium (37). Later, Godwin-Austen (38), summarizing 4 years of experience using levodopa, noted the intractable nature of the involuntary movements in many cases and the continued progression of the parkinsonian disability in most, despite early improvement in motor function in the majority. The high frequency of organic mental symptoms, including confusion and visual hallucinations, was also disturbing. These and other drug-related obstacles to effective treatment have not only frustrated treating physicians but also fueled the collective efforts of researchers to refine levodopa's cruder aspects and search for viable alternative therapies.

THE BIOCHEMISTRY AND METABOLISM OF LEVODOPA

Levodopa's complicated metabolism (Figure 38-1), a short (90 minutes) half-life, a diminishing capacity for a dying pool of nigrostriatal neurons to store and convert levodopa to dopamine, and other molecular

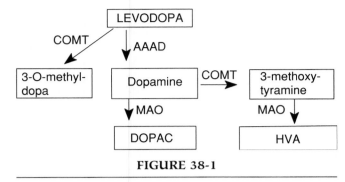

FIGURE 38-1

Levodopa metabolism. COMT = catechol-O-methyl transferase; MAO = monoamine oxydase; AAAD = aromatic amino acid decarboxylase; DOPAC = 3,4-dioxy-phenylacetic acid; HVA = homovanillic acid.

and pharmacodynamic reasons are responsible for the motor complications of long-term therapy. Levodopa is a large neutral amino acid (LNAA), which is absorbed in the proximal small intestine via an energy-dependent, carrier-mediated mechanism (38). The carrier is shared with other LNAAs and has saturation kinetics (39), which explains why dietary protein blocks the transport of individual oral doses of levodopa to the brain in some but not all patients. Cotzias reported this negative interaction in the early trials of levodopa in advanced PD. Peripherally, levodopa is rapidly metabolized to dopamine by the enzyme aromatic amino acid decarboxylase (AADC) and to 3-O methyl dopa by the enzyme catechol-O-methyl transferase (COMT). Its elimination half-life is approximately 90 minutes (40). The small amount of levodopa that eventually reaches the brain after a single oral dose—estimated at 1%—depends on the speed of gastric emptying, presence of competition for transport of the alternative amino acids, and, most of all, the degree of peripheral metabolism (41, 42). Coadministration of a peripheral AADC inhibitor (carbidopa or benserazide) doubles the bioavailability of levodopa without changing its elimination half-life (43) and allows more unchanged BBB-permissible levodopa to reach the brain (44). Increased bioavailability means at least an 80% reduction in the amount of levodopa required to achieve the same clinical effect as when levodopa is taken without an AADC inhibitor, as well as a decrease in peripheral dose-related side effects such as nausea, vomiting, and hypotension. After crossing the BBB, levodopa is taken up by the surviving striatal neurons and converted by intraneuronal AADC to dopamine (DA), which is, in turn, released presynaptically (45). According to this simplified model of levodopa's central metabolism, the response to a single dose of levodopa should decline in proportion to the progressive loss of nigral cells and the loss of their capacity to convert exogenous levodopa to DA. However, experience has shown that some PD patients, after many years of illness and near-total depletion of nigral neurons, still respond well to levodopa. There is some evidence to indicate that decarboxylation can occur in nondopaminergic striatal interneurons and in glia (46). Under physiologic conditions, dopamine is released at the synapse mainly through tonic activity in dopamine neurons (47). Released dopamine interacts in a complex fashion with dopamine receptors. Types D1 and D2 are the best characterized and are mainly represented in the motor striatum (48). Nigrostriatal denervation in PD is associated with upregulation of postsynaptic D2 receptors. It has been postulated that the combination of receptor upregulation, nonphysiologic pulsatile stimulation of receptors by exogenous DA, and abnormal signal transduction resulting from altered gene expression is responsible for the development of motor complications, specifically, "on-off" or wearing-off fluctuations and dyskinesia (49, 50). Dopamine is metabolized via the reuptake system or by the enzymes monoamine oxidase (MAO-B) and COMT (41). Oxidation via MAO-B converts dopamine to the stable, inactive byproduct homovanillic acid (HVA) (51). COMT methylates dopamine to produce 3-methoxytyramine (3-OMD), which is oxidized to HVA (44).

COMPLICATIONS OF LEVODOPA THERAPY

The immediate adverse effects of levodopa, particularly nausea and vomiting, were shown to be caused by the peripheral decarboxylation of levodopa to DA and were managed in the majority of cases by combining levodopa with carbidopa, a peripheral dopa decarboxylase inhibitor (DDI). In resistant cases, alternative peripheral dopamine antagonists (e.g., domperidone), which block dopamine receptors in the brainstem vomiting center, have been useful. However, the more insidious and ultimately disabling adverse drug effects generally emerge later, after several years of chronic use (see Chapters 38 and 39). Specifically, the evolution of motor fluctuations, drug-induced dyskinesia, and psychosis in the setting of advanced disease represents the most important challenge to the physician treating PD in the postlevodopa era. Cotzias and coworkers (27) described dyskinesia in 14 out of 28 patients treated with levodopa for up to 2 years. Since 1969, multiple volumes have been dedicated to the discussion of etiology and management of levodopa-induced complications, largely because the great majority of patients with PD must eventually learn to cope with the inevitable consequences of using an increasingly indispensable drug (52–56). For example, over 50% of the 352 patients enrolled in the DATATOP study of early PD developed fluctuations or wearing off. One-third of the sample reported dyskinesia within 20.5 (+8.8) months of starting levodopa therapy (54). The only study that provided a more optimistic profile of drug-induced complications was the CR FIRST clinical trial, which randomly compared the effects of initiating

treatment with standard-formulation carbidopa/levodopa versus the controlled-release formulation (57). In that study, only 22% of the patients developed fluctuations or dyskinesia during a 5-year prospective follow-up. The lower incidence of complications in CR FIRST can partly be explained by methodologic differences (fluctuations were recorded only if more than 20% of the day was spent in the "off" state and 10% of the day was spent with dyskinesia). Moreover, patients enrolled in CR FIRST, compared with other studies, required surprisingly low doses of standard and CR carbidopa/levodopa for a satisfactory response(158).

The most recent data on the incidence of dyskinesia in levodopa-treated patients with early PD come from the ELLDOPA study (Earlier versus Later Levodopa Therapy in Parkinson's Disease) (58). This study was designed to address the perennial debate of the impact of early initiation of levodopa therapy on the rate of progression of PD, which revolves around the possibility that levodopa might accelerate the progression of neurodegeneration because of its known ability to enhance oxidant stress in some in vitro experimental preparations (see below). In the ELLDOPA study, patients with recently diagnosed very early clinical parkinsonism and no prior exposure to long-term dopaminergic therapy were randomly assigned to four groups: placebo or carbidopa/levodopa at the daily levodopa dose of 150, 300, or 600 mg. Study duration was 40 weeks, followed by a 2-week washout period. The primary outcome measure was the rate of progression of PD based on the total score of the Unified Parkinson's Disease Rating Scale (UPDRS) performed by a blinded rater at the end of the washout period. Levodopa therapy reduced the worsening of PD symptoms in a dose–response pattern, with the greatest benefit seen in the group treated with the highest dose of levodopa, 600 mg daily. However, after less than a year's exposure, 16.5% of subjects treated with the 600-mg dose developed dyskinesia, and 30% developed wearing off by the end of the 40-week study period. The incidence of dyskinesia and wearing off in the groups receiving 150 and 300 mg was much lower and comparable to that in the placebo group.

The ELLDOPA study confirmed the high risk of levodopa-induced motor complications even early in the course of treatment, which correlated with the higher dose exposure. However, the study was not designed or powered either to quantify the degree of motor complications or to investigate the impact of motor complications on the patient's quality of life and the overall efficacy of therapy. The more interesting (and unexpected) finding of ELLDOPA was the inverse correlation between the dose of levodopa used during the study and the UPDRS score after the 2-week washout, thereby suggesting a potential *neuroprotective* (rather than adverse) effect of chronic levodopa therapy.

The pathogenesis of levodopa-associated motor fluctuations and dyskinesia is not fully understood, although two major pathophysiologic mechanisms are thought to be involved (50, 59, 60). First, progressive nigrostriatal degeneration reduces the capacity of the brain to store dopamine, and dopamine receptors increase in number as a result of denervation hypersensitivity. Second, intermittent or pulsatile stimulation (versus the more physiologic continuous stimulation) of dopamine receptors by exogenous levodopa appears to alter or heighten receptor sensitivity with untoward behavioral consequences, resulting in the emergence of motor complications. Third, the pathologic loss of dopamine causes significant disruption of intracellular signaling pathways linked to the healthy transcription of regulatory genes in the basal ganglia. As a result, altered gene expression can induce changes in the homeostatic biochemistry of neurotransmitters and neuropeptides, leading to unmodulated motor responses to drugs, especially levodopa, used to replace depleted dopamine. The precise nature of this common complication of chronic levodopa therapy is not known, especially because postmortem and positron emission tomographic (PET) studies in PD indicate that chronic levodopa therapy causes downregulation or a reduction in the number of dopamine receptors, the physiologic effect of which should be a lowered behavioral sensitivity (56). Experience in patients with PD and animals with MPTP-induced parkinsonism has shown that monotherapy with dopamine agonists in those previously untreated with levodopa is much less likely to induce dyskinesia, whereas dopamine agonists used to supplement levodopa where motor fluctuations are already present can easily induce dyskinesia (61, 62).

The duration of PD and the duration and amount of levodopa may influence the occurrence and timing of motor fluctuations (63). Early in the course of PD, patients experience a smooth response to levodopa treatment, with dosing only 2 to 3 times a day. Considering the short half-life of levodopa (90 minutes), this long-duration response (LDR) might be explained by presynaptic dopamine storage in unaffected axons and tonic release of the transmitter (41). As nigral degeneration progresses and nigrostriatal axons die back, storage capacity for dopamine becomes increasingly reduced and the LDR is transformed into a short-duration response, which conforms more or less with the pharmacokinetic short half-life of levodopa (64–66). This "storage hypothesis" is supported by a reduction in the striatal uptake of ^{18}F fluorodopa (an indicator of dopamine storage), on PET in fluctuating but not in stable PD patients (67). However, some patients develop fluctuations and dyskinesia soon after starting levodopa, irrespective of severity or duration of disease or of the dose of levodopa, as in the high-dose subgroup of ELLDOPA. Therefore loss of storage capacity may be necessary but is not sufficient to explain the complexities of motor fluctuations (56). The remarkably wide range of clinical variability among people who develop PD is a vivid reminder of how incompletely we understand the underlying basis

for many aspects of PD, especially the complications of levodopa therapy.

The evidence demonstrating a postsynaptic pharmacodynamic mechanism to explain motor fluctuations and dyskinesia has also been accumulating. Several studies have shown that the motor response to intravenous apomorphine, a direct dopamine agonist that does not depend on presynaptic storage and whose action is identical to that of dopamine, diminishes in proportion to the duration of illness and levodopa therapy (68, 69, 70). Similarly, in patients with asymmetric motor symptomatology, the duration of response to apomorphine is shorter on the more affected side (71). These experiments suggest that apomorphine's loss of efficacy is caused by the downregulation of postsynaptic receptors.

A number of studies have shown that chronic infusions of direct dopamine agonists, such as lisuride or apomorphine, ameliorate or significantly decrease on-off fluctuations and dyskinesias (72, 73). Similar results have been obtained with a continuous (nonpulsatile) infusion of levodopa (74, 75). These data suggest that motor fluctuations associated with chronic oral levodopa treatment are partly the result of nonphysiologic discontinuous delivery, in contrast to the tightly balanced mix of tonic and phasic release of dopamine in normal subjects (76).

The hypothesis of the relationship between pulsatile stimulation of postsynaptic dopamine receptors and induction of dyskinesia has been tested in two large randomized, double blind (RDB), placebo controlled clinical trials of dopamine agonists (DAs) versus levodopa for monotherapy of early PD. The primary endpoint of the studies was time of onset of motor complications. The design of the studies was based on the rationale that, compared to levodopa, DAs have a longer half-life and do not require presynaptic storage. Thus chronic use of DA should be associated with a lower risk of motor complications. Indeed, presently there is a solid body of clinical trials data with essentially all available DA demonstrating that treatment with DA produces fewer motor fluctuations and dyskinesia than levodopa (77–79). The two pivotal studies were conducted with two most commonly used DAs: pramipexole and ropinirole. The pramipexole-versus-levodopa study for patients with early PD (CALM PD) demonstrated a 24% incidence of dyskinesia in the pramipexole-treated group versus 54% in the levodopa-treated group over 4 years. (81). The ropinirole-versus-levodopa study had similar results in regard to dyskinesia: 20% in the ropinirole group versus 45% in the levodopa group over 5 years (82). The design of both studies allowed open-label levodopa supplementation in case the efficacy of the initial treatment agent was not sufficient. Patients who received DA and levodopa combination therapy still experienced fewer motor complications, which could have been a result of a lower dose of levodopa used in that subgroup compared to the group treated with levodopa monotherapy. The results of these studies could be interpreted as supporting the possibility that a longer half-life of dopaminergic agents leads to less dyskinesia.

It has been postulated that pulsatile stimulation of dopaminergic receptors can elicit long-term potentiation of excitotoxic glutamate-mediated responses because of disinhibition of the subthalamic nucleus, the major glutamatergic nucleus in the basal ganglia. The role of glutamate in causing motor fluctuations and dyskinesia is further supported by the observation that blockers of the NMDA (glutamate) receptor can ameliorate levodopa-induced dyskinesia in PD patients (61). For example, amantadine, a putative NMDA receptor blocker (80), has been demonstrated to reduce drug-induced dyskinesia when used at high dosages (83).

A CONTINUING CONTROVERSY: IS LEVODOPA TOXIC?

The Oxidant Stress Hypothesis

Despite its shortcomings, levodopa has stood the test of time and remains the most effective drug for treating the symptoms of PD. However, the pervasive, often disabling motor and mental complications associated with chronic levodopa usage have sustained an unresolved debate over the possibility that the drug itself is toxic and can accelerate neurodegeneration (84,85). It has been postulated that levodopa's toxicity is based on the formation of oxygen free radicals and other reactive oxygen species (Figure 38-2) (86), which can be destructive to the lipid substructure of cell membranes, among other areas, and may lead to cell death.

Oxidative reactions are ubiquitous in the human body and are an intrinsic part of the oxidative phosphorylation chain reactions resulting in the production of ATP. Hydrogen peroxide and free radical by-products can react with and damage not only cell membranes but also DNA and proteins (87). Normally, their production

is balanced by endogenous antioxidants, which effectively quench the toxic potential of these products. The most important of these intrinsic antioxidants are vitamins A, E, and C and the enzymes superoxide dismutase (SOD), catalase, and glutathione peroxidase (88). If the capacity of natural antioxidants is exceeded, cell death may result. Cells with high metabolic demand, such as the pigmented dopaminergic neurons in the SN, are particularly vulnerable to oxidative stress. Several characteristics peculiar to these neurons create a high risk for oxidative damage, including the presence of neuromelanin (89), iron (90), and MAO, all of which promote autooxidation. MAO catalyzes the oxidative deamination of dopamine in the SN and forms hydrogen peroxide (H_2O_2) in the process (Figure 38-2A) (91, 92). H_2O_2 itself is an oxidizing agent, but it also can react with ferrous iron (Fe^{2+}), to form the highly toxic hydroxyl radical (OH^-), a prime mediator of oxidative damage (Figure 38-2C). Iron is important in catalyzing oxidation reactions because of its ability to exist in 2 valence forms; thus it can donate a free electron, which promotes the formation of free radicals, including OH^- (88). H_2O_2 and oxygen radicals can also be generated nonenzymatically by the autooxidation of dopamine to form quinones (Q) and semiquinones (SQ) (Figure 38-2B) (93).

Neuromelanin, which is generated from dopamine autooxidation (93, 94), is associated with the generation of oxyradicals and hydrogen peroxide (95). Levodopa is a potential source of toxic free radicals as a result of its decarboxylation to dopamine and oxidation to neuromelanin. Under normal circumstances, the buffering capacity of the brain's antioxidants is sufficient to detoxify H_2O_2 and other free radicals. For example, glutathione is one of the most powerful naturally occurring antioxidants in the nervous system. Most tissue glutathione exists in the reduced form (GSH). Oxidation of glutathione is catalyzed by glutathione peroxidase, and this is the pathway by which H_2O_2 is cleared from the brain (Figure 38-2D). The average ratio of reduced glutathione to oxidized gluthathione (GSH:GSSG) in most normal tissues is more than 50:1. Although GSH is a potent antioxidant, GSSG can be potentially toxic. Levels of GSH have been shown to be selectively lowered in the SN of patients with early PD, compared with normal controls and patients with other neurodegenerative disorders (96–98). In addition, it is normal in other brain regions in PD. Even clinically normal subjects with incidental Lewy bodies in the SN (considered to be a marker of preclinical PD) on postmortem examination had decreased levels of GSH, similar to those in patients with advanced PD (99), but they showed no increase in GSSG, as might be predicted from Figure 38-2D if it were a mere consequence of increased hydrogen peroxide load. The latter observation suggests that GSH depletion is not a pure consequence of oxidant stress. Rather, it could be

(a). DOPAMINE–^{MAO} $\longrightarrow$ HVA + H_2O_2

Enzymatic oxidation of dopamine

(b). DOPAMINE + O_2 $\longrightarrow$ H_2O_2 + O_2^- + OH^- + SQ + Q

Dopamine autooxidation

(c). H_2O_2 + Fe^{2+} $\longrightarrow$ OH^- + $OH\cdot$ + Fe^{3+}

Production of OH free radicals

(d). 2GSH + H_2O_2 – glutathione peroxidase $\longrightarrow$ GSSG + $2H_2O$

The removal of hydrogen peroxide by glutathione

FIGURE 38-2

Oxidative stress hypothesis.

a primary biochemical defect leading to the programmed death of dopaminergic neurons. The use of exogenous levodopa may add further stress to an already overtaxed and inadequate supply of GSH. According to the oxidant stress hypothesis (see Chapter 28), this combination of a high rate of oxyradical formation (from dopamine) and insufficient levels of antioxidation (due to depleted GSH) is the metabolic mechanism responsible for accelerated cell death in PD.

A number of other possible mechanisms for levodopa-induced cell death have been reported and discussed; they include mitochondrial respiratory chain dysfunction (100, 101), apoptosis (102–107), and excitotoxicity (108) (see Chapters 27, 28, and 37).

Is Levodopa Neurotoxic in Vitro?

Levodopa is toxic to dopaminergic neurons in tissue culture (109–114). In these experiments, cells were exposed to levodopa concentrations ranging from 100 to 250 µM for 1 to 5 days. Postulated mechanisms by which levodopa enhanced cell death in these studies include the production of reactive oxygen radicals, which, in turn, cause cell death by either apoptosis or necrosis. Walkinshaw and Waters (104) showed that levodopa, not dopamine, was toxic and that toxicity was inhibited by antioxidants. In general, the concentration of levodopa used in tissue culture experiments has exceeded, by a large margin, the doses of levodopa used by patients with PD (5 to 50 µM) (115).

In a study of dopaminergic stimulation in a preparation of human lymphocytes, Blandini et al. (114) found mixed but mostly adverse effects of dopamine on antiapoptotic protein, Bcl-2, proapoptotic enzyme caspase-3, and antioxidant/antiapoptotic enzyme Cu/Zn superoxide dismutase.

Most in vitro experiments demonstrating levodopa toxicity have been conducted in neuronal cultures with few if any astrocytes—a major deficiency, since astrocytes have been shown to prevent autooxidation (116) and in vivo may help protect against the potential oxidative toxicity of dopamine. H_2O_2 resulting from the enzymatic metabolism of dopamine can be efficiently detoxified by abundant supplies of catalase and glutathione peroxidase located in glial cells (108). One astrocyte has the capacity to protect 20 neurons against the toxicity induced by the application of 100 µM of H_2O_2 (117). Dopaminergic neurons survive longer in glial-conditioned media, and this environment also protects them from the toxic effects of levodopa concentrations as high as 200 µM (118). Recent studies have demonstrated that the toxicity of levodopa in vitro is directly proportional to its concentration (119). In fact the addition of low concentrations of levodopa (50 µM) to cultures of fetal midbrain neurons increased survival and promoted neurite extension of dopaminergic

neurons (120). Exposure of cultures containing mesencephalic neurons and glia to levodopa actually *increased* the cell concentration of GSH (119) and enhanced neuronal protection.

There is another rationale for a possible neuroprotective, rather then neurotoxic, effect of levodopa therapy on dopaminergic neurons in PD. The hallmark of pathology in PD is presence of intracytoplasmic Lewy bodies (LB), which form as a result of the misfolding and abnormal fibrillization (aggregation) of the protein alpha synuclein. Dopamine combines with α-synuclein through oxidation to form dopamine-α-syn adducts, which can block the development of toxic amyloid fibrillization but instead form protofibrils that also can be neurotoxic (121). Therefore any intervention designed to protect vulnerable dopaminergic neurons and prevent neurodegeneration must block the formation of the entire fibrillization process. A more recent in vitro experiment documented that an intermediate by-product of dopamine oxidation, dopaminochrome, inhibits α-synuclein fibrillization by combining with the 125 to 129 amino acid residue of the α-synuclein molecule (122). Fully oxidized/polymerized dopamine is an ineffective inhibitor of α-synuclein fibrillization. The result is a conformational change in α-synuclein that leads to the formation of *nontoxic* oligomeric, soluble spheres which are unable to mature and are potentially toxic amyloid fibrils inside nigral neurons. In contrast to others, these investigators were unable to detect dopamine-α-synuclein adducts in their experimental model. Furthermore, in one transgenic animal model of PD, the α-synuclein A53T mutant mouse, insoluble synuclein aggregates were present in many parts of the brain but not the SN, where dopamine is primarily manufactured (122). Therefore, based on data from Norris and Giasson et al. (123), the presence of dopamine protects nigrostriatal neurons, and it is only when the cascade of factors responsible for the neuronal degeneration peculiar to PD begins to deplete dopaminergic cells that oxidant stress can gain an accelerating foothold to propel the degenerative process.

In summary, high concentrations of levodopa have been shown to be cytotoxic to pure dopaminergic neuron cultures and human lymphocytes; however, levodopa can also protect neurons in culture, especially when mixed with astrocytes in tissue cultures that approximate in vivo conditions more closely (124).

Is Levodopa Toxic in Normal Animals?

Exposure of normal animals to high concentrations of levodopa failed to demonstrate a neurotoxic effect (126–129). No reduction in the number of dopaminergic cells was observed in the substantia nigra of rats and mice fed with high doses of levodopa for 18 months (128). Administration of levodopa to normal rats did not increase the levels of striatal oxidized gluthathione (GSSG) despite a marked increase in dopamine turnover (130). GSSG, a by-product of the clearance of H_2O_2, could be considered a marker of increased oxidative load. The absence of an elevation in its concentration argues against the presence of levodopa-induced oxidative stress in normal animals. Primates given high doses of levodopa for 3 months showed no evidence of nigral degeneration or decrease in the density of striatal dopamine terminals (131). However, intrastriatal administration of high doses of levodopa to rats did produce degeneration of presynaptic dopaminergic terminals (132). Mytilineou et al, (133) explored the role of oxidative stress as an enhancer to the putative levodopa toxicity in dopaminergic cell culture and in neonatal rats: while glutathione inhibition enhanced levodopa-induced cell loss in tissue culture, there was no evidence of dopaminergic cell loss either with levodopa therapy or with glutathione inhibition in healthy neonatal rats. High concentrations of levodopa are potentially toxic to normal dopaminergic neurons in some species and not in others. No study has shown that systemic administration of levodopa in human-equivalent doses causes degeneration of dopaminergic cells in normal animals, although Pearce et al. (125) showed that dyskinesia can occur in normal monkeys given large doses of levodopa, thereby suggesting that exposure to supramaximal amounts of levodopa for any length of time can overwhelm the normal buffering capacity of striatal neurons for rapid reuptake and recycling of dopamine released at synaptic terminals.

Is Levodopa Toxic in Animals with a Lesioned Nigrostriatal System?

A number of studies have evaluated the effect of exposure to levodopa on the 6-hydroxy dopamine (6-OHDA) animal model of PD. Blunt et al. (134) lesioned the nigrostriatal pathway in rats and investigated the effect of chronic levodopa exposure on dopaminergic cell survival. Animals were assigned to a control group (lesion but no levodopa) and a treated group (lesion plus levodopa/carbidopa feedings for 27 weeks). The experiment demonstrated that the animals fed with levodopa/carbidopa had greater loss of dopaminergic cells on the lesioned side than control animals, especially in the ventral segmental area. The number of dopaminergic cells on the nonlesioned contralateral side was not affected in either group. The authors concluded that a damaged dopaminergic system is susceptible to further damage from levodopa-induced oxidative stress, which translates into an increased risk of treatment-related accelerated neurodegeneration.

The study by Murer and colleagues (136) used a similar design but expanded it considerably. Animals exposed to levodopa or placebo for 26 weeks had either a sham or actual unilateral 6-hydroxydopamine lesion that caused moderate or severe damage. When the various groups were compared, there was no significant difference in the number of surviving dopaminergic neurons between rats treated with levodopa versus rats treated with placebo. In contrast, surviving cells in the SN of the moderately lesioned rats treated with levodopa had a higher concentration of dopaminergic neurons compared with placebo-treated animals. The authors concluded that chronic levodopa exposure is not toxic to dopaminergic neurons of either healthy or 6-OHDA–lesioned rats. On the contrary, the authors postulated that levodopa can actually promote dopamine function and recovery in the rats with moderate degrees of 6-OHDA–induced damage. The difference between their results and those obtained by Blunt et al. was attributed to the variable degree of the 6-OHDA–induced lesion, which was more extensive in the Blunt study. The number of surviving dopaminergic cells before levodopa exposure was the key determinant of a neurotrophic levodopa effect. A number of more recent studies support that conclusion: Ferrario et al. (137) demonstrated no evidence of enhanced striatal cells degeneration with exposure to levodopa compared to a vehicle in 6-OHDA–lesioned rats. Reveron et al. (138) came to the same conclusion in the dopamine-depleted mouse model.

Is Levodopa Toxic in Humans?

There are no convincing data from human studies to assess a beneficial or detrimental effect of levodopa on the rate of PD progression or on nigral cell death in PD. The recently completed ELLDOPA study (cited earlier) was a pivotal attempt to address the issue of levodopa toxicity in PD patients and the impact of the drug on the rate of PD progression (58). The primary endpoint of the study was the rate of progression of PD over a 9½-month (40 weeks) period of exposure to a low (150 mg daily), medium (300 mg daily), and high (600 mg) daily dose of levodopa versus placebo in patients with early PD. The clinical marker of PD progression was the rate of change of the total UPDRS score over the duration of the study measured after 2 weeks of levodopa washout. Based on the short half-life of levodopa and previous clinical observations, the assumption was made that 2 weeks off medication was a sufficiently long time to wash out the symptomatic effect of the drug. The study enrolled 317 patients, and 86% completed the final clinical evaluation. The clinical outcome measures demonstrated that levodopa reduced the accumulation of PD disability in a dose–response fashion as measured by the UPDRS scale over the 40 weeks of observation. The effect was most robust in the high-dose levodopa (600 mg) group. After 2 weeks of washout, the scores in the levodopa-treated arms worsened but did not return to pretreatment baseline values. As discussed before, the high-dose levodopa arm also experienced the highest rate of adverse events, specifically motor complications, dyskinesias, and wearing off. The conclusion of the clinical arm of the study was that "levodopa either slows the progression of PD or has a prolonged effect on the symptoms of PD." The ELLDOPA study did not provide conclusive results on the impact of levodopa on the rate of progression of PD, since the benefit attributed to the highest-dose subgroup could have reflected greater storage capacity of the brain in early PD for exogenous levodopa, beyond the ability of a 2-week washout to measure. However, neither did the study demonstrated any clinical evidence of a detrimental effect of levodopa. There are a number of limitations of this study that make its interpretation difficult: (a) The short duration of the study provides limited insight into the long-term effect of the drug on the rate of progression of PD, and (b) The use of a washout in this study may be responsible for an unwarranted conclusion that levodopa is protective, since the persistence of a possible symptomatic effect of levodopa that exceeded the 2-week washout period could account for the improved status of the high-dose subgroup as a result of storage. There is no good information on how long exogenous levodopa can be "stored" in the brain, but it is not unreasonable to consider that it is still robust in patients with newly diagnosed PD. The unreliability of drug washouts must be considered in the design of future studies. The ELLDOPA-2 study is now planned to address these issues. In the interim, clinicians should be reassured that there is still no evidence that levodopa is toxic in humans with PD.

The Role of Dopamine Imaging in Evaluating the Impact of Levodopa on the Rate of PD Progression. One of the major constraints in defining the impact of levodopa on the natural history of PD has been lack of a reliable biomarker that can provide an accurate quantifiable estimate of progression of the disease and on which the symptomatic effect of treatment has no impact. Recent developments in the technology of in vivo neurotransmitter imaging and the assumption that these imaging modalities provide an accurate biomarker of the degree of preservation of the dopaminergic system have made imaging an attractive modality. Several ligands that utilize single photon emission computed tomography (SPECT) or positron emission tomography (PET) focused on the dopamine system have been developed (139). The 2 most commonly used ligands in PD measure the integrity of presynaptic dopamine function: ^{18}F fluorodopa PET labels dopa decarboxylase and β-CIT SPECT labels the dopamine transporter (140). Both ligands have been demonstrated to reliably separate subjects with normal dopaminergic function from those with a parkinsonian disorder(140). The degree of decline of ligand uptake correlates with the severity of PD symptoms and the degree of dopaminergic cell loss as demonstrated in postmortem

tissue (141, 142). These properties of the ligands make them an attractive research tool in measuring the rate of progression of PD and studying the impact of pharmacological agents as disease-modifying interventions.

The ELLDOPA study was one of a series of clinical trials performed over the last decade that attempted to use dopamine imaging as a surrogate marker to complement the clinical outcome measures (58). In addition to clinical evaluations, a subset of 142 study subjects underwent β-CIT SPECT imaging. The scans were performed before initiation of treatment and at week 40, before levodopa taper. The imaging substudy demonstrated that the patients treated with levodopa had a higher percent decrease in β-CIT uptake than the placebo-treated cohort. That analysis was performed after the exclusion of 19 subjects (14.5%) with normal β-CIT uptake. The conclusion of the imaging part of the ELLDOPA study was that "the neuroimaging data suggest that levodopa either accelerates the degree of dopaminergic cell loss or that its pharmacological effects modify the dopamine transporter." The major unanswered question is the pharmacological effect of the treatment agent (levodopa) on the level of transporter binding and how it affects the results of the scans.

Clinical trials of dopamine agonists versus levodopa in early PD also utilized dopamine imaging scans (143–145). REAL PET evaluated the impact of ropinirole versus levodopa on the results of ^{18}F fluorodopa PET scan obtained 4 weeks after the initiation of the treatment and again after 24 months of therapy (145). The study demonstrated a 34% relative reduction in the decline of tracer uptake in the ropinirole group compared to the levodopa group at 24 months. Clinical outcome measures demonstrated the superiority of levodopa treatment in controlling PD symptoms as measured by the motor UPDRS scale on medication. The pramipexole versus levodopa (CALM PD) study used β-CIT SPECT obtained at baseline and again at 24 and 46 months of treatment. At 24 months, there was no difference in imaging outcome between the treatment groups; but at 46 months there was a significant one-third reduction in the rate of tracer uptake decline in the pramipexole group (143, 144). The clinical outcome measure, motor UPDRS score off medication, did not differ between the treatment-assignment groups in the imaging substudy; but, as discussed previously, levodopa was superior to pramipexole in the whole CALM PD cohort. Both studies demonstrated a beneficial effect of dopamine agonists or detrimental effect of levodopa therapy on the imaging outcome measures, and these effects were consistent across the studies despite the use of different imaging ligands and different dopamine agonists. However, the interpretation of these studies is challenging due to potential direct pharmacological effect of the treatment agent on the level of ligand binding, which can influence the results of the scans (139, 146).

There is a concern of potential dopamine transporter upregulation by dopamine agonists but not by levodopa (146, 147). Levodopa and dopamine agonists can also have differential effects on metabolism of ^{18}F fluorodopa (146). Last, there is a discrepancy between the clinical outcomes that favor the effect of levodopa and the imaging outcomes that favor the effect of DA on the rate of disease progression. Provided that the intervention has a true neuroprotective effect, it should be expected to cause both outcome measures to point in the same direction.

In conclusion, the use of dopamine imaging as the surrogate marker of the rate of PD progression is presently premature. Additional data are necessary to clarify the impact of the treatment agents on the results of the imaging studies in the short and long term (139). Such studies are under way at present. In the interim, dopamine scans will continue to be used as exploratory tools in clinical trials, but the efficacy of the treatment interventions will still be based on clinical outcome measures. Imaging studies have not helped to clarify the issue of the protective versus detrimental effect of levodopa on the rate of progression of PD.

Another approach to assessment of the potential neuroprotective versus neurotoxic effect of long-term levodopa therapy is to evaluate the treatment effect on normal individuals and conduct large-scale epidemiological studies. Individuals treated with chronic levodopa as a result of a mistaken diagnosis of PD do not develop parkinsonism or changes in striatal metabolism on PET scans (148, 149), and nigral degeneration is not present at autopsy in these cases (148, 150). However, it can be argued that the normal brain is more resistant to oxidative stress than the parkinsonian brain. Autopsy data from patients with PD have not demonstrated any difference in the number of surviving nigral cells between levodopa-treated and levodopa-untreated patients (151), notwithstanding the difficulty of making quantitative comparisons in a SN severely depleted of neurons by end-stage PD. Moreover, active axonal outgrowth has been demonstrated in a fetal mesencephalic transplant performed on a levodopa-treated patient with PD who subsequently died of unrelated causes (152). Such active fetal tissue proliferation despite continuous levodopa treatment argues against drug toxicity in vivo.

Enhanced survival of PD patients in the postlevodopa era is used as another argument against levodopa-induced neurotoxicity. The landmark study of the natural history of PD in the prelevodopa era by Hoehn and Yahr (in about 1967) (36) reported a mortality rate 2.9 times greater than that in the age-matched population. Studies performed soon after the introduction of levodopa revealed a favorable but variable effect on mortality rates. Yahr (153) reexamined 597 of the patients who were treated with levodopa between 1967 and 1973 and showed that the mortality had decreased from 2.9 to 1.46

times the expected rate. Hoehn (154) reported a similar mortality ratio of 1.5 in 182 patients who were followed since the advent of levodopa therapy and concluded that life expectancy in the treated patients was close to that of the general population. Diamond and colleagues (155) demonstrated a positive correlation between early initiation of levodopa and reduced mortality. Other studies showed less optimistic results, and the mortality ratios ranged from 1.85 to 2.5 (156–160). One of the explanations for the discrepancy in mortality ratios between the early and later studies is that reduced mortality is a somewhat transitory benefit experienced during the first years of levodopa therapy but is partly reversed by the progressive nature of PD even in the face of optimal and sustained levodopa therapy (161). After a mean of 6 years of follow-up, Lees and Stern observed that the mortality ratio was 1.46 in a cohort of 178 patients treated with levodopa between 1969 and 1977, but it increased to 2.59 after a mean of 12 years of follow-up. Louis and colleagues (162) reported that the combination of PD and dementia was associated with the highest mortality, although the actual cause of death could not be separated into motor and mental components.

In conclusion, the question of levodopa's potential neurotoxicity remains unanswered (84, 163). In fact, levodopa may even be neuroprotective (85). However, since in vitro and in vivo models of human PD are imperfect, the practical impact of this debate devolves to a critical interpretation of the total body of clinical data.

REFINEMENT OF LEVODOPA THERAPY

Controlled-Release Levodopa/Carbidopa: Sinemet CR

The declining capacity of nigrostriatal neurons to store and physiologically release dopamine in progressive PD leads to a growing dependence on a rapidly metabolized, exogenous source of levodopa for effective motor control. This combination of forces may be responsible for the emergence of motor fluctuations and dyskinesia, whereby rapid cycling of exogenous dopamine at the synapse exposes the dopamine receptors to a less physiologic and potentially harmful pulsatile stimulation by the released neurotransmitter. One of the proposed ways to reverse the negative impact of pulsatile activation of the dopamine receptor and the associated motor fluctuations is to provide a steady levodopa plasma concentration and, consequently, a more continuous stimulation of these receptors (187). Multiple attempts to develop a controlled release (CR) preparation of levodopa/carbidopa were made during the 1970s, but the clinical effects were inconsistent. After numerous clinical trials, controlled-release (CR) carbidopa/levodopa (Sinemet) reached optimal development with the CR4 formulation. This was a slowly erodible matrix that released its contents in the most favorable temporal relationship with gastric emptying and offered the best kinetic advantage over immediate release (IR) Sinemet to offset CR's lower bioavailability (70% of IR) (188). The superiority of CR over IR was validated in phase III trials, and CR was approved by the FDA for marketing in the United States in the summer of 1991. Sinemet CR (in the United States) and Madopar HBS (in the United Kingdom and Canada), the CR preparations used today, produce a constant elevation of plasma levodopa levels for 3 to 4 hours longer than the IR preparation. Peak plasma levodopa levels are decreased and the half-life is prolonged (189). Several open-label and double-blind studies of CR have demonstrated a significant reduction in "off" time, improvement in clinical disability, and decreased frequency of dosing when compared with IR (190). However, two 5-year, randomized, double-blind trials comparing IR and CR in early untreated patients (134 in one study and 618 in the other) showed no major differences in the development of motor fluctuations or in performance on the UPDRS (57,191,192). The only statistically significant finding favoring CR (the Koller or CR FIRST study) was improvement in performance of ADLs and emotional reaction–social isolation scores on the Nottingham health profile (NHP), a measure of quality of life. CR was well tolerated. In one open-label study, 24 patients with advanced PD were converted from IR to CR and followed for 6 months (193). There was no significant difference in frequency of dosing, degree of fluctuations, and dyskinesias between the two groups, but a majority of patients preferred CR over IR and the NHP scores showed improvement in degree of social isolation, emotional reaction, and quality of sleep comparable to the favorable effect demonstrated by CR FIRST. In patients with early stages of PD and mild disability, the evidence from the CR FIRST clinical trial does not confer enough of an advantage to offset the higher expense of CR. Moreover, CR can cause increased and at times uncontrollable dyskinesias late in the day, as the concentration of levodopa in the blood increases.

REFINEMENT OF LEVODOPA THERAPY: ENZYME INHIBITION

Efforts to improve and refine levodopa's antiparkinsonian potential began in parallel with the earliest clinical trials. Enthusiasm for levodopa's phenomenal clinical success as an oral drug for PD was tempered by 2 major pharmacologic shortcomings: First, the short (90 minute) half-life caused the short duration response (SDR) to predominate over the long duration response (LDR) in many patients. Second, the high doses of levodopa that Cotzias found

necessary for the best suppression of parkinsonian symptoms and signs caused intolerable nausea because of the stimulating effect of dopamine (decarboxylated peripherally from levodopa) on the vomiting center in the floor of the fourth ventricle, which lies outside the BBB. Creative chemists at Hoffman–La Roche, the manufacturer of levodopa, saw 3 ways to manipulate levodopa's metabolic pathway to achieve clinical advantage: block peripheral conversion to dopamine (inhibit dopa decarboxylase) so that nausea could be prevented and a smaller amount of precursor would be required to enter the brain; prolong levodopa's duration of action by blocking the enzymes that degrade it (inhibit MAO and COMT); and retard intestinal absorption and thereby sustain bioavailability (controlled-release preparation).

Inhibitors of Dopa Decarboxylase

The earliest attempt to combine levodopa with a decarboxylase inhibitor (DDI) occurred when Roche sponsored Birkmayer's successful trial of levodopa and the DDI benserazide in the 1960s (164, 165). Cotzias et al. (27, 166) reported a similar effect with the L-isomer of an alternative DDI, alpha-methyldopahydrazine. In 1973, Rinne, Sonninen and Siirtola (167) demonstrated that levodopa and a DDI in a 4:1 ratio allowed a five-fold dose reduction of the dose of levodopa with comparable clinical benefit and significant amelioration of drug-induced nausea and vomiting. These unequivocally positive results convinced the Federal Drug Administration in the United States to approve a combination of levodopa and the DDI carbidopa for commercial distribution under the name of Sinemet (from the Latin: without nausea). Its counterpart in Europe, a combination of levodopa and benserazide, was released as Madopar. Optimists predicted that the reduced levodopa burden would greatly diminish the incidence of motor fluctuations, a central complication of long-term levodopa exposure. However, experience quickly showed that only the peripheral dopaminergic side effects (nausea and vomiting) were impacted.

Inhibitors of Enzymes that Degrade Dopamine: Monoamine Oxidase-B and Catechol-O-Methyl Transferase

The successful inhibition of MAO-B and COMT by safe and effective pharmaceuticals represents another advance in the refinement of levodopa as the premier agent for treating PD (see Chapters 33, 35). Birkmayer and Horniekiewicz (168), in the early 1960s, were the first to attempt to enhance levodopa's duration of action by combining it with a nonselective MAO inhibitor. The combination therapy potentiated the effect of levodopa but caused severe hypertension, tachycardia, and toxic delirium. The conclusion that a MAO inhibitor could not be used in conjunction with levodopa did not take into account—because it was not known at the time—that the adverse drug effects were manifestations of sympathetic overactivity caused by the catalytic action of MAO-A on norepinephrine (NE) and serotonin (5-HT), and not dopamine, which is metabolized by MAO-B. The toxic side effects observed by the investigators were precipitated by an increase in the concentration of tyramine (producing the "cheese" effect) because of the blockade of tyramine metabolism by MAO-A. Deprenyl, a selective MAO-B inhibitor, first introduced by Knoll et al. (169) as a "psychic energizer," is devoid of tyramine side effects in doses used in humans. It was subsequently shown to benefit patients with PD when used jointly with levodopa by modulating motor fluctuations while at the same time allowing for a reduction in the effective dose of levodopa (170). However, deprenyl is metabolized to methamphetamine and amphetamine, which may cause cognitive side effects.

In the presence of a DDI, COMT becomes the major enzyme responsible for the peripheral metabolism of levodopa (171). The principal by-product, 3-O-methyldopa (3-OMD), weakly competes with levodopa for uptake into the brain (172) but does not compromise its central therapeutic action. COMT inhibitors (COMTIs) can significantly decrease the peripheral metabolism of levodopa and boost central bioavailability of the drug. The initial attempts to develop COMTIs, in the early 1970s, were halted because of the toxic effects of the compounds and lack of efficacy (173). In the 1990s, 2 new COMTIs—tolcapone and entacapone—were developed to address the problem of motor fluctuations. A number of level I clinical trials (randomized, double-blind, placebo controlled) showed that COMTIs reduced "off" time by an average of 90 to 120 minutes per day while permitting a variable reduction in levodopa dosage by as much as 25% (174). Tolcapone is a more potent inhibitor of COMT, acting peripherally and centrally with a longer half-life, whereas entacapone inhibits only peripheral COMT and must be given more frequently with each dose of carbidopa/levodopa (175, 176). Both drugs improve the availability of levodopa as measured by the area under the plasma concentration–time curve without increasing the maximum concentration (Cmax) of plasma levodopa after single dose (177, 178, 186). However, with multiple doses, there is gradual escalation of the peak plasma concentration, which translates into increased potential to induce peak-dose dyskinesia. Indeed, dyskinesia was one of the most prominent adverse effects (along with nausea, diarrhea and insomnia) in the early trials of tolcapone. Tolcapone was associated with an asymptomatic and reversible elevation of hepatocellular enzymes in a small percentage of users in the trials, but the occurrence of 3 deaths from hepatic failure in patients using tolcapone forced its removal from the marketplace

in Canada and Europe and restriction of its use by the FDA in the United States (179). Current FDA regulation requires biweekly liver function tests for the first year of administration, followed by monthly testing.

The virtual demise of tolcapone in the aftermath of the hepatic deaths has allowed entacapone to become the dominant COMTI worldwide. A recent review of 8 level I clinical trials of carbidop/levodopa/entacapone compared with carbidopa/levodopa/placebo (1560 patients followed for 2 to 12 months) (180) concluded that entacapone reduced "off" time by 1 to 2 hours per day and levodopa dosage by 10% to 15%. Best motor function, ADLs, and quality of life were only modestly improved if at all.

The possibility that the combination of carbidopa/ levodopa and entacapone might be more effective than carbidopa/levodopa alone in *nonfluctuating* Parkinson's patients has been evaluated in 2 recent studies. Olanow et al. (181) conducted a 26-week, multicenter, randomized, double-blind, placebo-controlled, parallel trial of 750 patients (373 entacapone, 377 placebo) with mild to moderate (Hoehn and Yahr stage II), typical PD and a stable response to carbidopa/levodopa. Changes in the UPDRS (Part II-ADL, Part III-motor and total) and a quality-of-life (QOL) scale were the primary efficacy measures. There was no significant difference between the groups, although some items on the QOL scale trended positively. The results were confounded by a 25% dropout rate and an increased carbidopa/levodopa requirement in the placebo group.

In the second study of similar design, Brooks et al. (182) evaluated 172 fluctuators and 128 nonfluctuators over 6 months, with a 2:1 treatment:control ratio. The primary efficacy measure was change in part II of the UPDRS. As predicted, the fluctuators had significantly increased "on" time (average 1.3 hours per day) and reduced levodopa dosage. The nonfluctuators showed a modest (1-point) but significant improvement in UPDRS ADL score.

These 2 studies of nonfluctuating patients treated with carbidopa/levodopa and entacapone reached different conclusions, although differences in study design, the second study's small sample size, and the minimal absolute improvement in the primary efficacy measure could account for the variance. It was inferred from the use of entacapone combined with carbidopa/levodopa (marketed as Stalevo in the United States and Europe) in early, nonfluctuating patients that the combination produces more sustained blood levels of levodopa and less pulsatile, more physiologic delivery of the drug to the brain's dopamine receptors (135, 183) than carbidopa/ levodopa without entacapone. Hence it was felt that early use of the combination might prevent or at least postpone the time when motor fluctuations occurred in the chronic levodopa users. This hypothesis is supported by evidence in animal models of parkinsonism that early use of entacapone with carbidopa/levodopa therapy can prevent motor fluctuations when compared with carbidopa/levodopa alone (184, 185). An RDB, placebo-controlled clinical trial comparing Stalevo with regular Sinemet as initial pharmacotherapy is currently under way to test the hypothesis in humans.

Dopamine Agonists

Adverse events associated with levodopa's use as an antiparkinsonian drug prompted investigators to search for alternative treatment strategies. Dopamine agonists (DAs) (see Chapter 34) were appealing because they represented a fundamentally different and potentially advantageous approach to treatment. First, unlike levodopa, DAs act directly on postsynaptic dopamine receptors and are not dependent on a supply of presynaptic enzymes to convert levodopa to dopamine (194). Second, DAs have a longer half-life than levodopa, thereby providing the benefits of sustained instead of pulsatile stimulation of postsynaptic dopamine receptors (195). Third, DAs have a greater affinity for the D2 subgroup of dopamine receptors, which are not as likely to be involved with the generation of dyskinesia as the D1 subgroup (196). Fourth, DAs have the potential to decrease endogenous dopamine turnover through negative feedback to nigral neurons and can indirectly reduce the formation of dopamine-generated oxygen free radicals, which in turn have the capacity to accelerate neuronal cell death (194, 197).

Clinical trials in the early 1970s demonstrated the efficacy of the DA bromocriptine in PD, but experience quickly and clearly showed that DAs were effective mainly as modulators of and not as substitutes for levodopa except in the earliest phase of illness, when disability is mild (78, 79). The first generation of DAs (bromocriptine, pergolide) were derivatives of ergot alkaloid. In the few studies of these agents as monotherapy, a majority of patients required the addition of levodopa to the agonist within a year (195, 198). Such a short duration of benefit coupled with an average 30% rate of discontinuation of therapy in clinical trials because of immediate side effects (nausea, vomiting, hypotension) and lack of efficacy halted further studies in patients with newly diagnosed PD. Instead, these drugs were reserved as adjunctive therapy in advancing disease (195). Pergolide was reevaluated as monotherapy for early PD, and a 3-month double-blind, placebo-controlled trial demonstrated its efficacy and safety (199).

Pramipexole and ropinirole were developed in the early 1990s and approved by the FDA in 1997. Unlike the earlier DAs, these agents were evaluated systematically as monotherapy in early PD (195, 198). Long-term experience with ropinirole and pramipexole comes from the 2 pivotal RDB placebo-controlled studies discussed above: the Requip 056 study (82) and the CALM PD study (pramipexole) (81). Both studies were designed to compare DA and levodopa with respect to the potential to delay motor fluctuations and dyskinesia over a long-term treatment period: 5 years for ropinirole and 4 years for pramipexole. The Requip 056 study enrolled 268 patients with early PD. Patients were randomly assigned to receive ropinirole or levodopa, both of which were titrated to symptomatic effect. Physicians were allowed to supplement study patients with open-label levodopa in both groups if PD symptoms were not adequately controlled by the primary assigned drug. The ropinirole study demonstrated that 59.8% and 34% of patients, respectively, who completed the study remained on ropinirole monotherapy without the need for supplemental levodopa at 3 and 5 years of follow-up (82). The primary outcome measure was time to onset of drug-induced dyskinesia. There was a significant difference in the incidence of dyskinesia in favor of ropinirole regardless of levodopa supplementation: 20% in the ropinirole group and 45% in the levodopa group. Only 5% of study patients treated with ropinirole alone reported dyskinesia at the 5-year follow-up, although only 34% of the patients who completed the study were in this group (82). The efficacy of treatment based on the UPDRS motor scores favored levodopa. However, the statistically significant difference was small and did not translate into a change in activities of daily living (ADL) scores. The study had a nearly 50% dropout rate in both treatment groups. Withdrawal due to the side effects was also comparable in both groups. The study concluded that ropinirole monotherapy with as-needed levodopa supplementation provides adequate control of symptoms in early PD and reduces the risk of developing dyskinesia.

The role of pramipexole versus levodopa as initial treatment for PD was investigated in the CALM-PD study (81), which was designed like the ropinirole protocol, but the endpoint was incidence of *all* motor complications rather than dyskinesia only (81). The study again demonstrated the superiority of DA over levodopa in the incidence of motor complications: 52% in the pramipexole group versus 74% in the levodopa group. The incidence of dyskinesia was comparable to that in the ropinirole study: 24% in the pramipexole group, independent of levodopa supplementation, compared with 54% in the levodopa group. Levodopa was also superior to DA in the level of efficacy of treatment of PD symptoms based on the UPDRS motor score, but the quality-of-life scores did not differ between the groups. Pramipexole, like ropinirole, was effective as monotherapy early on. Approximately 70% of patients remaining in the study responded satisfactorily to monotherapy at the 2-year follow-up; by 4 years, however, 72% of the patients in pramipexole group required levodopa supplementation (81). Trials of open-label use of pramipexole report similar results, with about 50% of patients maintaining monotherapy for up to 36 months (200).

The results of these two studied unequivocally support the ability of DAs to delay the onset of motor complications for several years. However, there still remains a debate on the long-term significance of that effect (146). While DAs are associated with a lower risk of developing motor complications, they are less effective in controlling PD motor disability, associated with higher incidence of drug-related side effects (specifically somnolence, confusion, and leg edema), and substantially more expensive and complicated to use. Although the apparent advantages of using DAs as monotherapy in early PD have not been firmly proven, the appeal of postponing the use of levodopa is strong among neurologists (201). Even if there is no long-term benefit in a degenerative disease like PD, which runs a protracted course, the ability of DA monotherapy to reduce the risk of early motor fluctuations deserves serious consideration in the process of deciding which treatment is appropriate for an individual patient. The same reasoning applies to the earlier combination of levodopa and DA in patients who require increased motor benefit. The algorithm for the management of Parkinson's disease presented by Olanow and Watts (202) suggests a choice between DAs and levodopa as initial monotherapy: DAs in the "younger," fit patients with a milder burden of disease and levodopa in older patients with a higher burden of disease, especially if cognitive dysfunction is an issue,. There are compelling empirical arguments for initiating the treatment of PD with either a DA or with levodopa. The American Academy of Neurology's (AAN) Quality Standards Subcommittee and the International Movement Disorder Society (MDS) have each published reviews of the various pharmacologic therapies for PD to guide the treating physician through the proliferating and often conflicting literature on the subject. Each used standard biomedical databases (e.g., MEDLINE, Cochrane Library) to select publications that met high inclusion standards with emphasis on well-designed randomized controlled clinical trials (level I studies). Each also reached evidence-based conclusions on efficacy and safety. The MDS review (174) addresses each drug or class of drugs individually and compares efficacies where data permit. The AAN review (203) concludes with general recommendations for treating PD patients with the entire spectrum of drugs. In this report, the Quality Standards Subcommittee recommended the following: "For PD patients requiring initiation of symptomatic therapy, either levodopa or a dopamine agonist can be used. Levodopa provides superior motor benefit but is associated with a higher risk of dyskinesia" (203). Moreover,

none of the antiparkinson drugs reviewed were shown convincingly to have neuroprotective properties.

Continuous Levodopa Administration

The rationale for continuous drug delivery in PD is to simulate with exogenous levodopa the "normal" steady state of dopamine release at the striatal synapse. A number of such systems providing continuous delivery of levodopa to the brain have been evaluated. Patients receiving brief continuous enteral or intravenous infusions of levodopa have experienced excellent control or a significant reduction of fluctuations and dyskinesia (204). Shoulson and Chase (205) first used a constant intravenous infusion of levodopa in 5 patients with wearing off and demonstrated the ability to abolish motor fluctuations once a stable plasma levodopa concentration was achieved. Subsequently, other authors confirmed that continuous intravenous infusion of levodopa could effectively ameliorate complex fluctuations (206). However, long-term continuous intravenous delivery of the drug is not practical because of the corrosive effect of chronically infused levodopa on veins and soft tissue.

Continuous duodenal or jejunal infusion of levodopa has been employed as a way of neutralizing the contribution of erratic gastric emptying and uneven intestinal absorption to the problem of motor fluctuations in patients with advanced PD. Several open-label studies have demonstrated significant improvement in quality of life during "on" time (207,208). Kurth et al. (209) performed a small double-blind, placebo-controlled study of duodenal infusion of levodopa/carbidopa in 10 patients with advanced PD; 7 of the 10 improved, and 5 continued using duodenal infusion for 20 months after completion of the study. New gel preparation of carbidopa/levodopa for intraduodenal infusion was recently developed in Sweden (210–214), and the results of a 6-week randomized crossover study were reported (214). In a cohort of 24 patients with motor fluctuations, daytime inraduodenal infusion provided a 34% reduction of UPDRS motor scores compared to conventional PD medications. The infusion resulted in a 20% increase in "on" time without a corresponding increase in dyskinesia. PD quality-of-life scales also improved in the infusion group. At the end of the study, 16 patients elected to remain on the infusion. In that short-term study, the gel preparation was delivered via nasoduodenal tube. The same group reported their experience with long-term intraduodenal infusion (210). Between 1991 and 1998, a total of 28 patients with advanced PD were treated with intraduodenal carbidopa/levodopa infusion (210). They required insertion of an intraabdominal pump to deliver the drug and infusion was limited to the daytime hours due to concern of development of tolerance if it were continuous and around the clock. Patients were allowed to supplement the infusion with oral PD medications. Twenty-two patients remained on the infusion therapy long term, although the rate of pump-related complications was relatively high: 6 patients had tube infection, and gastroscopy-guided catheter adjustment was performed 35 times over the duration of follow-up. In summary, continuous duodenal drug delivery has been revived with advancing technology. However, each of the studies cited included small numbers of patients, and all authors agreed that the demands of maintaining the duodenal delivery system limit its use to a select subgroup of highly motivated patients with advanced disease who fail other treatment options.

A liquid suspension of carbidopa/levodopa, stabilized with ascorbic acid and taken orally, has been used as an alternative to cumbersome intraduodenal infusion. The mixture is stable for up to 72 hours at room temperature without specific handling (216). The results of this simple technique for facilitating oral–intestinal absorption have been modestly positive. In one study reported by Pappert et al. (216), some patients overcame unpredictable "off" symptoms by an earlier boost of the peak plasma levodopa level but otherwise realized no advantage over standard carbidopa/levodopa tablets. The frequency of dosing actually increased.

Parcopa, an orally dissolvable preparation of carbidopa/levodopa, was approved in 2005 (215). It offers the convenience of avoiding the need to swallow a pill, can be taken without water, but has no additional benefit over standard carbidopa/levodopa. It can be a useful alternative for postoperative and dysphagic patients and a convenient option if carbidopa/levodopa cannot be taken with a liquid beverage.

Levodopa methyl ester, a dispersable oral agent now in development as a liquid or tablet, contains the same active ingredients as standard carbidopa/levodopa but is more rapidly absorbed and has a shorter time to peak plasma concentration. It has no effect on the duration of on time but has the potential for quickly reversing severe early morning akinesia. Levodopa methyl ester has the same short half-life as standard carbidopa/levodopa and therefore is no less likely to be associated with the development of motor fluctuations (217). Alternative routes of delivery of levodopa methyl ester—including intranasal, subcutaneous, and intravenous—have also been investigated (218).

Another way to optimize levodopa therapy is to develop a levodopa compound that will circumvent the obstacles of gastrointestinal absorption and systemic metabolism encountered by the standard formulation. A number of new compounds are now being investigated. One such product, levodopa ethyl ester, is a levodopa prodrug, which, as a result of hydrolysis by esterases in the GI tract, has a faster onset of action and higher maximum concentration compared with standard carbidopa/levodopa. It can also be used parenterally as rescue therapy for severe "off" symptoms, especially in postoperative patients unable to take anything by mouth (219). An RDB study comparing levodopa ethyl ester and carbidopa/levodopa as a remedy for the reduction of morning "off" time and the latency between swallowing a pill and its onset of action showed no difference between the two drugs (220).

All of these pharmacologic strategies represent incremental progress, but they still fall short of disease modification, the holy grail of pharmacotherapy. Research on fetal cell transplantation has slowly and deliberately evolved for more than 2 decades (221), and early results were promising. However, the results of two recent RDB sham-controlled trials showed no difference between implanted patients and controls (222, 223) despite promising results of the open-label protocols (224, 225) (see Chapter 44 for further discussion). Levodopa or dopamine-secreting cell lines, encapsulated in slow-release polymer systems and implanted subcutaneously or directly into the striatum, are being investigated in animals and pilot human trials (226). Another approach is delivery of the growth factors to stimulate intrinsic nigrostriatal production of dopamine. A pilot open-label protocol with glial-derived neurotrophic factor (GDNF) demonstrated substantial benefit in 5 patients after 2 years of therapy (227). A subsequent double-blind randomized study was terminated prematurely at 6 months due to lack of efficacy and safety concerns. Finally, studies of gene therapy aimed at encoding enzymes responsible for dopamine biosynthesis, employing a variety of vectors, are on the near horizon (see Chapter 44). The most recent studies have focused on genes that offer neuroprotective or even neurorestorative function like production of growth factors (228, 229).

CONCLUSIONS

Forty years of experience have taught us much about the strengths, shortcomings, and travails of using levodopa to treat PD. As we move further into the new millennium and reflect on the remarkable story of this true pharmaceutical miracle, we conclude this chapter with a condensed list of lessons learned.

Levodopa remains the most effective drug for treating the symptoms of PD, notwithstanding the problems related to chronic use. Maximal levodopa efficacy is achieved by the concomitant use of inhibitors of the peripheral catabolic enzymes dopa decarboxylase, monoamine oxidase, and COMT.

- There is no evidence that levodopa is toxic to human beings, notwithstanding the experimental findings supporting toxicity in vitro. To the contrary, it may be neuroprotective!

- Motor complications associated with chronic oral levodopa therapy occur in most patients from the interaction between progressive nigrostriatal degeneration, unique pharmacodynamic properties of dopamine receptors, and altered molecular plasticity regulated by genes of the basal ganglia.
- The question of whether treatment with levodopa should be initiated early or later in the course of illness remains unanswered. The pendulum swings back and forth. That debate may continue into the twenty-second century.
- The fashion of treating "young" parkinsonians with dopamine agonists as a levodopa-sparing strategy has a sound theoretical and empirical basis. It is not yet clear that this strategy makes a difference over the long course of PD.
- Combination pharmacotherapy is a major advance in the management of PD. The evolution of this

practice is the result of major achievements in drug development and the emergence of the randomized clinical trial as the most rigorous measure of drug efficacy.
- The Achilles' heel of levodopa therapy is the drug's short half-life and erratic intestinal absorption, both of which produce a nonphysiologic pulsatile delivery of levodopa to the brain. A simple and effective system of continuous parenteral delivery has been pursued but not realized. A cure for PD is nowhere on the horizon but is still the ultimate dream of all researchers, no matter how they focus their investigative attention. Development of a completely new generation of antiparkinson drugs based on discoveries of mutated genes and their by-products may offer the best hope of major breakthroughs that will bring the dream closer to reality. Then and only then will levodopa be truly obsolete.

References

1. Parkinson J. *An Essay on the Shaking Palsy.* London: Sherwood, Neely, and Jones, 1817.
2. Charcot JM. *Lecons sur les malades de systeme nerveux: Faltes a la Salpetriere.* Paris, Delahaye et Lacrosmier,1871:155–188.
3. Lewy FH. Zue pathologischen Anatomie der Parlysis agitans. *Dtsch Z Nervenheilk* 1913; 50:50–55.
4. Tretiakoff C. *Contribution a l'etude de l'anatomie pathologiqaue du Locus Niger de Soemmering.* Paris: Thesis, 1919.
5. Ordenstein I. *Sur la paralysie agitante* Paris, Martinet. 1867.
6. Duvoisin R C. Cholinergic-anticholinergic antagonism in parkinsonism. *Arch Neurol* 1967; 17(2): 124–136.
7. Putman TJ. Treatment of unilateral paralysis agitans by section of the lateral pyramidal tract. *Arch Neurol Psychiatry* 1940; 44:950–976.
8. Cooper IS. Ligation of the anterior choroidal artery for involuntary movements of parkinsonism. *Arch Neurol* 1952; 75:36–48.
9. Svennilson E, Torvik A, Lowe R, et al. Treatment of parkinsonism by stereotactic thermolesions in the pallidal region: A clinical evaluation of 81 cases. *Acta Psychiatr Neurol Scand* 1960; 35:358–377.
10. Webster DD. Dynamic evaluation of thalamotomy in Parkinson's disease: Analysis of 75 consecutive cases. In: Gillingham FJ, Donaldson IML (eds). *Third Symposium on Parkinson's Disease.* Edinburgh: Livingstone, 1969:266–271.
11. Brodie BB, Comer MS, Costa E, et al. The role of brain serotonin in the mechanism of the central action of reserpine. *J Pharmacol Exp Ther* 1966; 152(2):340–349.
12. Carlsson A, Lindquist M, Magnusson T. 3, 4dihydroxyphenylalaninen and 5-hydroxytryptophan as reserpine antagonists. *Nature* 1957; 180:200.
13. Carlsson A, Lindquist M, Magnusson T, et al. On the presence of 3 hydroxytyramine in brain. *Science* 1958; 127:471–472.
14. Bertler A, Rosengren E. Occurrence and distribution of catecholamines in brain. *Acta Physiol Scand* 1959; 47:350–361.
15. Hornykiewicz O. Physiologic, biochemical and pathological backgrounds of levodopa and possibilities for the future. *Neurology* 1970; 20:1–5.
16. Ehringer H, Hornykiewicz O. Verteilung von Noradrenalin und Dopamin (3-Hydroxytyramin) im Gehirn des Menschen und ihr Verhalten bei Erkrankungen des extrapyramidalen Systems. *Wein Klin Wochensch* 1960; 38:1236–1239.
17. Bernheimer H, Birkmayer W, Hornykiewicz O, et al. Zur Differenzierung des Parkinson-Syndrome: Biochemisch-neurohistologische Vergleichsuntersuchungen. *Proc 8th Int Conf Neurol* (Vienna); 1965:145.
18. Hornykiewicz O. Parkinson's disease. From brain homogenates to treatment. *Fed Proc Fed Am Soc Exp Biol* 1973; 32:183–190.
19. Anden NE, Carlsson A, Dahlstrom A, et al. Demonstration and mapping of nigroneostriatal dopamine neurons. *Life Sci* 1964; 3:523–530.
20. Poirier LJ, Sourkes TL. Influence of the substantia nigra on the catecholamine content of the striatum. *Brain* 1965; 88:181–192.
21. Birkmayer W, Hornykiewicz O. Der 1–3,4 Dioxyphenylalanin (D DOPA)-Effekt bei der Parkinson-Akinese. *Wien J Klin Wochenschr* 1961; 73:787–788.
22. Barbeau A, Sourkes TL, Murphy CF. Les catecholamines dans la maladie de Parkinson, In: J de Ajuriaguerra (ed). *Monoamines et Systeme Nerveaux Central.* Geneva: Georg, 1962; 247–262.
23. Birkmayer W, Hornykiewicz O. Weitere experimentelle untersuchungen uber beim Parkinsonsyndrom und reserpine-parkinsonismus. *Arch Psychiatry Zeitschr Neurol* 1964; 206:367–381.
24. McGeer PL, Zeldowitz LR. Administration of dihydroxyphenylalanine to parkinsonian patients. *Can Med Assoc J* 1964; 90:463–466.
25. Duvoisin RC, Yahr MD, Cote L. Pyridoxine reversal of L-dopa effect in parkinsonism. *Trans Am Neurol Assoc* 1969; 94:81–84.
26. Cotzias GC, Van Woert MH, Schiffer LM. Aromatic amino acids and modifications of parkinsonism. *N Eng J Med* 1967; 276:374–379.
27. Cotzias GC, Papavasiliou PS, Gellene R. Modification of parkinsonism: Chronic treatment with L-dopa. *N Engl J Med* 1969; 280:337–345.
28. Yahr MD, Duvoisin RC, Schear MJ, et al. Treatment of parkinsonism with levodopa. *Arch Neurol* 1969; 21:343–354.
29. McDowell FH, Lee JE, Sweet R, et al. The treatment of Parkinson's disease with dihydroxyphenylalanine. *Ann Intern Med* 1970; 72:19–25.
30. Markham CH. Thirty months trial of levodopa in Parkinson's disease. *Neurology* 1972; 22:17–22.
31. Godwin-Austen RB, Tomlinson EB, Frears CC, et al. Effects of L-dopa in Parkinson's disease. *Lancet* 1969; 2:165–168.
32. Yahr MD, Duvoisin RC, Hoehn MM, et al. L-dopa (L-3,4-dihydroxyphenylanine): Its clinical effects in parkinsonism. *Trans Am Neurol Assoc* 1968; 93:56–63.
33. Cotzias GC, Papavsiliou PS, Steck A, et al. Parkinsonism and levodopa. *Clin Pharm Ther* 1970; 12:319–322.
34. Yahr MD, Duvoisin RC. Drug therapy of parkinsonism. *N Engl J Med* 1972; 287: 20–24.
35. Hoehn MM. Parkinson's disease: Progression and mortality. *Adv Neurol* 1987; 457–461.
36. Hoehn MM, Yahr MD: Parkinsonism: Onset, progression and mortality. *Neurology* 1967; 17:427–442.
37. Barbeau A, McDowell FH (eds). *L-Dopa and Parkinsonism.* Philadelphia: Davis, 1970.
38. Godwin-Austen RB. The long term therapeutic effect of levodopa in the treatment of parkinsonism. *Adv Neurol* 1973; 3:23–27.
39. Wade DN, Mearrick PT, Morris JL. Active transport of L-dopa in the intestine. *Nature* 1973; 242:463–465.
40. Hardie RJ, Malcom SL, Lees AJ, et al. The pharmacokinetics of intravenous and oral levodopa in patients with Parkinson's disease who exhibit on-off fluctuations. *Br J Pharmacol* 1986; 22:429–436.
41. Nutt JG, Feldman JH. Pharmacokinetics of levodopa. *Clin Neuropharm* 1984; 7:35–49.
42. Nutt JG, Woodward WR, Hammerstad JP, et al. The "on-off" phenomenon in Parkinson's disease: Relation to levodopa absorption and transport. *N Engl J Med* 1984; 310: 483–488.
43. Nutt JG, Woodward WR, Anderson JL. Effect of carbidopa on pharmacokinetics of intravenously administered levodopa: Implications for mechanism of action of carbidopa in the treatment of parkinsonism. *Ann Neurol* 1985; 13:537–544.
44. Wade LA, Katzman R. 3-O-Methyldopa uptake and inhibition of L-dopa at the blood-brain barrier. *Life Sci* 1975; 17:131–136.
45. Hefti F, Melamed E, Wurtman RJ. The site of dopamine formation in rat striatum after L-dopa administration. *J Pharmacol Exp Ther* 1980; 217:189–197.

46. Poewe W: L-dopa in Parkinson's disease: Mechanisms of action and pathophysiology of late failure. In: Jankovic J, Tolosa E (eds). *Parkinson's disease and Movement Disorders*. Baltimore: Williams & Wilkins, 1993:103–113.

47. Bunny BS, Walter JR, Roth RH, et al. Dopaminergic neurons: Effects of antipsychotic drugs and amphetamine on single cell activity. *J Pharmacol Exp Ther* 1973; 85:560–571.

48. Schwartz J-C, Giros B, Martres M-P, et al. The dopamine receptor family: Molecular biology and pharmacology. *Semin Neurosci* 1992; 4:99–108.

49. Obeso JA, Luquin MR, Grandas F, et al. Motor response to repeated dopaminergic stimulation in Parkinson's disease. *Clin Neuropharm* 1992; 15:75–79.

50. Widnell, K. Pathophysiology of motor fluctuations in Parkinson's disease. *Mov Disord* 2005; 20(Suppl 11): S17–S22.

51. Oreland L. Monoamine oxidase, dopamine and Parkinson's disease. *Acta Neurol Scand* 1991; 81(Suppl 136):60–65.

52. Marsden CD, Parkes JD, Quinn N. Fluctuations of disability in Parkinson's disease: Clinical aspects. In: Marsden CD, Fahn S (eds). *Movement Disorders*. London: Butterworth, 1982:96–119.

53. Quinn N, Critchley P, Marsden CD. Young onset Parkinson's disease. *Mov Disord* 1987; 2:73–91.

54. The Parkinson Study Group. Impact of deprenyl and tocopherol treatment on Parkinson's disease in DATATOP patients requiring levodopa. *Ann Neurol* 1996; 39:37–45.

55. Nutt J, Obeso JA, Stocchi F. Continuous dopamine-receptor stimulation in advanced PD. *Trends in Neroscience* 2000; 23 (Suppl):S109–S115.

56. Brooks DJ. PET studies and motor complications in PD. *TINS* 2000; 23(Suppl): S101–S108.

57. Block G, Liss C, Reines S, et al. Comparison of immediate-release and controlled-release carbidopa/ levodopa in Parkinson's disease: A multicenter 5 year study. The CR FIRST Study Group. *Eur Neurol* 1997; 37:23–27.

58. Fahn S, Oakes D, Shoulson, I, et al. Levodopa and the progression of Parkinson's disease. *N Engl J Med* 2004; 351(24):2498–2508.

59. De Jong GJ, Meerwaldt JD, Schmitz PI. Factors that influence the occurrence of response variations in Parkinson's disease. *Ann Neurol* 1987; 22: 4–7.

60. Bedard PJ, Blanchet PJ, Levesque D, et al. Pathophysiology of L-dopa induced dyskinesias. *Mov Disord* 1999; 14(Suppl 1):4–8.

61. Obeso JA, Lingzaroso G, Gorospe, et al. Complications associated with chronic levodopa therapy in Parkinson's disease. In: Olanow CW, Obeso JA (eds). *Beyond the Decade of the Brain*. Kent, UK: Wells Medical, 1997:11–35.

62. Rascol O. L-Dopa–induced peak-dose dyskinesias in patients with Parkinson's disease. A clinical pharmacologic approach. *Mov Disord* 1999; 14(Suppl 1):19–32.

63. Caraceni T, Scigliano G, Mussico M. The occurrence of motor fluctuations in parkinsonian patients treated long-term with levodopa: Role of early treatment and disease progression. *Neurology* 1991; 41:380–384.

64. Wooten GF. Progress in understanding the pathophysiology of treatment-related fluctuations in Parkinson's disease. *Ann Neurol* 1988; 24:366–371.

65. Fabbrini G, Mouradian MM, Juncos JL, et al. Motor fluctuations in Parkinson's disease: Central pathophysiological mechanisms: Part I. *Ann Neurol* 1988; 24:366–371.

66. Mouradian MM, Juncos JL, Fabbrini G, et al. Motor fluctuations in Parkinson's disease: Pathogenetic and therapeutic studies. *Ann Neurol* 1987; 22:475–479.

67. Leenders KL, Palmer AJ, Quinn N, et al. Brain dopamine metabolism in patients with Parkinson's disease measured with positron emission tomography. *J Neurol Neurosurg Psychiatry* 1986; 49:853–860.

68. Colosimo C, Merello M, Hughes AJ, et al. Motor response to acute dopaminergic challenge with apomorphine and levodopa in Parkinson's disease: Implications for the pathogenesis of the "on-off" phenomenon. *J Neurol Neurosurg Psychiatry* 1996; 60:634–637.

69. Gancher ST, Nutt JG, Woodward WR, et al. Time course of tolerance to apomorphine in parkinsonism. *Clin Pharmacol Ther* 1992; 52(5):504–510.

70. Gancher ST, Nutt JG, Woodward WR. Apomorphine infusional therapy in PD: Clinical utility and lack of tolerance. *Mov Disord* 1995; 10:37–43.

71. Rodriguez M, Lera G, Vaamonde J, et al. Motor response to apomorphine in asymmetric Parkinson's disease. *J Neurol Neurosurg Psychiatry* 1994; 57:562–566.

72. Vaamonde J, Luquin MR, Obeso JA. Subcutaneous lisuride infusion in Parkinson's disease: Response to chronic administration in 34 patients. *Brain* 1991; 114:601–614.

73. Kempster PA, Frankel JP, Stern JM, et al. Comparison of motor response to apomorphine and levodopa in Parkinson's disease. *J Neurol Neurosurg Psychiatry* 1990; 53:1004–1007.

74. Mouradian MM, Heuser IJE, Baronti F, et al. Modification of central dopaminergic mechanisms by continuous levodopa therapy for advanced Parkinson's disease. *Ann Neurol* 1990; 27:18–23.

75. Juncos JL, Engber TM, Raisman R, et al. Continuous and intermittent levodopa differentially affect basal ganglia function. *Ann Neurol* 1989; 25:437–478.

76. Grace AA. Phasic versus tonic dopamine release and the modulation of dopamine system responsivity: A hypothesis for the etiology of schizophrenia. *Neuroscience* 1991; 41:1–24.

77. Jenner P. The rational for use of dopamine agonists in Parkinson's disease. *Neurology* 1995; 45(Suppl 3):S6–S12.

78. Rinne UK. Early combination of bromocriptine and levodopa in the treatment of Parkinson's disease: A 5-year follow-up. *Neurology* 1987; 37:826–828.

79. Factor SA, Weiner WJ. Early combination therapy with bromocriptine and levodopa in Parkinson's disease. *Mov Disord* 1993; 8:257–262.

80. Metman LV, Del Doto P, Van den Munckhof P, et al. Amantadine as treatment for dyskinesias and motor fluctuations in Parkinson's disease. *Neurology* 1998; 50: 1323–1326.

81. Holloway RG, Shoulson I, Fahn S, et al. Pramipexole vs levodopa as initial treatment for Parkinson disease: A 4-year randomized controlled trial. *Arch Neurol* 2004; 61(7):1044–1053.

82. Rascol O, Brooks DJ, Korczyn AD, et al. A five-year study of the incidence of dyskinesia in patients with early Parkinson's disease who were treated with ropinirole or levodopa. 056 Study Group. *N Engl J Med* 2000; 342(20):1484–1491.

83. Metman VL, Del Doto P, Blanchet PJ, et al. Blockade of glutaminergic transmission as treatment of dyskinesias and motor fluctuations in Parkinson's disease. *Amino Acids* 1998; 14:75–82.

84. Fahn S. Is levodopa toxic? *Neurology* 1996; 47(Suppl 3):S184–S195.

85. Agid Y. Levodopa. Is toxicity a myth? *Neurology* 1998; 50:858–863.

86. Jenner P, Shapira AHV, Marsden CD. New insights into the cause of Parkinson's disease. *Neurology* 1992; 42:2241–2250.

87. Cross CE. Oxygen radicals and human disease. *Ann Intern Med* 1987; 107: 526–545.

88. Southorn PA, Powis G. Free radicals in medicine: Chemical nature and biological reactions. *Mayo Clin Proc* 1988; 63:381–389.

89. Fahn S, Cohen G. The oxidant stress hypothesis in Parkinson's disease: Evidence supporting it. *Ann Neurol* 1992; 32:804–811.

90. Olanow CW, Youdim MHB. Iron and neurodegeneration: Prospects for neuroprotection. In: Olanow CW, Jenner P, Youdim MHB (eds). *Neurodegeneration and Neuroprotection in Parkinson's Disease*. London: Academic Press, 1996:55–67.

91. Cohen G. The pathobiology of Parkinson's disease: Biochemical aspects of dopamine neuron senescence. *J Neural Transm* 1983; (Suppl 19):89–103.

92. Oreland L. Monoamine oxidase, dopamine and Parkinson's disease. *Acta Neurol Scand* 1991; 81(Suppl 136):60–65.

93. Graham DG. Oxidative pathways for catecholamines in the genesis of neuromelanin and cytotoxic quinones. *Mol Pharmacol* 1978; 14:633–643.

94. Graham DG. On the origin and significance of neuromelanin. *Arch Pathol Lab Med* 1979; 103:359–362.

95. Youdim MBH, Ben-Schachar D, Riederer P. Is Parkinson's disease a progressive siderosis of substantia nigra resulting in iron and melanin induced neurodegeneration? *Acta Neurol Scand* 1989; 80(Suppl 126):47–54.

96. Perry TL, Godin DV, Hansen S. Parkinson's disease: A disorder due to nigral glutathione deficiency. *Neurosci Lett* 1982; 33:305–310.

97. Sofic E, Lange KW, Jellinger K, et al. Reduced and oxidized glutathione in the substantia nigra of patients with Parkinson's disease. *Neurosci Lett* 1992; 142:128–130.

98. Sian J, Dexter DT, Lees AJ, et al. Alterations in glutathione levels in Parkinson's disease and other neurodegenerative disorders affecting basal ganglia. *Ann Neurol* 1994; 36:348–355.

99. Dexter DT, Sian J, Rose S, et al. Indices of oxidative stress and mitochondrial function in individuals with incidental Lewy body disease. *Ann Neurol* 1994; 35:38–44.

100. Pardo B, Mena MA, de Yebenes JG. L-dopa inhibits complex IV of the electron transport chain in catecholamine-rich human neuroblastoma NB69 cells. *J Neurochem* 1995; 64:576–582.

101. Ben-Shachar D, Zuk R, Glinka Y. Dopamine neurotoxicity: Inhibition of mitochondrial respiration. *J Neurochem* 1995; 64:718–723.

102. Kerr JFR, Wyllie AH, Currie AR. Apoptosis: A basic biological phenomenon with wide ranging implications in tissue kenetics. *Br J Cancer* 1972; 26:238–257.

103. Mochizuki H, Goto K, Mori H, et al. Histochemical detection of apoptosis in Parkinson's disease. *J Neurol Sci* 1996; 137:120–123.

104. Walkinshaw G, Waters CM. Induction of apoptosis in catecholaminergic PC12 cells by L-dopa: Implications for the treatment of Parkinson's disease. *J Clin Invest* 1995; 95:2458–2464.

105. Ziv I, Offen D, Barzilay A, et al. The protooncogene Bcl-2, a novel cellular protective mechanism against dopamine toxicity: Possible implications for Parkinson's disease (abstr). *Neurology* 1995; 45(Suppl 4):A279.

106. Hanrott K, Gudmunsen L, O'Neill, MJ, et al. 6-Hydroxydopamine-induced apoptosis is mediated via extracellular auto-oxidation and caspase 3-dependent activation of PKCdelta. *J Biol Chem* 2006 Mar 3; 281(9):5373–82.

107. Schulz JB, Gerhardt E. Apoptosis: Its relevance to PD. *Clin Neurosci Res* 2001; 1:427–433.

108. Masserana JM, Gong L, Kulaga H, et al. Dopamine induces apoptotic cell death of a catecholaminergic cell line derived from the central nervous system. *Mol Pharmacol* 1996; 50:1309–1315.

109. Michel PP, Hefti F. Toxicity of 6-hydroxydopamine and dopamine for dopaminergic neurons in culture. *J Neurosci Res* 1990; 26:428–435.

110. Pardo B, Mena MA, Fahn S, et al. Ascorbic acid protects against levodopa-induced neurotoxicity on a catecholamine-rich human neuroblastoma cell line. *Mov Disord* 1993; 8:278–284.

111. Mytilineou C, Han SK, Cohen G. Toxic and protective effects of L-dopa mesenchipal cell cultures. *J Neurochem* 1993; 61:1470–1478.

112. Pardo B, Mena MA, Casarejos MJ, et al. Toxic effects of L-dopa on mesenchipal cell cultures: Protection with antioxidants. *Brain Res* 1995; 682:133–143.

113. Ziv I, Melamed E, Nardin N, et al. Dopamine induces apoptosis-like cell death in cultured chick sympathetic neurons-a possible novel pathogenetic mechanism in Parkinson's disease. *Neurosci Lett* 1994; 170:136–140.

114. Blandini F, Mangiagalli A, Martignoni, E, et al. Effects of dopaminergic stimulation on peripheral markers of apoptosis: Relevance to Parkinson's disease. *Neurol Sci* 2003; 24(3): 157–158.

115. Cedarbaum JM. Clinical pharmacokenetics of anti-parkinsonian drugs. *Clin Phamacokinet* 1987; 13:141–178.

116. Pelton EW, Kimelberg HK, Shipherd SV, et al. Dopamine and norepinephrine uptake and metabolism by astroglial cells in culture. *Life Sci* 1981; 28:1655–1663.

117. Desagher S, Glowinski J, Premont J. Astrocytes protect neurons from hydrogen peroxide toxicity. *J Neurosci* 1996; 16:2553–2562.

118. Mena MA, Casarejos MJ, Carazo A, et al. Glia conditioned medium protects fetal rat midbrain neurones in culture from L-dopa toxicity. *Neuroreport* 1996; 7:441–445.

119. Han SK, Mytilineou C, Cohen G. L-dopa up-regulates glutathione and protects mesencephalic cultures against oxidative stress. *J Neurochem* 1996; 66:501–510.

120. Mena MA, Davila V, Sulzer D. Neurotrophic effects of L-dopa in postnatal midbrain dopamine/cortical astrocyte cocultures. *J Neurochem* 1997; 69:1398–1408.

121. Conway KA, Rochet JC, Biegannski, RM, et al. Kinetic stabilization of the alpha-synuclein protofibril by a dopamine-alpha-synuclein adduct. *Science* 2001; 294(5545):1346–1349.

122. Giasson, Duda JE, Quinn, SM, et al. Neuronal alpha-synucleinopathy with severe movement disorder in mice expressing A53T human alpha-synuclein. *Neuron* 2002; 16; 34(4):521–533.

123. Norris EH, Giasson BI, Hodara R, et al. Reversible inhibition of alpha-synuclein fibrillization by dopaminochrome-mediated conformational alterations. *J Biol Chem* 2005; 280(22):21212–21219.

124. Muller T, Hefter H, Hueber R, et al. Is levodopa toxic? *J Neurol* , 2004, 251(Suppl 6): VI/44–VI/6.

125. Pearce RK. L-dopa and dyskinesias in normal monkeys. *Mov Disord* 1999; 14(Suppl 1): 9–12.

126. Perry TL, Yong VW, Ito M, et al. Nigrostriatal dopaminergic neurons remain undamaged in rats given high doses of L-DOPA and carbidopa chronically. *J Neurochem* 1984; 43:990–993.

127. Cotzias GC, Miller ST, Tang LC, et al. Levodopa, fertility, and longevity. *Science* 1977; 196:549–551.

128. Hefti F, Melamed E, Bhawan J, et al. Long-term administration of L-dopa does not damage dopaminergic neurons in the mouse. *Neurology* 1981; 31:1194–1195.

129. Melamed E, Rosenthal J. Can chronic levodopa therapy accelerate degeneration of dopaminergic neurons and progression of Parkinson's disease? In: Nagtsu T, Fisher A, Yoshida M (eds). *Basic, Clinical, and Therapeutic Aspects of Alzheimer's and Parkinson's Diseases.* New York: Plenum Press, 1990:253–256.

130. Loeffler DA, DeMaggio AJ, Juneau PL, et al. Effects of enhanced striatal dopamine turnover in vivo on glutathione oxidation. *Clin Neuropharmacol* 1994; 17:370–379.

131. Jenner PG, Brinn MF. Levodopa neurotoxicity. Experimental studies versus clinical relevance. *Neurology* 1998; 50(Suppl 6): S39–S43.

132. Filloux F, Townsend JJ. Pre- and postsynaptic neurotoxic effects of dopamine demonstrated by intrastriatal injection. *Exp Neurol* 1993; 119:79–88.

133. Mytilineou C, Walker RH, JnoBaptiste R, et al. Levodopa is toxic to dopamine neurons in an in vitro but not an in vivo model of oxidative stress. *J Pharmacol Exp Ther* 2003; 304(2):792–800.

134. Blunt SB, Jenner P, Marsden CD. Suppressive effect of L-dopa on dopamine cells remaining in the ventral tegmental area of rats previously exposed to the neurotoxin 6-hydroxydopamine. *Mov Disord* 1993; 8:129–133.

135. Entacapone/levodopa/carbidopa combination tablet: Stalevo. *Drugs RD* 2003; 4(5): 310–311.

136. Murer MG, Dziwczapolsik G, Menalled LB, et al. Chronic levodopa is not toxic for remaining dopamine neurons but instead promotes their recovery in rats with moderate nigrostriatal lesions. *Ann Neurol* 1998; 43:561–575.

137. Ferrario JE, Delfino MA, Stefano AV, et al. Effects of orally administered levodopa on mesencephalic dopaminergic neurons undergoing a degenerative process. *Neurosci Res* 2003; 47(4):431–436.

138. Reveron ME, Savelieva KV, Tillerson JL, et al. L-dopa does not cause neurotoxicity in VMAT2 heterozygote knockout mice. *Neurotoxicology* 2002; 23(4–5): 611–619.

139. Ravina B, Eidelberg D, Ahlskog JE, et al. The role of radiotracer imaging in Parkinson disease. *Neurology* 2005; 64(2): 208–215.

140. Marek K, Jennings D, Seibyl J, et al. Imaging the dopamine system to assess disease-modifying drugs: studies comparing dopamine agonists and levodopa. *Neurology* 2003; 61(6 Suppl 3): S43–S48.

141. Niznik HB, Fogel EF, Fassos FF, et al. The dopamine transporter is absent in parkinsonian putamen and reduced in the caudate nucleus. *J Neurochem* 1991; 56(1): 192–198.

142. Snow BJ, Tooyama I, McGeer EG, et al. Human positron emission tomographic [18F]fluorodopa studies correlate with dopamine cell counts and levels. *Ann Neurol* 1993; 34(3):324–330.

143. Pramipexole vs levodopa as initial treatment for Parkinson disease: A randomized controlled trial. Parkinson Study Group. *JAMA* 2000; 284(15): 1931–1938.

144. Dopamine transporter brain imaging to assess the effects of pramipexole vs levodopa on Parkinson disease progression. Parkinson Study Group *JAMA* 2002; 287(13):1653–1661.

145. Whone AL, Watts RL, Stoessl AJ, et al. Slower progression of Parkinson's disease with ropinirole versus levodopa: The REAL-PET study. *Ann Neurol* 2003; 54(1):93–101.

146. Ahlskog JE. Slowing Parkinson's disease progression: Recent dopamine agonist trials. *Neurology* 2003; 60(3):381–389.

147. Albin RL, Frey KA. Initial agonist treatment of Parkinson disease: A critique. *Neurology* 2003; 60(3): 390–394.

148. Quinn N, Parkes D, Janoto J, et al. Preservation of the substantia nigra and locus ceruleus in a patient receiving levodopa plus decarboxylase inhibitor over a four-year period. *Mov Disord* 1986; 1:65–68.

149. Rajput AH, Fenton ME, Birdi S, et al. Is levodopa toxic to nondegenerating substantia nigra cells? Clinical evidence (abstr). *Neurology* 1996; 46(Suppl):A371.

150. Rajput AH, Fenton ME, Birdi S, et al. Is levodopa toxic to human substantia nigra? *Mov Disord* 1997; 12:634–638.

151. Yahr MD, Wolf A, Antunes JL, et al. Autopsy findings in parkinsonism following treatment with levodopa. *Neurology* 1970; 6(Suppl):55–56.

152. Kordower JH, Freeman TB, Snow BJ, et al. Neuropathological evidence of graft survival and striatal reinnvervation after the transplantation of fetal mesencephalic tissue in a patient with Parkinson's disease. *N Engl J Med* 1995; 332:1118–1124.

153. Yahr MD. Evaluation of long-term therapy in Parkinson's disease: Mortality and therapeutic efficacy. In: Birkmayer W, Hornykiewicz O (eds). *Advances in Parkinsonism.* Basel: Editiones Roche, 1976:444–445.

154. Hoehn MM. Parkinsonism treated with levodopa: Progression and mortality. *J Neural Transm* 1983; 19(Suppl):253–264.

155. Diamond SG, Markham C, Hoehn MM, et al. Multicenter study of Parkinson mortality with early versus later dopa treatment. *Ann Neurol* 1987; 22:8–12.

156. Curtis L, Lees AJ, Stern GM, et al. Effect of L-dopa on the course of Parkinson's disease. *Lancet* 1984; 2:211–212.

157. Uitti RJ, Ahlskog JE, Maraganore DM, et al. Levodopa therapy and survival in idiopathic Parkinson's disease. Olmstead County Project. *Neurology* 1993; 43:1918–1926.

158. Morgante L, Salemi G, Meneghini F, et al. Parkinson disease survival: A population-based study. *Arch Neurol* 2000; 57(4): 507–512.

159. Guttman M, Slaughter PM, Theriault ME, et al. Parkinsonism in Ontario: Increased mortality compared with controls in a large cohort study. *Neurology* 57(12): 2278–2282.

160. Bennett DA, Beckett LA, Murray AM, et al. Prevalence of and mortality from parkinsonism in a community population of older persons. *N Engl J Med* 1996; 334: 71–76.

161. Clarke CE. Does levodopa therapy delay death in Parkinson's disease? A review of the evidence. *Mov Disord* 1995; 10:250–256.

162. Louis ED, Marder K, Cote L, et al. Mortality from Parkinson's disease. *Arch Neurol* 1997; 54:260–264.

163. Weiner WJ. The initial treatment of Parkinson's disease should begin with levodopa. *Mov Disord* 1999; 14:716–724.

164. Birkmayer W, Mentasti M. Weitere experimentalle Untersuchungen uber den Catecholaminstoffwechsel bei extrapyramidalen Erkrankungen (Parkinson und chorea syndrome). *Arch Psychiatr Zschr Ges Neurol* 1967; 210:29–35.

165. Birkmayer W, Linauer W, Mentasti M. Traitement a la L-dopa combinee avec un inhibiteur de la dacarboxylase (RO4–4602). In: Ajuriaguerra J (ed.). *Monoamines noyaux gris centraux et syndrome de Parkinson.* Geneva: Georg, 1971:435–441.

166. Calne DB, Reid WF, Pletscher A. Idiopathic Parkinsonism treated with an extracerebral decarboxylase inhibitor in combination with levodopa. *Br Med J* 1971; 3:729–732.

167. Rinne UK, Sonninen V, Siirtola T. Treatment of Parkinsonian patients with levodopa and extracerebral decarboxylase inhibitor, Ro 4–4602. *Adv Neurol* 1973; 3:59–71.

168. Birkmayer W, Hornykiewicz O. Das Verhalten einiger Enzyme im Gehirn normaler und parkinsonkranker Menschen. *Arch Exp Pathol Pharmacol* 1962; 243:295.

169. Knoll J, Ecsery Z, Kelemen, et al. Phenylisopropylmethylpropinylamine (E-250), a new spectrum psychic energiser. *Arch Int Pharmacodyn* 1965; 155:154.

170. Birkmayer W, Birkmaer GD. Effect of (-) deprenyl in long-term treatment of Parkinson's disease. A 10 years experience. *J Neural Trans Suppl* 1986; 22:219–225.

171. Mannisto PT, Kaakkola S. New selective COMT inhibitors: Useful adjuncts for Parkinson's disease? *Trends Pharmacol Sci* 1989; 10:54–56.

172. Nutt JG, Woodward WR, Gancher ST, et al. 3-O-Methyldopa and the response to levodopa in Parkinson's disease. *Ann Neurol* 1987; 21:584–588.

173. Ericsson AD. Potentiation of the l-dopa effect by the use of catechol-O methyltransferase inhibitors. *J Neurol Sci* 1971; 14:193–197.

174. Management of Parkinson's disease: An evidence-based review. *Mov Disord* 2002; 17(Suppl 4): S1–S166.

175. Kaakkola S, Wurtman RJ. Effects of COMT inhibitors on striatal dopamine metabolism: A microdialysis study. *Brain Res* 1992; 587:241–249.

176. Limousin P, Pollak P, Gervason-Tournier CL, et al. Ro 40–7592, a COMT inhibitor, plus levodopa in Parkinson's disease. *Lancet* 1993; 341:1605.

177. Ahtila S, Kaakkola S, Gordin A, et al. Effect of entacapone, a COMT inhibitor, on the pharmacokinetics and metabolism of levodopa after administration of controlled-release levodopa-carbidopa in volunteers. *Clin Neuropharmacol* 1995; 18:46–57.

178. Dingemanse J, Jorga K, Zurcher G, et al. Pharmacokinetic–pharmacodynamic interaction between the COMT inhibitor, tolcapone and single dose levodopa. *Br J Clin Pharmacol* 1995; 40:253–262.

179. Assal F, Spahr L, Hadengue A, et al. Tolcapone and fulminant hepatitis. *Lancet* 1998; 352(9132):958.

180. Deane KH, Spieker S, Clarke CE, al. Catechol-O-methyltransferase inhibitors for levodopa-induced complications in Parkinson's disease. *Cochrane Database Rev* 2004; (4):CD004554.

181. Olanow CW, Kieburtz K, Stern M, et al. Double-blind, placebo-controlled study of entacapone in levodopa-treated patients with stable Parkinson disease. *Arch Neurol* 2004; 61(10):1563–1568.

182. Brooks DJ, Sagar H. Entacapone is beneficial in both fluctuating and non-fluctuating patients with Parkinson's disease: A randomised, placebo controlled, double blind, six month study. *J Neurol Neurosurg Psychiatry* 2003; 74(8):1071–1079.

183. Stalevo for Parkinson's disease. *Med Lett Drugs Ther* 2004; 46(1182):39–40.

184. Marin C, Aguilar E, Bonaste M, et al. (2005). "Early administration of entacapone prevents levodopa-induced motor fluctuations in hemiparkinsonian rats." *Exp Neurol* 192(1):184–193.

185. Smith LA, Jackson MJ, Barghouthy G, et al. Multiple small doses of levodopa plus entacapone produce continuous dopaminergic stimulation and reduce dyskinesia induction in MPTP-treated drug-naive primates. *Mov Disord* 2005; 20(3):306–314.

186. Kurth MC, Adler CH, St Hiliare M, et al. Tolcapone improves motor function and reduces levodopa requirement in patients with Parkinson's disease experiencing motor fluctuations: A multicenter, double-blind, randomized placebo-controlled trial. *Neurology* 1997; 48:81–87.

187. Sage JI, Mark MH. The rational for continuous dopaminergic stimulation in patients with Parkinson's disease. *Neurology* 1992; 42(Suppl 1):23–28.

188. Koller W, Pahwa R. Treating motor fluctuations with controlled-release levodopa preparations. *Neurology* 1994; 44(Suppl 6):S23–S28.

189. LeWitt PA, Nelson MV, Berchou RC, et al. Controlled-release carbidopa/levodopa (Sinemet 50/200 CR4): Clinical and pharmacokinetic studies. *Neurology* 1989; 39(Suppl 2):45–53.

190. Jankovic J, Schwartz K, Van der Linden C. Comparison of Sinemet CR4 and standard Sinemet: Double-blind and long-term open trial in Parkinsonian patients with fluctuations. *Mov Disord* 1989; 4:303–309.

191. Dupont E, Andersen A, Boas J, et al. Sustained-release Madopar HBS compared with standard Madopar in the long-term treatment of de novo parkinsonian patients. *Acta Neurol Scand* 1996; 93(1): 14–20.

192. Koller WC, Hutton JT, Tolosa E, et al. Immediate-release and controlled-release carbidopa/levodopa in PD: A 5-year randomized multicenter study. Carbidopa/Levodopa Study Group. *Neurology* 1999; 53(5): 1012–1019.

193. Hurtig HI, Skolnick BE, Matthews MR, et al. Post-market comparison of controlled-release Sinemet and standard Sinemet. A six-month follow-up study (abstr). *Mov Disord* 1996; 11(Suppl 1):158.

194. Olanow CW. A rationale for dopamine agonists as primary therapy for Parkinson's disease. *Can J Neurol Sci* 1992; 19:108–112.

195. Watts RL. The role of dopamine agonists in early Parkinson's disease. *Neurology* 1997; 49(Suppl 1):S34–S48.

196. Uitti RJ, Ahlskog JE. Comparative review of dopamine receptor agonists in Parkinson's disease. *CNS Drugs* 1996; 5:369–387.

197. Olanow CW, Jenner P, Brooks S. Dopamine agonists and neuroprotection in Parkinson's disease. *Ann Neurol* 1998; 44:S167–S174.

198. Factor SA. Dopamine agonists. *MedClin NorthAm* 1999; 83(2):415–443.

199. Barone P, Bravi D, Bermejo-Pareja F, et al. Pergolide monotherapy in the treatment of early PD. *Neurology* 1999; 53:573–579.

200. Carrion A, Weiner WJ, Shulman LM. A three and a half year experience with pramipexole monotherapy in patients with early Parkinson's disease. *Neurology* 1998; 50: A330.

201. Montastruc JL, Rascol O, Senard JM. Treatment of Parkinson's disease should begin with a dopamine agonist. *Mov Disord* 1999; 14:725–730.

202. Olanow CW, Watts RL, Koller WC, et al. An algorithm (decision tree) for the management of Parkinson's disease (2001): Treatment guidelines. *Neurology* 2001; 56(11 Suppl 5): S1–S88.

203. Miyasaki JM, Martin W, Suchowersky O, et al. Practice parameter: initiation of treatment for Parkinson's disease: an evidence-based review: Report of the Quality Standards Subcommittee of the American Academy of Neurology. *Neurology* 2002; 58(1): 11–17.

204. Marion MH, Stocchi F, Quinn NP, et al. Repeated levodopa infusion in fluctuating Parkinson's disease: Clinical and pharmacokinetic data. *Adv Neurol* 1986; 9:165–181.

205. Shoulson I, Glaubiger GA, Chase TN. On-off response: Clinical and biochemical correlations during oral and intravenous levodopa administration in parkinsonian patients. *Neurology* 1975; 25:1144–1148.

206. Nutt JG, Carter JH, Woodward W, et al. Does tolerance develop to levodopa? Comparison of 2-and 21-H levodopa infusion. *Mov Disord* 1993; 8:139–143.

207. Kurlan R, Rubin AJ, Miller CH, et al. Duodenal delivery of levodopa for on-off fluctuations in parkinsonism: Preliminary results. *Ann Neurol* 1986; 20:262–266.

208. Sage JL, Trooskin S, Sonsalla PK. Long-term duodenal infusion of levodopa for motor fluctuations in Parkinsonism. *Ann Neurol* 1988; 24:87–89.

209. Kurth MC, Tetrud JW, Tanner CM, et al. Double-blind, placebo-controlled, cross-over study of duodenal infusion of levodopa/carbidopa in Parkinson's disease patients with "on-off" fluctuations. *Neurology* 1993; 43:1698–1703.

210. Nilsson D, Nyholm D, Aquilonius SM, et al. Duodenal levodopa infusion in Parkinson's disease: Long-term experience. *Acta Neurol Scand* 2001; 104(6): 343–348.

211. Nyholm D, Lennernas H, Gomez-Trolin C, et al. Levodopa pharmacokinetics and motor performance during activities of daily living in patients with Parkinson's disease on individual drug combinations. *Clin Neuropharmacol* 2002; 25(2):89–96.

212. Nyholm D, Askmark H, Gomez-Trolin C, et al. Optimizing levodopa pharmacokinetics: intestinal infusion versus oral sustained-release tablets. *Clin Neuropharmacol* 2003; 26(3):156–163.

213. Nyholm D, Aquilonius SM. Levodopa infusion therapy in Parkinson disease: state of the art in 2004. *Clin Neuropharmacol* 2004; 27(5): 245–256.

214. Nyholm D, Nilsson Remahl AI, et al. Duodenal levodopa infusion monotherapy vs oral polypharmacy in advanced Parkinson disease. *Neurology* 2005; 64(2):216–223.

215. Parcopa: A rapidly dissolving formulation of carbidopa/levodopa. *Med Lett Drugs Ther* 2005; 47(1201):12.

216. Pappert EJ, Goetz CG, Niederman F, et al. Liquid lev-odopa/carbidopa produces significant improvement in motor function without dyskinesia exacerbation. *Neurology* 1996; 47:1493–1495.

217. Steiger MJ, Stocchi F, Bramante L, et al. The clinical efficacy of single morning doses of levodopa methyl ester: Dispersible Madopar and Sinemet Plus in Parkinson's disease. *Clin Neuropharmacol* 1992; 15:501–504.

218. Swope DM. Rapid treatment of "wearing off" in Parkinson's disease. *Neurology* 2004; 62(6 Suppl 4):S27–S31.

219. Djaldetti R, Ziv I, Melamed E. Impaired absorption of oral levodopa: A major cause for response fluctuations in Parkinson's disease. *Isr J Med* 1996; 32:1224.

220. Parkinson Study Group. A randomized controlled trial of etilevodopa in patients with Parkinson's disease who have motor fluctuations. *Arch Neurol.*2006; 63:210–216

221. Lindvall O. Update on fetal transplantation: The Swedish experience. *Mov Disord* 1998; 13(Suppl 1):83–87.

222. Freed CR, Greene PE, Breeze RE, et al. Transplantation of embryonic dopamine neurons for severe Parkinson's disease. *N Engl J Med* 2001; 344(10): 710–719.

223. Olanow CW, Goetz CG, Kordower JH, et al. A double-blind controlled trial of bilateral fetal nigral transplantation in Parkinson's disease. *Ann Neurol* 54(3): 403–414.

224. Freed C R, Breeze RE, Rosenberg NL, et al. Survival of implanted fetal dopamine cells and neurologic improvement 12 to 46 months after transplantation for Parkinson's disease. *N Engl J Med* 1992; 327(22):1549–1555.

225. Hoffer BJ, Leenders KL, Young D, et al. Eighteen-month course of two patients with grafts of fetal dopamine neurons for severe Parkinson's disease. *Exp Neurol* 1992; 118(3):243–252.

226. Lapchak PA. A preclinical development strategy designed to optimize the use of glial cell line–derived neurotrophic factor in the treatment of Parkinson's disease. *Mov Disord* 1998; 13(Suppl 4):49–54.

227. Patel NK, Bunnage M, Plaha P, et al. Intraputamenal infusion of glial cell line–derived neurotrophic factor in PD: A two-year outcome study. *Ann Neurol* 2005; 57(2): 298–302.

228. Kang UJ. Potential of gene therapy for Parkinson's disease: Neurobiologic issues and new developments in gene transfer methodologies. *Mov Disord* 1998; 13(Suppl 1):59–72.

229. Oransky I. Gene therapy trial for Parkinson's disease begins. *Lancet* 2003; 362(9385):712.

230. Cooper JR, Bloom FE, Roth RH. *The Biochemical Basis of Neuropharmacology*. New York: Oxford University Press, 1991.

39 Amantadine and Anticholinergics

Charles H. Adler

Before the discovery of levodopa for the treatment of Parkinson's disease (PD) the treatment of choice was trihexyphenidyl (Artane) or other anticholinergic medications. At about the same time that trials of levodopa demonstrated its efficacy, the finding that amantadine was beneficial in PD was published (1). Both groups of drugs continue to play important roles in the treatment of PD today.

AMANTADINE

The serendipitous discovery that amantadine (Symmetrel) had antiparkinsonian effects in improving rest tremor, rigidity, and akinesia was made by Schwab and colleagues (1) in 1968, when a PD patient took this drug as prophylaxis against influenza A. She improved during the 6 weeks that she took amantadine and deteriorated when it was discontinued. Since that time there have been numerous reports of amantadine's beneficial effects as monotherapy in early, untreated PD (1–6) and in stable, treated PD (4, 7) as well as in adjunctive treatment with levodopa for patients with more advanced, fluctuating disease (8–11). Although its mechanism of action of amantadine is not completely clear, its clinical role is established.

Pharmacology

Amantadine hydrochloride, 1-adamantanamine, is a tricyclic amine that is minimally metabolized and is excreted in the urine (dosing should be reduced in patients with decreased creatinine clearance) (12, 13). It is well absorbed when given orally. Maximum blood levels are reached between 1 and 4 hours; the half-life is approximately 15 hours in healthy patients, but it increases with age (14.7 hours in the young, 28.9 hours in the elderly) (12, 13). Amantadine sulfate can be administered orally or intravenously with equivalent motor effects in PD at a dose of 200 mg/d (14). The maximum concentration and area under the curve are greater when the drug is given intravenously; however, clinical efficacy of the orally administered formulation is equivalent (14). Amantadine sulfate is not available in the United States. However, in countries where it is available, it can be useful for patients who are unable to take medications orally.

The mechanism of action of amantadine in PD is not clear. Much evidence suggests that it's effect is mediated through the dopamine system: (a) It causes stereotypy and amphetamine-like turning behavior in rats (15); (b) it stimulates locomotor activity (16, 17) and reverses catalepsy (15) in catecholamine-depleted animals, suggesting a direct dopamine agonist effect; (c) its behavioral effect is not influenced by pretreatment with the presynaptic dopamine-depleting agents reserpine and tetrabenzine, both of which disrupt catecholamine storage vesicles, suggesting that amantadine may promote the release of extravesicular intraneuronal dopamine (Farnebo et al. 1971) (18); finally, (d) several studies have suggested that amantadine is a weak inhibitor of dopamine uptake (18, 19). In synthesizing the data regarding amantadine's effect on dopaminergic systems, it appears that its ability to release dopamine from extravesicular stores may be the most crucial effect, then its dopamine receptor agonist activity, and the least likely effect is the inhibition of dopamine reuptake (15). There is some evidence to suggest a possible anticholinergic effect (20).

The excitatory neurotransmitter glutamate may play a role in PD, and inhibition of the N-methyl-D-aspartate (NMDA) receptor subtype of glutamate receptors may be beneficial in treating PD patients (see Chapter 37). Amantadine has been shown to have NMDA antagonist activity, which may also provide some of its antiparkinsonian effect. NMDA antagonists block overactivity of the subthalamic nucleus, enhance striatal dopamine release and turnover, and protect nigral neurons from death in certain animal models (21). Further support for the benefits of an NMDA receptor antagonist in PD is found in the work of Klockgether and Turski (22) and Greenamyre and coworkers (23)In monoamine-depleted rats, NMDA antagonists potentiate the effects of levodopa even when levodopa is given in subtherapeutic doses (22, 23). Greenamyre and colleagues also demonstrated potentiation of levodopa's effect in parkinsonian monkeys while comparing remacemide hydrochloride (a glutamate antagonist) to placebo (23). There was no effect of NMDA receptor antagonist monotherapy in either the rat or the monkey models (21, 22). Engber and coworkers (24) have shown that NMDA receptor antagonists can reverse levodopa-induced motor fluctuations in a rat model, and Papa and Chase (25) have shown that levodopa-induced dyskinesias improve with glutamate antagonist treatment in MPTP-induced parkinsonian monkeys.

A placebo-controlled trial of dextromethorphan in 6 advanced PD patients showed reduced levodopa-induced dyskinesias without any change in levodopa's motor effects (26). However, dextromethorphan is not completely selective for the NMDA receptor (26). Results from placebo-controlled treatment trials suggest that the more specific NMDA receptor antagonist remacemide is beneficial when it is added to levodopa in PD (27). Whether amantadine's mechanism of action relates to the activity of NMDA receptor antagonists is not clearly established.

Clinical Use in Early Parkinson's Disease

The clinical benefit of amantadine in PD was first established by Schwab and associates in 1969 (1). In an open-

label study of 163 PD patients, 66% had improvement in bradykinesia and rigidity on 200 mg/d, with some tremor benefit as well (1). Although there was a decline in benefit after 4 to 8 weeks of treatment, patients continued to be improved when compared with baseline at 8 months. However, when amantadine was discontinued, patients who had lost the benefit over time had rebound worsening of symptoms (1). The investigators reviewed their 2-year experience with amantadine in 351 patients on 200 mg/d for 60 days (Schwab, Poskanzer et al. 1972). Maximum benefit occurred between 2 to 3 weeks, with 64% improving at 60 days. No correlation between the severity of PD and the effectiveness of amantadine was found and patients on no medication or on levodopa could also benefit (Schwab, Poskanzer et al. 1972).

Placebo-controlled trials have documented benefit with amantadine. Barbeau and colleagues (Barbeau, Mars et al. 1971) compared amantadine 100 mg bid with placebo in a crossover design and found significant improvement with amantadine in the 54 patients studied. When compared with a previous study of levodopa, only 44% had "moderate or better improvement" with amantadine, compared with 88% of those having received levodopa (Barbeau, Mars et al. 1971). Dallos and coworkers (Dallos, Heathfield et al. 1970) studied 62 patients, already on anticholinergic therapy, with a diagnosis of either PD or postencephalitic/arteriosclerotic parkinsonism. Some patients had prior thalamotomies. There was improvement in akinesia more than in rigidity and no change in tremor on amantadine. The maximum benefit occurred between 2 and 3 weeks, with some lessening of benefit at 4 weeks (Dallos et al. 1970). Butzer and associates (3) found that 20 of 26 PD patients preferred amantadine over placebo in a crossover study.

Zeldowicz and Huberman (6) found that 19 of 77 patients on amantadine alone improved for a mean duration of 21 months, and 46 patients had significant improvement with combined use of amantadine and levodopa as opposed to monotherapy with either drug (6). In a placebo-controlled crossover study, Savery (7) found that in 42 patients (Hoehn and Yahr stages II to IV) taking levodopa, 95% had improvement on 100 to 200 mg/d of amantadine. Comparing amantadine with the anticholinergic benzhexol, Parkes and associates (28) found that each drug produced a 15% reduction in disability as monotherapy and a 40% reduction when the drugs were combined. Koller (29) found that amantadine reduced tremor by 23%, compared with trihexyphenidyl's 59% benefit and levodopa's 55% benefit.

In contrast with its symptomatic effects, another potential reason to treat early PD patients with amantadine is the possibility that it may be "neuroprotective." Uitti and coworkers (30) reviewed the charts of all patients diagnosed with parkinsonism in their clinic from 1968 to 1990. A total of 836 parkinsonism cases were reviewed, 92% of which had PD. Amantadine treatment (for a minimum of 2 months) was found to be an independent predictor of improved survival. Of the 836 parkinsonism patients, 250 had been on amantadine 100 mg bid, and mean duration of treatment was 37 months (median 24 months). The mechanism by which this effect occurred is not clear, although the authors speculate that it is the NMDA antagonist activity of amantadine that may be critical (30). No controlled study of amantadine as a "neuroprotective" agent has been undertaken.

Crosby et al.(31, 32) performed a systematic review of amantadine as monotherapy in PD, concluding that there is not enough evidence to establish monotherapy with amantadine as safe or effective for treating PD. Further studies are needed.

Clinical Use in Advanced Parkinson's Disease

In addition to its role in early PD amantadine is useful in the treatment of advanced PD. Amantadine was first reported to benefit PD patients with postprandial motor fluctuations by DeDevitis and colleagues (9). They studied 19 patients, 16 of whom benefited from the addition of amantadine. In an open-label study of 20 patients with motor fluctuations (19, predictable wearing off; 1, unpredictable on-off), Shannon and coworkers (11) added amantadine 100 mg once or twice daily to levodopa taken with bromocriptine or pergolide. Eleven (55%) of the patients had subjective improvement in the severity of motor fluctuations at 2 months and a 30% improvement in their disability scores. Those who responded were initially more disabled and had more severe fluctuations than those who did not respond. The patient with unpredictable on-off fluctuations did not respond. The mean duration of improvement was 5.7 months (11).

Adler and coworkers (8) reported that amantadine's benefit—for predictable wearing off as well as a reduction in dyskinesias and dystonia—in 4 patients with advanced PD could last up to 2 years. They also found that a patient who had failed amantadine early in the course of the disease had benefit later in the disease (8). A study of MPTP-induced parkinsonism in monkeys demonstrated that levodopa-induced dyskinesias improved when treated with an NMDA antagonist (25).

Metman and associates (26) studied amantadine in 18 patients with advanced PD using a placebo-controlled crossover design. Treatment was for 3 weeks and 14 patients completed the study. Amantadine reduced dyskinesia severity by 60% compared with placebo, with no change in parkinsonian motor scores. The degree of dyskinesia reduction directly correlated with plasma amantadine concentration. The reduction in motor fluctuations and improvement in scores on activities of daily living (ADL) were significant. The average dose of amantadine was 350 mg/d (higher than normally used in clinic practice). Following the controlled trial, patients were placed on open-label amantadine, and most had sustained benefit for 12 months (26). Thus a potential advantage of adding amantadine to levodopa for dyskinesias is that there is no reduction in the motor effects of levodopa, a problem that often occurs using other dyskinesia-reducing strategies (26). In another short, randomized, double-blind, placebo-controlled, 3 week study of 18 PD cases (33) amantadine (200 mg/d) reduced the duration of levodopa-induced dyskinesias compared with placebo (33).

In a 12-month study of 40 patients randomized to receive amantadine chloridrate 300 mg/d or placebo, amantadine resulted in a 45% reduction in the total dyskinesia score (34). There were also reductions in the Unified Parkinson's Disease Rating Scale (UPDRS) dyskinesia rating scale and significant improvement based on the investigator global impression scale. However, the benefit lasted only 3 to 8 months in the 20 patients taking amantadine. When amantadine was stopped, there was a mild rebound worsening of dyskinesias.

A systematic review of the use of amantadine as add-on therapy to levodopa in PD concluded that there is not enough evidence that amantadine is safe or effective for treating advanced PD or levodopa-induced dyskinesias in advanced PD (31, 32).

Side Effects

GI discomfort, nausea, sleep disturbance, and nervousness are frequent acute side effects of amantadine (3, 6, 7, 15, 35). Chronic treatment with amantadine may result in livedo reticularis of the legs, characterized by reddish-purple skin discoloration, especially when the legs are dependent (6, 7, 15). Shealy and colleagues (36) first reported this in 10 of 18 women treated with 100 to 200 mg/d. Ankle edema was also found, both with and without livedo reticularis (36). In most cases symptoms resolve within 2 to 4 weeks of discontinuing the drug. The livedo reticularis is generally not associated with serious consequences. However, Shulman and colleagues reported a patient with amantadine-induced neuropathy associated with severe livedo reticularis (37).

In advanced PD, especially in patients with cognitive dysfunction or those already taking other antiparkinsonian drugs, hallucinations may be a significant problem with the addition of amantadine (15).

Neuroleptic malignant syndrome has been reported after withdrawal of amantadine in PD (38). Patients developed confusion, autonomic dysfunction, hyperthermia, leukocytosis, and elevation of creatinine kinase. Factor et al. (39) reported the development of acute delirium in 3 patients on long-term (4 to 18 years) amantadine who discontinued the drug. All 3 patients developed confusion, agitation, disorientation, and paranoia, and all required reinstitution of therapy with amantadine for resolution (39). All had advanced PD with dementia and a history of hallucinations; however, none had neuroleptic malignant syndrome.

Amantadine is contraindicated in patients with glaucoma, hepatic or renal disease, prostatic hypertrophy, and women who are pregnant or lactating (35). Because the drug is excreted unmetabolized in the urine, dosage must be reduced in patients with reduced creatinine clearance (12, 13).

Summary

Despite our incomplete knowledge of its mechanism of action in PD, amantadine may be an effective treatment for early and advanced patients. Monotherapy in early patients and adjunctive therapy to levodopa in patients with motor fluctuations or dyskinesias should be considered. Contrary to what has often been stated, amantadine may have prolonged benefit in both early and advanced disease (40). Dosing should start at 100 mg/d and can be increased to 100 mg tid, with most patients improving on 100 mg bid. Nausea, vomiting, livedo reticularis, and hallucinations may occur.

ANTICHOLINERGICS

Anticholinergic agents are compounds originally derived from plants of the Solanaceae family. The effects of belladona alkaloids were noted in the nineteenth century by Charcot, and their effects on PD were described by Ordenstein (41, 42). In the mid- to late 1920s, studies of cholinergic and anticholinergic agents in postencephalitic parkinsonism (43, 44), followed by Milhorat's studies in PD (45), supported the role of the cholinergic system in parkinsonism (46).

Pharmacology

Anticholinergic agents can be divided into those occurring in nature and those that are synthetically derived. Before the pharmacology of PD was understood, all naturally occurring "medications" were tested in patients with parkinsonism, but only those containing the belladonna alkaloids were effective. Feldberg (46–48) is credited with first postulating that atropine and scopolamine, both naturally occurring belladonna alkaloids, had their effect by central atropine-acetylcholine antagonism. Before the 1950s, atropine and scopolamine (the natural belladonna alkaloids) were primarily used in PD. In the 1950s, synthetic anticholinergic agents were introduced, including benztropine (Cogentin), trihexyphenidyl (Artane), procyclidine (Kemadrin), biperiden (Akineton), and ethopropazine (Parsidol) (46).

Anticholinergic drugs act by blocking acetylcholine receptors. There are 2 types of acetylcholine receptors, the muscarinic and the nicotinic. Distribution is quite different with the muscarinic receptors, which are located in the central nervous system (CNS), smooth muscle, cardiac muscle, and parasympathetically innervated glands, such as the salivary glands. Nicotinic receptors are located on striated muscle and in the autonomic ganglia. The beneficial effect of agents in PD is mediated by CNS muscarinic receptor blockade (41, 42).

The clinical effectiveness of anticholinergic agents has been correlated with multiple different in vitro effects, which include (a) antagonism of the central toxic effects in mice of the cholinomimetic agent oxotremorine (46, 49), (b) antagonism of drug-induced circling movements (50), and (c) antagonism of physostigmine's tremorigenic effect (51).

However, as often happens, patient trials appear to have preceded much of the traditional animal experimentation. In 1959, Nashold published a series of 11 PD patients demonstrating that direct infusion of acetylcholine into the globus pallidus caused an increase in contralateral tremor, while infusion of an anticholinergic agent, oxypheninium bromide, reduced contralateral tremor and rigidity (52). This led to Barbeau's hypothesis that PD was secondary to a deficit in dopamine, leading to a relative overactivity of cholinergic function in the CNS (53).

Ensuing studies in monkeys demonstrated that carbachol (a muscarinic cholinergic agonist) injected into the caudate nucleus induced contralateral rest tremor, which was inhibited by anticholinergic agents (54, 55). Further human studies demonstrated that the centrally active cholinergic agent physostigmine exacerbated PD signs, although centrally active anticholinergic agents (scopolamine or benztropine) reversed this effect (46, 47). Central and not peripheral anticholinergic action was crucial to the antiparkinsonian effect (47). The effects of the cholinergic agents affected only preexisting symptoms; thus a cholinergic mechanism was not likely the underlying etiology of PD (46, 47).

The only pharmacokinetic data available for an anticholinergic agent is for trihexyphenidyl. Its half-life is 1.7 hours in patients with dystonia (56). Studies of levodopa absorption in the presence or absence of chronic treatment with the anticholinergic orphenadrine revealed no significant difference for maximal levodopa concentration, time to maximal concentration, or area under the curve in 6 patients. One patient had an increase in plasma concentration of levodopa and 2 had a decrease (57).

Clinical Use

The scientific literature regarding the use of anticholinergics in PD is limited. Techniques used to study tremor and other symptoms, the type of anticholinergic used, daily dose, duration of treatment, and variable patient population all make the earlier studies difficult to interpret. Doshay and Constable (58) found that 77% of 117 patients with various forms of parkinsonism who were treated with open-label trihexyphenidyl had improvement, with rigidity being more responsive than tremor, with little effect on akinesia. Doshay and coworkers (59) reported the results for benztropine (Cogentin) in 20 patients with Parkinsonism (6 idiopathic, 8 arteriosclerotic, 6 postencephalitic). They found some benefit alone or with trihexyphenidyl, but no quantification is provided (59). The five-year summary of treatment in 302 patients found that 52% had improvement mostly in tremor and rigidity (60).

In 1965, Strang (61) reported the effects of open-label benztropine in 94 patients with parkinsonism (11 postencephalitic and 24 arteriosclerotic). Sixty patients were on benztropine alone, although 34 were on other medications including other anticholinergics. Less than 50% of those treated had benefit for tremor, rigidity, akinesia, or gait. Maximum benefit required dosing 3 to 4 times a day and a total dose of 3 to 6 mg/d (61).

Tourtellotte and colleagues (62) reported a double-blind, placebo-controlled crossover study of benztropine in 29 PD patients. All were on levodopa, and global assessments by the patient and physician showed improvement on benztropine. Rigidity, finger-tapping speed, and ADL scores improved 10% (62). Another double-blind study, procyclidine versus levodopa in 46 parkinsonian patients, revealed that levodopa was much more effective than procyclidine for rigidity and other clinical measures (63).

Koller (30) found, in 9 untreated PD patients, that trihexyphenidyl reduced tremor amplitude 59% compared with 23% for amantadine and 55% for levodopa. Five patients preferred trihexyphenidyl, although 4 preferred levodopa. Some studies of tremor using quantitative measures found benefit with anticholinergics (64), although other studies have not supported this effect (65).

Comparing benzhexol with amantadine, Parkes and coworkers (66) reported that each drug produced a 15% reduction in disability as monotherapy, with a 40% reduction when the drugs were combined. This combination had an equivalent effect when compared with giving levodopa, which caused a 36% reduction in disability scores (66). The anticholinergic procyclidine can be useful in PD patients with foot dystonia (67).

Individual Agents

Trihexyphenidyl (Artane) Trihexyphenidyl is a synthetic piperidine anticholinergic with efficacy in PD (68). Because of potential side effects, all anticholinergics should be started at a low dose and gradually titrated (69). The starting dose for trihexyphenidyl is 0.5 to 1 mg/d, and the dose should be increased no faster than every 7 to 14 days. Dose increases of 1 mg/d are reasonable and a dose of 2 mg 3 to 4 times per day is the usual goal.

Procyclidine (Kemadrin) Procyclidine is another piperidine agent that has similar efficacy to trihexyphenidyl. Some find fewer side effects with this agent. The dose is begun at 2.5 mg/d and increased gradually to a maximum of approximately 30 mg/d.

Benztropine (Cogentin) Benztropine is a synthetic agent that has both the benzhydryl group found in diphenhydramine and the tropine group found in atropine (59). It is more potent than trihexyphenidyl and less sedating than diphenhydramine. This drug is effective in PD and requires dosing 2 to 3 times per day (61). The dose is begun at 0.5 mg/d and can be raised to 4 to 8 mg/d.

Antihistamines This class of drugs has anticholinergic activity and they are mildly effective in PD (41). Diphenhydramine (Benadryl) and orphenadrine (Disipal, Norflex) have been most commonly used. However, both are sedating and are best used to help induce sleep. The starting dose is 25 mg/d; it can be titrated to 150 to 200 mg/d in divided doses. No data regarding the nonsedating antihistamines, such as astemizole (Hismanil) and loratadine (Claritin), exist for the treatment of PD.

Phenothiazines Phenothiazines primarily act as dopamine receptor antagonists with some anticholinergic activity. Thus most drugs in this family result in worsening of motor symptoms. The only agent in this class that is effective in PD is ethopropazine hydrochloride (Parsidol, Parsitan) (41). This drug is no longer available.

Side Effects

The use of anticholinergics in the treatment of PD is often difficult because of the multitude of side effects. In young patients this is less of an issue than in the elderly. Drug dose must be titrated very slowly and patients must be informed of the many side effects.

Anticholinergic agents block muscarinic acetylcholine receptors throughout the body. At low doses, blockade of these receptors in the salivary glands results in dry mouth, often the first side effect described (59, 61). Parenthetically, low dose anticholinergics can be helpful in treating the profound sialorrhea experienced by some patients. As the dose is increased, muscarinic receptor blockade in the smooth muscle of the GI tract results in constipation, which can progress to intestinal pseudo-obstruction and bowel dilation requiring aggressive intervention (47, 59, 61). Effects on the bladder can result in urinary retention, especially in male patients. Nausea, drowsiness, abdominal cramps, and mild tachycardia can occur (47). Dry skin and impaired sweating may lead to heat stroke. Anticholinergics are contraindicated in patients with closed-angle glaucoma (69). Some of these peripheral anticholinergic side effects may be counteracted by a low dose (30 to 60 mg/d) of pyridostigmine (Mestinon), an acetylcholinesterase inhibitor used in patients with myasthenia gravis.

The central side effects of the anticholinergic agents can be quite problematic. These drugs can cause confusion and memory loss (70, 71) and, in the more advanced and demented patients, hallucinations and disorientation (72). In a study of 27 hospitalized parkinsonian patients with dementia 6 of 13 (46%) not receiving an anticholinergic suffered confusional states, whereas 13 of 14 (93%) on an anticholinergic had confusional states (73). Neuropsychological testing revealed that trihexyphenidyl 2 mg tid given as monotherapy (6 patients) or added to levodopa (2 patients) or amantadine (4 patients) did not affect digit span; however, recall and learning tasks were worse after trihexyphenidyl (70, 71). Ataxia and dizziness may occur (59, 61). These agents can also cause orobuccal dyskinesias in PD patients (74).

Side effects can only be treated by lowering or discontinuing the drug. Withdrawal of anticholinergics should never occur quickly, given the potential for rebound worsening of symptoms (75, 76) As with other drugs, side effects with one anticholinergic do not predict side effects with all others (76).

SUMMARY

Anticholinergics may be useful as monotherapy in early, untreated PD and as adjunctive therapy to patients on levodopa. Although unclear from the data published, anticholinergics appear to benefit rigidity and tremor the most. PD patients with dystonia may respond to anticholinergics. Peripheral side effects include dry mouth, blurred vision, and constipation, whereas central side effects include dizziness, confusion, memory loss, hallucinations, and dyskinesia. All anticholinergic agents should be started at a low dose and gradually titrated, with elderly and more debilitated patients tolerating much lower doses than younger patients. The use of these drugs in patients above age 65 requires vigilance and caution.

REFERENCES

1. Schwab RS et al. Amantadine in the treatment of Parkinson's disease. *JAMA* 1969; 208:1168–1170.
2. Barbeau A et al. Amantadine-HCL (Symmetrel) in the management of Parkinson's disease: a double-blind cross-over study. *Can Med Assoc J* 1971; 105:42–62.
3. Butzer JF, Silver DE, Sahs AL. Amantadine in Parkinson's disease. A double-blind, placebo-controlled, crossover study with long-term follow-up. *Neurology* 1975; 25:603–606.
4. Dallos V et al. Use of amantadine in Parkinson's disease. Results of a double-blind trial. *Br Med J* 1970; 4:24–26.
5. Schwab RS et al. Amantadine in Parkinson's disease. Review of more than two years' experience. *JAMA* 1972; 222:792–795.
6. Zeldowicz LR, Huberman J, Long-term treatment of Parkinson's disease with amantadine, alone and combined with levodopa. *Can Med Assoc J* 1973; 109:588.
7. Savery F. Amantadine and a fixed combination of levodopa and carbidopa in the treatment of Parkinson's disease. *Dis Nerv Syst* 1977; 38:605–608.
8. Adler CH et al. Amantadine in advanced Parkinson's disease: Good use of an old drug. *J Neurol* 1997; 244:336–337.
9. DeDevitiis E et al. L'amantadina nel trattamento dell'ipokinesia transitoria di pazienti parkinsoniani in corso di terapia con L-dopa. *Minerva Med* 1972; 409:4007–4008.
10. Fahn S, Isgreen WP. Long-term evaluation of amantadine and levodopa combination in parkinsonism by double-blind crossover analyses. *Neurology* 1975; 25:695–700.
11. Shannon KM et al. Amantadine and motor fluctuations in chronic Parkinson's disease. *Clin Neuropharmacol* 1987; 10:522–526.
12. Aoki FY, Sitar DS. Clinical pharmacokinetics of amantadine hydrochloride. *Clin Pharmacokinet* 1988; 14:5135–5151.
13. Bleidner WE et al. Absorption, distribution and excretion of amantadine hydrochloride. *J Pharmacol Exp Ther* 1965; 150:484–490.
14. Muller T et al. Intravenous application of amantadine and antiparkinsonian efficacy in Parkinsonian patients. *J Neural Transm* 1995; 46:407–413.
15. Bailey EV, Stone TW. The mechanism of action of amantadine in parkinsonism: A review. *Arch Int Pharmacodyn* 1975; 216:246–262.
16. Lassen JB. The effect of amantadine and (+)-amphetamine on motility in rats wafter inhibition of monoamine synthesis and storage. *Psychopharmacology* 1973; 29:55–64.
17. Farnebo LO et al. Dopamine and noradrenaline releasing action of amantadine in the central and peripheral nervous system: A possible mode of action in Parkinson's disease. *Eur J Pharmacol* 1971; 16:3827–3838.
18. Stromberg U, Svensson TH, Waldeck B. The effect of amantadine on the uptake of dopamine and noradrenaline by rat brain homogenates. *J Pharm Pharmacol* 1970; 22:957–962.
19. Heimans RLH, Rand M, Fennessy MR. Effects of amantadine on uptake and release of dopamine by a particulate fraction of rat basal ganglia. *J Pharm Pharmacol* 1972; 24:875–879.

20. Nastuck WC, Pu PC, Doubilet P. Anticholinergic and membrane activities of amantadine in neuromuscular transmission. *Nature* 1976; 264:76–79.
21. Greenamyre JT, O'Brien CF. N-methyl-D-aspartate antagonists in the treatment of Parkinson's disease. *Arch Neurol* 1991; 48:977–981.
22. Klockgether T, Turski L. NMDA antagonists potentiate antiparkinsonian actions of L-dopa in monoamine-depleted rats. *Ann Neurol* 1990; 28:539–546.
23. Greenamyre JT et al. Antiparkinsonian effects of remacemide hydrochloride, a glutamate antagonist in rodent and primate models of Parkinson's disease. *Ann Neurol* 1994; 35:655–661.
24. Engber TM et al. NMDA receptor blockade reverses motor response alterations induced by levodopa. *Neuroreport* 1994; 5:2586–2588.
25. Papa SM, Chase TN. Levodopa-induced dyskinesias improved by a glutamate antagonist in parkinsonian monkeys. *Ann Neurol* 1996; 39:574–578.
26. Metman LV et al. Amantadine as treatment for dyskinesias and motor fluctuations in Parkinson's disease. *Neurology* 1998; 50:1323–1326.
27. Group PS. The glutamate antagonist remacemide improves motor performance in levodopa-treated Parkinson's disease. *Neurology* 1999; 52(Suppl 2):A262.
28. Parkes D. Amantadine. *Adv Drug Res* 1974; 8:11–81.
29. Koller WC. Pharmacologic treatment of parkinsonian tremor. *Arch Neurol* 1986; 43:126–127.
30. Uitti RJ. et al. Amantadine treatment is an independent predictor of improved survival in Parkinson's disease. *Neurology* 1996; 46: 1551–1556.
31. Crosby N, Deane KH, Clarke CE. Amantadine in Parkinson's disease. *Cochrane Database Syst Rev* 2003; (1):CD003468.
32. Crosby NJ, Deane KH, Clarke CE. Amantadine for dyskinesia in Parkinson's disease. *Cochrane Database Syst Rev* 2003; (2):CD003467.
33. Pereira da Silva F Jr et al. Amantadine reduces the duration of levodopa-induced dyskinesia: A randomized, double-blind, placebo-controlled study. *Parkinsonism Relat Disord* 2005; 11:449–452.
34. Thomas A et al. Duration of amantadine benefit on dyskinesia of severe Parkinson's disease. *J Neurol Neurosurg Psychiatry* 2004; 75(1): 141–143.
35. Danielczyk W. Twenty-five years of amantadine therapy in Parkinson's disease. *J Neural Transm* 1995; 46:399–405.
36. Shealy CN, Weeth JB, Mercier D. Livedo reticularis in patients with parkinsonism receiving amantadine. *JAMA* 1970; 212:1522–1523.
37. Shulman LM et al. Amantadine-induced peripheral neuropathy. *Neurology* 1999; 53(8):1862–1865.
38. Factor SA, Singer C. Neuroleptic malignant syndrome. In: Lang AE, Weiner WJ (eds). *Drug-Induced Movement Disorders.* Mount Kisco, NY: Futura, 1992:199–230.
39. Factor SA, Molho ES, Brown DL. Acute delirium after withdrawl of amantadine in Parkinson's disease. *Neurology* 1998; 50:1456–1458.

40. Factor SA, Molho ES. Transient benefits of amantadine in Parkinson's disease: The facts about the myth. *Mov Disord* 1999; .

41. Comella CL, Tanner CM. Anticholinergic drugs in the treatment of Parkinson's disease. In: Koller WC, Paulson G (eds). *Therapy of Parkinson's Disease.* New York: Marcel Dekker, 1995:109–122.

42. Ordenstein L. Sur la paralysie et la sclerose in plaque generalise. Paris: Martinet, 1867.

43. Marinesco G, Bourguignon G. Variations de la chronaxie et de l'attitude des membres sous l'influence de la scopolamine et de l'eserine dans deux cas de syndromes parkinsoniens post-encephalitiques. *C R Soc Biol (Paris)* 1927; 97:207.

44. Zucker K. Uber die Wirkung der Physostigmine bei Erkrankungen des extrapyramidalen Systems. *M Psych Neurol* 1925; 58:11.

45. Milhorat AT. Studies in diseases of muscle: IX. Effect of quinine and prostigmine methyl sulfate on muscular rigidity in paralysis agitans. *Arch Neurol Psychiatry* 1941: 45:74.

46. Duvoisin RC. Cholinergic-anticholinergic antagonism in parkinsonism. *Arch Neurol* 1967; 17: 124–136.

47. Duvoisin RC. The mutual antagonism of cholinergic an anticholinergic agents in parkinsonism. *Trans Am Neurol Assoc* 1966; 91:73–79.

48. Feldberg W. Present views on the mode of action of acetylcholine in the central nervous system. *Physiol Rev* 1945; 25:596.

49. Everett GM, Blockus LE, Shappard IM. Tremor induced by tremorine and its antagonism by antiparkinson drugs. *Science* 1956; 124:79.

50. Dejong MC, Funcke ABH. Sinistrotorsion in guinea pigs as a method of screening antiparkinson drugs. *Arch Int Pharmacodyn* 1962; 137:375.

51. Faucon G, Lavarenne J, Collard M. Mis en evidence de l'activite antiparkinonienne au moyen du tremblement eserinique. *Therapie* 1965; 20:37.

52. Nashold BS. Cholinergic stimulation of globus pallidus in man. *Proc Soc Exp Biol Med* 1959; 101:68–69.

53. Barbeau, A. The pathogenesis of Parkinson's disease: A new hypothesis. *Can Med Assoc J* 1962; 87:802–807.

54. Connor JD, Rossi GV, Baker WW. Antagonism of intracaudate carbachol tremor by local injections of catecholamines. *J Pharmacol Exp Ther* 1967; 155:545–551.

55. Velasco F, Velasco M, Romo R. Effect of carbachol and atropine perfusions in the mesencephalic tegmentum and caudate nucleus of experimental tremor in monkeys. *Exp Neurol* 1982; 78:450–460.

56. Burke R. Fahn S. Pharmacokinetics of trihexyphenidyl after acute and chronic administration. *Ann Neurol* 1982; 12:94.

57. Contin M et al. Combined levodopa-anticholinergic therapy in the treatment of Parkinson's disease. *Clin Neuropharmacol* 1991; 14:148–155.

58. Doshay LJ, Constable K. Artane therapy for parkinsonism: Preliminary study of results of 117 cases. *JAMA* 1949; 140:1317–1322.

59. Doshay LJ, Constable K, Fromer S. Preliminary study of a new antiparkinsonian agent. *Neurology* 1952; 2: 233–243.

60. Doshay LJ. Five-year study of benztropine (Cogentin) methanesulfate. *JAMA* 1956; 162:1031–1034.

61. Strang RR. Experiences with Cogentin in the treatment of parkinsonism. *Acta Neurol Scand* 1965; 145:413–418.

62. Tourtellotte WW et al. Parkinson's disease: Cogentin with Sinemet, a better response. *Prog Neuropsychopharmacol Biol Psychiatry* 1982; 6(1):51–55.

63. Timberlake WH. Double-blind comparison of levodopa and procyclidine in parkinsonism, with illustrations of levodopa-induced movement disorders. *Neurology* 1970; 20:31–35.

64. Agate FJ, Doshay LJ, Curtis FK. Quantitative measurement of therapy in paralysis agitans. *JAMA* 1956; 160:353–354.

65. Norris JW. Vas CJ. Mehixene hydrochloride and parkinsonian tremor. *Acta Neurol Scand* 1967; 43:535–538.

66. Parkes JD et al. Comparative trial of benzhexol, amantadine and levodopa in the treatment of Parkinson's disease. *J Neurol Neurosurg Psychiatry* 1974; 37:422–426.

67. Poewe WH, Lees AJ. The pharmacology of foot dystonia in parkinsonism. *Clin Neuropharmacol* 1987; 10:47–56.

68. Rix A, Fischer RG. Comparison of trihexyphenidyl and dihydromorphanthridine derivative in control of tremor of parkinsonism. *South Med J* 1972; 65:1305–1389.

69. Olanow CW. Koller WC. An algorithm (decision tree) for the management of Parkinson's disease: Treatment guidelines. *Neurology* 1998; 50(Suppl 3):S1–S57.

70. Koller WC. Disturbance of recent memory function in parkinsonian patients on anticholinergic therapy. *Cortex* 1984; 20:307–311.

71. Sadeh M, Braham J, Modan M. Effects of anticholinergic drugs on memory in Parkinson's disease. *Arch Neurol* 1982; 39:666–667.

72. Goetz CG, Tanner CM, Klawans HL. Pharmacology of hallucinations induced by long-term drug therapy. *Am J Psychiatry* 1982; 139:494–497.

73. de Smet Y et al. Confusion, dementia and anticholinergics in Parkinson's disease. *J Neurol Neurosurg Psychiatry* 1982; 45:1161–1164.

74. Hauser RA, Olanow CW. Orobuccal dyskinesia associated with trihexyphenidyl therapy in a patient with Parkinson's disease. *Mov Disord* 1993; 8: 512–514.

75. Hurtig HI. Advanced Parkinson's disease and complications of treatment. In: Stern MB, Hurtig HI (eds). *The Comprehensive Management of Parkinson's Disease.* New Yoek: PMA Publishing,1988:119–158.

76. Hurtig HI. Anticholinergics for Parkinson's disease. *Ann Neurol* 1980; 7:495.

40 Monoamine Oxidase Inhibitors

Alexander Rajput
Theresa A. Zesiewicz
Robert A. Hauser

mines are weakly basic organic compounds that contain a nitrogen group (1, 2). They are described as primary, secondary, or tertiary depending on whether 1, 2, or 3 carbon atoms are attached to the nitrogen atom (1). Primary amines are also called "monoamines" and include the catecholamines dopamine, norepinephrine, and 5-hydroxytryptamine (Figure 40-1). These chemicals play an integral role in neurotransmission. Many neuropsychiatric pharmaceutical agents act by inhibiting or promoting their formation, release, metabolism, or reuptake (3, 4).

Monoamine oxidases (MAOs) are intracellular enzymes that play a role in the catabolism of neuroactive amines (3). They are located in the outer mitochondrial membrane. MAOs catalyze the oxidative deamination of monoamines (5, 6) via a reaction between dioxygen and R-CH_2-NH_2 to form R-CHO, NH_3, and H_2O_2 (7). Monoamine oxidase inhibitors (MAOIs) inhibit the action of MAOs. Because of the ubiquitous nature of the enzyme, considerable inhibition must occur before any changes in monoamine concentrations are observed.

In the late 1800s, Schmiedeberg and colleagues (8) discovered that almost all monoamines containing the atomic grouping -CH_2-NH_2 are metabolized to ammonia (NH_3). The first MAO identified was tyramine oxidase in 1928 (9). Zeller later proposed the term *monoamine*

oxidase for the group of enzymes whose main function is the oxidative deamination of monoamines (10–12).

In the 1950s and 1960s, several drugs used to treat tuberculosis were noted to be mood elevators (13–15). Some patients experienced euphoria and were seen to "dance in the hall" during treatment (16). One antituberculosis medication, isonicotinic acid hydrazide, or iproniazid, was found to be a potent MAO inhibitor (17). Kline and coworkers (18) conducted an open-label trial of iproniazid in depressed, institutionalized patients and found that approximately 70% experienced significant improvement in mood. Iproniazid was later introduced as the first antidepressant medication (19).

The mood-elevating properties of iproniazid suggested that MAOIs could function as "psychic energizers." Knoll and Ecseri, seeking a compound with amphetamine-like stimulating effects and potent MAO inhibition, synthesized phenylisopropyl-N-methylpropinylamine, or E-250 (20, 21). E-250 was found to be a strong, irreversible inhibitor of MAO that metabolized benzylamine (21) and phenylethylamine (22). It also inhibited the metabolism of tyramine (22). The compound was separated into 2 isomers, and the L-form was named 'deprenyl' and later selegiline.

In 1968, Johnston synthesized 2, 3-dichlorophenoxypropyl-N-methylpropinylamine, or clorgyline, and found it to be similar in structure to deprenyl (23).

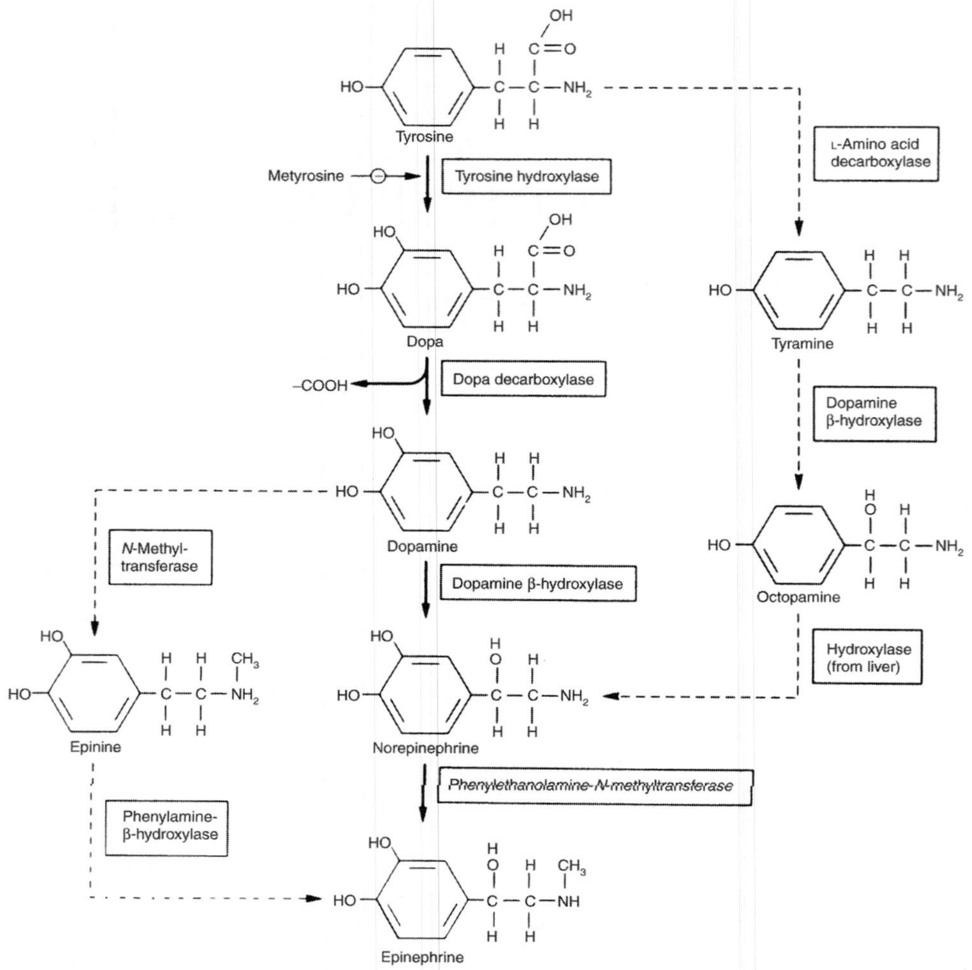

FIGURE 40-1

Biosynthesis of catecholamines. The rate-limiting step is the conversion of tyrosine to DOPA. [From Greenspan FS, Sterewler FJ (eds). *Basic and Clinical Endocrinology,* 5th ed. Stamford, CT: Appleton & Lange, 1996, with permission.]

He designated the form of MAO with greater affinity for clorgyline MAO A, and the type with lower affinity for clorgyline and greater affinity for deprenyl MAO B.

MONOAMINE OXIDASE: BIOCHEMISTRY AND MECHANISM OF ACTION

MAOs are a family of flavin-containing enzymes that catalyze the oxidative deamination of norepinepherine, epinephrine, dopamine, serotonin, and a variety of other monoamines to their corresponding aldehydes (24, 25) by the following reaction (26):

$$R\text{-}CH_2\text{-}NH_2 + O_2 + H_2O \rightarrow R\text{-}CHO + NH_3 + H_2O_2$$

The amine is oxidized to an iminium ion, and the flavin (FAD) is reduced (27). The iminium ion is then hydrolyzed to an aldehyde (26), and the reduced flavin is reoxidized with molecular oxygen (26).

MAO A and B show 71% sequence homology. The flavin sites on both forms of MAO are identical (28), thereby accounting for overlapping substrate specificities and inhibitor sensitivities (29). Although often described as selective, most MAO inhibitors are truly selective only at low concentrations (30).

MAO A primarily catabolizes serotonin and octopamine, whereas MAO B metabolizes benzylamine, phenylethylamine, milacemide, and N-methylhistamine. MAO B also deaminates long-chain diamines and tertiary cyclic amines such as 1-methyl-4-phenyl-1, 2, 3, 6-tetrahydropyridine (MPTP) (31). Both enzymes catabolize dopamine, epinephrine, norepinephrine, tyramine, tryptamine, 3-methoxytryamine, and kynuramine (common substrates) (31).

MONOAMINE OXIDASE: ANATOMY AND LOCALIZATION

MAO A and B are intracellular enzymes in the central nervous system (CNS) and peripheral tissues (32). Most MAO is tightly bound to the outer mitochondrial membrane (33, 34), although a small portion can be found in the microsomal fraction of the cell. MAO can exist as part of a membrane unit containing A and B forms embedded in a phospholipid structure. MAO A activity is thought to be phospholipid-dependent, whereas MAO B activity is not (35).

MAO is present in most peripheral organs, blood vessel walls, and ventricular surfaces but absent in red blood cells and blood plasma (36–39). MAO A constitutes a large portion of the enzyme in the pancreas, intestine, and spleen and is the sole form in the human placenta (40–42). In contrast, MAO B predominates in skin and skeletal muscle and is the sole form in platelets. The human liver contains both forms (43). The human brain contains predominantly MAO B (about 70% to 80%) (44–47), whereas the rodent brain contains predominantly MAO A (48).

In the brain, MAO A is primarily located in catecholamine cells and is usually situated intraneuronally in synaptosomes (49). MAO A–containing neurons include those in the locus ceruleus, nucleus subceruleus, periventricular regions of the hypothalamus, and dopaminergic neurons in the striatum (50, 51). Using specific antibodies to determine the immunocytochemical localization of MAO A, Westlund found that the MAO A content of primate substantia nigra is low relative to the number of cells that are tyrosine hydroxylase–positive (51).

MAO B is the predominant extraneuronal form of the enzyme (51). It is located in CNS astrocytes and in serotonergic neurons, including the raphe dorsalis in the midbrain. More than 80% of deamination in the frontal cortex is due to glial MAO B (52). Both protoplasmic and fibrillary astroctyes in the brain contain MAO B, whereas oligodendrocytes do not contain the enzyme. MAO B is also found in brain regions lacking a blood-brain barrier. It is found on either side of the midline in the medulla and pons, which includes cells in the raphe pallidus, raphe obscurus, raphe magnus, raphe pontis (53), and nucleus centralis superior.

Both MAO A and B activity is present in adrenergic nerve terminals in the hypothalamus, in the cortical projections from the posterior hypothalamus to the hippocampus, and paraventricular and supraoptic nuclei of the hypothalamus, medulla, and spinal cord (54).

In both rat and human brain (55), dopamine can be metabolized by either MAO A or MAO B. Yang and Neff (56) demonstrated that dopamine is metabolized by both in vitro, while Green and coworkers (57) observed similar findings in rat brain. Glial cells in the human substantia nigra contain both forms of the enzyme (58) and may be responsible for MAO activity in this area. Using dopamine as a substrate, the highest MAO activity is in the nucleus accumbens (59).

The half-life for turnover of MAO B in experimental animals is approximately 6 to 30 days. The half-life of MAO B in pig brain is approximately 6.5 days (60). Using 11Cl-deprenyl positron emission tomography (PET), Arnett and associates (60) determined the half-life for turnover of MAO B in baboons to be 30 days.

MONOAMINE OXIDASE INHIBITORS: REVERSIBLE AND IRREVERSIBLE

MAO inhibitors may be reversible or irreversible. Reversible inhibitors are competitive, mixed (noncompetitive), or uncompetitive (61). MAO B inhibitors are not sterically hindered from binding to MAO A and are therefore less selective than MAO A inhibitors (62, 63).

Selective MAO A inhibitors are formed by the substitution of the α-hydrogen by a methyl group on a monoamine (53, 54). Harmaline, mexiletine, procaine, debrisoquine, (±)α-methyltryptamine, and pirlindole are examples of reversible MAO A inhibitors (65). Other reversible MAO A inhibitors include amiflamine (66) and tolaxtone (67), which inhibit MAO A in vitro and in vivo. Many substances with other biological functions also act as reversible MAO A inhibitors, including amphetamine (1-methyl-2-phenylethylamine) (48), tetracaine, procainamide, propranolol, many formanilides (48), proflavine (68), salsolinol (69), and some xanthones (70). Moclobemide is also a reversible MAO A inhibitor (71). CGP 11305 (72) behaves as a short-acting MAO A inhibitor in vitro; befloxatone is a newer, reversible MAO A inhibitor (73). Potent irreversible MAO A inhibitors include clorgyline, cyclopropylamines, and the hydrazines (23).

There are far fewer MAO B inhibitors than MAO A inhibitors. Some examples of reversible MAO B inhibitors are benzyl alcohol, benzyl cyanide, and cyanophenol in vitro. The tricyclic antidepressants amitriptyline and imipramine (74) are MAO B inhibitors at lower concentrations than are needed for MAO A inhibition (75–77). MD 240928 and caroxazome are also reversible MAO B inhibitors (78). Lazabemide (Ro 19-6327) is a selective, rapidly reversible MAO B inhibitor (79). Irreversible MAO B inhibitors include the acetylenic compounds selegiline (deprenyl) and pargyline, the cyclopropylamines, and the hydrazines, which include phenylhydrazine and benzylhydrazine. Rasagiline [R(+)-N-propargyl-1-aminoindane] is a newer, selective irreversible MAO B inhibitor (80).

MONOAMINE OXIDASE INHIBITORS: HYPERTENSIVE CRISIS

Patients treated with early, nonselective MAO inhibitors including iproniazid, phenelzine, and tranylcypromine occasionally experienced dangerous hypertensive episodes when they ate foods rich in tyramine, such as aged cheese, yeast, chicken liver, snails, pickled herring, red wines, and broad beans or other indirectly acting amines (81). This phenomenon is known as "the cheese effect." Tyramine is a sympathomimetic amine that is normally metabolized by MAO A in the intestine; when absorbed, however, it results in the release of intraneuronal norepinephrine, leading to hypertensive crisis. Levodopa can also cause a hypertensive crisis when MAO A is inhibited. Therefore patients receiving nonspecific MAO or MAO A inhibitor medications must restrict tyramine in the diet and cannot take levodopa.

Selegiline, a relatively specific MAO B inhibitor, is free from the cheese effect when used in oral doses up to 10 mg/d. Knoll and colleagues (82) selected the levorotatory isomer of E-250 for further development because it inhibited the release of biogenic amines and acted in vivo and in vitro as a potent tyramine antagonist. It was later discovered that the cheese effect was generally not induced by this isomer even when administered with large amounts of tyramine. Elsworth and coworkers (83) found that individuals taking oral selegiline at a dose of 10 mg/d could tolerate 150 to 200 mg of tyramine without cardiovascular effects. However, there is increased sensitivity to tyramine with oral selegiline at a dose of 30 mg/d (58), and transient increases in blood pressure have been reported with oral selegiline at a dose of 20 mg/d. Thus, oral selegiline 10 mg/d or less does not necessitate a tyramine-restricted diet and can be given safely with levodopa. Significant MAO A inhibition may occur with oral selegiline doses of 20 mg/d or more and should ordinarily be avoided.

MONOAMINE OXIDASE INHIBITORS: PRECLINICAL NEUROPROTECTIVE EFFECTS

MAO-B inhibitors exhibit neuroprotective effects in a variety of cell culture and animal models (84–100). These effects are dependent on their pargylamine moiety and independent of MAO inhibition. For selegiline, its metabolite desmethylselegiline is primarily responsible for neuroprotective properties.

Both selegiline and rasagiline protect cell lines against apoptosis (programmed cell death) (87, 94, 95, 101–103) and both protect dopaminergic neurons from the toxic effects of salsolinol (89, 96, 104, 105). The selegiline metabolite L-metamphetamine inhibits the antiapoptotic effects of both selegiline and rasagiline, while aminoindan,

the primary metabolite of rasagiline, does not interfere with this effect (103).

Selegiline and rasagiline prevent apoptosis by upregulating antiapoptotic proteins Bcl-2 (B-cell CLL/lymphoma 2) and Bcl-XL, which stabilize the mitochondrial permeability transition pore complex (MPTp) (105, 106), thereby preventing mitochondrial release of cytochrome c and the consequent activation of the apoptotic pathway (107, 108). Closing the MPTp decreases signaling for proapoptotic caspases, including caspase-3, the primary effector caspase in the nervous system. In addition, selegiline and rasagiline downregulate the proapoptotic proteins Bad and Bax, which promote MPTp opening and collapse of the mitochondrial membrane potential (105).

Rasagiline activates protein kinase C (PKC) α and ε. This inhibits formation of Fas, the cleaved activated form of caspase-3, and the cleavage of poly (ADP-ribose) polymerase-1 (PARP-1), a caspase substrate. In addition, rasagiline and its derivatives convert amyloid precursor protein (APP) into the nonamyloidogenic soluble APPα, which also has neuroprotective and neurotrophic properties. This conversion is mediated by PKC and mitogen-activated protein kinase (MAPK)–dependent α-secretase activation (86). Selegiline and rasagiline both inhibit nuclear translocation of glyceraldehyde-3-phosphate dehydrogenase (88, 96).

Antioxidant enzymes and trophic factors increased by MAOIs include copper/zinc superoxide dismutase (SOD1), manganese superoxide (SOD2), and catalase (scavenger proteins); nerve growth factor (NGF), brain-derived neurotrophic factor (BDNF), ciliary neurotrophic factor (CNTF), glial-derived neurotrophic factor (GDNF), and basic fibroblast growth factor (FGF2) (neurotrophic factors) (109–111). Selegiline upregulates the antioxidant glutathione (92) and may itself act as a hydroxyl radical scavenger (112) at doses too low to inhibit MAO B.

Selegiline has demonstrated neuroprotective benefit in rat models of permanent middle cerebral artery occlusion (113), retinal ganglion cells in optic nerve crush injury (114), rescue of axotomized motoneurons (115) and of dorsal root ganglia sensory neurons following sciatic nerve transection (116). It also protects against the loss of anterior horn cells following intrathecal injection of cerebrospinal fluid from human patients with amyotrophic lateral sclerosis.

In vitro, rasagiline has demonstrated neuroprotection in multiple models, including increased survival of dopaminergic neurons under serum-free conditions (84), reduced glutamate toxicity in hippocampal neurons (117), and protection against cell death induced by oxygen and glucose deprivation in rat pheochromocytoma PC-12 cells (118). Rasagiline pretreatment is neuroprotective in primate 1-methyl-4-phenyl-1, 2, 3, 6-tetrahydropyridine (MPTP) (99) and rodent 6-hydroxydopamine (6-OHDA) models of PD (100). In postnatal anoxia-lesioned rats, rasagiline reduced deficits in memory and learning tasks (119) and in focal ischemic rat models, rasagiline reduced infarct volume by up to half compared with untreated controls (120). In a model of closed head injury in mice, both rasagiline and its S-enantiomer reduced cerebral edema and improved the recovery of motor function and spatial memory (121).

Thus, MAOIs provide neuroprotection by multiple mechanisms, including upregulation of antiapoptotic proteins, downregulation of proapoptotic proteins, increasing the quantity of antioxidant enzymes, and stabilizing the mitochondrial membrane. Neuroprotective benefits are mediated by the propargyl moiety and are not the result of MAO inhibition.

SELEGILINE

Pharmacokinetics

Selegiline is a relatively selective irreversible MAO B inhibitor. It is considered a "suicide inhibitor" because it forms a covalent bond with MAO, and loss of MAO inhibition is dependent on generation of new enzyme. Selegiline is lipophilic and readily absorbed from the gastrointestinal tract. The absolute bioavailability of selegiline is roughly 10% (122); 94% is bound to plasma proteins, with strong binding to macroglobulins (123, 124). Maximal concentrations are achieved approximately one-half to 2 hours after oral administration (125). Studies of platelets in PD patients have shown that within 2 to 4 hours after a single 5-mg dose of selegiline, MAO B activity is inhibited by 86%; within 24 hours of a 10-mg dose, MAO

B activity is inhibited by almost 98% (126). Selegiline readily crosses the blood-brain barrier and accumulates in brain regions rich in MAO B, including the striatum, thalamus, cortex, and brainstem (127). Brain MAO B must be inhibited by at least 85% to increase aminergic transmission (57, 128).

Selegiline has a tissue (liver or brain) half-life of 2 to 10 days (129, 130). It is metabolized in the liver by the microsomal cytochrome P-450 system to (−)- desmethylselegiline (DES) and to l-methamphetamine (l-MA) Figure 40-2 (131); the latter compound is further metabolized to amphetamine and p-hydroxylated metabolites (58). The metabolism of selegiline is depicted in Figure 40-2. These metabolites are conjugated with glucuronic acid to form inactive metabolites (58). Selegiline may also be metabolized outside the liver. Three metabolites have been identified in serum and urine: l-(−)-methamphetamine, l-(−)-amphetamine, and (−)-desmethylselegiline (DES) (132). Desmethylselegiline has activity as an irreversible MAO B inhibitor, but it is much less potent than selegiline (58, 133, 134).

Mechanisms of Action

Selegiline may provide symptomatic antiparkinsonian benefit through a number of mechanisms. Chronic administration increases striatal dopamine concentration in rats (135, 136). This is thought to be due to MAO B inhibition in striatal glia, as MAO B is essentially absent from nigrostriatal nerve terminals (137). Selegiline may also act by inhibiting dopamine reuptake (134) and by blocking presynaptic dopamine receptors (138). In rats, intraperitoneal selegiline increases 2-phenylethylamine

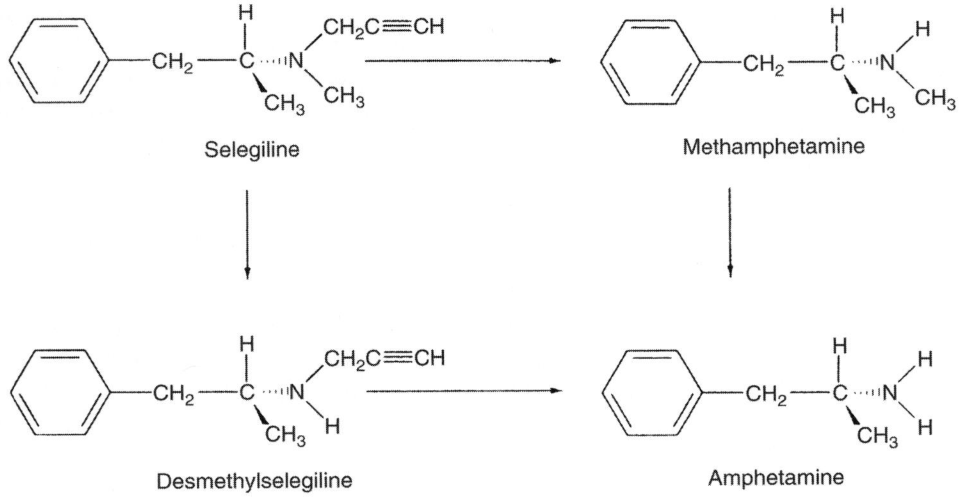

FIGURE 40-2

Metabolism of selegiline.

concentration (139), which may increase dopamine release. Metabolites of selegiline, including amphetamine, may also promote dopamine release, although the concentrations of these metabolites are probably too small to provide significant clinical benefit.

Side Effects

Selegiline is usually well tolerated. The most frequent side effect is an increase in dyskinesia when it is added to a levodopa regimen in patients who have already developed dyskinesia. Additional side effects include nausea, dizziness, dry mouth, sleep disturbances, confusion, anxiety, hallucinations, and orthostatic hypotension. When selegiline is combined with levodopa therapy, orthostatic hypotension may be marked and unassociated with compensatory tachycardia. This is reversible within days after stopping selegiline. Related to this is supine hypertension. Dopaminergic adverse reactions can typically be managed by lowering the levodopa dose (140). Gastric ulcer activation and urinary disturbances (141) have been reported (142, 143), and some patients may develop elevated liver function tests (102, 144). Psychiatric abnormalities with selegiline use, which include hypomania and paranoia, are rare (145–147).

Drug Interactions

Selegiline can interact with other drugs, resulting in a variety of complications. The constellation of stupor, muscular rigidity, severe agitation, and elevated temperature has been reported in some patients receiving the combination of selegiline and meperidine (148). This is typical of the interaction of meperidine and MAOIs. Selegiline is contraindicated for use with meperidine, and this contraindication is usually extended to other opioids. The combined use of selegiline and other MAO inhibitors may result in hypotension; their concomitant use is not recommended (149).

The combined use of selective serotonin reuptake inhibitor (SSRI) antidepressants and selegiline can cause the "serotonin syndrome," which results in some combination of mental status changes, myoclonus, diaphoresis, hyperreflexia, tremor, diarrhea, shivering, incoordination, and fever (150). The syndrome may, on rare occasions, progress to seizures, coma, or death (151). Treatment of the serotonin syndrome consists of discontinuation of the offending agent and supportive measures. The pathophysiology of the serotonin syndrome may be related to enhanced stimulation of 5-HT receptors in the brainstem and spinal cord (152).

Serotonin syndrome due to the combination of selegiline and an SSRI is rare. Two chart reviews of patients taking the combination of an SSRI and selegiline failed to detect side effects that had not already been reported with

each respective medication (152, 153). The Parkinson Study Group found that of 4568 PD patients treated with an antidepressant and selegiline, only 0.24% reported symptoms thought to be consistent with the serotonin syndrome (154). There were no fatalities. In routine clinical practice, oral selegiline at recommended dosages and SSRIs are commonly used together, but clinical monitoring appears warranted.

Clinical Trials of Selegiline

Early Parkinson's Disease. Selegiline monotherapy provides modest symptomatic benefit in early PD. In the DATATOP study, 800 patients were randomized to receive selegiline 10 mg/d or placebo. Total and motor scores on the Unified Parkinson's Disease Rating Scale (UPDRS) improved significantly at 1 and 3 months. Total UPDRS scores improved 2.07 ± 6.36 at 1 month in selegiline-treated patients compared with 0.11 ± 5.98 in placebo-treated patients ($P < .001$) and 1.56 ± 7.04 in selegiline-treated patients at 3 months; a worsening of 1.34 ± 6.70 was seen in placebo-treated patients ($P < .001$) (155). In a study of 157 patients, Palhagen and associates (156) noted significant improvement in total and motor UPDRS scores at 6 weeks and 3 months following the introduction of selegiline. At 3 months, total UPDRS scores improved 1.1 ± 4.3 in the selegiline group compared with a worsening of 0.4 ± 4.0 in the placebo group ($P < .05$). Although they studied only 93 patients, the French Selegiline Multicenter Trial also identified significant improvements in total and motor UPDRS scores at 1 and 3 months (157).

Several smaller studies were unable to identify early symptomatic effects, probably due to power limitations (157). In 54 patients, Tetrud and Langston found no symptomatic benefit at 1 month (158); and in a Finnish study of 52 patients, symptomatic benefit was not found at 3 weeks or 2 months (159). Thus, selegiline monotherapy in early PD provides minor symptomatic effects that are evident in larger studies by 4 to 6 weeks of therapy.

Withdrawal of selegiline results in a loss of symptomatic benefit that depends on the generation of new MAO B and may take several months. The half-life for human MAO B synthesis in the brain has been estimated to be as long as 40 days (156). In the DATATOP study, there was no significant loss of symptomatic benefit 1 month following selegiline withdrawal. However, at 2 months, total UPDRS scores had worsened 2.34 ± 4.95 points in selegiline-treated patients compared with 0.48 ± 5.72 in placebo-treated patients ($P < .001$) (155). Several smaller studies were unable to detect this effect. Tetrud and Langston did not find significant clinical changes during a 1-month washout in 54 patients (158), and Palhagen and colleagues (156) found no evidence of clinical deterioration during a 2-month washout in 157 patients.

Selegiline delays the need for additional symptomatic therapy in early PD. In the DATATOP study, selegiline significantly delayed the need for levodopa. The probability of reaching end point (need for levodopa) was significantly reduced in patients assigned to selegiline (hazard ratio, 0.50; 95% confidence interval, 0.41–0.62; $P < .001$). Subjects assigned to selegiline reached endpoint at a projected median of 719 days, compared with 454 days for subjects assigned to placebo, representing a difference of 9 months (156). Tetrud and Langston (158) found that patients taking selegiline required levodopa at a mean of 548.9 days, compared with 312.1 days for placebo-treated patients ($P < .002$). Palhagen and coworkers (156) noted that the median time for levodopa was 12.7 months in their selegiline group, compared with 8.6 months in the placebo group ($P = .028$). Myllyla and colleagues (159) found a mean of 545 ± 90 days in their selegiline group, compared with 372 ± 28 days in the placebo group ($P = .03$), a difference of almost 6 months. Selegiline monotherapy delays the need for additional symptomatic therapy by 6 to 9 months.

The mechanism by which selegiline delays the need for symptomatic therapy is not clearly defined. It is possible that the delay is entirely due to selegiline's symptomatic effect. However, it is not known whether this small symptomatic effect is sufficient to account for all of the delay in need for levodopa. The delay is potentially consistent with a neuroprotective effect, but this remains unproven. It is not possible to differentiate symptomatic and possible neuroprotective effects of selegiline in these studies.

During selegiline monotherapy, a slowing of progression of measures of parkinsonian disability is observed. Tetrud and Langston (158) identified a 50% decrease in the rate of progression in UPDRS motor scores in their selegiline group compared with placebo ($P = .002$). In the DATATOP trial, there was a significantly slower rate of decline in UPDRS scores in patients taking selegiline compared to those taking placebo through 6 months of follow-up (155). Palhagen and coworkers (156) reported a progression in total UPDRS score of 7.5 ± 8.4 points from baseline to start of washout (median time = 12.7 months) in the selegiline group compared with 10.6 ± 9.6 points (median time = 8.6 months) in the placebo group ($P = .042$). Myllyla and associates (159) also noted significantly less progression of disability in parkinsonian symptoms measured by the Columbia University Rating Scale in their selegiline group up to 1 year. The mechanism(s) underlying these observations are not clearly defined. A decline in the rate of progression of disability measured from an untreated baseline to a point during treatment may be due, wholly or in part, to symptomatic effects regardless of whether significant symptomatic benefit was observed.

Olanow and coworkers (160) reported significantly less progression in UPDRS scores from an untreated baseline to an untreated endpoint following medication washout. Patients were randomized to selegiline or placebo and to symptomatic treatment with bromocriptine or levodopa. Endpoint evaluation at 14 months was completed after a 2-month washout of selegiline and a 1-week washout of bromocriptine and levodopa. The change in total UPDRS scores from baseline to final visit was 0.4 ± 1.3 in the selegiline group compared with 5.8 ± 1.4 in the placebo group ($P < .001$). Palhagen and colleagues (156) assessed progression of UPDRS scores from an untreated baseline to an untreated endpoint following an 8-week washout of selegiline. Total UPDRS scores worsened significantly less in the selegiline group (11.3 ± 9.1) than in the placebo group (14.2 ± 10.9), when the length of time to reach the endpoint of need for levodopa was used as the covariate ($P = 0.033$). These observations are potentially consistent with a neuroprotective effect from selegiline, but it cannot be determined whether the washouts were of sufficient duration to allow resolution of all symptomatic effects.

Once patients require levodopa therapy, selegiline allows symptomatic control with lower levodopa doses. Myllyla and coworkers (159) randomized 27 newly diagnosed PD patients to selegiline 10 mg/d or placebo until initiation of levodopa, and then followed them for at least 2 years. Required doses of levodopa were significantly lower in the selegiline group than in the placebo group ($P < .001$). In selegiline-treated patients, the levodopa dose increased from 272 ± 75 to 358 ± 117 mg/d over 24 months, whereas in the placebo group the dose of levodopa almost doubled, from 293 ± 117 d to 543 ± 150 mg/d. Selegiline-treated patients also required significantly fewer levodopa doses per day (3.5 vs. 4.5, $P = .01$). DATATOP subjects who reached endpoint and required levodopa were invited to join an open-label extension in which they received selegiline 10 mg/d and levodopa as needed and were followed for an additional 18 months. Patients who had originally been assigned to selegiline took levodopa for a significantly shorter time ($P < .0001$) and received significantly lower total cumulative levodopa doses ($P < .02$). However, the total daily levodopa dose at final evaluation was similar between groups. These observations are consistent with the fact that selegiline delays the need for levodopa; moreover, with selegiline, patients on levodopa can be controlled with lower levodopa doses (155). In the DATATOP extension, levodopa dose requirements were equal once patients in both groups were taking selegiline (161). This suggests that the differences observed are likely to be due to symptomatic rather than neuroprotective effects.

Evaluation of other clinical endpoints in DATATOP extensions supports the idea that the effects of selegiline were symptomatic (162). Motor complications, including fluctuations, dyskinesia, and freezing, occurred at the same time and in the same proportion of patients originally treated with selegiline as those originally treated with selegiline placebo.

An independent second randomization was performed on 368 of the original DATATOP subjects on selegiline who had required levodopa (163). Half were assigned to continue selegiline 10 mg/d and the other half received placebo. Subjects were followed for an additional 2 years. The primary outcome measure was the occurrence of motor fluctuations; secondary outcome measures included time until motor fluctuations, freezing of gait, confusion, and dementia. Overall, there was no difference in the primary outcome measure between the 2 groups. Wearing off occurred in 52% of those on placebo compared with 41% on deprenyl, but this was not significant. However dyskinesias developed in 34% of those randomized to selegiline compared with 19% on placebo ($P = .006$). In contrast, freezing of gait was reported in 29% of the placebo group vs. 16% of selegiline-treated subjects ($P = .0003$). At an average follow-up of 2 years, there was significantly less decline in the total UPDRS ($P = .0002$), motor ($P = .0006$) and activities of daily living (ADL) ($P = .0045$) subscales in the selegiline group. Overall, these results may reflect a symptomatic effect, as selegiline-treated subjects experienced better UPDRS scores and less freezing but more dyskinesia.

Advanced Parkinson's Disease.   Selegiline affords mild to moderate symptomatic benefit as an adjunct to levodopa in advanced patients, and was approved by the U.S. Food and Drug Administration for this indication. In an early open-label trial, Rinne and associates (164) found that the addition of selegiline 10 mg/d in advanced patients on stable dosages of levodopa significantly improved tremor, rigidity, and bradykinesia. In double-blind controlled studies, Sivertsen and colleagues (165) noted significant improvement in tremor ($P = .02$), and Heinonen and coworkers noted significant improvement in tremor ($P = .010$), rigidity ($P = .027$), and hypokinesia ($P = .004$) (166).

In patients with motor fluctuations, selegiline prolongs the short-duration levodopa response and reduces "off" time. In an open-label trial, Rinne and colleagues (164) found that 68% of patients showed significant improvement, with less frequent and less severe motor fluctuations. In double-blind crossover trials, Heinonen and coworkers (166) and Lees and associates (167) reported significantly less end-of-dose akinesia in patients taking selegiline. In a larger double-blind, placebo-controlled, parallel-group trial of 96 fluctuating PD patients, Golbe and coworkers (168) observed better mean hourly symptom control in 58% of patients randomized to selegiline compared with 26.1% of patients randomized to placebo ($P < .01$). Improvement was also

noted in dressing, dysarthria, hypomimia, sialorrhea, and tremor ($P < .05$).

When used as an adjunct to levodopa, selegiline allows a reduction in daily levodopa dose of 10% to 25% (165–167). For example, Golbe and associates (168) found that mean daily levodopa dosages were decreased by 17% in the selegiline group compared with 7% in the placebo group.

Selegiline may worsen dyskinesia when initially added to levodopa, thereby necessitating levodopa dose reductions. Once the levodopa dosage is reduced, dyskinesia is usually no worse than at baseline. Golbe and colleagues (168) found that approximately 60% of patients taking selegiline and 30% of those taking placebo reported a worsening of dyskinesia 2 or 3 days after starting treatment. In most cases symptoms resolved after several days when the levodopa dosage was reduced.

Selegiline is useful as an adjunct to levodopa in patients with advanced disease to improve symptoms and reduce "off" time. If dyskinesia emerges or worsens, the levodopa dosage should be reduced.

Selegiline and Mortality

The Parkinson's Disease Research Group of the United Kingdom (169) reported a 60% increase in mortality rate in PD patients who were randomized to levodopa and selegiline vs. levodopa alone. A total of 624 patients were randomized to one of 3 groups: levodopa, levodopa plus selegiline, or bromocriptine. After a mean duration of 5.6 years, 44 (17.7%) deaths were observed in the levodopa group, compared with 76 (28%) deaths in the group receiving levodopa plus selegiline ($P = .05$). The mortality rate in the bromocriptine group was not provided. The increase in mortality became apparent after 2.5 to 3.5 years of treatment.

Questions have been raised regarding methodologic issues in this study and the validity of its conclusions. Multiple interim analyses were performed without apparent statistical adjustment in regard to mortality (170). In addition, the on-treatment analysis did not confirm the findings of the intention-to-treat analysis. Further, both treatment arms (levodopa and levodopa plus selegiline) experienced surprisingly high mortality rates. Mortality rates of 50.7 and 32.1/1000 were observed in the levodopa/selegiline and levodopa groups, respectively, while a meta-analysis of 5 long-term trials yielded mortality rates of 12.5 and 16.7/1000 (169).

Other long-term trials have not identified an increase in mortality with selegiline. In the DATATOP trial and a subsequent open-label extension, the overall death rate was 17.1% (137 of 800), or 2.1% per year, through a mean of 8.2 years of observation (171). Mortality rate was unaffected by any of the treatments. In another study, 3 (6%) deaths occurred in the selegiline group through a mean follow-up of 4.5 years, with no significant difference in mortality rate between groups, and no trend toward increased mortality with selegiline use (160). In a 13-year follow-up of the DATATOP cohort, cumulative exposure to selegiline was not associated with increased mortality (172). In a multivariate analysis, increased mortality was associated with: (a) disease severity; (b) rate of decline; and (c) poor levodopa response independent of disease severity or levodopa dosage. The findings were unchanged when the analysis was restricted to those with a likely diagnosis of PD at 6 years' follow-up (172).

Thus, although the U.K. study raised concern, the weight of evidence suggests that mortality is not increased and the drug can be considered safe.

Selegiline Use by Alternate Routes

Transdermal Selegiline. Selegiline delivery via other routes of administration has also been evaluated. The selegiline transdermal system provides relatively stable selegiline blood concentrations through the day and minimizes the formation of metabolites. Oral selegiline undergoes extensive first-pass metabolism and has an elimination half-life of about 2 hours. The transdermal system avoids the first-pass effect, thereby increasing bioavailability and decreasing metabolite production. Higher concentrations of selegiline in blood and brain may be achieved before MAO A in the gut is inhibited to the degree that a risk of hypertensive crisis is created. Higher concentrations of selegiline in brain might provide greater symptomatic benefit by completely inhibiting brain MAO B and possibly some MAO A. Inhibition of MAO A within the substantia nigra might increase intraneuronal dopamine pools and facilitate dopamine release.

Rohatagi and colleagues (80) administered selegiline transdermal system (STS) to 6 healthy male volunteers using 1 to 4 patches (delivering 1.83 mg/cm^2) daily for 5 days and observed higher blood concentrations of selegiline compared with oral tablets. Selegiline delivery increased proportionally from 7.7 ± 0.9 mg using one STS/d to 29.2 ± 5.2 mg following 4 STS/d. AUC increased linearly with dose.

Hauser and associates (173) evaluated the tolerability and safety of transdermal selegiline monotherapy in mild to moderate PD. Patients who were well controlled on levodopa underwent baseline evaluation following a 2-week levodopa washout. One selegiline transdermal system (delivering 8.5 mg/24 hours) was then applied each day for 8 weeks. The most common adverse events were dizziness (28%), headache (16%), and pruritus (16%). For patients completing 8 weeks on study medication, UPDRS total and motor scores improved significantly (−2.53 ± 4.37, P < .05; −1.80 ± 3.32, P = .05).

To our knowledge, transdermal selegiline is no longer being developed for an indication of PD.

Zydis Selegiline. Zydis selegiline is a freeze-dried tablet that dissolves rapidly when placed on the tongue. Properties of the Zydis formulation have been described in detail by Seager (174). In healthy volunteers, almost one-third of a Zydis seligiline 10-mg dose was absorbed pregastrically within 1 minute, with most absorption occurring in the buccal mucosa (175). The mean area under the curve (AUC) for plasma selegiline concentrations was nearly 5 times higher with Zydis selegiline 10 mg compared with oral selegiline, while plasma concentrations of selegiline metabolites were significantly lower (>90%) (175).

Clarke and associates reported 3 studies of Zydis seliginine (176) in which 197 stable PD patients on oral selegiline 10 mg/d, given as an adjunct to levodopa or dopamine agonist therapy, were randomized to 1 of 3 treatment arms: Zydis selegiline 1.25 mg/d, Zydis selegiline 10 mg/d, or oral selegiline 10 mg/d. Therapeutic equivalence, defined a priori as total UPDRS score ± 5, revealed both Zydis selegiline dosages to be comparable to oral selegiline 10 mg/d. The mean adjusted total UPDRS scores in those who switched from oral selegiline 10 mg/d to Zydis selegiline 1.25 mg/d was slightly improved at 12 weeks (−2.50; P = .01) (176). In the second study, a single-dose, randomized, 2-way crossover study, 148 PD patients received either Zydis selegiline 5 mg or matching placebo. Patients were stratified according to swallowing and salivation problems. Overall, 61% of subjects preferred Zydis selegiline 5 mg to oral selegiline. There was no difference between those with or without swallowing problems (176).

The third study (176) examined the tyramine pressor effect in 24 healthy volunteers, comparing Zydis selegiline 1.25 mg/d to oral selegiline 10 mg/d for 14 to 16 days. The pressor effect after 400 mg tyramine was unchanged from before to after 14 days of Zydis selegiline 1.25 mg. However, after 14 days of oral selegiline 10 mg/d, the threshold for pressor effect was reduced to 200 mg tyramine (176).

In a 3-month randomized placebo-controlled study, Zydis selegiline was reported to reduce "off" time in PD patients with motor fluctuations (177); 140 PD patients with at least 3 hours of daily "off" time were randomized to Zydis selegiline or placebo in a 2:1 ratio. Initially, subjects received Zydis selegiline 1.25 mg/d; at week 6, the dosage was increased to 2.5 mg/d. Overall, the drug was well tolerated. More than 90% of each group completed the trial, and drug-related events were noted by 32% of the Zydis selegiline–treated subjects compared with 21% of the placebo-treated subjects. The most frequent adverse events in the Zydis selegiline group were dizziness, dyskinesias, hallucinations, headache, and dyspepsia. "Off" time was significantly reduced at both weeks

4 to 6 and weeks 10 to 12 compared with placebo. For weeks 4 to 6 (Zydis selegiline 1.25 mg/d), "off" time was reduced 1.4 hours compared with 0.5 hours for placebo (P = .003) and for weeks 10 to 12 (Zydis selegiline 2.5 mg/d), "off" time was reduced by 2.2 hours compared with 0.6 hours for placebo (P < .001). Dyskinesia-free "on" time was significantly increased at week 6 (Zydis selegiline 1.25 mg/d, 1.6 hours, vs. 0.5 hours for placebo; P = .019); week 12 (Zydis selegiline 2.5 mg/d, 1.8 hours, vs. 0.4 hours for placebo; P = .006). Increase in daily "on" time with dyskinesias was similar in the Zydis and placebo groups at both week 6 (0.1 hour for Zydis selegiline 1.25 mg/d and 0.3 hour for placebo) and week 12 (0.4 hour for Zydis selegiline 2.5 mg/d and 0.3 hour for placebo) (177).

Zydis selegiline is now approved by the US FDA as an adjunct to levodopa in patients with wearing off fluctuations.

RASAGILINE

Pharmacokinetics

Rasagiline [R(+)-N-propargyl-1-aminoindan] is a selective irreversible MAO B inhibitor (178). Inhibition of platelet MAO-B is dose-dependent. One hour after rasagiline administration, platelet MAO-B inhibition is 35% with 1 mg and 99% with 10 mg. With repeated doses, rasagiline 2 mg/d inhibited over 99% of platelet MAO B by day 6. In a single-dose study, rasagiline 1 or 2 mg caused 50% to 70% inhibition of brain MAO-B, and 5 and 10 mg inhibited up to 99% (178).

The AUC and C_{max} of rasagiline increase linearly with the dose. The $t_{1/2}$ of rasagiline is approximately 3.5 hours, and the $t_{1/2}$ for 1(R)-aminoindan, its active metabolite, is approximately 11 hours. Because rasagiline is an irreversible MAO-B inhibitor, the serum (pharmacokinetic) half-life does not correlate with the functional (pharmacodynamic) half-life.

Side Effects

The safety and tolerability of rasagiline were established in phase I and phase II trials (179). In healthy male volunteers 18 to 40 years of age, doses up to 20 mg/d were well tolerated (179). Adverse effects were mild, consisting of dry mouth, headache, nausea, thirst, and abdominal discomfort. Rasagiline did not significantly affect vital signs, physical exam, lab values, or electrocardiographic (ECG) recordings.

In a phase III 26-week study of rasagiline as monotherapy in early disease (TEMPO: Rasagiline Mesylate [TVP-1012] in Early Monotherapy for Parkinson's Disease Outpatients), (180), adverse events (AEs) were no more common with rasagiline than with placebo. The 2 most common AEs were (a) infection, which occurred in 15.4% of the combined rasagiline groups (14.9% with 1 mg/d and 15.9% with 2 mg/d) compared with 15.9% in the placebo group, and (b) headache, which occurred in 13.2% of the combined rasagiline groups (14.2% with 1 mg/d and 12.1% with 2 mg/d) compared with 10.1% in the placebo group. Other AEs occurring with a frequency of greater than 5% were accidental injury, dizziness, asthenia, nausea, arthralgia, back pain, and pain. A total of 20 serious AEs were reported in this study (180), with 4 in the placebo group, 6 in the group receiving rasagiline 1mg/d, and 10 in the group taking rasagiline 2 mg/d. Three newly diagnosed cancers were detected only in the rasagiline 2 mg/d group (one each of malignant melanoma, prostate cancer, and squamous cell carcinoma of the skin). The delayed-start TEMPO study (181) followed subjects for a total of 12 months. In the first 6 months, subjects were randomized to receive rasagiline 1 mg/d, rasagiline 2 mg/d, or placebo (180). For the next 6 months, subjects were maintained on their initial treatment assignment of either rasagiline 1 mg/d or 2 mg/d, and those who had been on placebo were treated with rasagiline 2 mg/d (181). Infection (10.8%), headache (5.4%), unintentional injury (4.9%), and dizziness (4.6%) were the most common AEs reported among all subjects in the second 6 months of the study (no significant difference between groups). Five newly diagnosed neoplasms (squamous cell carcinoma n = 2, basal cell carcinoma n = 1, melanoma n = 1, colon cancer n = 1) and 17 hospitalizations for various reasons (vascular disease n = 6, gastrointestinal symptoms n = 4, unintentional injuries n = 3, syncope n = 1, bronchitis n = 1, cellulitis n = 1, vaginal prolapse n = 1) were reported as serious AEs in the second 6 months of this study, when all subjects were receiving rasagiline (181). Combining data over the 12 months, a total of 8 new malignancies were diagnosed, including 3 squamous cell carcinomas (skin), 2 cases of melanoma, and 1 basal cell carcinoma. Whether this exceeds the normal background rate is not clear; recent information suggests that PD patients experience more skin cancers than the general population (182). In a phase III study of rasagiline as an adjunct to levodopa in patients with fluctuations (PRESTO: A Randomized Placebo-Controlled Trial of Rasagiline in Levodopa-Treated Patients With Parkinson Disease and Motor Fluctuations) 183), AEs were reported in 87%, 91%, and 95% of participants receiving placebo, rasagiline 0.5 mg/d, and rasagiline 1 mg/d, respectively. Rasagiline 0.5 mg/d was more often associated with an adverse event of balance difficulty compared with placebo (5.5% vs. 0.6%, P = .03), and rasagiline 1 mg/d was more frequently associated with weight loss (9.4% vs. 2.5%, P = .02), vomiting (6.7% vs. 1.3%, P = .03), and anorexia (5.4% vs 0.6%, P = .04) (183). There were no dietary restrictions in the phase III studies and no episodes of hypertensive crisis occurred.

Clinical Trials of Rasagiline

Early PD. The TEMPO (Rasagiline Mesylate [TVP-1012] in Early Monotherapy for Parkinson's Disease Outpatients) study evaluated rasagiline in early PD. A total of 404 subjects were randomized to receive rasagiline 1 mg/d, rasagiline 2 mg/d, or placebo. The primary outcome was the change in total UPDRS scores between baseline and week 26. At 26 weeks, rasagiline provided significantly greater improvement than placebo; change in total UPDRS scores were –4.20 units for rasagiline 1 mg/d vs. placebo, and –3.56 units for rasagiline 2 mg/d vs. placebo ($P < .001$ for each comparison) (180). Significant differences in secondary endpoints, including UPDRS motor and ADL subscales and the Parkinson's disease quality of life scale (PDQUALIF), were observed favoring rasagiline compared with placebo. The secondary endpoint of need for levodopa, however, was not different among the groups (16.7% for placebo, 11.2% for rasagiline 1 mg, and 16.7% for rasagiline 2 mg). Nearly one-half (49%) of placebo-treated patients and two-thirds (66% for rasagiline 1 mg/d, 67% for rasagiline 2 mg/d) of subjects who received rasagiline were responders, defined as less than 3 units worsening in total UPDRS scores from baseline to week 26 ($P < .01$ for each active treatment group compared with placebo). Rasagiline was well tolerated, and 112 of 138 (81.1%) placebo-treated subjects , 111 of 134 (82.8%) subjects treated with rasagiline 1 mg, and 105 of 132 (79.5%) subjects treated with rasagiline 2 mg completed 26 weeks without needing additional medical therapy.

In the second 6 months of the TEMPO study (181), all subjects who completed the double-blind placebo-controlled phase (180) were placed on rasagiline. PD patients on either 1 or 2 mg/d of rasagiline from the start remained on that dosage for the full 12 months, while those who were initially on placebo for the first 6 months were then started on rasagiline 2 mg/d (delayed start) (181). A total of 380 subjects entered the active treatment phase, with 371 comprising the intention-to-treat cohort. The primary outcome measure was change in total UPDRS from baseline to 12 months. Subjects who received rasagiline 2 mg/d for one year had 2.29 units less worsening (increase) in total UPDRS score compared with those receiving placebo for 6 months followed by rasagiline for 6 months ($P = .01$). Subjects treated with rasagiline 1 mg/d for 1 year also experienced less worsening of total UPDRS scores than subjects who were treated with placebo for 6 months followed by rasagiline 2 mg/d for 6 months (1.82 units lower total UPDRS in the 1 mg/d group; $P = .05$). Nearly 70% (259 subjects) completed 12 months without the need for additional therapy.

Responders in this study were defined as subjects whose total UPDRS score worsened by less than 4 units over 12 months. Patients who received rasagiline 2 mg/d for 1 year were more likely ($P = .04$) to be responders than those who had a delayed start (placebo followed by rasagiline 2 mg/d), but there was no difference between the delayed-treatment group and those who received rasagiline 1 mg/d for 1 year (181).

Moderate to Advanced PD. Rasagiline was evaluated in moderate to advanced PD patients with motor fluctuations on levodopa in the PRESTO (A Randomized Placebo-Controlled Trial of Rasagiline in Levodopa-Treated Patients With Parkinson Disease and Motor Fluctuations) study (183). PD patients (n = 472) with a minimum 2.5 hours daily "off" time were randomized to rasagiline 0.5 mg/d, 1 mg/d, or placebo. The primary outcome measure was change in "off" time from baseline to 26 weeks as measured by patients' home diaries. Mean adjusted "off" time decreased by 1.85 hours with rasagiline 1 mg/d, 1.41 hours with rasagiline 0.5 mg/d, and 0.91 hours with placebo. There was approximately 1 hour less "off" time with rasagiline 1 mg/d, and one-half hour less "off" time with rasagiline 0.5 mg/d compared with placebo ($P < .001$, and $P = .02$, respectively). There was a small but significant increase in "on" time with troublesome dyskinesia in the rasagiline 1-mg group. The secondary endpoints of clinical global impression, UPDRS ADL "off", and motor UPDRS "on" were all significantly improved with both dosages of rasagiline (183). The 1-mg/d dosage was also associated with significant improvement on the Schwab and England (184) scale during "off" time (183).

The LARGO (Lasting effect in Adjunct therapy with Rasagiline Given Once daily) study evaluated 687 advanced PD patients in an 18-week double-blind, parallel-group trial (185). Patients were randomized to the addition of rasagiline 1 mg daily, entacapone 200 mg taken with each levodopa dose, or placebo. The primary outcome of change in "off" hours from baseline was significantly reduced in both the rasagiline (–1.18 hours; $P = .0001$) and entacapone (–1.2 hours; $P < .0001$) groups compared with placebo (–0.4 hours). Secondary outcomes of clinical global impression, UPDRS ADL scores in the "off" state, and UPDRS motor scores in the "on" state, were all improved in both active treatment groups compared with placebo (185). UPDRS dyskinesia scores were not worse with either rasagiline or entacapone. Three exploratory UPDRS subscores—postural instability–gait disorder (PIGD), freezing, and motor score in the practically defined "off state"—were each improved with rasagiline but not with entacapone (185). In addition, there was a small but significant reduction in daily levodopa dose with rasagiline (–24 mg) ($P = .0003$ vs. placebo) and entacapone (–19 mg) ($P = .0024$ vs. placebo) compared with a slight increase in daily levodopa requirement with placebo (+5 mg) (185). The benefits of rasagiline were independent of age and concomitant dopamine agonist treatment. Post hoc analysis revealed no increase in dopaminergic adverse effects in those above age 70 years. Rasagiline was well tolerated, and there were fewer early study terminations and fewer study withdrawals related to adverse effects compared to entacapone or placebo, although this was not significant (185).

An auxiliary study of LARGO evaluated freezing of gait in 454 advanced PD patients who had been randomized to rasagiline (1 mg/d; n = 150), entacapone (200 mg with each dose of levodopa; n = 150), or placebo (n = 154) (186). Compared with baseline, evaluation at 10 weeks demonstrated a mean improvement in FOG-Q (Freezing of Gait Questionnaire) in the rasagiline group of 1.2 points, compared with a 0.5-point worsening in the placebo group (P = .045). Subjects on entacapone had mean improvement of 1.1 points (P = .066 compared with placebo).

Rasagiline is now approved by the US FDA as monotherapy in early disease and as an adjunct to levodopa in patients with wearing off fluctuations. Although there were no dietary restrictions in the pivotal trials, it is currently recommended that patients receiving rasagiline avoid foods and beverages high in tyramine, pending results of additional tyramine studies.

OTHER MAO INHIBITORS

Lazabemide

Lazabemide (Ro 19-6327) is a selective, rapidly reversible MAO B inhibitor chemically unrelated to selegiline (187). It has a high degree of MAO B selectivity and is not metabolized to amphetamine or its derivatives. Even at high doses, lazabemide is devoid of any tyramine potentiation ("cheese effect") (188). Lazabemide does not cause dopamine release (189) or induce ipsilateral turning in 6-hydroxydopamine–lesioned rats (190).

In a 6-week double-blind trial, 201 early untreated PD patients were randomized to receive lazabemide 100 to 400 mg/d or placebo. Lazabemide treatment was associated with significant improvement in the ADL component of the UPDRS, but other scores were unchanged (187). A higher incidence of insomnia, decreased hematocrit, and elevated serum alanine aminotransferase levels were associated with lazabemide at the dose of 400 mg/d.

In another double-blind, placebo-controlled trial, 321 otherwise untreated patients were randomized to receive lazabemide 25 to 200 mg/d or placebo and were followed for up to 1 year (191). The primary endpoint was the time to reach functional disability severe enough to warrant levodopa therapy. The risk of reaching endpoint was reduced by 51% for patients receiving lazabemide compared with placebo (P = .008). No symptomatic effects were noted.

The Parkinson Study Group (192) conducted a tolerability study of lazabemide in 137 patients who experienced a stable response to levodopa. Subjects were randomized to receive lazabemide 100 to 400 mg/d or placebo for 8 weeks. Lazabemide was as well tolerated as placebo, but there was an increased frequency of dopaminergic side effects, including dyskinesia, nausea, and dystonia in lazabemide-treated groups.

To our knowledge, lazabemide is no longer being developed.

CONCLUSION

Monoamine oxidase plays an integral role in the metabolism of intracerebral dopamine, and inhibitors of the enzyme provide benefit in PD. Oral selegiline monotherapy provides modest symptomatic benefit in early PD and delays the need for dopamine replacement therapy by several months. Once levodopa is required, selegiline allows symptomatic control with lower levodopa doses. In advanced disease, selegiline provides mild to moderate symptomatic benefit as an adjunct to levodopa. Off time is reduced and symptom control is improved. If dopaminergic side effects emerge with the introduction of selegiline, the levodopa dose should be reduced. Zydis selegiline, an orally absorbed medication, is approved as an adjunct to levodopa in patients with wearing off fluctuations.

Rasagiline is more potent than oral selegiline and also appears to provide greater symptomatic benefit. It is approved as monotherapy in early PD and as an adjunct to levodopa in patients with wearing off fluctuations. The "delayed-start" TEMPO study suggests that the earlier introduction of rasagiline provides greater benefit than delayed introduction, and there is interest in whether this might reflect a neuroprotective or disease-modifying effect. Further studies are currently under way to confirm this result.

References

1. Hoffman BB, Lefkowitz RJ. Catecholamines, Sympathomimetic Drugs, and Adrenergic Receptor Antagonists. In: Hardman JG, Limbird LE, Goodman Gilman A, et al. (eds). In: *Goodman & Gilman's The Pharmacological Basis of Therapeutics*. New York: McGraw-Hill, 1996:199–248.
2. Smith AD, Datta SP, Howard Smith HG, et al (eds). *The Oxford Dictionary of Biochemistry and Molecular Biology*. Oxford, New York, Tokyo: Oxford University Press, 1997.
3. Nicoll RA. Introduction to the pharmacology of CNS. In: Katzung BG (ed). *Basic and Clinical Pharmacology*. Stamford, CT: Appleton & Lange, 1998.
4. (No authors specified) General aspects of neuropharmacology. In: Clark WG, Brater DC, Johnson AR (eds). *Goth's Medical Pharmacology*. St. Louis: Mosby, 1992.
5. Westlund KN. The distribution of monoamine oxidases A and B in normal human brain. In: Lieberman A, Olanow CW, Youdim MBH, et al (eds). *Monoamine*

Oxidase Inhibitors in Neurological Diseases. New York, Basel, Hong Kong: Marcel Dekker, 1994.

6. Lefkowitz RJ, Hoffman BB, Taylor P. Neurotransmission. The autonomic and somatic motor nervous systems. In: Hardman JG, Limbird LE, Molinoff PB, et al (eds). *Goodman & Gilman's The Pharmacological Basis of Therapeutics.* New York: McGraw-Hill, 1996.

7. Davison AN. Physiological role of monoamine oxidase. *Physiol Rev* 1958; 38:729–747.

8. Schmiedeberg O Ueber das Verhältniss des Ammoniaks. und der primären Monaminbasen zur . . . (1878) A History of Naunyn-Schmiedeberg's Archives of Pharmacology Author complete this reference

9. Hare MLC. Tyramine oxidase-1. A new enzyme system in liver. *Biochem J* 1928; 22:968–979.

10. Zeller EA. Uber den enzymatischen abbau von histamin und diaminen. *Helv Chim Acta* 1938; 21:881–890.

11. O'Brien EM, Tipton K. Biochemistry and mechanism of action of monoamine oxidases A and B. In: Lieberman A, Olanow CW, Youdim MBH, et al (eds). *Monoamine Oxidase Inhibitors in Neurological Disease.* New York, Basel, Hong Kng: Marcel Dekker, 1994:31–77.

12. Blaschko H. The natural history of amine oxidases. *Rev Physiol Biochem Pharmacol* 1974; 70:84–148.

13. Pletcher A. Monoamine oxidase inhibitors: Effects related to psychostimulation. In: Efron DH (ed). *Psychopharmacology. A Review of Progress 1957–1967.* Washington DC: US Government Printing Office, 1967.

14. Schiele BC. Antidepressants: Comparison of clinical effect in anergic schizophrenia and the depressed states. *Ann NY Acad Sci* 1963; 107:1131–1138.

15. Bryant JM, Schvartz N, Torosdag S, et al. Long-term antihypertensive effect of pargyline HCL with and without diuretic sulfonamides. *Ann NY Acad Sci* 1963; 107:1023–1032.

16. Pletscher A. The discovery of antidepressants: A winding path. *Experientia* 1991; 47:4–8.

17. Zeller EA, Barsky J. In vivo inhibition of liver and brain monoamine oxidase by 1-isonicotinyl-2-isopropyl hydrazine. *Proc Soc Exp Biol Med* 1952; 81:459–461.

18. Loomer HP, Saunders JC, Kline NS. A clinical and pharamcodynamic evaluation of iproniazid as a pyschic energizer. *Psychiatr Res Rep Am Psychiat Assoc* 1957; 135(8):129–141.

19. Loomer HP, Sauncers JC, Kline NS. Iproniazid, an amine oxidase inhibitor, as an example of a psychic energizer. *Congr Rec* 1957; 1382–1390.

20. Knoll J, Magyar K. Some puzzling pharmacological effects of monoamine oxidase inhibitors. *Biochem Psychopharmacol* 1972; 5:393–408.

21. Knoll H, Ecseri Z, Kelemen K, et al. Phenylisopropyl methylpropinylamine (E-250), a new spectrum psychic energizer. *Arch Int Pharmacodyn* 1965; 155:154–164.

22. Yang HYT, Neff NH. The monoamine oxidases of brain: Selective inhibition with drugs and the consequences for the metabolism of the biogenic amines. *J Pharmacol Exp Ther* 1974; 189:733–740.

23. Johnston JP. Some observations upon a new inhibitor of monoamine oxidase in brain tissue. *Biochem Pharmacol* 1968; 17:1285–1297.

24. Kearney EB, Salach JI, Walker WH, et al. Structure of the covalently bound flavin of monoamine oxidase. *Biochem Biophys Res Commun* 1971; 42:490–496.

25. Neff NH, Goridis C. Neuronal monoamine oxidase: Specific enzyme types and their rates of formation. *Adv Biochem Psychopharmacol* 1972; 5:307–323.

26. Yasunobu KI, Oi S. Mechanistic aspects of the bovine hepatic monoamine oxidase reaction. *Adv Biochem Psychopharmacol* 1972; 5:91–105.

27. Yasunobu KT, Gomes B. Mitochondrial amine oxidase (MAO) (beef liver). *Meth Enzymol* 1971; 17:709.

28. Nagy J, Salach JI. Identity of the active site flavin peptide fragments from the human "A"-form and the bovine "B"-form of monoamine oxidase. *Arch Biochem Biophys* 1981; 208:388–394.

29. Ramsay RR, Singer TP. The kinetic mechanisms of monoamine oxidases A and B. *Biochem Soc Trans* 1991;219–223.

30. Evidence for the existence of monoamine-containing neurons in the central nervous system. I. Demonstration of monoamines in the cell bodies of brainstem neurons. *Acta Physiol Scand* 1965; 62 (Suppl 232):1–55.

31. May T, Strauss S, Rommelspacher H. [3H] Harman labels selectively and with high affinity the active site of monoamine oxidase (EC1.4.3.4) subtype A (MAO-A) in rat, marmoset, and pig. *J Neural Transm* 1992; 32(Suppl):93–102.

32. Lewinsohn R, Glover V, Sandler M. Development of benzylamine oxidase and monoamine oxidase A and B in man. *Biochem Pharmacol* 1980; 29:1221–1230.

33. Pugh CEM, Quastel JH. Oxidation of aliphatic amines by brain and other tissues. *Biochem J* 1937; 31:2306–2321.

34. Quastel JH. Amine oxidases. In: Lajta A (ed). *Handbook of Neurochemistry.* New York: Plenum, 1970:285–312.

35. White HL, Stine DK. Monoamine oxidases A and B as components of a membrane complex. *J Neurochem* 1982; 38:1429–1436.

36. Blaschko H. Amine oxidase and amine metabolism. *Pharmacol Rev* 1952; 4:415–458.

37. Arai R, Kimura H, Maeda T. Topographic atlas of monoamine oxidase-containing neurons in the rat brain studies by an improved histochemical method. *Neurology* 1986; 19:905–925.

38. Kithama K, Denney RM, Maeda T, Jouvet M. Distribution of type B monoamine oxidase immunoreactivity in the cat brain with reference to enzyme histochemistry. *Neuroscience* 1991; 44:185–204.

39. Willoughby J, Glover V, Sandler M. Histochemical localization of monoamine oxidases A and B in rat brain. *J Neural Transm* 1988; 74:29–42.

40. Lewinsohn R, Glover V, Sandler M. Development of benzylamine oxidase and MAO-A and -B in man. *Biochem Pharmacol* 1980; 29:1220–1230.

41. Riederer P, Reynolds GP, Yodim MBH. Selectivity of MAO inhibitors in human brain and their clinical consequences. In: Youdim MBH, Paykel ES (eds). *Monoamine Oxidase Inhibitors: The State of the Art.* Chichester, UK: Wiley, 1981:63–76.

42. White HL, Tansik RL. Characterization of multiple substrate binding sites of MAO. In: Singer TP, von Korff RW, Murphy DL (eds). *Monoamine Oxidase: Structure, Function, Altered Functions.* New York: Academic Press, 1979:129–144.

43. Callingham BA. Substrate selective inhibition of monoamine oxidase by mexiletine. *Br J Clin Pharmacol* 1977;61:118.

44. Glover V, Sandler M, Owen F, et al. Dopamine is a monoamine oxidase B substrate. *Nature* 1979; 265:80–81.

45. Fowler CJ, Tipton KF. On the substrate specificities of the 2 forms of monoamine oxidase. *J Pharm Pharmacol* 1984; 36:111–115.

46. Reynolds GP, Riederer P, Rausch WD. Dopamine metabolism in human brain: effect of monoamine oxidase inhibition in vitro by (-)deprenyl and (+) and (−) tranylcypromine. *J Neural Transm* 1980; 16:173–178.

47. Murphy DL, Redmond D, Garrick N, et al. Brain region differences and some characteristics of monoamine oxidase type A and B activities in the vervet monkey. *Neurochem Res* 1979; 4:53–62.

48. Fowler CJ, Callingham BA, Mantle TJ, et al. Monoamine oxidase A and B: Aa useful concept? *Biochem Pharmacol* 1978; 27:97–101.

49. Oreland L. Monoamine oxidase, dopamine and Parkinson's disease. *Acta Neurol Scand* 1991; 84:60–65.

50. Levitt P, Pintar JE, Breakefield XO. Immunocytochemical demonstration of monoamine oxidase B in brain astrocytes and serotonergic neurons. *Proc Natl Acad Sci USA* 1982; 79:6385–6389.

51. Westlund KN, Kenney RM, Kochersperger LM, et al. Distinct monoamine oxidase A and B populations in primate brain. *Science* 1985; 230:181–183.

52. Oreland L, Arai Y, Stenstrom A, et al. Monoamine oxidase activity and localization in the brain and the activity in relation to psychiatric disorders. *Mod Probl Pharmacopsychiatr* 1982; 19:246–254.

53. Tipton KF, McCrodden JM, Kalir AS, et al. Inhibition of rat liver monoamine oxidase by alpha-methyl-and N-propargyl-amine derivatives. *Biochem Pharmacol* 1982; 31:1251–1255.

54. Wouterlood FG, Gaykema RPA. Innervation of histaminergic neurons in the posterior hypothalamic region by medial preoptic neurons. Anterograde tracing with *Phaselous vulgaris* leucoagglutinin combined with immunocytochemistry of histidine decarboxylase in the rat. *Brain Res* 1988; 455:170–176.

55. Youdim MBH, Green AR. Biogenic monoamine metabolism and functional activity in iron-deficient rats: Behavioral correlates. *Ciba Found Symp* 1976; 51:201–225.

56. Neff NH, Yang HY, Garelis E, Sampath SS. Biogenic amine-containing neurons: Biochemical mechanisms of synaptic transmission. *Psychother Psychosom* 1974; 23 (1–6):159–168.

57. Green AR, Youdim MB. Effects of monoamine oxidase inhibition by clorgyline, deprenyl or tranylcypromine on 5-hydroxytryptamine concentrations in rat brain and hyperactivity following subsequent tryptophan administration. *Br J Pharmacol* 1975; 55 (3):415–422.

58. Heinonen EH, Lammintausta RAS. A review of the pharmacology of selegiline. *Acta Neurol Scand* 1991; 84:44–59.

59. Kalaria RN, Mitchell MJ, Harik SI. Monoamine oxidases of the human brain and liver. *Brain* 1988; 111:1441–1451.

60. Arnett CD, Fowler JS, MacGregor RR, et al. Turnover of brain monoamine oxidase measure in vivo by positron emission tomography using L-(11C) deprenyl. *J Neurochem* 1987; 49:522–527.

61. Tipton KF, Fowlert CJ. In: Tipton KF, Dosteret P, Strolini Benedetti M (eds). *Monoamine Oxidase and Disease.* London: Academic Press, 1984.

62. Zeller EA, Arora KL, Gurne DH, et al. In: Singer TP, von Korff RW, Murphy DL (eds). *Monoamine Oxidase: Structure, Function, and Altered Functions.* New York: Academic Press, 1979.

63. Fowler CJ, Ross SB. Selective inhibitors of monoamine oxidase A and B: Biochemical, pharmacological, and clinical properties. *Med Res Rev* 1984; 4:323–358.

64. Ask AL, Hellstrom W, Norrman S, et al. Selective inhibition of the A form of monoamine oxidase by 4-dimethylamino-alpha-methylphenylalkylamine derivatives in the rat. *Neuropharmacology* 1982; 21:299–308.

65. Fowler CJ, Strolin Benedetti M. Cimoxatone is a reversible tight-binding inhibitor of the A form of rat brain monoamine oxidase. *J Neurochem* 1983; 40:510–513.

66. Ogren SO, Ask AL, Holm AC, et al. In: Youdim MBH, Paykel ES (eds). *Monoamine Oxidase Inhibitors. The State of the Art.* Chichester, UK: Wiley, 1981: 103–112.

67. Keane PE, Kan JP, Sontag N, et al. Monoamine oxidase inhibition and brain amine metabolism after oral treatment with toloxatone in the rat. *J Pharm Pharmacol* 1979; 31:752–754.

68. Urbaneja M, Knowles CO. Formanilide inhibition of rat brain monoamine oxidase. *Gen Pharmacol* 1979; 10:309–314.

69. Meyerson LR, McMurtrey KD, Davis VE. Neuro-amine-derived alkaloids: substrate-preferred inhibitors of rat brain monoamine oxidase in vitro. *Biochem Pharmacol* 1976; 25:1013–1020.

70. Suzuki O, Katsumata Y, Oya M, et al. Inhibition of type A and type B monoamine oxidase by naturally occurring xanthones. *Planta Med* 1981; 42:17–21.

71. Da Prada M, Keller HH, Schaffner R, et al. In: Kamijo K, Usdin E, Nagatsu T (eds). *Monoamine Oxidase: Basic and Clinical Frontiers.* Amsterdam: Excerpta Medica, 1981.

72. Rovei V, Caille D, Curet O, et al. Biochemical pharmacology of befloxatone (MD 370503), a new potent reversible MAO-A inhibitor. *J Neural Transm* 1994; 339–347.

73. Waldmeier PC, Felner AE, Tipton KF. The monoamine oxidase inhibiting properties of CGP 11305. *Eur J Pharmacol* 1983; 94:73–83.

74. Strolin Benedetti M, Destert P. Stereochemical aspects of MAO interactions: Reversible and selective inhibitors of monoamine oxidase. TIPS 1985; 246–251.

75. Roth JA, Gillis CN. Deamination of betaphenylethylamine by monoamine oxidase-inhibition by imipramine. *Biochem Pharmacol* 1974; 23:2537–2545.

76. Roth JA, Gillis CN. Some structural requirements for inhibition of type A and B forms of rabbit monoamine oxidase by tricyclic psychoactive drugs. *Mol Pharmacol* 1975; 11:28–35.

77. Edwards DJ, Change SS. Multiple forms of monoamine oxidase in rabbit platelets. *Life Sci* 1975; 17:1127–1134.

78. Dostert P, Strolin Benedetti M, Guffroy C. Different stereoselective inhibition of monoamine oxidase-B by the R-and S-enantiomers of MD 780236. *J Pharm Pharmacol* 1983; 335:161–165.

79. Henriot S, Kuhn C, Kettler R, et al. Lazabemide (Ro-19-6327), a reversible and highly sensitive MAO-B inhibitor: Preclinical and clinical findings. *J Neural Transm Suppl* 1994; 41:321–325.

80. Rohatagi S, Barrett JS, DeWitt KE, et al. Integrated pharamacokinetics and metabolic modeling of selegiline and metabolites after transdermal administration. *Biopharm Drug Dispos* 1997; 18:567–584.

81. Marley E, Blackwell B. Interactions of monoamine oxidase inhibitors, amines, and foodstuffs. *Adv Pharmacol Chemother* 1970; 8:186–239.

82. Knoll J, Vizi ES, Somogyi G. A phenyl-isopropyl-methylpropinylamine (E-250) tyraminantagonists hatasa. MTA V. *Oszt Kozl* 1967; 18:33–37.

83. Elsworth JD, Glover V, Reynolds GP. Deprenyl administration in man: A selective monoamine oxidase B inhibitor without the "cheese effect." *Psychopharmacology* 1978; 57:33–38.

84. Finberg JP, Takeshima T, Johnston JM, Commissiong JW. Increased survival of dopaminergic neurons by rasagiline, a monoamine oxidase B inhibitor. *Neuroreport* 1998; 9 (4):703–707.

85. Abu-Raya S, Tabakman R, Blaugrund E, et al. Neuroprotective and neurotoxic effects of monoamine oxidase-B inhibitors and derived metabolites under ischemia in PC12 cells. *Eur J Pharmacology* 2002; 434:109–116.

86. Mandel S, Weinreb O, Amit T, Youdim MBH. Mechanism of neuroprotective action of the anti-Parkinson drug rasagiline and its derivatives. *Brain Res Rev* 2005; 48:379–387.

87. Youdim MBH, Am OB, Yogev-Falach M, et al. Rasagiline: Neurodegenerative, neuroprotection, and mitochondrial permeability transition. *J Neurosci Res* 2005; 79:172–179.

88. Maruyama W, Akao Y, Youdim MBH, et al. Transfection-enforced Bcl-2 overexpression and an anti-Parkinson drug, rasagiline, prevent nuclear c\accumulation of glyceraldehyde-3-phosphate dehydrogenase induced by an endogenous dopaminergic neurotoxin, N-methyl(R)salsolinol. *J Neurochem* 2001; 78:727–735.

89. Maruyama W, Akao Y, Carrillo MC, et al. Neuroprotection by propargylamines in Parkinson's disease: Suppression of apoptosis and induction of prosurvival genes. *Neurotoxicol Teratol* 2002; 24:675–682.

90. Maruyama W, Nitta A, Shamoto-Nagai M, et al. N-Propargyl-1 (R)-aminoindan, rasagiline, increases glial cell line-derived neurotrophic factor (GDNF) in neuroblastoma SH-SY5Y cells through activation of NF-KB transcription factor. *Neurochem Int* 2004; 44:393–400.

91. Sanz E, Romera M, Bellik L, et al. Indolalkylamines derivatives as antioxidant and neuroprotective agents in an experiemental model of Parkinson's disease. *Med Sci Monit* 2004; 10(12):477–484.

92. Takahata K, Shimazu S, Katsuki H, et al. Effects of selegiline on antioxidant systems in the nigrostriatum in rat. *J Neural Transm* 2006; 113:151–158.

93. Seymour CB, Mothersill C, Mooney R, et al. Monoamine oxidase inhibitors l-deprenyl and chlorgyline protect nonmalignant human cells from ionising radiation and chemotherapy toxicity. *Br J Cancer* 2003; 89:1979–1986.

94. Szende B, Bokonyi Gy, Bocsi J, et al. Anti-apoptotic and apoptotic action of (−)-deprenyl and its metabolites. *J Neural Transm* 2001; 108:25–33.

95. Szende B, Magyar K, Szegedi ZS. Apoptotic and antiapoptotic effect of (−)deprenyl and (−)-desmethyl-deprenyl on human cell lines. *Neurobiology* 2000; 8(3–4):249–255.

96. Sharma SK, Carlson EC, Ebadi M. Neuroprotective actions of selegiline in inhibiting 1-methyl, 4-phenyl, pyridinium ion (MPP+)-induced apoptosis in SK-N-SH neurons. *J Neurocytol* 2003; 32:329–343.

97. Muralikrishnan D, Samantaray S, Mohanakumar KP. D-Deprenyl protects nigrostriatal neurons against 1-methyl-4-phenyl-1, 2, 3, 6-tetrahydropyridine-induced dopaminergic neurotoxicity. *Synapse* 2003; 50:7–13.

98. Mizuta I, Ohta M, Ohta K, et al. Selegiline and desmethylselegiline stimulate NGF, BDNF, and GDNF synthesis in cultured mouse astrocytes. *Biochem Biophys Res Commun* 2000; 279:751–755.

99. Kupsch A, Sautter J, Gotz ME, et al. Monoamine oxidase-inhibition and MPTP-induced neurotoxicity in the non-human primate: Comparison of rasagiline (TVP 1012) with selegiline. *J Neural Transm* 2001; 108:985–1009.

100. Blandini F, Armentero MT, Fancellu R, et al. Neuroprotective effect of rasagiline in a rodent model of Parkinson's disease. *Exp Neurol* 2004; 1987:455–459.

101. Naoi M, Maruyama W, Kasamatsu T, Dostert P. Oxidation of N-methyl-(R)-salsolinol: Involvement to neurotoxicity and neuroprotection by endogenous catechol isoquinolines. *J Neural Transm* 1998; 52(Suppl):125–138.

102. Tatton WG, Wadia JS, Ju WYH, et al. (−)-Deprenyl reduces neuronal apoptosis and facilitates neuronal outgrowth by altering protein synthesis without inhibiting monoamine oxidase. *J Neural Transm* 1996; 103(Suppl):48:45–59.

103. Am OB, Amit T, Youdim MBH. Contrasting neuroprotective and neurotoxic actions of respective metabolites of anti-Parkinson drugs rasagiline and selegiline. *Neurosci Lett* 2004; 355:169–172.

104. Ebadi M, Sharma S, Shavali S, et al. The multiple actions of selegiline. *Proc West Pharmacol Soc* 2002; 45:39–41.

105. Blandini F. Neuroprotection by rasagiline: A new therapeutic approach to Parkinson's disease? *CNS Drug Rev* 2005; 11(2):183–194.

106. Kluck RM. The release of cytochrome c from mitochondria: A primary site for Bcl-2 regulation of apoptosis. *Science* 1997; 275:1132–1136.

107. Reed JC. Cytochrome *c*: Can't live with it. can't live without it. *Cell* 1997; 91:559–562.

108. Eskes R, Amtonson B, Osensand A. Bax-induced cytochrome *c* release from mitochondria is independent of the mitochondrial transition pore but highly dependent on Mg2+ ions. *J Cell Biol* 1998; 143:217–224.

109. Shahani N, Gourie-Devi M, Nalini A, et al. (−)-Deprenyl alleviates the degenerative changes induced in the neonatal rat spinal cord by CSF from amyotrophic lateral sclerosis patients. *ALS Other Motor Neuron Disord* 2004; 5:172–179.

110. Carrillo MC, Minami C, Kitani K, et al. Enhancing effect of rasagiline on superoxide dismutase and catalase activities in the dopaminergic system in the rat. *Life Sci* 2000; 67(5):577–585.

111. Maruyama W, Yamamoto T, Kitani K, et al. Mechanism underlying anti-apoptotic activity of a (−)deprenyl-related propargylamine, rasagiline. *Mech Ageing Dev* 2000; 116 (2–3):181–191.

112. Wu RM, Chiueh CC, Pert A, Murphy DL. Apparent antioxidant effect of L-deprenyl on hydroxyl radical formation and nigral injury elicited by MPP+ in vivo. *Eur J Pharmacol* 1993; 243:241–248.

113. Simon L, Szilagyi G, Bori Z, et al. (−)-D-Deprenyl attenuates apoptosis in experimental brain ischaemia. *Eur J Pharmacol* 2001; 430:235–241.

114. Buys YM, Trope GE, Tatton WG. (−)-Deprenyl increases the survival of rat retinal ganglion cells after optic nerve crush. *Curr Eye Res* 1995; 14:119–126.

115. Tatton WG. Selegiline (−)-deprenyl can mediate neuronal rescue rather than neuronal protection. *Mov Disord* 1993; 8:S20–S30.

116. Hobbenaghi R, Tiraihi T. Neuroprotective effect of deprenyl in sensory neurons of axotomized dorsal root ganglion. *Clin Neuropharmacol* 2003; 26(5):263–269.

117. Finberg JP, Lamensdorf I, Weinstock M, et al. Pharmacology of rasagiline (N-propargyl-1R-aminoindan). *Adv Neurol* 1999; 80:495–499.

118. Abu-Raya S, Blaugrund E, Trembovler V, et al. Rasagiline, a monoamine oxidase-B inhibitor, protects NGF-differentiated PC12 cells against oxygen-glucose deprivation. *J Neurosci Res* 1999; 58(3):456–463.

119. Speiser Z, Katzir O, Rehavi M, et al. Sparing by rasagiline (TVP-1012) of cholinergic functions and behavior in the postnatal anoxia rat. *Pharmacol Biochem Behav* 1998; 60(2):387–393.

120. Speiser Z, Mayk A, Eliash S, Cohen S. Studies with rasagiline, a MAO-B inhibitor, in experimental focal ischemia in the rat. *J Neural Transm* 1999; 106(7–8):593–606.

121. Huang W, Chen Y, Shohami E, Weinstock M. Neuroprotective effect of rasagiline, a selective monoamine oxidase-B inhibitor, against closed head injury in the mouse. *Eur J Pharmacol* 1999; 366(2–3):127–135.

122. Mahmood I, Marinac JS, Wilsie S, et al. Pharmacokinetics and relative bioavailability of selegiline in healthy volunteers. *Biopharm Drug Dispos* 1995; 16:535–545.

123. Szoko E, Kalasz H, Kerecsen L, et al. Binding of (-) deprenyl to serum proteins. *Pol J Pharmacol Pharm* 1984; 36:413–421.

124. Kalasz H, Herescen L, Knoll J, Pucsok J. Chromatographic studies on the binding action and metabolism of (−)-deprenyl. *J Chromatogr* 1990; 499:589–599.

125. Benakis A. *Pharmacokinetic Study in Man of 14 C Jumex, A Study Report*. Orion Corporation. Farmos, Turku, 1981.

126. Ahola R, Haapalinna A, Heinonen E, et al. Protection by L-deprenyl of intact peripheral sympathetic neurons exposed to neurotoxin 6-hydroxy-dopamine (6-OHDA). *New Trends Clin Neuropharmacol* 1994; 7:287.

127. Fowler JS, MacGregor RR, Wolf AP, et al. Mapping human brain monoamine oxidase A and B with 11C labeled suicide inactivators and PET. *Science* 1987; 23:481–485.

128. Green AR, Mitchell BD, Tordoff AF, Youdim MB. Evidence for dopamine deamination by both type A and type B monoamine oxidase in rat brain in vivo and for the degree of inhibition of enzyme necessary for increased functional activity of dopamine and 5-hydroxytryptamine. *Br J Pharmacol* 1977; 60:343–349.

129. Gerlach M, Reichmann H, Riederer P. Die Parkinson-Krankheit, 3rd ed. New York: Springer, 2003.

130. Youdim MBH, Tipton KF. Rat striatal monoamine oxidase-B inhibition by 1-deprenyl and rasagiline: Its relationship to 2-phenylethylamine-induced stereotype and Parkinson's disease. *Parkinsonism Relat Disord* 2002; 8:247–253.

131. Yoshida T, Yamada Y, Yamamoto T, et al. Metabolism of deprenyl, a selective monoamine oxidase (MAO) B inhibitor in rat: Relationship of metabolism to MAO-B inhibitory potency. *Xenobiotica* 1986; 16:129–136.

132. Knoll J. R-(−)-deprenyl (selegiline, MoverganR) facilitates the activity of the nigrostriatal dopaminergic neuron. *J Neural Transm* 1987; 25:4566.

133. Borbe HO, Neibich G, Nickel B. Kinetic evaluation of MAO-B activity following oral administration of selegiline and desmethyl-selegiline in rat. *J Neural Transm* 1990; 32:131–137.

134. Knoll J. The possible mechanism of action of (-)deprenyl in Parkinson's disease. *J Neural Transm* 1978; 43:177–193.

135. Tipton KF. What is it that 1-deprenyl (selegiline) might do? *Clin Pharmacol Ther* 1994; 56:781–796.

136. Zsilla G, Foldi P, Held G, et al. The effect of repeated doses of (−) deprenyl on the dynamics of monoaminergic transmission. Comparison with clorgyline. *Pol J Pharmacol Pharm* 1986; 38:57–67.

137. Salo PT, Tatton WG. Deprenyl reduces the death of motoneurons caused by axotomy. *J Neurosci Res* 1992; 31:394–400.

138. Bronzetti E, Felici L, Ferrante F, et al. Effect of ethylcholine mustard axiridium (AF64A) and of the monoamine oxidase-B-inhibitor L-deprenyl on the morphology of rat hippocampus. *Int J Tissue React* 1992; 14:175–181.

139. Tatton WG, Seniuk NA. "Trophic-like" actions of (−)-deprenyl on neurons and astroglia. *Acad Biomed Drug Res* 1994; 7:238–248.

140. Myllylä VV, Sotaniemi K, Mäki-Ikola O, et al. Role of selegiline in combination therapy of Parkinson's disease. *Neurology* 1996; 47(Suppl)3:S200–S209.

141. Waters CH. Side effects of selegiline (Eldepryl). *J Geriatr Psychiatry Neurol* 1992; 5:31–34.

142. Yahr MD, Mendoza MR, Moros D, et al. Treatment of Parkinson's disease in early and late phases: Use of pharmacological agents with special reference to deprenyl (selegiline). *Acta Neurol Scand* 1983; 95:95–102.

143. Elizan TS, Moros DA, Yahr MD. Early combination of selegiline and low-dose levodopa as initial symptomatic therapy in Parkinson's disease: Experience in 26 patients receiving combined therapy for 26 months. *Arch Neurol* 1991; 48:31–34.

144. Golbe LI. Long-term efficacy and safety of deprenyl (selegiline) in advanced Parkinson's disease. *Neurology* 1989; 39:1109–1111.

145. Boyson SJ. Psychiatric effects of selegiline (letter). *Arch Neurol* 1991; 48:902.

146. Menza MA, Golbe LI. Hypomania in a patient receiving deprenyl (selegiline) after adrenal-striatal implantation for Parkinson's disease. *Clin Neuropharmacol* 1988; 1:549–551.

147. Kurlan R, Dimitsopulos R. Selegiline and manic behavior in Parkinson's disease. *Arch Neurol* 1991; 48:31–34.

148. Zornberg GL, Bodkin JA, Cohen BM. Severe adverse interaction between pethidine and selegiline. *Lancet* 1991; 337:246.

149. Pare CMB, Mousawi MA, Sandler M, et al. Attempts to attenuate the "cheese effect." *J Affect Disord* 1989; 9:137–141.

150. Sternbach H. The serotonin syndrome. *Am J Psychiatry* 1991; 148:705–713.

151. Feigher JP, Boyer WF, Tyler DL, et al. Adverse consequences of fluoxetine-MAOI combination therapy. *J Clin Psychiatry* 1990; 51:222–225.

152. Waters CH. Fluoxetine and selegiline. *Can J Neurol Sci* 1994; 21:259–261.

153. Toyama SC, Iacono RP. Is it safe to combine a selective serotonin reuptake inhibitor with selegiline? *Ann Pharmacother* 1994; 28:405–406.

154. Richard IH, Kurlan R, Tanner C, Parkinson Study Group, et al. Serotonin syndrome and the combined use of deprenyl and an antidepressant in Parkinson's disease. *Neurology* 1997; 48:1070–1077.

155. Parkinson Study Group. Effects of tocopherol and deprenyl on the progression of disability in early Parkinson's disease. *N Engl J Med* 1993; 328:176–183.

156. Palhagen S, Heinonen EH, Hagglund J, et al. Selegeline delays the onset of disability in de novo parkinsonian patients. *Neurology* 1998; 51:520–525.

157. Allain H, Cougnard J, Neukirch HC. Selgiline in de novo parkinsonian patients: The French Selegiline Multicenter Trial. *Acta Neurol Scand Suppl* 1991; 136:73–78.

158. Tetrud JW, Langston JW. The Effect of deprenyl (selegiline) on the natural history of Parkinson's disease. *Science* 1989; 245:519–522.

159. Myllylä VV, Sotaniemi KA, Vuorinen JA, et al. Selegiline in de novo parkinsonian patients: The Finnish study. *Mov Disord* 1993; 8(Suppl 1):41–44.

160. Olanow CW, Hauser RA, Gauger L, et al. The effect of deprenyl and levodopa on the progression of signs and symptoms in Parkinson's disease. *Ann Neurol* 1995; 38:771–777.

161. Parkinson Study Group. Impact of deprenyl and tocopherol treatment on Parkinson's disease in DATATOP subjects not requiring levodopa. *Ann Neurol* 1996; 39:29–36.

162. Parkinson Study Group. Impact of deprenyl and tocopherol treatment on Parkinson's disease in DATATOP patients requiring levodopa. *Ann Neurol* 1996; 39:37–45.

163. Shoulson I, Oakes D, Fahn S, et al. Impact of sustained deprenyl (selegiline) in levodopa-treated Parkinson's disease: A randomized placebo-controlled extension of the Deprenyl and Tocopherol Antioxidative Therapy of Parkinsonism Trial. *Ann Neurol* 2002; 51:604–612.

164. Rinne UK, Siirtola T, Sonninen V. L-deprenyl treatment on "on-off" phenomena in Parkinson's disease. *J Neural Transm* 1978; 43:253–262.

165. Sivertsen B, Dupont E, Mikkelsen B, et al. Selegiline and levodopa in early or moderately advanced Parkinson's disease: A double-blind controlled short and long-term study. *Acta Neurol Scand* 1989; 126:147–152.

166. Heinonen EH, Rinne UK. Selegiline in the treatment of Parkinson's disease. *Acta Neurol Scand* 1989; 126:103–111.

167. Lees AJ. Current controversies in the use of selegiline hydrochloride. *J Neural Transm* 1987; 25:157–162.

168. Golbe LI, Lieberman AN, Muenter MD, et al. Deprenyl in the treatment of symptom fluctuations in advanced Parkinson's disease. *Clin Neuropharmacol* 1988; 11:45–55.

169. Lees AJ, Parkinson's Disease Research Group of the United Kingdom. Comparison of therapeutic effects and mortality data of levodopa and levodopa combined with selegiline in patients with early mild Parkinson's disease. *BMJ* 1995; 311:1602–1607.

170. Olanow CW, Fahn S, Langston JW, et al. Selegiline and mortality: A point of view. *Ann Neurol* 1996; 40:841–845.

171. Parkinson Study Group. Mortality in DATATOP: A Multicenter Trial in Early Parkinson's Disease. *Ann Neurol* 1998; 43:318–325.

172. Marras C, Andrews D, Sime E, Lang AE. Botulinum toxin for simple motor tics. *Neurology* 2001; 56:605–610.

173. Hauser RA, Stern MC, Olanow CW, et al. Tolerability and safety of transdermal selegiline monotherapy in mild to moderate Parkinson's disease. *Mov Disord* 1998; 13:256.

174. Seager H. Drug-delivery products and the Zydis fast-dissolving dosage form. *J Pharm Pharmacol* 1998; 50:375–382.

175. Clarke A, Brewer F, Johnson ES, et al. A new formulation of selegiline: Improved bioavailability and selectivity for MAO-B inhibition. *J Neural Transm* 2003; 110:1241–1255.

176. Clarke A, Johnson ES, Mallard N, et al. A new low-dose formulation of selegiline: Clinical efficacy, patient preference and selectivity for MAO-B inhibition. J Neural Transm 2003; 110:1257–1271.

177. Waters CH, Sethi KD, Hauser RA, et al. Zydis Selegiline Study Group. Zydis selegiline reduces off time in Parkinson's disease patients with motor fluctuations: A 3-month, randomized, placebo-controlled study. *Mov Disord* 2004; 19(4):426–432.

178. Thebault JJ, Guillaume M, Levy R. Tolerability, safety, pharmacodynamics, and pharmacokinetics of rasagiline: A potent, selective and irreversible monoamine oxidase type B inhibitor. *Pharmacotherapy* 2004; 24(10):1295–1305.

179. Marek K, Friedman J, Hauser R, et al. Phase II evaluation of rasagiline mesylate (TVP-1012), a novel anti-parkinsonian drug in parkinsonian patients not using levodopa/carbidopa. *Mov Disord* 1997; 12:838–839.

180. Parkinson Study Group. A controlled trial of rasagiline in early Parkinson disease. *Arch Neurol* 2002; 59:1937–1943.

181. Parkinson Study Group. A controlled, randomized, delayed-start study of rasagiline in early Parkinson disease. *Arch Neurol* 2004; 61:561–566.

182. Elbaz A, Peterson BJ, Bower JH, et al. Risk of cancer after the diagnosis of Parkinson's disease: A historical cohort study. *Mov Disord* 2005; 20 (6):719–725.

183. Parkinson Study Group. A randomized placebo-controlled trial of rasagiline in levodopa-treated patients with Parkinson disease and motor fluctuations. *Arch Neurol* 2005; 62:241–248.

184. Schwab RS, England AC Jr. Projection technique for evaluating surgery in Parkinson's disease. In: Gillingham FJ, Donaldson IML (eds). *Third Symposium on Parkinson's Disease*. Held at the Royal College of Surgeons of Edinburgh on 20, 21, and 22 May 1968. Edinburgh: E & S Livingstone, 1969:152–157.

185. Rascol O, Brooks DJ, Melamed E, et al. Rasagiline as an adjunct to levodopa in patients with Parkinson's disease and motor fluctuations (LARGO, Lasting effect in Adjunct therapy with Rasagiline Given Once daily study): A randomised, double-blind, parallel-group trial. *Lancet* 2005; 365:947–954.

186. Giladi N, Rascol O, Brooks DJ, et al. Rasagiline treatment can improve freezing of gait in advanced Parkinson's disease: A prospective randomized, double blind, placebo and entacapone controlled study. *Neurology* 2004; 62(Suppl 5):A329–A330.

187. Parkinson Study Group. A controlled trial of lazabemide (RO19-6327) in untreated Parkinson's disease. *Ann Neurol* 1993; 33:350–356.

188. Dingemanse J, Wood N, Jorga K, et al. Pharmacokinetics and pharmacodynamics of single and multiple doses of the MAO-B inhibitor lazabemide in healthy subjects. *Br J Clin Pharmacol* 1997; 43:41–47.

189. Wachtel SR, Abercrombie ED. L-3, 4-dihydroxyphenylalanine-induced dopamine release in the striatum of intact and 6-hydroxydopamine-treated rats: differential effects of monoamine oxidase A and B inhibitors. *J Neurochem* 1994; 63:108–117.

190. Heeringa MJ, d'Agostini F, DeBoer P, DaPrada M, Damsma G. Effect of monoamine oxidase A and B and of catechol-O-methyltransferase inhibition on L-DOPA-induced circling behavior. *J Neural Transm* 1997; 104:593–603.

191. Parkinson Study Group. Effect of lazabemide on the progression of disability in early Parkinson's disease. *Ann Neurol* 1996; 40:99–107.

192. Parkinson Study Group. A controlled trial of lazabemide (Ro 19-6327) in levodopa-treated Parkinson's disease. *Arch Neurol* 1994; 51:342–347.

41 Dopamine Agonists

Puiu F. Nisipeanu
Amos D. Korczyn

Although levodopa affords considerable improvement in motor function in Parkinson's disease (PD), it does not prevent progression of the disease, and its long-term use is associated with undesirable motor complications and mental symptomatology (1, 2). The debate concerning levodopa neurotoxicity has resulted in a variety of therapeutic strategies conceived to prevent, delay, or diminish these complications by postponing or reducing the use of levodopa (3–7).

A number of drugs belonging to different classes and operating by distinct mechanisms have been shown to help patients with PD. Dopamine receptor agonists as well as MAO-B inhibitors and amantadine are effective as monotherapy in early disease or as adjunct to levodopa in later stages. The many therapeutic choices must be tailored to clinical decisions, considering the preferences and lifestyles of individual patients as well as the nature and severity of their disease symptoms, concurrent morbidity, and concomitant medication.

Dopamine and dopaminergic drugs interact with one or more of the 5 known subtypes of receptors: D1, D2, D3, D4, D5. These are grouped in 2 families on the basis of their homology and coupling with stimulatory G proteins (D1, D5)—that is, the D1 family, or with inhibitory G proteins (D2, D3, and D4 receptors), belonging to the D2 family (8–10).

The antiparkinsonian efficacy of levodopa, the metabolic precursor of dopamine, is predominantly due to stimulation of the D2 family of receptors, mainly D2. D2 postsynaptic receptors and presynaptic autoreceptors (see Chapter 23) have almost contrasting functions, and it is the activation of postsynaptic receptors that is thought to be essential to the effects of dopamine on motor behavior. The stimulation of D1 receptors, mainly expressed in the dorsal striatum, nucleus accumbens, and cortex with almost the same order of dopamine affinity as D2 receptors is considered necessary to achieve maximal dopaminergic effect. The affinity of dopaminergic drugs toward the D2 receptors is much greater than that toward the D1 receptors. The affinities of the most commonly used dopaminergic agents were recently studied (11–13) by using a multivariate analysis of their binding profile to human monoaminergic receptors (11–13). The investigators found a conspicuous heterogeneity in binding profiles, which may offer a partial explanation for differences in clinical activity in PD. However, although these studies give a clear picture of the agonists in the experimental system, it must be recognized that in vivo they interact with the endogenous dopamine. This could result not only in potentiation but, theoretically, also in competition, thus reducing the endogenous activity of dopamine. Moreover, since dopaminergic drugs have properties beyond motor modulation—which might be important to other characteristics of PD, such as affect, motivation, cognition, or pain—this heterogeneity could be of value.

One result of these studies was the separation of dopaminergic drugs into two major groups. The first group, which included ropinirole, pramipexole, and piribedil, displayed low affinities for D5 and D1 compared to D2 receptors and negligible affinity for nondopaminergic receptors. Within this group, ropinirole and pramipexole showed marked similarity. The second group included bromocriptine, pergolide, cabergoline, and lisuride—all ergot derivatives—as well as apomorphine. Its members manifested higher affinities for most sites. Some intragroup differences were noted. Bromocriptine had high affinity at α-1 adrenergic receptors (AR), while lisuride had affinity at 5-HT2a/2c and β1/β2 ARs. Cabergoline and pergolide expressed similar receptor binding profiles. Newman-Tancredi and colleagues (12, 13) showed that pramipexole, ropinirole, cabergoline, and pergolide were as efficacious as dopamine itself at D2 sites. Apomorphine was highly efficacious, while bromocriptine, lisuride, and piribedil showed intermediate efficacy. At D3 receptors, all displayed agonist activity, apomorphine and cabergoline being most efficacious. At D4 receptors, ropinirole showed relatively high efficacy, while pramipexole, cabergoline, lisuride, pergolide, and apomorphine had intermediate efficacy. Bromocriptine did not interact with D4 receptors at all. However, the clinical relevance of interaction with different subtypes of the D2 family is still unclear.

Cabergoline, bromocriptine, lisuride, and apomorphine shared antagonistic properties at α2 ARs, which may be beneficial for PD treatment.

Newman-Tancredi and coworkers (12, 13) also evaluated the efficacy of the ergot derivatives bromocriptine, pergolide, lisuride, and cabergoline as well as apomorphine and piribedil at human recombinant serotonin receptors 5-HT 1a, 5-HT 1b, 5-HT1d, 5-HT2a, 5-HT2b, and 5-HT2c. Notably only pergolide and cabergoline displayed high potency at 5-HT2b receptors, which may be of relevance in regulating heart valve fibrosis. This is consistent with recent studies (14). Thus, dopamine agonists display different patterns of interaction with monoamine receptors, and a better understanding of these patterns may be helpful in defining their therapeutic potential and adverse effects profile.

Numerous dopaminergic agents have been investigated in the treatment of patients with PD. Their development followed a typical sequence: (1) capability to elicit dopaminomimetic effects on the neuroendocrine system; (2) ability to bind to different dopamine receptors in vitro; (3) demonstration of dopamine-like action in animals and to reverse parkinsonism in experimental models; and finally (4) human studies in PD. This search for dopamine agonists occurred partly in order to avoid the adverse effects of long-term levodopa therapy, especially motor fluctuations and dyskinesias.

Dopamine agonists possess pharmacokinetic and pharmacodynamic properties that in theory are advantageous over levodopa (15–18). They act directly on dopamine receptors and bypass the need for conversion and storage in the degenerating nigrostriatal neurons. They do not depend (as levodopa does) on amino acid transporters for absorption across the gastrointestinal tract and later the blood-brain barrier and consequently may be taken with meals. Their metabolism in the liver is much more limited than that of levodopa; thus the hepatic first-pass effect is reduced. Most of them have longer half-lives than levodopa; they therefore provide more continuous dopaminergic stimulation, which may reduce the incidence of dyskinesias (20). Most exhibit low-protein binding, thus limiting the possibility of pharmacokinetic interactions with other drugs, and none adversely interfere with levodopa pharmacokinetics. Unfortunately, however, in addition to having lower potency, dopamine agonists are less well tolerated than levodopa, with a higher occurrence of side effects—including marked peripheral effects, such as nausea and orthostatic hypotension—which contribute to the higher rate of dropouts from dopamine agonist treatment. These effects also occur with levodopa, but since this drug is now always used with peripheral dopa decarboxylase inhibitors (and frequently with catechol-O-methyl transferase inhibitors), the amount of dopamine in the periphery is so small that these effects rarely occur.

Treatment with dopamine agonists must be initiated at low dosage and the titration period may extend for months, so as to improve tolerance to the peripheral side effects. Consequently the clinical benefit is delayed. Finally, the price of dopamine agonists is higher than that of levodopa preparations (in the United Kingdom, dopamine agonists cost about three times as much as levodopa), the evidence of its advantages must be compelling to consider it as the preferred option for initial treatment (21).

The most forceful argument for initial treatment with dopamine agonists is the reduction or delay of motor complications. The occurrence of motor complications is believed to be due to the combination of striatal denervation and intermittent stimulation of these dopamine receptors. Levodopa has a short half-life (60 to 90 minutes). It must be administered repeatedly, particularly to those patients who have lost the capacity to compensate for dopamine depletion from nigral neurons and synaptic terminals. Consequently dopamine receptors will be exposed to large oscillations in dopamine concentration. This pulsatile stimulation is theorized to contribute to an altered neuronal discharge pattern conducive to motor complications (22–24). The prevalence of motor complications is higher among patients who started levodopa shortly after symptom onset and among younger patients (perhaps because they use higher doses) (25). Because of their longer half-life, dopamine agonists cause more continuous occupancy and stimulation of dopamine receptors, thus in theory preventing or reducing these complications.

The appearance of motor complications dramatically increases the costs of care; therefore the higher initial cost of dopamine agonists therapy may thus be justified (26). The impact of dyskinesias on quality of life and related costs was recently evaluated in a prospective study in France, Germany, and the United Kingdom. Pechevis and colleagues (27) confirmed that dyskinesias adversely affect quality of life. Dyskinesias were also associated with significant health-related costs. It must be noted that the assessment of motor complications in clinical trials in early PD was not standardized, which makes the interpretation of results problematic. For example, the proportion of patients with dyskinesias at 5-year follow-up ranged from 5% to 41% in different studies (28). Van Gerpen and coworkers (29), in a retrospective study, showed that about 30% of levodopa-treated patients develop dyskinesias by 5 years and about 60% by 10 years of treatment. However, at 10 years, only 12% of patients had uncontrollable dyskinesias. This may weaken the case of dyskinesias as a major concern. In addition, dykinesias seen in early disease may not be clinically significant.

NEUROPROTECTION

A second rationale for the use of dopamine agonists as monotherapy is their supposed neuroprotective property. Over the years the concept that dopamine agonists may provide neuroprotection has repeatedly been proposed (30, 31). Neuroprotective compounds are claimed to slow neuronal degeneration and to rescue or protect vulnerable neurons, in this case the dopaminergic neurons of the nigrostriatal system. The Ad Hoc Committee to Identify Neuroprotective Agents in Parkinson's disease (CINAPS) retained the definition proposed by Shoulson (32) to "favorably influence the disease progress or underlying pathogenesis to produce enduring benefits for patients." CINAPS has specified criteria for choosing a putative neuroprotective agent: scientific rationale, evidence of penetration of the blood-brain barrier, adequate safety information, efficacy in animal models and/or preliminary efficacy data in patients (33).

The use of levodopa is associated, in experimental models, with the generation of metabolites able to induce oxidative stress in neurons (Chapter 30). Conversely, newer dopamine agonists exert an antioxidative effect, presumably protecting nigral cells exposed to oxidative injury (28). Both ergot derivatives and the nonergot dopaminergic drugs pramipexole and ropinirole have some protective effects in various experimental models of nigrostriatal degeneration.

A major issue is how to define and measure neuroprotection. In principle, neuroprotective agents could slow the degeneration of nigral dopaminergic neurons or slow other processes, such as cortical Lewy body deposition. Nigral degeneration is reflected by more rapid clinical deterioration. This cannot easily be measured directly because of the symptomatic effects of dopamine agonists. In the DATATOP study (34), to investigate potential neuroprotection, selegiline or placebo was administered for an extended period until the patient required levodopa. Although the results showed a significant delay in the selegiline group in reaching this endpoint, there were no definite conclusions because of its symptomatic effects. This complicates the analysis of a possible protective effect of any drug with symptomatic antiparkinsonian effect.

One consistent observation is that treatment with dopamine agonists delays the onset of motor complications, particularly dyskinesias (freezing, however, may become more common in patients treated de novo with dopamine agonists than in those given levodopa), when given to de novo cases (5). Whether this is considered neuroprotection is a matter of definition. A more direct demonstration is through imaging, using either positron emission tomography (PET) or single photon emission computed tomography (SPECT), both of which have hinted at a slower loss of dopaminergic terminals with the use of either ropinirole or pramipexole (35, 36). The trial conducted by the Parkinson Study Group included PD patients who were treated with pramipexole or levodopa and underwent radioimaging scans (β-CIT SPECT) (36). Whone and colleagues (35) reported the results obtained by using F-dopa PET in 162 patients with early PD treated with ropinirole or levodopa. In both studies, patients on agonists had "better" imaging results seemed to fare better than those on levodopa (pramipexole at 46 months scans and ropinirole at 24 months), with a one-third reduction in the rates of radiotracer imaging decline. However, in both trials levodopa-treated patients had better symptomatic control of motor manifestations. This discordance, together with the data provided by the ELL-DOPA trial (3), which also showed inconsistency between clinical benefits of levodopa and reduced rate of decline assessed by β-CIT SPECT at baseline and at 40 weeks makes interpretation uncertain (37).

CINAPS assessment considered only ropinirole and pramipexole among dopamine agonists as suitable candidates for phase II and III neuroprotection trials, while apomorphine, bromocriptine, and pergolide were excluded.

ADVERSE EFFECTS OF DOPAMINE AGONISTS

Because dopamine agonists differ from each other in structure, monoaminergic receptors affinity, potency, and other pharmacologic properties, it is reasonable to assume that they might have distinctive adverse-effect profiles. Nevertheless ergot and nonergot dopamine agonists share a variety of peripheral and central adverse effects.

The most common "peripheral" adverse effects are nausea, vomiting, and orthostatic hypotension, each having a mixed peripheral and central component. These effects are dose- and time-dependent, being highly prevalent during initiation of treatment and tending to diminish or disappear over weeks as peripheral tolerance develops.

The mechanism underlying the development of tolerance to these side effects is unknown. Interestingly, a similar effect occurs with cholinesterase inhibitors, where the initial exposure frequently produces nausea and vomiting, which subside with repeated administration. Nicotine may also have an analogous effect, since smoking commonly causes nausea with the first cigarettes. These adverse effects can be alleviated by domperidone, a peripheral D2 receptor antagonist, which does not cross the blood-brain barrier.

Nausea and vomiting result from direct dopaminergic stimulation of chemoreceptors located in the area postrema, which is outside the blood-brain barrier. Orthostatic hypotension, first reported by Calne and colleagues (38), probably occurs through inhibition of the sympathetic nervous system, with consequent venous and arterial dilation and hypotension (39). Orthostatic hypotension is also a feature of autonomic dysfunction, which is frequent in PD but can be asymptomatic. Kujawa and colleagues (40) showed that at the start of dopaminergic agonist treatment, 34% of patients developed orthostatic hypotension, while only 3% complained of light-headedness. This may suggest that many patients do not report subjective symptoms yet may be prone to instability and falls.

Somnolence is a common complaint during treatment with levodopa and dopamine agonists. Reports of sudden-onset of sleep in patients being treated with pramipexole or ropinirole triggered an intense debate (Chapter 62). Frucht and associates (41) described 8 patients who fell asleep while driving. The sleep attacks were sudden, unexpected, and irresistible; they abated after discontinuation of the dopamine agonists. A review by Homman and collaborators recorded 124 patients reported until May 2001 (42). However, the definition of sleep attacks varied greatly. By defining sleep attacks as overwhelming sleepiness that occurs too suddenly to allow for protective measures, 96 sleep attacks were recorded (5 definite, 8 probable, 83 possible). Most patients were taking pramipexole and ropinirole, while others received levodopa monotherapy, bromocriptine, piribedil, lisuride, cabergoline, or apomorphine. Some patients reported a more protracted onset, with tiredness and waves of sleepiness. Razmy and colleagues (43), using polysomnographic techniques, studied 80 dopamine agonist–treated patients. They found that subjective statements scored by the Epworth Sleepiness Scale did not relate to impaired sleepiness or wakefulness. Fifteeen patients (18.8%) had pathologic daytime sleep latency. The main risk factor was the total dose of agonist (pramipexole, ropinirole, or bromocriptine).

Sleep attacks were reported with all dopamine agonists in a survey of 2952 patients by Paus and coworkers (44). A comparable survey of 929 patients revealed that 22% of respondents reported events of uncontrollable somnolence, which were significantly more likely to occur in those treated with pramipexole, ropinirole, or pergolide (45). Another study assessed sleep quality, daytime somnolence, and sleep attacks in PD patients and age-matched controls. Ferreira and colleagues (46) found that PD patients report more abnormal daytime somnolence and poorer sleep quality, but the proportion of those reporting sleep attacks was almost the same (27% PD patients, 32% controls). However the episodes of sleep attacks were significantly more frequent in PD patients, and they were reported to occur more frequently in conditions demanding sustained attention. As almost all patients received levodopa, bromocriptine, or ropinirole, this study did not confirm the association of sleep attacks with a particular drug or class of drugs. Gjerstad and colleagues (47) examined the incidence of excessive daytime sleepiness in a community-based cohort of 232 PD patients. They concluded that although dopamine agonists play a part in inducing hypersomnolence, its development is multifactorial and mainly related to age and disease duration.

Central dopaminergic adverse effects are dominated by psychiatric symptomatology, with a spectrum similar to that of levodopa. The psychiatric manifestations include mood disturbances (depression, irritability, euphoria, and hypomania), vivid dreams, nightmares, sleep difficulties, inappropriate sexual behavior, hallucinations (visual, rarely auditory or tactile), delusions, agitation, confusional states, and paranoid psychosis (Chapter 48). In an extensive review, Factor (48) divided drug-induced psychoses into those occurring on a background of clear sensorium and those associated with confusion and impaired consciousness, fulfilling the criteria for delirium. The frequency of hallucinations and other psychotic symptomatology differed in various studies, probably reflecting the stage of the disease, comorbidity, or comedication. Additionally, the potential of dopamine agonists to induce mental adverse effects in patients with a psychiatric history or cognitive impairment or in elderly patients (who are usually excluded from therapeutic trials) remains to be assessed.

Hallucinations are commonly assumed to be drug-related. Fenelon and colleagues (49) reviewed the evidence in favor of this assumption. However, hallucinations were known to occur in PD patients before the levodopa era and were sometimes associated with anticholinergic drugs. Thus, hallucinations may constitute a part of the disease in certain situations, while dopamine plays a facilitating role (50). The early appearance of visual hallucinations in a parkinsonian patient—especially in association with fluctuations in mental status, cognitive dysfunction, milder parkinsonian symptoms, and absence of tremor—suggests alternative diagnoses. Goetz and colleagues (51) compared patients who developed hallucinations early after dopaminergic therapy was started with patients in whom hallucinations started beyond 1 year of treatment. They found that none of the early hallucinators—i.e., within 3 months of initiation of treatment—had PD only; most suffered from cognitive changes due to the cortical Lewy body disease or Alzheimer's disease with extrapyramidal features.

The implication of antiparkinsonian medication in the development of hallucinations was recently reassessed by Merims and colleagues (52). Their study compared antiparkinsonian therapy in 422 patients with and without hallucinations. The mean levodopa dose and additional medications did not differ, suggesting that other factors are more important in producing hallucinations than dopaminergic drugs.

Several points are clear:

1. In all drug studies where dopamine agonists were compared to levodopa, the frequency of hallucinations was higher in the dopamine agonists arm.
2. While initially it was believed that antiparkinsonian drugs caused hallucinations by interacting with serotonergic receptors, agents lacking 5-HT activity, such as ropinirole or pramipexole, seem to be associated with hallucinations to the same extent as are the older, nonselective dopamine agonists.
3. The relationship of the drugs to hallucinations is complex (53). The hallucinations are not dose-dependent, and there is a marked difference between them and, for instance, dyskinesias, since the latter will immediately disappear once the dopaminergic drugs are stopped or reduced in amount while the hallucinations will continue.
4. Dopamine agonists were only rarely linked to hallucinations when used in non-PD patients, which suggests that PD pathology plays an important role in the induction of hallucinations.

A new spectrum of dopaminergic adverse effects, initially named hedonistic homeostatic dysregulation and later dopamine dysregulation syndrome and recently considered with compulsive or impulse control disorders, was reported by Giovannoni and associates in 2000 (Chapter 19) (54). The core symptomatology was misuse of medication in patients with early-onset PD who took increasing amounts of levodopa and also apomorphine. Patients developed disabling dyskinesias, followed by hypomanic behavior and eventually manic psychosis. Other features seen in some patients were stereotyped motor behavior—punding—described by Evans and colleagues (55) as comprising intense fascination with a repetitive activity, hypersexuality, pathologic gambling and shopping, and eating disorders. Evans and Lees (56) suggested that the incidence of this syndrome is probably higher than reported, probably about 6% to 8%.

The most common reports concerned pathologic gambling, an uncontrollable impulse to gamble occurring after the onset of dopaminergic therapy. Dodd and coworkers (57) described 11 patients, 10 of them males, who developed pathologic gambling after a dopamine agonist was added to levodopa. About 20 patients had previously been reported and a survey of the FDA Adverse Event Reporting System database (AERS) added scores of patients (58). Bromocriptine, pergolide, cabergoline, ropinirole, and pramipexole have all been reported to be associated with pathologic gambling, but pramipexole was most often incriminated (73%). Voon and colleagues (59, 60) in prospective studies found that dopamine agonists induced pathologic gambling in 7.2%, pathologic hypersexuality in 2.4%, and compulsive shopping in 0.7% of treated PD patients. The association of impulse control disorders with dopaminergic therapy was confirmed recently by Pontone and coworkers (61). The propensity of pramipexole to lead to pathologic gambling was tentatively linked to excessive stimulation of limbic D3 receptors. Evans and colleagues (62) published PET data suggesting that the dopamine dysregulation syndrome is connected to increased dopaminergic activation of the ventral striatum.

Depression

Depression in PD is not uncommon (63, 64). A possible antidepressant influence of dopamine agonists has been suggested but not confirmed when agonists were used in depressed non-PD patients. The nonergot agonists have marked agonist activity at D3 receptors and may exert a beneficial antidepressant effect. Pramipexole was evaluated in depressed non-PD patients (65) and compared with sertraline in a randomized, parallel-group trial in PD patients with major depression (66). Both drugs ameliorated depression. The use of nonergot dopaminergic agonists could therefore be considered, particularly in depressed PD patients.

Fibrosis

Ergot derivatives have been associated with pleuropulmonary, pericardial, and retroperitoneal fibrosis (67, 68). Because bromocriptine was the first oral dopamine agonist and for years the most widely used, most reports related to this drug. The introduction of other agonists in different countries led to reports of adverse reactions associated with pergolide and cabergoline. The frequency of reports for a specific agonist is probably linked to the number of prescriptions dispensed. With the extension of indications for dopamine agonists, some reports have reflected the occurrence of pleuropulmonary disease as well in patients treated for restless legs syndrome (69). Pleuropulmonary fibrosis is still the most prevalent reported type. Rinne (67) reported it in 2% to 4% of patients at 5 years of treatment with bromocriptine. Clinically, patients had pleural inflammation with or without fever, cough, pleuritic pain, friction rubs, dyspnea, and pleural effusions. As in other types of fibrosis, the onset may be insidious and the symptomatology may appear many years later. Inflammatory markers—erythrocyte sedimentation rate (ESR) and C-reactive protein—are elevated, and some experts recommended their use in monitoring patients undergoing long-term therapy with ergot derivatives. Constrictive pericarditis and pericardial effusion were also associated with bromocriptine, pergolide and cabergoline (70–72).

Retroperitoneal fibrosis seems to be as frequent as pericarditis, but its diagnosis is more elusive (73). The pathologic process can entrap and obstruct retroperitoneal structures, notably the ureters, and induce renal failure. Clinical features may be nonspecific—poorly described back pain, low-grade fever, fatigue, anorexia, weight loss—and extensive investigations including surgical intervention may be required to establish the diagnosis. The prognosis of fibrotic reactions is usually favorable after elimination of the offending drug, but the improvement may be slow and surgery may be needed if the ureters are involved.

Peripheral edema, which is common in PD, has been observed more frequently in dopamine agonist–treated groups than in parallel placebo-treated groups or levodopa-treated patients. The mechanism is not known, and non-ergot agonists are also linked to edema. Unlike other peripheral effects of dopamine agonists, tolerance to edema does not develop. Edema usually resolves with discontinuation of the agonist but otherwise is unresponsive to diuretics. It appears mostly during the first months of treatment (74).

Other uncommon but potentially serious adverse effects related to ergot's vasoconstrictive properties are Raynaud's phenomenon, erythromelalgia, and possibly exacerbation of angina pectoris.

BROMOCRIPTINE

Bromocriptine (2-bromo-α–ergocryptine) was, in 1978, the first dopamine agonist licensed in the United States for the treatment of PD, following the pioneering work of Calne and coworkers (75). Bromocriptine was tried initially in patients with levodopa-induced motor complications; and its role in early PD as monotherapy or in combination with levodopa was explored later (76). This strategy has been employed in the therapeutic trials of successive dopamine agonists.

Bromocriptine has a marked preference for D2 receptors, has modest affinity and inactive properties at D4 receptors, and is antagonistic at D1 receptors. Bromocriptine has a high affinity for 5-HT1a, 5-HT1b, 5-HT2a, and 5-HT2b receptors and displays antagonist activity at α2 adrenergic receptors. Bromocriptine has a bioavailability of only 6%, being extensively metabolized in the liver. Its distribution half-life is 6 hours and its elimination half-life is 50 hours. However, after oral administration of single doses ranging from 12.5 to 100 mg, motor improvement was observed within 30 to 90 minutes and continued up to 4 hours.

Bromocriptine in Early Parkinson's Disease

Some of the early trials were conducted in the era before more rigorous methodologic rules for clinical trials were commonplace. Teychenne and colleagues (77) suggested that starting with a low dose and slow uptitration would increase bromocriptine tolerability. The addition of domperidone, a peripheral blocker of dopamine receptors, prevented many unpleasant adverse effects and permitted the use of higher doses of bromocriptine—results that also apply to newer dopamine agonists (78). Lees and Stern (79) demonstrated that levodopa is more effective than bromocriptine and also raised the possibility that the dopamine agonist may induce less dyskinesia and wearing off. Both of these observations were later confirmed with all other dopamine agonists. Ramaker and van Hilten (80) reviewed randomized trials (including published and unpublished data) that evaluated the efficacy of bromocriptine in delaying the onset of motor complications compared to levodopa. Due to heterogeneity of trials, a meta-analysis was not feasible; however, it was concluded that bromocriptine may be beneficial in delaying motor complications and dyskinesias. Nevertheless, the proportion of withdrawals due to perceived lack of efficacy or to side effects was significantly higher in the bromocriptine group. Two long-term studies by Lees and colleagues (81) and by Hely and colleagues (82) and a study of Montastruc and associates (83) examined the possible influence of initial bromocriptine treatment on disease progression, disability, and mortality. Hely and colleagues compared bromocriptine with levodopa monotherapy, where patients were followed for up to 18 years in an open manner (84). The rate of progression and mortality were similar, but dyskinesias and dystonia occurred later in the bromocriptine group. Survivors were plagued by non–levodopa responsive features such as cognitive decline, falls, and urinary incontinence.

Montastruc and colleagues (83) did not find a favorable effect of early use of bromocriptine in comparison with levodopa regarding long-term mortality. It thus seems that initial therapy with bromocriptine does not confer any long-term benefit except to delay of motor complications.

The efficacy of early combination of bromocriptine with levodopa to produce substantially fewer motor fluctuations and dyskinesias after a 5-year follow-up was reported in an open-label trial (85). A Cochrane review found no evidence in favor of this early combination in preventing or delaying the occurrence of motor complications (86).

Bromocriptine in Advanced Parkinson's Disease

Numerous open and double-blind placebo-controlled trials confirmed the early results of bromocriptine's use in PD. It was suggested that bromocriptine improved "off" features—reducing frequency, severity, and duration—and diminished dyskinesias subsequent to reduction of levodopa dosage. However, there were major methodological flaws in these early studies that precluded a firm conclusion about bromocriptine efficacy.

The advent of new dopaminergic agonists led to trials comparing them with bromocriptine in well-designed randomized studies. Bromocriptine was compared to ropinirole in 3 trials in PD patients with motor complications. Brunt and colleagues (87)—in a 6-month, randomized, double-blind, parallel group design—investigated ropinirole versus bromocriptine. The outcomes were Unified Parkinson Disease Rating Scale (UPDRS) motor score, reduction of levodopa dose, differences in "on/off," and Clinical Global Impression score. Both agonists improved the UPDRS motor score and the time spent "on," and both allowed levodopa dosage reductions. The safety data were not different and the withdrawal percentage was equal (19%). Im and coworkers (88) conducted a 16-week trial in 76 patients randomized to ropinirole or bromocriptine with an 8-week titration phase. The primary endpoint was the number of responders defined as patients who achieved at least a 20% levodopa reduction. Significantly more ropinirole patients achieved this reduction (54% versus 28%). Murayama and colleagues (89) randomized patients to ropinirole or bromocriptine in another 8-week trial. Drug efficacy assessed by improvement in Hoehn-Yahr scale was similar in both groups. Thus it seems that ropinirole does not offer significant advantages over bromocriptine.

Guttman and colleagues (90) and Mizuno and associates (91) conducted a 3-arm randomized, parallel-group, 36-week trial comparing bromocriptine to pramipexole and to placebo. The study was not powered to detect differences between agonists but rather improvement with either drug versus placebo.

Bromocriptine has been compared to cabergoline in 5 randomized, double-blind, parallel-group trials involving 1071 (92) patients. It should be noted that only one medium-term trial was published; the data from the other trials and supplementary data for all trials was provided to the reviewers by the drug manufacturer. Inzelberg and colleagues (93) reported the findings of a randomized, double-blind, parallel-group study of patients with motor complications. Both agonists achieved similar improvement on motor items and on the Schwab and England scale. Only the reduction in "off" time was statistically in favor of cabergoline. However, the other studies did not confirm this finding (92). Levodopa dose was reduced in all studies in a similar proportion. Adverse events differed only by more confusion with cabergoline. Considering the shorter duration of the other trials, the relatively moderate mean doses of both agonists, and methodologic problems, the lack of difference in both benefit and side effects must be taken with caution.

The newer dopamine agonist trials using bromocriptine as a comparator support the evidence suggesting that bromocriptine is an effective symptomatic adjuvant to levodopa in the treatment of advanced PD.

Two randomized clinical studies compared the efficacy of bromocriptine or lisuride to that of selegiline. The UK-PDRG (77 compared levodopa, levodopa plus selegiline and bromocriptine. After 9 years' follow-up. there was no difference in Webster scores as compared to the baseline between the last two groups. Caraceni and Mussico (94) randomized de novo patients to levodopa, bromocriptine, lisuride, or selegiline in an open long-term study (median follow-up 34 months). The main outcome was the occurrence of motor fluctuations and dyskinesias. There were no significant differences between the dopamine agonists and selegiline. However more patients assigned to selegiline needed levodopa supplementation earlier (after a median of 15 months vs. 30 months with dopamine agonists), and more withdrew due to lack of efficacy.

Based on these studies, it may be suggested that initial treatment with selegiline does not prevent motor complications. It is unclear whether rasagiline will be more beneficial in this respect.

There are no studies comparing MAO-B inhibitors to dopamine agonists in advanced PD.

Two randomized open studies compared bromocriptine or pergolide to tolcapone (95, 96). The first (95) trial was short-term (8 weeks) and entered levodopa-treated patients with wearing off. As expected, tolcapone allowed a significant reduction in levodopa dose, but this was not seen with bromocriptine. Other measures, such as the time "off," were similar in the two arms. Koller and coworkers (96) reported a 12-week open–label, blinded-rater trial of PD patients with motor fluctuations who were treated with pergolide or tolcapone. The primary outcome was a change in the proportion of "off" time, as assessed by home diaries. No differences were found in any measures except for a greater improvement reported by the tolcapone group in quality of life evaluated by PDQ-39. More nausea, constipation and orthostatic complaints were found in the pergolide and bromocriptine groups, while tolcapone-treated patients reported more muscle cramps and dystonia.

Thus, in head-to-head trials, there was no evidence of any drug superiority, and the evidence is insufficient to prefer catechol-O-methyl transferase (COMT) inhibitors over dopamine agonists. However, a report of the Quality Standards Subcommittee of the American Academy of Neurology (97) retained only the COMT inhibitor entacapone as effective in reducing "off" time, while pergolide, pramipexole, and ropinirole were considered as probably effective. Apomorphine and cabergoline were designated as possibly effective by the same subcommittee. The committee's recommendations were related to the strength of evidence for each drug and not as favoring one drug over the other.

PERGOLIDE

Pergolide mesylate is a semisynthetic ergoline compound. It has dose-dependent D2/D1 activities: selective D2 agonist stimulation at low dose mixed with D1 agonism at higher doses, with a high affinity for D2 autoreceptors at low dose. The receptor-binding profile of pergolide is similar to that of cabergoline, with a special note for its potent agonist activity at 5-HT 2b receptors. Pergolide is well absorbed; peak plasma concentration is obtained within a couple of hours and its terminal half-life is the second longest after cabergoline, about 21 hours (98, 99).

Pergolide in Early Parkinson's Disease

A few trials investigating the efficacy and safety of pergolide in de novo or early PD included small numbers of patients, most of whom could not be maintained on monotherapy for more than 1 year. Common adverse events included frequent gastrointestinal and psychiatric problems. Nevertheless, in those who tolerated the drug, wearing off, dyskinesias, and other motor fluctuations were rarely recorded and the motor deficit improved (100). A randomized, placebo-controlled trial was conducted by Barone and collaborators (101). Several outcomes were significantly in favor of pergolide: the percentage of responders (56.6% vs. 17.3%), UPDRS total score, activities of daily living (ADLs), motor score, and clinical global impression (CGI). Pergolide generated more nausea, anorexia, vomiting, and somnolence than placebo. Oertel and colleagues (102) reported a multi-

center, double-blind, randomized 3-year trial of pergolide versus levodopa in patients with early PD PELMOPET study. Primary endpoints were clinical efficacy assessed by UPDRS, UPDRS parts II and III, CGI, time to onset of motor complications, and progression of disease. Motor measures favored levodopa-treated patients, However, agonist-treated patients had significantly less severe motor complications. The withdrawal rate was higher in the pergolide-treated group.

Pergolide in Advanced Parkinson's Disease

The only large, randomized, placebo-controlled trial in patients with levodopa-induced complications was reported by Olanow and coworkers (103). The results showed a significant difference in favor of pergolide in the reduction of the mean time spent "off" (1.8 hours less per day as compared with 0.2 hours), in the motor and ADL parts of the modified Columbia scale, and in Hoehn-Yahr stage. Patients receiving pergolide reduced their mean levodopa dose by 235 mg, while the placebo-treated patients had a 51-mg reduction. The most common adverse effect was dyskinesia, which occurred or increased in 62% of pergolide-treated and in 25% of placebo-treated patients. Pergolide-treated patients suffered significantly more nausea, hallucinations, and withdrawals. This study failed to show amelioration of dyskinesias by pergolide. A dose of 3 mg/day was recommended for maintenance therapy, although higher doses may allow a greater reduction in levodopa dose, time spent "off," and dyskinesia.

In addition to the known side effects of ergot dopaminergic agonists, the use of pergolide in older patients was thought to be associated with cardiotoxicity and led to a temporary suspension of clinical trials. Subsequent studies did not prove a deleterious cardiac effect of pergolide (104). However, since 2002, pergolide has been increasingly connected to cardiac valvulopathy. These reports led the FDA to establish a registry of patients with pergolide-associated valvular heart disease (105). Pritchett and colleagues (106) reported severe tricuspid valve regurgitation combined with some degree of regurgitant left-sided valve disease in 3 adults treated chronically with pergolide. Histologic analysis in 2 patients who had undergone valve replacement surgery revealed fibrotic changes similar to those encountered in patients with carcinoid and in those treated with anorectic drugs (fenfluramine, dexfenfluramine) or ergot derivatives such as ergotamine and methysergide, thus suggesting a serotonin-mediated mechanism. Pergolide and other dopaminergic ergot compounds have been known to induce serosal, pericardial, retroperitoneal, and pleural fibrosis. Ergot derivatives are thought to act by direct stimulation of 5-HT 2b receptors, which are expressed in the fibroblasts of the heart valves. Both pergolide and cabergoline are full agonists of these receptors.

Before the publication by Pritchett and associates, the risk of pergolide-related valvular heart disease was estimated at less than 0.005%, which may translate to about 25 patients worldwide. However, a recent review of pergolide-associated heart valvulopathy counted almost 100 reported patients (107). It must be mentioned that prospective data on frequency, duration of treatment, dosage, typical clinical presentation, pattern of valvulopathy, severity, and potential reversibility are still being collected. The study of Van Camp and coworkers (108) of 78 pergolide-treated patients and 18 controls pointed to restrictive valvular heart disease in 33% of pergolide-treated patients compared with none in the control group; 15% of patients were considered to have important disease, and in 6 pergolide was stopped. Baseman and collaborators (109) found that 89% of 46 pergolide-treated patients had some degree of valvular insufficiency, most frequently tricuspid regurgitation. In another large study, Waller (110) and colleagues reviewed the medical records and 2-dimensional echocardiograms of pergolide-treated patients (both parkinsonians and patients with restless legs syndrome) and matched controls; no differences between groups in the overall frequency of mitral or tricuspid regurgitation were found. Aortic regurgitation was increased in pergolide-treated patients (45% versus 21%), which may be important, as the frequency of aortic regurgitation is less than 25% in people above 60 years of age. There was also some evidence of an association between higher doses of pergolide and moderate to severe aortic regurgitation. Recent studies assessing the risk of heart-valve regurgitation in patients chronically treated with antiparkinsonian drugs have again found that pergolide and cabergoline were associated with valvular heart disease (14, 111). The mechanisms by which pergolide and cabergoline, both full 5HT2b agonists, induce heart-valve disease is thought to be the inappropriate mitogenesis of normally quiescent valve cells, with consequent overgrowth valvulopathy. This may occur through activation of protein kinase C, extracellular kinases, and phosphorylation of retinoblastoma protein (112).

These data were considered by some regulatory bodies sufficient to lead to total withdrawal, or at least restrict the use of pergolide and bromocriptine to second-line agents after nonergot dopamine.

LISURIDE

Lisuride, a semisynthetic ergot derivative, is unique because its high potency allows it to be dissolved in water and administered in small volumes in subcutaneous or intravenous infusions. This property of lisuride has led to its development as a transdermal patch. Lisuride is a full agonist with high affinity for D2 receptors and for α2 AR (113). It is a potent 5-HT2B antagonist, which may explain why lisuride was not linked to fibrotic valvulopathy (114). Following oral ingestion, lisuride is rapidly and completely absorbed with a 1- to 3-hour terminal half-life.

Oral Lisuride in Early Parkinson's Disease

There are no good randomized trials of oral lisuride as monotherapy in early PD. One relatively large open-label study (115) randomized de novo patients to lisuride, levodopa, or both. After a 4-year follow-up, 17% of patients were still on lisuride monotherapy but with significantly lower benefit than seen in levodopa-treated patients. However, the lisuride-treated patients did not exhibit wearing off or dyskinesias. Significantly less dyskinesias and motor complications were also seen in the early combination of group as compared to patients on levodopa monotherapy.

Lisuride in Advanced Parkinson's Disease

Studies performed in the early eighties did not attain high methodologic quality. No randomized controlled study was identified in the literature that examined the role of oral lisuride in more advanced PD. Its effect in this setting is uncertain, and its use is no longer promoted. However, lisuride infusions may have a place in patients with major motor complications. The first trials, conducted by Vaamonde and colleagues (116) and by Baronti and associates (117), showed that round-the-clock infusions dramatically prolonged the antiparkinsonian effect of levodopa and widened its therapeutic window, supporting the view that continuous dopamine replacement greatly diminishes motor fluctuations and peak-dose dyskinesias. Marked reduction in "off" hours was sustained for many months at doses of 0.5 to 8 mg/day. Nevertheless, this improvement was later followed in most patients by severe dyskinesias and difficult-to-manage "off" periods. A major disadvantage was the frequent occurrence of psychiatric side effects in up to one-third of patients. A more recent study by Stocchi and coworkers (118) followed 40 patients with motor fluctuations and dyskinesias for 4 years who could not be sufficiently controlled by other medications. The patients were randomized to waking-day infusions of subcutaneous lisuride or to conventional oral treatment of levodopa and dopaminergic agonists. The study was open, with separate clinical evaluators for the main variables. Lisuride infusion treatment was better in reducing "off" time and in decreasing dyskinesias, nocturnal akinesia, and dystonia. Mean UPDRS motor scores during "off" and "on" periods remained stable in lisuride-treated patients and deteriorated in the other group. The psychiatric side effects were not major, and only 2 patients withdrew from the study, probably because the infusions were restricted to waking hours.

A dermal patch of lisuride is being studied (119), with positive initial results. The patch is relevant to this drug because of its short half-life.

CABERGOLINE

Cabergoline is a long-acting ergoline D2 agonist. Its very long terminal half-life (65 to 110 hours) permits once-daily (or even less frequent) oral administration. Its long half-life may be valuable in patients with nocturnal fluctuations, especially dystonic pain, nocturnal awakenings, and early-morning dystonia. Cabergoline provides more continuous dopaminergic stimulation than any other antiparkinsonian drug and potentially prevents or delays motor fluctuations (120, 121).

Cabergoline in Early Parkinson's Disease

Bracco and colleagues (121) reported the results of a 5-year, double-blind, randomized, levodopa-controlled trial. In de novo patients, the primary outcome was the time to motor complications. Other variables included changes in total UPDRS, ADLs, and motor function (part III of the UPDRS and CGI). Motor complications were delayed in the cabergoline group. There was a total risk reduction of > 50% in favor of cabergoline in the occurrence of dyskinesias (9.5% versus 21.2% for the levodopa group). However, levodopa was better than cabergoline in motor improvement. The adverse event profile was similar in both arms, the only significant difference being in peripheral edema: 17.5 % cabergoline versus 3.4% levodopa.

Cabergoline in Advanced Parkinson's Disease or as Adjunct to Levodopa

Cabergoline has been assessed versus placebo in 2 small short-term phase II trials and in one phase III trial (122). At entry, patients were suboptimally controlled and experiencing wearing off or other motor complications. Patients were titrated to a maximum 5mg/day dose of cabergoline. The results favored the actively treated group in the ADL and motor scores. "Off" hours were reduced by a mean of 1.32 hours and the mean dose of levodopa was also reduced. The results of this trial, short-term studies, and unpublished data provided by the manufacturer for the Cochrane review (123) imply that cabergoline may be used to reduce levodopa dose and to improve motor function and ADLs. It should be emphasized that the cabergoline

doses used in these studies were much lower than the maximal recommended dose (10 mg).

A retrospective, case-controlled study found a significantly increased prevalence of cardiac valvulopathy in cabergoline-treated patients compared to those treated with pergolide or pramipexole. This high frequency was correlated with higher cumulative dose and longer treatment with cabergoline (124).

ROPINIROLE

Ropinirole is a potent synthetic nonergoline D2 agonist with full intrinsic activity at the D2 and D3 receptors. Like pramipexole, ropinirole exhibits mild partial agonist activity at 5-HT1a receptors. Its affinity order for D2 receptors subtype is D3 > D2 > D4, similar to that of dopamine, but ropinirole is 20-fold more selective for human D3 than for D2 receptors. Ropinirole has negligible or no affinity for D1, benzodiazepine, GABA, cholinergic, and α or β adrenergic receptors. Ropinirole is rapidly absorbed after oral administration, its concentration peak occurs in less than 2 hours, and its elimination half-life is 5 to 7 hours (125–127).

Ropinirole in Early Parkinson's Disease

Several large prospective double-blind multicenter studies entered patients with early PD (Hoehn-Yahr stages I to III). Patients were enrolled if they had not been treated with levodopa (or had been treated for less than 6 weeks) and required symptomatic therapy. Selegiline was not an exclusion. In all trials, ropinirole and the control drug were titrated to a potential maximum dose of 24 mg for ropinirole. Very few patients achieved this dose.

Korczyn and coworkers (128, 129) reported a comparison of bromocriptine with ropinirole. The primary endpoint was the change in motor function measured with the UPDRS. The motor score was improved for both groups at 6 months, but ropinirole provided a more robust change than bromocriptine. An interesting finding was that when only the non-selegiline-treated patients were compared, ropinirole demonstrated a stronger relative response. However, when patients who received selegiline were compared, this difference between ropinirole and bromocriptine was not seen. This may suggest that selegiline in some way augmented the efficacy of bromocriptine but not the efficacy of ropinirole. At 3 years, UPDRS scores showed definite improvement in both groups, although ADLs were significantly better with ropinirole (at a mean dose of 12 ± 6 mg) than with bromocriptine (at a mean dose of 24 ± 8 mg). At 3 years, 60% of ropinirole-treated and 53% of bromocriptine-treated patients were still on agonist monotherapy. The

2 groups did not differ in adverse events, and there was a low incidence of dyskinesias.

Rascol and collaborators (130) compared the efficacy and safety of ropinirole with that of levodopa in a large 5-year study. The addition of levodopa in an open-label fashion was permitted if required for symptomatic control. Of the ropinirole group, 47% completed this 5-year trial, as did 51% of the levodopa group. Of the ropinirole completers, 34% remained on agonist monotherapy. There was a difference in favor of ropinirole in the incidence of dyskinesias (hazard ratio 2.82; CI 95% 1.78 to 4.44). Overall dyskinesias were present in 20% of the original ropinirole group and 45% of the levodopa group. Disabling dyskinesias were rarer in the ropinirole group. However, the change in motor function favored the levodopa group and the scores for ADLs were also better for the levodopa group. Another variable, the prevalence of freezing when walking, showed a higher percentage in the ropinirole group. The adverse events and the early withdrawals were similar in both groups. A subgroup of patients with early PD (15%) can be managed with ropinirole monotherapy for up to 5 years (131).

Ropinirole in Advanced Parkinson's Disease

Ropinirole was also tried as adjunctive therapy in the treatment of patients with levodopa-induced motor complications. The first major placebo-controlled trial, by Lieberman and colleagues (132) was a medium-term randomized, parallel-group study that used ropinirole 3 times a day. This study showed a reduction in "off" time in the ropinirole group. However, when additional data provided by the manufacturer were analyzed by Clarke and Deane for a Cochrane review (133), the difference in the reduction of "off" time, while greater with ropinirole, did not reach statistical significance, probably due to an imbalance of the groups at baseline. In supplementary data, Clarke and Deane found that significantly more patients were "improved" or "very much improved" on ropinirole as compared with placebo. Dyskinesias were significantly higher in those on ropinirole than those on placebo, but no other adverse effects were different.

PRAMIPEXOLE

Pramipexole (PPX), a synthetic amino-benzothiazole derivative, is another nonergot dopamine D2 full receptor agonist, acting preferentially at presynaptic D2 autoreceptors (in nondenervated striatum) with even stronger affinity for the D3 subtype than ropinirole. PPX occupies and activates the high-affinity state of D2 receptors. PPX has negligible affinity at D1 sites. It is rapidly absorbed, reaches peak concentrations in about 2 hours, and has a terminal half–life of 8 to 12 hours (134–136). Typical doses are 3 to 4.5 mg/day.

Pramipexole in Early Parkinson's Disease

Three double-blind, placebo-controlled studies using a gradual titration of up to 4.5 or 6 mg/day confirmed the efficacy and tolerability of PPX in early PD.

The Parkinson Study Group (137) reported on a dose-ranging trial that evaluated 4 doses of PPX (1.5 to 6 mg) and placebo. There was a 6-week dose-escalation period followed by 4 weeks of maintenance therapy. The primary outcome measure for efficacy was the total UPDRS score and tolerability as determined by the patients' capability to complete the study. There was a linear trend between mean response and dosage that was highly significant; however it was found that the magnitude of the mean response was similar across all active groups (20% improvement in UPDRS score), and all groups were significantly superior to placebo. PPX seemed to be more effective in more severely impaired patients. This study was unable to find a minimum effective dose, since even the 1.5-mg dose was significantly more effective than placebo.

The proportion of completers was significantly lower in PPX-treated patients with the exception of the group treated with 3 mg. The major adverse events were somnolence, nausea, and hallucinations as well as dizziness, and all of these increased with higher doses. On the basis of this trial it was thought that the optimal dose for monotherapy in early PD may be around 3 mg.

Shannon and coworkers reported the results of a large 6-month trial comparing PPX and placebo (138). More than 80% of patients completed the trial. There was a considerable (22% to 29%) improvement in the ADL score and a similar (25% to 31%) improvement in the motor score, both of which were significant and maintained for the entire 6 months. The most common adverse events—and ones that were significantly more frequent with active therapy—included nausea, insomnia, constipation, and somnolence. Visual hallucinations occurred in 9.7% of actively treated patients, more than in the control group.

PPX was compared to levodopa in early PD by the Parkinson Study Group in a multicenter, parallel-group, double-blind, randomized controlled trial (139). The patients were randomized to receive PPX 0.5 mg 3 times per day or 25/100 mg of carbidopa/levodopa 3 times a day, dose escalation being allowed in case of residual disability during the first 10 weeks. After this period and until the end of the study, the addition of open-label levodopa was permitted as needed. At 23.5 months, motor complications occurred in 28% of the PPX-treated patients compared with 51% of the levodopa group (hazard ratio 0.45). This reduced risk of developing motor complications replicates the findings obtained in similar trials with other dopaminergic agonists (pergolide, cabergoline, and ropinirole). In this study, motor improvement on the UPDRS was significantly greater in levodopa-treated patients. The adverse effects of somnolence, hallucinations, and edema were significantly more frequent in PPX–treated patients.

This trial was extended to 4 years, in an open-label design in which additional drugs or dose changes were allowed. Again, PPX produced a significant reduction in the appearance of dyskinesias (hazard ratio 0.37) and wearing off (hazard ratio 0.68). Patients who were initially treated with levodopa showed a greater improvement in the UPDRS score and a reduced risk of freezing.

Pramipexole in Advanced Parkinson's Disease

Two large double-blind, medium-term, placebo-controlled trials performed in advanced PD patients with motor complications showed marked improvement for PPX over placebo in motor disability as well as decreased "off" time.

Lieberman and coworkers (140) reported a trial with a 7-week titration phase followed by a 6-month maintenance period. The PPX group was allowed to escalate to 4.5 mg. The ADL score improved significantly and was maintained for the entire duration of study. The motor score was also better, with a decrease of about 25%. "Off" time was reduced (31% vs. 7%). The severity of "off" states was improved in the PPX group. The major adverse events included dyskinesias (61.3%), asymptomatic orthostatic hypotension (48.1%), dizziness (36.5%), insomnia (22.7%), hallucinations (19.3 %), nausea (17.7%), and symptomatic orthostatic hypotension (16%).

Guttman and associates (90) conducted a 9-month trial in PD patients suffering from wearing off which included three treatment groups: PPX (escalating dose up to 4.5 mg), bromocriptine (escalating dose up to 30 mg), and placebo. The study was not powered for a comparison of the 2 dopamine agonists. At an average daily dose of 3.36 mg, PPX treatment resulted in improvement in ADL scores (26.7% better than baseline) and in motor examination score (34.9% better than baseline). There was also an increase in "on" (2.5 hours) per day in the PPX group. There was a significant advantage of PPX in quality of life. The most frequent adverse effects in PPX patients were dyskinesias (40%), nausea (36%), orthostatic hypotension (40%), dizziness (33%), insomnia (28%), headache (20%), hallucinations (14%), and confusion (14%).

Four favorable short-term smaller double-blind placebo-controlled trials were reported (141–144). Clarke and colleagues (145), having reviewd these trials and data obtained from the manufacturer, concluded that PPX significantly reduced time spent "off" and improved

UPDRS ADL scores, motor scores, and quality of life. A significant reduction in levodopa dose also occurred. Withdrawal from the studies was higher in the PPX groups, among whom more adverse events were seen. However, these attained statistical significance only for hallucinations. Similar results were recently reported for a large double-blind placebo-controlled trial with an open extension phase (146).

These results confirmed the efficacy of PPX in diminishing "off" time and improving motor and ADL scores. In addition, the post hoc analysis suggested a tremorlytic action and improvement in motivation, initiative, and depression items.

Pogarell and coworkers (143) studied PD patients with "drug-resistant" tremor, and found a significant reduction was obtained by PPX of tremor items score of the UPDRS.

APOMORPHINE

Apomorphine hydrochloride, a nonaddictive derivative of morphine, is a nonergoline full dopaminergic agonist with high affinity for D4, D2, and D3 receptors. Its affinity for D1 receptors is lower, but the difference between D2 and D1 sites is the least among dopamine agonists.

Apomorphine is not effective in oral use due to extensive first-pass hepatic metabolism. Following subcutaneous injection, apomorphine is rapidly absorbed, plasma Tmax being less than 10 minutes. The equilibrium between plasma and brain is reached rapidly. Clinical improvement is reflected by the appearance of the drug in the CSF and starts within less than 20 minutes. Improvement on average does not extend beyond 90 minutes, corresponding to a terminal elimination half-life of about 40 minutes (147). The duration of improvement is shortened with disease progression, and steepening of dose-response relation may also occur (148). Apomorphine was the first agonist ever used in PD. It was synthesized by Matthiesen and Wright in 1869 and had been used in medicine because of its emetic and sedative properties (149, 150).The emetic effect is shared by all dopamine agonists, but because apomorphine is injected and has a short half-life, this effect is fast, pronounced, and brief. Almost immediately after its synthesis, Pierce reported good results in treating patients with chorea. Its value in PD was recognized by Weill in 1884 (151). Weill's idea was confirmed 65 years later by Schwab, Amador and Lettvin, who injected apomorphine subcutaneously and obtained a striking improvement in tremor and in rigidity in parkinsonian patients (152). This finding lay dormant until the 1970s, Cotzias and coworkers (153) showed, in the first double-blind controlled trial, that apomorphine improves motor features in parkinsonian patients chronically treated with levodopa.

The clinical effects of apomorphine start shortly after injection, become maximal at 30 to 60 minutes, and dissipate after approximately 2 hours. Unfortunately, patients experienced disturbing side–effect, including drowsiness, nausea, vomiting, hypotension, bradycardia, and syncope. A few years later Corsini and associates (154) demonstrated that domperidone prevents most of these side effects without impeding on the efficacy of apomorphine. At present in the United States, the combination of apomorphine with domperidone or trimethobenzamide is the mainstay of apomorphine initiation treatment.

Recently Factor (155) and LeWitt (156) reviewed apomorphine experience. Apomorphine was approved in the United States for the treatment of episodes of hypomobility, such as "end of dose" and "unpredictable on/off" in advanced PD unresponsive to other medications. Prefilled "Penject" syringes for intermittent bolus injection and minipumps (not in the US) for continuous subcutaneous infusions are available, both displaying an almost identical quality of response. Bolus injections are easier to use and better tolerated than the continuous infusions. These intermittent injections may be used up to 10 times per day; if more is required, patients should be switched to continuous infusions. Apomorphine treatment reduces the time spent "off," usually by more than 50%. The mean dose varied between 2 and 4mg. Continuous subcutaneous infusions showed, in addition, a reduction in peak-dose dyskinesias, duration of dyskinesias, disability, and levodopa dosage (147, 158).

A small number of double-blind controlled trials followed the pioneer study of Cotzias and colleagues (153). One recent study by Dewey and colleagues (159) confirmed the clinical effectiveness of subcutaneously injected apomorphine as demonstrated by significant improvement in UPDRS motor scores over placebo—the primary endpoint—and by reversing "off" states 95% the time as compared to 23% with placebo.

Another indication for apomorphine is in the treatment of hospitalized patients who have stopped oral intake (160). In addition, timely injections may ameliorate swallowing difficulties, "off"-period belching, "off" pain, painful dystonia, and perhaps constipation, anismus, adynamic bowel, and neurogenic hyperreflexic bladder.

Apomorphine can be safely and effectively used in patients receiving COMT inhibitors (161, 162).

Other Routes. Several routes and formulations for apomorphine have been reviewed (163). The sublingual use of apomorphine tablets is followed by a motor response of a magnitude identical to that of the subcutaneous route, with a longer latency (20 to 40 minutes). Intranasal apomorphine had a latency and duration of effect almost identical to those obtained by injecting apomorphine. Rectal administration may have a longer duration effect but is considered inconvenient for everyday use. The transdermal route was employed by Priano and coworkers (164). Apomorphine was included in a microemulsion, achieving therapeutic plasma levels with consequent long action and efficacy.

Intravenous administration was explored in a small trial (165). This included patients unable to continue subcutaneous treatment due to intolerable local side effects; they were switched to intravenous apomorphine via a long-term indwelling catheter. Manson (165) and colleagues demonstrated that this route is highly effective in controlling refractory motor fluctuations, reducing dyskinesias, and diminishing the need for other dopaminergic medication. However, the complication rate was very high, including intravascular thrombosis due to the deposition of apomorphine crystals. The available apomorphine injections are suitable only for subcutaneous use.

Side Effects. The most common side effects of apomorphine are similar to those of other dopamine agonists—nausea, vomiting, and hypotension. These can be ameliorated by prior and concomitant use of domperidone or trimethobenzamide. Many patients were able to discontinue the antinauseant drug as tolerance to the peripheral side effects developed. The use of other antiemetics like 5HT3 agonists is contraindicated due to possible profound hypotension. Neuropsychiatric complications increasingly occur with long-term treatment; however, they may be less common than with other dopamine agonists. Hallucinations were reported in 11% of patients in clinical trials (155–159). A stereotyped pattern consisting of unjustified increase of daily injections, severely disturbed sexual behavior, and acute psychomotor agitation has been described (166), suggesting that dependence may take place. Yawning was reported by 40% of the patients, and it may herald the beneficial effect of the drug. Drowsiness and somnolence were also frequent but apparently unrelated to yawning.

Other rare or exceptional adverse events included transient Coombs'-positive autoimmune hemolytic anemia, transient atrial fibrillation, cardiac arrest, penile erection or priapism, and precipitation of migraine attacks in migraineous patients.

The benefit of apomorphine is unfortunately marred in most patients by the appearance of local reactions: nodules—panniculitis—at subcutaneous injection sites. Ulcerations and necrosis with subsequent abdominal wall scarring at injection sites are often attributed to poor hygiene. These cutaneous reactions were more common in patients who received continuous infusions. Severe stomatitis or nasal vestibulitis were seen when other routes were used.

Another suggested use for apomorphine was as a diagnostic tool in differentiating PD from other parkinsonian syndromes. Rossi and colleagues (167) challenged patients with PD and with other degenerative parkinsonian syndromes with apomorphine (1.5 mg to 4.5 mg SC) and oral levodopa (250 mg). They remarked that the motor improvement according to part III of the UPDRS was significantly higher in PD than in non-PD patients. However, the change was not decisive in terms of sensitivity or specifity of diagnosis. The meta-analysis performed by Clarke and Davis (168) found that the sensitivity and specificity of both acute apomorphine and levodopa responsiveness did not differ from that of chronic levodopa therapy in parkinsonian patients. since as the common practice is to assess the long-term response to levodopa therapy, the use of these challenge tests for diagnostic purpose in early parkinsonians is probably not warranted.

PIRIBEDIL

Piribedil is a nonergoline selective D2 > D3 > D4 dopaminergic agonist. It possesses α2-adrenoceptor antagonist properties and weak partial agonist activity at 5HT1a receptors. Piribedil has been used in Europe from the early 1970s as add-on therapy. More recently, Ziegler and colleagues (169) showed in a randomized, double-blind, placebo-controlled trial that piribedil is better than placebo in levodopa nonfluctuating patients at a daily dose of 150 mg. Piribedil was well tolerated, the most frequent reported adverse events being gastrointestinal symptoms. However, like other dopamine agonists, piribedil induced sleep attacks in 6% of patients (170). Interestingly, Simon and associates demonstrated that intravenous infusion of piribedil may reverse end-of-dose akinesia (171). Currently piribedil is considered efficacious as add-on therapy to levodopa (172).

DIHYDROERGOCRIPTINE

Dihydroergocriptine (DHEC) is an ergot derivative structurally similar to bromocriptine. It is a potent D2 agonist and a partial D1 antagonist with no adrenergic or serotonergic activities (173). DHEC has been evaluated in open studies since the 1980s, but good-quality randomized studies are scarce. Bergamasco and colleagues (174) reported a randomized, double-blind, placebo-controlled trial in de novo parkinsonian patients. The study was designed as an 18-month trial but was stopped prematurely due to a significant difference in favor of active treatment at the 3-month interim analysis. DHEC was found to be significantly better than placebo for the primary outcome: the UPDRS total score. DHEC adverse events were mainly gastrointestinal symptoms. DHEC is not approved in the United States. In many other countries it is accepted as efficacious in symptomatic monotherapy.

ROTIGOTINE

Other potent D2 receptors agonists are aminotetralines, which are structurally unrelated to the ergolines. Two of them, N-0437 and its (-) enantiomer N-0923, were effective in rat and monkey models of PD. As N-0923 was found to be the active component, it was developed and became known as rotigotine (175, 176). Rotigotine is a D3 > D2 > D1-preferring agonist; it has antagonistic activity on α-2 receptors, agonistic activity at 5HT1A(a) receptors and no activity at 5HT2 receptors.

Rotigotine is administered as a transdermal patch (4.5 mg/10 cm²) once daily. It averts first-pass hepatic metabolism and delivers constant dopaminergic stimulation to the brain (177).

The efficacy and safety of rotigotine in early PD were reported in 2 randomized, multicenter, double-blind, placebo-controlled, parallel group trials. The PSG study (178) allocated patients to different doses of rotigotine with patching containing 4.5, 9, 13.5, or 18 mg of rotigotine or to placebo. The main outcome variable was the change in the sum of the UPDRS parts 2 and 3 (ADL and motor component) from baseline to 11-week assessment. The results showed a significant difference in favor of rotigotine as compared to placebo in the groups treated with 13.5 and 18 mg.

Watts and associates (179) randomized patients to receive rotigotine (titrated to an optimal response or to 13.5 mg (6 mg/day)) or placebo in a 2:1 ratio. The primary endpoint was similar with the addition of the proportion of responders, defined as patients achieving a decrease in the combined scores of UPDRS parts 2 and 3 of 20% or greater. Mean dose of rotigotine at the end of 27 weeks treatment was 13.5 mg in more than 90% of patients. Rotigotine was better than placebo at both primary endpoints, the UPDRS improvement and responders rate.

Rotigotine induced more nausea, vomiting, somnolence, dizziness, headache, and application site irritation than placebo.

Preliminary data regarding the efficacy and safety of rotigotine in fluctuating PD suggest that at 8 to 12 mg/daily, the drug may decrease "off" time, and it had good tolerability. Rotigotine patches can be used in patients who cannot swallow drugs, such as postoperatively (180).

DOPAMINE AGONISTS MONOTHERAPY

The choice of the first dopaminergic drug in de novo PD patients—levodopa or a dopamine agonist—has been much debated. The Quality Standards Subcommittee of the American Academy of Neurology (5), the Agency for Healthcare Research and Quality (181), the Task Force of the Movement Disorder Society (MDS)

(182), the joint task force of the European Federation of Neurological Societies and the Movement Disorder Society, and the National Institute for Clinical Excellence (NICE) (21) have provided the most valuable evidence intended to help treating physicians, patients, and health decision authorities.

There is no categorical recommendation endorsing the use of an initial dopamine agonist over levodopa as there is no convincing evidence for the best initial treatment of PD. The selection of which dopamine agonist to use is not much easier, as no adequately powered head-to-head trials have been conducted. However, some analyses of data may facilitate the decision. An example may be the hierarchy established by the MDS Task Force based on efficacy, safety and practice implications for every drug. The Task Force considered pramipexole, ropinirole, pergolide, and dihydroergocryptine to be efficacious and clinically useful, bromocriptine and lisuride as likely efficacious and possibly useful. The data concerning other drugs (cabergoline, piribedil, and apomorphine) were insufficient to allow any definite conclusions. NICE recommendations do not specify which drug is more efficacious, in contrast to those of the MDS task force. The task force did not consider agonist groupings in terms of ergot and nonergot. Consequently a nonergot agonist may be preferred. The Quality Standards Subcommittee did not discriminate between pramipexole, ropinirole and cabergoline regarding efficacy. More recent studies have compared dopamine agonists to levodopa not only for symptomatic benefit but also for the ability of dopamine agonists to forestall long-term motor complications associated with levodopa. The improved methodology of these modern trials supported the conclusion that dopamine agonists delay motor complications. This especially refers to pramipexole, ropinirole, and cabergoline, while bromocriptine is considered likely efficacious. However, in all these later studies, levodopa administration resulted in better motor scores.

The combination of low-dose levodopa with an older dopamine agonist at the initiation of dopaminergic therapy is more difficult to evaluate; a meta-analysis by the Agency of Healthcare suggested that in early PD the association resulted in better motor scores, but the studies were hampered by many flaws. At present, such combinations are not widely recommended.

DOPAMINE AGONISTS AS ADJUVANT THERAPY

Dopamine agonists were initially used as add-on therapy in patients with advanced disease. Apomorphine, pramipexole, ropinirole, and pergolide were considered efficacious and useful in late-stage PD, while bromocriptine and cabergoline were designated as likely efficacious and possibly useful by the MSD Task Force. NICE recommendations emphasized that the benefit shown by bromocriptine, cabergoline, pergolide, pramipexole, and ropinirole was obtained in short-term studies.

No head-to-head sufficiently powered study compared add-on dopamine agonist therapy therapy in PD (97).

The nonergot dopaminergic agonists ropinirole and pramipexole presented the option to switch patients from ergot derivatives, mainly bromocriptine and pergolide, to the newcomers. This argument became intense with the recognition of the cardiac lesions presumably caused by pergolide and cabergoline. The ensuing debate concerned the safest way to accomplish this switch: rapid overnight switch or slow titration over weeks (183–186). The feasibility of a rapid switch was convincingly demonstrated by multiple trials. The dose-equivalence ratios were bromocriptine to ropinirole 10:6, bromocriptine to pramipexole 5:1, pergolide to ropinirole 1:6, and pergolide to pramipexole 1:1 (187).

OVERVIEW

The dopamine agonists are a heterogenous group of drugs with unequal effects on different dopamine receptors and other receptors. They are safe and easy to use but are less efficacious than levodopa. Most have longer half-lives than levodopa, resulting in a lower frequency of daily administration.

The main advantage of dopamine agonists over levodopa in early disease is that they delay the onset of dyskinesias and motor fluctuations by 1 to 3 years. This effect may be related to their longer duration of action. It is unclear whether a similar effect can be achieved if levodopa is administered with COMT inhibitors, since the latter also provide a more continuous dopaminergic stimulation. It is also unclear whether this potential advantage is useful in all patients, since early dyskinesias are mild.

The longer duration of action of carbergoline and pergolide and also of transdermal patch preparations like rotigotine and lisuride makes them particularly useful for some patients, as in those with nocturnal symptoms or frequent "on-off" episodes during the day.

The neuroprotective effect of dopamine agonists is a potentially important although still unproven effect.

The main disadvantages of dopamine agonists are the following:

1. Lower efficacy compared to levodopa.
2. Significant side effects, such as hypotension, nausea and vomiting, which require a slow titration of the dose until tolerance develops.
3. Induction of unexpected, irresistible sleep episodes.
4. Induction of behavioral symptoms and the impulse control disorder
5. Induction of hallucinations and lower limb edema.

6. In the case of pergolide and cabergoline, the need for careful monitoring of possible cardiotoxic effects; for other ergot derivatives, attention to other fibrotic complications.

7. Not all dopamine agonists being the same, some authorities favor the use combinations of agonists in individual patients (188). The benefit of this approach needs to be studied.

References

1. Olanow CW. The scientific basis for the current treatment of Parkinson's disease. *Annu Rev Med* 2004; 55:41–60.
2. Nutt JG, Wooten GF. Diagnosis and initial management of Parkinson's disease. *N Engl J Med* 2005; 353:1021–1027.
3. Fahn S, Shoulson I, Kieburtz K, et al. Levodopa and the progression of Parkinson's disease. *N Engl J Med* 2004; 351:2498–2508.
4. Fahn S and the Parkinson Study Group. Does levodopa slow or hasten the rate of progression of Parkinson's disease? *J Neurol* 2005; 252(Suppl 4):iv37–iv42.
5. Miyasaki JM, Martin W, Suchowersky O, et al. Practice parameter: Initiation of treatment for Parkinson's disease: An evidence-based review. *Neurology* 2002; 58:11–17.
6. Weiner WJ. Initial treatment of Parkinson disease. *Arch Neurol* 2004; 61:1966–1969.
7. Suchowersky O, Gronseth G, Perlmutter J, et al. Practice parameter: Neuroprotective strategies and alternative therapies for Parkinson disease (an evidence-based review). *Neurology* 2006; 66:976–998.
8. Sibley DR, Monsma FJJ. Molecular biology of dopamine receptors. *Trends Pharmacol Sci* 1992; 13:61–69.
9. Sokoloff P, Schwartz JC. Novel dopamine receptors half a decade later. *Trends Pharmacol Sci* 1995; 16:270–275.
10. Missale C, Russel SN, Robinson SW, et al. Dopamine receptors: From structure to function. *Physiol Rev* 1998; 78:189–225.
11. Millan MJ, Maiofiss L, Cussac D, et al Differential actions of antiparkinsonian agents at multiple classes of monoaminergic receptor. A multivariate analysis of the binding profiles of 14 drugs at 21 native and cloned human receptors subtypes JPET. 2002; 303:791–804.
12. Newman-Tancredi A, Cussac D, Audinot V, et al. Differential actions of antiparkinsonian agents at multiple classes of monoaminoergic receptor: II. Agonist and antagonist properties at subtypes of dopamine D2-like receptor and α1/α2-adrenoreceptor. *JPET* 2002; 303:806–814.
13. Newman-Tancredi A, Cussac D, Quentric Y, et al. Differential actions of antiparkinson agents at multiple classes of monoaminoergic receptor: III. Agonist and antagonist properties at serotonin, 5-HT1 and 5-HT2, receptors subtypes. *JPET* 2002; 303:815–822.
14. Zanettini R, Antonini A, Gatto G, et al. Valvular heart disease and the use of dopamine agonists for Parkinson's disease. *N Engl J Med* 2007; 356:39–46.
15. Watts RL. The role of dopamine agonists in early Parkinson's disease. *Neurology* 1997; 49:S34–S38.
16. Factor S. Dopamine agonists. *Med Clin North Am* 1999; 83:415–433.
17. Clarke CE, Guttman M. Dopamine agonist monotherapy in Parkinson's disease. *Lancet* 2002; 360:1767–1769.
18. Schwarz J. Rationale for dopamine use as monotherapy in Parkinson's disease. *Curr Opin Neurol* 2003; 16(Suppl 1):S27–S33.
19. Bonuccelli U. Comparing dopamine agonists in Parkinson's disease. *Curr Opin Neurol* 2003; 16(Suppl 1):S13–S19.
20. Jenner P. Dopamine agonists, receptor selectivity and dyskinesia induction in Parkinson's disease. *Curr Opin Neurol* 2003; 16(Suppl 1):S3–S7.
21. National Institute for Clinical Excellence. Parkinson's disease: Diagnosis and management in primary and secondary care. *NICE Guidelines*, CG 35, June 2006.
22. Olanow CW, Obeso JA, Stocchi F. Continuous dopamine-receptor treatment of Parkinson's disease: Scientific rationale and clinical implications. *Lancet Neurol* 2006; 5:677–687.
23. Korczyn AD. Pathophysiology of drug-induced dyskinesias, *Neuropharmacology* 1972; 11:75–77.
24. Korczyn AD. The function of presynaptic dopamine receptors on nonadrenergic nerve terminals. *Med Hypoth* 1979; 5:1131–1132.
25. Kumar N, van Gerpen JA, Bower JH, Ahlskog JE. Levodopa-dyskinesia incidence by age of Parkinson's disease onset. *Mov Disord* 2005; 20:342–344.
26. Noyes K, Dick AW, Holloway RG, Group T. Pramipexole and levodopa in early Parkinson's disease: Dynamic changes in cost effectiveness. *Pharmacoeconomics* 2005; 23:1257–1270.
27. Pechevis M, Clarke CE, Vierrege P, et al. Effects of dyskinesias in Parkinson's disease on quality of life and health-related costs: A prospective European study. *Eur J Neurol* 2005; 12:956–963.
28. Ahlskog JE, Muenter MD. Frequency of levodopa-related dyskinesias and motor fluctuations as estimated from the cumulative literature. *Mov Disord* 2001; 16:448–458.
29. Van Gerpen JA, Kumar N, Bower JH, et al. Levodopa-associated dyskinesia risk among Parkinson disease patients in Olmsted County, Minnesota, 1976–1990. *Arch Neurol* 2006; 63:205–209.
30. Olanow CW. Dopamine agonists and neuroprotection in Parkinson's disease. *Ann Neurol* 1998; 44:S167–S174.
31. Koller WC. Neuroprotection for Parkinson's disease. *Ann Neurol* 1998; 44:S155–S159.
32. Shoulson I. Where do we stand on neuroprotection? Where do we go from here? *Mov Disord* 1998; 13(Suppl 1):46–48.
33. Ravina BM, Fagan SC, Hart RG, et al. Neuroprotective agents for clinical trials in Parkinson's disease. *Neurology* 2003; 60:1234–1240.
34. Parkinson Study Group. DATATOP: A multicenter controlled clinical trial in early Parkinson's disease. *Arch Neurol* 1989; 46:1052–1060.
35. Whone AL, Watts RL, Stoessl AJ, et al. Slower progression of Parkinson's disease with ropinirole versus levodopa: The REAL-PET study. *Ann Neurol* 2003; 54:93–101.
36. Parkinson Study Group. Dopamine transporter brain imaging to assess the effects of pramipexole vs levadopa on Parkinson disease progression. *JAMA* 2002; 287:1653–1661.
37. Ravina B, Eidelberg D, Ahlskog JE, et al. The role of radiotracer imaging in Parkinson disease. *Neurology* 2005; 64:208–215.
38. Calne DB, Brennan J, Spiers ASD, Stern GM. Hypotension caused by levodopa. *BMJ* 1960; 1:474–475.
39. Johns DW, Ayers CR, Carey RM. The dopamine agonist bromocriptine induces hypotension by venous and arteriolar dilatation. *J Cardiovasc Pharmacol* 1984; 6:582–587.
40. Kujawa K, Leurgans S, Raman R, et al. Acute orthostatic hypotension when starting dopamine agonists in Parkinson's disease. *Arch Neurol* 2002; 57:1461–1463.
41. Frucht S, Rogers JD, Greene PE, et al. Falling asleep at the wheel: Motor vehicle mishaps in persons taking pramipexole and ropinirole. *Neurology* 1999; 52:1908–1910.
42. Homman CN, Wenzel K, Suppan K, et al. Sleep attacks in patients taking dopamine agonists: Review. *BMJ* 2002; 324:1483–1487.
43. Razmy A, Lang AE, Shapiro CM. Predictors of impaired daytime sleep and wakefulness in patients with Parkinson disease treated with older (ergot) vs newer (nonergot) dopamine agonists. *Arch Neurol* 2004; 61:97–102.
44. Paus S, Brecht HM, Koster J, et al. Sleep attacks, daytime sleepiness, and dopamine agonists in Parkinson's disease. *Mov Disord* 2003; 18:659–667.
45. Avron J, Schneeweiss S, Sudarsky LR, et al. Sudden uncontrollable somnolence and medication use in Parkinson disease. *Arch Neurol* 2005; 62:1242–1248.
46. Ferreira JJ, Desboeuf K, Galitzky M, et al. Sleep disruption, daytime somnolence and sleep attacks in Parkinson's disease: A clinical survey in PD patients and age-matched healthy volunteers. *Eur J Neurol* 2006; 13:209–214.
47. Gjerstad MD, Alves G, Wentzel-Larsen T, et al. Excessive daytime sleepiness in Parkinson disease: Is it the drugs or the disease? *Neurology* 2006; 67:853–858.
48. Factor SA, Molho ES, Podskalny GD, Brown DL. Parkinson's disease: Drug-induced psychiatric states. *Adv Neurol* 1995;65:115–138.
49. Fenelon G, Mahieux F, Huon R, Ziegler M. Hallucinations in Parkinson's disease: Prevalence, phenomenology and risk factors. *Brain* 2000; 123:733–745.
50. Fenelon G, Goetz CG, Karenberg A. Hallucinations in Parkinson disease in the prelevodopa era. *Neurology* 2006; 66:93–98.
51. Goetz CG, Vogel C, Tanner CM, et al. Early dopaminergic drug-induced hallucinations in parkinsonian patients. *Neurology* 1998; 51:811–814.
52. Merims D, Shabtai H, Korczyn AD, et al. Antiparkinsonian medication is not a risk factor for the development of hallucinations in Parkinson's disease. *J Neural Transm* 2004; 111:1447–1453.
53. Korczyn AD. Hallucinations in Parkinson's disease. Lancet 2001; 358:1031–1032.
54. Giovannoni G, O'Sullivan JD, Turner K, et al. Hedonistic homeostatic dysregulation in patients with Parkinson's disease on dopanime replacement therapies. *J Neurol Neurosurg Psychiatry* 2000; 68:423–428.
55. Evans AH, Katzenschlager R, Paviour D, et al. Punding in Parkinson's disease: Its relation to the dopamine dyregulation syndrome. *Mov Disord* 2004; 19(4):397–405.
56. Evans AH, Lees AJ. Dopamine dysregulation syndrome in Parkinson's disease. *Curr Opin Neurol* 2004; 17:393–398.
57. Dodd ML, Klos JH, Bower JH, et al. Pathological gamling caused by drugs used to treat parkinson disease. Arch Neurol 2005; 63:1377–1384.
58. Szarfman A, Doraiswamy PM, Tonning JM, Levine JG. Association between pathologic gambling and parkinsonian therapy as detected in the Food and Drug Administration Adverse Event Database. *Arch Neurol* 2006; 63:299–200.
59. Voon V, Hassan K, Zurowski M, et al. Prospective prevalence of pathologic gambling and medication association in Parkinson disease. *Neurology* 2006; 66:1750–1752.
60. Voon V, Hassan K, Zurowski M, et al. Prevalence of repetitive and reward-seeking behaviors in Parkinson disease. *Neurology* 2006; 67:1254–1257.
61. Pontone G, Williams JR, Bassett SS, Marsh L. Clinical features associated with impulse control disorders in Parkinson disease. *Neurology* 2006; 67:1258–1261.
62. Evans AH, Pavese N, Lawrence AD, et al. Compulsive drug use linked to sensitized ventral striatal dopamine transmission. Ann Neurol 2006; 59:852–858.
63. Lieberman A. Depression in Parkinson's disease: A review. *Acta Neurol Scand* 2006; 113:1–8.
64. Treves TA, Paeacu D, Rabey JM, Korczyn AD. Depression inventories in Parkinson's disease. In: Kraus PH, Klotz P, Korczyn AD (eds). *Instrumental Methods and Scoring in Extrapyramidal Disorders*. New York: Springer, 1995:31–43.
65. Goldberg JF, Burdick KE, Endick CJ. Preliminary randomized, double-blind, placebo-controlled trial of pramipexole added to mood stabilizers for treatment-resistant bipolar depression. *Am J Psychiatry* 2004; 161:564–566.

66. Barone P, Scarzella L, Marconi R, et al. Pramipexole versus sertraline in the treatment of depression in Parkinson's disease. *J Neurol* 2006; 253:601–607.
67. Rinne UK. Early combination of bromocriptine and levodopa in the treatment of Parkinson's disease: a 5 year follow-up. *Neurology* 1987;37:826–828.
68. Tintner R, Manian P, Gauthier P, Jankovic J. Pleuropulmonary fibrosis after long-term treatment with the dopamine agonist pergolide in Parkinson's disease. *Arch Neurol* 2005;62:1290–1295.
69. Danoff SK, Grasso ME, Terry PB, Flynn JA. Pleuropulmonary disease due to pergolide use for restless legs syndrome. *Chest* 2001; 120:313–316.
70. Frans E, Dom R, Demedts M. Pleuropulmonary changes during treatment of Parkinson's disease with a long-acting ergot derivative, cabergoline. *Eur Respir J* 1992; 5:263–265.
71. Champagne S, Coste E, Peyriere H, et al. Chronic constrictive pericarditis induced by long-term bromocriptine therapy: Report of two cases. *Ann Pharmacother* 1999; 33:1050–1054.
72. Ling LH, Ahlskog JE, Munger TM, et al. Constrictive pericarditis and pleuropulmonary disease linked to ergot dopamine agonist therapy (cabergoline) for Parkinson's disease. *Mayo Clin Proc* 1999; 74:371–375.
73. Agarwal P, Fahn S, Frucht SJ. Diagnosis and management of pergolide-induced fibrosis. *Mov Disord* 2004; 19:699–704.
74. Tan EK, Ondo W. Clinical characteristics of pramipexole-induced peripheral edema. *Arch Neurol* 2000; 57:729–732.
75. Calne DB, Teychenne PF, Leigh PN, et al. Treatment of parkinsonism with bromocriptine. *Lancet* 1974; 2:1355–1356.
76. Przuntek H, Welzel D, Gerlach M, et al. Early institution of bromocriptine in Parkinson's disease inhibits the emergence of levodopa-associated motor side effects. Long-term results of the PRADO study. *J Neural Transm* 1996; 103:699–715.
77. Teychenne PF, Bergsrud D, Racy A, et al. Bromocriptine: Low-dose therapy in Parkinson disease. *Neurology* 1982; 32:577–583.
78. Agid Y, Pollak P, Bonnet AM, et al. Bromocriptine associated with a peripheral dopamine blocking agent in treatment of Parkinson's disease. *Lancet* 1979; 1:570–572.
79. Lees AJ, Stern GM. Sustained bromocriptine therapy in previously untreated patients with Parkinson's disease. *J Neurol Neurosurg Psychiatry* 1981; 44:1020–1023.
80. Ramaker C, van Hilten JJ. Bromocriptine versus levodopa in early Parkinson's disease. *Cochrane Database Syst Rev* 2000; (3):CD 002258.
81. Lees AJ, Katzenschlanger R, Head J, Ben-Shlomo Y. Ten-year follow-up of three different initial treatments in de novo PD. *Neurology* 2001; 57:1687–1697.
82. Hely MA, Morris JG, Reid WG, et al. The Sydney multi-center study of Parkinson's disease: A randomized, prospective five year study comparing low dose bromocriptine with low dose levodopa-carbidopa. *J Neurol Neurosurg Psychiatry* 1994; 57:903–910.
83. Montastruc JL, Rascol O, Rascol A. A randomized, controlled study of bromocriptine versus levodopa in previously untreated parkinsonian patients: A 3-year follow-up. *J Neurol Neurosurg Psychiatry* 1989; 52:773–775.
84. Hely MA, Morris JG, Reid WG, Trafficante R. Sydney Multicenter Study of Parkinson's disease: Non-levodopa-responsive problems dominate at 15 years. *Mov Disord* 2005; 20:190–199.
85. Rinne UK. Early combination of bromocriptine and levodopa in the treatment of Parkinson's disease. *Neurology* 1987; 37:826–828.
86. Ramaker C, van Hilten JJ. Bromocriptine/levodopa combined versus levodopa alone for early Parkinson's disease. *Cochrane Database Syst Rev* 2002; (2):CD 003634.
87. Brunt ER, Brooks DJ, Korczyn AD, et al. A six-month, multicentre, double-blind controlled study of the safety and efficacy of ropinirole in the treatment of patients with Parkinson's disease not optimally controlled by L-dopa. *J Neural Transm* 2002; 109:489–502.
88. Im JH, Ha JH, Cho IS, Lee MC. Ropinirole as an adjunct to levodopa in the treatment of Parkinson's disease: A 16-week bromocriptine controlled study. *J Neurol* 2003; 250:90–96.
89. Murayama S, Narabayashi H, Kowa H, et al. Clinical evaluation of ropinirole hydrochloride patients with Parkinson's: A double-blind comparative study versus bromocriptine mesylate. *Jpn Pharmacol Ther* 1996; 24:1939–2007.
90. Guttman M. International Pramipexole-Bromocriptine Study Group: Double-blind comparison of pramipexole and bromocriptine treatment with placebo in advanced Parkinson's disease. *Neurology* 1997; 49:1060–1065.
91. Mizuno Y, Yanagisawa M, Kuno S, et al. Randomized, double-blind study of pramipexole with placebo and bromocriptine in advanced Parkinson's disease. *Mov Disord* 2003; 18:1149–1156.
92. Clarke CE, Deane KD. Cabergoline versus bromocriptine for levodopa-induced complications in Parkinson's disease. *Cochrane Database Syst Rev* 2001; (1):CD 001519.
93. Inzelberg R, Nisipeanu P, Rabey M, et al. Double-blind comparison of cabergoline and bromocriptine in Parkinson's disease with motor fluctuations. *Neurology* 1996; 47:785–788.
94. Caraceni T, Musicco M. Levodopa or dopamine agonists, or deprenyl as initial treatment for Parkinson's disease. A randomized multicenter study. *Parkinsonism Relat Disord* 2001; 7:107–114.
95. Tolcapone Study Group. TSG Efficacy and tolerability of tolcapone compared with bromocriptine in levodopa-treated parkinsonian patients. *Mov Disord* 1999; 14:38–44.
96. Koller W, Lees AJ, Doder M, et al. Randomized trial of tolcapone versus pergolide as add-on to levodopa therapy in Parkinson's disease patients with motor fluctuations. *Mov Disord* 2001; 16:858–866.
97. Pahwa R, Factor SA, Lyons KE, et al. Practice parameter: Treatment of Parkinson disease with motor fluctuations and dyskinesia (an evidence-based review). *Neurology* 2006; 66:983–995.
98. Langtry HD, Clissold SP. Pergolide: A review of its pharmacological properties and therapeutic potential in Parkinson's disease. *Drugs* 1990; 39:491–506.
99. Brin O. The pharmacokinetics of pergolide in Parkinson's disease. *Curr Opin Neurol* 2003; 16(Suppl 1):S1–S12.
100. Storch A, Trenkwalder C, Oehlwein C, et al. High-dose treatment with pergolide in Parkinson's disease patients with motor fluctuations and dyskinesias. *Parkinsonism Relat Disord* 2005; 11:393–398.
101. Barone P, Bravi D, Bermejo-Pareja F, et al. Pergolide monotherapy in the treatment of early Parkinson's disease: A randomized controlled study. *Neurology* 1999; 53:573–579.
102. Oertel WH, Wolters E, Sampaio C, et al. Pergolide versus levodopa monotherapy in early Parkinson's disease patients: The PELMOPET study. *Mov Disord* 2006; 21:343–353.
103. Olanow CW, Fahn S, Muenter M, et al. A multicenter, double-blind placebo-controlled trial of pergolide as an adjunct to treatment in Parkinson's disease. *Mov Disord* 1994; 9:40–42.
104. Kurlan R, Millar C, Knapp R, et al. Double-blind assessment of potential pergolide-cardiotoxicity. *Neurology* 1986; 36:993–995.
105. Flowers CM, Racoosin JA, Lu SL, Beitz JG. The US Food and Drug Administration's Registry of patients with pergolide–associated valvular heart disease. *Mayo Clin Proc* 2003; 78:730–731.
106. Pritchett AM, Morrison JF, Edwards WD, et al. Valvular heart disease in patients taking pergolide. *Mayo Clin Proc* 2002; 77:1280–1286.
107. Corvol J-C, Schupbach M, Bonnet, A-M. Valvulopathies sous pergolide: Revue critique de la literature et conduite a tenir en pratique. *Rev Neurol (Paris)* 2005; 161:637–643.
108. Van Camp G, Flamez A, Cosyns B, et al. Treatment of Parkinson's disease with pergolide and relation to restrictive valvular heart disease. *Lancet* 2004; 363:1179–1183.
109. Baseman DG, O'Suilleabhain PE, Reimold SC, et al. Pergolide use in Parkinson disease is associated with cardiac valve regurgitation. *Neurology* 2004; 63:301–304.
110. Waller EA, Kaplan J, Heckman MG. Valvular heart disease in patients taking pergolide. *Mayo Clin Proc* 2005; 80:1016–1020.
111. Schade R, Andersohn F, Suissa S, et al. Dopamine agonists and the risk of cardiac-valve regurgitation. *N Engl J Med* 2007; 356:29–38.
112. Roth BL. Drugs and valvular heart disease. *N Engl J Med* 2007; 356:6–9.
113. Horowski R, Dorow R, Loschmann P, et al. Oral and parenteral use of lisuride in Parkinson's: Clinical pharmacology and implications for therapy in parkinsonism and ageing. In: Calne DB, Comi G, Crippa R (eds). *Parkinsonism and Ageing.* New York: Raven Press, 1989:269–286.
114. Hofmann C, Penner U, Dorow R, et al. Lisuride, a dopamine receptor agonist with 5-HT2B receptor antagonist properties: Absence of cardiac valvulopathy adverse drug reaction reports supports the concept of a crucial role for 5-HT2B receptor agonism in cardiac valvular fibrosis. *Clin Neuropharmacol* 2006; 29:80–86.
115. Rinne UK. Lisuride, a dopamine agonist in the treatment of Parkinson's disease. *Neurology* 1989; 39:336–339.
116. Vaamonde J, Luquin MR, Obeso JA. Subcutaneous lisuride infusion in Parkinson's disease. *Brain* 1991; 114:601–614.
117. Baronti F, Mouradian MM, Davis TL, et al. Continuous lisuride effects on central dopaminergic mechanisms in Parkinson's disease. *Ann Neurol* 1992; 32:776–781.
118. Stocchi F, Ruggieri S, Vacca L, Olanow CW. Prospective randomized trial of lisuride infusion versus oral elodea in patients with Parkinson's disease. *Brain* 2002; 125:2058–2066.
119. Woitalla D, Müller T, Benz S, et al. Transdermal lisuride delivery in the treatment of Parkinson's disease. *J Neural Transm* 2004; 68:89–95.
120. Fariello RG. Pharmacodynamic and pharmacokinetic features of cabergoline: Rationale for use in Parkinson's disease. *Drugs* 1998; 55:10–16.
121. Bracco F, Battaglia A, Chouza C, et al. The long-acting dopamine receptor agonist cabergoline in early Parkinson's disease: Final results of a 5-year, double-blind, elodea-controlled study. *CNS Drugs* 2004; 18:733–744.
122. Hutton JT, Koller WC, Ahlskog JE, et al. Multicentre, placebo-controlled trial of cabergoline taken once daily in the treatment of Parkinson's disease. *Neurology* 1996; 46:1062–1065.
123. Clarke CE, Deane KH. Cabergoline for levodopa-induced complications in Parkinson's disease. *Cochrane Database Syst Rev* 2001; (1)CD 001518.
124. Yamamoto M, Uesugi T, Nakayama T. Dopamine agonists and cardiac valvulopathy in Parkinson disease: A case-control study. *Neurology* 2006; 67:1225–1229.
125. Eden RY, Costall B, Domeney AH, et al. Preclinical pharmacology of ropinirole (SK&F 101468-A), a novel dopamine D2 agonist. *Pharmacol Biochem Behav* 1991; 38:147–154.
126. Tulloch IF. Pharmacologic profile of ropinirole: A nonergoline dopamine agonist. *Neurology* 1997; 49:558–562.
127. Dechant KL, Plosker GI. Ropinirole. *CNS Drugs* 1997; 8:335–341.
128. Korczyn AD, Brooks DJ, Brunt ER, et al. Ropinirole versus bromocriptine in the treatment of early Parkinson's disease: A 6-month interim report of a 3-year study. *Mov Disord* 1998; 13:46–51.
129. Korczyn AD, Brunt ER, Larsen JP, et al. A 3-year randomized trial of ropinirole and bromocriptine in early Parkinson's disease. *Neurology* 1999; 53:364–370.
130. Rascol O, Brooks DJ, Korczyn AD, et al. A five-year study of the incidence of dyskinesia in patients with early Parkinson's disease who were treated with ropinirole or levodopa. *N Engl J Med* 2000; 342:1484–1491.
131. Korczyn AD, Thalamas C, Adler CH. Dosing with ropinirole in a clinical setting. *Acta Neurol Scand* 2002; 106:200–204.
132. Lieberman A, Olanow CW, Sethi K, et al. A multi-center trial of ropinirole as adjunct treatment for Parkinson's disease. *Neurology* 1998; 51:1057–1062.
133. Clarke CE, Deane KH. Ropinirole for levodopa-induced complications in Parkinson's disease. *Cochrane Database Syst Rev* 2000; (3):CD 001516. Update in *Cochrane Database Syst Rev* 2001; (1):CD 001516.

134. Mierau J, Schingnitz G. Biochemical and pharmacological studies on pramipexole, a potent and selective dopamine D2 receptor agonist. *Eur J Pharmacol* 1992; 215: 161–170.

135. Piercey MF. Pharmacology of pramipexole, a dopamine D3–preferring agonist useful in treating Parkinson's disease. *Clin Neuropharmacol* 1998; 21:141–151.

136. Seeman P, Ko F, Willeit M, et al. Antiparkinson concentrations of pramipexole and PHNO occupy dopamine D2 (high) and D3 (high) receptors. *Synapse* 2005; 58:122–128.

137. Parkinson Study Group. Safety and efficacy of pramipexole in early Parkinson disease: A randomized dose-ranging study. *JAMA* 1997; 278:125–130.

138. Shannon KM, Bennett JP Jr, Friedman JH. Efficacy of pramipexole, a novel dopamine agonist, as monotherapy in mild to moderate Parkinson's disease. *Neurology* 1997; 49:724–728.

139. Parkinson Study Group. Pramipexole vs levodopa as initial treatment for Parkinson's disease: A randomized controlled trial. *JAMA* 2000; 284:1931–1938.

140. Lieberman A, Ranhosky A, Korts D. Clinical evaluation of pramipexole in advanced Parkinson's disease: Results of a double-blind, placebo-controlled, parallel group study. *Neurology* 1997; 49:162–168.

141. Wermuth L. A double-blind, placebo-controlled, randomized, multi-center study of pramipexole in advanced Parkinson's disease. *Eur J Neurol* 1998; 5(3):235–242.

142. Pinter MM, Pogarell O, Oertel WH. Efficacy, safety, and tolerance of the non-ergoline dopamine agonist pramipexole in the treatment of advanced Parkinson's disease: A double blind, placebo controlled, randomised, multicentre study. *J Neurol Neurosurg Psychiatry* 1999; 66:436–441.

143. Pogarell O, Gasser T, van Hilten JJ, et al. Pramipexole in patients with Parkinson's disease and marked drug resistant tremor: A randomized, double blind, placebo controlled, multicentre study. *J Neurol Neurosurg Psychiatry* 2002; 72:713–720.

144. Ka Sing Wong Lu Chin-Song Shan Din-E Yang Chih-Chao Tak Hong Tsoi MOK Vincent Efficacy, safety, and tolerability of pramipexole in untreated and levodopa-treated patients with Parkinson's disease. *J Neurol Sci* 2003; 216(1):81–87.

145. Clarke CE, Speller JM, Clarke JA. Pramipexole for levodopa-induced complications in Parkinson's disease. *Cochrane Database Syst Rev* 2000; (3):CD 002261.

146. Moller JC, Oertel WH, Koster J, et al. Long-term efficacy and safety of pramipexole in advanced Parkinson's disease: Results from a European multicenter trial. *Mov Disord* 2005; 20:602–610.

147. Gancher ST, Woodward WR, Boucher RB, et al. Peripheral pharmacokinetics of apomorphine in humans. *Ann Neurol* 1989; 26:232–238.

148. Metman LV, Locatelli MD, Bravi D, et al. Apomorphine responses in Parkinson's disease and the pathogenesis of motor complications. *Neurology* 1997; 48:369–372.

149. Foley PB. *Beans, Roots and Leaves: A History of the Chemical Therapy of Parkinsonism.* Marburg, Germany: Tectum Verlag, 2003.

150. Sneader W. *Drug Discovery: A History.* New York: Wiley, 2005.

151. Weill E. De l'apomorphine dans certains troubles nerveux. *Lyon Med* 1884; 48: 411–419.

152. Schwab RS, Amador LV, Lettvin JY. Apomorphine in Parkinson's disease. *Trans Am Neurol Assoc* 1951; 76:251–253.

153. Cotzias GC, Papavasilliou PS, Fehling C, et al. Similarities between neurologic effects of L-dopa and of apomorphine. *N Engl J Med* 1970; 282:31–33.

154. Corsini GV, Del Zompo M, Gessa GL, Mangoni A. Therapeutic efficacy of apomorphine combined with an extra cerebral inhibitor of dopamine receptors in Parkinson's disease. *Lancet* 1979; 1:954–956.

155. Factor S. Intermittent subcutaneous apomorphine therapy in Parkinson's disease. *Neurology* 2004; 62(Suppl 4):S12–S17.

156. Le Witt PA. Subcutaneously administered apomorphine. *Neurology* 2004; 62(Suppl 4): S8–S11.

157. Colzi A, Turner K, Lees AJ. Continuous waking-day subcutaneous apomorphine therapy in the treatment of levodopa-induced dyskinesias and "on-off" phenomena in Parkinson's disease. *Mov Disord* 1997; 12:428.

158. Katzenschlager R, Hughes A, Evans A, et al. Continuous subcutaneous apomorphine therapy improves dyskinesias in Parkinson's disease: A prospective study using single-dose challenges. *Mov Disord* 2004; 20:151–157.

159. Dewey RB, Hutton JT, Le Witt PE, Factor SA. A randomized, double-blind, placebo-controlled trial of subcutaneously injected apomorphine for parkinsonian off-state events. *Arch Neurol* 2001; 58:1385–1392.

160. Broussolle E, Marion MH, Pollak P. Continuous apomorphine as replacement for levodopa in severe parkinsonian patients after surgery. *Lancet* 1992; 340:859–860.

161. Ondo WG, Hunter C, Vuong KD, Jankovic J. The pharmacokinetic and clinical effects of tolcapone on a single dose of sublingual apomorphine in Parkinson's disease. *Parkinsonism Relat Disord* 2000; 6:237–240.

162. Zijlmans JCM, Debilly B, Rascol O, et al. Safety of entacapone and apomorphine coadministration in levodopa-treated Parkinson's disease patients: Pharmacokinetic and pharmacodynamic results of a multicenter, double-blind, placebo-controlled, cross-over study. *Mov Disord* 2004; 19:1006–1011.

163. Koller W, Stacy M. Other formulations and future considerations for apomorphine for subcutaneous injection therapy. *Neurology* 2004; 62(Suppl 4):S22–S26.

164. Priano L, Albani G, Calderoni S, et al. Transdermal apomorphine permeation from microemulsions: A new treatment in Parkinson's disease. *Mov Disord* 2004; 19: 937–942.

165. Manson AJ, Hanagasi H, Turner K, et al. Intravenous apomorphine therapy in Parkinson's disease: Clinical and pharmacokinetic observations. *Brain* 2001; 124:331–340.

166. Courty E, Durif F, Zenut M, et al. Psychiatric and sexual disorders induced by apomorphine in Parkinson's disease. *Clin Neuropharmacol* 1997; 20:140.

167. Rossi P, Colosimo C, Moro E, et al. Acute challenge with apomorphine and levodopa in parkinsonism. *Eur Neurol* 2000; 43:95–101.

168. Clarke CE, Davies P. Systematic review of acute levodopa and apomorphine challenge tests in the diagnosis of idiopathic Parkinson's disease. *J Neurol Neurosurg Psychiatry* 2000; 69:590–594.

169. Ziegler M, Castro-Caldas A, Del Signore S, Rascol A. Efficacy of piribedil as early combination to levodopa in patients with stable Parkinson's disease: A 6-month, randomized, placebo-controlled study. *Mov Disord* 2003; 18:418–425.

170. Tan EK Piribedil-induced sleep attacks in Parkinson's disease. *Fundam Clin Pharmacol* 2003; 17:117–119.

171. Simon N, Micallef J, Reynier JC, et al. End-of-dose akinesia after a single intravenous infusion of the dopaminergic agonist piribedil in Parkinson's disease patients: A pharmacokinetic, pharmacodynamic, randomized, double-blind study. *Mov Disord* 2005; 20:803–809.

172. Korczyn AD, Nisipeanu P. Newer therapies for Parkinson's disease. *Neurol Neurochir Pol* 1995; 30(Suppl 2):105–111.

173. Albanese A, Colosimo C. Dihydroergocriptine in Parkinson's disease: Clinical efficacy and comparison with other dopamine agonists. *Acta Neurol Scand* 2003; 107:349–355.

174. Bergamasco B, Frattola L, Muratorio A, et al. A-dihydroergocriptine in the treatment of de novo parkinsonian patients: Results of a multicentre, randomized, double-blind, placebo-controlled study. *Acta Neurol Scand* 2000; 101:372–380.

175. Jenner P. A novel dopamine agonist for the transdermal treatment of Parkinson's disease. *Neurology* 2005; 65(Suppl 1):S3–S5.

176. Reynolds NA, Wellington K, Easthope SE. Rotigotine in Parkinson's disease. *CNS Drugs* 2005; 19(11):973–981.

177. Morgan JC, Sethi KD. Rotigotine for the treatment of Parkinson's disease. *Exp Rev Neurother* 2006; 6(1):275–282.

178. The Parkinson Study Group. A controlled trial of rotigotine monotherapy in early Parkinson's disease. *Arch Neurol* 2003; 60:1721–1728.

179. Watts RL, Wendt RL, Nausied B, et al. Efficacy, safety, and tolerability of the rotigotine transdermal patch in patients with early-stage, idiopathic Parkinson's disease: A multi-center, multinational, randomized, double-blind, placebo-controlled trial. *Mov Disord* 2004; 19(Suppl 9):258.

180. Korczyn AD, Reichmann H, Boroojerdi B, Hack HJ. Rotigotine transdermal system for perioperative administration. *J Neural Transm* 2007; 114:219-221.

181. Levine CB, Fahrbach KR, Siderowf AD, et al. *Diagnosis and Treatment of Parkinson's Disease : A Systematic Review of the Literature.* Evidence Report/Technology Assessment Number 57, AHRQ Publication No 03-E040. Rockville, MD: Agency for Healthcare Research and Quality, 2003.

182. Rascol O, Goetz C, Koller W, et al. Treatment interventions for Parkinson's disease: An evidence based assessment. *Lancet* 2002; 359:1589–1598.

183. Canesi M, Antonini A, Mariani CB, et al. An overnight switch to ropinirole therapy in patients with Parkinson's disease. *J Neural Transm* 1999; 106:925–929.

184. Goetz CG, Blasucci L, Stebbins GT. Switching dopamine agonists in advanced Parkinson's disease: Is rapid titration preferable to slow? *Neurology* 1999; 52:1227–1229.

185. Reimer J, Kuhlmann A, Muller T. Neuroleptic malignant-like syndrome after rapid switch from bromocriptine to pergolide. *Parkinsonism Relat Disord* 2002; 9:115–116.

186. Grosset K, Needleman F, Macphee G, Grosset D. Switching from ergot to nonergot dopamine agonists in Parkinson's disease: A clinical series and five-drug dose conversion table. *Mov Disord* 2004; 19:1370–1374.

187. Thobois S. Proposed dose equivalence for rapid switch between dopamine receptor agonists in Parkinson's disease: A review of the literature. *Clin Ther* 2006; 28:1–12.

188. Reichmann H, Herting B, Muller A, Sommer U. Switching and combining dopamine agonists. *J Neural Transm* 2003; 110:1393–1400.

42 Catechol-*O*-Methyltransferase Inhibitors

Cheryl Waters

LIMITATIONS OF LEVODOPA

To appreciate the rationale for the use of catechol-*O*-methyltransferase (COMT) inhibitors, it is important to understand the metabolism of levodopa. The majority (70%) of oral levodopa is rapidly metabolized in the liver and intestinal mucosa to dopamine via dopa decarboxylase. Even while levodopa is being absorbed, it is undergoing decarboxylation. A second pathway of metabolism occurs via COMT to produce 3-*O*-methyldopa (3-OMD). Less than 1% of administered oral levodopa penetrates the brain. The peripheral production of dopamine results in side effects such as nausea, hypotension, and cardiac arrhythmias. With the use of peripheral dopa decarboxylase inhibitors (e.g., carbidopa and benserazide), the dose of levodopa is substantially reduced (about 70%) and peripheral side effects markedly attenuated (1).

Even with decarboxylase inhibitors, only 5% to 10% of oral levodopa reaches the brain. With the inhibition of dopa decarboxylase, other pathways are activated. In particular, COMT metabolizes levodopa to 3-OMD. The half-life of 3-OMD is about 15 hours, compared with about 1 hour for levodopa. It has been suggested that 3-OMD may compete with levodopa for the energy-dependent transport mechanism used for penetration into the brain. Large amounts of 3-OMD may decrease the efficacy of levodopa in animals and

patients with Parkinson's disease (PD). 3-OMD is of no benefit to the parkinsonian brain: whether it has deleterious properties is unknown. COMT is one of the main enzymes responsible for metabolism of levodopa and other catecholamines. It is located in the liver, kidney, and gut wall as well as in the central nervous system (CNS) neurons and glia (2).

RATIONALE FOR COMT INHIBITORS

COMT inhibitors are used in conjunction with levodopa/carbidopa in PD patients to lengthen levodopa's duration of action. Peripheral metabolism of levodopa is reduced by carbidopa and COMT inhibitors. This allows for a greater portion of the dose of levodopa to remain in the circulation for transport to the brain (Figure 42-1). In this way, COMT inhibitors lengthen levodopa's duration of action by prolonging its half-life in plasma and increasing the amount of levodopa available to enter the brain (2). This is an important development because the shortening of the duration of response to levodopa has been associated with the onset of motor fluctuations (3). Block and colleagues observed a low (20%) but definite prevalence of response fluctuations after 5 years of treatment with levodopa-carbidopa therapy [immediate release (IR) or controlled release (CR)] (4).

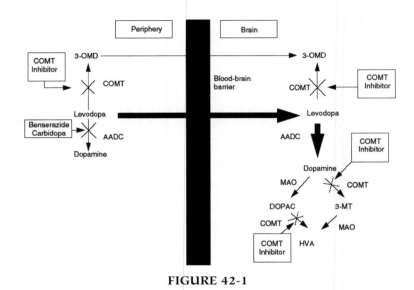

FIGURE 42-1

Metabolism of levodopa: Effects of peripheral and central COMT inhibition AADC, aromatic amino acid decarboxylase; COMT, catechol-O-methyltransferase, DOPAC, 3, 4-dihydroxyphenylacetic acid; HVA, homovanillic acid; MAO, monoamine oxidase; 3-MT, 3-methoxytyramine; 3-OMD, 3-O-methyldopa.

In addition, preclinical and clinical studies suggest that current therapeutic regimens provide only intermittent stimulation of dopamine receptors (5). This intermittent stimulation may lead to neuronal changes downstream that contribute further to the development of motor complications. Dopamine replacement regimens that provide continuous stimulation of dopamine receptors may prevent or ameliorate the motor complications of PD. Therefore patients should obtain significant advantages from adjunctive therapy with a COMT inhibitor, which may result in the stabilization or "smoothing out" of dopamine levels.

After a number of years, many patients treated with levodopa develop motor fluctuations (6). Motor fluctuations of the "wearing off" type are the most common. Because these fluctuations result from a shortening of levodopa's duration of action, they are also the known as end-of-dose deterioration. Eventually, progression of PD results in loss of terminals and the inability of the remaining neurons to store dopamine; both contribute to the increasing severity and unpredictability of the motor fluctuations. As this occurs, motor function fluctuates between 2 states: the "on" state, when plasma levodopa concentrations remain within the therapeutic range and optimally control bradykinesia, tremor, and rigidity; and the "off" state, when plasma levels decline, the medication's effect diminishes, and mobility is compromised.

As the disease advances and with long-term levodopa use, many patients show an enhanced sensitivity to even small fluctuations in blood concentrations of levodopa (1). They also may experience peak-dose dyskinesias (choreic or dystonic movements) that occur when plasma

concentrations of levodopa are at their highest (6, 7). Furthermore, disease progression can bring complications in motor response that may be unrelated to the dosing interval. These abrupt and often unpredictable fluctuations, also called random fluctuations or the "on-off" phenomenon, can become the most disabling symptoms of PD and are generally not amenable to therapeutic intervention.

Patients with early PD who have not developed fluctuations are categorized as having nonfluctuating, or stable, PD. As a rule, in these early stages, bid or tid administration of levodopa/carbidopa provides constant control of parkinsonian symptoms. Most patients experience the "on" and "off" states to some degree as the disease progresses. The goals of drug development in PD are symptomatic relief; delay or prevention of disease progression; avoidance of "wearing off" fluctuations; amelioration of such fluctuations when they do develop; and management of other associated problems of PD, such as psychosis, cognitive impairment, and depression (6). The challenge for the clinician is to use the range of pharmacologic interventions appropriately to achieve maximum benefit.

Patients with nonfluctuating disease seem to have sufficient presynaptic dopaminergic neurons to store and release dopamine, thus avoiding fluctuations in intrasynaptic dopamine levels and facilitating long-duration responses. In patients with advanced disease, residual neurons are thought to have a diminished capacity to take up levodopa and to store and release dopamine, thus shortening the duration of response. Intrasynaptic

TABLE 42-1
Strategies for Extending Levodopa's Effect

Increase amount of levodopa administered per dose
Increase frequency of levodopa doses
Switch to controlled-release preparations of levodopa
Provide direct intraduodenal infusion of levodopa
Inhibit peripheral catechol-O-methyltransferase
Inhibit monoamine oxidase

dopamine concentrations begin to reflect the fluctuating plasma levels of levodopa that correspond to periodic administration of levodopa.

Although controversial and by no means established, clinical evidence suggests that fluctuating levels of levodopa may be associated with motor complications, and continuous levels of levodopa may ameliorate these problems. Research is focusing on extending the duration of each dose of levodopa to sustain a more consistent plasma level. This may be achieved by administering levodopa infusions, substituting CR (controlled-release) formulations for IR (intermittent-release) formulations, and adding COMT or monoamine oxidase (MAO-B) inhibitors (Table 42-1).

Some believe that increasing the dose of levodopa or the frequency of dosing can lead to the development or worsening of dyskinesias. Either strategy steepens the dose-response curve for levodopa, narrowing the therapeutic index and heightening sensitivity to minute changes in drug availability (3).

CLINICAL STUDIES WITH COMT INHIBITORS

Tolcapone

Pharmacokinetics of Tolcapone Tolcapone is a COMT inhibitor that acts both peripherally and centrally, although clinical response seems to be primarily related to its peripheral effects. Tolcapone, like entacapone, was shown in several studies to increase the half-life of levodopa (2). Tolcapone increases the area under the curve (AUC) for levodopa. This occurs without a concomitant increase in peak plasma concentration. At a 200-mg dose of tolcapone, the AUC increases by 94%. Inhibition of 3-OMD formation is substantial and dose-dependent (8). The overall clearance of tolcapone is low, which translates to good bioavailability. The elimination half-life is 2.1 hours. The inhibition of erythrocyte COMT is stronger and considerably longer with tolcapone than with entacapone.

Studies in Patients with Fluctuating Parkinson's Disease In one study (9), tolcapone prolonged the time during which patients received clinical benefits from levodopa. In addition, patients were able to reduce their total levodopa dose requirements. This multicenter, double-blind, placebo-controlled study included patients (n = 51) who initially required at least 3 doses of IR levodopa/carbidopa daily. All patients had PD and were experiencing predictable "on" time in response to the first morning dose of levodopa/carbidopa and at least 2 predictable end-of-dose "off" episodes (with a combined "off" time > 2 hours). Primary efficacy measures were the investigators' 10-hour evaluation of "off" time and the Unified Parkinson's Disease Rating Scale (UPDRS) motor subscale (part 3). Clinical evaluations were made just before and after 6 weeks of treatment with tolcapone (50, 200, or 400 mg 3 times a day). At both evaluations, UPDRS motor subscale scores as well as "on-off" and dyskinesia assessments were made at 30-minute intervals over a 10-hour period. Compared with placebo, the difference between baseline and week 6 for all 3 doses of tolcapone significantly reduced "off" time by an average of 40%; [0.4% vs. 2.7% (placebo); 16.6% vs. 2.7% (50-mg tid group); 16.1% vs. 2.8% (200-mg tid group); and 18.1% vs. 3.0% (400-mg tid group); $P < 001$]. The change in AUC was statistically and significantly different from placebo for all tolcapone dosages from baseline to week 6 [11.4 vs. 8.6 (placebo); 44.8 vs. 8.9 (50-mg tid group); 37 vs. 8.9 (200-mg tid group); and 49.1 vs 10.1 (400-mg tid group); $P < .05$]. Both the total daily dose of levodopa/carbidopa and the dosing frequency were significantly reduced in patients receiving tolcapone either 200 or 400 mg tid.

Although well tolerated, tolcapone was associated with typical dose-related dopaminergic side effects in some patients. Dopamine-related adverse events increased during the first 2 weeks of treatment in all tolcapone groups but diminished as levodopa dosages were adjusted downward. The most frequently reported adverse event was dyskinesia; 21.4% in the placebo group and approximately 50% in the tolcapone-treated patients. Nausea was reported in 12% in the placebo group and in 25% in the tolcapone group. Postural hypotension was reported by 12% in the placebo group and between 7.5% and 18.4% in the tolcapone group. These side effects could be ameliorated or eliminated by reducing the dosage of levodopa/carbidopa. Dizziness (5.3% to 10% of tolcapone patients vs. 0% of placebo patients) and urine discoloration (4.9% to 23.7% of tolcapone patients vs. 0% of placebo patients) were also noted. No significant changes in the mean values of vital signs were observed. No abnormal laboratory tests results were reported related to tolcapone.

Welsh and colleagues assessed the effect of tolcapone (50, 200, or 400 mg tid) vs. placebo on quality of life (QOL) in patients who were receiving levodopa/carbidopa therapy over a 6-week period (10). This study was conducted in parallel with the double-blind, placebo-controlled, dose-response study previously described (10). Quality of life was measured by the Sickness Impact Profile (SIP) and adjustment to illness was measured by the Psychosocial Adjustment to Illness Scale–Self-Report (PAIS-SR). Objective assessment of the impact of PD was measured by the UPDRS. Patient ratings of total illness impact (PD .003), physical impact (PD .002), and psychosocial impact (PD .007) improved significantly in subjects in the 3 tolcapone groups (9).

In a double-blind, parallel group trial involving 11 centers, Rajput and colleagues studied 202 patients who were experiencing the "wearing off" phenomenon on levodopa; these patients were at least 30 years old and had been treated with levodopa for at least 1 year (11). At the start of the study, patients were taking at least four doses daily of levodopa/carbidopa (or 3 doses daily if 2 were a CR formulation). Patients were experiencing predictable motor fluctuations at the end of a dosing interval that could not be eliminated by adjusting their existing therapy.

The principal efficacy measurement was "off" and "on" time assessed by patient diaries. Investigators' global assessment (IGA) was used to evaluate change in the "wearing off" phenomenon and severity of PD symptoms. The UPDRS scale was used to assess parkinsonian symptoms, and QOL was measured. After baseline assessments, patients were randomized to receive either tolcapone (100 or 200 mg tid) or placebo in addition to levodopa/carbidopa. After 3 months of treatment with tolcapone, the patients' daily diaries were analyzed. Patients experienced reductions in the duration of "off" time—a mean reduction of 3.2 hours—compared with baseline when treated with tolcapone 200 mg tid ($P < .01$) (Table 42-2) (11). A subgroup of these patients received tolcapone for 12 months, during which further reductions in total daily levodopa dose were achieved and reduced "off" time was maintained. The dosage of levodopa was reduced in patients receiving either dosage of tolcapone compared with those receiving placebo ($P < .01$) and the number of daily doses was also reduced ($P < .01$) (11).

Tolcapone therapy was well tolerated; the most frequent dopaminergic adverse events were dyskinesias and nausea, which were transient and occurred early in the study. Dyskinesias were satisfactorily controlled by adjusting levodopa dose. Diarrhea and constipation were the most frequent nondopaminergic events and accounted for the majority of withdrawals from the trial (4% and 8% withdrew from the 100- and 200-mg tid groups, respectively, and 3% withdrew from the placebo group) (11). Tolcapone treatment was associated with elevated liver enzymes in 3 patients in the 100-mg tid group and 2 patients in the 200-mg tid group.

Baas and colleagues demonstrated that tolcapone reduces "off" time and levodopa requirements in patients ($n = 177$) experiencing predictable fluctuations (12). During the study, patients received either tolcapone (100 or 200 mg tid) or placebo for 3 months. At 3 months, changes in the frequency of "wearing off" fluctuations were assessed, along with other efficacy parameters. Compared with placebo, the addition of tolcapone 100 mg tid to the regimen produced statistically significant reductions in "off" time (31.5% decrease; $P < .05$); significant increases in "on" time (21.3% increase, $P < .01$); and significant reductions in the mean daily levodopa dose (decrease of 109 mg, $P < .05$). "On" time was increased by 20.6% ($P < .01$) and "off" time decreased by 26.2% (NS) with tolcapone 200 mg tid. Diarrhea resulted in withdrawals in 7% of the 100-mg tid group and 10% of the 200-mg tid group.

Another study of tolcapone in patients with fluctuating disease was reported by Adler and coworkers (13). This study was a placebo-controlled, double-blind, randomized trial involving 15 centers. Patients were on levodopa at least for 1 year and had to be using a minimum of 4 doses of standard formulation levodopa or 3 doses if 2 were of the controlled-release type. They had to have end-of-dose failure but not unpredictable "on–off" and had to be on a stable dose of levodopa for at least 4 weeks. Patients were randomized to receive placebo or tolcapone 100 mg tid or 200 mg tid. Primary efficacy measures were changes in "on" and "off" time measured by diaries. Secondary efficacy measures were UPDRS, IGA, dyskinesia scale, and SIP. A total of 215 patients enrolled: mean duration of PD was 10.5 years, mean duration of levodopa therapy was 8.5 years, and 76% had dyskinesias. A 6-week study showed significant increases in "on" time for both tolcapone groups (2.1 hours for 100 mg tid, 2.3 hours for 200 mg tid) vs. placebo (0.3 hours) ($P < .001$). "Off" time decreased by 2 hours in the 100-mg tid group, 2.5 hours in the 200-mg tid group; and 0.3 hours in the placebo group ($P < .005$). Levodopa dose decreased 23% in 100-mg tid group, 29% in 200-mg tid group compared to placebo ($P < .001$), and the number of doses per day decreased in active treatment groups. Adverse events were similar to those of previous studies.

Comparison to Dopamine Agonists

The relative effectiveness and tolerability of a COMT inhibitor vs. a dopamine agonist as adjunctive therapy

---

TABLE 42-2

Efficacy Data: Change from Baseline to Month 3

	PLACEBO	100 MG	200 MG
Daily "off" time	–1.4	–2.3	–3.2*
Percent of baseline	–20	–32	–48

*$P < .01$.
Source: From Rajput et al.(11). With permission.

to levodopa have been compared in a randomized single-blind study conducted in Europe (14). Over an 8-week period, investigators compared the effects of adjunctive therapy with tolcapone (200 mg tid) vs. bromocriptine (mean final dose, 22.4 mg/d) in 146 levodopa-treated patients with fluctuating disease. Tolcapone was shown to be more effective than bromocriptine for increasing the mean "on" time and decreasing the mean "off" time and was also better tolerated (Table 42-3). Patients treated with tolcapone required less levodopa and experienced fewer CNS adverse effects (psychosis and hallucinations) than patients treated with bromocriptine.

These results demonstrate that when used as an adjunct to levodopa therapy in patients with fluctuating disease, tolcapone is as effective or more so than the dopamine agonist bromocriptine. In addition, tolcapone has the advantage of not requiring titration at the start of treatment. Tolcapone also leads to significant reductions in the total daily dose of levodopa and to improvements in "wearing off" fluctuations. Tolcapone was associated with a much lower incidence of peripheral dopaminergic events (e.g., nausea) than bromocriptine.

In phase III tolcapone studies for patients with fluctuating disease, in which about one-third received a dopamine agonist concomitantly with tolcapone as an adjunct to levodopa and a dopa decarboxylase inhibitor, no serious safety concerns were identified. However, the incidence of orthostatic complaints and hallucinations was higher among those receiving dopamine agonists with tolcapone than those receiving only tolcapone (11). The incidence of dyskinesias was approximately 8% to 10% higher in the dopamine agonist group.

Patients With Nonfluctuating Parkinson's Disease

For patients who have not developed motor fluctuations (the "stable" patient), tolcapone has been studied to assess its ability to delay their development and improve ADL scores. It has been hypothesized that smooth and continued delivery of levodopa in patients with nonfluctuating disease, by using adjunctive therapy, may positively influence the development of motor fluctuations.

In a study of stable patients receiving levodopa, the major outcome variable was the percent change in the ability to perform ADL as measured by UPDRS subscale II. After 6 months, the patients receiving tolcapone 100 or 200 mg tid showed significant improvement on the ADL (subscale II) and motor function (subscale III) sections of the UPDRS, compared with patients who received placebo (15). There was an 18% (1.4 vs. .3) and a 20% (1.6 vs. .3) improvement in ADL scores in patients receiving tolcapone 100 mg tid (P < .05) or tolcapone 200 mg tid (P < .01). In contrast, there were no significant changes in the ADL or motor scores of patients receiving

TABLE 42-3

Efficacy and Tolerability of Bromocriptine Compared With Tolcapone as Adjunctive Therapies to Levodopa*

CLINICAL EFFECT	BROMOCRIPTINE (N = 74)	TOLCAPONE (N = 72)
Levodopa		
Reduction in total daily dose (mg)	−30.0 ± 20.3	−124.0 ± 21.5†
Patients reduced dosage per day	11%	−33%
"On-off" time		
Change in mean "off" time (hours)	−2.4 ± 0.4	−3.0 ±0.5
Mean change in "off" time/mean baseline "off" time	−37.9%	−43.7%
Change in mean "on" time (hours)	+ 2.1± 0.5	+ 2.8 ± 0.5
Mean change in "on" time/mean baseline "on" time	27.5%	36.6%
Investigators' global assessment		
Efficacy: patients improved	69%	82%‡
Tolerability: patients improved	9%	16%
UPDRS subscale II score Change in ADL	−0.1 ± 0.4	−0.9 ± 0.5
UPDRS subscale III score Change in motor function	−3.3 ± 1.0	−3.1 ± 1.05

UPDRS = Unified Parkinson's Disease Rating Scale; ADL = activities of daily living.
*In the open-label study, either tolcapone (200 mg tid) or bromocriptine (mean final dose, 22.4 mg/d) was administered to patients also receiving levodopa. Data are mean ± standard error of the mean (SEM) between baseline and week 8 or percentage of patients at week 8.
†P < .01
‡P < .05
Source: From Agid et al.(13). With permission.

placebo over the same 6-month period (C .1 vs. .6 change on subscales II and III).

Along with the improvements in motor function, patients receiving tolcapone 100 mg and 200 mg tid were able to reduce their total daily levodopa dose by 6% and 9%, respectively (P < .001 for both groups). In contrast, patients in the placebo group required an additional

47 mg of levodopa over the same 6-month period, which was not accompanied by a decrease in impairment.

Compared with placebo patients, a lower proportion of patients treated with 200 mg tid tolcapone developed evidence of motor fluctuations at 6 months.

In this study, patients treated with tolcapone 100 mg tid ($P < .01$ vs placebo) or 200 mg tid ($P < .05$ vs. placebo) also experienced significant improvements in the physical subscale of the SIP.

Dupont and colleagues assessed the effect of tolcapone on levodopa dose in patients with stable PD whose "wearing off" phenomena had been controlled with more frequent levodopa dosing (16). In this double-blind, placebo-controlled study, 97 patients were randomly assigned to receive placebo or tolcapone (200 or 400 mg tid) for 6 weeks. On the morning of the first day of the treatment period, the levodopa dose was reduced by 35% and subsequently titrated as needed. In case of dyskinesias, increasing the dose interval, mainly in the afternoon, was preferred to decreasing the size of a single dose except when the first daily dose was not tolerated (16). After 6 weeks of treatment, patients in the 200-mg-tid group crossed over to the 400-mg-tid group and vice versa for another 3 weeks. Patients receiving placebo remained on placebo until the end of the 9-week study. The primary efficacy parameter was change in levodopa dosage from baseline to week 6. Other efficacy parameters were IGA and UPDRS subscales I (mentation, behavior, mood), II (ADL), III (motor functions), and IVb (clinical fluctuations). Safety assessments included levodopa-induced symptoms, dyskinesia rating scale, UPDRS subscales IVa (dyskinesias) and IVc (other complications), IGA of tolerability, vital signs, ECGs, and laboratory analyses. Efficacy was analyzed via hypothesis testing for the first 6-week treatment period.

At the end of the 6-week treatment period, both tolcapone groups evidenced greater reduction in total daily dose (27% for 200-mg-tid group and 25% for 400-mg-tid group) and number of doses of levodopa (1.3 for 200-mg-tid group and 1.5 for 400-mg-tid group) compared with the placebo group (19% decrease in dose and 1.1 doses per day), but these differences did not reach significance. The tolcapone 200-mg-tid group demonstrated the greatest improvement in estimated mean scores for all efficacy parameters ($P < .05$ vs. placebo only for a change in UPDRS subscale II). The changes seen in the tolcapone 400-mg-tid group were nearly indistinguishable from those in the placebo group. However, the results indicate that a reduction in levodopa dosage in the tolcapone groups did not occur at the expense of other efficacy parameters.

Nnausea and dyskinesias were the most frequently reported dopaminergic adverse events. The most unexpected nondopaminergic event frequently reported was diarrhea, which was reported by 3 patients (9%) in the tolcapone 200-mg-tid treatment group and 6 patients (19%) in the 400-mg-tid treatment group. The majority of the adverse events reported were mild and reversible.

Entacapone

Pharmacokinetics of Entacapone   Entacapone is rapidly absorbed and exhibits linear pharmacokinetics up to a dose of 200 mg (8). The bioavailability of entacapone is low at 35%. It is rapidly metabolized in the liver. Entacapone has a greater volume of distribution than tolcapone and tolcapone is protein-bound. Therefore entacapone is cleared more rapidly from the body than tolcapone.

Early Studies of Entacapone   In a 4-week open-label trial, entacapone improved "on" time from 2.3 to 3.4 hours per dose of levodopa (17). Dyskinesias were seen as a side effect. These results were validated in a cross-over trial of entacapone and placebo (18). In this study, entacapone prolonged the duration of a motor response to an individual dose of levodopa by 34 minutes. Dyskinesia duration was similarly prolonged. From home diaries, "on" time was found to be prolonged by 2.1 hours per day.

Entacapone has been studied pharmacologically and was found to increase the area under the curve (AUC) for levodopa without enhancing T_{max} or C_{max} (19). It prolongs the elimination half-life of levodopa, thus extending its action. This was true when tested with either orally or intravenously administered levodopa (20). Entacapone increased the duration of action of single doses of levodopa by 56%. Plasma 3-OMD concentrations were reduced by 60%. During chronic administration of this drug (8 weeks), the daily requirements for levodopa were reduced 27%. Patients reported that the percentage of day "on" time was 77% during treatment with entacapone, dropping to 44% when this drug was withdrawn.

Parkinson Study Group and Nordic Study Group   In a large, multicenter placebo-controlled, double-blind, randomized 24-week study of entacapone was conducted by the Parkinson Study Group (21), 205 patients were randomized to receive either entacapone 200 mg or placebo with each dose of levodopa. The primary efficacy endpoint was the change in "on" time while awake. Entacapone treatment increased "on" time by 5% (approximately 1 hour) per day consistently throughout all 24 weeks of the study (21). The effect of entacapone treatment was especially dramatic in patients with the lowest amount of "on" time (< 55%) at baseline (i.e., patients who were most impaired). The total UPDRS score improved in 10% of patients treated with entacapone at week 24. Entacapone reduced patients' levodopa requirements by

100 mg/d on average. The investigators' global evaluations of the patients revealed a shift in the positive direction in those patients treated with entacapone compared with the placebo group, who shifted in a negative direction (PD .002) (Table 42-4). When entacapone was withdrawn in a blinded staggered drug withdrawal period, the beneficial effects were rapidly lost.

The most frequently reported adverse events in the entacapone group were dyskinesias, urine discoloration, dizziness, nausea, and constipation. Dyskinesias were most frequent during the first 8 weeks of the trial (30 of 33 patients in the placebo group; 53 of 55 patients in the entacapone group) (20). However, after the levodopa dosage was adjusted, dyskinesias resolved in one-third of the patients within 8 weeks. No differences were observed between entacapone and placebo groups in vital signs, laboratory tests, or ECG results.

Similar results with entacapone have been reported by the Nordic Study Group (n = 171) (22). This was a 6-month double-blind, placebo-controlled trial using patient diaries as the primary outcome measure. Treatment with entacapone increased daily "on" time. Baseline daily "on" time was 9 to 10 hours, which increased by 1.3 hours after entacapone treatment. Treatment with entacapone also reduced the mean total UPDRS scores when "on" by approximately 10% compared with scores for patients receiving placebo. The benefits of treatment with entacapone were lost within 2 to 3 hours of the last dose administered and before the beginning of the next scheduled dose cycle (21, 22).

The efficacy of entacapone in controlling motor fluctuations was evaluated in a 6-month, randomized, placebo-controlled trial in 301 levodopa-treated patients, of whom 260 had motor fluctuations (23). The primary outcome was absolute change in on hours at 6 months compared with baseline. Entacapone ($P < .05$) prolonged daily on time by a mean of 1.7 hours from 10.0 at baseline to 11.7 compared with an increase from 9.7 to 10.7 with placebo. The difference vs. placebo was greatest in the subgroup of 174 patients taking more than 5 daily doses of levodopa. UPDRS motor scores improved by 3.3 points with entacapone vs. 0.1 points with placebo ($P < .01$).

In a subsequent trial, Brooks and colleagues randomized 172 fluctuating and 128 nonfluctuating levodopa-treated patients to entacapone or placebo for 6 months (24). The primary endpoint in the nonfluctuating group was the change of the UPDRS ADL score at 4 and 6 months vs. baseline. The primary outcome in the fluctuating group was the proportion of daily on time while awake at 4 and 6 months vs. baseline. In the nonfluctuating group, there was ($P < .001$) greater improvement in UPDRS ADL scores with entacapone. In addition, the mean daily dose of levodopa increased by 7 mg with entacapone group compared with an increase of 47 mg with placebo ($P < .01$). In the fluctuating group, entacapone induced an increase in mean proportion of daily "on" time. Mean absolute "on" time increased by 1.3 hours on entacapone compared with 0.1 hours with placebo ($P < .001$).

Although transient dyskinesias and mild nausea are more common with entacapone treatment, this drug is well tolerated, with no abnormalities in vital signs or laboratory surveillance tests. The long-term safety and tolerability of entacapone were demonstrated in a 12-month safety study in 326 levodopa-treated patients with and without motor fluctuations, two-thirds of whom were randomized to entacapone and one-third to placebo (25). There was no significant difference between entacapone and placebo in the rate of discontinuation due to adverse events (14% vs. 11%, respectively). As expected due to dopaminergic enhancement, dyskinesia was a more frequent adverse event with entacapone than with placebo. Entacapone had no adverse effect on hepatic enzymes, ECG, or hemodynamic parameters, and there was no evidence of toxicity.

In a large community-based open-label trial, 30 days of treatment with entacapone added to levodopa

---

TABLE 42-4

Distribution of Responses on the Investigator's Global Evaluation of the Patient at Baseline and at Week 24*.

	VERY POORLY	POORLY	RATHER POORLY	NOT WELL, NOT POORLY	RATHER WELL	WELL	VERY WELL
Baseline							
Placebo	1	2	11	42	32	13	1
Entacapone	0	3	14	35	29	18	4
Week 24							
Placebo	1	7	28	30	26	7	3
Entacapone	1	4	9	30	33	14	2

*The investigator was asked to rate how the patient had been doing in terms of his or her PD during the week preceding the visit.
Source: From Parkinson's Study Group (20). With permission.

resulted in reduced frequency of levodopa administration and significant improvements in overall QOL (26). Nearly 20% of patients reported depression at baseline, but that incidence was reduced by 40% after just 30 days. Patients who were no longer depressed at study completion achieved the greatest improvement in quality-of-life scores (27).

Patients with Nonfluctuating Parkinson's Disease   One double-blind placebo controlled trial of entacapone failed to show any difference in motor function although some effect was noted in QOL measures (28).

For patient convenience, a new triple combination tablet (Stalevo) has been developed that contains 12.5 mg carbidopa/50 mg levodopa/200 mg entacapone (Stalevo 50), 25 mg carbidopa/100 mg levodopa/200 mg/entacapone (Stalevo 100), or 37.5 mg carbidopa/150 mg levodopa/200 mg entacapone (Stalevo 150). The indications for these formulations are the same as those for entacapone (i.e., for patients experiencing wearing off with carbidopa/levodopa).

Dosage and Administration   Entacapone should be given 200 mg with each dose of levodopa up to a total daily entacapone dose of 1600 mg.

SAFETY OF COMT INHIBITORS

Management of Dopaminergic Adverse Events

Both tolcapone and entacapone have the potential to increase dopaminergic adverse events in patients receiving levodopa. The most frequent adverse events associated with COMT inhibitors (those occurring in > 5% of treated patients) have been dopaminergic in nature, including peak-dose dyskinesias, nausea, or hallucinations. These have been mild, and reducing levodopa dose when tolcapone or entacapone is administered tends to minimize their occurrence (9, 11, 12, 22). Short-term studies have shown that administration of COMT inhibitors is safe and well tolerated in patients with PD (9, 29). In clinical trials of tolcapone, the majority of patients required a decrease in their daily levodopa dose if that dose initially was above 600 mg or if they had moderate or severe dyskinesias before beginning tolcapone treatment (11). In those patients who required a levodopa dose reduction, the average reduction in daily dosage was 30%.

Management of Nondopaminergic Adverse Events

Nondopaminergic adverse events such as diarrhea, headache, increased sweating, and abdominal pain have been observed. Diarrhea is the most frequent reason given for patients' withdrawing from the long-term tolcapone trials

(11, 15). However, Waters and colleagues reported that in 92% to 95% of patients, diarrhea abated or was mild enough that patients continued tolcapone on a long-term basis (15). With tolcapone, severe diarrhea affects approximately 5% to 10% of patients. Furthermore, almost all cases of severe diarrhea developed during the first 3 months of treatment. Approximately one-half of patients who experienced diarrhea elected to discontinue treatment with tolcapone. After 3 months, the incidence of diarrhea was equivalent to that in the placebo-treated patients. Thereafter, all patients tolerated tolcapone extremely well (12). If a patient does not develop diarrhea in the first 6 months, it is unlikely to occur. Entacapone has also been associated with hypotension and constipation, but the incidence of diarrhea (5%) and gastrointestinal cramping has been relatively low (20). The diarrhea can be severe. Nearly all patients who develop this problem will redevelop it if rechallenged with the drug.

Between 6 and 12 weeks after the start of tolcapone treatment, some patients had increased levels of alanine aminotransferase (ALT) and aspartate aminotransferase (AST) (> 3 times the upper limit of normal); this was observed in 3% receiving 200 mg tid and 1% receiving 100 mg tid. Within 2 to 4 weeks of discontinuing treatment, both AST and ALT levels tended to return to normal without any other hepatic adverse effects (12, 15). In patients who continued treatment, liver enzyme abnormalities resolved spontaneously without sequelae (15). Six patients were withdrawn from the studies because of elevated transaminases (11, 12, 15).

As of October 1998, 3 deaths from acute fulminant hepatic failure had been reported in association with the use of tolcapone. The occurrence of tolcapone-associated fatal hepatotoxicity led to marked restrictions in its use, and several countries withdrew tolcapone from their markets. In the United States, a "black box" warning was used by the FDA with restrictions on the use of tolcapone. These restrictions included using tolcapone only when patients' motor fluctuations no longer responded to other PD medications, using it only for a short period of time to be certain that there was efficacy, and implementing very frequent monitoring with liver function tests (LFTs). Patients were also required to sign a consent form prior to their use of the drug.

Postmarketing surveillance seems to indicate that hepatotoxicity due to tolcapone is a rare idiosyncratic drug reaction. This has led the FDA to issue new guidelines for the use of tolcapone.

The new labeling (2006) states that serum SGPT/ALT and SGOT/AST levels should be determined at baseline as well as every 2 to 4 weeks for the first 6 months of therapy. Further, periodic monitoring is recommended at intervals deemed clinically relevant after the first 6 months of therapy. Tolcapone should be discontinued if ALT or AST levels exceed twice the upper limit of normal. The consent form has been replaced by a much less onerous patient acknowledgment form (www.Tasmar.com). Since the introduction of liver monitoring, no new deaths have been reported with tolcapone. Patients should also be advised of the need for self-monitoring for the signs of liver failure. As the dose is increased from 100 to 200 mg tid, the monitoring should be repeated as if the patient had just been initiated. Because of the potential for rhabdomyolysis, it is recommended that this drug not be used in patients with severe dyskinesia. If it is necessary to discontinue tolcapone, it should be done with care, since sudden withdrawal may lead to worsening of PD, hyperpyrexia, or confusion (a neuroleptic malignant–like) syndrome (2). Entacapone has not been associated with liver toxicity. It has been approved by the FDA for use in fluctuating PD patients without the requirement of liver function monitoring. COMT inhibitors can change the color of the patients urine to bright yellow or orange. This is not a cause for alarm, but patients should be informed of this possibility.

Safety When Used with Selegiline Tolcapone has been shown to be effective and tolerable when used with selegiline and levodopa (29, 30).

DIFFERENCES BETWEEN TOLCAPONE AND ENTACAPONE

Both tolcapone and entacapone are peripheral inhibitors of COMT; however, several important distinctions need to be made between the two drugs.

Pharmacokinetics

Differences between the two drugs can be attributed to differences in their pharmacokinetic profiles (Table 42-5) (8). Both are rapidly absorbed and exhibit linear pharmacokinetics up to a dose of 200 mg (8). Since only a small

amount of tolcapone is lost during first-pass metabolism in the liver, the absolute bioavailability of tolcapone after oral administration is 70%. This is significantly higher than the bioavailability of entacapone (35%), which is rapidly metabolized in the liver. Entacapone has a greater volume of distribution than tolcapone and is metabolized rapidly, whereas tolcapone becomes protein-bound. Therefore entacapone is cleared more rapidly from the body than tolcapone (8).

Tolcapone and entacapone have similar half-lives (2.1 vs. 0.6 hours and 3.4 vs. 2.7 hours). Tolcapone is active in both the periphery and, in animal studies, in the brain, whereas entacapone inhibits only peripheral COMT activity. However, central COMT inhibition with tolcapone has not been proven to occur in humans (31), and any possible clinical advantage of central activity is not known.

Factor and others compared the results of 2 separate simultaneous long-term open-label extension studies, one for tolcapone and the other for entacapone (32). The inclusion/exclusion criteria were similar. Data were collected prospectively at 6, 12, 24, and 36 months. Efficacy measures included the UPDRS total score, subscores, items 32 (duration of dyskinesia) and 39 (duration of "off" time), and levodopa dose. The 2 groups were compared using a Mann-Whitney U test for change from baseline and analysis of variance. Tolerability was defined as the ability of patients to maintain therapy and was compared using a Kaplan-Meier analysis. Eleven patients enrolled in the entacapone study and 14 in the tolcapone study. The tolcapone group had more severe disease, with significantly higher UPDRS motor scores, duration of "off," and levodopa dose requirement. Tolcapone was more effective in lowering UPDRS motor and complication subscores, duration of "off" time, and levodopa doses. UPDRS motor scores and change in levodopa dose in the tolcapone group remained below baseline level for 36 months; however, they were above baseline in the entacapone group from 6 months on. Tolerability was the same for both treatments. Tolcapone appeared to have greater and longer efficacy with regard to motor symptoms, "off" time, and change in levodopa requirements than entacapone. The authors concluded that tolcapone continues to have a place in the treatment of advanced PD.

Switch Study

A second study evaluated tolcapone vs. entacapone in a "switch over" study of advanced PD (33). Forty patients were initially treated for 3 to 7 months with tolcapone as adjunctive therapy to levodopa until the drug was discontinued due to side effects (increase in liver enzymes, orthostasis, hypotension, diarrhea) or mandatory indications of the European drug authority. After tolcapone discontinuation, levodopa dosage was adjusted for 3 to 6 months, followed by a 3-month trial of entacapone.

TABLE 42-5

Pharmacokinetic Parameters of Entacapone and Tolcapone After Administration of 200 mg*

	TOLCAPONE	ENTACAPONE
Cmax (ug/mL)	6.3 ± 2.9	1.8 ± 0.8
Tmax (h)	1.8 ± 1.3	0.7 ± 0.2
AUC (h*ug/mL)	18.5 ± 5.2	1.6 ± 0.3
Half-life (h)	2.1 ± 0.6	3.4 ± 2.7

*Values are mean ± SD.
Source: From Jorga (8). With permission.

During tolcapone treatment, "off" time was decreased 16%, compared with 7% during entacapone treatment. "On" time was increased 15% ($P < .05$) with tolcapone, compared with 8% with entacapone. Although the results suggest that tolcapone is a more effective drug for treating motor complications in PD, the data may have been confounded by natural disease progression.

Dosing Regimens

The recommended dosing regimens are significantly different for tolcapone and entacapone. The schedule for tolcapone is 100 or 200 mg tid at 6-hour intervals. Entacapone 200 mg is administered simultaneously with each dose of levodopa (19).

Use With Different Formulations of Levodopa

Jorga and colleagues have demonstrated that adjunctive treatment with tolcapone potentiates the clinical effects of levodopa irrespective of the levodopa/carbidopa formulation (34). The results were obtained for all of the following formulations of levodopa/carbidopa after coadministration with tolcapone 200 mg: 100 mg/10 mg; 100 mg/25 mg; 200 mg/20 mg; 200 mg/50 mg; 250 mg/25 mg (IR); and 200 mg/50 mg (CR) (33). Comparable effects have been observed when tolcapone was administered with both single- and multiple-dose regimens (35).

The effects of entacapone combined with levodopa/carbidopa differ from those of tolcapone in combination with levodopa/carbidopa. In a study by Ahtila and colleagues, normal volunteers were treated simultaneously with entacapone (200 mg) and CR levodopa/carbidopa (36). Although entacapone extended the time that levodopa remained within the therapeutic range, the effect on levodopa bioavailability was less with the CR formulation than had been demonstrated previously with standard levodopa.

PATIENT SELECTION CRITERIA

COMT inhibitors are likely to play an important role in the long-term management of patients with PD. Therefore it is important to identify those patients who will be most responsive to this therapy.

Patients Residing Alone or in Nursing Homes

Because they may reduce or eliminate the need for other adjunctive therapies such as selegiline, amantadine, anticholinergic agents, and dopamine agonists, COMT inhibitors should be beneficial not only to those elderly PD patients living alone but also to PD patients living in nursing homes. COMT inhibitors, by extending the duration of action of each dose of levodopa, reduce the total number of daily levodopa doses that need to be administered to each patient (11, 21).

In many elderly patients, there are concerns about cognitive dysfunction with dopamine agonists (6, 37). Hallucinations and delusions are commonly assumed to complicate advanced PD when dopaminergic drug treatment has been given for an extended period and a high dosage is required to control motor symptoms. However, Graham and colleagues found that these behavioral problems were more prevalent among PD patients when a direct-acting dopamine receptor agonist was prescribed concomitantly with levodopa therapy regardless of age at onset of PD, stage of the disease, "on" motor disability, cognitive function, or dosage of levodopa (29).

If problems arise with cognition, physicians can reduce and/or eliminate anticholinergic agents, amantadine, selegiline, and dopamine agonists. The COMT inhibitors can be substituted if the motor fluctuations become troublesome.

CONCLUSION

Unique among the adjunctive therapies for PD, COMT inhibitors extend and enhance the duration and action of levodopa. COMT inhibitors increase "on" time, reduce "off" time, improve the patient's ability to perform ADL, increase motor function scores on UPDRS subscales, and may reduce the dosage of levodopa needed.

Unlike dopamine agonists, COMT inhibitors have an effect on levodopa pharmacokinetics after the first dose. If dopaminergic side effects occur with COMT inhibitors, the dose of levodopa can be reduced. COMT inhibitors do not require titration for optimal effect. COMT inhibitors are an option in the treatment of PD in patients with fluctuating motor responses.

References

1. LeWitt PA. Treatment strategies for extension of levodopa effect. *Neurol Clin* 1992; 10:511–527.
2. Kurth MC, Adler CH. COMT inhibition: A new treatment strategy for Parkinson's disease. *Neurology* 1998; 50:S3–S14.
3. Mouradian MM, Heuser IJ, Baronti F, et al. Modification of central dopaminergic mechanisms by continuous levodopa therapy for advanced Parkinson's disease. *Ann Neurol* 1990; 27:18–23.
4. Block G, Liss C, Reines S, et al. Comparison of immediate-release and controlled-release carbidopa/levodopa in Parkinson's disease. *Eur Neurol* 1997; 37:23–27.
5. Chase TN. Levodopa therapy: Consequences of the nonphysiologic replacement of dopamine. *Neurology* 1998; 50(Suppl):S17–S25.
6. Waters CH. Managing the late complications of Parkinson's disease. *Neurology* 1997; 49(Suppl 1):S49–S57.
7. Juncos JL. Levodopa: Pharmacology, pharmacokinetics, and pharmacodynamics. *Neurol Clin* 1992; 10:487–509.
8. Jorga KM. COMT inhibitors: Pharmacokinetics and pharmacodynamic comparisons. *Clin Neuropharmacol* 1998; 21:S9–S16.

9. Kurth MC, Adler CH, Saint Hilaire M-H, et al. Tolcapone improves motor function and reduces levodopa requirement in patients with Parkinson's disease experiencing motor fluctuations: A multicenter, double-blind, randomized, placebo-controlled trial. *Neurology* 1997; 48:81–87.

10. Welsh MD, Ved N, Waters CH. Psychosocial adjustment and illness impact in Parkinson's disease patients before and after treatment with tolcapone (Tasmar). Mov Disord 2000; 15:497–502.

11. Rajput AH, Martin W, Saint Hilaire M-H, et al. Tolcapone improves motor function in Parkinsonian patients with the "wearing-off" phenomenon: A double-blind, placebo-controlled, multicenter trial. *Neurology* 1997; 49:1066–1071.

12. Baas H, Beiske AG, Ghika J, et al. COMT inhibition with tolcapone reduces "wearing-off" phenomenon and levodopa requirements in fluctuating Parkinsonian patients. *J Neurol Neurosurg Psychiatry* 1997; 63:421–428.

13. Adler CH, Singer C, O'Brien C et al. Randomized, placebo-controlled study of tolcapone in patients with fluctuating Parkinson's disease treated with levodopa carbidopa. *Arch Neurol* 1998; 55:1089–1095.

14. Agid Y, Destee A, Durif F, et al. Tolcapone, bromocriptine, and Parkinson's disease. *Lancet* 1997; 350:712–713.

15. Waters CH, Kurth M, Bailey P, et al. Tolcapone in stable Parkinson's disease: Efficacy and safety of long term treatment. *Neurology* 1997; 49:665–671.

16. Dupont E, Burgunder J-M, Findley L, et al. Tolcapone added to levodopa in stable Parkinsonian patients: A double-blind, placebo-controlled study. *Mov Disord* 1997; 12:928–934.

17. Ruottinen HM, Rinne UK. A double-blind pharmacokinetic and clinical dose-response study of entacapone as an adjuvant to levodopa therapy in advanced Parkinson's disease. *Clin Neuropharmacol* 1996; 19:283–296.

18. Ruottinen HM, Rinne UK. Entacapone prolongs levodopa response in a one-month double-blind study in parkinsonian patients with levodopa-related fluctuations. *J Neurol Neurosurg Psychiatry* 1996; 6:36–40.

19. Kaakkola S, Teravainen H, Ahtila S, et al. Effect of entacapone, a COMT inhibitor, on clinical disability and levodopa metabolism in parkinsonian patients. *Neurology* 1994; 44:77–80.

20. Nutt JG, Woodward WR, Beckner RM, et al. Effect of peripheral catechol-O-methyltransferase inhibition on the pharmacokinetics and pharmacodynamics of levodopa in parkinsonian patients. *Neurology* 1994; 44:913–919.

21. Parkinson Study Group. Entacapone improves motor fluctuations in levodopa treated Parkinson's disease patients. *Ann Neurol* 1997; 42:747–755.

22. Rinne UK, Larsen JP, Siden A, et al. Entacapone enhances the response to levodopa in parkinsonian patients with motor fluctuations. *Neurology* 1998; 51:1309–1314.

23. Poewe WH, Deuschl G, Gordin A, et al. Celomen Study Group. Efficacy and safety of entacapone in Parkinson's disease patients with suboptimal levodopa response: A 6-month randomized placebo-controlled double-blind study in Germany and Austria (Celomen study). *Acta Neurol Scand* 2002; 105:245–255.

24. Brooks DJ, Sagar H, UK-Irish Entacapone Study Group. Entacapone is beneficial in both fluctuating and non-fluctuating patients with Parkinson's disease: A randomised, placebo controlled, double blind, six month study. *J Neurol Neurosurg Psychiatry* 2003; 74:1071–1079.

25. Myllyla VV, Kultalahti ER, Haapaniemi H, et al. FILOMEN Study Group. Twelve-month safety of entacapone in patients with Parkinson's disease. *Eur J Neurol* 2001: 8:53–60.

26. Hubble JP, Schumock GT, Markowitz J, Gutterman EM. Entacapone and quality of life in patients with Parkinson's disease: Results of the Response Initiative Program. *Neurol Rev* 2000; Oct(Suppl):11–16.

27. Hubble JP, Schumock GT, Markowitz J, Gutterman EM. Entacapone and feelings of depression in patients with Parkinson's disease. *Neurol Rev* 2000; Oct(Suppl): 17–20.

28. Olanow CW, Kiebertz K, Stern M, et al for the US01 Study team. Double-blind, placebo-controlled study of entacapone in levodopa-treated patients with stable Parkinson's disease. *Arch Neurol* 2004; 61:1563–1568.

29. Davis TL, Roznoski M, Burns RS. Acute effects of COMT inhibition on LEVODOPA pharmacokinetics in patients treated with carbidopa and selegiline. *Clin Neuropharmacol* 1995; 18:333–337.

30. Hauser R, Molho E, Shale H, et al. A pilot evaluation of the tolerability, safety, and efficacy of tolcapone alone and in combination with oral selegiline in untreated Parkinson's disease patients: Tolcapone De Novo Study Group. *Mov Disord* 1998; 13:643–647.

31. Roberts JW, Cora-Locatelli G, et al. Catechol-O-methyltransferase inhibitor tolcapone prolongs levodopa/carbidopa action in Parkinsonian patients. *Neurology* 1994; 44:2685–2688.

32. Factor SA, Molho ES, Feustel PJ, et al. Long-term comparative experience with tolcapone and entacapone in advanced Parkinson's disease. *Clin Neuropharmacol* 2001; 24:295–299.

33. Onofrj, M, Thomas, A, Iacono, D, et al. Switch-over from tolcapone to entacapone in severe Parkinson's disease patients. *Eur Neurol* 2001; 46:11–16.

34. Jorga K, Fotteler B, Sedek G, et al. The effect of tolcapone on levodopa pharmacokinetics is independent of levodopa/carbidopa formulation. *J Neurol* 1998; 245:223–230.

35. Jorga K, Dingemanase J, Fotteler B, et al. Pharmacokinetics-pharmacodynamics of a novel COMT inhibitor during multiple dosing regimens (abstract). *Clin Pharmacol Ther* 1993; 53(Suppl 2):II–40.

36. Ahtila S, Kaakkola S, Gordin A, et al. Effect of entacapone, a COMT inhibitor, on the pharmacokinetics and metabolism of levodopa after administration of controlled-release levodopa-carbidopa in volunteers. *Clin Neuropharmacol* 1995; 18:46–57.

37. Graham J, Grünewald R, Sagar H. Hallucinosis in idiopathic Parkinson's disease. *J Neurol Neurosurg Psychiatry* 1997; 63:434–441.

43 Excitatory Amino Acid Antagonists

James G. Greene

Despite the considerable advances in dopaminergic therapy for Parkinson's disease (PD), there remain significant personal and societal burdens associated with the disease from physical, emotional, and financial perspectives. There is no doubt that dopamine-centered therapy will remain the mainstay of symptomatic treatment for the foreseeable future; however, significant limitations of dopaminergic drugs continue to exist. These include inadequate or incomplete symptom control, intolerable side effects, and long-term complications (motor fluctuations and dyskinesias). As such, identification of other pharmacologic modalities for the symptomatic and neuroprotective treatment of PD is a priority.

Excitatory amino acid (EAA) antagonists have been thought for almost 20 years to have potential impact on the treatment of PD (1, 2). First-generation antagonists were "broad-spectrum" in that they affected multiple receptor types in essentially every brain region. This led to significant side effects that made EAA antagonist therapy intolerable. Conversely, drugs that had minimal side effects were ineffective symptomatically.

Extensive investigation into the role that EAAs play in normal and parkinsonian basal ganglia neurotransmission has led to the development and recognition of new compounds that modulate EAA function (3–5). A greater understanding of how EAAs affect the generation of parkinsonism, complications of dopaminergic therapy,

and degeneration of dopamine neurons has uncovered new and promising EAA agents and ways to use them effectively to potentially treat patients with PD (6–9).

EXCITATORY AMINO ACID NEUROTRANSMISSION

Excitatory amino acid neurotransmitters are the most prominent excitatory transmitters in the mammalian central nervous system (CNS), and a variety of amino acids, including glutamate and aspartate excite CNS neurons in vivo and in vitro. In addition to being abundant and critical for intermediary cellular metabolism, glutamate is thought to be the primary excitatory amino acid neurotransmitter in humans. Multiple putative glutamatergic pathways have been identified in the mammalian brain, including thalamocortical, corticocortical, corticostriatal, and extrapyramidal circuits (1).

As with most classic neurotransmitters, glutamate is specifically concentrated into synaptic vesicles in nerve terminals (10, 11), released during depolarization in a calcium-dependent manner (12), and inactivated by reuptake (13). However, unlike classic transmitters, glutamate uptake by glial cells is significant. Within glia, glutamate is transaminated by glutamine synthetase to form glutamine, which diffuses into nerve terminals and is converted back to glutamate by mitochondrial glutaminase (14, 15). In this way, glutamate is recycled from nerve terminal to glial cell and back to nerve terminal.

Glutamate acts on 2 broad categories of receptors, each with many subtypes. Ion channel glutamate receptors are termed *ionotropic* and G protein–coupled glutamate receptors are termed *metabotropic*. Ionotropic receptors are further divided into subtypes named for the agonists that stimulate them: N-methyl-D-aspartate (NMDA), α-amino-3-hydroxy-5-methyl-4-isoxzazole-propionic acid (AMPA), and kainate (KA). Excitatory postsynaptic potentials resulting from glutamate stimulation can generally be resolved into components contributed by multiple receptor subtypes (8).

AMPA receptors are primary mediators of fast excitatory neurotransmission. Most of these receptors exclusively transduce sodium, but some endogenous AMPA receptors, in a subunit–dependent manner, conduct calcium (16, 17). Kainate receptors mediate a slower component of excitatory postsynaptic transmission and are also involved in modulation of both excitatory and inhibitory neurotransmission (18). NMDA receptors have a very high calcium conductance and are activated (and deactivated) quite slowly. These differences have significant functional consequences. For example, the complicated pharmacodynamics of the NMDA receptor allow it to subserve several integrative neuronal functions, such as coincidence detection and synaptic plasticity (3, 8).

All ionotropic glutamate receptors are made up of combinations of subunits; AMPA receptors are thought to be tetrameric complexes. At present, there are 4 cloned AMPA receptor subunits (GluR1–4), each with at least 2 splice variants (8). The pharmacology, physiology, and anatomic distribution of individual subunits are distinct; it is therefore hypothesized that there are a great many unique endogenous AMPA receptors. In vitro, subunits can come together in either a homomeric (all the same subunit) or heteromeric (2 different subunits) combination to form functional channels. Whether the same is true in the brain and if there are limited or preferred combinations in vivo is not known.

In general, AMPA receptors are rapidly activated and desensitized by glutamate. Most AMPA receptors transduce sodium; however, AMPA receptors lacking the GluR2 subunit also have a high calcium conductance (16, 17). Regulation of GluR2 subunit expression is complex and not based solely on brain region or neuron type. GluR2 protein expression may be up- or downregulated in different disease states, after activation of certain postsynaptic receptors, or during plastic synaptic events, such as long-term potentiation (LTP) (19–21). As such, rapid calcium conductance associated with AMPA receptor activation can be controlled on a minute-to-minute basis in an individual neuron. Subunits also undergo significant posttranslational modifications by phosphorylation,

glycosylation, and proteolysis as well as interactions with other cellular proteins, all of which may affect receptor function and response to drugs (8, 22, 23). This "real time" alteration in receptor subunit expression and function obviously has significant consequences for the study of AMPA antagonists as therapeutic agents.

Five different kainate receptor subunits (GluR5–7, KA1–2) have been cloned, and each has several splice variants. GluR5–7 subunits can form homomeric receptors, but KA1–2 subunits only form functional receptor complexes in heteromeric combination with GluR5, 6, or 7 (18). Individual kainate receptors appear to be tetrameric, but the ratio of specific subunits is unknown. Kainate receptors can be located either pre- or postsynaptically on either excitatory or inhibitory neurons. This places them spatially in a unique position to modulate balance of inhibitory and excitatory neurotransmission in multiple brain regions. There are several endogenous modulators of kainate receptor function, including protons, zinc, and polyamines (24).

Like AMPA and kainate receptors, endogenous NMDA receptors are composed of several different subunits (NMDAR1, NMDAR2A–D, NMDAR3A–B), the regional expression patterns and posttranslational modifications of which result in a myriad of possible endogenous NMDA receptors with slightly different properties (3, 8, 25).

The NMDA receptor has binding sites for glutamate and glycine, both of which must be occupied for receptor activation to occur (26, 27). It also has several other modulatory sites, which include binding sites for zinc, protons, polyamines, and a site modulated by oxidation-reduction (8). As an example of the potential consequence of modulatory site function, protons inhibit receptor activation such that when extracellular pH is low (e.g., during ischemia or intense neuronal activity), NMDA receptors are less likely to open (28, 29).

The NMDA receptor ion channel is voltage-gated as well as ligand-gated (30). At resting membrane potential, the ion channel is blocked by extracellular magnesium, which prevents ion transduction even when agonist is bound to the receptor. Since this magnesium blockade is voltage-dependent, postsynaptic depolarization facilitates NMDA receptor activation. As a result, the NMDA receptor is activated only under conditions of coincident agonist binding and postsynaptic depolarization. This quality is vitally important for the physiologic functions of the NMDA receptor, such as learning and memory, and also for the induction of NMDA receptor–mediated toxicity (31, 32).

Unlike most AMPA and kainate channels, the NMDA receptor ion channel has a very high calcium conductance (33, 34), and calcium is thought to be the primary mediator of both the physiologic and toxic properties of the NMDA receptor.

TABLE 43-1
Metabotropic Glutamate Receptor Subtypes

GROUP	MEMBERS	SECOND MESSENGER	PUTATIVE FUNCTIONS
I	mGluR1 mGluR5	Stimulate PLC, PLA, and AC Modulate K$^+$ and Ca^{2+} channels	Postsynaptic excitation Modulate synaptic plasticity Modulate ionotropic receptors
II	mGluR2 mGluR3	Inhibit AC Modulate Ca^{2+} channels	Regulate glutamate release Regulate GABA release
III	mGluR4 mGluR6 mGluR7 mGluR8	Inhibit AC Modulate K$^+$ and Ca^{2+} channels	Regulate transmitter release Regulate postsynaptic excitability

PLC, phospholipase C; PLA, phospholipase A; AC, adenylate cylclase.

In contrast to ionotropic glutamate receptors, metabotropic glutamate receptors are G protein–coupled receptors linked to cellular second-messenger systems and are single proteins containing 7 membrane-spanning domains (35). Thus far, 8 metabotropic receptors have been cloned and designated mGluR1 through mGluR8; all have different, sometimes overlapping anatomic distributions (36). Metabotropic receptors have been categorized into 3 groups based on gene sequence, pharmacology, and second-messenger systems (Table 43-1). Group I mGluRs are primarily postsynaptic in a perisynaptic localization; group II mGluRs are located both pre- and postsynaptically; and group III mGluRs are predominantly presynaptic. Presynaptic mGluRs respond to glutamate on both glutamatergic and GABAergic terminals, thus modulating both inhibitory and excitatory neurotransmission (6, 35).

Depending on the cell and receptor subtype, metabotropic receptors may be linked through G proteins to multiple different second-messenger systems. Group I mGluRs exert most of their action through phospholipase C activation, liberating inositol triphosphate and diacylglycerol to release calcium from intracellular stores. They may also activate phospholipase A to liberate arachidonic acid or adenylate cyclase so as to increase cAMP production. Group II and III receptors inhibit adenylate cyclase. All 3 groups of metabotropic receptors modulate activity of cation channels through specific G proteins. Furthermore, metabotropic receptors may modulate activity of various tyrosine kinases in the neuron (35). Through these mechanisms, mGluR activation modulates ionotropic glutamate receptor function, suggesting significant cross talk between the two broad categories of glutamate receptors (37, 38).

Excitotoxicity

Glutamate neurotransmission is a paradox in that it is vital for essentially all excitatory synaptic transmission in the CNS, but excessive stimulation of glutamate receptors is toxic to neurons. This phenomenon, known as *excitotoxicity*, has been intensely studied and implicated as a potential pathogenic factor in a number of neurologic diseases, including PD. The ability of an agonist to stimulate its glutamate receptor correlates well with its propensity to induce neurodegeneration, and excitotoxicity can be prevented by glutamate antagonists; both indicate that it is truly a receptor-mediated event (39,40). All subtypes of glutamate receptors can mediate excitotoxic events (41–43).

Obviously, under normal circumstances, neurons are able to resist the potential toxicity associated with glutamate receptor activation. In fact, even high levels of extracellular glutamate are minimally toxic to neurons in vivo. However, neurons under metabolic stress, for instance hypoxia, are exquisitely sensitive to excitotoxicity. The mechanism of this enhanced susceptibility is thought, at least in part, to be related to impaired mitochondrial function. This results in diminished mitochondrial calcium buffering, less ATP production, and diminished ability to maintain neuronal membrane potential. Considering its voltage-dependent properties and large calcium conductance, the NMDA receptor is thought to play a key role linking energetic compromise to excitotoxic damage (44–46). Given the hypothesis that mitochondrial dysfunction may play a role in the pathogenesis of PD, these mechanisms of neurodegeneration may be particularly relevant in PD (see Chapter 30).

EXCITATORY AMINO ACIDS IN THE BASAL GANGLIA

Several extrapyramidal pathways employ glutamate as their primary neurotransmitter. The majority of cortical inputs into the basal ganglia are glutamatergic, including projections from cortical neurons to the caudate and putamen (STR), substantia nigra pars compacta (SNc), subthalamic nucleus (STN), and thalamus. Ascending glutamatergic projections from the pedunculopontine nucleus (PPN) innervate the internal globus pallidus (GPi) and the substantia nigra pars reticulata (SNR). The STN is the origin of a very important set of glutamatergic efferents to the GPi and external globus pallidus (GPe), SNR, and SNc. A highly simplified schematic drawing of this circuitry is presented in Figure 43-1. The STN plays a central role in regulating basal ganglia output to the thalamus (47, 48). From the available evidence, it is clear that there are numerous glutamatergic projections to the SNc, raising the possibility on a purely anatomic basis that excitotoxicity may be involved in damage to dopamine neurons in PD.

Glutamate receptors known to be expressed either pre- or postsynaptically in different regions of the basal ganglia are also shown in Figure 43-1 (3, 6, 49, 50). Although this is by no means an exhaustive list, it gives an idea of the potential complex interplay between different glutamate receptor subtypes located at basal ganglia synapses. Furthermore, anatomic variability in subunit expression coupled with the systems circuitry inherent in the basal ganglia means that, if possible, targeting specific receptors at specific synapses would be the ideal approach to glutamatergic pharmacotherapy for PD.

As an example of the potential for interplay between different glutamatergic and nonglutamatergic systems in the basal ganglia, schematic synapses onto a GABAergic projection neuron from the GPi are depicted in Figure 43-2. GPi neurons express many different AMPA and kainate receptor subunits, and NMDA receptors in these neurons are thought tocomprise predominantly of NR1 and NR2A or D subunits (3, 50). AMPA and NMDA receptors are thought to be postsynaptic, while kainate receptors are present both pre-and postsynaptically. At least mGluR1–5 are expressed as well; group I receptors are pre- and postsynaptic at excitatory synapses, as well as presynaptic at inhibitory synapses. There is also a significant number of extrasynaptic group I mGluRs. In addition, mGluR2–4 are present on glutamatergic inputs to the GPi (6, 50).

Functional Changes of Excitatory Transmission by Parkinson's Disease

The functional architecture of the basal ganglia has been an interesting and productive area of investigation for many years, culminating in the use of functional neurosurgical techniques for the management of PD (47, 51). Detailed descriptions of this functional anatomy are presented in Chapter 22, and models for the circuitry of the basal ganglia are constantly being refined. An overly simplistic model is described here merely to highlight the potential importance of excitatory amino acids in this circuitry and potential avenues for therapeutic glutamatergic intervention. Only the motor circuit is discussed.

Cortical excitatory inputs are filtered through the striatum to the basal ganglia output nuclei, the SNR, and the GPi. The output nuclei project to the motor thalamus (ventral anterior and ventrolateral nuclei), which closes the loop with an excitatory projection back to the cortex. GABAergic striatal projection neurons can be subdivided into 2 groups. Those expressing D1 dopamine receptors and using dynorphin and substance P as cotransmitters give rise to a direct projection to the GPi and SNR. Striatal projection neurons expressing D2 receptors and using enkephalin as a cotransmitter project indirectly to the output nuclei through the GABAergic GPe and glutamatergic STN. This model predicts that excitation of both pathways results in decreased inhibitory output from the basal ganglia, directly by striatal GABAergic inhibition, and indirectly by minimizing excitatory glutamate input from the STN. In this model, glutamate mediates neurotransmission at several critical points.

Using this model as a framework, the basic functional alterations occurring in this circuit in PD are relatively straightforward. There is a certain amount of subtlety to the interpretation of the circuit changes, including critical changes in firing patterns, which are not focused on here but are discussed in Chapter 22 (47). The primary cause of motor symptoms in PD is loss of dopaminergic innervation of the striatum (Figure 43-3). This results in decreased activity of D1-expressing (direct) striatal projection neurons and increased activity of D2-expressing (indirect) striatal projection neurons. Enhanced indirect pathway activity results in greater inhibition of GPe neurons. Since GPe neurons are themselves inhibitory, the result is less inhibition of excitatory glutamatergic STN neurons, leaving the STN neurons overactive in the parkinsonian state. This has been confirmed in animal studies showing increased mitochondrial activity, increased glucose utilization, and increased firing rates in the STN (52–54). Dramatic benefits seen with deep brain stimulation and ablative surgery in the STN confirm this hypothesis in PD patients (51, 55).

Overly active glutamate neurons from the STN project prominently to the SNR and GPi. This increased excitatory drive, coupled with reduced inhibition from underactive direct-pathway striatal neurons, contributes to a substantial increase in thalamic inhibition from the basal ganglia, causing less thalamic feedback to the cortex. These changes are coupled with abnormally enhanced

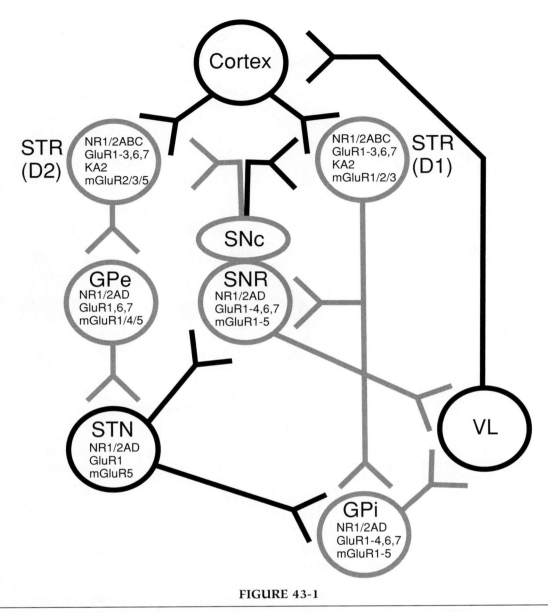

FIGURE 43-1

Schematic drawing of major circuitry of the basal ganglia. Excitatory pathways are depicted in black; inhibitory pathways are depicted in gray. Selected glutamate receptor subunits known to be expressed in a region, either pre- or postsynaptically, are listed (see text). Abbreviations: STR (D2), striatum (indirect D2 receptor expressing pathway); STR (D1), striatum (direct D1 receptor–expressing pathway); GPe, external globus pallidus; GPi, internal globus pallidus; STN, subthalamic nucleus; SNc, substantia nigra pars compacta; SNR, substantia nigra pars reticulata; VL, ventrolateral nucleus of the thalamus.

glutamatergic drive onto intrinsic striatal neurons by corticostriatal afferents as a direct result of striatal dopamine depletion (56, 57). Thus, loss of dopamine innervation to the striatum causes a profound alteration in the circuitry of the basal ganglia, in which glutamate plays a central role. Taking advantage of this therapeutically will require clever application of pharmacologic and physiologic techniques but may prove to be rewarding for PD therapy. It would seem—since the major glutamatergic

pathways to and in the basal ganglia (corticostriatal and subthalamic) are overactive—that blockade of glutamate neurotransmission would be a preferred strategy for PD treatment. This is likely true, but it pays to remember the other abundant pathways using glutamate as a transmitter, including basal ganglia pathways, may be unchanged or even hypoactive in PD, such as the pedunculopontine inputs and thalamic projections to cortex. These may also have significant implications for treatment and

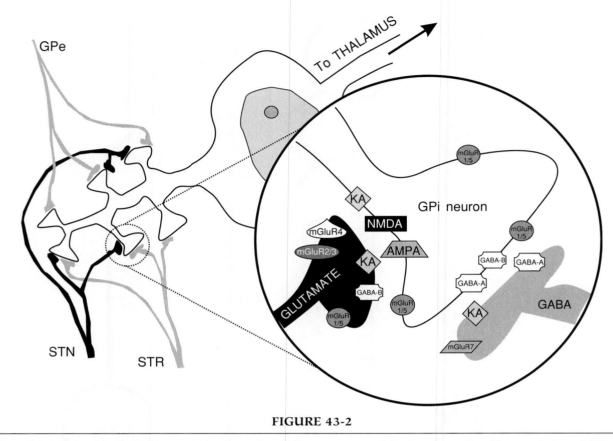

FIGURE 43-2

Cartoon of a GPi neuron, depicting synaptic inputs that influence output of the basal ganglia . Blowup: Spine of GPi neuron diagramming variety and localizations of glutamate receptors. Note pre-, post-, and extrasynaptic localization of receptors at both excitatory glutamatergic and inhibitory GABAergic synapses.

treatment-related side effects of glutamate antagonists. This issue will continue to benefit from detailed investigations into basal ganglia circuits.

Another complicating factor is the pathophysiologic response to increased glutamatergic stimulation. In animals and PD patients, STN hyperactivity causes downregulation of glutamate receptors in the areas to which it projects. Studies have demonstrated decreased AMPA and NMDA receptors in SNR in rats and decreased NMDA receptors in GPi in patients (53, 58), but data examining striatal glutamate receptors in PD are unclear at present (3). Evaluation of other types of glutamate receptors in PD has been inconclusive.

Circuitry alteration, receptor anatomy, and pharmacologic and biophysical properties of specific glutamate receptors suggest some potential rational methods for interfering with abnormal glutamate neurotransmission in PD. For instance, AMPA receptor blockade, based on the receptors' postsynaptic localization in output nuclei and rapid kinetics, could be effective at ameliorating PD symptoms by blunting the effects of an overactive STN,

but the reliance of other brain regions on fast excitatory transmission may be limiting with regard to the side-effect profile. In addition, rapid desensitization of AMPA receptors may make them a relatively fleeting target and hence effective for only short durations.

NMDA receptor blockade may be an effective therapy for motor symptoms, but the integrative properties of the receptor and its involvement in synaptic plasticity may make it a more appropriate target for interfering with the development of dyskinesias. Kainate receptors, given their unique locations (pre- and postsynaptic on inhibitory and excitatory terminals), may make an effective target for modulation of inhibitory-excitatory balance in the basal ganglia with potentially fewer side effects. Finally, mGluRs—given their multiple second-messenger systems, diverse but distinctive localizations, and modulatory effects on ionotropic receptors—also provide an attractive yet complex target for pharmacotherapy. For any of these strategies, mechanisms to antagonize glutamate transmission in a use-dependent manner would be an ideal way to provide more specific targeting of the overactive glutamate

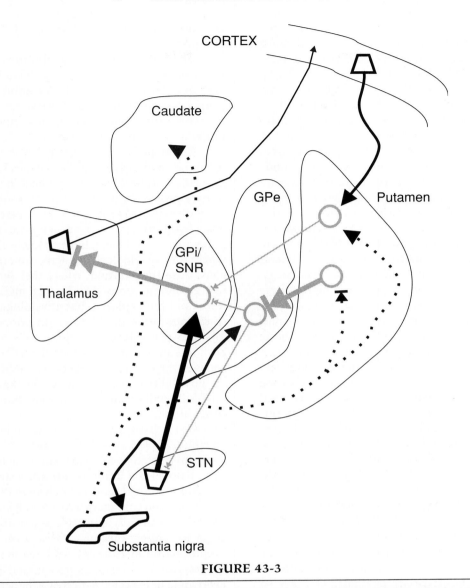

FIGURE 43-3

Simplified drawing of changes in the circuitry of the basal ganglia in PD. Loss of dopamine input to the striatum (caudate and putamen) results in decreased inhibition of GPi/SNR via both the direct and indirect pathways. The overactive glutamatergic STN plays a central role. The result is excessive inhibition of thalamic feedback to the cortex by the basal ganglia output nuclei. See text and Figure 43-1 for abbreviations.

pathways in the basal ganglia, thus widening the therapeutic window for antiglutamatergic treatment.

EXCITATORY AMINO ACID ANTAGONISTS AS THERAPY FOR PARKINSON'S DISEASE

This section is not intended as a comprehensive review of the effect of every glutamatergic drug that has been evaluated in animal model systems of PD. Early attempts, including those involving compounds with some human experience (discussed below), are cited, but the section focuses instead

on several categories of targeted pharmacologic interventions mentioned in the previous section. Mechanisms to decrease glutamatergic transmission in relevant areas of the basal ganglia, possibly by postsynaptic receptor antagonism but also by stimulating or antagonizing presynaptic receptors, are the focus of this discussion.

Animal Studies

Several AMPA receptor antagonists have shown efficacy in animal models of PD. Systemic administration of the selective AMPA antagonist NBQX (6-nitro-7-

sulfamoyl-benzo(f)quinoxaline-2,3-dione) has no anti-parkinsonian effect when given alone but significantly augments benefit when coadministered with L-dopa in rats and monkeys (59). Human experience with AMPA antagonists is primarily limited to stroke where there was significant morbidity due to global CNS effects (60).

NMDA antagonists have intriguing potential for therapy of PD, particularly because several NMDA antagonists have use-dependent properties. This means that they effectively block the NMDA receptor only under conditions of significant neuronal activity or excessive receptor activation. For example, uncompetitive NMDA receptor channel blockers have access to the NMDA receptor cation channel only when the channel is open, meaning that they are effective only in regions where NMDA receptors are activated. Initial experience with NMDA channel blockers such as MK-801 and phencyclidine were negative because these compounds have a very high affinity for the NMDA receptor and thus caused an essentially irreversible blockade (8). Conversely, low-affinity channel blockers have much faster kinetics and are much more likely to be released from the receptor, making their blockade reversible. As such, only neurons with high levels of NMDA receptor activation will experience strong blockade of the receptor, which would seem to be ideal for PD, where excessive activation of the glutamatergic STN causes high levels of NMDA receptor activation in the output nuclei. In fact, lower-affinity channel blockers, such as remacemide, are effective antiparkinsonian agents in animal models, including 6-hydroxydopamine-lesioned rats and MPTP-lesioned monkeys (61, 62).

Another method whereby one might take advantage of use-dependent blockade of NMDA receptors involves proton modulation of NMDA receptor function. Extracellular protons inhibit NMDA receptor activation, and this mechanism is active at physiologic pH (8). Additionally, there are dramatic changes to extracellular pH related to neuronal activity, such that regions with high synaptic activity have lower pH (63, 64). This suggests that there is a negative feedback loop between neuronal activity and NMDA receptors in an attempt to prevent pathologic NMDA receptor activation (29, 65). Most importantly, pH modulation of NMDA receptors has significant effects not only on receptor activation but also on the receptors' response to other agents. For example, protons enhance the affinity of the NMDA receptor for the polyamine channel blocker ifenprodil (5). This raises the possibility that agents like ifenprodil might have antiparkinsonian effects with minimal side effects because they block NMDA receptors in active areas with minimal blockade in areas that have normal activity. In fact, ifenprodil has significant antiparkinsonian effects in rats and nonhuman primates (66, 67). Other agents are currently being developed to take advantage of

this use-dependent mechanism of NMDA receptor antagonism.

The understanding of metabotropic glutamate receptor physiology and pharmacology has advanced considerably over the past 5 years. Delineation of the activation properties, anatomy, and selective drugs has increased the repertoire of pharmacotherapy aimed at modulation of glutamate neurotransmission (4, 6).

Compounds targeting group I mGluRs have been studied in rodent models of PD. The mGluR5 antagonist MPEP [2-methyl-6-(phenlethenyl)-pyridine] increases movement in parkinsonian rats when given chronically (68, 69). A related analog (MTEP) can have similar effects (70). The exact basal ganglia localization for the action of mGluR5 antagonists is not clear, but it is likely either in the STN, where they would decrease activation of glutamate neurons, or in the striatum, where they would inhibit cholinergic interneurons (68, 71, 72). mGluR1 antagonists have not been explored, but physiologic studies provide some interesting possibilities. In normal animals, only mGluR5 is involved in exciting STN neurons, whereas both mGluR1 and 5 stimulate the STN in parkinsonian rodents; the situation is reversed in SNR (73). This raises the possibility that concomitant blockade of both group I mGluRs will be more efficacious than the blockade of either alone.

Group II mGluRs are also altered in states of chronic dopamine depletion (74). Thus, although group II antagonism can be effective in situations of acute parkinsonism (e.g., haloperidol administration), it appears to be less effective in animal models of chronic PD (75–78).

Conn and colleagues have recently proposed group III mGluRs, specifically mGluR4, as a particularly tempting target for antiparkinsonian therapy (4, 6, 79). mGluR4 receptor activation reduces GABAergic inhibition in the GPe by presynaptic action on indirect striatal afferents (80, 81). This would be expected to decrease the activity of STN neurons in parkinsonian animals. In fact, the group III agonist L-AP4 (L-2-amino-4-phosphono-butanoate) has significant antiparkinsonian effects, to the point where it is nearly as efficacious as L-dopa (80, 82). The selective allosteric mGluR4 modulator PHCCC [N-phenyl-7-(hydroxylimino) cyclopropa[b]chromen-1a-carboxamide] also has potent antiparkinsonian effects in rodents by decreasing the activity of the STR-GPe synapse (83, 84).

Neuroprotection by Glutamate Antagonism in Models of Parkinson's Disease   As suggested above, glutamate may be involved not only in symptom generation in PD but also in pathogenesis. It has been hypothesized that glutamate receptor stimulation in the SNc contributes to dopamine neuron degeneration. The finding that the glutamatergic STN projects to SNc and is overactive in PD has further suggested a role for glutamate antagonists in preventing PD progression. Two notable early studies indicated that glutamate receptor antagonists could protect dopamine neurons from MPP$^+$ toxicity in rodents and primates (85, 86). More recently, ablation and pharmacologic inactivation of the STN in rodents made parkinsonian has been shown to limit dopamine neuron death (87–89). In one study of PD patients, STN deep brain stimulation did not slow disease progression, but the effects of DBS on STN output and the potential complexities of neuroprotection in advanced disease have not been completely explored (90). Despite this result, it is possible that glutamate antagonism may "kill two birds with one stone" in PD—namely, being both a symptomatic and a disease-modifying therapy.

Caveats Preclinical studies such as these have provided proof of principle that glutamate antagonism is a potentially effective therapeutic strategy for PD, but they have also pointed toward more effective approaches to that antagonism. Early preclinical and clinical trials were plagued by troubles with poor efficacy and significant side effects. One potential cause of that was the use of direct agonists and antagonists. Recent advances in understanding *allosteric* modulation of antagonism of glutamate receptors may have provided a way around these problems. An allosteric potentiator or antagonist binds to a different site on the receptor to modulate the effects of endogenous glutamate. This preserves the pulsatile, activity-dependent nature of receptor stimulation while minimizing side effects from excessive receptor activation (or blockade) or desensitization (or upregulation). The classic example is benzodiazepine-induced modulatory potentiation of GABAA receptor function. This technique is beginning to be taken advantage of by allosteric potentiation of mGluR4 receptors and modulation of proton-induced inhibition of NMDA receptors (4, 5). This suggests that optimism is warranted for the second generation of clinical trials of glutamate receptor modulation in PD.

Human Experience

Clinical experience with antagonists to glutamate neurotransmission is limited. Amantadine and memantine, commonly used in the treatment of PD, are NMDA receptor channel blockers, among other things, and can be effective against symptoms (91–93). Coadministration of amantadine with L-dopa can diminish the severity and duration of dyskinesias significantly while still maintaining the same level of antiparkinsonian effect (94–96). Dextromethophan is also a weak NMDA channel blocker that has been tried with little success for primary symptoms of PD but may be effective at ameliorating dyskineisas (97–100). Complicating these results is the fact that these agents have other effects, including anticholinergic properties, that make interpretation of the results difficult.

The more selective NMDA channel blocker remacemide has met with modest success in 2 clinical trials in PD patients. Although it showed no effect when administered alone, when given concomitantly with dopaminergic therapy, remacemide simultaneously reduced "off" time and improved motor symptoms without increasing side effects, such as dyskinesias or hallucinations (101, 102).

Ifenprodil, a noncompetitive NMDA antagonist that acts at the polyamine site, was not effective against PD symptoms in a pilot study (103). Since this agent binds to the amino terminus of the NR2B subunit, in retrospect it is perhaps not surprising that it had no effect, since NR2B is not highly expressed in human basal ganglia output nuclei (see above). However, NR2B is highly expressed in striatum, perhaps accounting for success of this agent in animals and warranting further exploration of dosing paradigms in humans (66).

The anticonvulsant agent lamotrigine is thought to inhibit glutamate release from nerve terminals; however, controlled clinical trials have revealed no beneficial effect of this agent in patients (104, 105).

Although none of these clinical trials hit the metaphoric "home run," there are some encouraging signs. In particular, the modest therapeutic effect and minimal side effects of the low-affinity NMDA channel blockers is reason for optimism. This type of drug is exactly what one might have predicted to be effective in treating parkinsonism. These agents target overactive glutamate pathways because they have access to block NMDA receptor channels only if the channel is already open. In addition, low-affinity binding is a sign of rapid kinetics, allowing the compound's blockade to be rapidly reversible and thus limiting detrimental effects. Further exploration of allosteric modulators of glutamate neurotransmission may well provide more useful clinical compounds for the treatment of PD.

CONCLUSION

As understanding of the circuitry of the basal ganglia and its perturbation in PD has advanced, it has become clear that excessive activation of the glutamatergic STN plays a central role in the generation of the motor symptoms of PD. Although functional neurosurgery can address this issue, it is not available to every patient and does not address other glutamatergic abnormalities in the basal ganglia that are relevant to symptom production. As understanding of the glutamatergic influences in the basal ganglia advances, targeted, effective pharmacotherapy directed against excitatory glutamate neurotransmission will become a useful option for the treatment of PD.

References

1. Blandini F, Porter RH, Greenamyre JT. Glutamate and Parkinson's disease. *Mol Neurobiol* 1996; 12(1):73–94.

2. Greenamyre JT, O'Brien CF. N-methyl-D-aspartate antagonists in the treatment of Parkinson's disease. *Arch Neurol* 1991; 48(9):977–981.

3. Hallett PJ, Standaert DG. Rationale for and use of NMDA receptor antagonists in Parkinson's disease. *Pharmacol Ther* 2004; 102(2):155–174.

4. Marino MJ, Conn PJ. Glutamate-based therapeutic approaches: Allosteric modulators of metabotropic glutamate receptors. *Curr Opin Pharmacol* 2006; 6(1):98–102.

5. Mott DD, Doherty JJ, Zhang S, et al. Phenylethanolamines inhibit NMDA receptors by enhancing proton inhibition. *Nat Neurosci* 1998; 1(8):659–667.

6. Conn PJ, Battaglia G, Marino MJ, Nicoletti F. Metabotropic glutamate receptors in the basal ganglia motor circuit. *Nat Rev Neurosci* 2005; 6(10):787–798.

7. Paquet M, Tremblay M, Soghomonian JJ, Smith Y. AMPA and NMDA glutamate receptor subunits in midbrain dopaminergic neurons in the squirrel monkey: An immunohistochemical and in situ hybridization study. *J Neurosci* 1997; 17(4):1377–1396.

8. Dingledine R, Borges K, Bowie D, Traynelis SF. The glutamate receptor ion channels. *Pharmacol Rev* 1999; 51(1):7–61.

9. Wu SS, Frucht SJ. Treatment of Parkinson's disease : What's on the horizon? *CNS Drugs* 2005; 19(9):723–743.

10. Naito S, Ueda T. Characterization of glutamate uptake into synaptic vesicles. *J Neurochem* 1985; 44(1):99–109.

11. Naito S, Ueda T. Adenosine triphosphate–dependent uptake of glutamate into protein I–associated synaptic vesicles. *J Biol Chem* 1983; 258(2):696–699.

12. McMahon HT, Nicholls DG. Transmitter glutamate release from isolated nerve terminals: Evidence for biphasic release and triggering by localized Ca2+. *J Neurochem* 1991; 56(1):86–94.

13. O'Shea RD. Roles and regulation of glutamate transporters in the central nervous system. *Clin Exp Pharmacol Physiol* 2002; 29(11):1018–1023.

14. Schousboe A. Role of astrocytes in the maintenance and modulation of glutamatergic and GABAergic neurotransmission. *Neurochem Res* 2003; 28(2):347–352.

15. Nicklas WJ. Glia-neuronal inter-relationships in the metabolism of excitatory amino acids. In: Roberts PJ, Bradford HF (eds). *Excitatory Amino Acids*. London: MacMillan, 1986:57–66.

16. Brorson JR, Bleakman D, Chard PS, Miller RJ. Calcium directly permeates kainate/alpha-amino-3-hydroxy-5-methyl-4-isoxazolepropionic acid receptors in cultured cerebellar Purkinje neurons. *Mol Pharmacol* 1992; 41(4):603–608.

17. Burnashev N, Khodorova A, Jonas P, et al. Calcium-permeable AMPA-kainate receptors in fusiform cerebellar glial cells. *Science* 1992; 256(5063):1566–1570.

18. Huettner JE. Kainate receptors and synaptic transmission. *Prog Neurobiol* 2003; 70(5):387–407.

19. Huang Y, Myers SJ, Dingledine R. Transcriptional repression by REST: Recruitment of Sin3A and histone deacetylase to neuronal genes. *Nat Neurosci* 1999; 2(10):867–872.

20. Myers SJ, Dingledine R, Borges K. Genetic regulation of glutamate receptor ion channels. *Annu Rev Pharmacol Toxicol* 1999; 39:221–241.

21. Jayakar SS, Dikshit M. AMPA receptor regulation mechanisms: Future target for safer neuroprotective drugs. *Int J Neurosci* 2004; 114(6):695–734.

22. Wang JQ, Arora A, Yang L, et al. Phosphorylation of AMPA receptors: Mechanisms and synaptic plasticity. *Mol Neurobiol* 2005; 32(3):237–249.

23. Duprat F, Daw M, Lim W, et al. GluR2 protein-protein interactions and the regulation of AMPA receptors during synaptic plasticity. *Philos Trans R Soc Lond B Biol Sci* 2003; 358(1432):715–720.

24. Mott DD, Washburn MS, Zhang S, Dingledine RJ. Subunit-dependent modulation of kainate receptors by extracellular protons and polyamines. *J Neurosci* 2003; 23(4):1179–1188.

25. Chatterton JE, Awobuluyi M, Premkumar LS, et al. Excitatory glycine receptors containing the NR3 family of NMDA receptor subunits. *Nature* 2002; 415(6873):793–798.

26. Kleckner NW, Dingledine R. Requirement for glycine in activation of NMDA-receptors expressed in *Xenopus* oocytes. Science 1988; 241(4867):835–837.

27. Johnson JW, Ascher P. Glycine potentiates the NMDA response in cultured mouse brain neurons. *Nature* 1987; 325(6104):529–531.

28. Traynelis SF, Cull-Candy SG. Proton inhibition of N-methyl-D-aspartate receptors in cerebellar neurons. *Nature* 1990; 345(6273):347–350.

29. Velisek L, Dreier JP, Stanton PK, et al. Lowering of extracellular pH suppresses low-Mg(2+)-induced seizures in combined entorhinal cortex-hippocampal slices. *Exp Brain Res* 1994; 101(1):44–52.

30. Nowak L, Bregestovski P, Ascher P, et al. Magnesium gates glutamate-activated channels in mouse central neurones. *Nature* 1984; 307(5950):462–465.

31. Riedel G, Platt B, Micheau J. Glutamate receptor function in learning and memory. *Behav Brain Res* 2003; 140(1–2):1–47.

32. Albin RL, Greenamyre JT. Alternative excitotoxic hypotheses. *Neurology* 1992; 42(4):733–738.

33. Dingledine R. N-methyl aspartate activates voltage-dependent calcium conductance in rat hippocampal pyramidal cells. *J Physiol* 1983; 343:385–405.

34. MacDermott AB, Mayer ML, Westbrook GL, et al. NMDA-receptor activation increases cytoplasmic calcium concentration in cultured spinal cord neurones. *Nature* 1986; 321(6069):519–522.

35. Balazs R, Bridges RJ, Cotman CW. Metabotropic glutamate receptors. In: Cotman CW (ed). *Excitatory Amino Acid Transmission in Health and Disease*. New York: Oxford University Press, 2006:115–166.

36. Pin JP, Acher F. The metabotropic glutamate receptors: Structure, activation mechanism and pharmacology. *Curr Drug Target CNS Neurol Disord* 2002; 1(3):297–317.

37. Marino MJ, Conn JP. Modulation of the basal ganglia by metabotropic glutamate receptors: Potential for novel therapeutics. *Curr Drug Target CNS Neurol Disord* 2002; 1(3):239–250.

38. Marino MJ, Conn PJ. Direct and indirect modulation of the N-methyl D-aspartate receptor. *Curr Drug Target CNS Neurol Disord* 2002; 1(1):1–16.

39. Olney JW, Adamo NJ, Ratner A. Monosodium glutamate effects. *Science* 1971; 172(980):294.

40. Sattler R, Tymianski M. Molecular mechanisms of glutamate receptor–mediated excitotoxic neuronal cell death. *Mol Neurobiol* 2001; 24(1–3):107–129.

41. Wang Q, Yu S, Simonyi A, et al. Kainic acid–mediated excitotoxicity as a model for neurodegeneration. *Mol Neurobiol* 2005; 31(1–3):3–16.

42. Petrovic M, Horak M, Sedlacek M, Vyklicky L Jr. Physiology and pathology of NMDA receptors. *Prague Med Rep* 2005; 106(2):113–136.

43. Greene JG, Porter RH, Eller RV, Greenamyre JT. Inhibition of succinate dehydrogenase by malonic acid produces an "excitotoxic" lesion in rat striatum. *J Neurochem* 1993; 61(3):1151–1154.

44. Greene JG. Mitochondrial function and NMDA receptor activation: Mechanisms of secondary excitotoxicity. *Funct Neurol* 1999; 14(3):171–184.

45. Olney JW. Excitotoxicity, apoptosis and neuropsychiatric disorders. *Curr Opin Pharmacol* 2003; 3(1):101–109.

46. Greene JG, Greenamyre JT. Bioenergetics and glutamate excitotoxicity. *Prog Neurobiol* 1996; 48(6):613–634.

47. Wichmann T, DeLong MR. Pathophysiology of Parkinson's disease: The MPTP primate model of the human disorder. *Ann N Y Acad Sci* 2003; 991:199–213.

48. Wichmann T, Bergman H, DeLong MR. The primate subthalamic nucleus: I. Functional properties in intact animals. *J Neurophysiol* 1994; 72(2):494–506.

49. Jin XT, Pare JF, Raju DV, Smith Y. Localization and function of pre- and postsynaptic kainate receptors in the rat globus pallidus. *Eur J Neurosci* 2006; 23(2):374–386.

50. Smith Y, Charara A, Paquet M, et al. Ionotropic and metabotropic GABA and glutamate receptors in primate basal ganglia. *J Chem Neuroanat* 2001; 22(1–2):13–42.

51. Boucai L, Cerquetti D, Merello M. Functional surgery for Parkinson's disease treatment: A structured analysis of a decade of published literature. *Br J Neurosurg* 2004; 18(3):213–222.

52. Bergman H, Wichmann T, Karmon B, DeLong MR. The primate subthalamic nucleus. II. Neuronal activity in the MPTP model of parkinsonism. *J Neurophysiol* 1994; 72(2):507–520.

53. Porter RH, Greene JG, Higgins DS, Jr, Greenamyre JT. Polysynaptic regulation of glutamate receptors and mitochondrial enzyme activities in the basal ganglia of rats with unilateral dopamine depletion. *J Neurosci* 1994; 14(11 Pt 2):7192–7199.

54. Mitchell IJ, Clarke CE, Boyce S, et al. Neural mechanisms underlying parkinsonian symptoms based upon regional uptake of 2-deoxyglucose in monkeys exposed to 1-methyl-4-phenyl-1,2,3,6-tetrahydropyridine. *Neuroscience* 1989; 32(1):213–226.

55. Bergman H, Wichmann T, DeLong MR. Reversal of experimental parkinsonism by lesions of the subthalamic nucleus. *Science* 1990; 249(4975):1436–1438.

56. Calabresi P, Mercuri NB, Sancesario G, Bernardi G. Electrophysiology of dopamine-denervated striatal neurons. Implications for Parkinson's disease. *Brain* 1993; 116(Pt 2):433–452.

57. Picconi B, Centonze D, Rossi S, et al. Therapeutic doses of L-dopa reverse hypersensitivity of corticostriatal D2-dopamine receptors and glutamatergic overactivity in experimental parkinsonism. *Brain* 2004; 127(Pt 7):1661–1669.

58. Lange KW, Kornhuber J, Riederer P. Dopamine/glutamate interactions in Parkinson's disease. *Neurosci Biobehav Rev* 1997; 21(4):393–400.

59. Klockgether T, Turski L, Honore T, et al. The AMPA receptor antagonist NBQX has antiparkinsonian effects in monoamine-depleted rats and MPTP-treated monkeys. *Ann Neurol* 1991; 30(5):717–723.

60. Walters MR, Kaste M, Lees KR, et al. The AMPA antagonist ZK 200775 in patients with acute ischaemic stroke: A double-blind, multicentre, placebo-controlled safety and tolerability study. *Cerebrovasc Dis* 2005; 20(5):304–309.

61. Greenamyre JT, Eller RV, Zhang Z, et al. Antiparkinsonian effects of remacemide hydrochloride, a glutamate antagonist, in rodent and primate models of Parkinson's disease. *Ann Neurol* 1994; 35(6):655–661.

62. Porter RH, Greenamyre JT. Regional variations in the pharmacology of NMDA receptor channel blockers: Implications for therapeutic potential. *J Neurochem* 1995; 64(2):614–623.

63. Chesler M. The regulation and modulation of pH in the nervous system. *Prog Neurobiol* 1990; 34(5):401–427.

64. Chesler M, Kaila K. Modulation of pH by neuronal activity. *Trends Neurosci* 1992; 15(10):396–402.

65. Tombaugh GC, Sapolsky RM. Evolving concepts about the role of acidosis in ischemic neuropathology. *J Neurochem* 1993; 61(3):793–803.

66. Nash JE, Fox SH, Henry B, et al. Antiparkinsonian actions of ifenprodil in the MPTP-lesioned marmoset model of Parkinson's disease. *Exp Neurol* 2000; 165(1):136–142.

67. Nash JE, Hill MP, Brotchie JM. Antiparkinsonian actions of blockade of NR2B-containing NMDA receptors in the reserpine-treated rat. *Exp Neurol* 1999; 155(1):42–48.

68. Breysse N, Amalric M, Salin P. Metabotropic glutamate 5 receptor blockade alleviates akinesia by normalizing activity of selective basal-ganglia structures in parkinsonian rats. *J Neurosci* 2003; 23(23):8302–8309.

69. Breysse N, Baunez C, Spooren W, et al. Chronic but not acute treatment with a metabotropic glutamate 5 receptor antagonist reverses the akinetic deficits in a rat model of parkinsonism. *J Neurosci* 2002; 22(13):5669–5678.

70. Ossowska K, Konieczny J, Wolfarth S,et al. Blockade of the metabotropic glutamate receptor subtype 5 (mGluR5) produces antiparkinsonian-like effects in rats. *Neuropharmacology* 2001; 41(4):413–420.

71. Oueslati A, Breysse N, Amalric M, et al. Dysfunction of the cortico-basal ganglia-cortical loop in a rat model of early parkinsonism is reversed by metabotropic glutamate receptor 5 antagonism. *Eur J Neurosci* 2005; 22(11):2765–2774.

72. Phillips JM, Lam HA, Ackerson LC, Maidment NT. Blockade of mGluR glutamate receptors in the subthalamic nucleus ameliorates motor asymmetry in an animal model of Parkinson's disease. *Eur J Neurosci* 2006; 23(1):151–160.

73. Marino MJ, Awad-Granko H, Ciombor KJ, Conn PJ. Haloperidol-induced alteration in the physiological actions of group I mGlus in the subthalamic nucleus and the substantia nigra pars reticulata. *Neuropharmacology* 2002; 43(2):147–159.

74. Picconi B, Pisani A, Centonze D, et al. Striatal metabotropic glutamate receptor function following experimental parkinsonism and chronic levodopa treatment. *Brain* 2002; 125(Pt 12):2635–2645.

75. Bradley SR, Marino MJ, Wittmann M, et al. Activation of group II metabotropic glutamate receptors inhibits synaptic excitation of the substantia nigra pars reticulata. *J Neurosci* 2000; 20(9):3085–3094.

76. Konieczny J, Ossowska K, Wolfarth S, Pilc A. LY354740, a group II metabotropic glutamate receptor agonist with potential antiparkinsonian properties in rats. *Naunyn Schmiedebergs Arch Pharmacol* 1998; 358(4):500–502.

77. Dawson L, Chadha A, Megalou M, Duty S. The group II metabotropic glutamate receptor agonist, DCG-IV, alleviates akinesia following intranigral or intraventricular administration in the reserpine-treated rat. *Br J Pharmacol* 2000; 129(3):541–546.

78. Murray TK, Messenger MJ, Ward MA, t al. Evaluation of the mGluR2/3 agonist LY379268 in rodent models of Parkinson's disease. *Pharmacol Biochem Behav* 2002; 73(2):455–466.

79. Marino MJ, Hess JF, Liverton N. Targeting the metabotropic glutamate receptor mGluR4 for the treatment of diseases of the central nervous system. *Curr Top Med Chem* 2005; 5(9):885–895.

80. Valenti O, Marino MJ, Wittmann M, et al. Group III metabotropic glutamate receptor-mediated modulation of the striatopallidal synapse. *J Neurosci* 2003; 23(18):7218–7226.

81. Matsui T, Kita H. Activation of group III metabotropic glutamate receptors presynaptically reduces both GABAergic and glutamatergic transmission in the rat globus pallidus. *Neuroscience* 2003; 122(3):727–737.

82. MacInnes N, Messenger MJ, Duty S. Activation of group III metabotropic glutamate receptors in selected regions of the basal ganglia alleviates akinesia in the reserpine-treated rat. *Br J Pharmacol* 2004; 141(1):15–22.

83. Maj M, Bruno V, Dragic Z, et al. (-)-PHCCC, a positive allosteric modulator of mGluR4: Characterization, mechanism of action, and neuroprotection. *Neuropharmacology* 2003; 45(7):895–906.

84. Marino MJ, Williams DL Jr, O'Brien JA, et al. Allosteric modulation of group III metabotropic glutamate receptor 4: A potential approach to Parkinson's disease treatment. *Proc Natl Acad Sci USA* 2003; 100(23):13668–13673.

85. Turski L, Bressler K, Rettig KJ, et al. Protection of substantia nigra from MPP+ neurotoxicity by N-methyl-D-aspartate antagonists. *Nature* 1991; 349(6308):414–418.

86. Zuddas A, Oberto G, Vaglini F, et al. MK-801 prevents 1-methyl-4-phenyl-1,2,3,6-tetrahydropyridine-induced parkinsonism in primates. *J Neurochem* 1992; 59(2):733–739.

87. Blandini F, Nappi G, Greenamyre JT. Subthalamic infusion of an NMDA antagonist prevents basal ganglia metabolic changes and nigral degeneration in a rodent model of Parkinson's disease. *Ann Neurol* 2001; 49(4):525–529.

88. Piallat B, Benazzouz A, Benabid AL. Subthalamic nucleus lesion in rats prevents dopaminergic nigral neuron degeneration after striatal 6-OHDA injection: Behavioural and immunohistochemical studies. *Eur J Neurosci* 1996; 8(7):1408–1414.

89. Maesawa S, Kaneoke Y, Kajita Y, et al. Long-term stimulation of the subthalamic nucleus in hemiparkinsonian rats: Neuroprotection of dopaminergic neurons. *J Neurosurg* 2004; 100(4):679–687.

90. Hilker R, Portman AT, Voges J, et al. Disease progression continues in patients with advanced Parkinson's disease and effective subthalamic nucleus stimulation. *J Neurol Neurosurg Psychiatry* 2005; 76(9):1217–1221.

91. Merello M, Nouzeilles MI, Cammarota A, Leiguarda R. Effect of memantine (NMDA antagonist) on Parkinson's disease: A double-blind crossover randomized study. *Clin Neuropharmacol* 1999; 22(5):273–276.

92. Muller T, Kuhn W, Quack G, Przuntek H. Intravenous application of amantadine and antiparkinsonian efficacy in parkinsonian patients. *J Neural Transm Suppl* 1995; 46:407–413.

93. Muller T, Kuhn W, Schulte T, Przuntek H. Intravenous amantadine sulphate application improves the performance of complex but not simple motor tasks in patients with Parkinson's disease. *Neurosci Lett* 2003; 339(1):25–28.

94. da Silva-Junior FP, Braga-Neto P, Sueli Monte F, de Bruin VM. Amantadine reduces the duration of levodopa-induced dyskinesia: A randomized, double-blind, placebo-controlled study. *Parkinsonism Relat Disord* 2005; 11(7):449–452.

95. Metman LV, Del Dotto P, LePoole K, et al. Amantadine for levodopa-induced dyskinesias: A 1-year follow-up study. *Arch Neurol* 1999; 56(11):1383–1386.

96. Verhagen Metman L, Del Dotto P, van den Munckhof P, et al. Amantadine as treatment for dyskinesias and motor fluctuations in Parkinson's disease. *Neurology* 1998; 50(5):1323–1326.

97. Bonuccelli U, Del Dotto P, Piccini P, Behge F, Corsini GU, Muratorio A. Dextromethorphan and parkinsonism. Lancet 1992; 340(8810):53.

98. Montastruc JL, Fabre N, Rascol O, et al. N-methyl-D-aspartate (NMDA) antagonist and Parkinson's disease: A pilot study with dextromethorphan. *Mov Disord* 1994; 9(2):242–243.

99. Verhagen Metman L, Blanchet PJ, van den Munckhof P, et al. A trial of dextromethorphan in parkinsonian patients with motor response complications. *Mov Disord* 1998; 13(3):414–417.

100. Verhagen Metman L, Del Dotto P, Natte R, et al. Dextromethorphan improves levodopa-induced dyskinesias in Parkinson's disease. *Neurology* 1998; 51(1):203–206.

101. Shoulson I, Penney J, McDermott M, et al. A randomized, controlled trial of remacemide for motor fluctuations in Parkinson's disease. *Neurology* 2001; 56(4):455–462.

102. A multicenter randomized controlled trial of remacemide hydrochloride as monotherapy for PD. Parkinson Study Group. *Neurology* 2000; 54(8):1583–1588.

103. Montastruc JL, Rascol O, Senard JM, Rascol A. A pilot study of N-methyl-D-aspartate (NMDA) antagonist in Parkinson's disease. *J Neurol Neurosurg Psychiatry* 1992; 55(7):630–631.

104. Shinotoh H, Vingerhoets FJ, Lee CS, et al. Lamotrigine trial in idiopathic parkinsonism: A double-blind, placebo-controlled, crossover study. Neurology 1997; 48(5):1282–1285.

105. Zipp F, Burklin F, Stecker K, et al. Lamotrigine in Parkinson's disease: A double blind study. *J Neural Transm Park Dis Dement Sect* 1995; 10(2–3):199–206.

44 Adenosine A$_{2A}$ Receptor Antagonists

Rukmini Menon
Mark A. Stacy

The mainstay of symptomatic treatment in Parkinson's disease (PD) is restoring dopamine deficiency in the nigrostriatal pathway. Therapeutic strategies are based on increasing dopaminergic activity through (a) dopamine precursors, such as levodopa; (b) dopamine receptor agonists, such as pramipexole or ropinirole; or (c) agents that alter the metabolism of levodopa, such as dopa-decarboxylase and catechol-O-methyltransferase inhibitors or dopamine with monoamine oxidase-b inhibitors. These drugs, while highly effective initially in ameliorating disability, require escalating dosages with disease progression. Because this dopaminergic approach to treating PD symptoms is eventually self-limiting, a newer treatment focus has shifted to compounds that are nondopaminergic or medications with neuroprotective or neurorestorative effects. Selective adenosine A$_{2a}$ receptor antagonists, such as istradefylline, hold promise for symptomatic nondopaminergic benefit as adjunctive medications to levodopa and as neuroprotective agents (1).

MECHANISM OF ACTION

Adenosine is a ubiquitous purine that participates in multiple fundamental functions at the cellular level. While originally recognized for its energy storage capacity in the metabolic pathway as the molecules adenosine triphosphate (ATP) and cyclic adenosine monophosphate (cAMP), receptor chemistry has also found that these molecules influence a wide range of physiologic activity (Table 44-1).

In the central nervous system, adenosine influences sleep and arousal, seizure susceptibility, locomotion, and nociception. In addition, possibly by mediating glutamate release from the subthalamic nucleus, A$_{2A}$ receptor antagonists may play an indirect role in cellular protection.

To date, 4 subtypes of adenosine receptors have been identified: A$_1$, A$_{2A}$, A$_{2B}$, and A$_3$. The A$_1$ and A$_{2A}$ receptors exhibit high affinity for adenosine, while A$_{2b}$ and A$_3$ demonstrate low adenosine affinity. A$_1$ receptors inhibit adenyl cyclase and A$_{2A}$ receptors stimulate adenyl cyclase (2). A$_1$ and A$_{2A}$ receptors also differ in their distribution in the brain, with A$_1$ receptors being expressed throughout the brain while A$_{2A}$ receptors are concentrated in the basal ganglia (3–5). This restricted distribution of A$_{2A}$ receptors may account for the relatively few neurologic side effects seen with A$_{2A}$ receptor antagonists (see Table 44-1).

A$_{2A}$ Receptors and Motor Control

The development of motor symptoms in PD may result from changes in relative activities between the direct and

TABLE 44-1
Adenosine Antagonists Divided by Activity and Potential Compounds for Investigation

	COMPOUND	ACTIVITY
Nonselective adenosine antagonists	Caffeine Theophylline Propentofylline	⇑ Cardiac rate[56]
Adenosine A1 antagonists	1,3-dipropyl-8-cyclopentylxanthine (DPCPX) 8-cyclopentyl-1,3-dimethylxanthine (8-CPT)	⇑ Cardiac rate[56] ⇑ Cerebral perfusion
Adenosine A2 antagonists	Istradefylline 7-(2-phenylethyl)-5-amino-2-(2-furyl)- pyrazolo-[4,3-e]-1,2, 4-triazolo[1,5-c] pyrimidine (SCH 58261) 8-(3-chlorostyryl) caffeine (CSC)	Activates D2 receptors in the indirect pathway
Adenosine A3 antagonists	3-ethyl-5-benzyl-2-methyl-4-phenylethynyl-6- phenyl-1,4-dihydropyridine-3, 5 dicarboxylate (MRS1191)	⇓ Growth rate of human melanoma cells[56]

⇑ = increase, ⇓ = decrease.

indirect pathways in the basal ganglia (6, 7). Loss of equilibrium results from nigral terminal dopamine deficiency, which produces direct (striatonigral) pathway underactivity and indirect (striatopallidal) pathway overactivity. In the direct system, the putamen and caudate receive excitatory input from the pars compacta of the substantia nigra and project inhibitory fibers to the medial globus pallidus and to the pars reticularis of the substantia nigra. The pars reticularis inhibits the ventrolateral nucleus of the thalamus (Figure 44-1). Thus, stimulation of the direct system disinhibits the ventrolateral nucleus of the thalamus, resulting in cortical excitation. In the indirect system, the putamen and caudate receive inhibitory input from the pars compacta of the substantia nigra and project inhibitory fibers to the lateral globus pallidus, which, in turn, inhibits the subthalamic nucleus. The subthalamic nucleus stimulates the medial globus pallidus, resulting in inhibition of the ventrolateral nucleus of the thalamus and cortical inhibition (Table 44-2).

The gamma-aminobutyric acid (GABA) neurons in the direct pathway bear dopamine D1 receptors and contain the peptides substance P and dynorphin. The neurons of the indirect pathway express the dopamine D2 receptors and contain the peptide enkephalin (8). A_{2A} receptors, which are expressed almost exclusively in the basal ganglia, are colocalized with dopamine D2 receptors in the indirect pathway (9–11). In the normal brain, dopamine inhibits D2 receptor and reduces the indirect pathway activity. Given that A_{2A} activation reduces the D2 receptor dopaminergic affinity, an A_{2A} receptor antagonist may increase the action of dopamine on D2 receptors and inhibit the indirect pathway. Thus, by restoring D1/D2 pathway equilibrium, A_{2A} receptor

antagonists may provide symptomatic benefit for the motor symptoms in PD (12–17).

A_{2A} Receptors, Dyskinesias, and Motor Fluctuations

Dyskinesias and motor fluctuations are associated with increasing disease severity, duration of PD, and duration of levodopa treatment. The frequency of levodopa induced dyskinesias (LID) ranges from 20% to 50% in 5 years (18–21). The underlying mechanisms, while poorly understood, are postulated to be due to progressive degeneration of the neurons in the nigrostriatal system with increasing sensitization of the postsynaptic receptors to dopamine.

In PD, the reduction in dopaminergic input into the striatum leads to decreased dynorphin expression in the direct (striatonigral) pathway and increased expression of enkephalin in the indirect (striatopallidal) pathway. Interestingly, while treatment with levodopa reverses the decrease of dynorphin mRNA levels in the striatonigral system, it has no effect on the elevated enkephalin mRNA expression in the striatopallidal system (22, 23). Thus, repeated dosing of levodopa corrects the abnormality in the direct pathway but leaves the abnormality in indirect pathway unchanged, contributing to the development of levodopa-induced dyskinesias and motor fluctuations (24–26).

Studies of rat and nonhuman primate parkinsonism models as well as postmortem human tissue suggest that it is the continued elevation of the mRNA enkephalin expression in the indirect pathway that leads to dyskinesias. Calon et al. found abnormally high levels of preproenkephalin mRNA, the precursor of the peptide

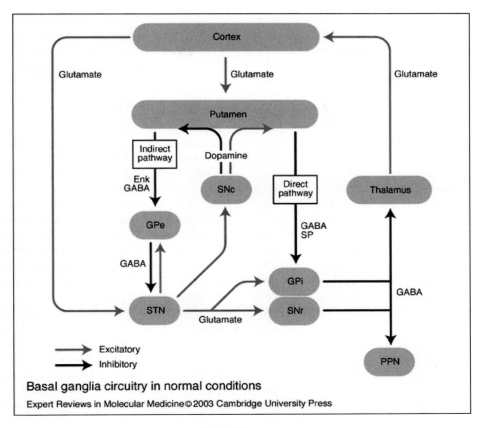

FIGURE 44-1

The schematic divisions in the direct and indirect pathways of the basal ganglia.

dynorphin, in postmortem analysis of striatonigral neurons of patients with PD (27,28). Henry et al. report similar findings in nonhuman MPTP primates with dyskinesias (29). In another nonhuman primate study, Aubert et al. demonstrated that D1 and not D2 receptors were mainly affected by dopamine replacement therapy.

These authors further suggest that dopamine replacement therapy increase both the number and the sensitivity of D1 receptors (30). Perhaps more importantly, given that A$_{2A}$ receptors and D2 receptors are colocalized in the basal ganglia, a number of studies suggest that A$_{2A}$ blockade may attenuate levodopa-associated sensitization of

TABLE 44-2

Neuromodulatory, Anatomic, and Physiologic Differences Between the Direct and Indirect Pathways of the Basal Ganglia

	DIRECT PATHWAY	**INDIRECT PATHWAY**
Neurotransmitter	Dopamine	Dopamine
Neuromodulatory peptides	Substance P, dynorphin	Enkephalin
Anatomic localization	Striatonigral	Striatopallidal
Afferent projection	(+) from SNpc	(−) from SNpc
Efferent projection	(−) to GPi, SNpr	(−) to GPe
Outcome	⇑ Thalamic, cortical activity	⇓ STN, thalamic, cortical activity

(+), excitatory; (−), inhibitory; SNpc, substantia nigra pars compacta; GPi, globus pallidus interna; SNpr, substantia nigra pars reticulata; GPe, globus pallidus externa; STN, subthalamic nucleus; ⇑, increase; ⇓, decrease.

the D2 axis. Bibbiani et al. report that coadministration of an A_{2A} antagonist with apomorphine prevented the development of apomorphine-induced dyskinesias in MPTP-treated monkeys (31). However, when the A_{2A} antagonist was discontinued, these animals gradually developed involuntary movements.

The current hypothesis for A_{2A} blockade preventing dopamine sensitization is based on both presynaptic and postsynaptic mechanisms (26). Presynaptically, A_{2A} receptor activation enhances the release of a variety of neurotransmitters—including dopamine, glutamate, GABA, and acetylcholine—known to stimulate dopaminergic neuron activity (32). Blocking of A_{2A} receptors decreases the sensitivity of striatal neurons to both direct and indirect dopaminergic stimulation. Postsynaptically, A_{2A} receptors modulate striatal and accumbal neurons, and A_{2A} receptor activation leads to suppression of D2 receptor–mediated inhibition of GABA in the globus pallidus (12, 16, 33). This antagonistic relationship between A_{2A}-D2 receptors on a background of loss of dopaminergic input also leads to decreased expression of dynorphin in the striatonigral neurons and increased expression of enkephalin in the striatopallidal neurons. While levodopa increases the expression on dynorphin mRNA, it has no effect on enkephalin expression, and dyskinesias may develop because of this mismatch. A_{2A} receptor blockade reverses the increased expression of enkephalin mRNA. It appears that the administration of levodopa along with an A_{2A} antagonist may simultaneously correct both the decreased dynorphin and increased enkephalin postsynaptically, thus preventing the development of dyskinesias (34–37). There are also data supporting A_{2A} antagonism as a modulator of levodopa-related increased dynorphin expression in PD (36–38).

Nondopamine systems also play a contributory role in the development of dyskinesias. The cortex and thalamus modulate the striatal activity via excitatory glutamatergic projections. These projections are in close interaction with dopamine and A_{2A} receptors. Through the ionotropic N-methyl-D-aspartate (NMDA) and gamma-amino-3 hydroxy-5-methyl-4-isoxazole aspartate (AMPA) receptors as well as metatropic receptors, glutamate stimulates striatal medium spiny neurons. With dopamine depletion, increases in spontaneous glutamate release, terminal size, and synaptic concentrations are seen. Nonphysiologic intermittent dopaminergic stimulation activates signal transduction pathways in the striatum and is thought to cause abnormal phosphorylation of NMDA receptors. This may contribute to the development of dyskinesias in PD patients receiving levodopa. A_{2A} receptors may alter NMDA receptor conductance and phosphorylation (39–41). A_{2A} receptor blockade is thought to attenuate the hyperphosphorylation of NMDA and AMPA receptors in the striatum and thus alleviate dykinesias (31, 42). Therefore A_{2A} receptors, both pre-synaptically and postsynaptically, potentially have a role in the development of dyskinesias and motor fluctuations; A_{2A} receptor blockade may be helpful in preventing development of these motor complications.

A_{2A} Receptors and Neuroprotection

Increasing emphasis has been placed on discovering neuroprotective agents in PD. A_{2A} receptor antagonists, such as istradefylline, have shown some potential in this area. Furthermore, large prospective studies have shown that consumption of coffee on a regular basis decreases the risk of developing PD (43, 44). Caffeine, a nonspecific adenosine receptor antagonist, initially pointed researchers in the direction of the potential neuroprotective effects of A_{2A} receptor antagonism. A_{2A} antagonists have been shown to have neuroprotective effects in the striatonigral system (45) as well as in neuronal populations outside the basal ganglia (46, 47).

The mechanism by which A_{2A} blockade is neuroprotective in the basal ganglia or in other locations in the brain is not well understood. The most likely mechanism involves blocking the release of glutamate. A_{2A} agonists enhance the release of glutamate, an excitatory neurotransmitter that may also be excitotoxic in the setting of increased metabolic demand. A_{2A} antagonists attenuate the release of glutamate and thus reduce neurotoxicity and neuronal cell death (48–51).

EVIDENCE FROM CLINICAL TRIALS

While clinical trials attempting to determine the efficacy of adenosine antagonists have been ongoing since the 1970s, it is only very recently that such trials have been conducted using selective A_{2A} antagonists. Phase 2 clinical trials have been completed using the A_{2A} antagonist istradefylline in advanced PD subjects exhibiting dyskinesias and motor fluctuations. Two trials that were reported almost simultaneously were by Bara-Jimenez et al. (52) and Hauser et al. (53). Both were similar in being small, placebo-controlled, double-blind studies in patients on standard medications who were experiencing motor fluctuations and dyskinesias. Bara-Jimenez et al. studied 15 subjects for a 6-week interval. After a 2-week placebo run-in, the study participants were randomized to active (n = 12) and placebo (n = 3) groups. Subjects received the drug in escalating doses of 40 mg/day for 2 weeks followed by 60 mg/day for 2 weeks. All patients were evaluated at the end of 2, 4, and 6 weeks for change in dyskinesias or motor fluctuations, overall PD severity, and adverse events. While both doses of the study drug failed to show efficacy either alone or in combination with optimal doses of levodopa, the higher dose (60 mg/day) of the drug when given with suboptimal doses of levodopa improved the motor benefits to a level similar to that seen in subjects optimally treated with levodopa, but with fewer dyskinesias. In addition, the duration of action of the optimal levodopa dose was prolonged when given along with the A$_{2A}$ antagonist. There were no major adverse events noted, with nausea being the commonest side effect.

The study reported by Hauser et al. also investigated the benefit of A$_{2A}$ antagonist therapy as an adjunct to standard PD therapy. In this study, 83 subjects were randomized into 3 groups: placebo, low dose, and high dose. All patients continued stable dosages of anti-Parkinson medications during the study. The patients were evaluated every 2 weeks using patient home diaries and in-office evaluations by clinicians as well as being monitored for any side effects. There was a significant decrease in "off" time as documented by patient home diaries (–1.2 hours for the active treatment group, +0.5 hours in the placebo control group) and a trend toward decreased "off" time as evaluated by the clinicians of the study groups in the office setting. Symptomatic benefit was first noted at the eighth week and increased with duration of treatment. Also noted was an increase in "on" time with dyskinesias but without an increase in severity of dyskinesias. There was no difference between the placebo and study groups on the Unified Parkinson's Disease Rating Scale (UPDRS) subset or total scores. The most common side effect was nausea.

Although these initial studies are promising, larger pivotal trials are near completion. The US-005/US-006 Clinical Investigator Group conducted two 12-week placebo-controlled, double blind, randomized, multicenter trials involving 591 Parkinson's patients with wearing off motor responses (54,55). The 591 patients were randomized into placebo, low-dose istradefylline (20 mg/day), and high-dose istradefylline (60 mg/day). The patients were evaluated using patient home diaries and in-office clinician evaluations and were monitored for adverse events at 2-, 4-, 8-, and 12-week intervals. In addition, subjects were required to characterize "on" time with dyskinesias into "on" time with troublesome dyskinesias and "on" time with nontroublesome dyskinesias. As in the previous studies, there was a significant decrease in "off" time (60 mg, 1.4 hours; 40 mg, 1.8 hours, 20 mg, 1.2 hours and placebo, 0.5 hours) and

increase in "on" time with dyskinesias in the study group patients. However, there was no significant difference between the placebo and treatment groups in "on" time with troublesome dyskinesias. There was also an increase in "on" time with nontroublesome dyskinesias noted in the treatment group. Although not reaching clinical significance, an improvement in the UPDRS subscale and total scores in the treatment group when compared to the placebo group was noted. There was no significant difference in adverse events between the two groups, with an increase in nontroublesome dyskinesias being the commonest side effect seen in the treatment group.

CONCLUSIONS

Most therapeutic options for treating PD have been based on strategies to increase dopaminergic activity in the central nervous system. Such treatments, while very effective initially, lead to complications later on due to motor fluctuations and abnormal motor responses. A$_{2A}$ antagonists are drugs that offer an alternative to standard PD therapy. Preclinical testing in animal models and initial clinical studies in PD subjects have been quite encouraging. As more is learned about the pathophysiology of the basal ganglia and, more importantly, the A$_{2A}$ receptor antagonists, perhaps more refined clinical populations will be identified for clinical study. In advanced PD patients with motor complications, adjunctive treatment with an A$_{2A}$ antagonist has shown benefit. Trials to assess the potential for an A$_{2A}$ antagonist to delay the onset of levodopa-related motor complications remain a potentially exciting area of investigation. In addition, assessing the effects of A$_{2A}$ antagonists on sleep, cognition, psychosis, and other nonmotor symptoms that commonly represent a continuing unmet need in PD treatment will be important. Furthermore, the potential for istradefylline monotherapy, in either symptomatic or neuroprotective investigation paradigms, have not been initiated. These trials will be important in determining the full spectrum of potential for the A$_{2A}$ antagonists. Last, given the ubiquitous nature of adenosine, A$_{2A}$ receptors are widely distributed throughout the body, and further research into other potential therapeutic arenas seems warranted.

References

1. Jenner P. Istradefylline, a novel adenosine A$_{2A}$ receptor antagonist, for the treatment of Parkinson's disease. *Exp Opin Invest Drugs* 2005; 14(6):729–738.
2. Fredholm BB, Ap IJ, Jacobson KA, et al. International Union of Pharmacology: XXV. Nomenclature and classification of adenosine receptors. *Pharm Rev* 2001; 53:527–552.
3. Albin RL, Young AB, Penney JB. The functional anatomy of basal ganglia disorders. *Trends Neurosci* 1989; 12:366–375.
4. Wichmann T, Delong MR. Functional neuroanatomy of the basal ganglia in Parkinson's disease. *Adv Neurol* 2003; 91:9–18.
5. Tohyama M, Takatsuji K. *Atlas of Neuroactive Substances and Their Receptors in the Rat.* New York: Oxford University Press, 1998.
6. Blandini F, Nappi G, Tassorelli C, Martignoni E. Functional changes of the basal ganglia circuitry in Parkinson's disease. *Prog Neurobiol* 2000; 62:63–88.
7. Dawson TM, Dawson VL. Molecular pathways of neurodegeneration in Parkinson's disease. *Science* 2003; 302:819–822.
8. Xu K, Bastia E, Schwarzschild M. Therapeutic potential of adenosine A$_{2A}$ receptor antagonists in Parkinson's disease. *Pharm Ther* 2005; 105:267–310.
9. Schiffmann SN, Jacobs O, Vanderhaeghen JJ. Striatal restricted adenosine A$_{2A}$ receptor (RDC8) is expressed by enkephalin but not by substance P neurons: An in situ hybridization histochemistry study. *J Neurochem* 1991; 57:1062–1067.
10. Fink JS, Weaver DR, Rivkees SA, et al. Molecular cloning of the rat A^{2A} receptor: Selective coexpression with D2 dopamine receptors in rat striatum. *Mol Brain Res* 1992; 14:186–195.

11. Schiffmann SN, Libert F, Vassart G, Vanderhaeghen JJ. Distribution of adenosine A$_2$ receptor mRNA in the human brain. *Neuroscience Lett* 1991; 130:177–181.

12. Ferre S, Fuxe K. Dopamine denervation leads to an increase in the intramembrane interaction between adenosine A$_2$ and dopamine D$_2$ receptors in the neostriatum. *Brain Res* 1992; 594:124–130.

13. Ferre S, von Euler G, Johansson B, et al. Stimulation of high-affinity adenosine A$_2$ receptors decreases the affinity of dopamine D2 receptors in the rat striatal membranes. *Proc Natl Acad Sci USA* 1991; 88:7238–7241.

14. Ferre S, O'Connor WT, Fuxe K, Ungerstedt U. The striatopallidal neuron: A main locus for adenosine-dopamine interactions in the brain. *J Neurosci* 1993; 13:5402–5406.

15. Ferre S, O'Connor WT, Snaprud P, et al. Antagonist interaction between adenosine A$_{2A}$ receptors and dopamine D$_2$ receptors in the ventral striopallidal system. Implications for treatment of schizophrenia. *Neuroscience* 1994; 63:765–773.

16. Ferre S, Schwarcz R, Li XM, et al. Chronic haloperidol treatment leads to an increase in intramembrane interaction between adenosine A$_2$ and dopamine D$_2$ receptors in the neostriatum. *Psychopharmacology* 1994; 116:279–284.

17. Fuxe K, Stromberg I, Popoli P, et al. Adenosine receptors and Parkinson's disease. Relevance of antagonistic adenosine and dopamine receptor interactions in the striatum. *Adv Neurol* 2001; 86:345–353.

18. Ahlskog JE, Muenter MD. Frequency of levodopa related dyskinesias and motor fluctuations as estimated from the cumulative literature. *Mov Disord* 2001; 16:448–458.

19. Miyawaki E, Lyons K, Pahwa R, et al. Motor complications of chronic levodopa therapy in Parkinson's disease. *Clin Neuropharm* 1997; 20:523–530.

20. Rajput AH, Fenton ME, Birdi S, et al. Clinical-pathological study of levodopa complications. *Mov Disord* 2002; 17:289–296.

21. Rascol O, Brooks DJ, Korczyn AD, et al. A five year study of the incidence of dyskinesias in patients with early Parkinson's disease who were treated with ropinirole or levodopa. 056 Study group. *N Engl J Med* 2000; 342:1484–1491.

22. Berke J, Paletzki RF, Aronson GJ, et al. A complex program of striatal gene expression induced by dopaminergic stimulation. *J Neurosci* 1998; 18:5301–5310.

23. Gerfen CR. D$_1$ and D$_2$ receptor-regulated gene expression of striatonigral and striatopallidal neurons. *Science* 1990; 250:1429–1432.

24. Lee T, Seeman P, Rajput A, et al. Receptor basis for dopaminergic supersensitivity in Parkinson's disease. *Nature* 1978; 273:150–151.

25. Gerfen CR. Molecular effects of dopamine on striatopallidal pathways. *Trends Neurosci* 1995; 23:S64–S70.

26. Steiner H, Gerfen CR. Dynorphin regulates D$_1$ dopamine receptor–mediated responses in the striatum: Relative contributions of pre- and postsynaptic mechanisms in the dorsal and ventral striatum demonstrated by altered immediate-early gene expression. *J Comp. Neurol* 1996; 376:530–541.

27. Calon F, Dridi M, Hornykiewicz O, et al. Increased adenosine A$_{2A}$ receptors in the brain of Parkinson's disease patients with dyskinesias. *Brain* 2004; 127:1075–1084.

28. Calon F, Birdi S, Hornykiewicz O, et al. Increase of preproenkephalin mRNA levels in the putamen of Parkinson's disease patients with levodopa induced dyskinesias. *J Neuropathol Exp Neurol* 2002; 61(2):186–196.

29. Henry B, Duty S, Fox SH, et al. Increased striatal pre-proenkephalin B expression is associated with dyskinesia in Parkinson's disease. *Exp Neurol* 2003; 183:458–468.

30. Aubert I, Guigoni C, Hakansson K. Increased D$_1$ dopamine receptor signaling in levodopa induced dyskinesia. *Ann Neurol* 2005; 57:17–26.

31. Bibbiani F, Oh JD, Petzer JP, et al. A$_{2A}$ antagonist prevents dopamine agonist induced motor complications in animal models of Parkinson's disease. *Exp Neurol* 2003; 184(1):285–294.

32. Vanderschuren LJ, Kalivas PW. Alterations in dopaminergic and glutamatergic transmission in the induction and expression of behavioral sensitization: A critical review in preclinical studies. *Pyschopharmacology* 2000; 151:99–120.

33. Ferre S, Snaprud P, Fuxe K. Opposing actions of an adenosine A$_2$ receptor agonist and a GTP analogue on the regulation of dopamine D$_2$ receptors in rat neostriatal membranes. *Eur J Pharmacol*. 1993; 244:311–315.

34. Lundblad M, Vaudano E, Cenci MA. Cellular and behavioral effects of the adenosine A$_{2A}$ receptor antagonist KW-6002 in a rat model of L-dopa induced dyskinesia. *J Neurochem* 2003; 84:1398–1410.

35. Chen JF, Xu K, Petzer JP, et al. Neuroprotection by caffeine and A$_{2A}$ adenosine receptor inactivation in a model of Parkinson's disease. *J Neurosci* 2001; 21:RC143.

36. Carta AR, Pinna A, Cauli O, Morelli M. Differential regulation of GAD67, enkephalin and dynorphin mRNAs by chronic intermittent L-dopa and A$_{2A}$ receptor blockade plus L-dopa in dopamine-denervated rats. *Synapse* 2002; 44:166–174.

37. Freduzzi S, Moratalla R, Monopoli A, et al. Persistent behavioral sensitization to chronic L-dopa requires A$_{2A}$ adenosine receptors. *J Neurosci* 2002; 22:1054–1062.

38. Chen JF, Freduzzi S, Bastia E, et al. Adenosine A$_{2A}$ receptors in neuroadaptation to repeated dopaminergic stimulation: Implications for the treatment of dyskinesias in Parkinson's disease. *Neurology* 2003; 61(11 Suppl 6):S74–S81.

39. Koles L, Wirkner K, Illes P. Modulation of ionotropic glutamate receptor channels. *Neurochem Res* 2001; 26:925–932.

40. Wirkner K, Gerevich Z, Krause T, et al. Adenosine A$_{2A}$ receptor induced inhibition of NMDA and GABAA receptor mediated synaptic currents in a subpopulation of rat striatal neurons. *Neuropharmacology* 2004; 46:994–1007.

41. Gerevich Z, Wirkner K, Illes P. Adenosine A$_{2A}$ receptors inhibit the N-methyl-D-aspartate component of excitatory synaptic currents in the rat striatal neurons. *Eur J Pharmacol* 2002; 451:161–164.

42. Chase TN, Bibbiani F, Bara-Jiminez W, et al. Translating A$_{2A}$ antagonist KW6002 from animal models to parkinsonian patients. *Neurology* 2003; 61(11 Suppl 6):S107–S111.

43. Ross GW, Abbott RD, Petrovich H, et al. Association of coffee and caffeine intake with the risk of Parkinson's disease. *JAMA* 2000; 283:2674–2679.

44. Ascherio A, Zhang SM, Hernan MA, et al. Prospective study of caffeine consumption and risk of Parkinson's disease in men and women. *Ann Neurol* 2001; 50:56–63.

45. Fink JS, Kalda A, Ryu H, et al. Genetic and pharmacological inactivation of the adenosine A$_{2A}$ receptor attenuates 3-nitropropionic acid induced striatal damage. *J Neurochem* 2004; 88:538–544.

46. Jones PA, Smith RA, Stone TW. Protection against kainite-induced excitotoxicity by adenosine A$_{2A}$ receptor agonists and antagonists. *Neuroscience* 1998; 85:229–237.

47. Stone TW, Jones PA, Smith RA. Neuroprotection by A$_{2A}$ receptor antagonists. *Drug Dev Res* 2001; 52:323–330.

48. Corsi C, Pinna A, Gianfriddo M, et al. Adenosine A$_{2A}$ receptor antagonism increases striatal glutamate outflow in dopamine-denervated rats. *Eur J Pharmacol* 2003; 464:33–38.

49. Pintor A, Quarta D, Pezzola A, et al. SCH 58261(an adenosine A$_{2A}$ receptor antagonist) reduces, only at low doses, K(+)-evoked glutamate release in the striatum. *Eur J Pharmacol* 2001; 421:177–180.

50. Popoli P, Pintor A, Domenici MR, et al. Blockade of striatal adenosine A$_{2A}$ receptor reduces, through a presynaptic mechanism, quinolinic acid induced excitotoxicity: Possible relevance to neuroprotective interventions in neurodegenerative diseases of the striatum. *J Neurosci* 2002; 22:1967–1975.

51. Marcoli M, Raiteri L, Bonfanti A, et al. Sensitivity to selective adenosine A$_1$ and A$_2$ receptor antagonists of the release of glutamate induced by ischemia in rats. *Neuropharmacology* 2003; 45:201–210.

52. Bara-Jiminez W, Sherzai A, Dimitrova T, et al. Adenosine A$_{2A}$ receptor antagonist treatment of Parkinson's disease. *Neurology* 2003; 61:293–296.

53. Hauser RA, Hubble JP, Truong DD. Randomized trial of the adenosine A$_{2A}$ receptor antagonist istradefylline advanced PD. *Neurology* 2003; 61:297–303.

54. Stacy MA and the 6002-US-005/US-006 Clinical Investigator Group. Istradefylline as adjunctive therapy in patients with advanced Parkinson's disease: A positive safety profile with supporting efficacy. *Mov Disord* 2004; 19(Suppl 9):S215, P605.

55. LeWitt PA and the 6002-US-005/US-006 Clinical Investigator Group. "Off" time reduction from adjunctive use of istradefylline(KW-6002) in levodopa-treated patients with advanced Parkinson's disease. *Mov Disord* 2004; 19(S9):S222, P624.

56. Jacobson KA, Gao ZG. Adenosine receptors as therapeutic targets. *Nat Rev Drug Disc* 2006; 5:247–264.

45 Complementary and Alternative Medicine

Jorge L. Juncos

The term *traditional medicine* refers to practices, substances, and beliefs used to protect and restore health before the advent of "modern medicine." This hand-me-down approach to health maintenance is still cultivated through traditions kept by a loosely knit community of practitioners found in most countries and ethnic groups (1). It is also the common ancestor to both modern medicine and complementary and alternative medicine (CAM). *Complementary and alternative medicine* refers to health interventions and beliefs not yet accepted as correct, appropriate, or consonant with the standards of the dominant group of medical practitioners in a given society (2). However, this terminology began to be rejected a decade ago, after Eisenberg and others pointed out that "the judgmental tone of this definition may inhibit the collaborative inquiry and discourse that is necessary to separate useful from useless practices and techniques" (3). Using National Institutes of Health terminology, CAM is now defined as "healthcare practices outside the realm of conventional medicine that remain to be validated using scientific methods" (4). In other words, once there is sufficient scientific evidence to support the claims of a particular CAM intervention, there is no further need make a distinction between that practice and modern medicine.

From a philosophic standpoint, many of the CAM practices today are based in part on eastern traditions that reject the western duality between mind and body. From an academic standpoint, CAM has also been defined as interventions neither taught widely in medical schools nor available in most hospitals (5). This definition of CAM is also becoming blurred as an increasing number of traditional medical and nursing schools begin to expand their curricula to include CAM teachings (6–8). In addition, an expanding number of hospitals and medical centers firmly grounded in modern medicine have begun to offer "integrative care" which often includes CAM.

Perhaps the biggest difference between CAM and modern medicine is that modern medicine has been more aggressive at embracing the evidenced-based scientific method and the principle of promoting outcomes-based therapies. This is not to say that modern medicine has stopped using interventions that have little to no evidence to support their use. The hope is that, with leadership, time, and money, evidence-based CAM will join forces with modern medicine to promote evidence-based therapies.

CAM and the Health Care Industry

The health care industry has also influenced the evolution of CAM practices in the United States. Under public pressure, and in some cases based on sound business and marketing decisions, many insurers have begun offering coverage for selected CAM practices like acupuncture for pain, nausea induced by chemotherapy, or as an anesthetic. Other offerings include massage therapy and a number of relaxation techniques (9). In academic circles, evidence has begun to accumulate suggesting that some of these practices, particularly those involving health maintenance, may be beneficial and more cost-effective than what modern medicine has to offer (10).

As with everything else in medicine, as information emerges claiming that a particular CAM procedure can be used to treat an illness, practice liability issues become an important consideration (11).

CAM and Regulatory Agencies

In the United States today, millions of adults use some form of CAM therapy to treat a variety of ailments. For instance, it is estimated 15 million American use herbal remedies or high-dose vitamins along with conventional medicines (12). From 1990 to 1997, the use of herbal remedies increased 380% and the use of high-dose vitamins by 130%, incurring an estimated out-of-pocket expenditure of $27 million in the United States (13). In the same period, the utilization of other forms of CAM grew from 25% to 42% (13).

These figures have raised concerns and captured the imagination of public health officials, the U.S. Food and Drug Administration (FDA), the health insurance industry, and practitioners. The sheer volume of unregulated products being used has opened the door to an increasing number of real and sometimes serious issues of drug contamination, toxicity, and adverse drug-drug interactions (14–16). Another danger has been posed by delays in the proper diagnosis and therapy of treatable conditions due to overreliance on practices and agents outside the purview of modern medicine. The FDA has become impatient with manufacturers of nutraceuticals and pharmaceuticals who try to promote the sale their products by disseminating unproven claims regarding their efficacy. Such claims, particularly in regard to the effectiveness of supplements for specific medical conditions, have triggered the FDA's more aggressive oversight.

Conventional drugs must be shown to be safe and effective before they can be marketed for a particular indication. In contrast, over-the-counter dietary supplements used in CAM are regulated under the Dietary Supplement Health and Education Act of 1994. This law removed these ingredients and products from regulatory oversight by the FDA. Therefore, when issues of public safety come up in relation to an unregulated product, to intervene, the FDA has to then demonstrate that the product presents a serious or unreasonable risk under the conditions of use on the label or as commonly consumed.

How does the community of CAM practitioners view these developments? Based on a number of personal communications with various CAM practitioners, they are both intrigued by and skeptical of the interest that academia, government, and the health insurance industry have taken in CAM. They are intrigued by the opportunities that this brings to provide validation for centuries-old practices that have gradually migrated from East to West and to offer services to a wider audience. On the other hand, they are skeptical about the ability of current scientific methods to explain and be fair to practices that in many instances have obscure mechanisms of action. For instance, science has yet to explain the *power of belief,* a force that seems to drive the core of some CAM practices and remains beyond the grasp of neurobiology.

The CAM community is also ambivalent about the interest the federal government has taken in their industry. With the potential for health care coverage for CAM interventions comes increasing oversight by the FDA and the Department of Health and Human Services. The business community, with its sometimes intrusive attempts to regulate costs, will certainly want a say in the utilization of CAM resources as soon as these interventions are offered as options to a health care plan. Considering the sometimes adversarial relationship that modern medicine and business have had in the last few decades (17), the CAM community remains uncertain about adopting the business model of modern medicine.

CAM and Medical Education

The decision to include CAM in mainstream medical school curricula has been driven by various factors, including public pressure and a growing interest and healthy curiosity on the part of both medical school faculty and students. A major tipping point in forcing the leadership of major medical schools to take CAM seriously began with congressional mandates that, from 1991 to 1998, eventually established the National Center for Complementary and Alternative Medicine (NCCAM at www.nccam.nih.gov). NCCAM's mission is to (a) explore complementary and alternative practices in the context of rigorous science, (b) train complementary and alternative medicine researchers, and (c) disseminate authoritative information to the public and professionals. The institute has created opportunities for the funding of many scientific studies seeking answers to a broad range of questions, from possible mechanisms of disease to objective outcomes studies that have helped to distinguish promising CAM interventions. Examples of early funding initiatives include the first controlled study on the use of St. John's wort for major depression and a study of the use of electroacupuncture to treat chemotherapy-induced nausea.

These federal initiatives notwithstanding, it is up to the medical and nursing school leadership and curriculum committees to make final decisions on whether to include the teaching of a particular CAM practices in crowded curricula. By and large these decision have been based on the epidemiologic, clinical, and scientific evidence that a particular practice or substance has been able to accumulate (7, 18, 19). There have been many calls for caution following the publication of several unanticipated toxic reactions apparently due to the use of untested and unregulated over-the-counter CAM remedies (20). A principle that reconciles these views is that neither modern medicine nor CAM should be given a free ride when it comes to evidence-based practice.

Finally, the exponential growth in the accessibility of the Internet, the availability of an ever-increasing number of websites related to CAM, and the efforts of the National Institutes of Health to funding scientific research and educational symposia in the field has led to the wide dissemination and a better understanding of the complex and heterogeneous body of knowledge that is CAM.

INTEREST IN CAM AMONG PATIENTS WITH PARKINSON'S DISEASE

In 2001, Rajendran et al. documented the prevailing interest in alternative medicine (or CAM) in a community of patients with PD in Baltimore (21). They administered a structured questionnaire in an effort to determine whether there was any correlation between the use of CAM and the demographics or disease characteristics of these patients. Forty one of the patients (81%) had used at least one CAM modality for a variety of reasons. In most cases they began using it after the diagnosis of PD. These CAM modalities generally comprised nutraceuticals, vitamin supplements, massage therapy, and acupuncture. Compared to nonusers, users of CAM tended to have an earlier age of onset, to be younger, to have a higher income, and to be better educated that those who did not use CAM (21). Symptom severity was not a predictor of CAM use among these patients. The finding simply validated the PD community's interest in these modalities and called attention to the need of physicians to become better informed about the risks and potential benefits of these practices. There was no attempt to examine issues of efficacy.

Much like the general population, patients with PD tend to use CAM for 3 main reasons: First they are seeking validation and autonomy for their symptoms and they tend to view CAM as more congruent to their views of health as holistic and their illness as a transformational experience (22). Although some patients may be dissatisfied with the limitations of modern medicine and its therapies, this is apparently not a prominent reason

for seeking out CAM (24). Instead, in our experience, a patient's disappointment with modern medicine more commonly stems from the way the attitudes of his or her treating physician are perceived. For instance, a statement such as "you have a progressive neurologic illness that has no cure, and the medications used to treat it tend to lose their efficacy over time" may be factual, but it fails to provide the validation and empowerment the patient is seeking and may hope to obtain from CAM.

Body Work and Exercise

Massage Therapy. The core motor symptoms of PD suggest that massage therapy may be beneficial. Patients can be disabled due to painful rigidity, muscle fatigue, back problems from postural abnormalities, all of which are targets of traditional massage therapy (23). From a nonmotor standpoint, massage therapy can help anxiety and mood. Benefits of some of these techniques have been reported in the rehabilitation literature (24). Unfortunately most of these studies have failed to control for the placebo effect (25, 26).

Some of the more common form of massage therapy are described below as an introduction to the terminology and techniques. The language used in these descriptions does not necessarily imply efficacy or even substantive differences between the techniques. When westerners think of massage, they think of *Swedish massage*. It is a classic technique that combines kneading and long, smooth massage strokes to improve circulation and relax and loosen muscles. Five basic strokes, all flowing toward the heart, are used to manipulate the soft tissues of the body. Therapists use a combination of gliding, tapping, and other motions aided by the application of oil to the skin to reduce friction. *Sports massage* uses a combination of the same strokes plus compression, friction, and vibration reach into deep muscle layers and promote relaxation and drainage of lymphatic fluid. *Neuromuscular therapy* (NMT) is a similar but more standardized form of massage that relies on direct compression of trigger points to alleviate muscle pain and spasms and on gliding, lengthening strokes applied with moderate compression parallel to muscle bundles in the neck, back, and extremities (27). Trigger points are small, painful areas throughout the body that contain soft tissue foci of decreased circulation, increased muscle contraction, and nerve sensitivity.

Other body-work modalities include *myotherapy,* which emphasizes various techniques aimed at releasing trigger points. *Shiatsu* is a traditional form of Japanese pressure-point massage that, like myotherapy, incorporates the use of pressure using the fingers, thumbs, palms, knees, forearms, elbows, and even feet to relieve tension from pressure points. *Acupressure* is best thought of as acupuncture without the needles. It is an ancient Chinese technique based on the principles of acupuncture and involves the use of finger pressure on specific points along the body. *craniosacral therapy* (CST) consists of gentle form of manipulation of the craniosacral system and is used to treat migraine headaches, chronic neck and back pain, scoliosis, and fibromyalgia, among other ailments. *Thai massage* may be best thought of as a form of assisted yoga in which the client typically remains fully clothed and the massage usually takes place on the floor or a mat rather than massage table.

Finally, *reflexology* is based on the belief that one's feet and hands are maps or mirrors of the body. By putting pressure on and massaging specific areas of the feet or hands, the reflexologist tries to relieve pain or tension in corresponding areas of the client's body. *Pohaku* ("hot stone") uses heated river stones or lava rocks to carry warmth deep into muscles, tissues, and joints, thus releasing tension and stress.

Several uncontrolled studies have suggested that massage therapy (mostly Swedish massage and NMT) is a beneficial adjunct in the symptomatic management of PD (28, 29). This view has received support from a recently published, randomized, controlled pilot study of NMT in PD (30). Investigators randomly assigned 36 patients with early to middle stages of PD to 4 weeks of biweekly NMT or to music relaxation (MR) provided in the same environment and by the same therapist administering NMT. They found that, although both groups were satisfied with their treatment assignment, only the NMT group evidenced significant improvement in the United Parkinson Disease Rating Scale (UPDRS) motor score ($P < 0.001$), most notably in the tremor score (30). Also improved were the Clinical Global Impression of Severity (CGIS) scores ($P < 0.007$) and finger-tapping speed ($P < 0.001$). The MR control group experienced a slight improvement in tremor but not in other measures. These effects were sustained after an 8-day washout following the last treatment; however, their magnitude and significance had begun to decline by then. Both groups exhibited a modest but significant improvement in the PD Quality of Life 39 item scale or PDQ-39. After the washout, the effect was sustained only in the NMT group, in which mood and anxiety also improved significantly. An initial improvement in anxiety in the MR group disappeared after the washout. Group differences between NMT and MR were apparent only for the motor UPDRS and QOL scores (30).

The authors concluded that NMT can improve motor and selected nonmotor symptoms in PD and that this effect is more durable for the motor symptoms. This study needs to be reproduced with a larger number of subjects to better examine group difference and investigate possible mechanisms.

Aerobic Exercise.   Although not strictly a CAM modality, aerobic exercise embodies many of the cardiovascular and neuromuscular benefits of CAM-oriented body work and exercise modalities. It has also been used in PD by physical medicine and in a few controlled studies (31–36). It is clear that, as in the general population, aerobic exercise can help to improve overall health, the sense of well-being, strength, and the viscoelastic properties of joints and muscles in patients with PD. It is also widely recommended for PD. Unfortunately, it is less clear that this translates into an improvement in parkinsonian motor symptoms (35, 37, 38).

The role of exercise in PD acquired added interest since the publication of an epidemiologic study suggesting that patients who exercise have an improved survival rate compared to those who do not (39, 40). In this study, 438 patients from Osaka, Japan, were followed for an average of 4.1 years. During the observation period, there were 71 deaths. The overall hazards ratio for observed/expected deaths was 1.8 in the group that did not exercise compared to the groups that did. By patient subgroup, the hazards ratio in patients who did not exercise at all was 2.47; for those who exercised but could not walk, it was 1.9; and for those able to walk independently it was 1.45.

In animal models of the dopa denervation of PD, aerobic exercise has been shown to improve cerebral blood flow, angiogenesis, response to dopamine agonists, and the expression of dopamine receptors in the striatum. In rats, chronic wheel running increases norepinephrine levels in the frontal cortex, hippocampus, amygdala, locus ceruleus, and spinal cord (41, 42). Exercise increases the expression of hippocampal brain-derived neurotrophic factor (BDNF) (43). In addition, experimental animals that exercised were more resistant to oxidative stress and less likely to develop dopamine cell death when exposed to prooxidants like MPTP (44). Taken together, these findings suggest the possibility that exercise may alter the course of symptoms in PD. The challenge now is to determine how exercise can alter the central oxidative state of dopamine and other neurons.

Skidmore et al. examined whether progressive treadmill exercise training can improve locomotor function and cardiovascular fitness in advanced PD (45). They exercised 5 of 8 eligible subjects 3 times a week for 3 months. These patients were able to achieve a 50% increase in metabolic equivalents (METs) ($P < 0.005$) and a 27% increase in peak ambulatory workload capacity ($P < 0.02$), indicating a significant improvement in fitness from a presumably low baseline. UPDRS motor scores also improved by 17%, but this improvement did not reach statistical significance (45). This study was limited by the small number of subjects and a 7% incidence of exercise-induced hypotension. It suggests that, in addition to its cardiovascular effects, aerobic training may benefit motor function in PD.

Another interesting aspect of the study is the "forced" nature of the treadmill exercise, compared with other modalities that allow patients to set their own pace. In a recent web report, Alberts of the Lerner research Institutes reports similar improvement in parkinsonian motor function in a patient who rode a tandem bicycle with him 450 miles in a week. He reports that patients "may need to be forced to exercise at rates beyond that which they can achieve on their own." He believes that this driving of the central nervous system may be necessary to produce the changes in brain biochemistry that would then mediate the clinical benefits to the patient (46).

Chinese Martial Arts

Tai chi chuan (TCC) incorporates some of the benefits of aerobic exercise and adds to it elements of mind modalities such as controlled breathing and meditation reinforced through the execution of slowly flowing forms derived from self-defense moves. Rodrigues de Paula et al. reviewed 31 original studies, published in Chinese or English journals, 9 of which examined TCC and contrasted it with aerobic exercise in non-PD subjects (47). These studies showed that TCC can provide moderate exercise intensity, with approximately 55% of the maximal oxygen intake and thus a significantly lower ventilatory equivalent (Ve/VO_{2max}) to that of aerobic exercise. A number of clinical studies suggest that in addition to its beneficial effects on the cardiorespiratory system, TCC improves muscle strength, musculoskeletal function, balance, mental control, and posture control, thus reducing the risk of falls in the elderly (47, 48).

Juncos et al. have presented data from a 3-month controlled study of TCC in PD in which 56 subjects were stratified by fitness and PD disability and then assigned to receive twice-a-week sessions of aerobic training (or AE, a walk-run exercise program), TCC (limited to less that half the METs achieved by the AE group and to 10 forms emphasizing posture and balance), or QiGong (QG), practiced as meditation in stillness with no aerobic value (active control for aerobic conditioning). In this study, unlike the initial open-label study of aerobic exercise in PD (37), parkinsonian motor function and QOL indices did not improve (49). Severity measured by the CGIS and severity improved only in the AE group ($P < 0.054$), and there was a significant trend for improvement by group as follows: AE > TCC > QG, $P = 0.01$. The most important changes were seen in the AE group, with improvement in aerobic capacity (measured as distanced walked in 6 minutes) and a reduction in the recorded falls and near falls (e.g., "I managed not to fall by holding onto X, or throwing myself on the sofa, bed. . . ."), which improved only in the AE group ($P < 0.01$). The conclusions were that the practice of TCC at very low intensities is not sufficient to improve parkinsonian motor function. Furthermore, 4 months of TCC was barely enough for this representative group of patients to learn the 10 forms. The results, rather than negating

a potential role for TCC in PD, point out that, like many elderly patients, PD patients have a steep learning curve in acquiring complex motor programs. The results also suggest that the UPDRS may not be the ideal tool to evaluate the effects of these modalities in PD.

In 2006 Schmitz-Hubsch et al. evaluated the immediate and sustained effects of QG on the motor and nonmotor symptoms of PD (50). Fifty-six patients with different levels of disease severity were recruited for a study comparing the effects of QG and placebo (no additional intervention) on the progression of such symptoms. QG exercises were applied in 90-minute weekly sessions of group instruction for 2 months, followed by a 2-months pause and a second 2-month treatment period. More patients improved in the QG group than in the control group at 3 and 6 months ($P = 0.008$ at 3 months and $P = 0.05$ at 6 months; Fisher's exact test). At 12 months, there was a sustained difference between groups only when changes in UPDRS motor subscale were normalized to baseline. Depression scores decreased motor subscores in both groups, whereas the incidence of several nonmotor symptoms decreased in the QG group only.

Unlike westerners, who often begin to learn these modalities after they retire, elderly practitioners of TCC and QG in eastern societies are more likely to have been practicing them from a young age, making the suspected learning curve a nonissue. Unlike the above short-term studies, in eastern societies these interventions are part of a lifestyle. The challenge to students in the field will be to show that the belated introduction of such a practice can be assimilated by a PD patient well enough to have an impact on advancing disability. The learning of TCC and QG by PD patients, compared with their age-matched counterparts, may be further complicated by the motor, intentional, and visuospatial defects of these patients (51). Finally, when it comes to PD and exercise, investigators are still at the stage of defining need to define which exercise, at what intensity, and for how long is necessary to obtain maximum benefit in PD.

Mind-Body Modalities

Mind-body interventions are important to CAM but have rarely been used in PD; thus there are very few data to report.

Meditation Techniques. Meditation techniques use deep-breathing techniques and a variety of sensory inputs, psychotropics, or artifacts (e.g., shamanism, active placebos, stone therapy) to reach a state of controlled relaxation. Controlled breathing is central to these modalities. The conscious control of this otherwise automatic function is thought to modulate the receptive state of the frontal lobes and increase its plasticity. From a neurologic standpoint, it is clear that hyperventilation causes massive electroencephalographic changes that can be entrained. This conditioning entrainment is thought to become functionally autonomous, providing benefits that extend beyond the practice sessions themselves. Scientific evidence for the power of these quasimeditative states comes from a multitude of physiologic studies demonstrating that achieving "that state" allows subjects to modify their vital signs, coronary blood flow, and metabolic rate. From a physiologic standpoint, the aim of these and other CAM modalities is to increase subjects' resiliency.

Reiki is a Japanese healing art whereby the practitioner places his or her hands upon the person to be healed and acts as a conduit, the intention being to channel the healing energy of the universe into the recipient to restore balance and harmony.

Nutraceuticals and Multivitamins

There is laboratory, biochemical, and genetic evidence indicating that PD is a disorder mediated in part by abnormalities in energy metabolism, specifically defects in complex I of the oxidative phosphorylation chain (52–55). Many of the nutraceuticals used for general health are antioxidants. It is therefore not surprising that investigators in this field have been interested in using these agents in PD.

The 3 antioxidants most commonly considered as potentially useful neuroprotective or disease-modifying agents in PD are vitamin E, coenzyme Q10, creatine, and carnitine. Biochemical and laboratory evidence suggests that antioxidants like these can protect dopamine neurons against various oxidants (e.g., MPTP, rotenone) used to create models of dopamine denervation in PD (54–57).

The first study of CAM in PD was the DATATOP study, in which vitamin E was conclusively shown not to have any therapeutic or disease-modifying effect in PD (58). It was thus surprising to find that vitamin E was the most commonly used nutraceutical in the 2001 survey of PD patients (21).

Coenzyme Q_{10} is an over-the-counter antioxidant that serves as a cofactor to complex I of the oxidative phosphorylation chain (59). It is also a mitochondrial membrane stabilizer that has been shown to be deficient in the mitochondria and plasma of patients with PD (60). In 2004, under the direction of Shults et al., the Parkinson Study Group published a randomized controlled pilot study of placebo versus 300, 600, and 1200 mg/day of CoQ_{10} in untreated patients with PD followed for 16 months (61). The endpoint was the change in total UPDRS score from baseline to the time the patient required dopaminergic therapy to control disability from symptom progression. The results showed that, although there was no difference in total UPDRS scores per se, patients receiving 1200 mg/day showed significantly less progression of disability (as measured in the activities of daily living or part II of the UPDRS) than patients on placebo or on the 2 other doses of CoQ_{10}. Patients on the 300- and 600-mg doses showed a trend intermediate from placebo and the 1200-mg dose, which did not reach statistical significance. CoQ_{10} offered no acute symptomatic motor benefit and was well tolerated (61). On the basis of these pilot results, a phase III trial with doses 1200 and 2400 mg/day of CoQ_{10} versus placebo and an otherwise similar design has been launched.

Creatine is another over-the-counter dietary supplement that has been shown to increase brain and muscle creatine and phosphocreatine concentrations and to improve muscular performance in adults. The mechanisms of performance enhancement may include increased intramuscular phosphocreatine, enhanced energy shuttling, and/or stimulation of protein synthesis (62). It has been shown to have a neuroprotective effect in a mouse model of Huntington's disease (63). In two pilot studies in PD, creatine was shown not to have any beneficial effects on the motor symptoms of PD, but it may have a beneficial effect on mood and an additive strength benefit in patients with PD who are lifting weight and taking 5 g of creatine per day (64, 65). In a phase II randomized, controlled trial of creatine in patients with untreated PD, data suggested that this compound is safe and may have a positive disease-modifying effect on the progression of PD symptoms (66). Based on this, a recent large, simple phase III trial was launched in which patients who had been treated for less than 2 years are to be followed on creatine (5 g/day) or placebo for 5 years to determine if creatine can slow symptom progression in this illness.

In the symptomatic treatment of PD, fava beans have been shown to be a rich source of levodopa, which may be of benefit in PD (67). Valerian extract in an over-the-counter herbal hypnotic was recently tested in a 31-day double-blind controlled study for sleep promotion in 68 PD patients (68). The study included polysomnography (PSG) with repeated measures. Valerian (600 mg at bedtime) was not associated with significant improvement in PSG measures or sleep. The rate of side effects did not differ in the valerian and placebo groups.

Instrumental Interventions

Acupuncture. Acupuncture consists of stimulation of various anatomic locations in the skin that correspond to traditional meridians as defined in Chinese tradition. Depending on the condition being addressed, small needles are inserted into these meridians and then manipulated by mechanical or electrical means (69). From the Chinese perspective, acupuncture is embedded in a complex theoretical framework that provides its conceptual and therapeutic direction (70). An explanation of this complexity is beyond the scope of the present chapter; thus the reader is referred to reviews on the topic and technique (70, 71).

In neuroscience, several lines of evidence suggest possible mechanisms of action for acupuncture. For instance, in man, acupuncture can change noradrenaline levels in CSF (72); in mice, it can change brain dopamine levels (73).

In the only controlled study of acupuncture in PD, Shulman et al. used an open-label, repeated measures design to examine the effect of traditional acupuncture on multiple domains of function in 20 PD patients who received 2 weekly treatments for 7 to 9 weeks (74). Acupuncture was administered by a licensed practitioner. The procedure was well tolerated but had no effect on parkinsonian motor or nonmotor symptoms (i.e., depression and anxiety), although patients reported discrete symptomatic improvement (74). A broad battery of tests suggested acupuncture may have helped sleep and rest only.

There are unsubstantiated claims from Germany that permanent implantation of an acupuncture needle into the earlobe provides substantial benefit to patients with PD. Werth provides a series of testimonials and diagrams of his own uncontrolled data as well as subjective explanations on how this may work. The nature of the information available makes it difficult to evaluate (75).

Finally, Kapchuck et al. offer a words of advice to students of this topic, suggesting that the placebo effect with devices such as acupuncture needles is at least as great as that seen with nutraceuticals (76).

Transcranial Magnetic Stimulation. Clinical depression occurs in up to 50% of all patients with PD (77). Electroconvulsive therapy (ECT) is a well-established treatment for medication-refractory depression in the general population. In PD, it is reported to ameliorate depression as well as motor symptoms for a variable period of time (78, 79). In the CAM domain, repetitive transcranial magnetic stimulation (rTMS) of the left dorsolateral prefrontal cortex (DLPFC) has emerged as a promising treatment for refractory depression (80). Its advantage over ECT is that it does not require general anesthesia and has a shorter recovery time, potentially making it more attractive, practical, and cost-effective.

Recent studies suggest that TMS may be beneficial in the management of treatment-resistant depression in PD (81, 82). In a personal communication based on open, repeated measures Epstein et al. report that, in addition to improvements in depression, their 14 PD inpatients with refractory depression also experienced improvement in motor function for as long as 3 to 6 weeks.

CAM and the Role of Placebo

The aim of this chapter is not to propose an integrative mind-body approach while ignoring placebo effects. Eastern traditions have occasionally emphasized the principle of mind-body integration at the expense of attending to underlying pathologic processes. This does not serve the public well. On the other hand, western medicine has been wedded to the perhaps naive construct that a placebo response can discriminate between organic ("real") and subjective ("psychogenic") symptoms. This is a product of the post–Charcot-Freud deterministic separation of mind and body. While searching *for true and real* clinical responses, western medicine has perhaps lost opportunities that result from an understanding of the physiology of placebo responses. These can be as real and sustained as any other biologic responses.

Part of this evidence comes from imaging studies in which the placebo effect is mediated by the dopaminergic reward mechanisms in the human brain. This mechanism can be linked to dopamine release in the striatum and is related to the expectation (belief) of clinical benefit on the part of the patient (83). These studies were conducted using radioligand techniques in which the release of dopamine is estimated using dopamine receptor radioligand displacement during, before, and after placebo positron emission tomography (PET) (83). In spite of the dopamine deficiency of this state, PD patients are able to generate placebo responses of high magnitude (17% and higher), and these can be sustained for 6 to 12 months or longer, mediated at least in part by dopamine release in the striatum (26, 84). In coming years, with our expanding understainding of the placebo response, perhaps we will learn to be less dismissive of this powerful variable in human response.

A lesson to be learned from experienced western medicine–based clinicians and perhaps from some of the practices of CAM, is that the placebo response should be viewed as another tool available to a caregiver to foster positive change in the ways a patient copes with illness and adversity—in effect, as a way of integrating the mind and the body for the purpose of promoting health. For investigators participating in clinical trials, controlling and equalizing expectation in randomized clinical trials will continue to be a difficult proposition (85).

SUMMARY AND CONCLUSIONS: FROM CAM TO INTEGRATIVE MEDICINE

CAM practices do not need western medicine to survive and thrive. They have done so on their own for centuries without our help. Wider dissemination of CAM knowledge inside and outside of their current constituency will stand to benefit a wider audience and enrich the field of health care. Modern medicine is skeptical, however, about giving CAM a free ride when it comes to scientific evidence and evidence-based practices. Western medicine was guilty of this far too long. It has since taken many years to uncover practices that were of no value and wasteful. We simply do not want to repeat these mistakes. The public expects and deserves practices that are safe and that deliver what they promise based on objective evidence—that is, randomized controlled trials and long-term evidenced-based outcome measures. The federal government and the health care industry are in agreement with these principles. Western medicine's adherence to scientific methods has kept it reasonably humble and on track with improving the health care of individuals and the public. It is the hope of modern medicine that, as an increasing number of CAM practitioners adhere to these principles, the public health will continue to improve and that medical care will become more affordable (86, 87).

A number of institutions have taken the lead in implementing practices that combine the best of conventional, and evidence-based CAM into an integrative approach that has become popular with the public and among those practitioners of modern medicine who have been exposed to it (86, 87). Making these combined practices cost-effective and widely available has its challenges. However, the main point of these efforts continues to be the promotion of scientific and evidence-based principles in all the healing arts so that these distinctions such as the medicine of the East versus that of the West or CAM versus modern medicine can evolve into a unified, integrative, evidenced-based form of medical practice.

Acknowledgment

Supported in part by NINDS RO-1 AT00612-03, P30AT00609, and the American Parkinson Disease Center for Research Excellence in Parkinson Disease at Emory University.

References

1. Manyam BV, Sanchez-Ramos JR. Traditional and complementary therapies in Parkinson's disease. *Advances in Neurology* 1999; 80:565–574.
2. Gevitz N. *Other Healers: Unorthodox Medicine in America.* Baltimore, MD: John Hopkins University Press, 1988.
3. Eisenberg DM, Kessler RC, Foster C, et al. Unconventional medicine in the United States. Prevalence, costs, and patterns of use. *N Engl J Med* 1993; 328(4):246–252.
4. Kaptchuk TJ, Eisenberg DM. Varieties of healing: 1. Medical pluralism in the United States. *Ann Intern Med* 2001; 135(3):189–195.
5. Eisenberg DM. The Institute of Medicine report on complementary and alternative medicine in the United States: Personal reflections on its content and implications. *Alt Ther Health Med* 2005; 11(3):10–15.
6. Wetzel MS, Eisenberg DM, Kaptchuk TJ. Courses involving complementary and alternative medicine at US medical schools. *JAMA* 1998; 280(9):784–787.
7. Maizes V, Schneider C, Bell I, Weil A. Integrative medical education: Development and implementation of a comprehensive curriculum at the University of Arizona. *Acad Med* 2002; 77(9):851–860.
8. Kligler B, Maizes V, Schachter S, et al. Core competencies in integrative medicine for medical school curricula: A proposal. *Acad Med* 2004; 79(6):521–531.
9. Cleary-Guida MB, Okvat HA, Oz MC, Ting W. A regional survey of health insurance coverage for complementary and alternative medicine: Current status and future ramifications. *J Alt Comp Med* 2001; 7(3):269–273.
10. Pelletier KR. A review and analysis of the clinical and cost-effectiveness studies of comprehensive health promotion and disease management programs at the worksite: 1995–1998 update (IV). *Am J Health Prom* 1999; 13(6):333–345, iii.
11. Cohen MH, Eisenberg DM. Potential physician malpractice liability associated with complementary and interactive medical therapies. *Ann Intern Med* 2002; 136(8):596–603.
12. Am Board on Health Promotion and Disease Prevention—Committee on the use of CAM in the US. *Complementary and Alternative Medicine in the United States.* Washington, DC: The National Academies Press, 2005.
13. Eisenberg DM, Davis RB, Ettner SL, et al. Trends in alternative medicine use in the United States, 1990–1997: Results of a follow-up national survey. *JAMA* 1998; 280(18):1569–1575.
14. LoVecchio F, Curry SC, Bagnasco T. Butyrolactone-induced central nervous system depression after ingestion of RenewTrient, a "dietary supplement." *N Engl J Med* 1998; 339(12):847–848.
15. Slifman NR, Obermeyer WR, Aloi BK, et al. Contamination of botanical dietary supplements by *Digitalis lanata*. *N Engl J Med* 1998; 339(12):806–811.
16. Lantz MS, Buchalter E, Giambanco V. St. John's wort and antidepressant drug interactions in the elderly. *J Geriatr Psychiatr Neurol* 1999; 12:7–10.
17. Mahar M. *Money-Driven Medicine: The Real Reason Healthcare Costs So Much.* New York: Harper Collins, 2006.
18. Kreitzer MJ, Mitten D, Harris I, Shandeling J. Attitudes toward CAM among medical, nursing, and pharmacy faculty and students: A comparative analysis. *Alt Ther Health Med* 2002; 8(6):44–47, 50–43.
19. Torkelson C, Harris I, Kreitzer MJ. Evaluation of a complementary and alternative medicine rotation in medical school. *Alt Ther Health Med* 2006; 12(4):30–34.
20. Angell M, Kassirer JP. Alternative medicine: The risks of untested and unregulated remedies. *N Engl J Med* 1998; 339(12):839–841.
21. Rajendran PR, Thompson RE, Reich SG. The use of alternative therapies by patients with Parkinson's disease. *Neurology* 2001; 57(5):790–794.
22. Astin JA. Why patients use alternative medicine: Results of a national study. *JAMA* 1998; 279:1548–1553.
23. Field T. Massage therapy effects. *Am Psychol* 1998; 53(12):1270–1281.
24. Ulm G. The current significance of physiotherapeutic measures in the treatment of Parkinson's disease. *J Neural Trans Suppl* 1995; 46:455–460.
25. Kaptchuk TJ. The placebo effect in alternative medicine: Can the performance of a healing ritual have clinical significance? *Ann Intern Med* 2002; 136(11):817–825.
26. Goetz CG, Janko K, Blasucci L, Jaglin JA. Impact of placebo assignment in clinical trials of Parkinson's disease. *Mov Disord* 2003; 18(10):1146–1149.
27. Travell J, Simons DG. *Myofascial Pain and Dysfunction: The Trigger Point Manual.* Baltimore: Williams & Wilkins, 1983.
28. Steefel L. Massage therapy as an adjunct healing modality in Parkinson's disease. *Alt Comp Ther* 1996; 6(Nov/Dec):377–382.
29. Miesler D. Parkinson's disease and massage therapy. *Massage Ther J* 1996; Winter:34–37.
30. Craig LH, Svircev A, Haber M, Juncos JL. Controlled pilot study of the effects of neuromuscular therapy in patients with Parkinson's disease. *Mov Disord* 2006; 21(12):2127–2133.
31. Palmer SS, Mortimer JA, Webster DD, Bistevins R. Exercise therapy for Parkinson's disease. *Arch Phys Med Rehabil* 1986; 67:741–745.
32. Bharucha A, Chitrit I, Patil S, et al. Exercise physiology in Parkinson's disease: Fatigue and efficiency studies before and after levodopa. *Neurology* 1992; 42:309.
33. Mouradian M, Juncos J, Serrati C, et al. Exercise and the antiparkinsonian response to levodopa. *Clin Neuropharmacol* 1987; 10:351–355.
34. Van-Oteghen SL. Exercise program for those with Parkinson's disease. *Geriatr Nurs* 1987; 8:183–184.
35. Schenkman M, Cutson T, Kuchibhatla M, et al. Exercise to improve spinal flexibility and function for people with Parkinson's disease: A randomized, controlled trial. *J Am Geriatr Soc* 1998; 46:1207–1216.
36. Protas EJ, Stanley RK, Jankovic J. Parkinson's disease: Exercise testing and prescription recommendations. In: *ACSM's Exercise Management for Persons with Chronic Diseases and Disabilities/American College of Sports Medicine.* Champaign, IL: Human Kinetics, 1997:212–217.
37. Juncos JL, Millard TL, Catlin PA. The effect of cardiovascular training on fitness and motor function in Parkinson's disease. *Neurology* 1993; 43:284.
38. Bridgewater KJ, Sharpe MH. Aerobic exercise in early Parkinson disease. *J Neurol Rehabil* 1996; 10(4):233–241.
39. Sasco AJ, Paffenbarger RS, Gendre I, Wing AL. The role of physical exercise in the occurrence of Parkinson's disease. *Arch Neurol* 1992; 49:600–605.
40. Kuroda K, Tatara K, Takatorige T, Shinsho F. Effect of physical exercise on mortality in patients with Parkinson's disease. *Acta Neurol Scand* 1992; 86(1):55–59.
41. Dunn AL, T.G. R, et al. Brain norepinephrine and metabolites after treadmill training and wheel running in rats. *Med Sci Sports Exerc* 2001; 28:204–209.
42. Dishman RK, Renner KJ, White-Welkey JE, et al. Treadmill exercise training augments brain norepinephrine responses to familiar and novel stress. *Brain Res Bull* 2001; 52:337–342.
43. Garcia C, Chen MJ, et al. The influence of specific noradrenergic and serotonergic lesions on the expression of hippocampal brain-derived neurotrophic factor transcripts following voluntary physical activity. *Neuroscience* 2003; 119:721–732.
44. Smith AD, Zigmond MJ. Can the brain be protected through exercise? Lessons from an animal model of parkinsonism (comment). *Exp Neurol* 2003; 184(1):31–39.
45. Skidmore FM, Patterson SH, Shulman LM, et al. Aerobic treadmill exercise in advanced Parkinson's disease. *Neurology* 2006; 66(Suppl 2):A314.
46. Alberts J. Forced exercise might improve the symptoms of Parkinson's disease. In: 2007.

47. Rodrigues de Paula F, Teixeira-Salmela LF, Coelho de Morais-Faria CD, Rocha de Brito P. Impact of an exercise program on physical, emotional, and social aspects of quality of life of individuals with Parkinson's disease. *Mov Disord* 2006; 21(8):1073–1077.

48. Li JX, Hong Y, Chan KM. Tai chi: Physiological characteristics and beneficial effects on health. *Br J Sports Med* 2001; 35(3):148–156.

49. Juncos JL, Haber M, Hass C, et al. A controlled study of aerobic exercise and Chinese exercise modalities in Parkinson disease. *Neurology* 2006; 66(5 Suppl 2):A314.

50. Schmitz-Hubsch T, Pyfer D, Kielwein K, et al. Qigong exercise for the symptoms of Parkinson's disease: A randomized, controlled pilot study. *Mov Disord* 2006; 21(4):543–548.

51. Owen AM, Iddon JL, Hodges JR, et al. Spatial and non-spatial working memory at different stages of Parkinson's disease. *Neuropsychologia* 1997; 35(4):519–532.

52. Schapira AHV. Oxidative stress in Parkinson's disease. *Neuropathol Appl Neurobiol* 1995; 21:3–9.

53. Jenner P, Olanow CW. Oxidative stress and the pathogenesis of Parkinson's disease. *Neurology* 1996; 47(Suppl 3):S161–S170.

54. Beal MF. Aging, energy, and oxidative stress in neurodegenerative diseases. *Ann Neurol* 1995; 38:357–366.

55. Sherer TB, Betarbet R, Stout AK, et al. An in vitro model of Parkinson's disease: Linking mitochondrial impairment to altered alpha-synuclein metabolism and oxidative damage. *J Neurosci* 2002; 22:7006–7015.

56. Roghani M, Behzadi G. Neuroprotective effect of vitamin E on the early model of Parkinson's disease in rat: Behavioral and histochemical evidence. *Brain Res* 2001; 892(1):211–217.

57. Hornsby PJ. Parkinson's disease, vitamin E, and mitochondrial energy metabolism. *Arch Neurol* 1989; 46(8):840–841.

58. Parkinson SG. Impact of deprenyl and tocopherol treatment on Parkinson's disease in DATATOP subjects not requiring levadopa. *Ann Neurol* 1996; 39:29–36.

59. Ebadi M, Govitrapong P, Sharma S, et al. Ubiquinone (coenzyme Q10) and mitochondria in oxidative stress of Parkinson's disease. *Biol Sign Recept* 2001; 10(3–4):224–253.

60. Shults CW, Haas RH, Beal MF. A possible role of coenzyme Q10 in the etiology and treatment of Parkinson's disease. *BioFactors (Oxford)* 1999; 9(2–4):267–272.

61. Shults CW, Flint Beal M, Song D, Fontaine D. Pilot trial of high dosages of coenzyme Q10 in patients with Parkinson's disease. *Exp Neurol* 2004; 188(2):491–494.

62. Benzi G, Ceci A. Creatine as nutritional supplementation and medicinal product. *J Sports Med Phys Fit* 2001; 41(1):1–10.

63. Matthews RT, Yang L, Jenkins BG, et al. Neuroprotective effects of creatine and cyclocreatine in animal models of Huntington's disease. *J Neurosci* 1998; 18(1):156–163.

64. Bender A, Koch W, Elstner M, et al. Creatine supplementation in Parkinson disease: A placebo-controlled randomized pilot trial. *Neurology* 2006; 67(7):1262–1264.

65. Hass CJ, Collins MA, Juncos JL. Resistance training with creatine monohydrate improves upper-body strength in patients with Parkinson disease: A randomized trial. *Neurorehab Neural Repair* 2007; 21(2):107–115.

66. NINDS NET-PD Investigators. A randomized, double-blind, futility clinical trial of creatine and minocycline in early Parkinson disease (see comment). *Neurology* 2006; 66(5):664–671.

67. Bejjani BP, Rahme R, Jabr M. Do fava beans, a natural source of levodopa for parkinonian patients, restore dopaminergic transmission? Paper presented at the World Congress of Neurology, London, 2001.

68. Bliwise SL, Saunders DS, Wood-Siverio C, et al. Double-blind, placebo-controlled, polysomnographic randomized clinical trial of valerian for sleep in Parkinson's disease. *Sleep* 2007; 30 (Suppl): A41.

69. Wu DZ. Acupuncture and neurophysiology. *Clin Neurol Neurosurg* 1990; 92(1):13–25.

70. Kaptchuk TJ. Acupuncture: Theory, efficacy, and practice (see comment). *Ann Intern Med* 2002; 136(5):374–383.

71. Rabinstein AA, Shulman LM. Acupuncture in clinical neurology. *Neurologist* 2003; 9(3):137–148.

72. Liu B, Zhu S, Chen Q, et al. The changes in noradrenaline content in CSF of patients under electroacupuncture. *Chen Tzu Yen Chiu* 1988; 13(3):243–246.

73. Zhu W, Xi G, Ju J. Effect of acupuncture and Chinese medicine treatment on brain dopamine level of MPTP-lesioned C57BL mice. *Chen Tzu Yen Chiu* 1996; 21(4):46–49.

74. Shulman LM, Wen X, Weiner WJ, et al. Acupuncture therapy for the symptoms of Parkinson's disease. *Mov Disord* 2002; 17(4):799–802.

75. Werth U. The discovery of implant acupuncture. From brochure published in Magdeburg, Germany; 2006. (http://www.renaris.de/docs/implant_acupuncture.pdf)

76. Kaptchuk TJ, Goldman P, Stone DA, Stason WB. Do medical devices have enhanced placebo effects? *J Clin Epidemiol* 2000; 53(8):786–792.

77. Tandberg E, Larsen J, Aarsland D, Cummings J. The occurrence of depression in Parkinson's disease. A community-based study. *Arch Neurol* 1996; 53:175–179.

78. Faber R, Trimble M. Electroconvulsive therapy in Parkinson's disease and other movement disorders. *Mov Disord* 1991; 6:293–303.

79. Brown G. Parkinsonism depression and ECT. *Am J Psychiatry* 1975; 132:1084.

80. Berman R NM, et al. A randomized clinical trial of repetitive transcranial magnetic stimulation in the treatment of major depression. *Biol Psychiatry* 2000; 47:332–227.

81. Avery D HP, Fawaz W, Russo J, et al. A controlled study of repetitive transcranial magnetic stimulation in medication-resistant major depression. *Biol Psychatry* 2006; 59(59):187–194.

82. Fregni F, Santos C, Myczkowski MM, et al. Repetitive transcranial magnetic stimulation is as effective as fluoxetine in the treatment of depression in patients with Parkinson's disease. *J Neurol Neurosurg Psychiatry* 2004; 75:1171–1174.

83. de la Fuente-Fernandez R, Schulzer M, Stoessl AJ. The placebo effect in neurological disorders. *Lancet Neurol* 2002; 1(2):85–91.

84. Goetz CG, Leurgans S, Raman R—the Parkinson Study Group. Placebo-associated improvements in motor function: Comparison of subjective and objective sections of the UPDRS in early Parkinson's disease. *Mov Disord* 2002; 17(2):283–288.

85. Stone DA, Kerr CE, Jacobson E, et al. Patient expectations in placebo-controlled randomized clinical trials. *J Eval Clin Pract* 2005; 11(1):77–84.

86. Cassileth BR. The Integrative Medicine Service at Memorial Sloan-Kettering Cancer Center. *Semin Oncol* 2002; 29(6):585–588.

87. Rees L, Weil A. Integrated medicine. *BMJ* 2001; 322(7279):119–120.

VIII

TREATMENT ISSUES

46 Motor Fluctuations and Dyskinesia

Steven A. Gunzler
John G. Nutt

Motor fluctuations are an important contributor to the disability of Parkinson's disease (PD). Fluctuations interrupt patients' activities and are associated with other fluctuating phenomena such as mood, sensory, and autonomic symptoms that add to the distress of this problem (see Chapter 40). Dyskinesia, a frequent accompaniment of motor fluctuations, further compounds the problem. Motor fluctuations are important not only to patients but also to the clinicians who treat them. Finally, motor fluctuations challenge our understanding of how the dopaminergic system functions and our concept of neurotransmitter replacement therapy for central nervous system disease.

PREVALENCE OF FLUCTUATIONS AND DYSKINESIA

Motor fluctuations are generally seen as an inevitable consequence of long-term levodopa therapy. Sweet and McDowell found that 47% of patients still alive and taking levodopa after 5 years had motor fluctuations and 49% had dyskinesia (1). Barbeau found that 55% of his patients had motor fluctuations and 55% dyskinesia after 6 years of treatment (2). These early studies, shortly after the introduction of levodopa, likely included patients with

more severe disease than the typical patient entering initiation of levodopa studies today. Also, these early studies employed higher doses of levodopa than is the practice today. As a result, these studies tended to show development of dyskinesia much sooner after levodopa initiation and at higher prevalences than more recent studies (3). Poewe and colleagues, in a more recent study, found that after 6 years, with low-dose levodopa (less than 500 mg/d with decarboxylase inhibitor), 52% of their patients had motor fluctuations and 54% had dyskinesia (4). With maximally tolerated doses after 6 years, the prevalence of motor fluctuations was 80% and that of dyskinesia 88% (4). Hely, *et al.* found that 41% of patients treated for 5 years with low-dose carbidopa/levodopa had motor fluctuations and 55% had dyskinesia (5), and Reardon, *et al.* found similar results in a 6-year study (6).

Age of onset of PD may influence the occurrence of fluctuations; 96% of patients with onset of PD before age 40 had fluctuations after 5 years of levodopa treatment, as opposed to 64% of case-matched patients with disease onset after age 40 (7). Other studies in young-onset PD have also found prevalence of more than 90% for fluctuations and dyskinesia (8, 9).

In contrast to these retrospective studies, which reported prevalence of fluctuations and dyskinesia of 40% to 96% after 5 or 6 years of levodopa therapy, a large, double-blind prospective study comparing 5 years of treatment with low-dose, immediate-release carbidopa/levodopa with controlled-release carbidopa/levodopa found an approximately 20% prevalence of motor fluctuations and dyskinesia by patient report or physician observation (10). One possible explanation for this low prevalence of motor complications is that subjects with relatively mild Parkinsonism were enrolled. A smaller, open prospective study observed fluctuations in 13 of 18 subjects and dyskinesia in 11 of 18 subjects monitored during a dose cycle after the first year of levodopa treatment (11). However, only 6 of the subjects reported fluctuations and 3 reported dyskinesia (11). Furthermore, analysis of patients randomized to levodopa in 2 more recent studies of levodopa vs. dopamine agonist as initial therapy for PD revealed a cumulative incidence of dyskinesia of 45% over 5 years in one study (12) and 54% over 4 years in the other (13). This discrepancy suggests that studies which depend on patient report to determine prevalence of these complications will underestimate their prevalence and give a different picture of the natural history of these complications. On the other hand, patient reports may better estimate the prevalence of clinically significant fluctuations and dyskinesia. Most studies indicate that motor complications are common after about 5 years of levodopa therapy. Excluding the older studies, in which subjects had delayed treatment because levodopa had not yet been available, the overall weighted median frequency of dyskinesia is about 36% by 4 to 6 years of levodopa treatment compared with about 27% at 2.5 to 3.5 years and about 88% past 9 years (3).

Denny and Behari found an association between dyskinesia and younger age of onset of PD as well as an association between both dyskinesia and motor fluctuations with earlier initiation and longer duration of levodopa exposure (14). In contrast, Schrag and Quinn found that frequency of dyskinesia was most influenced by duration of levodopa treatment, whereas fluctuations were most likely with greater disease duration and levodopa dose (15).

DEVELOPMENT OF MOTOR FLUCTUATIONS

The manner in which motor fluctuations develop is important for understanding the pathogenesis and designing therapies. The clinical impression of changes in levodopa response differs from the measured changes in motor function that occur during long-term levodopa therapy. An accurate definition of the natural history of the response to levodopa and how the response changes during long-term therapy is important, since the time course of changes may implicate or exclude various pathogenetic mechanisms for fluctuations and dyskinesia.

Motor fluctuations are commonly envisioned to occur because of a single effect of levodopa on motor function. However, there is evidence that the motor performance of a levodopa-treated PD patient represents the summation of several different responses to levodopa plus contributions from endogenous dopamine (11, 16). There are at least 3 different motor responses to levodopa. The *short-duration response* is a motor improvement that roughly parallels the elevation of plasma levodopa after a dose of drug, and is measured in minutes to hours. The short-duration response is responsible for the peak motor response—which has been the focus of attention in the clinic and in basic and clinical research. The *long-duration response*, first described by Cotzias (17) and Muenter (18), is a motor improvement that builds up over days and likewise decays over days. It has received relatively little attention. A *negative or inhibitory response* is a worsening of motor function that follows (and may also precede) a short-duration response (19–22). The negative response worsens the "off" condition for minutes up to an hour and is therefore sometimes termed the "*super off*." These 3 responses to levodopa are superimposed on a diurnal pattern of motor function that is evident in all PD patients, treated and untreated. The diurnal motor pattern is characterized by better motor performance in the morning, called sleep benefit (23–26), and worse function in the afternoon and evening (27). Finally, there is the residual endogenous dopaminergic function that presumably accounts for what motor function remains when a patient has been taken off levodopa for several weeks. This endogenous dopamine production may be virtually nil, as indicated by the virtual immobility of severely affected untreated PD patients. The endogenous dopamine plus the long-duration response are the main determinants of the "off" motor function. Currently there is no way of disassociating the contributions of the long-duration levodopa response and the motor function due to endogenous dopamine production without prolonged withdrawal from levodopa, which is usually precluded for ethical, medical, and logistic reasons.

The clinical definition of the stable response is a levodopa-induced improvement of motor function in the absence of motor fluctuations in a patient taking 4 or less doses of carbidopa/levodopa per day. The stable response is characteristically observed in patients early in the course of the disease and early in long-term levodopa therapy, the "honeymoon" period, which lasts several years. It is commonly envisioned that the stable response stems from the fact that the short-duration response to each dose of carbidopa/levodopa is sufficiently long that the effects of each dose overlap with the previous dose to produce a sustained response. However, measurement of motor performance in patients with a stable response suggests that the sustained improvement appears to be largely due to the long-duration response. If patients' motor function is measured in the morning after 12 hours without levodopa or even several days without medication, it can be seen that their motor function is still appreciably better than that before they began levodopa (11, 28). Stable-responding subjects do have motor fluctuations related to the short-duration response, which is superimposed on the long-duration response, but they are unaware of such fluctuations and untroubled by them (11). The negative response and diurnal variation are usually not important at this stage.

Motor fluctuations first appear clinically as "wearing off," when bradykinesia emerges at the ends of dose cycles or in the morning after the patient has been without levodopa overnight. This is commonly attributed to shortening of the short-duration response. Motor effects no longer seem to last the 4 to 6 hours between doses. The short-duration response is briefer in "wearing-off" patients (29–32), but there is neither a direct correlation with duration of action and presence of fluctuations nor are the differences between stable and fluctuating patients very great (30, 32). The often ignored characteristic of fluctuating patients is that there is a large, clinically appreciable difference in motor function between the "on" and "off" motor states (30, 32, 33). Thus another difference between fluctuating and stable patients is that the short-duration response, generally measurable from the beginning of therapy, becomes larger and clinically more significant. The peak levodopa response does not increase; rather, deterioration in the "off" motor function makes the magnitude of the short-duration response larger. Precisely how much of this deterioration in the "off" motor function is related to changes in the long-duration response and how much is related to further loss of endogenous dopaminergic function is not known. The long-duration response is still present in severely affected PD patients, although whether it is of the same magnitude as in patients with less severe PD is unclear (34–35), or whether it instead declines in duration and magnitude with disease progression (36–37). Loss of endogenous dopamine production seems more likely to explain the increasing "off" motor disability. The negative response may also appear at this time and further augment "off" disability. Finally, diurnal patterns of response become apparent with better function in the morning and poorer response to medications in the afternoon (38, 39).

The more marked motor fluctuations, termed "on-off," are clinically characterized by rapid switches between "on" and "off," which are seemingly unrelated to oral dosing with levodopa. This effect occurs in patients with severe PD, who experience large differences in "on" and "off" motor function and are on complex, frequent dosing regimens. The unpredictable response to oral levodopa is in contrast to the predictable, dose-responsive responses to intravenous boluses or brief infusions in these patients (33, 40). This observation indicates that the unpredictable "on-off" response is largely pharmacokinetic in origin. Unpredictability is enhanced by administering frequent small doses of levodopa in the

vain hope that this strategy will yield relatively constant plasma levodopa concentrations.

DEVELOPMENT OF LEVODOPA-INDUCED DYSKINESIA

Dyskinesia is almost an invariable component of motor fluctuations and a consideration in treating them. Dyskinesia occurring when the patient is "on" is frequently termed *peak-dose* dyskinesia. This term is misleading in that dyskinesia is generally present throughout the time the patient is "on" and is physically, emotionally, or cognitively active (i.e., dyskinesia is brought out by motor activity and any form of stress and, conversely, is reduced by relaxation and inactivity). Furthermore, many patients have an increase in dyskinesia at the beginning and end of a dose cycle—a mild form of the so-called *"diphasic"* dyskinesia (41).

The ways in which the dyskinesia dose-response relationship is altered during long-term levodopa therapy should offer clues to the pathogenesis of dyskinesia. The thresholds and time course for dyskinesia and antiparkinsonian effects are reported to be similar in patients with motor fluctuations (40, 42). The important question is what happens during the initial months of treatment as dyskinesia first appears. There are 3 hypotheses.

One hypothesis is that the threshold for dyskinesia is initially much higher than that for an antiparkinsonian effect and that the dyskinesia threshold is lowered by repeated dosing of levodopa until it approximates the antiparkinsonian effect threshold (40, 42). The threshold is a marker for the initial inflection of the dose-response curve or the equivalent of an "effective dose 05" (dose producing 5% of the maximum response). Thus lowering of the dyskinesia threshold would be equivalent to shifting the dose-response curve to the left. The slope of the dyskinesia dose-response curve and the maximum response (E_{max}) could also change, but the essential feature is the leftward shift and reduction of dose required to produce dyskinesia (often expressed as the reduction in ED_{50}, the dose producing 50% of the maximum response). The problem with this hypothesis is that there have been few (40) or no (42) subjects described with newly developed dyskinesia who fall between the subjects who have no dyskinesia at all (and in whom no threshold can be determined because they do not have dyskinesia) and the fluctuating subjects whose dyskinesia thresholds are similar to antiparkinsonian thresholds. Thus there are no subjects with dyskinesia in whom the initially high threshold postulated by this model can be demonstrated. In conclusion, although this hypothesis is intuitively attractive, the leftward shift of the dose-response curve constitutes an unproven model of how dyskinesia develops.

A second model proposes that rather than a leftward shift of the dose-response curve, an increase in E_{max} from clinically undetectable to clinically apparent explains the development of dyskinesia (43). The pattern of dyskinesia in early PD subjects is consistent with this hypothesis. The duration of dyskinesia was similar to the antiparkinson effects (37) and did not just appear at peak L-dopa concentrations, as suggested by the lowered threshold model. The E_{max} hypothesis would explain the increase in severity of levodopa-induced dyskinesia during long-term levodopa therapy.

The third model contradicts both of the above models and suggests that neither the ED_{50} nor the E_{max} of the dose (concentration)-response curve for dyskinesia change during levodopa therapy (44). These conclusions are based on longitudinal studies in 11 PD subjects who received levodopa for an average of 4 years and had dyskinesia for 1 year upon entry into the study. Concentration (as opposed to dose)-response curves were derived from pharmacokinetic-pharmacodynamic modeling. Instead of the dyskinesia concentration–response curve shifting, the antiparkinsonian concentration-response curve shifted to the right. That is, the threshold for the antiparkinsonian action increased during long-term therapy, whereas that for dyskinesia did not change. The severity of dyskinesia (E_{max}) also did not change over the 3 years of the study, although the scale used (45) was relatively insensitive to changes in severity of dyskinesia.

It is obvious that more careful observations, as dyskinesia initially appears, are critical to deciding between these different models of development of dyskinesia. Understanding the clinical course of events will indicate the type and time course of biochemical events that might underlie development of dyskinesia.

Three unproven concepts guide treatment of dyskinesia. The first concept is that there are different thresholds for dyskinesia and for antiparkinsonian actions of levodopa. Most studies using single parenteral doses of levodopa find that the thresholds for dyskinesia and antiparkinsonian actions are similar in "wearing-off" and "on-off" patients (33, 40). Thus the concept of dosing to exceed the antiparkinsonian threshold and not the dyskinesia threshold is problematic, particularly when the short half-life of levodopa is considered.

The second unproven concept is that severity of dyskinesia is dose-related. However, several studies indicated that severity of dyskinesia is not very dose-related and more of an all-or-nothing phenomenon (33, 42, 46). The duration of dyskinesia is, nonetheless, dose-related (33, 42, 46). Thus small doses of levodopa will not necessarily reduce the severity of dyskinesia, although they will shorten the time dyskinesia is present. By patient history, dyskinesia tends to have a diurnal pattern; if present, it tends to be more severe in the evening.

The third unproven concept is that pulsatile dopaminergic stimulation promotes the development of dyskinesia, as well as motor fluctuations (47, 48). Therefore

continuous dopaminergic stimulation may lessen or prevent the development of dyskinesia (48). Specifically, reduction in exposure to troughs in levodopa concentration may be important in preventing dyskinesia (49). Despite the lower frequency of motor complications with dopamine agonists as initial therapy for PD compared to carbidopa/levodopa, there are important differences between dopamine agonists and carbidopa/levodopa that confound this comparison (12, 13). Controlled release carbidopa/levodopa did not reduce motor complications when used as initial therapy in place of regular carbidopa/levodopa (50–52). Furthermore, addition of dopamine agonists or catechol-O-methyltransferase (COMT) inhibitors to carbidopa/levodopa did not decrease dyskinesia in a number of trials (53, 54). The experience with long-term subcutaneous or intravenous infusion of dopamine agonists has been mixed, often but not always reducing dyskinesia, although enteric levodopa infusions did reduce dyskinesia (52, 55, 56). Continuous dopaminergic stimulation and its effect on dyskinesia are reviewed in more detail elsewhere (57). Given the equivocal evidence that continuous dopaminergic stimulation prevents dyskinesia, further study is necessary to clarify this issue.

TREATMENT OF FLUCTUATIONS AND DYSKINESIA

Aims

The strategies for managing PD patients with motor fluctuations are dictated by the physician's clinical experience and his or her weighing of clinical studies and their interpretations. What follows is admittedly a personal algorithm and is a mixture of science and style.

Several principles guide treatment of a patient with fluctuations. First, educate the patient that fluctuations generally cannot be eliminated but may be made more bearable. Second, determine what fluctuates and what causes disability. Third, make responses predictable by controlling pharmacokinetic factors and administering adequate doses. Fourth, make the response to each dose sufficiently long such that it is useful to the patient. Fifth, reduce "off" disability. Sixth, avoid drug toxicity and tolerance by limiting cumulative doses of antiparkinsonian agents. Seventh, treat "on" dyskinesia and "off" dystonia. These principles are considered in the following sections.

Determining What Fluctuates

To treat fluctuations effectively, it is important to have a clear picture of what is fluctuating and in what pattern. A careful history in the clinic may be sufficient; if not, having the patient remain at the clinic for several hours may allow the clinician to see the "on" and "off" states. The clinician should be aware that the response to the first dose cycle may be different from the response to dose cycles later in the day. Home videos are another manner in which the "on" and "off" manifestations can be seen. Home diaries, with the patient, caregiver, and physician agreeing on what constitutes "off" and what constitutes "on" before the diary is filled out, may yield diurnal patterns of response. It is important to recognize that the motor fluctuations are often accompanied by fluctuations in anxiety, mood, autonomic function, and sensation. Anxiety and depression, as part of the "off" experience, are frequently major contributors to distress. Patients who reported motor fluctuations in one study were likely to also have diary evidence of mood and anxiety fluctuations, although they often fluctuated at different times (58). It may be that therapy needs to be directed to these non-motor phenomena, in addition to treating motor fluctuations.

Making Responses Predictable

Unpredictable levodopa responses are generally related to pharmacokinetic causes. The most important pharmacokinetic characteristic of levodopa is its short plasma half-life. This, in turn, makes the variable absorption and distribution of levodopa very important. The most common cause of unpredictable responses is frequent small doses of levodopa. The duration of response to each dose of levodopa is, as with other drugs, proportional to the size of the dose; larger doses give longer responses (59). Small levodopa doses will give brief periods of motor improvement and thereby increase the motor fluctuations. Furthermore, because small doses will produce plasma concentrations that are closer to the threshold for antiparkinsonian effects, delays or reductions in absorption may cause individual doses to fail to reach threshold. Controlled-release levodopa preparations are associated with lower plasma concentrations, more erratic absorption, and consequently erratic responses in many subjects. Because of these considerations, when a patient is manifesting a seemingly unpredictable response to controlled-release levodopa, a good strategy is to switch him or her to regular levodopa given at 3- to 4-hour intervals. The regular form of carbidopa/levodopa is typically administered at a 20% to 30% lower dose of levodopa than the controlled-release form because of incomplete absorption of the controlled-release formulation (60, 61). A caveat is that some patients with peak-dose dyskinesia or "off" dystonias have been found to benefit from the controlled-release form of carbidopa/levodopa (60). The schedule for administration of other antiparkinsonian agents should be adjusted so that they are given with levodopa. This will almost always convert the unpredictable response into a predictable response and provide a starting point for adjusting medications. There is another benefit of this regimen: a simpler regimen will increase compliance and reduce the variability caused by patients' efforts to titrate their medications with self-developed, complex formulas based on response.

The short half-life of levodopa (1 to 2 hours) makes it impossible to maintain relatively constant plasma concentrations. Further, the absorption of levodopa is largely in the small bowel, so that variations in gastric emptying or bowel transit time may alter absorption. Avoiding levodopa administration with meals (62–64) or with ferrous sulfate (65), reconsidering the need for anticholinergics that may slow gastric emptying (66), and possibly adding antacids or domperidone to enhance gastric emptying (67, 68) are methods to enhance absorption. Levodopa enters the brain via a saturable large neutral amino acid (LNAA) transporter, and its entry may be influenced by plasma concentrations of LNAAs. Increases in LNAA concentrations after meals and the tendency for these concentrations to increase during the day underlie some unpredictable motor fluctuations (62) and the diurnal pattern of declining response to levodopa during the day (39). The standard American diet contains about twice the recommended daily amount of protein. Restricted-protein diets will enhance levodopa effects (69) but are difficult to implement. Rather than a restricted-protein diet, avoiding meals with very high protein may be the best compromise. A dietician may be very helpful to patients in implementing such diets and also in helping them to avoid protein malnutrition.

Making Responses Usable

A predictable response that lasts for only a few minutes is of little use to the patient. The response must be of sufficient duration that the patient can accomplish various activities. Methods to prolong the response to each dose of the drug include giving larger doses of levodopa (33, 46), using controlled-release preparations in patients who do not have complicated fluctuations, and adding amantadine, dopamine agonists, selegiline, or COMT inhibitors. Amantadine may be helpful in some fluctuating patients. In addition to reducing "off" time, dopamine agonists may delay wearing off in early PD (12). COMT inhibitors have been shown in randomized controlled trials to significantly reduce "off" time (70, 71). There is a tendency to continue to escalate doses of antiparkinsonian agents to lengthen "on" time, but this is a strategy with diminishing returns. The most striking example of this phenomenon in the authors' clinic was a 50-year-old man who had been maintained on carbidopa/levodopa 25/250 every 3 hours and who, to cope with wearing off at the end of each dose cycle, progressively increased his carbidopa/levodopa to 25/250 every 45 minutes around the clock and still had wearing off. This case and some studies suggest that tolerance develops with continuous therapy (72–76). For this reason, it is worthwhile to try to limit the total drug intake and provide some drug-free periods, generally overnight. Another limitation to increasing antiparkinsonian medications is an exacerbation of dyskinesia, considered later.

Reducing "Off" Disability

Dopamine agonists are often considered to reduce "off" disability, although what has been measured in trials is a reduction in "off" time and "off" ADL (77). Pallidotomy reduces "off" severity in the hands of some investigators but not others (9, 78), and it is best to consider an improvement in "off" disability a bonus and not the indication for pallidotomy. Deep brain stimulation (DBS) of the pars interna of the globus pallidus (GPi) or subthalamic nucleus (STN), on the other hand, can reduce "off" severity (80–84). Compared with unilateral pallidotomy, bilateral STN or GPI DBS causes a greater reduction in both dyskinesia and Unified Parkinson's Disease Rating Scale (UPDRS) "off" motor score (83–85). It remains unclear whether one DBS site is superior to the other as far as improvement in "off" disability is concerned (83, 84, 86). Fetal mesencephalic grafting into the putamen has not shown clear efficacy in reducing "off" disability in 2 randomized controlled studies and has been associated with "off"-time dyskinesia (87, 88). Anxiety, panic attacks, and depression as "off" phenomena may be amenable to treatment with conventional therapies, thereby reducing distress in the "off" state.

Reducing Cumulative Drug Intake

There is a tendency to increase antiparkinsonian drugs during long-term treatment because an increase in levodopa will temporarily reduce "off" time. However, this benefit wanes over weeks to months, necessitating a further increase in levodopa. The authors try to keep their patients on 1200 mg/day of levodopa or less. Sometimes it is possible to get as good or better control of fluctuations with lower doses of levodopa, with less adverse effects (89). One strategy is to try to minimize levodopa use during the night and focus on other methods to give the patient a comfortable night's sleep. Trazodone or benzodiazepines may help with sleep, and therapy for restless legs, "off" dystonia, and nocturia may improve sleep.

Controlling "On" Dyskinesia

The first strategy for reducing dyskinesia is to reduce adjunctive antiparkinsonian medications that may contribute to dyskinesia. Selegiline can promote dyskinesia and is the first drug to consider for tapering and discontinuance if possible. Controlled-release levodopa preparations may increase dyskinesia; switching to an immediate-release formulation may reduce dyskinesia and increase the predictability of a motor response. Dopamine agonists rarely cause dyskinesia by themselves, but they may augment dyskinesia when added to levodopa. Therefore, stopping agonists may reduce dyskinesia. Levodopa itself may be reduced. As discussed earlier, efforts to prevent dyskinesia by using frequent small doses of levodopa are generally ineffective and lead to short, unpredictable motor responses. A second strategy is to add drugs. Amantadine may reduce dyskinesia while increasing "on" time, although amantadine may lose its beneficial effect by 8 to 12 months of treatment (90, 91). Successful treatment of dyskinesia with amantadine often allows higher doses of carbidopa/levodopa to be better tolerated, further increasing "on" time. Despite animal data indicating that levetiracetam has antidyskinetic properties (92), open-label studies of levetiracetam to suppress dyskinesia had mixed results and found a high incidence of somnolence (93, 94). The serotonin 5-HT1A agonist sarizotan was studied in clinical trials, with some promising results (95, 96). Buspirone was reported to reduce dyskinesia (97) but the effect is not dramatic in the authors' experience. Fluoxetine and propranolol have also been proposed to treat dyskinesia (98, 99), but no randomized blinded trials have been done. Adding dopamine agonists and reducing levodopa may be very effective, particularly if levodopa can be markedly reduced or stopped (100). A third strategy for severe disabling dyskinesia is pallidotomy contralateral to the most affected side (101, 102). Bilateral pallidotomy is effective at reducing dyskinesia bilaterally but with an unacceptable rate of speech, swallowing, and balance problems. A fourth strategy is DBS. Bilateral DBS surgery appears to reduce dyskinesia to a greater degree than unilateral pallidotomy when performed in either the GPi or STN (83–85). The reduction in dyskinesia with STN DBS seems to be at least partially related to postoperative reduction of dopaminergic drug doses, whereas GPi DBS seems to reduce dyskinesia directly (85, 86, 103).

Reducing "Off" Dystonia

"Off"-period dystonia is a painful posture or cramp, generally occurring in the foot or leg, that appears when plasma levodopa concentrations are low. For this reason, "off"-period dystonia is particularly common in the morning before the first dose of levodopa. It is also frequently brought on by movement, typically walking to the bathroom upon arising. There are several methods to cope with this problem. The easiest is to have the patient take the first dose of levodopa while in bed, perhaps dissolving the tablet in water to hasten absorption, and waiting 15 to 30 minutes before arising. A second method is to use a controlled-release levodopa preparation at bedtime that will sometimes carry over to the next morning. A third method is to add a dopamine agonist to the antiparkinsonian drug regimen. Antispasticity drugs such as baclofen have been of little use in the authors' experience. Finally, although "off"-period dystonia is rarely an indication for pallidotomy or DBS surgery by itself, this phenomenon, like "on" dyskinesia, is generally relieved by contralateral pallidotomy as well as either GPi or STN DBS (104).

Prevention of Motor Complications

The knowledge that levodopa-induced fluctuations and dyskinesia will ultimately complicate the management of a majority of patients with Parkinsonism is dictating treatment early in the course of the disease. As these complications are clearly related to levodopa and are rare to nonexistent with other drugs, including the dopamine agonists, one strategy is to delay levodopa use until absolutely necessary. This could preserve the patient's function and may subsequently reduce levodopa use by combining it with other antiparkinsonian drugs. There is no doubt that initiating dopaminergic treatment with dopamine agonists will delay the need for levodopa by about 1 to 3 years and that the incidence of motor complications during that time will be very low (105). In one study, 65% of early PD patients treated with cabergoline required the addition of levodopa within the 3- to 5-year follow-up (106); and in another study 66% of patients on ropinirole received levodopa within 5 years (12). In the CALM-PD study, 53% of early-PD patients in the pramipexole arm required some supplemental levodopa within the 23.5-month treatment period (107, 108), whereas about 17% of patients in the ropinirole arm in the REAL-PET study required levodopa within 2 years (109). It remains unclear whether the frequency of dyskinesia, when levodopa is ultimately added, is similar (106) or lower (12, 107) than it is in patients who have been on levodopa alone for the duration of therapy. However, when levodopa is added, motor complications will emerge with the same or shortened latency as when levodopa is the first dopaminergic treatment (105). This may be related to the observation that delaying initiation of levodopa shortens the interval to appearance of motor fluctuations (110), probably because emergence of motor complications is related to disease severity (111).

Another strategy for early treatment of Parkinsonism is based on the theoretical role of pulsatile administration of levodopa in the development of motor complications (47, 48, 112). An attempt to test this theory by comparing immediate-release carbidopa/levodopa and controlled-release preparations did not show any difference in motor complications after 5 years of treatment (10). Controlled-release carbidopa/levodopa does not produce constant dopaminergic stimulation; therefore it may be argued that the failure to show differences is not a test of the theory. However, it is also important to realize that the animal studies supporting this theory used levodopa doses that could be difficult to extrapolate to the clinic (113). Clinical studies of this concept have so far yielded conflicting data. In conclusion, there are strong feelings about the proper manner to manage early PD, but they are based more on interpretation of basic studies than proven clinical tenets (114, 115). Studies are under way with combinations of carbidopa/levodopa and entacapone to determine whether the more continuous dopaminergic stimulation produced by this strategy is a viable means of preventing dyskinesia.

Because motor fluctuations and dyskinesia are related to disease severity, another method of minimizing fluctuations is to reduce the "off" disability. This means preventing or reversing the further loss of the endogenous nigrostriatal dopaminergic system and either increasing or at least maintaining the long-duration response. Neuroprotective strategies are largely theoretical at this point (116) but are under active investigation. Deep brain stimulation of the pallidum (80, 81) and subthalamic nucleus (82, 117) does not slow progression, although it does reduce dyskinesia. Coenzyme Q10 (118) and rasagiline (119–121) are being investigated as possible neuroprotective agents. Neurotrophic factors such as glial cell line–derived neurotrophic factor (GDNF) constitute another active area of research (122). Finally, the mechanism underlying the long-duration response is completely mysterious; when understood, it may offer other strategies to improve function and reduce motor complications.

ACKNOWLEDGMENTS

Preparation of this manuscript is supported in part by the Parkinson's Disease Research, Education, and Clinical Center (PADRECC) at the Portland VA Medical Center, the National Parkinson's Foundation, and by NIH grant 5 R01 NS21062.

References

1. Sweet RD, McDowell FH. Five years treatment of Parkinson's disease with levodopa: Therapeutic results and survival of 100 patients. *Ann Intern Med* 1975; 83:456–463.
2. Barbeau A. High-level levodopa therapy in severely akinetic Parkinsonian patients: Twelve years later. In: Rinne UK, Klinger M, Stamm G (eds). *Parkinson's Disease:*

Current Progress, Problems and Management. Amsterdam/New York: Elsevier, 1980:229–239.
3. Ahlskog JE, Muenter MD. Frequency of levodopa-related dyskinesias and motor fluctuations as estimated from the cumulative literature. *Mov Disord* 2001; 16:448–458.

4. Poewe WH, Lees AJ, Stern GM. Low-dose L-dopa therapy in Parkinson's disease: A 6-year follow-up study. *Neurology* 1986; 36:1528–1530.
5. Hely MA, Morris JGL, Reid WGJ, et al. The Sidney multicentre study of Parkinson's disease: A randomized, prospective five year study comparing low dose bromocriptine with low dose levodopa-carbidopa. *J Neurol Neurosurg Psychiatry* 1994; 57:903–910.
6. Reardon KA, Shiff M, Kempster PA. Evolution of motor fluctuations in Parkinson's disease: A longitudinal study over 6 years. Mov Disord 1999; 14:605–611.
7. Kostic V, Przedborski S, Flaster E, et al. Early development of levodopa-induced dyskinesias and response fluctuations in young-onset Parkinson's disease. *Neurology* 1991; 41:202–205.
8. Quinn N, Critchley P, Marsden CD. Young onset Parkinson's disease. *Mov Disord* 1987; 2(2):73–91.
9. Schrag A, Ben-Shlomo Y, Brown R, et al. Young-onset Parkinson's disease revisited: Clinical features, natural history and mortality. *Mov Disord* 1998; 13:885–894.
10. Block GA, Liss CL, Reines S, et al. Comparison of immediate-release and controlled-release carbidopa/levodopa in Parkinson's disease. *Eur Neurol* 1997; 37:23–27.
11. Nutt JG, Carter JH, Van Houten L, et al. Short- and long-duration responses to levodopa during the first year of levodopa therapy. *Ann Neurol* 1997; 42:349–355.
12. Rascol O, Brooks DJ, Korczyn AD, et al. A five-year study of the incidence of dyskinesia in patients with early Parkinson's disease who were treated with ropinirole or levodopa. 056 Study Group. *N Engl J Med* 2000; 342:1484–1491.
13. Parkinson Study Group. Pramipexole vs levodopa as initial treatment for Parkinson disease: A 4-year randomized controlled trial. *Arch Neurol* 2004; 61:1044–1053.
14. Denny AP, Behari M. Motor fluctuations in Parkinson's disease. *J Neurol Sci* 1999; 165:18–23.
15. Schrag A, Quinn N. Dyskinesias and motor fluctuations in Parkinson's disease. *Brain* 2000; 123:2297–2305.
16. Nutt JG, Holford NHG. The response to levodopa in Parkinson's disease: Imposing pharmacological law and order. *Ann Neurol* 1996; 39:561–573.
17. Cotzias GC, Van Woert MH, Schiffer LM. Aromatic amino acids and modification of Parkinsonism. *N Engl JMed* 1967; 276:374–379.
18. Muenter MD, Tyce GM. L-dopa therapy of Parkinson's disease: Plasma L-dopa concentration, therapeutic response, and side effects. *Mayo Clin Proc* 1971; 46:231–239.
19. Nutt JG, Gancher ST, Woodward WR. Does an inhibitory action of levodopa contribute to motor fluctuations? *Neurology* 1988; 38:1553–1557.
20. Kempster PA, Frankel JP, Stern GM, et al. Comparison of motor response to apomorphine and levodopa in Parkinson's disease. *J Neurol Neurosurg Psychiatry* 1990; 53:1004–1007.
21. Contin M, Riva R, Martinelli P, et al. Response to a standard oral levodopa test in Parkinsonian patients with and without motor fluctuations. *Clin Neuropharmacol* 1990; 13:19–28.
22. Merello M, Lees AJ. Beginning-of-dose motor deterioration following the acute administration of levodopa and apomorphine in Parkinson's disease. *J Neurol Neurosurg Psychiatry* 1992; 55:1024–1026.
23. Marsden CD. "On-off" phenomena in Parkinson's disease. In: Rinne UK, Klinger M, Stamm G (eds). *Parkinson's Disease: Current Progress, Problems and Management*. Amsterdam and New York: Elsevier/North-Holland Biomedical Press, 1980:241–254.
24. Currie LJ, Bennett JP, Harrison MB, et al. Clinical correlates of sleep benefit in Parkinson's disease. *Neurology* 1997; 48:1115–1117.
25. Merello M, Hughes A, Colosimo C, et al. Sleep benefit in Parkinson's disease. *Mov Disord* 1997; 12:506–508.
26. Hogl BE, Gomez-Arevalo G, Garcia S, et al. A clinical, pharmacologic, and polysomnographic study of sleep benefit in Parkinson's disease. *Neurology* 1998; 50:1332–1339.
27. Bonuccelli U, Del Dotto P, Lucetti C, et al. Diurnal motor variations to repeated doses of levodopa in Parkinson's disease. *Clin Neuropharmacol* 2000; 23:28–33.
28. Fahn S, Oakes D, Shoulson I, et al. Levodopa and the progression of Parkinson's disease. *N Engl J Med* 2004; 351:2498–2508.
29. Fabbrini G, Mouradian MM, Juncos JL, et al. Motor fluctuations in Parkinson's disease: Central pathophysiological mechanisms, Part I. *Ann Neurol* 1988; 24:366–371.
30. Gancher ST, Nutt JG, Woodward WR. Response to brief levodopa infusions in parkinsonian patients with and without motor fluctuations. *Neurology* 1988; 38:712–716.
31. Contin M, Riva R, Martinelli P, et al. Longitudinal monitoring of the levodopa concentration–effect relationship in Parkinson's disease. *Neurology* 1994; 44:1287–1292.
32. Colosimo C, Merello M, Hughes AJ, et al. Motor response to acute dopaminergic challenge with apomorphine and levodopa in Parkinson's disease: Implications for the pathogenesis of the on-off phenomenon. *JNeurol Neurosurg Psychiatry* 1996; 61:634–637.
33. Nutt JG, Woodward WR, Carter JH, et al. Effect of long-term therapy on the pharmacodynamics of levodopa: Relation to on-off phenomenon. *Arch Neurol* 1992; 49:1123–1130.
34. Kaye JA, Feldman RG. The role of L-dopa holiday in the long-term management of Parkinson's disease. *Clin Neuropharmacol* 1986; 9:1–13.
35. Nutt JG, Carter JH, Woodward WR. Long duration response to levodopa. *Neurology* 1995; 45:1613–1616.
36. Zappia M, Oliveri RL, Montesanti R, et al. Loss of long-duration response to levodopa over time in PD: Implications for wearing-off. *Neurology* 1999; 52:763–767.
37. Nutt JG, Carter JH, Lea ES, et al. Evolution of the response to levodopa during the first 4 years of therapy. *Ann Neurol* 2002; 51:686–693.
38. Rusk GD, Siemers ER. Diurnal variation in motor ability in Parkinson's disease (abstract). *Ann Neurol* 1993; 34:266–267.
39. Nutt JG, Carter JH, Lea ES, et al. Motor fluctuations during continuous levodopa infusions in patients with Parkinson's disease. *Mov Disord* 1997; 12:285–292.
40. Mouradian MM, Juncos JL, Fabbrini G, et al. Motor fluctuations in Parkinson's disease: Central pathophysiological mechanisms, Part II. *Ann Neurol* 1988; 24:372–378.
41. Marconi R, Lefebvre-Caparros D, Bonnet A, et al. Levodopa-induced dyskinesia in Parkinson's disease: Phenomenology and pathophysiology. *Mov Disord* 1994; 9:2–12.
42. Metman LV, van den Mundkhof P, Klaassen AAG, et al. Effects of suprathreshold levodopa doses on dyskinesia in advanced Parkinson's disease. *Neurology* 1997; 49:711–713.
43. Nutt JG, Gancher ST, Woodward WR. Motor fluctuations in Parkinson's disease. *Ann Neurol* 1987; 25:633.
44. Contin M, Riva R, Martinelli P, et al. Relationship between levodopa concentration, dyskinesias, and motor effect in Parkinsonian patients: A 3-year follow-up. *Clin Neuropharmacol* 1997; 20:409–418.
45. Goetz CG, Stebbins GT, Shale HM, et al. Utility of an objective dyskinesia rating scale for Parkinson's disease: Inter-and intrarater reliability assessment. *Mov Disord* 1994; 9:390–394.
46. Nutt JG, Woodward WR. Levodopa pharmacokinetics and pharmacodynamics in fluctuating Parkinsonian patients. *Neurology* 1986; 36:739–744.
47. Olanow CW, Agid Y, Mizuno Y, et al. Levodopa in the treatment of Parkinson's disease: Current controversies. *Mov Disord* 2004; 19:997–1005.
48. Stocchi F, Olanow CW. Continuous dopaminergic stimulation in early and advanced Parkinson's disease. *Neurology* 2004; 62:S56–S63.
49. Stocchi F, Vacca L, Ruggieri S, et al. Intermittent vs continuous levodopa administration in patients with advanced Parkinson disease. *Arch Neurol* 2005; 62:905–910.
50. Koller WC, Hutton JT, Tolosa E, et al. Immediate-release and controlled-release carbidopa/levodopa in PD: A 5-year randomized multicenter study. Carbidopa/levodopa Study Group. *Neurology* 1999; 53:1012–1019.
51. Dupont E, Boas J, Boisen E, et al. Sustained-release Madopar HBS compared with standard Madopar in the long-term treatment of de novo parkinsonian patients. *Acta Neurol Scand* 1996; 93:14–20.
52. Olanow CW, Agid Y, Mizuno Y, et al. Levodopa in the treatment of Parkinson's disease: Current controversies. *Mov Disord* 2004; 19:997–1005.
53. Olanow CW, Fahn S, Muenter M, et al. A multicenter double-blind placebo-controlled trial of pergolide as an adjunct to Sinemet in Parkinson's disease. *Mov Disord* 1994; 9:40–47.
54. Parkinson Study Group. Entacapone improves motor fluctuations in levodopa-treated Parkinson's disease patients. *Ann Neurol* 1997; 42:747–755.
55. Manson AJ, Turner K, Lees AJ. Apomorphine monotherapy in the treatment of refractory motor complications of Parkinson's disease: Long-term follow-up study of 64 patients. *Mov Disord* 2002; 17:1235–1241.
56. Stocchi F, Vacca L, Ruggieri S, et al. Intermittent vs continuous levodopa administration in patients with advanced Parkinson disease: A clinical and pharmacokinetic study. *Arch Neurol* 2005; 62:905–910.
57. Nutt JG. Continuous dopaminergic stimulation: Is it the answer to the motor complications of levodopa? *Mov Disord* 2007; 22(1):1-9.
58. Richard IH, Frank S, McDermott MP, et al. The ups and downs of Parkinson disease: A prospective study of mood and anxiety fluctuations. *Cogn Behav Neurol* 2004; 17:201–207.
59. Levy G. Kinetics of pharmacologic effects. *Clin Pharmacol Ther* 1966; 7:362–372.
60. Linazasoro G, Grandas F, Martinez Martin P,et al. Controlled release levodopa in Parkinson's disease: Influence of selection criteria and conversion recommendations in the clinical outcome of 450 patients. STAR Study Group. *Clin Neuropharmacol* 1999; 22:74–79.
61. Manyam BV, Hare TA, Robbs R, et al. Evaluation of equivalent efficacy of Sinemet and Sinemet CR in patients with Parkinson's disease applying levodopa dosage conversion formula. *Clin Neuropharmacol* 1999; 22:33–39.
62. Nutt JG, Woodward WR, Hammerstad JP, et al. The "on-off" phenomenon in Parkinson's disease: Relation to levodopa absorption and transport. *N Engl J Med* 1984; 310:483–488.
63. Baruzzi A, Contin M, Riva R, et al. Influence of meal ingestion time on pharmacokinetics of orally administered levodopa in Parkinsonian patients. *Clin Neuropharmacol* 1987; 10:527–537.
64. Contin M, Riva R, Martinelli P, et al. Effect of meal timing on the kinetic-dynamic profile of levodopa/carbidopa controlled release in Parkinsonian patients. *Eur J Clin Pharmacol* 1998; 54:303–308.
65. Campbell NRC, Rankine D, Goodridge AE, et al. Sinemet–ferrous sulphate interaction in patients with Parkinson's disease. *Br J Clin Pharmacol* 1990; 30:599–605.
66. Algeri S, Cerletti C, Curcio M, et al. Effect of anticholinergic drugs on gastrointestinal absorption of L-dopa in rats and in man. *Eur J Pharmacol* 1976; 35:293–299.
67. Rivera-Calimlim L, Dujovne CA, Morgan JP, et al. L-dopa treatment failure: Explanation and correction. *BMJ* 1970; 4:93–94.
68. Soykan I, Sarosiek K, Shifflett J, et al. Effect of chronic domperidone therapy on gastrointestinal symptoms and gastric emptying in patients with Parkinson's disease. *Mov Disord* 1997; 12:952–957.
69. Pincus JH, Barry KM. Protein redistribution diet restores motor function in patients with dopa-resistant "off" periods. *Neurology* 1988; 38:481–483.
70. Adler CH, Singer C, O'Brien C, et al. Randomized, placebo-controlled study of tolcapone in patients with fluctuating Parkinson disease treated with levodopa-carbidopa. *Arch Neurol* 1998; 55:1089–1095.
71. Rinne UK, Larsen JP, Siden A, et al. Entacapone enhances the response to levodopa in parkinsonian patients with motor fluctuations. *Neurology* 1998; 51:1309–1314.
72. Coleman RJ, Quinn NP, Traub M, et al. Nasogastric and intravenous infusions of (C)-4-propyl-9-hydroxynaphthoxazine (PHNO) in Parkinson's disease. *J Neurol Neurosurg Psychiatry* 1990; 53:102–105.
73. Cedarbaum JM, Silvestri M, Kutt H. Sustained enteral administration of levodopa increases and interrupted infusion decreases levodopa dose requirements. *Neurology* 1990; 40:995–997.
74. Cedarbaum JM, Clark M, Toy LH, et al. Sustained-release of (C)-PHNO [MK-458 (HPMC)] in the treatment of Parkinson's disease: Evidence for tolerance to a selective

D2-receptor agonist administered as a long-acting formulation. *Mov Disord* 1990; 5:298–303.

75. Gancher ST, Nutt JG, Woodward WR. Time-course of tolerance to apomorphine in Parkinsonism. *Clin Pharmacol Ther* 1992; 52:504–510.

76. Nutt JG, Carter JC, Woodward WR. Effect of brief levodopa holidays on the short-duration response to levodopa: Evidence for tolerance to the anti-Parkinsonian effects. *Neurology* 1994; 44:1617–1622.

77. Lieberman A, Ranhosky A, Korts D. Clinical evaluation of pramipexole in advanced Parkinson's disease: Results of a double-blind, placebo-controlled, parallel-group study. *Neurology* 1997; 49:162–168.

78. Lozano AM, Lang AE, Galvez-Jimenez N, et al. Effect of GPi pallidotomy on motor function in Parkinson's disease. *Lancet* 1995; 346:1383–1387.

79. Johansson F, Malm J, Nordh E, et al. Usefulness of pallidotomy in advanced Parkinson's disease. *J Neurol Neurosurg Psychiatry* 1997; 62:125–132.

80. Gross C, Rougier A, Guehl D, et al. High-frequency stimulation of the globus pallidus internalis in Parkinson's disease: A study of seven cases. *J Neurosurg* 1997; 87:491–498.

81. Pahwa R, Wilkinson S, Smith D, et al. High-frequency stimulation of the globus pallidus for the treatment of Parkinson's disease. *Neurology* 1997; 49:249–253.

82. Limousin P, Pollak P, Benazzouz A, et al. Effect on Parkinsonian signs and symptoms of bilateral subthalamic nucleus stimulation. *Lancet* 1995; 345:91–95.

83. Anderson VC, Burchiel KJ, Hogarth P, et al. Pallidal vs subthalamic nucleus deep brain stimulation in Parkinson disease. *Arch Neurol* 2005; 62:554–560.

84. Deep-Brain Stimulation for Parkinson's Disease Study Group. Deep-brain stimulation of the subthalamic nucleus or the pars interna of the globus pallidus in Parkinson's disease. *N Engl J Med* 2001; 345:956–963.

85. Esselink RAJ, de Bie RMA, de Haan RJ, et al. Unilateral pallidotomy versus bilateral subthalamic nucleus stimulation in PD: A randomized trial. *Neurology* 2004; 62:201–207.

86. Krause M, Fogel W, Heck A, et al. Deep brain stimulation for the treatment of Parkinson's disease: Subthalamic nucleus versus globus pallidus internus. *J Neurol Neurosurg Psychiatry* 2001; 70:464–470.

87. Freed CR, Greene PE, Breeze RE, et al. Transplantation of embryonic dopamine neurons for severe Parkinson's disease. *N Engl J Med* 2001; 344:710–719.

88. Olanow CW, Goetz CG, Kordower JH, et al. A double-blind controlled trial of bilateral fetal nigral transplantation in Parkinson's disease. *Ann Neurol* 2003; 54:403–414.

89. Barbeau A. The clinical physiology of side effects in long-term L-dopa therapy. *Adv Neurol* 1974; 5:347–365.

90. Thomas A, Iacono D, Luciano AL, et al. Duration of amantadine benefit on dyskinesia of severe Parkinson's disease. *J Neurol Neurosurg Psychiatry* 2004; 75:141–143.

91. Shannon KM, Goetz CG, Carroll VS, et al. Amantadine and motor fluctuations in chronic Parkinson's disease. *Clin Neuropharmacol* 1987; 10:522–526.

92. Hill MP, Ravenscroft P, Bezard E, et al. Levetiracetam potentiates the antidyskinetic action of amantadine in the 1-methyl-4-phenyl-1, 2, 3, 6-tetrahydropyridine (MPTP)-lesioned primate model of Parkinson's disease. *J Pharmacol Exp Ther* 2004; 310:386–394.

93. Zesiewicz TA, Sullivan KL, Maldonado JL, et al. Open-label pilot study of levetiracetam (Keppra) for the treatment of levodopa-induced dyskinesias in Parkinson's disease. *Mov Disord* 2005; 20:1205–1209.

94. Meco G, Fabrizio E, Epifanio A, et al. Levetiracetam in L-dopa-induced dyskinesia. *Clin Neuropharmacol* 2005; 28:102–103.

95. Olanow CW, Damier P, Goetz CG, et al. Multicenter, open-label, trial of sarizotan in Parkinson disease patients with levodopa-induced dyskinesias (the SPLENDID Study). *Clin Neuropharmacol* 2004; 27:58–62.

96. Bara-Jimenez W, Bibbiani F, Morris MJ, et al. Effects of serotonin 5-HT1A agonist in advanced Parkinson's disease. *Mov Disord* 2005; 20:932–936.

97. Bonifati V, Fabrizio E, Cipriani R, et al. Buspirone in levodopa-induced dyskinesia. *Clin Neuropharmacol* 1994; 17:73–82.

98. Durif F, Vidailhet M, Bonnet AM, et al. Levodopa-induced dyskinesias are improved by fluoxetine. *Neurology* 1995; 45:1855–1858.

99. Carpentier AF, Bonnet AM, Vidailhet M, et al. Improvement of levodopa-induced dyskinesia by propranolol in Parkinson's disease. *Neurology* 1996; 46:1548–1551.

100. Facca A, Sanchez-Ramos J. High-dose pergolide monotherapy in the treatment of severe levodopa-induced dyskinesia. *Mov Disord* 1996; 11:327–341.

101. Lang AE, Lozano AM, Montgomery E, et al. Posteroventral medial pallidotomy in advanced Parkinson's disease. *N Engl J Med* 1997; 337:1036–1042.

102. Samuel M, Caputo E, Brooks DJ, et al. A study of medial pallidotomy for Parkinson's disease: Clinical outcome, MRI localization and complications. *Brain* 1998; 121:59–75.

103. Russmann H, Ghika J, Combrement P, et al. L-dopa-induced dyskinesia improvement after STN-DBS depends upon medication reduction. *Neurology* 2004; 63:153–155.

104. Loher TJ, Burgunder JM, Weber S, et al. Effect of chronic pallidal deep brain stimulation on off period dystonia and sensory symptoms in advanced Parkinson's disease. *J Neurol Neurosurg Psychiatry* 2002; 73:395–399.

105. Montastruc JL, Rascol O, Senard JM, et al. A randomized controlled study comparing bromocriptine to which levodopa was later added, with levodopa alone in previously untreated patients with Parkinson's disease: A five year follow up. *J Neurol Neurosurg Psychiatry* 1994; 1034–1038.

106. Rinne UK, Bracco F, Chouza C, et al. Early treatment of Parkinson's disease with cabergoline delays the onset of motor complications. Results of a double-blind levodopa controlled trial. The PKDS009 Study Group. *Drugs* 1998; 55(Suppl 1):23–30.

107. Parkinson Study Group. Pramipexole vs levodopa as initial treatment for Parkinson disease: A randomized controlled trial. *JAMA* 2000; 284:1931-1938.

108. Parkinson Study Group. A randomized controlled trial comparing pramipexole with levodopa in early Parkinson's disease: Design and methods of the CALM-PD Study. *Clin Neuropharmacol* 2000; 23:34–44.

109. Whone AL, Watts RL, Stoessl AJ, et al. Slower progression of Parkinson's disease with ropinirole versus levodopa: The REAL-PET study. *Ann Neurol* 2003; 54:93–101.

110. Cedarbaum JM, Gandy SE, McDowell FH. "Early" initiation of levodopa treatment does not promote the development of motor response fluctuations, dyskinesias, or dementia in Parkinson's disease. *Neurology* 1991; 41:622–629.

111. Langston WJ, Ballard P. Parkinsonism induced by 1-methyl-4-phenyl-1, 2, 3, 6-tetra-hydropyridine (MPTP): Implications for treatment and the pathogenesis of Parkinson's disease. *Can J Neurol Sci* 1984; 11:160–165.

112. Chase TN, Engber TM, Mouradian MM. Palliative and prophylactic benefits of continuously administered dopaminomimetics in Parkinson's disease. *Neurology* 1994; 44(Suppl 6):S15–S18.

113. Trugman JM, Hubbard CA, Bennett JP. Dose-related effects of continuous levodopa infusion in rats with unilateral lesions of the substantia nigra. *Brain Res* 1996; 725:177–183.

114. Ahlskog JE. Treatment of early Parkinson's disease: Are complicated strategies justified? *Mayo Clin Proc* 1996; 71:659–670.

115. Watts RL. The role of dopamine agonists in early Parkinson's disease. *Neurology* 1997; 49(Suppl 1):S34–S48.

116. Olanow CW. Attempts to obtain neuroprotection in Parkinson's disease. *Neurology* 1997; 49(Suppl):S26–S33.

117. Limousin P, Krack P, Pollak P, et al. Electrical stimulation of the subthalamic nucleus in advanced Parkinson's disease. *N Engl J Med* 1998; 339:1105–1111.

118. Shults CW, Oakes D, Kieburtz K, et al. Effects of coenzyme Q10 in early Parkinson disease. *Arch Neurol* 2002; 59:1541–1550.

119. Parkinson Study Group. A randomized placebo-controlled trial of rasagiline in levodopa-treated patients with Parkinson disease and motor fluctuations. *Arch Neurol* 2005; 62:241–248.

120. Parkinson Study Group. A controlled trial of rasagiline in early Parkinson disease. *Arch Neurol* 2002; 59:1937–1943.

121. Parkinson Study Group. A controlled, randomized, delayed-start study of rasagiline in early Parkinson disease. *Arch Neurol* 2004; 61:561–566.

122. Nutt JG, Burchiel KJ, Comella CL, et al. Randomized, double-blind trial of glial cell line–derived neurotrophic factor (GDNF) in PD. *Neurology* 2003; 60:69–73

47 Fluctuations of Nonmotor Symptoms

Jacob I. Sage

The majority of patients with Parkinson's disease (PD) begin to experience a fluctuating response to levodopa (LD) within 5 years of initiating treatment (1). The most common fluctuations consist of changes in motor function presumably associated with alterations in the concentration and efficacy of striatal dopamine (2). High-concentration motor effects usually consist of dyskinesias (peak dose dyskinesias, chorea, or dystonia) and are associated with the "on" state. Low concentration or reduced efficacy of striatal dopamine is associated with the reemergence of parkinsonian motor symptoms ("off" state, end-of-dose wearing off) and frequently with chorea (diphasic) and dystonia [early-morning dystonia, diphasic dystonia (3, 4)].

Although the treatment of patients with advanced PD places major emphasis on controlling or reducing motor fluctuations, it has become increasingly clear that nonmotor fluctuations may be equally or even more incapacitating and common (5). Riley and Lang have suggested that most nonmotor fluctuations can be classified into 3 groups: sensory, autonomic, and cognitive/psychiatric (6). In a study of 130 patients with motor fluctuations, it was shown that at least 17% had nonmotor fluctuations as well (5). In a significant number

of patients, these nonmotor phenomena were a major if not the major cause of discomfort or disability.

It is important to note that many of these nonmotor phenomena are present in PD patients as a constant complaint and not as a fluctuating problem. Paresthesias, pain, drooling, orthostatic hypotension, urinary frequency, hallucinations, depression, anxiety, and dementia—to name only the most obvious—are difficulties faced all the time by some patients. A number of these complaints, most commonly pain and depression, can even be seen as initial or early symptoms of PD.

However, this chapter focuses on situations in which these nonmotor problems appear in temporal patterns closely associated with fluctuating concentrations of dopaminergic medications and of resultant changes in motor function. The Riley and Lang classification of nonmotor phenomena occurring both in the "on" and "off" states is applied. Nonmotor complications occurring in association with the "on" state are better known and therefore more frequently diagnosed than those occurring in the "off" state. The recognition of all nonmotor fluctuations depends on the clinician's knowledge of all the phenomena that can occur and relating the individual event with either a hypodopaminergic or a hyperdopaminergic state. Nonmotor symptoms and signs must be related carefully to motor signs and symptoms and to the timing of medications so as to make an accurate judgment of whether the patient is experiencing an "on" or an "off" problem. Appropriate therapeutic adjustments can then be made (7).

NONMOTOR PHENOMENA ASSOCIATED WITH THE "ON" STATE (TABLE 47-1)

Akathisia

Akathisia is a feeling of inner restlessness associated with a need to move. Patients describe an experience in which they feel unable to remain at rest. They find relief of this uncomfortable sensation only when they move about, either by walking or sometimes, when seated or recumbent, by moving the trunk or limbs. Some patients experience this sensation in one limb or one-half of the body,

---

TABLE 47-1

Nonmotor Phenomena Associated with the "Off" State

Sensory

Limb pain
Abdominal pain
Facial pain
Dysesthesias
Akathisia
Dyspnea
Internal tremor

Autonomic

Malignant hyperthermia
Dysphagia
Belching
Drooling
Anismus
Facial flushing
Limb edema
Drenching sweats
Urinary frequency and urgency
Nausea
Abdominal bloating
Cough
Hunger
Stridor
Pupillary dilation

Cognitive psychiatric

Cognitive dysfunction
Depression
Panic
Anxiety
Hallucinations
Moaning/screaming

---

usually the side with worse parkinsonism. About half of the patients experiencing akathisia find that there is no relationship to the timing of medications or parkinsonian state, while the remainder are evenly divided between those with akathisia in the "on" state and those with this sensation in the "off" state (8).

When it occurs as a peak-dose phenomenon, akathisia generally starts from 30 minutes to 1 hour after a patient's "on" period has begun and may last until that patient goes "off." It begins with peak plasma levodopa (and presumably brain dopamine) concentration and abates as these levels go down. Ten percent of patients experience akathisia in the beginning of dose pattern, starting about 10 minutes after levodopa ingestion and lasting only for 15 to 30 minutes. Some of these patients have diphasic akathisia associated with suboptimal levodopa concentrations or an inhibitory effect of levodopa.

The sense of a need to move, which is true akathisia, probably should be distinguished from mild chorea. Many patients with mild chorea do not even realize they are moving and have no sensation of a need to move. In some fluctuators, however, akathisia is a prelude to chorea or dystonia. In such patients, slight increases in the dose of levodopa or other dopaminergic agents will produce obvious chorea, suggesting that the perception of akathisia may occasionally mark the beginning of choreiform movements. Anxiety, depression, or even claustrophobia may be expressed by a perceived need to move about during an "on" phase in a fluctuating patient. As with other types of fluctuations, akathisia can begin shortly after the onset of levodopa treatment or many years after initiation of therapy.

Pain Associated with Dystonia

Only 10% of PD patients with pain have it during the "on" state. Virtually all of these patients have pain associated with dystonia and only a few have it with chorea (9). Patients with "on" type pain usually have cramps or tightness, most commonly in the neck, face, or paraspinal muscles of the upper trunk. Face and neck pain associated with dystonia is obvious on inspection. Paraspinal dystonic pain may be mistaken for nonspecific back pain and must be looked for with careful inspection of the involved body parts during an "on" period. Foot and leg pain can sometimes be seen with "on" periods but is generally seen at times of maximal parkinsonism ("off" periods).

Sweating and Flushing

Profuse sweating and flushing during the "on" state is almost always associated with severe chorea (10). Since sweating during periods of choreiform movement is related more to excessive physical activity than to poor heat dissipation, the entire body sweats, although head and neck areas may be somewhat more involved than the limbs or lower trunk (11).

Nausea

Although nausea is not an uncommon problem with the initiation of dopaminergic therapy, it usually disappears or is minimized as treatment continues (12). Patients with advanced disease on long-term levodopa therapy rarely begin to experience nausea. Such patients are usually on high doses of levodopa and have nausea shortly after each dose in association with the peak plasma concentration. Nausea often occurs in these patients only with the first dose of the day, but it can also occur with every dose or get worse with each successive dose throughout the day.

Hypotension

Both the supine and standing blood pressures (BPs) in fluctuating PD patients are significantly lower in the "on" than in the "off" state (13). Since many patients with advanced PD have low blood pressure, further reduction in standing BP during an "on" can lead to symptomatic orthostatic hypotension (OH) and syncope. Although the majority of patients with measured OH on routine office examination (a drop in BP greater than 15 mm Hg) are asymptomatic, a major cause of unexplained dizziness during the "on" state in fluctuating parkinsonian patients is OH (14). These patients do not experience dizziness every time the BP drops or every time they are "on" but are only intermittently symptomatic, which makes the diagnosis difficult. Furthermore, such complaints of "dizziness" due to OH must be distinguished from those related to postural instability. Multiple BP measurements or even continuous ambulatory BP monitoring may be necessary to make a diagnosis in equivocal cases.

Cognitive or Psychiatric

In general, fluctuating PD patients do not have more psychopathology or increased cognitive deficits during the "on" state than patients without motor fluctuations. Most PD patients have more psychopathology during "off" states as compared with "on" periods. One should always be careful in assuming that a psychiatric or cognitive deficit in any given patient is an "on" phenomenon only. Despite this caveat, in rare patients, hallucinations, delusions, and even mania and punding may be seen as manifestations of the "on" state only or may be worsened during an "on" period.

Some patients with severe nighttime akinesia require bedtime levodopa to sleep comfortably. These patients are at increased risk for nighttime hallucinations. Such hallucinations are relatively frequent, and it is difficult to say whether this situation (taking bedtime levodopa) should be classified as a psychosis associated with the "on" state or is more accurately considered a levodopa associated psychosis occurring during the night.

Hypomania may occur in the "on" state (15). We have seen patients who went on buying sprees, gambled excessively, or were hypersexual during such "on" periods. Others have reported sexually deviant behavior such as masochism, exhibitionism, and bondage associated only with "on" states (16). Most of these patients become more rational and even repentant as the "on" state wears off.

Depression that occurs mainly with the "on" state is almost always associated with severe choreiform dyskinesias (17). Many patients whose mood fluctuates with their motor state also have depression when "off," but they feel normal during an "on" state without dyskinesias. This pattern of mood fluctuations argues for a reactive depression due to increased disability in such patients.

Punding is a stereotyped behavior characterized by repeated cleaning, polishing, taking things apart, and putting things together, to name a few. Fernandez and colleagues described several patients with this type of behavior during "on" time (18).

NONMOTOR FLUCTUATIONS ASSOCIATED WITH THE "OFF" STATE

Abnormalities of Sensation

Pain Without Dystonia. About 25% of patients with "off" state, nonmotor phenomena have sensory symptoms; most of these are complaints of pain (19–22). Commonly, these pains mimic a radicular or neuropathic distribution. Patients describe a shooting sensation from proximal leg or arm locations traveling distally to the fingers or toes. The sensation is usually constant (although it may be paroxysmal), beginning as the levodopa dose is wearing off and continuing until the next dose "kicks in." Other common types of pain include deep, boring pain perceived to be in the bones of the legs, usually distally but sometimes above the knee. This feeling has been likened to "ripping the flesh from the bone." Patients also describe superficial, burning dysesthesias that can be compared with a raw sunburn but more often is a tingling or a feeling of numbness in the distal leg or toes. Patients with pain from other causes, such as low back arthritis, also notice fluctuations in pain. Their pain, although present continuously, is worse in the "off" state than in the "on" state. In some, approaching the treatment of pain from this angle may be more successful than using pain relievers.

A number of syndromes are distinguished by the location of pain and are seen more rarely than those enumerated. Pain in the proximal arm and pectoral area (22), "whole body" pain, proximal limb burning, burning of the nipples, and pain similar to that of trigeminal neuralgia have all been seen as "off" phenomena (5). Abdominal pain is perhaps the most dramatic of these less common presentations. It occurs just as the "off" period begins, often doubling the patient over with an excruciating intra-abdominal cramp-like feeling. The patient reports the symptoms as if he or she were experiencing an acute abdomen without a sense of external cramping of the abdominal musculature. Inspection of the abdominal muscles reveals nothing unusual, and there is no visible bloating.

Pain with Dystonia. Pain may be associated with obvious dystonia (23). Since "off" dystonia commonly involves the leg and foot, this type of pain is usually associated with a severe cramp in the dorsiflexors of the great toe, the gastrocnemius, anterior tibial, or posterior tibial, although any muscles of the leg or foot may be involved. Some patients experience "off" dystonia in other parts of the body and report pain in the back, abdominal muscles, an arm, or even the head and neck. This is far less common than foot or leg involvement.

Akathisia. Two other sensory phenomena that occur with "off" periods are akathisia and sensory dyspnea. Akathisia has already been discussed as a peak-dose phenomenon, but it is more commonly seen in the "off" state. "Off" akathisia can be so severe that bradykinetic patients may require passive movement of the extremities to keep the discomfort levels tolerable. Akathisia should not be related to immobility alone. One must also exclude other causes of a need to move—such as severe rigidity; positive sensory phenomena like itching, burning, or paresthesias; restless legs syndrome; claustrophobia; anxiety or depression; and diphasic or end-of-dose dyskinesias—all of which can mimic akathisia.

Sensory Dyspnea. Sensory dyspnea is the distressing feeling that one cannot take another breath (5). During such periods there is no observable abnormality of breathing, which is in sharp contrast to dyspnea associated with peak-dose chorea, in which the respirations appear visibly chaotic (23). Because breathing patterns and rates are normal during these episodes, it is unlikely that chest muscle rigidity is responsible for the complaints. Despite the discomfort, most patients are not anxious. There is no evidence of autonomic or motor dysfunction during each episode other than the usual "off" phenomena characteristic of each patient. In particular, there is no stridor or other evidence of upper airway obstruction and no dystonia or chorea. It is a sensation of dyspnea; therefore the symptoms have been classified as sensory in nature. The dyspneic feeling usually disappears within minutes after a levodopa dose begins to take effect.

Internal Tremor

The term *internal tremor* describes an often encountered subjective complaint that patients with PD experience. This is a sensation of a tremor felt inside the limbs or axial regions with no associated observable tremor. A sensation of internal tremor has been reported in up to 44% of patients with PD. Internal tremor can be episodic, most often lasting between 5 and 30 minutes. It may occur on a daily basis or only 1 to 4 times per week. Eighty percent of patients who experience internal tremor report no predictable schedule to its occurrence. More than half of the patients report the sensation of internal tremor when they are feeling anxious. Internal tremor is described by patients as being unpleasant, uncomfortable, or painful. Internal tremor is most often experienced in the extremities. More than half of these patients are unaware of any association between the sensation of internal tremor and whether they are "on" or "off." Those patients who note an association of internal tremor and fluctuations usually experience it during an "off" period. Internal tremor is not terribly responsive to antiparkinsonian medications but is often relieved by anxiolytic agents (25).

Autonomic Dysfunction

Drenching Sweats. Sweating abnormalities have been noted in PD patients since the early descriptions of Gowers and Charcot (26, 27). Excessive intermittent head and neck sweating and patchy impairment of thermoregulatory sweating suggests that abnormal sweating patterns are primarily disease-related. After the introduction of levodopa therapy in 1967, it also became clear that episodes of profuse sweating occurred in a fluctuating pattern, similar to motor dysfunction (10). Excessive whole-body sweating can accompany severe peak-dose chorea and probably represents an impairment of thermoregulation during hard exercise. The most severe drenching sweats, however, occur as part of the spectrum of "off"-period levodopa-related fluctuations (28).

Profuse sweating during periods of subtherapeutic plasma levodopa concentrations suggests that this phenomenon results from inadequate central dopaminergic stimulation. The sweating, usually involving the head and neck, begins as plasma levels of levodopa fall below the threshold necessary to maintain the "on" state and may last for an hour or more if the patient does not take another dose of levodopa. Most often these episodes occur during the night, several hours after the last evening dose of levodopa. Patients may drench their clothing and the bedsheets, often necessitating a change of bedclothes and bed linen. Sweating, like diphasic dyskinesias, does not necessarily occur each time the levodopa level falls or even every night. Patients may experience night sweats for many months, only to have them disappear for no apparent reason.

That abnormal sweating is seen most often as an end-of-dose or nighttime-only pattern is probably related to the fact that most methods of levodopa administration produce rapid rises to peak levodopa concentrations followed by a gradual return to baseline. The concentration window at which sweating occurs may be reached briefly as levodopa levels rise, just before the dose becomes effective. Diphasic events such as profuse sweats are usually too fleeting to be noticed or may not occur at all before most "on" states, developing only as the medication is wearing off.

Urinary Frequency and Urgency. Patients with PD often have detrusor hyperactivity, which leads to urinary frequency, urgency, and nocturia (12, 29). Nocturia is the most common urinary complaint, followed by daytime symptoms. If daytime frequency or urgency occurs early, causes such as mechanical obstruction from prostatism should be considered. Significant problems with daytime frequency can be seen in the "off" state. Such patients are usually on a schedule of frequent levodopa doses and exhibit "wearing off" less than 3 hours after each dose. As a dose of medication wears off, patients develop urinary frequency and urgency that lasts until the next dose takes effect. The sense of urgency in these patients may be severe enough that they need to return to the bathroom every few minutes during an "off" period. In some patients, this sense of urgency recurs each time the levodopa wears off. This type of urgency and frequency may be seen in patients whose "off" symptoms are severe (marked bradykinesia, tremor, rigidity, and gait disturbance) but is also seen in patients with less severe "off" states.

Malignant Hyperthermia. Most reported cases of hyperthermia, tachycardia, tachypnea, sweating, and mental status deterioration occur in dopaminergic medication withdrawal and are thought to represent an abnormality of central dopaminergic thermoregulatory systems. The signs and symptoms occur within several days after discontinuation of therapy and may or may not be accompanied by elevations in serum creatine kinase. In rare patients, stupor, hyperthermia, and—to a variable extent—the other signs noted previously may occur repeatedly in association with "off" episodes in the context of severe motor fluctuations. A case has been reported in which this syndrome led to the patient's death (30).

Gastrointestinal Tract Dysmotility. Autonomic pathology and dysfunction in patients with PD is widespread and responsible for a number of problems related to different parts of the gastrointestinal tract. Some of these problems are exacerbated during "off" periods (31–35). Lewy bodies have been found within degenerating colonic neurons (myenteric plexus); the primary clinical correlates are slowed stool transit time and constipation, related to impaired colonic muscle contraction. Some patients may even develop sigmoid volvulus and megacolon (36). Vagal dysfunction may delay gastric emptying, especially of solids. Esophageal peristalsis, mediated by the dorsal motor nucleus of the vagus, is probably abnormal, with resultant segmental esophageal spasm and reflux in many cases. It has been noted that infusion of dopamine relaxes the gastroesophageal sphincter. Both parasympathetic and sympathetic inputs mediate small bowel motility, whereas salivation is primarily a parasympathetic phenomenon controlled by the cholinergic superior and inferior salivatory nuclei.

Dysphagia, in patients who do not normally complain of swallowing difficulty, or exacerbation of existing dysphagia during "off" periods, has several causes (37, 38). The most common cause of dysphagia during "offs" is a slowing down of the musculature that propels food from the mouth backward into the pharynx. This neural control system involves voluntary buccolingual striated muscle and is therefore a motor rather than a nonmotor phenomenon. Once food enters the esophagus, it is rapidly propelled via a complex reflex mechanism that carries food into the stomach. During "offs," patients may complain of a lump in the throat as food becomes lodged in the esophagus. This may occur only during an "off" or as an exacerbation of a complaint present to a lesser degree at other times as well. Transit of food is often slowed in the lower third of the esophagus, where peristalsis is most impaired. Some patients complain more of heartburn secondary to esophageal reflux during "off" periods. Two patients have been reported with paroxysmal belching associated with esophageal dysmotility and involuntary aerophagia during the "off" state. Subcutaneous apomorphine improved esophageal motility in these patients (as shown by radiologic evaluation), with resolution of belching and aerophagia for the duration of dopamine agonist–induced "on" time.

Drooling is a common complaint in patients with PD. Some patients with drooling find that they appear to have a marked overproduction of saliva during their "off" periods. A few patients with little or no drooling during "on" experience a sudden onset of drooling with each "off." These periodic increases in drooling often seem so excessive that it is hard not to infer a significant increase in saliva production as a dose of levodopa is wearing off, although no such increased production has ever been adequately documented. An alternative explanation is that increased drooling during "offs" reflects a decrease in the automatic, unconscious swallowing of saliva, with subsequent pooling in the mouth and drooling. The author has witnessed several such episodes where it seemed that there was some role for excessive saliva production.

Abdominal pain during "off" is usually associated with dystonia. A number of patients with abdominal complaints associated with the "off" state have disturbances related to the sudden onset of "intestinal gas pain" (39). These symptoms can occur as each levodopa dose wears off, or they may sometimes develop during the night after the last daytime dose of medication has been given, often after awakening the patient from sleep. Some rare patients have visible abdominal bloating during such episodes. Anismus has even been reported as a wearing-off phenomenon (40, 41).

There are a host of other infrequently reported symptoms and signs of autonomic dysfunction that can be seen during "off" periods (5); these include pupillary dilation, tachycardia, pallor, facial flushing, cough, hunger, stridor, and changes in body temperature. Although nausea is usually related to the effect of peak levodopa concentrations on the central vomiting mechanism, the author has seen at least one patient with "off" state nausea presumably associated with gastointestinal hypomotility and increased intestinal gas. Limb edema, although usually due to poor mobility, can be seen as an "off" phenomenon. In one case, hand swelling occurred as a dose of levodopa wore off and disappeared within an hour after the next dose took effect. In this patient, poor mobility of the limb is an unlikely explanation for the rapid onset and clearing of "off"-period edema, which was probably a result of autonomic dysfunction.

Cognitive or Psychiatric

Panic or Anxiety.   Panic attacks are the most debilitating nonmotor "off" symptoms. One study reported a frequency of 24% in PD patients (42). It usually occurs when wearing off has been present for a few years. Panic begins abruptly, with many patients describing an uncontrolled feeling that death or some other terrible event is imminent. It is often associated with other symptoms, including shortness of breath, palpitations, trembling, sweating, abdominal distress, and chest pain. This frightening sensation disappears just as suddenly with the onset of the next "on" state. Reports suggest that panic always occurs in the setting of generalized anxiety (43, 44). This is not necessarily true in all cases, since some personally observed patients with panic attacks were anxious only during "off" states.

Since these panic episodes can occur in the setting of severe bradykinesia, it is conceivable that the feeling of panic might be merely a consequence of the motor problem, with its associated fear and discomfort. This is probably not an adequate explanation for most patients. Many patients with end-of-dose panic have been seen whose "off" bradykinesia, rigidity, or other signs of parkinsonism were not that much more severe than in their "on" condition.

The distinction between panic and anxiety in these patients is somewhat arbitrary. Some patients for whom the word *panic* is not quite appropriate have severe anxiety as an end-of-dose phenomenon. There is probably a continuum from mild "off"-period anxiety to severe panic.

Depression.   Depression is common in patients with PD, occurring in as many as 50% (45, 46). Some PD patients experience mood swings of a large amplitude, which go in tandem with their motor fluctuations (47). The symptoms of depression in these patients are often out of proportion to their motor dysfunction and can be the most disabling part of the disease. In one survey, as many as two-thirds of fluctuating patients reported some mood swings (44).

Depressive symptoms and signs are usually linked to "off" periods, appearing abruptly as a dose of medication wears off and ceasing just as quickly as the next dose takes effect. In some patients, depression has been associated both with "off"-state bradykinesia and during "on" periods with severe dyskinesias, suggesting a reactive process linked to motor impairment rather than a biochemical state of the brain (17). In the majority of patients with mood swings related to motor fluctuations, significant depression is seen in "off" states only. A study comparing fluctuating parkinsonian patients and those similarly immobile from rheumatoid arthritis showed increased "off"-period depression in the PD patients (49). This suggests that the depressive symptoms are related to the underlying biochemical, molecular, and structural causes of fluctuations and are not psychological reactions to immobility.

Hallucinosis.   The abrupt onset of hallucinations and confusion can occur in "off" periods (50). In some personally observed cases, hallucinations began 30 to 60 minutes after levodopa wore off. The psychosis was accompanied by marked exacerbations of parkinsonism, both of which improved when the next dose began to take effect. A few cases of "off"-period moaning and screaming accompanying hallucinosis and pain have been reported (51). One case of "off"-state moaning alone has been seen without confusion, hallucinations, or screaming.

Cognitive Changes.   Cognitive function is difficult to assess accurately in fluctuating patients—a fact that may account for the differing opinions of various authors (52–56). Observations from the older studies are here described first. One such study finds that verbal recall ability is state-dependent; that is, when asked to recall a verbal task, it is better if they are in the same motor state as they were the previous day, regardless of whether they were "on" or "off." Some investigations report diminished mental ability in the "off" state. However, tests of high cortical function that depend on the integrity of motor systems skew results toward findings that suggests worsening mental ability during "off" states. At least one report demonstrates a deterioration in intellectual functioning during "off" states that was related to deterioration in affect and arousal scores. Another study suggests that some aspects of frontal lobe cognitive function may be improved in "off" states, while others are better during "on" periods. Most of the evidence and our own experience suggests that significant numbers of patients do have selective deficits in cognitive function during "off" states. These problems vary from patient to patient and are certainly not present in all patients with complaints of cognitive dysfunction during "off" periods. Delayed memory function, particularly for names, and perseveration or festination of speech are most frequently seen in these patients. Many complain of increased difficulty in concentrating, although this is difficult to measure. When there is a difference in cognitive functioning between "on" and "off" states, it is usually mild, although it may be troublesome.

We have studied the role of dopamine in cognitive sequence learning in PD patients during the "on" and "off" states (57). These studies were based on electrophysiologic and computational work that suggested a role for nigrostriatal dopamine in learning sequences of environmentally important stimuli, especially when this learning is based on step-by-step associations between stimuli. The hypothesis was that such sequentially dependent learning would be disrupted during the "off" state in patients with PD. Patients were given a "chaining task" in which each additional link in a sequence of stimuli leading to

a reward is trained step by step until the full sequence is learned. Parkinson's patients tested during the "off" state performed as well as controls when required to learn a simple stimulus response association but were impaired at learning the full sequence. This deficit was repaired during the "on" state. The fact that specific learning but not all types of learning are deficient during the "off" state is supported by other studies (58). We have shown that patients with PD are impaired on a feedback-based task but not on a nonfeedback version of the same task. Furthermore, PD patients and controls use different learning strategies, depending on the feedback structure.

TREATMENT

Treatment of nonmotor fluctuations is not always possible but should be aimed at diminishing "off" time or peak-dose effects, whichever is appropriate (see Chapter 40). There are a few special points worth noting. In several patients with severe "off" pain," the benefit derived from tolcapone, a catechol-O-methyl transferase (COMT) inhibitor, has been particularly impressive. Some of the patients with "off"-state depression who were not depressed during "on" periods and did not benefit from antidepressants were helped by pramipexole. Not much benefit has been found from botulinum toxin in patients with painful dystonia related to either "on" or "off." Anismus seems to be helped in a number of patients by injections of apomorphine. Drenching sweats in many patients appear to have a limited time course, lasting for several months and diminishing in intensity or even disappearing for long periods for seemingly no reason. Recognition of the symptoms and signs of nonmotor fluctuations will prevent unnecessary investigations and useless treatments.

References

1. Wooten GF. Progress in understanding the pathophysiology of treatment-related fluctuations in Parkinson's disease. *Ann Neurol* 1988; 24:363–365.
2. Sage JI, Mark MH. Basic mechanisms of motor fluctuations. *Neurology* 1994; 44(Suppl 6):S10–S14.
3. Muenter MD, Sharpless NS, Tyce GM, et al. Patterns of dystonia ("I-D-I" and "D-I-D") in response to L-dopa therapy for Parkinson's disease. *Mayo Clin Proc* 1977; 52:163–174.
4. McHale DM, Sage JI, Sonsalla PK, et al. Complex dystonia of Parkinson's disease: Clinical features and relation to plasma levodopa profile. *Clin Neuropharmacol* 1990; 13:164–170.
5. Hillen ME, Sage JI. Nonmotor fluctuations in patients with Parkinson's disease. *Neurology* 1996; 47:1180–1183.
6. Riley DE, Lang AE. The spectrum of levodopa-related fluctuations in Parkinson's disease. *Neurology* 1993; 43:1459–1464.
7. Sage JI, Mark MH, McHale DM, et al. Benefits of monitoring plasma levodopa in Parkinson's disease patients with drug-induced chorea. *Ann Neurol* 1991; 29:623–628.
8. Lang AE, Johnson K. Akathisia in idiopathic Parkinson's disease. *Neurology* 1987; 37:477–481.
9. Sage JI, Kortis HI, Sommer W. Evidence for the role of spinal cord systems in Parkinson's disease–associated pain. *Clin Neuropharmacol* 1990; 13:171–174.
10. Barbeau A. The clinical physiology of side effects of long-term L-dopa therapy. *Adv Neurol* 1974; 5:347–364.
11. Appenzeller O, Goss JE. Autonomic deficits in Parkinson's syndrome. *Arch Neurol* 1971; 24:50–57.
12. Tanner CM, Goetz CG, Klawans HL. Autonomic nervous system disorders in Parkinson's disease. In: Koller WC (ed). *Handbook of Parkinson's Disease*. New York: Marcel Dekker, 1992:185–215.
13. Weiner WJ, Bergen D. Prevention and management of the side effects of levodopa. In: Klawans HL (ed). *Clinical Neuropharmacology*. Vol 2. New York: Raven Press, 1977.
14. Hillen ME, Wagner ML, Sage JI. "Subclinical" orthostatic hypotension is associated with dizziness in elderly patients with Parkinson's disease. *Arch Phys Med Rehabil* 1996; 77:710–712.
15. Hardie RT, Lees AJ, Stern GM. On-off fluctuations in Parkinson's disease. *Brain* 1984; 107:487–506.
16. Quinn NP, Toone B, Lang AE, et al. Dopa dose–dependent sexual deviation. *Br J Psychiatry* 1983; 142:296–298.
17. Menza MA, Sage JI, Marshall E, et al. Mood changes and "on-off" phenomena in Parkinson's disease. *Mov Disord* 1990; 5:148–151.
18. Fernandez HH, Friedman JH. Punding on L-dopa. *Mov Disord* 1999; 14:836–838.
19. Snider SR, Fahn S, Isgreen WP, et al. Primary sensory symptoms in Parkinsonism. *Neurology* 1976; 26:423–429.
20. Koller WC. Sensory symptoms in Parkinson's disease. *Neurology* 1984; 34:957–959.
21. Goetz CG, Tanner CM, Levy M, et al. Pain in Parkinson's disease. *Mov Disord* 1986; 1:45–49.

22. Quinn NP, Lang AE, Koller WC, et al. Painful Parkinson's disease. *Lancet* 1986; 1:957–959.

23. Sage JI, McHale DM, Sonsalla PK, et al. Continuous levodopa infusions to treat complex dystonia in Parkinson's disease. *Neurology* 1989; 39:888–891.

24. Weiner WI, Goetz C, Nausieda PA, et al. Respiratory dyskinesias: Extrapyramidal dysfunction presenting as dyspnea. *Ann Intern Med* 1978; 3:134–140.

25. Shulman LM, Singer C, Bean JA, et al. Internal tremor in patients with Parkinson's disease. *Mov Disord* 1996: 11:3–7.

26. Gowers WR. *A Manual of Disease of the Nervous System.* Philadelphia: Blakiston, 1888.

27. Charcot JM. *Maladies du syteme nerveux.* Vol 1. Paris: Battaille, 1892.

28. Sage JI, Mark MH. Drenching sweats as an off phenomenon in Parkinson's disease: Treatment and relation to plasma levodopa profile. *Ann Neurol* 1995; 37:120–122.

29. Fitzmaurice H, Fowler CJ, Rickards D, et al. Micturition disturbance in Parkinson's disease. *Br J Urol* 1985; 57:652–656.

30. Pfeiffer RF, Sucha EL. "On-off"–induced lethal hyperthermia. *Mov Disord* 1989; 4:338–341.

31. Koller WC, Silver DE, Lieberman A (eds). An algorithm for the management of Parkinson's disease. *Neurology* 1994; 44(Suppl 10):S19–S27.

32. Edwards LL, Quigley EMM, Hofman R, et al. Gastrointestinal symptoms in Parkinson's disease: 18-month follow-up study. *Mov Disord* 1993; 8:83–86.

33. Edwards LL, Pfeiffer RF, Quigley EMM, et al. Gastrointestinal symptoms in Parkinson's disease. *Mov Disord* 1991; 6:151–156.

34. Edwards LL, Quigley EMM, Pfeiffer RF. Gastrointestinal dysfunction in Parkinson's disease: Frequency and pathophysiology. Neurology 1992; 42:726–732.

35. Edwards LL, Quigley EMM, Harned RK, et al. Defacatory function in Parkinson's disease: Response to apomorphine. *Ann Neurol* 1993; 33:490–493.

36. Caplan LH, Jacobson HG, Rubinstein BM, et al. Megacolon and volvulus in Parkinson's disease. *Radiology* 1965; 85:73–79.

37. Bushmann M, Dobmeyer SM, Leeker L, et al. Swallowing abnormalities and their response to treatment in Parkinson's disease. *Neurology* 1989; 39:1309–1314.

38. Edwards LL, Quigley EMM, Harned RK, et al. Characterization of swallowing and defecation in Parkinson's disease. *Am J Gastroenterology* 1994; 89:15–25.

39. Kempster PA, Lees AJ, Crichton P, et al. Off-period belching due to a reversible disturbance of oesophageal motility in Parkinson's disease and its treatment with apomorphine. Mov Disord 1989; 4:47–52.

40. Mathers SE, Kempster PA, Law PJ, et al. Anal sphincter dysfunction in Parkinson's disease. *Arch Neurol* 1989; 46:1061–1064.

41. Mathers SE, Kempster PA, Swash M, et al. Constipation and paradoxical puborectalis contraction in anismus and Parkinson's disease: A dystonic phenomenon? *J Neurol Neurosurg Psychiatry* 1988; 51:1503–1507.

42. Vasquez A, Jiminez-Jiminez FJ, Garcia-Ruiz P, et al. "Panic attacks" in Parkinson's disease: A long-term complication of levodopa therapy. *Acta Neurol Scand* 1993; 87:14–18.

43. Stein MB, Heuser IJ, Juncos JL, et al. Anxiety disorders in patients with Parkinson's disease. *Am J Psychiatry* 1990; 147:217–220.

44. Routh LC, Black JL, Ahlskog JE. Parkinson's disease complicated by anxiety. *Mayo Clin Proc* 1987; 62:733–735.

45. Marsden CD, Parkes JD. "On and off" variability and response swings in Parkinson's disease. In: Rose FC, Capildeo R (eds). *Research Progress in Parkinson's Disease.* Kent, UK: Pitman Medical, 1981:265–264.

46. Menza M, Forman N, Sage J, et al. Psychiatric symptoms in Parkinson's disease: A comparison between patients with and without "on-off" symptoms. *Biol Psychiatry* 1993; 33:682–684.

47. Keshavan MS, David AS, Narayanen HS, et al. "On-off" phenomena and manic depressive mood shifts: Case report. *J Clin Psychiatry* 1986; 47:93–94.

48. Nissenbaum H, Quinn NP, Brown RG, et al. Mood swings associated with the "on-off" phenomenon in Parkinson's disease. *Psychol Med* 1987; 17:899–904.

49. Cantello R, Gilli M, Riccio A, et al. Mood changes associated with "end of dose deterioration" in Parkinson's disease: A controlled study. *J Neurol Neurosurg Psychiatry* 1986; 49:1182–1190.

50. Sage JI, Duvoisin RC. Sudden onset of confusion with severe exacerbation of Parkinsonism during levodopa therapy. *Mov Disord* 1986; 1:267–270.

51. Steiger MJ, Quinn NP, Toone B, et al. Off-period screaming accompanying motor fluctuations in Parkinson's disease. *Mov Disord* 1991; 6:89–90.

52. Huber SJ, Shulman HG, Paulson GW, et al. Dose-dependent memory impairment in Parkinson's disease. *Neurology* 1989; 39:438–440.

53. Delis D, Direnfeld L, Alexander MP, et al. Cognitive fluctuations associated with on-off phenomenon in Parkinson's disease. *Neurology* 1982; 32:1049–1052.

54. Girotti E, Carella F, Grassi MP, et al. Motor and cognitive performance of parkinsonian patients in the on and off phases of the disease. *J Neurol Neurosurg Psychiatry* 1986; 49:657–660.

55. Gotham AM, Brown RG, Marsden CD. "Frontal" cognitive function in patients with Parkinson's disease "on" and "off" levodopa. *Brain* 1988; 11:299–321.

56. Poewe W, Berger W, Benke T, et al. High speed memory scanning in Parkinson's disease: Adverse effects of levodopa. *Ann Neurol* 1991; 29:670–673.

57. Shohamy D, Myers CE, Grossman S, et al. The role of dopamine in cognitive sequence learning: Evidence from Parkinson's disease. *Behav Brain Res* 2005; 156:191–199.

58. Shohamy D, Myers CE, Grossman S, et al. Cortico-striatal contributions to feedback-based learning: Coberging date from neuroimaging and neuropsychology. *Brain* 2004; 127:851–859.

48 Psychosis and Other Behaviors

Eric S. Molho

With the development of levodopa for the treatment of Parkinson's disease (PD) in the late 1960s came great optimism that dopamine replacement therapy might provide a cure or at least a lasting reversal of symptoms. It was soon realized, however, that levodopa therapy, though dramatically effective in controlling symptoms, was not a cure and that a number of long-term disabling complications were associated with its use. Among these problems were drug-induced behavioral and psychiatric syndromes. The most important of these is drug-induced psychosis (DIP) (1). Hallucinations in PD are a major risk factor for increased caregiver stress and strain (2) as well as nursing home placement (3). The occurrence of hallucinations and DIP heralds an alarmingly high mortality, particularly in the nursing home setting (4, 5). Psychosis in PD has received increased attention because of the demonstrated efficacy of clozapine (CLZ) in treating this problem (6, 7) and the availability of other alternative "atypical" antipsychotic medications that have been proposed as safe and effective alternative to CLZ. There has also been growing recognition that psychosis, its impact on the treatment of motor symptoms, and its interaction with cognitive dysfunction represent a major unmet need in the treatment of advanced PD. The history, clinical features, and mechanisms of DIP in PD, recent literature concerning the treatment of DIP,

and a practical approach to its treatment are reviewed below. Two other related behavioral syndromes in PD, mania and hypersexuality, are also discussed.

TERMINOLOGY AND HISTORY

The terms "levodopa psychosis," "drug-induced psychosis (DIP)," and "dopaminomimetic psychosis" have been used interchangeably to describe several different psychiatric syndromes in PD. The broad application of these terms has hindered our understanding of the frequency, pathophysiology, and treatment of these disorders. It is clear that there are several distinct psychiatric syndromes with psychotic features that occur in PD. Friedman (8) has pointed out that it is probably more accurate to refer to these syndromes as the levodopa psychoses. However, levodopa is not the only drug capable of causing psychosis. There are also questions as to whether psychosis is purely a dopaminergic phenomenon, so that the terms dopaminomimetic or levodopa psychosis may not be accurate. However, for the most part, psychosis does occur in treated patients. This chapter uses the term DIP.

These syndromes are divided into two broad categories: those associated with a clear sensorium and those occurring on a background of confusion. Patients with a clear sensorium may suffer from hallucinations, delusions, or both. By the criteria of the *Diagnostic and Statistical Manual of Mental Disorders* (DSM-III-R, these correspond to an organic delusional syndrome or an organic hallucinosis, respectively (9). The organic confusional psychosis is seen in patients with a clouded sensorium and can vary in intensity from a mild confusional state to a frank delirium. Although these terms are no longer utilized in DSM-IV, they are still useful in the discussion of psychosis in PD. There is agreement that, although all these syndromes can be induced by dopaminergic medications, they are distinct in their epidemiology and pathophysiology, including association with dementia and response to treatment (8, 10–12). The term DIP is used here to refer to psychotic symptoms (hallucinations and delusions) occurring on the background of a clear sensorium.

A historical review of psychosis in PD from the prel-evodopa era indicates that not all psychotic symptoms are drug-related. Coexistent and premorbid psychiatric disease can occur, including schizophrenia (8). Psychiatric symptoms including psychosis can also be a prominent feature of secondary parkinsonism, particularly the postencephalitic form (13). In dementia with Lewy bodies (DLB), psychosis can be the presenting feature (14). However, the occurrence of hallucinations, delusions, and other psychotic symptoms as part of the natural history of PD is controversial, especially since there is a clear overlap between PD and DLB, leading to speculation that these are the same disease (15, 16).

In James Parkinson's original description of the disease, he concluded, "...by the absence of any injury to the senses and to the intellect, we are taught that the morbid state does not extend to the encephalon (17)." This view of PD as a process that spares the intellect and psychological functioning was held for almost a century. In 1903, Regis (18) categorized the mental disorders associated with parkinsonism and specifically mentioned depression as an early phenomenon and hallucinations as a symptom associated with advanced disease. In 1922, a total of 140 patients with PD were reviewed in an attempt to exclude those with postencephalitic parkinsonism (19). Depression was found in these patients and was thought to be reactive in nature, but there was no mention of psychotic symptoms. Another review in 1923 presented several patients with "paralysis agitans" and prominent symptoms of psychosis (20). Early features such as sleep disturbance, withdrawal from social situations, and suspiciousness were mentioned. Also discussed were more dramatic symptoms such as paranoid delusions and even hallucinations, which were "...generally limited to the organic sensations and tactile sense..." (20). In 1950, Schwab et al. (21) described a number of psychiatric symptoms in "Parkinson's disease" including paroxysmal depression, paranoia, and schizoid reactions. However, it is clear from a review of the case histories in this paper that all the patients described had a history of encephali-

tis, oculogyric crisis, or both and likely had postencephalitic parkinsonism rather than PD.

Fenelon et al., who reviewed the historical literature on PD, found evidence that hallucinations may be a part of PD itself, in the absence of pharmacologic treatment, particularly in those with late dementia or depression (22). Iit appears, therefore, that psychosis may have occurred in PD prior to the levodopa era. It must have been rare, however, and a number of these cases might have had secondary forms, especially postencephalitic parkinsonism.

During the initial levodopa trials in the 1960s, it became apparent that various psychiatric syndromes were occurring with a much higher frequency in treated than in untreated PD patients. Unfortunately it is difficult to determine the incidence with which these problems occurred because the early studies varied with regard to inclusion criteria, the dosages of levodopa employed, and the classification of the psychiatric side effects reported. Studies that included patients with postencephalitic parkinsonism reported incidences of psychiatric symptoms as high as 55% (23). Most of the studies reporting a significant incidence of psychosis used levodopa dosages in excess of 4 g per day or did not specify the specific dosages used (24–31). On the other hand, Cheifetz et al. (32) reported no incidence of psychosis in 34 patients treated with 4 g per day or less. In addition, some authors included patients with preexisting psychiatric symptoms in their data while others excluded such patients. In reporting side effects, confusional states were sometimes lumped with other forms of psychosis, while other studies attempted to be more specific in their definitions.

Despite these limitations, Goodwin, in 1971, attempted to review the psychiatric side effects that occurred in 908 PD patients treated in the early clinical trials using levodopa (33). He found an average incidence of 20%, but the range was quite large, 10% to 50%. Confusional states including delirium were most common, with an overall incidence of 4.4%. Psychosis, including delusions and hallucinations, occurred with a frequency of 3.6%. These numbers are low but include only patient reports where the psychiatric side effects were clearly defined.

CURRENT EPIDEMIOLOGY AND RISK FACTORS

In the last 15 years, several studies have looked at the prevalence of hallucinations and psychosis among PD patients. Unlike older reviews on this topic, these studies reflect the modern era of PD treatment and the impact of the several adjunctive medications now available and in common use. Table 48-1 summarizes the results of 8 publications since 1990 (1322 patients) (34–41). The results are fairly consistent with the average incidence

TABLE 48-1

*Frequency of Psychosis in Parkinson's Disease:
Summary of Recent Studies*

AUTHOR, YEAR	PATIENT POPULATION	NO. OF PATIENTS	PERCENT PSYCHOSIS*
Factor, 1990	Clinic	78	22%
Sanchez-Ramos, 1996	Clinic	214	26%
Barclay, 1997	Clinic	227	31%
Graham, 1997	Clinic	129	25%
Inzelberg, 1998	Clinic	121	37%
Aarsland, 1999	Population-based	235	25%
Fenelon, 2000	Clinic	216	46%†
Holroyd, 2001	Clinic	102	29%
Total		1322	30.8%

* Some studies included lifetime and recent occurrence. Lifetime numbers shown.
† Included minor symptoms.

of psychotic symptoms, being 30.8%. All of these studies except one are based on movement disorder clinic populations and possibly overestimate the incidence of these problems due to selection bias. Fenelon et al. (40) found a particularly high incidence of 46% but included so-called minor symptoms of psychosis such as illusions and presence hallucinations. To avoid the problem of selection bias, Aarsland et al. (39) performed the first extensive community-based survey of patients with PD and found that 15.8% had active symptoms of DIP at the time of the survey and 9.8% had hallucinations. When asked whether the patient had ever had symptoms of DIP after the diagnosis of PD was made (lifetime prevalence) the frequency increased to 25%.

Recent reviews have recognized that all of the antiparkinsonian drugs in current use and not just levodopa are capable of causing DIP (1, 8, 10, 12). Individual reports on bromocriptine and pergolide have shown these agents to cause hallucinations, delusions, and confusional states with a frequency comparable to that of levodopa (42–45). The newest dopamine agonists, pramipexole and ropinirole, which are now in widespread use, have a similar tendency in advanced PD (46). However, in studies in early PD patients, when pramipexole and ropinirole were compared to levodopa, the agonists were associated with a higher frequency of DIP (47, 48). DIP has also been reported with other dopamine agonists such as cabergoline (49), lisuride (50), apomorphine (51), lergotrile, and mesulergine (52). Selegiline may be particularly likely to cause psychotic symptoms in susceptible individuals. This is most common when it is given concurrently with other antiparkinsonian medications (53, 54).

Nondopaminergic drugs are also known to cause psychosis in PD. Propranolol, which is occasionally used in PD to treat tremor, has been reported to cause hallucinations (55). Amantadine, an NMDA antagonist, and anticholinergic drugs have also been associated with confusional and nonconfusional psychotic syndromes in PD. When these drugs are given in isolation, the frequency of such problems is low (56, 57). However, when they are given in combination with dopaminergic medications, they are much more likely to cause an acute confusional psychosis (10–12, 58). The acute confusional syndromes seen with anticholinergic medications are more common in older or demented patients and can result in a frank delirium (12). Paradoxically, acute delirium has also been described with amantadine withdrawal in patients who had been treated chronically with this agent (59). It appears that this is particularly true if patients are demented and have been on doses of 300 mg or more per day.

The COMT (catechol-O-methyltransferase) inhibitors are a novel class of antiparkinsonian medication whose beneficial effect is achieved through increasing the bioavailability of concomitantly administered levodopa. Tolcapone was the first of these agents to be approved for use in PD. In clinical trials, tolcapone was shown to dramatically increase the duration of action and potency of levodopa, resulting in improvement of motor fluctuations (60, 61). Not surprisingly, patients treated with tolcapone experienced an increase in dopaminergic side effects, including hallucinations. Sometimes dramatic reductions in levodopa dose were required to treat this complication of tolcapone treatment (60, 61). Clinical practice has confirmed that tolcapone must be used with caution in patients prone to cognitive side effects from levodopa, and some patients will experience DIP for the first time when started on this medication.

Entacapone, another COMT inhibitor, was approved for the adjunctive treatment of PD in 1999. In clinical trials, hallucinations and other dopaminergic side effects have been encountered with a frequency similar to that seen with tolcapone (62).

Despite the fact that DIP is common, it has been clear since the early days of levodopa therapy that most patients do not experience this problem. Even in early reviews, the assertion is made that psychiatric side effects were much more likely to occur in patients with certain predisposing characteristics. Specifically, several authors mentioned dementia as a risk factor (28, 29, 33, 63). A confusional psychosis was thought to be particularly common in these patients. Other important risk factors mentioned in these early reviews were advanced age (30), premorbid psychiatric illness (28, 32, 33), and exposure to high daily doses of levodopa (32).

Several recent publications have also looked at the issue of risk factors for DIP. There has been consistent agreement that cognitive impairment (35, 36, 39–41, 64) and depression (35, 36, 39, 41, 64) are strong predictors of the development of hallucinations. More advanced age was found to be a risk in some studies (35, 39, 64) but not others (36, 65). Similarly, duration or severity of PD was associated with the presence of DIP in some reports (36, 40, 41, 64) but not all (35, 41, 65). Interestingly, none of these recent studies found a correlation between levodopa dose and DIP. There has also been growing interest in disorders of sleep, not only as a risk factor for hallucinations (35, 40, 64, 66) but also as a clue to the pathophysiology of hallucinations in PD (67). Similarly, visual loss has been found in three studies to be linked to hallucinations in PD (40, 41, 68). Combined with the fact that visual hallucinations that occur in the visually impaired (Charles Bonnet syndrome) (69) clinically resemble those experienced by PD patients, these findings have fostered speculation that visual impairment may contribute to the pathophysiology of DIP (40, 64, 70). In a recent prospective evaluation, the factors predictive of new-onset hallucination over a 1-year period were severe sleep disorder, visual impairment, and axial motor symptoms suggesting that involvement of the brain outside the nigrostriatal system is likely to increase the risk of psychosis in PD (71).

Although hallucinations can occur at any time in the course of illness, it is most commonly seen as a late complication of PD in susceptible individuals. Goetz et al. (72) suggested that early-onset hallucinations (within 3 months of starting levodopa therapy) are not typical of idiopathic PD. Rather, the occurrence of hallucinations early in the course of levodopa treatment suggests the presence of premorbid psychiatric illness or an atypical parkinsonian syndrome such as DLB or Alzheimer's disease with extrapyramidal signs.

There have been several attempts to evaluate the occurrence of genetic risk factors for hallucinations. A recent paper analyzing dopamine transporter gene polymorphisms found that a particular variant allele was more frequent in levodopa-treated PD patients experiencing dyskinesia and psychosis (73). The authors warned that this was a preliminary finding and that they could not exclude the possibility that other determinants such as ethnicity might account for the differences observed. Another group looked at the cholecystokinin (CCK) promoter polymorphisms. They found a trend toward more frequent representation of CCK-T in combination with the CCKAR-C polymorphism in hallucinators, but the differences compared to nonhallucinators were not significant (74).

CLINICAL FEATURES

The clinical features of DIP in PD are well defined and have been described in numerous publications. Visual hallucinations are the most common symptom (10), with recent estimates approximating 30% in treated individuals (see Table 48-1). Hallucinations can be defined as spontaneously fabricated perceptions occurring while awake (perceptions without stimulus). In PD, hallucinations usually occur on a background of a clear sensorium; however, a concomitant confusional state is not uncommon in older or demented patients (10, 11). Usually, hallucinations are fully formed, nonthreatening images of people, animals, or inanimate objects and tend to be recurrent, stereotyped, and reflecting each patient's past experience (10, 11). For most, the imagined figures seem familiar and friendly, such as family members or friends who have died, while for others, they appear to be innocuous strangers or foggy shadows seen in dim light. Some patients will see adults sitting around their home as if they belonged there. Others describe children wandering around the house. Another common scenario occurs when patients peer outside through a window and see children playing in the yard or men working (so-called kinetic scenes). One patient reported seeing a parade passing in front of her home on several occasions. Visions of animals are common. Cats, dogs, and other benign furry creatures are typical, but small bugs and reptiles might also be seen. Occasionally, there will be an erotic overtone to the visions (35), and about 28% of the time hallucinations will have a threatening or frightening quality (57). While the literature indicates that hallucinations are mostly nocturnal, they can occur at any time. Hallucinations are typically brief, lasting seconds to minutes, with variable frequency. They may be in color or black and white and figures may occasionally be miniature.

Oddly, many patients will claim to realize the fabricated nature of these images and yet describe them to family members and physicians in such neutral terms that they seem to be no more extraordinary than a visit from a neighbor. More severely affected patients may insist they are real, and hence the hallucinations will affect their behavior. One patient was setting rat traps while another was spraying bug spray to ward off the insects. The patients will often argue with their spouses about the real nature of the hallucinations. In most patients, hallucinations are fleeting and may disappear if they look directly at the image, move toward it, blink their eyes or try to touch it (35). In most cases, visions of people are silent and relatively passive. Patients without insight sometimes become frustrated because the hallucination (person) does not respond to their queries.

Two other forms of visual hallucinations have been well described. The "passage" hallucination is one seen out of the corner of the eye and passes by quickly. When the patient looks in that direction, it is usually gone. Another is the "presence" hallucination (extracampine). The patient usually has a sense that someone standing behind or nearby. Although they don't actually see anyone, they describe it as if they had (35, 40, 75).

Pure auditory hallucinations are rare in PD, but a secondary auditory component has been reported in up to 40% of patients with visual hallucinations (37, 40). The auditory hallucinations are usually unrelated to the visual hallucinations despite their simultaneous occurrence. Auditory hallucinations accompanied visions in 8% of patients (38) and were described as human voices, which were "nonimperative, nonparanoid, and often incomprehensible" like the background of voices at a party. In our clinic, two patients described hearing music periodically, unconnected to their other hallucinations. Both claimed that the music was of a particular style but could not identify a specific tune. One of these patients heard music along with muffled voices that seemed to emanate from the air-conditioning ducts in her house. She actually attempted to tape-record the sounds and play them back for her husband, who could not hear them. In prior studies, music was heard in 14% of patients (38, 40).

Other hallucinations have been reported. Tactile and olfactory hallucinations can occur but are extremely rare. Friedman et al. reviewed the data collected on 160 patients in two separate controlled clinical trials on the treatment of DIP in PD (76). In one study 9% of patients and in another 22% reported olfactory hallucinations; 21% and 24% reported tactile hallucinations, respectively. A patient with tactile hallucinations is often seen to be taking something out of his or her hand and putting it down. This is more likely to occur in those with dementia. In one report, a patient was described as "...feeling as if her bowels and bladder extruded from the distal parts of her upper limbs" (77). The authors interpreted this as a somatic hallucination of visceral origin (cenesthetic hallucination). True illusions, which are distortions or misperceptions of actual visual stimuli, can occur in some patients but are less common than true hallucinations (57). Typically, patients will report seeing faces in patterned fabric, misinterpret a curtain blown by the wind as a person moving or mistake crumbs on a tablecloth for small bugs. One patient intermittently reported that other people's faces appeared to be distorted in grotesque ways. Illusions often occur in patients who also experience bona fide visual hallucinations (40).

Hallucinations in PD are quite different from the well-known hallucinatory syndromes seen with mind-altering drugs. Absent are the flashing lights, elaborate shifting patterns, and bizarre distortions of time and space seen with illicit hallucinogenic drugs (78). Synesthesias such as seeing sounds as colors also do not occur in PD.

Abnormal dreaming and sleep disturbances seem to be closely related to the presence of hallucinations and other drug-induced psychiatric phenomena in PD patients. Nausieda et al. (79) showed that 98% of patients with psychiatric side effects from their medications also experienced sleep disturbance in the form of sleep fragmentation, excessive daytime sleepiness, altered dreams or parasomnias such as sleep talking, sleepwalking, and nocturnal myoclonus. They also found that hallucinations occurred in 39% of patients with sleep disturbance and only 4% of patients with normal sleep patterns. Indeed, it is not unusual for hallucinations to blend indistinguishably with dream phenomena possessing similar themes (11).

Delusions are not as common as hallucinations in PD, but they usually constitute a more serious problem for the patient and physician because their occurrence carries a greater risk of injury, hospitalization, or even suicide. Delusions are false beliefs based on incorrect inference; they are held despite evidence to the contrary and are not ordinarily accepted by other members of one's culture (9). In PD, delusions are usually paranoid in nature. They most often occur on a background of a clear sensorium without other elements of a thought disorder, as seen in schizophrenia (11). They can occur as a side effect of any of the currently used antiparkinsonian medications (10). Klawans (11) indicated that about 3% of patients treated with levodopa for 2 or more years experience this type of organic delusional syndrome. Friedman et al. (76) found that the most common delusional themes reported by patients with DIP participating in a clinical treatment trial involved stealing, spousal infidelity, abandonment, and the conviction that their spouse was an imposter or that they were not in their real home. Delusions of spousal infidelity and elaborate conspiracies on the part of family members and even physicians are particularly common. Other examples include fears of being injured, poisoned, filmed, and even delusions of grandeur.

Delusional misidentification syndromes are also described. The belief that family members or friends have been replaced by identical-appearing impostors (Capgras phenomenon) or a familiar person appearing in the guise of a stranger (Fregoli syndrome) has been reported (80). One patient, who was an artist, thought his paintings were being stolen and replaced by reproductions. Another delusional syndrome rarely described in PD is Cotards syndrome (81). It is a fixed and unshakable belief that the person does not exist. Another interpretation is that the person thinks that he or she is dead. Jenkins and Groh described one such case in 1970 (30). This patient became psychotic and had the delusion that her husband was dead. "It was pointed out to her that she had been speaking to him; thereupon she developed the delusion that she herself was dead." Factor and Molho reported a similar case (82). The patient was admitted by ambulance to the hospital because she was immobile. She had stopped taking her PD medications; when asked why, she claimed that she was dead and no longer had need for them. Her syndrome reversed with quetiapine therapy and PD medications were reinstituted.

Psychosis in PD is very different from that of schizophrenia. Verbal commands and ego-dystonic critical commentaries are usually not seen. Holroyd reported on 102 PD patients with DIP, none of whom had a schizophrenic-like syndrome (41); but this does occasionally occur. Two such cases have been reported (82), both with advanced PD. One heard voices telling her that she would be punished by having her PD medications withdrawn. This was very frightening to her, since her "off" times were characterized by severe immobility. The other patient was hearing the voice of God commanding her to stop all medications or she would be punished. Neither patient had typical visual hallucinations or was demented and neither had a history of premorbid psychotic disease. One was hospitalized. Both were treated successfully with atypical antipsychotics.

MECHANISMS OF PSYCHOSIS

The pathophysiology of DIP in PD is poorly understood. In some patients, medications precipitate acute psychiatric symptoms by unmasking a premorbid psychiatric state. This has been shown to occur in schizophrenics (83) and patients with manic-depressive illness (33) who were exposed to levodopa. For the majority of PD patients, however, there is no premorbid psychiatric disorder. Thus, other characteristics peculiar to PD patients, PD medications, or both must be important.

It has been known for many years that drugs that are structurally similar to dopamine, such as lysergic acid diethylamide (LSD), mescaline, and amphetamine, can cause elaborate hallucinations and other psychotic symptoms in otherwise healthy individuals (83). The discovery that levodopa could also precipitate psychiatric symptoms in animals and humans coupled with the dramatic efficacy of dopamine receptor blockers (neuroleptics) in treating endogenous psychosis has formed the basis for the dopamine theory of psychosis (83). Clinical evidence that supports this hypothesis includes the de novo, dose-related appearance of hallucinations in PD patients treated with levodopa, the reliable disappearance of these symptoms with dose reduction. and the efficacy of traditional neuroleptics in treating this problem.

More recent theories have been based on the altered dopamine receptor physiology associated with PD and the varied effects of dopaminergic drugs on different dopamine-mediated systems in the brain. It is well known that dysfunction of the nigrostriatal dopamine system and the resulting insufficiency of dopamine at the receptor sites of otherwise normal striatal neurons is responsible for the motor symptoms of PD. This process also results in denervation hypersensitivity of striatal dopamine receptors. The early appearance of psychotic symptoms in patients treated with dopaminergic medications has been attributed to stimulation of these hypersensitive receptors (57).

In order to explain the late appearance of psychosis in PD, Klawans et al. (84) introduced the concept of levodopa-induced dopamine receptor hypersensitivity. They demonstrated in animal models that chronic stimulation of dopamine receptors can cause stereotyped behavior to appear with subthreshold doses and with a shorter latency than in animals not chronically exposed to dopaminergic stimulation. Chronic exposure to dopamine agonists causes hypersensitivity of dopamine receptors rather than the expected result, downregulation. In applying this model to levodopa-induced psychosis, Moskovitz et al. (57) proposed that two populations of dopamine-sensitive neurons exist in the striatum and limbic cortex. These are the dopamine-facilitated and dopamine-inhibited neuronal populations. Dopamine-inhibited neurons predominate in the striatum and exhibit downregulation and hyposensitivity with chronic dopaminergic stimulation. On the other hand, dopamine-facilitated neurons respond to chronic stimulation by becoming hypersensitive. These observations suggest that this dopamine-facilitated neuronal population might predominate in limbic cortex and thus be responsible for the psychotic symptoms seen with chronic levodopa treatment.

Although the literature supporting the central role of dopamine in DIP seems compelling, Goetz et al. cast doubt on this concept (85). They gave 5 nondemented PD patients with daily visual hallucinations high-dose intravenous infusions of levodopa utilizing both steady and pulse infusions paradigms. None of the patients experienced hallucinations in response to the infusions, but some did experience an increase in dyskinesia. The investigators concluded that "Visual hallucinations do not relate simply to high levels of levodopa or to sudden changes in plasma levels." This conclusion is enhanced by epidemiologic studies showing no relationship between daily dose of levodopa and hallucinations (35, 40)

Dysfunction of central serotonergic pathways has also been explored as a cause of DIP. Postmortem studies have shown that patients with this complication have lower brainstem levels of serotonin (79). In addition, acute administration of levodopa reduces brain serotonin levels by several possible mechanisms. Including interference with the transport of L-tryptophan across the gut and blood-brain barrier, inhibiting tryptophan hydroxylase, and replacing serotonin in presynaptic storage sites, leading to increased dopamine formation (33, 79). In animals, levodopa caused a decrease in 5HT levels but increase in 5HIAA, suggesting an increase in release and turnover of serotonin that, in turn, leads to increased receptor stimulation (86). Dysfunction of serotonergic systems is also suggested by the frequent association of DIP with sleep disturbance and altered dreaming, both of which are thought to have a serotonergic basis (35, 66, 79). Comella et al. (87) compared PD patients with and without hallucinations using polysomnogaphy and found that hallucinators had reduced sleep efficiency, reduced total rapid-eye-movement (REM) sleep, and reduced percentage REM sleep. In another study, 24-hour ambulatory polysomnography was performed on 20 PD patients experiencing visual hallucinations (67). A close temporal link between 33% of the hallucinations and the occurrence of non-REM sleep during the day or REM sleep patterns at night was found. These findings suggest that serotonergic neural mechanisms involved in generating sleep and dream phenomena may play a role in the occurrence of DIP in PD. The serotonin hypothesis is further strengthened by data showing that ondansetron, a selective 5HT3 receptor antagonist, markedly improved psychotic symptoms in PD patients (86).

Cholinergic pathways have also been implicated. Older studies (88) suggested this possibility because of the occurrence of hallucinations as an adverse event to anticholinergic drugs, implying that anticholinergic drug therapy was a risk factor for the occurrence of psychosis, additionally, cholinergic deficiency was described in the brains of such patients. The recent finding that cholinesterase inhibitors provide relief of psychosis in PD also supports this possibility (89). Perry and Perry (90) advocated a more comprehensive appreciation of the role of cholinergic pathways in the organization and maintenance of normal consciousness. Based on findings in DLB, they propose that decreased cortical acetylcholine leads to breakdown of the boundaries maintaining the clarity of normal conscious thought. This, in turn, results in intrusion of subconscious intrinsic thoughts and sensory phenomena into consciousness, i.e., hallucinations and delusions.

Further insights into the pathophysiology of hallucinations have come from studies that suggest that hallucinations occurring in PD are similar to those of the Charles Bonnett syndrome (40). This syndrome, first described in 1769, describes fully formed hallucinations in patients who are blind from macular degeneration or other causes. Hallucinations occur in 21% of blind patients (68). It is thought to result from denervation hypersensitivity of the visual cortex (69). PD patients may be prone to this phenomenon because they develop retinal disorders with abnormalities of contrast-sensitivity measures and have a number of age-related problems such as macular degeneration. Fenelon et al. found that ocular pathology in PD was an independent risk factor for hallucinations (40). Functional neuroimaging in hallucinating PD patients has also demonstrated decreased activation in occipital, parietal, and temporoparietal regions and increased activity in the region of the frontal eye fields, suggesting more widespread dysfunction of the visual axis (91).

There has been some success in elucidating the functional neuroanatomy of hallucinations in parkinsonian disorders, although results have varied. Harding et al. (92) systematically reviewed the clinical features and neuropathologic findings in 63 patients with DLB or PD with dementia. They found a striking association between the density of Lewy bodies in the temporal lobe and the presence of hallucinations in patients with DLB. The density of Lewy bodies was particularly high in the amygdala and the parahippocampus. These regions are also important for dementia and the overlap is obvious. This paper looked specifically at DLB, a disorder of dementia, and parkinsonism. The fact that psychosis is so much a part of this disorder brings up the question of what the relationship is between dementia and its associated pathology and the occurrence of hallucinations. Dementia is the most robust risk factor for onset of hallucinations in PD, and hallucinations represent a possible risk factor for dementia (5, 35). Dementia may be a necessary comorbidity because it may promote misinterpretation of visual stimuli. In DLB, hallucinations often occur without medications, but otherwise the hallucinations are similar in both diseases. Indeed, it may be that Lewy body pathology itself is specifically associated with hallucinations in parkinsonian disorders. Strongly supporting this is a large retrospective autopsy study showing visual hallucinations to be specific to Lewy body parkinsonism as opposed to other pathologic forms of parkinsonism (93).

Other regions may play an important role in the onset of hallucinations in PD. In one report, visual hallucinations were reliably induced by deep brain stimulation of the subthalamic nucleus (STN-DBS) in a postsurgical PD patient who was off medications (94), suggesting a role of the STN. There is increasing evidence that altered occipital lobe function may also be important. Using functional magnetic resonance imaging (fMRI), Goetz et al. (91) found that PD patients with chronic hallucinations respond to visual stimuli with prominent cingulate cortex activation and loss of the expected visual cortex activation seen in normal individuals. The decreased occipital activity is also shown in positron emission tomography (PET) studies of PD dementia and DLB (95, 96) and with MRI spectroscopy, showing a diminished N-acetylaspartate peak in PD dementia (97). One study with fMRI suggested that different regions are abnormal depending on the type of hallucinations. For instance, facial hallucinations were associated with temporal lobe abnormalities, while objects and kinetic scenes were associated with occipital lobe changes (98).

The task of assimilating the various neurochemical, neuroanatomic, and treatment-related factors presented here into a single coherent explanation of the pathophysiology of psychosis in PD seems daunting. However, Diederich et al. (70) have made an attempt by incorporating these disparate findings into the theories of consciousness developed by Hobson (99). They suggest that visual hallucinations result from the dysfunction of cortical and subcortical systems responsible for the proper gating and filtering between external conscious perception and internal image production. Additionally, neurochemical changes in the brainstem are postulated to enhance the emergence of internally generated images via the ponto-geniculo-occipital system (cholinergic) and the intrusion of REM dream imaging into wakefulness (serotonergic). Finally, impaired modulation and separation of these external and internal stimuli result from the effects of the cortical dysfunction associated with dementia and exogenous dopaminergic overactivation of mesolimbic systems.

TREATMENT OF PSYCHOSIS

General Considerations

There are some PD patients with psychotic symptoms who do not require antipsychotic therapy. Those patients with hallucinosis on the background of a clear sensorium may not need or want therapeutic intervention, especially when the hallucinations are intermittent, brief, nonthreatening, and the patient has preserved insight. In fact, some patients actually claim to gain pleasure from the symptoms. These patients should be watched carefully, however, since escalation of psychotic symptoms may occur.

In patients with a sudden onset of psychotic symptoms, it is important to investigate for triggering events, such as urinary and pulmonary infections, metabolic disturbance, cerebrovascular events, or traumatic brain injury. Treatment of these underlying conditions is paramount and may be sufficient. Postoperative psychosis is another situation that may not require specific therapy. In one study (100), psychosis occurred in 60% of PD patients who had surgical intervention. Other possible causes of postoperative psychosis include the effects of anesthetics, pain medications, alteration in environment, and superimposed metabolic encephalopathy or infection.

If the patient has DIP and requires intervention, the first step is to decrease PD medications; this remains standard practice. It is clear that lowering medication dosages can be helpful and is usually well tolerated. Marsden and Fahn (101) suggested decreasing and then removing adjunctive medications before lowering levodopa. However, as medications are stripped away one by one and psychosis persists, eventually the patient will experience intolerable worsening of motor symptoms. It is at this point that the addition of antipsychotic medication is usually considered.

In the 1970s and early 1980s, some physicians utilized the "drug holiday" to treat PD patients with various late complications including psychosis. Medications were typically withdrawn for 5 to 14 days, and this led to significant physical disability (102–103). Many patients became bedridden, unable to move or even swallow. As Friedman noted (106) this was "not a holiday in the usual sense." It is now well recognized that there are major drawbacks to the drug holiday. First, it requires long-term hospitalization, which is costly. More importantly, patients have the terrifying experience of becoming profoundly immobile. Nursing care must be meticulous to prevent complications, which may include decubitus ulcers, compression neuropathies, contractures, aspiration pneumonia, deep venous thrombosis, pulmonary embolism, and depression (102). In addition, the sudden cessation of dopaminergic medications can lead to a potentially lethal syndrome similar to the neuroleptic malignant syndrome (102). Considering the gravity of these complications, such a drug holiday should not be promoted as a routine therapeutic measure and, in fact, has been abandoned in most medical centers.

Drug therapy for DIP in the past also included standard neuroleptics, particularly low-potency agents (101). Marsden and Fahn (102) indicated that although the use of these agents was "illogical," the addition of a small dose of thioridazine could allow a compromise between the relative disability imposed by psychosis or immobility. However, in most cases neuroleptics, including thioridazine, cause marked exacerbation of PD symptoms (103).

Treatment with Clozapine

Clozapine (CLZ) is a unique drug for the treatment of DIP in PD patients. It is an "atypical" antipsychotic because it does not cause increased in muscle tone and postural abnormalities in laboratory animals (104) and is associated with minimal risk of drug-induced parkinsonism, dystonia, and akathisia (103, 104). CLZ can effectively treat psychosis without causing parkinsonism, which led to the initial attempts to use this drug in PD. The safety and efficacy of CLZ in PD patients with DIP has been demonstrated in numerous open-label studies (105). This accumulated experience with CLZ has been remarkably uniform and has shown that it can be used in small, well-tolerated doses to rapidly reverse symptoms of psychosis.

In 1999, the results of two multicenter, 4-week, double-blind, placebo-controlled trials were published; these confirmed the results seen in previous open-label trials. The first was a North American trial organized by the Parkinson Study Group (6, 7). In this study, 30 patients with DIP were treated with CLZ and 30 were randomized to placebo. CLZ was started at a low dose of 6.25 mg at bedtime and increased as needed according to a standardized schedule to a maximum dose of 50 mg. Psychotic symptoms were measured with (a) a 7-point clinical global impression scale (CGI); (b) the Brief Psychiatric Rating Scale (BPRS); (c) a modified form of the BPRS to remove 4 items thought to be more reflective of parkinsonism than psychosis; and (d) the Survey Assessment of Positive Symptoms (SAPS). The motor subscale of the Unified PD Rating Scale (UPDRS) was used to assess worsening of parkinsonism. Psychotic symptoms were significantly improved in the CLZ group compared to placebo at a mean dose of 27 mg per day without worsening of motor function. The double-blind study was followed by a 3-month open-label extension that confirmed this effect (7). These results were confirmed in a second double blind, placebo-controlled study organized by the French Parkinson Study Group (106), which used a similar methodology and found very similar results. This drug remains the only one proven with controlled trials to improve DIP without worsening motor symptoms. Sedation is the most common side effect with CLZ, but its occurrence should be used to therapeutic advantage. Frequently, patients with DIP also have sleep disruption and some degree of reversal of their normal sleep-wake cycle. These patients often spend nights awake, agitated, hallucinating, and engaged in paranoid behaviors. As a result, they will be sleepy and more disoriented the next day. Caregivers also become sleep deprived, emotionally stressed, and physically exhausted. When CLZ therapy is started as a bedtime dose, the most dramatic initial benefit is usually restored sleep and normalization of the sleep-wake cycle. This is greatly appreciated by all involved and is generally also a sign that the CLZ dose is at or very near an effective antipsychotic dose. Dosing should begin at 6.25 mg at bedtime and increase every few days by 6.25 to12.5 mg. Most patients will obtain benefits with 50 mg or less. Occasionally acutely psychotic patients need to be given doses as high as 150 to 200 mg per day until their symptoms are under control. Then, a smaller maintenance dose can be used to prevent recurrence. Some patients on a single bedtime dose will experience breakthrough symptoms the next day, in the late afternoon or early evening. In this situation, a small additional daytime dose (usually ≤ 12.5 mg) is sufficient. If sedation is a problem in the morning, the bedtime dose can be lowered or moved 1 to 2 hours earlier in the evening.

Once psychotic symptoms are adequately controlled and the patient is sleeping through the night, it is usually possible to carefully increase the dosage of antiparkinsonian medications to improve motor functioning. Small increases in daytime levodopa doses are possible, but it is best to keep nighttime doses to a minimum. Adjunctive medications such as dopamine agonists or MAO or COMT inhibitors will usually have been dramatically reduced in dose or eliminated prior to starting CLZ. These medications need to be used with caution in patients requiring antipsychotic therapy; they should be avoided in those with a significant dementia.

The adverse effect of most concern with CLZ is agranulocytosis. In 1975, the occurrence of 8 deaths from septicemia out of 16 patients who developed agranulocytosis in Europe (103, 107) delayed the marketing of CLZ in the United States. The estimated risk of agranulocytosis in schizophrenic patients treated with CLZ is 1% to 2% (108), which is higher than that associated with standard psychotropic medications. This figure is about the same in PD (7), indicating that this adverse effect is idiosyncratic and not dose-related. An apparent prodrome of 29 days characterized by a gradual decrease in white blood cell (WBC) count has been observed (108). However, precipitous drops in the WBC count from the normal range can also occur.

Current guidelines in the United States require weekly monitoring of WBCs for the first 6 months of CLZ therapy, every other week monitoring for the next 6 months, and monthly monitoring thereafter. It is recommended that therapy be interrupted when the WBC count drops to less than 3000/mm^3 or the absolute neutrophil count drops to less than 1500/mm^3. These patients may be rechallenged with CLZ but must undergo weekly blood testing for the first 12 months. Permanent discontinuation is recommended if the WBC count drops below 2000/mm^3 or the absolute neutrophil count declines to less than 1000/mm^3. Also, patients with a baseline WBC count of less than 3500/mm^3, a neutrophil count of less than 2000/mm^3, or a history of immune deficiency should not be treated.

Apparently, these guidelines have been effective in reducing the risk of agranulocytosis. Honigfeld et al. (109) reviewed the incidence of agranulocytosis in 99,502 patients treated with CLZ according to these guidelines between 1990 and 1994. They found that 382 cases of this condition (0.38%) and 12 deaths had occurred; this was dramatically reduced from the 995 cases of agranulocytosis and 149 deaths that would have been predicted based on the preguideline incidence of 1% to 2%.

Other hematologic side effects that may occur with CLZ include mild asymptomatic eosinophilia, chronic leukocytosis that may be associated with a low-grade fever, and lymphopenia (less than 600 lymphocytes/mm^3), which is usually asymptomatic or may be associated with diarrhea and fever (104). The etiology of these problems is unknown (110). One other adverse event of concern is neuroleptic malignant syndrome. Although CLZ causes few extrapyramidal side effects, neuroleptic malignant syndrome has rarely been reported. One case was described in a patient with CLZ who was receiving carbamazepine therapy and the other in a patient with CLZ who was on lithium therapy (111).

CLZ can cause several other adverse effects in PD. Sialorrhea and delirium are the most frequent after sedation (8, 104). These appear to be dose-related adverse events and are a common cause of dose limitation. Orthostatic hypotension can also be a problem with PD patients, since many already suffer from this problem, caused either by PD medications or autonomic dysfunction. Seizures are of concern in schizophrenics, occurring in up to 4% of these patients (104, 112, 113); this is related to electroencephalographic (EEG) changes, which have been well described. Both seizures and EEG changes are dose-related phenomena. This would explain why no seizures have thus far been reported with the low doses used in PD. The incidence of seizures is less than 1% at doses under 300 mg per day, 2.7% at daily doses of 300 to 600 mg, and 4.4% at doses greater than 600 mg per day (112).

Serious but rare medical complications associated with CLZ use include venous thromboembolism (114), myocarditis (115, 116), and possibly sudden death (117). There have also been several reports of poor blood sugar control in diabetics and the increased risk of new-onset type 2 diabetes (118, 119). These reports involved schizophrenics treated with high doses. The same increases in blood glucose were not seen in a study of PD patients treated with much lower doses (120). Olanzapine and other neuroleptic medications have also been implicated, indicating that this may be a class effect (121–123).

The main obstacle to long-term success with CLZ therapy in PD is progression of underlying disease, particularly dementia. Greene et al. (124) found that of 4 patients with marked dementia treated with CLZ, only 1 improved and the rest experienced adverse events. Factor et al. (125), in a long-term trial, showed that as dementia progressed [indicated by a decreased score on the in mini-mental state examination (MMSE)], psychosis began to reemerge and adverse effects became more of a dose-limiting problem. It is believed that nondemented patients can tolerate long-term therapy well.

Treatment with Other Atypical Antipsychotics

Safe and effective alternatives for the treatment of DIP in PD have been sought because of the small but significant risk of agranulocytosis associated with CLZ and the need for mandatory blood monitoring. Six additional antipsychotic medications are now available that have "atypical" pharmacologic profiles and do not carry the risk of agranulocytosis. Four have been utilized in the treatment of PD; risperidone (RSP), olanzapine (OLZ), quetiapine (QTP), and aripiprazole (ARI). It is their atypical pharmacology that makes these drugs potential alternatives for PD patients. But, what is the definition of "atypical"? This has not been clearly defined pharmacologically. CLZ remains the prototype of this class of drugs and is the drug to which all others are compared. It is distinguished from typical antipsychotic drugs by its strong antipsychotic effect coupled with freedom from extrapyramidal syndromes. That is the clinical definition of "atypical."

The features most often discussed as defining the atypical classification of drugs, based on the unique pharmacology of CLZ, are listed in Table 48-2, along with an indication of how all currently available atypical agents fulfill these standards (126). It should be noted from this table that although RSP and OLZ share some features considered to define atypicality, it is QTP that is the most similar in these respects. However, at this point there does not appear to be a single pharmacologic trait that strictly defines this class of agents.

A compelling theory of the neurophysiologic basis of atypicality has been derived from studies examining the way in which CLZ interacts with dopamine receptors. In vitro experiments using cloned human dopamine D2 receptors have shown that CLZ and QTP are loosely bound and easily displaced from these receptors (127). All other antipsychotic drugs tested with this method—including RSP, OLZ, and traditional neuroleptics—show prolonged and tighter binding to D2 receptors (see Table 48-2). A second study utilizing in vivo PET scanning in 12 patients treated with QTP (128) demonstrated only transiently high occupancy of dopamine D2 receptors. It has been speculated that the atypical clinical and pharmacologic features seen most prominently in CLZ and QTP are due to this "loose" binding and fast

---

TABLE 48-2
Summary of Distinguishing Characteristics of Atypical Antipsychotics

CHARACTERISTICS	CLZ	RSP	OLZ	QTP	ZIP	ARI
Fails to induce catalepsy or antagonize amphetamine stereotypies	+	−	−	+	−	−
Inc. 5HT/D-2 binding	+	+	+	+	+	+
No prolactin elevation	+	−	±	+	−	+
Mesolimbic selectivity	+	−	+	+	?	−
Loose D2 binding	+	−	−	+	−	−*
Improves negative symptoms	+	+	+	+	+	+
Decreased EPS	+	−	+	+	+	+
Not associated with TD	+	−	±	+	?	?

EPS = extrapyramidal side effects; TD = tardive dyskinesia; CLZ = clozapine; RSP = risperidone; OLZ = olanzapine; QTP = quetiapine; ZIP = ziprasidone; ARI = aripiprazole; * = has partial dopamine agonist effects as well as antagonist effects, Inc. = increased.

TABLE 48-3
Summary of Open-Label Reports with Risperidone in the Treatment of Psychosis in Parkinson's Disease

AUTHOR, YEAR	NO. OF PATIENTS	DOSAGE*	PSYCHOSIS IMPROVED	PD WORSENED
Meco, 1994	6	0.67 mg/day	6	0
Ford, 1994	6	1.5 mg/day	6	6
Rich, 1995	6	0.5–4 mg/day	4	5
Allen, 1995	3	0.5–1 mg/day	3	0
McKeith, 1995	3	1 mg/day	0	3
Meco, 1997	10	0.73 mg/day	9	3
Workman, 1997	9	1.9 mg/day	8	0 (est)
Leopold, 2000	39	1.1 mg/day	33	6
Mohr 2000	17	.5–3 mg/day	16	0†

* = dosage is given as a mean or a range.
est = estimated number based on available information in the publication.
† Of 17 patients, 10 reported "hypokinesia" as an adverse event and 1 withdrew due to worsening of gait.

dissociation from D2 receptors. In addition, it is thought that loose binding allows for a more physiologic response to surges in endogenous dopamine, thus preventing the usual neuroleptic side effects, such as drug-induced parkinsonism (129). This feature may also contribute to mesolimbic selectivity and may be the reason for a faster relapse of psychosis in schizophrenia when the drugs are discontinued.

Risperidone   A summary of open-label studies published on the treatment of DIP in PD with RSP is shown in Table 48-3 (130–138). The first report of its effect in PD psychosis was an open-label trial in 6 patients reported in 1994, the year it was approved for use in schizophrenia (130). The results were promising, as all patients demonstrated improvement in psychosis, with total elimination in 3. No change in the UPDRS scores or levodopa dose was reported. Two subsequent publications reported contrasting results (131, 132). Both studies also treated 6 patients and found that RSP had effective antipsychotic properties in PD, but parkinsonism worsened in 11 of the 12, even at low doses. Some patients became more confused. Meco et al. followed up their initial report, with longer-term experience (133). This time 7 out of 10 subjects stopped using the drug within a year, despite improved psychosis in 9. Of the 3 patients had worsening of motor features, 2 dropped out. There have also been 2 reports of RSP treatment for psychosis in DLB. A total of 6 patients were treated in the 2 studies; 3 experienced severe worsening of motor symptoms (134, 135).

Based on these reports and clinical experience, most PD specialists were in agreement that the use of RSP was not appropriate in this setting. Surprisingly however, 3 recently published papers indicate positive experiences. Unfortunately each report has limitations that make the results difficult to interpret. Workman et al. (136)

reported that 9 demented, agitated, psychotic PD patients in a psychiatric hospital did well on RSP when followed for a mean of 37 days. Since 3 of these had been on typical neuroleptics at entry into the study and none of the patients had their motor examinations rated formally, the authors' conclusion that RSP did not worsen extrapyramidal symptoms could be questioned. In another report, Leopold (137) treated 39 parkinsonian patients (32 PD and 6 DLB) with a mean dose of 1.1 mg per day of RSP. Significant improvement in psychosis was seen in 23 patients and modest improvement in 10. Only 16 patients completed the 6-month trial; among these, no worsening was seen in the UPDRS motor scores at 3 or 6 months. However, of the other 23 patients, 6 were clinically diagnosed as having DLB and experienced severe worsening of motor function. No information regarding the motor examination was provided for the remaining 17 patients. In the most recent report, Mohr et al. (138) treated 17 patients with 0.5 to 2.0 mg per day over 12 weeks and found a substantial improvement in psychotic symptoms and no statistical worsening in the UPDRS motor subscale. However, since 10 of the 17 patients reported "hypokinesia" as an adverse event, the conclusion that RSP does not adversely affect the symptoms of PD is suspect.

In the only double-blind trial published on the use RSP in PD, by Ellis et al., compared RSP to CLZ in 10 patients with PD and DIP (139). Both medications improved psychosis, but RSP worsened motor features, while there was an improvement with CLZ. Although these changes did not reach statistical significance, the authors advised caution in using RSP in this setting, indicating that RSP is not well suited for use in PD.

Olanzapine   The next "atypical" antipsychotic medication that became available for use in PD patients was

TABLE 48-4

Summary of Open-Label Reports with Olanzapine in the Treatment of Parkinson's Disease with Psychosis

AUTHOR, YEAR	NO. OF PATIENTS	DOSAGE*	PSYCHOSIS IMPROVED	PD WORSENED
Wolters, 1996	15	6.5 mg/day	15 (est)	0
Jimenez, 1998	2	5 mg/day	1	2
Friedman, 1998	19	N/A	7	10
Friedman, 1998	12	4.4 mg/day	12	7
Weiner, 1998	21	5 mg/day	13	9
Graham, 1998	5	5 mg/day	5	4
Molho, 1999	12	6.3 mg/day	9	10
Stover, 1999	22	N/A	12	8

* Dosage is given as a mean or a range.
est = estimated number based on available information in the publication;
N/A = data not available.

OLZ, which was approved for use in schizophrenia in 1996. A summary of published open-label studies on the use OLZ in PD is shown in Table 48-4 (140–147). As with RSP, the initial report on the use of OLZ for DIP in PD was encouraging. Wolters et al. (140) found that OLZ was effective in 15 nondemented PD patients. No worsening of motor functioning was reported in this open-label prospective study. Unfortunately the subsequent literature concerning the use of OLZ in this setting has, once again, been less impressive. Several open-label studies found that disabling motor deterioration can be seen in some PD patients (141–143, 145–147). Our own experience with OLZ has also been disappointing. In a retrospective analysis of 12 patients we had treated with OLZ, symptoms of psychosis were improved in 9 patients (75%), but 9 patients (75%) also experienced significant motor deterioration (144). Only 1 of the original 12 subjects was still using OLZ successfully after a year, but even that patient stopped the drug soon thereafter because of symptom worsening and recurrence of psychosis.

The reason for the disparity between the initial favorable results and subsequent studies is unclear but may relate to the differences in patient population and the method of dose titration used in these studies. Wolters et al. (148) suggested that the poor results reported in subsequent studies were related to the inclusion of patients with atypical parkinsonian syndromes and dementia. In addition, the starting dose of OLZ in Wolters' report was 1 mg per day, which is less than half the initial dose of 2.5 to 5.0 mg per day used in subsequent studies (the lowest dose currently available in the United States is a 2.5-mg tablet).

Three well-designed double-blind trials using OLZ to treat DIP have been published, which resolved this confusion. In the first trial, Goetz et al. (149) compared OLZ to CLZ in blinded fashion. A total of 15 patients were randomized to one of the two drugs. Motor function was measured with the UPDRS at baseline and then weekly. After 15 patients completed the study (the study was powered for 28), an independent interim safety analysis was performed and safety-stopping rules were invoked because of significant worsening of parkinsonism in the OLZ group, where 6 of 7 patients withdrew. In the CLZ group there was actually a small improvement in UPDRS scores with no dropouts. The poor results in the OLZ group occurred despite the fact that patients with dementia were excluded. CLZ was more effective in improving psychosis. In the second trial, Ondo et al. (150) compared OLZ to placebo in 30 patients with PD and DIP. Psychosis did not significantly improve in the OLZ-treated patients compared to placebo. In addition, there was significant worsening of motor function (gait and bradykinesia) in the active treatment group. Most recently, the results of two large multicenter, randomized, placebo-controlled trials of OLZ in DIP were published together and reported strikingly similar results to the previous placebo-controlled trial (151). A total of 160 patients were randomized between the two trials. There was no significant improvement in psychosis in the OLZ group when compared to placebo. Motor worsening was seen in both studies on several different measures of PD functioning, and these differences did reach significance. OLZ is not well suited for use in PD.

Quetiapine Perhaps the most promising "atypical" antipsychotic medication introduced as an alternative to CLZ for PD is QTP, which was approved for schizophrenia in 1998. A summary of published open-label studies is shown in Table 48-5 (152–162). Several open-label studies show that it appears to be effective in treating DIP in PD at doses of 50 to 400 mg per day, with minimal impact on motor features.

Fernandez et al. (158) reported the results of an open trial of QTP in 35 PD patients; of these. 24 were neuroleptic-naive, while 11 switched from OLZ (3 patients) and CLZ

TABLE 48-5
Summary of Open Label Reports with Quetiapine in the Treatment of PD with Psychosis.

AUTHOR/REFERENCE YR	# PATIENTS	DOSAGE*	# PSYCHOSIS IMP	# PD WORSENED
Evatt 1996	10	50 mg/day	10 (est)	0
Parsa 1998	2	200,400 mg/day	2	1
Juncos 1998	15	70 mg/day	15 (est)	0
Juncos 1999	40	25-800 mg/day	40 (est)	8 (est)
Samanta 1998	10	37.5 mg/day	6	7
Fernandez 1999	35	40.6 mg/day	25	0
Friedman 1999	15	62.5 mg/day	12	4
Targum 2000	11	25-300 mg/day	6	0
Reddy 2002	43	54 mg/day	35	5
Fernandez 2003	106	60 mg/day	87	34
Juncos 2004	29	12.5-400 mg/day	18	NS

* dosage is given as a mean or a range
est = estimated number based on available information in the publication
NS = no significant worsening overall. Individual results not reported.

(8 patients). Of the neuroleptic-naive patients, 20 had a marked improvement or complete amelioration of psychosis at 4 weeks that was maintained through 8 weeks. Ten patients had baseline and week 4 BPRS measures and significant improvement was observed. There was no worsening of parkinsonism. Of the 11 switched to QTP, only 5 made the transition easily. In the other 6, there was an increase in erratic behavior, confusion, and hallucinations. These patients had to be switched back to their prior therapeutic agent. The authors concluded that the drug was a good antipsychotic agent for PD but that transition from another antipsychotic may be difficult. In a follow-up study (159), 15 patients were gradually switched from CLZ to QTP over an 8-week period. Patients tolerated this slower change more easily, and 12 made the transition successfully and stayed on QTP. Motor features did not worsen except for a transient worsening of tremor in 4 patients.

In a larger cohort, Fernandez et al. also provided long-term data in 106 PD patients treated with QTP (161). The mean duration of therapy was 15 months, and the average dose of QTP was 60 mg per day. Psychosis partially or completely remitted in 82%, while 18% did not improve. Some degree of motor worsening was seen in 32% of patients, but only 9% discontinued QTP because of this problem. The presence of dementia was associated with an increased likelihood of motor worsening as well as nonresponse in terms of psychosis.

In an open-label evaluation by Reddy et al. (160), 43 consecutive PD patients with DIP (mean duration 13 months) were treated with QTP at a mean dose of 54 mg. per day for a mean duration of 10 months. Of the total, 81% (35 patients) had improvement of psychotic symptoms (23 complete amelioration and 12 partial); 5 patients

(12.5%) experienced mild worsening of motor symptoms and 2 had to stop therapy. Twenty of the patients were demented and the rest were not. There was no difference in antipsychotic effect in both groups but mild worsening of motor symptoms was seen only in the demented group as measured by UPDRS. All five of the patients with definite worsening had some degree of dementia. None of the non-demented patients had worsening of motor symptoms.

Unfortunately, much as with other potential alternatives to CLZ, placebo-controlled clinical trials with QTP have been less positive. In one double-blind trial (163), 31 patients were followed for 12 weeks and treated with up to 200 mg per day of QTP or placebo. No significant improvements were seen with QTP treatment on measures of hallucinations or psychosis. There was no significant worsening of UPDRS motor scores. In another double-blind study, 58 patients were randomized and followed for 3 months (164). Again, no significant differences were seen between the two groups in measure of psychosis or PD motor function. Treatment had to be interrupted in 15 of the original 30 patients randomized to QTP largely due to lack of perceived benefit (10 subjects) and because of side effects (3 subjects). In both reports, the authors concluded that larger controlled trials were needed to see whether these disappointing results are confirmed.

QTP appears to be less potent than CLZ in relieving psychosis. The dose may need to be pushed aggressively into the range normally used to treat schizophrenia (400 mg per day or higher) in some patients. Even then, some patients with DIP may not respond to QTP. An occasional patiently a patient has experienced a paradoxical worsening of agitation and psychosis when QTP was added at the usual starting dose of 25 mg at bedtime. Increasing the dose only exacerbated the problem in these rare patients.

The two newest "atypical" antipsychotic medications available are aripiprazole (ARI) and ziprasidone. The literature on the use of ziprasidone for DIP in PD is scarce; however, it has dopamine receptor binding similar to that of RSP and other typical antipsychotics and thus may have a similar impact on PD (127). One open-label 12-week trial of ziprasidone was reported in 12 patients with PD and psychosis. Ten patients reported a significant improvement in psychiatric symptoms, 2 patients withdrew because of adverse events, 2 patients had a 20% decline in UPDRS (part III), and 1 had gait deterioration (128). ARI has been viewed as promising because of its pharmacology as a partial dopamine agonist. However, the one large-scale controlled clinical trial using low-dose ARI for DIP in PD was ended early due to a high dropout rate and worsening of PD motor symptoms in some patients (165).

An experimental antipsychotic agent, ACP-103, is currently in phase 2 clinical trials and is being tested specifically in PD patients with DIP. This agent is an inverse agonist without any dopamine receptor–blocking properties. In a small double-blind preliminary safety study, ACP-103 was found to be safe and well tolerated in 12 PD patients (166). No worsening of motor symptoms was seen.

In April 2005, on the basis of the results of clinical drug trial adverse-event reporting (much of which was unpublished), the U.S. Food and Drug Administration issued a health advisory warning of an increased risk of death with the use of atypical neuroleptics in patients with dementia. In a published meta-analysis of randomized trials, Schneider et al. (167) also found a small but significantly increased mortality risk with atypical neuroleptics and no apparent distinction between the various agents. The authors recommended that this risk be considered in the context of medical need, efficacy evidence, medical comorbidity, and the relative lack of alternative treatments. Conventional neuroleptics are not safer in this regard when compared to atypicals (168). There are as yet no adequate data specifically for the PD population. However, in this special population a well-documented morbidity is associated with the occurrence of psychosis in PD, including hospitalization and nursing home placement (3, 4). There are also substantial risks associated with the alternative approach of reducing PD medication to the point of immobility, such as deep venous thrombosis, aspiration pneumonia, falls, and loss of independence. At this point, a rational weighing of these risks still would seem to favor the careful use of CLZ or QTP in the treatment of DIP in PD.

Nonneuroleptic Therapies

Approaches to the treatment of DIP, other than atypical antipsychotic medications, have been used with some success. Ondansetron is one of these agents. It is a serotonin (5HT3) receptor antagonist that was approved by the Food and Drug Administration in 1991 for chemotherapy-induced emesis. This drug has been utilized successfully in the treatment of schizophrenia (169) and has only rarely caused dystonia or akathisia (170). It does not have significant dopamine receptor–blocking properties; presumably as a result of this, there have been no reports of ondansetron-induced parkinsonism. These features make this drug an appropriate candidate for use in PD and have led to early trials. Zoldan et al. (86) treated 16 PD patients with psychosis with ondansetron 12 to 24 mg per day in open-label fashion. All but one patient experienced a moderate to marked improvement in psychiatric symptoms and the drug was well tolerated. In one additional study, these optimistic findings were not fully reproduced (171). Further studies of this drug are needed. However, a major obstacle to more widespread testing and use of this medication is its high cost.

The cholinesterase inhibitors have been investigated for their potential to treat cognitive and psychiatric symptoms in PD. Donepezil (DPZ), rivastigmine (RVS), and galantamine (GLN) have all been shown to be beneficial in mild to moderate Alzheimer's disease in large double blind, placebo-controlled trials (172–174). The rationale for using these agents in parkinsonian disorders is based on the finding that more severe cholinergic deficits are seen in the neocortex of patients with DLB than are seen in Alzheimer's disease (175). It is also thought that these agents might be better tolerated in PD than antipsychotic medications, since they do not block dopamine receptors. A theoretical concern has been that these agents might worsen motor features of parkinsonism by increasing cholinergic tone and upsetting the balance between acetylcholine and dopamine in the brain.

The results of preliminary studies have been encouraging. Rivastigmine has been the most thoroughly studied of these agents. Initially, McKeith et al. (89) investigated the utility of RVS in DLB and reported improvements in delusions and hallucinations in a double blind, placebo-controlled trial involving 120 patients. Patients were treated with up to 12 mg per day of rivastigmine for 20 weeks. The improvements were noted from subscores of the neuropsychiatric inventory (NPI) scale. In PD, 3 open-label trials examining psychotic symptoms found similar improvements in a small number of patients (176–178). Significant worsening of motor symptoms was not seen in any of these studies. In the only large controlled clinical trial on the use of a cholinesterase inhibitor in PD dementia, Emre et al. reported the results of blinded, placebo-controlled treatment with RVS in 541 patients over 24 weeks (179). Modest but significant improvements were found in cognitive function and psychiatric symptoms as measured by the NPI. An increase in tremor was seen in the active treatment group, but this was not reflected in any change in the UPDRS motor score. These benefits were sustained over an additional 24 weeks of open-label treatment, but the meaningfulness of this is difficult to assess, since the number of patients with psychosis was small (2.1%) and the NPI was reported only as a total score and individual items reflecting hallucinations and delusions were not reported (180).

Donepezil was used to treat DIP in PD in 2 small open-label studies (181, 182). Bergman and Lerner reported on 6 patients with PD who were treated with 10 mg per day of donepezil for 6 weeks (181). Of these 6 patients, 5 experienced "clinically significant" improvement in symptoms of psychosis. No worsening of motor symptoms was observed. Fabbrini et al. reported similar results in 8 nondemented PD patients with DIP. However, in this study 2 of the 8 patients experienced worsening of motor function (40% and 60% respectively) as measured by the UPDRS (182). A single open-label trial has looked at the use of GLN in PD with dementia and DIP (183). Aarsland et al. treated 16 patients for 8 weeks with 8 mg twice daily and found that hallucinations improved in 7 of 9 patients. Here too, some worsening of parkinsonism was seen in 3 patients, but a formal motor scale was not used, and it is unclear how significant the worsening was. Clearly larger, well-designed trials are needed to fully assess the utility and safety of these medications in this setting.

It has also been suggested that electroconvulsive therapy (ECT) may be useful in the treatment of DIP (8,184). Hurwitz et al. (184) treated two PD patients suffering from chronic nonconfusional psychosis with bilateral ECT (1 received 6 treatments and the other 3). This not only cleared the psychosis but also allowed for the use of higher doses of dopaminergic medications. After 5 months, 1 patient had no recurrence; at 6 months, the other had only occasional visual illusions. It is likely that patients with confusional states will not achieve the same benefit; in fact, confusion is considered a contraindication for ECT (8, 185). There also seems to be interest in using ECT to treat PD patients because of its ability to improve motor symptoms (186–188). It is believed that this improvement is due to an enhancement of dopamine transmission caused by the ECT (189). It is hard to explain the antipsychotic effect of ECT on the background of increased responsiveness of dopamine receptors; Hurwitz et al. (184) suggest that improvement in psychosis may be due to nondopaminergic mechanisms.

The improvement of motor features of PD by ECT is most likely transient (186, 187). In addition, the antidepressant effects of ECT are also temporary; patients should be treated with antidepressant agents for long-term maintenance. This would not make ECT a primary agent in the treatment of DIP in PD. The adverse effects of memory loss and delirium are also of concern. However, in those situations where CLZ does not improve psychosis or when significant side effects occur at dose levels that are otherwise ineffective, ECT can be used as an adjunct; then low-dose CLZ may help to maintain the benefit (190).

Treatment Summary

The treatment of DIP in PD can be approached in a stepwise fashion. First, it is necessary to search for and treat any triggering factors, such as infection, that may have precipitated decompensation in an otherwise stable patient. If no such triggers are present and the symptoms are mild, a modest reduction in antiparkinsonian medication dose will usually be sufficient. In more severely affected patients, the next step is to decrease or stop adjunctive medications. This should be done one drug at a time in order of decreasing risk-to-benefit ratio. If psychosis continues, an attempt should be made to decrease the dose of levodopa. If there is an increase in disability, an antipsychotic medication will be required.

CLZ is the only antipsychotic medication that has been proven in controlled clinical trials to effectively control DIP without worsening parkinsonism. However, based on clinical practice and ease of use, QTP is a reasonable alternative first-choice agent. It is usually started with a bedtime dose, and then daytime doses are added if necessary. If QTP is not effective or if side effects prevent further increases in dose, we recommend CLZ. Patients treated in our clinic have been given up to 400 mg/day of QTP without benefit and then responded to as little as 6.25 mg of CLZ. It is important to remember that PD patients are particularly prone to sedation with these medications, and therapy should be initiated with a low dose and increased in small increments. Frequent communication between physician and the patient's caretakers is paramount during this difficult period. Once DIP is controlled, a smaller maintenance dose is usually possible and a careful optimization of antiparkinsonian medications can be attempted.

In the rare patient who does not respond to either of these medications, a trial of one of the other atypical agents may be justified, but the patient should be carefully monitored for worsening of parkinsonism. In PD patients with dementia, cholinesterase inhibitors may be a useful adjunct by helping to control both symptoms of psychosis and dementia. Occasional patients will not respond to the above measures and more drastic reductions in levodopa will be necessary. This will usually be associated with severe worsening of parkinsonism and should be done in a hospital setting under the supervision of a movement disorder specialist. Finally, in nondemented patients, a course of ECT can be used as a last resort.

LONG-TERM OUTCOMES

It has been suggested that, with the onset of hallucinations, the prognosis of PD declines significantly. Several studies have examined the long-term outcome of patients who have DIP. In addition, the question of whether treatment with atypical antipsychotics alters the outcome of hallucinating patients has been addressed in a limited way. Two studies examined the outcomes of such patients prior to the availability of atypical agents. The first study, by Sweet et al. in 1976, looked at the outcome of 18 PD patients followed for about 6 years (191). Of these, 5 (27%) were placed in nursing homes, 5 (27%) died, 6x (33%) were incapacitated but living at home, and only 2 (11%) were at home and semi-independent. In 1993, Goetz et al. (3) performed a case-controlled study to specifically examine the most frequent reason for nursing home placement in PD. They studied 11 patients who had been placed and compared them to 22 who were still living at home. Hallucinations were significantly more common in patients placed in a nursing home and motor impairment and dementia did not differentiate between the 2 groups, indicating that hallucinations were an independent cause of nursing home placement. This study was followed by a 2-year follow-up to examine outcome. All (100%) of the nursing home patients had died, with a mean duration of survival of 15.6 months (4). It was found that nursing home placement in these patients was permanent. These studies focused on hallucinations in relation to nursing home placement and likely involved the most severely affected cases.

Two studies have since examined outcome after the availability of atypical antipsychotics. In the first, Juncos et al. examined the long-term outcome of 27 PD patients treated with either quetiapine or clozapine for hallucinations (192). Over the 36-month observation period, 50% were placed in nursing homes. Mortality of patients in nursing homes was 62%, compared with 52% in those still living at home. Finally, Factor et al. (5) evaluated 59 patients who were originally enrolled in a double blind, placebo-controlled clinical trial examining CLZ therapy for DIP in PD. Long-term outcome data were collected a mean of 22 months after enrollment. These patients were more typical of those seen in practice, with most living at home, requiring antipsychotic therapy, and receiving clozapine. Over the follow-up period, many switched to other agents or discontinued antipsychotics. They were not the most severe of these cases because enrollment included those who could withstand a month of placebo therapy. At baseline, 12% were living in a nursing home, 95% had hallucinations, and 60% had paranoia. On follow-up, 25% were dead, nursing home placement occurred in 42%, psychosis was persistent in 69%, and dementia was diagnosed in 68%. Of those in a nursing home, 28% had died over the 2-year period, including 2 of the 7 in a nursing home at baseline. Of those with persistent psychosis, 97% had hallucinations and 27% had paranoia.

Comparison of the studies before and after the availability of atypical agents is limited, but there are data suggesting that they do have a positive effect on long-term outcome. The death rate in nursing home patients is clearly diminished, suggesting an improvement in survival. In addition, the study by Factor et al. (5) demonstrated a significant decrease in the percentage of patients with paranoia, a symptom complex associated with increased nursing home placement. It is interesting that persistence (or lack) of psychosis at follow-up did not have an impact on the final outcome of these patients. A similar percentage of psychotic and nonpsychotic patients died, were placed in a nursing facility, were treated with antipsychotics, and became demented. This may suggest that the hallucinations themselves are not necessarily associated with a poor outcome but may be indicators of the development of a high-risk stage of the disease.

Factor et al. (5) also examined possible risk factors (from baseline data) that might predict poor outcome in PD patients with DIP. Older age and the presence of paranoia were risk factors for nursing home placement, while older age and age of onset and lower baseline MMSE scores conferred greater risk for developing dementia. On the other hand, younger age of onset and longer duration of disease were risk factors for persistent psychosis.

In combination, the data indicated that older patients tend to end up in nursing homes with paranoia or to develop dementia with poor survival, while younger-onset patients tend to continue to have hallucinations and remain in the community. Our goal should be to alter the outcome of PD patients with DIP; the examination of predictors for the individual outcome measures might lead to improved treatment approaches. This was the first study to determine modifiable risk factors that could lead to such an alteration.

MANIA

Mania (53, 193–198), hypomania (27, 33, 199), and euphoria (24, 193) have all been reported as side effects of dopaminergic medications. Goodwin (33) reported that the incidence of hypomania was 1.5% in 908 patients treated with levodopa. In 1972, the same group (200) treated 11 depressed non-PD patients with levodopa to evaluate its possible effects on depression. Six patients, all with a history of previous manic or cyclothymic behavior, developed acute mania or hypomania when treated with 4 to 10 g per day. O'Brien and colleagues (201) reported an interesting man who developed episodes of inappropriate laughter and grandiosity occurring in cycles, approximately 90 minutes after each 6-gm dose of levodopa. Jouvent et al. (202) reported 2 of 10 patients with PD who developed hypomania on high doses of bromocriptine. Mania also occurred in two non-PD patients treated with bromocriptine for postpartum suppression of lactation (196, 197). Both patients were taking bromocriptine for approximately a week before developing manic symptoms. After the withdrawal of bromocriptine and treatment with haloperidol for 3 to 7 days, all signs of mania were resolved. Euphoria developed in a single patient after pergolide was added to their previous medication regimen (193). Recently, acute mania was reported in PD patients taking selegiline (53, 198). Boyson (53) described 5 women with PD who developed acute mania when selegiline was added to their anti-PD medications. Two of these patients had previous symptoms of cyclothymia but had not been diagnosed with this disorder. Mendez (203) described a single patient who became hypomanic on selegiline after adrenal cell transplantation. Other authors (198, 204) warned against the concomitant use of selegiline and antidepressants (especially fluoxetine) because of the possibility of precipitating acute mania. Recently, pramipexole has been noted to result in mood elevation in PD patients (205).

Mania, hypomania, and euphoria do not occur in untreated PD (12). These are rare, treatment-related adverse effects and have occurred in PD and non-PD patients treated with dopaminergic agents. Patients with previous signs of mania or hypomania may experience an acute exacerbation if given these medications.

HYPERSEXUALITY

Increased libido and return of penile erection after years of impotence have been reported in PD patients treated in early levodopa trials (25, 201). However, these cases were not associated with aberrant sexual behavior. Subsequently, other investigators confirmed a renewed interest in sex among patients treated with levodopa; in rare cases, this led to sexual desires out of proportion to their premorbid sexual profile and sexual activities outside personal and social norms (206). Some patients were reported to become voyeuristic or to experience a disinhibition of long-suppressed erotic fantasies involving public indecent exposure or sadomasochism (207). Some of these patients acted to fulfill their desires, causing great embarrassment to themselves and their families. In many of these patients, the increased sexual desire and preoccupation is not accompanied by a return of sexual function, and impotence remains common among these individuals (206). This has led to compulsive self-stimulation in some patients, although others made constant requests of the spouse for genital stimulation even if orgasm could not be achieved.

Hypersexuality seems to be a rare complication of PD therapy and is estimated to occur in 0.9% to 3% of patients (33, 208). It is more common in men and has been reported to occur with all dopaminergic medications (10, 206), including recent reports on apomorphine (209), pramipexole, and ropinirole (210). Uitti et al. (206) reported 2 cases of hypersexuality occurring in PD patients after thalamotomy. Some authors have reported an association between hypersexuality and psychosis or hypomania (33). However,

patients without signs of either disorder have developed this problem (207). In addition, premorbid sexual behavior does not always predict the presence or absence of drug-induced hypersexuality (206).

Preoccupation with sex and erotic fantasy usually resolves when PD medications are reduced, but they are likely to resume if the patient is rechallenged with similar doses (206, 207). Low-potency neuroleptics have been helpful in treating some PD patients with this complication. However, as expected, their use has been limited by worsening of motor functioning (207). Experience suggests that CLZ or QTP can be used successfully in patients with problematic sexual behavior, many of whom also have some degree of DIP. Fernandez et al. reported a case of zoophilia (sexual contact with the family dog) precipitated by dopaminergic medications that responded to CLZ therapy (211). Cyproterone, an antitestosterone agent, was mildly beneficial in one male patient, but additional medications were ultimately required to control the uncharacteristic behavior (207).

The exact mechanism of how antiparkinsonian medications cause hypersexuality is not known. It would be reasonable to think that dopaminergic mechanisms are responsible, but there is no direct evidence for this. One recent report found fluctuating penile erection corresponding to peak-dose effects of levodopa (212), but this does not directly relate to aberrant sexual behavior, particularly in patients who remain impotent. Uitti and colleagues (206) speculated that prolactin may play a role. They based this on the clinical observation that patients with prolactin-secreting tumors, who suffer a decline in sexual drive, can experience a reversal of this problem when given bromocriptine. Although hypersexuality remains a rare psychiatric complication of the treatment of PD, it can potentially limit therapy.

Impotence is reported in 40% to 60% of male PD patients, and sildenafil (Viagra) is used frequently by male PD patients with sexual dysfunction. There has been a report of 22 PD patients treated effectively with sildenafil without significant side effects (213). However, this medication needs to be prescribed with caution in PD because of the possibility that patients with impotence may also have some degree of DIP, hypersexuality, or deviant sexual behavior. The patient is unlikely to volunteer this information in asking for sildenafil. Any PD patient considering treatment with sildenafil should be carefully screened for the presence of DIP or hypersexuality. Further, the patient's sexual partner should be interviewed separately to be sure that he or she is also in favor of this treatment.

ACKNOWLEDGMENTS

This work was supported by the Albany Medical Center Parkinson's Research Fund and the Riley Family Chair in Parkinson's Disease (ESM).

References

1. Fischer P, Danielczyk W, Simanyi M, Streifler MB. Dopaminergic psychosis in advanced Parkinson's disease. In: Streifler MB, Korczyn AD, Melamed E, Youdim MBH (eds). *Advances in Neurology.* Vol 53. PD: *Anatomy, Pathology and Therapy.* New York: Raven Press, 1990:391–397.

2. Carter JH, Archbold PG, Stewart BJ. Family caregiving. In: Factor SA, Weiner WJ (eds). *Parkinson's Disease: Diagnosis and Clinical Management.* New York: Demos, 2002:627–637.

3. Goetz CG, Stebbins GT. Risk factors for nursing home placement in advanced Parkinson's disease. *Neurology* 1993; 43:2227–2229.

4. Goetz CG, Stebbins GT. Mortality and hallucinations in nursing home patients with advanced Parkinson's disease. *Neurology* 1995; 45:669–671.

5. Factor SA, Feustel PJ, Friedman JH, et al. Longitudinal outcome of Parkinson's disease patients with psychosis. *Neurology* 2003; 60:1756–1761.

6. The Parkinson Study Group. Low-dose clozapine for the treatment of drug-induced psychosis in Parkinson's disease. *N Engl J Med* 1999; 340:757–763.

7. Factor SA, Friedman JH, Lannon MC, Oakes D, Bourgeois K, and the Parkinson Study Group. Clozapine for the treatment of drug-induced psychosis in Parkinson's disease: Results of the 12 week open label extension in the PSYCLOPS trial. *Mov Disord* 2001; 16:135–139.

8. Friedman JH. The management of the levodopa psychoses. *Clin Neuropharmacol* 1991; 14:283–295.

9. American Psychiatric Association. *Diagnostic and Statistical Manual of Mental Disorders, Third Edition, Revised.* Washington, DC: American Psychiatric Association, 1987.

10. Cummings JL. Behavioral complications of drug treatment of Parkinson's disease. *J Am Geriatr Soc* 1991; 33:708–716.

11. Klawans HL. Levodopa-induced psychosis. *Psychiatr Ann* 1978; 8:447–451.

12. Mayeux R. PD: A review of cognitive and psychiatric disorders. *Neuropsychiatr Neuropsychol Behav Neurol* 1990; 3:3–14.

13. Hoehn MM, Yahr MD. Parkinsonism: Onset, progression and mortality. *Neurology* 1967; 17:427–442.

14. Mckeith IG, Galasko D, Kosaka K, et al. Consensus guidelines for the clinical and pathological diagnosis of dementia with Lewy bodies (DLB): Report of the consortium on DLB international workshop. *Neurology* 1996; 47:1113–1124.

15. Hurtig HI, Trojanowski JQ, Galvin J, et al. Alpha-synuclein cortical Lewy bodies correlate with dementia in Parkinson's disease. *Neurology* 2000; 54:1916–1921.

16. Apaydin H, Ahlskog JE, Parisi JE et al. Parkinson's disease neuropathology: Later-developing dementia and loss of the levodopa response. *Arch Neurol* 2002; 59:102–112.

17. Parkinson J. *An Essay on the Shaking Palsy.* London: Sherwood, Neely and Jones, 1817.

18. Regis E. *Precis de Psychiatrie.* Paris: Gaston Doiz, 1906.

19. Patrick HT, Levy DM. PD: A clinical study of one hundred and forty-six cases. *Arch Neurol Psychiatry* 1922; 7:711–720.

20. Jackson JA, Free GBM, Pike HV. The psychic manifestations in paralysis agitans. *Arch Neurol Psychiatry* 1923; 10:680–684.

21. Schwab RS, Fabing HD, Prichard JS. Psychiatric symptoms and syndromes in Parkinson's disease. *Am J Psychiatry* 1950; 107:901–907.

22. Fenelon G, Goetz CG, Karenberg A. Hallucinations in Parkinson disease in the prelevodopa era. *Neurology* 2006; 66:93–98l.

23. Calne DB, Stern GM, Laurence DR, et al. L-dopa in post-encephalitic parkinsonism. *Lancet* 1969; 1:744–746.

24. Celesia GG, Barr AN. Psychosis and other psychiatric manifestations of levodopa therapy. *Arch Neurol* 1970; 23:193–200.

25. Yahr MD, Duvoisin RC, Schear MJ, et al. Treatment of parkinsonism with levodopa. *Arch Neurol* 1969; 21:343–354.

26. Cotzias GC, Papavasilou PS, Gellene R. Modification of parkinsonism: Chronic treatment with L-dopa. *N Engl J Med* 1969; 280:337–345.

27. McDowell F, Lee JE, Swift T, et al. Treatment of Parkinson's syndrome with L-dihydroxyphenyl-alanine (levodopa). *Ann Intern Med* 1970; 72:29–35.

28. Damasio AR, Lobo-Antunes J, Macedo C. Psychiatric aspects in parkinsonism treated with L-dopa. *J Neurol Neurosurg Psychiatry* 1971; 34:502–507.

29. Mawdsley C. Treatment of parkinsonism with laevo-dopa. *Br Med J* 1970; 1:331–337.

30. Jenkins RB, Groh RH. Mental symptoms in parkinsonian patients with L-dopa. *Lancet* 1970; 2:177–180.

31. Celesia GG, Wanamaker WM. Psychiatric disturbances in Parkinson's disease. *Dis Nerv Syst* 1972; 33:577–583.

32. Cheifetz DI, Garron DC, Leavitt F, Klawans HL, Garvin JS. Emotional disturbance accompanying the treatment of parkinsonism with L-dopa. *Clin Pharmacol Ther* 1970; 12:56–61.

33. Goodwin FK. Psychiatric side effects of levodopa in man. *JAMA* 1971; 218:1915–1920.

34. Factor SA, McAlarney T, Sanchez-Ramos JR, Weiner WJ. Sleep disorders and sleep effect in Parkinson's disease. *Mov Disord* 1990; 5:280–285.

35. Sanchez-Ramos JR, Ortoll R, Paulson GW. Visual hallucinations associated with Parkinson's disease. *Arch Neurol* 1996; 53:1265–1268.

36. Barclay CL, Hildebrand K, Gray P, et al. Risk factor for the development of psychosis in Parkinson's disease (abstract). *Mov Disord* 1997; 12(Suppl 1):108.

37. Graham JM, Grunewald RA, Sagar HJ. Hallucinosis in idiopathic Parkinson's disease. *J Neurol Neurosurg Psychiatry* 1997; 63:434–440.

38. Inzelberg R, Kipervasser S, Korczyn AD. Auditory hallucinations in Parkinson's disease. *J Neurol Neurosurg Psychiatry* 1998; 64:533–535.

39. Aarsland D, Larsen JP, Cummings JL, Laake K. Prevalence and clinical correlates of psychotic symptoms in Parkinson's disease. *Arch Neurol* 1999; 56:595–601.

40. Fenelon G, Mahieux F, Huon R, Ziegler M. Hallucinations in Parkinson's disease: Prevalence, phenomenology and risk factors. *Brain* 2000; 123:733–745.

41. Holroyd S, Currie L, Wooten GF. Prospective study of hallucinations and delusions in Parkinson's disease. *J Neurol Neurosurg Psychiatry* 2001; 70:734–738.

42. Lipper S. Psychosis in patients on bromocriptine and levodopa with carbidopa. *Lancet* 1976; 2:571–572.

43. White AC, Murphy TJC. Hallucinations caused by bromocriptine. *Br J Psychiatry* 1977; 130:104.

44. Kurlan R, Miller C, Levy R, et al. Long-term experience with pergolide therapy of advanced parkinsonism. *Neurology* 1985; 35:738–742.

45. Stern Y, Mayeux R, Ilson J, et al. Pergolide therapy for Parkinson's disease: Neurobehavioral changes. *Neurology* 1984; 34:201–204.

46. Factor SA. Dopamine agonists. *Med Clin North Am* 1999; 83:415–443.

47. Parkinson Study Group. Pramipexole vs levodopa as initial treatment for Parkinson's disease: A randomized controlled trial. *JAMA* 2000; 284; 1931–1938.

48. Rascol O, Brooks DJ, Korczyn AD, et al. A five-year study of the incidence of dyskinesia in patients with early Parkinson's disease who were treated with ropinirole or levodopa. *N Engl J Med* 2000; 342:1484–1491.

49. Hutton JJ, Morris JL, Brewer MA. Controlled study of the antiparkinsonian activity and tolerability of cabergoline. *Neurology* 1993; 43:613–616.

50. Rinne UK. Lisuride, a dopamine agonist in the treatment of early Parkinson's disease. *Neurology* 1989; 39:336–339.

51. Frankel JP, Lees AJ, Kempster PA, Stern GM. Subcutaneous apomorphine in the treatment of Parkinson's disease. *J Neurol Neurosurg Psychiatry* 1990; 53:96–101.

52. Lieberman AN, Goldstein M, Gopinathan G, Neophytides A. D-1 and D-2 agonists in Parkinson's disease. *Can J Neurol Sci* 1987; 14:466–473.

53. Boyson SJ. Psychiatric effects of selegiline (letter). *Arch Neurol* 1991; 48:902.

54. Venezia P, Mohr E, Grimes D. Deprenyl in Parkinson's disease: Mechanisms, neuroprotective effect, indications and adverse effects. *Can J Neurol Sci* 1992; 19:142–146.

55. Fleminger R. Visual hallucinations and illusions with propranolol. *Br Med J* 1978; 1:1182.

56. Weiner WJ, Bergen D. Prevention and management of the side effects of levodopa. In: Klawans HL, ed. *Clinical Neuropharmacology,* vol. 2. New York: Raven Press, 1977:1–23.

57. Moskovitz C, Moses H, Klawans HL. Levodopa-induced psychosis: A kindling phenomenon. *Am J Psychiatry* 1978; 135:669–675.

58. Schwab RS, England AC, Poskanzer DC, Young RR. Amantadine in the treatment of Parkinson's disease. *JAMA* 1969; 208:1168–1170.

59. Factor SA, Molho ES, Brown DL. Acute delirium after withdrawal of amantadine in Parkinson's disease. *Neurology* 1998; 50:1456–1458.

60. Adler CH, Singer C, O'Brien C, et al. Randomized, placebo-controlled study of tolcapone in patients with fluctuating Parkinson's disease treated with levodopa-carbidopa. *Arch Neurol* 1998; 55:1089–1095.

61. Rajput AH, Martin W, Saint-Hilaire MH, et al. Tolcapone improves motor function in parkinsonian patients with the "wearing-off" phenomenon: A double-blind, placebo-controlled, multicenter trial. *Neurology* 1997; 49:1066–1071.

62. Parkinson Study Group. Entacapone improves motor fluctuations in levodopa-treated Parkinson's disease patients. *Ann Neurol* 1997; 42:747–755.

63. Sacks OW, Kohl MS, Messeloff CR, Schwartz WF. Effects of levodopa in parkinsonian patients with dementia. *Neurology* 1972; 22:516–519.

64. Barnes J, David AS. Visual hallucinations in Parkinson's disease: A review and phenomenological survey. *J Neurol Neurosurg Psychiatry* 2001; 70:727–733.

65. Goetz CG, Leurgans S, Pappert EJ, et al. Prospective longitudinal assessment of hallucinations in Parkinson's disease. *Neurology* 2001; 57:2078–2082.

66. Pappert EJ, Goetz CG, Niederman FG, et al. Hallucinations, sleep fragmentation, and altered dream phenomena in Parkinson's disease. *Mov Disord* 1999; 14:117–121.

67. Manni R, Pacchetti C, Terzaghi M, et al. Hallucinations and sleep-wake cycle in PD: A 24-hour continuous polysomnographic study. *Neurology* 2002; 59:1979–1981.

68. Lepore FE. Visual loss as a causative factor in visual hallucinations associated with Parkinson's disease. *Arch Neurol* 1997; 54:799.

69. Burke W. The neural basis of Charles Bonnet hallucinations: A hypothesis. *J Neurol Neurosurg Psychiatry* 2002; 73:535–541.

70. Diederich NJ, Goetz CG, Stebbins GT. Repeated visual hallucinations in Parkinson's disease as disturbed external/internal perceptions: Focused review and a new integrative model. *Mov Disord* 2005; 20:130–140.

71. De Maindreville AD, Fenelon G, Mahieux F. Hallucinations in Parkinson's disease: A follow-up study. *Mov Disord* 2005; 20:212–217.

72. Goetz CG, Vogel C, Tanner CM, Stebbins GT. Early dopaminergic drug-induced hallucinations in parkinsonian patients. *Neurology* 1998; 51:811–814.

73. Kaiser R, Hofer A, Grapengiesser A, et al. L-dopa–induced adverse effects in PD and dopamine transporter gene polymorphism. *Neurology* 2003; 60:1750–1755.

74. Goldman JG, Goetz CG, Berry-Kravis E, et al. Genetic polymorphisms in Parkinson's disease patients with and without hallucinations: An analysis of the cholecystokinin (CCK) system (abstract). *Neurology* 2003; 60(Suppl 1):A282.

75. Chan D, Rosser MN. "-but who is that on the other side of you?" Extracampine hallucinations revisited. *Lancet* 2002; 360:2064–2066.

76. Friedman JH, Messing S, Oakes D, et al. A descriptive and comparative analysis of psychotic symptoms in three placebo-controlled, double-blinded trials of atypical antipsychotic drugs in the treatment of drug-induced psychosis in Parkinson's disease (abstract). *Mov Disord* 2002; 17:1105.

77. Jimenez-Jimenez FJ, Orti-Pareja M, Gasalla T, et al. Cenesthetic hallucinations in a patient with Parkinson's disease. *J Neurol Neurosurg Psychiatry* 1997; 63:120.

78. Kluver H. Neurobiology of normal and abnormal perception. In: Hoch P, Zubin J (eds). *Psychopathology of Perceptions*. New York: Grune & Stratton, 1965.
79. Nausieda PA, Weiner WJ, Kaplan LR, et al. Sleep disruption in the course of chronic levodopa therapy: An early feature of the levodopa psychosis. *Clin Neuropharmacol* 1982; 5:183–194.
80. Roane DM, Rogers JD, Robinson JH, Feinberg TE. Delusional misidentification in association with parkinsonism. *J Neuropsychiatry Clin Neurosci* 1998; 10:194–198.
81. Pearn J, Gardner-Thorpe C. Jules Cotard (1840–1889): His life and the unique syndrome which bears his name. *Neurology* 2002; 58:1400–1403.
82. Factor SA, Molho ES. Threatening auditory hallucinations and Cotard syndrome in Parkinson disease. *Clin Neuropharmacol* 2004; 27:205–207.
83. Yaryura-Tobias JA, Diamond B, Merlis S. Psychiatric manifestations of levodopa. *Dis Nerv System* 1970; 31:60–63.
84. Klawans HL, Goetz CG, Nausieda PA, Weiner WJ. Levodopa-induced dopamine receptor hypersensitivity. *Ann Neurol* 1977; 2:125–129.
85. Goetz CG, Pappert EJ, Blasucci LM, et al. Intravenous levodopa in hallucinating Parkinson's disease patients: High-dose challenge does not precipitate hallucinations. *Neurology* 1998; 50:515–517.
86. Zoldan J, Friedberg G, Livneh M, Melamed E. Psychosis in advanced Parkinson's disease: Treatment with ondansetron, a 5-HT3 receptor antagonist. *Neurology* 1995; 45:1305–1308.
87. Comella CL, Tanner CM, Ristanovic RK. Polysomnographic sleep measures in Parkinson's disease patients with treatment-induced hallucination. *Ann Neurol* 1993; 34:710–714.
88. Tanner CM, Vogel C, Goetz CG, Klawans HL. Hallucinations in Parkinson's disease: A population study (abstract). *Ann Neurol* 1983; 14:136.
89. McKeith I, Del Ser T, Spano P, et al. Efficacy of rivastigmine in dementia with Lewy bodies: A randomized, double-blind, placebo-controlled international study. *Lancet* 2000; 356:2031–2036.
90. Perry EK, Perry RH. Acetylcholine and hallucinations: Disease-related compared to drug-induced alterations in human consciousness. *Brain Cogn* 1995; 28:240–258.
91. Goetz CG, Medina D Carrillo M, et al. Functional neuroimaging in Parkinson's disease with hallucinations (abstract). *Neurology* 2002; 58(Suppl 3):A201.
92. Harding AJ, Broe GA, Halliday GM. Visual hallucinations in Lewy body disease relate to Lewy bodies in the temporal lobe. *Brain* 2002; 125:391–403.
93. Williams DR, Lees AJ. Visual hallucinations in the diagnosis of idiopathic Parkinson's disease: A retrospective study. *Lancet Neurol* 2005; 4:605–610.
94. Diederich NJ, Alesch F, Goetz CG. Visual hallucinations induced by deep brain stimulation in Parkinson's disease. *Clin Neuropharmacol* 2000; 23:287–289.
95. Albin RL, Minoshima S, D'Amato CJ, et al. Fluoro-deoxyglucose positron emission tomography in diffuse Lewy body disease. *Neurology* 1996; 47:462–466.
96. Vanderborght T, Minoshima S, Giordani B, et al. Cerebral metabolic differences in Parkinson's and Alzheimer's diseases matched for dementia severity. *J Nucl Med* 1997; 38:797–802.
97. Summerfield C, Gomez-Anson B, Tolosa E, et al. Dementia in Parkinson's disease: A proton magnetic resonance spectroscopy study. *Arch Neurol* 2002; 59:1415–1420.
98. Santhouse AM, Howard RJ, Ffytche DH. Visual hallucinatory syndromes and the anatomy of the visual brain. *Brain* 2000; 123:2055–2064.
99. Hobson JA, Pace-Schott EF. The cognitive neuroscience of sleep: Neuronal systems, consciousness and learning. *Nat Rev Neurosci* 2002; 3:679–693.
100. Golden WE, Lavender RC, Metzer WS. Acute postoperative confusion and hallucinations in Parkinson's disease. *Ann Intern Med* 1989; 111:218–222.
101. Klawans HL, Weiner WJ. Attempted use of haldol in the treatment of L-dopa–induced dyskinesias. *J Neurol Neurosurg Psychiatry* 1974; 37:427–430.
102. Marsden CD, Fahn S. Problems in PD. In: Marsden CD, Fahn S (eds). *Movement Disorders*. London: Butterworth Scientific, 1981:1–7.
103. Friedman JH. "Drug Holidays" in the treatment of Parkinson's disease: A brief review. *Arch Intern Med* 1985; 145:913–915.
104. Weiner WJ, Koller WC, Pearlik SJ, et al. Drug holiday and management of Parkinson's disease. *Neurology* 1980; 30:1257–1261.
105. Koller WC, Weiner WJ, Pearlik ST, et al. Complications of long-term levodopa therapy: Long-term efficacy of drug holiday. *Neurology* 1981; 31:473–476.
106. Friedman JH, Lannon MC. Clozapine in the treatment of psychosis in Parkinson's disease. *Neurology* 1989; 39:1219–1221.
107. Baldesserini RJ, Frankenburg FR. Clozapine: A novel antipsychotic agent. *N Engl J Med* 1991; 324:740–754.
108. Factor SA, Friedman JH. The emerging role of clozapine in the treatment of movement disorders. *Mov Disord* 1997; 12:483–496.
109. French Clozapine Parkinson Study Group. Clozapine in drug-induced psychosis in Parkinson's disease. *Lancet* 1999; 353:2041–2042.
110. Scholz E, Dichgans J. Treatment of drug-induced exogenous psychosis in parkinsonism with clozapine and fluperlapine. *Eur Arch Psychiatr Neurol Sci* 1985; 235:60–64.
111. Alvir JMJ, Lieberman JA, Safferman AZ, et al. Clozapine-induced agranulocytosis: Incidence and risk factors in the United States. *N Engl J Med* 1993; 329:162–167.
112. Honigfeld G, Arellano F, Sethi J, et al. Reducing clozapine-related morbidity and mortality: 5 years experience with the Clozaril National Registry. *J Clin Psychiatry* 1998; 59(Suppl 3):3–9.
113. Gerson SL. Clozapine-deciphering the risks. *N Engl J Med* 1993; 329:204–205.
114. Factor SA, Singer C. Neuroleptic malignant syndrome. In: Lang AE and Weiner WJ (eds). *Drug-induced Movement Disorders*. Mount Kisco, NY: Futura, 1992:199–230.
115. Devinsky O, Honigfeld G, Patin J. Clozapine-related seizures. *Neurology* 1991; 41:369–371.
116. Alphs LD, Meltzer HY, Bastani B, Ramirez LF. Side effects of clozapine and their management. *Pharmacol Psychiatry* 1991; 24:46.
117. Hagg S, Spigset O, Soderstrom TG. Association of venous thromboembolism and clozapine. *Lancet* 2000; 355:1155–1156.
118. Kilian JG, Kerr K, Lawrence C, Celermajer DS. Myocarditis and cardiomyopathy associated with clozapine. *Lancet* 1999; 354:1841–1842.
119. La Grenade L, Graham D, Trontell A. Myocarditis and cardiomyopathy associated with clozapine use in the United States (letter). *N Engl J Med* 2001; 345:224.
120. Devarajan S, Kutcher SP, Dursun SM. Clozapine and sudden death (letter). *Lancet* 2000; 355:841.
121. Liebert KA, Markowitz JS, Caley CF. New onset diabetes and atypical antipsychotics. *Eur Neuropsychol* 2001; 11:25–32.
122. Henderson D, Cagliero E, Gray C, et al. Clozapine, diabetes mellitus, weight gain, and lipid abnormalities: A 5-year naturalistic study. *Am J Psychiatry* 2000; 157:975–981.
123. Fernandez HH, Friedman JH, Factor SA, et al. New onset diabetes among parkinsonian patients on long-term clozapine use (abstract). *Mov Disord* 2002; 17(Suppl 5):S47.
124. Gianfrancesco FD, Grogg AL, Mahmoud RA, et al. Differential effects of risperidone, olanzapine, clozapine, and conventional antipsychotics on type 2 diabetes: Findings from a large health plan database. *J Clin Psychiatry* 2002; 63:920–930.
125. Koro CE, Fedder DO, L'Italian GJ, et al. Assessment of independent effect of olanzapine and risperidone on risk of diabetes among patients with schizophrenia: Population based nested case-control study. *Br Med J* 2002; 325:243–247.
126. McCown K, Romrell J, Treischmann ME, et al. New-onset diabetes in parkinsonian patients on long-term quetiapine (abstract). *Mov Disord* 2005; 20(Suppl 10):S45
127. Greene P, Coté L, Fahn S. Treatment of drug-induced psychosis in Parkinson's disease with clozapine. *Adv Neurol* 1993, 60:703–706.
128. Factor SA, Brown D, Molho ES, Podskalny GD. Clozapine: A two year open trial in Parkinson's disease patients with psychosis. *Neurology* 1994; 44:544–546.
129. Friedman JH, Factor SA. Atypical antipsychotics in the treatment of drug-induced psychosis in Parkinson's disease. *Mov Disord* 2000; 15:201–211.
130. Seeman P, Tallerico T. Rapid release of antipsychotic drugs from dopamine D2 receptors: An explanation for low receptor occupancy and early clinical relapse upon withdrawal of clozapine or quetiapine. *Am J Psychiatry* 1999; 156:876–884.
131. Gomez-Esteban JC, Zarranz JJ, Velasco F, et al. Use of ziprasidone in parkinsonian patients with psychosis. *Clin Neuropharmacol* 2005; 28(3):111–114. Comment in *Clin Neuropharmacol* 2005; 28(5):254.
132. Kapur S, Seeman P. Does fast dissociation from the dopamine D2 receptor explain the action of atypical antipsychotics?: A new hypothesis. *Am J Psychiatry* 2001; 158:360–369.
133. Kapur S, Zipursky R, Jones C, et al. A positron emission tomography study of quetiapine in schizophrenia: A preliminary finding of an antipsychotic effect with only transiently high dopamine D2 receptor occupancy. *Arch Gen Psychiatry* 2000; 57:553–559.
134. Meco G, Alessandria A, Bonifati V, Giustini P. Risperidone for hallucinations in levodopa-treated Parkinson's disease patients. *Lancet* 1994; 343:1370–1371.
135. Ford B, Lynch T, Greene P. Risperidone in Parkinson's disease. *Lancet* 1994; 344:681.
136. Rich SS, Friedman JH, Ott BR. Risperidone versus clozapine in the treatment of psychosis in six patients with Parkinson's disease and other akinetic-rigid syndromes. *J Clin Psychiatry* 1995; 56:556–559.
137. Meco G, Alessandria A, Giustini P, Bonifati V. Risperidone in levodopa-induced psychosis in advanced Parkinson's disease: An open-label, long-term study. *Mov Disord* 1997; 12:610–611.
138. Allen RL, Walker Z, D'ath PJ, Katona LE. Risperidone for psychotic and behavioral symptoms in Lewy body dementia. *Lancet* 1995; 346:185.
139. McKeith IG, Ballard CG, Harrison RWS. Neuroleptic sensitivity to risperidone in Lewy body dementia. *Lancet* 1995; 346:699.
140. Workman RJ Jr, Orengo CA, Bakey AA, et al. The use of risperidone for psychosis and agitation in demented patients with Parkinson's disease. *J Neuropsychiatr Clin Neurosci* 1997; 9:594–597.
141. Leopold NA. Risperidone treatment of drug-related psychosis in patients with parkinsonism. *Mov Disord* 2000; 15:301–304.
142. Mohr E, MendisT, Hildebrand IC, DeDeyn PP. Risperidone in the treatment of dopamine-induced psychosis in Parkinson's disease: An open pilot trial. *Mov Disord* 2000; 15:1230–1237.
143. Ellis T, Cudkowicz ME, Sexton PM, Growdon JH. Clozapine and risperidone treatment of psychosis in Parkinson's disease. *J Neuropsychiatr Clin Neurosci* 2000; 12:364–369.
144. Wolters EC, Jansen ENH, Tuynman-Qua HG, Bergmans PLM. Olanzapine in the treatment of dopaminomimetic psychosis in patients with Parkinson's disease. *Neurology* 1996; 47:1085–1087.
145. Jimenez-Jimenez FJ, Tallon-Barranco A, Orti-Pareja M, et al. Olanzapine can worsen parkinsonism. *Neurology* 1998; 50:1183–1184.
146. Friedman JH. Olanzapine in the treatment of dopaminomimetic psychosis in patients with Parkinson's disease (letter). *Neurology* 1998; 50:1195–1196.
147. Friedman JH, Goldstein SM, Jacques C. Substituting clozapine for olanzapine in psychiatrically stable Parkinson's disease patients; Results of an open-label pilot trial. *Clin Neuropharmacol* 1998; 21:285–288.
148. Molho ES, Factor SA. Worsening of motor features of Parkinson's disease with olanzapine. *Mov Disord* 1999; 14:1014–1016.
149. Weiner WJ, Minagar A, Shulman LM. Olanzapine for the treatment of hallucinations/delusions in Parkinson's disease. *Mov Disord* 1998; 13:862.
150. Graham JM, Sussman JD, Ford KS, Sagar HJ. Olanzapine in the treatment of hallucinosis in idiopathic Parkinson's disease: A cautionary note. *J Neurol Neurosurg Psychiatry* 1998; 65:774–777.
151. Stover NP, Juncos JL. Olanzapine treatment of parkinsonian patients with psychosis (abstract). *Neurology* 1999; 52(Suppl 2):A215.
152. Wolters EC, Jansen ENH, Tuynman-Qua HG, Bergmans PLM. Olanzapine in the treatment of dopaminomimetic psychosis in patients with Parkinson's disease (letter). *Neurology* 1998; 50:1196.

153. Goetz CG, Blasucci CM, Leurgans S, Pappert EJ. Olanzapine and clozapine: Comparative effects on motor function in hallucinating Parkinson's disease patients. *Neurology* 2000; 55:789–794.

154. Ondo WG, Levy JK, Vuong KD, et al. Olanzapine treatment for dopaminergic-induced hallucinations. *Mov Disord* 2002; 17:1031–1035.

155. Breier A, Sutton VK, Feldman PD, et al. Olanzapine in the treatment of dopamimetic-induced psychosis in patients with Parkinson's disease. *Biol Psychiatry* 2002; 52:438–445.

156. Parsa MA, Bastani B. Quetiapine (Seroquel) in the treatment of psychosis in patients with Parkinson's disease. *J Neuropsychiatry Clin Neurosci* 1998; 10:1–4.

157. Evatt ML, Jewart D, Juncos JL. "Seroquel" (ICI 204,636) treatment of psychosis in Parkinsonism. *Mov Disord* 1996; 11:595.

158. Juncos JL, Evatt ML, Jewert D. Long term effects of quetiapine fumarate in parkinsonism complicated by psychosis (abstract). *Neurology* 1998; 50(Suppl 4):A70–A71.

159. Juncos JL, Arvanitis L, Sweitzer D, et al. Quetiapine improves psychotic symptoms associated with Parkinson's disease (abstract). *Neurology* 1999; 52(Suppl 2):A262.

160. Targum SD, Abbott JL. Efficacy of quetiapine in Parkinson's patients with psychosis. *J Clin Psychopharmacol* 2000; 20:54–60.

161. Samanta J, Stacy M. Quetiapine in the treatment of hallucinations in advanced Parkinson's disease (abstract). *Mov Disord* 1998; 13(Suppl 2):274.

162. Fernandez HH, Friedman JH, Jacques C, Rosenfeld M. Quetiapine for the treatment of drug-induced psychosis in Parkinson's disease. *Mov Disord* 1999; 14:484–487.

163. Friedman JH, Fernandez HH, Jacques C, Rosenfeld M. Quetiapine for the treatment of drug-induced psychosis in Parkinson's disease (abstract). *Neurology* 1999; 52(Suppl 2):A215.

164. Reddy S, Factor SA, Molho ES, Feustel PJ. The effect of quetiapine on psychosis and motor function in parkinsonian patients with and without dementia. *Mov Disord* 2002; 17:676–681.

165. Fernandez HH, Trieschmann ME, Burke MA, et al. Long-term outcome of quetiapine use for psychosis among parkinsonian patients. *Mov Disord* 2003; 18:510–514.

166. Juncos JL, Roberts VJ, Evatt ML, et al. Quetiapine improves psychotic symptoms and cognition in Parkinson's disease. *Mov Disord* 2004; 19:29–35.

167. Ondo WG, Tinter R, Voung KD, et al. Double-blind, placebo-controlled, unforced titration parallel trial of quetiapine for dopaminergic-induced hallucinations in Parkinson's disease. *Mov Disord* 2005; 20:958–963.

168. Rabey JM, Prokhorov T, Miniovich A, Klein C. The effect of quetiapine in Parkinson's disease psychotic patients: A double-blind labeled study of 3 months duration (abstract). *Mov Disord* 2005; 20(Suppl 10):S46.

169. Friedman JH, Berman R, Carson W, et al. Low dose aripiprazole for the treatment of drug induce psychosis in Parkinson's disease patients (abstract). *Mov Disord* 2005; 20(Suppl 10):S92.

1670. Weiner DM, Vanover KE, Hacksell U, et al. The tolerability of ACP-103, a $5HT_{2a}$ receptor inverse agonist in Parkinson's disease patients (abstract). *Mov Disord* 2005; 20(Suppl 10):S72.

171. Schneider LS, Dagerman KS, Insel P. Risk of death with atypical antipsychotic drug treatment for dementia: Meta-analysis of randomized placebo-controlled trials. *JAMA* 2005; 294:1934–1943.

172. Wang PS, Schneeweiss S, Avorn J, et al. Risk of death in elderly users of conventional vs atypical antipsychotic medications. *N Engl J Med* 2005; 353:2335–2341.

173. White A, Corn TH, Feetham C, Faulconbridge C. Ondansetron in treatment of schizophrenia. *Lancet* 1991; 337:1173.

174. Halperin JR, Murphy B. Extrapyramidal reaction to ondansetron. *Cancer* 1992; 69:1275.

175. Eichhorn TE, Brunt E, Oertel WH. Ondansetron treatment of L-dopa–induced psychosis. *Neurology* 1996; 47:1608–1609.

176. Rogers SL, Friedhoff LT, and the Donepezil Study Group. The efficacy and safety of donepezil in patients with Alzheimer's disease: Results of a US multicenter, randomized, double-blind, placebo-controlled trial. *Dementia* 1996; 7:293–303.

177. Rosler M, Anand R, Cicin-Sain A, et al. Efficacy and safety of rivastigmine in patients with Alzheimer's disease: International randomized controlled trial. *Br Med J* 1999; 31:633–640.

178. Raskind MA, Peskind ER, Wessel T, et al. Galantamine in AD: A 6-month randomized, placebo-controlled trial with a 6-month extension. *Neurology* 2000; 54:2261–2268.

179. Perry EK, Haroutunian V, Davis KL, et al. Neocortical cholinergic activities differentiate Lewy body dementia from classical Alzheimer's disease. *Neuroreport* 1994; 5:747–749.

180. Reading PJ, Luce AK, McKeith IG. Rivastigmine in the treatment of parkinsonian psychosis and cognitive impairment: Preliminary findings from an open trial. *Mov Disord* 2001; 16:1171–1174.

181. Van Laar T, de Vries JJ, Nakhosteen A, Leenders KL. Rivastigmine as anti-psychotic treatment in patients with Parkinson's disease (abstract). *Parkinsonism Relat Disord* 2001; 7(Suppl 1):S73.

182. Bullock R, Cameron A. Rivastigmine for the treatment of dementia and visual hallucinations associated with Parkinson's disease: A case series. *Curr Med Res Opin* 2002; 18:258–264.

183. Emre M, Aarsland D, Albanese A, et al. Rivastigmine for dementia associated with Parkinson's disease. *N Engl J Med* 2004; 351:2509–2518.

184. Poewe W, Wolters E, Emre M, et al. Long-term benefits of rivastigmine in dementia associated with Parkinson's disease: An active treatment study. *Mov Disord* 2006; 21:456–461.

185. Bergman J, Lerner V. Successful use of donepezil for the treatment of psychotic symptoms in patients with Parkinson's disease. *Clin Neuropharmacol* 2002; 25:107–110.

186. Fabbrini G, Barbanti P, Aurilia C, et al. Donepezil in the treatment of hallucinations and delusions in Parkinson's disease. *Neurol Sci* 2002; 23:41–43.

187. Aarsland D, Hutchinson M, Larsen JP. Cognitive, psychiatric and motor response to galantamine in Parkinson's disease with dementia. *Int J Geriatr Psychiatry* 2003; 18:937–941.

188. Hurwitz TA, Calne DB, Waterman K. Treatment of dopaminomimetic psychosis in Parkinson's disease with electroconvulsive therapy. *Can J Neurol Sci* 1988; 15:32–34.

188. Brown GI. Parkinsonism depression and ECT. *Am J Psychiatry* 1975; 132:1084.

189. Stern MB. Electroconvulsive therapy in untreated Parkinson's disease. *Mov Disord* 1991; 6:265.

190. Douyon R, Serby M, Klutchko B, Rotrosen J. ECT and Parkinson's disease revisited: A "naturalistic" study. *Am J Psychiatry* 1989; 146:1451–1455.

191. Abrams R. ECT for Parkinson's disease. *Am J Psychiatry* 1989; 146:1391–1393.

192. Fochtmann L. A mechanism for the efficacy of ECT in Parkinson's disease. *Convuls Ther* 1988; 4:321–327.

193. Factor SA, Molho ES, Brown DL. Combined clozapine and electroconvulsive therapy for the treatment of drug-induced psychosis in Parkinson's disease. *J Neuropsychiatr Clin Neurosci* 1995; 7:304–307.

194. Sweet RD, McDowell FH, Feigenson JS, et al. Mental symptoms in Parkinson's disease during chronic treatment with levodopa. *Neurology* 1976; 26:305–310.

195. Juncos JL, Jewart RD, Neparizde N, Hanfelt J. Long-term prognosis of hallucinating Parkinson's disease patients treated with quetiapine or clozapine (abstract). *Neurology* 2002; 58:A435.

196. Lang AE, Quinn N, Brincat S, et al. Pergolide in late-stage Parkinson's disease. *Ann Neurol* 1982; 12:243–247.

197. Ryback RS, Schwab RS. Manic response to levodopa therapy; Report of a case (letter). *N Engl J Med* 1971; 285:788–789.

198. Pearlman C. Manic behavior and levodopa (letter). *N Engl J Med* 1971; 285:1326–1327.

199. Vlissides D, Gill D, Castelow J. Bromocriptine-induced mania (letter)? *Br Med J* 1978; 1:510.

200. Brook NM, Cookson IB. Bromocriptine-induced mania (letter)? *Br Med J* 1978; 1:790.

201. Kurlan R, Dimitsopulos T. Selegiline and manic behavior in Parkinson's disease. *Arch Neurol* 1992; 49:1231.

202. Barbeau A, Mars H, Gill-Joffroy L. Adverse clinical side effects of levodopa therapy. In: McDowell FH, Markham CM (eds). *Contemporary Neurology: Recent Advances in Parkinson's Disease.* Philadelphia: Davis, 1971:204–237.

203. Goodwin F, Murphy D, Brodie K, et al. Levodopa: alterations in behavior. *Clin Pharmacol Ther* 1971; 12:383–396.

205. O'Brien CP, DiGiacomo JN, Fahn S, et al. Mental effects of high-dosage levodopa. *Arch Gen Psychiatry* 1971; 24:61–64.

206. Jouvent R, Abensour P, Bonnet A, et al. Antiparkinsonian and antidepressant effects of high doses of bromocriptine; An independent comparison. *J Affect Disord* 1983; 5:141–145.

207. Mendez MA, Golbe LI. Hypomania in a patient receiving deprenyl (selegiline) after adrenal-striatal implantation for Parkinson's disease. *Clin Neuropharmacol* 1988; 11:549–551.

208. Suchowersky O, deVries J. Possible interaction between deprenyl and Prozac (letter). *Can J Neurol Sci* 1990; 17:352–353.

209. Pogarell O, Kunig G, Oertel WH. A non-ergot dopamine agonist, pramipexole, in the therapy of advanced Parkinson's disease: Improvement of parkinsonian symptoms and treatment-associated complications. A review of three studies. *Clin Neuropharmacol* 1997; 20(Suppl):S28–S35.

210. Uitti RJ, Tanner CM, Rajput AH, et al. Hypersexuality with antiparkinsonian therapy. *Clin Neuropharmacol* 1989; 12:375–383.

211. Quinn NP, Toone B, Lang AE, et al. Dopa dose–dependent sexual deviation. *Br J Psychiatry* 1983; 142:296–298.

212. Lesser RP, Fahn S, Snider SR, et al. Analysis of the clinical problems in parkinsonism and the complications of long-term levodopa therapy. *Neurology* 1979; 29:1253–1260.

213. Courty E, Durif F, Zenut M, et al. Psychiatric and sexual disorders induced by apomorphine in Parkinson's disease. *Clin Neuropharmacol* 1997; 2:140–147.

214. Colcher A, Simuni T, Stern M, Hurtig H. Dopamine agonists produce hypersexuality (abstract). *Mov Disord* 1998; 13:122.

215. Fernandez HH, Durso R. Clozapine for dopaminergic-induced paraphilias in Parkinson's disease. *Mov Disord* 1998; 13:597–598.

216. Jimenez-Jimenez FJ, Tallon-Barranco A, Cabrera-Valdivia F, et al. Fluctuating penile erection related with levodopa therapy. *Neurology* 1999; 52:210.

217. Brewer M, Stacy M. Sildenafil citrate therapy in men with Parkinson's disease(abstract). *Mov Disord* 1998; 13:860.

49 Treatment of Dementia

Karen E. Anderson

Idiopathic Parkinson's disease (PD) is a progressive, neurodegenerative condition characterized clinically by the motor features of bradykinesia, tremor, rigidity, and postural abnormalities (1). As cognitive symptoms of PD gained wider recognition by clinicians, patients, and their families over the past 2 decades, treatment of cognitive change has become a part of comprehensive care for the disorder. Unfortunately, recognition of cognitive symptoms has outpaced the development of treatment options. However, the work done to date on the treatment of cognitive impairment in PD has laid the foundation for much needed future study in this area. Since the work thus far has focused on PD patients with dementia, treatment options are discussed in relation to this feature unless otherwise specified. The treatment of PD patients with early and mild cognitive changes will likely become an important area of research in the coming years, as the cause and character of these symptoms are better understood.

Understanding the relationship between neuropathological changes in PD and cognitive decline is an important guide to the development of rational treatment strategies. The neuropathology is characterized by loss of dopaminergic cells in the pigmented nuclei of the brainstem. Cognitive deficits in PD are likely due to both degeneration of subcortical ascending systems—involving loss of dopaminergic,

noradrenergic, serotonergic, and cholinergic function—and the direct impact of disease on the cortex, indicated by the presence of Lewy bodies and degeneration of synapses and neurons leading to limbic and cortical Alzheimer disease (AD)-like changes (2–4). Parkinson's disease dementia (PDD) may be part of a continuum including dementia with Lewy bodies (DLB) and dementia due to AD (4–6). Thus, agents found to be efficacious in DLB and AD are also studied for use in PDD.

Cognitive changes in PD include a broad spectrum of symptoms such as attentional, executive, and memory deficits and visuospatial dysfunction; these may result in widespread cognitive impairment in the absence of dementia or may evolve into PDD. Many of the subtle deficits are similar to those seen in patients with damage to the prefrontal cortex: a failure of executive systems, leading to impairment of anticipation, planning, initiation, and monitoring, which are all behaviors required in the performance of goal-oriented tasks (7, 8). Deficits in memory, attention, and visuospatial processing may also occur in the absence of dementia (9–13). These deficits are strongly linked to dysfunction of the dopamine system in PD and may be seen quite early in the illness in both young- and old-onset PD (14–17). PDD is characterized by progressive loss of executive function, with memory deficits more severe than those described in patients who develop mild cognitive dysfunction affecting social activities. Decline of attentional systems may play a particular role in PDD (17–19). Other associated behavioral changes, such as hallucinations, delusions, and apathy, often complicate management. The incidence and prevalence of PDD have been reported with widely varying frequencies; however, the average prevalence is approximately 30% (20). Some groups report that this prevalence rises to 70% in PD patients above age 80 (21–23).

The importance of educating both patients and family members regarding the occurrence of cognitive symptoms in PD must be stressed, since many laypersons and even some health care professionals do not fully appreciate that cognitive impairment can accompany this disorder. This is especially important when the issue is mild cognitive impairment rather than dementia, since executive deficits may lead the family to feel that the patient is not fully participating in his or her care or is "uncooperative" or "unhelpful" with household or other tasks.

TREATMENT OPTIONS

Effects of Medications used to Treat Motor Symptoms on Cognition

Levodopa has been reported to have varying effects on cognition, including improvement, impairment, or little effect. This may be due in part to the varying stages of disease at which patients were evaluated in various studies, since responsiveness of the dopaminergic system varies greatly throughout the course of the illness (see Chapter 24 for a comprehensive review). It is recognized that in addition to levodopa, all of the medications used to treat the motor symptoms of PD may have a deleterious effect on cognition. Confusion and hallucinations, both common side effects of many agents used to treat motor symptoms in PD, may also worsen overall cognitive status. Clinicians should consider reducing PD medications in patients with worsening cognition, recognizing that there may well be a trade-off of motor symptom exacerbation in return for improved cognitive status. Since many individuals with PD are elderly, a review of all medications is often warranted, with particular attention to possible interactions among medications that could contribute to cognitive deficits.

Cholinesterase Inhibitors

PDD has been associated with cortical cholinergic denervation (25); the severity of this cholinergic dysfunction has been shown to correlate with the severity of dementia (26). Functional imaging studies have shown deficits in the cholinergic system in PD and PDD (27, 28). A recent small functional imaging study suggested that treatment of PDD with a cholinesterase inhibitor resulted in increased cingulate and frontal perfusion, in addition to significant improvement on the ADAS-cog (29). Thus,

several of the cholinesterase inhibitors approved for the treatment of memory loss in AD have been evaluated in patients with PDD. These include tacrine, a reversible, noncompetitive inhibitor of both acetylcholinesterase and butyrocholinesterease; galantamine, an allosteric modulator of nicotinic acetylcholine receptors; donepezil, a reversible, noncompetitive cholinesterase inhibitor; and rivastigmine, an inhibitor of both acetylcholinesterase and butyrocholinesterease. Tacrine was the first cholinesterase inhibitor approved for use in the treatment of AD; its current use is limited due to side effects, including gastrointestinal symptoms, bradycardia, worsening of chronic obstructive pulmonary disease, and association with asymptomatic, reversible hepatic enzyme elevations. All of the cholinesterase inhibitors may also cause gastrointestinal side effects. Case series and small open-label studies have shown efficacy in both improving cognitive status and other behavioral symptoms such as agitation and psychosis using tacrine, donepezil, rivastigmine, and galantamine (30–35).

Aarsland and colleagues (36) performed the first double-blind, randomized, placebo-controlled crossover study of donepezil for PDD. Fourteen patients with PD and cognitive impairment [scores between 16 and 26 out of 30 points total on the Mini Mental State Examination (MMSE)] received donepezil (5 or 10 mg per day) or matching placebo during 2 sequential periods lasting 10 weeks each. After 10 weeks of treatment, the mean MMSE score was increased by 2.1(SD 2.7) points on donepezil and 0.3 (SD 3.2) points on placebo, and the CIBIC+ score was 3.3 (SD 0.9) on donepezil and 4.1 (SD 0.8) on placebo, both of which demonstrated significant effects of donepezil. Two patients on donepezil (14%) dropped out because of peripheral cholinergic side effects; otherwise the adverse effects were minimal. Neuropsychiatric Inventory (NPI) and motor scores on the United Parkinson's Disease Rating Scale (UPDRS) did not differ significantly between the 2 groups. The authors concluded that donepezil improves cognition, is well tolerated, and does not to worsen parkinsonism in patients with cognitive impairment.

A second double-blind, placebo-controlled, randomized study of donepezil was conducted by Leroi and colleagues (37). Donepezil was found to improve memory subscales of the Dementia Rating Scale in PDD, with a trend toward improvement of psychomotor speed and attentional performance. Psychiatric symptoms, motor functions, and activities of daily living (ADLs) did not differ between the donepezil and placebo groups before or after treatment. Four patients in the donepezil group withdrew early due to adverse events, including two with cholinergic side effects and one with worsening of motor symptoms. Side effects were noted to occur in conjunction with dosage increases.

A large, randomized, placebo-controlled trial of rivastigmine for PDD was conducted by Emre and colleagues (38). Only patients in whom dementia developed at least 2 years after they received a clinical diagnosis of PD were accepted into this trial in an attempt to exclude those with DLB. Patients received placebo or 3 to 12 mg of rivastigmine per day for 24 weeks. A total of 541 patients were enrolled, and 410 completed the study. Rivastigmine-treated patients had a mean improvement of 2.1 points in the score for the 70-point ADAS-cog as compared with a 0.7-point worsening in the placebo group, a significant difference on this primary outcome measure. Small but statistically significant differences were also seen on the Alzheimer's Disease Cooperative Study-Clinical Global Impression of Change (ADCS-CGIS) scores, with the rivastigmine-treated group showing improvement. Significantly better outcomes were seen for rivastigmine with respect to all secondary efficacy variables, including changes from baseline in scores for the NPI, MMSE, and ADLS-ADL (Alzheimer's Disease Cooperative Study–Activities of Daily Living). The most common side effects—nausea and vomiting—occurred with significantly higher frequency in the rivastigmine group compared with the placebo group. UPDRS motor scores did not differ significantly between groups, but more patients in the rivastigmine-treated group reported tremor as an adverse event than did those in the placebo group (10% versus 4%). Effect sizes were somewhat modest, which is similar to what has been reported in studies of rivastigmine for the treatment of AD.

These results suggest that there is definitely a role for cholinesterase inhibitors in treatment of PDD but that the effects are modest. More data are needed regarding long-term efficacy of these agents in slowing cognitive decline and on outcomes such as nursing home placement.

Glutamatergic Antagonists

As a result of the loss of dopaminergic modulation in PD, the glutamatergic system is no longer inhibited and therefore shows a relative increase in activity. N-methyl-D-aspartic acid (NMDA) receptor antagonists, which block glutamatergic input to the striatum, improve motor symptoms of PD and can be helpful in the treatment of dyskinesias (39, 40). Amantadine, an NMDA receptor antagonist, is used to treat motor symptoms of PD. No studies have examined its use to treat cognitive deficits in PD. However, precipitation of worsening cognitive status and confusion have been reported with amantadine withdrawal (41). Amantadine may cause other behavioral changes, especially with dose escalation, including restlessness and psychotic symptoms.

Memantine is a noncompetitive NMDA antagonist that has been shown to be efficacious in treatment of AD (42). It has also been shown to be well tolerated in PD, but studies to date have focused on assessment of its effects for the treatment of motor symptoms (43, 44). A case series of 3 PDD patients reported improvement in MMSE scores following memantine treatment (45).

Further work is needed to assess whether memantine will prove efficacious for PDD.

Neuroprotective Agents

Early treatment studies for PDD focused on the nootropics piracetam and phosphatidylserine, neither of which was found to be efficacious in controlled trials (46, 47) Selegiline, a selective inhibitor of MAO-B, which was shown to delay functional impairment in AD, was not found to be effective in delaying, improving, or preventing PDD in the DATATOP study (48). Tocopherol (vitamin E) at 2000 IU also did not improve performance on cognitive tests in the same analysis of DATATOP.

The development of neuroprotective agents continues to be an active area of research in all neurodegenerative disorders, and studies are in progress to look at potential neuroprotective agents that may slow PD in general and prevent cognitive impairment in particular. A large neuroprotection futility trial funded by the National Institute of Neurological Disorders and Stroke (NINDS), Neuroprotection Exploratory Trials in Parkinson's Disease (NET-PD), has completed testing of CoQ10 (also known as ubiquinone) and GPI-1485 (49). Data are currently being analyzed to determine whether either or both are safe, well tolerated, and have possible neuroprotective potential in the treatment of PD. In animal models of PD, both CoQ10 and GPI-1485 have been shown to protect the neurons, and GPI-1485 shows the ability to help these cells regenerate. Both agents are generally well tolerated and side effects are usually mild. CoQ10 is widely used as a dietary supplement. It can cause abdominal discomfort, decreased appetite, and gastrointestinal symptoms. GPI-1485 is an investigational drug that may promote regeneration following neurodegeneration. Its main side effects are also gastrointestinal. Two other compounds—minocycline and creatine—are also being evaluated in NET-PD. Creatine may counteract oxidative stress and mitochondrial dysfunction in PD. It is generally well tolerated; occasional side effects include weight gain, edema, nausea, vomiting, and diarrhea. Minocycline is an antibiotic with anti-inflammatory effects and may also prevent apoptosis. Side effects associated with minocycline are gastrointesinal upset, dizziness, rash, hypersensitivity reactions, and headache.

Nicotine

Postmortem studies have demonstrated a substantial loss of nicotinic receptors in PD, which may contribute to some of the motoric and behavioral symptoms seen in the disorder. Epidemiologic studies suggest that cigarette smoking is protective against development of PD (see Chapter 5). Two studies to date have looked specifically at the effects of nicotine on both cognitive and motor function in PD. Kelton and colleagues (50) administered nicotine by transdermal patch for 2 weeks to nondemented patients with early PD. Improvements after acute nicotine administration were reported in reaction time, central processing speed, and decreased tracking errors. Improvements were also seen in measures of motor function. Since a control group was not used, practice effects may explain the cognitive gains seen in this study. Lemay and others (51) administered transdermal nicotine patches to 22 nonsmoking, nondemented PD patients over 25 days in increasing titrated doses. Patients tolerated nicotine poorly; approximately 60% withdrew because of acute side effects. Compared to a control group, no improvement was seen in cognitive or motor symptoms in the 9 patients who remained in the study. It is possible that nicotine lacks specificity for the critical nicotinic receptors that might be involved in PD pathophysiology; use of more selective nicotinic agents may provide greater tolerability and show efficacy in future work.

Estrogen

Estrogen has been purported to increase cerebral blood flow, act as an anti-inflammatory agent, enhance activity at neuronal synapses, and exert direct neuroprotective and neurotrophic effects on brain tissue. Given the interest in estrogen for the prevention of cognitive decline in normal aging and in the treatment of AD, it was a logical agent to examine in women with PD. Observational work has thus far been used to address this issue. Marder et al. (52) examined the effects of estrogen replacement therapy on the risk of development of dementia in 87 women with PD without dementia, 80 women with PD with dementia, and 989 nondemented healthy women in a community study. Estrogen replacement therapy was found to be protective for the development of PDD but not for PD. Fernandez and Laplane (53) examined the role of estrogen in motor, cognitive, and behavioral functions in 10, 145 elderly women with PD using the Systematic Assessment in Geriatric drug use via Epidemiology (SAGE) database, which contains cross-sectional information on nursing home residents. Independent of age, estrogen users were found to be less cognitively impaired and more independent in ADLs. Estrogen users were also more likely to be depressed and to be receiving antidepressant therapy than nonusers. Based on these 2 studies, further work is needed to determine the role of estrogen in the prevention and treatment of cognitive decline associated with PD. An 8-week, double-blind pilot trial of estrogen including 23 postmenopausal women with fluctuating PD has demonstrated short-term safety. In addition, there was a trend toward improvement in the motor features of PD (54). This could set the stage for a long-term large-scale trial.

Noradrenergic Agents

Reduced levels of norepinephrine have been found in PDD patients compared to those with PD and no demen-

tia (55). Bradyphrenia in PD, measured by impairment of performance on attentional and vigilance tasks, may be associated with an alteration in norepinephrine metabolism (56). The selective noradrenergic alpha-1 antagonist naphtoxazine partially ameliorated attentional deficits in PD in a small trial of 9 patients (57). In addition, specific evoked potentials thought to reflect attentional processes were improved by naphtoxazine. Based on these studies, it has been proposed that atomoxetine, a selective norepinephrine reuptake inhibitor, may be useful for the treatment of executive dysfunction in patients with PD. Atomoxetine has been shown to be helpful in reduction of impulsivity and attentional deficits in patients with adult attention deficit disorder (58). However, studies assessing its safety and efficacy in PD are pending at this time.

Modafinil

Modafinil is an atypical stimulant that does not promote feelings of euphoria and is often described as a "wakefulness-promoting agent." It has been found to be modestly helpful for reducing fatigue in PD in some but not all of the limited studies available and may prove useful for the treatment of cognitive deficits in PD (59–61). Further study is required to evaluate this agent for use in patients with PDD.

Deep Brain Stimulation

The reported effects of deep brain stimulation (DBS) on cognition are variable. It is generally agreed that patients should be screened preoperatively to exclude those with actual dementia; there have even been reports of patients with borderline cognitive function becoming irreversibly demented following DBS (62–64). In addition, STN-DBS may be particularly likely to cause cognitive deterioration in patients above age 69 (65). An extensive review by Fields and Troster (66) examined prior work on the cognitive effects of DBS. It suggested that DBS did not have a negative impact on cognitive function with the exception of small but consistent declines in verbal fluency. Milder and less consistent changes in executive function and memory were also noted. Although the motor benefits of DBS tend to outweigh the fairly minimal cognitive decline, the authors suggested caution, in that the number of patients evaluated postoperatively has been small, so that data are limited. Comparisons are generally with stimulators "on" versus "off" rather than pre- and postoperative. Some of the other notable problems with studies of cognitive changes following DBS include small sample sizes and follow-up times limited to a year at most.

Smeding and colleagues (67) recently evaluated the cognitive and behavioral effects of bilateral subthalamic nucleus (STN) stimulation in 99 PD patients and a control group of 36. Patients were evaluated presurgically and 6 months after surgery, while nonsurgical controls were evaluated after 6 months. At baseline and follow-up, neuropsychological tests of language, memory, visuospatial function, mental speed, and executive functions were administered. Six months after surgery, the STN group showed a larger decline than the control group on measures of verbal fluency, color naming, selective attention, and verbal memory. On the other hand, the STN group showed an increase in quality of life and a slight decrease in depressive symptoms. The authors concluded that bilateral STN stimulation adversely affects executive function in PD. It will be important for future studies to look at larger numbers of patients and longer postsurgical periods. At this time, DBS does not have a role in treatment of cognitive decline in PD and can worsen cognition in patients with preexisting impairments.

Cognitive Rehabilitation

Programs to strengthen existing cognitive ability and teach strategies to counteract memory loss are used in some neurological conditions, such as stroke, but have received little formal study in PD. A small study involving a rehabilitation program of 6 weeks, with both motor and cognitive training, was conducted with 20 early PD patients who had mild cognitive deficits but no dementia. Patients showed significant improvement in verbal fluency, logic memory, and Raven's matrices tests as compared to baseline. Results were stable over the study. The authors propose that particular benefits for PD may involve enhancement of executive function (68). More work is needed to show how cognitive rehabilitation should be designed to meet the specific needs of PD patients and whether it could provide an alternative to pharamacological treatment in some PD patients.

Antidepressant Therapy

Given that cognitive impairment in PD is thought to be associated with depression (69–71), it has been proposed that antidepressant therapy may have a role in the treatment of cognitive deficits in PD. Boggio and colleagues compared the selective serotonin reuptake inhibitor (SSRI) fluoxetine to repetitive magnetic transcranial stimulation (rTMS) of the left dorsolateral prefrontal cortex in a randomized, double-blind study of 25 PD patients with depression (72). Neuropsychological assessment by a blinded rater found that patients in both groups showed improvement in performance of the Stroop, Hooper, and Wisconsin Card Sort tests after treatment. These results suggest that treatment of depression in PD may improve cognition, particularly with respect to executive function.

SUMMARY

Despite the increasing identification of cognitive deficits and dementia as a part of the clinical picture in PD, effective treatments for these symptoms are lacking. Reduction of medications used to treat motor symptoms and general avoidance of polypharmacy are the judicious first steps in the treatment of cognitive change in PD. The addition of cholinesterase inhibitors has proven helpful, although the effect is modest; one such agent, rivastigmine, has recently gained FDA approval for the treatment of PDD. There is a need to tailor treatments to fit the specific picture, such as treating depressive or psychotic symptoms with the hope that they too will of improve overall cognition. More specific agents are needed to target receptor systems and reduce the side effects of current treatments. Alternative strategies to medications, including cognitive remediation, may prove useful but need to be adapted for the specific picture of deficits seen in PD. Neuroprotection offers the future hope that, if PD progression can be slowed, cognitive decline can be prevented.

References

1. Marsden CD. Parkinson's disease. *J Neurol Neurosurg Psychiatry* 1994; 57(6):672–681.
2. Churchyard A, Lees AJ. The relationship between dementia and direct involvement of the hippocampus and amygdala in Parkinson's disease. *Neurology* 1997; 49(6):1570–1576.
3. Jellinger KA. Morphological substrates of dementia in parkinsonism. A critical update. *J Neural Transm Suppl* 1997; 51:57–82.
4. Hely MA, Reid WG, Halliday GM, et al. Diffuse Lewy body disease: clinical features in nine cases without coexistent Alzheimer's disease. *J Neurol Neurosurg Psychiatry* 1996; 60(5):531–538.
5. McKeith IG, Galasko D, Kosaka K, et al. Consensus guidelines for the clinical and pathologic diagnosis of dementia with Lewy bodies (DLB): report of the consortium on DLB international workshop. *Neurology* 1996; 47(5):1113–1124.
6. Kosaka K, Yoshimura M, Ikeda K, Budka H. Diffuse type of Lewy body disease: progressive dementia with abundant cortical Lewy bodies and senile changes of varying degree—a new disease? *Clin Neuropathol* 1984; 3(5):185–192.
7. Bowen FP, Kamienny RS, Burns MM, Yahr M. Parkinsonism: effects of levodopa treatment on concept formation. *Neurology* 1975; 25(8):701–704.
8. Dubois B, Pilon B, Lhermitte F, Agid Y. Cholinergic deficiency and frontal dysfunction in Parkinson's disease. *Ann Neurol* 1990; 28(2):117–121.
9. Warburton JW. Memory disturbance and the Parkinson syndrome. *Br J Med Psychol* 1967; 40(2):169–171.
10. Wilson RS, Kaszniak AW, Klawans HL, Garron DC. High speed memory scanning in parkinsonism. *Cortex* 1980; 16(1):67–72.
11. Boller F, Passafiume D, Keefe NC, et al. Visuospatial impairment in Parkinson's disease. Role of perceptual and motor factors. *Arch Neurol* 1984; 41(5):485–490.
12. Brown RG, Marsden CD, Quinn N, Wyke MA. Alterations in cognitive performance and affect-arousal state during fluctuations in motor function in Parkinson's disease. *J Neurol Neurosurg Psychiatry* 1984; 47(5):454–465.
13. Downes JJ, Roberts AC, Sahakian BJ, et al. Impaired extra-dimensional shift performance in medicated and unmedicated Parkinson's disease: evidence for a specific attentional dysfunction. *Neuropsychologia* 1989; 27(11–12):1329–1343.
14. Cooper JA, Sagar HJ, Jordan N, et al. Cognitive impairment in early, untreated Parkinson's disease and its relationship to motor disability. *Brain* 1991; 114(Pt 5):2095–2122.

15. Hietanen M, Teravainen H. The effect of age of disease onset on neuropsychological performance in Parkinson's disease. *J Neurol Neurosurg Psychiatry* 1988; 51(2):244–249.

16. Tsai CH, Lu CS, Hua MS, et al. Cognitive dysfunction in early onset parkinsonism. *Acta Neurol Scand* 1994; 89(1):9–14.

17. Wermuth L, Knudsen L, Boldsen J. A study of cognitive functions in young parkinsonian patients. *Acta Neurol Scand* 1996; 93(1):21–24.

18. Zeng XH, Hirata K, Tanaka H, et al. Insufficient processing resources in Parkinson's disease: evaluation using multimodal event-related potentials paradigm. *Brain Topogr* 2002; 14(4):299–311.

19. Woodward TS, Bub DN, Hunter MA. Task switching deficits associated with Parkinson's disease reflect depleted attentional resources. *Neuropsychologia* 2002; 40(12):1948–1955.

20. Emre M. Dementia associated with Parkinson's disease. *Lancet Neurol* 2003; 2(4):229–237.

21. Mayeux R, Stern Y, Rosenstein R, et al. An estimate of the prevalence of dementia in idiopathic Parkinson's disease. *Arch Neurol* 1988; 45(3):260–262.

22. Mayeux R, Denaro J, Hemenegildo N, et al. A population-based investigation of Parkinson's disease with and without dementia. Relationship to age and gender. *Arch Neurol* 1992; 49(5):492–497.

23. Tison F, Dartigues JF, Auriacombe S, et al. Dementia in Parkinson's disease: a population-based study in ambulatory and institutionalized individuals. *Neurology* 1995; 45(4):705–708.

24. Kulisevsky J. Role of dopamine in learning and memory: implications for the treatment of cognitive dysfunction in patients with Parkinson's disease. *Drugs Aging* 2000; 16(5):365–379.

25. Perry EK, Marshall E, Thompson P, et al. Monoaminergic activities in Lewy body dementia: relation to hallucinosis and extrapyramidal features. *J Neural Transm Park Dis Dement Sect* 1993; 6:167–177.

26. Nakano I, Hirano A. Parkinson's disease: neuron loss in the nucleus basalis without concomitant Alzheimer's disease. *Ann Neurol* 1984; 15(5):415–418.

27. Kuhl DE, Minoshima S, Fessler JA, et al. In vivo mapping of cholinergic terminals in normal aging, Alzheimer's disease, and Parkinson's disease. *Ann Neurol* 1996; 40(3):399–410.

28. Bohnen NI, Kaufer DI, Ivanco LS, et al. Cortical cholinergic function is more severely affected in parkinsonian dementia than in Alzheimer disease: an in vivo positron emission tomographic study. *Arch Neurol* 2003; 60(12):1745–1748.

29. Ceravolo R, Volterrani D, Frosini D, et al. Brain perfusion effects of cholinesterase inhibitors in Parkinson's disease with dementia. *J Neural Transm* 2006; 113(11):1787–90.

30. Hutchinson M, Fazzini E. Cholinesterase inhibition in Parkinson's disease. *J Neurol Neurosurg Psychiatry* 1996; 61:324–325.

31. Werber EA, Rabey JM. The beneficial effect of cholinesterase inhibitors on patients suffering from Parkinson's disease and dementia. *J Neural Transm* 2001; 108(11):1319–1325.

32. Giladi N, Shabtai H, Gurevich T, et al. Rivastigmine (Excelon) for dementia in patients with Parkinson's disease. *Acta Neurol Scand* 2003; 108:336–373.

33. Reading P, Luce A, McKeith I. Rivastigmine in the treatment of parkinsonian psychosis and cognitive impairment. *Mov Disord* 2001; 16:1171–1174.

34. Aarsland D, Hutchinson M, Larsen JP. Cognitive, psychiatric, and motor response to galantamine in Parkinson's disease with dementia. *Int J Geriatr Psychiatry* 2003; 18:937–941.

35. Bullock R, Cameron A. Rivastigmine for the treatment of dementia and visual hallucinations associated with Parkinson's disease: a case series. *Curr Med Res Opin* 2002; 18(5):258–264.

36. Aarsland D, Laake K, Larsen JP, Janvin C. Donepezil for cognitive impairment in Parkinson's disease: a randomised controlled study. *J Neurol Neurosurg Psychiatry* 2002; 72(6):708–712. Erratum in *J Neurol Neurosurg Psychiatry* 2002; 73(3):354.

37. Leroi I, Brandt J, Reich SG, et al. Randomized, placebo-controlled trial of donepezil in cognitive impairment in Parkinson's disease with dementia. *Int J Geriatr Psychiatry* 2004; 19:1–8.

38. Emre M, Aarsland D, Albanese A, et al. Rivastigmine in Parkinson's disease patients with dementia: a randomized, double-blind, placebo controlled study. *N Engl J Med* 2004; 351 2509–2518.

39. Blanchet PJ, Verhagen L, Metman M, et al. Acute pharmacologic blockade of dyskinesias in Parkinson's disease. *Mov Disord* 1996; 11(5)580–581.

40. Skuza G, Rogoz Z, Quack G, Danysz W. Memantine, amantadine, and L-deprenyl potentiate the action of L-dopa in monoamine-depleted rats. *J Neural Transm Gen Sect* 1994; 98(1):57–67.

41. Factor SA, Molho ES, Brown DL. Acute delirium after withdrawal of amantadine in Parkinson's disease. *Neurology* 1998; 50(5):1456–1458.

42. Winblad B, Poritis N. Memantine in severe dementia: results of the 9M-Best Study (Benefit and efficacy in severely demented patients during treatment with memantine). *Int J Geriatr Psychiatry* 1999; 14(2):135–146.

43. Rabey JM, Nissipeanu P, Korczyn AD. Efficacy of memantine, an NMDA receptor antagonist, in the treatment of Parkinson's disease. *J Neural Transm Park Dis Dement Sect* 1992; 4:277–282.

44. Merello M, Nouzeilles MI, Cammarota A, Leiguarda R. Effect of memantine (NMDA antagonist) on Parkinson's disease: a double-blind crossover randomized study. *Clin Neuropharmacol* 1999; 22(5):273–276.

45. Lokk J. Memantine can relieve certain symptoms in Parkinson disease. Improvement achieved in two out of three described cases with dyskinesia and cognitive failure. *Lakartidningen* 2004; 101(23):2003–2006.

46. Sano M, Stern Y, Marder K, Mayeux R. A controlled trial of piracetam in intellectually impaired patients with Parkinson's disease. *Mov Disord* 1990; 5(3):230–234.

47. Fünfgeld EW, Baggen M, Nedwidek P, et al. Double-blind study with phosphatidylserine (PS) in parkinsonian patients with senile dementia of Alzheimer's type (SDAT). *Prog Clin Biol Res* 1989; 317:1235–1246.

48. Kieburtz K, McDermott M, Como P, et al. The effect of deprenyl and tocopherol on cognitive performance in early untreated Parkinson's disease. Parkinson Study Group. *Neurology* 1994; 44(9):1756–1759.

49. The NINDS NET-PD Investigators. A randomized clinical trial of coenzyme Q10 and GPI-1485 in early Parkinson disease. *Neurology* 2007; 68(1):20–28.

50. Kelton MC, Kahn HJ, Conrath CL, Newhouse PA. The effects of nicotine on Parkinson's disease. *Brain Cogn* 2000; 43(1–3):274–282.

51. Lemay S, Chouinard S, Blanchet P, et al. Lack of efficacy of a nicotine transdermal treatment on motor and cognitive deficits in Parkinson's disease. *Prog Neuropsychopharmacol Biol Psychiatry* 2004; 28(1):31–39.

52. Marder K, Tang MX, Alfaro B, Mejia H, Cote L, Jacobs D, Stern Y, Sano M, Mayeux R. Postmenopausal estrogen use and Parkinson's disease with and without dementia. Neurology. 1998 Apr; 50(4):1141–1143.

53. Fernandez HH, Lapane KL. Estrogen use among nursing home residents with a diagnosis of Parkinson's disease. *Mov Disord* 2000; 15(6):1119–1124.

54. Shulman LM and the Parkinson Study Group. The POETRY study: the safety tolerability and efficacy of estrogen replacement therapy in post-menopausal women with Parkinson's disease. *Mov Disord* 2006; 21:1545.

55. Cash R, Dennis T, L'Heureux R, et al. Parkinson's disease and dementia: norepinephrine and dopamine in locus ceruleus. *Neurology* 1987; 37(1):42–46.

56. Mayeux R, Stern Y, Sano M, et al. Clinical and biochemical correlates of bradyphrenia in Parkinson's disease. *Neurology* 1987; 37(7):1130–1134. Erratum in *Neurology* 1987; 37(10):1693.

57. Bedard MA, el Massioui F, Malapani C, et al. Attentional deficits in Parkinson's disease: partial reversibility with naphtoxazine (SDZ NVI-085), a selective noradrenergic alpha 1 agonist. *Clin Neuropharmacol* 1998; 21(2):108–117.

58. Michelson D, Adler L, Spencer T, et al. Atomoxetine in adults with ADHD: two randomized, placebo-controlled studies. *Biol Psychiatry* 2003; 53(2):112–120.

59. Hogl B, Saletu M, Brandauer E, et al. Modafinil for the treatment of daytime sleepiness in Parkinson's disease: a double-blind, randomized, crossover, placebo-controlled polygraphic trial. *Sleep* 2002; 25(8):905–909.

60. Nieves AV, Lang AE. Treatment of excessive daytime sleepiness in patients with Parkinson's disease with modafinil. *Clin Neuropharmacol* 2002; 25(2):111–114.

61. Ondo WG, Fayle R, Atassi F, Jankovic J. Modafinil for daytime somnolence in Parkinson's disease: double blind, placebo controlled parallel trial. *J Neurol Neurosurg Psychiatry* 2005; 76(12):1636–1639.

62. Foncke E, van der LC, Vandewalle V, et al. Chronic bilateral stimulation of the subthalamic nucleus (STN) in 15 patients with advanced ideopathic Parkinson's disease previously treated with unilateral internal globus pallidus (GPi) stimulation. *Neurology* 2001; 56(Suppl 3):A272.

63. Hariz MI, Johansson F, Shamsgovara P. Bilateral subthalamic nucleus stimulation in a parkinsonian patient with preoperative deficits in speech and cognition: persisting improvement in mobility but increased dependency. A case study. *Mov Disord* 2000; 15:136–139.

64. Limousin P, Krack P, Pollak P, et al. Electrical stimulation of the subthalamic nucleus in advanced Parkinson's disease. *N Engl J Med* 1998; 339:1105–1111.

65. Saint-Cyr JA, Trepanier LL, Kumar R, et al. Neuropsychological consequences of chronic bilateral stimulation of the subthalamic nucleus in Parkinson's disease. *Brain* 2000; 123 (Pt 10):2091–2108.

66. Fields JA, Troster AI. Cognitive outcomes after deep brain stimulation for Parkinson's disease: a review of initial studies and recommendations for future research. *Brain Cogn* 2000; 42(2):268–293.

67. Smeding HM, Speelman JD, Koning-Haanstra M, et al. Neuropsychological effects of bilateral STN stimulation in Parkinson disease: a controlled study. *Neurology* 2006; 66(12):1830–1836.

68. Sinforiani E, Banchieri L, Zucchella C, et al. Cognitive rehabilitation in Parkinson's disease. *Arch Gerontol Geriatr Suppl* 2004; (9):387–391.

69. Kuzis G, Sabe L, Tiberti C, et al. Cognitive functions in major depression and Parkinson disease. *Arch Neurol* 1997; 54(8):982–986.

70. Mayeux R, Stern Y, Rosen J, Leventhal J. Depression, intellectual impairment, and Parkinson disease. *Neurology* 1981; 31(6):645–650.

71. Starkstein SE, Preziosi TJ, Berthier ML, et al. Depression and cognitive impairment in Parkinson's disease. *Brain* 1989; 112(Pt 5):1141–1153.

72. Boggio PS, Fregni F, Bermpohl F, et al. Effect of repetitive TMS and fluoxetine on cognitive function in patients with Parkinson's disease and concurrent depression. *Mov Disord* 2005; 20(9):1178–1184.

50 Status of Neuroprotective Therapies

Andrew D. Siderowf
Matthew B. Stern

Therapies for Parkinson's disease (PD) may be divided into three main categories: (a) symptomatic, (b) restorative, and (c) neuroprotective. Effective symptomatic therapy for PD has existed since the demonstration by Cotzias (1) that dopamine replacement with exogenous levodopa could reverse most of the clinical manifestations of PD. More recently, therapies such as neural transplantation, (2) have shown the potential to restore the capacity to produce dopamine in PD patients. However, therapy that actually alters the underlying process of neurodegeneration in PD remains a largely unattained goal in spite of a number of areas of active research. This chapter reviews the status of currently available and emerging therapies with potential neuroprotective activity (Table 50-1) and addresses some of the issues related to evaluating these agents in clinical trials.

DEFINITION OF NEUROPROTECTION AND RELEVANCE TO PARKINSON'S DISEASE

Neuroprotection is a therapeutic strategy intended to slow or halt the progression of neuronal loss (3) and thereby alter the natural history of disease. As contrasted with symptomatic therapy, neuroprotective therapies act on the pathogenic mechanisms underlying cell death. A partially neuroprotective therapy slows the course of disease, while a therapy that is fully neuroprotective completely arrests disease progression. Other terms have been used to address concepts related to neuroprotection. For example, "disease-modifying" or "course-modifying" has been used to refer to therapies that may alter the clinical course of PD in some way—such as reducing the incidence of motor complications—without having a direct impact on the survival of dopaminergic neurons in the substantia nigra.

The term "neurorescue" has recently been used to describe a distinct type of neuroprotection. Neurorescue is based on the concept that a population of cells is dysfunctional but not irreversibly injured and may be restored to normal function (4). In contrast to traditional neuroprotective therapies, which would be expected to have no immediate effect on symptoms, neurorescue therapies may improve clinical manifestations of disease while also slowing or stopping disease progression.

The concept of neuroprotection obviously has great relevance to PD. Since the rate of disease progression in PD is relatively slow and little disability is associated with the early stages of disease (5), therapies that slow but do not entirely arrest disease progression would result in significant reduction in the burdens of PD.

TABLE 50-1
Current Status of Agents with Possible Neuroprotective Activity in PD

COMPOUND	STAGE OF DEVELOPMENT
MAO-B inhibitors	
Selegiline	Approved by FDA
Lazabemide	Finished phase III trials*
Rasagiline	Finished phase III trials
TCH-346	Trials stopped due to lack of efficacy
Dopamine Agonists	
Bromocriptine	Approved by FDA
Pergolide	Approved by FDA
Pramipexole	Approved by FDA
Ropinirole	Approved by FDA
Glutamate antagonists	
Remacemide	Trials failed to show efficacy
Amantadine	Approved by FDA
Dextromethorphan	Approved by FDA
Riluzole	Trials stopped due to lack of efficacy
Vitamins/Nutritional supplements	
Coenzyme Q10	Available
Vitamin C (ascorbic acid)	Available
Vitamin E (alpha tocopherol)	Available
Creatine	Available
Caffeine	Available
Nicotine	Available
Emerging therapies	
Immunophillins	Clinical trials in progress
GDNF	Trials stopped due to safety concerns
CEP-1347	Trials stopped due to lack of efficacy

*Not currently marketed in the United States.

MECHANISMS OF NEURONAL INJURY IN PD (SEE CHAPTERS 29 TO 31)

Development of rational neuroprotective therapies is predicated on understanding the underlying causes of neuronal injury in PD. Although these causes remain largely unknown, several theoretical models to explain the degenerative process in PD have been put forward. These will be covered briefly here. One of the major results of recent scientific investigations, particularly genetic linkage studies, has been to emphasize that the syndrome of PD is likely to have multiple primary causes.

One interpretation of the problem of multiple primary etiologies is that patients with the clinical syndrome of PD will need specific identification of their individual cause and therapy tailored to that cause. Alternatively, some etiologies may be thematically related, allowing for neuroprotective therapies that would be of benefit to larger numbers of patients. Furthermore, the varied etiologies may lead up to a final common pathway of cell death which would also benefit a majority of PD patients.

One such theme emphasizes the pathogenic role of abnormal protein accumulation and aggregation. In several forms of hereditary PD (6–9), either the gene product accumulates pathologically in PD patients, or the function of the gene product appears to be related to protein degradation and clearance. Abnormal protein clearance also appears to be highly relevant to at least one experimental model of PD.(10) Another possible mechanism is that of oxidative stress and excitotoxicity. Perhaps the strongest evidence for oxidative stress comes from experiments showing impaired mitochondrial electron transport chain function, particularly in complex I, resulting in increased free radical production and cellular injury.(11–13) Another important pathophysiological mechanism, excitotoxicity, is closely related to oxidative stress. Excitotoxic injury results from a cascade of events initiated by pathologically high levels of excitatory neurotransmitters, particularly glutamate.(14) In particular, stimulation of the ionotropic N-methyl D-aspartate (NMDA) glutamate receptor allows the intracellular entry of large amounts of calcium that in turn may trigger the production of reactive oxygen species as well as a variety of other pathological processes.(15)

Other potential mechanisms of injury in PD include inflammatory injury and glial cell dysfunction. A possible role of inflammation in the pathogenesis of PD has been suggested by the finding that the substantia nigra pars compacta (SNc) from parkinsonian patients contains increased levels of inflammatory mediators such as interluken-1 beta, interferon-gamma, and tumor necrosis factor-alpha and microglia.(16) Glial involvement in PD has been suggested by studies showing that the concentration of reduced glutathione (GSH) and mitochondrial complex I activity are decreased by about 30% in SN homogenates from patients with PD. This result can not be explained by neuronal loss alone, because dopaminergic neurons probably account for no more than about 2% of tissue in such samples.(17) These mechanisms are additional rational targets for neuroprotective therapies.

NEUROPROTECTIVE THERAPY FOR PD

A broad range of compounds have been considered as possible neuroprotective agents for PD. In an effort to prioritize these compounds, the National Institute for

TABLE 50-2

Compounds Identified as Priority Agents for Future Trials by the CINAPS Committee

Caffeine	Minocycline
Coenzyme Q10	Nicotine
Creatine	Pramipexole
Estrogen	Rasagiline
Neuroimmunophillin-1	Ropinirole
GM-1 ganglioside	Selegiline

Neurological Disease and Stroke (NINDS) initiated a process to evaluate the available evidence. The purpose of this process, as defined by the Committee to Identify Neuroprotective Agents in Parkinson's (CINAPS) (18), is to identify agents that could be tested in a large-scale, simple clinical trial. The CINAPS process identified a total of 59 compounds. Of these 12 were felt to have sufficient merit to be tested in further studies. The list of compounds evaluated by the CINAPS process is shown in Table 50-2. We will address the 12 target compounds as well as a selection of others.

Levodopa

Although the benefits of levodopa on the clinical symptoms of PD are unquestionable, pre-clinical studies have suggested that levodopa may be neurotoxic through the capacity to generate reactive oxygen species.(19) To address this issue the ELLDOPA study randomized subjects to receive either placebo or three doses of levodopa.(20) This study demonstrated that subjects who received levodopa ended up with better motor performance, even after a two week washout, than subjects receiving placebo. This might actually suggest a neuroprotective effect. However, [^{123}I] β-CIT imaging, which was a secondary outcome measure, showed less decline in dopamine transporter density in subject receiving placebo than in those receiving levodopa. Because of these conflicting results, the ELLDOPA study has not resolved whether levodopa treatment has an effect on the status of neurodegeneration in PD, and the question remains whether levodopa is protective, toxic or neither. (For more detail on the impact of levodopa on PD, see Chapter 38).

Selegiline

Selegiline, at doses of 5 to 10 mg per day, is a selective MAO-B inhibitor and is thus devoid of the hypertensive "cheese effect" associated with non-selective MAO inhibition.(21) Selegiline has been the subject of more intensive study than any other potentially neuroprotective compound for PD. However, a great deal of controversy remains regarding whether it possesses a neuroprotective effect, and, if present, the mechanism of action by which it is neuroprotective.

A substantial body of research suggests several potential mechanisms by which selegiline may protect degenerating neurons from oxidative injury, and thus alter the underlying course of disease in PD. First, it may protect against the effects of oxidative environmental toxins that act via a mechanism similar to the neurotoxin 1-methyl-4 phenyl-1, 2, 3, 6-tetrahydropyridine (MPTP)(22) (see Chapter 34). The conversion of MPTP, which is a protoxin, to the active toxin 1-methyl-4-phenylpyridium (MPP+) is catalyzed by MAO-B and treatment with selegiline can block the conversion, protecting dopaminergic neurons from MPTP-mediated injury (23, 24). In addition, animal experiments (25–27) have shown that selegiline induces the expression of the free radical scavenger superoxide dismutase (SOD), and may thus improve the ability of cells to buffer against reactive oxygen species.

It has recently been proposed that the protective effects of selegiline could result from novel actions including inhibition of apoptosis. Tatton and Greenwood (28) reported that selegiline protects dopaminergic neurons against the neurotoxic action of MPTP even when it is given 3 days after MPTP treatment. Furthermore, these investigators showed that the drug can rescue dopaminergic neurons from cell death induced by MPP+ when the active toxin is administered directly (28). These findings suggest that the mechanism of protection is independent of MAO-B inhibition. Subsequently, Tatton and colleagues demonstrated that treatment with selegiline promotes the expression of genes known to prevent apoptosis (29). These findings suggest an alternative neuroprotective mechanism for selegiline.

Two large-scale prospective monotherapy studies have attempted specifically to assess the neuroprotective effect of selegiline in PD patients. Tetrud and Langston (30) studied 54 subjects with early PD who were randomized to receive either selegiline 10 mg per day or placebo and then followed until they either reached the study endpoint, requiring additional symptomatic therapy (levodopa), or had completed 3 years of evaluations. In this study, there was a delay in reaching endpoint of approximately 9 months, and clinical disease progression was slowed by 40% to 83% per year in the selegiline-treated group.

The DATATOP study (Deprenyl and Tocopherol Antioxidative Therapy of Parkinsonism) (31) randomized 800 subjects to receive selegiline or tocopherol (vitamin E) alone, in combination, or placebo in a 2 x 2 factorial design. During interim analysis of this study, a substantially reduced likelihood of reaching endpoint (need for levodopa therapy) was found in the selegiline but not in the tocopherol treated group, and the selegiline randomization was terminated prematurely. The hazard ratio for reaching endpoint was 0.43, and, due to the large sample size, the P value for this result was 10^{-10}. The initial conclusion from both the Tetrud and Langston study and DATATOP was of an apparent protective effect of selegiline on the progression of PD.

However, the validity of the results of both studies has been questioned over concern that the delay in need for additional therapy was due to a *symptomatic* effect rather than a *neuroprotective* effect (32). Tetrud and Langston noted no symptomatic wash-in or washout effect in their relatively small group of patients, suggesting no meaningful symptomatic effect of selegiline. The DATATOP investigators found a small but statistically significant wash-in effect after 1 and 3 months of treatment. Similarly, a small washout effect was noted in the final staggered blinded washout in DATATOP (33), raising the possibility that symptomatic effects were at least partly responsible for the differences in reaching endpoint. In addition, several short-term studies have noted a symptomatic effect of selegiline (34, 35). Given the long pharmacodynamic effect of selegiline, it has been suggested that a longer washout would have shown an even greater symptomatic effect (36) in the DATATOP study. Thus the question of whether selegiline is indeed protective has not been adequately resolved by these 2 studies.

More recently, Palhagen et al. (37) studied the effect of selegiline in 157 patients with early, untreated PD in a design that included an 8-week washout period. These investigators found a significant delay in progression of Unified Parkinson's Disease Rating Scale (UPDRS) scores and delay in the time until the emergence of disability significant enough to require levodopa therapy. Selegiline was noted to have a small initial symptomatic effect. However, after the 8-week washout period, no significant differences in the deterioration of disability between the groups was noted in any of the clinical rating scales. The authors interpreted their results as suggesting that, beside having a slight symptomatic effect, selegiline may have a neuroprotective effect as well.

Olanow and coworkers (38) used a different study design to address the issue of neuroprotection with selegiline. They carried out a 14-month prospective randomized double-blind, placebo-controlled study of 100 patients with early PD. Subjects were randomized to 1 of 4 groups: selegiline plus carbidopa/levodopa, placebo plus carbidopa/levodopa, selegiline plus bromocriptine, or placebo plus bromocriptine. To avoid confounding effects of treatment, at the end of the study subjects were washed out from selegiline for 20 months and from levodopa or bromocriptine for 1 week. The final evaluation, performed off all treatments, showed a statistically significant increase in the rate of progression of disease in the patients who had not received selegiline. Because of the long washout from selegiline, these results are more likely to be due to a neuroprotective rather than symptomatic

effect. However, because of the adjunct treatment design, it is difficult to compare results from this trial to the monotherapy trials; thus this study did not clarify the issue of a neuroprotective effect of selegiline.

More controversial still are the findings of the Parkinson's Disease Research Group of the United Kingdom (PDRG-UK) (39). This group found that patients randomized to receive levodopa plus selegiline in their long-term open study had a 60% *increase* in mortality when compared to those receiving levodopa alone. This is the only report of increased mortality with selegiline and is not consistent with previous studies in animals (40) and PD patients (41), suggesting that selegiline may prolong life expectancy. Analysis of other long-term studies of early PD and a meta-analysis have not shown a similar increase in mortality in association with selegiline (36, 42, 43). Several concerns have been raised (32) regarding the design of the PDRG-UK study. One concern is that mortality in this study was unusually high in both the group receiving selegiline (28%) and in the nonselegiline group (18%). Other problems include a large proportion of subjects who failed to complete the study in their original treatment assignment and relatively poor documentation of the causes of death. In spite of these concerns, the data from the PDRG-UK study must not be entirely dismissed, and further information regarding potentially increased mortality during selegiline therapy should be sought.

Other MAO-B Inhibitors

Lazabemide is a selective, reversible inhibitor of MAO-B (44) that is not currently available for use in the United States. Lazabemide has approximately 100-fold greater selectivity in inhibiting MAO-B compared with MAO-A, making the possibility of a tyramine reaction very unlikely. Unlike selegiline, it is not metabolized to potentially active compounds such as methamphetamine and amphetamine (45). Lazabemide has been the subject of 3 placebo-controlled clinical trials in patients with early PD (46, 47). These studies showed that lazabemide has barely detectable symptomatic effects and the ability to delay the need to introduce levodopa by about 50% compared to placebo, effects that are very similar to those obtained in clinical trials of selegiline.

Rasagiline (R(+)-N-propargyl-1-aminoindane) is a selective, irreversible inhibitor of MAO-B that is also not metabolized into amphetamine derivatives (48). It was approved by the FDA for use in the United States in 2006. Rasagiline has been shown to have neuroprotective effects in a variety of experimental systems (49). In clinical trials, rasagiline has been shown to have a symptomatic effect in early, untreated PD (50) and in advanced PD patients with motor fluctuations (51, 52). The clinical evidence most relevant to a neuroprotective effect of rasagiline is a "delayed-start" analysis of subjects with early PD. This study showed that subjects treated with rasagiline for a year had better long-term motor performance than those treated for placebo for 6 months followed by rasagiline for 6 months (53), suggesting that earlier or more prolonged treatment with rasagiline may be beneficial to patients with early PD. Further studies are warranted to determine whether the observed effect is due to neuroprotection or another mechanism. A new trial, referred to as ADAGIO, is under way to further examine rasagiline's potential for neuroprotection. In this delayed-start study, each portion is 9 months instead of 6 and 1100 patients will be studied.

TCH346 is a compound related to selegiline and rasagiline in that it belongs to the propargylamine family of molecules. However, TCH346 does not possess MAO-B inhibitory properties. In animal models, TCH346 may exert its neuroprotective properties by reducing mitochondrial membrane permeability, resulting in reduced release of cytochrome c and thus inhibiting apoptosis (54, 55). In spite of promising preclinical data, human trials of TCH346 failed to show an effect on progression of PD.

Dopamine Agonists Dopamine agonists have been used to treat PD since the early 1970s. Initially they were used as an adjunct to levodopa in patients who had developed motor fluctuations (56–58). More recently dopamine agonists have been used as monotherapy in the early stages of PD (59, 60) based on the idea that delaying the introduction of levodopa may delay the emergence of levodopa-related complications, including motor fluctuations and dyskinesias (see Chapter 40). Attention has also focused on the possibility that dopamine agonists may have neuroprotective effects. Several potential neuroprotective mechanisms have been proposed, including (a) reduction of the need for exogenous levodopa, resulting in reduced production of free radicals; (b) stimulation of autoreceptors, resulting in reduced dopamine turnover and catabolism; (c) direct antioxidant or neuroprotective properties; and (d) reduction of glutamatergic output by the subthalamic nucleus, resulting in reduced excitotoxicity.

Studies of dopamine agonists as adjunctive therapy have consistently demonstrated that combining a dopamine agonist with levodopa produces a comparable level of antiparkinsonian control but with a reduced levodopa dose requirement (61, 62). Initiating therapy with a dopamine agonist in patients with mild symptoms also permits a substantial delay before the introduction of levodopa (60). If it is true that higher cumulative exposure to levodopa accelerates the degenerative process in PD, then these levodopa-sparing effects may be neuroprotective. Dopamine agonists may also reduce the rate of dopamine metabolism. Carter (63) has shown that the addition of the dopamine agonist pramipexole to a cell culture of dopaminergic neurons reduces the concentration of dopamine in the medium. Similarly, in vivo studies have shown that several dopamine agonists may reduce the firing rates of dopaminergic neurons (64). Slowed dopaminergic metabolism may translate into reduced production of reactive oxygen species.

Evidence for direct neuroprotective effects has been produced for many dopamine agonists in excitotoxic and oxidative stress models of neurodegeneration. For example, bromocriptine has been shown to mitigate excitotoxic injury in several ways: by enhancing the ability of cells to buffer extracellular glutamate (65, 66), by reducing the susceptibility of cultured neurons to MPTP-mediated toxicity (67), and by acting as a free radical scavenger (68). Pramipexole has been shown to reduce cell loss in toxic and ischemic models of neuronal injury (69). In addition, pramipexole has been shown to attenuate the generation of oxygen radicals and to inhibit the opening of mitochondrial transition pores in a dose-dependent fashion (70). Felten (71) showed that low doses of pergolide protected against age-related loss of dopaminergic neurons in Fisher rats.

Clinical studies have indicated that initial treatment with dopamine agonists rather than levodopa may be associated with a reduced frequency of motor complications (72, 73). In two large-scale multicenter, randomized clinical trials, pramipexole (Mirapex) (74) and ropinirole (Requip) (75) were associated with a significantly lower incidence of motor complications over a 4- to 5-year period than levodopa. These results have been interpreted as "disease-modifying," since the normal course of events in PD was affected differentially by therapy. However, motor performance, based on UPDRS measures, was somewhat better over time in both trials in subjects receiving levodopa, which would be inconsistent with an increase in neuronal survival.

These findings are consistent with preclinical data from Pearce et al. (76) showing that MPTP-treated nonhuman primates are less likely to develop dyskinesias when treated with dopamine agonists such as ropinirole or bromocriptine than when treated with levodopa. It has been hypothesized that reduction in motor complications observed with dopamine agonists may be related to constant rather than pulsatile stimulation of dopamine receptors (77); however, the delay in the development of motor complications may also be evidence of a neuroprotective effect.

Few clinical studies have directly addressed the neuroprotective effects of dopamine agonists. Olanow et al. (38) evaluated the rate of deterioration in UPDRS over 14 months in patients randomized to receive either levodopa or bromocriptine with or without selegiline. At the end of the study, there was no significant difference in the degree of deterioration in UPDRS scores between the levodopa- and bromocriptine-treated groups, suggesting no substantial protective effect. In another prospective, double-blind study, Przuntek et al. (78) randomized patients to receive treatment with bromocriptine plus levodopa when necessary vs. levodopa monotherapy. This trial was suspended prematurely due to the observation of lower mortality in the bromocriptine-treated group. These results had not been observed previously and remain to be confirmed in other trials.

Two studies have used functional imaging of the dopaminergic system to evaluate the relative effects of dopamine agonists compared to levodopa on the integrity of nigrostriatal neurons (75, 79). In one study, subjects were randomized to either pramipexole or levodopa and imaged repeatedly for up to 4 years with $[^{123}I]$ β-CIT single photon emission computed tomography (SPECT). In the other study, subjects were randomized to either ropinirole or levodopa and imaged with fluorodopa positron emission tomography (PET) at baseline and at 2 years. Both of these studies showed an approximately 30% relative reduction in the loss of dopaminergic signal on the imaging measure in subjects receiving the dopamine agonists compared to those receiving levodopa. The large effects seen in these studies have prompted substantial debate. One interpretation suggests a significant neuroprotective effect of dopamine agonists relative to levodopa. Another interpretation has been to question the validity of the imaging biomarkers as a measure of dopamine cell counts in the substantia nigra. Current studies are attempting to address the validity of the imaging biomarkers.

In summary, several lines of reasoning suggest that dopamine agonists may have neuroprotective activity. A substantial body of preclinical evidence from studies in animal models of parkinsonism as well as in vitro systems shows that dopamine agonists have neuroprotective potential. Preliminary clinical studies show that early use of dopamine agonists may delay the emergence of motor complications. Definitive studies of the effect of early use of dopamine agonists on the emergence of motor complications as well as studies to assess the effect of these agents on disease progression using the delayed-start protocol are in progress.

Potential Protective Effects of Stereotactic Surgery

It has been suggested (80) that stereotactic surgical procedures which reduce outflow from the subthalamic nucleus (STN) may have neuroprotective as well as symptomatic effects. The STN is the principal source of glutamatergic output in the basal ganglia. In pathophysiologic models of PD, loss of dopaminergic input results in loss of inhibition of the STN. The result of this disinhibition may be excessive excitatory outflow with the potential for glutamate-mediated excitotoxic injury. There is preclinical evidence to support this line of reasoning. In rat and primate models, STN ablation induces reductions

in mitochondrial enzyme activity, glutamic acid decarboxylase (GAD) mRNA expression, and 2-deoxyglucose uptake in the ipsilateral SNr and globus pallidus (81–84). These metabolic changes may reflect a reduction in the potential for excitotoxic injury.

More direct experimental evidence for a protective effect of STN ablation is emerging but remains inconclusive. In a rodent model, STN ablation protected dopaminergic neurons from 6-OHDA toxicity (85). In a primate model, however, no protective effect of STN lesioning was observed. In this experiment, lesions were created in the STN prior to treatment with MPTP. Postmortem counting of dopaminergic neurons did not show differences in cell loss between the lesioned and unlesioned sides (83). However, large doses of MPTP were employed, and neuroprotection was not the primary aim of this study. Studies of nonhuman primates designed to evaluate the protective effects of STN ablation as well as clinical evaluation of parkinsonian patients who have undergone stereotactic ablation or stimulation of the STN may clarify the potential neuroprotective effects of STN ablation or stimulation.

Glutamatergic Agents

Based on the hypothesis that even slightly excessive glutamatergic activity may be neurotoxic (15), a number of agents that inhibit glutamatergic transmission by antagonizing the action of glutamate at NMDA receptors or by interfering with glutamate release would have neuroprotective potential. Some of these agents include dextromethorphan, amantadine, remacemide, and riluzole. Because glutamatergic transmission is an important part of basal ganglia physiology, these agents may have symptomatic effects as well. Although the conduct of trials with these agents had been supported by substantial preclinical data, the results have been uniformly disappointing.

Amantadine is a tricyclic amine that has been used as a treatment for PD for decades. Its mechanism of action is not certain, but anticholinergic and dopamine release and reuptake inhibition have been suggested (86). However, amantadine has recently been shown to be a weak NMDA antagonist as well (87), and it has been demonstrated that it to reduces levodopa-induced involuntary movements in advanced PD (88). In a retrospective study, Uitti et al. (89) found that treatment with amantadine was an independent predictor of survival in patients with PD. This has not been confirmed in a prospective trial.

The commonly available cough medication dextromethorphan has also been shown to be a weak NMDA antagonist. It has been shown to have effects similar to those of amantadine on levodopa-induced dyskinesia (90). Because of their antiglutamatergic activity, benign or beneficial clinical profile in PD, and history of safe use, both amantadine and dextromethorphan are logical candidates to be tested as neuroprotective agents, but they have not been subjected to scrutiny in well-designed clinical trials.

There were promising preclinical data for both remacemide and riluzole (91–96). Riluzole had also been shown to delay the progression of amyotrophic lateral sclerosis (ALS) in two placebo-controlled clinical trials (97, 98). However, both compounds failed to show efficacy in large-scale randomized, placebo-controlled clinical trials in PD patients (99, 100).

Antioxidants: Vitamins C and E

Vitamin E (alpha-tocopherol) has long been viewed as a therapeutic answer to the oxidative stress hypothesis in PD. It acts as an antioxidant by blocking lipid peroxidation and trapping peroxyl radicals (101) and has been shown to have neuroprotective effects in several experimental systems (102). A case-controlled, community-based study (103) suggested that high dietary intake of vitamin E may protect against the development of PD. However, other epidemologic studies (104, 105) have failed to find an association between vitamin E intake and PD. The effect of vitamin E at a dose of 2000 IU per day was evaluated in the DATATOP trial. After a mean of 14 months of treatment, no effect was observed in patients receiving vitamin E compared to placebo (33). This adequately powered negative trial suggests that vitamin E is not a neuroprotective agent at the dosages used in DATATOP. Nonetheless, proponents of vitamin E suggest that the negative results of this trial can be explained by the poor penetration of vitamin E into the central nervous system. One study (68) found no increase in vitamin E levels in cerebrospinal fluid despite dosing of 4000 IU per day. Therefore the possibility that it may have a mild effect cannot be entirely excluded, especially at high doses or over sustained periods of time.

Vitamin C (ascorbic acid) is another compound with antioxidant properties that has been considered as a potential neuroprotective agent in PD. Vitamin C protects against dopamine autooxidation in cell culture (106) and may act synergistically with selegiline (107) to protect against oxidative injury. Several epidemiologic studies have failed to find a relationship between intake of vitamin C and the risk of PD (105, 108). However, in an open trial, Fahn (109) found that the need to introduce levodopa therapy was delayed by up to 2.5 years in patients treated with high-dose combination therapy with vitamins C and E compared to concurrent controls not treated with antioxidants. This result has not been confirmed in a randomized, placebo-controlled trial. Based on current evidence, the neuroprotective effects of vitamin C, like those of vitamin E, are probably quite modest.

Coenzyme Q10

Coenzyme Q10 (CoQ), which is known as ubiquinone, is a lipid-soluble compound that acts as an electron acceptor in complexes I and II in mitochondria (110). CoQ has antioxidant properties and has been shown to scavenge free radicals generated within microsomal membranes more effectively than vitamin E (111). Brain levels of CoQ decline with age; they are about 50% greater in young adults than in the elderly (112, 113) and have been shown to be lower in PD patients compared to age-matched controls (114, 115). Favit et al. (116) found that CoQ protected against markers of neuronal death in two in vitro models. Treatment with CoQ has also been shown to be neuroprotective in rodent models (117). It has been studied in a number of human diseases in which mitochondrial defects are considered to be present and has been shown to improve myocardial function and exercise duration in congestive heart failure (118), It has also been shown to be safe in pilot studies in Huntington's disease (119) and mitochondrial encephalopathies (120). In a pilot study in PD (121), patients treated with CoQ showed normalization of mitochondrial complex I activity. However, because of the small sample size, the results did not reach statistical significance.

A subsequent randomized, placebo-controlled phase II study of 3 dosages of CoQ (300, 600, and 1200 mg/day) in early untreated patients found a statistically significant difference in change of UPDRS scores between the highest dosage of CoQ and placebo after 16 months of treatment and a statistically significant dose-response trend among the 3 dosages and placebo (122). This pilot study suggests that CoQ may have a beneficial effect in PD patients. However, additional studies are needed to confirm the results of this study and to determine whether the effects of CoQ are due to a symptomatic or neuroprotective mechanism.

Other Agents

The CINAPS committee identified several other compounds as attractive agents to study in future trials. Two of these, nicotine and caffeine, are readily available and widely consumed by the general public. The best evidence for these agents as "antiparkinsonian" comes from epidemiologic studies that consistently show an inverse relationship between use of caffeine and nicotine and the risk of acquiring PD (123–125). Caffeine is thought to act on the central nervous system through adenosine receptor antagonism (126), although the downstream mechanisms of remain unclear. Animal data support protective effects for caffeine and the more specific A2A receptor antagonist KW-6002 (127, 128). Nicotine has also been shown to prevent MPTP toxicity in animals. Although the putative neuroprotective mechanism of nicotine are not known, there is evidence that nicotine may act as an antioxidant (46) or prevent excitoxicity (129). Epidemiologic evidence showing a consistent male predominance for PD also supports the use of estrogen (17B estradiol) as a possible neuroprotectant.

Creatine is a widely available nutritional supplement that may have beneficial properties in a number of neurodegenerative and mitochondrial disorders. Creatine is converted to phosphocreatine, which in turn can function as an energy buffer by transferring a phosphoryl group to ADP. It may act as an indirect antioxidant by enhancing energy transduction and may inhibit the transition to mitochondrial permeability (130). In doses of 1% to 2% of diet by weight, creatine appears protective in MPTP rodent models (131). In a phase II "futility" study, creatine was found not to be substantially non-inferior to a historical benchmark of progression of PD (132). It is to be studied in a long-term trial as part of the NET-PD program.

In this same study, minocycline was also not inferior to historical benchmarks, but not to the same extent as creatine. Minocycline may have a protective effect through inhibition of microglial activation (133). However, preclinical data have not consistently shown a neuroprotective effect (69, 134). Because of these mixed preclinical data and modest clinical effects, there is probably a limited role for minocycline as a neuroprotective agent in PD.

GM-1 ganglioside has been shown to be both neuroprotective and neurorestorative in animal models. It is a component of neuronal membranes that has been proposed to facilitate the neurotrophic actions of brain and glial-derived neurotrophic factors (135, 136). There are data in PD patients showing that GM-1 ganglioside is well tolerated and may have short-term symptomatic benefits (137). The main limitation of GM-1 ganglioside is the requirement for parenteral administration. Concerns about the immunogenicity of bovine-derived gangliosides and the relationship to Guillain-Barré syndrome (138) may not be relevant to current preparations. Orally active, synthetic derivatives are being explored by U.S.-based pharmaceutical companies.

Immunophilins are a group of molecules related to cyclosporine, including FK 506 and rapamycin. The principal clinical role of immunophilins is as immunosuppressive agents in patients who have undergone organ transplantation (139). Many immunophilins are small, orally active molecules that have the ability to cross the blood-brain barrier (140). Nonimmunosuppressive derivatives of immunophilins have been developed that retain their effects on neurons. The notion that immunophilins may be neuroprotective came from studies showing that they could inhibit nitric oxide synthase (NOS) and thus prevent excitotoxic injury. Subsequently, FK 506 has been shown to reduce neuronal injury in animal models of cerebral ischemia (141).

Nonimmunosuppressive derivatives have been shown to protect against MPTP and 6-OHDA–mediated injury to dopaminergic neurons in experimental models (142). Based on these preclinical data, immunophilins appear to be promising potential neuroprotective agents. Clinical studies are currently on going to evaluate the potential effectiveness of immunophilins particularly GPI 1485 as neuroprotective agents in PD.

Neurotrophic factors are a group of naturally occurring molecules, many of which are not structurally related to each other, that are required for the survival and development of neurons (143). In theory, these molecules may possess both neuroprotective and restorative properties. The neurotrophic factor that has been of greatest interest in PD is glial cell line–derived neurotrophic factor (GDNF). It belongs to a distinct family of trophic factors distantly related to the transforming growth factor-beta superfamily (144). GDNF has been shown to protect from 6-OHDA–mediated injury in rodents (145) and to mediate recovery from such injury (146). In nonhuman primates, Gash et al. (147) demonstrated a marked increase in tyrosine hydroxylase staining and increased numbers of dopaminergic fibers in MPTP-treated rhesus monkeys following GDNF administration. These primates also showed marked behavioral improvement as a result of GDNF treatment.

Based on these results, a pilot study of direct infusion of GDNF into the striatum in 5 human subjects was conducted; it showed a 39% improvement of motor symptoms and 64% reduction of antiparkinsonian medications as well as increased uptake of [18F]-dopa (148). Based on these data, a randomized, controlled trial of intrastriatal GDNF infusion was conducted. However, in spite of substantial enthusiasm based on preclinical and pilot data, no difference was found between placebo and active treatment in this randomized, controlled trial (149). Furthermore, several patients developed antibodies to GDNF, raising significant safety concerns.

Several studies have explored novel delivery systems for neurotrophic factors. Tseng and colleagues(150) implanted genetically engineered hamster kidney cells adjacent to the midbrain of Wistar rats and demonstrated preservation of tyrosine hydroxylase–positive neurons following midbrain transsection. Choi-Lundberg and colleagues (151) utilized adenovirus vectors to transfect cells in adult rats to produce GDNF. These genetically engineered animals showed markedly reduced susceptibility to 6-OHDA toxicity compared to nontransfected animals. This study illustrates the potential to apply gene therapy techniques in PD. Other gene therapy strategies that have been explored include engineering cells to express antiapoptosis gene products or free radical scavengers such as superoxide dismutase (SOD) (152). Strategies such as these, in which both the therapeutic agent and the delivery system are products of advances

TABLE 50-3
Status of Evidence for Classes of Neuroprotective Therapies

CLASS OF COMPOUND	EVIDENCE FOR RATIONALE*	PRE-CLINICAL EVIDENCE†	CLINICAL EVIDENCE‡
MAO-B inhibitors	++	+++	±
Dopamine agonists	++	+++	±
Antiglutamate agents	++	++	−
Antioxidant vitamins	++	++	−
Coenzyme Q	+++	++	+
Neurotrophic factors	++	+++	−
Immunophilins	++	++	N/A
Creatine	++	+	+

*Two plus signs (++) indicate evidence for rationale from nonhuman primate models, three plus signs (+++) indicate evidence for rationale from human studies (e.g., pathologic studies or studies using tissue samples from PD patients).
†Two plus signs (++) indicate supportive evidence in animal models other than nonhuman primates. Three plus signs (+++) indicate supportive evidence in nonhuman primates.
‡Evidence for protective effect of MAO-B inhibitors (specifically selegiline) is controversial in spite of large-scale trials designed to detect neuroprotective effect. §Preliminary evidence suggests that dopamine agonists may delay the emergence motor complications (dyskinesia and motor fluctuations). A large-scale trial (25) showed no effect of vitamin E on the progression of PD. N/A indicates that no evidence is currently available.

in molecular biology, may be an important paradigm for the future (Table 50-3).

Issues in the Design of Neuroprotective Trials

Convincingly demonstrating a neuroprotective effect in clinical trials has proved to be as challenging and as crucial as identifying neuroprotective compounds in the laboratory. Because of the slow rate of disease progression, neuroprotective trials are necessarily of long duration, involve large numbers of subjects, and are relatively costly. Identifying methods for testing promising compounds in more efficient trials has been one challenge for clinical investigators. A second major challenge has been to separate symptomatic effects from neuroprotective effects. Suggested approaches to this problem have included novel experimental designs and the use of functional imaging as a biological marker for disease progression.

Although the DATATOP trial established many of the standard procedures for neuroprotective trials in PD, it is unlikely that resources will be available to carry out trials as large as this for more than a few very promising compounds. In order to evaluate the relatively large number of potential compounds, more efficient clinical trials methods must be found. One response (153) to this challenge is to identify subsets of patients who may be more likely to respond to a given intervention and to carry out small trials in these populations. It is possible to take advantage of recent advances in genetics, molecular biology, and imaging to identify such populations. For example, the discovery of a mutation in the

α-synuclein gene on chromosome 4 that is responsible for autosomally dominant inherited parkinsonism (7) in several Mediterranean kindreds and investigations with PET (154) and SPECT (155) have suggested that it is possible to identify asymptomatic at-risk individuals for trials of neuroprotective agents. Trials in such individuals offer the possibility of preventing the emergence of parkinsonian symptoms. In addition, Morrish et al. (156), using PET techniques, have suggested that the rate of neuronal loss may be more rapid in early PD than later in the course of disease. Therefore it may be easier to detect a neuroprotective effect in asymptomatic at-risk individuals or in patients with very early rather than well-established disease.

Certain interventions may be more likely to be neuroprotective in distinct subpopulations of PD patients. For example, as noted above (121), the mechanism of action of CoQ appears to be to normalize the mitochondrial activity of complexes I and II. With the use of platelet-mitochondrial cybrids and platelet samples obtained from peripheral blood (157), patients with defects in mitochondrial function can be identified. It may be reasonable to preferentially select patients with clearly defined defects in complex I and II activity for early clinical trials. The limitation of using enriched subgroups is that such studies do not necessarily generalize to all patients with clinically defined PD. Nonetheless, studies in subgroups could be used to screen potential agents before embarking on long and costly definitive trials.

Separating neuroprotective effects from symptomatic effects has proved to be a very difficult methodologic issue in designing neuroprotective trials. Clearly the DATATOP experience is the most prominent example of this challenge. However, many other potentially neuroprotective compounds—including dopamine agonists, glutamate antagonists, and surgical interventions—have established effects on parkinsonian symptoms that may interfere with the detection of small but clinically meaningful changes in the natural history of disease.

One approach to this problem has been to discontinue or "wash out" the study drug for a period of time prior to the final clinical evaluation. The rationale for this strategy is that protective effects are likely to remain after washout while symptomatic effects should dissipate. Several washout strategies have been employed in clinical trials. Olanow et al. (38) combined a long-term washout of selegiline with a short-term washout of levodopa and bromocriptine symptomatic therapy in an effort to improve patient compliance with the long duration of withdrawal of selegiline required by that compound's long pharmacodynamic half-life. In another study, a blinded, staggered washout strategy was devised (33) to prevent unblinding or a reverse placebo effect during washout.

A second proposed option to distinguish between symptomatic and neuroprotective effects is the "randomized start" trial (see Figure 50-1) (158). In this design, patients are randomized to begin active treatment either right away or after a specified time interval. Symptomatic effects will lead the group that started later to "catch up" in clinical performance to the first group, and no difference between the groups will be detectable. However, if there is a true neuroprotective effect and the separation in starting time is sufficient, the performance of the two groups will remain distinct even if a symptomatic effect

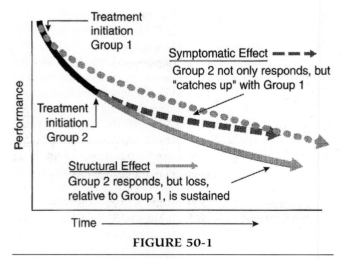

FIGURE 50-1

Schematic representation of randomized-start trial showing effects of symptomatic and neuroprotective therapies. Note that protective effects can be detected even in the presence of symptomatic effects. (From Koller, *Ann Neurol* 1998, with permission).

is present. Because all patients receive treatment at some time in this trial design, there is likely to be good patient acceptance while the essential elements of randomization, placebo-control, and blinding are retained. The randomized start design has been employed in neuroprotective trials of Alzheimer's disease (159). Although there is only one published report of a randomized start analysis in PD (53), this paradigm is increasingly being incorporated into trials intending to show results consistent with a neuroprotective action.

The Neuroprotection Exploratory Trials in Parkinson's Disease (NET-PD) program has taken the approach of conducting two phases of clinical trials (160). The first phase consists of "futility trials" in which potential agents are compared to a historical benchmark of disease progression. Agents that do not outperform the historical progression rate are considered futile and are not considered for future studies. The proposed second phase of the NET-PD program is a large, simple trial in which some or all of the nonfutile agents will be administered in a long-term (5 or more years in duration) trial in which mixtures of concomitant therapy are permitted. The concept behind this approach is that neuroprotective effects will become more prominent than symptomatic effects over longer periods of clinical follow-up.

The use of biological markers including PET and SPECT imaging represents another approach to demonstrating neuroprotection with compounds that may also have symptomatic effects. PET and SPECT have been refined to the point where they possess sufficient precision to be used as biological markers of nigral cell degeneration in clinical trials. Fluorodopa PET was the first functional imaging modality used to assess the integrity of dopamine terminal function in vivo. The loss of uptake observed with this technique appears to reflect dopaminergic terminal density and correlates with nigral cell counts obtained at autopsy (161). It is related to disease progression as measured by UPDRS and Hoehn and Yahr scales (162). Morrish et al. (154) estimated the rate of striatal dopamine loss at about 9% to 12% per year. Control patients showed no loss of dopaminergic uptake over 3 years.

SPECT imaging of the dopamine transporter may provide a more convenient and less expensive alternative to PET imaging. The dopamine transporter is located on the presynaptic membrane of dopaminergic terminals and provides a marker of dopaminergic innervation of the striatum (163). Imaging with radiolabeled compounds that bind to the dopamine transporter protein, including [123I] β-CIT, have demonstrated dopamine transporter loss in patients with early PD compared to controls (164) and that transporter loss in PD patients is correlated with disease severity (165). One disadvantage to [123I] β-CIT imaging is that the ligand must be administered 24 hours before imaging. As a result, other SPECT tracers with similar affinities for the dopamine transporter are being developed (166). As discussed above, these tracers have been used as outcome measures in clinical trials comparing dopamine agonists to levodopa and levodopa to placebo and have shown significant differences between the treatment groups. However, the interpretation of imaging measures remains controversial.

CONCLUSION

Neuroprotection remains a highly desirable but elusive goal in the treatment of PD. A number of potentially neuroprotective compounds are available, but none have been convincingly demonstrated to confer neuroprotection for PD patients. Significant advances in understanding the pathophysiologic processes underlying in PD and a body of preclinical evidence demonstrating neuroprotection in model systems for a number of candidate compounds raise the hope that neuroprotective therapy for PD is achievable. The challenges for the future will be to continue to develop promising compounds, to select the compounds that should be brought from the bench to the clinic, and to develop a sound and standardized clinical method to evaluate these compounds in PD patients.

References

1. Cotzias GC, Van Woert MH, Schiffer LM. Aromatic amino acids and modification of parkinsonism. *N Engl J Med* 1967; 276:374–379.
2. Freed CR, Greene PE, Breeze RE, et al. Transplantation of embryonic dopamine neurons for severe Parkinson's disease. *N Engl J Med* 2000; 344:710–719.
3. Shoulson I. Neuroprotective clinical strategies for Parkinson's disease. *Ann Neurol* 1992; 32(Suppl):S143–S145.
4. Shults CW. Neurotrophic factors. In: Watts RL, Koller WC (eds). *Movement Disorders: Neurologic Principles and Practice.* New York: McGraw-Hill, 1997:117–123.
5. Poewe WH, Wenning GK. The natural history of Parkinson's disease. *Ann Neurol* 1998; 44:S1–S9.
6. Trojanowski JQ, Goedert M, Iwatsubo T, Lee VM. Fatal attractions: Abnormal protein aggregation and neuron death in Parkinson's disease and Lewy body dementia. *Cell Death Differ* 1998; 5:832–837.
7. Polymeropoulos MH, Lavedan C, Leroy E, et al. Mutation in the alpha-synuclein gene identified in families with Parkinson's disease. *Science* 1997; 276:2045–2047.
8. Lucking CB, Durr A, Bonifati V, et al. Association between early-onset Parkinson's disease and mutations in the parkin gene. *N Engl J Med* 2000; 342:1560–1567.
9. Maraganore DM, Farrer MJ, Hardy JA, et al. Case-control study of the ubiquitin carboxy-terminal hydrolase L1 gene in Parkinson's disease. *Neurology* 1999; 53:1858–1860.
10. McNaught KS, Olanow CW, Halliwell B, et al. Failure of the ubiquitin-proteasome system in Parkinson's disease. *Nat Rev Neurol* 2001; 2:589–594.
11. Bowling AC, Beal MF. Bioenergetic and oxidative stress in neurodegenerative diseases. *Life Sci* 1995; 56:1151–1171.
12. Olanow CW. Oxidative reactions in Parkinson's disease. *Neurology* 1990; 40:22–29.
13. Inzelberg R, Shapira T, Korczyn AD. Effects of atropine on learning and memory functions in dementia. *Clin Neuropharmacol.* 1990; 13:241–247.
14. Choi DW. Glutamate neurotoxicity and diseases of the nervous system. *Neuron* 1998; 1:623–634.
15. Albin RL, Greenamyre JT. Alternative excitotoxic hypotheses. *Neurology* 1992; 42:733–738.
16. Kastner A, Anglade P, Bounaix C, et al. Immunohistochemical study of catechol-O-methyltransferase in the human mesostriatal system. *Neuroscience* 1994; 62(2):449–457.
17. Jenner P. The rationale for the use of dopamine agonists in Parkinson's disease. *Neurology* 1998; 45:6–12.
18. Ravina BM, Fagan SC, Hart RG, et al. Neuroprotective agents for clinical trials in Parkinson's disease: A systematic assessment. *Neurology* 2003; 60(8):1234–1240.
19. Fahn S. Is levodopa toxic? *Neurology* 1996; 47(Suppl 3): s184–s195.
20. Fahn S, Oakes D, Shoulson I, et al. Levodopa and the progression of Parkinson's disease. *N Engl J Med* 2004; 351(24):2498–2508.
21. Knoll J. Deprenyl (selegiline): The history of its development and pharmacological action. *Acta Neurol Scand* 1983; 68(Suppl 95): 57–80.
22. Langston JW, Ballard PA, Tetrud JW, Irwin I. Chronic parkinsonism in humans due to a product of meperidine analog synthesis. *Science.* 1983; 219:979–980.
23. Heikkila RE, Manzino L, Duvoisin RC, Cabbat FS. Protection against the dopaminergic neurotoxicity of 1-methyl-4- phenyl-1, 2, 3, 6-tetrahydropyridine (MPTP) by monoamine oxidase inhibitors. *Nature* 1984; 311:467–469.
24. Singer TP, Castagnoli NJ, Ramsay RR, Trevor AJ. Biochemical events in the development of parkinsonism induced by 1-methyl-4-phenyl-1, 2, 3, 6-tetrahydropyridine. *J Neurochem* 1987; 49:1–8.
25. Knoll J. Extension of life span of rats by long-term (-)deprenyl treatment. *Mt Sinai J Med* 1988; 55:67–74.
26. Carrillo M-C, Kanai S, Nokubo M. (-)Deprenyl induces activities of both superoxide dismutase and catalase but not of glutathione peroxidase in the striatum of young male rats. *Life Sci* 1991; 48:517–521.
27. Clow A, Hussain T, Glover V. (-)-Deprenyl can induce soluble superoxide dismutase in rat striata. *J Neural Transm Gen Sect* 1991; 86:77–80.
28. Tatton WG, Greenwood CE. Rescue of dying neurons: A new action for deprenyl in MPTP parkinsonism. *J Neurosci Res* 1991; 30:666–677.
29. Tatton WG, Chalmers-Redman RME. Modulation of gene expression rather than monoamine oxidase inhibition: (-)-Deprenyl-related compounds in controlling neurodegeneration. *Neurology* 1996; 47:S171–S183.
30. Tetrud JW, Langston JW. The effect of deprenyl (selegiline) in the natural history of Parkinson's disease. *Science* 1989; 245:519–522.
31. Parkinson Study Group. Effect of deprenyl on the progression of disability in early Parkinson's disease. *N Engl J Med* 1989; 321:1364–1371.
32. Olanow CW, Fahn S, Langston JW, Godbold J. Selegiline and mortality in Parkinson's disease. *Ann Neurol* 1996; 40:841–845.
33. Parkinson Study Group. Effects of tocopherol and deprenyl on the progression of disability in early Parkinson's disease. *N Engl J Med* 1993; 328:176–183.
34. Allain H, Pollak P, Neukirch HC, members of the French selegiline multicenter trial. Symptomatic effect of selegiline in de novo parkinsonian patients. *Mov Disord* 1993; 8:536–540.
35. Myllyla VV, Sontaniemi KA, Vuorinen JA, Heinonen EH. Selegiline as initial treatment in de novo parkinsonian patients. *Neurology* 1992; 42:339–343.
36. Olanow CW. Selegiline: Current perspectives on issues related to neuroprotection and mortality. *Neurology.* 1996; 47:S210–S216.
37. Palhagen S, Heinonen EH, Hagglund J, et al. Selegiline delays the onset of disability in de novo parkinsonian patients. Swedish Parkinson Study Group. *Neurology* 1998; 51:520–525.
38. Olanow CW, Hauser RA, Gauger L, et al. The effect of deprenyl and levodopa on the progression of Parkinson's disease. *Ann Neurol* 1995; 38:833–834.
39. Lees AJ, on behalf of the Parkinson's Disease Research Group of the UK. Comparison of therapeutic effects and mortality data of levodopa and levodopa combined with selegiline in patients with early mild Parkinson's disease. *BMJ* 1995; 311:1602–1607.
40. Knoll J. The striatal dopamine dependency of life span in male rats: Longevity study with (-)deprenyl. *Mech Ageing Dev* 1988; 46:237–262.
41. Birkmayer W, Knoll J, Riederer P. Increased life expectancy resulting from addition of L-deprenyl to Modopar treatment of Parkinson's disease: A long-term study. *J Neural Transm* 1985; 64:113–127.
42. Parkinson Study Group. Mortality in DATATOP: A multicenter trial in early Parkinson's disease. *Ann Neurol* 1998; 43:318–325.
43. Maki-Ikola O, Kilkku O, Heinonen E. Other studies have not shown increased mortality. *BMJ* 1996; 312:702.
44. Da-Prada M, Kettler R, Keller HH, et al. From moclobemide to Ro 19-6327 and Ro 41-1049: the development of a new class of reversible selective MAO-A and MAO-B inhibitors. *J Neural Transm* 1990; 29(Suppl):279–292.
45. Da-Prada M, Kettler R, Keller HH, Burkard WP. Ro 19-6327, a reversible, highly selective inhibitor of type B monoamine oxidase, completely devoid of tyramine-potentiating effects: Comparisons with selegiline. In: Dahlstrom A (ed). *Progress in Catecholamine Research.* New York: Liss, 1988:359–363.
46. Parkinson Study Group. Effect of lazabemide on the progression of disability in early Parkinson's disease. *Ann Neurol* 1996; 40:99–107.
47. Parkinson Study Group. A controlled trial of lazabemide (Ro 19-6327) in untreated Parkinson's disease. *Ann Neurol* 1993; 33:350–356.
48. Finberg JP, Lamensdorf I, Commissiong JW, Youdim MB. Pharmacology and neuroprotective properties of rasagiline. *J Neural Transm* 1996; 48 (Suppl):95–101.
49. Finberg JP, Takeshima T, Johnston JM, Commissiong JW. Increased survival of dopaminergic neurons by rasagiline, a monoamine oxidase B inhibitor. *Neuroreport* 1998; 9:703–707.
50. Parkinson Study Group. A controlled trial of rasagiline in early Parkinson's disease. *Arch Neurol* 2000; 59:1937–1943.
51. Parkinson Study Group. A randomized placebo-controlled trial of rasagiline in levodopa-treated patients with Parkinson disease and motor fluctuations: The PRESTO study. *Arch Neurol* 2005; 62(2):241–248.

52. Rascol O, Brooks DJ, Melamed E, et al. Rasagiline as an adjunct to levodopa in patients with Parkinson's disease and motor fluctuations (LARGO, Lasting effect in Adjunct therapy with Rasagiline Given Once daily, study): A randomised, double-blind, parallel-group trial. *Lancet* 2005; 365(9463):947–954.

53. Parkinson Study Group. A controlled, randomized, delayed-start study of rasagilinie in early Parkinson's disease. *Arch Neurol* 2004; 561–566.

54. Kragten E, Lalande I, Zimmermann K, et al. Glyceraldehyde-3-phosphate dehydrogenase, the putative target of the antiapoptotic compounds CGP 3466 and R-(-)-deprenyl. *J Biol Chem* 1998; 273(10):5821–5828.

55. Tatton WG, Chalmers-Redman RM, Ju WJ, et al. Propargylamines induce antiapoptotic new protein synthesis in serum- and nerve growth factor (NGF)-withdrawn, NGF-differentiated PC-12 cells. *J Pharmacol Exp Ther* 2002; 301(2):753–764.

56. Kartzinel R, Teychenne P, Gillespie MM, et al. Bromocriptine and levodopa (with or without carbidopa) in parkinsonism. *Lancet* 1976; 2:272–275.

57. Calne DB, Burton K, Beckman J, Martin, WR. Dopamine agonists in Parkinson's Disease. *Can J Neurol Sci* 1984; 11:221–224.

58. Olanow CW, Fahn S, Muenter MD, et al. A multi-center, double-blind, placebo-controlled trial of pergolide as an adjunct to Sinemet in Parkinson's disease. *Mov Disord* 1994; 9:40–47.

59. Shannon KM, Bennett JPJ, Friedman JH. Efficacy of pramipexole, a novel dopamine agonist, as monotherapy in mild to moderate Parkinson's disease. The Pramipexole Study Group *Neurology* 1997; 49:724–728.

60. Adler CH, Sethi KD, Hauser RA, et al. Ropinirole for the treatment of early Parkinson's disease. The Ropinirole Study Group. *Neurology*. 1997; 49:393–399.

61. Lieberman A, Ranhosky A, Korts D. Clinical evaluation of pramipexole in advanced Parkinson's disease: Results of a double-blind, placebo-controlled, parallel group study. *Neurology* 1997; 49:162–168.

62. Rascol O, Lees AJ, Senard JM, et al. Ropinirole in the treatment of levodopa-induced motor fluctuations in patients with Parkinson's disease. *Clin Neuropharmacol* 1996; 19:234–245.

63. Carter AJ, Muller RE. Pramipexole, a dopamine D2 antagonist receptor antagonist, decrease the extracellular concentration of dopamine in vivo. *Eur J Pharmacol* 1991; 200:65–72.

64. Piercey MF, Camacho-Ochoa M, Smith MW. Functional roles for dopamine-receptor subtypes. *Clin Neuropharmacol* 1995; 18:34–42.

65. Yamashita H, Kawakami H, Zhang YX, et al. Neuroprotective mechanism of bromocriptine *Lancet* 1995; 346:1305.

66. Sawada H, Ibi M, Kihara T, et al. Dopamine D2-type agonists protect mesencephalic neurons from glutamate neurotoxicity: Mechanisms of neuroprotective treatment against oxidative stress. *Ann Neurol* 1998; 44:110–119.

67. Muralikrishnan D, Mohanakumar KP. Neuroprotection by bromocriptine against 1-methyl-4-phenyl-1, 2, 3, 6-tetrahydropyridine-induced neurotoxicity in mice. *FASEB J* 1998; 12:905–9012.

68. Pappert EJ, Tangney CC, Goetz CG, et al. Alpha-tocopherol in the ventricular cerebrospinal fluid of Parkinson's disease patients: Dose-response study and correlations with plasma levels. *Neurology* 1996; 47:1037–1042.

69. Sethy VH, Wu H, Oostveen JA, Hall ED. Neuroprotective effects of the dopamine agonists pramipexole and bromocriptine in 3-acetylpyridine–treated rats. *Brain Res* 1997; 754:181–186.

70. Cassarino DS, Fall CP, Smith TS, Bennett, D. A. Pramipexole reduces reactive oxygen species production in vivo and in vitro and inhibits the mitochondrial permeability transition produced by the parkinsonian neurotoxin methylpyridium ion. *J Neurochem* 1998; 71:295–301.

71. Felten DL, Felten SY, Fuller RW, et al. Chronic dietary pergolide preserves nigrostriatal neuronal integrity in aged Fischer 344 rats. *Neurobiol Aging* 1992; 13:339–351.

72. Rinne UK. Early combination of bromocriptine and levodopa in the treatment of parkinson's disease: A 5 year follow-up. *Neurology* 1987; 37:826–828.

73. Montastruc JL, Rascol O, Senard JM, Rascol A. A randomized controlled study comparing bromocriptine to which levodopa was later added, with levodopa alone in previously untreated patients with Parkinson's disease: A five year follow-up. *J Neurol Neurosurg Psychiatry* 1994; 57:1034–1038.

74. Ondo W, Warrior D, Overby A, Calmes J, et al. Computerized posturography analysis of progressive supranuclear palsy: A case-control comparison with Parkinson's disease and healthy controls. *Arch Neurol* 2000; 57:1464–1469.

75. Whone AL, Watts RL, Stoessl AJ, et al. Slower progression of Parkinson's disease with ropinirole versus levodopa: The REAL-PET study. *Ann Neurol* 2003; 54:93–101.

76. Pearce RKB, Banerji T, Jenner P, Marsden CD. Effects of repeated treatment with L-dopa, bromocriptine and ropinirole in drug-naive MPTP-treated common marmosets. *Br J Pharmacol* 1996; 118:37.

77. Olanow CW, Jenner P, Brooks D. Dopamine agonists and neuroprotection in Parkinson's disease. *Ann Neurol* 1998; 44:S167–S174.

78. Przuntek H, Welzel D, Blumner E, et al. Bromocriptine lessens the incidence of mortality in L-dopa–treated parkinsonian patients: Prado-study discontinued. *Euro J Clin Pharmacol* 1992; 43:357–363.

79. Parkinson Study Group. Dopamine transporter brain imaging to assess the effects of pramipexole vs leovodpa on Parkinson disease progression. *JAMA* 2002; 287: 1653–1661.

80. Rodriguez MC, Obeso JA, Olanow CW. Subthalamic nucleus–mediated excitotoxicity in Parkinson's disease: A target for neuroprotection. *Ann Neurol* 1998; 44: S175–S188.

81. Blandini F, Greenamyre JT. Prospects of glutamate antagonists in the therapy of Parkinson's disease. *Fund Clin Pharmacol* 1998; 12:4–12.

82. Delfs JM, Ciaramitaro VM, Parry TJ, Chesselet MF. Subthalamic nucleus lesions: Widespread effects on changes in gene expression induced by nigrostriatal dopamine depletion in rats. *J Neurosci* 1995; 15:6562–6575.

83. Guridi J, Herrero MT, Luquin MR, et al. Subthalamotomy in parkinsonian monkeys. Behavioral and biochemical analysis. *Brain* 1996; 119:1717–1727.

84. Mitchell SL, Kiely DK, Kiel DP, Lipsitz LA. The epidemiology, clinical characteristics, and natural history of older nursing home residents with a diagnosis of Parkinson's disease. *J Am Geriatr Soc* 1996; 44:394–399.

85. Piallat B, Benazzouz A, Benabid AL. Subthalamic nucleus lesions on rats prevents dopaminergic nigral neuron degeneration after striatal 6-OHDA injection: Behavioral and immunohistochemical studies. *Eur J Neurosci* 1996; 1408–1414.

86. Goetz CG. New lessons from old drugs: Amantadine and Parkinson's disease. *Neurology* 1998; 50:1211–1212.

87. Stoof JC, Booij J, Drukalrch B. Amantadine as N-methyl-D-aspartaic acid receptor antagonist. *Clin Neurol Neurosurg* 1992; 94:S4–S6.

88. Verhagen ML, Del Dotto P, van den Munckhof P, et al. Amantadine as treatment for dyskinesias and motor fluctuations in Parkinson's disease. *Neurology* 1998; 50: 1323–1326.

89. Uitti RJ, Rajput AH, Ahlskog JE, et al. Amantadine treatment is an independent predictor of improved survival in Parkinson's disease. *Neurology* 1996; 46:1551–1556.

90. Verhagen ML, Blanchet PJ, van den Munckhof P, et al. A trial of dextromethorphan in parkinsonian patients with motor response complications. *Mov Disord* 1998; 13:414–417.

91. Palmer GC, Cregan EF, Borrelli AR, Willett F. Neuroprotective properties of the uncompetitive NMDA receptor antagonist remacemide hydrochloride. *Ann NY Acad Sci* 1995; 765:236–247.

92. Klockgether T, Turski L. NMDA antagonists potentiate antiparkinsonian effects of L-dopa in monoamine-depleted rats. *Ann Neurol* 1990; 28:536–539.

93. Greenamyre JT, Eller RV, Zhang Z, et al. Antiparkinsonian effects of remacemide, a glutamate antagonist, in rodent and primate models of Parkinson's disease. *Ann Neurol* 1994; 35:655–661.

94. Doble A, Hubert JP, Blanchard JC. Pertussis toxin pretreatment abolishes the inhibitory effect of riluzole and carbechol on D-3H-aspartate release from cultured cerebellar granule cells. *Neurosci Lett* 1992; 140(251):254.

95. Malgouris C, Bardot F, Daniel M, et al. Riluzole, a novel antiglutamate, prevents memory loss and hippocampal damage in ischemic gerbils. *J Neurosci* 1989; 9: 3720–3727.

96. Cheramy A, Barbieto L, Godeheu G, Glowinsky J. Riluzole inhibits the release of glutamate in the caudate nucleus of the cat in vivo. *Neurosci Lett* 1992; 147:209–212.

97. Bensimon G, Lacomblez L, Meininger V. A controlled trial of riluzole in amyotrophic lateral sclerosis. ALS/Riluzole Study Group (see comments). *N Engl J Med* 1994; 330:585–591.

98. Lacomblez L, Bensimon G, Leigh PN, et al. Dose-ranging study of riluzole in amyotrophic lateral sclerosis. Amyotrophic Lateral Sclerosis/Riluzole Study Group II *Lancet* 1996; 347:1425–1431.

99. Benazzouz A, Boraud T, Dubedat P, et al. Riluzole prevents MPTP-induced parkinsonism in the rhesus monkey: A pilot study. *Eur J Pharmacol* 1995; 284:299–307.

100. Boireau A, Miquet JM, Dubedat P, et al. Riluzole and experimental parkinsonism: Partial antagonism of MPP(+)-induced increase in striatal extracellular dopamine in rats in vivo. *Neuroreport* 1994; 5:2157–2160.

101. Halliwell B, Gutteridge JMC. Oxygen radicals and the nervous system. *Trends Neurosci* 1985; 8:22–26.

102. Gerlach M, Riederer P, Youdim MB. Neuroprotective therapeutic strategies. Comparison of experimental and clinical results. *Biochem Pharmacol* 1995; 50:1–16.

103. de Rijk MC, Breteler MM, den Breeijen JH, et al. Dietary antioxidants and Parkinson disease. The Rotterdam Study. *Arch Neurol* 1997; 54:762–765.

104. Scheider WL, Hershey LA, Vena JE, et al. Dietary antioxidants and other dietary factors in the etiology of Parkinson's disease. *Mov Disord* 1997; 12:190–196.

105. Logroscino G, Marder K, Cote L, et al. Dietary lipids and antioxidants in Parkinson's disease: A population-based, case-control study. *Ann Neurol* 1996; 39:89–94.

106. Offen D, Ziv I, Sternin H, et al. Prevention of dopamine-induced cell death by thiol antioxidants: Possible implications for treatment of Parkinson's disease. *Exp Neurol* 1996; 141:32–39.

107. Pardo B, Mena MA, Fahn S, Garcia DY. Ascorbic acid protects against levodopa-induced neurotoxicity on a catecholamine-rich human neuroblastoma cell line. *Mov Disord* 1993; 8:278–284.

108. Fernandez-Calle P, Jimenez-Jimenez FJ, Molina JA, et al. Serum levels of ascorbic acid (vitamin C) in patients with Parkinson's disease. *J Neurol Sci* 1993; 118:25–28.

109. Fahn S. A pilot trial of high-dose alpha-tocopherol and ascorbate in early Parkinson's disease. *Ann Neurol* 1992; 32(Suppl):S128–S132.

110. Frei B, Kim MC, Ames BN. Ubiquinol-10 is an effective lipid-soluble antioxidant at physiological concentrations. *Proc Natl Acad Sci USA* 1990; 87:4879–4883.

111. Stocker R, Bowry VW, Frei B. Ubiquinol-10 protects human low density lipoprotein more efficiently against lipid peroxidation than does alpha-tocopherol. *Proc Natl Acad Sci USA* 1991; 88:1646–1650.

112. Soderberg M, Edlund C, Kristensson K, Dallner G. Lipid composition in different regions of the human brain during aging. *J Neurochem* 1990; 54:415–423.

113. Erstner L, Dallner G. Biochemical, physiological and medical aspects of ubiquinone function. *Biochim Biophys Acta* 1995; 1271:195–204.

114. Matsubara T, Azuma T, Yoshida S, Yamagami T. Serum coenzyme Q-10 level in Parkinson syndrome. In: Folkers K, Littarru GP, Yamagami T (eds). *Biomedical and Clinical Aspects of Coenzyme Q*. Philadelphia: Elsevier, 1991:159–166.

115. Shults CW, Haas RH, Passov D, Beal MF. Coenzyme Q10 levels correlate with the activities of complexes I and II/III in mitochondria from parkinsonian and non-parkinsonian subjects. *Ann Neurol* 1997; 42:261–264.

116. Favit A, Nicoletti F, Scapagnini U, Canonico PL. Ubiquinone protects cultured neurons against spontaneous and excitotoxin-induced degeneration. *J Cereb Blood Flow Metab* 1992; 12:638–645.

117. Beal MF, Henshaw DR, Jenkins BH, et al. CoenzymeQ10 and nicotinamide block striatal lesions produced by the mitochondrial toxin malonate. *Ann Neurol* 1994; 36:882–888.

118. Wilson MF, Frishman WH, Giles T, et al. Coenzyme Q10 therapy and exercise duration in stable angina. In: Folkers K, Littarru GP, Yamagami T (eds). *Biomedical and Clinical Aspects of Coenzyme Q.* Philadelphia: Elsevier, 1991:339–348.

119. Kieburtz K, Feigin A, McDermott M, et al. A controlled trial of remacemide hydrochloride in Huntington's disease. *Mov Disord* 1996; 11:273–277.

120. Peterson PL. The treatment of mitochondrial myopathies and encephalomyopathies. *Biochim Biophys Acta* 1995; 1271:275–280.

121. Shults CW, Beal MF, Fontaine D, et al. Absorption, tolerability, and effects on mitochondrial activity of oral coenzyme Q10 in parkinsonian patients. *Neurology* 1998; 50:793–795.

122. Shults CW, Oakes D, Kieburtz K, et al. Effects of coenzyme Q10 in early Parkinson disease: Evidence of slowing of the functional decline. *Arch Neurol* 2002; 59(10):1541–1550.

123. Morens DM, Grandinetti A, Reed D, et al. Cigarette smoking and protection from Parkinson's disease: False association or etiologic clue. *Neurology* 1995; 45:1041–1051.

124. Tabenkin H, Gross R, Brammli S, Shvartzman P. Patients' views of direct access to specialists: An Israeli experience. *JAMA* 1998; 279:1943–1948.

125. Ascherio A, Zhang SM, Hernan MA, et al. Prospective study of caffeine consumption and risk of Parkinson's disease in men and women. *Ann Neurol* 2001; 50:56–63.

126. Schwarzschild MA, Xu K, Oztas E, et al. Neuroprotection by caffeine and more specific A2A receptor antagonists in animal models of Parkinson's disease. *Neurology* 2003; 61(11 Suppl 6):S55–S61.

127. Chen JF, Xu K, Petzer JP, et al. Neuroprotection by caffeine and A(2A) adenosine receptor inactivation in a model of Parkinson's disease. *J Neurosci* 2001; 21:RC143.

128. Ikeda K, Kurokawa M, Aoyama S, Kuwana Y. Neuroprotection by adenosine A2A receptor blockade in experimental models of Parkinson's disease. *J Neurochem* 2002; 80(2):262–270.

129. Meshul CK, Kamel D, Moore C, et al. Nicotine alters striatal glutamate function and decreases the apomorphine-induced contralateral rotations in 6-OHDA-lesioned rats. *Exp Neurol* 2002; 175(1):257–274.

130. Tarnopolsky MA, Beal MF. Potential for creatine and other therapies targeting cellular energy dysfunction in neurological disorders. *Ann Neurol* 2001; 49(5):561–574.

131. Shoulson I, Penney J, McDermott M, et al. A randomized, controlled trial of remacemide for motor fluctuations in Parkinson's disease. *Neurology.* 2001; 56:455–462.

132. The NINDS NET-PD Investigators (Ravina B, corresponding author). A randomized, double-blinded, futility clinical trial of creatine and minocycline in early Parkinson's disease. *Neurology* 2006; 66(5):669–671.

133. Tikka T, Fiebich BL, Goldstein G, et al. Minocycline, a tetracycline derivative, is neuroprotective against exitotoxicity by inhibiting activation and proliferation of microglia. *J Neurosci* 2001; 21:2580–2588.

134. Diguet E, Fernagut PO, Wei X, et al. Deleterious effects of minocycline in animal models of Parkinson's disease and Huntington's disease. *Eur J Neurosci* 2004; 3266–3276.

135. Fadda E, Negro A, Facci L, Skaper SD. Ganglioside GM1 cooperates with brain-derived neurotrophic factor to protect dopaminergic neurons from 6-hydroxydopamine-induced degeneration. *Neurosci Lett* 1993; 159(1–2):147–150.

136. Fusco M, Vantini G, Schiavo N, et al. Gangliosides and neurotrophic factors in neurodegenerative diseases: From experimental findings to clinical perspectives. *Ann NY Acad Sci* 1993; 695:314–317.

137. Schneider JS, Roeltgen DP, Mancall EL, et al. Parkinson's disease: Improved function with GM1 ganglioside treatment in a randomized placebo-controlled study. *Neurology* 1998; 50:1630–1636.

138. Odaka M, Yuki N, Nobile-Orazio E, et al. Antibodies to GM1(NeuGc) in Guillain-Barre syndrome after ganglioside therapy. *J Neuro Sci* 2000; 175(2):96–106.

139. Morris PJ. Cyclosporine, FK-506 and other drugs in organ transplantation. *Curr Opin Immunol* 1991; 3:748–751.

140. Snyder SH, Lai MM, Burnett PE. Immunophilins in the nervous system. *Neuron* 1998; 21:283–294.

141. Sharkey J, Butcher SP. Immunophilins mediate the neuroprotective effects of FK 506 in focal cerebral ischaemia. *Nature* 1994; 371:336–339.

142. Steiner JP, Connolly MA, Valentine HL, et al. Neurotrophic actions of nonimmunosuppressive analogues of immunosuppressive drungs FK506, rapamycin and cyclosporin A. *Nat Med* 1997; 3:421–428.

143. Tuszynski MH, Gage FH. Neurotrophic factors and diseases of the nervous system. *Ann Neurol* 1994; 35:S9–S12.

144. Gash DM, Zhang Z, Gerhardt G. Neuroprotective and neurorestorative properties of GDNF. *Ann Neurol* 1998; 44:S121–S125.

145. Kearns CM, Cass WA, Smoot K, et al. GDNF protection against 6-OHDA: Time dependence and requirement for protein synthesis. *J Neurosci* 1997; 17:7111–7118.

146. Hoffer BJ, Hoffmann A, Bowenkamp K, et al. Glial cell line–derived neurotrophic factor reverses toxin-induced injury to midbrain dopaminergic neurons in vivo. *Neurosci Lett* 1994; 182:107–111.

147. Lapchak PA, Gash DM, Jiao S, et al. Glial cell line–derived neurotrophic factor: A novel therapeutic approach to treat motor dysfunction in Parkinson's disease. *Exp Neurol* 1997; 144:29–34.

148. Gill SS, Patel NK, Hotton GR, et al. Direct brain infusion of glial cell line–derived neurotrophic factor in Parkinson disease. *Nat Med* 2003; 9(5):589–595.

149. Lang AE, Gill SS, Patel NK, et al. Randomized, controlled trial of intraputamenal GDNF infusion in Parkinson's disease. *Ann Neurol* 2006; 59:459–466.

150. Tseng JL, Baetge EE, Zurn AD, Aebischer P. GDNF reduces drug-induced rotational behavior after medial forebrain bundle transection by a mechanism not involving striatal dopamine. *J Neurosci* 1997; 17:325–333.

151. Choi-Lundberg DL, Lin Q, Chang Y-N, et al. Dopaminergic neurons protected from degeneration by GDNF gene therapy. *Science* 1997; 275:838–841.

152. Kang UJ. Potential of gene therapy for Parkinson's disease: Neurobiologic issues and new developments in gene transfer methodologies. *Mov Disord* 1998; 13(Suppl 1):59–72.

153. Marsden CD, Olanow CW. The causes of Parkinson's disease are being unraveled and rational neuroprotective therapy is close to reality. *Ann Neurol* 1998; 44:S189–S196.

154. Morrish PK, Sawle GV, Brooks DJ. Clinical and [18F] dopa PET findings in early Parkinson's disease. *J Neurol Neurosurg Psychiatry* 1995; 59:597–600.

155. Marek KL, Friedman J, Hauser R, et al,Phase II evaluation of rasagiline mesylate (TVP-1012), a novel anti-parkinsonian drug, in parkinsonian patients not using levodopa/carbidopa. *Mov Disord* 1997; 12:838.

156. Morrish PK, Rakshi JS, Bailey DL, et al. Measuring the rate of progression and estimating the preclinical period of Parkinson's disease with [18F]dopa PET. *J Neurol Neurosurg Psychiatry* 1998; 64:314–319.

157. Swerdlow RH, Parks JK, Miller SW, et al. Origin and functional consequences of the complex I defect in Parkinson's disease. *Ann Neurol* 1996; 40:663–671.

158. Leber P. Slowing the progression of Alzheimer disease: Methodologic issues. *Alzheimer Dis Assoc Disord* 1997; 11(Suppl 5):S10–S21.

159. Whitehouse PJ, Kittner BJ, Roessner M, et al. Clinical trial designs for demonstrating disease-course-altering effects in dementia. *Alzheimer Dis Assoc Disord* 1998; 12:281–294.

160. Tilley B. Utilizing futility designs in Parkinson's disease to optimize the ongoing search for new treatments. *Neurology.* 2006; 66(5):628–633.

161. Snow BJ, Tooyama I, McGeer EG, et al. Human positron emission tomographic [18-F] fluorodopa studies correlate with dopamine cell counts and levels. *Ann Neurol* 1993; 34:324–330.

162. Piccini P, Morrish PK, Turjanski N, et al. Dopaminergic function in familial Parkinson's disease: A clinical and 18F-dopa positron emission tomography study. *Ann Neurol* 1997; 41:222–229.

163. Kaufman MJ, Madras BK. Severe depletion of cocaine recognition sites associated with the dopamine transporter in Parkinson's-diseased striatum. *Synapse* 1991; 9:43–49.

164. Seibyl JP, Marek KL, Quinlan D, et al. Decreased single-photon emission computed tomographic [123I] β-CIT striatal uptake correlates with symptom severity in Parkinson's disease. *Ann Neurol* 1995; 38:589–598.

165. Marek KL, Seibyl JP, Zoghbi SS, et al. [123I] beta-CIT/SPECT imaging demonstrates bilateral loss of dopamine transporters in hemi-Parkinson's disease. *Neurology* 1996; 46:231–237.

166. Mozley PD, Schneider JS, Acton PD, et al. Binding of [99mTc]TRODAT-1 to dopamine transporters in patients with Parkinson's disease and in healthy volunteers. *J Nucl Med* 2000; 41:584–589.

51

Symptomatic Treatment Approaches for Early Parkinson's Disease

J. Eric Ahlskog

T here is no treatment proven to slow the progression of Parkinson's disease (PD); thus medical therapy is directed at treating the symptoms. In fact, symptomatic drugs typically produce gratifying responses, enabling people to remain in the mainstream of life for years. This chapter addresses the issues of when to start a medication, choice of the first drug, and appropriate doses, focusing on drugs approved by the U.S. Food & Drug Administration (FDA).

WHEN TO START TREATMENT

The treatment goal is to keep those patients with PD active and engaged in all the activities appropriate to their age: social, occupational, and recreational. If there are no limitations due to PD, as seen in very early disease, medical treatment may be deferred. The need for treatment varies not only with symptoms and severity but also with the social and occupational situation. For example, a prominent rest tremor may be of no consequence to a retiree but embarrassing and a source of distraction for a high school teacher lecturing to a class. That retiree may choose to take no medication but the teacher may elect to start a drug, even if other aspects of PD do not pose substantial problems. On the other hand, the decision is

straightforward when PD begins to limit physical activity or compromise gait. Patients who are becoming sedentary because of PD should be treated.

MEDICATION OPTIONS FOR EARLY PARKINSON'S DISEASE

Several chapters in this book addressed the different classes of medications used to treat PD. The reader is referred to them for detailed descriptions. The discussion here is subdivided into minor drugs vs. the primary medications.

Minor Drugs for Early Parkinson's Disease

Some clinicians start with a medication that is easy to dose when symptoms are mild. The usual drugs in this category are selegiline, rasagiline, and amantadine. None are highly efficacious, but when used as monotherapy they do not require complex dosing schemes and cause few side effects, making them reasonable first choices. The expectation is to maintain these for a few months or longer, with a more potent drug added when necessary.

Selegiline is a monoamine oxidase-B (MAO-B) inhibitor that is initiated and maintained at a dose of 5 mg in the morning and again at noon (it is not administered later in the day to avoid insomnia). Some clinicians simply prescribe a single 5-mg morning dose; this may be sufficient to fully inhibit brain MAO-B (1), which has a long half-life (40 days) (2).

Rasagiline is a newer MAO-B inhibitor that was recently approved for use by the FDA. In contrast to selegiline, it has no amphetamine metabolites, which potentially contribute to side effects such as insomnia. Indirect evidence suggests that it might slow PD progression (3), but this is controversial and unproven. Monotherapy with rasagiline modestly improves PD symptoms (3) and hence may be considered as initial treatment of PD. The standard dose is 0.5 to 1.0 mg in the morning.

Amantadine has been available to treat PD for approximately as long as levodopa. The mechanism of action was debated for many years; it is now attributed to inhibition of glutamate NMDA receptors (4–6). As monotherapy, it is modestly beneficial, but has some side effects (most notably mottling and swelling of the legs). It is typically started as a single 100-mg tablet taken once or twice daily, often escalated later to 100 mg 3 times daily.

Anticholinergic medications such as trihexyphenidyl and benztropine have a long track record in PD and previously were advocated as an initial treatment. However, they have limited efficacy (primarily against PD tremor and dystonia) plus numerous side effects (constipation, urinary hesitancy, mild memory impairment, blurred vision), especially in patients above age 60. With so many other better medication choices, they are now rarely prescribed as initial therapy.

Primary Medications for Early Parkinson's Disease

For parkinsonism that is compromising lifestyle, more potent medications are appropriate, specifically a dopamine agonist or levodopa (carbidopa/levodopa). Since the minor drugs discussed above typically provide only modest and transient symptomatic improvement, many clinicians simply start with an agonist or levodopa.

Levodopa is the most potent medication for the treatment of PD. With the availability of levodopa since 1970, the life span of PD patients has improved substantially (7–13). Levodopa will eventually be required for symptomatic treatment in nearly every PD patient, although it does not necessarily need to be started early in the course.

Levodopa is formulated with carbidopa, which blocks the premature conversion of levodopa to dopamine in the periphery; this prevents nausea, attenuates orthostatic hypotension and reduces the amount of levodopa that is required for benefit. The standard immediate-release formulation of carbidopa/levodopa is appropriate for initial therapy, but this agent also comes in a controlled-release formulation (Sinemet CR), which is the choice of some

clinicians. Carbidopa/levodopa is additionally formulated with the catechol-O-methyltransferase (COMT) inhibitor entacapone (Stalevo). As discussed in Chapter 42, the addition of entacapone prolongs the half-life of unmetabolized levodopa in the bloodstream by about an hour (14).

A dopamine agonist is the primary alternative to levodopa therapy in early PD; those available and most frequently used are pramipexole (Mirapex) and ropinirole (Requip). Bromocriptine (Parlodel) and pergolide (Permax) are also in the agonist class but carry a greater risk of side effects (see below); pergolide was recently removed from the market for this reason. Unlike levodopa, the agonists require no metabolic conversion and pass directly into the brain, where they bind to dopamine receptors.

Carbidopa/levodopa is the most effective drug for PD; moreover, it is among the least expensive. Why not simply start with that? In fact, many clinicians prescribe this as the initial medication; however, others argue that it should be deferred or limited. Some patients carry this to the extreme, caught up in what has been characterized as "levodopa phobia" (15). Since controversies relating to levodopa are central to the choice of drugs for early PD, we should examine the evidence.

IS LEVODOPA TOXIC?

The dopamine oxidant stress hypothesis of PD (16, 17) argues that oxidative metabolism of dopamine generates toxic free radical products, which cause neuronal degeneration of the substantia nigra. Evidence in favor of this theory is detailed in Chapter 30. Importantly, this hypothesis predicts that levodopa therapy fuels nigral neuronal death. Numerous lines of evidence, however, argue against substantial levodopa toxicity, as summarized below.

1. Coinciding with the introduction of levodopa therapy about 35 years ago was significant improvement in PD mortality rates (7–12); longevity remained significantly better when potential confounding variables were statistically controlled (13). Although one subsequent clinical trial suggested that levodopa increased mortality (compared to bromocriptine) (18), the outcome was uninterpretable due to confounding factors and has not been replicated (19).
2. The neuropathologic appearance of PD did not change with the introduction of levodopa therapy (20).
3. PD patients from the 1960s, whose levodopa therapy was delayed because of unavailability gained no advantage over post–levodopa era patients starting levodopa therapy early (matched for symptom duration) (21).

4. In two separate 9- to 12-month clinical trials, the rate of clinical progression on levodopa was the same as with bromocriptine monotherapy (22) and perhaps less than with placebo (23) (clinical scoring after drug washout, compared to baseline).

5. Levodopa treatment of other conditions has not been associated with evidence of clinical deterioration, the development of parkinsonism, or neuropathologic findings of substantia nigra toxicity (24–27).

6. Mice administered huge doses of levodopa daily for up to 18 months did not develop substantia nigra pathology (28–30).

7. Lipid peroxidation products (malondialdehyde) do not increase in the circulation with levodopa therapy, in contrast to diabetes mellitus, which is known to be associated with oxidant stress (31).

It should additionally be noted that the dopamine oxidant stress hypothesis is based on the presumption that substantia nigra degeneration and PD are essentially synonymous. Rather, it now appears that the dopaminergic substantia nigra is involved as an intermediate stage in the PD degenerative process (32, 33). Moreover, multiple predictions from the oxidant stress hypothesis are inconsistent with observations in PD (34). A consensus panel recently concluded that there is no compelling evidence for levodopa toxicity (35).

SHOULD LEVODOPA BE DELAYED?

Some argue that levodopa therapy should be deferred for as long as possible. This argument lost credibility with the growing consensus that levodopa is unlikely to be toxic. However, this admonition is also based on the presumption that delaying levodopa will forestall levodopa complications, dyskinesias, and motor fluctuations.

Deferring Levodopa Therapy to Delay Fluctuations or Dyskinesias: Retrospective Studies

Two early retrospective studies suggested that early levodopa initiation predisposes to wearing off and "on-off" phenomena (36, 37), but they were criticized due to patient selection bias (patients presenting with more severe and progressive disease are more likely to initiate levodopa) (38). Four subsequent retrospective studies failed to link early levodopa treatment to an increased frequency of wearing off and "on-off" phenomena (38–41); another study found only a transient effect, with similar frequencies after 5 years (42). One prospective well-designed study had similar results and concluded that there was no need to delay levodopa therapy (41). In the aggregate,

these trials fail to support delaying levodopa as a strategy to forestall short-duration motor responses.

Several retrospective clinical series have also failed to document a link between levodopa-dyskinesias and early initiation of levodopa therapy. Two studies actually suggested that delaying levodopa therapy increased the risk of dyskinesia (38, 39). Thus, dyskinesia frequency was not increased among patients starting levodopa early vs. later (38, 40, 42), nor was it associated with the duration of levodopa therapy (36).

Early Levodopa Trials

The retrospective studies cited above may be criticized for selection bias: enrollment of clinic patients with milder disease who are more likely to defer levodopa treatment. Studies from the early levodopa era, however, are not subject to that criticism; levodopa was delayed because it was not available. In an aggregate analysis of all the early levodopa trials (including many patients with long parkinsonism durations before levodopa treatment), half of the patients developed dyskinesias by 6 months; in contrast, only 7% of modern-era patients (short durations of parkinsonism) experienced dyskinesias by 1 treatment year (43). A study of patients beginning treatment in the 1969 Mayo Clinic levodopa trial documented similar results (44). In that series, the mean parkinsonism duration before levodopa was 7 years; dyskinesias occurred in nearly all patients by 1 treatment year and about 70% developed motor fluctuations by 2 years. Contrast that to the aggregate analysis of all modern-era levodopa trials through September 2000, where after 4 to 6 treatment years about 40% of all patients developed dyskinesias and 40% motor fluctuations (43).

These findings suggest that PD duration rather than levodopa treatment duration is the crucial factor; delaying levodopa may not substantially reduce the risk of dyskinesias or fluctuations once therapy is initiated. In practice, only a tiny minority of PD patients can defer levodopa treatment beyond several years unless they are willing to accept substantial disability.

SHOULD THE LEVODOPA DOSE BE LIMITED?

The rationale for limiting the levodopa dose is similar to that suggesting a delay in its initiation: concerns about toxicity and levodopa complications. There is no doubt that higher levodopa doses are more likely to elicit dyskinesias and allow motor fluctuations to become apparent. However, there is no compelling evidence to suggest that this is an irreversible event. Rather, it may simply represent a reversible threshold phenomenon (e.g., levodopa doses above the dyskinesia-threshold provoke dyskinesias, whereas dose reduction to below threshold does not).

Thus, a sensible general strategy is to administer levodopa doses that provide the greatest efficacy, but short of dyskinesias. However, this general strategy of dosage reduction is impractical for treating motor fluctuations, since lowering the dose sufficiently to abolish fluctuations will essentially abolish the short-duration response, with loss of efficacy.

Some argue that the doses should be kept low from the inception of levodopa therapy. Only a single prospective study has evaluated levodopa dosage ceilings as a means of limiting levodopa-related motor complications (45). In this 6-year trial, "low dose" therapy was ultimately associated with only a slightly lower frequency of clinical fluctuations and dyskinesias compared to "maximum tolerated dose" therapy. On balance, the slight reduction of these levodopa motor complications failed to offset the poor control of parkinsonian symptoms associated with low-dose therapy. Thus, low-dose levodopa monotherapy is not an acceptable longer-term strategy for most patients.

Summary: Levodopa Treatment

The available evidence suggests that levodopa therapy is not toxic. Ultimately, nearly all PD patients will require levodopa treatment, and when that time arrives, the risk of levodopa complications appears to primarily be a function of PD duration (and probably severity). Arbitrarily delaying levodopa may not result in any advantage once levodopa treatment is started. When it is prescribed, there appears to be no net benefit to restricting the dose, which might result in inadequate control of parkinsonism.

LEVODOPA VS. DOPAMINE AGONIST THERAPY

Carbidopa/levodopa is substantially more effective than dopamine agonist therapy. However, some clinicians start with an agonist for 2 primary reasons: (a) a lower risk of dyskinesias and motor fluctuations and (b) a possible neuroprotective effect, as suggested by brain dopamine imaging. These complex issues require further discussion.

Reduced Risk of Dyskinesias and Fluctuations With Dopamine Agonist Therapy

Every recent major clinical trial that has compared a dopamine agonist to levodopa has documented a lower risk of dyskinesias in the agonist arm (46–49). During the first year or two of these trials, when patients can be satisfactorily treated with an agonist alone, the motor complication risk with an agonist is extremely low, and much less than with levodopa therapy. These

trials allowed for adjunctive levodopa therapy, and even when that is added, the combination is associated with a significantly lower frequency of dyskinesias than with levodopa monotherapy (albeit not nearly as low as with agonist monotherapy). Somewhat surprising, however, was the finding that levodopa monotherapy consistently resulted in greater control of parkinsonism than combination agonist-levodopa therapy (despite allowing clinicians to adjust the dosage).

On the surface, it would seem that starting an agonist and later adding levodopa when required should reduce the longer-term risk of levodopa complications. However, there is a crucial unanswered question: Must the agonist be started initially? Is there a time-window early in the course of PD when the agonist must be initiated? If not started early, is the opportunity lost? It is not obvious why that should be the case. In fact, the conventional use of dopamine agonists for many years has been *after* levodopa motor complications developed (adding the agonist and reducing the levodopa dosage). Hence it may not be crucial to start with the agonist; the outcome might be the same if it were added later, in conjunction with levodopa adjustment.

Caveat: Reported Dyskinesia and Fluctuation Risk

All of the studies cited above that document the relative risks of dyskinesias or motor fluctuations are reporting *incident* motor complications. In other words, dyskinesias or fluctuations of any severity, occurring even transiently, are counted. This ignores the fact that motor fluctuations are often minor or easily controlled with medication adjustments. Moreover, dyskinesias are often mild and unobtrusive or are easily abolished by slight levodopa reduction. A recent community-based study looked beyond *incident* dyskinesias and tabulated prevalence (50): with Kaplan-Meier analysis, the risk of dyskinesias requiring medication adjustment was only 17% by 5 levodopa-treatment years and 43% after 10 years; the risk of dyskinesias that could not be controlled with medication adjustments was only 12% at 10 treatment years.

Age Influences Choice of Drug

Young-onset PD, defined as onset before age 40, is associated with an extremely high risk of both dyskinesias and motor fluctuations(51, 52); this approaches 100% incidence by 5 years on levodopa. PD patients in this age group might experience these motor complications during the first few years, when a dopamine agonist is often sufficient; hence they are preferably initially treated with a dopamine agonist unless there is some other compelling reason to use levodopa.

This begs the question whether PD onset slightly later than age 40 also should be initially treated with a dopamine agonist. If so, to what age does this high risk of motor complications persist? Only a single study bears directly on this issue (53). In a population-based cohort, the risk of dyskinesias diminished by decade:

Age of PD Onset	Percent With Dyskinesias After 5 Years of Treatment With Levodopa
40–49 years	40%
50–59	53%
60–69	26%
70–89	16%

Again, note that these were *incident* dyskinesias and not necessarily persistent, disabling, or uncontrollable. Parenthetically, the number of patients in this study within the 40- to 49-year-old group was too small to be very reliable.

Possible Neuroprotective Effect With Dopamine Agonist Therapy

In vitro and animal studies suggest that dopamine agonists might have a neuroprotective effect in PD. A challenge for clinician-investigators has been measurement of PD progression to confirm such an effect. Although clinical measures have been used in prior neuroprotective trials [e.g., the selegiline DATATOP trial (54, 55)], the symptomatic benefit from PD drugs had a confounding effect. As an alternative, investigators have used brain dopamine imaging, either [123I] β-CIT single photon emission computed tomography (SPECT) or 18fluorodopa positron emission tomography (PET). Each method provides a quantitative measure of striatal dopaminergic terminal density, which is known to decline with PD progression. Two clinical trials have employed this methodology (48, 56), each comparing carbidopa/levodopa monotherapy to dopamine agonist treatment (allowing for the addition of levodopa). In each study, the progressive loss of striatal imaging signal was significantly less rapid in the agonist arm (pramipexole (56) or ropinirole(48)) than in the levodopa arm. However, the clinical measures were just the opposite, significantly favoring the carbidopa/levodopa monotherapy arm in each trial. Superficial analysis focusing on the imaging data initially led to the conclusion that agonist therapy slowed the progression of PD. However, it was subsequently recognized that the administered drugs influence the regulation of proteins involved in the metabolism, transport, and binding of the imaging radioligands (57, 58). Thus these studies were seriously confounded and a consensus panel focusing on this

issue recently concluded that "current evidence does not support the use of imaging . . . as a surrogate endpoint in clinical trials" (59).

Advantages: Levodopa vs. Agonist

To summarize, the primary arguments for starting a dopamine agonist as initial therapy are twofold: (a) possible neuroprotective effect, based on imaging, and (b) less risk of subsequent motor complications. The ultimate prevalence of motor complications might be the same if the agonist were started later, after fluctuations developed, with corresponding adjustment of levodopa. Age, which influences motor complication risk, may also be a factor in the choice.

On the other hand, there are arguments for starting with carbidopa/levodopa: (a) significantly greater efficacy (46–49); (b) much less expense, especially when carbidopa/levodopa is prescribed as the generic formulation (60); (c) less complex dosing; (d) quicker response (2 to 4 weeks vs. about 6 to 8 weeks); (e) lower risk of hallucinations, somnolence, or leg edema and freezing of gait (46, 47).

Clinicians should weigh these arguments for each patient. Neither strategy is incorrect. Next we focus on how to administer these drugs.

INITIATING TREATMENT WITH LEVODOPA

Selection of the carbidopa/levodopa formulation and the dosage escalation scheme varies among clinicians. There is no single correct strategy; here we consider the options.

Immediate vs. Controlled Release

When controlled-release (CR) carbidopa/levodopa was first introduced, it was argued that the slower release is more physiologic and consequently may reduce the long-term risk of levodopa-related motor complications. A large multicenter clinical trial, however, failed to document any advantage to the CR formulation over immediate-release carbidopa/levodopa in preventing motor complications (61); motor scores and frequencies of levodopa motor complications were very similar after treatment for 5 years. A similar 5-year outcome was reported using the levodopa formulations available in Europe (sustained-release vs. standard benserazide-levodopa) (62).

There are several advantages to using the immediate-release formulation of carbidopa/levodopa: (a) it is considerably cheaper, comparing generics of each (60); (b) it has better bioavailability (99%, vs. 71% for CR) (63); and (c) it has more predictable interactions with meals, being taken on an empty stomach for maximum effect (64).

In contrast, the CR formulation has complex interactions with food, and it is unclear how it should be administered with respect to meals. CR carbidopa/levodopa enters the circulation more effectively when taken with food (63), but levodopa transport into the brain may be impeded by meal-derived amino acids (64). Use of the CR formulation can be problematic when there is a poor clinical response to increasing doses; the clinician is then left to ponder whether this may due to poor bioavailability or problems with meal effects and gastric emptying.

The CR formulation's advantage is the twice-daily dosing schedule vs. the usual thrice-daily dosing with immediate-release carbidopa/levodopa. However, this argument may be based more on convention than pharmacodynamics. Early PD patients starting levodopa typically experience a long-duration therapeutic response, in contrast to the short-duration, fluctuating responses experienced after several years or more (65). This long-duration response is cumulative over days and not dependent on frequent doses; it may be equally achieved by the same total dose distributed at longer dosing intervals. This was demonstrated in a cohort of early PD patients where immediate-release carbidopa/levodopa taken once every 3 days was as efficacious as doses divided into a thrice-daily regimen (66).

Should Levodopa Be Started With Entacapone?

Entacapone inhibits peripheral COMT and prolongs the serum half-life of levodopa by 30% to 40% (14). It now has been formulated with carbidopa/levodopa as brand-name Stalevo, and some advocate starting treatment with this combination therapy (67). The arguments for starting with this formulation are similar to those made years ago for Sinemet CR: the prolonged levodopa circulating half-life is more physiologic and may ultimately result in a lower risk of levodopa complications. To date no clinical trials have assessed this strategy. However, the half-life of circulating levodopa after a dose of entacapone-carbidopa/levodopa(14) is fairly similar to that of CR carbidopa/levodopa (63). The 5-year clinical trials comparing CR to immediate-release levodopa found no advantage to the formulation with the longer plasma half-life (61, 62), and one might predict a similar outcome in comparative trials of carbidopa/levodopa with and without entacapone.

Entacapone is much more expensive than generic carbidopa/levodopa, whether it is combined with carbidopa/levodopa in a single pill or taken separately (60). It does increase levodopa potency and a slightly lower dose of levodopa can be employed when adding entacapone; however, it can also exacerbate levodopa's side effects. There is no proven role for entacapone as initial therapy in PD in combination with carbidopa/levodopa.

What Dosage of Initial Carbidopa/Levodopa?

Immediate-release carbidopa/levodopa comes in three formulations: 25/100, 10/100, and 25/250. The 25/100 formulation is preferable given the larger amount or ratio of carbidopa, which reduces the risk of nausea and hypotension. The 10/100 form is slightly less expensive and is an acceptable alternative, but for some patients, 10 mg of carbidopa is insufficient to prevent nausea. Unless quartered, the 25/250 size provides too much initial levodopa to be used as the starting formulation. Whatever the formulation, the dosage should be started low and escalated slowly for two primary reasons: (a) less risk of side effects, especially nausea, and (b) gradual increments allow the patient to determine when optimum efficacy has been achieved.

Controlled-release carbidopa/levodopa is available in two forms, 25/100 and 50/200. The 25/100 formulation is preferred for initial treatment and titration.

Carbidopa/Levodopa: When and How Often?

Immediate-release carbidopa/levodopa is typically started with a thrice-daily schedule; it is taken on an empty stomach. Dietary amino acids compete for transport with levodopa (a large neutral amino acid) at the blood-brain barrier (64); to assure maximum passage into the brain, it should be ingested about an hour before meals; intervals of less than an hour may work for some patients provided that gastric emptying is not delayed.

CR carbidopa/levodopa is conventionally started with a twice-daily schedule; however, it is unclear whether it should be administered with meals or on an empty stomach. As mentioned, mealtime dosing increases levodopa bioavailability in the bloodstream (63), but this may be less important than the competitive inhibition by dietary amino acids at the blood-brain barrier (64). Whichever mealtime strategy is chosen for initial CR carbidopa/levodopa administration, it should be consistent, either always taken with meals or on an empty stomach. However, if mealtime dosing is associated with a poor response despite increasing doses, the timing can be switched to 2 hours before meals. Pharmacodynamic studies of the CR formulation indicate that the latency to clinical response is 2 hours in some patients (68), hence the suggestion to administer 2 hours before meals to avoid conflict with dietary amino acids.

Carbidopa/Levodopa Initiation and Escalation Scheme

A variety of dosing schedules can be utilized for initiating carbidopa/levodopa therapy. One common strategy for the immediate-release formulation is to start with one or one-half of a 25/100 tablet 1 hour before each of 3 meals and then to escalate this by half-tablet increments for all doses; these increments can be implemented every 1 to 2 weeks. Our practice is to raise the doses until substantial improvement, but not beyond 2½ to 3 tablets thrice daily (60). From experience with patients starting treatment, individual doses higher that 2½ to 3 tablets (taken on an empty stomach) do not provide further benefit, with very rare exceptions (such as malabsorption). Thus, in patients with recent-onset PD, the full benefit is captured with doses up to 2½ to 3 immediate-release 25/100 tablets 3 times daily on an empty stomach. More frequent dosing may be necessary later if fluctuations develop (short-duration levodopa response), but this is unexpected in early PD. The only exception is the occasional person who has trouble sleeping due to parkinsonism despite 3 doses during the day; in that case, a fourth dose at bedtime or during the night may be helpful. Some clinicians are reluctant to use more than small doses in early PD; however, there is no proven benefit to that strategy.

A similar strategy may be used for CR carbidopa/levodopa using the 25/100 formulation. It may be initiated with a single tablet twice daily and then increased weekly by adding a tablet to each of the 2 doses up to 3 to 4 tablets twice daily (i.e., 1 tablet twice daily, then 2 tablets twice daily, etc.). For convenience, a 50/200 tablet can be substituted for 2 of the 25/100 size. If there is insufficient clinical improvement despite 4 of the 25/100 CR tablets twice daily, this could be due to bioavailability problems with the CR formulation. In that case, one may consider dosing 2 hours before eating for 2 weeks. If there is still a poor clinical response, it may be wise to switch to the immediate-release formulation, which has excellent bioavailability and predictable responses when taken on an empty stomach (1 hour before meals). Obviously, a poor response to carbidopa/levodopa could occur because the diagnosis is non-PD parkinsonism (multiple system atrophy, progressive supranuclear palsy, etc.); however, before arriving at that conclusion, the levodopa trial must be sufficient to capture any potential responsiveness.

Common Side Effects in Initiating Carbidopa/Levodopa

Probably the two most common side effects in initiating carbidopa/levodopa are nausea and orthostatic hypotension. Dyskinesias are unexpected early in therapy; if the patient reports these, more than likely he or she has mistaken tremor or other symptoms for dyskinesias.

Nausea is usually not a significant problem; when it occurs with levodopa therapy, it is often mild and dissipates with continued treatment. Levodopa-induced nausea relates to circulating dopamine that stimulates the chemoreceptive trigger zone in the area postrema of the brainstem (which has no blood-brain barrier). This may be due to inadequate carbidopa, which blocks dopa decarboxylase in the periphery (the enzyme converting levodopa to dopamine). To counter this, additional carbidopa may be administered; this is available as plain carbidopa (Lodosyn) 25 mg. One or two carbidopa tablets may be taken just before or with each carbidopa/levodopa dose. Carbidopa/levodopa may also be taken with small amounts of nonprotein food, such as dry bread or soda crackers to counter nausea. If nausea is a substantial problem, a habituation strategy can be employed (60), starting with very low doses and escalating very slowly (e.g., beginning with one-fourth of a 25/100 tablet plus supplemental carbidopa 3 times daily and advancing this weekly by increments of one-fourth tablet for all doses).

Patients with low blood pressure or signs of orthostatic hypotension before starting carbidopa/levodopa are at risk for hypotensive symptoms. People with PD often have at least mild dysautonomia and some potential for orthostatic hypotension. This may be exacerbated by levodopa therapy. When levodopa drops the standing BP, it does this for 3 to 4 hours after each dose, followed by a return to baseline. It is wise to check the standing BP of patients before starting carbidopa/levodopa. If it is already low, levodopa may drop it lower. Some patients take medications that can be discontinued to avoid this (e.g., unnecessary diuretics, antihypertensives). If the standing BP is quite low (e.g., 90 systolic), it must be treated before starting carbidopa/levodopa; there are a variety of means to counter orthostatic hypotension (60); see Chapter 11.

DOPAMINE AGONIST AS THE FIRST DRUG

A dopamine agonist is a reasonable choice for initial therapy, especially in young PD patients. However, anticipate that most patients will find this insufficient in a few years or less; levodopa will then be necessary.

In committing to initial agonist treatment, it is probably wise to counsel the patient that the initial doses will not provide benefit and that adherence to the dosage escalation schedule, which spans many weeks, is important. A common problem is failure to advance the agonist dose into the therapeutic range. Thus it is important to see the patient back a few weeks after starting the agonist to ensure continuing compliance with the schedule.

Which Agonist to Choose for Initial Therapy?

Available orally administered agonists come in two classes, ergotamines (bromocriptine, pergolide, cabergoline) and non-ergotamines (pramipexole, ropinirole). The ergotamines have more potential for side effects, especially inflammatory-fibrotic reactions (69), which may damage heart valves (70–72); pergolide was recently withdrawn from the market because of cardiac valvulopathy and the other ergots also carry this risk. The ergotamine

TABLE 51-1
Dopamine Agonists for Initial Therapy

Agonist	Tablet Sizes, mg	Starting Dose	Typical Maintenance Doses	Time to Escalate to the Typical Maintenance Doses*	Usual Ceiling Dose
Pramipexole (Mirapex)	0.125, 0.25, 0.5, 1.0, 1.5	0.125 mg tid	1.0–1.5 mg tid	5–7 weeks	2 mg tid †
Ropinirole (Requip)	0.25, 0.5, 1.0, 2.0, 3.0, 4.0, 5.0	0.25 mg tid	3–5 mg tid	8–10 weeks	7 mg tid †

*Per the manufacturers' published schedules.
†Occasionally slightly higher doses are administered as tolerated.

agonists are considerably more expensive (60) and have no important advantages over non-ergot agonists. Hence they are not discussed further.

Either pramipexole ropinirole are appropriate for initial treatment in PD. They have a similar pharmacology (73, 74), with selective affinity for dopamine D3 receptors (especially pramipexole). Ropinirole and pramipexole cost about the same (60), and their efficacies appear to be similar, although there has been no head-to-head comparison in a clinical trial. Perhaps the major difference between these two drugs is that the pramipexole dosing scheme is less complex (60); unlike ropinirole, pramipexole tablets are scored, which allows fewer pill sizes to be used in dose escalation.

Specifics of Dopamine Agonist Therapy

All agonists are started in a low, subtherapeutic dose and slowly escalated over many weeks, as illustrated in Table 51-1. Unlike the case with levodopa therapy, there are no substantial interactions with food, and they are usually taken with each of 3 meals (thus reducing the potential for nausea). By convention, they are increased weekly to the maintenance dose, which is determined by the response. Since multiple pill sizes are necessary, the escalation is easiest for patients if they have printed instructions; the manufacturers provide these, and they also have been published for patients (60).

Common Side Effects With Non-ergot Agonist Therapy

Like levodopa therapy, agonists may also induce nausea; the risk is minimized by dosing after eating and the very slow dose increments, allowing habituation. Orthostatic hypotension may also occur, and a standing BP before

starting treatment is advisable; if the standing BP is already low, then close BP monitoring is appropriate.

Although any of the medications for PD may provoke hallucinations or sedation, these effects are substantially more likely with agonists than with levodopa (46, 47). Leg edema may also occur with the agonists (46, 47). Rarely, agonists provoke pathologic behaviors, such as gambling or hypersexuality (see Chapter 19); however, this is primarily due to the use of agonists in combination with carbidopa/levodopa (75, 76).

Newly-approved Dopamine Agonist Transdermal Patch: Rotigotine (Neupro)

Rotigotine (Neupro) is a dopine agonist that was FDA-approved and became available as this chapter was going to press. It is formulated as a transdermal preparation and has a pharmacology very similar to pramipexole and ropinirole (selective affinity for D_3 more than D_2 receptors (77)). Drug delivery is proportional to the size of the skin-patch, with stable plasma concentrations when administered once every 24 hours. Clinical trials in early PD patients revealed that rotigotine patch monotherapy ersulted in anti-parkinsonism efficacy and side effects very similar to what one would have expected with orally-administered pramipexole or ropinirole (78, 79). Thus, the role of rotigotine in clinical practice will be very similar to that of pramipexole and ropinirole.

Rotigotine is available in three skin patch sizes, with the following drug release rates: 2 mg per 24 hours (10 cm²); 4 mg per 24 hours (20 cm²) and 6 mg per 24 hours (30 cm²). According to the manufacturer's recommendations, therapy should be initiated with the 2 mg skin patch applied once daily. Guided by the response, it can then be increased after one week to the 4 mg/24 hours patch applied once daily, and a week later to the 6 mg/24 hours patch applied daily. Patients are advised to rotate the application sites on the body to avoid skin irritation.

Other Treatments for Early PD

Newly diagnosed PD patients occasionally ask whether neurosurgical procedures are appropriate. These, however, are reserved for advancing PD patients with motor fluctuations or dyskinesias that have become problematic.

Patients with early PD should be counseled to stay active, both physically and mentally, as appropriate for age and ability. Those with a sedentary lifestyle may be encouraged to engage in exercise or stretching classes or to consult a physical therapist for an appropriate program.

References

1. Oreland L, Johansson F, Ekstedt J. Dose regimen of deprenyl (selegiline) and platelet MAO activities. *Acta Neurol Scand* 1983; (Suppl 95):87–89.

2. Fowler JS, Volkow ND, Logan J, et al. Slow recovery of human brain MAO B after L-deprenyl (Selegiline) withdrawal. Synapse 1994; 18:86–93.

3. Parkinson Study G. A controlled, randomized, delayed-start study of rasagiline in early Parkinson disease. *Arch Neurol* 2004; 61:561–566.

4. Greenamyre JT, O'Brien CF. N-methyl-D-aspartate antagonists in the treatment of Parkinson's disease. *Arch Neurol* 1991; 48:977–981.

5. Stoof JC, Booij J, Drukarch B, Wolters EC. The anti-parkinsonian drug amantadine inhibits the N-methyl-D-aspartic acid-evoked release of acetylcholine from rat neostriatum in a non-competitive way. *Eur J Pharmacol* 1992; 213:439–443.

6. Lupp A, Lucking CH, Koch R, et al. Inhibitory effects of the antiparkinsonian drugs memantine and amantadine on N-methyl-D-aspartate-evoked acetylcholine release in the rabbit caudate nucleus in vitro. *J Pharmacol Exp Ther* 1992; 263:717–724.

7. Sweet RD, Mc Dowell FH. Five years' treatment of Parkinson's disease with levodopa: Therapeutic results and survival of 100 patients. *Ann Intern Med* 1975; 83:456–463.

8. Diamond SG, Markham CH. Present mortality in Parkinson's disease: The ratio of observed to expected deaths with a method to calculate expected deaths. *J Neural Transm* 1976; 38:259–269.

9. Zumstein H, Siegfried J. Mortality among Parkinson patients treated with L-dopa combined with a decarboxylase inhibitor. *Eur Neurol* 1976; 14:321–327.

10. Martilla RJ, Rinne UK, Siirtola T, Sonninen V. Mortality of patients with Parkinson's disease treated with levodopa. *J Neurol* 1977; 216:147–153.

11. Joseph C, Chassan JB, Koch ML. Levodopa in Parkinson's disease: A long-term appraisal of mortality. *Ann Neurol* 1978; 3:116–118.

12. Hoehn MM. Parkinsonism treated with levodopa: Progression and mortality. *J Neural Transm* 1983; 19(Suppl 1):253–264.

13. Uitti RJ, Ahlskog JE, Maraganore DM, et al. Levodopa therapy and survival in idiopathic Parkinson's disease: Olmsted County project. *Neurology* 1993; 43:1918–1926.

14. Holm KJ, Spencer CM. Entacapone. A review of its use in Parkinson's disease. *Drugs* 1999; 58:159–177.

15. Kurlan R. "Levodopa phobia": A new iatrogenic cause of disability in Parkinson's disease. *Neurology* 2005; 64:923–924.

16. Olanow CW. Oxidation reactions in Parkinson's disease. *Neurology* 1990; 40 (Suppl 3): 32–37.

17. Fahn S, Cohen G. The oxidant stress hypothesis in Parkinson's disease: Evidence supporting it. *Ann Neurol* 1992; 32:804–812.

18. Przuntek H, Welzel D, Blumner E, et al. Bromocriptine lessens the incidence of mortality in L-dopa-treated parkinsonian patients: Prado-study discontinued. *Eur J Clin Pharmacol* 1992; 43:357–363.

19. Ahlskog JE. The evaluation and treatment of Parkinson's disease. In: Lechtenberg R, Schutta HS (eds). *Neurology Practice Guidelines*. New York: Marcel Dekker, 1998:221–266.

20. Yahr MD, Wolf A, Antunes J-L, et al. Autopsy findings in parkinsonism following treatment with levodopa. *Neurology* 1972; 22(Suppl):56–71.

21. Markham CH, Diamond SG. Long-term follow-up of early dopa treatment in Parkinson's disease. *Ann Neurol* 1986; 19:365–372.

22. Olanow CW, Hauser R, Gauger L, et al. The effect of deprenyl and levodopa on the progression of Parkinson's disease. *Ann Neurol* 1995; 38:771–777.

23. Parkinson Study Group. Levodopa and the progression of Parkinson's disease. *N Engl J Med* 2004; 351:2498–2508.

24. Quinn N, Parkes D, Janota I, Marsden CD. Preservation of the substantia nigra and locus coeruleus in a patient receiving levodopa (2 kg) plus decarboxylase inhibitor over a four-year period. *Mov Disord* 1986; 1:65–68.

25. Nygaard TG, Marsden CD, Fahn S. Dopa-responsive dystonia: Long-term treatment response and prognosis. *Neurology* 1991; 41:174–181.

26. Rajput AH, Fenton ME, Dhand A. Is levodopa toxic to nondegenerating substantia nigra cells? Clinical evidence. *Neurology* 1996; 46(Suppl):A371.

27. Riley D. Is levodopa toxic to human substantia nigra? *Mov Disord* 1998; 13:369–370.

28. Sahakian BJ, Carlson KR, De Girolami U, et al. Functional and structural consequences of long-term dietary L-dopa treatment in mice. *Commun Psychopharmacol* 1980; 4: 169–176.

29. Hefti F, Melamed E, Bhawan J, Wurtman RJ. Long-term administration of L-dopa does not damage dopaminergic neurons in the mouse. *Neurology* 1981; 31:1194–1195.

30. Cotzias GC, Miller ST, Tang LC, et al. Levodopa, fertility and longevity. *Science* 1977; 196:549–551.

31. Ahlskog JE, Uitti RJ, Low PA, et al. Levodopa and deprenyl treatment effects on peripheral indices of oxidant stress in Parkinson's disease. *Neurology* 1996; 46:796–801.

32. Braak H, Del Tredici K, Rub U, et al. Staging of brain pathology related to sporadic Parkinson's disease. *Neurobiol Aging* 2003; 24:197–211.

33. Braak H, Ghebremedhin E, Rub U, et al. Stages in the development of Parkinson's disease–related pathology. *Cell Tissue Res* 2004; 318:121–134.

34. Ahlskog JE. Challenging conventional wisdom: The etiologic role of dopamine oxidative stress in Parkinson's disease. *Mov Disord* 2005; 20:271–282.

35. Agid Y, Ahlskog E, Albanese A, et al. Levodopa in the treatment of Parkinson's disease: A consensus meeting. *Mov Disord* 1999; 14:911–913.

36. Lesser RP, Fahn S, Snider SR, et al. Analysis of the clinical problems in parkinsonism and the complications of long-term levodopa therapy. *Neurology* 1979; 29:1253–1260.

37. DeJong GJ, Meerwaldt JD, Schmitz PIM. Factors that influence the occurrence of response variations in Parkinson's disease. *Ann Neurol* 1987; 22:4–7.

38. Cedarbaum JM, Gandy SE, Mc Dowell FH. "Early" initiation of levodopa treatment does not promote the development of motor response fluctuations, dyskinesias or dementia in Parkinson's disease. *Neurology* 1991; 41:622–629.

39. Blin J, Bonnet AM, Agid Y. Does levodopa aggravate Parkinson's disease? *Neurology* 1988; 38:1410–1416.

40. Roos RAC, Vredevoogd CB, van der Velde EA. Response fluctuations in Parkinson's disease. *Neurology* 1990; 40:1344–1346.

41. Caraceni T, Scigliano G, Musicco M. The occurrence of motor fluctuations in parkinsonian patients treated long-term with levodopa: Role of early treatment and disease progression. *Neurology* 1991; 41:380–384.

42. Trabucchi M, Appollonio I, Battaini F, et al. Influence of treatment on the natural history of Parkinson's disease. In: Calne DB (ed). *Parkinsonism and Aging*. New York: Raven Press, 1989:239–254.

43. Ahlskog JE, Muenter MD. Frequency of levodopa-related dyskinesias and motor fluctuations as estimated from the cumulative literature. *Mov Disord* 2001; 16:448–458.

44. Muenter MD, Ahlskog JE. Dopa dyskinesias and fluctuations are not related to dopa treatment duration. *Ann Neurol* 2000; 48:464.

45. Poewe WH, Lees AJ, Stern GM. Low-dose l-dopa therapy in Parkinson's disease: A 6-year follow-up study. *Neurology* 1986; 36:1528–1530.

46. Rascol O, Brooks D, Korczyn AD, et al. A five-year study of the incidence of dyskinesia in patients with early Parkinson's disease who were treated with ropinirole or levodopa. *N Engl J Med* 2000; 342:1484–1491.

47. Parkinson Study Group. A randomized controlled trial comparing the agonist pramipexole with levodopa as initial dopaminergic treatment for Parkinson's disease. *JAMA* 2000; 284:1931–1938.

48. Whone AL, Watts RL, Stoessl AJ, et al. Slower progression of Parkinson's disease with ropinirole versus levodopa: The REAL-PET study. *Ann Neurol* 2003; 54:93–101.

49. Holloway RG, Shoulson I, Fahn S, et al. Pramipexole vs levodopa as initial treatment for Parkinson disease: A 4-year randomized controlled trial. *Arch Neurol* 2004; 61: 1044–1053.

50. Van Gerpen JA, Kumar N, Bower JH, et al. Levodopa dyskinesia risk among Parkinson's disease patients in Olmsted County, Minnesota, 1976–1990. *Arch Neurol* 2006; 63: 205–209.

51. Quinn N, Critchley P, Marsden CD. Young onset Parkinson's disease. *Mov Disord* 1987; 2:73–91.

52. Schrag A, Ben-Shlomo Y, Brown R, et al. Young-onset Parkinson's disease revisited: Clinical features, natural history, and mortality. *Mov Disord* 1998; 13:885–894.

53. Kumar N, Van Gerpen JA, Bower JH, Ahlskog JE. Levodopa-dyskinesia incidence by age of Parkinson's disease onset. *Mov Disord* 2005; 20:342–344.

54. Parkinson Study Group. Effect of deprenyl on the progression of disability in early Parkinson's disease. *N Engl J Med* 1989; 321:1364–1371.

55. Parkinson Study Group. Effects of tocopherol and deprenyl on the progression of disability in early Parkinson's disease. *N Engl J Med* 1993; 328:176–183.

56. Parkinson Study Group. Dopamine transporter brain imaging to assess the effects of pramipexole vs levodopa on Parkinson disease progression. *JAMA* 2002; 287: 1653–1661.

57. Ahlskog JE. Slowing Parkinson's disease progression: Recent dopamine agonist trials. *Neurology* 2003; 60:381–389.

58. Albin RL, Frey KA. Initial agonist treatment of Parkinson's disease. A critique. *Neurology* 2003; 60:390–394.

59. Ravina B, Eidelberg D, Ahlskog JE, et al. The role of radiotracer imaging in Parkinson disease. *Neurology* 2005; 64:208–215.

60. Ahlskog JE. *The Parkinson's Disease Treatment Book: Partnering with Your Doctor to Get the Most from Your Medications.* New York: Oxford University Press, 2005.

61. Koller WC, Hutton JT, Tolosa E, et al. Immediate-release and controlled-release carbidopa/levodopa in PD. *Neurology* 1999; 53:1012–1019.

62. DuPont E, Andersen A, Boas J, et al. Sustained-release Madopar HBS compared with standard Madopar in the long-term treatment of de novo parkinsonian patients. *Acta Neurol Scand* 1996; 93:14–20.

63. Yeh KC, August TF, Bush DF, et al. Pharmacokinetics and bioavailability of Sinemet CR: A summary of human studies. *Neurology* 1989; 39(Suppl 2):25–38.

64. Nutt JG, Woodward WR, Hammerstad JP, et al. The "on-off" phenomenon in Parkinson's disease: Relation to levodopa absorption and transport. *N Engl J Med* 1984; 310: 483–488.

65. Muenter MD, Tyce GM. L-dopa therapy of Parkinson's disease: Plasma L-dopa concentration, therapeutic response, and side effects. *Mayo Clin Proc* 1971; 46:231–239.

66. Quattrone A, Zappia M. Oral pulse levodopa therapy in mild Parkinson's disease. *Neurology* 1993; 43:1161–1166.

67. Koller WC, Tse W. Unmet medical needs in Parkinson's disease. *Neurology* 2004; 62 (Suppl 1):S1–S8.

68. Ahlskog JE, Muenter MD, McManis PG, et al. Controlled-release Sinemet (CR-4): A double-blind crossover study in patients with fluctuating Parkinson's disease. *Mayo Clinic Proc* 1988; 63:876–886.

69. Uitti RY, Ahlskog JE. Comparative review of dopamine receptor agonists in Parkinson's disease. *CNS Drugs* 1996; 5:369–388.

70. Pritchett AM, Morrison JF, Edwards WD, et al. Valvular heart disease in patients taking pergolide. *Mayo Clin Proc* 2002; 77:1280–1286.

71. Baseman DG, O'Suilleabhain PE, Reimold SC, et al. Pergolide use in Parkinson disease is associated with cardiac valve regurgitation. *Neurology* 2004; 63:301–304.

72. Van Camp G, Flamez A, Cosyns B, et al. Treatment of Parkinson's disease with pergolide and relation to restrictive valvular heart disease. *Lancet* 2004; 363: 1179–1183.

73. Perachon S, Schwartz JC, Sokoloff P. Functional potencies of new antiparkinsonian drugs at recombinant human dopamine D1, D2 and D3 receptors. *Eur J Pharmacol* 1999; 366:293–300.

74. Gerlach M, Double K, Arzberger T, et al. Dopamine receptor agonists in current clinical use: Comparative dopamine receptor binding profiles defined in the human striatum. *J Neural Transm* 2003; 110:1119–1127.

75. Dodd ML, Klos KJ, Bower JH, et al. Pathological gambling caused by drugs used to treat Parkinson disease. *Arch Neurol* 2005; 62:1377–1381.

76. Klos KJ, Bower JH, Josephs KA, et al. Pathological hypersexuality predominantly linked to adjuvant dopamine agonist therapy in Parkinson's disease and multiple system atrophy. *Parkinsonism Relat Disord* 2005; 11:381–386.

77. Jenner P. A novel dopamine agonist for the transdermal treatment of Parkinson's disease. *Neurology* 2005; 65(2 Suppl 1):S3–S5.

78. The Parkinson Study G. A controlled trial of rotigotine monotherapy in early Parkinson's disease. Archives of *Neurology* 2003; 60(12):1721–1728.

79. Watts RL, Jankovic J., Waters C, Rajput A, Boroojerdi B, Rao J. Randomized, blind, controlled trial of transdermal rotigotine in early Parkinson disease. *Neurology* 2007; 68:272–276.

52 Progress in Gene Therapy

Hideki Mochizuki
M. Maral Mouradian

Currently, 3 phase I clinical trials are under way utilizing recombinant adeno-associated viral vectors for the treatment of Parkinson's disease (PD). In the first trial, the candidate gene is for aromatic amino acid decarboxylase (AADC), used to enhance dopamine production. The second employs a neuroprotective strategy to deliver the gene for the neurotrophic factor neurturin, a member of the glial cell–derived neurotrophic factor (GDNF) family. And the third trial is designed to deliver the gene for glutamic acid decarboxylase (GAD), the enzyme responsible for GABA synthesis, into the subthalamic nucleus to "quiet down" the nucleus and alleviate PD symptoms. If safety is confirmed, these clinical trials could pave the way to phase II to III studies in the near future to identify their clinical efficacies. Thus, the last several years have witnessed tremendous advances in the field of gene therapy for PD, and further progress is anticipated toward making this novel strategy a therapeutic option in the foreseeable future.

PD is particularly appropriate for gene therapy since (a) the brain pathology is well characterized and degeneration of nigrostriatal dopaminergic neurons accounts for the motor symptoms; (b) animal models are available allowing preclinical testing in proof-of principle experiments; and (c) several candidate genes known to favorably impact dopaminergic neurons both in vitro and in vivo have already been cloned. In addition, the search for genetic mutations responsible for causing familial forms of PD has accelerated in recent years, with several genes or loci being identified (1–6). Thus, gene transfer has the potential to become an adjunct to or a replacement for conventional pharmacotherapy currently used for this disease.

The development of gene-based therapy for PD requires 2 primary considerations: (a) what gene should be targeted and (b) how to deliver that gene. In general, the development of a rational strategy for gene-based therapy first requires identification of the defective gene and characterization of the normal gene product. Elucidation of the functional properties of a protein is essential before a feasible plan for gene delivery can be formulated. Finally, understanding the mechanism by which the mutation alters the phenotype is crucial, particularly knowing whether it results in loss of a normal function or gain of a toxic function. In case of the latter scenario, adding a normal copy of the gene would not eliminate the defective dominant mutant phenotype. While the genes responsible for PD are being identified and their functions and pathologic effects are still being investigated, alternative gene therapy approaches currently available include augmentation of dopaminergic neurotransmission or preservation of residual nigral dopamine neurons by targeting compensatory or secondary molecular pathways. The latter approach can potentially be achieved by delivering neuroprotective or neurorestorative proteins or by blocking toxic gene products. Thus, the goal of gene therapy for PD is not limited to replacement of a defective gene responsible for the basic disease process.

METHODS OF GENE TRANSFER TO THE BRAIN

Two main approaches to gene-based therapy are being pursued for PD. The first is the in vivo approach, which involves direct introduction of a therapeutic gene into an appropriate brain region such as the striatum or substantia nigra. The second approach is ex vivo, which involves the introduction of a therapeutic gene into an appropriate cell type in culture, selection of appropriate clones, and expansion to the necessary number of cells, followed by grafting the engineered cells into the brain.

The in vivo gene transfer can be achieved by viral vectors or by plasmids, although the former method remains the most efficient. In addition, viral vectors can be designed to accommodate one or more therapeutically relevant genes and can be sufficiently attenuated to prevent destructive infection in the brain. Plasmids, which can be used either as naked DNA or with cationic liposomes, result in shorter-lived gene expression than viral vectors and are therefore generally not useful for a chronic disorder like PD.

VIRAL VECTORS

Different viral vectors have been developed for somatic gene therapy (Table 52-1). In general, they are designed to be devoid of their cytopathogenic genes, which are replaced by the therapeutic gene(s). Many of these vectors have been used in experimental gene transfer studies in animal models of PD (7–10). These vectors vary with respect to their physical and biological characteristics as well as their tropism to the different cellular populations of the brain. Consequently these properties dictate the suitability of each vector system for in vivo vs. ex vivo gene transfer methods.

Viral vectors that can be used for gene transfer to the brain should be neuronotropic such as those derived from herpes simplex virus type 1, adenovirus, adeno-associated virus or lentivirus. Although retroviruses generally require replicating cells for their life cycle, a lentiviral vector based on the human immunodeficiency virus-1 capable of infecting striatal and cerebellar neurons in vitro and expressing the transgene in adult rats holds considerable promise (11, 12).

Herpes simplex virus type I (HSV-1) is a large neuronotropic virus that can infect a wide range of host cells and establishes indefinite latency within neurons. HSV-1–based vectors have been used in a variety of experimental systems (13). Two different techniques of exploiting HSV-1 have been developed: (a) recombinant HSV-1 with various deletions that render the virus replication defective and (b) HSV-1 amplicon based on plasmids containing transgenes with minimal HSV-1 sequences. Such plasmids are transfected into a complementing cell line along with a helper virus for packaging. The term "amplicon" refers to the fact that multiple repeats of the plasmid are packaged, allowing the delivery of several copies of the transgene into a single cell and hence amplifying the signal.

Although HSV-1-based vectors were the first successfully used vectors to introduce transgenes into postmitotic neurons, these vectors have many disadvantages, including the possible reversion from mutant to wild-type HSV-1, resulting in lytic encephalitis. Since a high percentage of people have latent HSV-1 residing in

TABLE 52-1
Viral Vectors for Gene Therapy

VIRUS	INTEGRATION IN HOST GENOME	TARGET CELLS	ADVANTAGES	DISADVANTAGES
HSV-1	No	Neurons	Large insert size, latency	Cytotoxic
Adenovirus	No	Glia > Neurons	High titer, efficient	Immunogenic
AAV	Ch 19, some episomal	Neurons > Glia	Nonpathogenic	Low titer
Retrovirus	Random integration	Dividing cells only	Most experience	For ex vivo gene transfer only
Lentivirus	Random Integration	Dividing and nondividing, neurons	Low immune reaction	No packaging cell line, concerns about HIV virus

the trigeminal ganglion, the theoretical possibility exists for a recombination event between latent HSV-1 and the engineered vector, resulting in lytic infection or reactivation of latent HSV-1 in the CNS. A number of studies also reported cytotoxicity associated with several HSV-1 vectors. Such cytotoxicity may be partly due to the fact that these defective vectors require the presence of a helper virus to provide the missing proteins needed to generate a virus stock. However, attempts have been made to attenuate these risks. Newer-generation vectors with multiple deletions to reduce the risk for neurovirulence and cytotoxicity (14–16) as well as an amplicon vector free of helper virus have been developed (17).

In clinical trials, direct injection of replication-competent HSV into brain tumors of patients has proven safe. Following a pilot clinical study of combined IL-2/HSV-TK gene therapy for recurrent glioblastoma multiforme, Colombo et al. (18) extended the protocol to a larger population of patients and confirmed the safety, feasibility, and biological activity of this treatment. This suggests that an HSV-1–based vector can be a candidate gene therapy vehicle for PD as well (19, 20).

Adenovirus is the common cold virus, which is considered a candidate for in vivo gene transfer in the brain due to its high-titer virus stocks, efficient infection of postmitotic neuronal cells, and the relatively benign course of its infection (21, 22). The adenoviral genome stays episomal (i.e., it is not integrated in host chromosomal DNA), which makes it less than ideal for long-term expression of transgenes. The predominant cell type in the brain that is infected with adenovirus vector appears to be the astrocyte (23). However, the main shortcoming of adenoviral vectors is their tendency to elicit an intense immune reaction from the host, associated with inflammation and gliosis. Thus, current adenovirus vectors are useful for short-term experimental studies but do not appear to be practical for long-term treatment. Attempts are under way to develop vectors with reduced immunogenicity and toxicity. Sadly, patient Jesse Gelsinger died in 1999 while participating in a clinical trial to treat ornithine transcarbamylase deficiency, a rare metabolic disease, using an adenovirus vector. His death galvanized support for greater regulatory oversight of the clinical trial enrollment process (24).

AAV is a nonpathogenic parvovirus that requires a helper virus such as adenovirus or HSV-1 for productive infection. It can infect both dividing and nondividing cells. AAV-derived vectors offer several advantages, including the fact that most of the wild-type viral genome is deleted and therefore has minimal deleterious consequences. AAV vectors that are entirely free of helper viruses and do not encode any viral proteins are currently available. This is a significant improvement over other viral vectors such as HSV-1 and adenovirus, which retain the ability to synthesize viral proteins. Thus the main advantage of AAV-based vectors is the apparent absence of significant cytotoxicity. In addition, AAV integrates into a specific site on chromosome 19, permitting increased DNA stability and prolonged expression time (25). Minor disadvantages include significantly lower viral titers than those obtained with adenovirus and the small insert size, which is generally not an issue for most currently known candidate therapeutic genes for PD. Importantly, the restricted tissue tropism of AAV and its low transduction efficiency have limited its further development as vector. Recent studies using vectors derived from alternative AAV serotypes—such as AAV1, 4, 5, and 6—have shown improved potency and broadened tropism of the AAV vector by packaging the same vector genome with different AAV capsids (26).

To date, more than 25 patients with PD have been reported worldwide to have received gene therapy with this vector. No side effects have been reported, but vigilance for possible adverse effects as a result of long-term transgene expression as well as the AAV vector itself is paramount.

Retroviruses are RNA viruses that require dividing cells for their reverse transcription and integration into host chromosomal DNA. Disabled Moloney murine leukemia viruses have been widely used for ex vivo gene transfer for many years. The main advantages include high infection rates and transgene expression as well as availability of packaging cell lines. Neuronal progenitor cells are particularly suited as the target population for ex vivo gene therapy and cellular therapy in PD. Efficient genetic modification of neuronal progenitor cells with retroviral vectors has yet to be achieved because of several problems inherent to current retroviral technology. One of these is the low transduction efficiency of neuronal progenitor cells with current retroviral vectors, most of which carry the Moloney murine leukemia virus–derived long terminal repeat, which is very susceptible to "shutting off/silencing" in immature cells such as embryonic stem (ES) cells or hematopoietic stem cells. Fetal bovine serum, which is a common component of the virus supernatant, is also a critical problem because it induces neuronal progenitor cells to differentiate into mature neurons and glial cells during the transduction procedure. To overcome these problems, a new retrovirus production system has been established in which the simplified retroviral vector engineered to be resistant to de novo methylation is packaged in the vesicular stomatitis virus G protein as a pseudotyped retrovirus production system (27). This virus can be concentrated to high titers, thereby permitting the use of much higher values of multiplicity of infection than had been possible previously. This allows the transgene to be easily introduced and traced in neuronal stem cells by removing fetal bovine serum from the virus supernatant (28, 29).

Lentiviruses, unlike other retroviruses, can infect nondividing cells such as neurons. A vector based on the human immunodeficiency virus has been shown to transduce nonproliferating adult neurons in vitro (11) and in vivo (12). Transgene expression is maintained over several months without appreciable decline, and no obvious pathogenic changes or immune responses have been detected.

To regulate transgene expression, an improved regulatable lentivirus vector has been generated, which is composed of a self-inactivating lentivirus vector–bearing inducible tet-responsive promoter elements (30). Inducible systems that allow the control of gene expression in mammalian cells are versatile tools for conditional gene expression and knockdown (31). Since human immunodeficiency virus interferes with host cell division, the development of packaged cell lines that can facilitate vector generation has been somewhat hampered.

CELL VEHICLES FOR EX VIVO GENE TRANSFER FOR PARKINSON'S DISEASE

Ex vivo engineering of cells containing cDNAs encoding candidate therapeutic proteins is also being explored in PD models. Several cell culture types have been used in preclinical studies to assess their suitability for engineering and subsequent transplantation into the brain to deliver secreted molecules (Table 52-2). Early studies that used cell lines (e.g., fibroblasts, Schwann cells, myoblasts, neuroblastoma, glioma and neuroendocrine cells) reported varying degrees of success and reproducibility (32, 33). Not surprisingly, such cells were quickly abandoned for gene transfer applications because they generally either form large expanding tumors or are killed by host immune defense mechanisms.

TABLE 52-2

Cell Types for Ex Vivo Gene Therapy in Animal Models of Parkinson's Disease

---

Fibroblasts
Myoblasts
Astrocytes
Schwann cells
Transformed cell lines
Carotid body
Bone marrow stromal cells
Neural progenitor cells
Embryonic stem cells
Olfactory ensheathing glial cells
Encapsulated cells
Human retinal pigment epithelial cells attached to
     gelatin microcarriers

The possibility of tumor formation as a result of grafting free-floating cell lines is a major source of concern. This situation has stimulated the development of encapsulated cell technology. A macroporous gelatin microcarrier system, which provides interior surfaces for cell attachment to protect cells from shear forces, is one of the candidates for ex vivo transplantation. Because such microcarriers are made of gelatin, which is derived from collagen, cells attach and grow in an environment that simulates the in vivo environment more closely than other carriers can. Indeed, implants of human retinal pigment epithelial cells attached to gelatin microcarriers appear to be safe and well tolerated and have been reported to improve motor symptoms in animal models and in a pilot study in PD patients (34, 35). Furthermore, human retinal pigment epithelial cells produce levodopa and can be isolated from postmortem human eye tissue, grown in culture, and implanted into the brain attached to microcarriers. Modification of this approach could be useful for other ex vivo gene therapy for PD.

Another means of circumventing the limitations of grafted cell lines is the application of molecular techniques of conditional immortalization using nontransforming oncogenes such as the temperature-sensitive allele of the SV40 large tumor antigen. This manipulation allows cell growth at low permissive temperatures (around 33°C) in culture but not at the body temperature of 37°C. Immortalization of rat fetal mesencephalic neurons by using this method has been tested in 6-hydroxydopamine (6-OHDA)–lesioned rats, demonstrating behavioral recovery without immune rejection or tumor formation (36). Delivery of the tyrosine hydroxylase (TH) cDNA using such cells increased L-dopa production in rodent and nonhuman primate models of PD (37). Alternatively, the use of cell lines that differentiate into neurons under appropriate conditions has also been tried. For example, PC12 cells engineered with nerve growth factor under the control of the zinc-inducible metallothionein promoter differentiate into neurons when grafted in the rat striatum (38).

The idea of an autologous source of cells that are easily obtained from the patient and readily transduced by therapeutic genes in vitro has stimulated the use of primary skin fibroblasts as vehicles for gene transfer (39–41). However, survival of these cells in the brain is not predictable. In addition, instead of integrating with host brain circuitry, they tend to displace the brain parenchyma by forming a globular clump of cells, which itself can disrupt rotational behavior in rodents (40). Astrocytes have also been tested owing to their natural supportive role in the brain, their efficient secretory mechanisms, their transducibility in vitro, and their tendency to migrate from the graft site, thus minimizing mass effect (42, 43). Furthermore, astrocytes potentially represent autologous source of cell vehicles (44). Immature astrocytes from rat brain transduced with TH cDNA and transplanted in the striatum of 6-OHDA–lesioned rats have been reported to survive and migrate. Although only few grafted cells expressed TH in vivo, some behavioral recovery was observed (45).

Astrocytes have also been used as cografts with embryonic ventral mesencephalic neuronal grafts, but results have been variable depending on the age of astrocytes used and whether they expressed recombinant bioactive brain-derived neurotrophic factor (BDNF) (46). An immortalized human fetal astrocyte cell line expressing TH injected in the striatum of 6-OHDA–lesioned rats reportedly resulted in behavioral recovery but poor graft survival (47). Lentivirus is a good tool for long-term transgene expression in astrocytes. Genetically modified astrocytes expressing GDNF by lentivirus vector provided neuroprotection in a rat model of PD following transplantation to the substantia nigra (48).

The bone marrow, including its stromal cells, exhibits multiple traits of a stem cell population with potential use as an autologous source (49, 50). Marrow stromal cells can be greatly expanded in vitro and induced to differentiate into multiple mesenchymal cell types such as bone, cartilage, myocytes, and hepatocytes as well as glial cells after transplantation (51, 52). In addition, human and mouse bone marrow stromal cells can be induced to differentiate into neural cells under experimental cell culture conditions (53). This suggests that a population of neuronal cells can be generated from bone marrow stromal cells and potentially used for neuroreconstructive purposes. Marrow cells can also seed the brain in vivo and reside in the parenchyma as astrocytes, microglia, and even neurons (54, 55). Further, marrow-derived astrocytes tend to home in to the site of brain injury, as with stroke (56). These properties of marrow-derived brain cells have been exploited to deliver the GDNF cDNA in the mouse MPTP model with evidence of neuroprotection (57).

The ideal cells for CNS somatic gene therapy would be of CNS origin with many neuronal features such as storage mechanisms, secretory pathways, second messengers and signal transduction pathways. Neural progenitor cells that could potentially develop these features have been isolated from fetal and adult brains, particularly from regions that undergo neurogenesis, such as the subventricular zone, the olfactory system, and the hippocampus (58). However, progenitor cells transplanted in the brain differentiate predominantly into the glial phenotype (58, 59).

Some genetically modified progenitor cells exhibit enhanced differentiation to dopaminergic neurons. For example, progenitor cells with the transduced von Hippel–Lindau gene efficiently differentiate into TH-positive neurons both in vitro and in vivo (60). This approach has the potential to produce universal donor cells with many of the desirable neuronal features. Among the different cell types tested experimentally, neural progenitors derived from embryonic mesencephalic cultures hold the best potential (61–65).

ES cells provide a potentially unlimited source of specialized cells for regenerative medicine. A high proportion of dopamine-producing TH-positive neurons are obtained from ES cells treated with stromal cell-derived inducing activity (66). Several studies demonstrated that transplanted ES cells can develop spontaneously into dopaminergic neurons. Transplantation of such dopaminergic neurons restored cerebral function and behavior in an animal model of PD (67, 68). Recent advances in coculture conditions allow rapid and efficient derivation of most central nervous system (CNS) phenotypes from ES cells (69). The effect of transplantation of dopaminergic neurons generated from monkey ES cells into 1-methyl-4-phenyl-1, 2, 3, 6-tetrahydropyridine-treated (MPTP)–treated monkeys was also examined. Behavioral and functional imaging studies revealed that the transplanted cells functioned as dopaminergic neurons and attenuated MPTP-induced neurologic symptoms (70).

The olfactory bulb is a structure of the CNS in which axonal growth occurs throughout the lifetime of the organism. A major difference between the olfactory bulb and the remaining CNS is the presence of ensheathing glia in the first 2 layers of the olfactory bulb. Olfactory ensheathing glia display properties suggestive of involvement in the process of regeneration, and they appear to be responsible for the permissibility of the adult olfactory bulb to axonal growth. In fact, olfactory ensheathing cells transplanted to the site of a spinal cord injury can promote axonal sparing/regeneration and functional recovery (71). Olfactory ensheathing cells are also a good candidate for an autologous source of cells for ex vivo transplantation for PD (72). Whether the mechanism(s) that kills nigral neurons in PD also affect the survival of transplanted cells remains unknown, and no evidence is available to address this issue. Overall, the outlook is optimistic, but important aspects still need to be worked out (73).

CANDIDATE THERAPEUTIC GENES FOR PARKINSON'S DISEASE

Two categories of candidate therapeutic genes are being considered for gene transfer studies in experimental parkinsonism. First, symptomatic molecules that relieve the phenotypic manifestations of the disorder, such as dopamine biosynthetic enzymes, without substantially influencing the underlying neurodegeneration. Second, restorative molecules that have the potential to retard the neurodegenerative process by one or more mechanisms (Table 52-3).

TABLE 52-3
Categories of Candidate Therapeutic Genes for Parkinson's Disease

Symptomatic
　Transmitter enzymes: TH, GTP-CH1, AADC
　Gene for inhibition of overactive neurons: GAD

Restorative
　Neurotrophic factors: GDNF, BDNF
　Antiapoptotic molecules: *bcl-2*, Apaf-1 dominant
　　negative inhibitor, X-chromosome-linked inhibitor
　Free radical scavengers: Cu/Zn SOD
　Anti-alpha-synuclein toxicity: heat-shock protein 70
　　(Hsp) 70, beta-synuclein, inhibitor of transglutamin-
　　ase, rybozime, RNAi of alpha-synuclein,
　　alpha-synuclein antibody

Replacement
PARK 2: parkin
PARK 6: PINK1
PARK 7: DJ-1

Symptomatic Gene Products

Since TH is the rate-limiting enzyme in dopamine biosynthesis, attempts to deliver the cDNA encoding this protein have been a focus of intense investigation (8). One method of delivering the TH cDNA into the striatum is transplantation of a tissue that endogenously expresses TH. The latter, in fact, has been one of the rationales for transplantation of human fetal mesencephalic tissue. However, due to the limitations of this approach, a more direct method for delivery of TH cDNA to the parkinsonian brain would be desirable. Carotid body autotransplants were also used in animal models of PD, with reportedly favorable results (74–76). A pilot clinical study indicates that carotid body autograft transplantation is a relatively simple, safe, and viable therapeutic approach for the treatment of patients with advanced disease (76).

Methods to deliver TH cDNA in animal models of PD initially used cell lines such as AtT-20 and NIH3T3, but subsequently primary cells such as fibroblasts, myoblasts, astrocytes, and Schwann cells were used in ex vivo gene transfer studies (33, 40, 45). Immortalized cell lines generated from embryonic mesencephalic cultures have been also utilized for the delivery of TH into the striatum of PD models (37). In addition, direct in vivo TH gene transfer has been tried with plasmid DNA using lipofectin (77–79). Several viral vectors have been used in proof-of-principle experiments to deliver the TH cDNA in the rat 6-OHDA model of PD. An HSV-1 based amplicon vector expressing TH in the striatum of lesioned rats has resulted in behavioral recovery over a period of

1 year (80). However, about 10% of the animals in that study died with evidence of HSV-1–mediated cytopathic effects, presumably due to the presence of helper virus or the production of cytotoxic or immunogenic viral proteins. In addition, reduction of TH expression was observed over time, perhaps due to downregulation of the viral promoter in the vector. TH cDNA has also been delivered using AAV to the rat striatum (81). Although most infected cells were neurons, transgene expression declined over 4 months and rotational recovery was reported for only 2 months. However, a 1-year-long expression of transgene was confirmed by the multiple administrations of either identical (readministration) or different (cross-administration) serotype-based AAV vectors (82). An adenovirus vector expressing TH resulted in functional recovery, but only for a short time, mainly due to the known short-lived expression of this vector (83). Interestingly, even TH expressed in glial cells under the influence of the glial fibrillary acidic protein promoter resulted in behavioral recovery in this model (79).

Another dopamine biosynthetic enzyme is aromatic amino acid decarboxylase (AADC), which converts L-dopa to dopamine. However, the importance of AADC in vivo is not clinically evident, since L-dopa is decarboxylated effectively in the brains of parkinsonian patients despite the loss of the majority of their dopaminergic neurons. Presumably, the required AADC function is provided by nondopaminergic cells such as glia, serotoninergic cells, or vascular endothelial cells. Coadministration of 2 separate AAV vectors for TH and for AADC in the striatum of rats resulted in more efficient dopamine production and behavioral recovery than TH alone (84). Furthermore, in nonhuman primates that were rendered parkinsonian by MPTP administration, TH and AADC delivery in the striatum resulted in TH-positive cells and biochemical but no consistent behavioral improvement (85). However, some reports also suggest a detrimental effect of AADC on dopamine production, perhaps due to endproduct inhibition of TH (86). This effect might be cell type–specific, perhaps seen in nonneuronal cells such as fibroblasts, which cannot sequester dopamine into synaptic vesicles, thus allowing it to interact with and inhibit cytoplasmic TH. To circumvent the problem of end-product inhibition, constructs having a truncation of the N-terminal regulatory domain of TH, leaving only its catalytic domain, have been developed (87).

TH is also critically dependent on the cofactor tetrahydrobiopterin (BH4) for its activity. The importance of BH4 has been demonstrated in fibroblast cell lines that do not produce sufficient amounts of BH4 to permit production of L-dopa in vitro or in vivo (88). The addition of BH4 to these cells is necessary for L-dopa synthesis and behavioral recovery. Thus, BH4 must be either supplemented exogenously or by coexpression of guanine 5′-triphosphate cyclohydrolase (GTP-CH1), the rate-limiting enzyme in BH4 production. The expression of both TH and GTP-CH1 in fibroblasts grafted in denervated striata is reportedly required for detectable basal L-dopa levels (40). In vivo microdialysis studies following gene transfer with AAV have shown that TH alone is not enough for L-dopa production and that GTH-CH1 is required in the absence of exogenous BH4 (89). Thus, the role of GTH-CH1 appears to apply to both in vivo and ex vivo gene transfer.

A phase I/II clinical trial (http://www.nwpf.org/articles.asp?id=1370) of an AAV vector (AV201) containing the AADC cDNA was initiated at the University of California San Francisco and the Lawrence Berkeley National Laboratory in late 2004 (90). The vector is delivered directly to the striatum of patients with advanced PD with the expectation that they would respond more readily to levodopa, since enhanced AADC expression should improve dopamine synthesis at the site of its action. The results from positron emission tomography (PET) brain scans of a few patients obtained 6 months after AV201 infusion reportedly revealed increased activity of AADC in the targeted area of the brain, compared with the patients' pre-treatment PET scans. After clearance of safety issues, a phase II/III clinical trial is planned to detect the efficacy of this gene therapy approach for advanced PD.

Genes for the Inhibition of Overactive Neurons

Glutamic Acid Decarboxylase. Many of the manifestations of PD are believed to be due to the downstream disinhibition of the subthalamic nucleus (STN), leading to pathologic excitation of its target nuclei, the internal segment of the globus pallidus and substantia nigra pars reticulata. Silencing the excitatory glutamatergic neurons of the STN by overexpressing GAD, the enzyme that catalyzes the synthesis of the inhibitory neurotransmitter GABA, by using an AAV vector is another gene therapy approach being examined for PD (91). In the rat model, neurons transduced with such a vector produce mixed inhibitory responses associated with GABA release. The same intervention appears to be neuroprotective against 6-OHDA–induced degeneration of dopaminergic neurons (92).

In the first FDA-approved clinical trial to test gene therapy in PD, (http://www.eurekalert.org/pub_releases/2005-09/bm-nap092305.php), an AAV vector carrying the human GAD cDNA was infused in the STN of patients with advanced disease. This open-label phase I study was carried out at the Weill Medical College of Cornell University. Interim results announced in 2005 were positive with respect to safety and efficacy in the 12-patient cohort. The treatment was safe and well tolerated, with no evidence of adverse effects or immunologic reaction to the

virus. Clinical assessments at 1 year revealed a statistically significant 27% improvement in motor function (measured by the UPDRS) on the side of the body that correlated with the treated side of the brain. In contrast, the untreated side showed no significant improvement. Activities of daily living also showed a trend toward improvement. Furthermore, fluorodeoxyglucose-PET scans obtained at 1 year revealed that the treated side of the brain exhibited a statistically significant decline in abnormal metabolism while the untreated side showed a further increase in abnormal metabolism. These encouraging results need confirmation with a more vigorous trial design.

Neurorestorative Genes

Since L-dopa associated motor response complications arise in the context of severe neuronal loss in the substantia nigra, preservation of these dopaminergic neurons would be the optimal strategy for preventing the development of late complications and minimizing disease severity as well. Thus, the delivery of transgenes that enhance the survival of these cells should accomplish both objectives. At present, candidate genes include those that encode neurotrophic or antiapoptotic factors or genes that reduce oxidative stress.

Because neurotrophic factors cannot cross the blood brain barrier, and because of problems associated with intracerebroventricular delivery of proteins, gene transfer approaches have been attempted in animal models of PD. To date, GDNF family proteins and BDNF have been examined for this purpose (93, 94). GDNF delivered *in vivo* with an adenoviral vector into the rat substantia nigra (95) or striatum (96, 97) protected against subsequent 6-OHDA lesions. A similar approach of delivering GDNF also restored neural function even in rats with established 6-OHDA lesions (98). Adenovirus vector mediated GDNF delivery was also effective in a mouse MPTP model (99). In addition, an AAV vector was used to deliver the GDNF cDNA to the rat substantia nigra and resulted in functional recovery (100).

Neurturin is a member of the same protein family as GDNF and they have similar pharmacological properties. Neurturin exerts potent actions on the survival and function of midbrain dopaminergic neurons (101, 102), and provides efficient neuroprotection of lesioned nigral dopaminergic neurons, similar to GDNF, using an *in vivo* gene therapy approach (103).

In September 2005, a phase I clinical trial to deliver neurturin cDNA via an AAV type 2 vector (CERE-120) for PD was announced (http://www.ceregene.com/news-pr.html). The goal of this study was to determine the safety and efficacy of this approach using standardized clinical assessments and brain imaging (104). Primary outcomes of the study design, safety and tolerability, were successfully met. This study including 12 patients showed a clinical improvement of 40% in the UPDRS motor off score compared to baseline by 9 months. In September 2006, plans for a phase II randomized, double-blind, sham surgery-controlled study (CERE-120) for PD was announced. The design of this study calls for approximately 34 participants to receive CERE-120 and approximately 17 participants to receive sham surgery. Participants in this trial will be followed for one year after the neurosurgical procedure.

Gene Replacement Therapy for Familial Parkinson's Disease

About 15% of patients with PD have an inherited form of the disease. Several causal genes for familial PD have been identified in recent years (1–6). Early development efforts in gene therapy in the 1980s targeted uncommon single-gene disorders using wild-type gene replacement of the defective gene. In PD, 3 genes have been identified to cause autosomal recessive disease. These are mutations in *parkin* (PARK2) (2), *PINK1* (PARK6) (4), and *DJ-1* (PARK7) (5). Loss of function of a single gene product can lead to the degeneration of dopaminergic neurons and clinical manifestations of parkinsonism. Thus, the mechanism of cell death in the substantia nigra in these families is the loss of function of these candidate genes. Normal wild-type gene replacement therapy for PD patients with these mutations should be ideal for protection against cell death. In familial disease, *parkin* mutations are the most common cause of autosomal recessive early-onset parkinsonism, including the autosomal recessive juvenile disease. The frequency of the mutation is estimated at 50% in families with autosomal recessive early-onset parkinsonism. The Parkin protein functions as a ubiquitin ligase targeting specific proteins for degradation (105).

Since *parkin*-associated PD is recessively inherited—that is, loss of function of parkin leads to the development of *parkin*-associated PD—substrates for Parkin (for its E3 function) would be expected to accumulate in the brain. Therefore Parkin replacement therapy for such patients should decrease the toxicity of these substrates. Studies of parkin-null mice should define the effect of Parkin replacement using a viral vector for PARK2.

Other in vitro studies have shown that parkin exhibits cytoprotective effects against the toxic effects of α-synuclein overexpression (106). Alpha-synuclein is present in Lewy bodies, the pathologic hallmark of PD, and point mutations in the α-synuclein gene (PARK1) and triplication of the wild-type α-synuclein locus (PARK4) can be pathogenetic in rare cases of dominantly inherited PD (107). Two studies have reported that parkin gene therapy using viral vectors is effective against α-synucleinopathy, suggesting its potential suitability for patients with sporadic PD as well (108, 109).

DJ-1 (PARK7) has been identified as another causative autosomal recessive gene for PD. While the mechanism of action of DJ1 is unknown, it has been found to be associated with oncogenic mechanisms, control of gene transcription, regulation of mRNA stability, and a sensor of oxidative stress (5). DJ-1 null mice show hypolocomotion when subjected to amphetamine challenge and increased susceptibility to MPTP. With regard to replacement gene therapy for PARK7 patients, restoration of DJ-1 expression in DJ-1 null mice or cells via adenoviral vector delivery mitigated all phenotypes. The same group of investigators found that wild-type mice receiving adenoviral delivery of DJ-1 resisted MPTP-induced striatal damage and that neurons overexpressing DJ-1 were protected from oxidative stress in vitro (110). Thus DJ-1 gene therapy could potentially have a rescue effect against cell death of nigral dopaminergic neurons in patients with sporadic PD.

PINK1, which is the causative gene for PARK6, is also responsible for a recessive form of PD (4). Most mutations have been reported to cluster in or around the putative kinase domain of this protein, suggesting that loss of PINK1 kinase activity may cause the disease. PINK1 reduces basal neuronal proapoptotic activity and protects neurons from staurosporine-induced apoptosis (111). Thus, PINK1 gene therapy may also be useful not only for PARK6 patients as a replacement therapy but as protective therapy for sporadic PD.

Other Neuroprotective Genes

Several potential cascades culminating in dopaminergic cell death in the substantia nigra have been described. Inhibiting such a cascade is one of the options for gene therapy in PD. One of these pathways is triggered by cytochrome c released from mitochondria, which promotes the activation of caspase-9 through apoptotic protease activating factor-1 (Apaf-1). A recent study demonstrated that an AAV-derived Apaf-1 dominant negative inhibitor (as an antiapoptotic gene therapy) prevented MPTP toxicity (112). In another study, adenoviral gene transfer of a protein caspase inhibitor, X-chromosome-linked inhibitor of apoptosis, also prevented MPTP-induced cell death of dopaminergic neurons in the substantia nigra pars compacta of mice (113). A major issue in antiapoptotic gene therapy is the potential adverse effect of oncogenesis. Thus, transient expression of antiapoptotic molecules may be a better strategy than long-term expression.

Fibrillization and aggregation of α-synuclein may play a critical role in PD. The chaperone heat-shock protein 70 (Hsp70) strongly inhibits α-synuclein fibril formation via preferential binding to prefibrillar species (114). Several compounds can suppress the toxicity of α-synuclein, such as β-synuclein, inhibitors of tissue transglutaminase (115), rybozime, RNAi of α-synuclein

(116), and α-synuclein antibody (117). Some of these are also candidate genes suitable for neuroprotective gene therapy for PD.

Reactive oxygen species are implicated in the pathogenesis of PD. The antioxidant enzyme glutathione peroxidase has neuroprotective potential. A viral vector carrying the human glutathione peroxidase-1 gene was reported to provide protection against 6-OHDA–induced neurotoxicity of dopaminergic neurons in the substantia nigra pars compacta of rats (118). This indicates that antioxidative gene therapy strategies may be relevant.

DEALING WITH PROBLEMS RELATED TO GENE THERAPY

Different aspects of gene therapy should be addressed and important practical problems overcome, particularly those related to oncogenesis and immunologic rejection before this strategy becomes commonplace.

Gene therapy research faces various ethical issues and controversies that need to be carefully managed. Of special note, the use of human embryonic stem cells is surrounded by a number of ethical controversies, the extent of which is partly dependent on their source. The availability of any eventual embryonic stem cell therapies will likely pose a dilemma for those countries and people that have declared stem cell research to be unacceptable. The second ethical problem is the risk of sham surgery in a double-blind gene therapy trial. A placebo-controlled study is the gold standard for evaluating new therapies including gene therapy. The question whether surgery to deliver an empty viral vector is safe enough to be used as a comparison group for evaluating surgical gene therapy for PD is debatable. A few studies involving PD patients have examined the risk of sham surgery in clinical trials (119, 120). While placebo surgeries were generally safe and well tolerated, the number of subjects who received these procedures was small (119). One of these studies demonstrated that half of the researchers believed that an unblinded control efficacy trial would be unethical because it might lead to a falsely positive result (120). This brings up another problem: the placebo effect of surgery in uncontrolled trials. For example, this was shown for GDNF intrastriatal infusion therapy; the negative results of a placebo-controlled randomized trial contradicted the impressive results of a previous open-label uncontrolled trial (121). The placebo effect is a psychobiological phenomenon that can be attributed to different mechanisms, including expectation of clinical improvement and Pavlovian conditioning. A PET study using the ability of endogenous dopamine to compete for [¹¹C]raclopride binding demonstrated substantial dopamine release in response to placebo in PD patients (122). The strong placebo responses in PD patients who are implanted with electrodes for deep brain stimulation have been exploited recently by recording from single neurons after placebo treatment. These studies showed that placebo treatment reduced the activity of single neurons in the subthalamic nucleus in placebo-responsive patients (123). Thus, there is a need to monitor the placebo effect in any gene therapy protocol designed for patients with PD.

In conclusion, judging from the phenomenal advances in experimental gene therapy for PD in the past few years, the future looks more promising than ever barring unforeseen hurdles in the early clinical trials.

References

1. Polymeropoulos MH, Lavedan C, Leroy E, et al. Mutation in the α-synuclein gene identified in families with Parkinson's disease. *Science* 1997; 276:2045–2047.
2. Kitada T, Asakawa S, Hattori H, et al. Mutations in the Parkin gene cause autosomal recessive juvenile parkinsonism. *Nature* 1998; 392:605–608.
3. Leroy E, Boyer R, Auburger G, et al. The ubiquitin pathway in Parkinson's disease. *Nature* 1998; 395(6701):451–452.
4. Valente EM, Abou-Sleiman PM, Caputo V, et al. Hereditary early-onset Parkinson's disease caused by mutations in PINK1. *Science* 2004; 304(5674):1158–1160.
5. Bonifati V, Rizzu P, van Baren MJ, et al. Mutations in the DJ-1 gene associated with autosomal recessive early-onset parkinsonism. *Science* 2003; 299(5604):256–259.
6. Zimprich A, Biskup S, Leitner P, et al. Mutations in LRRK2 cause autosomal-dominant parkinsonism with pleomorphic pathology. *Neuron* 2004; 44(4):601–607.
7. Mouradian MM, Chase TN. Gene therapy of Parkinson's disease: An approach to the prevention or palliation of levodopa-associated motor complications. *Exp Neurol* 1997; 144:51–57.
8. Mouradian MM, Chase TN. Gene therapy for Parkinson's disease: Current knowledge and future perspective. *Gene Ther* 1997; 4:504–506.
9. Mochizuki H, Mizuno Y. Gene therapy for Parkinson's disease. *J Neural Transm Suppl* 2003; (65):205–213.
10. Freese A, Stern M, Kaplitt MG, et al. Prospects for gene therapy in Parkinson's disease. *Mov Disord* 1996; 11:469–488.
11. Mochizuki H, Schwartz JP, Tanaka K, et al. High-titer human immunodeficiency virus type 1-based vector systems for gene delivery into nondividing cells. *J Virol* 1998; 72:8873–8883.
12. Naldini L, Blomer U, Gallay P, et al. In vivo gene delivery and stable transduction of nondividing cells by a lentivirus vector. *Science* 1996; 272:263–267.
13. Kennedy PG. Potential use of herpes simplex virus (HSV) vectors for gene therapy of neurological disorders. *Brain* 1997; 120:1245–1259.
14. Glorioso JC, DeLuca NA, Fink DJ. Development and application of herpes simplex virus vectors for human gene therapy. *Annu Rev Microbiol* 1995; 49:675–710.
15. Marconi P, Krisky D, Oligino T, et al. Replication-defective herpes simplex virus vectors for gene transfer in vivo. *Proc Natl Acad Sci USA* 1996; 93:11319–11320.
16. Fink DJ, Poliani PL, Oligino T, et al. Development of an HSV-based vector for the treatment of Parkinson's disease. *Exp Neurol* 1997; 144:103–112.
17. Geller AI, Yu L, Wang Y, Fraefel C. Helper virus–free herpes simplex virus-1 plasmid vectors for gene therapy of Parkinson's disease and other neurological disorders. *Exp Neurol* 1997; 144:98–102.
18. Colombo F, Barzon L, Franchin E, et al. Combined HSV-TK/IL-2 gene therapy in patients with recurrent glioblastoma multiforme: Biological and clinical results. *Cancer Gene Ther* 2005; 12(10):835–848.
19. Sun M, Kong L, Wang X, et al. Comparison of the capability of GDNF, BDNF, or both, to protect nigrostriatal neurons in a rat model of Parkinson's disease. *Brain Res* 2005; 1052(2):119–129.
20. Fink DJ, Glorioso J, Mata M. Therapeutic gene transfer with herpes-based vectors: Studies in Parkinson's disease and motor nerve regeneration. *Exp Neurol* 2003; 184(Suppl 1): S19–S24.
21. Horellou P, Bilang-Bleuel A, Mallet J. In vivo adenovirus-mediated gene transfer for Parkinson's disease. *Neurobiol Dis* 1997; 4:280–287.
22. Barkats M, Bilang-Bleuel A, Buc-Caron MH, et al. Adenovirus in the brain: Recent advances of gene therapy for neurodegenerative diseases. *Prog Neurobiol* 1998; 55: 333–341.
23. Horellou P, Vigne E, Castel M-N, et al. Direct intracerebral gene transfer of an adenoviral vector expressing tyrosine hydroxylase in a rat model of Parkinson's disease. *NeuroReport* 1994; 6:49–53.
24. Somia N, Verma IM. Gene therapy: Trials and tribulations. *Nat Rev Genet* 2000; 1(2):91–99.

25. Linden RM, Ward P, Giraud C, et al. Site-specific integration by adeno-associated virus. *Proc Natl Acad Sci USA* 1996; 93:11288–11294.

26. Gao G, Vandenberghe LH, Wilson JM. New recombinant serotypes of AAV vectors. *Curr Gene Ther* 2005; 5(3):285–297.

27. Suzuki A, Obi K, Urabe T, et al. Feasibility of ex vivo gene therapy for neurological disorders using the new retroviral vector GCDNsap packaged in the vesicular stomatitis virus G protein. *J Neurochem* 2002; 82(4):953–960.

28. Yamada M, Onodera M, Mizuno Y, Mochizuki H. Neurogenesis in olfactory bulb identified by retroviral labeling in normal and 1-methyl-4-phenyl-1, 2, 3, 6-tetrahydro-pyridine-treated adult mice. *Neuroscience* 2004; 124(1):173–181.

29. Yoshimi K, Ren YR, Seki T, et al. Possibility for neurogenesis in substantia nigra of parkinsonian brain. *Ann Neurol* 2005; 58(1):31–40.

30. Pluta K, Luce MJ, Bao L, et al. Tight control of transgene expression by lentivirus vectors containing second-generation tetracycline-responsive promoters. *J Gene Med* 2005; 7:803–817.

31. Szulc J, Wiznerowicz M, Sauvain MO, et al. A versatile tool for conditional gene expression and knockdown. *Nat Methods* 2006; 3(2):109–116.

32. Freed WJ, Geller HM, Poltorak M, et al. Genetically altered and defined cell lines for transplantation in animal models of Parkinson's disease. In: Dunnett SB, Richards S-J (eds). *In Progress Brain Research*. Philadelphia: Elsevier, 1990:11–21.

33. Wolff JA, Fisher LJ, Xu L, et al. Grafting fibroblasts genetically modified to produce L-dopa in a rat model of Parkinson disease. *Proc Natl Acad Sci USA* 1989; 86:9011–9014.

34. Stover NP, Bakay RA, Subramanian T, et al. Intrastriatal implantation of human retinal pigment epithelial cells attached to microcarriers in advanced Parkinson disease. *Arch Neurol* 2005; 62(12):1833–1837.

35. Doudet DJ, Cornfeldt ML, Honey CR, et al. PET imaging of implanted human retinal pigment epithelial cells in the MPTP-induced primate model of Parkinson's disease. *Exp Neurol* 2004; 189(2):361–368.

36. Prasad KN, Clarkson ED, La Rosa FG, et al. Efficacy of grafted immortalized dopamine neurons in an animal model of parkinsonism: A review. *Mol Genet Metab* 1998; 65:1–9.

37. Anton R, Kordower JH, Maidment NT, et al. Neural-targeted gene therapy for rodent and primate hemiparkinsonism. *Exp Neurol* 1994; 127:207–218.

38. Rohrer DC, Nilaver G, Nipper V, Machida CA. Genetically modified PC12 brain grafts: Survivability and inducible nerve growth factor expression. *Cell Transplant* 1996; 5(1):57–68.

39. Kawaja MD, Gage FH. Morphological and neurochemical features of cultured primary skin fibroblasts of Fischer 344 rats following striatal implantation. *J Comp Neurol* 1992; 317:102–116.

40. Bencsics C, Wachtel SR, Milstein S, et al. Double transduction with TP cyclohydrolase I and tyrosine hydroxylase is necessary for spontaneous synthesis of L-DOPA by primary fibroblasts. *J Neurosci* 1996; 16:4449–4456.

41. Lee WY, Lee EA, Jeon MY, et al. Vesicular monoamine transporter-2 and aromatic L-amino acid decarboxylase enhance dopamine delivery after L-3, 4-dihydroxyphenylalanine gene therapy prevents development of motor complications in parkinsonian rats after chronic intermittent L-3, 4-dihydroxyphenylalanine administration. *Exp Neurol* 2006; 197(1):215–224.

42. Yoshimoto Y, Lin Q, Collier TJ, et al. Astrocytes retrovirally transduced with BDNF elicit behavioral improvement in a rat model of Parkinson's disease. *Brain Res* 1995; 691:25–36.

43. Ljungberg MC, Stern G, Wilkin GP. Survival of genetically engineered, adult-derived rat astrocytes grafted into the 6-hydroxydopamine lesioned adult rat striatum. *Brain Res* 1999; 816:29–37.

44. Ridet JL, Corti O, Pencalet P, et al. Toward autologous ex vivo gene therapy for the central nervous system with human adult astrocytes. *Hum Gene Ther* 1999; 10:271–280.

45. Lundberg C, Horellou P, Mallet J, Bjorklund A. Generation of dopa-producing astrocytes by retroviral transduction of the human tyrosine hydroxylase gene: In vivo characterization and in vivo effects in the rat Parkinson model. *Exp Neurol* 1996; 139:39–53.

46. Krobert K, Lopez-Colberg I, Cunningham LA. Astrocytes promote or impair the survival and function of embryonic ventral mesencephalon co-grafts: Effects of astrocyte age and expression of recombinant brain-derived neurotrophic factor. *Exp Neurol* 1997; 145:511–523.

47. Tornatore C, Baker-Cairns B, Yadid G, et al. Expression of tyrosine hydroxylase in an immortalized human fetal astrocyte cell line; In vitro characterization and engraftment into the rodent striatum. *Cell Transplant* 1996; 5:145–163.

48. Ericson C, Georgievska B, Lundberg C. Ex vivo gene delivery of GDNF using primary astrocytes transduced with a lentiviral vector provides neuroprotection in a rat model of Parkinson's disease. *Eur J Neurosci* 2005; 22(11):2755–2764.

49. Brazelton TR, Rossi FM, Keshet GI, Blau HM, From marrow to brain: expression of neuronal phenotypes in adult mice. Science. 2000 Dec 1; 290(5497):1775–1779.

50. Nakano K, Migita M, Mochizuki H, Shimada T. Differentiation of transplanted bone marrow cells in the adult mouse brain. *Transplantation* 2001; 71(12):1735–1740.

51. Azizi SA, Stokes D, Augelli BJ, et al. Engraftment and migration of human bone marrow stromal cells implanted in the brains of albino rats: Similarities to astrocyte grafts. *Proc Natl Acad Sci USA* 1998; 95(7):3908–3913.

52. Munoz JR, Stoutenger BR, Robinson AP, et al. Human stem/progenitor cells from bone marrow promote neurogenesis of endogenous neural stem cells in the hippocampus of mice. *Proc Natl Acad Sci USA* 2005; 102(50):18171–18176.

53. Dezawa M, Kanno H, Hoshino M, et al. Specific induction of neuronal cells from bone marrow stromal cells and application for autologous transplantation. *J Clin Invest* 2004; 113(12):1701–1710.

54. Eglitis MA, Mezey E. Hematopoietic cells differentiate into both microglia and macroglia in the brains of adult mice. *Proc Natl Acad Sci USA* 1997; 94: 4080–4085.

55. Mezey E, Chandross KJ, Harta G, et al. Turning blood into brain: Cells bearing neuronal antigens generated in vivo from bone marrow. *Science* 2000; 290(5497):1779–1782.

56. Eglitis MA, Dawson D, Park KW, Mouradian MM. Targeting of marrow-derived astrocytes to the ischemic brain. *Neuroreport* 1999; 10(6):1289–1292.

57. Park KW, Eglitis MA, Mouradian MM. Protection of nigral neurons by GDNF-engineered marrow cell transplantation. *Neurosci Res* 2001; 40(4):315–323.

58. Gage FH, Coates PW, Palmer TD, et al. Survival and differentiation of adult neuronal progenitor cells transplanted to the adult brain. *Proc Natl Acad Sci USA* 1995; 92:11879–11883.

59. Lundberg C, Field PM, Ajayi YO, et al. Conditionally immortalized neural progenitor cell lines integrate and differentiate after grafting to the adult rat striatum. A combined autoradiographic and electron microscopic study. *Brain Res* 1996; 737:295–300.

60. Yamada H, Dezawa M, Shimazu S, et al. Transfer of the von Hippel–Lindau gene to neuronal progenitor cells in treatment for Parkinson's disease. *Ann Neurol* 2003; 54(3):352–359.

61. McKay R. Stem cells in the central nervous system. *Science* 1997; 76:66–71.

62. Martinez-Serrano A, Bjorklund A. Immortalized neural progenitor cells for CNS gene transfer and repair. *Trends Neurol Sci* 1997; 20:530–538.

63. Svendsen CN, Caldwell MA, Shen J, et al. Long-term survival of human central nervous system progenitor cells transplanted into a rat model of Parkinson's disease. *Exp Neurol* 1997; 148:135–146.

64. Studer L, Tabar V, McKay RD. Transplantation of expanded mesencephalic precursors leads to recovery in parkinsonian rats. *Nat Neurosci* 1998; 1:290–295.

65. Shihabuddin LS, Ray J, Gage FH. Stem cell technology for basic science and clinical applications. *Arch Neurol* 1999; 56:29–32.

66. Kawasaki H, Mizuseki K, Nishikawa S, et al. Induction of midbrain dopaminergic neurons from ES cells by stromal cell–derived inducing activity. *Neuron* 2000; 28(1):31–40

67. Barberi T, Klivenyi P, Calingasan NY, et al. Neural subtype specification of fertilization and nuclear transfer embryonic stem cells and application in parkinsonian mice. *Nat Biotechnol* 2003; 21(10):1200–1207

68. Bjorklund LM, Sanchez-Pernaute R, Chung S, et al. Embryonic stem cells develop into functional dopaminergic neurons after transplantation in a Parkinson rat model. *Proc Natl Acad Sci USA* 2002; 99(4):2344–2349.

69. Kim JH, Auerbach JM, Rodriguez-Gomez JA, et al. Dopamine neurons derived from embryonic stem cells function in an animal model of Parkinson's disease. *Nature* 2002; 418(6893):50–56.

70. Takagi Y, Takahashi J, Saiki H, et al. Dopaminergic neurons generated from monkey embryonic stem cells function in a Parkinson primate model. *J Clin Invest* 2005; 115(1):102–109

71. Ramon-Cueto A, Plant GW, Avila J, Bunge MB. Long-distance axonal regeneration in the transected adult rat spinal cord is promoted by olfactory ensheathing glia transplants. *J Neurosci* 1998; 18(10):3803–15.

72. Johansson S, Lee IH, Olson L, Spenger C. Olfactory ensheathing glial co-grafts improve functional recovery in rats with 6-OHDA lesions. *Brain* 2005; 128(Pt 12):2961–2976.

73. Ibrahim A, Li Y, Li D, et al. Olfactory ensheathing cells: Ripples of an incoming tide? *Lancet Neurol* 2006; 5(5):453–457.

74. Espejo EF, Montoro RJ, Armengol JA, Lopez-Barneo J. Cellular and functional recovery of Parkinsonian rats after intrastriatal transplantation of carotid body cell aggregates. *Neuron* 1998; 20:197–206.

75. Toledo-Aral JJ, Mendez-Ferrer S, Pardal R, et al. Trophic restoration of the nigrostriatal dopaminergic pathway in long-term carotid body-grafted parkinsonian rats. *J Neurosci* 2003; 23(1):141–148.

76. Arjona V, Minguez-Castellanos A, Montoro RJ, et al. Autotransplantation of human carotid body cell aggregates for treatment of Parkinson's disease. *Neurosurgery* 2003; 53(2):321–328.

77. Cao L, Zheng Z-C, Zhao Y-C, et al. Gene therapy of Parkinson disease model rat by direct injection of plasmid DNA-lipofectin complex. *Hum Gene Ther* 1995; 6:1497–1501.

78. Imaoka T, Date I, Ohmoto T, Nagatsu T. Significant behavioral recovery in Parkinson's disease model by direct intracerebral gene transfer using continuous injection of a plasmid DNA-lipsome complex. *Hum Gene Ther* 1998; 9:1093–1102.

79. Segovia I, Vergara P, Brenner M. Astrocyte-specific expression of tyrosine hyrdoxylase after intracerebral gene transfer induces behavioral recovery in experimental parkinsonism. *Gene Ther* 1998; 5:1650–1655.

80. During MJ, Naegele JR, O'Malley KL, Geller AI. Long-term behavioral recovery in parkinsonian rats by an HSV vector expressing tyrosine hydroxylase. *Science* 1994; 266:1399–1403.

81. Kaplitt MG, Leone P, Samulski RJ, et al. Long-term gene expression and phenotypic correction using adeno-associated virus vectors in the mammalian brain. *Nature Genet* 1994; 8:148–154.

82. Riviere C, Danos O, Douar AM. Long-term expression and repeated administration of AAV type 1, 2 and 5 vectors in skeletal muscle of immunocompetent adult mice. *Gene Ther* 2006; 13(17):1300–1308.

83. Horellou P, Mallet J. Gene therapy for Parkinson's disease. *Mol Neurobiol* 1997; 15:241–256.

84. Fan DS, Ogawa M, Fujimoto KI, et al. Behavioral recovery in 6-hydroxydopamine-lesioned rats by cotransduction of striatum with tyrosine hydroxylase and aromatic L-amino acid decarboxylase genes using two separate adeno-associated virus vectors. *Hum Gene Ther* 1998; 9:2527–2535.

85. During MJ, Samulski RJ, Elsworth JD, et al. In vivo expression of therapeutic human genes for dopamine production in the caudates of MPTP-treated monkeys using an AAV vector. *Gene Ther* 1998; 5:820–827.

86. Wachtel SR, Bencsics C, Kang UJ. Role of aromatic L-amino acid decarboxylase for dopamine replacement by genetically modified fibroblasts in a rat model of Parkinson's disease. *J Neurochem* 1997; 9:2055–2063.

87. Moffat M, Harmon S, Haycock J, N'Malley KL. L-dopa and dopamine-producing gene cassettes for gene therapy approaches to Parkinson's disease. *Exp Neurol* 1997; 144:69–73.

88. Uchida K, Tsuzaki N, Nagatsu T, Kohsaka S. Tetrahydrobiopterin-dependent functional recovery in 6-hydroxydopamine-treated rats by intracerebral grafting of fibroblasts transfected with tyrosine hydroxylase cDNA. *Dev Neurosci* 1992; 14:173–180.

89. Mandel RJ, Rendahl KG, Spratt SK, et al. Characterization of intrastriatal recombinant adeno-associated virus-mediated gene transfer of human tyrosine hydroxylase and human GTP-cyclohydrolase I in a rat model of Parkinson's disease. *J Neurosci* 1998; 18:4271–4284.

90. Mandel RJ, Burger C. Clinical trials in neurological disorders using AAV vectors: Promises and challenges. *Curr Opin Mol Ther* 2004; 6(5):482–490.

91. During MJ, Kaplitt MG, Stern MB, Eidelberg D. Subthalamic GAD gene transfer in Parkinson disease patients who are candidates for deep brain stimulation. *Hum Gene Ther* 2001; 12(12):1589–1591.

92. Luo J, Kaplitt MG, Fitzsimons HL, et al. Subthalamic GAD gene therapy in a Parkinson's disease rat model. *Science* 2002; 298(5592):425–429.

93. Olson L. The coming of age of the GDNF family and its receptors: Gene delivery in a rat Parkinson model may have clinical implications. *Trends Neurol Sci* 1997; 20:277–279.

94. Bohn MC. A commentary on glial cell line-derived neurotophic factor (GDNF). From a glial secreted molecule to gene therapy. *Biochem Pharmacol* 1999; 57:135–142.

95. Choi-Lundberg DL, Lin Q, Chang YN, et al. Dopaminergic neurons protected from degeneration by GDNF gene therapy. *Science* 1997; 75:838–841.

96. Bilang-Bleuel A, Revah F, Colin P, et al. Intrastriatal injection of an adenoviral vector expressing glial-cell-line-derived neurotrophic factor prevents dopaminergic neuron degeneration and behavioral impairment in a rat model of Parkinson's disease. *Proc Natl Acad Sci USA* 1997; 94:8818–8823.

97. Choi-Lundberg DL, Lin Q, Schallert T, et al. Behavioral and cellular protection of rat dopaminergic neurons by an adenoviral vector encoding glial cell line-derived neurotrophic factor. *Exp Neurol* 1998; 154:261–275.

98. Lapchak PA, Araujo DM, Hilt DC, et al. Adenoviral vector-mediated GDNF gene therapy in a rodent lesion model of late stage Parkinson's disease. *Brain Res* 1997; 777:153–160.

99. Kojima H, Abiru Y, Sakajiri K, et al. Adenovirus-mediated transduction with human glial cell line-derived neurotrophic factor gene prevents 1-methyl-4-phenyl-1, 2, 3, 6-tetrahydropyridine-induced dopamine depletion in striatum of mouse brain. *Biochem Biophys Res Commun* 1997; 238:569–573.

100. Mandel RJ, Spratt SK, Snyder RO, Leff SE. Midbrain injection of recombinant adeno-associated virus encoding rat glial cell line-derived neurotrophic factor protects nigral neurons in a progressive 6-hydroxydopamine-induced degeneration model of Parkinson's disease in rats. *Proc Natl Acad Sci USA* 1997; 94:14083–14088.

101. Kotzbauer PT, Lampe PA, Heuckeroth RO, et al. Neurturin, a relative of glial-cell-line-derived neurotrophic factor. *Nature* 1996; 384(6608):467–470.

102. Horger BA, Nishimura MC, Armanini MP, et al. Neurturin exerts potent actions on survival and function of midbrain dopaminergic neurons. *J Neurosci* 1998; 18(13):4929–4937.

103. Rosenblad C, Kirik D, Devaux B, et al. Protection and regeneration of nigral dopaminergic neurons by neurturin or GDNF in a partial lesion model of Parkinson's disease after administration into the striatum or the lateral ventricle. *Eur J Neurosci* 1999; 11(5):1554–66.

104. Fjord-Larsen L, Johansen JL, Kusk P, et al. Efficient in vivo protection of nigral dopaminergic neurons by lentiviral gene transfer of a modified neurturin construct. *Exp Neurol* 2005; 195(1):49–60.

105. Shimura H, Hattori N, Kubo S, et al. Familial Parkinson disease gene product, parkin, is a ubiquitin-protein ligase. *Nat Genet* 2000; 25(3):302–305.

106. Petrucelli L, O'Farrell C, Lockhart PJ, et al. Parkin protects against the toxicity associated with mutant alpha-synuclein: proteasome dysfunction selectively affects catecholaminergic neurons. *Neuron*. 2002; 36(6):1007–1019.

107. Singleton AB, Farrer M, Johnson J, et al. Alpha-synuclein locus triplication causes Parkinson's disease. *Science* 2003; 302(5646):841.

108. Yamada M, Mizuno Y, Mochizuki H. Parkin gene therapy for alpha-synucleinopathy: A rat model of Parkinson's disease. *Hum Gene Ther* 2005; 16(2):262–270.

109. Lo Bianco C, Schneider BL, Bauer M, et al. Lentiviral vector delivery of parkin prevents dopaminergic degeneration in an alpha-synuclein rat model of Parkinson's disease. *Proc Natl Acad Sci USA* 2004; 101(50):17510–17515.

110. Kim RH, Smith PD, Aleyasin H, et al. Hypersensitivity of DJ-1-deficient mice to 1-methyl-4-phenyl-1, 2, 3, 6-tetrahydropyrindine (MPTP) and oxidative stress. *Proc Natl Acad Sci USA* 2005; 102(14):5215–5252.

111. Petit A, Kawarai T, Paitel E, et al. Wild-type PINK1 prevents basal and induced neuronal apoptosis, a protective effect abrogated by Parkinson disease-related mutations. *J Biol Chem* 2005; 280(40):34025–34032.

112. Mochizuki H, Hayakawa H, Migita M, et al. An AAV-derived Apaf-1 dominant negative inhibitor prevents MPTP toxicity as antiapoptotic gene therapy for Parkinson's disease. *Proc Natl Acad Sci USA* 2001; 98(19):10918–10923.

113. Eberhardt O, Coelln RV, Kugler S, et al. Protection by synergistic effects of adenovirus-mediated X-chromosome-linked inhibitor of apoptosis and glial cell line–derived neurotrophic factor gene transfer in the 1-methyl-4-phenyl-1, 2, 3, 6-tetrahydropyridine model of Parkinson's disease. *J Neurosci* 2000; 20(24):9126–9134.

114. Dedmon MM, Christodoulou J, Wilson MR, Dobson CM. Heat shock protein 70 inhibits alpha-synuclein fibril formation via preferential binding to prefibrillar species. *J Biol Chem* 2005; 280(15):14733–14740.

115. Junn E, Ronchetti RD, Quezado MM, et al. Tissue transglutaminase-induced aggregation of alpha-synuclein: Implications for Lewy body formation in Parkinson's disease and dementia with Lewy bodies. *Proc Natl Acad Sci USA* 2003; 100(4):2047–2052.

116. Hayashita-Kinoh H, Yamada M, Yokota T, et al. Down-regulation of alpha-synuclein expression can rescue dopaminergic cells from cell death in the substantia nigra of Parkinson's disease rat model. *Biochem Biophys Res Commun* 2006; 341(4):1088–1095.

117. Masliah E, Rockenstein E, Adame A, et al. Effects of alpha-synuclein immunization in a mouse model of Parkinson's disease. *Neuron* 2005; 46(6):857–868.

118. Ridet JL, Bensadoun JC, Deglon N, et al. Lentivirus-mediated expression of glutathione peroxidase: Neuroprotection in murine models of Parkinson's disease. *Neurobiol Dis* 2006; 21(1):29–34.

119. Frank S, Kieburtz K, Holloway R, Kim SY. What is the risk of sham surgery in Parkinson disease clinical trials? A review of published reports. *Neurology* 2005; 65(7):1101–1103.

120. Kim SY, Frank S, Holloway R, et al. Science and ethics of sham surgery: A survey of Parkinson disease clinical researchers. *Arch Neurol* 2005; 62(9):1357–1360.

121. Lang AE, Gill S, Patel NK, et al. Randomized controlled trial of intraputamenal glial cell line-derived neurotrophic factor infusion in Parkinson disease. *Ann Neurol* 2006; 59(3):459–466.

122. de la Fuente-Fernandez R, Ruth TJ, Sossi V, et al. Expectation and dopamine release: Mechanism of the placebo effect in Parkinson's disease. *Science* 2001; 293(5532):1164–1166.

123. Benedetti F, Colloca L, Torre E, et al. Placebo-responsive Parkinson patients show decreased activity in single neurons of subthalamic nucleus. *Nat Neurosci* 2004; 7(6):587–588.

53 Genetic Testing

John Hardy
Aideen McInermey-Leo

arkinson's disease (PD) poses a unique and complex series of problems for clinicians seeking to use and explain genetic data to patients and their families. This is a relatively new challenge, since PD has historically been considered a nongenetic disease. The annual incidence of PD ranges between 16 and 19 individuals per 100,000 (1). To date, 6 genes have been established and associated with the disease. The challenges of interpreting molecular data and counseling families identified with hereditary forms of PD is important, since commercial genetic tests have become available and additional genes will almost certainly be identified in the near future.

Parkinsonism has been shown to have a variety of etiologies, including vascular insults (2, 3), toxic substance exposures (4–7), infectious disorders (8), frontal lobe tumors (9–11), and defects or variations in metabolic pathways (12–16). In the face of such evidence, the common assumption that PD had a primarily environmental etiology was tenable. Although familial PD was reported in the literature as early as 1880 (17), it has been the growing knowledge of molecular genetics that has resulted in the broader consideration of PD as a disorder with a complex etiology combining varying contributions of genetic and environmental factors. At one end of the spectrum, there are families in which PD

is inherited in a Mendelian pattern; at the other end, there are individuals with toxin-induced parkinsonism with no identifiable contributing family history. Recurrence risks for relatives in the case of typical PD with an age of onset above 60 years is modest, with first-degree relatives of such individuals being probably 2 to 3 times more likely than the relatives of controls to develop the disease (18–20). However, families where individuals present with an early onset of symptoms (before age 50) in the presence of other affected relatives suggest a greater potential for a hereditary basis for PD (19–21). It is within this subset of PD that formal risk assessments by relationship may be possible in the foreseeable future, as additional genes are identified and clinical genetic testing and specifically presymptomatic testing becomes available.

To date, 11 genetic linkage loci have been reported for PD; they have been labeled PARK-1 to PARK-11, respectively. Three of these loci are no longer in parlance in the field (the family who originally mapped to PARK-4 actually maps to PARK-1 (22), PARK-5 is probably wrong, and PARK-9 is readily distinguishable from PD (23). Among the remaining 9 loci, 5 genes have been identified: PARK-1 (*α-synuclein*), PARK-2 (*parkin*), PARK-6 (*PINK1*), PARK-7 (*DJ-1*), and PARK-8 (*LRRK2/dardarin*). In addition, 4 additional genes have been identified in hereditary disorders with phenotypes that overlap clinically with PD: frontotemporal dementia with parkinsonism linked to chromosome 17 (FTDP-17) (24), X-linked dystonia parkinsonism (XDP), and 2 of the spinocerebellar ataxias (SCA)—that is, SCA-2 (especially in those of Asian origin) (23) and SCA-3 (Machado-Joseph disease; especially in those of African origin) (25). A gene has also been identified for dopa-responsive dystonia (also known as Segawa's disease) (26), a phenotypically variable condition in which some of the affected individuals exhibit signs of parkinsonism in the absence of classic symptoms of dystonia. Although the number of patients with family histories clearly consistent with Mendelian inheritance is relatively small in comparison to the number of sporadic cases, identification of the genetic factors contributing to PD in these rare families provides us with important clues to the etiology of idiopathic PD and helps to establish a paradigm. Below is a brief synopsis of the current state of knowledge for the 5 genes identified thus far.

PARK-1

In 1997, a large family of Italian ancestry with autosomal dominant PD showed genetic linkage to the long arm of chromosome 4 (4q) (27). A point mutation was identified in the PARK-1 (α–synuclein) gene in this family (A53T), and the same mutation was subsequently found in 6 pedigrees from Greece (28), reflecting an ancient founder effect. A year later, a second mutation (A30P) was described in an autosomal dominant family from southern Germany (29). More recently, inherited PD in a large dominant Iowan kindred was found to be attributable to a triplication of the α-synuclein gene such that affected individuals carried 4 normal copies of the gene (22). The discovery of α-synuclein, which was shown to be a major component of Lewy bodies (30), was the first unequivocal proof that genetics played a role in PD, and research accelerated thereafter.

In the families reported with an A53T mutation, the average age of onset was 46 years, which is a decade younger than typical sporadic PD; however, the clinical picture was typical with regard to presentation, progression, and responsiveness to levodopa (27, 28), although dementia appears to be more frequent (31). Within the A53T kindreds, the disease appears to be fully penetrant (27) (i.e., those who have the mutation will definitely develop the condition assuming that they live into late adulthood). In contrast, in the small German family reported with an A30P mutation, the age of onset was slightly later, and there appeared to be a lower degree of penetrance (29). Triplication of α-synuclein is associated with an early onset (also averaging around the fifth decade) and rapidly progressive dopa-responsive parkinsonism, often followed by (or in some cases accompanied by) dementia at onset (22, 32, 33). This gene alteration

also results in a fully penetrant dominant form of the condition. Once again, this appears to be a rare cause of PD, as recent analysis of a large number of cases with familial PD, sporadic PD, or dementia with Lewy bodies did not detect any other cases of multiplication of α-synuclein (22). A further mutation, E46K, has been found in a Spanish kindred with dominant parkinsonism and Lewy body dementia (34). Within this family, symptoms begin between the ages of 50 and 65 years and dementia typically presents within 2 years of diagnosis. Of further interest and possible future complication is that some studies suggest that α-synuclein promoter (the DNA sequence that regulates transcription of the gene) variants may contribute to the lifetime risk of typical sporadic PD (35–38) whereby polymorphisms associated with higher α-synuclein expression are associated with increased risk.

PARK-2

PARK-2 (parkin) is located on the long arm of chromosome 6 (6q). Parkin mutations were first described in Japanese patients with autosomal recessive juvenile parkinsonism. The clinical picture differs from classic PD, as dystonia is typically present at onset and the features also include hyperreflexia, slow progression, and early complications from L-dopa therapy (39–41). Mutations have subsequently been reported in young-onset PD (age of onset below 40 years) and even among later-onset, familial PD from a large variety of ethnic backgrounds (42–45). Early-onset cases with no known family history of PD were also found to have mutations in parkin; the probability of finding a mutation dramatically increased when the patient was under 20 years of age and/or had consanguineous parents (44, 46). Parkin mutations have been reported in a wide variety of other conditions including but not limited to parkinsonism associated with dopa-responsive dystonia (47) and peripheral neuropathy (48).

Khan and colleagues (45) described 24 patients with parkin mutations, 14 of whom had a characterized mutation in 2 alleles; the remainder had only 1 mutation identified. Age of onset varied from 7 to 54 years of age with most presenting in the second or third decade. Patients survived on average for 10 to 20 years after the disease was diagnosed, although 1 patient lived to age 56 with the condition. These individuals had clinical features consistent with those of other patients carrying parkin mutations, such as dystonia, freezing, retropulsion, autonomic failure, responsiveness to anticholinergics and L-dopa, L-dopa–induced dyskinesias, and recurrent psychosis. The authors also reported behavioral and mood disorders before the onset of PD. Many of the same features were seen in a separate study in which 146 patients with parkin mutations were compared to 250 individuals with early-onset parkinsonism in whom no mutations were detected (41). Aside from the slow progression, hyperreflexia, and dystonia, those with parkin mutations were more likely to have a more symmetrical onset and a more marked response to L-dopa. As in the case of α-synuclein, the parkin gene promoter has several functional variants; those that have lower transcriptional activity have been reported to be associated with increased risk of PD (49).

PARK-6

Analysis of three large families from Sicily, Italy, and Spain led to the discovery of the PINK1 (*PTEN-induced kinase 1*) gene at the PARK-6 locus (50). All 3 families shared a common haplotype, demonstrating a shared ancestry. The clinical course closely resembled that of classic PD, with early onset of drug-induced dyskinesias but a good response to levodopa (51). Positron emission tomography (PET) studies showed a reduction of ^{18}F-dopa uptake in the putamen (52). There were no reports of dementia. A study of early-onset (before 50 years of age) idiopathic PD in Italy has revealed 2 patients homozygous for mutations in PINK1, with 5 others carrying a missense mutation. One percent of healthy, unrelated controls carried a single missense mutation (53). Another study of 289 individuals with PD, of whom approximately 50% had early-onset PD, found 2 individuals homozygous for mutations in the PINK1 gene. Both developed symptoms at an early age and had a family history consistent with autosomal recessive inheritance (54).

PARK-7

The PARK-7 locus on 1q has recently been cloned and shown to be due to the loss of function of a previously identified protein, DJ-1 (55). Mutations at this locus appear to be a rare cause of PD; histopathologic examination of cases with mutations at this locus have yet to be reported. However, PET studies demonstrated presynaptic dopaminergic cell loss in these patients. Clinically, these patients develop symptoms at an early age, but the disease course is typically insidious and shows good responsiveness to dopamine replacement therapy (55).

PARK-8

Dardarin, the protein encoded by *LRRK2*, is 2527 amino acids long and contains leucine-rich repeat, WD40, RAS, and kinase domains (56, 57). The function of dardarin is as yet unknown, but the presence of the kinase domain appears to be crucial to the toxic actions of the protein (58).

PARK-8 is an autosomal dominant form of PD. Mutations in *LRRK2* have now been linked to large numbers of cases of both familial and sporadic PD. In Caucasians, a single mutation, G2019S, has been established as the most common known genetic cause of PD, responsible for more than 1% of typical sporadic disease and 5% of cases with a family history of PD (59–61). Despite disparate ethnic backgrounds, genetic analysis of all G2019S individuals examined so far is consistent with 2 separate founder events; a single common founder who lived more than 2000 years ago and a second less common, more recent one (62). Similarly, a high proportion of cases with Chinese ethnicity have a single mutation (63, 64). Clinically, the majority of LRRK2 cases are indistinguishable from typical sporadic PD; neuropathologic examination reveals pathology consistent with PD, including nigral degeneration and the presence of brainstem α-synuclein–positive Lewy bodies. The notable exceptions to this are 3 families in which the clinical or pathologic phenotype varies considerably. Affected members of some families (57) present clinically with a range of phenotypes, including PD, dementia, and amyotrophy. Neuropathologic assessment of affected members from these families shows strikingly disparate pathologies: some have nonspecific neuronal loss with ubiquitin-reactive inclusions, 1 has tau pathology reminiscent of progressive supranuclear palsy, and some have α-synuclein–positive brainstem and cortical inclusions (57).

While the first families who were ascertained showed almost full penetrance of the disease mutations, even the early data on the Basque population suggested that the mutations were not fully penetrant (56). More recent and epidemiologically based assessments have suggested that the mutations have a lifetime penetrance of less than 35%. The reasons for this low penetrance are not clear, but they pose considerable challenges for clinical and presymptomatic testing (65).

THE IMPLICATIONS OF THESE FINDINGS FOR CLINICAL PRACTICE

The major current implication of these findings is with respect to genetic testing: is diagnostic or presymptomatic testing appropriate? This is a complex issue without a simple answer. A high proportion (estimated at up to 50%) of early-onset cases are believed to have recessive inheritance of *parkin, DJ-1 or PINK1*; however, it is not clear that screening of such cases for mutations is of clinical utility at present. The presence or absence of mutations in any of these genes would not alter the clinical management of the case, nor would it have quantifiable implications for the children of the patient, since the likelihood would be that they would be heterozygotes and thus at comparatively low risk. The issue of risk related to one mutation in recessive forms of PD is currently unresolved (66). The only relatives whose risk status might be substantively altered would be sibs who, in the case of a recessive disease, would be at one-quarter a priori risk. While conceivably a couple would want testing for the purpose of family planning, it is unlikely that the unaffected parent would be a heterozygous mutation carrier except in the case of consanguineous marriages. Screening for mutations in recessive diseases is a nontrivial problem because some mutations are difficult to find for technical reasons and not inexpensive. Thus, all 3 outcomes of a genetic test (2 mutations in trans, one mutation, or no finding) are not simply interpretable. However, should treatment regimes that are beneficial to one specific genotypic group be discovered, this advice will change; one may hope the technology for finding and interpreting mutations will have improved by that time too.

> My current recommendation (02/07), therefore, is that clinical testing for these recessive genes is not useful.

Some pedigrees with autosomal dominant inheritance in which mutations in α-synuclein have been found have been offered the Huntington's protocol, and certainly many of these kindreds have a fulminant course of disease, similar to the severity and rate of decline of Huntington's disease itself. Similarly, those kindreds with the dominant parkinsonisms caused by *MAPT* or *SCA2* or *SCA3* mutations pose similar problems.

> Currently, these kindreds are appropriately being offered the Huntington's protocol.

Although they are autosomal dominant, *LRRK2* mutations have genetic features for which an approach by clinicians and genetic counselors remains to be developed.

These include that they are common but not completely penetrant, and they appear to be associated with a rather benign disease course with a slower rate of progression than is typical of PD and with less prevalent dementia, although this requires confirmation. This combination of factors is difficult to legislate, especially since screening for the most common mutations is relatively simple, inexpensive (compared to recessive forms), and could be applied to all PD cases. A mutation in such a case may be associated with a benign outcome, but it will, of course, imply that the patient's children are at marginally increased risk of disease, albeit with unknown onset age and unpredictable natural history. Also, it would not change the approach to therapy. The large number of individuals who would be reasonably eligible for screening means that it is probably impractical to apply the Huntington's protocol before genetic testing; equally clearly, however, the children of mutation-positive cases will need counseling.

> At present it is not clear whether LRRK2 testing has a clinical role. Given the very large number of cases with easily identified mutations but the reduced penetrance and generally benign outcome of these mutations, the Huntington's protocol may not be practical or appropriate. More discussion on this issue is required.

CONCLUSION

Genetic analysis of kindreds with PD is clearly affecting the Parkinson research agenda. It is also now directly affecting clinical practice, especially in terms of who should be genetically tested and how they should be counseled. This is a time of great flux, as technologies improve and information about risk assessments become more certain. The question of how this should be managed in clinical practice needs annual reassessment (67, 68).

References

1. Twelves D, Perkins KS, Counsell C. Systematic review of incidence studies of Parkinson's disease. *Mov Disord* 2003; 18:19–31.
2. Demirkiran M, Bozdemir H, Sarica Y. Vascular parkinsonism: A distinct, heterogeneous clinical entity. *Acta Neurol Scand* 2001; 104:63–67.
3. Horner S, Niederkorn K, Ni XS, et al. [Evaluation of vascular risk factors in patients with Parkinson syndrome]. *Nervenarzt* 1997; 68:967–971.
4. Langston JW, Ballard P, Tetrud JW, Irwin I. Chronic parkinsonism in humans due to a product of meperidine-analog synthesis. *Science* 1983; 219:979–980.
5. Aquilonius SM, Hartvig P. A Swedish county with unexpectedly high utilization of anti-parkinsonian drugs. *Acta Neurol Scand* 1986; 74:379–382.
6. Semchuk KM, Love EJ, Lee RG. Parkinson's disease and exposure to agricultural work and pesticide chemicals. *Neurology* 1992; 42:1328–1335.
7. Tanner CM, Langston JW. Do environmental toxins cause Parkinson's disease? A critical review. *Neurology* 1990; 40(Suppl 3):17–30; discussion 30–31.
8. Poskanzer DC, Schwab RS. Studies in the epidemiology of Parkinson's disease predicting its disappearance as a major clinical entity by 1980. *Trans Am Neurol Assoc* 1961; 86:234–235.
9. Imai H, Hirayama K. [Hemiparkinsonism with forced grasping produced by frontal tumor]. *Rinsho Shinkeigaku* 1975; 15:736–742.
10. Kaijima M, Fukui M, Shima F, et al. [Epidermoid in the middle cranial fossa presenting hemiparkinsonism—A case report (author's transl)]. *No Shinkei Geka* 1978; 6:1103–1108.
11. Majchrzak H, Wencel T, Majchrzak R, Bazowski P. [Hemiparkinsonism in a patient with frontal lobe tumor]. *Pol Tyg Lek* 1979; 34:1799–1800.
12. Barbeau A, Cloutier T, Roy M, et al. Ecogenetics of Parkinson's disease: 4-Hydroxylation of debrisoquine. *Lancet* 1985; 2:1213–1216.
13. Steventon GB, Heafield MT, Waring RH, Williams AC. Xenobiotic metabolism in Parkinson's disease. *Neurology* 1989; 39:883–887.
14. Tanner CM. Abnormal liver enzyme–mediated metabolism in Parkinson's disease: A second look. *Neurology* 1991; 41(Suppl 2):89–92.
15. Armstrong M, Daly AK, Cholerton S, et al. Mutant debrisoquine hydroxylation genes in Parkinson's disease. *Lancet* 1992; 339:1017–1018.
16. Johnson S. Is Parkinson's disease the heterozygote form of Wilson's disease: PD = 1/2 WD? *Med Hypoth* 2001; 56:171–173.

17. Leroux PD. *Contribution á l'étude des causes de la paralysie agitante.* Paris: Parks, 1880.

18. Marder K, Tang MX, Mejia H, et al. Risk of Parkinson's disease among first degree relatives: A community-based study. *Neurology* 1996; 47:155–160.

19. Elbaz A, Grigoletto F, Baldereschi M, et al. Familial aggregation of Parkinson's disease: A population-based case-control study in Europe. Europarkinson Study Group. *Neurology* 1999; 52:876–1882.

20. Payami H, Zareparsi S, James D, Nutt J. Familial aggregation of Parkinson disease: A comparative study of early-onset and late-onset disease. *Arch Neurol* 2002; 59:848–850.

21. Tanner CM, Ottman R, Goldman SM, et al. Parkinson disease in twins: An etiologic study. *JAMA* 1999; 281:341–346.

22. Singleton AB, Farrer M, Johnson J, et al. Alpha-synuclein locus triplication causes Parkinson's disease. *Science* 2003; 302:841.

23. Gwinn-Hardy K, Chen JY, Liu HC, et al. Spinocerebellar ataxia type 2 with parkinsonism in ethnic Chinese. *Neurology* 2000; 55:800–805.

24. Hutton M, Lendon CL, Rizzu P, et al. Association of missense and 5-splice-site mutations in tau with the inherited dementia FTDP-17. *Nature* 1998; 393:702–705.

25. Subramony SH, Hernandez D, Adam A, et al. Ethnic differences in the expression of neurodegenerative disease: Machado-Joseph disease in Africans and Caucasians. *Mov Disord* 2002; 17:1068–1071.

26. Ichinose H, Ohye T, Takahashi E, et al. Hereditary progressive dystonia with marked diurnal fluctuation caused by mutations in the GTP cyclohydrolase I gene. *Nat Genet* 1994; 8:236–242.

27. Polymeropoulos MH, Higgins JJ, Golbe LI, et al. Mapping of a gene for Parkinson's disease to chromosome 4q21-q23. *Science* 1996; 274:1197–1199.

28. Polymeropoulos MH, Lavedan C, Leroy E, et al. Mutation in the alpha-synuclein gene identified in families with Parkinson's disease. *Science* 1997; 276:2045–2047.

29. Kruger R, Kuhn W, Muller T, et al. Ala30Pro mutation in the gene encoding alpha-synuclein in Parkinson's disease. *Nat Genet* 1998; 18:106–108.

30. Spillantini MG, Schmidt ML, Lee VM, Trojanowski JQ, et al. Alpha-synuclein in Lewy bodies. Nature 1997; 388:839–840.

31. Spira PJ, Sharpe DM, Halliday G, et al. Clinical and pathological features of a Parkinsonian syndrome in a family with an Ala53Thr alpha-synuclein mutation. *Ann Neurol* 2001; 49:313–319.

32. Muenter MD, Forno LS, Hornykiewicz O, et al. Hereditary form of parkinsonism-dementia. *Ann Neurol* 1998; 43:768–781.

33. Farrer M, Kachergus J, Forno LS, et al. Comparison of kindreds with Parkinsonism and alpha-synuclein genomic multiplications. *Ann Neurol* 2004; 55:174–179.

34. Zarranz JJ, Alegre J, Gomez-Esteban JC, et al. The new mutation, E46K, of alpha-synuclein causes Parkinson and Lewy body dementia. *Ann Neurol* 2004; 55:164–173.

35. Holzmann C, Kruger R, Saecker AM, et al. Polymorphisms of the alpha-synuclein promoter: Expression analyses and association studies in Parkinson's disease. *J Neural Transm* 2003; 110:67–76.

36. Farrer M, Maraganore DM, Lockhart P, et al. Alpha-synuclein gene haplotypes are associated with Parkinson's disease. *Hum Mol Genet* 2001; 10:1847–1851.

37. Tan EK, Matsuura T, Nagamitsu S, et al. Polymorphism of NACP-Rep1 in Parkinson's disease: An etiologic link with essential tremor? *Neurology* 2000; 54:1195–1198.

38. Tan EK, Tan C, Shen H, et al. Alpha synuclein promoter and risk of Parkinson's disease: Microsatellite and allelic size variability. *Neurosci Lett* 2003; 336:70–72.

39. Yamamura Y, Sobue I, Ando K, et al. Paralysis agitans of early onset with marked diurnal fluctuation of symptoms. *Neurology* 1973; 23:239–244.

40. Kitada T, Asakawa S, Hattori N, et al. Mutations in the parkin gene cause autosomal recessive juvenile parkinsonism. *Nature* 1998; 392:605–608.

41. Lohmann E, Periquet M, Bonifati V, et al. How much phenotypic variation can be attributed to parkin genotype? *Ann Neurol* 2003; 54:176–185.

42. Klein C, Schumacher K, Jacobs H, et al. Association studies of Parkinson's disease and parkin polymorphisms. *Ann Neurol* 2000; 48:126–127.

43. Abbas N, Lucking CB, Ricard S, et al. A wide variety of mutations in the parkin gene are responsible for autosomal recessive parkinsonism in Europe. French Parkinson's Disease Genetics Study Group and the European Consortium on Genetic Susceptibility in Parkinson's Disease. *Hum Mol Genet* 1999; 8:567–574.

44. Lucking CB, Durr A, Bonifati V, et al. Association between early-onset Parkinson's disease and mutations in the parkin gene. French Parkinson's Disease Genetics Study Group. *N Engl J Med* 2000; 342:1560–1567.

45. Khan NL, Graham E, Critchley P, et al. Parkin disease: A phenotypic study of a large case series. Brain 2003; 126(Pt 6):1279–1292.

46. Periquet M, Latouche M, Lohmann E, et al. Parkin mutations are frequent in patients with isolated early-onset parkinsonism. *Brain* 2003; 126(Pt 6):1271–1278.

47. Tassin J, Durr A, Bonnet AM, et al. Levodopa-responsive dystonia. GTP cyclohydrolase I or parkin mutations? *Brain* 2000; 123(Pt 6):1112–1121.

48. Tassin J, Durr A, de Broucker T, et al. Chromosome 6–linked autosomal recessive early-onset Parkinsonism: Linkage in European and Algerian families, extension of the clinical spectrum, and evidence of a small homozygous deletion in one family. The French Parkinson's Disease Genetics Study Group, and the European Consortium on Genetic Susceptibility in Parkinson's Disease. *Am J Hum Genet* 1998; 63:88–94.

49. West AB, Maraganore D, Crook J, et al. Functional association of the parkin gene promoter with idiopathic Parkinson's disease. *Hum Mol Genet* 2002; 11:2787–2792.

50. Valente EM, Salvi S, Ialongo T, et al. PINK1 mutations are associated with sporadic early-onset parkinsonism. *Ann Neurol* 2004; 56:336–341.

51. Bentivoglio AR, Cortelli P, Valente EM, et al. Phenotypic characterisation of autosomal recessive PARK6-linked parkinsonism in three unrelated Italian families. *Mov Disord* 2001; 16:999–1006.

52. Khan NL, Valente EM, Bentivoglio AR, et al. Clinical and subclinical dopaminergic dysfunction in PARK6-linked parkinsonism: An 18F-dopa PET study. *Ann Neurol* 2002; 52:849–853.

53. Rogaeva E, Johnson J, Lang AE, et al. Analysis of the PINK1 gene in a large cohort of cases with Parkinson's disease. *Arch Neurol* 2004; 61:1898–1904.

54. Valente EM, Abou-Sleiman PM, Caputo V, et al. Hereditary early-onset Parkinson's disease caused by mutations in PINK1. *Science* 2004; 304:1158–1160.

55. Bonifati V, Rizzu P, van Baren MJ, et al. Mutations in the DJ-1 gene associated with autosomal recessive early-onset parkinsonism. *Science* 2003; 299:256–259.

56. Paisán-Ruiz C. et al. Cloning of the gene containing mutations that cause PARK8 linked Parkinson disease, *Neuron* 2004; 44:595–600.

57. Zimprich A et al. Mutations in LRRK2 cause autosomal-dominant parkinsonism with pleomorphic pathology, *Neuron* 2004; 44:601–607.

58. Greggio E, Lewis PA, van der Brug MP, et al. Kinase activity is required for the toxic effects of mutant LRRK2/dardarin. *Neurobiol Dis* 2006; 23:329–341.

59. Gilks WP et al. A common LRRK2 mutation in idiopathic Parkinson's disease, *Lancet* 2005; 365:415–416.

60. Di Fonzo A et al. A frequent LRRK2 gene mutation associated with autosomal dominant Parkinson's disease, *Lancet* 2005; 365:412–415.

61. Nichols WC et al. Genetic screening for a single common LRRK2 mutation in familial Parkinson's disease. *Lancet* 2005; 365:410–412.

62. Zabetian CP, Hutter CM, Yearout D, et al. *LRRK2* G2019S in families with Parkinson's disease originating from Europe and the Middle East: Evidence for two distinct founding events beginning two millennia Ago. *Am J Hum Genet* 2006; 79:752–758.

63. Di Fonzo A, Wu-Chou YH, Lu CS, et al. A common missense variant in the LRRK2 gene, Gly2385Arg, associated with Parkinson's disease risk in Taiwan. *Neurogenetics* 2006; 7(3):133–138.

64. Fung HC, Chen CM, Hardy J, et al. A common genetic factor for Parkinson disease in ethnic Chinese population in Taiwan. *BMC Neurol* 2006; 22(6):47.

65. Goldwurm S, Zini M, Mariani L, et al. Evaluation of LRRK2 G2019S penetrance. *Neurology* 2007 Jan 10; 68:1141–1143.

66. Kay DM, Moran D, Moses L, et al. Heterozygous parkin point mutations are as common in control subjects as in Parkinson's patients. *Ann Neurol* 2007; 67:47–54.

67. McInerney-Leo A, Hadley DW, Gwinn-Hardy K, Hardy J. Genetic testing in Parkinson's disease. *Mov Disord* 2005; 20:1–10.

68. Hardy J, Cai H, Cookson MR, et al. Genetics of Parkinson's disease and parkinsonism. *Ann Neurol* 2006; 60(4):389–398.

IX

SURGERY

54 Deep Brain Stimulation

Norika Malhado-Chang
Ron L. Alterman
Michele Tagliati

The last 20 years have witnessed a resurgence of interest in functional neurosurgery for Parkinson's disease (PD) and other movement disorders, including tremor, dyskinesias, and dystonia. This revival has been spurred by the temporal limitations of levodopa therapy (1), the improved understanding of the pathophysiology of the basal ganglia (2), and technological advances, most importantly the development of deep brain stimulation (DBS). When used for the treatment of movement disorders, DBS is currently targeted to 3 areas of the brain: the ventral intermediate nucleus of the thalamus (Vim), the globus pallidus pars interna (GPi), and the subthalamic nucleus (STN). As Vim DBS almost exclusively improves contralateral tremor, it has been progressively replaced by DBS at the 2 other targets for the treatment of PD, even when tremor predominates.

Successful DBS therapy depends on the proper implementation of a series of procedures, which include accurate candidate selection, proper anatomic and electrophysiologic targeting, proficient electrode programming, expert medication adjustments, management of side effects, and, last but not least, patient education and support. DBS requires a delicate balance of electrical and medical treatment that includes a critical understanding of the principles of pulse generator programming. Successful postoperative management necessitates detailed knowledge of the anatomy and physiology of the target area, expertise in the pharmacologic treatment of PD, and familiarity with the protocols for setting optimal stimulation parameters.

After a brief historical overview of the development of DBS, this chapter reviews the cardinal steps leading to successful DBS therapy as well as the published results and known complications in PD. It also addresses some of the current controversies, including the mechanism of action of DBS. Finally, possible future developments that may further improve the clinical impact of DBS in PD are discussed.

HISTORY OF DBS FOR PARKINSON'S DISEASE

The history of DBS dates back to the original surgical procedures for movement disorders of the early twentieth century. In the 1930s, Penfield used electrical stimulation to disclose the existence of detailed cortical function maps (3). While it had become clear that large-scale resection of key elements of the motor pathways yielded unacceptable loss of function, it was not until human stereotactic frames were developed in the late 1940s that neurosurgeons could begin to safely approach the basal ganglia and other deeper cerebral structures (4). Initially, electrical stimulation was used almost exclusively to identify target structures during ablative procedures (5). In the 1950s, controversial work by Robert G. Heath proposed that brain stimulation with the use of electrodes was useful in treating various ailments such as chronic pain. In the early 1960s, Hassler reported an observation that marked the beginning of the modern era of DBS for movement disorders: high-frequency (100-Hz) stimulation of the ventrolateral thalamus could reduce tremor (6, 7). However, for decades, DBS was used only transiently for targeting surgical lesions (8). The earliest report of DBS via chronically implanted electrodes comes from the work of Sem-Jacobsen, who first developed a method for leaving DBS electrodes in place, although still for the purpose of improving lesioning techniques (9).

Surgery for PD took a back seat to levodopa after its emergence in 1967. It was not until the long-term adverse effects of levodopa, such as dyskinesias and motor fluctuations, emerged that focus was redirected to surgical techniques. In the meanwhile, the 1970s witnessed the initial experimental use of chronic stimulation for treating pain (10), epilepsy, and movement disorders other than PD (11). While the spinal cord was targeted for the treatment of pain, the cerebellum was targeted for cerebral palsy. However, after initial enthusiasm (12), cortical cerebellar stimulation in cerebral palsy fell out of favor when controlled studies failed to replicate the initial success (13). In 1980, Brice and McLellan reported the first experience treating severe intention tremor with stereotactically placed bipolar electrodes in the contralateral midbrain and basal ganglia (14). Finally, in 1987, Benabid demonstrated that the nucleus ventralis intermedius (Vim) of the thalamus was an effective target for treating tremor with DBS (15) (Figure 54-1).

The evolution of modern DBS for PD is rooted in the development of new technologies, like imaging techniques and the implantable pacemaker, and the improvement of our understanding of the pathophysiology of the basal ganglia. The advent of computed tomography (CT) and magnetic resonance imaging (MRI) made visualization of implantation sites within the brain easier and stereotaxic surgery safer. The discovery of 1-methyl-4-phenyl-1,2,3,6-tetrahydropyridine (MPTP) in 1983 (16) created the first reliable primate model of PD and spurred enormous interest in the study of its pathophysiology (17). Pronounced subthalamic overactivity was found in the basal ganglia–thalamocortical loops of MPTP-treated monkeys (18). In 1990, experimental lesioning of subthalamic nuclei in monkeys was shown to completely and permanently reverse the effects of MPTP (19, 20).

The STN became a natural target of surgical therapy for PD in humans, and the development of implantable

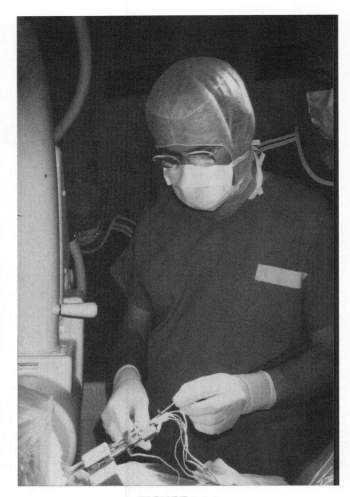

FIGURE 54-1

Dr. Alim-Louis Benabid, one of the pioneers of functional neurosurgery, developed deep brain stimulation (DBS) for Parkinson's disease.

pacemaker technology allowed skirting the potential danger of causing hemiballismus by lesioning the nucleus. It was postulated that electrical current applied to the STN would inhibit its activity, reproducing the experimental effects of the STN lesion in the monkey. In 1993, the group of Dr. Benabid in Grenoble published the first results of bilateral STN DBS in 3 patients with advanced akinetic-rigid PD with disabling, unpredictable motor fluctuations and severe "off" periods who were free of dementia (21). Improvement in activities of daily living (ADLs) and motor scores of the Unified Parkinson's Disease Rating Scale (UPDRS) at 3 months after surgery was dramatic (21) and confirmed by many groups in the following years (22). Coupled with such brilliant clinical results, the benefits of DBS over conventional ablative surgery (reversibility, adjustability, and the ability to affect bilateral structures without prohibitive side effects) led to the current popularity of electrical therapy for advanced medication-refractory PD.

PATIENT SELECTION: THE SECRET OF SUCCESS

Many elements are involved in successful DBS surgery, but the first and fundamental step is patient selection. Choosing the appropriate candidate for this procedure is the most significant factor determining postoperative benefit. A retrospective analysis revealed that over 30% of patients labeled as "DBS failures" were actually not good candidates (23). The best DBS candidate is the one who will reap the greatest benefit; however, only a few clear outcome predictors have been established, including a diagnosis of advanced PD, response to levodopa, and absence of cognitive deterioration (24). The role of other variables such as age and concurrent nonmotor symptoms is less well defined.

A sustained preoperative response to levodopa is considered the best predictor of outcome after DBS, and a recent consensus statement concluded that levodopa responsiveness must be assessed in each patient considered for this procedure (24), using a sufficient dose of levodopa to reproduce the patient's best "on" response; this dose is given after a medication-free interval of 12 hours (usually overnight). Levodopa response is usually defined as a 30% improvement in UPDRS motor scores (part III) as compared to the "off" state (25, 26), although there is no consensus on what constitutes an appropriate challenge dose of levodopa. A suprathreshold dose has been variably defined (24), while others have supported the use of the normal first dose of the day (27), a fixed 200-mg test dose (28), or even apomorphine (29). In our experience, however, patients with well-defined idiopathic PD can benefit from DBS of the STN even when their motor response is indeterminate due to intolerance to levodopa (30).

Only patients with a well-established diagnosis of advanced PD (31) should be considered for DBS therapy, as results in atypical parkinsonism have been very disappointing (32–36). Several case reports demonstrated the ineffectiveness of DBS in multiple system atrophy (MSA), even when the patient was responsive to levodopa, either using STN (32–35, 37) or GPi DBS (36). DBS can improve levodopa-responsive bradykinesia, rigidity, or dystonia but usually aggravates difficulties with speech, swallowing, and gait. Motor fluctuations do not improve and levodopa dose remains unchanged (32, 34). Even when initial improvement is observed, this is not sustained (33, 37). These cases emphasize the need for diagnostic modalities that distinguish PD from MSA and other parkinsonian syndromes in which the levodopa response pattern resembles that observed in PD (34).

DBS therapy primarily treats motor disability, which can be related to the duration and severity PD symptoms. *Disease duration*, although strictly not an outcome predictor (24, 25), has an important role in ruling out atypical PD. PD patients typically develop motor complications requiring DBS therapy after 5 to 10 years of disease, so those with advanced parkinsonism less than 5 years after onset should be further evaluated for atypical PD before being considered for DBS. Similarly, although not an outcome predictor, PD *severity* is an important consideration. In general, only patients with advanced, medication-refractory symptoms should be considered for surgery, although there is no consensus on specific UPDRS score thresholds (24). Severe PD disability generally coincides with UPDRS motor scores around 30 (out of a maximum of 108), and this would be a reasonable severity cutoff. Available experience with STN or GPi DBS has been mostly with levodopa-responsive patients having "off"-period UPDRS motor scores higher than 40 or 50 (24). In other words, the ideal PD surgical candidate is severely disabled when *off* levodopa while doing well (with or without dyskinesias) *on* medications (Table 54-1).

There is some controversy over the role of *age* as an outcome predictor for DBS (25, 38, 39), and various age cutoffs have been arbitrarily established by different authors. While chronological age has not been established as a significant predictor for postoperative benefit (24), advanced age is correlated with negative outcome predictors such as cognitive decline (40), axial symptoms, and gait instability. In general, DBS candidates above age 70 should be evaluated with particular care. The role of age is further discussed among the controversies at the end of the chapter.

TABLE 54-1
Features Defining the "Ideal" DBS Candidate

- Age: 40–75
- Established diagnosis of Idiopathic PD
- Symptom duration of 5 years or more
- Good response to levodopa
- Marked "on/off" phenomena
  - Frequent medication cycles (q3h or less)
  - Substantial disability during "off" periods
    - UPDRS motor score ≥ 30
  - Minimal "on" time without dyskinesias
  - Severe dyskinesias
- Intact cognition
- Absence of untreated psychiatric conditions
  - Depression, suicidal risk
  - Visual hallucinations
- Realistic expectations
- Access to programming of stimulators

Next, in selecting the appropriate patient for DBS, consideration must be given to general features that may contraindicate surgery. Patients with uncontrolled hypertension or diabetes, coronary artery disease, cardiac pacemakers, liver or kidney failure, seizure disorders, or coagulopathies may be poor candidates, though the risk/benefit ratio of DBS surgery should be assessed individually. Normal preoperative cognitive status is also very important, as the prevalence of dementia in PD is high (41) and preoperative dementia is a risk factor for permanent cognitive decline after DBS (42). Although there is insufficient evidence about the predictive validity of any given neuropsychological assessment, interview, or cognitive test (24), several tests are used in the selection of surgical candidates with the goal of excluding patients with dementia or severe deficits in executive function (43). Finally, a full psychiatric evaluation is essential for those patients who pass cognitive screening, as depression is prevalent in PD, with figures ranging between 2.7% and 70% according to a recent review (44). In particular, untreated depression, anxiety, apathy, dopaminergic dysregulation syndrome, medication-induced hypomania/mania, psychotic symptoms, and suicide risk should be carefully assessed (24). Visual hallucinations are not an absolute contraindication to DBS surgery; however, these commonly portend a poor cognitive prognosis. Visual hallucinations can affect up to 50% of PD patients (45), and several medications such as anticholinergics, dopamine agonists, and levodopa may contribute to this symptom. Good cognition and emotional state also play a role in the patient's outlook after surgery. It is important for DBS candidates to have an educated, realistic view of what can be expected from the procedure. It is important to remind patients that DBS is not a cure for PD and is not likely to halt progression of the disease. Optimal results may take months to achieve and may be different for each patient. Finally, adequate social support is crucial for DBS candidates. The process of stimulator programming is a concerted effort between patient, neurologist/programmer, and caretaker. Often, frequent visits are required postoperatively to discern the optimal settings for each electrode. During this process, the caretaker is essential to provide transportation, emotional support, and encouragement.

What emerges from this brief review of the DBS patient selection process is the importance of a multidisciplinary team approach, which includes the patient. A neurologist—possibly a movement disorder specialist—is in charge of meticulously reviewing the selection criteria to make sure that the patient is a proper candidate. A functional neurosurgeon reviews neuroimaging studies and general surgical eligibility. An internist tests for conditions that may preclude clearance for the procedure, while a neuropsychiatrist helps with interpreting the results of formal neuropsychiatric batteries and addresses eventual psychiatric comorbidities, including depression. Needless to say, no decision regarding DBS surgery is appropriate without an informed discussion of the risks and benefits related to the different phases of the procedure (e.g., functional neurosurgery, hardware implant, programming, and stimulation). A detailed review of the potential complications related to DBS is presented further on.

SURGICAL TECHNIQUE

Target Localization Methods

The best method for targeting deep brain structures has been a matter of debate since the very beginning of stereotactic neurosurgery. The advent of modern imaging techniques and compatible stereotactic frames made it possible to directly or indirectly locate targets deep within the brain. However, even current MRI technology is not always able to visualize deep brain nuclei with adequate resolution and is prone to reflect geometric distortions. Although usually small, these distortions can affect ideal anatomic targeting. Therefore, intraoperative neurophysiologic recordings are normally employed to confirm correct targeting. The role of single-unit recordings in the operating room has been emphasized by recent advances in the understanding of basal ganglia circuitry, which have shown that the structures targeted for movement disorders therapy are as much physiologic as they are anatomic. Imaging and neurophysiologic targeting methods currently used in functional neurosurgery for movement disorders are summarized below.

Anatomic Targeting: Neuroimaging Techniques

Advances in streotactic targeting have always followed advances in neuroimaging. In the early era of human stereotactic surgery (from about 1947 to 1973), positive-contrast ventriculography was the radiographic standard for targeting deep brain structures. Although it is incapable of demonstrating various deep brain structures directly, ventriculography is used to locate the foramen of Monro and the anterior and posterior commisures. Coordinates for the desired target can then be determined indirectly, deriving guidance from human stereotactic atlases, which demonstrate the relationships of deep brain structures to the imaginary intercommissural plane (46, 47). Ventriculography is still utilized in several centers but is diminished in importance due to the widespread use of MRI and CT, noninvasive imaging techniques that allow for more direct targeting of specific structures.

The introduction of CT reduced morbidity and mortality and expanded the role of stereotactic surgery by enabling a less invasive targeting technique (48, 49). Later, in the 1970s and early 1980s, MRI was developed and proved superior to CT due to its greater tissue resolution and multiplanar imaging. Furthermore, there is no exposure to ionizing radiation with MRI, and, unlike CT-compatible frames, MRI-compatible frames create no visible artifact (50). As applied to functional neurosurgery, nonreformatted MR images provide better anatomic resolution and visualization of the commissures, thalamus, and some of the basal ganglia structures than CT (51). Recently, investigators have been able to image both the internal pallidum and STN with MRI and to target these structures directly (52–57).

MRI is not without disadvantages. Most concerning is the potential geometric distortion introduced by nonlinearity of the magnetic field and by items that cause the field distortion (58). Distortions of the magnetic field, and in turn of the final image, can be generated by a number of factors, including the presence of ferromagnetic objects, magnetic imperfections, and, most commonly, patient movements (51, 58, 59). CT scanning maintains linear accuracy, while MRI can result in mean 2-dimensional vector differences between 1.2 and 2 mm (51, 60). These inaccuracies may introduce unacceptable targeting errors for small areas surrounded by vital structures, such as the GPi, STN, and Vim (61, 62). The magnitudes of MRI distortion error appear to be sequence-related (54); fast spin-echo inversion recovery may be less susceptible to such distortions than other sequences (53).

Although the development of CT and MRI has dramatically improved our ability to visualize deep intracranial structures accurately, image-based targeting is not foolproof, so that some form of intraoperative physiologic confirmation of correct targeting is necessary.

Physiological Targeting: Recording Techniques

While it is generally accepted that some form of physiologic localization is necessary to refine image-derived coordinates for functional neurosurgical targets, there is still debate about the best technique to accomplish this. The literature demonstrates wide variation in the percentage of patients who require correction of the anatomically chosen target, ranging from 12% to 67% (53, 61, 63). The combined use of imaging technologies and neurophysiologic targeting optimizes placement of the DBS electrode and minimizes potential complications (53, 61, 63–66). There are 4 neurophysiologic approaches to target localization: (a) impedance measurements; (b) macroelectrode recordings and stimulation; (c) semi-microelectrode recording (and/or stimulation); and (d) microelectrode recording (and/or stimulation).

Tissue impedance is the simplest and crudest form of functional localization and takes advantage of the differences in the electrical conductivity of gray and white matter. Gray matter impedances typically exceed 400 Ω, while white matter impedances are 300 Ω or less. Impedance recordings are used mostly in the location of large white matter bundles, nuclear groups, and spaces containing cerebrospinal fluid (67, 68).

Macroelectrode recording provides more detailed information than do impedance measurements (67, 69, 70). These techniques generate recordings that are similar to electroencephalographic (EEG) signals (71). The main advantage of using this approach is that the electrode can be advanced faster through the neural structures, since the recordings are limited to "neural noise" and there is no need to collect and analyze detailed cellular discharges. The obvious disadvantage is the lack of detailed definition, which is needed to characterize single-cell firing features inside the structure under study.

Microelectrode recordings (MERs) provide the most detailed picture of the neural elements (69, 72–87) and can localize the targeted brain structures more precisely than any other available technique. By recording individual neuronal activity, MER allows precise mapping of the target areas involved in movement and sensation by determining function at a cellular level. A potential disadvantage of MERs is the longer time required to record. However, we feel that the microelectrode technique is indispensable for final target localization during DBS surgery for PD. Target refinement with MER reduces the need to revise lead position due to incorrect anatomic targeting, which can affect as many as 12% of patients (23, 88).

Intraoperative Procedures

DBS implantation is performed in 2 stages. During the first stage, the DBS lead(s) is (are) stereotactically implanted into the functional target. During the second stage, the lead is connected subcutaneously to an implantable pulse generator (IPG), which, like a pacemaker, is inserted into a pocket beneath the skin of the chest wall. As with most stereotactic procedures for movement disorders, the first stage is performed with the patient awake in order to monitor his or her neurologic status and facilitate physiologic localization. The stereotactic head frame is applied on the morning of surgery and a targeting MRI is performed. Alternatively, the MRI can be performed days prior to surgery and merged to a stereotactic CT scan on the day of surgery. This technique is believed to reduce targeting errors due to MRI distortion, but it has never been proven. A combination of MER and macroelectrode stimulation is then used to physiologically refine the desired target. Details of the technique employed by our surgical team can be found in a prior publication (89). The DBS lead is about 1.3 mm in diameter and flexible, so that it moves with the brain and does not damage it. It is implanted and anchored to the skull with a burr-hole "cap." A brain MRI is obtained immediately postoperatively to confirm proper electrode placement and make sure that there is

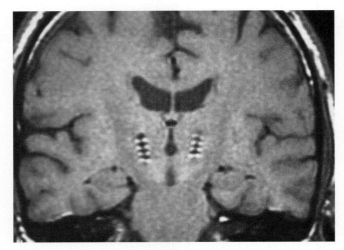

FIGURE 54-2

Postoperative coronal brain MRI section illustrating bilateral placement of DBS electrodes in the subthalamic nucleus (STN).

no hemorrhage (Figure 54-2). If the MRI is acceptable, the patient is returned to the operating room, where the remainder of the device is implanted under general anesthesia. This second stage may be performed on the same day as the lead implant; however, if bilateral leads are implanted during one operative procedure, we prefer to wait 1 to 2 weeks before implanting the generators in order to allow the brain to recover from bilateral frontal lobe penetrations before being subjected to general anesthesia.

Frame vs. Frameless

While frame-based targeting remains the "gold-standard" for DBS lead placement, frameless techniques are gaining popularity (90). The main advantage of these techniques is the enhancement of patient comfort due to the elimination of the stereotactic frame, which can be confining for some patients because it both surrounds and immobilizes the head. The 2 commercially available frameless technologies are in fact miniframes, which, rather than surrounding the head, are mounted on top of it. Neither technology requires the patient's head to be immobilized, so that he or she can move periodically during the procedure. In addition to patient comfort, miniframe technologies can improve operative efficiency by disconnecting surgical planning from the procedure itself. The targeting MRI and creation of the surgical plan can be performed well in advance of the procedure, saving up to 2 hours on the day of the lead implant.

The main disadvantages to miniframe technologies are cost and the fact that their accuracy remains unproven. While they enhance efficiency on the day of surgery,

the total time required for the surgeon to perform the operation is not reduced and may actually be increased. More importantly, these technologies involve expensive disposable components, thus increasing the cost of the operation to the institution. Finally, while preliminary studies do suggest that both miniframe technologies can be as accurate as a stereotactic frame, our own experience suggests that they can be erratic in their performance and require further improvement before they are ready for widespread use.

POSTOPERATIVE MANAGEMENT

Following proper patient selection and accurate lead location, competent programming of the implanted device is essential to optimized DBS therapy. Indeed, a perfectly implanted lead in a well-selected patient is useless without the proper stimulation settings. In a recent study, over one-third of patients referred to a movement disorders center for "DBS failures" were not properly programmed (23).

The primary goals of DBS programming are to maximize symptom suppression and minimize adverse effects. Minimization of battery drain and optimization of medication regimens are significant secondary goals. In order to achieve these, one must take a systematic, multi-step approach to DBS programming. These steps include the acquisition of pertinent surgical data, selection of the optimal contact and appropriate stimulation parameters, adjustment of dopaminergic medications, and the eventual management of side effects. Although DBS programming may vary slightly among different targets (e.g., STN, GPi, Vim), the general principles summarized below are applicable to any of them.

Preprogramming Data

Before programming begins, it is fundamental to obtain information regarding the patient's medical history, neurologic status, and medication regimen in order to assess the effects of stimulation. In addition, it can be valuable to obtain the surgeon's estimate of electrode placement and optimal electrode(s) as established with MER and DBS testing in the operating room. This information can be used to guide optimal programming and aid in eventual troubleshooting process. In this regard, we advocate routine post operative MRI to confirm lead position.

Two DBS lead types are currently available: the model 3387 (Medtronic, Inc., Minneapolis, MN) with widely spaced electrodes, spanning 10.5 mm, and the model 3389, which has closely spaced contacts with a span of 7.5 mm. In addition, two types of neurostimulator are currently available: Soletra and Kinetra. The Soletra neurostimulator

(Medtronic, Inc.) accomodates 1 extension/lead. Therefore 2 Soletra neurostimulators are required for bilateral therapy. The Kinetra (Medtronic, Inc.) accommodates 2 extensions/leads and thus provides bilateral neurostimulation from a single neurostimulator.

Selecting the Optimal Contact

We recommend postponing initial programming for about 2 to 4 weeks postsurgery in order to allow for tissue healing and microlesioning effects (the transient improvement of parkinsonian symptoms often observed after electrode implantation) to subside. The patient should be scheduled for a morning visit, when possible, with medication withheld overnight or longer ("off" condition).

The DBS device can be programmed to deliver stimulation in monopolar or bipolar fashion employing any of the 4 electrode contacts alone or in combination. Thus, a great deal of therapeutic flexibility is provided, permitting customized stimulation for each patient. Stimulation parameters can be adjusted at any time using a transcutaneous programmer.

After recording impedance and current drain for each contact to assess device function, the first step of DBS programming is to determine the "therapeutic window" of each contact—i.e., the voltage range between the initial observation of reliable antiparkinsonian effects and the threshold for adverse events. With an initial pulse width of 60 µs for STN and 90 for GPi and a frequency of 130 to 185 Hz, the effects of stimulation at each of the 4 contacts are assessed as voltage is slowly increased from 0 to 4 V or more. The contact that yields the greatest antiparkinsonian effects and/or exhibits the greatest therapeutic window should be selected for chronic stimulation. Amplitudes between 2.5 and 3.5 V provide the best results in the majority of cases (91).

If amplitudes higher than 3.5 V are needed, it is useful to remember that the DBS programmable variables (V, PW, and F) are mutually dependent in producing the energy of stimulation according to the formula:

$$\text{Energy} \cong [(\text{Voltage}^2 \times \text{Pulse width} \times \text{Frequency})/(\text{Impedance})]$$

Although the relationship between pulse width, frequency, and voltage is nonlinear (92), a higher pulse width allows the use of lower voltage to deliver the same energy, so that similar amounts of stimulation can be delivered. Rarely, pulse widths higher than 120 µs are needed for STN stimulation, but they can be effectively used for GPi or Vim stimulation. In many cases, increasing the frequency of stimulation up to 185 Hz will provide additional benefit. Furthermore, using higher frequencies (within the range of 130 to 185 Hz) may permit the use of lower voltages. Typical

PARAMETER	VIM	STN	GPI
Amplitude	2.5–3.6 V	2.0–3.6 V	2.5–3.6 V
Pulse width	90–120 µs	60–90 µs	90–120 µs
Rate	130–185 Hz	130–185 Hz	130–185 Hz
Electrode configuration	Unipolar bipolar	Unipolar bipolar	Unipolar bipolar

TABLE 54-2 *Typical Stimulation Parameters*

stimulator parameters for different targets are shown in Table 54-2.

If a single contact fails to provide satisfactory results, it may be useful to add an adjacent contact in monopolar configuration (e.g., 1−, 2−, C+) in order to broaden the effective field of stimulation. On the other hand, if the use of 2 or more contacts causes unwanted adverse events, a bipolar setting can be used in order to achieve a more focused field of stimulation ("field shaping"). To do so, the contact with the best therapeutic window should still be set as the active electrode (cathode) with an adjacent contact set as the anode (4). If no significant improvement is observed or stimulation-induced adverse events overwhelm clinical benefits, correct electrode position should be verified and technical troubleshooting started (92). An algorithm summarizing the fundamental steps in STN DBS programming is presented in Figure 54-3.

When assessing the clinical effects of stimulation, it is useful to remember a few key concepts relative to the response of parkinsonian symptoms to DBS: (a) *Rigidity* is considered the most reliable symptom to evaluate (93), because it has a short response time (20 to 30 seconds),

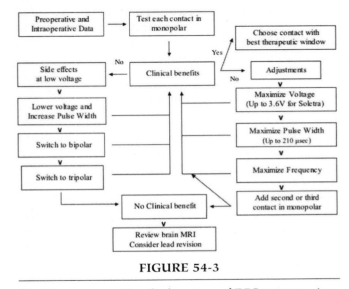

FIGURE 54-3

Algorithm summarizing the key steps of DBS programming.

is assessed with little patient cooperation and it is relatively stable as compared to tremor and bradykinesia. (b) *Tremor* is also a very good target symptom, particularly in tremor-predominant PD, with an extremely short latency of response (usually a few seconds). However, tremor can be variable and influenced by the emotional state of the patient. (c) *Bradykinesia* has generally the slowest latency of improvement, which may occur after several hours or even days. For this reason, it is typically the least useful symptom to monitor for initial programming. (d) *Off-drug dystonia* is also relieved by subthalamic stimulation, when present (46). (e) Levodopa-induced *dyskinesias* can be tremendously improved by subthalamic or pallidal stimulation (46, 93). However, dyskinesia cannot provide guidance at the initial programming session because patients are normally off medications.

This systematic yet empirical approach to programming is necessary because it is very difficult to predict which contacts will have maximum benefit. Even though the STN is the implanting target, the therapeutic area may expand beyond the nucleus itself. Herzog and colleagues found that stimulation of the dorsolateral border zone of the STN was more effective than that of the subthalamic white matter, such as the zona incerta (94). On the other hand, the dorsal/dorsomedial zona incerta may be a more effective target to relieve parkinsonism (95–97).

In stimulating the GPi, variable responses between different pallidal areas need to be taken into account. Stimulation of the ventral GPi may improve dyskinesias but worsen bradykinesia, while stimulation of the dorsal GPi has the opposite effect (52, 98).

In programming bilaterally, the additive effects of bilateral stimulation may require further adjustments after both devices are activated. Furthermore, before completing the first programming session, the patient should be observed after taking at least one standard dose of levodopa in order to determine and address potential additive effects of medication and stimulation and to assess the impact of the selected stimulation parameters on medication-induced dyskinesias.

Refining Stimulation Parameters

In a routine situation, the patient is sent home with the initial settings in monopolar configuration using the contact with the best therapeutic window at the lowest effective voltage or slightly above. Over the following few weeks, however, it is not uncommon to observe a recurrence of parkinsonism, due either to further healing of the brain (and consequent increased resistance to stimulation spread) or to the loss of the levodopa long-duration response secondary to medication reduction. In fact, we advocate very cautious reduction or even no change of antiparkinsonian medications after initial programming. If parkinsonian symptoms reappear, adjustments of the initial parameters of stimulation are needed. The initial approach in adjusting DBS settings is to increase the amplitude of stimulation until an improvement comparable to the "on" levodopa state is observed.

Medication Adjustments

Pallidal and thalamic stimulation usually does not allow dramatic changes in medication. However, the antiparkinsonian effect of subthalamic DBS should, over time, approximate or ideally match the benefits of levodopa therapy while eliminating or greatly reducing the associated motor fluctuations (99). Because the beneficial effects of DBS relate to all the cardinal symptoms and signs of PD, dopaminergic medication can usually be reduced after STN DBS. On average, levodopa and other dopaminergic agents are reduced 40% to 50% (93–99, 100) and rarely patients even discontinue their pharmacologic therapy (101). In general, discontinuation of dopaminergic medications should never be set as a primary goal of subthalamic DBS. In cases where levodopa doses were kept to a minimum because of severe dyskinesias, levodopa use may actually increase thanks to the elimination of this side effect.

Dyskinesias are the primary additive effect of dopaminergic and DBS therapy (93, 102, 103), but nonmotor phenomena such as hypomanic states, sedation, sleepiness, and confusion have also been observed. Dyskinesias may be induced by stimulation within the STN proper (100, 103) and several groups consider the intraoperative induction of dyskinesias a marker for good lead placement and a predictor of a positive response to chronic stimulation.

Failure to decrease dopaminergic medications sufficiently during chronic STN stimulation may predispose the patient to sedation, excessive daytime sleepiness, and mild confusional states. These side effects are well described in association with dopaminergic drugs (104) and are reversible in the vast majority of cases with proper medication adjustment. On the other hand, overly aggressive or rushed medication reductions can lead to the unwanted reemergence of the motor and nonmotor symptoms typical of low dopaminergic states. Temporary worsening of motor symptoms, particularly akinesia and freezing of gait, may be observed in these circumstances, as well as depressive symptoms or apathy (93). Similarly, depressive symptoms or apathy may be an indication of excessive reduction of antiparkinsonian medications (93, 105, 106). Patients who have received very high doses of levodopa (i.e., more than 1500 mg per day) for many years usually do not tolerate quick reductions in their regimens. Addiction to dopaminergic drugs is a controversial but fairly well described entity (107, 108) and needs to be taken into account in these cases. Apathy can be an independent symptom of PD, a symptom

TABLE 54-3
Vim DBS Results

STUDY (REF. #)	PERCENTAGE TREMOR IMPROVEMENT (NO. OF SUBJECTS)					
	3 MONTHS	6 MONTHS	12 MONTHS	2 YEARS	5 YEARS	6–7 YEARS
Koller W et al., 1997 (114)	85% (24)	82% (24)	78% (24)			
Limousin P et al., 1999 (116)	78.5% (73)		74.6% (73)			
Schuurman PR et al., 2000 (115)		91% (33)				
Rehncrona S et al., 2003 (117)				78% (16)		55% (12)
Pahwa R et al., 2006 (118)					82% (9)* 90–100% (5)†	
Mean (total pts)	80% (97)	86.5% (77)	75.5% (97)	78% (16)	86% (14)	55% (12)

* Unilateral.
† Bilateral.

of dopaminergic "withdrawal," or part of a depressive syndrome. Depression generally improves after STN DBS (109, 110). However, a minority of patients can develop severe postoperative depression, and sporadic suicidal attempts have been reported (93, 105, 110). Increased dopaminergic stimulation generally improves depression, but acute depression might result from stimulation of the subthalamic area as well (see later on). Finally, we have observed a new onset of restless legs after successful DBS, likely related to excessive decrease of dopaminergic therapy; this responded to small doses of a dopamine agonist (111).

RESULTS

The published experience with DBS for PD spans a period of almost 20 years and comprises hundreds of papers that have used different study methods, stimulation targets, and patient populationsThis review is limited to large series of patients, and the results are subdivided by the 3 main surgical targets for DBS implants. Following a historical path, the impact of thalamic DBS on PD symptoms is addressed first. Then, the published outcomes of subthalamic and pallidal DBS are evaluated.

Thalamus (Vim)

Electrical stimulation of the thalamus was initially employed for tremors from causes other than PD, such as essential tremor and multiple sclerosis (112). DBS of the nucleus ventralis intermedius (Vim) became an attractive therapeutic option in PD patients with a previous (contralateral) thalamotomy because it could spare the severe motor and neuropsychological deficits associated with bilateral thalamotomy (113). Several studies confirmed

the efficacy of thalamic DBS in achieving tremor resolution, with fewer adverse effects than lesioning (114, 115) (Table 54-3). A large European study, enrolling 73 PD patients, showed a significant reduction in upper and lower limb tremor. Contralateral rest tremor was reduced at least 2 UPDRS points in 85% of the electrodes. Akinesia and rigidity scores were moderately but significantly reduced by 34% and 16% respectively, while axial scores were unchanged (116).

There is convincing evidence that high-frequency thalamic stimulation can efficiently suppress severe tremor in PD for several years after electrode implant (117, 118). In a 5-year follow-up study evaluating the long-term effects of Vim DBS in 19 PD patients, Pahwa et al. reported that unilateral implants yielded an 85% improvement in the targeted hand tremor, while bilateral implants provided a 100% improvement in the left hand and 90% improvement in the right (118). Interestingly, the side-effect profile was dramatically different in patients receiving unilateral vs. bilateral stimulation. Adverse events in patients receiving unilateral implants were paresthesia (45%) and pain (41%), while patients receiving implants bilaterally complained mostly of dysarthria (75%) and balance difficulties (56%). PD patients seem to experience the tolerance phenomenon (the reemergence of tremor after several months of effective stimulation) less frequently than patients with essential tremor (115).

Despite its dramatic effects on resting tremor, Vim stimulation has fallen out of favor for the treatment of PD because of its relative lack of efficacy for bradykinesia, rigidity, dyskinesia, and gait (116). Improvement of contralateral rigidity and levodopa-induced dyskinesias after thalamic DBS has been reported (119) but seldom replicated. Obviously alleviation of tremor alone can be extremely helpful, as it often improves subjective dexterity and functionality of the hands. However, PD patients rarely have tremor in isolation, and stimulation of targets such as the STN or GPi that do improve a variety of parkinsonian motor symptoms in addition to tremor has surpassed DBS of the thalamus in clinical relevance. Therefore the role for Vim targeting in DBS patients is currently limited to those who cannot undergo STN or Gpi stimulation.

Subthalamic Nucleus

The next target investigated for stimulation was the STN. In 1993, Dr. Benabid's group in Grenoble published the first case report of a 51-year-old patient with advanced akinetic-rigid PD who underwent unilateral DBS of the subthalamic nucleus with intraoperative alleviation of contralateral symptoms (21). Five years later, the same group published a 1-year follow-up study of 24 PD patients treated with bilateral STN stimulation, reporting a 60% improvement of the UPDRS parts II and III scales. All cardinal PD features improved. The on-medication UPDRS motor subscores improved by 10%, even though dopaminergic drug dosages were reduced by half (46). In the following years, many other case series confirmed and validated the safety and efficacy of STN DBS in advanced PD (22) (Table 54-4).

In 2001, the Deep Brain Stimulation for Parkinson's Disease Study Group reported the first prospective, multicenter, double-blind, crossover study of STN DBS in 96 patients with advanced PD (100). At 6 months, STN DBS had provided a mean improvement of 44% in UPDRS ADL scores and 51% in UPDRS motor scores off medications compared to baseline. The most marked improvement was found in tremor, which diminished by

79%. There was also significant improvement in rigidity (58%), bradykinesia (42%), gait (56%), and postural instability (50%). Most importantly, daily "on/off" fluctuations were dramatically reduced: subjective "off" time was decreased by 61%, daily "on" time was increased by 64%, and dyskinesias decreased by 70%. A European randomized trial recently compared STN DBS with best medical treatment in 156 patients with advanced PD and motor complications (120). Six months after surgery, STN stimulation resulted in a significant improvement in quality of life and motor function with fewer dyskinesias compared to medications alone. Cognition, mood, and psychiatric function were unchanged. While serious adverse events, including death from a perioperative intracerebral hemorrhage, were more common in the neurostimulation group, the overall incidence of adverse events was higher in the medication arm (120).

Data on long-term outcomes of bilateral STN DBS in patients with advanced PD are providing reassuring evidence for the stability of this therapy in preserving patients' quality of life. A 5-year prospective study of the first 49 consecutive patients treated with STN DBS in Grenoble reported encouraging results (121). In this study, off-medication motor scores at 5 years were still 54% better than baseline, while ADL scores improved 49%. Speech was the only motor function with no improvement in off-medication scores. Moreover, dopaminergic medications and levodopa-induced dyskinesia were significantly reduced compared to baseline. The average scores for cognitive performance and mean depression remained unchanged, although one patient committed suicide. Worsening of on-medication akinesia, speech, postural stability, and freezing of gait between the first and the fifth years was interpreted as consistent with the

TABLE 54-4
STN DBS Results

STUDY (REF. #)	PERCENTAGE UPDRS–III IMPROVEMENT (NO. OF SUBJECTS)					
	3 MONTHS	6 MONTHS	12 MONTHS	24 MONTHS	36 MONTHS	60 MONTHS
Limousin et al. 1998 (46)			60% (20)			
Burchiel et al., 1999 (171)			44% (5)			
DBS Study Group 2001 (100)	49% (96)	52% (96)				
Volkmann et al., 2001 (141)		67% (16)	60% (16)			
Ostergaard et al., 2002 (233)	57% (26)		64% (26)			
Romito et al., 2002 (234)				49% (10)	49% (7)	
Vingerhoets et al., 2002 (28)	46% (19)	49% (19)	49% (19)	53% (10)		
Kleiner–Fisman et al., 2003 (235)			51% (25)			
Krack et al., 2003 (121)			65.8% (43)		59% (40)	53.7% (39)
Anderson et al., 2005 (171)			48% (10)			
Schupbach et al., 2005 (122)		59% (37)		69% (37)		54% (37)
Deuschl et al., 2006 (120)		40.8% (71)				
Mean (total pts)	47% (227)	58% (108)	54% (248)	50% (29)	58% (49)	54% (42)

TABLE 54-5
GPi DBS Results

STUDY (REF. #)	PERCENTAGE UPDRS–III IMPROVEMENT (NO. OF SUBJECTS)							
	3 MONTHS	6 MONTHS	9 MONTHS	12 MONTHS	24 MONTHS	36 MONTHS	48 MONTHS	60 MONTHS
Ghika et al., 1998 (125)		53% (6)	52% (6)	55% (6)	50% (6)			
Krack et al., 1998 (106)		39% (5)						
DBS Study Group 2001 (100)	37% (38)	33% (38)						
Scotto di Luzio et al., 2001 (236)	49% (5)	44% (5)		42% (5)				
Volkmann et al., 2001 (141)	56% (11)			51% (11)				
Durif et al., 2002 (237)		36% (6)		26% (6)	38% (6)			
Loher et al., 2002 (238)	36% (10)			41% (10)				
Lyons et al., 2002 (127)							37% (9)	
Volkmann et al., 2004 (126)				55% (10)		49% (9)		23% (6)
Anderson et al., 2005 (171)			39% (10)					
Mean (total pts)	45% (64)	41% (60)	46% (16)	45% (48)	44% (12)	49% (9)	37% (9)	23% (6)

natural history of PD (121). Schupbach et al. reported similar sustained benefits—also associated with moderate motor and cognitive decline—in 37 PD patients followed for 5 years after DBS surgery (122).

Finally, a comprehensive meta-analysis of published STN DBS studies gathered results from 921 patients with an average age of 58.6 ± 2.4 years (range 53 to 63) and mean disease duration of 14.1 ± 1.6 years (range 8.4 to 16.4). Aside from confirming on a larger scale the postoperative symptomatic improvements and medication reductions previously described, this study integrated 34 individual reports to arrive at uni- and multivariable metaregression models. According to this analysis, improvements in UPDRS motor and ADL scores after STN DBS were predicted by higher baseline UPDRS scores, shorter follow-up time (6 months vs. >12 months), longer disease duration, and levodopa responsiveness (123).

Globus Pallidum Pars Interna

The first study of DBS targeted to the GPi in PD patients was published in 1994, shortly after the initial experience with STN. Sigfried and Lippitz reported satisfactory clinical results in 3 patients with advanced PD, motor fluctuations, and dyskinesias (47). Although it appears to be an obvious target given the prior clinical success of pallidotomies, the GPi was never consistently adopted as a prime DBS target for PD (see more below on this controversy). Nevertheless, as with STN DBS, stimulation of the GPi has resulted in attractive symptomatic control without the severe speech, balance, and cognitive impairments that often accompany bilateral lesioning procedures (Table 54-5).

The consistent effect of pallidal stimulation is a marked reduction of contralateral levodopa-induced dyskinesias (22, 124). Improvement of "off"-period symptoms of parkinsonism is significant in most studies and in the range of 30% to 50% for bilateral stimulation. Similar to STN DBS, the easing of dyskinesias and the reduction of off-period disability provides patients significant improvement in self-perceived motor fluctuations. In 2001, the prospective, multicenter, double-blind, crossover study conducted by the Deep Brain Stimulation for Parkinson's Disease Study Group also evaluated 41 atients treated with GPi DBS (100). At 6 months, tremor improved by 59%, rigidity by 31%, and bradykinesia by 26% when baseline off-medication UPDRS motor scores were compared to the off-medication/on-stimulation state after 6 months. Furthermore, gait, postural stability, and subjective dyskinesia-free "on" time were all increased by about 35%. Similarly, the patient's interpretation of "off" time was decreased by 13%.

Long-term studies with GPi stimulation have provided less consistent results. A 2-year follow-up revealed diminished GPi DBS effectiveness after 12 months, leading to the return of dyskinesias due to an obligatory increase in medications, although a 32% improvement in off-medication motor scores was still observed at 24 months (125). Similar results were reported by Volkmann et al. in 11 PD patients followed for 5 years (126). While dyskinesias remained significantly reduced until the last assessment, the initial improvement of "off"-period motor symptoms and fluctuations gradually declined after the first year of stimulation. Replacement of pallidal electrodes into the subthalamic nucleus in 4 patients restored the initial benefit of DBS and allowed a significant reduction of dopaminergic drug therapy. However, in another long-term follow-up study, Lyons et al. reported sustained improvements in UPDRS, motor, and ADL scores, dyskinesias, as well as "on" and "off" times after 4 years of pallidal DBS (127).

COMPLICATIONS OF DBS

Adverse events related to DBS are classified into 3 categories: procedure-related, device- or hardware-related, and stimulation-related (Table 54-6).

Procedure-Related Adverse Events

Because of the invasive nature of the surgery, there is a risk of intraparenchymal hemorrhage, which has been reported in 1% to 5% of cases (128–130). The severity of hemorrhage can vary greatly from small, subclinical bleeds along the implantation tract to large, life-threatening accumulations. Only 5 of 86 patients (6%) sustained persistent neurologic sequelae in one study (128). In our experience, the rate of significant neurologic events directly following surgery is approximately 1% to 2% (131). There is no particular indication in the literature on how to handle hemorrhagic complications related to DBS surgery (132).

There are few data in the literature regarding the incidence and most frequent location of misplaced leads, which may be implanted outside the target nucleus and even in the cerebral ventricles (133). In a series of 41 patients referred for "DBS failure," we found that 19 (46%) had suboptimally placed electrodes (23). The consensus is that lead misplacement can be prevented using reliable stereotactic technique, including MERs (132). Misplaced leads usually result in suboptimal clinical outcome and unwanted side effects at low-voltage stimulation. They can be diagnosed radiographically and revised as soon as possible in order to minimize patient discomfort.

Hardware-Related Adverse Events

More common are the risks related to the implanted hardware, which have been reported with frequencies varying from 2.7% to 50% of patients (128–130, 132–135). A

TABLE 54-6
Complications of DBS

- **Procedure-related**
  - Intracranial hemorrhage (128–130)
  - Misplaced lead (23,133)
  - Seizures
  - Confusion
- **Device-related**
  - Skin erosion/infection (132)
  - Lead fracture (132)
  - Lead migration (132)
  - Extension wire failure (132)
  - Foreign body reaction/granuloma (132)
  - Seroma (132)
  - Pulse generator malfunction (132)
- **Stimulation-related (reversible)**
  - **Vim**
    - Paresthesias (118)
    - Pain (118)
    - Muscle contractions (118)
    - Dysarthria (118)
    - Postural instability/ataxia (118)
    - Dysphagia (118)
  - **STN**
    - Dyskinesias/hemiballismus (93)
    - Paresthesias
    - Muscle contractions
    - Dysarthria/dysphonia (46, 93, 155)
    - Hypotonia
    - Gait/postural instability (156)
    - Abnormal eye movements, diplopia (93)
    - Apraxia eyelid opening (46, 93, 141, 142)
    - Acute depression (143–146,157)
    - Hypomania (147–148, 153–154)
    - Impaired verbal fluency (143, 183–187)
  - **GPi**
    - Muscle contractions
    - Dysarthria
    - Visual phenomena

---

retrospective analysis of 124 electrodes in 79 patients revealed that 20 (25%) had hardware-related complications involving 23 electrodes: 4 lead fractures, 4 lead migrations, 3 short or open circuits, 12 erosions/infections, and 1 cerebrospinal fluid leak (130). We reported a 15.3% incidence of hardware-related complications in our initial 131 cases (131).

Infections after DBS implants have been reported with rates varying from 1% to 15%, depending on the diagnostic criteria, which are not well defined in the literature (132). They can present at variable locations (burr-hole site, generator pocket, connecting wires) and at variable times after implantation, but there have not been any reported cases of sepsis or death from an infected DBS electrode (132). Therapeutic strategies can also vary greatly, and there is no consensus on how to deal with infections once they occur. In cases of active infection, we almost invariably advocate hardware removal, since attempts at providing antibiotic therapy without doing so have a high rate of failure (136). If the infection is restricted to the IPG, the battery and extension cable can be removed with the DBS electrode left in place (134). A new IPG and extension cable can be replaced after 6 to 8 weeks of antibiotic therapy (137).

Other hardware-related complications include electrode fracture, extension-wire failure, lead migration, skin erosion, foreign-body reaction, granuloma, seroma, IPG malfunction, and pain over the pulse generator (132). The literature regarding diagnosis, prevention, and treatment of hardware-related complications is limited (132, 138).

Stimulation-Related Adverse Events

Electrical brain stimulation evokes behavioral effects that depend on the location of the electrodes, the stimulation parameters, and the type of neural tissue stimulated (i.e., cells vs. axons). Stimulation-related adverse events are strictly dependent on the anatomic location of the therapeutic target. They can be further categorized as side effects that are specific to stimulation of the intended surgical target and side effects related to current diffusion into adjacent areas of the central nervous system (93).

Target-Specific Adverse Events

Vim. The target of therapeutic stimulation in the thalamus is the nucleus ventralis intermedius (Vim), which is the thalamic area receiving cerebellar input. The Vim is located next to the ventral caudal (Vc) nucleus of the thalamus, the main somatosensory receiving area of the thalamus (Figure 54-4). Not surprisingly, the most frequent side effects encountered during thalamic DBS are paresthesias and pain (118). These will complicate Vim DBS if the DBS lead is located too posteriorly or if stimulation parameters are spreading the electrical field posteriorly into the somatosensory region. Less frequently, tetanic muscle contractions can result from costimulation of the pyramidal tract in the adjacent internal capsule. Other side effects include disequilibrium or balance difficulties, dysphagia, cognitive difficulties, and abnormal gait (118), which can normally be managed by adjusting the stimulation settings. Interestingly, when thalamic stimulation is applied bilaterally, the primary adverse effects are dysarthria and postural instability (118), suggesting the involvement of the internal capsule and possibly cerebellar afferent tracts. Dysphagia and increased salivation have also been reported. In general, lowering the stimulation voltage or switching to a different active contact (if still therapeutic) can resolve these complications.

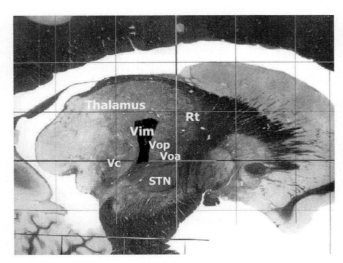

FIGURE 54-4

Sagittal section of the thalamus, illustrating the relationship of the nucleus ventralis intermedius (Vim) with the ventral caudal (Vc) nucleus and other neural structures. Rt = reticular thalamus; STN = SUBTHALAMIC Nucleus; Vc = ventral caudal nucleus; Vim = nucleus ventralis intermedius; Voa = nucleus ventro-oralis anterior; Vop = nucleus ventro-oralis posterior. (Courtesy of Dr. Jay Shils). See color section following page 356.

Subthalamic nucleus. The exact therapeutic mechanism(s) and anatomic location of the electrodes is still a matter of debate (96, 97, 139, 140). Nevertheless, the STN itself remains the anatomic target for subthalamic DBS, and adverse events resulting from its stimulation may be used to confirm proper lead placement.

The typical target-related adverse event is the development of *dyskinesias*, which are clinically similar to levodopa-induced dyskinesias and may, in fact, be worsened by levodopa therapy. Stimulation-induced dyskinesias can develop slowly over a period of minutes to hours (93) and can be managed with decreases in both stimulation voltage and levodopa dose. With chronic stimulation and levodopa reductions, the threshold for inducing dyskinesias seems to increase over time, allowing for progressive increases in voltage. As dyskinesias can either be caused or ultimately treated by STN DBS, this symptom is addressed further on, with other controversial issues.

A particularly troublesome adverse event related to target stimulation is *hypotonia*. Successful resolution of rigidity can predispose the parkinsonian patient to rapid loss of tone of antigravity muscles of the lower limbs, resulting in impairment of gait and postural stability. A complaint of "jelly legs" or falls that were not experienced before the surgery is not uncommon in the first few weeks of DBS therapy. Usually these symptoms are exacerbated by levodopa and should be managed with either a reduction in levodopa dose or stimulation voltage. Gait rehabilitation that strengthens the antigravity muscles can provide further stabilization of these symptoms.

Apraxia of eyelid opening (AEO) is a rare condition in which patients have difficulty opening otherwise normal eyelids. It is commonly associated with blepharospasm and some neurodegenerative disorders (e.g., PD and progressive supranuclear palsy). It has been occasionally described after STN DBS (46, 141, 142). The specific cause or control center for both blepharospasm and AEO is poorly understood, as is the mechanism by which DBS causes or aggravates this problem. The fact that AEO is associated with good motor responses suggests that it may be a direct consequence of STN stimulation, possibly secondary to the involvement of the oculomotor loop (93). A case report implicated electrical current spread to the dorsal trigeminothalamic tract, which is located just caudal and medial to the STN (142). If using dorsal contacts is not effective, AEO can be treated with botulinum toxin injections or myectomy.

A wide range of *neuropsychiatric and cognitive complications* of STN DBS surgery have been reported (143). A recent meta-analysis including a total of 1,398 patients who underwent bilateral STN DBS found cognitive problems in 41%, depression in 8%, and hypomania in 4% of the patients. Anxiety disorders were observed in less than 2%, and personality changes, hypersexuality, apathy, anxiety, and aggressiveness in less than 0.5% of the reported cases. Notably, about half of the patients did not experience behavioral changes (144). Acute transient depressive and euphoric mood states as well as the subacute onset of major depression, mania, and anxiety have been described in response to subthalamic stimulation (145, 146). Stimulation-induced hypomanic conditions may include mirthful laughter, euphoria, logorrhea, overactivity, and increased sexual drive (147, 148). As levodopa and dopamine agonists can induce similar mood elevations in PD patients (149–151), one might mistake these as medication-induced effects and reduce dopaminergic therapy when, in fact, stimulator adjustments may be more appropriate.

Behavioral changes observed during programming are considered to be a consequence of the interaction with dopaminergic medications or secondary to stimulation of an unintended target. Additional factors that may contribute to the onset of psychiatric symptoms in DBS patients include prolonged implantation procedures with multiple electrode passes through the frontal lobes and the psychosocial consequences of an outstanding response (i.e., loss of the "sick role") commonly seen in patients with chronic disabilities (145). However, the fact that similar behavioral disturbances have not been documented following surgery at other DBS targets (152) suggests that at least some of these neuropsychiatric effects may be related to stimulation of the limbic STN, which is located in the most medial area of the nucleus in primates (153, 154). While further physiologic and imaging studies are needed to better define the pathogenesis of these phenomena, it

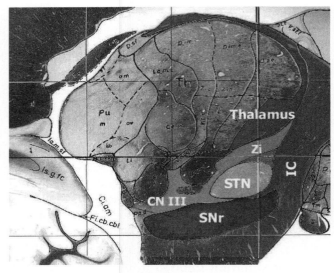

FIGURE 54-5

Sagittal view of the subthalamic area, illustrating the anatomic relationships of the subthalamic nucleus (STN). CN III = oculomotor nerve fibers; IC = internal capsule; SNr = substantia nigra pars reticulata; Zi = zona incerta. (Courtesy of Dr. Jay Shils). See color section following page 356.

may be appropriate to avoid the deepest and most medial contacts and carefully adjust dopaminergic medications in patients showing behavioral abnormalities during subthalamic DBS programming. Because their relationship with STN stimulation is still poorly defined, cognitive and mood complications are discussed further on, with other controversial issues.

The STN is nestled in an area dense with important cellular and white matter structures (Figure 54-5), and stimulation of these can cause several unwanted side effects. Assuming that the DBS lead is correctly placed, these problems can be prevented in most cases by appropriate programming strategies. Manipulations of PW or amplitude as well as the appropriate use of mono- or bipolar settings allow the programmer to control the volume of neural tissue affected by DBS therapy. If adverse events clearly related to structures surrounding the STN persist and overwhelm DBS benefits despite proper adjustments of the field and energy of stimulation, lead placement should be checked and eventual lead revision should be considered. Table 54-7 summarizes the most frequently encountered stimulation-related adverse events and the most likely area affected by stimulation in each case.

Similar to what has been observed for thalamic DBS, *dysarthria* is probably the single most frequent adverse event interfering with successful subthalamic DBS in PD. Speech problems such as hypophonia; monotone pitch; hoarse, breathy, or tremulous voice; and slurred, hesitating or fast speaking (festination of speech)are frequently encountered in patients with PD. It may be difficult to

---

TABLE 54-7
Probable Lead Location for Some Stimulation-Related Adverse Events

STN

ADVERSE EVENT	DBS LEAD IS LIKELY	STRUCTURE STIMULATED
Dysarthria/dysphagia	Too anterior and lateral	Corticobulbar fibers
Tonic muscle contractions	Too lateral or anterior	Corticospinal fibers
Diplopia / eye deviations	Too medial and ventral	Oculomotor fibers
Ataxia Too medial and ventral	Cerebellar fibers	
Persistent dysesthesias	Too posterior and medial	Medial lemniscus
Acute depression	Too ventral	Substantia nigra
Dyskinesias	On target	Subthalamic nucleus

GPi

ADVERSE EVENT	DBS LEAD IS LIKELY	STRUCTURE STIMULATED
Dysarthria	Too posteromedial	Corticobulbar fibers
Tonic muscle contractions	Too posteromedial	Corticospinal fibers
Visual phenomena	Too ventral	Optic tract
No effect at high voltage	Too superior, anterior, or lateral	

---

differentiate what is an adverse event related to stimulation and what is simply an unresolved or progressive symptom of the disease. In fact, as they are relatively resistant to levodopa therapy, speech abnormalities are often unaffected by subthalamic DBS (46).

Nevertheless, specific speech difficulties temporally related to subthalamic stimulation are frequently encountered during programming and are likely related to unwanted stimulation of adjacent corticobulbar fibers. Corticobulbar fibers pass directly anterior, lateral, and ventral to the STN and are particularly affected the most ventral contacts, 0 and 1, are being used. Speech impairment secondary to stimulation is characterized subjectively by an increased effort to speak and objectively by hypophonia, hesitation, slurring of words, and rapid fatigue (93). Because there is no habituation, the patient is sometimes faced with the dilemma of choosing between PD improvement and normal speech. However, careful adjustments of stimulation settings—including lowering the amplitude, switching to more dorsal contacts, and/or to bipolar configuration—prevent severe speech impairment in the vast majority of cases. In our experience using the 3387 lead, speech problems can be often avoided using contacts 2 and 3 unless tremor represents the major PD symptom to treat. Speech therapy and in particular the Lee Silverman Voice Technique can provide further improvement in these cases (155).

Occasionally, we have encountered patients complaining of *dysphagia* after successful STN programming. Like speech abnormalities, dysphagia can be a symptom of untreated PD, and it may be only the temporal association with STN suggesting an etiologic correlation. The pathogenesis of dysphagia after STN DBS is probably similar to that of dysarthria. Swallowing abnormalities may result from unwanted interference with signals carried by corticobulbar fibers to the swallowing muscles. Significant improvement of dysphagia can be obtained by lowering stimulation amplitude or by switching to more dorsal contacts and/or to bipolar configuration.

Tonic muscle contractions of the contralateral face, hand, and, more rarely, arm and leg, can be observed after subthalamic stimulation. These symptoms need to be clinically differentiated from off-medication dystonia in patients with PD. Reduction of the amplitude and switching to another clinically effective contact are usually effective in preventing the unwanted activation of the pyramidal system. If these adjustments provide little relief, lead revision should be considered.

Diplopia, blurred vision, and *abnormal eye movements* can be observed in patients with STN DBS. These are not symptoms usually seen in PD and clearly suggest current diffusion toward the fibers of the oculomotor nerve, which sweep medially, ventrally, and posteriorly to the STN. When stimulation affects the oculomotor nerve, adduction or downward movement of the ipsilateral eye can be seen. In these cases, it is imperative to switch to a more dorsal contact and eventually lower the amplitude or change the configuration to bipolar (field shaping). If abnormal eye movements are observed at unusually low voltages, lead revision should be considered.

Postural instability is another symptom frequently encountered in patients with PD that can occasionally worsen or present de novo after subthalamic DBS. Preexisting postural instability is generally improved by subthalamic DBS (156) unless it had not responded to levodopa therapy. In some cases, postural instability may derive from hypotonia caused by the additive effects of successful stimulation and levodopa therapy. In other cases, the patient may complain of distinct truncal ataxia, a sensation of retropulsion, and possible falls that were never experienced before DBS. In these instances, the current is likely spreading to the cerebello-rubro-thalamic fibers medial to the STN or to the red nucleus positioned medially and ventrally (93). Decreasing amplitude and PW, moving to more dorsal contacts, and/or to bipolar configuration can improve balance in most cases.

Transient contralateral "tingling" sensations resembling "electrical currents" are usually predictive of good lead location and positive stimulation outcome. However, persistent *paresthesias* indicate current spread to the medial lemniscus or sensory thalamus, located ventrally and posterior to the STN. In most cases, programming adjustments such as decreasing the amplitude and focusing the field with bipolar stimulation relieves sensory symptoms. If the patient reports persistent dysesthesias at unusually low voltages, lead revision should be considered.

Transient *acute depression* has been reported during STN DBS and may be related to stimulation of the substantia nigra (157). It is speculated that the pathogenesis of depression and mood liability with stimulation of the SN may be related to its anatomical connections with the amygdala and the limbic system (157). In these cases, using more dorsal contacts will avoid this dramatic adverse effect of stimulation.

Globus pallidum.   Unlike the STN, the GPi is a relatively large nuclear mass that can accommodate the DBS lead and its therapeutic electrical field. In fact, the complications of pallidal stimulation are relatively rare (125–127). Ideally the lead should be positioned in the posteroventral portion of the internal pallidum (158); thus two main anatomic boundaries need to be taken into account: (a) the corticospinal tracts sweeping posteromedially and (b) the optic tract passing ventrally to the GPi border. Based on these anatomic correlations (Figure 54-6), it is easy to explain why the most frequently reported stimulation-related side effects in the GPi are contralateral contractions of tongue, throat, face, or limbs as well as dysarthria, gagging, and facial tightness. Interestingly, a subjective tingling sensation may occur before any visible muscle contraction, providing a warning signal of side-effect threshold. Rarely, tonic limb contraction and cramping can be observed. As noted for the other DBS targets, reducing stimulation amplitude or switching to a

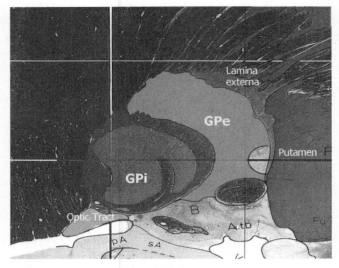

FIGURE 54-6

Sagittal view of the globus pallidum. GPe = globus pallidum pars externa; GPi = globus pallidum pars interna. (Courtesy of Dr. Jay Shils). See color section following page 356.

different active contact normally resolves these problems. If they persist at low (subclinical) voltages, lead position should be questioned and lead revision eventually planned.

As contact 0 is normally positioned very close to the optic tract (OT), visual side effects can be expected when this contact is used for therapeutic stimulation. Phosphenes, flashes, or sparkles of light in the contralateral visual field are reported by the patient when the stimulation spreads to the OT. Usually visual symptoms are transient unless the stimulation voltage is very high (more than 5 V), well beyond the therapeutic range of amplitudes (2.5 to 3.5 V). If visual complaints occur at lower voltages, an alternative contact should be used or a lead revision planned.

MECHANISMS OF ACTION

Throughout its history, the clinical possibilities—and at times revolutionary applications—of DBS have been much more clearly elucidated than the mechanisms whereby it works. Several theories have been published trying to explain the neurophysiology underlying the success of stimulation. However, we have yet to arrive at an unequivocal theory encompassing the various clinical and experimental findings associated with DBS of the basal ganglia. Indeed, it is possible that the truth lies in a combination of several theories (140). Needless to say, further clarification of the mechanism(s) of action of DBS may yield immense benefits to our knowledge of basal ganglia pathophysiology and to its clinical effectiveness. Understanding how DBS works will make us more adept at manipulating the active contacts and stimulation parameters, so that we may ultimately achieve optimal and enduring symptomatic control. The currently proposed theoretical mechanisms of DBS for PD are reviewed below.

It would be intuitive to conclude that electrical stimulation of a cell body or axon produces activation of that neuron. Indeed, there are increased levels of glutamate during STN stimulation in the rat, which implies activation of glutamatergic neurons projecting to the globus pallidus (159). We know that pallidal stimulation using ventral contacts in proximity to the optic nerve causes positive visual phenomena such as flashes of light, while subthalamic stimulation of dorsal contacts near thalamus may yield sensory phenomena such as paresthesias. Similarly, tetanic contractions in the face and limbs often result from stimulation of various targets in the vicinity of the internal capsule. These examples suggest that the introduction of electrical current via DBS *activates* the target regions and facilitates the release of neurotransmitters.

On the other hand, it has been observed that DBS of basal ganglia structures results in effects similar to surgical lesioning. Positron emission tomography (PET) studies show that metabolic activity within the cortex is very similar after pallidotomy and DBS (160). How, then, are the mechanisms of DBS not *inhibitory*? When the STN of rats is stimulated, there appears to be decreased neuronal activity of the SNr and Gpi (161). Perhaps DBS ultimately leads to inhibition via activation of inhibitory afferents. The release of GABA, resulting in inhibition, may originate from afferents of the thalamic reticular nucleus in Vim or from the globus pallidum pars externa (Gpe) or putamen in STN and Gpi (162).

In an attempt to rectify these seemingly disconjugate findings, 4 general hypotheses have been described: depolarization blockade, synaptic inhibition, synaptic depression, and stimulation-induced modulation of pathologic network activity (163). The early concepts of *depolarization blockade*, introduced by Beurrier et al. in 2001, and synaptic inhibition, proposed by Dostrovsky et al. in 2000, have helped to explain the connection between the therapeutic benefits of ablation and DBS (164, 165). Depolarization blockade describes the block of neural outputs near the stimulating electrode via activation of voltage-gated currents by changes in stimulation (164). *Synaptic inhibition* is a more indirect mechanism, whereby neuronal outputs are inhibited by activation of efferent neurons connecting with neurons near the stimulating electrode (165). These early hypotheses have fallen out of favor because they do not consider the possible independent activation of local neurons and their axons. The single-unit recordings used as the basis for developing these 2 ideas focus on the soma and not the axon. This is concerning because, during extracellular stimulation,

the axon plays a more important role in activating surrounding cells (166), and the soma's response does not always match that of the axon (167).

The theory of *synaptic depression* was also aimed at conciliating the clinical effects of DBS and ablation (168). It postulates that depletion of neurotransmitter after a stimulus train makes neurons unable to maintain high-frequency firing. In this way, transmission of signals could be blocked between nuclei by high-frequency stimulation (168). However, subsequent studies have consistently shown increases in transmitter release following activation of postsynaptic neurons. Therefore synaptic depression cannot be the sole mechanism whereby DBS exerts effect (163).

Finally, DBS may simply alter abnormal subcortical firing patterns in a more synchronized fashion. It has been hypothesized that DBS functions by substituting pathologic output "noise" from the basal ganglia with a "noise" that is more "pleasing" to cortex. In 2003, Hashimoto et al. described the transmission blockade of altered neuronal activity patterns by high-frequency stimulation of the subthalamic nucleus (169). By replacing abnormal low-frequency oscillatory activity (170) with tonic high-frequency output, DBS may facilitate the unaffected components of the basal ganglia-thalamocortical pathways (163).

It is most likely that DBS modulates neural activity on a much larger scale than can be explained by excitation or inhibition at the cellular level. The mechanisms underlying the positive therapeutic benefit probably involve all of the above theories to various extents. Further research, using in vivo recordings and computer modeling is needed to elucidate DBS mechanisms of action and possibly improve our understanding of PD pathophysiology.

CONTROVERSIAL ISSUES

Optimal Target: STN vs. Gpi

Both the Gpi and the STN are effective targets for DBS, but which target should be preferentially chosen to treat PD remains a controversial topic. There is a relative paucity of research (in particular large prospective randomized trials) directed at comparing the results of each target, but some conclusions can be drawn from the data available. A randomized, blinded study in 20 PD patients studied the outcomes of bilateral STN or Gpi DBS with blinded evaluations conducted 3, 6, and 12 months postoperatively (171). At the 1-year mark, rigidity, bradykinesia, tremor, speech, gait, posture, and postural stability were all improved in both groups, although bradykinesia and axial symptoms improved to a slightly greater degree in the STN group. Off-medication motor scores were improved by 39% in the Gpi group and 48% in the

STN group, although UPDRS ADL scores were improved by 23% in all patients, regardless of the surgical target. There were no significant changes in cognition or behavior in either group, but the levodopa dosage was reduced by 38% in the STN group vs. 3% in the Gpi group. The on-medication/off-stimulation scores deteriorated in both groups similarly. Dyskinesias were markedly improved in both groups at 12 months (89% for Gpi and 62% for STN). The differences in these targets were statistically small but appeared to be consistent with previous reports citing greater efficacy of STN stimulation for bradykinesia (106, 41). The Deep Brain Stimulation for Parkinson's Disease Study Group conducted a prospective, double-blind, crossover study in which 96 patients were (not randomly) implanted in the STN and 38 patients were implanted in the GPi (100). Three months postoperatively, motor scores were improved 49% in the STN group and 37% in the GPi group. At 6 months, daytime mobility without involuntary movements improved from 27% to 74% in the STN group and from 28% to 64% in the GPi group ($P < 0.001$ for all comparisons).

There is emerging evidence suggesting that patients treated with STN DBS may experience more frequent neuropsychiatric complications than those receiving pallidal stimulation (172), although such evidence is inconclusive (143). In fact, STN stimulation may improve other neuropsychiatric symptoms, either directly or as a consequence of the reduction of dopaminergic medications. Ongoing large, randomized, controlled studies will hopefully provide further data to decide whether preoperative neuropsychiatric comorbidity should play a role in target selection (143).

In considering cost, STN stimulation seems to have an advantage because it generally uses 2 to 3 times less electrical energy (99, 141) and decreases medication requirements 65% (173). This cost benefit may be offset by the need for more rigorous postoperative programming visits and side effects on mood and motivation secondary to levodopa withdrawal (141).

It appears that the STN is the preferred target for PD patients at most centers because it provides better efficacy in reducing motor symptoms in the "off" state, better stimulation energy conservation, and more pronounced medication reduction. Pallidal stimulation may be useful in older patients, for whom levodopa withdrawal may be difficult, cognitive profile more vulnerable and programming requirements too time-consuming (124, 172).

Dyskinesias

Optimal surgical treatment of dyskinesias is a subplot of the STN vs. Gpi controversy. Severe levodopa-induced dyskinesias are considered a prime indication for Gpi DBS. Indeed, the effects of pallidal stimulation on dyskinesias are usually remarkable (22, 100, 126, 171). Dyskinesias

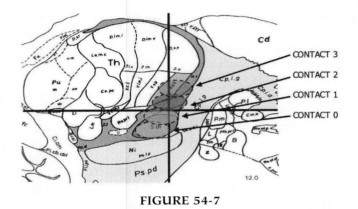

FIGURE 54-7

Schematic representation of the 3387 DBS electrode placement in the subthalamic area, illustrating the extended anatomic area that can be stimulated by its 4 contacts. (Courtesy of Dr. Jay Shils). See color section following page 356.

are among the adverse events of STN stimulation (93, 100, 102, 103). We know that the intraoperative induction of dyskinesias is considered one of the markers for good lead placement in the STN and a predictor of a positive response to chronic stimulation.

Somewhat surprisingly, STN DBS provides outstanding improvement of dyskinesias, comparable to that observed after pallidal stimulation (22, 46, 100, 120). Such a remarkable outcome is usually attributed to reduced levodopa requirements (102). However, we and others have observed it as an immediate effect of stimulation, particularly with the activation of the 2 most dorsal electrodes that likely stimulate an area outside the STN, such as the zona incerta and pallidothalamic fibers (174–176). The pathophysiologic relevance of this needs to be elucidated, but it suggests that the entire subthalamic area and not only the STN itself may be a target of successful stimulation in PD (Figure 54-7). Support for this interpretation comes from a recent study reporting that DBS differentially affects fibers crossing the subthalamic area, activating the subthalamic-pallidal pathway while inhibiting pallidothalamic output (177).

Both GPi and STN DBS seem to successfully control levodopa-induced dyskinesias. Given the additional benefits of PD symptom control and medication reduction, we advocate the use of subthalamic DBS even when dyskinesias are the major indication for surgery.

The Role of Age

Advanced age (greater than 70 years) is considered by some to be a poor outcome predictor or even a contraindication for DBS surgery (25, 26). However, given that the average age of onset of PD is 60 years and the mean illness duration is 10 to 15 years at the time of surgery, a large proportion of potential DBS candidates are 70 years of age or older. Age and duration of symptoms influence the natural history of PD independently (178), and aging effects on nigrostriatal dopaminergic neurons are considered unresponsive to levodopa (179). In addition, the incidence of cognitive dysfunction is progressively greater in PD patients above age 70 (180). Saint-Cyr et al. reported that a post-DBS decline in several spheres of mental processing (particularly frontal executive function) was more common in patients above age 69 (40). As a result of this important but relatively small study, many neurologists tend to shy away from recommending DBS to patients above age 70.

In a study of 52 levodopa-responsive PD patients undergoing STN-DBS, Russmann et al. reported that postoperatively those above age 70 experienced similar improvement of motor fluctuations and dyskinesia as did younger patients and that surgery was equally well tolerated (38). These results suggest that older patients may benefit from DBS as well as younger ones. However, older patients had a less dramatic improvement in their off-medication motor UPDRS score and a smaller reduction in levodopa dose. More discouraging was an actual decline in "on" motor UPDRS score and ADLs after surgery. Axial scores in particular seemed to be adversely effected by DBS in older patients. Twenty-five percent of patients above age 70 were institutionalized at the 48-month follow-up. The authors concluded that age itself is probably an independent risk factor in predicting poor DBS outcomes in PD patients.

In reality, there are patients above age 70 who do very well after DBS (38, 39). Of the 13 elderly patients in Russmann's study, 5 (38%) did well after surgery (38). In our experience, the average off-medication motor improvement of patients above age 70 (n = 18) was 48.0%, and this did not differ statistically from that observed in patients below age 70 at time of surgery (39, 181). Our cohort of patients above age 70 could be divided into 2 subsets: one that had satisfactory postoperative improvement in the off-medication state (n = 13) and another that had a less than optimal response (n = 5). Identification of the former subset preoperatively can provide a great service to elderly patients suffering from the motor complications of advanced PD. Currently it appears that abnormal results of neuropsychological testing and preoperative axial scores in the "on" state may be of higher predictive value than strict age criteria in excluding poor candidates for DBS.

Effects of Deep Brain Stimulation on Nonmotor Symptoms

It is becoming clear that the disability caused by PD extends far beyond its motor symptoms (i.e., tremor,

slowness, stiffness, or gait problems). Cognitive decline, depression, behavioral problems, dysautonomia, sleep disturbance, and pain are prominent nonmotor symptoms that often reflect the widespread neurodegeneration of PD, which extends beyond the striatal dopaminergic loss. Poorly responsive to pharmacologic treatments, these nonmotor symptoms remain a major cause of disability and loss of independence (182). While the results of properly applied DBS on motor symptoms have been outstanding, the ability to alleviate these challenging nonmotor symptoms has been far less impressive.

Cognition and Mood. One of the main obstacles in evaluating the effects of DBS on cognition and mood is the frequent occurrence of dementia and depression in the natural progression of the disease. A community-based population study found a prevalence of dementia in excess of 40% in patients with PD, with values approaching 70% in patients above age 80 (180). Although this can be attributed to the natural course of the neurodegenerative process, other factors such as medication side effects, pseudodementia secondary to depression, and excessive fatigue must be considered to play a role in cognitive decline.

Most of the studies describing *neuropsychological* outcome following DBS for PD were conducted on patients who underwent STN DBS. Transient postoperative confusion has been reported in 1% to 36% of patients (100, 101, 121, 141, 143, 146), most often after bilateral implants with multiple microelectrode passages. Beyond that, there is relatively little cognitive impairment reported in well-selected patients undergoing STN DBS. In fact, mild improvements in mental flexibility, working memory, visuomotor sequencing, conceptual reasoning, and overall cognitive function were described in some cases (143). There are, however, case reports describing severe cognitive deterioration after DBS surgery (42, 121, 183).

The most frequently reported cognitive side effect appears to be a decline in verbal fluency (40, 99, 105, 109, 110, 183–187). Older age and moderate cognitive impairment prior to surgery are associated with greater risk of developing cognitive deficits (40, 146, 185, 188), although this has not been unequivocally demonstrated (143). In addition, since dementia is an exclusion criterion in most DBS studies, there are virtually no data available on the potential effect of STN DBS on the cognitive function of patients with dementia prior to surgery.

Unfortunately, little is known about potential cognitive risk factors for patients undergoing DBS, and only a few studies have systematically examined the role of stimulation and/or medications on cognitive performance. Either no significant cognitive effects (183) or some improvement in processing speed, working memory, and problem solving were reported on stimulation

(186, 189). On the other hand, a decline in performance on a conditional associative learning task (189) and impairments in response inhibition measures have been documented on stimulation (190). A decline in working memory and response inhibition measures under high-cognitive-demand conditions has also been described (191). Interestingly, cognitive function did not change either "on" or "off" dopaminergic medications during STN stimulation in one study (192).

Similar to the case of STN stimulation, the majority of studies addressing neuropsychological changes following GPi DBS failed to reveal any significant cognitive decline (143). Mild declines in semantic word fluency (126, 193) and visuoconstruction scores (193) have been reported, while a significant but partially reversible executive dysfunction was described following bilateral pallidal stimulation (194). Finally, very few studies have addressed the neuropsychological consequences of Vim DBS, which appears to have no significant effect on cognitive abilities in PD patients (143).

The incidence and nature of *psychiatric* complications of DBS has been mostly documented with STN DBS. Apathy, depression, and hypomania are the most common psychiatric symptoms observed. *Apathy* can be associated with excessive dopaminergic withdrawal, although its incidence is not known. One longitudinal study found the incidence of apathy to grow from 9% at baseline to 25% at 3 years (105), while another reported permanent apathy in 12% of patients (121). *Hypomania* has been reported in 4% to 15% of patients, most frequently within the first 3 months of stimulation (121, 187, 195, 196). Several investigators have addressed the incidence of *depression* after STN DBS, with results ranging from 1.5% to 25% (143). Both baseline depression and withdrawal of dopaminergic medications may contribute to these figures (105, 141). Two large studies found the incidence of suicide attempts to range between 0.5% and 3% (197, 198). This wide range of neuropsychiatric symptoms suggests a multifactorial etiology that likely includes preoperative morbidity, dopaminergic therapy manipulation, surgical and stimulation effects, underlying PD-related factors, and psychosocial factors (143).

Neuropsychiatric complications of pallidal DBS seem to be less frequent. Several small studies comparing STN and GPi stimulation found that virtually none of the GPi patients developed psychiatric symptoms versus the 15% to 20% incidence in the STN group (141, 171, 199). Larger controlled studies are required to clarify this issue. Other studies of GPi DBS have reported improvement of depression and anxiety scores with isolated cases of mania and hypersexuality (143).

Autonomic Dysfunction. The autonomic dysfunction suffered by many PD patients is likely multifactorial and in most cases predates DBS surgery. It can be challenging to differentiate the impact of DBS on dysautonomia. Indeed, the basal ganglia project to several nuclei that may modify autonomic outflow, including the PPN, which, when stimulated in animals, increases heart rate and blood pressure (200). Kaufmann et al. noted, in 3 patients implanted with STN DBS, heart rate increased significantly when high-frequency (185 Hz) stimulation was initiated (200). The sympathetic activation of 5 patients receiving bilateral STN stimulator implants was studied intraoperatively (201). Marked and reproducible changes in blood pressure regulation, sweating, and respiratory patterns were detected when the electrode was placed just outside the STN. When in proximity to the posterior hypothalamus, stimulation yielded a sweating disturbance, while when near the dorsomedial hypothalamus, tachycardia, hyperthermia, and heightened stress responses were observed (201). These findings underscore the importance of accurate surgical targeting and postoperative imaging, because patients whose electrodes are located more posteriomedially to the STN may deserve additional monitoring for sympathetic side effects (201). There is a paucity of data describing the long-term effects of DBS on autonomic control. A 12-month follow-up study after bilateral STN DBS in 14 PD patients did not show any difference in the power spectra of heart rate variability frequency bands analyzed from 24-hour ECG recordings (202).

Sleep Disturbance. Asking PD patients specific questions about daytime fatigue and nighttime sleep habits often unveils an undiagnosed sleep disorder in 60% to 98% (203). Obstructive sleep apnea (OSA), periodic limb movements of sleep (PLMS), restless legs syndrome (RLS), circadian rhythm disorders, insomnia, sleep fragmentation, and rapid-eye-movement (REM) sleep behavior disorder (RBD), all have been described in PD patients. About 40% of patients with PD take sleeping pills, and the degree of sleep disturbance correlates with disease severity, UPDRS motor score, and levodopa dose (203).

A few studies have assessed sleep in PD patients who have undergone STN DBS. Using multiple investigative techniques including polysomnography, clinician ratings, and self-report questionnaires, these studies suggest that sleep is improved by from STN DBS. Reducing the dosages of potentially sedating antiparkinsonian medications may be the first way DBS improves energy levels in addition to improving sleep quality by way of improved mobility in bed and reduction of sleep fragmentation (204, 205). Subjective and objective improvement of night sleep quality during STN DBS was reported by several studies (206–208), while daytime sleepiness seem to be less affected (206, 209).

In addition, PLMS and RBD symptoms were not alleviated by stimulation, suggesting alternative pathways involved in these conditions (204, 206). In one of the few long-term studies of DBS effect on sleep, Romito et al. found that night sleep improved in all patients 3 years after surgery (210). Well-designed longitudinal studies are needed to fully understand the long-term effects of DBS on sleep.

Pain. Approximately half of all PD patients complain of pain, which can be associated with "off" dystonic spasms and other conditions such as musculoskeletal or rheumatic pain, neuritic or radicular pain, primary or central pain, and akathitic discomfort (211). Because both STN and Gpi DBS result in decreased amounts of time spent "off," pain is usually better controlled post-stimulation. In particular, *"off"* dystonia is alleviated by both procedures (102, 212). The effects of DBS on other types of PD-associated pain (e.g., central pain) have not been studied.

Patients with Previous Ablative Procedures

Animal models of MPTP-induced parkinsonism supported the experimental notion that controlling over-active pallidal output, due in part to hyperactive STN neurons projecting to, and exciting the GPi, can reduce excessive thalamic inhibition. This enhances thalamo-cortical transmission and serves to reverse PD symptoms (124). An important limitation of pallidotomy therapy has been the excessive morbidity encountered with bilateral procedures (213). Moreover, PD disability eventually returns after an extended period of time after pallidotomy (214), while high-frequency stimulation has been found to yield longer-lasting albeit reversible benefits (121, 122).

A number of studies have addressed the cases of PD patients with previous pallidotomies who were subsequently implanted with DBS electrodes (215–218). Kleiner-Fisman et al. performed pairwise comparisons of 6 patients receiving bilateral STN DBS an average of 3.5 years after successful pallidotomy and 25 patients with STN DBS with no prior lesioning procedure (215). UPDRS III motor scores "off med/on stim" were improved by 42.1% in the pallidotomy group after STN DBS, although ADL scores in the off-medication state and dyskinesias overall remained unchanged. The control group displayed similar improvement in UPDRS motor scores, ADL scores, and levodopa requirement; however, there was a greater reduction in dyskinesias (215). Revilla et al. conducted a similar study, finding 34% reduction in UPDRS III scores in postpallidotomy patients treated with STN DBS vs. 53% reduction in nonlesioned patients 3 months postoperatively (216). Levodopa medications were decreased by 36%

and 57% respectively. Postpallidotomy patients experienced clinically significant improvement, although not as impressively as did their lesion-naive cohorts (216, 217). This and other results support the safety and efficacy of bilateral STN DBS in patients who have undergone unilateral pallidotomy. Similarly, residual PD disability in tremor-predominant patients with previous thalamotomy can be greatly improved by bilateral STN stimulation (218).

An interesting controversy stemming from these studies is whether pallidal lesioning affects neuronal firing within the STN. Hyperactive STN is considered a pathophysiologic hallmark of PD and STN firing is used intraoperatively for target localization. Mogilner and colleagues analyzed the cellular activity of 6 patients undergoing STN DBS after previous unilateral palli-dotomies. In their experience, STN firing rates were significantly lower on the side ipsilateral to the previous pallidotomy, manifesting a decrease in activity (219). However, Kleiner-Fisman's group could not reproduce this finding when they studied 94 STN cells from 8 PD patients with previous unilateral pallidotomy (215). In their experience, the STN firing rates were similar to those recorded from the contralateral, nonlesioned side as well as to STN neurons from patients without previous surgery.

Is Deep Brain Stimulation Neuroprotective?

Neuroprotection is a major goal of research in neurode-generative diseases. Although not a primary focus of this research, STN DBS may theoretically alter the natural course of nigral cell loss and slow disease progression. As in other neurodegenerative diseases (220, 221), glu-tamatergic excitotoxicity appears to underlie the mechanisms of cell death leading to PD (222). In particular, it is speculated that glutamatergic output from the hyper-active STN in PD may cause excitotoxic degeneration of the pallidum, substantia nigra, and pedunculopontine nucleus, perpetuating the progression of the disease. If this is true, surgical lesioning and high-frequency stimulation of the STN, by decreasing its glutamatergic drive and resultant excitotoxicity, may slow the progression of PD (222). It would not be unreasonable to hypothesize that DBS could be neuroprotective by blocking pallidal and nigral destruction (222, 223). Unfortunately, this theory is based on the assumption that DBS has an inhibitory effect on the STN, an assumption that is itself under criticism (140). In addition, there is little clinical evidence thus far to support a neuroprotective effect of STN DBS in PD patients.

Using ^{18}F-fluorodopa PET, a surrogate marker of PD progression (224, 225), Hilker et al. conducted a prospective study of 30 patients with bilateral STN DBS to determine whether successful stimulation improved measures of PD severity (226). Despite a 52% clinical improvement in UPDRS scores compared to baseline, there was a significant decrease in striatal F-dopa uptake over the 16-month follow-up period. This translates to a 9.5% to 12.9% loss of baseline radiotracer binding per year, a rate of progression that is in line with published rates for PD patients treated pharmacologically (225). While these data suggest continued decline of dopaminergic function in the face of effective STN stimulation, other studies suggest that the progression of PD may decelerate over the long term. In a study of 22 patients who underwent successful STN DBS, Ostergaard and Sunde reported that at 4 years their motor UPDRS scores did not appear to worsen compared to baseline when kept off both medication and stimulation (227). While the lack of PD progression may be attributed to a number of factors, including possible artifacts related to the design of the study, these data need to be confirmed (or dispelled) by larger longitudinal studies.

FUTURE DIRECTIONS

The treatment of PD has been revolutionized by DBS. As more patients are implanted, the benefits and limitations of this modality are becoming better understood.

There are several device improvements in progress. The relatively large internal pulse generator implanted in the subclavicular chest area has a battery life of approximately 3 to 5 years depending on each patient's individual settings. Creation of a more compact, miniature IPG would undoubtedly be more comfortable and less cumbersome for patients. In addition, battery life extending for longer than 5 years would be more convenient. Alternatively, the ability to recharge the batteries from an external energy source would spare patients additional morbidity from another invasive surgical procedure. Finally, accessing the IPG remotely would enable physicians and DBS programmers to make small changes in settings without having to bring the patient into the office. Clearly, the importance of periodic physical examination of DBS patients cannot be overemphasized. However, remote access to IPGs would be important for urgent conditions and could prevent unnecessary and often laborious trips to emergency rooms.

One of the most significant factors impeding optimal symptomatic improvement after DBS is access to proper programming. This can be the result of a lack of competent programmers in the patient's vicinity or a physical barrier to making the frequent office visits. This issue can be addressed on several levels. There is a call for an educational initiative to make stimulator programming more pervasive within movement disorder practices across the country. There must be basic competency among physicians to make stimulator adjustments confidently. To be performed properly, both doctor and patient must agree to a committed relationship. Because this is a time-intensive undertaking, it is often efficient for practices to have specialized nurse practitioners and physician assistants dedicated to the laborious task of programming. Research is ongoing to explore "shortcuts," such as electrophysiologic or imaging markers that can lead to the optimal setting parameters and drug dosages for each patient (228).

Indeed, a better understanding of DBS mechanisms of action will likely lead to a more accurate selection of therapeutic targets and improved efficacy as clinicians move away from current generic methods of stimulation based on trial-and-error selection of the active parameters. In addition, specific electrode design and alternative deliveries of the electrical pulse (e.g., constant-current, asymmetrical pulses) may bring about parameters of stimulation customized to individual patients and specific neuropsychiatric disorders.

Assuming that each patient has access to care and the ideal individual settings, there are certain symptoms that elude even the most optimal DBS implants. Nonmotor symptoms like cognitive impairment, psychiatric disturbances, and dysautonomia, may be particularly disabling. These problems may not be related to dopaminergic stimulation and are thus refractory to DBS. We have also seen that disorders of gait and postural stability may not be particularly responsive to GPi or STN stimulation. In comparison to the other cardinal PD symptoms, the improvement is less impressive and briefer.

The frustrations of these limitations of STN and Gpi DBS have laid the groundwork for exploration into DBS of novel structures involved in modulation of locomotor activity. In conjunction with the basal ganglia, the pedunculopontine nucleus (PPN) is a deep brain structure involved in the control of motor function (229). It has been established that the PPN degenerates in Parkinson's disease as it does in related neurodegenerative disorders with extrapyramidal features, such as multiple system atrophy (MSA). Stimulation within this collection of neurons in the rostral tegmentum causes stepping movements, while lesioning results in akinesia (230). Nandi and colleagues have demonstrated the spectrum of responses when a PPN-implanted primate was stimulated at a variety of frequencies. Stimulation at 100 Hz resulted in severe loss of postural stability, while akinesia was more pronounced at frequencies above 45 Hz than at lower frequencies (229). Two groups have reported initial studies of the feasibility of PPN DBS in advanced PD (231, 232). In addition to improvement in UPDRS motor scores, Plaha and Grill demonstrated improvement in gait dysfunction and postural stability in both the on- and off-medication states with low-frequency (20 to 25 Hz) stimulation (231). This is in contrast to GPi and STN DBS, where the improvement in "off" medication gait stability is often modest and usually equivalent to that obtained with levodopa alone (231). Because improvements were seen in gait, postural stability, and other cardinal signs of PD in both the on- and off-medication states, these preliminary reports deserve further scrutiny with expanded studies. The PPN may represent an exciting new target for DBS therapy.

ACKNOWLEDGMENTS

The authors thank Caitlin Martin for her technical assistance. Dr. Malhado-Chang was supported in part by a Medtronic Fellowship.

References

1. Jankovic J. Levodopa strengths and weaknesses. *Neurology* 2002; 58(Suppl 1): S19–S32.
2. Wichmann T, DeLong MR. Models of basal ganglia function and pathophysiology of movement disorders. *Neurosurg Clin North Am* 1998; 9:223–236.
3. Penfield W, Boldrey E. Somatic motor and sensory representation in the cerebral cortex of man as studied by electrical stimulation. *Brain* 1937; 60:389–443.
4. Spiegel EA, Wycis HT, Marks M, Lee AJ. Stereotaxic apparatus for operations on the human brain. *Science* 1947; 106:349–350.
5. Spiegel EA, Wycis HT. Thalamotomy and pallidotomy for treatment of choreic movements. *Acta. Neurochir (Wien)* 1952; 2:417–422.
6. Hassler R, Riechart T, Munginer F, et al. Physiological observations in stereotaxic operations in extrapyramidal motor disturbances. *Brain* 1960; 83:337–350.
7. Ohye C, Kubota K, Hongo T, et al. Ventrolateral and subventrolateral thalamic stimulation. *Arch Neurol* 1964; 11:427–434.
8. Bergstrom MR, Johansson GG, Laitinen LV, et al. Electrical stimulation of the thalamic and subthalamic area in cerebral palsy. *Acta Physiol Scand* 1966; 67:208–213.
9. Sem-Jacobsen CW. Depth-electrographic observations related to Parkinson's disease. Recording and electrical stimulation in the area around the third ventricle. *J Neurosurg* 1966; 24(Suppl):388–402.
10. Hosobuchi Y, Adams JE, Rutkin B. Chronic thalamic stimulation for the control of facial anesthesia dolorosa. *Arch Neurol* 1973; 29:158–161.
11. Cooper IS. Effect of chronic stimulation of anterior cerebellum on neurological disease. *Lancet* 1973; 1:206.
12. Cooper IS, Riklan M, Amin I, et al. Chronic cerebellar stimulation in cerebral palsy. *Neurology* 1976; 26:744–753.
13. Penn RD. Chronic cerebellar stimulation for cerebral palsy: A review. *Neurosurgery* 1982; 10:116–121 .
14. Brice J, McLellan L. Suppression of intention tremor by contingent deep-brain stimulation. *Lancet* 1980; 1:1221–1222.
15. Benabid AL, Pollak P, Louveau A, et al. Combined (thalamotomy and stimulation) stereotactic surgery of the Vim thalamic nucleus for bilateral Parkinson disease. *Appl Neurophysiol* 1987; 50(1–6):344–346.
16. Langston JW, Ballard P, Tetrud JW, et al. Chronic parkinsonism in humans due to a product of meperidine-analog synthesis. *Science* 1983; 219:979–980.
17. Burns RS, Chieuh CC, Markey SP, et al. A primate model of parkinsonism: Selective destruction of dopaminergic neurons in the pars compacta of the substantia nigra by MPTP. *PNAS* 1983; 80:4546–4550.
18. Alexander GE, Crutcher MD, DeLong MR. Basal ganglia-thalamocortical circuits: Parallel substrates for motor, oculomotor, prefrontal and limbic functions. *Prog Brain Res* 1990; 85:119–146.
19. Bergman H, Wichmann T, DeLong M. Reversal of experimental parkinsonism by lesions of the subthalamic nucleus. *Science* 1990; 249:1436–1438.
20. Aziz TZ, Peggs D, Sambrook MA, et al. Lesion of the subthalamic nucleus for the alleviation of 1-methyl-4-phenyl-1,2,3,6-tetrahydropyridine (MPTP)–induced parkinsonism in the primate. *Mov Disord* 1991; 6:288–292.
21. Pollak P, Benabid AL, Gross C, et al. Effects of the stimulation of the subthalamic nucleus in Parkinson disease. *Rev Neurol (Paris)* 1993; 149):175–176.
22. Walter BL, Vitek JL. Surgical treatment for Parkinson's disease. *Lancet Neurol* 2004; 3:719–728.
23. Okun MS, Tagliati M, Pourfar M, et al. Management of referred DBS failures: A retrospective analysis from two movement disorders centers. *Arch Neurol* 2005; 62: 1250–1255.
24. Lang AE, Houeto JL, Krack P, et al. Deep brain stimulation: Preoperative issues. *Mov Disord* 2006; 21(Suppl 14):S171–S196.
25. Welter ML, Houeto JL, Tezenas du Montcel S, et al. Clinical predictive factors of subthalamic stimulation in Parkinson's disease. *Brain* 2002; 125:575–583.
26. Charles PD, Van Blercom N, Krack P, et al. Predictors of effective bilateral subthalamic nucleus stimulation for PD. *Neurology* 2002; 59:932–934.
27. Pahwa R, Wilkinson SB, Overman J, Lyons KE. Bilateral subthalamic stimulation in patients with Parkinson disease: Long-term follow up. *J Neurosurg* 2003; 99:71–77.
28. Vingerhoets FJ, Villemure JG, Temperli P, et al. Subthalamic DBS replaces levodopa in Parkinson's disease: Two-year follow-up. *Neurology* 2002; 58:396–401.
29. Pinter MM, Alesch F, Murg M, Helscher RJ, Binder H. Apomorphine test: A predictor for motor responsiveness to deep brain stimulation of the subthalamic nucleus. *J Neurol* 1999; 246:907–913.
30. Katayama Y, Kasai M, Oshima H, et al. Subthalamic nucleus stimulation for Parkinson disease: Benefits observed in levodopa-intolerant patients. *J Neurosurg* 2001; 95:213–221
31. Hughes AJ, Daniel SE, Kilford L, Lees AJ. Accuracy of clinical diagnosis of idiopathic Parkinson's disease. A clinico-pathological study of 100 cases. *J Neurol Neurosurg Psychiatry* 1992; 55:181–184.
32. Tarsy D, Apetauerova D, Ryan P, Norregaard T. Adverse effects of subthalamic nucleus DBS in a patient with multiple system atrophy. *Neurology* 2003; 61:247–249.
33. Tagliati M, Shils J, Miravite-Ingram J, et al. Subthalamic nucleus stimulation in two cases of multiple system atrophy. Proceedings of the Quadriennal Meeting of the ASSFN, New York, May 18–21, 2003:120.
34. Chou KL, Forman MS, Trojanowski JQ, et al. Subthalamic nucleus deep brain stimulation in a patient with levodopa-responsive multiple system atrophy. Case report. *J Neurosurg* 2004; 100:553–556.
35. Lezcano E, Gomez-Esteban JC, Zarranz JJ, et al. Parkinson's disease–like presentation of multiple system atrophy with poor response to STN stimulation: A clinicopathological case report, *Mov Disord* 2004; 19:973–977.
36. Patrick S, Kristl V, Miet DL, et al. Deep brain stimulation of the internal pallidum in multiple system atrophy. *Parkinsonism Relat Disord* 2006; 12:181–183
37. Visser-Vandewalle V, Temel Y, Colle H, van der Linden C. Bilateral high-frequency stimulation of the subthalamic nucleus in patients with multiple system atrophy parkinsonism. Report of four cases. *J Neurosurg* 2003; 98:882–887.
38. Russmann H, Ghika J, Villemure JG, et al. Subthalamic nucleus deep brain stimulation in Parkinson disease patients over age 70 years. *Neurology* 2004; 63:1952–1954.
39. Tagliati M, Pourfar MH, Alterman RL. Subthalamic nucleus deep brain stimulation in Parkinson disease patients over age 70 years. *Neurology* 2005; 65:179–80.
40. Saint-Cyr JA, Trepanier LL, Kumar R, et al. Neuropsychological consequences of chronic bilateral stimulation of the subthalamic nucleus in Parkinson's disease. *Brain* 2000; 123:2091–108.
41. Mayeux R, Denaro J, Hemenegildo N, et al. A population-based investigation of Parkinson's disease with and without dementia. Relationship to age and gender. *Arch Neurol* 1992; 49:492–497.
42. Hariz MI, Johansson F, Shamsgovara P, et al. Bilateral subthalamic nucleus stimulation in a parkinsonian patient with preoperative deficits in speech and cognition: Persistent improvement in mobility but increased dependency: A case study. *Mov Disord* 2000; 15:136–139.
43. Pillon B. Neuropsychological assessment for management of patients with deep brain stimulation. *Mov Disord* 2002; 17(Suppl 3):S116–S122.
44. Burn DJ. Beyond the iron mask: Towards better recognition and treatment of depression associated with Parkinson's disease. *Mov Disord* 2002; 17:445–454.
45. Williams DR, Lees AJ. Visual hallucinations in the diagnosis of idiopathic Parkinson's disease: A retrospective autopsy study. *Lancet Neurol* 2005; 4:605–610.
46. Limousin P, Krack P, Pollak P, et al. Electrical stimulation of the subthalamic nucleus in advanced Parkinson's disease. *N Engl J Med* 1998; 339:1105–1111.
47. Siegfried J, Lippitz B. Bilateral chronic electrostimulation of ventroposterolateral pallidum: A new therapeutic approach for alleviating all parkinsonian symptoms. *Neurosurgery* 1994; 35:1126–1130.
48. Lunsford LD, Latchaw RE, Vries J. Stereotaxic implantation of deep brain electrodes using computed tomography. *Neurosurgery* 1983; 13:280–286.
49. Lunsford LD, Martinez AJ. Stereotactic exploration of the brain in the era of computed tomography. *Surg Neurol* 1984; 22:222–230.
50. Lunsford LD, Martinez AJ, Latchaw RE. Stereotaxic surgery with a magnetic resonance and computed tomography–compatible system. *J Neurosurg* 1986; 64:872–878.
51. Kondziolka D, Dempsey PK, Lunsford LD, et al. A comparison between magnitude resonance imaging and computed tomography for stereotactic coordinate determination. *Neurosurgery* 1992; 30:402–407.
52. Bejjani B, Damier P, Arnuff I, et al. Pallidal stimulation for Parkinson's disease. Two targets? *Neurology* 1997; 49:1564–1569.
53. Alterman, RL, Reiter GT, Shils J, et al. Targeting for thalamic deep brain stimulation implantation without computer guidance: Assessment of targeting accuracy. *Stereotact Func Neurosurg* 1999; 72:150–153.

54. Taren JA, Ross DA, Gebarski SS. Stereotactic localization using fast spin-echo imaging in functional disorders. *Acta Neurochir* 1993; 58(Suppl):59–60.

55. Starr PA, Vitek JL, DeLong M, et al. Magnetic resonance imaging–based stereotactic localization of the globus pallidus and subthalamic nucleus. *Neurosurgery* 1999; 44:303–314.

56. Reich CA, Hudgins PA, Sheppard SK, et al. A high-resolution fast spin-echo inversion-recovery for preoperative localization of the internal globus pallidus. *Am J Neuroradiol* 2000; 21:928–931.

57. Zonenshayn M, Rezai AR, Mogilner AY, et al. Comparison of anatomic and neurophysiologic methods for subthalamic nucleus targeting. *Neurosurgery* 2000; 47:282–294.

58. Sumanaweera TS, Adler JR, Napel S, et al. Characterization of spatial distortion in magnetic resonance imaging and its implications for stereotactic surgery. *Neurosurgery* 1994; 35:696–704.

59. Gerdes JS, Hitchon PW, Neerangun W, et al. Computed tomography versus magnetic resonance imaging in stereotactic localization. *Stereotact Funct Neurosurg* 1994; 63:124–129.

60. Holtzheimer PE, Roberts DW, Darcey TM. Magentic resonance imaging versus computer tomaography for target localization in functional stereotactic neurosurgery. *Neurosurgery* 1999; 45:290–298.

61. Guridi J, Gorospe A, Ramos E, et al. Stereotactic targeting of the globus pallidus internus in Parkinson's disease: Imaging versus electrophysiological mapping. *Neurosurgery* 1999; 45:278–289.

62. Carlson JD, Iaconoa RP. Electrophysiologcal versus image-based targeting in the posteroventral pallidotomy. *Comput Aid Surg* 1999; 4:93–100.

63. Forster A, Eljamel MS, Varma TR, et al. Audit of neurophysiological recording during movement disorder surgery. *Stereotact Funct Neurosurg* 1999; 72:154–156.

64. Kelly PJ. Pallidotomy in Parkinson's disease (editorial). *Neurosurgery* 1995; 36: 1154–1157.

65. Brierly JB, Beck E. The significance in human stereotactic brain surgery of individual variation in the diencephalon and globus pallidus. *J Neurol Neurosurg Psychiatry* 1959; 22:287–2998.

66. Iacono RP, Lonser R, Morenski JD. Stereotactic surgery for Parkinson's disease. *Mov Disord* 1994; 2:470–472.

67. Tasker RR, Kiss ZHT. The role of the thalamus in functional neurosurgery. *Neurosurg Clin North Am* 1995; 6:73–99.

68. Organ WL, Tasker RR, Moody NF. The impedance profile of the human brain as a localization technique in stereoecephalotomy. *Confin Neurol* (Madrid) 1967; 29:192–196.

69. Tasker RR, Organ LW, Hawrylyshyn PA. *The Thalamus and Midbrain of Man. A Physiological Atlas Using Electrical Stimulation.* Springfield, IL: Charles C Thomas, 1982.

70. Yoshida M, Yanagisawa N, Shimazu H, et al. Physiological identification of the thalamic nucleus. *Arch Neurol* 1964; 11:435–443.

71. Nakajima H, Fukamachi A, Isobe I, et al. Estimation of neural noise. *Appl Neurophysiol* 1978; 41:193–201.

72. Guridi J, Lozano AM. A brief history of pallidotomy. *Neurosurgery* 1997; 41: 1169–1180.

73. Bakay RA, DeLong MR, Vitek JL. Posteroventral pallidotomy for Parkinson's disease (letter). *J Neurosurg* 1992; 77:487–488.

74. Dogali M, Beric A, Sterio D, et al. Anatomic and physiologic considerations for Parkinson's disease. *Stereotact Funct Neurosurg* 1994; 62:53–60.

75. Ohye C, Narabayashi H. Physiological study of presumed ventralis intermedius neurons in the human thalamus. *J Neurosurg* 1979; 50:290–297.

76. Hardy J. Electrophysiological localization and identification. *J Neurosurg* 1966; 24: 410–414.

77. Hutchison WD, Allan RJ, Opitz H, et al. Neurophysiological identification of the subthalamic nucleus in surgery for Parkinson's disease. *Ann Neurol* 1998; 44: 622–628.

78. Lenz FA, Tasker RR, Kwan HC, et al. Selection of the optimal site for the relief of parkinsonian tremor on the basis of spectral analysis of neuronal firing patterns. *Appl Neurophysiol* 1987; 50:338–343.

79. Lenz FA, Dostrovsky JO, Tasker RR, et al. Single-unit analysis of the human ventral thalamic nuclear group: Somatosensory responses. *J Neurophysiol* 1988; 59:299–316.

80. Lenz FA, Tasker RR, Kwan HC, et al. Single unit analysis of the human ventral thalamic nuclear group: Correlation of thalamic tremor cells with the 3- to 6-Hz component of parkinsonian tremor. *J Neurosci* 1988; 8:754–764.

81. Lenz FA, Kwan HC, Dostrovsky JO, et al. Single unit analysis of the human ventral thalamic nuclear group. *Brain* 1990; 113:1795–1821.

82. Taha JM, Favre J, Baumann TK, et al. Functional anatomy of the pallidal base in Parkinson's disease. *Neurosurgery* 1996; 39:1164–1168.

83. Taha JM, Favre J, Baumann TK, et al. Characteristics and somatotopic organization of kinesthetic cells in the globus pallidus of patients with parkinson's disease. *J Neurosurg* 1996; 85:1005–1012.

84. Dogali M, Fazzini E, Kolodny E, et al. Stereotactic ventral pallidotomy for Parkinson's disease. *Neurology* 1995; 45:753–761.

85. Lozano A, Hutchison W, Kiss Z, et al. Methods for microelectrode-guided posteroventral pallidotomy. *J Neurosurg* 1996; 84:194–202.

86. Hirai T, Miyazaki M, Nakajima H, et al. The correlation between tremor characteristics and the predicted volume of effective lesions in stereotaxic nucleus ventralis intermedius thalamotomy. *Brain* 1983; 106:1001–1018.

87. Gillingham FJ. Depth recording and stimulation. *J Neurosurg* 1966; 24:382–387.

88. Alterman RL, Sterio D, Beric A, et al. Microelectrode recording during posteroventral pallidotomy: Impact on target selection and complications. *Neurosurgery* 1999; 44:315–323.

89. Shils J, Tagliati M, Alterman R. Neurophysiological monitoring during neurosurgery for movement disorders, In: Deletis V, Shils J (eds). *Neurophysiology in Neurosurgery.* San Diego CA: Academic Press, 2002:393–436.

90. Holloway KL, Gaede SE, Starr PA, et al. Frameless stereotaxy using bone fiducial markers for deep brain stimulation. *J Neurosurg* 2005; 103:404–413.

91. Moro E, Esselink RJ, Xie J, et al. The impact on Parkinson's disease of electrical parameter settings in STN stimulation. *Neurology* 2002; 59:706–713.

92. Volkmann J, Herzog J, Kopper F, et al. Introduction to the programming of deep brain stimulators. *Mov Disord* 2002; 17(Suppl 3):S181–187.

93. Krack P, Fraix V, Mendes A, et al. Postoperative management of subthalamic nucleus stimulation for Parkinson's disease. *Mov Disord* 2002; 17(Suppl 3):S188–S197.

94. Herzog J, Fietzek U, Hamel W, et al. Most effective stimulation site in subthalamic deep brain stimulation for Parkinson's disease. *Mov Disord* 2004; 19:1050–1054.

95. Tagliati M, Shils J, Rogers J, Alterman R. What is the true therapeutic target of subthalamic deep brain stimulation for Parkinson's disease? *Neurology* 2001; 56(Suppl 3):A278.

96. Voges J, Volkmann J, Allert N, et al. Bilateral high-frequency stimulation in the subthalamic nucleus for the treatment of Parkinson disease: Correlation of therapeutic effect with anatomical electrode position. *J Neurosurg* 2002; 96:269–279.

97. Plaha P, Ben–Shlomo Y, Patel NK, Gill SS. Stimulation of the caudal zona incerta is superior to stimulation of the subthalamic nucleus in improving contralateral parkinsonism. *Brain* 2006; 129:1732–1747.

98. Krack P, Pollak P, Limousin P, et al. Opposite motor effects of pallidal stimulation in Parkinson's disease. *Ann Neurol* 1998; 43:180–192.

99. Moro E, Scerrati M, Romito LM, et al. Chronic subthalamic nucleus stimulation reduces medication requirements in Parkinson's disease. *Neurology* 1999; 53:85–90.

100. The Deep-Brain Stimulation for Parkinson's Disease Study Group. Deep-brain stimulation of the subthalamic nucleus or the pars interna of the globus pallidus in Parkinson's disease. *N Engl J Med* 2001; 345:956–963.

101. Molinuevo JL, Valldeoriola F, Tolosa E, et al. Levodopa withdrawal after bilateral subthalamic nucleus stimulation in advanced Parkinson disease. *Arch Neurol* 2000; 57:983–988.

102. Krack P, Pollak P, Limousin P, et al. From off-period dystonia to peak-dose chorea. The clinical spectrum of varying subthalamic nucleus activity. *Brain* 1999; 122:1133–1146.

103. Limousin P, Pollak P, Hoffmann D, et al. Abnormal involuntary movements induced by subthalamic nucleus stimulation in parkinsonian patients. *Mov Disord* 1996; 11: 231–235.

104. O'Suilleabhain PE, Dewey RB Jr. Contributions of dopaminergic drugs and disease severity to daytime sleepiness in Parkinson disease. *Arch Neurol* 2002; 59:986–989.

105. Funkiewiez A, Ardouin C, Caputo E, et al. Long term effects of bilateral subthalamic nucleus stimulation on cognitive function, mood, and behaviour in Parkinson's disease. *J Neurol Neurosurg Psychiatry* 2004; 75:834–839.

106. Krack P, Pollak P, Limousin P, et al. Subthalamic nucleus or internal pallidal stimulation in young onset Parkinson's disease. *Brain* 1998; 121:451–457.

107. Gschwandtner U, Aston J, Renaud S, et al. Pathologic gambling in patients with Parkinson's disease. *Clin Neuropharmacol* 2001; 24:170–172.

108. Sanchez-Ramos J. The straight dope on addiction to dopamimetic drugs. *Mov Disord* 2002; 17:223–225.

109. Ardouin C, Pillon B, Peiffer E, et al. Bilateral subthalamic or pallidal stimulation for Parkinson's disease affects neither memory nor executive functions: A consecutive series of 62 patients. *Ann Neurol* 1999; 46:217–223.

110. Berney A, Vingerhoets F, Perrin A, et al. Effect on mood of subthalamic DBS for Parkinson's disease: A consecutive series of 24 patients. *Neurology* 2002; 59:1427–1429.

111. Kedia S, Moro E, Tagliati M, et al. Emergence of restless legs syndrome (RLS) during subthalamic stimulation for Parkinson's disease. *Neurology* 2004; 63:2410–2412.

112. Brice J, McLellan L. Suppression of intention tremor by contingent deep-brain stimulation. *Lancet* 1980; 1:1221–1222.

113. Benabid AL, Pollak P, Gao D, et al. Chronic electrical stimulation of the ventralis intermedius nucleus of the thalamus as a treatment of movement disorders. *J Neurosurg* 1996; 84:203–214.

114. Koller W, Pahwa R, Busenbark K, et al. High frequency unilateral thalamic stimulation in the treatment of essential and Parkinsonian tremor. *Ann Neurol* 1997; 42:292–299.

115. Schuurman PR, Bosch DA, Bossuyt PM, et al. A comparison of continuous thalamic stimulation and thalamotomy for suppression of severe tremor. *N Engl J Med* 2000; 342:461–468.

116. Limousin P, Speelman JD, Gielen F, et al. Multicentre European study of thalamic stimulation in Parkinsonian and essential tremor. *J Neurol Neurosurg Psychiatry* 1999; 66:289–296.

117. Rehncrona S, Johnels B, Widner H, et al. Long–term efficacy of thalamic deep brain stimulation for tremor: Double–blind assessments. *Mov Disord* 2003; 18:163–170.

118. Pahwa R, Lyons KE, Wilkinson SB, et al. Long term evaluation of deep brain stimulation of the thalamus. *J Neurosurg* 2006; 104(4):506–512.

119. Caparros–Lefebvre D, Blond S, et al. Chronic thalamic stimulation improves tremor and levodopa induced dyskinesias in Parkinson's disease. *J Neurol Neurosurg Psychiatry* 1993; 56:268–273.

120. Deuschl G, Schade-Britten C, Krack P, et al. A randomized trial of deep-brain stimulation for Parkinson's disease. *N Engl J Med* 2006; 355:896–908.

121. Krack P, Batir A, Van Blercom N, et al. Five-year follow-up of bilateral stimulation of the subthalamic nucleus in advanced Parkinson's disease. *N Engl J Med* 2003; 349: 1925–1934.

122. Schupbach M, Gargiulo M, Welter ML, et al. Stimulation of the subthalamic nucleus in Parkinson's disease: A 5 year follow up. *J Neurol Neurosurg Psychiatry* 2005; 76: 1640–1644.

123. Kleiner–Fisman G, Herzog J, Fisman D, et al. Subthalamic nucleus deep brain stimulation: Summary and meta-analysis of outcomes. *Mov Disord* 2006; 21(Suppl14): S290–S304.

124. Volkmann J. Deep brain stimulation for the treatment of Parkinson's disease. *J Clin Neurophysiol* 2004; 21:6–17.

125. Ghika J, Villemure JG, Fankhauser H, et al. Efficiency and safety of bilateral contemporaneous pallidal stimulation (deep brain stimulation) in levodopa-responsive patients with Parkinson's disease with severe motor fluctuations: A 2 year follow-up review. *J Neurosurg* 1998; 89:713–718.

126. Volkmann J, Allert N, Voges J, et al. Long-term results of bilateral pallidal stimulation in Parkinson's disease. *Ann Neurol* 2004; 55:871–875.

127. Lyons KE, Wilkinson SB, Troster AI, Pahwa R. Long-term efficacy of globus pallidus stimulation for the treatment of Parkinson's disease. *Stereotact Funct Neurosurg* 2002; 79(3–4):214–220.

128. Beric A, Kelly PJ, Rezai A, et al. Complications of deep brain stimulation surgery. *Stereotact Funct Neurosurg* 2001; 77:73–78.

129. Hariz MI. Complications of deep brain stimulation surgery. *Mov Disord* 2002; 17: 162–166.

130. Oh MY, Abosch A, Kim SH, et al. Long–term hardware–related complications of deep brain stimulation. *Neurosurgery* 2002; 50:1268–1276.

131. Poulad D, Shils J, Tagliati M, et al. Surgical complications of DBS surgery: The Beth Israel experience. Proceedings of the Quadriennal Meeting of the American Society Stereotactic and Functional Neurosurgery, New York, 2003:120.

132. Rezai AR, Kopell BH, Gross RE, et al. Deep brain stimulation for Parkinson's disease: Surgical issues. *Mov Disord* 2006; 21(Suppl 14):S197–S218.

133. Joint C, Nandi D, Parkin S, et al. Hardware-related problems of deep brain stimulation. *Mov Disord* 2002; 17:175–180.

134. Umemura A, Jaggi JL, Hurtig HI, et al. Deep brain stimulation for movement disorders: Morbidity and mortality in 109 patients. *J Neurosurg* 2003; 98:779–784.

135. Hariz MI, Johansson F. Hardware failure in parkinsonian patients with chronic subthalamic nucleus stimulation is a medical emergency. *Mov Disord* 2001; 16:166–168.

136. Oh MY, Hodaie M, Kim SH, et al. Deep brain stimulator electrodes used for lesioning: Proof of principle. *Neurosurgery* 2001; 49:363–367.

137. Yamada M, Takeuchi S, Shiojiri Y, et al. Surgical lead–preserving procedures for pacemaker pocket infection. *Ann Thorac Surg* 2002; 74:1494–1499.

138. Deuschl G, Herzog J, Kleiner-Fisman G, et al. Deep brain stimulation: Postoperative issues. *Mov Disord* 2006; 21 (Suppl.14): S219–S237.

139. Benabid AL, Benazzouz A, Pollak P. Mechanisms of deep brain stimulation. *Mov Disord* 2002: 17(Suppl 3):S73–S74.

140. Vitek JL. Mechanisms of deep brain stimulation: Excitation or inhibition. *Mov Disord* 2002; 17(Suppl 3):S69–S72.

141. Volkmann J, Allert N, Voges J, et al. Safety and efficacy of pallidal or subthalamic nucleus stimulation in advanced PD. *Neurology* 2001; 56:548–551.

142. Shields DC, Lam S, Gorgulho A, et al. Eyelid apraxia associated with subthalamic nucleus deep brain stimulation. *Neurology* 2006; 66:1451–1452.

143. Voon V, Kubu C, Krack P, et al. Deep brain stimulation: Neuropsychological and neuropsychiatric issues. *Mov Disord* 2006; 21(Suppl 14):S305–S327.

144. Temel Y, Kessels A, Tan S, et al. Behavioural changes after bilateral subthalamic stimulation in advanced Parkinson disease: A systematic review. *Parkinsonism Relat Disord* 2006; 12:265–272.

145. Mayberg HS, Lozano AM. Penfield revisited? Understanding and modifying behavior by deep brain stimulation for PD. *Neurology* 2002: 59:1298–1299.

146. Houeto JL, Mesnage V, Mallet L, et al. Behavioral disorders, Parkinson's disease and subthalamic stimulation. *J Neurol Neurosurg Psychiatry* 2002; 72:701–707.

147. Krack P, Kumar R, Ardouin C, et al. Mirthful laughter induced by subthalamic nucleus stimulation. *Mov Disord* 2001: 16:867–875.

148. Kulisevsky J, Berthier ML, Gironell A, –et al. Mania following deep brain stimulation for Parkinson's disease. *Neurology* 2002; 59:1421–1424.

149. O'Brien CP, DiGiacomo JN, Fahn S, Schwarz GA. Mental effects of high–dosage levodopa. *Arch Gen Psychiatry* 1971: 24:61–64.

150. Sporn J, Ghaemi SN, Sambur MR, et al. Pramipexole augmentation in the treatment of unipolar and bipolar depression: A retrospective chart review. *Ann Clin Psychiatry* 2000: 12:137–140.

151. Voon V, Hassan K, Zurowski M, et al. Prospective prevalence of pathologic gambling and medication association in Parkinson disease. *Neurology* 2006; 66:1750–1752.

152. Vingerhoets G, van der Linden C, Lannoo E, et al. Cognitive outcome after unilateral pallidal stimulation in Parkinson's disease. *J Neurol Neurosurg Psychiatry* 1999; 66:297–304.

153. Alexander GE, Crutcher MD, De Long MR. Basal ganglia–thalamocortical circuits: Parallel substrates for motor, oculomotor, "prefrontal" and "limbic" functions. *Prog Brain Res* 1990; 85:119–146.

154. Nakano K, Kayahara T, Tsutsumi T, Ushiro H. Neural circuits and functional organization of the striatum. *J Neurol* 2000; 247(Suppl 5):V1–V15.

155. Ramig LO, Sapir S, Countryman S, et al. Intensive voice treatment (LSVT) for patients with Parkinson's disease: A 2 year follow up. *J Neurol Neurosurg Psychiatry* 2001; 71:493–498.

156. Shivitz N, Koop MM, Fahimi J, Heit G, Bronte-Stewart HM. Bilateral subthalamic nucleus deep brain stimulation improves certain aspects of postural control in Parkinson's disease, whereas medication does not. *Mov Disord* 2006; 21(8):1088–1097.

157. Bejjani BP, Damier P, Arnulf I, et al. Transient acute depression induced by high-frequency deep-brain stimulation. *N Engl J Med* 1999; 340:1476–1480.

158. Starr PA. Placement of deep brain stimulators into the subthalamic nucleus or globus pallidus internus: Technical approach. *Stereotact Funct Neurosurg* 2002; 79(3–4):118–145.

159. Windels F, Bruet N, Poupard A, et al. Effects of high frequency stimulation of subthalamic nucleus on extracellular glutamate and GABA in substantia nigra and globus pallidus in the normal rat. *Eur J Neurosci* 2000; 12:4141–4146.

160. Limousin P, Greene J, Pollack P, et al. Changes in cerebral activity pattern due to subthalamic nucleus or internal pallidum stimulation in Parkinson's disease. *Ann Neurol* 1997; 42:283–291.

161. Benazzouz A, Gao DM, Ni ZG, et al. Effect of high frequency stimulation of the subthalamic nucleus on the neuronal activities of the substantia nigra pars reticulata and ventrolateral nucleus of the thalamus in the rat. *Neuroscience* 2000; 99: 289–295.

162. Dostrovsky J, Lozano A. Mechanisms of deep brain stimulation. *Mov Disord* 2002; 17(Suppl 3):S63–S68.

163. McIntyre C, Savasta M, Walter B, et al. How does deep brain stimulation work? Present understanding and future questions. *J Clin Neurol* 2004; 21:40–50.

164. Beurrier C, Bioulac B, Audin J, et al. High-frequency stimulation produces a transient blockade of voltage-gated currents in subthalamic neurons. *J Neurophysiol* 2001; 85:1351–1356.

165. Dostrovsky JO, Levy R, Wu JP, et al. Microstimulation-induced inhibition of neuronal firing in human globus pallidus. *J Neurophysiol* 2000; 84:570–574.

166. Grill WM, McIntyre CC. Extracellular excitation of central neurons: implications for the mechanisms of deep brain stimulation. *Thalamus Rel Syst* 2001; 1:269–277.

167. McIntyre CC, Grill WM, Sherman DL, et al. Cellular effects of deep brain stimulation: Model–based analysis of activation and inhibition. *J Neurophysiol* 2004; 91: 1457–1469.

168. Urbano FJ, Leznik E, Llinas RR. Cortical activation patterns evoked by afferent axons stimuli at different frequencies: An in vitro voltage-sensitive dye imaging study. *Thalamus Rel Syst* 2002; 1:371–378.

169. Hashimoto T, Elder CM, Okun MS, et al. Stimulation of the subthalamic nucleus changes the firing pattern of pallidal neurons. *J Neurosci* 2003; 23:1916–1923.

170. Brown P. Oscillatory nature of human basal ganglia activity: Relationship to the pathophysiology of Parkinson's disease. *Mov Disord* 2003; 18:357–363.

171. Anderson VC, Burchiel K, Hogarth P, et al. Pallidal vs subthalamic nucleus deep brain stimulation in Parkinson's disease. *Arch Neurol* 2005; 62:554–560.

172. Okun MS, Foote KD. Subthalamic nucleus vs globus pallidus interna deep brain stimulation, the rematch: Will pallidal deep brain stimulation make a triumphant return? *Arch Neurol* 2005; 62:533–536.

173. Pollak P, Fraix V, Krack P, et al. Treatment results: Parkinson's disease. *Mov Disord* 2002; 17(Suppl 3):S75–S83.

174. Figueiras-Mendez R, Marin-Zarza F, et al. Subthalamic nucleus stimulation improves directly levodopa induced dyskinesias in Parkinson's disease. *J Neurol Neurosurg Psychiatry* 1999; 66:549–550.

175. Tagliati M, Huang N, Shils JL, et al. Immediate relief of levodopa-induced dyskinesias after deep brain stimulation of the subthalamic nucleus in Parkinson's disease. *Mov Disord* 2002; 17(Suppl 5):S199.

176. Katayama Y, Oshima H, Kano T, et al. Direct effect of subthalamic nucleus stimulation on levodopa-induced peak-dose dyskinesia in patients with Parkinson's disease. *Stereotact Funct Neurosurg* 2006; 84:176–179.

177. Stefani A, Fedele E, Galati S, et al. Deep brain stimulation in Parkinson's disease patients: Biochemical evidence. *J Neural Transm Suppl* 2006; 70:401–408.

178. Lee CS, Schulzer M, Mak EK, et al. Clinical observations on the rate of progression of idiopathic parkinsonism. *Brain* 1994; 117:501–507.

179. Newman RP, LeWitt PA, Jaffe M, et al. Motor function in the normal aging population: treatment with levodopa. *Neurology* 1985; 35:571–573.

180. Mayeux R, Chen J, Mirabello E, et al. An estimate of the incidence of dementia in idiopathic Parkinson's disease. *Neurology* 1990; 40:1513–17.

181. Tagliati M, Miravite J, Koss A, et al. Is advanced age a poor predictor of motor outcome for subthalamic DBS in Parkinson's disease? *Neurology* 2004; 69:A345.

182. Adler CH. Nonmotor complications in Parkinson's disease. *Mov Disord* 2005; 20(Suppl 11):S23–S29.

183. Morrison CE, Borod JC, Perrine K, et al. Neuropsychological functioning following bilateral subthalamic nucleus stimulation in Parkinson's disease. *Arch Clin Neuropsychol* 2004; 19:165–181.

184. Moretti R, Torre P, Antonello RM, et al. Neuropsychological changes after subthalamic nucleus stimulation: A 12 month follow–up in nine patients with Parkinson's disease. *Parkinsonism Relat Disord* 2003; 10:73–79.

185. Alegret M, Junque C, Valldeoriola F, et al. Effects of bilateral subthalamic stimulation on cognitive function in Parkinson disease. *Arch Neurol* 2001; 58:1223–1227.

186. Pillon B, Ardouin C, Damier P, et al. Neuropsychological changes between "off" and "on" STN or GPi stimulation in Parkinson's disease. *Neurology* 2000; 55:411–418.

187. Daniele A, Albanese A, Contarino MF, et al. Cognitive and behavioural effects of chronic stimulation of the subthalamic nucleus in patients with Parkinson's disease. *J Neurol Neurosurg Psychiatry* 2003; 74:175–182.

188. Dujardin K, Defebvre L, Krystkowiak P, et al. Influence of chronic bilateral stimulation of the subthalamic nucleus on cognitive function in Parkinson's disease. *J Neurol* 2001; 248:603–611.

189. Jahanshahi M, Ardouin CM, Brown RG, et al. The impact of deep brain stimulation on executive function in Parkinson's disease. *Brain* 2000; 123:1142–1154.

190. Witt K, Pulkowski U, Herzog J, et al. Deep brain stimulation of the subthalamic nucleus improves cognitive flexibility but impairs response inhibition in Parkinson disease. *Arch Neurol* 2004; 61:697–700.

191. Hershey T, Revilla FJ, Wernle A, et al. Stimulation of STN impairs aspects of cognitive control in PD. *Neurology* 2004; 62:1110–1114.

192. Perozzo P, Rizzone M, Bergamasco B, et al. Deep brain stimulation of the subthalamic nucleus in Parkinson's disease: Comparison of pre- and postoperative neuropsychological evaluation. *J Neurol Sci* 2001; 192:9–15.

193. Tröster AI, Fields JA, Wilkinson SB, et al. Unilateral pallidal stimulation for Parkinson's disease: Neurobehavioral functioning before and 3 months after electrode implantation. *Neurology* 1997; 49:1078–1083.

194. Dujardin K, Krystkowiak P, Defebvre L, et al. A case of severe dysexecutive syndrome consecutive to chronic bilateral pallidal stimulation. *Neuropsychologia* 2000; 38: 1305–1315.

195. Herzog J, Volkmann J, Krack P, et al. Two-year follow-up of subthalamic deep brain stimulation in Parkinson's disease. *Mov Disord* 2003; 18:1332–1337.

196. Romito LM, Raja M, Daniele A, et al. Transient mania with hypersexuality after surgery for high frequency stimulation of the subthalamic nucleus in Parkinson's disease. *Mov Disord* 2002; 17:1371–1374.

197. Burkhard PR, Vingerhoets FJ, Berney A, et al. Suicide after successful deep brain stimulation for movement disorders. *Neurology* 2004; 63:2170–2172.

198. Voon V, Moro E, Saint-Cyr JA, et al. Psychiatric symptoms following surgery for Parkinson's disease with an emphasis on subthalamic stimulation. In: Anderson KE, Weiner WJ, Lang AE (eds). *Advances in Neurology: Behavioral Neurology of Movement Disorders*, 2nd ed. Philadelphia: Lippincott Williams & Wilkins; 2005:147.

199. Rodriguez-Oroz MC, Obeso JA, Lang AE, et al. Bilateral deep brain stimulation in Parkinson's disease: A multicenter study with 4 years follow-up. *Brain* 2005; 128: 2240–2249.

200. Kaufmann H, Bhattacharya KF, Voustianiouk A, et al. Stimulation of the subthalamic nucleus increases heart rate in patients with Parkinson disease. *Neurology* 2002; 59:1657–1658.

201. Lipp A, Tank J, Trottenberg T, et al. Sympathetic activation due to deep brain stimulation in the region of the STN. *Neurology* 2005; 65:774–775.

202. Erola T, Haapaniemi T, Heikkinen E, et al. Subthalamic nucleus deep brain stimulation does not alter long-term heart rate variability in Parkinson's disease. *Clin Auton Res* 2006; 16:286–288.

203. Adler C, Thorpy M. Sleep issues in Parkinson's disease. *Neurology* 2005; 64(Suppl 3): S12–S20.

204. Arnulf I, Bejjani BP, Garma L, et al. Improvement of sleep architecture in PD with subthalamic nucleus stimulation. *Neurology* 2000; 55:1732–1734.

205. Monaca C, Ozsancak C, Jacquesson JM, et al. Effects of bilateral subthalamic stimulation on sleep in Parkinson's disease. *J Neurol* 2004; 251:214–218.

206. Antonini A, Landi A, Mariani C, et al. Deep brain stimulation and its effect on sleep in Parkinson's disease. *Sleep Med* 2004; 5:211–214.

207. Iranzo A, Valldeoriola F, Santamaria J, et al. Sleep symptoms and polysomnographic architecture in advanced Parkinson's disease after chronic bilateral subthalamic stimulation. *J Neurol Neurosurg Psychiatry* 2002; 72:661–664.

208. Cicolin A, Lopiano L, Zibetti M, et al. Effects of deep brain stimulation of the subthalamic nucleus on sleep architecture in parkinsonian patients. *Sleep Med* 2004; 5:207–210.

209. Hjort N, Ostergaard K, Dupont E. Improvement of sleep quality in patients with advanced Parkinson's disease treated with deep brain stimulation of the subthalamic nucleus. *Mov Disord* 2004; 19:196–199.

210. Romito LM, Scerrati M, Contarino MF, et al. Bilateral high frequency subthalamic stimulation in Parkinson's disease: Long-term neurological follow-up. *J Neurosurg Sci* 2003; 47:119–128.

211. Tinazzi M, Del Vesco C, Fincati E, et al. Pain and motor complications in Parkinson's disease. *J Neurol Neurosurg Psychiatry* 2006; 77:822–825.

212. Loher TJ, Burgunder JM, Weber S, et al. Effect of chronic pallidal deep brain stimulation on off period dystonia and sensory symptoms in advanced Parkinson's disease. *J Neurol Neurosurg Psychiatry* 2002; 73:395–399.

213. Hua Z, Guodong G, Qinchuan L, et al. Analysis of complications of radiofrequency pallidotomy. *Neurosurgery* 2003; 52:89–99.

214. Fine J, Duff J, Chen R, Long–term follow–up of unilateral pallidotomy in advanced Parkinson's disease. *N Engl J Med* 2000; 342:1708–1714.

215. Kleiner–Fisman G, Fisman DN, Zamir O, et al. Subthalamic nucleus deep brain stimulation for Parkinson's disease after successful pallidotomy: Clinical and electrophysiological observations. *Mov Disord* 2004; 19:1209–1214.

216. Revilla FJ, Mink JW, Rich KM, et al. Clinical outcome of bilateral subthalamic nucleus stimulation in patients with Parkinson's disease and previous pallidotomy. *Mov Disord* 2002; 17(Suppl 5):S189.

217. Ondo WG, Silay Y, Almaguer M, Jankovic J. Subthalamic deep brain stimulation in patients with a previous pallidotomy. *Mov Disord* 2006; 21:1252–1254.

218. Fraix V, Pollak P, Moro E, et al. Subthalamic nucleus stimulation in tremor dominant parkinsonian patients with previous thalamic surgery. *J Neurol Neurosurg Psychiatry* 2005; 76:246–248.

219. Mogilner A, Sterio D, Rezai A, et al. Subthalamic nucleus stimulation in patients with a prior pallidotomy. *J Neurosurg* 2002; 96:660–665.

220. Van Den Bosch L, Van Damme P, Bogaert E, et al. The role of excitotoxicity in the pathogenesis of amyotrophic lateral sclerosis. *Biochim Biophys Acta* 2006; 1762: 1068-1082.2006.

221. Mamelak M. Alzheimer's disease, oxidative stress and gammahydroxybutyrate. *Neurobiol Aging* 2006; Jul 10; [Epub ahead of print].

222. Rodriguez MC, Obeso JA, Olanow CW. Subthalamic nucleus–mediated excitotoxicity in Parkinson's disease: A target for neuroprotection. *Ann Neurol* 1998; 44(3 Suppl 1): S175–S188.

223. Warnke PC. STN stimulation and neuroprotection in Parkinson's disease: When beautiful theories meet ugly facts. *J Neurol Neurosurg Psychiatry* 2005; 76:1186–1187.

224. Borghammer P, Kumakura Y, Cumming P. Fluorodopa F 18 positron emission tomography and the progression of Parkinson disease. *Arch Neurol* 2005; 62:378–382.

225. Morrish PK, Sawle GV, Brooks DJ. An ^{18}F dopa–PET and clinical study of the rate of progression in Parkinson's disease. *Brain* 1996; 119:585–591.

226. Hilker R, Portman AT, Voges J, et al. Disease progression continues in patients with advanced Parkinson's disease and effective subthalamic nucleus stimulation. *J Neurol Neurosurg Psychiatry* 2005; 76:1217–1221.

227. Ostergaard K, A Sunde N. Evolution of Parkinson's disease during 4 years of bilateral deep brain stimulation of the subthalamic nucleus. *Mov Disord* 2006; 21:624–631.

228. Lozano A, Hamani C. The future of deep brain stimulation. *J Clin Neurophysiol* 2004; 21:68–69.

229. Nandi D, Liu X, Winter J, et al. Deep brain stimulation of the pedunculopontine region in the normal non-human primate. *J Clin Neurosci* 2002; 9:170–174.

230. Aziz TZ, Davies LE, Stein JF, et al. The role of descending basal ganglia connections to the brainstem in parkinsonian akinesia. *Br J Neurosurg* 1998; 12:245–249.

231. Plaha P, Gill S. Bilateral deep brain stimulation of the pedunculopontine nucleus for Parkinson's disease. *Neuroreport* 2005; 16:1883–1887.

232. Mazzone P, Lozano A, Stanzione P, et al. Implantation of human pedunculopontine nucleus: A safe and clinically relevant target in Parkinson's disease. *Neuroreport* 2005; 16:1877–1881.

233. Ostergaard K, Sunde N, Dupont E. Effects of bilateral stimulation of the subthalamic nucleus in patients with severe Parkinson's disease and motor fluctuations. *Mov Disord* 2002; 17:693–700.

234. Romito LM, Scerrati M, Contarino MF, et al. Long-term follow up of subthalamic nucleus stimulation in Parkinson's disease. *Neurology* 2002; 58:1546–1550.

235. Kleiner-Fisman G, Fisman DN, Sime E, et al. Long-term follow up of bilateral deep brain stimulation of the subthalamic nucleus in patients with advanced Parkinson's disease. *J Neurosurg* 2003; 99:489–495.

236. Scotto di Luzio AE, Ammannati F, Marini P, et al. Which target for DBS in Parkinson's disease? Subthalamic nucleus versus globus pallidus internus. *Neurol Sci* 2001; 22:87–88.

237. Durif F, Lemaire JJ, Debilly B, Dordain G. Long-term follow-up of globus pallidus chronic stimulation in advanced Parkinson's disease. *Mov Disord* 2002; 17:803–807.

238. Loher TJ, Burgunder JM, Pohle T, et al. Long-term pallidal deep brain stimulation in patients with advanced Parkinson disease: 1-year follow-up study. *J Neurosurg* 2002; 96:844–853.

55 Neural Transplantation: Yesterday, Today, and Tomorrow

Paul Greene

The recent excitement surrounding the potential use of stem cells to replace ailing tissues in the body has once again focused attention on the attempt to treat degenerative brain diseases using cell transplant therapy. This goal dates at least to the end of the nineteenth century, with the unsuccessful attempts by Thompson in 1890 to transplant adult cortex to adult cortex in cats and dogs (1). For the next 80 years, advances in brain transplantation therapy were not frequent: for example, the demonstration in 1917 that immature brain could survive after transplantation, the demonstration in 1940 that fetal tissue could survive transplantation into the brain, and the demonstration in 1962 that grafts could establish functional connections with the host brain (grafted pituitary tissue into the hypothalamus of rats) (1). Modern transplant efforts accelerated after the demonstration in 1976 that rat fetal monoaminergic neurons could survive after transplantation into adult rat brain (2).

Currently, Parkinson's disease (PD) is the only neurodegenerative disease that has shown benefit from cell transplantation. Medical therapy is very effective in treating the motor symptoms of PD, and deep brain stimulation (DBS) has proven to be effective in treating dyskinesias, one of the major side effects of antiparkinson medications. In order to be a viable treatment in the future, cell transplantation must show benefit over current therapy in at least one of the following three areas:

1. Slowing or stopping the progression of PD. There have been a series of studies indicating that selegiline or rasagiline may slow the progression of PD. There have also been single studies suggesting that pramipexole, ropinirole, coenzyme Q10, or levodopa might have a protective effect. But none of these medications is universally accepted as protective, and the effects seem modest. An agent with substantial protective effect is a major goal (3).

2. Relieving or preventing motor fluctuations. DBS has proven effective in substantially reducing dyskinesias and may moderate motor fluctuations in many patients. However, many older patients are not good candidates for DBS and motor fluctuations/dyskinesias continue to be a major concern of patients and their doctors (4).

3. Relieving symptoms of PD that do not respond to current therapy. Gait freezing and loss of postural reflexes leading to falling are problems that cannot always be treated by current medications or DBS. Dementia becomes a major problem in many patients as PD progresses and is poorly controlled by medications. Other symptoms, such as dysphagia and various forms of autonomic instability, can also

be refractory to treatment, leading to both morbidity and mortality (5).

ADRENAL MEDULLARY TRANSPLANTS

Adrenal medullary cells removed from the influence of cortisol can release dopamine and form neuron-like processes (6). In animals, transplantation of adult adrenal medullary tissue into the striatum resulted in poor graft survival except when nerve growth factor was added (7). Transplanted adult adrenal tissue did not show significant fiber outgrowth, and most surviving cells did not show evidence of dopamine production (8, 9). Despite this, in the early 1980s, several patients with PD received implants of their own adrenal medullary tissue. None of these patients experienced dramatic or long-lasting improvement, and it is likely that adrenal medullary transplants would have disappeared if not for the report in 1987 by Madrazo and colleagues that 2 patients improved dramatically after adrenal medullary autografts (10). Within a year, at least 135 additional patients with PD received adrenal medullary autografts, and the initial reports were interpreted as promising (11, 12). By the early 1990s, it was apparent that as a group, patients receiving adrenal medullary transplants did not have substantial or long-term benefit. In 1991, Goetz and coworkers summarized the results of adrenal medullary grafting in 61 Canadian and U.S. patients operated in 13 centers; they concluded that only 19% were considered improved at 2 years and that this was comparable to what would have been seen with a dopamine agonist (13). In addition, there was considerable short-term morbidity as well as deaths attributable to the surgery in the 2 years after transplantation (13). Despite the questionable preclinical basis for this procedure, initial enthusiasm was maintained for several years because of the lack of controlled trials and considerable variation in posttransplantation patient evaluation in the open-label studies.

HUMAN FETAL MESENCEPHALIC TRANSPLANTS

Open-Label Trials

The initial reports of fetal tissue implantation for PD came from China in 1987 (14), followed a year later by reports from Sweden (15) and Mexico (16). By 1998 over 200 patients throughout the world had received fetal mesencephalic grafts for parkinsonism (17). By 2001 the figure had climbed to about 300 patients (18). Based on extensive animal data and a small number of autopsies in PD patients receiving fetal grafts, it seems likely that at least some effects of fetal grafts come about because of specific neural connections that release dopamine (19).

Techniques for fetal tissue transplantation in humans have been adapted from techniques used in animals, but the optimal techniques in humans are not known and there have been differences in various aspects of the procedure that may significantly affect the outcome. There is general agreement, based on survival of human fetal tissue implants into adult rat brain, that optimal cell survival is at approximately 5.5 to 8 weeks' gestational age for cell suspensions or 6.5 to 9 weeks' gestational age for solid grafts (20). Animal studies and a human autopsy suggest that with current techniques, 5% to 10% of transplanted dopaminergic neurons survive, but survival is not uniform along the implantation tracks (21, 22). Some of the differences in preparation and implantation of fetal tissue are:

1. Whether to culture the fetal tissue and assay for the presence of tyrosine hydroxylase or production of dopamine metabolites before transplantation (23, 24).
2. Transplanting within hours of collection of fetal tissue vs. storing tissue prior to implantation, either cultured for several days, cultured for many days, or frozen (23–25).
3. Transplanting cell suspensions vs. transplanting solid fragments of tissue (19).
4. The amount of tissue to transplant (26).
5. Whether to transplant tissue into the putamen alone or also into the caudate nucleus (19).
6. Whether to transplant tissue using multiple needle tracks in a ventrodorsal direction through the putamen or a smaller number of needle tracks in an anteroposterior direction (27, 28).
7. Whether to use short-term immunosuppression, long-term immunosuppression, or no immunosuppression (19).

Despite these many variations in technique, the open-label results of transplantation were substantially promising in almost all groups. A review of almost 300 patients in 2001 concluded that about 2 out of 3 of these patients had at least a moderate improvement [greater than or equal to 35% improvement in the Unified Parkinson's Disease Rating Scale (UPDRS) rating scale] that persisted for at least 2 years of follow-up (29). In addition, patients had a mean 25% reduction in levodopa usage after the transplant. The review also noted that the mean age at time of transplantation was 52 years, whereas the mean age at onset for PD is about 60 years (29). In addition to these trials, there were 2 reports using fetal porcine mesencephalic tissue in patients with PD; these were also promising (30, 31).

Controlled Trials

There have been 3 double-blind, sham-surgery controlled studies of transplantation of fetal mesencephalic cells into patients with PD: 2 using human fetal tissue from elective abortions and 1 using fetal porcine tissue. These studies were organized because of the growing number of reports of successful open-label transplants and were carried out by groups that had previously reported benefit in open-label trials. The outcome of these 3 studies was surprising and had an unsettling effect on the whole field of neural transplantation for PD. Two studies (one using human fetal tissue and the other using porcine fetal tissue) showed complete lack of benefit (28, 32), and the remaining study showed no benefit for the entire cohort but did show statistically significant benefit in a preplanned analysis of patients who were younger at time of transplantation (27). Because of the impact of these studies, it is worth examining them in some detail.

Efficacy. The University of Colorado–Columbia University–North Shore University study (in which I participated) was the first sham surgery–controlled, prospective, randomized trial of mesencephalic fetal cell transplantation for advanced, medication-refractory PD; it was published in 2001 (27). Forty patients were recruited with PD of at least 7 years' duration with disabling motor symptoms despite optimal drug management. Patients were recruited so that half were over age 60 and half were 60 years old or younger at the time of recruitment. Patients were randomized to fetal tissue transplant or sham surgery. The sham consisted of a burr hole through the outer table of the skull but no penetration of the dura or brain. Operating room procedures were carefully orchestrated to be identical for fetal tissue and sham patients. The actual transplant consisted of tissue from 2 fetuses per side extruded into strands and implanted into the putamen through 2 needle tracks on each side along the long (anteroposterior) axis of the putamen. No immunosuppression was used. Patients underwent extensive testing twice at baseline and 3 times over the year after transplantation, including multiple "on" and "off" UPDRS exams, use of the Schwab and England disability scale (S&E scale) and a subjective global rating scale, neurophysiologic and neuropsychological testing, home diaries to record amount of "on" and "off" time, and 2 fluorodopa PET scans. The blind was broken at 1 year and patients who had received the sham procedure had the option of undergoing implantation immediately.

There was no statistically significant difference between operated and sham groups in the primary outcome variable: a subjective comparative global rating 1 year after surgery. The total mean UPDRS "off" score improved more in the operated group (13.8%) than in the sham group (4.5%), but this was of borderline significance ($P = .055$). There were some subscores (such as the "off" total motor, bradykinesia, and rigidity subscores of the UPDRS and the S&E scale) that were significantly more improved in the operated than the sham group

(P ranging from .00001 to .017), but this improvement occurred primarily in the group of younger patients. The younger group, in a preplanned analysis, did improve markedly in the "off" UPDRS total score and motor, rigidity, and bradykinesia subscores and S & E scales compared with placebo (P ranging from .0003 to .02). Walking did not improve significantly on examination or by history in any age group and there was a significant worsening of walking and balance in the group over 60 years of age. There were no significant differences between operated and sham patients in either age group in any "on" measure or the amount of time "off," "on," "on" without dyskinesias, or in the total daily dose of medication taken.

Of 19 implanted patients, 12 had improvement greater than any sham-operated patient in PET striatal/occipital ratio (SOR) on at least one side of the brain. However, this improvement did not correlate with improvement in PD ratings in the "off" state, since the older group had similar mean improvement in PET to the younger group but did not show a comparable improvement in UPDRS rating.

A second study of human fetal tissue transplants for PD was published in 2003 (28). In that study, 34 patients with medication-refractory PD were randomized to receive tissue from 1 fetus per side, tissue from 4 fetuses per side, or placebo. The sham also consisted of a burr hole through the outer table of the skull but no penetration of the dura or brain. Grafts were diluted so that all patients received the same volume of material, which was deposited through 8 needle tracks per side from the crown of the head into the posterior putamen bilaterally. Patients were immunosuppressed with cyclosporine for 6 months after the procedure. Patients underwent testing at baseline and at 1, 3, 6, 9, 12, 15, 18, 21, and 24 months after transplantation. Evaluations were similar to the first study, including multiple "on" and "off" UPDRS exams, home diaries to record amount of "on" and "off" time, and fluorodopa PET scans at baseline and at 1 and 2 years after transplantation. Dyskinesias were evaluated by a blinded rater viewing "on" and "off" videos from each visit.

There was no significant difference between operated and sham groups in the primary outcome variable: the "off" UPDRS motor score. There were also no significant improvements in multiple other variables, including time "off," time with dyskinesia, and medication usage. In post hoc analyses, there was no improvement in the group of younger patients, but there was statistically significant improvement in patients with milder disease (UPDRS < 49) that persisted for 2 years. There was also significant improvement in both transplanted groups compared to placebo at 6 and 9 months after transplantation, which then returned to placebo levels. There was a significant improvement in PET SOR in both transplanted groups compared with placebo.

The results of the porcine transplant double-blind study have been published only in abstract form (32). A total of 10 patients received porcine fetal mesencephalic cells at 1 site in the caudate nucleus and 5 sites in the putamen bilaterally. Patients were immunosuppressed for 75 days after surgery with cyclosporine and prednisone. There was no significant improvement in the primary outcome: total "off" UPDRS 18 months after surgery (both groups improved by 20% to 25%). Several secondary outcomes were measured, including "on" and "off" time, but only percentage of time spent with dyskinesias showed significant improvement in the operated group compared with the placebo group.

Despite promising open-label trials, each of 3 groups failed to confirm benefit in prospective sham-surgery controlled studies. Each group reported significant improvement in some measures or in some subgroups, but most of these were post hoc analyses after multiple comparisons. The finding of significant improvement in younger patients in the first study was a preplanned analysis but was not confirmed by post hoc analysis in the second study. Either the studies were badly flawed, the open-label literature substantially overestimated the amount of benefit, or some combination of these.

There have been a variety of attempts to explain why the studies might have been flawed. These were summarized in a 2005 review (33) as follows:

1. Lack of chronic immunosuppression. One study did not use immunosuppression and the others used short-term immunosuppression. Although this could have influenced outcome, it did not differ from prestudy technique in each group.
2. Change in technique. In the first blinded study, the surgical technique used in open-label studies was modified to reduce the risk of intracerebral hemorrhage. In order to minimize the risk of hemorrhage, which should be proportional to the number of needle passes, they switched from the 8 ventrodorsal needle passes used in the open-label studies to 4 sagittal needle passes through the forehead along the long axis of the putamen (27). That could have influenced the outcome in this study but not in the other studies.
3. Improper patient selection. In the second human fetal tissue study, preoperative levodopa usage was lower in open-label studies than in the controlled study, suggesting a consistent difference in patient selection (28). This would not apply to the other human study. The available data are too sparse to enable a comparison of patient selection in the porcine open-label and blinded studies.
4. Improper tissue processing. Both blinded human fetal tissue studies used solid grafts. Some have argued that cell suspension may produce a better outcome.

A pathologic study using glial cell line–derived neurotrophic factor (GDNF) treated cell suspensions found long-term survival and dense reinnervation of the putamen in 2 patients (34). Of these, one also received midbrain transplants of fetal tissue, and neither patient developed graft-related dyskinesias. It is also worth noting that these patients received only 6 months of immunosuppression, and were still felt to have substantial improvement with little inflammatory response noted on pathologic examination. Improper tissue processing would not explain why the 2 blinded studies failed to confirm benefit observed with the same solid tissue grafts used in open-label trials.

Many other factors have also been discussed as possible explanations for the lack of benefit in these studies, such as preoperative storage of tissue and transplantation of inadequate amounts of viable tissue. Most of these either do not apply to all 3 studies or fail to explain the difference between open-label and controlled results from the same groups. A simpler explanation is that open-label studies exaggerate the benefit from fetal tissue transplantation due to long-term placebo response and other explanations, such as regression to the mean (recruitment of patients who are worse than their average state and who improve to their average state after recruitment into a study).

Some have argued that placebo effect does not play a role in these controlled studies, since there was no change in mean ratings in the placebo groups in controlled studies using human fetal tissue (there may have been significant improvement in motor ratings in the more severely affected group in the second study) (35). This is a mistaken interpretation. The porcine controlled study did show placebo effect (32). It is possible that there is negative as well as positive placebo effect (worsening of patients who believe they did not get the real treatment), so that absence of mean change does not indicate absence of placebo effect. Even when there is no net placebo effect, the placebo effect increases the variability (standard deviation) in both groups, making a significant difference more difficult to obtain.

Based on the controlled studies alone, it is hard to avoid the conclusion that fetal tissue transplantation as currently performed does produce a dopaminergic effect, but that the effect is unpredictable and on average quite small. Another conclusion suggested by the blinded trials is that improvement in fluorodopa PET does not necessarily predict clinical improvement. This was true in both the human fetal tissue transplant studies and was also observed in the recent blinded study of intraputamenal GDNF (36). A final conclusion is that studies of surgical procedures in PD without sham controls can produce very misleading results. It has been asserted that "Sustained and consistent placebo effects do not typically occur in patients with PD" (37). But, as argued above, this is a misinterpretation. The sham control produced a storm of controversy about the ethics of sham-controlled surgical trials. The organizers of one of the trials argued that the risk of subjecting large numbers of patients to an ineffective surgical procedure (as has been done multiple times in the past) justified some risk to the participants receiving sham surgery (38). This is reasonable, since the potential benefit is generally considered to justify the risk to the participants receiving the actual surgery. A survey of 103 PD researchers found that over 80% were in favor of sham-surgical controls if the risk were low (39).

Safety   Lack of efficacy was not the only surprise in the double-blind studies. Prior to these studies, there were few reports of serious risks of fetal tissue transplantation. The risk of symptomatic intracerebral hemorrhage during stereotactic tissue implantation is difficult to estimate directly from the published literature, since not all patients are reported. One review of 60 patients reported 3 symptomatic intracerebral hemorrhages or a risk of 5% (40). Overall, there have been very few reports of symptomatic hemorrhage. For comparison, the risk of stereotactic DBS in a roughly similar population ranges from 1% to 3% (41, 42). Transient change in mental status immediately after grafting and a small number of seizures have been reported. There have been a number of reports of persistent or progressive mental deterioration after grafting, but it is not clear whether this is attributable to the transplant procedure. There have been reports of opportunistic infections presumably related to immunosuppression (43). Other perioperative complications, such as brain abscess and other infections, have been reported only rarely. There were also two troubling reports of uncontrolled growth of nonneuronal tissue after transplantation (44, 45). It was felt that both of these resulted from inclusion of nonneural tissue in the graft.

Surprisingly, both controlled studies involving human fetal tissue identified another, previously unrecognized problem: severe dyskinesias or dystonia. In the first study, 5 of 34 implanted patients developed dyskinesias and/or dystonia after transplantation despite marked reduction and even discontinuation of anti-PD medications (27). The involuntary movements were severe in 4 of these patients and 3 ultimately received bilateral pallidal DBS with some benefit. In the second study, 13 of 23 patients developed dyskinesias after medicine withdrawal overnight (28). The dyskinesias were severe in 3 patients and required another surgery, presumably DBS (28). The second study did not comment on whether the dyskinesias in the 3 severely affected patients improved with reduction in medication, but presumably they either did not improve or the patients were unable to tolerate adequate medication reduction.

Although dyskinesias had been noted since the earliest reports of neurotransplantation, these usually responded to reductions in levodopa dose. Prior to the first double-blind transplant trial, no attention was given to disabling involuntary movements after cell transplantation. There were reports of 2 patients with dyskinesias who did not respond to medication reduction, 1 of whom improved with pallidotomy (40, 46). There have been several other reports of graft-related dyskinesias that may not have responded to medication adjustment, but the descriptions were not detailed enough to be sure (40). Subsequent to the publication of the controlled studies, a video review of 14 patients previously transplanted in open-label studies found that dyskinesias or dystonia in the "off" state either appeared or worsened after transplant in 9 patients but were severe in only 1 (47, 48). That patient had all PD medications withdrawn for 9 weeks with no improvement in dyskinesias, but no further clinical details were provided.

Despite improvement after DBS or pallidotomy in patients with graft-related involuntary movements, this problem caused deep concern in the transplant community after the blinded studies. The major concern is that other forms of tissue transplantation for PD, such as stem cell transplantation, might also produce severe involuntary movements. One critical issue is whether the dyskinesias are due to excess dopamine. Analysis of the first double-blind study indicated that these dyskinesias were in fact caused by focal areas of excess dopamine. This was based on the following observations:

1. The dyskinesias/dystonias were similar to presurgical involuntary movements except that the preoperative movements resolved with a reduction in medications.
2. This subgroup of patients had the best clinical response and thus presumably the largest delivery of dopamine by the grafts.
3. Patients with dyskinesias had patchy increased fluorodopa signal on positron emission tomography (PET) compared with patients without dyskinesias (49).
4. Autopsy results showed patchy survival of transplanted tyrosine hydroxylase–positive cells.
5. The dyskinesias improved with antidopaminergics such as tetrabenazine and alpha-methyl para tyrosine (although PD symptoms worsened).
6. The dyskinesias worsened with levodopa.

Others in the transplant community disagreed. A review in 2005 argued that the dyskinesias were not due to excess dopamine (48). The authors offered the following observations and alternatives:

1. In their review of 14 patients, there was no correlation between postgraft dyskinesias and benefit.

2. Lower extremity dyskinesias predominated in their patients, which is not typical of levodopa-induced dyskinesias.

3. Dystonia, which was a prominent postgraft problem in the first double-blind study, is less common as a peak dose phenomenon than as a diphasic or "off" phenomenon. In that case, increased supply of dopamine to the striatum may not necessarily produce more dyskinesias.

4. The patchy fluorodopa signal previously mentioned suggests that patchy or insufficient dopamine release might explain the dyskinesia, by analogy with the "low-level" dyskinesia seen in diphasic dyskinesias.

5. If dyskinesias are caused by release of dopamine gradually reaching supersensitive dopamine receptors, this should normalize over time. In fact, the graft-related dyskinesias worsen or remain constant over time.

6. Release of other neurotransmitters or chemicals from the graft might provoke dyskinesias. This is a theoretical possibility, but there are no data to support it.

7. Trauma to the putamen somehow predisposes patients to dyskinesias. This would explain why the dyskinesias in the first study are the most symptomatic, since the needle tracks were the longest.

8. Host immune response might predispose to dyskinesias. This fails to explain why patients in the second controlled study did not do as well as patients treated by the same group in its open-label studies with the same immunosuppression regimen.

Although all these hypotheses are plausible, there is no more evidence for them than for the dopaminergic hypothesis. There is currently no explanation for the difference in the rate of severe graft dyskinesias between the controlled and uncontrolled studies. Efforts are now under way to create animal models of graft-related dyskinesias (50).

Can the Problems Be Fixed?

Although the results of the blinded trials were a disappointment to many neurologists, the transplant community saw this as a temporary if significant setback. One response has been to look for reasons that the controlled studies did not reflect the full potential of cell replacement therapy. Others have tried to suggest new directions that might overcome what are perceived as shortcomings of current practice. In 2004, Lindvall and Björklund identified the following potential problems with current fetal tissue transplants (19):

1. Insufficient graft survival and outgrowth. This has been recognized as a problem for a long time. Most investigators believe that improved cell survival and more robust outgrowth of processes will improve clinical outcome, and there has been research into solving this problem. Improving neuronal survival and increasing axonal outgrowth would allow for the use of less tissue and also possibly improve the magnitude of the response to grafting. Several trophic factors have been used to improve graft growth and survival. GDNF has been the most extensively studied of these factors. It increases neuronal survival, neuronal size, and density of tyrosine hydoxylase–positive fibers after ventral mesencephalic grafting in animal models (51, 52). Two patients with PD underwent grafting with GDNF-treated fetal ventral mesencephalon and seemed to show both clinical improvement and improvement in fluorodopa PET (53). Other trophic factors that enhance survival of grafted dopaminergic neurons in animal models include brain-derived neurotrophic factor (BDNF) (54) and neurotrophin-3 (55). Attempts have also been made to improve cell survival using antioxidants such as the lazaroid tirilazad (56) and flunarizine (57).

2. Inadequate patient selection. Several researchers have suggested that more restrictive selection of candidates might improve the outcome after transplantation: younger and/or milder patients may do better, but the data are sparse. Each of the double-blind studies reached different conclusions about which group of patients is most likely to improve after transplantation: younger patients or patients with a better response to levodopa (27, 28). Patients requiring less levodopa may also be in a milder stage of disease and might benefit more for that reason (19). So far, no study has examined the effects of cell transplantation in mildly ill patients. In any case, if cell transplantation were limited to younger or less severely affected patients, it might exclude a large percentage of patients with PD.

3. Graft placement was not tailored to individual needs. The authors suggest the use of high-resolution PET so that grafts could be placed in the most denervated areas (19). They also speculate that patients with greater denervation in mesolimbic areas may not do as well after transplantation. There is only a small amount of animal data supporting these suggestions.

4. Lack of standardization of the graft tissue. There is wide variability in the duration of storage of fetal tissue for grafting, methods of storing the tissue, and preparation of the tissue for transplantation. The optimal methods could be determined, at least in animals.

5. Lack of a standard immunosuppressive regimen. The role of the immune response after grafting

remains controversial, even with a growing number of autopsy studies. The authors of the review suggest long-term immunosuppression. At this time, there are insufficient data to determine what immunosuppression if any is necessary to optimize transplantation.

6. Strategy to avoid dyskinesias. The authors suggest further experimentation with animal models. There are many hypotheses about the etiology of this problem, but the data are sparse and contradictory.

DIRECTIONS FOR THE FUTURE

Stem Cells

Fetal cell transplants to treat PD were never conceived as a practical means to treat large numbers of patients with PD. There is not only controversy about the use of aborted tissue but also insufficient tissue from elective abortions to treat more than a small number of patients: it has been estimated that less than 0.01% of the tissue from all elective abortions is available for research use (58). Neither adult adrenal medullary tissue or porcine fetal mesencephalic tissue seems promising. Several other tissues, including extra-adrenal chromaffin cells (59) and human retinal pigment epithelial cells cultured from postmortem tissue (60) have been proposed as alternatives to fetal tissue. Despite promising open-label data for retinal pigment epithelial cells in patients with PD, the cells that have caused the most excitement in the transplantation community are stem cells. A variety of stem cells are candidates for cell therapy: embryonic stem cells, genetically engineered embryonic stem cells, embryonic stem cells with nuclear transfer, nonneural stem cells, fetal and adult neural stem cells, and in situ substantia nigra (SN) stem cells (61). The most attractive of all these possibilities is to induce stem cells already residing in the SN to differentiate into dopamine-producing cells and to establish connections with the striatum. Although glial precursor cells have been demonstrated in the SN of rats, these cells have not been shown to produce a dopaminergic phenotype, and it is far from clear whether newly generated dopaminergic cells in the SN would be able to establish functional connections in the adult (62). For every challenge, ingenious solutions have been proposed. For example, most stem cell transplantation runs the risk of immune rejection. This could be circumvented by the use of somatic nuclear transfer, in which a nucleus from a patient's own cells replaces the nucleus of the embryonic stem cell. Unfortunately this is difficult to achieve and generates several serious problems of its own (61). Although any of these techniques may ultimately be adequate for human therapeutic use, currently only the use of embryonic stem cells seems sufficiently advanced to be ready for human use (61). The technical problems involved in producing successful cells for transplantation are far too numerous to be reviewed here, and there are many transplantation-oriented stem cell reviews in the literature (61–63). One major challenge is that transplantation of undifferentiated stem cells creates a risk of teratoma formation (the cells would have to be induced to differentiate into dopamine-producing cells after transplantation), but stem cells that have fully differentiated in vitro have very low survival rates after transplantation (61). Nonetheless, initial experiments using stem cells in animal models of PD are promising, and it is likely that human trials will follow (for an example in a primate model, see ref. 64). Because of the large variety of techniques, it is difficult to predict whether stem cell transplantation is likely to provide an attractive alternate treatment for PD. We can, however, measure stem cell transplantation against the proposed requirements for successful fetal cell transplantation. How well do the new candidate techniques, and stem cells in particular, address these issues? Stem cells have the potential to produce large quantities of standardized dopamine-producing cells. However, the introduction of large amounts of dopamine producing tissue have the potential for producing uncontrollable dyskinesias. It is not obvious that stem cell technology can solve the problems of uneven cell survival and incomplete reinnervation of the striatum. The use of stem cells can be expected to provide large amounts of relatively homogeneous tissue producing only dopamine. The use of stem cells will not solve the problems of patient selection and individualized transplantation. It is impossible to predict at this time whether stem cell transplantation can overcome the known problems with fetal cell transplantation and whether it will supplement or complement existing treatments for PD.

Use of Genetically Modified Cells

Although most efforts at gene therapy have involved introduction of genes via the use of viral vectors or liposomal DNA transfer, there have been animal experiments involving the use of viral-transfected cells to introduce a variety of factors in an attempt to improve the symptoms of PD or to achieve neuroprotection (65). This has been done to enhance the survival of fetal mesencephalic cells, enhance the production of dopamine, and provide potentially protective trophic factors. For example, cografting of polymer-encapsulated baby hamster kidney cells transfected with the gene for GDNF was found to improve fetal mesencephalic transplants in parkinsonian rats; myoblasts transfected with tyrosine hydroxylase produced prolonged improvement in a rat model of PD; and fibroblasts transfected with the gene for BDNF seemed to be protective in a rat model of PD (65). Encapsulation of the transfected cells in a polymer sheath has been used to prevent rejection and answer concerns about potential tumor formation, but loss of expression of the transgenes and other technical difficulties still limit the use of this technology (65).

SUMMARY

We are faced with a dilemma. There is a large body of open-label data suggesting that fetal cell transplants may produce dramatic results in some patients with PD—that they have the potential to reduce dyskinesias and solve some of the problems of medical therapy. There are 3 blinded, controlled studies (2 with fetal tissue and the other with porcine fetal tissue) that fail to confirm net benefit in typical PD and identify the potentially serious problem of increased dyskinesias, which may not be controllable by medication reduction. It is possible that a change in technique, use of stem cells, or some other innovation may overcome the lack of consistent response and graft related dyskinesias. At this time, however, cell transplants using fetal mesencephalic tissue cannot be recommended as therapy for PD. A recent evidence-based review of pharmacologic and surgical treatments of PD concluded that fetal mesencaphalic transplants were nonefficacious and that, because of the potential for dyskinesias, the risk was unacceptable (66). The review recommended that fetal transplantation be continued on an investigational basis, since the basic science might be improved. We do not know whether stem cell transplants or other emerging technologies can provide more predictable benefit in PD while avoiding the problem of dyskinesias. Based on current hypotheses about the problems with fetal cell transplant, stem cell transplants and other techniques can circumvent some but not all of the identified problems. Although proponents of transplant therapy for PD suggest a number of potential solutions, there are currently no data to reassure the medical community that these problems will be overcome in the near future. Until much more research has been done, the promise of tissue replacement for PD remains a distant hope.

References

1. Björklund A, Stenevi U. Intracerebral neural grafting: A historical perspective. In: Björklund A, Stenevi U (eds). *Neural Grafting in the Mammalian CNS.* Elsevier; New York, NY, 1985:3–14.
2. Stenevi U, Björklund A, Svengaard NA. Transplantation of central and peripheral monamine neurons to the adult rat brain: Techniques and conditions for survival. *Brain Res* 1976; 114:120.
3. Fahn S, Sulzer D. Neurodegeneration and neuroprotection in Parkinson disease. *NeuroRx* 2004; 1:139–154.
4. Thobois S, Delamarre-Damier F, Derkinderen P. Treatment of motor dysfunction in Parkinson's disease: An overview. *Clin Neurol Neurosurg* 2005; 107:269–281.
5. Lang AE, Obeso JA. Challenges in Parkinson's disease: Restoration of the nigrostriatal dopamine system is not enough. *Lancet Neurology* 2004; 3:309–316.
6. Freed WJ. Functional brain tissue transplantation: Reversal of lesion induced rotation by intraventricular substantia nigra and adrenal medulla grafts with a note on intracranial retinal grafts. *Biol Psychiatry* 1983; 18:1205–1267.
7. Brundin P, Duan WM, Sauer H. Functional effects of mesencephalic dopamine neurons and adrenal chromaffin cells grafted to the rodent striatum. In: Dunnett SB, Björklund A (eds). *Functional Neural Transplantation.* New York: Raven Press, 1994:946.
8. Bohn MC, Marciano F, Cupit L, Gash DM. Recovery of dopaminergic fibers in striatum of the MPTP treated mouse is enhanced by grafts of adrenal medulla. In: Gash DM, Sladek JR (eds). *Progress in Brain Research.* Vol 78. Amsterdam: Elsevier, 1988:535–542.
9. Bankiewicz KS, Plunkett RJ, Kopin IJ, et al. Transient behavioral recovery in hemiparkinsonian primates after adrenal medullary allografts. In: Gash DM, Sladek JR (eds). *Progress in Brain Research.* Vol 78. Amsterdam: Elsevier, 1988:543–549.
10. Madrazo I, DruckerColin R, Diaz V, et al. Open microsurgical autograft of adrenal medulla to the right caudate nucleus in two patients with intractable Parkinson's disease. *N Engl J Med* 1987; 316:831–834.
11. Fahn S. Status of Transplantation in Patients With Parkinson's Disease. Soriano lecture. Philadelphia: American Neurological Association, 1988.
12. Goetz CG, Tanner CM, Penn RD, et al. Adrenal medullary transplant to the striatum of patients with advanced Parkinson's disease: 1-year motor and psychomotor data. *Neurology* 1990; 40:273–276.
13. Goetz CG, Stebbins GT, Klawans HL, et al. UPF Neural Transplantation Registry. United Parkinson Foundation Neurotransplantation Registry on adrenal medullary transplants: Presurgical and 1- and 2-year follow-up. *Neurology* 1991; 41:1719–1722.
14. Jiang N, Jiang C, Tang Z, et al. Human fetal brain transplant trials in the treatment of parkinsonism. *Acta Acad Med Shangai* 1987; 14:77.
15. Lindvall O, Rehncrona S, Gustavii B, et al. Fetal dopamine-rich mesencephalic grafts in Parkinson's disease. *Lancet* 1988; 2:1483–1484.
16. Madrazo I, Leon V, Torres C, et al. Transplantation of fetal substantia nigra and adrenal medulla to the caudate nucleus in two patients with Parkinson's disease. *N Engl J Med* 1988; 318:51.
17. Lindvall O. Update on fetal transplantation: The Swedish experience. *Mov Disord* 1998; 13(Suppl 1):8387.
18. Clarkson ED. Fetal tissue transplantation for patients with Parkinson's disease: A database of published clinical results. *Drugs Aging* 2001; 18:773–785.
19. Lindvall O, Björklund A. Cell therapy in Parkinson's disease. *NeuroRx* 2004; 1:382–393.
20. Freeman TB, Sanberg PR, Nauert GM, et al. Influence of donor age on the survival of solid and suspension intraparenchymal human embryonic micrografts. *Cell Transplant* 1995; 4:141–154.
21. Brundin P, Strecker RE, Widner H, et al. Human fetal dopamine neurons grafted in a rat model of Parkinson's disease: Immunological aspects, spontaneous and drug-induced behaviour and dopamine release. *Exp Brain Res* 1988; 70:192–208.
22. Kordower JK, Rosenstein RM, Collier TJ, et al. Functional fetal nigral grafts in a patient with Parkinson's disease: Chemoanatomic, ultrastructural and metabolic studies. *J Comp Neurol* 1996; 370:203–230.
23. Spencer DD, Robbins RJ, Narftolin F, et al. Unilateral transplantation of human fetal mesencephalic tissue into the caudate nucleus of patients with Parkinson's disease. *N Engl J Med* 1992; 327:1541–1548.
24. Freed CR, Breeze RE, Rosenberg NL, et al. Survival of implanted fetal dopamine cells and neurologic improvement 12 to 46 months after transplantation for Parkinson's disease. *N Engl J Med* 1992; 327:1549–1555.
25. Freeman TB, Olanow CW, Hauser RA, et al. Bilateral fetal nigral transplantation into the postcommissural putamen in Parkinson's disease. *Ann Neurol* 1995; 38:379–388.
26. Tabbal S, Fahn S, Frucht S. Fetal tissue transplantation in Parkinson's disease. *Curr Opin Neurol* 1998; 11:341–349.
27. Freed CR, Greene PE, Breeze RE, et al. Embryonic dopamine cell transplantation for advanced Parkinson's disease A double-blind neurosurgical trial. *N Engl J Med* 2001; 344:710–719.
28. Olanow CW, Goetz CG, Kordower JH, et al. A double-blind controlled trial of bilateral fetal nigral transplantation in Parkinson's disease *Ann Neurol* 2003; 54:403–414.
29. Clarkson ED. Fetal tissue transplantation for patients with Parkinson's disease: A database of published clinical results. *Drugs Aging* 2001; 18:773–785.
30. Deacon T, Schumacher J, Dinsmore J, et al. Histological evidence of fetal pig neural cell survival after transplantation into a patient with Parkinson's disease. *Nature Med* 1997; 3:350–353.
31. Schumacher JM, Ellias SA, Palmer EP, et al. Transplantation of embryonic porcine mesencephalic tissue in patients with PD. *Neurology* 2000; 54:1042–1050.
32. Watts RL, Freeman TL, Hauser RA, et al. A double-blind, randomized, controlled, multicenter clinical trial of the safety and efficacy of stereotaxic intrastriatal implantation of fetal porcine ventral mesencephalic tissue (Neurocell-PD) vs imitation surgery in patients with Parkinson's disease (PD). *Parkinsonism Rel Disord* 2001; 7(Suppl):S87.
33. Winkler C, Kirik D, Björklund A. Cell transplantation in Parkinson's disease: How can we make it work? *Trends Neurosci* 2005; 28:86–92.
34. Mendez I, Sanchez-Pernaute R, Cooper O, et al. Cell type analysis of functional fetal dopamine cell suspension transplants in the striatum and substantia nigra of patients with Parkinson's disease. *Brain* 2005; 128:1498–1510.
35. Björklund A, Dunnett ST, Brundin P, et al. Neural transplantation for the treatment of Parkinson's disease. *Lancet Neurol* 2003; 2:437–445.
36. Lang AE, Gill S, Patel NK, et al. Randomized controlled trial of intraputamenal glial cell line-derived neurotrophic factor infusion in Parkinson disease. *Ann Neurol* 2006; 59:459–466.

37. Slevin JT, Gerhardt GA, Smith CD, et al. Improvement of bilateral motor functions in patients with Parkinson disease through the unilateral intraputaminal infusion of glial cell line–derived neurotrophic factor. *J Neurosurg* 2005; 102:216–222.

38. Freeman TB, Vawter DE, Leaverton PE, et al. Use of placebo surgery in controlled trials of a cellular-based therapy for Parkinson's disease. *N Engl J Med* 1999; 341:988–992.

39. Kim SYH, Frank S, Holloway R, et al. Science and ethics of sham surgery: A survey of Parkinson disease clinical researchers. *Arch Neurol* 2005; 62:1357–1360.

40. Wenning GK, Odin P, Morrish P, et al. Short and long term survival and function of unilateral intrastriatal dopaminergic grafts in PD. *Ann Neurol* 1997; 42:95–107.

41. Benabid AL, Pollak P, Gao D, et al. Chronic electrical stimulation of the ventralis intermedius nucleus of the thalamus as a treatment of movement disorders. *J Neurosurg* 1996; 84:203–214.

42. Lyons KE, Wilkinson SB, Overman J, Pahwa R. Surgical and hardware complications of subthalamic stimulation: A series of 160 procedures. *Neurology* 2004; 63:612–616.

43. Lopez-Lozano JJ, Bravo G, Brera B, et al. Long-term improvement in patients with severe Parkinson's disease after implantation of fetal ventral mesencephalic tissue in a cavity of the caudate nucleus: 5-year follow up in 10 patients. *J Neurosurg* 1997; 86:931–942.

44. Folkerth RD, Durso R, Survival and proliferation of nonneural tissues, with obstruction of cerebral ventricles, in a parkinsonian patient treated with fetal allografts. *Neurology* 1996; 46:1219–1225.

45. Mamelak AN, Eggerding FA, Oh DS, et al. Fatal cyst formation after fetal mesencephalic allograft transplant for Parkinson's disease. *J Neurosurg* 1998; 89:592–598.

46. Defer GL, Geny C, Ricolfi F, et al. Long-term outcome of unilaterally transplanted parkinsonian patients. *Brain* 1996; 119:4150.

47. Hagell P, Piccini P, Björklund A, et al. Dyskinesias following neural transplantation in Parkinson's disease. *Nature Neurosci* 2002; 5:627–628.

48. Hagell P, Cenci MA. Dyskinesias and dopamine cell replacement in Parkinson's disease: A clinical perspective. *Brain Res Bull* 2005; 68:4–15.

49. Ylong M, Feigin A, Vijay D, et al. Dyskinesia after fetal cell transplantation for parkinsonism: A PET study. *Ann Neurol* 2002; 52:628–634.

50. Winkler C, Kirik D, Björklund A, Cenci MA. L-DOPA-induced dyskinesia in the intrastriatal 6-hydroxydopamine model of Parkinson's disease: Relation to motor and cellular parameters of nigrostriatal function. *Neurol Dis* 2002; 10:165–186.

51. Rosenblad C, Martinez-Serrano A, Björklund A. Glial cell line-derived neurotrophic factor increases survival, growth and function of intrastriatal fetal nigral dopaminergic grafts. *Neuroscience* 1996; 75:979–985.

52. Granholm A-C, Mott JL, Bowenkamp K, et al. Glial cell line–derived neurotrophic factor improves survival of ventral mesencephalic grafts to the 6-hydroxydopamine lesioned striatum. *Exp Brain Res* 1997; 116:29–38.

53. Mendez I, Dagher A, Hong M, et al. Enhancement of survival of stored dopaminergic cells and promotion of graft survival by exposure of human fetal nigral tissue to glial cell line-derived neurotrophic factor in patients with Parkinson's disease. *J Neurosurg* 2000; 92:863–869.

54. Yurek DM, Lu W, Hipkens S, Wiegand SJ. BDNF enhances the functional reinnervation of the striatum by grafted fetal dopamine neurons. *Exp Neurol* 1996; 137:105–118.

55. Espejo M, Cutillas B, Arenas E, Ambrosio S. Increased survival of dopaminergic neurons in striatal grafts of fetal ventral mesencephalic cells exposed to neurotrophin-3 or glial cell line-derived neurotrophic factor. *Exp Neurol* 1997; 148:324–333.

56. Björklund A, Spenger C, Stromberg I. Tirilazad mesylate increases dopaminergic neuronal survival in the in Oculo grafting model. *Exp Neurol* 1997; 148:324–333.

57. Schierle GSK, Hansson O, Brundin P. Flunarizine improves the survival of grafted dopaminergic neurons. *Neuroscience* 1999; 94:17–20.

58. Lawson HW, Atrash HK, Saftlas AF, et al. Abortion surveillance, US 1984–1985. *MMWR* 1988; 38:1142.

59. Fernandez-Espejo E. Pathogenesis of Parkinson's disease. *Mol Neurobiol* 2004; 29: 15–30.

60. Stover NP, Bakay RAE, Subramanian T, et al. Intrastriatal implantation of human retinal pigment epithelial cells attached to microcarriers in advanced Parkinson disease. *Arch Neurol* 2005; 62:1833–1837.

61. Correia AS, Anisimov SV, Li J-Y, Brundin P. Stem cell–based therapy for Parkinson's disease. *Ann Med* 2005; 37:487–498.

62. Levy YS, Stroomza M, Melamed E, Offen D. Embryonic and adult stem cells as a source for cell therapy in Parkinson's disease. *J Mol Neurosci* 2004; 24:353–386.

63. Sonntag K-C, Simantov R, Isacson O. Stem cells may reshape the prospect of Parkinson's disease therapy. *Mol Brain Res* 2005; 134:34–51.

64. Takagi Y, Takahashi J, Saiki H, et al. Dopaminergic neurons generated from monkey embryonic stem cells function in a Parkinson primate model. *J Clin Invest* 2005; 115: 102–109.

65. Eberhardt O, Schulz JB. Gene therapy in Parkinson's disease. *Cell Tissue Res* 2004; 318:243–260.

66. Goetz CG, Poewe W, Rascol O, Sampaio C. Evidence-based medical review update: Pharmacological and surgical treatments of Parkinson's disease: 2001–2004. *Mov Disord* 2005; 20:523–539.

56 Stereotactic Pallidotomy and Thalamotomy

Robert E. Gross
Andres M. Lozano

Over the last 2 decades, the surgical treatment of Parkinson's disease (PD) and other movement disorders has evolved to a level of importance in the armamentarium of treatment for patients with advanced disease. This progress has been based mainly on advances in understanding the pathophysiology of the basal ganglia, improvements in computer technology, and access to better imaging and stereotactic equipment that make neurosurgical procedures more accurate and safe. Most important, the increased acceptance of these treatments has related to the success of several prospective controlled trials demonstrating the safety and effectiveness of surgical therapy. As a result, patients with advanced levels of disability despite optimized medical treatment now have recourse to a treatment that adds years of improved quality of life.

Generally, there are three main surgical approaches for PD: ablative surgery, deep brain stimulation (DBS), and "restorative" therapies, predominantly neural transplantation and now also gene therapy. These therapies are usually reserved for patients with advanced disease refractory to medications or who experience significant adverse effects, most notably motor complications, such as fluctuations and dyskinesias. This chapter focuses on ablative surgery, specifically stereotactic pallidotomy and thalamotomy, which, in spite of the increased safety and acceptance of DBS, still has an important role, especially in less developed regions.

HISTORICAL BACKGROUND

The first report of surgery for movement disorders was published more than a century ago and consisted of resection of the premotor area to treat choreoathetosis (1). Surgical procedures for PD early in this century included lesioning the cerebral cortex or corticospinal system and replacing tremor with motor deficits (2–4). Meyers (5) first introduced surgical lesions directed at the basal ganglia in 1940. He found that sectioning of pallidofugal fibers could improve parkinsonism, particularly tremor, without creating a pyramidal deficit. This pioneering work was followed by the development of more precise and safer methods using stereotactic guidance. Spiegel et al. (6) performed the first acknowledged stereotactic pallidotomy for movement disorders in the end of the 1940s. Soon Leksell (7), Cooper (8), Guiot (9), and Narayabashi (10), developed their own instruments and surgical approaches to the globus pallidus and its output fibers. Because of the perceived variable and inconsistent results on tremor with pallidotomy as practiced at that time, Hassler introduced surgery of the ventrolateral (VL) nucleus of the thalamus (11). The procedure was based on a study of the anatomic connections between the pallidum and the thalamus. Beginning in the mid- to late 1950s and reaching a peak in the 1960s, stereotactic neurosurgery, especially thalamotomy, became a prominent mode of therapy for PD. Microelectrode recording, first utilized in the 1960s, allowed the groups of Guiot (12) and Narabayashi (13, 14) to define the ventral intermediate (Vim) nucleus of the thalamus as the best target to control the tremor in PD. But the Vim target was still disappointing for akinesia and rigidity. This provided a rationale for combining pallidotomy with thalamotomy, with the surgeon performing the second procedure as necessary depending on the response to the initial lesion (15).

About a half-century after the first discovery of dopamine by Guggenheim in 1913, levodopa treatment for PD was introduced in 1961 and was widely available by 1968. As it gained worldwide popularity, stereotactic neurosurgery declined, and the number of stereotactic procedures soon decreased dramatically (16). However, despite the striking benefits provided by levodopa, it quickly became evident that it too had shortcomings. As PD progresses and with prolonged administration of levodopa, symptoms become refractory to the drug and disabling, abnormal, involuntary movements (dyskinesias) and "on-off" fluctuations appear. Because of these problems, stereotactic neurosurgery was revisited and gained an increasing role. This new era was ushered in by advances in the understanding of basal ganglia pathophysiology (17, 18) coincident with the work of Laitinen and coworkers (19, 20), who reintroduced Leksell's pallidotomy, and the development of better brain imaging and intraoperative electrophysiologic techniques. Through the 1990s, pallidotomy (and to a lesser extent thalamotomy) was increasingly evaluated for PD and other movement disorders (21). However, the resurgence of radiofrequency ablation techniques was short-lived, as they were quickly supplanted by deep brain stimulation, which offers similar benefits but also an improved safety profile, especially when used bilaterally (22, 23).

RATIONALE OF SURGERY

Pallidotomy

Together with the substantia nigra pars reticulata (SNr), the internal segment of the globus pallidus (GPi) constitutes the source of the final output of the basal ganglia. As a result of the dopamine deficiency, the GABAergic output of the GPi is increased in PD (24–29). Two main mechanisms are believed to contribute to this: (a) increased drive from the excitatory glutamatergic subthalamic nucleus (STN) via the indirect pathway, which derives from the striatum through the external segment of globus pallidus (GPe), and (b) decreased inhibition

(dysinhibition) via a direct pathway from the motor striatum (28, 30). Hyperactivitiy of the GPi is considered to be a hallmark of PD physiology and exerts an excessive inhibitory influence on the thalamus, downstream cortical motor systems, and brainstem motor areas, which are thought to be responsible for the disrupted and impoverished movement that characterizes PD. In addition, the output from GPi is more irregular in PD, at least in part contributing to the downstream dysregulation of the thalamocortical projections (31). The surgical strategy is to make lesions selectively in the sensorimotor portions of the GPi so as to decrease the inhibitory influence of basal ganglia output, thus releasing brainstem motor areas and normalizing thalamocortical activity. It is believed that lesions should be limited to the sensorimotor portions of the Gpi, as it is defined by the area populated by neurons that respond to movement. Lesions should spare the limbic and associative territories of the GPi to avoid unwanted complications, and they should also avoid injury to the other adjacent territories including the GPe, optic tract, and internal capsule.

Vim Thalamotomy

The Vim nucleus of the thalamus receives predominantly contralateral cerebellar inputs and projects to the ipsilateral primary motor cortex, premotor, and supplementary motor cortical areas. Early investigations involving the motor thalamus in PD patients revealed that many of its cells have a discharge pattern synchronized to the patient's tremor (32–34). These "tremor cells" were found in sites presumed to correspond to the Vim and Vop nuclei—the cerebellar and pallidal receiving areas respectively. As a result, additional studies (35–38) focused on the role of these ventral nuclear groups of the thalamus in the pathogenesis of tremor in PD. Moreover, intraoperative electrical stimulation in the regions where these tremor cells were recorded produced tremor arrest, and lesions at these same sites produced long-term tremor relief (39, 40).

Vim thalamotomies, however, have little effect on rigidity, bradykinesia, or the gait disturbances characteristic of PD (see below). For this reason, the Vim target is of limited use in PD and should be restricted to a small subgroup of patients, who have medication-resistant tremor-dominant PD (41).

INDICATIONS AND PATIENT SELECTION FOR SURGERY

In general, stereotactic surgery for PD is indicated in patients who respond only suboptimally to dopaminergic therapy and who are experiencing "off" periods and dyskinesias that impair the quality of their lives. Patients must be sufficiently healthy to undergo a lengthy surgical procedure while awake. The presence of neuropsychiatric complications such as dementia and unstable medical conditions are contraindications to surgery. In addition, since the main complication of surgery is intracranial hemorrhage, all patients should be screened for bleeding tendency, coagulopathy, and hypertension. Furthermore, antiplatelet agents such as acetylsalicylic acid should be discontinued for at least a week before surgery. Hypertensive patients should have their blood pressure strictly controlled before and during surgery. Patients with cardiac disease should be proven stable by undergoing a cardiac stress test and other procedures; the surgical procedure may be the most stressful experience the patient has undergone for some time and thus poses the risk of myocardial infarction. Special consideration should be given to those with significant cerebral atrophy because of the increased risk of subdural hematoma from traction injury to bridging veins.

Pallidotomy

Early in the course of PD most patients respond well to dopaminergic agents, such as dopamine agonists or levodopa, and symptoms are controlled without the development of significant "off" time or dyskinesia. This is due in large measure to an adequate reserve of dopaminergic nerve terminals in the striatum, which can take up the dopamine precursor, synthesize and store dopamine, and release it over long periods of time. However, for a variety of incompletely understood reasons, including progressive nerve terminal loss and postsynaptic changes such as sensitization of receptors and tolerance, complications of medical treatment may develop (42, 43). These are characterized by "wearing off" and peak-dose dyskinesia, leading to periods of the day spent in the "off" state or in the "on" state with dyskinesia, with marked decreases in good-quality "on" time. The "off" state is generally characterized by the presence of bradykinesia, rigidity, tremor, and gait disturbance. Pallidotomy is then indicated for the following: treatment of levodopa-induced dyskinesias, severe wearing off or "on-off" fluctuations characterized by rigidity, bradykinesia, and tremor; "off"-period dystonia; and gait disturbance, in that order of preference. The presence of a good response to levodopa predicts a good response to pallidotomy (44). Conversely, "midline" symptoms persisting in "on" periods (i.e., swallowing difficulty, hypophonic speech, postural instability, and freezing) are resistant and may even worsen with pallidotomy. The exceptions to this are tremor and dyskinesia; both may be present in the "on" condition, but they respond well to pallidotomy.

The ideal candidate for pallidotomy (a) has asymmetrical symptoms, (b) is young, (c) has bradykinetic PD with symptoms responsive to levodopa but continues to have significant motor impairment during "off" times, (d) is cognitively intact, and (e) has reasonable expectations from surgery. Preoperative assessments include neurologic, psychiatric, neuroradiologic, and neuropsychological evaluations to screen out secondary forms of parkinsonism or Parkinson-plus syndromes and other problems that would contraindicate surgery. Patients who do not respond to levodopa for example, are unlikely to have PD or to derive substantial benefit from pallidotomy. It is important to distinguish between PD and other causes of parkinsonism [e.g., multiple system atrophy (MSA), progressive supranuclear palsy (PSP), diffuse Lewy body disease, parkinsonism secondary to multifocal ischemic white matter disease] because these disorders are much less likely to benefit from pallidotomy and may actually worsen.

Magnetic resonance imaging (MRI) evidence of severe brain atrophy or multiple lacunar infarcts may also be a relative contraindication. The presence of linear high signal in the posterolateral putamen (on T2 or proton MRI scans) sometimes combined with evidence of low signal on T2, indicative of iron disposition in the lenticular nucleus, strongly suggests a diagnosis of MSA (45). Fluorodeoxyglucose positron emission tomography (FDG-PET) may also be used for patient selection, as patients who show lentiform hypometabolism should be excluded; this finding suggests a Parkinson-plus syndrome, whereas PD exhibits lentiform hypermetabolism and reduced striatal ^{18}F-dopa uptake, particularly in the posterior putamen (46–48). Moreover, Eidelberg and colleagues (49) reported that preoperative FDG/PET measurements of lentiform glucose metabolism showed significant correlation with clinical outcome following pallidotomy.

Age is not an absolute selection criterion, although some authors (50–52) suggest that younger patients derive more benefit than older patients; there has even been a study showing a positive correlation of age with outcome (53). This also raises the controversial issue of when in the course of the illness surgery is best performed. Surgery is generally reserved for patients who have reached a level of impairment that prevents them from carrying out important activities of daily living (e.g., work or self-care) despite (or because of, as in the case of dyskinesias) optimal medical therapy. Pallidotomy is not offered to end-stage, wheelchair-bound, or bedridden patients, based on the early experience of the limited benefits they derive and their often disabling associated features that are unresponsive to medication or surgery (54).

Pre- and postoperative patients should be assessed according to the Core assessment program for intracerebral transplantation (CAPIT) protocol (55, 56), which incorporates the Unified Parkinson's Disease Rating Scale (UPDRS) and Hoehn and Yahr staging scale, or the more recently developed Core assessment program for surgical interventional therapies in PD (CAPSIT-PD), which incorporates, in addition, cognitive and behavioral evaluation and increased emphasis on quality of life (57).

Evaluations of patients on and off medication, a series of timed motor tasks, and cognitive assessment of potential surgical candidates are also very important. Patients who score 25 or less out of 30 on the Folstein Mini-Mental Status Examination (58) or less that 116 out of 144 on the Mattis Dementia Rating Scale (59) are generally not considered to be good candidates. These patients may not be fully cooperative for the surgery, may be more prone to cognitive side effects from pallidal lesions, and—because of their cognitive impairment—may derive less overall benefit associated with an improved motor status. Arguably all patients, but at least in patients that appear "at risk" based on screening tools, more detailed neuropsychological evaluation should be performed before and after surgery (60–73).

Because the benefits of pallidotomy are predominantly unilateral, surgery is directed toward the patient's worst side. When the disease is symmetrical, the dominant hemisphere is surgically treated. Although the issue has not been evaluated in extensive controlled trials, the risk to speech and cognition of bilateral pallidotomies is regarded by most to be too great to be an option in patients with PD (see below), although the same may not be true in patients with dystonia.

In summary, unilateral pallidotomy is relatively safe and effective for patients with PD who are experiencing complications of medical treatment including dyskinesia, wearing off, and "on-off" with off periods characterized by the presence of bradykinesia, rigidity, and/or tremor. The greatest and most consistent benefit is amelioration of dyskinesia. Other major advantages, compared to other surgical strategies such as deep brain stimulation, are its wide availability, no implantation-related problems, and immediate benefit. The major drawbacks of pallidotomy are that it is irreversible and nonmodifiable. In this sense, a previous pallidotomy may thereafter preclude the full benefit of other therapeutic modalities; thus patients should be informed that they may be ineligible for certain other medical and surgical therapeutic trials. Moreover, when a second procedure is contemplated on the opposite side, a series of complications and side effects are more common than with a single unilateral procedure.

Thalamotomy

Thalamotomy directed to the Vim nucleus is indicated for asymmetrical, severe, medically intractable tremor, especially when the patient is not affected by significant disabilities from other features of PD. Vim thalamotomy is not effective for bradykinesia, micrographia, or disturbances of gait or speech (74). There is evidence, however, that lesioning Vop, the nucleus situated anterior

to Vim, which is a pallidal receiving area, can result in improvement of rigidity and dyskinesia, possibly through the mechanisms described earlier (75, 76). Some patients develop *Benign tremulous parkinsonism* and may progress slowly with little difficulty from other motor symptoms. The frequency of this form of PD is unclear, and it is currently not possible to predict that this will be the course. Having said that, it should be stressed that the majority of patients with PD eventually develop disabling symptoms other than tremor. Therefore, although thalamotomy may be an ideal therapeutic measure to treat the tremor, many patients will later require consideration of an additional procedure(s) for other disabilities. This is reflected by the recent slow decline in the number of thalamotomies being performed in patients with PD. The same applies to thalamic DBS (see Chapter 54). Thalamotomy on the second side is effective in ameliorating tremor but results in a high incidence of speech and balance problems, and thus has largely been abandoned in favor of Vim DBS and DBS of GPi and STN, procedures that have the potential to treat all major motor manifestations of PD.

Selection criteria for thalamotomy include patients with (a) primarily tremor, (b) highly asymmetrical tremor, (c) drug-resistance or intolerance, (d) lack of significant cognitive dysfunction, and (e) disabilities due to tremor such that its amelioration could result in an improved quality of life. Medical contraindications for thalamotomy are similar to those for pallidotomy (e.g., uncontrollable hypertension, diabetes mellitus, bleeding tendency, cancer, etc.).

SURGICAL TECHNIQUES FOR PALLIDOTOMY AND THALAMOTOMY

The surgical procedures for pallidotomy and thalamotomy are described together because the basic techniques are similar (detailed procedures are outlined in Refs. 77 through 80). Here only a brief description of stereotactic pallidotomy and thalamotomy is presented. It is divided into 3 phases. First is stereotactic imaging; second, neurophysiologic mapping; and third, lesion making.

Imaging is used to obtain the location of the tentative surgical target in 3-dimensional (3D) stereotactic space. Currently, computed tomography (CT) and MRI are being used most commonly for this purpose, but ventriculography has been extensively used in the past and continues to be used in certain centers. Initially, the stereotactic frame is applied to provide the terms of reference for the target in stereotactic space. This is done under local anesthesia. Generally the patient is kept in an "off" state, the medications having been withheld for 12 hours overnight to accentuate the pathophysiologic cellular activity in the basal ganglia and allow direct observation of the effects of incremental lesions in either the thalamus or pallidum. On the other hand, if the patient is extremely uncomfortable (e.g., because of painful "off"-period dystonia), it may be necessary to give some short-acting antiparkinson medications first thing in the morning, perform the imaging with the patient "on" or partially "on," and then allow the medication to wear off before performing the physiologic mapping. Target coordinates are chosen directly from the images or in relation to standard landmarks, such as the anterior and posterior commissures. The pallidal target usually corresponds quite closely to the target initially described by Laitinen and coworkers (81) and is usually 2 to 3 mm anterior to the midcommissural point, 3 to 6 mm below the intercommissural (IC) line, and 20 to 21 mm lateral to the midline. The thalamic target is usually 25% of anterior commissure to posterior commissure l(AC-PC) length posterior to midcommissural point on the IC plane and 13 to 17 mm from midline.

For the neurophysiologic mapping, a burr hole or twist-drill opening just anterior to the coronal suture on the side opposite the worse parkinsonian symptoms is made to allow the introduction of a macroelectrode or cannula to guide a microelectrode. There are currently 2 widely used techniques for physiologic mapping, microelectrode recording/stimulation and macroelectrode stimulation mapping (82). The macroelectrode technique permits mapping based on the interpretation of macrostimulation responses. It has the advantage of being rapid and requiring minimal equipment, but it does not allow the recording of neuronal activity. The microelectrode technique permits the acquisition of direct measures of cellular activity from individual neurons, offering a high level of physiologic resolution of nuclei based on the pattern of neuronal activity and the determination of their receptive fields. These advantages come at the price of extra time, extra equipment, and a high level of expertise.

The information required to place GPi lesions safely includes the identification of the optic tract, the internal capsule, and the sensorimotor GPi, defined as that portion containing movement-responsive neurons (Figure 56-1). Additionally, to take into consideration that the location of GPi can differ from medial to lateral based in part on the width of the third ventricle (83), the lateral border of the GPi is best determined and the final target adjusted accordingly (84). For thalamotomy, important considerations in selecting the optimal target include the following. Lesions should be placed (a) at least 2 to 3 mm anterior to the border of the tactile sensory relay thalamic nucleus, (b) in areas containing kinesthetic (movement-related) cells with receptive fields corresponding to the distal upper extremity and cells that fire in synchrony with upper extremity tremor, (c) in areas where electrical stimulation produces arrest of upper extremity tremor,

and (d) at the base of the thalamus to deafferent the entire dorsal-ventral extent of Vim from incoming cerebellar fibers.

Pallidotomy and thalamotomy lesions are made with a radiofrequency generator that heats a 1-mm-diameter probe with a 2- or 3-mm exposed tip. First a test lesion is made at 60°C for 60 s, followed by the formal lesioning by heating the electrode to 70°C, 80°C, and up to 90°C for 60 s. In the thalamus, 4-mm-diameter lesions are made, whereas larger, 6-mm-diameter lesions are usually made in the GPi by repeating the lesion in 1 or 2 additional tracks (77, 84). A spherical lesion that measures approximately 6 mm in height and 4 mm in diameter in the GPi is demonstrated on a T1-weighted MR image after surgery (Figure 56-2). Other groups make multiple smaller lesions on one or more electrode tracts. Some attempt to make the lesion depending on the somatotopic findings and the clinical distribution of signs and symptoms (85). On the other hand, there is no convincing evidence that the clinical outcome is any better using this approach than with the single larger lesion. Throughout lesion making, the patient's speech, vision, and motor functions are tested. Although the optimal lesion size and location are as yet unclear, the lesion must to be sufficiently large to produce a long-standing clinical benefit but small enough to avoid unwanted side effects. The benefits of pallidotomy and thalamotomy are seen immediately in the operating room.

CLINICAL RESULTS

Pallidotomy

Clinical Benefits of Pallidotomy. The results of pallidotomy have been reported in nearly 2000 patients from 40 centers in 12 countries (86). By far the most striking effect of pallidotomy is the nearly complete and sustained amelioration of drug-induced involuntary movements on the contralateral side (52, 53, 81, 87–107). After pallidotomy, patients are better able to tolerate similar or even higher doses of dopaminergic medication than before surgery because of the striking diminution in contralateral and, to a lesser extent, ipsilateral dyskinesias. This translates into more dyskinesia-free "on" time and a striking improvement in quality of life.

The effects of pallidotomy on rigidity, tremor, and bradykinesia in the "off" condition are also quite significant. The results of unilateral pallidotomy from nonduplicated reports of series of greater than 5 patients followed with the UPDRS for at least 6 months are shown in Table 56-1. This includes 528 patients who underwent surgery in 22 centers, and followed for 6 to 12 months (51, 53, 87, 88, 90–94, 97–104, 106–111). The major impact of unilateral pallidotomy is seen during

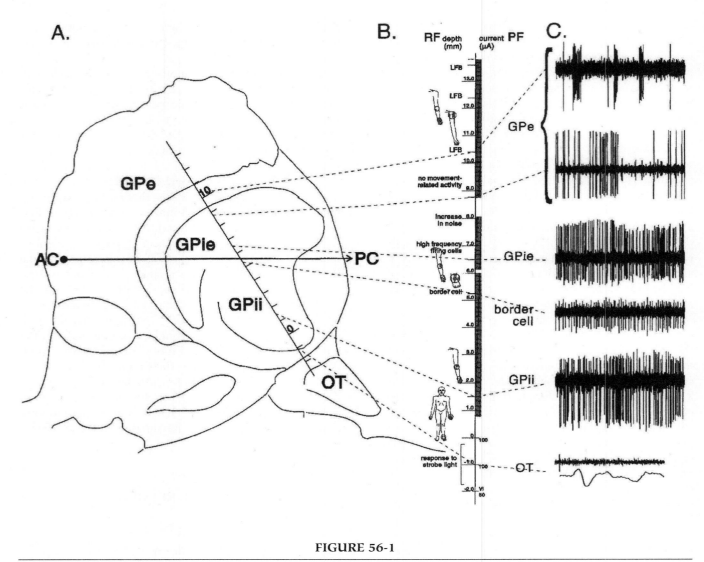

FIGURE 56-1

A. Physiologic data obtained from one trajectory through the globus pallidus and optic tract (OT) plotted on the 20-mm sagittal map from the Schaltenbrand and Wahren stereotactic atlas. B. Locations of neurons and their responses as well as intraoperative observations of the characteristics of recordings can be seen. Thick lines represent the cellular areas and thin lines represent the acellular (quiet) regions. Receptive fields (RFs) are shown to the left of the line along with the depth of the recordings along the trajectory. Projection fields (PFs), or the effects of microstimulation, are shown to the right of the line along with the current used. C. Oscilloscope traces of representative examples of the neuronal types. GPe neurons have two distinct patterns of spontaneous firing: a low-frequency discharge (10 to 20 Hz) punctuated by rapid bursts (so-called low-frequency burst neurons) and an irregular pattern at a relatively slow frequency (30 to 60 Hz), also with intervening brief pauses (termed slow-frequency discharge-pause neurons). Neurons in GPi fire on average at a higher frequency (82 ± 32 Hz, with ranges of 20 to 200 Hz) than that found in the Gpe, and they normally lack audible pauses (termed high-frequency discharge neurons). Some of these neurons, termed "tremor cells," discharge in a rhythmic fashion in synchrony with peripheral tremor. Tremor cells tend to be found in the ventral half of the GP but have been found in some patients in the dorsal GPi as well. The white matter laminae that separate the GPe from GPi and GPi,e from GPi,i are flanked by "border cells," which often have wide spikes with a long afterpotential. Border cells have the unique property of firing in a regular pattern at rates on the order of 20 to 40 Hz. The position of the internal capsule is determined with microelectrodes by its characteristic absence of somatodendritic action potentials and the tetanization produced by stimulating corticospinal tract fibers. The somatotopic organization of the corticospinal system (face is medial, followed by the upper limb and leg most laterally) provides information on the laterality of the trajectory. For the OT (optic tract), a single-pass recording is shown above the multisweep potential responses to strobe light stimulation. LFB = low-frequency burst neurons; AC = anterior commissure; PC = posterior commissure. [Reprinted from Lozano A et al. (77), with permission.]

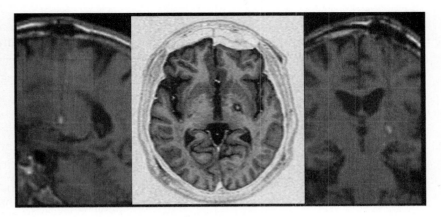

FIGURE 56-2

Postoperative MRI confirming the location of globus pallidus lesion in a patient with idiopathic Parkinson's disease in coronal (A), sagittal (B), and horizontal (C) planes. [Reprinted from Lozano A et al. (77), with permission.]

"off" motor examination scores (part 3 of the UPDRS) with a weighted average of 31% improvement across all series (range 11% to 65%) at short-term follow-up, whereas "on" medication scores decreased by 19% overall. Activities of daily living (ADLs) (part 2 of the UPDRS) scores did not improve as much in the "off" state (19% overall) and minimally in the "on" state (3% overall). These changes are reflected in other measures such as the Schwab and England scale and Hoehn and Yahr staging scale, although fewer centers have reported these particular scales.

The vast majority of studies of pallidotomy are retrospective case series or prospective uncontrolled trials. However, several prospective controlled trials have now been reported, including 3 controlled, randomized, observer-blind trials yielding class I clinical data (51, 59, 102, 108, 111, 112) (Table 56-2). In 2 trials, patients undergoing unilateral pallidotomy were compared to patients randomly assigned to best medical therapy, and in each case patients in the surgical group experienced a statistically significant decrease of the "off" UPDRS score compared to controls, ranging from 31% (108) to 34% (59) at 6 months. These results are consistent with the open-label results. Similarly, "off" ADL scores decreased significantly, and there was no significant change in the "on" motor or ADL scores. In addition, in these 2 class I studies, significant improvements were seen in motor fluctuations (59) and the PDQL, a quality-of-life scale (108). Thus the results of controlled trials validate the far greater data from noncontrolled trials.

Improvements in UPDRS motor exam scores in the "on" state tend to be more modest than those seen "off" medications and are not generally significant (see Tables 56-1 and 56-2). There are probably several reasons for this. First, surgical candidates are patients who still receive substantial benefit from levodopa treatment with regard to amelioration of motor symptoms. Hence it is difficult to improve on their "best on" state. In contrast, patients undergoing surgery generally are experiencing incapacitating "off" times and dyskinesia. These features are not assessed directly in the UPDRS motor exam scale but can affect the ADL portion and part IV, the complications portion of the UPDRS, and other quality-of-life measures. UPDRS ADL scores in the "on" state tend to improve because of a decrease in dyskinesia. This is demonstrated, for example, by Vitek et al., who showed a 75% decrease in contralateral (and 30% decrease in ipsilateral) dyskinesia and a 32% decrease in "off" time, which reflect on individual items in the "on" UPDRS ADL scale and complications scale (59). This magnitude of decrease of dyskinesia has been shown in every retrospective trial of pallidotomy and is the single most robust effect of pallidotomy on the disability of patients undergoing surgery (the heterogeneity of the scales used to assess dyskinesia precluded their easy synopsis, but the fact that they all show significant improvement is a testament to the robustness of the improvement in this complication) (see Table 56-2). Decreased dyskinesia during the "on" state is independent of medication changes, as doses generally remain stable following pallidotomy. Other studies also demonstrate an increase in "on" time without dyskinesia by 20% to 25% and a decrease in "off" time (90, 105), although in one long-term study these improvements reverted to baseline after 4 years (106). Another reason why "on" functioning is not improved is that the symptoms that are nonresponsive to medication also do not respond to surgical treatment. These symptoms include "on"-period gait disturbance (including freezing), postural instability, and speech disturbance.

TABLE 57-1
Outcome Using Standardized Measures of Contemporary Unilateral Pallidotomy Series

Author	N	F/u	UPDRS Motor Off			UPDRS ADL Off			UPDRS Motor On		
			Pre	Post	%	Pre	Post	%	Pre	Post	%
6–12 MONTHS											
Adelaide[109]	12	6	38.1	33.9	−11	18.4	19	3.2	nr	nr	nr
Amsterdam[89]	26	7.5	47.5	33.0	−30	26.5	20.5	−21	17.5	15	−14
Atlanta[87]	10	12	50.1	37.3	−26	28.2	21.9	−33	30.6	26.3	−15
Barcelona[106]	17	12	51.4	35.6	−31	25.8	22.3	13.7	21.7	17.7	−18.4
Boston[90]	45	6	(1)	nr	nr	25.5	21	−18	nr	nr	nr
Buenos Aires[101]	10	12	32	17	−45	36	63	75	16	10	−38
Chicago (Rush)[104]	22	6	49	41.7	−15	nr	nr	ns	24.5	27.3	12
Cordoba[94]	13	16	49.7	31.8	−38	nr	nr	nr	nr	nr	nr
Dallas[91]	27	6	42	29.4	−30	nr	nr	nr	nr	nr	nr
Houston[99]	62	12	57.2	34.4	−40.4	30.9	19.6	−36.6	31.5	17.5	−44.5
Kaohsiung[107]	9	12	37.7	28.6	−24	17.4	11	−37	27.4	21.6	−22
Kerala[97]	20	6	58.2	35.2	−40	nr	nr	nr	nr	nr	nr
Kumamoto[92]	19	6	50	28	−41	nr	nr	nr	30	21	−30
New York (CUMC)[88]	12	12	nr	nr	nr	nr	nr	nr	nr	nr	nr
New York (NYU)[51]	18	12	35	12	−65	19	8	−58	nd	nr	nr
Oxford[103]	25	12	45	35	−22	24	18	−23	20	17	−16
Pittsburgh[98]	58	9	95.8	77.6	−23	25.2	23.7	−6	39.6	34.1	−14
San Francisco[101]	29	6	52.4	43.9	−16	21.4	19.6	−8	nr	nr	nr
San Sebastian[93]	35	12	49	32.5	−33.7	nr	nr	nr	nr	nr	nr
Taipei[100]	9	12	44.6	33	−26	nr	nr	nr	nr	nr	nr
Toronto[110]	39	6	44.4	30.7	−31	24.6	17.2	−30	17.4	16.5	−5
Vancouver[53]	11	12	47.3	25.5	−46	23.6	17.2	−27.1	16.9	18.5	9.5
Weighted average	**528**				**−31.3%**			**−18.7%**			**−18.7%**
24–36 MONTHS											
Atlanta[59]	20	24	39.2	29.4	−25	23.9	21.7	−19	16	17.2	7.5
Boston[99]	25	24	(1)	nr	nr	25.5	22.5	−12	nr	nr	nr
Houston[99]	41	26.6	57.2	37.7	−35.7	30.9	20.9	−32	31.5	20.1	−36
New York (NYU)[132]	10	36	32	7.5	−77	16	4	−75			
Taiwan[107]	9	24	37.7	30.6	−18	17.4	11	−37	27.4	25.1	−9
Toronto[126]	17	24	41.7	~33	−21	24.5	~20	−18	15	17.9	19
Vancouver[131]	20	36	(2)	nr	nr	21	26	23	nr	nr	nr
Weighted average	**142**				**−33.5%**			**−20.6%**			**−12.5%**
>40 MONTHS											
Atlanta[87]	10	48	50.1	44.8	−11	28.2	30.6	8	30.6	30.7	7
Barcelona[106]	17	48	51.4	39.6	−23	25.8	20.9	−19	21.7	23.9	10.1
Toronto[130]	20	52	41.7	33.8	−18	24.5	22.1	−9.8	15	17.9	19.3
Weighted average	**47**				**−18.3%**			**−9.3%**			**13.6%**

(1) Inability to reliably obtain practically-defined off states prevented motor evaluations; (2) not reported due to poor inter-rater reliability.

Abbreviations: UPDRS, Unified Parkinson's Disease Rating Scale; S & E, Schwab and England scale; H & Y, Hoehn and Yahr scale; f/u, follow-up in months; pre, pre-operative; post, post-operative; nr, not reported.

Improvements in "off" functioning following unilateral pallidotomy occur mostly contralateral to the lesion. The greatest improvements in individual items are in contralateral bradykinesia, rigidity, and tremor (Table 56-3). This is associated with improved hand pronation/supination and tapping (see Table 56-1), both alone (113) and when performed simultaneously (114). Improvements in axial features including tests of gait and postural stability, as evaluated by the UPDRS, respond less well to unilateral pallidotomy. Gait and postural instability have been studied by several groups using computerized dynamic posturography, where improvements

UPDRS ADL On			S & E Off			S & E On			H & Off			H & Y On		
Pre	Post	%	Pre	Post	%	Pre	Post	%	Pre	Post	%	Pre	Post	%
nr	nr	nr	71.9	78.8	9.5	nr	nr	nr	3.4	2.8	−18	nr	nr	nr
12	11	−8	50	65	30	80	85	6	4	3	−13	2.5	2	−20
10.2	10.1	0	44.3	78.5	77.2	nr	nr	nr	nr	nr	nr	nr	nr	nr
12.5	11.4	−8.8	49.4	49.9	1	67.9	67.9	0	3.5	3.4	−2.9	2.7	2.7	0
10.5	10	−5	nr	nr	nr	nr	nr	nr	nr	nr	nr	nr	nr	nr
52	71	36.5	nr	nr	nr	nr	nr	nr	nr	nr	nr	nr	nr	nr
nr	nr	ns	nr	nr	nr	nr	nr	nr	nr	nr	ns	nr	nr	ns
nr	nr	nr	nr	nr	nr	nr	nr	nr	3.5	3	−14.3	nr	nr	nr
nr	nr	nr	nr	nr	nr	nr	nr	nr	nr	nr	nr	nr	nr	nr
17.1	9.3	−46.6	43.1	59.8	38.7	72.7	85.6	17.3	4	3.1	−22.5	2.8	2	−28.6
14.7	9.3	−36	nr	nr	nr	nr	nr	nr	3.8	3.2	−16	nr	nr	nr
nr	nr	nr	nr	nr	nr	nr	nr	nr	nr	nr	nr	nr	nr	nr
nr	nr	nr	nr	nr	nr	nr	nr	nr	nr	nr	nr	nr	nr	nr
nr	nr	nr	45	64.2	43	81.7	83.3	2	nr	nr	nr	nr	nr	nr
nr	nr	nr	nr	nr	nr	nr	nr	nr	nr	nr	nr	nr	nr	nr
12	9	−26	nr	nr	nr	nr	nr	nr	nr	nr	nr	nr	nr	nr
15.4	16.4	6.4	44.1	48.5	9.9	81.5	76	−7	nr	nr	nr	nr	nr	nr
nr	nr	nr	nr	nr	nr	nr	nr	nr	3.5	3.4	−2.9	nr	nr	nr
nr	nr	nr	nr	nr	nr	nr	nr	nr	nr	nr	nr	nr	nr	nr
nr	nr	nr	64.5	74.4	15	nr	nr	nr	4.1	3.3	−20	nr	nr	nr
10.3	17.2	67	39	65.1	67	78.2	85.2	9	nr	nr	nr	nr	nr	nr
7.5	7.3	−2.7	nr	nr	nr	nr	nr	nr	nr	nr	nr	nr	nr	nr
		3.4%			32.3%			6.0%			−14.7%			−21.8%
12.9	12.2	−5.5	52.5	63	20	78.1	82.2	5	4.1	3.6	−12	3	2.5	−17
10.5	11.5	10	nr	nr	nr	nr	nr	nr	nr	nr	nr	nr	nr	nr
17.1	10.1	−41	43.1	56.2	30	72.7	84	16	4	3.3	−17.5	2.8	2.1	−25
14.7	11.6	−22	nr	nr	nr	nr	nr	nr	3.8	3.3	−14	nr	nr	nr
8.5	11.1	31	44.5	53.5	20	81.3	80.8	−1	nr	nr	nr	nr	nr	nr
8	16	94	nr	nr	nr	nr	nr	nr	3.4	4	20	nr	nr	nr
		5.1%			25.3%			9.5%			−7.6%			−22.4%
10.2	19.6	92.1	44.3	61.5	38.8	nr	nr	nr	nr	nr	nr	nr	nr	nr
12.5	11.9	−5	49.4	50	1.2	67.9	69.4	2.2	3.5	3.5	0	2.7	2.6	−3.7
8.5	11.1	30.6	44.5	53.5	20.2	81.3	80.8	−0.7	nr	nr	nr	nr	nr	nr
		30.8%			17.3%			0.6%			0.0%			−3.7%

have been found by some (115–117) but not others (101), and effects on posture may be transient (118, 119). Beneficial effects on walking speed and stride length have also been observed (120). Speech intelligibility and volume have also been studied in depth, demostrating lack of improvement (121) or deterioration in speech (122).

Schulz et al. (123) found that vocal sound pressure level increased in mildly dysarthric patients but deteriorated in patients with preoperative moderate or severe dysarthria. Hypophonic or dysarthric patients need to be informed of the lack of beneficial effects on speech and the possibility of deterioration even from a unilateral procedure.

TABLE 57-2
Outcome in Controlled Trials of Unilateral Pallidotomy for Parkinson's Disease

Authors	Class	Design (Follow-up)	Groups	N	UPDRS Total Score				UPDRS III Motor			
					Pre	Post	%	P-value	Pre	Post	%	P-value
Vitek[58]	1	Randomized Observer blind 6 month	U/L palli	18	80.4	54.9	−32.7	0.0001	OFF 43.2	28.7	−34	0.0002
			Med ther	18	72.8	76.6	5.2		36.9	38.4	4.1	
			U/L palli	18					ON 18.4	16.6	−10	0.32
			Med ther	18					16.2	16.4	1	
de Bie[107]	1	Randomized Observer blind (6 month)	U/L palli	18					OFF 47	32.5	−31	0.0004
			Med ther	15					52.5	56.5	7.6	
			U/L palli	18					ON 19	22	16	0.24
			Med ther	15					18	22	22	
Esselink[111]	1	Randomized Observer blind (6 month)	U/L palli	13					OFF 46.5	37	−20	0.002
			B/L STN DBS						51.5	26.5	−48.6	
			U/L palli						ON 15.5	19	23	0.02
			B/L STN DBS						21	13	−38	
Dogali[50]	3	Control group (12 month)	U/L palli	18					OFF 35	12	−65	<0.001
			Med ther	7					28	32	14	ns
Merello[101]	3	Randomized Non-blinded (3 month)	U/L palli	7					OFF 27.8	19.5	−19.7	<0.05
			U/L GPi DBS	6					28.5	20.3	−28.7	<0.05
			U/L palli	7					ON 13	12.5	−3.8	ns
			U/L GPi DBS	6					17.3	16	−7.5	ns
Merello[110]	3	Control group (12 month)	U/L palli	10					OFF 32	17.5	−55	<0.005
			Med ther	10					26	27	4	ns
			U/L palli	10					ON			
			Med ther	10					16	10	−37	<0.05
									14	14.5	4	ns

The relationship between lesion characteristics, improvement in the UPDRS overall, and individual parkinsonian features has been examined by several groups. Some have found no association between lesion location and outcome (124, 125) or, grossly, that location within the GPi is associated with better outcomes (44). Kishore et al. (97) found that ventral lesion volume was associated with improved dyskinesia but that there was no relationship between lesion size and location with other signs. These studies are limited by insufficient patient numbers, lack of variance or too much variance with respect to lesion location, or inadequate statistical techniques. However, the authors found that a lesion location within the GPi was statistically correlated with improvement in selective symptoms such that anteromedial, central, and posterolateral lesions of the GPi more significantly improved rigidity, akinesia, and tremor, respectively (Figure 56-3) (85). In agreement, Eskandar et al. (90) found that tremor was improved more with posterolateral lesions, and dyskinesia more with more medial lesions. Improvements in postural stability and akinesia were seen, albeit transiently, with more centrally located lesions (85).

Improvements in "off" period parkinsonian features on the ipsilateral side to the pallidal lesion have been reported (50, 51, 127, 128), but these changes are not

UPDRS II ADL				DYKSINESIA RATING SCALE				SCHWAB AND ENGLAND			
PRE	POST	%	P-VALUE	PRE	POST	%	P-VALUE	PRE	POST	%	P-VALUE
OFF				*Contralateral (from UPDRS)*				*OFF*			
24.7	18.9	−23	0.0001	2.4	0.6	−75	0.0001	50.3	71.5	42	0.0001
24.3	25.6	5		2.1	2.2	4.8		51	50.9	−0.2	
ON				*Ipsilateral (from UPDRS)*				*ON*			
11.5	10.3	−10	0.11	2.2	1.4	−30	0.0001	79.3	86.2	6.9	0.0001
12	14.3	19		1.6	1.7	6.3		75.9	72.5	−4.5	
OFF				*DRS (Goetz)*				*OFF*			
30	21	−30	0.002	2	1	−50	0.02	35	70	50	0.0009
32	35	9		2	2	0		35	30	−16.6	
ON								*ON*			
12	12	0	0.09					80	80	0	0.09
10	12	20						80	80	0	
OFF				*CDRS*				*OFF*			
27.5	18	−35	0.15	9	3	−66.7	0.62	50	80	60	0.08
27	14.5	−46		8	3.5	−56		55	80	45.5	
ON								*ON*			
10	11	10	0.16					90	90	0	0.82
10	7.5	−25						90	90	0	
OFF											
19	8	−58	<0.001								
14	19	36	ns								
OFF				*Contralateral upper limb*							
40	58.5	46	<0.05	2	0.13	−93.5	<0.05				
38	6	−57.8	<0.05	2.9	1.8	−37.9					
ON				*Ipsilateral upper limb*							
55	62.5	13.6	ns	0.2	0.13	−35	ns				
53	65	22	ns	0.3	0.17	−43	ns				
				Contralateral (from UPDRS)							
				1.6	0.25	−84	<0.05				
				1.8	1.6	−11	ns				
				Ipsilateral (from UPDRS)							
				0.75	0.4	−47	ns				
				1.2	0.9	−25	ns				

as striking or consistent with the possible exception of a moderate reduction in bradykinesia. On the other hand, ipsilateral dyskinesias are consistently improved in up to 50% of patients (52, 53). However, the authors have found that this benefit is lost between 1 and 2 years following surgery.

Related to the improvements in "on"-period dyskinesia, pallidotomy significantly improves "off"-period painful dystonia, the presence of which is an appropriate indication for surgery (59, 88, 129).

Predictors of good response to pallidotomy have been examined in a few studies. Van Horn and colleagues (44) found that young age, tremor, unilateral predominance, levodopa responsiveness, the presence of fluctuations with dyskinesia, and good lesion placement predicted better response to surgery. However, Kishore (53) found that older patients actually improved more, whereas de Bie (124) found no relationship with age. The only predictor in the latter study was lower medication dosages.

Long-term follow-up (36 months or more) was tabulated in 179 patients (59, 87, 90, 99, 106, 107, 130–132) (Table 56-1). Improvements in motor UPDRS "off"-period scores decline to a weighted average of 18% in studies by 4 years (48 months) and beyond. The apparent maintenance of the benefit up to 36 months is driven by one outlying study (132); without this study

TABLE 57-2
(Continued)

Authors	Class	Design (Follow-up)	Groups	N	Hoehn and Yahr Pre	Post	%	P-value	Other Pre	Post	%	P-value
Vitek[58]	1	Randomized Observer blind	U/L palli	18	4.1	3.2	OFF −22	0.0001	Motor fluctuations 4.38	3	−32	
<0.0001		6 month	Med ther	18	4.1	4.1	0		4.23	4.25	0.5	
			U/L palli	18	2.8	2.5	ON 10.7	0.047				
			Med ther	18	2.9	3	3.4					
de Bie[107]	1	Randomized Observer blind (6 month)	U/L palli	18					PDQL 113	88	−22.1	0.004
			Med ther	15					104	108	3.8	
			U/L palli	18								
			Med ther	15								
Esselink[111]	1	Randomized Observer blind (6 month)	U/L palli	13					PDQL 111.5	104	−6.7	0.15
			B/L STN DBS						99	76	−23.2	
			U/L palli									
			B/L STN DBS									
Dogali[50]	3	Control group (12 month)	U/L palli	18								
			Med ther	7								
Merello[101]	3	Randomized Non-blinded (3 month)	U/L palli	7					PIGDS ON 5.1	3.2	−37	ns
			U/L GPi DBS	6					5	4	−20	ns
			U/L palli	7					PIGDS OFF 2.7	2.7	0	ns
			U/L GPi DBS	6					4	3.6	−10	ns
Merello[110]	3	Control group (12 month)	U/L palli	10					ADL OFF* 37	63	70	<0.05
			Med ther	10					50	51	2	ns
			U/L palli	10					ADL ON*			
			Med ther	10					52.5	71	35	<0.05
									61	57	−7	ns

Primary outcome measure denoted by bold lettering; P-values reflect difference between the two groups.
*ADL is not from UPDRS; larger values are better.
Abbreviations: UPDRS, Unified Parkinson's Disease Rating Scale; U/L palli, unilateral pallidotomy; Med ther, medical therapy; CDRS, Chicago Dyskinesia Rating Scale; PDQL, Parkinson's Disease Quality of LIfe scale; PIGDS, postural instability and gait disturbance score.

patients experienced a 28% benefit at 18 to 36 months after surgery. Improvement in "off"-period ADL scores also declined (to −9.3%), while on-period motor and ADL UPDRS scores actually are worse after 40 months as compared to baseline (13.6% and 30.8% worse than preoperative baseline, respectively). This reflects the worsening of patients' responses to medications with more advanced disease and the failure of pallidotomy to affect "on"-period dysfunction with the notable exception of dyskinesia.

The effect of pallidotomy on response to levodopa has been evaluated beyond the simple assessment of "on"-period clinical scores. Merello and coworkers (133) found a nonsignificant reduction (by 50%) in the latency to benefit from a single oral dose of levodopa, although the duration of benefit was significantly prolonged bilaterally. Generally the dose of dopaminergic medication remains the same postoperatively. However, this may vary, since some patients are able to increase levodopa dosage because of an improvement in dose-limiting dyskinesias, whereas

TABLE 56-3
Changes in Individual Measures of after Unilateral Pallidotomy

TEST (AND REFERENCES)	PERCENT CHANGE	
	Mean	Range
CAPIT		
Walk times[31,89,108]	−29%	−13, −24, −50
Pronation-supination[31,59,89,97]	−33%	−18 − −46
Finger dexterity[31,59,89,97,108,110]	−27%	−14 − −42
Hand/arm[31,59,97]	−39%	−33 − −48
Pro/sup + Fing dex + Hand/arm)[132]	−42%	−40, −44
UPDRS		
Tremor[53,59,87−89,92−94,97−100,106,107,110,111,130,131]	−69%	−33 − −100
Rigidity[53,59,87,89,92−94,97−100,106,107,110,111,130]	−49%	−22 − −64
Brady[53,59,87,89,92−94,97−100,106,107,109−111,130,131]	−36%	−9 − −67
Tremor + Rigidity + Bradykinesia[93,104]	−43%	−26, −60
Axial[93,106,107]	−19%	−9 − −38
Postural Stability[53,59,94,100,87,97,130]	−17%	+8 − −42
Gait[53,59,87,94,97,98,100,103,110,130]	−26%	−4 − −32
Postural Instability and Gait Disturbance[88,89,92,100,110,111,130]	−27%	−10 − −41
Speech[89]	−42%	−32, −50
Freezing[59,98,100,110,130]	−13%	+4 − −39
Motor fluctuations[53,59,109]	−20%	−12, −16, −32
Pain Visual Analog Scale[108]	−48%	−48
Barthell Index[108]	71%	71%
PDQL On Medication[108]	−22%	−22

CAPIT, Consensus Assessment Protocol for Intracerebral Transplantation; UPDRS, Unified Parkinson's Disease Rating Scale; PDQL, Parkinson's Disease Quality of Life scale; Mean % Change: Average of the % Changes reported in each of the referenced papers for this item; Range of % Changes: if more then 3 references contained this data, the range is shown; if 3 or less, each reported % change is given.

others may reduce their daily drug intake because of an improvement in "off" periods. Studying responses to single oral doses and intravenous infusions of levodopa, Skalabrin and coworkers (134) found changes in motor benefit and dyskinesias suggesting that pallidotomy significantly widens the therapeutic window of levodopa in PD.

The issue of performing bilateral pallidotomy in patients is still controversial. The need for bilateral surgery is usually driven by appendicular symptoms on both sides and also the notion that axial symptomatology such as gait and postural disturbance requires bilateral intervention. However, Jankovic and coworkers (118, 119) found that unilateral surgery improved gait and balance in both "on" and "off" states and that this was maintained. However, after bilateral pallidotomies, "off" period measures which had improved initially returned nearly to preoperative levels in the long term and no "on" period improvements were seen. Despite the beneficial effects described by some authors (20, 95, 135), most investigators have either avoided this approach or given it up, primarily because of the accompanying complications of speech deterioration, worsening of cognitive deficits, and gait disorders (136, 137), which are usually more frequent and more serious than with unilateral

surgery. For patients with bilateral symptomatology, alternatives to bilateral pallidotomy include unilateral pallidotomy and contralateral GPi DBS (138), bilateral GPi, or bilateral subthalamic nucleus (STN) stimulation. Merello et al. (139) randomized patients to bilateral pallidotomy or unilateral pallidotomy with contralateral GPi DBS. The bilateral pallidotomy arm was halted after all 3 patients experienced serious adverse effects including apathy and depression and marked worsening in motor performance, whereas the pallidotomy/contralateral GPi DBS group all experienced improved motor performance without adverse effects. With the safer alternatives available, the issue of the safety vs. effectiveness of bilateral pallidotomy has all but disappeared except in developing nations that may not have access to DBS technology.

Neuropsychological Effects of Pallidotomy. The neuropsychological effects of unilateral pallidotomy have been extensively studied. One randomized controlled trial found small but significant declines in verbal fluency with respect to nonsurgical controls and decreases in Boston Naming Task and California Verbal Learning Test at 3 months but not at 6 months (59), whereas another (124) found decreased verbal fluency and increased perseveration in

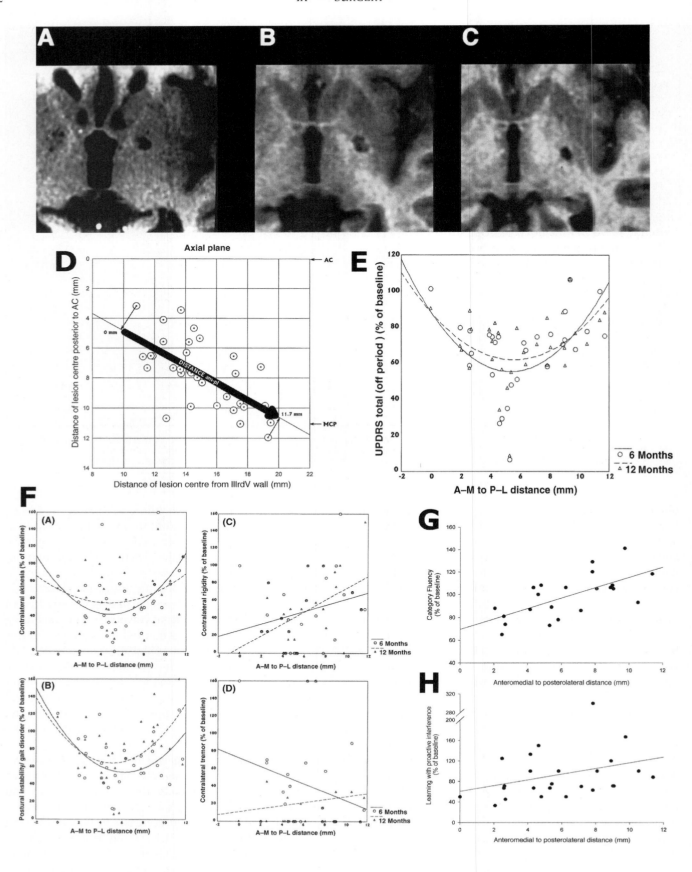

left-sided lesions, with decreased perseveration following right sided lesions. The most consistent findings across studies are changes in frontal lobe function, likely related to the frontosubcortical circuitry involving the GPi (see Figure 56-4). Verbal fluency is consistently decreased following left-sided pallidotomies (60, 61, 65–68, 105, 124, 140–150). Stebbins et al. (146, 151) found that all measures sensitive to frontostriatal dysfunction showed significant declines after pallidotomy, but not in a nonsurgical control group. These included tasks assessing working memory capacity and other aspects of frontal executive functioning and visuoconstructional functions studied 1 year after surgery. Scott et al. (63) and Perrine et al. (62) reported a decline in verbal memory postoperatively in 18% to 25% of patients. Similarly, Jahanshahi et al. (152), using a control group to control for improvements related to practice effects, found declines in measures of working memory and executive function. Further analysis of the decline in verbal fluency by Troster et al. (153) showed that a decrease in switching occurs following pallidotomy, which is consistent with the declines observed by others in the Wisconsin Card Sorting Test, and which is a frontal executive function. Other groups have found decreases in learning (154, 155), which may relate to impaired novelty detection, a function of frontosubcortical circuits involving the ventral striatum (154). These results support a role for frontobasal ganglia circuits in lexical and semantic search and access processes (147).

While many of the changes noted are not very robust albeit statistically significant and may not affect individual patients' daily function, frontostriatal dysfunction might not be so benign in certain cases. Trepanier and coworkers (65) reported frontal behavioral dyscontrol in 25% of patients, which interfered with patients' ability to function properly at work or in social settings. Lack of insight into these changes was noted in some patients, making behavioral management more difficult. However, these changes were outweighed by the positive clinical benefits obtained following the surgery. Frontal

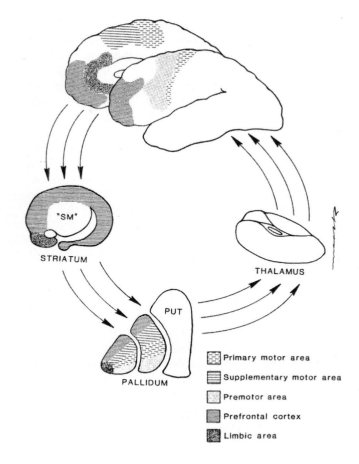

FIGURE 56-4

Model of frontosubcortical circuitry. Five segregated circuits through the basal ganglia are illustrated, each originating in a distinct area of the frontal lobes. The anatomic arrangement of the 5 circuits through each of the structures is shown. In the globus pallidus, the cognitive regions from the premotor cortex lie more dorsomedial than the motor regions from the supplementary and premotor regions, which are ventrolateral. SM = sensorimotor regions of the putamen; PUT = putamen. [Reprinted from Lombardi WJ et al. (144), with permission.]

FIGURE 56-3

The relationship of lesion location along the anteromedial-to-posteroventral axis of the globus pallidus internus to outcome following pallidotomy in Parkinson's disease. A to C show representative axial MR images of pallidotomies that are relatively more anteromedial (A), central (B), or posterolateral (C) within the GPi. The relative location along this axis (D) was quantified for 34 patients who underwent prospective evaluation of the effects of pallidotomy on both motor and cognitive function. A significant relationship was seen between motor function on the motor subscale of the UPDRS in the "off" state and location (E), such that patients with more centrally located lesions had greater improvement than those with more anteromedial or posterolateral lesions. Relationships to individual items on the motor scale (F) further revealed that more centrally located lesions improved akinesia and postural instability/gait disturbance to a greater extent, whereas anteromedial lesions had a greater impact on rigidity (and dyskinesia, not shown); posterolateral lesions had a greater impact on tremor. With respect to cognitive outcome, as expected because of the organization of cognitive and motor circuitry in GPi, more anteromedial lesions led to a decline in certain measures of cognitive function such as category fluency (G) and learning with proactive interference (H) as compared to more posterolateral lesions, which actually improved performance in these areas. [Reprinted from Gross RE et al. (83) and Lombardi WJ et al. (144), with permission.]

behavioral dyscontrol has also been rarely observed by others (104, 125, 132). There are few long-term follow-up studies of neuropsychological changes after pallidotomy, however, so it is not clear how long-lasting these findings are. Several studies have found that short-term changes (e.g., 3 months) did not translate into permanent changes after pallidotomy (67, 70, 150, 156).

Lesion side and location seem to be important determinants of cognitive effects of pallidotomy (67, 147). In a review, Green and Barnhart (142) concluded that frontal lobe deficits are associated with left-sided lesions. Indeed, right-sided lesions have sometimes been found to improve certain frontal functions, such as visual memory (65, 145), visuospatial function (157), word recall during proactive interference (144), and verbal fluency (68). These authors (142) posited that effects on frontal lobe function result from impingement on nonmotor regions of the GPi or GPe. Indeed, this was supported by the authors, who showed that lesion location was related to neuropsychological outcome following pallidotomy (see Figure 56-3) (144). More anteromedial lesions within GPi, which may impinge on the cognitive frontal-basal ganglionic circuits (Figure 56-4), led to declines in category fluency, continuous mental arithmetic (a measure of working memory), and the second list-learning on the California Verbal Learning Test (CVLT) (proactive interference), whereas more posterolateral lesions led to improvements in these measures.

While a number of studies have found short- and/or long-term neuropsychological deficits, others have found no change (50, 64, 67, 73, 156, 158–160), while still others have reported improvements (67, 68, 70, 144, 157). However, there are many methodologic issues that contribute to inconsistencies and affect interpretation across neuropsychological studies, including differences in selection criteria, sample sizes, the use of control groups, length of follow-up, battery of tests performed, technique of pallidotomy, and statistical methods (73, 161). Nevertheless, the overall picture that emerges is fairly consistent, with left-sided pallidotomies leading to mostly transient declines in lexical frontal lobe functions; some patients, especially older (71, 143, 145) or more cognitively impaired patients at baseline (71, 145), experiencing more disturbing changes in behavior related to frontal lobe dysfunction (71).

Complications of Pallidotomy. Adverse effects and complications of pallidotomy are common. de Bie (162) performed a comprehensive review of all studies from 1992 through 2000. When only prospective series screened for various stringent inclusion criteria were considered, of 334 patients treated, 30% experienced adverse effects and nearly 14% experienced "permanent" complications (lasting more than 3 months). A similar figure was reported in a review of 1510 patients (Table 56-4) (86). Interestingly, the group of retrospective series, which included 359 patients, revealed an overall rate of 20% of patients experiencing adverse effects with only 6.4% permanent complications, demonstrating

that retrospective studies probably underestimate complication rates. Symptomatic (permanent) hemorrhage or infarction, the most ominous complication, occurred in 4% of patients in the prospective group. The most frequent adverse effects were in speech (dysarthria, hypophonia, dysphasia), which was permanently affected in 6% of patients. Acute confusion occurred in approximately 10% (162) but varied greatly (86). Personality or behavioral changes that lasted more than 3 months occurred in nearly 4% of patients. Longer-term follow-ups would likely show that at least some of these problems resolve with time. Facial paresis (2%) or visual field defects (2%) due to lesioning of the internal capsule or optic tract, respectively, likely decreased in the course of time with increasing experience (84). Mortality was 1.2% in the prospective series, 0.3% in the retrospective series (162), and 0.4% in another review of 1959 patients (86). Other less frequent (1% or less) complications include hypersalivation, memory loss, depression, seizure, psychosis, and urinary incontinence. Although comprehensive reviews of complication rates are invaluable for their estimate of the range and incidence of historical consequences of pallidotomy, decreased incidence with progressive experience is not generally assessed. Vitek et al. (84), for example, noted a marked decrease in their complication rate with experience. They had 2 symptomatic hemorrhages in their first 23 patients and none in the next 137 patients.

A controversial issue has been the relative benefits and consequences of the microelectrode recording technique. Comprehensive literature reviews have shown a higher rate of symptomatic intracranial bleeding in series reporting the use of microelectrode recording (1.3% and 2.7%) vs. macroelectrode stimulation (0.25% and 0.5%) (86, 163), or 4.9% higher (162). The overall rate of complications was higher with microelectrode recording in some reviews (86, 162), but not in others (163), and the rate of persistent complications was not significantly different in 2 reviews (86, 163). Differences in reporting in retrospective series limit the conclusions that can be drawn from them. In the end, complications of microelectrode recording must be considered in the context of possible improvements in targeting and outcome.

In 5 reports regarding bilateral pallidotomy reviewed by de Bie et al. (162), all historical cohort series, 70% of patients had complications, and in 60% they were permanent, including 25% of patients with speech problems and 20% with cognitive decline. Inasmuch as these were retrospective series and the rate of complications is underestimated in such series as compared to prospective series by almost 50%, the true complication rate is likely even higher. Nevertheless, others have performed bilateral pallidotomies, either staged or contemporaneously, with few complications. The largest experience is that of Iacono and colleagues (137). In a retrospective review of their own experience in 796 consecutive cases, they did not find any significant difference in speech and swallowing in patients undergoing bilateral simultaneous pallidotomy as

TABLE 56-4
Complications of Unilateral Pallidotomy

Type of studies reviewed	ALKHANI AND LOZANO[86]	DE BIE ET AL.[162]		
	All	Historical	Prospective	Combined
Number of patients	1510	359	334	693
		Percent of Patients		
Symptomatic Infarciton or Hemorrhage		2.0	3.9	2.9
Infarction		0.9		
Cerebral hemorrhage	1.7			
Deep		1.5		
Superficial		1.2		
Paresis, visual loss				
Visual field defect (persistent)	1.5		2.4	
Facial weakness (persistent)	1.3		2.4	
Limb weakness	0.9		0.3	
Contralateral neglect		0.6		
Behavioral, neuropsych, mood				
Postop confusion	2.6		0	
Postop psychosis	0.5		0.9	
Changes in personality or behavior		3.9		
Impaired memory	0.9			
Worsened dementia		0.3		
Depression	0.9		0	
Speech, language				
Hypophonia	1.3		1.2	
Dysarthria (persistent)	1.6		3.6	
Anarthria		0.3		
Dysphagia (persistent)	0.5		2.4	
Dysphasia		0.9		
Other				
Postop Seizure	0.5		0.3	
Postural instability		1.2		
Urinary incontinence		0.3		
Deep vein thrombosis		0		
Hypersalivation	0.6		2.1	
Other	2			
Percent with any adverse effect	23.1	20.3	30.2	25.1
Percent with persistent adverse effects	14.3	6.4	13.8	10.0

compared to unilateral pallidotomy. Bilateral pallidotomy was, however, a significant risk factor for acute postoperative confusion in this series. Unfortunately, the authors did not report on the incidence of permanent cognitive decline in their patients (137). The other published series are very small. Schuurman et al. (164) performed staged bilateral pallidotomies on 3 patients without significant speech and swallowing difficulties or cognitive sequelae. In 4 patients, Ghika et al. (136) reported that 2 patients experienced mood disturbance (depression, obsessive-compulsive disorder), 2 experienced frontoexecutive disturbance, and 1 had memory loss. One patient experienced both severe apraxia of eyelid opening and "psychic akinesia," thought to be related to corticobulbar damage. Finally, Merello

et al. (139), in their prospective randomized evaluation of bilateral pallidotomy vs. unilateral pallidotomy with contralateral GPi DBS, found that all 3 bilateral pallidotomy patients experienced severe adverse effects, including unintelligible speech, marked sialorrhea, swallowing difficulties requiring nasogastric feeding tubes, apathy, and severe loss of initiative, motivation, and motor drive. Moreover, these patients experienced a deterioration of gait freezing that was resistant to levodopa treatment. These adverse effects were persistent at 3 months; no such adverse effects were found with unilateral pallidotomy and contralateral GPi DBS.

More detailed neuropsychological assessment has been reported in a small number of papers regarding bilateral pallidotomy. In a study of 8 patients, Scott et al.

found generally well-preserved cognitive abilities, with selective loss of verbal fluency (as with unilateral left-sided lesions) (63) and loss of the ability to shift attention to novel dimensions (a frontal executive function) (165). The only deficit seen in a group of 17 postbilateral pallidotomy patients by Turner et al. was also in a frontal-executive function (Tower of London task) (166). Finally, in 6 patients, Whelan et al. (167) did not see any groupwise statistical changes in neuropsychological function but did observe clinically meaningful changes in language function on a case-by-case basis.

In sum, the issue of the safety of bilateral pallidotomy is unresolved, with some groups finding serious adverse effects unrelated to whether the procedure was staged or contemporaneous and others seemingly observing little in the way of long-term sequelae. However, with the advent of nondestructive procedures such as DBS performed either bilaterally or contralateral to a pallidotomy, this topic will likely become moot.

Quality of Life following Pallidotomy. All of the above factors (i.e., degree of improvement, neuropsychologic effects, and complications/adverse effects) summate to affect the quality of patients' lives following surgery and influence the decision of patients to consider surgery. Quality-of-life (QOL) measures are increasingly being incorporated into prospective and retrospective evaluations of the outcome of surgery such as pallidotomy. The ADL subsection (part II of the UPDRS) addresses QOL to some extent. Aside from this, the most utilized QOL measure for PD is the PDQ-39 questionnaire. Following unilateral pallidotomy, significant improvements have been seen in the ADL (168–170) and mobility (169, 170) measures of this instrument. Improvements in other measures (emotions, bodily pain) were significant (169) or tended to change in the right direction (170). The global "summary index" improved significantly in only 1 study (169). In a prospective study using the PDQ-L, de Bie and colleagues (124) found improvements on all psychosocial and physical subscales. Other indices also manifest improvement. The Sickness Inventory Profile (SIP) has documented physical, psychosocial, and total functioning improvement (170), including alertness and social interaction. Similarly, the Medical Outcomes Study short form (SF-36) showed improved physical role, energy/vitality, and general health (168). In a controlled study, Carr et al. (141) showed improvements in SF-36 measures of bodily pain and social functioning but not physical functioning or mood in operated patients as compared to wait-listed controls. Improvements in depression and anxiety (59, 170) also have been shown. Interestingly, despite the associated complications shown by some, bilateral pallidotomy has been found to lead to marked improvements in the PDQ-39 (mobility, ADLs, emotional well-being, cognition, communication, bodily discomfort, summary index) (168, 171), which was largely maintained 2 years following surgery in one study (172).

Thalamotomy

Clinical Benefits of Thalamotomy. Thalamotomy has been performed almost universally for tremor-dominant PD. However, rigidity and/or dyskinesia may be an indication for some investigators (76, 173). One difficulty in evaluating the reported results of thalamotomy for PD arises from differences in target selection. Vim is the preferred target for thalamotomy for tremor of various etiologies, including PD and essential tremor. However, this target, which interrupts the cerebellar afferent pathway to the thalamus, may not be the best target for other PD symptomatology. In contrast, more anterior target location within the pallidal receiving area [i.e., ventralis oralis anterior and posterior (Voa, Vop)] may provide greater benefits for rigidity, akinesia, and/or dyskinesia (174–176). Confusion arises because both Voa/Vop and Vim are contained within the VL thalamus of the so-called American nomenclature (essentially equivalent to the anterior and posterior divisions, VLa and VLp, respectively) (177). Thus, some VL thalamotomies might target Voa/Vop whereas others might target Vim and still others may target other regions or combinations thereof. Lesions performed by differing groups have varied in location by up to 7 mm (178).

Numerous reports suggest that up to 80% of patients achieve total abolition or marked reduction of contralateral tremor after unilateral thalamotomy for PD (Table 56-5) (36, 40, 76, 79, 179–192). A more posterior location near the Vop/Vim border was more effective than more anteriorly located lesions (193). A recent prospective randomized trial compared Vim thalamotomy to Vim DBS for severe tremor of various types (187). In patients with PD, a measure of functional status (Frenchay activities index) improved significantly more following DBS than thalamotomy after 6 months. It should be noted that thalamotomy is most effective in relieving appendicular tremor. Midline symptoms, such as head tremor and voice tremor (more typical of essential tremor), seem to respond less well and may progress relentlessly, limiting function in about 25% of patients (194–196). VanBuren et al. (195) found that impairment from the midline symptoms and speech deficits due to surgery exceeded any gains from the reduced limb tremor; their average patient functioned less well after thalamotomy. Therefore, before making a final decision to

TABLE 56-5	
Published Results of Unilateral Thalamotomy	
for Tremor in Parkinson's Disease	

Tremor	% of patients
Total Abolition	45 – 93
Significant reduction	66 – 100

*Percent of patients based on data reported in literature (36, 40, 76, 79, 179–192).

proceed to surgery, patients should be informed of what they can reasonably expect.

Several groups have demonstrated that Voa/Vop thalamotomy improves dyskinesia (197, 198); Narabayashi actually showed near complete resolution of dyskinesia, but not with Vim thalamotomy. However, there is little reliable confirmation of these claims (199, 200). Rigidity has also been shown by some groups to improve following Voa/Vop thalamotomy (200). Recently, Moriyama et al. (184) demonstrated that rigidity but not akinesia improved following thalamotomy, and this effect was sustained for up to 15 years. Nevertheless, ADL improvement fell off with time, associated with progression of symptoms including akinesia. Bilateral thalamotomy in 4 patients failed to recapture benefits.

Although a blinded long-term follow-up study by Diederich et al. (180) showed significant persistent improvement or amelioration of the tremor, other studies with follow-up periods up to 10 years indicated that as many as 48% of patients returned to their preoperative state and only 22% to 44% continued to show improvement from their preoperative baseline (179, 201). Also, as thalamotomy does not arrest general disease progression and has little effect on other parkinsonian features, it is usually necessary to continue pharmacologic therapy.

Complications of Thalamotomy. Published complications of unilateral thalamotomy for PD are listed in Table 56-6 (74, 79, 181, 189, 192, 194, 196, 202–205). The mortality rate is approximately 0.5% (range 0% to 5%), with intracranial hemorrhage being the major cause of death (incidence of intracranial hematoma, 1.5% to 6%). Other complications include dysarthria, cognitive difficulties, persistent hemiparesis or limb weakness, dystonia, unilateral auditory neglect, neglect of the contralateral extremities, arm dyspraxia, and "cerebellar" complications, including limb ataxia and astasia. Side effects such as paresthesias or numbness with a predominant hand-mouth distribution may be seen often, but these usually subside spontaneously (74, 79, 181, 189, 192, 194, 196, 202–205). Facial paresis has also been reported but is usually transient in the majority of cases. Memory and language dysfunctions following thalamotomy are probably more common than traditionally thought or recognized. They occur in about one-third of patients and up to double this figure with bilateral thalamotomy. One-half of these patients can be expected to recover to baseline within several months (206). However, a recent review of neurocognitive studies indicated that, rather than impairing cognitive status, unilateral thalamotomy can be associated with improvements in some measures, including verbal memory (207).

Bilateral Thalamotomy

Among patients who have undergone unilateral thalamotomy, many will eventually develop sufficiently disabling

TABLE 56-6
Published Complications of Unilateral Thalamotomy for Parkinson's Disease

	PERCENTAGE OF PATIENTS*	
SYMPTOM	TRANSIENT	PERSISTENT
Death		0 – 5
Hemorrhage		1.5 – 6
Cognitive	1 – 43	0.8 – 14
Hemiparesis	0 – 26	0 – 9
Dysphasia	1 – 29	0 – 3
Dysarthria	1 – 43	0.8 – 11.2
Hand ataxia	5 – 61	1.3
Gait	1 – 30	1.2 – 6
Equinovarus deformity	2.7	3.5 – 5.3
Hyperkinesia		0.3 – 9
Numbness	1 – 20	0.5 – 3.3
Confusion	0 – 16	0 – 1
Blepharospasm	0 – 2	0 – 1
Hypertonia	0 – 9	
Dystonia	0 – 3	
Seizure	0.5 – 8	
Dsyphagia/ pseudobulbar symptoms	0.3 – 0.3	
Infection	0.5 – 4	

*Percentages based on data reported in the literature (74, 79, 181, 192, 194, 196, 202–205).

tremor in the opposite limb to consider contralateral surgery. Table 56-7 lists the outcome data for bilateral thalamotomy reported in the literature (36, 183, 201–203, 208). Although its effect on abolishing tremor has been reported to be similar to that of the unilateral procedure (205), there has generally been significant reluctance to perform bilateral thalamotomy because of the high incidence of adverse effects. Most surgeons prefer bilateral or contralateral thalamic DBS over bilateral thalamotomy. Table 56-8 reviews the published complications of bilateral thalamotomy for PD (36, 79, 183, 190, 201–203, 208). The incidence of complications tends to be two- to threefold higher than that for unilateral thalamotomy. The predominant complication is speech and language

TABLE 56-7
Published Results of Bilateral Thalamotomy for Parkinson's Disease

Tremor	% of Patients
Complete abolition	33 – 100
Significant reduction	67 – 71

*Percentage of patients based on data reported in the literature (36, 54, 183, 201, 203, 208).

TABLE 56-8

Published Complications of Bilateral Thalamotomy for Parkinson's Disease

	PERCENTAGE OF PATIENTS*	
SYMPTOM	TRANSIENT	PERSISTENT
Death		0 – 4.3
Cognitive	1.8 – 34.8	
Hemiparesis	0.8 – 1.8	
Dysphasia	5.5	3.6
Dysarthria	1.8 – 50	18 – 60
Dysphagia	3.6 – 5.4	
Gait	48	17.4
Equinovarus deformity	2.2	
Hyperkinesia	5 – 7.2	
Foot dystonia	0 – 1.8	
Infection	0 – 3.6	

*Percentages based on data reported in the literature (36, 79, 183, 190, 201–203, 208).

impairment, characterized by hypophonia, dysarthria, and dysphasia. Significant dysphagia and transient confusion may also be seen in up to 10% of cases. Cognitive dysfunction is also much more common and concerning following bilateral thalamotomy than after unilateral surgery.

Radiosurgical Thalamotomy. Ohye and colleagues (209–211) reported the results in 53 patients, including 32 tremor-dominant PD patients and 3 PD patients treated for rigidity with thalamotomy using the gamma knife. Tremor response took 12 months to become manifest, although a shorter time course was found following reloading of the device. Insufficient quantitative information has been reported to determine its effectiveness except to note that about 80% to 85% of patients (not stratified by diagnosis) experienced reduction of tremor to less than one-third of the preoperative level (but no quantitative data have been presented). Young et al. (212) reported on 102 PD patients treated for tremor. At 12 months, 76.5% were tremor-free and an additional 2.7% nearly so; at 48 months, 89.2% maintained this response. Tremor scores from the UPDRS significantly decreased from 6 to 48 months. Complications from gamma thalamotomy include contralateral paresthesia, paresis, dysphasia, dysarthria, and balance difficulties as well as incoordination (210–214). Given the case-series nature of the published reports, the rate of adverse effects is hard to gauge, although Young et al. (212) reported an incidence of 1.3%. It has been argued that the true rate of complications may be underreported (215), although this is true of any retrospective series. Care in the use of this procedure, utilizing current standards of radiosurgical

practice, must be exercised. Most practitioners limit the use of gamma thalamotomy to patients in whom invasive surgical procedures are contraindicated (216).

Subthalamotomy

Although ischemic or hemorrhagic lesions of the STN may lead to hemiballism, recent work has shown that stereotactic radiofrequency ablation of the STN may be safe and effective in the treatment of PD (Table 56-9). Several series, comprising a total of 96 lesions performed in 78 patients (18 bilateral lesions), have been reported (217–220). Contralateral lesion–induced dyskinesia has occurred in a significant number of patients but is usually mild and transient. More severe dyskinesia has occurred in 3 of 18 bilaterally lesioned patients (217) and, following unilateral lesions, in 5 of 60 patients (218–220). In 2 of the series, the dyskinesia resolved with either DBS or thalamotomy. In addition, in 2 series, the dyskinesia resolved spontaneously in 5 of 6 patients, but 1 patient died due to aspiration pneumonia possibly related to the severe dyskinesia. Alvarez et al. (217) performed bilateral (staged or simultaneous) subthalamic nucleotomy in 18 patients, resulting in a decrease in "off" UPDRS motor score of 50% and also a decrease of 36% in the "on" motor score. ADL scores were also significantly decreased, and dyskinesia declined by 50%, probably due to a 50% drop in medications doses. Complications included dysarthria/ataxia/disequilibrium in 3 patients but no significant cognitive impairments. Three trials involved unilateral lesions, with contralateral DBS if there were bilateral indications for surgery (218–220). Significant decreases in contralateral motor scores were observed in each trial (Table 56-9). As in the experience of Alvarez et al. (217), improvements in motor on functioning was seen in each study. This could be due in part to improvement in dyskinesia (in all 4 studies, medication doses were reduced by approximately 50%) but also to improvements in gait and tremor that were not completely responsive to dopaminergic therapy. Aside from infrequent lesion-induced dyskinesia, complications were rare. Patel (218) noted few neurocognitive adverse effects on detailed neuropsychological testing aside from some decrease in frontal functioning and verbal fluency, not unlike that seen with unilateral pallidotomy. Despite these preliminary findings, given the risk of ablative surgery, especially when performed bilaterally, at this stage subthalamic nucleotomy should be considered only when the implantation of DBS hardware is contraindicated or the economic burdens associated with it are prohibitive.

CONCLUSION

Unilateral stereotactic pallidotomy results in unequivocal clinical benefits and is generally well tolerated in

TABLE 56-9
Results of Radiofrequency Ablation of the Subthalamic Nucleus (Subthalamic Nucleotomy)

		SURGERY TYPE			UPDRS	
AUTHOR	F/U	U/L	B/L	U/L + DBS	OFF SCORES	ON SCORES
Alvarez et al.[217]	3 – 4 yrs		18		49.5% decrease in Motor subscale (III)	35.5% decrease in Motor subscale (III)
Patel et al.[218]	6 mo	17		4	36.8% decrease in c/l Motor subscale (III)	39.0% decrease c/l Motor subscale (III)
Su et al.[219]	6 mo	7		5	55.3% decrease in c/l tremor, rigidity, bradykinesia	56.1% decrease in c/l tremor, rigidity, bradykinesia
Vilela Filho et al.[220]	n/r	21*			75% decrease in c/l tremor, rigidity, bradykinesia	

*8/21 had ipsilateral thalamotomy.
Abbr.: UPDRS, Unified Parkinson's Disease Rating Scale; III, UPDRS Motor Scale; c/l, contralateral; n/r, not reported.

correctly selected patients; it has therefore has become an important treatment modality in patients with later-stage PD who, despite optimal medical therapy, are disabled by levodopa-responsive "off"-period symptoms or levodopa-induced dyskinesias. Unilateral thalamotomy is also effective but primarily for tremor; therefore its usefulness in PD is limited and its use disappearing. Neither procedure is well tolerated when administered bilaterally. However, pallidotomy and thalamotomy have, in the developed world, been essentially replaced by either unilateral or bilateral deep brain stimulation of the STN or GPi because of an improved safety profile. Moreover, the safety of bilateral DBS offers improved outcomes for patients with bilateral symptoms. "The best fate of a new treatment is to be replaced by an even better treatment" (A-L Benabid, personal communication), and pallidotomy certainly met this fate after less than a decade had

lapsed since its renaissance. Only time will tell whether DBS itself is fated to be replaced by another novel surgical therapy, such as human fetal cell transplantation (221–224), implantation of encapsulated cells (225–227) or of retinal pigment epithelial cells (228, 229), infusion of trophic factors (230–236), or gene therapy (237–249). Although many of these approaches are in current clinical trials, it will be some time before their safety and effectiveness are established. On the other hand, STN and GPi DBS have been shown to be at least as safe and effective as pallidotomy (23, 102, 112, 250, 251), so it is reasonable to offer this nondestructive approach to most patients, keeping in mind the potential for a response to new treatments as they become available. However, practical issues—including availability, cost, and the extensive amount of time required to optimize DBS—may still persuade some patients to undergo pallidotomy.

References

1. Horsley V. Remarks on the surgery of the central nervous system. *Br Med J* 1890; 2:1286–1292.
2. Bucy P, Buchanan D. Athetosis. *Brain* 1932; 55:479–492.
3. Bucy P, Case T. Tremor: Physiologic mechanism and abolition by surgical means. *Arch Neurol Psychiatry* 1939; 41:721–746.
4. Klemme R. Surgical treatment of dystonia, paralysis agitans and athetosis. *Acta Neurol Psychiatry* 1940; 44:926.
5. Meyers R. Surgical procedure for postencephalitic tremor, with notes on the physiology of the premotor fibres. *Arch Neurol Psychiatry* 1940; 44:455–459.
6. Spiegel E, Wycis H, Marks M. Stereotaxic apparatus for operations on the human brain. *Science* 1947; 106:349–350.
7. Leksell L. A stereotaxic apparatus for intracerebral surgery. *Acta Chir Scand* 1949; 99:229–233.
8. Cooper IS. Ligation of the anterior choroidal artery for involuntary movements: Parkinsonism. *Psychiatr Q* 1953; 27:317–319.
9. Guiot G, Brion S. Traitement des mouvements anormaux par la coagulation pallidal. *Rev Neurol (Paris)* 1953; 89:578–580.
10. Narabayashi H, Okuma T. Procaine oil blocking of the globus pallidus for the treatment of rigidity and tremor of parkinsonism. *Psychiatr Neurol Jpn* 1953; 56:471–495.
11. Hassler R. The pathological and pathophysiological basis of tremor and parkinsonism. In: *Second International Congress of Neuropathology*. Amsterdam: Excerpta Medica, 1955:2940.
12. Guiot G, Hardy J, Albe-Fessard D. Precise delimination of the subcortical structures and identification of thalamic nuclei in man by stereotactic electrophysiology. *Neurochirurgia* 1962; 5:1–18.
13. Narabayashi H, Surgical approach to tremor. In: Marsden C, Fahn S (eds). *Movement Disorders*. London: Butterworth Scientific, 1982:292–299.
14. Narabayashi H, Ohye C. Parkinsonian tremor and nucleus ventralis intermedius of the human thalamus. In: Desmedt JE, ed. Physiological tremor. Pathological tremors and clonus. Basel: S. Karger, 1978:165–172.
15. Gillingham F. Surgical management of the dyskinesis. *J Neurol Neurosurg Psychiatry* 1960; 23:347–348.
16. Gildenberg PL. Whatever happened to stereotactic surgery? *Neurosurgery* 1987; 20:983–987.
17. Alexander GE, Crutcher MD, DeLong MR. Basal ganglia–thalamocortical circuits: Parallel substrates for motor, oculomotor, "prefrontal" and "limbic" functions. *Prog Brain Res* 1990; 85:119–146.
18. Filion M, Tremblay L. Abnormal spontaneous activity of globus pallidus neurons in monkeys with MPTP-induced parkinsonism. *Brain Res* 1991; 547:142–151.

19. Laitinen LV. Pallidotomy for Parkinson's disease. *Neurosurg Clin North Am* 1995; 6:105–112.

20. Laitinen LV, Bergenheim AT, Hariz MI. Ventroposterolateral pallidotomy can abolish all parkinsonian symptoms. *Stereotact Funct Neurosurg* 1992; 58:14–21.

21. Hariz MI. From functional neurosurgery to "interventional" neurology: Survey of publications on thalamotomy, pallidotomy, and deep brain stimulation for Parkinson's disease from 1966 to 2001. *Mov Disord* 2003; 18:845–853.

22. Benabid AL, Deuschl G, Lang AE, et al. Deep brain stimulation for Parkinson's disease. *Mov Disord* 2006; 21(Suppl 14):S168–S170.

23. Kleiner-Fisman G, Herzog J, Fisman DN, et al. Subthalamic nucleus deep brain stimulation: Summary and meta-analysis of outcomes. *Mov Disord* 2006; 21(Suppl 14):S290–S304.

24. Albin RL, Young AB, Penney JB. The functional anatomy of basal ganglia disorders. *Trends Neurosci* 1989; 12:366–375.

25. Bankiewicz KS, Plunkett RJ, Jacobowitz DM, et al. The effect of fetal mesencephalon implants on primate MPTP-induced parkinsonism. Histochemical and behavioral studies. *J Neurosurg* 1990; 72:231–244.

26. Bergman H, Wichmann T, DeLong MR. Reversal of experimental parkinsonism by lesions of the subthalamic nucleus. *Science* 1990; 249:1436–1438.

27. Blanchet PJ, Konitsiotis S, Hyland K, et al. Chronic exposure to MPTP as a primate model of progressive parkinsonism: A pilot study with a free radical scavenger. *Exp Neurol* 1998; 153:214–222.

28. DeLong MR. Primate models of movement disorders of basal ganglia origin. *Trends Neurosci* 1990; 13:281–285.

29. Miller W, DeLong MR. Altered tonic activity of neurons in the globus pallidus and subthalamic nucleus in the primate MPTP model of parkinsonism. In: Carpenter M, Jayaraman A (eds). *The Basal Ganglia II: Structure and Function: Current Concepts.* New York: Plenum Press, 1987:415–417.

30. Obeso JA, Rodriguez MC, DeLong MR. Basal ganglia pathophysiology. A critical review. *Adv Neurol* 1997; 74:3–18.

31. Hashimoto T, Elder CM, Okun MS, et al. Stimulation of the subthalamic nucleus changes the firing pattern of pallidal neurons. *J Neurosci* 2003; 23:1916–1923.

32. Bertrand G, Jasper H, Wong A, et al. Microelectrode recording during stereotactic surgery. *Clin Neurosurg* 1969; 16:328–355.

33. Lenz FA, Dostrovsky JO, Kwan HC, et al. Methods for microstimulation and recording of single neurons and evoked potentials in the human central nervous system. *J Neurosurg,* 1988; 68:630–634.

34. Lenz FA, Kwan HC, Martin RL, et al. Single unit analysis of the human ventral thalamic nuclear group. Tremor-related activity in functionally identified cells. *Brain* 1994; 117(Pt 3):531–543.

35. Jasper H, Bertrand G. Thalamic units involved in somatic sensation and voluntary and involuntary movements in man. In: Purpura D, Yarh M (eds). *The Thalamus.* New York: Columbia University Press, 1966:365–390.

36. Narabayashi H. Stereotaxic Vim thalamotomy for treatment of tremor. *Eur Neurol* 1989; 29(Suppl 1):29–32.

37. Raeva S. Unit activity of some deep nuclear structures of the human brain during voluntary movement. In: Somjen G (ed). *Neurophysiology Studied in Man.* Amsterdam: Excerpta Medica, 1972:64–78.

38. Tasker RR. Tremor of parkinsonism and stereotactic thalamotomy. *Mayo Clin Proc* 1987; 62:736–739.

39. Hirai T, Miyazaki M, Nakajima H, et al. The correlation between tremor characteristics and the predicted volume of effective lesions in stereotaxic nucleus ventralis intermedius thalamotomy. *Brain* 1983; 106(Pt 4):1001–1018.

40. Lenz FA, Normand SL, Kwan HC, et al. Statistical prediction of the optimal site for thalamotomy in parkinsonian tremor. *Mov Disord* 1995; 10:318–28.

41. Josephs KA, Matsumoto JY, Ahlskog JE. Benign tremulous parkinsonism. *Arch Neurol* 2006; 63:354–357.

42. Nutt JG. Continuous dopaminergic stimulation: Is it the answer to the motor complications of levodopa? *Mov Disord* 2007; 22:1–9.

43. Olanow CW, Agid Y, Mizuno Y, et al. Levodopa in the treatment of Parkinson's disease: Current controversies. *Mov Disord* 2004; 19:997–1005.

44. Van Horn G, Hassenbusch SJ, Zouridakis G, et al. Pallidotomy: A comparison of responders and nonresponders. *Neurosurgery* 2001; 48:263–271; discussion 271–273.

45. Vitek JL, Bakay RA, DeLong MR, Posteroventral pallidotomy for Parkinson's disease. In: Obeso J, DeLong M, Ohye C, et al (eds). *The Basal Ganglia and Surgical Treatment of Parkinson's Disease.* Philadelphia: Lippincott Williams & Wilkins, 1997:183–198.

46. Brooks DJ. PET studies on the early and differential diagnosis of Parkinson's disease. *Neurology* 1993; 43:S6–S16.

47. Eidelberg D. Positron emission tomography studies in parkinsonism. *Neurol Clin* 1992; 10:421–433.

48. Eidelberg D, Takikawa S, Moeller JR, et al. Striatal hypometabolism distinguishes striatonigral degeneration from Parkinson's disease. *Ann Neurol* 1993; 33:518–527.

49. Eidelberg D, Moeller JR, Ishikawa T, et al. Regional metabolic correlates of surgical outcome following unilateral pallidotomy for Parkinson's disease. *Ann Neurol* 1996; 39:450–459.

50. Baron MS, Vitek JL, Bakay RA, et al. Treatment of advanced Parkinson's disease by posterior GPi pallidotomy: 1-year results of a pilot study. *Ann Neurol* 1996; 40:355–366.

51. Dogali M, Fazzini E, Kolodny E, et al. Stereotactic ventral pallidotomy for Parkinson's disease. *Neurology* 1995; 45:753–761.

52. Lang A, Lozano A, Montgomery E. Posteroventral medial pallidotomy in advanced Parkinson's disease (see comments). *N Engl J Med* 1997; 337:1036–1042.

53. Kishore A, Turnbull IM, Snow BJ, et al. Efficacy, stability and predictors of outcome of pallidotomy for Parkinson's disease. Six-month follow-up with additional 1-year observations. *Brain* 1997; 120(Pt 5):729–737.

54. Lozano A, Hutchison W, Pallidotomy: Indications and techniques. In: Germano I (ed). *Neurosurgical Treatment of Movement Disorders.* Park Ridge, IL: AANS Publications Committee, 1998:131–141.

55. Lang AE, Benabid AL, Koller WC, et al. The core assessment program for intracerebral transplantation. *Mov Disord* 1995; 10:527–528.

56. Langston J, Winder H, Goetz C. The core assessment program for intracerebral transplantation (CAPIT). *Mov Disord* 1992; 7:2–13.

57. Defer GL, Widner H, Marie RM, et al. Core assessment program for surgical interventional therapies in Parkinson's disease (CAPSIT–PD). *Mov Disord* 1999; 14:572–584.

58. Folstein MF, Folstein SE, McHugh PR. "Mini–mental state." A practical method for grading the cognitive state of patients for the clinician. *J Psychiatr Res* 1975; 12:189–198.

59. Vitek JL, Bakay RA, Freeman A, et al. Randomized trial of pallidotomy versus medical therapy for Parkinson's disease. *Ann Neurol* 2003; 53:558–569.

60. Masterman D, DeSalles A, Baloh RW, et al. Motor, cognitive, and behavioral performance following unilateral ventroposterior pallidotomy for Parkinson disease. *Arch Neurol* 1998; 55:1201–1208.

61. Rilling L, Filoteo J, Roberts J. Neuropsychological functioning in patients with Parkinson's disease pre- and post-pallidotomy. *Arch Clin Neuropsychol* 1996; 11:442.

62. Perrine K, Dogali M, Fazzini E, et al. Cognitive functioning after pallidotomy for refractory Parkinson's disease. *J Neurol Neurosurg Psychiatry* 1998; 65:150–154.

63. Scott R, Gregory R, Hines N, et al. Neuropsychological, neurological and functional outcome following pallidotomy for Parkinson's disease. A consecutive series of eight simultaneous bilateral and twelve unilateral procedures. *Brain* 1998; 121(Pt 4):659–675.

64. Soukup VM, Ingram MC, Schiess MC, et al. Cognitive sequelae of unilateral posteroventral pallidotomy. *Arch Neurol* 1997; 54:947–950.

65. Trepanier LL, Saint-Cyr JA, Lozano AM, et al. Neuropsychological consequences of posteroventral pallidotomy for the treatment of Parkinson's disease. *Neurology* 1998; 51:207–215.

66. Demakis GJ, Mercury MG, Sweet JJ, et al. Motor and cognitive sequelae of unilateral pallidotomy in intractable Parkinson's disease: Electronic measurement of motor steadiness is a useful outcome measure. *J Clin Exp Neuropsychol* 2002; 24:655–663.

67. Green J, McDonald WM, Vitek JL, et al. Neuropsychological and psychiatric sequelae of pallidotomy for PD: Clinical trial findings. *Neurology* 2002; 58:858–865.

68. Lacritz LH, Cullum CM, Frol AB, et al. Neuropsychological outcome following unilateral stereotactic pallidotomy in intractable Parkinson's disease. *Brain Cogn* 2000; 42:364–378.

69. Marshall LF, Tung H. Pallidotomy and neuropsychological outcome. *J Neurosurg* 2000; 93:527–528.

70. Rettig GM, York MK, Lai EC, et al. Neuropsychological outcome after unilateral pallidotomy for the treatment of Parkinson's disease. *J Neurol Neurosurg Psychiatry* 2000; 69:326–336.

71. Trepanier LL, Kumar R, Lozano AM, et al. Neuropsychological outcome of GPi pallidotomy and GPi or STN deep brain stimulation in Parkinson's disease. *Brain Cogn* 2000; 42:324–347.

72. Vingerhoets G, van der Linden C, Lannoo E, et al. Cognitive outcome after unilateral pallidal stimulation in Parkinson's disease. *J Neurol Neurosurg Psychiatry* 1999; 66:297–304.

73. York MK, Levin HS, Grossman RG, et al. Neuropsychological outcome following unilateral pallidotomy. *Brain* 1999; 122(Pt 12):2209–2220.

74. Tasker RR, Siqueira J, Hawrylyshyn P, et al. What happened to VIM thalamotomy for Parkinson's disease? *Appl Neurophysiol* 1983; 46:68–83.

75. Narabayashi H. Surgical treatment in the levodopa era. In: Stern G (ed). *Parkinson's Disease.* London: Chapman and Hall, 1990.

76. Ohye C. Thalamotomy for Parkinson's disease and other types of tremor. In: Gildenberg PL, Tasker R (eds). *Textbook of Stereotactic and Functional Neurosurgery.* New York: McGraw-Hill, 1997:1167–1178.

77. Lozano A, Hutchison W, Kiss Z, et al. Methods for microelectrode-guided posteroventral pallidotomy. *J Neurosurg* 1996; 84:194–202.

78. Lozano AM, Hutchison WD, Dostrovsky JO. Microelectrode monitoring of cortical and subcortical structures during stereotactic surgery. *Acta Neurochir Suppl* 1995; 64:30–34.

79. Tasker RR. Thalamotomy. *Neurosurg Clin North Am* 1990; 1:841–864.

80. Tasker RR, Lang AE, Lozano AM. Pallidal and thalamic surgery for Parkinson's disease. *Exp Neurol* 1997; 144:35–40.

81. Laitinen LV, Bergenheim AT, Hariz MI. Leksell's posteroventral pallidotomy in the treatment of Parkinson's disease. *J Neurosurg* 1992; 76:53–61.

82. Gross RE, Krack P, Rodriguez–Oroz MC, et al. Electrophysiological mapping for the implantation of deep brain stimulators for Parkinson's disease and tremor. *Mov Disord* 2006; 21(Suppl 14):S259–S283.

83. Gross RE, Lombardi WJ, Hutchison WD, et al. Variability in lesion location after microelectrode-guided pallidotomy for Parkinson's disease: Anatomical, physiological, and technical factors that determine lesion distribution. *J Neurosurg* 1999; 90: 468–477.

84. Vitek JL, Bakay RA, Hashimoto T, et al. Microelectrode-guided pallidotomy: Technical approach and its application in medically intractable Parkinson's disease. *J Neurosurg* 1998; 88:1027–1043.

85. Gross RE, Lombardi WJ, Lang AE, et al. Relationship of lesion location to clinical outcome following microelectrode-guided pallidotomy for Parkinson's disease. *Brain* 1999; 122(Pt 3):405–416.

86. Alkhani A, Lozano AM. Pallidotomy for parkinson disease: A review of contemporary literature. *J Neurosurg* 2001; 94:43–49.

87. Baron MS, Vitek JL, Bakay RA, et al. Treatment of advanced Parkinson's disease by unilateral posterior GPi pallidotomy: 4-year results of a pilot study. *Mov Disord* 2000; 15:230–237.

88. Dalvi A, Winfield L, Yu Q, et al. Stereotactic posteroventral pallidotomy: Clinical methods and results at 1-year follow up. *Mov Disord* 1999; 14:256–261.
89. de Bie RM, Schuurman PR, de Haan PS, et al. Unilateral pallidotomy in advanced Parkinson's disease: A retrospective study of 26 patients. *Mov Disord* 1999; 14:951–957.
90. Eskandar EN, Shinobu LA, Penney JB Jr, et al. Stereotactic pallidotomy performed without using microelectrode guidance in patients with Parkinson's disease: Surgical technique and 2-year results. *J Neurosurg* 2000; 92:375–383.
91. Giller CA, Dewey RB, Ginsburg MI, et al. Stereotactic pallidotomy and thalamotomy using individual variations of anatomic landmarks for localization. *Neurosurgery* 1998; 42:56–62; discussion 62–65.
92. Goto S, Hamasaki T, Nishikawa S, et al. Temporal sequence of response to unilateral GPi pallidotomy of motor symptoms in Parkinson's disease. *Stereotact Funct Neurosurg* 2000; 75:160–166.
93. Guridi J, Gorospe A, Ramos E, et al. Stereotactic targeting of the globus pallidus internus in Parkinson's disease: Imaging versus electrophysiological mapping. *Neurosurgery* 1999; 45:278–287; discussion 287–289.
94. Herrera EJ, Viano JC, Caceres M, et al. Posteroventral pallidotomy in Parkinson's disease. *Acta Neurochir (Wien)* 2000; 142:169–175.
95. Iacono RP, Shima F, Lonser RR, et al. The results, indications, and physiology of posteroventral pallidotomy for patients with Parkinson's disease. *Neurosurgery* 1995; 36:1118–1125; discussion 1125–1127.
96. Johansson F, Malm J, Nordh E, et al. Usefulness of pallidotomy in advanced Parkinson's disease. *J Neurol Neurosurg Psychiatry* 1997; 62:125–132.
97. Kishore A, Panikar D, Balakrishnan S, et al. Evidence of functional somatotopy in GPi from results of pallidotomy. *Brain* 2000; 123(Pt 12):2491–2500.
98. Kondziolka D, Bonaroti E, Baser S, et al. Outcomes after stereotactically guided pallidotomy for advanced Parkinson's disease. *J Neurosurg* 1999; 90:197–202.
99. Lai EC, Jankovic J, Krauss JK, et al. Long-term efficacy of posteroventral pallidotomy in the treatment of Parkinson's disease. *Neurology* 2000; 55:1218–1222.
100. Lu CS, Weng YH, Wu T, et al. Posteroventral pallidotomy for advanced Parkinson's disease. *Chang Gung Med J* 2001; 24:409–417.
101. Melnick ME, Dowling GA, Aminoff MJ, et al. Effect of pallidotomy on postural control and motor function in Parkinson disease. *Arch Neurol* 1999; 56:1361–1365.
102. Merello M, Nouzeilles MI, Kuzis G, et al. Unilateral radiofrequency lesion versus electrostimulation of posteroventral pallidum: A prospective randomized comparison. *Mov Disord* 1999; 14:50–56.
103. Parkin SG, Gregory RP, Scott R, et al. Unilateral and bilateral pallidotomy for idiopathic Parkinson's disease: A case series of 115 patients. *Mov Disord* 2002; 17:682–692.
104. Shannon KM, Penn RD, Kroin JS, et al. Stereotactic pallidotomy for the treatment of Parkinson's disease. Efficacy and adverse effects at 6 months in 26 patients. *Neurology* 1998; 50:434–438.
105. Uitti RJ, Wharen RE Jr, Turk MF, et al. Unilateral pallidotomy for Parkinson's disease: Comparison of outcome in younger versus elderly patients. *Neurology* 1997; 49:1072–1077.
106. Valldeoriola F, Martinez-Rodriguez J, Tolosa E, et al. Four year follow-up study after unilateral pallidotomy in advanced Parkinson's disease. *J Neurology* 2002; 249:1671–1677.
107. Yen CP, Wu SJ, Su YF, et al. Unilateral stereotactic posteroventral globus pallidus internus pallidotomy for Parkinson's disease: Surgical techniques and 2-year follow-up. *Kaohsiung J Med Sci* 2005; 21:1–8.
108. de Bie RM, de Haan RJ, Nijssen PC, et al. Unilateral pallidotomy in Parkinson's disease: A randomised, single–blind, multicentre trial. *Lancet* 1999; 354:1665–1669.
109. Kimber TE, Tsai CS, Semmler J, et al. Voluntary movement after pallidotomy in severe Parkinson's disease. *Brain* 1999; 122(Pt 5):895–906.
110. Lang AE, Lozano AM, Montgomery E, et al. Posteroventral medial pallidotomy in advanced Parkinson's disease. *N Engl J Med* 1997; 337:1036–1042.
111. Merello M, Nouzeilles MI, Cammarota A, et al. Comparison of 1-year follow-up evaluations of patients with indication for pallidotomy who did not undergo surgery versus patients with Parkinson's disease who did undergo pallidotomy: A case control study. *Neurosurgery* 1999; 44:461–467; discussion 467–468.
112. Esselink RA, de Bie RM, de Haan RJ, et al. Unilateral pallidotomy versus bilateral subthalamic nucleus stimulation in PD: A randomized trial. *Neurology* 2004; 62:201–207.
113. Hayashi R, Hashimoto T, Tada T, et al. Effects of unilateral pallidotomy on voluntary movement, and simple and choice reaction times in Parkinson's disease. *Mov Disord* 2003; 18:515–523.
114. Levy R, Lang AE, Hutchison WD, et al. Simultaneous repetitive movements following pallidotomy or subthalamic deep brain stimulation in patients with Parkinson's disease. *Exp Brain Res* 2002; 147:322–331.
115. Bronte-Stewart HM, Minn AY, Rodrigues K, et al. Postural instability in idiopathic Parkinson's disease: The role of medication and unilateral pallidotomy. *Brain* 2002; 125:2100–2114.
116. Hagiwara N, Hashimoto T, Ikeda S. Static balance impairment and its change after pallidotomy in Parkinson's disease. *Mov Disord* 2004; 19:437–445.
117. Westerberg BD, Roberson JB, Stach BA, et al. The effects of posteroventral pallidotomy on balance function in patients with Parkinson's disease. *Stereotact Funct Neurosurg* 2002; 79:75–87.
118. Jankovic J, Lai EC, Ondo WG, et al. Effects of pallidotomy on gait and balance. *Adv Neurol* 2001; 87:271–281.
119. Roberts-Warrior D, Overby A, Jankovic J, et al. Postural control in Parkinson's disease after unilateral posteroventral pallidotomy. *Brain* 2000; 123(Pt 10):2141–2149.
120. Bastian AJ, Kelly VE, Perlmutter JS, et al. Effects of pallidotomy and levodopa on walking and reaching movements in Parkinson's disease. *Mov Disord* 2003; 18:1008–1017.
121. Mourao LF, Aguiar PM, Ferraz FA, et al. Acoustic voice assessment in Parkinson's disease patients submitted to posteroventral pallidotomy. *Arq Neuropsiquiatr* 2005; 63:20–25.
122. Schrag A, Samuel M, Caputo E, et al. Unilateral pallidotomy for Parkinson's disease: Results after more than 1 year. *J Neurol Neurosurg Psychiatry* 1999; 67:511–517.
123. Schulz GM, Greer M, Friedman W. Changes in vocal intensity in Parkinson's disease following pallidotomy surgery. *J Voice* 2000; 14:589–606.
124. de Bie RM, Schuurman PR, Bosch DA, et al. Outcome of unilateral pallidotomy in advanced Parkinson's disease: Cohort study of 32 patients. *J Neurol Neurosurg Psychiatry* 2001; 71:375–382.
125. Krauss JK, Desaloms JM, Lai EC, et al. Microelectrode-guided posteroventral pallidotomy for treatment of Parkinson's disease: Postoperative magnetic resonance imaging analysis. *J Neurosurg* 1997; 87:358–367.
126. Gross CE, Boraud T, Guehl D, et al. From experimentation to the surgical treatment of Parkinson's disease: Prelude or suite in basal ganglia research? *Prog Neurobiol* 1999; 59:509–532.
127. Laitinen L, Hariz M. Movement disorders. In: Yomans J (ed). *Neurological Surgery*. Philadelphia: Saunders, 1996:3575–3609.
128. Lozano A, Lang AE, Galvez-Jimenez N. GPi pallidotomy improves motor function in patients with Parkinson's disease. *Lancet* 1995; 346:1383–1386.
129. Honey CR, Stoessl AJ, Tsui JK, et al. Unilateral pallidotomy for reduction of parkinsonian pain. *J Neurosurg*, 1999; 91:198–201.
130. Fine J, Duff J, Chen R, et al. Long-term follow-up of unilateral pallidotomy in advanced Parkinson's disease. *N Engl J Med* 2000; 342:1708–1714.
131. Pal PK, Samii A, Kishore A, et al. Long term outcome of unilateral pallidotomy: Follow up of 15 patients for 3 years. *J Neurol Neurosurg Psychiatry* 2000; 69:337–344.
132. Fazzini E, Dogali M, Sterio D, et al. Stereotactic pallidotomy for Parkinson's disease: A long-term follow-up of unilateral pallidotomy. *Neurology* 1997; 48:1273–1277.
133. Merello M, Nouzeilles MI, Cammarotta A, et al. Changes in the motor response to acute L-dopa challenge after unilateral microelectrode-guided posteroventral pallidotomy. *Clin Neuropharmacol* 1998; 21:135–138.
134. Skalabrin EJ, Laws ER Jr, Bennett JP Jr. Pallidotomy improves motor responses and widens the levodopa therapeutic window in Parkinson's disease. *Mov Disord* 1998; 13:775–781.
135. Shima F, Ishido K, Sun SJ, et al. Surgical control of akinesia in Parkinson's disease. *Eur Neurol* 1996; 36(Suppl 1):55–61.
136. Ghika J, Ghika-Schmid F, Fankhauser H, et al. Bilateral contemporaneous posteroventral pallidotomy for the treatment of Parkinson's disease: Neuropsychological and neurological side effects. Report of four cases and review of the literature. *J Neurosurg* 1999; 91:313–321.
137. Higuchi Y, Iacono RP. Surgical complications in patients with Parkinson's disease after posteroventral pallidotomy. *Neurosurgery* 2003; 52:558–571; discussion 568–571.
138. Galvez–Jimenez N, Lozano A, Tasker R, et al. Pallidal stimulation in Parkinson's disease patients with a prior unilateral pallidotomy. *Can J Neurol Sci* 1998; 25:300–305.
139. Merello M, Starkstein S, Nouzeilles MI, et al. Bilateral pallidotomy for treatment of Parkinson's disease induced corticobulbar syndrome and psychic akinesia avoidable by globus pallidus lesion combined with contralateral stimulation. *J Neurol Neurosurg Psychiatry* 2001; 71:611–614.
140. Alegret M, Vendrell P, Junque C, et al. Effects of unilateral posteroventral pallidotomy on "on–off" cognitive fluctuations in Parkinson's disease. *Neuropsychologia* 2000; 38:628–633.
141. Carr JA, Honey CR, Sinden M, et al. A waitlist control-group study of cognitive, mood, and quality of life outcome after posteroventral pallidotomy in Parkinson disease. *J Neurosurg* 2003; 99:78–88.
142. Green J, Barnhart H. The impact of lesion laterality on neuropsychological change following posterior pallidotomy: A review of current findings. *Brain Cogn* 2000; 42:379–398.
143. Kubu CS, Grace GM, Parrent AG. Cognitive outcome following pallidotomy: The influence of side of surgery and age of patient at disease onset. *J Neurosurg* 2000; 92:384–389.
144. Lombardi WJ, Gross RE, Trepanier LL, et al. Relationship of lesion location to cognitive outcome following microelectrode-guided pallidotomy for Parkinson's disease: Support for the existence of cognitive circuits in the human pallidum. *Brain* 2000; 123(Pt 4):746–758.
145. Obwegeser AA, Uitti RJ, Lucas JA, et al. Predictors of neuropsychological outcome in patients following microelectrode-guided pallidotomy for Parkinson's disease. *J Neurosurg* 2000; 93:410–420.
146. Stebbins GT, Gabrieli JD, Shannon KM, et al. Impaired frontostriatal cognitive functioning following posteroventral pallidotomy in advanced Parkinson's disease. *Brain Cogn* 2000; 42:348–363.
147. Troster AI, Woods SP, Fields JA. Verbal fluency declines after pallidotomy: An interaction between task and lesion laterality. *Appl Neuropsychol* 2003; 10:69–75.
148. Marsden C, Olanow CW. The causes of Parkinson's disease are being unraveled and rational neuroprotective therapy is close to reality. *Ann Neurol* 1998; 44:S189–S196.
149. Trepanier L, Saint-Cyr J, Lang A, et al. Hemisphere-specific cognitive and motor changes after unilateral posteroventral pallidotomy. *Arch Neurol* 1998; 55:881–883.
150. Yokoyama T, Imamura Y, Sugiyama K, et al. Prefrontal dysfunction following unilateral posteroventral pallidotomy in Parkinson's disease. *J Neurosurg* 1999; 90:1005–1010.
151. Stebbins GT, Goetz CG. Factor structure of the Unified Parkinson's Disease Rating Scale: Motor Examination section. *Mov Disord* 1998; 13:633–636.
152. Jahanshahi M, Rowe J, Saleem T, et al. Striatal contribution to cognition: Working memory and executive function in Parkinson's disease before and after unilateral posteroventral pallidotomy. *J Cogn Neurosci* 2002; 14:298–310.
153. Troster AI, Woods SP, Fields JA, et al. Declines in switching underlie verbal fluency changes after unilateral pallidal surgery in Parkinson's disease. *Brain Cogn* 2002; 50:207–217.
154. Brown RG, Jahanshahi M, Limousin–Dowsey P, et al. Pallidotomy and incidental sequence learning in Parkinson's disease. *Neuroreport* 2003; 14:21–24.

155. Sage JR, Anagnostaras SG, Mitchell S, et al. Analysis of probabilistic classification learning in patients with Parkinson's disease before and after pallidotomy surgery. *Learn Mem* 2003; 10:226–236.

156. Alegret M, Valldeoriola F, Tolosa E, et al. Cognitive effects of unilateral posteroventral pallidotomy: a 4-year follow-up study. *Mov Disord* 2003; 18:323–328.

157. Junque C, Alegret M, Nobbe FA, et al. Cognitive and behavioral changes after unilateral posteroventral pallidotomy: Relationship with lesional data from MRI. *Mov Disord* 1999; 14:780–789.

158. Fukuda M, Kameyama S, Yoshino M, et al. Neuropsychological outcome following pallidotomy and thalamotomy for Parkinson's disease. *Stereotact Funct Neurosurg* 2000; 74:11–20.

159. Gironell A, Kulisevsky J, Rami L, et al. Effects of pallidotomy and bilateral subthalamic stimulation on cognitive function in Parkinson disease. A controlled comparative study. *J Neurol* 2003; 250:917–923.

160. Merello M. Subthalamic stimulation contralateral to a previous pallidotomy: An erroneous indication? *Mov Disord* 1999; 14:890.

161. Miyawaki E, Troster AI. Introduction to neurobehavioral issues in pallidotomy and pallidal stimulation. *Brain Cogn* 2000; 42:309–312.

162. de Bie RM, de Haan RJ, Schuurman PR, et al. Morbidity and mortality following pallidotomy in Parkinson's disease: A systematic review. *Neurology* 2002; 58:1008–1012.

163. Palur RS, Berk C, Schulzer M, et al. A metaanalysis comparing the results of pallidotomy performed using microelectrode recording or macroelectrode stimulation. *J Neurosurg* 2002; 96:1058–1062.

164. Schuurman PR, de Bie RM, Speelman HD, et al. Bilateral posteroventral pallidotomy in advanced Parkinson's disease in three patients. *Mov Disord* 1997; 12:752–755.

165. Scott RB, Harrison J, Boulton C, et al. Global attentional-executive sequelae following surgical lesions to globus pallidus interna. *Brain* 2002; 125:562–574.

166. Turner KR, Reid WG, Homewood J, et al. Neuropsychological sequelae of bilateral posteroventral pallidotomy. *J Neurol Neurosurg Psychiatry* 2002; 73:444–446.

167. Whelan BM, Murdoch BE, Theodoros DG, et al. Redefining functional models of basal ganglia organization: Role for the posteroventral pallidum in linguistic processing? *Mov Disord* 2004; 19:1267–1278.

168. Gray A, McNamara I, Aziz T, et al. Quality of life outcomes following surgical treatment of Parkinson's disease. *Mov Disord* 2002; 17:68–75.

169. Martinez–Martin P, Valldeoriola F, Molinuevo JL, et al. Pallidotomy and quality of life in patients with Parkinson's disease: An early study. *Mov Disord* 2000; 15:65–70.

170. Straits-Troster K, Fields JA, Wilkinson SB, et al. Health-related quality of life in Parkinson's disease after pallidotomy and deep brain stimulation. *Brain Cogn* 2000; 42:399–416.

171. D'Antonio LL, Zimmerman GJ, Iacono RP. Changes in health related quality of life in patients with Parkinson's disease with and without posteroventral pallidotomy. *Acta Neurochir (Wien)* 2000; 142:759–767; discussion 767–768.

172. Zimmerman GJ, D'Antonio LL, Iacono RP. Health related quality of life in patients with Parkinson's disease two years following posteroventral pallidotomy. *Acta Neurochir (Wien)* 2004; 146:1293–1299; discussion 1299.

173. Ohye C. Use of selective thalamotomy for various kinds of movement disorder, based on basic studies. *Stereotact Funct Neurosurg* 2000; 75:54–65.

174. Narabayashi H, Maeda T, Yokochi F. Long-term follow-up study of nucleus ventralis intermedius and ventrolateralis thalamotomy using a microelectrode technique in parkinsonism. *Appl Neurophysiol* 1987; 50:330–337.

175. Hassler R. Sagittal thalamotomy for relief of motor disorders in cases of double athetosis and cerebral palsy. *Confin Neurol* 1972; 34:18–28.

176. Okun MS, Vitek JL. Lesion therapy for Parkinson's disease and other movement disorders: Update and controversies. *Mov Disord* 2004; 19:375–389.

177. Macchi G, Jones EG. Toward an agreement on terminology of nuclear and subnuclear divisions of the motor thalamus. *J Neurosurg* 1997; 86:77–92.

178. Laitinen LV. Brain targets in surgery for Parkinson's disease. Results of a survey of neurosurgeons. *J Neurosurg* 1985; 62:349–351.

179. Broggi G, Giorgi C, Servello D. Stereotactic neurosurgery in the treatment of tremor. *Acta Neurochir Suppl (Wien)* 1987; 39:73–76.

180. Diederich N, Goetz CG, Stebbins GT, et al. Blinded evaluation confirms long-term asymmetric effect of unilateral thalamotomy or subthalamotomy on tremor in Parkinson's disease. *Neurology* 1992; 42:1311–1314.

181. Fox MW, Ahlskog JE, Kelly PJ. Stereotactic ventrolateralis thalamotomy for medically refractory tremor in post-levodopa era Parkinson's disease patients. *J Neurosurg* 1991; 75:723–730.

182. Jankovic J, Cardoso F, Grossman RG, et al. Outcome after stereotactic thalamotomy for parkinsonian, essential, and other types of tremor. *Neurosurgery* 1995; 37:680–686; discussion 686–687.

183. Matsumoto K, Shichijo F, Fukami T. Long-term follow-up review of cases of Parkinson's disease after unilateral or bilateral thalamotomy. *J Neurosurg* 1984; 60:1033–1044.

184. Moriyama E, Beck H, Miyamoto T. Long-term results of ventrolateral thalamotomy for patients with Parkinson's disease. *Neurol Med Chir (Tokyo)* 1999; 39:350–356; discussion 356–357.

185. Nagaseki Y, Shibazaki T, Hirai T, et al. [Long-term follow-up study of selective VIM-thalamotomy]. *No To Shinkei* 1985; 37:545–554.

186. Osenbach R, Burchiel KJ, Thalamotomy: Indications, techniques, and results. In: Germano I (ed). *Neurosurgical Treatment of Movement Disorders.* Park Ridge, IL: AANS Publications Committee, 1998:107–130.

187. Schuurman PR, Bosch DA, Bossuyt PM, et al. A comparison of continuous thalamic stimulation and thalamotomy for suppression of severe tremor. *N Engl J Med* 2000; 342:461–468.

188. Speelman JD, Bosch DA. Resurgence of functional neurosurgery for Parkinson's disease: A historical perspective. *Mov Disord* 1998; 13:582–588.

189. Tasker RR. Ablative therapy for movement disorders. Does thalamotomy alter the course of Parkinson's disease? *Neurosurg Clin North Am* 1998; 9:375–380.

190. Tasker RR, DeCarvalho GC, Li CS, et al. Does thalamotomy alter the course of Parkinson's disease? *Adv Neurol* 1996; 69:563–583.

191. Valalik I, Sagi S, Solymosi D, et al. CT-guided unilateral thalamotomy with macroelectrode mapping for the treatment of Parkinson's disease. *Acta Neurochir (Wien)* 2001; 143:1019–1030.

192. Wester K, Hauglie-Hanssen E. Stereotaxic thalamotomy: Experiences from the levodopa era. *J Neurol Neurosurg Psychiatry* 1990; 53:427–430.

193. Atkinson JD, Collins DL, Bertrand G, et al. Optimal location of thalamotomy lesions for tremor associated with Parkinson disease: A probabilistic analysis based on postoperative magnetic resonance imaging and an integrated digital atlas. *J Neurosurg* 2002; 96:854–866.

194. Riechert T. Stereotaxic surgery for treatment of Parkinson's syndrome. *Progr Neurol Surg* 1973; 5:1–78.

195. Van Buren JM, Li CL, Shapiro DY, et al. A qualitative and quantitative evaluation of parkinsonians three to six years following thalamotomy. *Confin Neurol*, 1973; 35:202–235.

196. Van Manen J. Long-term results of stereotaxic operations for Parkinson's disease. *Psychiatry Neurol Neurochir* 1970; 73:365–374.

197. Nakajima T, Nimura T, Yamaguchi K, et al. The impact of stereotactic pallidal surgery on the dopamine D2 receptor in Parkinson disease: A positron emission tomography study. *J Neurosurg* 2003; 98:57–63.

198. Ohye C, Shibazaki T. Lesioning the thalamus for dyskinesia. *Stereotact Funct Neurosurg* 2001; 77:33–39.

199. Goetz CG, Poewe W, Rascol O, et al. Evidence-based medical review update: Pharmacological and surgical treatments of Parkinson's disease: 2001 to 2004. *Mov Disord* 2005; 20:523–539.

200. Metman LV, O'Leary ST. Role of surgery in the treatment of motor complications. *Mov Disord* 2005; 20(Suppl 11):S45–S56.

201. Matsumoto K, Asano T, Baba T, et al. Long-term follow-up results of bilateral thalamotomy for parkinsonism. *Appl Neurophysiol* 1976; 39:257–260.

202. Kelly PJ, Gillingham FJ. The long-term results of stereotaxic surgery and L-dopa therapy in patients with Parkinson's disease. A 10-year follow-up study. *J Neurosurg* 1980; 53:332–337.

203. Krayenbuhl H, Siegfried J. [Treatment of Parkinson's disease: L-dopa or stereotaxic technics?]. *Neurochirurgie* 1970; 16:71–76.

204. Ohye C, Choice of patient, localization with microelectrodes and long–term results, in Neurosurgery: State of Art Reviews. Stereotactic Surgery., Tasker R, Editor. 1987, Hanley and Belfus: Philadelphia. p. 193–208.

205. Tasker R, The outcome of thalamotomy for tremor, in Textbook of Stereotactic and Functional Neurosurgery, Gildenberg PL and Tasker R, Editors. 1998, McGraw–Hill: New York. p. 1179–1198.

206. Rossitch E, Jr., Zeidman SM, Nashold BS, Jr., et al. Evaluation of memory and language function pre– and postthalamotomy with an attempt to define those patients at risk for postoperative dysfunction. *Surg Neurol*, 1988; 29:11–16.

207. Hugdahl K, Wester K. Neurocognitive correlates of stereotactic thalamotomy and thalamic stimulation in Parkinsonian patients. *Brain Cogn*, 2000; 42:231–252.

208. Smith M. Stereotactic operations for Parkinson's disease: Anatomical observations. *Mod Trends Neurol*, 1967; 4:21–52.

209. Ohye C, Shibazaki T, Ishihara J, et al. Evaluation of gamma thalamotomy for parkinsonian and other tremors: Survival of neurons adjacent to the thalamic lesion after gamma thalamotomy. *J Neurosurg* 2000; 93(Suppl 3):120–127.

210. Ohye C, Shibazaki T, Sato S. Gamma knife thalamotomy for movement disorders: Evaluation of the thalamic lesion and clinical results. *J Neurosurg*, 2005; 102(Suppl):234–240.

211. Ohye C, Shibazaki T, Zhang J, et al. Thalamic lesions produced by gamma thalamotomy for movement disorders. *J Neurosurg* 2002; 97:600–606.

212. Young RF, Jacques S, Mark R, et al. Gamma knife thalamotomy for treatment of tremor: Long-term results. *J Neurosurg* 2000; 93(Suppl 3):128–135.

213. Duma CM, Jacques S, Kopyov OV. The treatment of movement disorders using gamma knife stereotactic radiosurgery. *Neurosurg Clin North Am* 1999; 10:379–389.

214. Friedman DP, Goldman HW, Flanders AE, et al. Stereotactic radiosurgical pallidotomy and thalamotomy with the gamma knife: MR imaging findings with clinical correlation—Preliminary experience. *Radiology* 1999; 212:143–150.

215. Okun MS, Stover NP, Subramanian T, et al. Complications of gamma knife surgery for Parkinson disease. *Arch Neurol* 2001; 58:1995–2002.

216. Kondziolka D. Gamma knife thalamotomy for disabling tremor. *Arch Neurol* 2002; 59:1660; author reply 1662–1664.

217. Alvarez L, Macias R, Lopez G, et al. Bilateral subthalamotomy in Parkinson's disease: Initial and long–term response. *Brain* 2005; 128:570–583.

218. Patel NK, Heywood P, O'Sullivan K, et al. Unilateral subthalamotomy in the treatment of Parkinson's disease. *Brain* 2003; 126:1136–1145.

219. Su PC, Tseng HM, Liu HM, et al. Treatment of advanced Parkinson's disease by subthalamotomy: One-year results. *Mov Disord* 2003; 18:531–538.

220. Vilela Filho O, da Silva DJ. Unilateral subthalamic nucleus lesioning: A safe and effective treatment for Parkinson's disease. *Arq Neuropsiquiatr* 2002; 60:935–948.

221. Bjorklund A, Dunnett SB, Brundin P, et al. Neural transplantation for the treatment of Parkinson's disease. *Lancet Neurol* 2003; 2:437–445.

222. Freed CR, Greene PE, Breeze RE, et al. Transplantation of embryonic dopamine neurons for severe Parkinson's disease. *N Engl J Med* 2001; 344:710–719.

223. Olanow CW, Goetz CG, Kordower JH, et al. A double-blind controlled trial of bilateral fetal nigral transplantation in Parkinson's disease. *Ann Neurol* 2003; 54:403–414.

224. Lindvall O. Update on fetal transplantation: The Swedish experience. *Mov Disord* 1998; 13(Suppl 1):83–87.

225. Christenson L, Emerich DF, Sanberg PR. Encapsulated cell implantation for Parkinson's disease. *Mov Disord* 1992; 7:185–186.

226. Kordower JH, Liu YT, Winn S, et al. Encapsulated PC12 cell transplants into hemiparkinsonian monkeys: A behavioral, neuroanatomical, and neurochemical analysis. *Cell Transplant* 1995; 4:155–171.

227. Lindner MD, Emerich DF. Therapeutic potential of a polymer-encapsulated L-dopa and dopamine-producing cell line in rodent and primate models of Parkinson's disease. *Cell Transplant* 1998; 7:165–174.

228. Bakay RA, Raiser CD, Stover NP, et al. Implantation of Spheramine in advanced Parkinson's disease (PD). *Front Biosci* 2004; 9:592–602.

229. Stover NP, Bakay RA, Subramanian T, et al. Intrastriatal implantation of human retinal pigment epithelial cells attached to microcarriers in advanced Parkinson disease. *Arch Neurol* 2005; 62:1833–1837.

230. Arenas E. GDNF, a multispecific neurotrophic factor with potential therapeutic applications in neurodegenerative disorders. *Mol Psychiatry* 1996; 1:179–182.

231. Date I, Ohmoto T. Neural transplantation and trophic factors in Parkinson's disease: Special reference to chromaffin cell grafting, NGF support from pretransected peripheral nerve, and encapsulated dopamine-secreting cell grafting. *Exp Neurol* 1996; 137:333–344.

232. Grondin R, Gash DM. Glial cell line–derived neurotrophic factor (GDNF): A drug candidate for the treatment of Parkinson's disease. *J Neurol* 1998; 245:P35–P42.

233. Sautter J, Meyer M, Spenger C, et al. Effects of combined BDNF and GDNF treatment on cultured dopaminergic midbrain neurons. *Neuroreport* 1998; 9:1093–1096.

234. Gill SS, Patel NK, Hotton GR, et al. Direct brain infusion of glial cell line–derived neurotrophic factor in Parkinson disease. *Nat Med* 2003; 9:589–595.

235. Lang AE, Gill S, Patel NK, et al. Randomized controlled trial of intraputamenal glial cell line–derived neurotrophic factor infusion in Parkinson disease. *Ann Neurol* 2006; 59:459–466.

236. Patel NK, Bunnage M, Plaha P, et al. Intraputamenal infusion of glial cell line–derived neurotrophic factor in PD: A two–year outcome study. *Ann Neurol* 2005; 57:298–302.

237. Bankiewicz KS, Bringas JR, McLaughlin W, et al. Application of gene therapy for Parkinson's disease: Nonhuman primate experience. *Adv Pharmacol* 1998; 42:801–806.

238. Barkats M, Bilang-Bleuel A, Buc-Caron MH, et al. Adenovirus in the brain: Recent advances of gene therapy for neurodegenerative diseases. *Prog Neurobiol* 1998; 55:333–541.

239. Bowers WJ, Howard DF, Federoff HJ. Gene therapeutic strategies for neuroprotection: Implications for Parkinson's disease. *Exp Neurol* 1997; 144:58–68.

240. Cao L, Zheng ZC, Zhao YC, et al. Gene therapy of Parkinson disease model rat by direct injection of plasmid DNA–lipofectin complex. *Hum Gene Ther* 1995; 6:1497–1501.

241. Mouradian MM, Chase TN. Gene therapy for Parkinson's disease: An approach to the prevention or palliation of levodopa-associated motor complications. *Exp Neurol* 1997; 144:51–57.

242. Redmond DJ. Gene therapy approaches to Parkinson's disease: Preclinical to clinical trials, or what steps to take to get there from here. *Exp Neurol* 1997; 144:160–167.

243. Betchen SA, Kaplitt M. Future and current surgical therapies in Parkinson's disease. *Curr Opin Neurol* 2003; 16:487–493.

244. During MJ, Kaplitt MG, Stern MB, et al. Subthalamic GAD gene transfer in Parkinson disease patients who are candidates for deep brain stimulation. *Hum Gene Ther* 2001; 12:1589–1591.

245. Emborg ME, Carbon M, Holden JE, et al. Subthalamic glutamic acid decarboxylase gene therapy: Changes in motor function and cortical metabolism. *J Cereb Blood Flow Metab* 2007; 27:501–509.

246. Luo J, Kaplitt MG, Fitzsimons HL, et al. Subthalamic GAD gene therapy in a Parkinson's disease rat model. *Science* 2002; 298:425–429.

247. Sanftner LM, Sommer JM, Suzuki BM, et al. AAV2-mediated gene delivery to monkey putamen: Evaluation of an infusion device and delivery parameters. *Exp Neurol* 2005; 194:476–483.

248. Kordower JH, Herzog CD, Dass B, et al. Delivery of neurturin by AAV2 (CERE–120)–mediated gene transfer provides structural and functional neuroprotection and neurorestoration in MPTP-treated monkeys. *Ann Neurol* 2006; 60:706–715.

249. Kordower JH, Emborg ME, Bloch J, et al. Neurodegeneration prevented by lentiviral vector delivery of GDNF in primate models of Parkinson's disease. *Science* 2000; 290:767–773.

250. Deuschl G, Schade-Brittinger C, Krack P, et al. A randomized trial of deep-brain stimulation for Parkinson's disease. *N Engl J Med* 2006; 355:896–908.

251. Smeding HM, Esselink RA, Schmand B, et al. Unilateral pallidotomy versus bilateral subthalamic nucleus stimulation in PD—A comparison of neuropsychological effects. *J Neurol* 2005; 252:176–182.

X

SUBTYPES OF PARKINSONISM

57 Parkinson's-plus Disorders

Meredith Broderick
David E. Riley

Over the last several decades we have come to appreciate that James Parkinson described a syndrome, not a disease, in his famous 1817 monograph (1). This syndrome is known by the name *parkinsonism*. What we now call Parkinson's disease (PD) is a form of parkinsonism that, like other diseases, has characteristic clinical features, epidemiology, clinical course, prognosis, pathology, and treatment. The concept of "Parkinson's-plus" disorders arises from the realization that there are a variety of diseases that mimic PD in some respects but produce unique additional features that are not seen in PD (Table 57-1). Unfortunately, one of the problems we must address for these disorders, as with PD, is a lack of knowledge regarding etiology and an absence of curative therapies.

Parkinson's-plus diseases share many of the symptoms and signs of PD; in addition, they affect people of a similar age group and, at least at first, tend to develop in the same insidious, progressive manner. Thus they are often mistaken for the more common and more familiar PD. Pathologic studies indicate this is no small problem. Up to 25% of patients who are thought to have PD on a clinical basis, not just initially but until death, have another pathologic explanation for their neurologic problems (2, 3). Our inability to identify these patients promptly after presentation means, first, that the opportunity to study these other diseases is lost and, second, that inclusion of these patients confounds the results of PD studies. Both PD and Parkinson's-plus patients suffer as a result.

We acknowledge at the outset that "Parkinson's-plus" is a poor term with which to describe the major diseases discussed in this chapter. The implication of this phrase is that these diseases look just like PD but with some added features, which is certainly not the case. The parkinsonism seen in so-called Parkinson's-plus diseases differs in relation to the frequency of individual features, their distribution, and their chronological occurrence in the course of the disease. For example, a resting tremor is a relatively rare finding in patients with any of the Parkinson's-plus diseases, while they develop disequilibrium and falls much earlier in their course. Because they usually lack the responsiveness to levodopa that characterizes PD, Niall Quinn has suggested that "Parkinson's-minus" might be a more appropriate designation for these diseases (4). In other words, PD is not a diagnosis of default that depends solely on the absence of other findings. There are both characteristic and relatively exclusionary clinical features for all of these disorders.

This chapter should be regarded as one category in the differential diagnosis of PD. The chief disorders under consideration here are progressive supranuclear palsy (PSP), multiple system atrophy (MSA), cortical-basal ganglionic degeneration (CBGD), and dementia with Lewy bodies

TABLE 57-1
General Features of Parkinson's-Plus Syndromes

Features in common with PD
Insidious onset in middle to late life
Progressive course measured in years
Akinesia and rigidity
Lack of diagnostic laboratory tests
Definitive diagnosis requires appropriate data from both clinical and pathologic sources
Lack of knowledge regarding etiology, prevention, and cure
Only symptomatic treatment is available

Features distinctive from PD
Rest tremor unusual or rare
Frequent corticobulbar/corticospinal tract signs
Early postural instability
Frequent abnormal imaging studies
Poor response to antiparkinsonian medication
More rapid progression, shorter life expectancy
Pathology involves brain areas not typically involved in PD

(DLB). Also reviewed briefly is frontotemporal dementia and parkinsonism linked to chromosome 17 (FTDP-17).

PROGRESSIVE SUPRANUCLEAR PALSY

Progressive supranuclear palsy was first described in 1964 by 3 Canadian neurologists whose names have been honored in the British eponym for this disease, the Steele-Richardson-Olszewski syndrome (5). Although in retrospect there were previous case reports, these authors merited this distinction by virtue of having placed PSP on the parkinsonian map.

Clinical Findings

While the ocular motility disorder that Steele and colleagues chose to highlight remains the most distinctive feature of the clinical syndrome of PSP, strict reliance on this single physical sign leads to a lack of sensitivity, or at least a delay, in diagnosis. Most patients do not present with symptoms or signs related to their eyes. The most common initial feature of PSP is a disturbance of gait and a history of falling, which typically begins within 12 months of onset (6).

The parkinsonism of the classic syndrome of PSP differs from that of PD in the lack of tremor, the relative sparing of limb movement (except writing), the greater rigidity in the neck than the limbs, and the early development of freezing and marked micrographia. The speech disturbance shares the hypophonia and lack of modulation of PD speech but differs in the frequent additional presence of spastic dysarthria and dysphonia. Nevertheless, in one large series of pathologically confirmed PSP cases, a subset comprising 32% of patients was found to have a syndrome more consistent with PD, including tremor, asymmetric onset, and modest responsiveness to levodopa (7).

The distinctive supranuclear gaze palsy (SNGP) begins with slowing of vertical saccades, followed by a limitation of their range. Pursuit movements are affected later. Horizontal gaze is eventually impaired, but vertical gaze palsies always precede and predominate. Other ocular motor findings include saccadic intrusions into fixation ("square-wave jerks"), loss of convergence, blepharospasm, abnormal vertical optokinetic nystagmus and eyelid freezing, also known as apraxia of eyelid opening or closure.

Other clinical clues indicative of PSP include stuttering, palilalia, early dysphagia, personality changes, sleep disturbances, apraxia, and dementia. One characteristic feature is a facial expression of perpetual astonishment due to continuous frontalis contraction and a low blink rate. Another is extensor neck posturing, although this dystonia has come to represent to PSP what coprolalia has to Gilles de la Tourette syndrome: both were features described by the original authors that have been stressed by subsequent authors but actually occur in fewer than 25% of cases. An "applause sign," where patients perseverate in clapping beyond a requested total of 3 handclaps, may be specific for PSP (8). Other clinical findings in PSP include action tremor, pseudobulbar palsy, hyperreflexia, and Babinski signs. Infrequent occurrences in PSP that lead to problems in differential diagnosis include an absence of ocular motor abnormalities, resting tremor, hemidystonia, asymmetric apraxia, and urinary incontinence. Autonomic dysfunction may be more common than is generally appreciated, resulting in misdiagnosis of PSP as MSA. Patients who present with apraxia or aphasia also present a diagnostic challenge, as they run the risk of being mislabeled as having CBGD or Alzheimer's disease (AD).

Symptoms invariably begin insidiously and progress gradually. Golbe and colleagues surveyed the clinical course of PSP and found that it took a mean of 3 years for patients to require gait assistance, 8 years to become confined to a wheelchair or bed, and 10 years to die (9). However, the duration of illness varies widely, from 2 to more than 15 years (10). The isolated triad of hypophonic stuttering speech, micrographia, and freezing of gait known as "pure akinesia" is associated with a more benign course (11). Common causes of death include pulmonary and urinary tract infections, pulmonary emboli, head trauma, and complications of hip fractures.

Diagnostic criteria for clinical research into PSP were established at an international workshop in 1995 (12). These criteria were validated retrospectively with pathologically confirmed cases. The published report appended helpful descriptions of clinical and neuropsychological testing methods. Considered the most important clinical features in favor of the diagnosis of PSP were a vertical SNGP, slowing of vertical saccades, and prominent postural instability with falls within a year of onset (12).

Epidemiology and Genetics

Patients with PSP are more uniformly aged than those with PD. The mean age of onset is in the early seventh decade. Males outnumber females by as much as 2:1. Incidence rates in population studies indicate one can expect up to 11 new cases per million per year (13), approximately one-fifth the incidence of PD. However, the shorter life expectancy means that PSP patients make up a correspondingly lower proportion of patients in parkinsonism clinics. The prevalence of PSP is around 6 per 100,000 (14). No specific occupational or other environmental risk factors are known. Hypertension may be a risk factor (15).

A number of families are known in which PSP is transmitted in an autosomal dominant fashion (16). Genetic analysis has detected a high frequency of the allele A0 of the *tau* gene in patients with PSP (17, 18) but also in asymptomatic relatives of PSP patients. A novel *tau* gene mutation was found in one pedigree with early-onset familial PSP (19). In another family, a linkage locus at 1q31.1 was discovered (20). Mutations in *LRRK2* may also produce a PSP-like pathologic picture (21).

Investigations

There are no helpful indicators in common laboratory tests. Routine magnetic resonance imaging (MRI) studies may demonstrate atrophy of the midbrain (22–24) and superior cerebellar peduncles (25). Longitudinal MRI studies show accelerated midbrain and whole-brain volume loss compared to controls (26, 27). Formal neuropsychological testing indicates disproportionate impairment of frontal lobe function (28–30).

Pathology

There are no striking gross abnormalities in PSP. Atrophy of the midbrain, milder cortical atrophy, pallor of the substantia nigra, and enlargement of the third ventricle and Sylvian aqueduct may all be present. Microscopically, the characteristic features of PSP are neurofibrillary tangles (NFTs), tufted astrocytes, threads, and oligodendroglial coiled bodies distributed in varying densities throughout subcortical and brainstem structures (31). The most consistently affected regions are the basal ganglia and particularly the substantia nigra, subthalamic nucleus, and internal globus pallidus. Other parts of the brainstem

commonly affected in PSP include the superior colliculi, pretectal nuclei, periaqueductal gray matter, and pontine tegmentum. Involvement of the cerebral cortex may be a prominent feature (32, 33). Aside from the neuronal loss and gliosis common in degenerative diseases, NFTs are cytoplasmic inclusions found in surviving neurons. They are not specific to PSP, also being found in AD, postencephalitic parkinsonism, dementia pugilistica, and the parkinsonism-dementia complex of Guam, among others. Ultrastructurally, the NFTs of PSP are mainly composed of single straight filaments (34), in contrast to the paired helical filaments that predominate in AD.

The major structural element of NFTs in PSP appears to be abnormally phosphorylated tau, a protein associated with the microtubules responsible for axonal transport. Tau exists in multiple isoforms consisting of complete or partial translations of a single gene on chromosome 17. Its ability to promote formation of microtubules and stabilize them is thought to derive from its state of phosphorylation. It is speculated that abnormal phosphorylation of tau interferes with microtubule function, impairs axonal transport, and leads to tau aggregation as NFTs. Tau-positive inclusions are also common in oligodendroglia in PSP and may cause the formation of "tufted" astrocytes. Thus, abnormal tau modifications in both neurons and glia may be central to the pathophysiology of PSP. However, tau pathology is also seen in cortical-basal ganglionic degeneration (CBGD), Pick's disease, and other degenerative diseases. In fact, the 4-repeat pattern of tau isoform accumulation in PSP is identical to that seen in CBGD, suggesting strong pathogenetic bonds between the two conditions (35).

Among patients diagnosed with PSP during life, 76% to 78% have had the diagnosis confirmed postmortem (36, 37). The main sources of false-positive diagnoses of PSP have been diffuse Lewy body disease, MSA, and CBGD.

Management

The treatment of PSP can be difficult, as there is no cure and no symptomatic medications work in a majority of individuals (38); When they do work, their effects are usually modest at best (39, 40). Nevertheless, many symptoms can be relieved in a variety of ways (Table 57-2). The primary goals of management are to identify the patient's major problems, decide which can be remedied, and treat them.

Most studies involving medication have focused on the movement disorders present in PSP, where dopaminergic medications are much less useful than in PD because of the neuroanatomic substrate including striatum and globus pallidus. In a retrospective review of treatment of 381 PSP patients, amitriptyline and other antidepressants, levodopa and dopamine agonists were the least ineffective (41). Perhaps not unexpectedly in a disease that is complex

TABLE 57-2

Symptomatic Treatment of Parkinson's-Plus Syndromes

MOTOR PROBLEMS	AVAILABLE TREATMENTS
Blepharospasm	Botulinum toxin, eye crutches, surgery
Disequilibrium, falls	Gait and safety training, canes, weighted walkers, handrails, grab bars, low-heel nonstick shoes
Drooling	Conscious swallowing, drying medications, botulinum toxin
Dysarthria	Facial exercises, speech therapy, written communication, talking keyboard
Dysphagia	Head posturing, dietary changes, gastrostomy
Dystonia	Anticholinergic drugs, clonazepam, botulinum toxin, surgery
Freezing of gait	Visual cues, rhythmic cues, arc (not pivot) turns
Hypophonia	Speech therapy (posture, breathing, swallowing, speaking), voice amplifiers
Micrographia	Change pen or wrist position, keyboard device
Myoclonus	Clonazepam, valproate
Oculomotor palsy	Prisms, pursuit (not saccade) movements, levodopa
Parkinsonism	Exercise, levodopa, dopamine agonists, amantadine, other medications, physical and occupational therapy
Tremor (action type)	Primidone, propranolol, metazolamide, gabapentin

AUTONOMIC PROBLEMS	AVAILABLE TREATMENTS
Constipation	Increase fluids and fiber, exercise, bulk-forming agents, laxatives, suppositories, enemas
Postural hypotension	Eliminate causative drugs, increase salt and fluid intake, elevate head of bed, eat smaller meals, physical maneuvers, schedule afternoons for activity, midodrine, fludrocortisone, other medications, elastic stockings
Sexual dysfunction	Sildenafil, vardenafil, tadalafil, yohimbine, papaverine, vacuum pump, penile implant
Urinary incontinence/ retention	Treat infection, oxybutinin, tolterodine, incontinence pads/diapers, catheterization

OTHER PROBLEMS	AVAILABLE TREATMENTS
Cognitive impairment	Simplify routines, reminders, rivastigmine, donepezil, galantamine, memantine, tacrine
Psychosis	Quetiapine and clozapine
Dental care	Avoid dry mouth, electric toothbrush
Depression	Psychotherapy, antidepressant medication
Hypersomnia	Treat insomnia, treat obstructive sleep apnea, stimulant medication
Insomnia	Treat depression, behavioral treatment, hypnotics
REM-sleep behavior disorder	Clonazepam
Restless legs syndrome	Dopamine agonists, levodopa, clonazepam, gabapentin, opiates
Stridor	Tracheostomy

and poorly understood, contradictory medications may yield benefit in different patients. Methysergide, a serotonin antagonist (in contrast with serotonergic antidepressants), initially resulted in success when used in some PSP patients; however, with further experience it has been abandoned as ineffective. Similarly, anticholinergic drugs may occasionally improve motor symptoms, while the cholinesterase inhibitors may support cognitive function. Amantadine is less effective than other antiparkinsonian drugs, but worth trying. In the now discarded category of noradrenergic agonists, idazoxan was somewhat effective for PSP but poorly tolerated, while efaroxan was better tolerated but ineffective. Limited studies of electroconvulsive therapy suggest that it offers some benefit for the parkinsonism, but practical difficulties and posttreatment confusion limit its usefulness. The multifocal pathologic nature of PSP thwarts potential benefit from stereotactic surgery, as it does for medications.

Exercise is an important measure for motor symptoms. Physical and occupational therapy may be valuable for limitations of gait and motor independence. Hypophonia is best treated with breathing exercises, which may be taught by a speech therapist. Drooling patients need to be reminded to swallow consciously. The side effect of dry mouth caused by anticholinergic drugs such as atropine and glycopyrrolate can be exploited to relieve drooling. Botulinum toxin injections into the parotid and submandibular glands may also be helpful. Changing pens, stiffening the wrist, or typing may circumvent handwriting difficulties. Balance problems are poorly responsive to any intervention, although patients and families occasionally state that they benefit from canes or walkers. Patients need frequent reminders to take precautionary measures against falls.

Dysarthria may be helped by facial exercises, but written or keyboard communication is often a necessary substitute. A formal swallowing evaluation is mandatory for dysphagia, which is best managed in early stages by a speech therapist who will advise patients and families regarding the mechanics of swallowing and possibly advantageous changes in the consistency of foods. In later stages, gastrostomy is often required. The leading cause of death in PSP is aspiration pneumonia (42). Dystonia is typically poorly responsive to medication (clonazepam, anticholinergics), but botulinum toxin may be very helpful, especially for blepharospasm. Management of nonmotor complications such as depression is similar to that of depressed patients without PSP.

MULTIPLE SYSTEM ATROPHY

From a tentative beginning 4 decades ago in the discussion of a single case report (43), the concept that striatonigral degeneration (SND), sporadic olivopontocerebellar atrophy (OPCA), and Shy-Drager syndrome (SDS) are variants of one and the same disease has taken firm hold. Multiple system atrophy (MSA) has emerged as the most difficult disease to distinguish from PD. The name not only describes the pathology but also helps keep in mind the various combinations of clinical manifestations encountered in MSA.

Clinical Findings

The clinical manifestations of MSA are often divided into motor and autonomic categories, the latter reflecting the involvement of the autonomic nervous system that is emphasized in descriptions of SDS. The motor syndromes can be subdivided into basal ganglia (chiefly parkinsonism) and cerebellar types, known as MSA-P and MSA-C, respectively reflecting the presence of SND and OPCA. The most common presentation of MSA is parkinsonism, but cerebellar or autonomic symptoms may also predominate as initial features. These distinctions become arbitrary over time, since one sees all permutations of disease manifestations as MSA evolves. Ultimately, over 85% of MSA patients develop parkinsonism, about 75% have autonomic problems, and over 50% show evidence of cerebellar degeneration (44). Thus, categorization as MSA-P or MSA-C is usually relevant only to the initial presentation, and sometimes the referral pattern through the health care system is affected until the time of diagnosis. However, the concept of dividing MSA into clinical subtypes is useful for purposes of research and management.

As with the other diseases discussed in this chapter, the parkinsonism of MSA tends to manifest as akinesia, rigidity, and early postural instability, with tremor being uncommon. However, MSA mimics PD more closely than PSP in the prominence of limb involvement, often asymmetric, and the less striking postural instability. Cerebellar findings in MSA include limb ataxia, a wide-based gait, dysarthric and scanning speech, and nystagmus. Dystonia is often quite prominent, with the most common manifestations being antecollis, limb dystonia, and levodopa-induced action dystonia of facial muscles (45). Other motor signs (spasticity, hyperreflexia, Babinski signs) are attributable to involvement of the corticospinal tract as it courses through the pons. Common autonomic symptoms include orthostatic light-headedness, syncope, urinary retention or incontinence, impotence (in males) or anorgasmia (in females), fecal incontinence, loss of sweating, and paroxysmal bursts of excessive sweating. Other clinical features of MSA may include action myoclonus, respiratory stridor (46), dysphonia, Raynaud's phenomenon, pain, contractures, and rapid-eye-movement (REM) sleep behavior disorder, which may precede motor manifestations (47).

A consensus committee published formal criteria for the clinical diagnosis of MSA (48). The essential elements of diagnosis were felt to be a combination of autonomic dysfunction and either cerebellar ataxia or parkinsonism poorly responsive to levodopa.

Epidemiology and Genetics

The mean age of onset of MSA, at 54 years, is slightly younger than that for PD and considerably younger than that for PSP. The youngest reported age of onset was 31. The prevalence has been determined to approximate 3 per 100,000 population (49).

Current criteria specify that the diagnosis of MSA should be restricted to patients with sporadic disease (48, 50); thus familial cases are unknown. Although adherence to this diagnostic principle enhances the specificity of criteria for clinical research purposes, it closes off what has been a fruitful avenue of research for PD and PSP. In part, the reasons for adopting this posture are historical. Authorities in this field have only recently managed to persuade medical orthodoxy to accept that sporadic OPCA occurring in the context of MSA is a different disease from hereditary OPCA (also known as spinocerebelllar ataxia). It may simply be too soon to turn around and advance the argument that some cases of MSA are inherited but still distinct from familial OPCA. One can predict, however, that familial cases of MSA will eventually be discovered, as has occurred with nearly every other common degenerative neurologic disease. Identification of a biological marker for MSA would naturally make this task much easier.

Investigations

There is no definitive diagnostic test for MSA. We have available a "battery of nonspecific tests in which abnormal results help to sway the balance of diagnostic probability" (50). "Two types of investigations are particularly useful in supporting a diagnosis of MSA, autonomic studies and imaging. Formal autonomic testing can provide evidence of widespread autonomic dysfunction in a patient with a single autonomic symptom or sign, or it can detect dysautonomia in a patient with a pure parkinsonian or cerebellar syndrome. A cardiovascular battery, including tilt table testing and measurement of cardiac responses to deep breathing and the Valsalva maneuver, and urodynamic testing are common tools for such clinical situations." However, autonomic testing cannot reliably distinguish MSA from PD in individual patients (51). Anal sphincter electromyography (EMG) may show denervation signifying degeneration of Onuf's nucleus, but this too has proven to be nonspecific.

Imaging studies may be of diagnostic value. Computed tomography (CT) scans are relatively insensitive to changes in MSA but may detect evidence of cerebellar, pontine or putaminal atrophy. Far more helpful has been MRI, which is not only more sensitive to changes in structural appearance but also may show evidence of metabolic dysfunction. A variety of MRI abnormalities have been associated with MSA. Putaminal atrophy, a hyperintense lateral putaminal rim, and infratentorial signal change (hyperintense middle cerebellar peduncles, transverse pontine fibers and midline raphe) on T2-weighted or proton density images are thought to be highly sensitive findings in MSA (52). Degeneration of pontine fibers is thought to be the basis for the "hot cross bun" sign (53). A combination of dorsolateral putaminal hypointensity with a lateral linear hyperintensity on T2-weighted studies may be particularly characteristic (54).

Nerve conduction studies may disclose a mild sensorimotor polyneuropathy, although clinical evidence is much less common than upper motor neuron signs. Sleep studies in the majority of MSA patients demonstrate abnormalities consisting of REM sleep behavior disorder, obstructive sleep apnea, and periodic limb movements during sleep (55).

Pathology

The gross findings at autopsy can include atrophy and darkening of the putamina and atrophy of the pons and cerebellum. Depigmentation of the substantia nigra may be present but is not universal. Microscopic examination reveals a distribution of degenerative changes (neuronal loss, astrocytosis) involving the putamen, substantia nigra, pontine nuclei, Purkinje cell layer of the cerebellum, inferior olives, locus ceruleus, and intermediolateral columns of the spinal cord. Involvement of the basal ganglia (SND) is more common than that of the cerebellum (OPCA) (56).

The hallmark of the microscopic pathology of MSA is the finding of oligodendroglial inclusions known as glial cytoplasmic inclusions (GCIs) (57). These are found not only in the areas of greatest neuronal degeneration but also in the frontal cortex, globus pallidus, and cerebral and cerebellar white matter. Electron microscopy reveals that GCIs are composed of tubular filaments 20 to 30 nm in diameter. Immunostaining identifies α-synuclein as a major constituent of GCIs, as it is of Lewy bodies.

Management

The management of MSA is more difficult than that of PD because of the greater resistance of its motor manifestations to medications, and the wider assortment of problems usually encountered. Nevertheless, many of its symptoms are amenable to therapy (Table 57-2). Ten percent of MSA patients may show a dramatic response to levodopa, comparable to that of patients with PD (50). Overall, however, only one-third of MSA patients show any response to levodopa, and then the response is almost always atypical in some way. If levodopa is unsuccessful or poorly tolerated, it is worth pursuing treatment with dopamine agonists or amantadine, because individual patients may respond better to one of these agents. There is no consistently effective treatment for the cerebellar manifestations, but isoniazid, clonazepam, or wrist weights occasionally dampen an ataxic tremor. Spasticity almost never reaches the point of requiring therapy.

Autonomic disturbances are the most amenable to treatment (58). A variety of measures are effective for orthostatic hypotension (59, 60). A priority is to identify and reduce or eliminate medications that may be contributing to the problem. Nonpharmacologic measures include elevating the head of the bed, increasing salt and fluid intake, avoiding heat, and adopting specific body postures such as crossing the legs or squatting. Elastic stockings are effective but poorly tolerated due to the annoyance of constant pressure on the legs and the heat of summer. Orthostatic hypotension is most pronounced on getting up after prolonged recumbence, as in the morning, and best in the middle of the day. Slow, staged arising from bed is advised, and activities are best scheduled during afternoons. Smaller meals make lower demands on the circulatory system. The most effective medications for orthostatic hypotension are the peripheral alpha-adrenergic antagonist midodrine and the mineralocorticoid fludrocortisone. Other potentially useful medications include low-dose propranolol, pyridostigmine, desmopressin, phenylpropanolamine, yohimbine, and indomethacin.

Urinary incontinence may be related to detrusor hyperreflexia, which may respond to anticholinergics such as oxybutinin or tolterodine. Urinary retention usually can be managed by intermittent catheterization. Either of these problems may ultimately require indwelling catheterization. Consultation with a urologist to diagnose and treat these ailments is highly recommended. Male sexual dysfunction may also be treated with a variety of pharmacologic and nonpharmacologic measures, which are also best directed by a urologist. Patients with parkinsonism are frequently constipated. There are numerous measures to relieve this: increased fluid intake, exercise, a high-fiber diet, bulk-forming agents, laxatives, and others. Respiratory stridor demands a consultation with an otolaryngologist. Tracheostomy may be indicated.

CORTICAL-BASAL GANGLIONIC DEGENERATION

In 1968, a report entitled "corticodentatonigral degeneration with neuronal achromasia" (61) described 3 cases of the disorder we now know as corticobasal ganglionic degeneration (CBGD), often abbreviated as corticobasal degeneration. No further attention was paid to CBGD until 1985. Since then, however, it has generated a level of interest comparable to that of PSP and MSA.

Clinical Findings

The most striking aspect of the clinical picture of CBGD is the asymmetry with which it presents and pursues its course. In this it resembles PD more than any other type of degenerative parkinsonism. However, the addition of other motor findings such as dystonia, myoclonus, and apraxia (62) to the akinesia and rigidity results in CBGD being the least likely of the disorders discussed in this chapter to be mistaken for PD. As is typical of degenerative diseases, CBGD develops insidiously and progresses gradually.

The clinical findings in CBGD can be divided into 3 categories: movement disorders (usually reflecting dysfunction in the basal ganglia), cerebral cortical signs, and others. Parkinsonism in the limbs consist almost exclusively of akinesia and rigidity, with rest tremor being extremely rare. Other evidence of basal ganglia involvement includes dystonia (usually fixed and often causing pronounced and/or painful deformities), postural instability, athetosis, and orofacial dyskinesias. Signs of cerebrocortical dysfunction consist of apraxia, cortical sensory loss, the alien limb phenomenon, dementia, and frontal lobe reflexes. Other manifestations of other or uncertain localization include an action tremor, focal reflex-action myoclonus, hyperreflexia, Babinski signs, and impaired ocular and eyelid motility.

The above description pertains to "classic" CBGD with a predominantly motor presentation. A variety of proposals for clinical diagnostic criteria have been published, the latest being by Kumar and colleagues (63). The key concept in all these schemes is that patients must demonstrate a combination of signs pointing to both basal ganglia and cerebral cortical involvement. Authors of one pathologic series have suggested that dementia may be the most common clinical syndrome associated with the pathologic picture of CBGD (64). Presentations can also include speech apraxia and progressive aphasia. It should also be noted that the "classic" CBGD picture described above is not specific to CBGD and has been associated with a variety of other pathologic findings (65). Thus, for a variety of reasons, the definitive diagnosis of CBGD requires compatible findings in both clinical and pathologic domains.

Epidemiology and Genetics

CBGD is the least understood of the Parkinson's-plus disorders. Its relatively delayed rise to prominence has led to a lower profile among physicians in general and a presumably high rate of false-negative diagnoses. Nevertheless, it is likely that CBGD is somewhat less common than either PSP or MSA. The average patient with CBGD is similar to one with PSP, a little older than a typical patient with PD. No cases with onset below age 40 have been recognized. The mean life expectancy from onset is 8 years (66). There are no known risk factors.

The hereditary status of CBGD is unclear. One report describes 2 brothers with typical motor findings, but there has been no pathologic confirmation. Two families were reported where the pathology was characteristic of CBGD, but the clinical presentation consisted almost exclusively of cognitive and behavioral deterioration with only rare basal ganglia manifestations (67).

Investigations

The most helpful type of study is brain imaging, either by CT or MRI. This will detect asymmetric atrophy of the cerebral cortex greater on the side opposite that more clinically involved, but this is seen in less than half the cases. Symmetric atrophy occurs in a like number. Signal hyperintensities on T2-weighted MRI in subcortical white matter may be found; these have been attributed to gliosis (68). A few patients will have normal imaging (69). Other routine studies are normal. Positron emission tomography (PET) may demonstrate asymmetric striatal uptake of fluorolevodopa, and reduction of cortical metabolism using fluorodeoxyglucose as a marker.

Pathology

The clinical findings and imaging studies presage the pathologic findings. The cerebral cortex and basal ganglia, particularly the substantia nigra, carry the burden of disease. Macroscopically, there is usually visible cerebral atrophy, often asymmetric and predominating in the medial areas of the frontal and parietal lobes. Sectioning of the brain usually reveals pallor of the substantia nigra.

Under the microscope the abnormalities follow the same pattern. In the cerebral cortex—particularly the superior frontal, precentral, and postcentral gyri—are abundant swollen ("ballooned") poorly staining ("achromatic") neurons amid nonspecific degenerative changes. These abnormal neurons are the most characteristic pathologic finding of CBGD. They do not contain discrete inclusion bodies such as neurofibrillary tangles or Pick bodies, but some surviving nonswollen cortical neurons do contain tau-positive inclusions. However, CBGD distinguishes itself from other tauopathies in that tau immunoreactivity predominates in cellular processes rather than in cell bodies, and these processes are mainly of glial origin. Tau-positive "astrocytic plaques" in CBGD (70) are distinct from the "tufted astrocytes" of fellow tauopathy PSP (71). Oligodendroglial inclusions, known as coiled bodies, may be identified. In the substantia nigra, neuronal loss, depig-

mentation, extraneuronal melanin, and gliosis are found. Some residual nigral neurons contain inclusions known as corticobasal bodies that are morphologically similar to NFTs. Tau-positive cell processes and glial abnormalities are abundant here as well. The putamen, caudate nucleus, globus pallidus, and subthalamic nucleus usually show similar changes to a more modest degree. The tau that accumulates in CBGD contains the same 4-repeat isoforms as seen in PSP.

Management

As with the other disorders discussed, there is no specific treatment for CBGD; therapy is currently purely symptomatic (see Table 57-2) (40). Parkinsonism in CBGD is particularly resistant to treatment, and medication rarely provides any meaningful benefit. Somewhat more amenable to therapy are the myoclonus (with clonazepam or valproate) and dystonia (with botulinum toxin) (72), but treatment of CBGD is usually a dismal exercise in frustration for patients, families, and physicians.

DEMENTIA WITH LEWY BODIES

Of all these disorders, dementia with Lewy bodies (DLB) is the one that most deserves the appellation "Parkinson's plus." DLB is best regarded as one facet of a triad of dementia, parkinsonism, and dysautonomia with underlying degenerative and Lewy body pathology (73–75), often called "diffuse Lewy body disease." When dementia is the presenting feature, this disease is diagnosed as DLB; when it begins as parkinsonism, we recognize it as PD; when dysautonomia is the initial manifestation, it is called pure autonomic failure (76). Much like MSA, the 3 component disorders of DLB can be seen in any sequence or combination (77).

Although some investigators maintain a division between DLB and the dementia that complicates preexisting PD (Parkinson's disease dementia, or PDD) (78), the consensus committee that originally drew this distinction stated from the start that this was an arbitrary distinction intended to define a research cohort rather than reflect any true clinical or pathologic difference (79). The notion of the identity of DLB and PDD is supported by their common clinical (80, 81), neuropsychological (82–84), anatomic (85), and metabolic (86–88) imaging, and pathologic (89–92) manifestations. Reported differences between the two disorders are sequential, quantitative, and topographic rather than qualitative. Most authors currently accept the concept that DLB and PDD are the same disorder with differing presentations (80, 93, 94).

Indeed, the intraneuronal inclusions that give DLB its name were first described by Friederich Lewy in the basal forebrain and dorsal motor nucleus of patients with PD (95). Tretiakoff would later name these inclusions "Lewy bodies." It was not until 1961 that a syndrome associating cortical Lewy bodies with dementia was described (96). Recent advances in ubiquitin and alpha-synuclein immunocytochemistry have led to the emergence of an increasingly well-defined syndrome, DLB. Owing to the complex nature of this syndrome, a consensus committee was organized to draw up diagnostic guidelines. First published in 1996 (79), the consensus criteria have already undergone 2 revisions (97, 98).

Clinical Findings

The defining clinical feature of DLB is dementia. The cognitive impairment in DLB can manifest itself in numerous ways, including memory impairment, problems in executing multistepped tasks, losing one's train of thought, or spatial disorientation. Major distinguishing features from Alzheimer's-type dementia include the much greater incidences of psychosis and cognitive fluctuations in DLB. Hallucinations are typically visual in nature, and the subjects are usually human and mute. In mild cases, patients retain insight into the hallucinations; they can describe them and ignore their presence. In more advanced cases, patients may feel alarmed or threatened; they may telephone police or emergency services for help. Even when patients later acknowledge the absurdity of their psychosis, the utter realism that these hallucinations manifest may make it difficult for patients to accept their imaginary nature. DLB psychosis can also manifest as delusions, typically with a paranoid theme such as theft or infidelity. Cognitive fluctuations in DLB can involve variations in level of alertness or lucidity (99). Patients with DLB suffer from excess somnolence (100) and often spend the majority of their time in sleep. They frequently exhibit episodes of staring unresponsiveness (sometimes called "zoning out" episodes, or similar names, by caregivers) or times when their flow of ideas seems disorganized, unclear, or illogical, punctuating periods of relatively intact cognitive function (101).

In addition to cognitive and psychiatric features, the manifestations of clinical DLB include parkinsonism consistent with PD, REM sleep behavior disorder, and autonomic dysfunction (98). Although it is often stated that DLB patients do not respond well to levodopa, this likely reflects the conflicting effects of levodopa on cognition (102), which is also true of PD patients with subsequent dementia and limitations on dosage due to mental side effects. From a motor standpoint, 75% of DLB patients improve on levodopa (103). Historically, dysautonomia has been more closely related to PD than DLB but nevertheless is clearly associated with DLB as well (104–107). Indeed, autonomic dysfunction is common in DLB, where it may be even more pronounced than in PD (105, 108), suggesting that DLB can be associated with more widespread Lewy body pathology than PD. Patients with DLB demonstrate the same postganglionic cardiac sympathetic denervation as those with PD (109–111); paroxysmal orthostatic hypotension may be responsible for many of the cognitive fluctuations reported in DLB, particularly as characterized by staring unresponsiveness (104). The most common autonomic manifestation in DLB is orthostatic intolerance or the inability to tolerate standing upright, typically due to a loss of blood pressure in that position (105).

The above clinical description is reflected in the diagnostic criteria developed by the DLB Consortium (98). The consortium outlined criteria for (a) probable, (b) possible, and (c) no diagnosis of DLB. According to these criteria, any diagnosis of DLB requires the "central" feature of dementia, typically associated with deficits on tests of attention, executive function, and visuospatial ability. For a diagnosis of "probable" DLB, 2 of 3 "core" features—namely fluctuating cognition, recurrent visual hallucinations, and spontaneous (i.e., not drug-induced) parkinsonism—are required. Alternatively, a diagnosis of probable DLB may be made in the presence of one core feature and one of the following "suggestive" features: REM sleep behavior disorder, severe neuroleptic sensitivity, or low dopamine transporter uptake in basal ganglia (all phenomena associated with PD) on single photon emission computed tomography (SPECT) or PET. Any core or suggestive feature in isolation in a demented patient leads to a diagnosis of "possible" DLB. Clinical features "supportive" of the diagnosis of DLB are common but lack diagnostic specificity and include repeated falls, syncope, transient losses of consciousness, autonomic dysfunction, delusions, and depression. Factors weighing against a diagnosis of DLB are cerebovascular disease, other physical illness, neurologic disorders, or onset of parkinsonism at a severe stage of dementia (the arbitrary distinction discussed above). Diagnostic accuracy using previous versions of the DLB Consortium criteria has consistently combined high specificity with low sensitivity (112).

Epidemiology and Genetics

Accurate epidemiologic data regarding DLB are sparse. Clinical recognition and diagnostic pathologic studies are relatively recent in origin. Thus incidence and prevalence estimates continue to grow; they vary widely in the limited number of available studies (113). DLB is now recognized as the second most common cause of dementia, probably responsible for 10% to 20% of all cases (112). There is a mild but consistent male predominance. The age of onset is typically between 50 and 80 years. No epidemiologic studies have established any identifiable environmental risk factors. Although most cases of DLB are not familial, pathologic studies have determined that having a parent with cortical Lewy body disease confers a risk of developing dementia in offspring of up to 20% (91). The E46K mutation of the *alpha-synuclein* gene may produce a syndrome of DLB as well as PD (114, 115).

Investigations

There is no definitive laboratory test for DLB, although several studies can aid in diagnosis, particularly in distinguishing DLB from AD. Low dopamine transporter (DAT) uptake in the basal ganglia, as assessed by SPECT or PET imaging, favors a diagnosis of DLB over AD (116, 117). Metaiodobenzoguanidine (MIBG), which quantifies postganglionic sympathetic innervation to the heart, is reduced in DLB and normal in AD (109, 110). Anatomic MRI findings in DLB should reflect relative preservation of hippocampal and medial temporal lobe volume with atrophy of the putamen.

Pathology

The fundamental pathologic finding in DLB is the presence of abundant Lewy bodies in cerebral cortex (91). The classic Lewy body is a microscopic structure 5 to 30 μm in diameter. It is a cytoplasmic (intracellular and extranuclear) inhabitant with a dense eosinophilic center and a pale outer region on hematoxylin and eosin staining. Under the electron microscope, the core is composed of dense granular material, while the halo contains radially arrayed filaments. In recent years, we have come to recognize that Lewy bodies of the cerebral cortex have a less stratified and more homogeneous appearance, essentially resembling a core without a halo. The chemical composition of Lewy bodies remained largely a mystery until 1997, when Polymeropoulos and colleagues discovered that the gene carrying the mutation in a family with autosomal dominant PD coded for the protein α-synuclein (118). Further study led to the discovery that Lewy bodies, even in sporadic cases, consist of dense aggregations of α-synuclein along with a multitude of other proteins including parkin, ubiquitin, ubiquitin C-terminal hydrolase L1 (UCH-L1), synphilin 1, torsin A, Pael-R, a number of other components of the ubiquitin-proteasome system, and heat-shock proteins (119–121). Perhaps equally notable is the absence of other major proteins such as DJ-1 (122) and non-alpha forms of synuclein. Tau is usually considered absent as well, although it has been spotted in the periphery of some Lewy bodies (123).

The DLB Consortium revised its recommendations for identifying cortical Lewy bodies and Lewy neurites to include immunohistochemical staining for α-synuclein (89). The consortium also emphasized semiquantitative grading of inclusion density into 5 categories: none, mild, moderate, severe, and very severe. At autopsy, coinciding neuropathologic findings consistent with AD (cortical amyloid plaques and neurofibrillary tangles) are frequently seen (124).

Management

Effective management of DLB rests on the prerequisites of accurate diagnosis and prompt recognition of complications. As with other degenerative diseases, treatment is symptomatic in nature. The main symptoms amenable to treatment are cognitive decline, psychosis, REM sleep behavior disorder, parkinsonism, and autonomic complications.

First-line treatment for cognitive impairment consists of cholinesterase inhibition (125, 126), which is sometimes felt to be more effective in DLB than AD (103). Cholinesterase inhibitors may improve not only cognitive impairment but also hallucinosis, delusions, and sleep disturbances (93, 127). Psychosis can be treated with quetiapine or clozapine with minimal risk of aggravating parkinsonism (126, 128).

Levodopa therapy is the most appropriate therapy for parkinsonism in DLB owing to its efficacy (103) and relatively low incidence of cognitive side effects. Anticholinergic medications, on the other hand, have the highest propensity among antiparkinsonian medications to cause cognitive and psychiatric side effects and should be avoided. Treatment of depression is identical to that of depression outside of DLB. Clonazepam at bedtime can be helpful for REM sleep behavior disorder. For a discussion of management of autonomic complications, see Table 57-2. In all cases, owing to the precarious cognitive state of patients, care should be given to starting pharmacologic therapy with small doses and keeping dosage adjustments small. Nonpharmacologic treatments involve patient and caregiver awareness, increased daily stimulation, and supplemental aids for activities of daily living, including weighted utensils and writing devices and physical and speech therapy.

FRONTOTEMPORAL DEMENTIA WITH PARKINSONISM

The term *frontotemporal dementia and parkinsonism linked to chromosome 17* (FTDP-17) has been coined to unify a group of hereditary disorders that share important clinical and pathologic features (129) as well as a genetic basis of mutations in the *tau* and *progranulin* genes on the long arm of chromosome 17. FTDP-17 is included in this chapter because of the link to tauopathies, PSP, and CBGD. However, it is the obvious exception among these diseases in that there are confirmatory diagnostic tests, even though gene sequencing is not yet routine or widely available.

Although individual kindreds express seemingly distinctive clinical features, the presentation of FTDP-17 can be roughly categorized as either dementia or parkinsonism. If cognitive changes predominate, other manifestations including parkinsonism tend to occur late or not at all. In these patients behavioral abnormalities may be striking, including aggression, disinhibition, irritability, withdrawal, and paranoid actions. If an akinetic-rigid syndrome develops first, dementia soon follows, and there are a greater variety of additional features such as amyotrophy, dystonia, spasticity, and ocular motor dysfunction. This broad division may reflect the presence of mutations in different regions of the *tau* and *progranulin* genes. However, this is likely an oversimplification in view of the clinical heterogeneity within families. For example, in one family with FTDP-17, the father developed a typical dementia while his son presented with a motor syndrome suggestive of CBGD (130).

The pathologic findings of FTDP-17 reflect the clinical features. The most consistent abnormality is atrophy, often with spongiform changes, of the cerebral cortex, predominating in the frontal and temporal lobes. Depigmentation, neuronal loss, and gliosis in the substantia nigra are common. Degeneration of other basal ganglia—including the caudate nucleus, putamen, and subthalamic nucleus—may be prominent (131). A variety of tau-positive neuronal and glial inclusions are present.

Recognition of FTDP-17 is a recent phenomenon, and cases remain rare.

CONCLUSION

Growing interest in Parkinson's-plus diseases has resulted in the accumulation of an impressive body of information about PSP, MSA, CBGD, and DLB. Yet we are unable to make fundamental changes in the outlook for patients because the etiology and pathogenesis have eluded the grasp of research so far, and it appears that we remain a long way from developing definitive treatments. Fortunately, frustration has not set in, and efforts at untangling this mysterious area of neurology have intensified. Never has the degree of interest in these disorders been as great as it is at present.

Much of the recent scientific excitement surrounding Parkinson's-plus diseases stems from the realization that mutations in the *tau* gene produce nervous system disease that is not far removed from PSP and CBGD. The potential that the study of FTDP-17 holds for shedding light on the etiology and pathophysiology of PSP and CBGD is enormous. Furthermore, the discovery of FTDP-17 has accelerated a paradigm shift in the nosology of degenerative diseases, moving from clinicopathologic entities to clinicopathogenetic correlations. Unfortunately, this has reminded us that although genetic knowledge gives us crucial information regarding the identity or multiplicity of hereditary conditions, it is insufficient to predict either clinical or pathologic effects on the nervous system. Production of seemingly disparate clinical and pathologic syndromes from identical mutations is common to many genes other than that coding for tau (132). Clearly we will need to understand more than simply the genetic trigger to explain how members of the same family with the same mutations develop different clinicopathologic "entities."

Nevertheless, optimism that we are near to solving a major riddle of this complex puzzle is difficult to restrain. The identification of biological markers for specific diseases, which is among the most coveted of research goals, seems almost within our grasp. Perhaps the closest of these diseases to being understood is PSP, because of the number of well-documented affected families. The information we derive from them should enlighten us to a great degree about the pathogenesis and pathophysiology of PSP in general. The most encouraging development in this field has been the increasing dedication to study of all the diseases discussed in this chapter.

References

1. Parkinson J. *An Essay on the Shaking Palsy.* London: Sherwood, Neely, and Jones; 1817.
2. Rajput AH, Rozdilsky B, Rajput A. Accuracy of clinical diagnosis in parkinsonism—Aa prospective study. *Can J Neurol Sci* 1991; 18(3):275–278.
3. Hughes AJ, Daniel SE, Kilford L, Lees AJ. Accuracy of clinical diagnosis of idiopathic Parkinson's disease: A clinico-pathological study of 100 cases. *J Neurol Neurosurg Psychiatry* 1992; 55(3):181–184.
4. Quinn N. Multiple system atrophy—The nature of the beast. *J Neurol Neurosurg Psychiatry* 1989; (Suppl):78–89.
5. Steele JC, Richardson JC, Olszewski J. Progressive supranuclear palsy. *Arch Neurol* 1964; 10:333–359.
6. Williams DR, Watt HC, Lees AJ. Predictors of falls and fractures in bradykinetic rigid syndromes: A retrospective study. *J Neurol Neurosurg Psychiatry* 2006; 77(4):468–473.
7. Williams DR, de Silva R, Paviour DC, et al. Characteristics of two distinct clinical phenotypes in pathologically proven progressive supranuclear palsy: Richardson's syndrome and PSP-parkinsonism. *Brain* 2005; 128(Pt 6):1247–1258.
8. Dubois B, Slachevsky A, Pillon B, et al. "Applause sign" helps to discriminate PSP from FTD and PD. *Neurology* 2005; 64(12):2132–2133.
9. Golbe LI, Davis PH, Schoenberg BS, Duvoisin RC. Prevalence and natural history of progressive supranuclear palsy. *Neurology* 1988; 38(7):1031–1034.
10. Litvan I, Mangone CA, McKee A, et al. Natural history of progressive supranuclear palsy (Steele-Richardson-Olszewski syndrome) and clinical predictors of survival: A clinicopathological study. *J Neurol Neurosurg Psychiatry* 1996; 60(6):615–620.
11. Riley DE, Fogt N, Leigh RJ. The syndrome of "pure akinesia" and its relationship to progressive supranuclear palsy. *Neurology* 1994; 4(6):1025–1029.
12. Litvan I, Agid Y, Calne D, et al. Clinical research criteria for the diagnosis of progressive supranuclear palsy (Steele-Richardson-Olszewski syndrome): Report of the NINDS–SPSP international workshop. *Neurology* 1996; 47(1):1–9.
13. Bower JH, Maraganore DM, McDonnell SK, Rocca WA. Incidence of progressive supranuclear palsy and multiple system atrophy in Olmsted County, Minnesota, 1976 to 1990. *Neurology* 1997; 49(5):1284–1288.
14. Kawashima M, Miyake M, Kusumi M, et al. Prevalence of progressive supranuclear palsy in Yonago, Japan. *Mov Disord* 2004; 19(10):1239–1240.

15. Sibon I, Macia F, Vital A, et al. Hypertension and progressive supranuclear palsy: Is everything so clear? *Mov Disord* 2004; 19(10):1259–1261.

16. Tetrud JW, Golbe LI, Forno LS, Farmer PM. Autopsy-proven progressive supranuclear palsy in two siblings. *Neurology* 1996; 46(4):931–934.

17. Bennett P, Bonifati V, Bonuccelli U, et al. Direct genetic evidence for involvement of tau in progressive supranuclear palsy. European Study Group on Atypical Parkinsonism Consortium. *Neurology* 1998; 51(4):982–985.

18. Morris HR, Janssen JC, Bandmann O, et al. The tau gene A0 polymorphism in progressive supranuclear palsy and related neurodegenerative diseases. *J Neurol Neurosurg Psychiatry* 1999; 66(5):665–667.

19. Ros R, Thobois S, Streichenberger N, et al. A new mutation of the tau gene, G303V, in early-onset familial progressive supranuclear palsy. *Arch Neurol* 2005; 62(9):1444–1450.

20. Ros R, Gomez Garre P, Hirano M, et al. Genetic linkage of autosomal dominant progressive supranuclear palsy to 1q31.1. *Ann Neurol* 2005; 57(5):634–641.

21. Zimprich A, Biskup S, Leitner P, et al. Mutations in LRRK2 cause autosomal-dominant parkinsonism with pleomorphic pathology. *Neuron* 2004; 44(4):601–607.

22. Soliveri P, Monza D, Paridi D, et al. Cognitive and magnetic resonance imaging aspects of corticobasal degeneration and progressive supranuclear palsy. *Neurology* 1999; 53(3):502–507.

23. Adachi M, Kawanami T, Ohshima H, et al. Morning glory sign: A particular MR finding in progressive supranuclear palsy. *Magn Reson Med Sci* 2004; 3(3):125–132.

24. Oba H, Yagishita A, Terada H, et al. New and reliable MRI diagnosis for progressive supranuclear palsy. *Neurology* 2005; 64(12):2050–2055.

25. Paviour DC, Price SL, Stevens JM, et al. Quantitative MRI measurement of superior cerebellar peduncle in progressive supranuclear palsy. *Neurology* 2005; 64(4):675–679.

26. Josephs KA, Whitwell JL, Boeve BF, et al. Rates of cerebral atrophy in autopsy-confirmed progressive supranuclear palsy. *Ann Neurol* 2006; 59(1):200–203.

27. Paviour DC, Price SL, Jahanshahi M, et al. Longitudinal MRI in progressive supranuclear palsy and multiple system atrophy: Rates and regions of atrophy. *Brain* 2006; 129(Pt 4):1040–1049.

28. Litvan I, Mega MS, Cummings JL, Fairbanks L. Neuropsychiatric aspects of progressive supranuclear palsy. *Neurology* 1996; 47(5):1184–1189.

29. Paviour DC, Winterburn D, Simmonds S, et al. Can the frontal assessment battery (FAB) differentiate bradykinetic rigid syndromes? Relation of the FAB to formal neuropsychological testing. *Neurocase* 2005; 11(4):274–282.

30. Millar D, Griffiths P, Zermansky AJ, Burn DJ. Characterizing behavioral and cognitive dysexecutive changes in progressive supranuclear palsy. *Mov Disord* 2006; 21(2):199–207.

31. Josephs KA, Mandrekar JN, Dickson DW. The relationship between histopathological features of progressive supranuclear palsy and disease duration. *Parkinsonism Relat Disord* 2006; 12(2):109–112.

32. Verny M, Jellinger KA, Hauw JJ, et al. Progressive supranuclear palsy: A clinicopathological study of 21 cases. *Acta Neuropathol* 1996; 91(4):427–431.

33. Bergeron C, Pollanen MS, Weyer L, Lang AE. Cortical degeneration in progressive supranuclear palsy. A comparison with cortical-basal ganglionic degeneration. *J Neuropathol Exp Neurol* 1997; 56(6):726–734.

34. Duyckaerts C, Verny M, Hauw JJ. [Recent neuropathology of parkinsonian syndromes]. *Rev Neurol (Paris)* 2003; 159(5 Pt 2):S11–S18.

35. Sergeant N, Wattez A, Delacourte A. Neurofibrillary degeneration in progressive supranuclear palsy and corticobasal degeneration: Tau pathologies with exclusively "exon 10" isoforms. *J Neurochem* 1999; 72(3):1243–1249.

36. Josephs KA, Dickson DW. Diagnostic accuracy of progressive supranuclear palsy in the Society for Progressive Supranuclear Palsy brain bank. *Mov Disord* 2003; 18(9):1018–1026.

37. Osaki Y, Ben–Shlomo Y, Lees AJ, et al. Accuracy of clinical diagnosis of progressive supranuclear palsy. *Mov Disord* 2004; 19(2):181–189.

38. Nieforth KA, Golbe LI. Retrospective study of drug response in 87 patients with progressive supranuclear palsy. *Clin Neuropharmacol* 1993; 16(4):338–346.

39. Kompoliti K, Goetz CG, Litvan I, et al. Pharmacological therapy in progressive supranuclear palsy. *Arch Neurol* 1998; 55(8):1099–1102.

40. Lang AE. Treatment of progressive supranuclear palsy and corticobasal degeneration. *Mov Disord* 2005; 20(Suppl)12:S83–S91.

41. Litvan I, Chase TN. Traditional and experimental therapeutic approaches. In: Litvan I, Agid Y (eds). *Progressive Supranuclear Palsy*. New York: Oxford University Press, 1992:254–269.

42. Nath U, Thomson R, Wood R, et al. Population based mortality and quality of death certification in progressive supranuclear palsy (Steele-Richardson-Olszewski syndrome). *J Neurol Neurosurg Psychiatry* 2006; 76(4):498–502.

43. Graham JG, Oppenheimer DR. Orthostatic hypotension and nicotine sensitivity in a case of multiple system atrophy. *J Neurol Neurosurg Psychiatry* 1969; 32(1):28–34.

44. Wenning GK, Tison F, Ben Shlomo Y, et al. Multiple system atrophy: A review of 203 pathologically proven cases. *Mov Disord* 1997; 12(2):133–147.

45. Boesch SM, Wenning GK, Ransmayr G, Poewe W. Dystonia in multiple system atrophy. *J Neurol Neurosurg Psychiatry* 2002; 72(3):300–303.

46. Glass GA, Josephs KA, Ahlskog JE. Respiratory insufficiency as the primary presenting symptom of multiple-system atrophy. *Arch Neurol* 2006; 63(7):978–981.

47. Gagnon JF, Postuma RB, Mazza S, et al. Rapid-eye-movement sleep behaviour disorder and neurodegenerative diseases. *Lancet Neurol* 2006; 5(5):424–432.

48. Gilman S, Low PA, Quinn N, et al. Consensus statement on the diagnosis of multiple system atrophy. *J Auton Nerv Syst* 1998; 74(2–3):189–192.

49. Vanacore N. Epidemiological evidence on multiple system atrophy. *J Neural Transm* 2005; 112(12):1605–1612.

50. Quinn N. Multiple system atrophy. In: Marsden CD, Fahn S (eds). *Movement Disorders 3*. Oxford, UK: Butterworth-Heinemann, 1994:262–281.

51. Riley DE, Chelimsky TC. Autonomic nervous system testing may not distinguish multiple system atrophy from Parkinson's disease. *J Neurol Neurosurg Psychiatry* 2003; 74(1):56–60.

52. Schrag A, Kingsley D, Phatouros C, et al. Clinical usefulness of magnetic resonance imaging in multiple system atrophy. *J Neurol Neurosurg Psychiatry* 1998; 65(1):65–71.

53. Abe K, Hikita T, Yokoe M, Mihara M, Sakoda S. The "cross" signs in patients with multiple system atrophy: A quantitative study. *J Neuroimaging* 2006; 16(1):73–77.

54. Kraft E, Trenkwalder C, Auer DP. T2–weighted MRI differentiates multiple system atrophy from Parkinson's disease. *Neurology* 2002; 59(8):1265–1267.

55. Plazzi G, Corsini R, Provini F, et al. REM sleep behavior disorders in multiple system atrophy. *Neurology* 1997; 48(4):1094–1097.

56. Ozawa T, Paviour D, Quinn NP, et al. The spectrum of pathological involvement of the striatonigral and olivopontocerebellar systems in multiple system atrophy: Clinicopathological correlations. *Brain* 2004; 127(Pt 12):2657–2671.

57. Lantos PL. The definition of multiple system atrophy: A review of recent developments. *J Neuropathol Exp Neurol* 1998; 57(12):1099–1111.

58. Wenning GK, Geser F, Poewe W. Therapeutic strategies in multiple system atrophy. *Mov Disord* 2005; 20(Suppl 12):S67–S76.

59. Riley DE. Orthostatic hypotension in multiple system atrophy. *Curr Treat Options Neurol* 2000; 2(3):225–230.

60. Colosimo C, Tiple D, Wenning GK. Management of multiple system atrophy: State of the art. *J Neural Transm* 2005; 112(12):1695–1704.

61. Rebeiz JJ, Kolodny EH, Richardson EP Jr. Corticodentatonigral degeneration with neuronal achromasia. *Arch Neurol* 1968; 18(1):20–33.

62. Zadikoff C, Lang AE. Apraxia in movement disorders. *Brain* 2005; 128(Pt 7):1480–1497.

63. Kumar R, Bergeron C, Lang AE. Corticobasal degeneration. In: Jankovic J, Tolosa E (eds). *Parkinson's Disease and Movement Disorders*. 4th ed. Philadelphia: Lippincott Williams & Wilkins, 2002:185–198.

64. Grimes DA, Lang AE, Bergeron CB. Dementia as the most common presentation of cortical-basal ganglionic degeneration. *Neurology* 1999; 53(9):1969–1974.

65. Boeve BF, Maraganore DM, Parisi JE, et al. Pathologic heterogeneity in clinically diagnosed corticobasal degeneration. *Neurology* 1999; 53(4):795–800.

66. Wenning GK, Litvan I, Jankovic J, et al. Natural history and survival of 14 patients with corticobasal degeneration confirmed at postmortem examination. *J Neurol Neurosurg Psychiatry* 1998; 64(2):184–189.

67. Brown J, Lantos PL, Roques P, et al. Familial dementia with swollen achromatic neurons and corticobasal inclusion bodies: A clinical and pathological study. *J Neurol Sci* 1996; 135(1):21–30.

68. Tokumaru AM, O'Uchi T, Kuru Y, et al. Corticobasal degeneration: MR with histopathologic comparison. *AJNR* 1996; 17(10):1849–1852.

69. Ballan G, Tison F, Dousset V, et al. [Study of cortical atrophy with magnetic resonance imaging in corticobasal degeneration]. *Rev Neurol (Paris)* 1998; 154(3):224–227.

70. Feany MB, Dickson DW. Widespread cytoskeletal pathology characterizes corticobasal degeneration. *Am J Pathol* 1995; 146(6):1388–1396.

71. Komori T, Arai N, Oda M, et al. Astrocytic plaques and tufts of abnormal fibers do not coexist in corticobasal degeneration and progressive supranuclear palsy. *Acta Neuropathol (Berl)* 1998; 96(4):401–408.

72. Kompoliti K, Goetz CG, Boeve BF, et al. Clinical presentation and pharmacological therapy in corticobasal degeneration. *Arch Neurol* 1998; 55(7):957–961.

73. de Vos RA, Jansen EN, Stam FC, et al. "Lewy body disease": clinico-pathological correlations in 18 consecutive cases of Parkinson's disease with and without dementia. *Clin Neurol Neurosurg* 1995; 97(1):13–22.

74. McKeith IG. Clinical Lewy body syndromes. *Ann N Y Acad Sci* 2000; 920:1–8.

75. McKeith IG, O'Brien JT, Ballard C. Diagnosing dementia with Lewy bodies. *Lancet* 1999; 354(9186):1227–1228.

76. Kaufmann H, Hague K, Perl D. Accumulation of alpha-synuclein in autonomic nerves in pure autonomic failure. *Neurology* 2001; 56(7):980–981.

77. Riley DE. Lewy body disease. *Arch Neurol* 2002; 59(6):1043.

78. Tsuboi Y, Dickson DW. Dementia with Lewy bodies and Parkinson's disease with dementia: Are they different? *Parkinsonism Relat Disord* 2005; 11(Suppl 1):S47–S51.

79. McKeith IG, Galasko D, Kosaka K, et al. Consensus guidelines for the clinical and pathologic diagnosis of dementia with Lewy bodies (DLB): Report of the consortium on DLB international workshop. *Neurology* 1996; 47(5):1113–1124.

80. Padovani A, Costanzi C, Gilberti N, Borroni B. Parkinson's disease and dementia. *Neurol Sci* 2006; 27(Suppl 1):S40–S43.

81. Janvin CC, Larsen JP, Salmon DP, et al. Cognitive profiles of individual patients with Parkinson's disease and dementia: Comparison with dementia with Lewy bodies and Alzheimer's disease. *Mov Disord* 2006; 21(3):337–342.

82. Aarsland D, Litvan I, Salmon D, et al. Performance on the dementia rating scale in Parkinson's disease with dementia and dementia with Lewy bodies: Comparison with progressive supranuclear palsy and Alzheimer's disease. *J Neurol Neurosurg Psychiatry* 2003; 74(9):1215–1220.

83. Noe E, Marder K, Bell KL, et al. Comparison of dementia with Lewy bodies to Alzheimer's disease and Parkinson's disease with dementia. *Mov Disord* 2004; 19(1):60–67.

84. Collerton D, Burn D, McKeith I, O'Brien J. Systematic review and meta-analysis show that dementia with Lewy bodies is a visual-perceptual and attentional-executive dementia. *Dement Geriatr Cogn Disord* 2003; 16(4):229–237.

85. Burton EJ, McKeith IG, Burn DJ, et al. Cerebral atrophy in Parkinson's disease with and without dementia: A comparison with Alzheimer's disease, dementia with Lewy bodies and controls. *Brain* 2004; 127:791–800.

86. Firbank MJ, Colloby SJ, Burn DJ, et al. Regional cerebral blood flow in Parkinson's disease with and without dementia. *Neuroimage* 2003; 20(2):1309–1319.

87. Kasama S, Tachibana H, Kawabata K, Yoshikawa H. Cerebral blood flow in Parkinson's disease, dementia with Lewy bodies, and Alzheimer's disease according to three-dimensional stereotactic surface projection imaging. *Dement Geriatr Cogn Disord* 2005; 19(5–6):266–275.

88. Colloby SJ, Williams ED, Burn DJ, et al. Progression of dopaminergic degeneration in dementia with Lewy bodies and Parkinson's disease with and without dementia assessed using 123I-FP-CIT SPECT. *Eur J Nucl Med Mol Imaging* 2005; 32(10):1176–1185.

89. Duda JE. Pathology and neurotransmitter abnormalities of dementia with Lewy bodies. *Dement Geriatr Cogn Disord* 2004; 17(Suppl 1):3–14.

90. Camicioli R, Fisher N. Progress in clinical neurosciences: Parkinson's disease with dementia and dementia with Lewy bodies. *Can J Neurol Sci* 2004; 31(1):7–21.

91. Harding AJ, Das A, Kril JJ, et al. Identification of families with cortical Lewy body disease. *Am J Med Genet* 2004; 128B(1):118–122.

92. Guo L, Itaya M, Takanashi M, et al. Relationship between Parkinson disease with dementia and dementia with Lewy bodies. *Parkinsonism Relat Disord* 2005; 11(5):305–309.

93. Williams-Gray CH, Foltynie T, Lewis SJ, Barker RA. Cognitive deficits and psychosis in Parkinson's disease: A review of pathophysiology and therapeutic options. *CNS Drugs* 2006; 20(6):477–505.

94. McKeith IG, Mosimann UP. Dementia with Lewy bodies and Parkinson's disease. *Parkinsonism Relat Disord* 2004; 10(Suppl 1):S15–S18.

95. Lewy FH. *Paralysis Agitans: I. Pathologische Anatomie*. Berlin: Springer, 1912.

96. Galvin JE. Dementia with Lewy bodies. *Arch Neurol* 2003; 60(9):1332–1335.

97. McKeith IG, Perry EK, Perry RH. Report of the second Dementia With Lewy Bodies International Workshop: Diagnosis and treatment. Consortium on Dementia with Lewy Bodies. *Neurology* 1999; 53(5):902–905.

98. McKeith IG, Dickson DW, Lowe J, et al. Diagnosis and management of dementia with Lewy bodies: Third report of the DLB Consortium. *Neurology* 2005; 65(12):1863–1872.

99. Geser F, Wenning GK, Poewe W, McKeith I. How to diagnose dementia with Lewy bodies: State of the art. *Mov Disord* 2005; 20(Suppl 12):S11–S20.

100. Grace JB, Walker MP, McKeith IG. A comparison of sleep profiles in patients with dementia with Lewy bodies and Alzheimer's disease. *Int J Geriatr Psychiatry* 2000; 15(11):1028–1033.

101. Ferman TJ, Smith GE, Boeve BF, et al. DLB fluctuations: Specific features that reliably differentiate DLB from AD and normal aging. *Neurology* 2004; 62(2):181–187.

102. Cools R. Dopaminergic modulation of cognitive function: Implications for L-dopa treatment in Parkinson's disease. *Neurosci Biobehav Rev* 2006; 30(1):1–23.

103. Lebert F, Le Rhun E. [Treatment of dementia with Lewy bodies]. Rev Neurol (Paris) 2006; 162(1):131–136.

104. Horimoto Y, Matsumoto M, Akatsu H, et al. Autonomic dysfunctions in dementia with Lewy bodies. *J Neurol* 2003; 250(5):530–533.

105. Thaisetthawatkul P, Boeve BF, Benarroch EE, et al. Autonomic dysfunction in dementia with Lewy bodies. *Neurology* 2004; 62(10):1804–1809.

106. Allan LM, Ballard CG, Allen J, et al. Autonomic dysfunction in dementia. *J Neurol Neurosurg Psychiatry* 2006.

107. Kashihara K, Ohno M, Kawada S, Okumura Y. Reduced cardiac uptake and enhanced washout of 123I–MIBG in pure autonomic failure occurs conjointly with Parkinson's disease and dementia with Lewy bodies. *J Nucl Med* 2006; 47(7):1099–1101.

108. Suzuki M, Kurita A, Hashimoto M, et al. Impaired myocardial 123I–metaiodobenzylguanidine uptake in Lewy body disease: Comparison between dementia with Lewy bodies and Parkinson's disease. *J Neurol Sci* 2006; 240(1–2):15–19.

109. Yoshita M, Taki J, Yamada M. A clinical role for [(123)I]MIBG myocardial scintigraphy in the distinction between dementia of the Alzheimer's-type and dementia with Lewy bodies. *J Neurol Neurosurg Psychiatry* 2001; 71(5):583–588.

110. Estorch M, Camacho V, Fuertes J, et al. [Dementia with Lewy bodies and Alzheimer's disease: Differential diagnosis by cardiac sympathetic innervation MIBG imaging]. *Rev Esp Med Nucl* 2006; 25(4):229–235.

111. Orimo S, Amino T, Itoh Y, et al. Cardiac sympathetic denervation precedes neuronal loss in the sympathetic ganglia in Lewy body disease. *Acta Neuropathol (Berl)* 2005; 109(6):583–588.

112. McKeith I, Mintzer J, Aarsland D, et al. Dementia with Lewy bodies. *Lancet Neurol* 2004; 3(1):19–28.

113. Zaccai J, McCracken C, Brayne C. A systematic review of prevalence and incidence studies of dementia with Lewy bodies. *Age Ageing* 2005; 34(6):561–566.

114. Zarranz JJ, Alegre J, Gomez–Esteban JC, et al. The new mutation, E46K, of alpha–synuclein causes Parkinson and Lewy body dementia. *Ann Neurol* 2004; 55(2):164–173.

115. Hardy J, Lees AJ. Parkinson's disease: A broken nosology. *Mov Disord* 2005; 20(Suppl 12):S2–S4.

116. Costa DC, Walker Z, Walker RW, Fontes FR. Dementia with Lewy bodies versus Alzheimer's disease: Role of dopamine transporter imaging. *Mov Disord* 2003; 18(Suppl 7):S34–S38.

117. McKeith I, O'Brien J, Walker Z, et al. Sensitivity and specificity of dopamine transporter imaging with 123I–FP–CIT SPECT in dementia with Lewy bodies: A phase III, multicentre study. *Lancet Neurol* 2007; 6(4):305–313.

118. Polymeropoulos MH, Lavedan C, Leroy E, et al. Mutation in the alpha-synuclein gene identified in families with Parkinson's disease. *Science* 1997; 276(5321):2045–2047.

119. Jellinger KA. Neuropathological spectrum of synucleinopathies. *Mov Disord* 2003; 18(Suppl 6):S2–S12.

120. Murakami T, Shoji M, Imai Y, et al. Pael-R is accumulated in Lewy bodies of Parkinson's disease. *Ann Neurol* 2004; 55(3):439–442.

121. Olanow CW, Perl DP, DeMartino GN, McNaught KS. Lewy-body formation is an aggresome-related process: A hypothesis. *Lancet Neurol* 2004; 3(8):496–503.

122. Neumann M, Muller V, Gorner K, et al. Pathological properties of the Parkinson's disease–associated protein DJ-1 in alpha-synucleinopathies and tauopathies: Relevance for multiple system atrophy and Pick's disease. *Acta Neuropathol (Berl)* 2004; 107(6):489–496.

123. Ishizawa T, Mattila P, Davies P, et al. Colocalization of tau and alpha-synuclein epitopes in Lewy bodies. *J Neuropathol Exp Neurol* 2003; 62(4):389–397.

124. Weisman D, McKeith I. Dementia with Lewy bodies. *Semin Neurol* 2007; 27(1):42–47.

125. Maidment I, Fox C, Boustani M. Cholinesterase inhibitors for Parkinson's disease dementia. *Cochrane Database Syst Rev* 2006(1):CD004747.

126. Miyasaki JM, Shannon K, Voon V, et al. Practice parameter: Evaluation and treatment of depression, psychosis, and dementia in Parkinson disease (an evidence-based review): Report of the Quality Standards Subcommittee of the American Academy of Neurology. *Neurology* 2006; 66(7):996–1002.

127. Wesnes KA, McKeith I, Edgar C, et al. Benefits of rivastigmine on attention in dementia associated with Parkinson disease. *Neurology* 2005; 65(10):1654–1656.

128. Poewe W. Treatment of dementia with Lewy bodies and Parkinson's disease dementia. *Mov Disord* 2005; 20(Suppl 12):S77–S82.

129. Foster NL, Wilhelmsen K, Sima AA, et al. Frontotemporal dementia and parkinsonism linked to chromosome 17: A consensus conference. Conference Participants. *Ann Neurol* 1997; 41(6):706–715.

130. Bugiani O, Murrell JR, Giaccone G, et al. Frontotemporal dementia and corticobasal degeneration in a family with a P301S mutation in tau. *J Neuropathol Exp Neurol* 1999; 58(6):667–677.

131. Nasreddine ZS, Loginov M, Clark LN, et al. From genotype to phenotype: A clinical pathological, and biochemical investigation of frontotemporal dementia and parkinsonism (FTDP–17) caused by the P301L tau mutation. *Ann Neurol* 1999; 45(6):704–715.

132. Bird TD. Genotypes, phenotypes, and frontotemporal dementia: Take your pick. *Neurology* 1998; 50(6):1526–1527.

58 Symptomatic Parkinsonism

Sanjay S. Iyer
William T. Garrett
Kapil D. Sethi

arkinson's disease (PD) is an idiopathic condition resulting from degeneration of the pigmented nuclei in the brain, particularly the substantia nigra. The pathologic hallmark is the presence of intracytoplasmic eosinophilic inclusions called Lewy bodies (see Chapter 21). The symptoms are typically asymmetrical and insidious in onset, with gradual progression.

The term "parkinsonism" refers to a variable clinical combination of signs including bradykinesia, tremor, rigidity, and postural instability. Bradykinesia plus 1 of the other 3 signs meets the criteria for parkinsonism. Symptomatic parkinsonism describes a heterogeneous group of disorders due to an identifiable agent or etiology. A variety of etiologies may cause parkinsonism, including infections, drugs, toxins, and structural lesions. In some cases, it may be impossible to distinguish PD from symptomatic parkinsonism by clinical features alone. An extensive review of the medical history and diagnostic tests, such as neuroimaging, can aid in making the correct diagnosis. A classification of symptomatic parkinsonism appears in Table 58-1. The discussion of more widespread central nervous system degenerative diseases causing parkinsonism has been excluded, as they are covered in Chapter 53. In this chapter, various etiologies of symptomatic parkinsonism, their evaluation, and their treatment are discussed.

INFECTION

In 1893, Blocq and Marinesco first reported parkinsonism secondary to infection in a patient with a tuberculoma residing in the substantia nigra (1). In the 1920s, infection with the influenza type A virus was associated with the development of postinfectious parkinsonism in a large number of patients. Since that time, there have been sporadic reports of other infectious processes causing parkinsonism. At present, infectious causes of parkinsonism are very rare.

Encephalitis Lethargica and Postencephalitic Parkinsonism

From 1919 to 1926, there were several pandemic outbreaks of encephalitis lethargica (EL; also known as Von Economo's encephalitis), which presented with headache, fever, somnolence, and ophthalmoplegia (2). After a variable delay, a number of patients developed parkinsonism associated with psychiatric abnormalities, ophthalmoplegia, oculogyric crisis, blepharospasm, and tics (3, 4). In postencephalitic parkinsonism (PEP), tremor tends to be less prominent than in PD, and other movement disorders, like dystonia, may be seen. Oculogyric crisis (OGC) does not occur in PD and is characterized by forceful deviation of the eyes, usually down or upward and laterally (5).

TABLE 58-1
A Classification of Parkinsonism

1. **Infections**
   Encephalitis lethargica and postencephalitic
       parkinsonism
   Other encephalitids
       Western equine encephalitis
       Japanese B encephalitis
       Cytomegalovirus
       West Nile virus
   Human immunodeficiency virus
   Creutzfeldt-Jakob's disease
   Fungal infections
   Mycoplasmal pneumonia
   Tuberculosis
2. **Drug-Induced Parkinsonism (Table 58-2)**
3. **Toxin-Induced Parkinsonism**
   Manganese
   Carbon monoxide
   Cyanide
   Carbon disulfide
   Methyl alcohol
4. **Structural lesions**
   Hydrocephalus
   Brain tumors
   Intracranial hemorrhage
   Multiple infarcts
5. **Miscellaneous**
   Posttraumatic parkinsonism
   Demyelinating disease
   Alcohol withdrawal
   Sjögren's syndrome
   Psychogenic parkinsonism

The attacks are sometimes accompanied by obsessional thoughts, fear, and anxiety. The parkinsonism tends to follow a relatively static course, but the worsening of signs and symptoms is well documented (6).

The clinical features and pathologic findings are similar to those of progressive supranuclear palsy (PSP) (7–9). However, in contrast to PSP, PEP has an earlier age of onset, a history of encephalitis, a longer disease course, OGC, and responsiveness to levodopa (4). The pathology includes devastation of the zona compacta of the substantia nigra and less often the locus ceruleus. Microscopically, Lewy bodies are not seen; instead, neurofibrillary tangles are found. In patients who died soon after disease onset, perivascular cuffing with lymphocytes was seen. Although EL is associated with the influenza type A virus of 1918–1919, the relationship has never been definitively proven.

Parkinsonism is rarely associated with other forms of viral encephalitis, including the arboviruses, measles, polio, coxsackievirus, echoviruses, herpes simplex, varicella, Japanese encephalitis, and Western equine encephalitis (2, 10, 11). Parkinsonian features such as masked

facies, tremor, rigidity, and gait impairment can be seen during the acute infection but usually resolve following recovery from the encephalitis. If parkinsonian symptoms persist, neuroimaging may demonstrate lesions in the substantia nigra, thalamus, and basal ganglia (10).

Before the advent of levodopa, PEP was treated with amphetamines and belladona. Levodopa was shown to be of benefit in a double-blind study (12). The response to levodopa in PEP is inconsistent and may wane after excellent improvement. In a follow-up of 50 patients, one-third continued to benefit, one-third showed no response, and the other patients could not tolerate levodopa (13). OGC may respond to anticholinergics and levodopa. However, levodopa may sometimes worsen OGC.

Other Infectious Etiologies

Neurologic complications, including parkinsonism, may occur in patients with acquired immunodeficiency syndrome (AIDS) (14). The parkinsonian features may be caused by secondary AIDS-associated cerebral infections or primary cerebral infection with human immunodeficiency virus (HIV) alone (14, 15). In addition, AIDS patients are particularly sensitive to neuroleptics and may develop severe drug-induced parkinsonism very quickly and on low doses. Some patients, including children with HIV-associated progressive encephalopathy and parkinsonism, may respond to levodopa (16).

Other infectious processes may also rarely be associated with parkinsonism. Adler et al. described a case of an intravenous drug user with subacute parkinsonism secondary to bilateral fungal striatal abscesses (17). Mycoplasmal pneumonia may lead to bradykinesia and chorea in some children (18). Parkinsonism associated with syphilis and cryptococcal and cysticercal infection has also been described (19–22). Eleven patients have also been reported with parkinsonism as a neurologic manifestation of West Nile virus (23).

DRUG-INDUCED PARKINSONISM

Drug-induced parkinsonism (DIP) is the most common cause of symptomatic parkinsonism. DIP is often misdiagnosed as PD because the clinical features of these conditions may be indistinguishable. Although several medications may be associated with DIP (Table 58-2), dopamine-blocking agents (DBA) are the most common offenders.

Dopamine-Blocking Agents

Parkinsonism may be secondary to DBAs, such as neuroleptics (25, 26) and metoclopramide (27). All classes of neuroleptics have been implicated. Veralipride, a benzamide derivative now used more commonly to treat hot

TABLE 58-2
Drugs Inducing Parkinsonism

Inhibitors of Dopamine Synthesis or Formation of a False Neurotransmitter
Alpha methyl-paratyrosine
Alpha methyldopa

Inhibitors of Presynaptic Dopamine Storage
Reserpine
Tetrabenazine

Blockade of Postsynaptic D2 Receptors:
Neuroleptics

TRADE NAME	GENERIC NAME
1. Phenothiazines	
Compazine	Prochlorperazine
Etrafon (Triavil)	Perphenazine and Amitriptyline
Mellaril	Thiordazine
Phenergan	Promethazine
Prolixin	Fluphenazine
Serentil	Mesoridazine
Stelazine	Trifluoperazine
Thorazine	Chlorpromazine
Torecan	Thiethylperazine
Trilafon	Perphenazine
2. Butyrophenones	
Haldol	Haloperidol
3. Thioxanthenes	
Navane	Thiothixene
4. Benzamides	
Reglan	Metoclopramide
Agreal	Veralipride
5. Dihydroindolone	
Moban	Molindone
6. Dibenzoxazepine	
Loxitane	Loxapine
Miscellaneous D2 Blocking Agents	
Tetrabenazine	
Flunarizine	
Amoxapine	
Trimetazidine	

All motor parkinsonian features may be seen in DIP, including rigidity, bradykinesia, tremor, and a gait disturbance (26, 31). Some authors suggest that symmetric signs and the absence of tremor are typical of DIP (31); however, asymmetric tremor may be seen in 33 to 50 percent of patients (26, 31). In contrast to PD, rigidity is more common than tremor in DIP, but a tremor-dominant disorder may also be seen (26).

The exact pathophysiologic mechanism of DIP is not clear, but it is probably related to direct D2 dopamine receptor blockade. The majority of patients treated with neuroleptic medications will not develop DIP; this suggests that individual susceptibility exists. Risk factors include age, female gender, the use of a higher-potency DBA, and possibly previous brain injury. There is some evidence that patients who develop DIP may have subclinical Lewy body PD, in which disease onset is hastened by the DBA. This unmasking may be the reason that parkinsonism fails to resolve in some patients following withdrawal of the DBA. In a clinicopathologic study of 2 patients with presumed DIP, Lewy bodies were found at autopsy even though the symptoms and signs of parkinsonism had resolved after the DBA was stopped (32). An F-dopa PET study demonstrated similar findings. Patients with DIP and normal putamenal uptake of F-dopa had subsequent improvement in their parkinsonism following neuroleptic cessation, while those with reduced uptake in the putamen had continued or progressive disease despite stopping the offending agent (33).

Treatment of DIP depends largely on the ability to withdraw the offending medication. If it is not possible to withdraw it, patients should be placed on the lowest efficacious dose or changed to an atypical agent such as clozapine or quetiapine. Levodopa treatment has not been studied systematically and the concern is that it may worsen existing psychosis (26). Although anticholinergics may be beneficial, amantadine proved to be superior in one double-blind study (34).

Other Medications Associated with Parkinsonism

Dopamine-depleting agents, such as reserpine and tetrabenazine, may also produce DIP (35). These medications are currently used in the treatment of hyperkinetic movement disorders such as chorea and dystonia. Flunarizine and cinnarizine, calcium channel blockers chemically related to neuroleptics (currently unavailable in the United States), are also associated with parkinsonism. The parkinsonism may persist for long periods (36). Possible mechanisms include prevention of striatal cell activation due to the inhibition of calcium influx vs. direct dopamine receptor antagonism (37). Other calcium channel blockers—including amlodipine, diltiazem, and verapamil (38–40)—have also rarely been associated

flushes, can induce parkinsonism (28). Additionally, reports have implicated two newer atypical antipsychotics, ziprasidone and aripiprazole, as causing DIP (29, 30). DIP may be indistinguishable on physical examination from PD; therefore it may not be recognized (25, 26). The incidence of DIP is between 15% and 40% in patients receiving neuroleptics, and its prevalence increases with age (26). DIP tends to occur subacutely after drug exposure. However, the length of time from the initiation of a neuroleptic drug to the onset of symptoms is variable; in one series, the mean length of exposure was as much as 6.3 years (26).

with parkinsonism. The existence of lithium-induced parkinsonism is debatable (41). While the patients treated with lithium often have tremor and myoclonic jerks, typical parkinsonism appears to be rare. The symptoms resolve after discontinuation of the drug. Trimetazidine, an antianginal agent, has also been reported to cause parkinsonism (42).

A variety of other medications have been rarely associated with parkinsonism. These include chemotherapeutic agents (5-fluorouracil, doxorubicin, and vincristine), cardiac medications (amiodarone, alpha methyldopa), histamine-2 (H2) antagonists (cimetidine), immunosuppressants (cyclosporine), antiepileptics (valproic acid), and antidepressants, including the serotonin-specific reuptake inhibitors trazodone and bupropion (43–52).

TOXIN-INDUCED PARKINSONISM

Parkinsonism may be caused by a variety of toxins, including carbon monoxide, 1-methyl-4-phenyl-1,2,5, 6-tetrahydropyridine (MPTP), manganese, and cyanide. The onset of symptoms is usually subacute following exposure to the toxin and the course may be progressive. Historical clues can suggest possible toxin exposure leading to an appropriate diagnosis.

Carbon Monoxide

Carbon monoxide is a colorless, odorless, nonirritating toxic gas. Sources of carbon monoxide that may lead to poisoning include natural gas, smoke, automobile exhaust, and methylene chloride in paint remover (53). The diagnosis of carbon monoxide exposure is usually suggested by the history and clinical suspicion. The diagnosis is confirmed by elevated carboxyhemoglobin levels in the blood (54).

Clinically, patients with carbon monoxide poisoning present with tachycardia, tachypnea, headache, nausea, syncope, seizures, or coma. The classic findings of cyanosis—cherry-red lips and retinal hemorrhages—rarely occur (54). Delayed clinical presentations include neuropsychiatric symptoms such as cognitive and personality change, psychosis, dementia, and parkinsonism (55). Although all features of parkinsonism may be observed, rigidity, bradykinesia, and postural instability may be more common than tremor (54).

Carbon monoxide is easily absorbed from the lungs and competes with oxygen for binding to hemoglobin. The toxicity appears to result not only from hypoxia but also from direct cellular injury (54). The most common findings on computed tomography (CT) are symmetrical, diffuse, low-density lesions in the globus pallidus and cerebral white matter (53). Changes seen on magnetic resonance imaging (MRI) may be dramatic, with pallidal lesions, representing necrosis, being the dominant feature.

In the acute setting, the patient should be quickly removed from the source of carbon monoxide exposure and treated with 100% oxygen. A carboxyhemoglobin level should be checked; however, that level does not correlate with clinical symptoms. Patients with respiratory compromise may require mechanical ventilatory support. Other than coma, the indications for hyperbaric oxygen therapy are controversial (54). The parkinsonism responds poorly to levodopa. The delayed clinical symptoms may resolve over time (54).

MPTP

MPTP (see Chapter 34) is a chemical by-product of 1-methyl-4-phenyl-4-propionoxy-piperidine (MPPP) synthesis and can contaminate MPPP manufactured in illicit drug operations. In fact, this adulteration is what led to the appearance of MPTP-induced parkinsonism. Irreversible parkinsonism associated with MPTP exposure was originally reported in a drug addict in 1979 (56) and was characterized more fully in 1983 (57).

Acute MPTP intoxication produces symptoms that differ from those due to heroin, such as severe burning at the injection site, dimming of vision during drug injection, and a different feeling of euphoria (57). Individuals exposed to MPTP may develop all the classic features of parkinsonism subacutely, with the onset of symptoms approximately 2 weeks following exposure (56). The most common clinical features include bradykinesia, rigidity, and postural instability. Rest tremor can occur but is much less common than in PD (57). The parkinsonism becomes severe very quickly.

MPTP toxicity results in parkinsonism by selectively damaging dopaminergic neurons in the substantia nigra. After intravenous injection, MPTP crosses the blood-brain barrier and is then converted to 1-methyl-4-phenyl-pyridine (MPP^C) by monoamine oxidase B in the glia. MPP^C is taken up by dopamine-containing cells in the substantia nigra, where it causes degeneration by inhibiting mitochondrial energy production (58). This selective destruction of nigrostriatal neurons led to the development of animal models that have become a research tool in PD (58).

Patients with MPTP-induced parkinsonism respond to levodopa in a manner similar to that seen in those with PD. However, these patients may develop levodopa-induced side effects including dyskinesia, fluctuations, and hallucinations very early (59).

Manganese

Manganese is used in the manufacture of chlorine gas, dry-cell batteries, paints, varnish, enamel, linoleum, and as an antiknock agent in gasoline. Manganese enters the body through the inhalation of dust particles or by ingestion (60).

The effects of chronic manganese intoxication were first described by Couper in 1837 (61). The clinical presentation is stereotypical and includes bradykinesia, postural instability, and rigidity. The gait is characterized by extension of the spine, elbow flexion, and toe-walking (cock-walk). Tremor is less frequent and may have a flapping quality similar to that seen in Wilson's disease (61). A psychiatric prodrome of irritability, emotional instability, psychosis (locura manganica), and dystonia occur, typically from manganese dust inhalation in miners; however, these features are not seen in industrial manganese intoxication (62).

The severity of the clinical features of manganese intoxication does not correlate with tissue manganese levels (61, 62). Pathologic studies have demonstrated degeneration in the internal segment of the pallidum, caudate nucleus, putamen, and rarely of the substantia nigra (60, 61). Possible mechanisms of manganese toxicity include dopaminergic toxicity, free radical production, or 6-hydroxydopamine production (61). MRI scans generally show high signal in the globus pallidus on T1-weighted images.

Treatment with chelating agents has proven ineffective, possibly because tissue injury may occur even when tissue levels of manganese are low (61, 62). Removal of the manganese source may lead to stabilization or improvement of the symptoms. Levodopa may be beneficial in some patients, although in most the improvement is transient. Severely affected patients may not respond to levodopa (62).

Carbon Disulfide

Carbon disulfide is a solvent used as a fumigant in the grain storage and rayon industries (63). Patients exposed to carbon disulfide may clinically exhibit cerebellar dysfunction, hearing loss, peripheral neuropathy, chorea, and parkinsonism. The parkinsonian features include rest tremor, gait and postural instability, rigidity, and bradykinesia (64).

The exact mechanism by which carbon disulfide toxicity occurs is not known, but it may involve the binding of trace metals that interrupt certain enzymatic activities (64). Brain MRI may reveal findings consistent with central demyelination (64).

Other Toxins

A variety of other toxic exposures have also been associated with parkinsonism. These rare causes include petroleum waste, hydrocarbons (n-hexane), diquat, paraquat, cyanide, and methanol (65–68).

STRUCTURAL LESIONS

Structural lesions that, either directly or indirectly, affect the basal ganglia may produce parkinsonism. Lesions secondary to hypoxia, hydrocephalus, tumors, vascular disease (including strokes and vascular malformations), and demyelination have been associated with parkinsonism.

Hydrocephalus

Hydrocephalus has been reported as a cause of parkinsonism (69). Patients may develop parkinsonian symptoms months or years after their initial presentation with hydrocephalus, or the parkinsonism may develop acutely from shunt failure. Revision of the shunt results in amelioration of the acute exacerbation (70). Clinically, patients may manifest tremor, rigidity, and bradykinesia. They can also have a characteristic shuffling gait with postural instability. Patients often develop Parinaud's syndrome prior to the onset of parkinsonism (69).

Normal-pressure hydrocephalus (NPH) is a condition characterized by the triad of gait apraxia, mental status changes, and urinary incontinence. Poor postural reflexes and flexed posture may be seen (71). NPH should be differentiated from dementia with atrophy and hydrocephalus ex vacuo.

The hydrocephalus should be treated either by shunting or by shunt revision in the case of malfunction. If the parkinsonian symptoms do not respond to shunting, some patients will respond to dopaminergic therapy with a dopamine agonist or levodopa. Most patients will achieve adequate control of their symptoms and some may eventually be weaned off dopaminergic therapy (69).

The mechanism that leads to parkinsonism from hydrocephalus is not known; however, it is believed that pressure on the white matter tracts or striatum plays a role.

Tumors

Tumors, appropriately placed, can be a rare cause of parkinsonism. The tumors associated with parkinsonism may occur in several regions of the brain including the striatum, frontal lobe, temporal lobe, parietal lobe, thalamus or hypothalamus, substantia nigra, midbrain, and third ventricle (72, 73). A variety of tumor types have been reported, including glioma, meningioma, lymphoma, fibrosarcoma, and metastasis (72).

The pathologic mechanism leading to parkinsonism may be either the direct infiltration of tumor cells or indirect mass effect causing impaired metabolism of the striatum. Rarely, direct or indirect compression of the midbrain leads to parkinsonism (72).

Vascular Disease

The concept of vascular or arteriosclerotic parkinsonism was introduced by Critchley in 1929 (74) and has been a matter of debate for decades. The existence of this phenomenon now appears to be supported by both clinical and pathologic studies (75–77).

Vascular parkinsonism may have a variety of clinical presentations and may be acute or subacute in onset. The symptoms may include all the classic motor features of PD. Symptoms are usually bilateral but may be unilateral (78). Unlike those with PD, the majority of patients with hemiparkinsonism due to a focal ischemic lesion do not exhibit tremor (79). The course of vascular parkinsonism may be stable from onset, may be progressive, or may resolve spontaneously (80). A subgroup of patients may present with lower body parkinsonism—minimal upper extremity involvement with predominant lower extremity symptoms, including a freezing gait (81). The symptoms may occur as the result of multiple small vessel infarcts or a large single one (74, 77). These patients have risk factors for stroke, including hypertension and diabetes mellitus.

Vascular parkinsonism may result from interruption of the nigrostriatal pathway or by direct involvement of the striatum or globus pallidus externa, causing decreased inhibitory input to the globus pallidus interna. This cascade would lead to excessive inhibition of the thalamus by the globus pallidus interna, thus producing parkinsonism (77).

Some patients with persistent symptoms may respond to levodopa, especially if the vascular lesion interrupts the nigrostriatal pathway. Cases secondary to direct striatal involvement may not respond (77).

Intracranial Hemorrhage

Intracranial hemorrhage may occur secondary to head trauma, arteriovenous or other vascular malformations, or aneurysm. They may be subdural, epidural, intracerebral, or subarachnoid in location. The first report of a chronic subdural hematoma producing parkinsonism was by Samily in 1968 (82). This problem may also aggravate the symptoms already present in PD.

Clinically, patients may exhibit any of the classic features of parkinsonism (82). Patients with hemorrhagic lesions may complain of headache or have other findings, such as altered mental status, suggestive of a diagnosis other than PD (82). Hemorrhagic lesions may cause parkinsonism by anatomically distorting the basal ganglia and midbrain structures. This may affect metabolic function of the involved neurons (82). It is important to realize that sudden worsening in a patient with PD may be due to a subdural hematoma caused by negligible trauma.

Surgical intervention, such as draining a subdural hematoma, or spontaneous resolution of the hemorrhage may result in improvement in the patient's symptoms. Levodopa may be useful in some patients with persistent symptoms (82).

Posthypoxic Parkinsonism

Anoxic brain injury from cardiac arrest or other events may result in parkinsonism. Neuroimaging may reveal lesions in the striatum or the globus pallidus.

Demyelinating Disease or Multiple Sclerosis

A few cases reported in which parkinsonian symptoms emerged in patients with multiple sclerosis (MS). However, most of these are attributable to the coincidental occurrence of PD in patients with MS; a clear anatomic lesion correlating with the parkinsonian features could not be identified (83). There is one case of a patient with MS who developed bilateral cogwheel rigidity and akinesia associated with a demyelinating lesion in the substantia nigra. This patient's symptoms resolved with corticosteroid treatment (83).

Posttraumatic Parkinsonism

An isolated head injury usually does not lead to parkinsonism unless it is severe enough to cause loss of consciousness and significant brain damage, especially to the basal ganglia (84). However, multiple minor (subconcussive) head injuries may cause cumulative damage to the brain, resulting in characteristic dysarthria, parkinsonism (all features), and dementia. This syndrome occurs in boxers who have experienced multiple knockouts (i.e., dementia pugilistica) (85). In this situation, the severity of symptoms correlates with length of career, number of fights, and number of blows. The damage may be due to rotatory forces of the skull and brain in opposite directions and tearing of neurons. Despite cessation of boxing, the encephalopathy usually progresses to very severe levels (86). Radiologically, this is characterized by diffuse brain atrophy and a large cavum septum pellucidum. Pathologically, diffuse neurofibrillary tangles and neuronal loss are seen. The parkinsonism may not respond to levodopa. Rarely, parkinsonism has been described following electrical injury (87).

Psychogenic Parkinsonism

Psychogenic parkinsonism is not common; however, psychogenic tremor is often seen (88). This tremor is usually complex (occurring at rest as well as with changes in posture and action) and of variable frequency, direction, and location. The bradykinesia takes the form of a deliberate slowness, with no change in amplitude of movement, and can be variable. These patients often have bizarre gait disorders, deliberate stiffness, and dramatic, catastrophic responses to shoulder pull without falling. Psychogenic disorders usually have an abrupt, severe onset and secondary pain may be present. A normal neurologic examination and distractability further support a functional problem. Detailed history often reveals underlying psychiatric illness or secondary gain. Prolonged careful observation may be necessary to make the diagnosis of psychogenic parkinsonism. Normal β-CIT single photon emission computed tomography may help to exclude PD in difficult cases (89). Early diagnosis, confrontation, and psychiatric therapy offer the best chance for recovery.

MISCELLANEOUS CAUSES OF SECONDARY PARKINSONISM

Parkinsonism may occur transiently during alcohol withdrawal (90). Metabolic causes include hypoparathyroidism with basal ganglia calcifications and hypothyroidism (91). There are a few reports of Sjögren's syndrome with associated parkinsonism. Whether parkinsonism is related to Sjögren's syndrome directly or the association is coincidental is not clear (92). Parkinsonian features have been reported in central pontine and extrapontine myelinolysis (93), following a wasp sting (94), and in Behçet's disease (95). Reversible parkinsonism has also been described as a manifestation of CNS lupus (96).

References

1. Blocq P, Marinesco G. Sur un cas tremblement Parkinsonien hemiplegique symptomatiqued, une tumeur de pedoncule cerebral. *CR Cos Biol* (Paris) 1893; 45:105–111.
2. Duvoisin RC, Yahr MD. Encephalitis and parkinsonism. *Arch Neurol* 1965; 12: 227–239.
3. Wilson SAK. Epidemic encephalitis in neurology. London: Arnold, 1940: 99–104.
4. Litvan I. Parkinsonism-dementia syndromes. In: Jankovic J, Tolosa E (eds). *Parkinson's Disease and Movement Disorders.* Baltimore: Williams & Wilkins, 1998:827–828.
5. Oeckinghaus W. Encephalitis epidemica und Wilsonisches Krankenheit. *Dtsch Z Nervenkr* 1921; 72:294.
6. Calne DB, Lees AJ. Late progression of postencephalitic Parkinson's syndrome. *Can J Neurol Sci* 1988; 15:135–138.
7. Geddes JF, Hughes AJ, Lees AJ, et al. Pathological overlap in cases of parkinsonism associated with neurofibrillary tangles: A study of recent cases of postencephalitic parkinsonism and comparison with progressive supranuclear palsy and Guamanian parkinsonism-dementia complex. *Brain* 1993; 116:281–302.
8. Pramstaller PP, Lees AJ, Luxon LM. Possible clinical overlap between postencephalitic parkinsonism and progressive supranuclear palsy. *J Neurol Neurosurg Psychiatry* 1996; 60(5):589–590.
9. Litvan I, Agid Y, Jankovic J, et al. Accuracy of clinical criteria for the diagnosis of progressive supranuclear palsy (Steele-Richardson-Olszewski syndrome). *Neurology* 1996; 46:922–930.
10. Shoji H, Watanabe M, Itoh S, et al. Japanese encephalitis and parkinsonism. *J Neurol* 1993; 240:59–60.
11. Solbrig MV, Nashef L. Acute parkinsonism is suspected herpes simplex encephalitis. *Mov Disord* 1993; 8(2):233–234.
12. Calne DB, Stern GM, Laurence DR, et al. L-dopa in postencephalitic parkinsonism. *Lancet* 1969; 12:744.
13. Hunter KR, Stern GM, Sharkey J. L-dopa in postencephalitic parkinsonism. *Lancet* 1970; 2:1366.
14. Nath A, Jankovic J, Pettigrew LC. Movement disorders and AIDS. *Neurology* 1987; 37:37–41.
15. Carrazana EJ, Rossitch E, Samuels MA. Parkinsonian symptoms in a patient with AIDS and cerebral toxoplasmosis. *J Neurol Neurosurg Psychiatry* 1989; 52:1445–1447.
16. Mintz M, Tardieu J, Hoyt L, et al. Levodopa therapy improves motor function in HIV-infected children with extrapyramidal syndromes. *Neurology* 1996; 47:1583–1585.
17. Adler CH, Stern MB, Brooks ML. Parkinsonism secondary to bilateral striatal fungal abscesses. *Mov Disord* 1989; 4(4):333–337.
18. Kim JS, Choi IS, Lee MC. Reversible parkinsonism and dystonia following probable *Mycoplasma pneumoniae* infection. *Mov Disord* 1995; 10:510–512.
19. Neill KJ. An unusual case of syphilitic parkinsonism. *Br Med J* 1953; 2:320.
20. Milton WJ, Atlas SW, Lavi E, et al. Magnetic resonance imaging of Creutzfeldt-Jacob disease. *Ann Neurol* 1991; 29:438–440.
21. Wszolek Z, Monsour H, Smith P, et al. Cryptococcal meningoencephalitis with parkinsonian features. *Mov Disord* 1988; 3(3):271–273.
22. Verma A, Berger JR, Bowen BC, et al. Reversible parkinsonism syndrome complicating cysticercus midbrain encephalitis. *Mov Disord* 1995; 10(2):215–219.
23. Sejvar JJ, Haddad MB, Tierney BC, et al. Neurologic manifestations and outcomes of West Nile virus infection. *JAMA* 2003; 290(4):511–515.
24. Lehmann HE, Hanrahan GE. Chlorpromazine: New inhibiting agent for psychomotor excitement and manic states. *Arch Neurol Psychiatry* 1954; 71:227.
25. Hardie RJ, Lees AJ. Neuroleptic-induced Parkinson's syndrome: Clinical features and results of treatment with levodopa. *J Neurol Neurosurg Psychiatry* 1988; 51:850–854.
26. Sethi KD, Zamrini EY. Asymmetry in clinical features of drug-induced parkinsonism. *J Neuropsychiatry Clin Neurosci* 1990; 2(i):64–66.
27. Sethi KD, Patel B, Meador KJ. Metoclopramide induced parkinsonism. *South Med J* 1989; 82:1581–1582.
28. Masmoudi K, Gras-Champel V, Lemaire-Hurtel AS, et al. Extrapyramidal adverse effects of veralipride (Agreal), a drug used to treat hot flushes: A propos of 17 cases. *Rev Med Interne* 2005; 26(6):453–457.
29. Bilal L, Tsai C, Gasper JJ, Ndlela JC. Parkinsonism with intramuscular ziprasidone. *Am J Psychiatry* 2005; 162(12):2392–2393.
30. Sharma A, Sorrell JH. Aripiprazole-induced parkinsonism. *Int Clin Psychopharmacol* 2006; 21(2):127–129.
31. Hausner RS. Neuroleptic-induced parkinsonism and Parkinson's disease: Differential diagnosis and treatment. *J Clin Psychiatry* 1983; 44:13–16.
32. Rajput AH, Rozdilsky B, Hornykiewicz O, et al. Reversible drug-induced parkinsonism: Clinicopathologic study of two cases. *Arch Neurol* 1982; 39:644–646.
33. Burn DJ, Brooks DJ. Nigral dysfunction in drug-induced parkinsonism: A ^{18}F-dopa PET study. *Neurology* 1993; 43:552–556.
34. Kelly JT, Zimmerman RL, Abuzzahab FS, et al. A double-blind study of amantidine hydrochloride versus benztropine mesylate in drug-induced parkinsonism. *Pharmacology* 1974; 12:65–73.
35. Jankovic J, Beach J. Long-term effects of tetrabenazine in hyperkinetic movement disorders. *Neurology* 1997; 48:358–362.
36. Marti-Masso JF, Poza JJ. Cinnarizine-induced parkinsonism: Ten years later. *Mov Disord* 1998; 13(3):453–456.
37. Micheli F, Pardal M, Gatto M, et al. Flunarizine and cinnarizine-induced extrapyramidal reactions. *Neurology* 1987; 37:881–884.
38. Sempere AP, Duarte J, Cabezas C, et al. Parkinsonism induced by amlodipine. *Mov Disord* 1995; 10(1):115–116.
39. Dick RS, Barold SS. Diltiazem-induced parkinsonism. *Am J Med* 1989; 87:95–96.
40. García-Albea E, Jiménez FJ, Ayuso-Peralta L, et al. Parkinsonism unmasked by verapamil. *Clin Neuropharmacol* 1993; 16(3):263–265.
41. Shopsin B, Gershon S. Cogwheel rigidity related to lithium maintenance. *Am J Psychiatry* 1975; 132:536–538.
42. Marti Masso JF, Marti I, Carrera N, et al. Trimetazidine induces parkinsonism, gait disorders and tremor. *Therapie.* 2005; 60(4):419–422.
43. Bergevin PR, Patwardhan VC, Weissman J, et al. Neurotoxicity of 5-fluorouracil. *Lancet* 1975; 1:410.
44. Boranic M, Raci F. A Parkinson-like syndrome as side effect of chemotherapy with vincristine and Adriamycin in a child with acute leukaemia. *Biomedicine* 1979; 31:124–125.
45. Sechi GP, Demontis G, Rosati G. Relationship between Meige syndrome and alpha-methyldopa-induced parkinsonism. *Neurology* 1985; 35:1668–1669.
46. Dotti MT, Federico A. Amiodarone-induced parkinsonism: A case report and pathogenetic discussion. *Mov Disord* 1995; 10:233–234.
47. Handler CE, Besse CP, Wilson AO. Extrapyramidal and cerebellar syndrome with encephalopathy associated with cimetidine. *Postgrad Med J* 1982; 58:527–528.
48. Bird GLA, Meadows J, Goka J, et al. Cyclosporine-associated akinetic mutism and extrapyramidal syndrome after liver transplantation. *J Neurol Neursurg Psychiatry* 1990; 53:1068–1071.
49. Armon C, Shin C, Miller P, et al. Reversible parkinsonism and cognitive impairment with chronic valproate use. *Neurology* 1996; 47:626–635.
50. Di Rocco A, Brannan T, Prikhojan A, et al. Sertraline-induced extrapyramidal side effects may be related to interference with dopamine metabolism. *Mov Disord* 1997; 12(Suppl 1):66.
51. Albanese A, Rossi P, Altavista MC. Can trazodone induce parkinsonism? *Clin Neuropharmacol* 1988; 11(2):180–182.
52. Szuba MP, Leuchter AF. Falling backward in two elderly patients taking bupropion. *J Clin Psychiatry.* 1992; 53(5):157–159.
53. Miura T, Mitomo M, Kawai R, et al. CT of the brain in acute carbon monoxide intoxication: Characteristic features and prognosis. *AJNR* 1985; 6:739–742.
54. Ernst A, Zibrak JD. Carbon monoxide poisoning. *N Engl J Med* 1998; 339(22):1603–1608.
55. Min SK. A brain syndrome associated with delayed neuropsychiatric sequelae following acute carbon monoxide intoxication. *Acta Psychiatry Scand* 1986; 73:80–86.
56. Davis GC, Williams AC, Markey SP, et al. Chronic parkinsonism secondary to intravenous injection of meperidine analogs. *Psychiatry Res* 1979; 1:249–254.
57. Langston JW, Ballard P, Tetrud JW, et al. Chronic parkinsonism in humans due to a product of meperidine-analog synthesis. *Science* 1983; 219:979–980.
58. McCrodden JM, Tipton KF, Sullivan JP. The neurotoxicity of MPTP and the relevance to Parkinson's disease. *Pharmacol Toxicol* 1990; 67:8–13.
59. Tetrud JW, Langston JW, Garbe PL, et al. Mild parkinsonism in persons exposed to 1-methyl-4- phenyl-1,2,3,6-tetrahydropyridine (MPTP). *Neurology* 1989; 39:1483–1487.

60. Huang CC, Chu NS, Lu CS, et al. Chronic manganese intoxication. *Arch Neurol* 1989; 46:1104–1106.

61. Barbeau A. Manganese and extrapyramidal disorders. *Neurotoxicology* 1984; 5(1):13.

62. Mena I, Court J, Fuenzalida S, et al. Modification of chronic manganese poisoning: Treatment with L-dopa or 5-OH tryptophane. *N Engl J Med* 1970; 282(1):5–10.

63. Peters HA, Levine RL, Matthews CG, et al. Extrapyramidal and other neurologic manifestations associated with carbon disulfide fumigant exposure. *Arch Neurol* 1988; 45:537–540.

64. Pezzoli G, Strada O, Silani V, et al. Clinical and pathological features in hydrocarbon-induced parkinsonism. *Ann Neurol* 1996; 40:922–925.

65. Tetrud JW, Langston JW, Irwin I, et al. Parkinsonism caused by petroleum waste ingestion. *Neurology* 1994; 44:1051–1054.

66. Sechi GP, Agnetti V, Piredda M, et al. Acute and persistent parkinsonism after use of diquat. *Neurology* 1992; 42:261–263.

67. Sanchez-Ramos JR, Hefti F, Weiner WJ. Paraquat and Parkinson's disease. *Neurology* 1987; 37:728.

68. Rosenow F, Herholz K, Lanfermann H, et al. Neurological sequelae of cyanide intoxication: The patterns of clinical, magnetic resonance imaging, and positron emission tomography findings. *Ann Neurol* 1995; 38:825–828.

69. Zeidler M, Dorman PJ, Ferguson IT, et al. Parkinsonism associated with obstructive hydrocephalus due to idiopathic aqueductal stenosis. *J Neurol Neurosurg Psychiatry* 1998; 64:657–659.

70. Keane JR. Tremor as the result of shunt obstruction: Four patients with cysticercosis and secondary parkinsonism: Report of four cases. *Neurosurgery* 1995; 37:520–522.

71. Krauss JK, Regel JP, Droste DW, et al. Movement disorders in adult hydrocephalus. *Mov Disord* 1997; 12:53–60.

72. Waters CH. Structural lesions and parkinsonism. In: Stern MB and Koller WC (eds). *Parkinsonian Syndromes.* New York: Marcel Dekker, 1993:137–145.

73. Cicarelli G, Pellecchia MT, Maiuri F, et al. Brain stem cystic astrocytoma presenting with "pure" parkinsonism. *Mov Disord* 1999; 14(2):364–366.

74. Critchely M. Arteriosclerotic parkinsonism. *Brain* 1929; 52:23–83.

75. Murrow RW, Schweiger GD, Kepes JJ, et al. Parkinsonism due to a basal ganglia lacunar state: Clinicopathological correlation. *Neurology* 1990; 40:897–900.

76. Hughes AJ, Daniel SE, Kilford L, et al. Accuracy of clinical diagnosis of idiopathic Parkinson's disease: A clinico-pathological study of 100 cases. *J Neurol Neurosurg Psychiatry* 1992; 55:181–184.

77. Hurtig HI. Vascular parkinsonism. In: Stern MB, Koller WC (eds). *Parkinsonian Syndromes.* New York: Marcel Dekker, 1993:81–93.

78. Fenelon G, Houeto JL. Unilateral parkinsonism following a large infarct in the territory of the lenticulostriate arteries. *Mov Disord* 1997; 12(6):1086–1089.

79. Morgan JC, Sethi KD. Midbrain infarct with parkinsonism. *Neurology* 2003; 60(12):E10.

80. Tolosa ES, Santamarıa J. Parkinsonism and basal ganglia infarcts. *Neurology* 1984; 34:1516–1518.

81. FitzGerald PM, Jankovic J. Lower body parkinsonism: Evidence for vascular etiology. *Mov Disord* 1989; 4(3):249–260.

82. Turjanski N, Pentland B, Lees AD, et al. Parkinsonism associated with acute intracranial hematomas: A [18F] dopa positron-emission tomography study. *Mov Disord* 1997; 12(6):1035–1038.

83. Federlein J, Postert T, Allgeier A, et al. Remitting parkinsonism as a symptom of multiple sclerosis and the associated magnetic resonance imaging findings. *Mov Disord* 1997; 12(6):1090–1091.

84. Jankovic J. Posttraumatic movement disorders: Central and peripheral mechanisms. *Neurology* 1994; 44:2006–2014.

85. Koller WC, Wong, GF, Lang A. Posttraumatic movement disorders: A review. *Mov Disord* 1989; 4:20–36.

86. Factor SA. Posttraumatic parkinsonism. In: Stern MB, Koller WC (eds). *Parkinsonian Syndromes.* New York: Marcel Dekker, 1993:95–110.

87. Morris HR, Moriabadi NF, Lees AJ, et al. Parkinsonism following electrical injury to the hand *Mov Disord* 1998; 13(3):600–602.

88. Lang AE, Koller WC, Fahn S. Psychogenic parkinsonism. *Arch Neurol* 1995; 52:802–810.

89. Factor SA, Seibyl J, Innis R, et al. Psychogenic parkinsonism: Confirmation of diagnosis with β-CIT SPECT scans. *Mov Disord* 1998; 13:860.

90. Shandling M, Carlen PL, Lang AE. Parkinsonism in alcohol withdrawal: A follow-up study. *Mov Disord* 1990; 5:36–39.

91. Sweeney PJ. Metabolic causes of parkinsonism. In: Stern MB, Koller WC (eds). *Parkinsonian Syndromes.* New York: Marcel Dekker, 1993:195–200.

92. Walker RH, Spiera H, Brin MF, et al. Parkinsonism associated with Sjogren's syndrome: Three cases and a review of the literature. *Mov Disord* 1999; 14(2):262–268.

93. Seiser A, Schwarz S, Aichinger-Steiner MM, et al. Parkinsonism and dystonia in central pontine and extrapontine myelinolysis. *J Neurol Neurosurg Psychiatry* 1998; 65(1):119–121.

94. Leopold NA, Bara-Jimenez W, Hallett M. Parkinsonism after a wasp sting. *Mov Disord* 1999; 14(1):122–127.

95. Bogdanova D, Milanov I, Georgiev D. Parkinsonian syndrome as a neurological manifestation of Behcet's disease. *Can J Neurol Sci* 1998; 25(1):82–85.

96. Tan EK, Chan LL, Auchus AP. Reversible parkinsonism in systemic lupus erythematosus. *J Neurol Sci* 2001; 193(1):53–57.

XI

OTHER ISSUES

59 Outcome Measures

Lisa M. Shulman

edical progress, resulting in increased life expectancy and mobility for people with Parkinson's disease (PD), has led to difficulty in finding meaningful and valid outcome measures. When acute illness was more prevalent than chronic conditions, the impact of disease was traditionally measured in terms of life expectancy or mortality. Advances in the management of PD have resulted in marked extensions of life expectancy; it is not uncommon to see patients 2 to 3 decades after the onset of symptoms. In the current era, where chronic illness predominates, impairment, disability, and quality of life have replaced longevity as more practical and meaningful endpoints. This chapter compares these 3 outcome measures for the assessment of patients with PD.

Impairment, Disability, and Quality of Life in Parkinson's Disease

The terminology utilized for outcome measures can be confusing. Terms such as *disease severity, symptoms, impairment, function, disability,* and *quality of life* are often used interchangeably in the medical literature, although their definitions are distinct. *Impairments* are the symptoms and signs of a disease process. The impairments of PD include tremor, bradykinesia, freezing of gait, depression, and fatigue. Information about impairment comes from both subjective and objective sources (history and physical examination). The World Health Organization defines *disability* as "any restriction or lack of ability to perform an activity within the range considered normal for a human being due to an impairment" (1). Disability can also be assessed based on subjective and objective data. Inquiries about performance of basic activities of daily living (ADLs), including dressing and bathing, or instrumental activities of daily living (IADLs), such as shopping and preparing food, give the patient or family perspective on disability. Objective data about disability are often also assessed during the office visit, as when patients are unable to undress themselves for the exam or handle toileting independently. Objective quantitative data regarding function may be collected with physical performance measures, including timed gait testing or simulations of daily activities.

Quality of life is a complex measure that comprises elements of impairment and disability but also encompasses patients' subjective perception of their health and well-being. By definition, quality of life is a subjective measure; understanding the subjectivity of quality of life data is the key to understanding its strengths and weaknesses as an outcome measure. The individual's view of his or her health is influenced by numerous factors including expectations, mood, responsibilities, and personal goals. Similar levels of disease severity in PD are likely to have different impacts on the lives of a 43-year-old husband and father as compared to a 67-year-old retiree, and their quality-of-life reporting is likely to be markedly different in spite of similar impairment ratings. The idiosyncratic nature of quality-of-life assessment can result in perplexing and seemingly contradictory data. Nevertheless, it is difficult to quarrel with patients being the final arbiters of the success or failure of their health care.

Assessment of all three outcome measures (impairment, disability, and quality of life) has limitations in terms of the accuracy and precision of measurement. Two neu-

rologists may have different assessments of the severity of rigidity or bradykinesia. Yet objective assessment of the cardinal impairments of PD is likely to be more reproducible than are assessments of disability or quality of life. The motor impairments of PD are a direct manifestation of the neurodegenerative process, whereas disability is less directly related to the underlying disease, since other influences including medical comorbidity and age are likely to contribute. Quality of life can be thought of as being even more remote from the disease process, since it is gauged through the filter of the patient's personal viewpoint.

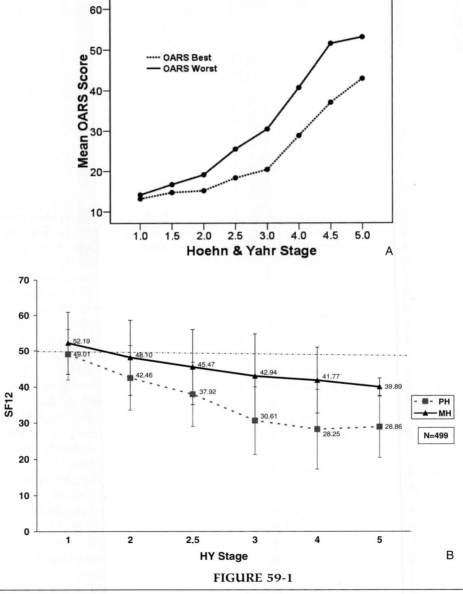

FIGURE 59-1

A. Self-reported disability on the Older Americans Resource and Services Scale (OARS) is shown at progressive stages of Parkinson's disease at both best function and worst function. B. Health-related quality of life on the SF12 Health Status Survey is shown at progressive stages of Parkinson disease for both the Mental Health and Physical Health Summary scores. The horizontal line at the 50th percentile shows the mean score of a normative population in the United States.

It is well recognized that disease severity in PD is correlated with both disability and quality of life. At the University of Maryland PD and Movement Disorders Center, visiting patients are routinely assessed for impairment with the Unified Parkinson's Disease Rating Scale (UPDRS) (2), disability with the Older Americans Resource and Services Scale (OARS) (3), and quality of life with the SF-12v2 Health Status Survey (4). Based on cross-sectional data on about 800 PD patients, disease progression represented by advancing Hoehn and Yahr stages (HY) is accompanied by progressive increased disability (Figure 59-1A) and reduced quality of life (Figure 59-1B). The development of motor fluctuations in PD is represented by the progressive increase in disparity between patient reports of best function vs. worst function over the previous week (see Figure 59-1A). The SF-12 yields 2 summary scores, Physical Health (PH) and

Mental Health (MH). These scores are expressed as a percentile, where the 50th percentile is the average score of a U.S. adult normative population. Patients with unilateral parkinsonism (HY 1) have no reduction in quality of life; but progressive decline is seen with each advancing HY stage, with the greatest slope of decline observed between HY 2.5 and 3, with the onset of loss of balance. The impact on PH quality of life is greater than MH quality of life at all stages, with advanced stage 5 PD associated with about the 30th percentile on the PH summary score and the 40th percentile on MH.

When the relationships between impairment, disability, and quality of life are shown as individual data points for each of nearly 800 patients, a different picture emerges (Figures 59-2 to 59-4). Although all 3 outcome measures are correlated with each other ($P < .001$), the degree of scatter of the data is revealed. In Figure 59-2B,

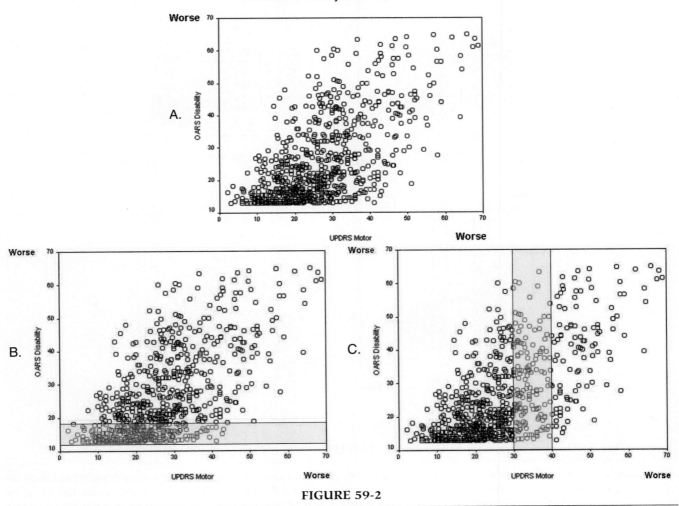

FIGURE 59-2

A. A scatterplot of 759 subjects with Parkinson's disease showing the individual data points of self-reported disability on the OARS scale and the objective physician rating of impairment on the UPDRS Motor examination ($r = 0.635$, $P < 0.001$). B. The horizontal bar highlights those subjects with either no disability or early disability. C. The vertical bar highlights those subjects with moderate to severe impairment (UPDRS = 30 to 40).

Disease Severity & Quality of Life in PD

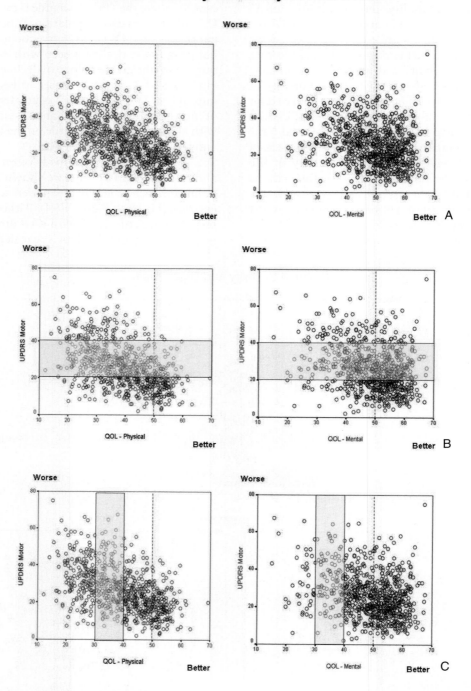

FIGURE 59-3

A. A scatterplot of 776 subjects with Parkinson's disease showing the individual data points of self-reported quality of life on the SF-12 Health Status Survey and the objective physician rating of impairment on the UPDRS Motor examination. Quality of life is reported as both physical and mental health summary scores. Physical health quality of life is depicted in the left panel ($r = -0.483, P < .001$) and mental health in the right panel ($r = -0.300, P < .001$). The vertical line at the 50th percentile shows the mean score of a normative population in the United States. B. The horizontal bars highlight individuals with UPDRS motor scores of 20 to 40. C. The vertical bars highlight individuals reporting SF-12 scores of in the 30th to 40th percentiles (reduced quality of life).

the horizontal band at the lower portion of the graph highlights the patient subgroup reporting the lowest level of disability. Indeed, even among patients reporting no disability, the UPDRS motor examination (part III) score ranges from 5 to 40. Similarly, if we focus only on the patients scoring between 30 to 40 on the UPDRS motor exam (Figure 59-2C), the subjective OARS disability ratings range from the lowest possible score of 14 to over 50, from normal function to loss of independence. The scatterplots of the relationship between impairment and quality of life also depict a broad range of quality-of-life ratings at a given level of impairment (Figure 59- 3A to C). For example, in Figure 59-3B, patients with UPDRS motor exam ratings of 20 to 40 report PH quality-of-life ranging from the 20th to the 55th percentiles and MH quality of life from the 25th to the 65th percentiles. Since the 50th percentile is the population norm, PD subjects with similar disease severity report a quality of life that ranges from markedly reduced to moderately increased.

Impairment ratings (UPDRS part III, the motor exam) have a stronger correlation with disability than with quality of life [$r = 0.64$ (OARS) vs. 0.48 (SF12 PH) or 0.30 (SF12 MH)]. And quality of life has a stronger correlation with disability than with impairment [$r =$ PH: 0.62 (OARS) vs. 0.48 (UPDRS III) and MH: 0.46 (OARS) vs. 0.30 (UPDRS III)]. These comparisons emphasize the significance of choosing suitable outcome measures targeted to specific needs. Is the assessment being done in the context of clinical evaluation, a clinical trial, or a needs assessment for social services? Clinical trials also have varying needs based on the study aims, the particular intervention under study, and even the changing regulatory environment. It is not uncommon to find that an intervention results in a significant change in 1 but not all 3 types of outcome measures.

To illustrate this point, contrast the needs of three different clinical trials that are assessing the efficacy of (1) an antiparkinsonian medication, (2) an antidepressant, and (3) a rehabilitation program. The antiparkinsonian medication under study is particularly efficacious for tremor. The rehabilitation program focuses on the use of various assistive devices that enhance daily activities. In the first example, the antiparkinsonian medication results in improvement in ratings of impairment (tremor), but the changes in disability and quality of life ratings do not achieve significance. The antidepressant results in improvements on a validated scale of depression and the mental health quality-of-life ratings but no change in PD severity or disability. The rehab program emphasizes the use of assistive devices and results in marked improvements in ratings of disability and quality of life but no change in the PD motor examination (impairment). A better understanding of the performance of these different outcome measures is necessary to guide the choice of clinical outcome measures and their positioning as primary or secondary endpoints.

The Impact of Parkinson's Disease Impairment on Disability and Quality of Life

Many studies have focused on the relationship between PD and quality of life and, increasingly, both general health status and disease-specific qualify-of-life scales are being

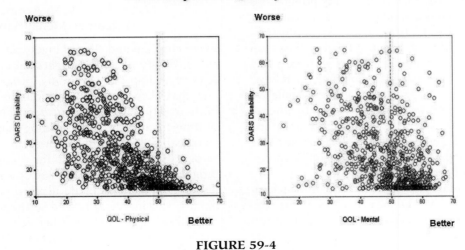

Disability and Quality of Life

FIGURE 59-4

A scatterplot of 744 subjects with Parkinson's disease showing the individual datapoints of self-reported disability on the OARS scale and health-related quality of life on the SF12 Health Status Survey (physical health summary score $r = -0.620, P = 0.001$ and mental health summary score $r = -0.457, P = <.001$).

included as outcome measures in clinical research trials. Assessment of the impact of PD on disability is included in most clinical trials, although the most commonly used scales have limitations. The Schwab and England Activities of Daily Living (S&E) (5) is a single measurement of dependency in ADLs. The UPDRS part II ADL combines a subset of ADLs (walking, dressing, handwriting) with some impairment ratings (sensory complaints, tremor, salivation, and gait disorder) and omits the major ADL of toileting. IADLs include shopping, meal preparation, housework, medication and money management, and these are not covered in the UPDRS part II scale. Assessment of IADLs is less commonly used in studies of PD, although they may be more sensitive to early disability than ADLs and are a good indicator of dependency with the need for social services.

A review of more than a dozen studies of PD and quality of life shows that depression has a robust correlation with reduced quality of life (6–27). Disease severity and disability are, as expected, common determinants of quality of life, although disease duration is not. Complications of advanced PD—including motor fluctuations, dyskinesia, cognitive impairment, and psychosis—have also been associated with poor quality of life. Most studies have found that age and gender are not significant correlates, although a study by Schrag et al. (26), which focused on young- vs. older-onset PD, concluded that young-onset patients more frequently experience loss of employment, disruption of family life, greater perceived stigmatization, and greater depression, resulting in greater reduction of quality of life.

Studies of PD reveal a complex and even contradictory relationship between levodopa and quality of life, with some studies showing a detrimental effect and others demonstrating improvement. These inconsistencies suggest differences in the disease stage of the study populations as well as the measurement of quality of life applied. For example, in the CALM-PD study (28), early results indicated that quality of life was better in the levodopa than in the pramipexole group among patients with early PD, but this discrepancy resolved with more time for follow-up. Variables such as levodopa dosage and cumulative levodopa exposure are inextricably linked to disease severity and duration. When the variable was levodopa response, Schrag and Quinn (14) found that quality of life was significantly better among those with a good response than those with a moderate or poor response.

Some factors that have a prominent influence on quality of life have rarely been measured, including self-efficacy, mastery, and personality attributes of optimism and locus of control. Unexpected correlates are likely to continue to be identified such as "satisfaction with explanation at time of diagnosis," as was reported by the Global Parkinson Disease Survey (22).

Depression also has a strong correlation with disability in PD (29–32). Disease severity and complications of advanced PD have also been associated with disability. Rubenstein et al. (10) reported that disability was highly correlated with motor fluctuations and dystonia, moderately correlated with dyskinesia, and weakly correlated with orthostatic hypotension and sleep disturbance. Interestingly, Diamond et al. (33) highlighted the association between later age of onset of PD with both disability and mortality, while younger age of onset was associated with worse quality of life by Schrag et al (26).

Recent studies of disability and quality of life at the University of Maryland PD Center show that both motor and nonmotor symptoms are important determinants (34–36). Gait impairment, postural instability, and bradykinesia are the motor symptoms that have the strongest correlation with disability and quality of life. Tremor showed no correlation with either of these outcome measures. Among the nonmotor symptoms, cognitive dysfunction, psychotic ideation, urinary incontinence, motivation, and depression all had strong correlation with either disability or quality of life. However, sleep disturbance and orthostatic hypotension were weakly correlated. When a comparison was performed of the impact of advanced PD symptoms—including cognitive dysfunction, psychosis, motor fluctuations, and dyskinesia—on disability and quality of life, it was found that cognition and psychosis have a stronger influence than motor fluctuations or dyskinesia (36). Self-efficacy, defined as the sense of confidence an individual has to manage selected activities, was shown to be an unexpectedly strong determinant of both disability and quality of life (34, 35). Self-efficacy to manage PD in general or do the household chores proved to be as potent an influence on disability and quality-of-life ratings as any of the motor or nonmotor factors.

Impediments to Accuracy of Outcomes Measurement

Every clinician and clinical investigator has experienced the difficulty of collecting accurate and reproducible data regarding PD symptoms, progression of disease, and disability. There are pitfalls in the collection of both objective and subjective data. The phenomenology of movement disorders including parkinsonism can be changeable. Important factors that can alter the neurologic examination include the timing of medications, fatigue, and patient effort. Assessments of impairment, disability, and quality of life all rely upon patient-reported data to varying degrees, and self-reported data have a number of important limitations. In a recent study of subjective vs. objective assessments of ADLs in PD, we found discordance between these assessments in the majority of patients (37). While most of the study subjects underrated their objective disability, there was a tendency for those with early PD to underrate while those with advanced PD tended to overrate their disability.

Outcomes data are commonly collected from both patient and family, yet many studies have shown that there is discordance between patient- and "proxy"- generated data, with proxies tending to rate disability higher and quality of life lower than do patients (38). Response shift is another important factor in the accuracy of self-reported data. "Response shift" refers to a change in self-reporting of health information overtime related to diminished expectations and recalibration of internal standards (39, 40). This phenomenon is likely to occur in the context of a chronic condition like PD, when people gradually adjust to progressive symptoms. Response shift results in the tendency for the person with PD to report a higher quality of life than a healthy person would assign to the same level of function. Notably, when data from a population with a chronic condition are compared to those from a healthy population, the presence of response shift tends to depress the size of the disease effect. Similarly, recognition of disability in PD may be hindered by a very gradual alteration in function that may not be apparent to the patient or family.

Accuracy in outcomes measurement is integral to clinical decision making, clinical trials, and public policy. Yet methodologies for the assessment of outcomes for chronic medical conditions have a number of shortcomings. Efforts are in progress to develop better scales for the assessment of PD-related impairments, disability, and quality of life, but there is growing interest and debate regarding the meaningfulness of these outcome measures. Should our health care dollar be focused on amelioration of PD-related impairments, delay of disability, or improved quality of life? Societal values are likely to play a role in determining the relative importance of the various measures of outcomes of disease.

References

1. World Health Organization. *International Classification of Impairments, Disabilities, and Handicaps.* Geneva: WHO, 1980.
2. Fahn S, Elton RL, Members of the UPDRS Development Committee. Unified Parkinson's Disease Rating Scale. In: Fahn S, Marsden CD, Calne DB, Goldstein M (eds). *Recent Developments in Parkinson's Disease.* Vol 2. Macmillan Health Care Information, 1987:153–164.
3. Duke University Center for the Study of Aging and Human Development. *Multidimensional Functional Assessment: The OARS Methodology. A Manual.* 2nd ed. 1978.
4. Ware JE Jr, Kosinski M, Keller SD. A 12-item short-form health survey: Construction of scales and preliminary tests of reliability and validity. *Med Care* 1996; 34(3):220–233.
5. Schwab JF, England AC. Projection technique for evaluating surgery in Parkinson's disease. In: Gillingham FJ, Donaldson MC (eds). *Third Symposium on Parkinson's Disease.* Edinburgh: Livingston, 1969:152–157.
6. Longstreth WT Jr, Nelson L, Linde M, Munoz D. Utility of the sickness impact profile in Parkinson's disease. *J Geriatr Psychiatr Neurol* 1992; 5(3):142–148.
7. Jenkinson C, Peto V, Fitzpatrick R, et al. Self-reported functioning and well-being in patients with Parkinson's disease: Comparison of the short-form health survey (SF-36) and the Parkinson's Disease Questionnaire (PDQ-39) *Age Ageing* 1995; 24(6):505–509.
8. Wallhagen MI, Brod M. Perceived control and well-being in Parkinson's disease. *West J Nurs Res* 1997; 19(1):11–25; discussion 25–31.
9. Karlsen KH, Larsen JP, Tandberg E, Maland JG. Quality of life measurements in patients with Parkinson's disease: A community-based study. *Eur J Neurol* 1998; 5(5): 443–450.
10. Rubenstein LM, Voelker MD, Chrischilles EA, et al. The usefulness of the Functional Status Questionnaire and Medical Outcomes Study Short Form in Parkinson's disease research. *Qual Life Res* 1998; 7(4):279–290.
11. Koplas PA, Gans HB, Wisely MP, et al. Quality of life and Parkinson's disease. *J Gerontol A Biol Sci Med Sci* 1999; 54(4):M197–M202.
12. Schrag A, Jahanshahi M, Quinn N. What contributes to quality of life in patients with Parkinson's disease? *J Neurol Neurosurg Psychiatry* 2000; 69(3):308–312.
13. Schrag A, Jahanshahi M, Quinn N. How does Parkinson's disease affect quality of life? A comparison with quality of life in the general population. *Mov Disord* 2000; 15(6):1112–1118.
14. Schrag A, Quinn N. Dyskinesias and motor fluctuations in Parkinson's disease. A community-based study. *Brain* 2000; 123(Pt 11):2297–2305.
15. Schrag A, Selai C, Jahanshahi M, Quinn NP. The EQ-5D—a generic quality of life measure—is a useful instrument to measure quality of life in patients with Parkinson's disease. *J Neurol Neurosurg Psychiatry* 2000; 69(1):67–73.
16. Karlsen KH, Tandberg E, Arsland D, Larsen JP. Health related quality of life in Parkinson's disease: A prospective longitudinal study. *J Neurol Neurosurg Psychiatry* 2000; 69(5):584–589.
17. Kuopio AM, Marttila RJ, Helenius H, et al. The quality of life in Parkinson's disease. *Mov Disord* 2000; 15(2):216–223.
18. Damiano AM, McGrath MM, Willian MK, et al. Evaluation of a measurement strategy for Parkinson's disease: Assessing patient health-related quality of life. *Qual Life Res* 2000; 9(1):87–100.
19. Caap-Ahlgren M, Dehlin O. Insomnia and depressive symptoms in patients with Parkinson's disease. Relationship to health-related quality of life. An interview study of patients living at home. *Arch Gerontol Geriatr* 2001; 32(1):23–33.
20. Keranen T, Kaakkola S, Sotaniemi K, et al. Economic burden and quality of life impairment increase with severity of PD. *Parkinsonism Relat Disord* 2003; 9(3):163–168.
21. Siderowf A, Ravina B, Glick HA. Preference-based quality of life in patients with Parkinson's disease. *Neurology* 2002; 59(1):103–108.
22. Global Parkinson's Disease Survey Steering Committee. Factors impacting on quality of life in Parkinson's disease: Results from an international survey. *Mov Disord* 2002; 17(1):60–67.
23. Cubo E, Rojo A, Ramos S, et al. The importance of educational and psychological factors in Parkinson's disease quality of life. *Eur J Neurol* 2002; 9(6):589–593.
24. Scaravilli T, Gasparoli E, Rinaldi F, et al. Health-related quality of life and sleep disorders in Parkinson's disease. *Neurol Sci* 2003; 24(3):209–210.
25. Morimoto T, Shimbo T, Orav JE, et al. Impact of social functioning and vitality on preference for life in patients with Parkinson's disease. *Mov Disord* 2003; 18(2):171–175.
26. Schrag A, Hovris A, Morley D, et al. Young- versus older-onset Parkinson's disease: Impact of disease and psychosocial consequences. *Mov Disord* 2003; 18(11):1250–1256.
27. Marras C, Lang A, Krahn M, et al. Quality of life in early Parkinson's disease: Impact of dyskinesias and motor fluctuations. *Mov Disord* 2004; 19(1):22–28.
28. Parkinson Study Group. Pramipexole vs levodopa as initial treatment for Parkinson disease: A randomized controlled trial. *JAMA* 2000; 284(15):1931–1938.
29. Brown RG, MacCarthy B, Gotham AM, et al. Depression and disability in Parkinson's disease: A follow-up of 132 cases. *Psychol Med* 1988; 18(1):49–55.
30. Starkstein SE, Mayberg HS, Leiguarda R, et al. A prospective longitudinal study of depression, cognitive decline, and physical impairments in patients with Parkinson's disease. *J Neurol Neurosurg Psychiatry* 1992; 55(5):377–382.
31. Liu CY, Wang SJ, Fuh JL, et al. The correlation of depression with functional activity in Parkinson's disease. *J Neurol* 1997; 244(8):493–498.
32. Siderowf A, Ravina B, Glick HA. Preference-based quality of life in patients with Parkinson's disease. *Neurology* 2002; 59(1):103–108.
33. Diamond SG, Markham CH, Hoehn MM, et al. Effect of age at onset on progression and mortality in Parkinson's disease. *Neurology* 1989; 39(9):1187–1190.
34. Shulman LM, Anderson KE, Gruber-Baldini AL, et al. Disease-specific or co-morbid factors: Which has the greatest impact on quality of life in Parkinson's disease? *Neurology* 2006: 66(Suppl 2):A116.
35. Shulman LM, Anderson KE, Gruber-Balidini AL, et al. Disease-specific or co-morbid factors: Which has the greatest impact on disability in Parkinson's disease? *Mov Disord* 2006; 21(Suppl 15):S509.
36. Shulman LM, Anderson KE, Vaughan CG, et al, The impact of symptoms of advanced Parkinson's disease on daily function and quality of life. *Neurology* 2004; 62(Suppl 5):A335.
37. Shulman LM, Pretzer-Aboff I, Anderson KE, et al. Subjective report versus objective measurement of activities of daily living in Parkinson's disease. *Mov Disord* 2006; 21(6):794–799.
38. Fleming A, Cook KF, Nelson ND, Lai EC. Proxy reports in Parkinson's disease: Caregiver and patient self-reports of quality of life and physical activity. *Mov Disord* 2005; 20(11):1462–1468.
39. Kern RZ, Brown AD. Disease adaptation may have decreased quality-of-life responsiveness in patients with chronic progressive neurological disorders. *J Clin Epidemiol* 2004; 57(10):1033–1039.
40. Schwartz CE, Sprangers MAG, Carey A, Reed G. Exploring response shift in longitudinal data. *Psychol Health* 2004; 19:51–69.

60 Family Caregiving

Julie H. Carter
Barbara J. Stewart
Patricia G. Archbold

Caregiving is part of all relationships. It is the act of providing assistance to someone with whom one has a personal relationship. It is usually an extension of caring and a reciprocal act. In conditions of chronic progressive disease such as Parkinson's disease (PD), the act of caregiving is primarily from one person, and reciprocal caregiving is diminished. In these situations, caregiving can become stressful and threaten the well-being of the caregiver and the care recipient, with significant negative economic, social, and psychological impact.

DEMOGRAPHIC TRENDS IN FAMILY CAREGIVING FOR THE TWENTY-FIRST CENTURY

Growth of the Elderly Population

During the past century the United States experienced unprecedented growth in the population 65 years of age and older. Indeed, the rate of growth for this subpopulation exceeded the rate of growth for the country as a whole: there was an 11-fold increase in elders between 1900 and 1994, compared with a 3-fold increase in the population below age 65 (1). A further dramatic increase in the actual numbers and relative percentage of elders

is expected as the baby boomers enter old age between 2010 and 2030. The elderly are projected to grow from the current 35 million (12.8%) to 70 million (20%). In addition, the percentage of racial and ethnic minority elders will increase at a much higher rate. From 2000 to 2005, it is projected that white elderly will double, African-American elderly will quadruple, and Hispanic elderly will increase 7-fold (2).

The elderly population is most at risk for functional loss and declines in health. The percentage of community-dwelling elders needing help with one or more activities of daily living (ADLs) (e.g., bathing and dressing) increases with age. Among those aged 65 to 74, only about 10% need help with such activities; but by age 85, about 50% need help (1). In 1990, some 4.5 million elders needed assistance with one or more ADLs.

IMPORTANT ROLE OF FAMILY CAREGIVING IN CHRONIC ILLNESS

The family is the linchpin of the health and long-term-care system for patients in this country. Families provide 80% to 90% of the care received by community-dwelling chronically ill elders. Because families are the main providers of care and support to chronically ill persons, including persons with PD, the need for family care is growing unprecedently as the number of persons with chronic illness increases.

This can be expressed quantitatively as the parent-support ratio, or the number of persons 85 years of age and older divided by the number of persons 50 to 64 years old times 100. In 1993 the parent-support ratio was 10; by 2050, it is projected to triple (1). Having living parents who are 85 of age or older will become commonplace in just over 50 years.

In 1996, a national phone survey of randomly selected English-speaking families was conducted to identify caregivers who provided unpaid assistance to a relative or friend 50 of age or older. Nearly 25% of households contained at least one caregiver. Three-quarters of these caregivers were providing care at the time of the phone survey and the remaining 24% had provided such care in the year preceding the survey (3). About half of the family caregivers who participated in the Caregiver Supplement of the National Long-Term Care Survey had been providing unpaid assistance to an elder for 1 to 4 years; another quarter had been providing assistance for 5 years or more (4). Eighty percent of these caregivers provided unpaid assistance 7 days a week and spent an average of 4 hours per day, or more than a half-time job, on caregiving tasks (4). In a report of the economic burden of PD, Whetten-Goldstein and colleagues found that hidden costs of PD included the significant costs of uncompensated informal care ($M = \$5386$ per family per year); these are costs that would be borne by society if the family did not provide care (5, 6).

THE RISKS ASSOCIATED WITH FAMILY CAREGIVING

Not only are the number of potential caregivers not increasing as fast as the elders in our society but clinicians and researchers are also concerned that the strain of caregiving can bring with it health risks that may threaten a caregiver's ability to continue in that role. In their 1995 review of the caregiving literature related to psychiatric and physical effects of dementia caregiving, Schulz and colleagues found that all studies reported elevated levels of depressive symptoms in caregivers (7). In Pinquart and Sörensen's 2003 meta-analysis comparing the health of caregivers and noncaregivers, caregivers had worse ratings on depression, stress, self-efficacy, and general subjective well-being (8). The present authors found a 27.1% prevalence rate of depressive symptoms in spouses of persons with late-stage PD, not quite as high as the 27.9% to 55% prevalence rates found with Alzheimer's disease (AD) caregivers (9). Pinquart and Sörensen found that the evidence for physical health effects in caregivers was weaker than the psychological effects noted above (8). In their 2003 meta-analysis comparing the physical health of dementia caregivers with that of demographically matched noncaregivers, Vitaliano and colleagues found

that there was a slightly greater risk of health problems in caregivers, with the largest risks involving increased stress hormones, decreased antibodies, and poorer global reported health (10). One of the most concerning findings from the Caregiver Health Effects Study is that caregiving in and of itself is not harmful, but that spouses who experience high strain are at greater risk for mortality (11).

PREDICTORS OF CAREGIVER STRAIN

Most clinicians have had the experience of seeing patients with similar symptoms and dependencies, yet one family caregiver is coping well whereas another is visibly on the verge of burnout. An understanding of this disparity may provide insight into how to help struggling families. A focus of many researchers has been to look at factors that predict strain and factors that reduce or buffer strain as well as, more complexly, the interaction between the two. Various models with theoretical underpinnings, offering ways to conceptualize this multifactorial problem, have been developed (12). Rather than choosing a specific model, this chapter synthesizes the research on strain and the various factors linked to it and organizes them into 3 categories: (1) caregiver strain (i.e., perceived difficulty), (2) characteristics of the caregiver, and (3) the caregiving situation. Inherent in this thinking is that the greater the strain, the greater the risk for negative outcomes such as decreased physical and emotional health of the caregiver, nursing home placement, and economic burden. Most caregiving research has been done in dementia. Research that is specific to PD is also discussed.

Caregiver Role Strain

Caregiver strain is defined as the perceived difficulty of fulfilling the caregiving role. Strain can lead to negative outcomes that may prevent a family member from continuing in this role. Research in family caregiving has identified a number of variables associated with strain. Some of these predict more strain and some less. These factors are reviewed below, under "Caregiver Characteristics" and "The Caregiving Situation." An understanding of the predictors of strain makes it possible to identify caregivers who are at risk for higher strain. It also holds the potential for developing interventions that may reduce strain.

In addition to understanding factors linked to strain, it is important to recognize that within the global concept of strain there are subtypes. Archbold, Stewart, and colleagues identified nine subtypes of strain that include strain from worry, tension, frustration from communication, direct care, role conflict, mismatched expectations, economic burden, lack of personal resources, and feelings of being manipulated (13). If a clinician knows that a caregiver's frustration from communication is greater than the strain from lack of personal resources (e.g., exhaustion), he or she might refer that individual to a specialist in augmentative communication techniques rather than for respite care.

In PD, strain increases as the disease progresses (9, 14). By ferreting out types of strain, it becomes clear that strain occurs at all stages of disease and accumulates with each advancing stage. In early-stage disease, when motor signs are minimal and before direct-care activities have started, worry emerges as an area of significant strain. In middle-stage disease, worry continues, but now there is the addition of tension, frustration from communication problems, strain from direct care, and role conflict. By late disease, significant levels of strain from lack of personal resources, economic burden, feelings of being manipulated, and mismatched expectations are added to the strain seen at earlier stages (9). For clinicians, having a general profile of the types of strain that a family member might be experiencing at different stages of disease may be helpful in considering referral to appropriate resources. A longitudinal study in PD spouses who had been providing care for over 10 years looked for warning signs early in caregiving that might predict those at greatest risk for increased strain and declining health. The study used predictive variables of health status, depression, strain, optimism, pessimism, mutuality, early changes in these variables (a change over 2 years), and late changes (change over 10 years). Early deterioration was found to predict spouse caregivers who were at the greatest risk for increased strain and declining health (15). The ability to identify warning signs in early disease may help to focus interventions on high-risk families.

Caregiver Characteristics

The response to caregiving is directly influenced by characteristics of the caregiver. These include (1) age and gender, (2) economic status, (3) physical and emotional health, (4) whether the caregiver is a spouse or adult child, (5) ethnicity, (6) personality, (7) mutuality (i.e., positive quality of the relationship), and (8) preparedness (how prepared one feels for the caregiving role). Most of these variables cannot be influenced by interventions, but their relationship to caregiver burden is important in identifying people at risk.

Age and Gender

Caregiver age has been inversely correlated with caregiver strain (7, 16–18). It has been suggested that younger caregivers experience more strain because they are subjected to multiple, often conflicting role demands as well as greater economic burdens. In caring for a spouse with PD, young caregivers (40 to 55 years of age) reported

more strain than did older caregivers (70 to 87 years of age) from lack of resources as well as more difficulty in handling symptoms such as hallucinations; however, these groups did not differ in terms of strain from worry or tension (18).

In general, women caregivers report more negative emotional and physical responses to caregiving than do men (19, 20). This may be because of women's greater awareness of their emotions, differences in coping styles, differences in the amount and type of direct care tasks that women perform, or differences in social support (20–22). Although most of the research examining gender differences has been done in caregiving for patients with dementia, the limited comparison of PD to AD would suggest that the findings are similar (23). Gender differences are important because the majority of caregivers are women.

Economic Status

The association of lower economic status and increased caregiver strain is more equivocal (16, 17, 24, 25). A clear understanding of this relationship is difficult to achieve because better education is usually seen with better economic status. More education may result in better problem-solving and coping skills, whereas more economic stability may allow for more paid support and opportunities for respite (19).

Preexisting Health

The relationship of a family member's precaregiving physical and emotional health to caregiver outcomes has been difficult to study because most research is done after caregiving has begun. Poor health is a predictor of higher strain. It is understandable that poor physical and emotional health might limit an individual's capacity to respond to the demands of caregiving and that caregiving might exacerbate underlying vulnerabilities (24–26). What is not clear is whether this is reinforcing, with more strain producing worse health and worse health resulting in more strain. Longitudinal studies are needed to answer this question.

Relationship to Patient

The majority of caregivers are either spouses or adult children of the care recipient. Spouses compared with adult children experience more strain in the caregiver role (27). In spite of this, it should be kept in mind that adult children have unique characteristics that contribute to their strain and which may limit side-by-side comparison to a spouse caregiver. Some of these are (1) a sense of filial responsibility, (2) employment demands, (3) conflict with other siblings regarding care of a parent, (4) responsibility to their own spouses and children, (5) prior relationship with parent, and (6) role reversals (28–31).

Ethnicity

Ethnic differences influence the long-term outcomes of family caregiving. With predictions that the proportion of minority elders will increase 23% by the year 2020, knowledge of these differences will be important in care delivery to families (32).

A review article of 116 studies evaluated what is known about ethnic differences in family caregiving. These studies included primarily caregivers of demented or frail elderly. The ethnic minorities included in this meta-analysis were African Americans, Hispanics, and Asian Americans. Comparisons were made to white caregivers. Differences in background characteristics, stressors, social resources, coping processes, caregiver rewards, and the health outcomes of caregiving were compared (33).

In summary, ethnic minorities provided more hours of care, had less education, and had fewer financial resources than white caregivers. At the same time they had more informal support and more cognitive and emotion-focused coping than whites. In regard to health outcomes, minorities had poorer physical health but were varied in their responses of depression and perceived strain. The benefit of better psychological health was seen most among African Americans, who were less depressed and reported less strain than did white caregivers, while Hispanics and Asian Americans reported more depression than did white caregivers (33).

Poorer physical health outcomes and, nevertheless, better psychological health outcomes among minorities might be explained on the basis that poorer physical health is a result of worse health care, racial discrimination, and lower levels of insurance coverage rather than the effect of caregiving. Better psychological health among African Americans may be due to the fact that their motivation to provide care is stronger based on cultural beliefs of filial responsibility and the greater use of informal support systems such as extended family and faith in God. These factors may buffer the emotional impact of caregiving, resulting in less perceived strain and depression (34).

Personality

Personality traits of optimism and pessimism have been examined in relation to caregiver strain and depression. Pessimism has been related to less effective coping and more depression, while optimism has been related to more effective coping in spouse caregivers (35). In addition, a higher level of caregiver sense of coherence—which includes dimensions of comprehensibility, manageability, and meaningfulness—has been associated with less caregiver burden (36). Because coping styles are modifiable,

this has important implications for interventions. Education or cognitive therapy directed toward coping skills can reduce strain and depression (37, 38).

Among 311 spouses of people with early PD, optimism and pessimism were examined as predictors of negative health outcomes over a 10-year period. On the basis of the Life Orientation Scale, it was found that high caregiver pessimism early in the caregiver role is a warning sign for poor current and future caregiver health (39). The negative effect for pessimism was seen in higher depression, worse physical health, and a faster decline in health over the 10-year period. Of interest was the finding that optimism was not a powerful predictor of the decline of mental or physical health compared to pessimism (40). It may be that optimism is more important in predicting the rewards of caregiving. Caregiver reward or uplift has been identified as having a buffering effect on the perception of strain. These concepts hold potential importance for caregiver interventions. Martin Seligman has championed the potentially useful concept of "learned optimism," which teaches people to cope with their negative "self-talk" when they experience setbacks as well as how to reframe their thinking and thereby increase their optimism (41).

Mutuality

Mutuality, the positive quality of the relationship between the caregiver and care receiver, is predictive of less caregiver strain. Archbold and coworkers found that high levels of mutuality were associated with low levels of strain even after controlling for other variables (i.e., gender, relationship, impairment level, and amount of direct care) (13). Mutuality in PD was extremely high for a sample of 380 spouse caregivers. Nonetheless, mutuality declined significantly across stages of disease, suggesting that the protective quality of a positive relationship eroded as the disease progressed (9).

Preparedness

Family caregivers' self-perception of how well they provide care has received attention as a predictor of strain. The concept of doing caregiving well has been described as preparedness (13) and mastery (42, 43). *Preparedness* describes how well prepared one feels for the tasks and stresses of caregiving. *Mastery* refers to the belief that one is able to control life events and is competent in managing these events (44). The possibility of improving preparedness or mastery among family caregivers in order to decrease or prevent strain holds promise. One study found a moderate level of preparedness among PD caregivers that remained similar across all stages of disease (9). Interventions to improve preparedness may be helpful to caregivers who perceive themselves as not well prepared. A recent qualitative study by Davey and colleagues (14) examined the experiences of wife caregivers of repeat fallers with PD. They described methods used by the wives to get their husband up from the floor and found that wife caregivers often injured themselves and received little information about managing falls safely. It will be important, through further study, to find ways in which families can provide care more skillfully (46).

The Caregiving Situation

The caregiving situation includes variables that stem from the care needs and demands of the patient and the caregiving required to fulfill these needs. The underlying assumption in PD is that these needs will intensify over time. They include (1) the physical and cognitive health problems of the patient, (2) the kind and amount of direct care, (3) the unpredictability of the situation, and (4) the amount of paid and unpaid social support.

Patient Characteristics

Patient characteristics are usually divided into three categories; (1) cognitive impairment, (2) functional impairment, and (3) behavioral disturbance. A review of 228 studies looked at the association between the caregiver's strain and depression and the care receiver's clinical features. Behavioral disturbance is the characteristic most consistently linked to caregiver strain and depression. When problems such as agitation, disinhibition, and hallucinations exist, families have a hard time. On the other hand, increased cognitive and functional impairment does not consistently correlate with increased strain (47). In other words, some families experience a great deal of strain while others in the same situation experience very little. This may be explained on the basis of moderator variables embedded in the characteristics of the caregiver, such as mutuality or personality (e.g., optimism). Other studies have suggested that perceived rewards, feeling useful, or experiencing increased closeness to the care receiver may also buffer the perception of strain (48).

Research focused on the impact of Parkinson's disability on caregiver strain is extremely limited (49–51). Most studies have had small sample sizes (94, 54, 65) and used different instruments to measure caregiver strain as well as different measurements for clinical variables. Aarsland et al. divided caregiver strain into emotional and social distress and correlated these with both physical and mental (i.e., depression and cognitive) patient variables. They found that mental disturbances in PD predicted both emotional and social distress in the caregiver. Using the Unified Parkinson's Disease Rating Scale (UPDRS) motor and ADL scores, these investigators found that functional status (ADL scores) predicted social strain but not emotional strain and that motor

scores did not contribute significantly (49). Miller found that depression in the patient was the strongest predictor of psychological strain and that functional impairment predicted strain from physical burden (50). Calder et al. found a bigger contribution from functional disability than from mental symptoms. They found that cognitive impairment independent of parkinsonian functional disability had no effect on cognitive strain levels. In contrast, PD disability predicted relatives' strain independently from cognitive impairment (51). This may be partially explained by the difference in severity of disease between the different studies. The severity of disease was greater in the Aarsland and Miller studies [Hoehn and Yahr (HY) 2.9 and 3.0] vs. the Calder study, which was HY 2.0.

A recent study in PD by Carter et al. correlated the clinical features of motor score, cognition, and depression in early PD with strain in 206 spouse caregivers. Using regression analysis, clinical features explained 9% to 16% of the variance in caregiver strain and 10% of caregiver depression. The motor features explained 0% to 6.0% and the psychological/cognitive symptoms explaining 7% to 13% (52).

This finding suggests that although the clinical features of PD are association with strain, there are other variables that play a role in explaining or mediating the perception of strain. These variables may be rooted in the traits of the caregiver, such as quality of the caregiver/care receiver relationship, or in the caregiving situation, such as the amount of social support.

Direct Care

Caregiver strain has been correlated with the number of tasks performed in a day and the duration of caregiving. Pinquart's meta-analysis identified that the more assistance a caregiver provides, the greater the burden and depression they experience (47). The types of tasks performed in addition to their sheer number may provide further insight into caregivers who are at the most risk for strain. Investigators have categorized types of tasks in a number of ways. Some have looked at the difference between tasks that require physical work such as toileting, bathing, and feeding vs. tasks that require emotional work, such as dealing with depression or hallucinations (53). Albert identified categories by asking caregivers to sort 25 tasks into common groups. The result was a triple classifications of tasks: (1) tasks that are dictated by type of impairment (physical vs. cognitive), (2) location of tasks (at home vs. outside the home), and (3) tasks that respond to care receiver competency (fostering independence vs. guardianship) (54). Still others have used factor analysis to group tasks. Examples of categories are tasks that require physical care, tasks that require supervision, help with transportation, household care, financial responsibilities, or help with health care arrangements (24, 54). In examining a list of 51 PD tasks, the mean number of tasks was found to triple from early disease (11 tasks) to late disease (30 tasks). Although the concept of doing an average of 15 to 20 tasks a day seems daunting, it was not until late disease (mean 30) that the strain from direct care became clinically significant for the average caregiver (9).

Predictability

The predictability of the family care situation is directly related to caregiver strain. Even with physical or mental limitations, if the care situation and everyday life are predictable, a family can count on what to expect, make plans, and have some sense of control. Predictability is a particular problem in the later stages of PD, when motor fluctuations become prominent. A person may be mobile and able to engage in activities one moment and rendered completely immobile the next. These "off" periods may last minutes or hours and are not always related to the timing of medication. This results in the disruption of routine and loss of control. Predictability has been shown to decline as PD progresses (9).

Social Support

Social support has been defined as an exchange that provides physical assistance, social contact, or emotional support. The concept of social support and its relationship to caregiver strain is complex. It includes the following aspects; (1) the caregiver's satisfaction with the quality of support, (2) the structure (number and relationship of people in the support network), and (3) the kind of support (emotional vs. physical). The one consistent finding is that the greater the caregiver's perceived satisfaction with support, the less the burden, the less the depression, and the fewer health problems. This inverse relationship is seen more with informal networks such as friends and families but is less well correlated with formal sources of support such as paid providers (7, 55–57). In addition, how this social support holds up as caregiving demands increase is important in assessing its value (57). In a comparison of social support in AD and PD, the caregivers of persons with AD gave more care but had fewer social supports available to them (23).

Assessment

A thorough assessment of caregiver issues must be completed before appropriate interventions can be implemented. Health care personnel face 2 hurdles in the assessment of families: (1) traditional medical training has focused on diagnosis and treatment of the patient, so that many clinicians do not consider caregiver issues in their purview, and (2) time is limited in the clinical setting, and clinicians need an efficient and systematic way of assessing these issues.

The first step is to determine whether caregiver strain exists. The second step is to gather information about the caregiving situation, as this may help in selecting the most useful interventions. Four areas that should be explored with family caregivers include (1) the degree of strain, (2) the emotional and physical health of the caregiver, (3) the caregiver's knowledge of the illness and its treatment, and (4) the need for additional social support.

Caregiver Strain

Clinicians should start by asking a global question about the degree of perceived strain. One example is to ask the family caregiver to rate on a scale from 0 to 4 (0 = no stress, 4 = overwhelming stress), how much stress they feel from all their obligations. It is then helpful to determine the causes of strain. One useful screening tool is the 18-question Multi-dimensional Caregiver Strain Scale Index (MCSI) (59) (Table 60-1), Where most caregiver screening tools look only at strain, the MCSI addresses 6 areas; physical strain, social constraints, financial strain, interpersonal strain, elder demanding behavior and time constraints. This questionnaire can be quickly administered and scores of 29 or higher should alert the clinician to problem areas that need further exploration or referral.

Psychological and Physical Health

It is useful to have caregivers self-rate their physical health on a scale of 1 to 5 (1 = poor, 5 = excellent) and then rate their current health compared to a year earlier (1 = much worse, 5 = much better). It is also helpful to inquire about any other medical conditions, such as arthritis or heart disease, that may limit the caregiver's ability to provide care.

Psychological health should be evaluated in terms of depression and anxiety. Simply asking whether a caregiver experiences any of these emotions is the first step. If depression is a major concern, it is worth evaluating by using a self-report measure such as the Center for Epidemiologic Studies Depression Scale (CES-D) (60). This instrument has good normative data, and a score of 16 or greater suggests the possibility of clinically significant depression that requires further evaluation and treatment.

Knowledge Base and Preparedness

The caregiver's understanding of the illness, expected course, and medications should be assessed. Lack of knowledge can cause considerable frustration and tension in a relationship. As an example, fluctuations in mobility can be misunderstood as an intentional lack of

TABLE 60-1
The Multidimensional Caregiver Strain Index*

CIRCLE THE NUMBER WHICH MOST CLOSELY REFLECTS YOUR FEELINGS ABOUT CARING FOR YOUR PARTNER, RELATIVE, OR FRIEND.	NEVER	A LITTLE	MODERATE	A LOT	A GREAT DEAL
1. I feel I have less energy now that I am caring for my spouse or family member.	0	1	2	3	4
2. I feel physically strained because of caring for my spouse or family member.	0	1	2	3	4
3. I feel that my physical health has suffered because of caring for my spouse or family member.	0	1	2	3	4
4. I feel that my social life has suffered because of caring for my spouse or family member.	0	1	2	3	4
5. I have had to give up vacations or trips because of caring for my spouse or family member.	0	1	2	3	4
6. I am able to go out when I want.	0	1	2	3	4
7. I have had to make adjustments in my work or personal schedule.	0	1	2	3	4
8. Caring for/providing help for my spouse or family member is a financial strain.	0	1	2	3	4
9. I resent the extra cost of caring for my spouse or family member.	0	1	2	3	4
10. I have enough time to do the things I need to do (such as chores and helping).	0	1	2	3	4
11. I have a lot of time to myself.	0	1	2	3	4
12. I feel resentful toward my spouse or family member.	0	1	2	3	4
13. I feel angry toward my spouse or family member.	0	1	2	3	4
14. I feel pleased about my relationship with my spouse or family member.	0	1	2	3	4
15. My relationship with my spouse or family member is strained.	0	1	2	3	4
16. I am glad that I can provide care my spouse or family member.	0	1	2	3	4
17. I feel that my spouse or family member tries to manipulate me.	0	1	2	3	4
18. I feel that my spouse or family member is overly demanding.	0	1	2	3	4

*Total score (reverse code 6, 10, 11, 14, and 16).
Adapted from Stull. DE. *J Clin Geropsychol* 1996; 2(3).

initiative. Understanding that this is part of the disease and not intentional can shift the energy from frustration with the family member to acceptance and more creative problem solving. Improving knowledge can also reduce the anxiety of being poorly prepared for the tasks of caregiving, improve observations of symptoms and medication response, and in general result in better care of the person with PD. To assess preparedness, one might ask: "How well prepared do you think you are (a) to take care of your family member's physical needs? (b) to take care of your family member's emotional needs? (c) to find out about and set up services for him or her? (d) for the stress of caregiving?" (13).

Social Support and Interpersonal Relations

Because social support has the potential to reduce strain, it is important to assess for the type of assistance a family member is receiving. The first step in assessing social support is to determine whether there is a need. Many caregivers are reluctant to acknowledge that they need help. The following question can elicit this information: "Many people in your situation find support from others helpful; are you receiving adequate help in caring for (name of person with PD)?" This can be followed with a second question to help understand the types of help needed. "Some people find they need help in the home with physical activities, some need time away, and others need someone to talk to about their feelings. How would you describe your needs?"

Inherent in a consideration of support is usually a discussion about help from other family members. One caveat is an awareness of the quality of past family relationships. A disease that results in dependence on family members can provoke unresolved competitions and conflicts that can cause tension and even elder abuse. It is helpful to inquire whether the family is working together or is conflicted about the right approach to care. To assess family conflict, one might ask: "How much family conflict has occurred because of your family member's health situation and need for help?" The past quality of the relationship between the caregiver and care receiver can also be significant in terms of the caliber of care given. A strong prior relationship is a buffer of strain, and a prior unhealthy relationship may result in more strain and poor care. As an example, past anger toward an abusive parent or spouse can easily alter the desire to provide adequate or involved care. These types of issues might help the clinician rethink the kind of support that would be most beneficial to the family and person with PD. To assess the quality of a past relationship, the clinician might ask: "Before your family member had Parkinson's disease, (a) to what extent did you enjoy the time you spent together? (b) how close did you feel to him or her at that time? (c) how much emotional support did he or she give you?"

INTERVENTIONS

Over the years, sensitive clinicians have responded to observed family needs by developing interventions for their patient or family population. Much work is still needed in this area, both in developing interventions but also in evaluating their effectiveness. In this section, family caregiver interventions that have received systematic evaluation and interventions that have practical value and need formal evaluation are reviewed. Many of the family and caregiver interventions described have been evaluated with families in which one member has a chronic illness that seriously impairs function. These samples may include PD, AD, and other illnesses. More studies specific to the care of persons with PD are needed. Five types of interventions reported in the literature will be discussed: psychoeducational, respite care, support groups, telephone and computer care, comprehensive in-home interventions, and interventions to improve the competence of the care receiver. In addition, some interventions have evaluated combinations of these approaches.

Psychoeducational and Psychotherapeutic Interventions

Psychoeducational interventions are directed toward reducing caregiver stress, moderating other negative consequences of caregiving, and increasing the caregiver's problem-solving skills. The psychoeducational approach goes beyond the more usual educational or emotional support model in that it teaches specific psychological skills that can be used by caregivers to manage stress on an ongoing basis (38). These interventions may be delivered individually or in group sessions (usually 1 to 2 hours per session for 6 to 10 sessions). They are typically led by a trained professional and include written materials.

Examples of interventions that have been evaluated with caregivers include a life-satisfaction class, a problem-solving class, and an anger-management class. For example, Gallagher-Thomson et al. found that some caregivers are easily angered and others very reserved (denying their feelings), and that both these patterns were associated with elder abuse and neglect (38).

On the basis of these findings, they developed a course in "coping with frustration" (anger management) for caregivers. Class content included (a) presentation of the cognitive-behavioral model and treatment rationale; (b) discussion of sources of frustration and anger in caregiving and the typical ways people respond; (c) teaching relaxation skills; (d) teaching cognitive techniques (e.g., self-talk); (e) helping individuals to develop a series of self-statements that work in coping with frustration; (f) teaching the difference between assertive, passive, and aggressive behavior; (g) teaching specific assertiveness skills; (h) encouraging individuals to practice self-assertion with family members and others in the caregiving situation; and (i) dealing with termination. The course included 8 classes and 2o booster sessions (61).

In PD, cognitive behavioral therapy was evaluated in family caregivers to see whether improvements in cognitive and behavioral skills could also improve the psychological outcomes associated with the current stressors of caregiving. Family caregivers were randomized into either a course of 12 to 14 sessions or to a no-treatment group. Sessions included education about the disease, accessing community resources, health self-enhancement activities, relaxation and sleep, working with negative thoughts and feelings, challenging maladaptive rules and beliefs, and planning for the future. A clinical psychologist taught the sessions. Results were evaluated using the General Health Questionnaire (GHQ-28). It was found that caregivers in the treatment group had significantly greater improvement than the no-treatment group and that this improvement was sustained over a 3-month period (62).

Another example of a psychoeducational intervention that has not received systematic evaluation is a caregiver educational series called *Powerful Tools for Caregivers*. This program is built on the concept of training the trainer with the purpose of a wider dissemination of information to caregivers who do not have access to professional psychoeducational programs. The curriculum is designed so that it can be taught by a non–health care professional who is trained to teach the curriculum with structured supportive written materials (63). This program has reached caregivers in many rural environments and has been self-sustaining because of ongoing demand.

In their meta-analysis, Sorenson and colleagues looked at the effectiveness of caregiver interventions by synthesizing 78 caregiver intervention studies (64). The analysis included 6 types of interventions; psychoeducational, supportive, respite-based, psychotherapy, care receiver–focused (e.g., memory clinics for patients with dementia), and multicomponent interventions. These interventions were evaluated using 6 outcome variables; caregiver burden, depression, subjective well-being, caregiver rewards, ability and knowledge, and care receiver outcomes.

Psychotherapeutic and psychoeducational interventions showed the most consistent improvement on all 6 outcome variables. Multicomponent interventions had significant effect on burden, well-being, and ability/knowledge but not on depression and care receiver symptoms. Support interventions reduced burden and increased ability/knowledge. Training of care recipients was effective in increasing caregivers' well-being and reducing care receivers' symptoms, but the effects on burden, depression, and ability/knowledge were not significant (64).

Respite Care and Adult Day Care

Respite care is designed to provide the caregiver with relief from caregiving activities; it includes such interventions as adult day care, in-home respite, and night care. Respite can be accomplished by hiring in-home care or by short-term placement of the care receiver to a nursing home or foster care facility. Adult day care offers respite for the caregiver and at the same time restorative activity programs for the care receiver. Analysis of respite care across 13 studies showed that respite and day care interventions were effective on burden, depression, and well-being but not significant for caregiver rewards, knowledge/ability, or care receiver symptoms (64). Clinicians should consider recommending respite care to families who need relief from care activities. Obtaining respite can be difficult for families when it involves hiring a person or people to care for their loved one. The checklist in Table 60-2 might be helpful to families.

Telephone and Computer Care

For over 15 years, telephone monitoring and support interventions have been successful in a wide range of

---

TABLE 60-2
Steps to Hire In-Home Respite Care

Hiring on your own
Create a job description
Conduct a search
Conduct interviews
Check references and public records
  for criminal history
Write an employee agreement
Set a work schedule
Talk with your insurance company
Talk with a tax accountant
Keep work records

TABLE 60-3
Parkinson's Disease Hotlines*

National Parkinson Foundation, Inc.
1501 NW 9th Ave./Bob Hope Rd.
Miami, FL 33136
Tel: 305-547-6666
Fax: 305-243-4403
Website: www.parkinson.org

WE MOVE: Worldwide Education and Awareness for
  Movement Disorders
204 West 84th Street
New York, NY 10024
Tel: 212-241-8567
Fax: 212-987-7363
Website: www.wemove.org

The American Parkinson's Disease Association
1250 Hylan Blvd.
Staten Island, NY 10305
Tel: 800-223-2732/718-981-8001
Fax: 718-981-4399
Website: www.apdaparkinson.com

Michael J. Fox Foundation for Parkinson's Research
20 Exchange Place, Suite 3200
New York, NY 10005
TEL: (212) 509-1650
FAX: (212) 509-2390
Website: www.michaeljfox.org

Parkinson's Action Network (PAN)
1025 Vermont Ave. NW, Suite 1120
Washington DC, 20005
Tel: 202-638-4101/800-850-4726
Fax: 202-638-7257
Website: www.parkinsonsaction.org

Parkinson's Disease Foundation
1359 Broadway, Suite 1509
New York, NY, 10018
Tel: 212-923-4700/800-457-6676
Fax: 212-923-4778
Website: www.pdf.org

*All the national organizations have free literature, a newsletter, and support group information.

---

health care situations, including cardiac disease (65, 66) and oncology (67, 68). More recently, computer-based information and support interventions have been found effective for caregivers of persons with chronic illnesses, including AD (69). Telehealth technologies provide access to health advice and monitoring in the home for family-initiated questions or for provider-initiated monitoring. National PD organizations sponsor hotlines for people with PD and their families. These telephone intervention systems provide information and referral services, connecting persons with local and national PD resources. A list of hotlines is given in Table 60-3.

In-Home Interventions

A few studies have evaluated the effects of comprehensive, in-home interventions on elders and families; most involve extensive interdisciplinary in-home care along with telephone support (70–77). Each of these studies evaluated a new model of care for frail elders and their families. In each, an intervention that changed the nature of health care delivery and the mix of health care providers was evaluated. Two comprehensive in-home interventions, PREP and the comprehensive support program, are reviewed.

PREP was a comprehensive program of expanded in-home and telephone care for elders and their families referred for home health. PREP focused on three goals: increasing (1) preparedness, (2) enrichment, and (3) predictability in family care. PREP involved care planning and management, a PREP advice line (PAL) whereby families could receive telephone advice about care when needed, and the Keep-in-touch (KIT) system, through which nurses could monitor families. A pilot study of PREP found that mean levels of preparedness, enrichment, and predictability in PREP families were significantly higher than in control families ($P < .05$) and that PREP reduced mean health care costs per family by $3800 over a 3-month period (70, 78).

The comprehensive support program of Mittelman and colleagues was designed to treat the primary caregivers of persons with AD over the course of the disease (74, 75). The intervention included treatments to maximize formal and informal support for the caregivers and included individual and family counseling sessions directed at increasing the support of the primary caregiver by other family members.

In addition, the intervention included availability of a weekly support group and ad hoc consultation by project staff when needed by the caregiver. The intervention was designed to provide continuous support for the caregiver and family as long as it was needed. Over the period of a year, caregivers in the control group became more depressed; however, caregivers in the treatment group remained stable. After 8 months of the intervention, treated caregivers were significantly less depressed than control-group caregivers.

Although comprehensive in-home interventions are not widely available, they hold great promise for persons with PD and their families. They provide highly individualized care to families, focus on developing family care skills, attend to long-term and acute problems, and monitor for transitions in health and care so that early intervention is possible.

Support Groups

Support groups may be led by professionals or peers. They are usually focused on building rapport among participants and creating a forum for the discussion problems and feelings. They are built on the concept that support from others with similar problems can be invaluable and provides an opportunity to exchange ideas and strategies that can help others cope better. Although support groups are the most available interventions for caregivers, there is great variability in the purpose and structure of these groups. Rigorous evaluation of support groups has been hampered by their enrollment practices; in general, caregivers self-select to join a support group when they are ready. Most evaluations of support groups in the literature depend on anecdotal comments from participants. In spite of limitations in comparing studies of support group effectiveness, Sörensen et al. concluded that this intervention reduced caregiver burden and increased ability/knowledge but had no effect on the other 4 outcome variables of depression, subjective well-being, caregiver rewards, and care receiver outcomes (64, 79, 81, 82).

In some situations (e.g., involving people who are newly diagnosed with PD), support groups can be more frightening than comforting. In these cases, it may be desirable to refer such individuals and their families for peer support, typically to a person with a similar experience who is coping well. Such an approach is grounded in findings from Pillemer and Suitor, who highlighted the beneficial effects of interactions with people who have the same condition or experience (80). There has also been an evolution of targeted support groups. Examples are groups for newly diagnosed people and their family members, people with early-onset disease, or support groups that are solely for caregivers. Targeted support groups have not received systematic evaluation.

CONCLUSION

For the estimated 1.5 million persons in the United States who have PD, family and friend caregivers are important mainstays. These caregivers are also valuable resources for physicians, nurses, and other clinicians who provide health care to these persons. With the projected future increases in the elderly population and the corresponding anticipated increases in the number of persons with PD, collaboration between family caregivers and health care providers may be the key to improving the quality of care and quality of life of persons with PD. Such collaboration between families and providers may have the additional benefit of reducing caregiver strain and improving the satisfaction that families derive from caregiving. In the coming decades, we look forward to a growing number of creative interventions conducted by teams of clinicians and researchers to improve the health and well-being of persons with PD and of the families who care for them.

References

1. Hobbs FB, Damon BL. *Current Population Reports, Special Studies, 65C in the United States.* Washington, DC: U.S. Bureau of the Census, U.S.Government Printing Office, 1996:23–190.

2. U.S. Bureau of the Census. Projections of the total resident population by 5-year age group, race, and Hispanic origin with special age categories: Middle series 1999–2000; middle series 2050–2070. From http://www.census.gov/population/projections/nation/summary/np-t4-a.txt.

3. National Alliance for Caregiving and the American Association of Retired Persons. *Family Caregiving in the United States: Findings from a National Survey.* National Alliance for Caregiving and the American Association of Retired Persons. Washington, DC, 1997.

4. Stone R, Cafferata GL, Sangl J. Caregivers of the frail elderly: A national profile. *Gerontologist* 1987; 27:616–626.

5. Whetten-Goldstein K, Sloan F, Kulas E, et al. The burden of Parkinson's disease on society, family, and the individual. *JAGS* 1997; 45:844–849.

6. Rubenstein LM, DeLeo A, Chrischilles EA. Economic and health-related quality of life considerations of new therapies in Parkinson's disease. *Pharmacoeconomics* 2001; 19(7):729–752.

7. Schulz R, OBrien AT, Bookwala J, et al. Psychiatric and physical morbidity effects of dementia caregiving: Prevalence, correlates, and causes. *Gerontologist* 1995; 35:771–791.

8. Pinquart M, Sorensen S. Associations of stressors and uplifts of caregiving with caregiver burden and depressive mood: A meta-analysis. *J Gerontol B Psychol Sci Soc Sci* 2003; 58(2):P112–128.

9. Carter JH, Stewart BJ, Archbold PG, et al. Living with a person who has Parkinson's disease: The spouse's perspective by stage of disease. *Mov Disord* 1998; 13:20–28.

10. Vitaliano PP, Zhang J, Scanlan JM. Is caregiving hazardous to one's physical health? A meta-analysis. *Psychol Bull* 2003; 129(6):946–972.

11. Schulz R, Beach SR. Caregiving as a risk factor for mortality: The Caregiver Health Effects Study. *JAMA* 1999; 282(23):2215–2219.

12. Pearlin LI, Mullan JT, Semple SJ, et al. Caregiving and the stress process: An overview of concepts and their measures. *Gerontologist* 1990; 30(5):583–594.

13. Archbold PG, Stewart BJ, Greenlick MR, et al. Mutuality and preparedness as predictors of caregiver role strain. *Res Nursing Health* 1990; 13:375–384.

14. Berry RA, Murphy JF. Well-being of caregivers of spouses with Parkinson's disease. *Clin Nursing Res* 1995; 4:373–386.

15. Lyons, KS, Carter JH, Stewart BJ, Archbold, PG. *Spousal Caregiving to Patients with Parkinson's Disease: A Follow-up Study.* OR: Medical Research Foundation of Portland, OR, 2003.

16. Montgomery RJV, Stull DE, Borgatta EF. Measurement and the analysis of burden. *Res Aging* 1985; 7(1):137–152.

17. Meshefedjian G, McCusker J, Bellavance F, et al. Factors associated with symptoms of depression among informal caregivers of demented elders in the community. *Gerontologist* 1998; 38(2):247–253.

18. Lyons, KS, Stewart BJ, Archbold PG, Carter JH. Comparing young vs. older caregiver spouses in early-middle stage Parkinson's disease. 55th Annual Scientific Meeting of the Gerontological Society of America, 2002.

19. Rose-Rego SK, Strauss ME, Smyth KA. Differences in the perceived well-being of wives and husbands caring for persons with Alzheimer's disease. *Gerontologist* 1998; 38:224–230.

20. Miller B, Cafasso L. Gender differences in caregiving: Fact or artifact? *Gerontologist* 1992; 32:498–507.

21. Lutzky SM, Knight BG. Explaining gender differences in caregiving distress: The role of emotional attentiveness and coping styles. *Psychol Aging* 1994; 9:513–519.

22. Lynch SA. Who supports whom? How age and gender affect the perceived quality of support from family and friends. *Gerontologist* 1998; 38(2):231–238.

23. Monahan DJ, Hooker K. Caregiving and social support in two illness groups. *Social Work* 1997; 42(3):278–287.

24. Bull MJ. Factors influencing family caregiver burden and health. *West J Nursing Res* 1990; 12(6):758–776.

25. Schulz R, Williamson GM. The measurement of caregiver outcomes in Alzheimer disease research. *Alzheimer's Dis Assoc Disord* 1997; 11(6):117–124.

26. Poulshock SW, Deimling GT. Families caring for elders in residence: Issues in the measurement of burden. *J Gerontol* 1984; 39:230–239.

27. George LK, Gwyther LP. Caregiver well-being: A multidimensional examination of family caregivers of demented adults. *Gerontologist* 1986; 26:253–259.

28. Doty P, Jackson ME, Crown W. The impact of female caregivers' employment status on patterns of formal and informal eldercare. *Gerontologist* 1998; 38:331–341.

29. Strawbridge WJ, Wallhagen MI. Impact of family conflict on adult child caregivers. *Gerontologist* 1991; 31(6):770–777.

30. Harrison DS, Cole KD. Family dynamics and caregiver burden in home health care. *Geriatr Home Care* 1991; 7(4):817–829.

31. Jarrett WH. Caregiving within kinship systems: Is affection really necessary? *Gerontologist* 1985; 25(1):5–10.

32. Williams DR, Wilson, CM. Race, ethnicity, and aging. In: Binstock RH, George LK (eds). *Handbook of Aging and the Social Sciences.* San Diego, CA: Academic Press, 2001:160–178.

33. Pinquart M, Sorensen S. Ethnic differences in stressors, resources, and psychological outcomes of family caregiving: A meta-analysis. *Gerontologist* 2005; 45(1):90–106.

34. Dilworth-Anderson P, Williams IC, Gibson BE. Issues of race, ethnicity, and culture in caregiving research: A 20-year review (1980–2000). *Gerontologist* 2002; 42(2): 237–272.

35. Pinquart M, Duberstein PR. Optimism, pessimism and depressive symptoms in spouses of lung cancer patients. *Psychol Health* 2005; 20(5):565–578.

36. Caap-Ahlgren M, Dehlin O. Factors of importance to the caregiver burden experienced by family caregivers of Parkinson's disease patients. *Aging Clin Exp Res* 2002; 14(5): 371–377.

37. Hooker K, Frazier LD, Monahan DJ. Personality and coping among caregivers of spouses with dementia. *Gerontologist* 1994; 34(3):386–392.

38. Gallagher-Thompson D, Lovett S, Rose J. Psychotherapeutic interventions for stressed family caregivers. In: Myers WA (ed). *New Techniques in the Psychotherapy of Older Patients.* Washington, DC: American Psychiatric Press, 1991:61–75.

39. Scheier MG, Carver CS. Optimism, coping and health: Assessment and implications of generalized outcome expectancies. *Health Psychol* 1985; 4(3):219–247.

40. Lyons KS, Stewart BJ, Archbold PG, et al. Pessimism and optimism as early warning signs for health decline in Parkinson's disease caregiving. *Nur Res* 2004; 53:354–362.

41. Seligman M. *Learned Optimism: How to Change Your Mind and Your Life.* New York: Knopf, 1991.

42. Myers WA (ed). *New Techniques in the Psychotherapy of Older Patients.* Washington, DC: American Psychiatric Press, 1991:61–75.

43. Lawton MP, Kleban MH, Moss M, et al. Measuring caregiving appraisal. *J Gerontol* 1989; 44(3):P61–P71.

44. Christensen KA, Stephens MAP, Townsend AL. Mastery in women's roles and well-being: Adult daughters providing care to impaired parents. *Health Psychol* 1998; 17(2):163–171.

45. Schumacher KL, Stewart BJ, Archbold PG. Conceptualization and measurement of doing family caregiving well. *J Nurs Schol* 1998; 30(1):63–69.

46. Davey C, Wiles R, Ashburn A, Murphy C. Falling in Parkinson's disease: The impact on informal caregivers. *Disabil Rehabil* 2004; 2;26(23):1360–1366.

47. Pinquart M, Sorensen S. Differences between caregivers and noncaregivers in psychological health and physical health: A meta-analysis. *Psychol Aging* 2003; 18(2):250–267.

48. Dorfman LT, Holmes CA, Berlin D. Wife caregivers of frail elderly veterans. *Fam Relat* 1996; 45:46–55.

49. Aarsland D, Larsen JP, Lim NG, et al. Mental symptoms in Parkinson's disease are important contributors to caregiver distress. *Int J Geriatr Psychiatry* 1999; 14(10):866–874.

50. Miller E, Berrios GE, Politynska BE. Caring for someone with Parkinson's disease: Factors that contribute to distress. *Int J Geriatr Psychiatry* 1996; 11:263–268.

51. Calder SA, Ebmeier KP, Stewart L, et al. The prediction of stress in carers: The role of behaviour, reported self-care and dementia in patients with idiopathic Parkinson's disease. *Int J Psychiatry* 1991; 6(10):797–742.

52. Carter JH, Stewart BJ, Lyons KS, et al. Do Motor and Non-Motor Symptoms in PD Patients Predict Caregiver Strain and Depression? *Movement Disorders*, 2007 (In press)

53. Montgomery RJV, Gonyea JG, Hooyman NR. Caregiving and the experience of subjective and objective burden. *Fam Relat* 1985; 34:19–26.

54. Albert SV. Cognition of caregiving tasks: Multi-dimensional scaling of the caregiver task domain. *Gerontologist* 1991; 31(6):726–734.

55. Given BA, Given CW. Family caregiving for the elderly. In: Fitzpatrick JJ, Tauton RC, Jacox AK (eds). *Annual Review of Nursing Research.* Vol 9. New York: Springer, 1991:77–92.

56. Vrabec NJ. Literature review of social support and caregiver burden, 1980 to 1995. *J Nurs Schol* 1997; 29(4):383–388.

57. Haley WE, Levine EG, Brown SL, et al. Psychological, social, and health consequences of caring for a relative with senile dementia. *JAGS* 1987; 35:405–411.

58. OReilly F, Finnan F, Allwright S, et al. The effects of caring for a spouse with Parkinson's disease on social, psychological and physical well-being. *Br J Gen Prac* 1996; 46:507–512.

59. Stull DE. The Multidimensional Caregiver Stain Index (MCSI): Its measurement and structure. *J Clin Geropsychol* 1996; 2(3)175–196.

60. Radloff LS. The CES-D Scale: A self-report depression scale for research in the general population. *Appl Psychol Meas* 1977; 1:385–401.

61. Gallagher-Thompson D, DeVries HM. "Coping with frustration" classes: Development and preliminary outcomes with women who care for relatives with dementia. *Gerontologist* 1995; 34(4):548–552.

62. Secker DL, Brown RG. Cognitive behavioural therapy (CBT) for carers of patients with Parkinson's disease: A preliminary randomised controlled trial. *J Neurol Neurosurg Psychiatry* 2005; 76(4):491–497.

63. Schmall VL, Cleland M, Sturdevant M. *The Caregiver Helpbook: Powerful Tools for Caregiving.* Legacy Health Care Systems, Portland, OR, 2000.

64. Sorensen S, Pinquart M, Duberstein P. How effective are interventions with caregivers? An updated meta-analysis. *Gerontologist* 2002; 42(3):356–72.

65. Beckie T. A supportive-educative telephone program: Impact on knowledge and anxiety after coronary artery bypass graft surgery. *Heart Lung* 1989; 18:46–55.

66. Gortner SR, Gilliss CL, Shinn JA, et al. Improving recovery following cardiac surgery: A randomized clinical trial. *J Adv Nurs* 1998; 13:649–661.

67. Hagopian, GA, Rubenstein JH. Effects of telephone call interventions on patients' well-being in a radiation therapy department. *Cancer Nurs* 1990; 13:339–344.

68. Nail LM, Greene D, Jones LS, et al. Nursing care by telephone: Describing practice in an ambulatory oncology center. *Oncol Nurs Forum* 1987; 16:387–395.

69. Brennan PF, Moore SM, Smyth KA. The effects of a special computer network on caregivers of persons with Alzheimer's disease. *Nurs Res* 1995; 44:166–172.

70. Archbold PG, Stewart BJ, Miller LL, et al. The PREP system of nursing interventions: A pilot test with families caring for older members. *Research in Nursing and Health* 1995; 18:3–16.

71. Cummings JE, Hughes SL, Weaver FM, et al. Cost-effectiveness of Veterans Administration hospital-based home care. *Arch Intern Med* 1990; 150:1274–1280.

72. Hughes SL, Cummings J, Weaver F, et al. A randomized trial of Veterans Administration home care for severely disabled veterans. *Med Care* 1990; 28(2):135–145.

73. Mohide EA, Pringle DM, Streiner DL, et al. A randomized trial of family caregiver support in the home management of dementia. *J Am Geriatr Soc* 1990; 38:446–454.

74. Mittelman MS, Ferris EM, Shulman E, et al. A comprehensive support program: Effect on depression in spouse-caregivers of AD patients. *Gerontologist* 1995; 35: 792–802.

75. Mittelman MS, Ferris SH, Shulman E, et al. A family intervention to delay nursing home placement of patients with Alzheimer's disease: A randomized controlled trial. *JAMA* 1996; 276(21):1725–1757.

76. Oktay JS, Volland PJ. Posthospital support program for the frail elderly and their caregivers: A quasi-experimental evaluation. *Am J Public Health* 1990; 80:39–46.

77. Zimmer JG, Groth-Juncker A, McCusker J. A randomized controlled study of a home health care team. *Am J Public Health* 1985; 75:134–141.

78. Miller LL, Hornbrook M, Archbold PG, et al. Development of use and cost measures in a nursing intervention for family caregivers and frail elderly patients. *Res Nurs Health* 1996; 19:273–285.

79. Gonyea JG. Alzheimer's disease support group participation and caregiver well-being. *Clin Gerontol* 1990; 10(2):17–34.

80. Pillemer K, Suitor JJ. "It takes one to help one:" Effects of similar others on the well-being of caregivers. J *Gerontol Soc Sci* 1996; 51B:S250–S257.

81. Herbert R, Lederc G., Bravo G, et al. Efficacy of a support group program for caregivers of demented patients in the community: A randomized controlled trial. *Arch Gerontol Geriatr* 1994, 18:1–14.

82. Demers A, Lavoie JP. Effect of support groups on family caregivers to the frail elderly. *Can J Aging* 1996; 15:129–144.

61 Economics

E. Ray Dorsey
Andrew D. Siderowf
Robert G. Holloway

Health care expenditures in the United States have continued to rise. From 1993 to 2003, national health expenditures nearly doubled, from $0.9 trillion to $1.7 trillion (1). As a percentage of gross domestic product (GDP), expenditures have risen from 13.3% of GDP in 2003 to 15.3% in 2005 (1). The principal reason postulated for the high level of expenditures in the United States relative to other countries is the greater intensity of services provided (e.g., more specialist care, more amenities, lower utilization of capital equipment, higher administrative costs, higher physician incomes) (2). The principal driver for the high rate of growth in health care expenditures is technology, either the development of new technology or new applications of existing technology (2). While health care expenditures continue to rise, concerns mount that the benefit (or value) of these expenditures is not keeping pace. This mismatch between increased expenditures and marginal health benefit affects all of health care, including that related to Parkinson's disease (PD).

Health services research is the field of medical inquiry concerned with evaluating the delivery, financing, and quality of health care. This research can help determine whether expenditures in health care are generating value for patients and society (3). This chapter considers economic evaluation in health care and its relevance to PD. It reviews estimates of the overall economic burden of PD and discusses methods for economic evaluation of interventions in PD.

GLOBAL ECONOMIC BURDEN

Estimates of the annual economic burden of PD in the United States range from a 1992 estimate of $5.6 billion ($7.8 billion in 2005 dollars adjusted for inflation using the U.S. Consumer Price Index–All Urban Consumers) (4) to a 1997 estimate of $25 billion ($30 billion in 2005 dollars) (5, 6). To put this figure into context, in 1992, dementing illnesses were estimated to cost over $100 billion ($139 billion in 2005), whereas stroke cost approximately $17 billion ($24 billion in 2005), and epilepsy cost approximately $600 million per year ($800 million in 2005) (7).

In Europe, the burden of PD is similarly large. A 2004 study, *Costs of Disorders of the Brain in Europe*, estimated the direct and indirect costs associated with neurologic, neurosurgical, and psychiatric disorders. In the study, the direct health care (e.g., physician, hospital, pharmaceutical costs) associated with PD was 4.6 billion euros in 2004. Among neurologic disorders, only stroke and dementia imposed a greater cost burden. The "direct nonmedical costs" (e.g., social services, transportation) were even higher, at 6.1 billion euros, and were second only to dementia. Together, the total direct costs were 10.7 billion euros in 2004, trailing only dementia (55.2 billion euros) and stroke (16.2 billion euros). Insufficient data precluded an estimate of the indirect costs (e.g., lost productivity) associated with PD (8, 9).

As suggested by the economic data from the United States and Europe, PD is a common presenting disease to neurologists. Data from the 1991–1992 National Ambulatory Medical Care Survey (NAMCS) (10) showed that PD was the third most common presenting diagnosis (after headache and seizures) at neurology outpatient visits. For patients over 65 years of age, PD was the most common diagnosis, accounting for 16.9% of total neurology outpatient visits in this age group. In another study, PD was the second most common neurologic reason (after Alzheimer's disease) for home health care visits in patients over age 65. An estimated 11,800 patients receive such services annually in the United States (11). In addition, patients with PD account for between 2.2% and 6.8% of the U.S. nursing home population. Thus, the frequency of institutionalization among patients with PD is substantially in excess of the prevalence of the disease (12).

As the population ages, the prevalence and burden of PD are likely to increase. Using age-specific prevalence rates for PD (13) in the United States combined with demographic projections from the U.S. Census Bureau, the burden of PD in the United States will increase by approximately 80% from 2005 to 2030 (14). The worldwide burden is likely to grow at an even higher rate as maturing population and economies in China and India increasingly contribute to the global burden of PD.

DIRECT AND INDIRECT COSTS

The economic impact of PD includes both direct and indirect costs. Direct costs are the formal medical services, home care, institutional care, and medications attributed to a particular condition. Indirect costs reflect the value of output (e.g., labor productivity) lost because individuals with a given disorder are impaired and unable to work. The division between direct and indirect costs is not always clear, as some costs, such as informal care provided by family members, are treated by some investigators as direct costs and by others as indirect costs. The critical determination is not whether a cost is direct or indirect but that all costs from a societal perspective are captured. The components included in each study, variability in estimates of the cost of these components, and the estimate of the population prevalence of PD all contribute to differences between estimates. These cost categories are summed to produce a cost per subject; then the cost per subject is often multiplied by an estimate of the prevalence of PD to arrive at an overall cost estimate.

As early as 1973, Singer (15) examined a number of economic factors in her detailed analysis of the social and economic impact of PD. Among the findings in this study were that employment was substantially reduced among PD patients and that income from disability payments was increased compared to controls. There were also reductions in the ability to perform housework tasks and engage in leisure activities. More recent studies have attempted to quantify the annual costs associated with PD.

A detailed report on the economic impact of PD was prepared in 1998 for the Parkinson's Disease Foundation (6). This study estimated the per-individual yearly cost of PD in 1997 at $24,041 ($29,047 in 2005 dollars). Based on a prevalence of 1 million affected individuals (6) (other prevalence studies(13, 16) lead to lower estimates of the prevalence), the total economic burden in this study was calculated as $24 billion in 1997 ($29 billion in 2005 dollars). Direct medical costs contributed $8872 or about one-third of the per-patient cost. These direct costs included physician visits and hospitalizations as well as use of allied medical professionals such as physical therapists, costs of assisted living, and nursing home costs. The estimate of drug costs of $2137 used in this study may be an overestimate, since the investigators used retail prices rather than wholesale costs. The remaining $15,169 per patient was made up by indirect costs including lost productivity in patients under 65 years of age and a fraction of patients between 65 and 74 years of age.

More detailed reports of the costs associated with PD continue to be published in the medical literature. In one such study, Whetten-Goldstein et al. (17) interviewed 109 PD patients in central North Carolina. Measures in this study included direct medical costs, lost wages, and an estimate of the economic effect on family caregivers. The total costs per PD patient were estimated at $25,001 per year in 1994 ($32,813 in 2005 dollars). Direct medical costs account for only $4026 ($5284 in 2005 dollars) of this cost, while lost wages both of patients and family caregivers make up the remaining portion of the costs.

Rubenstein et al. (18) used data from the National Medical Expenditures Survey of 1987 to estimate the economic burden of PD. From a survey of 14,000 households, they identified 58 individuals with PD, of whom 43 had cost and health status estimates for an entire year. These individuals were compared to a control group matched for age, gender, race, urban-rural status, and presence of specific target conditions known to be highly associated with health resource use. Patients with PD were significantly more likely than controls to report lost productivity due to health problems, greater use of hospital visits, and longer duration of hospitalization for similar diagnoses. Such patients were also more likely to visit physicians, use home health care services, and take

TABLE 61-1
Direct and Indirect Costs per Individual with Parkinson's Disease

Investigator	Study Year	Country	Monetary Value Year	Currency	Direct Cost	Indirect Cost	In 2005 USD Direct Cost	In 2005 USD Indirect Cost
Rubenstein et al.	1997	United States	1987	USD	10,392		17,862	
Whetten-Goldstein et al.	1997	United States	1994	USD	4,026	20,975	5,284	27,530
Dodel et al.	1998	Germany	1995	DM	20,840		18,563	
John Robbins Associates	1998	United States	1997	USD	8,872	15,169	10,720	18,328
LePen et al.	1999	France	1996	Euros	4,710		7,482	
Hagell et al.	2002	Sweden	1998	Euros	7,920	5,810	10,324	7,573
Findley et al.	2003	United Kingdom	1998	Euros	3,360		4,380	
Keranen et al.	2003	Finland	1998	Euros	4,900	6,900	6,387	8,994

USD = U.S. dollars; DM = Deutsche mark

significantly more prescription medications. Total direct medical expenditures in 1987 were $10,392 ($17,862 in 2005 dollars) per year for PD patients and $5648 ($9708 in 2005 dollars) more than for controls. The authors commented that their estimates were somewhat imprecise because of their small sample. After adjusting for inflation, their estimate is also somewhat higher than the $4026 estimate derived by Whetten-Goldstein et al. (17) and the $8872 estimate used in the PDF study.

Dodel et al. (19) conducted a 3-month prospective analysis of direct health care costs of PD including drug costs, hospitalization costs, office visits, diagnostic procedures and nursing care among 20 PD patients in Germany. Informal care and lost productivity were not included in their estimate. Overall, these investigators found a 3-month mean direct costs of 5210 DM or $3400 in 1995 ($4,336 in 2005). This annualized estimate ($14,556) is higher than those mentioned above and approximately 30% higher than an earlier estimate by the same investigators (20) based on a (retrospective) review of medical records of 273 patients. Prospective measurements may lead to higher estimates of overall cost for several reasons. Prospective data collection may be more accurate as a result of more complete recall of resource use. However, prospective studies may also systematically inflate estimates because they tend to be made up of subjects who have recently come to medical attention. As a result, the study sample may be biased toward patients with greater resource use. The ideal study would collect data on resource use prospectively from a sample of patient identified from a population of community-dwelling individuals with PD. This information should also be validated by comparison with insurance claims. Table 61-1 summarizes many of the studies (6, 17–19, 21–24) published on the direct and indirect costs associated with PD. However, comparisons across studies are difficult due to different patient populations and methodologies, including the scope of direct and indirect costs.

INFLUENCE OF CLINICAL FEATURES ON RESOURCE USE

Many factors may influence the costs associated with PD (Table 61-2). Chief among them are the characteristics and severity of the disease. The study by Dodel et al. (19) also

TABLE 61-2
Determinants of Parkinson's Disease Cost

Patient-level factors:
  Disease severity
    Motor symptoms
    Nonmotor symptoms
  Comorbidities
  Age
  Socioeconomic status
Physician factors:
  Specialty of treating physician
  Setting of physician (academic vs. community)
Health system factors:
  Access to care
  Quality of care
  Financial (reimbursement) incentives

examined the impact of specific disease characteristics on resource use. These investigators found that patients with early disease [Hoehn and Yahr (H&Y) stage 1] had substantially lower costs than those with advanced disease ($1250 per year vs. $6330 per year). They also found that patients experiencing motor fluctuations had substantially higher costs ($4260) than those who did not have motor fluctuations ($1960).

Several other studies have evaluated the effect of disease severity on resource use. Chrischilles et al. (25) conducted a detailed study of resource use in 193 patients with PD attending 2 University-based neurology clinics in Iowa. These investigators measured a number of economic factors, including use of formal medical services, ancillary and community services, and durable medical equipment. Days out from work and premature retirement due to PD were recorded as measures of lost productivity. Caregiver burden was not assessed. There was a strong relationship between disease severity as measured by H&Y stage and use of resources. For example, 3 times as many patients with H&Y stage 3 disease reported use of emergency room services compared to those with stage 1 or 1.5 (14.8% vs. 40.7%) over a 12-month period. Other studies have also found that expenditures increase with disease severity (22–24).

We (unpublished data) conducted a survey of resource use of 428 patients attending a movement disorders clinic. Patients and caregivers completed a detailed questionnaire including items on disability for activities of daily living, use of direct medical services, drug use, and employment status. As in the study by Chrischilles et al. (25), we found a strong relationship between disease status and resource use. We also found that certain PD symptoms such as motor fluctuations, hallucinations, and confusion were strongly associated with resource use and negatively associated with employment. This is consistent with a previous study showing that the presence of visual hallucinations was strongly associated with the need for nursing home placement (26). Our survey, although limited by lack of verification of patient self-report of resource use, suggests that nonmotor symptoms are an important patient-level factor associated with resource use in PD. Future research employing population-based studies that use prospective and verifiable methods to ascertain costs will help better characterize the economic burden of PD.

COST OF MEDICATIONS AND SURGERY

Expenditures on prescription drugs have risen sharply. From 1993 to 2003, U.S. expenditures on prescription drugs rose an average of 13.3% per year (by comparison, inflation rose 2.4% per year over the same time period) from $51.3 billion to $179.2 billion (1). Relative to total U.S. health expenditures, prescription drugs accounted for 10.7% of expenditures in 2003, up from 5.8% in 1993 (1). Pharmacologic treatment is among the largest contributors in the overall direct medical costs associated with PD (20).

New agents and new formulations of existing agents have increased the therapeutic options available for PD and have increased the costs. Annual cost of treatment with nonergot dopamine agonists can easily exceed $2000 per year. By comparison, treatment with generic carbidopa/levodopa costs approximately one-third as much. Table 61-3 shows the prices of commonly prescribed medications for PD.

Surgical therapies, including pallidotomy and deep brain stimulation (DBS), have very high initial costs (27) but could be associated with long-term savings. Cost-effectiveness research provides a means to assess the costs and health consequences of these new medical and surgical interventions.

COST-EFFECTIVENESS RESEARCH

Cost-effectiveness research embodies a set of research methods to assess the efficiency with which health care technologies make use of limited resources to produce health outputs. The drivers of these studies are the principles that all resources (including those for health) are limited and that health benefit should be maximized subject to those limitations. The goal of cost-effectiveness research is to compare incrementally the costs and benefits of alternative courses of action to show the relative value of alternative health-related interventions. The methodologic underpinnings and the importance of formal economic evaluations in analyzing neurologic issues have been reviewed elsewhere (28, 29). Cost-effectiveness analysis is increasingly used to evaluate interventions for PD (27, 30).

COST-EFFECTIVENESS OF MEDICATIONS

One study has assessed the cost-effectiveness of pramipexole in both the early and late stages of PD (30). In this study, the investigators modeled the potential health and cost effects of adding pramipexole compared to standard treatment with levodopa for patients in both the early and late stages of disease. For both early- and late-stage patients, the pramipexole strategy was both more costly and more effective than the baseline levodopa strategy. For early PD patients, it was estimated that the pramipexole strategy costs an additional $8837 (United States, 1997) to gain an additional quality-adjusted life year (QALY) compared to the baseline treatment. For advanced PD patients, it costs an additional $12,294 to gain an additional QALY. These cost-effectiveness ratios were sensitive to many of the input variables in the model. For example, the cost-effectiveness of pramipexole becomes more

TABLE 61-3
Average Wholesale Prices of Commonly Prescribed Drugs for Parkinson's Disease

DRUG	DOSE	MANUFACTURER	AVERAGE WHOLESALE PRICE	UNITS
Carbidopa/levodopa				
Carbidopa/levodopa	25/100 mg	Alpharma	$80.00	per 100 tablets
Sinemet CR	25/100 mg	Bristol-Myers Squibb	$104.59	per 100 tablets
Sinemet CR	50/200 mg	Bristol-Myers Squibb	$201.71	per 100 tablets
Stalevo (carbidopa/ entacapone/levodopa)	25/200/100 mg	Novartis	$219.45	per 100 tablets
Parcopa	25/100	Schwarz	$102.70	per 100 tablets
Dopamine agonists				
Bromocriptine	2.5 mg	Mylan	$218.25	per 100 tablets
Pergolide	1 mg	Ivax Pharmaceuticals	$401.65	per 100 tablets
Mirapex (pramipexole)	1 mg	Boehr Ingelheim	$216.64	per 90 tablets
Requip (ropinirole)	5 mg	GlaxoSmithKline	$240.86	per 100 tablets
COMT inhibitors				
Comtan (entacapone)	200 mg	Novartis	$203.16	per 100 tablets
Tasmar (tolcapone)	100 mg	Valeant Pharmaceuticals	$255.04	per 100 tablets
Anti-cholinergics				
Trihexyphenidyl	2 mg	Consolidated Midland	$15.00	per 100 tablets
Benztropine	0.5 mg	Upsher-Smith	$18.42	per 100 tablets
Amantadine	100 mg	Upsher-Smith	$59.06	per 100 capsules

Sources: Average wholesale price determined from Red Book. Pharmacy's Fundamental Reference. 2005 edition. Prices are in 2005 U.S. dollars

attractive (greater effect for less cost) if one assumes a slower rate of change over time in Unified Parkinson's Disease Rating Scale (UPDRS) scores for those patients receiving pramipexole treatment (i.e., neuroprotection). Under certain assumptions, for example, when the annual rate of UPDRS change in the pramipexole group was reduced to 2 units or less, the pramipexole strategy actually leads to cost savings. The potential cost savings associated with a neuroprotective agent in PD was noted over a decade ago (31).

COST-EFFECTIVENESS OF SURGERY

Cost-effectiveness analyses have also evaluated surgical treatments of PD. A 2001 study used a decision model comparing DBS to best medical treatment in individuals over age 50 with PD and found that the incremental cost-effectiveness from DBS treatment was $49,000 per quality-adjusted life year (QALY). However, because the long-term efficacy of DBS is unknown, the authors had to make assumptions regarding the duration and magnitude of effect. The need for these critical assumptions highlights "the need for randomized, controlled, prospective DBS experiments including quality of life and economic components" (32). Table 61-4 summarizes the results of

cost-effectiveness analyses listed for PD in the Harvard School of Public Health's Cost Effectiveness Analysis Registry (33).

IMPLICATIONS OF COST-EFFECTIVENESS RESEARCH

The central measure used in cost-effectiveness research is the cost-effectiveness ratio (C/E ratio), or the incremental costs associated with using one technology compared with another to achieve a gain in a unit of health. Costs are counted in the numerator of the C/E ratio and health outcomes in the denominator. The denominator in a C/E ratio is often expressed in QALYs. The QALY is the most comprehensive and universal measure of health benefit (34). The summary measure of these studies is expressed in terms of a cost in dollars to achieve one QALY. Comparing C/E ratios obtained from analyses of different interventions can assist decision makers in valuing these competing health interventions. Moreover, because the dollars per QALY units of the C/E ratio are not specific to any given disease, the ratio obtained in the analysis of an intervention for one condition can be directly compared to an intervention in an entirely different condition, as in Table 61-5 (35). For example, the one study reviewed

TABLE 61-4

Results of Cost-Effectiveness Analysis Studies in Parkinson's Disease

INVESTIGATOR	YEAR	INTERVENTION EVALUATED	RESULT (IN $/QALY)*
Hoerger et al.	1998	Pramipexole in early PD vs. Standard of care, levodopa in patients with PD not already on levodopa	9,900
Hoerger et al.	1998	Pramipexole in late PD vs. Standard of care, levodopa in patients with PD not already on levodopa	14,000
Shimbo T et al	2001	Dopamine agonists plus levodopa vs. Levodopa alone in 60-year-old men with PD in Hoehn-Yahr stage II in Japan	190,000
Nuitjen MJ et al	2001	Entacapone vs. Usual care in patients with PD with motor fluctuations	Cost-saving
Tomaszewski KJ et al	2001	Deep brain stimulation vs. Best medical management in PD patients 50 years or older in later stages of disease	50,000

Source: Harvard Cost-Effectiveness Analysis Registry
QALY = quality-adjusted life year
*Standardized to 2002 U.S. dollars

above found that it costs $8837 to gain a QALY when using pramipexole rather than levodopa in patients with early PD (30). The results of this study can be directly compared with those of another study looking at the screening and treatment of patients with asymptomatic carotid stenosis; it found that intervention cost $120,000 per QALY (36). The implication of comparing one ratio to another is that those treatments or technologies with lower cost-per-QALY estimates represent better investments in health care resources compared to those with higher cost-per-QALY estimates. It is generally accepted that health care interventions with cost-effectiveness ratios of less than $50,000 to $100,000 per QALY are reasonable investments (see Table 61-5) (37).

Many controversies, challenges, and limitations remain in applying the results of cost-effectiveness research to help allocate resources. Recent attempts have been made to standardize the conduct and reporting of cost-

TABLE 61-5

Comparison of Cost-Effectiveness Ratios for Various Medical Interventions

PROGRAM	REFERENCE	COST-EFFECTIVENESS RATIO ($/QALY)*
Seat belt laws	Kaplan (1988)	0
Coronary artery bypass grafting surgery for lesion of left main coronary artery	Weinstein (1982)	6,616
Oral gold in rheumatoid arthritis	Thompson et al. (1987)	16,206
Treatment of mild hypertension in 40-year-old males	Weinstein and Stason (1976)	29,831
Screening for asymptomatic carotid stenosis	Lee et al. (1997)	145,132

QALY, quality-adjusted life year.
Source: Kaplan RM, Anderson JP. The general health policy model: An integrate approach, In: Spilker B (ed). *Quality Of Life and Pharmacoeconomics in Clinical Trials*, 2nd ed. Philadelphia: Lippincott-Raven, 1996:309–322.
*Standardized to 2002 U.S. dollars.

effectiveness analyses so as to minimize the effects of potential biases and improve the validity of the study results (38–39).

SUMMARY

By all metrics used, the economic burden of PD is large in the United States and Europe. With the aging of western populations and the economic and demographic maturation of the East, this burden is likely to grow substantially over time and become a more global issue. The burden extends beyond medical care to other direct costs, such as long-term care, and to indirect costs, such as lost productivity. It will be challenging to develop, within economic constraints, therapies and policies that meet the needs of individuals with PD.

Health services research, in particular cost-effectiveness research, provides new insights into the economics of PD and the value of PD interventions. Because PD is highly disabling and expensive, even modestly effective interventions are likely to be of good value. The burden of proof, however, depends on the careful conduct of cost-effectiveness analyses of PD-related interventions and critical appraisal of the results. Only then can the medical community translate the knowledge gained from these studies into strategies for promoting improvements in the prevention and treatment of PD.

References

1. Smith C, Cowan C, Sensenig A, Catlin A. Health spending growth slows in 2003. *Health Affairs* 2005; 24(1):185–194.
2. Fuchs VR. Health care expenditures reexamined. *Ann Intern Med* 2005; 143(1): 76–78.
3. Moses H, Dorsey ER, Matheson DHM, Thier SO. Financial anatomy of biomedical research. *JAMA* 2005; 294(11):1333–1342.
4. Consumer Price Index: All Urban Consumers. U.S. Department of Labor Bureau of Labor Statistics 2005 [cited 2005 Nov 16]; Available from: http://data.bls.gov/cgi-bin/surveymost
5. *Parkinson's Disease: Hope Through Research*. Bethesda, MD: Office of Communication and Public Liaison, NINDS, 1994.
6. *The Average Per-Patient Costs of Parkinson's Disease*. New York: John Robbins Associates, 1998.
7. *The Cost of Disorders of the Brain*. Washington, DC: National Foundation for Brain Research, 1992.
8. Andlin-Sobocki P, Jonsson B, Wittchen HU, Olesen J. Costs of disorders of the brain in Europe: Foreword. *Eur J Neurol* 2005; 12:VIII–VIIX.
9. Olesen J. Costs of disorders of the brain in Europe: Preface. *Eur J Neurol* 2005; 12:VI–VII.
10. Schappert S. Office visits to neurologists: United States, 1991–1992. *Adv Data* 1995; 267:1–20.
11. Haupt B. An overview of home health and hospice care patients: 1996 national home and hospice care survey. *Adv Data* 1998; 291:1–36.
12. Mitchell SL, Kiely DK, Kiel DP, Lipsitz LA. The epidemiology, clinical characteristics, and natural history of older nursing home residents with a diagnosis of Parkinson's disease. *J Am Geriatr Soc* 1996; 44(4):394–399.
13. Mayeux R, Marder K, Cote LJ, et al. The frequency of idiopathic Parkinson's disease by age, ethnic group, and sex in northern Manhattan, 1988–1993. *Am J Epidemiol* 1995; 142(8):820–827.
14. Dorsey ER, Constantinescu R, Thompson JP, Biglan KM, Holloway RG, Kieburtz K, Marshall FJ, Ravina BM, Schifitto G, Siderowf A, Tanner CM. Projected number of people with Parkinson's disease in the most populous nations, 2005–2030. *Neurology* 2007; 68:384–386.
15. Singer E. Social costs of Parkinson's disease. *J Chronic Dis* 1973; 26(4):243–254.
16. Mayeux R, Denaro J, Hemenegildo N, et al. A Population-based investigation of Parkinson's disease with and without dementia: Relationship to age and gender. *Arch Neurol* 1992; 49(5):492–497.
17. Whetten-Goldstein K, Sloan F, Kulas E, et al. The burden of Parkinson's disease on society, family, and the individual. *J Am Geriatr Soc* 1997; 45(7):844–849.
18. Rubenstein LM, Chrischilles EA, Voelker MD. The impact of Parkinson's disease on health status, health expenditures, and productivity: Estimates from the National Medical Expenditure Survey. *Pharmacoeconomics* 1997; 12(4):486–498.
19. Dodel RC, Singer M, Kohne-Volland R, et al. The economic impact of Parkinson's disease: An estimation based on a 3-month prospective analysis. *Pharmacoeconomics* 1998; 14(3):299–312.

20. Dodel RC, Eggert KM, Singer MS, et al. Costs of drug treatment in Parkinson's disease. *Mov Disord* 1998; 13(2):249–254.
21. Lepen C, Wait S, Moutaud-Martin F, et al. Cost of illness and disease severity in a cohort of French patients with Parkinson's disease. *Pharmacoeconomics* 1999; 16(1):59–69.
22. Hagell P, Nordling S, Reimer J, et al. Resource use and costs in a Swedish cohort of patients with Parkinson's disease. *Mov Disord* 2002; 17(6):1213–1220.
23. Findley L, Aujla M, Bain PG, et al. Direct economic impact of Parkinson's disease: A research survey in the United Kingdom. *Mov Disord* 2003; 18(10):1139–1145.
24. Keranen T, Kaakkola S, Sotaniemi K, et al. Economic burden and quality of life impairment increase with severity of PD. *ParkinsonismRelat Disord* 2003; 9(3):163–168.
25. Chrischilles EA, Rubenstein LM, Voelker MD, et al. The health burdens of Parkinson's disease. *Mov Disord* 1998; 13(3):406–413.
26. Goetz CG, Stebbins GT. Risk Factors for nursing home placement in Parkinson's disease. *Ann Neurol* 1992; 32(2):250.
27. Siderowf A, Holloway R, Mushlin A. Cost-effectiveness of pallidotomy and add-on medical therapy in advanced Parkinson's disease. *Ann Neurol* 1998; 44(3):517.
28. Holloway RG. Cost-effectiveness analysis: What is it and how will it influence neurology? *Ann Neurol* 1996; 39(6):818–823.
29. Eisenberg JM. Clinical economics: A guide to the economic-analysis of clinical practices. *JAMA* 1989; 262(20):2879–2886.
30. Hoerger TJ, Bala MV, Rowland C, et al. Cost effectiveness of pramipexole in Parkinson's disease in the U.S. *Pharmacoeconomics* 1998; 14(5):541–557.
31. Kurlan R, Clark S, Shoulson I, Penney JB. Economic impact of protective therapy for early Parkinson's disease. *Ann Neurol* 1988; 24(1):153.
32. Tomaszewski KJ, Holloway RG. Deep brain stimulation in the treatment of Parkinson's disease: A cost-effectiveness analysis. *Neurology* 2001; 57(4):663–671.
33. The CEA Registry. Harvard School of Public Health 2005. Accessed December 9, 2005 at www.tufts-nemc.org/cearegistry/Drummond MF, O'Brien B, Stoddard GI, et al. *Cost-Utility Analysis. Methods for the Economic Evaluation of Health Care Programmes*. New York: Oxford University Press, 1997.
34. Kaplan RM, Anderson JP. The general health policy model: An integrated approach. In: Spilker B (ed). *Quality of Life and Pharmacoeconomics in Clinical Trials*, 2nd ed. Philadelphia: Lippincott-Raven, 1996:309–322.
35. Lee TT, Solomon NA, Heidenreich PA, et al. Cost-effectiveness of screening for carotid stenosis in asymptomatic persons. *Ann Intern Med* 1997; 126(5):337–346.
36. Phelps CE, Mushlin AI. The (near) equivalence of cost-effectiveness and cost-benefit-analysis. *Med Decision Making* 1987; 7(4):286.
37. Weinstein MC, Siegel JE, Gold MR, et al. Recommendations of the panel on cost-effectiveness in health and medicine. *JAMA* 1996; 276(15):1253–1258.
38. Russell LB, Gold MR, Siegel JE, et al. The role of cost-effectiveness analysis in health and medicine. *JAMA* 1996; 276(14):1172–1177.
39. Siegel JE, Weinstein MC, Russell LB, Gold MR. Recommendations for reporting cost-effectiveness analyses. *JAMA* 1996; 276(16):1339–1341.

62 Driving

Stewart A. Factor
William J. Weiner

D riving is a complicated task that nearly all members of society now learn at a young age (15 to 20 years). To perform safely, a variety of psychomotor activities including perception, information processing, judgment, decision making, sequential and simultaneous movements of limbs, reaction-time tasks, continuous tracking, and attentional tasks are utilized. These functions subserve appropriate judgment of distance and speed, application of control forces for braking and accelerating, and the negotiation of curves and hazards that may come up unexpectedly while driving. Driving ability becomes deeply ingrained with continuous practice, so that mild to moderate loss of motor and cognitive function may not necessarily alter one's ability to drive. Determining when a disease has progressed to the point of impairing driving can be difficult. Although assessment of the ability to drive in elderly people with and without neurodegenerative disease is complicated in and of itself, there are other concerns that add to the complexity, including the social and political ramifications. Driving is such an important social issue because the car provides a means to visit family and friends, attend social and cultural events, shop, and visit health care providers, among other things. There is also a culturally engendered value where the car and a driver's license represent symbols of independence. If they are

lost, so is independence. Alternative travel options may not always be available. Some patients will not give up their license even if they do not use it. Pullen and coworkers (1) demonstrated that a significant number of elderly people maintained their driver's license even when they had given up driving on their own years before. When interviewed, the elderly voiced that the loss of the car was a sign of becoming more dependent and required them to stay closer to home and have less social interactions. Many elderly patients became quite upset when faced with the prospect of life without a car (2).

The concerns of Parkinson's disease (PD) patients are similar to those of patients with other neurodegenerative diseases. In fact, the need for mobility and independence may be more important to the disabled than the healthy. They also voice concern regarding the increased reliance on other family members to take time to help them even when the family member volunteers to do so. Patients with PD experience motor symptoms such as tremor, slowness, muscle stiffness, dyskinesias, and motor fluctuations, which can potentially interfere with driving. Psychological problems in PD may include executive dysfunction, impaired information processing, difficulties carrying out multiple tasks simultaneously, memory difficulties, visuospatial and visuoperceptive problems, and in some cases frank dementia (3). Finally, drugs prescribed for PD can cause somnolence, visual hallucinations, and confusion. Patients with PD will often, to the best of their ability, hide their illness from the motor vehicle bureau so as to maintain a license. Gimenez-Roldan and coworkers (4) found that at renewal time, 63% of PD patients did not volunteer information on their disease for fear of losing their license.

On almost a daily basis, movement disorder specialists are faced with the issue of whether a PD patient should still drive. This issue is often broached by spouses or children, and it frequently causes a family rift. Attempts are made on both sides to sway the treating neurologist to see their point of view. Even after the issue is addressed and a license is lost, the patient continues to push for renewal. How can neurologists deal with this issue in an educated manner? In this review, we discuss important issues regarding driving and the elderly, since most PD patients are in this age group. Then we discuss what is known about driving performance in PD. Excessive daytime somnolence and "sleep attacks" are covered. We also provide the neurologist with a plan to follow when dealing with this situation in practice.

DRIVING AND THE ELDERLY

Individuals over age 65 make up 13% to 17% of licensed drivers (5). In the traffic safety literature, there is extensive study related to investigation of the safe elderly driver (2). Driving performance may be affected by several factors that relate to the physiologic changes of aging, disease processes, and the medications used to treat them. Although there has been criticism about the effort to study aging drivers because it is too focused on narrow measurable parameters not consistent with the overall everyday reality drivers face, it is of more than passing interest to recognize studies that have examined sensory decrements, muscular degeneration, visual deficits, perceptual changes, attention problems, dichotic listening decrements, reaction times, psychomotor slowing, and glare impairment.

These studies establish facts concerning driving in the elderly and may form the basis of future public policy decisions concerning driving in North America. The major conclusions regarding the elderly healthy driver include the following: (a) elderly drivers are underrepresented in accident statistics; (b) studies based on actual miles driven in a year show that elderly drivers are the second most-accident prone group, second only to teenagers; (c) when the elderly are involved in automobile accidents, the most frequent problems include turning improperly, particularly to the left, failure to yield the right of way, starting up improperly in traffic, and ignoring traffic signals; (d) the elderly have a far better record with regard to alcohol-related motor vehicle accidents; (e) physical frailty makes the elderly more prone to

become traffic fatalities (6). Motor vehicle accidents are the leading cause of death by unintentional injury in the 65- to 74-year age group; the second leading cause of death (first is falling), for those 75 years of age or older, (7). Finally, elderly people are poor judges of their own ability to drive; this is especially true when health issues come into play (1).

Although medical conditions and their associated morbidity, including visual and cognitive deficits, lead to decreased driving activity and driving cessation (8, 9), many impaired patients continue to drive. In one study of patients seen in a geriatric clinic (10), drivers, as compared with nondrivers, were younger, more often male, and scored higher on a mental status exam. Even so, 40% of drivers were diagnosed with Alzheimer's disease and 26% were impaired with regard to activities of daily living. In another study comprising inpatients (1), 37 of 498 of those interviewed were active drivers and only 5 of these met the established medical criteria for safe driving. These findings underscore safety concerns related to the fact that unqualified people are driving and the difficulty of determining which of the elderly should not drive and how this decision can be established. There is evidence that the elderly compensate for increasing driving impairment. These compensations include (a) driving less at night, (b) avoiding unfamiliar roads, (c) avoiding rush hours, (d) avoiding poor weather conditions, and (e) driving more slowly (6, 8). Although these people still drive frequently, they do so under familiar, safer surroundings. Despite this behavior and the fact that they are guilty of fewer traffic violations, evidence indicates that their risk of involvement in a motor vehicle accident remains higher. Slower driving may lead to more prolonged exposure to high-risk situations (6). This may be the reason left turns appear to be so hazardous.

Specific correlates that may lead to increased risk of motor vehicle accidents for drivers over the age of 64, and particularly over the age of 74, include the claim that the proportion of accidents occurring on poor road conditions at night, which is exaggerated (2). Also, data on the relative probability of accident responsibility by age in a large data set involving over 88,000 accidents clearly delineates that drivers over the age of 75 are more likely to be the cause of accidents (2).

What explains the deterioration in driving seen in the elderly? Two broad areas are of particular concern in relation to the physiology of aging. The first is visual disturbances, which are an increasing problem for elderly drivers. Poor vision is the most common reason for cessation of driving. Sorting relevant information from a wide array of competing influences becomes increasingly difficult in the elderly. Recognition-response activities become harder, and when additional tasks are superimposed—for example, turning on a car radio or speaking on a cellular phone—responsiveness becomes even more compromised. The second problem area is the decision-making process following extraction of pertinent information from the driving environment. Elderly drivers require more time to make decisions. Elderly drivers are better able to maintain the direction of their vehicles than to change direction on short notice. This is reflected by the increasing involvement of elderly drivers in motor vehicle accidents at intersections. A test used to evaluate combined visual and cognitive changes is referred to as the "Useful Field of View" (UFOV). This is a computer-administered test of visual attention that is divided into three parts: (a) central vision and processing speed; (b) divided attention and recognizing objects both centrally and peripherally; and (c) selective attention, which utilizes distracters and forces the driver to focus on the object that is of greater significance. The score leads to a measure of risk for motor vehicle accidents. This test has been used to evaluate driving ability in those at risk (11).

Elderly drivers are also confronted with deterioration in information processing, depth judgment, and reaction speed. However, the degree of these difficulties and the age at which they become significant in any given individual is quite variable, and the exact relationships between these changes and accident risk are not understood. Therefore there is resistance to limiting driver licenses by a set age or even to determine a specific age of mandatory retesting.

Driving difficulties in the elderly may also relate to medical illness, functional disabilities, or medications. Several studies have examined these issues. Medical conditions frequently associated with motor vehicle accidents and ultimate driving cessation include cardiac disease, diabetes mellitus, Alzheimer's disease, PD, seizure disorders, stroke, and sleep apnea (5). One study (11) suggests that functional disabilities and non-specific diagnoses or age predict at-fault motor vehicle accidents. In addition to visual difficulties measured by UFOV, falling was associated with increased accidents. The authors suggest that risk factors for accidents and falling are similar. Falling with fractures was also associated with cessation of driving in women, perhaps due to osteoporosis (8). Another study found that foot abnormalities and decreased range of motion of the neck were important (5). In this study, association analyses demonstrated a strong predictive value of three factors: poor near vision (usually associated with poor distant vision as well), poor visual attention, and poor range of motion of the neck. These were retrospective studies, and one author felt that the results might lead to an office-based screening tool; however, prospective evaluations would be needed to confirm the usefulness of such an approach. Drug therapy (tricyclics, hypnotics, opiates) also plays an important role in the occurrence of automotive accidents involving the elderly, especially males (12). The side effects of these drugs and resultant effect on driving

ability may be enhanced with advancing age, illness, or other concomitant medication. Sims and coworkers (11) found that the use of beta blockers was associated with fewer accidents. It may be that these drugs reduce anxiety and tremor, thus decreasing the risk of accidents. Many patients have more than one ailment or are taking several drugs, so comorbidity is important, but proper studies have not been completed.

It is clear that there are several concerns about the safe driving of elderly individuals. Further study is needed to determine what factors result in increased risk for accidents and how steps can be taken to counsel drivers appropriately. When PD is associated with motor and cognitive features, these issues are further complicated, and neurologists must often participate in evaluating them.

DRIVING AND PARKINSON'S DISEASE

Although it is known that PD is a common cause of driving cessation (13), the issue of driving has not been well examined in this patient population. Patients with PD experience a number of abnormalities of function vital to driving safety. Motor function, visual perception, reaction time, attention maintenance, and information processing are all abnormal in PD patients, even in those without dementia. Dementia adds another dimension to the problem. Although the question of whether a PD patient should drive is frequently addressed in movement disorder clinics, there are limited data to helps us to make appropriate decisions. The social issues make the decision to withdraw a patient's driving privileges difficult.

Assessment of Driving Performance

Simulator Studies. Driving ability in PD patients has been evaluated using both simulators and on-road driving tests with a series of computer-aided laboratory tests. Relatively few studies with small numbers of subjects have been reported, and there is no standardized method of examining performance. Nevertheless, those studies have demonstrate clearly that driving is impaired in PD. Simulator studies are easier and safer than on-road studies to administer in PD patients. Four studies have been reported using both PD and control subjects.

Madeley et al. (14) measured the ability of subjects to react with steering adjustments, respond to light changes, and utilize foot pedals. They examined 10 PD patients classified in stages 1 to 3 according to Hoehn and Yahr (H&Y): 6 active drivers and 4 who had given up driving as well as 10 age- and sex-matched controls. In the PD patients, accuracy, driving reaction time, and light recognition were found to be impaired.

Lings and Dupont (15) evaluated driving in 28 PD patients, 18 with a driver's license (5 no longer driving) and 10 without (5 gave it up and 5 never had one), and 109 controls. Controls were not age-matched and were, in fact, younger (median age 49) than the PD patients (median age 65). The duration of disease was 8.75 years and mean H&Y stage was 2.2. Of the total, 21 had mild motor fluctuations, 14 had mild dyskinesia, and none had "on-off" symptoms. The authors specified that patients were selected by their lack of major complicating problems. The simulator used measured the following: grip strength, force applied by hand and foot, isometric force while turning the steering wheel, reaction time to audio and visual stimuli in hand and foot, choice reaction times, direction and speed of steering wheel turning, patterns of steering wheel movement, and erroneous reactions. PD patients had the following findings: (a) reduced grip strength; (b) significantly reduced speed of movement; (c) significantly increased reaction times, the consequence of which was a prolonged reaction length; (d) increased frequency and more serious errors, mostly directional in nature (wrong turns). Overall, 61% of PD patients compared with 32% of controls had 1 error while 21% of PD patients and 6% controls had 2 or more errors; in addition, 57% of PD patients made directional errors compared to 22% in controls. Some patients completely failed to react to signals. When only licensed drivers were analyzed, the results were similar.

Zesiewicz et al. (16) examined 39 PD patients and 25 controls. The primary endpoint was the number of collisions for day and night conditions. Among the 39 patients, 56% were still driving their usual amount, 26% had reduced their driving, and 18% had stopped. The main reason for discontinuing driving was difficulty concentrating. The mean H&Y stage was 2.2. Controls were comparable for age and miles driven per month. Those with PD had significantly lower scores on the Mini-Mental State Examination (MMSE) than controls (23.6 vs. 28.6; $P < .001$). When examining all PD patients and then just those still actively driving driving, the total number of collisions was significantly higher among PD patients verus controls ($P < .01$). Those with accidents had lower MMSE score and were older.

One additional study (17) reported on internally guided cognition and the impact of the use of external cues. It examined approach speed to traffic lights, deceleration point, stopping point, curve speed, and lane positioning using 2 paradigms; one advanced preparation with maps and another with no opportunity for advanced internal cueing. External cues were varied. PD patients suffer from dysfunction of internal cueing and require external cues in several cognitive domains, such as verbal learning and visuospacial orientation. It was hypothesized that patients would have significant difficulty with internal cueing and would improve with external cues.

The simulator measured the use of the steering wheel, accelerator, and brake pedals. Among the 18 patients and 18 controls studied, there was no significant difference in age, education, or driving experience; however, the PD group drove less distance at the time of the study. All subjects were active drivers. PD was mild to moderate and patients were tested in the medication "on" state to optimize capability. The results demonstrated that PD patients had significantly more trouble with time to deceleration, stopping on time, and driving on curves with slower speed and speed variance as well as difficulty maintaining a constant lateral position. There was a trend toward slower speed in approaching a traffic light. In the absence of external cues, patients were less able to internally cue approach speed adjustment and deceleration. They were more likely to run through traffic signals. They also had difficulty adjusting curve speed appropriately. Patients relied on external cues even when given advanced preparation for the test. They were, overall, less able to adapt to changing conditions than were controls.

On-Road Studies.   Although simulators are very useful in measuring driving performance because they make it possible to test hazardous situations that would otherwise be unsafe in real time on the road, they do not fully predict performance with on-road testing. Subjects may have trouble adjusting to the simulator and they may not react with urgency because of the fabricated setting. Some have suggested that this procedure may be utilized as a screening procedure. The gold standard is the on-road test. Despite that, only 2 studies in PD using this test situation have been reported.

The first, performed by Heikkila and coworkers (18), studied driving ability in PD patients using a 45-minute driving test and a series of computer-aided lab tests, including visual short-term memory, perceptual flexibility and decision making, vigilance, complex-choice reaction times, information-processing capacity, and stress-tolerance. They tested 20 men with PD H&Y stages 1 to 3 and 20 age-matched controls. The PD patients were regular drivers with no motor fluctuations. The driving test demonstrated an increase in risky faults that could lead to danger and infractions of the law. The patients had difficulty driving in traffic, difficulty turning left, and greatest difficulty in urban conditions. Highway driving was not impaired when compared with controls, perhaps because there was no need for changes in direction or lane. There was wide individual variation of driving ability in the PD group: overall, 35% of the drivers were unfit. The laboratory studies demonstrated more difficulties in the PD group with visual memory testing, choice reaction time, and information-processing capacity. These findings were seen even in mild to moderate stages of disease, and they correlated with driving test difficulties, particularly the number of risky faults. The conclusions were that PD significantly influenced driving ability even in mild to moderate disease, although the milder patients were considered to be competent.

Wood et al. (19) examined driving performance in 25 PD patients and 21 controls (community volunteers). The average age of patients was 63.7 years and that of controls 65.2 years. In the PD group, the mean H&Y stage was 2.3, duration of PD 6.2 years, mean levodopa dose 673 mg/day, and Unified Parkinson's Disease Rating Scale (UPDRS) score 27.4. Both groups of subjects had similar driving experience, frequency of driving, and self-reported accidents. The PD patients drove fewer kilometers and were less confident driving alone. In this study, there was a driving instructor in the front seat and an occupational therapist specifically trained in driving assessment in the back seat. Seven aspects were rated at 147 locations in the driving course and the driver was given an overall rating on a scale of 1 to 10. (A score 1 to 3 indicated that the instructor had to act to avoid an accident or that the driver actually hit an object. This rating indicated that the driver should cease driving. A score of 4 to 5 indicated poor driving and observational skills; 6 to 8 indicated an average driver with some bad habits; and 9 to 10 pointed to an excellent driver.) Both occupational therapist and instructor rated the driver and both were highly correlated. The subjects also completed a 57-item questionnaire for drivers' perceived difficulty in 24 situations. The PD patients were significantly less safe than controls (mean PD score 4.8 vs. 6.6 for controls). Overall, 14 PD and 5 controls scored at 5 or below, indicating that they would have failed a driver test. Types of errors seen included those involving self-directed navigation (internal cueing),, lane keeping, monitoring blind spot, traffic light and intersection navigation, lane changing, driving in reverse, and parking. The authors concluded that PD patients are less safe than controls and probably should be assessed by an occupational therapist at regular intervals.

In all these on-road and simulator studies, patients with mild to moderate PD were selected and examined when medication response was optimal. Nevertheless, it is worrisome to find that driving impairment is detectable and significant and that more than 50% of patients would actually fail driving tests. In all studies, PD patients were found to be less safe behind the wheel than age-matched controls. Many of the patients tested were active drivers, indicating, as also seen in the well elderly, that some patients with substantial impairment remain behind the wheel.

Incidents of Motor Vehicle Accidents or Moving Violations

Information on rates of motor vehicle accidents involving PD patients is sparse (20). Only a few studies examining this issue (separate from falling asleep at the wheel) have been reported. There is no information on the types of accidents or outcomes. One study from Germany found that patients caused fewer accidents and were ticketed for moving violations less often than the national average (21). Of 156 PD patients who were still active drivers, 7.7% registered with the state traffic commission for traffic offenses or accidents as compared to 25% in the general population. Infractions reported included a minor motor vehicle accident, 7 minor violations, and 2 major offenses which led to 3 revocation of the driver's license. There were no repeat offenses. A review of the records of the United Kingdom department of transportation also indicates that PD is not an important cause of motor vehicle accidents (22). Data from other countries also suggests that fewer, not more, accidents than expected are seen with PD because of the limitations and adjustments patients impose on themselves in driving. Dubinsky and coworkers (23) found that PD patients were infrequently involved accidents; however, it was discovered that PD patients did experience more accidents per mile of driving, 80 versus 14.3 for controls. Meindorfner et al. (24) reviewed 6620 questionnaires completed by PD patients regarding accident frequency; among these, 82% had a license at some time, 60% were still driving, 14.5% of licensed drivers had been involved in an accident over the previous 5 years (18% of restricted drivers), and 10.8% reported causing one. Younger PD patients were more likely to cause an accident than the age-matched controlled population, but these figures converged with advancing age. Accident involvement was associated with sudden-onset sleep, disease severity, and kilometers driven per year.

Correlates to Driving Performance

Several attempts have been made to find clinical features that might predict poor driving performance in PD. This would enhance decision making in the office setting. But the outcome has been unclear because PD is heterogeneous and a variety of features may play a role in the development of driving trouble, including motor features, executive functioning abnormalities involving planning and sequencing movements, inability to perform dual tasks, dementia, psychosis and other psychiatric features, and visual abnormalities. Several investigators have attempted to correlate motor abnormalities and diminished driving ability. Zesiewicz et al. (16) showed that UPDRS motor scores correlated with total collisions on a simulator test, Madeley and coworkers (14) demonstrated a correlation between the results of simulator testing and the Webster severity scale. On the other hand, Wood et al. (19) and Heikkila et al. (18), on the basis of on-road tests, found no correlation between UPDRS, H&Y stage, or levodopa dose and driving capability. The same is true for 2 other simulator studies (15, 17). In a questionnaire study, Dubinsky and coworkers (23) demonstrated poor correlation between the Northwestern University Parkinson's Disease Rating Scale and the Schwab and England scale with driving ability and number of motor vehicle accidents. However, they did show that there was correlation between H&Y stage and motor vehicle accidents and that more occurred at stage 3. The lack of a consistent relationship between disease severity and driving difficulties suggests that other aspects of disease play an important role and that the motor examination cannot, by itself, be used as a guide to decision making.

Another area of interest relates to age and duration of disease. In an unpublished study (Weiner, personal communication), patients with PD who were still driving were younger (age 66 vs. 74) and had a shorter duration of disease (5 vs. 8 years) compared with nondrivers. Another study also demonstrated that older age was associated with poor driving performance in the PD group but not in controls (17). Cognition, often controlled for in studies by allowing an MMSE score in the normal range, is likely important. Several studies (16, 18, 23) showed a correlation of total accidents or poor driving performance and MMSE score, and these patients were not considered to be demented. Stolwyk (17) demonstrated that internally guided cognition with the use of internal cues is abnormal. While the fundamental mechanism underlying this cognitive function is unknown, it may relate to executive function or attentional processing loads.

Worringham and colleagues (25) specifically studied predictors of poor performance in PD. They were the only authors to take into account the heterogeneity of PD features. They performed 2 days of functional tests before the on-road test on 25 PD patients and 21 controls. Three domains were examined; visual function, cognition, and motor performance. The results indicated that a combination of 3 tests, one from each domain, was highly and significantly correlated with driving safety. These tests were Pelli-Robson contrast sensitivity, symbol digit, and Perdue pegboard. These tests examine low-contrast sensitivity to visual stimulation, efficient attention shifting, and motor dexterity. The sensitivity (correct prediction of a passing driver's test) was high and the specificity (correct identification of a failure) was moderate. These results were enhanced when age of the subject was accounted for in the analysis, and the investigators found that they could predict results for PD subjects and controls. The authors suggest that these tests are widely available, portable, and easy to administer and should be used periodically in the clinic.

Clinical Features Impairing Driving Ability

Several clinical features of PD may impair driving. Motor features that appear to have the greatest impact on driving include dyskinesia, fluctuations, tremor, and falling. In nonparkinsonian elderly, a correlation was observed between falling and motor vehicle accidents (8, 11). Meindorfner et al. (24) reported 19 patients in whom freezing of gait or motor blocks were important causes of accidents. Visual dysfunction plays a key role. Patients with PD suffer from abnormalities of visual acuity, contrast sensitivity, speed processing and perception, spatial and motion perception, and visuoconstructional ability (26). Hallucinations, confusion, depression, anxiety, and poor impulse control can all affect driving. Drug therapy and aging may also play a role. Few of these issues have been studied.

Dementia occurs in more than 30% of PD patients (3), and it has a progressive nature, as in Alzheimer's disease; in fact, some patients have Alzheimer's disease associated with their PD. The role of dementia in the driving difficulties of PD patients has not been studied. Most studies purposely include patients with mild to moderate disease and no cognitive deficits. Considering that these mild to moderate PD patients already have problems with driving for a variety of reasons, it is clear that adding dementia to the mix could be very problematic. We can learn from the substantive literature on Alzheimer's disease (27), and the information gathered could provide some insight into the influence of dementia on driving problems in PD. Although all Alzheimer's patients eventually stop driving, several questions surround the issue, especially in the early years. During on-road tests, early Alzheimer's patients demonstrated significant concern. One study of 19 patients with an average duration of disease of 4 years demonstrated a failure rate greater than 60% (28). Another demonstrated a 19% failure rate in "very mild" patients and a 41% failure rate in those considered "mild" compared with 3% in controls, indicating that driving impairment occurs very early in the course of disease (29). In another study of 50 patients with a clinical dementia rating (CDR) of 0.5 (very mild) or 1 (mild), 9 subjects were rated unsafe, 19 marginal, and 22 safe (30). The abnormalities seen included delayed pedal release, lane boundary crossing, lane changing, signaling, and selection errors (31). Other on-road and simulator studies demonstrate similar findings (for review see Ref. 27), indicating that patients with very mild and mild dementia already have significant difficulties. While this indicates that Alzheimer's disease impacts driving early on, as with PD, some authors have suggested that the finding indicates that, since some pass, a diagnosis of Alzheimer's disease does not mean immediate discontinuation of driving (27). However, an increased rate of motor vehicle accidents has been demonstrated by simulator tests (32). One survey study (33) demonstrated that the increased risk for accidents in the first 2 to 3 years of Alzheimer's disease is modest, and the yearly rate is lower than that in young people up to the middle twenties. In addition, the accident rate is within the accepted risk for all registered drivers. However, after 3 years, the risk of accidents rises significantly. Approximately 50% of AD patients stop driving by 3 years of disease (33).

There is marked variability in driving in the early years. Medical assessment and duration of disease do not correlate directly with the occurrence of unsafe driving. Several attempts have been made to develop a battery of neuropsychological tests to predict unsafe driving in demented patients. Several studies suggest that the MMSE may be predictive and scores of 18, 22, and 24 have been suggested as cutoffs for driving, but this association is modest at best (27). Adler et al. (27) suggest that anyone with a score of 24 or less should be tested. Other studies suggest that trailmaking part B, visual tracking, visual perception, and visuospatial skills correlate (34), and these tests have been recommended for use in screening drivers (27). Other studies included tests of attention processing, such as the UFOV, Benton visual retention, and digit span (35); these too seem to be good measures of dementia severity. In the final analysis, there has been no consensus on a standard neuropsychological test that would be predictive of unsafe driving. Drachman and coworkers (33) recommended the use of direct driving tests to judge the individual's competence. Others have suggested periodic reevaluation every 6 months in patients with dementia.

Several studies examined driving-related tests to predict unsafe driving. These include the Traffic Sign Recognition Test, Driving Performance Test (DPT), and Driving Advisement System (DAS) (31, 36) as well as a battery of executive function tests, particularly visuospatial studies (30); these too, however, need further study. The American Academy of Neurology suggests that all demented patients with a CDR of 1 (mild impairment) or worse should stop driving and those with 0.5 should be tested (37).

Dementia alone can be a significant obstacle to guiding a motor vehicle safely. The addition of those visual aspects associated with aging and PD compounded with dementia and the motor features and one can begin to realize the complexity of assessing driving in patients with PD.

Excessive Daytime Somnolence and "Sleep Attacks"

A particular symptom complex of interest in relation to driving safety is excessive daytime sleepiness (EDS) and sleep attacks. It has been well known for years that some PD patients suffer from EDS (38). Spontaneous dozing is significantly more common in PD patients (49%) than in controls (26%) (38). It has also been shown that daytime somnolence occurs in primates with MPTP-induced parkinsonism (39). But it was not until 1999, after Frucht and coworkers (40) reported that 8 patients with PD had fallen asleep at the wheel, that concerns about the impact

of EDS on driving safety arose. These patients were taking a wide variety of medications, including the dopamine agonists pramipexole and ropinirole, and it was suggested that these medications were the cause. This report was not a study of sleep or driving problems in PD and did not account for the many variables that could also have played a role in falling asleep at the wheel. Several reports followed, indicating that pergolide and levodopa could cause the same problems (41). These reports engendered an unusual amount of interest, response, and controversy (42–44). Based on the report by Frucht et al. (40), the FDA and health organizations around the world required amendments to package inserts, including a black box warning in the United States with a statement that patients should not drive until "they have gained sufficient experience to gauge whether or not pramipexole affects their mental performance adversely." In Germany, patients were instructed not to drive (45). The restrictions were tighter than those for known sedative drugs. This led to considerable concern about the driving capability of PD patients in general. As a result, considerable interest in the mechanisms of sleep disturbance in PD and the effect of drugs on sleep in PD occurred.

The controversy concerned whether these patients had true sleep attacks, as seen with narcolepsy, or drug-induced somnolence. Terminology from this literature indicates the presence of 2 types of episodes: (a) "sleep attacks" occurring without warning and unrelated to somnolence and (b) "unintended sleep episodes" or "sleep events," which are events with premonitory sleepiness. "Sudden-onset sleep" includes both groups. Investigations with polysomnography have demonstrated that both occur. Of importance is that sleep attacks do occur, albeit rarely. Tracik et al. (46) reported a single patient on cabergoline, budapine, levodopa, and entacapone with sudden-onset sleep with demonstrated electroencephalographic (EEG) slowing within 10 seconds and stage 2 sleep in 60 seconds. Rye et al. (47) examined 27 patients, none of whom were on pramipexole or ropinirole, and 13 controls for EDS with polysomnography and a multiple sleep latency tests (MSLTs). They found that 19% of PD patients had pathologic sleepiness and MSLTs below 5 minutes. In this study, 30% of all MSLTs measured resulted in pathologic sleepiness. Six patients had episodes of sudden-onset rapid-eye-movement (REM) sleep similar to those seen in narcolepsy. These findings were present in both treated and untreated PD patients. An additional aspect of the controversy related to whether the presence of nocturnal sleep disorders led to increased somnolence during the day with sudden onset of sleep. It was actually shown with polysomnography that higher levels of daytime alertness were associated with poor sleep (decreased total sleep and sleep efficiency) (47). In another study of 6 patients with sudden-onset sleep, polysomnography and MSLT demonstrated insufficient nocturnal sleep (decreased total sleep time and sleep fragmentation as well as reduced slow-wave and REM sleep) (45). None of these patients experienced sudden-onset REM sleep; no control subjects were examined. These authors performed a driving simulator test and a checkerboard test, both demonstrating early fatigue in all patients. They concluded that EDS was caused by nocturnal sleep fragmentation and that dopamine agonists increased this tendency. These issues still need to be resolved.

The characteristics of the two types of sudden-onset sleep differ. For sleep events where the subjects have prodromal sleepiness, the sleepiness comes in waves, and when they fall asleep, they remain asleep for about 60 minutes. These are episodes of slow, irresistible dozing off, and patients have poor awareness of their sleepiness. Sleep attacks involve no prodromal sleepiness and the episodes are irresistible but brief, lasting for a few minutes only. Some subjects report this phenomenon to be more like a short circuit than falling asleep (45). The type of accident that occurs while falling asleep at the wheel differs from that which occurs during active awake driving. Those who fall asleep at the wheel do so when the task is monotonous, with a low degree of difficulty. Such accidents are due to driving off the road (84% of the time) and generally involve a single vehicle (82%) (24). Accidents unrelated to sleep occur in more complicated situations, such as at crossroads and in parking areas (97% of the time) and generally involve other drivers (92%).

The frequency of sudden-onset sleep has been examined in several studies. Homan et al. (48) reviewed the literature of cases of sleep attacks in patients taking dopamine agonists. Of 1787 patients, 6.6% (range 0% to 30%) had sudden-onset sleep and two-thirds were male. Seventeen cases occurred with driving and resulted in 10 accidents. Twenty patients had recurrent events. Meindorfner et al. (24), through a questionnaire study, found that 8% of 5210 patients experienced at least one episode of sudden-onset sleep; 57% had unintended sleep episodes and 26% had sleep attacks. Overall 2.3% of patients with a driver's license reported an accident due to sudden-onset sleep and 8% of all accidents recorded happened for this reason. Sudden-onset sleep was often reported in association with change in medications and, in half, was due to the addition of dopamine agonists. A consortium of 18 Canadian sites (49) examined 638 patients, including 420 who were active drivers, with a questionnaire. EDS was present in 51% of patients [similar to the 49% reported in 1990 (38)], but sudden-onset sleep occurred in 3.8% and actual sleep attacks were reported in 0.7%.Only one minor accident was reported. The investigators failed to show a relationship with any particular group of drugs. Avorn et al. (50) examined 929 patients and questioned them about sleep events in the preceding 6 months. These authors combined all episodes of sudden-onset sleep and did not sepa-

rate unintended sleep episodes from sleep attacks. Of this population, 22% had uncontrolled somnolence. In this particular study, those treated with dopamine agonists had a 3-fold greater risk of sudden-onset sleep, and pergolide, pramipexole, and ropinirole were similar in their effects. There was also a dose-related response. Patients on neither levodopa nor an agonist had no sudden-onset sleep. In a single-center study, Brodsky et al. (51) examined 101 patients and controls, finding EDS to be present in 76% of patients and 47% controls. Sleep episodes while driving occurred in 21% of patients and 6% controls.

EDS is a common problem in PD. Sudden-onset sleep of both types does occur in 4 to 20%, with sleep attacks being less common, occurring in about a quarter of thos with sudden onset sleep. Accidents related to sleep events in PD patients are generally minor and uncommon (estimated at 0% to 2%) (24, 42, 49). These events appear to be a dopaminergic phenomenon because of their more frequent occurrence with agonists and levodopa, although Rye et al. (47) demonstrated their occurrence in untreated patients as well. While Avorn et al. (50) seem to show a direct relationship to dopamine agonists, other studies do not. The data at this point are not reliable enough to establish a direct relationship. The numbers are too low for drug-to-drug comparisons, the methodology is problematic—uncontrolled and retrospective, and the data are incoherent. preventing combined analysis or generalizable conclusions. Clinical trials such as the CALM-PD trial (52) and 056 trial (53) have demonstrated a greater rate of somnolence with dopamine agonists as compared to levodopa in early PD patients. When therapy with levodopa or dopamine agonists is initiated, patients should be cautioned about the possibility of somnolence and the operation of any dangerous machinery, including automobiles (54).

It should be noted that falling asleep at the wheel is not an uncommon complaint in the general population. A number of causes relate to its occurrence in healthy people, including disturbed sleep, long work hours, long-distance and monotonous driving, the use of sedatives or alcohol, and others (55). In a survey study, 29% of drivers reported that they nearly fell asleep at the wheel at some time during the prior year; approximately 15% of accidents on main roads and 20% on secondary roads were attributed to this phenomenon (55). This problem correlates with degree of daytime sleepiness, occupation, annual driving distances and proportion of highway driving as well as disturbed nocturnal sleeping habits and sleep disorders such as sleep apnea. It is not uncommon for drivers involved in motor vehicle accidents due to falling asleep to indicate that they had no warning. However, it has been shown in simulator studies that drivers do experience tiredness about 40 minutes before falling asleep and that that tiredness worsens over time

(55, 56). Actual sleep attacks appear to be rare in the general population.

Risk factors for the development of sudden-onset sleep in PD are difficult to predict based on available data, and those found have not been consistent. The best appears to be the score on the Epworth sleep scale (44, 49, 51), but in most studies the measure is taken at a remote time after the crash, so it is difficult to draw this conclusion with certainty. Others have suggested the presence of autonomic dysfunction (48), poor nocturnal sleep (45), duration of disease, and severity of disease (54).

It is interesting to note that the appearance of sudden-onset sleep does not lead to the decision to restrict driving on the patient's part; therefore physicians need to take an active role in addressing this issue. Many subjects with sudden-onset sleep fail to assess wakefulness correctly; hence they tend to believe that the event occurred suddenly.

The Patient's Perspective

Several authors have questioned PD patients formally regarding their driving and evaluated how they deal with their difficulties. Such patients seem to be more likely to give up driving than others (24). Dubinsky and coworkers (23) reported on the results of a retrospective survey of 150 PD patients and 100 controls with regard to driving ability. They found that 32 out of 150 (21%) stopped driving, 18 because they were concerned with their own safety and 10 because of safety concerns of the family. It was also noted that PD patients compensate for their difficulties by driving larger vehicles, driving under the speed limit, and avoiding rush-hour traffic and hazardous weather conditions. Gimenez-Roldan and coworkers (57) used a semistructured questionnaire in 166 PD patients and age-, sex-, social background–matched controls to assess this question. Of the PD patients, only 37% (62 patients) still had their driver's license; 19.2% (32 patients) were still active drivers. Only 40% of the patients were still driving after 5 years of disease. Most (80%) of the of the former drivers quit because of PD, while 53% of active drivers were aware of difficulties with driving, including managing foot pedals and judging distances. Meindorfner et al. (24) provided a self-administered questionnaire to 6620 PD patients, of whom 82% had a driver's license at some time, 40% had given up driving, 37% restricted driving, and 23% were still driving without change or restriction. The investigators found that men held their licenses 1.5 times more often than women. Logistic regression examining correlates of quitting driving found association with age, more advanced disease, female gender, and higher level of daytime sleepiness. Reasons given by patients for quitting or restricting driving were disease progression (52%),, driving being effortful (31%), traffic too dangerous (26%),

no longer able to drive (14%), sleepiness at the wheel (7%), experience of near accident (4%), and experience of accident (3%). The increased likelihood of men to hold onto their licenses has been demonstrated in other studies (21). Wood et al. (19) demonstrated that patients drive fewer kilometers and note that they have trouble with reading signs, moving the foot from accelerator to brake and back, and steering. In general, these drivers rated themselves more poorly than non-PD controls. They also tend to drive less often alone. It has been suggested that the decrease in driving implemented by PD patients may lead to further deterioration of performance (17). These particular patients also made adjustments in their driving habits to compensate, including reducing speed and decreasing the number of hours behind the wheel. Thus these patients seem to have an awareness of their difficulties and limitations. In all likelihood, some continue to drive actively, although they should not, and many know that they should not. Even an episode of sudden-onset sleep at the wheel does not cause patients to stop driving. The need for independence seems to be a strong impetus to continue driving despite perceived impairment.

Assessing Driver Competence

A major question that faces society is how to assess driving competence appropriately. Legislation often leaves this to be decided on an individual basis (55). One example of the language used regarding assessment is the following: "An individual is deemed unable to drive a car safely only if there is an immediate likelihood, supported by facts, of injury or damage," and "A hazardous situation exists if a driver is expected within the foreseeable period to be subject to the risk of sudden loss of physical or mental capability" (55). However, with PD and other neurodegenerative diseases, a gradual deterioration, not a sudden loss of function, makes this decision more difficult. Who makes the decision? And how? It is interesting that even though PD patients are aware of driving difficulties and alter their habits, they are often incapable of deciding to stop on their own. This is true of patients with dementia as well where these patients underestimate their cognitive dysfunction, whereas healthy elderly tend to overestimate it (27). Possible reasons include denial, diminished insight, and the desire to remain independent for as long as possible even if it means using deception and placing themselves and others in danger (18, 30). Patients usually believe that they can judge, but they are very inaccurate when compared to driving instructors (18, 19, 46). The ability of caregivers to appropriately assess driving in PD has not been tested; but in patients with dementia, they are at best modestly predictive (30). Even if they are very concerned about the ability of the patient to drive, they will often not verbalize their concern because they are concerned about alienating the patient.

Caregivers will sometimes discuss with the physician their concerns about the patient's driving ability in private but will not take the next step, discussing it with the patient and taking away the car keys or reporting the patient to the proper authorities. They leave that to the neurologist. However, the neurologist is actually not able to assess the patient's driving ability accurately either. Although they are better predictors than patients and caregivers (30), physicians are not able to assess driving as well as a driving instructor (18). One author indicates that physicians are "too optimistic" about the driving abilities of their patients (18). Since motor dysfunction is not predictive of driving ability, the decision is even more difficult (23). In Alzheimer's disease, one study examined the ability of several types of physicians (based on experience with demented patients) to predict driving ability and compared their determination to that of a driving instructor who took the patients for an on-road test (the "gold standard") (30). These were 50 patients with very mild or mild Alzheimer's disease who had active driver's licenses. There were 5 physicians and 1 nurse practitioner who based their assessments on medical records; a dementia specialist (25 years of experience), a second dementia specialist (16 years of experience), a general practitioner, a geriatric nurse practitioner, a geriatric neurology fellow, and a geriatric psychiatry fellow. The dementia specialists (including fellows) were accurate 72% to 78% of the time (duration of experience did not have a big effect); general practitioners and nurse practitioner were accurate 62% to 64% of the time. But there was wide variability in sensitivity and specificity between raters. The authors indicate that consistency was insufficient to justify making the physicians the final arbiters of the decision to revoke driving privileges, especially primary care physicians. Finally, driving instructors using simulators or actual driving tests and occupational therapists with expertise in driving issues appear to be the best judges of patients' driving ability.

Many hospitals or rehabilitation centers have driving test programs run by driving rehabilitation specialists. The programs are usually part of the occupational therapy program and seem to be increasing in number as concern about driving ability in this population has grown. These programs not only assess driving ability but provide education, appropriate adaptive equipment, and training. They teach compensatory techniques. Some provide neuropsychological testing as part of the assessment. Some use simulators and some use on-road tests. Some have utilized the Washington University protocol (29, 58) but there is no standardized program that is used throughout the country. Some programs do the assessment as a three-step process. First there is a screening phase, in which a detailed review of the medical status, functional disability, medical history, and driving history is obtained. This is done through a direct interview and record review. Included is a series of visual tests and examinations of mobility, strength, range of motion, and cognitive-perceptual deficits. The second phase includes a neuropsychological testing battery including cognitive-perceptual function, examination of sensory (particularly vision and hearing) and motor function (including reaction time, range of motion, head control), and driving knowledge (including location and function of automobile controls). Cognitive testing includes attention span, decision-making ability, perceptual skills, and analytic abilities. These assessments lead to a profile of the driver including his or her strengths and weaknesses relative to the task of driving. Finally, the dynamic test is the actual road test, in which instructors assess such activities as controlled acceleration and braking, turning, following traffic markers, and responding to traffic signals. This type of comprehensive examination should be used if available to the physician.

The most difficult aspect of assessing driving is when to send patients for the first test. There is no standardized strategy for this. But one thing is certain, driving assessment programs are underutilized. It is generally an accident that leads to the end of driving. Testing routinely would avoid that accident and perhaps save lives and costs and would avoid embarrassment for the patient. The physician must question the patient and family from the earliest stages of disease and, at any suggestion of difficulty, recommend testing. Since a large portion of PD patients stop driving by 5 years of disease, it is reasonable to start testing no later than at that time. With dementia, testing should begin at 3 years. Since PD is progressive, it is reasonable to recheck patients every 6 to 12 months. In those with dementia, more frequent assessment is wise. In our experience, if a patient is having trouble with driving and is unsafe, the physician's suggestion of testing has either of 2 effects. Either the driver will stop driving because of fear of failing or will stop after failure occurs. Either way, the recommendation helps to make the roads safer. Occasionally, patients will resist testing and continue to drive. The issue must be readdressed frequently with emphasis on safety for the patient and others on the road. Each state may have different physician obligations regarding impaired drivers.

CONCLUSION

Parkinson's disease impairs driving ability secondary to motor and visual symptoms, cognitive dysfunction, and medication side effects. This leads to an increase in accidents per miles driven. In the mild-to-moderate stages, some patients remain competent, whereas others do not. Many continue to drive despite disabilities even in advanced stages because of the issue of independence and the social impact of cessation. Eventually, all must give up this privilege, but when and how the decision is made remains an issue. There are no consistent guidelines, and there is considerable disagreement on how to approach, assess, and address driving in PD and other neurodegenerative diseases. There is no standardized in-office evaluation, and the assessments at rehabilitation centers vary. There are no uniform federal laws to guide us, and state laws are variable. Much of the responsibility for determining driving competence in early- to midduration PD patients falls to physicians as does counseling in this regard. However, physicians are not properly trained to make driving recommendations (59) and, as it turns out, neurologists are poor judges of driving ability. Despite that, it is the physician's responsibility to recognize impairments in patients that translate to unsafe driving. When the patient is adamant about continuing to drive, even when it seems obvious that he or she cannot do so, the key is to take advantage of resources available, including neuropsychological testing and a proper driving assessment by an experienced driver rehabilitation specialist. This could be completed with a simulator or on-road test. The use of such testing helps to make the patient realize that he or she is impaired and allows for appropriate choices. It also provides the physician with an assessment that will make the final decision easier because it will be based on factual findings.

Some key issues for physicians include the need for them to be aware of state laws. This information is available at the Department of Motor Vehicles or from several publications (60). Many physicians are unaware of the laws in their states (59). State laws differ with regard to required reporting. In California, Oregon, and Pennsylvania, physicians are required to report unsafe drivers and can be found legally responsible if they fail to do so and the patient ends up in an accident. Also, the issue of anonymity of those reporting differs between states. In Georgia there is none and in Maryland there is confidentiality if requested by the reporter. Reporters are protected from legal action in Maryland, not in Georgia. The physician must disclose to the patient what his or her responsibilities are and can use that to negotiate with them and to develop a responsible plan.

In assessing driving, the physician should consider each case individually, obtaining a complete detailed motor and cognitive assessment and a driving history, including accidents, near misses, and violations. Based on these findings, a driving test can be offered. It should be indicated that the results of the test will be sent to the physician, not the Motor Vehicle Bureau. Because of the sensitivity of the issue, the approach to the patient should be tactful but candid, and the family should be present. All results and discussions should be documented. In the end, all involved should make a valid, responsible decision.

References

1. Pullen R, Harlacher R, Fusgen I. Driving performance in older in-patients. *J Am Geriatr Soc* 1997; 45:781–782.
2. Rothe JP. *The Safety of Elderly Drivers: Yesterday's Young in Today's Traffic.* New Brunswick, NJ: Transaction Publishers, 1990.
3. Barba AL, Molho ES, Higgins DS, et al. Dementia. In: Ebadi M, Pfeiffer R (eds). *Parkinson's Disease.* Boca Raton, FL: CRC Press, 2005:347–366.
4. Gimenez-Roldan S, Mateo D, Dobato JL. Renovacio de la licencia conducir vehiculos en personas con enfermedad de Parkinson. *Rev Neurol* 1997; 25:1337–1342.
5. Marottoli RA, Richardson ED, Stowe MH, et al. Development of a test battery to identify older drivers at risk for self-reported adverse driving events. *J Am Geriatr Soc* 1998; 46:562–568.
6. Cox AB, Cox DJ. Compensatory driving strategy of older people may increase driving risk. *J Am Geriatr Soc* 1998; 46:1058–1059.
7. Reuben DB, Korner Y, Traines M. The aging driver: Medicine, policy, and ethics. *J Am Geriatr Soc* 1988; 36:1135–1142.
8. Forrest KYZ, Bunker CH, Songer TJ, et al. Driving patterns and medical conditions in older women. *J Am Geriatr Soc* 1997; 45:1214–1218.
9. Stutts JC. Do older drivers with visual and cognitive impairments drive less? *J Am Geriatr Soc* 1998; 46:854–861.
10. Carr D, Jackson T, Alquire P. Characteristics of an elderly driving population referred to a geriatric assessment center. *J Am Geriatr Soc* 1990; 38:1145–1150.
11. Sims RV, Owsley C, Allman RM, et al. A preliminary assessment of the medical and functional factors associated with vehicle crashes by older adults. *J Am Geriatr Soc* 1998; 46:556–561.
12. Dahl ML, Holmgren P, Viitanen M. Traffic dangerous drugs are often found in fatally injured older male drivers. *J Am Geriatr Soc* 1997; 45:1034–1035.
13. Marrottoli R, Ostfeld A, Merrill S, et al. Driving cessation and changes in mileage driven among elderly individuals. *J Gerontol Soc Sci* 1993; 48:S255–S260.
14. Madeley P, Hulley JL, Wildgust H, et al. Parkinson's disease and driving ability. *J Neurol Neurosurg Psychiatry* 1990; 53:580–582.
15. Lings S, Dupont E. Driving with Parkinson's disease: A controlled laboratory investigation. *Acta Neurol Scand* 1992; 86:33–39.
16. Zesiewicz TA, Cimino CR, Malek AR, et al. Driving safety in Parkinson's disease. *Neurology* 2002; 59:1787–1788.
17. Stolwyk RJ, Triggs TJ, Charlton JL, et al. Impact of Internal versus external cueing on driving performance in people with Parkinson's disease. *Mov Disord* 2005; 20:846–857.
18. Heikkila VM, Turkka J, Korpelainen J, et al. Decrease driving ability in people with Parkinson's disease. *J Neurol Neurosurg Psychiatry* 1998; 64:325–330.
19. Wood JM, Worringham C, Kerr G, et al. Quantitative assessment of driving performance in Parkinson's disease. *J Neurol Neurosurg Psychiatry* 2005; 76:176–180.
20. Homann CN, Suppan K, Homann B, et al. Driving in Parkinson's disease: A health hazard? *J Neurol* 2003; 250:1439–1446.
21. Ritter G, Steinberg H. Parkinson's and driving fitness. *Munch Med Wochenschr* 1979; 121:1329–1330.
22. Driving and Parkinson's disease. *Lancet* 1990; 336:78.
23. Dubinsky RM, Gray C, Husted D, et al. Driving and Parkinson's disease. *Neurology* 1991; 41:517–520.
24. Meindorfner C, Korner Y, Moller JC, et al. Driving in Parkinson's disease: Mobility, accidents and sudden onset of sleep at the wheel. *Mov Disord* 2005; 20:832–842.
25. Worringham CJ, Wood JM, Kerr GK, Silburrn PA. Predictors of driving assessment outcome in Parkinson's disease. *Mov Disord* 2006; 21:230–235.
26. Uc EY, Rizzo M, Anderson SW, et al. Visual dysfunction in Parkinson's disease without dementia. *Neurology* 2005; 65:1907–1913.
27. Adler G, Rottunda S, Dysken M. The older driver with dementia: Aan updated literature review. *J Safety Res* 2005; 36:399–407.
28. Fox GK, Bowden SC, Bashford GM, et al. Alzheimer's disease and driving: Prediction and assessment of driving performance. *J Am Geriatr Soc* 1997; 45:949–953.
29. Hunt LA, Murphy CF, Carr D, et al. Reliability of the Washington University road test: A performance-based assessment for drivers with dementia of the Alzheimer type. *Arch Neurol* 1997; 54:707–712.
30. Ott BR, Anthony D, Papandonatos GD, et al. Clinician assessment of the driving competence of patients with dementia. *J Am Geriatr Soc* 2005; 53:829–833.
31. Rebok GW, Keyl PM, Bylsma FW, et al. The effects of Alzheimer's disease on driving related abilities. *Alzheimer Dis Assoc Disord* 1994; 8:228–240.
32. Rizzo M, Reinach S, McGehee D, et al. Simulated car crashes and crash predictors in drivers with Alzheimer's disease. *Arch Neurol* 1997; 54:545–551.
33. Drachman DA, Swearer JM, Collaborative Study Group. Driving and Alzheimer's disease: The risk of crashes. *Neurology* 1993; 43:2448–2456.

34. Reger MA, Welsh RK, Watson GS, et al. The relationship between neuropsychological functioning and driving ability in dementia: A meta-analysis. *Neuropsychology* 2004; 18:85–93.

35. Duchek JM, Hunt L, Ball K, et al. Attention and driving performance in Alzheimer's disease. *J Gerontol Psychol Sci* 1998; 53:130–141.

36. Carr DB, LaBarge E, Dunnigan K, et al. Differentiating drivers with dementia of the Alzheimer type from healthy older persons with a traffic sign naming test. *J Gerontol Med Sci* 1998; 53:135–139.

37. Dubinsky RM, Stein AC, Lyons K. Practice parameter: Risk of driving and Alzheimer's disease (an evidenced based review): Report of the Quality Standards Subcommittee of the American Academy of Neurology. *Neurology* 2000; 54:2205–2221.

38. Factor SA, McAlarney T, Sanchez-Ramos J, Weiner WJ. Sleep disorders and sleep effect in Parkinson's disease. *Mov Disord* 1990; 5:280–285.

39. Daley J, Turner R, Bliwise D, Rye D. Nocturnal sleep and daytime alertness in the MPTP-treated primate. *Sleep* 1999; 22(Suppl):S218–S219.

40. Frucht S, Rogers JD, Greene PE, et al. Falling asleep at the wheel: Motor vehicle mishaps in persons taking pramipexole and ropinirole. *Neurology* 1999; 52:1908–1910.

41. Schapira AHV. Sleep attacks (sleep episodes) with pergolide. *Lancet* 2000; 355:1332–1333.

42. Hauser RA, Gauger L, McDowell A, Zesiewicz TA. Pramipexole-induced somnolence and episodes of daytime sleep. *Mov Disord* 2000; 15:658–663.

43. Weiner WJ. Letter to the editor. *Neurology* 2000; 54:274–275.

44. Olanow CW, Schapira AHV, Roth T. Waking up to sleep episodes in Parkinson's disease. *Mov Disord* 2000; 15:212–215.

45. Moller JC, Stiasny K, Hargutt V, et al. Evaluation of sleep and driving performance in six patients with Parkinson's disease reporting sudden onset of sleep under dopaminergic medication: Aa pilot study. *Mov Disord* 2002; 17:474–481.

46. Tracik F, Ebersbach G. Sudden daytime sleep onset in Parkinson's disease: Polysomnographic recordings. *Mov Disord* 2001; 16:500–506.

47. Rye DB, Bliwise DL, Diphenia B, Gurecki P. Daytime sleepiness in Parkinson's disease. *J Sleep Res* 2000; 9:63–69.

48. Homann CN, Wenzel K, Suppan K, et al. Sleep attacks in patients taking dopamine agonists: Review. *BMJ* 2002; 324:1483–1487.

49. Hobson DE, Lang AE, Martin WRW, et al. Excessive daytime sleepiness and sudden-onset sleep in Parkinson's disease: A survey by the Canadian Movement Disorders Group. *JAMA* 2002; 287:455–463.

50. Avorn J, Schneeweiss S, Sudarsky LR, et al. Sudden uncontrollable somnolence and medication use in Parkinson's disease. *Arch Neurol* 2005; 62:1242–1248.

51. Brodsky MA, Godbold J, Roth T, Olanow CW. Sleepiness in Parkinson's disease: A controlled study. *Mov Disord* 2003; 18:668–672.

52. Parkinson Study Group. Pramipexole vs levodopa as initial treatment of Parkinson's disease: A 4 year randomized controlled trial. *Arch Neurol* 2004; 61: 1044–1053.

53. Rascol O, Brooks DJ, Korczyn AD, et al. A five-year study of the incidence of dyskinesia in patients with early Parkinson's disease who were treated with ropinirole or levodopa. 056 Study Group. *N Engl J Med* 2000; 342:1484–1491.

54. Adler CH, Thorpy MJ. Sleep issues in Parkinson's disease. *Neurology* 2005; 64(Suppl 3): S12–S20.

55. Lachenmayer L. Parkinson's disease and ability to drive. *J Neurol* 2000; 247(Suppl 4): IV/28–IV/30.

56. Reyner LA, Horne JA. Falling asleep whilst driving: are drivers aware of prior sleepiness? *Int J Legal Med* 1998; 111:120–123.

57. Gimenez-Roldan S, Dobato JL, Mateo D. Conductores de vehiculos con enfermedad de Parkinson: Pautes de comportamiento en una muestra de pacientes de la comunidad de Madrid. *Neurologia* 1998; 13:13–21.

58. Duchek JM, Carr DB, Hunt L, et al. Longitudinal driving performance in early stage dementia of the Alzheimer type. *J Am Geriatr Soc* 2003; 31:1342–1347.

59. Yale SH, Hansotia P, Knapp D, Ehrfurth J. Neurologic conditions: Assessing medical fitness to drive. *Clin Med Res* 2003; 1:177–178.

60. American Medical Association. *Physician's Guide to Assessing and Counseling Older Drivers.* Washington DC: National Traffic Safety Administration, 2003.

63 The Patient's Perspective

David S. Heydrick

DOCTOR AND PATIENT

In 2002, I was a general neurologist enjoying private practice in suburban Maryland. In August of that year I just did not feel right and noticed that the finger movements on my (dominant) right hand were slow. Several months later, a postural and resting tremor developed in my right hand. My partners and I considered Parkinson's disease (PD), as my grandfather had suffered from it, but denial was my friend. The diagnosis was confounded by a herniated disk in my neck, also on the right, causing arm weakness and neck pain; despite surgery for the disk and subsequent rehabilitation, my tremor progressed and my handwriting deteriorated into micrographia. Circumstances were chipping away at my denial; I recall seeing one of my favorite PD patients, thinking how similar my symptoms were to hers. Eventually, imitators of PD were ruled out and dopamine agonist therapy improved my micrographia considerably, but less so my tremor (unfortunately it also caused severe intractable nausea and fatigue). Finally, I arranged for an F-dopa positron emission tomography (PET) scan as part of a research study (because insurance does not cover PET scans for PD diagnosis), wanting to "see the dopamine problem." The result was a colorful scan showing decreased dopamine uptake in the left basal ganglia (corresponding to my right tremor); it was consistent with "early Parkinson's."

Having diagnosed and treated PD patients, I now was one. My state of semidenial was over and my journey was just beginning.

DIFFICULTIES IN DIAGNOSIS

"Idiopathic" PD is a clinical diagnosis, which commands a role for both patient and physician. If most of the motor symptoms match the cardinal parkinsonian symptoms of tremor, rigidity, and bradykinesia; if confounding causes of parkinsonism such as normal-pressure hydrocephalus are ruled out; and if there is a good clinical response to dopaminergic therapy, the diagnosis is presumed. But part of the difficulty with making the diagnosis with certainty is the heterogeneity of the disease; like its victims, PD comes in many shapes and sizes, and it changes unpredictably. I remember reading one study in which arm pain (of unknown etiology) preceded the cardinal parkinsonian symptoms by 2 years! I have met many patients who have gone years (after symptoms began) before being accurately diagnosed; this speaks to the fact that patients and doctors alike often do not recognize important but subtle early clues, such as nonmotor symptoms. Compound this with the thought that dopaminergic neuronal demise in PD may actually start many years earlier, and one can see that until imaging or other biomarkers are widely available, diagnosis of PD will still rely dually on a patient's awareness that something is not right and an astute physician.

What do patients want? First, patients want a name for their disorder. Probably the sensible way to approach the occasional diagnostic dilemma is to have a low threshold for keeping PD on the differential diagnosis of an unclear diagnosis, especially if there is any family history. In the right clinical setting, "panels" of risk factors may provide additional helpful clues, such as midlife difficulty with the sense of smell, rapid-eye-movement (REM) sleep behavior disorder, constipation, prolonged QT interval on the electrocardiogram (ECG), obesity—even unexplained fatigue and/or asymmetric pain. PET and single photon emission computed tomography (SPECT) scans are expensive diagnostic tools and probably not cost-effective for general screening. As I found out, however, they can be useful in cases that are unclear or when the educated patient is in denial.

DIFFICULTIES IN TREATMENT

The second thing a patient wants is to know how to treat the disorder so as to preserve quality of life (QOL). The medical and surgical options are covered in this textbook; but these must be communicated effectively to the patient. I was having lunch with a PD patient who told me that he was going to be started on medication at his next visit to the neurologist. Unfortunately he had no idea what the medical (or surgical, for that matter) possibilities were. I listed them for him on a napkin, discussing each one. He later contacted me and told me how helpful that napkin had been when he went to the doctor, who was unable to spend as much time with him as I had. He knew his options and felt good about the treatment initiated.

In addition to knowing the medical options, patients want to take as few pills as possible, at the lowest effective dose, as few times a day as possible, without side effects, and with resulting maintenance or restoration of QOL. This is a somewhat idealistic but not unreasonable attitude. Patients want to know that the treating neurologist has considered this in making his or her recommendations. Listening to the patient is yet another challenge.

Listen to Me: Nonmotor Symptoms and Medication Side Effects are Significant

I was being seen by a movement disorder fellow who questioned my claim of profound fatigue, concluding that I was simply "tired." I had been a college athlete and made it through the rigors of graduate school and medical training: I know what it means to be tired. With my PD, I battle profound fatigue and pain, the kind that—(unpredictably day to day—seeps into your whole being, making your limbs feel heavy and unmanageable. And more or better sleep is not the answer.

Nonmotor symptoms are many times more debilitating than motor symptoms. The list—encompassing constitutional symptoms, brainstem disturbances, neuropsychiatric disturbances, and dysautonomia—is long and well documented in this text. From the patient's perspective, pain, as from rigid muscles or dystonia, can be devastating and fatigue debilitating; obviously so can depression, apathy, and anxiety. It's hard not to feel anxious about PD—about the daily symptoms, caregiver burden, and the expected course of the disease, including the possibility of dementia. One may compensate for this anxiety simply by not caring about anything. Depression must be recognized and acknowledged by both patient and physician and appropriately treated in order even to begin optimizing QOL. Many patients I know who are depressed seem to also be angry at their disease and anyone associated with their care, so consider an angry PD patient in your clinic as a red flag for depression. I would like to emphasize that a lowered threshold for stress is a given, and not well recognized by clinicians. Every PD patient I've ever met reports this symptom. Having worked in many high-pressure situations prior to my PD diagnosis, I now find it challenging even to go to my sons' baseball games, although these are a passion of mine, as my neck becomes tight and my tremor emerges uncomfortably in public, cyclically causing more stress. When these issues are combined with executive dysfunction such as diminished ability to multitask, poor ability to write, and the unpredictability of motor fluctuations, most jobs and even complex activities of daily living ultimately become unmanageable. Recent surveys have uncovered further complaints often unmentioned by PD patients, including diplopia, dribbling, and dysgeusia.

Finally, the side effects—e.g., motor, cognitive, gastrointestinal, and fatigue—of dopaminergic and other "antiparkinsonian" medications are "thorns in the side" of patients, who must learn to live with them. Motor side effects involve primarily dyskinesia. Studies have also concluded that PD patients don't mind dyskinesia—given the alternative of immobility—but most dyskinetic patients I know find these jerky, abnormal movements socially if not physically debilitating. Cognitive side effects involve essentially a drug-induced encephalopathy. Patients often have to adjust their medication dose to trade off motor control for cognitive performance. Imagine trying to work while your mind is in slow motion. Some dopaminergic drugs if not PD itself can cause compulsive behavior, which may destroy relationships.

Gastrointestinal side effects include nausea and constipation. Constipation is not pleasant, and unless you've experienced it, you'll just have to take my word for it that patients with constipation really suffer. Also, I experienced almost 24-7 nausea while on dopamine agonists, which was debilitating in and of itself; the nausea was eventually diminished by domperidone (obtained from Canada), but the tradeoff was sleepiness.

This brings me back to fatigue. In addition to PD itself "causing" fatigue in many but not all patients, most of the medications used in PD also have "tiredness" as a side effect.

Furthermore, unpredictable symptomatology is often the rule; one long-standing patient aptly said, "Parkinson's is a different disease every day," and some would even say "every hour." Although PD patients expend great effort planning their days around their medication, irregular fluctuations always seem to appear. If it's not clear yet that nonmotor symptoms are debilitating, especially in combination with the motor symptoms, imagine trying to get through a day being unpredictably fatigued, in pain from dystonia, constipated, and cognitively fuzzy—in addition to being bradykinetic, dyskinetic, unstable on your feet, and tremoring. All the while your speech is so soft and forced that no one can understand you and you know that your sleep tonight will be fractured. Daunting isn't it? But that's what some of PD patients are experiencing. The multiplicity of these factors often puts a capital "D" in disability.

The patient's job in the doctor's office—to convey meaningful symptomatology efficiently—is not easy. Even with my experience as a medical practitioner, I find it challenging as a patient to communicate to my neurologist, within a few minutes, the complexity of my motor and nonmotor symptoms, including probable medication side effects, and the variable degree to which they adversely affect my QOL. It is really only the patient who can truly appreciate the comprehensive nature of his or her issues, including comorbidities, and, generally what is a priority in order to maintain an acceptable QOL. The bottom line: patients need to prepare for their doctor visit as though they were visiting an accountant, with symptoms and questions concisely written down. For their part, neurologists need to ask about the litany of possible PD symptoms and medication side effects and really listen in order to understand how these are affecting their patients' lives.

What about Getting Deep Brain Stimulation Earlier Rather than Later?

In 2005, having found myself poorly tolerant of dopaminergic therapy and experiencing a declining QOL due to asymmetric tremor and bradykinesia, I had staged deep brain stimulation (DBS) surgeries, with electrodes placed in the subthalamic nucleus bilaterally. Since I was relatively young and in good health, my recovery was swift. In the first year after DBS, my QOL increased far beyond my expectations, allowing me to exercise more efficiently and to rejoin the workforce. Prior to DBS, my right face-arm-leg

tremor had progressed to the point that I could not write, drive, use a keyboard, button shirts, tie my shoes, give talks, or even go out in public comfortably, as to restaurants. The stress on my wife was tremendous and my relationship with my children became superficial, as I spent all my cognitive and physical energy just trying to make it through each day, with little energy or patience left over to be husband and dad. Struggling at the office, I recall that one patient told my colleague, "I think Dr. Heydrick is sicker than I am." I had to quit my private practice and use my private disability policy (which has been a blessing). But after DBS and lifestyle changes—comprising lowered stress, more focused nutrition, and a variety of exercises (such as stretching, weight lifting, running, biking, and tai chi) —my ability to function as well as my QOL were restored almost miraculously. I have regained the ability to exercise, drive, write and type, get dressed at reasonable speed, give talks, go out to restaurants, and work, coming off disability. I have changed my work to be low-stress, including being the science advisor to the Parkinson's Action Network, a public policy research advocacy organization, some consulting, and even practicing neurology again, though in the form of doing electromyography (EMG) and nerve conduction studies (NCS). Happily, my functional restoration has also included being able to play baseball with my sons once again; in fact, my fastball was recently clocked at 60 mph (no kidding!).

I know a fair number of patients with DBS who manifested a wide variety of symptoms prior to their DBS surgery. These patients were debilitated by bradykinesia, motor complications, or intractable tremor. None were demented or depressed, all had their DBS surgery at a center that used an interdisciplinary team, and all have had their QOL dramatically improved. However, it is my personal observation that the responders who benefited the most, compared with medical therapy alone, were either those whose most debilitating problem was tremor, which is often difficult to treat with medications, or those who were not on much medicine to begin with. All the DBS patients I know have lowered their medication intake, but those on the most medication prior to DBS (typically those with profound bradykinesia in the "off" state and often with dyskinesia) seem to have had the hardest time decreasing their dependence on L-dopa after DBS. The side effects I incurred from bilateral DBS have been mild speech and balance difficulties, both of which have improved with rehabilitation therapies. Although my DBS fraternity reports that they generally have the same function as in their best "on" state, it is my experience that unlike medication, DBS works around the clock, without fluctuations, and without systemic side effects. It is hard to put into words what profound difference DBS has made in my QOL. I therefore think that it should be considered more frequently and earlier, especially for certain young-onset patients.

Below are the partial contents of an unpublished letter coauthored by (and published here with permission from) neurologist Gerald Vitek, MD, PhD (Director of Functional Neurosciences at the Cleveland Clinic Foundation), Carol Walton (Executive Director of the Parkinson Alliance and Director of DBS-STN) and me:

> There are early-stage PD patients who are good surgical candidates, who cannot tolerate or fully benefit from conventional dopaminergic or other antiparkinsonian therapy, and whose QOL has declined to such a state that, to them, the potential benefits of surgery outweigh its risks. These patients are the "exception to the rule." A recent QOL survey by the organization DBS-STN (www.dbs-stn.org) has shown that "The relationship between disease duration and satisfaction with overall severity of the movement disorder was correlated in the non-DBS group but not the DBS group. In other words, as the Parkinson's disease process continues, individuals in the non-DBS group reported dissatisfaction with the severity of their "movement disorder"; this, however, was not the case with the case with the DBS group, where patients' level of satisfaction following DBS surgery did not relate to disease duration." As for cost, it is difficult to assign a monetary value to QOL; additionally, after DBS surgery, some patients can once again rejoin the workforce, at least for the near future.

> Until the next breakthrough in functional restoration for PD patients is developed and widely available, possibly the neurology community should consider DBS surgery (performed by a competent interdisciplinary team) in *appropriate* "nonadvanced PD" patients, before severe motor fluctuations and dyskinesia develop. Although this may be deemed as taking undue risk and "not necessary" by some, there are others who wonder whether neurologists wait "too long" (to recommend DBS), allowing the abnormal pathophysiological changes that take place in Parkinson's disease to continue unchecked. While such a philosophy is not advocated without well-controlled studies to warrant its use, there should be more discussion regarding this approach and for future consideration of such a study in patients with idiopathic PD.

DIFFICULTIES IN SOCIAL ADJUSTMENT

Young-onset PD (YOPD) patients may have a harder social adjustment to their disease and its visible and invisible symptoms than typical-onset (older) PD patients. In addition to the plethora of other motor and nonmotor symptoms, YOPD patients battle public misinformation and lack of information about PD and the fact that PD is still not widely recognized as affecting persons less than 50 years old. Furthermore, a YOPD patient may have significant anxiety about how he or she is going to deal with the sequelae of the disease for 30 or more years, including

practical concerns about the impact of potential disability on job, income, family (including risk of PD in parents and siblings) and social life, long-term-care planning, retirement nest egg, and college savings for their children. At least these are the things that keep me awake at night.

The treating physician can help with these issues simply by proactively bringing them up in conversation with patients. Asking them about what the impact PD has been on the practical aspects of their daily lives as well as what worries them about the future can allow the physician to figure out how to help in make these patients' lives better. This may mean identifying which referrals to make to various multidisciplinary team members, including psychiatrists and financial planners.

THE PARKINSON'S PYRAMID™

From the day of diagnosis of PD onward, a patient must respect the disease process, because PD ultimately has the upper hand. But there are 8760 hours in a year and neurologist visits for the year may total less than 2 hours, so patients would do well to realize that, during the other 8758 hours, they have some ability to take charge of their health by fighting back sensibly, subsequently improving their symptoms, possibly slowing the disease process, and maybe even to some extent rewiring their brains. Patients should be encouraged to be proactive in managing their health. The strategy I developed to take charge of my own health, essentially integrated medicine for PD, and which seems to be working, is what I call the Parkinson's Pyramid, a takeoff on the food pyramid, as and illustrated in Figure 63-1.

Stress Management

At the base of the pyramid, to the right, is stress management, showing (a) that environmental stress can cause oxidative stress; (b) that parkinsonian symptoms worsen with stress in a vicious cycle, (c) and that PD patients have a lower threshold for stress. This equation compels a solution that will reduce stress, most effectively through behavior modification. This starts with a commitment by patients to rearrange their priorities, putting their health first, including getting their bodies and brains in shape in order to take full advantage of future therapeutics. Neurologists should encourage and be appreciative of a patient's decision to put his or her health first, realizing that this may mean supporting the patient's decision to leave a stressful job, which may also mean applying for disability.

Symptom Management

Also at the base of the pyramid is symptom management. This applies to managing physical and psychological symptoms, which many practitioners may claim is obviously

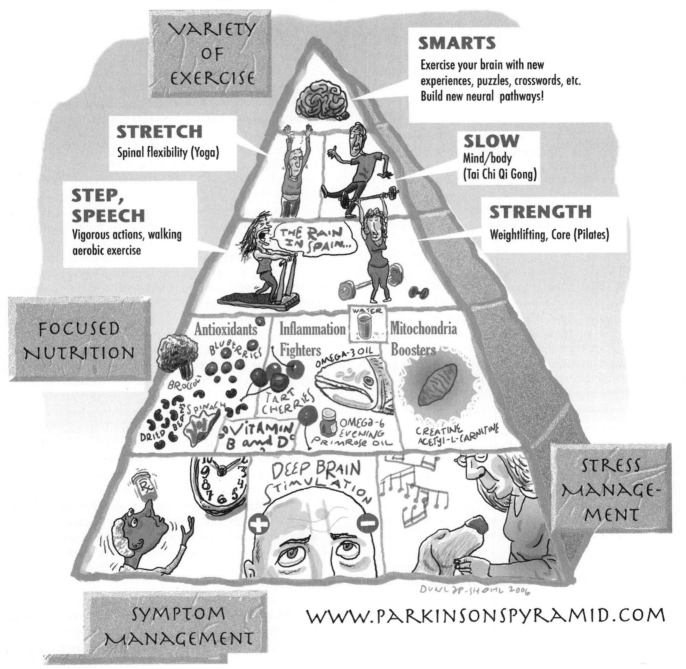

FIGURE 63-1

The Parkinson's Pyramid.

their mission. But from a patient's perspective, the ramifications of suboptimal management are far-reaching. For example, unless depression is diagnosed and treated appropriately, the rest of the health paradigm is useless. Other PD nonmotor symptoms should be identified and treated as well as possible; in fact, sometimes a significant step toward symptom relief can be achieved if the doctor simply acknowledges and validates the symptom. The management of motor symptoms involves normalizing the motor circuit(s) and patient function by prescribing medication at the lowest effective dose and/or by arranging for surgical therapy such as DBS. Finally, be aware that dyskinesia is, for most patients, an unwanted side effect of dopaminergic therapy.

Focused Nutrition

As I see it, neuroprotection is the immediate goal of health restoration—that is, to slow or stop disease progression; without neuroprotection, future neurorestoration will be useless. I want to emphasize that this is my personal approach; it does not necessarily represent the opinion of any PD researcher or organization and is not intended as medical advice. What makes sense to me is a focused nutritional strategy aimed at fighting back against cell death. Yes, I know this brings chills to all neurologists whose exclusive view is one of evidence-based medicine and who want to see evidence from class I clinical trials before making any recommendations. But PD patients appreciate an open-minded physician who can talk knowledgably about healthy lifestyles, acknowledging that there is not always class I evidence to back up everything that he or she may discuss. The premise is that there are many probable ways in which cells can die or become debilitated (e.g., by oxidative stress and inflammation or via abnormal protein aggregation or mitochondrial dysfunction). So it is logical that *multiple* different therapeutics (including exercise) are necessary to fight back.

Antioxidant-rich (and thus anti-inflammation–rich) foods such as dark berries [e.g., acai (Euterpe oleracea) and blueberries] and vegetables, dried beans, properly balanced unsaturated fatty acid–rich foods, and green tea, for example, can be recommended without guilt. Given that many PD patients often do not get sufficient sunlight for institutional or geographic reasons, supplementing with vitamin D (800 to 1000 mg daily), which has strong antioxidant qualities, may be advised. Finally, general health can often be enhanced by a taking a multivitamin (without iron) that contains selenium and the B vitamins. Be aware that vitamin B_6 should be limited to 5 mg/d, since it may interfere with L-dopa metabolism.

Evidence is mounting for so-called mitochondrial medicine. Patients will be asking about it if they aren't already. Supplements are often difficult to justify if there is no physiologic deficiency or sufficient clinical trial evidence of efficacy (which there usually is not). But some supplements are worth knowing about because patients are reading and hearing about them. Most PD patients know that their brains are damaged and are willing to take some risks, ahead of the years involved in "proving" efficacy, if the science is leaning toward seeing a generally safe compound as helpful therapeutically. As a result of the Neuroprotection Exploratory Trials–Parkinson's Disease (NET-PD Phase II trials), creatine (10 g/d) was recently declared "not futile to study further" by National Institutes of Health. Creatine not only stabilizes mitochondrial function but may also inhibit abnormal protein aggregation and help diminish sarcopenia, the worrisome loss of muscle from less mobile PD patients. However, it is a large molecule, and renal function would have to be monitored. Like creatine in being a mitochondrial "metabolic inhibitor" is acetyl-L-carnitine. Finally, there is the potent antioxidant and mitochondrial respiratory chain cofactor ubiquinone or coenzyme Q10 (Co-Q10). This is the coenzyme for at least 3 mitochondrial enzymes (complexes I, II, and III) as well as enzymes in other parts of the cell. In very preliminary trials, it has shown some promise at 1200 mg/day in slowing the progression of PD. Co-Q10 at 2400 mg/d, a dose at which more definitive results would be expected, is being tested in the NET-PD with regard to whether it is neuroprotective and thus whether it would warrant further study.

Although some of these foods and compounds may eventually be studied for efficacy in treating PD, it seems reasonable to at least be knowledgeable about them and to discuss their possible incorporation now into a patient's therapeutic regimen. Some drawbacks to using "unproven" supplements are (a) not knowing whether side effects are due to a supplement or interaction with a medication, (b) an increased number of pills to swallow daily, and (c) the cost, which can run to hundreds of dollars per month, especially if Co-Q10 is used. Nonetheless, a neurologist's thoughtful discussion with the patient about possibly employing a healthy, natural, multipronged strategy may be appreciated and helpful. But the best "supplement" of all may be exercise.

Exercise

Probably, the most underprescribed therapy is exercise in all its forms. Studies, originally reported on stroke patients, are accumulating on PD. These studies describe significant motor recovery with exercise in the form of treadmill training (e.g., as a part of physical therapy). Exercise in moderation raises the body's natural antioxidant function and is therapeutic for many nonmotor symptoms too. Thus, one goal of optimal symptomatic management should be to allow the PD patient to exercise more ably, thus taking better charge of his or her health. One PD patient I know, a member of the same tai chi class I attend, cut his L-dopa use in half over the course of 2 years by way of regular swimming and training in the martial arts.

Motor circuits are undeniably complicated and likely need to be stimulated in a variety of ways in the hope of rewiring motor pathways effectively. Thus, as in the case of the multipronged nutritional strategy outlined above, patients would benefit from engaging in different forms of exercise weekly (the "S's"): (a) stretching, as via yoga; (b) strengthening, as via supervised weight training; (c) step exercises or large, repetitive movements, which might initially be supervised by a physical therapist or trainer and would categorically include repetitive voice therapy; and (d) slow, controlled movements, as via tai chi or qi gong; and (e) smarts, i.e., regularly exercising the brain with mental challenges (e.g., sodoku).

The Parkinson's Pyramid is an empowering health strategy, not a specific program, that can be used by neurologists in encouraging their PD patients to take charge of their own health, with the goals of increasing patient QOL, helping the patients feel that they are fighting back, and optimistically improving the chances that they will be functioning better within a year. More information can be obtained from the website www.parkinsonspyramid.com.

Index